CURRENT
OPERATIVE
UROLOGY

Edited by

E. Douglas Whitehead, M.D.

ASSISTANT CLINICAL PROFESSOR OF UROLOGY,
MOUNT SINAI SCHOOL OF MEDICINE;
ASSOCIATE ATTENDING UROLOGIST,
DEPARTMENT OF UROLOGY,
BETH ISRAEL MEDICAL CENTER
NEW YORK, NEW YORK

Elliot Leiter, M.D.

DIRECTOR OF UROLOGY,
BETH ISRAEL MEDICAL CENTER;
PROFESSOR OF UROLOGY,
MOUNT SINAI SCHOOL OF MEDICINE
NEW YORK, NEW YORK

235 Contributors

CURRENT OPERATIVE UROLOGY

SECOND EDITION

HARPER & ROW, PUBLISHERS

PHILADELPHIA

Cambridge
New York
Hagerstown
San Francisco

1817

London
Mexico City
São Paulo
Sydney

Sponsoring Editor: Richard Winters
Manuscript Editor: Rosanne Hallowell
Indexer: Julie Schwager
Art Director: Maria S. Karkucinski
Designer: Rita Naughton
Production Supervisor: J. Corey Gray
Production Assistant: Barney A. Fernandes
Compositor: Monotype Composition Co.
Printer/Binder: Halliday Lithograph Corp.

The authors and publisher have exerted every effort to ensure that drug selection and dosage set forth in this text are in accord with current recommendations and practice at the time of publication. However, in view of ongoing research, changes in government regulations, and the constant flow of information relating to drug therapy and drug reactions, the reader is urged to check the package insert for each drug for any change in indications and dosage and for added warnings and precautions. This is particularly important when the recommended agent is a new or infrequently employed drug.

3 5 6 4 2

Library of Congress Cataloging in Publication Data
Main entry under title:

Current operative urology.

Includes bibliographies and index.
1. Genito-urinary organs—Surgery. I. Whitehead,
E. Douglas. II. Leiter, Elliot. [DNLM: 1. Urogenital
system—Surgery. WJ 168 C976]
RD571.C87 1984   617'.46   83-22228
ISBN 0-061-42684-9

To our contributors for their patience and understanding.

To our patients for all they have taught us.

But most of all to our wives and children for their love and support.

CONTRIBUTORS

RICHARD ABLIN, M.D.
Senior Scientific Officer, Cook County Hospital, Hektoen
Institute for Medical Research, Chicago, Illinois
(Chapter 69 Commentary)

JESSE I. ABRAHAMS, M.D.
Associate Professor of Urology, SUNY Downstate Medical
Center, Brooklyn, New York; Chief Urologist, VA Hospital,
Brooklyn, New York
(Chapter 71 Overview)

SALAH AL-ASKARI, M.D.
Professor of Urology, New York University School of Medicine,
New York, New York; Director of Urology, Bellevue Hospital
Center, New York, New York; Consultant Urologist, Veterans
Administration Hospital, New York, New York
(Chapter 32 Commentary)

TERRY D. ALLEN, M.D.
Professor of Urology, The University of Texas Southwestern
Medical School, Dallas, Texas
(Chapter 93 and 94 Overview)

ARJAN D. AMAR, M.D., M.S., F.R.C.S.(C.)
Chief, Department of Urology, Kaiser Permanente Medical
Center, Walnut Creek, California; Associate Clinical Professor,
Department of Urology, University of California School of
Medicine, San Francisco, California
(Chapter 34 Commentary)

RICHARD D. AMELAR, M.D.
Professor of Clinical Urology, New York University Medical
Center, New York, New York
(Chapter 124 Overview)

MOHAMMAD AMIN, M.D.
Professor and Chief, Division of Urology, Department of
Surgery, University of Louisville School of Medicine, Louisville,
Kentucky
(Chapter 28 Commentary)

E. EVERETT ANDERSON, M.D.
Professor, Division of Urology, Duke University Medical Center,
Durham, North Carolina
(Chapter 94 Commentary)

JULIAN S. ANSELL, M.D.
Professor and Chairman, Department of Urology, University of
Washington, Seattle, Washington
(Chapter 92 Overview)

MICHAEL HANDLEY ASHKEN, B.Sc., M.S., F.R.C.S.
Department of Urology, Norfolk and Norwich Hospital,
Norwich, England
(Chapter 107 Commentary)

ROGER BARNES, M.D. (deceased)
Distinguished Service Professor of Urology, Loma Linda
University School of Medicine, Loma Linda, California
(Chapter 75 Commentary)

ARNOLD M. BELKER, M.D.
Clinical Professor of Surgery (Urology), University of Louisville
School of Medicine, Louisville, Kentucky
(Chapter 124 Commentary)

A. BARRY BELMAN, M.D.
Chairman, Department of Pediatric Neurology, Children's
Hospital, Washington, D.C.; Professor of Urology and Child
Health & Development, National Medical Center, Washington,
D.C.
(Chapter 45 Commentary)

ALAN H. BENNETT, M.D.
Professor of Surgery, and Head, Division of Urological Surgery,
Albany Medical College, Albany, New York
(Chapter 1 Commentary)

HARRY BERGMAN, M.D.
Clinical Professor of Urology, New York Medical College,
Valhalla, New York; Clinical Professor of Urology, University of
Miami Medical School, Miami, Florida
(Chapter 30 Commentary)

JOHN P. BLANDY, M.A., D.M., M.Ch., F.R.C.S.
Professor of Urology, University of London, The London
Hospital Medical Center, London, England
(Chapters 6 through 9 Overview)

WILLIAM W. BONNEY, M.D.
Associate Professor, Department of Urology, University of Iowa
Hospital, Iowa City, Iowa; Chief, Urology Section, Veterans
Administration Medical Center, Iowa City, Iowa
(Chapter 88 Commentary)

NOEL J. BONNIN, M.D., F.R.C.S., F.R.A.C.S.
Consulting Surgeon, Queen Elizabeth Hospital, Adelaide,
Australia; Formerly, Urologist, Royal Adelaide Hospital,
Adelaide, Australia
(Chapter 71 Commentary)

WILLIAM T. BOWLES, M.D.
Associate Professor of Urology (Clinical), Washington University
School of Medicine, St. Louis, Missouri
(Chapter 65 Commentary)

RICHARD J. BOXER, M.D.
Clinical Instructor, Department of Urology, The Medical College
of Wisconsin, Milwaukee, Wisconsin; Chief, Section of
Urology, Department of Surgery, Mount Sinai Medical Center,
Milwaukee, Wisconsin
(Chapter 101 Commentary)

WILLIAM H. BOYCE, M.D.
Professor and Chairman, Section of Urology, Department of
Surgery, Bowman Gray School of Medicine, Wake Forest
University, Winston-Salem, North Carolina
(Chapter 6 Commentary)

ULRICO BRACCI, M.D.
Chief of Urological Department, University of Rome, Rome,
Italy
(Chapter 57 Commentary)

WILLIAM BRANNAN, M.D.
Chairman, Department of Urology, Ochsner Clinic and Ochsner
Foundation Hospital, New Orleans, Louisiana; Clinical Professor
of Urology, Tulane University School of Medicine, New
Orleans, Louisiana
(Chapter 69 Overview)

STANLEY BROSMAN, M.D.
Clinical Professor of Urology, UCLA Center for the Health
Sciences, Los Angeles, California
(Chapter 121 Commentary)

JORDON S. BROWN, M.D.
Professor of Clinical Urology, New York University School of
Medicine, New York, New York; Director, Section of Urology,
New York Veterans Administration Medical Center, New York,
New York.
(Chapter 123 Overview)

REG BRUSKEWITZ, M.D.
Assistant Professor of Surgery/Urology, University of Wisconsin
Hospital, Madison, Wisconsin
(Chapter 114 Commentary)

ANTON J. BUESCHEN, M.D.
Professor and Director, Division of Urology, Department of
Surgery, University of Alabama in Birmingham School of
Medicine, Birmingham, Alabama
(Chapter 96 Commentary)

IRVING M. BUSH, M.D.
Professor of Surgery (Urology), The University of Health
Sciences, The Chicago Medical School, Chicago, Illinois; Senior
Consultant, Center for Study of Genitourinary Diseases,
Burlington, Illinois; Senior Attending Urologist, Cook County
Hospital, Chicago, Illinois; and Urologist, Sycamore Municipal
Hospital, Sycamore, Illinois
(Chapter 69 Commentary)

MARCO CAINE, M.S. (Lond.), F.R.C.S.
Head, Department of Urology, Hadassah University Hospital,
Jerusalem, Israel; Professor of Urology, Hebrew University,
Jerusalem, Israel
(Chapter 8 Commentary)

ANTHONY A. CALDAMONE, M.D.
Director, Pediatric Urology, Rainbow Babies' and Children's
Hospital, Rochester, New York; Assistant Professor in Urology,
Case Western Reserve University, Rochester, New York
(Chapter 22 Overview)

CHARLES CARDANY, M.D.
Sibley Memorial Hospital, Chevy Chase, Maryland; Suburban
Hospital, Bethesda, Maryland; Washington Hospital Center,
Washington, D.C.
(Chapter 99 Commentary)

C. EUGENE CARLTON, Jr., M.D.
Chairman, Department of Urology, Baylor College of Medicine,
Houston, Texas
(Chapter 72 Overview)

SAMUEL S. CLARK, M.D.
Clinical Professor of Urology, Stritch School of Medicine,
Loyola University, Chicago, Illinois
(Chapter 51 Overview)

ABRAHAM T. K. COCKETT, M.D.
Professor of Urological Surgery, and Chairman, Division of
Urology, Rochester Medical Center, Rochester, New York
(Chapter 22 Overview)

ARNOLD H. COLODNY, M.D.
Senior Surgeon and Associate Director, Division of Urology,
Children's Hospital, Boston, Massachusetts; Associate Clinical
Professor of Surgery, Harvard Medical School, Boston,
Massachusetts
(Chapter 55 Overview)

JOHN MARQUIS CONVERSE, M.D. (deceased)
Lawrence D. Bell Professor of Plastic Surgery, New York
University Medical Center, New York, New York
(Chapters 99 and 100 Overviews)

JOSEPH N. CORRIERE, Jr., M.D.
Professor of Surgery and Director of Urology, Division of
Urology, The University of Texas Medical School at Houston,
Houston, Texas
(Chapter 4 Commentary)

LUIS R. COS, M.D.
Major, Medical Corps, United States Army, Division of Organ
Transplantation, Walter Reed Army Medical Center,
Washington, D.C.
(Chapter 22 Overview)

MALCOLM D. COSGROVE, M.D., F.R.C.S.
Associate Professor of Surgery/Urology, University of Southern California School of Medicine, Los Angeles, California
(Chapter 23 Commentary)

KIRAN KENNY CROOKS, M.D. (deceased)
Associate Professor of Urology, Children's Hospital, Ohio State University, Columbus, Ohio
(Chapter 55 Commentary)

DAVID A. CULP, M.D.
Professor and Head, Department of Urology, College of Medicine, University of Iowa, Iowa City, Iowa; Attending Urologist, University Hospitals, Iowa City, Iowa
(Chapter 59 Commentary)

JOSEPH E. DAVIS, M.D.
Clinical Professor of Urology, New York Medical College, New York, New York
(Chapter 126 Overview)

CHARLES J. DEVINE, Jr., M.D.
Professor and Chairman, Department of Urology, Eastern Virginia Medical School, Norfolk, Virginia
(Chapters 95 and 99 Commentaries)

PATRICK C. DEVINE, M.D.
Professor of Urology, Eastern Virginia Medical School, Norfolk, Virginia; Director of Urology Residency Program, Eastern Virginia Graduate School of Medicine, Norfolk, Virginia
(Chapters 108 through 110 Overview)

JAMES H. DeWEERD, M.D.
Anson L. Clark Professor of Urology, Emeritus, Mayo Medical School, Emeritus Staff, Mayo Clinic, Rochester, Minnesota
(Chapter 29 Commentary)

JOHN P. DONOHUE, M.D.
Professor and Chairman, Department of Urology, Indiana University Medical Center, Indianapolis, Indiana
(Chapters 121 and 122 Overview)

LEONARD R. DOURMASHKIN, M.D.
Clinical Assistant Urologist, Albert Einstein School of Medicine, New York, New York; Associate Urologist, Beth Israel Hospital, New York, New York; Associate Urologist, Montefiore Hospital, Bronx, New York
(Chapter 42 Commentary)

JOSEPH B. DOWD, M.D.
Chairman, Department of Urology, Lahey Clinic, Burlington, Massachusetts; Clinical Assistant Professor of Surgery, Harvard Medical School, Boston, Massachusetts
(Chapter 83 Overview)

JOHN W. DRAPER, M.D.
Clinical Professor of Urology, Cornell University Medical College, New York, New York; Attending Urologist, New York Hospital, Cornell Medical Center, New York, New York
(Chapter 80 Commentary)

STEPHEN P. DRETLER, M.D.
Assistant Professor of Urology, Harvard Medical School, Boston, Massachusetts; Massachusetts General Hospital, Boston, Massachusetts
(Chapter 55 Commentary)

LAWRENCE DUBIN, M.D.
Professor of Clinical Urology, New York University School of Medicine, New York, New York
(Chapter 124 Overview)

JOHN W. DUCKETT, M.D.
Director, Division of Pediatric Urology, Children's Hospital of Philadelphia, Philadelphia, Pennsylvania; Professor of Urology, Department of Surgery, University of Pennsylvania School of Medicine, Philadelphia, Pennsylvania.
(Chapter 112 Overview)

H. B. ECKSTEIN, M.A., M.D., M.Chir., F.R.C.S.
Consultant Surgeon, The Hospital for Sick Children, London, England
(Chapters 44 and 45 Overview)

MILTON T. EDGERTON, M.D.
Professor and Chairman, Department of Plastic and Maxillo-facial Surgery, University of Virginia Medical Center, Charlottesville, Virginia
(Chapters 101 and 102 Overviews)

RICHARD M. EHRLICH, M.D.
Professor, Division of Surgery/Urology, UCLA Medical Center, Los Angeles, California
(Chapter 11 Commentary)

ARTHUR T. EVANS, M.D.
Professor and Director, Division of Urology, University of Cincinnati Medical Center, Cincinnati, Ohio
(Chapter 37 Overview)

WILLIAM R. FAIR, M.D.
Professor of Surgery and Chairman, Division of Urology, Washington University School of Medicine, St. Louis, Missouri; Urologist-in-Chief, Barnes and Allied Hospitals, St. Louis, Missouri
(Chapter 43 Overview)

EDUARDO M. FARCON, M.D.
Clinical Associate Professor of Urology, New York University Medical Center, New York, New York
(Chapter 7 Commentary)

MANUEL FERNANDES, M.D.
Associate Director, St. Luke's Hospital Urology Service, New York, New York; Associate Clinical Professor of Urology, College of Physicians and Surgeons, Columbia University, New York, New York
(Chapter 110 Commentary)

CASIMIR F. FIRLIT, M.D., Ph.D.
Professor of Urology and Chairman, Division of Urology,
Northwestern University Medical School, Chicago, Illinois;
Head, Renal Transplantation, and Acting Surgeon-in-Chief,
Children's Memorial Hospital, Chicago, Illinois
(Chapter 50 Overview)

ELWIN E. FRALEY, M.D.
Professor and Chairman, Department of Urologic Surgery,
University of Minnesota College of Health Sciences,
Minneapolis, Minnesota
(Chapter 19 Commentary)

SELWYN Z. FREED, M.D.
Professor and Chairman, Einstein/Montefiore Department of
Medicine, Bronx, New York; Chairman, Department of Urology,
Montefiore Medical Center, Bronx, New York; Professor,
Department of Urology, Albert Einstein College of Medicine,
Bronx, New York
(Chapter 13 Commentary)

HUBERT G. W. FROHMÜLLER, M.D., M.S.
Professor and Chairman, Department of Urology, University of
Würzburg Medical School, Würzburg, West Germany
(Chapter 73 Overview)

BERNARD FRUCHTMAN, M.D.
Associate Clinical Professor of Urology, Albert Einstein College
of Medicine, Bronx, New York; Attending Urologist, Beth Israel
Medical Center, New York, New York
(Chapter 120 Overview)

WILLIAM L. FURLOW, M.S., M.D.
Professor of Urology, Mayo Medical School, Mayo Clinic,
Rochester, Minnesota
(Chapter 104 Commentary)

WILLIAM B. GARLICK, M.D.
Clinical Professor of Surgery (Urology), Albany Medical College,
Albany, New York
(Chapter 84 Overview)

ROBERT A. GARRETT, M.D.
Professor of Urology, Indiana University School of Medicine,
Indianapolis, Indiana
(Chapters 95 and 96 Overviews)

GEORGE L. GARSKE, M.D.
Chief of Urology, St. Mary's Hospital, Minneapolis, Minnesota;
Clinical Associate Professor, University of Minnesota Medical
School, Minneapolis, Minnesota; Consultant, Veterans' Hospital,
Minneapolis, Minnesota
(Chapter 58 Commentary)

KENNETH I. GLASSBERG, M.D.
Associate Professor, Department of Urology, and Director,
Division of Pediatric Urology, State University of New York
(Downstate Medical Center, Kings County Hospital Center, and
Long Island College Hospital), Brooklyn, New York
(Chapter 92 Commentary)

MIRCEA N. GOLIMBU, M.D.
Associate Professor of Urology, New York University Medical
Center, New York, New York
(Chapter 51 Commentary)

MAURICE J. GONDER, M.D.
Department of Urology, State University of New York at Buffalo
School of Medicine, Buffalo, New York
(Chapter 83 Commentary)

PAUL GONICK, M.D.
Professor of Surgery (Urology), Hahnemann University,
Philadelphia, Pennsylvania
(Chapter 23 Overview)

EDMOND T. GONZALES, JR., M.D.
Director of Pediatric Urology, Texas Children's Hospital,
Houston, Texas; Professor of Urology, Baylor College of
Medicine, Houston, Texas
(Chapter 40 Overview)

WILLARD E. GOODWIN, M.D.
Professor of Surgery/Urology, UCLA School of Medicine, Los
Angeles, California
(Chapter 56 Overview)

HARRY GRABSTALD, M.D.
Professor of Surgery, Chief of Urology, University of South
Florida Medical College, Tampa, Florida
(Chapters 26 and 27 Overview)

SAM D. GRAHAM, JR., M.D.
Assistant Professor of Urology, Emory University School of
Medicine, Atlanta, Georgia
(Chapter 68 Commentary)

EDUARDO S. GRANATO, B.S.
Columbia University College of Physicians and Surgeons, New
York, New York
(Chapter 102 Commentary)

ROBERTO C. GRANATO, M.D., F.R.C.S.
Columbia University College of Physicians and Surgeons, New
York, New York
(Chapter 102 Commentary)

JOHN T. GRAYHACK, M.D.
Professor and Chairman, Department of Urology, Kretschmer
Laboratories, Northwestern University Medical School, Chicago,
Illinois
(Chapters 89 and 90 Overview)

STANLEY H. GREENBERG,M.D.
Clinical Assistant Professor of Surgery in Urology, University of
South Carolina School of Medicine, Columbia, South Carolina
(Chapter 123 Commentary)

W. L. GREGOIR, M.D.
Professor of Urology, University of Brussels, Brussels, Belgium
(Chapter 33 Commentary)

W. GRAHAM GUERRIERO, M.D.
Associate Professor of Urology, Baylor College of Medicine, Houston, Texas
(Chapter 24 Commentary)

PATRICK D. GUINAN, M.D.
Associate Professor of Surgery (Urology), University of Illinois School of Medicine, Chicago, Illinois
(Chapter 69 Commentary)

DONALD B. HALVERSTADT, M.D.
Clinical Professor of Urology and Pediatrics, and Vice-Chairman, Department of Urology, University of Oklahoma College of Medicine, Oklahoma City, Oklahoma; Executive Chief of Staff, State of Oklahoma Teaching Hospitals, Oklahoma City, Oklahoma; Special Assistant to the President for Hospital Affairs, University of Oklahoma, Oklahoma City, Oklahoma
(Chapter 118 Overview)

JOHN S. HANSON, B.Sc., F.R.C.S.I.
Consultant Urologist and Renal Transplant Surgeon, The Charitable Infirmary, Jervis Street, Dublin, Ireland
(Chapter 15 Commentary)

LLOYD H. HARRISON, M.D.
Professor of Surgery (Urology), Division of Urology, Department of Surgery, Bowman Gray School of Medicine, Wake Forest University, Winston-Salem, North Carolina
(Chapters 18 through 20 Overview)

CHARLES E. HAWTREY, B.A., M.D.
Professor of Urology, University Hospitals, Iowa City, Iowa
(Chapter 100 Commentary)

HUBERT HECHT, M.D.
Assistant Clinical Professor of Urology, Albert Einstein College of Medicine, Bronx, New York; Attending Urologist, Beth Israel Medical Center, New York, New York
(Chapter 119 Overview)

W. HARDY HENDREN, M.D.
Professor of Surgery, Harvard Medical School, Boston, Massachusetts; Chief of Pediatric Surgery, Massachusetts General Hospital, Boston, Massachusetts
(Chapter 35 Commentary)

TERRY W. HENSLE, M.D.
Director, Pediatric Urology, Babies Hospital, New York, New York; Associate Professor of Urology, Columbia University College of Physicians and Surgeons, New York, New York
(Chapters 52 through 54 Overview)

HARRY W. HERR, M.D.
Associate Attending Surgeon, Memorial Sloan-Kettering Cancer Center and The New York Hospital, New York, New York; Associate Professor of Surgery, Cornell University Medical College, New York, New York
(Chapter 87 Commentary)

FRANK HINMAN, Jr., M.D.
Clinical Professor of Urology, University of California at San Francisco, San Francisco, California; Chief of Urology, Children's Hospital, San Francisco, California
(Chapters 57 through 59 Overview)

PAUL HOCHSZTEIN, M.D.
Clinical Instructor of Urology, Mount Sinai School of Medicine, New York, New York; Assistant Attending Physician, Department of Urology, Beth Israel Medical Center, New York, New York; Staff Attending Physician Department of Urology, St. Luke's–Roosevelt Hospital, New York, New York
(Chapter 74 Overview)

CLARENCE V. HODGES, M.D.
Professor of Surgery/Urology, J. A. Burns School of Medicine, University of Hawaii, Honolulu, Hawaii
(Chapters 28 and 29 Overview)

NORMAN B. HODGSON, M.D.
Clinical Professor, Department of Urology, Medical College of Wisconsin, Milwaukee, Wisconsin
(Chapter 97 Commentary)

WILLIAM W. HOFFMAN, B.S., M.D., D.A.B.U., F.I.C.S.
Associate Clinical Professor of Urology, University of Texas Southwestern Medical School, Dallas, Texas; Chief of Urology, Baylor University Medical Center, Dallas, Texas
(Chapter 79 Commentary)

RUDOLF HOHENFELLNER, M.D.
Professor and Chairman, Department of Urology, University of Mainz, Mainz, West Germany
(Chapter 76 Commentary)

CHARLES E. HORTON, M.D., F.R.C.S.(G.)(Hon.)
Professor, Department of Plastic Surgery, Eastern Virginia Medical School, Norfolk, Virginia
(Chapters 95 and 99 Commentaries)

ROBERT S. HOTCHKISS, M.D.
Emeritus Professor of Urology, New York University College of Medicine, New York, New York
(Chapter 91 Overview)

MARK A. IMMERGUT, M.D.
Associate Clinical Professor of Urology, Georgetown University College of Medicine, Washington, D.C.
(Chapter 44 Commentary)

ALAIN JARDIN, M.D.
Professor of Urology, Hospital de la Pitié, Paris, France
(Chapter 63 Commentary)

HUGH J. JEWETT, M.D.
Professor Emeritus of Urology, Johns Hopkins University School of Medicine, Brady Urological Institute, Johns Hopkins Hospital, Baltimore, Maryland
(Chapter 86 Commentary)

J. H. JOHNSTON, M.B., F.R.C.S., F.R.C.S.I.
Urological Surgeon, Alder Hey Children's Hospital, Liverpool,
England; Lecturer in Paediatric Urology, University of Liverpool,
Liverpool, England
(Chapters 34 and 35 Overviews)

JOHN S. JOSE, M.A., F.R.C.S., F.R.A.C.S.
Senior Visiting Urologist, Royal Adelaide Hospital, Adelaide,
Australia
(Chapter 71 Commentary)

GEORGE W. KAPLAN, M.D.
Clinical Professor of Urology and Pediatrics, and Chief of
Pediatric Urology, University of California at San Diego, San
Diego, California; Attending Urologist, Children's Hospital, San
Diego, California
(Chapter 60 Commentary)

D. K. KARANJAVALA, M.S., F.R.C.S., F.I.C.S.
Professor of Urology, King Edward VII Memorial Hospital,
Bombay India; Visiting Urologist, Tata Memorial Hospital,
Bombay Hospital, and Breach Candy Hospital, Bombay, India
(Chapter 22 Commentary)

FLOYD A. KATSKE, M.D.
Clinical Assistant Professor of Surgery/Urology, UCLA Center of
Health Sciences, Los Angeles, California; Attending in Urology,
Los Angeles County–Mid Valley Medical Center, Van Nuys,
California
(Chapter 11 Commentary)

JOSEPH J. KAUFMAN, M.D.
Professor of Surgery/Urology, and Chief, Division of Urology,
UCLA Medical Center, Los Angeles, California
(Chapters 16 and 17 Overview)

PANAYOTIS P. KELALIS, M.D.
Professor of Urology, Mayo Medical School, and Chairman,
Department of Urology, Mayo Clinic and Mayo Foundation,
Rochester, Minnesota
(Chapter 53 Commentary)

JEAN B. deKERNION, M.D.
Associate Professor of Surgery/Urology, Head of Urologic
Oncology, and Director for Clinical Programs, UCLA Jonsson
Cancer Center, Los Angeles, California
(Chapter 32 Overview)

WALTER S. KERR, Jr., M.D.
Clinical Professor of Surgery, Harvard Medical School, Boston,
Massachusetts; Senior Urologist, Massachusetts General
Hospital, Boston, Massachusetts
(Chapter 73 Commentary)

WILLIAM K. KERR, M.D., F.R.C.S.(C)
Staff Surgeon, Urology, Toronto General Hospital, Toronto,
Ontario
(Chapter 61 Commentary)

ZAFAR KHAN, M.D., F.R.C.S.
Physician-in-Charge, Urodynamic Laboratory, Beth Israel
Medical Center, New York, New York; Assistant Professor,
Department of Urology, Mount Sinai School of Medicine, New
York, New York
(Chapter 42 Commentary)

LOWELL R. KING, M.D.
Professor of Urology, Associate Professor of Pediatrics, and
Head of Section on Pediatric Urology, Duke University Medical
Center, Durham, North Carolina
(Chapters 97 and 98 Overview)

STANLEY J. KOGAN, M.D.
Co-Director, Pediatric Urology Section, Westchester County
Medical Center, Valhalla, New York; Attending Pediatric
Urologist, Albert Einstein Hospital, Montefiore Hospital, Jacobi
City Hospital, and North Central Bronx Hospital, Bronx, New
York; Visiting Associate Professor of Pediatrics, Albert Einstein
College of Medicine, Bronx, New York; Adjunct Professor of
Urology and Surgery, New York Medical College, Valhalla, New
York
(Chapter 118 Commentary)

F. PETER KOHLER, M.D.
Chief, Division of Urology, Lankenau Hospital, Philadelphia,
Pennsylvania; Associate Professor of Clinical Urology, Thomas
Jefferson University, Philadelphia, Pennsylvania
(Chapter 90 Commentary)

R. LAWRENCE KROOVAND, M.D.
Associate Professor of Urology, Wayne State University School
of Medicine, Detroit, Michigan; Associate Director of Pediatric
Urology, Children's Hospital of Michigan, Detroit, Michigan
(Chapter 39 Commentary)

RENÉ KÜSS, M.D.
Professor of Urology, Centre Hospitalo-Universitaire de la
Pitie-Salpetriere à Paris, Paris, France
(Chapter 63 Commentary)

RUSSELL W. LAVENGOOD, M.D.
Clinical Professor of Surgery (Urology), Cornell University
Medical College, and College of Physicians and Surgeons,
Columbia University, New York, New York; Attending Urologist,
New York Hospital, Cornell Medical Center, and St. Luke's-
Roosevelt Hospital Center, New York, New York; Adjunct
Clinical Professor of Urology, New York Medical College, New
York, New York
(Chapters 30 and 31 Overviews)

GUY W. LEADBETTER, Jr., M.D.
Professor of Surgery, and Chairman, Division of Urology,
University of Vermont Medical School, Burlington, Vermont
(Chapter 113 Overview)

ECTOR LeDUC, M.D. (deceased)
Associate Clinical Professor of Surgery/Urology, University of California at San Diego Medical School, La Jolla, California
(Chapter 70 Commentary)

ELLIOT LEITER, M.D.
Director of Urology, Beth Israel Medical Center, New York, New York; Professor and Acting Chairman, Department of Urology, Mount Sinai School of Medicine, New York, New York
(Chapter 14 Commentary, Chapter 46 Overview, and Chapters 85 and 86 Overview)

HARRY H. LeVEEN, M.D.
Professor of Surgery, Medical University of South Carolina, Charleston, South Carolina
(Chapter 105 Overview)

BERNARD LEVINE, M.D.
Attending Urologist, Beth Israel Medical Center and Cabrini Medical Center, New York, New York
(Chapter 36 Commentary)

STANLEY R. LEVINE, M.D.
Clinical Associate Professor, Department of Surgery, University of Health Sciences, Chicago Medical School, North Chicago, Illinois; Attending Staff, Highland Park Hospital, Highland Park, Illinois; Attending Staff, Lake Forest Hospital, Lake Forest, Illinois
(Chapter 21 Commentary)

SELWYN B. LEVITT, M.D.
Co-Director, Section of Pediatric Urology, Westchester Medical Center, Valhalla, New York; Attending Pediatric Urologist, Albert Einstein College Hospital, Montefiore Hospital and Medical Center, and Bronx Municipal Hospital Medical Center, Bronx, New York; Adjunct Clinical Professor of Urology, New York Medical College, Valhalla, New York; Visiting Clinical Professor of Pediatrics, Albert Einstein College of Medicine, Bronx, New York
(Chapter 117 Overview)

JOHN LIBERTINO, M.D.
Vice Chairman of Surgery, Lahey Clinic Medical Center, Burlington, Massachusetts
(Chapter 113 Commentary)

ROBERT LICH, Jr., M.D. M.S. (Path.)
Emeritus Professor of Urology, University of Louisville School of Medicine, Louisville, Kentucky
(Chapter 28 Commentary)

OTTO M. LILIEN, M.D.
Professor and Chairman, Department of Urology, Upstate Medical Center, Syracuse, New York
(Chapter 82 Commentary)

LARRY I. LIPSHULTZ, M.D.
Professor of Urology, Department of Urology, Baylor College of Medicine, Houston Texas
(Chapter 125 Overview)

RICHARDS P. LYON, M.D.
Clinical Professor of Urology, University of California School of Medicine, San Francisco, California
(Chapter 112 Commentary)

BERNARD LYTTON, M.B., F.R.C.S.
Professor and Head, Section of Urology, Yale University School of Medicine, New Haven, Connecticut
(Chapter 60 Overview)

RICHARD J. MACCHIA, M.D.
Associate Professor and Vice Chairman, Department of Urology, Downstate Medical School, Brooklyn, New York
(Chapter 41 Commentary)

JOHN L. McCORMACK, M.D.
Staff Urologist, The Swedish Hospital Medical Center, Seattle, Washington; Clinical Associate Professor, Department of Urology, University of Washington, Seattle, Washington
(Chapter 119 Commentary)

DAVID L. McCULLOUGH, M.D.
Clinical Professor of Urology, University of South Alabama College of Medicine, Mobile, Alabama
(Chapter 3 Commentary)

DONALD F. McDONALD, M.D.
Professor, Division of Urology, University of Texas Medical Branch, Galveston, Texas
(Chapter 27 Commentary)

JOHN H. McGOVERN, M.D.
Professor of Clinical Surgery (Urology), James Buchanan Brady Foundation, Cornell University Medical College/The New York Hospital, New York, New York
(Chapter 107 Overview)

ANDREW J. McGOWAN, Jr., M.D.
Chief, Division of Urology, St. Vincent's Hospital and Medical Center, New York, New York; Associate Clinical Professor of Urology, State University of New York, Downstate Medical Center, Brooklyn, New York
(Chapter 120 Commentary)

EDWARD J. McGUIRE, M.D.
Professor of Surgery (Urology), Yale University School of Medicine, New Haven, Connecticut
(Chapter 74 Commentary)

MARTIN G. McLOUGHLIN, M.D., F.R.C.S.(C).
Professor and Chairman, Division of Urology, Brady Urological Institute, The Johns Hopkins Hospital, Baltimore, Maryland
(Chapter 18 Commentary)

TERRENCE R. MALLOY, M.D.
Chief of Urology, Pennsylvania Hospital, Philadelphia, Pennsylvania; Associate Professor of Urology, University of Pennsylvania, Philadelphia, Pennsylvania
(Chapter 104 Overview)

MICHAEL MARBERGER, M.D.
Head, Department of Urology, Krankenanstalt Rudolfstiftung,
Vienna, Austria
(Chapter 38 Commentary)

PAUL MARSIDI, M.D.
Staff Urologist, Baptist Memorial Hospital, Union City,
Tennessee; Consultant Urologist, Volunteer Hospital, Martin,
Tennessee
(Chapter 108 Commentary)

J. TATE MASON, M.D.
Clinical Professor of Urology, University of Washington Medical
School, Seattle, Washington
(Chapter 25 Overview)

WILLY MATHISEN, M.D.
Professor and Chairman, Department of Urology, Oslo
University Hospital, Rikshospitalet, Oslo, Norway
(Chapter 77 Overview)

DAVID M. MAZOR, M.D.
Attending Urologist, North Shore University Hospital, New York,
New York; Clinical Assistant Professor of Surgery (Urology),
Cornell University Medical College, New York, New York
(Chapter 117 Commentary)

WINSTON K. MEBUST, M.D.
Professor and Chairman, Section of Urology, Kansas University
Medical Center, Kansas City, Kansas
(Chapter 84 Commentary)

ARNOLD MELMAN, M.D.
Associate Director of Urology, Beth Israel Medical Center, New
York, New York; Associate Professor of Urology, Mount Sinai
School of Medicine, CUNY, New York, New York
(Chapter 103 Overview)

CLAUDE E. MERRIN, M.D.
Clinical Associate Professor of Urology, Loyola University
Medical School, Chicago, Illinois; Chief, Urologic Oncology
Services, Swedish Covenant Hospital, Chicago, Illinois
(Chapter 2 Commentary)

VÁCLAV MICHAL, M.D., DrSc. (med.)
Clinical Scientific Office, Cardiovascular Research Centre and
Department of Surgery, Institute for Clinical and Experimental
Medicine, Prague, Czechoslovakia
(Chapter 105 Commentary)

RICHARD G. MIDDLETON, M.D.
Professor of Surgery and Chairman, Division of Urology,
University of Utah School of Medicine, Salt Lake City, Utah
(Chapter 89 Commentary)

DAVID I. MILLSTEIN, M.D.
Assistant Attending Physician, Department of Urology, Beth
Israel Medical Center, New York, New York
(Chapter 106 Commentary)

DAVID T. MININBERG, M.D.
Associate Professor of Clinical Urology/Surgery, and Director,
Pediatric Urology, The New York Hospital–Cornell University
Medical Center, The James Buchanan Brady Foundation, New
York, New York
(Chapter 93 Commentary)

J. P. MITCHELL, C.B.E., T.D., M.S., F.R.C.S.(Ed.), F.R.C.S.
Honorable Professor of Surgery (Urology), University of Bristol,
Bristol, England; Consultant Urological Surgeon, United Bristol
Hospitals and Southmead General Hospital, Bristol, England
(Chapter 111 Overview)

P. MOLLARD, M.D.
Chirurgiem des Hopitaux, Professeur de Chirurgie Infantile,
Hopital Debrousse, Lyon, France
(Chapters 78 and 79 Overview)

DROGO K. MONTAGUE, M.D.
Head, Section of Urodynamics and Prosthetic Surgery,
Department of Urology, Cleveland Clinic Foundation,
Cleveland, Ohio
(Chapter 10 Commentary)

PABLO MORALES, M.D.
Professor and Chairman, Department of Urology, New York
University School of Medicine, New York, New York
(Chapter 7 Commentary)

DOUGLAS D. MOREHOUSE, M.D., F.R.C.S.(C.)
Senior Urologist, Royal Victoria Hospital, Montreal, Quebec;
Associate Professor of Surgery (Urology), McGill University
Faculty of Medicine, Montreal, Quebec
(Chapter 72 Commentary)

PHILIP MOSCA, M.D., Ph.D.
Clinical Assistant Professor of Urology and Adjunct Clinical
Assistant Professor of Pediatrics, University of Oklahoma College
of Medicine, Oklahoma City, Oklahoma
(Chapter 118 Commentary)

EDWARD C. MUECKE, M.D.
Clinical Professor of Surgery (Urology), Cornell University
Medical College, New York, New York; Attending Surgeon
(Urology), The New York Hospital, New York, New York
(Chapter 78 Commentary)

GERALD P. MURPHY, M.D., D.Sc.
Director, Roswell Park Memorial Institute, and Professor of
Surgery, State University of New York at Buffalo, Buffalo, New
York
(Chapters 87 and 88 Overviews)

JOHN J. MURPHY, M.D.
Professor of Urology, Hospital of the University of Pennsylvania,
Philadelphia, Pennsylvania
(Chapters 48 and 49 Overview)

JOHN S. NAJARIAN, M.D.
Professor and Chairman, Department of Surgery, University of Minnesota Affiliated Hospitals, Minneapolis, Minnesota
(Chapter 11 Overview)

JOHN B. NANNINGA, M.D.
Associate Professor of Urology, Northwestern University Medical School, Chicago, Illinois
(Chapter 116 Overview)

DAVID J. NARINS, M.D.
Clinical Assistant Professor of Urology, New York University Medical Center, White Plains, New York; Attending Urologist, White Plains (N.Y.) Hospital and New York University Hospital, White Plains, New York
(Chapter 20 Commentary)

ANDREW C. NOVICK, M.D.
Head, Section of Renal Transplantation, Department of Urology, Cleveland Clinic Foundation, Cleveland, Ohio
(Chapter 16 Commentary)

VINCENT J. O'CONOR, Jr., M.D.
Professor of Urology, Northwestern University Medical School, Chicago, Illinois; Chief of Urology, Northwestern Memorial Hospital, Chicago, Illinois
(Chapters 75 and 76 Overview)

CARL A. OLSSON, M.D.
Lattimer Professor and Chairman, Department of Urology, College of Physicians and Surgeons, Columbia University, New York, New York
(Chapter 77 Overview)

JOHN M. PALMER, M.D.
Professor of Urology, Davis School of Medicine, University of California, Sacramento, California
(Chapters 2 through 5 Overview)

DAVID F. PAULSON, M.D.
Professor and Chief, Division of Urology, Department of Surgery, Duke University Medical Center, Durham, North Carolina
(Chapter 68 Commentary)

HARPER D. PEARSE, M.D.
Associate Professor of Surgery/Urology, and Head, Urologic Oncology, University of Oregon Health Sciences Center, Portland, Oregon
(Chapter 47 Commentary)

LESTER PERSKY, M.D.
Clinical Professor of Urology, Case Western Reserve School of Medicine, University Hospitals of Cleveland, Cleveland, Ohio
(Chapter 91 Commentary)

PAUL C. PETERS, M.D.
Professor and Chairman, Division of Urology, The University of Texas Southwestern Medical School, Dallas, Texas
(Chapter 36 Overview)

PROFESSOR DR. SAVA D. PETKOVIĆ
Retired Professor and Chairman of Urology, Medical Faculty of Belgrade, Belgrade, Yugoslavia; Member, Academy of Sciences of Serbia
(Chapter 26 Commentary)

BERNARD D. PINCK, M.D. (deceased)
Clinical Professor of Urology, New York University School of Medicine, New York, New York; Attending Urologist, Bellevue Hospital, New York, New York; Associate Attending Urologist, University Hospital, New York, New York
(Chapter 56 Overview)

W. REID PITTS, Jr., M.D.
Assistant Professor (Clinical) Urology, New York Hospital–Cornell Medical School, New York, New York; Associate Professor (Clinical) Urology, St. Lukes-Roosevelt Hospital and Columbia University College of Physicians and Surgeons, New York, New York
(Chapter 80 Commentary)

A. PUIGVERT, M.D.
Institute de Urologia, Nefrologia y Andrologia, Hospital de la Santa Cruz y San Pablo, Barcelona, Spain
(Chapter 5 Commentary)

BISWAMAY RAY, M.D.
Assistant Clinical Professor, Surgery/Urology, Abraham Lincoln School of Medicine, University of Illinois Hospital, Chicago, Illinois
(Chapter 122 Commentary)

SHLOMO RAZ, M.D.
Associate Professor of Surgery-Urology, University of California School of Medicine, Los Angeles, California
(Chapter 114 Commentary)

ALAN B. RETIK, M.D.
Professor of Surgery (Urology), Harvard Medical School, Boston, Massachusetts; Chief, Division of Urology, Children's Hospital Medical Center, Boston, Massachusetts
(Chapters 38 and 39 Overview)

ROBERT K. RHAMY, M.D.
Professor of Urology, Vanderbilt University School of Medicine, Nashville, Tennessee
(Chapter 47 Overview)

FRANCIS H. RICHARDSON, M.D.
Attending Urologist, Victory Memorial Hospital, St. Therese Hospital, Waukegan, Illinois
(Chapter 116 Commentary)

JEROME P. RICHIE, M.D.
Associate Professor of Urological Surgery, Harvard Medical School, Boston, Massachusetts; Chief of Urologic Oncology, Brigham and Women's Hospital, Boston, Massachusetts; Consultant, Sidney Farber Cancer Center, Boston, Massachusetts
(Chapter 50 Commentary)

JAMES A. ROBERTS, M.D.
Professor of Urology, Tulane University School of Medicine, New Orleans, Louisiana; Senior Research Scientist, Delta Regional Primate Research Center, Covington, Louisiana
(Chapter 21 Overview)

MYRON S. ROBERTS, M.D.
Associate Clinical Professor, Columbia University College of Physicians and Surgeons, New York, New York; Director of Urology, Mount Vernon Hospital, New York, New York
(Chapter 49 Commentary)

JOEL W. ROSENBERG, M.D.
Assistant Professor of Urology, Department of Urology, New York University, New York, New York
(Chapter 31 Commentary)

STEPHEN N. ROUS, A.B., M.D., M.S. (Urology)
Professor and Chairman, Department of Urology, Medical University of South Carolina, Charleston, South Carolina
(Chapter 115 Overview)

RONALD W. SADLOWSKI, M.D.
Clinical Associate Professor of Surgery, Division of Urology, University of South Florida College of Medicine, Tampa, Florida
(Chapter 45 Commentary)

NADER SADOUGHI, M.D.
Professor, Division of Urology, Rush Presbyterian Hospital–St. Luke's Medical Center, Chicago, Illinois; Chief of Urology, Mount Sinai Medical Center, Chicago, Illinois
(Chapter 69 Commentary)

OSCAR SALVATIERRA, Jr., M.D.
Professor of Surgery & Urology, and Chief, Transplant Service, University of California, San Francisco, California
(Chapter 17 Commentary)

PETER L. SCARDINO, M.D.
Professor of Surgery/Urology, Medical College of Georgia, Savannah, Georgia; Director of Education for Urology, Memorial Medical Center, Savannah, Georgia
(Chapter 42 Overview)

PETER T. SCARDINO, M.D.
Associate Professor of Urology, Baylor College of Medicine, Houston, Texas
(Chapter 64 Commentary)

PAUL F. SCHELLHAMMER, M.D.
Associate Professor of Urology, Eastern Virginia Medical School, Norfolk, Virginia
(Chapter 66 Commentary)

MARTIN SCHIFF, Jr., M.D.
Professor, Section of Urology, Yale University School of Medicine, New Haven, Connecticut
(Chapter 12 Commentary)

JOSEPH D. SCHMIDT, M.D.
Professor of Surgery/Urology, and Head, Division of Urology, School of Medicine, University of California, San Diego, California; Consultant, Urology Section, Veterans Administration Medical Center, San Diego, California; Consultant Urologist, Naval Regional Medical Center, San Diego, California; Consulting Staff, Department of Surgery (Urology), Mercy Hospital and Medical Center, San Diego, California
(Chapter 52 Commentary)

STANWOOD S. SCHMIDT, M.D.
Research Associate in Urology, University of California Medical School, San Francisco, California
(Chapter 126 Commentary)

F. BRANTLEY SCOTT, M.D.
Professor of Urology, Baylor College of Medicine, Houston, Texas; Chief of Urology, St. Luke's Episcopal Hospital, Houston, Texas
(Chapter 114 Overview)

MANMEET SINGH, M.B.B.S., F.R.C.S.
Consultant Urologist, Whipps Cross Hospital, London, England; Late Senior Lecturer, Department of Urology, The London Hospital Medical College, London, England
(Chapter 109 Commentary)

DONALD G. SKINNER, M.D.
Professor of Surgery, and Chairman, Division of Urology, USC School of Medicine, Los Angeles, California
(Chapter 64 Commentary)

ROY W. SKOGLUND, Jr., M.D.
Clinical Assistant Professor, Department of Urology, University of Washington, Seattle, Washington
(Chapter 48 Commentary)

NORMAN SLADE, M.B., Ch.B., F.R.C.S.
Consultant Urologist, Southmead General Hospital, Bristol, England
(Chapter 111 Commentary)

MICHAEL P. SMALL, M.D.
Clinical Professor of Urology, University of Miami School of Medicine, Miami, Florida
(Chapter 103 Commentary)

ARTHUR D. SMITH, M.D.
Chief, Division of Urology, Department of Surgery, Long Island Jewish-Hillside Medical Center, Stony Brook, New York; Associate Professor, State University of New York at Stony Brook, Stony Brook, New York
(Chapter 25 Overview and Chapter 43 Commentary)

E. DURHAM SMITH, M.D., M.S., F.R.A.C.S.
Consultant Paediatric Surgeon, Royal Children's Hospital, Melbourne, Australia
(Chapter 98 Commentary)

THOMAS E. STARZL, M.D., Ph.D.
Professor of Surgery, University of Pittsburgh, Pittsburgh, Pennsylvania; Attending Surgeon, Veterans Administration Hospital, Children's Hospital of Pittsburgh, and Presbyterian University Hospital, Pittsburgh, Pennsylvania
(Chapters 12 through 15 Overview)

BRUCE H. STEWART, M.D. (deceased)
Chairman, Division of Surgery, and Member, Department of Urology, Cleveland Clinic Foundation, Cleveland, Ohio
(Chapter 16 Commentary)

STEVAN B. STREEM, M.D.
Assistant Professor of Surgery, Division of Urology, Ohio State University College of Medicine, Columbus, Ohio
(Chapter 1 Commentary)

JACQUES G. SUSSET, M.D.
Department of Surgery, Roger Williams General Hospital, Providence, Rhode Island
(Chapter 74 Overview)

ARTHUR N. TESSLER, M.D.
Professor of Clinical Urology, New York University School of Medicine, New York, New York
(Chapter 70 Overview)

SEIGI TSUCHIDA, M.D.
Professor and Chairman, Department of Urology, Akita University School of Medicine, Akita, Japan
(Chapter 25 Commentary)

DAVID T. UEHLING, M.D.
Professor of Surgery (Urology), University of Wisconsin Medical School, Madison, Wisconsin
(Chapter 40 Commentary)

E. DARRACOTT VAUGHAN, Jr., M.D.
Professor and Chairman, Division of Urology, The New York Hospital–Cornell Medical Center, New York, New York
(Chapters 80 through 82 Overview)

RALPH J. VEENEMA, M.D.
Professor of Clinical Urology, Columbia University College of Physicians and Surgeons, New York, New York
(Chapter 85 Commentary)

ROBERT S. WALDBAUM, M.D.
Clinical Associate Professor of Surgery (Urology), Cornell University Medical School, New York, New York; Director of Urology, North Shore University Hospital, Manhasset, New York
(Chapter 106 Overview)

DAVID M. WALLACE, C.B.E., M.S., F.R.C.S.
Former Consulting Surgeon, Royal Marsden Hospital, London, England; Former Professor of Urology, Riyadh Medical College, Riyadh, Saudi Arabia
(Chapters 64 through 68 Overview)

ANTHONY WALSH, F.R.C.S.I.
Senior Consultant Urologist, Jervis Street Hospital, Dublin, Ireland; Lecturer in Urology, Royal College of Surgeons, Dublin, Ireland
(Chapter 46 Commentary)

JOSEPH N. WARD, M.D., F.R.C.S. (Eng.), F.R.C.O.G.
Associate Clinical Professor, Columbia University College of Physicians & Surgeons, New York, New York
(Chapter 115 Commentary)

KEITH WATERHOUSE, M.A., M.B., B.Chir. (Cantab.), F.R.C.S.
Professor and Chairman, Department of Urology, Downstate Medical Center, Brooklyn, New York
(Chapter 24 Overview)

MICHAEL WECHSLER, M.D.
Assistant Professor of Clinical Urology, Columbia University College of Physicians and Surgeons, New York, New York; Assistant Attending Urologist, Presbyterian Hospital, New York, New York
(Chapter 85 Commentary)

RICHARD WEIL III, M.D.
Professor of Surgery and Director of Organ Transplantation, University of Colorado Medical Center, Denver, Colorado
(Chapters 12 through 15 Overview)

SIDNEY R. WEINBERG, M.D.
Chief of Urology, The Jewish Hospital and Medical Center of Brooklyn; Clinical Professor of Urology, Downstate Medical College, Brooklyn, New York
(Chapter 31 Commentary)

ROBERT M. WEISS, M.D.
Professor, Yale University School of Medicine, Section of Urology, New Haven, Connecticut
(Chapter 12 Commentary)

ROBERT H. WHITAKER, M.Chir., F.R.C.S.
Consultant Urologist, Addenbrooke's, Hospital, Cambridge, England; Associate Lecturer, University of Cambridge
(Chapter 41 Overview)

RALPH deVERE WHITE, M.D., F.R.C.S. (Edin.)
Associate Professor of Urology, Columbia University College of Physicians and Surgeons, New York, New York; Associate Attending Urologist, Columbia Presbyterian Hospital, New York, New York
(Chapter 77 Commentary)

E. DOUGLAS WHITEHEAD, M.D.
Assistant Clinical Professor of Urology, Mount Sinai School of Medicine, New York, New York; Associate Attending Urologist, Department of Urology, Beth Israel Medical Center, New York, New York
(Chapters 67 and 125 Commentaries)

J. E. A. WICKHAM, M.S., M.B., B.Sc., F.R.C.S
Director of the Academic Unit, Institute of Urology, University of London; Consultant Surgeon, St. Peter's Hospital, and Senior Consultant Urologist, St. Bartholomew's Hospital, London, ·England; Consulting Urologist to the Royal Air Force
  (Chapter 9 Commentary)

DONALD F. WILLIAMS, M.D.
Clinical Instructor, Department of Urology, UCLA School of Medicine, Los Angeles, California
  (Chapter 56 Commentary)

CHESTER C. WINTER, M.D.
Louis Levy Professor of Urology, Ohio State University Medical Center, Columbus, Ohio
  (Chapters 61 through 63 Overview)

GILBERT J. WISE, M.D.
Director of Urology, Maimonides Medical Center, Coney Island Hospital; Clinical Professor, Department of Urology, Downstate Medical Center, State University of New York, Brooklyn, New York
  (Chapter 10 Overview)

HENRY A. WISE II, M.D.
Director, Division of Urology, Ohio State University, Columbus, Ohio
  (Chapter 108 Commentary)

PETER H. L. WORTH, M.A., M.B., B.Chir., F.R.C.S.
Consultant Urological Surgeon, University College Hospital and St. Peter's Hospitals, London, England
  (Chapter 62 Commentary)

MENDLEY A. WULFSON, M.D., F.R.C.S.
Associate Attending Urologist, Passaic General Hospital and Beth Israel Hospital, Passaic, New Jersey; Assistant Clinical Professor, The Mount Sinai Medical Center, New York, New York
  (Chapter 81 Commentary)

JOHN D. YOUNG, Jr., M.D.
Professor and Head, Division of Urology, University of Maryland Hospital, Baltimore, Maryland
  (Chapter 1 Overview)

HARVEY A. ZAREM, M.D.
Professor of Surgery, UCLA School of Medicine; Chief, Division of Plastic and Reconstructive Surgery, UCLA Medical Center, Los Angeles, California
  (Chapter 101 Commentary)

THOMAS ZAYDON, Jr., M.D.
Clinical Instructor (Plastic Surgery), Louisiana State University Medical School, New Orleans, Louisiana
  (Chapter 99 Commentary)

ERNST J. ZINGG, M.D.
Professor of Urology and Head, Department of Urology, Inselspital, University of Berne, Switzerland
  (Chapter 33 Overview)

LEONARD ZINMAN, M.D.
Urological Consultant, Lahey Clinic Foundation, Boston, Massachusetts; Assistant Professor of Surgery, Harvard Medical School, Boston, Massachusetts
  (Chapter 54 Commentary)

ADRIAN W. ZORGNIOTTI, M.D.
Professor of Clinical Urology, New York University School of Medicine, New York, New York
  (Chapter 37 Commentary)

FOREWORD

It is a pleasure to provide these introductory remarks to the second edition of *Current Operative Urology* and to echo the comments of Dr. Robert S. Hotchkiss, who offered the foreword to the first edition. In common with Dr. Hotchkiss, I share concern over the volume of urologic literature and our individual abilities to comprehend and encompass the mounting mass of medical and surgical information available today. There exists a continuing need for synthesis of thought in urology as in other disciplines, and a comprehensive effort to codify current information on urologic surgical procedures is welcome indeed.

The stated objectives of *Current Operative Urology* in this expanded format are similar to those of the first edition: Drs. Whitehead and Leiter have given exhaustive scrutiny to the advances in urologic surgery of the past decade, assembled noteworthy and landmark papers in the respective areas, then gathered a panel of acknowledged experts for both commentary and overview of the many aspects of our specialty that command our careful attention. The editors are to be congratulated on their perception in choice of subject matter, their judicious selection of contributors, and—perhaps most of all—their diligence and attention to detail in compiling this information in the most useful manner. Readers will appreciate the substantial expansion in scope of this edition as compared with its predecessor, as well as the timeliness of the material included, since virtually every contribution in this volume reflects work accomplished within the past 10 years.

From the vantage point of personal experience, I can state categorically that it is impossible to provide complete or total attention to every aspect and nuance of urologic surgery. On the other hand, this volume treats a broad and sweeping panorama of a vast segment of our specialty in a thorough and gratifying fashion. All urologic surgeons can be grateful for this significant achievement.

James F. Glenn, M.D.
Professor of Urology and President
The Mount Sinai Medical Center
New York, New York

FOREWORD
TO THE FIRST EDITION

The huge mass of medical literature relating to urology has become so overwhelming that no individual has the time to accomplish a comprehensive review of all the material. Much valuable information in both English and foreign languages to be found in books, periodicals, reports of scientific symposia, and even in abstracts often escapes the attention of the student of urology, who becomes frustrated by an inability to review properly this gigantic and complex body of information. The loaded shelves of every institutional library give ample testimony to this impossible task. Those isolated from such facilities must cope with the additional disadvantage of an unavailability of current literature.

A special problem confronts the medical student and the physician engaged in a busy residency training program. Their limited exposure and experience has not yet given them the perspicuity to evaluate some of the material of a controversial character; they need some guidance and advice. Furthermore, every urologist is confronted with the problem of devoting a large segment of available time to patient care at the expense of reserving an adequate amount for reading and progressive self-education.

Dr. Whitehead became keenly aware of these problems while a resident in urology at the New York University Medical Center where he conceived the novel idea of collecting classical works of proven value in regard to urologic surgical principles. He denied himself the privilege of selecting articles of his own choice, but wisely resorted to the opinions of recognized experts, each of whom had developed special skill and expertise in regard to the topics assigned to them. Each of these contributing authors was asked to designate for reproduction the most valuable and significant report he had encountered in his own exhaustive review of the world literature. Each author was also requested to submit a commentary on the report and to supply annotations of other significant reports on the same topic, thereby giving balance and personal evaluation to the subject.

The discussions of surgical methods and techniques contained in these pages are noteworthy for their current practicality and applicability. Most procedures are within the scope and routines of every modern urologic surgeon, yet he will benefit by reviewing or becoming acquainted with the best descriptions on methodology culled from the recent literature.

This volume on operative urology in no way attempts to cover the multitude of important contributions on other aspects of experimental and clinical urology. The format, however, offers promise for similar treatment of other disciplines which likewise require the attention of urologists. There is ample justification to anticipate a complimentary reception of this text. It is hoped that Dr. Whitehead will be stimulated by success and will extend his efforts to treat other areas of urologic knowledge in a similar style.

Robert S. Hotchkiss, M.D.
Professor Emeritus of Urology
New York University School of Medicine
New York, New York

PREFACE

The second edition of *Current Operative Urology* is being published less than 10 years after the first edition, primarily because of the many recent surgical advances in our specialty. Subjects absent from the first edition but covered in this second edition include anatrophic nephrolithotomy; renal autotransplantation; percutaneous nephrostomy and cyst puncture; arterial embolization for renal carcinoma; surgical treatment of chyluria; renal and prostate biopsy techniques; retroperitoneal fibrosis; ureterostomy *in situ*; jejunal and ileocecal conduit diversions; urinary undiversion; continent vesicostomy; salvage cystectomy; infravesical diversion; internal urethrotomy; interstitial irradiation of prostatic carcinoma; endoscopic surgery of kidney, ureter, and urethra, and of bladder calculi; circumcision; Peyronie's disease; meatal reconstruction; external urethroplasty; surgery of testicular and testicular appendage torsion; treatment of urethral carcinoma; microsurgical vasovasostomy and epididymovasostomy. In addition, the recent changes in the surgical management of neurogenic bladder, intersex states, hypospadias, male transsexual surgery, and surgical treatment of erectile impotence and urinary incontinence are included.

The format of the first edition has been retained. Each author of a Commentary and Annotated Bibliography has selected one highly significant and outstanding paper in his area of expertise for reproduction *in toto,* and has critically reviewed his assigned subject and commented upon it, using the selected paper as the basis for his Commentary. With this format, newer operative procedures can be placed in perspective and compared with widely employed, established surgical methods of managing urologic problems. Each subject has then been reviewed by an Overviewer.

All of the contributing authorities have provided thoughtful, incisive, and, when necessary, provocative and controversial observations in presenting the current management of each of their subjects. Although most of the contributing authorities are from the United States, we have again solicited contributions from many urologists and notable non-urologists from out of the United States. The vast majority of the reproduced papers have been published within the last 10 years.

Within these covers, 235 recognized authorities have contributed 126 Commentaries and 88 Overviews that bring the reader up to date from the time of the original appearance of the 126 selected papers, to the present. In addition, over 750 additional papers have been reviewed in the Annotated Bibliographies and approximately 4000 references have been included. The expertise provided by the contributing authorities assures the quality of the 126 chapters.

We would like to express our gratitude to all of the contributing authorities; to our secretaries for their secretarial and photocopy assistance; to the Seymour J. Phillips Health Science Library of the Beth Israel Medical Center–Hospital for Joint Diseases Orthopaedic Institute; and to the J. B. Lippincott Company, for their continuing assistance and cooperation in the preparation of this publication.

E. Douglas Whitehead, M.D.
Elliot Leiter, M.D.

CONTENTS

PART ONE

SURGERY OF THE ADRENAL GLAND

1

HYPERPLASIA AND TUMORS OF THE ADRENAL CORTEX

J. H. Harrison, D. Jenkins and A. H. Bennett

Division of Urology, Department of Surgery, Harvard Medical School, Peter Bent
Brigham Hospital, Boston, Mass.

Urologia Internationalis
Secretarius generalis: GEORGES MAYOR, Zürich
S. KARGER—BASEL/NEW YORK (Printed in Switzerland)
SEPARATUM

Urol. int. 27: 81–117 (1972)

ABSTRACT—An outline of the important historical events relative to surgery of the adrenals since Thomas Addison's brilliant description in 1855 will be brought up-to-date. The pathologic physiology of hyperadrenocorticism due to both hyperplasia and neoplasm of the adrenal cortex will be described. Biochemical abnormalities of each type of pathology will be summarized. The changes in inorganic metabolism, organic metabolism, cellular effects and sexual effects will be outlined in detail. Various methods of laboratory valuation of the adrenal cortical function will be described. Biochemical techniques for differentiation of the various hyperfunctioning states of the adrenal cortex from both hyperplasia and tumor are described in detail. The diagnosis and treatment of hyperadrenocorticism due to hyperplasia is considered and followed by a similar discussion of neoplasms both malignant and benign of the adrenal cortex causing hyperadrenocorticism. The syndromes of hyperaldosteronism, the adrenogenital syndrome and the feminizing adrenogenital syndrome in male are each discussed in detail. The experience of the Peter Bent Brigham Hospital urologic service during the last twenty years in collaboration with the metabolic service of Dr. George W. Thorn is summarized with reference to the management of hyperadrenocorticism. During this period, there were 63 patients operated upon for hyperadrenocorticism due to adrenocortical hyperplasia, 74 patients were explored for adrenal tumors both cortex and medulla. Currently there have been 23 patients having pheochromocytoma from whom a total of 28 tumors have been removed. This latter series will be reported elsewhere.

Author's address: J. Hartwell Harrison, M.D., F. A. C. S., Division of Urology, Department of Surgery, Harvard Medical School, Peter Bent Brigham Hospital, 721 Huntington Avenue, *Boston, MA 02115* (USA)

Key Words
Hyperadrenocorticism
Hyperplasia of the adrenal cortex
Adenoma of the adrenal cortex
Carcinoma of the adrenal cortex
Aldosterone adenoma
Cyst of the adrenal cortex
Pathophysiology of hyperadrenocorticism
Biochemical alterations in hyperadrenocorticism

HISTORICAL EVENTS WITH RELATION TO THE ADRENALS

The first clinical intimation of the function of the adrenal glands occurred in 1855 when Thomas Addison[1] gave his brilliant description of the condition which bears his name. He correlated the findings at autopsy of destruction of the adrenal glands by tuberculosis with symptoms of severe wasting, fatigue, and pigmentation noted during life. In 1895 Oliver and Schaefer[2] demonstrated the pressor effect of adrenal medullary extract by showing its ability to raise the blood pressure and pulse of a cat. Cannon[3] in 1914 discovered the close relationship of the action of the thoracolumbar autonomic nervous system to that of adrenal medullary extract and found that adrenin-like substances were secreted at the nerve endings. Holmes[4] described the first removal of an adrenal tumor by Thornton in 1899. This tumor weighed 20 pounds, recurrence did not occur, the patient's state of virilism reverted to normal and she continued in good health thereafter. Holmes' description of this tumor showed that it was derived from the adrenal cortex by histologic criteria. Identification of epinephrine and later norepinephrine as products of the adrenal medulla and the sympathetic ganglion constituted a most important discovery. Cushing[5] in 1912 and in 1932[6] described the syndrome which now bears his name and attributed the pathologic physiology to a basophilic adenoma of the anterior pituitary. His work has great importance in relation to both primary and secondary operations of the adrenal glands. Mayo[7] in 1927 removed the first pheochromocytoma, and Pincoffs[8] in 1929 made the first preoperative diagnosis of pheochromocytoma. Crile[9] manifested an intensive interest in the comparative anatomy and physiology of the adrenal glands as well as the relation of these organs to hypertension in human beings. Young[10] in 1937 summarized the literature available at that time on surgery of the adrenal cortex, summarizing the results of surgical intervention in 33 adults and 31 children having tumors of the adrenal cortex. Thorn[11] in 1940 showed the efficacy of desoxycorticosterone acetate in the treatment of patients having Addison's disease. Reichstein and Shoppee[12] at Basle and Kendall et al.[13] at the Mayo Clinic in 1936 simultaneously isolated, identified and synthesized cortisone

acetate. It remained, however, for Hench et al.[14] at the Mayo Clinic in 1950 to illustrate the physiologic benefits of this substance in the treatment of rheumatoid arthritis and for Thorn et al.[15] subsequently in 1952 to show that cortisone acetate and desoxycorticosterone acetate furnished substitution therapy adequate for survival and normal existence after bilateral total adrenalectomy in human beings. Huggins[16] in 1944 carried out the first bilateral total adrenalectomy in man and temporary survival was accomplished with Thorn's assistance by means of adrenocortical extract and desoxycorticosterone acetate. Li et al.[17] working with Armour Laboratories isolated adrenocorticotrophic hormone from beef pituitary. In 1947 Goldenberg et al.[18] published their work with benzodioxane showing its transitory effect in producing a fall in blood pressure in patients having sustained hypertension due to pheochromocytoma. In 1952 Gifford et al.[19] described the similar effects of phentolamine and elaborated the importance of this substance in differentiating hypertension due to pheochromocytoma. In 1954 Simpson et al.[20] accomplished the isolation and crystallization of aldosterone. In 1955 Conn[21] at the University of Michigan described the clinical condition of hyperaldosterone and emphasized the significance of alkalosis and hypokalemia clinically in patients having hypertension, suggesting the possibility of the presence of this condition. It is now 19 years since the first bilateral total adrenalectomy was performed at the Peter Bent Brigham Hospital and the patient treated successfully with prolonged survival because of cortisone acetate and desoxycorticosterone-acetate therapy.[22] Since then the indications for total and subtotal adrenalectomy have been clearly defined.[23]

HYPERADRENOCORTICISM DUE TO HYPERPLASIA AND NEOPLASMA OF THE ADRENAL CORTEX

The adrenal glands have attained a growing importance in the practice of urology due to the anatomic location in the natural domain of the urologic surgeon, the availability of adequate adrenocortical substitution therapy, increased knowledge of the pathophysiology of adrenal disorders, greater appreciation of the effects of adrenocortical disorders on sexual differentiation and new insight into renal-adrenal interrelations in the regulation of blood pressure and blood volume.

Surgical Anatomy. For a detailed review of the surgical anatomy of the adrenals the reader is referred to Campbell's 'Urology'.[24]

Hormone Secretion of the Adrenal Cortex. Although more than 40 steroids have been isolated from the adrenal cortex only a few are actively secreted. The major secretory product in man having glucocorticoid action is cortisol. Corticosterone has been isolated but only in small amounts. Aldosterone is the major mineral corticoid. Quantitatively dehydroepiandrosterone sulfate is the main androgen. Smaller amounts of 11β-hydroxy-Δ5-androstenedione and dehydroepiandrosterone are also secreted. While compounds having estrogenic and progestational activity may be released in minute amounts by normal adrenals the contribution is so small that they are not ordinarily classified as adrenal cortical hormones. In certain abnormalities of biosynthesis those steroids may be secreted in relatively large amounts to cause hormonal disturbances. This is certainly the case in the rare instances of feminizing tumors of the adrenal cortex.

Steroid Metabolism. The major circulating glucocorticoid is cortisol. According to Daughaday[25] most of the circulating cortisol is bound to a specific *a*-globulin, transcortin or corticosteroid-binding globulin (CBG). The bound cortisol is in reversible equilibrium with a small part of presolution and in all likelihood it is the latter fraction which is directly involved in the biologic actions of the hormone. When the binding sites of CBG become saturated at plasma cortisol levels of 20–27 μg/100 mil, the quantity present in free solution rises significantly. One effect of protein binding is to reduce the glomerular filtration of cortisol. In contrast, the hormonally inactive metabolites of cortisol, conjugated mainly as water-soluble glucuronides, are not protein bound and are excreted much more efficiently by the kidneys. The half-life of free cortisol in plasma is 60–100 min; this relatively rapid rate of removal is accompanied by the liver. Cortisol and cortisone are interchangeable via reversible reduction oxydation at C-1. The reduction of cortisone produces tetrahydrocortisone and cortilone. In adults the average daily urinary excretion of these metabolites is tetrahydrocortisone 5 mg; tetrahydrocortisol 3 mg; cortol plus cortilones 3 mg; and 11-hydroxylated 17-ketosteroids 1–2 mg. Only a very small fraction of cortisol is excreted unchanged into the urine: 20–125 μg/day.

The metabolic turnover of aldosterone is more rapid, possibly because it is only weakly bound to protein. Aldosterone undergoes reduction to tetrahydro derivatives in conjunction with glucuronic acid. However, a small fraction appears in the urine probably as a glucuronide conjugated at C-18 which is usually estimated in the clinical laboratory and, on the average, amounts to 5–15 μg/day.

Dehydroepiandrosterone and Δ5-androstenedione are reduced to androsterone and etiocholanolone. These 17-ketosteroids are also conjugated at the C-3 position in the liver and excreted in the urine as sulfates or glucuronides. Testosterone is the most important androgen

in man and its output primarily reflects testicular activity and serves as an excellent index of Leydig cell function. However, in some adrenal disorders overt virilization occurs reflecting potent androgen is testosterone. It appears that much of the testosterone originates from peripheral (probably hepatic) metabolism of normal adrenal cortical products to testosterone rather than from adrenal secretion of testosterone.[26] Just as the placenta may utilize the adrenal dehydroepiandrosterone derivatives to produce estrogen, the liver can also utilize adrenal androgens to produce testosterone. It has been shown that dehydroepiandrosterone and its sulfate can be converted by the liver to testosterone but only in minute amounts. Present evidence indicates that Δ + 5-androstenedione is the main peripheral precursor,[27] forming both testosterone glucuronide and testosterone, some of which reenters the circulation as active hormone. In normal females as much as 50% of the small amount of circulating testosterone may be derived from androstenedione of adrenal and ovarian origin.[28]

Functions of the Adrenal Cortex. The cortical hormones influence the function of all body cells in both inorganic and organic metabolism. The inorganic functions comprise sodium retention and an increased excretion of potassium and hydrogen ions. Steroids controlling these functions have been called mineralocorticoids. The organic functions related to the control of carbohydrate, fat and protein metabolism are controlled by glucocorticoids. The distinction between mineralocorticoids and glucocorticoids is by no means complete because cortisol has a significant effect on electrolyte metabolism in addition to its other actions. Other hormones exhibit their full actions only in the presence of small amounts of glucocorticoids such as fat mobilization by epinephrine or vasoconstriction by norepinephrine requiring the presence of small amounts of cortisol for these actions to take place.

Inorganic Metabolism. The absence of the adrenal cortex results in sodium chloride and water loss leading to hyponatremia, dehydration, a reduction of plasma volume, hypotension and, in extreme cases, vascular shock. In addition, the excretion of potassium may be inadequate to prevent the accumulation of circulating as well as tissue potassium. Excessive secretion may result in lowered blood and tissue levels of potassium which can be severe enough to produce characteristic abnormalities of neuromuscular and cardiac function. Hypokalemia may be accompanied by hypochloremia and an elevated level of plasma CO_2. Regulation of electrolyte secretion is influenced predominantly by aldosterone acting on the ion exchange mechanism of the distal renal tubules.

Organic Metabolism. Adrenal cortical failure causes inability to maintain normal blood sugar concentration during fasting. The defect results primarily from a decrease in hepatic gluconeogenesis normally regulated by cortisol. Aldosterone is largely devoid of this action at physiologic levels. An excess of cortisol produces hyperglycemia and glycosuria (steroid diabetes in some patients).

Regulation of gluconeogenesis depends primarily on the influence of cortisol on the balance between synthesis and degradation of proteins: Synthesis from amino acid precursors is diminished and it is possible that the breakdown of cellular proteins is accelerated. The amino acid residues are deaminized in the liver with the resulant decrease in the production of urea and in the formation of liver glycogens. The net result is a deviation of body proteins to available carbohydrates.

Cellular Effects. With excessive levels of cortisol the changes in protein metabolism impair body growth, interfere with the formation of osteoid tissue resulting in osteoporosis and interfere with wound healing. Muscular strength simultaneously is diminished.

Cortisol overdosage produces neutrophilic leucocytosis, eosinopenia, lymphopenia and reduction in fixed lymphoid tissue. The structure of all connective tissue elements including reticular cells, fibrils and gland substance may be affected. The reactivity of mesenchymal tissues to irritants, foreign protein and bacteria is impaired. As a result of these deleterious effects the ability to withstand injury and particularly infection may be seriously deranged. Large doses of cortisol reduce the production of antibodies presumably by the lysis of fixed plasma cells and lymphocytes. Cortisol increases gastric acidity and pepsin production. Psychiatric disturbances may occur when it is given in excess. The production of angiotensinogen is enhanced by cortisol leading to higher levels of angiotensin, an extremely potent vasoconstrictor and stimulator of aldosterone production. In addition, cortisol sensitizes the arterioles to the pressor effects of norepinephrine. Primary adrenal failure is associated with increased deposition of melanin in the skin. The increased pigmentation is due to elevated plasma levels of ACTH. One portion of the corticotrophin molecule is identical in structure with the melanocyte-stimulating hormone.

Sexual Effects. The adrenal cortex secretes steroids which are weakly androgenic normally. The growth of axillary hair and pubic hair in females appears to be partially controlled by adrenal androgens. It is probable that in females the adrenal androgens provide a weak anabolic effect enhancing protein synthesis from amino acids. However, with hyperplasia of the zona reticularis or tumors involving this segment of the cortex excessive hair growth, oligomenorrhea, amenorrhea and greatly increased muscularity will occur from the increased production of potent androgen by the lesion of the adrenal cortex. Extensive studies have showed that the adrenal cortex plays a significant role in the normal response to major stress.[29] The importance of an adequate adrenal response to changes in the external environment and to dislocations of the internal milieu is best demonstrated by the marked vulnerability of the patients with adrenocortical insufficiency to stress of all types. Engle has showed that a normal circulating level of cortisol may be adequate to resist brief stresses of moderate intensity. However, with prolonged or severe insults the pituitary adrenal cortical system is activated, primarily as a results of neurohormonal stimuli involving the hypothalmus with resultant acceleration of cortisol production. It has been repeatedly demonstrated that major surgical procedures constitute a serious stress eliciting a marked increase in adrenocortical secretion. Therefore it is evident:

(a) Activation of the pituitary adrenal cortical system is requisite to the safe conduct of major surgery; (b) patients with adrenocortical insufficiency cannot be safely subjected to surgical procedures unless adequate quantities of cortisol are administered; (c) surgery directed toward the removal of the adrenal glands can only be safely performed when cortical steroid substitution therapy is available; (d) the resection of functioning adrenocortical tumors and the performance of either subtotal or total adrenalectomy require preoperative corticosteroid preparation and postoperative hormonal maintenance.

Control of Adrenocortical Function. Growth and maintenance of normal adrenocortical structure are controlled by corticotrophin from the anterior pituitary gland as demonstrated by the influence of ACTH on the incorporation of C-14 acetate into adrenal proteins. Corticotrophin regulates the synthesis and secretion of cortisol and the adrenocortical sex steroids. This hormone alphcorticotrophin has been isolated and is a polypeptide with 39 amino acids and a molecular weight of 4,540. Human corticotrophin has been purified and is almost identical with ACTH from animal sources.[30] Certain basophilic cells in the anterior pituitary gland appear to be the source of corticotrophin since fluorsine-labeled antibodies to corticotrophin are found by these cells.

Schally and Bowers[31] and others have extracted from hypothalamic tissue corticotrophin-releasing factors which augment ACTH secretion by the pituitary gland. Since the hypothalamus has long been regarded as the head ganglion of the autonomic nervous system it is probable that the emergency stress responses of both the adrenal medulla and the adrenal cortex are regulated and correlated by the hypothalamus. Ganong[32] has shown that cortisol has an important role in regulating the rate of corticotrophic secretion, probably through its effects on the hypothalamic production CRF. A fall in plasma cortisol leads to a rise in corticotrophin output and conversely a rise in cortisol inhibits corticotrophin secretion. This servomechanism maintains the level of plasma cortisol within stable limits. Protracted administration of cortisol may so effectively inhibit hypothalmic pituitary function that adrenocortical atrophy ensues. This has been observed in patients with carcinoma of the prostate and carcinoma of the breast treated with steroids.

Several mechanisms have been recognized in the control of an aldosterone output:

(a) Corticotrophin does increase aldosterone secretion but the effect is far less than that on cortisol output and is not sustained so that the secretion rate returns to previous levels despite continued corticotrophin administration.

(b) An elevated serum potassium level appears to lead directly to increased aldosterone secretion.

(c) The primary mechanisms for control of aldosterone production appear to reside in a feedback system involving the kidney rather than the hypothalamic pituitary system. The sensor apparatus resides in the juxtaglomerular apparatus and decreased renal blood flow causes an increased release of renin which acts on the circulating globulin to produce angiotensin I and the latter is converted into angiotensin II by a specific plasma enzyme. Angiotensin II is a stimulator of the zona glomerulosa of the adrenal cortex resulting in increase of aldosterone output. The common stimuli of increased aldosterone secretion are sodium restriction, reduction in intravascular volume, hemorrhage and dehydration.

Laboratory Evaluation of Adrenocortical Function.
For years measurement of the urinary 17-ketosteroids was a major method for evaluating adrenocortical activity and was viewed as the index of adrenal androgen secretion. Although the procedure does reflect the output of steroids with androgenic activity, the implied correlation with androgenicity is often lacking because testosterone is the most potent androgen and is not a 17-ketosteroid while etiocholanolone is one of the major 17-ketosteroids and has very weak androgenic activity. The measurement of the urinary 17-ketosteroids does provide a reliable index of adrenocortical secretion of cortisol. Normal range for adult males is 7–20 mg/24 h and for females 5–15 mg/24 h. Over the age of 40 the excretion gradually declines. One-third of the urinary 17-ketosteroids in males arises in the testis. The urinary 17-ketosteroids often fail to provide a good index for adrenal function and hyperadrenocorticism. In Cushing's syndrome normal levels are found in many patients with adrenocortical hyperplasia or adrenal adenoma but high values usually accompany adrenal carcinoma. In adrenal tumors producing only virilizing effects urinary 17-ketosteroids are significantly elevated.

Urinary 17-hydroxycorticoids are measured by the Porter-Silber[33] technique and measure chiefly tetrahydrocortisone and tetrahydrocortisol. While the excretion of urinary 17-hydroxycorticoids does not always reflect the plasma cortisol level, the correlation in most circumstances is excellent and affords a reasonably good guide to adrenocortical activity. Patients with hyperadrenocorticism leading to increased cortisol secretion show in most instances elevated urinary 17-hydroxycorticoids. These patients may also show an increase in urinary corticoid levels but plasma cortisol values are often normal which reflects an increased rate of cortisol catabolism. Normal values for excretion of 17-hydroxycorticoids in adult males are 4–12 mg/day and in the female 2–10 mg/day.

Many prefer Norimbursky's technique for measuring a larger fraction of urinary cortisol metabolites known as the urinary 17-ketogenic steroids. Normal values are higher. Adult males excrete 8–22 mg/day and adult females 5–18 mg/day. The urinary 17-ketogenic steroids are said to show a higher correlation with actual cortisol secretion rates than Porter-Silber chromagens.

The plasma cortisol level is an important index of adrenocortical activity and measures the 17-hydroxycorticoid steroids of the plasma. Approximately 85% of the material in human plasma reacts with phenylhydrazine in sulphuric acid as cortisol. In normal subjects the normal concentration ranges from 5–20 μg/100 ml. Plasma cortisol shows diurnal fluctuations, the highest values being found at 6–9 a.m. with a slow decline thereafter to a minimum between midnight and 2 a.m. Alteration in the diurnal pattern may be important in interpreting the physiologic significance of plasma hormone levels. It is clear that the concentration of plasma cortisol does not always reflect the rate of secretion by the adrenal cortex. A normal plasma level in the presence of a decreased rate of disposal suggests decreased secretion of steroid while a normal level and the presence of an increased rate of degradation suggest increased secretion. In order to resolve such uncertainties isotopic cortisol can be utilized to obtain a more quantitative measure of adrenal cortical secretion.[34,35] Cortisol production rate in normal adults is 16 ± 6 mg/24 h. Isotopic methods of estimating actual production rates of steroids are very informative and specific diagnostic techniques.

Aldosterone. Plasma levels of aldosterone are so low as to be of limited practical value. Urinary aldosterone determinations are presently used and constitute the three oxometabolites which are measured. This represents about 10% of the aldosterone secreted daily. Normal values range from 5–20 μg/day. Accuracy in the measurement of this small moiety has been greatly enhanced by using the double isotope derivative dilution technique of Peterson.[36] It is important to remember that sodium depletion stimulates an increased secretion of aldosterone and thus evaluation requires circumstances with a normal salt intake.

Testosterone. The most potent naturally occuring androgen is testosterone from the testis. However, in certain virilizing disorders significant quantities of this hormone or its immediate precursors which can be converted to testosterone in the liver are secreted from the adrenal. Methods involving gas liquid chromatography[37] or double isotope derivative dilution[38] are available for the measurement of testosterone in plasma or urine. The plasma concentration appears to be the most useful method because urinary values may be deceptive because of the conversion of steroids to urinary conjugates of testosterone. Plasma testosterone in the normal adult male ranges from 0.3–1 μg/100 ml. Urinary values for testosterone glucuronide vary with the methodology employed but most authors have found 30–150 μg/24 h in adult males and only 4–15 μg/24 h in normal females.

Adrenal Cortical Stimulation. The response to corticotrophin is a specific test of adrenocortical reserve function. ACTH is given intravenously, 20–40 USP units of lyophilized hormone in a 6–8 hour infusion. It may be given intramuscularly, 60–80 units of ACTH Gel. Normal subjects show the following responses to an 8-hour infusion of ACTH: Urinary 17-ketogenic steroids increase to a level of 30–55 mg/24 h, 17-hydroxycorticosteroids rise to 15–30 μg/100 ml. A rapid screening test can be done using plasma cortisol values before and after a 1–2 hour infusion of ACTH: The values rise to 30–40 μg/100 ml.

Adrenocortical Suppression. Elevated levels of plasma cortisol suppress pituitary secretion of corticotrophin and adrenocortical function falls to a low level. The administration of very potent synthetic glucocorticoids inhibits adrenal activity but will not contribute significantly to the results of corticosteroid measurement. Dexamethazone is usually used since its ACTH-suppressing activity is approximately 30 times that of cortisol. The dosage is 5 mg orally every 6 h for 2–3 days. Normally the urinary 17-ketogenic steroids decline to less than 6 mg/24 h, the 17-hydroxycorticoids fall below 3 mg for 24 h and plasma cortisol to a level under 5 μg/100 ml. A more rapid procedure consists of 1 mg of dexamethazone given orally at midnight, plasma cortisol is drawn

the following morning and is normally less than 10 μg/100 ml and usually less than 3 μg/100 ml. From the foregoing facts an understanding of the underlying biochemistry in hyperplasia, adenoma and carcinoma of the adrenal cortex is greatly increased. By means of the foregoing laboratory measurements differentiation of these conditions in the clinic is accomplished.

Hyperadrenocorticism is a state of increased adrenocortical hyperfunction which may be caused by hyperplasia, adenoma or carcinoma. A variety of clinical syndromes may result from each of these lesions.

HYPERADRENOCORTICISM OR INCREASED ADRENAL CORTICAL HYPERFUNCTION

The adrenal cortex secretes cortisol, aldosterone and other corticosteroids, androgens, estrogens and progesterone. In different clinical disorders the gland may secrete an excess of one or more of these compounds. A variety of clinical syndromes may occur as a result of different lesions such as bilateral cortical hyperplasia, benign tumor or malignant tumor.

Cushing's Syndrome. Cushing's syndrome properly defined refers to the clinical picture described in 1932 by Cushing. The disease is comparatively rare, occurs mostly in young adults and is 3–5 times more common in females than males. The clinical features of this syndrome reflect the metabolic phenomena resulting from excessive levels of cortisol.

Pathogenesis. In 75% of patients having Cushing's syndrome no adrenal neoplasm is present but hyperfunction of the adrenal cortex occurs as a result of hyperplasia. Cushing postulated that in these cases the disorder rose from a pituitary basophilic adenoma. At the same time he recognized the fact that adrenal tumors could cause the identical clinical picture and stated that when the same features characterized the syndrome of basophile adenoma they in all probability are secondarily ascribable to a hypersecretory influence of the adrenal cortex even in the absence of any histologically appreciable abnormality. Subsequent studies failed to confirm the pituitary basophilic tumors as the important cause of the disease and opinion swung to the view that the adrenocortical hyperplasia could be primary. However, it is now clear that the anterior pituitary gland is indeed importantly involved. There are cases of basophilic pituitary adenomas found, but more often a chromophobe tumor is encountered leading to the suggestion that the apparent chromophobe cells are very actively secreting cells of chromophilic origin. In 25% of cases an adrenocortical neoplasm is found. Somewhat more than one half of these tumors are benign. Benign tumors may or may not be independent of corticotrophic control. Malignant tumors are usually autonomous. Rarely an adrenal rest tumor arises in ectopic adrenocortical tissue, most commonly located in the perinephric area but also found near the celiac axis, ovaries, testis, or elsewhere. When an adrenal tumor is the primary source of excess cortisol, pituitary ACTH output is suppressed and nontumorous adrenal tissue is atrophic. In 1967 Liddle[39] has showed direct and indirect evidence that the majority of patients with Cushing's syndrome due to adrenocortical hyperplasia had increased secretion of ACTH. In most cases plasma corticotrophin levels are moderately elevated, in others the concentration is in the upper normal range. Patients with Cushing's disease do not show a normal decline in plasma corticotrophin late in the day, explaining a lack of diurnal variation in plasma cortisol excretion. It would appear to be an increased pituitary production of ACTH that leads to adrenocortical hyperplasia and increased secretion of cortisol in hyperadrenocorticism. It has been shown that reduction in cortisol output by adrenalectomy results in further elevation of ACTH while the administration of additional cortisol produces a fall in plasma ACTH. Therefore, it has been suggested that the primary defect in Cushing's disease may reside in the hypothalamus whereby the center controlling corticotrophin-releasing factor is reset so that higher than normal levels of plasma cortisol are required to inhibit CRF output.

Paraendocrine tumors such as oat-cell bronchogenic carcinoma, carcinoma of the liver, carcinoma of the prostate, carcinoma of the breast may be responsible for hyperadrenocorticism simulating Cushing's syndrome. These patients have elevated plasma levels of a material which is biologically, chemically and immunologically indistinguishable from ACTH. The source of this substance is the malignant tumor; pituitary corticotrophin is suppressed. The adrenal lesion is adrenocortical hyperplasia.

Signs and Symptoms. Cushing described the syndrome including a truncal type of obesity, amenorrhea in females or impotence in males, hypertrichosis in females, purplish cutaneous striae, plethora, hypertension, muscular weakness, a buffalo hump due to cervical kyphosis, osteoporosis, glycosuria, erythemia, edema, proteinuria and a marked susceptibility to infection.

The obesity produces classic moon fascies and prominent fat deposits in the dorsocervical, supraclavicular and subscapular areas. Suppression of gonadal function is common and hirsutism occurs in many females but true virilization is unusual. Hypertension is frequently present and sometimes persists in long standing cases despite cure of other signs and symptoms. The effects of excess cortisol produces muscle weakness, osteoporosis with decalcification of the bones, easy bruisability and ecchymoses. Purplish striae are found in about ⅔ of the patients. Mental disturbances ranging from emotional lability to major psychoses usually of a depressive or paranoid type appear frequently.

Laboratory Findings. Circulating eosinophiles are below 100 cells/ml³ in 90% of patients and moderate neutrophilic leucocytosis is often found. The hematocrit is usually within normal range but mild elevation is occasionally present particularly in those patients producing excessive androgens. Hypokalemia sometimes accompanied by hypochloremia and metabolic alkalosis is usually restricted to those with severe disease. Three-fourths of the patients exhibit intermittent glycosuria but overt diabetes occurs in a much smaller number. There is an increased incidence of nephrolithiasis as a result of the enhanced urinary calcium excretion secondary to progressive osteoporosis. Occasionally hyperuricemia and uric acid calculi are found. Osteoporosis is most marked in the spine and pelvis but in severe long standing cases even the skull may be involved and fractures of vertebrae, ribs and pelvis can occur from mild trauma.

Diagnosis. The diagnosis of Cushing's syndrome may be confirmed by measurement of an increase in adrenocortical production of cortisol. It is desirable to obtain information concerning the underlying lesion-bilateral adrenocortical hyperplasia or neoplasia. Direct measurement of cortisol by isotope dilution of cortisol production rate is preferably accomplished with urinary metabolite method. The value exceeds 30 mg/day in most patients with Cushing's syndrome. The chromatographic isolation of free cortisol in urine and quantitation by the Porter-Silber procedure gives values in excess of 150 mg/day. Measurement of the 24-hour excretion of 17-ketogenic steroids or 17-hydroxycorticoids shows levels are increased in the majority of patients but in mild cases borderline or normal results may be encountered. Plasma cortisol concentrations are usually elevated but in some patients are only in the upper range of normal. The best evidence in favor of the diagnosis comes from a demonstration that the feedback control of adrenocortical function is abnormal: (a) The diurnal variation of plasma cortisol levels is lost so that morning and evening values fall within the same range; (b) a single oral dose of dexamethasone (1.0 mg) given at midnight, fails to elicit the normal degree of pituitary-adrenocortical suppression; plasma cortisol measured the following morning is above 10 μg/100 ml and often above 20 μg/100 ml; (c) while cortisol production is regularly suppressed in normal subjects given small doses of dexamethasone (0.5 mg every 6 h for 48 h) little or no suppression occurs in patients with Cushing's syndrome.[40] A normal response is a decrease of urinary 17-hydroxycorticoids to less than 3 mg/day or of urinary 17-ketogenic steroids to less than 6 mg/day, demonstrating that the hypothalamic pituitary system responds appropriately to an increase in plasma glucocorticoid levels. Lack of suppression in patients with adrenal hyperplasia appears to indicate that the hypothalamic pituitary axis is reset to a higher threshold.

Determination of the type of causative adrenal lesion is accomplished by pharmacologic tests: (a) pituitary adrenal suppression with dexamethasone, (b) adrenocortical stimulation by ACTH and (c) pituitary activation by metyrapone.

Suppression of urinary corticoid excretion values to less than half the baseline can be demonstrated in patients with adrenal hyperplasia. Patients with adrenal neoplasms, either benign or malignant, ordinarily fail to show a significant fall of plasma or urinary steroids even with large doses of dexamethasone.

Patients with adrenocortical hyperplasia usually demonstrate increased reactivity to exogenous adrenocorticotrophic hormone. Following a standard 8-hour intravenous infusion of corticotrophin a hyperactive response is evidenced by an excessive rise in plasma cortisol and urinary 17-hydroxycorticosteroids or 17-ketogenic steroids. The response of benign adenomas is variable. Adrenal carcinoma is usually resistant to stimulation reflecting the autonomy of the tumor tissue and atrophy of the contralateral gland.[41]

Patients with adrenal hyperplasia demonstrate a hyperactive response to metyrapone reflected by an excessive rise in urinary 17-hydroxycorticoids or 17-ketogenic steroids. In contrast, patients with benign or malignant adrenocortical tumors show a failure of the urinary steroids to rise because after the administration of metyrapone corticotrophin is not released in the normal manner. Very high levels of urinary corticosteroids and 17-ketosteroids suggest the presence of an adrenocortical tumor. Gross increase in dehydroepiandrosterone occurs in most of these cases. In the case of nonendocrine tumors producing corticotrophin of ACTH like peptides, baseline plasma cortisol and urinary steroid values are often markedly elevated. These are difficult to differentiate from hyperplasia of the adrenal cortex. These patients usually exhibit responsiveness to ACTH unless endogenous ACTH secretion by the tumor approaches the level at which maximal adrenocortical activation occurs but no suppression with dexamethasone, even in high dosage levels. No increase in urinary corticosteroids follows metyrapone administration. Plasma ACTH levels are also significantly elevated.

The major difficulty in differential diagnosis arises in patients with obesity, hypertension and diabetes mellitus, especially in females with these disorders accompanied by hirsutism. Extreme obesity is uncommon in Cushing's syndrome and in exogenous obesity the distribution of excess fat is generalized and not truncal. The baseline urinary steroid values in exogenous obesity are often moderately elevated but the diurnal variation is intact. Very obese patients may show a hyperactive response to ACTH but dexamethasone suppression occurs normally. Patients with chronic active hepatic disease or carcinoma of the liver may exhibit clinical changes reminiscent of Cushing's syndrome probably because of an impaired ability to metabolize cortisol. Plasma cortisol secretion rates are within the normal range.

Hyperpigmentation in patients with Cushing's syndrome points to an extraadrenal neoplasm producing excessive quantities of corticotrophin. The responsible lesion may be a pituitary tumor most commonly a chromophobe adenoma. The sella turcica may be enlarged depending upon the size of the lesion. In some cases these tumors have actually been invasive producing severe headaches and visual disturbances including ophthalmoplegia. Hyperpigmentation occurs in paraendocrine lesions producing corticotrophin-like polypeptides. These tumors may be bronchogenic in origin, the adrenal medulla, thymus, pancreas, liver, ovary, thyroid, parotid gland, prostate and other organs also have been involved. Obesity is usually absent in these patients and hypokalemic alkalosis is often severe.

Techniques for Visualization of the Adrenal Glands. Radiologic evidence of adrenal tumors should be sought initially on the plain film of the abdomen followed by excretory urography. A greatly increased yield will be obtained by combining excretory urography with tomography or laminography. The insufflation of air or gas with tomography is no longer necessary. In fact, evidence now points to the fact that erroneous conclusions have been drawn more often from pneumograms than not. Fifty-eight deaths have occurred with air, oxygen or helium whereas none have occurred with carbon dioxide or nitrous oxide because of the latters high solubility.

Adrenal angiography, both arterial and venous, have added the most active radiologic visualization of the adrenal glands and have furnished the most accurate visual differentiation of hyperplasia, adenoma and carcinoma. The refined selective characterization of the arteries and veins of the adrenal gland have furnished not only more accurate visualization but also the possibility of carrying out biochemical measurements of steroids in the venous effluent. Great care must be taken during venography because of the fragility of the gland and the possibility of hemorrhage and rupture. Increasing experience is being obtained by the radiologist in the characterization of the vessels of both the kidney and the adrenal. The biochemical measurements of the venous effluent are becoming increasingly accurate and add immeasurably to the radiographic visualization attained simultaneously. Preoperative utilization of these studies are being increasingly used with good results.

Surgical exploration constitutes the final diagnostic procedure. It permits the direct visualization of a tumor, of aberrant adrenal lesions and the differentiation of hyperplasia and tumor is easily made at the operating table with confirmation of the preoperative biochemical and pharmacologic studies. Unless the surgeon has had extensive experience with adrenocortical lesions in his training he should not undertake the exploration of these cases. However, such training is not always available and the necessity for exploration by the inexperienced should be preceded with all of the preoperative diagnostic parameters which have been outlined. The recognition of adrenocortical hyperplasia may be difficult at the operating table but knowledge regarding the preoperative tests will always reinforce the operative finding and serve as a guide to the surgical decisions. Repeatedly we have had to reoperate patients who had previously been operated and adrenal glands found without tumor and no tissue had been removed. Perpetuation of hyperadrenocorticism had existed and demanded the reoperation with bilateral total adrenalectomy. On the other hand, we have seen patients who have had bilateral total adrenalectomy when their primary lesion was either an ovarian tumor or the Stein-Leventhal polycystic ovary lesion.

Preoperative decisions concerning treatment should be based on a specific diagnosis established on the basis of studies of pituitary adrenocortical function. At times it is impossible to differentiate between adenoma and hyperplasia preoperatively and exploration is the final step.

In mild cases without enlargement of the sella turcica and no radiologic evidence of a suprarenal mass but showing a defective suppression of urinary corticoids by dexamethasone and significant elevation of these by ACTH stimulation or by metyrapone, pituitary irradiation may be indicated as the initial treatment. It is emphasized that transitory improvement after pituitary irradiation may occur when the causative adrenal process is either hyperplasia or adenoma. The five-year mortality of the untreated Cushing's disease approaches 50%.[42] It is to be emphasized that the management of Cushing's syndrome involves procedures of considerable magnitude entailing some risk. Many patients are converted from a state of hyperadrenocorticism to a state of permanent adrenal insufficiency. The latter, however, can be adequately and intelligently controlled by the administration of hydrocortisone, cortisone acetate and fluorohydrocortisone. Nonetheless, it is hazardous to make a diagnosis of Cushing's syndrome when it does not exist.

Patients with adrenocortical hyperplasia having enlargement of the sella turcica have usually been treated with irradiation using a telecobalt source to deliver 4,000 to 4,500 r to the pituitary through multiple ports; with a-particles delivered by linear accelerator, it is possible to deliver 8,000 r to the pituitary gland with reasonable safety.[43] Internal pituitary irradiation has also been employed using stereotaxic implantation of Yttrium-90 by the transphenoidal route; use of this procedure is limited by potential deleterious effects of irradiation on perisellar structures. Tumors exhibiting progressive expansion and producing visual field defects and other signs should be surgically removed. When sellar enlargement is only moderate and signs are limited, the surgical procedure of choice may well be transphenoidal cryohypophysectomy. With more extensive involvement the transfrontal approach should be employed. These patients require not only adrenocortical substitution therapy but gonadal and thyroid replacement treatment as well.

Patients without sellar enlargement have been treated in the past by subtotal bilateral adrenalectomy. However, subtotal adrenalectomy entailed certain serious disadvantages; eventual relapse can be expected in 30% or more patients; and the status and the fate of the adrenal remnant are often problematic, as demonstrated by the eventual occurrence of adrenal insufficiency in approximately 50% of the patients. Intercurrent stress may precipitate adrenal crisis in patients who have only sufficient adrenal tissue to meet the hormone requirements for normal existence.

Total bilateral adrenalectomy is the surest method of controlling Cushing's syndrome.[44] The procedure is indicated in those patients who have severe disease with advancing hypertension, diabetes, progressive osteoporosis, psychosis, or other potentially serious complications. The procedure is also indicated in those patients who have not responded to treatment aimed at the pituitary gland. Patients having a mild degree of Cushing's syndrome may have a subtotal adrenalectomy followed by very close surveillance in the future. Total adrenalectomy has been performed during the last 18 years in the treatment of Cushing's syndrome. During this time an unexpected complication in 10–15% of patients has been the appearance of a pituitary tumor. All of these tumors that have been reported were chromophobe adenomas. One cannot always be certain that they were not present prior to the adrenalectomy but it is possible that some have occurred subsequent to it.

Adrenal Tumor. The treatment of a primary adrenocortical tumor is complete surgical resection. In most cases the condition is unilateral so that the involved adrenal gland can be removed and the contralateral atrophic gland left intact. The ultimate recovery of normal adrenocortical function in the remaining gland eliminates the need for hormone replacement therapy. Bilateral aldosterone adenomas have been found infrequently.

The preparation of the patient must adhere to the usual principles of gaining maximal preoperative renal and cardiorespiratory function. If the patient has congestive heart failure, profound potassium depletion or infection, appropriate measures must be taken with these complications before surgery is undertaken. Once surgical treatment has been elected, whether the diagnosis is tumor or hyperplasia, the following considerations are fundamental:

(1) All patients must be adequately prepared preoperatively and firmly supported postoperatively by adrenal hormone replacement. Full-scale hormone treatment should be employed irrespective of the extent of adrenal resection since the incidence of complications attributable to proper hormone therapy has been almost negligible. Adequate quantities of cortisol are necessary during and following surgery.

(2) Water-soluble preparations of cortisol can be given intravenously, intramuscularly or subcutaneously, 100 mg every 8 h beginning with preoperative medication and continuing for 24 h postoperatively.

(3) During the ensuing 7–10 days the dosage is gradually decreased towards physiologic levels.

(4) When a large tumor has been localized unilateral adrenal resection is carried out through a posterolateral incision with resection of the 11th rib for a subdiaphragmatic extrapleural extraperitoneal approach.

(5) If the tumor is very large, a transthoracic exposure by a thoracoabdominal incision is judicious because it facilitates exposure and makes the operation much more safe.

(6) If the tumor has not been localized, a decision must be made concerning an approach through an anterior incision across the epigastrium or a bilateral posterior approach simultaneously with resection of the 11th rib on each side. The abdominal approach gives the added advantage of further exploration with regards to ectopic tissue. With increasing experience it is the author's feeling that the approach should be determined by the size of the tumor, the physical attributes of the patient, as well as the basic pathogenic process present. Hyperaldosteronism demands bilateral exploration in most cases. The anterior approach is less desirable in cases of marked obesity. Osteoporosis with or without multiple vertebral compression fractures makes the posterolateral approach more hazardous. When simultaneous bilateral posterolateral incisions are to be employed exploration of the left adrenal is usually undertaken first since the surgical hazards are less on this side (the vena cava and liver being on the right). In the presence of obvious

adrenocortical atrophy a hyperfunctioning tumor on the opposite side is highly probable. If both adrenal glands appear atrophic the likelihood of aberrant hyperexcreting adrenal cortical tissue is high.

(7) Postoperatively, the patient is maintained on dosage of cortisol sufficient to prevent symptoms of adrenocortical insufficiency and fluorohydrocortisone 0.1–0.2 mg daily. Recovery of the remaining adrenal gland can be facilitated by the intramuscular administration of corticotropin 20–40 U daily for a few weeks. This has seldom been necessary. Ordinarily hormone treatment can be withdrawn completely in less than three months. Many malignant tumors can be completely resected and their management is then identical with benign adenoma. If total resection of an adrenal carcinoma cannot be accomplished subtotal removal should be performed and subsequently chemotherapy carried out. In one patient reoperation has yielded a more complete removal after the lapse of several months because of biologic encapsulation of the residual tumor. Chemotherapy of adrenal cortical carcinoma will be discussed in further detail later.

Primary Aldosteronism. In 1952 the isolation and identification of electrocortin or aldosterone was accomplished by a group working at the University of Basle and the University of London in a cooperative effort. These were Simpson, Tait, Wettstein, Neher, von Euw, and Reichstein. In 1955 a new clinical syndrome was described by Conn at the University of Michigan which was characterized by benign arterial hypertension, hypokalemia, alkalosis, muscle weakness and vasopressin-resistant polyuria. The first aldosterone-producing adenoma was removed by Baum at the University of Michigan. The majority of cases reported to date have resulted from an autonomous aldosterone adrenal secreting adenoma. Three-fourths of these tumors have measured less than 3 cm in diameter and have weighed less than 6 g. In some cases the diameter has been 1 cm or less and the weight below 2 g. These tumors have been much more common on the left than on the right and in more than 90% of cases there has been a single tumor; in the remainder multiple tumors have been found usually in only one gland but rarely both adrenals have been involved. In a small number of patients an adrenal carcinoma has been encountered but the true incidence is not known. 80% of the patients have been between the ages of 30–60 and there have been twice as many females as males.

In an increasing number of reports of all of the typical clinical findings have been present but at operation adrenal hyperplasia or normal appearing adrenal glands have been found. In 1961 Conn and Conn[45] suggested that this might represent a separate category of juvenile aldosteronism. In contrast to the usual syndrome, these patients were young, usually male and often presented with malignant hypertension and frequently gave a history of polyuria and polydipsia beginning in childhood. It is now clear that in a significant number of adult patients who fulfill all accepted diagnostic criteria for primary aldosteronism no adrenal tumor is present. Many of these cases may be a secondary type of aldosteronism. In a series of 38 adult patients, ⅔ of whom were females, a typical solitary cortical adenoma was found in 26 while in 5 the tumor was associated with multiple microadenomata. In 7 patients no tumor was found; adrenocortical hyperplasia was present in 6 and no abnormality could be identified in the remaining glands. When nodular or diffuse cortical hyperplasia is present, it is possible that all zona glomerulosa cells have undergone a primary metabolic derangement leading to autonomous oversecretion of aldosterone but, in view of the pathophysiology of other known adrenocortical disorders, this is unlikely. It seems more reasonable to postulate that the glomerulosa is responding to an abnormal trophic stimulus; since cortisol production is normal and plsma renin levels were low, it is unlikely that either ACTH or angiotensin are involved in these cases. Secondary aldosteronism of unknown etiology may prove to be a more suitable description of such cases.

Pathophysiology of Aldosteronism. Aldosterone in excess increases the distal renal tubular reabsorption of sodium and the excretion of potassium, hydrogen, ammonium, and magnesium ions. Sodium retention leads to expansion of extracellular and plasma volumes followed by increase in glomerular filtration rate, renal plasma flow, and concomitant decrease in renin production. Eventually the kidney escapes from the sodium-retaining action but not from effects on potassium secretion. As a result, a progressive depletion of total body intracellular potassium ensues. The decreased intracellular action is partially compensated by a movement into cells of hydrogen ions leading to systemic alkalosis. The latter, particularly in the presence of hypokalemia, may cause paresthesias and even tetany. Mild weakness progressing to frank paralysis may occur from this potassium loss. Poor concentrating ability of the kidney and a reduced capacity to acidify the urine results from the kaliopenic tubular nephropathy. The urine is alkaline and contains a high content of ammonia. There may be an exaggeration of the normal postural sodium diuresis secondary to an expanded extracellular fluid volume in the presence of hypertension, and in some patients a marked sodium diuresis and nocturia occurs.

The exact mechanism by which excess aldosterone causes hypertension is not defined, but it appears to be secondary to changes in sodium metabolism since salt restriction prevents the rise in blood pressure. The administration of aldosterone and salt decreases plasma renin levels which indicates that a mechanism other than the renin angiotensin system is involved. Tobian[46] has suggested that increased sodium and water content of the arteriolar wall which followed mineral corticoid administration may increase peripheral vascular resistance thereby raising the blood pressure.

Signs and Symptoms. The incidence of symptoms in the first 145 cases reported in the literature have been summarized by Conn et al.[47] and are recorded in the table below:

Symptoms in Primary Aldosteronism

Muscle weakness	73%	Visual disturbance	21%
Nocturia, polyuria	72%	Intermittent paralysis	21%
Headache	51%	Tetany	21%
Polydipsia	46%	Muscle discomfort	16%
Paresthesias	24%	(Asymptomatic)	6%

Physical findings in 145 cases summarized by Conn are listed in the following table:

Signs in Primary Aldosteronism

Hypertension	100%
Retinopathy	50%
Cardiomegaly	41%
Positive Trousseau	17%
Tetany	9%
Paralysis	4%

Laboratory Findings. The following table lists the major biochemical abnormalities encountered in hyperaldosteronism.

Laboratory Abnormalities in Primary Aldosteronism

A. Blood	B. Urine
1. Hypokalemia	1. Decreased concentrating ability
2. Hypernatremia	2. Decreased ability to acidify
3. Hypomagnesemia	3. Increased potassium excretion (high urine potassium at low plasma potassium levels)
4. Alkalosis	4. Normal 17-OHCS, 17-KGS and 17-KS
5. Increased plasma volume	5. Increased aldosterone excretion secretion rate

It is to be emphasized that these biochemical abnormalities may be psychical and early cases the serum potassium concentration will be consistently normal but diminished with potassium deprivation and increased with potassium administration.

There exists a renal-adrenal mechanism for the normal maintenance of sodium balance and systemic renal perfusion pressure. Through this mechanism the kidney releases renin when its perfusion is threatened, and renin generates angiotensin. Angiotensin stimulates aldosterone secretion which causes retention of sodium and tends to restore renal perfusion. In 1964 Conn suggested that this system, functioning through feedback mechanisms, might result in subnormal plasma renin activity in primary aldosteronism and that this finding could provide an additional diagnostic criterion. It has now been confirmed that when aldosterone is secreted the mechanisms normally involved in aldosterone stimulation are suppressed and plasma renin activity is low. Furthermore, procedures which are known to elicit a significant rise in plasma renin levels in normal subjects (the maintenance of upright posture and sodium deprivation are usually much less effective in patients with primary aldosteronism).

Diagnosis. The autonomous secretion of aldosterone by an adrenal adenoma is indicated by an elevated secretion rate in plasma and urine of aldosterone. At the same time the excess hormone suppresses renal production of renin. An increase of aldosterone output while the patient receives a liberal salt intake, and a decrease in plasma renin in the face of salt deprivation are two changes which provide the major criteria for the diagnosis of primary aldosteronism.[48]

The present major criteria for the diagnosis of primary aldosteronism are: (a) Hypertension which is not malignant; (b) hypokalemia which tends to improve with sodium restriction, gets worse with sodium loading and which is not the result of diuretic therapy; (c) increased aldosterone output which persists despite high sodium intake or mineralocorticoid administration; (d) suppressed plasma renin levels which fail to rise normally during the maintenance of the upright position and the restricted sodium intake.

Improved techniques of renal-adrenal tomography, selective adrenal angiography and venography have delineated some lesions as small as 1–2 cm in diameter. Conn, Sutton, and Egdahl have all reported on the successful use of adrenal phlebography in demonstrating these tumors. The measurement of aldosterone in the adrenal venous effluent has been successful in reports by Conn et al.[48] and Egdahl et al.[49]

Differential Diagnosis. In the differential diagnosis of primary aldosteronism one must consider all those conditions causing hypertension, hypokalemia and any condition which causes elevation of aldosterone output. Among these conditions are patients with hypertension or primary aldosteronism, secondary aldosteronism due to malignant hypertension, diuretic therapy of hypertension, congenital defects in the biosynthesis of corticoids resulting in a mineral corticoid excess, Cushing's syndrome, malignancies causing ACTH increase, pseudoaldosteronism and licorice ingestion. In the nomotensive states in the differential diagnosis the syndrome of juxtaglomerular hyperplasia of Bartter et al.[50] renal tubular acidosis and familial periodic paralysis must be considered.

Treatment. The cause of primary aldosteronism is an aldosterone-producing adrenocortical adenoma, the proper treatment of which is surgical removal. The minimal criteria before adrenal exploration are hypertension, elevated aldosterone output which is not suppressed by sodium loading, or mineralocorticoid administration; low plasma renin levels which do not rise normally in response to sodium restriction and the upright posture. Even with these requirements fulfilled, 10–15% of the patients explored will have diffuse or nodular bilateral adrenocortical hyperplasia rather than a tumor; the source of the stimulus repsonsible for the hyperplasia is not now known, but these patients are considered to have a form of secondary aldosteronism and their response to adrenalectomy is not reliably predictable. Finally, in an occasional patient bilateral tumors will be found. When X-rays and the studies of the venous effluent from the two adrenal glands localize the tumor one may be satisfied temporarily at least with only exploration and removal of the tumor on that side. Usually the approach has been bilateral and the simultaneous bilateral posterior approach is the approach of choice. Some have preferred an anterior transverse and upper abdominal incision with oblique extension downward toward the iliac crest in thin subjects. The morbidity is considered to be lower through the bilateral posterior approach, in all but heavily muscular individuals. Preoperative management centers around correction of the potassium deficit using supplemental potassium chloride in doses of 40–120 mEq/day. A low sodium diet will aid potassium repletion and in severe cases aldosterne antagonists (spironolactones) or agents which interfere with renal tubular ion transport (triamterene) may be helpful.

When a tumor is found, it should be removed by unilateral adrenalectomy; this is in contrast to the policy of those who favor discrete resection of the tumor by partial adrenalectomy. Because of their small size the tumor will not be immediately apparent in some cases, but by very careful palpation and complete surgical exposure very small adenomata can be identified. Nodular hyperplasia may simulate a single adenoma; at times it has not been identified correctly except by histologic examination. If no tumor is found at exploration of one gland the opposite gland must be explored. In patients with adrenocortical hyperplasia the procedure of choice is controversial. Subtotal adrenalectomy is preferred by most authors in an effort to interrupt the cycle of aldosterone overproduction. However, the chance that a small adenoma will be left in the remnant indicates that total adrenalectomy may be the more desirable procedure. Simultaneous renal biopsy is carried out in order to measure the extent of renal damage.

Postoperatively, there is an expected urinary diuresis of sodium; potassium is retained and the carbon dioxide content and pH of the blood returns to normal. Polyuria and polydipsia usually disappear promptly but the biochemical shifts are not complete until the second or third postoperative week. At times patients will develop azotemia, hyponatremia and hyperkalemia during the immediate postoperative period reflecting a transient aldosterone deficiency. In such instances replacement therapy with fluorohydrocortisone will be required temporarily. In patients with extensive renal disease azotemia may persist indefinitely. In Conn's experience about 15% of the patients show only a temporary decline in pressure and a subsequent gradual rise to preoperative levels. In 85% of patients blood pressure either returns to normal within four months following the operation or significantly declines but does not reach the normal level. This has occurred even in patients in whom all defects of electrolyte metabolism have been completely obliterated making it appear that in some patients the hypertension is fixed, presumably on a renal basis. The studies in most clinics would indicate that hyperaldosteronism is not a common cause of hypertension. This is in contradistinction to the findings of Conn and his group at the University of Michigan.

Adrenogenital Syndrome. The adrenogenital syndrome includes all cases of sexual precocity and heterosexual abnormalities due to adrenocortical dysfunction. Except for the relatively rare feminizing tumors in males, the clinical features of the disorder are the result of an excessive adrenal production of androgens, producing heterosexual virilizing changes in females and isosexual precocity in males.

The problem of heterosexual development in infants or small children is that of differentiating cases due to genetic intrauterine influence from cases due to abnormal secretion of sex hormones by the fetal endocrine system, including the adrenal cortex. The former include true hermaphroditism in which both ovarian and testicular tissue are present; male pseudohermaphroditism, in which the gonads are testes but the genital ducts, urogenital sinus, and external genitalia exhibit ambisexual differ-

The Adrenogenital Syndrome: Classification

1. Prenatal (congenital virilizing adrenocortical hyperplasia)
   Pseudohermaphroditism in females
   Macrogenitosomia praecox in males
2. Postnatal (adrenocortical hyperplasia or tumor)
   Prepubertal
       heterosexual precocity in females
       isosexual precocity in males
   Postpubertal
       virilism in females
       feminization in males

entiation; and the femal pseudohermaphroditism due to maternal masculinizing hormones (*e.g.* virilizng ovarian tumor). It is important to note that in true hermaphroditism and male pseudohermaphroditism secondary sexual characteristics do not develop prior to the normal time of puberty, and once initiated, development of the external genitalia and genital ducts is largely unpredictable and may or may not correspond to the sex of the gonads. In contrast, heterosexual abnormalities of adrenal origin are often prepubertal in onset and sexual differentiation occurs along a fairly predictable pattern, for example, in female pseudohermaphroditism development of the genital tubercle is masculine, while the genital ducts are always feminine. The principal objective in dealing with problems of isosexual precocity, such as macrogenitosomia praecox, is to establish the source of the stimulus and, i.e. whether the development of secondary sex characteristics is the results of adrenal or gonadal hormones. The disturbance may arise in a primary tumor of adrenal or gonad or results secondarily from precocious-adrenal or pituitary-gonadal activation.

Congenital Virilizing Adrenal Hyperplasia. This is the most common disorder of adrenocortical function in childhood. Four clinical types of virilizing adrenal hyperplasia have been identified as: (a) simple virilism; (b) virilism and sodium loss; (c) virilism and hypertension; and (d) the 3β-hydroxysteroid dehydrogenase defect; (e) a fifth congenital disorder involving the 17-hydroxylation system has been described. 60% of the patients show simple virilism alone and one-third have exhibited salt loss, but the actual occurrence of this form may be higher since, in some cases, patients can die undiagnosed. Approximately 5% have developed hypertension and the 3β-hydroxysteroid dehydrogenase defect is apparently very rare. Three times as many females as males have been described with this disorder. In all four types of the disorder virilism results from the excessive production of adrenal androgens. The primary fact is a deficiency of one or more specific enzymes necessary for the biosynthesis of cortisol. The decrease in cortisol output activates the mechanism regulating the hypothalmic-pituitary-adrenocortical function, and increased quantities of ACTH are released. Stimulation by this corticotrophin brings about adrenal hyperplasia and accelerates the synthesis of adrenal steroids. As a result, cortisol production approaches normal levels but precursors of cortisol accumulate behind the enzyme block and are secreted. The pathways leading to androgen production are not impeded, and androgen secretion rises.

The most common form of the disease is due to a relative deficiency of 21-hydroxylase and results in simple virilism. The major urinary metabolites of progresterone are pregnanolone and pregnanediol; or 17-hydroxyprogesterone, 17-hydroxypregnanolone and pregnanetriol; of 21-deoxycortisol, they are 11-hydroxypregnanetriol and 11-ketopregnanetriol. The demonstration of significantly increased quantities of these metabolites in the urine identifies the site of the partial enzymatic deficiency. Pregnanetriol is most conveniently measured and provides a simple key to the diagnosis. Increased quantities of dehydroepiandrosterone sulfate are excreted directly into the urine; $\Delta 4$-androstenedione is converted in the adrenal or in the liver into testosterone. When the disorder is severe, aldosterone synthesis is also materially impaired, as demonstrated by an inadequate rise in aldosterone production rate in response to sodium restriction. In addition to virilization, significant sodium loss occurs in these patients.

With the C-11-hydroxylase defect the key urinary metabolites are tetra-hydrodeoxycorticosterone and tetrahydro-S. The unblocked androgen pathway again produces excessive quantities of Δ^4-androstenedione, resulting in increased testosterone and 17-ketosteroid production. Aldosterone synthesis is depressed but abnormal sodium loss does not occur because of the accumulation of 11-deoxycorticosterone which also may account for the hypertension.

The enzymatic defect is due to a non-sex-linked recessive mutant gene which is expressed clinically only in the homozygous offspring. Multiple cases occur in one generation, and the affected siblings always have the same form of the disease; the parents show no evidence of endocrine dysfunction.

Signs and Symptoms. In the female infant congenital virilizing adrenal hyperplasia is manifested as pseudo-hermaphroditism. The gonads are ovaries and the mullerian ducts differentiate normally into the uterus, oviduct and vagina; the urogenital sinus persists and excessive development of the genital tubercle occurs. One ordinary encounters at birth a large clitoris resembling a hypospadiac penis, hypertrophic labia majora, atrophic labia minora, and a urogenital sinus opening at the base of the clitoris. On rectal examination the uterus may be palpable but prostatic tissue is absent. Endoscopy reveals both urethra and vagina opening into a common passage, a uterine cervix, and absence of the verumontanum and ejaculatory ducts. Pubic and axillary hair usually appear by the age of 3–4 years. Skeletal and muscular growth are accelerated. Acne may occur and the voice deepens. Menstruation and breast development do not occur at puberty.

In the male infant, prematue virilization occurs but the patient may reach 2–4 years before genital growth becomes abnormal. Pubic, axillary and eventually facial hair develop. Acne appears and enlargement of the larynx accompanies deepening of the voice. It is important to note that the testes typically remain small. Penile and prostatic size reach adult proportions in late childhood. Rarely do testes become enlarged and regression occurs with suppressive steroid treatment which indicates that the scrotum contains aberrant adrenocortical tissue.

The most common cause of female pseudohermaphroditism and isosexual precocity in males is congenital adrenocortical hyperplasia. The diagnosis should be considered in all infants exhibiting vomiting, dehydration or other signs of acute adrenal insufficiency. It is important in the differential diagnosis of hypertension in children having sustained hypertension. One must document the elevation of urinary 17-ketosteroids and of the abnormal urinary metabolites. It is essential to show that the excretion of urinary 17-ketosteroids and of the urinary metabolites is suppressed by the administration of dexamethazone. The suppression tests indicate the basic pathologic process is adrenal hyperplasia and not neoplasia. Virilizing adrenal tumors produce large amounts of urinary 17-ketosteroids mainly 17-dehydroepiandrosterone sulfate and the administration of dexamethazone does not return the values to normal.

The principle of therapy of congenital adrenal hyperplasia is suppression of adrenocortical activity by supplying cortisol or other glucocorticoids, inhibiting corticotropin output and preventing the secretion of adrenal androgens. Intramuscular administration is more effective than oral administration. Inaccurate dosage has been responsible for failure of suppression and restoration to a normal pattern of growth and development. Initial doses are 10–20 mg/day of cortisol for infants; 20–40 mg/day of cortisol for older children and 60–80 mg/day for adolescents or adults. The necessary maintenance dosage must be measured specifically in individual cases using the level of urinary 17-ketosteroids or specific urinary metabolities such as pregnanetriol as a guide. The results are measured in terms of growth rate and osseous development. With inadequate suppression of adrenal function bone age advances and leads to premature epiphyseal fusion. Failure to suppress may result in adrenocortical hyperplasia persisting for many years that may results in neoplasia. Therefore, continued suppressive therapy must be maintained both in females and males.

Postnatal Adrenogenital Syndrome. Postnatal adrenal virilism in females prior to puberty may result from adrenal hyperplasia but is usually due to adrenal tumor. Tumors have been discovered in the first six months of life, or in the postpubertal period. When a neoplasm is causative, the external genitalia are normal at birth but virilization is usually progressive; pubic and axillary hair develop and the clitoris enlarges. Excessive somatic development in growth is accelerated. The output of urinary 17-ketosteroids is high and the urinary dehydro-epiandrosterone sulfate is usually elevated. The diagnosis depends upon the exclusion of congenital adrenal hyperplasia by failure of dexamethasone inhibition. Pyelography and tomography are valuable in the preoperative localization of the tumor. Arteriography and measurement of the hormones in the venous effluent of the adrenal represent refined coordinated advances in diagnosis. The adrenogenital syndrome in adult females occurs before the menopause and either hyperlasia or tumor may be responsible but tumor is unfortunately more often the cause. The earliest event is the appearance of hirsuitism of the face and extremities and the conversion of the pubic hair line into a male pattern. Hair of the scalp becomes thin and actual baldness ensues with temple recession being common. Menses become scanty and cease. Libido is diminished and the breasts, ovaries and uterus diminish in size as the clitoris undergoes hypertrophy. The voice deepens as the larynx enlarges and the musculature of the body until body configuration may approach the male form. High levels of urinary 17-ketosteroids are measured. Syndromes with characteristics of Cushing's and the adrenogenital syndrome may be caused by either hyperplasia or tumor but the latter should always be suspected.

In the differential diagnosis polycystic disease of the ovaries, arrhenoblastomas, and luteinizing granulosa cell tumors must be considered. Pelvic exploration may be necessary to establish the presence or absence of primary ovarian pathology. Differentiation between bilateral adrenocortical hyperplasia and adrenocortical tumors is essential. A plain film of the abdomen, adrenal tomography with excretory urography and selective angiography both arterial and venous may serve to localize the tumor. Venography is not without hazard and must be done with the greatest care. Dexamethasone suppression will cause a fall in the urinary metabolites when adrenocortical hyperplasia is the cause of their increase. This will not occur when a malignant tumor is the cause. Some adenomas do show suppression and also an elevation in response to ACTH stimulation.

The treatment of virilizing adrenal tumor is imme-

diate removal. When the tumor has been localized preoperatively, the approach is determined very much by its size and direction of growth. When the predominant growth seems to be inferiorly down into the abdomen, transverse abdominal incision extending down to the iliac crest is a very adequate exposure. Tumors of less great size may be approached through the classical flank incision with resection of the 11th rib. This is an extrapleural, subdiaphragmatic approach. When the tumors are quite large a posterolateral thoracoabdominal approach is definitely the procedue of choice. When the tumor has not been accurately localized, transabdominal approach by a transverse incision with oblique extension, as necessary inferiorly, is preferable.

Feminizing Adrenogenital Syndrome in Males. The feminizing adrenogenital syndrome in males is nearly always due to tumor. Feminization has not been described as the presenting picture in congenital adrenocrotical hyperplasia. Feminization appearing in the adult male always raises the question of malignant adrenocortical neoplasm. In 1965 Gabrilove reviewed 52 cases of feminizing adrenocortical tumors. They occur between the ages of 22–50. Gynecomastia is the most frequent change and is usually bilateral. Diminished libido and testicular atrophy occur in one-half of the patients. Oligospermia, obesity, feminine hair distribution, penile atrophy, arterial hypertension and edema may also be occasionally found. Some patients have shown moon face, cutaneous striae, osteoporosis and steroid diabetes similar to Cushing's syndrome. These tumors are typically large and palpable in more than 50% of the patients. In most cases death occurs within two years following the onset of symptoms. Metastases appear in the liver, lungs, and pancreas by direct extension. Estrogenic excretion is much greater in malignant tumors than with adenomas. Estrone, estradiol and estriol are similar to the distribution found in normal males. Very high values for 17-ketosteroids and urinary estrogens are found. Radical operation for cancer is necessary, removing all periadrenal fat, fascia and lymphatics. The kidney is often invaded and must be removed on that side. In addition, the spleen and tail of the pancreas have been involved in some cases and required removal. If the tumor can be removed, gynecomastia regresses, libido returns, and the testes increase in size. Excessive excretion of urinary estrogens, 17-ketosteroids and 17-hydroxycorticoids fall. Persistence of symptoms and elevated steroid levels are an indication of functioning metastases. The administration of $o'p'DDD$ has reduced steroid output in some cases but not in all.

Functional Tumors of the Adrenal: Adenoma. Adrenocortical tumors are found in approximately one-fourth of patients with Cushing's syndrome, and about one-half of these neoplasms are benign. Tumors weighing over 200 g have been reported as true adenomas but usually the adenoma is a small lesion. The differentiation between adenoma and carcinoma in these large tumors may be quite difficult histologically. The benign tumors usually produce the hyperglucocorticoid state in contrast to the state of virilization of feminization. Primary aldosteronism is due to an adenoma usually though in a few instances carcinoma has occurred.

Carcinoma of the adrenal cortex is a rare malignancy, accounting for less than 0.2% of deaths from all cancer. It occurs at any age but the highest incidence is between the ages of 20–50. A significant number of cases have occurred before the age of 10. Virilization in females with and without Cushing's syndrome and aldosteronism are produced by carcinoma and emphasize their tendency to produce a mixed picture or intergrade type of lesion. In addition to surgical removal, the treatment has involved reoperation after radiation therapy of metastases and chemotherapy as well. $o'p'$DDD has been effective in causing inhibition of growth of adrenocortical carcinoma.

The compound $o'p'$DDD has the chemical formula 1,1- dichloro - 2(o - chlorophenyl) - 2(p - chlorophenyl) - ethane and has been shown to produce a marked decrease in the secretion of steroids by the adrenal cortex, often associated with focal degenerative lesions of the zona reticularis and the zona fasciculata. Recently, Hutter and Kayhoe[51] summarized the results of $o'p'$DDD treatment of 138 patients with adrenal carcinoma. Initial dosage for adults is 2–6 g in divided doses and subsequently the level is increased until toxicity becomes a limiting factor. Maximum daily dose in most patients is 8–10 g. Unfortunately toxic side effects are noted in 90% of patients. Drug reaction predominantly involve the gastrointestinal tract, neuromuscular system, and the skin. Anorexia, nausea, vomiting and diarrhea are the gastrointestinal disturbances. Central nervous system depression manifested as lethargy and somnolence occurs in about one-fourth of the treated patients but is usually reversible with reduction of dosage. Dizziness, vertigo, muscle tremors, headache, and confusion have occurred. Cutaneous eruptions appear in 15% of the ptients and are not always dose related. Bone marrow depression and liver damage have not been noted. In 70% of patients urinary steroid values are decreased during treatment. It may require 3–4 weeks before any fall is noted. 35% of treated patients may be expected to show objective signs of tumor regression including the reduction in the size of palpable masses, disappearance of pulmonary metastatic lesions, a decrease in the intensity of hormone-induced effect, diminished pain and improved strength.

Survival for as long as three years has occurred in the presence of hepatic metastases following removal of a large adrenocortical carcinoma when chemotherapy has been utilized in the above mentioned form. Recently, a new agent has been introduced for the control of metabolic derangements resulting from steroid-producing lesions. This compound is aminoglutethimide, originally used as an anticonvulsant. *In vitro* and *in vivo* studies indicate that the drug inhibits adrenal steroid synthesis by interfering with the conversion of cholesterol to pregnenolone. The adrenal cortex undergoes hypertrophy through increased corticotrophin secretion by the feedback system. The usefulness seems to be the management of pituitary-dependent adrenocortical hyperplasia. However, the drug has produced favorable responses in patients with metastatic adrenocortical carcinoma. Dosage of 0.75–2 g/day. At dose levels of 1.2 g/day or less, minimal side effects occur but doses of 1.5 g/day cause anorexia, somnolence, fever, vomiting, ataxia and skin rashes. These untoward effects have disappeared following withdrawal of the drug.

Great progress has been made in the study and care of disorders of the adrenal cortex since Addison's first publication in 1855. Parallel progress has been made in advances with regard to the adrenal medulla. The synthesis of cortisone, the demonstration of its life-saving substitutional effects, the discovery of ACTH and desoxycorticosterone acetate as well as the synthetic mineralocorticoids such as fluorohydrocortisone followed by the isolation and synthesis of electrocortin and Conn's description of aldosteronism constitute the chief advances in the biochemistry and physiology of the adrenal cortex. The striking improvements in radiography of the adrenal and the simultaneous improvements in anesthesiology and surgical technique all indicate great progress in the management of surgery of the adrenals in the last 21 years.

The urologic service of the Peter Bent Brigham Hospital has been most fortunate in having the privilege of collaborating with Dr. George W. Thorn and his service in the management of hyperadrenocorticism due to hyperplasia or tumor during the last twenty-five years. Most of these cases were treated during the last twenty years which is, since this group demonstrated the survival of man after bilateral total adrenalectomy, sustained by substitution therapy with cortisone acetate and desoxycorticosterone acetate. A review of the studies of the primary pathology of the adrenal cortex and medulla at the Peter Bent Brigham Hospital in the last three decades reveals that 63 patients have been operated upon for hyperadrenocorticism due to adrenocortical hyperplasia and 74 patients have been explored for adrenal tumors of various sorts. In the latter group, there were 16 patients with adenomas which produced Cushing's syndrome, 14 patients had adenoma causing primary aldosteronism, 18 patients had adrenocortical carcinoma, 5 patients had large cysts of the adrenal and 23 patients had pheochromocytoma.

There were 38 patients having bilateral total adrenalectomy in a one-stage operation and 7 patients had bilateral total adrenalectomy in a two-stage operation. Unilateral adrenalectomy and pituitary radiation was carried out in 3 patients; total unilateral adrenalectomy and partial opposite adrenalectomy in 5 patients. Bilateral subtotal adrenalectomy was done in 3 and unilateral adrenalectomy in 1. Reoperation for adrenocortical remnants due to recurrent hyperadrenocorticism of patients having subtotal adrenalectomy elsewhere was carried out on 4 patients and removal of ectopic adrenocortical ovarian tissue was carried out in 2 patient. One of the latter had had a previous bilateral total adrenalectomy and one had been treated for the adrenogenital syndrome with dexamethazone as suppressive adrenocortical therapy. The complications of surgery in this latter group were: inferior vena cava tear 1, wound infection 4, phlebitis 2, cerebral vascular accident 1, pneumonia 4, urinary tract infection 2, psychosis 1, Addisonian crisis after leaving the hospital 4. There were seven deaths in this group of patients operated on for adrenocortical hyperplasia, and these were due to: cardiovascular origin 2, gastrointestinal hemorrhage 1, persistent hyperadrenocorticism 2, pneumonia complicated by septic shock 1, suicide 1. Nine of these patients had significant psychiatric disease, 42 had hypertension, 3 renal calculi, and 11 osteoporosis. There were 3 patients who were found after adrenalectomy to develop pituitary tumors and all of these survived after pituitary radiation and hypophysectomy.

Hyperadrenocorticism due to functioning adrenal adenomas were found in 16 patients, 15 were female and one a male. The average age in this group was 33 years with a range of 17–65 years. Fourteen of the patients with adenomas were studied with ACTH stimulation test which was positive in 10 which, of course, raised the question of the possibility of adrenocortical hyperplasia in each of these patients. Excretory urography demonstrated a tumor in 11 of the 16 patients. Arteriography was used only once and helped to localize an adenoma 3 cm in diameter in the right adrenal gland. All of the operations were performed from the flank using either a subcostal 11th or 12th rib approach. Seven patients underwent bilateral explorations and in only one patient were small bilateral adenomas discovered. Eight adenomata were found on the left side and one on the right. The average diameter was 3.6 cm with a range of 1.5–6 cm. Postoperative complications consisted of urinary tract infections 2, peptic ulcer 1, and a fatal myocardial infarction occurred in one patient three years after surgery. The followup of 15 survivors range from 6 months to 20 years and all reported having normal blood pressure. Three of these patients required maintenance steroid therapy after discharge from the hospital. All were subjected to measurement of basal steroid levels prior to discharge by measuring their response to adrenocorticotrophic hormone.

There were 18 patients having adrenocortical carcinoma, 14 of whom were females and 4 were males. The age distribution was from 7 to 70 years and the average age was 44 years. The tumor was easily palpable in 12 patients and excretory urography showed the tumor in 13 of the 18 patients. Arteriography is extremely useful in outlining the blood supply of these tumors and helpful in giving a roadmap for surgery. The patients underwent thoracoabdominal incisions and 6 were operated through flank incisions. One patient underwent bilateral subcostal incisions and one patient was not subjected to surgery because of advanced metastatic disease. Six nephrectomies, 2 splenectomies, 1 partial pancreatectomy and 2 resections of solitary lung metastases were carried out. Two patients developed wound infections, two developed urinary tract infections, one had a nonfatal pulmonary embolus. Eleven patients died subsequently as a result of metastatic disease and one from shock secondary to primary rupture of the tumor. The average survival of those who died was 2 years with the longest survivor being 9 years after surgery. Five patients are living without metastasis 3½ to 21 years after removal of carcinoma of the adrenal cortex. One patient is alive with metastatic disease 3½ years after removal of the primary tumor. Five patients were treated with o'p'DDD because of metastatic disease. Three have had excellent palliation with evidence of tumor regression. One patient is alive with metastases under treatment with o'p'DDD more than 3 years after primary surgery. Cysts of the adrenal were discovered in 5 patients during an excretory urogram, as part of a hypertensive study in 3 patients and as a part of a workup for abdominal pain in 2. The preoperative diagnosis of cysts of the adrenal was made in all 5 cases. Adrenal angiography was carried out in only one case and this confirmed the impression obtained from the excretory urogram. Calcium was demonstrated in the wall of the cyst in 3 patients. Intensive studies for adrenocortical insufficiency should be made in the patients having cysts as well as other members of the family.

The details of the patients undergoing surgery for pheochromocytoma are being published elsewhere. The importance of arteriography and vena caval sampling needs further emphasis in the preoperative diagnosis.

REFERENCES

1. ADDISON, T.: On the constitutional and local effects of disease of the suprarenal capsules (Highley, London 1855)

2. OLIVER, G. and SCHAEFER, A. E.: Physiological effects of adrenal extracts. J Physiol Lond 18:230, 1895

3. CANNON, W. B.: The emergency function of the adrenal medulla in pain and the major emotions. Amer J Physiol 33:356–372, 1914

4. HOLMES, G.: A case of virilism associated with a suprarenal tumor recovery after its removal. Quart J Med 18:143, 1924/25

5. CUSHING, H.: The pituitary body and its disorders, p 341 (Lippincott, Philadelphia 1912)

6. CUSHING, H.: Basophil adenoma of pituitary body and their clinical manifestations (pituitary basophilism). Bull Johns Hopk Hosp 50:137–195, 1932

7. MAYO, C. H.: Paroxysmal hypertension with tumor of retroperitoneal nerve. Report of case. J Am Med Ass 89:1047, 1927

8. PINCOFFS, M. C.: A case of paroxysmal hypertension associated with suprarenal tumor. Trans Ass Am Physicians 44:295, 1929

9. CRILE, G.: Denervation of the adrenal glands for neurocirculatory asthenia. Surg Gynec Obstet 54:294, 1932

10. YOUNG, H. H.: Genital abnormalities, hermaphroditism and related adrenal diseases (Williams & Wilkins, Baltimore 1937)

11. THORN, G. W.; HARRISON, J. H.; CRICITIELLO, M. G., and FRAWLEY, T. F.: Physiological changes following bilateral total adrenalectomy in patients with advanced hypertensive vascular disease. Abstract. Trans Ass Am Physicians 64:126, 1951

12. REICHSTEIN T. VON and SHOPPEE, C. W.: The hormones of the adrenal cortex. Vitamins Hormones N Y 1:345, 1943

13. KENDALL, E. C.; MASON, L. L., and MYERS, C. S.: Concerning the chemical nature of the hormones of the adrenal cortex. Proc Staff Meet Mayo Clin 11:351, 1936

14. HENCH, P. S.; KENDALL, E. C.; SLOCUMB, C. M., and POLLEY, M. F.: Effects of cortisone acetate and pituitary ACTH on rheumatoid arthritis, rheumatic fever, and certain other conditions. Arch Intern Med 85:545–666, 1950

15. THORN, G. W.; HARRISON, J. H.; MERRILL, J. P.; CRISCITIELLO, M. G.; FRAWLEY, T. F., and FINKENSTAEDT, J. T.: Clinical studies on bilateral adrenalectomy in patients with severe hypertensive vascular disease. Ann Intern Med 37:972, 1952

16. HUGGINS, C, and BERGENSTAL, D. M.: Inhibition of human mammary and prostatic cancer by adrenalectomy. Cancer Res 12:134–142, 1952

17. LI, C. H.; EVANS, H. M., and SIMPSON, M. E.: Adrenocorticotrophic hormone. J Biol Chem 149:413–424, 1943

18. GOLDBERG, M.; SNYDER, C. Y., and ARANOW, H.: New test for hypertension due to circulating epinephrine. J Am Med Ass 135:971, 1947

19. GIFFORD, R. W. jr.; ROTH, G. M., and KVALE, W. F.: Evaluation of new adrenolytic drug (Regitine) as test for pheochromocytoma. J Am Med Ass 146:1628–1634, 1952

20. SIMPSON, S. A.; TAIT, J. F.; WETTSTEIN, A.; NEHER, F.; EUW, J. VON; REICHSTEIN, T. V. und SCHINDLER, O.: Konstitution des Aldosterons, des neuen Mineralocorticoids. Experienta 10:132, 1954

21. CONN, J. W.: Primary aldosteronism. A new clinical syndrome. J Lab Clin Med 45:3–17, 1955

22. HARRISON, J. H.; THORN, G. W., and CRISCITIELLO, M. G.: A study of bilateral total adrenalectomy in malignant hypertension and chronic nephritis. J Urol, Baltimore 67:405, 1952

23. JENSKINS, D. and HARRISON, J. H.: The adrenals; in Campbell Urology, vol 3, chap 63 (Saunders, Philadelphia/London 1963)

24. JENKINS, D. and HARRISON, J. H.: The adrenals; in Campbell and Harrison Urology, vol 3, chap 67 (Saunders, Philadelphia/London 1970)

25. DAUGHADAY, W. H.: The binding of cortico-steroids by plasma protein; in Eisenstein The adrenal cortex, p 385 (Little, Brown, Boston 1967)

26. CAMACHO, A. M. and MIGEON, C. J.: Testosterone excretion and production rate in normal adults and in patients with congenital adrenal hyperplasia. J Clin Endocrin Metabol 25:893, 1966

27. KORENMAN, S. G. and LIPSET, M. B.: Is testosterone glucuronide uniquely derived from plasma testosterone? J Clin Invest 43:2125, 1964

28. TAIT, J. F. and HORTON, R.: The *in vivo* estimation of blood production and interconversion rates of androstenedione and testosterone and the calculation of their secretion rates; in Pincus and Nakao Dynamics of steroid metabolism, p 393 (Academic Press, New York 1965)

29. SELYE, H.: Textbook of endocrinology (University of Montreal, Montreal 1947)

30. LI, C. M.; EVANS, H. M., and SIMPSON, M. E.: Adrenocorticotrophic hormone. J Biol Chem 149:413–424, 1943

31. SCHALLY, A. V. and BOWERS, C. Y.: Corticotrophin-releasing factor and other hypothalamic peptides. metabolism 136:1190, 1964

32. GANONG, W. F.: The central nervous system and the synthesis and release of adrenocorticotrophic hormone; in Nalbandov Advances in neuroendocrinology (University of Illinois Press, Urbana, Ill. 1963)

33. PORTER, C. C. and SILBER, R. H.: A quantitative color reaction of cortisone and related 17,21-dihydroxy-20-ketosteroids. J Biol Chem 185:201–207, 1950

34. PETERSON, R. E.: Metabolism of adrenocorticosteroids in man. Ann NY Acad Sci 82:846, 1959

35. TAIT, J. F.: The use of isotopic steroids for the measurement of production rates *in vivo*. Review J Clin Endocrin Metabol 23:1285, 1963

36. PETERSON, R. E.: Metabolism of adrenocorticosteroids in man. Ann NY Acad Sci 82:846, 1959

37. DORFMAN, R. and SHIPLEY, R. A.: Androgens, p 564 (Wiley, New York; Chapman & Hall, London 1956)

38. RIONDEL, A.; TAIT, J. F.: GUT, M.; TAIT, S. A. S.: JOACHIM, H., and LITTLE, B.: Estimation of testosterone in human peripheral blood using S-35-thiosemicarbazide. J Clin Endocrin Metabol 23:620, 1963

39. LIDDLE, G. W.: Cushing's syndrome; in Eisenstein The adrenal cortex, p 523 (Little, Brown, Boston 1967)

40. LIDDLE, G. W.: Test of pituitary-adrenal suppressibility in the diagnosis of Cushing's syndrome. J Clin Endocrin Metabol 20:971, 1952

41. LAIDLAW, J. C.; GOETZ, F. C.; JENKINS, D.; MUNSON, P. L.; HARRISON, J. H. and THORN, G. W.: 17-Ketosteroid and androgen excretion in orchiectomized, adrenalectomized patients. J Clin Endocrin 12:971, 1952

42. PLOTZ, C. M.; KNOWLTON, A. I., and RAGAN, C.: The natural history of Cushing's syndrome. Am J Med 13:597, 1952

43. LAWRENCE, J. H.; TOBIAS, C. A., and BORN, J. L.: Acromegaly. Trans. Amer Clin Climat Ass 73:176, 1961

44. HARRISON, J. H.; THORN, G. W., and JENKINS, D.: Further observations of bilateral adrenalectomy in man. AMA Genito-Urin Surg 44:85, 1952

45. CONN, J. W. and CONN, E. S.: Primary aldosterone versus hypertensive disease with secondary aldosteronism. Recent Progr Hormone Res 17:389, 1961

46. TOBIAN, L.: Interrelationships of electrolytes, juxtaglomerular cells and hypertension. Physiol Rev 40:280, 1960

47. CONN, J. W.; KNOPF, R. F., and NESBIT, R.: Primary aldosteronism. Present evaluation of its clinical characteristics and of the results of surgery; in Baulieu and Robel Aldosterone, p 327 (Davis, Philadelphia 1964)

48. CONN, J. W.; COHEN, E. L., and ROVNER, D. R.: Suppression of plasma renin activity in primary aldosteronism. Distinguishing primary from secondary aldosteronism in hypertensive disease. J Am Med Ass 190:213, 1964

49. EGDAHL, R. H.; KAHN, P. C., and MELBY, J. C.: Role of angiography in surgery of the adrenal. Amer J Surg 117:480–484, 1969

50. BARTTER, F. C.; PRONOVE, P.; GILL, J. R., jr., and McCARDLE, R. C.: Hyperplasia of the juxtaglomerular complex with hyperaldosteronism and hypokalemic alkalosis. Amer J Med 33:811, 1962

51. HUTTER, A. M. and KAYHOE, D. E.: Adrenal cortical carcinoma. Results of treatment with o'p'DDD in 138 patients. Am J Med 41:581, 1966

52. THORN, G. W.; HOWARD, R. P.; EMERSON, K., jr., and FIOR, W. M.: Treatment of Addison's disease. Bull Johns Hopk Hosp 64:339, 1939

Commentary: The Adrenal Gland

Stevan B. Streem and Alan H. Bennett

Multiple surgical approaches to the adrenal glands have been described in the preceding article. Each approach has specific indications and advantages, depending on the presenting pathologic entity. A thoracoabdominal approach remains favored for bulky unilateral lesions, usually carcinoma. A lateral incision with resection of the 11th or 12th rib is indicated for small tumors that have been accurately localized preoperatively. Adrenal cysts may be particularly amenable to this approach. Bilateral flank incision, with rib resection, remains the procedure of choice when total bilateral adrenalectomy is required to control Cushing's syndrome due to bilateral hyperplasia.[1] As an alternative to flank incision, the posterior approach has been advocated for unilateral or bilateral exposure of the adrenal glands. This is best performed as an oblique incision through the bed of the 11th or 12th rib with the patient prone and the table flexed to 35°. Although the advantage of this approach is perhaps shorter operative time and earlier postoperative ambulation and recovery, the limited exposure makes inadvertent injury to the great vessels a distinct possibility. This is especially true of the vena cava when right adrenalectomy is performed.

A transabdominal approach has been extensively used for pheochromocytomas, which are frequently multiple and ectopic, and for adenomas, which are often small but were previously difficult to localize preoperatively. For exploration of pheochromocytomas not adequately localized before surgery, the inverted U or "frown" continues to be our incision of choice, since it allows good bilateral exposure of both adrenal glands and sympathetic chains.[2] However, several variations of both vertical and transverse approaches have been used successfully. Accessibility of the adrenal glands through any transabdominal incision may be limited, however, and this approach requires extensive mobilization of abdominal viscera.[3] Additionally, exploration for tumors such as pheochromocytomas or adenomas not adequately localized preoperatively is often time consuming and occasionally unrewarding.

Advances in surgical therapy of most adrenal lesions have thus resolved around refinement of techniques for better preoperative localization and, often, for recognition of specific pathology. In part, this technology should enable the physician to choose the operative approach with the least morbidity and mortality and, at times, to find surgical intervention unnecessary. Previously, the diagnostic armamentarium for these lesions included adrenal tomography, venography, arteriography, and inferior vena caval sampling of epinephrine, norepinephrine, cortisol, and aldosterone. During the last decade, however, a revolution in diagnostic capabilities has occurred. The greatest achievements have been made through the use of adrenal scintigraphy, computed tomography (CT scannning), and reliable radioenzymatic assays for neurotransmitters and minute quantities of plasma hormones.

Scintillation scanning of the adrenal glands was first accomplished *in vivo* in 1970 with ^{131}I-19-iodocholesterol. Although the agent saw some clinical use, the target–background ratio was often suboptimal. ^{131}I-6-beta-Iodomethyl-19-norcholesterol, a radiochemical impurity in ^{131}I-19-iodocholesterol, eventually developed as the agent of choice. Applications of adrenal scanning span the entire range of adrenal pathology, but it is most useful clinically when combined with other diagnostic modalities.

In patients with Cushing's syndrome, the adrenal scan may distinguish hyperplasia, carcinoma, or adenoma in 95% of patients and will lateralize adenomas when present.[4] In this setting, one of four findings will be noted:

1. Symmetric visualization is almost invariably due to bilateral adrenal hyperplasia, of which Cushing's disease is the most common etiology. Symmetric uptake is also seen in healthy adrenal glands, with Cushing's disease being distinguishable only by biochemical documentation of excessive glucocorticoids. A "low-dose" dexamethasone suppression test is of obvious value in borderline instances. Patients with ectopic production of adrenocorticotropic hormone (ACTH) may have identical scans. However, these patients generally have a distinctly different clinical presentation and may often be identified on the basis of extremely high plasma ACTH levels alone or by administration of metyrapone.

2. Asymmetric visualization may be a normal finding on a posterior scan and is related in part to the variable depth of the right and left adrenal glands. This finding in healthy glands can readily be distinguished with an anterior scan, which will reverse the seemingly asymmetric uptake. For the same reason, asymmetry may be seen in bilateral hyperplasia. Rarely, asymmetry is caused by the coexistence of a Cushing's adenoma with hyperplasia. This is suggested when the difference in uptake is greater than 50%. Finally, asymmetry may be due to previous subtotal adrenalectomy and is therefore useful for evaluating patients after attempted surgical control of their disease.[5]

3. Unilateral visualization may similarly be seen unexpectedly after "bilateral total adrenalectomy" if a remnant was left behind. In the absence of a surgical history, however, this finding is caused by a functioning adenoma with suppression of the contralateral adrenal gland. Previous unilateral adrenalectomy must also be considered with this finding in any patient who has undergone nephrectomy on the nonvisualized side.

4. Bilateral nonvisualization may be due to technical reasons or exogenous hormonal therapy. However, in the face of excessive endogenous glucocorticoids, this finding is generally caused by adrenocortical carcinoma. Although the tumor concentrates radiocholesterol, the uptake and secretion per gram of tissue is less than in the healthy gland. The opposite adrenal gland is again suppressed. On the other hand, non-cortisol-secreting adrenal carcinomas cause no suppression. The contralateral adrenal gland is normal, and the ipsilateral gland is distorted or destroyed.

Adrenal scintigraphy has also proved a valuable adjunct in the diagnostic evaluation of primary aldosteronism. The usual cause is a single adrenal adenoma, with multiple adenomas, usually on the same side, occurring in some patients. However, bilateral hyperplasia (idiopathic hyperaldosteronism) is the etiology in 15% to 25% of patients.[6] Although surgical treatment for adenomas is generally curative, it is unreliable for hyperplasia, which is best managed medically. Unfortunately, in the past the distinction between these pathologic entities was made at the time of exploration. Although adrenal scintigraphy with dexamethasone suppression may alone accurately identify the type and location of the lesion in 80% of patients, a multifactorial analysis including adrenal venography, caval sampling, and suppressed adrenal scanning will increase this accuracy to 95%.[4] Postural changes in plasma aldosterone levels have also been advocated to clarify the pathologic process. Healthy persons and those with idiopathic hyperaldosteronism will have a significant rise in plasma aldosterone after 4 hours of upright posture between 8 AM and 12 noon. Most patients with adenomas have a decreased level, although some will have only a mild increase.[6]

The dexamethasone-suppressed scan was introduced to overcome the lack of specificity in the standard adrenal scan. Since an aldosteronoma is not suppressed by dexamethasone, the classic finding in the patient with a unilateral adenoma is early visualization on the side of the lesion and nonvisualization of the contralateral gland, which is suppressed by dexamethasone. In patients with bilateral hyperplasia, bilateral visualization begins by 4 days after injection. Most impressive is the fact that adenomas have been found at the time of surgery in 94% of patients who underwent lateralizing scans.[4] Similarly, suppression scans are being evaluated for use in patients with excess adrogen production. In those with adrenal adenomas, the scan may again lateralize the lesion.

With CT scans the normal adrenal gland may be visualized bilaterally in 90% of patients using 1-cm intervals, and either gland alone may be visualized in an additional 1%.[7] When adrenal pathology is suspected, intervals of 0.5 cm may increase the likelihood of visualization. Failure of visualization is often the result of inadequate retroperitoneal fat required for sharp delineation. CT scans are capable of identifying adrenal tumors as small as 1 cm and, equally important, often rule out an adrenal tumor. Absolute measurements of size of the adrenal gland may not be as valuable an indicator of pathology as change in shape; the margin of a normal gland is usually concave or straight, and a convex or spherical gland implies a pathologic condition.

In patients with Cushing's syndrome, CT scanning may contribute to the diagnostic evaluation. Even though it will reliably differentiate patients with bilateral hyperplasia from those with unilateral lesions (adenoma or carcinoma), it remains difficult to distinguish bilateral hyperplastic glands from healthy ones.

Experience with CT scanning in patients with primary aldosteronism is small, and surgical or autopsy confirmation of its diagnosis is even more limited. The goal remains to distinguish those patients with the surgically curable adenoma from those with bilateral hyperplasia. Contributing to the lack of operative confirmation is the fact that patients suspected of having bilateral hyperplasia by biochemical and CT findings are treated medically. However, a high degree of reliability has been proved surgically when CT scanning suggests a unilateral mass.[8]

Although carcinoma of the adrenal cortex may be recognized on CT scans, differentiation of the organ of origin as the adrenal gland rather than the kidney or the liver is often impossible without biochemical evidence of abnormal steroid production. Because these lesions are often bulky and metastatic at the time of diagnosis, CT scanning will primarily determine involvement of the mass with surrounding structures. Identification of lesions as cystic has considerable implications in management. Previously, surgical exploration of cystic lesions of the adrenal gland was recommended in all but high-risk patients.[9] More recently, diagnostic techniques including angiography, adrenal scintigraphy, and ultrasonography have been successfully combined with cyst puncture for accurate, nonoperative diagnoses.[10,11] CT scanning is especially useful in identifying cystic lesions because of their sharply marginated round configuration and homogenous fluid density. Although some believe that lesions meeting the CT criteria for benign adrenal cysts in adults require no further evaluation,[7] we recommend performing cyst puncture with cytologic examination. Furthermore, although nonoperative management of these lesions is being reported in a greater number of patients, one must consider that the pathologic spectrum of these "cysts" is not analogous to that in the kidney, and no large series has yet proved superiority of this over a surgical approach.

Perhaps the greatest role of CT scanning for adrenal gland lesions lies in accurate localization of pheochromocytomas. Previous diagnostic regimens have been complex and generally have included invasive procedures such as inferior vena caval sampling and arteriography, which may be hazardous in these patients. Recent reports of simplified diagnostic approaches have therefore been enthusiastically received. Although adrenal gland lesions such as adenomas smaller than 1.5 cm may be missed by CT scanning, the vast majority of pheochromocytomas are larger.[12] Therefore, with increasing experience, CT scanning has become the procedure of choice for localization of biochemically proven pheochromocytomas, including those of extra-adrenal origin. In surgically confirmed cases, the tumor had been accurately demonstrated in 84% to 88% of patients.[7,13] The preoperative diagnostic evaluation may be simplified further by recent reports of clinically useful radioenzymatic assays of plasma catecholamines obtained through simple venipuncture. The diagnostic accuracy has been reported to be as high as 100%, with all the patients proved to have pheochromocytomas showing elevated levels; overlap of values with other hypertensive patients is apparently minimal.[13,14]

. . .

With multiple operative approaches to the adrenal gland available, the surgeon must choose the most appropriate one for the patient's condition. This decision is based largely on preoperative diagnosis and localization of the lesion, a task that has been complex, invasive, expensive, and occasionally inaccurate.

Adrenal scintigraphy, CT scanning, and radioenzymatic assays are highly accurate and nonvasive diagnostic tests that allow the physician to choose more confidently an approach offering the greatest accessibility of the adrenal gland(s) with the least morbidity to the patient. Transabdominal and bilateral flank or posterior explorations might often be supplanted by unilateral operations or, at times, no operation at all.

ANNOTATED BIBLIOGRAPHY

Thrall JH, Freitas JE, Beierwaltes WH: Adrenal scintigraphy. Semin Nucl Med 8:23, 1978.

Presented in this paper is a comprehensive review of adrenal scintigraphy at the University of Michigan Medical Center from the first successful *in vivo* scan to the most recent clinical trials. Included are discussions of radiocholesterol and other technical aspects of scanning, the role of dexamethasone suppression, and limitations of adrenal scintigraphy. Most impressive are the clinical correlations in large groups of patients with adrenal pathology.

Karstaedt N, Sagel SS, Stanley RJ, Melson GL, Levitt RG: Computed tomography of the adrenal gland. Radiology 129:723, 1978, and Korobkin M, White EA, Dressel HY, Moss AA, Montagne JP: Computed tomography in the diagnosis of adrenal disease. Am J Radiol 132:231, 1979.

Both papers review the role of computed tomography for the diagnosis of adrenal pathology. Limitations of this technique are better appreciated following the discussion in Karstaedt's paper of CT scanning and the normal adrenal gland. Clinical correlations of CT findings including surgical and autopsy confirmations have been excellent, although the number of patients studied is somewhat limited. Also presented are brief comparisons of CT scanning with other diagnostic techniques such as adrenal venography, arteriography, and scintigraphy, thus allowing the diagnostician to choose complementary studies where indicated.

Gonzalez–Serva L, Glenn JF: Adrenal surgical techniques. Urol Clin North Am 4:327, 1977, and McGuffin WL, Gunnels JC: Primary aldosteronism. Urol Clin North Am 4:227, 1977.

Although only these two articles have been singled out for mention, the entire monograph from the Urologic Clinics, edited by James Glenn, provides an excellent review of all aspects of the adrenal gland. Included are chapters on anatomy, physiology, most medical and surgical adrenal lesions, specific problems in patient management, diagnostic evaluations, and surgical techniques. All chapters are well indexed and provide recent, comprehensive bibliographies.

REFERENCES

1. Bennett AH, Cain JP, Dluhy RG, Tynes WV, Harrison JH, Thorn GW: Surgical treatment of adrenocorticol hyperplasia: 20 years experience. Urol 109:321, 1973
2. Bennett AH, Harrison JH, Thorn GW: Neoplasms of the adrenal gland. J Urol 106:607, 1971
3. Gonzalez–Serva K, Glenn JF: Adrenal surgical techniques. Urol Clin North Am 4:327, 1977
4. Thrall JH, Freitas JE, Beierwaltes WH: Adrenal scintigraphy. Semin Nucl Med 8:23, 1978
5. Herwig KR, Sonda LP: Usefulness of adrenal venography and iodocholesterol scan in adrenal surgery. Urol 122:7, 1979
6. McGuffin WL, Gunnels JC: Primary aldosteronism. Urol Clin North Am 4:227, 1977
7. Karstaedt N, Sagel SS, Stanley RJ, Melson GL, Levitt RG: Computed tomography of the adrenal gland. Radiology 129:723, 1978
8. Korobkin M, White EA, Dressel HY, Moss AA, Montagne JP: Computed tomography in the diagnosis of adrenal disease. Am J Radiol 132:231, 1979

9. Kearney GP, Mahoney CM, Maher E, Harrison JH: Functioning and nonfunctioning cysts of the adrenal cortex and medulla. Am J Surg 134:363, 1977
10. Gross MD, Freitas JE, Silver TM: Letter: Documentation of adrenal cysts by adrenal scanning techniques. J Nucl Med 19:1092, 1978
11. Scheible W, Coel M, Siemers PT, Seigel H: Percutaneous aspiration of the adrenal cysts. Roentgenology 128:1013, 1977
12. Stewart BH, Bravo EL, Haaga J, Meaney TF, Tarazi R: Localization of pheochromocytoma by computed tomography. N Engl J Med 299:460, 1978
13. Stewart BH, Bravo EL, Meaney, TF: A new simplified approach to the diagnosis of pheochromocytoma. J Urol 122:579, 1979
14. Gangly A, Henry DP, Yune HY, Pratt H, Grim CE, Donohue JP, Weinberger MH: Diagnosis and localization of pheochromocytoma. Am J Med 67:21, 1979

Overview: Surgery of the Adrenal Gland

John D. Young, Jr.

The 1972 publication by Harrison, Jenkins, and Bennett is replete with well-organized historical information on current concepts of cause and management of adrenal endocrinopathies. The essay remains quite current. The authors of the Commentary have adequately updated the diagnostic adjuvants that help identify anatomical abnormalities of the adrenal gland and determine alterations in the biochemical products resulting from these disorders.

As the authors indicate, significant biologic disturbances are often caused by the altered amounts of biochemicals (hormones) from adrenal glands of nearly normal size or by very small tumors. Severe paroxysmal hypertension resulted from a 9-g pheochromocytoma in one of our patients. Scintigraphic and CT findings recently were, at best, equivocal in demonstrating a small aldosterone-producing adenoma in the left adrenal gland. Adrenal scintigrams, phlebography, and even CT scans too frequently fail to identify a small intra-abdominal tumor or an ectopic steroid-producing neoplasm. Our colleagues in nuclear medicine and CT scanning often are more aware of these techniques' limitations than those of us anxiously awaiting the precise localization of any lesion 1 cm or larger anywhere in the human body. What was thought to be left adrenal gland tumor on a CT scan of a recent patient apparently was the tail of the pancreas, and "metastases to retroperitoneal lymph nodes" could not be discerned by the pathologist in the resected nodes of another patient. Yet this imaging is far more accurate than any previous technique, and there is little doubt that those skilled in the use of various imaging devices are accumulating experience and criteria that will lead to greater precision in diagnosis. For the moment, however, we must not rely entirely on imaging. If assays for steroids and catecholamines and their metabolites indicate a surgically treatable endocrinopathy, determination of catecholamines and adrenocorticotrophins from various levels of the vena cava is mandatory, particularly when the adrenal and pituitary glands show no abnormality by imaging. It is estimated that 10% of pheochromocytomas may be extra-adrenal or multiple, or both, and this neoplasm has been identified in sites extending from the neck to the urinary bladder. High levels of ACTH in the superior vena cava helped us locate a thymoma that produced both ACTH and melanocyte-stimulating hormone. A urologic surgeon should be prepared to search the intraperitoneal and retroperitoneal spaces for these hormone-producing tumors.

The surgeon treating adrenal and extra-adrenal hormonally active lesions should be capable of a variety of surgical approaches. Perhaps I would recognize fewer disadvantages of the transabdominal approach than proposed in the Commentary. A transverse upper abdominal incision made from the inferior margin of one 9th costal cartilage straight across the upper abdomen to the other obtains excellent exposure of the adrenal and retroperitoneal areas. One can extend the incision into the 10th rib bed on the side of the suspected lesion, but this usually is not needed. However, the exposure through this approach will be completely unsatisfactory unless the lift on the operating table is elevated under the patient's upper lumbar spine to slightly accentuate the normal lumbar lordotic curve. This flares the costal margin and rotates the liver slightly superiorly. Reflect the hepatic flexure of the colon and second portion of the duodenum medially by incising the peritoneum over the right kidney. Then open Gerota's fascia, exposing the kidney and the adrenal gland. This exposure recently was particularly helpful in the extirpation of a 4.5-cm pheochromocytoma from beneath the vena cava. Approach the left adrenal gland by incising the gastrocolic omentum below the lateral half of the stomach, reflecting the transverse colon downward, reflecting the stomach and pancreas upward, and opening Gerota's fascia over the upper pole of the kidney and adrenal gland. These maneuvers obviate some of the drawbacks to the transabdominal approach, such as the extensive mobilization of the abdominal viscera mentioned earlier in this chapter. I prefer this anterior route over the bilateral flank incisions for suspected lesions on both sides or for bilateral adrenalectomy. Exploration along the great vessels, at the root of a small bowel mesentery, and at the bifurcation of the aorta have led to discovery of ectopic pheochromocytomas. I would agree that the flank approach is appropriate for a well-localized unilateral tumor of the adrenal gland, but I prefer the transabdominal approach over bilateral flank incisions. The thoracoabdominal incision is the approach of choice if there is a very large unilateral adrenal lesion. However, such a mass often can be exposed adequately through the transabdominal incision described above. For reasons mentioned in the Commentary, I am wary of the bilateral posterior approach, although this may be done more quickly in most instances. The hazard of caval injury the authors described is very real, and the surgeon is in a less favorable position to cope with this possibility through the posterior approach.

After adrenalectomy or removal of a hormone-producing neoplasm, changes from the patient's preoperative pathophysiologic state must be carefully monitored and treated. The metabolic sequelae of changing adrenal hormone concentration are accentuated in a postoperative patient. For example, the vasodilatation after removal of a pressor-producing pheochromocytoma may result in persistent hypotension. Volume replacement above the measured loss often will be necessary to compensate for the relative increase in intravascular space.

Both the Harrison, Jenkins, and Bennett paper and the Commentary are useful references for management of surgical lesions of the adrenal gland.

PART TWO

SURGERY FOR RENAL ADENOCARCINOMA

2

THE SURGICAL MANAGEMENT OF RENAL CELL CARCINOMA

Donald G. Skinner,* Clinton D. Vermillion and Robert B. Colvin

From the Department of Urology and Pathology, Massachusetts General Hospital, Boston, Massachusetts

The Journal of Urology
Copyright © 1972 by The Williams & Wilkins Co.
Vol. 107, May
Printed in U.S.A.

The incidence of renal cell carcinoma is 3.5 per 100,000 population per year. This represents approximately 1.7 percent of cancer occurring in male subjects and 1.0 percent of cancer in female subjects.[1]

In 1883 Grawitz first described this tumor when he noted the striking gross resemblance of the yellow renal mass to the adrenal cortex and suggested that it might be derived from adrenal rests.[2] The term hypernephroma was introduced by Birch-Hirschfeld in 1892 as an appropriate name for the Grawitz tumors.

Gradually urologists and pathologists realized that most renal parenchymal tumors arise from renal tubular epithelial cells—a fact supported by light and electron microscopy,[3,4] Thus, the term renal cell carcinoma or renal cell adenocarcinoma seems most appropriate. These parenchymal tumors, the renal cell carcinomas, constitute approximately 85 percent of all renal tumors. The remaining 15 percent include tumors of the renal pelvis and tumors of the renal capsule. Herein we shall deal only with renal cell carcinomas.

HISTORICAL DATA

In 1871 Walcott performed the first nephrectomy for renal cell carcinoma.[5] In 1932 Hand and Broders reported a 23 percent 5-year survival for patients with renal parenchymal tumors treated by nephrectomy at the Mayo Clinic. Operative mortality was 12 percent.[6]

Since Walcott's bold adventure there have been numerous reports on results of treatment of renal cell carcinoma by nephrectomy. Before 1950 the reported 5-year survivals ranged from 13 to 40 percent.

In 1948 Mortensen described a transthoracic approach for the removal of an extremely difficult left renal tumor[7] and in 1949 Chute and associates reported on 39 cases in which a radical nephrectomy was performed via the thoracoabdominal approach.[8] Since it has been demonstrated that the direct extension of tumor into the perinephric fat occurs in 13 to 25 percent of

Accepted for publication June 25, 1971. Read at annual meeting of American Urological Association, Chicago, Illinois, May 16–20, 1971.
* Current address: Department of Surgery/Urology, U.C.L.A. School of Medicine, Los Angeles, California 90024.

cases of renal cell carcinoma, the principles of cancer surgery dictate that nephrectomy be done in such a way as to include the complete removal of Gerota's fascia with its contents intact along with early ligation of the renal artery and vein.[9,10] This generally constitutes a radical nephrectomy.

In 1963 and again in 1968 Robson indicated that extensive radical nephrectomy plus regional lymph node dissection would markedly improve survival.[11,12] However, despite the trend toward more radical operation, the published 5-year survival results have remained in the 25 to 50 percent range, although few investigators have reported either the method of treatment or the pathologic extent of the tumors treated.

In the past 20 years several investigators have suggested that irradiation either preoperatively or postoperatively could favorably affect survival in patients with renal cell carcinoma. Flocks and Kadesky and subsequently Riches and associates have given support for the adjunctive use of irradiation.[13–15] Their total number of patients treated with irradiation is small, however, and Peeling's recent data derived from a larger series indicate that the adjunctive use of irradiation actually decreased survival in those patients as compared to patients treated by nephrectomy alone.[16]

Recently a nationwide cooperative study involving the random assignment of preoperative irradiation to patients with renal call carcinoma has been established to specifically answer the question of whether preoperative irradiation does in fact alter survival. It will be some time before the longterm results of that study are known.

Table 1 is an attempt to summarize the published results of the surgical management of renal cell carcinoma with and without preoperative or postoperative irradiation. This is a comparison of results in all patients surgically treated except those with metastases present at hospitalization or those whose primary tumor histologically involved contiguous visceral organs.[6,12–14,16–20]

It is our purpose herein to report the results of a 30-year experience in the surgical management of renal cell carcinoma, according to pathologic stage and histologic grade as relating to 5 and 10-year survival and type of treatment employed.

MATERIALS AND METHODS

Between 1935 and 1965, 329 patients with renal cell carcinoma were surgically treated at this hospital. All patients underwent renal exploration and all except 10 underwent nephrectomy.

Between 1935 and 1948 simple nephrectomy via the lumbar or the transperitoneal approach was the usual form of therapy. Since 1948 radical nephrectomy, usually via the thoracoabdominal approach, has become the standard operation. This approach has been designed to

TABLE 1. Summary of Published Results of Treatment of Renal Cell Carcinoma, Comparing Nephrectomy Alone to Nephrectomy Plus Irradiation Therapy. Pathologic Stage I to III Tumors Includes All Patients Surgically Treated Except Those with Metastases Present on Admission

| Series | No. Cases | 5-Year Survival | | | 10-Year Survival | | |
		Nephrectomy Alone No. (%)	Nephrectomy Plus Irradiation No. (%)	Over-All No. (%)	Nephrectomy Alone No. (%)	Nephrectomy Plus Irradiation No. (%)	Over-All No. (%)
Flocks and Kadesky[13] Iowa, 1926–1950	96	27/56 (48)	21/40 (52)	48/96 (50)	9/39 (23)	9/27 (33)	18/66 (27)
Riches and associates[14] British Isles, 1935–1950	398	105/345 (30)	26/53 (49)	131/398 (33)	30/177 (17)	4/15 (27)	34/192 (17)
Peeling and associates[16] London, 1940–1965	164	50/96 (52)	17/68 (25)	67/164 (10)			
Hand and Broders[6] Mayo Clinic, 1901–1923	193	14/193	0	41/193 (23)			
Foot and associates[17] New York, 1926–1949	104	33/81 (40)	0	33/81 (10)	9/40 (22)		9/40 (22)
Myers and associates[18] Mayo Clinic, 1940–1955	479	250/479 (54)	0	259/479 (54)	183/479 (38)		183/479 (38)
Middleton[19] New York Hospital, 1932–1965	334		25% received irridation	112/320 (35)		25% received irridation	19/108 (18)
Kaufman and Mims[20] UCLA, 1966	79	37/79 (17)	0	37/79 (47)	27/79 (34)	0	27/79 (34)
Robson and associates[12] Toronto, 1949–1964	70	40/70 (57)	0	40/70 (57)	18/34 (53)	0	18/34 (53)
Skinner and associates Boston, 1935–1965	232	109/190 (57)	9/18 (50)	118/208 (57)	61/139 (44)	0	61/139 (44)

include the removal of Gerota's fascia and its contents intact with early ligation of the renal artery and vein. Regional lymph node dissection has been done in most of these cases. The term radical nephrectomy will refer to this operation with or without lymph node dissection.

Of these 329 patients, 20 could not be traced and their hospital records were not sufficiently complete to permit evaluation. These 20 patients were excluded, leaving 309 patients for evaluation. In calculating survival we have included those patients who died at operation or during the immediate postoperative period (operative mortality). Patients who died within 5 years of unrelated causes (24) but had autopsy or good clinical evidence of freedom from metastatic renal cell carcinoma were excluded from the 5-year survival calculations. Ten-year survival calculations were based on those patients who were at risk at least 10 years from the date of their operation. The operative mortality was included in this calculation but patients who died within 10 years of unrelated causes were excluded.

As others have found also, male subjects dominated this series by a 2 to 1 ratio. Only 9 percent of these patients presented with a combination of gross hematuria, pain and an abdominal mass, the so-called classic triad. A combination of any 2 of these 3, however, occurred in 36 percent and hematuria was noted in 60 percent.

Ten patients had secondary polycythemia (hematocrit greater than 50 percent or hemoglobin greater than 15.5) at hospitalization which returned to nornal following nephrectomy. On the other hand, anemia (hematocrit less than 33 percent or hemoglobin less than 10) was a common finding and was noted in 64 patients (21 percent). Secondary hyperparathyroidism with hypercalcemia (serum calcium greater than 10.5) was found at hospitalization in 11 patients. Seven male patients were referred because of the sudden onset of a varicocele, 6 of these 7 occurring on the left side. One patient with tumor involving the vena cava presented with an acute right varicocele.

One other patient presented with a large hematoma in the right flank following spontaneous rupture of a carcinoma. While 10 percent of patients presented because of clinical symptoms secondary to metastases, 77 of 309, or nearly 25 percent, had x-ray or clinical evidence of metastases when first seen for therapy. In 7 percent of our patients renal cell carcinoma was an incidental finding, usually discovered during the course of another operative procedure.

With the exception of those patients who presented with metastases and those in whome renal cell carcinoma was an incidental finding, no significant prognostic relation could be found between various presenting symptoms or laboratory abnormalities and the over-all survival.

In these 309 patients, 93 simple nephrectomies were performed and 203 patients underwent radical nephrectomy. Three heminephrectomies were performed in patients with either a solitary kidney or hypoplastic contralateral kidney. Ten patients with extensive metastases underwent exploration and were regarded as inoperable.

Fifteen of the 309 patients died at operation or in the immediate postoperative period. This is an over-all operative mortality of 5 percent. Irradiation was used as adjunctive therapy in only 19 of the 232 patients who were without metastases when first seen for therapy.

Operations for removal of an apparent solitary metastasis were performed on 34 patients and 7 others underwent 2 operations for removal of 2 metastatic foci.

RESULTS

To analyze the outcome of therapy, surgical staging according to the plan of Robson and associates was employed.[11,12] Briefly, this divides the over-all group of tumors into 4 stages dependent upon specific pathologic involvement.

Stage I. Tumor is confined to the kidney—perinephric fat, renal vein and regional nodes are negative. There were 102 patients with this stage tumor treated, resulting in a 65 percent 5-year survival and a 56 percent 10-year survival (see Fig. 2-1). Radical nephrectomy produces slightly but not statistically better results at 5 and 10 years. Adjunctive irradiation was given to 6 of 102 patients; 2 of these 6 patients survived beyond 5 years.

Stage II. Tumor involves the perinephric fat but is confined within Gerota's fascia—renal vein and regional nodes are negative. There were 22 patients with this stage tumor treated, resulting in a 5-year survival of 47 percent and a 10-year survival of 20 percent (see figure). This group is small but a 10 percent improvement in the 5-year survival was noted with radical nephrectomy. Three patients were treated with adjunctive irradiation therapy, all of whom survived more than 5 years.

Stage III. umor involves renal vein and/or regional nodes, with or without involvement of the vena cava or perinephric fat. There were 108 patients with this stage tumor treated, with a 5-year survival of 51 percent and a 10-year survival of 37 percent (see figure). Table 2 further shows 5 and 10-year survival according to various specific combinations of histologic involvement. While a statistically significant improvement in over-all survival between radical nephrectomy and simple nephrectomy cannot be demonstrated, 2 of 6 patients with positive regional nodes survived 5 years following radical nephrectomy as the only form of therapy, and one of these

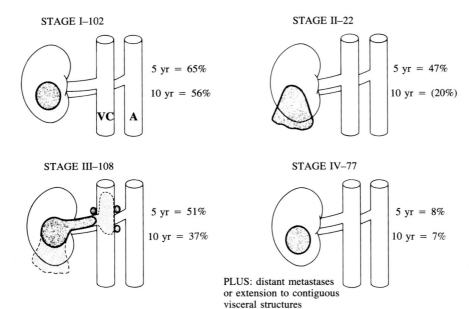

Fig. 1. Five and ten-year survival of 309 surgically treated patients according to specific pathologic stage. Parentheses indicate too few patients to be significant.

TABLE 2. Summary of Survival According to Extent of Pathologic Involvement by Tumor

	Histologic Extent of Tumor	5-Year Survival No. (%)	10-Year Survival No. (%)
Confined to kidney (stage I)		59/91 (65)	34/61 (56)
Renal vein involvement	Renal vein only	34/48 (66)	17/35 (49)
	Renal vein plus perinephric fat	16/33 (50)	7/21 (33)
	Renal vein plus regional nodes	0/6 (0)	0/3 (0)
	Renal vein plus perinephric fat plus regional nodes	0/4 (0)	0/2 (0)
	Total	48/81 (59)	24/61 (40)
Perinephric fat involvement	Perinephric fat only	8/17 (47)	2/10 (20)
	Perinephric fat plus renal vein	16/33 (50)	7/21 (33)
	Perinephric fat plus regional nodes	1/3 (33)	0/1 (0)
	Perinephric fat plus renal vein plus regional nodes	0/4 (0)	0/2 (0)
	Total	25/57 (44)	9/34 (26)
Regional node involvement	Regional nodes only	2/6 (33)	1/6 (17)
	Regional nodes plus renal vein	0/6 (0)	0/3 (0)
	Regional nodes plus perinepheric fat	1/3 (33)	0/1 (0)
	Regional nodes plus renal vein plus perinepheric fat	0/4 (0)	0/2 (0)
	Total	3/19 (16)	1/12 (8)
Direct extension of tumor to contiguous visceral structures		0/15 (0)	0/12 (0)

is well more than 10 years following surgical treatment. Irradiation was used as adjunctive therapy in 10 patients, 4 of whom survived more than 5 years.

Vascular involvement, by itself, does not statistically alter the prognosis at either 5 or 10 years compared to stage I tumors (Table 2). Five of these 48 patients with vascular involvement only had extension of tumor into the vena cava. All 5 of these survived 5 years and 3 of the 4 survived more than 10 years.

Stages I through III. Patients in these stages are those who are potentially curable by a surgical procedure. Table 3 summarizes the results of therapy in these 232 patients. As noted by Peeling[16] the adjunctive use of irradiation did not improve survival at 5 years compared to nephrectomy alone.

Stage IV. There are distant metastases secondary to renal cell carcinoma present at hospitalization or histo-

TABLE 3. Over-All Summary of Results of Surgical Treatment According to Pathologic Stage

Pathologic Stage	No. Cases	Dead Within 5 Years Free of Tumor-Excluded from Study	Op. Mortality No. (%)	5-Year Survival No. (%)	10-Year Survival No. (%)	Dead Beyond 10 Years Due to Renal Cell Carcinoma
Stage I	102	11	4/102 (4)	59/91 (65)	34/61 (56)	1
Stage II	22	5	0	8/17 (47)	2/10 (20)	1
Stage III	108	8	3/108 (3)	51/100 (51)	25/68 (37)	5
Total (stages I–III)	232	24	7/232 (3)	118/208 (57)	61/139 (44)	7
Stage IV	77	0	8/77 (10)	6/77 (8)	4/56 (7)	1
Total (stages I–IV)	309	24	15/309 (5)	124/285 (44)	65/195 (33)	8

logic involvement by tumor of contiguous visceral structures. There were 77 patients who presented with a stage IV tumor. The 5-year survival was 8 percent and 10-year survival was 7 percent with an operation mortality of 10 percent (see figure). All but one of the long-term survivors in this group had excision of an apparently solitary metastasis. One other patient had multiple pulmonary nodules on chest x-ray that were considered to represent metastatic renal cell carcinoma. Following nephrectomy these lesions disappeared and this patient is currently well. The nature of these pulmonary lesions was never proved histologically.

There were 15 patients in whom carcinoma directly invaded contiguous visceral structures. None of these 15 survived 5 years (Table 2).

Table 3 shows the over-all results of the surgical treatment of renal cell carcinoma for the entire 309 patients, regardless of pathologic involvement.

Excision of metastatic renal cell carcinoma. Since 1935 there have been 48 operations for the removal of metastatic lesions of renal cell carcinoma in 41 patients. Of these 41 patients 5 are alive and 4 died free of disease more than 10 years following excision of the metastasis. Of the 32 deaths from renal cell carcinoma in this group, 23 patients died within 2 years, 6 patients died between 2 and 5 years and 3 patients survived more than 5 years but subsequently died with widespread metastases. Of the 5 patients who are alive and of the 7 who survived more than 5 years following removal of an apparent solitary metastasis, 9 underwent operation for the removal of metastasis more than 4 years after nephrectomy.

Seven patients had 2 separate metastases excised; 3 of these 7 patients are alive although one has recurrent disease. One other patient who died of metastases lived more than 6 years following the excision of the second metastasis.

HISTOLOGIC GRADING

All available microscopic sections were independently reviewed by a pathologist (R. C.).

Numerous microscopic features were recorded and the means of grading was chosen for its ease of appli-

cation. Ours is somewhat similar to Hand and Broders' approach.[6] Two important differences are that our classification is concerned only with nuclear morphology and not with cytoplasmic products or histological organization, and that the worst area of the tumor, rather than an over-all impression, defines the grade. Grade 1 tumors consisted of cells with small nuclei indistinguishable from those seen in normal tubular epithelial cells. Grade 2 tumors had slightly irregular and frequently pyknotic nuclei but were without abnormal nucleoli. Grade 3 tumors consisted of enlarged irregular and pleomorphic nuclei often with prominent nucleoli. Grade 4 tumors included those with extremely bizarre giant nuclei.

Table 4 is a brief summary of survival according to histologic grade and its relation to pathologic stage. Grade significantly affects survival but to a lesser degree than does pathologic stage. Because tumors may include a great variety of cell types, grades and histologic patterns, microscopic examination can define only the minimum malignant potential, since more malignant areas may not be sampled. This may be one reason why staging generally correlates better with survival, since it is based upon the most malignantly behaving portion of the tumor.

The influence of the cytoplasmic appearance of these tumors on survival also was analysed (Table 5). While pure spindle cell tumors significantly decreased survival, the prognosis of pure clear cell tumors compared to pure granular or mixtures of granular and clear cell was only slightly better at 5 and 10 years.

In most cases with biopsies of metastases, the metastases appeared at least equal to the grade of the worst portion of the primary tumor, and no grade 1 tumors were noted in metastases or in the renal vein.

A more detailed study of the histologic grade and its relation to stage and survival is presented elsewhere.[21]

DISCUSSION

In 1939 Mintz and Gaul reported the results of simple nephrectomy on survival in 127 patients treated at this hospital between 1900 and 1935. Of these 127 patients

TABLE 4. Summary of Survival According to Histologic Grade of Tumor and Its Relation to Pathologic Stage

		Stage I	Stage II	Stage III	Stage IV	Overall Total
Grade 1	No. cases	8	1	0	0	9
	1-year survival (%)	88	(100)	0	0	
	5-year survival (%)	(75)	(100)	0	0	77
	10-year survival (%)	(75)	—	0	0	(75)
Grade 2	No. cases	40	8	31	9	88
	1-year survival (%)	95*	88	96	89	
	5-year survival (%)	81	38	70	22	65
	10-year survival (%)	73	—	55	(11)	55
Grade 3	No. cases	36	9	39	32	118
	1-year survival (%)	78	100	77	31	
	5-year survival (%)	58	62	40	3	56
	10-year survival (%)	53	42	36	(—)	48
Grade 4	No. cases	9	2	23	17	57
	1-year survival (%)	78	(100)	61	20	
	5-year survival (%)	67	(33)	27	(5)	26
	10-year survival (%)	67	—	19	0	22

* Underlined survivals are significantly different within each stage (p < 0.05). (Parentheses indicate groups with less than 5 at risk.

TABLE 5. Influence of Cytoplasmic Appearances and Cell Type on Survival (%)*

Cell Type	No. Cases	1-Year Survival (%)	5-Year Survival (%)	10-Year Survival (%)
Pure clear	67	87	58	54
Clear and/or granular	169	73	46	38
Spindle	36	47	23	16

* p < 0.01 for all types except 5-year and 10-year survivals of pure clear and clear/granular combinations which have p < 0.03 and p < 0.10, respectively.

only 17 (13 percent) survived 5 years.[5] While our report shows a marked improvement in the results of surgical management over the succeeding 30 years, surgical technique, advancement in postoperative management and patient selection have changed so markedly that further comparison is not warranted.

In a retrospective study such as this, it is difficult to draw significant conclusions regarding the best form of surgical treatment. Over-all results suggest that radical nephrectomy does not improve the survival compared to simple nephrectomy. Such a conclusion does not seem justified because of patient selection. Early in this series the operative findings and surgical ability of the operator would often dictate the form of treatment—that is the more extensive tumor was often treated by a more extensive operation and vice versa. Fifty-two percent of the simple nephrectomies were performed for stage I tumors whereas only 24 percent of radical nephrectomies were done for tumors of this low stage.

The perinephric fat or regional nodes were involved in nearly 30 percent of potentially curable patients in this series. Survival in this group of patients was improved by radical nephrectomy. The principles of cancer surgery would dictate that because of extension of renal cell carcinoma to the perinephric fat and regional nodes in a significant percentage of cases, the best operation should include the removel of Gerota's fascia with its contents intact together with the early ligation of the renal artery and vein, followed by regional lymph node dissection. We prefer to do this through the thoracoabdominal approach.

Contrary to other reports, tumor invasion of the renal vein, by itself, did not significantly alter prognosis compared to stage I tumors.[18,20]

The operative mortality cannot be considered independent of stage and grade. The operative mortality of stage IV tumors was 10 percent and that of grade 4 was 10.5 percent as opposed to 5 percent over-all in this series. We have elected to include the operative mortality in calculating the survival figures. If operative mortality were excluded the 5 and 10-year survival calculations for potentially curable patients would be 59 percent and 46 percent, respectively.

Our study tends to confirm the previous observations by Petkovic, Arner and recently Böttiger that division by pathologic stage correlates better with survival than does division by grade.[22-24] Grading according to nuclear morphology was more meaningful than division according to cytoplasmic "differentiation".

Several investigators have alluded to the possibility that irradiation therapy, either preoperatively or postoperatively, can improve survival.[13-15,25] This report, as well as those by Robson, Peeling and Böttiger, has demonstrated that to date the results of the surgical management of renal cell carcinoma are as good as or better than any results in which irradiation has been used as adjunctive therapy.[11,12,16,24]

In carefully selected cases an aggressive approach to apparently solitary metastases seems justified.[19] In our study it was apparent that patients operated on for an apparent solitary metastasis did better if a significant period of time elapsed between nephrectomy and removal of the metastasis.

Previous 5-year survival figures reported in the literature vary between 30 and 60 percent for patients without obvious metastatic disease. This variation in survival has undoubtedly occurred because the majority of authors fail to correlate prognosis with pathologic stage and many have not even reported method of treatment. It has been our purpose to attempt to correlate survival with pathologic staging in a large series, so that it might be possible to form a rational opinion as to the prognosis of individual cases.

SUMMARY

The results of a 30-year experience in the surgical management of renal cell carcinoma have been reported according to pathologic stage as relating to 5 and 10-year survival and the type of treatment used.

Between 1935 and 1965, 329 patients with renal cell carcinoma underwent renal exploration at this hospital. Of these 309 patients were followed and analyzed. There were 93 simple nephrectomies and 203 patients underwent radical nephrectomy. Three heminephrectomies were performed and the remaining 10 patients had only biopsies of the primary tumor.

Operative mortality was 5 percent and over-all survival was 44 percent at 5 years and 33 percent at 10 years. Excluding those patients with metastases present when first seen for treatment, the 5-year survival was 57 percent and the 10-year survival was 44 percent.

Division by pathologic stage was noted to correlate better with survival than did division by grade, and no significant prognostic relations could be found between various presenting symptoms or laboratory abnormalities and the over-all survival of these patients.

It is noteworthy that vascular involvement, by itself, did not statistically alter the prognosis at either 5 or 10 years compared to stage I tumors.

In selected cases an aggressive approach to apparently solitary metastases seems justified.

REFERENCES

1. MacDonald, E. J.: Present incidence and survival picture in cancer and promise of improved prognosis. Bull Amer Coll Surgeons 33:75, 1948

2. Melicow, M. M.: Classification of renal neoplasms: a clinical and pathological study based on 199 cases. J Urol 51:333, 1944

3. Carter R. L.: The pathology of renal cancer. JAMA 204:221, 1968

4. Pinals R. S. and Krane, S. M.: Medical aspects of renal carcinoma. Postgrad Med J 38:507, 1962

5. Mintz, E. R. and Gaul, E. A.: Kidney tumors; some causes of poor end results. New York State J Med 39:1405, 1939

6. Hand J. R. and Broders, A. C.: Carcinoma of the kidney: the degree of malignancy in relation to factors bearing on prognosis. J Urol 28:199, 1932

7. Mortensen, H.: Transthoracic nephrectomy. J Urol 60:855, 1948

8. Chute, R., Soutter, L. and Kerr W. S., Jr.: Value of thoraco-abdominal incision in removal of kidney tumors. New Engl J Med 241:951, 1949

9. Foley, F. E. B., Mulvaney, W. P., Richardson, E. J. and Victor, I.: Radical nephrectomy for neoplasm. J Urol 68:39, 1952

10. Beare, J. B. and McDonald, J. R.: Involvement of the renal capsule in surgically removed hypernephroma: a gross and histopathologic study. J Urol 61:857, 1949

11. Robson, C. J.: Radical nephrectomy for renal cell carcinoma. J Urol 89:37, 1963

12. Robson, C. J., Churchill, B. M. and Anderson, W.: The results of radical nephrectomy for renal cell carcinoma. J Urol 101:297, 1969

13. Flocks, R. H. and Kadesky, M. C.: Malignant neoplasms of the kidney: an analysis of 353 patients followed five years or more. J Urol 79:196, 1958

14. Riches, E. W., Griffiths, I. H. and Thackray, A. C.: New growths of the kidney and ureter. Brit J Urol 23:297, 1951

15. Riches, E.: The place of radiotherapy in the management of parenchymal carcinoma of the kidney. J Urol 95:313, 1966

16. Peeling, W. B., Mantell, B. S. and Shepheard, B. G. F.: Post-operative irradiation in the treatment of renal cell carcinoma. Brit J Urol 41:23, 1969

17. Foot, N. C., Humphreys, G. A. and Whitmore, W. F.: Renal tumors: pathology and prognosis in 295 cases. J Urol 66:190, 1951

18. Myers, G. H., Jr., Fehrenbaker, L. G. and Kelalis, P. P.: Prognostic significance of renal vein invasion by hypernephroma. J Urol 100:420, 1968

19. Middleton, R. G.: Surgery for metastatic renal cell carcinoma. J Urol 97:973, 1967

20. Kaufman, J. J. and Mims, M. M.: Tumors of the kidney. In: Current Problems in Surgery. Chicago: Year Book Medical Publishers, Inc., pp 1–44, 1966

21. Skinner, D. G., Colvin, R. B., Vermillion, C. D., Pfister, R. C. and Leadbetter, W. F.: The diagnosis and management of renal cell carcinoma: a clinical and pathologic study of 309 cases. Cancer 28:1165, 1971

22. Petkovic, S. D.: An anatomical classification of renal tumors in the adult as a basis for prognosis. J Urol 81:618, 1959

23. Arner O., Blanck, C. and Schreek, T., von: Renal adenocarcinoma: morphology—grading of malignancy—prognosis. A study of 197 cases. Acta Chir. Scand., suppl. 346, p 1, 1965

24. Böttiger, L. E.: Prognosis in renal carcinoma. Cancer 26:780, 1970

25. Cox, C. E., Lacy, S. S., Montgomery, W. G. and Boyce, W. H.: Renal adenocarcinomas: 28-year review, with emphasis on rationale and feasibility of preoperative radiotherapy. J Urol 104:53, 1970

Commentary: Radical Nephrectomy

Claude E. Merrin

PREOPERATIVE PROCEDURES

Evaluation of the Tumor. The success of radical nephrectomy is based on a careful preoperative evaluation that allows for a detailed mapping of the tumor and its relationship with surrounding anatomic structures. This evaluation consists of the following procedures.

1. *Intravenous urography (IVP)*. IVP evaluates the size of the tumor and its relationship with the pyelocaliceal system of the kidney and with the ureter.
2. *Nephrotomography*. Nephrotomography complements IVP and permits a more precise definition of the tumor. Tomographic cuts are often done with IVP.
3. *Selective renal angiography*. The injection of radiopaque dye in the renal artery helps define the extent of tumor vascularity.
4. *Venacavography*. Inferior cavography and, when necessary, simultaneous superior cavography permit a clear delineation of a possible tumor thrombus in the vena cava.
5. *Renal scan*. The renal scan (Fig. 2) may permit diagnosis of avascular intrarenal tumoral masses. It is useful when tumor size is larger than 2 cm.

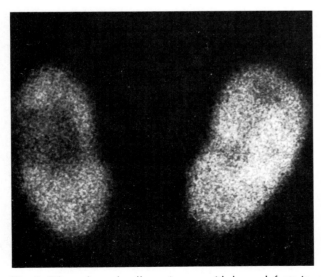

Fig. 2. Bilateral renal cell carcinoma with large defects in both kidneys. IVP and angiogram were normal. The patient presented with multiple metastases. Bone biopsy first revealed the renal origin of the tumors.

6. *Bilateral pedal lymphography*. Bilateral pedal lymphography permits the evaluation of the regional lymph nodes when gross tumor is present. When there is microscopic invasion, this study is not helpful. Controversy exists on its value. In my experience, it has an accuracy of approximately 80%.
7. *Gastrointestinal (GI) studies*. Very large tumors may invade the colon, pancreas, or small bowel, or a combination of these organs. Therefore, investigation of these structures with upper GI series and barium enema may give valuable preoperative information and allow for adequate surgical planning (bowel resection).
8. *Computed tomography (CT scanning)*. CT scanning shows the sagittal relationship of the tumor and its surrounding structures and often complements the aforementioned studies that give a longitudinal view of the tumor. It should always be done in conjunction with the previous diagnostic studies.
9. *Ultrasonography*. Ultrasonography is of value in determining grossly the size and the consistency of the tumor.
10. *Simultaneous aortography and inferior venacavography*. Simultaneous aortography and venacavography (Fig. 3), when performed after lymphography, gives a view of the tumor and its relationship to the regional lymphatics, the vena cava, and the aorta (in a series of films). It is also possible to visualize the celiac axis and to rule out the presence of hepatic metastases.

These preoperative studies give the surgeon a tridimensional picture of the tumor and its surroundings, thus allowing for a better planning of the surgical approach.

Evaluation of the Patient. Many patients diagnosed with renal cell carcinoma are in their fifth, sixth, and seventh decades, ages when latent alterations of the cardiovascular and pulmonary systems are present. In addition, renal cell carcinoma often has metabolic and hormonal manifestations that may complicate surgery. Therefore, the following preoperative studies are indicated.

1. *Electrocardiography (with stress test when indicated)*. Electrocardiography (ECG) permits the physician to rule out latent myocardial ischemia.
2. *Pulmonary function tests*. Pulmonary function tests complement the ECG and permit the physician to measure pulmonary lung reserve. In my experience, a decrease in pulmonary function accurately predicts cardiovascular postoperative complications, especially in chronic smokers.
3. *Biochemical studies*. Emphasis should be put on certain biochemical studies, for example, the evaluation of the

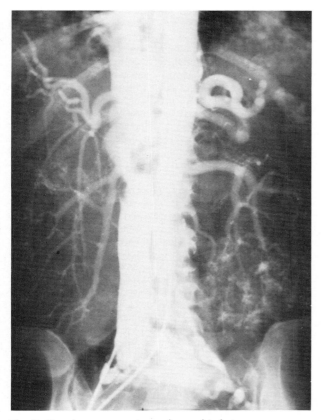

Fig. 3. Simultaneous aortography and inferior venacavography after lymphography. Bilateral renal tumors can be seen. Irregularities in the lateral border of the vena cava as well as filling defects suggest caval invasion by the tumors.

renal function of the contralateral kidney (blood urea nitrogen [BUN], serum creatinine, creatinine clearance, electrolytes). Since some of the renal cell carcinomas may produce hypercalcemia, calcium and phosphorous determinations in serum are mandatory to evaluate the tumor's endocrinologic potential.

4. *Coagulation studies.* Since renal cell carcinoma may produce erythrocytosis (due to secretion of erythropoietin), with increased platelets and hypercoagulability, coagulation studies are important to determine preoperatively such an alteration because of the increased incidence of thromboembolic accidents that it may produce. On occasion, preoperative heparinization is necessary.

5. *Liver function studies.* Alterations of liver function can sometimes be observed; therefore, enzyme determinations, for example, serum glutamic-oxaloacetic transaminase (SGOT), serum glutamic-pyruvic transaminase (SGPT), and lactic dehydrogenase (LDH), the sulfobromophtalein test, and serum bilirubin measurements are recommended.

6. *Glucose metabolism.* Subclinical diabetes may decompen-

sate after surgery, and it is thus advisable to perform a glucose determination and, when indicated, a glucose tolerance test. In addition, the presence of subclinical diabetes may mandate modification of the intravenous (IV) fluids administered postoperatively and insulin coverage.

7. *Blood volume and hemoglobin (Hb) studies.* Some patients with renal cell carcinoma are anemic because of hematuria; therefore, evaluation of the degree of Hb depletion will allow for adequate preoperative replacement. The combination of subclinical cardiac ischemia with a minimal decrese in pulmonary function and moderate anemia may precipitate myocardial infarction postoperatively. It is therefore important to have the patient in the best condition of oxygen perfusion by restoring an adequate Hb level before surgery.

Preparation. Preoperative preparation includes the following procedures.

1. *Bowel preparation.* The patient should receive a low-residue diet, enemas, and nonreabsorbable sulfanomide.
2. *Good hydration.* If necessary, administer IV fluids 24 hours in advance to ensure adequate hydration.
3. *Breathing exercise.* In my experience, preoperative breathing exercise will allow for better postoperative ventilation and prevent postoperative atelectasis.
4. *Heparinization.* When hypercoagulation states are present, heparinization will decrease the incidence of postoperative emboli.

SURGICAL TECHNIQUES

The surgical treatment of renal cell carcinoma consists of the *en bloc* excision of the kidney, the perirenal fat, Gerota's fascia, part of the ureter, and the regional lymph nodes. Ligation of the renal vascular pedicle should be accomplished initially to prevent tumor emboli during the intraoperative manipulation of the kidney and the surrounding structures. Some authors recommend the routine excision of the homolateral adrenal gland, but I prefer not to remove it unless metastases exist or are suspected. Two approaches are used.

Transabdominal Transperitoneal Approach. Two incisions are used in the transabdominal transperitoneal approach (Fig. 4): the midline incision going from the symphysis pubis to the xyphoid process (Fig. 4*B*) and the bilateral subcostal incision (chevron; Fig. 4*A*). I prefer the midline incision, since it provides as good an operative field and is easier to perform.

Once the peritoneum has been opened, the operation is identical no matter which incision is used.

Retroperitoneal Lymphadenectomy. The retroperitoneal lymphadenectomy is performed first, since it prepares the renal pedicle for ligation before the kidney is manipulated (Fig. 5). The small bowel is retracted laterally to the right, exposing the root of the mesentery. An incision is made from the angle of Treitz down and around the cecum and is continued upward along the right gutter. The right colon is mobilized, exposing the retrocolonic space and its contents (kidney, ureter, and vena cava). The posterior parietal peritoneum is then dissected

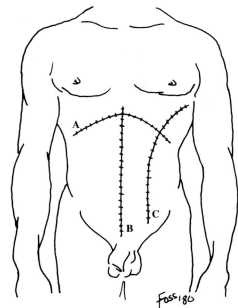

Fig. 4. (*A*) Subcostal chevron incision (transperitoneal). (*B*) Midline transperitoneal incision. (*C*) Thoracoabdominal incision (extraperitoneal).

in the left side to complete the exposure of the aorta, the left ureter, and the left renal vein. The lymphadenectomy is started at the level of the left renal vascular pedicle, and continued to the right and then downward along the aorta and the vena cava. The tissue is completely excised surrounding these structures anteriorly, posteriorly, and laterally. Lumbar vessels can be ligated, but it is advisable to leave as many as possible intact to prevent possible spinal cord ischemia. The inferior mesenteric artery is ligated and transected in patients under 50 years of age. It is spared in older patients, since ischemia and gangrene of the colon may occur because of arteriosclerotic vascular disease. The ligation is continued down to the level of the bifurcation of the aorta and vena cava.

Left-Sided Lesions. In the process of the retroperitoneal lymphadenectomy the renal artery has been previously dissected. It is therefore easy to ligate and transect it at its junction with the aorta (Fig. 6). The left renal vein (also previously dissected) can then be ligated and transected at its junction with the vena cava. Caution is exercised in dissecting the left spermatic and adrenal veins, since they can be torn inadvertently. They are ligated and transected at the junction with the renal vein, and the dissection is continued along the aorta separating the devascularized kidney and its surrounding tissues laterally and posteriorly. The left gutter is opened, and the left colon is mobilized medially to expose the most lateral aspect of the kidney. Dissection can then proceed with ease, with the

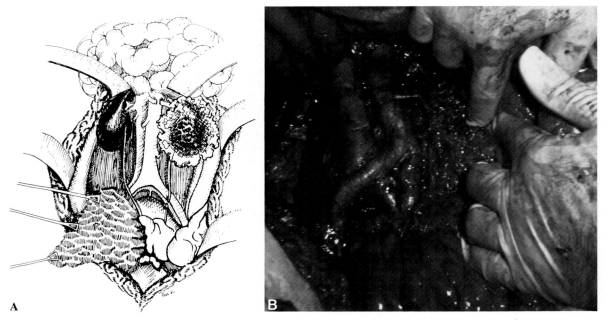

A   B

Fig. 5. Retroperitoneal lymphadenectomy. (*A*) Tissues surrounding both renal vascular pedicles, the aorta, and the vena cava are removed *en bloc*. (*B*) Intraoperative view in a patient who underwent bilateral nephrectomies for bilateral renal cell carcinomas. The inferior mesenteric artery has been dissected and preserved to prevent possible ischemia of the colon.

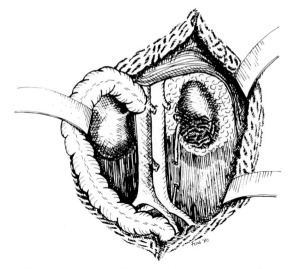

Fig. 6. After retroperitoneal lymphadenectomy, the left kidney has been devascularized and can be excised *en bloc* with its surrounding tissues.

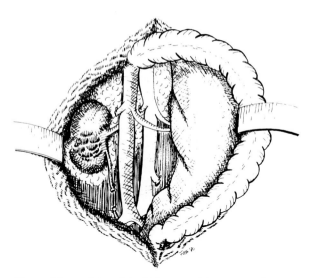

Fig. 7. View of the right kidney and its tumor after lymphadenectomy and ligation of the renal pedicle.

kidney and its surrounding tissues being excised under complete visual control.

Right-Sided Lesions. The right renal artery is isolated and ligated at its junction with the aorta (Fig. 7). The largest part of this artery is located under the inferior vena cava, and its dissection therefore requires vena caval mobilization. This is generally accomplished at the time of lymphadenectomy.

The right renal vein is ligated and transected at its junction with the inferior vena cava. Once the kidney is devascularized, it is easy to proceed with the dissection from the midline laterally and posteriorly and to remove the kidney *en bloc* with its surrounding tissues. If there is any evidence of intracaval thrombus, caval control (for the removal of the thrombus or partial resection of the vena cava) can be accomplished through this approach. If the thrombus extends into the superior vena cava or into the right atrium, the incision is prolonged into the chest through a midline sternotomy to expose the mediastinum and gain control of the superior vena cava and to eventually established a cardiac bypass with extracorporeal circulation.

Thoracoabdominal Approach. The thoracoabdominal approach (Figs. 4*C* and 8) was first used by Chute in 1949 to resect large renal cell carcinomas. More recently it has been popularized by Skinner. The operation is essentially the same as in the transabdominal approach, but this approach gives a better field when lesions are large and localized in the kidney's superior pole.

The patient is positioned in a modified kidney position so that he forms an angle of 30° with the operation table (Fig. 9). The contralateral leg is flexed and protected from the homolateral leg with adequate padding. The kidney rest is elevated, then the table broken. An incision is made over the eighth or ninth rib and continued medially through the costochondral cartilage to the epidgastrium. A paramedian incision is continued downward along the lateral border of the rectus muscle. To gain more field in the midline, the incision can be continued more medially through the rectus muscle. As in the classic flank approach, the rib can be resected or the chest entered through the intercostal space.

The pleura is opened and the diaphragm incised in the direction of its fibers. The rectus muscle is transected at the level of the epigastrium (medial incision) or retracted (lateral approach). The posterior sheath of the rectus fascia is separated from the peritoneum, and retroperitoneal space is thus developed, separating the posterior parietal peritoneum from Gerota's fascia superiorly and posteriorly first. The dissection is continued in the left side until the superior mesenteric artery and the celiac axis are encountered. The root of these vessels is dissected in order to retract the peritoneum and its contents to a maximum (Fig. 10), thus exposing the retroperitoneal space. The dissection is continued downward to find the inferior mesenteric

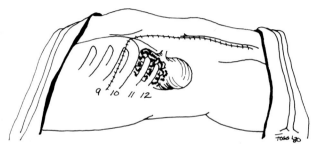

Fig. 8. View of the incision for the thoracoabdominal approach to a renal cell carcinoma in the right kidney.

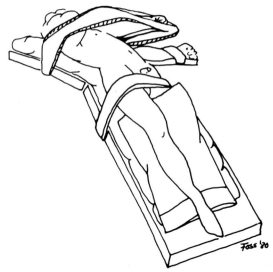

Fig. 9. Modified kidney position for the thoracoabdominal approach to kidney tumors. The patient forms an angle of 30° with the table and lies in hyperextension.

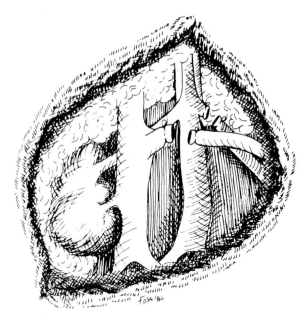

Fig. 10. The superior mesenteric artery, the vena cava, the aorta, and both renal pedicles as seen in the thoracoabdominal approach for a left-side tumor.

artery arising from the distal part of the aorta before its bifurcation. In young patients it is ligated and divided, liberating the peritoneum and allowing maximal (right) lateral retraction of the peritoneal sac and its contents. In older patients, it is dissected in order to preserve vascularization of the lower part of the colon. The peritoneal mobilization exposes the retroperitoneal space. The tissue surrounding the aorta, vena cava,

and renal vessels is dissected and excised. The dissection is started at the level of the diaphragm and continued downward around the superior mesenteric artery and the celiac axis and down to the left renal artery, which should be ligated and transected at its junction with the aorta. The left renal vein is dissected, then ligated and transected. The kidney is devascularized and dissected along the aorta. The tissues are excised anteriorly, posteriorly, and laterally. Lumbar vessels should be individualized and, when necessary, ligated and transected. When possible, they should be preserved. The tissues between the aorta and the vena cava are excised and the right renal artery is dissected free. The anterior vertebral ligament is exposed, and the vena cava is freed from the surrounding tissues anteriorly, laterally, and posteriorly. Dissection is continued down to the level of the bifurcation of the iliac vessels. When possible (and when there is no evidence of tumor involvement), the adrenal gland is preserved. The kidney and its surrounding tissues, which have been previously severed from their vascular attachment, can now be dissected from the midline toward the left and removed *en bloc*. The ureter is transected and ligated near its vesical junction.

In the right side the incision is the same, but it is preferable to open the peritoneum in order to retract the liver more easily. The right colon is mobilized, and the retroperitoneal space is exposed. In doing so, dissection is continued medially, the duodenum is mobilized, and the retroperitoneal structures are further exposed. The inferior mesenteric artery is dissected, ligated, and transected. The parietal peritoneum mobilization is continued upward to the level of the superior mesenteric artery. The tissues surrounding this artery, the aorta, and vena cava in the suprahilar area of the kidney are excised. Dissection is continued along the right renal artery, then ligated and transected. The right renal vein is ligated and transected. At this stage, dissection is continued around the vena cava and the aorta down to the bifurcation of the iliac vessels in the same fashion as in the left side. The right kidney and surrounding tissues are dissected and excised (this can be done with ease). Care is taken to control parasitic veins, which are often present between the tumor and the abdominal wall, by using hemoclips. The ureter is transected (as in the left side) near its junction with the bladder. A chest tube is inserted in the chest, and the incision is closed with nonreabsorbable sutures for the diaphragm and chest wall. The abdominal part of the incision is closed in three layers, using nonreabsorbable sutures for the fascia.

POSTOPERATIVE CARE

The maintenance of adequate electrolyte and fluid balance, intensive breathing exercises, and early ambulation are emphasized.

COMMENTS

The anterior transabdominal approach is very adequate for tumors located in the middle or inferior portion of the kidney, but large tumors located in the superior pole of the kidney are better approached through a thoracoabdominal incision. Adequate retroperitoneal lymphadenectomy can be performed with either approach.

For the past 8 years I have routinely used preoperative

embolization of the tumors 12 hours before surgery. Such a procedure facilitates surgery by decreasing the number of parasitic vessels and therefore decreasing blood loss. In addition, the renal devascularization is equivalent to renal artery ligation and allows for early intraoperative manipulation of the tumor with possible decrease of tumor cell embolization.

ANNOTATED BIBLIOGRAPHY

Robson CJ, Churchill BM, Anderson W: The results of radical nephrectomy for renal cell carcinoma. Trans Am Assoc Genitourin Surg 60:122, 1968.

Eighty-six patients with renal cell carcinoma operated on at the Toronto General Hospital between 1949 and 1964 were followed from 3 to 15 years. The mean age was 53 years; 76% were male, 24% were female, and 75% underwent transperitoneal or thoracoabdominal approaches with the initial ligation of the renal artery and *en bloc* excision of the kidney and its surroundings. Retroperitoneal lymphadenectomies were performed from the diaphragmatic crus to the bifurcation of the aorta. Perirenal fat was invaded by tumor in 45.5% of patients. Adrenal metastases were present in 5.7%. In 91% there was involvement of surrounding organs, and lymph nodes were positive for tumor in 22.7%. In 91% distant metastases were found. Survival by stage was as follows:

Stage I (kidney only): 73% alive at 3 years, 66% at 5 years, and 60% at 10 years

Stage II (perirenal fat): 67% alive at 3 years, 64% at 5 years, and 67% at 10 years

Stage III (vascular or lymphatic invasion): 59% alive at 3 years, 42% at 5 years, and 38% at 10 years.

Stage IV (distant metastases): 25% alive at 3 years, 11% at 5 years, and 0% at 10 years

Survival by grade showed the following:

Grade I: 64% alive at 3 years, 57% at 5 years, and 58% at 10 years

Grade II: 58% alive at 3 years, 47% at 5 years, and 33% at 10 years

Grade III: 53% alive at 3 years, 40% at 5 years, and 29% at 10 years

Postoperative mortality was 3.3%; average hospital stay was 20 days. No chest tubes were left in patients undergoing the thoracoabdominal approach. Thoracocentesis was required in only 4 patients. The authors review the necessary studies to evaluate the tumor before surgery. They recommend routine lung tomographies, mediastinoscopies, aortography, and inferior venacavography.

Middleton RG, Presto AJ: Radical thoracoabdominal nephrectomy for renal cell carcinoma. J Urol 110:36, 1973.

Sixty-one patients with renal cell carcinoma (39 men and 22 women) without evidence of distant metastases underwent radical thoroacoabdominal nephrectomy with *en bloc* removal of the kidney, perinephric fat, and adrenal gland, and retroperitoneal lymphadenectomy; 69% were alive at 3 years, 59% at 5 years, and 40% at 10 years. Thirty-five patients had their tumor limited to the kidney, 14 patients had renal vein involvement, 3 patients had lymphatic involvement (only), and 4 additional patients had simultaneous venous and lymphatic involvement.

The distribution of survival according to the extension of the tumor was as follows:

Kidney only: 80% alive at 3 years. 71% at 5 years, and 70% at 10 years

Renal vein involvement: 57% alive at 3 years, 50% at 5 years, and 33% at 10 years

Lymphatic involvement: 100% alive at 3 years, 67% at 5 years, and 0% at 10 years

Venous and lymphatic involvement: 50% alive at 3 years, 25% at 5 years, and 0% at 10 years

The authors review the experiences of other surgeons and conclude that radical thoracoabdominal nephrectomy improves survival when compared with simple nephrectomy.

Waters WB, Richie JP: Aggressive approach to renal cell carcinoma: Review of 130 cases. J Urol 122:306, 1979.

One hundred and thirty patients with renal cell carcinoma operated on at Peter Bent Brigham Hospital between 1957 and 1977 were reviewed. The mean age was 56.5 years, with a male: female ratio of 1.5:1. Radical nephrectomy was performed in 115 patients, regional lymphadenectomy was done in 67 patients, 8 patients underwent partial nephrectomy, 5 patients underwent a simple nephrectomy, and 2 patients had renal biopsies. In the last 10 years thorocoabdominal approaches were used with the majority of the patients: 5 patients underwent vena caval resections, 3 patients underwent removal of solitary lung metastases, 17 patients received radiation, and 16 patients had chemotherapy. Survival by stage was as follows:

Stage I: 51% alive at 5 years

Stage II: (with renal vein involvement): 58.5% alive at 5 years

Stage II: (with vena cava involvement): 53% alive at 5 years

Stage III: 12.3% alive at 5 years

Stage IV: 0% alive at 5 years

Of the patients who underwent lymphadenectomy, 24% had involvement of he lymph nodes.

Recurrences occurred in 21 patients (57%). The initial site of recurrence was in the pulmonary area in 57%, locally in 19%, and in other sites in 24%. There was no correlation between lymphocyte count and survival. The authors review the literature and the experiences of other surgeons. They conclude that an aggressive approach to tumors involving the renal vein or the vena cava seems to increase survival, but they cannot assess the real value of retroperitoneal lymphadenectomy.

Boxer RJ, Waisman J, Lieber MN, Mampaso FM, Skinner DG: Renal carcinoma: computer analysis of 96 patients treated by nephrectomy. J Urol 122:598, 1979.

Ninety-six patients with renal cell carcinoma were treated by simple or radical nephrectomy at the University of California, Los Angeles, from 1956 to 1976. One hundred and nine items of pathologic, clinical, and survival data were submitted to computer analysis. There were 67 men and 29 women; mean age was 55.7 years. Signs, symptoms, and metabolic alterations were anayzed. Survivals by stage were as follows:

Stage I: 94% alive at 1 year, 56% at 5 years, and 20% at 10 years

Stage II: 100% alive at 1 year, 100% at 5 years, and 66% at 10 years

Stage III: 89% alive at 1 year, 50% at 5 years, and 25% at 10 years

Stage IV: 68% alive at 1 year, 8% at 5 years, and 0% at 10 years

Correlation existed between increased survival and 50% of clear cells present on pathologic examination. Presence of fusiform cells reduced survival significantly. The incidence of local extension without evidence of metastatic disease was similar to that reported by others and supports the use of radical nephrectomy with early ligation of renal vessels and regional lymphadenectomy.

3

VENA CAVA RESECTION FOR RENAL CELL CARCINOMA

D. L. McCullough and Ruben F. Gittes

From the Department of Surgery, Division of Urology, University Hospital, University of California School of Medicine, San Diego, California

The Journal of Urology
Copyright © 1974 by The Williams & Wilkins Co.
Vol. 112, August
Printed in U.S.A.

Inferior vena cava obstruction by a renal cell carcinoma thrombus is occasionally diagnosed ante mortem, especially since venacavography has become available. However, successful surgical removal of these renal tumors en bloc with the involved vena cava has been reported in only in a few cases. We recently cared for 4 such patients.

CASE REPORTS

Case 1. R.E.D., UH 546848, a 58-year-old man, had nagging low back pain and a heavy feeling in the lower extremities which had developed during the previous month. Physical examination was negative except for slight pitting edema of the lower extremities. Urinalysis showed 1 plus protein with a negative sediment.

An excretory urogram (IVP) demonstrated a mass in the right kidney. The hemogram, renal function and liver function tests were normal. The bone scan was negative. Arteriographic studies revealed a mass in the right kidney consistent with renal cell carcinoma. Vena-

Accepted for publication January 11, 1974.
Read at annual meeting of Western Section, American Urological Association, Honolulu, Hawaii, June 24–30, 1973.

cavography showed occlusion of the inferior vena cava from the iliac bifurcation to the level of the hepatic veins.

Surgical exploration was through an 8th rib thoracoabdominal incision. The liver was reflected away from the diaphragm by dividing the right coronary and triangular ligaments. The liver was then rotated anteriorly, thereby exposing the vena cava with 5 to 6 hepatic veins emptying into it. The veins, whose inflow into the cava was occluded by tumor, were ligated and divided. The 2 large hepatic veins which were most cephalad were isolated and preserved. The inferior vena cava was isolated and proximal control was obtained with a cardiac tourniquet loop. Occlusion of the hepatic veins and inferior vena cava at the right atrium caused a decrease in blood pressure and the measured cardiac output decreased to dangerous levels. There was considerable bleeding from large collateral veins which deterred consideration of anticoagulating the patient at this point for a cardiopulmonary bypass. The right renal artery was ligated and divided. Lumbar branches of the inferior vena cava were ligated and divided, and the left renal vein was ligated at its junction with the inferior vena cava. The cava was then cross-clamped just above the tumor and below the inflow of the 2 upper hepatic veins, divided and sutured transversely. The lower vena cava was ligated and divided upon the iliac bifurcation. The kidney and cava were lifted out en bloc.

Pathologic examination revealed positive hilar nodes, invasion of the renal vein and inferior vena cava, and extension into the perinephric fat. There was an organized blood thrombus in the cava caudal to the tumor thrombus. There was only 55 mg protein in a 24-hour urine specimen 3 days after ligation of the left renal vein.

The patient left the hospital 12 days postoperatively. He is currently working, doing well 1 year postoperatively but has several suspicious areas on a chest film. The serum creatinine level is 1.7 mg percent.

Case 2. M. M., MGH 177-18-23, a 63-year-old white man, was hospitalized with gross hematuria. Physical examination revealed only fullness in the right upper quadrant and edema of the left leg. Laboratory studies revealed a hematocrit of 32 percent, a blood urea nitrogen of 43 mg percent and a creatinine of 1.9 mg percent. Serum glutamic oxaloacetic transaminase (SGOT) and alkaline phosphatase were slightly elevated. Urinalysis revealed 2 to 3 white and red blood cells per high power field and no proteinuria. Urine cytology was positive for malignant cells. IVP revealed a poorly functioning right kidney. Renal angiography showed right upper pole mass consistent with renal cell carcinoma. The inferior vena-cavogram revealed occlusion of the lower vena cava from the bifurcation to the hepatic vein level with many collateral channels. Other radiographic studies were normal, including metastatic survey, chest x-ray, barium enema and liver scan. Chest tomograms revealed a questionable 2.5 cm density in the right mid lung. The patient was given a 4,500 R preoperative irradiation to the kidney as part of a protocol. During irradiation right shoulder pain developed and roentgenograms revealed an osteolytic bone lesion in the right humerus and rib.

A palliative nephrectomy was considered to be indicated. The specimen containing kidney, nodes and cava was resected en bloc as described in case 1 except the hepatic diaphragmatic attachments were left intact. The left renal vein was ligated at its entrance to the cava. Pathologic examination revealed capsular invasion, of the diaphragm, inferior vena cava, right renal vein and hilar lymph nodal metastases.

Convalescence was uneventful and the left kidney fuctioned well. The patient did well for several months but then progressively deteriorated despite chemotherapy and further radiotherapy, and died 5 months postoperatively.

Case 3. R. G., UH 529745, a 66-year-old women, had a history of fever and fatigue for 3 months with frequent temperature spikes to 102°F accompanied by night sweats.

IVP revealed a lower pole mass. Renal angiographic studies were consistent with renal cell carcinoma and cavography revealed a large tumor thrombus occluding the inferior vena cava. The admission hematocrit was 28 percent. Urinalysis revealed microscopic hematuria and pyuria with a 2 plus protein. Klebsiella was cultured from the urine. Renal function tests were normal. The liver function tests were abnormal with an elevated SGOT, lactic dehydrogenase, bromsulphthalein and alkaline phosphatase.

An operation was performed through an 8th rib thoraco-abdominal incision. The pericardium was opened and the inferior vena cava–atrial junction was secured with a cardiac tourniquet loop. Occlusion of the vena cava at the right atrial level decreased the cardiac output to 2 L per minute and blood pressure to 65 per mm Hg systolic. The inflow from hepatic veins was obviously quite significant. Cross-clamping of the inferior vena cava below the main hepatic inflow did not affect the blood pressure. The suprarenal cava was resected en bloc with the tumor thrombus, which extended into the vena cava through the right renal vein. The remaining cava was oversewn just below the level of the hepatic inflow and a caudal strip was tubularized to drain the left renal vein. Pathologic examination of the specimen revealed positive lymph nodes, adrenal involvement, direct extension into the wall of inferior vena cava, renal vein and perinephric fat. The patient left the hospital 10 days later.

In a retrospective review several small bony lesions and a left lung nodule were seen on radiographic survey. Three months later cerebral metastases were noted and the patient died 6 months postoperatively.

Case 4. R. V., UH 564895, a 70-year-old man, exhibited gross painless hematuria several times in the 6 weeks prior to hospitalization. Physical examination was entirely negative.

Several urinalyses showed 2 to 3 red and white blood cells per high power field and 1 to 2 plus proteinuria with a specific gravity around 1.020. Preoperative creatinine clearance was 67 cc per minute and the serum creatinine was 1.3 mg percent. Liver function tests were normal.

IVP revealed a right renal mass and the arteriogram revealed a mass consistent with renal cell carcinoma. Inferior cavography revealed a filling defect causing almost total obstruction of the cava at the level of the right renal vein with numerous collateral veins (Fig. 1A). Caudal to the tumor thrombus was a large filling defect thought to represent a bland thrombus (Fig. 1B). A bone scan was normal.

During the operation a left ureteral catheter was placed cystoscopically to monitor the left renal urinary output. The surgical technique described in case 1 was used. No major blood pressure aberrations were noted. Indigo carmine dye (given intravenously after clamping the left renal vein) was visible in the left renal urine after 5 minutes.

Pathologic examination revealed no nodal metastases and no extension through the capsule or into perirenal fat. There was invasion of the renal vein and vena cava. Postoperatively there was a period of oliguria for about 3 days during which time the creatinine rose to 5.9 mg

percent (Fig. 2). The patient was heparinized for 3 days and fluids were restricted after an initial fluid push and furosemide were unsuccessful in increasing urine output. The urine output gradually rose and the creatinine decreased. There was considerable proteinuria initially as well and serum renin levels were transiently elevated as well as the blood pressure. These fell to normal levels by the time the patient left the hospital 9 days postoperatively, with a serum creatinine of 2.0 mg percent and no lower extremity edema. This patient is well 7 months later. The physiologic postoperative changes will be reported in detail in a subsequent manuscript.

COMMENT

These cases illustrate several important points in diagnosis and surgical management. All patients had tumors on the right side. Two patients had lower extremity edema, metastases, anemia and hematuria. Only 1 patient had a palpable mass. Fever was a component in only 1 case as was flank pain.

Precise localization of the tumor thrombus in the cava, especially the upper limits, was invaluable in formulating the surgical plan. Kaufman stressed the importance of cavography in patients with renal cell carcinoma.[1] Cavography is also indicated for Wilms tumor and malignant adrenal tumors. In our patients cavography (using the femoral and superior vena caval routes) was necessary for precise definition of the upper limits of the thrombus (Figs. 3 and 4). Fortunately, the tumors did not extend into the atrium. The cardiopulmonary bypass team was available for 2 cases but their service was not required. Certainly, the heparinization of patients which is required for use of the cardiopulmonary bypass carries some risk after the extensive dissection required during a radical procedure.

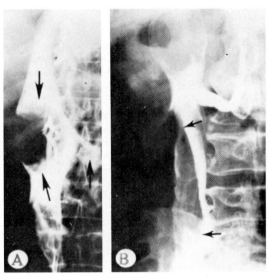

Fig. 1. Case 4. (*A*) Interior venacavogram shows nearly total obstruction by tumor thrombus. The arrow points to left renval vein. (*B*) Inferior venacavogram demonstrates large bland thrombus in cava caudad to tumor thrombus. Collateral lumber vessel is immediately above.

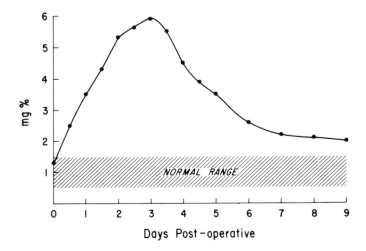

Fig. 2. Case 1. Postoperative creatinine following ligation of left renal vein.

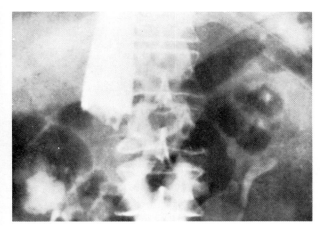

Fig. 3. Inferior venacavogram through superior vena cava demonstrates tumor thrombus at level of hepatic veins.

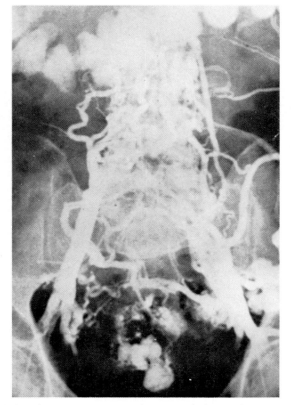

Fig. 4. Interior venacavogram shows total obstruction with extensive collateral.

Ligation of the left renal vein at the caval junction was not accompanied by renal dysfunction except for case 4 in which temporary renal dysfucntion was compatible with venous congestion. Marshall reported a case

in which renal failure lasted for 24 days following occlusion of the left renal vein for only 30 minutes.[2] Several other authors reported temporary renal dysfunction after ligation of the left renal vein[3,4] while another author found none.[5] Obstruction of the cava at the level of the left renal vein had obviously encouraged collateral venous flow in our first 3 cases. The left adrenal, gonadal and a lumbar vein are regularly available for collateral drainage of the left renal vein (Fig. 5). This does not apply to the right renal vein which is usually devoid of collaterals. If the left renal vein and cava require resection for a left renal cell carcinoma then a right renal vein-portal vein anastomosis would provide the most feasible venous drainage for the right kidney.[6]

In 1 patient a strip of cava was preserved from the lower inferior vena cava to the left renal vein and closed as a tube for venous drainage (case 3). This method has doubtful merit on the left side but may be useful on the right side when the entire caval wall is not invaded and a strip can be preserved.

The technique of dividing the ligaments which connect the right lobe of the liver and diaphragm is worthy of special mention. After dividing these ligaments one may rotate the liver medially like turning the page of a book. This exposes the infrahepatic vena cava and enables one to inspect and control the hepatic veins as well as divide the cava closer to the atrium than would otherwise be possible (Fig. 6).

There are usually 2 or more right hepatic veins and 1 main left hepatic vein which drain into the infrahepatic cava in its more cephalad position, while smaller, usually right hepatic veins drain in more caudally. Some of these smaller hepatic veins can be sacrificed to enhance the caval removal as in cases 1 and 4.

The various contributions to cardiac venous return include 25 to 33 percent from the lower inferior vena cava, 25 percent from renal veins and 25 percent from hepatic veins.[7] In case 3 it was obvious that occlusion of the hepatic inflow lowered cardiac output rather dramatically but occlusion of the cava immediately below the hepatic inflow had little effect. In all these patients there was already considerable bypass collateral venous flow from the subdiaphragmatic cava by way of the lumbar, azygos and hemiazygos system.

DISCUSSION

The vena cava is involved by direct vascular tumor thrombus extension in roughly 5 percent of reported nephrectomies for renal cell carcinoma.[2,5] Extension via the right renal vein is present in about 70 percent of reported cases of caval involvement.[8] This undoubtedly occurs because the right renal vein is shorter than the left renal vein. About 80 percent of patients with caval

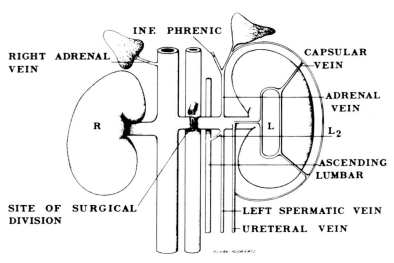

Fig. 5. Collateral venous drainage of left kidney and site of division close to cava.

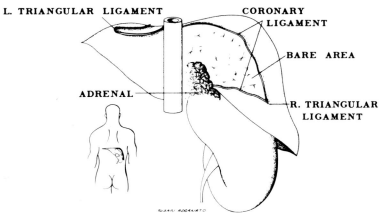

Fig. 6. Posterior view of hepatic ligaments and relationship of vena cava to liver.

involvement are male subjects.[8,9] The incidence of extension into the right atrium in patients with caval extension ranges from 14 to 41 percent.[8–10] The tumor thrombus tends to be led in a cardiac direction by the caval blood flow initially. After complete occlusion this influence is lost and tumor growth may proceed in either direction. Occasionally a Budd-Chiari syndrome develops owing to ingrowth of a tumor into the hepatic veins or by secondary thrombosis.[7,9,11] The rather significant venous flow from the hepatic veins tends to resist this occurence. The syndrome may be recognized by the presence of hepatic pain, an enlarged and tender liver, ascites, vomiting and jaundice.

The diagnosis of caval extension may occasionally be made by recognizing arterialization of tumor thrombus seen at the time of selective renal arteriography and aided by the use of epinephrine.[5,12]

Involvement of the vena cava by tumor thrombus has generally been thought to carry a grim prognosis[2]

but if there is no perinephric fat or nodal involvement the prognosis is quite acceptable.[5]

The presence of edema of the lower extremities without a history of previous venous insufficiency should make one suspect middle vena caval obstruction.[7] This, plus albuminuria and hematuria, strongly suggests caval involvement by a renal cell carcinoma thrombus. Isolated albuminuria is not uncommon.[9] A left varicocele which does not collapse when a patient is supine suggests left renalvein occlusion, while a right varcocele suggests caval obstruction.

There are a few reported cases of successful removal of renal cell carcinomas with caval neoplastic thrombi.[1,2,5,13,14] However, we are only aware of 3 case reports of patients who underwent successful excision of a right renal tumor with en bloc excision of the suprarenal and infrarenal cava with complete interruption of the cava as well as ligation of the left renal vein.[3–5] To these cases we add 3 additional cases (cases 1, 2 and

4). Only 1 of our patients had temporary renal dysfunction (case 4) while 2 of the other 3 reported cases did. Case 3 is not included in this strictly defined group because a bridge of lower inferior vena cava was left attached and closed as a tube to the left renal vein.

Resection of the cava is not always necessary when the tumor merely extends into the caval lumen and a cavotomy may be sufficient to enable one to remove an intact specimen. One author reported such a case but the patient died of an air embolus.[9] When the tumor thrombus may be invading or is densely adherent to the cava, as was found in all of our cases, caval resection seems desirable, although a few long-term survivals have been reported when the entire tumor was not removed.[9] However, all patients in Marshall's series who had mere ligation of the renal vein (leaving intraluminal cancer in place) demonstrated carcinomatosis within 12 months.[2]

The indication for an operation in an individual case with caval involvement, with or without evident metastases, should not differ from those in a case without caval involvement as long as adequate surgical facilities are available. The role of nephrectomy in a patient with metastases remains controversial.[15,16] The long-term prognosis depends on the stage of the disease which exists at the time of surgical intervention.

SUMMARY

Four cases demonstrating invasion of the right renal vein and inferior vena cava by renal cell carcinoma were treated by thoraco-abdominal radical nephrectomy, including en bloc resection of the vena cava without extracorporeal circulatory assistance. Three patients underwent complete excision of the suprarenal cava up to the main hepatic veins, and ligation and division of the left renal vein. They are cases 4, 5 and 6 to be reported in the literature. Only 1 of these 3 cases had temporary renal dysfunction.

Helpful technical adjuncts described include: (1) division of the right hepatic triangular ligaments (which facilitates hepatic mobilization and exposure of the infrahepatic vena cava) and (2) ligation and division of the lower hepatic veins.

REFERENCES

1. Kaufman, J. J., Burke, D. E. and Goodwin, W. E.: Abdominal venography in urological diagnosis. J urol 75:160, 1956
2. Marshall, V. F., Middleton, R. G., Holswade, G. R. and Goldsmith, E. I.: Surgery for renal cell carcinoma in the vena cava. J Urol 103:414, 1970
3. Clark, C. D.: Survival after excision of a kidney, segmental resection of the vena cava, and division of the opposite renal vein. Lancet 2:1015, 1961
4. Pathak, I. C.: Survival after right nephrectomy, excision of infrahepatic vena cava and ligation of left renal vein: a case report. J Urol 106:599, 1971
5. Skinner, D. G., Pfister, R. F. and Colvin R.: Extension of renal cell carcinoma into the vena cava: the rationale for aggressive surgical management. J Urol 107:711, 1972
6. Lome, L. G. and Bush, I. M.: Resection of the vena cava for renal cell carcinoma: an experimental study. J Urol 107:717, 1972
7. Leiter E.: Inferior-vena-caval thrombosis in malignant renal lesions. JAMA 198:1167, 1966
8. Ney, C.: Thrombosis of the inferior vena cava associated with malignant renal tumors. J Urol 55:583, 1946
9. Svane, S.: Tumor thrombus of the inferior vena cava resulting from renal carcinoma. A report on 12 autopsied cases. Scand J Urol Nephrol 3:245, 1969
10. Arkless, R.: Renal carcinoma: how it metastasizes. Radiology 84:496, 1965
11. Parker, R. G.: Occlusion of the hepatic veins in man. Medicine 38:369, 1959
12. Kahn, P. C.: The epinephrine effect in selective renal angiography. Radiology 85:301, 1965
13. Riches, E. W.: Factors in the prognosis of carcinoma of the kidney. J Urol 79:190, 1958
14. Gleason, D. M., Reilly, R. J., Anderson, R. M., O'Hare, J. E., Kartchner, M. M. and Komar, N. N.: Removal of hypernephroma and inferior vena cava: right atrial tumor thrombus. Arch Surg 105:795, 1972
15. Garfield, D. H. and Kennedy, B. J.: Regression of metastatic renal cell carcinoma following nephrectomy. Cancer 30:190, 1972
16. Middleton, R. G.: Surgery for metastatic renal cell carcinoma. J Urol 97:973, 1967

Commentary:
The Inferior Vena Cava and Atrium in Radical Nephrectomy

David L. McCullough

Since the preceding article was written, several important observations have become more apparent as more cases are reported. First, vena cava resection, or even vena cavotomy, for renal cell carcinoma in the face of metastatic disease to regional nodes or to other areas of the body is contraindicated. It does not prolong survival, and it subjects the patient to unjustified potential operative mortality and morbidity. Second, the vena cava can be resected or cavotomy performed with low operative mortality and morbidity if the surgeon is familiar with vascular techniques and pays meticulous attention to surgical detail. Third, precise information on the location of the tumor thrombus and its relationship to the cava, major and minor hepatic veins, opposite renal vein, and right atrium is absolutely necessary in the planning and carrying out of the operation. Occasionally, vena cavagraphy through the superior vena cava is required to obtain this information. Finally, renal failure is possible after ligation of the *left* renal vein at the *caval* junction when a right-sided tumor, its tumor thrombus, and the cava are resected. If the tumor is not actually growing into the wall of the cava, a cavotomy is preferred for extraction of the thrombus, *en bloc,* with the attached kidney. If the tumor thrombus invades the cava in a small area adjacent to the right renal vein–caval junction, that area of the cava can be resected, and a strip of suprarenal or infrarenal cava can be rolled into a tube with the attached left renal vein. Allowing the left renal vein to drain into the cava diminishes the chance of transient or prolonged left renal failure.[1]

SELECTION OF PATIENTS

As mentioned above, exclude patients with demonstrable metastatic disease from surgery. Make every effort to exclude metastatic disease with lung tomograms, technitium bone and computed tomography (CT) scans, and renal angiography of the opposite kidney.

SURGICAL TECHNIQUE

The thoracoabdominal incision is admirably suited for this procedure. If the pericardium is to be opened because of intra-atrial extension, some authors prefer a median sternotomy.

As the preceding article describes, incision of the coronary ligaments that attach the liver to the diaphragm greatly facilitates exposure of the intrahepatic cava; short hepatic veins can thus be divided with impunity. Preserve at least two of the major hepatic veins in the upper intrahepatic cava to prevent liver failure.

Complete control of the caval blood supply with tapes or clamps on all tributaries in the field is imperative. When the tumor thrombus has extended into the supradiaphragmatic cava, some authors have found the Pringle maneuver (in which the porta hepatis is clamped with a soft-bladed occlusive clamp) useful to help control the hepatic blood flow. The liver can apparently withstand 30 minutes of warm ischemia without functional impairment. If resection of the cava is not required because the tumor projects into, but does not invade, the caval wall, a Foley catheter with a 30 cc balloon is quite helpful. The balloon can be inflated and gentle traction applied to pull the thrombus down and out of the cavotomy site. A recent case of supradiaphragmatic caval tumor extension was managed with the Pringle maneuver and cross clamping of the aorta at the esophageal hiatus.[2]

Take extreme care to avoid an air embolus; release tapes or clamps so that blood is allowed to well up in the cavotomy site, so that air and debris may be evacuated before closing the cavotomy.

As mentioned above, if cava resection is required, sometimes a strip of infrarenal or suprarenal cava is rolled into a connecting tube with the attached left renal vein. This helps prevent left renal failure. However, complete resection of the cava from the major hepatic veins distally to the bifurcation of the cava and its junction with the left renal vein has been carried out successfully on a numer of occasions without sequelae.

Another important consideration is the possible development of hypotension when the cava is obstructed acutely. If caval collaterals are developed and occlusion of the cava at the time of surgery is done gradually, hypotension may not develop, especially if the cava has been occluded by thrombus below the level of the major hepatic vein inflow. Ordinarily the renal veins contribute about 25% of venous return to the heart; the hepatic veins, 25%; and the lower inferior cava, 25%–33%. If hypotension is not easily controlled, or if the atrium contains tumor thrombus, the patient can be placed on cardiopulmonary bypass.

I have found the vascular autostapler to help in rapidly dealing with "suture lines" in the cava.

Finally, the vascular anatomy of the vena cava, the hepatic circulation, and the collaterals of the cava and of the left renal vein are extremely important in this particular type of surgery. Fortunately, most of these tumors that involve the cava originate in the right kidney. The left kidney is well endowed with collateral vessels, namely, the gonadal, adrenal, and lumbar branches, which allows one to ligate the left renal vein at the caval junction, if required, and usually to avoid serious insult to the left kidney.

SURGICAL RESULTS

Most surgeons dealing with these types of tumors would agree that this type of extensive surgery is worthwhile if performed on patients without evidence of metastatic disease.[2-6] A number of patients from the combined series above have survived a year or more without evidence of metastatic disease and with a good quality of life. If good chemotherapeutic adjunctive therapy were available (such as with testis tumors), the indications for this surgery could be extended.

REFERENCES

1. McCullough DL, Talner LB: Inferior venal caval extension of renal carcinoma: A lost cause? Am J Roentgenol 121:819, 1974
2. Cummings KB, Li WI, Ryan JA, Horton WG, Paton RR: Intraoperative management of renal cell carcinoma with supradiaphragmatic caval extension. J Urol 122:829, 1979
3. Skinner DG, Pfister RF, Colvin R: Extension of renal cell carcinoma into the vena cava: The rationale for aggressive surgical management. J Urol 107:711, 1972

4. Abdelsayed MA, Bissada NK, Finkbeiner AE, Redman JF: Renal tumors involving the inferior vena cava: Plan for management. J Urol 120:153, 1978
5. Schefft P, Novich AC, Stratton RA, Stewart BH: Surgery for renal cell carcinoma extending into the inferior vena cava. J Urol 120:28, 1978
6. Beck AD: Renal cell carcinoma involving the inferior vena cava: Radiologic evaluation and surgical management. J Urol 118:533, 1977

ANNOTATED BIBLIOGRAPHY

Skinner DG, Pfister RF, Colvin R: Extension of renal cell carcinoma into the vena cava: The rationale for aggressive surgical management. J Urol 107:711, 1972

The Massachusetts General Hospital experience with vena cava involvement by renal cell carcinoma from 1935–1965 is reviewed. Eleven of 232 patients (5%) had gross extension of tumor into the vena cava at the time of nephrectomy. A 5-year survival rate of 55% and a 10-year survival rate of 43% was reported. Survival with caval extension in the absence of perinephric fat or regional node involvement was thought to be much more likely than had previously been reported. A case report is well described, complete with excellent radiographs, anatomic diagram, and operative technique.

McCullough DL, Gittes RF: Ligation of the renal vein in the solitary kidney—effects on renal function. J Urol 113:295, 1975

This paper reviews the experience of renal dysfunction in reported cases of vena cava extension of renal cell carcinoma and also reviews experimental data. One patient with incomplete cava obstruction from renal cell carcinoma underwent ligation of the left renal vein at the caval junction and developed temporary renal dysfunction (lasting 9 days) similar to that seen with renal vein thrombosis. This paper is a good review of the physiology of renal vein ligation and should be read before one considers ligating the renal vein in the remaining solitary kidney.

Schefft P, Novich AC, Stratton RA, Stewart BH: Surgery for renal cell carcinoma extending into the inferior vena cava. J Urol 120:28, 1978

The Cleveland Clinic surgical experience with 21 patients who had renal cell carcinoma extension into the cava and underwent cavotomy or cavectomy is presented. Six of 12 patients diagnosed with localized neoplasm were alive at the time the manuscript was written. The patients with preoperative metastatic disease fared quite poorly; this strengthens the argument against surgery in the face of metastatic disease. The operative mortality in this series was 14%; it is one of the largest series reported.

Marshall VF, Middleton RG, Holswade AR, Goldsmith E: Surgery for renal cell carcinoma in the vena cava. J Urol 103:414, 1970

The authors present their experience with caval extension of renal cell carcinoma. All patients with ligation of the renal vein (leaving intraluminal cancer in place) demonstrated carcinomatosis within 12 months. Eight of 11 patients operated on were dead or dying 1 year postoperatively.

Abdelsayed MA, Bissada NK, Finkbeiner AE, Redman JF: Renal tumors involving the inferior vena cava: Plan for management. J Urol 120:153, 1978

Twelve cases of caval involvement are presented. One patient, who died 2 days postoperatively, had widespread metastatic disease preoperatively—another reminder that one should avoid surgery in this type of patient. One patient had temporary renal dysfunction. The Pringle maneuver is discussed and recommended for control of the hepatic circulation. Two-thirds of the patients free of metastatic disease at the time of surgery were alive at the time of the manuscript's publication, although half these patients had metastatic disease.

Cummings KB, Li WI, Ryan JA, Horton WG, Paton RR: Intraoperative management of renal cell carcinoma with supradiaphragmatic caval extension. J Urol 122:829, 1979

This paper delves into specialized technical steps that were successfully carried out in a patient with tumor in a solitary left kidney who underwent nephrectomy and subsequent hemodialysis. Temporary circulatory arrest of the lower extremities, the use of the Pringle maneuver, and a method of tumor extraction from the intrapericardial vena cava with a Foley catheter are well described with text and diagrams.

This paper explains quite well a number of useful technical adjuncts in this very specialized area of urologic surgery.

4

PERCUTANEOUS TRANSFEMORAL RENAL ARTERY OCCLUSION IN PATIENTS WITH RENAL CARCINOMA

Preliminary Report

R. B. Bracken, D. E. Johnson, H. M. Goldstein, S. Wallace, and A. G. Ayala

From the Department of Surgery, Section of Urology, and Departments of Diagnostic Radiology and Pathology, The University of Texas System Cancer Center, M. D. Anderson Hospital and Tumor Institute, Houston, Texas

Urology / July 1975 / Volume VI, Number 1

ABSTRACT—Twenty-four patients have undergone percutaneous transfemoral selective renal artery occlusion as part of their management for renal carcinoma. Preoperative infarction was performed in 7 cases. This facilitated surgery by eliminating the major blood supply to the tumor and resulted in collapse of the large collateral veins and created edema within the perirenal tissue. In 17 patients with visceral metastases, tumor infarction was performed in lieu of nephrectomy for control of the primary lesion and in hopes of stimulating an autoimmune response. The current status of this procedure is discussed in light of its indications, complications, and preliminary results.

Advanced renal carcinoma has generally proved refractory to chemotherapeutic agents,[1,2] and nephrectomy performed in the presence of metastatic disease has yielded disappointing results.[3] Failure to achieve a consistent and meaningful increase in survival rates for patients with metastatic renal carcinoma has prompted

us to explore the use of renal artery embolic occlusion*
as a means of controlling the primary tumor.

Therapeutic arterial embolization has been utilized
in the past in treatment for cerebral arteriovenous malformations,[4,5] aneurysms,[6] postbiopsy arteriovenous renal
fistulas,[7] control of gastrointestinal and pelvic bleeding,[8-10] and management of bone tumors.[11] Recently,
Almgard *et al.*[12] reported promising results in the treatment of massive renal tumors by embolic occlusion of
the larger renal vessels. This report presents our preliminary experience with the procedure as an adjunct to the
over-all management of patients with advanced renal
carcinoma.

MATERIAL AND METHODS

Twenty-four patients with advanced renal carcinoma
evaluated at this center between November, 1973, and
April, 1975, have undergone percutaneous transfemoral
selective renal artery occlusion as a part of the management for their disease. The diagnosis of renal carcinoma
was established in all patients on the basis of arteriographic findings and was later confirmed histologically
in the 9 instances in which tissue was available for
examination. There were 20 men and 4 women ranging
in age from thirty-five to seventy-seven years, with an
average age of 58.6 years.

Initially, embolization was performed with autologous tissues (skin, subcutaneous tissue, and muscle),
clot, and the use of small pieces of stainless steel wire.
When this technique proved unsatisfactory, surgical type
gelatin sponge (Gelfoam) was substituted as the embolic
material and has been utilized in 22 patients.[13] After
completion of the peripheral arterial infarction with
gelatin sponge, a small stainless steel coil inserted into
the major renal artery has recently been utilized in 4
patients (Fig. 1). The coil serves as a nidus for thrombosis
of the major renal vessels and has allowed for a more
permanent infarction of the kidney and tumor. This latter

* An end hold catheter, 6 F, is inserted well into the renal artery
as close to the neoplasm as possible to infarct the neoplasm more
selectively and to minimize the possibility of reflux. A gelatin sponge
(Gelfoam) pad which is cut into 3 by 3 mm emboli or 5 mm strips is
used to occlude the peripheral renal vascular bed. One to two pads
are usually adequate to infarct most renal neoplasms. A number of
emboli, approximately five at a time, are packed into a 2 cc syringe
which is then filled with normal saline and/or contrast material. This
combination is injected slowly and carefully into the renal artery
followed by a saline flush. Injection of emboli will initially and
selectively go with the arterial blood flow to the neoplasm. This is
continued and checked until reflux of the contrast material is identified.

In addition to the gelatin sponge, a wire coil with wool strands
is utilized for a more permanent occlusion of renal artery centrally.
This is accomplished by exchanging the initial polyethylene catheter
with a 7 F non-tapered Teflon catheter and introducing the mechanical
device as described in the package insert.

modification resulted from research seeking more permanent occluding devices[14] after repeat arteriographic
examination performed in 2 patients revealed recanalization of their vessels five and six months following
infarction. The procedure is performed under local
anesthesia and sedation, with injection and infarction
monitored by television and periodic roentgenograms.

POSTINFARCTION SYNDROME

Pain, localized to the affected renal area beginning
almost immediately after infarction, was noted in 22 of
the 24 patients. Severity was usually directly related to
the degree of infarction achieved by the procedure and
inversely related to the amount of collateral and parasitic
arterial supply to the tumor. Parenteral narcotics were
required for relief in all instances for twelve to ninety-
six hours after completion of the procedure. Elevation
of the patient's preinfarction diastolic blood pressure in
excess of 10 mm Hg was noted in only 2 instances and
returned to pretreatment levels within four hours. Temperature elevations ranging from 99.5° to 103°F occurred
in all patients, with the duration of pyrexia varying from
twelve hours to seven days. Hematuria was notably
absent in all patients. Mild to moderate gastrointestinal
symptoms of nausea, vomiting, and paralytic ileus lasting
from twelve to seventy-two hours were experienced by
all patients. Intravenous fluids were usually required to
maintain adequate hydration during this period. The
postinfarction symptoms induced by the procedure averaged three days and necessitated hospitalization during
this period. No permanent side effects directly attributable to the tumor occlusion were documented.

Renal failure developed in 2 patients following renal
artery occlusion, but it is believed that the considerable
amount of contrast media (350 cc of 76 percent Reno-
grafin) used during the combined diagnostic and therapeutic angiographic procedures was a contributing factor.
Renal failure was temporary in 1 patient and cleared
completely without dialysis within ten days. In the other
patient death supervened, and necropsy revealed a massive tumor thrombosis totally occluding the inferior vena
cava and opposite renal vein. Careful histologic examination of the "normal" kidney failed to demonstrate
any foreign substances or arteritis to suggest a causal
relationship with the infarction procedure. However,
there was evidence of tubular necrosis.

PATHOLOGY

Eight kidneys (7 nephrectomy specimens; 1 necropsy
specimen) were available for careful pathologic examination two to eight days following renal artery occlusion.
The tumors were large, ranging in size from 5.5 to 10

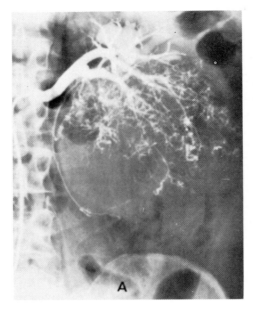

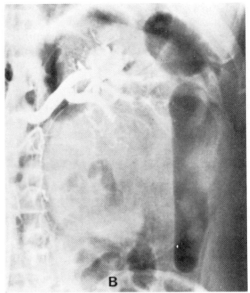

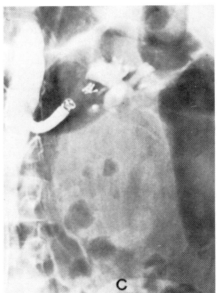

The most striking histologic finding was the presence of an acute necrotizing arteritis associated with the gelatin sponge (Fig. 3A). The inflammatory infiltrate consisted of polymorphonuclear leukocytes which were infiltrating the entire thickness of the arterial wall, periarterial zone, and also the gelatin sponge. Edema and disruption of the internal elastica was also present (Fig. 3B).

RESULTS

Seventeen patients with metastatic renal carcinoma underwent renal artery embolization without subsequent surgical removal (Table 1). Five patients died within

Fig. 1. (A) Selective renal arteriogram demonstrates large, hypervascular renal carcinoma. (B) Selective renal angiography after embolic occlusion of peripheral renal vessels and (C) after embolic occlusion of major renal artery.

cm. In 4 cases there was direct invasion of the renal hilum, and in 3 instances renal vein invasion was present. The severity of renal infarction varied according to the number and degree of peripheral renal arteries occluded. However, in no case was there complete infarction of the renal parenchyma and tumor (Fig. 2).

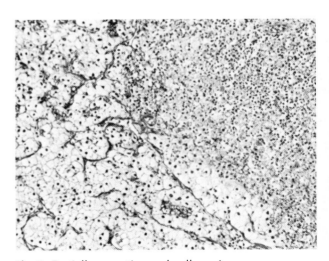

Fig. 2. Partially necrotic renal cell carcinoma.

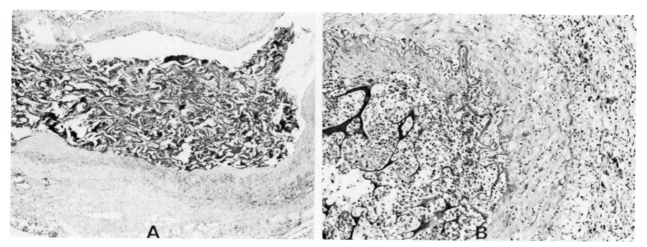

Fig. 3. (A) Branch of renal artery is occluded with gelatin sponge; inflammatory cells are present in arterial wall. (B) Gelatin sponge with inflammatory cells present within lumen of vessels; intima and elastica are partially destroyed and permeated with polymorphonuclear leukocytes which are also seen within muscle and adventitia.

TABLE 1. Clinical Summary of Patients with Metastatic Renal Carcinoma Undergoing Renal Artery Embolization Without Subsequent Nephrectomy

Age	Sex	Site of Metastasis	Therapy	Response*	Current Status
65	M	Lungs	Medroxyprogesterone acetate	N	Dead, 7 months
68	M	Liver/lungs	Medroxyprogesterone acetate	S	Alive, 10 months
48	M	Lungs/liver	Vincristine; hydroxyurea	N	Dead, 4 months
77	M	Liver	None	S	Alive, 8 months
72	M	Lymph nodes	None	N	Dead, 2 weeks
59	F	Lung/lymph nodes	Vincristine; hydroxyurea	N	Dead, 3 months
77	M	Lungs/bone	Vincristine; hydroxyurea	N	Alive, 4 months
67	M	Lungs/liver	None	N	Dead, 2 weeks
47	F	Lungs	Vincristine; hydroxyurea	N	Alive, 2 months
58	F	Lungs/bones	Vincristine; hydroxyurea	N	Alive, 5 months
67	M	Lungs/bone	Vincristine; hydroxyurea	S	Alive, 5 months
65	M	Lung/bone	Vincristine; hydroxyurea	NE	Alive, 2 weeks
52	M	Lung/brain	Vincristine; hydroxyurea	NE	Alive <4 weeks
35	F	Lung	Streptozotocin	NE	Alive <4 weeks
46	M	Liver	Medroxyprogesterone acetate	NE	Alive <4 weeks
48	M	Lung/scalp	Streptozotocin	NE	Alive <4 weeks
45	M	Lung/liver	Medroxyprogesterone acetate	NE	Alive <4 weeks

* N = no response; S = stable; NE = nonevaluable.

eight days to seven months following the procedure as a result of their malignant disease. Three patients are currently alive at two, four, and five months postinfarction but have progressive metastatic disease. In 6 patients renal artery occlusion has been performed too recently for adequate evaluation. In the remaining 3 patients, however, metastatic disease has remained stable. One patient is clinically asymptomatic five months postinfarction with no progression in his pulmonary metastases. Pleural metastases have remained stable in 1 patient ten months postinfarction, and in the other patient there has been no progression of liver metastases after eight months.

Renal artery occlusion was performed in 7 patients within a week prior to nephrectomy for removal of their primary tumor. In 6 of these patients surgery was believed simplified because of the collapse of the engorged and fragile tumor vessels usually encountered. Edema induced by the infarction tended to make tissue planes more distinct and thereby facilitated the dissection of the tumor-containing kidney. Concomitantly, there has been a reduction in the expected blood loss and operative time. In 1 patient no surgical benefit could be attributed to the preoperative infarction. In this case embolization was hampered because of a short main renal artery, and surgery was delayed for seven days resulting in probable

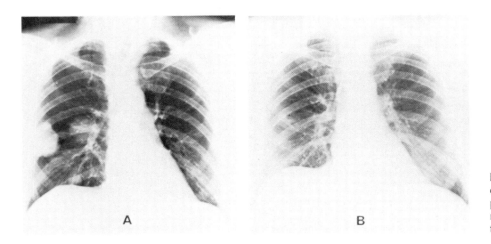

Fig. 4. (*A*) Metastatic renal carcinoma in right lung. (*B*) Complete resolution of metastases 9 months following renal infarction.

recanalization of many of the vessels. In addition the splenic artery contributed to the tumor blood supply, and this parasitic source of vascularity may have increased in the seven-day interval between the infarction and surgery. The 4 patients in this group who had no evidence of metastatic disease at the time of nephrectomy are alive and free of disease five to twelve months postinfarction.

Three patients with metastases had nephrectomy following infarction; 2 with pulmonary metastases and 1 with skeletal lesions. The latter patient died six months postinfarction of progressive metastatic disease. The 2 patients with pulmonary metastases treated with selective artery embolization and subsequent nephrectomy were placed on medroxyprogesterone acetate (Depo-Provera), and both have had complete resolution of their pulmonary metastases (Fig. 4). One patient is alive at eleven months and the other at seventeen months without evidence of demonstrable disease.

COMMENT

Our preliminary experience in treating 24 patients with renal carcinoma by percutaneous transfemoral renal artery occlusion confirms Almgard's[12] earlier report that the procedure (1) leads to a reduction of the total body tumor, and (2) facilitates surgical removal of large, locally advanced vascular tumors. Although total necrosis of the kidney was not produced by the procedure in either series, pathologic examination of the excised specimens and the postinfarction clinical picture strongly suggest that significant necrosis of the primary tumor rapidly ensues following the embolic occlusion. Whether or not a specific immune response is associated with the necrosis remains speculative. However, it is noteworthy that the metastatic disease was essentially stabilized in 6 of 13 patients in Almgard's series[12] and in 5 of 20 patients in our series. The complete resolution of pulmonary metastases reported in the series in 2 patients placed on progesterone therapy after infarction and nephrectomy strongly suggests further evaluation of this combination approach.

Acute renal failure developing immediately after renal infarction in 2 patients is of concern. Although the embolization procedure per se could not be incriminated, we believe it emphasizes the possible dangers of excessive amounts of contrast media used in performing both diagnostic and therapeutic procedures concurrently. We, therefore, recommend that infarction not be performed within forty-eight hours of extensive diagnostic arteriographic procedures.

REFERENCES

1. JOHNSON, D. E., and SAMUELS, M. L.: Chemotherapy for metastatic renal carcinoma. Cancer Chemotherapy—Fundamental Concepts and Recent Advances. Chicago, Year Book Medical Publishers, Inc., 1975

2. JOHNSON, D. E., CHALBAUD, R. A., SAMUELS, M. L., and HOLOYE, P. Y.: Clinical trial of bleomycin for metastatic renal carcinoma. Cancer Chemother Rep 59:433, 1975

3. JOHNSON, D. E., KAESLER, K. E., and SAMUELS, M. L.: Is nephrectomy justified in patients with metastatic renal carcinoma? (in press)

4. LEUSSENHOP, A. J., and SPENCE, W. T.: Artificial embolization of cerebral arteries: report of use in a case of arteriovenous malformation. JAMA 172:1153, 1960

5. KRICHEFF, I. I., MADAYAG, M., and BRAUNSTEIN, P.: Transfemoral catheter embolization of cerebral and posterior fossa arteriovenous malformations. Radiology 103:107, 1972

6. ALMGARD, L. E. and FERNSTROM, I.: Embolic occlusion of an intrarenal aneurysm: a case report. Br J Urol 45:485, 1973

7. BOOKSTEIN, J. J., and GOLDSTEIN, H. M.: Successful management and postbiopsy arteriovenous fistula with selective arterial embolization. Radiology 109:535, 1973

8. PROCHASKA, J. M., FLYE, M. W. and JOHNSRUDE, I. S.: Left gastric artery embolization for control of gastric bleeding: complication. Ibid 107:521, 1973

9. ROSCH, J., DOTTER, C. T., and BROWN, M. J.: Selective arterial embolization: new method for control of acute gastrointestinal bleeding. Ibid 102:303, 1972

10. RING, E. J., et al.: Arteriographic management of hemorrhage following pelvic fracture. Ibid 109:65, 1973

11. FELDMAN, F., CASARILLA, W. J., DICK, H. M., and HOLLANDER, B. A.: Selective intra-arterial embolization of bone tumors. Am J Roentgenol Radium Ther Nucl Med 123:130, 1975

12. ALMGARD, L. E., FERNSTROM, I., HAVERLING, M., and LJUNG-QVIST, A.: Treatment of renal adenocarcinoma by embolic occlusion of the renal circulation. Br J Urol 45:474, 1973

13. GOLDSTEIN, H. M., et al.: Transcatheter embolization of renal cell carcinoma. Am J Roentgenol Radium Ther Nucl Med 123:557, 1975

14. GANTURCO, C., ANDERSON, J., and WALLACE, S.: Mechanical devices for arterial occlusion. Ibid, (in press)

Commentary: Arterial Embolization in Radical Nephrectomy

Joseph N. Corriere, Jr.

Since the preceding article was written, preoperative transcatheter embolization of the kidney has become an acceptable and widespread addition to the treatment of both resectable and disseminated renal cell carcinoma. Numerous agents have been tried (autologous blood clots and muscle, clot modified with thrombin, isobutyl-2-cyanoacrylate, polyvinyl alcohol, ferromagnetic silicone microspheres, balloon catheter, glass beads, stainless steel pellets, and barium), but the method reported by Gianturco and associates is the most popular.[1-8]

In this method, small pieces of gelatin sponge (Gelfoam) are injected through an angiographic catheter to occlude the peripheral arterioles and main renal artery. If further or long-term blocking of the vessels is desired, several stainless steel coils with entwined wool strands are placed into the main renal artery.

INTRAOPERATIVE ADVANTAGES

At present, the main indication for renal artery embolization is to facilitate the surgical removal of renal carcinoma. Preoperatively occluding the renal artery markedly reduces tumor size and vascularity, with collapse of the large renal and perirenal collateral veins. When the surgeon approaches the kidney anteriorly, the main renal vein can be secured early on, facilitating ligation of the renal artery, which is usually easily exposed after the vein has been transected and retracted. The kidneys can then be removed *en bloc* with Gerota's fascia intact.

Perihilar edema is induced by the infarction and actually helps define tissue planes, aiding in the dissection. Theoretically, there should also be less tumor cell dissemination, since the intrarenal vasculature has been decompressed. The procedure is particularly helpful in patients with hilar adenopathy, renal vein or vena cava tumor invasion, or both. Blood loss and operative time in operations on large and difficult tumors are markedly reduced.

POSTINFARCTION COMPLICATIONS

Nephrectomy has been performed anywhere from a few hours to over a week after embolization. A postinfarction syndrome usually develops after the occlusion procedure. Pain requiring injectable narcotics and fever in the range of 99°F to 103°F virtually always occur. Nausea and vomiting is common, and paralytic ileus necessitating nasogastric suction has been reported.

Patients with a history of urinary tract infection should probably receive prophylactic antibiotics before the procedure. Under no circumstances should patients with a positive urine culture be infarcted. Retroperitoneal infection resulting in death has been reported on two occasions in patients who had infected urine.

Renal failure after infarction has been reported and is probably due to the high dose of contrast material necessary to combine both extensive diagnostic arteriographic procedures and a vascular occlusion procedure. Do not, therefore, perform infarction within 48 hours of extensive diagnostic arteriography.

The major complication of this procedure seems to be associated with the escape of the embolic material into the systemic circulation, resulting in peripheral vessel occlusion. Interestingly enough, hypertension has been only a transient problem.

ADJUNCTIVE TUMORICIDAL EFFECTS

The demonstration of metastatic tumor regression or stabilization after renal infarction and subsequent nephrectomy, as discussed in the preceding article, is the most exciting development associated with this technique. Almgard and associates have postulated that embolic occlusion of the renal circulation in patients with metastatic renal carcinoma might enhance an immunologic action on the metastases through widespread necrosis of the primary tumor and subsequent reduction in tumor volume by nephrectomy. Note that renal artery occlusion performed in the face of metastatic disease without subsequent nephrectomy does little to increase these patients survival.[1,9,10]

The largest group of patients so studied is the follow-up study of the preceding article. Johnson and co-workers at the M.D. Anderson Hospital and Tumor Institute have evaluated 50 patients with metastatic renal cell carcinoma with a combination of selective renal artery embolization, radical nephrectomy within 3 to 12 days, and medroxyprogesterone acetate (400 mg administered intramuscularly [IM] twice a week).[11] Seven had complete responses; five, partial responses; and six, prolonged stabilization of their disease.

This 36% overall response rate far exceeds any results obtained to date with surgery or with hormonal or cytotoxic drug therapy used alone or in various combinations. The mechanism for this response is unclear. It has been proposed that an alteration in the host-immune response, possibly cell mediated, may play a role, although explanations of its exact nature remain speculative at best.

CONCLUSION

Renal artery embolization performed before radical nephrectomy for renal cell carcinoma facilitates surgical removal of large and difficult tumors. In patients with metastatic disease, renal infarction with subsequent nephrectomy in conjunction with progestogen therapy seems to provide additional survival time for over half the patients so treated.

REFERENCES

1. Almgard LE, Slezak P: Treatment of renal adenocarcinoma by embolization. Eur Urol 3:279, 1977

2. Arkell DG, Cotter KP, Fitz–Patrick JD, Shaw RE: Pre-operative arterial embolisation in renal carcinoma. Br J Urol 50:469, 1978

3. Marberger M, Georgi M: Balloon occlusion of the renal artery in tumor nephrectomy J Urol 114:360, 1975

4. Turner RD, Rand RW, Bentson JR, Mosso JA: Ferromagnetic silicone necrosis of hypernephromas by selective vascular occlusion to the tumor: A new technique. J Urol 113:455, 1975

5. Gianturco C, Anderson JH, Wallace S: Mechanical devices for arterial occlusion. Am J Roentgeno 124:428, 1975

6. Ben-Menachem Y, Crigler CM, Corriere JN Jr: Elective transcatheter renal artery occlusion prior to nephrectomy. J Urol 114:355, 1975

7. Bergreen PW, Woodside J, Paster SB: Therapeutic renal infarction. J Urol 118:372, 1977

8. Goldstein HM, Medellin H, Beydoun MT, Wallace S, Ben-Menachem Y, Bracken RB, Johnson DE: Transcatheter embolization of renal cell carcinoma. Am J Roentgenol 123:557, 1975

9. Almgard LE, Fernstrom I, Haverling M, Ljungqvist A: Treatment of renal adenocarcinoma by embolic occlusion of the renal circulation. Br J Urol 45:474, 1973

10. Johnson DE, Bracken RB, Goldstein HM, Wallace S: Percutaneous transfemoral renal artery occlusion in patients with renal carcinoma. Kimbrough Urol Semin 9:123, 1975

11. Swanson DA, Wallace S, Johnson DE: The role of embolization and nephrectomy in the treatment of metastatic renal carcinoma. Urol Clin North Am 7:719, 1980

ANNOTATED BIBLIOGRAPHY

Almgard LE, Slezak P: Treatment of renal adenocarcinoma by embolization. Eur Urol 3:279, 1977

This article is an update of Almgard's previous series, which now includes 38 patients with renal adenocarcinoma who underwent renal embolization with an autologous muscle suspension for control of hematuria or metastases. Twenty-nine of the patients underwent nephrectomy 8 to 42 days later. Nine patients are alive up to 6 years after embolization. Patients who had nephrectomies survived longer than those who only underwent embolization. However, the embolization-only patients were much more seriously ill than those who had subsequent surgical removal of the primary tumor. Widespread necrosis of the kidney and tumor was present in all the surgical specimens.

Gianturco C, Anderson JH, Wallace S: Mechanical devices for arterial occlusion. Am J Roentgenol 124:428, 1975

This article describes the development of two mechanical devices for transcatheter vascular occlusion. In the first device, eight strands of cotton thread are attached to segments of steel tubing; it is used to occlude vessels of 2 mm or less. In the second device, four woollen strands are attached to a segment of steel guidewire; it is used to occlude larger vessels. These devices are passed through a no. 6 or 7 French thin-wall Teflon catheter into the vessel selected for embolization. Occlusion has been shown to be complete for as long as 2 weeks after the procedure and is felt to be permanent.

Johnson DE, Bracken RB, Goldstein HM, Wallace S: Percutaneous transfemoral renal artery occlusion in patients with renal carcinoma. Kimbrough Urol Semin 9:123, 1975

This report compares the survival of 21 patients who underwent renal artery embolization alone to 21 patients who underwent renal artery embolization followed by radical nephrectomy. In the embolization-alone group, only two patients had their disease stabilized; half were dead 7 months after the procedure. In the operated group, only two had died of their disease within 6 months of surgery; two who also received medroxyprogesterone acetate had complete regression of their disease. These preliminary results suggest that the combination of renal infarction, nephrectomy, and progestogens may cause regression or stabilization of metastatic renal cell carcinoma.

Marberger M, Georgi M: Balloon occlusion of the renal artery in tumor nephrectomy. J Urol 114:360, 1975

Before radical nephrectomy for renal cell carcinoma in 26 patients, these authors occluded the renal artery of the kidney to be removed by percutaneously placing a Swan–Ganz catheter in the vessel and inflating the catheter balloon. Only one catheter placement failed because of a burst balloon. This technique's advantages are mainly technical, but the fact that the occlusion is potentially reversible makes the procedure attractive if a planned nephrectomy must be aborted before completion.

5

PARTIAL NEPHRECTOMY FOR RENAL TUMOUR: 21 CASES

A. PUIGVERT

Instituto de Urologia, Barcelona

Eur. Urol. 2:70–78 (1976)

ABSTRACT—Partial nephrectomy has been performed in 21 cases of kidney tumours. It can be used for well-limited parenchymatous tumours and obligatory in patients with a soltary kidney, but is not advisable for tumours originating in the urothelium. These results are compared with the parallel experience with radical surgery and followed during 46 years in the same centre, they give a greater value to this study and encourage the reasoned practice of partial nephrectomy for tumours especially in the solitary kidney.

Key Words
Renal carcinoma
Nephrectomy
Partial nephrectomy
Urothelial tumour

Renal tumours originating in the parenchyma may be circumscribed but extirpation of the tumour is not the usual treatment. Some authorities employ what they call 'radical nephrectomy', with the addition of wide dissection of the surrounding fat. In addition, extirpation of the suprarenal gland, the periaortic and iliac lymph node and any clots in the vena cava, even up to the right auricle, are removed. When there are indications of metastases, this form of therapy cannot be effective.

Mr. A. Puigvert, Fundacion Puigvert, Appartado 24005, Barcelona (Spain)

In certain cases and conditions, depending on the type and spread of the tumour, limited extirpation of the lesion is possible, conserving the remaining non-affected part of the kidney. The usefulness of this procedure which becomes obligatory when the patient has only one kidney, has been confirmed by results.

MATERIAL

The present study is based on an analysis of 575 cases of renal tumour from the Instituto de Urologia; 308 arising in the renal parenchyma, 283 in the urothelium and 84 which were not operated on or disappeared from follow-up, so that the exact origin of the tumour was never determined.

In 21 of the 308 cases operated on for tumours of the parenchyma the lesion was locally extirpated, conserving the rest of the kidney. These 21 cases represent 6.7% of the total, showing the limited use of this procedure (Table 1). There were 35 operations employing conservative surgery for tumour of the urothelium (pyelectomy 5, partial nephrectomy 2, and partial ureterectomy 28), which are omitted from this report.

METHOD

When a renal tumour has been diagnosed, the site and size of the lesion may make partial nephrectomy possible or advisable. It is necessary to have a urographical examination showing how much of the kidney is functioning properly and the state of the excretory tract. An angiographic survey is done to provide fuller information about the lesion, its relation with the kidney and the vascular distribution. On this information, the possibility of local excision of the tumour will be determined.

Isotopic renography contributes little useful information, unless it shows areas of lesser condensation, indicative of parenchymatous dissemination when partial nephrectomy is not advisable.

Again, if cavography shows intravenous involvement, partial nephrectomy is not advisable. When there is a single kidney in spite of endovascular involvement, it may be justifiable.

INDICATIONS

Partial nephrectomy can be used for circumscribed or encapsulated tumours originating in the renal pyrenchyma. When there is only one kidney partial nephrectomy will be obligatory and should be decided on exploration. Also, if the other kidney is functioning poorly, partial nephrectomy should again be considered.

Certain tumours have special characteristics which make partial nephrectomy easier. Such are the cystic tumours whose clear delimitation facilitates enucleation and removal from the kidney. Excision of these gives excellent results as renal functioning is not affected. These tumours are morphological or cystic in origin, without parenchymatous spread. They are filled with papillary tumour, of a structure similar to Grawitz's carcinoma, with bleeding, and contain blood clot. The swollen wall of the cyst has a fibrous consistency which facilitates separation of the tumor.

Although in some cases these cysts may appear on angiogram to be solid, their easy enucleation encourages conservation of the kidney with results that are good. It should not be forgotten that removal of a renal tumour is symptomatic treatment, the aetiology and extend of the lesion are unknown. Hence recurrence of lesions may occur immediately after removal of the kidney.

SURGICAL TECHNIQUE

This year marks the hundredth anniversary of the first lumbar nephrectomy, which was performed on a woman by *Langebuch*.

After the extent of the lesion has been determined, the vascular supply should be identified, especially if the lesion is intrarenal. Selective arteriography is particularly useful and vessels can then be ligated separately. In the case of encapsulated or cystic tumour, separation from the kidney is usually very easy. A small incision is made in the capsule and in the parenchyma adjoining the tumour. Enucleation of the tumour is commenced initially through this opening. If a small blood vessel in the parenchyma begins to bleed, it should be ligated by transfixion and the raw surface of the kidney covered with a pediculated flap of perirenal fatty capsule. The kidney is then replaced within its cavity.

When it is not possible to enucleate the tumour because it has developed within the parenchyma, the latter is cut through and the raw surface treated in the usual way. After removal, haemostasis is controlled and a drainage tube left in, the abdominal wall being sutured in the usual way.

RESULTS

Although operative mortality for total nephrectomy for tumors has been reduced to an extraordinary degree (in the statistics of our institute, the figure is 13.2%) since the post-operative period is lengthened to 1 month, the cure at 5 years after total nephrectomy is 22.3% and at 25 years 5.5%. These survival figures are affected by speediness of diagnosis and removal of the lesion before extrarenal spread occurs. This spread passes unnoticed in the early stage and may not be evident until operation or during the post-operative period.

Recurrence occurs most frequently as pulmonary metastases and least frequently as local lymphatic spread. Recurrence may be seen after removal or not until after serveral years. A complication has been observed in 31% of the nephrectomy cases and only 19% of partial. The longer incidence in partial nephrectomy is that it is only performed in the absence of any signs of spread (Table 4).

Although pre-operative irradiation of large tumours may facilitate their removal without improving the ultimate result, irradiation after nephrectomy is of doubtful

(*Text continues on page 64*)

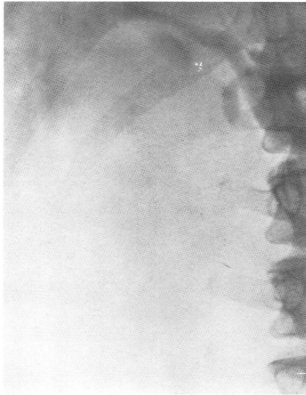

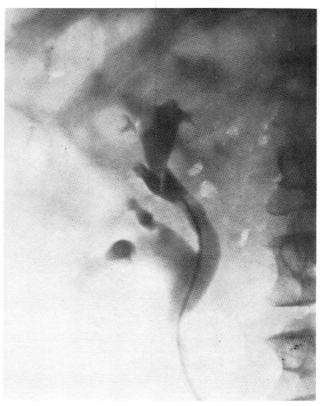

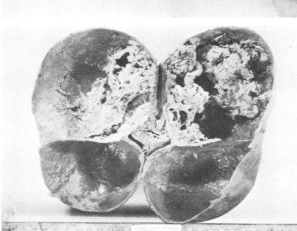

Fig. 1. (H.C., 3,085) 1947: renal displacement by large tumoural mass invading the excretory system. 1951: Retrograde pyelography 4 years after partial nephrectomy (PN). Sample: walled cystic tumour with liquid contents and putrid masses. Renal adenocarcinoma. Weight 1,330 g.

TABLE 2. Malignant Tumours of the Renal Parenchyma (1928–1974)

	n	%
Total nephrectomy	287	93.2
Partial nephrectomy	21	6.7
Total patients operated	308	

TABLE 3. Malignant Tumours of the Renal Parenchyma (1928–1974); Results (January 1975)

	Total Nephrectomy (287 = 93.2%)		Partial Nephrectomy (21 = 6.7%)	
	n	%	n	%
Survival	80	27.8	8	38.1
Exitus	158	55	8[1]	38.1
Immediate	38		1	
Subsequent	120		7	
Not controlled	48	17	5	23.8

[1] Two single-kidney patients through tumour.

TABLE 1. Malignant Kidney Tumors (1928–1974)

	n	%
Renal parenchyma	308	50
Excretory tract	183	34.2
Non-extirpable	84	14.8
Total case histories	575	

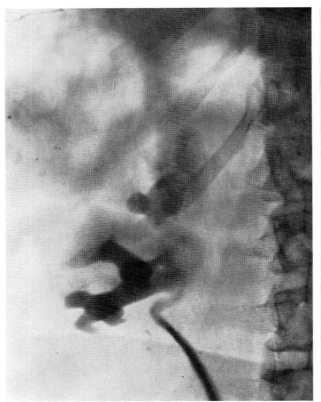
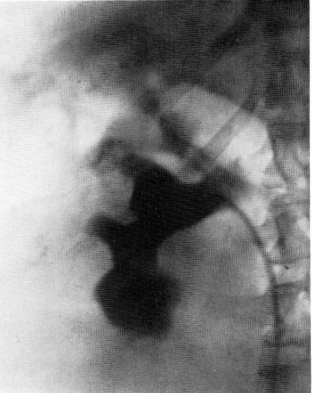

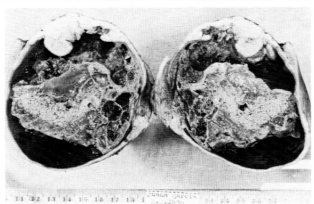

Fig. 2. (H.C., 4,636) 1946: displacement and pelvic flattening with calyectasia through tumour of the upper pole. 1946: Retrograde pyelography 7 months after PN. Sample: cystic tumour with hematoputaceous content; swelling of the wall. Renal adenocarcinoma. Weight 580 g.

TABLE 4. Malignant Tumours of the Renal Parenchyma (1928–1974); Exitus (January 1975)

		Total Nephrectomy (n = 287)		Partial Nephrectomy (n = 21)	
		n	%	n	%
Immediate		38	13.2	1	4.7
Metastasis		98	34.5	5	23.8
years					
−1	36			—	
+1	20			1[1]	
+2	18			—	
+3	4			—	
+4	4			—	
+5	9			2[2,3]	
	91		31.7	3	14.2
+10	4			1	
+15	1			1	
+20	2			—	
	7		2.5	2	9.5
Other causes		13	4.5	—	—
Unknown causes		9	3.2	2	9.5
Exitus		158	55	8	38.1

[1] Single-kidney.
[2] One single-kidney.
[3] Recurrence in single-kidney.

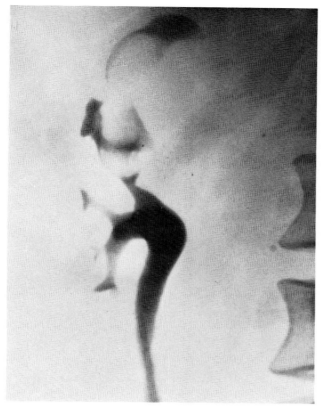

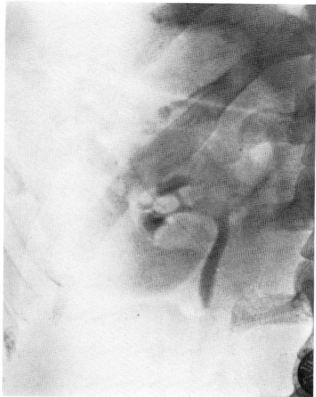

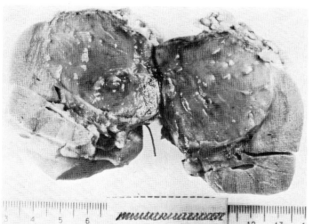

Fig. 3. (H.C., 17,323) 1955: Extreme lengthening of the upper calyx through tumour of the parenchyma. 1959: Pyelography 4 years after PN. Sample: tumour of the upper pole and part of the renal parenchyma. Renal adenocarcinoma. Weight 107 g.

TABLE 5. Malignant Tumours of the Renal Parenchyma (1928–1974); Survival (January 1975)

	Total Nephrectomy (n = 287)		Partial Nephrectomy (n = 21)	
	n	%	n	%
Survival	80	27.8	8	38.1
− 1 year	16		2	
+ 1 year	11		—	
+ 2 years	14		—	
+ 3 years	4		1	
+ 4 years	5		—	
+ 5 years	14		2	
	64	22.3	5	23.8
+ 10 years	7		1	
+ 15 years	6		2	
+ 20 years	2		—	
+ 25 years	1		—	
	16	5.5	3	14.2

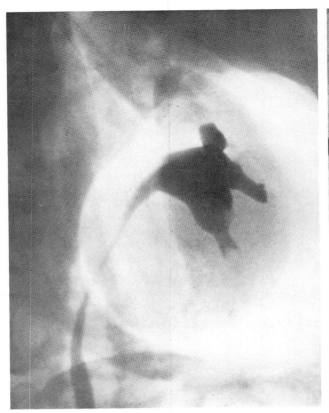

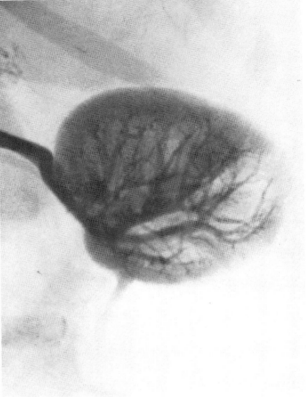

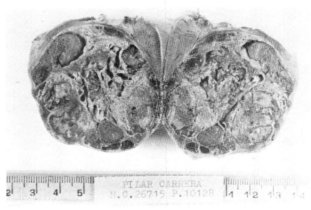

Fig. 4.(H.C., 26,715) 1957: cystic mass superimposed on the lower pole of the kidney with slight pelvic repercussion. 1962: renal arteriography of the upper half of the kidney 15 years after PN. Sample: encapsulated renal adenocarcinoma. Weight 95 g.

TABLE 6. Malignant Tumours of the Renal Parenchyma; Conservative Surgery (Control: January 1975)

Operation	Survival (good at)
September 1955	19 years, 2 months
July 1957	17 years, 6 months
November 1963	12 years, 2 months
August 1966	8 years, 5 months
June 1969	6 years
September 1971	3 years, 6 months
October 1973	8 months
October 1974	2 months
Without further controls	
March 1946	3 years, 9 months
August 1964	9 years, 5 months
September 1967	5 months
November 1967	6 years, 2 months
August 1968	5 years, 5 months

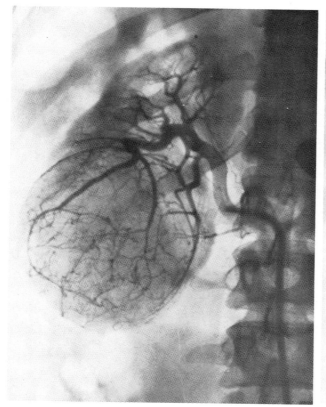

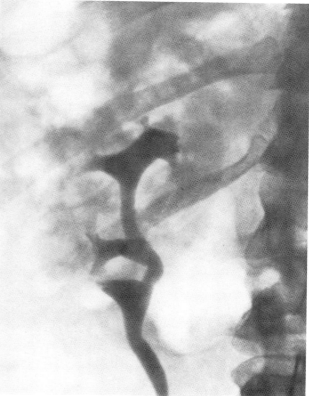

Fig. 5. (H.C. 44,005) 1966: tumour of the lower pole with extensive parietal irrigation and without venous openings. 1968: pyelography 1 year after PN. Sample tumour of cystic appearance and solid contents with piece of renal parenchyma on the external edge. Renal adenocarcinoma. Weight 275 g.

TABLE 7. Malignant Tumours of the Renal Parenchyma (1928–1974); Conservative Surgery (Control: January 1975)

Operation	Age at Operation	Exitus Through
August 1951	18 years	hepatitis
August 1947	10 years	ictus
March 1955	7 years	recidivism in situ[1]
June 1956	7 years	unknown cause
March 1957	7 years	hepatitis metastasis
December 1963	5 years	unknown cause
January 1964	13 months	cerebral metastasis
March 1969	4 days	diabetic coma

[1] Single-kidney

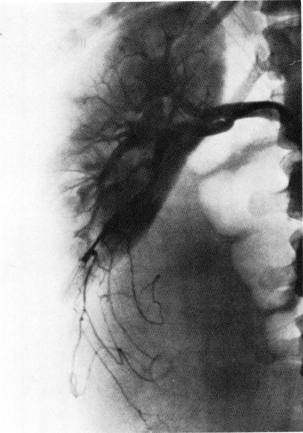

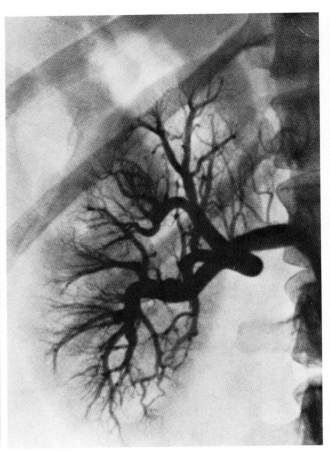

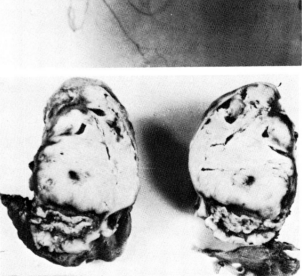

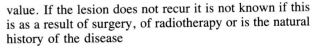

Fig. 6. (H.C. 49,283) 1968: lower polar mass irrigated by perforating blood vessels coming from the kidney. 1969: arteriography 1 year after PN. Sample: solid tumour with a small portion of renal parenchyma from the lower poles. Weight 200 g.

was given radiotherapy (4,000 rad) to the lumbar region; the patient tolerated it well. At the age of 70, soon after a cholecystectomy, he developed urinary retention, making prostatectomy necessary. A 30 gram adenomatous tumour was extirpated, within which were found foci or a atypical hyperplasia. During the operation, examination of the vesical cavity and the ureteric meatus were done. Two years later, he had painless haematuria with slight clotting. Cytological examination of the urine revealed epithelial elements suspicious of malignancy. Cystoscopy showed the trigone on the side of the nephrectomy erect like the finger of a glove. The mucosa was unchanged and blood was oozing from the meatus. The patient refused further operation and a few months later died with symptoms of hepatic and pulmonary neoplasia with no other urinary disturbances except occasional painless, well-tolerated haematuria.

It is important to note that 27 years elapsed between removal of the renal tumour and irradiation, and the appearance

value. If the lesion does not recur it is not known if this is as a result of surgery, of radiotherapy or is the natural history of the disease

The following case history makes one wonder. A nephrectomy was performed on a man of 46 years, in 1946, for a renal adenocarcinoma of the lower pole. After operation he

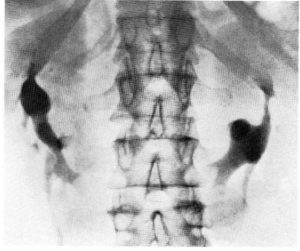

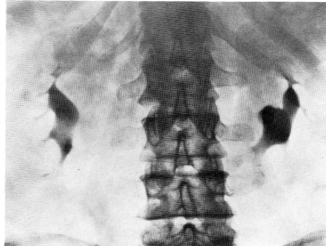

Fig. 7. (H.C. 92,883) 1973: horseshoe kidney with calculus in lower left calyx giving an image of lighter contrast 1975: separation of the pelvises by section of the isthmus and amputation of the lower left-hand pole. Sample: renal pole in which the two dissected surfaces and a cortical neoplastic nodule can be seen. Renal adenocarcinoma. Weight 25 g.

of the ureteric tumour. Doubt remains as to the histology of this ureteric tumour.

Though some authors have observed temporary improvement in metastases following treatment with antimitotic drugs, these are not really very satisfactory. Similarly, hormonal treatment with progesterone or testosterone cannot be recommended because of the bivalent activity of these hormones. The removal of the tumour with conservation of the rest of the kidney, is justified whenever the topography of the lesion permits it, with two-kidney patients, and is an obligatory procedure with single kidney patients.

CONCLUSIONS

The most important information is summarised in Table 3. Of the 308 operations, 287 were total nephrectomies, and 21 partial. Survival rate after total nephrectomy was 27.8%, after partial nephrectomy 38.1%; mortality 55% for total nephrectomy, and 28.1% for partial nephrectomy. Three figures require analysis.

The 55% mortality with total nephrectomy includes 34.5% from metastasis, which is not surprising as in some nephrectomies the existence of lymphatic and vascular metastases was discovered. As for partial nephrectomy, the metastasis in 3 operated patients represents 23%.

In 1 patient recurrence occurred in the remainder of the kidney 7 years after the partial nephrectomy, in the second, hepatic metastasis appeared 7 years later, and in the third recurrence took the form of cerebral metastasis 13 months post-operatively.

The only explanation offered for this difference is the earliness, of institution of therapy. The immediate mortality rates of 13.2 and 4.7%, respectively can be explained in the same way.

Survival rates after 5 years are similar for the two procedures: 22.3 and 23.8%. This confirms that apart from post-operative mortality through metastasis (higher for total nephrectomy, and the discovery of which makes partial nephrectomy prohibitive), the long-term cure is similar for the two procedures.

Finally, thanks to partial nephrectomy, the patient retains a mass of renal parenchyma which may even allow removal of the other kidney should this become necessary.

REFERENCES

Albarran J: Les tumeurs du rein (Masson, Paris 1903)

Dufour A: La nephrectomie partielle. Rep. Ass. Française d'Urologie, Paris 1951

Fey B, Dossot R, Quenu L: Traie de technique chirurgicale; 2nd ed, vol 8 (Masson, Paris)

Foley FEB, Mulvaney WP, Richardson, EJ, Victor I: Radical nephrectomy for neoplasm. J Urol 68:38–49, 1952

Lunggren E: Partial nephrectomy in renal tumour. Acta Chir Scand Suppl 253, p 37 (1960)

Kay S: Renal carcinoma. A 10 year study. Am J Clin Path 50:428–432, 1968

Mims MM, Cristenson B: 10 years evaluation of nephrectomy for extensive renal-cell carcinoma. J Urol 95:10–15, 1966

Riches E: Surgery of renal tumors; in Tumors of the kidney and ureter, pp 275–290 (Livingstone, Edinburgh 1964)

Robson CJ: Partial nephrectomy for renal cell carcinoma. J Urol 89:37, 1963

Robson CJ, Churchill BM, Anderson W: The results of radical nephrectomy for renal cell carcinoma. J Urol 101:297–301, 1969

Smith BA, Jr: Partial nephrectomy for hypernephroma in a solitary kidney. J Urol 86:196, 1961

Smithers DW: Tumours of the kidney and ureter. Sir Eric Riches, M.C. section 6: The treatment of renal tumour in adults. Partial nephrectomy (1964)

Wahlquist L: Factors of importance for primary surgical therapy in renal carcinoma nephrectomy and kidney resection. Scand J. Urol Nephrol Suppl 4 (1969)

Wermooten V: Indications for conservative surgery in certain renal tumours: a study based on the growth patterns of the clear cell carcinoma. J Urol 64:200, 1950

Commentary: Partial Nephrectomy for Renal Carcinoma

A. Puigvert

Because physicians are still ignorant of the etiology of renal carcinoma and the mechanism of metastasis secondary to this disease, current treatment is surgical and essentially symptomatic. However, it is hoped that the etiology of renal carcinoma will soon be discovered, allowing changes in therapeutic management. Due to the present state of knowledge, physicians can only remove the lesion when it is discovered or, if that is not possible, treat the patient symptomatically for local and systemic metastasis.

For the above reasons, surgical excision of the tumor is performed as soon as it is discovered. If it seems to be circumscribed and well delineated, proceed with its removal in the least traumatic way. In the solitary kidney, partial nephrectomy is mandatory, but there appears to be no significant reason why partial nephrectomy should not be employed in patients with both kidneys, since the situation is otherwise the same in both instances (*i.e.*, the true extension of the disease is not known). In my experience of 23 partial nephrectomies for malignant tumor, only 1 patient with partial nephrectomy developed local recurrence 6½ years after I had performed a lower-pole partial nephrectomy. In 3 other patients, metastases occurred between 8 months and 2 years after partial nephrectomy, without any kind of local recurrence.

GENERAL INFORMATION

Historical Background. During 1975, the centenary of Langebuch was celebrated, commemorating the first lumbar nephrectomy for tumor performed in a woman. Subsequently, nephrectomy has been employed in the treatment of renal tumors. In 1908, Albarran and Imbert reviewed 456 cases of kidney tumors in their book Tumeurs du Rein, 413 of the tumors were parenchymal. Nephrectomy was performed in 381 patients, and in 7 patients (2%) only the tumors were excised (partial nephrectomy).

Within that series was included the first case of partial nephrectomy for a malignant sarcoma, performed by Czerny in 1887. Despite this, surgical excision of kidney tumors with preservation of the noninvolved kidney has not been widely employed to date. Therefore, I shall describe my data from this operation and compare it to total nephrectomy.

Usual Treatment. The usual treatment for renal tumors originating in the tubular epithelium, regardless of size, is surgical excision of the kidney with surrounding fat (including the adrenal gland), removal of the para-aortic and iliac lymph nodes, and, when there is venous extension, excision of the renal vein up to and, if necessary, including the inferior vena cava. When these signs of tumor extension are present, any treatment or modality will fail. However, when other favorable conditions are present and the size, shape, and location of the tumor are considered, local excision of the tumor and conservation of the rest of the kidney is possible. This is the only therapeutic modality available in patients with solitary kidneys, but its results have confirmed its usefulness and, in view of the enigma of the disease and the process by which metastasis occurs, have led to its use in patients with both kidneys.

Data. My experience consists of 602 renal tumors, with 322 tumors occurring in the renal parenchyma, 280 tumors in the renal urothelium, and 84 patients in whom I could not determine the exact origin of the tumor.

Of the patients with tumors of the renal parenchyma, I excised the tumor *per se,* conserving the rest of the kidney, in 23 patients (partial nephrectomy). This represents 6.7% of all operated patients and demonstrates how infrequently I used this therapeutic procedure. In addition, 35 patients with tumors of the renal urothelium underwent partial nephrectomy; the results were unsatisfactory in 2.

INVESTIGATIONS

Once the diagnosis of renal tumor has been established, and after the morphologic and topographic conditions of the tumor in relation to the kidney have been determined, one can consider partial nephrectomy. Besides good renal function on excretory urography, the integrity and condition of the rest of the urinary tract system must be noted. Perform renal angiography to determine the nature of the lesion, its relationship with the rest of the kidney, and the renal vasculature of the kidney. All these factors can influence the proposed surgical excision.

The radioisotope enogram has given little useful information. Only when there is a zone of irregular parenchymal condensation, proving that the tumor is metastatic, will partial nephrectomy not be considered feasible. In addition, inferior venocavography demonstrating intravenous (IV) extension of the tumor is a bad prognostic sign that precludes partial nephrectomy.

INDICATIONS

Perform partial nephrectomy for tumors originating in the renal parenchyma when they are circumscribed or encapsulated and when the anatomic and morphologic characteristics permit such surgical excision. In patients with solitary kidneys, partial nephrectomy is necessary. Likewise, if the contralateral kidney is not functioning fully, partial nephrectomy is justified to conserve the remaining functioning renal mass of the neoplasm-containing kidney.

I must stress several anatomic considerations of the renal anatomy that facilitate partial nephrectomy: duplication of the collecting system, horseshoe kidney, and cystic carcinomas whose capsule the tumor has not invaded (the fibrous consistency of the capsule facilitates the enucleation of the tumor from the renal parenchyma). Although on some occasions angiography of these cystic tumors shows characteristics of a solid tumor, its easy enucleation facilitates conservation of the rest of the kidney and justifies partial nephrectomy.

One cannot avoid the fact, however, that surgical excision of the tumor-containing kidney is symptomatic, particularly in view of the local recurrences of malignancy after such excisions and subsequent metastasis.

SURGICAL TECHNIQUE

Partial nephrectomy for renal tumors involves the same technique used for other renal lesions (Figs. 8–16). I prefer the

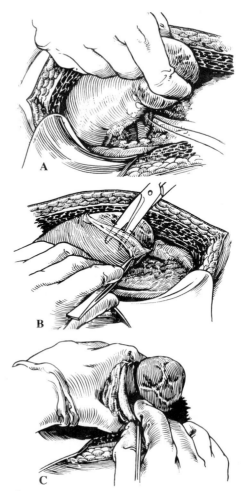

Fig. 8. (A) Liberate the kidney, and ligate a lower pole renal artery before resecting the pole. (B) Encapsulate the lower pole, and reflect the capsule toward the rest of the kidney. (C) Further reflect the capsule with the scalpel, and make a parenchymal incision circumscribing the pole to be removed.

usual lumboiliac incision with resection of the lower rib. On occasion, resection of the 12th rib is required, but normally it is only necessary to articulate the rib to enlarge the operating field. To proceed: mobilize Gerota's perirenal fat forward, and, as a result of this manuever, note Zuckerkand's aponeurotic fascia very near the lumbar mass. Identify the kidney. Extend the incision of the aponeurosis in both directions with scissors and carefully free the kidney, handling it as little as possible. Confirm the size and shape of the renal lesion in order to determine the feasibility of partial nephrectomy. Afterward, examine the renal vessels in the hilum and palpate the regional lymph nodes for gross abnormalities. Suspected vascular or lymph node metastasis precludes partial nephrectomy except

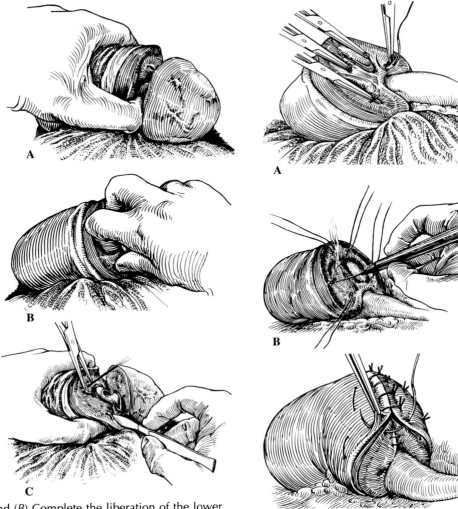

Fig. 9. (*A*) and (*B*) Complete the liberation of the lower pole by blunt finger dissection. (*C*) Once the parenchyma is separated, stop the parenchymal arterial bleeding points with hemostatic forceps and cut the lower calyx with a scalpel.

Fig. 10. (*A*) and (*B*) Methods of obtaining hemostasis of the renal parenchyma. (*C*) Capsular closure with parenchymal **U** sutures.

in patients with one kidney. If the lesion is well demarcated, identify the venous and arterial vessels to be ligated individually before performing the partial nephrectomy.

When dealing with encapsulated or cystic tumors, separate the renal tumor from the noninvolved kidney by initially making a little incision in the renal parenchyma at the edge of the tumor. This is generally easy to do. Through this hole, detach the tumor from the kidney *per se*. If small bleeding vessels are present, ligate them with transfixtion sutures with fine catgut. When enucleation of the tumor is not possible,

incise the parenchyma itself, being careful not to enter the tumor mass. Repair the raw surface of the kidney in a routine fashion, and obtain hemostasis as usual. Finally, cover the raw surface of the kidney with a pedicle flap of perirenal fat.

When the operation is complete, check hemostasis again, cover the cut surface of the kidney, and replace the kidney into its original position. Place a catheter next to the raw surface of the kidney. Afterward, suture Zuckerkand's aponeurosis with one or two catgut sutures and close the muscular wall and skin as usual.

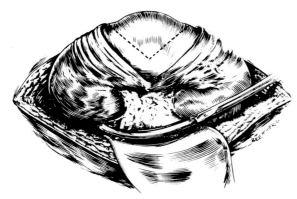

Fig. 11. Parenchymal tumor producing a deformation of the outer border of the kidney. Dotted line shows the proposed incision.

Fig. 12. Cuniform excision of a tumor in the central renal area.

Fig. 13. The kidney after suture closure of the fibrous capsule.

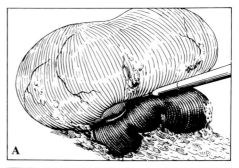

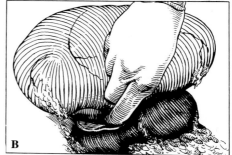

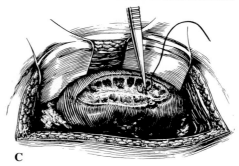

Fig. 14. (A) Tumor occurring on the convex border of the kidney. (B) Dissection with an electric scalpel of the renal parenchyma bordering the tumor, which is then detached with the finger. (C) Placement of hemostatic sutures on renal parenchymal vessels.

Fig. 15. Scalpel and finger dissection of a large renal tumor of the lower pole of the kidney.

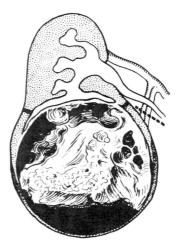

Fig. 16. Schema of line of dissection of parenchyma and taking of vascular supply of large renal tumor of the lower pole of the kidney.

ANNOTATED BIBLIOGRAPHY

Novick AC, Stewart BH, Straffon RA, Banowsky LH: Partial nephrectomy in the treatment of renal adenocarcinoma. J Urol 118:932, 1977

In this series from the Cleveland Clinic, 17 patients are reported who underwent partial nephrectomy during a 20-year period for primary curative therapy for renal adenocarcinoma. Fifteen of these 17 patients (88%) underwent partial nephrectomy *in situ* with free margins of resection for tumors situated at either renal pole or at the kidney's lateral midaspect. They performed a right radical nephrectomy in one of their patients with a adenocarcinoma in the right kidney and a nonfunctioning left kidney. The kidney was flushed with Collins (solution submerged in iced saline) before they performed *ex vivo* partial nephrectomy. The kidney was reconstituted and autotransplanted into the contralateral iliac fossa. This patient was alive 18 months postoperatively. The authors note that occlusion of the renal artery with local hypothermia will allow at least 3 hours of safe protection from ischemia. However, they caution that extracorporeal partial nephrectomy involves a greater potential for morbidity and should be reserved for the small number of patients with centrally located tumors that are large and unresectable *in situ*. In the authors' experience, there was no operative mortality, and postoperative complications were limited to 3 patients (17%) who had urinary fistulas. They conclude that their data support the efficacy of partial nephrectomy when it can be performed with free margins of resection. In addition, they indicate that as extracorporeal surgical techniques become more refined, and as newer forms of adjuvant therapy evolve, it may assume an even greater role in the future of patients with renal carcinoma.

Viets DH, Vaughan ED Jr., Howards SS: Experience gained from the management of nine cases of bilateral renal cell carcinoma. J Urol 118:937, 1977

Because the presence of bilateral simultaneous renal cell carcinoma or subsequent development of a renal cell carcinoma in a remaining kidney necessitates modification of the traditional therapy to preserve renal function, the authors report their experience in management of synchronous and asynchronous

bilateral renal cell carcinoma in nine patients with potentially resectable bilateral disease to illustrate the value of aggressive surgical therapy. They noted that in two of their nine patients an inapparent contralateral renal tumor was present. Therefore, they suggest that bilateral selective renal artiography be performed in all patients with renal cell carcinoma. Their aggressive approach consists of *in vivo* resection of bilateral renal cell carcinoma (heminephrectomy) and a contralateral procedure. They state that there has been no operative mortality or necessity for *ex vivo* bench surgery and that life-sustaining renal function and a reasonable long-term survival rate have been achieved in all patients. They stress that by avoiding bench surgery and autotransplantation, they avoided these procedures' potential complications.

Palmer JM, Swanson DA: Conservative surgery in solitary and bilateral renal carcinoma: Indications and technical considerations. J Urol 120:113, 1978

Seven patients with solitary or bilateral renal carcinoma are reported. Four patients treated with partial nephrectomy are well and free of disease at 24 to 32 months. The authors note that a review of other series reveals a survival of 78% in patients with solitary renal tumors who underwent partial nephrectomy; compared with survival in patients who underwent chronic hemodialysis for the same time interval it is only 65%. Thus, the authors suggest that when technically feasible, one should perform partial nephrectomy in patients with solitary renal carcinoma. They note that in patients with bilateral lesions, the survival rate after partial nephrectomy is similar to that of patients receiving hemodialysis.

Finkbeiner A, Moyad R, Herwig K: Bilateral simultaneously occurring adenocarcinoma of the kidney. J Urol 116:26, 1976

The authors report their experience with three patients with simultaneously-occurring hypernephromas who underwent simultaneous-directed therapy on both kidneys. They review the past management of this problem, namely, a staged procedure with radical nephrectomy of the more seriously involved kidney first and contralateral partial nephrectomy shortly after. However, because the staged procedure was supposed to decrease the risk of renal insufficiency or even renal failure, the current availability of dialysis, transplantation, and better postoperative care render these considerations invalid reasons to choose this approach, in the authors' opinion. They prefer a transabdominal approach with early control of the renal pedicle, which allows more rapid and accurate dissection and simultaneous removal of the tumors. They do not advise using bench operations unless absolutely necessary.

Malek RS, Utz DC, Culp OS: Hypernephroma in the solitary kidney, experience with 20 cases and review of the literature. J Urol 116:553, 1976

This report from the Mayo Clinic analyzes factors pertinent to management and survival of these patients and 66 other well-documented patients in the literature. The authors note that most patients were unusually young and that a significant number had had a nephrectomy for contralateral renal cell carcinoma. In addition, they stress that the earlier presence of malignant disease in the other kidney is closely related to survival and that the interval between detection of the two neoplasms and the stage of the lesion in the solitary kidney is also closely related to survival. They conclude that partial nephrectomy was the most effective treatment; mean survival in their series was 6 years. They state that partial nephrectomy has produced results as impressive as those after nephrectomy for hypernephroma in one of a pair of otherwise normal kidneys.

Gittes RF, McCullough DL: Bench surgery for tumor in a solitary kidney. J Urol 113:12, 1975

Gittes RF: Partial Nephrectomy and Bench Surgery, Techniques and Applications. In Libertino JA, Zinnan L (eds): Reconstructive Urologic Surgery: Pediatric and Adult. Baltimore, Williams & Wilkins, 1977

In both the article and chapter Dr. Gittes presents his experience with bench surgery and partial nephrectomy. Because of the chapter's thorough treatment of this subject, I strongly suggest it for those considering bench surgery and autotransplantation. The chapter presents techniques and applications of these procedures clearly and uses well-illustrated figures.

Skinner DG, deKernion JB: Clinical manifestations and treatment of renal parenchymal Tumors. In Skinner, DG, deKernion JB (eds): *Genitourinary Cancer*, pp 123–129. WB Saunders, Philadelphia 1978

This chapter discusses the management of patients with tumor in a solitary kidney or tumors appearing bilaterally and simultaneously. Basically, three alternative treatment modalities (*in vivo* partial nephrectomy with regional hypothermia, *ex vivo* ("bench") excision and autotransplantation, and complete removal of renal tissue with subsequent chronic hemodialysis) are considered in detail.

Graves FT: The Arterial Anatomy of the Kidney—the Basis of Surgical Technique. Baltimore, Williams & Wilkins, 1971

This small but comprehensive book presents an anatomic basis for partial nephrectomy and devotes a whole chapter to renal hypothermia as an aid to partial nephrectomy. The author states that this technique is essential in the performance of partial nephrectomy where resection is done on the only functioning kidney. The last chapter documents the author's results of partial nephrectomy with hypothermia in 52 patients since 1969.

OVERVIEW: SURGERY FOR RENAL ADENOCARCINOMA

John M. Palmer

In Chapters 2 to 5, four recognized authorities on the treatment of renal adenocarcinoma present their current opinions and annotated bibliographies in areas of their special interest. Three of these approaches represent the cutting edge of current therapy: preoperative renal arterial embolization, retrieval of tumor from the venous return to the heart, and the role of partial nephrectomy. Ancillary methods of therapy in renal cell carcinoma, such as radiation therapy or chemotherapy, are conspicuous by their absence. The surgeon remains in the dominant role in the treatment of these lesions, which are potentially curable only by surgery in the 75% of patients with renal carcinoma who do not have apparent metastatic disease.

CHAPTER 2

In Chapter 2, Dr. Claude Merrin outlines a detailed approach to the patient with operable disease and presents his preoperative work-up and operative technique. At the University of California, Davis School of Medicine, the usual progression of studies begins with intravenous (IV) urography and tomography. At times, ultrasonography is obtained to confirm the presence of a solid tumor. Almost all patients are now studied by computed tomography (CT scanning), which is quite valuable in establishing the presence of a parenchymal tumor but, in my experience, is less effective than the (IV) pyelogram (IVP) in outlining the extent of the lesion. There appear to be many false-positive observations of regional adenopathy with CT scanning, so that currently I give little credence to these findings preoperatively. I no longer use lymphangiograms in evaluating this tumor. The aortogram with or without selective studies and (in most right-sided lesions and large left tumors) simultaneous vena cavography are the final pivotal studies.

Intra-arterial injection of 6 μg to 8 μg of norepinephrine during venography enhances the definition of the renal venous system. Careful search for metastatic disease must then be carried out, often including lung tomography, which is indicated despite its expense by the predilection of this tumor for pulmonary metastases.

Alterations in liver function tests must not be overinterpreted, since, as Stauffer reported in 1961, an hepatic dysfunction syndrome can be present in renal cell carcinoma in the absence of liver metastases.[1]

Merrin then outlines the various surgical techniques in approaching renal adenocarcinoma. These principles are familiar to most urologic surgeons accustomed to dealing with renal cancer and should be reviewed with care. I agree with Merrin that retroperitoneal lymphadenectomy should precede nephrectomy when possible. This facilitates careful ligation of the renal artery and vein and is (in smaller lesions) more consistent with good surgical extirpative principles. In tumors that cross the midline, this may, of course, be impossible. The inferior mesenteric artery probably should be transected with care in older individuals. Similarly, the anterior spinal artery usually originates from the aorta above the crus at the T8–T12 level and is rarely damaged, but there are tragic exceptions. At our center the thoracoabdominal approach is often used. The great improvement in exposure and reassuring nature of the cephalad approach to the renal artery and vein lend effectiveness to this approach in almost all large lesions, regardless of polarity. Unlike Merrin, I incise the diaphragm circumferentially about 5 cm from the chest wall rather than in the direction of its fibers. The former incision greatly reduces injury to the phrenic nerve, which, when divided, can lead to increased postoperative pulmonary morbidity. I try to preserve

TABLE 1. Results of Partial Nephrectomy in 10 Patients with Renal Adenocarcinoma

Age/Sex	Tumor Interval	Surgical Treatment	Local Recurrence	Follow-up (mo)	Status
Solitary					
52 M		Partial nephrectomy	None	45	Dead of myocardial infarction; no *M*
65 F		Partial nephrectomy	None	53	Alive; no *M*
50 M		Partial nephrectomy	None	39	Alive; no *M*
Bilateral					
46 M	Simultaneous	Bench partial nephrectomy autotransplant	None	52	Dead; *M*
65 F	Simultaneous	Partial nephrectomy	None	61	Alive; no *M*
73 F	4 Years	Partial nephrectomy	None	36	Dead; *M*
53 F	10 Years	Partial nephrectomy	None	28	Alive; *M*
55 F	8 Years	Nephrectomy	Hemodialysis	None	?
54 F	Simultaneous	Bilateral nephrectomy	Hemodialysis		Dead
52 F	7 Years	Partial nephrectomy	Yes hemo-dialysis	9	Dead; *M* and renal failure

M, metastases.

TABLE 2. Solitary Renal Cancer since 1971 (Excluding Wickham[6]), 16 Males and 13 Females

Surgical treatment	
In situ partial nephrectomy	26
Bench partial nephrectomy, autotransplant	3
Local recurrence (3 of 29)	10%
Median survival	48 mo
Alive, no disease	22 (75%)
Alive with disease	1
Dead, natural cause	5
Dead of disease	1
Total	29

TABLE 3. Bilateral Renal Carcinoma since 1971 (Excluding Wickham[6]), in 14 Males and 15 Females

Surgical treatment	
In situ partial nephrectomy	23
Tumor enucleation	3
Bench partial nephrectomy autotransplant	3
Local recurrence (3 of 29)	10%
Median survival for both sequential (13) and simultaneous (16) tumors	30 mo
Alive, no disease	19 (65%)
Alive with disease	2
Dead, natural cause	1
Dead of disease	7
Total	29

More patients with solitary lesions are alive without disease.

More patients with bilateral tumors appear to die of their disease.

Knowledge of bench surgery is not a prerequisite in managing these patients (used in only 10% of cases).

Local tumor recurrence is constant at 10% in each group of patients.

These data establish a place for partial nephrectomy in the treatment of renal adenocarcinoma. Local tumor recurrence rates are lower than the expected death rate from metastatic disease, and far more patients die from peripheral metastases than from recrudescence of cancer. Even patients who develop metastases frequently enjoy a long period of survival before dying of their disease. If the added burden of hemodialysis is not placed unnecessarily upon their shoulders, this can often be a rewarding period for surgeon and patient alike. Finally, it appears that the overall yearly attrition of hemodialyzed patients calculated over a 5-year period is greater than the expected death rate of patients with renal adenocarcinoma in a solitary kidney who undergo partial nephrectomy.[7]

REFERENCES

1. Warren MM, Kelalis PP, Utz DC: The changing concept of hypernephroma. J Urol 104:376, 1970
2. Skinner DG, Colvin RB, Vermillion CD, Pfister RD, Leadbetter WF: Diagnosis and management of renal cell carcinoma. Cancer 28:1165, 1971
3. Humphreys GA, Foot NC: Survival of patients (235) following nephrectomy for renal cell and transitional cell tumors of the kidney. J Urol 83:815, 1960
4. Skinner DG, deKernion JB: Clinical manifestations and treatment of renal parenchymal tumor. In Skinner DG, deKernion JB (eds): Genitourinary Cancer, p 120. Philadelphia, WB Saunders, 1978

5. Almgard LE, Fernstrom I, Haverling M, Ljungvist A: Treatment of renal adenocarcinoma by embolic occlusion of the renal circulation. Br J Urol 45:474, 1973
6. Wickham JEA: Conservative renal surgery for adenocarcinoma. The place of bench surgery. Br J Urol 47:25, 1975
7. Palmer JM, Swanson DA: Conservative surgery in solitary and bilateral renal carcinoma: Indications and technical considerations. J Urol 120:113, 1978

PART THREE

THE SURGERY
OF RENAL CALCULI

6

THREE KEY METHODS ADVANCE RENAL REPAIR

Contemporary Surgery / Vol. 3 No.3

Three techniques, developed largely at the Bowman Gray School of Medicine, have greatly facilitated the removal of renal calculi and the repair of kidneys and calyces damaged by stones.

Reviewing 100 consecutive cases of renal calculi treated over a period of six years, Dr. William H. Boyce, professor of urology, comments, "Ten years ago, the majority, if not all, of these kidneys would have been removed. But we were able to salvage all but one."

Only one of the patients in this series eventually required unilateral nephrectomy, and one died postoperatively, following acute coronary occlusion. The success rate in this series, Dr. Boyce feels, is due mostly to the three techniques he and his associates at the Winston-Salem, N.C., school have been working on for the past 15 years.

Dr. Boyce began introducing methylene blue dye around 1958 to demarcate exactly the boundary between the kidney's anterior and posterior segments, providing a "map" for incision. Shortly before that, he began to use local hypothermia to reduce the risks of the prolonged ischemia required for stone removal and kidney repair. At the same time, the Bowman Gray surgeons were beginning to apply the techniques of plastic surgery to damaged or constricted calyces.

None of these techniques, Dr. Boyce points out, is new to general surgery. But application to renal surgery has been slow to develop.

In the past, the best care for a kidney with a severe infection or large stone was often simply unilateral nephrectomy. "It is still good medicine to remove some kidneys," says Dr. Boyce, "but now we're saying that techniques are available to reconstruct and preserve kidneys, and salvage should be attempted whenever possible."

USING METHYLENE BLUE

Defining precisely the boundaries between the anterior and posterior kidney segments has always been a problem for the renal surgeon. The main renal artery divides into a smaller posterior segment and a large anterior one, which divides again into four smaller arteries. The renal vessels are all end arteries, with no collateral circulation. Incisions should follow the planes between the kidney segments, Dr. Boyce explains. "If you get off the line between the two segments as you are cutting into the kidney, the tissue between the incision and the actual arterial division will always atrophy."

With incisions placed exactly along the line between the segments, healing is prompt, secondary hemorrhage and necrosis rarely occur, and cicatrization is minimized. Mattress or other constrictive parenchymal sutures are thus unnecessary and, if all else is done properly, urine leakage is minimal.

Finding where the kidney's segments divide, however, can be difficult. Angiograms and surface markings do not always accurately show the arterial anatomy. For this reason, Dr. Boyce and his associates now use the methylene dye technique routinely.

After mobilizing the kidney and identifying the arterial branches, the surgeons clamp off the anterior division of the main renal artery. The anesthesiologist

(*Text continues on page 82*)

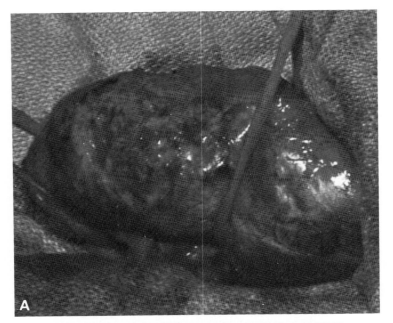

Fig. 1. For nephrolithotomy and reconstructive renal surgery, the kidney is first mobilized and suspended on traction tapes. With the anterior division of the main renal artery temporarily occluded, the anesthesiologist administers 20 cc of methylene blue dye solution intravenously. In 1 to 2 minutes, the posterior renal segment, its circulation still intact, turns blue (A). The blue posterior segment is visible adjacent to tape at left side of photograph. For hypothermia, the kidney, its blood supply now completely cut off, is surrounded with a rubber ''dam'' and packed with supercooled physiologic saline crystals (B). The kidney will be completely covered with the slush for about 10 minutes. Once hypothermia is achieved, the surgeon makes the incision into the capsule along the division between the posterior and anterior renal segments following the color demarcation (C). With the aid of specially developed small retractors, the incision is developed down a posterior calyx and into the renal pelvis, exposing the stone (D). By extending the incision into an anterior and a basilar calyx, the surgeon can remove the calculus intact (E). If necessary, before the nephrotomy is closed, film is inserted behind the kidney and an x-ray taken to check for stone fragment. When all calculi have been removed, the surgeon sutures each of the incised calyces and the renal pelvis with 7-0 chromic suture, using microsurgical techniques. A continuous lock stitch of 4-0 chromic closes the renal capsule (F). No mattress, belting, or other sutures are necessary.

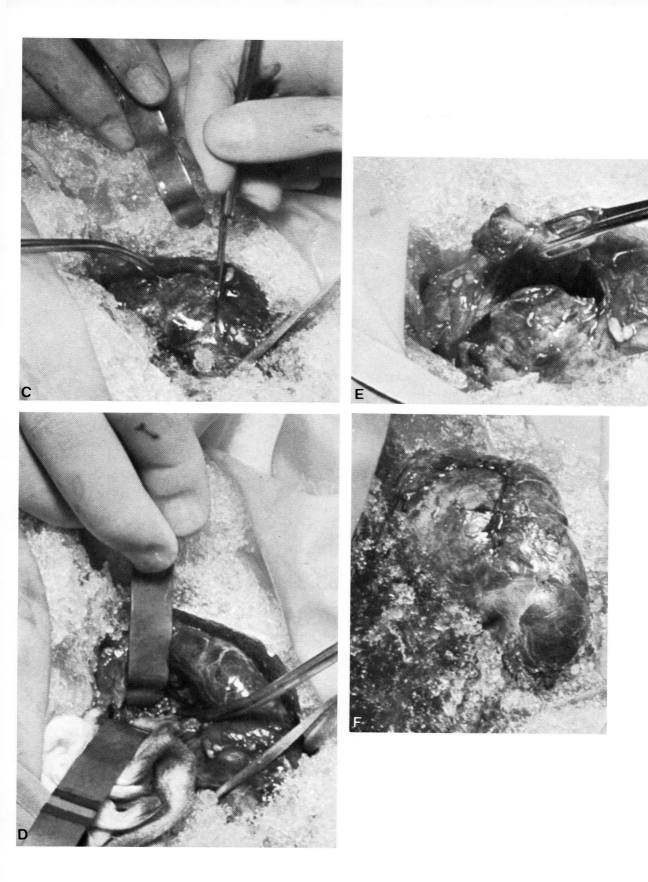

then injects 20 cc of dye intravenously. In one to two minutes, the still-vascularized posterior renal segment turns blue. The line between the blue segment and the pink ischemic anterior portion is clearly delineated.

The procedure has no true contraindications, although at one time methylene blue was somewhat suspect because of its previous use as a urinary antiseptic. "This is one of the oldest drugs around," comments Dr. Boyce. "When it was used for other purposes, there were some hematologic problems, anemias, which were attributed to toxins or heavy metal impurities. Zinc was incriminated. But in the small one-shot dose we use for this procedure, no complications have appeared."

In some patients, the intravenous administration of the dye fails to demarcate the renal segments. The kidney's surface may be so scarred from previous infections or operations that the dye does not show clearly. Or the kidney's circulation may be impaired. In such cases, the surgeons may inject 10 cc of methylene blue into the aorta just above the renal artery's posterior segment, giving a much greater local concentration of dye.

A less desirable alternative to this is injection of 1 cc or 2 cc of dye directly into the renal artery. This, however, is technically difficult and poses some risk. The intima of the small vessel may be injured, Dr. Boyce warns. If the needle's point elevates the intima up from the submucosa, the procedure may predispose to thrombosis. For most patients, intravenous injection suffices.

"If the kidney doesn't blue up after direct injection of dye in the aorta or renal artery," he comments, "you can be sure there is no circulation in that part of the organ. This may be confirmed by direct measurement with the electromagnetic flowmeter."

The discovery that part of the kidney has no circulation may well take place during the operation. Dr. Boyce comments, because preoperative pyelography or even, sometimes, angiography may not reveal a segmental infarct, usually the cause of the condition. Accordingly, the surgical procedure may be altered to meet this finding.

If it is decided to excise part of the kidney, special methods of repair may be necessary. Dr. Boyce and his colleagues may cover the raw portion of the kidney with a synthetic gel, or surgical or absorbable gauze, made from processed human albumin. Or they may cover the area with thin silicone sheeting, tailored to fit the defect. Quilting stitches are used to hold the covering material in place.

LOCAL HYPOTHERMIA

Although hypothermia has long been used in a variety of surgical procedures, Dr. Boyce and his colleagues were, he feels, the first to use it specifically and locally for the kidney. "However," he is quick to say, "it's nice to note that the English developed methods for cooling the kidney locally, quite independently of us, although certainly years later.

"Our first, tentative use of hypothermia was in about 1955," he reports, "and then only in unilateral procedures. We were testing it in animals before that time."

To provide local hypothermia, the mobilized kidney is surrounded with a rubber sheet, or dam, then packed with a slush of supercooled physiologic saline ice crystals. The ideal temperature to which to lower the kidney is near 7°C, although a wide range of temperatures may exist from the renal cortex to medulla. The Bowman Gray surgeons have learned to eliminate the temperature gradient by opening the kidney almost immediately after application of the slush. This allows the coolant to enter the pelvis and the calyces and bring the kidney to the desirable 7° throughout.

At one time, the surgeons used 1 mm thermocouples to monitor the temperature and keep it between 7°C and 17°C. Now, however, this is not usually done, because the time-termperature curves are well established and reproducible, except for grossly anatomically distorted kidneys. For such cases, Dr. Boyce still recommends thermal monitoring.

Before the artery is clamped off and the hypothermia achieved, the patient receives 25 gm of IV mannitol to prevent ice crystals forming in the kidney. Heparin is also administered locally to reduce the possibility of intravascular thrombosis.

Dr. Boyce feels there is room for improvement in the present hypothermic techniques. A simple method for producing the sterile slush would be especially desirable. Now it is prepared by covering bottles of sterile physiologic irrigation solution with ice and rock salt, in a ratio of eight pounds of ice to one of rock salt. The solution supercools and then crystalizes when poured into a container. A sterile, mechanical method for preparation of this slush of extremely small crystals is greatly needed.

"Any kid," Dr. Boyce comments, "can go out and buy a Slurpy—which is really just the same thing as a supercooled solution. But surgeons can't get access to a similar, sterile machine to have in the operating room. And it would help a great deal."

Eventually, perhaps, nontoxic coolants might be developed for circulation through the renal pelvis or even, using bypass, through the occluded blood vessels to cool and preserve the kidney.

DRUGS AND RENAL ISCHEMIA

There are no known contraindications to using local hypothermia in renal surgery. But Dr. Boyce has found he must exercise caution in using certain medications in conjunction with ischemic surgery.

"After all," he says, "any kidney that is occluded, with or without hypothermia, is for a time a sick kidney; it has to recover some of its function and enzymatic activity."

The effect of certain drugs is exaggerated during ischemia, he explains. "Some diuretics, particularly furosemide, are very powerful stimulants to the renal tubules. And some of our best antibiotics, particularly those used against *Pseudomonas,* including kanamycin, polymyxin, and colistin, are potentially nephrotoxic. We feel that, if used at all, these should be administered with great caution in the immediate postoperative period." Furthermore, some drugs used in anesthesia, including autonomic blocking agents, may enhance the diuretic's and antibiotic's toxic activity. "If certain lingering anesthetics are used along with postoperative diuretics and postoperative antibiotics," he comments, "there can be serious trouble."

Accordingly, the surgeons at Bowman Gray administer antibiotics before surgery. Their aim is to reduce the bacterial population to an absolute minimum and them to time the surgery to coincide with this low bacterial population. "In the first 24 to 48 hours after surgery, we coast," Dr. Boyce continues.

"The level of nephrotoxic drugs is reduced until we're sure, by monitoring its function, that this kidney is beginning to pick up and go again."

REPAIRING THE CALYCES

Even before Dr. Boyce and his colleagues were using the methylene dye and hypothermia, they were working on procedures that went beyond stone removal to actual reconstruction of obstructed areas inside the kidney. "Quite often," Dr. Boyce relates, "we found that the infection and irritation caused by stones had resulted in the cicatrization of the calyx. In the late 1940s and early 1950s, we were doing nephrolithotomies that exposed and opened the calyx so that it could be repaired with a truly plastic procedure."

A number of techniques are used to rebuild the kidney's internal drainage system. These include shortening and widening of calyces that have become dilated because of calculi. With methylene blue to demarcate the anterior and posterior calyces, the surgeon can approach the renal pelvis between the two.

Dr. Boyce reports the development of some unique techniques for special situations. "Sometimes, if we have a very narrow calyx, instead of reclosing it back, we anastomose it to an adjacent one. By combining two drainage tubes we promote promote better drainage and eliminate the obstruction."

Another technique that involves shortening is applied when two sides of the renal pelvis are opened and there is only one calyx. In that case, the surgeons shorten the calyx by sliding a flap of pelvic mucosa into the partially closed calyx, thus leaving it shortened and a littler larger.

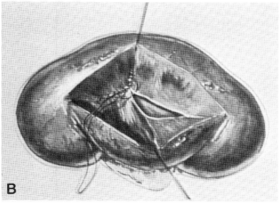

Fig. 2. Repair of anatomically paired calyces (*A*), involves foreshortening and enlargement of their diameter. A continuous 7-0 chromic suture joins the epithelial margins of the adjacent calyces. The papillae of the pink anterior calyces can be seen, and the effect of the repair is demonstrated by direct presentation of these papillae into the renal pelvis. The posterior calyces have been similarly repaired. Note suture line in blue segment. A running 7-0 chromic suture will close the pelvis. Starting at the end of the pelviotomy and continuing along the pelvic margins, this suture tents the pelvic wall into any calyx that requires enlargement of its diameter. These procedures completely re-epithelialize pelvic and calyceal surfaces. When anatomically paired calyces are not available, the calyx is partially resutured. Then the pelvis from the opposite renal segment is tented into the calyx. This procedure produces a shortened and enlarged calyx (*B*).

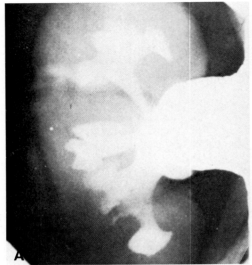
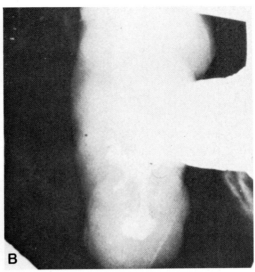
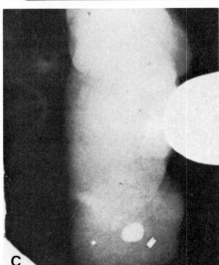

Fig. 3. Taken during surgery but before incision into renal pelvis, x-rays demonstrate calyces and calculi. Pyelograms in AP view (*A*) and lateral view in coronal plane (*B*) were made after injection of contrast material into renal pelvis. Plane film (*C*) shows calculi in lower pole and anterior calyces. To make these x-rays, film is inserted behind the kidney and the x-ray beam positioned at right angles to it.

In some patients, the renal pelvis may be split into two large divisions. When this occurs, the two divisions are opened and the halves sutured together to form a single pelvis.

RECENT EXPERIENCE

The combined methylene dye, hypothermia, and plastic reconstructive techniques have yielded good results in Dr. Boyce's series of 100 consecutive patients. All were seriously ill; 17 were in renal failure. Dr. Boyce recalls that some "had lost kidney function to a point where, had we been able to find suitable matched kidneys, these patients would have been candidates for transplantation. Their creatinine clearances were in the range of about 12 cc per minute.

"We told all the patients that the best treatment might be to remove the kidney, but, if they agreed, we would attempt repair. If that did not work, we would remove the kidney later. We were gambling the risk of two operations against the chance of keeping a kidney. Every patient agreed to try repair."

The problem of whether stopping renal circulation and applying hyothermia produces hypertension remains a key question. In this series of patients, the answer appears to be negative. Thirteen had hypertension before surgery. After the operation, five of these had normal blood pressures while the others continued to show some elevation. Of the 77 patients with normal preoperative blood pressures, three showed a slight postoperative elevation. "Considering the patients we were dealing with," Dr. Boyce says, "we do not feel this clearly indicates a cause and effect relationship between the procedure and the blood pressure. As a matter of fact, the incidence of hypertension in our series is about the same as that for the general population in this age group, without kidney stones."

For some patients, however, nephrolithotomy and reconstructive surgery are contraindicated. When intrarenal calcification makes removal of the entire stone impossible, Dr. Boyce tries to delay surgery until obstruction or some other cause necessitates operation. "For such patients," he concludes, "nephrectomy remains necessary."

Commentary: Anatrophic Nephrolithotomy

William H. Boyce

The term *anatrophic* was chosen to describe a concept of transparenchymal approach to the intrarenal portions of the urinary collecting system by separation of the arterial segments of the kidney. Since these segments have no collateral circulation, and since any injury to their blood supply results in ischemic atrophy, the technique is thus "opposed to atrophy." Calirhaphy denotes the closure of calices (and infundibulae) by simple suturing. Plastic calirhaphy or calicoplasty describes the reconstruction of these parts through various principles of plastic surgery, that is, the combination of adjacent calices, sliding flaps of pelvis, Z-plasty, Y-V-plasty, and related techniques.[1] Since the publication of the preceding article, my experience suggests that the following aspects deserve reemphasis or revision.

RENAL ANATOMY

In 1967, the techniques for identifying the parenchymal planes of the renal arterial segtments were, in general, investigative procedures. The surgeon estimated the position of the plane between anterior and posterior segments, which was the most generally employed transparenchymal incision.[1] Attempts to make slight modifications in the nephrotomy either to avoid splitting a compound papilla or to accommodate the nephrotomy to the underlying intrarenal pathology resulted in several nephrotomy incisions, described in the preceding article. Subsequent experience has suggested that variation among patients in position and configuration of the parenchymal boundaries of the renal arterial segments is very significant and that estimates of this position are not precise enough. Furthermore, postoperative complications are greatly reduced by strict adherence of the nephrotomy to the intersegmental planes, regardless of their tortuosity.[2]

Definition of the arterial segments can be accomplished in each surgically exposed kidney. An effective measure is to occlude temporarily selected branches of the renal artery and administer methylene blue intravenously (IV). I do not recommend direct injections into the renal artery. Injections into the aorta cephalad to the renal arteries will effectively perfuse the kidney. Thermal gradients as defined by thermocouples or liquid crystals sandwiched between plastic sheets depict the intersegmental boundaries. However it is accomplished, it is vital to define the planes between arterial segments in *each* and *every kidney* at the time of surgery and to make the parenchymal incisions follow them precisely. The nephrotomy sites so developed are positioned relative to the intrarenal pathology. The versatility of this approach is such that any intrarenal pathologic condition can be surgically exposed for adequate removal or repair.[3]

CONTROL OF BLOOD FLOW

The total renal arterial blood flow must be occluded with an atraumatic thermally insulated clamp. I do not recommend occlusion of the renal vein, since venous thrombosis or parenchymal injury may ensue if the vein is occluded before the artery is clamped or after it is unclamped. The most common cause of ooze from a nephrotomy is not "venous backflow" but an unidentified accessory artery. The pelvic artery is a common offender.

The sterile ultrasonic doppler probe* is an invaluable aid in detecting the position of the segmental renal arteries, aberrant renal arteries, and intrarenal arteriovenous fistulae or the peristence of intrarenal blood flow after the main artery is clamped. This instrument also provides reassurance of blood flow as opposed to transmitted pulsation in the renal circulation after completion of the surgical procedure. No renal surgeon who has become familiar with this instrument will wish to be deprived of its ready availability.

---

* Blood velocimeter, BV380. Manufactured by Sonicaid Ltd., Bognor Regis, Sussex, England. Distributed in the United States by Sonicaid, 321 Wallace Lane, Fredricksburg, VA 22401.

PRESERVATION OF RENAL FUNCTION DURING PROLONGED ISCHEMIA

Hypothermia in the range of 7°C to 14°C is unquestionably the most effective currently available method for preserving functional integrity in the ischemic kidney. Indeed, it is so effective for up to 12 hours of continuous ischemia that physicians have been unable to devise acceptable protocols for experimental evaluation of possible ancillary methods. Chemical inhibition of cellular respiration and preservation of intact enzyme systems may someday supplant the discomfort of cooling one's fingers and the aggravation of ice crystals within the operative field.

The majority of such ancillary techniques are used with considerable empiricism. I have administered a mannitol load before clamping the renal artery, hoping to lower the freezing point of fluid in the cortical nephrons and to prevent ice crystallization. Certain drugs preserve renal lysosomal membranes during ischemia (*e.g.,* allopurinol, phenoxybenzamine, and chlorpromazine). Methylprednisolone in a single preoperative dose of 13 mg/kg of body weight may prevent "sludging" of blood elements in renal capillaries. Inosine as an energy precursor in the adenosine triphosphate (ATP) system may benefit the ischemic kidney if the load is administered before arterial occlusion. In general, I do not give any drug to patients with impaired renal function unless the indications are precise and the results subject to quantitation.

REMOVAL OF ALL FRAGMENTS DURING NEPHROTOMY FOR CALCULI

Intraoperative radiography of adequate quality is an imperative ancillary service to surgery for renal calculi.[4] There is no truly satisfactory substitute for direct visual inspection of the papillae and calices, but this requires opening the infundibulae. The surgeon must judge whether, in a specific instance, the radiograph or the nephroscope is an acceptable alternative to opening the collecting system.

RECONSTRUCTIVE RENAL SURGERY

Complete closure of the collecting system is essential to proper wound healing with minimal cicatrization. Urinary extravasation by error or by vent or tube is undesirable. Microsurgical techniques and sutures are basic requirements.

One should limit *partial nephrectomy* to removal of diseased kidney tissue; it should not be planned solely on a polar or segmental basis. Obviously, all tissue supplied by an injured or ligated branch of a segmental artery should be removed, but it is not necessary to remove whole segments routinely. Renal diseases, for instance, cancer in solitary kidneys, are rarely segmental in distribution. By combining adjacent calices and folding the residual parenchyma, the capsule can be reclosed in most instances. I have successfully removed the entire anterior renal segment with portions of adjacent segments in this manner by combining the basilar and apical calices. Suture of the calices and hilar capsule maintains the folded kidney in its new configuration without the need for belting sutures. The advantages of thus dispensing with hemostatic mattress sutures and capsular grafts of peritoneum, collagen sheets, or tissue adhesives (isobutyl cyanoacrylate) are obvious.

The compound renal papilla is, on occasion, split by the nephrotomy that precisely follows the intersegmental plane, and diseased papillae may require resection.[5] Do not suture the papilla in either instance; suture of the adjacent calices is all that is required to maintain the divided papilla in apposition. Resection of the papilla should be considered as a developing concept and, at present, should be limited to papillary ducts distal to a plane drawn through the tips of the caliceal cusps.[5]

The ultimate objective in restructure and repair of the kidney and its collecting system is to provide unobstructed conduits for the remaining functional renal parenchyma. The obvious combinations of established techniques of plastic surgery include the following:

Sliding flaps of pelvis into strictured infundibulae
Combinations of adjacent infundibulae into a single conduit of large caliber
YV-plasty whereby a flap of dilated calix is incorporated into an infundibulum or even into the pelvis
Calicocalyostomy between adjacent hydrocalyces
Calicoureterostomy as a supplemental procedure

The techniques for relief of ureteral and pelvic obstruction are not, strictly speaking, components of intrarenal surgery. These include the various methods for pyeloureteroplasty, calicoureterostomy as a bypass for a nonfunctional pelvis, and ureteral replacement. These procedures may be necessarily employed in conjunction with intrarenal surgery.

Whatever procedures are employed, it is essential to minimize cicatrization during the healing process. This requires suturing all conduits to prevent leakage of urine, to eliminate foreign bodies, and to guard against the subsequent introduction of bacteria. All techniques for temporary diversion of urine compromise these objectives.

EXTRACORPOREAL (BENCH) SURGERY AND AUTOLOGOUS RENAL TRANSPLANTATION

In my experience, the vast majority of kidneys requiring intrarenal surgery may be as effectively treated and repaired *in situ* as *ex vivo,* or "on the bench." Autologous renal transplantation is a most satisfactory technique for bringing the kidney close enough to the bladder to eliminate a portion or all of an irreparably damaged ureter. If the kidney requires transplantation for this reason or for replacement of the renal artery, and if intrarenal surgery is also required, there is no disadvantage to performing the intrarenal surgery extracorporeally while the kidney is in transit.

REFERENCES

1. Smith MJV, Boyce WH: Anatrophic nephrotomy and plastic calyrhaphy. Trans Am Assoc Genitourin Surg 59:18, 1967
2. Boyce WH, Harrison LH: Complications of renal stone surgery.

In Smith RB, Skinner DG (eds): Complications of Urologic Surgery. Prevention and Management, p 87. Philadelphia, WB Saunders, 1976
3. Boyce WH: Reconstructive renal surgery for infectious staghorn

stones. In Topics in Urology, pp 4–13, 1979 (Shering)
4. Boyce WH: The localization of intrarenal calculi during surgery. J Urol 118:152, 1977
5. Boyce WH, Webb RT, Russell JM: Management of the papillae during intrarenal surgery. Trans Am Assoc Genitourin Surg 71:76–82, 1979
6. Russell JM, Webb RT, Harrison LH, Boyce WH: Long-term follow-up of 100 anatrophic nephrolithotomies. Proc Int Conf Stones, Perth, Australia, 1979

7. Metzner PJ, Boyce WH: simplified renal hypothermia: An adjunct to conservative renal surgery. Br J Urol 44:76, 1972
8. Boyce WH, Whitehurst AW: Hypoplasia of the major renal conduits. J Urol 116:352, 1976
9. Boyce WH, Stubbs AJ, Resnick MI: Intrarenal nephrolithotomy and reconstruction of the solitary kidney. Trans Am Assoc Genitourin Surg 69:118, 1978

ANNOTATED BIBLIOGRAPHY

Smith MJV, Boyce WH: Anatrophic nephrotomy and plastic calyrhaphy. Trans Am Assoc Genitourin Surg 59:18, 1967

The authors describe the technique of intersegmental nephrotomy in which the kidney is not bivalved; rather, the nephrotomy incision is placed between the junction of the anterior and posterior arterial segments. Correction of caliceal stenosis is achieved by calicoplasty, and a new method of using vertical mattress sutures and water-tight closure is discussed. This procedure was developed over 12 years; the 138 patients operated on during this time had large staghorn calculus or multiple calculi. Thirty-six percent of these kidneys had been operated on before. Follow-up studies are based on patients who had been followed for more than 1 year postoperatively. The results of this procedure are thoroughly reviewed.

Boyce WH, Harrison LH: Complications of renal stone surgery. In Smith RB, Skinner DG (eds): Complications of Urologic Surgery. Prevention and Management, p 87. Philadelphia, WB Saunders, 1976

The probability of untoward reactions occurring in association with surgery becomes apparent when one considers the variable factors associated with the diversity of endocrinologic, infectious, metabolic, malignant, and congenitally determined and degenerative disease states that are associated with urinary calculi. These problems are compounded by the complexity and the often contradictory features of therapeutic measures which must be applied within the peculiar environment of renal anatomy, blood flow, and functions (filtrative, resorptive, secretory, and endocrinologic). In a series of 256 consecutive patients undergoing complicated nephrotomy, encompassing a period of 20 years, serious complications were found to be relatively infrequent. A compilation of adverse or untoward reactions is divided into two categories: (1) problems encountered in the application of techniques described by Boyce in 1975 and (2) interpretive assessment of problems encountered in patients when these techniques were not employed.

Boyce WH: Reconstructive renal surgery for infectious staghorn stones. In Topics in Urology, pp 4–13, 1979 (Shering)

A case history is presented as an illustration of the thorough metabolic and urologic evaluation carried out in each patient with urinary calculus disease. Possible contributory factors to both the stones and urinary infection were determined. Once these were identified and corrected, the surgical and medical programs were combined to clear the urinary system of obstruction, foreign bodies, and bacteria. The chapter provides a photographic review in color of the use of intersegmental nephrotomies and of some of the more useful ancillary procedures in the treatment of staghorn calculi due to infection.

Boyce WH: The localization of intrarenal calculi during surgery. J Urol 118:152, 1977

This article reviews past and present technology for accurate anatomic localization of calculi within the surgically exposed kidney and relates the position of the intersegmental planes of the kidney to the collecting system or to intrarenal pathology. It briefly describes units, film and accessories, radiographic techniques, and surgical techniques.

Boyce WH, Webb RT, Russell JM: Management of the papillae during intrarenal surgery. Proc Soc Genitourin Surg, 1979

The papillae are involved in renal disease and hence are an inextricable consideration in intrarenal surgical procedures. Guidelines for their management are newly emergent and consequently tentative. If papillae are divided along intra-arterial planes, they appear to heal with little functional impairment. Resections of papillae limited to the intracaliceal portions involve no medullary structures and heal without apparent dysfunction. The authors describe the anatomic and experimental data on management of the renal papilla that may be unavoidably split or electively resected during intrarenal surgery.

Russell JM, Webb RT, Harrison LH, Boyce WH: Long-term follow-up of 100 anatrophic nephrolithotomies. Trans Am Assoc Genitourin Surg 71:76–82, 1979

This study provides a long-term follow-up of a group of patients who had anatrophic nephrolithotomies with extensive caliceal reconstruction. A critical analysis has been made of each patient with recurrent nephrolithiasis in order to determine the underlying factors contributing to recurrent stone formation and to the identity of high-risk groups. Eighty patients underwent 100 consecutive anatrophic nephrolithotomies between January 1967 and January 1972, with a mean follow-up period of 8.9 years. The long-term recurrence rate is 22%, emphasizing the effectiveness of complete stone removal and meticulous caliceal repair. The article describes several groups of patients with a high-risk of stone recurrence.

Metzner PJ, Boyce WH: Simplified renal hypothermia: An adjunct to conservative renal surgery. Br J Urol 44:76, 1972

Hypothermia of the surgically exposed kidney is now recognized as being practical, beneficial, and safe; it allows the surgeon to clamp the renal artery for an extended period and ensures against the effects of long-term renal ischemia. The method described in this article differs from other clinical applications of regional hypothermia in that the cooling process is maintained throughout the procedure and ''ischemic time'' is not lost in waiting for basal temperatures or for the recooling of the previously cooled kidney that has warmed during a long procedure. Slush cooling offers a simple technique for regional hypothermia. It is effective, without complications, requires no specialized monitoring equipment, and remains efficient for the duration of the operative procedure. The articles reports a series of 300 patients subjected to this procedure over 10 years.

Boyce WH, Whitehurst AW: Hypoplasia of the major renal conduits. J Urol 116:352, 1976

This is an unusual case report of a girl aged 15 who survived a bilateral congenital anomaly of the major renal conduits. Anatomic features of this case, considered with present embryologic ideas in mind, support the concept of a continuum of disorders of the major renal conduits. The article reviews the literature and discusses interesting microsurgical techniques with hypothermia that enable reconstruction of the collecting systems and renal preservation. There are descriptions of calicocalyostomy and calicoureterostomy techniques where calicoplasty is impossible to achieve.

Boyce WH, Stubbs AJ, Resnick MI: Intrarenal nephrolithotomy and reconstruction of the solitary kidney. Trans Am Assoc Genitourin Surg 69:118, 1978

A documented review of 30 patients with solitary kidneys containing staghorn calculi who underwent neophrolithotomy with extensive plastic revision of strictured calices with local renal hypothermia. These patients were followed for 8 months to 16 years; all had a recent in-hospital evaluation of renal function and recurrent stone formation. The authors report that no surgical mortality (death within 3 months of operation) occurred. Seven patients died postoperatively, only one of whom had associated progressive deterioration of renal function as a contributory cause of death.

7

EXTENDED PYELOLITHOTOMY FOR RENAL CALCULI

J. P. Blandy, M.Ch., F.R.C.S., and G. C. Tresidder, F.R.C.S.

From the Department of Urology, The London Hospital

British Journal of Urology / 1967 / Vol 39

When renal calculi are too large to be easily removed through an incision in the renal pelvis or when the extrarenal part of the renal pelvis is very small, it has been usual to approach the stone through an incision in the renal parenchyma. Developed to its extreme limit, this becomes the renal bivalve operation (Baker *et al.*, 1964; Marshall *et al.*, 1965). In practice, however, this renal bivalve procedure is neither easy nor bloodless. Considerable damage to the parenchyma is caused by the sutures used to secure hæmostasis, and to close the kidney. Because it is necessary to occlude the renal pedicle, a strict time limit is imposed on the operation despite methods for cooling the kidney *in situ*. In published series the mortality ranges from 5 to 8 percent.

There are also many cases where a stone is difficult to localise in an outlying calyx, even with the aid of radiographs at operation. To find and extract such a calculus it may be necessary to make quite a large incision through healthy renal parenchyma with hæmorrhage and kidney damage in consequence. Although this may not be a problem when a lower pole partial nephrectomy is necessary, in other cases to explore each calyx under direct vision would have obvious advantages, but unless the pelvis is large and extrarenal it is not possible to get a sufficiently good view of the openings of the individual calyces.

The idea of increasing the exposure of the renal pelvis, by dissecting into the renal sinus, is not a new one; Surraco (1939) described a technique which involved stripping off the renal capsule and dissecting between capsule and parenchyma into the sinus. Hellström (1949) described a technique of "pyelolithotomy *in situ*" which allowed him to extract stones from the pelvis and calyces without mobilizing the kidney. Similar ideas are expressed by McIver (1960), Hellström and Franksson (1960) and Aboulker (1961). Gil-Vernet (1964 *a*) gave a vivid presentation of a method for reaching the kidney pelvis through a vertical lumbotomy. An excellent ciné film illustrated his technique and was supported by his large personal experience (1964 *b*). This presentation drew attention to the advantages of this kind of approach, and since that time the present authors have developed a method freely based on that of Gil-Vernet. Instead of using a vertical lumbotomy, routine approach to the kidney is used through the bed of the twelfth rib, and instead of leaving the kidney *in situ* as Hellström advises, we recommend full mobilization of the kidney whenever possible, so as to permit control of the predicle and to allow X-rays to be taken on the table. The present technique has been used particularly for large staghorn calculi, but it has also been found most useful for stones in the pelvis or calyces, which cannot easily be removed through an ordinary pyelolithotomy. The technique has been found to be of great value, but as would be expected with any surgical method there are certain difficulties and dangers. It was with the object of pointing out these difficulties that the present report was written, so that what is undoubtedly a most valuable contribution to surgery of kidney stones should not fall into disrepute for want of simple precautions.

Method. In the present series the patient has been placed in the usual lateral position with the table "broken," or the loin angled over inflatable cushions. The conventional incision through the anterior half of the resected twelfth rib is extended forward as far as the build of the patient renders it necessary.

Whenever possible the kidney has been fully mobilised, not only to secure the predicle if necessary, but also to enable X-rays to be taken *in situ*. There have, however, been several occasions when extensive adhesions from previous operations have made it difficult completely to mobilise the kidney, but this has not made it impossible to utilise this extended pyelolithotomy, which is in fact a real advantage of the technique. Usually the renal pelvis was approached from its posterior aspect,

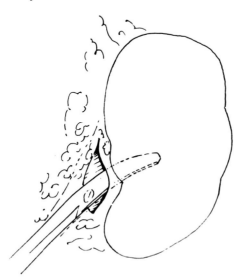

Fig. 1. The plane of cleavage is developed with curved scissors between the peri-renal fat and the muscle of the kidney pelvis.

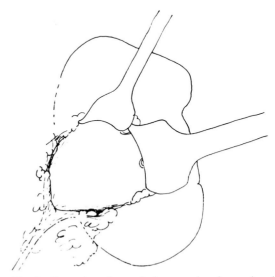

Fig. 3. Once the plane of cleavage has been developed the kidney parenchyma is lifted up with special retractors to display almost the whole of the intrarenal pelvis.

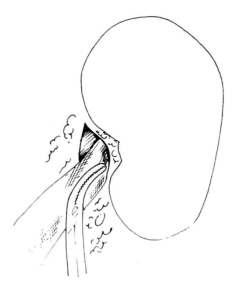

Fig. 2. The plane of cleavage is further developed by packing with a moist gauze ribbon.

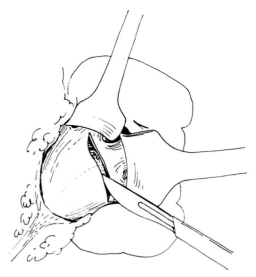

Fig. 4. With the intrarenal pelvis fully displayed the incision is made on to the stone.

unless the presence of abnormal vessels made it easier to reach it from the front.

The success or failure of the entire operation depends on finding the correct plane of cleavage between the pelvic fat and the actual muscle of the pelvis or ureter (Fig. 1). When this plane has been correctly located, it is enlarged by curved scissors and by the insertion of moist ribbon gauze towards the hilium of the kidney (Fig. 2). If the correct plane is not found at the start, however, this dissection may be difficult and bloody. The dissection should be completed if possible before any incision is made into the pelvis.

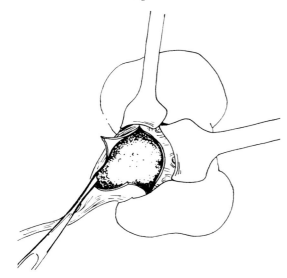

Fig. 5. The calculus is liberated from the renal pelvis.

After this dissection has been completed the packing is withdrawn, when there is usually only a trivial loss of blood. The renal parenchyma is now lifted up and away from the pelvis with specially designed retractors (Fig. 3) which give a good exposure of the entire intrarenal pelvis. This can now be incised in whichever direction will make it easiest to remove the stone (Fig. 4). The calculus is then gently separated from the lining of the pelvis (Fig. 5) and eased out (Fig. 6). The retractors are then readjusted so as to lift up the cut edge of the kidney pelvis (Fig. 7).

It is now possible to see right into the orifice of each major calyx. Large outlying calculi can often be seen and picked out, smaller ones have to be found with probe or forceps. Each calyx can then be irrigated in turn with a syringe and catheter, and finally, to make sure that no stones have been left behind, a radiograph is taken on the table. The incision in the pelvis is then closed with interrupted sutures of fine, plain catgut. When the retractors are withdrawn the renal parenchyma falls back over the suture line in the pelvis. The wound is then closed in the usual way with drainage.

Results. The technique has been used in 30 kidneys in 28 patients (Table 1). Some of the stones have been large, friable and adherent, and others have been very hard. It has been suggested that this type of approach is useful only when the stone could easily be removed in any event. This is not so. It is obviously more difficult to find the correct plane between parenchyma and pelvis when there are many previous operative adhesions, but

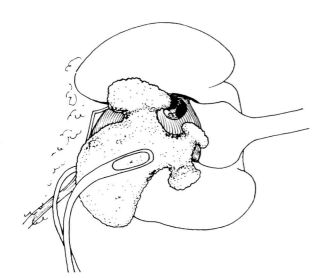

Fig. 6. The calculus is extracted.

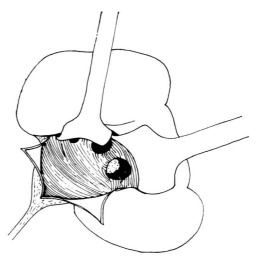

Fig. 7. Having readjusted the retractors a good view is obtained of the interior of the kidney pelvis and stones lying in the calyces may be removed under direct vision.

TABLE 1

Sex	Age	Side	Comment
M	40	L	Stag. Cystinuria. Solitary kidney
M	47	L	Calyx. Hypercalciuric
F	40	R	Stag. Urine infected proteus
F	35	R	Stag. Hyperparathyroid.
F	35	L	Stag. Hyperparathyroid
F	59	L	Stag. (Bilateral) also stone in ureter
F	37	L	*E. coli*. Staghorn
M	48	L	Calyx and ureter. Hyperparathyroid
M	21	R	Recumbency staghorn. Proteus infect.
F	50	L	Proteus Staghorn. Hypercalciuria
F	50	R	. . .
F	44	R	Cystinuria. Staghorn
F	39	L	Upper calyx: entirely intrarenal
F	46	L	Small stone (L) renal pelvis was entirely intrarenal
F	40	L	Middle calyx. Intrarenal infected. Also stone in ureter
M	58	L	Pelvis intrarenal and calyx
M	59	R	Calyceal
M	47	L	Small calculus. Intrarenal, solitary kidney
M	60	L	Staghorn
F	34	L	Staghorn. Hypercalciuria
F	47	L	Staghorn
M	42	L	Superior calyx. Mushroom extensions
F	46	L	Inferior calyx
F	56	L	Bilateral staghorns
F	56	R	Infected urine
M	52	L	Pelvis mainly intrarenal
F	24	R	Staghorn two previous operations died of cardio-respiratory failure from post-polio paralysis with gross chest deformity
M	37	R	Staghorn calculus
F	74	R	Pyelo- and nephro-lithotomy for mushroom extension
M	53	L	Peripelvic fat and adhesions, intrarenal pelvis. Small calyceal calculi

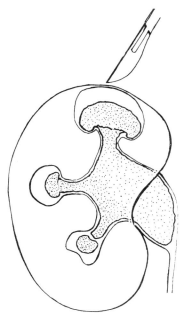

Fig. 8. If there is a large mushroom extension to the stone it cannot be safely removed through the extended pyelolithotomy. A small incision should be made through the thin overlying cortexon to the calculus which should be broken through at the neck of the stone.

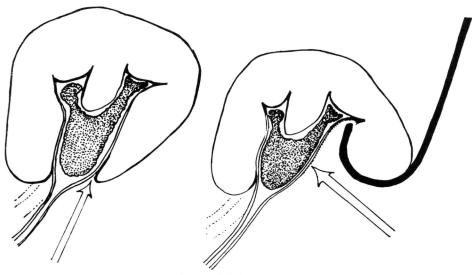

Fig. 9. The principle of the extended pyelolithotomy operation.

even then it is not impossible and these difficulties apply with even more force to renal bivalve operations.

Because this method offers such as excellent view of the interior of the renal pelvis, it has made it easier to ensure the complete removal of large as well as small

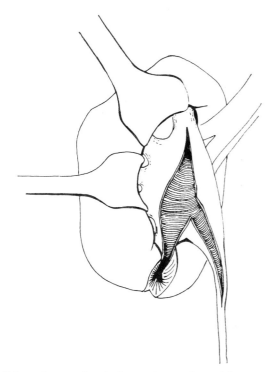

Fig. 10. If there is associated obstruction at the pelvi-ureteric junction this may be overcome by carrying out a lateral anastomosis between the pelvis, lower calyx and ureter.

outlying calculi, and in this series very few stones were overlooked only to be demonstrated by radiography, with a valuable saving of time.

Hæmorrhage has been minimal with all these cases. Post-operative leakage of urine has occurred for the first few days, but has not been a problem.

No method is without disadvantages or dangers. In this technique one disadvantage in particular must be emphasised. Often a staghorn calculus will form a large mushroom-shaped extension into a calyx, and in this event no attempt should be made to remove the stone in one piece or the calyx will split and rupture adjacent vessels. This took place in one case early in the present series, and although the bleeding was easily controlled by passing mattress sutures through the parenchyma, these lead to the very necrosis which it is the object of the present method to avoid. The renal parenchyma overlying large extensions of a staghorn calculus is usually thin and atrophic, so that if it is incised there is little bleeding and only a negligible amount of paren-chyma is rendered ischæmic by subsequent sutures. This type of extension should be broken off at its neck, and the main part of the staghorn removed through the extended pyelolithotomy (Fig. 8).

If the kidney is surrounded by particularly dense adhesions, it is more difficult to find the correct plane between fat and kidney pelvis (Fig. 9) and there is a temptation to begin the dissection into the kidney sinus, before the right plane has been clearly identified. It is helpful to begin the dissection a little distance away from the edge of the kidney, either on the ureter itself, or on the extrarenal part of the pelvis. If necessary, in the subsequent dissection it is better to open into the pelvis rather than trespass on to the veins of the renal sinus. The rule is to stay close to the pelvis when making this exposure.

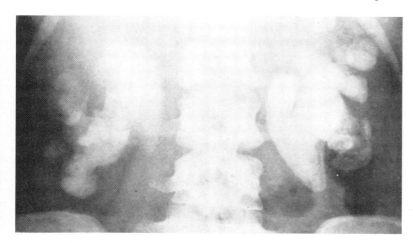

Fig. 11. Bilateral staghorn calculi in a patient with parathyroid tumour.

After removal of the stones it is sometimes difficult accurately to close the laceration made in the kidney pelvis, but in these cases there is little post-operative leakage of urine, probably because the renal parenchyma falls over the suture line to seal it off.

The question sometimes arises how best to deal with a stenosis at the pelvi-ureteric junction associated with a staghorn calculus. After this exposure has been made it is simple to anastomose the ureter side-to-side to the incision which has been carried down into the lower calyx, if necessary dividing a small part of overlying parenchyma (Fig. 10). This procedure was performed in three cases of the present series with uneventful recovery.

Post-operative pyelograms (Figs. 11 and 12) suggest

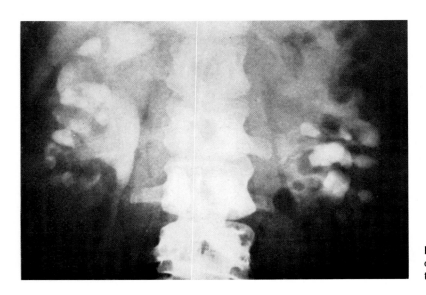

Fig. 12. Both kidneys completely cleared of calculi with return of excretory function.

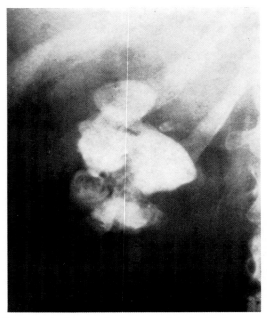

Fig. 13. Typical staghorn calculus associated with long-standing urinary infection due to *B. proteus*.

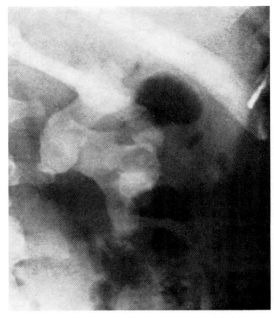

Fig. 14. Staghorn calculus associated with long-standing *E. coli* urinary infection.

that little if any damage is done to the kidney parenchyma by this operation. No necrotic kidney parenchyma is left behind and much less catgut has to be buried than after a renal bivalve procedure, but of course only time and experience will show whether these points are of value in preventing subsequent stone formation.

The approach, being technically easy, is quick.

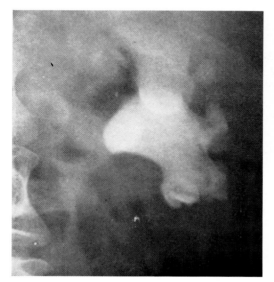

Fig. 15. Staghorn calculus associated with *E. coli* urinary infection.

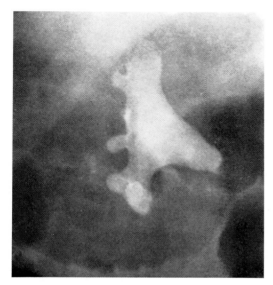

Fig. 16. Recumbency calculus in a young woman following a road accident. Removed through extended pyelolithotomy followed by eradication of urinary infection.

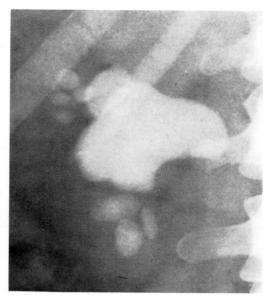

Fig. 17. Staghorn cystine calculus removed through extended pyelolithotomy from a homozygous cystinuric female patient. Patient now on penicillamine. No recurrence of calculus in 18 months.

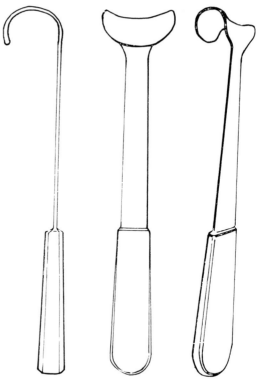

Fig. 18. The special retractors developed for extended pyelolithotomy based on Gil-Vernet's retractor.

There is little bleeding and few patients have needed blood at operation. It offers such a good exposure of the interior of the kidney that large stones with their branches and satellites can be rapidly removed under direct vision. In the present series the calculi encountered have included some very difficult ones (Figs. 12 to 17). As long as care and common sense are used in dealing with the large mushroom-shaped extensions, all these stones can be removed with minimal bleeding, injury to the kidney or morbidity.

There has been one death in this series, in a young girl with gross chest deformity following severe polio-myelitis in infancy. Her death was not due to the immediate effects of the operation, but to post-operative respiratory inadequacy.

None of these kidneys has been cooled at operation and in no case has it been necessary to occlude the vessels, though we continued to make certain that this could be done if unexpected hæmorrhage were to arise.

The only special instruments which had to be obtained for this operation were specially designed retractors,* which were based on those illustrated by Gil-Vernet (Fig. 18). Those used in the present series had been given a malleable stem, which has advantages in practice. The cheek retractor used by oral surgeons will be found to have a suitable shape if these special retractors are not available. The present technique differs from that described by Gil-Vernet in only minor details: we use an ordinary incision instead of his vertical lumbotomy; we use drainage rather than closure of the wound without a drain.

* Obtainable from The Genio-Urinary Manufacturing Company Ltd.

SUMMARY

Extended pyelolithotomy offers a method for removing large or multiple renal stones with negligible bleeding or drainage to the parenchyma. Experience based on 30 cases is described.

REFERENCES

ABOULKER, P: J Urol Med Chir 66:407 (1961)

BAKER R., MAXTED, W.C., KELLY, T., LAICO, J., LONGFELLOW, D: J Urol 92:589, (1964)

GIL-VERNET, J.M., Jr: New surgery in renal calculus. Film, 13th Congress International Society of Urology, London (1964 a)

————An Med Cirug Barcelona 40:391 (1964 b)

HELLSTRÖM, J: Acta Chir Scand 98:442 (1949)

HELLSTRÖM, J., and FRANKSSON, C: In "Operative Urology I, Ency- clopedia of Urology," Vol. 13. Ed. by Alken, C., Dix, V. W., Weyrauch, H. M., and Wildbolz, E. (Berlin: Springer Verlag) (1960)

McIVER, R.B: In "Treatment of Urinary Lithiasis," p. 178. Ed. by Butt, A.J. (Springfield, Ill.: C.C. Thomas) (1960)

MARSHALL, V.F., LAVENGOOD, R.W., and KELLY, D: Ann Surg 162:366 (1965)

SURRACO, L.A: J Urol Med Chir 48:217 (1939)

Commentary:
Technique of Extended
Pyelolithotomy

Eduardo M. Farcon and Pablo Morales

The Gil–Vernet approach for surgical removal of staghorn calculi uses a posterior vertical lumbotomy and an intrasinusal exposure of the pelvis and calices. The method has proved to be effective, with minimal tissue damage and bleeding prob- lems. Blandy modified the approach by using a standard oblique lumbotomy and by mobilizing the kidney completely to allow intraoperative renal x-ray films and placement of a pedicle clamp in case of unexpected bleeding. The success of the technique depends on the surgeon's developing the correct cleavage plane between the posterior surface of the renal pelvis and calices and the overlying peripelvic renal parenchyma. Additional nephrotomies may be necessary to extract large, mushroom-shaped caliceal stones. Attendant bleeding from the nephrotomies is generally minimal because the parenchyma covering the stone is usualy thin and atrophic.

To perform good renal stone surgery, one should strive

to (1) remove all the stones completely, (2) preserve renal tissue, (3) provide unimpeded urinary drainage, and (4) maintain sterile urine. One can remove a solitary stone in the renal pelvis successfully by simple pyelolithotomy, but a large staghorn calculus or stones lodged in the calices are best removed by the extended pyelolithotomy, as described by Gil–Vernet and Blandy, unless one resorts to renal bisection.

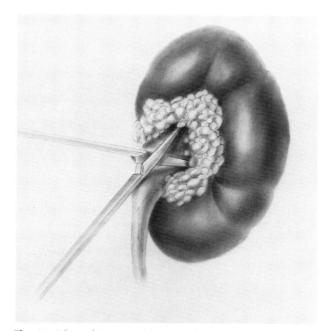

Fig. 19. Blunt dissection between the peripelvic fat and the posterior surface of the renal pelvis up to the renal sinus.

PREOPERATIVE EVALUATION

All patients should undergo careful metabolic screening before surgery. Preoperative control of infection with specific antibiotics is without doubt advisable. Accurate localization of the calculi in relation to the different calcices can facilitate the surgery. This can be achieved by tomograms of the kidney in anteroposterior, lateral (75°), and oblique views, before and during excretory urography.

SURGICAL PROCEDURE

The surgical approach is usually a flank incision, either subcostally or with resection of the 12th and 11th rib. Completely mobilize the kidney to allow for intraoperative radiograms and for access to the renal pedicle in case of unexpected bleeding.

To proceed: begin dissection just above the ureteropelvic junction. Bluntly reflect the peripelvic fat from the posterior surface of the renal pelvis up to the entrance to the renal sinus (Fig. 19). (The renal sinus is the intraparenchymal space containing the intrarenal portion of the pelvis and calices, vessels, lymphatics and nerves, and adipose tissue. The entrance to the sinus is sealed by a fibrous diaphragm that arises from the renal capsule and adheres to the pelvis.) Carefully follow the adventitia of the pelvis, using blunt pointed scissors to get in between the fibrous diaphragm and the renal pelvis, and enter the renal sinus (Fig. 20). With the malleable neurosurgical retractor, reflect the peripelvic fat and the inner surface of the renal parenchyma away from the intrarenal portion of the pelvis (Fig. 21). There is little danger of tearing the parenchyma during this maneuver because it is protected by the capsule and peripelvic fat. Achieve a wider exposure of the calices by bluntly separating the inner-surface of the parenchyma from the renal collecting system and by placing another malleable retractor so that the posterior half of the kidney can be lifted up, allowing a complete view of the pelvis and major calices. With careful dissection, one can do this without significant bleeding. In certain patients, as a result of severe perihilar inflammation or previous surgery, it is difficult to dissect the

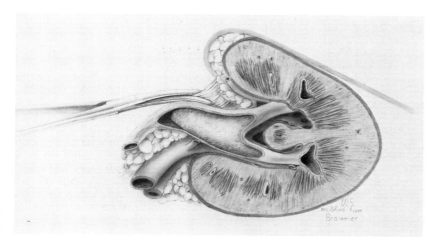

Fig. 20. Severance of fibrous diaphragm connecting adventitia of the pelvis and the renal capsule.

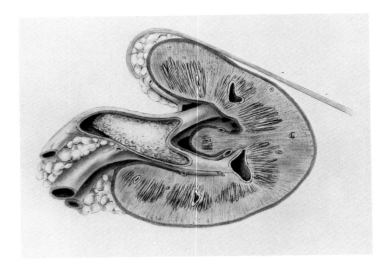

Fig. 21. Malleable neurosurgical retractor lifts the peripelvic fat and inner surface of the renal parenchyma away from the intrarenal collecting system.

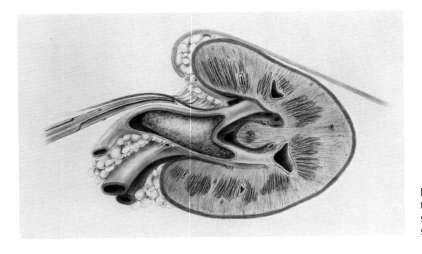

Fig. 22. Blunt dissection beneath the adventitial layer of the renal pelvis in cases of severe perihilar inflammation or previous surgery.

pelvis because the peripelvic fat densely adheres to the pelvis adventitia of the pelvis. One must then perform the dissection beneath the adventitial layers (Fig. 22).

Make the incision in the pelvis with a hooked scalpel; it should conform to the size and location of the stone. A simple pelvic stone usually requires a transverse incision, and branched calculi require an arciform incision that follows the course of the upper and lower branches of the staghorn calculus (Fig. 23).

Free the stone with gentle manipulation, and dislodge the vertex of the stone with a simple blunt stylet. The next branch for delivery through the incision should be the most mobile, the shortest, and the most easily accessible. Gentle pulling, pushing, and rotating along the axis of the branch will avoid tears in the incision or damage to the endothelial lining. Avoid pulling hard so as not to fragment the calculus and lacerate the calix. If the caliceal branch is larger than the infundibulum, a longitudinal incision through the obstructing infundibulum

may be required before the stone can be extracted. Sometimes it is necessary to break the branch at its neck and remove the distal part through an additional nephrotomy (Fig. 24). Blind probing with forceps and repeated attempts to extract large caliceal stones through a narrow infundibulum can cause annoying bleeding and secondary scar tissue. Removal through a nephrotomy is preferable, since the renal parenchyma overlying this large caliceal extension of a staghorn calculus is usually thin and atrophic. When the parenchyma is too thick for the stone to be palpable over the renal surface, pass a small probe under direct vision through the infundibulum that leads to the stone in the calix. Push this probe alongside the stone and out through the renal surface. Make a parenchymal incision along the course of the probe (Fig. 25), and deepen it until the stone is reached. One alternative is to press the stone against the thick renal tissue with an instrument (Fig. 26); it can then readily be located by palpation from the outer surface of the kidney.

After extracting the stone, thoroughly irrigate the entire collecting system. A flexible nasal irrigator or dental pulse-jet water irrigation system (Water-Pik) (Fig. 27) can direct a vigorous jet of saline into every calix. This ensures removal of small fragments either left during manipulation or undetected on the preoperative films. Intraoperative renal radiography is essential in confirming complete removal of the stones. Insert a soft Robinson catheter Fr. 8–10 through the pyelotomy and down the ureter to ensure free passage.

Close the renal pelvis incision with interrupted 4–0 chromic catgut. The infundibular incisions do not have to be closed. After removal of the renal sinus retractors, the renal hilus and posterior edge of the renal parenchyma will fall down on the infundibula and pelvis and cover the remaining openings (Fig. 28).

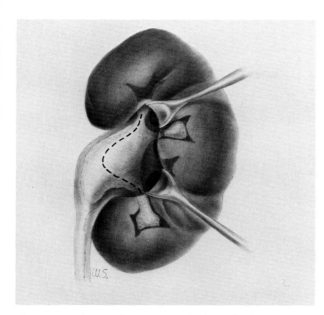

Fig. 23. Arciform pelvis incision for branched calculus (*dotted line*).

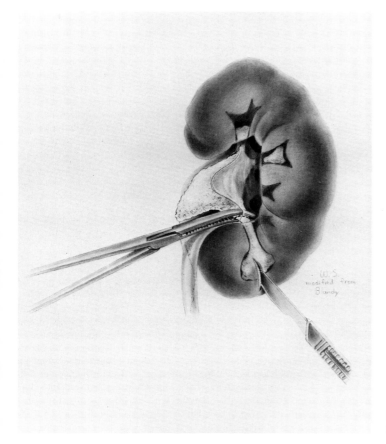

Fig. 24. Breaking the calculus calyceal extension at its neck before delivery through a nephrotomy.

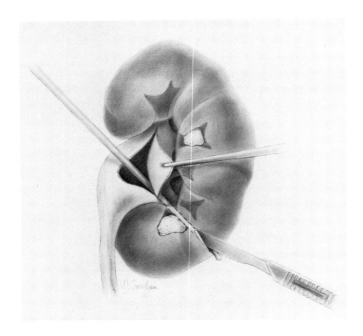

Fig. 25. Small probe to localize the calyceal stone along the course of the probe before nephrotomy.

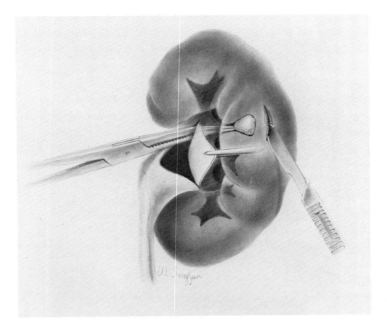

Fig. 26. Instrument pressing the calyceal stone against renal tissue, and parenchymal incision made over the stone.

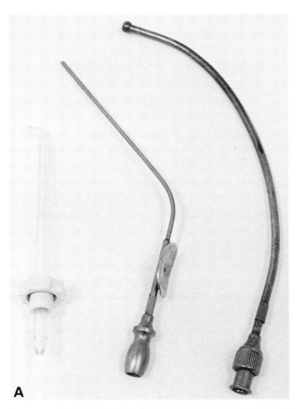

A

Fig. 27. (*A*) Flexible nasal irrigators. (*B*) Dental pulse jet water irrigation system.

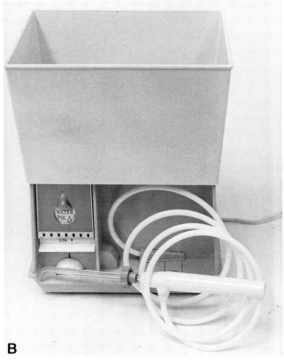

B

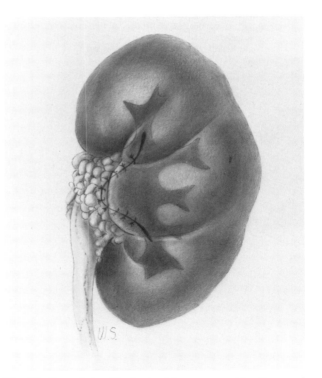

Fig. 28. Open infundibular incisions covered by the renal hilus, and posterior edge of the renal parenchyma after removal of sinus retractors.

ANNOTATED BIBLIOGRAPHY

Gil–Vernet JM Jr: New surgical concepts in removing renal calculi. Urol Int 20:255, 1965

This paper describes in detail the surgical approaches to complete removal of renal calculi. The surgical procedures consist of a posterior vertical lumbotomy, surgery of the kidney *in situ,* an intrasinusal approach to the pelvis and renal calices, transverse pyelotomy, and longitudinal calicotomy. Dissection of the renal hilum affords the surgeon direct access to all main infundibula and calices, so that staghorn calculus could be removed without difficulty. Additional nephrotomies were needed in large caliceal stones that could not pass the infundibulum. Gil–Vernet's surgical technique is regarded as the best and least traumatic approach in removal of renal calculi. The article discusses the applications and advantages of the different technical procedures and illustrates the techniques. Singh M, Tresidder GC, Blandy J: The long term results of removal of staghorn calculi by extended pyelolithotomy without cooling or renal artery occlusion. Br J Urol 43:658, 1971

This paper cites the authors experience with the modified Gil–Vernet extended pyelolithotomy for removal of staghorn calculus. They have found that new stones may form in kidneys completely cleared and, more often, in kidneys incompletely cleared. Small fragments left behind may remain unchanged for years and may pass down the ureter. Their results showed that majority of branched staghorn calculi could be removed by Gil–Vernet's extended pyelolithotomy and combined with selective nephrotomy in few cases, without renal hypothermia or renal artery occlusion. Fifty-four large, branched staghorn calculi were removed from 45 patients who were followed for up to 7 years. There was no mortality, no secondary hemorrhage, and no secondary nephrectomy. Renal function improved in 43 of 45 patients. Infection was controlled in 80% of patients from whom all stone fragments were removed and in 66% of those in whom small fragments were left behind.

Blandy J: Surgery of renal cast calculi. In Libertino JA, Zinman L (eds): Reconstructive Urologic Surgery, p 17. Baltimore, Williams & Wilkins, 1977

The surgical approach for branched staghorn calculus Blandy uses is a modification of the technique first described by Gil–Vernet in 1964: a long oblique lumbotomy and complete mobilization of the kidney. This technique could remove large staghorn calculus with less tissue damage and bleeding problems. Caliceal calculi are removed in a variety of ways depending on the calculus's size and nature. Additional nephrotomies with or without renal hypothermia are sometimes needed. In 100 consecutive cases Blandy reports no operative mortality. He advocates removal of asymptomatic staghorn calculus because of its life-threatening complications, and clearly elucidates that it is best to remove all the calculi; to leave a fragment behind after a thorough attempt to remove it, however, is not a tragedy.

Kerr WS Jr: Surgical management of renal stones with emphasis on infundibulotomy. J Urol 103:130, 1970

The author explains that good renal stone surgery includes a preoperative knowledge of the anatomic and functional status of the kidneys. The objectives are preservation of renal tissue, provision of a normal urinary drainage, and maintenance of sterile urine. Pyeloinfundibulotomy has proved to be an effective surgical approach in complete removal of renal calculi, with less need of nephrotomies associated with renal tissue damage and bleeding problems. Continued postoperative follow-up study by the urologist is imperative, with emphasis on high fluid output (specific gravity 1.010), detection and control of infection, and programs for prevention or recurrences.

8

PARTIAL NEPHRECTOMY FOR RENAL LITHIASIS
Experience with 208 Cases

A. Puigvert, M.D., F.I.C.S.

Director of the Institute of Urology, Santa Cruz and San Pablo Hospitals, Barcelona

International Surgery,
December 1966,
Vol. 46 · No. 6

Among the local factors influencing calculus disease and favoring recurrence are the papillocalyceal inflammatory lesions, the congenital tubulomedullary lesions that can act as a lithogenous element, and those lesions secondary to the presence of a calculus in a calyceal cavity; also the obstructive lesions at the kidney outlet which because of the retention stasis produced, influence the development of new stones. Frequently, these factors are enhanced by the presence of some commonly unknown infection (hyperparathyroidism, diseased tooth acting as a foci of infection, a colloidcrystalloid disorder, vitamin A-D disturbances, etc.). The above mentioned elements can by themselves or jointly favor the development of new and successive renal calculi.

Neither the spontaneous passage, nor the endoscopic or surgical removal of a calculus excludes the possibility of a recurrence of renal calculus disease, which in a majority of cases is already favored by localized factors within the kidney itself.

Presented in Barcelona on the Mediterranean Tour of the International College of Surgeons, May 24, 1966. Accepted for publication July 18, 1966.

This evidence justifies the complete removal of the stone together with the correction of local lithogenous factors. Papillocalyceal and tubulomedullary lesions are fully corrected by partial nephrectomy (P.N.), and obstructive lesions by appropriate plastic procedures.

In 1929, I first performed P.N. for renal lithiasis in a female patient with a solitary kidney and a large pelvic calyceal calculus which had developed into a calculous pyonephrosis of the lower third. The results were excellent, the patient being alive 17 years following operation.

My personal experience, up to the present time, exceeds 500 P.N. from different causes; of these, 208 cases were for renal calculi. The age of the patients varied between 20 and 70 years of age, the practice of P.N. being unusual after 65 years of age because it is only justifiable in the case of a poor condition of the opposite kidney or its absence. Its peak incidence is seen between 40 and 50 years of age.

In polar renal calculi, P.N. is almost a "must"; the most frequent site being the lower pole which accounts for more than 80% of the cases. Possibly this site is

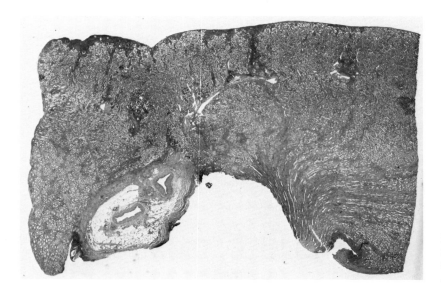

Fig. 1. Ulcerated papillocalyceal fornix and papillary apex, that constitute a permanent lithogenous focus (C.H. 34669).

favored by the loosening of a stone nucleus from a papillocalyceal genesial focus (Randall's plaque) or from a tubulomedullary one (Carr's microlithis). Freed in the pelvic calyceal system, it is stored in a calyx, preferably the lower one, where it is being developed, thus creating in situ a new lithogenous focus from decubitus which may even endure the preexistence of the papillary focus; this most dependent portion explains the frequent localization of a stone in the lower calyx.

The finding of a lithogenous renal focus (papillocalyceal or tubulomedullary) is important in treatment of this disease; its operative identification is not easy, because a straight observation of the kidney rarely discloses these lithogenous lesions; only a great callyceal dilation from retention or cortical cicatricial retractions can be appraised during a surgical intervention.

When we suspect the presence of a lithogenous focus, either calyceal or medullary, we must resort for proof to an intravenous pyelogram (I.V.P.) with double dose contrast medium or by a drip infusion technic—methods which can demonstrate with greater probability a papillocalyceal lesion or a medullary dysplasia that is the origin of possible recurrences. The presence of parenchymatous microliths which are a sign of a lithogenous tubulomedullary dysplasia must be appraised in the plain film.

Selective renal angiography in its arterial, arteriolar and nephrographics phases constitutes a complementary form for the interpretation of the urographic disturbances produced by the aforementioned lesions. The arteriolar modifications coincident with the papillocalyceal lesions that were seen in the I.V.P. are the parenchymatous

evidence of a segmentary lithogenous pyelonephritis and this contributes to the confirmative diagnosis of the kidney focus. As far as the medullary dysplasias are concerned, renal angiography gives very little information. A careful operative hemostasis is of prime importance if excellent results are to be obtained in P.N. The most reliable method consists of ligature of the prelocular arterial branch pertaining to the segment to be excised. Selective renal angiography expedites the understanding of the arterial architecture for ulterior operative identification. This information becomes much more important when upper pole resection is contemplated because the arteries entering from above may descend to the lower pole.

Under these circumstances, the ligature of a main renal branch produces the ischemia of a renal half together with the loss of a kidney portion we were attempting to preserve.

In a partial ectomy, renal morphology must always be remembered. If the segment to be excised is clearly seen as in a pyonephrotic calyceal dilatation or in a bifid pelvis, the surgical technic becomes easier. When the renal surface retains its normal morphology, the limits of the segment to be excised, previously identified by a radiographic examination, are corroborated by an ischemic zone following a hemostatic suture ligature; the surface changes color and becomes pale when the artery is tied or red-bluish when the draining vein is tied.

Just at the line of demarcation, cortical division is carried out with an electrosurgical unit and then by blunt intersegmentary dissection, cutting deeper until the calyx where the stone is lodged is reached, its neck then being

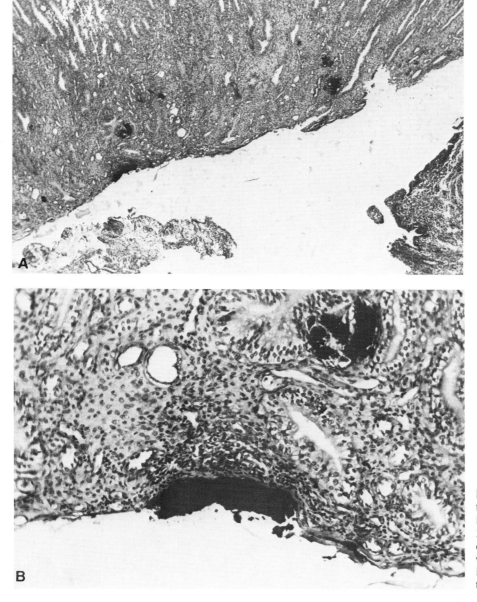

Fig. 2. (*A*) Randall's plaque at the papillary apex; tubular and interstitial microliths (C.H. 36966). (*B*) Randall's plaque increased in size. Microlith which because of its increase in size has gone through the tubular wall (C.H. 36966).

incised either with the electrosurgical unit or with scissors, removing the renal pole together with the lithogenous lesion and calculi.

Occasionally P.N. is complemented with a small nephrotomy incision or a ureterolithotomy procedure, so as to remove stone remaining in a calyx or in the ureter. In others, a ureteropyeloplasty is done in order to correct or widen the kidney outlet. Some other technical details without importance (ureterocalyostomy, pyelotomy, etc.) are also complements of P.N.

The perirenal sclerolipomatosis which frequently accompanies calculus disease, more severe in a case of a recurrence, usually makes disseciton of the renal vascular pedicle more difficult. To exteriorize the kidney, it is necessary to identify the renal vessels as well as its hilar distribution for a good preventive hemostasis.

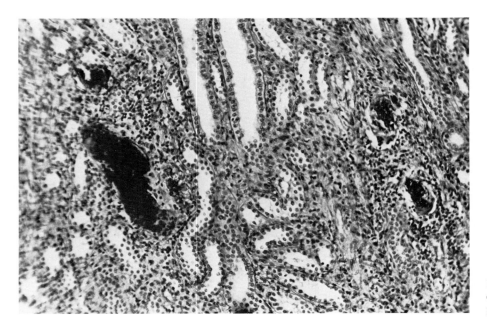

Fig. 3. Tubulo-interstitial microliths in a pyramid of Malpighi (C.H. 35408).

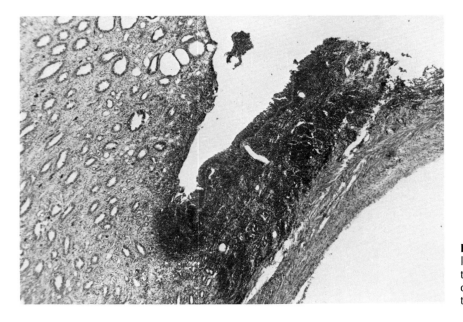

Fig. 4. Lithogenous lesion from a calyceal fornix showing ulceration of the papillary epithelium. Tubulomedullary dysplastic dilatation. Interstitial microliths (C.H. 36801).

Because of this difficulty, hemostasis is directly carried out at the level of the raw surface of the kidney by a transfixion suture ligature of each bleeding vascular point.

The histological examination of specimens obtained from P.N. has revealed in a number of cases, renal lesions which would be very difficult to cure; pyelonephritic or interstitial sclerosis, ulcerations of the papillocalyceal fornix, Randall's plaques, tubulomedullary dysplasias, etc., which favor the development of microliths and ulterior development of new calculi.

Other lesions have been discovered upon examination of the operative specimens. Among those, some new growths are Grawitz's tumor, adenocarcinoma, hamartoma, etc.

When renal calculi occur together with a pyelorenal

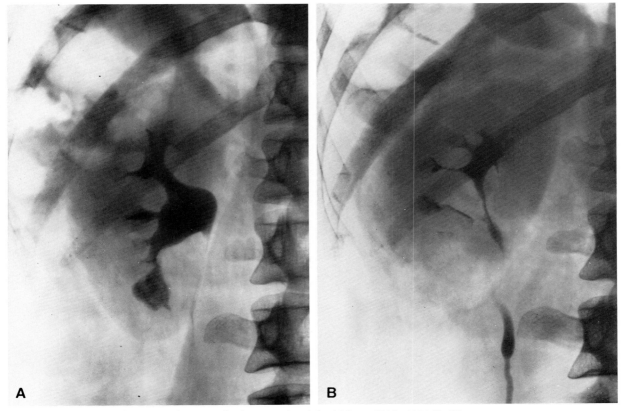

Fig. 5. (A) Calyceal lithogenous focus at the lower pole of the kidney (C.H. 63571). (B) Intravenous pyelogram one month following lower pole resection of the lithogenous focus (C.H. 63571).

malformation which can favor calculus disease, the latter expedites the practice of P.N. Under these circumstances, the anomalous vascular distribution expedites a main branch hemostasis.

Before P.N. is done and the remaining portion of the kidney is restored into the kidney fossa, a radiographic control must be undertaken, by radiotelevision when ever possible, in order to assure the nonexistence of stone fragments in the pyelocalyceal system of the preserved kidney.

Following resection and hemostasis, irrigation is done either through the calyceal neck or through the pelvic incision with normal saline solution of the pyelocalyceal system in order to remove possible remaining stone fragments.

The operations of segmental resection of the kidney for renal lithiasis can be arranged in the following manner: 208 operations done in 204 patients, P.N. being performed on both kidneys in four of them.

Localization	Cases	%
P.N. upper pole	33	15.9
P.N. lower pole	169	81.25
Horseshoe kidney	6	2.9

Solitary Kidneys	Cases	%
Surgical	8	
Congenital	1	
Total	9	4.3

There were three deaths (1.4%) in the immediate postoperative period: one three days later from uremia, one six hours later from shock, with a severe hemoperitoneum found at autopsy and one 12 days later from cerebral thrombosis.

Operations Done Before P.N.	Cases
Boari's operation (opposite side)	1
Partial cystectomy and ureteroneocystostomy	1
Litholapaxy	2
Ureteral meatotomy (endoscopic)	3
Nephrectomy	8
Nephrostomy, as a diversion procedure	5
Pyelotomy	23
Lumbo-iliac ureterotomy	11
Ureterectomy and ureteroneocystostomy	3
Lumbotomy	1
Cystostomy	3
Ureteropyeloplasty	1
Prostatic adenomectomy	3

Complementary Operations to P.N.	
P.N. + pyelotomy	34
P.N. + ureteropyeloplasty	5
P.N. + ureterocalyostomy	1
P.N. + ureterotomy	9
P.N. + nephrotomy	2
P.N. + excision of a cyst	4

Operations Done Following P.N.	
Partial cystectomy	1
Gastroenterostomy	1
Closure of lumbar incision	3
Pyelotomy	4
Pyelostomy	1
Ureterotomy	1
Pyelonephrolithotomy	1
Ureteropyeloplasty	2
Ureterectomy and ureteroneocystostomy	1
Secondary nephrectomy	1

Postoperative Period	Days
Average confinement in bed	7
Average hospitalization	14
Lumbar urinary drainage	4–7

Complications		Cases
Severe hypotension		4
a. recovery	3	
b. death	1	
Hemorrhage through the operative incision		3
Urinary retention		4
Severe intestinal paralysis		6
Phlebitis, lower extremity		4
Pulmonary infarction		1
Purulent retention from the incision		10
Operative pneumothorax		18

Lithiasic Evolution		Cases
Postoperative spontaneous passage of calculi (a month and a half)		4
Painless in 2 cases and painful in 2 cases.		
Recurring of calculus following P.N.		6
6 years later	1	
3 years later	1	
After 1 year	3	

Histological Examination of Operative Specimens	Cases
Pyelonephritis with nephrolithiasis	82
Pyonephritis plus renal cyst	17
Papillitis + inflammatory lesions of calices and tubular dysplasia	94
Interstitial nephritis and hydrocalyx	1
Nephrosis and nephritis	3
Renal atrophy	1
Grawitz's tumor	1
Intrarenal tubular papilloma	1
Trabecular adenocarcinoma	1
Cystic microadenoma and multilocular	2
Sponge medullary dysplasia	1
Medullary dysplasia and hamartoma	3
Calyceal dysplasia	1
Total	208

Chemical Examination of Calculi	Cases
Uric acid and urates	26
Urates and calcium phosphate	5
Calcium phosphate	46
Oxalates + calcium phosphate	23
Oxalates + uric acid	2
Calcium phosphate	11
Phosphates and alkaline carbonates	63
Phosphates bicalcium	9
Triphosphates (ammonium magnesium phosphate)	13
Total	198

Urinary Fistula (Lumbar). In approximately 50% of cases, leakage of urine was seen from the drainage tube for four to eight days; in the large majority of cases, the leakage of urine ceased as soon as they were out of bed; only in 2% of them, did leakage last a few weeks. In two patients, indwelling ureteral catheterization was necessary, with no leakage from the fistula a week later.

Azotemia. Usually the blood urea nitrogen (BUN) does not exceed the preoperative value and only in a very rare case did the BUN exceed 1 gr/1000 ml.

Fever. During the first few days, it may oscillate from 37.5°C to 38°C, rarely up to 39.5°C but decreasing rapidly. Protection with antibiotics is a routine but it must be used in accordance with previously done sensitivity tests.

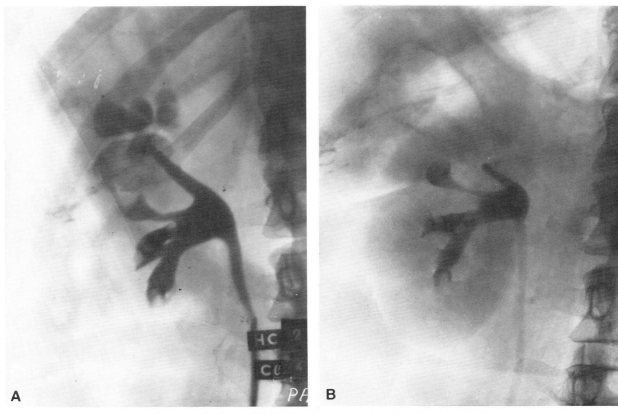

Fig. 6. (*A*) Upper caliectasis from a calculus embedded at the calyceal neck (C.H. 2631). (*B*) Intravenous pyelogram 14 years following upper nephrectomy (C.H. 2631).

Hematuria. Very scanty during the first few days; rarely after the fifth day. In one case, hematuria reappeared for 24 hours, ten days after the operation. In another case, hematuria persisted for about ten days, ceasing spontaneously.

Four deaths (1.4%) were seen from 15 months to 17 years after operation. One case with a solitary kidney died 17 years later from renal failure, one case two years later from neoplastic cachexia (Ca of the bladder), another six years later from senility, and one 15 months later from Ca metastases of the brain—a right nephrectomy being done for carcinoma and three months later partial nephrectomy being done for renal calculi together with a neoplastic lesion (Grawitz's tumor) in the plower pole which was found at operation and removed.

CONCLUSIONS

P.N., because of its effectiveness and curative properties, is justifiable when renal calculi are accompanied by a well circumscribed papillocalyceal or medullary lesion which is a true lithogenous site or the renal portion which lodges the stone cannot be saved. The obstructive dilatated calyceal lesions cannot be mistaken, from the stand point of recovery, for the retractile ones that lodge the stone; the latter are not modified after removal of a calculus and an interstitial and calyceal sclerosing gradually develops, thus creating a lithogenous element for recurrence. On the contrary, the calyceal dilatation tends to regress and the immediate recovery of the kidney parenchyma is excellent.

The pyelographic identification of the lithogenous papillocalyceal and tubulomedullary disturbances, as much or more than the morphologic and topographic characteristics of the stone, justify P.N.

The deficit in iodine excretion during I.V.P. through the renal reniculi that empty into it or into the calices that lodge the stone reveals the functional disturbance of this kidney portion, thus establishing an indication for the removal of this renal segment.

(*Text continues on page 112*)

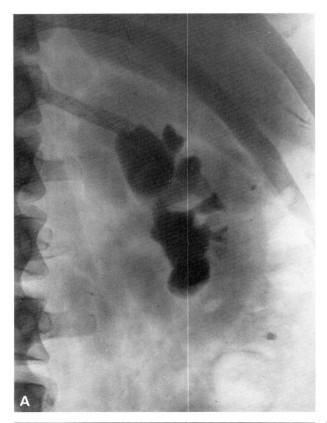

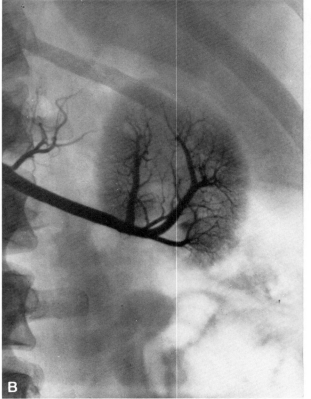

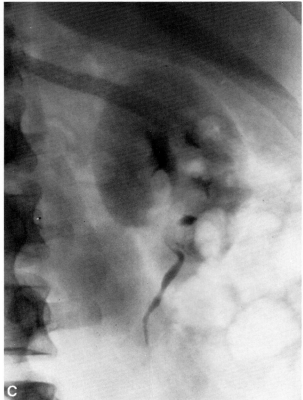

Fig. 7. (*A*) Upper caliectasis due to obstruction; renal pelvis and lower calyces completely filled with calculi (retractile pyelitis) (C.H. 61573). (*B* and *C*) Selective arteriogram and secondary pyelogram 5 years following lower pole nephrectomy. Normal apppearance of the calyceal cavities pertaining to the upper and middle group (C.H. 61573).

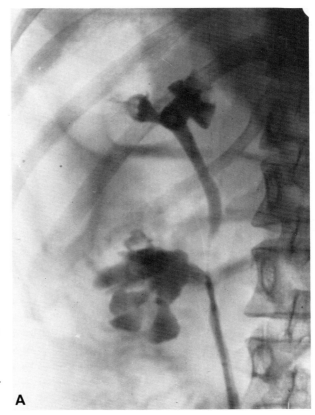

Fig. 8. (A) Bifid renal pelvis with calculi seen in the lower pelvis (C.H. 2262). (B and C) Selective arteriogram and secondary pyelogram 24 years following lower pole nephrectomy. Because of a slight bout of cystitis, an I.V.P. was done and because of the atypical appearance of the renal pelvis, removal of the well preserved remainder of the kidney shown in the arteriogram was advised (C.H. 2262).

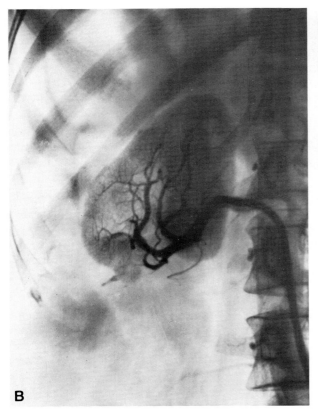

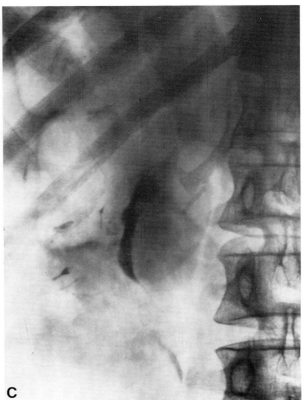

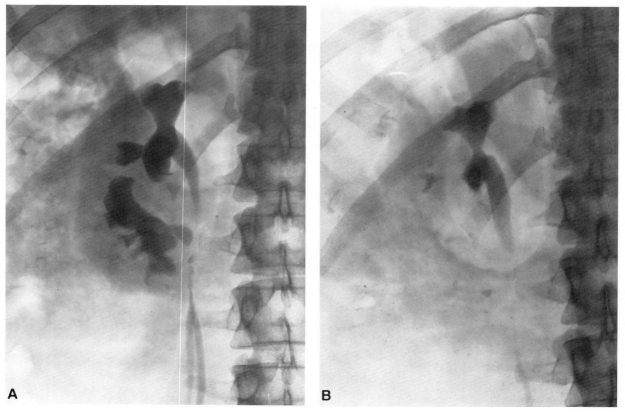

Fig. 9. (A) Calculus recurrence in the lower renal pelvis (C.H. 64971). (B) Intravenous pyelogram one momth following lower pole nephrectomy. A calculous nucleus at the level of the kidney cicatrix is seen showing no changes 5 years later (C.H. 64971).

The morphologic disturbances of the renal papillae and the corresponding calyceal cup seen in the I.V.P. confirm the aforementioned statement.

If selective renal angiography shows a decrease in the arteriolocapillary circulatory network corresponding to the reniculus pointed out in the intravenous pyelogram as compared with the normal arteriolar texture of the remaining kidney, the reniculus disease is confirmed and its removal is justified in order to prevent the recurrence of calculus.

Selective suture ligature of the vascular branches corresponding to the portion of the kidney to be removed is the most efficacious hemostatic procedure. It is an easy maneuver, when we are dealing with a lower pole resection or one that coincides with a polar vessel supplying this segment. When the contemplated resection is an upper one, even if it coincides with a polar vessel, we must be sure that it does not reach the middle third or especially the lowest one supplying a renal half, in which case suture ligature will be done only to the lobular branch or branches shown by renal angiography in order to preserve the blood supply from the remaining artery. For this reason, preoperative arteriographic identification is essential since occasionally the superior branch is apt to descend to the lower pole of the kidney.

In resection of the middle third of the kidney, preventive main branch hemostasis is practically impossible. In P.N. of the lower pole, main branch hemostasis is easier, the risk of renal ischemia in the preserved kidney being much less.

The temporary hemostatic methods, through occlusion of the vascular pedicle either with a rubber band or with an elastic or flexible clamp whenever possible, are not always effective. Even if occlusion is complete for the renal vein, it may be inadequate for the artery, thus allowing leakage of blood to the kidney due to a lack in backflow, inducing blood raw surface oozing on the preserved kidney.

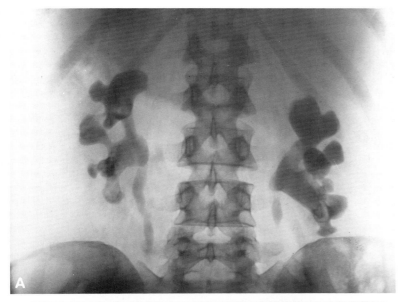

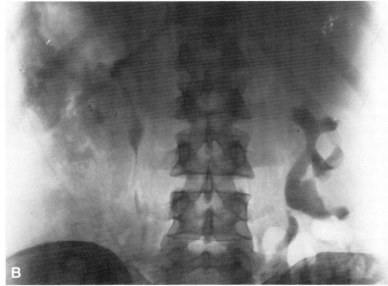

Fig. 10. (*A*) Preoperative intravenous pyelogram; calculus recurrence in the left side and a right pyelocalyceal stone (C.H. 54094). (*B*) Intravenous pyelogram 18 months following bilateral lower pole nephrectomy. The extrarenal lithogenous factors were not modified but the lithogenous focus from each kidney was removed, therefore, there was no recurrence (C.H. 54094).

The operative accidents as well as the postoperative hemorrhage complications of P.N. are the same as in any other type of renal surgery done for the same reason. In the 208 cases of P.N. done for renal calculi, not a single case of postoperative renal hemorrhage has been observed, thus making unnecessary an emergency procedure.

An intrarenal drainage, which is forbidden in P.N. is more especially so in the case of renal calculi. Drainage of the renal fossa in order to evacuate the serohematic oozing and possibly the leakage of urine during the first few days is paramount. A possible leakage of urine through the operative wound stops easily. If it persists, it usually stops as soon as the patient is out of bed; standing favors fistula closure.

The recurrence of calculi following P.N. are few (5%) due to the fact that in the case of renal lithiasis, some not too wellknown general factors are implicated

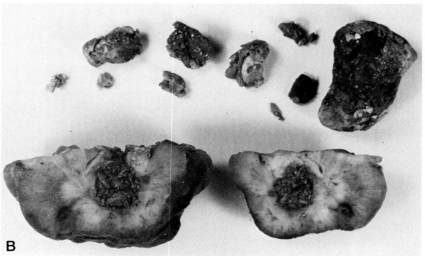

Fig. 11. (*A*) Right and left lower pole of the kidney removed from a female patient who had a left pyelotomy for a stone but had a recurrence 3 months later. (*B*) No recurrence seen 18 months following bilateral P.N. (C.H. 54094).

and only the local lithogenous factors can be eradicated by P.N. Thus the coefficient for a recurrence tends to diminish.

To be mentioned here are two cases in which an unidentified calyceal stone was overlooked but did not contribute to the formation of new ones.

The persistence of some calculus remnant on the cicatricial cut surface of the kidney which an intravenous pyelogram showed with an extracanalicular localizaton, implies no future risk.

The histological studies done on P.N. specimens reveal very frequently irreversible lesions leading to renal sclero-atrophy of the kidney portion removed; for this

reason, P.N. constitutes no mutilation of a useful nephron unit because it only removes kidney parenchyma already condemned to be functionless.

Postoperative sterilization of the urine is almost constant; in a small number of patients, slight pyuria persists. Recovery is determined by sensitivity tests and supported by the use of the proper antibacterial agent and dosage, thus eradicating the residual infection, which tends so much to influence recurrence.

The periodic follow-up of patients shows good function from the preserved kidney. Only in one patient operated on for renal calculi, was it necessary to remove the remaining portion of the kidney, because of a severe bout of pyelonephritis following a retrograde pyelogram, 40 days after P.N.

Every angiographic study of the preserved kidney has revealed a normal vascular pattern as well as a good renal function; an excellent patency of the evacuating pathways is observed on the secondary pyelogram.

Following P.N., no increase in blood pressure has been observed in any of the patients reviewed.

When there are circumscribed tubulomedullary dysplasic disturbances seen in the removed renal portion, effective cure is the rule; but if the dysplasia involves multiple Malpighian pyramids, late results are more uncertain.

SUMMARY

A selected series of cases of partial nephrectomy for renal calculi, based on a wide personal experience (over 500 cases) is presented. Two hundred and eight operations were done in 204 patients, nine of them with a solitary kidney. In four patients, this operation was carried out on both kidneys.

The indications for partial nephrectomy for renal lithiasis, together with the localized renal lesions that constitute the lithogenous focus and thus the site for a recurrence following the mere removal of a calculus from the kidney pelvis or a calyx, have been emphasized.

No operative accidents were observed in accordance with his statistics, the postoperative being discussed in detail.

There have been three deaths within the first postoperative 12 days, only one being attributable to the operation.

One case required a secondary nephrectomy because of a pyelonephritic infection one month following partial nephrectomy.

In order to perform a pole resection of the kidney he proceeds with a main stem ligature of the arterial branches proper to the segment to be removed which were previously identified by selective renal arteriography.

Nephrostomy has been abandoned by the author in all cases of renal resection.

Recurrences do not exceed 5% of the cases.

Commentary:
Partial Nephrectomy and
Pyelocalicolithotomy

Marco Caine

It seems desirable to stress at the outset that this commentary refers to the use of partial nephrectomy for renal calculi only and that some of the comments do not necessarily apply to partial nephrectomy for such conditions as tumor, renal hypertension, or tuberculosis, which do not fall in the terms of reference of this chapter.

INDICATIONS FOR OPERATION

One of the interesting developments in the subject of partial nephrectomy in recent years relates to the indications for this operation. When Dr. Puigvert wrote his article, most authorities on the subject would probably have agreed that most calculi were related to a localized "lithogenous focus" and that removal of this region of the kidney together with the stone was advisable in order to reduce the incidence of recurrent ipsilateral stone formation. Serious doubt, however, has been cast on the validity of this concept of a localized lithogenous region in the kidney by Anderson's finding that calcification in kidneys removed at autopsy is uniformly distributed throughout the whole organ.[1] Thus, although mineralized renal tissue might be removed by partial nephrectomy, tissue that is just as heavily mineralized will remain. The majority of publications tended to support the belief that partial nephrectomy reduces the incidence of recurrence, but on careful analysis it becomes clear that many of the series are unsatisfactory because there was too short a period of follow-up studies in too few cases or because no routine radiography of all patients had been performed irrespective of the presence or absence of symptoms.

More recently, a number of papers have cast additional doubt on this belief. Thus, Pedersen reported a recurrence rate of 20.6% in a series with a mean follow-up of 3.9 years, and Myrvold and Fritjofsson reported a recurrence rate of 43% over a mean of 9 years follow-up.[2,3] In our series, with a mean follow-up of 5.85 years and a maximum of 16 years, we found an ipsilateral recurrence rate of 26%, which was almost identical to the recurrence rate in a very comparable series of pyelolithotomies.[4] Although the comparison with the recurrence rate after pyelolithotomy is frequently used as a criterion, note that this comparison is not strictly valid because of the preselection of the two groups of patients for the different operations, especially in the same department. Generally speaking, those in whom pyelolithotomy was performed were adults with calculi in the renal pelvis without evidence of a localized origin or localized disease in a specific kidney region, whereas if the latter existed, a partial nephrectomy was usually preferred. If the latter group of patients had been treated by pyelolithotomy, it is quite possible that the recurrence rate would have been higher.

Nonetheless, the overall results do tend to cast doubt upon the value of partial nephrectomy in preventing recurrent calculus in many patients, and in our paper we attempted to determine if any factors could guide one to or away from this operation. Our results indicated that a history of previous ipsilateral or contralateral calculi, or of multiple or scattered calculi, are points against, rather than for, partial nephrectomy. The composition of the stone, and the presence or absence of infection before or at the time of operation, did not appear to be important in this respect. We concluded that the use of partial nephrectomy for stone is logical and indicated where there is a diseased or deformed kidney segment that it would be unwise to leave behind according to general surgical principles, but that the operation could no longer be recommended in the hope of removing a hypothetic localized stoné-bearing region of the kidney.

One of the indications for the use of partial nephrectomy in renal calculi is in certain cases of staghorn calculi. We have drawn attention to the fact that sequential studies of the development of staghorn calculi can sometimes clearly demonstrate the growth of the stone by progressive extension from one segment of the kidney, generally the lower pole.[5] When in such cases the originating segment is likely to remain deformed, a good case can be made for its removal at the same time the staghorn calculus is removed. Not only does this probably reduce the risk of recurrence, but it often makes the operation much easier technically.

In some patients, an alternative to partial nephrectomy is *pyelocalicolithotomy,* in which an incision in the renal pelvis is extended into a calix, usually the lower one, and cuts through the overlying renal parenchyma. The pelvicaliceal system is thus opened wide, enabling the removal of large calculi and a good visualization of the interior of the kidney. This operation has the advantage over partial nephrectomy of conserving functioning renal parenchyma but the disadvantage of leaving any deformed or diseased kidney tissue. If combined with a ureterocalicostomy, as outlined below, any such segment will be provided with maximal drainage. In view of the increasing evidence, referred to above, that partial nephrectomy does not entirely live up to surgeons' earlier expectations in preventing stone recurrence, it would seem that pyelocalicolithotomy should be more widely employed, especially with staghorn calculi, when it will enable the additional preservation of functioning renal tissue. In certain patients, this operation can be combined with partial nephrectomy to facilitate removal of intracaliceal extensions of a large staghorn calculus.[6]

PREOPERATIVE CARE

Generally speaking, no special preoperative preparations or investigations, other than those common to all major operations, are required for either of the operations. If there is stubborn renal infection that cannot be eliminated preoperatively, it is wise to start appropriate antibiotic treatment with a loading parenteral dose immediately before the operation to obtain high blood and tissue levels at the time of a possible bacteremia (during the operation). In certain patients, especially those with already impaired renal function, radioisotope studies of the kidneys before operation may provide information on the function of a segment of the affected kidney and thus help one to decide whether to save or sacrifice it. Preoperative renal angiography is required in those patients undergoing a partial nephrectomy for tumors or segmental renal vascular hypertension, but, as indicated below, it is not necessary as a routine in the case of partial nephrectomy for stone.

SURGICAL TECHNIQUE

The approach to the kidney for either operation is normally by one of the standard loin incisions, preferably with resection of the 11th or 12th rib. I have found that a lumbotomy incision, although excellent for a simple or extended pyelolithotomy, does not give an adequate exposure for these operations. In a partial nephrectomy, mobilize the kidney until the pedicle is isolated but not skeletonized; keep a protective layer of fat and place on it an atraumatic vascular clamp, taking care to avoid the pelvis and the ureter. Despite Dr. Puigvert's emphasis on the dissection of the individual main arterial branches and ligation of a segmental artery with resection of the relevant renal segment, I question whether anything is gained by this in the specific case of partial nephrectomy for calculus disease. In these instances, the segment of the kidney to be removed is related more to the architecture of the collecting system than to the intrarenal distribution of the blood vessels, and the line of section of the kidney should correspondingly be related to the findings on the pyelogram, supplemented in some patients by additional information from an intraoperative pyelogram obtained by direct injection of contrast material into the collecting system.[7]

What is undoubtedly vital in a lower partial nephrectomy is to ensure that the whole of the involved calix is resected and that no caliceal stump remains. That such a stump could allow stasis and an increased danger of recurrent ipsilateral stone formation was suggested by Stewart; we have confirmed this.[4,7] This does not apply to the same extent in an upper partial nephrectomy, where, on the one hand, the better drainage reduces the danger of recurrent calculus formation, and, on the other hand, the close proximity of the posterior branch of the renal artery to the caliceal neck makes this hazardous.

I prefer to section the kidney straight across in a "guillotine" manner rather than to cut it in the form of a "wedge." The wedge approach is not only apt to result in devascularised renal parenchyma being left, but also makes the subsequent closure of the pelvicaliceal system more difficult. Hemostasis is obtained by suture–ligation of the individual vessels on the cut surface with 4–0 catgut before the vascular clamp is removed. After its removal, treat any remaining vessels in the same manner and control any residual oozing with hot packs. Never use deep mattress sutures to control hemorrhage. These are not only unnecessary but will almost inevitably result in ischemia and necrosis of renal parenchyma.

The renal parenchyma is most expeditiously cut with a scalpel, although other methods such as blunt division with the knife handle or transection of the parenchyma with one or more loops of catgut have been suggested in order to facilitate identification and ligature of the intrarenal blood vessels.[8] I cannot recommend the electrocautery unit, as suggested in the preceding article, in order to reduce the amount of oozing from the raw surface, since this can cause appreciable thermal damage to the adjacent renal parenchyma. Recently, cutting the kidney with the surgical CO_2 laser beam has been used both experimentally and clinically in a few urologic departments, including my own, with encouraging results.[9] The laser does only minimal damage to the adjacent renal tissue and seals the smaller blood vessels, hence reducing the time required for hemostasis and the amount of blood lost by oozing from the raw surface. On the other hand, the actual cutting of the tissue is slower than with the scalpel, and it is necessary to isolate the arterial supply to the kidney and occlude it alone to avoid engorging the kidney with blood—a condition that interferes with the effectiveness of the laser beam. All in all, although promising, it is too early to assess the advantages and disadvantages of the laser and to determine its place in surgery of the renal parenchyma. From a practical view point, much may depend on the successful development of a much more compact and convenient machine than is now available.

It is quite unnecessary to reflect capsular flaps in order to use them afterward to cover the cut surface of the kidney. On the contrary, it appears more satisfactory to leave the surface exposed to ensure free drainage of any blood or serum that may escape in the postoperative period. If, nonetheless, one decides to cover the raw surface with the capsule, it is important to buttonhole it in a number of places to prevent the accumulation of a subcapsular hematoma. Attempts have been made to prevent oozing from the surface by applying tissue adhesives, but a suitable adhesive has not yet been found and the method has not entered into clinical use.[10]

The question arises of the necessity or advisability of employing renal hypothermia for this operation (see Chapter 9). I think that although hypothermia is undoubtedly vital in prolonged and complicated kidney operations in which the blood supply must be interrupted, the ischemic time normally necessary for a straightforward partial nephrectomy for stone does not necessitate this refinement. In special cases of this operation where prolonged ischemia is necessary, and particularly when a solitary kidney is being operated on, renal hypothermia can certainly be a most valuable adjunct and can considerably increase the safety margin.

Both the irrigation of the pelvicaliceal system and the control by intraoperative radiography mentioned by Dr. Puigvert are very important technical details for minimizing the danger of leaving stone fragments in the kidney; do not omit them. Close the pelvicaliceal system by a continuous locking suture of 3–0 catgut, loosely approximate the perinephric tissue, and leave a corrugated drain down to the region of the cut surface. I fully agree that no nephrostomy should be used in a straightforward partial nephrectomy. When operating on a solitary kidney, leave a catheter in the bladder for about 24 hours in order to monitor urinary output.

In pyelocalicolithotomy, good mobilization of the kidney is required, but interruption of the main blood supply is not usually necessary.[11] To proceed: extend an incision in the renal pelvis through the caliceal neck into the relevant calix, cutting through the overlying parenchyma to open it completely. One can make the incision through a relatively avascular region by delineating the segmental arterial supply with an intravascular injection of methylene blue. Obtain temporary control of bleeding by local pressure or temporary sutures, remove the stones, and inspect the interior of the kidney with an illuminated sucker or a pyeloscope. Irrigation and x-ray control, as in the case of partial nephrectomy, are then mandatory. Conclude the operation by simple closure or by a ureterocalicostomy. In the former, following surface hemostasis as described in the discussion on partial nephrectomy, close the calix and renal parenchyma with absorbable sutures, taking care not to cause ischemia, and close the pelvis in the normal manner. In the latter, extend the opening in the pelvis into the ureter and suture it side to side to the open calix. In this case, unless the tissue is very thin, one must pare away the sides and the tip of the parenchymal incision and splay out the calix by suturing its edges to the renal capsule to prevent adhesions and scarring of the renal tissue around the anastomosis. With simple closure no nephrostomy is normally necessary, but when a ureterocalicostomy is fashioned, it is wiser to leave a fenestrated stent through the anastomosis for about 10 days, which will necessitate a nephrostomy. In both cases, leave a corrugated drain down to the operation site.

POSTOPERATIVE CARE

After partial nephrectomy, I keep the patient in bed for the first 24 hours after operation in order to minimize the risk of reactionary hemorrhage from the cut kidney surface. Similarly, in case secondary bleeding should occur, I do not remove the drain until the 10th postoperative day. If a urinary tract infection was present before the operation, make every effort to eradicate such infection in the postoperative period with appropriate antibiotics, chosen in accordance with the bacterial sensitivity. As indicated above, administer the initial dose immediately before the operation.

Impairment of function of the operated kidney in the postoperative period is transient as long as the ischemic time was kept within the accepted limits, with or without hypothermia, and in the patient with a satisfactory contralateral kidney it is of no clinical importance. Where surgery has been performed on a solitary kidney, the rare patient may be encountered in whom a period of impaired renal function or even of renal shut down may necessitate careful supervision of the fluid and electrolyte balance, or even dialysis, during the postoperative period until satisfactory renal function is restored.

After a pyelocalicolithotomy with simple closure, follow a similar post-operative regimen. After a ureterocalicostomy, the stent can normally be removed on the 10th day. The following day, perform a nephrostogram to confirm patency of the anastomosis and the absence of leakage and then remove the nephrostomy tube.

COMPLICATIONS

As Dr. Puigvert indicated, the operation of partial nephrectomy as practiced today is relatively free of complications. Those that may be regarded as specific to the operation are hemorrhage from the cut surface of the kidney, urinary fistula, or severely impaired renal function. The former two may also be seen after pyelocalicolithotomy.

A rare complication is vascular thrombosis due to intimal damage caused by the vascular clamp. Minimize the danger by leaving a protective layer of fat on the renal pedicle and avoiding excessive closure of the clamp.

Reactionary or secondary hemorrhage is still occasionally encountered; hence, adequate drainage of the operation site is important. Most cases are relatively mild and will respond to rest and blood transfusion.

Temporary leakage of urine for a few days is a not-uncommon complication, but it soon ceases spontaneously unless there is any impediment to free urinary drainage down the ureter. In our series of 158 operations, only 1 patient had urinary leakage for more than 10 days. As mentioned above, temporary impairment of renal function may occur, but permanent absence of function in the operated kidney, as disclosed by subsequent pyelography, is rare as long as the warm ischemic time was kept to 20 minutes or less.

. . .

These two operations for renal stone undoubtedly have an important place in the urologist's surgical repertoire. Each combines the aim of complete removal of the stones with eradication of any known or putative anatomic factors that would predispose to a recurrence. The evidence that stone recurrence after partial nephrectomy is by no means negligible should incline one more toward a maximal preservation of reasonably healthy renal tissue, as afforded by pyelocalicolithotomy, especially when combined with ureterocalicostomy. However, the removal of diseased and deformed kidney tissue associated with stones still remains an important operation. The indications for the two operations undoubtedly overlap, and the decision of which to employ in a given patient will certainly depend to some extent on the surgeon's personal preference.

REFERENCES

1. Anderson CK: Partial nephrectomy—a pathological evaluation. Proc R Soc Med 67:459, 1974

2. Pedersen JF: Partial nephrectomy for nephrolithiasis. Scand J Urol Nephrol 5:171, 1971

3. Myrvold H, Fritjofsson A: Late results of partial nephrectomy for renal lithiasis. Scand J Urol Nephrol 5:57, 1971

4. Wald U, Caine M, Solomon H: Partial nephrectomy in surgical treatment of calculous disease. Urology 11:338, 1978

5. Caine M, Rubin S: The management of staghorn calculi. Proc Cong Int Soc Urol 2:77, 1970

6. Barzilay BI, Kedar SS: Surgical treatment of staghorn calculus by lower partial nephrectomy and pyelocalicolithotomy. J Urol 108:689, 1972

7. Stewart HH: The surgery of the kidney in the treatment of renal stone. Br J Urol 32:392, 1960

8. Kim SK: New techniques of partial nephrectomy. J Urol 102:165, 1969

9. Barzilay BI, Perlberg S, Caine M: The use of CO_2 laser beam for kidney surgery. Experimental and clinical experience. Preliminary report. Proceedings of the second International Symposium on Laser Surgery, 1977, p 164

10. Rathert P, Lymberopoulos S, Gierlichs H–W, Breining H: Fluorpropylcyanoacrylat: Ein neuer Gewebeklestoff. Urol Int 28:154, 1973

11. Stephenson TP, Bauer S, Hargreave TB, Turner Warwick RT: The technique and results of pyelocalycotomy for staghorn calculi. Br J Urol 47:751, 1976

ANNOTATED BIBLIOGRAPHY

Anderson CK: Partial nephrectomy—a pathological evaluation. Proc Soc Med 67:459, 1974

Calcification in the kidney substance is common. It can best be delineated by contact radiography of thin kidney slices. Detection by this method is limited by the degree of mineralization rather than by the size of the deposit, since even the smallest deposits can be demonstrated with appropriate techniques. Using this method, two types of radiologically positive calcification have been identified. One consists of large, dense deposits of up to 2 mm, which are aggregates of calcium phosphate and occasionally oxalate, situated within the terminal collecting tubules and ducts of Bellini. They are, in essence, small incipient stones. The other type is small feathery deposits, situated both around the large bodies and deeper in the parenchyma. These are tubular deposits of calcium phosphate in the collecting tubules and Henle's loop. The deposition may be found in the lumen, the epithelial cells, or the adjacent interstitial tissue. Examination of the distribution of these two types of calcification in whole kidneys, obtained at autopsy, shows a much greater incidence in stone-formers than in non-stone-formers. The finding of radiopaque microcalculi was extremely common in recurrent stone formers (91% of 45 cases) and very rare in non-stone-formers (7% of 108 cases). The calcification was usually uniformly distributed throughout the kidney, and no difference could be detected between one area and another. Thus, it would appear that although heavily mineralized tissue may be removed at partial nephrectomy, just as heavily mineralized tissue will remain. The author concludes that any effect that partial nephrectomy may have on reducing renal stone recurrence must therefore rest on other factors.

Hans J–P, de Backer E: La nephrectomie partielle. Acta Urol Belg 40:804, 1972

This is a good general paper on the subject of partial nephrectomy. The authors review their results in 95 partial nephrectomies, 72 of which were performed for stone. Their mean follow-up time was only 26.6 months, and their calculus recurrence rate was 6.94%. They emphasize that the longer the follow-up, the higher the incidence of stone recurrence. Their technique consists of a wedge excision with electric cautery, after they isolate and clamp the renal pedicle, and suture–ligation of the vessels on the cut surface. In certain cases they leave in a nephrostomy through which irrigation can be performed. Their complication rate of secondary nephrectomy and fistula is relatively high and may perhaps be related to certain aspects of their technique, as mentioned in the Commentary. A large bibliography is appended.

Myrvold H, Fritjofsson A: Late results of partial nephrectomy for renal lithiasis. Scand J Urol Nephrol 5:57, 1971

A report is given of 65 patients who underwent partial nephrectomy for stone and were followed for up to 18 years, with a mean of 9 years. The authors report a recurrence of stone in 37 patients, but in 9 of these the recurrence was in the contralateral kidney; thus the true ipsilateral recurrence rate was 28 out of 65 patients (43%). Six of these ipsilateral recurrences were symptomless. The authors stress the importance of the length of the follow-up time in the evaluation of recurrence. Infection did not play a decisive part in stone formation. The incidence of postoperative complications was relatively high, and loss of fucntion in the ipsilateral kidney occurred in 6.6%. The authors conclude that only exceptionally does partial nephrectomy eradicate the causal factors in lithiasis and that it should be reserved for strictly selected patients in whom the lithiasis is accompanied by local pathologic changes or the kidney contains a group of calculi.

Rose MB, Follows OJ: Partial nephrectomy for stone disease. Br J Urol 49:605, 1977

The results of 227 partial nephrectomies for stone in 209 patients are reviewed. Sixty-three patients came for follow-up examination, at which new x-rays films were performed; data on the remaining 146 patients were obtained from the hospital records. The mean follow-up time was 11.9 years, and the series appears to be the largest reported in the English literature. The recurrence rate was related to the number of years of follow-up and was defined as the number of kidneys with true recurrences expressed as a percentage of kidneys under surveillance and at risk of recurrences, at any given time after operation. The overall true ipsilateral recurrence rate was 20%, increasing with time up to 34% at 20 years. The ipsilateral and contralateral recurrence rates were the same, whereas recurrence in the affected kidney would have been expected to be more frequent. Ipsilateral recurrence was about half that found after nephrolithotomy, pyelolithotomy, and ureterolithotomy, as reported in another series. The authors conclude that anatomic factors are important in stone formation and that partial nephrectomy is of value in the management of renal stones.

Wald U, Caine M, Solomon H: Partial nephrectomy in surgical treatment of calculous disease. Urology 11:338, 1978

This is a report on a detailed follow-up of 131 of 158 partial nephrectomies for stone up to 16 years, with a mean follow-up time of 5.85 years. Routine x-rays studies were performed on all patients, irrespective of symptoms. All relevant data from the patients' hospital records and follow-up examinations and all roentgenograms from before operation until follow-up were suitably coded and subjected to computer analysis to identify any significant correlations between various parameters recorded. A total incidence of 26% ipsilateral true recurrence was found, which can compare with an incidence of 28% in a comparable series of pyelolithotomies reported from the same department. Analysis of the parameters showed a correlation of recurrence with a residual caliceal stump, with a history of previous calculi passed spontaneously or removed from the same or the contralateral kidney, and with the presence of multiple or scattered stones in the same kidney. There was no correlation with urinary tract infection at or before the partial nephrectomy. The authors conclude that partial nephrectomy for stone is indicated with the specific aim of removing a locally deformed or diseased kidney segment, but not in the general hope of removing a theoretic localized stone-forming region of the kidney.

9

ONE HUNDRED CASES OF NEPHROLITHOTOMY UNDER HYPOTHERMIA

J. E. A. Wickham, N. Coe and J. P. Ward

From the Department of Urology. St. Bartholomew's Hospital, London, England

The Journal of Urology
Copyright © 1974 by The Williams & Wilkins Co.

Regional renal hypothermia for complicated nephrolithiasis has been described previously.[1,2] Between 1968 and 1973 more than 130 kidneys have been operated upon under regional cooling. Results of the first 100 consecutive cases are reported herein. The dry field technique provided by renal artery occlusion and local cooling provides a clean and detailed view of the intrarenal anatomy, minimizes the risk of damage to the finer vasculature and avoids subsequent loss of renal function. The procedure also allows ample time to perform a planned and detailed operation without anxiety over deteriorating renal function in an ischemic situation.

OPERATIVE TECHNIQUE

A standard loin incision is used to excise the anterior end of the 12th rib. A specially contoured ring retractor is then inserted (Fig. 1). The retractor provides a good operative exposure and allows the assistant's hands to be completely free. When the kidney is fully mobilized size B gauze elastic bandage is stretched over the kidney to provide an atraumatic sling for the organ, preventing

bruises from handling during the operation (Fig. 2). The renal artery is then exposed and isolated with nylon tape. A small bulldog clamp is placed on the artery to arrest circulation. Complete pedicle clamping is not necessary and produces intrarenal congestion. Heat exchanger coils are then placed on either side of the mobilized kidney and cooled water is circulated from an external cooling unit (Fig. 3). The cooling unit is basically a refrigerated reservoir of water at 1°C (Fig. 4). From this large reservoir of 16 L capacity, water is conveyed to the coils at a rate of about 1½ L per minute by a high speed pump and serves to maintain a coil surface temperature of 1°C to 2°C.* A telethermometer unit is built into the unit and is supplied complete with a needle probe to monitor intrarenal temperature during cooling. Cooling is continued until the deep core renal temperature is betwen 15°C and 20°C. For the average-sized kidney cooling takes about 8 minutes. The coils are then removed and the operation can proceed in a clear dry field without the encumbrance of curshed ice, saline slush or plastic ice water bags.

During the operation rewarming to 30°C occurs in

Accepted for publication March 22, 1974

* Pye Dynamics Ltd., Cambridge, England.

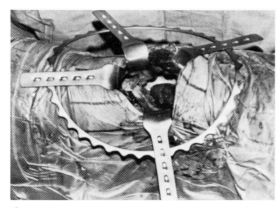

Fig. 1

Fig. 3

Fig. 2

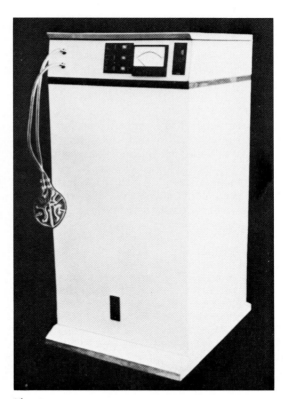

Fig. 4

about 35 to 40 minutes but simple re-application of the coils will lower the temperature to 15°C if further extension of ischemia time is necessary.

In cases involving complete staghorn calculi the pelvic portion of the stone is removed through a posterior pyelotomy incision. Caliceal calculi are then removed through multiple small radially disposed nephrotomies in the renal parenchyma. Because of the dryness of the field the major intralobar vessels can be seen and displaced to one side with a blunt dissector. A small fiberlight caliceal speculum is then inserted into the calix and a thorough search for all stone fragments is done under direct vision (Fig. 5).

For a high pressure flush 1.0 L bags of sterile normal saline are pre-cooled in a domestic refrigerator. When saline is needed it is placed in a bag compressor and connected to a malleable antrum cannula by a sterile drip extension tube. The bag is then compressed to give a high pressure irrigating jet by means of which small crumbs of calculus may be flushed from the calices onto swabs packed in the base of the wound.

After all macroscopic calculi are removed, Cushing silver clips are attached to the gauze as localizing markers and close contact x-rays are taken to exclude the presence of residual stone fragments. If fragments are discovered they are removed via further nephrotomy. When all stones have been removed the nephrotomies are closed by simple suture of the renal capsule with 4-zero chromic catgut stitches. Because major intralobar vessels are avoided during the incision deep and damaging hemostatic sutures are not required. Finally, a 12F nephrostomy tube is placed in the lower calix, the pyelotomy is closed and the wound is closed with drainage.

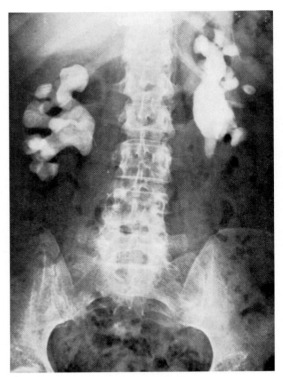

Fig. 6

PATIENTS

A consecutive and random group of 100 patients with nephrolithiasis such that complete removal of calculi could not be achieved except by incision of the renal parenchyma were included in the study (Fig. 6). Many patients had had staghorn calculi knowingly present for long periods, in 1 case for at least 30 years. The majority of these patients had been troubled with recurrent urinary tract infections and symptoms of fever, loin pain (often severe), frequency, hematuria and recurrent dysuria. In a number of cases the collecting system of the kidney was completely, or almost completely, obstructed by the position of the stone at the pelvioureteral junction and in 2 patients the kidney was pyonephrotic.

The patients ranged in age from 16 to 67 years, with a mean of 40.5 years. There were 34 men and 66 women. In 70 patients the stones were unilateral, while in 15 they were bilateral and the patients needed bilateral operations. Followup of these 100 patients ranged from 2 months to 4 years 1 month, with a mean of 1 year 4 months.

All patients were screened for metabolic abnormalities known to contribute to calculous formation. Dupli-

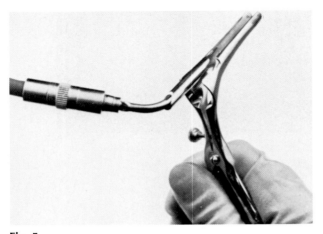

Fig. 5

cate estimations were made of serum calcium, phosphorus and 24-hour urinary calcium and phosphorous excretion, plasma uric acid and urinary screening for cystine. Whenever possible 2, 24-hour endogenous creatinine clearance tests were performed before and after operation and at 3-month followup. Serum creatine was estimated at similar times and at 1-month followup.

All patients had an excretory urogram preoperatively and 3 months postoperatively. Contact films were taken at the time of operation and a nephrostogram and plain renal x-ray were taken about 8 days postoperatively to exclude residual calculi in the ureter or kidney.

RESULTS

There were no deaths in this series. One patient underwent secondary nephrectomy for persistent bleeding from a kidney subsequently found to contain multiple Staphylococcal abscesses. However, no urinary fistulas were noted. Less than 500 ml. of blood was lost in 76 percent of the patients, between 500 and 1,000 ml in 20 percent and more than 1,000 ml in 4 percent. The average ischemia time for the group was 53 minutes, with a range of 9 to 118 minutes.

No detectable abnormality was noted on metabolic screening in 66 percent of the patients, while the remainder had some detectable metabolic abnormality.

The principal stone types analyzed are shown in Table 1. The effect of the operation coupled with appropriate antibiotic treatment is shown in Table 2 and Fig. 7. Patients with sterile urine at the end of followup were not on antibiotic therapy. All calculi removed were cultured bacteriologically. When the preoperative midstream urine was infected in all but 2 cases the organism grown from the stone matched exactly the organism grown from the urine. In 10 cases in which the preoperative midstream urine was sterile, organisms were grown from the excised calculus.

Radiologically, 76 percent of these cases had complete evacuation of all stones, while 24 percent had small

TABLE 1. Type of Stone

	No.
Triple and mixed phosphatic	74
Calcium oxalte	13
Cystine	9
Uric acid	2
Others	1

TABLE 2

	Preop.	1 Mo Postop.	Completion of Followup	Stone
Sterile	51	72	91	38
Proteus	24	14	0	31
Coliform	21	8	6	27
Pseudomonas	4	6	3	4

EFFECT OF OPERATION ON URINARY INFECTION

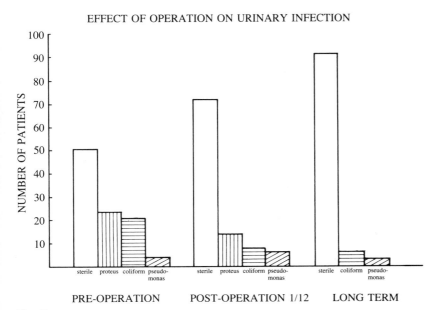

Fig. 7

residual fragments of stones but only 9 of this group had stone fragments that were considered removable by an operation. In the remaining 15 patients the fragments were minute and probably within the parenchyma of the papillae or medulla and not amenable to surgical extraction.

In 7 percent of the patients in this series recurrent calculi developed by the end of followup and all exhibited metabolic abnormality: 4 had cystinuria and 3 had hypercalciuria. None of this group had urinary infection preoperatively or postoperatively. In no patient with calculi suspected of having an infective origin did a stone recur.

Duplicate creatinine clearance studies were performed in 68 percent of the patients preoperatively and 2 weeks postoperatively. A paired T test between the values preoperatively and 2 weeks postoperatively revealed a mean reduction of clearance of 3.78 ml per minute with a standard deviation of 24.5 ml per minute (T equals 1.272, p equals 0.208—a non-significant reduction in renal function). Duplicate creatinine clearance studies were performed in 56 percent of the patients at the long-term followup. A paired T test between the preoperative and long-term followup values showed a mean improvement in clearance of 9.38 ml per minute, with a standard deviation of 24.5 ml per minute (T equals 2.184, p equals 0.0332—a significant increase over preoperative function).

Duplicate serum creatinine studies were performed in 85 percent of the patients preoperatively and 2 weeks postoperatively. A paired T test between the preoperative and 2-week postoperative values showed a mean increase of 0.21 mg percent, with a standard deviation of 2.34 mg percent (T equals 0.844, p equals 0.4011—a non-

significant decrease in renal function). Duplicate serum creatinine studies were performed in 63 percent of the patients preoperatively and at the long-term followup. A paired T test between preoperative and long-term values showed a mean decrease of 0.18 mg percent, with a standard deviation of 0.66 mg percent (T equals 2.209, p equals 0.0309—a significant improvement in function).

CONCLUSIONS

The technique appears to be a surgically safe and accurate procedure for the patient and kidney. Blood loss is usually slight, and postoperative wound infection and fistulization are not problems. In some cases renal function may be slightly depressed after the operation but this has recovered to its initial value in all except 3 cases. There has been significant improvement in creatinine clearance and serum creatinine levels in the majority of patients. In nearly all cases with preoperative urinary infection, the infection may be cured if all calculi are removed. With perseverance a high pecentage of complete stone clearance can be achieved.

Throughout the period of followup calculous recurrence appears low especially in cases in which the stones were of infective origin. Metabolic abnormality usually dictates a higher rate of stone recurrence. A clearer differentiation should be made between patients with calculi of metabolic origin and those whose disease appears to be determined by a preceding urinary tract infection. There is absolutely no indication for the performance of lower polar amputation of renal tissue, especially in cases in which the stones are of infective origin.

SUMMARY

The long-term followup of 100 patients with complicated nephrolithiasis treated by regional renal hypothermia is reported. The procedure is safe, resulting in little blood loss and permitting good clearance of calculi from the kidney. Renal function as measured by endogenous creatinine clearance was not significantly reduced immediately after the operation but was significantly improved after 3 months. Persistent urinary infection and its associated symptoms were cleared in 84 percent of the patients. Recurrent stones occurred in patients with a metabolic abnormality but there was no recurrence in patients with stones having an infective origin. There is no indication for a multilating polar nephrectomy in cases in which the calculi appear to have arisen following a urinary tract infection.

REFERENCES

1. Wickham J. E. A., Mathur V. K.: Hypothermia in the conservative surgery of renal disease. Brit J Urol 43:648, 1971

2. Wickham, J. E. A., Hanley H. G., Joekes A. M.: Regional renal hypothermia, Brit J Urol 39:727, 1967

Commentary: Regional Hypothermia in the Treatment of Renal Stone Disease

J. E. A. Wickham

Since the preceding article was published in 1974, more than 250 patients with complicated nephrolithiasis have been treated with an ischemic technique and their renal function protected by hypothermia. During the 10-year period in which these patients have been treated, a better evaluation of the place of hypothermia in renal surgery has been possible, and its value in comparison with other techniques of nephrolithotomy can now be defined. Several points are worth discussing.

ISCHEMIC TECHNIQUE IN RENAL CALCULUS SURGERY

Obviously an ischemic technique is not necessary in all renal calculus surgery, since it is clearly foolish to invoke a complicated operative procedure for treatment of a simple calculus lying within the pelvis of the kidney and with no extension into the peripheral renal collecting system. Such cases may be easily dealt with by simple pyelolithotomy with no need for dissection of the renal pedicle or renal artery. While a few of the earlier cases in our series may have been better dealt with in this way, our criterion for the use of ischemia has, in recent years, become much more strict, and the technique is now reserved for those cases of nephrolithiasis with peripheral caliceal calculi lying in a relatively undilated intrarenal collecting system.

THE EXTENDED PYELOLITHOTOMY OPERATION

Professor Gil–Vernet has elegantly demonstrated the possibilities of his extended pyelolithotomy operation for the extraction of complicated renal calculi with peripheral caliceal involvement.[1] This must be the preferred method of surgical treatment of the staghorn calculus in the dilated and hydronephrotic collecting system. The bulk of the stone may be easily extracted through a transverse pyelotomy, and peripheral caliceal calculi can be removed through the dilated necks of the hydrocalycosis. When, however, the collecting system of the kidney is not dilated, and, more imortant, when there is a normal thickness of renal parenchyma, it is extremely difficult to extract caliceal calculi through the caliceal neck without considerable local trauma to either calix or papilla. Here counternephrotomy is almost always required, especially if the contained caliceal stone is large or especially hard. In this instance, control of the renal circulation by arterial occlusion is indicated. Short-term arterial clamping of no more than 15 minutes may allow sufficient time for accurate extraction of a stone, but normally with multiple caliceal extensions a much longer period of occlusion is required, and this is where a functional protective system is necessary. Professor Gil–Vernet estimates that counternephrotomy is necessary in about 25% of all patients with staghorn calculi whom he has operated on.[2] In such operations, he uses short periods of vascular occlusion with intermittent reflow of blood at approximately 10-minute intervals. There is some experimental evidence, however, that intermittent normothermic occlusion may have a more damaging effect on renal function than a continuous period of circulatory arrest.[3]

There is also the consideration of preventable blood loss in this technique, which, although in most patients is easily replaced, may on occasion be a considerable and significant factor in prolonging postoperative morbidity.

ALTERNATIVE METHODS OF PRODUCING RENAL HYPOTHERMIA

The method of protecting renal function by hypothermia described in our article has served very well in over 300 patients who underwent renal surgery and required vascular arrest.[4] The use of small heat-exchanger coils through which a coolant solution is circulated from an external reservoir has the advantage of maintaining a totally dry operative field while making the entire kidney accessible to surgery. One may remove and replace the coils as necessary to maintain a core temperature of 15°C to 20°C. Usually this is done 3 times or so during an ischemia of about 1 hour, each cooling period taking between 4 and 8 minutes and the coils being repositioned during radiography while film development is awaited.

Our method has been criticized because it requires specialist apparatus that, although relatively inexpensive, may not be generally available to the surgeon performing occasional ischemic renal surgery. One may make a simple copy of the system, however, with an ice water reservoir—a simple electric pump of the bilge or washing-machine type coupled with self-wound coils of Silastic tubing cemented with elastic adhesive. I used such a system very satisfactorily in the early days of hypothermia.[4] Alternative methods of achieving renal cooling are, however, described below for surgeons wishing to use hypothermia with a minimum of specialist equipment.

First, Graves' method consists of invaginating a sterile plastic bag over the mobilized kidney, securing it around the pedicle with an elastic band, and then pouring sterile ice water into the gully formed around the kidney,[6] Core temperature is measured with a telethermometer probe. When a working temperature of 20°C is reached, remove the bag and start the operation. Recooling is, of course, difficult.

Second, the slush–ice method of achieving renal hypothermia developed by Professor W. H. Boyce is an excellent way of producing renal cooling.[7] It is described in detail in Chapter 6 but does, of course, entail an entirely different concept of operating technique insofar as the kidney remains completely buried in a slush–ice coolant for the duration of the ischemia, with temperatures falling below the optimum 15°C to 20°C. Burying the kidney completely in ice predicates that surgery must always be done through the parenchyma of the kidney, and Boyce has developed the intrasegmental concept of approach to the collecting system. This entails an initial dissection of the posterior branch of the renal artery, which may well be difficult in recidivist cases.

Again, although the technique is excellent for the removal of the pelvic portion of a staghorn calculus, large caliceal stones in a kidney with a thick parenchyma are difficult to extract without dividing the caliceal neck. Also, to reach the intrarenal collecting system, one must divide and meticulously ligate large intrarenal veins to avoid serious hemorrhage on declamping. Finally, long-term slush–ice cooling of this degree can result in significant whole-body cooling and may confront the anesthesiologist with a considerably more complicated management problem.

In a recent study of the effect of various operative approaches to the intrarenal collecting system, we have demonstrated that the functional effect of such operations on the dog kidney has a definite gradation, when measured at 48 hours postoperatively, such that there is little or no reduction in function with he sinus approach.[8] With the multiple nephrotomy paravascular approach, using three nephrotomies, there is a 20% reduction in function; with the intersegmental approach, a 50% reduction in function; and with a bivalve nephrotomy, an 80% functional loss.

INOSINE AND PROTECTION OF RENAL FUNCTION

In the last 3 years, following extensive animal experimentation by Dr. A. R. Fernando on the preservative effects of the basic nucleotides upon renal function during ischemia, we were able to demonstrate to our satisfaction that the dog kidney would withstand up to 1 hour of ischemia with little depression of

renal function.[9] Similarly, the rat kidney could survive a 3-hour period of normothermic vascular occlusion with good functional preservation and animal survival. Encouraged by these results, we have to date preformed about 40 operations on patients using the basic nucleotide inosine to preserve renal function during ischemias up to 1 hour with good results. The nucleotide has been given as a 2 g bolus injection in 80 ml of diluent into the renal artery after clamping and more recently by peripheral intravenous (IV) infusion 10 minutes before arterial occlusion in a similar dose. I have used Trophicardyl, a commercially available pharmacological preparation of inosine.[5]

The advantages of this method are that no cumbersome hypothermic equipment is required and that the operation can be performed in a clear field. No side-effects of this technique have been noted, apart from a transient rise in serum uric acid levels for a few hours after the operation. We therefore prefer to use this method when ischemia is not expected to exceed 1 hour.

. . .

In summary I would say, therefore, that my attitude to the operative surgery of the difficult nephrolithotomy is as follows. First, it is vital to remove all fragments of stone from the intrarenal collecting system, especially when dealing with the infected phosphatic stone. Patients with a pyocyaeneus infection are particularly prone to recurrence if all the stone is not removed and the infection eradicated. Second, remove the stone(s) by the Gil–Vernet sinus technique if at all possible. This entails no ischemic episode and causes the least depression of renal function. There are, however, some limitations to this technique, as described above. Third, if, to remove all calculi, the parenchyma must be incised, use an ischemic technique. There is, nowadays, no place for blind nephrolithotomy carried out in a pool of blood. With an ischemic technique, protect function by hypothermia or by inosine preservation. My preferred method of access to the calices is through the radial paravascular nephrotomy, which I suggest, if executed carefully to avoid transection of interlobar vessels, produces less depression of function than the intersegmental method of Boyce.[5] Finally, whatever method is used to work upon the intrarenal collecting system, it is becoming increasingly evident that physicians are now moving into the field of meticulous microsurgery and, happily, away, from the sanguinous sorties of yesteryear.

REFERENCES

1. Gil–Vernet JM Jr: New surgical concepts in removing renal calculi. Urol Int 20:255, 1965
2. Gil–Vernet JM Jr: Indications, surgical techniques, post-operative control and later results of staghorn calculi. Report of International Symposium on Staghorn Calculi, Vienna, 1979, p 105
3. Steueber PJ, Koletsky S, Perksky L: The effect of intermittent clamping of the renal pedicle. Surg Forum 10:857, 1959
4. Wickham JEA, Hanley HG, Joekes AM: Regional renal hypothermia. Br J Urol 39:727, 1967
5. Wickham JEA: Intravenous inosine for protection of renal function in ischaemic renal surgery. Br J Urol (in press)

6. Graves FT: Renal hypothermia: An aid to partial nephrectomy. Br J Surg 50:362, 1963
7. Boyce WH: In Glenn JF (ed): Renal Calculi in Urologic Surgery, 2nd ed, pp 169–189. Hagerstown, Harper & Row, 1975
8. Fitzpatrick J, Marburger M, Koo M, Wickham JEA: Intrarenal access (in press)
9. Fernando AR, Griffiths JR, O'Donoghue EPN, Ward JP, Armstrong DMG, Hendry WF, Perrett D, Wickham JEA: Enhanced preservation of the ischaemic kidney. Lancet 1:555, 1976

ANNOTATED BIBLIOGRAPHY

Boyce WH: In Glenn JF (ed): Renal Calculi in Urologic Surgery, 2nd ed, pp 169–189. Hagerstown, Harper & Row, 1975

This chapter describes Dr. Boyce's method of nephrolithotomy, including the slush–ice method of inducing renal hypothermia, together with details of the determination of the intersegmental plane between the anterior and posterior renal branch artery territories. Also described is Dr. Boyce's method of caliceal reconstruction for caliceal neck stenosis, a corrective maneuver all too often neglected by the urologist who is intent on calculus removal alone. This chapter is required reading for all physicians interested in renal calculus surgery.

Fernando AR, Griffiths, JR, O'Donoghue, EPN, Ward JP, Armstrong DMG, Hendry WF, Perrett D, Wickham JEA: Enhanced preservation of the ischaemic kidney. Lancet 1:555, 1976

This paper describes our initial experimental results with the basic nucleotide inosine as a preservative of renal function during an ischemic episode. As far as we can determine, inosine, a precursor metabolite of adenosine monophosphate and, ultimately, ATP provides a boost to the cellular energy mechanisms compromised by a period of ischemia. Animals treated with this compound did significantly better in terms of subsequent renal function than did control animals. This is basically a background experimental paper written before the clinical development of the use of inosine.

Fitzpatrick J, Marberger M, Koo M, Wickham JEA: The effects of renal function and morphology of the commonly used methods of intrarenal access. Br J Urol (in press)

This paper describes our attempt to quantitate experimentally the effects of the four standard methods for the extraction of staghorn calculi from the canine kidney. We performed functional and anatomic studies on dog kidneys subjected to either a sinus operation or multiple nephrotomy with intersegmental and bivalve approaches. Besides functional studies at 48 hours after operation, we made plastic resin casts of the kidneys, which demonstrate the degree of parenchymal loss. The main message from this paper is that "bivalve nephrotomy along Brödel's line should be abandoned forthwith and consigned to the history books."

Graves FT: British Journal of Surgery, 50, p. 362. Renal hypothermia: An aid to partial nephrectomy. Br J Surg 50:362, 1963

This article describes Graves's initial work on regional renal hypothermia with a "plastic bag–iced saline" technique. It describes ten clinical cases so treated. This is a good method for producing renal cooling with a minimum of equipment, but it is difficult to recool half-way through an operation with the kidney partially dissected.

Gil–Vernet JM Jr: Indications, surgical techniques, post-operative control and later results of staghorn calculi. Report of International Symposium on Staghorn Calculi. Vienna, 1979, p 105

This article brings up to date Professor Gil–Vernet's excellent results with the sinus pyelonephrolithotomy. These results are surely the sort of standard against which all surgery for staghorn calculi should be measured. I must admit to a sense of relief when I found that even Professor Gil–Vernet needed to perform peripheral nephrotomy in 25% of all patients to achieve complete stone removal.

Gil–Vernet JM Jr: New surgical concepts in removing renal calculi. Urol Int 20:255, 1965

This is the classic initial paper on Professor Gil–Vernet's sinus techniques and should be essential reading for the trainee interested in renal stone surgery. It gives an excellent description of the method of the sinus approach and of the posterior lumbotomy incision.

Steueber PJ, Koletsky S, Perksky L: The effect of intermittent clamping of the renal pedicle. Surg Forum 10:857, 1959

This is one of the significant early papers on the effects of different periods of ischemia upon renal function. There is now a vast and well-documented literature upon subsequent renal function, particularly in the dog. Surely there is no need to perform another set of control studies each time a worker investigates a new method of renal preservation. A few hours spent in the library could well obviate the unnecessary sacrifice of many animals.

Wickham JEA, Fernando AR, Hendry WF, Whitfield HN, Fitzpatrick JM: Inosine for ischemic renal surgery. Br J Urol 51:47, 1979

This short paper describes our initial clinical experiences with inosine administered intravenously 10 minutes before renal artery occlusion in a human. The results confirm our experience with animals and also define the method's possible limits. We are using inosine protection as our principal method of choice now, rather than hypothermia, for up to 1 hour of ischemia.

Wickham JEA, Hanley HG, Joekes AM: Regional renal hypothermia. Br. J Urol 39:727, 1967

This paper describes our initial observation of the optimum temperature for regional renal hypothermia at around 15°C to 20°C in animals. It also describes an initial experimental heat-exchanger coil for animal and human hypothermia and our initial clinical results of an ischemia technique with hypothermic functional protection. At the time, we were delighted with the diminution in operative blood loss and the consequent extraordinary lack of morbidity in our patients, compared with previous methods of nephrolithotomy. This paper gives a comprehensive bibliography on early work on renal ischemia and preservation.

OVERVIEW: METHODS FOR REMOVING STONES

John P. Blandy

Today there are several excellent methods for removing stones of any size and shape from the kidney without damaging the renal parenchyma and usually without significant blood loss. From times to time, physicians must remind themselves that these operations are not always necessary; quite often, the patient's interests will be better served by nephrectomy (when the contralateral kidney is stone free and has perfect function), but when nephrectomy is not an option, the surgeon must do his best to remove the stone. Surgeons still have to defend the position that surgical removal of the stone is safer than leaving it *in situ,* since the myth still lingers that some stones are silent and innocent; there is ample ammunition with which to refute this hoary piece of nonsense.[1-5]

The next question is, Which way is best to remove the large, branched, difficult stone? Obsession with cleverness in surgical technique sometimes obscures the underlying problem, which is usually very simple: inside the renal pelvis is the main body of the stone, to which are attached, usually by narrow arms, several peripheral branches. These branches expand into mushroom-shaped caliceal knobs. The knobs are too big to go through the neck of the calix without splitting it. If the caliceal neck is split, then a main segmental artery will be torn or a large vein laid open. In planning the surgical attack on the stone, there are two quite distinct problems and, hence, two distinct steps to the operation. The first step is to remove the body of the stone, and the second step is to remove its peripheral stalked knobs. When trying to choose between Boyce's method or Gil–Vernet's and mine, of approaching these two steps, consider briefly the arrangement of the arterial supply to the kidney (Fig. 1). There are five segmental arteries, and the territory of parenchyma supplied by each is distinct from that supplied by its neighbor—hence the possibility of

Boyce's bloodless or anatrophic incision.[6] But a second glance at the diagram of the arrangement of the arteries shows two other equally important facts: (1) adjacent to each caliceal neck are several large segmental vessels and (2) the vessels in the periphery are more sparse than those in the middle. Clearly, a radially directed incision, placed well out in the periphery of the kidney, is less likely to injure large segmental vessels than any incision that cuts through the neck of a calix.

How do these considerations apply to Gil–Vernet's method and Boyce's technique? In Boyce's anatrophic incision (Fig. 2) a bloodless incision is made, skirting the parenchymal territory supplied by the posterior segmental vessel. This brings the surgeon down along the knobs of the posteriorly directed branches of the staghorn calculus (Fig. 3*B*), which are readily exposed and lifted out from their calices (Fig. 3), but in order to free them entirely, one must cut the neck of the calix and the necks of the calices that face anteriorly. After complete removal of the body and branches of the stone, every single calix that has been opened must be closed or anastomosed together. (Fig. 4). Clearly, with experience, patience, and skill (as Dr. Boyce and colleagues have admirably shown), this formidable technical exercise can be accomplished with excellent results. However, it differs in an important and fundamental way from the Gil–Vernet technique (as adapted over the last 16 years by myself and my colleagues).[7-9]

In Gil–Vernet's approach to the renal pelvis, one must lift the parenchyma up off the muscle of the pelvis, and in difficult and previously operated on patients, one may have to use sharp dissection to get into the bloodless plane. Gil–Vernet draws attention to white line of Brödel, where the sinus fat sometimes densely adheres to the muscle of the pelvis (Fig. 5). Once in the right plane, it is not difficult to get good

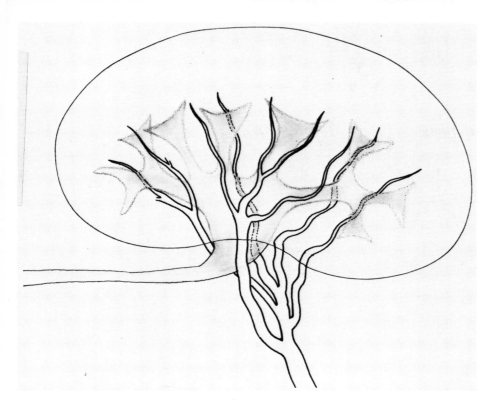

Fig. 1. The arterial anatomy of the kidney. There are five main segmental arteries to the kidney. They fan out radially from the hilum, and many of the larger vessels pass very close to the necks of the calices. Incision through the neck of a calix is therefore more likely to cut a large segmental artery than is a nephrotomy placed out toward the periphery of the renal parenchyma and made in a radial direction. (After Graves FT: The Arterial Anatomy of the Kidney. Bristol, John Wright & Sons, 1971)

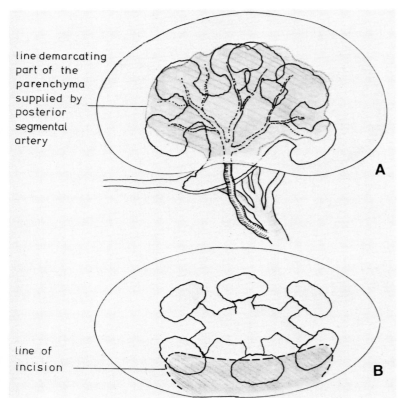

line demarcating part of the parenchyma supplied by posterior segmental artery

line of incision

Fig. 2. The basis of the anatrophic incision into the renal parenchyma is that one can show the "geographic" demarcation line between the territory supplied by the posterior segmental vessel and the remainder of the kidney. Cutting along this line (A) in a bloodless hypothermic field will not divide any major vessels and will bring one down upon the knobs of staghorn that project posteriorly (B).

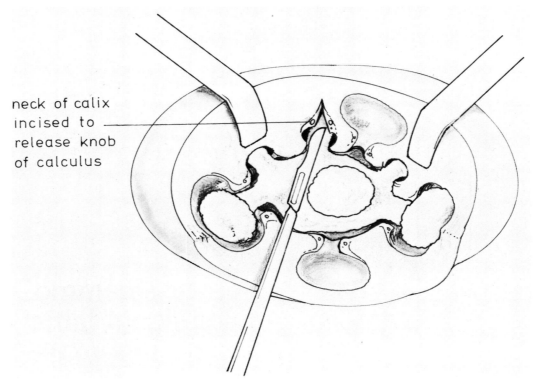

neck of calix
incised to
release knob
of calculus

Fig. 3. Anatrophic nephrotomy. A cut along the line separating the territory of the posterior segmental artery from that of its neighboring segmental vessels easily frees the knobs that project posteriorly from their calices, but to get at the body of the stone, the caliceal necks and the necks of the calices of the anteriorly facing knobs of stone must be cut across.

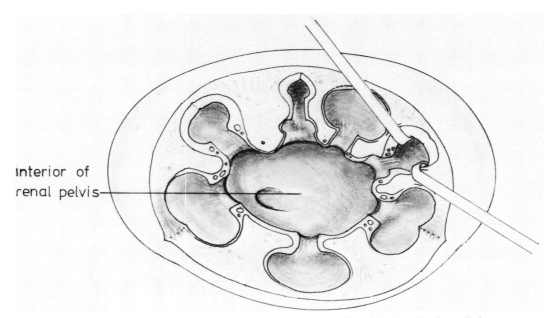

interior of
renal pelvis

Fig. 4. Anatrophic nephrotomy. All the stone has been removed *en bloc* by dividing all the necks of all the calices. These now must be repaired. Divided vessels must be secured by suture ligature. Narrow calices can be anastomosed to their neighbors to overcome obstruction.

130

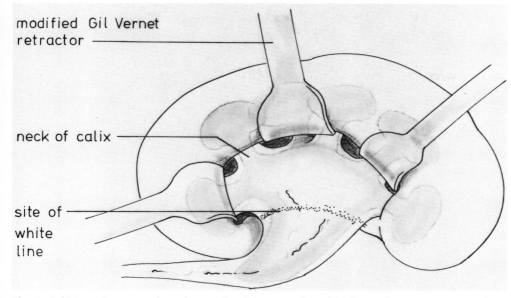

modified Gil Vernet
retractor

neck of calix

site of
white
line

Fig. 5. Gil-Vernet's approach to the renal pelvis. Note the *white line,* where, in a previously operated on patient, the sinus fat sometimes adheres to the muscle of the renal pelvis and may require separation by sharp dissection. Once in Gil-Vernet's bloodless plane, lift the parenchyma up and away from the renal pelvis to show the necks of the major calices.

access to the entire pelvis and, in most patients, to the principal calices.

To proceed: after incising the pelvis from the superior calix to the inferior one, allow the main body of the stone to deliver itself through the incision in the pelvis (Fig. 6). Deliberately fracture the stalks of the peripheral mushroom-shaped extensions of the stone when the mushrooms are obviously too large (as shown on the original radiograph) to be pulled out through the neck of the calix. Remove the knobs of the stone through separate incisions placed as far toward the periphery of the kidney as possible and made in a radial direction to run parallel with and, if possible, in between the segmental arteries (Fig. 7). When the parenchyma over these knobs has become atrophic and thin, there is no need to occlude the renal artery or cool the kidney, but when the parenchyma is thick and vascular, render the kidney ischemic. In this respect, Gil–Vernet's operation has no great advantage over Boyce's; the advantage lies in its avoidance of any need to incise the neck of the calix. There is no need to repair the calix; no major blood vessels have been divided, and the only incision in the collecting system requiring formal closure is the incision in the renal pelvis.

METHODS OF COOLING THE KIDNEY

There are several good methods of cooling the kidney from which the surgeon may choose. Probably the most elegant and least messy is that of Wickham (see Chap. 9), but it is expensive and not widely available. Just as good are the techniques using sterile ice or saline slush, as used by Boyce and at many centers, and the cold irrigating system devised

by Politano and brought to my attention by Marshall.[9] This simple system has the great advantage of needing no special apparatus other than the blood-warming coils used by every anesthesiologist, some sterile blood-giving extension tubes, and a bucket of (unsterile) ice from the hospital kitchen. Saline, water, or glycine is allowed to trickle through the blood-warming coils under the ice, emerges at about 5°C, and is allowed to play over the surface of the kidney and into the renal pelvis after one has removed the main body of the stone. As with all surface methods of cooling, it takes about 10 minutes for kidney temperature to fall to the safe range of 10° to 20°C, at which more than 1 hour of ischemia is tolerable. This simple method deserves to be more widely known, since it is so easy to set up. It also has the slight advantage of allowing the surgeon to go ahead with the nephrotomies without waiting the initial 10 minutes for the kidney to cool down.

I object to methods that inject cold solutions into the renal artery, because they may damage the intima of the artery.

One hopes that in time, Wickham's interesting claims for the protective value of an intravenous injection of inosine will be confirmed by other groups, since that would do away with the necessity of cooling altogether.[10]

COAGULUM PYELOLITHOTOMY

The technique of coagulum pyelolithotomy has been available for several years, but it is only recently that I have come to adopt it; my experience with it has made me enthusiastic about the following simplified version.[11]

To proceed: Freshly dissolve 2 g of fribrinogen in 75 ml of sterile water without shaking the solution, thus avoiding the

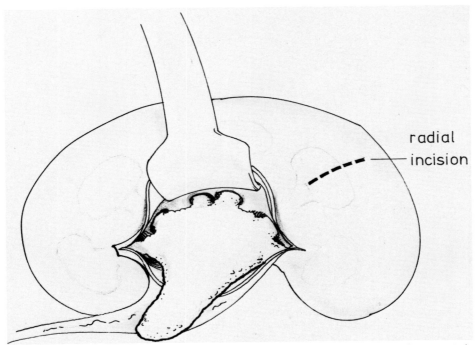

Fig. 6. Make a long sagittal incision from the most superior caliceal neck to the most inferior one, and pry out the body of the calculus, still attached to its stalked, peripheral, mushroom-shaped knobs. The stalks will be fractured at their most narrow parts; remove the peripheral knobs through radial incisions in the parenchyma. Note that no incision is made through any of the caliceal necks.

formation of air bubbles. Dissolve topical thrombin (5000 U) in 100 ml of sterile physiologic saline. Expose the renal pelvis through the Gil–Vernet approach, insert two butterfly needles, and withdraw the surplus urine. Place a bulldog clip on the ureter. With an assistant's help, inject the fibrinogen (conveniently stained with a drop of methylene blue) at the same time as the thrombin: my team uses two syringes and injects in the ratio of 2 ml of fibrinogen:1 ml of thrombin. We leave the coagulum 8 minutes to set firm and then proceed with the Gil–Vernet incision and delivery of the body and outcrops of the calculus. In staghorn surgery the jelly not only allows one to remove small outlying fragments of stone, but it lubricates the larger lumps and dilates the calices, making outlying knobs easier to withdraw. The blue color makes subsequent identification of calices through nephrotomy incisions more easy and keeps a friable calculus in one piece. In Britain the risk of hepatitis from the small-pool fibrinogen is negligible; elsewhere, cryoprecipitate may be considered safer.

ADJUNCTS TO STAGHORN STONE SURGERY

The search for the missing fragment of stone still proves to be a real difficulty, although with the regular use of the coagulum it has become less of a nuisance than formerly. It goes without saying that one must have good-quality radiographs on the table, with small films capable of being placed behind the kidney in the wound. If, after completing what one thinks is a good clearance of the kidney, there are still one or two small bits left behind, I have come to accept that the most reliable and most sensitive way of finding them is to use forefinger and thumb—finger in the lumen of the renal pelvis and thumb on the parenchyma. To make this easier, occlude the renal artery in order to allow the kidney to shrink down and become flaccid. With this additional assistance, it is very rare not to be able to feel even minute fragments of stone.

I have tried to use the flexible bronchoscope to search for missing bits of stone, but the view was always obscured by blood and the instrument was useless. The right-angled nephroscope still seems somewhat thick and clumsy for those tiny caliceal openings, which, at this stage of the operation, are often edematous and difficult to negotiate. In some patients an ordinary small-caliber cystoscope can be useful, and as long as the preliminary mobilization of the kidney has been complete, it will afford an excellent view into all but the most awkward calices.

Once one has found a missing bit of stone, it is seldom very difficult to wriggle it out with forceps or finger, and in practice I have not found the Water-Pik to have any advantage over an ordinary narrow-nozzled, hand-operated bulb syringe of the kind regularly used by neurosurgeons. With these Dakins

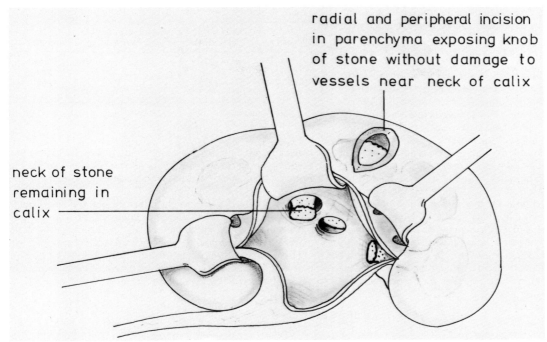

radial and peripheral incision
in parenchyma exposing knob
of stone without damage to
vessels near neck of calix

neck of stone
remaining in
calix

Fig. 7. Once the body of the stone has been removed, after, if necessary, fracturing the stalks of the peripheral knobs of stone, remove the large knobs through peripherally sited radial incisions. These are nearly always made through already thinned-out parenchyma that does not bleed.

syringes one can irrigate small fragments of calculus from quite small calices in the same way that wax is washed out from children's ears.

NEPHROSTOMY AND IRRIGATION WITH RENACIDIN OR SOLUTION G

It is my practice to leave a nephrostomy in every kidney whose function is precious to the patient's survival, but I am ultra-cautious in the use of irrigating solutions for the purpose of dissolving fragments of calculus left *in situ*. I am aware that some authors have obtained excellent results, but I am equally aware of the occasional tragedy where pyonephrosis and septicemia have complicated the inadvertent introduction of infection along with the irrigating system. No doubt these solutions have a place when used with exceptional care, but they are no substitute for a meticulous and complete removal of all the bits of stone.

REFLECTIONS

The Place for Common Sense

In the past I have been reproached for suggesting that there comes a time, in some patients, when the surgeon should stop and accept the fact that he cannot get all the bits of stone out.

Of course, this is not the result to aim for; nevertheless, stones do come back even in the patients of the most clever and experienced surgeons, and even when all the bits of stone have been removed. And, by the same token, small fragments often clear themselves spontaneously during the first few weeks after the operation.[12] One should aim, in every patient, to remove every last scrap of calculus, knowing that to leave a stone behind means leaving a hiding place for bacteria. As the same time, after 90 minutes of ischemia and 10 nephrotomies, the prudent surgeon does well to remember that he is trying to preserve nephrons, not treat a radiograph.

The Place for Partial Nephrectomy

There is unquestionably a place for partial nephrectomy when one or the other kidney pole is so scarred and contracted that it can serve no useful purpose. Unquestionably also, a partial nephrectomy of a scarred lower pole may make a subsequent calicoureterostomy easier in those patients in whom postoperative scarring has led to narrowing of the pelviureteric junction, but to perform a partial nephrectomy to prevent stone recurrence is very questionable. In one series, the results led to the conclusion that partial nephrectomy was only useful when polar stones were large, multiple, or accompanied by much parenchymal scarring.[13] Caine's very important study (see Chap. 8) showing that recurrence of stone was not prevented significantly by partial nephrectomy has at last put an end to the concept, never well founded, of the stone nest.

PROSPECTS

The story of stone surgery does not end with the successful removal of all the stone. Today, when in fewer than 10% of uninfected patients can one find any cause for calculus disease other than alleged idiopathic hypercalciuria and when infected patients are so often the haunt of resistant strains of *Proteus* or *Pseudomonas* that not even the most vigorous and protracted antibiotic regimen can utterly extinguish, the aftercare of the patient with a staghorn calculus is every bit as important as the care on the operating table. Moreover, what should force the surgeon to be modest about his claims for successful eradication of the calculus is the truthful reporting of his results during a long-term follow-up study (Table 1). Nobody expects a recurrence of calculus in the clean uninfected kidney without a metabolic cause for the stone when it is easy to permanently rid the kidney of infection afterward. In the young woman whose staghorn calculus is detected in the course of an investigation of a urinary tract infection during pregnancy, it

TABLE 1. Reported Recurrence Rate of Staghorn Calculi

Kidneys	Duration of Follow Up	Recurrence Rate (%)	Reference
100	1967–1972	22	No. 6, Chapter 6 Commentary
189	1964–1979	22.8	No. 5, Overview
100	1968–1973	14.5	No. 14,

is usually possible to remove the stone before the kidney has become permanently scarred by pyelonephritis and before the *Proteus* infection has become incurable. But many other patients have gigantic stones, badly scarred parenchyma, and *Proteus* infections unresponsive to the most diligent courses of antibiotics. In Egypt and other tropical countries, dehydration and schistosomiasis add additional causes for recurrence of stone disease. In clinical practice the causes of recurrent calculi are multiple, and the follow up of every patient must be patient, protracted, and perservering; the treatment of calculus disease does not end with removal of the calculus.

REFERENCES

1. Priestley JT, Dunn JH: Branched renal calculus. J Urol 61:194, 1949

2. Marshall VF, Lavengood RW Jr, Kelly D: Complete longitudinal nephrolithotomy and the Shorr regimen in the management of staghorn calculi. Ann Surg 162:366, 1965

3. Singh M, Chapman R, Tresidder GC, Blandy JP: The fate of the unoperated staghorn calculus. J Urol 45:581, 1973

4. Blandy JP, Singh M: The case for a more aggressive approach to staghorn stones. J Urol 115:505, 1976

5. Woodhouse CRJ, Farrell CR, Paris AMI, Blandy JP: The place of extended pyelolithotomy (Gil-Vernet operation) in the management of renal staghorn calculi. Br J Urol 53:520, 1981

6. Graves FT: The Arterial Anatomy of the Kidney. Bristol, John Wright & Sons, 1971

7. Blandy JP: Operative Urology p. 38. Oxford, Blackwell Scientific Publications, 1978

8. Blandy JP: The management of renal calculi. Ann R Coll Surg Engl 48:159, 1971

9. Marshall VR, Blandy JP: Simple renal hypothermia Br J Urol 46:253, 1974

10. Wickham JEA, Fernando R, Hendry WF, Watkinson LE, Whitfield HN: Inosine: Clinical results of ischaemic renal injury. Br J Urol 50:465, 1978

11. Patel VJ: Coagulum pyelolithotomy. Br J Surg 60:230, 1973

12. Singh M, Marshall VR, Blandy JP: The residual renal stone. Br J Urol 47:125, 1975

13. Marshall VR, Singh M, Tresidder GC, Blandy JP: The place of partial nephrectomy in the management of renal calyceal calculi. Br J Urol 47:759, 1976

14. Sleight MW, Wickham JEA: Long term follow-up 100 cases of renal calculi. Br J Urol 49:601–604, 1977

PART FOUR

NEPHRECTOMY FOR NONMALIGNANT DISEASES

10

NEPHRECTOMY: INDICATIONS AND COMPLICATIONS IN 347 PATIENTS

Martin Schiff, Jr.* and Wayne B. Glazier

From the Section of Urology, Department of Surgery, Yale University School of Medicine, New Haven, Connecticut

Copyright © 1977 by The Williams & Wilkins Co.
Vol. 118, December
Printed in U.S.A.

ABSTRACT—The indications, complications and mortality rate in a recent 12-year experience with 347 nephrectomies were reviewed. Renal tumor is the most frequent condition requiring nephrectomy, probably because of the improved, non-ablative methods to treat inflammatory, obstructive, calculous and hypertensive renal disease. The over-all mortality rate was 1.4 percent but was almost nil in the absence of malignancy.

Review of the literature failed to reveal data on the fate of patients undergoing nephrectomy during the last decade. The 2 most recent reports, one from a university center and the other from a private urological practice, are derived from norms that are now 10 to 20 years old.[1,2] The last decade has witnessed significant refinements in the preoperative diagnostic evaluation, as well as improvements in anesthetic and surgical techniques, and postoperative management. Therefore, we thought that it was pertinent to note the effect, if any, of these

Accepted for publication April 1, 1977.
* Requests for reprints: Section of Urology, Yale University Medical Center, New Haven, Connecticut 06505.

changes on patients undergoing nephrectomy, in terms of the indications for the procedure as well as subsequent complications and mortality rates.

METHODS

A retrospective study weas done on all nephrectomies performed at a single institution between 1964 and 1975. The patients were cared for by a heterogeneous group of urologists, including private practitioners, full-time faculty members and resident staff. All nephrectomy patients were included except for those undergoing bilateral nephrectomy for end stage renal disease, transplant recipients requiring removal of a rejected allograft, patients subjected to complete nephroureterectomy with removal of a bladder cuff and suprapubic cystostomy and patients undergoing several major surgical procedures, as exemplified by the patient with trauma to other abdominal viscera.

RESULTS

Records of 347 patients undergoing nephrectomy during the 12-year period were available for analysis. Most patients were in the 5th and 6th decades of life, with the youngest patient being a 1-day-old newborn and the oldest an 86-year-old woman (table 1).

Neoplastic disease accounted for almost 40 percent of the total group of patients (table 2). Renal adenocarcinomas were by far the most common tumors found (68 percent), with urothelial tumors of the kidney and upper ureter accounting for the majority of the rest (16 percent). This latter group was included since only nephrectomy and upper ureterectomy were performed through a single incision. At times it was difficult to separate obstructive, infectious and calculous etiologies into mutually exclusive categories. However, the diagnoses as listed are thought to represent the predominant disease process.

The cases were separated according to the surgical approach to the kidney (table 2). All nephrectomies accomplished by placing the patient in the lateral decubitus position, whether through a subcostal incision or with resection of a rib in an extrapleural fashion, were designated flank approaches. The 225 patients in this group (65 percent) were mainly patients whose kidney was infected and/or obstructed but, surprisingly, 41 of 89 patients undergoing nephrectomy for adenocarcinoma of the kidney were operated through the flank approach. Patients undergoing the transperitoneal approach to the kidney were considered a single group irrespective of the type of incision. There were 68 patients in this group. An anterior retroperitoneal approach was used in 44 patients and a thoracoabdominal nephrectomy was done in 10.

Postoperative complications were grouped into 4 major categories (table 3). Included among the pulmonary complications were patients with atelectasis, pneumonia and pneumothorax but not those with thromboembolic disorders, which were considered cardiovascular. The infectious complications included all postoperativae wound infections, deep and superficial, episodes of sepsis and retroperitoneal abscesses but not uncomplicated urinary tract infections, which respond to a single course of antibacterial therapy.

The highest complication rate (25 percent) were found in patients whose nephrectomy was performed via the flank approach. Initially, this fact was attributed to a higher rate of wound infections, presumably because patients with pre-existing renal parenchymal inflammatory and calculous disease are operated on primarily through the flank. However, subgrouping the data revealed that patients whose flank operation was performed for reasons not related to pre-existing infection (neoplasia, hypertension and kidney donor) had a similar postoperative complication rate (23.5 percent) when compared to the group as a whole. Moreover, patients undergoing the flank approach for nephrectomy had a higher rate of cardiovascular and pulmonary complications (26 of 225 patients or 11.5 percent) than the remainder of the group (7 of 122 patients or 5.7 percent). If the 68 nephrectomies performed on patients less than 21 years old, a group in whom cardiovascular and/or pulmonary complications would be unexpected, are excluded then these problems occurred at a rate of 13.6 and 6.9 percent in flank and non-flank operations, respectively.

There were 5 deaths in the entire group (1.4 percent). Four of the 5 involved patients undergoing radical nephrectomy for renal cell carcinoma: 2 died of pulmonary emboli, 1 of myocardial infarction and 1 of hepatic necrosis. The fifth patient died of a cerebrovascular accident while undergoing an exploration and nephrectomy for what proved to be a renal cyst. This patient never regained consciousness after the operation. Therefore, the mortality rate of patients undergoing nephrectomy for renal neoplasm was 3 percent, as opposed to 0.4 percent for those undergoing nephrectomy for non-malignant disease.

DISCUSSION

Our most common indication for nephrectomy during the last decade has been a renal tumor. This fact is at variance with the 2 most recently reported series, in

TABLE 1. Age and Sex Distribution of Patients Undergoing Nephrectomy

	0–10	11–20	21–30	31–40	41–50	51–60	61–70	71–80	80+	Totals
Male pts.	32	4	11	12	26	45	31	17	5	183
Female pts.	25	7	14	20	28	25	21	17	7	164
Total										347

TABLE 2. Indications for Nephrectomy and Operative Approach

	Flank	Trans-peritoneal	Anterior Retroperitoneal	Thora-coab-dominal	Totals
Neoplasia	60	48	14	9	131
Hydronephrosis	54	8	8	1	71
Infection	37	—	7	—	44
Hypertension	19	4	10	—	33
Living related kidney donor	27	—	—	—	27
Staghorn calculus	20	2	—	—	22
Multicystic	3	1	2	—	6
Miscellaneous	5	5	3	—	13
Totals	225	68	44	10	347

TABLE 3. Postoperative Complications

	No. Pts.	Pulmonary	Cardiovascular	Gastrointestinal	Infectious	Totals (%)
Flank	225	15	11	8	23	57 (25.3)
Transperitoneal	68	4	1	4	4	13 (19.1)
Anterior retroperitoneal	44	—	1	—	2	3 (6.8)
Thoracoabdominal	10	—	1	—	1	2 (20.0)

which neoplasia accounted for a smaller proportion of nephrectomies.[1,2] The change may possibly be caused solely by the differences in patient populations. However, it would seem more likely that it is merely a reflection of improved methods to manage patients with obstructive, inflammatory, hypertensive and calculous renal disease by measures short of nephrectomy.

The over-all mortality rate after nephrectomy of 1.4 percent offers no evidence of recent improvement, despite more sophisticated methods of patient monitoring during and after the operation. Of patients treated between 1953 and 1962 at a university hospital, Sakati and Marshall reported a 2 percent mortality rate in 622 nephrectomies.[3] However, in the present series only a single death occurred in the absence of renal malignancy. Nephrectomy for relief of severe hypertension, for example, was accomplished without mortality and with minimum mor-

bidity on 33 patients. This finding was somewhat reassuring when compared to the 3.3 percent mortality rate found for this type of nephrectomy by the Cooperative Study Group of Renovascular Hypertension.[4]

In a retrospective study such as the one reported conclusions in regard to the benefits and risks of one treatment modality compared to another are not justified. The flank approach remains the predominant surgical route to the kidney and it is used almost exclusively for patients with infection or calculous disease. Hydronephrotic kidneys also are generally approached in this manner, the few exceptions involving neonates and small children operated upon by pediatric surgeons who favor the transperitoneal approach.

The anterior retroperitoneal approach, performed through a subcostal extraperitoneal incision, was almost devoid of complications. This approach is particularly adaptable to children and small adults, and combines the advantages of avoiding the abdominal cavity, the deleterious physiological effects of the lateral positioning of the patient, as well as a large, painful incision through major muscles.

It was somewhat surprising that almost half of the patients undergoing nephrectomy for renal adenocarcinoma had their operation performed via the flank approach, since this diagnosis is now almost invariably made preoperatively. Although the case for radical nephrectomy in improving the survival of patients with this disease remains to be proved[5,6] the principle of early ligation of the renal vessels is reasonable and usually cannot be accomplished with the flank approach.

Nephrectomy in the living related kidney donor is a singular category, since it is an operation that bestows no benefit upon the patient. Therefore, it was believed at the outset of the renal transplantation program that it should be performed in a fashion designed to create the least risk to the donor and, intuitively, the flank approach was chosen to avoid possible gastrointestinal complications. The present data would not seem to support our initial bias. Perhaps operations for donor nephrectomy might best be selected on the basis of the individual's renal anatomy and body habitus.

REFERENCES

1. Scott, R. F., Jr. and Selzman, H. M.: Complications of nephrectomy: review of 450 patients and a description of a modification of the transperitoneal approach. J Urol 95:307, 1966
2. Pearlman, C. K. and Kobashigawa, L.: Nephrectomy: review of 200 cases. Am Surg 34:438, 1968
3. Sakati, I. A. and Marshall, V. F.: Postoperative fatalities in urology. J Urol 95:412, 1966

4. Franklin, S. S., Young, J. D., Jr., Maxwell, M. H., Foster, J. H., Palmer, J. M., Cerny, J. and Varady, P. D.: Operative morbidity and mortality in renovascular disease. JAMA 231:1148, 1975
5. Robson, C. J., Churchill, B. M. and Anderson, W.: The results of radical nephrectomy for renal cell carcinoma. J Urol 101:297, 1969
6. Skinner, D. G., Vermillion, C. D. and Colvin, R. B.: The surgical management of renal cell carcinoma. J Urol 107:705, 1972

Commentary: Approaches in Nephrectomy

Drogo K. Montague

If the 131 nephrectomies done for neoplasia are eliminated from the retrospective review of 347 nephrectomies performed at a single institution over a 12-year period 216 nephrectomies for nonmalignant disease remain. Schiff and Glazier have divided the nephrectomies according to operative indications and operative approaches. They discuss and analyze postoperative complications according to operative approach.

SURGICAL APPROACHES

Flank. Flank incisions were used for 225 of the 347 nephrectomies in Schiff and Glazier's series. In most institutions, the flank approach probably still is the most common operative approach for simple nephrectomy. However, whether this is because of tradition or because of the superiority of this approach is not entirely clear.[1,2] Schiff and Glazier point out that the postoperative complication rate was highest in patients in whom the flank approach was used. In these patients, they experienced a 25.3% complication rate. If only those patients who had a flank nephrectomy for indications other than infection are considered, the complication rate still remains high (23.5%). The reasons for these relatively high complication rates after simple flank nephrectomy are not immediately clear. Perhaps the patient's lateral position on the operating table has an adverse effect on cardiopulmonary function during the operative procedure; also, the amount of postoperative wound discomfort in patients with flank incisions appears to be considerable and may approach that of patients with anterior subcostal incisions. Because of this discomfort, patients tend to breath shallowly and cough poorly; this certainly contributes to a relatively high incidence of pulmonary complications.

A complication frequently overlooked by the urologist, but not by the patient, is the denervation of flank muscles that occurs when a subcostal nerve is damaged during a flank approach. Although great care may be taken to identify the subcostal nerve and to dissect it free, inadvertent stretching and tearing of the nerve often occurs when retractors are placed in the flank wound to gain sufficient exposure. These patients have a bulge in their flank postoperatively. Many patients, particularly women, find this detectable even through clothing and may want to modify their dressing habits accordingly.

An advantage of the flank approach is that the peritoneal cavity is not entered; consequently, any infection is usually confined to the retroperitoneal space. In the markedly obese patient, most of the large panniculus falls forward when the patient is in the flank position, with exposure through the flank being surprisingly easy.

Anterior Transperitoneal. The anterior transperitoneal approach is an approach for a simple nephrectomy that has gained favor in recent years.[1-4] It has become especially popular in radical nephrectomies for malignant disease, since it allows preliminary division of the renal artery and renal vein before manipulation of the neoplasm-containing kidney. However, many surgeons also use the anterior transperitoneal approach increasingly in nephrectomies for nonmalignant disease. The principal advantage of the transperitoneal approach for renal surgery is that exposure in the area of the renal pedicle, aorta, and vena cava is optimal. This is the most critical anatomic area of any nephrectomy procedure, since one may inadvertently injure these vessels more readily if exposure is poor. Also, if these vessels are injured and exposure is poor, control of bleeding and subsequent repair is difficult.

Initially physicians feared that the transperitoneal approach to the kidney would result in an unacceptably high incidence of postoperative short- and long-term gastrointestinal (GI) complications. However, this was not borne out in the series reported by Schiff and Glazier nor in a recent report from my institution on this approach for living-related kidney–donor nephrectomies.[5] Schiff and Glazier noted a 19.1% complication rate for this approach.

An important consideration in using the transperitoneal approach is that exposure is more critical at the medial aspect of the incision than at the lateral aspect. To obtain proper exposure in the region of the great vessels, one must extend the incision across the midline; transect the entire contralateral rectus muscle to obtain the best exposure. The urologist using this incision for the first time often extends it too far laterally and not far enough medially.

Exposure with this approach is excellent and easily maintained if one uses a Smith ring retractor.[6] By using this retractor, the surgeon and one assistant can readily perform the operation.

Anterior Retroperitoneal. Schiff and Glazier reported the lowest complication rate in patients in whom a nephrectomy was performed through an anterior retroperitoneal approach (6.8%). However, they note that this approach is most suitable for children and smaller (thin or average) adults, and it is in this group that one would expect to see the lowest complication rate. I too have used this exposure to good advantage, primarily in children and thin adults. The patient is placed in the supine position, and a roll is placed under the patient to elevate the side to be operated on. Should inadequate exposure be obtained during the course of this operation, one can extend the incision and deliberately enter the peritoneum.[1,2,7]

Thoracoabdominal. The thoracoabdominal approach to the kidney is reserved primarily for large neoplasms.[8,9] In Schiff and Glazier's series it was used for one case of hydronephrosis;

presumably this was a giant hydronephrosis. I have found it more convenient to remove giant hydronephrotic kidneys through either a flank or a transperitoneal approach. Once a portion of the kidney is exposed, the contents of the kidney are aspirated through a trocar; remove the trocar after placing a pursestring suture around it. Subsequent mobilization and removal of the kidney are then readily accomplished from any type of infradiaphragmatic approach.

Posterior An operative approach not used in Schiff and Glazier's series is the posterior approach.[10,11] This approach is particularly good for the removal of small kidneys. The principal advantage of this approach is that the kidney lies close to the surface. An additional advantage is that the patient experiences very little incisional discomfort or ileus. Coughing, deep breathing, and ambulation are easier, and the patient is usually able to eat a regular diet on the first postoperative day.

With the posterior approach, exposure in the retroperitoneum is limited. For this reason, take care not to injure the great vessels. Injury to these vessels through a posterior approach usually is difficult to control; rarely, it is necessary to pack the posterior wound, turn the patient on his back, and gain vascular control through a transperitoneal approach.

SURGICAL PROCEDURE

Regardless of the approach used to the kidney, the performance of a simple nephrectomy is basically the same. In many instances in which a diseased kidney must be removed, the so-called simple nephrectomy is really not so easy. Intense perinephric inflammation may exist, and mobilization of the kidney may proceed with great difficulty. Under these circumstances, it is best to use sharp dissection under direct vision. During a difficult nephrectomy, if the dissection suddenly becomes easy, the surgeon has probably broken through the capsule of the kidney. Unless one wishes to perform a subcapsular nephrectomy, re-establish an extracapsular plane.

Occasionally it is necessary to perform a subcapsular nephrectomy, and in these patients the capsule is deliberately entered along the lateral convex portion of the kidney.[1,12] To proceed: strip the capsule and the fibrotic perinephric tissues from the kidney toward the renal hilus. This may be the only way to remove a severely diseased kidney, and on some occasions the kidney may fragment and be removed in pieces. In these difficult nephrectomies it is usually necessary to apply pedicle clamps to the renal artery and vein together. On the right side, it is particularly important to ensure that the duodenum has been reflected medially before applying the pedicle clamps to avoid injury to its retroperitoneal segment.

Ordinarily, if there is no significant inflammation, once Gerota's fascia has been entered, quickly mobilize the kidney, largely by blunt dissection. At the upper pole of the kidney stay close to the kidney to avoid injuring the adrenal gland. If the adrenal gland is injured, leave it until after the kidney is removed; inspection will then reveal whether a running suture along its injured edge will be enough to control hemostasis or whether an adrenalectomy is necessary.

Whenever possible, I prefer to isolate the renal artery and the renal vein and to secure and divide these vessels separately. Of course, divide the renal artery first in order to minimize blood loss with the removal of the kidney. The separate ligation and division of the renal artery and renal vein makes the postoperative development of an arteriovenous fistula much less likely.

PATIENT PREPARATION

Finally, a word on preparation of the patient for a nephrectomy is needed. Patients brought to the operating room who have not eaten or drank since the previous evening are already dehydrated. This is poor preparation for any major surgery, and it is particularly bad when the surgery will leave the patient with only one kidney. These patients should reach the operating room in an already well-hydrated state, and, for this reason, we usually begin intravenous (IV) fluids the night before surgery. Proper replacement of blood, colloids, and fluids during the operative procedure is also important. Diuretics may be given along with these fluids to maintain a liberal urine output before and immediately after removal of the kidney. This should lessen the incidence of postoperative renal failure.

REFERENCES

1. Montague DK, Straffon RA: Complications of renal surgery. In Smith RB, Skinner DG (eds): Complications of Urologic Surgery: Prevention and Management. Philadelphia, WB Saunders, 1976

2. Montague DK, Stewart BH: Incisions; Simple nephrotomy. In Stewart BH (ed): Operative Urology: The Kidneys, Adrenal Glands, and Retroperitoneum. Baltimore, Williams & Wilkins, 1975

3. Chute R, Baron JA Jr, Olsson CA: The transverse upper abdominal "chevron" incision in urological surgery. J Urol 99:528, 1968

4. Stewart BH, Hewitt CB, Kiser WS, Straffon RA: Anterior transperitoneal operative approach to the kidney. Cleve Clin Q 36:123, 1969

5. Ruiz R, Novick AC, Braun WE, Montague DK, Stewart BH: Transperitoneal live-donor nephrectomy. J Urol 123:819, 1980

6. Smith DP: An anchored mechanical retractor. Am J Surg 83:717, 1952

7. Lyon R: An anterior extraperitoneal incision for kidney surgery. J Urol 79:383, 1958

8. Chute R, Soutter L, Kerr WS Jr: Value of thoracoabdominal incision in removal of kidney tumors. N Engl J Med 241:951, 1949

9. Robson CJ: Radical nephrectomy for renal cell carcinoma. J Urol 89:37, 1963

10. Freed SZ, Veith FJ, Soberman R, Gliedman ML: Simultaneous bilateral posterior nephrectomy in transplant recipients. Surgery 68:468, 1970

11. Patil J, Bennett AH, Bailey GL, Mahoney EM, Harrison JH: Simultaneous bilateral nephrectomy from a posterior approach. Surg Gynecol Obstet 134:764, 1972

12. Kittredge WE, Fridge JC: Subcapsular nephrectomy. JAMA 168:758, 1958

ANNOTATED BIBLIOGRAPHY

Montague DK, Straffon RA: Complications of renal surgery. In Smith RB, Skinner DG (eds): Complications of Urologic Surgery: Prevention and Management. Philadelphia, WB Saunders, 1976

This chapter describes various operative approaches to the kidney. The relative advantages and disadvantages of each approach are discussed, as are the various indications for the use of each approach. Techniques of simple and subcapsular nephrectomies are described and illustrated. Emphasis is on the prevention of complications; management of the complications that can occur is discussed.

Montague DK, Stewart BH: Incisions; Simple nephrectomy. In Stewart BH (ed): Operative Urology: The Kidneys, Adrenal Glands and Retroperitoneum. Baltimore, Williams & Wilkins, 1975

Chapter 3, illustrates the various approaches to the kidney. The flank (subcostal and 11th and 12th rib), anterior extraperitoneal, anterior subcostal transperitoneal, throacoabdominal, midline transperitoneal, and posterior approaches are among those illustrated.

Chapter 8 describes the techniques of simple and subcapsular nephrectomies.

Stewart BH, Hewitt CB, Kiser WS, Straffon RA: Anterior transperitoneal operative approach to the kidney. Cleve Clin Q 36:123, 1969

The authors prefer subcostal or bilateral subcostal incisions for most anterior approaches to the kidney. The bilateral subcostal incision provides better exposure for the obese patient. A vertical midline incision gives rapid access to the abdomen and retroperitoneum in trauma cases and has also frequently been used for bilateral nephrectomies in patients with end stage renal disease. Renovascular surgery is best accomplished through anterior transperitoneal approaches, since they provide optimal exposure of the great vessels and their branches. For radical nephrectomies, anterior transperitoneal approaches allow ligation and division of the renal artery and vein before the neoplasm is manipulated. In performing pyeloplasties, the anterior transperitoneal approach preserves anatomic relationships and often permits repair without extreme renal mobilzation and subsequent repositioning. These approaches are often preferable for many types of adrenal surgery,

since early vascular control is permitted and bilateral adrenal exposure may be accomplished. The authors emphasize that these approaches are poorly suited for kidneys with infected hydronephrosis, perinephric abscess, or multiple calculi.

Freed SZ, Veith FJ, Soberman R, Gliedman ML: Simultaneous bilateral posterior nephrectomy in transplant recipients. Surgery 68:468, 1970

This paper discusses a technique for simultaneous bilateral posterior nephrectomy in transplant recipients. Vertical incisions at the lateral margins of the paraspinous muscles are employed. These procedures can usually be accomplished within 1 hour and are well tolerated by these chronically ill patients. Results in 35 patients are presented. The only complication was a subcutaneous hematoma requiring drainage; there were no deaths. The technique described may obviously be used for unilateral nephrectomy in other disease states, but I do not recommend its use in nephrectomies for neoplasm or in nephrectomies for large kidneys. It may also be difficult to perform a nephrectomy through this approach in the obese patient.

Patil J, Bennett AH, Bailey GL, Mahoney EM, Harrison JH: Simultaneous bilateral nephrectomy from a posterior approach. Surg Gynecol Obstet 134:764, 1972

Simultaneous bilateral nephrectomies through 12th rib incisions are described; 10-cm incisions are employed and the 12th ribs are resected. The authors note that this technique requires nearly 1 hour less operating time than the transabdominal operations and nearly 2 hours less time than the flank procedure, which requires changing the patient's position. The authors now use this approach for all bilateral nephrectomies, except those done for polycystic kidneys. Their last 100 consecutive cases are reviewed. There were no deaths or major complications.

Overview: Reasons for Nephrectomy for Nonmalignant Disease

Gilbert J. Wise

The nonmalignant renal diseases that mandate nephrectomy include minimal or nonfunctioning kidneys that are a source of pain, infection, anemia, or hypertension. The kidney may be chronically infected, hypoplastic, or massively enlarged by hydronephrosis or polycystic disease. Recurrent stone disease and multiple surgical procedures are often indications for nephrectomy. In certain cases, nephrectomy may be the expeditious cure in the elderly or debilitated patient with a chronic urinary fistula.

The surgical approach for nephrectomy for nonmalignant disease may differ among patients depending on kidney size and location, previous surgery, and the patient's physiognomy. Although the short-statured, obese, endomorphic patient is a

suitable candidate for the flank approach, the lean, ectomorphic patient may require a nephrectomy for the same condition through an extraperitoneal anterior approach. Previous surgical scars, musculoskeletal deformities such as scoliosis, and ectopic kidney location will influence the surgeon's decision on the proper operative approach.

Renal arteriography is often advisable before surgery for nonmalignant renal conditions.[1] The renal arteriogram is helpful in determining diagnosis and in defining the location and number of major renal arteries, which is critical when surgical dissection is through an inflamed and fibrotic retroperitoneum. In cases of suspect renal carbuncle, renal arteriography will often localize the abscess.[2]

Most pyonephrotic kidneys will require nephrectomy. Many urologists believe that preliminary nephrostomy or drainage will improve the surgical results and thus decrease the morbidity and mortality associated with nephrectomy for this condition. Recent observation suggests that this is not necessarily the case. Jimenez and colleagues from Barcelona, Spain, reported their observations in comparison of treatment used in the management of 97 patients with pyonephrosis.[3] These patients were divided into three groups: (1) patients in whom primary nephrectomy was done, (2) patients in whom nephrectomy was performed secondary to nephrostomy, and (3) patients in whom nephrectomy was performed secondary to drainage through a translumbar percutaneous puncture. Nephrectomy was subsequently performed in all patients through either a subcostal or an intercostal extroperitoneal lumbotomy. In two patients a transperitoneal incision was used without complications. The surgery was technically easier and the complication rate was no greater in the group of patients in whom primary nephrectomy was performed. Although the authors did not cite detailed data on the preoperative management or antimicrobial treatment, they concluded that preliminary kidney drainage need not be performed before nephrectomy for pyonephrosis.

Irrespective of the indication for nephrectomy for nonmalignant conditions, a variety of surgical approaches may be used for successful removal of the kidney. Dr. Montague has presented an excellent précis. The high complication rate of 25.3% associated with flank incision as reported by Shiff and Glazier appears at first to be surprisingly high.[4] Much of the morbidity associated with the flank approach is related to the cardiovascular, pulmonary, and infectious complications. A significant number of GI complications were noted but not clearly defined. It is my opinion that inhibition ileus is variably associated with retroperitoneal surgery. For this reason, oral intake should be restricted for 4 to 5 days after nephrectomy. The flank approach requires greater operating time and surgical dissection through muscle and ultimately requires greater time for closure than the anterior approach. As Dr. Montague indicated, damage to the subcostal nerve may inadvertently occur while the flank incision is developed. Unless the kidney is unusually low, I do not recommend the flank approach through a subcostal incision. I prefer the 12th rib resection, which offers excellent exposure in most patients and minimizes damage to the subcostal nerve. Patients have less postoperative discomfort with a transcostal approach than with the subcostal incision.

One can minimize postoperative atelectasis and other pulmonary complications by prolonging tracheal intubation in the immediate postoperative anesthetic recovery. The elderly, critically ill, or volume-depleted patient may develop hypotension when placed in the flank position. This is believed to be secondary to compression of the great vessels following flexion of the operating table. In these patients, the anterior approach may be more appropriate if technically feasible. Despite disadvantages of the flank approach, this incision is still the most suitable in many patients requiring a nephrectomy. Improved exposure can be obtained by resection of a segment of the 11th rib or division of the lumbocostal ligament, as described by Turner–Warwick.[5] If necessary, extensive exposure can be further obtained by the osteoplastic flap of Nagamatsu.[6] In an analysis of 100 consecutive patients requiring bilateral nephrectomy for end-stage renal disease, Viner and associates noted that the bilateral flank approach produced fewer complications than did the transperitoneal approach (23% vs 66%).[7] There was a greater incidence of ileus, significant infection, and death in the transperitoneal approach group. Included in the transperitoneal group of 39 patients were 15 patients with polycystic disease who required more anesthesia time and intraoperative transfusion. Inclusion of the polycystic patients increased the morbidity associated with transperitoneal approach for nephrectomy. It was evident that kidney size and underlying pathologic process influenced the surgical result.

The anterior extraperitoneal approach offers the best of both worlds, that is, flank vs transperitoneal. It is particularly useful for nephroureterectomy in patients with congenital anomaly such as hypoplastic or chronically infected refluxing renal units. The anterior subcostal incision obviates the need for change of patient position required for lower ureterectomy. The extraperitoneal approach also minimizes the morbidity associated with excision of an infected renal unit. However, the anterior extraperitoneal approach is technically more difficult in the obese, short-statured individual with a narrow intercostal angle.

The presence of inflammatory reaction due to previous surgical approach or chronic infection makes surgical removal of the kidney most difficult irrespective of the approach. As Dr. Montague indicated, separate ligation of the renal artery and vein is most desirable. Patients with marked inflammatory reaction may require massive ligatures. Several suture ligatures should be used, since ties can slip when there is an inflammatory reaction or excessive fat.

Rarely, loss of control of the vascular pedicle may require the surgeon to place and leave vascular clamps *in situ* several days after surgery.[8] Although this technique is rarely used today, it was useful in the preantibiotic era, when one often encountered extensive inflammatory reaction.

The posterior incision is most applicable for bilateral removal of small, atrophic kidneys. Although the kidney is a posterior organ, the surgeon will find the kidney at greater depth than anticipated.

When performing a nephrectomy, the surgeon should choose an approach based on kidney size and location and, most important, on his experience with a particular approach.

REFERENCES

1. Lytton B: Surgery of the kidney. In Gittes RF, Perlmutter AD, Stamey TA, Walsh PC (eds): Campbell's Urology, Vol 3, 4th ed, Chap 65, pp 1993–2046. Philadelphia, WB Saunders, 1979

2. Craven JD, Hardy B, Stanley P, Orecklin JR, Goodwin WE: Acute renal carbuncle: The importance of preoperative angiography. J Urol 111:727, 1974

3. Jimenez JF, Lopez Pacios MA, Llamazares G, Conejero J, Sole-Balcells F: Treatment of pyonephrosis: A comparative study. J Urol 120:287, 1978

4. Schiff M, Glazier WB: Nephrectomy: Indications and complications in 347 patients. J Urol 116:930, 1977

5. Turner–Warwick R: The supracostal approach to the renal area. Br J Urol 37:671, 1965

6. Nagamatsu GR: Dorsolumbar approach to the kidney and adrenal with osteoplastic flap. J Urol 63:569, 1952

7. Viner NA, Rawl JC, Braren V, Rhamy RR: Bilateral nephrectomy: An analysis of 100 consecutive cases. J Urol 113:291, 1975

8. Smith DR, Schulte JW, Smart WR: Surgery of the kidney. In Campbell MF, Harrison JH (eds): Urology, Vol 3, 3rd ed. Philadelphia, WB Saunders, 1970

PART FIVE

RENAL TRANSPLANTATION

11

LONG-TERM RESULTS OF RENAL TRANSPLANTATION IN CHILDREN

Richard N. Fine, M.D., Mohammad H. Malekzadeh, M.D., Alfred J. Pennisi, M.D., Robert B. Ettenger, M.D., Christel H. Uittenbogaart, M.D., Vida F. Negrete, R.N., M.S., *and* Barbara M. Korsch, M.D.

From the Department of Pediatrics, University of Southern California School of Medicine, and the Dialysis and Transplant Program, Childrens Hospital of Los Angeles

Pediatrics Vol. 61
No. 4 April 1978

During the past decade, as hemodialysis and renal transplantation have become more available, the outlook for children with irreversible renal insufficiency has changed dramatically. Prior to that time, no programs were devoted exclusively to the treatment of children with end-stage renal disease (ESRD), and a limited number of children received treatment in adult facilities. In light of very limited experience there were those who claimed[1,2] that the rigors of the treatment program were

Received July 12; revision accepted for publication October 4, 1977.

ADDRESS FOR REPRINTS: (R.N.F.) 4650 Sunset Boulevard, Los Angeles, CA 90027.

so catastrophic for both child and family, and the outlook so dismal, that dialysis and transplantation should not be offered to children.

Despite these warnings a program was initiated in 1967 at Childrens Hospital of Los Angeles (CHLA) to provide dialysis and transplantation for children with ESRD. The program was designed to include a component for long-term medical and psychosocial evaluation.

Subsequently, other programs were developed in the United States, Canada, and western Europe. The latest report on Regular Dialysis and Transplantation of Children in Europe, 1975,[3] of the European Dialysis and

Transplant Association Registry included 1,111 children who were less than 15 years of age at the initiation of therapy, and the last report of the ACS/NIH Transplant Registry[4] included data on 987 children, 0 to 15 years of age. In addition, numerous articles[5-25] describing experience with transplantation in children attest to the increasing acceptance of this therapeutic modality for children. However, there are few reports of children surviving with a functioning graft for more than five years.[13,14,21-23,25] Only the reports of DeShazo et al.[21] and Weil et al.[25] include data on the long-term results of renal transplantation in a large number of pediatric patients. During the past ten years (February 1967 to February 1977), 157 children have received 207 renal transplants at our institution. Of this number, 69 children received 81 transplants during the first five years of the program. This report describes the long-term results of patients treated during the first five years of the program with respect to patient and graft survival, growth, psychosocial adaptation, and rehabilitation.

MATERIALS AND METHODS

Between February 1967 and February 1972, a total of 69 children received 81 renal allografts. Sixty-eight of the grafts were first transplants (1 patient received an initial graft at another institution) and 13 were second transplants. Twenty-six of the first transplants were from live related donors (LDs) and 42 from cadaver donors (CDs); all of the second transplants were from CDs. The ages of the patients at the time ESRD developed and dialysis was required are shown in Figure 1, and the primary diseases leading to renal failure in these patients are listed in Table 1.

With one exception (the first recipient received peritoneal dialysis only), all patients were treated with hemodialysis before transplantation.[26] The surgical technique of transplantation was similar to that used for adult recipients with extraperitoneal placement of the graft in the iliac fossa and anastomoses of the renal artery and vein to the external or common iliac artery and hypogastric vein. Revascularization of kidneys from pediatric CDs was facilitated by a "cuff" of aorta and vena cava. Kidneys from pediatric donors as young as 6 months of age provided adequate function for adolescent recipients, and kidneys from adult donors were transplanted without difficulty into recipients weighing 10 kg.[27,28] The donor ureter was reimplanted into the bladder via a ureteroneocystotomy unless it was too short, at which time a ureteroureteral anastomosis was performed.

Immunosuppressive therapy consisted of prednisone and azathioprine exclusively in the dosage schedule delineated in Tables 2 and 3. One year after transplant, the dosage of prednisone was maintained at 7.5 to 15 mg daily and azathioprine at 2 to 3 mg/kg/day. Since August 1974, in recipients with good allograft function the therapy has been changed to alternate-day corticosteroid therapy at approximately twice the daily dose.

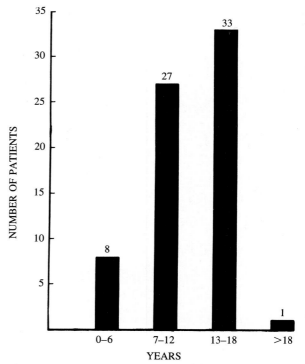

Fig. 1. Patients' ages at initiation of dialysis.

TABLE 1. Primary Renal Disease

Disease	No. of Cases
Acquired	
Glomerular disease	
Chronic glomerulonephritis (GN)	25
Membranoproliferative GN	5
Nephrotic syndrome with focal sclerosis	4
Rapid progressive GN	1
Shunt nephritis	1
Membranous nephritis	1
Lupus nephritis	1
Other	
Cortical necrosis	2
Bilateral Wilms' tumor	1
Hemophilia with ? renal disease	1
Congenital/hereditary	
Obstructive uropathy	16
Hypoplasia	2
Oligomeganephronia	1
Medullary cyst disease	1
Familial nephritis	3
Polycystic disease	2
Cystinosis	2

TABLE 2. Immunosuppressive Therapy

Time	Azathioprine (mg/kg/24 hr)	Prednisone (mg/kg/24 hr)
Preoperative (3 days)	2–3	3
Postoperative	2–3	3
Postoperative with oligoanuria	0.5–1	3
Rejection		
Acute	2–3	30 × 3 days (IV)
Chronic	0.5–2	. . .

TABLE 3. Tapering Prednisone Dosage Schedule

Time Posttransplant	Patient Weight (kg)			
	<20	20–35	35–50	>50
3 wk*	2	2	2	2
6 wk*	1	1	1	1
9 wk*	0.5	0.5	0.5	0.5
6 mo†	10	12.5	15	20
1 yr†	7.5	10	12.5	15

* Milligrams per kilogram per 24 hours.
† Milligrams per day.

No patient received antilymphocytic serum, irradiation, or actinomycin C, and no patient underwent thymectomy or splenectomy.

Prospective histocompatibility testing was performed in the laboratory of Dr. Paul I. Terasaki at the Center for the Health Sciences, University of California at Los Angeles.[29] The only prerequisite was ABO blood group compatibility and a negative microlymphocytotoxic antibody cross-match.[30] Only two of the grafts were between HLA identical siblings.

RESULTS

Patient Survival. Of the 69 children who received transplants before February 1972, 54 (78%) are currently alive. A total of 47 (68%) are surviving with a functioning graft—32 first, 12 second, and 3 third; 7 (10%) are undergoing dialysis after having rejected one or more grafts, 4 at home and 3 in center; and 15 (22%) have died. Nine of the 15 deaths occurred as a result of a complication following transplantation; six of these deaths were caused by infection. Seven deaths occurred during the first year after transplant. The remaining six patients died while undergoing dialysis, 2 to 24 months (mean, 12.7 months) after graft rejection, from complications unrelated to transplantation. The cause of death of these 15 patients is shown in Table 4.

Graft Survival. The actual (real rather than potential) five-year graft survival of the 81 grafts is shown in Figure 2. The one-year graft survival rate for the 26 LD first grafts was 85% (22/26) with minimal subsequent

TABLE 4. Cause of Death

Treatment	Cause	Time Since Transplant/ Graft Loss (mo)
Transplant	Gram-negative septicemia	2
	Gram-negative septicemia	36
	Cytomegalovirus infection	8
	Agranulocytosis	1
	Unknown	1
	Gastrointestinal hemorrhage	4
	Candida infection	6
	Pneumocystis carinii	65
	Cytomegalovirus infection	1
Dialysis	Endocarditis	15
	Suicide	4
	Cerebral edema	9
	Cerebrovascular accident	24
	Aspiration after seizure at home	1
	Endocarditis	24

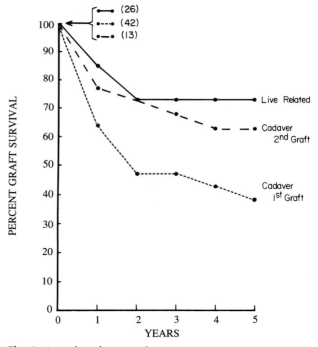

Fig. 2. Actual graft survival (years).

attrition. At five years, 73% (19/26) of these grafts were functioning. Four grafts failed during the first posttransplant year, and one each during the second and third posttransplant years. There was no loss between the third and fifth posttransplant years. One graft was subsequently lost after five years. Currently, 69% (18/26) of the LD grafts are functioning five years one month to ten years (mean, six years nine months) following transplantation.

The one-year graft survival of CD first grafts was 64% (27/42) with a significant attrition rate to 39% (16/42) at five years. Fifteen grafts failed during the first posttransplant year, seven during the second, and two each during the third and fourth posttransplant years. Two grafts failed after the fifth year and, at the present time, 33% (14/42) of the CD first grafts are functioning five years to eight years nine months (mean, seven years nine month) following transplantation.

The one-year and five-year survival rates of the CD second grafts were 77% (10/13) and 62% (8/13), respectively. Three grafts were lost during the first posttransplant year, and one each during the second and third posttransplant years. One graft failed after the fifth posttransplant year and, currently, 54% (7/13) of the CD second grafts are functioning five years one month to seven years (mean, six years) following transplantation.

Of the 81 grafts, 43 (53%) survived a minimum of five years. The maximum loss occurred during the first posttransplant year. Twenty-two (27%) grafts were lost during the first posttransplant year, nine (11%) during the second, two (2.5%) during the third, three (4%) during the fourth, and two (2.5%) during the fifth posttransplant year. Four grafts (5%) were lost after the fifth posttransplant year.

Etiology of Graft Failure. Hyperacute rejection accounted for 1 and acute rejection accounted for 12 of the 22 grafts lost during the first posttransplant year. Two grafts were lost due to technical failures; one from a 5-day-old anencephalic infant infarcted because of high venous pressure resulting from an arteriovenous cannula in the thigh; one had a persistent ureteral leak. Two grafts were removed following discontinuation of immunosuppressive therapy because of severe systemic infection; one with cytomegalovirus and the other with *Clostridium perfringens*. Five patients died either with graft function or in the immediate postoperative period while the graft was recovering from acute tubular necrosis.

Chronic rejection accounted for 14 of the 16 grafts lost between the first and fifth posttransplant years. One patient died from infection while undergoing chronic rejection. The remaining graft was lost following an unsuccessful attempt to repair a renal artery stenosis. Noncompliance with immunosuppressive drug therapy contributed to graft loss from chronic rejection in six recipients, five of whom were adolescent females. All four graft failures after five years were due to chronic rejection, two of which were related to noncompliance; both were in adolescent females.

Growth. Of the 43 patients who survived with a functioning graft for more than five years, 23 had a bone age of less than 12 years and 20 had a bone age of more than 12 years at the time of transplantation. Those recipients with a bone age of more than 12 years grew minimally after transplantation. No growth occurred in ten patients with fused epiphyses. In the remaining ten recipients, an increment in height of only 2 to 3 cm occurred in the five- to nine-year follow-up period.

There were 10 boys and 13 girls in the group of recipients with a bone age of less than 12 years. Growth retardation was present at transplantation in 17 of these children; their height was at the third percentile or less for their chronological age. All recipients with a bone age of less than 12 years grew following transplantation. However, normal growth (>80% of that expected for bone and height age) as observed in only three patients (Figs. 3 and 4).

Corticosteroid therapy was changed to alternate-day therapy in ten of the 23 recipients (Figs. 3 and 4). Each recipient had a bone age of less than 12 years at initiation of alternate-day therapy and was previously growing at less than 80% of that expected for bone and height age while receiving daily corticosteroid therapy. During the subsequent 24 to 30 months of alternate-day therapy the growth rate improved in four, but was more than 80% of that expected in only one of these four recipients.

It is beyond the scope of this report to detail all the potential factors that affect posttransplant growth. These have been discussed in depth in a separate communication.[31]

Psychosocial Adaptation. Psychosocial assessment of the patients has been an integral part of the dialysis and transplant program at CHLA since its inception. Systematic follow-up data on patient and family obtained one to ten years following transplantation are currently available for approximately 100 patients. The data concerning 41 of the 43 (two patients were too young to undergo testing) who survived with a functioning graft for more than five years are not essentially different from those obtained in respect to the entire sample. These 41 patients were included in the samples analyzed and described in previous publications.[32,33]

Systematic personality testing of patients one year after transplant included California Test of Personality (CTP), a test for which controls are available from large populations of sick and well children in various circumstances. The Piers-Harris scale for self-esteem was selected because self-esteem is known to be one feature of personality function which is especially vulnerable to the ravages of any chronic disease and its complex treatment.

In general, personality test results one year after transplant were not grossly deviant. Figure 5 shows the distribution of results of the CTP for the total personality

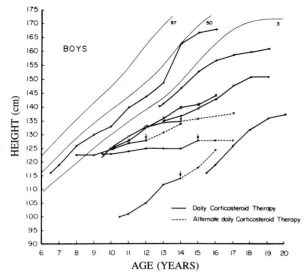

Fig. 3. Growth curves following transplants in ten boys with bone age less than 12 years at time of transplant. *Arrow* indicates initiation of alternate-day therapy.

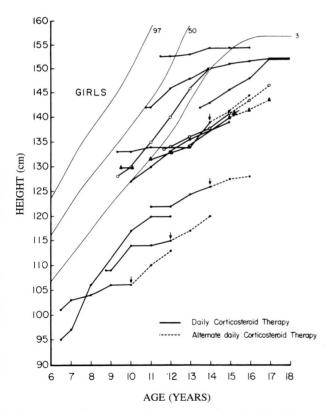

Fig. 4. Growth curves following transplants in 13 girls with bone age less than 12 years at time of transplant. *Arrow* indicates initiation of alternate-day therapy.

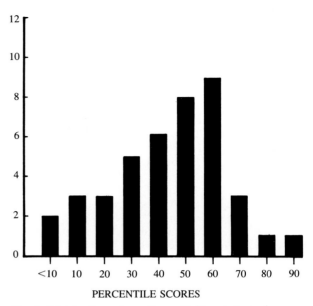

Fig. 5. Distribution of results on California test of personality total adjustment (n = 41). Two of the 43 patients were excluded because they were below school age.

score of the 41 children. This test is scored on a percentile basis. The distribution of scores is not significantly different from a normal population.

The CTP scores for "social adaptation" (Fig. 6), however, were significantly different from a group of normal children of the same ages ($P < .005$). It is not difficult to understand why these children would show defects in their social adaptation. The experiences with chronic renal disease, the many hospitalizations, the multiple surgical procedures, the period of hemodialysis, and finally the renal transplant itself all contribute to gross restriction in socialization and social activities.

Likewise, the self-esteem scores can be seen to include a high proportion of children with more "deviant" responses than is considered normal (Fig. 7). The complications of chronic renal disease such as short stature and osteodystrophy, accompanied by the many invasions of privacy and physical trauma that are necessary in dialysis and transplantation, readily explain why the patient's body image and self-esteem would be suboptimal. In our experience, the immunosuppressive treatment following transplantation adds another significant stress because of the cushingoid features, growth problems, and the tendency to obesity that are associated with the corticosteroid treatment.

Systematic assessment of family function with special emphasis on communication patterns within the family (about the illness and in general) and with

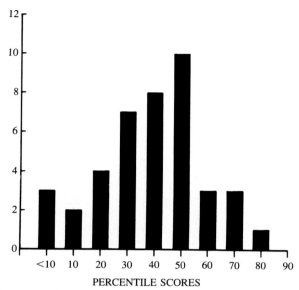

Fig. 6. Distribution of results on California test of personality social adjustment (n = 41). Two of the 43 patients were excluded because they were below school age.

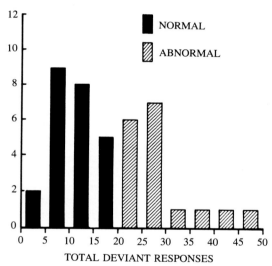

Fig. 7. Distribution of results of Piers-Harris self-esteem scale (n = 41). Two of the 43 patients were excluded because they were below school age.

emphasis on the family's coping mechanisms were also part of the follow-up study. In general, it was found that unless there were overwhelming medical and surgical complications following transplantation, family equilibrium and family function had usually returned to preillness levels by one year after transplant. As would be expected, the stress of the illness experience exaggerated preexisting problems or made manifest potential problems in family function rather than producing new problems. Similarly, for the child patients themselves, those personality attributed that had been weak or vulnerable before the exposure could be predicted to become exaggerated or even pathological under the stress of illness and treatment. Thus, most of the psychosocial effects of the treatment program were nonspecific. The most consistent specific problem reported by transplant patients and their families was fear or rejection of the allograft.

One of the distressing and dramatic results of poor psychosocial adaptation to the treatment program has been the significant incidence of noncompliance with immunosuppressive medication after transplantation. This led to irreversible reduction in allograft function or allograft failure. In the total sample there were 14 cases of documented noncompliance. Among the 43 cases that have been followed up for more than five years, there were eight noncompliant patients. Most of these were adolescent girls. Noncompliance was suspected with sudden diminution in cushingoid features or unexplained elevations of the BUN and serum creatinine levels noted on routine clinic visits. The noncompliance was confirmed by an interview with a psychosocial team member. When asked why they interrupted their immunosuppressive therapy, some of the patients reported that they could not bear the cosmetic side effects of the corticosteroid treatment even though they had been assured that these side effects were only temporary. In other instances there seemed to be a significant element of adolescent rebellion or depression, or the wish to deny the entire experience.

On the basis of selected family function items and certain personality test scores, it is currently possible to identify compliant and noncompliant patients by computer (B. M. Korsch et al., unpublished data). Efforts are currently under way to predict noncompliance on the basis of this kind of information so that appropriate preventive measures can be instituted to minimize this heretofore neglected cause of allograft failure.

Other types of gross maladaptation to illness and treatment also tend to be observed in those patients with personality test scores at the lower end of the spectrum. It is these patients who have needed psychiatric consultation and treatment and who have been the greatest problem to the treatment team.

Rehabilitation. The degree of rehabilitation following transplantation was assessed in two ways. Educational achievement of the 43 recipients who survived with a functioning graft for more than five years was evaluated and the current status of the 54 patients who are currently surviving was determined.

At the time of transplantation, 3 young (aged 1½

to 5 years) children were preschool age, 17 children were attending elementary school, and 1 recipient had graduated from high school. Twenty-one patients who were in primary or secondary school at the time of transplantation have graduated from high school; only three recipients failed to graduate. Of the high school graduates, 14 subsequently attended college and 4 became involved in a vocational rehabilitation program. In addition, one patient who did not graduate from high school entered a vocational rehabilitation program. The remaining 18 children progressed in their schooling (a school for handicapped for 2 patients with significant mental retardation) and are attending primary or secondary school.

Of the 54 recipients currently alive, 47 are surviving with a functioning graft, and 7 are undergoing dialysis (4 at home and 3 in center). Twenty-eight of the 47 patients are of "job market" age. Of these 28, seven are attending a university, four are in vocational training programs, eight are employed full-time (seven appropriately), two are at home with their infants, and six are unemployed. The remaining 19 recipients are in primary or secondary schools appropriate for their age. School performance in these 19 children is above average in six, average in ten, below average in one, and two children are in programs for the mentally retarded. Therefore, only six (13%) of the 47 recipients are not engaged in meaningful activity.

Eight recipients (five men and three women) are married; four young women have given birth to normal children and two young men have fathered normal children. In addition, one young woman has had two elective abortions.

Long-Term Graft Function. Serial serum creatine levels of the 43 recipients whose grafts functioned for a minimum of five years are shown in Figures 8 and 9. Of 19 recipients of LD grafts, 15 currently have good function as evidenced by a serum creatinine level of less than 2.0 mg/100 ml. Four have deteriorating graft function; one of these recently failed. In three of the four recipients the serum creatinine level rose above 2.0 mg/100 ml between the fourth and seventh posttransplant years.

Seventeen of the 24 patients with CD grafts have good function. Chronic rejection occurred in seven grafts, three of which failed between the fifth and sixth posttransplant years. The serum creatinine level exceeded 2.0 mg/100 ml between the fourth and eighth posttransplant years in six of the seven recipients.

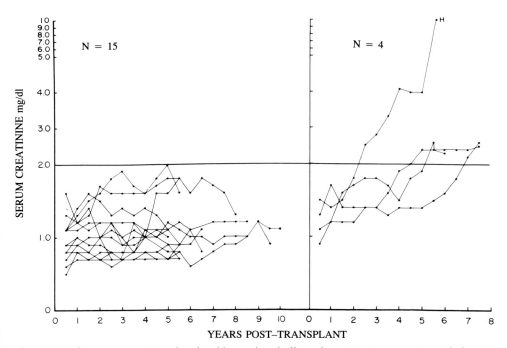

Fig. 8. Serial serum creatinine levels of live related allograft recipients surviving with functioning graft for more than five years. Recipients with stable allograft function as indicated by serum creatinine level <2.0 mg/100 ml are depicted on left, and recipients with declining allograft function on right.

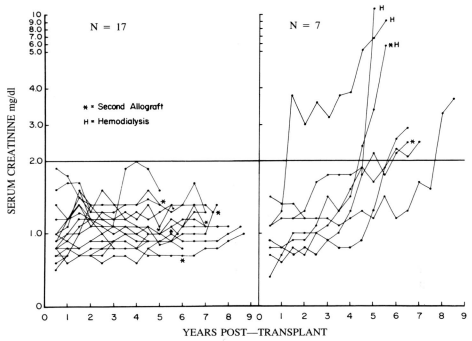

Fig. 9. Serial serum creatinine levels of cadaveric allograft recipients surviving with functioning graft for more than five years. Recipients with stable allograft function as indicated by serum creatinine level <2.0 mg/100 ml are depicted on left, and recipients with declining allograft function on right.

DISCUSSION

DeShazo et al.[21] reported the results of transplantation in 96 children performed between 1963 and 1973. Twenty-six patients received a graft prior to 1968. The projected actuarial ten-year patient and graft survival for the LD grafts was 77% and 74%, respectively, and for CD grafts, 63% and 44%, respectively. No specific information was included on the 26 patients at risk for a minimum of five years. However, the report of Weil et al.[25] included a follow-up period of 6 to 13 years on 57 children (47 LD and 10 CD grafts) who received their initial graft between 1962 and 1969. Thirty-five (61%) of the patients were alive and 32 (60%) had a functioning graft. Retransplantation was necessary in 16 children, and 10 of the survivors had either a second, third, fourth, or fifth graft.

Scant long-term follow-up of predominantly adult graft recipients is available.[34,35] Thomas et al.[34] reported an overall actual patient survival of 48% in 99 patients (66 LD, 54 CD, 4 live unrelated donor grafts) who received an initial graft 8 to 12 years previously. All of the survivors had a functioning graft; however, 25 retransplants were performed on this group of recipients. In 1974, Starzl et al.[35] gave a decade follow-up of 64 transplants performed between 1962 and 1964. Some of

the recipients were children and are included in the report of Weil et al.[25] After 10 to 11½ years, 52% (24/46) of the recipients of LD grafts were alive with a functioning graft. Twenty-one patients had their original graft. However, only two of 18 recipients of live unrelated donor grafts were alive, and only one had a functioning original graft.

Our 78% (54/69) patient survival is attributable to increased availability of dialysis facilities for patients who reject an initial or subsequent graft during the past decade. This availability has permitted us to save the patient rather than make heroic efforts to salvage the graft. Although 68% (47/69) of the survivors have a functioning graft, only 32 recipients are surviving with their original graft. The virtue of retransplantation is evident in that 15 patients have a functioning second (12) or third (3) graft, 6 of which have been functioning for more than five years.

Retransplantation is necessary for patient survival with a functioning graft. This is especially true if CD grafts are used for the initial transplant. In the present report, 73% (19/26) of the LD grafts were functioning at five years, whereas only 39% (16/42) of the CD grafts were functioning at five years ($P < .05$). The results with CD grafts have not improved during the past five years either at our institution[36] or in other centers throughout the world.[37]

Survival of grafts between HLA identical siblings is superior to that of nonidentical siblings, parental, or cadaver donors. It was anticipated that improved CD graft survival would result from improved histocompatibility matching between donor and recipient. The results have been contradictory,[38,39] and in our experience the degree of HLA histocompatibility has not affected graft outcome.[36]

The attrition rate of first CD grafts is disconcerting, whereas the outcome of CD second grafts is somewhat encouraging. The five-year graft survival of 62% (8/13) approached that of the LD first grafts, expecially if the two HLA identical sibling transplants are excluded (71%),

A functioning allograft makes patient survival possible; however, all of the consequences of renal failure are not improved. In children, the most serious one of these is persistent growth retardation. Growth failure is a frequent occurrence in children with chronic renal insufficiency. The etiology is multifactorial with acidosis,[40] osteodystrophy,[41] and insufficient caloric intake[42] proposed as possible contributing causes.

Normal growth following transplantation is variable. Potter et al.[43] reported that no recipeint receiving corticosteroids daily grew normally, whereas Lilly et al.[13] described normal growth in 57% of their recipients. In a previous report from our institution, we noted that 42% of our patients with growth potential (bone age < 12 years at transplantation) grew normally following transplantation.[44] However, the period of posttransplant follow-up in that group of patients was only one to three years.

Long-term growth following transplantation in the present series was disappointing. No patient showed significant catch-up growth. Recipients with a bone age of more than 12 years at transplantation and open epiphyses grew minimally following transplantation. All recipients with a bone age of less than 12 years at transplantation had an increase in height; however, normal growth was present in only three (13%). The difference in the present long-term results from our previous report which had a shorter follow-up period is possibly related to two factors. These are the rapid advancement in bone age with subsequent epiphyseal closure during sexual maturation in children with a retarded bone age at transplantation, and the development of reduced graft function resulting from chronic rejection.[31]

It is possible that the growth retarding effects of corticosteroids contribute to posttransplant growth retardation. Consequently, alternate-day corticosteroid therapy has been advocated in attempt to improve growth.[43–47] No improvement has been noted in the recipient with a bone age of more than 12 years.[47] Increased growth has been reported in recipients with growth potential; however, the follow-up period has been insufficient to assess the ultimate long-term beneficial effects. We currently change from daily to alternate-day therapy 12 to 18 months after transplantation in recipients with stable graft function. A modest increment in height has been noted with minimal adverse effect on graft function.[48] Further long-term follow-up is necessary to determine if alternate-day therapy improves the recipient's ultimate adult height.

Persistent short stature as well as the other complications of chronic renal disease such as osteodystrophy account for some of the psychosocial problems following transplantation. The rigors of the entire treatment program and specifically the side effects of corticosteroids are also impediments to normal posttransplant psychosocial adaptation. However, in general, we have found in a systematic follow-up study that the patient and family return to preillness equilibrium by one year after transplantation.[32,33] Personality testing at that time, however, did indicate that a significant number of recipients had evidence of defective social adaptation and low self-esteem.

Following transplantation, the major psychosocial problems are related to fear of rejection and the visual consequences of corticosteroid therapy. A significant result of poor psychosocial adaptation is noncompliance with immunosuppressive drugs. This leads to irreversible reduction in graft function or graft loss or both. In adolescent recipients the noncompliance may be a manifestation of adolescent rebellion or may result from severe depression. Noncompliance has also been reported in adult recipients and has accounted for graft loss in a number of long-term recipients.[35]

In spite of the persistent growth failure and occasional psychosocial maladaptation, long-term rehabilitation is excellent. Only 13% of the 47 recipients with a currently functioning graft are not engaged in any meaningful activity. Adolescents who survived with a functioning graft for five to ten years have graduated from high school and entered college or vocational rehabilitation programs. Another example of the satisfactory adaptation of the long-term survivors is their ability to marry and have children.

Since few, if any, of the causes of ESRD in children are currently preventable, dialysis and transplantation will be necessary in the foreseeablefuture for patient survival. The long-term results of transplantation which we have reported justify the continued use of this therapeutic modality. Five to ten years after development of ESRD, 78% of the patients with transplants are surviving and 68% have a functioning graft. The quality of the life is acceptable, although persistent difficulties with psychosocial adaptation exist.

REFERENCES

1. Riley CM: Thoughts about kidney homotransplantation in children. J Pediatr 65:797, 1964

2. Reinhart JB: The doctor's dilemma. J Pediatr 77:505, 1970

3. Combined report on regular dialysis and transplantation of children in Europe, 1975. Proc Eur Dial Transplant Assoc 13:60, 1976

4. The 12th report of the human renal transplant registry. JAMA 233:787, 1975

5. Startzl TE, Marchioro TL, Porter KA, et al: The role of organ transplantation in pediatrics. Pediatr Clin North Am 13:381, 1966

6. Williams GM, Lee HM, Hume DM: Renal transplants in children. Transplant Proc 1:262, 1969

7. Martin LW, Gonzalez LL, West CD, et al: Clinical problems encountered in renal homotransplantation in children. J Pediatr Surg 5:207, 1970

8. Fine RN, Korsch BM, Stiles Q, et al: Renal homotransplantation in children. J Pediatr 76:347, 1970

9. Potter D, Belzer FO, Rames L, et al: The treatment of chronic uremia in childhood: I. Transplantation. Pediatrics 45:432, 1970

10. Gonzalez LL, Martin L, West CD, et al: Renal homotransplantation in children. Arch Surg 101:232, 1970

11. La Plante MP, Kaufman JJ, Goldman R, et al: Kidney transplantation in children. Pediatrics 40:665, 1967

12. Lawson RK, Campbell RA, Hodges CV: Renal transplantation in infants and small children. Transplant Proc 3:358, 1970

13. Lilly JR, Giles G, Hurwitz R, et al: Renal homotransplantation in pediatric patients. Pediatrics 47:548, 1971

14. Najarian JS, Simmons RL, Tallent MB, et al: Renal transplantation in infants and children. Ann Surg 174:583, 1971

15. Boulton-Jones JM, Bewick CM, Ogg CS, et al: Treatment of terminal renal failure in children by home dialysis and transplantation. ArchDis Child 46:457, 1971

16. Hulme B, Kenyon JR, Owen K, et al: Renal transplantation analysis of 25 consecutive transplants in 19 recipients. Arch Dis Child 47:486, 1972

17. Belzer Fo, Schweitzer RT, Holliday M, et al: Renal homotransplantation in children. Am J Surg 124:270, 1972

18. Cerilli J, Evans WE, Sotos JF: Renal transplantation in infants and children. Transplant Proc 4:633, 1972

19. Fine RN, Korsch BM, Brennan LP, et al: Renal transplantation in young children. Am J Surg 125:559, 1973

20. Mauer SM, Kjellstand CM, Buselmeier TJ, et al: Renal transplantation in the very young child. Proc Eur Dial Transplant Assoc 11:247, 1974

21. DeShazo CV, Simmons RL, Bernstein DM, et al: Results of renal transplantation in 100 children. Surgery 76:461, 1974

22. Henriksson C, Andersen HJ, Gustafsson A, et al: Renal transplantation in children. Acta Paediatr Scand 64:833, 1975

23. Talwalkar YB, Harner MH, Musgrave JE, et al: Pediatric renal transplantation. West J Med 123:1, 1975

24. Lawson, RK, Talwalkar YB, Musgrave JE, et al: Renal transplantation in pediatric patients. J Urol 113:225, 1975

25. Weil R, Putman CW, Porter KA, et al: Transplantation in children. Surg Clin North Am 56:467, 1976

26. Fine RN, Korsch BM, Grushkin CM, et al: Hemodialysis in children. Am J Dis Child 119:498, 1970

27. Fine RN, Brennan LP, Edelbrock HH, et al: The use of pediatric cadaver kidneys for homotransplantation in children. JAMA 210:477, 1969

28. Fine RN: Renal transplantation in children. Adv Nephrol 5:201, 1975

29. Terasaki PI, Mickey MR, Driesler M: Presensitization and kidney transplant failures. Postgrad Med J 47:89, 1971

30. Patel R, Terasaki PI: Significance of the positive cross match test in kidney transplantation. N Engl J Med 280:735, 1969

31. Pennisi AJ, Phillips LS, Costin G, et al: Linear growth in long term renal allograft recipients. Clin Nephrol, to be published

32. Korsch BM, Negrete VF, Gardner JF, et al: Kidney transplantation in children: Psychosocial followup study on child and family. J Pediatr 83:399, 1973

33. Korsch BM, Fine RN, Negrete VF, et al: Noncompliance in female adolescents with kidney transplants. Pediatr Res 10:440, 1976

34. Thomas F, Lee HM, Wolf JS, et al: Long-term (8-12 years) prognosis in related and unrelated renal transplantation. Transplant Proc 7:707, 1975

35. Starzl TE, Porter KA, Halgrimson CG, et al: A decade followup in early cases of renal homotransplantation. Ann Surg 180:606, 1974

36. Fine RN, Malekzadeh MH, Pennisi AJ, et al: Cadaver renal transplantation in children. Transplant Proc 9:133, 1977

37. Terasaki PI, Opelz G, Mickey MR: Analysis of yearly kidney transplant survival rates. Transplant Proc 8:139, 1976

38. Belzer FO, Fortmann JL, Salvatierra O, et al: Is HL-A typing of clinical significance in cadaver renal transplantation? Lancet 1:774, 1974

39. Dausset J. Hors J, Busson M, et al: Serologically defined HL-A antigens and long term survival of cadaver kidney transplants. N Engl J Med 290:979, 1974

40. Cooke RE, Boyden DG, Haller E: The relationship of acidosis and growth retardation. J Pediatr 57:326, 1960

41. Broyer M, Kleinknecht C, Loirat C, et al: Growth in children treated with long term hemodialysis. J Pediatr 84:642, 1974

42. Chantler C, Holliday MA: Growth in children with renal disease with particular reference to the effects of calorie malnutrition: A review. Clin Nephrol 1:230, 1973

43. Potter DE, Holliday MA, Wilson CJ, et al: Alternate-day steroids in children after renal transplantation. Transplant Proc 7:79, 1975

44. Grushkin CM, Fine RN: Growth in children following renal transplantation. Am J Dis Child 125:514, 1973

45. McEnery PT, Gonzalez LL, Martin LW, et al: Growth and development of children with renal transplants: Use of alternate-day steroid therapy. J Pediatr 83:806, 1973

46. Reimold EW: Intermittent prednisone therapy in children and adolescents after renal transplantation. Pediatrics 52:235, 1973

47. Hoda Q, Hasinoff DJ, Arbus GS: Growth following renal transplantation in children and adolescents. Clin Nephrol 3:6, 1975

48. Pennisi AJ, Negrete VF, Malekzadeh M, et al: Daily and alternate day corticosteroid therapy and linear growth in long-term renal allograft recipients. Abstract WDTS, Seattle, Oct 1976

Commentary: Renal Transplantation in Children

Richard M. Ehrlich and Floyd A. Katske

Pediatric patients with end-stage renal disease occur in the population from 1.5 to over 3:1 million. These patients, because of age, social maturity, and physical habitus, are frequently poor candidates for long-term hemotoneal or peritoneal dialysis; in the last 10 years, however, there has been renewed research and dedication to demonstrate that children are acceptable transplant candidates. With recent advances in surgical technique and immunosuppressive therapy and a better understanding of the intricate psychosocial changes that take place, pediatric transplantation offers not only improvement in the child's quality of life, but potential reversal of the effects of chronic renal failure.

Doctor Fine and co-authors describe the largest series of pediatric transplantation to date. Their article covers, in depth and with substantial statistics, the major considerations that go into decision making in the care of pediatric transplant recipients. Particular emphasis has been given to criteria of acceptability and the deliberation necessary before considering a child for transplantation. It is a fascinating story indeed. Patients with diseases that formerly excluded them from consideration, such as diabetes and oxalosis, are now considered acceptable for transplantation.

SURGICAL PROCEDURE

It has been our practice to use a retroperitoneal rather than a transperitoneal approach. To gain adequate exposure, one must reflect or incise (or do both) the rectus muscles near their pubic attachment. Venous anastomoses are done end to side to the vena cava or occasionally to the iliac vein. The arterial anastomosis is done using the aorta, common, or internal iliac artery. We use 6–0 cardiovascular suture for all vascular anastomoses. Interrupted sutures are commonly employed to allow for radial growth of the artery; continuous sutures tend to act as a pursestring and retard potential growth. Vascular problems can usually be dealt with using standard vascular techniques and ingenuity with the employment of vein and Dacron patches in difficult management situations.

We generally anastomose the ureter to the bladder in a modified Leadbetter–Politano method, creating an adequate submucosal tunnel. We have not used the Lich–Gregoir method. Meticulous attention to detail is crucial, since anastomotic leaks or urologic complications, as in all transplant series, carry a high morbidity and mortality. This cannot be overemphasized.

It is indeed fascinating to transplant kidneys in children previously diverted because of "bladder dysfunction." Important advances in urodynamic testing have facilitated physicians' ability to identify this important subgroup, whose members were diverted with poor or fallacious indications. Many bladders have been resurrected and undiversion performed to the great advantage of the afflicted child; many unfortunately go into irreversible renal failure during their adolescent growth spurt but later are acceptable transplant candidates with an intact and properly functioning lower urinary tract.

Transplantation into a conduit does, however, seem to be an acceptable alternative in special situations. Time alone will tell whether the antireflux colon conduit is superior to an iliac conduit. In the interim, we employ the colon conduit whenever feasible. We prefer to perform enteric surgery before transplantation because of the possibility of a vascular blowout from mycotic infection.

We strongly concur with Doctor Fine's group in his stated criteria for acceptability. Mentally retarded or physically handicapped patients do not fare well with their transplants. Diabetic patients also present multiple problems, many of which can now be surmounted. It has been our experience that the glomerular diseases do not contraindicate transplantation. We further suggest that age is not a contraindication, but those patients under 1 year of age present complex managerial problems.

The use of bilateral nephrectomy is somewhat controversial, but we concur that the presence of persistent unyielding hypertension, before or after transplantation, is an indication for nephrectomy. Grossly infected or hydronephrotic kidneys, or those with reflux, are usually removed preoperatively. Splenectomy is no longer routinely performed because of recent reports of significant postoperative sepsis, plus the absence of firm data that it improves graft survival.

Angiography should be performed in patients with moderately severe hypertension. Recently we have been using Saralasin intravenous (IV) bolus testing to identify renin-mediated hypertension, which, in conjunction with renal vein renin studies, selects out patients with renovascular disease. We particularly stress the use of oblique arteriographic views to aid in visualizing stenotic areas often not seen in the AP projection.

COMPLICATIONS

The development of lymphoceles, although uncommon, presents a diagnostic dilemma in many instances. The differences between hematoma, lymphocele, urinary leakage, and abscess, particularly when rejection is present, are frequently confusing. The cardinal features of lymphoceles included deterioration of graft function, swelling over the graft site, and edema of the genitalia or ipsilateral extremity. Management depends on the size of the collection. Formal incision and drainage is preferred; intraperitoneal marsupialization has not been performed for fear of inducing septic peritonitis.

Doctor Fine's group describes the alarmingly high number of patients who do not take their steroid medication as prescribed, causing either loss of graft function or rejection and necessitating its removal. This problem, particularly noted in teenaged girls, adds a unique dimension to the postoperative management of the pediatric transplant patient. Korsch and colleagues describe attempts at psychosocial identification in management of these patients. Identification of noncompliance is based on changes in physical appearance in terms of loss of the cushinoid state, weight loss, or unexplained deterioration in graft function. Certain behavioral tests (*e.g.,* the California Test of Personality) appear to be of some predictive value in identifying the potential noncompliant patient, even with reinstitution of therapy. However, these patients fare poorly; 50% of noncompliant renal transplant patients lose their graft to rejection, and the remainder show marked diminution of renal function. It appears that a team approach to aid in the identification in these patients, as well as careful monitoring of the high-risk patient, may help to avert this unfortunate complication.

ANNOTATED BIBLIOGRAPHY

Levey RH, Ingelfinger J, Grupe WE, Toper M, Eraklis AJ: Unique surgical and immunologic features of renal transplantation in children. J Pediatr Surg 13:576, 1978

This paper summarizes experience from Boston Children's Hospital in pediatric transplantation. In that period, 93 transplants were performed in 89 patients with a mean age of 13 years. There was an equal number of males and females. Sixty-four transplants were live related; 29 were cadaver donors. One third of the patients had obstructive disease, and two thirds had acquired pathology. The authors offer a short description of operative technique. Antilymphocytic serum was used on selected patients. The avoidance of steroid pulsing appeared to reduce mortality. Results show 75% were functioning 6 months to 7 years after transplantation. Complications included urine leak from the bladder in two patients and from the renal pelvis in one. There were no reports of vascular stenosis.

Martin LW, McEnery PT, Rosenkrantz JG, Cox JA, West CD, LeCoultre C: Renal homotransplantation in children. J Ped Surg 14:571, 1979

Ninety-six renal transplants in 77 pediatric patients are reported, with follow-up study as long as 12½ years. Thirteen of the first 14 patients are living with a functioning kidney after 8 to 12½ years. The patient survival for the entire group is 78%. Sixty-four percent are living with a functioning transplanted kidney. Anencephalic newborn infants have been found to be a satisfactory source of cadaver-donor kidneys. Growth and development have been satisfactory when the transplant is performed before 12 years of age if it functions well and if an alternate-day regimen of steroid administration is followed. Both boys and girls have now passed through puberty with their transplanted kidneys, have married, have become parents, and are leading essentially normal lives. A plea is made for earlier transplantation in small children with irreversible progressive renal failure before their growth is stunted severely and before the need for prolonged dialysis arises.

Grushkin CM, Fine RN: Growth in children after renal transplantation. Am J Dis Child 125:514, 1973

Twenty-six children (aged 18 months to 18 years) surviving from 1 to 4 years after renal transplantation were evaluated to identify predictable methods to ascertain growth potential. The authors conclude that males grow better than females; the reason for this is unclear. The patients' bone age at the time of surgery appears to be a valuable indicator. Those patients with radiographic bone ages less than 12 years grew, whereas those with bone age greater than 12 years did not. The effect of steroid immunosuppression is variable. Doses of prednisone greater than 10 mg/m² did not preclude growth. The origin of the graft, that is, live vs cadaver, did not affect growth rate. The authors suggest that alternate-day steroid therapy may help patients attain normal height.

Korsch BM, Fine RN, Negrete VF: Noncompliance in children with renal transplants. Pediatrics 61:872, 1978

This article, also by the group from Los Angeles Children's Hospital, reviews a series of 14 patients who did not comply with their immunosuppressive medication regimens. Thirteen of the 14 patients were adolescents. Suspicion of noncompliance based on physical changes or dimunition of renal function was confirmed by interview. Common among the noncompliant patients was a ''vulnerable personality'' as defined by a group of psychologic tests and a concern over the cosmetic changes associated with steroid use. The authors question the benefit of a psychologic team approach to identification, since many of the patients exhibited deep-seated personality problems, possibly amenable only to intensive psychiatric therapy.

McEnery PT, Flanagan J: Fulminant sepsis in splenectomized children. Transplantation, 24:154, 1977

The authors question whether the use of splenectomy is worthwhile as a routine procedure. Sixty-nine children received 80 grafts; 69% (46 patients) underwent splenectomy. Nine percent (four patients) developed fulminant sepsis, and three patients died. The authors noted that no infection occurred in the nonsplenectomized group matched for age, sex, and renal disease. This paper provides supportive evidence that splenectomy as a routine procedure is contraindicated in the pediatric transplant recipient.

Overview: Indications and Preparation for Renal Transplantation in Children

John S. Najarian

With experience of over 200 kidney transplants in children, I find that kidney transplantation is the best way to treat end-stage kidney disease. Children usually tolerate dialysis poorly, and, as a result, one should make every attempt at transplantation whenever end-stage kidney disease is present.

TIMING AND PREPARATION

Several unique criteria on the timing of transplantation in children must be considered. Because uremia results in general slowing of the growth process, it may be necessary to consider transplantation before the patient with absolute end-stage kidney disease requires dialysis and transplantation. In addition, various conditions in children necessitate early transplantation, for instance, congenital nephrotic syndrome, because the loss of protein is so great that the patient cannot be adequately managed until the source of that protein loss (the kidneys) is removed.

I feel that children are acceptable candidates for transplantation unless extreme mental deterioration is present. The only absolute contraindications to transplant are (1) ABO blood group incompatibility, (2) cytotoxic antibodies against donor lymphoid cells, (3) active infection, and (4) uncontrollable malignancy.

Because I feel that the limits of psychomotor potential are currently undefined, I therefore give the patient the benefit of the doubt and accept children with psychomotor retardation of undefined etiology as transplantation candidates. Children with severe retardation from a specific cause, such as birth asphyxia, structural abnormalities, and mental disorders, are excluded.

In preparing the patient for transplantation I do not do bilateral nephrectomies on children unless they have nephrotic syndrome with protein loss, infectious disease, infected kidneys, ureteral reflux, kidney tumor, or hypertension that cannot be controlled by hemodialysis. In the past I performed routine splenectomies and felt that this procedure was responsible for good kidney survival statistics. The consideration of potential sepsis after splenectomy, however, made me reassess this position, epecially in children. The results of a randomized, prospective, double-blind study on splenectomies and kidney transplantation, done 2 years ago, showed a significant improvement of graft survival with splenectomy compared with equally matched patients without splenectomy. Thus, I am

again doing routine splenectomies on all transplant recipients, including children. Splenectomy patients receive a small dose of either oral penicillin or a sulfonamide to prevent sepsis. I have not seen septic problems related to asplenia.

SURGICAL PROCEDURE

A concerted effort is made to find living–related kidney donors. Only 30% of our children have received cadaveric kidney transplants. Children tolerate dialysis so poorly that an elective operation at an early date allows better management of the patient than does waiting for a cadaver donor. Since most of the living–related donors used are parents, I have carefully evaluated the results of parent transplants into children. In general, the survival of these transplants is no better than those for equally matched cadaver kidneys into children. When looking at individual parents, however, the father–donor graft does better than cadaveric kidney grafts, but grafts from mothers do rather poorly. There is approximately a 10% to 15% difference in kidney survival statistics between kidneys donated by the mother and by the father. Because of this difference, I have switched my immunosuppressive regimen so that it is much stronger for recipients of grafts from mothers than for routine related–donor transplants; I use the same immunosuppressive regimen used for cadaveric kidney transplants. With this new program I hope to improve overall parent–kidney graft survival so that it is closer to sibling–graft survival than to cadaver–graft survival.

Additionally, I feel strongly that the use of HLA typing to select donors is worthwhile. Since I began using only donors with a two-antigen serologic HLA match, whether the donor is a cadaver or a living relative, a significant improvement in graft survival over one or less antigen-matched donor kidney transplants has been noted.

My general immunosuppressive therapy includes azathioprine and prednisone, as described by Dr. Fine; however, all transplant patients also receive antilymphocyte globulin (ALG). This added immunosuppressive agent has provided an opportunity to lower corticosteroid levels most dramatically and has resulted in better graft results as well as in fewer steroid complications. In addition, when rejection episodes occur, I increase steroid therapy and administer 150 rads of local radiation to the graft every other day, for a total of three doses.

In general, my policy is similar to that discussed in Dr.

Fine's paper. However, I prefer the intra-abdominal approach in children who weigh less than 10 kg because it provides an opportunity to place even an adult-size kidney directly into the potential recipient's aorta and inferior vena cava. I have used parent kidneys in 18 children who weighed less than 10 kg; these kidneys have done well with direct anastomosis to the cava and the aorta.

I have not hesitated to do second transplants and even third and fourth transplants. Dr. Fine mentions that third and fourth transplants in his group have done rather poorly and that he feels it would be better for the patient to return to dialysis. I am now investigating the use of a possibly better method of immunosuppression—total lymphoid irradiation (TLI). I have used TLI on 11 patients who have lost either one or two transplants by rejection in their first posttransplant year. Under these circumstances, the use of TLI without ALG and with the accompaniment of modest doses of azathioprine and prednisone has resulted in satisfactory graft survival without rejection. This is a remarkable finding, considering that all these patients were at a high risk for rejection, having previously rejected either one or two grafts.

It has been my experience that one must transplant patients early in their uremia if growth is a problem, especially in children under age 10, in whom most linear growth occurs. When undergoing transplantation early, these children generally achieve parallel growth and occasionally "catch up" to their peers. Because the cadaver transplant may be difficult to maintain and can require higher doses of steroids, these recipients have poor growth rates. Some selected patients have received alternate-day doses of steroids. Although those patients have not experienced a uniform improvement in growth, in general it has been better than when prednisone is given daily.

I agree with Dr. Ehrlich that many urinary diversions are carried out in patients who have salvageable bladders. Unless a true neurogenic bladder is present (*i.e.,* meningomyelocele), most bladders can be resurrected and used for the eventual transplant. I have removed more ileal loops than I have constructed, but when necessary, implantation of the kidney into an ileal loop has been successful in patients who do not have a functioning bladder.

Psychologic, social, and physical rehabilitation of pediatric patients with renal transplantation can be extremely good, especially if the factors relating to growth, the avoidance of excessive doses of steroids, and the maintenance of a supportive physician-patient relationship continue throughout the post-transplantation period.

12

CURRENT STATUS OF RENAL TRANSPLANTATION AT THE CLEVELAND CLINIC

Andrew C. Novick,* William E. Braun, Magnus Magnusson and Nicholas Stowe

From the Departments of Urology, and Hypertension and Nephrology, The Cleveland Clinic Foundation, Cleveland, Ohio

The Journal of Urology
Copyright © 1979 by The Williams & Wilkins Co.
Vol. 122, October
Printed in U.S.A.

During the last 15 years renal transplantation has become an effective method to treat patients with end stage renal failure. The pool of potential transplant recipients continues to increase with the advent of federal funding and improved patient survival rates. In 1977 approximately 37,000 patients with end stage renal disease were treated with either dialysis or transplantation. The first patient to undergo a renal transplant at this institution received a cadaver kidney in January 1963 and since then >600 renal transplants have been performed here. Herein are summarized our current philosophies regarding medical and surgical care of renal transplant patients.

* Requests for reprints: Department of Urology, Cleveland Clinic Foundation, 9500 Euclid Ave., Cleveland, Ohio 44106.

SELECTION AND PREPARATION OF RECIPIENTS

During the last several years the criteria for acceptance into most transplant programs, including our own, have expanded significantly to encompass many high risk patients with end stage renal failure. These include conditions such as age <10 or >45 years, an abnormal lower urinary tract, prior cured malignancy, coronary artery disease, persistent hepatitis B-antigenemia, tuberculosis or systemic diseases, such as diabetes mellitus, systemic lupus erythematosus, cystinosis, polyarteritis, scleroderma or Wegener's granulomatosis. Renal transplantation currently is contraindicated only in the management of chronic renal failure owing to oxalosis, or in patients with active infection, uncontrolled or recently treated malignancy, or such severe extrarenal disease as to render prohibitive the risk of anesthesia for a major operation.

In most cases renal transplantation is not performed until chronic dialysis has been initiated. Patients maintained on chronic peritoneal dialysis are now acceptable candidates but should dialysis be necessary in these patients immediately after transplantation this is achieved with hemodialysis until the surgical incision has healed. Transplantation for chronic renal failure is recommended before dialysis in patients with diabetic nephropathy to obviate progression of extrarenal manifestations of this disease, such as retinopathy or neuropathy.[1] In patients who present before dialysis with an HLA-identical living related donor, transplantation often is scheduled for the time when the patient would otherwise require initiation of chronic dialysis.

Before transplantation all candidates undergo a residual urine determination and a voiding cystourethrogram, while a cystometrogram also is obtained in diabetic patients. No other urologic studies are done routinely unless the history suggests an abnormality of the upper or lower urinary tract. We have had only 7 patients in whom the bladder could not be used for transplantation, either because of severe neurogenic disease or severe post-inflammatory contracture. In these cases transplantation was done into a pre-fashioned ileal or sigmoid conduit.

All transplant candidates with diabetes, symptoms of coronary artery disease or age >40 years undergo coronary arteriography. During the last 5 years 102 such patients with end stage renal disease have been studied.[2] In followup of these patients coronary artery disease has accounted for 75 percent of the deaths occurring in patients having >50 percent narrowing of the coronary vessels on angiography (Table 1). There were 31 patients who had received renal allografts after evaluation with coronary arteriography, and only 2 of 11 recipient deaths were owing to coronary disease. A coronary artery bypass operation has been performed safely in several end stage renal disease patients, and these patients can undergo transplantation successfully. This approach has allowed renal transplantation to be done more safely in older or diabetic patients.

In patients with documented remote or active peptic ulcer disease an acid reducing gastric procedure is done before transplantation to lessen the potential for postoperative steroid-induced gastrointestinal hemorrhage.[3] Recently, selective vagotomy has become the operation of choice and these patients also are treated with cimetidine during the initial transplant hospitalization.[4] Splenectomy has not been done in the preparation of transplant recipients since 1969 and analysis of pooled data has shown no significant beneficial effect on graft survival.[5] Likewise, thymectomy is no longer performed, although analysis by internal comparison of our earlier patient data suggested improved long-term graft survival in thymectomized patients, most of whom also had splenectomies.[6]

The indications for pre-transplant bilateral nephrectomy must be balanced with the advantages derived from retained native kidneys in patients on dialysis. Definite indications for preliminary nephrectomy are pyeloemphritis, structural abnormalities of the urinary tract, renin-mediated hypertension and polycystic kidneys that have led to urinary infection or significant hematuria. Less common indications are renal malignancy. immunologically active renal disease, severe proteinuria or the unusual syndrome of cachexia, hypertension and ascites experienced by some chronic dialysis patients. Also of significance are data from the Transplant Registry, indicating improved graft survival in nephrectomized patients,[5] and evidence from Corry and associates that this phenomenon may be independent of the effect of blood transfusions.[7] When preliminary nephrectomy is indicated a bilateral posterior surgical approach is preferred and is now being used in the majority of patients undergoing this operation. Contraindications to this method are the presence of enlarged kidneys, bilateral ureteral reflux or the need for an adjunctive abnormal procedure. In a comparison of the transperitoneal and posterior surgical approaches to performing bilateral nephrectomy the latter has proved far superior in terms of more rapid patient recovery and diminished operative morbidity.[8]

SELECTION OF DONORS

Living Related Donors. The prospective donor must be motivated properly and free of any conditions that would increase the risk either of an operation or of losing a significant fraction of renal function. Histocompatibility testing of the donor and recipient must indicate a good probability of graft survival. In our experience approximately 25 percent of apparently healthy potential donors

TABLE 1. Coronary Arteriography in Evaluation of 102 Patients with End Stage Renal Disease

	No. Pts.	Survival No. (%)	Coronary Deaths No. (%)
Non-diabetic patients			
No significant disease	42	31 (74)	0/11 (0)
>50 percent stenosis of major vessels	30	20 (67)	7/10 (70)
Diabetic patients			
No significant disease	17	11 (65)	0/6 (0)
>50 percent stenosis of major vessels	13	8 (62)	4/5 (80)

have been found to have serious, previously undetected, abnormalities that precluded organ donation. We do accept live donor candidates who are less than ideal because of multiple renal vessels, multiple ureters, unilateral calicectasis or megaureter, benign renal cysts, unilateral medial fibroplasia, obesity, benign elevation of the serum bilirubin, mild alterations in glucose metabolism or a history of urinary infections from cystitis.

When a live donor nephrectomy is performed the anterior transperitoneal surgical approach is preferred since this provides optimum exposure for atraumatic dissection of the renal vessels. Analysis of >200 transperitoneal live donor nephrectomies performed at this institution has revealed this to be a safe and effective operation with low risk to the donor.[9]

Cadaver donors. Our criteria for acceptance and preparation of cadaveric donors differ in no significant way from those used at other institutions.[10] Heart-beating donors are preferred and all cadaver kidneys are harvested *en bloc* with the aorta and vena cava to ensure preservation of multiple renal vessels. The importance of preserving ureteral blood supply during donor nephrectomy cannot be over-emphasized. Since there continues to be a shortage of cadaver organs in relation to the number of potential recipients it also is imperative that suitable kidneys not be discarded for anatomic or technical reasons. Extracorporeal microvascular reconstructive techniques now enable use of most cadaver organs with diseased, damaged or multiple vessels.

IMMUNOLOGIC CONSIDERATIONS

The correlation between HLA matching and allograft survival has been accepted widely for living related transplants. Its acceptance in cadaver allografting is strengthening with evidence from nearly 1,000 cadaver allografts reported from France,[11] >600 from England[12] and a large single center experience from the University of Minnesota,[13] all showing significant correlations between HLA matching, particularly for 2 or more A and B series antigens, and a successful allograft. Our policy is to transplant only those cadaver kidneys that match for 2 or more of these antigens with the recipient. Preliminary data from several transplantation centers have suggested that the recently described D-locus related series HLA antigens may have an even stronger influence on cadaver allograft survival.[14-16] Prospective studies of D-locus related matching currently are underway in this[17] and several other centers.

Compatibility for D-locus antigens measured by the mixed lymphocyte culture has been examined in living related transplant pairs in 2 clinical situations. Initially, the mixed lymphocyte culture was used just to detect those serologically identical siblings who were D-locus

recombinants. A broader application of mixed lymphocyte culture testing has been found by Cochrum and associates, who first reported that serologically non-identical living related pairs could be divided by a 2-way mixed lymphocyte culture stimulation index of 8 into groups with a high probability of transplant success (stimulation index >8) and with a low probability of success (stimulation index >8).[18] Our own data now show in 63 living related transplants that the best discrimination can be obtained by using a combination of serologic haplotype matching and a 2-way mixed lymphocyte culture stimulation index of 10 (p >0.001). As shown in Table 2 no failures occurred among the 17 recipients with 2-way mixed lymphocyte cultures having a stimulation index >10 and 2 haplotype matched, whereas 20 percent of the 30 patients with only one of these criteria lost their allografts to rejection in >1 year.

Pre-sensitization of allograft recipients by itself does not appear to affect adversely allograft outcome.[19,20] The presence of donor-specific preformed antibody, of course, still constitutes a contraindication to transplantation. Increased sensitivity of cross-match techniques for detecting such donor specific antibody plus the more frequent testing of waiting recipients' serum for samples with antibody to be used in cross-matches has sharply reduced the occurrence of hyperacute rejections.

Numerous studies have demonstrated improved allograft survival rates in patients receiving blood transfusions before cadaver transplantation.[21] However, blood transfusions, in addition to transmitting viral hepatitis, also may lead to sensitization and render less likely the chance of finding a cross-match negative kidney for a potential recipient. For this reason we have been reluctant to adopt a policy of deliberate pre-transplant blood transfusions in patients awaiting a cadaver allograft. When blood is necessary frozen washed red cells or leukocyte poor packed cells are administered.

Pre-treatment of cadaver donors with cyclophosphamide and methylprednisolone is another controversial area. Guttman's original series of patients continues to show an advantage for recipients of pre-treated donor

TABLE 2. Combined Haplotype and Mixed Lymphocyte Culture Correlation with Allograph Survival in 63 Living Related Transplant Recipients

	2-Haplotype Match and SI* < 10 No. (%)	Either 2-Haplotype Match or SI* < 10 No. (%)	Neither 2-Haplotype Match nor SI* < 10 No. (%)
No. pts.	17	30	16
Allograft success	17 (100)	24 (80)	7 (44)
Allograft failure	0	6	9

* Stimulating index with 2-way mixed lymphocyte culture.

organs.[22] While another major center concurs,[23] others have failed to find any improvement with pre-treatment.[24] Because of the need to initiate treatment of the donor several hours before harvesting the kidneys pretreatment has not been feasible in our cadaver donors.

The cornerstone of current immunosuppression of the recipient remains corticosteroids and azathioprine. High dose methylprednisolone generally is accepted as a reasonably effective way of treating acute cellular rejection. However, over the years we have reduced the amount that is used for any single patient. Nevertheless, with careful monitoring of the patient for infection and other steroid-induced complications, high doses may be used safely in selected patients. Our continuing study of cytomegalovirus infections has helped to identify infected patients, many of whom are leukopenic, in time to modify their immunosuppression.[25] Because of the success achieved with antilymphocyte globulin by the University of Minnesota Transplant Center[26] we presently are engaged in a prospective, controlled, multi-center evaluation of their antilymphocyte globulin preparation in first cadaver allografts. The morphologic and immunochemical evidence that fibrin and platelet thrombi are involved in allograft rejection has been the basis for using low dose heparin and anti-platelet drugs in treating rejection.

RENAL PRESERVATION

Preservation of the cadaver kidney before transplantation can be achieved either by simple cold storage or continuous hypothermic pulsatile perfusion. With cold storage the period of preservation usually is limited to 24 hours, especially if any warm renal ischemia has occurred. Of interest is a recent report suggesting that preservation up to 40 hours may be achieved in some cases with this method.[27] All cadaver kidneys harvested in Northeastern Ohio are flushed with Collins' intracellular electrolyte solution and immediately placed on the Mox 100 pulsatile perfusion unit. Since 1969 >800 human cadaver organs have undergone pulsatile perfusion in our organ preservation laboratory. It has been suggested that perfusion preservation may cause pathologic changes that adversely affect renal allograft function.[28,29] We recently evaluated 87 consecutive 1-hour cadaver allograft biopsies and found no evidence of perfusion-related or immunologic allograft damage.[30] Although cryoprecipitated plasma has been the time-honored pulsatile preservation perfusate several reports have shown that albumin or plasma protein fraction is equally as effective.[31,32] Since cryoprecipitated plasma is cumbersome to prepare and carries the risk of hepatitis transmission or cytotoxic antibody-induced immunologic damage to the graft we are now using plasma protein fraction as the preservation perfusate in our laboratory.

In review of 90 consecutive cadaver renal transplants performed at the Cleveland Clinic a significant correlation was found between postoperative acute tubular necrosis and the period of warm renal ischemia sustained before implantation (Table 3). In contrast, the periods of cold storage, pulsatile perfusion or allograft revascularization exerted no discernible effect on the need for dialysis immediately after transplantation. Since ischemic allograft damage is predominantly a function of warm ischemia time and since renin has been implicated in the pathogenesis of acute tubular necrosis we have evaluated experimentally several drugs with anti-renin properties for the ability to prevent renal failure resulting from warm ischemia. By far the most promising of these agents has been propranolol and, in particular, its D-isomer.[33] By pre-treatment of the canine kidney with D-propranolol periods of warm renal ischemia up to 120 minutes have been tolerated safely. The protective effect of D-propranolol may as well be a function of membrane stabilizing properties similar to local anesthetic agents, such as quinidine or chlorpromazine. Since D-propranolol, unlike the racemic compound, is relatively free of β-adrenergic (cardiogenic) blocking activity there should be no untoward side effects and we are now preparing to use this protective agent in our clinical transplant program.

TRANSPLANT OPERATION

There has been little change in the standard surgical technique for renal transplantation and ureteroneocystostomy remains the method of choice for management of the ureter.[34] In small pediatric recipients or in patients with an intestinal conduit a transabdominal incision is used and the graft is placed retrocecally with anastomoses of the renal vessels to the aorta and vena cava. In multiple artery renal transplants, when a Carrel aortic patch is not available, extracorporeal donor arterial repair under surface hypothermia has proved most effective.[35] The 3 basic techniques to perform such repairs are 1) the conjoined arterial anastomosis, 2) end-to-side reimplantation of a small renal artery into a larger one and 3)

TABLE 3. Comparison of Kidney Graft Ischemia Times in Dialyzed *versus* Non-Dialyzed Cadaver Recipients

Ischemia Times	Dialyzed Patients (48)	Non-Dialyzed Patients (42)
	Hrs.	Hrs.
Warm ischemia	0.26 ± 0.04*	0.12 ± 0.02†
Cold storage	2.27 ± 0.15	2.50 ± 0.36
Perfusion time	17.03 ± 1.29	18.07 ± 1.06
Revascularization time	0.78 ± 0.04	0.77 ± 0.07
Total time	20.34 ± 1.28	21.46 ± 0.95

* Significantly different (p < 0.01).
† Values represent mean ± S.E.M.

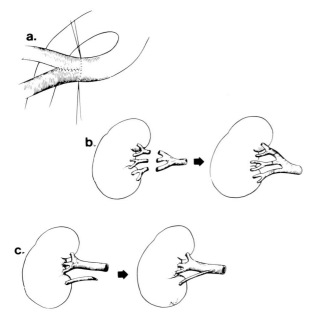

Fig. 1. Three methods of extracorporeal donor arterial repair for multiple artery transplants. (a) Conjoined anastomosis of 2 equal caliber arteries with end-to-end anastomosis to recipient hypogastric artery. (b) Repair with branched autogenous vascular graft. (c) End-to-side reimplantation of small renal artery into larger one.

use of a branched autogenous vascular graft to fashion a single renal artery (Fig. 1). These techniques are uncomplicated and widely applicable. Since the kidney is kept cold throughout the extracorporeal repair transplantation is performed as with a single renal artery with no increase in revascularization time. Kidneys with double ureters also can be transplanted successfully (Fig. 2).

Surgical complications occur in >10 percent of transplant recipients and rarely are the cause for graft loss today. From March 1977 to March 1979, 115 renal transplants were performed at the Cleveland Clinic (60 cadaver and 55 living related), including 23 kidneys transplanted with multiple arteries. During this period there were no vascular complications and 3 (2.6 percent) urologic complications occurred, 2 ureteral fistulas and 1 bladder fistula. In this recent series a single graft was lost because of a technical problem and this occurred in 1 patient who had a ureteral fistula.

Serial isotope renography with ^{131}I-orthoiodohippurate is obtained in all transplant recipients postoperatively and can reliably differentiate acute tubular necrosis from rejection.[36] This has proved to be an accurate, noninvasive technique to evaluate early post-transplant dysfunction and has reduced significantly the indications for open renal biopsy or transplant angiography. In patients with anuria after transplantation, when scintiscanning

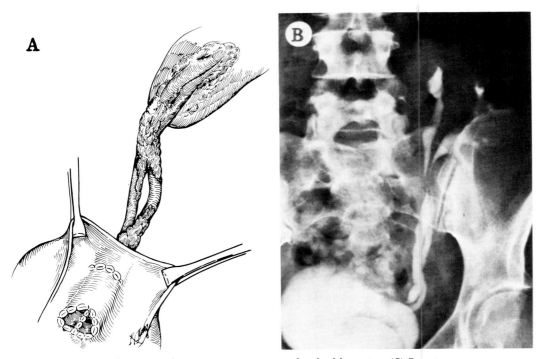

Fig. 2. (A) Method of conjoined ureteroneocystostomy for double ureter. (B) Excretory urogram after successful transplantation of cadaver kidney with 2 ureters.

shows minimal uptake of isotope by the allograft, angiography is obtained to rule out hyperacute rejection or vascular occlusion. In transplant recipients with acute rejection unresponsive to high dose steroid therapy, angiography and renal biopsy are useful complimentary studies in determining whether further attempts to salvage the allograft are warranted.[37]

RESULTS

Although graft survival rates after renal transplantation have not altered appreciably in the last decade, patient survival rates have improved steadily. This has resulted from fewer technical complications postoperatively, better management of those complications that do occur and, most importantly, a less aggressive approach to immunosuppressive therapy. During the last 2 years (1976 and 1977) 1-year patient survival rates at the Cleveland Clinic after living related and cadaver transplantation have been 93 and 89 percent, respectively. Similar results have been reported by other transplant centers[38,39] and, hence, survival of patients with end stage renal failure after transplantation is now comparable to that obtained with chronic dialysis.[40,41]

We continue to give preference to well matched living related donors because of the higher rate of success and because of a continuing shortage of cadaver organs. During the last 2 years (1976 and 1977) our 1-year allograft survival rates have been 64 percent with cadaver donors and 72 percent with live donors (HLA-identical and non-identical combined). Based on our results with the mixed lymphocyte culture in living related transplantation[17] we are now accepting as live donors only 2 haplotype matches or 1 haplotype matched donors with a 2-way mixed lymphocyte culture stimulation index < 10. We anticipate improved graft survival rates in our live donor recipient population with implementation of this policy.

TABLE 4. Results of 65 Transplants at Cleveland Clinic (1963 to February 1978)

Transplant No.	No. Kidneys	Donor Source	1-Yr Graft Survival No. (%)
Second (1963–1969)	30	Cadaver, 28 Live donor, 2	13 (43)
Second (1970–1978)	29	Cadaver, 28 Live donor, 1	15 (52)
Third	6	Cadaver, 6	3 (50)

Patients who receive a graft from an HLA-identical live donor comprise an immunologically privileged group with a greater likelihood of immediate and long-term function. From 1969 to 1977, 38 HLA-identical living related transplants were performed at this institution with 1 and 5-year graft survival rates of 94 and 78 percent, respectively. A significantly reduced incidence of steroid-related complications also was observed in this group, since anti-rejection therapy was less often necessary.

Opelz and Terasaki recently reported that transplant patients who lose a primary allograft to rejection can be re-transplanted with an almost equivalent chance of success.[42] From February 1963 to February 1978, 65 re-transplants were performed at the Cleveland Clinic (Table 4) and our data are in agreement. In our recent series of second transplants (1970 to 1978), most of which were cadavergrafts, 1-year graft survival is 52 percent.

Most patients with long-term functioning allografts achieve a high degree of rehabilitation approaching their pre-renal failure status. In comparison with chronic dialysis renal transplantation also is a more cost-effective method of management for patients with end stage renal disease.[43] Although advances in tissue typing and immunosuppression are needed to achieve better graft survival rates, renal transplantation remains an effective form of therapy that can be applied safely to the majority of patients with end stage renal disease.

REFERENCES

1. Najarian JS, Sutherland DE, Simmons RL, Howard RJ, Kjellstrand CM, Mauer SM, Kennedy W, Ramsey R, Barbosa J, Goetz FC: Kidney transplantation for the uremic diabetic patient. Surg Gynec & Obst 144:682, 1977

2. Braun WE, Phillips D, Vidt DG, Novick AC, Nakamoto S, Pohl MC: Coronary angiography in end-stage renal disease. Ann Intern Med in press 1979

3. Spanos PK, Simmons RL, Rattazzi LC, Kjellstrand CM, Buselmeier, TJ, Najarian JS: Peptic ulcer disease in the transplant recipient. Arch Surg 109:193, 1974

4. Jones RH, Rudge CJ, Bewick M, Parsons V, Weston MJ: Cimetidine: prophylaxis against upper gastrointestinal haemorrhage after renal transplantation. Brit Med J 1:398, 1978

5. Advisory Committee to the Renal Transplant Registry: The 13th Report of the Human Renal Transplant Registry. Transplant Proc 9:9, 1977

6. Banowsky, LH: The role of adjuvant operations in renal transplantation. Urol Clin N Amer 3:527, 1976

7. Corry RJ, Freeman RM, Thompson JS: Influence of blood transfusion and bilateral nephrectomy on survival of renal transplants. Dialy Transpl 6:50, 1977

8. Novick AC, Braun WE, Nakamoto S, Magnusson, M: Reduced morbidity with posterior surgical approach for pretransplant bilateral nephrectomy. In press, 1979

9. Novick AC, Ruiz R, Braun WE, Montague DK, Stewart BH: Transperitoneal live-donor nephrectomy. J Urol in press, 1979

10. Salvatierra O Jr., Olcott C IV, Cochrum KC, Amend WJ Jr, Feduska NJ: Procurement of cadaver kidneys, Urol Clin N Am 3:457, 1976

11. Dauset J, Hors J, Busson M, Festenstein H, Oliver RTD, Paris AMI, Sachs JA: Serologically defined HL-A antigens and long-term survival of cadaver kidney transplants. A joint analysis of 918 cases performed by France-Transplant and the London Transplant Group. New Engl J Med 290:979, 1974

12. Sachs JA, Festenstein H, Tuffnell VA, Paris AMI: Collaborative scheme for tissue typing and matching in renal transplantation. IX. Effect of HLA-A, -B, and -D locus matching, pretransplant transfusion, and other factors on 612 cadaver renal grafts. Transplant Proc. 9:483, 1977

13. Simmons RL, Thompson EJ, Yunis EJ, Noreen H, Kjellstrand CM, Fryd DS, Condie RM, Mauer SM, Buselmeier TJ, Najarian JS: 115 patients with first cadaver kidney transplants followed two to seven and a half years: a multifactorial analysis. Amer J Med 62:234, 1977

14. Ting, A, Morris PJ: Matching for B-cell antigens of the HLA-DR series in cadaver renal transplantation. Lancet 1:575, 1978

15. Persijn GG, van Leeuwen A, Hoogebooon J, Gabb BW, Nagtegaal A, van Rood JJ: Matching for HLA antigens of A, B, and DR loci in renal transplantation by eurotransplant. Lancet 1:278, 1978

16. Terasaki PL, Ayoub G, Opelz G, Park MS: HLA-DR matched transplants. Dialy Transpl 7:1152, 1978.

17. Braun WE, Jayavant J, Dejelo C, Zachary A, Novick AC: MLC, PHA, HLA and Drw: studies in renal allografting. Transplant Proc in press, 1979

18. Cochrum KC, Salvatierra O, Belzer FO: Correlation between MLC stimulation and graft survival in living related and cadaver transplants. Ann Surg 180:617, 1974

19. Ferguson RM, Simmons RL, Noreen H, Yunio EJ, Najarian JS: Host presensitization and renal allograft success at a single institution: first transplants. Surgery 81:139, 1977

20. Salvatierra O Jr, Perkins HA, Amend W Jr, Feduska N, Duca RN, Potter DE, Cochrum KC: The influence of presensitization on graft survival rate. Surgery 81:146, 1977

21. Opelz G, Sengar DPS, Mickey MR, Terasaki PI: Effect of blood transfusions on subsequent kidney transplants. Transplant Proc 5:253, 1973

22. Guttman RD, Morehouse DD, Meakins JL, Klassen J, Knaack J, Beaudoin JG: Donor pretreatment in an unselected series of cadaver renal allografts. Kidney Int Suppl 8 13:99, 1978

23. Zincke H, Woods JE: Donor pretreatment in cadaver renal transplantation. Surg Gynec & Obst 145:183, 1977

24. Jeffrey JR, Downs A, Grahame JW, Lye C, Ramsey E, Thomson AE: A randomized prospective study of cadaver donor pretreatment in renal transplantation. Transplantation, 25:287, 1978

25. Braun WE, Nakervis A, Banowsky LH, Protiva D, Biekert E, McHenry MC: A prospective study of cytomegalovirus infections in 78 renal allograft recipients. Proc Clin Dial Transpl Forum 1:8, 1976

26. Najarian JS, Simmons RL, Condie RM, Thompson EJ, Fryd DS, Howard RJ, Matas AJ, Sutherland DER, Ferguson RM, Schmidtke JR: Seven years' experience with antilymphoblast globulin for renal transplantation from cadaver donors. Ann Surg 184:352, 1976

27. Barry JM, Metcalfe JB, Farnsworth MA, Bennett WM, Hodges CV: Comparison of intracellular flushing and cold storage to machine perfusion for human kidney preservation. J Urol in press, 1979

28. Hill GS, Light JA, Perloff LJ: Perfusion-related injury in renal transplantation. Surgery 79:440, 1976

29. Spector D, Limas C, Frost JL, Zachary JB, Sterioff S, Williams GM, Rolley RT, Sadler JH: Perfusion nephropathy in human transplants. New Engl J Med 295:1217, 1976

30. Novick AC, Braun WE: Unpublished data

31. Mendez-Picon G, Belle C, Pierce JC, Thomas F, Murai M, Wolf J, Lee HM: Use of plasma protein fraction in preservation of cadaveric kidneys. Surgery 79:364, 1976

32. Feduska NJ, Collins GM, Amend WJ, Vincenti F, Duca RM, Stieper, KW, Mitchell JW, Cochrum, KC, Salvatierra O: Comparative study of albumin solution and cryoprecipitated plasma for renal preservation: a preliminary report Transplant Proc 11:472, 1979

33. Stowe NT, Emma J, Magnusson M, Loening S, Yarimizu S, Ocon J, Khairallah P, Straffon R: Protective effect of propranolol in the treatment of ischemically damaged canine kidneys prior to transplantation. Surgery 84:265, 1978

34. Banowsky, LH: Renal transplantation. In: Operative Urology. Edited by B.H. Stewart. Baltimore: The Williams & Wilkins Co. Chap 14, pp 215–246, 1975

35. Novick AC, Magnusson M, Braun WE: Multiple-artery renal transplantation: emphasis on extracorporeal methods of donor arterial reconstruction, J Urol in press, 1979

36. Salvatierra O Jr, Powell MR, Price DC, Kountz SL, Belzer FO: The advantages of ^{131}I-orthoiodohippurate scintiphotography in the management of patients after renal transplantation. Ann Surg 180:336, 1974

37. Hamway S, Novick AC, Braun WE, Levin H, Banowsky L, Alfidi R, Magnusson M: Impaired renal allograft function: a comparative study with angiography and histopathology. J Urol 122:292, 1979

38. Tilney NL, Strom TB, Vineyard GC,. Merrill JP: Factors contributing to the declining mortality rate in renal transplantation. New Engl J Med 299:1321, 1978

39. Salvatierra O Jr, Potter D. Cochrum KC, Amend WJC, Duca R, Sachs BL, Johnson RWJ, Belzer FO: Improved patient survival in renal transplantation. Surgery, 79:166, 1976

40. Burton BT, Kruegger KK and Bryan FA: National registry of long-term dialysis patients. JAMA 218:718, 1971

41. Popowniak KL, Nakamoto S, Magnusson MO: Home dialysis: eight years experience. Cleveland Clin Quart 42:225 1975.

42. Opelz G, Terasaki PI. Absence of immunization effect in human-kidney retransplantation. New Engl J Med 299:369, 1978

43. Salvatierra O, Jr., Feduska N, Vincenti F, Duca R, Potter D, Nolan J, Cochrum KC, Amend WJC: Analysis of coists and outcomes of renal transplantation at one center. Its implications. JAMA 241:1469, 1979

Commentary:
Renal Transplantation in Adults

Martin Schiff, Jr., and Robert M. Weiss

The vast majority of patients who develop end-stage renal disease will be initially stabilized and maintained by chronic hemodialysis. Although some individuals adapt well to this treatment modality on a long-term basis, many develop a plethora of problems, both physiologic and emotional, that are difficult or impossible to manage. For these patients, chronic dialysis is merely the first step in their treatment program, and only successful renal transplantation offers a reasonable hope for return to a normal life. Although the success rate of a functioning graft has not changed dramatically over the past decade, refinements and modifications in the management of patients with kidney transplants, together with a better appreciation of the risks of immunosuppression, have succeeded in markedly diminishing the danger of dying after renal transplantation. It is now possible to reduce the mortality within the first year after transplantation to below 5%, a figure that is less than the 1-year mortality for chronic hemodialysis.[1,2]

The frequency with which preliminary bilateral nephrectomy has been performed in prospective renal transplant recipients has markedly decreased over the past decade, largely because of the development of newer pharmacologic agents for the treatment of renin-dependent hypertension. Perhaps this procedure should be more strongly considered in a greater number of patients with suboptimum control of their hypertension while on dialysis, since, especially with small kidneys, it is now performed with minimal morbidity through bilateral posterior lumbotomy incisions.[3] After transplantation and the administration of high doses of steroids, with their attendant propensity for resultant salt and water retention, many such patients with borderline blood pressure control before surgery become extremely difficult management problems. Furthermore, the previously compelling reason for attempting to spare patients from the anephric state, namely, the requirement for more frequent blood transfusions, has now been well shown to be advantageous rather than deleterious to the ultimate fate of the graft.[4] Many transplant centers, including our own, have, in fact, recommended intentional repetitive transfusion of prospective recipients of cadaveric kidneys in order to maximize their likelihood of a favorable outcome after transplantation.[5]

Although the need for cadaveric donors remains acute, ever more stringent criteria are being made on their suitability and on the circumstances under which cadaveric donor nephrectomy is performed. Removal of kidneys after cardiac arrest is no longer performed in most instances, since acceptance of the concept of brain death has become commonplace. The removal of kidneys from "heart-beating cadavers," performed in the operating room under nearly normal physiologic circumstances, should minimize the possibility of anatomic or physiologic damage to the kidneys and any subsequent impediment to their acceptance by transplant surgeons not directly involved with their removal. It is somewhat dismaying to note, however, that in our own experience, approximately 40% of the cadaveric kidneys not used are discarded, not because of any inherent problem with either the kidney or its donor, but simply because no suitable recipient could be identified during its period of *ex vivo* viability.

To extend this period of *ex vivo* viability beyond 24 hours, the use of continuous hypothermic pulsatile perfusion, with one of a number of possible perfusates, is required. However, of potential concern are structural changes within the glomerular capillary loops, consisting primarily of fibrin deposition, which have been reported after some instances of hypothermic pulsatile perfusion. The actual pathogenesis of the lesion remains unclear, and the real significance of the morphologic changes on the ultimate fate of the graft is difficult to assess because of the wide variety of additional variables present. Future studies, employing serial renal biopsies obtained at the time

of donor nephrectomy, during and following pulsatile perfusion, and after revascularization may help to clarify the situation.

The use of living–related donors for patients awaiting a kidney transplant has continued at a relatively steady rate in the United States, accounting for approximately 25% to 35% of transplants, although European and Australian centers have decried their use on ethical and moral grounds. Their unquestioned higher success rate, however, remains a persuasive argument for those 15% to 20% of prospective recipients who have a suitable parent or sibling willing and able to serve as a donor. This option is especially relevant for children with end-stage renal disease, in whom prompt transplantation from a well-matched donor minimizes problems with physical, emotional, and sexual development, which are commonplace with chronic dialysis. Transplantation from living–related donors also permits a more rapid reduction in the dosage of postoperative steroids, which have growth-retarding properties.

A sibling with complete HLA identity and nonstimulation on mixed lymphocyte culture is the ideal donor, short of an identical twin. One-haplotype-match living related donors can now also be used, with almost as high a success rate, provided the prospective recipient is pretreated with donor-specific transfusions and does not become sensitized in the process.[6]

The authors' expertise in renovascular surgery is well known and further shown by the absence of any vascular complications in this latest series of patients, despite a 20% incidence of kidneys with multiple renal arteries. With a single-donor renal artery and vein, an end-to-end anastomosis of the renal artery to the internal iliac artery and an end-to-side anastomosis of the renal vein to the external iliac vein is preferable. With multiple renal arteries, a Carrel aortic patch or various methods of combining the renal arteries with subsequent anastomosis into the internal iliac artery may be used. We usually prefer to avoid, wherever possible, an end-to-side anastomosis into the external iliac artery because of the potential risk of a major vascular complication in those patients who subsequently undergo removal of the renal allograft. Additionally, however, one must consider the potential risk of sexual impotence developing when a male receives a second renal transplant into the internal iliac artery when the initial transplant also involved an end-to-end anastomosis to the contralateral internal iliac artery.[7]

Several points on the reconstruction of the urinary collecting system are worth emphasizing, since urologic complications after transplantation remain a serious and potentially lethal problem.[8] Despite sporadic enthusiasm for alternatives and numerous minor modifications, most surgeons favor a primary ureterovesical anastomosis using a portion of the allograft ureter. The creation of an adequate submucosal tunnel is important, not so much as an antireflux mechanism, but as a method of preventing urinary extravasation from the ureterovesical junction. The caliber of the tunnel should be generous enough to guard against ureteral obstruction in the postoperative period when reactive hyperemia and edema may occur in the allograft ureter. A small relaxing incision in the vesical adventitial layer adjacent to the entering ureter may help to prevent undue tension from developing at this critical junction. The new ureteral orifice should be placed well down on the trigone, adjacent to, but without damage to, the recipient's own ipsilateral ureter. This maximizes the possibility of successful ureteral catheterization, should it subsequently prove necessary. It also serves to prevent progressive ureteral obstruction at late onset, which may result from high ureteral reimplantation without bladder fixation.

The long-standing uremia and anemia common to transplant recipients, their immunosuppressed status, and the lack of adequate vesical drainage postoperatively are factors that combine to leave little margin for surgical error. The ureterovesical anastomosis must be performed with meticulous attention to every detail in order to avoid disastrous postoperative complications.

REFERENCES

1. Tilney NL, Strom TB, Vineyard GC, Merrill MD: Factors contributing to the declining mortality rate in renal transplantation. N Engl J Med 299:1321, 1978
2. Bonney S, Finkelstein FO, Lytton B, Schiff M, Steele TE: Treatment of end-stage renal failure in a defined geographic area. Arch Intern Med 138:1510, 1978
3. Freed SZ: The present status of bilateral nephrectomy in transplant recipients. J Urol 115:8, 1976
4. Opelz G, Terasaki PI: Improvement of kidney graft survival with increased numbers of blood transfusions. N Engl J Med 299, 799, 1978

5. Oei LS, Thompson JS, Corry RJ: Effect of blood transfusions on survival of cadaver and living-related renal transplants. Transplantation 28:482, 1979
6. Salvatierra O, Vincenti F, Ameno W et al: Deliberate donor specific blood transfusions prior to living related renal transplantation. Ann Surg 192:543, 1980
7. Gittes RF, Waters WG: Sexual impotence: The overlooked complication of a second renal transplant. J Urol 121:719, 1979
8. Schiff M, McGuire EJ, Weiss RM, Lytton B: Management of urinary fistulas after renal transplantation. J Urol 115:251, 1976

ANNOTATED BIBLIOGRAPHY

Opelz G, Terasaki PI: Improvement of kidney graft survival with increased numbers of blood transfusions. N Engl J Med 299:799, 1978

In a study of 1360 cadaveric renal transplants from a group of transplant centers, graft survival appeared to be improved by pretransplant blood transfusions. The 1-year graft survival for recipients receiving more than 20 transfusions was 71 ± 5%, compared to a 1-year graft survival of 42 ± 2% for those receiving no transfusions. At 4 years the respective rate of graft survivals was 65 ± 5% and 30 ± 3%. These differences were statistically significant. Frozen blood was less effective than nonfrozen blood in achieving this beneficial effect, and a single pretransplant transfusion or transfusion during the transplant operation did not affect graft survival statistics.

Tilney NL, Strom TB, Vineyard GC, Merrill JP: Factors contributing to the declining mortality rate in renal transplantation. N Engl J Med 299:1321, 1978

The authors note a decrease in mortality after renal transplantation. The most dramatic decrease, in the mortality from sepsis, was related to the decrease in overall immunosuppression as well as to the routine use of antibiotics during all surgical procedures. They have noted improvement related to the use of ultrasonography in diagnosing perinephric collections and a lower complication rate with percutaneous needle biopsy rather than with open renal biopsy. Two thirds of failed allografts were left *in situ* without the need for nephrectomy.

Gittes RF, Waters WG: Sexual impotence: The overlooked complication of a second renal transplant. J Urol 121:719, 1979

In a group of 20 men who received two kidney transplants, the incidence of impotence after the second renal transplant was 65%, compared to a 10% incidence after the first transplant. The authors propose that sequential ligation of both internal iliac arteries could explain the high incidence of impotence in patients receiving two renal transplants.

Weil R III, Schröter, GPJ, West JC, Starzl TE: A 14-year experience with kidney transplantation. World J Surg 1:145, 1977

In a review of 668 kidney transplants done in 556 consecutive patients from 1962 to 1975, the authors noted that patient survival after unrelated donor grafts approximated that after related donor transplants. This improvement in the survival statistics with regard to cadaveric grafts was related to the inception of a policy that excessive immunosuppression, in an attempt to prolong cadaveric graft survival, was an unreasonable risk to life. Retransplantation has provided a functioning graft in the majority of patients, and the results of pediatric transplantation were similar to that in adults.

Salvatierra O Jr, Potter D, Cochrum KC, Amend WJC, Duca R, Sachs BL, Johnson RWJ, Belzer FO: Improved patient survival in renal transplantation. Surgery 79:166, 1976

Survival was improved in those patients who did not have prolonged high-dose immunosuppression. Immunosuppression was not increased after the first rejection if renal function did not return to near-normal levels and was not increased for chronic rejection after the second rejection. Furthermore, immunosuppression was reduced with infection and when the white blood cell (WBC) count was 2,000 or less. With this policy, deaths from infection have decreased. Graft survival was not jeopardized by low-dose immunosuppression, and patient survival was significantly improved.

Schiff M Jr, McGuire EJ, Weiss RM, Lytton B: Management of urinary fistulas after renal transplantation. J Urol 115:251, 1976

Urinary fistulas developed in 13 of 134 patients (9.7%) after renal transplantation. Bladder fistulas originating from the anterior suture line developed in six patients and were satisfactorily treated with urethral or paravesical drainage. Although living-related donors accounted for only 23% of the total transplants, 4 of the 6 patients with vesical fistulas had received a living-donor transplant and had experienced an immediate diuresis. Four patients developed ureteral fistulas; wherever possible, these were best treated by surgical repair using the recipient's own ureter. Caliceal fistulas developed in three patients; they are most frequently related to segmental renal infarction resulting from failure to recognize or inability to reanastomose an accessory renal artery. These were successfully treated with nephrostomy drainage.

13

BILATERAL NEPHRECTOMY IN TRANSPLANT RECIPIENTS

Selwyn Z. Freed, M.D.

Chief, Division of Urology, Montefiore Hospital; Director of Urology, North Central
Bronx Hospital; Professor of Urology, Einstein College of Medicine; Urologist in
Charge, Transplant Program, Montefiore Hospital and Medical Center, Einstein
College of Medicine, Bronx, New York

Supplement to Urology / July 1977 / Volume X, Number 1

Increasing appreciation of the nonexcretory functions of the kidney challenges the old assumption that end stage kidneys are expendable. Routine pretransplant bilateral nephrectomy has therefore been superseded by selective indications. There is also better understanding of the problems in the management of anephric patients.

Survival figures with and without removal of indigenous kidneys are controversial. Several reviews of posttransplant complications in patients without prior bilateral nephrectomy suggest that routine removal of kidneys is not justified.[1-3] A comparison of 29 grafts with pretransplant bilateral nephrectomy with 55 transplants without nephrectomy indicated a better survival and fewer rejection episodes in the latter group.[4] On the other hand, a review of more than 6,500 transplants with nephrectomy to almost 7,000 patients without showed improved survival in the former. Functional survival of those patients receiving a cadaver graft, with nephrectomies, was significantly higher at all time intervals through four years for patients with glomerulonephritis, through three years with polycystic disease, and through two years for those patients with pyelonephritis and nephrosclerosis. Functional survival of those patients receiving a living donor kidney was also better in those who had pretrans-

111 East 210th Street
Bronx, New York 10467

plant nephrectomies, but statistically only those who had glomerulonephritis showed a significant difference through four years.[5] The controversy must also concern itself with the considerable morbidity and mortality which varies with the technique of the procedure. Eventually, therefore, the decision to perform bilateral nephrectomy rests with the specific indications.

INDICATIONS FOR BILATERAL NEPHRECTOMY

The clearest indication for pretransplant bilateral nephrectomy is hypertension which is not controlled by hemodialysis, maintenance of dry weight, and antihypertensive medication.[6] Removal of both kidneys will usually lower the elevated blood pressure of end stage renal disease, especially in patients whose peripheral plasma renin activity is elevated.[7] Short-term malignant hypertension of end stage renal failure is promptly reversible by bilateral nephrectomy.[8] On the other hand, mortality from the operation is highest in this group of patients[1] and hypertension persists in some. Renin activity was reported to be present in the sera of several patients for more than three years after bilateral nephrectomy.[9] Control of blood pressure in the absence of a functioning renin-angiotensin system is at the mercy of even minor volume changes.[10]

Pyelonephritis is listed in most transplant centers as the second most common indication for bilateral nephrectomy. This also requires precise justification. Ineradicable or recurrent bacterial infection of the kidneys poses a serious threat to the post-transplant immunosuppressed patient and should certainly be eliminated. However, bacterial pyelonephritis is often an elusive diagnosis, both clinically and pathologically. Many of our patients with end stage kidneys had a long clinical history of pyelonephritis, but cultures of the urine and renal tissue rarely yielded any growth. Perhaps these kidneys represent a burned-out infection. If so, does this kidney, presently sterile, represent a threat? Probably not. Nephrolithiasis, so diagnosed, also resists categorical discard. Kidneys that contain large calculi, especially of the staghorn variety, are almost all infected and should properly be removed. However, a small stone tucked away in a calyx is often present in the absence of infection. Routine nephrectomy for all such patients is not justified. The relevant issue is persistent bacteriuria.

Judgment must also be exercised in the case of vesicoureteral reflux. Massive reflux with intractable infection clearly mandates nephroureterectomy, but less blatant examples may be controversial. Wisps of reflux are usually clinically innocuous. However, true reflux, even in the absence of infection, acts essentially as a bladder diverticulum in the post-transplant state and represents a definite hazard.

Anatomic defects of the kidney and ureter should be evaluated urologically. Obstructive lesions such as strictured ureter which has caused a large hydronephrosis are ominous. However, nonobstructive conditions such as renal cysts, segmental megaureter and the like, are usually harmless and pose no post-transplant threat. Polycystic kidneys constitute a special controversy. Indications for their removal include their huge bulk which preempts the abdominal cavity, excessive hematuria, infection, and pain. Hypertension accompanying this syndrome is rarely an indication because it is usually well controlled by conservative measures. Some centers do bilateral nephrectomy routinely[11] while others favor it only if there is a history of pyelonephritis or gross hematuria.[12] It would appear logical to remove the offending kidney only, but this is usually followed shortly by the need to remove the second kidney.[13] Our view is that excision of polycystic kidneys should be avoided if possible since the operation is formidable and hematopoiesis is especially vigorous in these kidneys.

A rapidly progressive glomerulonephritis characterized by antibodies positive to glomerular basement membrane may also cause severe hemoptysis, pulmonary dysfunction, and threaten life itself. (Goodpasture's syndrome). Dramatic cessation of the pulmonary hemorrhage may be achieved by bilateral nephrectomy.[14]

However, spontaneous recovery of renal function and subsidence of pulmonary hemorrhage without nephrectomy has been observed, so forebearance for a time may be rewarded here as well.[15,16]

One of the earliest motivations of the transplant teams has been the prevention in the transplanted kidney of the original renal pathology. Does the antigen-antibody complex responsible for the demise of the old kidneys attack the new one? It must be conceded that the grafted kidney is vulnerable to the persisting immune mechanism. This is clearly demonstrated by the high incidence of recurrent glomerulonephritis in renal transplants between identical twins when no immunosuppressive drugs are used.[17] Histochemical techniques have documented the recurrence of the original glomerular lesion in renal allografts.[18]

It was hoped that bilateral nephrectomy would lower the risk of such recurrent disease, and even rapidly progressive glomerulonephritis has been so treated without recurrence.[19] However, anephric patients have persistent circulating antibasement membrane antibodies which, after transplantation, may be found on the basement membranes of the transplanted kidneys.[20] One must conclude that it is the immunosuppressive regimen that protects against the recurrence of glomerulonephritis in the grafted kidney, not the removal of the original renal pathology. Bilateral nephrectomy is not justified on this basis.

Bilateral renal malignancy, especially nephroblastoma, may be successfully treated by surgical extirpation and transplantation.[21] Nevertheless, if polarization of the tumor and the renal vessels lend themselves to at least a single partial nephrectomy, maintenance of this indigenous tissue is to be preferred.[22]

Additional uncommon situations which appear to respond to bilateral nephrectomy crop up. We have had occasion to perform binephrectomy for the relief of severe hypoproteinemia secondary to massive urinary protein loss. Control of cachexia and ascites in hemodialysis patients in this manner has been reported[23] and also the reversal of an otherwise uncontrollable hypercoagulable state.[24]

Most other popular indications for bilateral nephrectomy do not fare well when exposed to close scrutiny. Diabetic patients manifest a decrease in insulin requirement as renal failure progresses and a sharp fall in this requirement after bilateral nephrectomy, no doubt a function of metabolism of insulin by the kidney.[25] The benefit of bilateral nephrectomy, however, is countered by the sharp rise in insulin requirement after transplantation.

Even less defensible is the compulsion to gather information regarding these radiologically nonvisualized kidneys by nephrectomy. Although one series of 200 bilateral nephrectomies disclosed 5 cases of previously undiagnosed renal carcinoma, it is conceded that the over-all incidence is too small to justify the operation for this purpose.[3] It was also popular in the past to remove the native kidneys to avoid confusion regarding the source of the post-transplant urine, but there are obviously better ways to evaluate the function of the new kidney. Finally, since the overwhelming trend for disposition of the transplanted ureter is toward ureteroneocystostomy, nephrectomy merely to provide a ureter for ureteroureterostomy may be deferred until required for a secondary repair.

CLINICAL CONSEQUENCES OF BILATERAL NEPHRECTOMY

Shrinking indications and the surgical risks of bilateral nephrectomy must also take into account its clinical consequences. The kidney is the major site of erythropoietic-stimulating factor.[26] Although androgenic hormones have a beneficial hematologic effect on the anemia of uremic patients, they have no value in the anephric state.[27] They therefore require multiple transfusions which predispose to cytotoxicity and the risk of hepatitis.[28]

The management of blood pressure can be very difficult because excretion of water, sodium, and potassium as well as the patient's drinking are obviously severely limited in the absence of kidneys. Renal prostaglandins may actually function as antihypertensive hormones.[29] Also, the loss of the psychologic benefit of voiding is sometimes felt keenly.

The state of uremia predisposes to osteodystrophy whether the kidneys are present or not, but bilateral nephrectomy may precipitate an acute onset of hypocalcemia and secondary hyperparathyroidism. A true hormone, 1,25-dihydrocholecalciferol, is secreted by the kidney and is the most active form of vitamin D_3 in promoting intestinal calcium absorption and skeletal calcium mobilization.[30] Finally, in addition to excreting and secreting, the kidney also metabolizes certain substances, such as myoinositol, a toxic metabolite responsible for uremic polyneuropathy.[31]

When the issues for and against bilateral nephrectomy have been assessed in favor of the procedure, the surgeon assumes the obligation to minimize the hazards in these poor risk patients. Unfortunately, many serious complications, including pneumonia, atelectasis, retroperitoneal abscess, splenic and adrenal lacerations, prolonged ileus, peritonitis, peritoneal cutaneous fistula, and significant blood loss, bedevil an anterior abdominal approach to the kidneys,[32-34] while flank incisions yield only slightly better results.[35] Mortality is significant. However, when these end stage kidneys are removed

via simultaneous posterior incisions, the complications are far fewer (Table 1). Other advantages include the sparing of the anterior abdominal wall from scarring and infection that may delay or endanger transplantation, a reduced operating room time that rarely exceeds one hour, less blood loss (average 100 cc.), and a minimal discomfort that allows the patient to be up and about the next day.

TECHNIQUE

The technique of simultaneous posterior bilateral nephrectomy, adapted from Young's exposure of the adrenals[36] and first reported in 1962,[37] has been barely modified since its original publication.[38] The prone position is used with bolster support beneath the chest and pelvis so that the peritoneum and its contents sag anteriorly and away from the retroperitoneal structures (Fig. 1A). The patient is flexed to increase the distance between the pelvis and the ribs. The incisions are usually made simultaneously with one surgeon and one assistant on each side. Each incision is begun just above the twelfth rib about 5 cm. from the midline and extended in a gentle curve to the iliac crest 8 cm. from the midline (Fig. 1A). It is deepened through the subcutaneous tissue and lumbodorsal fascia (posterior lamella), exposing the sacrospinalis muscle. Occasionally, a portion of the latissimus dorsi muscle which takes origin from the lumbodorsal fascia intrudes into the line of exposure and must also be incised (Fig. 1B). The sacrospinalis muscle, which is not adherent to the incised overlying lumbodorsal fascia, can now be retracted medially against the spine. This is facilitated by detaching its musculofibrous attachment to the twelfth rib (Fig. 2A). The presently exposed middle lamella is now incised in the line of the incision up to the twelfth rib. At this point the operating resident is habitually cautioned to beware of the pleura which can be protected by inserting a finger beneath the middle lamella. However, we favor visual inspection

TABLE 1. Comparison of Complications and Mortlity of Anterior and Posterior Incision

| Cases Reported | Number of Patients | Complications (percent) | | Mortality |
		Anterior and Flank Incisions	Posterior Incisions	
Konnak, Hyndman, and Cerny[32]	54	42	. . .	1.8
Van Blerk and Lissoos[33]	52	42	. . .	5.1
Talley et al.[34]	60	86.7	. . .	11.7
Viner et al.[35]	100	40	. . .	4
Freed, 1976	141	. . .	3	0

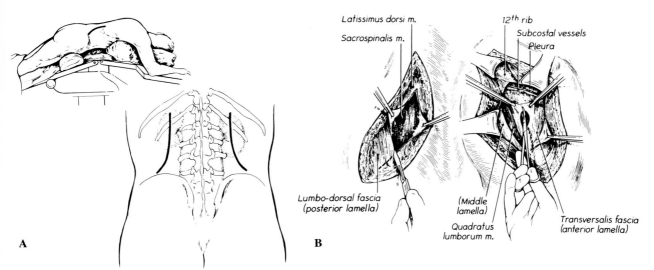

Fig. 1. (*A*) Patient lies prone on bolsters, allowing intraperitoneal contents to fall anteriorly. The incisions begin just above the twelfth rib approximately 5 cm from the midline and extend in a gentle curve to the iliac crest 8 cm from the midline. (*B*) The simultaneous bilateral dissection is relatively bloodless. The pleura should be identified to avoid perforation. (Printed with permission from J Urol 115:1, 1976.)

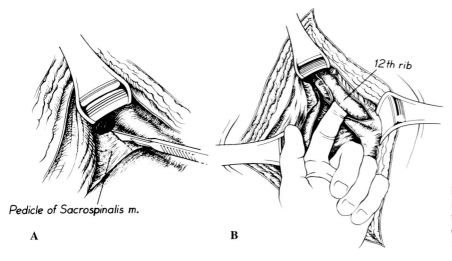

Fig. 2. (*A*) Musculofibrous attachment of sacrospinalis muscle to twelfth rib is divided. (*B*) Pleura is dissected free and retracted superiorly beneath the twelfth rib.

for its identification and preservation. The pleura can then be gently dissected free and retracted superiorly (Fig. 2B).

The twelfth rib is not removed but it is now freed from its ligamentous attachment to the vertebra so that it can be retracted superiorly and laterally (Fig. 3). Care should be taken to avoid injury to the subcostal vessels. The exposed transversalis fascia (anterior lamella) is now incised, and also the posterior layer of the renal fascia (Gerota's). The sacrospinalis and quadratus lum-

borum muscles in both wounds can be retracted medially by the use of a Burford retractor or a Finochietto retractor with the blades reversed (Fig. 4). The end stage kidneys in these patients are usually quite small, facilitating their delivery but occasionally making identification momentarily difficult. The ligated ureter is depressed inferiorly for possible subsequent anastomosis to the transplant ureter. Care should be taken to avoid injury to the spleen and liver, and also the adrenal vein on the right. These potential injuries have not occurred in our series, but on

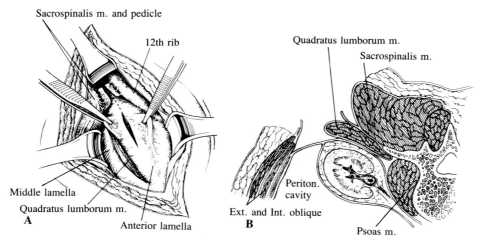

Sacrospinalis m. and pedicle
12th rib
Middle lamella
Quadratus lumborum m.
Anterior lamella
A

Quadratus lumborum m.
Sacrospinalis m.
Periton. cavity
Ext. and Int. oblique
B
Psoas m.

Fig. 3. (*A*) Anterior lamella is incised and retroperitoneum is entered. (*B*) Relevant anatomy is diagrammed in *cross-section.*

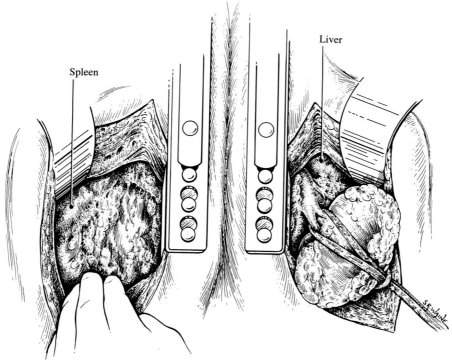

Spleen

Liver

Fig. 4. Self-retaining retractor is in place. Care should be taken to avoid injury to spleen on left and liver and adrenal vein on right. (Printed with permission from J. Urol 115;8–11, 1976.)

three occasions the pleura was inadvertently opened. In each instance it was repaired locally and a chest tube was not used. A postoperative chest x-ray film showed the lung fully expanded. The wounds are closed in layers without drainage after meticulous hemostasis, since these patients must undergo heparinization for dialysis in the postoperative period.

The operation is preceded routinely by cystoscopy and retrograde pyelography to establish the presence and position of radiographically nonvisualized kidneys. The exposure is not suitable for polycystic kidneys, which are too large, nor for the nephroureterectomy required by massive vesicoureteral reflux. In the latter situation simultaneous posterior bilateral nephrectomy is advocated nevertheless, ipsilateral ureterectomy at the time of the transplant and contralateral ureterectomy at later time if it is deemed necessary.

The time sequence to the transplantation may vary.

Some centers report a lower complication rate if the patient is sustained by a functioning homograft and advise transplantation first.[39] We favor bilateral nephrectomy first rather than in the post-transplant immunosuppressed state but have performed several at that time without event. We discourage the performance of the nephrectomies at the same time as the transplantation.

Our series of 141 posterior nephrectomies (135 bilateral and 6 unilateral) has incurred no mortality and only three minor postoperative complications—two wound hematomas and one wound abscess—all responding promptly to incision and drainage.

REFERENCES

1. Rosenberg JC, et al.: Indications for pretransplant nephrectomy. Arch Surg 107:233, 1973

2. Mitchell TS, Halasz NA, and Gittes RF: Renal transplantation: selective preliminary bilateral nephrectomy. J Urol 109:796, 1973

3. Ball JH: et al.: Transplantation without bilateral nephrectomy. Ibid 112:706, 1974

4. Bennett WM: Cost-benefit ratio of pretransplant bilateral nephrectomy. JAMA 235:1703, 1976

5. Newsletter: American College of Surgeons/National Institutes of Health, April, 1976

6. Vertes V: Management of hypertension associated with chronic renal failure including the role of bilateral nephrectomy. Postgrad Med 52:123 1972

7. Schiff M Jr., Brown RS, and Lytton B: The role of bilateral nephrectomy in the treatment of hypertension of chronic renal failure. J Urol 109:152, 1973

8. Donohue JP, Bohnert WW, Shires DL, and Bradley KP: Bilateral nephrectomy: its role in management of the malignant hypertension of end-stage renal disease. Ibid 106:488, 1971

9. Del Greco F, and Burgess JL: Hypertension in terminal renal failure: observations pre and post bilateral nephrectomy. J Chronic Dis 26:471, 1973

10. Coleman TG, Bower JD, Langford HG, and Guyton AC: Regulation of arterial pressure in the anephric state. Circulation 42:509, 1970

11. Amamoo DG, Woods JE, and Anderson CF: Renal transplantation in end stage polycystic renal disease. J Urol 112:443, 1974

12. Mendez R, Mendez RG, Payne JE, and Berne TV: Renal transplantation in adult patients with end stage polycystic kidney disease. Urology 5:26, 1975

13. Bennett AH, Stewart W, and Lazarus JM: Bilateral nephrectomy in patients with polycystic renal disease. Surg Gynecol Obstet 137:819, 1973

14. Shires DL et al.: Pulmonary hemorrhage and glomerulonephritis. Treatment of two cases by bilateral nephrectomy and renal transplantation. Arch Surg 97:699, 1968

15. Munro JF, Geddes AM, and Lamb WL: Goodpasture's syndrome: survival after acute renal failure. Br Med J 4:95, 1967

16. Strauch BS, Charney A, Doctorouff S, and Kashgarian M: Goodpasture's syndrome with recovery after renal failure. JAMA 219:444, 1974

17. Glassock RJ et al.: Human renal isografts: a clinical and pathologic analysis. Medicine 47:411, 1968

18. Gale P, Hinglais N, and Crosnier J: Recurrence of original glomerular lesion in 3 renal allografts. Transplant Proc 3:368, 1971

19. Richardson JA, Rosenau W, Lee JC, and Hopper J, Jr: Kidney transplantation for rapidly progressive glomerulonephritis. Lancet 2:180, 1970

20. Dixon FJ, McPhaul JJ, Jr, and Lerner R: Recurrence of glomerulonephritis in the transplanted kidney. Arch Intern Med 123:554, 1969

21. deLorimier AA, Belzer FO, Kountz SL, and Kushner J: Treatment of bilateral Wilms' tumor. Am J Surg 122:275, 1971

22. Ehrlich RM, Goldman R, and Kaufman JJ: Surgery of bilateral Wilms' tumors: the role of renal transplantation. J Urol 111:277, 1974

23. Feingold LN, Gutman RA, Walsh FX, and Gunnells JC: Control of cachexia and ascites in hemodialysis patients by binephrectomy. Arch Intern Med 134:989, 1974

24. Feldman SM, Libertino JA, and Zinman L: Reversal of hypercoagulable state by bilateral nephrectomy. Urology 6:84, 1975

25. Rubenstein AH, and Spitz I: Role of the kidney in insulin metabolism and excretion. Diabetes 17:161, 1968

26. Murphy GP, Mirand EA, and Kenny GM: Renal and extrarenal erythropoietin in man. NY State J Med 69:2007, 1969

27. Fried W, Jonasson O, Lang G, and Schwartz F: The hematologic effect of androgen in uremic patients. Ann Intern Med 79:823, 1973

28. Van Ypersele de Strihou C, and Stragier A: Effect of bilateral nephrectomy on transfusion requirements of patients undergoing chronic dialysis. Lancet 2:705, 1969

29. Zins GR: Renal prostaglandins. Am J Med 58:14, 1975

30. Kodicek E: The story of vitamin D: from vitamin to hormone. Lancet: 1:325, 1974

31. Clements RS, Jr, DeJesus PV, Jr, and Winegrad AL: Raised plasmamyoinositol levels in uraemia and experimental neuropathy. Ibid 1:1137, 1973

32. Konnak JW, Hyndman CW, and Cerny JC: Bilateral nephrectomy prior to renal transplantation. J Urol 107:9, 1972

33. Van Blerk PJ, and Lissoos I: Bilateral anterior extraperitoneal nephrectomy. S Afr J Surg 10:21, 1972

34. Talley TE et al.: Bilateral nephrectomy and splenectomy in renal failure. Urology 4:378, 1974

35. Viner NA, Rawl JC, Braren V, and Rhamy RK: Bilateral nephrectomy: an analysis of 100 consecutive cases. J Urol 113:291, 1975

36. Young HH: A technique for simultaneous exposure and operation on the adrenals. Surg Gynecol Obstet 54:179, 1936

37. Goodwin WE et al.: Human renal transplantation. II. A successful case of homotransplantation of the kidney between identical twins. Calif Med 97:8, 1962

38. Freed SZ, Veith FJ, Soberman R, and Gliedman ML: Simultaneous bilateral posterior nephrectomy in transplant recipients. Surgery 68:468, 1970

39. Aronian JM et al.: Bilateral nephrectomy in chronic dialysis and renal transplant patients. Am J Surg 126:635, 1973

Commentary: Indications for Bilateral Nephrectomy

Selwyn Z. Freed

Bilateral nephrectomy in transplant recipients, a routine procedure in the first decade of renal transplantation, has become uncommon and critically selective. However, uncontrolled hypertension, chronic pyelonephritis, and bleeding polycystic kidneys are still considered to be absolute indications for bilateral nephrectomy in most transplantation centers.[1] Indications for this procedure at the adult renal transplant service of Montefiore Hospital and Medical Center continue to involve patients with unremitting hypertension despite optimum maintenance hemodialysis and those with persistent bacteriuria. I have avoided nephrectomy in most patients with polycystic renal disease because the surgery is formidable in these poorrisk candidates, but I was nevertheless compelled to do so in one instance because of intractable hemorrhage. I do not consider a history of pyelonephritis to be an indication for bilateral nephrectomy unless active infection proves ineradicable. It is now well established that although glomerulonephritic antibodies put the transplanted kidney at risk, it is not bilateral nephrectomy but immunosuppressive medication that minimizes the danger. Some controversy persists on long-term survival of transplanted kidneys with or without routine prior bilateral nephrectomy, but significant advantage has yet to be proved. Some transplant centers continue the procedure in a relatively high percentage of recipients. I advocate bilateral nephrectomy only according to specific indications.

When indicated, I am convinced of the overwhelming superiority of the posterior approach. Comparison of mortality and morbidity between anterior and posterior incisions demonstrates striking differences (see the preceding article). In addition, the anterior abdominal wall is spared for the transplantation itself. Unaccountably, some surgeons continue to use anterior abdominal incisions. In a review of the morbidity of pretransplant nephrectomy and splenectomy in patients with juvenile onset diabetes, Khan and colleagues report a mortality of 7%, sepsis in 10%, abdominal complications in 17%, and vascular complications such as stroke in 5%.[2] On the other hand, pretransplant nephrectomy, using posterior incisions, was performed on 163 patients, including 11 juvenile diabetic patients in my center; none of the diabetic patients had any significant complications from the procedure.

Posterior incisions for pretransplant bilateral nephrectomy has also demonstrated its value in pediatric patients. Dr. Selwyn Levitt and coauthors, in the pediatric renal transplant division of of Einstein–Montefiore, report its use in 13 children with only minimal morbidity.[3] They emphasize the freedom from nasogastric tube drainage, the absence of prolonged ileus in the postoperative period, minimal analgesic requirement in addition to a virgin peritoneal cavity for subsequent renal transplantation.

The surgical technique remains essentially as described in the preceding article. However, although the operation was formerly routinely preceded by cystoscopy and retrograde pyelography to establish the presence and position of radiographically nonvisualized kidneys, present modalities obviate this. Localization of the kidneys can be effectively demonstrated by ultrasonography or radionuclide imaging.

REFERENCES

1. Twelfth Report of Human Renal Transplant Registry: JAMA 233:787, 1975
2. Khan AV, Zincke H, Leary FJ: Morbidity of pre-transplant nephrectomy and splenectomy in juvenile onset diabetics. Presented at the 74th Annual Meeting of the American Urology Association, New York City, 1979

3. Levitt SB, Delph WI, Kogan SJ, Hanna MK, Paruk S, Hardy MA: The posterior approach for bilateral nephrectomies in children with end-stage renal failure. J Pediatr Surg 16(5), 1981

ANNOTATED BIBLIOGRAPHY

Kropp KA: Posterior approach to the kidney. Surg Clin North Am 51:251, 1970

The author reports that the posterior lumbar approach to the kidney represents an ideal incision when dealing with a small kidney. He advocates an extension of this approach to bilateral nephrectomy before renal transplantation. He feels the operation is much less traumatic than other approaches. No major body cavity need be entered, and postoperative discomfort is minimal.

Ward JP: Synchronous bilateral lumbotomy. Eur Urol 2:102, 1976

The author reports on 40 unilateral lumbotomies and 10 bilateral procedures—9 nephrectomies and 1 nephrolithotomy. No significant paralytic ileus was encountered, and all 10 patients were mobile on the second postoperative day and ate well on the third. The lack of muscle cutting allowed mobilization sooner. He advised that the renal pedicles not be tied simultaneously, since even light traction on one pedicle can move the vena cava. Only three minor complications were reported: temporary anesthesia about the anterior superior iliac spine in one patient, and two cases of small unilateral pleural effusions that did not require treatment.

14

RENAL TRANSPLANTATION: PREPARATION OF LIVE AND CADAVER DONORS AND TECHNIQUES OF NEPHRECTOMY

Elliot Leiter, Irwin Gelernt, Changyul Oh, Allan Kark, Lewis Burrows, Sheldon Glabman, Lenard Jacobson, and Herbert Brendler

From the Departments of Urology, Surgery and Medicine, The Mount Sinai School of Medicine, New York, New York

The Journal of Urology
Copyright © 1971 by The Williams & Wilkins Co.
Vol. 106, No. 2, August

Immunologic factors will ultimately determine the survival of a transplanted kidney. However, the initial functional capacity of the transplanted organ depends upon the harvesting of a kidney whose function has been maintained, as nearly as possible, at a normal level. Herein are described the methods we have used in evaluating potential donors (live and cadaver) from the point of view of renal function, underlying disease processes and anatomic abnormalities. These considerations, as well as techniques of nephrectomy and organ perfusion, have a major effect on the eventual functional integrity of the transplanted kidney.

Accepted for publication November 1970.
Read at annual meeting of American Medical Association, New York, New York, July 13–17, 1969.

GENERAL CONSIDERATIONS

It is generally agreed that transplantation should not be performed if the ABO blood groups of the donor and recipient are incompatible.[1] The principles of ABO compatibility are identical to those involved in blood transfusion and need not be reviewed here. However, with live donors more stringent criteria are used and every attempt is made to use pairs with identical major blood groups.

Other absolute contraindications to consideration as a donor include a history of diabetes, hypertension, renal disease or malignancy other than primary brain tumors. No donor in our series has been more than 58 years old and, generally, we would not consider any patient more than 60 years old as a suitable donor.

The eventual outcome of any organ transplantation clearly depends upon the degree of histocompatibility between donor and recipient. While present methods of leukocyte typing may not accurately delineate the degree of histocompatibility in all donor-recipient pairs, there seems little doubt that transplants performed between well-leukocyte-matched pairs generally will do better than those between patients who are poorly matched.[2] Accordingly, leukocyte typing is performed on all donors.

With live donors, typing is always performed prior to transplantation and all potential donors are matched with the recipient. Cadaver donors are likewise typed. The kidney is then transplanted to the best matched recipient.

In histocompatibility testing a major mismatch exists when the recipient lacks an antigen that is present in the donor. This donor antigen—present in the donor kidney—will elicit a recipient reaction to the graft.

If an antigen is present in the recipient which is lacking in the donor, a minor mismatch is present. While the transplanted kidney theoretically may contain cells that will react against the recipient's, practically speaking such "graft versus host" reactions have not been observed in whole organ transplants.

Leukocyte typing has been performed at the New York Blood Center against a bank of approximately 70 antisera using microagglutination and microcytotoxicity tests. The figure shows a typical report from that center. The recipient shows a common antigen (IILA-2) with all potential donors. In this example, a single minor mismatch is present for all donors. In addition, a major mismatch exists between the recipient and her father. However, the major mismatch that is present involves only a weak antigen (4b). Hence all potential donors are judged to be well matched. In addition, preformed antibodies to donor tissue are tested for in the column marked "crossmatch." A positive crossmatch contraindicates use of that particular donor.[3]

LIVING DONORS

Donor Selection. All potential living related donors are sought. At an initial interview with the entire potential donor pool, the objectives and hazards of the transplant procedure are outlined.

The potential donors submit blood specimens for ABO red cell and leukocyte antigen typing, and the best donor-recipient pair is determined. If the suitable relative is willing to be considered as a donor, thorough psychiatric, social and medical evaluations follow.

Psychiatric and social evaluations are directed towards assessing the operative familial pressures and interpersonal relationships. Since a certain risk is inherent in all operations, we have tended to avoid parental donors when the death of that donor would disrupt the remainder of the family unit—as would be the case, for example, if several small dependent children are part of the family unit.

The medical evaluation includes a careful check for hypertension, diabetes, cardiovascular disease and systemic diseases (such as lupus erythematosus, vasculitis, gout and others) that might involve the kidneys. The laboratory procedures include a complete blood count, urinalysis, blood urea nitrogen (BUN), serum creatinine and electrolytes and a 2-hour post-prandial blood sugar. In addition, a chest roentgenogram and electrocardiogram are obtained. If, after this initial assessment, no abnormalities have been detected, an excretory urogram (IVP), urine culture and colony count are obtained. If these tests are normal the potential donor is admitted to the hospital for renal angiography and creatinine clearance.

Renal angiography demonstrates the presence of multiple renal arteries, an important technical consideration. If single arteries are present bilaterally, we have tended to use the left kidney as the donor organ because of the greater length of the left renal vein. If renal artery duplication is present on one side only, the kidney with a single artery is removed. The presence of more than 2 renal arteries or major renal anomalies such as horseshoe or crossed renal ectopia has precluded the use of that particular donor. Whenever there is a discrepancy of more than 1 cm in the long axis of the 2 kidneys, the smaller kidney is removed.

Live Donor Nephrectomy. The removal of a kidney for renal transplantation differs from ordinary nephrectomy in several ways. Obviously, the procedure must be as safe as possible for the donor; but most importantly, it must produce a kidney with maximum vessel length, minimal disturbance of renal function and maximal preservation of ureteral blood supply.

The patient is instructed to force oral fluids until 8 hours prior to the operation. At that time an intravenous infusion of lactated Ringer's solution is started and adjusted to run at 150 cc per hour. One hour before the operation the rate of infusion is increased to 500 cc per hour. The patient voids before going to the operating room. No indwelling catheter is placed. Donor nephrectomy is started about 30 minutes before operation is begun on the recipient, unless the recipient is to undergo bilateral nephrectomy. In that case donor nephrectomy is begun at about the time the second nephrectomy is being performed on the recipient. Fifteen minutes before the renal vessels are clamped, 25 gm mannitol are given intravenously. At the conclusion of the operation the suprapubic area is carefully percussed. If bladder disten-

LEUKOCYTE ANTIGEN TYPING REPORT

Requested by: _____   Purpose of typing: *Kidney Transplant*

_____

_____

Donor or Recip.	NAME McCall	ABO Genotype	Leukocyte Antigens from the HL-A locus (circled antigens are mismatched to recipient)											Cross-match	Matching Grade
			HLA 1	HLA 2	HLA 3	HLA 11	HLA 5	HLA 7	HLA 8	Da4	4a	4b	6a		
Father	Robert	A/B		+		+						+		Neg	B
Mother	Elizabeth	O/P		+				+						Neg	B
Recip	Barbara	A/C		+		+		+							
Sib	Sandra	B/C		+				+						Neg	B

Remarks: $A = HL-A_{11}$ $B = HL-A_2$ $C = HL-A_{2,7}$ $D = ?$

Previous nomenclature

| LA1 | LA2 | LA3 | LA4 | Da5 | 4d / 6b/7c | 7d | | Te3 | Te7 | |

approx. correspondence with other groups

A = identical sib only   C = 1 group mismatch
B = no group mismatch   D = 2 or more group mismatches
          E = positive crossmatch

Date: 5. 1. 69   By _____

Leukocyte Laboratory
Dept. of Surgery and Genetics
The New York Blood Center
310 East 67th Street
New York, New York 10021

This report is based on results of approximately 70 antisera, using both microagglutination and microcytotoxicity tests.

tion is evident, a urethral catheter is passed, the bladder is drained and the catheter is removed before the patient leaves the operating room.

If transplantation to the recipient's right iliac fossa is planned, a left donor nephrectomy is performed. Conversely, right donor nephrectomy usually requires transplantation into the recipient's left renal fossa. Except for the differences in dissection fo the renal veins, the approach for either nephrectomy is basically similar.

Nephrectomy is performed through a standard flank incision, with subperiosteal resection of the twelfth rib. The lateral border, the upper and lower poles, as well as the anterior and posterior surfaces to within 2 cm of the hilum are freed. With gentle traction on the kidney, dissection over the renal vein is begun at least 2 to 3 cm medial to the renal hilus. All hilar fat lateral to this dissection is left undisturbed to insure maximal ureteral blood supply.

On the left side the ovarian or spermatic vein enters inferiorly, the adrenal vein enters superiorly and one or more lumbar veins usually enter posteriorly. Their junc-

tions with the renal vein are carefully identified and each vein is clamped and ligated with 4-zero silk. The right renal vein is short and receives no tributaries. It is cleanly dissected to its junction with the vena cava. The renal artery is traced as nearly as possible to its junction with the aorta. The ureter is identified at the lower pole of the kidney and gently dissected upward toward the hilum, taking great care to leave intact as much peripelvic fat and periureteral areolar tissue. This method of nephrectomy is designed to limit dissection around the renal hilum and to restrict it largely to the sites of transection.

When the recipient surgical team is ready for the donor kidney, the ureter is tied as inferiorly as possible with a 2-zero chromic catgut ligature and cut free. Vascular right angle clamps are applied first to the artery and then to the vein. The artery and vein are transected with a scalpel, leaving 3 mm for tying. The kidney is then placed directly on a separate sterile table and a 2-man team starts hypothermic perfusion.

The donor's vessels are doubly tied with 1-zero silk ligatures. Some investigators prefer suture closure of these proximal stumps. Drains are not used ordinarily. The wound is closed in layers using interrupted 2-zero silk throughout. Followup urinalysis, urine culture and creatinine clearance are obtained from the donor.

Renal Perfusion. Hypothermic perfusion is performed in the donor operating room, on a sterile table with separate instruments. As soon as the kidney is received it is immersed in cold Ringer's lactate solution (4°C). A blunt-tipped needle or plastic catheter is inserted into the open end of the renal artery and tied in place with a silk ligature. Perfusion is performed with a previously prepared cold solution containing 1,000 cc Ringer's lactate at 4°C, 10 cc 1 per cent lidocaine (xylocaine-Astra), 50 mg heparin and 12.5 gm salt-poor human albumin.

The perfusate is placed at a height of about 100 cm. Usually, 200 to 300 cc solution are necessary before the efflux from the renal vein becomes clear. While the perfusion is running, further fine dissection and trimming around the vessels and ureter are done. The area around the hilum is left undisturbed. Occasionally, a tiny vessel is noted to be leaking perfusate and it is ligated with a fine silk tie. The kidney is then covered with a sterile drape and transferred to an adjacent operating room where the recipient is waiting.

CADAVER DONORS

Donor Selection. The principles of donor selection have been outlined. Patients with malignancies (other than primary brain tumors), sepsis, hypertension, diabetes or evidence of renal disease are automatically excluded. While an elevated BUN or serum creatinine ordinarily indicates renal function impairment, certain clinical situations that produce these abnormalities do not exclude the use of these patients as cadaveric donors. Thus, for example, we have transplanted kidneys from patients with hepatorenal failure, post-perfusion cardiorenal failure and a patient with thrombocytopenic, hemorrhagic shock. In all these patients serum creatinine values ranged from 3 to 5 mg percent. In each case renal function was re-established within 7 to 10 days following transplantation. Premorbid normal chemistry studies in these patients were apparently an accurate guide to their subsequent successful use as cadaveric donors.

Ethical and Moral Considerations. Many difficult moral, ethical and legal problems have arisen as a result of cadaver organ procurement for transplantation.[4] The most critical problem has been the clinical definition of death. Other sensitive areas have included the extent of involvement of the transplant team in the ante mortem care of the organ donor and the legal problems relating to organ procurement, organ donation and permission of next of kin. Many difficulties in these areas have not been resolved. Hence, we shall outline what we have found to be a practical working solution, fully aware of the fact that future developments may necessitate changes of varying degrees.

The dying donor should be cared for by nontransplant physicians. The transplant team can proceed with certain investigations, provided that these will not interfere with the patient's ongoing medical care. Occasionally, the transplant team may suggest supportive measures but under no circumstances should these measures adversely affect the dying patient. The patient's own physician may or may not elect to follow as many or as few of these recommendations as he sees fit. Permission, in general, is obtained by the transplant team, in advance of death, after having been introduced to the next of kin by the patient's physician.

Traditionally, clinical death has been equated with circulatory arrest. Considerable discussion has centered on the redefinition of death to include irreversible death of the nervous system.[5] We have tended to follow a middle path. In most of our patients clinical death has been defined as cardiac death. However, in situations involving severe head injury or massive cerebral hemorrhage that has caused irreversible and extensive cerebral damage, we have subscribed to the view that artificial supportive means can be discontinued.[6,7]

The diagnosis of death must be made by the patient's own physician. The transplant team is notified immediately. External cardiac massage with full heparinization and artificial respiration with 100 percent oxygen via the endotracheal tube are performed on the way to the operating room.

Cadaver Nephrectomy. Swift, atraumatic removal of the kidney is essential. Both kidneys are always removed. Whenever possible, each kidney is used for a separate recipient. If only 1 recipient is available the most suitable kidney is used.

Under strict aseptic technique, a mid-epigastric transverse incision is made from one midaxillary line to the opposite midaxillary line. The left kidney is approached first by mobilizing the descending colon. The entire perirenal fat is then gently separated from the renal capsule by blunt finger dissection. The anterior and posterior surfaces are thus cleared to the aorta and vena cava. Large Kelly clamps are applied to the aorta and vena cava. The kidney is removed with a cuff of these great vessels. Since double renal arteries commonly arise from the aorta in close proximity, this cuff procedure will often avoid the need for a double arterial anastomosis. The ureter is divided close to the ureterovesical junction. Care should be taken to preserve the periureteral blood supply.

Right nephrectomy is similarly performed after mobilization of the ascending colon.

Perfusion is performed as described for live donor nephrectomy. Further careful dissection and ligation of arterial and venous tributaries are obviously necessary and accomplished during perfusion. When perfusion is complete the kidneys are placed in sterile, tied, double plastic bags and immersed in ice. When the recipient is ready the inner sterile bag is given to the recipient team. Alternatively, the kidney can be thus transported for placement on a perfusion apparatus.

RESULTS

We have performed 20 transplants with the techniques described. Fifteen patients have received kidneys from cadaveric donors while 5 patients have received kidneys from live related donors.

All 5 patients receiving kidneys from live donors had good immediate renal function. Eleven of 15 patients receiving cadaveric kidneys had immediate renal function sufficient to maintain them without post-transplant dialysis. Four patients receiving cadaveric kidneys had oliguric periods ranging from 3 to 15 days after the transplantation. These patients required between 1 and 4 hemodialysis treatments before transplant function recovered sufficiently to maintain them without dialysis.

Of the 20 patients who received transplants, 2 have had ureteroneocystostomy. In 18 patients the urinary tract has been reconstructed with a pyeloureteral anastomosis. There have been no urinary leaks or strictures in this series.

DISCUSSION

The most important factor influencing renal function in the immediate post-transplant course appears to be the warm ischemia time.[8,9] In the case of cadaver donors warm ischemia time is defined as the time from the moment of donor death to the start of renal perfusion, plus the time required to re-establish renal blood flow in the recipient. With live donors the warm ischemia time consists primarily of the anastomotic time. The period of renal perfusion at 4°C as well as the time the kidney is immersed in ice is called the cold time. While cold times may extend as long as 3 to 4 hours with subsequent immediate function, in no instance in our series did the cold time exceed 2 hours.

The warm ischemic time for cadaveric kidneys which functioned immediately varied between 28 and 79 minutes. The warm time for those patients who did not have immediate satisfactory function ranged from 68 to 129 minutes. In general, the shorter the warm time the better the function. While other investigators have suggested that warm times less than 85 minutes appeared to result in good renal function,[10] we have had several patients with warm ischemic times less than 85 minutes who have not had good renal functions in the immediate post-transplant period. This suggests that factors other than the ischemic time also influence the satisfactory resumption of function.

Primary among these other factors is the mode of death of the donor. A donor who has had a prolonged agonal phase during which renal perfusion is diminished will probably provide a kidney which will not function adequately for several days. In our donors, situations adversely affecting renal function included hypotension, vasopressor drugs, hepatorenal syndrome and prolonged extracorporeal left heart bypass.

In an attempt to minimize these adverse agonal effects we have instituted various measures designed to reduce the incidence of posttransplant tubular necrosis. We have been impressed by the efficacy of mannitol in re-establishing urine flow in oliguric terminal patients. Ethacrynic acid also has been used with mannitol in some patients as an adjunct in the prevention of oliguric renal failure. To reduce tissue oxygen consumption several donors have been made hypothermic, with rectal temperatures approximating 90°F.

Our success with urinary reconstruction is attributable, in part, to the care which is taken to preserve ureteral blood supply, with minimal dissection of peripelvic and hilar fat.

SUMMARY AND CONCLUSIONS

Eleven of 15 transplant recipients receiving kidneys from cadaveric donors had immediate renal function. Four patients had oliguric periods ranging from 3 to 15 days post-transplant and required supportive hemodialysis. All 5 patients receiving kidneys from live donors had good immediate renal function. The principles that have guided us in donor selection and management are presented.

When cadaveric donors are used, the time of death is defined as accurately as possible. Immediate nephrectomy is performed under strictly aseptic conditions. The period of warm ischemic time prior to perfusion with cold modified Ringer's lactate is thus kept to a minimum. Proper patient selection, maintenance of renal function integrity during the agonal phase and rapid kidney removal help to minimize renal tubular damage.

Problems of timing are less important when live donors are used. However, the added difficulties inherent in placing a healthy donor at risk assume greater significance. Blood and leukocyte typing will determine a donor's suitability. Adequate renal reserve and the absence of major anatomic variations are confirmed by IVP, renal function assessment, urine culture and renal angiography.

The care and management of the donor directly affect the quality of the transplanted organ and will profoundly influence its functional integrity.

REFERENCES

1. Gleason, R. E. and Murray, J. E.: Report from kidney transplant registry: analysis of variables in the function of human kidney transplants. I. Blood group compatibility and splenectomy. Transplantation 5:343, 1967

2. Lee, H. M., Hume, D. M., Vredevoc, D. L., Mickey, M. R. and Terasaki, P. I.: Serotyping for homotransplantation. IX. Evaluation of leukocyte antigen matching with the clinical course and rejection types. Transplantation 5:1040, 1967

3. Hume, D. M., Leo, J., Rolley, R. T. and Williams, G. M.: Some immunological and surgical aspects of kidney transplantation in man. Transplant Proc 1:171, 1969

4. Appel, J. Z.: Ethical and legal questions posed by recent advances in medicine. JAMA 205:513, 1968

5. Wolstenholme, G. E. W. and O'Connor, M.: Foundation Symposium: Ethics in Medical Progress, with Special Reference to Transplantation. Boston: Little, Brown and Co, p 72, 1966

6. Hamburger, J. and Crosnier, J.: Moral and ethical problems in transplantation. In: Human Transplantation. Edited by F. T. Rapaport and J. Dausset. New York: Grune & Stratton, Inc, p 43, 1968

7. Wolstenholme G. E. W. and O'Connor, M.: Foundation Symposium: Ethics in Medical Progress, with Special Reference to Transplantation. Boston: Little, Brown and Co, p 14, 1966

8. Pletka, P., Cohen, S. L., Hulme, B., Kenyon, J. R., Owen, K., Thompson, A. E., Snell, M., Mowbray, J. F., Porter, K. A., Leigh, D. A. and Peart, W. S.: Cadaveric renal transplantation. An analysis of 65 cases. Lancet 1:1, 1969

9. Straffon, R. A., Kiser, W. S., Stewart, B. H., Hewitt, C. B., Gifford, R. W., Jr. and Nakamoto, S.: Four years' clinical experience with 138 kidney transplants. J Urol 99:479, 1968

10. Mowbray, J. F., Cohen, S. L., Doak, P. B., Kenyon, J. R., Owen, K., Percival, A., Porter, K. A. and Peart, W. S.: Human cadaveric renal transplantation. Report of twenty cases. Brit Med J 2:1387, 1965

Commentary: Donor Nephrectomy in Renal Transplantation

Elliot Leiter

Although the transplantation of kidneys is limited to a relatively few medical centers, urologists at any institution may be called on to harvest such kidneys, particularly from cadaver donors. Accordingly, it is vital that all urologists be familiar with the techniques employed as well as with the principles relating to donor selection and procurement, organ preservation, and the like. Since the differences relating to live and cadaver donors are substantial, these two areas will be considered separately. It is, perhaps, superfluous to point out that in each case the result should be an organ that is harvested as swiftly and as atraumatically as possible so that it will function optimally when transplanted into the recipient.

LIVE DONOR NEPHRECTOMY

Live donors will continue to be an important source of transplantable kidneys. Not only are cadaveric sources unable to meet the demand, but, in addition, the results of transplantation from living–related donors continue to be superior to those of cadaver–donor transplantation. The importance of live donors varies from country to country. In the United States, live donors furnish almost 50% of the kidneys for transplantation, while in other countries fewer kidneys come from live donors.[1]

The kidney transplant donor obviously assumes multiple risks. Most obvious is that of nephrectomy, although there is also a small rate of complication secondary to angiography and at least some theoretic psychologic complications as well. In general, though, these risks have been minimal, and there are relatively few reported instances of death after nephrectomy.[1,2] Of course, all the complications that one can expect after major surgery have been reported, including myocardial infarction, pneumonia, urinary tract and wound infection, and prolonged ileus.[3–7] In a recent review of the experience of more than 350 donor transplant operations at Peter Bent Brigham Hospital, mortality was 0.29% and the overall complication rate was 28.6%.[8] Most of the selection process, therefore, is geared to reducing these problems to a minimum as well as to optimizing the probability of harvesting a good organ.

In the harvesting of a viable organ, the most important preoperative consideration seems to be the prevention of preoperative dehydration. All institutional protocols reviewed emphasize initiation of intravenous (IV) fluids on the evening before surgery to maintain donor hydration. Additionally, all stress the importance of maintaining a diuresis during surgery, either with mannitol or with furosemide.

Although the suggested surgical approach can consist

either of a transabdominal approach or of a flank approach subcostally (with rib resection) or supracostally, the *sine qua non* of successful live donor nephrectomy is gentle renal mobilization and careful preservation of ureteral blood supply.[3-9] More and more surgeons are advocating the intraoperative use of heparin, reversed by IV administration of protamine after the kidney is removed.

The surgical technique of kidney removal, except as noted above, differs little from that of standard nephrectomy. Often it is not necessary to leave a drain in place. Where a supracostal or 11th rib resection is employed and the pleura is entered, a chest tube has been used successfully. Postoperative care is standard.

CADAVER DONOR NEPHRECTOMY

There has been increasing use of cadaveric kidneys for renal transplantation. Human Transplant Registry reports indicate that 56% of the grafts performed in 1967 were from cadavers, while the proportion of cadaver donors had increased to 70% by 1973.[10] The method of kidney harvest obviously will have a direct effect on the quality of the organ obtained. Although many modifications of the technique are described in the preceding article, all are geared toward rapid, simple, atraumatic removal of a kidney with its ureteral blood supply intact. Since the incidence of multiple renal vessels may be as high as 20%, most modifications suggest the *en bloc* removal of both kidneys attached to the aorta and vena cava. This modification is, of course, essential in pediatric cadaver situations.[11-16] The most controversial point on cadaver kidney harvest revolves around the prenephrectomy organ perfusion some workers suggest.[15,16] Although this technique does have the advantage of minimizing warm ischemic time, it makes the harvesting technique somewhat more cumbersome and lengthy.

REFERENCES

1. Bergan JJ: Current risks to the kidney transplant donor. Transplant Proc 5:1131, 1973

2. Bennett AH, Harrison JH: Experience with living familial renal donors. Surg Gynecol Obstet 139:894, 1974

3. Smith RB III et al: Operative morbidity among 40 living kidney donors. J. Surg Res 3:199, 1972

4. Leary FJ, Deweerd JH: Living donor nephrectomy. J Urol 109:947, 1973

5. Uehling DT, Malek GH, Wear JB: Complications of donor nephrectomy. J Urol 111:745, 1974

6. McLaughlin MG: Related living donor nephrectomy. J Urol 116:304, 1976

7. Jacobs SC, McLaughlin AP III, Halasz NH, Gittes RF: Live donor nephrectomy. Urology 5:175, 1975

8. Harrison JH, Bennett AH: The familial living donor in renal transplantation. J Urol 118:166, 1977

9. Barry JM, Hodges CV: The supracostal approach for live donor nephrectomy. Arch Surg 109:448, 1974

10. The 12th Report of the Human Renal Transplant Registry: JAMA 233:787, 1975

11. Stuart FP, Hall JL, Simonian SJ: The cadaver kidney donor—selection, management, nephrectomy and short-term renal preservation. Surg Clin N Am 56:7, 1976

12. Lee HM, Sulkin M, Heime D: A standard technique for procurement of cadaver donor organs. Transplant Proc 4:583, 1972

13. Freed SZ, Veith FJ, Tellis V, Whittaker J, Gliedman ML: Improved cadaveric nephrectomy for kidney transplantation. Surg Gynecol Obstet 137:101, 1973

14. Linke CA, Linke CL, Davis RS, Fridd CW: Cadaver donor nephrectomy. Urology 6:133, 1975

15. Lou ES, Tellis VA, Veith FJ, Gliedman, ML, Freed SZ: Emergency cadaveric donor en bloc nephrectomy by in-corpora perfusion technique. Urology 7:363, 1976

16. Salvatierra O Jr, Olcott C, Cochrum KC, Amend WJ, Feduska NJ: Procurement of cadaver kidneys. Urol Clin N Am 3:457, 1976

ANNOTATED BIBLIOGRAPHY

Smith RB III, Walton K, Lewis EL, Perdue GD, Herndon EG: Operative morbidity among 40 living donors. Surg Res 3:199, 1972

An excellent review of the 5-year experience ending in February 1971 with 40 live–donor nephrectomies at the Emory University School of Medicine. The authors review the operative technique and analyze the postoperative complications that one can expect in any transplant experience. The most common complication, urinary tract infection, occurred in 25% of the donors in this series.

Uehling DT, Malek GH, Wear JB: Complications of donor nephrectomy. J Urol 111:745, 1974

This article is a similar review of the complications at the University of Wisconsin on 66 living–related donors. It is of particular historical interest, since the mortality reported was apparently the first such death following live–donor nephrectomy.

Harrison JH, Bennett AH: The familial living donor in renal transplantation. J Urol 118:166, 1977

The authors review the 20-year experience with more than 300 living donors at Peter Bent Brigham Hospital, describing the surgical technique employed, listing the complications, and analyzing the results. This article is particularly noteworthy because, as is well known, the first kidney transplant was done at this hospital on December 23, 1954. The circumstances leading to this historic first transplantation are described with masterful understatement.

Barry JN, Hodges CV: The supracostal approach for live donor nephrectomy. Arch Surg 109:448, 1974

This article is most notable for its complete description of the technique of nephrectomy and the excellent diagrams. Whether one approaches supracostally, as the authors described or not, the description of the renal dissection applies to all live–donor situations.

Salvatierra O Jr, Olcott C, Cochrum KC, Amend WJ, Feduska NJ: Procurement of cadaver kidneys. Urol Clin North Am 3:457, 1976

This is the most complete exposition I have found in the literature on the subject of cadaveric kidney donors. The authors explore such important areas as the development of donor sources, donor selection, donor procurement and its relationship to the referring hospital, pharmacologic management of the cadaver donor, cadaver donor nephrectomy, and pediatric cadaver kidneys. This is required reading for any surgeon who may be called upon to secure a kidney from a cadaveric donor.

Linke CA, Linke CL, Davis RS, Fridd CW: Cadaver donor nephrectomy. Urology 6:133, 1975

This article is primarily concerned with the technical aspects of cadaveric renal harvest. The diagrams of the method employed, a modification of Ackerman's *en bloc* procedure, are excellent and are complemented nicely by the description of the operative technique.

Stuart FT, Hill JL, Simonian SJ: The cadaver kidney donor: selection, management, nephrectomy and short term renal preservation: Surg Clin North Am 56:7, 1976

These authors review their criteria for selection of cadaver donors, their preparation of the cadaver donor, their method for determining death, their technique of donor nephrectomy by a standard technique similar to that described in the preceding article, and methods for temporary renal preservation. This is an excellent review.

Lou ES, Tellis VA, Veith FJ, Gliedman ML, Freed SZ: Emergency cadaveric donor en bloc nephrectomy by in-corpora perfusion technique. Urology 7:363, 1976

These authors describe their technique of donor nephrectomy using in-corpora perfusion, which they feel has the advantages of minimizing warm ischemic time and avoiding damage to accessory renal arteries, if present. The diagrams and description are excellent and should be read by those considering prenephrectomy *in situ* perfusion.

15

URETEROCYSTOSTOMY IN RENAL TRANSPLANTATION: COMPARISON OF ENDO- AND EXTRAVESICAL ANASTOMOSES

L. Hooghe, M.D., P. Kinnaert, M.D.,
C. C. Schulman, M.D., C. Toussaint, M.D.,
J. Van Geertruyden, M.D., and P. Vereerstraeten, M.D.

Departments of Surgery, Medicine, and Urology, Brugmann Hospital, Université
Libre de Bruxelles, Brussels, Belgium

World J Surg 1:231–235, 1977

ABSTRACT—Among 241 renal transplants with implantation of the ureter into the urinary bladder, the endovesical technique of Politano and Leadbetter (PL) was used in 108 cases and the extravesical technique of Grégoir and Lich (GrL) was used in 133. Urinary fistulas occurred in 10 patients (9.3%) with the PL technique and in only 1 patient (0.8%) with the GrL technique. The difference was highly significant ($p < 0.01$). Stenosis of the ureter developed in 3 patients (2.8%) following the PL technique and in 9 patients (6.8%) after the GrL technique, an insignificant difference ($p > 0.10$). None of the complications resulted in death or failure of transplantation. It is concluded that the extravesical technique of Grégoir and Lich is the best method of avoiding urinary leakage, which is the most dangerous urologic complication of kidney transplantation.

Supported by research projects from the Veterans Administration; by United States Public Health Service Grants AM-17260 and AM-07772; and by Grants RR-00051 and RR-00069 from the General Clinical Research Centers Program of the Division of Research Resources, National Institutes of Health.

Reprint requests: Professor Jean Van Geertruyden, Department of Surgery, Hôpital Brugmann, 4, place van Gehuchten, B-1020 Brussels, Belgium.

Some of the urologic complications of the surgical procedure of renal transplantation are life threatening. Fistulas and stenosis of the ureter often lead to loss of the graft or even to death of the patient. To avoid fistulas, most surgical teams now recommend the ureterovesical anastomosis, in which a submucosal tunnel is created in the bladder as described by Politano and Leadbetter,[1] or one of the variants.[2-4] However, even with this technique the frequency of fistulas ranges from 1 to 25%.[5-13] In the most recent literature, several authors have advocated use of the Grégoir and Lich procedure,[14,15] which avoids the complications of a cystotomy and at the same time provides an antireflux mechanism by a submucosal tunnel. We have compared the results of these two techniques with regard to the frequency of the two serious urologic complications, fistula and stenosis of the ureter.

MATERIALS AND METHODS

Between March, 1965 and December, 1975, the same surgical team performed 241 renal transplantations. Except for the reconstruction of the urinary tract, the operative procedure was the same in all cases. The ureterovesical implantation was accomplished in 108 cases using the Politano and Leadbetter technique (PL), as described by Starzl et al.[2] in 1964. In 133 cases the Grégoir and Lich technique (GrL) was used for implantation of the ureter (Fig. 1).

The Grégoir and Lich technique involves a vertical incision along the lateral margin of the bladder, 5 cm in length. The serosal and muscular layers are opened completely but the mucosa is not entered. At the end of

the dissection an outward herniation of the mucosa must be observed. At the inferior extremity of the incision, an opening of 5 mm in diameter is made into the mucosa. The ureter, cut to appropriate length, is then cradled into the incision, protruding about 0.5 to 1 cm into the bladder lumen. The ureter is secured by a U-form transfixing suture through the bladder wall. The muscular and serosal layers are then sutured over the ureter in two layers with 3–0 chromic catgut suture, thereby creating the antireflux mechanism.

Treatment before, during, and after the transplantation operation, including immunosuppression therapy (azathioprine, steroids, ALG), was the same for both groups of patients. The Foley catheter was removed 24 hours after transplantation. Table 1 compares the two groups of patients with regard to age, sex, renal disease, source of the kidney graft, and duration of graft survival. The follow-up period ranged from 14 months to 8 years for the PL technique, and from 5 months to 6 years for the GrL technique.

RESULTS

A total of 11 urinary fistulas (4.6%) and 12 ureteral stenoses (5.0%) occurred after the 241 renal transplantations (Table 2). None of these complications resulted in death of failure or transplantation. In 1 case, a patient who received a pair of baby kidneys, a renal pelvis rupture required ablation of one of the two kidneys.

Fistula. The 11 fistulas (Table 3) occurred between the 1st and the 56th day after transplantation. Ten followed the PL technique and 1 followed the GrL technique. Of the 10 leaks resulting from the PL technique, 4 were at

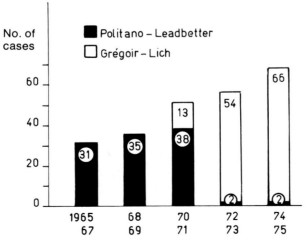

Fig. 1. Frequency by use, by year, of the two surgical techniques of ureterovesical anastomosis in 241 renal transplantations.

TABLE 1. Age, Sex, Renal Disease, Source of the Kidney Graft, and Graft Survival

| | Politano-Leadbetter | | Grégoir-Lich | |
	Cases	%	Cases	%
Total cases	108	100	133	100
Age—mean and range (years)	32 (6–53)		36 (12–64)	
Sex				
Male	68	63	82	62
Female	40	37	51	38
Renal disease*				
CGN	65	60	78	59
CIN	35	32	26	19
Others	8	8	29	22
Source of kidney				
Cadaver	86	80	128	96
Living donor	22	20	5	4
Graft survival ≥ 30 days	95	88	114	86

* CGN, chronic glomerulonephritis; CIN, chronic interstitial nephritis; others, polycystic kidneys, nephroangiosclerosis, renal hypoplasia, Alport syndrome, oxalosis, cortical necrosis, Kimmelstiel-Wilson syndrome.

TABLE 2. Frequency of Urinary Fistula and Stenosis of Ureter

| | Politano-Leadbetter | | Grégoir-Lich | | |
	Cases	%	Cases	%	p
Total cases	108	100	133	100	
Urinary fistula					
Total	10	9.3	1	0.8	<0.01
Due to the implantation technique	7	6.5	1	0.8	<0.05
Stenosis of ureter					
Total	3	2.8	9	6.8	>0.10
Due to the implantation technique	1	0.9	5	3.8	>0.10

TABLE 3. Patients with Urinary Fistulas

Patient Sex/Age	Anastomosis Technique	Time After Operation of First Symptoms (Days)	Site/Etiology*	Treatment
M 23	PL	9	UVI	Drainage
M 39	PL	2	C	Suture
F 22	PL	20	C	Suture
M 14	PL	12	NU	Reimplantation
M 44	PL	13	?	Drainage
M 31	PL	11	C	Suture
M 31	PL	15	RP	Ureteroureterostomy
M 32	PL	56	RP	Excision 1 of 2 kidneys
F 32	PL	11	C	Drainage
F 38	PL	3	?	Foley catheter
M 30	GrL	1	UVI	Reimplantation

* UVI, ureterovesical implantation; C, cystomy; NU, necrosis of terminal portion of ureter; RP, rupture of renal pelvis; ?, site unknown.

TABLE 4. Patients with Stenosis of Ureter

Patient Sex/Age	Anastomosis Technique	Time After Operation of First Symptoms (Days)	Site/Etiology*	Treatment
M 20	PL	277	IM	Reimplantation
M 31	PL	1475	PA	Ureterolysis
M 31	PL	15	PA	Pyeloureterostomy
F 14	GrL	115	IM	Reimplantation
F 21	GrL	18	G	Endoscopic resection
F 27	GrL	404	IM	Reimplantation
M 25	GrL	209	PA	Ureterolysis
M 25	GrL	688	PA	Ureterolysis
F 29	GrL	289	IM	Ureterovesicoplasty
M 28	GrL	184	PA	Ureterolysis
F 25	GrL	144	G	Endoscopic resection
M 12	GrL	19	SpC	Section spermatic cord

* IM, intramural stenosis; PA, periureteral adhesions, bands, or fibrosis; G, endovesical granuloma; SpC, compression by spermatic cord.

Of the 11 patients with fistulas, 9 were operated on or treated within 24 hours following the first symptoms. One patient showed unobtrusive signs of fistula, consisting only of edema of the vulva, which caused a 3-day postponement in diagnosis and operation. In 1 other patient, a 2-day delay in reoperation was caused by a primary diagnosis of rejection. The treatment used in each case is shown in Table 3. In all cases, the treatment was successful without loss of transplant function.

Stenosis. The 12 cases of stenosis of the ureter (Table 4) arose between the 15th day and the 48th month after transplantation. Nine occurred after the 4th month. Three were observed after the PL technique and 9 after the GrL reconstruction. Following the PL procedure 1 obstruction was located at the site of the anastomosis and 2 resulted from adhesions or periureteral fibrous reactions.

In the GrL group, 2 stenoses were caused by a granuloma at the extremity of the ureter, 3 were at the site of the anastomosis, 3 were due to adhesions and periurteral fibrosis, and in 1 case, the ureter had been passed behind the spermatic cord which compressed it. Thus, the GrL technique was responsible for 5 (3.8%) cases of stenosis, and the PL type of reconstruction caused 1 (0.9%) case. Strictures due to adhesions or fibrous reactions were most probably the consequence of hematomas or low-grade infections, and the obstruction by the spermatic cord was not specifically related to one or the other technique.

The treatment used in each case is shown in Table 4. In 10 patients, after reoperation all radiologic signs of hydronephrosis disappeared and there was no alteration of renal function. In 1 patient, periureteritis recurred and a second ureterolysis was performed 11 months later.

the cystotomy suture line, 1 was at the point of penetration of the ureter into the bladder, 1 was in the body of the ureter, 2 were in the renal pelvis, and the location of 2 was not determined because they were treated by simple drainage or indwelling bladder catherization. The fistula from the body of the ureter resulted from necrosis of the terminal portion of the ureter with a 3-mm perforation 2 cm above the vesical implantation. The fistulas from the renal pelvis resulted from necroses and rupture due to adhesions around the ureter at the ureteropelvic junction in 1 case and perhaps in the other. The single fistula resulting from the GrL technique was due to malpositioning of the ureter within the submucosal tunnel: the end of the ureter had not been drawn far enough into the vesical lumen. Thus, 7 (6.5%) of the fistulas were due to the PL technique and 1 (0.8%) to the GrL procedure. The other causes of urinary leakage cannot be attributed with certainty to either one or the other implantation technique.

This patient regained fair renal function with a serum creatinine level of 1.7 mg% 20 months after the second reoperation. In 1 patient radiologic signs of moderate hydronephrosis have persisted, without signs of worsening during the last 28 months, and renal function remains good with a serum creatinine level of 1.4 mg%.

DISCUSSION

The 2 groups of patients are not comparable because of the overlapping nature of the study. However, the same team performed all renal transplantations and the same treatment was used. Only the ureterovesical anastomosis techniques were different. Age and sex distribution and graft survival were similar in both groups. There were a few differences in primary renal disease and in graft donors, but these factors are not believed to influence the rate of urologic complications.[13,16] We used the GrL technique for the first time in 1970. During the following 18 months we had no urinary fistulas, whereupon we decided not to continue further the comparison of the GrL and PL procedures. After January, 1972, the PL technique was used in only 4 instances: 3 cases in which the bladder mucosa was accidentally opened during the muscular incision of the GrL procedure, and 1 patient who received a pair of baby kidneys. This last reason, however, is not an absolute indication for the PL technique, since 4 other transplantations have been performed with paired infant kidneys and GrL implantations without any operative difficulty or postoperative complications. The GrL procedure avoids the most frequent and most dangerous urologic complication of

kidney transplantation, namely, urinary leakage. Urinary fistula occurred in 0.8% of the cases in our GrL group. In other series, the incidence of urinary fistula has ranged from 0 to 8% with the GrL technique,[9,13,16,17] and from 1 to 25% after the PL type of reconstruction.

Ureteral obstruction resulting from the GrL technique was more frequent, but the difference compared to the PL technique was not significant. Only 3 stenoses were located at the site of the anastomosis, and another 2 resulted from granuloma formation. We have observed 3 other cases of such granulomas, 1 during investigations for hematuria (cured by transureteral coagulation) and 2 others in asymptomatic patients during routine pyelography. Some authors who perform the GrL technique do not pull the ureter into the bladder but suture its end to the vesical mucosa. We are not certain whether the transverse U-shaped suture used to anchor the ureter or the excessive endovesical ureteral length is responsible for the granuloma formation. However, since September, 1974 the anchorage has been performed by passing the suture longitudinally through the end of the ureter only one time, and the intraluminal portion of the ureter does not exceed 5 mm in length. In the last 42 transplantations performed with this modified technique, we have observed no case of granuloma formulation.

In our experience the technique described by Grégoir and Lich is the best method to avoid urinary leakage, the most dangerous urologic complication of kidney transplantation. It creates as good as antireflux mechanism as the PL procedure. It is easy to perform. It requires no large paravesical dissection or cystomy, and thereby reduces the danger of infection in immunodepressed patients.

REFERENCES

1. Politano, V.A., Leadbetter, W.F.: An operative technique for the correction of vesicoureteral reflux. J Urol 79:932, 1958
2. Starzl, T.E., Marchioro, T.L., Dickinson, T.C., Rifkind, D., Stonington, O.G., Waddell, W.R.: Technique of renal homotransplantation. Experience with 42 cases. Arch Surg 89:87, 1964
3. Anderson, E.E., Glenn, J.F., Seigler, H.F., Stickel, D.L.: Ureteral implantation in renal transplantation. Surg Gynecol Obstet 134:494, 1972
4. Kenefick, J.S., Fernando, O.N., Hopewell, J.P., Moorhead, J.F.: Ureteric implantation in renal transplantation. Br J Urol 44:328, 1972
5. Anderson, E.E., Glenn, J.F., Seigler, H.F., Stickel, D.L.: Urologic complications in renal transplantation. J Urol 107:187, 1972
6. Belzer, F.O., Kountz, S.L., Najarian, J.S., Tanagho, E.A., Hinman, F., Jr.: Prevention of urological complications after renal allotransplantations. Arch Surg 101:449, 1970
7. Dreikorn, K., Röhl, L.: Urological complications in renal transplantation. Eur Urol 1:170, 1975
8. Hricko, G.M., Birch, A.G., Bennett, A.H., Wilson, R.E.: Factors responsible for urinary fistula in the renal transplant recipient. Ann Surg 178:609, 1973
9. Konnak, J.W., Herwig, K.R., Turcotte, J.G.: External ureteroneocystostomy in renal transplantation. J Urol 108:380, 1972
10. Leary, F.J., Woods, J.E., De Weerd, J.H.: Urologic problems in renal transplantation. Arch Surg 110:1124, 1975

11. Malek, G.H., Uehling, D.T., Daouk, A.A., Kisken, W.A.: Urological complications of renal transplantation. J Urol 109:173, 1973
12. Starzl, T.E., Groth, C.G., Putnam, C.W., Penn, I, Halgrimson, C.G., Flatmark, A., Gecelter, L., Bretschneider, L., Stonington, O.G.: Urological complications in 216 human recipients of renal transplants. Ann Surg 172:1, 1970
13. Van Geertruyden, J., Alexandre, G., Derom, F., DeRoose, J., Grosjean, O., Kinnaert, P., Lejeune, G., Maquinay, C., Otte, H., Otte, J.B., Ringoir, S., Toussaint, C., Troch, R., Van Ypersele, C., Vereerstraeten, P.: Les complications urologiques de la transplantation rénale. Prévention. Traitement. Expérience de 306 cas. Minerva Chir 28:866, 1973
14. Lich, R., Jr., Howerton, L.W., Davis, L.A.: Recurrent urosepsis in children. J Urol 86:554, 1961
15. Grégoir, W.: Traitement chirurgical du reflux congénital et du mégauretère primaire. Urol Int 24:502, 1969
16. Campos Freire, G., Jr., Goes, G.M., Campos Freire, G: Extravesical ureteral implantation in kidney transplantation. Urology 3:304, 1974
17. McKinnon, K.J., Oliver, J.A., Morehouse, D.D., Taguchi, Y.: Cadaver renal transplantation: emphasis on urological aspects. J Urol 99:486, 1968

INVITED COMMENTARY

Samuel L. Kountz, M.D.

State University of New York, Downstate Medical Center, Brooklyn, New York, U.S.A.

It has been well established that urological complications may contribute greatly to the morbidity as well as the mortality of patients following kidney transplantation. The paper of Hooghe et al. describes experience in 241 renal transplants with implantation of the ureter into the bladder using two techniques, extravesical in 133 cases and endovesical in 108 cases. This experience extended over several years and the operations were done by the same operating team. The fact that no deaths or graft loss could be attributed to urological problems attests to the superior technical skill used in these operations. The investigators demonstrate that the extravesical technique of Grégoir and Lich was superior to the endovesical technique of Politano and Leadbetter. The simplicity of the extravesical technique suggests that this procedure is the best method for establishing urological drainage following kidney transplantation. It has the advantage of being much simpler to perform and it avoids the necessity of opening the bladder where a fistula could develop. Furthermore, the technique has another attraction in that only 50% of patients with cadaver transplantation have a successful transplant on the first try, so that many patients are now receiving retransplantation. This procedure is much easier to perform at retransplantation as it does not require repeated long incisions in the bladder. It requires less dissection around the bladder and can be performed by those who have minimum experience in urological techniques. Although for many years I had used the endovesical technique of Politano-Leadbetter, I have recently changed to the extravesical technique of Grégoir and Lich and find it to be much simpler. It is my impression and belief that the technique of Grégoir and Lich will become the procedure of choice in kidney transplantation.

Commentary: Advisability and Methods of Ureterocystostomy

John S. Hanson

The ultimate decision for the patient with end-stage renal failure and his attending physician is whether to continue indefinitely on some form of regular dialysis therapy or to attempt transplantation. The patient being offered a renal allograft should not be exposed to grave danger or an increased mortality risk but should expect independence from dialysis and a superior quality of life with total personal and occupational rehabilitation. In the event of graft failure, he can be returned to dialysis to await a subsequent transplantation.

Early postoperative urinary fistulas with associated inevitable sepsis carry a high mortality and graft loss, while stricture formation is delayed and less hazardous to the patient and causes impairment of renal function and possible graft loss. Either complication exposes the patient to secondary and often extremely difficult surgery. All renal transplant recipients have deficient reparative and defensive mechanisms. In the postoperative period, there are also the deleterious effects of immunosuppressive agents. Therefore, any technique used to provide urinary continuity challenges the surgeon's skill.

Vascular complications occur infrequently; therefore, all surgeons should avoid the tragedy of death or of a failed allograft by avoiding preventable technical urological complications.

I have chosen to discuss Hooghe's article, in which two established techniques are compared and discussed and in which none of the urologic complications resulted in death or transplant failure.

In 1969, Woodruff in Edinburgh and Rohl in Germany advocated the use of ureteroneocystostomy to provide urinary continuity in renal transplantation.[1] In 1971, Robson and Calne confirmed the reliability and the usefulness of the technique.[2] Within my transplant service, the Leadbetter ureterosigmoidostomy technique was adopted for ureterocystostomy in the early 1960s and has remained the standard method of urinary reconstruction.[3]

The original Lich technique, as an antireflux procedure, required opening the bladder and introducing a guide ureteral catheter.[4] Extravesical dissection freed the terminal ureter to its mucosal attachment. A proximal muscular trough was created in the natural ureteric line, and the bladder muscle and serosa were resutured over the ureter. The ureter remained intact.

The Grégoir antireflux technique also retains ureteric continuity and is conducted in similar fashion without cystotomy. The Grégoir and Lich technique, as described, employs a transfixing suture and protrusion of the terminal ureter into the bladder lumen with the attendant complications (see preceding article). I prefer to achieve precise mucosa-to-mucosa apposition of the spatulated ureter with interrupted or continuous fine chromic catgut sutures. I always employ a nonirritant ureteric splint and closed continuous bladder drainage. This technique is, to my knowledge, best illustrated in Robson's and Calne's article.[2]

It is my practice to close over the bladder muscle defect with extramucosal, nonabsorbable silk, interrupted sutures. Where possible, I suture the extravesical fascia separately with fine chromic catgut, thus providing a two-layer closure.

Adequate ureteral length with an intact blood supply to its distal end must be available. The ureter should be allowed to take a sigmoid course to its bladder insertion, thus allowing shortening to occur after revascularization without exerting tension on the anastomotic area, yet the ureter must run a vertical course to prevent kinking of the ureter on bladder filling. Therefore, the site of insertion is not at a convenient and accessible area on the bladder dome, but on the lateral bladder wall, exposed with minimal dissection and disturbance of extravesical areolar tissues.

A Grégoir–Lich-type technique excludes the need for a cystotomy incision. They report that 10 of 11 fistulas in their series were associated with the endovesical technique of Politano and Leadbetter, 4 being from the cystotomy incision. No urinary fistulas occurred in their series when they used an extravesical technique exclusively.

As reported by Hooghe and co-workers, distal ureter strictures occur more frequently with the extravesical approach. In the absence of excessive perinephric fibrosis from previous hematoma, urine leak, or sepsis, extravesical reimplantation at a new site is feasible in the majority of patients. Where ureteric sloughing occurs or an adequate length of donor ureter is not available, a pyeloureterostomy can readily be performed with the ipsilateral recipient ureter. One can do this procedure as a primary procedure or after an initial period of kidney and wound drainage if perinephric or wound sepsis is present.

Ipsilateral recipient nephrectomy before transplantation or at the time of surgeryis not required with a primary or secondary pyeloureterostomy.

It has been my practice to ligate the recipient ureter with silk well above the iliac vessels. One wound fistula has resulted 2 years after operation, requiring an ipsilateral nephrectomy of a hydronephrotic infected kidney.

REFERENCES

1. Woodruff MR, Nolan B, Robson JS, MacDonald MK: Renal transplantation in man: Experience in 35 cases. Lancet 1:6, 1969
2. Robson AJ, Calne RY: Complications of urinary drainage following renal transplantation. Br J Urol 43:586, 1971
3. Leadbetter GW Jr, Monaco AP, Russell PS: A technique for reconstruction of the urinary tract in renal transplantation. Surg Gynecol Obstet 123:839, 1966
4. Lich R Jr, Howerton LW, Davis LA: Recurrent urosepsis in children. J Urol 86:554, 1961

ANNOTATED BIBLIOGRAPHY

Lich, R Jr, Howerton LW, Davis LA: J Urol 86:554, 1961

This article describes the Lich antireflux technique.

Woodruff, MF, Nolan B, Robson JS, MacDonald MK: Lancet 1:6, 1969, and Robson AJ, Calne RY: Br J Urol 43:587, 1971

These two articles give excellent descriptive and illustrated accounts of the procedure of ureteroneocystostomy.

Leadbetter GW Jr, Mandea AP, Russell PS: Surg Gynecol Obstet 123:839, 1966, and Greenberg SH, Wein AJ, Perloff LJ, Barker CF: J Urol 118:17, 1977

Both these articles advocate the use of ureteropyelostomy as the primary method of urinary reconstruction after transplantation, but Greenberg admits that ureteroneocystostomy remains the preferred method in most transplant centers. He wisely recommends that the technique of ureteropyelostomy be familiar to all surgeons for use in patients with major urologic complications after ureteroneocystostomy. Indeed, the surgeon may be required to perform ureteropyelostomy as a primary procedure where the ipsilateral ureter is not available because of previous pathology.

Salvatierra O Jr, Olcott C IV, Amend WJ Jr, Cochrum KC, Feduska NJ: J Urol 117:421, 1977

This article stresses once again the importance of preserving ureteral vascularity. The removal of a large conical mass of hilar tissue en bloc with the kidney and the preservation of lower polar vessels must be the surest method of maintaining ureteric vascular supply. Ideally, a member of the transplant team should be available to perform all donor nephrectomies. The authors recommend an individualized approach to the patient who has an urinary fistula or obstruction and confirm that with early diagnosis and surgical exploration, good kidney salvage and patient survival can be attained. They recommend the judicious use of ^{131}I-hippurate scintiphotography in the early diagnosis of urologic complications.

Tilney NL, Strom TB, Vineyard GC, Merrill JP: N Engl J Med 299:1321, 1978

These authors comment on the use of ultrasound in discriminating between patients with acute rejections and those with obstructive nephropathy or perinephric fluid collections.

Cook GT, Cant JD, Crassweller PO, Deveber GA: J Urol 118:20, 1977

These authors comment on the vascular qualities of the bladder wall. The mobility of the bladder dome permits implantation of a short ureter or direct anastomosis of a bladder flap to the transplant pelvis or to a calix.

Linke, CA, Cockett ATK, Lai MK, Youssef AM: J Urol 120:532, 1978

This paper discusses the use of pedicled grafts of omentum in the repair of transplant-related urinary tract problems. The presence of impaired tissue healing and infection in these situations makes it essential that all surgeons be familiar with this excellent technique.

McLoughlin MG, Williams GM: J Urol 114:527, 1978, Schweizer RT, Bartus SA, Khan CS: J Urol 117:125, 1977, and Karmi SA, Dager FJ, Ranos E, Young JD Jr: Urology 11:380, 1978

The above three papers are included to make the reader aware of the many and varied causes of late ureteric obstruction. Late perirenal lymphocele, rejection fibrosis, and obstruction caused by the spermatic cord are the factors described.

Castro JE, Mustapha N, Mee AD, Shackman R: Br J Urol 47:603, 1975, and Lenitt SB, Caberwal D, Kogan SJ, Ronas NA, Hardy MA: Urology 13:377, 1979

These two papers stress that in the presence of uncorrectable abnormalities of the lower urinary tract, it is feasible and compatible with long-term graft function to divert the urine into an intestinal conduit or a pre-existing cutaneous ureterostomy.

Lucas BA, McRoberts JW, Curtis JJ, Luke RG: J Urol 121:156, 1979

These authors describe two techniques of ureteroneocystostomy, one of which provides an antireflux mechanism. However, although the importance of reflux in long-term graft failure remains unconfirmed, it is desirable, where possible, to employ a technique or ureteroneocystostomy that will, in the majority of patients, prevent reflux.

OVERVIEW: NEW PROCEDURES IN RENAL TRANSPLANTATION: IMPROVED QUALITY OF LIFE

Richard Weil III and Thomas E. Starzl

The articles in Chapters 12 to 15 were originally published between 1971 and 1979. The most recent of the four (Chapter 12, published in 1979) summarizes the state of the field at that time; the other three articles describe technical aspects of bilateral nephrectomy in transplant recipients, donor nephrectomy in living related kidney donors, donor nephrectomy in cadaver kidney donors, and ureterovesical anastomosis with intravesical and extravesical approaches.

These clinical and technical articles are useful for urologists and for all surgeons who do kidney transplants. The four commentaries, with annotated bibliographies, provide meaningful perspective on the four primary subjects. Although our practices in Denver vary from those of the authors in a number of details (*e.g.,* we do not require pretransplant coronary angiography for all patients of a certain age, we do recipient nephrectomies through an anterior and usually transperitoneal approach, we have usually done pretransplant splenectomy for leukopenia associated with hypersplenism, and we remove cadaver donor kidneys with single vessels individually rather than *en bloc*), we nevertheless regard the principles and the methods described in the preceding articles and commentaries as sound and effective.

During the last 2 years, surgeons performing clinical kidney transplantation, for the first time in more than 10 years have begun to realize the possibility of improving the quality of patient service, which has been long awaited but equally long delayed by lack of improvement in immunos

Until very recently, the basic tools of immunosuppression have been those defined in the early and middle 1960s, in Denver as well as elsewhere: corticosteroids, azathioprine, and sometimes an antilymphocyte (ALG) or antithymocyte (ATG) globulin.[1] In the United States, for many years the 1-year function of first cadaver kidney grafts has been essentially fixed at approximately the 50% mark in most centers, even with the use of ATG, although a few institutions with especially potent globulins have been able to exceed this unsatisfactory record.[2-5] A quantum improvement in the result of kidney transplantation, particularly cadaver kidney transplantation, has been made to wait for improvements in the immunosuppressive tools, so that better graft survival could be achieved without increased risk of mortality.[6]

Successful kidney transplantation, for most patients, offers a better quality of life than chronic hemodialysis. A minority of patients have a living relative who can donate a kidney for transplantation; therefore, any real upgrading of the service offered by kidney transplantation must have as its centerpiece improved graft and patient survival in cadaver kidney transplantation.

Supported by research projects from the Veterans Administration; by United States Public Health Service Grants AM-17260 and AM-07772; and by Grants RR-00051 and RR-00069 from the General Clinical Research Centers Program of the Division of Research Resources, National Institutes of Health.

There are now on the horizon at least five areas of applied immunology that are likely to have strong impact on kidney transplantation and, singly or in combination, to enable cadaver kidney homotransplantation with a high probability of success and a low probability of debilitating side-effects.

HISTOCOMPATIBILITY TESTING

For 15 years, since the introduction of clinical histocompatibility testing, it has been hoped that this tool would make it possible to provide each kidney transplant recipient with a well enough matched graft that only small amounts of immunosuppressive agents would be needed to achieve satisfactory kidney function. However, in the United States the HLA matching system has been disappointing in its ability to predict outcome after cadaver transplantation.

In a recent large survey of more than 100 North American transplant centers with data on 6226 primary cadaver kidney transplants, the 1-year kidney graft function was 51%, with 0–1 mismatched HLA antigens and 43% with 4 mismatched HLA antigens.[7] This small (8%) difference, and only a 51% success rate with well-matched kidneys, illustrates the extremely limited value of HLA matching in a highly outbred population that depends on azathioprine and corticosteroids as the main immunosuppressive agents.

It is possible that a relatively newly defined HLA locus, the HLA–DR locus, may prove to correlate more closely with cadaver graft outcome than the longer established HLA–A and HLA–B loci. The HLA–DR locus is thought to reflect cellular immunity more than humoral immunity, and the HLA–DR matching could therefore be expected to reflect cellular immune differences between kidney recipient and donor. Preliminary data indicate that there is some correlation between matching at least one HLA–DR antigen and cadaver transplant function; however, more experience with this method is necessary before any broad conclusions about its efficacy can be drawn.[8]

Improvements in the characterization of cytotoxic antibodies have made possible more accurate direct crossmatching between recipient and donor with identification of false-positive results. Ayoub and colleagues have demonstrated that recipient anti-B-lymphocyte antibodies will not cause hyperacute rejections and do not contraindicate transplantation even when specifically directed against donor B-lymphocyte antigens.[9] The presence of cold anti-B-lymphocyte antibodies before transplantation has, in fact, been associated with a more favorable prognosis than the absence of cytotoxic antibodies.[10] These cold anti-B-lymphocyte antibodies appear to be enhancing antibodies, and their induction may, in the future, become a method for preconditioning recipients in order to increase the probability of successful transplantation.

BLOOD TRANSFUSIONS

Opelz and Terasaki have demonstrated in a large retrospective study of 1852 patients that increasing numbers of packed red blood cell (RBC) transfusions, given before transplantation, increase first cadaver kidney survival at 1 year; with no transfusions the 1-year graft function was 41%, whereas with more than 20 transfusions, it was 75%.[11] The risk of this method, however, is that elective blood transfusions may, in some patients, produce such high titers of cytotoxic antibodies that transplantation for those individuals may no longer be possible. Salvatierra and associates recently transfused 45 candidates with 1-haplotype-identical related kidney donors; each recipient received 3 infusions of 250 ml of blood from that individual's prospective related donor in preparation for related transplantation. Thirteen (29%) of these 45 patients developed such high titers of cytotoxic antibodies that related transplantation was no longer considered safe and was not carried out. Of the 30 patients who did receive related grafts after the transfusions, 29 had excellent results.[12] Elective blood transfusion is therefore capable of improving the results of transplantation, but this improvement may also decrease the probability of successful transplantation in those individuals who develop cytotoxic antibodies in response to the transfusions.

TOTAL LYMPHOID IRRADIATION

Pretransplantation total lymphoid irradiation (TLI) was shown by Slavin and colleagues to provide effective and specific immunosuppression in rats. This central lymphoid irradiation is delivered through ports that are similar in design to the radiotherapy sometimes given for Hodgkin's disease and is safer than total body irradiation (TBI). In the rats, using pretransplantation TLI combined with infusions of donor bone marrow, Slavin and co-workers induced acceptance of heart and skin homografts from the animal that had donated the bone marrow, without ablating the recipient animal's ability to respond immunologically to grafts from third-party donors.[13] This form of pretreatment is currently being evaluated in patients at the University of Minnesota.*

THORACIC DUCT DRAINAGE

The fourth recent direction in applied immunology for transplantation, thoracic duct drainage, is an approach that was abandoned by most of the centers that had previously employed it until a new technique, with a double lumen catheter and heparin instillation, was described in 1978 by Machleder and Paulus of the University of California at Los Angeles (UCLA).[14] The procedure had previously been technically unreliable in a majority of patients. In 1978, in Denver, Koep and associates developed a modification of the UCLA thoracic duct drainage method,[15] which has permitted effective thoracic duct drainage in more than 90% of patients, including small children. Sixty-five primary cadaver kidney transplant recipients received thoracic duct drainage between April 1978 and December 1979, with follow-up study of 6–26 months to date. Twenty-five patients began their thoracic duct drainage at the time of transplantation, 18 patients had thoracic duct drainage pretreatment for fewer than 28 days before transplantation, and 22 patients had thoracic duct drainage pretreatment for 28 or more days before transplantation. The results in these cases have been reported, and continuing follow-up has confirmed our impression that at least 28 days of thoracic duct drainage

---

* Najarian JS: Personal communication.

pretreatment are necessary for the procedure to have maximum benefit.[16] The actuarial 1-year patient survival in the group of patients who received at least 28 days of thoracic duct drainage pretreatment is 82%, and the actuarial 1-year cadaver–graft survival is 73%.

Although thoracic duct drainage is safe and effective if carried out for at least 28 days before, as well as for a short time after, transplantation, the procedure requires an additional operation and an additional period of hospitalization. During the last 6 months we in Denver have therefore been working with a new pharmacologic agent in an effort to provide improved patient service without the necessity for additional hospitalization or operation.

CYCLOSPORIN A

Cyclosporin A, a polypeptide, is extracted from a fungus by the Sandoz Company of Basel, Switzerland. The initial clinical trials were carried out by Calne and colleagues at Cambridge, England.[17] In Denver, during the last 6 months, 36 patients received cadaver kidney transplants with Cyclosporin A immunosuppression. All these patients also received corticosteroids, but in smaller amounts than in the past, when azathioprine and prednisone were the immunosuppressive agents. Eleven of the patients received thoracic duct drainage as well as Cyclosporin A and corticosteroids; 25 patients were treated with Cyclosporin A and corticosteroids without thoracic duct drainage. Two of those 36 patients have died: 1 of pneumonia, and one of hemorrhage after coronary artery bypass, 6 weeks after transplantation, with a normal kidney transplant. Two kidneys have been rejected. Not all the kidney transplants are functioning normally, but 32 of the 36 patients (89%) currently have transplants that can sustain life without dialysis. We are optimistic about the long-term effectiveness of Cyclosporin A as an immunosuppressant for transplantation.[18]

. . .

The 17½ years since the first kidney homograft was done in Denver have been characterized by short periods of application of new technologies to improve results, followed by longer periods of consolidation of gains. During the 1970s, the main obstacle to providing patients with better transplantation undoubtedly was unsatisfactory immunosuppression.

In the 1980s, the development of more effective and less toxic immunosuppression appears more probable than at any previous time. This probability carries with it the hope that kidney transplant patients, including those without living–related donors, will be able to look forward to long lives that are not threatened by the morbid side effects of corticosteroids.

REFERENCES

1. Starzl TE: Experience in Renal Transplantation. Philadelphia, WB Saunders, 1964
2. The 13th Report of the Human Renal Transplant Registry: Transplant Proc 9:9, 1977
3. Wechter WJ, Brodie JA, Morrell RM, Rafi M, Schultz JR: Antithymocyte globulin (ATGAM) in renal allograft recipients: Multicenter trials using 14-dose regimen. Transplantation 28:294, 1979
4. Najarian JS, Simmons RL, Condie RM, Thompson EJ, Fryd DS, Howard RJ, Matas AJ, Sutherland DER, Ferguson RM Schmidtke JR: Seven years' experience with antilymphoblast globulin for renal transplantation from cadaver donors. Ann Surg 184:352, 1976
5. Thomas F, Mendez–Picon G, Thomas J, Peace K, Flora R, Lee HM: Effect of antilymphocyte-globulin potency on survival of cadaver renal transplants. Lancet 2:671, 1977
6. Weil R III, Schröter GPJ, West JC, Starzl TE: A 14-year experience with kidney transplantation. World J Surg 1:145, 1977
7. Oriol R, Opelz G, Chun C, Terasaki PI: Combined effects of HLA matching and age in renal transplantation. Transplantation 29:125, 1980
8. Cross DE, Coxe–Gilliland R, Weaver P: DR w antigen matching and B-cell antibody cross matching: Their effect on clinical outcome of renal transplants. Transplant Proc 11:1908, 1979
9. Ayoub G, Park MS, Terasaki PI, Iwaki Y, Opelz G: B-cell antibodies and crossmatching. Transplantation 29:227, 1980
10. Iwaki Y, Terasaki PI, Weil R III, Koep LJ, Starzl TE: Retrospective tests of B-cold lymphocytotoxins and transplant survival at a single center. Transplant Proc 11:941, 1979
11. Opelz G, Terasaki PI: Dominant effect of transfusions on kidney graft survival. Transplantation 29:153, 1980

12. Salvatierra O Jr, Vincenti F, Amend W, Potter D, Iwaki Y, Opelz G, Terasaki P, Duca R, Cochrum K, Hanes D, Stoney RJ, Feduska NJ: Deliberate donor-specific blood transfusions prior to living related renal transplantation: A new approach. Ann Surg 192:543, 1980
13. Slavin S, Reitz B, Bieber CP, Kaplan HS, Strober S: Transplantation tolerance in adult rats using total lymphoid irradiation: Permanent survival of skin, heart, and marrow allografts. J Exp Med 147:700, 1978
14. Machleder HI, Paulus H: Clinical and immunological alterations observed in patients undergoing long-term thoracic duct drainage. Surgery 84:157, 1978
15. Koep LJ, Weil R III, Starzl TE: The technique of prolonged thoracic duct drainage in transplantation. Surg Gynecol Obstet 151:61, 1980
16. Starzl TE, Weil R, III, Koep LJ, Iwaki Y, Terasaki PI, Schröter GPJ: Thoracic duct drainage before and after cadaveric kidney transplantation. Surg Gynecol Obstet 149:815, 1979
17. Calne RY, Rolles K, White DJG, Thiru S, Evans DB, McMaster P, Dunn DC, Craddock GN, Henderson RG, Aziz S, Lewis P: Cyclosporin A initially as the only immunosuppressant in 34 recipients of cadaveric organs: 32 kidneys, 2 pancreases, and 2 livers. Lancet 2:1033, 1979
18. Starzl TE, Weil R. III, Iwatsuki S, Klintmalm G, Schröter GPJ, Koep LJ, Iwaki Y, Terasaki PI, Porter KA: The use of cyclosporin A and prednisone in cadaver kidney transplantation. Surg Gyecol Obstet 151:17, 1980

PART SIX

RENAL AUTOTRANSPLANTATION, *EX VIVO* RENAL SURGERY, AND RENAL ARTERY SURGERY

16

RENAL AUTOTRANSPLANTATION: CURRENT PERSPECTIVES

Bruce H. Stewart, Lynn H. Banowsky, Clarence B. Hewitt and Ralph A. Straffon

From the Department of Urology, Cleveland Clinic Foundation, Cleveland, Ohio

The Journal of Urology
Copyright © 1977 by The Williams & Wilkins Co.
Vol. 118, September
Printed in U.S.A.

ABSTRACT—Autotransplantation, with or without an extracorporeal renal operation, has been done 39 times in 37 patients. Indications for the procedure included severe ureteral injury in 4 patients, failed supravesical diversion in 2, renal carcinoma in a solitary kidney in 1, renovascular hypertension in 1 and donor arterial reconstruction before renal transplantation in 29. Success was obtained in all but 2 procedures, both of which involved previously operated kidneys with severe inflammation and adhesions involving the renal pelvis and pedicle.

Based on our experience and a review of currently available literature we believe that renal autotransplantation and extracorporeal reconstruction can provide the best solution for patients with severe renovascular and ureteral disease not correctable by conventional operative techniques. The technique can be of particular value in removing centrally located tumors in solitary kidneys and in preparing donor kidneys with abnormal arteries for renal transplantation.

The role of autotransplantation in the management of advanced renal trauma and calculus disease is less clear. A long-term comparison of patients treated by extracorporeal nephrolithotomy versus conventional lithotomy techniques will be necessary before a conclusion is reached in these disease categories.

Accepted for publication December 23, 1976.

The development of any major new surgical procedure can be divided into 3 separate phases. 1) The procedure is conceived, researched and tried in a few selected patients by innovative surgeons. 2) If the procedure seems to have merit it is taken up by many other surgeons and used in an increasing variety of clinical situations. With this wave of initial enthusiasm the procedure often is attempted in many patients who would have been managed better by more conventional methods of therapy. 3) As rapidly expanding experience with the new procedure is gained more specific indications and contraindications are defined and the extent to which the procedure is used stabilizes at a level commensurate with its true value.

In the case of renal autotransplantation we are now well into the second phase. It is time to evaluate carefully the advantages and disadvantages, and more precisely to define the role of the procedure in urological operations. Therefore, our experience with renal autotransplantation and extracorporeal renal operations in 37 patients during the last 5 years has been reviewed and is compared to the reports of other investigators in this field.

INDICATIONS

Vascular Disease. To date the vast majority of renal autotransplantations, with or without extracorporeal repair, has been performed for extensive renovascular disease.[1] However, we would agree with Poutasse and others that many patients treated by autotransplantation could be managed as well or better by conventional revascularization techniques.[2-4] Consequently, of more than 600 patients who have undergone renal revascularization at our hospital only 1 has been managed by renal autotransplantation.

On the other hand, extracorporeal reconstruction of the renal artery in preparation for renal transplantation has been a more common indication for bench surgery in our experience. From January 1963 through February 1976, 453 kidneys have been transplanted, 180 of which were from live donors and 273 from cadavers. Since 1969, 586 kidneys have been perfused in our organ preservation laboratory. Of these 391 were believed to be suitable for transplantation, 117 of which were transplanted at our hospital. Of this group arterial reconstruction before transplantation was necessary in 26 kidneys: 25 for multiple renal vessels and 1 involving excision of a renal artery aneurysm with branch reconstruction and subsequent transplantation. Therefore, about 20 percent of the kidneys that we have taken from nonliving donors have required extracorporeal arterial repair to render them suitable for transplantation. In addition,

3 vessels damaged during live donor nephrectomy were repaired by extracorporeal microvascular technique.

Ureteral Disease. Although the first successful renal autotransplants were done for ureteral injury[5,6] relatively few autotransplants have been done since for correction of extensive ureteral disease. However, as experience has been gained with this new surgical procedure a sizable number of cases have been reported. Iatrogenic ureteral trauma,[7-9] retroperitoneal fibrosis,[10,11] bilateral ureteral tumors,[12,14] recurrent ureterolithiasis,[15] ureteral tuberculosis,[9] ureteral cholesteatoma[16] and failed supravesical diversion[17] all have constituted indications for ureteral reconstruction by the autotransplantation technique. Since 1970 we have reconstructed 8 ureters in 6 patients with extensive ureteral disease: 3 were done for postoperative ureteral injury, 1 followed ureteral avulsion from attempted basket extraction and 2 patients underwent bilateral autotransplantation for correction of complications after previous supravesical diversion.

Renal Neoplasia. Extracorporeal partial nephrectomy and autotransplantation for renal carcinoma in a solitary kidney are being used with increasing frequency, particularly when the tumor is extensive and conventional in situ procedures seem to be hazardous.[18-21] It is surprising how frequently one can achieve satisfactory exposure in situ, and a satisfactory partial nephrectomy for carcinoma can be done with the use of a temporary vascular occlusion and local hypothermia (Fig. 1). From 1956 through 1976, 17 partial nephrectomies have been done for carcinoma in a solitary kidney. Seven of these patients had extensive carcinoma of the contralateral kidney treated by radical nephrectomy. Only 1 patient has been treated by extracorporeal partial nephrectomy, renal reconstruction and autotransplantation. In retrospect, 1 patient who was operated on in 1966, before the advent of extracorporeal perfusion techniques, ultimately died of renal failure from vascular thrombosis after a most difficult in situ partial nephrectomy—he would have been treated better by autotransplantation. A second patient later had a local recurrence in the operated kidney—he, too, might have been managed better by extracorporeal resection and autotransplantation. Eleven patients have done well. A review of our somewhat limited experience indicates that roughly 20 percent of patients with carcinoma in a solitary kidney should be considered candidates for autotransplantation.

Renal Trauma and Calculus Disease. Extracorporeal repair of severely traumatized kidneys and the removal of calculi from extensively involved kidneys have constituted indications for autotransplantation in several recent reports.[4,22-24] Isolated cases of severe trauma

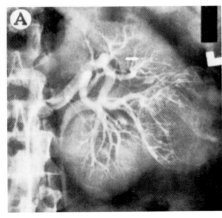

Fig. 1. (*A*) Solitary left kidney with centrally located renal cell carcinoma. (*B*) In situ exposure demonstrates partial resection of central located carcinoma in solitary left kidney. Renal artery had been temporarily occluded and perfused with chilled electrolyte solution, an operation was performed in local hypothermic field. Patient currently remains free of metastases and maintains normal renal function.

undoubtedly will be reported in the future, in which it would seem to be advisable to remove the kidney and repair it, leaving the kidney on pulsatile perfusion until the general condition of the patient stabilizes and allows satisfactory reimplantation of the repaired kidney. To date, we have not encountered any case in which autotransplantation seemed to offer a significant advantage over in situ procedures using temporary vascular occlusion and local hypothermia. Although isolated cases of extensive nephrolithiasis may constitute indications for ex vivo operations the in situ anatrophic nephrotomy developed by Boyce has eliminated, to a great extent, the need for extensive extracorporeal procedures. The interesting case reported on by Olsson involved autotransplantation with pyelovesicostomy for recurrent intractable ureteral colic that was unresponsive to medical management. Whether the long-term effects of a direct vesicocaliceal anastomosis will be an improvement over the relief of colic and/or recurrent obstruction by conventional therapy remains to be seen.

RESULTS

Vascular. Our single case of autotransplantation for renovascular hypertension was done because of extensive aortic atherosclerosis with proximal occlusion of the right renal artery in a patient who had autonephrectomized the left kidney owing to arteriosclerotic vascular obstruction. The kidney was autotransplanted to the right iliac fossa, leaving the ureter intact and anastomosing the renal artery end-to-side to a relatively normal right common iliac artery. Blood pressure and renal function remained normal 6 months postoperatively. Recently, another patient with extensive renovascular disease has been treated successfully by extracorporeal repair and autotransplantation. During the same period 26 other patients underwent renal revascularization by conventional in situ procedures.

Twenty-nine kidneys were prepared by extracorporeal arterial reconstruction before renal transplantation. Of these 25 had multiple renal arteries and, in each instance, a conjoined anastomosis of 2 vessels was done under hypothermic conditions just before revascularization (Fig. 2). The kidney was taken off the pulsatile preservation unit and the 2 vessels were joined with the kidney that was submerged in iced saline. The kidney was then implanted into the donor in standard fashion. Optical magnification has not been necessary. There were no kidneys lost owing to vascular thrombosis and only 1 patient has had late stenosis at the suture line. In 3 kidneys there was damage to the segmental vasculature during donor nephrectomy and reconstruction was satisfactorily performed just before transplantation. In these procedures optical magnification was necessary, using 7 or 8-zero vascular sutures and microvascular instruments. In 1 final case a renal artery aneurysm was present in the donor kidney, which as resected and the distal branches were repaired under optical magnification, anastomosing the main renal artery of the donor kidney to conjoined distal branches, with subsequent transplantation into a suitable recipient 12 hours later.

Ureteral Disease. Of the 3 patients with ureteral injury after a previous operation all kidneys have been salvaged

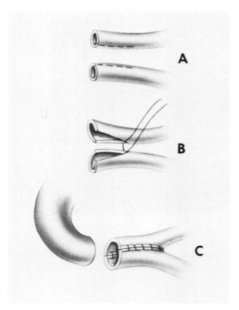

Fig. 2. Conjoined arterial anastomosis used in reconstruction of multiple renal arteries before renal revascularization of transplantation.

successfully after renal autotransplantation. One kidney had sloughed nearly the entire ureter after a complicated ureterolithotomy and was found to have 2 main renal arteries. The kidney was transplanted into the contralateral iliac fossa, with 1 artery anastomosed end-to-end to the hypogastric artery and 1 end-to-side into the common iliac artery. The ureter was implanted into the bladder by a modified Paquin technique and the patient has had an excellent result for 5 years postoperatively. The second patient suffered massive ureteral injury as a complication of left colectomy for perforated diverticulitis and ultimately underwent successful autotransplantation into the contralateral iliac fossa after temporary nephrostomy drainage. The renal and iliac fossae were prepared simultaneously and the kidney was transplanted without the need for extracorporeal perfusion. The third case involved an attempted transureteroureterostomy in a patient with right ureteral stenosis and hydronephrosis after ureterolithotomy. Massive leakage occurred at the suture line, resulting in slough of the upper third of the transplanted ureter, in addition to an ischemic segment about 1 cm. long involving the normal ureter at the site of anastomosis. The involved kidney was removed and placed on pulsatile perfusion, while the normal contra-

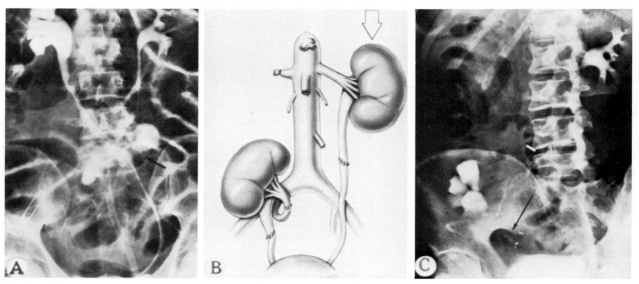

Fig. 3. (*A*) Excretory urogram (IVP) in patient with massive ureteral leakage and right ureteral necrosis after transureteroureterostomy. Original operation was done to correct right ureteral stricture secondary to previous ureterolithotomy. (*B*) Operative correction included downward mobilization of left kidney with excision of short ischemic segment left mid ureter and elliptical ureteroureterostomy. Right kidney was removed and placed on extracorporeal pulsatile perfusion apparatus while right iliac fossa was prepared, after which right renal autotransplantation was done in usual fashion. (*C*) Postoperative IVP demonstrates normal left upper urinary tract but mild residual hydronephrosis. Right ureter appears patent (*arrow*) and residual hydronephrosis may represent irreversible changes present before original operation.

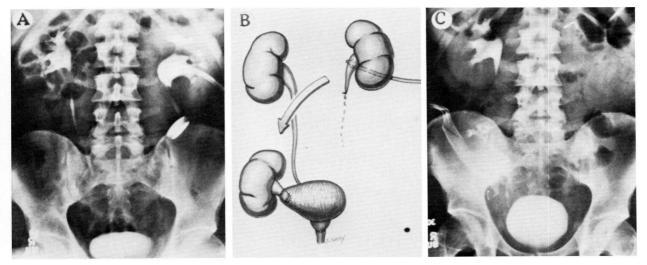

Fig. 4. (*A*) IVP shows temporary nephrostomy drainage after avulsion of left ureter as result of attempted basket extraction. (*B*) Schematic representation of left kidney autotransplanted into right iliac fossa, with direct ureteroneocystostomy because of short ureteral length. (C) Postoperative IVP shows satisfactory function of transplanted kidney.

lateral kidney was mobilized downward and an end-to-end spatulated ureteroureterostomy was performed at the site of the ureteral injury. The right kidney was then transplanted into the ipsilateral iliac fossa and the upper ureter was anastomosed end-to-end into the remnant of the lower ureter (Fig. 3). The patient remains asymptomatic 1 year postoperatively, although mild residual hydronephrosis remains in the transplanted kidney.

One patient had avulsion of the entire left ureter as a result of an ill-advised attempt to extract a small stone from the upper ureter by the endoscopic basket technique. Temporary nephrostomy drainage had been established after the injury, which made the definitive autotransplant procedure much more difficult. The kidney was finally removed, perfused and transplanted into the contralateral iliac fossa. Because of the short length of ureter available a spatulated direct ureteral anastomosis into the dome of the bladder was necessary (Fig. 4).

Bilateral renal autotransplantation because of previously failed supravesical diversionary procedures has been done in 2 patients, who have been described in detail elsewhere.[17] One patient had undergone ileal conduit diversion for retroperitoneal fibrosis and underwent staged bilateral renal autotransplantation because of recurrent pyelonephritis and poor drainage of the upper tracts. The first procedure was entirely successful, although mild vesicoureteral reflux persists owing to the extensive disease of the ureter and an inability to achieve a satisfactory submucosal tunnel at the time of autotransplantation. Because of extensive inflammation around

the pedicle of the second kidney the kidney has functioned poorly, although ureteral patency is good. Presumably, vascular spasm during the difficult resection at the time of nephrectomy resulted in poor perfusion and ultimate impairment of function in this kidney (Fig. 5). The second patient underwent autotransplantation because of a failed ileal conduit diversion (intractable stomal leakage) and because of subsequent ureteral slough after attempted ureterosigmoidostomy. The first autotransplant was successful, implanting the ureter into the lower sigmoid colon—the first reported case of autotransplantation combined with ureterosigmoidostomy. The removal of the second kidney resulted in severe vascular spasm; the kidney never perfused satisfactorily and, therefore, had to be discarded. Failure here was thought to be caused by severe inflammation in and about the renal pedicle associated with previous nephrostomy drainage and recurrent pyelonephritis.

Renal Neoplasia. A 56-year-old woman with a large hypernephroma in a solitary right kidney was found on renal angiography to have neoplasm involving the upper and middle portions of the kidney with medial extension over the hilus. At the time of surgical exploration it was not believed that in situ removal was feasible because of the intimate relationship of the tumor to small vessels within the hilus of the kidney. Right radical nephrectomy and regional lymphadenectomy were performed and the kidney was flushed with Collins' C-3 solution and then submerged on a platform in iced saline solution. With

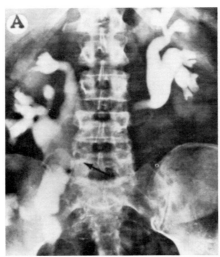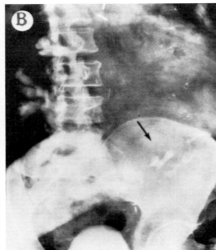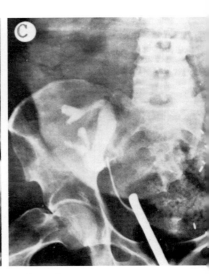

Fig. 5. (A) Preoperative IVP in patient with failed ileal conduit originally done for correction of retroperitoneal fibrosis. Patient had intractable pyelonephritis despite revision of conduit, with direct anastomosis of left ureter to right renal pelvis and construction of a short conduit from lower right renal pelvis to skin (*arrow*). Bladder function remained normal and renal autotransplantation was considered. (B) IVP after left renal autotransplantation in left iliac fossa shows good function of transplanted kidney (*arrow*). (C) Retrograde pyelogram after right renal autotransplantation into right iliac fossa demonstrates patent right ureteroureterostomy. Right kidney continues to function poorly, presumably because of irreversible vascular spasm and ischemia at time of difficult nephrectomy and autotransplantation.

optical magnification the tumor was excised and the kidney was reconstructed. After reconstruction the kidney was placed in the Mox-100 organ preservation unit and potential major bleeding points were suture ligated. It was impossible to control completely parenchymal oozing while on the machine because of lack of clotting ability of the perfusate. The oozing stopped immediately after autotransplantation into the contralateral iliac fossa of the recipient, with total ischemia time about 2 hours. The patient had an uneventful convalescence and continued to have normal blood pressure, normal renal function and no sign of metastatic disease 1 year postoperatively.

DISCUSSION

As experience with renal autotransplantation and/or bench surgery is accumulated its place in the urological surgeon's armamentarium can be defined better. Whether this new therapeutic modality should be chosen must depend on the disease process that is present and the clinical situation with which one is confronted.

As a general rule, most cases of renovascular disease are managed best by either conventional revascularization techniques, some form of ablative operation or by antihypertensive medication. Good risk patients with progressive lesions involving only the main renal artery or its major branches can be managed satisfactorily by local resection, endarterectomy or bypass grafting in situ, especially when the Smith-Ring self-retaining retractor and optical aids are used. In patients with uncontrollable hypertension in whom the operative risk is high or severe ischemic atrophy or focal infarcts are present nephrectomy becomes the treatment of choice. Most cases with extensive branch disease and good renal reserve are caused by medial fibroplasia, a disease that rarely progresses in patients more than 40 years old, does not result in renal infarction and usually is managed best medically. In the rare case of uncontrollable hypertension and significant branch disease in situ bypass grafting usually is possible, using the conjoined branch repair technique under optical magnification or simply dilating the diseased branches distal to the main arterial anastomosis. As Belzer and associates have concluded recently, extracorporeal arterial reconstruction and renal autotransplantation should be reserved for good risk patients with progressive disease involving segmental branches and in whom hypertension cannot be controlled well by drug therapy.[3] Other indications include patients with the middle aortic syndrome[25] and the rare case of severe aortic atherosclerosis in which conventional by-pass procedures are not technically possible.[26] Distally progressing arterial dissections that are not reparable by standard bypass procedures also should be managed by extracorporeal microvascular repair and autotransplantation if the patient's general condition permits. After a review of the literature on autotransplantation for renovascular disease one can say safely that at least half of the cases could just as well have been managed by conventional revascularization techniques, with significantly reduced operative time and postoperative morbidity.

Extracorporeal vascular repair is, on the other hand, rather commonly indicated in the preparation of donor kidneys for transplantation into patients with chronic renal failure.[27] The increasing shortage of suitable cadaver donors has made it mandatory to use every kidney possible and the reconstruction of diseased, damaged or multiple arteries has resulted so far in normally functioning allografts in the majority of patients. Also, it is now recognized that there is an increased incidence of caliceal fistulas resulting from segmental infarction, presumably owing to segmental vascular injury at the time of transplantation. So far, there have been no urinary fistulas in our series related to ureteral slough or renal infarction and, therefore, it would appear reasonable and safe to use kidneys with multiple vessels whenever possible.

Under special circumstances renal autotransplantation can provide the best long-term solution for patients with the problem of extensive ureteral disease. Successful restoration of upper tract integrity already has been well documented in patients with ureteral trauma, multiple tumors, calculus disease, tuberculous ureteritis and in some cases with retroperitoneal fibrosis. In the future rehabilitation of patients who have had previous supravesical diversion and who retain normal bladder function may well become a frequent indication for renal autotransplantation. However, autotransplantation should not be considered in poor risk patients with good contralateral renal function, in patients with severe iliac atherosclerosis or in patients in whom more conventional operative techniques can provide equally good results. Also, a relatively high incidence of failure has been reported in patients with severe inflammation of the kidney and/or renal pedicle—these kidneys do not perfuse well and the vascular spasm associated with a difficult nephrectomy may render them unsuitable for autotransplantation.[9,17,24,28] Either supravesical diversion or other forms of ureteral reconstruction should be used in these cases. A note of caution should be sounded in patients with retroperitoneal fibrosis, in whom the fibrotic process also may involve the iliac veins and result in poor venous return from the autograft. Olsson already has observed 1 such failure and believes autotransplantation is, therefore, contraindicated in patients with this disease.[21]

Extracorporeal resection, renal reconstruction and autotransplantation may be the only therapeutic solutions in patients with centrally located or large tumors of a solitary kidney. Again, it must be recognized that polar lesions are managed better by segmental arterial ligation and partial nephrectomy, and that the majority of smaller tumors, even when centrally located, can be removed quite easily by using in situ vascular control, local perfusion and hypothermia.[29] Prolonged operating time and the risk of vascular or ureteral complications are simply not necessary in the majority of these cases.

The future of extracorporeal nephrolithotomy and autotransplantation in patients with extensive calculus disease is less certain at this time. Most patients with renal calculi can be managed very nicely by an extended pyelotomy[30] or by the anatrophic nephrolithotomy of Smith and Boyce,[31] using vascular control and local hypothermia, portable operative radiography, nephroscopy and pulsatile irrigation. Only in severe cases, in which prolonged ischemia or extensive parenchymal damage is anticipated, would ex vivo nephrolithotomy and autotransplantation seem to offer a significant advantage. Again, the relatively poor perfusion of severely inflamed or excessively manipulated kidneys must be borne in mind.

The rare problem of recurrent ureteral obstruction requiring excessive narcotic therapy and/or repeated ureterolithotomy possibly could be solved by autotransplantation with direct pyelovesicostomy. However, the long-term results of this procedure will have to be compared to those of ileal substitution, with or without supravesical diversion, before this particular indication can be supported fully.

Although experience with the extracorporeal repair of traumatized kidneys is limited its use in selected cases is intriguing. Removal of such kidneys in the patient with multiple injuries theoretically would allow time for meticulous reconstruction and organ perfusion until the patient stabilized, thus allowing autotransplantation to be done as a secondary procedure if the condition of the patient were satisfactory. This philosophy of management might be particularly useful in poor risk patients with multiple injuries who have sustained severe trauma to a solitary kidney.

Finally, it must be emphasized that the entire field of renal transplantation is still in its relative infancy and that long-term evaluation of vascular patency and function of the reimplanted ureter must be accomplished before the final rule of autotransplantation can be defined satisfactorily.

REFERENCES

1. Milsten, R., Neifeld, J. and Koontz, W. W. Jr.: Extracorporeal renal surgery. J Urol 112:425, 1974
2. Poutasse, E. F.: Personal communication, 1975
3. Belzer, F. O., Salvatierra, O., Palubinskas, A. and Stoney, R. J.: Ex vivo renal artery reconstruction. Ann Surg 182:456, 1975
4. Sullivan, M. J., Joseph, E. and Taylor, J. C.: Extracorporeal renal parenchymal surgery with continuous perfusion. JAMA 229:1780, 1974
5. Hardy, J.D.: High ureteral injuries. Management by autotransplantation of the kidney. JAMA 184:97, 1963
6. Marshall, V. F., Whitsell, J., McGovern, J. H. and Miscall, B. G.: The practicality of renal autotransplantation in humans. JAMA 196:1154, 1966
7. Banowsky, L. H. and Stewart, B. H.: Renal transplantation. In: Operative Urology. Edited by B. H. Stewart, Baltimore: The Williams & Wilkins Co, chapt 14, pp 215–246, 1975
8. Rockstroh, H. and Schulze, R.: Autotransplantation der Niere bei ausgedehnter Harnleiteruerletzung. Z Urol 62:331, 1969
9. Van Cangh, P. J., Otte, J. B., Van Ypersele De Strihou, C., Coche, E. and Alexandre, G. P.: Renal autotransplantation for widespread ureteral lesions: report of 4 cases. J Urol 113:16, 1975
10. Brisset, J. M.: Cited by Dufour, B.: Les obstructions de L'uretère lombo-iliague. Rapport pour le 67ème Congrès français d'Urologie, Paris, France, 1973
11. Linke, C. A. and Mayu, A. G.: Autotransplantation in retroperitoneal fibrosis. J Urol 107:196, 1972
12. Murphy, G. P., Staubitz W. J. and Kenny, G. M.: Renal autotransplantation for rehabilitation of a patient with multiple urinary tumors. J Urol 107:199, 1972
13. Rhame, R. C.: Application of renal autotransplantation to the treatment of simultaneous bilateral ureteral tumours. Brit J Urol 45:388, 1973
14. Saltzstein, E. C. and Fine, S. W.: Renal autotransplantation and partial resection of the ureter for recurrent benign ureteral tumor. Surgery 77:67, 1975
15. Olsson, C. A.: Personal communication, 1975
16. Krane, R. J., Cho, S. I., Klugo, R. C. and Olsson, C. A.: Laboratory and clinical experience with extra-corporeal renal surgery. Trans. Amer. Soc. Artif. Intern. Organs, 20B:538, 1974

17. Stewart, B. H., Hewitt, C. B. and Banowsky, L. H. W.: Management of extensively destroyed ureter: special reference to renal autotransplantation. J Urol 115:257, 1976
18. Calne, R. Y.: Tumor in a single kidney: nephrectomy, excision and autotransplantation. Lancet 2:761, 1971
19. Gelin, L-E., Claes, G., Gustafsson, A. and Storm, B.: Total bloodlessness for extracorporeal renal organ repair. Rev Surg 28:305, 1971
20. Gittes, R. F. and McCullough, D. L.: Bench surgery for tumor in a solitary kidney. J Urol 113:12, 1975
21. Olsson, C. A.: Personal communication, 1976
22. Lim, R. C., Jr., Eastman, A. B. and Blaisdell, F. W.: Renal autotransplantation. Adjunct to repair of renal vascular lesions. Arch Surg 105:847 1972
23. Corman, J. L., Anderson, J. T., Taubman, J., Stables, D. P., Halgrimson, C. G., Popovtzer, M. and Starzl, T. E.: Ex vivo perfusion, arteriography, and autotransplantation procedures for kidney salvage. Surg Gynec & Obstet 137:659, 1973
24. Gil-Vernet, J. M., Caralps, A., Revert, L., Andreu, J., Carretero, P. and Figuls, J.: Extracorporeal renal surgery. Work bench surgery. Urology 5:444, 1975
25. Kaufman, J. J.: The middle aortic syndrome: report of a case treated by renal autotransplantation. J Urol 109:711, 1972
26. Straffon, R. A.: Personal communication, 1975
27. Banowsky, L. H. W., Stewart, B. H. and Straffon, R. A.: Autotransplantation, ex vivo surgery, and satisfactory surgical alternatives. Ann Surg in press
28. Sullivan, M. J. and Palmer, J. M.: Pitfalls at "the bench". Urol Digest pp. 15–17, January 1976
29. Gibbons, R. P., Correa, R. J., Jr., Cummings, K. B. and Mason, J. T.: Surgical management of renal lesions using in situ hypothermia and ischemia. J Urol 115:12, 1976
30. Gil-Vernet, J.: New surgical concepts in removing renal calculi. Urol Int 20:255, 1965
31. Smith, M. J. V. and Boyce, W. H.: Anatrophic nephrotomy in plastic calyrhaphy. J Urol 99:521, 1968

Commentary: Indications for Renal Autotransplantation

Andrew C. Novick and Bruce H. Stewart

Transferral of a kidney from one site to another in the same patient evolved as a logical extension of the field of renal allotransplantation. Early attempts at autotransplantation resulted in failure until, in 1962, Hardy successfully transferred a kidney into the ipsilateral iliac fossa in a patient whose ureter had been severely damaged by previous aortic surgery.[1] Effective methods of renal preservation and microvascular surgical techniques have also resulted in the advent of extracorporeal

renal surgery as a form of treatment for several complex renal disorders. In 1967, Ota reported the first successful extracorporeal renal arterial repair combined with autotransplantation in a patient with renovascular hypertension.[2] Since then, many other cases have been reported, employing varying methods of renal preservation and surgical repair, including an earlier review from the Cleveland Clinic that has been reprinted.

The indications for extracorporeal renal surgery and

autotransplantation now appear to have stabilized and include selected patients with renovascular disease, ureteral disease, carcinoma in a solitary kidney, renal trauma, extensive renal calculus disease, and reconstruction of donor kidneys with vascular anomalies before allotransplantation. The commentary summarizes the current state of the art regarding these operations and discusses the operative techniques that have proved most effective in achieving their successful performance.

OPERATIVE TECHNIQUES

In evaluating patients for renal autotransplantation, one should perform preoperative renal and pelvic arteriography to define renal arterial anatomy, to ensure relatively disease-free iliac vessels, and, in patients with branch renal artery lesions, to assess the hypogastric artery and its branches as a reconstructive graft. The same preoperative and intraoperative measures should be taken as in live–donor nephrectomy for allotransplantation to ensure minimal renal ischemia and immediate function after revascularization. These include adequate preoperative hydration, prevention of hypotension during the period of anesthesia, intraoperative administration of mannitol, minimal surgical manipulation of the kidney, and rapid flushing and cooling of the kidney after its removal. The operation has usually been performed through an anterior subcostal transperitoneal incision combined with a separate, lower quadrant, transverse, semilunar incision. Occasionally, in nonobese patients, a single midline incision extending from the xyphoid to the symphysis pubis has been used. Patients with a solitary kidney are informed about the possibility of hemodialysis postoperatively.

Renal Autotransplantation. In some patients, renal autotransplantation without extracorporeal repair is indicated, as for ureteral disease or renovascular lesions confined to the main renal artery. In these patients, the removed kidney is flushed by gravity flow with 500 ml of chilled Ringer's lactate to which 5 ml of 2% procaine, 10,000 u of aqueous heparin, and 1 ml of sodium bicarbonate have been added. Although 150 to 200 ml of flushing solution is usually sufficient to obtain clear effluent from the renal vein, one can obtain more uniform renal cooling by using a larger amount of chilled solution. Anastomosis of the renal artery and vein to the prepared iliac vessels is then performed, and circulation to the kidney is restored within 30 to 60 minutes.

When autotransplantation is done for renovascular disease, the ureter is left intact, and, although it may follow a redundant course to the bladder, normal ureteral peristalsis provides effective drainage of urine from the kidney. In such cases, take care not to rotate the kidney in moving it so as to produce an obstructive torsion of the ureter. In patients with ureteral disease, a variety of methods are available for restoring urinary continuity after autotransplantation, including ureteroneocystostomy, ureteroureterostomy, ureteropyelostomy, and pyelovesicostomy with or without a Boari flap. Nephrostomy tube drainage is not routinely employed, and a Penrose drain is positioned extraperitoneally, well away from the vascular anastomoses.

Extracorporeal Renal Surgery and Autotransplantation. When an extracorporeal renal operation is performed in conjunction with autotransplantation, flush the removed kidney with 500 ml of chilled Collin's intracellular electrolyte solution and then submerge it in a basin of ice–slush saline to maintain hypothermia. Under these conditions, if there has been minimal warm renal ischemia, the kidney can safely tolerate periods outside the body far in excess of the time needed to perform even the most complex renal repair. In performing extracorporeal partial nephrectomy for renal carcinoma, leave the ureter attached to preserve important collateral vascular supply to the renal pelvis and ureter. Here, do the repair under hypothermia on the abdominal wall with the ureter temporarily occluded to prevent retrograde blood flow to the kidney. In performing extracorporeal vascular reconstruction without resection of renal parenchyma, the ureter may be transected and the kidney placed on a separate workbench to perform the repair. This method is somewhat less cumbersome, and, since urologic complications after ureteroneocystostomy are rare, is an acceptable alternative approach.[3]

When extracorporeal renal revascularization is performed for branch renal artery disease, a branched hypogastric arterial autograft is the optimum material for vascular reconstruction (Fig. 6).[4] If this is not available, use a prefashioned branched saphenous vein graft, with separate end-to-end anastomosis of each graft branch to a distal renal arterial branch.[5] Other techniques that may be applicable are end-to-end anastomosis of a graft branch to two conjoined renal artery branches or direct implantation of a renal artery branch end-to-side into a limb of the graft. Such vascular repairs are performed under surface hypothermia with 7–0 or 9–0 suture material with microvascular instruments and optical magnification. The latter can generally be achieved with 3.5× opthalmologic loupes; however, in unusual cases, the operating microscope may be helpful. When extracorporeal arterial repair has been completed, before autotransplantation, the kidney is placed on the Mox 100 hypothermic pulsatile perfusion unit (Fig. 7). With the perfusion pressure set at the patient's systolic pressure, any arterial anastomotic leaks can be readily identified and controlled. Another useful adjunct is to instill 2 ml of indigo carmine into the arterial cannula, and, if this is evenly distributed throughout the perfused kidney, patency of all branch anastomoses is thus verified. Figure 8 illustrates extracorporeal repair and autotransplantation in a patient with hypertension caused by renovascular disease and involving four branches of the renal artery.

Extracorporeal partial nephrectomy for renal carcinoma is performed after radical nephrectomy, with the flushed kidney in ice–slush saline. To appreciate the full extent of the neoplasm, first divest the kidney of all perinephric fat. Since such tumors are generally centrally located, begin dissection in the renal hilus and carry it out to the periphery of the kidney. Secure and divide arterial and venous channels directed toward the neoplasm, but preserve those vessels supplying uninvolved renal parenchyma (Fig. 9). Progressively incise the overlying capsule and parenchyma to preserve a 2-cm margin of normal renal tissue around the tumor. Again, microvascular techniques and optical magnification are invaluable aids in securing transected blood vessels and closing the collecting system.

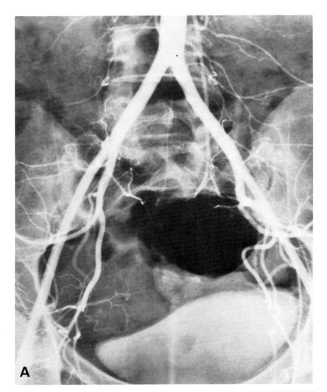

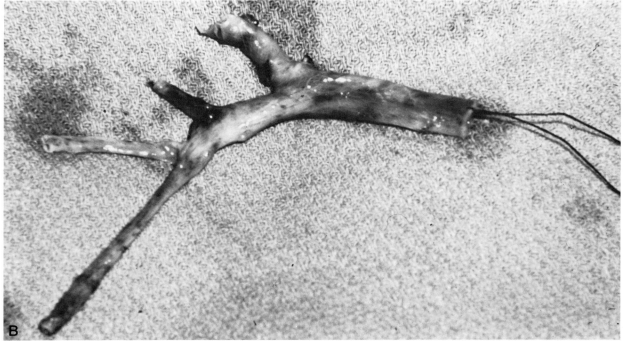

Fig. 6. (*A*) Normal pelvic arteriogram shows disease-free iliac arteries and, in particular, the hypogastric artery and its branches. (*B*) Operative photograph of hypogastric artery removed intact with four branches.

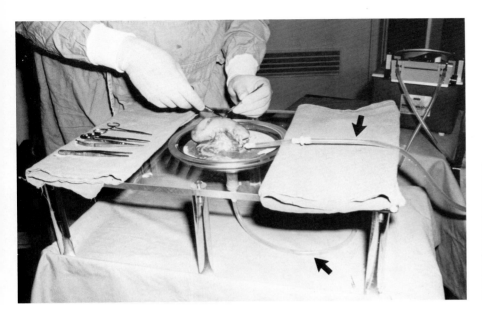

Fig. 7. After extracorporeal repair, use hypothermic pulsatile perfusion to assess vascular patency and hemostasis. Place the kidney on a separate workbench, with connecting tubing (*arrows*) running to and from the pulsatile perfusion unit. (Reproduced from Journal of Urology with permission of Williams & Wilkins Co.)

After completion of the resection, tumor-free margins may be verified by frozen sections, extacorporeal arteriography, or both. If arteriography is done, immediately reflush the kidney to avoid toxicity of contrast agents or their cold-induced precipitation.[6] Place the reconstructed kidney on the pulsatile perfusion unit to assess pressure–flow relationships and to permit suture ligation of remaining potential bleeding points. At this stage, to facilitate arterial and venous hemostasis, alternately perfuse the kidney through the renal artery and renal vein. Since the perfusate lacks clotting ability, there may continue to be some mild parenchymal oozing, which can safely be ignored. If possible, close the defect created by the partial nephrectomy by suturing the kidney upon itself to further ensure a watertight repair. When removal of the neoplasm has necessitated dissection of vascular supply to the renal pelvis or the upper ureter, as in extensive lower-pole tumors, leave in a nephrostomy tube for postoperative drainage.

Extracorporeal Donor Arterial Repair Before Allotransplantation. There are three basic methods for extracorporeal donor arterial repair that, singly or combined, are readily applicable to most anatomic variants presented by kidneys with diseased, damaged, or multiple arteries (Fig. 10). These repairs are performed before transplantation, with the kidney preserved by surface hypothermia in ice–slush saline. When two adjacent renal arteries of comparable size are present, perform a conjoined (side-to-side) anastomosis of the two vessels to create a common ostium. For kidneys supplied by two renal arteries of disparate calibre, perform end-to-side anastomosis of the smaller artery to the larger one. A third method for transplanting kidneys with more than two renal arteries involves extracorporeal repair with a branched graft of autogenous hypogastric artery or saphenous vein. These techniques have been described in detail; they allow transplantation to be performed as with a single renal artery, with no increase in revascularization time.[7]

SURGICAL EXPERIENCE

From January 1971 to March 1979, renal autotransplantation, an extracorporeal renal operation, or both were performed 67 times in 65 patients at the Cleveland Clinic.

Renovascular Disease. Ten patients underwent renal autotransplantation as surgical treatment for renovascular hypertension. These included one child with aortic hypoplasia, two patients with severe aortic atherosclerosis, and seven patients with branch renal artery disease not amenable to *in situ* repair (Table 1). In the latter group, autotransplantation was performed after extracorporeal microvascular branch arterial repair.

Nine of ten patients were cured of hypertension postoperatively. One patient with bilateral disease improved, but will probably undergo revascularization of the heretofore unoperated on contralateral kidney. There were no cases of postoperative arterial stenosis or occlusion, and no complications resulted from the ureteroneocystostomy that was performed in seven patients undergoing extracorporeal branch renovascular repair.

Ureteral Disease. Ten renal autotransplants were performed in eight patients with extensive ureteral disease. Six patients had iatrogenic ureteral injury, while two patients underwent bilateral autotransplantation to correct complications from previous supravesical urinary diversion.

In this group, 8 autotransplants where successful, with excellent function of the involved kidney 1 to 8 years postoperatively. The two failures in this group occurred in patients undergoing urinary diversion who had severe inflammation and fibrosis around the kidney and its vascular pedicle.

Carcinoma in a Solitary Kidney. Three patients with renal carcinoma in a solitary kidney underwent extracorporeal partial

(*Text continues on p. 210.*)

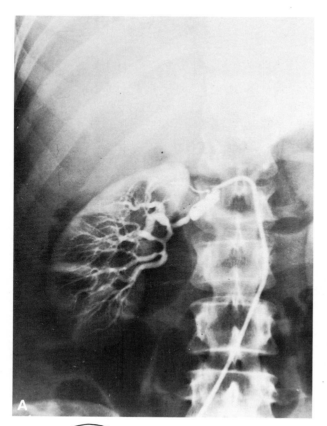

Fig. 8. (*A*) Preoperative right renal arteriogram demonstrates perimedial fibroplasia involving the main renal artery and four distal branches. (*B*) Autotransplantation after extracorporeal repair with branched hypogastric arterial autograft. Note that kidney was supplied by two renal veins of equal caliber. (*C*) Operative photograph of completed extracorporeal repair with arrow indicating branch arterial anastomoses. (*D*) Operative photograph of completed autotransplant with arrow indicating vascular anastomoses. The renal artery is anastomosed to common iliac artery, and renal veins are anastomosed separately to common iliac vein. (Reproduced from Journal of Urology with permission of Williams & Wilkins Co.)

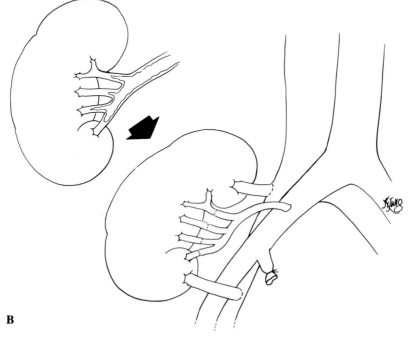

B

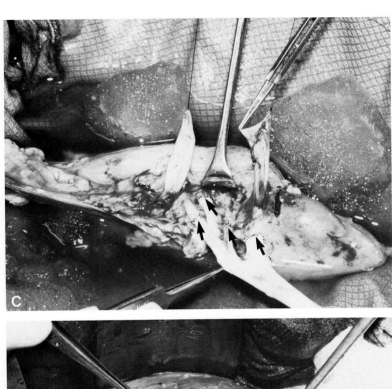

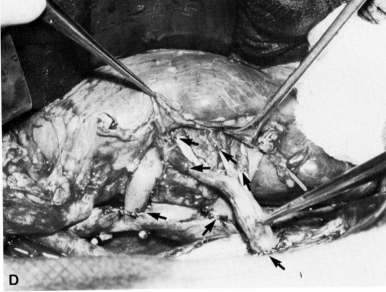

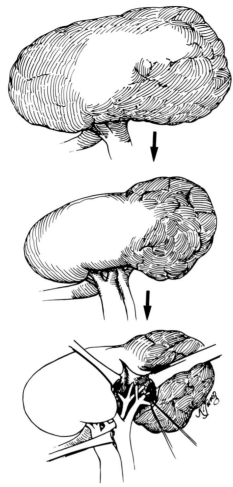

Fig. 9. Method of extracorporeal partial nephrectomy for renal carcinoma. The dissection begins in the renal hilus; all vascular channels supplying the neoplasm are ligated and divided. (Reproduced from Journal of Urology with permission of Williams & Wilkins Co.)

TABLE 1. Results of Autotransplantation in Treatment of Renovascular Hypertension

Patient	Age (Yr)	Pathologic Diagnosis	Indication for Autotrans-plantation	Outcome
1	54	Atherosclerosis	Severe aortic disease	Cured
2	59	Atherosclerosis	Severe aortic disease	Cured
3	10	Aortic hypoplasia	Aortic hypoplasia	Cured
4	15	Intimal fibroplasia	Branch disease	Cured
5	62	Atherosclerosis	Branch disease	Cured
6	40	Perimedial fibro-plasia	Branch disease	Cured
7	44	Medial fibroplasia	Branch disease	Cured
8	40	Perimedial fibro-plasia	Branch disease	Cured
9	48	Medial fibroplasia	Branch disease	Improved
10	47	Expanding aneu-rysm	Branch disease	Cured

nephrectomy and autotransplantation (Table 2). One of these patients (O.W.) developed cardiac arrhythmias during the bench procedure, which required termination of the operation. The repaired kidney was maintained on pulsatile perfusion overnight, and, when the patient's condition stabilized, autotransplantation was performed 24 hours later.

All three patients are curently alive, with functioning autografts, and tumor free 10 to 48 months postoperatively. One patient (C.D.), in whom a generous and technically complicated resection was performed, required hemodialysis for 6 months postoperatively. Resolution of postoperative acute tubular necrosis and hypertrophy of the renal remnant subsequently allowed dialysis to be discontinued, and this patient's serum creatinine level is now 3.9 mg/dl. One patient (O.W.), in whom the lower half of the kidney was excised, developed a postoperative urine leak from ischemic necrosis of the renal pelvis and upper ureter. This resolved after secondary repair and nephrostomy tube insertion; however, with healing, a stricture of the ureteropelvic junction developed. This patient remains on nephrostomy drainage with a serum creatinine level of 2.6 mg/dl, and a reconstructive procedure to restore urine flow to the bladder is being considered.

TABLE 2. Extracorporeal Partial Nephrectomy and Autotransplantation for Renal Carcinoma in a Solitary Kidney

Patient	Age (yr)	Sex	Tumor Location	Amount of Kidney Resected (%)	Period Renal Preservation (hr)	Current Serum Creatinine (mg/dl)	Outcome
R.Y.	56	Female	Upper third kidney	40	2.5	1.6	Alive 48 mo postoperatively, tumor free
C.D.	48	Female	Central	65	3	3.9	Alive 13 mo postoperatively, tumor free
O.W.	55	Male	Lower half kidney	60	24	2.6	Alive, 10 mo postoperatively, tumor free, with nephrostomy tube

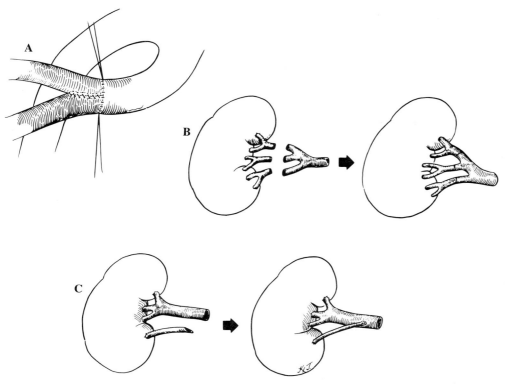

Fig. 10. Three methods for extracorporeal donor arterial repair before renal allotransplantation. (*A*) Conjoined arterial anastomosis. (*B*) Repair with a branched autogenous vascular graft. (*C*) End-to-side reimplantation of small renal artery into larger one. (Reproduced from Journal of Urology with permission of Williams & Wilkins Co.)

Renal Calculus Disease. A single patient with multiple recurrent renal calculi from cystinuria was treated by extracorporeal pyelolithotomy and autotransplantation (Fig. 11). Although extracorporeal pyelolithotomy was performed, these stones could have been readily removed with standard *in situ* methods. The rationale for removing the kidney here was to perform autotransplantation with Boari flap pyelovesicostomy, thus enabling subsequent calculi to pass directly to the bladder.

This patient has a serum creatinine level of 1.1 mg/dl 6 months after operation. Intravenous pyelography (IVP) shows excellent unobstructed function of the autograft, and, during this short follow-up interval, there has been no further stone formation.

Donor Arterial Repair Before Allotransplantation. Extracorporeal arterial repair was performed in 43 donor kidneys with vascular anomolies before allotransplantation. The indications and specific techniques employed in these repairs are outlined in Table 3.

In this group, there were no cases of arterial thrombosis or hemorrhage from vascular anastomoses. One patient developed late arterial stenosis at a suture line, with resulting hypertension that has been controlled medically. There were

TABLE 3. Extracorporeal Donor Arterial Repair Before Renal Allotransplantation

Technique of Repair	Number of Kidneys	Indications
Conjoined arterial anastomosis	29	Multiple renal arteries
End-to-side arterial anastomosis	8	Multiple renal arteries (5) Damaged renal arteries (3)
Repair with branched vascular graft	3	Multiple renal arteries
End-to-end arterial anastomosis	2	Damaged renal artery branches
Resection of renal artery and reanastomosis	1	Renal artery aneurysm
Total	43	Kidneys repaired

no other cases of severe posttransplant hypertension, and no graft ruptures occurred. Two patients developed urine leaks at the site of ureteroneocystostomy. However, they were both considered technical failures, and the leaks were not considered the result of devascularization with ureteral necrosis.

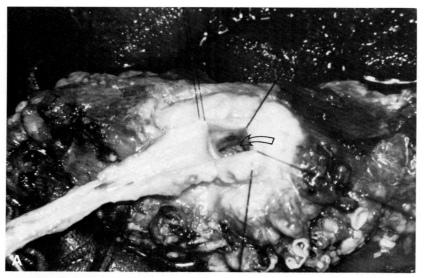

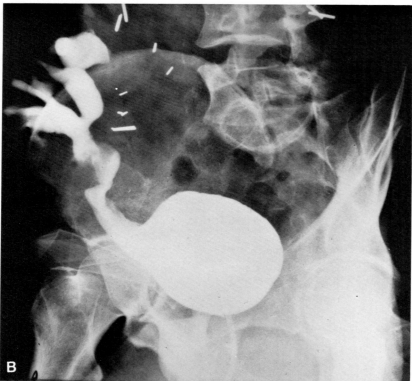

Fig. 11. (*A*) Operative photograph of extracorporeal pyelolithotomy. Staghorn renal calculus can be seen (*arrow*) before removal through pyelotomy incision. (*B*) Gravity cystogram following renal autotransplantation with Boari flap pyelovesicostomy in this patient. (Reproduced from Journal of Urology with permission of Williams & Wilkins Co.)

DISCUSSION

Extracorporeal renal surgery, autotransplantation, or both have become the treatments of choice for several difficult urologic problems. The advantages of performing extracorporeal repair of the kidney include optimum exposure and illumination, a bloodless surgical field, greater protection of the kidney from ischemia, more facile employment of microvascular techniques and optical magnification, and diminished risk of tumor spillage in cases of carcinoma. Nevertheless, since these operations are technically complex, they are best reserved for problems that are not amenable to repair *in situ* with conventional methods.

In our experience, the most common indication for an extracorporeal renal operation has been the preparation of donor kidneys for allotransplantation with diseased, damaged, or multiple arteries. Multiple renal arteries occur unilaterally and bilaterally in 23% and 10% of the population, respectively, and have comprised the most frequent indication for such vascular repairs, when a Carrel aortic patch is unavailable. The three extracorporeal methods of donor arterial repair described here are technically uncomplicated; they are readily applicable to most anatomic situations, they allow performance of a precise repair between arteries of similar thickness, and the repair can be carefully examined upon completion. In addition, since the kidney is kept cold throughout the bench procedure, transplantation is then performed as with a single renal artery with no increase in revascularization time. For these reasons, extracorporeal arterial repair is preferable to methods of transplantation that require performance of multiple arterial anastomoses *in situ*.

Renal autotransplantation is infrequently indicated in the surgical treatment of renovascular disease. Significantly, of over 350 patients who have undergone renal revascularization at our institution since 1969, only 10 of them (3.5%) have required management by autotransplantation. It has been our experience that branch renal artery lesions can often be repaired *in situ* when disease-free branches occur outside the renal hilus.[8] The size of the involved branches has not been a determining factor, and, with microvascular instruments with optical magnification, vessels as small as 1.5 mm can be repaired *in situ*. Extracorporeal branch arterial repair and autotransplantation is thus indicated only when preoperative angiography demonstrates intrarenal extension of renovascular disease. Although some have recommended using pulsatile perfusion exclusively to achieve renal preservation during such repairs, this involves an obligatory period of ischemia to each renal segment during repair of its corresponding branch.[9] In difficult cases, this may lead to prolonged acute tubular necrosis or nonfunction of the autograft, and hence we recommend that the flushed kidney be protected with external cooling throughout these repairs.[10] Renal autotransplantation is also indicated when renovascular disease is associated with the middle aortic syndrome or, in some patients, with a surgically difficult aorta and relatively disease-free iliac arteries.[11,12]

A recent review has shown that satisfactory results can occur after partial nephrectomy for bilateral synchronous renal neoplasms or carcinoma occurring in a solitary kidney.[13] In our experience, the majority of these tumors (82%) have been situated at either renal pole or on the lateral midaspect of the kidney, enabling *in situ* partial nephrectomy with free margins of resection (Table 4). Only three patients with large, centrally located tumors have required extracorporeal partial nephrectomy and autotransplantation. Although the follow-up study on these patients has been relatively short, they are all currently tumor free with adequate renal function. These operations may

TABLE 4. *In situ* vs Extracorporeal Partial Nephrectomy in 22 Patients with Renal Carcinoma in Solitary Kidney

Tumor Location	No. of Patients	*In Situ* Excision	Extracorporeal Excision
Polar or lateral	18	18	0
Central	4	1	3

be particularly complicated, and, to preserve collateral ureteral vascular supply, it is best to leave the ureter attached. As our third case (O.W.) illustrates, if complete removal of the neoplasm requires extensive hilar dissection of vessels supplying the renal pelvis or ureter, leave in a nephrostomy tube postoperatively.

Renal autotransplantation continues to provide an effective form of management for patients with extensive ureteral disease or selected patients undergoing urinary diversion.[14] We continue to advise caution in performing autotransplantation of kidneys that are severely inflamed, excessively manipulated, or involved with significant parenchymal disease. Ureteral replacement by intestinal segments or supravesical diversion is preferable in most of these complex cases.

In patients with recurrent obstructing ureteral calculi and intractable colic, autotransplantation with pyelovesicostomy can provide an excellent alternative to ileal ureteral replacement in permitting direct passage of subsequent stones into the bladder.[15] Olsson has also emphasized the advantages of a specially constructed Boari bladder flap in functioning as a nonrefluxing, large-caliber urinary conduit in these patients.[16]

Guttman and colleagues recently reported successful extracorporeal repair and autotransplantation after an avulsion injury to the renal pedicle.[17] Although such injuries are uncommon and require early operative intervention for attempted renal salvage, this is an ideal area for the application of extracorporeal microvascular renal reconstruction and autotransplantation. In one of our patients with carcinoma in a solitary kidney (O.W.), the repaired kidney was maintained on pulsatile perfusion for 24 hours before autotransplantation, until the patient's condition stabilized. This approach might also be employed in the critically ill patient with multiple injuries and severe renal trauma, in whom renal salvage is felt to be important.

Finally, we remain skeptical about the role of extracorporeal pyelonephrolithotomy and autotransplantation in patients with extensive renal calculus disease. It would thus far appear that the vast majority of these patients can be satisfactorily managed either by anatrophic nephrolithotomy or by extended pyelolithotomy. Despite increasing familiarity with methods of renal preservation and vascular reconstruction, autotransplantation should continue to be employed only in selected patients and when *in situ* surgical management is not technically possible.

REFERENCES

1. Hardy JD: High ureteral injuries: Management by autotransplantation of the kidney. JAMA 184:97, 1963

2. Ota K, et al: Ex vivo repair of renal artery for renovascular hypertension Arch Surg 94:370, 1967

3. Novick AC, Braun WE, Magnusson MO, Stowe N: Current status of renal transplantation at the Cleveland Clinic. J Urol 122:433, 1979

4. Novick AC, Stewart BH, Straffon RA: Autogenous arterial grafts in the treatment of renal artery stenosis. J Urol 118:919, 1977

5. Novick AC, Pohl MA: Atherosclerotic renal artery occlusion extending into branches: Successful revascularization in situ with a branched saphenous vein graft. J Urol 122:240, 1979

6. Alfidi RJ, Magnusson MO: Arteriography during perfusion preservation of kidneys. Am J Roentgenol 114:690, 1972

7. Novick AC, Magnusson M, Braun WE: Multiple-artery renal transplantation: Emphasis on extracorporeal methods of donor arterial reconstruction. J Urol 122:731, 1979

8. Novick AC, Straffon RA, Stewart BH: Surgical management of branch renal artery disease: In situ vs extracorporeal methods of repair. J Urol 123:311, 1980

9. Salvatierra O Jr, Olcott C, Stoney RJ: Ex vivo renal artery reconstruction using perfusion preservation. J Urol 119:16, 1978

10. Berkoff H: Discussion of paper by Stoney RJ et al: Ex vivo renal artery reconstruction. Arch Surg 113:1272, 1978

11. Kaufman JJ: The middle aortic syndrome: Report of a case treated by renal autotransplantation. J Urol 109:711, 1973

12. Novick AC, Banowsky LH, Stewart BH, Straffon RA: Renal revascularization in patients with severe atherosclerosis of the abdominal aorta or a previous operation on the abdominal aorta. Surg Gynecol Obstet 144:211, 1977

13. Novick AC, Stewart BH, Straffon RA, Banowsky LH: Partial nephrectomy in the treatment of renal adenocarcinoma, J Urol 118:932, 1977

14. Stewart BH, Hewitt CB, Banowsky LH: Management of extensively destroyed ureter: Special reference to renal autotransplantation. J Urol 115:257, 1976

15. Goodwin WE, Cockett ATK: Surgical treatment of multiple, recurrent, branched renal (staghorn) calcium by pyelo-nephro-lieo-vesical anastomosis. J Urol 85:214, 1961

16. Olsson CA, Idelson B: Renal autotransplantation for recurrent renal colic. J Urol 123:467, 1980

17. Guttman FM, Homsy Y, Schmidt E: Avulsion injury to the renal pedicle: successful autotransplantation after bench surgery. J Trauma 18:469, 1978

ANNOTATED BIBLIOGRAPHY

DeWeerd JH, Paulk SC, Tomera FM, Smith LH: Renal autotransplantation for upper ureteral stenosis. J Urol 116:23, 1976

This article illustrates the efficacy of autotransplantation in bridging extensive ureteral disease to salvage a functioning renal unit. In the cases described, autotransplantation was performed after conventional reconstructive surgery had failed to relieve upper ureteral stenosis. Our experience has also shown that autotransplantation is an effective form of management in these cases. Renal autotransplantation represents no more formidable a surgical task than ileal ureteral replacement and often obviates postoperative problems associated with the latter method such as electrolyte reabsorption, mucous secretions, persistent urinary tract infections, vesicorenal reflux, and progressive hydronephrosis.

Stoney RJ, Silane M, Salvatierra O Jr: Ex vivo renal artery reconstruction. Arch Surg 113:1272, 1978

Twenty-four patients underwent extracorporeal renal revascularization and autotransplantation for hypertension resulting from fibrous dysplasia of the renal artery, with excellent results. Renal preservation during the extracorporeal repair is achieved exclusively with hypothermic pulsatile perfusion. This involves an obligatory period of ("rewarming") ischemia to each renal segment during repair of its corresponding branch, which, we believe, can be avoided by adjunctive external cooling of the removed kidney. The authors perform autotransplantation into the renal fossa with vascular anastomoses to the aorta and inferior vena cava. This is somewhat more difficult than replacing the kidney into the iliac fossa, where the exposure is superior and the vascular anastomoses are easier to perform.

Guttman FM, Homsy Y, Schmidt E: Avulsion injury to the renal pedicle: successful autotransplantation after "bench surgery." J Trauma 18:469, 1978

This article describes a patient who underwent successful extracorporeal renal repair and autotransplantation after an avulsion injury to the renal pedicle from blunt trauma. There have been few reports of extracorporeal repair of traumatized kidneys, and its use in cases such as this is intriguing. Prompt diagnosis of the renal injury and early operative intervention are essential for salvage of the involved kidney. Established methods of renal preservation and newly developed microvascular techniques indeed enable repair of extensive renal parenchymal and vascular damage heretofore not considered possible. The patients' overall condition and the amount of damaged renal tissue should be important guides to therapy in such injuries. In patients with severe unilateral renal trauma and multiple other injuries, simple nephrectomy remains an appropriate method of management.

Gil–Vernet JM, Caralps A, Rivert L, Andreu J, Carretero P, Fuguls J: Extracorporeal renal surgery. Urology 5:444, 1975

This article reviews the indications for extracorporeal renal surgery; 12 cases are reported, 10 of them successful. Several of these cases involved repair of kidneys with severe cicatricial scarring of the pelvis, ureteral pelvic junction, or both. The authors also propose extracorporeal removal of recurrent staghorn calculi where conventional surgery does not enable complete removal of the calculi. We have yet to encounter a patient with extensive renal calculus disease who could not be satisfactorily managed with either anatrophic nephrolithotomy or extended pyelolithotomy. Nevertheless, for difficult renal calculi associated with severe infundibular or pyeloureteral strictures, an extracorporeal approach may be the most effective method both of removing all calculi and of ensuring unobstructed drainage of the collecting system.

17

AUTOGENOUS TISSUE REVASCULARIZATION TECHNICS IN SURGERY FOR RENOVASCULAR HYPERTENSION

Edwin J. Wylie M.D., Dorothee L. Perloff, M.D., Ronald J. Stoney, M.D.

From the Department of Surgery and Department of Medicine, University of California School of Medicine, San Francisco, California

Reprinted from Annals of Surgery, Vol. 170, No. 3, September 1969
Copyright © 1969 by J. B. Lippincott Company
Printed in U. S. A.

The discovery that obstructive lesions of the renal artery are a common cause of hypertension and that an operation which either removes or revascularizes an ischemic kidney may cure hypertension has led to numerous studies directed toward two major objectives. The first objective is the establishment of clinical or laboratory criteria to identify hypertension of renovascular origin, and the second is the development of safe, effective, and durable surgical technics to restore normal renal blood flow. The present report describes our efforts toward the latter objective. So far clinical testing of laboratory technics has not led to a uniformly accurate method of defining surgical candidates. The indications

for operation in the surgical methods described in this report were based primarily on the findings of renal arteriography. A hypertensive patient was considered to be a candidate for renal revascularization if operable obstructive lesions judged to be sufficiently advanced to impair blood flow in one or more renal arteries were identified by arteriography and if the potential benefit from a successful operation was believed to outweigh the surgical risk.

The anatomical adequacy of arterial reconstructive operations was evaluated by the postoperative arteriographic demonstration of the renal vasculature. The immediate physiological result of operation was determined by comparing the average preoperative blood pressure to the blood pressure six months after operation. The durability of favorable results was evaluated by

Presented at the Annual Meeting of the American Surgical Association, April 30–May 3, 1969, Cincinnati, Ohio.

measuring the blood pressure at 6-month intervals. A patient was classified as cured if blood pressure was consistently below 150 mm systolic and 90 mm Hg diastolic. Patients were classified as improved if (1) mild systolic hypertension (<170 mm Hg) persisted in the presence of normal diastolic pressures or (2) if previously refractory hypertension was relieved by mild antihypertensive medications (i.e., Reserpine and thiazides alone).

The renal artery obstructive lesions of the patients in this report were caused by atherosclerosis or by fibromuscular hyperplasia. The arteriographic diagnosis was confirmed by pathological examination in the 90% of patients in whom the lesion was available for microscopic study. Operations for the two disease categories will be considered separately. Patients who required a second operation appear twice in the evaluation, once for each operation.

FIBROMUSCULAR HYPERPLASIA

An arteriographic diagnosis of fibromuscular hyperplasia of the renal arteries was made in 136 hypertensive patients. In 25 the lesions were minimal and hypertension was easily controlled by medication. In 31 there were bilateral occlusive lesions in either secondary branches of the main renal artery or in accessory arteries. These patients were considered to be inoperable. Eighty patients had major operable lesions and hypertension had been difficult to control. In these the distribution of lesions determined the selection of operation. Primary nephrectomy was performed in 14 patients with unilateral disease of branch or accessory arteries not amenable to arterial reconstruction. Revascularization operations were performed in 62 patients with unilateral and nine patients with bilateral disease of the main renal arteries. In two patients with bilateral involvement a reconstruction was feasible only on one side. In these patients a two-stage operation was performed. The first procedure was limited to arterial repair on the side with the operable lesion. Contralateral nephrectomy for the treatment of persistent hypertension was performed after arteriographic confirmation of an adequate repair, and split-function studies demonstrated decreased blood flow on the inoperable side at the end of one year.

NEPHRECTOMY

Nephrectomy was the primary operation in 14 patients. Nephrectomy was chosen when arteriography demonstrated obstructive lesions or aneurysms in branch or small accessory arteries, or when exploration showed pathological thinning of the arterial wall at the bifurcation of the main renal artery. Secondary nephrectomy was performed in five patients: in three it followed late arterial stricture of a previous reconstruction and in two it was the second operation of a two-stage approach following successful revascularization of the opposite kidney. Nephrectomy resulted in cure of hypertension in 14 and improvement in four. The one patient who failed to respond was a 47-year-old woman with associated coronary, cerebral and ilio-femoral atherosclerosis.

SEGMENTAL RENAL ARTERY RESECTION AND REANASTOMOSIS

Resection of the diseased arterial segment and simple reanastomosis was the method we presented to this association in a previous report.[3] This was performed as a unilateral procedure in 23 patients and bilateral in five. The result in the 28 patients 6 months postoperatively was 19 patients cured of hypertension, five improved, and three unchanged. One patient died on the tenth postoperative day from rupture of an intracranial aneurysm.[2] This patient, a 35-year-old woman, had become normotensive following operation. Postoperative arteriograms, obtained in two of the three early failures, showed suture line stenosis.

Three patients who were normotensive six months after operation and who were originally classified as cured, had recurrence of hypertension nine months, 14 months, and four years after operation. Arteriograms in each of these patients at the time of recurrence showed stenosis of the main renal artery. In all of the early or late failures, lengthy segments of the renal artery had been excised. In four of the five patients in whom stenosis was demonstrated, the narrowing of the lumen, maximum at the suture line, extended symmetrically both proximal and distal to the site of anastomosis, suggesting the influence of abnormal tension on the full length of the renal artery (Fig. 1). The three patients with late recurrence of hypertension have undergone a successful second operation (nephrectomy in two and autograft bypass in one) (Fig. 2).

SPLENO-RENAL GRAFT

In two patients with disease in the left renal artery, the proximal end of the transected splenic artery was anastomosed to the distal left renal artery transected beyond the zone of stenosis. Both patients were normotensive 6 months postoperatively but one developed suture line stenosis and recurrence of hypertension after one year. This patient became normotensive after nephrectomy.

VEIN PATCH ANGIOPLASTY

An on-lay vein patch was used in seven patients. In three patients stenotic disease extended from the main

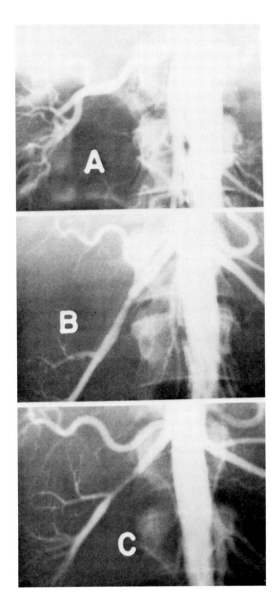

Fig. 1. Preoperative aortograms in a 41-year-old woman with hypertension and fibromuscular hyperplasia of the right renal artery at expiration (A) and inspiration (B). The inspiration film, aside from being the one which more clearly shows the stenotic zone, illustrates the tension on the renal artery that mobility of the kidney produces. The patient was normotensive. (C) Aortogram (when hypertension recurred) 14 months after operation showing lengthy stenosis of the shortened renal artery.

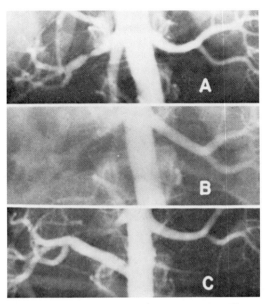

Fig. 2. Preoperative (A) and postoperative (B) arteriograms in a patient with fibromuscular hyperplasia of the right renal artery showing postoperative stenosis at the suture line. Hypertension was eventually cured by autograft replacement of the right renal artery (C).

renal artery into one of the primary branches. Five patients were cured and one was improved. The seventh patient, normotensive postoperatively, died from a ruptured intracranial aneurysm 2 weeks after operation. One patient, originally classified as cured, had recurrence of hypertension 24 months after operation. An arteriogram showed stenosis at one end of the patch (Fig. 3).

SAPHENOUS VEIN GRAFT REPLACEMENT

A free graft of the saphenous vein, anastomosed to the side of the aorta proximally and to the distal end of the divided renal artery distally, was used in one patient. Hypertension persisted and a postoperative arteriogram showed stenosis of the proximal one fourth of the graft. A second patient, not included in this series, was studied here for persistent hypertension following a vein graft bypass operation at another hospital. Stenosis in the proximal one fourth of the graft and a poststenotic graft aneurysm were demonstrated. This patient was cured after nephrectomy.

RENAL ARTERY RE-IMPLANTATION

Anastomosis of the transected distal end of the renal artery to the side of the aorta was attempted in only one patient, who is still hypertensive. Arteriograms 1 year and 3 years after operation show patent anastomoses without stenosis or occlusion.

ARTERIAL AUTOGRAFT RENAL ARTERY REPLACEMENT

Arterial autograft replacement for main renal artery lesions has been used in 27 of the last 35 reconstructive operations. Two patients required bilateral grafts, which were performed at the same operation. A delayed contralateral nephrectomy for residual inoperable disease in arteries to the contralateral kidney was performed in two patients (Fig. 3). The donor artery was the hypogastric artery in 25 operations and the external iliac artery (replaced by a dacron graft) in two.

The proximal aortic anastomosis is made slightly posteriorly on the lateral surface of the aorta and midway between the renal and inferior mesenteric artery origins. Anastomoses at this level avoid traction on the suture lines as the kidney descends when the patient is in the erect position. A disc of the aortic wall is removed which is equal in diameter to the external diameter of the donor artery measured before the donor artery is removed. The end to side anastomosis proximally and the end to end anastomosis distally are made with interrupted sutures

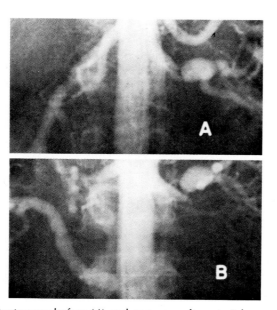

Fig. 3. Aortogram before (*A*) and one year after arterial autograft replacement of the right renal artery (*B*) in a patient with bilateral fibromuscular hyperplasia. Stenosis at the proximal end of a previous vein patch arterioplasty of the left renal artery is shown. Hypertension was cured by a subsequent left nephrectomy.

to allow the artery to dilate uniformly to its normal size following recovery from operative spasm.

Twenty-five patients with a total of 27 grafts were studied by arteriography one week or more following operation.* All but one of the grafts showed normal patency (Figs. 2, 3, 4). Early thrombosis of the graft occurred in one patient in whom the distal anastomosis at the level of the renal bifurcation was compromised by arterial disease at that point.

The average period of follow-up for the 25 patients is two and a half years. All of them have been observed for at least 6 months. Hypertension has been cured in 16 and improved in eight. There have been no late recurrences. Hypertension has persisted in the one patient noted above with postoperative graft thrombosis. He has refused nephrectomy.

DISCUSSION

Twenty-four patients have now undergone an anatomically successful renal arterial autograft operation; two of these patients subsequently had contralateral nephrectomy. Seventeen other patients have had unilateral primary nephrectomy which removed all demonstrable renal artery lesions. In only one of these 41 patients was hypertension unimproved. This suggests that arteriographic criteria alone are adequate for the selection of surgical candidates in hypertensive patients with fibromuscular hyperplasia of the renal arteries. Postoperative arteriograms were obtained in all but one patient with residual hypertension following other operations. The almost uniform presence of postoperative arterial defects in these patients suggests that technical deficiencies rather than improper selection of patients was the principal cause of failure.

A review of the results of the various arterial reconstructive operations indicates that in our hands autograft bypass is less susceptible to technical failure than the other methods. The nature of the postoperative arterial stenotic lesions in the patients who developed this complication after partial renal artery resection and reanastomosis or a spleno-renal bypass operation suggests that abnormal tension on the foreshortened traumatized artery contributes to stenosis.

The results from the small number of patients with veinon-lay patch or vein bypass operations do not permit an adequate analysis of these operations. In three patients the patch technic was used to correct stenosis extending beyond the main renal artery and in this circumstance it

* Two additional patients not as yet included in this series are awaiting nephrectomy for inoperable contralateral disease following an anatomically adequate arterial autograft replacement operation.

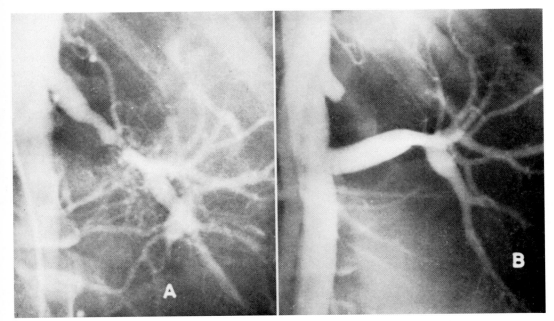

Fig. 4. Preoperative (A) and postoperative (B) aortograms in a 10-year-old girl with fibromuscular hyperplasia of the distal third of the left renal artery and congenital absence of the right kidney. The patient remains normotensive five years after autograft replacement of the left renal artery.

appears to be the most suitable method. Foster's experience with saphenous vein bypass operations suggests that this operation, carefully performed, yields good results.[1] We have found that an adequate anastomosis is relatively easier to accomplish when a normal artery is used.

ATHEROSCLEROSIS

Of 228 patients with hypertension studied by arteriography and found to have atherosclerotic obstructive lesions in one or more renal arteries, the lesions were judged sufficient to impair blood flow in 165. Operations for relief of hypertension were performed in 110 patients. Twenty-eight of the surgically treated patients had another major indication for operation—aorto-iliac occlusive disease in 19, aortic aneurysm in six, and symptomatic visceral artery disease in three. Total renal function was impaired in 12 patients. In eight of these the primary objective of operation was the prevention of early death from renal failure.

The mean age of the surgically treated patients was 51. The operative technics included nephrectomy or one of four types of revascularization operations, either alone or in combination.

NEPHRECTOMY

Unilateral nephrectomy was performed in 19 patients. Nephrectomy was selected as the primary operation in 16 patients who, because of age, obesity or associated disease, were judged to be poor candidates for a major arterial reconstruction operation. Nephrectomy was performed secondarily in three patients who previously had had an unsuccessful reconstructive operation. In both groups there was no arteriographic evidence of disease in arteries to the other kidney. Six months postoperatively, hypertension was cured in eight, improved in seven and unchanged in four.

SPLENO-RENAL SHUNTS

A left spleno-renal anastomosis was performed singly in three patients and combined with a right transrenal endarterectomy in one. Two patients were cured, one was improved, and one was unchanged. The postoperative arteriogram in the patient whose hypertension persisted showed a patent anastomosis and residual obstructive lesions, not recognized preoperatively, in both of two arteries to the right kidney. The blood pressure in the patient with postoperative improvement

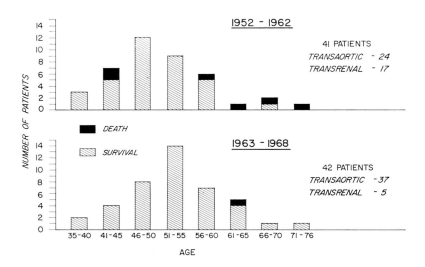

Fig. 5. Age distribution, operative deaths, and surgical approach in 83 patients undergoing renal endarterectomy for atherosclerotic occlusive lesions of main renal arteries.

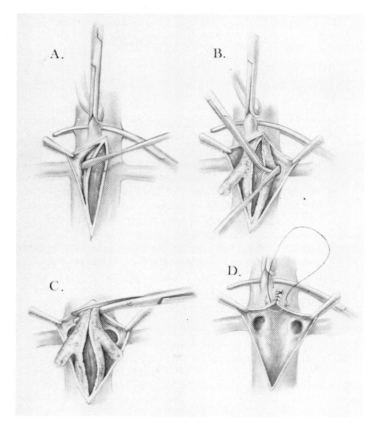

Fig. 6. Artist's drawing of the procedure for transaortic endarterectomy of the renal arteries in which the renal lesions are removed with a sleeve of aortic intima. This method is applicable when there is diffuse involvement of the aortic intima.

returned to preoperative levels after 9 months. Suture line stenosis was demonstrated by arteriography.

FREE BYPASS GRAFTS

Two patients had dacron bypass grafts and in one hypertension was improved. The other patient, whose other kidney had been previously removed, died in uremia following late thrombosis of the graft 5 months after operation. Arterial autografts from endarterectomized hypogastric arteries were used in three patients. One died from irreversible shock after hemorrhage from disruption of the aortic suture line. One patient was improved and the third, who had an arteriographically adequate result, was unchanged.

ENDARTERECTOMY

Renal endarterectomy was performed in 83 patients. The obstructing lesions were unilateral in 47 patients and bilateral in 36. The approach was through a renal arteriotomy in 22 operations and a longitudinal aortotomy in 61. The mean age of the 83 patients was 52 years and 80 percent were under 60 (Fig. 5).

Transrenal endarterectomy, although now abandoned in favor of the transaortic operation, is suitable for the removal of short proximal lesions in normal sized renal arteries when the aorta is free of intimal thickening or aneurysmal degeneration. A transverse arteriotomy, made at the distal end of palpable disease, allows extraction of the thickened intima from the proximal artery and from a limited extent of the aorta adjacent to the renal orifice. Closure of the arteriotomy with interrupted sutures restores a lumen slightly larger than normal at the site of endarterectomy.

The transaortic approach to the renal orifices, although particularly suitable for patients with bilateral lesions of the main and accessory renal arteries, is now used for even single main renal artery lesions. Complete mobilization of the mid-abdominal aorta to the level between the celiac and superior mesenteric artery orifice is required. Exposure is facilitated by division of the ligamentous surfaces of the crura of the diaphragm on each side of the aorta proximal to the origins of the renal artery. An 8–9 cm longitudinal anterior aortotomy extending superiorly to a point adjacent to and to the left of the superior mesenteric artery provides excellent exposure of the renal orifices. It is extended inferiorly if exposure of more distal accessory renal arteries is required. (Nine of the 36 patients with bilateral lesions had atherosclerotic stenosis of accessory arteries as well.) Endarterectomy may then be performed either by removing a sleeve of the entire aortic intima (Figs. 6, 7)

or by elevating a disc of aortic intima about specific renal arteries (Figs. 8, 9). Gentle traction on the specimen as the dissection is extended into each renal artery everts the distal renal media into the aortic lumen and allows the surgeon to approach the end point under direct vision without separating the intima beyond this point. In several patients almost the entire renal artery was everted to reach an end-point near the bifurcation of the renal artery. A loose distal flap requiring renal arteriotomy for its removal was observed in only two operations.

The average period of total renal and aortic occlusion was 18 minutes and the maximum was 24 minutes. In 25 patients the operation was extended to the lower abdominal aorta and iliac arteries for the management of occlusive or aneurysmal lesions. During this portion of the operation the proximal aortic clamp was transferred to a position distal to the renal arteries.

The effect of renal endarterectomy in reducing hypertension is shown in Table 1. When the second part of the series is compared to the earlier part, a sharp reduction in operative mortality is seen as a result of our increasing experience. Moreover, the number of patients whose hypertension was reduced after operation rose

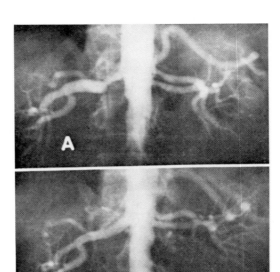

Fig. 7. (*A*) Preoperative aortograms in a 52-year-old man with hypertension of recent origin showing atherosclerotic stenosis of the right main renal artery and of paired renal arteries to the left kidney. (*B*) The postoperative aortogram following transaortic sleeve endarterectomy shows a normal lumen in each of the three renal arteries. The patient had been normotensive for three years.

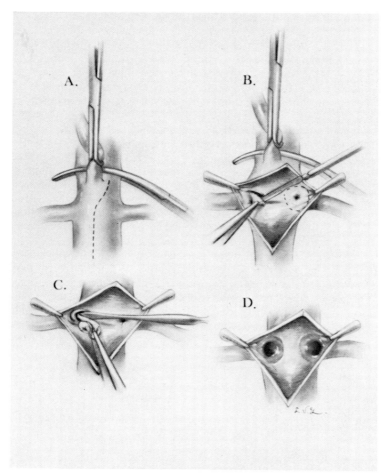

Fig. 8. Artist's drawings of the procedure for transaortic renal endarterectomy in which only a disc of aortic intima surrounding the renal artery orifice is removed. A tapered renal artery orifice is assured by cutting a disc with a diameter twice the external diameter of the renal artery.

from 66 percent in the early part of the series to 76 percent in the second part of the series.

The six operative deaths in the first half of the endarterectomy experience were caused by technical errors, resulting in renal artery thrombosis and death from uremia in two patients and uncontrolled hemorrhage from aortic tears in four patients. The mean age of these six patients was 62 years. Advanced degenerative change in the aortic wall was a characteristic finding and in two patients a previous operation on the aorta had been performed. The one operative death in the 42 patients operated upon by endarterectomy in the last 6 years was caused by cerebral infarction on the tenth postoperative day secondary to carotid artery thrombosis.

Follow-up aortograms have been obtained in 18 of the 22 patients whose hypertension. Twelve of the 18 of the 22 patients whose hypertension persisted after

operation and in the three patients who developed late recurrence of hypertension. Twelve of the 18 aortograms in the immediate failures showed no visible arterial defect. The defects in the six with residual obstructive lesions were minimal proximal stenosis in one, advanced stenosis at the endarterectomy end-point in two, distal branch artery occlusion in two, and stenosis of a pre-operatively normal accessory artery at the site of the operative application of a vascular clamp in one.

Aortograms in three patients with late recurrence of hypertension showed stenosis of the operated segment in two and occlusion in one.

One of the three patients with recurrent renal artery stenosis is of particular historical interest, since her operation is believed to be the first successful renal revascularization operation for renal artery stenosis. An aorto-iliac and renal endarterectomy was performed on

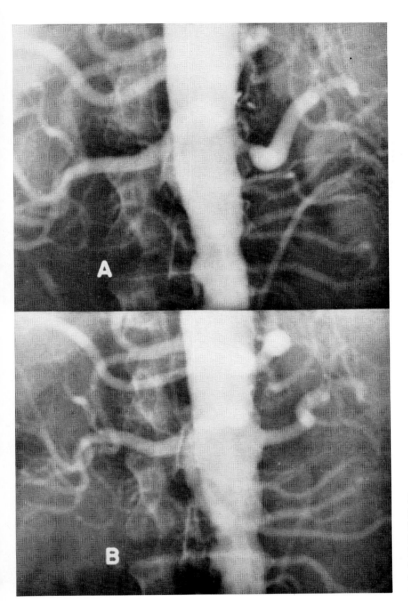

Fig. 9. (*A*) Preoperative aortogram in a 47-year-old hypertensive man showing atherosclerotic stenosis at the origin of the left renal artery. (*B*) Postoperative aortogram following a transaortic disc endarterectomy of the left renal artery showing restoration of a normal lumen. The patient has had normal blood pressure for five years.

November 10, 1952 by one of us (E. J. W.) on a 46-year-old woman with hypertension, left renal artery stenosis and aortic occlusion caused by atherosclerosis. She developed recurrent renal artery stenosis and hypertension 7 years later. Nephrectomy restored normal blood pressure but hypertension recurred three years later. Stenosis of a previously normal right renal artery was demonstrated. A dacron bypass graft was inserted which

occluded 5 months later. The patient died from uremia.

An associated indication for renal endarterectomy in eight patients was the improvement of depressed total renal functions. Preoperative serum creatinine levels averaged 2.6 mg/100 ml. Stenosis involved both renal arteries in six of these patients. Postoperatively hypertension was cured in two and improved in four. Creatinine levels fell postoperatively in five patients and became

TABLE 1. The Results of Renal Endarterectomy for the Surgical Management of Hypertension in Patients with Atherosclerosis of the Renal Arteries

	1952–62 41 Patients		1963–68 42 Patients	
Cure	9	56%	11	74%
Improved	14		20	
Dead	6	44%	1	26%
Unchanged	12		10	
Recurrence	2		1	

normal in two. Except for one patient who died from uremia after 8 months, all five are living with a mean follow-up period of 4 years.

DISCUSSION

A review of the results of operation in the 112 atherosclerotic patients operated upon for renovascular hypertension shows that of 104 survivors blood pressure was not reduced in 28. Residual or iatrogenic renal arterial lesions were demonstrated in 11 of the failures. The absence of residual arterial lesions in 17 patients (artery repair—13, nephrectomy—4) reflects the occasional fallibility of arteriography as the only prognostic and screening test for patients with hypertension and atherosclerosis of the renal arteries.

Renal endarterectomy through a transaortic approach has become the most generally applicable surgical technic. Multiple lesions may be removed simultaneously during a period of total renal ischemia which is well tolerated.

SUMMARY

The results of nephrectomy and revascularization operations for the treatment of renovascular hypertension in 190 patients are reported. The obstructive lesions of the renal artery were caused by fibromuscular hyperplasia in 80 patients and by atherosclerosis in 110 patients.

For patients with fibromuscular hyperplasia, arteriographic criteria alone were adequate for the selection of surgical candidates. Of the various reconstructive procedures, arterial autograft replacement of the main renal arteries has provided the most successful and durable result.

Transaortic endarterectomy has become the most reliable reconstructive operation for atherosclerotic lesions of the main renal artery. Seventy-six per cent of patients in whom arteriographic findings alone were the indication for operation have had a favorable blood pressure response.

REFERENCES

1. Foster, J. H., Oates, J. S., Rhamy, R. K., Klatte, E. C., Burko, H. C. and Michelakis, A. M.: Hypertension and fibromuscular dysplasia of the renal arteries. Surgery 65:157, 1969
2. Wylie, E. J., Binkley, F. M. and Palubinskas, A. J.: Extrarenal fibromuscular hyperplasia. Am J Surg 112:149, 1966
3. Wylie, E. J., Perloff, D. and Wellington, J. S.: Fibromuscular hyperplasia of the renal arteries. Ann Surg 156:592, 1962

DISCUSSION

Dr. John H. Foster (Nashville): I certainly enjoyed Dr. Mannick's and Dr. Wylie's presentation. I would like to speak specifically to Dr. Mannick's presentation.

Our hypertension study group at Vanderbilt has also been interested in renal venous renin assays. This slide shows 47 patients who have had renin assays and who have undergone operative treatment for renovascular hypertension. It has been our experience that if the renin activity from the involved kidney exceeds that from the uninvolved kidney by 50 percent or more the patient is likely to benefit from operative treatment. The renal venous blood samples were drawn with the patient in the supine position without any special stimulation as Dr. Mannick and his associates have done.

There were 39 patients who had a 50 percent or greater elevation in renin activity from the involved kidney. Of the 39 patients thirty were cured, five unequivocally improved, and four were failures. Of the four failures one was death in the early post-operative period and two were technical failures: one was due to a thrombosis of a graft and the other a stenosis at the graft anastomosis. These three patients never had the opportunity to be benefited. If they are eliminated from the prognostic analysis, you will find then that 35 of 36 with elevated renin activity were either cured or improved.

In the other eight patients the renin activity from the two kidneys was equal. Two patients with unilateral stenosis and satisfactory operative treatment were failures and remain hypertensive. Three patients with equal renins were clearly improved. All three had bilateral renal artery stenosis but only unilateral operative correction. Finally there were three patients with equal renins who were cured. Two had bilateral lesions and bilateral reconstructions. That leaves us with one false-negative result. This patient had a unilateral stenosis. Renin activity from each kidney was equal but quite high. Perhaps an explanation for the false-negative result is found in the next slide. This slide shows three patients with right renal artery stenosis. With the patient in the supine position the renin activity was elevated in all three patients. With catheters still in each renal vein, the patient is tilted to the upright position. Like Dr. Mannick's use of hydralazine this also stimulates renin release. The renin activity from both kidneys increases and the difference is magnified. The point I would like to emphasize is what happens when the patient is returned to the supine position. Renin release is shut off and the curves of the renin activity from each kidney falls. As the curves slope downward we find a point where the two curves are essentially superimposed. If one assays renin at this point there will be no difference in the renin activity from the two kidneys. This is the result of prolonged recirculation of high levels of renin which were released in the upright position. Thus if one casually draws renal venous blood samples without carefully controlling the patient's posture, unreliable results may be obtained. This work was done by Drs. Liddle and Michelakis of our Endocrinology Division and was published in the March 1969 issue of *Archives of Internal Medicine,* 123:359, 1969.

I would like to ask Dr. Mannick if he has any untoward effects from hydralazine. My question is prompted by our clinical pharmacologist's apprehension about the use of this drug intravenously, and I wonder if there has been any problem.

In regard to the work of Dr. Wylie and Dr. Stoney they have long led the way in the surgical treatment of renovascular hypertension and their use of autologous artery grafts represents another valuable contribution. We too have used autologous grafts—autologous saphenous vein—and have been quite pleased with the results.

Dr. Howard A. Frank (Boston): The very nice technics and results that we have been shown here are applicable, as the authors have pointed out, to stenoses of the renal artery or its major branches.

My associates, Drs. Edward Friedman and Peter Lambert and I have been interested in the possibility of revascularizing kidneys whose arterial lesions do not permit direct reconstruction.

For this we have implanted vascular pedicle.

[Slide] A pedicle formed of artery, vein, and fine vessel plexus remains patent in many tissues and forms connections with the local arterial bed.

Here in a dog a pedicle is prepared by isolation of the splenic artery and vein with preservation of the intervening fine vessels. The pedicle is implanted into a kidney, the artery of which is simultaneously narrowed. Three weeks later the division of the artery is completed.

[Slide] Two or three weeks thereafter examination of vascular interconnection by injection entirely through the implant artery shows patency of the implanted artery and complete filling of the renal arterial bed as well as of spontaneous collateral arteries.

[Slide] The longitudinal section shows the uniformity of filling of the vasa recta, the arcuate and the interlobular and capsular arteries

and of glomeruli, and in this cross-section [slide] we can see the nature of the connection between the implant artery here seen in section and an intralobar artery. This collateral inflow can be shown to be useful in maintaining renal function and in correcting renal hypertension. Our work thus far has been experimental only, but the method seems applicable to appropriate clinical situations.

Dr. John A. Mannick (Closing): I would agree with Dr. Foster that if one has a positive renin assay from the renal venous blood under basal conditions, the patient is very likely to be cured of his hypertension if one corrects the responsible lesion by surgery.

Our problem has been that we have found a number of patients who have negative assays under basal conditions who are equally amenable to cure by surgery. This is the reason for the hydralazine stimulation test.

In answer to his question, we have had no untoward effects of hydralazine administration. We are not giving very much hydralazine. In fact, in the majority of the patients, this has not been enough hydralazine to alter the systemic blood pressure at all.

Dr. Edwin J. Wylie (Closing): Dr. Foster modestly declined to describe his experiences with the use of saphenous vein grafts for renal artery replacement in fibromuscular hyperplasia. From my most recent information he is now having a 95 percent success rate. It seems clear that autogenous vessels, vein or artery, are performing better than synthetic grafts in this particular situation.

Dr. Frank has described an ingenious approach to patients with fibromuscular hyperplasia when the disease extends into the distal arteries. Dr. Folkert Belzer in our own department is exploring another approach with encouraging results in experimental preparations. In this method, he removes the kidney prior to transplantation and, while the kidney is being perfused, he applies various microsurgery technics to the distal renal artery branches. He has demonstrated normal arterial function after reimplantation of the kidney.

Commentary: Elaboration of Recent Techniques in the Management of Renovascular Hypertension

Oscar Salvatierra, Jr.

Renovascular hypertension has emerged as a recognized remedial clinical entity, and surgical techniques have advanced to the point that revascularization can be performed with a high degree of success and concommitant low morbidity and mortality. A spectrum of technology is currently available, permitting increased precise tailoring of therapy to the specific lesion. In regard to *in vivo* revascularization techniques, the preceding article represents the initial report of the Univeristy of California, San Francisco (UCSF), preference for arterial autografts and transaortic renal endarterectomy. On the other

hand, the articles by Dean and colleagues, Novick and colleagues, and Stanley and colleagues (see the annotated bibliography) represent contrasting approaches with aortorenal saphenous vein grafts. Wylie and co-workers' 1969 report has withstood the test of time and currently represents the preferred procedures for revascularization in renovascular hypertension at UCSF. This article, and the three describing the use of saphenous vein grafts, deal primarily with *in vivo* techniques for correction of renal arterial lesions. Since there is already considerable familiarity with these techniques, the commentary will be reserved for further elaboration of two more recently employed techniques in the management of renovascular hypertension: *ex vivo* renal arterial surgery and percutaneous transluminal angioplasty.

EX VIVO RENAL ARTERY SURGERY

It was against the background of renovascular hypertension, as managed at UCSF, that *ex vivo* renal artery reconstruction was initiated by Belzer and associates and later further developed. I will consider (1) the advantages of perfusion preservation in the UCSF experience, (2) technical aspects of the procedure, (3) specific indications for the procedure, and (4) advantages of the arterial autograft as renal arterial replacement material.

Advantages of Perfusion Preservation. Either cold storage or perfusion preservation may be used for extracorporeal preservation of the kidney requiring renal artery reconstruction. At UCSF, perfusion preservation has proved to be a very satisfactory method of extracorporeal preservation in that members of the operating team and, in addition, perfusion technicians have had an ongoing experience of preserving and transplanting more than 100 cadaver kidneys alone each year since 1974. Thus, the extension of this procedure to *ex vivo* renal artery reconstruction has posed no difficulty but has, in fact, enhanced workers' ability to satisfactorily repair some otherwise impossible renal artery lesions.

There are several distinct advantages of continuous hypothermic perfusion preservation in *ex vivo* renal artery reconstruction. First, dissection of the renal arterial vascular tree as it ramifies into primary and secondary branches is greatly simplified because these vessels are distended with the continuous perfusion. This greatly facilitates the dissection where considerable hilar and perivascular cicatricial reaction exists from previous arterial reconstructive procedures. Particularly in kidneys with previous surgery, the distension of the vessels and the ability to execute the dissection under close vision permits accurate and adequate skeletonization of the vascular tree for the necessary arterial repair.

Second, if any injury occurs to the small vessels during dissection, perfusion preservation permits immediate and exact identification of the injury, and, in addition, allows precise repair.

Third, the kidney is continuously perfused throughout the procedure, maintaining a constant cold core temperature. Only that portion of the kidney supplied by the branch artery being anastamosed to the arterial autograft is temporarily excluded from perfusion. This method permits a precise reconstruction and eliminates concern on ischemic time limitation.

Fourth, at the end of reconstruction, perfusion pressure is set at the patient's systolic pressure to identify and control any branch vessel anastomotic leaks before removing the repaired kidney from the perfusion circuit. Excessive blood loss from leaks at the small branch vessel anastomotic sites are thus avoided. Additionally, if attempts at hemostasis were left to be made after reimplantation of the kidney, the branch artery repairs might be injured because their location deep in the renal hilus obstructs proper exposure.

Finally, we have avoided postoperative tubular necrosis in the operated kidney in nearly all patients. This has been verified by normal renograms on the first postoperative day in almost 90% of these patients. In the remaining instances, only mild transient impairment of function in the operative kidney was present, as shown by some renal cortical retention of the radioisotope, but the excretory phase of the renogram has always shown a downhill slope.

Operative Technique. Initially, the entire kidney with the ureter was removed for the vascular reconstruction and then reimplanted in the iliac fossa, similar to a renal transplant. Later we found two distinct advantages for exteriorizing only the kidney on the lower abdomen and leaving the ureter intact (Fig. 10). The operative procedure now requires less time without the necessity of a ureteroneocystostomy for re-establishment of continuity of the urinary tract. Some patients have extensive collateral circulation along the ureter, and an intact ureter ensures that these collaterals are preserved, not disrupted.

Soon after the division of the renal artery and vein and exteriorization of the kidney to undergo *ex vivo* repair, the kidney is flushed through the renal artery, which, in our practice, has been accomplished with cold Ringer's lactate with various additives. The renal artery or branch arteries are cannulated and then connected to the outlets on the dissecting and perfusion platform. The needed dissection of the renal artery and its branches can then be easily accomplished with the vessels distended from the continuous perfusion. The internal iliac artery with its branches is then usually harvested as the arterial autograft to be used for the reconstruction. We replace the diseased renal artery and its branches with the autograft by serially dividing the renal artery branches and anastomoses of these branches to branches of the internal iliac artery autograft. Perfusion preservation is maintained for the entire kidney except for that segment dependent on the isolated branch then undergoing anastomoses to the autograft. In sequential fashion, the anastamosed branch is returned to perfusion, while the next branch artery is temporarily excluded from perfusion, so as to be anastomosed to the appropriate branch of the arterial autograft.

The distal ends of the divided branches of the renal artery are anastomosed in end-to-end fashion to the appropriate branches of the arterial autograft with interrupted cardiovascular sutures (6–0 or 7–0). If a renal artery branch cannot be matched to the autograft configuration for an end-to-end anastomoses, the end of this branch can be beveled and attached to the side of the autograft at an appropriate site. When all the renal artery branches have been transposed to the autograft, the kidney is maintained on perfusion while the appropriate sites on the vena cava and aorta are prepared for the reimplantation into the renal fossa. The renal vein is reanastomosed on the left, and on the right it is attached to the side of the vena cava, slightly caudad to the oversewn stump of the right renal vein. The renal artery autograft is most often anastomosed to the side of the aorta, 2 cm to 4 cm caudad to the original renal artery orifice, which has been oversewn. To facilitate the arterial anastomosis, the aorta is doubly clamped to isolate a 2 cm to 3 cm segment. A circular defect is created in the posterolateral wall of this aortic segment that approximates the diameter of

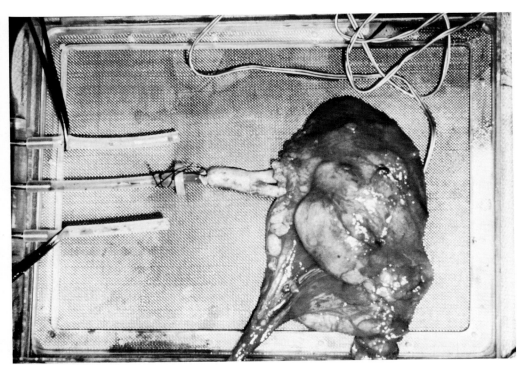

Fig. 10. Dissecting and perfusion platform placed on lower abdomen. The visualized kidney has already been reconstructed with an internal iliac arterial autograft. The branch vessel anastomoses are deep in the renal hilus and cannot be visualized. The inact ureter can be seen extending from the abdominal wound. Two other perfusion tubing outlets were used to maintain perfusion of the branch vessels during arterial reconstruction.

the autograft. The end of the autograft is then anastomosed to the defect with interrupted 5–0 cardiovascular sutures.

The time required for the *ex vivo* renal artery reconstruction would probably be less than that required for *in vivo* repair of the same lesion because the small-vessel anastomoses can be easily accomplished accurately under direct vision. This same attention to small-vessel anastomoses in the *in vivo* situation would most likely not be possible and would be more time consuming. In analyses of the total microanastomoses and macroanastomoses performed in the *ex vivo* technique, only one extra anastomosis is required in the *ex vivo* procedure— the renal vein anastomosis. This anastomosis is the easiest and quickest of all the anastomoses performed.

Indications. Indications for the procedure are quite limited and primarily involve patients with uncontrollable renovascular hypertension due to lesions that are inoperable by *in situ* methods. Primary among these is extensive fibromuscular dysplasia extending into primary and secondary branches. Every attempt should be made to repair an extensive fibromuscular dysplasia lesion in young females, since the incidence of eventual bilateral disease approaches 50%. Nephrectomy should be reserved only for cases of severe renal atrophy, particularly in older patients, in whom the chances of occurrence

or progression of disease in the opposite normal renal artery is unlikely.

Indications for *ex vivo* reconstruction other than for vascular lesions are rare. For example, an operation for a staghorn calculus can be handled effectively by local *in situ* techniques in almost all instances. *Ex vivo* reconstructive operations should be used only when *in situ* surgical repair is considered impossible or hazardous.

Use of Arterial Autografts. Several reports identifying the long-term fate of autologous saphenous veins for renal artery reconstruction have led us to continue using arterial autografts for renal artery replacement. Autologous, saphenous vein, aortorenal grafts have developed dilation, aneurysmal formation, and stricture in carefully followed series. We at UCSF have used the arterial autograft as an arterial substitute since 1964, and experience has demonstrated prolonged satisfaction with its use in a variety of sites of commonly treated arteriosclerotic obstructive lesions and fibromuscular dysplasia.

The durability of the autogenous arterial grafts has primarily accumulated from experience with autogenous aortorenal grafting. Late graft function of 45 aortorenal autografts performed from 1964 to 1972 has revealed only 1 early graft occlusion and no late graft occlusions. In one child, initial slight graft dilitation occurred, which remained stable on subsequent angiography performed 11 years postoperatively.

Because of this excellent record of function, our preferred graft for *ex vivo* renal arterial repair is the autogenous internal iliac artery whenever possible. There are several advantages other than those enumerated above:

The size of the internal iliac artery closely approximates that of the renal artery both in adults and children.

The internal iliac artery usually ends in several branches, which is particularly useful when distal renal artery reconstruction is required.

The iliac arteries are accessible in the same operative field.

Arterial autografts are suitable for renal artery repair in children, since their growth parallels the child's somatic growth.

PERCUTANEOUS TRANSLUMINAL ANGIOPLASTY

As an alternative to renovascular surgery, there has been increasing enthusiasm about the use of percutaneous transluminal angioplasty, initially reported by Grüntzig as a conservative way to manage selected renal arterial lesions. To proceed, one advances a dilatation catheter through the stenosing lesion over a guidewire. The dilatation is performed after the infusion of heparin into the renal artery. There are now increasing reports of successful management of arterial lesions by this technique. However, follow-up study is still quite short, and I must reserve definitive comment until more long-term follow-up studies are available. In addition, the true incidence of potential complications, such as dissection and thromboses,

can only be ascertained on the evaluation of a larger experience. Moreover, its place in the management of multiple branch vessel lesions, as in cases managed by *ex-vivo* surgery, remains to be determined. The interested reader is referred to reports appearing in *Lancet* and *New England Journal of Medicine* (see annotated bibliography).

PROSPECTS

The incidence of hypertension in the U.S. population is estimated to range from 5 to 22 million. In turn, the actual incidence of hypertension on a renovascular basis involves at least 6% of all hypertensive patients. The variation depends in good part on the referring pattern of the reporting centers. There now appear to be several alternatives to treatment, which may be used singly or in combination in the management of renovascular hypertension.

There is now good experience in several U.S. centers to indicate that *ex vivo* renal artery reconstruction can be employed with reasonable expectation of good outcome in patients otherwise inoperable by *in situ* methods. Other therapeutic considerations relate to recently used percutaneous luminal angioplasty and, of course, to the time-proven pharmacotherapy, with recent experience in newer and more effective drugs. These management alternatives appear to present distinct advantages to the patient with renovascular hypertension; this, in turn, would permit greater opportunity for surgeons to achieve the desired goals for the management of the wide spectrum of symptomatic renal artery lesions: cure or control of hypertension with concommitant maximum preservation of renal function.

ANNOTATED BIBLIOGRAPHY

Dean RH, Wilson JP, Burko H, Foster JH: Saphenous vein aortorenal bypass grafts: Serial arteriographic study. Ann Surg 180:469, 1974

This report presents the outcome and follow-up study of 108 autologous saphenous veins used to construct an aortorenal bypass in 94 patients. Problems with graft thrombosis, suture line stenosis, graft dilatation, and aneurysmal formation are described in detail. Another observation encountered in the study was the relative high frequency of development of new or progressive stenotic lesions in the contralateral renal artery. This further underscores the importance of avoiding nephrectomy if possible in patients with renovascular hypertension.

Novick AC, Straffon RA: Aortorenal bypass with a branced saphenous vein graft for renal artery disease extending into the branches. Surgery 85:225, 1979

This article gives a detailed impressive description of the various anastomoses effected in two patients who underwent aortorenal bypass with a saphenous vein graft. The longest follow-up study is 3 years, but without apparent angiographic reevaluation. In addition, this paper gives an alternative to the surgical approaches used in the UCSF series.

Stanley JC, Ernst CB, Fry WJ: Fate of 100 aortorenal vein grafts: Characteristics of late graft expansion, aneurysmal dilatation, and stenosis. Surgery 74:931, 944, 1973

One hundred autogenous saphenous vein aortorenal grafts were evaluated with detailed postoperative arteriographic studies. Aneurysmal dilatations and stenoses were demonstrated in 16%

of late follow-up studies. The authors point out the "discrepancy between very acceptable clinical results and a significant number of unsatisfactory appearing vein grafts." This elaborate manuscript was presented at the Annual Meeting of the Society for Vascular Surgery in 1973 and includes the extensive discussion that followed the presentation. This is certainly required reading for the renovascular surgeon.

Stoney RJ, Silane M, Salvatierra O Jr: Ex-vivo renal artery reconstruction. Arch Surg 113:1272, 1978

This report summarizes the UCSF *ex vivo* renal artery experience from the initial procedure in 1972 until 1978. A bibliography of the initial and earlier reports in this series is included for the interested reader. More important, this paper was presented at the 26th Scientific Meeting of the International Cardiovascular Society in 1978 and includes all the discussion that occurred after the presentation. For example, Dr. Stanley raised the question of temporary cold storage.

Millan VG, Madias NE: Percutaneous transluminal angioplasty for severe renovascular hypertension due to renal artery medicofibroplasia. Lancet 1:993, 1979

This report provides an early experience with extensive documentation of percutaneous transluminal angioplasty (modified from Grüntzig).

Millan VG, Mast WE, Madias NE: Nonsurgical treatment of severe hypertension due to renal-artery intimal fibroplasia by percutaneous transluminal angioplasty. N Engl J Med 300:1371, 1979

This represents another well-documented case by Millan's group.

OVERVIEW: RENOVASCULAR LESIONS AND *EX VIVO* RENAL SURGERY WITH AUTOTRANSPLANTATION

Joseph J. Kaufman

Part 6 examines two subjects: the treatment of renovascular lesions by *in situ* and *ex vivo* methods and the general subject of *ex vivo* renal surgery with autotransplantation. These two subjects are ripe for critical review and new perspectives. During the last 40 years, physicians have seen renovascular surgery evolve from the initial experience with nephrectomy followed by endarterectomy, bypass surgery using native vessels such as the splenic artery, free grafts of autogenous tissue, and synthetics to, more recently, autotransplantation and *ex vivo* repair. Now the pendulum is swinging to nonsurgical treatment with transarterial dilation and the development of effective antirenin drug therapy. The article by Wiley, Perloff, and Stoney, although written some 11 or 12 years ago, is a good review of the state of the art at that time. Its authors recognized that there were two distinct groups of patients with renal hypertension—the atherosclerotic and the fibrous dysplastic arterial involvement. These two entities share some features in terms of history, diagnosis, and treatment, but they vary widely in their response to surgical treatment as well as in natural history. These authors espouse the transaortic method of endarterectomy and boast an enviable record with this technique. The other technique these authors popularized is the free hypogastric autograft. Their results with this method were excellent. My own experience, which is approximately equal to that of the UCSF group in the use of autologous hypogastric arterial autografts (see Salvatierra's commentary)

confirms that this is an ideal tissue to use, particularly in young patients and primarily for nonatherosclerotic renal artery occlusive disease.

Doctor Salvatierra chooses to elaborate on *ex vivo* repair for renovascular lesions and is still advocates the continuous perfusion type of preservation popularized at his institution by Belzer. He is one of the few remaining surgeons who still thinks that continuous perfusion offers definite advantages to initial flush with cold, hyperosmolar, intracellular, electrolyte solution for *ex vivo* vascular repair. He makes valid comments on the advantages of the perfusion techniques's and boasts a high percentage of immediate function of the repaired kidneys. It is, therefore, impossible to criticize the method as it is used at his institution and in his hands. Most urologists and vascular surgeons prefer simpler preservation techniques, because they are entirely adequate for the 2- or 3-hour repair that is necessary and because they eliminate the expensive and cumbersome apparatus that is not now commonly employed at most hospitals for the harvesting and preservation of kidneys for allografts. Doctor Salvatierra has modified the *ex vivo* technique to maintain the continuity of the ureter, which most urologic surgeons performing autotransplantation prefer.

He is correct, however, in stating that the indications for *ex vivo* repair are quite limited and that the technique should be reserved for cases of uncontrollable renovascular hypertension secondary to lesions inoperable by *in situ* methods. I

229

endorse his statment that *ex vivo* reconstructive operations, including all disorders other than difficult renal arterial lesions, should be used only when *in situ* surgical repair is impossible or hazardous.

I agree with Doctor Salvatierra that the hypogastric artery, popularized by Wiley and colleagues at UCSF, and by my team at University of California, Los Angeles (UCLA), is preferable to autogenous saphenous vein grafts in that late aneurysmal dilatations and stenoses are extremely uncommon.

Doctor Salvatierra mentions percutaneous transluminal angioplasty, developed by Grüntzig, and credits it with good early results. He maintains some skepticism of the long-term results and the possibility of complications. Although it is true that experience with this technique is relatively recent, the technique of arterial dilation is not new and appears to have withstood the test of some 6 or 7 years, since described by Dotter, on the maintenance of patency. Surprising as this may seem, and perhaps frustrating to surgeons who have worked long to develop revascularization techniques, I believe that the method is going to replace surgery for the majority of stenosing lesions of the renal artery causing hypertension, particularly the fibrous lesions in young adults. In the United States alone, there are now well over 300 or 400 cases of transfemoral intraluminal "angioplasty" with excellent results and few complications.

Based on my own experience, I have made the following observations. Transfemoral angioplasty is easy and is cost effective. It certainly carries less risk of life and loss of renal function than surgery. It should be used with extreme caution in patients in whom renal artery dissection is suspected on arteriography. It may not be of lasting value for the dilation of atherosclerotic plaques, but since many of these occur in poor-risk patients, even short-term or intermediate-term good results may offer a distinct advantage over surgery in morbidity and mortality. In some cases, segmental lesions of the renal artery that formerly may have required partial nephrectomy can be satisfactorily treated by segmental embolization and infarction.

In the techniques of autotransplantation, with or without extracorporeal renal surgery, performed at the Cleveland Clinic, I agree with the technique of kidney flush with chilled, intracellular, electrolyte solution. Our own laboratory research has proved that this provides physiologic clemency for extracorporeal repair for 2 to 3 hours. I further agree that in the case of branch renal arterial disease, the hypogastric arterial graft is the optimal material; the saphenous vein graft is second best but nonetheless acceptable. The $3\frac{1}{2}$X magnification lenses optimize the technique and the results of arterial and venous anastomoses on small vessels.

I believe that renovascular disease is the best indication for *ex vivo* surgery. My results with the use of intestinal segments to replace *long ureteral defects* has been so gratifying that I seldom resort to autotransplantation. Yet in the hands of surgeons who are familiar with the technique of the vascular anastomoses, I agree that autotransplantation is an acceptable method of managing such conditions.

Carcinoma in the solitary kidney or bilateral carcinoma requiring extracorporeal resection is probably not a good indication for extracorporeal surgery. If a patient can be cured of a tumor in a solitary kidney, it is usually one that is located in a portion of the kidney that can be resected *in situ*. The idea of morcellating a kidney in order to remove several foci of cancer is unappealing and rarely, if ever, provides long-term freedom from recurrent cancer.

Renal calculus disease will never be widely treated by autotransplantation, even in the presence of extensive branch calculi. The anatrophic nephrolithotomy is such a satisfactory procedure and the infections associated with this type of calculi are so hazardous to the integrity of vascular anastomosis that I would consider all but the most exceptional patient improper for the application of autotransplantation. Recently Olsson described his method of handling recurrent stones in order to facilitate their passage in a patient with sponge kidney or primary oxalosis. He has suggested autotransplantation with direct anastomosis of the renal pelvis to the bladder or to a Boari flap. I have not employed this method, but I can see that this might be a situation where the autotransplantation could be useful.

PART SEVEN

RECONSTRUCTIVE SURGERY OF THE KIDNEY

18

URETEROCALYOSTOMY: A NEW SURGICAL PROCEDURE FOR CORRECTION OF URETEROPELVIC STRICTURE ASSOCIATED WITH AN INTRARENAL PELVIS

Sam G. Jameson, J. Schuler McKinney and Joe F. Rushton

The Journal of Urology
Vol. 77, No. 2, February 1957
Printed in U.S.A.

Surgical treatment of hydronephrosis has brought forth many varied procedures in an attempt to improve drainage of the renal pelvis. In reviewing the literature on this subject, all of the operative procedures described are specifically designed for the extrarenal pelvis. Nowhere in the literature, to the best knowledge of the authors, is any specific operation described for the occasional, or rare, ureteropelvic stricture associated with a complete intrarenal pelvis. This problem has been unexpectedly encountered in a solitary kidney of an 8-month-old male infant, making it mandatory that a procedure be devised whereby drainage would be improved.

CASE REPORT

J.L.C., 8-month-old-white boy, was always in good health when he suffered an acute episode of gastroen-teritis. Because of diarrhea and vomiting with dehydration, the patient was hospitalized and given subcutaneous fluids and antibiotics followed by improvement. He was discharged 4 days after admission. However, during the 24 hours after leaving the hospital, the mother noted that patient did not void. Generalized edema was also noted, and patient was again hospitalized.

Physical examination: Temperature 100.2 degrees; pulse 140; abdomen revealed large, firm, questionably tender mass in right upper quadrant. Moderate generalized edema was present.

Laboratory determiantions: Hemoglobin 10.6 gm; red blood cells 4,660,000; white blood cells 15,000; blood urea nitrogen 65.0; sodium 135 mEq/liter; potassium 5.0 mEq/liter; chlorides 90 mEq/liter; and CO_2 combining power 26 volumes percent. No urine could be obtained upon admission for urinalysis.

In spite of supportive therapy, including M/6 sodium lactate, the general condition of patient became worse during the following 24 hours and generalized edema increased. Because there was no urinary output, it was felt that cystoscopy with passage of ureteral catheters was indicated to rule out obstructive uropathy. Cystoscopy revealed congenital absence of left half of trigone and left ureteral orifice. Protruding from right ureteral orifice were several brownish colored crystals which microscopically were found to be uric acid. A 4F ureteral catheter was passed to the right renal pelvis several times. Upon removing the catheter from the ureter each time, one or more waves of urine were seen to come from the ureteral orifice. Because of the poor condition of the patient, anesthesia and instrumentation were not prolonged in order to do retrograde pyelograms at this time. It was felt that the obstruction had been relieved and the patient was returned to his room. In retrospect, it was felt that diarrhea with dehydration and acidosis had produced precipitation of uric acid crystals with subsequent blockage of ureter.

Twenty-four hours following cystoscopy, it was noted that the patient still had not voided, and catheterization revealed no urine in the bladder. Cystoscopy was again performed under general anesthesia, and a 4F ureteral catheter was passed to the renal pelvis and left indwelling. A retrograde pyelogram at this time revealed a large filling defect in the right renal pelvis, felt to be due to uric acid crystals. This catheter was left in place and the patient was returned to his room. During the following 12 hours diuresis was profuse through the catheter, which was irrigated frequently with sodium bicarbonate solution in an effort to further dissolve the uric acid crystals. Because the temperature by this time had risen to 105.8 degrees, the patient was started on antibiotics and chemotherapy.

Three days later there was marked generalized improvement of the patient and the ureteral catheter was removed after making a retrograde pyelogram, which revealed considerable decrease in filling defect, although it was still present. Following removal of catheter, the patient voided frequently with a large 24-hour volume. During the following 14 days, the patient was continued on supportive therapy, chemotherapy, and antibiotics with much improvement. The white blood cell count fell from 29,800 to 13,600. After receiving whole blood transfusions, the hemoglobin rose from 8.5 gm to 10.1 gm, and the red blood cells rose from 3,000,000 to 4,260,000.

Twenty days after admission the patient appeared to be in good general condition, at which time an excretory urogram was made to determine whether any underlying pathological process might be present, which, in addition to the dehydration and acidosis resulting from the diarrhea, could have caused precipitation of uric acid crystals. This excretory urogram confirmed the previous diagnosis of congenital absence of left kidney. On the right side there was a large hydronephrotic sac, obviously secondary to a stricture of the ureteropelvic junction (Fig. 1A). There was no evidence of uric acid crystals in the renal pelvis or calyceal system at this time.

Surgical correction of this stricture was recommended to the parents, but because of the constant vigil during the preceding illness, they requested that surgery

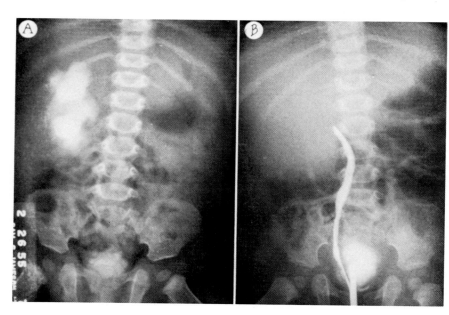

Fig. 1. (A) Excretory urogram 20 days after admission to hospital reveals right hydronephrosis secondary to stricture of ureteropelvic junction. Congenital absence of left kidney. (B) Retrograde ureterogram 8 days following intravenous pyelogram reveals complete blockage of ureteropelvic junction secondary to inflammatory reaction and edema at site of stricture.

be postponed for 2 weeks in order to allow them to get away from the hospital for a few days. It was felt this would not be detrimental to patient, and therefore he was discharged.

The patient did well for about 8 days, but then fever and generalized edema developed. There days later he ceased voiding and was readmitted to the hospital.

Physical examination: Temperature 104; pulse rate 140; respiratory rate 30; abdomen revealed right kidney enlarged and tender, easily palpable below right costal margin. There was marked generalized edema.

Laboratory findings: Hemoglobin 8.7 gm; red blood cells 2,640,000; white blood cells 26,000; blood urea nitrogen 45.

It was felt that inflammatory reaction at site of ureteropelvic stricture resulted in enough edema to completely block drainage from the kidney.

Cystoscopy was again performed under general anesthesia. A 4F catheter was introduced into the right ureter, at which time a ureterogram was made (Fig. 1B). Following this a catheter was introduced into the renal pelvis and a retrograde pyelogram made. The catheter was left indwelling; there was immediate diuresis with prompt clinical improvement of patient.

First operation (Fig. 2): Eight days after admission, the right kidney was exposed in order to repair the ureteropelvic stricture. Upon dissecting hilum of kidney completely free, a marked narrowing of ureter was found immediately adjacent to the kidney for a distance of about 1 cm. This stricture became more pronounced the closer the ureter approximated the kidney. At this point the ureter was very pale and friable in appearance. There was no evidence whatsoever that any portion of the renal pelvis extended outside the renal parenchyma. To further

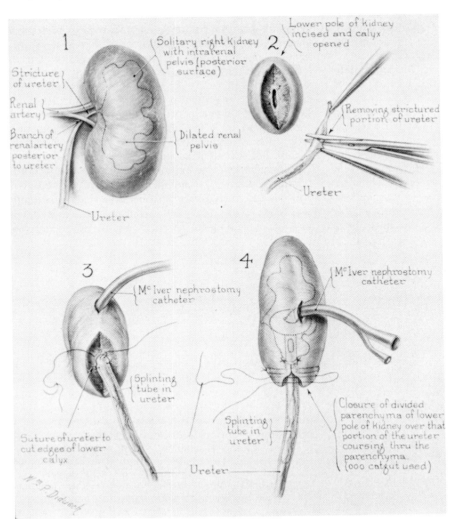

Fig. 2. Findings and procedure at time of first operation. The mistake made was closure of lower pole nephrostomy over that portion of ureter coursing through it, later resulting in compression of ureter by fibrosis and contracture of parenchyma. In retrospect, lower pole amputation at site of ureterocalyceal anastomosis should have been performed.

complicate this finding, the renal artery was divided into two branches, with the slightly smaller of the two branches coursing posterior to ureter and supplying the posterior one-third of kidney. Temporary occlusion of this vessel caused marked cyanosis of the posterior one-third of the kidney. Therefore, it was felt that this artery could not be sacrificed in order to split the medial surface of parenchyma so that the renal pelvis could be exposed. Because of marked friability of the stricture, associated with marked inflammatory reaction of this area, it was felt that an intubation type procedure would not succeed.

Rather than do a nephrostomy, which certainly would have been permanent, the decision was made to divide the ureter and approximate the free end to the lower calyx. With a Doyen clamp on the renal vessels, the lower pole of the kidney was divided on the convex surface down to the lower calyx. The lower calyx was opened large enough to have a circumference about twice the size the circumference of the ureter. The strictured and friable portion of ureter was excised, after which a No. 18 McIver nephrostomy tube with 12F splint was brought through the kidney into opening of lower calyx. The splinting portion of this catheter was introduced into the ureter, after which the upper free edge of the ureter was sutured to the mucous membrane of the calyx with 3 interrupted sutures of 4-0 chromic catgut. Whether to amputate the lower pole of kidney up to site of anastomosis or whether to close the lower pole of kidney over that portion of ureter coursing through the parenchyma was debated, and it was felt that in all probability a better anastomosis could be obtained by closing the parenchyma over the ureter. Therefore, several mattress sutures of 3-0 chromic catgut were taken through the parenchyma closing the nephrostomy of the lower pole

of the kidney over that portion of the ureter coursing through it. A rubber drain was left down to the kidney, after which the wound was closed in the usual manner.

The patient tolerated the procedure very well, and postoperative course was essentially uneventful. There was considerable urinary drainage by way of the tissue drain onto the dressing, but a major portion of urine drained satisfactorily through the nephrostomy tube. The patient was discharged from the hospital on the tenth postoperative day and followed as an outpatient.

The nephrostomy tube was removed on the twenty-second postoperative day and an excretory urogram made on the twenty-third postoperative day (Fig. 3A). This pyelogram revealed essentially no change from the excretory urogram made prior to surgery. It was felt that in all probability there was either compression of ureter by renal parenchyma, or else a stricture was forming at site of anastomosis.

Following removal of the nephrostomy tube, the patient began to have low grade fever and pyuria which continued in spite of specific chemotherapy and antibiotics as indicated by urine culture and sensitivity tests.

On the thirty-second postoperative day cystoscopy was performed and a 4F catheter was introduced into ureter and ureterogram made (Fig. 3B), revealing compression of that portion of ureter coursing through the parenchyma. The catheter was passed into the renal pelvis and left indwelling 36 hours. During this time the patient became afebrile. After removal of the catheter, the low grade fever promptly reappeared in spite of continued antibiotics and chemotherapy.

On the thirty-ninth postoperative day, cystoscopy was repeated and a 5F catheter introduced to renal pelvis and left indwelling for 48 hours. Again, during a period

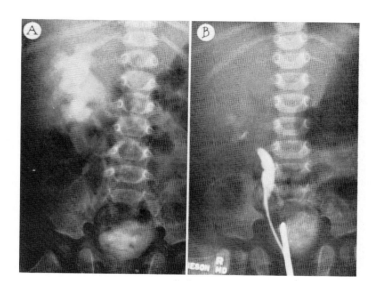

Fig. 3. (A) Excretory urogram on 23rd postoperative day. Essentially no change from preoperative film. (B) Retrograde ureterogram on 32nd postoperative day. Note filling of ureter up to point where ureter enters renal parenchyma. At this point there is no evidence of contrast medium because of compression of ureter by fibrosis and contracture of lower pole of kidney.

of ureteral catheter drainage there was no elevation of temperature, but low grade fever and promptly reappeared upon removal of the catheter.

Low grade fever and pyuria continued until the sixtieth postoperative day, at which time cystoscopy was repeated and a 6F catheter introduced into the renal pelvis with no difficulty. Twenty-five cubic centimeters of grossly infected residual urine were obtained from the pelvis. The catheter was left indwelling in order to decompress the kidney completely. The patient was readmitted to the hospital and antibiotics and chemotherapy were continued. The patient became completely afebrile in 48 hours.

Second operation (Fig. 4): On the sixty-second postoperative day, the patient was taken to the operating room and the right kidney exposed. The ureter was identified and freed by sharp and blunt dissection from point of exit from lower pole of kidney down to a point about 5 cm. distally. The lower pole of the kidney was found to be markedly scarred, indurated, and contracted from previous surgery and infection. The lower pole was excised using sharp dissection, care being taken to leave the ureter intact at the site of anastomosis to the lower calyx. The infundibulum of the lower calyx was opened and a right angle clamp introduced through calyx into upper ureter, with no evidence whatsoever of stricture at the site of the previous anastomosis. It was then obvious that impaired drainage following the first operation resulted from fibrosis and contracture of lower pole parenchyma and compressed that portion of the ureter coursing through it. The ureter was divided completely from the calyx, and the opening into the calyx was made

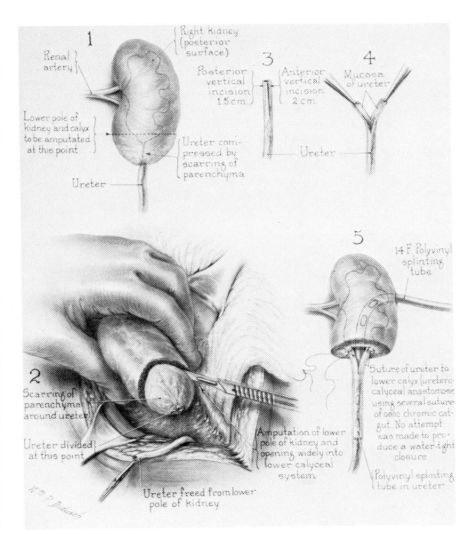

Fig. 4. Findings and procedure at time of second operation. Lower pole of kidney was fibrotic and contracted. Amputation of lower pole with revision of ureterocalyostomy was performed.

larger by extending it into the infundibulum. The entire fibrotic and contracted lower pole was amputated. Using curved nephrostomy hook, a 14F polyvinyl catheter was brought through the convex surface of upper portion of kidney into the intrarenal pelvis and out the lower calyx and infundibulum. A longitudinal incision was made on the posterior surface of the ureter for a distance of about 1.5 cm, and a similar incision made on the anterior surface of the ureter for a distance of about 2.0 cm. After making several holes in that portion of catheter which was to be left in renal pelvis, the distal portion of the catheter was introduced into the ureter. The free edges of ureter were sutured to the mucous membrane of the calyx and infundibulum with interrupted sutures of 4-0 chromic catgut. No attempt was made to make a water tight closure. After completion of anastomosis, a rubber drain was left down to the kidney and the wound closed in layers in the usual manner.

The patient tolerated this procedure well and was returned to room in good condition. He was continued on antibiotics and other supportive therapy. The convalencence was most satisfactory and again uneventful, and patient was discharged on tenth postoperative day.

There was considerable urinary drainage onto the dressing for 15–20 days, but this soon became minimal. The polyvinyl splint was removed on the thirty-sixth postoperative day, being replaced with a 12F nephrostomy tube. A pyelogram was made through this nephrostomy tube on the fifty-ninth postoperative day (Fig. 5A). The nephrostomy tube was removed on the sixty-third postoperative day. There was no urinary drainage from the flank following removal of the tube, and the nephros-

tomy site healed promptly. Excretory urogram was made 9 months postoperatively (Fig. 5C).

The patient has remained afebrile since removing the nephrostomy tube, and the urine has become negative. He has continued to do extremely well in general, and at this time is completely asymptomatic.

DISCUSSION

This patient has presented a multitude of problems. First, the decision had to be made whether to do a nephrostomy in order to evacuate the uric acid crystals from the renal pelvis, or whether conservative therapy in the form of an indwelling ureteral catheter with alkaline irrigations would suffice. The latter was found to be most satisfactory and is recommended as treatment of choice for this particular trouble.

Second, at time of the first operative procedure the ureter was found to enter renal parenchyma without any evidence whatsoever of pelvis being located externally. The upper ureter, because of friability and inflammatory reaction, was certainly not the ideal type tissue with which to do a successful pyeloureteroplasty. Longitudinal incision of the ureter into the renal parenchyma and renal pelvis was considered, with intubation over a prolonged period of time. However, the marked amount of inflammatory reaction, along with the large aberrant renal artery, made this, in the opinion of the authors, doomed from the onset. In lieu of doing a nephrostomy, which certainly would have been permanent and progressively fatal, it was felt that ureterocalyostomy should be given a chance. The error made at the first operation

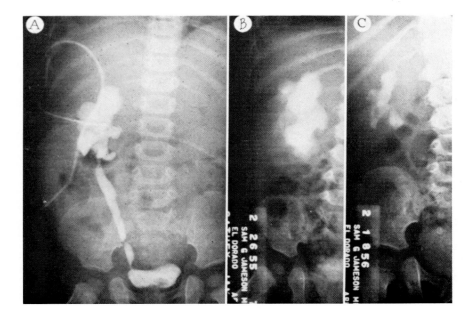

Fig. 5. (A) Pyelogram made through nephrostomy tube on fifty-ninth postoperative day. No evidence of extravasation of contrast medium at site of anastomosis, indicating complete epithelization at site of anastomosis. (B) Preoperative excretory urogram and 9-month postoperative excretory urogram. Note decrease of hydronephrosis.

was the closing of that portion of the parenchyma through which the ureter coursed, resulting in compression externally of the ureter by fibrosis and contracture. If the lower pole had been amputated up to the opening of the lower calyx at time of the first operation, it is believed that the ureterocalyostomy would have been successful from the onset.

Third, at time of second operation, the lower pole had to be amputated in order to release compression of that portion of ureter coursing through it. Slightly more renal tissue had to be removed at this procedure than would have had to be removed if the lower pole had been amputated at the first operation. In other words, if this particular procedure is used in the future, the amount of kidney tissue which would be sacrificed by lower pole amputation would be much less than that which was amputated in this particular case.

Fourth, as evidenced by the prolonged nephrostomy drainage even though the ureter was patent, there was temporary loss of peristalsis of the ureter, including both the frequency of peristaltic waves and the amplitude of each wave. Swenson[1,2] has done much investigative work on ureteral peristalsis, and because of his reports considerable confidence was obtained that the ureter would eventually regain its peristaltic properties. This was evidenced several weeks later by the fact that the bladder output became more and more, and the output through the nephrostomy tube became less and less, even with the nephrostomy tube being left open continuously.

Last, the authors are most cognizant of the fact that one case or one operation proves nothing. However, because ureteropelvis stricture associated with a complete intrarenal pelvis is not too common, because there is no specific operative procedure designed for this type anomaly, and because in this particular case our end results were most satisfactory, we believe that our experience with lower pole amputation and ureterocalyostomy may well be of benefit to others who encounter this type anomaly. It is for this reason that this one-case report has been prepared.

SUMMARY

A case of congenital stricture with complete blockage of the ureteropelvic junction is presented. This case was complicated by absence of the opposite kidney, the presence of a complete intrarenal pelvis, and the coursing of a large aberrant artery posterior to the ureter.

A method of dissolution or uric acid crystals in the ureter and renal pelvis is presented.

A technique of lower pole amputation of the kidney with ureterocalyostomy is presented, and is recommended as the procedure of choice in the presence of hydronephrosis secondary to ureteropelvic stricture associated with a complete intrarenal pelvis.

REFERENCES

1. Swenson, Orxar and Marchant, Douglas: Ureteropelvic obstruction in infants and children. J Urol 73:945–950, 1955
2. Swenson, Orxar: Personal communications, 1955

Accepted for publication September 12, 1956.

El Dorado, Ark. (S.G.J. and J.S.McK.)
Magnolia, Ark. (J.F.R.)

Commentary: Ureterocaliostomy Reconstruction

Martin G. McLoughlin

To restore continuity in an obstructed intrarenal pelvis in the patient who has had previous ureteropelvic surgery, has a thinned lower-pole parenchyma, and may have lower-pole calculi, an infrequently used surgical technique may be necessary. The length of the normal ureter is important in one's choice of procedure in any reconstructive technique where a scarred ureteropelvic junction must be reconstructed. If the kidney is encased in scar, is inaccessible, or both, then the standard ureteropelvic reconstructive procedures, autotransplantation, the Davis intubated ureterostomy, and an ileal segment interposition do not always lend themselves to the clinical situation.[1-4] The placement of a permanent nephrostomy tube is an alternative that may be accompanied by many complications. The use of nephrectomy in a patient with a scarred intrarenal pelvis and failed reconstruction should be a last resort, and, in many instances, the patient with this clinical picture has often already undergone contralateral nephrectomy or has an atrophic kidney on the other side.

Ureterocaliostomy reconstruction provides the means of dependent drainage to a kidney whereby an adequate funnel with a wide diameter to the caliceal ureteral anastomosis may prevent future scarring and stenosis. This procedure requires the adequate removal and tapering of the surrounding renal tissue to prevent future scarring and stenosis. The principle of the anastomosis in this procedure should be the same as for any dismembered pyeloplasty with a wide suture line between the infundibulum and the split ureter.

This procedure should be used infrequently—reserved for the patient in whom standard ureteropelvic reconstructive procedures have been tried and have failed. The patient should have a diverting nephrostomy tube and internal stent; recently I have used Dexon sutures, since most of the patients have had a previous reconstructive procedure with chromic sutures and therefore may benefit from the delayed absorption of the Dexon.

REFERENCES

1. Smart WR: Surgical correction of hydronephrosis. In Harrison JH (ed): Campbell's Urology. Vol 3, p 2047, Philadelphia, W B Saunders, 1979

2. McLoughlin MG, Williams GM, Stonesifer GL: Ex vivo surgical dissection. JAMA 235:1705, 1976

3. Davis DM: The process of ureteral repair: A recapitulation of the splinting question. J Urol 79:215, 1958

4. Goodwin WE, Winter CC, Turner RD: Replacement of the ureter by small intestine. Clinical application and results of the "ileal ureter." J Urol 81:406, 1959

ANNOTATED BIBLIOGRAPHY

McLoughlin MG: Ureterocalyostomy. Br J Urol 48:328, 1976

This article presents a case report of a woman aged 28 with a solitary kidney with a nephrostomy tube in place. She had a serum creatinine level of 2.8 mg/dl and a urine culture showing greater than 100,000 colonies of *Pseudomonas hydrogenase*. I exposed her kidney through a transperitoneal approach and resected the ureter just below the ureteropelvic junction, then removing the lower pole of the kidney to exose the dilated inferior calix. The renal parenchyma around the exposed calix was then shaved off so that no parenchyma could be found. After removing a small calculus from this exposed inferior calix, I fashioned a funneled ureterocalyostomy and used nephrostomy tube drainage. The nephrostomy tube was removed after 3 weeks, and she has been seen in follow-up examination with a creatinine level of 1.6 mg/dl. I discuss the technical aspects of this operation and the need to remove the parenchyma surrounding the lower poles so that scar tissue cannot result in stenosis. This is a rarely used procedure that should only be contemplated after other standard techniques fail to provide adequate drainage in a dependent position with adequate lumen size.

Kuss R, Chatelain C: Surgery of the Ureter, p 44–50. Berlin, Springer-Verlang, 1975

The authors describe the operative technique for ureterocaliceal anastomosis. They favor approaching the ureter and kidney through the anterior transperiteoneal pouch because it provides a different and wider exposure to the lesion but also permits intestine ureteroplasty if the ureterocaliceal anastomosis cannot be carried out. The technique of exposing the ureter and lower calix is outlined; the authors emphasize that one must remove all scar tissue and renal parenchyma to develop a wide crater in the renal parenchyma down to the caliceal wall. The ureter is then spatulated and anastomosed to the calix. Urinary drainage is provided by an *in situ* ureterostomy that remains for 12 to 14 days. A temporary nephrostomy tube is often used to provide adequate drainage. In order for the anastomosis to succeed, the disease must be limited to the first part of the ureter; the rest of the ureter and the lower urinary tract should be normal, and there must be free communication between the caliceal system. This procedure should be carried out when there is destruction and where the scarred stenotic renal pelvis cannot be handled by routine reconstructive procedures. In general, the best results occur when the renal parenchyma is thin and there is adequate exposure for a direct ureterocaliceal anastomosis.

19

DISMEMBERED INFUNDIBULOPYELOSTOMY: IMPROVED TECHNIQUE FOR CORRECTING VASCULAR OBSTRUCTION OF THE SUPERIOR INFUNDIBULUM

Elwin E. Fraley

From the Surgery Branch, National Cancer Institute, National Institutes of Health, Bethesda, Maryland

The Journal of Urology
Copyright © 1969 by The Williams & Wilkins Co.
Vol. 101, February
Printed in U.S.A.

Although both radiologists and urologists long have recognized that renal arteries and renal veins can produce radiographic filling defects by impinging upon the infundibula,[1-4] only recently has it been appreciated that these crossing vessels may have clinical significance. In 2 recent papers the author described 5 cases of a previously unrecognized syndrome of nephralgia caused by intrarenal vascular obstruction of the superior infundibulum.[5,6] These reports detailed the anatomic and radiographic findings in this abnormality and outlined the surgical techniques used to correct the obstructions.

Accepted for publication March 15, 1968.

The purpose of this communication is to record two additional cases of vascular obstruction of the superior infundibulum and to describe an improved technique for correcting one form of this abnormality.

CASE REPORTS

Case 1. P.M., a 52-year-old woman, entered the hospital with a 12-year history of intermittent right flank pain. The patient was in good health until pain developed mainly in the right costovertebral angle and flank but occasionally radiated to the groin. Also, at times, the discomfort was felt in the right upper quadrant anteriorly.

Because of the persistence of the pain without apparent cause a cholecystectomy was done, but symptoms remained unchanged. A subsequent excretory urogram revealed a right renal abnormality. The patient was told that she had a birth defect in her kidney and that, if discomfort persisted, she would need a nephrectomy. The patient denied all other urinary tract symptoms.

Physical examination revealed only mild right costovertebral angle tenderness. The cholecystectomy incision was well-healed. The hemogram, urinalysis and basic chemistries were all within normal limits. A urine culture was sterile.

The excretory urogram showed a long right superior infundibulum that was somewhat dilated proximal to a filling defect in its mid-portion (Fig. 1A). The upright film indicated that the obstruction was accentuated by kinking of the infundibulum as the kidney descended even though there was only minimal renal mobility (Fig. 1B).

Cystoscopy was unremarkable and a right retrograde pyelogram again demonstrated a well-defined filling defect in the infundibulum that did not disappear with over-distention of the proximal collecting system. There was retention of dye in the infundibulum proximal to

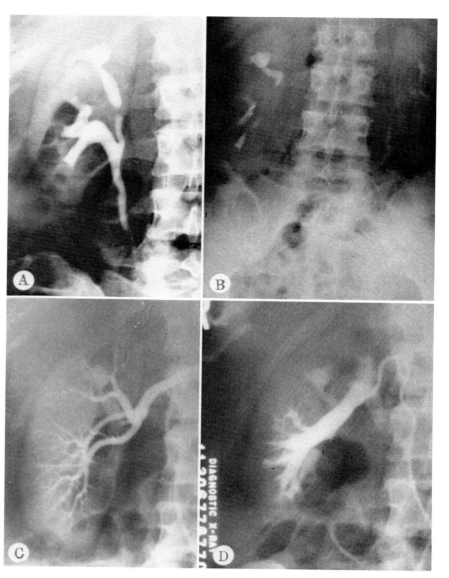

Fig. 1. Case 1. (A) Excretory urogram shows right superior calycectasis proximal to persistent midinfundibular filling defect. (B) Upright film of excretory urogram demonstrates kinking of infundibulum and accentuation of infundibular obstruction associated with mild renal ptosis. (C) Selective right renal arteriogram illustrates artery to posterior renal vascular segment crossing superior infundibulum at site of pyelographic filling defect. (D) Right renal venogram. Main renal vein also crosses infundibulum at site of obstruction.

the filling defect on the 30-minute drainage film of the retrograde pyelogram. This delay in drainage from the superior calyx was approximately equal in both supine and upright positions.

A cine excretory urogram showed interference with the delivery of dye from a proximal superior calyx and infundibulum into the renal pelvis. The infundibular obstruction again appeared to be increased when the patient was upright.

Selective right renal arteriography and venography demonstrated an artery crossing the infundibulum in the area of the filling defect (Fig. 1C and D). A lateral projection on the arteriogram indicated that the artery crossed dorsally to the infundibulum and that the infundibulum was caught in a vascular vise between the artery and the main renal vein.

A diagnosis of vascular obstruction of the superior infundibulum was made and the patient was explored. The anatomical basis of the obstruction was exactly as predicted from the preoperative arteriogram; that is, the superior infundibulum was compressed between the artery supplying the posterior renal vascular segment and the overlying main renal vein (Fig. 2). The site of the obstruction was essentially extrarenal. To relieve this obstruction, the infundibulum was transected at the infundibulopelvic junction and then it was placed dorsal to the artery. A small catheter was passed into the infundibulum to rule out intrinsic obstruction. The lumen of the infundibulum was also visualized clearly by rolling the infundibulum back on itself to expose the point of obstruction. The infundibulum was then anastomosed to the pelvis with a single running layer of 5-zero chromic catgut suture (Fig. 2).

The patient was asymptomatic 6 months postoperatively. The excretory urogram showed less superior calycectasis and no infundibular filling defect.

Case 2. J.C., a 22-year-old man, entered the hospital with a 1-year history of intermittent right flank pain. The patient was well until the onset of low back and right costovertebral angle pain. The discomfort became progressively worse and just prior to admission to the hospital acute exacerbation was associated with the passage of tea-colored urine.

Physical examination was unremarkable except for right costovertebral angle tenderness. Routine laboratory studies including urinalysis were all within normal limits. The urine was sterile.

An excretory urogram showed right superior calycectasis and a persistent filling defect on the right superior infundibulum (Fig. 3). There was no abnormal mobility in the upright position.

Cystoscopy was unremarkable. A retrograde pyelogram demonstrated entrapment of dye in the right

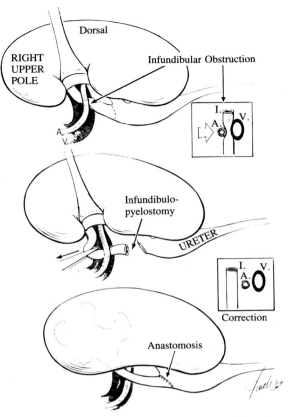

Fig. 2. Case 1. Right kidney completely mobilized as seen dorsally. Artery to posterior vascular segment is obstructing superior infundibulum by compressing it ventrally against main renal vein. To correct obstruction, infundibulum was transected at infundibulopelvic junction and then infundibulum was transposed dorsally to artery. Infundibulum was anastomosed to pelvis with single running suture. Kidney was turned and fixed in position so artery remained away from infundibulum.

superior calyx after 30 minutes even though the patient was kept in steep reverse Trendelenberg position to facilitate drainage. The previously noted filling defect also was clearly demonstrated.

A cine excretory urogram showed marked hold up of dye and interference with infundibular peristalsis in the area of the infundibular filling defect. A selective right renal angiogram demonstrated what appeared to be the artery to the posterior renal vascular segment compressing the infundibulum and producing the persistent radiographic filling defect. We concluded that the patient also had obstruction of the right superior infundibulum that was causing pain from periodic over-distention of the calyx.

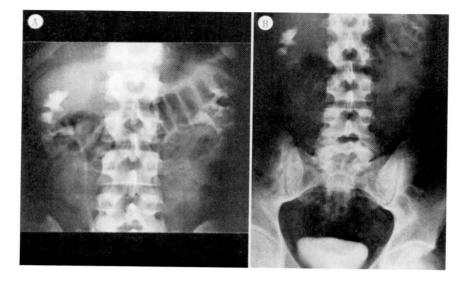

Fig. 3. Case 2. Excretory urograms show persistent filling defect in infundibulum and marked right superior calycectasis.

Surgical exploration revealed that the artery to the posterior vascular segment was compressing the infundibulum against overlying renal substance and the main renal vein (Fig. 4). The obstruction was intrarenal in location. The abnormality was exposed by careful dissection in the pyelorenal sinus. Surgical repair consisted of a dismembered infundibulopyelostomy similar to that performed in case 1.

One year postoperatively the patient was without symptoms. The excretory urogram showed less superior calycectasis and no infundibular filling defect.

DISCUSSION

It is well known that pain can result from obstruction to urine flow and stretching of the ureter or renal pelvis. Similarly, pain associated with obstruction of the infundibulum probably is caused by periodic over-distention of the calyx major and its surrounding smooth muscle. Although pain secondary to obstruction in the proximal urinary tract is usually referred to the flank or costovertebral angle it may be vaguely localized in the right upper quadrant. Case 1 clearly illustrates how nephralgia can be confused with the pain of biliary tract disease, and thus this case emphasizes the importance of considering nephralgia in the differential diagnosis of right upper quadrant pain.

The most frequent benign causes of chronic flank pain are probably pyelonephritis, stones and gross anatomical abnormalities such as ureteropelvic junction obstruction. All of these conditions usually are easily diagnosed. However two common causes of chronic nephralgia, nephroptosis and vascular obstruction of the

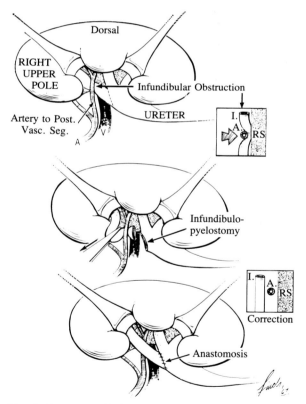

Fig. 4. Case 2. Right kidney completely mobilized and viewed dorsally. Site of obstruction was intrarenal in location. Artery to posterior vascular segment was compressing infundibulum against overlying renal substance. Surgical correction of abnormality was essentially as described in figure 2.

infundibulum, may go undetected unless subtle abnormalities in the excretory urogram are properly interpreted. In fact, the excretory urogram from patients with nephroptosis may be essentially normal and renal ptosis will not be seen unless upright films are obtained. The radiographic findings in vascular obstruction of the infundibulum consist of calycectasis, a well-defined radiographic filling defect in the infundibulum and delayed emptying of the obstructed calyx on the late drainage films of the retrograde pyelogram. Further specialized studies such as cine excretory urography and angiography are of course helpful in substantiating this diagnosis. A more complete description of the radiographic findings in vascular obstruction of the infundibulum has been presented elsewhere.[7]

The operative procedure used to relieve vascular obstruction of the infundibulum varies depending upon the anatomy.[5,6] For example, if the offending vessel is a vein, simply dividing it will usually correct the abnormality. However, renal arteries are end-arteries and they cannot be interrupted without death of a significant amount of renal tissue. The operative technique presented herein was conceived for cases in which an artery coursing dorsally to the infundibulum causes an obstruction by compression of the infundibulum ventrally against either renal veins (case 1) or overlying kidney (case 2). Because the artery cannot be divided the infundibulum must be repositioned away from the obstructing vessel. This maneuver can be accomplished by transecting the mid-portion of the infundibulum and performing an infundibuloinfundibulostomy ventral to the artery. However, in the one previous case in which the procedure was done,[6] technical difficulty was encountered because of the small size of the mid-infundibulum and its relative inaccessibility. An infundibulopyelostomy on the other hand is easy to perform because of the greater size and extrarenal location of the structures. In addition, an infundibulopyelostomy is probably less likely to stricture.

There are several other important aspects of surgical technique relating to these cases that should be mentioned briefly. Adequate exposure of the upper pole and renal pedicle is absolutely essential and can usually only be achieved through an 11th or 12th rib incision. An intrinsic obstruction of the infundibulum must be ruled out. We have always checked the patency of the infundibulum with a small straight rubber catheter if the infundibulum is normal by palpation. Also, the lumen of the infundibulum usually can be exposed at some time during the surgical procedure. The kidney should be fixed in a position so that the previously obstructing vessel is held away from the infundibulum permanently.

SUMMARY

Two cases of vascular obstruction of the superior infundibulum are presented. The technique of infundibulopyelostomy which is outlined is suitable for correcting vascular obstruction of the infundibulum caused by an artery compressing the superior infundibulum ventrally against either the main renal vein or kidney. Infundibulopyelostomy is preferred to infundibuloinfundibulostomy because it is easier technically and the anastomosis is probably less prone to stricture. The importance of considering the kidney as a possible source of vague abdominal pain is emphasized.

REFERENCES

1. Baum, S., Gillenwater, J. Y.: Renal artery impressions on the renal pelvis. J Urol 95:139–145, 1966
2. Kreel, L. and Pyle, R.: Arterial impressions on the renal pelvis. Brit J Radiol 35:609–613, 1962
3. Meng, C. H. and Elkin, M.: Venous impressions on calyceal system. Radiology 87:878–882, 1966
4. Tille, D.: Nicht pathologische Fullungsdefekte des Nierenbeckens and der Nierenkelche. Deutsch Med Wschr 85:1414–1415, 1960
5. Fraley, E. E.: Vascular obstruction of superior infundibulum causing nephralgia: a new syndrome. New Engl J Med 275:1403–1409, 1966
6. Fraley, E. E.: Surgical correction of intrarenal disease. I. Obstructions of the superior infundibulum. J Urol 98:54–64, 1967
7. Nebesar, R. A., Pollard, J. J. and Fraley, E. E.: Renal vascular impressions: incidence and clinical significance. Amer J Roentgen 101:719–727, 1967

Commentary: The Fraley Syndrome

Elwin E. Fraley

The syndrome of nephralgia caused by obstruction of the superior infundibulum by renal blood vessels, which other physicians have since called the Fraley syndrome, was first reported in 1966.[1] Its incidence is not known, but clearly it is not rare. I have treated 20 patients for it, and several other physicians have reported 1 or more cases.[2-14] Also, Freed has described a patient whose middle infundibulum was obstructed, causing incapacitating pain.[15]

Any of several anatomic abnormalities may be responsible for the obstruction. The infundibulum may be compressed against the renal parenchyma, often by the artery to the upper pole; this is especially likely when the collecting system is almost entirely intrarenal. In other patients, the infundibulum is trapped between two blood vessels as if by scissors. In such cases, the crossing vessels may be drawn more tightly when the patient is upright, both by the descent of the kidney and by its dorsal-to-ventral rotation on its long axis.[16]

The differential diagnosis of nephralgia can be difficult. Among the possible causes of the pain, other than infundibular obstruction, are obstruction of the ureteropelvic junction (which may be intermittent), renal ptosis, vesicoureteral reflux, calculi, and tumors. Too often, these patients are evaluated by one clinical department after another, eventually being seen by a psychiatrist because no physical cause for the pain can be found.

The evaluation begins with an infusion urogram, which must include supine, prone, and upright views, because many intrarenal obstructions and obstructions of the ureteropelvic junction are evident only when the patient is in a particular position. The diuresis accompanying the procedure often accentuates the pain, and some authors have suggested provocative tests such as forced diuresis or retrograde ureteral catheterization with distension of the renal pelvis to increase or precipitate pain.[17-19] In my experience, provocative tests often fail. Certainly, if the pain is intermittent, the evaluation is not complete until a urogram has been obtained during an episode of pain.

Other tests are needed as well. A voiding cystourethrogram is especially important in children, in whom vesicoureteral reflux may cause nephralgia. A renogram with ^{131}I-hippuran also is useful, and, again, both supine and upright views may be needed.[20] When it is not clear whether the obstruction is intrinsic or extrinsic, and when abnormal blood vessels are suspected, an arteriogram with oblique views is useful.[21] The differential diagnosis of renal pain has been reviewed by DeWolf and Fraley.[22]

It is important to note that approximately 10% of patients reveal vascular impressions on the superior infundibulum at radiography.[16] I believe that these findings are significant only when there are symptoms, such as infection or pain. All the patients I have seen with this syndrome have had clear radiographic signs: persistent infundibular filling defects on excretory and retrograde pyelography and delayed drainage of the superior calix (confirmed by renogram).[1,16,23] Cineradiography often showed a lack of peristalsis across the obstruction. Certainly, the diagnosis of infundibular obstruction should not be one of last resort.

Treatment varies, depending on the particular abnormality. If the obstruction is caused by a vein, or by an artery and a vein, division of the offending vein may suffice. However, if the infundibulum is trapped between two arteries, or compressed against the kidney by an artery, it may be necessary to transpose the infundibulum. I believe that the best technique for this is the dismembered infundibulopyeloplasty, as described in the preceding article. (This also was the technique used to correct obstruction of the middle infundibulum.[15]) In those patients in whom there is insufficient space through which to bring the infundibulum, it may be necessary to divide one branch of the artery and, perhaps, to remove a wedge of kidney so that the infundibulum can be transposed.

Certain points of the operative technique require comment. In early cases, I approached the infundibulum through a small nephrotomy. Experience showed that careful removal of the connective tissue covering the vessels and the collecting system releases the infundibulum, which can be pulled toward the surgeon for a better look at the problem. During the corrective procedure, I usually retract the infundibulum with a small rubber drain or umbilical tape. Also, the renal hilum is easier to see if the medial edge of the kidney is retracted with a small or medium-size vein retractor. Because extensive dissection usually is necessary, the kidney should be fixed in position as part of the operation; otherwise, the patient may suffer postoperatively from pain caused by renal ptosis. Fixation also holds the kidney away from structures that could impinge on the collecting system.

Usually the most that can be expected from the operation is relief of pain and improved drainage. In most patients, the obstruction will have been longstanding, and irreversible dilatation of the calix can be expected. Delayed drainage films of the retrograde pyelogram will thus show improved emptying, but continued caliectasis is likely.

REFERENCES

1. Fraley EE: Vascular obstruction of the superior infundibulum causing nephralgia. N Engl J Med 275:1403, 1966

2. D'Alò R, Severini A: Impronte vasali sulla pelvi renale. Radiol Med 53:225, 1967

3. Deckers PJ, Fraley EE, Paulson DF, Harbert JC: Vascular obstruction of the superior renal infundibulum in children. Surgery 67:856, 1970

4. Michel JR, Barsamian J: Les empreintes vasculaires sur les calices et le bassinet. Ann Radiol 14:15, 1971

5. Johnston JH, Sandomirsky SK: Intrarenal vascular obstruction of the superior infundibulum in children. J Pediatr Surg 7:318, 1972

6. Joffre F, Carcy JB, Putois J: Obstructions calicielles par compression infundibulaire vasculaire (syndrome de Fraley). J Radiol Electrol 53:485, 1972

7. Johnston JH: Intrarenale Gefassstenose des obern Kelchhalses bei Kindern. Actuel Urol 3:219, 1972

8. Gold JM, Bucy JG: Fraley's syndrome with bilateral infundibular obstruction. J Urol 112:299, 1974

9. Benz G, Willich E: Das Syndrom des obern Kelches bei Kindern mit chronischen Pyelonephritis. Fortschr Geb Röntgenstr Nuklearmed 121:445, 1974

10. Raymond G, Toubol J: Décroissement du calice supérieur pour syndrome de Fraley. J Urol Nephrol 82:516, 1976

11. van Helsdingen PJRO, Felderhof J: The superior calix syndrome (Fraley's syndrome). Vascular compression of the infundibulum of the superior calix of the kidney as a cause of lumbar pain. Ned Tijdschr Geneeskd 120:773, 1976

12. Peruzzi PF, Tucci PL: Ematuria persistente da compressione vascolare del pedunculo dei calici renali superiori in età pediatrica. Minerva Pediatr 29:603, 1977

13. Fryczkowski M, Zaluczkowski K, Kobierska–Szczepańska A, Rawski W: Results of operative treatment of Fraley's syndrome. Int Urol Nephrol 10:103, 1978

14. Koyanagi T, Takamatsu T, Terashima M, Nonomura N, Tsuji I: Intrarenal vascular obstruction of superior ureteropelvic junction causing nephralgia in a woman with complete duplex kidney. Int Urol Nephrol 10:267, 1978

15. Freed SZ: Infundibulopyeloplasty for vascular obstruction of a middle infundibulum. J Urol 118:99, 1977

16. Nebesar R, Pollard J, Fraley EE: Renal vascular impressions. Am J Roentgenol 101:719, 1967

17. Harrold BP: Bilateral loin pain after oral furosemide. Lancet 1:888, 1973

18. Olsson C, Moyer JD, Chute R: Oral diuretics and renal pain—a provocative test. J Urol 108:25, 1972

19. Kendall AR, Karafin L: Intermittent hydronephrosis: Hydration pyelography. J Urol 98:653, 1968

20. Harbert JC, Fraley EE: Scintillation camera renography in superior infundibular obstruction. JAMA 207:2433, 1969

21. Doppmen JL, Fraley EE: Arteriography in the syndrome of superior infundibular obstruction. A simplified technic for identifying the obstructing vessel. Radiology 91:1039, 1968

22. DeWolf WC, Fraley EE: Renal pain. Urology 6:403, 1975

23. Fraley EE: Surgical correction of intrarenal disease. I. Obstruction of the superior infundibulum. J Urol 98:54, 1967

ANNOTATED BIBLIOGRAPHY

Fraley EE: Vascular obstruction of the superior infundibulum causing nephralgia. A new syndrome. N Engl J Med 275:1403, 1966

This article, which includes four case reports, was the first demonstration that compression of the infundibulum by blood vessels can have clinical significance. The operative technique, in which the intrarenal structures are approached through a nephrotomy, has since been modified, as described in the preceding article and commentary. In one patient, an upper-pole nephrectomy was necessary because the superior infundibulum could not be anastomosed to the renal pelvis without obstructing the middle collecting system. All patients were asymptomatic postoperatively.

Fraley EE: Surgical correction of intrarenal disease. I. Obstruction of the superior infundibulum. J Urol 98:54, 1967

This article reports further experience correcting intrinsic and extrinsic obstruction of the superior infundibulum.

Deckers PJ, Fraley EE, Harbert J, Paulson DF: Vascular obstruction of the superior infundibulum causing nephralgia in children. Surgery 67:856, 1970

Intrarenal obstruction in children may be subtle, and other symptoms, in addition to pain, are needed for the diagnosis. The use of radiolabeled compounds with renography is discussed.

Dufour B: Le calice superieur du rein. Anatomie—voies d'abord—pathologie. J Chir. 100:7, 1970

This article reviews the embryology, anatomy, and physiology of the normal superior calix and the anatomy, evaluation, complications, and correction of several abnormal forms. The abundant illustrations make the article useful even to readers whose French is not very good. (Unfortunately, there is no English abstract.)

DeWolf WC, Fraley EE: Renal pain. Urology 6:403, 1975

This article reviews the pathophysiology of renal pain and of the techniques for differential diagnosis of the cause. In most patients, a specific cause can be found, making effective treatment possible.

20

HORSESHOE KIDNEY: A REVIEW OF TWENTY-NINE CASES

A. M. Dajani, M.B., B.Ch., F.R.C.S.(Glasg.)

Surgical Registrar, Urological Department, Meath Hospital and County Dublin Infirmary, Dublin.

Reprinted from *British Journal of Urology,* Vol. 37, pp. 388–402, 1966. Copyright 1966 by E. & S. Livingstone, London.

Among the great varieties of kidney anomalies the horseshoe kidney is of special interest. Campbell (quoted by Lowsley, 1952) reported it at 1 in 405 autopsies. Davidsohn (quoted by Lowsley, 1952) reported an incidence of 1 in 1,000, while Allen (1951) gave 1 in 719 to 1 in 376. Sherwood *et al.* (1956) examined 12,160 newborn infants and reported twenty-four genito-urinary anomalies, four of which were horseshoe kidneys.

At the Duke Medical Center Hospital and Clinics (quoted by Glenn, 1959) the incidence was less than 0.01 per cent. of all patients seen during a period of twenty-five years.

In Lowsley's series (Lowsley, 1952) our of 13,080 pyelograms there were forty-six cases (1 in 284). Judd, Braash, and Scholl (quoted by Lowsley, 1952) found

I should like to express my gratitude to both Mr D. O'Flynn and Mr V. Lane for letting me review their cases and for their help in preparing this paper.

I am also grateful to Dr S. J. Douglas, Head of the Radiological Department, for his selection of suitable films which were photographed; to Dr R. Jordan for her kind help; to the Photographic Department at Steven's Hospital for taking the pictures published in this series; and to Dr J. Mullaney, Pathologist at the Meath Hospital, for her kind help in selecting the slides.

the incidence among 2,424 kidney operations to be 1 in 142.

During the period from 1956 to 1964, 6,099 new patients were seen at this department, and twenty-three proved to have horseshoe kidneys, *i.e.,* an incidence of 1 in 265.

It is the general opinion that this anomaly is found at least two and a half times as often in males as in females* (Lowsley, 1952).

From 1912 until 1953, 106 patients with true horseshoe kidney had renal operations at the Mayo Clinic (Culp and Winterringer, 1955); males predominated in a ratio of 4 to 1. In our series the ratio was 4.8 to 1.

While the youngest and oldest in the Mayo Clinic series were 5 and 65 years of age, in this series they were 4 and 75 years of age respectively. Over half the cases occurred in the third and fourth decades (Table 1, 323)

Out of 117 horseshoe kidneys observed at autopsy, reduplication of the ureters occurred in ten cases (Campbell, quoted by Menville, 1955).

* J. F. Glenn (1959) disagrees with this opinion and believes that the incidence is almost equal in either sex.

TABLE 1. Incidence According to Age Group

Age (years)	Number of Cases
1 to 10	3
11 to 20	4
21 to 30	7
31 to 40	5
41 to 50	4
51 to 60	3
61 to 70	2
71 to 80	1
Total	29

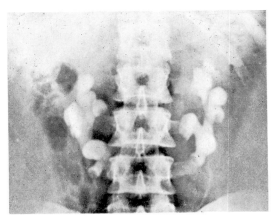

Fig. 1. Intravenous pyelogram of a typical case of horseshoe kidney; note isthmus across spine, the lowermost calyx pointing inwards and the concavity of horseshoe upwards.

Among the rarer abnormalities is the horseshoe kidney with ureteral ectopia. Up to January 1955 only three cases had been found in the literature; in two the left ureter ended in the colliculus seminalis (Thom, quoted by Menville, 1955), and in the other it ended in the vestibule (Massari, quoted by Menville, 1955). All cases were discovered at necropsy. Menville (1955) added a fourth case which was believed to be the first recorded case which was recognised clinically and treated.

Embryology and Description of the Anomaly. Horseshoe kidney anomaly is the result of an embryological fault that occurs between the fourth and eighth weeks of foetal life. The two renal blastemas fuse together before migration and rotation. Improper ascent and rotation of the kidneys ensue and the total renal mass tends to anchor at a lower level than normal with the pelvis remaining in the anterior position.

The horseshoe kidney thus lies astride the vertebral column, usually at the level of the third or fourth lumbar vertebra. Ninety-five percent of the cases exhibit fusion of the lower poles with the concavity of the horseshoe pointing upwards (Fig. 1).

The isthmus is usually composed of parenchymatous tissue, rarely it is represented by a fibrous strand. Usually it lies in front of the aorta and the vena cava, very rarely behind them, and according to Young (quoted by Lowsley, 1952) still more rarely between them.

Not only are the kidneys displaced downwards but also they lie closer to the spine than do separate organs. The pelves usually face anteriorly or medially, or they may face laterally and away from each other with the ureters far apart.

The calyces are atypically arranged, depending on the nature of the malrotation, and may point inwards towards the spinal column, or downwards, or both.

The ureters enter the pelvis higher up than in non-fused kidneys, arising from the inner border of the upper part of each kidney and passing over the anterior surface of the renal isthmus, hence ureteropelvic obstruction of varying degree is not uncommon.

There is a great variation in the origin, number, and size of the arteries supplying each renal mass, as well as in the veins. The vessels may arise from the nearest great vessel, and this fact must be borne in mind when operating upon a horseshoe kidney. Arterial branches from the inferior mesenteric, common iliac, and external and internal iliac arteries supply the fused kidneys in addition to those from the aorta (Lowsley, 1952).

Guiterrez (quoted by Glenn, 1959) stresses the fact that asymmetric fusion is not a true horshoe kidney and must, therefore, be classified as fused renal ectopia or crossed fused renal ectopia. It is similarlly true that a fused pelvic kidney cannot be classified as a horseshoe kidney.

Diagnosis. This is usually made from pyelographic data, although rarely the presence of an umbilical mass may suggest it. Excretory urograms will usually establish the diagnosis unless there is a serious destruction of the parenchyma; retrograde pyelograms are rarely necessary. The pathological horseshoe kidney, especially if it contains stones, can sometimes be recognised on a plain film.

The radiographic criteria are irregular pelves and most characteristically the lower-most calyx points inwards (Fig. 1). The whole renal mass is usually low in position and the pyelographic angle constructed by drawing a line from the midpoint of the vertebral column at the level of the crest of the ilia to the lowermost calyces is 20 to 30 degrees in the horseshoe kidney, as compared to 90 degrees in the normally situated kidney.

The ureters in a large percentage of cases take on a "flower vase" appearance (Scott, 1952). The presence of calculi in the oblique or transverse position near or over the spine should arouse suspicion. Abnormalities of urine are those of the complicating disease process.

The importance of diagnosis cannot be over-emphasised. It is not as simple as some writers have implied. Too many horseshoe kidneys have been explored because of a palpable mass in the abdomen. These patients deserve a thorough study, and excretory urograms do not always suffice (Culp *et al.*, 1962).

Clinical Findings. Most symptoms are caused by secondary renal disease rather than by fusion. This is the most common form of horseshoe kidney diagnosed clinically. Usually the clinical findings are those of infection, calculi, obstruction, or a tumour. Sometimes pain may be the presenting symptom. On other occasions it may be an incidental finding, or gastro-intestinal symptoms (renodigestive reflex) mimicking peptic ulcer, gallstones, or appendicitis may be obtained.

Occasionally secondary renal changes may produce symptoms which are not referable to the kidney itself.

Physical examination is usually negative. Very rarely an umbilical mass may be palpated over the lower lumbar spine (the isthmus).

Urine analysis is normal unless infection is present. Renal function is normal unless disease co-exists in each of the fused segments.

Guiterrez (quoted by Glenn, 1959) in his classical monograph on the subject, classified these patients into three groups:

1. Patients who have the anomaly but no signs and symptoms referable to it.
2. "Horseshoe kidney disease"—consisting of nausea, abdominal discomfort, a feeling of fullness and occasional pain on hyperextension of the spine—the so-called Rovsing syndrome.
3. "Diseased horseshoe kidney"—which includes patients with urinary obstruction, infection or calculi, or any combination of these. The most common complication is hydronephrosis.

Group I. This is the most common type and is discovered accidentally or at autopsy. It is advisable to observe these patients in case complications develop.

Group II. These cases which are apparently not numerous were thoroughly discussed by Foley (1940). Symptoms are due to pressure on the great vessels and adjoining nerves by the isthmus or the ectopic renal masses. The diagnosis is made by not finding any extrarenal lesion causing the symptoms and no renal disease other than the anomaly. Such patients have frequently been operated upon for the relief of symptoms ascribed to the appendix, gall-bladder, etc., without relief of their symptoms, and in many cases horseshoe kidney has been diagnosed accidentally during non-renal abdominal surgery. Therefore it would seem advisable that patients with unexplained epigastric pain, especially if accompanied by gastro-intestinal disturbances, should have an excretory urogram before an exploratory operation is done. Surgical treatment is seldom necessary, though division of the isthmus and nephropexy have been performed.

Group III. Horseshoe kidneys with secondary renal lesions, with or without symptoms referable to the kidney. This is the most common form of horseshoe kidney diagnosed clinically. Hydronephrosis, infection, and calculi are the most frequent lesions with tuberculosis relatively common and rarer instances of polycystic disease, solitary cyst, pyonephrosis, nephritis, tumour (including Wilms' tumour), and trauma. Hypertension may result from unilateral disease of a horseshoe kidney and may be cured by renal surgery.

The frequency of secondary lesions may be due to several factors:

1. The unusual position and curvature of the ureters due to their abnormal insertion and course over the isthmus, resulting in pressure upon them.
2. The regularly anomalous vessels which predispose to obstruction of the ureters by direct pressure.
3. Fixation of the fused kidney by its isthmus to the surrounding structures and vessels, resulting in the lack of renal mobility and pressure or drag upon the vessels.

Prognosis. It has been stated that the existence of a horseshoe kidney strongly predisposes to serious renal disease, and the vast majority of articles in the literature suggest that the condition is not only prevalent but also has serious sequels.

Experience in this department in the long-term care of patients with horseshoe kidney leads to the conclusion that many of them survive to old age without the grave complications attributed to the condition. This study shows that the mere presence of the anomaly need not have serious sequelae. Thus seven cases, or about 25 percent, presented when the patient was 50 years of age or more. Three of these (57, 70, and 63 years of age) presented with acute retention due to prostatic enlargement. Another three cases (75, 55, and 50 years of age) were treated conservatively and one died from carcinoma of the lung about five years later while only one case was complicated by a hypernephroma. In all these seven cases the blood urea at the time of the first examination ranged from 33 to 78 mg percent.

It therefore appears that the complications and morbidity rates indicated in other studies are disproportionately high.

Treatment. Most of these anomalies do not require surgical treatment unless symptoms or evidence of secondary pathological process is present. According to Latham and Smith (1962), surgical intervention is required in 25 percent of cases. During the fifteen years from 1939 to 1954 approximately one-fourth of the horseshoe kidneys that were diagnosed at the Mayo Clinic were subjected to some type of operation (Culp and Winterringer, 1955).

Once a horseshoe kidney becomes diseased there is little hope of permanent relief except by surgical intervention (Lowsley, 1952).

Socin (quoted by Lowsley, 1952) in 1888 was the first successfully to perform heminephrectomy in a horseshoe kidney, removing the hydronephrotic half.

Usually a lumbar incision is employed, but according to Culp *et al.* (1962) a transperitoneal approach is preferable. This, they claim, permits resection of the isthmus under better vision as well as simultaneous bilateral operation.

In order to ensure success and avoid troublesome complications, removal of one-half of a horseshoe kidney should include excision of all cortical tissue to the adjacent pole of the remaining kidney rather than simple division at a convenient level. If the isthmus cannot be freed easily, subcapsular enucleation over the great vessel will simplify the procedure.

Subsequent excessive bleeding usually comes from the cut surface of the remaining kidney. It is imperative, therefore, that haemostasis be complete. Simple mattress sutures tied over pads of fat usually suffice, or, as frequently done here, the capsule is closed over a piece of muscle.

The blood supply can be evaluated by direct observation and by injecting the arteries with indigo-carmine. Aortography, particularly in children, carries many hazards and is very difficult to interpret. Occasionally the isthmus has a separate blood supply which can be ligated. One must remember, however, that the entire blood supply to both segments of the horseshoe kidney may enter via the isthmus.

The large ill-defined isthmus that extends well beyond the midline has probably been the greates pitfall. There is reason to suspect that this can be managed more accurately by transperitoneal exposure despite the continued popularity of the incisions confined to the flank (Culp and Winterringer, 1955).

Various operations are performed depending upon the complicating pathological process.

Indications for Operation. (1) Hydronephrosis (without calculi); (2) calculi (with or without hydronephrosis); (3) pyonephrosis; (4) tuberculosis; (5) renal cyst; (6) tumour; (7) post-operative fistula; (8) pain (none of our series was operated upon because of pain only).

Operations for Hydronephrosis. (1) The affected half of the kidney is removed; (2) conservative operations.

The following plan is adopted by Culp *et al.* (1962) in the management of hydronephrosis in a horseshoe kidney:—

If there is bilateral hydronephrosis and one side is beyond repair, a pyeloplasty is performed on the salvageable kidney, followed later by nephrectomy on the other side. If the hydronephrosis is unilateral the isthmus is divided or resesected and the involved component is rotated into a more normal axis to provide dependent drainage. If there is additional obstruction at the ureteropelvic junction, a pyeloplasty is performed.

In the series of Culp and Winterringer (1955), three of the four failures subsequent to pyeloplasty followed reimplantation of the ureter, and all of the four patients with a Foley Y-plasty had gratifying results.

Operations for Calculi. (1) Simple pyelolithotomy; (2) nephrolithotomy; (3) pyelolithotomy and pyeloplasty, or nephropexy, or both.

In the series of Culp and Winterringer (1955), calculi recurred only when the isthmus was left intact. In this series five cases had pyelolithotomy for stones and two had recurrence (one case was treated outside this department).

Heminephrectomy is performed for disease of major import (such as tumour, tuberculosis, and extensive destruction as in pyonephrosis, etc.).

The treatment of Wilms' tumour in the horseshoe kidney does not differ in principle from that of Wilms' tumour occurring in normally separated kidneys. Provided that the lesion is resectable by heminephrectomy, the prognosis is not adversely affected by the presence of the underlying anomaly of fusion and the treatment does not differ. Latham and Smith (1962) reported eight years' survival following removal of a Wilms' tumour in a horseshoe kidney.

The treatment of horseshoe kidneys and duplicated pelves and ureters consists in the treatment of the complications. In ectopic ureter the treatment of choice is heminephrectomy and ureterectomy. If the opposite kidney functions satisfactorily the pathological segment of the kidney draining into the ectopic ureter should be removed with the ureter. All infected, dilated, ectopic ureters and all ectopic ureters opening into the urethra should be removed completely; in the former instance a pyro-ureter may develop, whereas in the latter a urethral diverticulum may result (Menville, 1955).

Operations for Pain. Pain is never due to horseshoe kidney alone, and most operations performed solely for the relief of pain seem to be doomed to failure. The following operations, however, have been done: (1) Division of isthmus and nephropexy; (2) division of isthmus alone; (3) ureterolysis; (4) nephrectomy.

Operative Hazards. Hæmorrhage and fistula appear to be the greatest hazards of nephrectomy for horseshoe kidney.

Because of the frequency of the anomalous vessels there is a great chance of injuring them, and every care shold be taken in dealing with them.

Before a large vessel is clamped its circulation should be interrupted by gentle pressure for a few minutes to determine the location and amount of the kidney tissue that may be affected.

Rarely the isthmus lies behind or between the great vessels. This should be determined before it is attempted to free the isthmus.

A small percentage of horseshoe kidneys (about 5 percent) are fused at their upper poles. This departure from the usual should be recognized during the pre-operative examination and the operation planned accordingly.

To avoid a fistula the cut surface should be inspected carefully, and any open calyces should be sutured. For many years Culp *et al.* (1962) have used fat pads in the loops of mattress suture, but during the past five years they have substituted oxidised cellulose "oxycel or gel foam" and have found both much more satisfactory. The sutures can be tied more firmly.

CLINICAL MATERIAL

From 1942 unti 1964, twenty-nine patients with horseshoe kidney were seen and treated at the Urological Department, Meath Hospital, Dublin. Males (twenty-four) predominated in the ratio of 4.8 to 1 which is similar to what was reported by Culp and Winterringer (1955) of the Mayo Clinic (4 to 1).

The youngest patient was 4 years of age, and the oldest 75 years of age. The majority presented during the third and fourth decades (Table 1).

Sixteen patients complained of pain which was either typical of renal colic or else a dull pain in the loin, back, or hypogastrium. Eleven patients had hæmaturia which in two cases was precipitated by trauma and in one case was perhaps associated with deficiency of vitamin C. Eleven patients presented with urinary infection. The other presenting symptoms were as shown in Table 2.

In four cases the anomaly was an incidental finding.

Without exception the past and the family history were irrelevant. Two patients had hypertension.

Table 3 shows the complicated cases in this series.

Fourteen cases or 48.3 percent were treated conservatively by eradication of infection or attention to the other incidental complaints (enuresis, epididymo-orchitis, enlarged prostate), while keeping careful observation of the condition of the kidneys.

Fifteen patients were operated upon; of these five had more than one operation. One patient had a cyst removed before he was seen, another had a neoplasm which proved to hypernephroma and the tumour-bearing segment was removed. Two cases had tuberculosis and the affected segment of the horseshoe kidney was resected. A plastic repair for a hydronephrotic segment was carried out as will be described later in detail.

The operations performed are show in Table 4.

TABLE 2. Presenting Symptoms

Symptom	Number
Pain (renal)	16
Frequency	11
Hæmaturia	11
Dysuria	5
Epididymo-orchitis	3
Acute retention	3
Enuresis	1
Anuria	1

TABLE 3. Complicated Cases

Complication	Number
Hydronephrosis	6
Hydropelvis	9
Hydro-ureter	5
Stones	5
(Recurrent stones)	1
Pyonephrosis	2
Hypernephroma	1
Cyst	1
Infection (non-tuberculous)	7
Tuberculosis	2

TABLE 4. Types and Number of Operations on the Kidney Proper

Operation	Number
Division of isthmus and nephropexy	4
Resection (partial nephrectomy of one segment)	2
Pyelithotomy	5
Heminephrectomy	6
Nephrotomy	1
Nephrostomy	1
Plastic repair	1

TABLE 4a. Other Operative Procedures

Operation	Number
Cystoscopy and dilatation of ureteric stricture	1
Exposure and dilatation of ureteric stricture	1
Prostatectomy	3
Epididymectomy	1
Cystodiathermy of cyst of bladder neck	1

TABLE 5. Results after Operation

	Number of Cases
Improved	7
Satisfactory	7
Deteriorated	1
Total number operated on	15

Findings at Operation. The usual extraperitoneal loin approach was used in all cases except in one where an anterior short transverse subcostal incision was done. Smith (Culp *et al.*, 1962) recommends the transperitoneal approach which he claims give good exposure and permits division of the isthmus with everything under control as well as simultaneous bilateral operation. The lumbar approach is criticised on the grounds that during division of the isthmus once it is let go the contralateral segment retracts from view. (In a previous paper Culp and Winterringer (1955) used the lumbar approach in 128 out of 137 cases.)

The isthmus consisted of parenchymatous tissue in all cases with the exception of one. In this case there was a definite demarcation of the renal tissue but the renal capsule was continuous. In all cases the isthmus was anterior to the great vessels except in one where it was posterior to both the aorta and the inferior vena cava.

After division of the isthmus the cut surface was covered with a part of the capsule and a pad of fat, except in one case where fibrin foam was used.

Abnormal blood supply was found in three cases. The vessels had to be secured before resection.

In one case subcapsular resection of a segment was performed because of the presence of dense adhesions.

Two cases of duplication of the pelvis of one segment was found, but each had only one ureter.

In one of the cases, a female child aged 6 years, an abdominal mass was felt and at operation a cyst was resected from one of the poles of a horseshoe kidney. This patient proved to have Turner's syndrome.

Complications. Bleeding after division of the bridge was difficult to control in one case. A urinary fistula complicated another case of division of the isthmus and nephropexy; it was cured by nephrectomy. One case, the description of which will follow, was complicated by a recurrent collection of urine under the subcutaneous tissue following a nephrectomy for neoplasm, and which required repeated aspirations.

Wound infection complicated two cases and paralytic ileus a third. Two patients developed post-operative bronchopneumonia.

Results. The progress of these cases and the results of treatment were judged by the following criteria: (1) Kidney function and configuration on intravenous urograms; (2) blood urea and clearance tests: (3) presence or absence of infection; (4) the statement of the patient himself; (5) clinical examination.

Follow-Up. The results in this series are based upon a previous follow-up by the two surgeons in charge of this department, or by a personal interview and examination of the patients, or through an enquiry to their home doctors.

As stated before, fifteen patients had major surgical procedures and one had only a dilatation of his left ureter. The period of postoperative follow-up ranged from three months to twenty-one years; while in those treated conservatively it ranged from six months to nine years.

Among those operated upon, one patient lived for ten years with no urinary trouble, and died from carcinoma of the colon. Table 5 shows the results.

Those who improved are the ones where dilatation of the pelvis or calyces became less, or who developed no recurrent stones and had good renal function and no infection. The other seven cases are considered to be satisfactory because of good renal function and less dilatation of the pelvicalyceal system, but two cases had persistent urinary infection and one persistent leakage of urine into the subcutaneous tissues. Another patient lived with a good renal function before dying from another disease (carcinoma of the colon). The three remaining cases still had some degree of dilatation of the calyceal system but with good kidney function.

Those cases which improved had undergone the following operations: (1) Nephrectomy (partial); (2) division of the isthmus and nephropexy with or without resection of diseased pole; (3) prostatectomy; (4) repair of a hydronephrosis.

Those cases classified as satisfactory had either pyelolithotomy or nephrostomy. One case which had division of the isthmus together with nephropexy and nephrectomy has a persistent urinary infection. A case which needs frequent aspiration of a collection of urine from the subcutaneous tissues had a nephrectomy for a hypernephroma.

Three patients treated conservatively cannot be traced. One patient died after six years, from carcinoma of the lung, but during those six years he had recurrent stones (fifteen years before being seen at this department he had had pyelolithotomy elsewhere).

A study of the remaining ten cases shows that eight cases have improved, and two are satisfactory.

The overall results of the whole series after excluding the three untraced cases are:

Improved—fifteen.

Unchanged—nine (including the dead patient).

Deteriorated—two (including the dead patient who developed recurrent stones).

This shows an improvement in 57.7 percent of cases; adding these cases to the satisfactory ones, the overall percentage of cases leading a satisfactory life with a good renal function is about 92 percent.

Some of the interesting cases in this series are the following:

Case 1. J. M., a male aged 26 years, was admitted on 23rd December 1942 complaining of increasing frequency and urethral pain on micturition, but no haematuria. Clinical examination was negative except for slight tenderness in the right renal area. His urine contained pus (+ + +) and albumin (+ +). Blood urea was 38 mg percent.

X-rays on 10th December 1942:

K.U.B.—One large stone-like shadow and several smaller ones in the right renal field. At lest nine stone-like opacities in the left renal field.

I.V.P.—Horseshoe kidney. Pyelectasis on both sides.

On 18th January 1943 division of the isthmus and excision of the lower pole of the right kidney was done, and a stone

was removed. Then nephropexy was performed. At operation the isthmus was behind the great vessels which is very rare. The right ureter was opened up to the inferior calys, curetted and closed.

The post-operative period was complicated by broncho-pneumonia and wound sepsis. He was discharged on 19th February 1943.

On 27 September 1943 he reported again with frequency and dysuria. Resection of the lower pole of the left kidney and part of the left hydronephrosis was performed; many stones were removed and a nephrostomy was done.

On 22nd October 1943 he had left nephrotomy, the kidney was pyonephrotic and contained a stone.

Since then he has persistent urinary infection (Gram-negative vacilli). He was last seen on 9th April 1964 when I.V.P. was satisfactory, haemoglobin 82 percent., and blood urea 56 mg, percent. (Figs. 2 and 3).

Comment. This was the only case where the isthmus was behind the great vessels. In spite of infection his right segment is still satisfactory twenty-one years after operation.

Case 2. M. W., a female aged 17½ years, on 20th June 1962 had a sudden onset of pain in the left loin and left groin. Apart from some tenderness in the left renal angle the clinical examination was negative.

Urine contained a trace of albumin and pus (+), no organisms, and it was negative for tubercle.

Blood urea was 38 mg percent., haemoglobin 86 percent., and white blood count 8,400 per cmm

X-rays on 25th June 1962:

IVP—Horseshoe kidney. Left calyces and pelvis dilated (Fig. 4).

On 29th June 1962 exploration of the left kidney and division of aberrant vessels and nephropexy.

Just below the pelvi-ureteric junction a band of vessels appeared to be the cause of the obstruction. After it was severed the pelvis emptied immediately. One stitch was put to

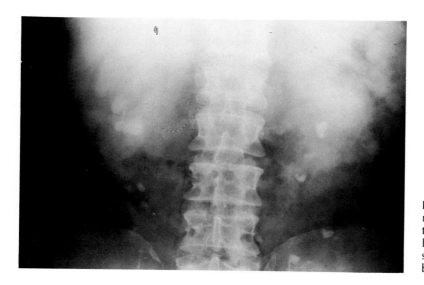

Fig. 2. Intravenous pyelogram on 13th February 1964 showing right pelvis concentration reduced and delayed, calyces also dilated Grade III, with loss of cortical substance; left side only represented by blobs of dye.

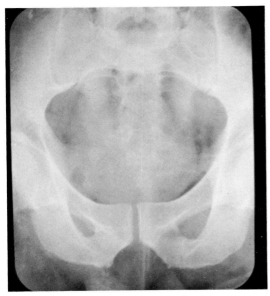

Fig. 3. Same case; bladder empties completely, ureters grossly dilated down to bladder.

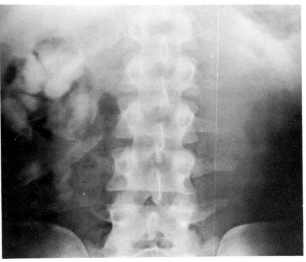

Fig. 5. Intravenous pyelogram of Case 3 showing no function on the left side and gross hydronephrosis on the right.

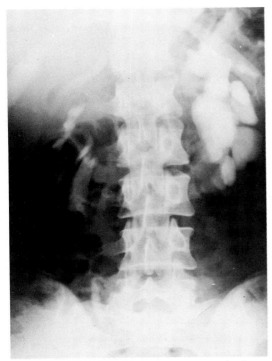

Fig. 4. Pre-operative IVP of Case 2 showing gross hydronephrosis of left segment.

the lower pole and held laterally in order to keep the cut ends of the vascular band apart.

She made a smooth recovery. Six months later she complained of pain in the left loin. Her urine was sterile.

X-rays on 3rd January 1963 (K.U.B and I.V.P):

Right pelvis—normal.

Left pelvis—concentration reduced and dilatation (+ +) with loss of cortical substance.

Left nephrectomy was done and histopathology showed marked hydronephrosis with focal chronic pyelonephritic scarring.

She was seen on 29th August 1964 and her condition was satisfactory; blood urea 37 mg percent, right pelvis normal on I.V.P

Comment. Removal of the cause of the hydronephrosis gave only temporary relief and nephrectomy had to be performed, but in spite of that she is leading a normal life.

Case 3. P. F., a male aged 23 years, was treated first at St Peter's Hospital, London, where on 6th November 1960 he was admitted with pain in the left loin and hæmaturia. I.V.P showed a horseshoe kidney with marked hydronephrosis and no function on the left side (Figs. 5 and 6). Division of the isthmus and nephropexy was performed.

Nearly three months later he developed sudden retention of urine and was admitted to Navan Hospital and was catheterised. The next day he had a right nephrostomy.

On 9th March 1961 he reported for the first time at our department. His blood urea was 93 mg percent, hæmoglobin 60 percent, and urine contained albumin (+ +), Gram-positive cocci, and Gram-negative bacilli. His blood-pressure was 130/85 mm Hg. There was a tenderness in the left loin.

The infection was treated and since then he has attended regularly to have the nephrostomy tube changed. He was last

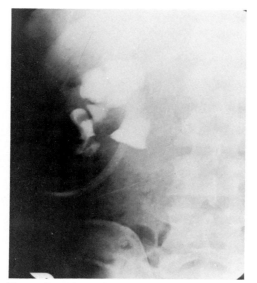

Fig. 6. Dye through nephrostomy tube.

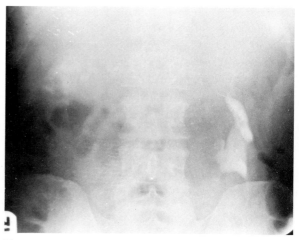

Fig. 7. Intravenous pyelogram of Case 4 showing almost no concentration on the right side; the left side is normal.

seen on 8th July 1964 when he reported that he felt well. Blood urea was 43 mg percent and the urine still contained Gram-positive cocci and Gram-negative bacilli.

Comment. There is loss of function of the left segment and the right side has advanced hydronephrosis. There is no alternative to a permanent nephrostomy.

Case 4. D. T., a male aged 36 years, in February and later in June 1956, had pain in the hypogastrium, frequency and hæmaturia. He was admitted on 28th September 1956. Although *M. tuberculosis* was not found in his urine, antituberculous drug treatment was prescribed because the X-ray appearances suggested tuberculosis.

Physical examination showed an enlarged and non-tender right kidney.

On 22nd October 1956 right nephrectomy was done when a large pyonephrotic kidney with a big abscess cavity at the lower pole was found. The duodenum and the large bowel were adherent to the pelvis; subscapsular dissection was done. A considerable amount of debris was evacuated from the pelvis. Oozing from the left lower pole was controlled by thrombin gauze.

Histopathology showed advanced tuberculosis with caseation and considerable destruction of renal parenchyma.

He made a smooth recovery and was discharged on 11th November 1956.

Repeated guinea-pig inoculation tests were negative. He was last seen on 28th July 1964 when his I.V.P. and general condition were satisfactory (Figs. 7 and 8).

Case 5. W. T., a male aged 40 years, had, on 12th May 1945, an attack of left renal colic after which he passed a stone.

Clinical examination was negative.

His urine was acid and contained a trace of albumin but no organisms.

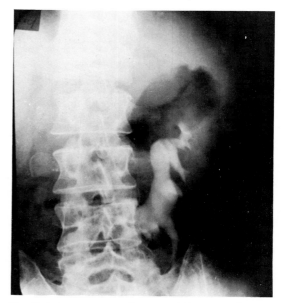

Fig. 8. Intravenous pyelogram of Case 4 eight years later showing good concentration in left segment.

X-ray on 26th April 1945:

K.U.B.—Stone-like opacities in renal areas, two on the right and one on the left.

I.V.P.—Right pelvis calyces dilated Grade II and III. Left pelvis calyces dilated Grade II. Lower calyces inverted on both sides. Horseshoe kidney.

On 18th May 1945 division of the isthmus and resection of the lower pole of the right kidney was done and two stones were removed. Nephrostomy and Deming nephropexy were done.

Post-operative recovery was smooth, the nephrostomy wound healed up on 19th June 1945.

On 31st July 1945 left anterior pyelolithotomy was done and a stone was removed.

On 2nd November 1946 a penile urethral stricture was dilated.

On 17th December 1946 exposure and dilatation of the left ureter was done. This was complicated by purulent discharge from the wound for a little more than two months.

In 1949 he came back with pain in the right loin.

On 7th July 1949 right nephrectomy was done. The kidney, which was full of pus (14 oz), was thin-walled and ruptured during dissection. Histopathology showed it to be a tuberculous kidney with virtually complete destruction of renal tissue.

Guinea-pig inoculation test of urine was negative.

In January 1955 he was treated conservatively for urinary infection, and was discharged on 11th January 1955 when his blood urea was 47 mg percent.

In June 1955 he developed oliguria due to low fluid intake which improved on rehydration.

In July he died of extensive carcinoma of the colon.

Comment. This patient survived for ten years after the first operation and six years with a blood urea of 47 mg percent after he had a nephrectomy and an attack of urinary infection.

Case 6. D. C., a male aged 19 years, was admitted on 6th October 1963 following an attack of pain in the right loin of four days' duration, together with frequency but no other urinary symptoms.

On examination there was tenderness in the right loin. Blood-pressure 160/100 mm Hg.

Urine.—Contained amorphous debris, occasional RBC's and very occasional Gram-negative bacilli.

Blood.—Hæmoglobin 106 percent, P.C.V. 48 percent, M.C.H.C. 32 percent. White blood count 8,000 per cmm B.U. 23 mk percent.

He received a course of Urolucosil.

X-rays on 6th October 1963:

K.U.B.—No clear renal outline.

I.V.P.—Right pelvis: no concentration.

Left pelvis: malrotated and appears to be the left component of a horseshoe kidney.

On 15th October 1963 a plastic repair of a right hydro-nephrosis (Michon's operation) was done.

He made a smooth recovery and was last seen on 29th January 1964 when he was well.

X-rays on 24th January 1964:

K.U.B.—Negative.

I.V.P.—Horseshoe kidney (Fig. 9).

Right pelvis—Concentration improved since 7th November 1963 and less dilated. Calyces now substantially normal. Pelvis proper dilated. Grade II at twenty minutes.

Left pelvis—Unchanged from 8th October 1963.

Comment. This was the only case with hypertension. The long-term result of the repair has to be watched and awaited for.

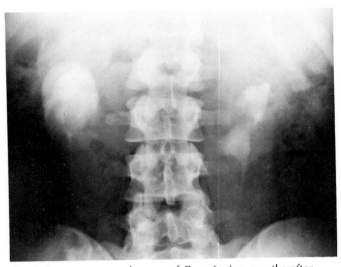

Fig. 9. Intravenous pyelogram of Case 6 nine months after operation, showing that the concentration on the right side has improved, the pelvis is less dilated and the calyces are substantially normal. The left pelvis is malrotated, otherwise normal.

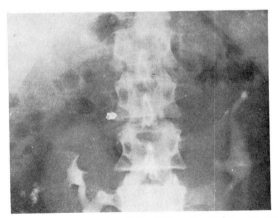

Fig. 10. Pre-operative IVP of Case 7. Right segment normal. Left, slight flattening of upper calyces with a faint curved line of calcification in mid-renal region.

Case 7. W. M., a male aged 53 years, had on 31st January 1962 a sudden violent pain in the left loin radiating to the groin with frank hæmaturia. Before he was seen here he was found to have a horseshoe kidney.

Clinical examination was negative. Blood urea was 35 mg percent, and the urine was sterile.

X-rays on 19th March 1963:

I.V.P.—Horseshoe kidney. The right segment appears normal but there is one calyx far to the left and slightly below the third lumbar vertebra (Fig. 10).

Left pelvis—The upper calyces have not filled and there

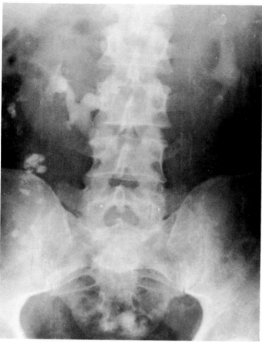

Fig. 11. Intravenous pyelogram of Case 7 shows flattening and crescentic deformity of upper calyces suggesting space-occupying lesion. Note right calyx across the midline.

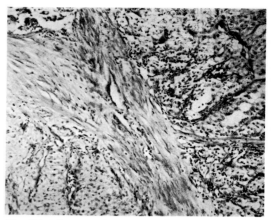

Fig. 12. Microscopic picture of the tumour in Case 7, showing it to be a hypernephroma.

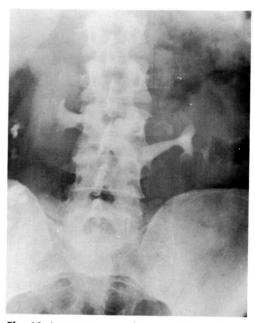

Fig. 13. Intravenous pyelogram of Case 7 four months after operation showing right segment normal.

is a suggestion of a space-occupying lesion involving the upper pole.

Left retrograde—Flattening and crescentic deformity of the upper calyx (Fig. 11). Appearance confirms I.V.P. findings of a space-occupying lesion at the upper pole.

On 27th March 1963 left nephrectomy was done. A neoplasm was found in the convex border and in the upper pole. There was no definite bridge of tissue.

In mobilising the lower segment an inward-pointing calyx was opened and neoplastic tissue extruded through it.

Renal tissue was divided roughly at the line of demarcation and this was quite vascular. A large calyx from the right side was opened and closed. Good hæmostasis was obtained. There was not enough capsule to cover the kidney and a patch of fat was pulled over it.

Pathological report: "That tumour is a hypernephroma which is infiltrating into the pelvis at one point. There is no invasion of the renal vein" (Fig. 12).

His post-operative period was complicated by atelectasis of the base of the left lung.

On 16th April 1963 the wound healed apart from a small sinus from which 5 oz of bloodstained fluid was evacuated. That was probably a urinary leak. He went home on 31st July 1963.

In April 1964 he was seen because of reaccumulation of fluid at the site of the left nephrectomy, and since then aspiration of clear urine has been done every six to eight weeks.

The excretory and retrograde pyelograms did not show any leakage.

On 13th April 1964 his right retrograde was substantially normal (Fig. 13).

Comment. The difficulty in covering the divided bridge of tissue due to excessive vascularity and the condition being neoplastic led, perhaps, to the disruption of part of the closure line and hence to leakage.

SUMMARY

Horseshoe kidney anomaly is the result of an embryonic fault occurring between the fourth and eighth week of fœtal life. The two renal blastemas become fused before migration and rotation. This accounts for the abnormal relation of the renal pelvis and parenchyma.

This review includes twenty-nine cases admitted to the Urological Department, Meath Hospital, Dublin, since 1942. The length of the follow-up varied from three months to twenty-one years. Fifteen cases had one or more surgical procedures and fourteen were treated conservatively. Three cases could not be traced for the follow-up, and two cases died from other diseases after living for six and ten years.

Fifteen cases showed definite improvement after treatment, nine cases were considered satisfactory, and two cases had shown some deterioration.

Seven interesting cases are described in detail.

REFERENCES

CULP, O. S., RUSCHE, C. F., JOHNSON, S. H., and SMITH, D. R. (1962). J Urol 88:442
CULP, O. S., and WINTERRINGER, J. R. (1955). J Urol 73:747
GLENN, J. F. (1959). J Med 261:684
LATHAM, J. E., and SMITH, K. H. (1962). J Urol 88:25

LOWSLEY, O. (1952). J Urol 67:565
MENVILLE, J. G. (1955). J Urol 73:747
SCOTT, W. W. (1952). "Year Book of Urology." (Chicago: Year Book Medical Publishers)

Commentary: Operative Considerations in Patients Requiring Surgery for Horseshoe Kidney

David J. Narins

Horseshoe kidney is one of the more common congenital urologic anomalies and, with the widespread use of excretory urography, is frequently diagnosed.[1] The horseshoe kidney is especially susceptible to hydronephrosis, infection, and calculi. Other renal fusion anomalies (cake kidney, crossed fused renal ectopia, and disk kidney) are all extremely rare, and their bizarre anatomy makes generalizations on surgical procedures upon them impossible. This commentary will concern itself with the selection of candidates for surgery, the preoperative evaluation (with emphasis on aortography both as a diagnostic tool and as an aid to the urologist in planning surgery and anticipating technical difficulties), and the specific surgical techniques involved in operations on horseshoe kidney.

SELECTION OF PATIENTS FOR SURGERY

Guiterrez, in his classic monograph, divided patients with horseshoe kidney into three groups:

1. Asymptomatic horseshoe kidney, comprising 75% of patients with the anomaly. The diagnosis is made incidentally or at autopsy.
2. Horseshoe kidney disease, in which the symptoms include nausea, abdominal discomfort, and pain on hyperextension of the spine (Rovsing's sign). Their symptoms are all ascribed to pressure of the fixed isthmus upon underlying nerves and great vessels, with no disease in the kidney itself.
3. Diseased horseshoe kidney, a condition that requires therapy. Hydronephrosis is most common, and pyonephrosis or calculi are frequently seen. Several factors related to the anomalous anatomy are thought to play a role. These include pressure on the ureter by the isthmus as the ureter courses over it and ureteral compression by aberrant blood vessels. Ureteropelvic junction obstruction due to abnormal insertion in the malrotated pelvis is frequent; incomplete drainage of abnormally placed calices, especially the lowermost ones draining the isthmus, contributes to pathology and symptomatology.[2]

A subgroup should be added to the third group to include renal parenchymatous diseases that are unrelated to the horseshoe kidney. Tuberculosis, renal cell carcinoma, Wilms' tumor, solitary cysts, and multicystic disease have all been reported in association with horeshoe kidney.[3,4] Surgical results in the second group of patients (operation for pain alone) have been disappointing.[4,5] Surgery should be considered only in those patients who demonstrate disease.

PREOPERATIVE EVALUATION

Since there are unique problems in performing surgery on the horseshoe kidney, an accurate preoperative assessment of the renal anatomy is essential. The diagnosis usually can be made on excretory urography. Retrograde pyelography, infusion nephrotomography, renal scan, and renal arteriography are useful adjuncts. Some distinguishing features are (1) low-lying mass on KUB, (2) collecting systems closer than normal to the midline on intravenous pyelography (IVP), (3) lower pole of kidneys angulated medially with parenchyma seen crossing the midline (IVP), (4) calices pointing posteriorly or medially, especially the lower ones, which often overlie the vertebral column (in rare patients they may communicate), and (5) abnormal course of the ureters, with the ureter lying lateral to the lower calices.

Retrograde pyelography is useful in delineating the anatomy of nonfunctioning or poorly functioning renal segments. It is important not to confuse horseshoe kidney with bilateral malrotation without fusion, since the surgical approach may be completely different. Renal scan can demonstrate the presence of fusion of parenchyma across the midline. Its primary value is to determine the extent of functioning parenchyma within the isthmus (Fig. 14). Ultrasound and computed tomography (CT) scans may also help in visualizing a horseshoe kidney and associated lesions. Aortography and renal angiography help demonstrate the number of vessels and the distribution of the arterial blood supply before surgery as well as the presence of aberrant vessels that may be producing ureteral obstruction (Fig. 15).[6] In addition, the thickness of parenchyma is demonstrated on the neophrographic phase of the aortogram (Fig. 16).

Children should receive a thorough urologic investigation, including cinecystography and cytoscopy, since they have a high incidence of reflux and other anomalies. The surgeon should also investigate other organ systems.[7]

OPERATIVE CONSIDERATIONS

There are three major considerations in surgery of the horseshoe kidney: (1) choice of incision, (2) division of the isthmus (symphysiotomy), and (3) aberrant blood supply.

Incision. Lowsley, Culp and Winterringer, and Dajani used an extraperitoneal flank incision in almost all cases.[4,8,9] Dahlen and Schlumberger and Culp and colleagues have recommended a transperitoneal procedure.[6,10] I prefer an anterior midline transperitoneal approach; it provides better access to the isthmus and control of the blood supply and permits simultaneous bilateral procedures if necessary. With a flank incision, the isthmus is in the depth of the wound and, once transected, retracts away from the surgeon, while with an anterior approach it is easily accessible for good hemostasis.

To proceed: make a midline incision and enter the peritoneal cavity. Pack the omentum, transverse colon, and small bowel superiorly. A self-retaining retractor such as the Smith ring* helps maintain exposure. The root of the small bowel mesentery extends diagonally from the left of the second lumbar vertebra to the right sacroiliac area; the isthmus can be palpated at its base. Incise the posterior peritoneum in an avascular area parallel to the root of the mesentery, affording good exposure of the isthmus and pelves. If necessary, carry the incision beneath the cecum and up the right colic gutter to

* Manufactured by Codman and Shurtleff, Inc.

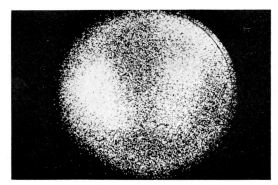

Fig. 14. Renal scan. Note renal axis of horseshoe kidney and little functional tissue at the isthmus. A fibrous isthmus was found at surgery.

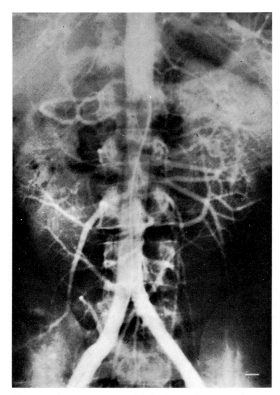

Fig. 15. Aortogram, arterial phase. Note major arterial supply arising from the common iliac artery bilaterally.

permit the ascending colon to be reflected superiorly. Due to the malrotation, the pelves and ureter lie in an accessible ventral position. Calices are often "extrarenal," and a separate pelvis may drain the isthmus.†

† Unpublished data.

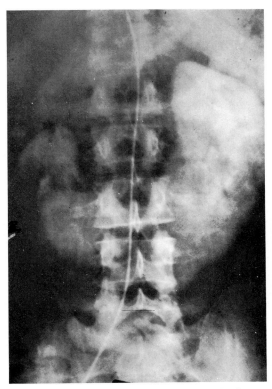

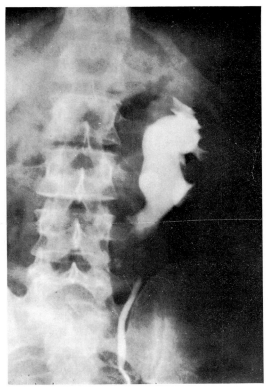

Fig. 16. Aortogram, nephrographic phase. Note thick functioning isthmus. This was confirmed at surgery.

Fig. 17. Occlusive tip retrograde pyelogram. Note segment of ureter compressed as it passes over isthmus. This area never filled with contrast material. At surgery this segment lay in a groove in the isthmic parenchyma.

Division of the Isthmus. Surgical procedures on the horseshoe kidney may require dividing the isthmus. Some urologists believe that dividing the isthmus is not necessary, since the kidney remains held by the vascular structures and surrounding tissues. In my experience, however, symphysiotomy has appeared to result in better drainage and has been free of complications.[11] The isthmus may vary from a thin fibrous band to a thick functioning renal mass. One must be aware that the pyelocaliceal system may cross the midline and that division must be at the line of demarcation and not necessarily at a convenient midline location. Failure to recognize this could result in postoperative urinary fistula.

I have used the guillotine technique of partial nephrectomy as described by Williams and coauthors in all recent cases.[12] To proceed: identify the area of demarcation and strip the capsule after carefully mobilizing the isthmus. Place two 1–0 chromic catgut sutures circumferentially on either side of the proposed site of transection. When these sutures are tied, they cut through the renal blood vessels. Sharply divide the isthmus between the two sutures. Place an additional chromic catgut suture around each cut end to reinforce the hemostatic sutures. If necessary, bleeding points can be suture ligated with 4–0 chromic catgut figure-of-eight sutures. Suture the renal capsule over the resected surface of the kidney and place retroperitoneal fat over this suture line. In no patient have I caused secondary

hemorrhage or fistula with this technique. If the isthmus is a fibrous band, division and transfixion are all that is required.

Anomalous Vasculature. Multiple and anomalous blood supply is common in horseshoe kidney,[13,14] There is persistence of the more primitive arterial blood supply arising from the iliac arteries and lower aorta. Venous drainage is similarly inconsistent. Often the isthmus has a separate blood supply, and these vessels may be only 1 cm to 2 cm and arise posteriorly. Aortography can aid in preoperative planning and in anticipating technical difficulties due to anomalous vessels. Lower vessels must sometimes be sacrificed to permit rotation of the separated renal masses to a more normal axis. Before dividing these arteries, occlude them with small bulldog clamps to determine the extent of parenchyma supplied and to define the amount of ischemic cortex that must be excised. Intra-arterial indigo carmine or methylene blue injection may also be used for this purpose. The parenchyma supplied by the vessel is stained blue.

OTHER CONSIDERATIONS

Specific operations (pyeloplasty, pyelolithotomy, nephrolithotomy, and nephrectomy) have been described elsewhere in this text. In patients with horseshoe kidney, pyelocaliectasis exist in the absence of intrinsic ureteropelvic junction obstruction or external vascular compression of the ureter. This is due to compression of the ureter as it courses over the isthmus (Fig. 17). If, after symphysiotomy and rotation of the involved segment to a more normal axis, there is dependent drainage and a patent ureteropelvic junction, no further reconstructive surgery is required.[10] If there is a high insertion of the ureter or a ureteropelvic junction obstruction, perform a suitable pyeloplasty. Decisions on the use of nephrostomy tubes or stenting ureteral catheters are similar to those in any pyeloplasty and are discussed elsewhere. If used, they are brought out retroperitoneally with the drain. Nephropexy should be done to fix the kidney in optimal position.[6,14] Close the incision in the posterior peritoneum.

REFERENCES

1. Farmen F: Fusion anomalies of the kidney. In Alken CE, Dix VW, Goodwin WE, Wildbolz E (eds): Encyclopedia of Urology, Vol 7, pp 66–71. New York, Springer-Verlag, 1968

2. Guttierrez R: The Clinical Management of Horseshoe Kidney. New York, Paul B Hoeber, 1934

3. Blackard CE,, Mellinger GT: Cancer in a horseshoe kidney. Arch Surg 97:616, 1968

4. Culp OS, Winerringer JR: Urological treatment of horseshoe kidney: Comparison of results after various types of operations. J Urol 73:747, 1955

5. Glenn JF: Analysis of 51 patients with horseshoe kidney. N Engl J Med 261:684, 1959

6. Dahlen CP, Schlumberger FC: Surgery of the diseased horseshoe kidney. Am J Surg 93:405, 1957

7. Segura JW, Kelalis PP, Burke EC: Horseshoe kidney in children. J Urol 108:333, 1972

8. Lowsley O: Surgery of the horseshoe kidney. J Urol 67:565, 1952

9. Dajani AM: Horseshoe kidney: A review of twenty-nine cases. Br J Urol 38:388, 1966

10. Culp OS, Rusche CF, Johnson SH III, Smith DR: Hydronephrosis and hydroureter in infancy and childhood—a panel discussion. J Urol 88:443, 1962

11. Pitts WR, Muecke EC: Horseshoe kidney: A 40 year experience. J Urol 113:743, 1975

12. Williams DF, Schapiro AE, Arconti JS, Goodwin WE: A new technique of partial nephrectomy. J Urol 97:955, 1967

13. Eisendrath DN, Phifer FM, Culver HB: Horseshoe kidney. Ann Surg 82:735, 1925

14. Graves FT: The arterial anatomy of the congenitally abnormal kidney. Br J Surg 56:533, 1969

15. Foley FEB: Surgical correction of horseshoe kidney. JAMA 115:1945, 1940

ANNOTATED BIBLIOGRAPHY

Culp OS, Winterringer TR: Surgical treatment of horseshoe kidney: Comparison of results after various types of operations. J Urol 73:747, 1955

This article analyzes 106 patients with horseshoe kidney operated on at the Mayo Clinic over a 41-year period. Approximately 25% of horseshoe kidneys diagnosed clinically required operative treatment, and 87% had hydronephrosis, calculi, or both. The authors stress the importance of meticulous care of anomalous vessels and division of the isthmus. Postoperative hemorrhage and fistula were the main complications. Results were better in patients with symphysiotomy and not good in Guiterrez type–2 patients.

Graves FT: The arterial anatomy of congenitally abnormal kidney. Br J Surg 56:533, 1969

This anatomic study defines several variations of arterial blood supply of normal, ectopic, and fused kidneys. The blood supply to horseshoe kidneys is studied in 13 patients. Postmortem resin casts and arteriograms are described. The author lists seven variations of arterial blood supply. The article is illustrated with photographs of the resin casts and line drawings.

Dahlen CP, Schlumberger FC: Surgery of the diseased horseshoe kidney. Am J Surg 93:405, 1957

This paper briefly describes a transperitoneal approach to the horseshoe kidney. The use of aortography is also described.

Gutierrez R: The Clinical Management of Horseshoe Kidney. New York, Paul B Hoeber, 1934

This classic monograph first described horseshoe kidney disease as a clinical entity. There are sections on embryology, anatomy, pathology, diagnosis, and treatment. Twenty-five cases are described. Illustrations, including many by William Didusch, are excellent.

Pitts WR, Muecke EC: Horseshoe kidney: A 40-year experience. J Urol 113:743, 1975

The experience at New York Hospital is detailed. The embryology as well as clinical presentation, associated urologic findings, and results of therapy are described. These authors believe that division of the isthmus is unnecessary.

OVERVIEW: SPECIAL INTRAOPERATIVE TECHNIQUES IN RECONSTRUCTIVE SURGERY OF THE KIDNEY

Lloyd H. Harrison

The majority of patients requiring surgical reconstruction of the ureteropelvic junction have large hydronephrotic extrarenal pelves.

There are many diverse obstructive situations that cause hydronephrosis, with equally as many variations in operative procedures and surgical techniques available for their correction.[1] The commentaries in Chapters 18 and 19 describe two operative techniques to correct intrarenal ureteropelvic obstruction (infundibuloplasty and calicoureterostomy). This type of obstruction is uncommon; however, the urologic surgeon seeking continued preservation of residual renal function should have a working knowledge of the basic principles of these procedures and should know when to apply them.

With an intrasinus approach and using special instruments (vein retractor, malleable brain retractor, or Gil–Vernet's retractor), many intrarenal pelves can be mobilized and a dismembered pyeloplasty performed in much the same manner as is done in an extrarenal pelvis.

There are some patients in whom this cannot be carried out adequately because of cicatrization, and it is in this circumstance that knowledge of special intraoperative techniques dealing with difficult intrarenal techniques becomes essential.

Horseshoe kidneys are usually associated with large extrarenal pelves and have been managed surgically with a wide variety of techniques.[2]

INFUNDIBULOPLASTY

Nephralgia caused by vascular obstruction of the superior infundibulum was first reported in 1966 by Fraley. Although the x-ray findings (vascular impression on the superior infundibulum) have been reported in approximately 10% of excretory urograms, the majority of these patients do not have the associated renal pain described in the Fraley syndrome.[3] Therefore, the preoperative diagnostic evaluation becomes critical before any type of surgical intervention.

As Fraley mentions, excretory urograms with cinefluoroscopy and renograms are performed routinely. Voiding cystourethrograms are done in children to rule out reflux. I have found provocative tests such as the hydrated excretory urogram with furosemide washout to be extremely helpful in accentuating the superior infundibulum obstruction and in reproducing renal pain in the patient. Where such tests are equivocal and furosemide does not produce pain, I repeat the intravenous pyelogram (IVP) during a bout of acute colic.

Should the patient have evidence of superior infundibulum obstruction but no evidence of chronic pyelonephritis, renal calculi, or any other gastrointestinal (GI) complaint, renal arteriography is the next step. This allows the surgeon to determine preoperatively the relationship between renal arteries and the site of infundibular obstruction, thereby acting as a road map during the intrahilum dissection.

The surgical success of this procedure is based on adequate exposure of the entire kidney with its renal pedicle. I prefer an 11th or 12th rib flank approach. Once the kidney is completely mobilized and positioned on tapes, dissection of the main renal artery and its segmental branches is begun. Microsurgical instruments and retractors (vein, malleable brain, or Gil–Vernet's retractors) aid in the meticulous dissection that is necessary for this stage of surgery. If localization of the renal vasculature proves difficult, I find that the sonic Doppler probe is useful in pinpointing the site of major division in the renal artery.

Infundibulopyelostomy is the logical procedure of choice once adequate mobilization is accomplished. The transposed infundibulum is in an accessible position, and a precise infundibular pelvic reanastomosis can be performed with 6–0 absorbable suture. I place a Silastic stent extending from the superior infundibulum down the pelvis and ureter into the bladder. If the stent does not pass spontaneously, it should be removed cystoscopically on the fifth postoperative day. The only other drain that I use is a Penrose drain, which is left inside Gerota's fascia for 48 hours. My own experience will not settle the controversy between the stent vs nonstent factions, but I would point out that the stent acts as a conduit, keeping urine within the urinary tract, and also functions as a mold while the infundibulum is sutured to the pelvis.

Judicious selection of patients to undergo this procedure is the only way to ensure a good surgical result.

URETEROCALIOSTOMY

Clinical situations requiring ureterocaliostomy are infrequent. In fact, most intrarenal ureteropelvic junction obstructions can be repaired despite previously failed surgical procedures.

Criteria for this procedure include lower-pole cortical atrophy and a patent lower-pole infundibulum. This allows removal of the lower-pole cortex without significant parenchymal loss and permits accurate dependent anastomosis between the lower-pole calix and the ureter. Once again, I would stent such an anastomosis and, by removing the parenchyma over the calix, thus reduce the possibility of ureterocalyceal obstruction.

I have found two clinical situations in which ureterocaliostomy is my procedure of choice: (1) the patient without stone disease in whom repeated ureteropelvic procedures and cicatrization have made an ileal substitution the only alternative corrective procedure and (2) a cadaver-donor kidney in which the pelvis and part of the lower pole have been destroyed. One should also appreciate the fact that the lower-pole calix is not always the most dependent portion of the kidney (*e.g.*, when the patient is supine) and that anything other than a functioning ureteropelvic junction compromises urinary drainage. Ureterocaliostomy will remain an infrequently used procedure, and thus patient selection requires great care and consideration.

SURGERY FOR HORSESHOE KIDNEY

The horseshoe kidney results from an anomaly of renal ascent and is one of the most frequently diagnosed congenital urologic

disorders.[4] It is certainly the most common anomaly of renal fusion. Traditionally, these patients are predisposed to urinary tract infection, ureteropelvic junction obstruction, and urolithiasis, yet many remain asymptomatic and often undiagnosed. Current data suggest that the relationship of upper urinary tract infection to the horseshoe kidney is tenuous and may, in fact, be related to instrumentation. A recent analysis of one medical center's population of patients with this type of kidney and concomitant renal calculi reveals their stone disease to be primarily metabolic.[5] Surgery in these patients may be indicated for removal of urolithiasis or correction of symptomatic ureteropelvic junction obstruction; however, I have found that surgery simply for relief of pain in these patients should be considered very carefully, since the results of such surgery are usually mixed.

My preoperative assessment, other than IVP and retrograde pyeloureterogram, always includes a renal arteriogram. I recommend a complete metabolic profile before any surgical procedure, especially surgery for calculi. I no longer use flank incisions in these patients, and I believe that an anterior midline transperitoneal approach provides superior access. Once the omentum, transverse colon, and small bowel have been packed superiorly, the posterior peritoneum is opened over the kidney and below the inferior mesenteric artery. The isthmus is usually located over the third or fourth vertebrae, and the anterior surface of the kidney can be easily mobilized; take care not to damage either ureter as it is draped over the kidney. The renal arteriogram aids in the dissection of the renal blood supply, which is segmental.[6] Here also, the sonic Doppler probe has proved useful in localizing these vessels precisely and in minimizing an unnecessarily wide dissection of such a critical area. Plastic arterial tapes define principal arterial supplies, and selective application of disposable bulldog clamps with peripheral IV injection of methylene blue allows the surgeon to identify points of segmental demarcation around the isthmus. In my experience, the majority of isthmi do contain functioning parenchyma worthy of preservation.

A Boyce-type anatrophic nephrolithotomy cannot be performed in a patient with an undivided horseshoe kidney.[7] Stone removal is most efficiently accomplished by a pyelolithotomy. In the presence of any evidence of ureteropelvic junction obstruction, the pyelotomy should be positioned so that a stented dismembered pyeloplasty can be performed after stone removal. I also believe that one can divide the horseshoe kidney at the same time; this is carried out along the intersegmental plane of the isthmus. Carefully position the divided kidneys based on the analogous blood supply, and perform nephropexy to the psoas muscle once the kidney is positioned satisfactorily.

Complications from this surgical approach to the horseshoe kidney have been rare. The patient generally requires nasogastric suction for 24 to 48 hours postoperatively, and the stents are removed later, as described previously. I have not observed any urinary leakage or fistula formation and believe that this is more likely to occur with the old ''guillotine''-type separation of the isthmus. A calix is rarely encountered during intersegmental division.

REFERENCES

1. Lich R, DeWeerd JH: Reconstructive surgery of the ureteropelvic junction. In Whitehead ED, Leiter E (eds): Current Operative Urology, Hagerstown, Harper & Row, 1982

2. Woodard JR: Renal ectopia and fusion anomalies. In Glenn JF, Boyce WH (eds): Urologic Surgery, 2nd ed, pp 143–153. Hagerstown, Harper & Row, 1975

3. Nebesar R, Pollard J, Fraley EE: Renal vascular impressions. Am J Roentgenol 101:719, 1967

4. Farmen F: Fusion anomolies of the kideny. In Alken CE, Dix VW, Goodwin WE, Wildbolz E (eds): Encyclopedia of Urology, Vol 7, pp 66–71. New York, Springer-Verlag, 1968

5. Evans WP, Boyce WH, Resnick MD: Horseshoe kidney and urolithiasis. Presented at the American Urological Association Meeting, San Francisco, May, 1980

6. Boatman DL, Cornell SH, Kolln C–P: The arterial supply of hourseshoe kidneys. J Urol 113:447, 1971

7. Harrison LH: Anatrophic nephrolithotomy: Update 1978. In Bonney WW (ed): AUA Courses in Urology, pp 1–23.Baltimore, Williams & Wilkins, 1979

PART EIGHT

SURGICAL TREATMENT OF RENAL CYST AND PERCUTANEOUS RENAL CYST PUNCTURE

21

CO-EXISTENCE OF RENAL CYST AND TUMOUR: INCIDENCE IN 1,007 CASES[1]

By John L. Emmett, M.D., Stanley R. Levine, M.D., and Lewis B. Woolner, M.D.

Section of Urology and Section of Surgical Pathology, Mayo Clinic and Mayo Foundation, Rochester, Minnesota.

Reprinted from *British Journal of Urology*, Vol. 35, pp. 403–410, 1963. Copyright 1963 by E. & S. Livingstone, London.

Refinement in roentgen diagnosis of cysts and tumours of the kidney by aortography and nephrotomography has raised new problems in the management of ''mass lesions'' of the kidney. Whereas previously surgical exploration was mandatory in all cases, its necessity as a routine procedure in every case is now being seriously questioned.

The limitations of aortography (especially by the translumbar method) have been adequately documented (Creevy and Price, 1955; Olsson, 1961; Uson, Melicow, and Lattimer, 1963). Errors usually consist of making a diagnosis of cyst when the lesion is actually a tumour. This occurs principally in large necrotic, infarcted, or degenerated tumours in which it is difficult or impossible to demonstrate pathological vascularisation (puddling, pooling, laking, and tumour staining). Olsson (1961) has demonstrated that the accuracy of diagnosis can be improved by the use of selective angiography. For this

the retrograde catheterisation method of aortography with the Seldinger technique is employed. A catheter of the Odman type is used because its tip is moulded so that it can be introduced directly into the renal artery. In addition to more complete visualisation of the small blood-vessels, Olsson also relied on the early nephrographic phase to aid in diagnosis.

Nephrotomography has now proved to be an accurate and helpful roentgenological method of differentiating cyst and tumour. The nephrotomogram combines (1) opacification of the renal parenchyma (nephrogram) with tomography (body section roentgenography). It provides an almost three-dimensional picture of the kidney, focused at any desired level and free of confusing overlying shadows of soft tissues or intestinal gas. Most nephrotomograms are made by means of intravenous injection of contrast medium because this is the simplest method. It should be pointed out, however, that excellent nephrotomograms may be obtained during aortography simply by exposing films later (during the nephrographic phase), using the tomographic apparatus. Although the vascular

[1] Read at the Nineteenth Annual Meeting of the British Association of Urological Surgeons at Leeds, July 1963.

supply of the kidney may be fairly well visualised in the intravenous nephrotomogram during the early "vascular" phase, it is distinctly inferior to that obtained during the vascular phase of an aortogram.

There is difference of opinion concerning the accuracy and reliability of the nephrotomograms for differentiating cyst and tumour. The New York hospital group (Southwood and Marshall, 1958; Chynn and Evans, 1960) have indicated that a diagnostic accuracy of approximately 95 percent is possible provided that only technically satisfactory films are considered. Our experience at the Mayo Clinic with almost 1,000 nephrotomographic examinations has also been most encouraging.[2] We have been sufficiently impressed with our ability to distinguish cyst from tumour (Fig. 1, *see also* Fig. 4) from a technically good nephrotomogram that for the past two years we have discontinued the diagnostic use of percutaneous needle aspiration and are no longer recommending surgical exploration in every case. The appearance in the literature from time to time of case reports concerning cysts and tumours co-existing in the same kidney, however, has caused us some uneasiness and prompted this study.

Pathogenesis and Terminology. According to Gibson (1954) there are four possible combinations of cyst and tumour co-existing in the same kidney as follows: (1) widely separated lesions of unrelated origin, so-called chance occurrence (obviously the incidence of tumour should be no higher than in a kidney without cysts); (2) a cyst originating within a tumour, so-called cystic degeneration, or regression or healing of a hypernephroma (Bartley and Hultquist, 1950; Bartley and Helander, 1962) (this appears to be a fairly common occurrence); (3) a tumour originating within a cyst (rare); and (4) a cyst originating distal to a tumour (often described as a tumour in the base of the cyst).

The last two types require comment. With regard to the origin of a tumour within a cyst (category 3), there appears to be considerable confusion in the literature. It is our opinion that many of these reported cases in the literature represent simply advanced cystic degeneration, regression, or healing of a tumour in which only a small amount of viable tumour tissue remains. Sometimes this may be as little as a 1 percent or less. As regards category 4, Gibson advanced an interesting concept of the origin of a cyst distal to a tumour or the presence of a tumour in the base of a cyst. On the basis of Hepler's (1930) experimental work, demonstrating that the mechanical obstruction of both renal tubules and

[2] Our experience with the first 336 nephrotomograms has already been reported (Witten, Greene, and Emmett, 1963; Green, Witten, and Emmett, 1964).

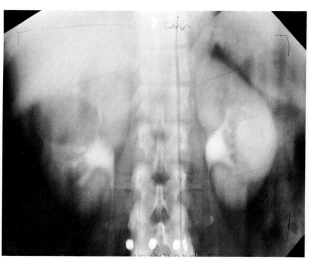

Fig. 1. Nephrotomogram. Simple solitary cyst in right kidney. Note homogeneous radiolucent character and well-defined thin wall of cyst with sharp demarcation from renal cortex, which forms an acute crescentic angle at junction of cortex and cyst wall. (Compare with solid renal tumour in Figure 4.)

blood-vessels in a localised area of the renal cortex will result in the development of a cyst distal to the lesion, Gibson postulated that a tumour of the renal cortex may provide this mechanical obstruction. This may result in a cyst distal to the tumour. As the cyst enlarges it tends to "engulf" the tumour. As a result the tumour appears to be in the "base" of the cyst, although in reality it is separated from it by the cyst lining. In other cases the tumour appears to be only adjacent to the base of the cyst. Judging from the literature, lesions of this category are uncommon.

Opinions in the Literature Concerning the Incidence of Cyst and Tumour in the Same Kidney. An attempt to determine the incidence of cyst and tumour in the same kidney encounters a literature burdened with discussions of methods of determining whether a "mass lesion" in a kidney were cyst or tumour. With the advent of nephrotomography much of this discussion is no longer relevant. The hæmorrhagic "cyst" with a thick capsule covered with thick shaggy grumous and gelatinous exudate usually does not cause great diagnostic difficulty; in our opinion these usually represent primary tumours with advanced cystic degeneration, spontaneous regression, or healing. Ordinarily they are not too difficult to identify with nephrotomography. The difficult diagnostic problem concerns the co-existence of a tumour and a simple serous cyst which has a thin wall of fibrous tissue, lined by flat mesothelium and filled with a clear transudate of plasma (Clarke, Hurwitz, and Dubinsky, 1956).

In this regard there are many loose and inadequately documented statements in the literature. One of the most interesting concerns the type of fluid in a cyst as a means of determining whether or not tumour is present. Three figures stand out which for many years have been quoted and copied from one article to another, all of which state that (1) the general incidence of tumours associated with cysts is 7 percent; (2) if the cyst fluid is clear, the incidence drops to 2 percent; and (3) if the cyst fluid is hæmorrhagic, it rises to 30 percent. The 7 percent figure was originally given in 1951 by Walsh, who stated that he had collected 500 cases of renal cyst *from the literature* and "found undoubted malignant tumour to be present in 7 percent." We have been unable to trace the source of the 2 percent figure. The 30 percent figure (with hæmorrhagic fluid) originated in 1936 from an article by Whitmore, a pathologist in Philadelphia. He stated: "In a study of cysts of the kidney, up to about eighteen mouths ago, Dr LeCompte and I have found that of forty-two reported cases of hæmorrhagic cysts . . . collected from the literature, tumour tissue was found in . . . thirteen cases." It seems likely that many of these cases would now be classified as cystic degeneration of tumour.

The actual incidence of tumour and simple serous cyst in the same kidney is impossible to determine from the literature. Some writers have considered the co-existence of these lesions rare to the point of being almost non-existent. Among those adhering to this belief may be mentioned Ainsworth and Vest (1952), Hamm (1956), Baker and Graf (1957), Southwood and Marshall (1958), and DeWeerd (1961). Also our pathologists at the Mayo Clinic maintain that they never see a tumour located within a simple serous cyst (either in the free wall or base of the cyst).

To other writers, however, this is a sufficiently significant problem that they recommend surgical exploration in every case of cyst regardless of the available diagnostic data. Most of the data concerning the co-existence of cyst and tumour come from isolated reports of single cases or, at most, a series of only two or three cases. For this reason, estimates of incidence have been meagre. One recent series was reported by Brannan, Miller, and Crisler (1962) who found three cases of associated tumour in 104 cases of renal cyst encountered at the Ochsner Clinic, New Orleans, from 1941 to 1961, an incidence of 2.9 percent. In one of the three cases the tumour was located adjacent to the base of the cyst, in another it was "in the base of the cyst," while the third case was a horseshoe kidney in which the base of the cyst was filled with "gelatinous material" and there

was tumour present in the base. It is questionable whether this last case could be classified as a simple serous cyst with the typical thin walls and clear fluid (transudate).

Rehm, Taylor, and Taylor (1962) reported three cases encountered in the Department of Urology at Ohio State University during a seven-year period (1954 to 1961). They did not estimate incidence. In one of their three cases tumour cells were found within the "free" cyst wall. (As far as we know, this is the only case ever reported in which tumour was found within the free cyst wall and covered with unbroken mesothelium of the lining of the cyst wall.) In one case they found a tumour in the base of a cyst, while in the third case they found a small papillary tumour in the base of the cyst.

Reports of single cases in the literature are difficult to evaluate. Many will not stand critical evaluation because descriptions of the lesion are incomplete and not standardised. For instance, often no mention is made of the character of the cyst wall or of the cyst fluid, or the relationship of the tumour to the cyst may be impossible to determine from lack of detailed data. Many cases appear to be simply examples of tumours in which cystic degeneration, necrosis, or infarction has occurred. Also the descriptions of the microscopic examination of the tumour often leave much to the imagination. Other cases, however, are well described and documented and can be accepted as valid. Melicow's study (1944), which mentioned fourteen cases, involves the problem of terminology considered previously. In these cases the pathological entities of cystadenoma and cystadenocarcinoma seem to be a primary concern. Parenthetically it is our opinion that such cases would not present an insurmountable problem in differential diagnosis by nephrotomography; most would be diagnosed either as tumour or as indeterminate, and surgical exploration would be carried out. The same is probably true of Lattimer's (1962) "cyst carcinomas."

Before this subject is left, one other problem should be mentioned, namely, the ability of the pathologist to distinguish small benign renal adenoma from carcinoma (hypernephroma). Top-flight pathologists admit that often this may not be possible even on careful microscopic examination. No less an authority than Bell (1946) has made the statement that a renal adenoma larger than 3 cm in diameter should be considered a hypernephroma.

MATERIAL FOR STUDY

We studied all case records at the Mayo Clinic in which the diagnosis of either cyst or tumour had been made during the thirteen-year period, 1950 through 1962. We then excluded all cases in which neither surgical exploration nor diagnostic needle aspiration had been done. This gave us 1,078 cases. We then excluded seventy-one cases in which needle aspiration only had been done without surgical exploration. This left us with 1,007 cases in all of which surgical exploration had been carried out. These may be considered as essentially consecutive cases. We considered increasing the number of cases studied by going further back in our files (previous to 1950). The Section of Biometry and Medical Statistics of our clinic discouraged this procedure as they stated that the sampling of 1,000 cases was adequate; more cases should not significantly change our findings. Of the 1,007 cases, 428 (43 percent) were cases of cysts; 579 (57 percent) were cases of tumour.

Cysts. Of the 428 cases of "simple" cysts, 314 were cases of solitary cyst, fifty-four of multiple cysts, fifty-eight of peripelvic cyst (insinuated deep in the sinus renalis), and two of multilocular cyst. It is of interest that in nine cases in our files the diagnosis was listed as multilocular cyst. We re-examined the gross specimens in these nine cases and found that only two satisfied the criteria for multilocular cyst suggested by Boggs and Kimmelstiel (1956) and Frazier (1951). This observation substantiates Uson and Melicow's recently expressed opinion (1963) that true multilocular cysts of the kidney are rare.

Tumours. There were 579 cases of tumour. Five hundred and forty-five were typical solid-type tumours (renal carcinoma or so-called hypernephroma); twenty-four were cases of "cystic" hypernephroma (so-called cystic degeneration). Tumour and cyst were found to be present in the same kidney in only ten cases.

Cystic Hypernephroma (Cystic Degeneration). We re-examined the gross specimens in the twenty-four cases considered to be cystic hypernephroma or cystic degeneration of tumour. The most common type (or garden variety) consisted of a solid-type tumour with multiple cystic areas often filled with hyaline material, an example of which is shown in Figure 2. This is no doubt the type of lesion that Willis (1953) described as being "an integral part of the habit of growth of the particular tumour, parts or the whole of which may assume a regular honeycombed or polycystic pattern." Unusual types were encountered, however, in which the degree of degeneration (or regression or healing) was so advanced that the tumours appeared more like thick-walled cysts covered with necrotic shaggy exudate with a minimal amount of viable tumour remaining (Fig. 3). It is our belief that this latter type of lesion is often described erroneously as tumour occurring in the wall of a cyst.

Tumour and Cyst Co-existing in the Same Kidney. As mentioned previously, there were ten cases in which

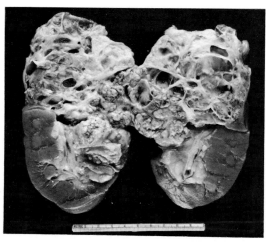

Fig. 2. Hypernephroma with "cystic degeneration." Most common type.

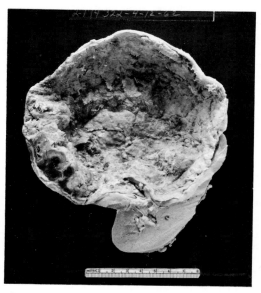

Fig. 3. Hypernephroma with advanced cystic degeneration, infarction, or "regression or healing." Less than 1 percent of viable tumour remains. This is the type of lesion which is often called "tumour occurring in a cyst." (*Reprinted with permission from G. J. Thompson and O. S. Culp (1962). Trans. Amer. Ass. Gen.-Urin. Surg., 54, 89.*)

tumour and cyst were present in the same kidney. This is an incidence of approximately 1 percent of the entire series of 2.3 percent of the 438 cases of cyst (428 + 10). This compares favourably with the incidence of 2.9 percent reported by Brannan and associates (1962). All ten gross specimens were carefully re-examined. One proved to be a multiple cystadenoma which had become malignant. In eight cases the cysts and tumours were widely separated with no apparent common basis of origin; their association must be considered as accidental or of chance occurrence. In the remaining case the tumour was close enough to the base of the cyst that it could possibly meet the postulates of Gibson (1954) that it was the cause of the cyst. We found no cases of tumour inside a typical simple serous cyst which had a thin wall and was filled with clear fluid (transudate of plasma).

DISCUSSION

This study indicates that the co-existence of cyst and tumour in the same kidney is infrequent. Computed on the basis of both cysts and tumours the incidence is about 1 percent; based on cysts alone it appears to be between 2 and 3 percent. These figures agree with those of Brannan and co-workers (1962).

The question may be asked if our ten cases could have been accurately diagnosed clinically without surgical exploration. Unfortunately nephrotomograms were made in only two of the ten cases because most of the patients were seen before we began using nephrotomography. In one of these cases a diagnosis of "indeterminate lesion" of the kidney was made, and surgical exploration was recommended. In the other case an accurate preoperative diagnosis was made of tumour in the upper pole and cyst in the lower pole and was confirmed at operation.

In Table 1 the ten cases have been listed with data concerning the presence or absence of the most suggestive clinical stigmata of renal tumour, namely, gross hæmaturia, unexplained fever, significant loss of weight, marked anæmia (less than 10.5 g of hæmoglobin per 100 ml of blood), and elevated sedimentation rate. In all cases except Case 9, and possibly Case 2, surgical exploration would have been carried out regardless of the roentgenological findings.

When one is trying to improve diagnostic accuracy, dogmatic rules and procedures may be of questionable value and are not always in the interest of the patient; each patient should be considered individually. For instance, in patients of advanced age (more than 65 years old) who are prone to the usual physical and mental disabilities incident to age, one must always weigh the incidence of possible post-operative mortality and morbidity against the apparently minimal risk of missing a tumour which may or may not be a serious threat to the patient if his normal life expectancy is taken into consideration. One must also ponder on the actual curative value of nephrectomy in each individual case.

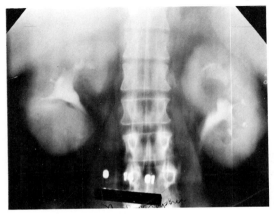

Fig. 4. Nephrotomogram to investigate a lesion in upper pole of left kidney, which in the excretory urogram suggested simple cyst or cysts. The cysts were demonstrated, but in addition a solid tumour of the lower pole of the right kidney was discovered. (The cysts of the left kidney were demonstrated better in another "cut" not shown here.)

TABLE 1. Cyst and Carcinoma in Same Kidney: Clinical Data More Suggestive of Renal Carcinoma than of Renal Cyst

Group	Case	Gross Hæmaturia	Fever	Loss of Weight	Anæmia*	Increased Sedimentation Rate†	Number of Stigmata of Tumour Present
Cystadeno-carcinoma (one case)	1	+	+	−	+	+	4
Carcinoma and cyst not in close association (eight cases)	2	−	−	−	−	+	1
	3	−	+	+	+	+	4
	4	−	−	+	−	+	2
	5	+	−	−	−	+	2
	6	−	+	+	+	+	4
	7	+	−	−	−	+	2
	8	−	−	+	−	+	2
	9	−	−	−	−	−	0
Carcinoma and cyst in close association (one case)	10	−	−	−	+	−	1

* Haemoglobin: <10.5 g per 100 ml of blood.
† Sedimentation rate from 36 to 134 mm in one hour.

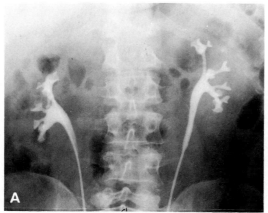

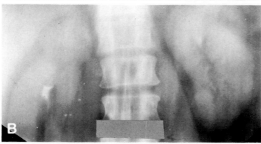

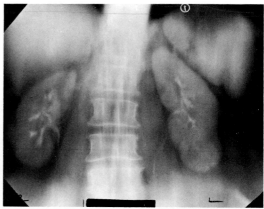

Fig. 6. Nephrotomogram. Hypernephroma of lower pole of left kidney, which does not distort pelvis or calyces.

Fig. 5. Patient was a man who had pain in ribs. Biopsy of rib disclosed metastatic adenocarcinoma, and pathologist suspected kidney as source of primary lesions. (A) Bilateral pyelograms interpreted as normal. (B) Nephrotomogram: rather large hypernephroma of upper pole of right kidney, which does not distort the pelvis or calyces. Note increased density of mass in comparison to radiolucent character of cyst in Figure 1.

What is the chance of prolonging comfortable life in an aged patient with a renal tumour? Is the tumour highly malignant or is it a low-grade, slowly growing lesion that may remain asymptomatic for years? The economic status of the patient must be taken into consideration also. If the security of a family is seriously jeopardised and their financial independence is lost because of an expensive period of hospitalisation that has not clearly improved the patient's health or significantly prolonged comfortable life, it may be difficult in retrospect to justify the decision to operate.

It should also be appreciated that the previous conventional practice of routine surgical exploration of all mass lesions of the kidney (that have been detected by excretory or retrograde urography only) is also open to a certain amount of diagnostic error. For instance, as has been pointed out elsewhere (Greene, Witten, and Emmett, in press), in the first 147 nephrotomograms made at the Mayo Clinic to distinguish renal cyst from tumour (because a ''mass'' lesion had been found with conventional urographic methods), one case was encountered in which a suspected *cyst* in the upper pole of the *left* kidney was substantiated, but an unsuspected *carcinoma* of the lower pole of the *right* kidney was also found (Fig. 4). Subsequent experience which now includes more than 1,000 nephrotomograms makes us believe that such unsuspected lesions may be found in at least 1 percent of cases because a tumour may be of such size and in such a location that it does not distort the pelvis or calyces (Figs. 5 and 6).

SUMMARY

Nephrotomography has provided a helpful diagnostic method of differentiating cysts and tumours of the kidney. It is our opinion that the problem of tumours in or associated with renal cysts has been exaggerated. In a study of 1,007 consecutive cases of surgically proved renal cysts or tumours at the Mayo Clinic, we found only ten cases in which cyst and tumour occurred in the same kidney. This was an incidence of 1 percent of the entire series, or 2.3 percent if based only on the cases of cyst. In none of these cases was the tumour situated within the cyst.

REFERENCES

AINSWORTH, W. L., and VEST, S. A. (1951). J Urol 66:740

BAKER, W. J., and GRAF, E. C. (1957). Prac North Cent Sect Amer Urol Ass, p 1

BARTLEY, O., and HELANDER, C. G. (1962). Acta Radiol Stockh 57:417

BARTLEY, O., and HULTQUIST, G. T. (1950). Acta Path Microbiol Scand 27:448

BELL, F. T. (1946). "Renal Diseases." (Philadelphia: Lea & Febiger)

BOGGS, L. K., and KIMMELSTIEL, P. (1956). J Urol 76:530

BRANNAN, W., MILLER, W., and CRISLER, M. (1962). Sth Med J 55:749

CHYNN, K. Y., and EVANS, J. A. (1960). J Urol 83:21

CLARKE, B. G., HURWITZ, I. S., and DUBINSKY, E. (1956). J Urol 75:772

CREEVY, C. D., and PRICE, W. E. (1955). Radiology, 64:831

DEWEERD, J. H. (1961). Trans Amer Ass Gen-Urin Surg 53:104

FRAZIER, T. H. (1951). J Urol 65:351

GIBSON, T. E. (1954). J Urol 65:241

GREENE, L. F., WITTEN, D. M., and EMMETT, J. L. (1964). J Urol 91:184

HAMM, F. C. (1956). New York J Med 56:2983

HEPLER, A. B. (1930). Surg Gynec Obstet 50:668

LATTIMER, J. K. (1961). Trans Amer Ass Gen.-Urin Surg 53:110

MELICOW, M. M. (1944). J Urol 51:333

OLSSON, O. (1961). In "Angiography," vol 2. Ed by HL Abrams. (Boston: Little, Brown & Co)

REHM, R. A., TAYLOR, W. N., and TAYLOR, J. N. (1961). J Urol 86:307

SOUTHWOOD, W. F. W., and MARSHALL, V. F. (1958). Brit J Urol 30:127

THOMPSON, G. J., and CULP, O. S. (1962). Trans Amer Ass Gen.-Urin Surg 54:89

USON, A. C., and MELICOW, M. M. (1963). J Urol 89:341

USON, A. C., MELICOW, M. M., and LATTIMER, J. K. (1963). J Urol 89:554

WALSH, A. (1952). Brit J Urol 23:377

WHITMORE, E. R. (1936). Sth Med J 29:1051

WILLIS, R. A. (1953). "Pathology of Tumours," 2nd ed. (London: Butterworth & Co. Ltd)

WITTEN, D. M., GREENE, L. F., and EMMETT, J. L. (1963). Amer J Roentgenol 90:115

Commentary: Renal Cysts: When to Operate

Stanley R. Levine

Since I last wrote about the low incidence of renal cell carcinoma associated with simple renal cyst, great advances have been made in the differential diagnosis of renal masses. Still, scattered reports cause concern.[1-6] One report resulted in some very interesting letters to the editor.[2] A most advanced article is discussed in the annotated bibliography; it is required reading for all urologists.[7]

The history of the diagnosis and treatment of renal masses is the development of the specialty of urology. Today, urologists are responsible for implementing the time-honored admonition to physicians: *primum non nocere* (first don't hurt). Clayman and associates state that "with modern radiologic technics and analysis of cyst fluid, an asymptomatic renal mass can be diagnosed accurately. The nonoperative approach is precise, has almost no morbidity and costs half as much as operative evaluation. Surgical exploration is rarely indicated."[3]

The patient who comes for an examination usually has no history that would make a physician suspect a renal mass. This mass is usually insidious. If one is lucky, hematuria, either gross or microscopic, is present early enough for a cure. The palpation of a renal mass usually is not a good diagnostic finding. Therefore, most renal masses are found by serendipity. The excretory urogram or sonogram or computed tomography (CT) scan first calls attention to the renal mass. Evans has pointed out the 95% accuracy of nephrotomography, a most valuable addition to the excretory urogram.[8] One should insist on using nephrotomography on all excretory urograms.

The next noninvasive technique should be the ultrasonic investigation of the renal mass. The diagnostic accuracy of ultrasound averages 95%. If a simple renal cyst is found, then cyst puncture, cystography, and cyst fluid analysis should be performed. Cyst puncture can be accomplished in 96% of lesions. The most feared complication of renal mass puncture—tumor growth along the needle track—has been reported twice in the last 15 years. Also, I never worry about needle biopsy of prostates in terms of tumor growth. As Clayman says, "In the series of Von Schreeb and Dean more than 200 suspected neoplasms were punctured without any seeding, and Von Schreeb noted no decrease in the five-year survival rate of patients who had had percutaneous puncture of their neoplasms." I disagree with Clayman about using CT scans to diagnose renal masses. The CT scanner has great ability to discriminate small lesions from normal renal tissue (*i.e.*, association of renal cysts and tumor 1%). Next, the use of angiography aortography, selective renal arteriography, and vena cavagrams are indicated if the diagnosis of a simple renal cyst has not been made.

The surgery of renal cystic disease creates the problem of whether to operate. All physicians agree that polycystic kidney disease is treated without surgery unless complications supervene. However, simple renal cysts (solitary or multiple), papillary cystadenoma, and hemorrhagic, calcified, and pararenal cysts present problems in surgical management. Wahlquist presents an excellent classification of cystic disorders.[7]

Physicians' obligation is to provide the best medicine that is "practical" and reasonably priced. As an example, physicians recommend an annual physical examination for all persons over age 50. How complete should that examination be? Should every patient undergo a complete gastrointestinal (GI) x-ray examination? Obviously, that is not practical, and few, if any, physicians would go to such lengths. But if physicians do not advise a complete examination, what risks do they take of overlooking some important lesion? For instance, if complete GI x-ray and proctoscopic examination were done yearly in every patient, how many early asymptomatic malignant lesions would be found? Would it be 0.5%, 1%, or 2%? Are physicans then remiss for "taking a chance" or overlooking these occasional lesions? The fact that physicians generally do not advise such complete routine examinations supplies the answer to the question. Apparently, such elaborate yearly examinations are not considered practical.

Essentially, physicians face a similar problem in the diagnosis of "mass lesions" of the kidney, which concerns itself chiefly with the differentiation of cyst and tumor. To follow the dogmatic advice "operate on all renal cysts" seems a gross oversimplification of a difficult problem. It is also an admission that diagnosis has not progressed much since the era before excretory urography, when bilateral renal exploration was often done in cases of renal tuberculosis to find out which kidney was involved.

The decision whether to explore a "mass lesion" of a kidney seems to require individual consideration in each case. If satisfactory nephrotomograms and subsequent renal arteriograms show a renal cyst with better than 99% accuracy, the risk of renal cell tumor is 1%; if the surgical morbidity and mortality is 1%, it follows that one need not explore all "mass lesions" of the kidney.

The criteria for surgical exploration of renal cysts should take into account all aspects of diagnosis. The assessment of clinical and laboratory observations—such as hematuria, elevation of temperature, erythrocyte sedimentation rate, and LAD content of urine—assists in the differentiation of benign cysts from renal tumors. Intravenous pyelograms (IVPs) and possibly retrograde pyelograms are scrutinized for calcifications, amputations, or distortions of the calices and infundibula, filing defects protruding into the pyelocaliceal system, or distortions of the renal outline. When any of the foregoing abnormalities is noted, consider nephrotomography. If the renal mass is completely avascular, and the mass exhibits sharp margins in its entire contour with a thin and perfectly smooth wall, it is almost certainly a benign cyst. If these nephrotomographic criteria are not met, perform renal arteriography with or without epinephrine-enhanced angiography. The use of epinephrine-enhanced angiography aids in intensifying opacification of renal vessels of a necrotic or cystic tumor that would otherwise appear as an avascular mass. Further refinement in the differential diagnosis of renal cysts and tumors includes cyst puncture, aspiration, and analysis of cyst contents for fat.

Surgical exploration of renal masses should be performed when, despite all the preceding techniques, the diagnosis is indeterminate. At surgery, if a cyst is found, open it and carefully examine and palpate the inner surface to rule out tumor. There are reported cases of tumor in the free wall margin. Obtain a frozen section if there is thickening of the cyst wall.

The operative technique is simple. The edges of the cyst are excised adjacent to the renal tissue and oversewn with a running suture of 4–0 chromic catgut or, more recently, 4–0 Dexon. If the cavity is large, some fat may be placed in it. Drain the area for 48 hours.

REFERENCES

1. Ambrose SS: Unsuspected renal tumors associated with renal cysts. J Urol 117:704, 1977
2. Hinman F Jr: Obstructive renal cysts. J Urol 119:681, 1978
3. Zelch J: Complications of renal cyst exploration versus renal mass aspiration. Urology 7:244, 1976
4. Stewart BH: Aspiration and cytology in the evaluation of renal mass lesions. Cleve Clin Q 43:1, 1976
5. Sherwood T: Needling renal cysts and tumors. Cystology and radiology. Br Med J 3:755, 1975
6. Lang EK: Renal cyst puncture and aspiration: A survey of complications. Am J Roentgenol 128:723, 1977
7. Clayman RV: Current Concepts: The pursuit of the renal mass. N Engl J Med 300:72, 1979
8. Chynn KY, Evans JA: Nephrotomography in the differentiation of renal cyst from neoplasm: A review of 500 cases. J Urol 83:21, 1960

ANNOTATED BIBLIOGRAPHY

Ambrose SS: Unsuspected renal tumors associated with renal cysts. J Urol 117:704, 1977

The abstract states, "A series of renal tumors associated with renal cysts is presented. Prior to surgical exploration, appropriate diagnostic studies failed to indicate evidence of the presence of neoplastic lesions. The importance of surgical exploration of avascular "benign" renal masses is emphasized." I question the statement "appropriate diagnostic studies." The authors specifically state that nephrotomography was performed in two of their seven patients, and they did not perform ultrasonography in any of these patients. Although cyst puncture revealed straw-colored fluid on several occasions with negative cytologic results, specific chemistry studies were not performed on any of the cystic fluid, except that from one patient which indeed proved to be a benign cyst adjacent to a solid tumor in the upper pole. I would advise reading this article, keeping in mind the importance of a complete preoperative work-up for the renal mass.

Hinman F Jr: Obstructive renal cysts. J Urol 119:681, 683, 1978

I suggest this article so that one can see an indication for surgical treatment of a renal cyst. Dr. Hinman states:

Rental cysts usually are asymptomatic, produce no harm to the kidney and require no treatment once diagnosed. However, an occasional expanding cyst causes progressive obstruction to caliceal or pelvic outflow. Herein is reported observations on 4 patients in whom cysts produced significant obstruction to the pelvis or major caliceal outflow. In 3 cases treatment was by decompression, with resolution of the obstruction. Two requirements must be met for a cyst to obstruct: 1) it must lie at or near the hilus and 2) it must have turgor sufficient to overcome the pressure of the intrapelvic urine. In contrast to most renal cysts those producing significant obstruction require operation.

Dr. J. D. Joubert of Cape Town, South Africa, added an addition three cases to this observation in the letters to the editor section (J Urol 121:258, 1978).

Zelch J: Complications of renal cyst exploration versus renal mass aspiration. Urology 7:244, 1976

This report compares the complications of surgical exploration with unroofing and renal cyst puncture. Two hundred and fifty five patients were operated on, with a mortality of 1% and a morbidity rate of 28%. The complications in 63 patients examined by mass aspiration included a morbidity rate of 6.4% and no mortality. The possibilities of overlooking carcinomas through cyst aspiration are weighed against the demonstrated morbidity of surgical exploration and found to be much less significant. The authors recommend that an asymptomatic renal mass that radiographically appears to be a cyst and is unaccompanied by urine changes or clinical stigmas of renal neoplasia be treated by cyst aspiration and not subjected to surgical exploration.

Stewart BH: Aspiration and cytology in the evaluation of renal mass lesions. Cleve Clin Q 43:1, 6, 1976

This paper presents practical management of a given patient with a renal mass. It confirms the findings I presented in 1963. "Levine et al in a review of 438 operated cysts, found no cases of malignancy in the cyst if the aspirated fluid was clear. Our data have shown similar results." Also, they state that operative exploration of renal cysts should be considered only when roentgenographic or clincal studies indicate a distinct possibility of neoplasm or if the cyst is causing significant obstruction of the collecting system. Routine nephrectomy should not be done in most patients with bloody cyst aspirate, since the incidence of carcinoma in these patients is relatively low. In such cases, the cyst should first be exposed, and if there is no gross evidence of carcinoma, the cyst should be opened and biopsy performed before nephrectomy is contemplated.

Sherwood T: Needling renal cysts and tumors. Cystology and radiology. Br Med J 3:755, 1975.

This is an excellent presentation of the approach to the renal mass.

Lang EK: Renal cyst puncture and aspiration: A survey of complications. Am J Roentgenol 128:723, 1977

This article reviews 5674 cyst puncture and aspiration complications. Major complications occurred in 78 of 5674 patients (1.4%), with perirenal hemorrhage by far the most common. Pneumothorax, arteriovenous fistulae, infection, and traumatic urinomas are other complications. Extensive laceration or rupture of the kidney, although frequently cited as arguments against cyst puncture and aspiration, was reported only once in this survey. Complications attributable to inadvertent puncture, lacerations of other parenchymal or hollow viscus organs, or both were also rare. There is a good discussion of minor complications.

Clayman RV: Current concepts: The pursuit of the renal mass. N Engl J Med 300:72, 1979

This entire article is required reading on the renal mass. Clayman has outlined, with substantiation from the world's literature, how to pursue a renal mass.

Overview: Techniques to Determine Renal Cyst

James A. Roberts

It used to be simple: find a renal mass and then operate! This is no longer true. Improvements in radiologic techniques not only help in diagnosis but also find more masses. This is especially true where a nephrotomogram cut is taken during all routine excretory urograms. My previous calculations suggest that 300,000 renal cysts and 15,000 renal tumors could be found in the U.S. population each year. They probably will not, since excretory urography is no longer routine. Reports of renal failure after this examination in patients with diabetes mellitus, the definite possible mortality from contrast anaphylaxis, and cost-benefit awareness for all have led to a change in the frequency of excretory urograms.

Now when a mass is found on excretory or retrograde urography, the nephrotomogram often determines the diagnosis, but only of tumor vs avascular mass. If the latter, ultrasound is the next step to confirm that it is cystic. When such a mass is only partially cystic, I prefer both arteriography and, if avascular, CT scanning to pick up the 5% of masses that are avascular tumors. If, however, ultrasound shows a renal cyst, percutaneous puncture of the cyst is necessary to find the 1% of cysts that contain tumors. Those who suggest surgery for all renal cysts are aiming for the same tumors but with the risk of operative mortality equaling the yield of discovered tumors.[1] I know of no mortality from percutaneous puncture of a renal cyst. Before puncture, evaluate the patient for bleeding tendency, as in renal biopsy.

After puncturing many cysts with fluoroscopic guidance, I turned to ultrasound; its comparative ease of puncture is amazing. I prefer the regular probe to locate and determine the depth of the cyst because the hollow probe fixes the needle too firmly, preventing it from moving with the kidney; this could lead to renal laceration. Some workers now feel that cystography is not really needed, since if the fluid is clear and is analyzed for fat, lactic dehydrogenase (LDH) and cytological examination will show a tumor.[2] I still do cystography with sodium diatrizoate to prove that the mass seen on cystogram is the same size as that on nephrotomogram and to rule out any irregularity of the wall. When the wall is irregular, it must be seen, and for this purpose I use percutaneous puncture with a larger needle to allow endoscopy of this area rather than surgical exploration and visualization with my eye.[3] This seems reasonable, since in a similar situation—the urinary bladder—surgeons diagnose endoscopically rather than by surgical exploration. The use of this larger needle has led to no increase in morbidity.

Thus, the surgical treatment of renal cyst is percutaneous in all but one further situation, that in which the cyst is obstructing, since preservation of renal function is the urologist's prime goal. This is infrequent and can now be diagnosed by functional evaluation rather than by radiography. I have shown, in a study of 27 consecutive renal cysts using quantitative renal scintillation camera studies, that renal function is not affected by a benign renal cyst, even when it appears obstructing on excretory urography.[4] I am sure that an occasional cyst will obstruct and decrease function, but I am happy that this further advance in surgeons' noninvasive armamentarium will allow intelligent decisions on which cysts need surgery.[5]

REFERENCES

1. Kropp KA, Grayhack JT, Wendel RM, Dahl DS: Morbidity and mortality of renal exploration for cyst. Surg Gynecol Obstet 125:803, 1967

2. Lang EK, Johnston B, Chance HL, et al: Assessment of avascular renal mass lesions: The use of nephrotomography, arteriography, cyst puncture, double contrast study and histochemical and histopathologic examination of the aspirate. South Med J 65:1, 1972

3. Roberts JA: Renal cystoscopy. Urology 8:537, 1976

4. Roth JK Jr, Roberts JA: Benign renal cysts and renal function. J Urol 123:625, 1980

5. Hinman F Jr: Obstructive renal cysts. J Urol 119:681, 1978

PART NINE

SURGICAL TREATMENT OF CHYLURIA

22

TECHNIQUE OF CLEARANCE (OR DISCONNECTION) OF DILATED LYMPHATICS IN THE RENAL HILUM AND LOWER URETER AND BLADDER IN CASES OF INTRACTABLE CHYLURIA OR HAEMOCHYLURIA

D. K. Karanjavala

Bombay

British Journal of Urology (1979), 51, 440–442

SUMMARY—The indications, investigations and techniques for treating patients with chyluria are presented. Thirty-eight patients were treated by lymphatic disconnection either at renal hilum or at lower ureter and bladder level. Pedal lymphangiography was essential to decide upon the level of operation. Results were satisfactory in the majority when chyluria was intractable.

In India chyluria and haemochyluria are features of filarial infestation. In about 20% of cases the disease takes a relentless course. Patients lose a considerable amount of weight and suffer from intermittent retention due to chylous or haemochylous clots. These patients can be treated by the lymphatic disconnection technique. At many centres this operation is undertaken only at the renal hilum after cystoscopy to detect the side of the greater leak and a retrograde pyelogram to demonstrate the exaggerated pyelolymphatic backflow. At times this operation fails since the exact site of the leak has not been determined. We have been using pedal lymphangiography to determine the exact site of the leak and then to decide on the approach for surgery.

PATIENTS AND METHODS

Thirty-eight patients with intractable chyluria or haemochyluria were treated by the lymphatic disconnection technique. Thirty of them had leaks around the renal hilum, while the rest had leaks around the lower ureter and the bladder; in 2 cases the cord lymphatics were grossly dilated.

Lymphangiography. The 8 lower tract lesions would have been missed if pedal lymphangiography had not been done (Table 1). Lymphangiography was indicated when the patient had not responded to prolonged treatment with antifilarial drugs and urinary antiseptics, had lost weight from loss of protein and fat in the urine, or had repeated episodes of urinary infection or clot retention due to haemochylous clots.

Usually, the lymph varices around the renal vein and artery were responsible for the leak of lymph into the urinary tract, but if the lymphatic varices were predominantly around the lower ureter and bladder, this area might need a separate clearance through a separate incision in the iliac region.

Lymphangiography was done through cannulated lymphatics in the dorsum of the foot, or in some cases of grossly dilated lymphatics of the inguinal region or in the spermatic cord by exposure and direct injection. The lymphangiogram demonstrated the leak convincingly by outlining the caliceal lymphatics and also the grossly dilated lymphatics around the renal hilum (*i.e.* around the renal vein and artery) (Fig. 1); this could be demonstrated at operation by pre-operative injection of these lymphatics with patent blue violet. The same was true in cases where the lymphatics around the lower ureters and bladder were to be cleared (Fig. 2). These lymphatics lay over the iliac vessels and after adequate clearance the iliac vein and artery were seen bare and clean.

Operative Technique. The pedal lymphatics were cannulated on the side to be operated about an hour before

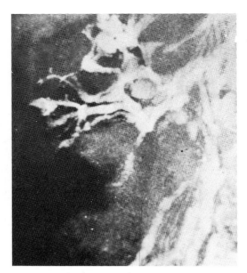

Fig. 1. Varicose lymphatics in the right renal hilum demonstrated by pre-operative lymphangiography.

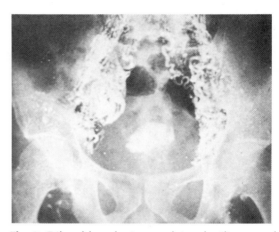

Fig. 2. Dilated lymphatics overlying the iliac vessels producing ethiodol cystogram.

the start of the operation; injection of blue dye was started and continued till the area of clearance was exposed and the abnormal (dilated) lymphatics well demonstrated (Figs. 3, 4 and 5).

It was important to secure or seal off even the tiniest blood vessels and keep the field from getting stained with blood so that the lymphatics could be clearly demonstrated. The dilated lymphatics overlying the ureter and the spermatic or ovarian vessels could be followed right into the renal hilum around the renal vein and artery. The lymphatics were easily isolated, tied and sectioned and some of the varicosities excised, leaving

TABLE 1. Site of Chylous Leak

Total number of patients with chyluria	38
Leak around renal hilum	30
Leak around lower ureter and bladder and 2 with dilatation of the spermatic cord lymphatics	8

Fig. 3. Dilated lymphatics around the ureter were demonstrated by the blue dye (*outlined in white*).

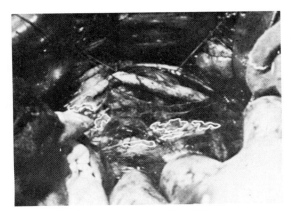

Fig. 4. Part of the lymphatics excised and the ureter retracted to show further lymphatics going up to the renal hilum (*outlined in white*).

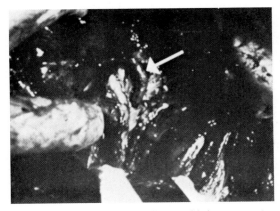

Fig. 5. A large lymphatic entering the renal hilum (*arrow*). Note that its caliber looks larger than the ureter.

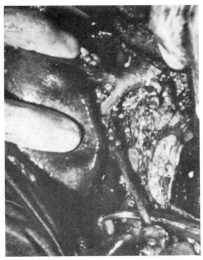

Fig. 6. The renal hilum cleared of varicose lymphatics showing renal vein clean and bare at the end of the operation.

the vein and artery looking bare and clean at the end of the dissection (Fig. 6).

The incision was closed, without drains, but postoperative antibiotic cover was given to prevent infection of any small lymph collection.

RESULTS

Twenty-eight of the 38 patients who underwent operation were cured. Twenty-two had leaks around the renal hilum while 6 patients had a leak around the lower ureter and bladder.

In the remaining patients symptomatic relief was obtained. They were passing significantly less chyle in their urine and were otherwise in good health.

DISCUSSIONS

Although this condition in the majority of cases responds to treatment with diethyl carbamazine, the refractory ones may require surgical disconnection. This type of management is not expected to lead to a cure but gives long periods of remission in many cases.

The final answer to this problem of filarial chyluria belongs in the domain of the epidemiologist and the public health services, but the surgeon can give relief from distress in some cases.

THE AUTHOR

D. K. Karanjavala, FRCS, Mayfair Gardens, Little Gibbs Road, Bombay 400006, India.

Commentary: Symptoms and Treatment of Chyluria

D. K. Karanjavala

The cardinal presenting symptoms of chyluria, apart from milky urine, are repeated episodes of urinary tract infection, hematuria or hemochyluria, and the associated weight loss due to the passage of proteins and fat in the urine. In India, the predominant cause is filariasis, which is endemic along the coastline where the Culex mosquito thrives. Filarial infestation and secondary streptococcal infection of the retroperitoneal lymph nodes leads to perinodal fibrosis and blockage of the lymphatics, resulting in secondary lymphatic hypertension and retrograde flow of chyle from the intestines to the kidneys and in chyluria. Other equally common genitourinary manifestations of filariasis in India are chylous or clear hydrocele (Fig. 11), lymphadenovarix (Fig. 7), lymph scrotum (Fig. 8), elephantiasis of scrotum, and lymphangiocele of the spermatic cord (Figs. 9 and 10).

I would like to thank Dr. Harshad Punjani, M.S., my assistant and colleague at the Bombay Hospital, for all the lymphangiograms and other investigations he has carried out on my cases and also for his assistance at surgery and after care.

INDICATIONS FOR SURGERY

Initially chyluria occurs intermittently, is of varying severity, and can usually be controlled by conservative measures. Unless the chyluria is affecting the patient's health (*i.e.,* severe loss of weight, recurrent infection, retention of urine due to chylous clots), and the patient is not responding to medical treatment (*i.e.,* diethylcarbamazine, 100 mg 3 times a day, omitted for 3 weeks and repeated for 6 months to 1 year), surgery is not warranted.

PREOPERATIVE INVESTIGATION

Preoperative investigation should include *repeated examination of urine smears* to spot red blood cells (RBCs), pus cells, chylomicrons, and microfilariae. Eosinophilia is common and is one of the more reliable confirmatory findings. A peripheral blood smear for microfilariae is positive only in a few patients and is not required to diagnose filariasis. I was lucky to see them in many of my patients. Serum proteins are usually normal but are lowered in intractable cases.

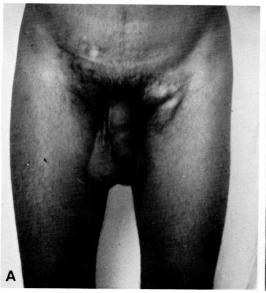 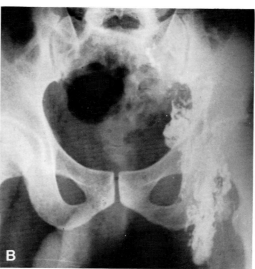

Fig. 7. (*A*) Swellings in the inguinofemoral region can be mistakenly diagnosed as a hernia, since there is usually an impulse on coughing, but the lymph nodes are palpably enlarged and surrounded by large lymphatics (*B*).

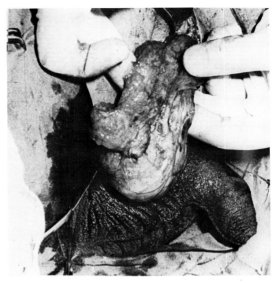

Fig. 8. The scrotal skin is often thickened and sometimes has bullae or vesicles.

Fig. 9. Lymphangiography done either by the conventional technique or by direct injection of grossly dilated inguinal or cord lymphatics is quite feasible, since these lymphatics have a good muscle coat and are not very friable. Grossly dilated cord lymphatics are exposed for direct injection lymphangiogram and later excision.

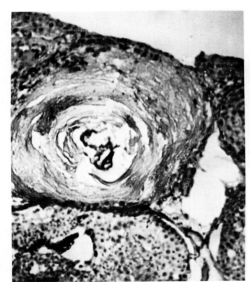

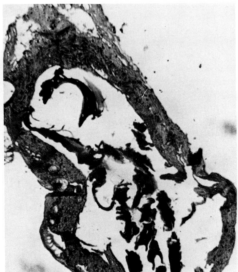

Fig. 10. In cases of recurrent and refractory epididymitis, epididymal and spermatic cord lymphatic nodules can, by a careful histologic examination, be shown to contain microfilaria. (Courtesy of Dr. S. S. Rao)

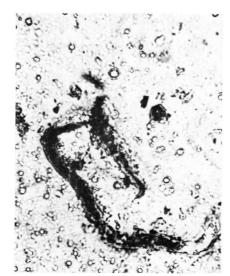

Fig. 11. A hydrocele, even with clear fluid, frequently has a chylous element, and it is only when one looks diligently for chylomicrons in the fluid that one also sees microfilaria on some occasions. (Courtesy of Dr. S. S. Rao)

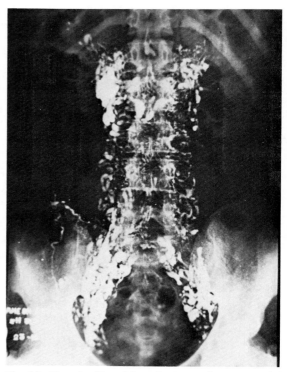

Fig. 12. Grossly dilated lymphatics in the region of the renal hilum and lower ureter demonstrated by lymphangiogram.

Lymphangiography: Technique and Interpretation. Lymphangiography is the anchor of our management. I use a modified Kinmonth technique under local anesthesia. After an initial interdigital web injection of 1% of patent blue violet mixed with an equal amount of 1% of lidocaine on both sides, lymphatics are nicely visible on the dorsum of the foot near the metatarsotarsal joints. These are dissected and cannulated with a no. 30-gauge needle attached to a long polyethelene tubing. Using a slow injector, 6 ml to 10 ml of ultrafluid lipiodol (Ethiodol) is injected over 60 minutes.

Serial radiograms are taken at the end of injection from the foot to the chest. These are repeated at 4 hours and 12 hours. In cases of severe lymphangiectasis, stasis of dye is noticed in the lymphatics even after 4 days. Pelvic lymphangiograms showed (1) massively dilated and vermiform plexus of lymphatic vessels (Fig. 12) and (2) absence of filling of pelvic and retroperitoneal lymph nodes. In some patients, these dilated lymphatics cross over the midline in pelvis and produced an Ethiodol cystogram (Fig. 13), while in others tortuous vessels climbed around the ureter (Fig. 14) or arborized around the pelvis to produce a pyelographic pattern (Fig. 15). Thus, in several cases the site of the leak was well demonstrated. Absence or paucity of lymph nodes in lymphangiography strengthened the hypothesis of secondary lymphatic hypertension and retrograde flow.

Whenever the patient had lymphadenovarix, direct cannulation of these lymphatics was done after exposing them through a small inguinal or scrotal incision. In many bilateral cases of lymphagiectasis, the thoracic duct was markedly dilated in the terminal 10 cm, with abrupt narrowing at the junction with subclavian vein. Retrograde flow into supraclavicular nodes was seen on a few occasions (Fig. 16).

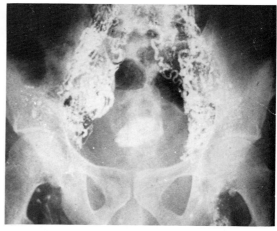

Fig. 13. Dilated lymphatics overlying the iliac vessels and producing an Ethiodol cystogram.

Cystoscopy. Cystoscopy was done in all patients and helped to determine which kidney hilum should be dealt with first. Also, whenever the bladder is the major site of the leak, I have seen chylous clots hanging from the bladder wall or as blebs under the mucosa. Whenever pedal lymphangiography

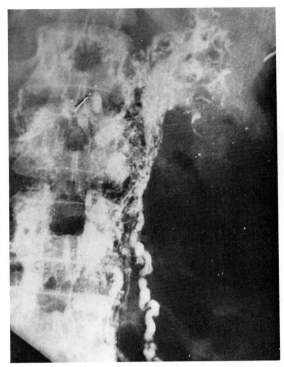

Fig. 14. IVP simultaneous with the lymphangiogram to demonstrate the relation of dilated lymphatic to ureter pelvis and calices.

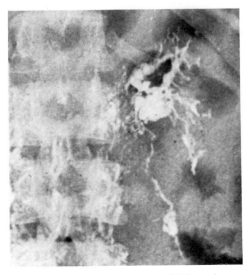

Fig. 15. Varicose lymphatics in the left renal hilum demonstrated by preoperative lymphangiography.

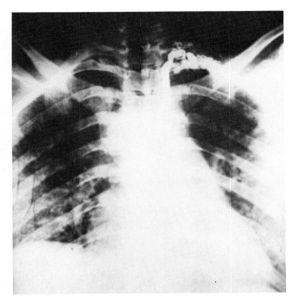

Fig. 16. Dilated terminal thoracic duct at its junction with the jugular vein.

has failed because of technical difficulty in cannulating a lymphatic, I have combined cystoscopy with retrograde ureteropyelogram with a cuffed catheter. This shows the pyelolymphatic backflow and demonstrates the caliceal leak.

SURGICAL TECHNIQUE: LYMPHATIC DISCONNECTION

To proceed: half an hour before the operation, cannulate the lymphatics of the dorsum of the foot and inject patent blue violet, which is continued throughout the operation. This gives a beautiful demonstration of the lymphatic varices in the affected area, but it is not an absolute necessity, now that I can identify these lymphatics without the blue dye. Expose the kidney and upper ureter through a standard renal incision, including resection of the 12th rib. Keep the operative field bloodless to see the lymphatics well. Lymphatic tributaries around the renal vein and artery are seen coming from the main lymphatic trunk lying near the venacava (Figs. 17 to 19). These are severed and ligated. I did not see dilated lymphatics in the peripheral area, and this probably accounts for failure of the operation of decapsulation.

For the lower ureter and bladder lymphatic disconnection: the oblique-muscle-cutting extraperitoneal approach is adequate, with the incision reaching up to the midline just above the pubic symphysis.

In some of my earlier cases for bilateral lymphangiectasis and dilated thoracic duct with abrupt ending I did ductojugular anastamosis. This was done by Professor Bhalerao, who is keenly interested in liver and portal hypertension work. The immediate effect was excellent, but relapses did take place. In this technique, the patient is given a small quantity of cream to drink an hour before the operation. This renders the thoracic

Fig. 17. Dilated lymphatics around the ureter demonstrated by blue dye.

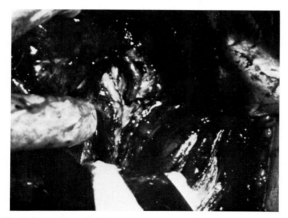

Fig. 18. A large lymphatic entering the renal hilum. Note that its caliber looks larger than the ureter.

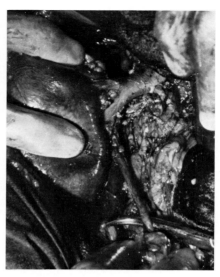

Fig. 19. Renal hilum cleared of varicose lymphatics and showing the renal vein clean and bare at the end of the operation.

changes seen in my patients, this method did not appeal to me.

MATERIAL AND RESULTS

Thirty eight patients with intractable chyluria or hemochyluria were treated by the lymphatic disconnection technique. Thirty of these had leaks around the renal hilum, while the rest had leaks around the lower ureter and the bladder; and in two patients the cord lymphatics were grossly dilated. These eight patients would have been missed if lymphangiography (pedal) had not been done (Table 1).

TABLE 1

Patients with chyluria	38
Patients with leak around renal hilum	30
Patients with leak around lower ureter and bladder (two had gross dilatation of spermatic cord lymphatics)	8

DISCUSSION

Lymphatic obstruction in these patients is widespread throughout the retroperitoneal nodes and tissues, which is why the nodes are usually not visualized. The blockage of the normal passage of chyle through the nodes leads to lymphatic hypertension with consequent development of abnormal and dilated collateral channels. The chyle then flows toward the kidneys in a retrograde manner, causing chyluria. If the iliac nodes are predominantly involved and if there are large channels around the bladder, there may be a direct leak in the bladder. But even the patients who primarily showed epididymitis and

duct white and easily identifiable. The terminal portion of the duct is exposed through a left supraclavicular incision, and the narrowed end where it opens into the vein is sectioned and tied off. The dilated proximal end is then anastomosed end-to-side with the jugular vein. Recently we have done the classic renal hilar lymphatic disconnection on the more affected side only as described above, in patients showing bilateral changes, with good results.

I do not believe in injecting sclerosing agents in the ureter and renal pelvis, since these agents give rise to severe chemical irritation and sometimes septicemia. I also do not like to operate on any one side based only on cystoscopic examination and retrograde studies. As seen from our lymphangiographic studies, ureteric and vesical leaks will be overlooked in such patients, and postoperative results may be vitiated.

Cockett and Goodwin have advocated a shunt between a single vericose lymphatic and the testicular or ovarian vein for the relief of lymphatic hypertension, but in view of the extensive chylous hydrocele also showed no filling of the retroperitoneal nodes and had abnormal renolymphatic communications. It is my belief, therefore, that the basic pathologic state starts in the retroperitoneal nodes and leads to lymphatic hypertension.

Resection of these renolymphatic communications is a good palliative procedure and, in a few cases, has given prolonged relief, although it does not do away with the basic hypertension. In patients with bilateral changes, surgery on the termination of the thoracic duct appears more logical.

In India, chyluria and hemochyluria are manifestations of filarial infestation. In about 20% of patients the disease takes a relentless course. Patients lose a considerable amount of weight and suffer from retention on and off due to chylous or hemochylous clots. Such patients are treated by the lymphatic disconnection technique. At many centers this operation is undertaken only at renal hilum level after doing cystoscopy to know the side of the greater leak and with a retrograde pyelogram to demonstrate the exaggerated pyelolymphatic backflow. At times this operation fails, since the exact site of the leak is not determined. I have, therefore, been using pedal lymphangiography to determine the exact site of the leak before deciding on the approach for surgery.

ANNOTATED BIBLIOGRAPHY

Sen SB, Ellappan E: Filarial chyluria. Ind Med Res 56:1535, 1968

This article reports one of the manifestation of filariasis as chyluria. Positive past history is available in only 50% of patients, and an equal number show recovery of microfilariae from the blood or urine. Also stressed here is the importance of lymphangiography. The exact site of lymphatic leak and various abnormalities of the thoracic duct are discussed. The most satisfactory treatment in intractable cases still remains surgical disconnection of the lymphatics around the renal hilum.

Sen SB, Chatterjee H, Ramprasad S: Chylous manifestation of filariasis: A clinical and lymphangiographic study in lymphadenovarix, chylocoele and chylous lymph scrotum. Ind Med Res 57:1738, 1969

This article described in detail lymphangiographic studies carried out in four cases of chylocoele, four cases of lymph adenovarix, and one case of lymph scrotum. The authors believe that early development of lymphadenovarix provides enough space for lymphatic stasis and that chyluria is an uncommon finding with the above manifestations.

Dedhia CN, Rao SS, Prabhu SR: Aetiology of idiopathic Hydrocele. Presented at the Urological Society of India Meeting, Hyderabad, September 1979

In this interesting article the author has pointed to the major etiologic factors causing hydrocele in India. It is not necessary to have chylous fluid or a positive blood smear to stamp hydrocele as of filarial origin. Positive clinical history, microfilaria in the spermatic cord, and tunica vaginalis or testis are equally important, as is the finding of chylomicrons in the urine.

Karanjavala DK: Lymphangiography in the management of filarial chyluria. Ann R Coll Surg 46:267, 1970, and Technique of clearance (or disconnection) of dilated lymphatics in the renal hilum and lower ureter and bladder in cases of intractable chyluria or haemochyluria. Br J Urol 51:440, 1979

These two articles are discussed in depth in the commentary.

Overview: Chyluria

Anthony A. Caldamone, Luis R. Cos, and Abraham T. K. Cockett

Hippocrates was probably the first to mention chyluria, although in 1653 Jean Pecquet described in detail the lymphatic circulation. It was Morgagni who, in 1741, associated chyluria with a disturbance in lymphatic circulation. Since that time, there have been debates in the literature over the exact mechanism that causes chyluria. Basically, two theories have predominated. The first is the "generalized obstruction and rupture" theory, which states that obstruction occurs between the lacteals of the small intestine and the thoracic duct, resulting in lymphatic hypertension, lymph stasis with lymphatic valvular incompetence, varices, and rupture of lymphatics into the urinary system. A second hypothesis, the "local obstruction" theory, proposes that local blockage from retroperitoneal lymph node fibrosis and replacement results in chylous reflux into the urinary tract; actual rupture is not necessary. The latter theory is more appealing and is based on lymphangiography demonstrating that the thoracic duct is not universally involved.

The major cause of chyluria is retroperitoneal obstruction of lymphatic vessels due to filariasis; this parasite is endemic to certain parts of India, Southeast Asia, and the Middle East—especially Egypt. A serologic test for filariasis is not widely available, and the diagnosis is based on finding the ova in the excised tissue where inflammation is evident. Our own experience includes three patients from geographic areas mentioned above: a Chinese immigrant, a patient of Japanese ancestry, and an Indian from an endemic area in his country.

The renal lymphatics are thought to be composed of two networks: the perinephric vessels, including the subcapsular vessels, and the intrarenal network. The perinephric network does not communicate with kidney parenchyma except through the capsular vessels, which freely communicate with cortical lymphatic vessels and drain into the hilar lymphatic vessels, finally joining larger tributaries near the cisterna chyli. The subcapsular vessels join four to seven parenchymal trunks at the renal hilum and follow the course of the renal vein to end in the para-aortic lymphatic glands near the cisterna chyli. Some of the subcapsular lymphatic vessels communicate with the cortical parenchymal network based on canine kidney injection studies. Investigators have demonstrated that renal parenchymal vessels encompass both medullary and cortical channels, which merge to form larger tributaries as they course toward the hilum. Whether intrarenal venous–lymphatic communications exist remains controversial. Nonetheless, the renal lymphatics act as "safety valves" capable of balancing extra fluid loads under conditions of overload, as in renal pelvic or ureteral obstruction. In addition, intrarenal lymphatics play a role in maintaining a low interstitial oncotic pressure, allowing the urine to become concentrated from the reabsorption of solutes and water through the lymphatic pathway.

RADIOLOGIC DIAGNOSIS

The goal of radiologic investigation is to delineate the site of lymphatic obstruction and backflow between the lymphatic system and the urinary tract. This can occur at the level of the renal lymphatics, ureteral lymphatics, or bladder lymphatics. The excretory urogram is of limited value. It is usually normal except in the late stages of the disease process, in which obstruction due to chronic pyelonephritis is evident. In some cases, pyelocaliceal backflow of contrast or ureteral deviation from enlarged para-aortic lymph nodes or varicosed lymphatic vessels may be present. Although some reports have described urinary–lymphatic backflow with retrograde pyelography, this has been of limited value for most investigators.

The most efficacious study, according to the majority of reports, is pedal lymphangiography. It is estimated that urinary–lymphatic fistulas are demonstrable in 50% of patients by pedal lymphangiography. In addition, the combination of simultaneous excretory urography or retrograde pyelography and pedal lymphangiography has been reported as successful in the demonstration of these communications.

MEDICAL TREATMENT

The medical treatment of chyluria falls into three categories: (1) dietary restriction of fats, (2) substitution of fat with medium-chain triglycerides, and (3) diethylcarbamazine for active filarial chyluria. In the majority of patients, diethylcarbamazine is capable of arresting mildly to moderately active filarial chyluria. The dosage used is 0.5 mg to 2 mg per kg three times daily for 1 to 3 weeks. In some patients, repeated courses of therapy are indicated. Because of secondary bacterial infections, antibiotics have also proved helpful. Diethylcarbamazine is only effective when active filarial disease is present. In all likelihood, once chyluria is established, diethylcarbam-

azine is of limited value. With nonparasitic chyluria, dietary alteration is the only nonsurgical therapy available. This consists of reducing dietary fat intake. There have been reports in the literature attesting to the beneficial effect of medium-chain triglyceride substitution; however, this effect is not universally accepted. Bed rest and the use of a tight corset to raise intraabdominal pressure have been reported as successful in some patients.

SURGICAL TREATMENT

The surgical treatment of chyluria is indicated only where the process is unrelenting, resulting in large losses of protein and fat from the urine with loss of body weight; chyluria-fibrous clots may result in ureteral obstruction or urinary retention, necessitating surgical intervention. This severe form of disease occurs in approximately 20% of reported cases. In evaluating the results of surgical treatment, one must consider that there have been reported instances of spontaneous remission, although the exact incidence is difficult to determine.

Surgical options can be divided into five categories: (1) caustic irrigation of the renal pelvis, (2) renal hilar lymphatic stripping, (3) hilar lymphatic stripping coupled with renal decapsulation, (4) internal drainage by surgical means, and (5) nephrectomy. Stripping of the renal hilar lymphatics (with or without renal decapsulation) has been the most popular technique used in the majority of reported cases. Most investigators believe that complete dissociation of renal hilar lymphatics precludes the necessity of renal decapsulation. Caustic irrigation of the renal pelvis, the ureter, or both may cause chemical irritation with septicemia.

Dr. Cockett previously reported on the treatment of chyluria by diversion of a single hilar lymphatic vessel to the spermatic vein by an end-to-side lymphatic–spermatic vein anastomosis. The remaining lymphatics were stripped and ligated. Theoretically, this would obviate the difficulty of achieving a complete stripping of renal hilar lymphatics; in effect, it would provide a "safety-valve" mechanism for renal lymphatic hypertension, which is the basis for chyluria. In the case previously reported, the success of the procedure was difficult to evaluate. Although the patient no longer had chyluria, the kidney operated on never regained function, most likely because of renal vascular damage. With an internal drainage system, the possible development of a lymphocele or a cutaneous fistula is reduced. There are potential complications of renal hilar lymphatic stripping, although the exact incidence in reported series has not been determined. A frequently reported cause for recurrence of chyluria, after renal hilar stripping, results from failure to fully ligate or disconnect all lymphatic channels. With an internal drainage procedure, the effect of incomplete stripping may be minimized. Anastomosis of a lumbar lymphatic vessel to the spermatic vein is a technically difficult procedure. In the reported case it was accomplished with the use of loupe magnification. Today, a higher anastomotic patency rate would be possible if one used the operating microscope to anastomose a lymphatic vessel with a venous tributary of similar size. More urologists are gaining this expertise through using the microscope to reattach the previously ligated ends of the vas deferens.

PART TEN

RENAL BIOPSY

23

A COMPARATIVE STUDY OF OPEN SURGICAL AND PERCUTANEOUS RENAL BIOPSIES

Warren K. Bolton* and Edwin D. Vaughan, Jr.

From the Departments of Internal Medicine and Urology, University of Virginia School of Medicine, Charlottesville, Virginia

The Journal of Urology
Copyright © 1977 by The Williams & Wilkins Co.
Vol. 117, June
Printed in U.S.A.

ABSTRACT—Percutaneous renal biopsy was performed on 171 patients during the same interval as an open surgical biopsy was done on 100 patients in the same hospital. Patients who underwent an open biopsy had more severe renal dysfunction and hypertension than those who had a percutaneous biopsy. Tissue adequate for diagnosis was obtained in 100 per cent of the open biopsies. The kidney was reached in 88 per cent of all percutaneous biopsies with tissue adequate for diagnosis in 82.5 per cent. Of 87 patients biopsied with image-amplification fluoroscopy renal tissue was obtained in 97 percent with tissue adequate for diagnosis in 92 per cent. No nephrectomies were done and no deaths occurred in either group. Our complications and yield by percutaneous biopsy compared favorably to those of other series. Further, open biopsy in a high risk population was associated with a high yield of tissue adequate for diagnosis with no increase in complications. Procurement of renal tissue need rarely be denied a patient if a biopsy is clinically indicated.

Accepted for publication September 17, 1976.

Read at annual meeting of Mid-Atlantic Section, American Urological Association, White Sulphur Springs, West Virginia, October 29–November 1, 1975.

*Requests for reprints: Box 133, Department of Internal Medicine, University of Virginia School of Medicine, Charlottesville, Virginia 22901.

Percutaneous and surgical renal biopsies have been used widely to study various diseases of the kidney.[1-5] Numerous advances have been made in the technique of percutaneous renal biopsy since it was first popularized by Iversen and Brun.[6] The blind method generally has been replaced by image-amplication fluoroscopy[7-12] and, in some cases, by image-amplification fluoroscopy combined with ultrasonographic localization.[13] Procurement of adequate tissue from percutaneous biopsy has ranged from 80 to 96 percent in most series and has been quite variable.[1,2,14,15] While many investigators have reported the results of percutaneous renal biopsy, little information regarding open surgical renal biopsy is available.[16,17] Moreover, there are no comparative studies of these 2 techniques. In the present retrospective study we describe the results of open and percutaneous renal biopsies from the same hospital during the same interval and compare the advantages and complications of these 2 techniques.

METHODS

Patients were scheduled routinely for percutaneous biopsy unless: 1) antihypertensive therapy was unsuccessful in lowering diastolic blood pressure consistently to less than 110 mm Hg without severe postural signs, 2) patients were uremic, 3) a skip or focal lesion was anticipated, 4) the patient was unable to tolerate the supporting roll under the abdomen or could not maintain apnea for a sufficient time to perform a biopsy, 5) the patient was unable to cooperate, 6) the patient refused a percutaneous biopsy, 7) massive obesity was present or 8) a unilateral, ectopic or horseshoe kidney was demonstrated. In these cases an open biopsy was performed. An arbitrary period was chosen relative to 100 consecutive surgical renal biopsies. All of the percutaneous biopsies performed during this interval were then included in the study. The records of the patients were examined in detail and the blood chemistry, studies, renal function, prothrombin time, partial thromboplastin time, platelet count and fibrinogen levels were noted. Systemic diseases, blood pressure and type of anesthesia also were registered. Any complications encountered either during or after biopsy were determined from the progress notes. Tissue was judged adequate for diagnosis if 5 or more glomeruli per section were found or if the specific diagnosis could be made with fewer glomeruli. Percutaneous biopsies were executed using either measurements from a flat plate excretory urogram (IVP) or image-amplification fluoroscopy, while open surgical biopsies were performed by a flank incision with routine techniques.

RESULTS

During the study 100 open surgical and 171 percutaneous renal biopsies were performed. The characteristics of the 2 patient populations are given in Table 1. No differences were noted in age, sex, race or serum albumin values. Systolic and diastolic blood pressures were significantly higher and hematocrit values were lower in patients who underwent an open biopsy compared to those biopsied percutaneously. The proportion of patients biopsied per year was similar for each technique, except for a 5-month period in 1970 when a slightly greater proportion of open biopsies was performed. Serum creatinine levels of patients not on dialysis were 3.9 plus or minus 0.6 mg per dl for open biopsies and 2.6 plus or minus 0.2 mg per dl for percutaneous biopsies (p less than 0.01). These differences can be seen more clearly in Figure 1. The proportion of patients with normal creatinine values was significantly higher in the percutaneous group. Most patients with severe uremia were biopsied using the surgical approach.

Tissue adequate for diagnosis was obtained in all of the open procedures and in 141 of the 171 closed attempts. Since the study 1 patient has had an open biopsy in which hepatic instead of renal tissue was obtained. Patients with membranous nephropathy and mild proliferative or focal lesions were biopsied more frequently percutaneously, while patients with vasomotor nephropathy, chronic renal failure and hypertensive lesions were biopsied more often by an open operation. Patients with potentially life-threatening diseases, such as disseminated intravascular coagulation and gastrointestinal bleeding, underwent open biopsies.

Complications of the biopsies are listed in Table 2. Three deaths occurred in the surgical group but were not related to the biopsy. Only minor postoperative problems were encountered. The mean operative time was 67 plus or minus 1.8 minutes and halothane was the most commonly administered anesthetic agent. Use of the lateral flank position did not result in hypotensive difficulties. Minimal postoperative decreases in hematocrit

TABLE 1. Characteristics of Patient Population*

	Biopsies	
	Open (100)	Closed (171)
Age (yrs)	34.3 ± 1.8	36.2 ± 1.4
Sex (%):		
Male	53	52
Female	47	48
Race (%):		
Black	77	76
White	23	24
Blood pressure:		
Systolic	156 ± 4.0	132 ± 1.4†
Diastolic	96 ± 2.2	83 ± 0.9†
Serum albumin (gm %)	3.0 ± 0.1	3.1 ± 0.1
Hematocrit:		
Pre-biopsy	29.8 ± 0.8	34.7 ± 0.5†
Post-biopsy	28.2 ± 0.8	—

* Mean plus or minus standard error of the mean.
† p less than 0.001.

were noted (Table 2). In the percutaneous group retro-peritoneal bleeding occurred in 3 percent, with surgical exploration in 1 percent. Of these patients 3 percent required transfusions. Five percent of all patients biopsied percutaneously had gross hematuria. There were no nephrectomies or deaths. Eight patients underwent a second percutaneous biopsy after inadequate tissue was obtained in the first attempt, and 5 of these were successful in obtaining tissue adequate for diagnosis. A third of all patients biopsied percutaneously requiring transfusions were included in the group with inadequate tissue and half of all cases of gross hematuria occurred in this group.

Kidney tissue was obtained in 88 percent of all patients biopsied percutaneously and was adequate for diagnosis in 82.5 percent. Analysis of the results of the closed technique revealed a sharp demarcation between biopsies performed prior to the use of image-amplification fluoroscopy and those done afterward. Renal tissue was obtained in 97 per cent of patients using image-amplification fluoroscopy but only 81 percent without this technique. Tissue adequate for diagnosis similarly was obtained in 92 percent with image-amplification fluoroscopy and 73 percent without. Serum creatinine values greater than 4 mg per dl and non-visualization were found in 57 percent of the inadequate tissue group using image-amplification fluoroscopy, and 39 percent prior to that time.

DISCUSSION

Procurement of tissue adequate for diagnosis with a minimum of morbidity and mortality is the ultimate goal of renal biopsies. Certain risks always are present and increase in proportion to the severity of illness of the patient. A high ratio of open to closed biopsies (1 to 1.7) was present in our series. Our indications for open biopsy presented previously may account for this in part. In addition, the patients sent to our hospital usually have been evaluated elsewhere and either present with diagnostic problems or have severe clinical renal disease. In series of 100 patients biopsied surgically and described by Patil and asociates[16] 46 were azotemic with 27 of these severely uremic. Nine of the latter 27 patients required dialysis. The over-all mortality rate was 6 percent in this series, with all deaths occurring in the severely uremic group. Four percent of the patients died

TABLE 2. Complications

	No.
Open biopsies (100):	
Prolonged drainage	1
Ileus	1
Pneumothorax	1
Wound infection	3
Bleeding requiring transfusion	3*†
Hematuria	1
Atelectasis	1
Closed biopsies (171):	
Retroperitoneal bleeding	5
Retroperitoneal bleeding with surgical exploration	2
Transfusions	5
Gross hematuria	8

* All patients were on hemodialysis.
† Later deaths during hospitalization: 1) gastrointestinal bleeding, bilateral nephrectomies and gastrectomy—dialysis; 2) gastrointestinal bleeding, sepsis secondary to peritoneal catheter—dialysis and 3) intracranial hemorrhage 1.5 months after biopsy—dialysis.

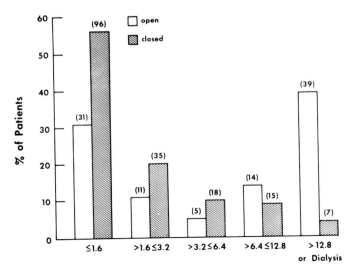

Fig. 1. Distribution of patients according to serum creatinine classes, each of which represents progressive 50 percent decrements in creatinine clearance with serum creatinine of 1.6 mg per dl taken as upper limit of normal. Significantly more patients (p less than 0.0005) with severely depressed renal function were biopsied surgically, while significantly more patients with serum creatinine less than 3.2 mg per dl (p less than 0.0005) were biopsied percutaneously.

during the natural course of their illness and 2 percent of the whole series, or 4 percent of the severely uremic patients, died of causes directly attributable to the biopsy procedure. In our series of 100 patients biopsied by the open method mild to moderate azotemia was present in 16 percent, with moderate to severe azotemia in 14 percent and uremia or dialysis in 39 percent of patients. Despite the greater number of patients with significant renal dysfunction the morbidity from open biopsy was minimal and no deaths were attributable to the procedure (Table 2).

Image-amplification fluoroscopy was first used for biopsy localization at this institution in September 1972. Prior to that time percutaneous biopsies were performed using measurement techniques from an IVP. Renal tissue was obtained in 81 per cent of the former patients and tissue adequate for diagnosis in only 73 percent. Repeat successful closed biopsies increased the yield for diagnosis in that patient group to 77 percent. This stands in marked contrast to the group of patients biopsied after image-amplification fluoroscopy began to be used. More than half of the patients unsuccessfully biopsied with image-amplification fluoroscopy (4 of 7) had serum creatinine values of 4.0 mg per dl or greater and/or showed essentially no visualization of fluoroscopy. If these patients had been excluded the yield of tissue adequate for diagnosis would have increased from 92 to 96 percent. The procurement of tissue adequate for diagnosis in 92 percent of closed biopsies with image-amplification fluoroscopy is similar to the best results in other studies.[8,13] In the recent series of 1,000 percutaneous biopsies reported by Diaz-Buxo and Donadio[15] no difference in obtaining tissue was found using image-amplification fluoroscopy for localization compared to other methods. However, the indications for image-amplification fluoroscopy were not given and, thus, it is not possible to ascertain if the patients were comparable. Furthermore, some patients missed by other methods were then biopsied with image-amplification fluoroscopy. All of our patients biopsied since 1972 have had renal localization by image-amplification fluoroscopy as described previously. Unlike the results reported by Diaz-Buxo and Donadio, this localization has improved significantly our yield of tissue adequate for diagnosis. Based on these observations we would add "failure to visualize by image-amplification fluoroscopy" to our list of indications for open biopsy that were described previously.

The complications of percutaneous renal biopsy in this study ae similar to other series.[2,4] No predisposing factors were noted in those patients wth biopsy-associated complications. However, since a third of the patients requiring transfusion were individuals from whom inadequate tissue was obtained it is possible that repeated attempts to procure tissue during a single procedure was a contributory factor. Although clotting parameters were normal and hypertension was not present at the time of biopsy 3 of the 5 patients with bleeding requiring transfusions had hypertension after the biopsy and this may well have contributed to the bleeding. Episodes of serious bleeding were not related to the type of localization procedure for precutaneous biopsy.

Our study demonstrates comparable results among our series and numerous other published series of patients biopsied percutaneously. In addition, it clearly establishes the low risk associated with open surgical biopsies even in hypertensive, uremic, seriously ill patients. Many physicians hesitate to obtain diagnostic tissue in patients in clinical situations that otherwise would indicate the need for a histologic diagnosis. This hesitancy usually is associated with the belief that open biopsy is not worth the risk of the operative procedure in circumstances under which percutaneous tissue cannot be obtained. Our findings demonstrate that this reluctance is unwarranted. Open biopsy is a safe procedure, even in patients with medical contraindications to closed renal biopsy, and should be considered as the logical alternative in situations requiring obtainment of renal tissue.

The Department of Urology and the Renal Section permitted us to study their patients.

REFERENCES

1. Muehrcke, R. C., Kark R. M. and Pirani, C. L.: Biopsy of the kidney in the diagnosis and management of renal disease. New Engl J Med 253:537, 1955
2. Kark, R. M., Muehrcke, R. C., Pollack, V. E., Pirani, C. L. and Kiefer, J. H.: An analysis of five hundred percutaneous renal biopsies. Arch. Intern Med 101:439, 1958
3. Ciba Foundation Symposium on Renal Biopsy: Clinical and Pathological Significance. Edited by G. E. W. Wolstenholme and M. P. Cameron. Boston: Little, Brown and Co, 1961
4. Dodge, W. F., Daeschner, C. W., Jr., Brennan, J. C., Rosenberg, H. S. Travis, L. B. and Hopps, H. C.: Percutaneous renal biopsy in children. I. General considerations. Pediatrics 30:287, 1962
5. Kark, R. M.: Renal biopsy and prognosis. Ann Rev Med 18:269, 1967
6. Iversen P. and Brun, C.: Aspiration biopsy of the kidney. Am J Med 11:324, 1951
7. Lusted, L. B., Mortimore, G. E. and Hooper, J., Jr.: Needle renal biopsy under image amplifier control. Am J Roentgen 75:953, 1956
8. Ginsburg, I. W., Durant, J. R. and Mendez, L.: Percutaneous renal biopsy under direct radiologic direction. JAMA, 181:211, 1962
9. Kark, R. M. and Buenger, R. E.: Television-monitored fluoroscopy in percutaneous renal biopsy. Lancet 1:904, 1966
10. Haddad, J. K. and Mani, R. L.: Percutaneous renal biopsy: an

improved method using television monitoring and high-dose infusion pyelography. Arch Intern Med 119:157, 1967

11. Lindholm, T., Hagstam, K. E. and Kjellstrand, C. M.: Some instrumental and methodological modifications of the technique for percutaneous renal biopsy. Acta Med Scand 181:245, 1967

12. Lindqvist, B.: Vasopressin as an aid in locating the kidney in roentgen television for renal biopsy. Acta Med. Scand 181:97, 1967

13. Bolton, W. K., Tully, R. J., Lewis, E. J. and Ranniger, K.: Localization of the kidney for percutaneous biopsy. A comparative study of methods. Ann Intern Med 81:159, 1974

14. Kark, R. M.: Renal biopsy. JAMA, 205:220, 1968

15. Diaz-Buxo, J. A. and Donadio, J. V., Jr.: Complications of percutaneous renal biopsy: an analysis of 1000 consecutive biopsies. Clin Nephrol 4:221, 1975

16. Patil, J., Bailey, G. L. and Mahoney, E. F.: Open-renal biopsy in uremic patient. Urology 3:293, 1974

17. Burrington, J. D.: Technique and results of fifty-five open renal biopsies in children. Surg Gynec & Obst 140:613, 1975

Commentary: Percutaneous *vs.* Open Renal Biopsy

Malcolm D. Cosgrove

Although biopsy of the kidney has been an established clinical procedure in the investigation of certain patients with renal disease for more than 20 years, remarkably few papers are devoted to the practical technical aspects of obtaining renal tissue by open and percutaneous methods.

Although it is perhaps entirely reasonable that more time, thought, and writing are expended in discussing the indications for renal biopsy, the nature of the information gleaned from the tissue, and the value of the knowledge gained from the biopsy in determining treatment and prognosis, the technologic aspects of renal biopsy are nevertheless required knowledge for all nephrologists and urologists.

I wish to suggest here that there may be reasons to re-examine the prevailing conventional wisdom that states that since it is an easier and safer procedure, a percutaneous needle biopsy should be done whenever possible, and that the open biopsy should be reserved for patients in whom the closed procedure is not safe or technically feasible.

The article by Bolton and Vaughan has been selected because, in a dispassionate and objective manner, a nephrologist and a urologist have collaborated to present their experience with both open and percutaneous renal biopsies. The authors have provided much needed comparative data that can help every physician make clinical decisions.

PREOPERATIVE PROCEDURE

My own procedure for open biopsy is to have the patient in as good fluid and electrolyte balance as possible preoperatively and to optimize hemoglobin (Hb) level, coagulation mechanism, and cardiorespiratory status. Since many patients undergoing biopsy receive regular dialysis treatment, some of these objectives can be realized quite easily and effectively by the nephrologist. It is mandatory to have available two units of fresh packed cells at the time of biopsy.

With x-ray studies, radionuclide scans, ultrasound, and, if necessary, computed tomography (CT) scans, I determine preoperatively kidney number, location, size, and relative function. Generally, my plan is to biopsy the larger, more accessible, and better functioning kidney. Where there is no obvious difference between the two kidneys, I biopsy the lower pole of the right kidney, since usually it is slightly lower and thus more accessible than the left.

SURGICAL PROCEDURES

Open Renal Biopsy. Although Gonick and Grau have recommended local anesthesia for open renal biopsy, I prefer a general anesthetic because a delicate procedure is being performed in a high-risk patient on a relatively inaccessible organ.[1] I wish to achieve my objective as safely and an quickly as possible without the added encumbrance of pain, movement, or muscle spasm and the possibility of inadequate exposure. Also, in the event of a surgical problem such as renal laceration or bleeding, I believe that the absence of general anesthesia might be a significant handicap.

To proceed: using suitable general inhalation anesthesia with muscle relaxation as necessary, position the patient in the flank position with the kidney rest up, and enter the perirenal space through a 7.5-cm incision below the tip of, and parallel to, the 12th rib. Where possible, split muscles in the line of their fibers and avoid nerves. Insert a self-retaining retractor, incise Gerota's fascia posteriorly, and expose the lower pole of the kidney by blunt finger and sponge dissection. Do not attempt to mobilize the rest of the kidney. Facilitate exposure of the lower pole by gentle downward traction with an empty sponge forcep on the perirenal fat and fascia. Do not incise the kidney until the containers for specimen collection for histopathology, electron microscopy (EM), and immunofluorescence studies are ready in the operating room and a needle holder loaded with a 2–0 chromic catgut suture on a round-bodied genitourinary needle is available. Excise a 1-cm × 0.5-cm elliptic wedge of renal tissue with a long-handled scalpel and, if possible, deliver it without forceps on the flat of the scalpel blade. Divide the biopsy specimen with the scalpel into three portions for appropriate analyses, and close the kidney defect carefully with interrupted chromic catgut sutures. If good capsule approximation is obtained, it is rarely necessary to incorporate additional material such as muscle, fat, or Gelfoam in the renal closure. Close the flank incision in layers with no. 0 Vicryl suture. Leave in a Penrose drain for 48 hours.

Percutaneous Needle Biopsy. For percutaneous needle biopsy, the preoperative patient preparation is identical to that for the open procedure, including ensuring the availability of blood for transfusion. The needle biopsy is done in the hospital with the patient fasting in order to lower the risk of vomiting and to enable general anesthesia to be safely given in the event of a major problem. Percutaneous needle biopsy is performed under sterile conditions with the patient conscious and lightly sedated, lying prone on the fluoroscopic x-ray table with pillows under the upper abdomen.

To proceed: visualize the lower pole of the kidney after intravenous (IV) urographic contrast infusion by image amplification fluoroscopy, and mark the optimum site for skin puncture on the back with a sterile marker pen. In cases of allergy to iodine contrast or in severe azotemia, perform renal localization by ultrasound scanning. Inject 1% lidocaine into the skin and the intended path of the needle and then nick the skin with the scalpel to facilitate the unimpeded passage of a narrow no. 22 probing spinal needle. Pass this needle under fluoroscopic guidance to the kidney. When the kidney is reached, ask the patient to hold his breath in inspiration and pass the needle into the kidney. The fact that the needle has indeed entered the kidney is confirmed by asking the patient to breath and by noting the cranial–caudal needle excursion with respiration. *Never* touch the needle while it is in the kidney during respiratory movements for fear of causing a renal laceration. Ask the patient once more to hold his breath in inspiration and, after noting the precise direction and depth of the probing needle, remove it and immediately replace it with the biopsy needle. I use either the disposable needle made by Travenol or the Franklin modification of the Vim–Silverman needle. Allow the patient to breath, and confirm the needle position both by noting its movements with respiration and by its location on x-ray film. Then, while the patient's breath is held in inspiration, cut a biopsy and remove the needle.

If the tissue looks adequate, divide it longitudinally into three narrow strips for histology, immunofluorescence, and EM analyses. Do not cut a needle biopsy specimen transversely for comparative studies because one portion will contain cortex while another will consist only of medulla. If inadequate tissue is obtained, try one, or at most two, more times to obtain tissue from the same or the contralateral kidney. Repeated biopsies enhance the risk of parenchymal and capsular tearing, major vessel injury, and bleeding.

Bolton and Vaughan noted with concern that one third of their patients who required blood transfusions after percutaneous needle biopsy were those in whom inadequate tissue was obtained for diagnosis and had repeated biopsies. Also, half the cases of gross hematuria after needle biopsy came from this same small group who underwent repeated biopsies.

POSTOPERATIVE PROCEDURE

After both open and percutaneous biopsy procedures, keep the patient in bed, well-hydrated, for 24 hours. Observe the voided urine carefully for blood, check the vital signs and the hematocrit regularly, and examine the flank to detect any signs of bleeding. Discharge the patient when his condition is satisfactory, usually 1 to 2 days after percutaneous biopsy and 2 to 3 days after open renal biopsy. Skin sutures are not removed in open biopsy cases until the eighth day.

COMMENTS AND COMPLICATIONS

The open and needle biopsy techniques just described are probably, with minor modifications, the procedures used most commonly by urologists and nephrologists. Gonick's open method under local anesthesia has already been commented upon.[1] Lofgren and Snellman, in 1957, were probably the first to use the needle to obtain cores of renal tissue after formally exposing the kidney surgically under general anesthesia.[2] Although several authors, including Hamburger and Burrington, have espoused this method, I see no advantage in it compared with wedge excision and, indeed, believe that the latter technique is safer and guarantees the acquisition of adequate tissue.[3,4]

The percutaneous biopsy technique described by Kark and colleagues in 1958 is the one used by most clinicians.[5,6] Current technical debate is limited to the choice of needle and methods for optimising marksmanship.[7] Standard intravenous pyelography (IVP), radionuclide scans, renal ultrasound, and image intensification fluoroscopy all have their proponents and places.[8] In the United States, fluoroscopy and ultrasound are probably the methods most commonly used to localize the biopsy site.

From a review of some of the larger published series from the major centers, it appears that the success rate in garnering renal tissue of diagnostic quality by percutaneous needle biopsy varies from 80% to 96%,[7,9–12] Open surgical wedge excision biopsy, on the other hand, never fails to yield adequate renal tissue.[1,13,14]

Many authors have developed tables listing the "absolute" and "relative" contraindications to percutaneous needle biopsy. Most would recommend open surgical biopsy for uncooperative, obese, or pregnant patients and those with solitary, horseshoe, or very small kidneys, hydronephrosis, renal mass lesions, severe hypotension, azotemia, arteriosclerosis, or a coagulation problem. Unquestionably, the poor-risk patient is selected for open biopsy.

The reported complications of renal biopsy are as interesting as they are varied. They include pain, fever, early and late hematuria, renal laceration, perirenal hematoma and abscess, and renal arteriovenous fistulae and aneurysm. Also reported are obstructive uropathy due to blood clot, calicealcutaneous and ureterocutaneous fistula, hypertension, hypotension, oliguria, systemic infection, and renal scarring. Perforation of other viscera such as liver, pancreas, spleen, bowel, pleura, and peritoneum and even loss of part of the biopsy needle have been reported. Most of the above complications have been documented in relation to needle biopsy. The complications unique to the open procedure are incisional pain and infection.

The rate of complications and the need for blood transfusion, renal exploration, and nephrectomy are certainly not greater with the open procedure, and this is borne out in Bolton's and Vaughan's comparative study of the two techniques.

Deaths directly related to renal biopsy are fortunately most rare (about 0.1%) and have occurred with both techniques—generally in very sick patients.

Thus, although the higher-risk patient is selected for open renal biopsy, the probability of complications and death is no greater for him than for the better-risk patient undergoing percutaneous needle biopsy. This point was also made by Almkuist and Buckalew in a recent review article.[7] One could well argue from this premise that perhaps the open procedure is indeed the safer one. Open surgical biopsy of course has its own drawbacks—increased cost, discomfort, and hospitalization—but, on the other hand, it has the undeniable advantage of 100% retrieval rate of diagnostic quality tissue.

I should emphasize that the justification for subjecting a high-risk patient to a biopsy procedure that carries substantial morbidity and mortality demands careful clinical consideration. Failure to retrieve tissue under these circumstances is more than unfortunate—it is a potential disaster.

It is my feeling, after reviewing the data from the literature in general and from the preceding article in particular, that urgent efforts should be made to achieve a 100% success rate for percutaneous biopsies. Until that goal is reached, surgeons should be more liberal in their use of open surgical excision biopsy.

REFERENCES

1. Gonick P, Grau J: Open Renal Biopsy Technique: Results in 202 patients. Urology 11:568, 1978

2. Lofgren S, Snellman B: Instrument and technique of kidney biopsy. Acta Med Scand 157:93, 1957

3. Hamburger J: La technique de biopsie renale utilisee a l'hospital Necker. Presse Med 66:1451, 1969

4. Burrington JD: Techniques and results of 55 open renal biopsies in children. Surg Gynecol Obstet 140:613, 1975

5. Kark RM, Muehrcke RC, Pollak VE, Pirani CG, Kiefer JH: An analysis of five hundred percutaneous renal biopsies. Arch Intern Med 101:439, 1958

6. Kark RM: Renal biopsy. JAMA 205:220, 1968

7. Almkuist RD, Buckalew UM: Techniques of renal biopsy. Urol Clin North Am 6:503, 1979

8. Bolton WH, Tully RJ, Lewis EJ, Ranniger K: Localization of the kidney for percutaneous biopsy: A comparative study of methods. Ann Intern Med 81:159, 1974

9. Arisz L, Brentjens JR, Vastenburg G, van der Hem GK, Hoedemaeker PJ, Arends A, Mandema E: At the 25th anniversary of the percutaneous renal biopsy: The state of the art. Neth J Med 19:29, 1976

10. Carvajal HF, Travis LB, Srivastava RN, de Beukelaer M, Dodge WF, Dupree E: Percutaneous renal biopsy in children—an analysis of complications in 890 consecutive biopsies. Tex Rep Biol Med 29:253, 1971

11. Chen BT: An Analysis of 400 percutaneous renal biopsies. Singapore Med J 12:166, 1971

12. Diaz–Buxo JA, Donadio JV: Complications of percutaneous renal biopsy: An analysis of 1000 consecutive cases. Clin Nephrol 4:223, 1975

13. Patil J, Bailey GL, Mahoney EF: Open renal biopsy in uremic patients. Urology 3:293, 1974

14. Schmidt A, Bauer R: Renal biopsy in children. Analysis of 61 cases of open wedge biopsy and comparison with percutaneous biopsy. J Urol 116:79, 1976

ANNOTATED BIBLIOGRAPHY

Almkuist RD, Buckalew UM: Techniques of renal biopsy. Urol Clin North Am 6:503, 1979

A recent review article concentrating mainly on percutaneous needle biopsy, but acknowledging that the complication rate is similar for percutaneous and open biopsies.

Arisz L, Brentjens JR, Vastenburg G, van der Hem GK, Hoedemaeker PJ, Arends A, Mandema E: At the 25th anniversary of the percutaneous renal biopsy: The state of the art. Neth J Med 19:29, 1976

In a review of 1000 biopsies, 1 death is reported.

Bolton WH, Tully RJ, Lewis EJ, Ranniger K: Localization of the kidney for percutaneous biopsy: A comparative study of methods. Ann Intern Med 81:159, 1974

Ultrasound is almost as effective as fluoroscopy in localizing the lower pole of the kidney. It is accurate, less expensive, and safer, especially during pregnancy.

Burrington JD: Techniques and results of 55 open renal biopsies in children. Surg Gynecol Obstet 140:613, 1975

The author has modified the Hamburger technique of exploring the kidney under general anesthesia and then taking biopsies with a disposable needle in children deemed unsuitable for standard percutaneous needle biopsy. Adequate tissue was obtained in all instances, and there were no serious complications.

Carvajal HF, Travis LB, Srivastava RN, de Beukelaer M, Dodge WF, Dupree E: Percutaneous renal biopsy in children—an analysis of complications in 890 consecutive biopsies. Tex Rep Biol Med 29:253, 1971

A success rate of 83% at the first biopsy attempt, rising to 96% after two attempts. There were no deaths and no nephrectomies.

Chen BT: An analysis of 400 percutaneous renal biopsies. Singapore Med J 12:166, 1971

A success rate of 82.5% is reported. There was one death attributed to the needle biopsy procedure; five patients required blood transfusions after biopsy.

Diaz–Buxo JA, Donadio JV: Complications of percutaneous renal biopsy: An analysis of 1000 consecutive cases. Clin Nephrol 4:223, 1975

In this series from the Mayo Clinic, adequate tissue was obtained in 94.9% of patients. The complication rate of 8.1% was related to patient age, presence of renal insufficiency, and arterial hypertension.

Gonick P, Grau J: Open renal biopsy technique: Results in 202 patients. Urology 11:568, 1978

> This article describes graphically the technique of renal biopsy through a muscle-splitting incision. General anesthesia was given in only 13% of patients, with IV droperidol or valium together with local anesthesia being used for the vast majority. There were no deaths attributable to the procedure. Three severely azotemic patients had to be re-explored because of bleeding. Adequate tissue for diagnostic purposes was obtained in 100%.

Hamburger, J. La technique de biopsie renale utilisee a l'hopital Necker. Presse Med 66:1451, 1969

Kark RM, Muehrcke RC, Pollak VE, Pirani CG, Kiefer JH: An analysis of five hundred percutaneous renal biopsies. Arch Intern Med 101:439, 1958

> The classic article written by one of the pioneers of needle biopsy of the kidney.

Kark RM: Renal biopsy. JAMA 205:220, 1968

> An excellent review article that carries the answers to a questionnaire on renal biopsies that Dr. Louis Welt sent to 21 leading nephrology centers.

Lofgren S, Snellman B: Instrument and technique of kidney biopsy. Acta Med Scand 157:93, 1957

> The authors were probably the first to describe the method of open surgical exposure of the kidney followed by a needle biopsy.

Patil J, Bailey GL, Mahoney EF: Open renal biopsy in uremic patients. Urology 3:293, 1974

> The authors reviewed 100 consecutive open renal biopsies mostly done under general anesthesia. Satisfactory tissue was obtained in all instances. There were two deaths in uremic patients, one attributed to anesthesia and the other to a late secondary hemorrhage. There were no deaths in the nonuremic cases. Excellent guidelines for the care of uremic patients undergoing biopsy are presented.

Schmidt A, Bauer R: Renal biopsy in children. Analysis of 61 cases of open wedge biopsy and comparison with percutaneous biopsy. J Urol 116:79, 1976

> The authors report a 100% success rate in obtaining tissue for diagnosis. No deaths, nephrectomies, or serious complications occurred with the open biopsy excision procedure under general anesthesia.

Overview: Comparing Surgical Biopsy and Needle Biopsy

Paul Gonick

Safe renal biopsy techniques have aided the urologist, nephrologist, and pathologist in sorting out the *potpourri* of disease processes that damage the kidney. Both needle biopsy and open surgical biopsy are relatively safe procedures. As a surgeon, I am biased toward the surgical approach, while nephrologists would probably tend toward needle biopsy.

SURGICAL BIOPSY

The technique I use for surgical biopsy is basically the one Cosgrove describes. Several points need emphasis. I use local anesthesia because I consider it safer than general anesthesia for two major reasons. First, the uremic patient has difficulty clearing bronchial secretions and is subject to atelectasis and pneumonitis with a general anesthetic. Second, the blood pressure in the hypertensive patient is not labile with changes in position under local anesthesia. I inject bupivacaine hydrochloride in a 0.5% solution into the 11th and 12th thoracic nerves at the angle of the rib. I use 0.5% lidocaine for the site of the incision, since its onset of anesthesia is faster. The bupivacaine can control pain for several hours after the biopsy. IV neuroleptic agents provide additional sedation. In over 200 biopsies, I never had to stop the procedure because of pain or convert to a general anesthetic. Relaxation and exposure, in all patients, were satisfactory.

To proceed: make the incision 1 cm below the tip of the 12th rib. A depression can be palpated in the area where the lumbodorsal fascia and the abdominal muscles insert into the fascia. This indentation is used as the midpoint of the 5-cm to 7.5-cm incision. Cut the fascia over the latissimus dorsi or serratus posterior–inferior, and spread the muscles by blunt dissection until the underlying lumbodorsal fascia is exposed. Incise the lumbodorsal fascia at right angles to the direction of the fibers, taking care to avoid the 12th thoracic nerve. Mobilize the lower pole of the kidney by blunt dissection and bring it into view by placing a Kelly clamp on the capsule or on adherent fat. This clamp may then be used to manipulate the lower pole of the kidney both to excise a small section for biopsy and to place hemostatic sutures. End-stage kidneys are usually fibrotic, do not bleed readily, and are easily sutured.

Nephrotic kidneys are swollen and friable, so that sutures must be placed following the curve of the needle. Sometimes a buttress of fat is placed under the suture; this prevents the suture, when tied, from tearing through the kidney.

NEEDLE BIOPSY

In needle biopsy, fluoroscopy with IV contrast material aids in visualizing the kidney. An ultrasound transducer with a central hole, through which the needle is passed, can be used to locate the kidney in the allergic patient. Experience in evaluation of ultrasound pictures is essential for safe needle placement. When doing a needle biopsy of the kidney, avoid the medial portion to prevent lacerating a major blood vessel.

Another technique recently described for the azotemic, nonallergic patient uses arteriographic control for visualizing the kidney before and after the biopsy.[1] Biopsy is performed with the patient in the prone position. To proceed: selectively place the catheter in the renal artery by the Seldinger technique.

The advantages of this method are precise localization of the kidney, smaller dose of contrast material (about 40% of that used for infusion pyelography), and immediate assessment of postbiopsy bleeding. Three patients had serious hemorrhage that ceased abruptly upon direct arterial vasoconstriction with epinephrine hydrochloride. It has been learned from postbiopsy studies that a needle cut beyond 2 cm from the periphery is the most likely to lead to significant hemorrhage. Under direct visualization, it is safest to introduce the biopsy needle from the center toward the periphery of the kidney.

If both kidneys are of equal size and function, biopsy the most accessible. I prefer the lower kidney (usually the right) for surgical biopsy and the left for needle biopsy. When one kidney is smaller or has less function than the other, my team's renal pathologist has assured us that an adequate histologic diagnosis can be made from this smaller kidney. From the preceding article and commentary, it is obvious that needle biopsy and open surgical biopsy are equally safe procedures. The skill, experience, training, facilities, patient's condition, and cost should determine the method of biopsy used.

REFERENCE

1. Swartz C, Starrs J, Wilson A, Richards P: Lessons from angiographic control of percutaneous renal biopsy. Presented at the American Society of Nephrology's 12th Annual Meeting, 1979

PART ELEVEN

SURGERY FOR RENAL TRAUMA

24

INTERMEDIATE-DEGREE BLUNT RENAL TRAUMA

Norman E. Peterson, M.D.

From the Division of Urology, Denver General Hospital, and the Department of Urology, University of Colorado Medical Center, Denver

The Journal of Trauma
Copyright © 1977 by The Williams & Wilkins Co.
Vol. 17, No. 6
Printed in U.S.A.

ABSTRACT—One hundred four cases of blunt renal trauma have been reviewed and analyzed, yielding 71 minor, 13 major, and 20 intermediate-degree injuries. Of the latter group, urinary extravasation (60%) and parenchymal laceration (100%) appear to be the dominant features exhibited by conventional radiographic maneuvers, neither of which suggest a de novo need for operation or interference with spontaneous resolution. Nephrectomy[9] and heminephrectomy[2] may often have been performed unnecessarily in this group, since nine such patients managed either nonoperatively,[7] or undergoing negligible operative procedures[2] responded with total functional and anatomic restoration. Arteriography is endorsed as an important contributor of information encouraging confidence in the conservative management of such cases.

Further experience with traumatic renal injuries has underscored the importance of basic principles of management, adherence to which has proved effective in simplifying a previously confusing issue, as well as improving overall results.

Presented at the Thirty-fifth Annual Session of the American Association for the Surgery of Trauma, 13 September 1975, Scottsdale, Arizona.

Address for reprints: Norman E. Peterson, M.D., Division of Urology, Department of Surgery, Denver General Hospital, Denver, CO 80204.

At one end of the scale of traumatic renal lesions is the relatively larger percentage (70–90%) of so-called "minor" injuries characterized by hematuria which is commonly mild or transient, by urographic function which tends to be essentially normal or with perhaps some delay or diminution in concentration and/or excretion of contrast medium, and by vital signs which are stable or easily stabilized (Table 1). Little controversy exists regarding the tendency of these injuries to respond favorably to conservative (nonoperative) management. At the opposite end of the scale are the "major" injuries

TABLE 1. DGH Blunt Renal Injuries

	Minor	Inter-mediate	Major
Hematuria	Mild, remitting		Severe, unremitting; none
Urography	Normal, delayed/ diminished function	?	Nonfunction
Vital signs	Normal, stable		Unstable, unaccept-able

TABLE 2. DGH Renal Trauma Series, Major Blunt Injuries

	Pedicle (9)	Shattered (3)
No X-ray	3	1
Nonfunction	6	3
Arteriography	2	1
Severe nonrenal injury	6	3
Extravasation	1	0
Nephrectomy	7	2
Heminephrectomy	1	1

characterized by hematuria which may be severe and unremitting, or virtually absent, by total urographic nonfunction, and by vital signs which are unstable or unacceptable. Such injuries comprise a much smaller segment of the total (5–15%), and debate is again limited regarding the need for further evaluation in the form of renal arteriography, or prompt exploration exclusively for the kidney injury or at laparotomy for nonrenal trauma.

Those injuries that remain are typically uncharacterized by clinical features which consign them conclusively to either the major or minor category, and it is with such injuries that confusion may exist regarding appropriate management.

Our local experience with renal trauma has been reviewed and is presented, with special emphasis given to intermediate-degree injuries, including features considered helpful in classifying such injuries. Consistent with a prior report of a local conservative philosophy of management of all nonmajor renal trauma[19,30] examples have been selected of conservatively managed intermediate-degree kidney injuries.

MATERIALS AND METHODS

Case records of the Denver General Hospital were reviewed for the period spanning 1967–1975, yielding 104 cases of blunt renal trauma. Subclassification according to the degree of injury (minor, intermediate, major) was made according to clinical, radiographic, and operative data, and cases were further critically assessed regarding the nature and necessity of surgical intervention.

RESULTS

Seventy-one patients with minor renal injuries had 62 contusions and nine lacerations. Only one renal contusion was explored, during splenectomy. Of the nine patients with renal lacerations, one died in shock from liver trauma, with a renal injury discovered at autopsy. Three patients underwent renal repair (during laparotomy for bowel injury, exploration of retroperitoneal hematoma,

and splenectomy), all retrospectively considered unnecessary due to the nature of the parenchymal repair. Of five unoperated patients with parenchymal fracture, three exhibited grade II extravasation which subsided spontaneously.

Thirteen renal injuries were considered of major severity owing to pedicle damage[9] or severe parenchymal fragmentation.[3] The thirteenth patient sustained parenchymal fracture of a severe congenital hydronephrosis and is omitted from statistical considerations. Table 2 summarizes the important clinical features of this subgroup. Preoperative urography was obtained in only 67% of this group, and arteriography in only 25%, both figures reflecting the frequent preclusion of these studies by surgical priorities ascribed to the renal injury per se, or to associated nonrenal injuries. Severe nonrenal injuries occurred in 75% of this group, including seven of the nine patients not undergoing arteriography, and support is thereby given to prior observations that isolated renal injuries are uncommon, and that the incidence and degree of renal injuries correlate directly with the degree of renal trauma.[20] Urographic nonfunction occurred in 100% of those studied; although numbers are too limited to be definitive, and pedicle injuries warrant a different predictive value, these figures nonetheless suggest the clinical significance of post-traumatic urographic nonfunction. Urinary extravasation occurred in only one of the eight patients studied. Twelve kidneys were explored; nephrectomy was performed in nine, heminephrectomy in two, repair of a pedicle injury in one (expiring at laparotomy), and no renal surgery in one (expiring in shock).

The remaining 20 patients exhibited renal injuries considered to be of intermediate degree due to inappropriate assignment to either the major or minor subgroup, and dominant features of this group are summarized in Table 3. Preoperative urography was not performed in six patients (30%), and arteriography was done in only eight patients (40%). However, seven of these latter patients occurred late in our series when an evaluation was being made of conservative management of such injuries, allowance for which yields a figure for arteri-

TABLE 3. DGH Renal Trauma Series, Intermediate Blunt Injuries (20)

No IVP	6
Nonfunction	1
Extravasation	8
Parenchymal fracture	19
Arteriogram	8 (7*)
Serious nonrenal injury	8 (6†)
Nephrectomy	9
Heminephrectomy	2
Nondefinitive surgery	2†

* Nonoperative.

† No arteriography.

ography of 15% (2/13). Again, these figures reflect preclusion of these studies by an initial assignment of surgical urgency relating to the renal injury itself, or to coexisting nonrenal injuries. Such injuries occurred in eight patients (40%), six of whom were not studied arteriographically. Although numbers are small, the disparity in percentage incidence of associated nonrenal injuries with major (75%) and intermediate (40%) renal injuries appears significant.

Of 14 patients who underwent urography, nonfunction occurred in only one, again in striking contrast to the major subgroup.

The dominant radiographic features of the intermediate subgroup included parenchymal fracture, occurring in 100%, and urinary extravasation in eight of 14 (40% of the overall group, but more appropriately, 60% of those patients studied urographically).

Of 12 patients with kidneys explored, nine underwent nephrectomy, two heminephrectomy, and two received repair which realistically added little to anticipated spontaneous recovery (exploration and suture; wedge resection). Both of the latter occurred during laparotomy for nonrenal injuries, and has not been studied arteriographically.

All patients managed conservatively (nonoperatively) recovered without incident or significant detectable functional or radiographic deficit.

ILLUSTRATIVE CASE REPORTS

Case 1. (DGH 259529) A 5-year-old male fell from a tree, sustaining right flank trauma and gross hematuria. Evaluation included right flank mass, tenderness, and guarding, normal vital signs, and diminishing hematuria. Excretory urogram revealed aparent right lower pole mass and extravasation, and poor upper pole visualization. Arteriography demonstrated parenchymal fracture along vascular planes, with significant diastasis, satisfactory fragment function, and unobstructed ureteral drainage (Fig. 1A). Bedrest was followed by resolution

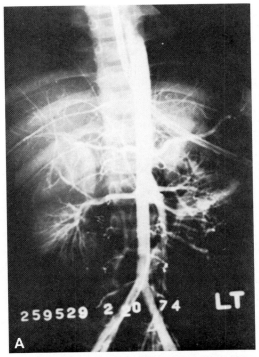

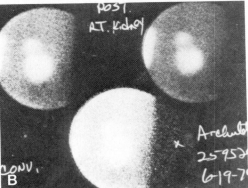

Fig. 1. (A) Arteriographic demonstration of right parenchymal fracture along vascular planes with persistent adequate fragment vascularization. (B) Renal scan at 4 months indicating modest reduction in right midparenchymal function only.

of microhematuria, flank mass, and tenderness. Urography at 4 months demonstrated satisfactory function and resolution of diastasis, verified by renal scan (Fig. 1B), at which time urine was clear, and the patient was asymptomatic and normotensive.

Case 2. (DGH 104545) A 49-year-old male was kicked in the left flank, followed by 48 hours of gross hematuria

before he sought medical attention, at which time vital
signs were stable and gross hematuria was modest.
Excretory urogram revealed rib fracture, prompt left
concentration/excretion, and extracapsular extravasation.
Arteriography demonstrated parenchymal fracture along
vascular planes with significant diastasis and satisfactory
fragment function (Fig. 2A). Bedrest was followed by
prompt resolution of microhematuria. Urography at 4
weeks demonstrated satisfactory left renal function despite architectural distortion, and resolution of extravasation and diastasis (Fig. 2B), which urinalysis was
normal and the patient was asymptomatic and normotensive.

Case 3. (DGH 536449) a 22-year-old male was kicked
in the left flank during a karate lesson, followed by local
pain and gross hematuria. Vital signs were stable, and
gross hematuria was diminishing at presentation. Excretory urogram demonstrated left lower pole parenchymal
fracture and extracapsular extravasation (Fig. 3A). Bedrest was associated with prompt resolution of tenderness
and microhematuria. Urography at 2 months revealed
satisfactory left renal function and resolution of the
extravasation (Fig. 3B), at which time urinalysis was
normal, and the patient remained normotensive and free
of symptoms.

Case 4. (DGH 188527) A 34-year-old male fell while
intoxicated, sustaining right flank trauma, followed by
local discomfort and gross hematuria. Medical attention
was sought 24 hours later at which time hematuria was
clearing and vital signs were stable, and examination
revealed only right flank mass and tenderness. Excretory
urogram described a large lower pole mass with extracapsular extravasation (Fig. 4A). Arteriography demonstrated parenchymal fracture along vascular planes
with significant diastasis, satisfactory vascularization of
fracture fragments, and unobstructed ureteral drainage
(Fig. 4B). Bedrest was followed by prompt resolution
of microhematuria and rapidly resolving physical findings
at the time of his voluntary transfer to another hospital.

Case 5. (DGH 477506) A 26-year-old female sustained
multiple injuries in an auto accident, including lower
left rib fracture, with local tenderness and gross hematuria. Excretory urography described delayed and diminished left lower pole function, with no evidence of upper
pole activity. Arteriography revealed satisfactory vascularization and function of the lower pole segment,
truncation of the upper pole vascular supply with no
demonstrable upper pole vascularization, and apparent
severe diastasis reflected in extensive superior displacement of the upper pole capsular vessel (Fig. 5A). Bedrest
was followed by gradual resolution of microhematuria

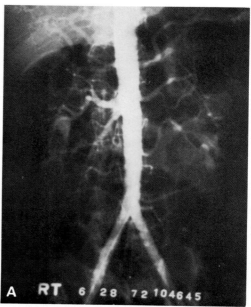

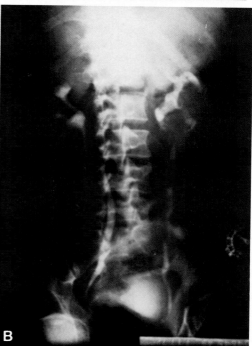

Fig. 2. (A) Renal arteriographic demonstration of severe
diastasis and sustained fragment vascularization by duplicate main renal arteries. (B) IVP at 4 weeks demonstrating, despite intrarenal architectural distortion, satisfactory
total renal function and unobstructed ureteral drainage.

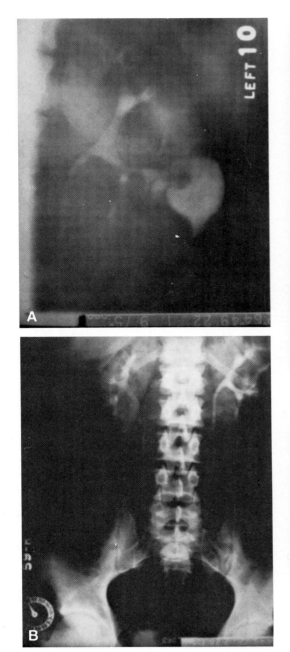

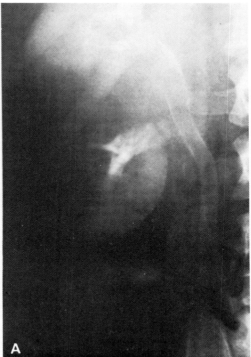

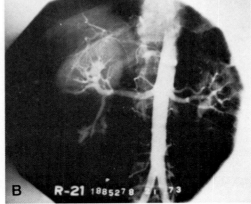

Fig. 4. (A) Plain abdominal film following right flank trauma, revealing large right lower polar mass. (B) IVP revealing large mid-parenchymal diastasis, satisfactory function of both fragments, grade I extravasation, and a normal draining, clot-filled ureter.

Fig. 3. (A) IVP following a karate kick to the left flank, revealing grade II extravasation. (B) IVP at 8 weeks demonstrating total resolution to normal.

and local symptoms, at which time she was discharged to outpatient supervision. Urography at 2 months revealed satisfactory lower pole function and unobstructed drainage, with apparent obliteration of the previous diastasis by the functionless upper pole fragment (Fig. 5B). Renal scan verified normal lower pole activity and upper pole inactivity (Fig. 5C). At 24 months the patient remained asymptomatic and normotensive, with normal urinalysis.

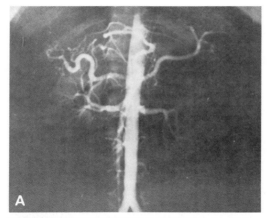

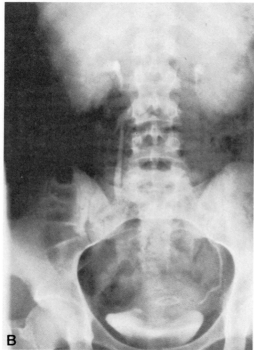

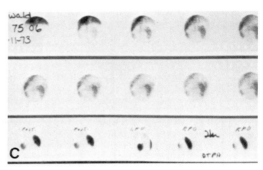

Fig. 5. (*A*) Renal arteriographic demonstration of adequate lower left renal vascularization, truncation of upper fragment blood supply, and suspicion of large diastasis due to severe displacement of upper capsular artery. (*B*) IVP at 8 weeks revealing satisfactory lower polar function, normal ureteral drainage, and mild grade I extravasation. (*C*) Renal scan at 8 weeks verifying urographic features.

with questionable upper pole activity, no extravasation, and apparent obliteration of diastasis. Subsequent renal scan demonstrated slightly reduced, but total renal activity, suggesting collateral supply of the upper pole segment, or vasospastic ischemia at the time of the initial study (Fig. 6*B*). Normal urinalysis, normotension, and absence of symptoms persisted.

Case 7. (CGH 511299) A 10-year-old female sustained extensive trauma in an auto accident, including gross hematuria. Right flank tenderness prompted right renal arteriography at the time of hepatosplenography (both normal), revealing significant parenchymal fracture along vascular planes with satisfactory vascularization and function of both fragments (Fig. 7*A*). Bedrest was followed by resolution of hematuria and local symptoms. Excretory urography at 2 weeks demonstrated extensive intrarenal extravasation, but continued function of both fragments, normal ureteral drainage, and apparent diminution of diastasis. Repeat urography at 6 weeks defined resolution of extravasation, continued normal function and drainage despite modest distortion of intrarenal architecture, and apparent total obliteration of diastasis (Fig. 7*B*). Urinalysis and blood pressure were normal, and symptoms were absent.

DISCUSSION

Evaluation of traumatic renal injuries is limited primarily to overall clinical status and stability, degree and duration of hematuria, and urographic assessment. Classification of renal injury is simplified by the tendency of these parameters to parallel one another in denoting trauma of

Case 6. (CGH 512458) A 4-year-old male was hit by an auto, sustaining left flank trauma and gross hematuria. Vital signs were stable, and hematuria had cleared to microscopic dimensions at emergency presentation. Urography indicated left upper polar nonfunction with delayed/diminished lower pole function. Arteriography revealed significant parenchymal fracture and diastasis, normal lower fragment vascularity, and apparent interruption of upper fragment blood supply (Fig. 6*A*). Observation and bedrest were attended by prompt resolution of local symptoms and microhematuria. Urography at 10 months revealed satisfactory lower pole function,

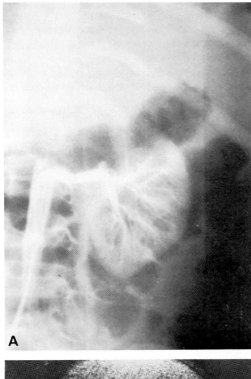

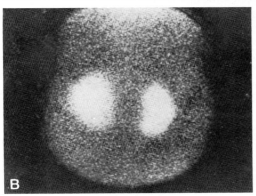

Fig. 6. (A) Renal arteriographic demonstration of satisfactory lower polar vascularization, and apparent upper segment devascularization. (B) Renal scan at 10 months verifying return of upper left renal function.

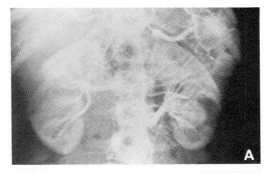

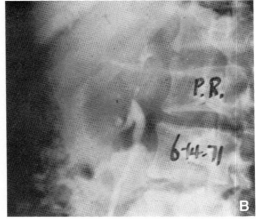

Fig. 7. (A) Right renal arteriographic demonstration of parenchymal fracture along vascular planes. (B) IVP at 6 weeks demonstrating, despite intrarenal architectural distortion, satisfactory total renal function and prompt ureteral drainage.

major or minor severity. Circumstances in which these parameters may not agree (*e.g.*, satisfactory renal function in the presence of severe, unremitting hematuria), would naturally warrant active intervention in the form of more definitive evaluation (arteriography), or immediate exploration as dictated by the threat of further delay. Agreement is virtually universal regarding these matters. Similar agreement exists as to the appropriate management (nonoperative) of injuries of minor degree.

Contradictory published data have, however, contributed to confusion relating to recommended policies of management of intermediate-degree renal injuries, more specifically to the significance of urinary extravasation and parenchymal fracture, and to the need for arteriography and the advisability of surgical intervention.

Urinary Extravasation. While several authors have considered any urinary extravasation an absolute indication for surgical intervention,[3,5,7,13,14,17,18,23,24] such data are often modified to the degree that uninfected extravasation confined within the renal capsule may be considered a benign phenomenon.[2,14,17,18,23,24] Most of these authors, however, as well as others opposing this latter view, agree that extracapsular extravasation requires exploration and drainage, and/or attempted repair.[3,5,7,13,14,23]

Our experience encourages correlation of the significance of uninfected urinary extravasation with anatomic localization (Fig. 8). Grade I extravasation is intraparenchymal, confined within the renal capsule; grade II escapes the renal capsule, but is confined within Gerota's fascia; grade III extravasation is retroperitoneal, escaping Gerota's fascia. Grades I and II extravasation have proved largely innocuous in the absence of any obstruction to ureteral drainage, and therefore prompt urographic visualization of a distal ureter of normal caliber is a reassuring factor in appraising such injuries. Retroperitoneal extravasation suggests a more significant injury, and therefore deserves further evaluation and probable intervention; however, its occurrence is uncommon. Infected urinary extravasation, documented obstruction to drainage (ureteropelvic obstruction, ureteral stricture, and the like), or proximal ureteral or renal pelvic injury (commonly requiring retrograde studies for confirmation) will seldom subside spontaneously or without toxic or cicatricial complications.

Parenchymal Fracture. Parenchymal fracture or laceration tends to develop according to shearing forces transmitted along the interface of tissues of different density. The kidney is composed of only four tissue compartments: renal capsule, collecting system, vascular system, and parenchyma, with the latter comprising the bulk of the total, as well as offering the least resistance to traumatic injury.

Blunt, or tangenital penetrating, forces therefore commonly produce fractures along vascular planes, the result of which is the tendency for vascularization and function of the fracture fragments to remain intact despite a potentially wide diastasis. The exposed nephrons cease urine production, reflected in the infrequency of resultant urinomas, while gradual resorption of the bridging hematoma results in progressive obliteration of the diastasis and restoration toward urographic normalcy (or occasional architectural distortion unaccompanied by significant functional deficit). Undocumented allusion to these phenomena appeared in an earlier report,[20] and numerous

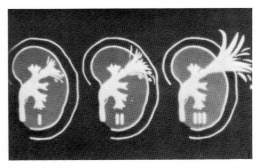

Fig. 8. Grading of urinary extravasation. *I*, intraparenchymal; *II*, extracapsular; *III*, retroperitoneal.

examples are present in the literature.[2,3,10,14] By no means is it a unique or uncommon event, and clear examples are provided by Cases 1, 2, 4, 6, and 7.

Segmental Nonfunction. A measure of insecurity attaches itself to the matter of segmental renal nonfunction, despite the success attendant upon conservative management of Cases 5 and 6. An avascular fragment includes the possibility of vascular avulsion with clinical stability provided only by hematoma tamponade or vasospasm, and potential complications include delayed hemorrhage, hypertension (assuming ischemic rather than avascular fragmentation), and abscess formation. Sargent and Marquardt cited the development of hypertension in only one of their collection of 70 conservatively managed cases of parenchymal fracture,[2] while Lang reported this complication in five of 13 patients with segmental infarction.[10] Despite the occurrence of post-traumatic hypertension only once in our series (polar artery thrombosis cured by heminephrectomy), this matter warrants further assessment until which time surgical excision of avascular fragments may advisably be considered the current management of choice.

Clinical reviews advocating operative intervention for traumatic renal injuries are numerous,[7,13,15,23,24,28] and are exemplified by the often cited reports of Hodges et al.,[7] and Scott and associates.[23]

The report of Hodges et al. was influenced by a prior report by Swan in which was described a 21% mortality of 1,232 cases of renal trauma. Further factors influencing their (Hodges) recommendations included an eagerness to avoid the sequelae of infection and protracted convalescence, frequently inferior radiological data in comparison with operative assessment, and an excessive delayed complication rate, including cyst, calculus, and nonfunction. However, of nine patients explored immediately, four underwent nephrectomy, and of three seen promptly and observed, two remained normal or stable (the third lost to followup). Despite an unacceptable delayed complication rate, this series was admittedly selected owing to their referral because of their sequelae.

Our own experience includes a mortality of 4% (all nonrenal causes), radiographic assessment much more reliable than commonly obtainable at laparotomy, and rarity of post-traumatic infection.

The report by Scott and associates subdivided 111 cases of blunt renal trauma according to severity, and cited a 2% complication rate in their nonoperated, less-severely traumatized patients, as opposed to a 50% complication rate in the nonoperated group IV patients. However, group IV was comprised of only four unexplored patients (two complications). Furthermore, all three patients explored underwent nephrectomy.

Cass and Ireland suggested that surgical management

resulted in less morbidity, but added that such management was three times more likely to result in nephrectomy.[1] Krahn and Axenrod presented two cases supporting their enthusiasm for surgical intervention, but illustrative data included arteriographic evidence of well-vascularized parenchymal fragments suggesting to us excellent healing potential.[10] Similar examples are not uncommon in the literature.

Proponents of a conservative policy of management have described the underestimated ability of the injured kidney to restore itself, as well as the difficulty in limiting surgery with less severe renal injuries. As early as 1939 Priestly suggested that conservative operations had little to offer, and that medical management was often attended by satisfactory functional results despite the possibility of persistent anatomic abnormalities.[21] Glenn and Harvard reported in their experience with 84 cases an 80–90% rate of spontaneous functional restoration with nonoperative management, a minimal tendency for significant sequelae, and a likelihood that mere parenchymal suturing accomplished little.[6] A similar opinion was held by Sargent and Marquardt, who observed no sequelae in 27 patients managed conservatively for 3–17 years.[22] Of 28 patients explored for renal trauma by Nation and Massey, renal injury was observed but not treated in 21, all patients recovering completely.[18] Only four nephrectomies were required by 93 patients sustaining blunt renal trauma collected by Waterhouse and Gross.[29] Twenty-one of 23 patients with "significant parenchymal lacerations treated conservatively by Morrow and Mendez responded favorably.[16] Lucey et al. suggested a 50% nephrectomy rate for patients explored for renal trauma, and added further their impression that delayed sequelae were uncommon.[2,14] Vermillion and associates considered unnecessary any early surgery performed with the intention of avoiding late sequelae.[27] A similar attitude has been reported by others.[12,19,25]

Other reasons proposed in favor of conservatism include a frequent inability to assess accurately the degree of renal damage at laparotomy,[25] and the diagnostic and prognostic reliability of arteriography in selecting patients for conservative management.[8,11] Finally, as already suggested, surgical procedures such as "exploration," "debridement," "repair," "suture," and so forth, may objectively accomplish nothing not realistically anticipated from nonsurgical management.[6,19,21]

Several features of blunt renal injury exhibited in the current series deserve emphasis. Seventy per cent of the total number were indisputably of minor degree, sustaining renal contusion or minor parenchymal fracture. Twelve percent were of major degree, characterized by pedicle injury or severe parenchymal fragmentation. The remaining intermediate-degree injuries comprise 19% of the total number, with parenchymal fracture (100%) and urinary extravasation (60%) as dominant clinical features.

Discounting modest orthopedic injuries, significant nonrenal trauma occurred in only 30% of the minor group, as opposed to 75% of the major, and 40% of the intermediate groups. The minor group was further characterized by a predominance of interpretable urograms and therefore a lack of need for arteriography, as well as the absence of indications for surgical intervention. Arteriography was obtained in only three of 13 patients with major renal injuries, with seven of the 10 unstudied patients having sustained nonrenal injuries of such severity as to contribute to the omission of this study. Similarly, 10 of 13 patients with intermediate-degree injuries were not evaluated arteriographically, eight of whom demonstrated significant nonrenal trauma. These data emphasize the factors which may contribute to inadequate assessment of renal trauma, namely, severe associated injuries and overestimation of the degree of renal damage, thereby possibly resulting in unnecessary exploration and, too often, nephrectomy. An analysis of 13 patients explored in our intermediate group (nine nephrectomy, two heminephrectomy) applied conservatively against the severity of the injury, as well as our subsequent observation of spontaneous recovery, suggests that most, if not all, of these procedures may have been unnecessary. Furthermore, heminephrectomy has not been performed by us during the past 3 years due to the tendency for fracture fragments to remain vascularized, as well as our experience with the benign course of devascularized segments in at least three instances.

The purpose of this description is not to debate the relative merits of conservative vs. surgical management of traumatic renal injuries. The purpose is, however, to illustrate the kidney's potential for spontaneous recovery after sustaining parenchymal fracture or injuries resulting in urinary extravasation. Knowledge of this fact may serve to protect the patient from unnecessary operation either specifically for the kidney injury, or incidentally during laparotomy for nonrenal injuries. The attainment of primary renal pedicle control, while enthusiastically endorsed, may nonetheless add significantly to operative time and surgical trauma when abbreviation of surgical and anesthesia time may be advisable, while nephrectomy during such surgery continues to be a too common result, often unnecessary in retrospect.

If one were to designate a single parameter as the most significant reflector of renal integrity, it would certainly be urographic function, regardless of apparently severe depression in comparison with its opposite. The presence of such function suggests a severity of injury somewhat less than major, and therefore optimism for full recovery, while nonfunction suggests a major-degree injury, and therefore warrants further evaluation (arteriography) or operative intervention. For this reason, every effort should be made to obtain interpretable urograms preoperatively, when permissible, or intraoperatively where preoperative studies were unobtainable, or when unexpected renal trauma is encountered at laparotomy. Once function is assessed, rational appraisal can be given to modifying factors such as degree of hematuria and retroperitoneal hemorrhage.

Whereas renal arteriography is seldom indicated in the presence of interpretable urograms (minor-degree injury), and often precluded by the urgency surrounding major-degree renal injuries or associated nonrenal trauma,[20] the indications for renal arteriography (persistent urographic nonfunction, unremitting severe hematuria, significant delayed hematuria) may be expanded to include those intermediate-degree injuries in which doubt may exist as to the advisability of nonoperative management, an opinion shared by others.[11]

Remarks herein have been deliberately confined to blunt renal trauma in an effort to clarify the principles emphasized, since the potential ramifications of the successful management of penetrating renal injuries necessarily introduce factors which may often create exceptions to such principles, or tend to establish priorities relegating definitive urologic assessment to a secondary or tertiary status. As previously stated, however, penetrating renal injuries also commonly respond with similarly favorable results to nonoperative management.[30]

It is therefore recommended that circumstances in which preoperative urologic assessment is omitted (a state of extremis accompanied by hematuria, intraoperative discovery of a retroperitoneal hematoma, and the like) may prudently include propitious intraoperative urography or renal arteriography in an effort to obtain information necessary to substantiate the need, or lack of need, for pedicle control and renal exploration. Parenthetically, what may appear to be exsanguinating hematuria at presentation will often subside dramatically within the time necessary to stabilize the patient and/or mobilize surgical facilities, and although such patients obviously require routine careful urologic evaluation, the degree of renal injury is commonly less than major. Finally, evidence or suspicion of significant renal trauma accompanied by slight or temporary gross hematuria or by microhematuria only, and/or by a small and stable retroperitoneal hematoma raises the spectre of pedicle damage. Urographic nonfunction is virtually invariably confirmatory, and immediate attempt at repair is one's only hope for renal salvage.[26]

REFERENCES

1. CASS AA, IRELAND GW: Comparison of the conservative and surgical management of the more severe degrees of renal trauma in multiple injured patients, J Urol 109:8, 1973
2. CHOVNICK SD, NEWMAN HR: Management of renal injuries. J Urol 83:330, 1960
3. COCKETT ATK, FRANK IN, DAVIS RS et al: Recent advances in the diagnosis and management of acute renal trauma. J Urol 113:751, 1975
4. DOWSE JLA: Renal injuries. Br J Surg 50:353, 1903
5. ELKIN M, MENG C, DE PAREDES RG: Correlation of intravenous urography and renal angiography in kidney injury. Radiology 86:496, 1966
6. GLENN JG, HARVARD BM: The injured kidney. JAMA 173:1189, 1960
7. HODGES CV, GILBERT DR, SCOTT WW: Renal trauma: A study of 71 cases. J Urol 66:627, 1951
8. ISWARIAH JD, KITTREDGE RD, DRAPER JW: Aortography as an adjunct in diagnosis and treatment of renal trauma. J Urol 95:146, 1966
9. KAZMIN MH, BROSMAN SA, COCKETT ATK: Diagnosis and management of renal trauma. J Urol 101:783, 1969
10. KRAHN HP, AXENROD R: The management of severe renal lacerations. J Urol 109:11, 1973
11. LANG EK: Arteriography in the assessment of renal trauma. J Trauma 15:533, 1975
12. LANG EK, TRICHEL BE, TURNER CW et al: Arteriographic assessment of injury resulting from renal trauma. J Urol 106:1, 1971
13. LICH R JR: Injury of the solitary kidney. J Urol 81:382, 1959
14. LUCEY DT, SMITH MJV, KOONTZ WW JR: A plea for the conservative treatment of renal injuries. J Trauma 11:390, 1971

15. LUCEY DT, SMITH MJV, KOONTZ WW JR: Modern trends in the management of urologic trauma. J Urol 107:641, 1972
16. MORROW JW, MENDEZ R: Renal trauma. J Urol 104:647, 1970
17. MORSE TS, SMITH JP, HOWARD WHR et al: Kidney injuries in children. J Urol 98:539, 1967
18. NATION EF, MASSEY BD: Renal trauma: Experience with 258 cases. J Urol 89:775, 1963
19. PETERSON NE, KIRACOFE HD: Renal trauma: When to operate. Urology 3:537, 1974
20. PETERSON NE, NORTON LW: Injuries associated with renal trauma. J Urol 109:766, 1973
21. PRIESTLEY JR: Renal trauma. Surg Clin No Amer 19:1033, 1939
22. SARGENT JC, MARQUARDT CR: Renal injuries. J Urol 63:1, 1950
23. SCOTT R JR, CARLTON CE JR, ASHMORE AJ et al: Initial management of non-penetrating injuries. J Urol 90:535, 1963
24. SCOTT R JR, CARLTON CE JR, GOLDMAN M: Penetrating injuries of the kidney. J Urol 101:247, 1968
25. SPENCE HM, BAIRD SS, WARE EW: Management of kidney injuries. JAMA 154:198, 1954
26. STABLES DP, FOUCHE RF, deVILLIERS VAN NIEKIRK JP et al: Traumatic renal artery occlusion: 21 cases. J Urol 115:229, 1976
27. VERMILLION CD, McLAUGHLIN AD, PFISTER RC: Management of renal trauma. J Urol 106:478, 1971
28. del VILLAS RG, IRELAND GW, CASS AS: Management of renal injury in conjunction with the immediate surgical treatment of the acute severe trauma patient. J Urol 107:208, 1972
29. WATERHOUSE K, GROSS M: Trauma to the genitourinary tract. J Urol 101:241, 1969
30. WHITNEY RE, PETERSON NE: Penetrating renal injuries. Urology 7:711, 1976

DISCUSSION

Dr. John H. Morton (601 Elmwood Avenue, Rochester, New York 14642): I enjoyed Doctor Peterson's paper very much, and rise merely to ask a question about the possible development of later hypertension in the patient who retains a portion of a kidney without apparent blood supply. I wonder, Doctor Peterson, what you have found in long-term evaluation of this problem. Does hypertension develop?

Dr. Norman Peterson (closing): In our total 190-odd patients we have had one delayed hypertensive patient, a child who was in an automobile accident and who sustained a segmental arterial interruption.

It is true that if a patient is going to get hypertension afterward, it will usualy happen with segmental nonfunction. There aren't many of these, but we have four or five now, with a maximum followup of 3 years, and we haven't so far observed hypertension in any. It still exists, however, and perhaps until we know more about the results of conservative management in these patients, it might be prudent to remove the functionless segments. I wouldn't be surprised, however, in view of our experience, if they could often be left in with impunity, recalling that it is ischemic, rather than infarcted parenchyma that is responsible for renindependent hypertension.

Commentary: Operative *vs.* Nonoperative Management of Renal Trauma

W. Graham Guerriero

The current controversy in urology between proponents of operative and nonoperative management of renal trauma is probably unwarranted. Conflict has occurred because of the absence of controlled series in the literature. In addition, most studies are retrospective, containing little information on indications for nephrectomy in operated patients or on the length of hospitalization and morbidity in patients treated conservatively. Those patients who are seriously injured and those with more minor injury are inadequately distinguished.

The incidence of hypertension and late sequelae, such as loss of renal mass, is rarely mentioned. Rarely is this the fault of the authors, since these patients are frequently lost to follow-up studies. Instead of trying to build a case for one or another form of management, physicians should ask, What are the indications for operative intervention? Would surgery prevent undesirable sequelae? Can I actually reduce mortality, reduce the incidence of nephrectomy, prevent abscess, loss of renal function, and hypertension, and decrease the economic consequences of injury by definitive surgical care?''

CAUSES

The kidney may be damaged by blunt or penetrating trauma. Blunt trauma compresses the kidney, which produces rupture of parenchyma, the renal pelvis, or renal fornices. Injury may also occur as a result of rapid deceleration, such as fall from height, which causes arterial intimal disruption leading to thrombosis or actual avulsion of arteries, veins or the collecting system.

Penetrating injuries may be a result of high-or low-velocity missiles or stab wounds. High-velocity injuries cause significant cortical necrosis, or "explosion" of the parenchyma and late hemorrhage, as the inadequately debrided tissue dies. Stab wounds may be minor but can frequently be deceiving, since the assailant may twist the knife after penetrating the flank or abdomen, creating large wounds of the kidney.

In addition to these mechanisms, one must remember that renal injury rarely exists by itself. Associated injuries to other organs occur as often as 80% in some series of penetrating trauma, and in up to 57% in cases of blunt trauma.[1,2]

EVALUATION

Evaluation of renal injury is inadequate when based on clinical signs and symptoms. The clinical history is frequently clouded by unconsciousness, confusion, drunkenness, shock, and pain. The physical examination is usually inadequate because of guarding of abdominal muscles and associated interabdominal injuries. The emergent nature of other injuries may make it difficult to examine the patient adequately. This is particularly true when other disciplines, such as orthopaedics and general surgery, are pressing for a solution to their own responsibilities.

Laboratory studies, such as urinalyses, are notoriously unreliable. No hematuria may be present, even with serious problems such as pedicle injury or major cortical laceration. Conversely, hematuria may be present as a result of injudicious urethral catheterization or lower urinary tract injury.

The best screening test for renal injury is the infusion intravenous pyelogram (IVP), although CT scanning is becoming increasingly important. All patients with abdominal trauma of more than minimal degree, with penetrating abdominal or flank injuries, with blunt flank injuries, who fell from a height or were thrown from a moving vehicle, with pelvic and femur fractures, and with lumbar process, lower rib fractures, and lower thoracic penetrating injuries should have an IVP once stable. Early recognition of injury does not preclude nonoperative treatment.

Visualization of the entire renal outline and collecting

system is imperative. If overlying gas or poor perfusion interferes with IVP quality, nephrotomography may be used to improve visualization of the renal outline and calices.

The purpose of all examinations of the kidney is to discover injury and to determine if treatment is needed, and, if so, what type. Kidney injuries may be classified as minor or major.

Minor renal injuries are those that may be safely observed and probably will not at any time require surgical intervention. They include renal contusions, shallow cortical lacerations, forniceal extravasation, and minor stab wounds. These injuries are characterized by an IVP demonstrating intact cortical outlines. Swelling of the kidney with an intact outline may be noted but is not usually seen in the first 12 hours. A large kidney should make one think of contained hematoma, congenital disease, or compensatory hypertrophy. If the parenchyma is damaged, compression of the calices and delayed function may be present. In most cases, the IVP is "normal." Treatment of these patients can be limited to bedrest until the hematuria clears, followed by avoidance of contact sports for 6 to 8 weeks. Some of these patients may develop hypertension, but this is very rare and usually suggests missed vascular injury. Arteriograms are usually not necessary to classify these patients.

Major renal injuries include cortical lacerations extending into the collecting system, avulsion or disruption of the renal pelvis or calices, renal pedicle injuries, multiple renal fractures, and gunshot or major stab wounds. Diagnosis may be made by IVP in most patients. If the kidney does not function in its entirety, or major injury cannot be excluded with certainty by IVP, an arteriogram should be performed, even if the physician feels he would initially follow a course of nonoperative management. To elect to observe a renal injury that may be of major consequence to the patient without obtaining studies such as an arteriogram is to deny the patient the benefits of definitive diagnosis, such as recognition of thrombosis of portions of the arterial tree or of major renal cortical injury. Recognition of associated injury to the aorta inferior vena cava and other major vessels, spleen, or liver is possible if celiac injection of contrast media is done at the time of aortogram for renal trauma. If arteriography is performed early and the patient should require eventual exploration after watchful waiting, delay will not occur at that time because further studies were needed. Information on the blood supply of the kidney may greatly benefit the surgeon facing exploration of a bleeding, highly vascular organ. Arteriography is the definitive test for renal injury.

TREATMENT

Once the extent of renal injury has been determined, the physician can choose operative or nonoperative management. Eighty-five percent of all blunt renal injuries are minor. Of the remaining 15%, less than half these patients will require nephrectomy or operative treatment. The decision on whether to operate should be made on the basis of expected benefits of surgery and the likelihood of serious sequelae such as hypertension.

Hypertension is seen most frequently in patients who have suffered major renal trauma and is said by some authors to occur only in those patients who have significant loss of renal parenchymal size secondary to vascular injury. Glenn and Harvard reported in 1960 that 5 of their 84 patients eventually became hypertensive.[3] Grant and co-workers reported that 13 of 33 patients with documented renal trauma developed hypertension.[4] When studied, 11 of their 13 patients had definitely abnormal IVPs and arteriograms. Only one patient had a normal IVP or arteriogram. The onset of hypertension was from as soon as 37 days after injury to as late as 16 years after trauma. Of interest is that 10 of the 11 patients were asymptomatic at the time their hypertension was discovered. Five of the 11 patients had parenchymal compression secondary to subcapsular hematoma (Page kidney), Six of the patients had vascular lesions (*i.e.*, traumatic thromboses). Nephrectomy was used to treat six of the seven patients who became normotensive in their study. Partial nephrectomy and endarterectomy was successful in only one patient. Thus, avoidance of early operation in the hope of avoiding nephrectomy is probably unwarranted. Hypertension following trauma is probably mediated by renin release and can be due either to thrombosis of the renal vasculature or to constriction of the kidney secondary to scar.[5] In 1939, Irving Page demonstrated that experimental hypertension could be produced by wrapping one of the kidneys of a dog in cellophane.[6] In 1944, Engel and Page reported a clinical case of hypertension secondary to parenchymal compression in a youth aged 19.[7]

The incidence of hypertension in trauma patients is low and, in fact, may be greater statistically than the general population. Maling and associates compared 63 patients who had suffered renal trauma with 63 age-and sex-matched control patients.[8] Six to 138 months after injury, 13 of the trauma patients and 12 of the control patients had hypertension. They concluded that it was unlikely that permanent hypertension would occur as a result of acute renal injury unless sufficient vascular disruption occurred to produce a decrease in renal size.

Thus, to prevent hypertension, surgeons must do whatever possible to prevent perfusion of devitalized renal parenchyma and to minimize the consequences of hematoma and extravasation.

I will now examine the various types of major renal injuries that can occur to the kidney and select those that should be explored. Deep polar lacerations extending into the collecting system should be repaired or resected primarily. This will significantly decrease the chance of late hemorrhage, abscess, and hypertension. These injuries frequently are detached from the collecting system, but the blood supply is completely or partially preserved, since the fracture line with blunt trauma extends between the vessels in most patients. Expectant treatment of these injuries usually results in eventual exploration for hemorrhage or abscess; late exploration is difficult, since the hematoma by this time is organized. Instead of a partial nephrectomy, complete nephrectomy may be necessary if exploration is carried out in the period of secondary healing.

Pedicle injury or injury to a major vascular segment should

be explored immediately, since serious sequelae from these injuries will almost certainly occur if definitive treatment is not promptly undertaken.

Multiple renal fractures should be observed if the capsule appears intact, since there is little that can be done except nephrectomy. Some of these patients may avoid nephrectomy with this policy, although a significant number may end up hypertensive. Major collecting system injuries, such as a ruptured renal pelvis and avulsion of the ureteropelvic junction, should be repaired primarily. Avulsion of the calices, fortunately, is a rare injury, but it requires immediate nephrectomy. Deep parenchymal lacerations in the kidney midportion of the kidney with good preservation of blood supply to the polar segments should be treated with watchful waiting as long as extravasation is not too great. If hemorrhage continues or abscess occurs, the patient must be explored at that time. Repair of these injuries, although possible occasionally, is frequently very difficult, and nephrectomy is more likely with early exploration of these patients. All gunshot wounds should be explored. Drainage of the kidney may be all that is required for low-velocity injury. High-velocity injuries may require extensive debridement and partial or complete nephrectomy. The incidence of associated injury is high in this group of patients.

Anterior stab wounds, or those associated with extravasation on IVP or with significant hematuria, should be explored. Superficial stab wounds of the flank should be observed.

Combined injury of the kidney and pancreas, or duodenum, is noted for producing significant complications such as hemorrhage, fistula, and pseudocyst and abscess. Extensive debridement of questionably viable tissue and liberal use of stents, nephrostomy, and drains is necessary in these patients.

If exploration is required, this should take place through a midline incision to permit evaluation of associated injuries. Preliminary control of the vascular pedicle is mandatory. With this approach, nephrectomy for intraoperative hemorrhage can be minimized. Meticulous hemostasis and the liberal use of drains, capsular or peritoneal flaps over the injury and omental wrap of the ureter, or interposition of the omentum between the injured pancreas, colon, and kidney helps in preventing postoperative complications.

Most important in the treatment of renal injuries is a logical, reasoned approach. Exploration must be based on the surgeon's technical ability, the extent of injury, and the patient's expected course. Blind adherence to operative or nonoperative treatment can only result in mismanagement of some patients.

REFERENCES

1. Carlton CE Jr, Scott R Jr, Goldman M: The management of penetrating injuries of the kidney. J Trauma 8:1071, 1968
2. Del Villar RG, Ireland GW, Cass AS: Management of renal injury in conjunction with the immediate surgical treatment of the acute severe trauma patient. J Urol 107:208, 1972
3. Glenn JF, Harvard BM: The injured kidney. JAMA 173:93, 1960
4. Grant RP, Gifford RW, Pudvan WR, Meoney TF, Staffon RA, McCormack LJ: Renal trauma and hypertension. Am J Cardiol 27:173, 1971

5. Braasch WF, Strom GW: Renal trauma and its relation to hypertension. J Urol 50:543, 1943
6. Page IH: The production of persistent arterial hypertension by cellophane perinephritis. JAMA 113:2046, 1938
7. Engel WJ, Page IH: Hypertension due to renal compression resulting from subcapsular hematoma. J Urol 73:735, 1955
8. Maling TJB, Little PJ, Maling TMJ, Gunesekera A, Bailey RR: Renal trauma and persistent hypertension. Nephron 16:173, 1976

ANNOTATED BIBLIOGRAPHY

Carlton CE Jr, Scott R Jr, Goldman M: The management of penetrating injuries of the kidney. J Trauma 8:1071, 1968

This paper develops criteria for classifying renal injury and discusses principles of management of renal injuries. In addition, the fallacy of depending on a negative excretory urogram to rule out major renal injury is pointed out.

Del Vilar RG, Ireland GW, Cass AS: Management of renal injury in conjunction with the immediate surgical treatment of the acute severe trauma patient. J Urol 107:208, 1972

These authors favor an aggressive approach to the management of blunt renal injuries. In this paper they present patients managed both by the conservative approach and by immediate aggressive radiologic evaluation and operation. They believe that the conservative approach resulted in increased morbidity and increased loss of renal tissue.

Glenn JF, Harvard BM: The injured kidney. JAMA 173:93, 1960

These authors conclude that the management of renal injury can only be based on thorough knowledge of the exact nature of the injury. In their series, 80% to 90% of renal injuries could be

treated conservatively. This is one of the few series of patients with blunt trauma in which an attempt is made to correlate subsequent hypertension with the original renal injury.

Grant RP, Gifford RW, Pudvan WR, Meoney TF, Staffon RA, McCormack LJ: Renal trauma and hypertension. Am J Cardiol 27:173, 1971

In this paper, which is a retrospective examination of 33 cases of renal injury, hypertension developed in 13 patients. Of the 13 patients, 11 were found to have definite abnormality by IVP and renal arteriogram, and all underwent operative treatment in an attempt to relieve hypertension. Nephrectomy ameliorated hypertension in seven of eight patients, six of whom became normotensive. No therapy other than nephrectomy appeared to be successful in the tretment of hypertension in these patients.

Grim C, Mullins MF, Nilson JP, Ross, G Jr: Unilateral "Page kidney" hypertension in man. JAMA 231:42, 1975

In this paper, studies were performed on a youth aged 17 one year after flank injury. He was found to have an ischemic kidney with abnormal renal vein ratios and split function studies. Nephrectomy cured the hypertension.

Page IH: The production of peristent arterial hypertension by cellophane perinephritis. JAMA 113:2046, 1939

> In 1939, Page first produced hypertension in the dog by wrapping one kidney in cellophane, which led to formation of a dense, fibrous encapsulation of the kidney.

Engel WJ, Page IH: Hypertension due to renal compression resulting from subcapsular hematoma. J Urol 73:735, 1955

> This paper presents a clinical case similar to Page's cellophane-wrapped dog kidney.

Maling TJB, Little PJ, Maling TMJ, Gunesekera A, Bailey RR: Renal trauma and persistent hypertension. Nephron 16:173, 1976

> In this very interesting paper, the authors conclude that it is unlikely that permanent hypertension would recur as a result of an acute renal injury unless sufficient vascular disruption occurred to produce a decrease in kidney size.

Overview: The Need for Cost-Effective Management of Renal Trauma

Keith Waterhouse

In his commentary on surgery for renal trauma, Dr. Guerriero remarks that "the current controversy in urology between proponents of operative and nonoperative management of renal trauma is probably unwarranted." In 1974, I was invited to discuss injuries to the urinary tract in *Reviews In Pediatric Urology*.[1] My opening remarks on parenchymal injuries were very similar to Dr. Guerriero's:

Despite apparent differences of opinion in the literature, I believe that the management of renal trauma does not vary much from center to center at this time. Non-operative management is relied upon for children with renal contusions and in most instances of cortical and calyceal lacerations. Occasionally in patients with cortical or calyceal lacerations special circumstances lead to the need for surgical repair, usually either repair of the laceration or partial nephrectomy. It is rare for nephrectomy to be needed.

In children with complete fractures having an injury involving the calyces, parenchyma, and capsule, although surgery is rarely very urgent, it is almost always required. Surgery should not be delayed any longer than is necessary to investigate thoroughly the problem. We prefer transperitoneal exploration of the patient with early control of the vascular pedicle allowing careful toilet of the kidney and estimation as to whether repair is possible or nephrectomy indicated. Control of the renal pedicle may be obtained either by the technique described by Scott, et al or by the method described by Waterhouse and Gross.

Some patients are, of course, so badly injured that immediate surgical exploration is necessary. We would again stress the importance of excretory urography in these patients to assess the status of the injured kidney.

These remarks apply equally to adults, and my views on this matter have not changed in the past 6 years. During this period, however, there have been great changes in social aspects of the delivery of medical care, and the phrase *cost effectiveness* has become commonplace. An interesting approach to the cost-effective care of renal trauma has been that of Eric Lang of New Orleans.* In the past, patients with contusions of the kidney have remained hospitalized with bed rest for 10 days while the hematuria cleared. Lang pointed out that although this was a conservative form of management, it was, in fact, rather expensive. He therefore proposed that patients with contusions should have a renal angiogram performed to demonstrate that the kidney was bruised and not lacerated. If there ws no laceration, he suggested that these patients could quite safely be discharged from the hospital to rest at home, with a great saving in the use of hospital beds. Patients with lacerations of the parenchyma or rupture of the calyceal system must, of course, remain under careful medical observations, since if conservative management is elected, a number of these patients require surgical intervention. With the advent of computed tomography (CT) scans, it is probable that the relatively invasive technique of arteriography may be replaced by this much less invasive examination.

It would appear to me that the indications for various forms of management have been well worked out in the past 15 years and that surgeons should now focus on developing the least invasive and most cost-effective form of investigation that will allow the selection of appropriate therapy.

* Personal communication.

REFERENCES

1. Waterhouse K: Injuries to the urinary tract in children. In Johnston JH, Goodwin WE (eds): Previews in Pediatric Urology, pp 241–267. New York, Elsevier–Dutton, 1974

PART TWELVE

ENDOSCOPIC SURGERY OF THE KIDNEY

25

A NEW OPERATIVE FIBERPYELOSCOPE

Seigi Tsuchida

From the Department of Urology, Akita University School of Medicine, Akita, Japan

The Journal of Urology
Copyright © 1977 by The Williams & Wilkins Co.
Vol. 117, May
Printed in U.S.A.

ABSTRACT—We describe a flexible fiberpyeloscope with which it is possible to extract renal pelvic and caliceal stones easily. The tip of the fiberpyeloscope can be deflected 90 degrees up or down from the basic position with a hand-manipulated angle deflector knob on the fiberpyeloscope grip. This flexibility allows the inside of the renal pelvis to be observed clearly from every direction. Specially designed stone forceps can be inserted through the channel of the fiberpyeloscope into the renal pelvis to grasp pelvic stones under direct visual observation. The fiberpyeloscope has been used in 4 cases of renal pelvic stones in which the pelvis was exposed by a subcostal flank incision. The stones were extracted successfully with the fiberpyeloscope, which was introduced through a small incision on the pelvis.

In 1941 Rupel and Brown were the first to observe the renal pelvis and calix through an endoscope during a surgical operation.[1] Since then various types of endoscopes have been developed to visualize renal stones and filling defects inside the pelvis and calix. However, those endoscopes were not very pratical.

Previously, we developed a flexible fibercystoscope and later an operative fiberpyeloscope that provided an inner channel sufficient to pass a stone-grasping forceps.[2,3] This pyeloscope has been improved recently for easier handling. Herein are explained its particulars and clinical uses.

MATERIAL AND METHOD

The total length of the fiberpyeloscope (500 mm) has been reduced from that of the previous model so that it may be handled more easily (Fig. 1). The outside diameter of the fiberpyeloscope is 8.5 mm, with a 70 degree foroblique field of vision, compared to the

Accepted for publication July 2, 1976.
Read at annual meeting of American Urological Association, Las Vegas, Nevada, May 16–20, 1976.

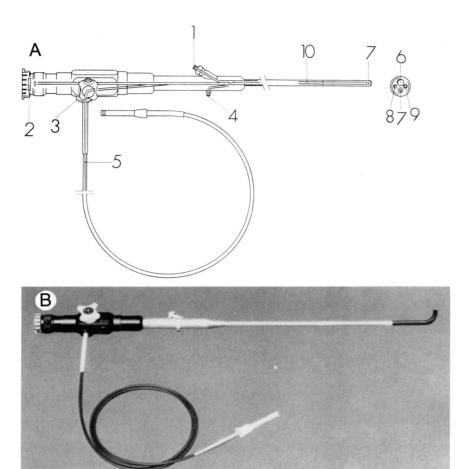

Fig. 1. (*A*) Schematic illustration of flexible fiberpyeloscope. *1*, biopsy forceps inlet. *2*, eyepiece lens. *3*, angle deflector dial (up and down). *4*, suction outlet. *5*, light guide cable. *6*, biopsy forceps and suction channel. *7*, objective lens. *8*, air outlet. *9*, light guide illumination. *10*, fiber image bundle. (*B*) Complete fiberscope unit.

straightforward vision of the earlier model. The foro-blique field of vision helps to visualize the tip of the forceps when it protrudes 2 mm from the tip of the pyeloscope. The fiberpyeloscope consists of a 220 mm long grip for controlling the instrument, a rigid part, a flexible part and an apical objective lens system equipped with a remote illuminating system and a universal cord. The eyepiee has an eyesight ring that can be adjusted to visualize objects from 2 to 30 mm from the fiberpyeloscope tip. Below this eyesight adjuster ring is an angle deflector dial that provides the control. The channel for fluid/air passage has an inside diameter of 1.5 mm, through which physiological sodium chloride solution, washing solution or air can be introduced into the renal pelvis.

The inside diameter of the forceps channel of the fiberpyeloscope is 4.0 mm, providing an opening to manipulate the forceps. The rigid part, covered with a metal sheath 220 mm long, can be held with the left hand for easy handling of the fiberpyeloscope in endoscopy. The flexible part is covered for 60 mm with a desmopane tube, which allows smooth insertion of the fiberpyeloscope into the renal pelvis. At a distance of 30 mm from the tip of the flexible part the fiberpyeloscope can be bent 90 degrees up or down by controlling the angle deflector dial on the grip. The tip of the pyeloscope is covered with a smooth metal cap so that the mucosa will not be damaged while the fiberpyeloscope is inserted into the renal pelvis. The tip consists of the objective lens system, illumination window, fluid/air outlet and forceps outlet. Light is transmitted through a light-carrier fiber bundle that is connected to a xenon lamp. Figure 2 shows the construction of the 3-hook stone-grasping forceps and basket catheter. The 3 hooks or basket tip can be pushed out from or withdrawn into their respective compartments by simple manipulation of the handles.

The operating procedure is as follows. 1) The flexible fiberpyeloscope is sterilized with ethylene oxide gas. 2)

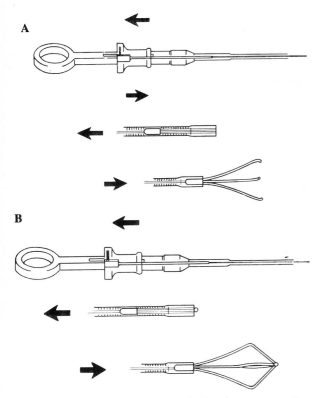

Fig. 2. (A) Schematic illustration of 3-hook stone-grasping forceps. (B) Schematic illustration of basket catheter.

The renal pelvis is exposed operatively by a standard subcostal flank incision, followed by a small incision on the exposed renal pelvis through which the fiberpyeloscope is inserted. 3) Physiological sodium chloride solution or air is sent into the pelvis in order to expand the pelvis a little. Observation of the interior renal pelvis and calix is started systematically, making full use of the angle deflection of the fiberpyeloscope tip. When a pelvic stone 3 to 12 mm in diameter is found the 3-hook forceps is used. When a caliceal stone within 5 mm in diameter is found the basket catheter is used to collect it. When it is confirmed that the 3-hook forceps or basket catheter has grasped the stone tightly the fiberpyeloscope is taken out from the incision site, with the forceps remaining inside the channel of the fiberpyeloscope.

CLINICAL RESULTS

We have used this fiberpyeloscope successfully in 4 patients with stones 4 to 12 mm in diameter in the renal pelvis and calix (Fig. 3). However, it was difficult to grasp a stone larger than 13 mm in diameter with the forceps. The blind search and extraction of such larger stones were done with a usual stone-grasping forceps.

DISCUSSION

As mentioned previously the sizes of the renal calculi successfully extracted with the forceps are within 12 mm in diameter. For larger stones the usual stone-grasping forceps can be used in the blind search and extraction method. Therefore, operative fiberpyeloscopy seems to be most effective in collecting and extracting renal pelvic and caliceal stones that remain after the usual pyelolithotomy. In addition, this fiberscope can be applied effectively when the existence of a tumor is suspected in the renal pelvis and calix, and clear observation of a tumor or bleeding ulcerous lesion can be obtained by introducing air into the pelvis through the fiberpyeloscope channel.

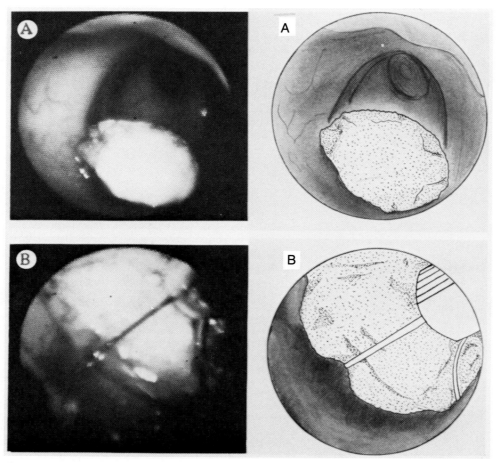

Fig. 3. (*A*) Endoscopic illustration of renal pelvic stone. (*B*) Endoscopic illustration shows 3-hook forceps grasping stone. Extracted stone measures 0.8 by 0.5 by 0.3 cm.

REFERENCES

1. Rupel, E. and Brown, R.: Nephroscopy with removal of stone following nephrostomy for obstructive calculous anuria. J Urol 46:117, 1941

2. Tsuchida, S. and Sugawara, H.: A new flexible fibercystoscope for visualization of the bladder neck. J Urol 109:830, 1983

3. Tsuchida, S.: A new operative fiberpyeloscope. Tohoku J Exp Med 116:369, 1975

Commentary: Accessories for Renal Surgery

Seigi Tsuchida

In 1950, Leadbetter reported the design and development of the first basic practical model of the rigid right-angle nephroscope with a lens system for clinical use.[1] The indications for the use of the nephroscope were reported in detail in 1976 by Gittes.[2] Recently, many attempts have been made to develop a flexible nephropyeloscope using optical glass fibers as the image-transmitting means because of the great advantage of flexibility; flexibility is enough to compensate for the disadvantage of slightly inferior image resolution in comparison with the lens system used with the rigid endoscope.[3–5]

In 1973, I reported on the flexible fibercystoscope with a tip deflection of 90° on a vertical plane, which made it possible to observe any internal part of the bladder and the neck of the bladder.[6] Furthermore, in 1977, as shown in the preceding article, an operative optical fiber pyeloscope was developed as an improved model of the fibercystoscope.[7] This instrument proved to be very useful in its clinical applications, having an image resolution scarcely inferior to that of the rigid operative pyeloscope with lens system. In addition, this fiberoptic instrument provides the possibility of operative applications.

For the image-transmitting means of the fiberoptic endoscope, several thousand optical glass fibers of a few microns in diameter are aligned in such an accurate way that each single fiber is clearly distinguishable even at both ends of the bundle (image bundle of glass fiber); the bundle is bound and fixed at both ends with a special cement. Through an objective lens at one end of the fiberoptic glass fiber image-transmitting bundle, each emitted light point of the image at that end is transmitted to the other end by each single fiber in the bundle. The image transmitted through the objective lens is observed through the eyepiece lens at the other end, since such a picture is the *blip* of the assembled light points from the original image.

Because of the special features of the glass fibers, the clearness of the image resolution transmitted through the glass fiber bundle depends on the density of the fibers in the bundle, and the resolution does not reach the level of the nephroscope with a rigid lens system. If one thoroughly examines the image ·observed through a fiberscope, the tessellated pattern of the glass fibers will appear, and the image observed is similar to the pictue on a television screen. The recent rapid improvements in optical technology have resulted in there being almost no practical difference between the resolution of the fiberscope and that of the endoscope with a rigid lens system. Therefore, the operative fiber pyeloscope seems to have more possible value in general clinical practice than the rigid type.

This commentary will discuss accessories developed since 1976 as well as indications and techniques not covered in the article.

NEW ACCESSORIES

In addition to the three-hook grasping forceps, a two-hook forceps has been designed (Fig. 4). This forceps is sufficient to grasp a stone smaller than 6 mm, while the three-hook forceps is used for bigger stones. Additionally, one can use standard cystoscopic biopsy forceps and fulgurating electrodes with various tips in specific instances.

INDICATIONS

As reported by Leadbetter and by Gittes, the pyeloscope can be used in cases of calculi, renal hematuria, and renal papillary tumors.[1,2]

Calculi. The pyeloscope has a major and a supplemental role during the surgical operation for renal calculus. Its major role is the procedure in which one removes the stone with the forceps after introducing the scope into the collecting system during the pyelotomy. In this procedure, the simple caliceal calculi of less than 1 cm will be the prime target for removal with the scope. For such small stone removal, blind probing and manipulation are quite difficult. In addition, there are several clinical hazards in attempting to catch such small stones blindly with the grasping forceps during pyelotomy; for instance, the renal parenchyma might be mistakenly damaged by to forceps or the neck of the pelvis might be ruptured by the finger, used for touch examination in the pelvis and the calix. These maneuvers may result in massive bleeding that may be difficult, or impossible, to control. Furthermore, the grasping forceps may injure the pelvis so extensively that there will be late stenosis of the pelviurenteric junction. The pyeloscope is especially effective for discovering and removing those stones floating in the pelvis and the calix.

Its supplemental role is to study stone location and number and other conditions in the pelvis and the calix when the stones are too big to be grasped by the forceps through the scope, making subsequent blind probing and manipulation for the

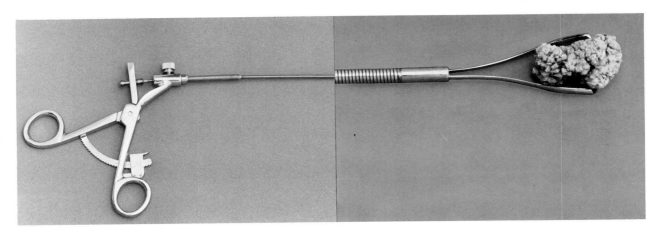

Fig. 4.

removal of the stones easier. Open surgery is necessary for large staghorn calculi located in the calix. However, in these cases, the pyeloscope is often quite effective for confirming and removing residual fragments.

For the aforementioned reasons, it is always wise to have the pyeloscope close at hand, even when operative pyeloscopic removal of stones is not planned. The sterilization and manipulation of the pyeloscope are rather easy, and the examination of the pelvis and calix takes under 10 minutes.

Renal Hematuria. Patients with persistent, unilateral, essential hematuria are considered for open pyeloscopy after all studies and findings are negative (*i.e.*, retrograde pyelography, renal arteriography, and repeated cytologic examination of the urine). Open pyeloscopy should be carried out before nephrectomy when the retrograde catheter study confirms that the hematuria is not from the ureter but from the renal pelvis. Gittes reported that when these studies are negative, an open nephroscopic exploration during a persistent bleeding episode allows one to determine the source of bleeding and to treat the patient with partial nephrectomy or fulguration.[2]

Renal Papillary Tumors. Only carefully selected patients with low-grade positive cytologic results or brush biopsy of an intrarenal lesion should be subjected to biopsy, fulguration, and resection of intrarenal papillary tumors with the nephroscope. Gittes reported on a patient in whom the fulguration was carried out on a tumor located in the upper calix of the solitary kidney. It is widely reported that nephroscopy should never be attempted in a patient with a high-grade malignancy.

SURGICAL PROCEDURE

To proceed: expose the renal pelvis through a standard subcostal flank incision. Make the vertical posterior pyelotomy between two points on the surface; suture than with silk. Limit the incision to under 1 cm so that the irrigation water or air will not flow out from the pyelotomy; it should be just large enough to introduce the pyeloscope. Darken the operating room slightly for effective pyeloscopic examination. When air is to be used as the irrigation material for observation with the scope, use the suction tube to remove all the urine in the renal collection system. Introduce the pyeloscope through the incision; the air will be continually supplied with slight pressure through the passage channel of the scope in order to distend the pelviocaliceal system for detailed inspection. Should it be difficult to carry out the observation because of the air flowing through an overlarge pyelotomy incision, stabilize the inner air pressue in the pelvis by bringing the scope into close contact with the incised surface of the pelvic wall; this is done by adjusting the sutures. This maneuver is of the greatest advantage in fiberoptic pyeloscopy when using air as the irrigation material. With this procedure, the observation area is not disturbed even when there is slight bleeding inside, and it allows the inside of the renal collecting system to be examined dynamically *in vivo*.

First observe the interior of the collecting system, and then the basal area of the renal pelvis at its superior, middle, and inferior sections, to observe the condition of the mucosa and the ocation of a stone, a tumor, or a bleeding site.

Generally, it is more difficult to observe the inferior calix than the upper calix. When a lesion is located in the inferior caliceal area, it is sometimes necessary to release the kidney from the surrounding tisue to make the kidney mobile, so that the tip of the scope can be easily introduced into the inferior calix. However, in contrast to the procedure with the rigid scope, renal mobilization is usually unnecessary for fiberoptic examination, because all-around inspection is possible with the use of the tip deflection of the fiberscope.

When a stone is observed, note whether (1) the stone is simple or multiple, (2) the stone can be removed pyeloscopically because a part or all of the stone is obstructing the calix, an (3) the surface of the stone is rough or smooth. When a stone less than 1 cm is floating in the pelvis and the calix, the best procedure is to remove it with the grasping forceps endoscopically. When the flexible pyeloscope is used, introduce either the three-hook or two-hook stone grasping forceps, selected according to the size of the stone, through the forceps channel of the scope, and bring the grasping forceps under direct visualisation close to the stone. Open the hook to catch the store. What is important in removing the stone with the grasping forceps is to push forward the forceps shaft 1 or 1.5 cm more in the direction of the stone, simultaneously closing the hook to grasp the stone, since the hook will be withdrawn into the forceps shaft when it is in a closed position (Fig. 5).

Handling the grasping forceps correctly is crucial because sometimes the stone cannot be grasped tightly even when it is clearly in sight. There are some patients in whom the stone cannot be removed with the grasping forceps, even though the stone is partially hooked by the forceps, because the greatest part of the stone is molded into the calix and only a small part of the stone is observed endoscopically at the neck of the calix. Furthermore, in some patients, the stone is totally in the calix and cannot be hooked with the grasping forceps. In these cases, I recommend bringing the scope tip into contact with the stone, pushing it toward the renal capsule, and, using the illumination coming out through the scope as the guide light, making a nephrotomy on the luminating surface of the capsule and introducing the grasp forceps for blind lithotomy to remove the stone. This procedure will minimize damage to the renal parenchyma.

When a tumor is suspected, even though cytologic studies are negative, it is better to do pyeloscopy through the pyelotomy. If a lesion located in the interior of the collecting system is suspected of being a tumor, biopsy the area under conditions where the flow of the urine or irrigation fluid from the pelvis is held to the minimum so as to prevent tumor spillage. I recommend immediate diagnosis of the biopsy specimen in order to confirm if the lesion is a tumor, and, if so, its grade of malignancy.

COMPLICATIONS

Complications in this procedure do not exceed 2%, which is almost the same incidence as through a subcostal incision. The amount of bleeding is decreased compared with normal open surgery for stone removal, since there is only a small possibility of causing bleeding by blind manipulation of the grasping forceps for stone removal. No mortality has been reported.

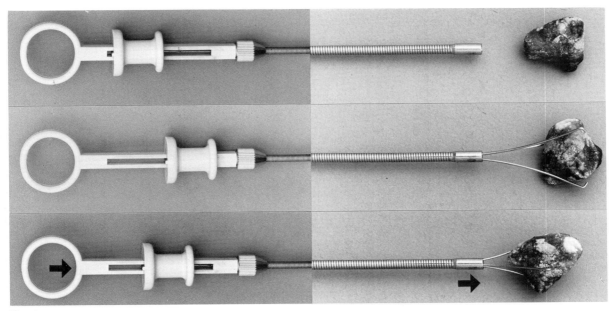

Fig. 5.

REFERENCES

1. Leadbetter WF: Instrumental visualization of the renal pelvis at operation as an aid to diagnosis. Presentation of a new instrument. J Urol 63:1006, 1950
2. Gittes RF: Operative nephroscopy. J Urol 116:148, 1976
3. Takayasu H, Aso Y, Takagi T, Go T: Clinical application of fiberoptic pyeloureteroscope. Urol Int 26:97, 1971
4. Stuart AE: Operative nephroscopy using bronchofiberscope. J Urol 111:9, 1974

5. Miki M, Inaba Y, Machida T: Operative nephroscopy with fiberoptic scope. J Urol 119:166, 1978
6. Tsuchida S, Sugawara H: A new flexible fibercystoscope for visualization of the bladder neck. J Urol 109:830, 1973
7. Tsuchida S: A new operative fiberpyeloscope. J Urol 117:643, 1977

ANNOTATED BIBLIOGRAPHY

Gittes RF: Operative nephroscopy. J Urol 116:148, 1976

The history of the improvements of the rigid-type operative nephroscope is reported. The author mentions that the present model of the right-angle operative nephroscope of rigid type was designed by W. F. Leadbetter in 1950. The details of the indications, technique, and results are reported for the nephroscope, which is presently available from the Storz Company. The indications for use of the nephroscope are in cases of renal calculi, renal hematuria, and renal papillary tumors.

Takayasu H, Aso Y, Takagi T, Go T: Clinical application of fiberoptic pyeloureteroscope. Urol Int 26:97, 1971

The authors have succeeded in passing the fiberscope up to the kidney transurethrally and taking photographs and movies of the renal pelvis and ureter. The fiberscope used for these purposes is 75 cm long and 2.5 cm in diameter and has both optical and illuminating systems. The optical system is an image-transmitting fiber bundle consisting of several thousand glass fibers. The authors succeeded in passing the fiberscope transurethrally with the use of a no. 24 operating cystoscope in 32 patients. Photographs and movies were taken in 14 and 12 patients, respectively.

The authors indicate that this fiberscope needs several improvements, namely: (1) glass fibers that are smaller in diameter, (2) better image resolution power of stronger quality, and (3) an improved steath around the insertion tube of the fiberscope that the operator can pass easily through the ureter. It is also desirable to include the irrigation in the sheath, since the irrigation is not provided in this fiberscope.

Miki M, Inaba Y, Machida T: Operative nephroscopy with fiberoptic scope. J Urol 119:166, 1976

The fiberoptic scope, originally designed for biliary tract operations, was used in 23 patients after pyelolithotomy to remove residual calculi for an examination of the renal pelvis and the ureter. At an open operation, the scope was introduced into the renal pelvis through the pyelotomy. The observation of the interior and the forceps manipulation were performed under water irrigation. Three kinds of forceps were used—those for stone removal, general biopsy, and coagulation. Of four cases of stones, three were successfully removed endoscopically, but one failed because a small calculus was trapped in the minor calix, there was not enough space for forceps manipulation, and bleeding occurred easily.

Overview: The Flexible Nephroscope and Endoscopic Surgery of the Kidney

INTRODUCTORY COMMENTS

J. Tate Mason

The advent of the flexible nephroscope has opened new vistas for the urologist. As of March 1980, the accessories and instrument so well described by Seigi Tsuchida have not been used outside of Japan. The author has noted his continued enthusiasm for the instrument.* The indications for the use of the instrument as proposed by Tsuchida appear valid, and his reported technique is most commendable. The complication rate is acceptable. Further evaluation and trials with his instrument should soon be forthcoming.

Extensive use of the flexible nephroscope (A.C.M.I. Regiflex Nephroscope) has been reported by McAninch, Bush and colleagues, and others who find it far superior to the rigid nephroscope.†,[1] Its major advantage is its ability to let the surgeon visualize all calices without trauma.† Visualization with the instrument is excellent, and the optics are very good. McAninch notes that "it offers the urologic surgeon the ability to fully inspect the intrarenal collective system and localize lesions."† Present grasping forceps go through the same opening as the irrigating fluid, making visualization somewhat difficult because of decreased irrigation flow, and the grasping forceps bear improvement; A.C.M.I. is currently working on this problem.

The advent of nephropyeloscopy and, shortly, uretopyeloscopy are clearly two of the important advances in urologic instrumentive technique.

ENDOSCOPIC SURGERY OF THE KIDNEY

Arthur D. Smith

The introduction of continuous real-time imaging methods such as fluoroscopy has made it possible to use the percutaneous nephrostomy tract in the same manner that urologists have long used the urethra, that is, as a route for performing many diagnostic and therapeutic procedures without open operation. The new field this has created, which has been named endourology, is already the subject of two published books.[2,3,4]

---

* Personal communication.
† Personal communication.

One of the greatest achievements of this new field is the nonoperative removal of most kidney, and many ureteral, calculi. Many methods are available, some of which are as simple as flushing and others of which require complex and costly equipment. I have reviewed these methods elsewhere.[5,6]

At present, it appears that two methods are going to dominate this approach to stones, which Dr. Ralph Clayman calls "nephrostolithotomy." The first is nephroscopy.[7] Many renal pelvic stones can be removed with forceps or the three-pronged Storz grasper by way of a rigid instrument such as the McCarthy panendoscope. Stones in the calices are usually more easily reached with one of the new flexible nephroscopes, such as that described by Dr. Tsuchida, that may also be used to retrieve some urethral stones. An additional advantage of nephroscopy is the opportunity it provides for examining the collecting system under direct vision. Sometimes, this will reveal stone fragments not visible by tomography or, alternatively, show that small calcifications not visible radiographically are in fact not stones but rather Randall's plaques.

The other type of method that seems likely to dominate the field of nephrostolithotomy is stone destruction. This can be done either ultrasonically or electrohydraulically, and makes it possible to remove even branched and staghorn stones.[8,9]

As urologists began removing renal stones percutaneously, it was inevitable that they would encounter calculi trapped in calices or diverticula, or impacted at the ureteropelvic junction. Clayman and associates have fashioned a cutting instrument from a small wire within a whistle-tip catheter, which is passed through a nephroscope.[10] Use of this method requires a thorough knowledge of renal arterial anatomy and great skill, and is thus not recommended for the beginning nephrostolithotomist.

Endourologic procedures on the kidney require new skills on the urologist's part, including the ability to visualize the kidney in three dimensions from the two-dimensional images of the radiographs.[11] At the same time, it offers us marvelous opportunities to provide care for our stone patients while causing them less pain and disability, and at generally lower cost than is possible with traditional methods of stone removal. In addition, for some patients, such as those in poor condition or those who have undergone several previous stone operations, endourology promises stone removal that might otherwise be difficult or impossible.

REFERENCES

1. Bush N, Goldberg E, Javadpour N, Chakrobortty H, Morelli F: Chicago Med School Q 30:1, 1970

2. Smith AD, Lange PH, Fraley EE: Letter to the editor: Percutaneous nephrostomy: New challenges and opportunities in endo-urology. J Urol, 121: 382, 1979

3. Smith AD (ed): Symposium on endourology. Urol Clin North Am 9(1): 1–196, 1982

4. Wickham JEA, Miller RA: Percutaneous Renal Surgery. Edinburgh, Churchill Livingstone, 1983

5. Smith AD, Clayman R, Castaneda-Zuniga WR et al: The endourological management of renal stones. Surg Rounds 6(3(:20–29, 1983

6. Smith AD, Lee WJ: Percutaneous stone-removal procedures including irrigation. Urol Clin North Am (in press)

7. Clayman RV, Miller RP, Reinke DB et al: Nephroscopy: Advances and adjuncts. Urol Clin North Am 9:51–60, 1982

8. Alken P: Percutaneous ultrasonic destruction of renal calculi. Urol Clin North Am 9:145–151, 1982

9. Clayman RV, Surya V, Miller RP et al: Percutaneous nephrolithotomy: An approach to branched and staghorn renal calculi. JAMA (in press)

10. Clayman RV, Hunter DH, Surya V: Percutaneous intrarenal electrosurgery. (submitted)

11. Kaye KW: Renal anatomy for endourologic stone removal. J Urol (in press)

PART THIRTEEN

SURGICAL TREATMENT OF CARCINOMA OF THE RENAL PELVIS AND URETER

26

CONSERVATION OF THE KIDNEY IN OPERATIONS FOR TUMOURS OF THE RENAL PELVIS AND CALYCES: A REPORT OF 26 CASES[1]

Sava D. Petković

Professor of Urology, Urological Clinic, Medical Faculty, University of Belgrade, Yugoslavia

British Journal of Urology (1972), 44, 1–8

In the last 20 years we have had the unpleasant advantage of being able to observe a large number of cases of tumours of the renal pelvis and ureter.

Table 1 shows the material observed in the Urological Clinic compared with tumours of the renal parenchyma.

The increase and frequency of the appearance of the kidney pelvis and ureteral tumours became particularly obvious about 1953. The number of cases of these tumours has increased since then and they now appear more frequently than tumours of the renal parenchyma. From personal communications (Puigvert, Barcelona; Nagel, Berlin; Alkin, Hamburg; and Bracci, Rome), it seems that kidney pelvis and ureteral tumours have been appearing in the last 2 decades more frequently all over the Continent.

Whilst the relative incidence of kidney pelvis tu-mours to those of the parenchyma is generally around 8 percent (7 percent Albarran, 1903; 9 percent Riches, 1951), the incidence in the Belgrade Urological Clinic is 42 percent. From 1961 to 1970 the incidence of kidney pelvis tumours exceeded that of the renal parenchyma tumours (Table 2).

From an inquiry among our colleagues in Yugoslavia we have succeeded in collecting for our statistics almost all the cases observed in the country in the last 20 years. To the end of 1970 the number of cases totalled 450 cases of renal pelvis tumours (Belgrade Urological Clinical, 220) and 257 cases of ureteral tumours (Belgrade Urological Clinic, 116). As it seemed that a particular frequency of these tumours corresponded to certain regions of Yugoslavia we plotted the geographical distribution of all the 707 cases according to the patient's usual place of residence.

Some villages along particular rivers (Sava, Drina, Kolubara, Morava, Mlava) have 1 case of kidney pelvis

---

[1] Read at the Twenty-seventh Annual Meeting of the British Association of Urological Surgeons in London, June 1971.

TABLE 1

Period	Kidney Parenchyma	Kidney Pelvis	Ureter
1921–1943	26	3	2
1944–1952	62	4	9
1953–1960	89	72	27
1961–1970	116	142	78
	293	221	116

TABLE 2

Authors	Tumours of Kidney Pelvis	Tumours of Kidney Parenchyma	%
Albarran-Imbert (1903)	42	505	7.0
Hunt (1927)	23	318	7.0
Bell (autopsies, 1946)	7	149	4.5
Caulc (collective, 1937)	. . .	1,785	8.5
Riches (collective, 1951)	189	1,935	9.0
Petković (1970)	220	293	42.0

TABLE 3

	Population	Tumour Kidney Pelvis and Ureter	Incidence
Cvetovac	1,338	7	1/200
Petka	943	6	1/157
Sopići	1,927	9	1/222
Belgrade	1,000,000	46	1/22,000
Novi Sad	180,000	4	1/45,000
Subotica	80,000	2	1/40,000

TABLE 4

Tumours	Total	With Renal Insufficiency	From Endemic Nephropathy Regions	Other Regions
Kidney pelvis	220	98 (45%)	54:98 = 54%	44:121 = 36%
Ureter	116	56 (48%)	27:43 = 63%	29: 73 = 40%

tumour per 200 inhabitants (the village Cvetovac) or even 1 per 157 (the village Petka), while in towns only 1 case of this tumour is seen per 22,000 (Belgrade) or even 45,000 (Novi Sad) inhabitants, as Table 3 clearly shows.

In the same regions and villages we have noticed the appearance of a special chronic nephropathy called endemic nephropathy or "Balkan Nephropathy". This nephropathy has been the subject of particular researches; we are here concerned only with its correlation with our tumour cases. A large number of our patients with tumours show symptoms of this nephropathy, by the gradual development of renal insufficiency, only mild proteinuria and a progressive and inevitable lethal course, but without hypertension.

We are now inclined to consider that this is caused by a toxic agent in the particular regions from the food or water.

There is, however, an increase in the number of these tumours in other regions as well—much more than is observed with other tumours. The kidney pelvis tumours in those other regions are also accompanied by renal insufficiency, though with a lower incidence than in those cases in the regions where nephropathy is endemic.

A considerable number of our cases of renal pelvis tumours and ureteral tumours are bilateral. In our series of 336 tumours, 34 (10 percent) were bilateral.

The first important factor making conservation of the kidney essential was the renal insufficiency in the high percentage of cases as shown in Table 4.

To our knowledge no other authors report such a high percentage of renal insufficiency in cases of these tumours; only Bloom and his collaborators (1970) reported, "Blood urea nitrogen was elevated in 42%", which was the result of observations of 102 cases of tumours seen in 13 hospitals. This renal insufficiency necessarily modifies our indications for nephrectomy in cases of kidney pelvis and ureteral tumours.

The factors against nephrectomy are:
1. The possibility (10 percent) of the development of a tumour on the other side.
2. Development of renal insufficiency in about 45 percent of cases, more frequently in cases with the endemic nephropathy, less frequently in cases of tumours from other regions.
3. The large number in our series of cases of small comparatively benign tumours with a narrow pedicle, without deep infiltration.
4. It is true that conservation of the kidney carries the risk of a recurrence of the tumour at the same site or of the ureters or of the bladder. But we fear a recurrence of the tumour on the other side as much as one in the bladder if the patient's expectation of life is long.

Our indications for the conservative procedures in 26 operations were:

Absolute: Renal insufficiency (17)
Solitary kidney (5)
Bilateral tumours (7)
Relative: Small tumour with a narrow pedicle.

Ferris and Daut (1948) were the first—in 1941—to perform a renal conserving operation in a case of a renal pelvis tumour and Vest (1945) was the first to perform such an operation in a case of a ureteral tumour. In 1957 we reported conservation of the kidney in 5 cases of ureteral tumours. Küss and Quenu (1959) were decidely against a systemic application of nephrectomy to cases of small tumours of the renal pelvis or of the ureter.

Our first conserving operation in a case of a kidney pelvis tumour was in 1962; since then we have performed similar operations in 26 cases. The results can be seen in Table 5.

The length of survival after operation is shown in Table 6.

In the 5 cases of solitary kidneys, the other kidney had been previously removed on account of kidney pelvis or ureteral tumours. In the 17 cases with renal insufficiency before operation this was the absolute indication for the conservation. A considerable number of the tumours had no deep infiltration into the wall of the kidney pelvis and had a narrow pedicle. If the tumour covers a large part of the kidney pelvis or is infiltrating, conservation is either impossible or at least inadvisable.

The results in cases of the kidney pelvis tumours treated by nephrectomy compared with cases treated by total nephro-ureterectomy (all before 1964) are shown in Table 7.

If to the number of living patients we add the number of those who died more than 5 years after operation, the percentage survival over 5 years is 48 percent.

Serious cases where conservation was essential are illustrated by the following:

Case 3. S. E., female, age 53. Left nephrectomy in 1963 for a severe hæmorrhage (probably from tumour) in a country hospital. On 7th November 1966 a right kidney pelvis tumour and 2 small tumours of the upper part of the ureter were excised. The blood urea was normal until 1970, but now (1971) the blood urea is about 120 mg per 100 ml (Fig. 1).

Case 4. L. A., female, age 43. Right nephrectomy on 11th March 1964 for a carcinoma of the renal pelvis. On 8th July 1964 lower pole of the left kidney was resected for papillary carcinoma. Since 1970 the patient has been living with a blood urea of about 150 mg per 100 ml but in good general health.

Case 5. K. P., female, age 49. In 1962 left nephrectomy for kidney pelvis tumour. The right superior calyx was resected on 15th May 1964 for papillary carcinoma. She was still alive in April 1971 with a blood urea of 120 mg per 100 ml (Fig. 2).

Operative Mortality. There has been no operative mortality in spite of 5 of the operations being on the solitary kidney.

Late Mortality. Out of 26 patients, 4 died (2 within 1 year after operation and 2 after 2 years). The cause of death was largely renal insufficiency, but not metastases.

TABLE 5

(a)	Satisfactory results (function maintained without relapse, without uræmia)	15
(b)	Without relapse but with uræmia	4
(c)	Secondary nephrectomy (unsatisfactory results)	3
(d)	Died (2 in less than a year after the operation and 2 after 2 years)	4

TABLE 6

(a)	Survived over 5 years (3 with uræmia)	5
(b)	Survived 4–5 years	3
(c)	Survived 2–4 years	5
(d)	Survived over 1 year	4
(e)	Recent operation	2
(f)	Survived with secondary nephrectomy	3
(g)	Died	4

TABLE 7

Operation	Total	Dead (after 5 years)	Alive
Nephro-ureterectomy	47	32 (8)	15 (32%)
Nephrectomy	72	49 (7)	23 (32%)

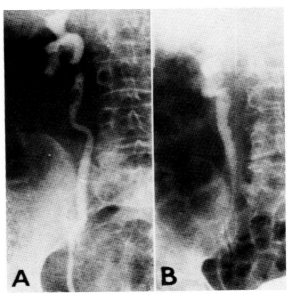

Fig. 1. Case 3. S. E. (A) Pre-operative (1965): tumour in kidney pelvis and ureter of a solitary kidney. (B) Post-operative follow-up April 1971: mild uraemia without recurrence of growth.

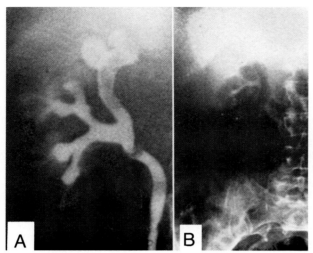

Fig. 2. Case 5. P. K. (*A*) Pre-operative: tumour in upper calyx of right solitary kidney 1964. (*B*) Post-operative follow-up April 1971: blood urea 62 mg per 100 ml. No recurrence.

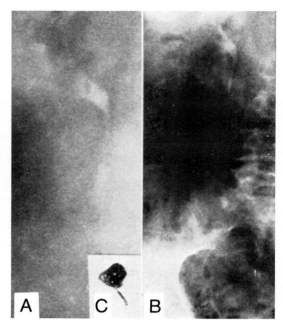

Fig. 4. Case 21. E. V. (*A*) Pre-operative: defect in middle of kidney pelvis 1968. (*B*) Post-operative follow-up April 1971: good kidney function. (*C*) Extirpated tumour.

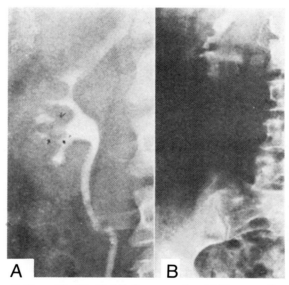

Fig. 3. Case 23. Dj. C. (*A*) Pre-operative 1969: a small pedunculated tumour in middle calyx of right kidney. (*B*) Post-operative follow-up in June 1971: normal blood urea. Left nephrectomy for atrophic kidney after resection of kidney pelvis for a tumour in June 1969.

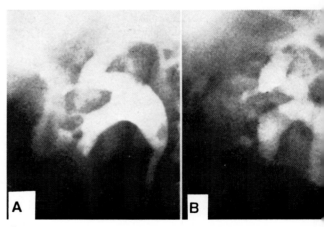

Fig. 5. Case 18. A. S. (*A*) Pre-operative: two small tumours in the right kidney pelvis 1967 (a large tumour was present in the left kidney for which nephrectomy was performed in 1968). (*B*) Post-operative follow-up April 1971: good kidney function.

In some cases in addition there might have been a small local recurrence.

It is noteworthy that in the series of 177 nephrectomies renal insufficiency was the cause of death as often as metastases.

Operative Technique. This is basically quite simple but a good and wide exposure is necessary. The access to the tumour can be:

1. By pyelotomy.

2. By nephrotomy and wide splitting of the calyx.

3. By partial nephrectomy required where the tumour involves a calyx or if early infiltration is suspected.

The exposure must provide a good view for excision of the base of the tumour. The pedicle must not be pulled off unless its base is visible; adequate access through the kidney pelvis alone is impossible if the base of the tumour lies deep in the calyx.

Throughout operation the neighbouring tissues are covered by gauze soaked in a disinfectant (Cetavlon 2 percent solution) to protect them from implantation by tumour cells. There were no recurrences in the perirenal tissue after these procedures.

SUMMARY

There is a vast number of kidney pelvis and ureteral tumours in Yugoslavia. They arise particularly frequently in the regions where an epidemic nephropathy occurs and develop in association with this which leads to slowly progressive renal insufficiency. In about 40 percent of the tumours in our series there is renal insufficiency. In about 10 percent of cases the tumours are bilateral. A considerable proportion of the cases have small tumours on narrow pedicles. These were considered decisive reasons for operations conserving the kidney.

In 26 cases of tumours of the renal pelvis or of the calyx only the tumours were removed, the kidney being conserved.

The results are encouraging.

REFERENCES

ALBARRAN, J. and IMBERT, L. (1903). "Les Tumeurs du Rein". Paris: Masson.

BELL, E. T. (1946). "Diseases of the Kidney." London: Kimpton.

BLOOM, N. A., VIDANE, R. A. and LYTON, B. (1970). Primary carcinoma of ureter: report of 102 new cases. J Urol 103:590–598.

CAULC, J. R. (1937). Tumours of the renal pelvis and ureter. Ann Surg 106:68–84.

FERRIS, D. O., and DAUT, R. V. (1948). Epithelioma of the pelvis of a solitary kidney treated by electrocoagulation. J Urol 59:577–579.

KÜSS, R., and QUENU, L. (1959). Chirurgie conservatrice chez les tumeurs des voies excrétrices du rein. J Urol Neph 65:1–10.

PETKOVIĆ, S. (1970). Nierenbecken and Harnleitertumoren. Actuelle Urologie 1:265–273.

PETKOVIĆ, S., and MUTAVDŽIĆ, M. (1970). Les interventions sur le rein unique portant la tumeur du bassinet ou de l'uretère. Urologie Treviso 37:252–260.

PETKOVIĆ, S., MUTAVDŽIÉ, M. PETRONIĆ, V, and MARKOVIĆ, V. (1968). Geographical distribution of cancer of urothelium in Yugoslavia. Urologia Treviso 35:425–433.

PETKOVIĆ, S., TOMIĆ, M., and MUTAVDŽIĆ, M. (1966). Quelques considerations sur l'étiologie et al clinique du cancer du bassinet. J Urol Néph 72:429–444.

RICHES, SIR ERIC (1964). "Tumours of the Kidney and Ureter." Edinburgh: Livingstone.

VEST, S. A. (1945). Conservative surgery in certain benign tumours of the ureter. J Urol 53:97–122.

DISCUSSION

Sir Eric Riches (London) could not recall any bilateral cases in the B.A.U.S. series of 1951. In Macalpine's series there was only one case and that was in a dye worker. In his own series of 63 cases (43 males, 20 females) there were no bilateral cases but in 15 the kidney, ureter and bladder were affected. He therefore preferred radical removal of the kidney and ureter with part of the bladder.

He thought that Dr Petkovic had done a valuable service in drawing attention to the endemic nephropathy of the Balkans; it appeared to a be a precursor of tumours of the renal pelvis and ureter with which we were unfamiliar.

He also emphasized the need for investigation of the upper urinary tract in all cases of papillary tumour of the bladder.

Commentary: Techniques of Conservative Surgery

Sava D. Petković

In the last 30 years an increase in the frequency of renal, pelvic, and ureteral tumors has been noted. In contrast to the early contributions of Swift–Jolly (337 cases in the literature of renal pelvic tumors) and Scott (182 cases in the literature of ureteral tumors), there are papers dealing with 67 personal cases of renal pelvic tumors (Dufour), 102 cases of ureteral tumors (Bloom and associates), and 40 cases of ureteral tumors (McIntare).[1–3]

The pathology of these tumors probably did not change, but earlier diagnostic investigations and methods of management of very small tumors encouraged the authors to attempt conservation of the kidney by local treatment. It is not acceptable to generalize in terms of one's preference for radical operation or for conservative treatment of these tumors, but one should individualize the choice of treatment for each patient.

The first conservative operation on the kidney for renal pelvic carcinoma was performed by Ferris and Daut in 1948, and the first conservative operation for a case of ureteral tumor was done by Vest in 1945.[4] In 1958, Kuss, in Paris, succeeded in conserving the kidney in some cases of renal pelvic and ureteral tumors, and I was able to report on 12 personal cases at the 12th Congress of International Society of Urology (Rio de Janeiro, 1961).

I was obliged to consider conservation of the kidney in my series for three principal reasons: (1) a high percentage of renal insufficiency (see the preceding article on the importance of endemic nephropathy in the etiology of the tumors), (2) many very small, mostly pedunculated tumors, and (3) a high percentage (10%) of bilaterality of tumors.

INDICATIONS

The absolute indications for attempting conservation of the kidney are (1) the solitary kidney, (2) the bilaterality of the tumor (attempt conservation of the kidney on at least one side), and (3) renal insufficiency. The factors one must consider in deciding on conservative treatment are (1) the presence of the tumor on a narrow base or on a small pedicle, (2) large exophytic tumors with no infiltrating tendency, and (3) no infiltration or minimal infiltration if the tumor is not on such a small base.

Nevertheless, each patient must be considered individually, and the possibility of reconstructive surgery of the pelvis and ureter must also be taken into account. For example, tumor position could be a decisive factor for or against conservative surgery. If a renal pelvic tumor occupies a large part of the intrahilar pelvis, reconstructive surgery is probably not possible.

OPERATIVE TECHNIQUE

Renal Pelvic Tumors. *Kidney Polar Resection.* To perform a kidney polar resection, proceed as follows: make a large lumbotomy. Liberate the kidney and the renal vascular pedicle. Temporarily clamp the renal pedicle with soft clamps (note the time!). Incise the renal fibrous capsule on the upper or lower poles, or even the middle part of the kidneys, and denude the kidney by peeling away the renal capsule as much as possible in order to allow for necessary resection.

If I am sure of my diagnosis at this point, which is very frequently the case, I resect part of the kidney without opening the calix and remove it *en bloc* with the tumor. If I must confirm the diagnosis of a tumor of the calix, I can open the parenchyma after denuding the capsule by incising the calix containing the tumor. By opening the kidney and the calix, I can see and confirm the diagnosis that the tumor is amenable

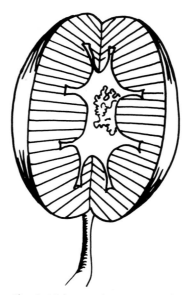

Fig. 6. Kidney polar resection for caliceal carcinoma. The renal capsule is peeled back. Renal tissue is opened, and caliceal tumor is visible. Either polar resection or tumor excision is chosen.

for polar resection (or for local resection). Make the opening under strict protection of the operative field to prevent tumor implantation. In the past, this was considered forbidden. This protection can be accomplished with many sponge gauzes soaked in an antiseptic solution (*e.g.*, 0.5% Asepsol). Now, explore the base of the tumor and the infiltration, if it is present. Thereafter, resect the kidney pole (or middle part) completely with the base of the tumor.

Obtain hemostasis by clamping the intrarenal vessels separately. The calix may be sutured, but this is not obligatory. Both kidney edges and the cut ends of the calices should be well coapted. Put the ends of the conserved renal capsule back in place on the surface and suture them. Release the renal pedicle clamps. Wash the whole field with antiseptic solution. Place a small drain and reconstruct the lumbotomy incision.

I employ kidney polar resection for those caliceal tumors with small bases and little or no parenchymal infiltration.

Resection of the Calix With Tumor or Local Excision. To perform a resection of the calix with tumor or local excision, follow the preparatory steps described above. Make a transverse incision of the kidney parenchyma, viewing the calix with the tumor (Fig. 6). Open the calix and inspect the tumor. The tumor must have a very narrow base or be pedunculated. Resect a small part of the caliceal wall or of the very narrow pedicle, and excise the tumor. A small defect of the mucosa after the excision of the tumorous base is unimportant. Finally, lavage the kidney and the operative field with antiseptic solution, and close the kidney with a transverse incision (Fig. 7). No nephrostomy is employed; lavage the renal pelvis with antiseptic solution through needle puncture. Lavage the bladder with a urethral catheter.

Fig. 7. Situation after closing the kidney.

There must be a small base or a pedunculated tumor if one is to use this technique. A view of the base is necessary; ensure that the circumcision of the base or section of the pedicle has completely removed the tumorous tissue.

Segmental Resection of the Renal Pelvis. In segmental resection of the renal pelvis, perform the large lumobotomy and isolate the kidney as described above. It is not necessary to clamp the renal pedicle, but it is absolutely necessary to have a good view of the renal pelvis by sufficiently freeing it. If the tumor is expanding toward the calix, prepare access to the calix by the technique of Gil–Vernet or Aboulker by an extended pyelotomy. Create exposure to the end of the calix, lower, middle or upper, by raising the edges of the renal parenchyma protruding over the renal pelvis; in this way, it is possible to enlarge the exposure greatly. If it is impossible to have a free border of the tumor by this exposure, abandon the conservative operation or perform a hilar nephrotomy. *Never* tear the tumor in order to root out the pedicle without viewing the base deep in the calix, since relapse will inevitably follow.

The *hilar nephrotomy* is easier and is best done in the lower segment toward the lower calix, in the middle of the kidney from the renal pelvis down along the lower calix, because in this part one will have to cut only small renal vessels. In the middle of the kidney, or alongside the upper calix, cut the great vessels.

After wide exposure of the renal pelvis, gently palpate the tumor to see if the tumor has no infiltration and whether it is soft or hard and to determine the vascularization of the tumor and its surroundings. If the vascularization is extensive, consider the progression of the malignancy, which places the use of a conservative operation in question.

Protect the operative field by sponge gauzes soaked in antiseptic solution and placed around the future opening of the pelvis in multiple layers; change them during manipulation of the tumor.

Open the pelvis a little to the side of the base of the tumor and not in the base itself. Evacuate the blood clots, and lavage the renal pelvis with antiseptic solution. The exposure must be large enough to see the tumor clearly. Excise the base of the tumor and a small quantity of normal mucosa. Inspect and lavage the renal pelvis. Perform the nephrotomy several times if the resection is large.

Local Excision of Renal Pelvis Tumor Through Pyelotomy. Local excision of the renal pelvis tumor through pyelotomy employs resection of the tumor by simple pedicle cutting instead of the resection (circumcision of the base of the tumor) previously described. Perform lumbotomy, isolate the kidney and renal pelvis, and protect the operative field as described above. As determined by palpation, movable, soft, and small tumors are suitable for this operation. Tumors with a hard base are unsuitable. After opening the pelvis on the side of the tumor, aspirate blood clots (Fig. 8). Grasp the tumor and gently pull it with soft forceps in order to see and manipulate the pedicle (Fig. 9). Cut the pedicle, and, if there is some hemorrhage, use simple electrocauterization or a very fine catgut suture on the edges. Check to exclude an additional tumor. Perform this technique only on very pedunculated tumors.

Ureteral Tumors. *Local Excision of Ureteral Tumor Through Ureterotomy.* In local excision of a ureteral tumor through ureterotomy, employ a lumbotomy at the level of the ureteral tumor or midlower abdominal incision. Free the ureter by general manipulation, and protect the operative field as described above. After opening the ureter by a 2-cm to 3-cm longitudinal ureteral incision, the proliferative ureteral tumor is immediately seen protruding through the incision. Gently

Fig. 8. Opening of the renal pelvis and demonstration of a small tumor in it. The retractor pushes aside the protruding parenchyma of the kidney in order to expose widely the renal pelvis.

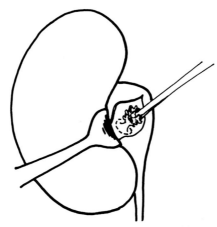

Fig. 9. The tumor is grasped with special forceps, and the pedicle is demonstrated before excision.

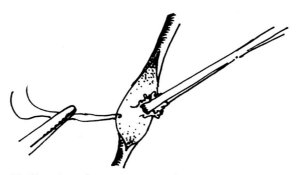

Fig. 10. Situation after ureterotomy for ureteral tumor. Local ureteral dilatation facilitates resection of the tumor base.

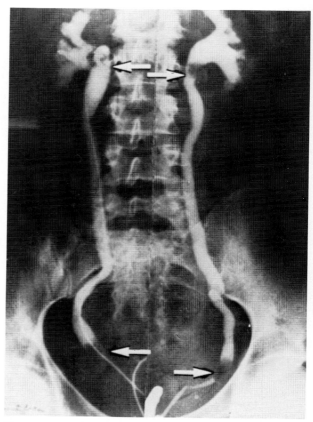

Fig. 11. Patient with four tumors of both ureters. The first operation (December 1959) included ureterotomy and upper left excision of tumor by left lumbotomy. On the same day a medial suprapubic incision was performed with excision of the left lower tumor through a ureterotomy and resection of the lower part of the right ureter and ureterovesical reimplantation. The second operation (February 1960) included excision of right subpyelic tumor through the ureterotomy. There was subsequent slight renal failure (endemic nephropathy).

grasp the tumor with soft clamps to see the pedicle. Cut the pedicle, and remove the tumor. Suture the opening of the ureter. Perform this technique only on very small and very pedunculated ureteral tumors (Fig. 10).

Resection of Ureteral Tumor With Small Base. Resecting a ureteral tumor with a small base is a little different. The surgeon is obliged to resect the base because the tumor is beginning to have a moderately large base without apparent infiltration. The resection can be accomplished only if too much circumferential ureteral wall is not involved with tumor. If that is the case, change the type of operation and perform resection of the whole circumference of the ureter—segmental resection of the ureter (Figs. 11 and 12).

To proceed: after opening the ureter (incision and protection are described above), gently grasp the tumor and pull it away to see the base. Perform local circumcision around the small base of the tumor and resect the mucosa or the entire wall of the ureter for a limited extent. Close the ureter with one or two sutures.

Segmental Resection of the Ureter. Segmental resection of the ureter involves excision of a segment of the whole circumference of the ureter. Perform lumbotomy or midabdominal incision for very low tumors, and protect the operative field as described above. To proceed: free the ureter extensively while preserving the longitudinal vascularization. Some inflammatory adhesions might be present. If there are extensive adhesions, suspect neoplastic infiltration around the ureter. In this case, it would be better to perform a radical nephroureterectomy and a very large local excision. If I am absolutely obliged to conserve the kidney, I perform a large local excision of the tissue around the tumor. Cutting the ureter some 1 cm to 2 cm above and the same below, remove the ureter *en bloc* with the tumor.

The radical nature of the technique is important in

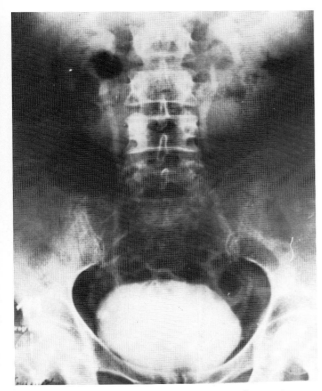

Fig. 12. Same patient as in Fig. 11, 7 years later. The patient was last seen in 1978 in good health but excretory urograms show the slow evolution of endemic nephropathy and renal failure.

considering extensive transverse excision of tissue due to lymphatic spread rather than extensive vertical incision of the tissue. Further mobilize the ureter and perform an oval end-to-end ureteroureterostomy. Nephrostomy is necessary if the lumen of the ureter is very narrow. if, on the contrary, there is a large ureteral lumen at the level of the anastomosis, omit the nephrostomy. No stent is used.

Segmental Distal Resection of Ureter and Ureterovesical Reimplantation. Segmental distal resection of the ureter and ureterovesical implantation is always preferable to ureteroureterostomy, and, if there is a ureteral tumor in the distal 6 cm of the ureter, it would be preferable to perform, after the ureteral resection and together with circumcision of the ureteral orifice through a cystostomy, a ureterovesical reimplantation or even a Boari procedure.

RESULTS

Renal Pelvic Carcinoma. In 1974 I reviewed my results with 26 patients with renal pelvic carcinoma treated with conservative surgery with a minimum of 3 years of follow-up study. After the operation, 13 patients (50%) survived for more than 5 years. Of these patients, 2 died between 5 and 10 years postoperatively and 3 died after 10 years. Counting only the patients followed for more than 5 years, there are 16 patients, 13 of whom survived more than 5 years (81%). However, 1 patient in this group required a secondary nephrectomy. Therefore, this is a 74% survival rate of more than 5 years in patients treated with conservative surgery.

After conservative surgery, 10 patients lived from 3 to 5 years, 3 of them in excellent health. In 1974, all 10 patients were alive. Five secondary nephrectomies were required for loss of kidney function, mostly without relapse of the tumor.

Ureteral Carcinoma. I operated on 49 patients before 1971, providing a follow-up study of a minimum of 3 years. Thirty patients of 49 were alive in 1974 (61%). Eight patients died after 5 years. Thirty one patients were operated on before 5 or more years had elapsed. There are now 18 patients alive (60%) 5 or more years. Of the 19 patients who died, 16 died of uremia and only 3 died of a relapse of the tumor. I fear uremia much more than a relapse, and that is the principal reason for my use of conservative surgery.

REFERENCES

1. Swift JJ: Tumors of the pelvis and ureter. Br J Urol 5:327, 1933
2. Scott WW: Primary carcinoma of the ureter. Surg Gynecol Obstet 58:215, 1934
3. Bloom NA, Vidone R, Lytton B: Primary carcinoma of the ureter. J Urol 105:590, 1970

4. Vest SA: Conservative surgery in certain benign tumors of the ureter. J Urol 45:97, 1945

ANNOTATED BIBLIOGRAPHY

Angervall I, Bengston U, Zetterlund CG: Renal pelvic carcinoma in a Swedish district with abuse of a phenacetin containing drug. Br J Urol 41:401, 1969

The abusers of analgesics in Sweden suffered from renal pelvic tumors in a high proportion, and the frequency of sex distribution corresponded to the frequency of male and female abusers. No other kind of nephropathy (88 cases) was followed by renal pelvic tumors.

Bloom NA, Vidone RA, Lytton B: Primary carcinoma of the ureter, a report of 102 cases. J Urol 105:590, 1970

The authors note the increase in frequency of ureteral tumors in the past 30 years. They noted in 42% of patients the elevation of blood urea nitrogen. The kidney was not visualized in 47% on intravenous pyelogram (IVP). The normal function on IVP certifies in 84% a stage I lesion, but only 11% of the group having a stage III lesion had visualization of the kidney. Sixty of 102 patients underwent a total nephroureterectomy, and 12 had kidney-conserving procedures. Recurrence occured in 20%. The overall 5-year survival rate was 42% and was influenced primarily by the tumors invasiveness and degree of anaplasia. The prognosis was better than previously suggested.

Gittes RF: Tumors of the Ureter and Renal Pelvis: In Campbell's Urology, 4th ed, p 1010. Philadelphia, W B Saunders, 1979

The etiologic problem with Balkan (endemic) nephropathy and with analgesic nephropathy are discussed, as well as the conserving, segmental surgery.

Petković SD: A plea for conservative operation for ureteral tumors. J Urol 107:220, 1972

The author performed 51 radical and 44 conservative operations in 100 cases of ureteral tumors seen in the Urological Clinic of Belgrade and advocates the conserving surgery under strict conditions. Twenty-two patients survived 5 years (6 of 22 patients were dead after 5 years); 17 survived from a total of 25 patients followed over 5 years (68%).

Petković SD: Epidemiology and treatment of renal pelvic and ureteral tumors. J Urol 114:858, 1975

The review of these tumors in Yugoslavia and their relation to endemic (Balkan) nephropathy in a series of 972 tumors (416 from the Urological Clinic) is discussed in this paper. The renal insufficiency was present in 63% of cases originating from regions of endemic nephropathies and in 40% from outside. The article presents a series of 188 patients operated on by nephrectomy and 75 patients operated on with kidney conservation (49 ureteral and 26 renal pelvic tumors). In patients undergoing conserving operations, the author fears renal insufficiency more than local relapse. The results of conserving operations are quite favorable, but strict indications for such operation were followed.

Petković SD: Treatment of bilateral renal pelvis and ureteral tumors. Eur Urol 4:397, 1978

From a series of 308 renal pelvic and 187 ureteral tumors seen in the Urological Clinic of Belgrade, 45 patients (some 9%) were bilateral, requiring the author to practice a conserving operation at least on one side. This operation was performed in 28 patients (8, both sides, and 20, one side). Nineteen patients survived more than 5 years, and 10 patients survived more than 10 years. Later uremia caused death in 29 of 45 patients.

Strauss MB,, Welt LG: Diseases of the Kidney, pp 678–679, 1265–1266. Boston, Little, Brown & Co, 1971

The most important signs of Balkan (endemic) nephropathy are presented.

27

TECHNIQUE OF NEPHROURETERECTOMY WITH REGIONAL LYMPH NODE DISSECTION

Donald G. Skinner, M.D., F.A.C.S.

From the Department of Surgery, Division of Urology, University of California School of Medicine, Los Angeles, California.

The Craft of Urologic Surgery
Donald G. Skinner, M.D., *Consulting Editor*
Gwynne M. Gloege, *Art Editor*

Nephroureterectomy is generally the procedure of choice in the management of epithelial tumors of the renal pelvis or ureter. The ideal surgical treatment for these tumors involves the removal of Gerota's fascia with its contents intact, together with early ligation of the renal artery and vein, and complete removal of the ureter, including the cuff of bladder surrounding the ureteral orifice. Regional retroperitoneal lymph node dissection is routinely performed as part of this procedure even though there are no solid data supporting its efficacy in improving survival.

Grabstald[4] has reported a 75 percent incidence of regional lymph node involvement in patients with invasive primary renal pelvic carcinoma; Williams and Mitchell[9] noted a five year survival rate of 48 percent for patients with superficial tumors, and a rate of only 11 percent for those with invasive disease, many of whom undoubtedly had associated regional node involve-ment. Although long term survival has not been reported for patients with transitional cell carcinoma of the renal pelvis or ureter metastatis to regional nodes, few centers have performed regional node dissection in conjunction with nephroureterectomy. Moreover, recent experience with locally metastatic transitional cell carcinoma of the bladder suggests that it should be possible to salvage some patients who have a few positive nodes.[2] In our hands, the lymph node dissection has not increased morbidity or operative mortality.

My own preference is the thoracoabdominal approach to radical nephroureterectomy. This technique was originally described by Sweet[8] for the surgical management of lower esophageal or high gastric carcinoma. Under the influence of Leadbetter, as reported by Cooper and associates,[1] this approach has been modified and is the one I now use almost exclusively for the surgical resection of primary renal parenchymal tumors

343

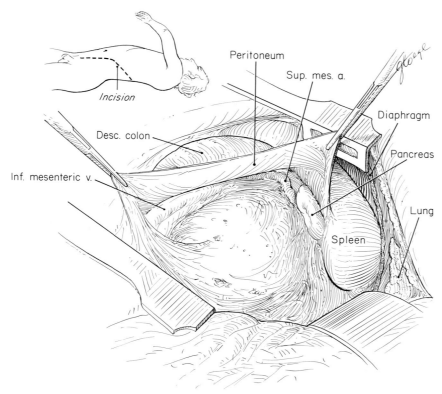

Fig. 1

and in the resection of all retroperitoneal tumors, especially large metastatic tumors of testicular origin.[6]

TECHNIQUE

Proper positioning of the patient is extremely important; salient features of the technique include positioning the patient as close to the ipsilateral edge of the operating table as possible. The pelvis should be nearly supine, with the shoulders angled about 40 degrees. A pad placed under the contralateral or ''down'' axilla serves to prevent any trauma to the brachial plexus.

The incision is begun at the midaxillary line over the eighth, ninth, or tenth rib, depending on the extent of the retroperitoneal disease; the larger the mass, the higher the incision. The incision extends over the rib, across the costochondral junction into the high epigastrium, where it courses inferiorly as a paramedian incision toward the pubis. A subperiosteal resection of the appropriate rib is then performed and the costochondral junction divided. The rectus muscle should be divided in the epigastrium and retracted laterally to prevent denervation of the rectus with postoperative weakness or diastasis of the ipsilateral abdominal wall.

Once the costochondral junction is divided, the

plane between the parietal peritoneum and the transversus abdominus fascia becomes apparent, and the peritoneum should be mobilized off the transversus abdominus fascia laterally, the diaphragm superiorly, and the posterior rectus fascia anteriorly by a combination of blunt and sharp dissection. The peritoneum is usually firmly attached to the junction of the lateral abdominal aponeuroses where they join to form the rectus fascia; sharp dissection is often required at that point. It usually is possible, however, to strip the peritoneum completely off the posterior rectus fascia as well as the transverse abdominus fascia. The peritoneum should also be dissected off the diaphragm superiorly so that the liver can be mobilized and retracted medially for right-sided tumors, and the spleen and pancreas can likewise be mobilized and reflected medially for left-sided tumors.

The peritoneum may or may not be entered, depending on the surgeon's preference, but it often helps to be able to explore the intraabdominal contents, including the liver, and also to palpate the regional lymph nodes to determine in advance the extent of the primary tumor. Moreover, it it useful to open the peritoneum inasmuch as this allows the surgeon accurately to determine the plane between the lateral peritoneal reflection and the anterior surface of Gerota's fascia (Fig. 1).

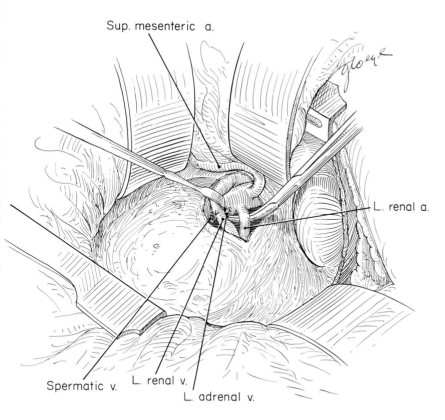

Sup. mesenteric a.

L. renal a.

Spermatic v.   L. renal v.

L. adrenal v.

Fig. 2

Definition of this plane is one of the important aspects of this operation; its proper identification is heralded by the finding of avascular loose fibroareolar tissue that separates the anterior surface of Gerota's fascia from the posterior peritoneum. Once this plane is identified, it is further developed medially beyond the great vessels by both sharp and blunt dissection. Medial and superior retraction of the peritoneal envelopes around the liver on the right side and spleen on the left side facilitates and enhances the exposure to the ipsilateral kidney and retroperitoneum.

For left-sided tumors, the only limiting factor that prevents one from completely crossing the midline in this plane is the inferior mesenteric artery, which is usually ligated and divided to facilitate exposure. Once development of this plane has been completed on either side, certain important landmarks must be identified. The inferior mesenteric vein can be traced to its junction with the splenic vein immediately identifying the region of the superior mesenteric artery, the most important landmark for both right and left-sided dissections. In all cases, the location of this artery must be identified where it originates from the anterior surface of the aorta and may be partially obscured by the crura of the diaphragm

often surrounding the aorta at this level. Immediately beneath or posterior to the superior mesenteric artery is the left renal vein, which should be dissected at this time. For left-sided tumors, ligation of the gonadal vein, the adrenal vein, and the normally present lumbar vein that enters posteriorly facilitates retraction of the renal vein and exposure of the left renal artery at its origin from the aorta (Fig. 2). For right-sided tumors, sufficient mobility of the left renal vein can usually be achieved to expose the aorta and right renal artery without ligating or dividing the left gonadal, adrenal, or lumbar vessels.

The renal artery should then be ligated and divided, followed by prompt ligation of the ipsilateral renal vein at its insertion into the vena cava.

At this point the surgeon has completely controlled the blood supply to the primary tumor and attention is directed to the region of the diaphragm where en bloc nephroureterectomy with regional lymph node dissection is performed. Initially the posterior surface of Gerota's fascia is mobilized off the posterior lumbar muscles and the psoas muscle, thus creating an envelope of Gerota's fascia containing the kidney, adrenal, renal pedicle, and regional nodes around the great vessels. The dissection then begins at the diaphragm where the communicating

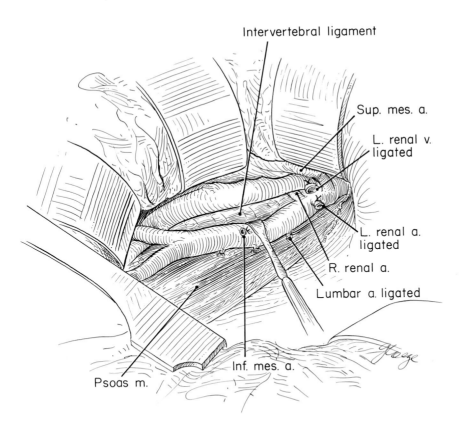

Intervertebral ligament

Sup. mes. a.

L. renal v. ligated

L. renal a. ligated

R. renal a.

Lumbar a. ligated

Inf. mes. a.

Psoas m.

Fig. 3

vessels between the adrenal and diaphragm are clipped and divided. The celiac ganglion is dissected off the ipsilateral crura of the diaphragm with care being taken to protect the superior mesenteric artery and clip the abundant lymphatic vessels draining the mesentery. For right-sided tumors, a finger can be gently inserted bluntly behind the vena cava, stripping all areolar and lymphatic tissue off the right crura. All tissue is then divided over the top of the vena cava, beginning at the insertion of the first hepatic vein superiorly. The adrenal vein is carefully secured, ligated and divided, and all lumbar veins are ligated and divided down to the bifurcation of the vena cava.

Again on the right side the dissection is continued over the top of the left renal vein over the aorta and then sweeps the areolar and lymphatic tissue off the top of the aorta down to the origin of the inferior mesenteric artery, which is usually left intact. The medial lumbar arteries are ligated and divided, allowing the surgeon to sweep all tissue from behind the aorta under the vena cava as an en bloc resection, thus cleaning and exposing the intervertebral ligaments. Retraction of the mobilized vena cava and use of large hemoclips along the contra-lateral peripheral margins of the dissection facilitates

this part of the operation and controls bleeding from divided lumbar vessels.

On the left side, once the crura have been dissected, all tissue is swept off the top of the vena cava from the ligated stump of the left renal vein down to the insertion of the right spermatic vein into the vena cava. From this point the dissection extends more medially down to the area in which the right common iliac artery crosses the left common iliac vein. Several medial lumbar veins are usually ligated. All areolar tissue over the top of the aorta is then divided and the lumbar arteries distal to the renal pedicle are ligated so that all lymphatics and fibroareolar tissue from behind the aorta and between the aorta and vena cava can be dissected off the inter-vertebral ligaments and brought to the ipsilateral side. The right renal artery must be carefully identified and protected and the cisterna chyli secured with a large hemoclip at the point at which it passes behind the right renal artery and medial to the right crus of the diaphragm.

The upper part of the operation now being complete (Fig. 3), attention is focused on the pelvic area. It is initially helpful to irrigate and fill the bladder with distilled water or Furacin solution as advocated by Fraley[3] through a Foley catheter placed prior to the operation.

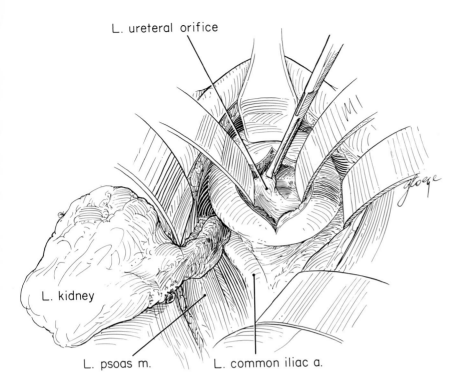

L. ureteral orifice

L. kidney

L. psoas m.   L. common iliac a.

Fig. 4

This lyses any possible tumor cells present in the urine and provides easy identification of the bladder as it distends out of the pelvis. A large clip is placed on the ureter at the point at which it crosses the common iliac vessel and the bladder is then opened in the dome, care being taken to immediately suction all solution from the bladder and further reduce the risk of possible tumor spill.

A circumferential incision is then made around the ipsilateral ureteral orifice with great care being taken to identify the contralateral ureter and see that the orifice is in no way damaged (Fig. 4). The ureter is sewn closed and the intramural ureter is mobilized in a manner similar to that for mobilizing the ureter to perform a ureteral reimplantation. The ureter is then dissected out of the deep pelvis by dividing the obliterated hypogastric ligament, separating the spermatic cord, and removing the entire en bloc nephroureterectomy specimen along with regional retroperitoneal lymph nodes. No effort is made to do an ipsilateral pelvic lymph node dissection unless there is evidence of a distal ureteral involvement by tumor. In those instances an ipsilateral pelvic iliac lymph node dissection is performed as described in *Urologic Surgery*.[5]

Thereafter the bladder is carefully closed, with caution exercised to prevent injuring the contralateral ureteral orifice. At the discretion of the urologist, a cystotomy tube may be left, although we prefer to simply leave the indwelling urethral Foley catheter.

We must emphasize that it is almost impossible to be certain that a cuff of the bladder has been removed unless a formal cystotomy is made with the ureteral orifice surgically circumscribed. Efforts have been made in the past to tent up the intramural ureter and place a large clamp on the bladder base in order to avoid opening the bladder, but in the author's experience a segment of intramural ureteral cuff is likely to be left, or possibly the contralateral ureteral orifice may be injured. Recent evidence reported by Strong and Pearse[7] clearly demonstrates that if any portion of the intramural ureter is left behind, the incidence of recurrence within the intramural portion approaches 25 percent following nephroureterectomy for primary renal pelvic tumors.

A drain is placed in the area of cystotomy and brought out through a separate stab incision in the lower abdominal wall. Closure of the thoracic part of the incision is facilitated by using No. 2 figure 8 through-and-through buried silk sutures, after the diaphragm has been carefully closed by interrupted 20 silk sutures, a rapid and satisfactory technique developed by Sweet.[8] A No. 32 French chest tube is routinely inserted and left in place for 48 to 72 hours until significant drainage ceases, after which it is removed. The posterior fascia and peritoneum are closed with a running 0 chromic suture, and the anterior fascia is closed with interrupted 0 Dexon figure 8 sutures. Anterior retention sutures may be used at the discretion of the surgeon.

Several comments concerning this operative technique should be emphasized. First, proper patient selection and surgical judgment are essential prerequisites. An operation of this extent is generally indicated only for those patients in good medical condition with a life expectancy of at least five to 10 years had they not developed cancer of the renal pelvis. Radical surgery is probably not advisable for poor risk patients in whom only a palliative nephrectomy is appropriate to control pain or bleeding. Occasionally diarrhea may result from ischemia to the large bowel following ligation of the inferior mesenteric artery, but this is rare in younger patients and can be successfully managed conservatively without long term sequelae.

The aorta is mobilized unless there is extensive evidence of atherosclerosis, in which case an attempt at regional lymph node dissection is probably not indicated. Ligation and division of the lumbar arteries distal to the renal pedicle facilitate aortic mobilization. Troublesome bleeding from an avulsed lumbar vessel may occur but can be avoided by individual ligation and division of each pair of arteries distal to the renal pedicle. Placement of hemoclips on the distal portion of the vessel facilitates this part of the operation, but it is best to ligate the origin from the aorta and vena cava because clips may be dislodged later in the procedure, causing troublesome bleeding behind the great vessels. Occasionally, troublesome bleeding from a torn lumbar vein or artery will develop despite all precautions. Use of an Allis clamp is very helpful, and fine arterial silk should be available in all cases.

The cisterna chyli should be identified behind the right renal artery located in the region medial to the right crus of the diaphragm between the aorta and vena cava. This should be ligated or secured with a large hemoclip to prevent significant loss of protein during the postoperative period and possible chylous ascites.

The thoracoabdominal approach to the management of these tumors has been successfully tolerated by patients of all ages. In a review of more than 300 patients undergoing radical nephrectomy for primary renal parenchymal tumors, we have found that the period of postoperative hospitalization, complication rate, morbidity, and mortality of the thoracoabdominal approach compares very favorably with transabdominal or lumbar approaches in which the thoracic cavity is not entered.

It should be emphasized, however, that this is a major surgical procedure requiring a thorough knowledge of the retroperitoneum and considerable expertise on the part of the surgeon. In qualified hands, it is safe, extremely well tolerated by the patient, and should provide maximum curability for those afflicted by primary epithelial tumors of the renal pelvis and ureter.

REFERENCES

1. Cooper, J. F., Leadbetter, W. F., and Chute, R.: The thoracoabdominal approach for retroperitoneal gland dissection—its application to testis tumors. Surg Gynec Obstet 90:496, 1950
2. Dretler, S. P., Ragsdale, B. D., and Leadbetter, W.F.: The value of pelvic lymphadenectomy in the surgical treatment of bladder cancer. J Urol 109:414, 1973
3. Fraley, E. E.: Cancer of the Renal Pelvis In Skinner, D. G. and de Kernion, J. (Eds): Genitourinary Cancer. Philadelphia, W B Saunders Company, in press for publication 1978
4. Grabstald, H., Whitmore, W. F., and Melamed, M. R.: Renal pelvic tumors. JAMA 218:845, 1971
5. Skinner, D. G.: Pelvic lymphadenectomy. In Glenn J (Ed): Urologic Surgery. Hagerstown, Harper & Row, 1975, 589–595
6. Skinner, D. G.: Considerations for management of large retroperitoneal tumors: use of the modified thoracoabdominal approach. J Urol 117:605, 1977
7. Strong, D. W., and Pearse, H. D.: Recurrent urothelial tumors following surgery for transitional cell carcinoma of the upper urinary tract. Cancer 38:2178, 1976
8. Sweet, R. H.: Carcinoma of the esophagus and the cardiac end of the stomach. JAMA 135:485, 1947
9. Williams, C. B., and Mitchell, J. P.: Carcinoma of the renal pelvis—a review of 43 cases. Br J Urol 45:370, 1973

Commentary:
Approaches in Nephroureterectomy

Donald F. McDonald

It is commonly appreciated that nephroureterectomy with a cuff of bladder offers the best prognosis for longevity in patients with tumors of the renal pelvis and ureter. However, radical nephroureterectomy including perinephric fat, Gerota's fascia, lymph nodes, and adrenal glands is not a common procedure for carcinomas of the renal pelvis and ureter.

In the preceding article, Dr. Skinner offers a surgical approach applicable to those patients in whom this more complete procedure could offer a superior prognosis. His technique can be adapted to the extent of the tumor as found on pyelography, arteriography, and computer tomography (CT) scans. For those patients demonstrating a very large tumor, with perinephric extension, or both, his extensive transthoracic exposure with excision of pernephric fat and lymph nodes is applicable.

Against this radical operation are the observations by Grabstald and coauthors that removal of tumor-involved lymph nodes failed to cure.[1] They think that survival correlates better with stage and grade than with type of surgery performed.

This view is shared by Rubenstein and colleagues, who found that tumor grade was the single most important determinant for survival.[2] Interesting also is their observation that bladder tumors were more commonly found in patients with lower-grade renal tumors and that survival was not adversely affected by the presence of bladder tumors. Five of 32 patients not undergoing total ureterectomy (16%) developed recurrent tumor in the ureteral stump, thus reaffirming the need for total ureterectomy with a bladder cuff.

Another relevant article describes a single paramedian incision for total nephroureterectomy with a cuff of bladder.[3] The approach may be practical in a slender person with a ureteral lesion. In my hands, the approach is too limited for a renal tumor.

There is little recent information of an optimistic nature concerning adjunctive treatment for transitional cell renal carcinoma. X-ray therapy and chemotherapy have not been of much benefit.

REFERENCES

1. Grabstald H, Whitmore WF, Melamed MR: Renal pelvic tumors. JAMA 218:845, 1971
2. Rubenstein MA, Walz BJ, Bucy JG: Transitional cell carcinoma of the kidney: 25 year experience. J Urol 119:594, 1978

3. Tessler AN, Yuvienco F, Farcon E: Paramedian extraperitoneal incision for total nephroureterectomy. Urology: 5,397 1975

ANNOTATED BIBLIOGRAPHY

Grabstald H, Whitmore WF, Melamed MR: Renal pelvic tumors. JAMA 218:845, 1971

> Survival in 70 patients depended more on tumor stage and grade than on type of surgery performed. Lymph node dissection in high-stage and high-grade tumors (7 patients, in which 6 had positive nodes) did not prevent death in less than 12 months from metastatic spread.

Rubenstein MA, Walz BJ, Bucy JG: Transitional cell carcinoma of the kidney: 25 year experience. J Urol 119:594, 1978

> Stage of tumor as seen on IVP correlated well with stage at surgery and survival rate, but survival in 70 patients appeared to be more related to tumor grade. Patients with grade I and II tumors had 5-year survivals of 80% and 33%, respectively, whereas patients with grade III and IV tumors were 11% and 0%, respectively. Occurrence of bladder tumors did not adversely affect survival.

Tessler AN, Yuvienco F, Farcon E: Paramedian extraperitoneal incision for total nephroureterectomy. Urology 5:397, 1975

> A single incision method for nephroureterectomy with a cuff of bladder is described.

Skinner DG: Considerations for management of large retroperitoneal tumors: Use of the modified thoraco abdominal approach. J Urol 117:605, 1977

> This article presents additional valuable suggestions on the technical details of the thoracoabdominal approach.

OVERVIEW: IMPORTANCE OF TUMOR STAGE AND GRADE IN TECHNIQUES FOR RENAL CARCINOMA

Harry Grabstald

CHAPTER 26

Recommendations based on Petković's experience with endemic pelvic tumors may not be applicable to the pelvic urothelial tumors seen in the United States, except in the very broadest terms. Theirs is a common renal tumor, undoubtedly of a different etiology (see Chaper 26). Second-generation Yugoslavs in this country very likely have the same incidence of this disease as non-Slavic U.S. citizens.

Before 1953, Petković indicates that he saw renal pelvic: renal cell cancer at a ratio of 3:26 (1921–1943) and 4:62 (1944–1952), probably the same incidence as seen in the United States. Interestingly enough, the incidence of endemic (Balkan) nephropathy is higher in areas where renal pelvic tumors are more common. All his reasons for conservative surgery are not totally applicable in the United States. They include (1) a 10% possibility of tumor on the opposite side, (2) renal insufficiency in almost half the patients, (3) a large number of benign tumors with a narrow pedicle, easily manageable by conservative means, and (4) awareness that the opposite kidney is at risk when nephrectomy is performed and that this risk is as real as the fact that a renal pelvic tumor treated conservatively still leaves that particular kidney at risk.

Regarding Petković's vs the United States' renal pelvic tumor population, I feel that there is not a 10% incidence of bilaterality in the Unisted States. If renal pelvic tumors were bilateral 50% of the time, all surgeons would be more expert in conservative management. Bilateral renal pelvic tumors, whether synchronous or asynchronous, are rare. In my experience, I had no patients with bilateral renal pelvic tumors unless they had—or were destined to get—bladder tumors, thereby proving that these patients had a multifocal urothelial tumor diathesis.[1] Five of 35 patients (14%) with pelvic and bladder tumors had bilateral renal pelvic tumors.[1] Renal insufficiency as an accompaniment of renal pelvic tumors is not seen unless it is a manifestation of progressive hydronephrosis. U.S. surgeons do not, unfortunately, see as many ''thin-pedicle'' tumors as the Yugoslavs do. U.S. surgeons are aware of the vulnerability of the opposite kidney when nephrectomy is performed and of the fact that the conservatively treated tumor leaves that kidney at risk. In my opinion, U.S. surgeons have not pursued a conservative enough course. Until fairly recently, the standard treatment recommended in all texts and journals for renal pelvic and ureteral tumors was complete nephrectomy and ureterectomy with resection of a cuff of bladder to ensure removal of the intraversial portion of the very distal ureter. These earlier texts and journals rarely mentioned anything less than ablative surgery except, obviously, in patients with solitary tumors.

I think several points should be emphasized when discussing conservative management of renal tumors, whether they are renal pelvic or renal parenchymal tumors. I feel that there is little that cannot be done *in vivo* that can be done with bench surgery. Among the areas I should emphasize are the use of mannitol diuresis, local cooling by means of local ice–slush or by other techniques, and wound irrigations.

Wound irrigation after conservative management to prevent implantation is extremely important. Except for the very real possibility of radiation nephritis, one might consider preoperative radiation therapy as in the fashion of preoperative radiation therapy for open, nonablative bladder tumor surgery when conservative management of pelvic and ureteral tumors was planned.[2]

Van der Werf–Messing reduced the incidence of local wound seeding from 24% to 0% after open-bladder radium-seed treatment of primary tumors.[2] The potential disadvantages of conservative management of renal pelvic tumor may be minimized by proper case selection and by the use of adjuvant treatment before and after surgery.

The nephroscope and the ureteroscope at present remain wishful thoughts. Research has been done and certainly should continue to be done in this area. At present, vision is limited even with a flexible scope. A narrow infundibulum prevents complete resection of distal caliceal tumors.

Operative nephroscopy has been used more recently to define the position and configuration of renal pelvic tumors when conservative surgery is contemplated, for example, on the basis of negative cytologic findings and low-grade histology as determined by brush biopsy.[3] Gittes felt that when brush biopsy and cytology were normal and there was persistence of a filling defect, operative nephroscopy might provide the decisive information on surgery. By direct observation and biopsy, one might even avoid nephrectomy. With improvement in instrumentation, I think his opinion will be further justified; certainly with more experience it will be.

CHAPTER 27

What *can* be done is not necessarily what *should* be done. A renal cell cancer clot may be removed from the superior vena cava extending to or in the heart. What, however, are the survival figures for this surgical exercise requiring great technical expertise, including vascular or pump surgery? They are the same for an exended node dissection for renal pelvic and ureteral tumors. Yes, it is possible and not difficult. I do the same general operation for testis tumors. The difference lies in the existence of ancillary therapeutic methods—chemotherapy, for instance, for testis tumors. Such ancillary chemo-

therapy does not exist for urothelial tumors. The fact is that patients with testis tumors containing nodes may frequently be cured by surgery alone. The same certainly may not be said for pelvic and ureteral or any urothelial tumors when node dissection is for cancer in lymph nodes.

Skinner refers to the paper in which I presented a 75% incidence of regional lymph node involvement in patients with invasive cancer of the renal pelvis.[1] Skinner then proceeds to mention in the same paragraph that ''longterm survival has not been reported for patients with transitional call carcinoma—metastatic to regional nodes.'' One point that he mentions is true, and that is that very few centers have performed a systematic regional lymph node dissection. He indicates that the procedure of choice is the thoracoabdominal approach. In my opinion, the question is not the approach one chooses, but whether one bothers doing a radical node resection at all, except for staging and prognosis purposes and as that staging relates to the potential use of other therapeutic modalities, such as chemotherapy, if nodes are positive. (One would do nothing if nodes were negative.)

My feeling about node dissection in general is that it is performed for one of four reasons. First, it is done for cure. There are very few urologic tumors for which this can be said. Tumors of the testis and penis are among these. Second, node dissection can be done for palliation, but this would be very rare. Third, it would be done to better define the extent of disease to facilitate further therapy; for example, it would help tell where radiation therapy might be directed. Finally, node dissection is done for staging and prognosis. In my opinion, that would be the indication for node dissection for transitional cell tumors of the pelvis.

It is often the pathologic staging of the bladder tumor rather than the renal pelvic tumor that dictates prognosis; indeed, associated bladder disease may help the surgeon to decide if conservative renal pelvic surgery is needed.

Gittes felt that ''if a tumor is of low grade (Grade I or Grade II), conservative segmental surgery of the kidney, pelvis or ureter is indicated.''[4] The problem obviously relates to the fact that one does not know the grade until one has committed oneself to either definitive ablative surgery or conservative surgery. What if conservative surgery is done, for example, and the pathologist reports grade IV carcinoma? According to this philosophy, the patient would have to be operated on for a nephrectomy if conservative surgery were done in the first place.

REFERENCES

1. Grabstald H, Whitmore WF, Melamed MR: Renal pelvic tumors. JAMA 218:845, 1971
2. Van der Werf–Messing B: Carcinoma of the bladder treated by suprapubic radium implants—the value of additional external irradiation. Eur J Cancer 5:277, 1969

3. Gittes RF: Operative nephroscopy. J Urol 116:148, 1976
4. Gittes RF: Tumors of the ureter and renal pelvis. In Campbell's Urology, Vol 2, p 1026. Philadelphia, WB Saunders, 1979

PART FOURTEEN

RECONSTRUCTIVE SURGERY OF THE URETEROPELVIC JUNCTION

SOME OBSERVATIONS ON CONGENITAL URETEROPELVIC JUNCTION OBSTRUCTION

Moneer K. Hanna, M.D.

From the Division o Pediatric Urology, The Hospital of Albert Einstein College of Medicine, and Montefiore Hospital and Medical Center, Bronx, New York

Urology / August 1978 / Volume XII, Number 2

The pathologic features of congenital ureteropelvic junction obstruction (UPJO) have been variously described. A variety of operations are available to correct the abnormality and preserve renal tissue. Certain aspects of the problem have been the subject of recent research or continue to present problems in management. Recently, the capability for postoperative functional recovery of the kidney and dilated collecting system has received much attention. However, in general, the extent of anatomic and functional recovery remains difficult to predict. An area of difficulty in management is the hydronephrosis associated with an incompetent ureterovesical junction (UVJ). The surgeon must decide whether the defect is primarily a faulty ureteropelvic or ureterovesical junction. Furthermore, bilateral obstructions may make difficult the selection as to which side should be operated on first.

Better understanding of the pathophysiology of UPJO allows the surgeon to choose the type of surgery more rationally and thereby reduce the morbidity and improve the results.

Moneer K. Hannah, M.D.
1825 Eastchester Road
Bronx, New York 10461

NORMAL URETEROPELVIC JUNCTION

Anatomic Considerations. The UPJ is the distal end of the pelvic funnel. It consists of muscle arranged mainly in spirals which are extending from the renal pelvis through the UPJ to the upper ureter. Both the renal pelvis and ureter contain muscle fibers running in all directions. More recent descriptions indicate that these structures are clearly nonlayered muscular tubes.[1,2] The muscle bundles are the anatomic units and each bundle contains heterogeneously oriented muscle cells. Functional continuity is maintained via the nexus which serve as sites for transmission of impulses from one muscle cell to another.[3]

Muscle cell contraction demands healthy myofilaments as well as a supply of energy from the mitochondria within the cell. The integrity of these intracellular organelles determine the quality of muscle cell performance. Under light microscopy the UPJ is an undefinable structure, however, with electron microscopy, the morphologically distinct pale muscle cells are more frequently observed. These pale "P" muscle cells extend in lesser numbers throughout the ureter and may represent the pacemaker cell population of the normal ureter in man.[3]

Functional Considerations. *Drainage System.* The renal pelvis and the ureter constitute one functional unit. Cine fluoroscopic examination has shown that the emptying of the renal pelvis demands relaxation of the UPJ to allow filling of the ureteral cone.[4] The harmony between pelvic systole and UPJ diastole ensures a pelvic ureteral contraction ratio of 1:1.[5] Hanley[6] reviewed over 1,000 excretory pyelograms and distinguished the "funnel"-shaped renal pelvis from the closed or "box" type. The latter is rounded and therefore urodynamically inferior to the funnel type. The better emptying capacity of the funnel pelvis than the box pelvis has been demonstrated in human cadavers.[7] Reconstructing a funnel is one of the objects of corrective surgery for UPJO.

Although the role of the autonomic nervous system in ureteral motility is a controversial subject, the autonomy of the ureter can be demonstrated soon after restoration of the circulation to the transplanted kidney, and clinical experience has shown that ureteral denervation does not alter ureteral function.

The Kidney. The formation of the nephrons is completed by the thirty-sixth week of intrauterine life.[8] Morphologic development of the tubules lag behind that of the glomeruli[9] as evidenced by the kidneys of normal infants and young children having a limited capacity for urine concentration. UPJO results early on in flattening of the renal papilla and consequently tubular damage, thereby interfering with the mechanism for urine concentration. In long-standing cases, thinning of the renal parenchyma is also evident and glomerular as well as tubular function is compromised.[10,11]

Excess sodium loss not uncommonly leads to salt depletion in babies with bilateral obstructions. These infants require rehydration and correction of salt deficit prior to surgery. One should also be aware of the potentiality of postobstructive diuresis following bilateral pyeloplasties on tense hydronephrotic kidneys. It should be noted, however, that Ghazali and Barratt[12] have provided evidence that postoperative naturesis is a favorable prognostic sign with regard to renal recoverability. Studies by Suki *et al.*[13] clearly demonstrated the difference between the functional recovery of acutely and chronically obstructed kidneys. The former is apt to be more complete and more rapid than the latter. Although congenital UPJO is a chronic form of obstruction, it is conceivable that episodes of high pressures associated with intermittent diuresis simulate multiple acute obstructions.

PATHOLOGY OF UPJO

UPJO Under Light Microscope. Congenital hydronephrosis is the most common ureteral obstruction en-

TABLE 1. Pathology of Congenital UPJO

Naked Eye Examination and Light Microscopy
  Extrinsic
    Bands and kinks
    High insertion
    Polar vessels
  Intrinsic
    Stricture
    Muscle reduction
    Muscle malorientation (replacement of spirals by longitudinal fibers)
    Mucosal folds

Electron Microsopy
  Excessive collagen throughout UPJ
  Excessive collagen between muscle cells and compromised muscle cells

countered in infants and children. Despite numerous reports of varying pathologic findings at the UPJ in congenital hydronephrosis, there is a widespread conviction that the actual process is a functional obstruction. Table 1 summarizes the causes of congenital UPJO reported during the past three decades.

It is unlikely that a single cause will be found to account for all cases of congenital UPJO. Indeed a spectrum of abnormalities was observed in 35 obstructed segments under light microscopy by Hanna *et al.*[14] There were three groups. Eight specimens were entirely normal. Reduced muscle bulk at the UPJ was observed in 13 specimens. The third group of 14 cases exhibited muscular malorientation, thickened adventitia, and a variable degree of inflammatory cell infiltration.

UPJO Under Electron Microscope. The high magnification of the electron microscope allows accurate assessment of detailed cellular morphology which cannot be resolved with the light microscope. Notley[15] demonstrated abundant collagen fibers in the obstructed UPJ. This was confirmed in a detailed study by the present author.[14] Excessive collagen between the muscle cells of the obstructed UPJ and compromised muscle cells in the area immediately proximal to the junction were noted.

In moderately dilated pelves a progressive improvement of muscle cell quality was observed as sections were taken in a more cephalad direction from the UPJ (Figs. 1 and 2). In gross hydronephrosis there were severe muscle cell damage and increased collagen and ground substance deposition over a much wider area of the renal pelvis. The nexus were markedly attenuated or ruptured accounting for structural and functional discontinuity between the muscle cells (Fig. 3). It is believed that these abnormalities have a prognostic impact on the results of surgical repair.

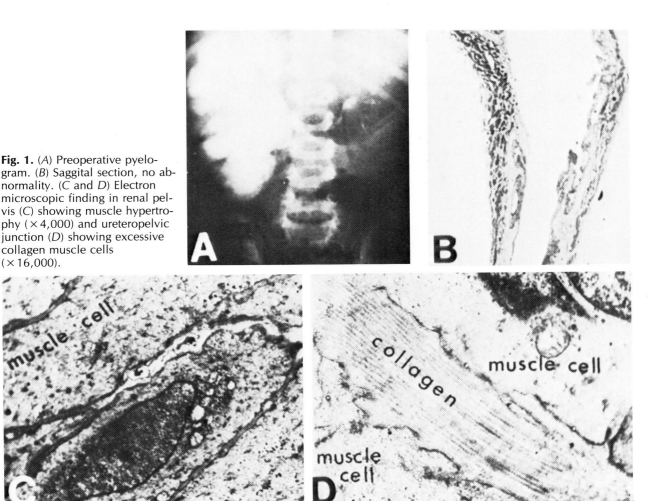

Fig. 1. (A) Preoperative pyelogram. (B) Saggital section, no abnormality. (C and D) Electron microscopic finding in renal pelvis (C) showing muscle hypertrophy ($\times 4,000$) and ureteropelvic junction (D) showing excessive collagen muscle cells ($\times 16,000$).

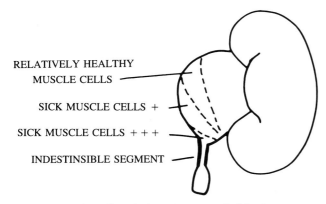

RELATIVELY HEALTHY MUSCLE CELLS

SICK MUSCLE CELLS +

SICK MUSCLE CELLS + + +

INDESTINSIBLE SEGMENT

Fig. 2. Muscle cell pathology in congenital hydronephrosis.

OBSTRUCTIVE POLAR VESSEL, FACT OR MYTH

An abberant lower polar artery, vein, or both have been implicated as being obstructive. Uson, Cox, and Lattimer[16] reported an abnormally located vessel in 28 of 154 hydronephrotic kidneys. Hellstrom[17] believed that obstruction occurs when a large redundant pelvis bulges over a vessel. Although a vessel may have played a role in the development of the abnormality as proposed by Allen,[2] the primary defect is likely one of muscle conduction and the vessel may occlude the ureter secondarily after the pelvis has become dilated. An intraoperative perfusion test (vide infra) after dissection of the vessel from the ureter will help to clarify the matter. The present author's experience suggests that the pressure flow relationships observed are compatible with intrinsic ureteral obstruction, and that the vessel is of secondary importance.

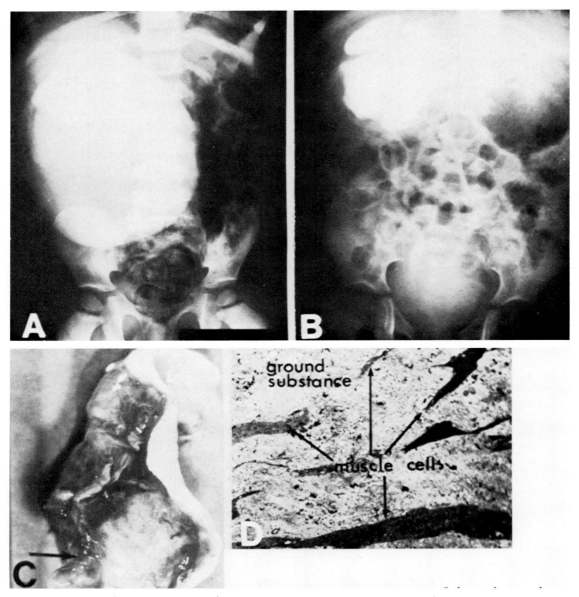

Fig. 3. (*A*) Preoperative intravenous pyelogram. (*B*) Postoperative intravenous pyelogram. (*C*) Operative specimen. (*D*) Electron microscopic findings in renal pelvis show muscle cell atrophy and excessive ground substance (×4,000).

Ureteropelvic Obstruction and Vesicoureteral Reflux. It has been postulated that the high intravesical pressure generated during voiding and transmitted to the renal pelvis in the presence of free vesicoureteral reflux causes pyelocalyceal dilatation and nephron destruction. This may explain the obstructive atrophy of kidneys in cases with seemingly sterile gross reflux. At times, the renal pelvic distention during reflux appears to be out of proportion to the degree of ureteral dilatation, and the radiographs simulate UPJO. Differentiation of primary UPJO from UPJO concomitant with associated reflux, necessitates careful examination of the intravenous pyelogram and voiding cystourethrogram. Where hydronephrosis is secondary to reflux, the obstruction is relative.

The combined urine volume from damaged polyuric kidneys together with that from the incompetent uretero-vesical junction exceeds the emptying capacity and distensibility of the normal UPJ. Furthermore, since the compliance of the renal pelvis and UPJ are different, the voiding pressure generated by the bladder may be transmitted cephalad leading to dilatation of the renal pelvis and to kinking of the UPJ.

Early intravenous pyelograms with an empty bladder and the cystogram at the height of micturition are the key films in the differential diagnosis. The early excretory urograms in secondary or relative UPJO usually fail to demonstrate classic holdup at the UPJ, as is seen in primary obstruction. During cystography, as the contrast material refluxes freely, it causes ballooning of the pelvis and tortuosity of the UPJ. Maximal distention of the pelvis is observed during voiding. Fluoroscopic screening during voiding and for a few minutes after voiding, to demonstrate complete emptying of the renal pelvis, is apt to be diagnostic. Clearly, the sequence of events are best demonstrated on cine fluoroscopic or videotape recording. The latter involves much less radiation exposure to the patient.

DIAGNOSTIC STUDIES

The degree of obstruction varies greatly from case to case. A greatly enlarged hydronephrotic kidney occasionally presents difficulty during delivery of the fetus. Feeding problems, failure to thrive, and pyrexia are not uncommon manifestations in infants. Pyuria, urinary infection, and an abdominal mass are clear indications of urinary tract involvement. Older children often localize the pain to the flank area. Hematuria may frequently occur following minor trauma to a hydronephrotic kidney. A history of recurrent attacks of abdominal pain and vomiting in a child should prompt a hydration high-dose intravenous pyelogram. Renal failure due to bilateral obstructions in young infants and stone formation in older children are not uncommon complications.

Clinical. In some infants, who present with an abdominal mass, the ballooned renal pelvis can be transilluminated. This requires a relatively large renal pelvis, a fiberoptic light source and complete darkness. Ultrasonography often proves useful in the differential diagnosis of an abdominal mass in the neonate.

Intravenous pyelography is the most frequently used method for confirming and diagnosing congenital hydronephrosis. High-dose urography with careful attention to technique should visualize most hydronephrotic kidneys. However, some urologists favor retrograde pyelography and in many clinics the examination is performed routinely. It should be remembered that instru-

mentation of the urethra of the male infant is not without morbidity. Furthermore, there is the risk of introducing infection in an obstructed system where bacterial elimination is impaired. When early films show a negative bodygram and the delayed films of an intravenous pyelogram fail to visualize the kidney of a neonate with an ultrasonographically cystic mass, radioisotopic scanning should be considered. Percutaneous direct puncture of the renal pelvis and antigrade pyelography also may be useful diagnostic procedures in selected cases.

Voiding cystourethrography should be performed routinely in those children with hydronephrosis who present with urinary infection in order to identify hydronephrotic kidneys secondary to vesicoureteral reflux.

Radioisotopic Study. Determination of the glomerular filtration rate (GFR) in children often poses a difficult problem. Chantler et al.[18] showed that the renal clearance of ^{51}Cr EDTA does not differ from the clearance of inulin over a wide range of clinical conditions. The GFR can be measured by analyzing the rate of fall of the plasma concentration of ^{51}Cr EDTA after a single intravenous injection of the isotope. Blood samples are obtained two and four hours after the injection of ^{51}Cr EDTA. This test was found to be safe, simple, and reliable (95 percent confidence limits).[19]

In bilateral obstructions it is unnecessary to introduce catheters into the renal pelvis for functional assessment. Determination of individual renal function may be achieved by measuring the rate of uptake of $^{131}Iodohippuran$ which correlates with the effective renal plasma flow which is directly proportional to the nephron population in each kidney. The accuracy of the test can be improved by computer-assisted blood background subtraction.[20]

Pieretti, Gilday, and Jeffs[21] studied a group of children whose urine was diverted via nephrostomies or ureterostomies. Conventional creatinine clearances of each kidney and differential renal scans were performed. Quantitative analysis of radioisotopic activity of each kidney correlated fairly well with the individual creatinine clearance, and they were able to express the functional contribution of each renal unit as a percentage of the total clearance value. Form the growing literature on isotope renography, it can be safely stated that these methods have a great potential for the assessment of total and individual renal function in hydronephrosis. They are particularly useful in monitoring progress after surgical correction and deliver much less radiation to the patient than does conventional urography.

Pressure Studies in Congenital Hydronephrosis. Pressure flow studies in cases of hydronephrosis may be performed preoperatively, during surgery, or postoperatively. A simple method is herein outlined. The kidney is located by high-dose intravenous urography. Under fluoroscopic control, two angiocatheters are threaded via 16- or 18-gauge needles into the renal pelvis. One inflow tube is connected to an infusion pump which delivers normal saline at a selected rate. The second tube is connected to a pressure transducer. a single tube connected to a Y connection alternatively may be used provided the intrinsic resistance of the tube to a given flow rate is recorded and subtracted from the measured values, in order to obtain absolute values.

A simpled version may be used which employs an intravenous drip set incorporating a burette for saline inflow and a central venous pressure water manometer. The normal basal pressure in the renal pelvis is below 10 cm water at a low flow rate of 1–2 ml minute. In human cadavers the emptying capacity of the UPJ is over 10 ml/minute in the adult[7] and up to 3–5 ml/minute in children between one and six years of age.

Johnston[22] noted low basal pressures in most hydronephrotic kidneys (5–20 cm of water). Struthers[23] suggested that the low pressure may be due to preoperative dehydration and the antidiuretic effect of anesthetic agents.

Preoperative perfusion of the renal pelvis may be helpful in the diagnosis of a radiographically nonvisualizing kidney which proves cystic on ultrasonography. The test is particularly useful in determining whether residual pelvic dilatation remaining after pyeloplasty is due to an atonic pelvis or persistent obstruction.

The use of the perfusion test intraoperatively can be useful in assessing intermittent hydronephrosis where the UPJ appears grossly normal. Pelvic distention with a high perfusion flow rate provides convincing evidence of the obstructive nature of the UPJ. Similarly, when a polar vessel is encountered, the perfusion test may be performed before and after dissection and retraction of the vessel away from the UPJ. Using this technique, Johnston[22] demonstrated that the abnormality was extrinsic in one third of his patients.

Postoperatively, the nephrostomy tube provides access to cine-pressure-flow assessment of the operative repair. These tests are unnecessary in the majority of cases, however, in the reoperated on and the complicated cases, visual and urodynamic testing may be useful.

SURGICAL REPAIR

Over twenty different operations have been described for salvageable hydronephrotic kidneys.[24] The operative approach to the UPJ in children may be through an anterior transverse subcostal incision, oblique incision from the tip of the twelfth rib, standard posterior flank incision, or transperitoneally. In the young child, resec-

tion of a rib is unnecessary. The extraperitoneal transverse subcostal incision provides an undisturbed view of the anatomy and can be extended intraperitoneally if indicated.

The arguments for dismembered and nondismembered pyeloplasty have been presented by Hinman[25] and Culp.[26] It is clear that in either operation, Foley's criteria[27] must be met, namely: (1) formation of a funnel; (2) dependent drainage; (3) no shortening of the suture line; and (4) watertight anastomosis, be it closely placed, interrupted, or running sutures.

The use of stents and nephrostomy tubes is controversial. The arguments for an unstented, undiverted repair are based on clinical and experimental observations. These include the fact that the renal pelvic blood supply runs in every direction, and surgical incisions rarely interfere with the vasculature of the renal pelvis.[28] Furthermore, the ureter heals by regeneration of the muscularis[29,30] and foreign bodies within the kidney predispose to infection. On the other hand, stenting and diversion are advocated by most in cases where the pelvis is markedly dilated, where infection is present, and where the procedure constitutes a reoperation or repair of a solitary kidney.

It is important to understand the indications and limitations of the various operative procedures. The urologist should be familiar with both the dismembered Anderson-Hynes[31] and the nondismembered Culp[32] procedures. The first is simple and highly successful. The latter is more suitable when a long stricture involves the UPJ and the upper ureter. The rationale for the commonly performed operations is outlined in Figure 4. It is clear that from a pathologic and urodynamic standpoint the Anderson-Hynes pyeloplasty is most appropriate. Additionally, the greater omentum may be used in cases in which previous unsuccessful pyeloplasty has been performed. The omentum may be extraperitonealized to prevent adhesions to the posterior bed of the kidney, and its unique lymphatic and vascular network allows for more sound healing of the ureteropelvic anastomosis.

Secondary calicoureterostomy has been described as an alternative to nephrectomy in difficult situations in which the nondiseased ureter could not reach the renal pelvis, or the pelvis was inaccessible due to severe peripelvic scarring or because of its intramural location. More recently, Levitt, Jervaid, and Kogan[33] presented the case for primary ureterocalicostomy in markedly dilated collecting systems where the lowermost calyx appeared to be the most dependent position of the collecting system rather than the pelvis itself. This situation is often seen in horseshoe kidneys with hydronephrosis. Their results in this small series of cases were most impressive in terms of decompression of the collecting system. Indeed, ureterocalicostomy may prove

Y V PYELOPLASTY

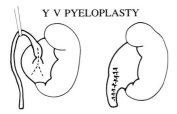

1) ADVANCEMENT OF A FLAP CONTAINING MANY SICK CELLS
2) MINIMAL REDUCTION OF DEAD SPACE

SPIRAL FLAP PYELOPLASTY

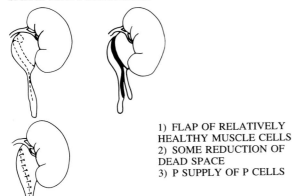

1) FLAP OF RELATIVELY HEALTHY MUSCLE CELLS
2) SOME REDUCTION OF DEAD SPACE
3) P SUPPLY OF P CELLS

ANDERSON HYNES PYELOPLASTY

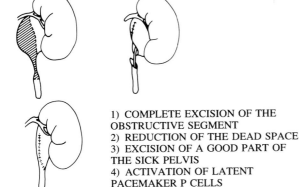

1) COMPLETE EXCISION OF THE OBSTRUCTIVE SEGMENT
2) REDUCTION OF THE DEAD SPACE
3) EXCISION OF A GOOD PART OF THE SICK PELVIS
4) ACTIVATION OF LATENT PACEMAKER P CELLS

Fig. 4. Rationale of pyeloplasty.

to be the procedure of choice in massively dilated hydronephroses secondary to ureteropelvic obstruction.

In bilateral UPJO an exhaustive study of renal function as outlined by Pieretti and co-workers[21] is appropriate to determine the percentage of functional contribution by each kidney and to plan the management of the infant. If the general condition and metabolic status of the patient are stable, bilateral pyeloplasty through a midline or transverse transperitoneal approach can be accomplished safely.[34] If it appears to be safer to stage the operation, one can use the following as a rough guide: if one kidney is severely impaired and contributes less than 20 percent of the total renal function, operation on the better side first is appropriate to improve the general condition of the child. The poorer side may be approached four to eight weeks later to allow recovery of the better kidney from operative trauma and to avoid further deterioration of the poorer side.

If the functional difference between the two kidneys is 20 percent or less, the conventional approach would be to treat the worst side first, in accordance with the principle of renal counterbalance. The author acknowledges the fact that a totally convincing argument for renal counterbalance, in humans, is lacking.

The acutely obstructed kidney should be corrected first regardless of the status of the contralateral kidney since in acute obstruction, the speed of deterioration and extent of recovery are greater. If a kidney is extremely scarred or dysplastic, it appears ill advised to preserve the kidney unless total renal function is so impaired that excision of any renal parenchyma is hazardous.

PROGNOSTIC FACTORS IN RENAL AND URETERAL RECOVERY AFTER PYELOPLASTY (POSTOPERATIVE RESIDUAL DILATATION)

In general, pyeloplasty is a successful procedure. Nevertheless, every sizeable series of patients include failures. Some of these failures are due to technical errors, whereas others are related to the preoperative status of the kidney and collecting system.

Factors in Renal and Ureteral Recovery. *Tense Ballooned Pelvis Versus the Small Flabby Pelvis With or Without Renal Dysplasia.* One form of congenital hydronephrosis occurring in the neonate consists of a greatly distended extrarenal pelvis which has spared the relatively less dilated calyces which are covered by caps of good parenchyma. This characteristic form usually presents as a palpable transilluminating mass and is not uncommonly bilateral. Pyeloplasty is usually successful, although return to normal appearance is unusual.[35]

Williams[36] has pointed out another type of hydronephrosis in which the renal pelvis and upper ureter are flabby and dysplastic. Cystic dysplasia of the kidney may be associated, and he has noted that the results of surgical correction are often disappointing in these cases.

Intermittent Hydronephrosis. This entity is characterized by the intravenous pyelogram often being unimpressive between episodes of pain. The diagnosis demands a high index of suspicion and high-dose contrast injection without dehydration. Since this form represents a relatively minor degree of obstruction, pyeloplasty gives excellent results.

Sterile and Infected Systems. Teague and Boyarsky[37] have demonstrated that bacterial toxins are capable of paralyzing ureteral musculature. In an electron microscopic study of the ureter Hanna and associates[38] have documented the severe morphologic damage to ureteral muscle cells and irreversible collagen deposition which results from repeated infections. With such structural damage to the renal pelvis, one would expect a lower rate of success for pyeloplasties performed in cases complicated by repeated infections.

In the ill child with infected urine, the question of temporary nephrostomy may arise. The author's preference is for a percutaneous needle nephrostomy by the method outlined by De Weerd,[39] since the surgical exposure for a formal nephrostomy is almost as extensive as that for pyeloplasty and the dissection may render subsequent reconstruction more difficult.

Urine Flow. The ureter can transport a limited volume of urine per unit of time. The UPJ is the first point of increased resistance to increased urine flow or, in a sense, it becomes a point of obstruction more particularly when operated upon since it may have decreased elasticity. It has been pointed out previously that in some hydronephrotic kidneys the countercurrent mechanism in the renal papilla may be compromised. The polyuric kidney may produce too much urine for a wide open UPJ. The increased urine flow may account for residual pelvic dilatation following a successful pyeloplasty.

Dilatation of the contralateral renal pelvis after excision of unilateral hydronephrosis has been observed and may appear years after the nephrectomy. In the case reported by Hutch and Tanagho[40] a unilateral nephrectomy unmasked the inability of the contralateral UPJ, below a box type renal pelvis, to handle a large urine volume. Although urine flow through the pelviureteral unit is hard to quantitate, one should be aware of the limitation of the normal drainage system and the anatomic-physiologic factors in the genesis of hydronephrosis. Radiologic assessment of the contralateral kidney after nephrectomy is therefore crucial.

Compromised Pelvic Musculature. Under the magnification of the electron microscope the integrity of pelvic and ureteral muscle cells can be examined. In a clinicopathologic study Hanna *et al.*[14,41] showed a correlation between the quality of muscle cells obtained from the excised pelves and ureters, and the postoperative recovery of the dilated system. When the ureteral and pelvic biopsies contained severely damaged muscle cells,

the postoperative result was unsatisfactory and significant pelvic dilatation persisted. It would appear that the severity of secondary changes in the collecting system proximal to the point of obstruction contributes to the poor results of reconstructive surgery.

Compensatory Hypertrophy of Contralateral Kidney. This phenomenon is often a poor prognostic sign and indicates that the better kidney has taken over the functional demands; thus, the likelihood of recovery of the diseased kidney following repair is diminished.

COMMENT

The utilization and application of a number of new techniques have greatly expanded our knowledge of the normal and abnormal ureteropelvic junction. Radioisotopic studies, ultrasonography, and in some cases, percutaneous puncture of the renal pelvis have a definite place in the preoperative workup of infants and children with congenital ureteropelvic junction obstruction.

Constant infusion pressure flow measurements have added another dimension to the diagnostic capabilities and allow differentiation of obstruction from nonobstructive pyelocalyceal dilatation. At present, urodynamic evaluation is most appropriate in cases in which considerable pelvic dilatation persists after a technically successful pyeloplasty.

Electron microscopic study of the collecting system in obstructive uropathy has an important potential. The effectiveness of ureteral contraction observed on fluoroscopy and the degree of dilatation in the pyelogram are functions of muscle cell integrity which can be directly observed under the electron microscope.

Recent studies utilizing the electron microscope have contributed significantly to our understanding of the underlying histopathology. The extent of structural abnormalities appear to be variable and can be more extensive than generally believed. Retrospective studies have provided evidence that the degree of muscle cell damage as seen with electron microscopy is relevant to the outcome of surgical correction. Hopefully, prospective study will provide more information to justify using the electron microscope as a prognostic tool in obstructive uropathy in children.

Radioisotopic renal scanning can demonstrate "nonfunctioning kidneys" when conventional intravenous urography fails to visualize them. Moreover, it has become clear that most hydronephrotic kidneys are amenable to reconstructive surgery and can be restored to useful function. Long-term postoperative results on large numbers of patients are now available. The excellent short-term results which have been reported by most authors can now be confidently described as so-called cures.

REFERENCES

1. Murnaghan GF: Renal pelvis and ureter, in Wells, C., and Kyle, J., Eds.: Scientific Foundation of Surgery, New York, American Elsevier, 1974, p. 653

2. Allen TD: Congenital ureteral strictures, J Urol 104:196 (1970).

3. Hanna MK, Jeffs RD, Sturgess JM, and Barkin M: Ureteral structure and ultrastructure, Part I. The normal human ureter, *ibid.* 116:718, 1976

4. Kiil F: The function of the ureter and renal pelvis, Philadelphia, W B Saunders Co., 1957, pp 87–88

5. Waterhouse RK and Hackett RE: Congenital anomalies of the kidney, ureter and bladder, in Karafin L and Kendall AR Eds: Urology, Scranton, Pa., Harper and Row, chap 1, vol 1, 1971

6. Hanley HG: Pelviureteric junction: cine pyelography study. Br J Urol 31:377, 1959

7. Hanna MK, and Wyatt JK: Urodynamics of the upper urinary tract in man: a method of clinical assessment, in press

8. Potter EL, and Thierstein ST: Glomerular development in the kidney as an index of fetal maturity. J Pediatr 22:695, 1943

9. Fetterman GH, Shuplock NA, Phillips FJ, and Gregg HS: The growth and maturation of the human glomerulus and proximal convolutions from term to adulthood: studies by microdissection. Pediatrics 35:60, 1965

10. Ericsson NO, Winberg J, and Zetterstrom R: Renal function in infantile obstructive uropathy. Acta Pediatr Scand 44:444, 1955

11. Barratt DM, and Chantler C: Obstructive uropathy in infants. Proc R Soc Med 63:1248, 1970

12. Ghazali S, and Barratt TM: Sodium excretion after relief of urinary tract obstruction in children. Br J Urol 46:163, 1974

13. Suki W, Eknoyang, Rector FC, and Seldin DW: Patterns of nephron perfusion in acute and chronic hydronephrosis. J Clin Invest 45:122, 1966

14. Hanna MK, Jeffs RD, Sturgess JM, and Barkin M: Ureteral structure and ultrastructure, Part II. Congenital ureteropelvic junction obstruction and primary obstructive megaureter. J Urol 116:725, 1976

15. Notley RG: The structural basis for normal and abnormal ureteric motility. The innervation and musculature of the human ureter. Ann R Coll Surg Engl 49:250, 1971

16. Uson AC, Cox LA, and Lattimer JK: Hydronephrosis in infants and children. JAMA 205:323, 1968

17. Hellstrom J: Relation of abnormally running renal vessels to hydronephrosis and an investigation of the arterial condition of 50 kidneys. Acta Chir Scand 61:289, 1927

18. Chantler C, Garnett ES, Parsons V, and Veali N: Glomerular filtration rate measured in man by single injection method using ^{51}Cr EDTA. Clin Sci 37:169, 1969

19. Chantler C, and Barratt TM: Estimation of glomerular filtration rate from plasma clearance of ^{51}chromium edetic acid. Arch Dis Childh 47:613, 1972

20. Britton DE, and Brown NJG: Clinical Renography, London, Lloyd-Luke Ltd, 1971, p 15

21. Pieretti RV, Gilday, and Jeffs RD: Differential kidney scan in pediatric urology. Urology 4:665, 1974

22. Johnston JH: Pathogenesis of hydronephrosis in children. Br J Urol 41:724, 1969

23. Struthers NW: The role of the manometry in the investigation of pelvi-ureteral function. Ibid 41:129, 1969

24. Creevy CD: Noncalculous obstruction at the ureteropelvic junction, in Landers RR, Bush RB, and Zorgniotti AW, Eds: Perspectives in Urology, New York, American Urological Association, Inc. and Roche Laboratories, 1976, vol 1, p 177

25. Hinman F: Dismembered pyeloplasty with diversion, in Scott R. Jr et al, Eds: Current Controversies in Urologic Management, Philadelphia, W B Saunders Co, 1972, p 253

26. Culp DA: Non-dismembered pyeloplasty with urinary diversion. p 256, op cit[25]

27. Foley FEB: Renal discussion on hydronephrosis. Urol Surg 7:91, 1957

28. Douville E, and Hollinshead WH: Blood supply of the normal renal pelvis. J Urol 73:906, 1955

29. Oppenheimer R, and Hinman F Jr: Ureteral regeneration: contracture vs hyperplasia of smooth muscle. Ibid 74:476, 1955

30. Kiviat MD, Russell R, and Ansell JS: Smooth muscle regeneration in the ureter: electron microscopic and autoradiographic observations. Am J Pathol 72:403, 1973

31. Anderson JC, and Hynes W: Retrocaval ureter: a case diagnosed pre-operatively and treated successfully by plastic operation. Br J Urol 21:209, 1949

32. Culp OS, and DeWeerd JH: A pelvic flap operation for certain types of ureteropelvic obstruction: preliminary report. Proc Mayo Clin 26:483, 1951

33. Levitt SB, Jervaid M, and Kogan SJ: The case for primary calicoureterostomy. Presented to the Society for Pediatric Urology meeting. Chicago, April, 1977

34. Ekstein HB: Bilateral simultaneous pyeloplasty for bilateral hydronephrosis review of 10 patients in series of 90 patients with UPJ obstruction: verbal presentation. International Pediatric Urological Seminars, Philadelphia, 1976

35. Williams DI, and Karlaftis CM: Hydronephrosis due to pelviureteric obstruction in the newborn. Br J Urol 38:138, 1966

36. Williams DI: Personal communication, 1970

37. Teague N, and Boyarsky S: Further effects of coliform bacillus on ureteral peristalsis. J Urol 99:720, 1968

38. Hanna MK, Jeffs RD, Sturgess JM, and Barkin M: Ureteral structure and ultrastructure, Part III. The congenitally dilated ureter (megaureter). Ibid 117:24, 1977

39. DeWeerd JH: Surgery of the renal pelvis and ureteropelvic junction, in Glenn JS and Boyce WH, Eds: Urologic Surgery, Scranton, Pa., Harper and Row, 1969, chap 4

40. Hutch JA, and Tanagho EA: Etiology of non-occlusive ureteral dilatation. J Urol 93:177, 1965

41. Hanna MK, Jeffs RD, Sturgess JM, and Barkin M: Ureteral structure and ultrastructure, Part IV. The dilated ureter, clinicopathologic correlation. Ibid 117:28, 1977

Commentary: Technique of Dismembered Pyeloplasty

Mohammad Amin and Robert Lich, Jr.

The preceding article is a comprehensive and up-to-date review of the subject. The basic technique of dismembered pyeloplasty has not changed over the past 20 years, although modifications are limited only by surgeons' imaginations.

SURGICAL PROCEDURE

We employ the conventional flank approach to dissect the renal pelvis and upper ureter extraperitoneally. To proceed: dissect free and preserve any excessory vessels to the lower pole of the kidney. Overdistending the pelvis with normal saline through a hypodermic needle will usually demonstrate the intrinsic obstruction at the ureteropelvic junction, and this test can be used in the form of hydration pyelogram preoperatively in patients with intermittent hydronephrosis. Use three stay sutures of 4–0 silk to mark the line of excision in the renal pelvis and upper ureter for orientation purposes (Fig. 5). Excise the ureteropelvic junction as well as the redundant pelvis. Gently explore the renal collecting system to remove any calculus that may not have been visible in the pyelograms. Spatulate the ureter, which is transected immediately below the strictured site, for approximately 2 cm in its lateral aspect, keeping the anterior stay suture for orientation purposes. Anastomose the spatulated end of the ureter to the most dependent part of the open renal pelvis with 4–0 chromic catgut sutures. After completing the posterior suture line, insert a nephrostomy and a ureteral catheter that acts as a stent. Complete the anterior suture line between the spatulated ureter and cut edge of pelvis on the top of this stent. Use additional sutures to close the pelvis above the ureteral anastomosis. It is important to replace the kidney in its original position without causing any kinks in the ureter. No nephropexy is necessary, since the nephrostomy will prevent any further kidney movement in the postoperative period. Use a Penrose drain for any leakage from the anastomotic site. Remove the ureteral stent after 5 to 7 days, and, if the urogram performed through the nephrostomy does not show any leakage, also remove the nephrostomy. The nephrostomy can be left for a few extra days, but we prefer the urine to start flowing down to keep the anastomosis open after the removal of ureteral stent. In the majority of our patients we remove the ureteral stent as well as the nephrostomy catheter at the same time. Exception can be made in operations on patients with solitary kidneys or in operations that are redone. The pathologist should cut the ureteropelvic junction longitudinally; we have consistently found intrinsic valvelike structures microscopically (Fig. 6).[1,2]

RESULTS

We have been satisfied with the results of dismembered pyeloplasty, which we have used in the great majority of patients with ureteropelvic obstruction. It is extremely rare to find a patient in whom an alternative technique is preferable. Our failures have been the result of errors in judgment. The degree of infection may sometimes be more penetrating than is apparent either from preoperative studies or at the time of surgery. In these instances, anastomotic healing is disturbed, and the secondary fibrosis may occlude the ureteral lumen. Another cause for failure is greater renal damage, both structurally and functionally, than was preoperatively apparent with a lack of postoperative restitution. In our opinion, experience alone can avoid these pitfalls, since laboratory tests and radioisotope studies are not infallible. Proper selection of patients is of paramount importance. Surgical alternatives to pyeloplasty are nephrectomy, nephrostomy, or continued observation. On occasion, initial nephrectomy may be the most conservative therapeutic consideration. The solitary kidney has a better chance for survival after the operation because of total body stimulus and large urine volume.

. . .

The following list summarizes procedural considerations:
1. Adequate surgical exposure is essential. An extraperitoneal 11th intercostal space incision gives adequate exposure.
2. Place stay sutures at the corners of resection for orientation purposes (see Fig. 5).
3. Explore the open renal pelvis for stones that did not appear on urograms.
4. Apply the plastic surgery principles of atraumatic tissue handling, no tension, and fine suture material.
5. Take extreme care in suturing the angle of spatulated ureter to the renal pelvis. A ureteral stent in place will avoid compromising the lumen.
6. At the completion of the procedure, replace the kidney and ureter so as not to cause any kinks.
7. It is advisable to remove or to clamp the nephrostomy soon after the removal of ureteral stent, so that the bolus of urine keeps the ureteropelvic junction open.

The disappearance of symptoms is the best guide to a successful operation. The x-ray findings may not improve for an extended period.

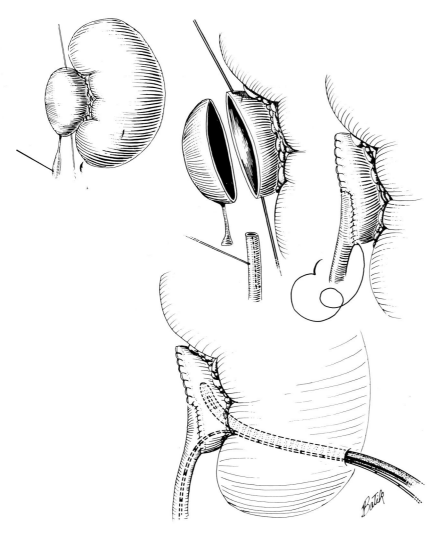

Fig. 5. Technique of dismembered pyeloplasty.

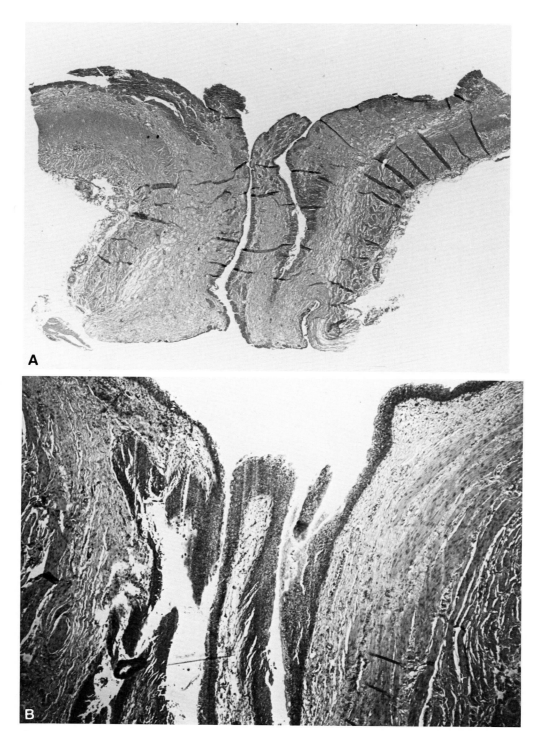

Fig. 6. Longitudinal section of ureteropelvic junction showing valvelike structures. (A) Low power. (B) High power.

REFERENCES

1. Lich R Jr, Barnes ML: A clinicopathologic study of ureteropelvic obstructions. Trans Am Assoc Genitourin Surg 48:143, 1956

2. Lich R Jr: The obstructed ureteropelvic junction. Radiology 68:337, 1957

ANNOTATED BIBLIOGRAPHY

Anderson JC, Hynes W: Rectrocaval ureter. A case diagnosed pre-operatively and treated successfully by a plastic operation. J Urol 21:209, 1949

The technique of dismembered pyelopasty the authors describe is illustrated in this article, and a case of retrocaval ureter is described where this technique was used successfully without splints or nephrostomy. The illustration shows excision of redundant renal pelvis with a V-flap made for anastomosis to the spatulated ureter. They advocated extraperitoneal approach to the kidney and are strongly against using any splinting. A comment was made that they have not employed nephrostomy in several patients and had only one patient develop urinary extravasation, but lately they were employing nephrostomy as a safety valve for a few days.

Kelalis PP, Culp OS, Stickler GB, Burke EC: Ureteropelvic obstruction in children: Experience with 109 cases. J Urol 106:418, 1971

The management of 109 children with ureteropelvic obstruction undergoing 120 operations is reviewed in this paper.The most impressive observation was the ability of the ureteropelvic junction obstruction to simulate gastrointestinal (GI) disease in the form of vague abdominal pain and vomiting. The most common urologic complaint was gross painless hematuria; symptoms of urinary tract infection were rare. The diagnosis was established by excretory urography. Voiding cystourethrograms were advised in all patients to rule out vesicoureteral reflux, which may simulate stasis in the renal pelvis. Four patients in this series were proved to have both vesicoureteral reflux as well as ureteropelvic obstruction requiring surgical repair. Spiral flap and YV-plasty were performed more frequently than dismembered pyeloplasty. Dismembered pyeloplasty was performed in 16 patients and gave the best results. The authors concluded that dismembered pyeloplasty had a distinct advantage over the other methods, at least in children.

Persky L, Tynberg D: Unstented, unsplinted pyeloplasty. Urology 1:32, 1973

Dismembered pyeloplasty, free of tubes, was performed in 32 children. A watertight closure and Penrose drain were used at the repair site. Better end results were obtained in the form of early clearing of infection, patient comfort, and shorter hospital stay.

Bard RH, Kirk RM: Caution urged in unsplinted, unstented pyeloplasty. Urology 3:701, 1974

Three patients had four operations for the ureteropelvic junction obstruction. Only two of these operations were dismembered pyeloplasty, but all patients had prolonged postoperative urinary drainage and prolonged hospitalization requiring further instrumentation. The authors believed that the morbidity rate in this small series of unsplinted, unstented pyeloplasties was unacceptable and recommend nephrostomy drainage, splinting across the repaired ureteropelvic junction, or both.

Whitaker RH: Equivocal pelvi-ureteric obstruction. J Urol 47:771, 1976

This is one of a series of articles by Whitaker giving his method of assessing the obstruction in the upper urinary tract with dynamic means. Since both radiographic and radioisotope methods may be deceptive, this dynamic method of assessing the obstruction is very useful. A cannula is introduced into the renal pelvis either percutaneously or at the time of surgery, and a fast perfusion of 10 ml or 5 ml/min is commenced. The back pressure to perfusion as well as the simultaneous bladder pressure are measured. The latter subtracted from the former produces a relative pressure, which is the pressure drop across the pelviureteric junction at a steady perfusion rate. The normal relative pressure at 10 ml/min perfusion rate should not exceed 10 cm to 12 cm of water. A series of 40 studies was performed to assess the degree of obstruction at the pelviureteric region. In 10 of 11 kidneys with typical ureteropelvic obstruction, the dynamic study gave higher than normal pressures. In one patient the pressure was normal. This method was used successfully to assess the results of pyeloplasty in the postoperative period. In 11 patients with equivocal ureteropelvic junction obstruction, this dynamic study showed obstruction in 5 patients who subsequently underwent operation. In six patients normal pressures were found; follow-up of these patients provided no evidence to refute the finding of this test. A recent article by the author (An evaluation of 170 diagnostic flow studies of the upper urinary tract. J Urol 121:602, 1979) gives normal absolute renal pelvic pressure as under 25 cm of water and relative pressure as under 15 cm of water at a flow rate of 10 ml/min.

Bratt CG, Aurell M, Nilsson S: Renal function in patients with hydronephrosis. Br J Urol 49:249, 1977

This paper reports the changes in renal function and drainage in 50 patients after 2 to 5 years (mean 3 years). In addition to routine laboratory and radiologic investigations, glomerular filtration rate (GFR) and isotope renography were performed in these patients. Twenty-eight patients had dismembered pyeloplasty, with 16 patients having normal GFR both preoperatively and postoperatively. The renal function improved in 6 of 12 kidneys and deteriorated in 2 kidneys postoperatively. Twelve patients had no operation because of minimal symptoms. Eleven of these patients had normal renal parenchymal function throughout the observation period. One patient with moderately decreased renal function deteriorated in this group. Ten patients had nephrectomy, and there was no change in preoperative and postoperative renal function, reflecting the greatly impaired function of the removed kidney. The drainage function improved after operation in 14 kidneys, remained unchanged in 13, and deteriorated in 1. In the nonoperated group, the drainage function remained unchanged in 9 and deteriorated in 3 kidneys. Two patients in the nonoperated group also developed calculi in the hydronephrotic kidneys during the observation period. The authors concluded that renal function is not decreased in the majority of patients with ureteropelvic obstruction. The indications for operation in these patients must therefore be based on factors other than the possible threat to the renal function.

29

MANAGEMENT OF URETEROPELVIC OBSTRUCTION*

Ormond S. Culp

Chief, Section of Urology, Mayo Clinic and Mayo Foundation, Rochester, Minn.

Bulletin of the New York Academy of Medicine
Vol. 43, No. 5
May 1967

Prolific literature on ureteropelvic obstruction, replete with platitudes, admonitions, innovations, and technical minutiae, has pointed up two irrefutable facts: 1) not all obstructions are amenable to the same type of operation, and 2) the ideal, foolproof technique for any type remains elusive.

From August 1950 to January 1966 my colleagues (Drs. J. H. DeWeerd, D. C. Utz, and P. P. Kelalis) and I performed 708 operations on 652 patients because of ureteropelvic obstruction. Our combined experiences have raised several pertinent questions regarding this clinical entity. These constitute the nucleus of this presentation. It is quite improbable that the same answers ever will be elicited from all urologists. Consequently it is hoped that our concepts and convictions will be provocative as well as informative.

Diagnosis of ureteropelvic obstruction usually is obvious during excretory or retrograde pyelographic studies, but *are urographic impressions dependable?* Some kidneys are able to cope with the reduced urinary volume that ensues during dehydration preparation for excretory urography and, therefore, appear relatively normal roentgenographically. The same kidneys may exhibit spectacular differences during diuresis. Both types of excretory urograms will be advisable when the nature of the patient's discomfort suggests renal origin.

Children with presumptive ureteropelvic obstruction warrant studies to exclude ureteral reflux. Frequently they have simulated stasis in the renal pelvis due to the decompensating column of regurgitated urine. Elimination of the reflux can result in dramatic reversion to a normal ureteropelvic transition.

It is best to have thorough knowledge regarding the *entire* ureter before formulating definitive therapy. The calculated risk of iatrogenic infections in these cases can be minimized if retrograde pyelographic studies are deferred until the patient is hospitalized and ready for operation during the same anesthetic period.

WHEN IS SURGICAL INTERVENTION INDICATED?

When renal function is excellent and calyces are well preserved, and when the patient has no pain, pyuria, or

---

* Presented at a combined meeting of the Section on Urology, The New York Academy of Medicine, with the New York Section of the American Urological Association, Inc., New York, N. Y., held at the Academy, March 30, 1966.

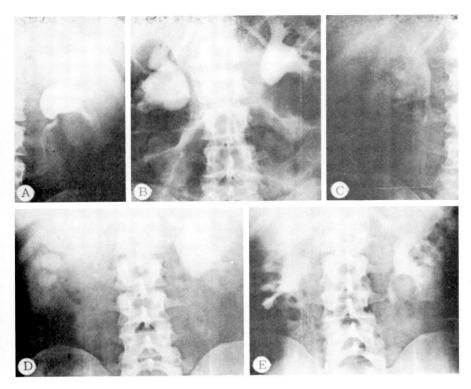

Fig. 1. Excretory urograms showing ureteropelvic obstruction. (A) Solitary left kidney with pyelectasis only, which has not changed in 25 years. (B) Bilateral pyelectasis but only right kidney symptomatic. (C) Same patient as in (B) after successful repair of right ureteropelvic obstruction; left pyelectasis has not changed during 15 years. (D) Both kidneys obstructed and symptomatic. (E) Same patient as in (D), showing post-operative changes. Left kidney was operated on 3 months after right pyeloplasty.

calculi, it is foolhardy to tamper with the ureteropelvic region (Fig. 1A). Yet, patients continue to be subjected to unpredictable operations solely because of pyelectasis and bizarre complaints.

Admittedly, renal pain can simulate a great variety of disorders, notably gastrointestinal disease. Evaluation of the discomfort can be extremely difficult. Relief by temporary indwelling-ureteral-catheter drainage is much more pathognomic than reproduction of the pain by retrograde pyelography. Too frequently the unstable victim is a fertile field for suggestion.

When in doubt, it will be prudent to "watch" the kidney with periodic urographic and urinary studies. Some obviously obstructed ones without cortical damage will never change.

An especially tempting situation is the case of bilateral obstruction in which the more advanced symptomatic side has been repaired successfully (Figs. 1B and C). Despite an overwhelming desire to correct the quiet, incipient, contralateral ureteropelvic obstruction, it will be wise to wait and be sure that such measures are justified.

But this admonition to be cautious must not be misconstrued as endorsement of needless procrastination. When both kidneys are obstructed and symptomatic, both sources of obstruction must be eliminated (Figs.

1D and E). Hopefully the delay between operations will not exceed 3 to 6 months.

WHEN PATIENT HAS BILATERAL OBSTRUCTION, SHOULD THE MORE ADVANCED SIDE ALWAYS BE CORRECTED FIRST?

Table 1 summarizes treatment to date in 152 patients with bilateral ureteropelvic obstruction. More than half the nephrectomies in the group with unilateral pyeloplasty were performed elsewhere. Many of the 67 untreated contralateral kidneys will require some type of operation eventually, including selected nephrectomies. Of the 31 patients with only nephrectomy to date, minimal pyelectasis predominates in the untreated kidneys. But it is imperative to follow these kidneys carefully because the degree of dilatation often progresses with the increased postoperative functional load.

Some obviously useless kidneys must be removed initially because of sepsis or pain. Others must be sacrificed because of trauma, neoplasm, debilitating symptoms, and a variety of diseases.

One must digress from comprehensive considerations to make a special plea for those patients who are operated on primarily to remove calculi. Too frequently the responsible ureteropelvic obstruction continues to be

TABLE 1. Bilateral Ureteropelvic Obstruction

Treatment		Patients
Bilateral pyeloplasty		17
Both sides at Mayo Clinic	13	
One side done elsewhere	4	
Unilateral pyeloplasty		104
Opposite side: Nephrectomy	34	
Nephrostomy	3	
Untreated	67	
Nephrectomy: other side untreated		31
Total		152 (23%)

TABLE 2. Previous Operation(s) on Same Kidney

Initial Procedure	Total	Subsequent Treatment	
		Pyeloplasty	Nephrectomy
Pyeloplasty	26	13	13
Removal of calculi	18	14	4
Nephrostomy	11	9	2
Nephropexy	5	3	2
Division of vessels	4	2	2
Partial nephrectomy	1	1	0
Total	65	42 (65%)	23 (35%)

TABLE 3. Age and Sex

Years	Males	Females	Total	%
>1	6	0	6	1
1–9	30	17	47	7
10–19	47	27	74	11
20–29	49	38	87	13
30–39	53	58	111	17
40–49	66	64	130	20
50–59	50	68	118	18
60–69	33	30	63	10
70–79	8	8	16	2
Total	342	310	652	

ignored. Secondary pyeloplasties can be disgustingly difficult, if not impossible.

HOW CAN ONE BE CERTAIN THAT THE URETEROPELVIC JUNCTURE IS TRULY COMPETENT?

Careful dissection may reveal high insertion of the ureter, localized constriction, a narrow ureter that tapers over a variable distance, or a long diminutive segment. But less than one third of the ureteropelvic obstructions in this series had demonstrable mechanical barriers. Calibration was deceiving and virtually useless. Many junctures accommodated large instruments but the pelves failed to empty promptly. Physiologic obstructions were more common than anatomic ones.

Some very sophisticated measures are being utilized for evaluation of the ureteropelvic juncture. Pressure gradients between the pelvis and the ureter have been especially illuminating. For practical purposes, any abrupt transition between pelvis and ureter indicates obstruction. When in doubt, simple distention of the pelvis with saline and observation of peristalsis and emptying ability usually will be diagnostic. Indeed, any time the ureteropelvic juncture can be identified, a pathologic state exists. Transition between the normal pelvis and ureter always is funnel-shaped.

The risk of unnecessary revision of the ureteropelvic juncture seems to be significantly less than the risk of difficulties inherent in secondary operations. Table 2 summarizes experiences with 65 kidneys

that had been operated on previously. Although 65 percent were salvaged eventually, far too many earlier procedures were devoted solely to removal of calculi, nephropexy, or division of aberrant vessels. One patient with only two thirds of one kidney remaining still had untreated ureteropelvic obstruction.

DOES ANY PARTICULAR TYPE OF PATIENT PREDOMINATE IN A LARGE SERIES OF URETEROPELVIC OBSTRUCTIONS?

Ages of the patients varied from 10 days to 79 years (Table 3). It is noteworthy that 50 percent of the individuals were 40 years old or older when they were first seen. Twice as many males as females were operated on under the age of 20 years. Yet there was no significant difference in total sex distribution. Right and left kidneys were affected about equally.

When the 652 patients included in this study were first seen, their renal status varied tremendously. Some were azotemic; others had uncontrollable infection; some had mild symptoms but severe hydronephrosis; others had severe symptoms and mild hydronephrosis.

HOW DOES ONE CHOOSE BETWEEN NEPHRECTOMY, NEPHROSTOMY, AND SOME TYPE OF PYELOPLASTY AS THE INITIAL TREATMENT OF CHOICE?

Such decisions can be difficult. Many obvious factors and other less tangible ones must be weighed differently in comparable clinical situations. It is unlikely that the choice of operations can ever be based on arbitrary rules, rigid prerequisites, or didactic formulas.

Of all patients treated by pyeloplasty, 74 (19 percent) had only one kidney capable of sustaining life, because the contralateral one had been removed in 23 cases, was functionless in 23, was diminutive in 11, and was congenitally absent in the remaining 17.

Extenuating circumstances left little or no therapeutic latitude in 30 percent of the entire series. Many kidneys

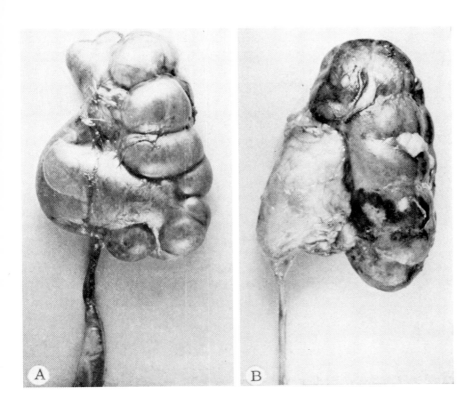

Fig. 2. Kidneys with ureteropelvic obstruction. (*A*) Useless because of complete cortical destruction. (*B*) Equivocal degree of hydronephrosis.

undoubtedly would have been sacrificed if there had been a reasonably normal-appearing one on the other side.

WHAT ARE ACCEPTABLE INDICATIONS FOR PRIMARY NEPHRECTOMY?

When one kidney is useless (Fig. 2A) and the other appears normal, choosing nephrectomy entails no mental gymnastics. Hydronephrotic sacs in this series contained as much as 8,000 ml. of urine. When an unexpected neoplasm is encountered, as was true in five patients, the wisdom of nephrectomy is obvious if the other kidney is capable of sustaining life. If the kidney is studded with cortical abscesses, as in 10 instances in this series, nephrectomy is highly desirable. If unanticipated leukoplakia threatens to compromise the result and the kidney is expendable, as in four cases, it should be removed. Other unique situations, including some bizarre anomalies, may point up nephrectomy as the procedure of choice despite reasonably good renal function.

When the benign hydronephrotic kidney seems to have equivocal value (Fig. 2B), thereapeutic decisions can be truly soul-searching. There are no infallible indices of salvageability of kidneys. Saving patients will continue to be more important than saving a few extra nephrons.

Two seldom-mentioned factors warrant serious consideration when there is a good contralateral kidney.

Rehabilitation. Too frequently surgeons forget that the patient should again be able to be a useful citizen. Executives do not have to face the same physical demands that confront laborers. The poor man's urinary tract should not be sold short because of his social or economic position, but surgeons must look farther ahead than the day John Doe can leave the hospital. Technical triumphs do not necessarily assure the most practical results. Multiple operations on the same kidney have created a host of urologic cripples. Nephrectomy will continue to be prudent in many instances.

Age. Although chronologic age can be most deceiving, one should be reluctant to perform any type of pyeloplasty if the patient is more than 60 years of age. Indeed, doubts exist about the virtues of such procedures after the age of 50 if the other kidney has good function. Infections can be deep-seated and refractory, vascular lesions are common, results are unpredictable, and risks of secondary nephrectomy in the older age groups cannot be ignored.

Influence of age in this series is summarized in Table 4. Not all the 465 patients with grossly normal

TABLE 4. Patients with Normal Other Kidney

Age (years)	Total	Pyeloplasty Patients	%	Nephrectomy Patients	%
<1	1	0		1	
1–9	28	16	79	12	58
10–29	113	63		50	
30–49	175	93		82	
Total	317	172	(54%)	145	(46%)
50–59	89	37		52	
60–69	49	7	21	42	41
70–79	10	1		9	
Total	148	45	(30%)	103	(70%)
Grand Total	465	217	(47%)	248	(53%)

contralateral kidneys had the same functional potential in the obstructed one. Although pyeloplasties outnumbered nephrectomies in the entire series, more kidneys were removed than were saved in the unilateral group. In patients of 50 or more years there were more than twice as many nephrectomies as pyeloplasties. Seventy-nine percent of the plastic procedures were on patients less than 50 years of age.

In the entire series, 313 kidneys were removed, including the secondary nephrectomies.

WHAT IS THE LEGITIMATE ROLE OF PRELIMINARY NEPHROSTOMY?

Attitudes regarding simple drainage of an obstructed kidney have changed. Unless the patient's general condition is truly precarious, it is wise to correct the obstruction during the primary operation. Usually this requires astonishingly little more operating time and it is unlikely that the surgeon will ever have a better opportunity to foster a good result.

There is one notable exception. Occasionally a kidney that cannot be sacrificed is so large that anatomic relationships are widely distorted. A plastic operation is not feasible until the entire renal mass shrinks and appropriate deployment of tissues can be made precisely. Even extensive resection of the dilated renal pelvis will not suffice in these situations.

Preliminary nephrostomy alone was employed for 14 kidneys in 10 patients. None of these seemed to be expendable at that time. Several pelves contained more than 1,000 ml. A few calculi were removed simultaneously. Blood-urea values ran as high as 339 mg/100 ml. In that particular case the value dropped to 48 within 8 months.

Plastic needles, customarily employed for parenteral administration of fluids, have been especially useful as nephrostomy tubes in infants, children, and young adults. They can be inserted under local anesthesia.

Of the 14 kidneys with preliminary nephrostomy drainage in this series, 10 have been salvaged by pyeloplasties that were performed from 1 week to 4 years later. Three patients with bilateral nephrostomies had such good results after pyeloplasty on the better kidney that the other one was removed. One patient awaits further treatment.

WHAT TYPE OF PYELOPLASTY OFFERS BEST RESULTS?

It is generally agreed that any acceptable pyeloplasty must provide: 1) dependent drainage, 2) good funneling, and 3) adequate caliber. Failure to fulfill all these prerequisites permits continued urinary stasis and compromises the result.

Furthermore, he who elects to treat ureteropelvic obstructions must be prepared to cope with five basic situations that pose dissimilar technical problems: 1) high insertion of the ureter on an extrarenal pelvis, 2) an obstructed juncture that already occupies a dependent position, 3) aberrant vessels or fibrous bands, 4) postoperative stenoses, and 5) "microureter." The last entails variable segments of diminutive ureter that may taper just below the ureteropelvic juncture or extend throughout the lumbar region. To date, "microureters" seem to e normal structurally and are best described as "sending a boy to do a man's job." Additional anatomic and physiologic studies of these oddities are under way and will be reported later.

Choice of operations for these five categories offers as much individuality as the selection of a club for a particular shot on a favorite golf course. The wood or iron best suited to one man's ability may be inadequate for his partner. But even so, there are limits to this flexibility if one ever hopes to shoot par. Furthermore, the sharpest distinction between the amateurs and the professionals is the ability to "pitch from the rough to the green." It is axiomatic that any surgeon should utilize those techniques that serve him best, provided his results are comparable to those of others.

When the ureter has a high insertion on an enlarged extrarenal pelvis, the well-known Y-plasty has been preferred (Fig. 3). The conversion of a Y-shaped incision to a V-type closure was not new, but Foley was the first to project this concept into a three-dimensional operation.

When performed properly the Y-plasty creates a V-flap that literally falls into its new position. Unfortunately, the Foley Y-plasty has been abused. Many surgeons have failed to appreciate its fundamental mechanical principles. One limb of the Y must be on the *anterior* surface of the pelvis and the other on the *posterior* surface. Both limbs must be generous to create a truly dependent V-shaped flap. Dainty localized revi-

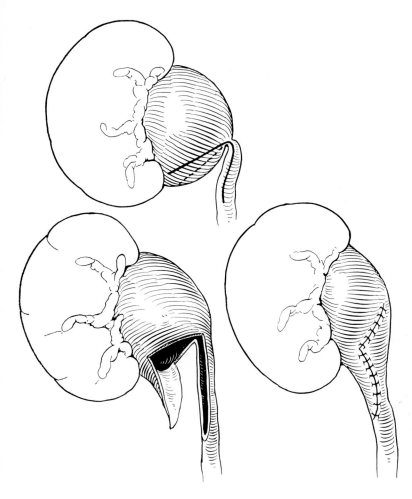

Fig. 3. Foley Y-plasty for high insertion of ureter. (Figures 3, 4, 5, 7, 9, and 10 are reproduced by permission of the Canadian Medical Association from Culp, O. S., "Choice of Operations for Ureteropelvic Obstruction: Review of 385 Cases," *Canad. J. Surg.* 4:157–65, 1961.)

sion of the high insertion per se does not suffice. The tail or stem of the Y must be on the *lateral* aspect of the ureter and carried on to a point well below the lower limit of the extrarenal pelvis, regardless of the adequate caliber of the upper portion of the ureter.

Some enterprising surgeons have attempted to use the Y-plasty in situations that were not suitable for this type of repair. It must be remembered that the Y-plasty was designed for and should be confined to kidneys with high insertion of the ureter.

Many constricted ureteropelvic junctures already occupy a dependent position, as shown in Figure 4. The Y-plasty would create angulation or tension. Dissatisfaction with other plastic procedures in cases of this type prompted the evolution of the "spiral flap" that incorporates commendable features of the three-dimensional Foley operation.

The converging incisions have a broad base, are slightly longer than the ureteral constriction, and follow the spherical contour of the pelvis to avoid undesirable angulation at the base.

Scardino was thinking along the same lines when he proposed his vertical-flap operation. But the spiral method affords opportunities for longer flaps to bridge longer narrowings.

When performed properly the "spiral flap" operation likewise creates a new, dependent, funnel-shaped juncture free of tension. Many questions and even more doubts have been raised regarding the practical ratio between length and width of such flaps. Intensive studies were made of the blood supply of the renal pelvis and upper end of the ureter in both normal and hydronephrotic kidneys. A consistently rich anastomotic pattern of vessels was found in all cases. It is doubtful whether any exacting proportions are necessary when creating flaps of pelvic wall. I have employed some that were 10 to 15 cm long with only 2 cm bases and had no problems. Nevertheless, it is wise to avoid sharply

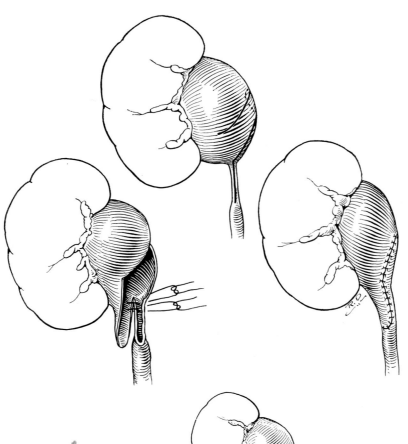

Fig. 4. Spiral-flap technique for dependent ureteropelvic obstruction.

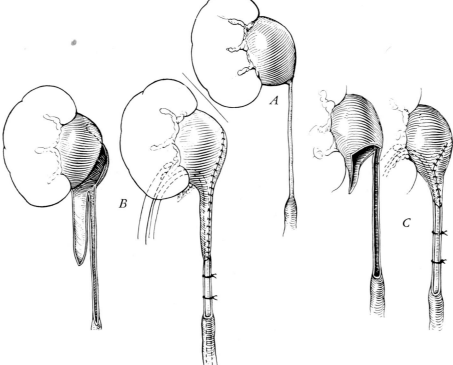

Fig. 5. (A) Typical long stricture or "microureter." (B) Intubation ureterotomy combined with spiral-flap procedure. (C) Davis's operation combined with Y- plasty.

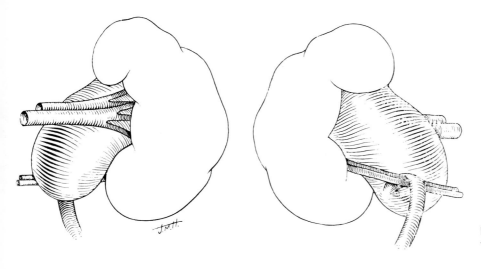

Fig. 6. Hydronephrosis aggravated by aberrant renal vessels.

pointed tips. Even an overlapping rounded end is preferable.

Some constrictions are far too long to be amendable to any type of revision of existing tissues (Fig. 5A). The temptation to stretch a short flap must be avoided. Problems of this type have been managed best with Davis's intubated ureterotomy.

Intubation alone sometimes still leaves an abrupt transition from the pelvis to the ureter. To ensure adequate funneling, it is preferable to combine intubated ureterotomy with the spiral-flap procedure (Fig. 5B) or with the Y-plasty (Fig. 5C).

Admittedly, there are a few well-documented examples of ureteropelvic obstruction due entirely to aberrant vessels. But more commonly they aggravate rather than produce obstruction (Fig. 6). The policy in this series has been to preserve anomalous blood supply. Two patients had only division of aberrant vessels. Both patients were relieved of pain but their renal pelves remained unchanged. In general, revision of the ureteropelvic juncture also will be advisable.

Frequently the ureteropelvic region is encased in scar tissue (Fig. 7). If the pelvis and ureter can be freed sufficiently, one of the previously described techniques is preferred. But too often the entire fibrotic mass must be excised. Reimplantation becomes imperative. The manner in which this is accomplished depends upon the amount of ureter that can be freed. Every effort should be made to create a funnel between pelvis and ureter. Simple approximation (Fig. 7B) must be deplored because results have been atrociously poor. If pelvis and ureter can be freed for only short distances, simple spatulation (Fig. 7A) can create a satisfactory new transition.

There has been considerable championing of the dismembered Y-plasty (Fig. 8), not only for cases of this type but also for *primary* revision of the ureteropelvic region. This technique requires a substantial amount of mobile pelvic and ureteral tissue.

Further cineradiographic studies should resolve conflicting views regarding the virtues of preserving ureteropelvic continuity.

Y-plasties, spiral flaps, intubated ureterotomy, and reimplantation accounted for 97 percent of the pyeloplasties in this study. In 10 cases, unique situations were treated by unorthodox measures.

Obstruction confined to the lower segment of a duplicated pelvis was remedied by joining the two segments of pelvis and partially duplicated ureters (Fig. 9).

A solitary, grotesque, cake kidney had obstruction high in the renal sinus. Some of the medial cortex was resected so that the side-to-side anastomosis could be extended into the dependent portion of the pelvis. This failed and nephrostomy drainage was continued. Similar principles were employed with good results in four horseshoe kidneys after each isthmus had been divided.

A simple Heinecke-Mikulicz operation was tried in two early cases. Only one was successful. The failure was rectified later by a spiral-flap procedure. It is regrettable that this was not employed initially. The Heinecke-Mikulicz is a treacherous maneuver because it tends to replace one type of obstruction with an equally dangerous one.

As mentioned previously, two patients had only division of aberrant vessels with questionable results.

None of the last four procedures could truly be considered an operation of choice.

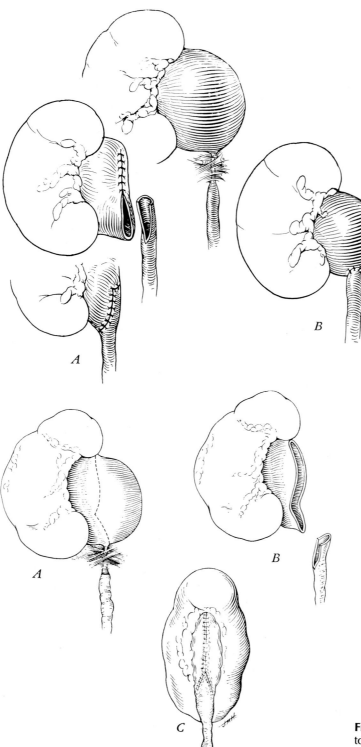

Fig. 7. (*Inset*) Postoperative or inflammatory ureteropelvic obstruction. (*A*) Reimplantation with spatulation of ureter. (*B*) Simple approximation of ureter to dependent portion of pelvis.

Fig. 8. Dismembered Y-plasty. (*A*) Outline of portion to be excised. (*B*) Configuration of remaining pelvis and spatulated end of ureter. (*C*) Inverted Y-type of anastomosis.

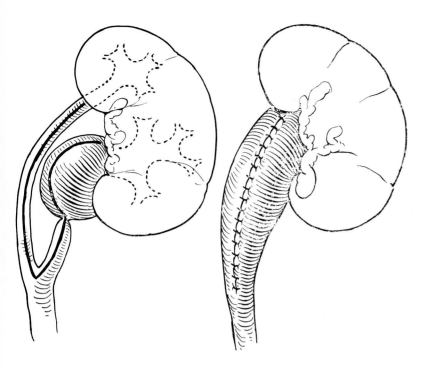

Fig. 9. Elimination of ureteropelvic obstruction in lower segment of duplicated renal pelvis by anastomosis of pelves and ureters.

TABLE 5. Results of 381 Pyeloplasties

Basic Type	Total	Died	Failures		Now Normal		Others	
			Patients	%	Patients	%	Patients	%
Spiral flap	171	2	10	6	64	37	95	56
Y-plasty	139	0	6	4	53	38	80	53
Intubation ureterotomy	37	1	5	14	9	24	22	59
Reimplantation	24	0	3	13	6	25	15	63
Others	10	1	2	20	2	20	5	50
Total	381	4	26	7	134	35	217	57

HOW CAN POSTOPERATIVE RESULTS BE EVALUATED?

All formulas for gradation of postoperative results have been inadequate. None is flexible enough to compensate for the original renal status of the individual or for the indeterminate recuperative power of the affected kidney. Isotope renograms have been promising but disappointing.

Although 35 percent of the patients subjected to plastic procedures now have normal pyelograms and no pain, infection, or calculi (Table 5), the most spectacular results were in individuals with kidneys incapable of resuming normal size or configuration because of permanent cortical damage. For example, a man aged 37 had advanced hydronephrosis and a blood-urea value of 146. The latter dropped to 34 after pyeloplasty. The solitary kidney drains promptly but the pelvis is not normal and remains infected. The operation obviously was successful but the patient can hardly be considered well.

Probably the most significant confirmation of success has been the fact that 107 patients with calculi in their obstructed kidneys have had no recurrences to date following simultaneous pelviolithotomy and pyeloplasty.

Failures usually are evident soon after operation. Additional elapsed time generally reveals further improvement rather than belated deterioration. For example, a 21-year-old Brazilian consistently had 500 ml of residual urine in her solitary kidney after a Y-plasty and was assumed to have a poor result. After 1 year of continued nephrostomy drainage the renal pelvis emptied promptly and completely when the tube was clamped. She now is free of tube, symptoms, and infection.

There were two late failures. These kidneys were removed 3 and 7 years after pyeloplasties because of persistent infections and increasing drug allergies despite less hydronephrosis. Perhaps nephrectomy was the initial operation of choice in both cases.

Results of 381 pyeloplasties are shown in Table 5. The four hospital deaths were due to rupture of an aneurysm of the circle of Willis (one case), coronary occlusion (one case) and renal insufficiency (two cases). Both of the last two patients were azotemic on admission and had multiple calculi. One had been operated on previously elsewhere. Their operations on the ureteropelvic juncture did not prolong the procedures unduly. They probably were doomed from the beginning.

Two late failures due to uncontrollable infection were mentioned previously. Of the other 24 that were evident early, one is in a patient who has a functionless kidney and has refused further treatment because of lack of symptoms. Five kidneys were salvaged by repeat pyeloplasties. These were performed from 3 weeks to 6 months after initial efforts. Secondary plastic procedures seem to be most promising when a substantial time interval can be interposed between operations.

Thirteen kidneys were removed. Many of these probably should have been extirpated initially. Perhaps some could have been salvaged; but the effort did not seem to be justified under the circumstances.

Nephrostomy drainage was continued in the remaining five cases because the kidneys were not expendable. This proved to be a poor solution to a bad problem. Three patients died of renal insufficiency in 2, 3, and 5½ years respectively. One patient was converted to an ileal ureteral substitute 7 years later and is still alive 14 years after the initial procedure. The fifth patient in this small group removed his nephrostomy tube at home soon after dismissal from the hospital and is alive but not well 12 years later. Nevertheless he may have added to his own longevity.

Despite all extenuating circumstances, seven failures occurred under seemingly ideal conditions.

WHY DO FAILURES OCCUR AFTER PYELOPLASTY?

All failures, especially the inexplicable ones, have been studied in detail in hope of finding a responsible and controllable common denominator. Ureteritis and periureteritis produced ureteral stenosis in each patient who underwent subsequent exploration. But the cause of this fibrosis remains obscure. Failures occurred with and without splints, infection, and calculi, and with all degrees of postoperative drainage from the incision. None of the strictures occurred at the end of the splint. Theories have been advanced regarding possible allergies to absorbable sutures; composition of tubes, and so forth. None is tenable.

It is especially noteworthy that 111 consecutive pyeloplasties were performed without a failure. Then there were two failures in rapid succession. Inexperience is not the explanation.

Histologic study was made of 50 normal ureteropelvic regions in kidneys that were removed because of hypernephroma and of 50 obstructed junctures obtained by nephrectomy or autopsy. Many types of special tissue stains were used. All degrees of hydronephrosis were included.

The obstructed juncture invariably was accompanied by hypertrophy of the muscularis of the pelvis, but occasionally the pelvic musculature was replaced by diffuse fibroelastic tissue. It was concluded that perhaps intrinsic alterations of the pelvic wall might preclude normal healing and function. But so far this theory has not accounted for all subsequent failures, despite routine biopsy of the renal pelvis. To date, one can merely conclude that the healing properties of some ureters and pelves are unpredictable.

SHOULD URETERAL SPLINTS (OR STENTS) BE EMPLOYED AND SHOULD URINE BE DIVERTED?

In recent years there has been increasing enthusiasm for abandoning ureteral splints and diversion of urine. The wisdom of abruptly discarding *all* tubes in *all* cases is viewed with skepticism. Of late, about 50 percent of patients have been treated by tubeless methods.

These patients were selected on the basis of the caliber of ureter with which the flap of pelvis was to be anastomosed. Some had infection. A few had calculi. Most had bulbous dilatation just below the obstruction (Fig. 10A). This permitted accurate approximation of tissues in contrast to the difficulties encountered when only a thin ribbon of ureteral tissue was available for a significant distance (Fig. 10B). In the latter situation the two parallel rows of sutures can be so close to each other that viability of the intervening tissue may be jeopardized. Splinting still seems to be prudent in these cases.

Despite careful selection of candidates for the tubeless techniques, four failures occurred. Two of these followed spiral-flap operations and two were the aftermath of Y-plasties. One of the latter kidneys was saved later by *intubation ureterostomy combined with Y-plasty*.

A few other pertinent facts became self-evident in this group. When all goes well there is no question about the reduction in postoperative morbidity, despite the slower return of pelvis and calyces to normal. A few patients never leaked urine, had no infection, and were out of the hospital within 1 week. Others were less fortunate.

Urinary drainage persisted for as long as 28 days,

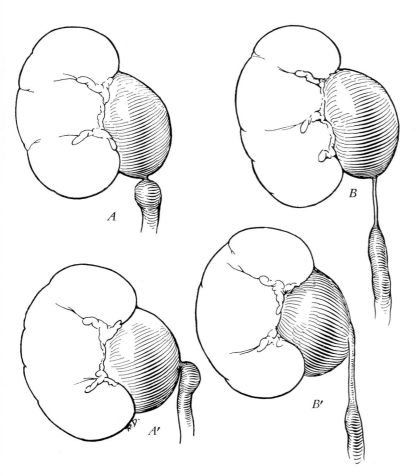

Fig. 10. Types of upper end of ureter. Bulbous dilatation associated with (A) dependent juncture and (A') high insertion of ureter. Narrow ureteral segment with (B) dependent juncture and (B') high insertion.

with an average of 12 days, despite meticulous suturing. A constant urinary poultice is annoying, uneconomical, and demands continued hospitalization. Indwelling ureteral catheters reduce this morbidity but they usually must be kept in place for several days and they preclude customary ambulation. Ureteral catheters were inserted because of copious flank leakage in 12 cases. They usually were dramatically effective, but they defeated the basic therapeutic concept.

In recent years, constant seepage of urine from the incision has been avoided by inserting a Hemovac tube with multiple openings through a stab wound below the incision and attaching it to suction. The patients have been dry and more comfortable but the duration of drainage has not been reduced even though the gradual decrease could be measured accurately.

With nephrostomy, ureteral splinting, and a leg receptacle for urine, most patients have been ambulatory the next day and out of the hospital on or about the seventh postoperative day, but their urine has been infected.

Delayed intrarenal bleeding can be especially harassing. One patient was ready to leave the hospital on the eighth postoperative day when excretory urography failed to visualize the operated kidney. Retrograde pyelography revealed a pelvis filled with blood clot. A nephrostomy tube would have been welcomed at this point. Indeed, it might have prevented this predicament. After 10 days of lavage with streptokinase-streptodornase (Varidase) through indwelling ureteral catheters, the pelvis became free of clot. Fortunately, the kidney appeared normal a year later. Another such experience was encountered; but that kidney eventually had to be removed.

IF ONE DECIDES TO SPLINT URETER AND DIVERT URINE, WHAT METHOD IS PREFERRED AND FOR HOW LONG?

Soft rubber splints (10 to 16 F) have been much more satisfactory than plastic ones. It is imperative to avoid excessively large splints because they can produce ischemia. An extra aperture is made in the intrapelvic portion. This has been a welcome auxiliary outlet for urine when the nephrostomy tube has become dislodged or obstructed.

With Y-plasties and spiral-flap operations a whistle-tip urethral catheter of appropriate size is pased down the ureter a reasonable distance and left in place for 2 weeks. One must remember that a Robinson or solid-end catheter will serve as a cork instead of a conduit!

With intubated ureterotomy and reimplantation, a Levin tube of proper size is used to splint the *entire* ureter for 4 to 8 weeks. In recent months, Silastic-coated tubes have been employed and much less edema has seemed to develop at the operative site.

It is wise to pass Braasch bulbs and calibrate the *entire* ureter from above to be sure that other segments of relative narrowing do not exist. Any that are detected should be incised as advocated by D. R. Smith, W. R. Smart, and others.

All splints are brought out through a lower calyx adjacent to a nephrostomy tube. The latter usually is a 22 F urethral catheter that is removed 24 hours after removal of the splint, provided clamping of the nephrostomy tube is not followed by pain, fever, leakage, or residual urine in the pelvis. It is noteworthy that delayed pyelograms made after injection of contrast medium through the nephrostomy tube do not always reflect the true result because of edema at the operative site and the viscosity of the contrast medium.

During the period of splinting and diversion, the nephrostomy tube is attached to a plastic receptacle on the leg during the day and to a bedside bottle at night. The splint is occluded with heavy silk and is incorporated in the dressing. It is thereby less likely to be dislodged than if it is connected to the drainage system.

Interrupted ooo or oooo chromic sutures are used throughout the closure of the urinary tract. Mannitol is administered as soon as closure has been completed. Some type of sulfonamide or antibiotic is given during convalescence, especially after removal of all tubes, in hope of sterilizing the urine.

SHOULD ONE ANTICIPATE ANY SPECIAL COMPLICATIONS?

Except for the flagrant failures after plastic procedures and the varying degrees of urinary infection that accompanied splinting and diverting catheters, these operations were followed by the same major complications that can be anticipated in any large surgical series. There was nothing unique in the successful management of sequelae. For example, patients with presumptive or obvious phlebothrombosis in a lower extremity did not develop hematuria during controlled anticoagulation therapy.

WHAT TYPE OF FOLLOW-UP STUDY IS INDICATED?

An excretory urogram usually is made before the patient is dismissed from the hospital. Another at home 6 months later is advised and a request is made to have the films forwarded for comparison. The patient is urged to return for thorough study 1 year later–sooner if symptoms referable to the urinary tract develop.

Every effort should be made to sterilize the urine. This invariably entails cooperation with the home-town physician. It may necessitate early return of the patient if the response to antibacterial drugs is diappointing.

Cine and retrograde radiographic studies usually are deferred until the patient returns and are governed by clinical indications.

CONCLUSION

No one harbors any illusions that the therapeutic plan outlined in this presentation is the best. Nevertheless, my associates and I have found that the Y-plasty and the spiral-flap operation seem to have comparable value, and intubation ureterotomy is so effective, even in adverse situations, that splints cannot be condemned.

Reimplantation was employed mostly in disheartening predicaments but served a most useful purpose. Less orthodox methods ae justifiable infrequently.

The ureteropelvic juncture always has been and no doubt always will be treacherous ground that should command everyone's respect. It is not the realm of the faddist. In the parlance of the horsey set, injudicious selection of patients and poor choice of operations constitute a daily double that will pay off only with grief and disappointment.

Commentary: Flap Pelvioplasty in Ureteropelvic Obstruction

James H. DeWeerd

Hydronephrosis secondary to ureteropelvic juncture dysfunction typically presents as a combination of extrarenal pyelectasis and caliectasis. At the turn of the century, surgeons, encouraged by their experience with enteroanastomosis and plastic revisions to increase the lumen of the intestine, applied their newly acquired knowledge to operations designed to improve drainage from the dilated kidney. Although successful end-to-side ureteropelvioplasty was described by Küster in 1891, subsequent publications by Fenger, Finney, Schwyzer, and others introduced techniques that, in one way or another, deployed renal pelvis tissue to enlarge the ureteropelvic juncture.[1] Modification and refinement of the basic principles embodied in these historic procedures have led to flap pelvioplasty as used today.

In 1937, Dr. Fred Foley astutely moved the limbs of the Y incision that Schwyzer in 1923 had patterned after the Durante pyeloplasty.[2] The Foley YV operation soon became the classic flap procedure. The principles embodied are important in that the incisions do not embarrass the blood supply and alteration of contour is accomplished with minimal distortion. The operation is the obvious solution when hydronephrosis is associated with high insertion of the ureter on the medial aspect of the pelvis. The high insertion ensures enough pelvic tissue between the ureteropelvic juncture and the renal hilus to allow creation of a flap of adequate length. The procedure can be applied to an obstructed insertion at the inferior level of the dilated pelvis provided that there is at least 2 cm of pelvic tissue between the ureter and the hilus.

Although the classic Foley YV procedure can be used effectively to correct many obstructive lesions at the ureteropelvic juncture, the dependent juncture with minimal pelvic tissue intervening laterally and the lengthy ureteral narrowing are problems that cannot be resolved by this procedure. In 1951, Ormond S. Culp and I devised a procedure that successfully enlarged a 4-cm segment of narrow ureter below a dependent ureteropelvic juncture.[3] The procedure, which we preferred to call the *spiral flap ureteropelvioplasty,* used the spherical contour of the dilated extrarenal pelvis to provide a long, broad flap of pelvic tissue based laterally and inferiorly. This flap of pelvic tissue was deployed into a longitudinal defect in the ureteropelvic juncture and narrow ureter made by inferior extension of the medial limb of the incisions that created the flap.

The vertical flap operation—an independently conceived variation of the spiral flap—was devised by Scardino and Prince and was described in 1953.[4] Adequate pelvic tissue is required between the dependent ureteropelvic juncture and the renal hilus.

Both operations provide dependent, large-caliber renal pelvis outlets and place the new ureteropelvic juncture at the distal point of the longitudinal incision in the ureter. Accessory or polar vessels that may be present are well removed from the new ureteropelvic juncture, crossing what actually becomes dependent renal pelvis. Maintenance of continuity of tissue inherent in flap operations may provide a bridge for transmission of peristaltic waves and thus enhance transport of urine in the early postoperative period.

The use of free patch grafts of renal pelvis to repair strictures and obstructions of the ureteropelvic juncture and ureter has enjoyed a measure of success, according to reports by Dorsey in 1968 and by Macauley and Frohbose in 1970.[5,6]

The use of ureteral stents and nephrostomy drainage has been considered an integral part of flap ureteropelvioplasty. Hamm and Weinberg in 1955 demonstrated that tubes and stents need not be used routinely.[7] This authoritative report and others, including those of Webb and associates and of Smith and co-workers, are indeed persuasive.[7,8] I continue to be a stanch advocate of the use of tubes and stents to provide adequate drainage of urine, to maintain alignment of structures, to prevent adherence of opposing suture lines, and to ensure patency of the newly enlarged ureteropelvic juncture and upper ureter until tissue fixation associated with the healing process can provide this protection. A whistle-tipped latex catheter in a size that can easily be introduced into the ureter negates the allegation that strictures result. Bacilluria, should it occur, responds to treatment if transport of urine is satisfactory. Advocates of tubeless techniques usually revert to use of stent and nephrostomy tube when dealing with a solitary kidney or a difficult bilateral problem. *I believe every renal unit treated should enjoy the confidence that stenting and drainage provide for the solitary or difficult unit.* Prolonged stenting and urinary drainage, that is, for more than 10 to 12 days, are generally unnecessary.

Every case requires careful study of the problem it presents, and one must choose a surgical approach with circumspect deliberation and sound judgment. A thorough knowledge of proved methods greatly complements surgical skill. Regardless of the method of correction selected, I cannot overemphasize the need for meticulous care in the handling of tissues while the pelvis and ureter are incised and the edges are reapproximated with accurately placed, delicate stitches of fine, absorbable suture material.

REFERENCES

1. DeWeerd JH: Renal pelvis and ureteropelvic surgery. In Glenn JF (ed): Urologic surgery, 2nd ed, pp 90–119. Hagerstown, Harper & Row, 1975
2. Foley FEB: A new plastic operation for stricutre at the uretero-pelvic junction: Report of 20 operations. J Urol 38:643, 1937
3. Culp OS, DeWeerd JH: A pelvic flap operation for certain types of ureteropelvic obstruction: Preliminary report. Proc Staff Meet Mayo Clin 26:483, 1951
4. Scardino PL, Prince CL: Vertical flap ureteropelvioplasty: Preliminary report. South Med J 46:325, 1953
5. Dorsey JW: Pyeloplasty by modified ureteroneopyelostomy. J Urol 100:353, 1968
6. Macauley RJ, Frohbose WJ: The surgical correction of ureteropelvic junction obstruction using a free graft of renal pelvis wall. J Urol 104:67, 1970
7. Hamm FC, Weinberg SR: Renal and ureteral surgery without intubation. J Urol 73:475, 1955
8. Webb EA, Smith BA Jr, Price WE: Plastic operations upon the ureter without intubation. J Urol 77:821, 1957
9. Smith BA Jr, Webb EA, Price WE: Ureteroplastic procedures without diversion. J Urol 83:116, 1960

ANNOTATED BIBLIOGRAPHY

Foley FEB: A new plastic operation for stricture at the uretero-pelvic junction: Report of 20 operations. J Urol 38:643, 1937

The December 1937 issue of the *Journal of Urology* was devoted largely to hydronephrosis (10 of 13 articles). All 10 papers, presented at the annual meeting of the American Urological Association in Minneapolis on June 29, 1937, provide informative reading for anyone interested in the ureteropelvic juncture. The most outstanding article is that by Dr. Fred Foley. In this detailed classic, Dr. Foley succinctly addresses hydronephrosis and its causes and effects, including differential renal function and the indications for surgical correction instead of nephrectomy when advanced hydronephrotic atrophy has occurred. The author reviews the evolution of ureteropelvio plasty as adaptations of general surgical principles and procedures and logically develops the principles involved in the YV-plasty. He used his procedure first in 1923 and on 19 additional renal units successfully through 1936. Twenty units at risk for 1 to 14 years were the basis of his report. The basic principle is placement of diverging limbs of the Y on the anterior and posterior surfaces of the pelvis and of the stem on the lateral surface of the ureter. The tip of the flap is carefully sutured into the lower end of the ureteral incision, and the closure is completed as a V. A soft rubber stent remains in place for 1 week, and a nephrostomy tube is removed after 1 week if the outlet is patent.

Culp OS, DeWeerd JH: A pelvic flap operation for certain types of ureteropelvic obstruction: Preliminary report. Proc Staff Meet Mayo Clin 26:483, 1951

The authors were stimulated to devise a method to resolve the problem created by a 4-cm, narrowed ureteral segment below a dependent ureteropelvic juncture in a child aged 3. The problem was resolved by fashioning a long flap of tissue from the spherical contour of the extrarenal pelvis. This broad-based flap composed of tissue from anterior, medial, and posterior surfaces of the pelvis rotated nicely to fill a longitudinal defect in the ureter. The inferolateral position of the broad-based flap, which is clearly illustrated, afforded the vascular supply necessary to maintain tissue viability. The medial incision in the renal pelvis was extended inferiorly through the ureteropelvic juncture and down the ureter until normal caliber was reached. A stent and a nephrostomy tube were used in this and 11 other cases cited in this preliminary report.

Scardino PL, Prince CL: Vertical flap ureteropelvioplasty: Preliminary report. South Med J 46:325, 1953

The vertical flap operation evolved during an operative procedure on a young female who had a 2-cm segment of ureter below a dependent ureteropelvic juncture. This operation is a variation of the spiral flap procedure, except that the anterior or posterior surface of the dilated pelvis is used rather than all surfaces of the spherical pelvis. A McIver or Cummings catheter was inserted to stent the reconstructed juncture and drain the renal pelvis. Nephropexy was performed when indicated in the six cases reported.

DeWeerd JH: Ureteropelvioplasty. In Glenn JF (ed): Urologic Surgery, 3rd ed, pp 227–252. Philadelphia, JB Lippincott, 1983

This comprehensive treatise reviews renal pelvis and pelvic outlet surgery and deals extensively with reconstruction of the obstructed ureteropelvic juncture. Strong support is given to the thesis that several factors or causes may occur alone or in combination to produce hydronephrosis. The need for careful study of each problem is emphasized. "Circumspect deliberation" coupled with "sound surgical judgment" is enhanced by "an accurate comprehension of proved [surgical] methods" to "greatly complement surgical skill and ingenuity" to reduce the risk of disappointing surgical results. Proved, widely accepted variations of flap reconstructions, as well as procedures combining dismembered operations with flap procedures, are diagrammatically illustrated. Reduction pelvioplasty and alternative management of duplicated systems are described in detail. Ligation and division of accessory blood vessels to the lower hilus or pole are condemned, and relocation of the ureteropelvic juncture below or inferior to the vessels is stressed as the proper method of management. Transposition of the ureter achieved by dismembered ureteropelviostomy ordinarily does not remove the hazard of blood vessel compression or angulation. Transposition of the ureter is rarely indicated. Surgical techniques, including exquisite care in handling tissues, are emphasized. Adjuvants, including stents and drainage tubes, are urged for all circumstances anything less than optimal. Routine use of stents and diversion tubes is advised, since it may not be possible to predict that they will not be needed during the postoperative course. Important postoperative care measures are (1) Hemovac drainage of parapelvic and paraureteral spaces to prevent the accumulations of urine or serum that predispose to infections and excessive fibrosis and (2) routine use of chemotherapeutic or antibiotic agents as an antibacterial screen. Complications include those related to postoperative hemorrhage and resultant clot retention, suture line disruption, and infection. The late sequences include stone formation after clot retention or infection and failure to eradicate deep-seated infection. Both these problems are accentuated by persisting hydronephrosis due to such conditions as poor urine transport and postoperative stenosis.

Hanna MK: Some observations on congenital ureteropelvic junction obstruction. Urology 12:151, 1978

On the logical premise that "better understanding of the patho-physiology of UPJO [ureteropelvic juncture obstruction] allows the surgeon to choose the type of surgery more rationally and thereby reduce the morbidity and improve the results," the author presents a detailed discussion beginning with anatomic and functional consideration of the normal ureteropelvic juncture. Discounting widespread acceptance of the theory of functional obstruction, Dr. Hanna presents a spectrum of abnormalities found in 35 obstructed segments when representative tissues were examined under light microscopy. His findings support the "no-single-cause" thesis: 8 specimens were normal, 13 had reduced muscle bulk, and 14 exhibited muscular malorientation with thickened adventitia and different degrees of inflammatory cellular infiltration. Electron microscopy (EM) revealed an excessive amount of collagen between the muscle fibers of the obstructed ureteropelvic juncture. The role of the aberrant or accessory vessel or vessels is considered to be secondary, and vesicoureteral reflux may produce renal pelvis distention out of proportion to the degree of ureteral dilatation. In these circumstances, the obstruction is relative, and differentiation of this ureteropelvic junction obstruction associated with relfux from primary ureter-opelvic junction obstruction is necessary. Diagnostic studies include clinical evaluation, intravenous pyelography, and voiding cystourethrography. Radioisotope and pressure flow studies by percutaneous renal puncture may be helpful in some instances. Numerous surgical procedures have been described. They can be put into two general categories: dismembered pyeloplasty and nondismembered pyeloplasty. Dr. Hanna believes that irrespec-tive of method, Foley's four criteria must be met, namely, formation of funnel, dependent drainage, no shortening of suture line, and watertight anastomosis. A plea is made for a prospective study by EM to help determine structural abnormalities within the cells at the ureteropelvic juncture and thereby to provide a basis for prognosis after surgical correction.

OVERVIEW: CONGENITAL HYDRONEPHROSIS: MEDICAL EVALUATION AND SURGICAL TECHNIQUE AND JUDGMENT

Clarence V. Hodges

The treatment of congenital hydronephrosis continues to be made up of a fascinating combination of medical evaluation and surgical technique and judgment. The commentary in Chapter 28 cites the interesting article "Some Observations on Congenital Ureteropelvic Junction Obstruction." This paper considers some of the theoretic possibilities associated with the cause of ureteropelvic junction obstruction and postulates that "sick cells" at the ureteropelvic junction interfere with the passage of peristalsis from the renal pelvis into the upper ureter. This helps to rationalize the difficulty that I have had in accepting "functional" obstruction of the ureteropelvic junction as a cause for obstruction not manifestly due either to intrinsic stricture or to extrinsic obstruction, as by fascial or vascular bands, and also makes it logical to exclude the "sick" portion of the ureteropelvic junction from the surgical repair.

The commentary by Dr. James DeWeerd on "flap pyeloplasty" is a distillation of the long and extensive experience that the late Dr. Ormond S. Culp and he have had in treating a large number of patients with hydronephrosis.

PREOPERATIVE EVALUATION

The indications for pyeloplasty have been summarized as the demonstration of an obstruction on radiologic examination at the ureteropelvic junction, usually accompanied by symptoms of pain on the ipselateral side and sometimes, particularly in children, by GI symptoms of upper abdominal pain, nausea, and vomiting. Sometimes, hydronephrotic kidneys will bleed, particularly if there is infection. Infection is also often accompanied by increased pain, fever, chills, and white blood cells (WBCs) and bacteria in the urine. Some hydronephroses may be asymptomatic; some, and for some reason this appears to be most common in women, may be *compensated* (a term coined by the late Dr. Spencer Hoyt) and remain at the same state of functional activity without increase or decrease in distension for many years. Also, in distinction to the usual belief that hydronephrosis is a progressive condition, some hydronephroses seem to improve with observation and time and to regain a normal or near-normal state.

Contraindications to treatment by surgery of hydronephrosis include (1) a patient who is too ill to undergo surgery, (2) infected kidney that require drainage either by ureteral catheter or by percutaneous nephrostomy until the infection is controlled by drainage and appropriate antibiotics, and (3) the relative contraindication of repeated operations that have left a kidney encased in scar and with compromised renal vasculature and function. Dr. F. E. B. Foley, under whom Dr. Culp, Dr. William Smart, and I served an apprenticeship, believed that a history of stone formation was a relative contraindication to pyeloplasty.

The work-up includes, in addition to a careful history

and physical examination, the laboratory evaluation of the urine for infection and evidence of chronic renal disease. Intravenous urography will usually give a good representation of the degree and kind of ureteropelvic junction obstruction as well as indication of the amount of impairment of renal function. Delayed and drainage films are very helpful in estimating to what degree renal function has suffered. Sometimes, the osmotic diuresis that accompanies excretory urography will tend to accentuate the degree of obstruction present by presenting an unusual fluid load to the kidney. It has also been noted that the removal of one kidney may result in the decompensation of a borderline obstruction of the other kidney pelvis when an unusual fluid load is applied.

Quantitative evaluation of the ureteropelvic junction obstruction has been facilitated by the development and improvement of techniques for percutaneous flank nephrostomy and the introduction of the Whitaker test. It is now possible to place a plastic catheter directly into the renal pelvis, to introduce contrast material that will greatly improve on the image of the poorly functioning kidney, and to submit the kidney to a functional test in which a known amount of fluid is required to be passed on by the ureteropelvic junction each minute. The third test consists of measuring the pressures brought about in the renal pelvis by the ability or lack of ability of the ureteropelvic junction to transmit the fluid load. The use of the renal scan is also important to evaluate renal function, renal blood flow, and tubular capacity of the ailing kidney. It often may be necessary and quite advisable to do a preoperative nephrostomy in order to allow renal function to improve and to gain control of renal infection. Percutaneous nephrostomy has many advantages over open surgical nephrostomy, which formerly was employed.

OPERATIVE TECHNIQUE

The operative approach I have come to favor is a supra-12th rib approach in which the incision is placed directly over the 12th rib and then allowed to slide off the upper edge of the rib and through the intercostal muscles to the perinephric fascia. Incision can then be extended forward onto the abdominal muscles with relative freedom from trauma to the intercostal nerves above or below the incision. This incision is readily closed by approximating the 11th and 12th ribs, and injury to the 11th and 12th nerves with the loss of functional capacity of the muscles and a weakness simulating herniation is usually avoided. In my experience, this incision is less painful than a rib resection or the conventional subcostal loin incision. for many years I have injected the proximal 11th and 12th intercostal nerves near their junction with the angle of the rib with a solution of Marcaine or a similar long-acting analgesic and have found that usually there is less postoperative pain.

When both kidneys are involved, I usually select the most symptomatic kidney first or the one that is most badly damaged if the other one has relatively good function. In cases of equal degree of damage and loss of function, one may elect to do both kidneys either through a single transverse abdominal incision or, perhaps more ideally, through separate flank incisions at the same sitting.

Stenting has been a subject of controversy for a number of years. I have done it both since my experience with Dr. Foley, who always used both a stent and a nephrostomy tube, and since the advent of proponents of nonstenting "slash-in-the-pelvis" drainage. It is difficult to believe that profuse and prolonged urinary drainage can do anything but cause harmful scarring. In addition, a stent helps to position the ureter and to prevent it from being drawn backward and against the lower pole of the kidney by postsurgical scarring. This type of angualtion has been the cause of a number of incidences of postoperative scarring, in my experience. I believe that all patients should be treated as "complicated," in an effort to prevent the operation from becoming complicated, by using stents routinely. This usually involves placing the stent through a nephrostomy site and having it extend down the ureter and into the bladder, using the largest tube that will fit comfortably in the ureteropelvic anastomosis. The stent can be removed in 5 to 6 days. As soon as one is satisifed that the clamping of the nephrostomy tube does not cause undue pain, fever, or an increase in drainage along the drain site, the nephrostomy tube can be removed as well. I have put Penrose drains in the majority of patients but the Hemovac drain is somewhat more tidy. If there is profuse drainage from the drain site, an ileostomy bag over the drain site will help to keep the patient dry and provide an estimate of the amount of drainage.

POSTOPERATIVE EVALUATION

Complications noted in the early postoperative period are almost always headed by fever, which tends to go up in a spike on the evening or day after surgery and then gradually subside over 2 to 3 days. This can be minimized by the use of a nephrostomy tube so that urine does not extravasate through the perirenal tissues. Pain is variable and will depend on the patient and the use, as described above, of perioperative installation of an intercostal blocking agent.

Infection is seldom encountered as a significant complication as long as preoperative sepsis has been controlled. Usually, after catheters are withdrawn, the patient will require chemotherapy, if cultures are positive, to promote rapid healing and minimize scarring. Prolonged urinary drainage may be allowed to persist for at least 1 week without the need for a ureteral catheter by retrograde means. After this time, it is a matter of judgment whether an ileostomy bag applied over the general drain site or an indwelling ureteral catheter, which may be hard to maintain in place, will fit the patient's needs better.

Late complications include stricture, which may be due to an inadequate repair, devascularization, or its being bound to the lower pole of the kidney by fibrous adhesions, as described above. Most strictures will require reoperation and may require ureterocalycostomy, since the ureter may now be too short to reach the ureteropelvic junction without undue tension. The calculus, unrecognized at surgery or more recently formed (probably unusual) in the postoperative period, may result in prolonged drainage and will require retrograde evaluation by urographic means and sometimes reoperation. Chronic pain may occur as a result of recurrence of obstruction, inflammatory and scar tissue involvement of one or more of the intercostal nerves, or both. This may require several stratagems to differentiate. The most valuable may be the water loading or diuretic test to determine if the pain is actually due to the inability of the ureteropelvic junction to pass urine down into the ureter. The use of intercostal blocks may help point out the pain resulting from intercostal nerve involvement.

Criteria for a successful operation are (1) an asymptomatic patient, (2) freedom from infection, and (3) evidence of good renal function or, at least, no loss of renal function on excretory urography. Many authors have emphasized that the results will never be perfect on x-ray study, but they may be judged satisfactory if the above criteria are met.

Indications for reoperation are persistent infection, pain that appears to be due to persistent obstruction at the ureteropelvic junction, or evidence of decreasing renal function that appears to be due to an unsuccessful procedure. Such reoperation is often fraught with difficulty because of extensive scarring around the kidney and requires careful, patient dissection of the kidney to maintain the integrity of the ureter and free up the kidney and the ureteropelvic junction to the point where a successful operative reanastomosis can be made. It is sometimes necessary to free the kidney entirely, including the renal pedicle, in order to mobilize the kidney downward to gain additional length. It is in these operations that ureterocalicostomy should receive very serious consideration.

Chapters 28 and 29 have described the three types of ureteropelvic junction obstruction: (1) a persistent obstruction with dependent funneling, (2) a persistent obstruction with a high insertion of the ureter, and (3) the so-called miniureter described by Culp, in which a variable portion of the upper ureter is simply much smaller than the remainder of the ureter. At present, most writers favor dismembered pyeloplasty, the so-called Anderson–Hynes procedure, as being applicable to the first two types of obstruction. The third type, much rare, will require either a Davis type of intubated ureterotomy with long-term stenting or, possibly, autotransplantation of the kidney and ureteropyelostomy, as is sometimes done for renal transplant.

The surgical conduct of the operation for hydronephrosis has been stressed by all authors to consist of careful, superlatively gentle handling of delicate tissues, the construction of accurate suture lines by meticulous and fine-material suturing, the careful regard for the vascularity of the kidney, and the judicial handling of stents, nephrostomy tubes, and infections in the postoperative period. The evaluations mentioned above make it possible to quantify the degree of obstruction and relative loss of renal function and to predict with more certainty those kidneys, a substantial percentage, in which nephrectomy will be the most logical and most economical method of handling the problem. The degree of judgment and skill required to handle single kidneys is even more demanding; the same is true for those complicated by the presence of stones or ureteral strictures. All these conditions require thorough preoperative evaluation of the patient, the best in surgical expertise, and a plentiful, helpful degree of philosophy to recognize, accept, and counteract the complications that beset every extensive surgical experience.

PART FIFTEEN

SURGERY
OF THE URETER

30

AN EVALUATION OF INTUBATION URETEROTOMY WITH A DESCRIPTION OF SURGICAL TECHNIQUE

William R. Smart

From the Department of Surgery, Division of Urology, University of California School of Medicine, San Francisco 22, Cal.

Reprinted from Journal of Urology, Vol. 85, pp. 512–524, 1961. Copyright 1961 by The Williams & Wilkins Company, Baltimore.

Intubation ureterotomy is a highly successful method of correcting strictures of the lumbar ureter. Recent articles in the urological literature have described other methods and have indicated dissatisfaction with splinting and nephrostomy. Yet most investigators admit that in the more formidable obstructions of the lumbar ureter, no other technique is applicable. The author believes that failures of the intubation operation are preventable for the most part if an orderly system of preoperative study, surgical technique and postoperative care is followed. Incorrect splinting and inadequate urinary diversion are two common causes of failure. Both of these subjects will be dealt with in detail. The indentification and elimination of segments of nonobstructive "relative stenosis" in the lumbar ureter, distal to the stricture, are discussed as a means of preventing strictures secondary to splinting.

Read at annual meeting of Mid-Atlantic Section of American Urological Association, Inc., White Sulphur Springs, W. Va., November 11–14, 1959.

The work of David M. Davis in his pioneering efforts to perfect intubation ureterotomy has been a significant step forward in the correction of a defect that, for the most part, is not amenable to any other procedure.

BASIC DIAGNOSTIC EVALUATION

The essential diagnostic steps should determine the location and length of the ureteral stricture, and assay the degree of obstruction and extent of the renal damage.

1. Intravenous pyelography is used to determine:
   a. The status of the contralateral kidney and ureter.
   b. The proximal limits of the stricture. (However, this gives us a little information on the status of the ureter distal to the stricture.)
   c. The degree of upper tract distortion.
   d. A rough estimate of differential renal function.

   In suspected obstructive lesions of the upper urinary tract, lower ureteral compression should not be used during intravenous pyelography since it introduces an artificial obstruction which may distort the true picture.

2. A retrograde study should be done following bilateral ureteral catheterization to obtain:
   a. The volume of residual urine in the renal pelvis, if possible.
   b. Examination and culture of urine from both kidneys and from the bladder.
   c. Visual evidence of correct placement of the catheters by plain roentgenogram.
   d. Differential renal function by phenolsulfonpthalein (P.S.P.) test.
   e. Retrograde pyelograms after complete filling of all calyces with radiopaque solution. (An inspection of the intravenous urograms should be made to obtain a rough estimate of the amount of solution needed for each side. Overdistention is to be avoided.)
   f. Roentgenographic visualization of the entire ureter is obtained by slow withdrawal of the ureteral catheters, during continuous dye injection, well down into the lower third of the ureters. In many cases an additional film is taken with the patient in a 45 degree oblique or lateral position with the affected side down. Complete withdrawal of the catheters is not done in the event that a second instillation of dye is required for adequate filling. The reason for visualizing the entire ureter by retrograde means is to determine the length and degree of the primary stricture and to be certain that there are no other abnormalities in the distal ureteral segment that would interfere with the satisfactory placement of the ureteral splint.
   g. Abnormal pelvic emptying by noting residual dye on a delayed film taken at fifteen to thirty minutes. (Delay in emptying after retrograde pyelograms is more significant than similar findings in intravenous pyelography because continuing dye excretion is eliminated. Care should be taken in evaluating abnormal dye retention in the delayed erect films in patients with renal ptosis. If the pelvis empties when the patient is returned to a supine position, the cause of the obstruction is due to the ptosis and not to intrinsic obstructive factors.)

3. Retrograde ureterograms
   Excellent visualization of the ureteral segment distal to a stricture can be obtained by a retrograde ureterogram using an acorn-tipped catheter. This is especially useful in cases in which angulations in the intramural and lower ureteral segments make catheterization of the ureter impossible. This method also avoids the abnormal ureteral spasm that could result from catheterization which may give roentgeno-

graphic evidence of constrictions (''phantom strictures''). The technique is as follows:
   a. One part of indigo carmine is added to five parts of the radiopaque solution.
   b. The tip of the acorn catheter is placed snugly into the ureteral orifice, through a panendoscope; care is taken not to use excessive pressure on the catheter which could kink the intramural ureter and result in unsatisfactory dye injection.
   c. With the catheter in place and under direct vision an assistant slowly injects 3 to 5 cc (adult dose) of the prepared solution. Any leakage or reflux of dye into the bladder can be seen and the necessary adjustments made. Here again care must be taken not to overdistend the ureter.
   d. The roentgenogram is taken immediately after the termination of dye instillation, with the catheter tip still in place.

SURGICAL EVALUATION

Surgically, hydronephrosis can be divided roughly into two clinical groups, extrarenal and intrarenal, although many cases are a mixture of both types (Fig. 1). In extrarenal hydronephrosis nearly perfect anatomic and functional results are obtained by the successful correction of the primary obstruction and adequate reconstruction of the renal pelvis (Fig. 1). In intrarenal hydronephrosis the loss of renal tissue is permanent as a rule; despite complete eradication of the primary obstruction, residual urine may persist in the calyces resulting in chronic infection that is most difficult to control. The subsequent pyelonephritis eventually destroys the kidney. These patients often are never completely cured. However, the functional recovery of such kidneys may be surprisingly good, especially in cases of solitary kidney, bilateral lesions, and in young persons.

1. Surgical choice in bilateral hydronephrosis:
   a. In uninfected hydronephrosis of equal degree either side may be repaired first. In cases of unequal degree the more damaged side should be repaired first. In both instances the repair of the other kidney should follow as soon as practicable.
   b. If the better of the two kidneys is infected it should be repaired first, after the infection has been controlled. The repair of the more advanced side should follow as soon as is practical so its function is not further depleted through the forces of renal counterbalance. This plan of surgical attack conforms with the proved theory of renal counterbalance advanced by Frank Hinman, Sr.
   c. If one kidney is hydronephrotic, but salvageable, (sic) and the other extensively damaged beyond hope of surgical repair, but still has function,

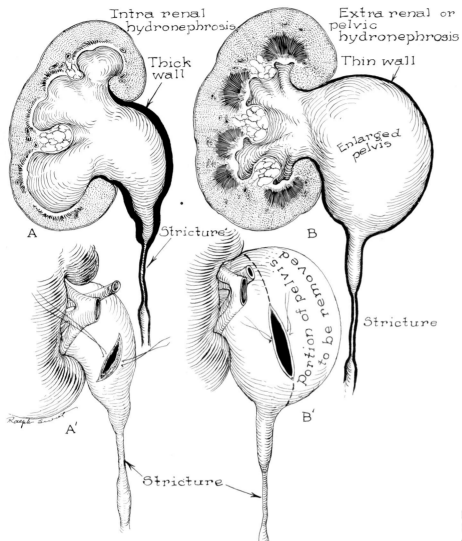

Fig. 1. Types of hydronephrosis. Placement of pyelotomy when redundant pelvic wall is to be resected.

nephrectomy should not be done until the better kidney has been successfully repaired. Nephrostomy drainage of the more damaged kidney will conserve as much renal function as possible while its mate is being surgically restored (Fig. 2). It may then either be re-evaluated or removed depending upon the functional recovery of its mate.

2. Contraindications to intubation ureterotomy.

No single operation will correct the wide variety of obstructive lesions found in this area. Despite the diagnostic findings the final decision as to the type of plastic repair required in a given case can only be made at the time of operation.

a. Pure extrinsic obstruction.

If extrinsic obstructions such as blood vessels, fibrous bands, or kinking adhesions are found they must either be eliminated or rendered nonobstructive. When an essential blood vessel is obstructive, reimplantation of the ureteropelvic junction to a dependent nonobstructive position may be considered. In such cases if a marginal cuff of pelvic wall is taken with the ureter it greatly simplifies the repair. The removal of an obvious extrinsic obstruction does not mean that the ureteral problem has been solved; there may be an associated congenital intrinsic stenosis which, if not corrected, will result

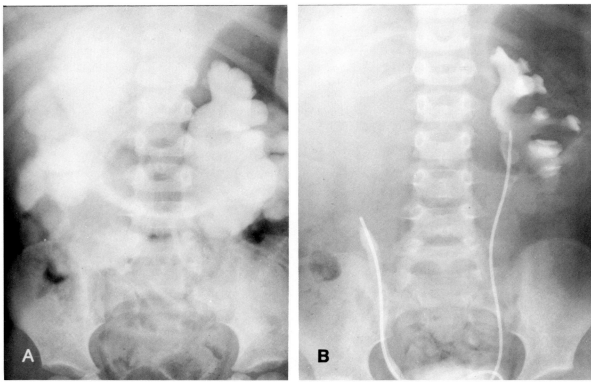

Fig. 2. Retrograde pyelograms in case of 3-year-old boy with bilateral ureteropelvic obstruction. (*B*) Right kidney is beyond repair but still has function. Left kidney is sustaining life. Right nephrostomy preceded repair on left side. (*B*) Left pyelogram 1 year after operation. Function normal and urine sterile. Right nephrectomy was performed 2 months after surgical repair on left side.

in clinical failure. All patients should have ureteral calibration with Braasch bulbs through a small pyelotomy incision.

b. High ureteropelvic insertion.

At times what appears on the roentgenogram to be a dependent ureteral obstruction is in reality a high insertion of the ureter in which the upper ureteral segment is tightly bound to the renal pelvis by layers of thick enveloping fibrous tissue. In such cases a Foley Y-plasty is indicated.

c. Ureteral stricture adjacent to a dependent ureteropelvic junction.

Here we have a choice between the Culp-Scardino type of ureteropelvioplasty or intubation ureterotomy. The Culp-Scardino procedure is excellent if the stricture is of such a length that an adequate flap of pelvic wall can be turned down. There are two benefits from this procedure: 1) better pelvic drainage is obtained through the resultant funneling of a dependent ureteropelvic junction, 2) the re-

sulting per primam healing requires a much shorter period of urinary diversion and splinting (2 to 3 weeks). These two advantages are also present in the Foley Y-plasty procedure.

However, in patients with a small extrarenal pelvis or an intrarenal pelvis, in which an adequate flap is not obtainable, the intubstion ureterotomy is the operation of choice.

d. Ureteral strictures with dense avascular scarring. It is not uncommon to find the strictured segment deeply imbedded in dense avascular scar tissue following the failure of previous surgical procedures for correction of ureteral obstruction. After dissection of the involved segment, if its blood supply is deemed insufficient for the necessary tissue regeneration required for healing after intubation ureterotomy, segmental resection should be considered provided adequate ureteral length can be obtained. The resection is made through viable ureter above and below the stricture cutting the ureter on a 45 degree angle and approximating it with four or five 4-0 atraumatic chromic catgut sutures over an adequate splinting catheter without tension on the suture line. The same technique of ureteral calibration and selection of splint and nephrostomy tube should be used as will be outlined later. The use of T-tubes or other "short cuts" as substitutes for proper ureteral splinting and urinary diversion should be avoided if at all possible since they increase the chances of fialure through malfunction. In this group of cases we have the most adverse conditions and comparatively poor functional results.

SURGICAL TECHNIQUE

1. Approach

Exposure of the entire kidney and lumbar ureter is obtained through a generous flank incision either

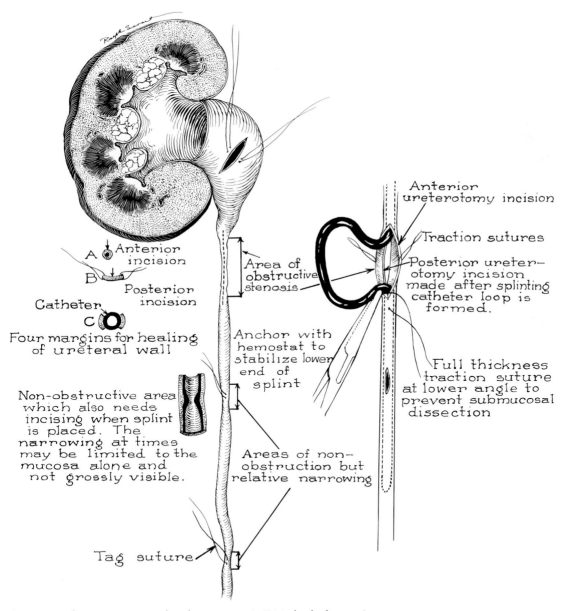

Fig. 3. Nonobstructive areas of "relative stenosis." Method of posterior ureterotomy.

just below or through the bed of the twelfth rib. Gerota's fascia is open posterolaterally. Care is taken not to disturb any fat lying between the ureter and the psoas muscle. This layer of fat assures mobility of the ureter postoperatively.

2. Exposure of the ureter.

The pelvis and ureteropelvic junction are evaluated only after the removal of redundant perirenal fat and areolar tissue, which at times may be quite fibrous and adherent. As a rule the obstructive segment can be easily seen at this time. When exposing the ureter there should be minimal dissection of this structure from its bed. If the ureter must be removed from its bed, care should be taken to leave as much periureteral tissue intact as possible. The investing periureteral tissues carry the blood vessels and nerves that supply the ureter in a segmental fashion with anastomosis to adjacent segments. Any excessive impairment of these two vital systems will defeat the purpose of this procedure at the outset. Only persistent arterial bleeders should be point-clamped and tied with fine catgut; venous or capillary bleeding, if excessive, can be controlled by warm packs. Hemostatic electrocoagulation should not be used on the ureter.

3. Pyelotomy, anterior ureterotomy, ureteral calibration.

Placement of the pyelotomy incision should conform with the data shown in Fig. 1, *B* if redundant pelvic wall is to be resected. The incision is made between stay sutures in the pelvic wall. A progression of whistle-tip or coudé ureteral catheters, well lubricated with sterile olive oil, are passed down the ureter through the obstructive segment until a snug fit is obtained. Forcing any bulb or dilating catheters through the stricture will only serve to traumatize the mucosa and damage the ureteral wall. After the stabilizing ureteral catheter is in place the entire strictured segment is cleanly incised longitudinally through all layers starting 4 to 6 mm. above the stricture and extending that much below (Fig. 3). A 4-0 atraumatic chromic stay suture is now carefully placed through all layers of the ureteral wall at the lower angle of the ureterotomy incision to prevent submucosal dissection during ureteral calibration and splint placement (Fig. 3). Stay sutures are placed on either edge of the anterior ureterotomy margins in the midportion, and the ureteral catheter is withdrawn.

Lubricated Braasch bulb catheters are passed through the anterior ureterotomy 4 to 5 inches down the ureter in increasing sizes until the average caliber of the ureteral lumen is determined. In the adult this will vary from size 10 to 14F. Any area of resistance to the downward passage of the bulb, with hanging or dragging on its withdrawal, is tagged with a 5-0

atraumatic chromic suture for subsequent incision (Fig. 3). These represent the areas of "relative stenosis" which if not corrected may result in clinical strictures secondary to splinting. (These nonobstructive segments with decreased caliber have been found in 15 to 20 percent of the cases in this series.)

4. Ureteral splinting, posterior ureterotomy.

An assortment of soft, red rubber Robinson

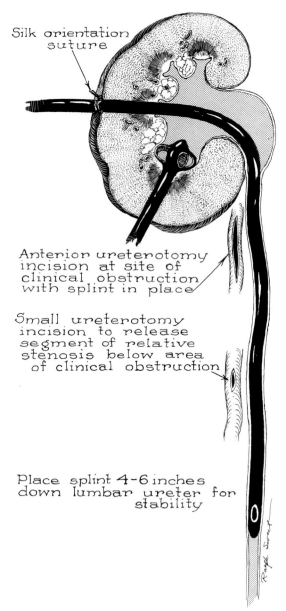

Silk orientation suture

Anterior ureterotomy incision at site of clinical obstruction with splint in place

Small ureterotomy incision to release segment of relative stenosis below area of clinical obstruction

Place splint 4-6 inches down lumbar ureter for stability

Fig. 4. Nephrostomy and splint placement.

catheters in sizes 8 through 14F should be available to be used as splints. All splints used are well lubricated with sterile olive oil. Using the information obtained from bulb calibration the largest splint is passed, through the pyelotomy, that will slide down the ureter without drag. Then it is removed and the *next smallest size* splinting catheter is put in place as the *permanent splint*. Although in most adults the

TABLE 1. Intubation Ureterotomy Technique (20 Cases)

Patient	Age	Sex	Date (sic) Surgery Date Last Seen	Kidney	Type of Obstruction and Other Data	Size Splint Size Nephrostomy Tube	Length of Ureterotomy Incision	PreOp. Infection	Duration of Splinting	Results
J.E.	25	M	(4/5/49)	Right	Intrinsic obst., pelvic resection.	#14–#30	2.5 cm	No	5 wks	Good
C.H.* (Figs. 5 and 6)	27	M	(5/9/50) (10/7/53)	Left	Intrinsic stenosis, extrinsic vessels. (non-obst. area)	#14–#30	2.5 cm	No	6 wks	Good
M.D. (Fig. 7)	36	F	(3/21/51) (6/27/57)	Right	Intrinsic stenosis, extrinsic bands.	#12–#30	2.0 cm	No	6 wks	Good
R.L. (Fig. 8)	36	F	(6/20/51) (4/13/59)	Left	Intrinsic stenosis, intrarenal hydronephrosis.	#12–#28	5.0 cm	No	6 wks	Poor
							(left nephrectomy 2/8/55)			
J.J.	42	M	(2/2/55) (5/27/57)	Left	Intrinsic stenosis, pelvic resection.	#12–#30	1.5 cm	Yes	6 wks	Good
S.C.	29	M	(2/3/53) (8/5/59)	Right	Surgical failure elsewhere 1951. Intrinsic stenosis, extrinsic obst., intense scarring.	#10	4.0 cm	Yes	6 wks	Good
O.L.	39	M	(3/5/53) (4/18/55)	Right	Intrinsic stenosis	#10–#28	2.5 cm	No	6 wks	Fair
P.G.	24	F	(12/3/53) (6/1/55)	Right	Intrinsic stenosis. Extrinsic vessels & bands.	#14–#28	1.0 cm	No	4 wks	Good
T.G.	43	F	(3/22/54) (6/25/55)	Right	Intrinsic stenosis	#10–#24	1.5 cm	No	5 wks	Good
C.N.	19	M	(6/8/55) (12/21/55)	Left	Intrinsic stenosis	#12–#30	2.0 cm	No	6 wks	Good
E.C.	38	F	(8/26/54) (5/6/57)	Right	Intrinsic stenosis	#12–#26	2.5 cm	No	6 wks	Good
H.F.	46	M	(1/6/55) (10/28/59)	Right	Intrinsic stenosis, extrinsic vessels & bands.	#12–#26	2.0 cm	No	6 wks	Good
M.B.*	38	F	(6/23/55) (8/19/55)	Right	Intrinsic stenosis, non-obst. area 8 cm distal to obst.	#12–#30	2.5 cm	No	4½ wks	Good
							(post-op right pneumothorax)			
I.B.	39	F	(6/28/56) (5/14/59)	Right	Intrinsic stenosis, extrinsic bands.	#10–#28	2.0 cm	No	5½ wks	Good
A.A.* (Figs. 9 and 10)	25	M	(5/16/55) (5/19/57)	Left	Intrinsic stenosis, non-obst. area	#12–#30	2.5 cm	No	5½ wks	Good
M.P. (Figs. 11 and 12)	40	F	(6/4/58) (8/4/59)	Left	Surgical failure elsewhere 1953, no splint or tube used. Intrinsic stenosis, dense extrinsic scarring.	#12–#28	4.0 cm	Yes	7 wks	Good
							(unable to drain from below)			
B.G.	44	M	(11/5/57)	Left	Solitary kidney. Intrinsic stenosis, pyonephrosis, cortical abscesses, acidosis, pneumonia, uremia.	#12–#26	1.5 cm	Yes		
									Expired 2 wks post-op	
M.M.	32	F	(11/8/57) (4/16/58)	Right	Intrinsic stenosis	#10–#28	1.5 cm	No	5½ wks	Good

Two patients operated on San Quentin Prison Hosp. (records not available). One good result, one fair. Both followed about two years. One had preoperative infection.

Good result is defined as (1) unobstructed pelvic drainage, (2) no persistent postoperative infection, (3) no subjective symptoms, (4) adequate renal function.

* Those cases in which an area of nonobstructive ''relative stenosis'' was found and corrected if intubation was done.

internal caliber of the ureter will vary from 10 to 14F, the actual test of snugness of the splint in the ureter is paramount irrespective of the size of the splint finally used. The larger the splint that can be safely used, the greater are the chances of success. Once the permanent splint is in place all tagged areas of "relative stenosis" are carefully incised through all layers of the ureteral wall. With the tension thus relieved these areas should cause no further to concern.

The splint is grasped with a forceps at the lower angle of the anterior ureterotomy and a loop is formed (Fig. 3). As lateral traction is placed on the ureteral stay sutures a clean midline posterior ureterotomy incision is made without removing the ureter from its bed. The splint "loop" is eliminated by upward traction leaving the splint lying in effective approximation throughout the originally strictured segment (Fig. 3, *A, B, C*).

5. Nephrostomy and splint.

The largest right-angle Malecot catheter should be used that will fit satisfactorily in the lower major calyx or lower art of the pelvis. In adults sizes 26 to 30F usually can be used. Smaller sizes are used in children or adults with small major calyces, and one wing of the catheter head may be cut off for better

TABLE 2. Other Types of Ureteropyeloplasty (14 Cases)

Patient	Age	Sex	Date of Surgery Date Last Seen	Kidney	Type of Surgery Type and Location of Obstruction	Size Splint Size Nephrostomy Tube	PreOp. Infection	Duration of Splinting	Results
F.E.	45	F	(1/31/50) (6/20/50)	Right	Foley Y-plasty, high insertion with obst.	#12–#24	No	4 wks	Good
H.D.	45	F	(7/9/52) (5/19/55)	Right	Foley Y-plasty, high insertion	#12–#24	No	5 wks	Good
J.H.*	27	F	(1/12/54) (2/5/59)	Right	Pelvic & ureterolysis, dense bands; pyelotomy, non-obst. stenosis 4 cm below U-P junction. Nephropexy.	None	No	—	Good
B.S.	38	F	(5/23/55) (11/9/55)	Right	Pure extrinsic obst. bands; ureterolysis, pyelotomy, nephropexy.	None	No	—	Good
K.E. (Fig. 2)	3	M	(8/25/55) (10/15/58)	Left	Culp-Scardino, intrinsic U-P junction obst.	#8–#16	Yes	3½ wks	Good
B.P.	29	F	(9/3/55) (5/15/57)	Right	Foley Y-plasty, pelvic resection. Solitary kidney; high insertion, intrinsic obst. & extrinsic adhesions.	#14–#30	Yes	3 wks	Good
C.N.	19	M	(10/2/55) (12/21/55)	Right	Uretero-ureteral anastomosis. Intrinsic & extrinsic dense scarring lumbar ureter. Two previous surgical failures elsewhere with nephrostomy drainage 1 year.	#12–#30	Yes	3 wks	Good
K.E.* (Fig. 2)	3	M	(12/10/56) (10/15/58)	Right	Culp-Scardino, intrinsic obst. 2 cm below U-P junction; non-obst. area in lumbar ureter. Dense scar.	#8–#16	Yes (nephrectomy 2/9/56)	3 wks	Poor
R.M.	31	M	(4/22/57) (9/12/58)	Right	Foley Y-plasty; intrinsic obst., high insertion. Marked intrarenal hydronephrosis.	#12–#28	No	3 wks	Good
S.G.	7	M	(7/6/57) (8/3/59)	Right	Culp-Scardino, intrinsic obst.	#8–#18	No	3 wks	Good
M.K.	3	F	(8/16/57) (6/15/58)	Left	Foley Y-plasty, high insertion.	#6–#14	No	3½ wks	Fair
L.H.	23	F	(8/21/57) (9/3/58)	Right	Ureterolysis, pyelotomy. Nephropexy. Pure extrinsic kinking adhesions.	None	Yes	—	Good
F.S.	18	F	(10/12/57) (1/16/59)	Right	Foley Y-plasty, intrinsic obst., high insertion.	#10–#30	No	2½ wks	Good
G.H.	25	F	(10/15/59) (10/15/59)	Left	Foley Y-plasty, solitary kidney, intrinsic obst., high insertion. (Short followup; doing very well to date 12/15/59.)	#12–#26	No	2 wks	Good

A good result is defined as (1) unobserved pelvic drainage, (2) no persistent postoperative infection, (3) no subjective symptoms, (4) adequate renal function.
* These cases in which an area of nonobstructive "relative stenosis" was found and corrected if intubation was done.

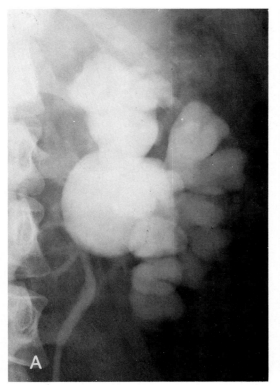

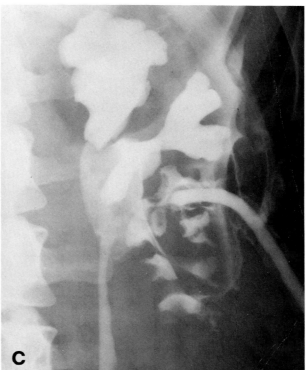

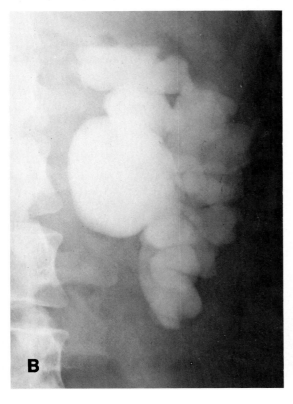

Fig. 5. Case 2, C. H. (table 1). (*A*) Preoperative retrograde ureteropyelogram (April 24, 1950). (*B*) Preoperative retrograde pyelogram, erect, 2 hour delayed emptying film (April 24, 1950). (*C*) Postoperative (6 weeks) nephrostogram done immediately after splinting catheter was removed. Note unobstructed ureteropelvic junction with adequate funnelling (June 20, 1950).

placement without impairment of its retaining or draining qualities.

During the routine placement of the nephrostomy tube three steps should be noted:

a. If the tube is stretched taut when drawn through the renal parenchyma and is then released, the expanded diameter will control much of the bleeding.

b. The head of the tube should be drawn well up into the renal pelvis to prevent its being trapped beneath an everted flap of calyceal mucosa; it is then withdrawn into the calyx or lower pelvis to a position of unobstructed drainage.

c. As a final test saline should flow through the tube rapidly at gravity pressure.

By using interlocking Kocher clamps the splint is brought through a middle major calyx and a silk orientation suture is tied tightly around the catheter at the level of the renal capsule to serve as a check point for any future displacement of the splint (Fig. 4).

6. Closure of the pyelotomy.

If pelvic resection is necessary it should be done at this time by extension of the pyelotomy incision (Fig. 1). The margins of the pelvic wall are approximated with interrupted 4-0 chromic sutures, inverting the mucosa.

7. Drainage of the wound, closure of the abdominal wall.

Unstuffed Penrose drains are placed as follows: under the upper pole of the kidney, under the lower pole and extending down and parallel to the course of the ureter, but not against it, and anteriorly across the midportion of the kidney and pelvis. All tubes and drains are brought out through the posterior angle of the wound or through a stab wound. The nephrostomy tube can be used to maintain the kidney in a high position with the lower pole tilted laterally. Fixation sutures for a nephropexy are not necessary and may prevent adequate perirenal drainage.

In children and adults with poor abdominal musculature or respiratory conditions that cause chronic coughing, it is advisable to use retention sutures in the anterior two thirds of the incision. The fascia of the muscle layers is approximated with interrupted catgut sutures. After complete closure of the wound all drains and tubes are loosely sutured with black silk to the lower wound margin, which is anesthetic. The exposed part of the splinting catheter is folded on itself, tied and buried in the dressings. As a last precaution, to secure the nephrostomy tube, a piece of 2 inch adhesive tape is placed around it, about 3 inches from the end, the tape is then adhered to itself for about an inch and firmly applied to the benzion-prepared skin parallel to and below the crest of the ilium, extending to the midline front and back. The nephrostomy tube is the "renal life-line" in this procedure and must be protected against malfunction.

CARE OF THE NEPHROSTOMY TUBE

1. Irrigation of the nephrostomy tube.

Due to the small size of the renal pelvis in those cases requiring excision of redundant pelvic wall (Fig. 1), any attempt at "closed system" irrigation, with large syringes or rubber bulbs, is futile and will serve only to blow out the pelvic suture lines and extravasate irrigating fluid throughout the entire sur-

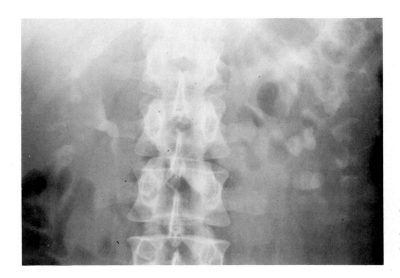

Fig. 6. Case 2, C. H. (table 1). Three year postoperative followup intravenous urogram (25 minute film) shows complete emptying of pelvis with reduction in calcyceal size. Persistent calyceal residual can be expected in such cases of intrarenal hydronephrosis.

gical wound. Infection by contamination usually results. If irrigation is needed, which it seldom is, the angle of the tube is gently straightened and a size 6 ureteral catheter can then be easily passed down the nephrostomy tube to its tip and slipped between the wings. Warm saline is introduced through the ureteral catheter, thus effectively irrigating the pelvis with an ''open system'' without pressure build-up at any time.

2. Insurance against trouble with the nephrostomy tube.

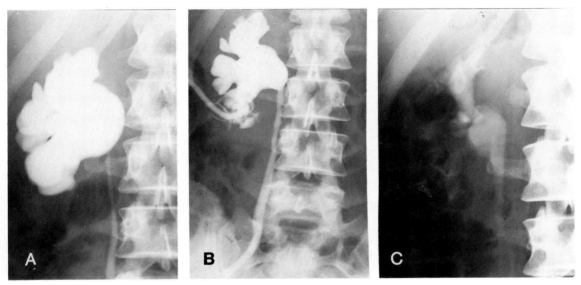

Fig. 7. Case 3, M. D. (table 1). (A) Preoperative retrograde pyelogram. (B) Postoperative (6 weeks) nephrostogram. (C) One year postoperative urogram (15 minute film).

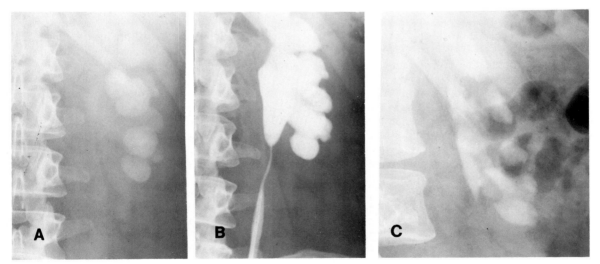

Fig. 8. Case 4, R. L. (table 1). (A) Preoperative intravenous urogram (15 minute film). Note marked intrarenal type of hydronephrosis. (B) Preoperative retrograde pyelogram shows long, intrinsic upper ureteral stenosis. Effort was made to save this kidney because of history of 2 stones on right side. (C) Intravenous urogram (30 minute film) 3½ years after plastic repair. Nephrectomy was performed because of chronic pyelonephritis secondary to persistent calyceal residual, despite adequate repair of original ureteral obstruction.

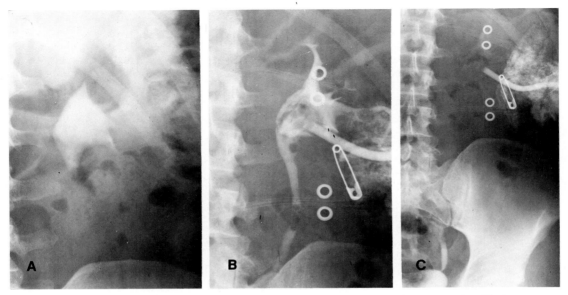

Fig. 9. Case 15, A. A. (table 1). (*A*) Preoperative intravenous urogram (1½ hour emptying film). Patient's chief complaints were recurrent infection and pain, although urine was sterile at time of surgery. (*B*) 5½ week postoperative nephrostogram. (*C*) Nephrostogram (5 minute delayed emptying film with tube clamped). Nephrostogram is done immediately after removal of splint and if pelvis empties completely, or without obvious obstruction, nephrostomy tube is removed without delay.

A large intake of water (3,000 cc per 24 hours) is the most essential single factor in assuring a smooth postoperative course. This not only produces good mechanical flushing, but dilates all urinary elements necessary to calculus formation.

An acid urine is a "clean" urine when rubber tubes are present. An alkaline urine, even though it be sterile, can soon foul tubing. Urinary acidifiers which may be used are: ammonium chloride 15 g (enteric coated) 4 times daily, acid ash and low calcium diet and cranberry juice as a diet additive. If there is evidence of a urea-splitting infection intensive antibiotic therapy, based on drug sensitivity studies, should be used. Prophylactic antibiotics are of no specific value if pelvic and perirenal drainage is satisfactory.

The nephrostomy tube must be carefully watched for the formation of "urinary sand" which will progressively obstruct the tube if allowed to go undetected. To remove this sand safely a size 6 ureteral catheter is passed down the tube which is then compressed and rolled between the thumb and forefinger, a flushing irrigation is then made through the ureteral catheter with half-strength solution G. If sand deeper in the nephrostomy tube is to be removed a glass Y-tube is attached with the ureteral catheter placed through a water-tight nipple on one arm and a gravity tube on the other arm. A continuous slow drip of half-strength solution G is directed into the depths of the nephrostomy tube, via the ureteral catheter, with "open system" drainage. Mucous and protein material may be cleared by alternating the irrigation with dilute proteolytic agents.

The ambulatory patient is instructed never to clamp or plug the nephrostomy tube at any time. When a gravity tube is not attached the nephrostomy tube should drain freely into an open mouth bottle or receptacle secured to a belt or strap around the patient's waist. No "closed system" rubber or plastic bags are allowed. An uncooperative or uninformed patient could jeopardize the entire procedure.

3. Removal of the tubes.

The splint should stay in place from 4 to 6 weeks depending on the degree and length of the stenotic segment.

a. A plain roentgenogram of the abdomen is taken to show the relative status of the splinting catheter and nephrostomy tube. Any accumulation of calcereous incrustations will be noted.

b. The splinting catheter is removed.

c. The splint opening is compressed with sterile cotton. The nephrostomy tube is held in a vertical position and an ounce of radiopaque solution is poured in. The tube is clamped and a second roentgenogram is taken which should outline the pelvis, most of the calyces and the entire ureter. The patient can often feel the dye running down the ureter. With the nephrostomy tube still clamped a third film is taken in 5 to 8 minutes which should show satisfactory drainage of the pelvis and calyces with the bladder containing most of the dye (Fig. 9, *B, C*).

d. When the ureter is seen to be patent throughout, with free drainage, the nephrostomy tube may be removed without further delay. In most cases the fistulas are dry within 2 to 24 hours.

4. Long-term evaluation (Tables 1 and 2).

If all goes well the diet may be liberalized at the time of the removal of the tubes. If there is any calcereous debris in the pelvis dairy products should be withheld until it has passed. Emphasis is still placed on a large fluid intake and the desirability of an acid urine. A followup intravenous pyelogram is obtained in 6 to 9 months, unless difficulties develop earlier. A second pyelogram may be obtained in 18 to 24 months and if the results are satisfactory the chances of success are good.

DISCUSSION

1. Ureteral anatomy and splinting.

It is an anatomical fact that the lumbar ureteral lumen may normally vary in its internal caliber, yet splints are of uniform diameter. It is suggested that many of the strictures resulting from ureteral splints have originated from the mucosal ischemia and necrosis in these unrecognized areas of "relative stenosis"; especially those against which the tip of the catheter has been forced and constant pressure maintained. The pressure against the mucosa only has to exceed its capillary pressure for necrosis to result. It is not reasonable that a soft, smooth, rubber catheter lying free in the ureter should cause a stricture at its tip, or anywhere else, if the steps outlined in the section on Surgical Technique in this article have been followed.

The practice of splinting the entire ureter is not necessary for satisfactory healing at the ureterotomy site, and is contraindicated because a large splint is needed in the strictured segment than can be accommodated safely in the intramural segment of the ureter.

2. Nephrostomy versus pyelostomy.

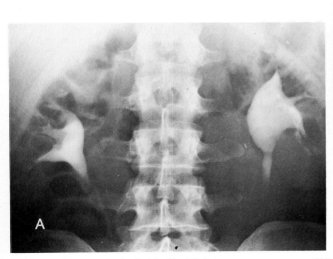

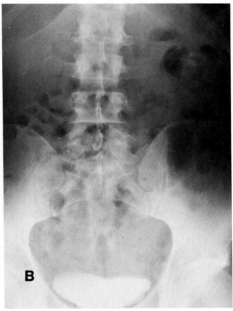

Fig. 10. Case 15, A. A. (table 1). (*A*) Intravenous urogram (15 minute film) 2 years after surgery. Case shows that extrarenal type of hydronephrosis with normal calyces can be intrarenal in position, thus making surgical reduction of such a pelvis impractical. (Compare outline of left kidney with that of right kidney.) (*B*) Intravenous urogram (30 minute film) 2 years after surgery. Rapid emptying when compared with preoperative pyelograms. Patient completely asymptomatic.

Pyelostomy is mentioned only to condemn it as a method for urinary diversion in intubation ureterotomy.

Nephrostomy has the following advantages:

a. A large tube can be used with a more direct access to the pelvis and better resultant drainage.

b. The tube is less likely to become displaced during the convalescent ambulatory period.

c. The end of the nephrostomy tube is recessed away from the pelvic suture lines and the splinting catheter.

d. The Malecot catheter seldom becomes plugged with prolapsing mucosa and tends to maintian itself properly inside a hollow viscus.

e. After 6 weeks the nephrostomy fistula closes much more quickly than a pyelostomy fistula.

3. The Foley bag catheter should not be used as a nephrostomy tube for the following reasons:

a. If the bag is defective and breaks or deflates in the early postoperative period before a fistulous tract has formed, its replacement may be impossible without surgical intervention.

b. The tip of the Foley catheter is too easily bent or kinked in the confinement of so small a hollow viscus.

c. If the emptying mechanism becomes defective the deflation of the bag poses a serious problem.

d. Following spontaneous rupture the removal of any portion of the bag wall, lying free in the pelvis, is an unnecessary hazard.

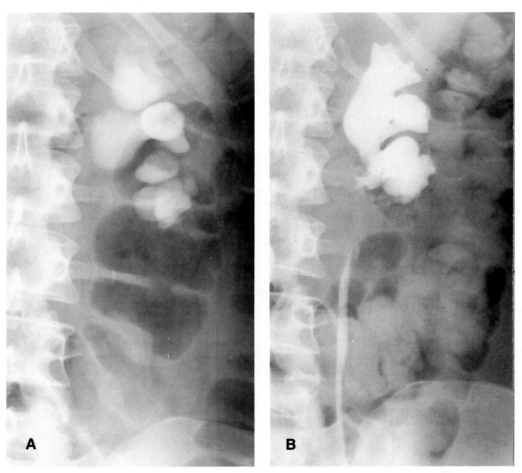

Fig. 11. Case 16, M. P. (table 1). (*A*) Preoperative intravenous urogram (30 minute film). Patient had acute infection with delayed appearance of dye. Corrective surgery followed control of infection by ureteral catheter drainage and intensive antibiotic therapy. (*B*) Preoperative retrograde ureteropyelogram shows long obstructive ureteral segment due to combination of intrinsic stenosis and extensive extrinsic scarring.

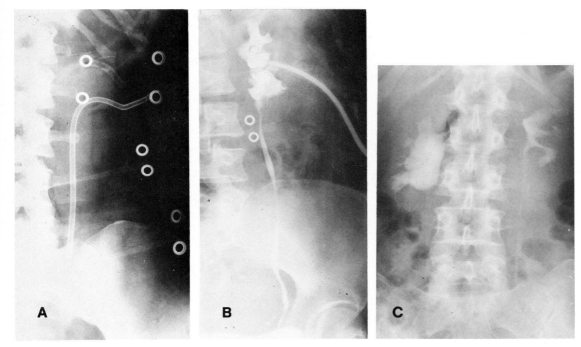

Fig. 12. Case 16, M. P. (table 1). (*A*) Postoperative x-ray shows placement of splinting catheter. (*B*) 7 week postoperative nephrostogram shows unobstructed lumbar ureteral segment with rapid emptying of radiopaque solution into bladder. (*C*) 1 year postoperative intravenous urogram (30 minute film). Adequate drainage on left with normal function and no infection. Operation elsewhere 8 years ago for nonprogressive right hydronephrosis.

SUMMARY

In the various types of ureteropelvioplasties, involving pelvic wall flaps with per primam healing, ureteral splinting is not completely essential to success. However, in plastic procedures involving ureterotomy and healing by secondary intention, two basic requirements are necessary: 1) an adequately sized splint through the involved segment during the healing period, and 2) complete unrestricted urinary diversion (nephrostomy) for this entire period. The fear of complications from splints and nephrostomy tubes, expressed by some authors, is not borne out in our series of plastic repairs (all types) when the technique of splint and nephrostomy preparation, outlined here, has been used.

The diagnostic steps and surgical technique of intubation ureterotomy are discussed in detail. The following points are made:

a. By ureteropyelography the entire ureter is visualized so that the exact extent of the stricture is seen and the absence of ureteral disease and deformity elsewhere is proved.

b. Intubation ureterotomy is selected for those patients with obstructive segments in the lumbar ureter that are not amendable to other plastic operations.

c. At operation nonobstructive areas of "relative stenosis" are detected in the ureteral segment distal to the stricture by Braasch bulb calibration and are incised. This important step assures satisfactory ureteral tolerance to the splint and prevents secondary strictures.

d. A simple technique for making the posterior ureterotomy incision is described.

e. Ureteral splints are used to splint and stabilize only the involved portion of the ureter.

f. Nephrostomy is used in preference to pyelostomy because it assures better urinary diversion over a long period of time with fewer complications.

g. A simple method of "open system" irrigation and maintaining open drainage of the nephrostomy tube is described.

The conclusions in this article are drawn from 34 consecutive cases, 20 intubation ureterotomies and 14 using either the Foley Y-plasty, Culp-Scardino or uretero-ureteral anastomosis technique. In this series there were three failures. There was one postoperative death and the other two required nephrectomy. There were 29 cases considered good results and two fair results. A good result is defined as: unobstructed pelvic drainage, no persistent postoperative urinary infection, no subjective symptoms and adequate renal function.

REFERENCES

Culp, O. S. and DeWeerd, J. H.: Pelvic flap operation for certain types of ureteropelvic obstructions. J Urol 71:523. 1954

Davis, D. M.: Intubation ureterotomy: A new operation for ureteral and ureteropelvic strictures. Surg Gynec & Obstet 76:513, 1943

Davis, D. M. and associates: Intubation Ureterotomy: Experimental work and clinical results. J Urol 59:851, 1948

Davis, D. M.: The unsuitability of polyvinyl plastic for ureteral splinting. J Urol 73:747, 1955

DAVIS, D. M: Process of ureteral repair: A recapitulation of splinting question. J Urol 79:215, 1958

FOLEY, F. E. B.: A plastic operation for structures at ureteropelvic junction. J Urol 38:643, 1937

GIBSON, T. E.: The ureteral splint. J Urol 42:1169–1175, 1939

GIBSON, T. E.: Hydronephrosis: Newer concepts of treatment. J Urol 76:708, 1956

HINMAN, F.: Renal counterbalance. Arch Surg 12:1105–1223, 1926

SCARDINO, P. L. AND PRINCE, C. L.: Vertical flap ureteropelvioplasty: Preliminary report. South Med J 46:325–331, 1953

Commentary: Indications for Intubated Ureterotomy

Harry Bergman

The indications for intubated ureterotomy have essentially remained the same since its introduction by D. M. Davis in 1943.[1] The surgical technique has been essentially unchanged since the description by Dr. Smart in 1961 in his classic article reproduced here. However, with the introduction of newer diagnostic modalities, such as urodynamics, which provide a "true" evaluation of a ureteral stricture and its effect on ureteral pressure–flow studies and peristalsis, the indications for this procedure have, under certain circumstances, been modified so that other operations have sometimes replaced intubation.

Among these operations are (1) partial or complete ureteral resection of a mid- or difficult-positioned stricture and end-to-end anastomosis, (2) ureteral replacement of such an area with intestine, (3) renal autotransplantation with bypassing of a large ureteral stricture, (4) resection of the stricture and anastomosis of the lower ureter to the bladder with a Psoas hitch, and (5) resection of the stricture and anastomosis of the lower ureter to the bladder with a Boari flap, usually in conjunction with a Psoas hitch. Despite all these newer techniques, Dr. Smart stated that good results are obtainabale in intubated ureterotomy "if an orderly system of preoperative study, surgical technique and postoperative care is followed. Incorrect splinting and inadequate urinary diversion are two common causes of failure."[2] The term *relative stenosis* is worthy of attention and should be studied urodynamically.

Like Dr. Smart, in bilateral involvement, if no infection exists, I also prefer to do the damaged side first. However, if infection is present, I prefer to do the best side first and to try to control the infection. Renal salvage is the ultimate aim. At the time of surgery, any well-known method of repair may be required depending on the patient's condition. Contraindications to intubation are very specific, and its indications are limited. Diagnostically, internal ureteral calibration is important. The classic lumbar approach is preferred, and care should be taken not to denude the ureter excessively of its periureteral blood and nerve supply. Calibration of the stricture and establishment of longitudinal incisions are necessary. Dr. Smart's statement on the "snugness of the splint" is important.

Silicone-covered Foley or Wolf catheters are now used for nephrostomy drainage. It is always advisable to test the "bag" at the time of surgery. Malecot catheters are not preferred for nephrostomy. Dependent renal nephrostomy drainage and midcaliceal stents without nephropexy must be re-emphasized. Drainage must be adequate, and puddling of urine completely prevented. Proper renal drainage and stenting and prevention of "sanding" in the catheter lumen are the *sine qua non* of successful intubation. Correct stenting time is between 4 and 6 weeks postoperatively, and proper care of the catheter, such as acidification of the urine, prevents undue complications. Adequate postoperative evaluations, including urodynamic and radiographic investigations, are important in ascertaining the true results of surgery.

REFERENCES

1. Davis DM: Intubated ureterostomy: A new operation for ureteral and ureteropelvic stricture. Surg Gynecol Obstet 76:513, 1943

2. Smart WR: An evaluation of intubation ureterotomy with description of surgical technique. J Urol 85:512, 1961

ANNOTATED BIBLIOGRAPHY

Davis DM: Intubated ureterotomy: A new operation for ureteral and ureteropelvic stricture. Surg Gynec Obstet 76:513, 1943

In this series of cases, one drainage catheter in association with pyelostomy drainage was used. Splinting time was shorter than now accepted, but prevention of ureteral ischemia by pressure or denudations of important vasculature was stressed. This article, a classic in urology, started a long chain of investigation concerning the nature of ureteral healing.

Hamm FC, Weinberg SR: Renal and ureteral surgery without intubation. Trans Am Assoc Genitourin Surg 46:109, 1954

The authors performed ureterotomy without the use of splints or nephrostomy tubes. Adequate drainage was provided by a renal pelvic rent, and a linear incision was made through the strictured area. Drainage was provided by a rubber drain placed down to the site of the ureteral incision and to the site of the rent. Adequate-calier ureteral healing by primary intention resulted. These investigators started a whole new approach to the mechanism of ureteral healing. In other types of plastic repair, we have found it very efficacious. In intubated ureterotomy, splinting is mandatory for over all adequate results.

Lapides J, Caffrey EL: Observations on the healing of ureteral muscle: relationship to intubated ureterotomy. J Urol 73:47, 1955

These authors stated that if a large defect in the ureter is to be bridged, it is imperative that the splinting tube remain in place at least 6 weeks. It takes that long for the muscle to completely enclose the ureter, whereas the mucosal layer will completely encircle the ureter in 3 weeks. Periureteral fibrosis must be prevented, and this can be obviated by enclosing the incised portion of ureter in retroperitoneal fat and by preventing prolonged leakage of urine into the operative area.

Davis DM: The process of ureteral repair: A recapitulation of the splinting question. J Urol 79:215, 1958

The purpose of the splint in intubated ureterotomy is to provide a mold around which healing takes place, and results in a larger tube than the original one. Exactly how smooth muscle and other ureteral components regenerate is not definitive. It is known that the incised ureter must *not* come in contact with solid tissue such as muscle, kidney, or peritoneum. It should be provided with adequate fat pads and well drained to prevent kinking and periureteral adhesions. Davis used splints through the entire length of ureter to prevent strictures at the lowermost part of the catheter. (Smart describes how this problem can be prevented and how to properly apply the principle of relative ureteral stenosis.) He discusses his methods of preventing infection, stone formation, and types of splints to be used. The difference in healing in a longitudinal incision, where complete reconstitution results, versus a transverse incision where only the epithelium will regenerate is discussed. If left intact, to increase the size of the ureteral lumen, splints must be used.

Gibson TE: Hydronephrosis, its treatment in the solitary kidney. J Urol 81:374, 1959

The intubated ureterotomy, requiring splints, is reserved for very specific types of lesions: (1) when the ureteropelvic junction is badly scarred; (2) in the presence of marked inflammatory changes in and about the ureteropelvic junction; (3) cases of partial or complete separation or avulsion of the kidney pelvis and ureter as a result of previous surgical injury; (4) in persons of middle age or older where there may be delay in healing; (5) where there are multiple, unusually long constrictions.

Persky L, Krause J: Splinting versus nonsplinting in ureteral surgery.

In Bergman H (ed): The Ureter, 2nd ed, p 187. New York, Springer Verlag, 1981

Reconstruction of the ureter depends on prompt epithelialization into tubular shape, which precedes the formation of muscular elements. If the normal epithelial layer can not be laid down, the other ureteral coats have no guide, and will be grossly abnormal. The process of regeneration is the same whether or not splints are used, provided there is nothing to hinder the epithelialization process and the tube formation. The primary purpose of the splint is to guide and orient regeneration of the ureteral wall. It must be nonallergenic. The silicone splint seems to be practically inert and causes no tissue reaction. Whether to splint or not will depend on the type of case, infection, and surgeon's own preference.

Hinman F, Jr: Experimental evidence for ureteral reconstitution. In Bergman H (ed): The Ureter, 2nd ed, p 179. New York, Springer Verlag, 1981

In the basic process, the cut edges fall closely together, a small amount of connective tissue forms between, contracs to approximate the edges, and a delicate scar not interfering with function results. If the cut edges of the ureteral muscle are not adjacent to the gaps, no true regeneration of muscular wall occurs. It was found that ureteral epithelium, itself, will not induce muscle regeneration about a splint. The muscle must be adjacent to the area of repair. The urinary flow will provide a more adequate lumen and stimulate muscle growth. It will, however, distract the newly formed epithelium. the ureter is reconstituted as follows: (1) There is a spreading growth of epithelium to line the new portion of the ureteral tube. (2) Simultaneously, the defect is filled with new connective tissue. (3) This fibrous portion matures and contracts, drawing the preexisting muscle around the lumen; this stimulates new smooth muscle formation by traction on tissue adjacent to the cut edge. These stages are adversely affected by early flow of urine through the defect, but promoted if urinary flow occurs after epithelialization is complete. They are distracted by a rigid bed about the healing ureter.

Ackermann R, Frohmuller H: Experiences with intubated ureterotomy and its indications. Urologe A 12:112, 1973

These authors report 68 cases of ureteral intubation. Their indications are ureteral stenosis at the ureteral pelvic junction with a small intrarenal pelvis, subpelvic stenosis of the ureter in association with secondary operations, and a long narrow ureteral segment. They advise long-term antibiotic therapy and have a 70% satisfactory result.

Borkowski A: Irregular regeneration and diverticulum formation after intubated ureterotomy. Eur Urol 1:91, 1975

In 179 cases of intubated ureterotomy this author reports his indications for the procedure as stricture resulting from unsuccessful plastic operations at the ureteropelvic junction, presence of intensive inflammatory reaction at the ureteropelvic junction, injury to the ureteror renal pelvis during operation on inflamed or fragile tissue at the ureteral pelvic junction, and cases of multiple or long areas of ureteral stenosis. Poor results are usually due to urinary extravasation or stagnation. Diverticula may result at the sites of healing if this occurs. Poor muscle and connective tissue regeneration are the probable cause.

Overview: Intubated Ureterotomy

Russell W. Lavengood

Intubated ureterotomy has stood the test of time but rarely is indicated. It is always preferable to make an anastomosis of the ureter with the renal pelvis. In some patients, this can be accomplished by completely dissecting the kidney and pedicle vessels and by moving up the periureteral tissue as described by Hendren and Hensle.[1] They accomplish this by dividing the gonadal vessels just above the ovary in the female and at the internal ring in the male. By doing this, they sweep the retroperitoneal tissue toward the ureter and prevent devascularizing the ureter.

With the great success of autotransplantation and the interposition of the small intestine, these upper ureteral defects can be overcome without intubated ureterostomy.

I prefer the through-and-through nephrostomy tube, which is brought through the renal parenchyma in the lower pole calix and out through the renal pelvis. This tube can be repositioned or replaced with greater accuracy and ease than a large nephrostomy tube. I prefer a polyethylene feeding tube as a splint instead of a latex catheter.

I leave the splinting tube in place for 6 weeks and, after its removal, carry out urodynamic studies such as intrapelvic pressures and drainage time of the kidney through the nephrostomy.

The Shorr regimen is an excellent way to prevent the deposits of phosphates in the renal pelvis and nephrostomy tube. This consists of double strength basic aluminum carbonate gel (Basaljel), 15 ml 4 times a day, a moderately low calcium and prosphorous diet, 700 mg and 1200 mg, respectively, for 24 hours, and a minimum of 2500 ml of fluid daily. The 24-hour urinary phosphorous level should be kept below 300 mg; this is accomplished by regulating the dose of the gel.

REFERENCE

1. Hendren WH, Hensle T: Transureterostomy: Experience with 75 cases. J Urol 123:826, 1980

31

END-TO-END URETERAL ANASTOMOSIS: A SIMPLE ORIGINAL TECHNIQUE

F. C. Hamm, S. R. Weinberg and R. K. Waterhouse

From the Department of Surgery, Division of Urology, State University of New York, Downstate Medical Center, Brooklyn, 3, N.Y.

Reprinted from *Journal of Urology*, Vol. 87, pp. 43–47, 1962. Copyright 1962 by The Williams & Wilkins Company, Baltimore.

The anastomosis of a ureter which has been severed, either deliberately or accidentally, has so often led to failure because of stricture and resultant hydronephrosis that Moore[1] in 1954 stated that anastomosis was probably not worth while as "in the majority of cases stricture at the site of anastomosis is almost inevitable." Marion[2] believed that section of the ureter causes the peristalsis in the two segments to become asynchronous and that whether or not a stricture occurred the final result of end-to-end anastomosis was hydronephrosis and death of the kidney. He collected 62 cases from the literature, of which only three were certain good results, and concluded that the bad results of anastomosis depended not on technical failure but on the physiological properties of the ureter.

In 1952 we began to study the physiology of the ureter in the animal laboratory. By means of a pressure transducer, a specially designed extraluminal ureteral electrode and a D.C. amplifier, the activity of the ureter was recorded during and after anastomosis. It was demonstrated that following transection peristalsis of the upper segment is active while the lower segment becomes relatively static. However, if the urine is diverted by performing a linear vertical ureterotomy at least 5 cm. proximal to the area of suture the segment below the ureterotomy and the anastomotic site are quiescent, allowing healing and preventing extravasation of urine through the anastomosis. Further experiments showed that once the anastomosis healed, about the fourteenth postoperative day, peristalsis was uniform throughout the length of the ureter.[3,4]

Using the dog, an acceptable surgical technique of end-to-end anastomosis was developed which was then applied clinically. In 1956 a 13-month followup report was presented on one patient who had had a severed ureter repaired with a satisfactory result.[5] The purpose of this paper is to confirm the technique and to present eight more patients in whom this method of anastomosis has been used.

The technique is simple and has 3 essentials (Fig. 1):

Read at annual meeting of American Urological Association, Inc., Los Angeles, Cal., May 22–25, 1961.

This work was supported in part by grant No. H2908C4 of the United States Public Health Service.

450 Clarkson Ave., Brooklyn, NY.

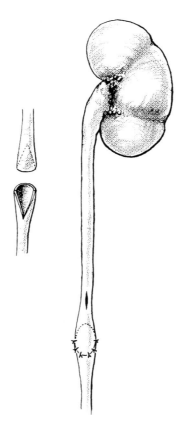

1) The urine is diverted by linear ureterotomy. 2) An oblique oval anastomosis is made. 3) No splints or catheters are used.

Urinary diversion by a longitudinal incision about 2.5 cm. in length well above the proposed site of operation has proved satisfactory, both in the laboratory and on the wards. No catheter is placed in the ureterotomy but free drainage of urine is encouraged by leading a penrose drain extraperitoneally down to the site of the ureterotomy. Usually about 8 or 10 days are required for the ureterotomy to close and give ample time for the anastomosis to heal. We withdraw this drain on the ninth day as by that time a tract has been established and, should further urinary drainage occur, there is no tendency for it to collect retroperitoneally.

The two ends of the ureter are joined, as in all plastic operations, without tension. Care should be taken not to free up the ureter more than is absolutely essential and it is better for the surgeon to work at a slight disadvantage in the depths of the wound than, by too extensive a mobilization, to prejudice the blood supply. Direct anastomosis of a ureter which has been sectioned transversely leads to a circular scar. As this contracts some stenosis of the ureter is unavoidable. Therefore, we prefer to perform an oblique anastomosis which

Fig. 1. Method of oblique end-to-end anastomosis of ureter with proximal diverting ureterotomy.

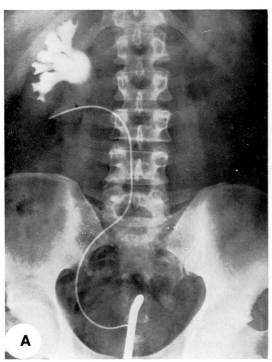

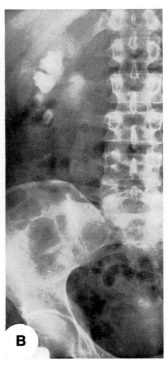

Fig. 2. M. F. (A) Preoperative retrograde pyelogram shows right retrocaval ureter with hydronephrosis. (B) 2 Months after repair by transection and anastomosis of ureter. Hydronephrosis is still present but patient is uninfected and symptom-free. (Hamm, F. C., Weinberg, S. R. and Waterhouse, K.: Repair of the injured ureter. Surg., 45:575–584, 1959.)

produces an oval scar of greater circumference than the ureter. Shrinkage of this scar can then occur without compromising the lumen of the ureter. This principle of oblique anastomosis of tubular organs is of general application and Soresi[6] described a method of intestinal anastomosis using it. Everidge[7] in England and Tsuchiya[8] in Japan suggested its use in end-to-end anastomosis of the ureter. The two ends of the ureter are spatulated by incising them for about 1.5 cm. The proximal segment is incised anteriorly and the distal segment posteriorly. Between 6 and 8 interrupted sutures of chromic 000 catgut are used and we do not attempt to make the anastomosis water-tight as we believe that excessive suturing may be a cause of stricture.

No splints or indwelling catheters are used as we have found them to be unnecessary and think that, especially if they are large, they may cause stricture at the site of anastomosis.[9]

If the anastomosis has been performed transperitoneally the posterior layer of peritoneum is carefully closed. The site of the anastomosis is drained extraperitoneally with a Penrose drain which is also removed on the ninth day.

CASE ABSTRACTS

Of our 9 cases (Table 1) five were surgical accidents, one was an injury and three were deliberate surgical transections. Cases 1 to 4 have already been presented in detail elsewhere and will not be discussed further except to say that their progress continues to be satisfactory.[10] No ureteral dilatations are required and the urine is not infected.

Case 5. M. F. had a retrocaval ureter and the kidney was hydronephrotic with poor function. Transposition of the ureter was performed with end-to-end anastomosis. The patient has been followed 2½ years. Function has

returned to this kidney and the degree of hydronephrosis has diminished (Fig. 2).

Case 6. A. L. During anterior resection of the sigmoid colon the left ureter was unintentionally divided. The ureter was anastomosed at the time of the original operation with a satisfactory result and 2½ years' followup (Fig. 3). The patient is symptom-free and has a normal excretory urogram. Study 2 months after repair showed peristalsis to abe uniform throughout the ureter (Fig. 4).

Case 7. A. L. The surgeon mistook the left ureter for the left sympathetic chain. He freed up the ureter from the level of L5 to the renal pelvis where he transected it. We were called and suggested anastomosis, although the ureter appeared to have been badly traumatized, as no excretory urograms were available and nothing was known about the other kidney. The anastomosis was a

TABLE 1

No. and Name	Operation	Follow-up	Results
1 M. S.	Right ureter accidentally severed during ligation of vena cava	6 yrs	Good
2 D. P.	Excision diverticulum left ureter	4 yrs	Good
3 M. G.	Hysterectomy, accidentally severed left ureter	4 yrs	Good
4 E. A.	Hysterectomy, accidentally severed left ureter	4 yrs	Good
5 M. F.	Retrocaval right ureter	2½ yrs	Good
6 A. L.	Anterior resection of sigmoid, accidentally cut left ureter	2½ yrs	Good
7 A. L.	Sympathectomy, accidentally cut left ureter	Zero	Failure
8 F. O.	Bullet wound right ureter	1½ yrs	Good
9 J. S.	Transuretero-ureterostomy	3 mos	Good

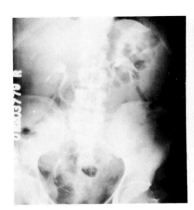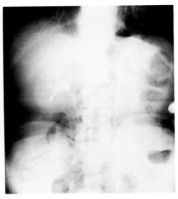

Fig. 3. A. L. (*A*) Preoperative excretory urogram prior to anterior resection of sigmoid. (*B*) Excretory urogram 2 years after anastomosis of left ureter.

failure; a urinary fistula developed and nephrectomy was performed.

Case 8. F. O., a 17-year-old boy, was accidentally struck in the abdomen by a bullet. The cecum and small intestine were perforated and the bullet lodged in the left pelvis. Surgical repair of the perforated bowel was successful, but the patient began to drain urine because of an unsuspected transection of the right ureter by the bullet. Surgical repair by end-to-end anastomosis has given an excellent result with normal excretory urograms (Fig. 5). The patient has been followed 18 months.

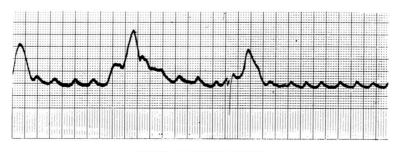

ABOVE ANASTOMOSIS

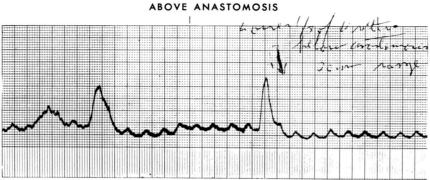

BELOW ANASTOMOSIS

Fig. 4. Patient A. L. Record of pressure fluctuations in ureter obtained by electro-manometer 2 months after end-to-end anastomosis (range of pressure varies from 0 to 20 mm mercury). Note similarity of peristaltic waves in segments of ureter above and below anastomosis.

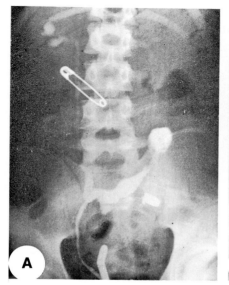

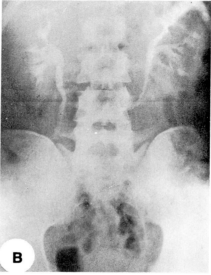

Fig. 5. F. O. (*A*) Retrograde pyelogram demonstrates fistula of right ureter due to bullet wound. (*B*) Excretory urogram 18 months postoperatively demonstrates normal morphology and function of right kidney and ureter.

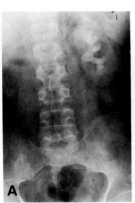
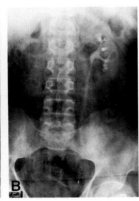
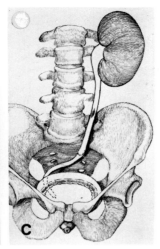

Fig. 6. J. S. (*A*) Excretory urogram shows hydronephrosis of solitary kidney after resection of bladder tumor and insertion of radon seeds. (*B*) Improvement after transuretero-ureteral anastomosis. (*C*) Sketch of operative procedure.

Case 9. J. S. had his right kidney removed for carcinoma. Carcinoma subsequently developed in his bladder, overlying the orifice of a solitary left kidney. Hydronephrosis occurred and the blood urea rose. Partial cystectomy was performed and the left ureter was anastomosed to the stump of the right ureter. The operation has been successful so far but the period of followup is short (Fig. 6).

SUMMARY

Synchronous peristalsis can be demonstrated in a successfully repaired ureter.

Diversion of the urine by proximal linear ureterotomy and extraperitoneal drainage allows healing at the site of anastomosis.

Oblique end-to-end anastomosis of the ureter has given satisfactory results in eight of 9 patients.

REFERENCES

1. Moore, T.D.: Surgery of the ureter, in Urology, ed. by Campbell. Philadelphia: W B Saunders Co, 1954, vol 3, p 1864

2. Gouverneur, R. and Marion, H.: La suture de l'uretère, Etude expérimentale. J Chir 33:621, 1929

3. Weinberg, S. R. and Siebens, A. A.: Activity of the ureter after surgery. J Urol 80:336, 1958

4. Weinberg, S. R., Peng, B., Kamhi, B., Ullman, A. and Hamm, F. C.: Improved regeneration of the ureter after diversion of urine by proximal ureterotomy. J Urol 85:749–758, 1961

5. Hamm, F. C. and Winberg, S. R.: Management of the severed ureter. J Urol 77:407–413, 1957

6. Soresi, A. L.: A new method of lateral (side-to-side) intestinal anastomosis. Surg Gynec & Obst 20:225–227, 1915

7. Everidge, J.: Injuries of the ureter. Brit J Urol 12:234, 1940

8. Tsuchiya, F. and Toyoda, Y: Treatment of injuries of ureter in hysterectomy. Operation 10:86–99, 1956

9. Hamm, F. C. and Weinberg, S. R.: Renal and ureteral surgery without intubation. Trans Am Assn Genito-Urin Surg 46:109–114, 1954

10. Hamm, F. C., Weinberg, S. R. and Waterhouse, K.: Repair of the injured ureter. Surg 45:575–584, 1959

Commentary: Principles of Ureteroureterostomy

Sidney R. Weinberg and Joel W. Rosenberg

The method of ureteroureterostomy described in the preceding article has so far withstood the test of time and is widely used today (albeit with minor variations in some quarters) with good results. It is difficult for a urologist entering practice in the 1980s to appreciate the apprehension with which urologic surgeons approached this procedure just three decades ago. At that time, the prognosis for success was so poor that most urologists preferred immediate nephrectomy.

The physiologic principles that dictated ureteroureterostomy are quite simple. First, physiologic study of the ureter indicates that after ureteroureterostomy, asynchronous peristalsis divides the upper from the lower segment. This causes a functional obstruction to the flow of urine. To prevent this it is necessary to divert urine from the anastomatic site until healing is complete. Second, the ureter is a retroperitoneal organ, and urine is not reabsorbed from this space. Any urine escaping into the area that is not properly drained becomes infected and can lead to stricture at the anastomatic site. Third, circumferential anastomosis of a round organ can produce a stricture at the operative site secondary to scarring. Therefore, it is far preferable to make an oblique anastomosis to ensure that healing occurs at different planes so that strictures do not occur. This is facilitated by spatulating the ends of the two segments.

Most urologists will agree with the aforementioned points. In addition, there can be little argument on several other points. First, adequate debridement should be accomplished whenever indicated, for instance, with trauma secondary to missiles. Second, tension on the suture line must be avoided, and mobilization of the ureter and kidney can be carried out to gain adequate length. When adequate length cannot be obtained, choose a different procedure. Transverse ureteroureterostomy is gaining popularity, but interposition of a segment of bowel the psoas hitch procedure, or the Boari bladder flap can be used. Finally, use fine, absorbable suture material and attempt a water-tight anastomosis.

One point that still uniformly evokes controversy is the use of splints. Much has been written on this subject, and evidence has been brought forward both for and against splinting.

A general surgical maxim states "never leave a foreign body across an anastomosis." This principle is equally true for urologists. Ureteral splints introduce irritation and infection at the site of anastomosis and can also cause ischemia by simple compression against soft tissues, which must contribute to scarring and stricture formation.

ANNOTATED BIBLIOGRAPHY

Weinberg SR: Physiology of the ureter. In Bergman H (ed): The Ureter. New York, Harper & Row, 1967, Chap. 4.

The physiologic principles dealt with in this chapter comprise the underlying basis for the current discussion of ureteral anastomosis.

Caine M, Hermann G: The return of peristalsis in the anastomosed ureter. Br J Urol 42:164, 1970

This study uses x-ray (cine) techniques to evaluate transmission of peristaltic waves across an anastomosed ureter. There is no transmission at all in the early postoperative phase, and only after weeks does it return to normal. The rationale of using a split T tube as a means of proximal diversion is discussed.

Carlton CE Jr, Scott R Jr, Guthrie AG Jr: Initial management of ureteral injuries: Report of 78 cases. J Urol 105:335, 1971

These authors stress adequate debridement, mobilization to avoid tension, spatulation to avoid circular anastomosis, watertight approximation with fine catgut, proximal diversion through ureterosotmy, and avoidance of splints. They emphasize the need for a watertight anastomosis, which in their opinion, is the single most important factor in obtaining a good result.

DeWeerd JH, Henry JD: Z-plastic ureteroureterostomy. J Urol 93:690, 1965

A technique is described that will result in the formation of the largest possible ureteral diameter. It is far more difficult than a straightforward oblique anastomosis and is probably indicated in only a small number of selected cases.

Braman W: Useful applications of transureteroureterostomy in adults and children. J Urol 113: 460, 1975

This author reports on 17 patients who underwent transureteroureterostomy. There were no deleterious effects on the contralateral kidney, and function of all transposed ureters and kidneys has been maintained or improved.

Hoch WH, Kursh ED, Persky L: Early agressive management of intraoperative ureteral injuries. J Urol 114:530, 1975

These authors stress the need for early, direct, and agressive management whenever possible. They used a variety of techniques; six patients had ureteroureterostomy.

Mendez R, McGinty DM: The management of delayed recognized ureteral injuries. J Urol 119:192, 1979

Late recognition of ureteral injury is associated with poor prognosis for repair. The authors quote Higgins: "The venial sin is injury to the ureter but the mortal sin is failure of recognition."

Stutzman RE: Ballistics and the management of ureteral injuries from high velocity missiles. J Urol 118:947, 1977

Ureteral trauma after high-velocity missiles is discussed. Principles of treatment emphasized include debridement, spatulation, avoidance of tension on the suture line, watertight anastomosis *with* a stent, proximal urinary diversion, adequate drainage at the site of anastomoses, and control of infection.

Overview: Ureteroureterostomy

Russell W. Lavengood

Drs. Weinberg and Rosenberg cover the subject of ureteroureterostomy well. They make the point that asynchronous peristalsis in the distal segment of the ureter requires temporary diversion through a ureterotomy above the anastomosis. This permits a certain amount of extravasation of urine into the retroperitoneum despite drainage with Penrose drains. I prefer to make a watertight anastomosis in a circumferential manner between the spatulated ends. I do this over a polyethylene feeding tube of adequate diameter to drain the kidney. The tube is placed into the renal pelvis and led down the ureter into the bladder. Two weeks later, the cathether is removed with the aid of a panendoscope and a grasping forceps.

Hendren and Hensle, reporting on 75 cases of transure-teroureterostomy, make several important observations that can be used in any form of ureteroureterostomy.[1] They stress the importance of not dissecting the surrounding retroperitoneal tissue in order to prevent devascularization of the ureter. They accomplish this by sweeping the surrounding retroperitoneal tissues toward the ureter. They divide the gonadal vessels just above the ovary in the female and at the internal ring in the male and leave the vessels in the periureteral tissue for additional collateral circulation. This had been reported earlier by Aledia.[2] When large segments of the ureter are destroyed, bladder wall flaps with a psoas hitch and autotransplantation can be used to bridge the gap.

REFERENCES

1. Hendren WH, Hensle TW: Transureterostomy: Experience with 75 cases. J Urol 123:826, 1980

2. Young JD Jr, Aledia FT: Further observations on flank ureterostomy and cutaneous transureteroureterostomy. J Urol 95:327, 1966

32

URETERAL SUBSTITUTION

Richard J. Boxer, M.D., Steven F. Johnson, M.D., and Richard M. Ehrlich, M.D.

From the Department of Surgery, Division of Urology, UCLA School of Medicine, and the Veterans Administration Wadsworth Hospital Medical Center, Los Angeles, California

Urology / September 1978 / Volume XII, Number 3

The capacity of the ureter to regenerate and heal is good when the continuity is maintained even by a narrow strip of the wall. However, a secondary stricture often results in hydroureteronephrosis with subsequent renal damage. Thus, the need for urinary diversion, ureteral replacement, or nephrectomy confronts the genitourinary surgeon. When only one functioning kidney is present or there is disease in the other, effective ureteral substitution is mandatory as the only alternative to permanent nephrostomy.

In the early 1890s, Van Hook was the first to use a bladder flap to bridge a lower ureteral defect.[1] Boari,[2a] and later Boari and Casati[2b] were the first successfully to replace the distal portion of the ureter in animals. They used a tubed bladder flap. They also experimented and failed using segments of arteries, glass tubes, uterine horns, and bowel. In the last seventy years attempts at replacing the ureter with synthetic material as well as free grafts from the cardiovascular and genitourinary systems have usually failed. The most successful method of ureteral replacement has been with pedicle flaps from the bladder or intestine. Transureteroureterostomy, as discussed in a preceding article in this symposium, can also be used with success, although several reports of complications have been reported recently.[3,4]

Ureteral substitutes may be classified as (1) synthetic prostheses, (2) free grafts, and (3) pedicle grafts. The first two are still in the experimental stage although sporadic reports of success in humans have appeared. The type of ureteral loss often determines the type of operative repair. If the ureteral injury or disease is in the distal third, a vesicopsoas hitch or bladder flap is the treatment of choice. Penetrating injuries can usually be repaired by primary ureteroureterostomy.[5] However, damage to long segments of the proximal third, recurrent renal calculi (with or without ureteral strictures), ureteral carcinoma in a solitary kidney, and certain congenital conditions are best treated with intestinal substitution, specifically the ileal ureter.

SYNTHETIC PROSTHESES

Synthetic prostheses are used as either stents and templates for ureteral regeneration or as simple conduits bridging a large ureteral gap. Boari in 1895[2a] was the first to use a synthetic prosthesis (glass tube) in animals. Various other synthetic materials have been used and all have been failures because of anastomotic leaks, stone formation, reflux, hydronephrosis, or migration of the prosthesis. Attempts have included the use of vitallium,[6] tantalum,[7] polyethylene,[8,9] dimethylpolysiloxane,[10,11] silver,[12] Ivalon,[13] polyvinyl,[14] Teflon,[15–17] Dacron[18,19] and silicone rubber.[11,20,21] Synthetic materials usually interfere with normal peristalsis and thus are poor substitutes for the ureter. Notwithstanding these disappointing results to date, there is promise that newer types of synthetic tubes may be used successfully in the future.[22]

The use of synthetic prostheses as stents and templates has been more successful. Studies show that even extensive defects will heal if the ureteral ends remain connected with at least a narrow strip of the wall.[23–26] However, strictures often occur.[27–30] Regeneration of the circular muscle has been shown[23–32] although it is uncertain whether or not longitudinal muscle regenerates. This phenomenon is the basis of the intubated ureterotomy of Davis.[33] Although cases of complete loss of ureteral wall and regeneration along a synthetic tube have been reported,[34] most defects fail to heal unless a portion of the wall is intact.[35,36]

FREE GRAFTS

Free autologous or homologous grafts have been used to replace a portion of the ureter. Hovnanian and associates[37,38] have been the most successful using bladder mucosal grafts fashioned into a tube over an indwelling stent. They found regeneration of longitudinal and circular fibers, but due to the disruption of the normal peristalsis, hydronephrosis resulted. However, other materials have been singularly unsuccessful including peritoneum,[39] stomach,[40,41] placenta,[42] lyophilized homologous ureter,[43,44] split-thickness skin,[45] veins and arteries,[7,46–50] and collagen.[51,52] Vistnes and Lilla[53] used homologous and autologous ureters as free grafts in dogs. The grafts functioned well for six weeks but thereafter rejection and subsequent stenosis occurred. The ideal free graft as replacement for the ureter has not yet been found. With rare exception, most experiments have failed. Thus, in clinical practice the pedicle graft is the procedure of choice.

PEDICLE GRAFTS

Melnikoff in 1912[54] and Schein, Sanders, and Hurwitt in 1956[55] used the fallopian tube and appendix on pedicles as substitutes for the ureter. Although the latter had a viable graft, both experiments failed physiologically, resulting in hydronephrosis. Strauss[56] and others[57,58] fashioned full-thickness abdominal wall into a tube to replace the ureter. This method, however, is not a practical approach to the problem. The proximal ureter has been experimentally replaced by a flap of renal capsule.[59] This method can be used to enlarge the ureteropelvic junction if dismembered or pelvic flap pyeloplasty does not permit a long, large funneled outlet.[60] However, the method has not proved applicable

for ureteral replacement. Thus, the pedicle grafts that have proved predictably successful in replacing the ureter are the Boari bladder flap with or without the vesicopsoas hitch and the intestine (ileal ureter).

Bladder Flap (Boari-Ockerblad) and Vesicopsoas hitch. The Boari bladder flap,[2a] popularized in this country by Ockerblad,[61] is an effective method of replacing the distal ureter when primary ureteral reimplantation is not possible. However, the psoas bladder hitch as described by Harrow[62] and others[63–66] can replace at least the distal third of the ureter, with relative ease. This procedure involves suturing the posterior bladder to the psoas tendon with chromic catgut. The reimplantation can then be performed without tension on the ureterovesical anastomosis. If even more extensive length is needed, a Boari flap in combination with a psoas hitch can be done. In one report, 18 cm of distal ureter were successfully replaced with this combination.[67] The use of the submucosal tunnel technique of ureteroneocystostomy minimizes the likelihood of reflux.[68]

The vesicopsoas hitch is performed through a midline incision. The peritoneum overlying the bladder should be mobilized carefully. A curvilinear U-shaped incision on the anterior surface is made with the base of the flap directed toward the involved side. Two fingers placed within the lumen can then displace the bladder upward and over the iliac vessels. The mobility of the bladder is then easily determined, and a decision made as to whether or not further vesical mobilization by take-down of the opposite vesical pedicle is necessary. Satisfactory length can usually be obtained without pedicle ligation in all but the most extensive ureteral injuries.

Our preference is to excise a button of muscularis at the tip of the tube and to create a long submucosal tunnel (at least 3 to 4 cm) prior to placing 2-0 or 1-0 chromic anchoring sutures into the psoas muscle from the posterior portion of the bladder. Care is taken to avoid injury to the genitofemoral nerve or incorporating the nerve within the sutures.

The bladder can then be anchored as high as possible without tension and the ureter led through the submucosal tunnel with a traction suture. The ureter is then spatulated and anastomosed to the bladder with 4-0 or 5-0 chromic sutures (Fig. 1). Stents are not mandatory but can be employed in difficult cases or if prior irradiation has been used.

It is mandatory to insure that the ureter is not angulated or twisted as it enters the tunnel, that the myotomy is adequate in caliber, and that the tunnel is of sufficient length to prevent reflux. Preoperative determination of adequate bladder neck and urethral caliber is important or simultaneous Y-V-plasty may be necessary to prevent distal obstruction. This is particularly

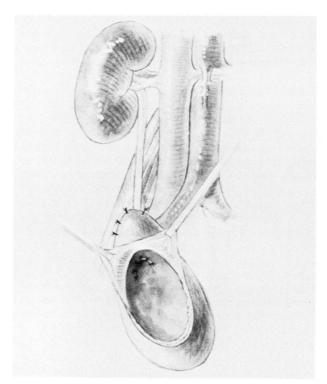

Fig. 1. Bladder reaches well above ileac vessels; long submucosal tunnel prevents reflux.

important in those cases in which the vesicopsoas hitch is used in conjunction with an ileal ureter.

Bilateral vesicopsoas horns can also be created in a similar manner but bilateral pedicle interruption is, of course, contraindicated.

The bladder is then closed vertically by means of a running mucosal suture of 3-0 chromic and a second layer of interrupted sutures of 2-0 chromic through the muscularis. A suprapubic tube is placed and adequate Penrose drainage is performed (Fig. 2) This procedure has been graphically illustrated in a recent film.[66]

Contraindications to the vesicopsoas hitch include a small thick-walled contracted bladder and those in which multiple operations have been performed making mobilization technically impossible. Pelvic irradiation, neurogenic bladder disease, uncorrectable bladder outlet obstruction, and urethral strictures are further contraindications. As in all urologic anastomoses, poor blood supply and tension usually lead to stricture and subsequent failure.

The operative technique of the Boari flap is not difficult. The base of the flap, most readily taken from the posterior wall, must have a width of 4 cm, whereas the apex should have a width no less than 3 cm. To gain

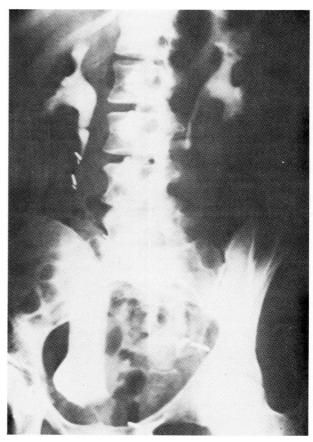

Fig. 2. Intravenous urogram demonstrates mobility of bladder; excellent vesical emptying is, however, preserved.

greater length, a tube can be fashioned by spiraling the flap across the anterior surface of the bladder. Up to 12 cm of bladder tube can be obtained in this fashion. The ureter is brought through the posterior wall and through a 1.5-cm submucosal tunnel. The ureter can be made to enter the submucosal tunnel of the bladder flap at its apex or it can be brought in a short distance from the cut end of the pedicle. The ureter is spatulated and sutured as in a ureteral reimplantation. The flap is then fashioned into a tube and closed with a continuous locked suture of chromic catgut.[69] The ureterovesical anastomosis may be stented.

Transureteroureterostomy. The transureteroureterostomy (TUU) is discussed elsewhere in this symposium. However, the complications are germane to this discussion. In well over 200 reported cases minimal morbidity has resulted. However, Ehrlich and Skinner[3] reported the first complications of transureteroureterostomy and specifically damage to the recipient ureterorenal unit in their 5 cases. One ileal ureter, one residual hydronephrosis, and one ureteral stricture resulted. Of the donor kidneys, three nephrectomies and one ileal ureter were necessary and one hydronephrotic kidney remains. More recently Sandoz, Paull, and Macfarlane[4] added four more injuries to the recipient ureter.

The aforementioned complications have two common denominators: poor blood supply and anastomotic tension. It has been emphasized that it is essential to accomplish the anastomosis without tension, and it is critical to have an adequate blood supply accompany the transplanted ureter. We fully endorse this concept. Mobilization of the recipient ureter toward the midline is contraindicated.

The donor ureter must be free from tension and allowed to lie in a gentle, unobstructed course. A tangential rather than perpendicular anastomosis is preferred, and the donor ureter should be cut obliquely and/or spatulated. If the donor ureter cannot easily reach the unmobilized recipient, alternative forms of reconstruction are mandatory, and it is urged that transureteroureterostomy not be performed. It is further emphasized that if the blood supply is questionable, the procedure should be abandoned.

While we fully recognize that transureteroureterostomy deserves a respected place in urologic surgery and do not suggest that its use be abandoned, it is nevertheless surprising that the vesicopsoas hitch has not been more relied upon in difficult ureteral injuries. In all of the 5 previously reported cases,[3] the vesicopsoas hitch could have been the procedure of choice, thus completely eliminating any possible injury to the recipient ureterorenal unit.

It is our considered opinion that nephrectomy is often a conservative option that should be chosen more often in less than optimum situations.

TUU is appealing from the standpoint of its simplicity, but it cannot be safely applied to the correction of defects of the upper one fourth to one third of ureter. Its primary indication is for problems affecting the middle third of the ureter. For extensive ureteral defects and for problems affecting the upper ureter autotransplantation to the iliac fossa or ureteral replacement by ileum has proved most successful. The application of renal autotransplantation for ureteral disease is currently viewed as a viable alternative in selected cases. However, since this chapter is devoted to ureteral replacements, autotransplantation is mentioned only for sake of completeness.

Replacement of Ureter by Intestine. The small intestine has been used for partial or complete replacement of a diseased or injured ureter for ninety years. In 1888, Foggi performed the first experiments of anastomosing a segment of ileum to the ureter and bladder.[70] Subsequent studies by Urso and Fabii in 1900[71] and Melnikoff in 1912[54] showed the procedure to be applicable in clinical surgery. Shoemaker in 1906 first performed an ileal ureter in two stages on an eighteen-year-old girl with urinary tuberculosis.[54] Thirty years later Nissen[72] reported the successful use of the ileal ureter for a ureteral fistula. Muller[73] and Lonquet[74] described cases of ileal replacement of an injured ureter during a Wertheim operation. The same operation was used by Rack[75] for replacement of a ureter that had been removed with a large adenocarcinoma of the colon. The indications for the ileal ureter were expanded to treatment of giant hydronephrosis,[76] recurrent renal calculi,[77–85] retroperitoneal fibrosis,[86] ureterovaginal fistula, megaureter, and ureteral tumor.[87]

An inherent property and potential drawback of the ileum is its absorptive capacity. Pyrah and associates[88] noted that hyperchloremic acidosis did not occur because of increased absorption of chloride, but they did find that potassium was absorbed from the loop, and that hyperkalemia can become a major problem if renal function is impaired. They concluded that electrolyte imbalance would not significantly affect the nonazotemic patient with an ileal ureter. However, Couvelaire[89] has advocated that the segment should not exceed 25 cm to prevent excessive electrolyte absorption. Acidosis and excessive blood ammonia can result in the patient with an ileal conduit or ileal ureter if intrahepatic disease interferes with urea synthesis.[90] In our experience[91] of 89 patients undergoing the ileal ureter procedure, no electrolyte problems have occurred if the patient's preoperative serum creatinine was below 2 mg/100 ml; 87.5 percent had a successful outcome* whereas only 5 (45 percent) of the 11 patients with greater than 2 mg/100 ml creatinine had a successful long-term result (Table 1). The failures were a direct result of the inability of the compensated kidneys to excrete the excess absorbed electrolytes. Although only preliminary reports are available, tapering of the ileal segment may be beneficial in decreasing the mucosal absorptive surface, and thus this may be indicated when preexisting mild azotemia is present.[92]

The ileum can be interposed into the urinary tract in various ways. The proximal anastomosis may be ureteroileal, pyeloileal, calycoileal, or nephroileal.

---

* The operation was considered successful if the renal function on the affected side was preserved, recurrent calculi were no longer troublesome, subsequent diversion was not necesssary, serum electrolytes were not abnormal (hyperchloremic acidosis did not occur), pyelographic appearance was unchanged or improved, and the patient was without pain.

TABLE 1. Comparative Renal Function—Data on 75 Patients, with Operative Success and Failure Results[91]

| No. of Patients | Serum Creatinine (mg/100 ml) | | | | | Results | |
| | Preoperative | Postoperative | | | | Success | Failure |
		0–0.9	1–1.9	2–2.2	≥3		
19	0–0.9	13	6	0	0	17 (89.5)	2 (10.5)
45	1–1.9	7	28	6	4	39 (86.7)	6 (13.3)
9	2–2.9	0	1	5	3	6 (66.7)	3 (33.3)
2	≥3	0	0	0	2	0	2 (100)

* Figures in parentheses represent percents

Goodwin recommends that when the indication for surgery is recurrent calculi, the anastomosis should be fashioned to the ureter, pelvis, and lower pole calyx and infundibulum.[77–83] Four very important technical points are: (1) that the ileum must be used in an isoperistaltic manner; (2) that the bladder is capable of emptying; (3) that the bladder neck be open to allow the passage of mucus produced by the ileum; and (4) distal obstruction should be vigorously searched for and corrected prior to or during the procedure.

Although the greatest experience is with the ileum, other segments of bowel may interpose between the bladder and kidney. Richie and Skinner[93] demonstrated that the emptying ability of the colon was equivalent to that of the ileum when used for urinary conduits. Goldschmidt and Dayton[94] reported no significant differences in absorption between equivalent segments of ileum and colon. In our series, 1 patient required bilateral ileal ureters for recurrent staghorn calculi. On the right side ileum was used and on the left side descending colon was anastomosed to the pelvis, lower pole calyces, and bladder. Both kidneys are functioning equally well. Struthers and Scott[95] reported the similar use of colon in a patient with a large defect in the pelvis and proximal ureter. The patient was doing very well five years after the operation.

The indications for the ileal ureter have become expanded as more urologists become familiar with the operation. At UCLA we have used the operation in the treatment of basically five types of problems (Table 2). The presence of recurrent calculi (44 patients) was the most frequent indication. Other indications were ureteral stricture or fistula (88.5 percent were iatrogenic), physiologic or anatomic obstruction of the ureter, ureteral carcinoma in a solitary kidney, and miscellaneous undiversion of cutaneous ileal urinary conduits. The operation was successful in 80.9 percent of these 89 patients. The majority of failures occurred in patients with congenital genitourinary tract disease. Only 45 percent of these patients were managed successfully by this operation. We believe the reason for this is twofold: the patient was either incapable of emptying his bladder

TABLE 2. Indications for Operation, with Operative Success and Failure Results[91]

Surgical Indications	No. of Patients	Success*	Failure*
Recurrent calculi	44†	38 (88.4)	5 (11.6)
Ureteral stricture or fistula	26	22 (84.6)	4 (15.4)
Urologic operation (7)			
Gynecologic operation (15)			
General surgical operation (2)			
Tuberculosis (2)			
Retroperitoneal fibrosis (1)			
Congenital obstruction	11	5 (45)	6 (55)
Ureteral carcinoma (solitary kidney)	2	2 (100)	0
Miscellaneous (including undiversion)	6	5 (83)	1 (17)
Totals	89	72 (80.9)	17 (19.1)

* Figures in parentheses indicate percents.
† One operative death.

because of a neuropathic or obstructed bladder, and/or renal function was poor at the time of the operation.

The patient in the "miscellaneous undiversion" category presented with ureterovaginal or vesicovaginal fistulas or intractable interstitial cystitis. These women required temporary diversion, but their basic bladder mechanics were intact. Undiversion would not only resolve the ureteral disease but would also expand the size of the bladder if desired (ileocystoplasty). This group of patients had an 83-percent long-term success rate. Some of these patients had bladder augmentation at the time of undiversion (ileocystoplasty).

The ileal ureter is an excellent treatment for severe ureteral disease; therefore, it has been used for ureteral stricture caused by tuberculosis or bilharzia,[70,87,96] radiation ureteritis,[96] retroperitoneal fibrosis,[91] megaureter,[87,91] severe vesicoureterorenal reflux causing atonic ureters,[70] as well as ureteral injury, stricture, or fistula.

Surgical Technique. The incision is made in the midline if a bilateral ileal ureter is needed. We prefer a modified flank torque position if the ileum is to be anastomosed to the renal pelvis or kidney. A paramedian incision can be employed if partial replacement of the ureter is needed.

The segment of ileum is selected approximately 15 to 20 cm proximal to the ileocecal valve and about 25 cm in length. The exact length is measured by laying the intestine in its future position. By palpation or transillumination, at least two arterial arcades should be defined to supply the segment. Care must be exercised to preserve the mesenteric vessels and at the same time gain maximum mobility of the segment.

If the surgeon is concerned about the vascular supply to the ileal segment, a method has been described to increase the collateral supply to the intestine.[97] A segment of ileum twice as long as needed is chosen. Approximatley 6 cm of bowel on both ends of the segment is separated from the mesentery. This leaves the necessary length of ileal segment with twice as much mesentery, allowing increased blood flow to the segment.

A one or two-layer ileoileostomy using 4-0 silk suture restores the continuity of the intestine. If the proximal end is not to be anastomosed to the kidney or renal pelvis, it is closed immediately or tagged with a silk suture. If the procedure is for recurrent calculi, the authors recommend that the nephrolithotomy be performed first. This guarantees the surgeon that a pyeloileal anastomosis is possible.

The success of the ureteroileal anastomosis is determined by an adequate blood supply to the ureter and an anastomosis without tension. Stents generally are not used. A single layer of 3-0 interrupted chromic catgut is used for the end to side, mucosa to mucosa anastomosis.

If the ileum is to be anastomosed to the renal pelvis or kidney, the proximal end is spatulated. A full-thickness, end to end pelvioileal anastomosis is done using 3-0 chromic catgut. If the indication for operation is recurrent calculi, a calycoileal anastomosis is used (Fig. 3). This gives maximum drainage to the kidney. A lower pole partial nephrectomy can be done to remove calculi or a diseased portion of the kidney and to optimize drainage. This is not usually recommended in order to preserve the maximum number of nephrons. Seven patients in our series had the procedure, and all had successful long-term outcomes.

The ileovesical anastomosis is usually a one-layered union using 3-0 chromic catgut. Goodwin recommends a plug of bladder be removed in the posterior aspect near the trigone for the best ileovesical anastomosis. Because the ileum produces mucus, it is absolutely essential to ensure preoperatively that the bladder neck is open, that the bladder empties to completion, and that no distal obstruction is present. Originally we thought that a Y-V plasty or an open or transurethral bladder neck resection should be performed; this may not be

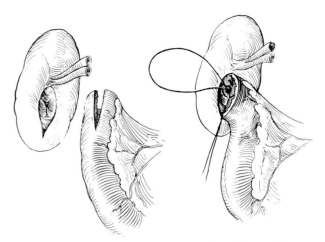

Fig. 3. Lower pole of kidney is opened widely and ileum is carefully sutured in mucosa to mucosa anastomosis; this allows excellent dependent drainage.

TABLE 3. Bladder Neck Revision and Operative Success of Failure Results[91]

Procedure	No. of Patients	Success*	Failure*
Y-V-plasty and/or transurethral resection bladder neck	24	19 (79)	5 (21)
Psoas hitch	7	7 (100)	0
No revision (operative death excluded)	57	46 (80.7)	11 (19.3)

* Figures in parentheses indicate percents.

necessary (Table 3). However, the vesicopsoas hitch may be advantageous for three reasons: (1) it opens the bladder slightly; (2) the length of intestine ad its absorptive surface area are reduced;[65] and (3) deep pelvic surgery is obviated (Fig. 4). At UCLA, 7 patients had a vesicopsoas hitch and all were treated successfully in the long-term.

It is desirable, although not necessary, to place the intestinal segment in the retroperitoneum. When the left ureter is to be replaced, the descending color is mobilized medially and the ileal segment is placed in the retroperitoneum through a window in the mesentery (Fig. 5). Inferiorly, the ureter must then reenter through the mesosigmoid or it may be brought over the sigmoid to enter the bladder. For right ureteral replacement, it is necessary to produce a 90-degree rotation of the mesentery to make the segment isoperistaltic. The window is then closed carefully, avoiding strangulation of the mesentery of the segment. The remainder of the peritoneum is closed with running absorbable suture. Drains are placed and brought out through a lower lateral stab.

The authors strongly recommend that the ileal ureter

should have proximal protection with nephrostomy to protect the anastomosis.

Surgical Results. Between 1956 and 1976 at the UCLA Hospital, 89 patients had partial or complete replacement of their ureter. The follow-up was at least six months, and only 5 patients were lost. Thirty-six patients were

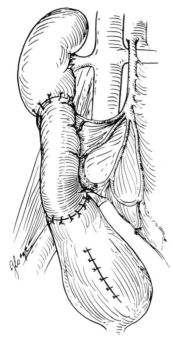

Fig. 4. Psoas hitch allows shorter ileal segment and thus reduces intestinal absorptive surface.

followed up for more than five years and 25 for ten years or longer.

The type of ileal ureter performed on the patient was dictated by the indication for surgery (Fig. 6), the most frequent indication being recurrent calculi. An 87-percent success rate with this procedure has been attained. The same procedure was done on 7 additional patients who also had a lower pole partial nephrectomy, all of whom did well.

The patients were evaluated by physical examination, renal function (serum creatinine), intravenous urograms, and voiding cystograms. The over-all success rate was 80.9 percent. Renal function, recorded in 75 patients pre- and postoperatively, was unchanged or decreased in 74.7 percent of the cases. In the 64 patients who had a creatinine of less than 2 mg/100 ml, 87.5 percent had successful outcomes. However, of the 11 patients who had a creatinine greater than 2 mg/100 ml, only 6 (54.5 percent) had successful operative therapy (Table 1). This cutoff point at 2 mg/100 ml creatinine substantiates our view that the procedure should not be performed on patients with poor renal function. A success rate of 66 percent can be expected if the serum creatinine is between 2 and 3 mg, and it continues to be our view that the operation should not be performed if the serum creatinine is over 3 mg/100 ml. Hyperchloremic acidosis was seen in most of the failures.

Pyelographic appearance, parenchymal thickness, and recurrent or residual calculi were the three criteria used in evaluating the IVPs. The pyelogram showed decreased dilatation or no change in the pelves and calyces in 62 of the 65 patients evaluated. Of the 62 patients, 55 (89 percent) had successful outcome. In the 62 patients who had parenchymal thickness measured, 59 were unchanged and 86 percent of these cases were

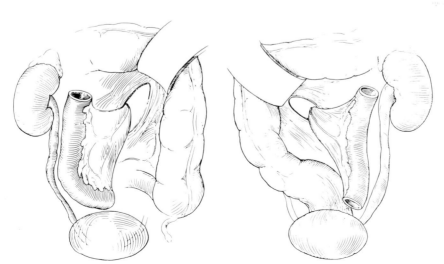

Fig. 5. Isolated ileal segment in place prior to anastomosis.

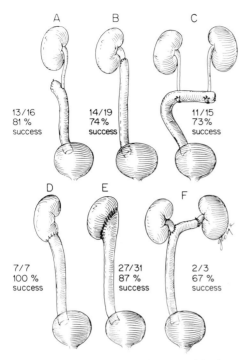

Fig. 6. Summary schema showing several types of ileal ureter employed in authors' series and respective success rates.

A
13/16
81 %
success

B
14/19
74%
success

C
11/15
73%
success

D
7/7
100 %
success

E
27/31
87 %
success

F
2/3
67 %
success

TABLE 4. Vesicoileal Reflux Evaluation Data on 55 Patients, with Operative Success or Failure Results[91]

Evaluation	Success*	Failure*
Reflux	39 (71)	1 (1.8)
No reflux	9 (16.4)	6 (10.8)

* Figures in parentheses indicate percents.

anastomosis. This allows reflux urine from the ileum to return to the bladder, thus decompressing the system.

Urinary infection is frequent after the ileal ureter. Twenty-eight patients had positive cultures of their urine, but 25 (89.3 percent) had no change or improvement in their renal function and pyelographic appearance.

One patient died as a result of the operation, a mortality rate of 1.1 percent. It must be emphasized that this is usually a difficult, long operation. The patients always have had previous operations, frequently have renal calculi or infection, or both. Pre- and postoperative antimicrobial therapy measurably adds to lessened morbidity and postoperative problems. The postoperative management can be difficult. However, the operative results of 80.9 percent success rate in patients who were extremely ill or were on permanent external drainage are gratifying and our enthusiasm is shared by other urologists.[72–76,86,87,89,95–108]

Contraindications to this procedure are ileal disease, creatinine greater than 2 mg/100 ml, neuropathic bladder, and bladder outlet or distal obstruction. If one follows these admonitions, a successful outcome can usually be expected. The reservation expressed by Tanagho[109] toward the incorporation of bowel segments into a closed urinary tract indicates the importance of strict patient selection and precise operative technique. Goodwin,[110] however, continues to be a strong advocate of this most versatile procedure.

Los Angeles, California 90024
(DR. BOXER)

Acknowledgment. This article is dedicated to Dr. Ian M. Thompson who made substantial contributions to the field of ureteral surgery, and to Dr. Willard E. Goodwin who has taught us the ileal ureter.

successful. Although 18 patients had residual or new calculi developed postoperatively, 17 (94.4 percent) were treated successfully by the operation. Of the 47 who had no calculi, 39 were considered successes. Thus, the presence or absence of calculi was of little prognostic value.

Reflux into the ileal segment was seen in 40 of 55 patients. Thirty-nine of these patients (97.5 percent) had successful operative therapy. However, only 9 of 15 patients (60 percent) with no postoperative reflux were successes (Table 4). Therefore, it appears that reflux may be beneficial. Davis and Nealon[98] have pointed out that the "damping" effect of the ileac segment may protect the kidney from reflux atrophy. Goodwin stresses that the ureter should be incorporated into the pyeloileal

REFERENCES

1. Reed RH: A review of ureteral surgery. Columbus Med J 15:492, 1895

2ª. Boari A: Cited by Spies JW, Johnson CW, and Wilson CS: Reconstruction of the ureter by a bladder flap. Proc Soc Biol Med 30:425, 1932

2ᵇ. Boari A, and Casati A: Cited by Spies JW, Johnson CW, and Wilson CS[2a]

3. Ehrlich RM, and Skinner DG: Complications of transureterureterostomy. J Urol 113:39, 1975

4. Sandoz Il, Paul DP, and Macfarlane CA: Complications with transureteroureterostomy. *Ibid.,* 117:39, 1977

5. Carlton CE, Scott R, and Guthrie AG: The initial management of ureteral injuries: A report of 78 cases, Trans Am Assoc Genitourin Surg 62:114, 1970

6. Lord JW, Jr, and Eckel JH: The use of Vitallium tubes in the urinary tract of the dog. J Urol 48:412, 1942

7. Lubash S: Experiences with tantalum tubes in the reimplantation of the ureters into the sigmoid in dogs and humans. J Urol 57:1010, 1947

8. Hardin CA: Experimental repair of ureters by polyethylene tubing and ureteral and vessel grafts. Arch Surg 68:57, 1957

9. Scher AM, Erickson RV, and Scher M: Polyethylene as partial ureteral prosthesis in dogs. J Urol 73:987 1955

10. Djurhuus JC, Gyrd-Hansen N, Nerstrom B, and Svenson O: Total replacement of ureter by a Scurasil prosthesis in pigs. Br J Urol 46: 415, 1974

11. Blum J, Skemp C, and Reisner M: Silicone rubber ureteral prosthesis. J Urol 90:276, 1963

12. Schein CJ, Sanders AR, and Hurwitt ES: Experimental reconstruction of ureters. Arch Surg 73:47, 1955

13. Dufour A, and Thellier G: Cited by Kočvara S, and Žák E.[18]

14. Ulm AH, and Lo M-C: Total bilateral polyvinyl ureteral substitutes in the dog. Surgery 45:313, 1959

15. Ulm AH, and Krauss L: Total unilateral Teflon substitutes in the dog. J Urol 83:575, 1960

16. Warren JW, Jr. Coomer T, and Fransen H: The use of Teflon for replacement of ureters. Ibid. 89:164, 1963

17. Warren JW, Jr, Brandura WP, Beltran FA, and Horochowski A: Use of Teflon grafts for replacement of ureters. Ibid 85:265, 1961

18. Kočvara S, and Žák F: Ureteral substitution with Dacron and Teflon prostheses. Ibid 88:365, 1962

19. Griffith DP, Moseley WG, and Beach PD: Experimental studies in ureteral substitution. Invest Urol 11:239, 1973

20. Dufour B, and Blondel P: The prosthetic replacement of the ureter. Europ Urol 1:134, 1975

21. Blum JA: Permanent Silastic ureteral prostheses. Surg Forum 13:501, 1962

22. Baum N, Mobley DF, and Carlton CE: Ureteral replacements. Urology 5:165, 1975

23. Davis DM: The process of ureteral repair: a recapitulation of the splinting question. J Urol 79:215, 1958

24. Davis DM, Strong GH, and Drake WM: Intubated ureterotomy. Ibid 59:581, 1948

25. Hamm FC, and Weinberg SR: Experimental studies of regeneration of the ureter without intubation. Ibid 75:43, 1956

26. Weaver RG: Ureteral regeneration: experimental and clinical. Ibid 79:31, 1958

27. Boyarsky S, and Duque O: Ureteral regeneration in dogs; an experimental study bearing on the Davis ureterotomy. Ibid 73:53, 1955

28. Kimborough JC, Furst JN, Worgan DK, and Denslow JC: Intubated ureterotomy, animal, clinical and experimental cases. Ibid 64:74, 1950

29. Tautner K, and Raaschou F: Histological examination of the regeneration of the ureter in dogs after intubated ureterotomy. Ibid 71:274, 1954

30. Weaver RG, and Henderson JH: Ureteral regeneration: experimental and clinical. Ibid 72:350, 1954

31. Hinman F, Jr, and Oppenheimer R: Smooth muscle regeneration in repair of experimental ureteral defects: the significance of the double lumen. Ibid 75:428, 1956

32. Oppenheimer R, and Hinman F, Jr: Ureteral regeneration: contracture vs. hyperplasia of smooth muscle. Ibid 74:476, 1955

33. Davis DM: Intubated ureterotomy: a new operation for ureteral and ureteropelvic stricture. Surg Gynecol Obstet 76:514, 1943

34. Borkowski A, and Kazon M: Regeneration of 2.5 cm of the ureter. Europ Urol 1:245, 1975

35. Huffman WL, McCorkle HF, and Persky L: Ureteral regeneration following experimental segmental resection. J Urol 75:796, 1956

36. Baker R, et al: Regeneration of the total length of the ureter in the dog. Ibid 92:621, 1964

37. Hovnanian AP, Javadpour N, and Gruhn JG: Reconstitution of the ureter by free autologous bladder mucosa graft. Ibid 93:455, 1965

38. Hovnanian AP, and Kingsley IA: Reconstruction of the ureter by free autologous bladder mucosa graft. Ibid 96:167, 1966

39. Esposti PL: Regeneration of smooth muscle fibers of the ureter following plastic surgery with free flaps of the parietal peritoneum. Minerva Chir 11:1208, 1956

40. Morelle VR: Replacement of the ureter by a segment of the stomach in pigs and dogs. Arch Chir Neerl 15:293, 1963

41. Tosatti E: Relocations of the small and large intestine for substitution of the stomach (and esophagus) and of the urinary bladder (and ureter). Rass Clin Sci 39:233, 1963

42. Minardi C: The use of placenta in experimental plastic surgery of the ureter. Riv Patol Clin 14:163, 1959

43. Harvard M, Camilleri JA, Nadig PW, and Glenn JF: Experimental transplantation of freeze-dried homologous and autologous ureteral segments. J Urol 86:385, 1961

44. Banonome A, and Begani R: Reconstruction of ureter by means of lyophilized tissue grafts, an experimental study. Arch Ital Chir 76:372, 1953

45. Horton CE, and Politano V: Ureteral reconstruction with split skin grafts; an experimental study. Plast Reconstr Surg 15:261, 1955

46. Blasucci E: Substitution of segments of ureters with arterial homografts. Minerva Chir 12: 1590, 1957

47. Itibere JL: Cited by Baum N, Mobley DF, and Carlton CE, Jr: Ureteral replacements. Urology 5:165, 1975

48. Rosenberg ML, and Dahlen GA: Autogenous vein grafts and venous valves in ureteral surgery, an experimental study. J Urol 70:434, 1953

49. Sewell WH: Failure of freeze-dried homologous arteries used as arteria grafts. J Urol 74:60, 1955

50. Fantino M, and Rangoni AG: Arterial and venous autoplastic grafts in reparative surgery of the ureter, experimental research. Arch Sci Med 107:640, 1959

51. Momose T: Urinary tract substitutions. Jap J Urol 58:935, 1967

52. Kaufman JJ, and Stoutz HL: Unpublished data on experimental use of collagen tubular prosthesis for ureteral replacements in dogs. Personal communication, April, 1978

53. Vistnes LM, and Lilla JA: Free grafts of autologous and homologous ureter: a functional study. Invest Urol 13:255, 1976

54. Melnikoff AE: Sur le replacement de l'uretère par une anse isolée de l'intestine grêle. Rev Clin d'Urol 1:601, 1912

55. Schein CJ, Sanders AR, and Hurwitt ES: Experimental reconstruction of the ureters. Arch Surg 73:47, 1956

56. Strauss AA: An artificial ureter made from abdominal wall. Surg Gynecol Obstet 18:78, 1914

57. Keshin JG, and Fitzpatrick TJ: A new technique for urinary diversion using a full thickness skin tube as a conduit. J Urol 88:631, 1962

58. Bettman AG: Anastomosis between the ureter and urinary bladder by means of a subcutaneous skin tube. Plast Reconstr Surg 2:80, 1947

59. Thompson IM, Kovacsi L, and Porterfield J: Reconstruction of the ureteropelvic junction with pedicle grafts and renal capsule. J Urol 89:573, 1963

60. Thompson IM: Repair of ureteropelvic junction and upper ureteral injury with renal capsule flap. Urol Clin North Am 4:45, 1977

61. Ockerblad NF: Reimplantation of the ureter into the bladder by a flap method. J Urol 57:845, 1947

62. Harrow BR: A neglected maneuver for ureterovesical reimplantation following injury at gynecologic operations. Ibid 100:280, 1968

63. Gross M, Peng B, and Waterhouse K: Use of mobilized bladder to replace the pelvic ureter. Ibid 101:40, 1969

64. Turner-Warwick R, and Worth PHH: The psoas bladder-hitch procedure for the replacement of the lower third of the ureter. Br J Urol 41:701, 1969

65. Ehrlich RM, Melman A, and Skinner DG: The use of the vesicopsoas hitch in urologic surgery. J Urol 119:322, 1978

66. Skinner DG, and Ehrlich RM: Use of the vesico-psoas hitch to facilitate ureteral reimplantation (film), Eaton Laboratories. Presented at the Western Section, A.U.A., San Francisco, March 13, 1977

67. Kelâmi A, et al: Replacement of the ureter using the urinary bladder. Urol Res 1:161, 1973

68. Kaufman JJ, Ehrlich RM, and Boxer RJ: Ureteral replacements, in Bergman H, Ed: The Ureter, 2nd ed, Springer-Verlag, New York, in press

69. Thompson IM: Bladder flap repairs of ureteral injuries. Urol Clin North Am 4:57, 1977

70. Küss R, and Chatelain C: Surgery of the ureter, in Anderson L, et al, Eds: Handbuch der Urologie, Springer-Verlag, New York, 1975, pp 95–129

71. Urso G, and Fabii A: Cited by Goldstein AE, Abeshouse BS, Yildiran C, and Siberstein H: Experimental studies of ileoureteral substitutes in dogs. J Urol 76:371, 1956

72. Nissen R: Reconstruction of the ureter. J Int Coll Surg 3:99, 1940

73. Muller K: Harnleiterverlängerung durch Dünndarmzwischenschaltung bei Harnleitnecrose. Dtsch Z Chir 264:588, 1950

74. Longuet YJ: On the possibility of replacing a segment of the pelvic ureter by a pedunculated graft of excluded small intestine in uretero-ileo-cystoplasty. Urol Cutan Rev 52:322, 1948

75. Rack RJ: Ureteroileal neocystostomy. JAMA 152:516, 1953

76. Küss R: L'ileó-urétéroplasties totale dans le traitement des hydronéphroses géantes. J Urol Med Chir 63:732, 1957

77. Goodwin WE, Winter CC, and Turner RD: Replacement of the ureter by small intestine. Clinical application and results of the "ileal ureter." J Urol 81:406, 1959

78. Goodwin WE, and Cockett ATK: Surgical treatment of multiple recurrent, branched, renal (staghorn) calculi by pyelo-nephro-ileo-vesical anastomosis. Trans Am Assoc Genitourin Surg 52:102, 1960; J Urol 85:214, 1961

79. Goodwin WE: The use of the ileal ureter for recurrent renal calculi. Urologists' Correspondence Club 36:47, 1971

80. Skinner DG, and Goodwin WE: Indications for the use of intestinal segments in management of nephrocalcinosis. J Urol 113:436, 1975

81. Goodwin WE: Replacement of the ureter by small intestine, in Cooper P, Ed: The Craft of Surgery, Boston, Little, Brown and Co., 1964, pp 1357–1366

82. IDEM: The uses of intestine in urology (a "gut reaction" for W.W.S.). Papers presented in honor of William Wallace Scott, New York, Plenum Publishing Corp., 1972, pp 75–80

83. IDEM: Replacement of the ureter by small intestine—the ileal ureter, in Riches E, Ed: Modern Trends in Urology, London, Butterworth and Co., 1960, pp 172–189

84. Barzilay BI, and Goodwin WE: Clinical application of an experimental study of ureteroileal anastomosis. J Urol 99:35, 1968

85. Fritzsche P, et al: Long-term radiographic changes of the kidney following ileal ureter operation. Ibid 114:843, 1976

86. Morales PA, Askari S, and Hotchkiss RS: Ileal replacement of the ureter. Ibid. 82:304, 1959

87. Wells CA: The use of the intestine in urology. Br J Urol 28:335, 1956

88. Pyrah LN, Care AD, Reed GW, and Parsons FM: The migration of sodium, chloride, and potassium ions across the mucous membrane of the ileum. Br J Surg 42:357, 1955

89. Couvelaire R: Les ressources du greffon intestinal en urologie. Urol Int (Basel) 2:1, 1956

90. McDermott WV, Jr: Diversion of urine to the intestines as a factor in ammoniagenic coma. N Engl J Med 256:460, 1957

91. Boxer RJ, et al: Replacement of the ureter by small intestine: clinical application and results of the ileal ureter in 89 patients. J Urol (in press)

92. Middleton AW, Jr: Tapered ileum as ureter substitution in severe renal damage. Urology 9:509, 1977

93. Richie JP, and Skinner DG: Urinary diversion: the physiological rationale for non-refluxing colonic conduits. Br J Urol 47:269, 1975

94. Goldschmidt S, and Dayton AB: Studies of the mechanism of absorption from the intestine. Am J Physiol 48:419, 1919

95. Struthers NW, and Scott R: Reconstruction of the upper ureter with colon. J Urol 112:179, 1974

96. Amin AH: Experience with the ileal ureter. Br J Urol 48:19, 1976

97. Ehrlich RM: An improved method of creating an ileac conduit: the importance of a better blood supply. J Urol 109:993, 1973

98. Davis DM, and Nealon TF, Jr: Complete replacement of both ureters by an ileal loop. Ibid 78:748, 1957

99. Baum WC: The clinical use of terminal ileum as a substitute ureter. Ibid 72:16, 1954

100. Bitker MP: Les urétéro-iléo-plasties. J d'Urol 60:473, 1954

101. Lachland AL: Sur les replacements totaux de l'uretere, Paris, Foulon and Co., 1970, pp 71–148

102. Moore EV, et al: Isolated ileal loops for ureteral repair. Surg Gynecol Obstet 102:87, 1956

103. DeFreitas R, and Sadi A: Neo-uretero-ileo-cystostomy, substitution of the ureter by an isolated segment of the terminal ileum. Urol Int 3:223, 1956

104. Monnig JA, Dale G, and Bicknell SL: The ileal ureter in recurrent urolithiasis. J Urol 116:699, 1976

105. Prout GR, Jr, Stuart WT, and Wittus WS: Utilization of ileal segments to substitute for extensive ureteral loss. Ibid 90:541, 1963

106. Gil-Vernet JM, Jr: The ileocolic segments in urologic surgery. Ibid 94:418, 1965

107. Dowd JB, and Chen F: Ileal replacement of the ureter in the solitary kidney. Surg Clin North Am 51:739, 1971

108. Dowd JB: Ileum- here and there. Urologists' Correspondence Club 41:32, 1976

109. Tanagho EA: A case against incorporation of bowel segments into the closed urinary tract. J Urol 113:769, 1975

110. Goodwin WE: Comment on Monnig JA, Dale G, and Bicknell SL. J Urol 116:702, 1977

Commentary: Ileum Substitution

Salah Al-Askari

Isolated segments of small bowel have been used in urologic surgery since 1900, either to form a conduit for urinary diversion or to replace part or all of one or both ureters. In 1888, Tizzoni and Foggi used isolated segments of ileum to replace the ureter in experimental animals.[1] In 1909, Shoemaker used a segment of ileum to replace a diseased ureter in a young girl with genitourinary tuberculosis.[2] However, the operation did not become popular until the 1950s, when several authors reported their series of successful replacement of all or part of the ureter by ileum.[3-6] Since then, the procedure has become an accepted therapeutic modality in urologic surgery.

The ileum is a dynamic tube by virtue of its peristalsis, which prevents accumulation of urine in its lumen and minimizes absorption of waste products and electrolytes. Also, its large lumen acts as a damper or shock absorber, which reduces the hydrostatic effect of reflux, usually encountered in ileal ureter. Countering these useful attributes of the ileum are the absorptive characteristics of its mucous membrane. Pyrah has demonstrated that the absorption of sodium and chloride from the ileum is milliequivalent for milliequivalent, which tends to minimize hyperchloremic acidosis, while potassium ion was shown to move simultaneously across the ileal wall.[6,7] A net movement of potassium from the ileum to the bloodstream was observed when the potassium concentration in the ileal segment was three times that in the plasma. Thus, absorption of potassium from the urine will take place whenever ileum is incorporated into the urinary tract. However, it seems that with adequate renal function, normal homeostasis can be achieved despite absorption of urinary electrolytes by the ileum. In a large group of patients with ileal ureters, Boxer and colleagues encountered no problems with electrolyte imbalance when the preoperative serum creatinine level was under 2 mg/dl.[8]

Thus, despite the limits imposed by ileum size, the high incidence of vesicoileal reflux, and the absorption of electrolytes and other waste products, ileal ureters, under certain conditions, offer a viable alternative to nephrectomy or peremanent nephrostomy.

The most common indications for ileal ureters are loss or damage of an extensive segment of ureter after urologic or gynecologic surgery, recurrent renal calculi, ureteral fistula, intrinsic or extrinsic ureteral obstruction due to inflammatory diseases such as tuberculosis, schistozomiasis, retroperitoneal fibrosis, and radiation ureteritis, ureteral carcinoma in a solitary kidney, and congenital physiologic or anatomic obstruction with loss of peristalsis.

Skinner and Goodwin pioneered the use of ileal ureter in the treatment of recurrent renal calculi.[9] In such cases, the wide bore of the ileal ureter facilitates the passage of newly formed calculi into the bladder, thus preventing their retention and growth in the kidney.

The essential prerequisites for replacement of the ureter by ileum are the presence of normally functioning bladder, absence of bladder outlet obstruction and urethral stricture (any such obstruction must lend itself to surgical correction before or during the operation), and adequate renal function with a serum creatinine level under 2.5 mg/dl. The types and techniques for partial or complete replacement of one or both ureters by ileum have been well described in the preceding article and in other publications.[9,10] However, certain points deserve emphasis. Most workers prefer an end-to-side ureteroileal anastomosis. The separate closure of the proximal end of the ileal segment without incorporation of the ureter decreases the risk of urinary leakage and anastomatic stricture. The ileal ureter must always be isoperistaltic to promote urinary drainage from the kidney. In cases of bilateral subtotal replacement of the ureters, I perform the left ureteroileal anastomosis first near the proximal end of the ileum, swing the ileal segment to the right, perform the right ureteroileal anastomosis, and then connect the ileum to the bladder. As an alternative, I use one long segment of ileum to replace the left ureter and another short ileal segment to connect the right renal pelvis to the left ileal ureter. This approach maintains isoperistalsis and directs the urine toward the bladder. I routinely place the ileal ureter intraperitoneally, except for the anastomotic areas, to avoid fixation of the ileum by fibrosis and subsequent restriction of the ileal peristalsis. Goodwin and others, however, recommend retroperitoneal placement of the ileal ureter.

The ileovesical anastomosis can be easily performed from within the bladder. To proceed: open the bladder anteriorly, excise a small button from the posterior bladder wall, and pull in the terminal end of the ileum and suture it to the bladder wall with an inner layer of full-thickness 3–0 chromic catgut. Place a second layer of interrupted 3–0 chromic catgut from outside the bladder, approximating the seromuscular layers of both organs. I no longer use silk in anastomosis involving the urinary tract for fear of suture exposure in the lumen and stone formation. Right ureteral replacement can be achieved by gentle rotation of the mesentery, so that the proximal end of the ileum is anastomosed to the renal pelvis.[11,12] Hendren recommends performing an antireflux ileovesical anastomosis in children.[13] In this procedure, the terminal portion of the ileal ureter is tapered along its antimesenteric border and implanted into the bladder through a 5-cm tunnel. I have used this approach in adults satisfactorily. Finally, the ileal ureter should be made as short as possible to avoid excessive absorption of electrolytes and other waste products.

Drain the bladder through a large suprapubic cystostomy

tube to avoid blockage by mucus. In addition, Boxer and colleagues recommend nephrostomy drainage, while Mc-Cullough and colleagues use a small stent for ureteroileal anastomosis. During the postoperative period, pay attention to signs and symptoms that might result from overdistention of the ileal segment after blockage of the cystostomy tube or bladder outlet with mucus. Under such circumstances, nausea, vomiting, central abdominal pain, and other signs of small bowel obstruction may develop. These symptoms are immediately relieved after bladder drainage. This point is of special importance in males, in whom prostatic obstruction may result in urinary retention and the presenting signs and symptoms may be those of intestinal obstruction.

The complications associated with replacement of the ureter by ileum are similar to those after any major abdominal surgery involving resection and reconstruction of the intestinal and urinary tracts. No doubt, bowel resection and anastomosis are apt to be followed by complications in some patients, but it is obvious that statistics given for purely surgical cases do not apply to ileal ureters, since the latter involves normal bowel that is not mutilated by disease or injury. Moreover, my patients are placed on a regimen of bowel preparation before surgery to provide optimal conditions for bowel resection. The usual list of complications after ileal ureter operation includes wound infection, intestinal obstruction, enteric fistula, and urinary leakage.

In general, the results of ileal substitution of the ureter have been satisfactory. In the presence of adequate renal function, there have been no difficulties with hyperchloremic acidosis or azotemia. Also, long-term follow-up studies showed no radiographic evidence of loss of renal parenchyma.[14] Although vesicoileal reflux is present in most instances, the ileum appears to act as a damper, preventing renal damage. Positive urine cultures are frequently encountered in patients with ileal ureters, but they do not seem to adversely affect renal fucntion.

The age of the patient is not a deterrent to this operation provided that there are no other contraindications to major surgery. In children, take special care to make the ileal segment as short as possible in order to avoid redundancy during adult life because of disporportionate growth of ileum.

REFERENCES

1. Tizzoni G, Foggi A: Die Wiederherstellung der Harnblase. Experimentelle Untersuchungen. Zentralbl F Chir 15:921, 1888

2. Shoemaker (cited by Hinman and Weyrauch): Critical study of different principles of surgery which have been used in uretero-intestinal implantation. Trans Am Assoc Genitourin Surg 29:15, 1936

3. Goodwin WE: Replacement of the ureter by small intestine—the ileal ureter. In Riches, E (ed): Modern Trends in Urology (second series). Scarborough, Ont, Butterworth & Co, 1960

4. Rack FJ, Simeone FA: Ureteroileal and pyeloileal neocystostomy in man. Ann Surg 140:615, 1954

5. Baum WC: The clinical use of terminal ileum as a substitute ureter. J Urol 72:16, 1954

6. Pyrah LN: Use of segments of small and large intestine in urologic surgery, with special reference to problem of ureterocolic anastomosis. J Urol 78:683, 1957

7. Davis DM, Nealon TF Jr: Complete replacement of both ureters by an ileal loop. J Urol 78:748, 1957

8. Boxer RJ, Fritzsche P, Skinner DG, Kaufman JJ, Belt E, Smith RB, Goodwin W: Replacement of ureter by small intestine: Clinical application and results in 89 patients. J Urol 121:728, 1979

9. Skinner DG, Goodwin WE: Indications for the use of intestinal segments in management of nephrocalcinosis. J Urol 113:436, 1975

10. Morales PA, Al-Askari S, Hotchkiss RS: Ileal replacement of the ureter. J Urol 82:304, 1959

11. Boyarsky S: Surgery of the ureter. In Glenn JF, Boyce WH (eds): Urologic Surgery. New York, Harper & Row, 1969

12. Hendren WH: Some alternatives to urinary diversion in children. J Urol 119:652, 1978

13. Fritzsche P, Skinner DG, Craven JD, Cahill P, Goodwin W: Long term radiographic changes of the kidney following ileal ureter operation. J Urol 114:843, 1975

ANNOTATED BIBLIOGRAPHY

Morales PA, Al-Askari S, Hotchkiss RS: Ileal replacement of the ureter. J Urol 82:304, 1959

This is one of the early papers describing replacement of the ureter by intestine. The authors review their experience with partial or complete substitution of the ureter by ileal segments in 9 patients, whose ages ranged from 7 to 66 years of age. The etiology of ureteral damage included radical pelvic surgery for carcinoma of the cervix, neurogenic bladder, chronic perinephric infection, retroperitoneal fibrosis, megaureter, and bladder extrophy. Three of these patients had solitary kidneys. The pelvioileal anastomoses were performed in an end-to-end or end-to-side fashion, using one layer of interrupted 3–0 chromic catgut. The ureteroileal anastomoses were performed on the antimesenteric border of the ileum, using the single layer of interrupted, fine, chromic catgut sutures. The ileovesical anastomoses were performed in two layers—an inner layer of continuous chromic catgut and an outer layer of interrupted silk for the seromuscular layer of both organs. The ileal ureters were placed intraperitoneally except for the pelvioileal anastomoses. All anastomatic sites were drained, and the bladder was drained by a cystostomy tube and a urethral Foley during the early postoperative course. The pelvioileal anastomoses were protected by nephrostomy drainage. Follow-up study revealed no evidence of deterioration of renal function or hyperchloremic acidosis. Postoperative excretory urograms showed improvement over the preoperative status or no change. There was one mortality due to massive sepsis, and another patient developed intestinal fistula, which was treated successfully.

McCullough DC, McLaughlin AP, Gittes RF, Kerr WS Jr: Replacement of damaged neoplastic ureter by ileum. J Urol 118:375, 1977

The ureter was replaced by ileum in 12 patients, 7 of whom had solitary kidneys. Three ileal ureters were exteriorized. The average age of the patients was 52 years, and the follow-up period ranged from 1 to 13 years. The complications included one case each of stenosis of ileocalyceal anastomosis, temporary obstruction by mucus, colocutaneous fistula, and deterioration of renal function, and three cases of prolonged flank drainage. The ileal ureters were placed either extraperitoneally or intraperitoneally without affecting outcome. A nephrostomy was placed in cases of pelvioileal anastomosis, while ureteroileal anastomoses were stented with small polyethylene tubes. The results were satisfactory in that the authors did not encounter difficulties with hyperchloremic acidosis; none of their patients with solitary kidneys exhibited this complication. There were no instances of recurrent infection caused by refluxing ileal ureters. The authors believe that the ileum protects the kidneys from the damaging effects of relux.

Hendren WH: Some alternatives to urinary diversion in children. J Urol 119:652, 1978

The author presents his approach to the management of patients with complex ureteral pathologic conditions involving dilated and short ureters on one or both sides. The remodeling of the urinary tract is achieved by transureteroureterostomy, psoas hitch, cecal cystoplasty, and ileal ureters. Only ileal ureters will be discussed here. The ureter was replaced by ileum in 29 patients. The author attempted to prevent vesicoileal reflux by tapering the entire ileum, especially the lower end, and implanting it into the bladder through a very long tunnel running diagonally across the trigon. In cases where the ureter was dilated and the bladder tunnel not sufficient to prevent reflux, a long ureteral nipple was incorporated into the ureteroileal anastomosis. The author does not provide statistical analysis of the results or the length of postoperative follow-up study of his series.

Prout GR, Stuart WT, Witus WS: Utilization of ileal segments to substitute for extensive ureteral loss. J Urol 90:541, 1963

In this study, the authors review their experience with 7 cases of ureteroileocystostomy, 2 cases of pyeloileocystostomy, and 1 case of infundibuloileocystostomy. The operation was performed for extensive ureteral damage secondary to treatment of cancer of the cervix in 6 cases, renal calculi in 2 cases, and pelvic inflammatory disease and ureteropelvic obstruction in the remaining cases. The follow-up period ranged from 1 to 52 months. Serial cystograms showed vesicoileal reflux in 9 of the 10 cases, and the reflux occurred at low intravesical pressure (less than 20 cm of water) in 7 cases. Four of seven ureteroileal anastomoses did not show ileoureteral reflux, with bladders containing from 175 to 600 ml of contrast material. Blood chemistry studies in nine patients followed from 5 to 52 months showed normal blood urea nitrogen (BUN) in seven patients and azotemia in 2. In the

same group, 3 patients had evidence of hyperchloremic acidosis. It seems that patients with good renal function before surgery did not experience deterioration in renal function after incorporation of ileum in their urinary tract. The authors conclude that although the operation leaves much to be desired, it is the best available approach under the circumstances, since the alternatives are less desirable.

Creevy DD: Misadventures following replacement of the ureters with ileum. Surgery 58:497, 1965

Nineteen ureters were partially or completely replaced by ileal segments in 15 patients. The criteria for success was a 2-year survival without symptoms or deterioration of renal function. Six patients had successful results and did well but were labeled apparent successes because they were followed for less than 2 years. There were four failures. One patient died from gastric hemorrhage due to stress ulcer. One patient had pyeloileocystostomy and was continued on nephrostomy drainage because the urine did not drain into the ileum; the renal pelvis was thought to be too rigid. This patient died from progressive renal failure. In two patients, the ileal segment became dilated and had to be disconnected from the bladder and exteriorized. Dr. Creevy stresses the need for thorough evaluation of the bladder function and its capacity to empty before surgery. Also, he considers poor renal function a contraindication for ileal ureter.

Baum WC: The clinical use of terminal ileum as a substitute ureter. J Urol 72:1633, 1954

This was one of the first papers to appear in the early 1950s with successful results. Four female patients aged 6 to 60 years underwent partial or total replacement of the ureter. The operation was performed for ureteral stricture in three patients and radiation injury to the ureter in one patient. Two patients had partial replacement of the ureter, while in the other two, the entire ureter was replaced by anastomosis of the proximal end of the ileum to the renal pelvis in one case and to a calix in the other. The ileal ureter was placed either intraperitoneally or extraperitoneally, and the ileal segments were 30 cm and 40 cm when the entire ureter was replaced. There was no morbidity or mortality, and the outcome was successful in every patient. Asymptomatic pyuria was present in two patients but did not affect renal function. Despite the rather long ileal segments in two patients, there was no electrolyte imbalance or azotemia.

Overview: Ureteroileocystotomy

Jean B. deKernion

The ileal ureter operation, although not a new procedure, is still not commonly performed. Indications for it are few, and operations of less magnitude, such as transureteroureterostomy or bladder hitch, must be considered well before this formidable procedure. The unkind reputation that the ileal ureter has gained in some centers is almost certainly due to patient selection. As with most reconstructive operations, the most straightforward

and physiologic procecdure is preferable to organ system substitution, which should be reserved for the more desperate situations. The narrow applicability of the operation is attested to by Boxer and colleagues, who reported 89 ileal ureter procedures at one center over a 20-year period, or fewer than 5 each year.

The ileal ureter operation has had its greatest application

in the management of recurrent calculus disease and iatrogenic ureteral damage, and the specific indications and points of technique are best discussed under these headings.

RECURRENT CALCULUS DISEASE

Imposition of the ileal segment from the renal pelvis to the bladder in the patient with chronic recurrent calculus disease has met with a high incidence of success, as shown by the preceding article and commentary. The underlying reasons for success have been attributed to various factors, especially changes in pH of the urine or mechanical washing of the renal pelvis by the refluxing urine. However, the only certain effect of the ileal ureter operation performed for this problem is to facilitate the ready passage of calculi, obviating recurrent severe colic, obstruction, and the need for repeated ureteral or renal pelvis surgery. The operation then should logically be limited to patients who have had recurrent episodes of colic, requiring repeated operations, for whom no metabolic cause or cure can be identified. Such a patient is unusual indeed. However, in this situation the operation has proved successful in most patients and should be in the armamentarium of the surgeon who treats difficult urinary tract calculus problems.

The technical point of the ileal ureter operation in the patient with recurrent calculi have been amply outlined, but specific points of the procedure in the stone patient should be emphasized. An absolute contraindication is poor renal function. The patient should have adequate renal function, most simply expressed as a creatinine level below 2.5 mg/dl. The quantitative gamma camera scan has not been used extensively to measure function in these patients before and after surgery, but it certainly would add a great deal of accuracy to the determination of function in the renal unit and improve the probability of success. Bladder function must be normal, and obstruction due to bladder neck contracture, urethral strictures, or prostatic enlargement should be corrected before interposition of an ileal segment. Finally, heavily radiated or diseased ileum makes the operation technically hazardous and unlikely to be successful.

The proximal anastomosis is the most difficult portion of the procedure when the surgeon is operating for recurrent stone disease, and it is often hazardous and surgically taxing. Most such patients have had multiple operations on the renal pelvis and renal parenchyma with resultant dense perinephric and peripelvic scarring. It is prudent to avoid extensive dissection of the kidney and to limit the dissection to the inferior portion of the pelvis and parenchyma, avoiding the renal vasculature. Many patients have in-dwelling nephrostomy or pyelostomy tube drainage with well-established tracts, and the maneuver to identify the renal pelvis, suggested by Goodwin, is very helpful. Insert a sterile clamp through the nephrostomy tube tract to identify the renal pelvis; it is then simple to cut down through the scar tissue to the point of the clamp, entering the renal pelvis without extensive and hazardous dissection.

Ligation or removal of the ureter seems inappropriate and unnecessary. The ureter provides an added route of egress of urine produced in the kidney and of urine refluxing up the ileal segment. The proximal end of the ileum can best be attached to the inferior aspect of the renal pelvis, near the ureteropelvic

junction, extending laterally along the inferior infundibulum. Occasionally it is necessary or advantageous to remove a small portion of the lower pole of the kidney, but usually the cortex inferior to the infundibulum can simply be incised with the infundibulum. It is then helpful to suture the cut edge of the infundibulum to the cortex before anastomosing to the ileum. I prefer 3–0 chromic interrupted suture for the proximal ileal anastomosis and have not been pleased with the handling characteristics of Dexon—more a matter of preference than a specific requirement. Always insert a nephrostomy tube before completing the anastomosis of the ileum to the renal pelvis and infundubulum.

Carefully choose the ileal segment, and preserve a broad-based blood supply. It is important that the segment be as short as possible but still allow the anastomosis to be made without tension. On the right side, the curvature of the isoperistaltic segment of ileum brings the distal end quite easily down to the point of anastomosis to the bladder. On the left side, the obliquity of the mesentery tends to bring the distal end of the isoperistaltic segment to a sharp curve medially, especially in the patient with a relatively short or scarred mesentery. This problem can be obviated by employing the psoas hitch before the ileovesical anastomosis, and I routinely do so on the left side. Bilateral psoas hitch may impair bladder vasculature and interfere with bladder function and should be avoided.

Anastomosis to the bladder is best done near a fixed point either at the point of attachment to the psoas or near the trigone. This will prevent kinking during bladder distention. When operating for recurrent calculi, I have not felt it beneficial to prevent reflux, since, as mentioned earlier, the buffering effect of the urine, which recycles in a circular fashion through the ileal segment, ureter, and bladder, may have an inhibitory effect on the stone diathesis. Furthermore, any form of narrowing of the anastomosis may defeat the major purpose of the operation (i.e., to facilitate passagae of stones). I use a single layer of interrupted 3–0 chromic suture to suture the full thickness of the inner bladder wall. This should be buttressed by several seromuscular sutures on the outside, at the point of entry of the bowel into the bladder wall.

Routine YV-plasty of the bladder neck has been advocated in these patients to facilitate the passage of ileal mucus. However, I have found this necessary only when outlet obstruction is evident, and I have not regretted selecting patients in whom I had to perform this portion of the operation routinely.

Ileal mucus secretion is especially problematic in the early postoperative phase, and maximum drainage is therefore essential. In addition to the nephrostomy tube, insert a suprapubic cystostomy tube and a urethral catheter. Drain each anastomosis extraperitoneally. Impatience about the removal of tubes and drains is a major cause of postoperative mishaps. Remove the urethral catheter on the seventh day if drainage at the anastomotic site has subsided, and then employ a schedule of voiding, measurement of residual bladder urine, and frequent irrigation of mucus. Only after all drainage has ceased and the patient is voiding with minimal residual urine, clamp and later remove the suprapubic tube. After the patient has voided for several days, study the continuity of the reconstructed urinary tract with a nephrostogram. If no leaks are detected and function of the ileal replacement is adequate, clamp and later remove the nephrostomy tube. I then recommend intravenous pyelography (IVP) 3 months and again at 12. Again, the gamma camera quantitative scan is a more accurate, safer, and less invasive method of serially measuring the function in each renal unit.

Drs. Boxer, Johnson, and Erlich do not specifically indicate the reasons for failure in all patients. Although poor preoperative renal function is a major cause of failure, numerous other potential complications, mainly technical, can occur. The possibility of morbidity can be markedly reduced by limiting the operation to patients with good renal function and by temporarily diverting and draining the renal pelvis and bladder. A careful bowel preparation is essential. Although the role of prophylactic antibiotics in this operation has not been defined, it appears reasonable to use the short-term preoperative and interoperative prophylaxis that is now widely recommended for major surgical procedures. Finally, performance of bilateral ileal ureter procedures for recurrent calculi is almost never necessary unless one is persuaded to use the ''backward 7'' technique. I prefer to perform the operation in stages, one side at a time, and have not regretted this more conservative approach.

Electrolyte imbalance secondary to absorption across the ileal mucosa is the major long-term complication that has been reported, and it should not be a problem if a short segment of ileum is used and if renal function is adequate. Stenosis either at the bladder or at the renal pelvis anastomosis should be unusual. Ischemia and narrowing of the ileal segment can also occur, usually due to a technical misadventure, with resultant impairment of blood supply to the conduit. Indeed, the relative paucity of long-term complications from the operation is somewhat surprising.

The type of procedure will influence the ultimate chance of success. When the indication is recurrent stones, it seems unreasonable to interpose bowel between ureter and bladder, and the proximal ileum should invariably be sutured to the inferior infundibulum and renal pelvis. A similar procedure is indicated in the unusual circumstance in which the ureter is completely excised for ureteral neoplasms. Here the basic operative principle is to excise as much of the urothelium at risk as feasible. Although tumors may subsequently form in the remaining urothelium of the infundibula or calices, the theoretic advantage of excision of the entire ureter is apparent.

IATROGENIC URETERAL DAMAGE

The second major indication for the ileal ureter operation is in the patient with ureteral fistula or stricture, usually iatrogenically imposed. In this situation, continuity of the upper tract with the bladder is the only goal intended. Often an operation of less magnitude will accomplish the same end with equal or greater certainty. The combination of a psoas bladder hitch with a posteriorly based tubularized bladder flap is often sufficient to replace even part of the middle third of the ureter. The reach can be further extended by a reverse nephropexy. When necessary, however, the ileal ureter can be a highly successful approach to an extremely confounding problem.

The *potpourri* of operations designed for such a purpose has been well enumerated in the preceding article and commentary. Complete excision or bypass of the ureter is not necessary, and normal ureter should be preserved and implanted into the interposed ileal segment. It seems reasonable and desirous to prevent reflux into the remaining proximal ureteral segment; attempt an antereflux implantation into the ileum. I have not had sufficient experience with antereflux ureteroileal anastomosis to support or decry its use. Note that the remaining proximal ureteral segment should be functionally and anatomically normal or the operation will eventually fail. It also is unwise to interpose ileum between segments of ureter proximally and distally. The distal end of the ileum should always be implanted into the bladder rather than anastomosed to ureter.

When operating for other than recurrent passage of stones, attempts at an antereflux bladder anastomosis are reasonable. This is best accomplished by tapering the distal 4 cm or 5 cm and implanting in an antereflux submucosal tunnel with fixation at the trigone. An alternative approach is fixation of an inverted nipple of ileum to the fixed portion of the bladder, which will be compressed with bladder filling and thereby prevent reflux. Either approach is satisfactory as long as implantation is in a fixed portion of the bladder and the vascularity of the distal portion of the ileum is carefully preserved.

33

THE BOARI-KUSS OPERATION
A 96 Cases Experience with 28 Years of Follow-up

R. Kuss and C. Chatelain

Hôpital La Pitié Salpétrière, Paris

When the pelvic ureter is destroyed and the kidney must be preserved, the use of a bladder flap is one of the possible techniques to replace the missing ureteral segment.

In 1951, one of us developed a ureteroplasty reconstructing the pelvic ureter. 8 operations have been performed since then allowing us to give a clear evaluation of the technique.

HISTORY

Van Hook in 1893 was the first to propose the use of a bladder flap[79] but his experiences were limited to the cadaver. Casati and Boari were the first to experiment successfully in dogs in 1894; their works paved the way to all further attempts.[7,9]

Many other experimental works have confirmed the validity of the technique: Schmidt in 1912,[71] demel in 1924 who created a sort of diverticulum with a large flap of the bladder dome,[17] Spies and colleagues in 1933, Barnes and Farley in 1948, R. Kuss and J. P. Binet in 1951 and H. F. Chauvin in 1953.[72,5,45,12]

During the first half of this century very few operations were performed. The unsuccessful experience of NYSTROM in 1917 was not very encouraging. However Baidin in 1926 obtained an excellent result with the technique proposed by Demel[4]; Rohde in 1937 follows approximately the same procedure.[68] For the first time in 1936 Ockerblad uses a real bladder flap, 10 cm long and 4 cm wide for the reconstruction of the pelvic ureter in a case of uretero-vaginal fistula.[60,61] The same type of operation was performed by Gaughlan in 1941.[25] The two next cases were published by Flocks in 1945 and in 1948 by St Clair and Henderson, respectively for lithiasic ureteritis and ureteral steonosis after hysterectomy.

After 1951 the operation was greatly developed and improved. In 1953, J. Holzer could in his thesis make an excellent report of our first 13 cases.[34]

In 1968 A. Lhez at the French Congress of urology had collected more than 350 cases in our country.

OPERATIVE TECHNIQUE

Our procedure borrows from Boari and Casati the mobilization of a bladder flap but is however rather a ureteral substitution than a uretero-cystoneostomy. It allows to replace the whole pelvic ureter up to the promontory by a vescial tube of a proper size anastomosed directly to the ureter by a direct end-to-end anastomosis. The end-to-end anastomosis allows alter free catheterization of the ureter.

The *approach* can be extra-or transperitoneal in organized lesions like stenoses, fistulae, etc.; we prefer the extra-peritoneal road by an inguinal incision in unilateral cases and a midline incision for a bilateral reconstruction in one session. Transperitoneal approach however is preferred to replace the ureter early after a surgical injury.

After a lateral iliac incision, the epigastric arteries and veins are ligated and the lateral peritoneum is liberated. The ureter is freed from the main iliac artery as far down as possible as the tissular inflammation or sclerosis allows. It is not necessary to go too deep, it might even be dangerous when the ureter is adherent to the internal iliac arteries and veins. The ureter should be transsected where its walls are still healthy. It will always be easy to replace it up to the promontory. A catheter is then inserted into the ureteral lumen to avoid wetting the operative field and to empty the kidney.

Preparation of the Flap. A uretral catheter has been placed and allows to fill the bladder half way, it will facilitate the extra-peritonization of its lateral walls. The peritoneum recovering the lateral aspect of the bladder is freed and pushed upwards. The flap is then prepared, it should be as long as necessary. Its anterior extremity lies somewhat above the bladder neck and its basis lies behind on the posterior bladder wall above the trigone.

The base of the flap is richly vascularized, it receives branches from the main vesical artery, the blood supply to the flap should be excellent. The bladder should be somewhat wider at the basis, its average width is 20 mm; its length according to the loss of ureteral substance, may reach up to 15 cm in a good capacity bladder (Figs. 1 and 2).

Tubulization of the Flap and Anastomosis. When it has been assessed that the bladder flap reaches without any undue traction the lower end of the severed ureter, the tube is constituted by a series of separated stitches over a large size ureteral caliber as a stent. The suture material is chromic gut. The needle will charge the whole thickness of the muscularis and take very little of the mucosa.

When the tube has been constituted, an end-to-end anastomosis is made between its upper extremity and the lower end of the ureter, always with separated stitches and the same suture material (Figs. 3 and 4).

If for some reason like inflammatory adhesions or neoplastic cellulitis, it seems difficult or even dangerous to liberate the pelvic ureter, it is possible to short-circuit the lower ureter by anastomosing directly the extremity of the bladder tube with the anterior face of the dilated ureter above the obstruction by a terminolateral anastomosis (Fig. 5).

Closure of the Bladder and Abdominal Wall. Before closing the bladder, one must verify that the ureteral indwelling catheter is well in place into the renal pelvis.

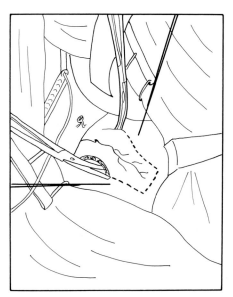

Fig. 1

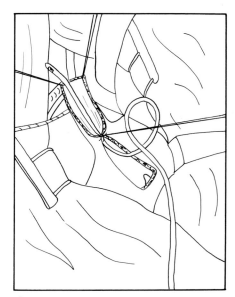

Fig. 2

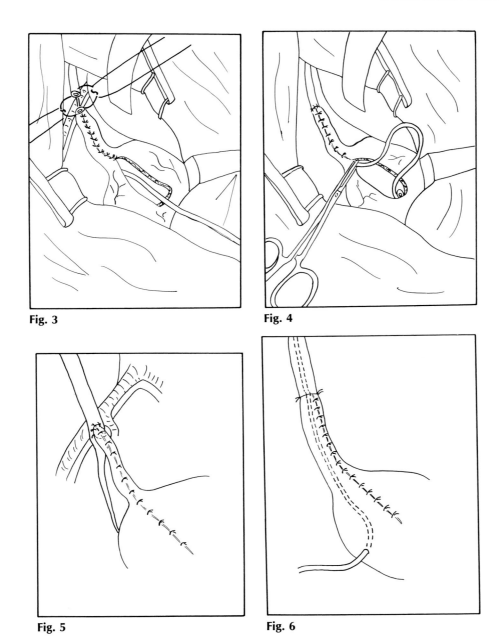

Fig. 3

Fig. 4

Fig. 5

Fig. 6

Its lower extremity may be slipped alongside the indwelling urethral catheter (in women) but if this is difficult (in men) it may be carried through the opposite bladder wall and the anterior abdominal wall like in an "in situ" ureterostomy. This will give it an excellent stability and allows early mobilization of the patient (Fig. 6).

The bladder is closed by separate chromic gut stitches. The latero-peritoneal space is drained during a few days and the ureteral catheter is removed on the 14th post-operative day.

TECHNICAL VARIATIONS

Ureteral Invagination. It is the experimental operation proposed by Boari-Casati. A small bladder flap is prepared on the anterior wall of the bladder and the distal end of the ureter is invaginated inside of the bladder cuff. The procedure is very simple, it has been advocated to avoid leakage and stenosis. Boeminghaus modified that procedure by fixing the lower end of the obliquely transsected ureter on a surface of the bladder flap where the mucosa had been removed. To prevent reflux one may create a submucosal tunnel at the extremity of the flap, the ureter passing through the tunnel before being anastomised to the bladder mucosa (Gil Vernet) (Figs. 7 and 8).

The latter procedure although quite ingenious, reduces the length of the whole system and may render catheterization of the ureter after the operation difficult if not impossible.

Bilateral Uretero-Cystoplasty. Bilateral reconstruction can be performed in one or two sessions by a bilateral extra-peritoneal approach. But it can also be performed through a midline transperitoneal incision. The two flaps may be completely distinct and separated or be each one the half of a transversal breach obtained by two parallel incisions as proposed by W. Gregoir (Fig. 9).

OBSERVATIONS AND RESULTS

Ninety-six patients underwent a bladder flap ureteroplasty after our procedure between 1951 and 1978 during a period of 28 years.

The indications are summarised in diagram I. Com-

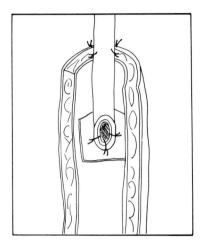

Fig. 7

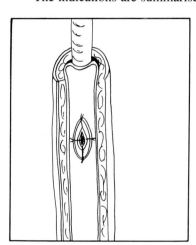

Fig. 8

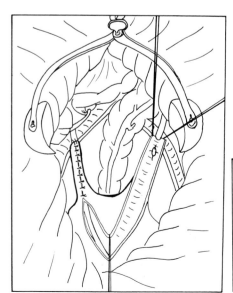

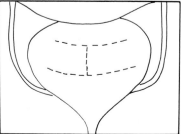

Fig. 9

plications of gyneacologic surgery (stenoses, fistulae, early reparations) are the most common (39 cases), if we include the complications of the surgical treatment combined with radiotherapy in cervical cancer (13 cases). Tuberculous ureteritis is the second indication in frequency: four times ureteral substitution was done on a solitary kidney; two times other surgical procedures were made at the same time on the same excretory system: one segmentar resection of the lumbar ureter and one partial nephrectomy (Figs. 10 to 12).

Other indications are the surgery of megalo-ureter in the case of complications or bad results of primary reconstruction. It was also successfully performed in a case of bilateral reflux with wide pelvic megalo-ureters. More exceptional indications were ureteral stenosis after colo-rectal surgery, lithiasic stenosis or stenosis secondary to endoscopic extractions or ureterotomies.

Some exceptional indications: in two cases the operation was performed for a ureteral tumor in the lower third on a solitary kidney; in one case ureteral stenosis was secondary to bilharzia. Three cases of neoplastic peri-ureteritis were also operated, the two first cases developed 7 and 15 years after hysterectomy for carcinoma of the cervics, in the third case the obstruction appeared 3 years after operation for a cancer of the recto-sigmoid.

Totally in 96 cases, the bladder flap was realized 7 times on a solitary kidney and 5 times on both sides in one or two sessions.

POST-OPERATIVE COURSE

There was no post-operative mortality. In 70% of the cases, the post-operative course was quite uneventful. In 20% of the cases we noted mild incidents without consequences like transient febrility after removal of the catheters or iliac leakage during the first post-operative days. It is our opinion that leakage does not develop at the level of the anastomosis or the tube but well at the bladder suture on the bladder dome, it subsides spontaneously if the bladder indwelling catheter is free; in five cases however it was necessary to replace the ureteral

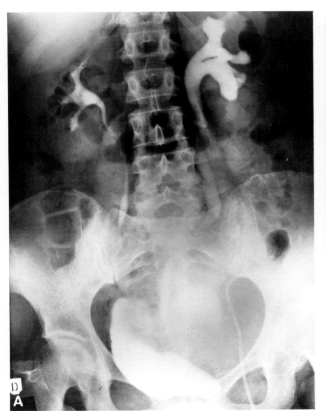
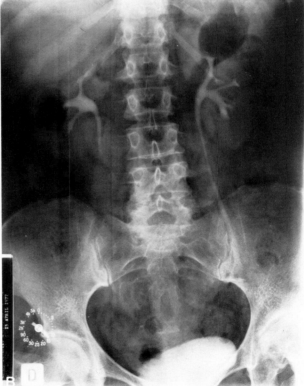

Fig. 10. (*A*) In a 52-year-old woman, ureteral necrosis on the left side after hysterectomy for endometriosis; fistula and large latero-vesical collection, ureteral dilatation. (*B*) IVP two years after reconstruction by a bladder flap; as usual the tube is hardly visible.

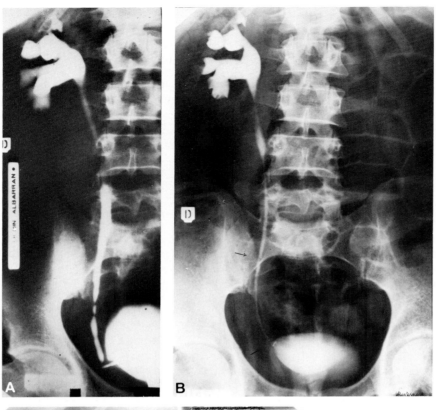

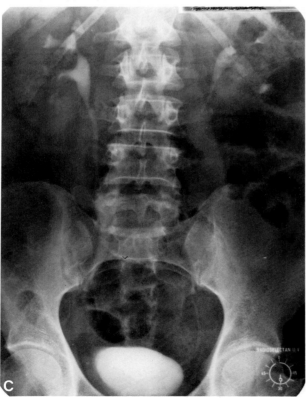

Fig. 11. (*A*) Tuberculous stenosis in a 44-year-old man, plug ureterography. (*B*) IVP 14 days after the operation; the *arrows* indicate the length of the tube. (*C*) IVP 20 years later.

stent (with a direct vision optical), the stent was left from 5 to 10 days before the wound was definitively dry.

In ten cases (10, 4%) the complications were responsible for early failure (see diagram II). In six cases, leakage could not be dried and led to secondary nephrectomy when the opposite kidney was normal. In two other cases when we were dealing with a solitary kidney we had to perform in one case a cutaneous ureterostomy and in the other an uretero-ileo-neocystostomy. In three cases where a ureteral dilatation was extreme before the operation, sepsis of the kidney led to secondary nephrectomy. In a last case an early stenosis developed, the case was severely infected before the operation.

Evolution During the First Year. Six cases developed in 2 failures during the first year, there is 8.1% on 74 cases (on 96 cases, 10 were early failures and 12 other cases were lost from sight after their discharge (diagram III). If early post-operative failures are mainly due to fistulae and leakage, secondary failures are mostly due to the stenoses: 3 stenoses developing during the first year after operation for tuberculous stenoses (one performed on a solitary kidney) led to a temporary nephrostomy and later ileo-uretero-cystoneostomy and 3 stenoses on lithiasic ureteritis (1 of the cases had been operated several times).

Late Results. If after one year the result is satisfactory it will most probably remain so indefinitely. The prognosis will depend from:

the nature of the causal lesion and its evolution (malignancy, tuberculosis).

the intensity of renal lesions and pyelonephritis at the time of the operation; evolution towards renal failure may be favoured by the presence of a vesicoureteral reflux.

intercurrent diseases.

The results of ureteral reconstruction after gynaecological surgery for benign lesions give excellent results since the ureteral damage occurs under a healthy kidney. They are however very difficult to follow-up after a while, the patients being symptomfree do not understand the necessity of regular checkups. It is easier to follow the tuberculous patients who are aware of their disease and understand the necessity of regular controls. A good result after reconstruction for tuberculous stenosis can be counterbalanced by an unfavourable evolution of the renal lesions. In cases of malignancies, none of our operated patients survived more than 5 years.

We have moreover noted 5 late failures:

3 cases of late renal atrophy by chronic pyelonephritis after from 4 to 8 years: 2 cases after reconstruction

for tuberculous stenosis and 1 after lithiasic ureteritis; in the 3 cases pyelonephritis was already present at the time of operation.

2 total nephro-ureterectomies had to be performed for late renal atrophy and intermittent crisis of pyelonephritis with pain, temperature and pyuria:

one was operated 23 years after reconstruction for tuberculous ureteritis made in 1952; a renal scan indicated a 48% function on the operated side against 130% on the opposite side.

the other one 12 years after reconstruction in 1962 for a uretero-vesicovaginal fistula after hysterectomy.

These 5 later failures represent a proportion of 11.4% (on an overall of 44 operated cases if we exclude 10 other patients who were lost from sight and all the malignancies). These 44 patients have been followed-up during a period ranging from 2 to 25 years.

Our series show 39 very good results after a very long follow-up, *i.e.* 52.7% of all the operated patients (including the early failures, the late failures and the malignancies, but excluding the 22 patients lost of sight). If one excludes the malignancies, the overall percentage of good results is 76.5%.

Some intercurrent incidents may have no consequence at all; for instance one of our patients developed a ureteral stone 7 years after the operation for tuberculous stenosis. The stone was blocked in the bladder flap tube, it was easily removed and the post-operative course was very simple, 12 years after the operation the patient was always in perfect conditions.

COMMENTARY

Technical Considerations. The technique that we have described is a complete substitution of the pelvic ureter. It can even go higher towards the lumbar ureter; when the bladder is large the tube can easily reach a total length of 12 cm; with such a length the anastomosis can be carried outside the pelvis well above the iliac vessels. The longer will be the bladder flap, the more one must be careful in appreciating and preserving the blood supply to the bladder wall and the widest must be the basis of the flap. The basis of the flap should lie in a postero-lateral position in that part of the bladder that does not move very much, and not on the bladder dome; with the basis of the flap in such a position one might loose a few cm but the total length of the flap can be much greater.

Bladder flap reconstruction during the years 1950–1960 was practically the unique procedure of replacement of the lower third of the ureter. Then came the technique

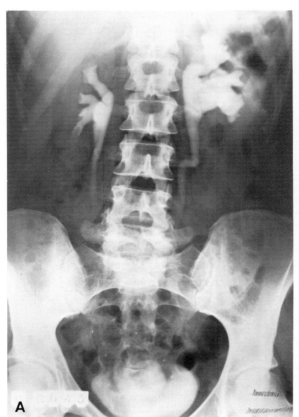

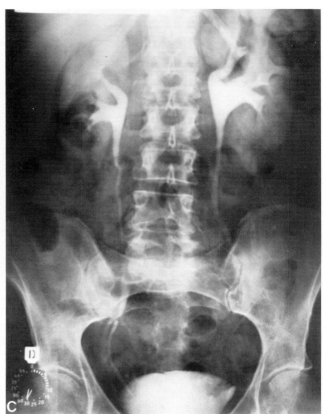

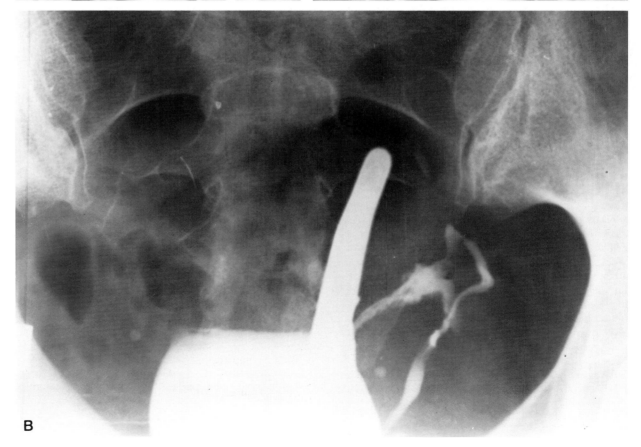

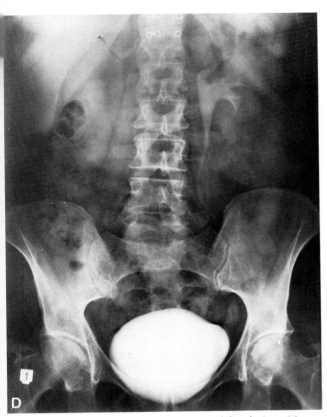

Fig. 12. (A) and (B) Left uretero-vaginal fistula in a 39-year-old woman after hysterectomy. (C) IVP 20 years later. No clinical symptoms, no infection, no impairment of renal function; there is, however, a reflux in the tube and the ureter (D).

of "vesical splitting" presented by Magder, 1963[51] and later the psoas hitch proposed by Tuner-Warwick in 1969.[79] To carry out these procedures in good conditions the bladder should be large and healthy without pericystitis; X-ray therapy is not favourable but is not an absolute counter-indication. Eventually the choice between these different procedures depends upon the local conditions, the state of the vesical and perivesical tissues; it depends also for a large part on the training of the surgeon in one or the other technique. Each one of them offers practically the same possibilities of replacing the ureter uni- or bilaterally and associating the operation to an anti-reflux procedure. They can however be combined: the mobilization of the bladder for instance associating a psoas hitch to a long bladder flap allows to replace practically the total length of the ureter, lowering the kidney if necessary to gain a few cm.[1]

The other procedures of ureteral substitution (enteroplasty, prosthesis, renal autotransplantation, transure-tero-ureterostomy) find their main indications in the impossibility to use a bladder flap when the bladder is not healthy or too small.[10]

The Problem of Vesico-Ureteral Reflux. It is perfectly possible to associate a bladder flap reconstruction to a submucosal tunnel.[26] Considering however that the risk of a stenosis was higher than the risk caused by an eventual reflux, we have always made a direct termino-terminal anastomosis between the tube and the ureter. It allows a perfect adaptation of the tube to the ureteral caliber, also the reconstructed ureter can be easily catheterized afterwards.

Post-operative reflux in the tube only or in the tube and in the ureter is quite frequent, but is very rarely badly tolerated. The kidney is protected by the tonicity and peristalsis of the lumbar ureter. It seems therefore little indicated to replace the pelvic dilated ureter in primary megalo-ureter by a bladder flap since the lumbar ureter is most of the time very dilated and atonic. In the majority of the cases an unfavourable evolution and the development of a chronic pyelonephritis with a secondary renal atrophy are much more the consequence of pre-existing lesions in the renal parenchyma as of the post-operative reflux. Reflux is however not always present and in many cases does not interest the lumbar ureter and remains limited to the tube.

The Causes of Failure. With the exception of acute infectious complications, the early post-operative failures are due to the development of a fistula; apparently the consequence of a necrosis of the distal part of the bladder flap. Reintervention is possible but identification of the lesions is uneasy and the best solution is often a secondary nephrectomy. Necrosis of the distal tube can be imputed to X-ray therapy, bladder sclerosis by inflammatory lesions or scar tissue. Pre-operative cystoscopy is compulsory, if the blood supply does not seem perfect another way of reconstruction should be performed.

Secondary stenoses mainly during the first post-operative year can be due to a sclerosis of the ureteral walls or bladder flap walls; they can also be the consequence of a peri-ureteral sclerosis, suppuration into the loose cellular tissue of the pelvis leading to late fibrosis. A surgical correction can sometimes be performed[50] but most of the time deterioration of the renal function is such that it is more advisable to remove it. In two cases of solitary kidney we had to perform an ileo-uretero-neocystostomy.

Later than one year after the operation the risks of deterioration of an initial good result seem to depend much more on the pre-existing renal lesions and their evolution.

The conditions for a good result can be summarised

as follows: bladder large and healthy, no or little infiltration of the cellular pelvic tissue, moderately dilated ureter with good peristalsis, no or mild lesions to the renal parenchyma. It is of course mandatory that the lower urinary tract be free of any type of obstruction. In one of our cases the bladder flap operation was associated to a prostatectomy.

The Indications and Their Evolution. The frequency of the indications for bladder flap reconstruction never stopped to decrease during the 28 years of our experience. The decrease was about 50% between each one of the three great periods: during the 5 first years (1951–1955), we found the most indications and published 38 cases[43]; during the 12 following years (1956–1967) we operated only 39 cases which allowed us to publish 77 case reports in the report presented by A. Lhez at the 62 French Congress of Urology in 1968[50]; since then, in 11 years (1968–1978) we have operated only 19 cases more (diagram IV). All during that time the overall surgical activity of our department has considerably increased, the relative diminution of the indication for a bladder flap has thus been much more considerable.

a. The treatment of ureteral injury in gyneacologic surgery is and remains the principal indication although the number of these cases has considerably decreased by the improvement of gyneacologic surgery and immediate repair by the gyneacologists themselves.

b. Ureteral injuries after surgery for carcinomas with or without radiotherapy constitute a much less favourable indication. In advanced cases of carcinomatous cellulitis the use of ureteral prosthesis is preferable. Ureteral injuries after colo-rectal surgery are in regression today.

c. Tuberculous stenoses constituted the second indication for bladder flap reconstruction during our two first periods. Since then their number has considerably decreased and no single operation for such an indication was performed in our department during the last 5 years. The disparition of urinary tuberculosis in our country make these indications quite exceptional.

d. Relatively, post-lithiasic ureteristis have somewhat increased, some cases occuring after stone baskets manoeuvres were treated by a bladder flap.[1,28,31]

e. Bilharzial ureteritis is not a good indication for reconstruction with a bladder flap since it does not seem advisable to reconstruct the ureter with a tissue affected by the same disease. However in a few rare cases where the bladder dome was healthy and the bladder had a large capacity, the operation was performed successfully.

f. Tumors of the pelvic ureter are not good indications either and for the same reasons. Moreover conservative surgery in ureteral tumors is frequently and with good reasons criticized. We had made the operation in two such cases and we had two failures.

g. Pelvic megalo-ureters were the third indication in our second serie. The operation should be strictly limited to those cases where the lumbar ureter is not dilated. However progresses realized during the last ten years in reconstruction of megalo-ureters and reimplantation invited us to descard that sort of indication altogether.

Thus the principal indications of uretero-substitution by a bladder flap seem to be limited today to the immediate repair of surgical injuries to the ureter, to the treatment of ureteral fistulae or stenoses after gyneacologic surgery without previous radiotherapy or carcinomatous cellulitis and to ureteral stenoses related to lithiasis and its treatment.

REFERENCES

1. Abdelsayed M., Onal E., Wax S.H. A vulsion of the ureter caused by stone basket manipulation. J Urol 118 (5), 868–70, 1977

2. Acconcia A. L'operazione di Casati e Boari. Minerva Chir 10, 504–505, 1950

3. Amsler E. Indication for Boari's surgery. Helv Chir Acta 37 (4), 481–8, 1970

4. Baidin A. L'autoplastie urétérale de Demel à l'aide de la vessie pratiquée chez l'homme. Z Bl Gynäk, 54, 3237–39, 1930

5. Barnes R.W., Farley S.L. Reconstruction of lower segment of ureter with tube made from bladder flap; preliminary report. J Urol (Baltimore) 59, 466–470, 1948

6. Bischoff P.F. Boari plasty and vesico renal reflux. Z Urol Nephrol 59 (3), 169–83, 1966

7. Boari A. L'urétéro-cystonéostomie. Etude clinique et expérimentale. Ann Mal Org Gén.-Urin. (Paris) 14, 1059–1088 et 1141–1170, 1899

8. Boeminghaus H. Chirurgie des organes génito-urinaires. Werk Verlag edit. (Bad Worishofen) 1, 197–204, 1950

9. Casati E., Boari A. Contributo sperimentale alla plastica dull'uretere. Comunicazione preventiva. Atti della accademia delle scierze mediche e naturali in Ferrara. Anno 68, Fasc. 3, 27 Mai 1894, pp 149–154

10. Chatelain C. Management of ureteric injuries and replacement of ureteric defects, in "Operative Surgery" (urology) pp 112–121 (CR et R. Smith) Butterworths, London, 1977

11. Chatelain C. L'urétéroplastie par lambeau vésical tubulé dans la bilharziose uro-génitale. in "la bilharziose uro-génitale." J Urol Nephrol 83, Suppl. I, p 239, 1977

12. Chauvin H.F. Etude expérimentale de l'opération de Boari. J Urol Med Chir 59, 219–228, 1953

13. Couvelaire R. Sur l'urétéro-néocystostomie avec lambeau vésical tubulé. J Urol Med Chir 58, 386–388, 1952

14. Couvelaire R., Cokier J., Abourachid H. Remarques sur l'opération de Boari-Casati (àpropos de 75 observations). J Urol Néphrol, 71, 805–833, 1965

15. Cukier J. L'opération de Boari—A propos de 63 cas. Acta Urol Belg. 34 (1), 15–28, 1966

16. Dellas G., Fischer W. Therapy of bilateral lesions of the ureter during or after surgery for gynecologic carcinoma. Zentralbl Gynaekol 99 (13), 808–11, 1977

17. Demel R. Remplacement de l'uretère par une plastie prélevée sur la vessie. Zbl Chir 51, 37, 2008–11, 1924

18. Deuticke P., Schimatzeh A. Die Blasenlappenplastik nach Boari-Küss, Technik, Indikation, Resultate. Urol Int (Basel), 18, 100, 1964

19. Dillon J.R. Use of bladder pedicles as substitutes for the lower ureter. J Urol (Baltimore) 83, 583–592, 1960

20. Firstater M. Unintubated Boari's ureterocystoplasty. J Urol (Baltimore) 93, 567–568, 1965

21. Firstater M. Boari's operation for the treatment of megaureter. J Urol (Baltimore) 93, 569, 1965

22. Flocks R.H. Anastomose uretero-vésicale quand la portion proximale de l'uretère est ccurte. Canad Med Ass J, 55, 574–77, 1946

23. Frick J., Greber F. Antirefluxmechanismen bei Modifikation der Boari-Plastik (Tierversuch). Urologe 7, 169, 1968

24. Garibaldi B. Contributo allo studio della tecnica delgi risultati della operazione di Boari Considerazioni su 12 casi. Urologia (Treviso) XXIII, fas VI, 1956

25. Gaughlan V. Uretero-vaginale fistula: repair of ureteral defect by use of bladder flaps. J Urol (Baltimore) 58, 428–443, 1947

26. Gil Vernet J.M. Uretero-vésicoplastie sous-muqueuse. Modification à la technique de Boari. J Urol Méd Chir 65, 504–508, 1969

27. Golimbu M., Block N., Morales P.A. Uretero vesical flap operation for middle and upper ureteral repair. Invest Urol 10 (4), 313–7, 1973

28. Grasset D. Intervention de Boari motivée par un accident de la sonde de Dormia. J Urol Néphrol 74, 851, 1968

29. Gregoir W. L'anastomose urétéro-vésicale latéro-latérale et la plasties tubulée. Acta Urol Belg 23, 32–37, 1955

30. Haga J.J., Scholtmeijer R.J. Some experiences with the modified Boari bladder flap operation. Arch Chir Neerl 22 (3), 155–64, 1970

31. Haliasses D., Mostronikolas E. Sur un cas d'opération de Boari nécessitée par un accident de la sonde lasso (Zeiss). J Uro Nephrol 76 (7), 673–5, 1970

32. Henderson D.S.L. Boari's operation: reimplantation of the ureter utilising a bladder flap. Urol Cutan Rev 55, 80–83, 1951

33. Higgins R.B. A new ureteroplasty: advancement of the ureter by a vesico-ureteral pedicle graft. J Urol (Baltimore) 70, 376–384, 1953

34. Holzer J. L'opération de Boari (réfection de l'uretère terminal par un lambeau vésical pédiculé et tubulé). Technique, indications, résultats. These Paris, n° 89, 1953

35. Ivancevic L.D., Hohenfellner R., Wulff H.D. Total replacement of the ureter using a bladder flap and cinematographic studies on the newly constructed ureter. J Urol (Baltimore) 107, 576–579, 1972

36. Kan D.V. Results of 83 cases of Boari's operation. Urol Nefrol (Mosk), 6, 28–30, 1974

37. Kinchi D., Wiesenfeld A. Injuries to the lower third of ureter treated by bladder flap plasty: Boari-Küss technique; report of two cases. J Urol (Baltimore) 89, 800, 1963

38. Kislrev S.V. Indications for combined psoas bladder hitch procedure with Boari vesical flap. Urology, 6 (4), 447–52, 1975

39. Koingsberg H., Blunt K.J., Muecke E.C. Use of Boari flap in lower ureteral injuries. Urology, 5 (6), 751–5, 1975

40. Küss R. Néo-uretère terminal par plastie vésicale pour fistule urétéro-vaginale. J Urol Méd Chir 58, 176–178, 1952

41. Küss R. Chirurgie plastique et réparatrice de la voie excrétrice du rein. Paris, Masson et Cie, 1954

42. Küss R. Sténose urétérale tuberculeuse bipolaire. Opération de Küss associée à une résection urétérale segmentaire. Urologia (Treviso) XXI, 280, 1954

43. Küss R. Urétéroplastie par lambeau vésical. A propos de 38 cas personnels. Urol Int (Basel) 3, 175–189, 1956

44. Küss R., Chatelain C. Ureteroplasty with a tubed bladder flap. In

Surgery of the ureter, pp 74–86. Encyclop. of Urol, XII/3, Springer Verlag, Berlin Heidelberg, New York (1975)

45. Küss R., Holzer J. Plastie urétérale par lambeau vésical tubulé (opération de Boari) à propos de 10 cas. Mém Acad Chir 79, 159–161, 1953

46. Küss R., Holzer J. Reconstitution de l'uretère pelvien par l'opération de Boari. Considérations techniques à propos de 18 cas personnels. J Urol Méd Chir 59, 578–595, 1953

47. Küss R., Quenu L. Tuberculose rénale. Urétérite segmentaire. Vessie saine: nouvelle orientation thérapeutique. Presse Méd 61, 191, 1953

48. Küss R., Sifalakis J., Legrain M. A propos de 85 observations de chirurgie de l'urétérite stánosante tuberculeuse. J Urol Méd Chir 65, 358, 1959

49. Lenz P., Meridies R. Report on experience with 107 Boari plastic operations. Urol Int 25 (3), 245–51, 1970

50. Lhez A. Urétéroplastie par lambeau vésical tubulé in "Les remplacements de l'uretère," pp 28–42. J Urol Nephrol, 74, n° 9bis, 1968

51. Magder M.E. La bipartition de la vessie. Sa place dans les anastomoses urétérovésicales. P.V. Mem Discuss 57è Cong. Fs Urol, Paris, Masson ed., 551, 1963

52. Marion. Traité d'Urologie—lère ed (1924) T. II, p. 879

53. Massaza M. La tecnica di Boari-Casati d'uretero-cistoneostomia. Minerva ginec. 14, 74–86, 1962

54. Melchior H., Lutzeyer W. Reconstruction of the ureter—A review of operative and functional aspects. Europ Urol 1, 216, 1975

55. Methfessel H.D., Methfessel G. Remote results following Boari's method of plastic surgery. Zentralbl Gynaekol 95 (20), 680–8, 1973

56. Methfessel H.D., Ropke F. Functional studies on the implanted ureter. Zentralbl Gynaekol 97 (6), 351–60, 1975

57. Migliardi L. Ureteroplasty with a bladder graft according to the Casati Boari method. Minerva Urol 21 (1), 13–5, 1969

58. Mobilio G., Mazza G. Réflexions sur l'urétérocystoméostomie utilisant un lambeau vésical tubulé. J Urol Nephrol, 82 (10–11, 837–44, 1976

59. O'Bayle P.J., Galli E.M., Gow J.G. The surgical management of tuberculous lower ureteric stricture. Brit J Urol, 48 (2), 101–5, 1976

60. Ockerblad N.F. Reimplantation of the ureter into the bladder by a flap method. J Urol (Baltimore) 57, 845–847, 1947

61. Ockerblad N.F. Garlson H.E. Surgical treatment of uretero-vaginal fistula. J Urol (Baltimore) 42, 263–268, 1939

62. Osterhage H.R. Urological complications following gynecological surgery. Geburtshilfe Frauenheilkd 37 (10), 857–63, 1977

63. Pearson B.S. Experiences with the Boari flap. Brit J Urol 42 (6), 740, 1970

64. Poetzel W. Primäres Ureterkarzinom; Ureteramputation und Boari-Plastik. Z Urol 50, 351, 1957

65. Quenu L. Les anastomoses urétérales (Urétérostomies cutanées et intestinales exclues). Rapt 53e Cong Franç Urol Paris 1959

66. Radavichius A.I. Ten year follow up after Boari Lopatkin operation. Urol Nefrol (Mosk) 1, 67–8, 1977

67. Raymond G. Intervention de Boari-Küss pour lithiase urétérale (indication d'exception). J Urol Néphrol 70, 278–279, 1964

68. Rohde C. Plastie urétérale à partir de la vessie. Zentr für Chir 64/I (7), 409–412, 1937

69. Sanadizadeh S,M., Mc Cagne N.J. Repair of lower ureteral injuries using bladder flap. J Urol 98 (1), 81–5, 1967

70. Schimatzek A. Late results of flap plastic surgery according to Boari Küss. Helv Chir Acta 37 (4), 491–3, 1970

71. Schmidt J.E. A propos de l'urétéroplastie. Zentr für Chir 39/I, 5–6, 1912

72. Spies J.W., Johnson C.E., Wilson C.S. Ureteric reconstruction by bladder flap technique. Proc Soc Exp Biol Med (New York) 30, 425–426, 1932–1933

73. St Clair D. et Henderson L. Operation de Boari: réimplantation de l'uretère dans la vessie à l'aide d'un lambeau vésical. Urol Cut Rev 55, 80–83, 1951

74. Stolzer K.J. Boari plastic operation and reflux. Int Urol Nephrol 4 (1), 21–4, 1972

75. Thiermann E. Modification à l'opération de Boari. Acta Urol Belg 25, 440–445, 1957

76. Thompson I.M. Bladder flap repair of ureteral injuries. Urol Chir North Am 4 (1), 51–7, 1977

77. Thompson I.M., Ross G. Jr. Long term results of bladder flap repair of ureteral injuries. J Urol 3 (4), 483–7, 1974

78. Tsugi I. A new method for the reconstruction of the urinary tract: bladder flap tube. XIe Cong Soc Int Urol (Stockholm) 2, 362–368, 1958

79. Turner-Warwick R., Worth P.H.L. The psoas bladder hitch procedure for the replacement of the lower third of the ureter. Brit J Urol, 41, 701, 1969

80. Tyloch F. Boari's operation in the light of cases recorded at the urology department of the Provincial hospital in Bydgoszcz. Pol Przegl Chir 49 (6a), 727–31, 1977

81. Van Hook W. la chirurgie des uretères—Recherches cliniques, bibliographiques et expérimentales. JAMA, 21, 911–16 et 965–73, 1893

82. Vierk N.F., Uhlman R.C. Open bladder flap ureteroneocystotomy. J Urol (Baltimore) 105, 209–210, 1971

83. Weems, W.L. Combined use of bladder flap and trans uretero ureterostomy: report of a case. J Urol 103 (1) 50–2, 1970

84. Weselowski S., Ambroz W. Boari's operation. Pol Przegl Chir 41 (4), Suppl. 4 a, 508, 1969

85. Williams J.L., Porter R.W. The Boari bladder flap in lower ureteric injuries. Brit J Urol 38 (5), 528–33, 1966

86. Yow J.G. The results of the reimplantation of the ureter by the Boari technique. Proc R. Soc Med, 61 (2), 128–30, 1968

Commentary: Bladder Flap: Indications and Technique

W. L. Gregoir

In Europe, the substitution of the pelvic ureter with a bladder flap was introduced by Kuss in clinical surgery nearly 30 years ago. It soon became a popular operation on the continent and was probably more frequently performed there than anywhere else during a time when there was practically no other alternative but nephrectomy.

TECHNIQUE

The approach can be extraperitoneal or transperitoneal, through a midline or a lateroinguinal incision, according to the case. When the laterovesical space is the seat of urine infiltration or acute inflammatory processes, begin the operation by simply leaving an extraperitoneal drainage and continuing transperitoneally, the bladder flap being mobilized from the bladder dome and entirely recovered by the peritoneum. Free the ureter at the level of the promontory by a small incision on the posterior peritoneum, on the right side where it can be seen by transparency and on the left side in the laterocolic groove. On the left side, the bladder tube will bridge the anterior face of the sigmoid. Do not leave any intraperitoneal drainge but take great care to avoid postoperative intestinal obstruction by suturing the lateral aspect of the tube to the lateral peritoneum alongside the promontory. Volvulus or intestinal incarceration is then impossible. Then suture the lips of the small incision that was made on the posterior peritoneum to free the ureter over the upper end of the tube just below the anastomosis to

extraperitonize it completely. Leakage can occur without danger, since the lateroperitoneal space is drained. I have never seen an intraperitoneal leakage occur. The suture on the tube and the bladder dome heals very quickly by the presence of the peritoneum and is probably occluded a few hours after the operation by spontaneous adhesions with the neighboring bowel.

Extraperitoneal dissection of the pelvic ureter surrounded by acute inflammatory cellulitis is a dangerous procedure and can lead to damage of the internal iliac vessels, giving rise to profuse bleeding. Tearing open the internal iliac vein is a very dangerous accident; dissection of the vein is impossible because of the cellulitis and its deep position behind the artery. By trying to free the internal iliac vein in order to suture it, one can even widen the opening to the main iliac trunk. The situation becomes disastrous and imposes a long and tedious dissection of the main trunks from the bifurcation downwards; in some cases hemostasis will be obtained only by matress sutures in the internal iliac territory. It is thus always much safer to avoid the depth of an inflamed lateroperitoneal space; keep well above and cut the ureter high enough where the tissues are healthy and make a bladder tube adpated to the size of the section.

When the ureters have been severely damaged or tied during a transvaginal operation, the upper part of the laterovesical and lateroperitoneal spaces are generally free, and the operation can be performed in ideal conditions by an inguinal incision without opening of the peritoneum. The same applies for tuberculous stenosis and lithiasic strictures, where no or little periureteritis is found.

The total length of a bladder flap can indeed reach up to 15 cm when a large bladder is disposed. I do not, however, agree entirely with Chatelain and Kuss on the location of the basis of the flap. It should not lie too deep, too near the bladder plate and trigone, since that opens the possibility of the accidental section of one of the main branches of the middle vesical artery, precisely that branch that could be indispensable for flap vitality. The vascularization or a poor blood supply to the flap leads to a complete sclerosis and retraction of the tube.

After the flap has been completely free and mobilized, carefully inspect its edges. They should bleed everywhere, principally around the extremity. If this does not occur, resect the extremity of the flap until the new section starts to bleed. If, after doing so, the tube is too short, mobilize the bladder by liberating its opposite face from the pelvic wall and the peritoneum; attach it over the promontory and fix it into position with two or three separate stitches to the psoas muscle. Place the stitches on the posterior bladder wall or somewhere near the base of the tube where they fit best. The tube is then brought up high enough to allow an anastomosis with the ureter without any undue traction.

A point of weakness is the angle formed by the tube and the bladder wall. Leakage is more apt to occur there than on the tube, and suture at that site must be made with great care and solidity.

Bilateral Cases. When dealing with a bilateral case, it is rather simple to make a double tube in one session. After a transvaginal operation, it is quite probable that the injuries lie very low on the ureter and are relatively short. A comfortable length of healthy ureter can thus be obtained. Perform the operation extraperitoneally through a midline incision; make a 2.5-cm vertical incision on the midline in the anterior part of

the dome just below the peritoneal reflection. From that incision, cut a 6- to 7-cm flap on each side. The tubes lie in a rather high and anterior position, but they come very easily into contact with the ureters.

After an abdominal operation, it is safer to make a midline transperitoneal approach, which offers a larger scope of technical possibilities and gives the surgeon more space to face any unsuspected situation. A double flap can be made by a simular procedure right on the bladder dome, which allows the tubes to be rather short.

Antireflux Procedure. Reflux is certainly one of the drawbacks of the operation. Frequently it will be well tolerated for a long time; it is true, nevertheless, especially with widely dilated ureters, that it will lead to permanent massive backflow and be responsible for a progressive renal failure with a late indication for secondary nephrectomy. This is particularly true in children. It is therefore advisable, whenever possible, instead of making an end-to-end anastomosis as proposed by Chatelain and Kuss, to reimplant the ureter inside the bladder tube through a 2-cm submucosal tunnel. A higher percentage of stenoses does not seem to have been reported in the literature. The tube should, of course, be somewhat longer, but that is available in most of the cases. The objection that it will not be so easy afterward to catheterize the ureter is theoretic.

It is also possible to combine the Boari operation to a Bischof antireflux procedure; after an end-to-end anastomosis, build a mucosal tube around the stent as in a Bischof's antireflux procedure. The tube can be practically as long as the flap, but 2 cm or 3 cm should suffice (Figs. 13 to 16).

ALTERNATIVES

Vesical splitting, as proposed by Magder (Fig. 17) in 1963, does not seem to have attracted many adherents. On the contrary, the psoas–hitch operation, described for the first time

Fig. 13. A rectangular bladder flap has been liberated from the bladder dome; two parallel incisions are made in the mucosa downward over 2–3 cm.

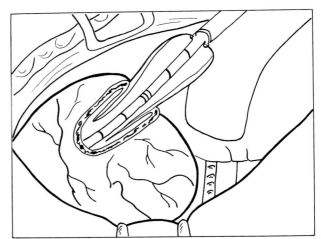

Fig. 14. A ureteral catheter has been inserted into the lower end of the ureter, which is sutured with separate stitches to the upper end of the flap.

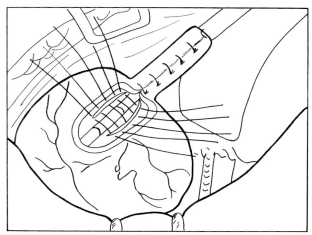

Fig. 15. The bladder flap is sutured to make a tube; around the ureteral stent a mucosal tunnel realized with separate stitches continues the tube downward.

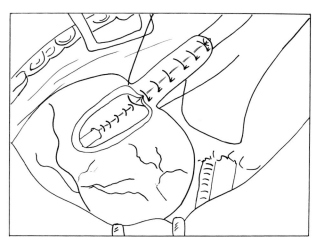

Fig. 16. The submucosal tube after completion. The bladder will now be closed.

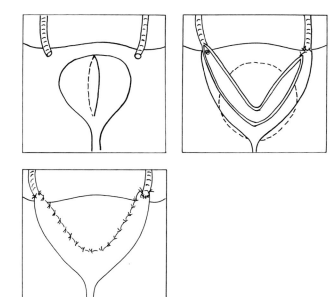

Fig. 17. The different stages of complete splitting of the bladder in bilateral cases.

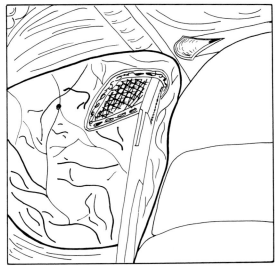

Fig. 18. The Psoas-Hitch procedure: the bladder has been opened, and the dome of the bladder is brought into contact with the psoas and the lower end of the ureter.

by Turner–Warwick in 1969, was widely accepted to the point that some surgeons have dropped the bladder flap altogether. The choice between a bladder flap or a psoas hitch can be made during the operation according to the local conditions (Figs. 18 to 21).

More recently, a totally different type of operation, the transureteroureterostomy, seems to take for itself many of the indications for a bladder flap or a psoas hitch. It is curious to note that Casati described that operation practically at the same time as Boari described the bladder flap substitution. The technique, however, was considered with great reluctance by the surgeons of the early century and was not adopted until recently because of an instinctive fear of damaging the opposite ureter. That fear was probably justified in a time when

antibiotics did not exist and the suture materials were not what they are today. Recent statistics, however, seem to indicate that today the fear is not justified and that in proper situations, the statistics and the results are better than after a bladder flap reconstruction. The operation has the great advantage of being performed high in the abdomen, above the promontory and

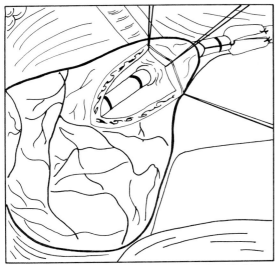

Fig. 19. An oblique tunnel is made through the bladder wall, and a catheter is inserted into the lower end of the ureter, where a nipple has been prepared.

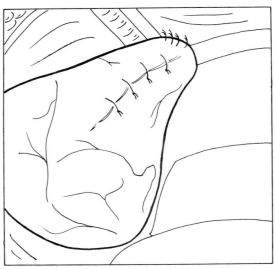

Fig. 21. The bladder has been sutured to the psoas by four separate stitches made of nonabsorbable material. The anterior bladder wall is closed.

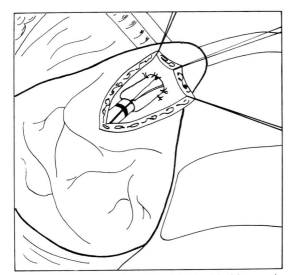

Fig. 20. The nipple is introduced inside the bladder, and the ureter is attached to the bladder mucosa.

away from the foci of infection, neoplastic processes, and radiotherapeutic cellulitis.

Serious technical problems can arise when the surgeon is dealing with important losses of substance. If the tube is too short to meet the ureter without traction, always try to liberate the kidney from the surrounding fat tissue and pull it down. This will generally allow a gain of 2 cm or 3 cm. If that is not enough, it is possible, on the right side, to bring down the kidney and gain around 8 cm by a renal vein transplantation.

Dissect the renal vein and artery free. Clamp the artery as well as the renal vein after severing it from the vena cava at the level of its implantation. Sever the two vertebral veins running below the renal pedicle; tie them to allow mobilization of the renal artery, which is slipped behind the vena cava into a lower position. Then reimplant the renal vein into the vena cava above the bifurcation. The tube can then be implanted directly into the renal pelvis. It is, however, always advisable to keep a short segment of lumbar ureter; as short as it may be; it will allow a submucosal reimplantation and protect the renal pelvis. On the left side, autotransplantation would, in such cases, be necessary.

A little-known operation is the reverse bladder flap substitution, used in patients with a large loss of substance of the middle portion of the ureter. Extensive destruction of the middle ureter can occur after operations for retrocecal appendicitis or on the ovary or the left colon. An inversed bladder flap involving the corresponding ureteral meatus and with its basis on the bladder dome is created and mobilized upward with the corresponding pelvic portion of the ureter. It easily covers a lack of substance of 10 cm (Figs. 22 to 26).

CATHETERS AND STENTS

Everybody agrees that a stent should be left into the tube and ureter a certain number of days. One can use a common ureteral catheter and slip it alongside the in-dwelling bladder catheter into the uretra, which is quite easy in women, or pull it outside by a puncture through the opposite bladder wall and a small abdominal stabwound. Large-size Cummings or McIver catheters are very convenient and require little care. A long, Silastic, multiperforated tube can also be left in place; it is, however, difficult to maintain in the proper place when the patient is mobilized.

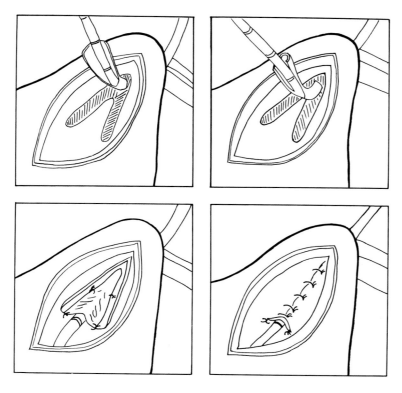

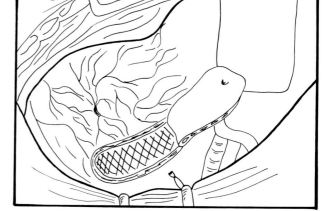

Fig. 22. Another way to reconstruct a submucal ureteral valve.

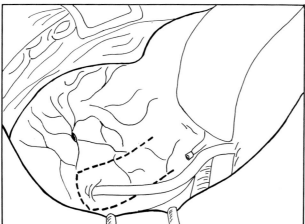

Fig. 23. The "inversed" Boari operation: the *dotted line* shows the incision around the meatus.

Fig. 24. The bladder flap and lower ureter are mobilized *en bloc* and brought upward.

The 14 days of splinting advocated by Kuss and Chatelain are probably a remnant of the early pioneer work in that sort of surgery; in my experience, 9 or 10 days is quite enough.

POSTOPERATIVE CARE

In the majority of patients, the immediate postoperative course is easy. Leakage has become extremely rare when sutures are done correctly and with the proper material. In the early days, sutures were made with chromic gut. Dexon and Vicryl have proved to be excellent material; their slow reabsorption probably confers more safety to the procedure.

Sclerosis of the upper extremity of the tube seems more frequent than stenosis of the anastomosis itself; it is no doubt the consequence of an inadequate blood supply.

Although not mentioned by Kuss and Chatelain, a com-

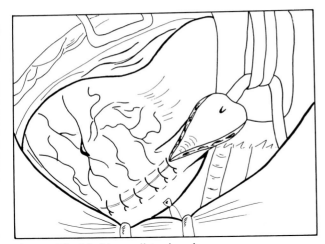

Fig. 25. The bladder wall is closed.

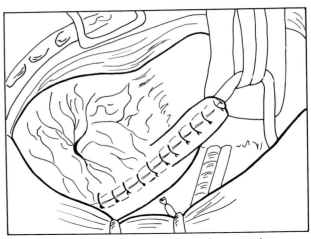

Fig. 26. The bladder flap is transformed into a tube.

plication that seems to be not too infrequent (I saw it 4 times in 25 years) is the late development of a lateroperitoneal abcess deep in the pelvis. It corresponds to a late awakening of a deep focus of infection. and destroys the tube completely by an intense process of periureteritis and a subsequent sclerosis, whether drained or not. In my four patients, the accident happened after an early excellent result. One should thus be careful in making a definitive prognosis, especially if there is some legal involvment.

INDICATIONS

Little can be said about the indications after the excellent comments of Kuss and Chatelain. I consider radiotherapy an absolute countraindication to the operation. Indeed, in 30 cases after various types of pelvic surgery preceded or followed by radiotherapy, the percentage of failures amounted to 33% (10 cases). With such an exorbitant rate, it is preferable to make a nephrectomy or, when conservation of the kidney is mandatory, to consider a transureteroureterostomy or some other type of substituion.

Bladder flap substitution is not a good operation in congenital megaloureters. Most of the time these ureters are widely dilated. The tube gives rise, especially in children, to a massive reflux even when a submucosal reimplantation has been performed. Paradoxally, the procedure can be used with complete success in cases of failures by recurrence or stenosis after surgery for reflux; in two such cases I reimplanted the moderately dilated ureter into a bladder flap with a 2.5-cm submucosal tunnel. The result was excellent both times.

Regarding the indications in lithiasic disease, it is remarkable to note that when I had to perform the operation in five patients in whom a stone basket was used successfully or unsuccessfully, I had to perform it only one time for a stenosis after surgical ureterotomy. This seems to indicate that endoscopic manoeuvres in ureteral stones are not so benign as many people think.

Indications for bladder flap substitution are fortunately becoming less frequent by improved public health and modern surgery. Whereas once it was the only available operation to preserve the kidney, it is now been partly replaced by more simple or more comfortable procedures. It has, however, survived and will certainly remain a classic operation in carefully selected patients.

ANNOTATED BIBLIOGRAPHY

Abourachid H, Beurton D, Vacant J, Cukier J: Les réimplantations urétéro-vésicales par l'intermédiaire de tubes vésicaux, opération de Boari et bipartition vésicales. J Urol Nephrol 78: 416, 1972

The authors report the results of bladder flap operation or bipartition in a total of 36 patients: 18 children and 18 adults. In children the indications were pelvic megaloureters in 11 instances. The results were quite satisfactory in 5; improvement on IVP, absence of reflux, clinical improvement, and disparition of the infection. They were fair in 3; improvement of IVP but persistence of a reflux, improvement of clinical signs, and pyuria. They were bad in the three remaining patients. The remaining seven operations were performed after failure of ureterovesical reimplantation. The results were excellent in five patients. In adults, the indications were ureteral fistulae or stenoses after gynecologic surgery, ureteral stenoses related to lithiasis, megaloureters, tuberculous stenoses, or secondary stenoses after surgery on the lower third of the ureter. In the 18 operated cases, the results were excellent in 10, fairly good in 3, and mediocre in 1; 3 cases were total failures. The authors conclude that the bladder flap operation or the bipartition of the bladder is a fairly good operation and is particularly indicated in long stenoses of the lower third when the stenosis is too long to allow reimplantation in good conditions.

Pearson BS: Experience with the Boari flap. Br J Urol 17:740, 1970

The Boari bladder flap operation was performed in 25 patients; 23 very good results were obtained. The two failures were due to a late stenosis and to a hematoma that brought about a disruption of the anastomosis. The indications were ureteric damage after Wertheim's or standard hysterectomy, ureteric strictures, retroperitoneal fibrosis, megaloureter, and tuberculous stenosis. When the ureter was dilated, the reconstruction was made by an end-to-end anastomosis between the newly formed tube and the ureter. When the ureteral caliber was normal, it was reimplanted into the tube through a submucosal tunnel. In patients with bilateral ureteric obstruction, both ureters were joined to a single bladder tube. However, when ureteric length proved inadequate on one side, ureteroureterostomy was carried out, and a single ureteric limb was anastomosed to the bladder tube. The psoas–hitch procedure was also applied when the bladder was of adequate size and capacity. The author notes that vesicoureteric reflux was commonly present after the operation and was of minor degree and without symptoms.

Chatelain C: La bilharziose uro-génitale: L'urétéroplastie par lambeau vésical tubulé. J Urol Nephrol 83:239, 1977

The paper refers to a rather exceptional indication of bladder flap operation: long stenosis of the lower third of the ureter by bilharzia. In five patients, three very good results were obtained, one patient was unchanged, and the last patient had failure due to reflux and ascending pyelonephritis. It seems that the main factor for success is the adequate size and elasticity of the bladder wall. When the bladder capacity is reduced and the bladder wall thickened and fibrous, the operation will lead to disaster. These conclusions can be applied to any other type of bladder retraction.

Ivancevic LD, Hohenfellner R, Wulff HD: Total replacement of the ureter using a bladder flap and cinematographic studies on the newly constructed ureter. J Urol 107:576, 1972

This interesting paper refers to an experimental work performed in dogs to obtain a long tube to replace practically the full length of the ureter. A 2-stage technique was successful in 8 of 12 dogs. In the first-stage, a long tube was prepared from the lateral wall of the bladder. In the second stage, the tube was mobilized to replace the ureter. Reflux was prevented by the use of a Politano–Leadbetter reimplantation. In the 8 surviving animals, bladder capacity was normal after 2 months. All animals had unimpaired kidney function, no reflux, and good peristalsis. The authors believe that the technique could be used in humans and that it would even be possible to replace the full length of the ureter by using a long tube–graft from the lateral bladder wall without significantly diminishing the capacity of the bladder. Whether this was realized later or not was not documented.

Thompson IM, Ross G Jr: Long-term results of bladder flap repair of ureteral injuries. J Urol 3:483, 1974

The authors consider that bladder flap reconstruction is indicated when it appears from preoperative study that 25% or more of the lower ureter has been lost; in other words, when the point where the ureter can be cut in healthy tissues is too distant from the bladder to permit reimplantation or when the lower ureter appears devitalized. In their series, 23 patients had 24 bladdder flap repairs (1 case was bilateral) for a wide variety of injuries (hysterectomy, large bowel resection, stone basket manipulation,

and aortofemoral bypass operations). The cases were followed for 4 to 14 years postoperatively. All patients have had complete vesicoureteral reflux on each cystographic study although the appearance of many of the bladder flaps had changed considerably: the upper portion of the tube becomes almost ureteral in character after varying periods. Secondary reflux thus seems to be well tolerated, infection was absent, and renal function and architecture remained stable.

Firstater M: Unintubated Boari's ureterocystoplasty. J Urol 93:567, 1965

An unintubated Boari's ureterocystoplasty was accomplished successfully in 9 patients; all the cases support the trend to eliminate splints and intracavitary drainage in plastic operations on the kidney and ureter. An end-to-end oblique anastomosis is accomplished over a catheter, which is passed through the urethra and placed inside the vesical tube and the ureter. After completion of the anastomosis, the catheter is withdrawn as far as the bladder and left inlying. a vent is opened in the ureter, some distance above the suture line, to provide a safety valve against excessive increase of intravesical pressure. This paper is one of the rare papers that advocates the Hamm–Weinberg vent rather than splinting.

Koningsberg H, Blunt KJ, Muecke EC: Use of Boari flap in lower ureteral injuries. Urology 5:751, 1975

The authors quote that Boari first described the operation in 1894, when it was then realized in a dog. The first description in the American literature was that of Ockerblad in 1947. By 1969, a total of 138 cases were reported, mostly in Europe, where the Boari flap had an earlier acceptance. They stress the fact that the tunnel technique reduces the incidence of reflux, but the ultimate success of the flap is related to type of anastomosis as well as other factors like bladder trabeculation, complete emptying of the bladder, vesical and ureteral blood supply, and degree of ureteral dilatation. The Boari flap was used 23 times in 21 patients; 1 patient had bilateral flaps and another had a second flap on the same side after stricture developed in the first. The indications for operation were bladder or ureteral tumor, ureterolithiasis, hysterectomy or radiation, ureterocelectomy, and postreimplantation surgery. Ureterovesical anastomosis was made by a Paquin-type technique in all patients except two, where an end-to-end procedure was used. The average follow-up time was 27 months. Eight patients had poor results; three of them had previously undergone x-ray therapy. Another had carcinoma of the bladder, which recurred in the flap. Two of the failures resulted from complete early stricture of the flap itself and were probably caused by devitalization. Reflux was common in patients with fair and poor results but rare in those with good results. Overall, acceptable results were obtained in two thirds of the surgical procedures. The authors believe it is useful to fix the tube to the psoas muscle in order to prevent tension on the anastomosis. Recently it has been reported that preoperative radiation constitutes a poor indication for bladder flap substitution. From 20% to 30% failure can be expected. In such cases, transureteroureteric reimplantation or ileal substitution is prefered.

Overview: Bladder Flap Ureteroneocystotomy

Ernst J. Zingg

Nowadays the ureterovesical flap procedure is rarely performed in general urologic practice, and it would be an overstatement to stress its popularity except among some enthusiasts. Timely handling of ureteric injuries sustained during gynecologic surgery or ureterolithotomy before scar formation occurs and improved medical management of urologic tuberculosis are two factors limiting the range of indications for this operation. However, its usefulness is diminished further by the availability of simpler procedures to permit a tension-free anastomosis between a foreshortened ureter and the bladder, such as the psoas hitch. This technique was described many years before Turner–Warwick popularized it.[1,2]

In other situations where the lower ureter has been damaged by injury and fibrosis after infection or fistulation or, above all, by irradiation, internal diversion by transureteroureterostomy is more appropriate. It hardly must be emphasized that for adequate mobilization of the bladder and construction of the Boari flap, the bladder itself must not be fibrotic and should have an adequate capacity. Previous pelvic irradiation will, of course, prejudice the healing of the long incision in the bladder. Furthermore, pathologic processes affecting the lower ureter will often extend to the bladder and render the operation impossible.

A flap procedure should hardly ever be necessary in the treatment of obstructive megaureter where adequate ureteric length is available in the first instant and since modern techniques for tapering the wide ureter and for constructing an antireflux neocystostomy are so adequate. As a last resort, it may have to be considered when previous attempts at reimplantation have been unsuccessful, but I cannot recommend it for the primary treatment of refluxing megaureters even if it is apparently feasible. Moreover, the reported high success rate of the operation for its devotees has not been obtained in pediatric urologic practice.[3]

As to operative technique, the question of whether to construct a nonrefluxing anastomosis is always controversial. The long-term effects of vesicoureteric reflux beginning in adulthood are still uncertain. Until definite information becomes available, ureteric reimplantation in whatever circumstances should be done by an antireflux technique. The potential drawbacks of the submucosal tunnel, namely, diminished ureteric length at operation and, subsequently, an increased incidence of preanastomotic stenosis are insignificant. I acknowledge the difficulty that may be encountered in retrograde ureteric catheterization, but it must be a very obscure disadvantage of using an antireflux technique.

Whether the definitive approach to the bladder is intraperitoneal or extraperitoneal is often determined by the extent of scarring of the lower ureter and surrounding retroperitoneal space. In any case, never follow the ureter into the scar, since this may seriously impair its distal blood supply. The positioning of the base of the flap is probably not critical, but if it is near the trigone one can be more confident that the main vascular supply is from the larger branches of the inferior vesical artery. In any event, filling the bladder and inserting stay sutures at the corners of the flap facilitate planning its appropriate dimensions.[4]

In conclusion, I endorse Professor Gregoir's observations. The Boari flap procedure (and its modifications) is a classic and elegant urologic plastic technique. Unfortunately, perhaps, it has become dated and, for many urologists, virtually obsolete. However, it still has a place in restricted circumstances where the distal ureter is extensively destroyed but the bladder is healthy. The articles by Kuss and Gregoir should therefore provide a helpful reminder of the indications and technical details of the operation.

REFERENCES

1. Witzel O: Extraperitoneale Ureterocystoneostomie mit Schrägkanalbildung. Zentralbl Gynaekol 20:289, 1896

2. Dolff C: Verbesserung der Ergebnisse der Ureterimplantation in die Blase mit Hilfe einer elastischen Fixation der Blase. Zentralbl Gynaekol 74:1777, 1952

3. Hohenfellner R: In Eckstein HB, Hohenfellner R, Surgical paediatric Urology, p 235. Williams DI (eds): Stuttgart, Georg Thieme, 1977

4. Zingg EJ: In Mayor G, Zingg EJ (eds): Urology Surgery, p 203. Stuttgart, Georg Thieme, 1976

34

REFLUX IN DUPLICATED URETERS: TREATMENT IN CHILDREN

By Arjan D. Amar and Kamla Chabra

From the Departments of Urology and Pediatrics, The Permanente Medical Groups, Kaiser Foundation Hospital, Walnut Creek; and the Division of Urology, University of California Medical Center, San Francisco. Calif.

J Pediat Surg 5:419–430, 1970

The primary goal of treatment for reflux in children with ureteral duplication is to eliminate conditions that contribute to chronic urinary infection and the implacable progress of pyelonephritis. Reflux, a major contributing cause of destruction of the renal parenchyma, is amenable to surgical correction in the majority of children with ureteral duplication.

Within the present decade, advances have been made in both the diagnosis and the treatment of ureteral duplication and associated reflux. Among the new or improved diagnostic methods are the indigo carmine cystoscopic test,[1] comparison of renal size,[2] urography utilizing an increased amount of contrast medium,[3] aortography, cineradiography, and radioisotopic renal scan.[4,5]

The specific contribution of vesicoureteral reflux to the development of pyelonephritis has been a major focus of concern among urologists since it was first

Arjan D. Amar, M.B., M.S., F.A.C.S., F.R.C.S.(C): Department of Urology, The Permanente Medical Group, Kaiser Foundation Hospital, Walnut Creek, Calif.; Division of Urology, University of California School of Medicine, San Francisco, Calif.; Kamla Chabra, M.B., B.S.: Department of Pediatrics, The Permanente Medical Group, Kaiser Foundation Hospital, Walnut Creek, Calif.

stressed by Hutch[8] in 1958. Reflux and stasis, whether in a duplicated or a single ureter, foster bacterial growth; and their early correction often averts progression of pyelonephritis, with its grave sequelae. Reflux has been shown to occur more often in duplicated than in non-duplicated ureters.[4,6,9–11] If only one of completely duplicated ureters in a child is refluxing, the renal segment to which the refluxing ureter is attached is usually the one that is pyelonephritic. For reasons that will be mentioned later, this is the lower segment in most instances (Fig. 1). Both ureters opening into the bladder may, however, reflux (Fig. 2).

Ureteral duplication is not always radiographically apparent on initial excretory urography. Pyelonephritis may have destroyed function in the affected renal segment, and rendered it atrophic. In such an instance, the discovery of reflux may furnish the only definitive clue to the presence of ureteral duplication (Fig. 3).

TYPES OF REFLUX IN DUPLICATED URETERS

The anatomic structure of duplicated ureters may permit any of three types of reflux:

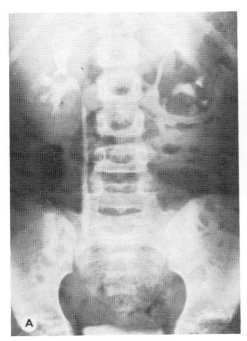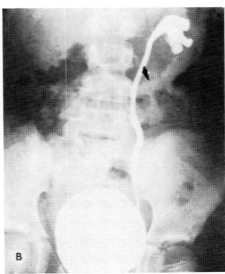

Fig. 1. Eight-year-old girl with recurrent urinary tract infection. (*A*) Excretory urogram showing ureteral duplication on the left. Normal single kidney on the right. (*B*) Cystogram showing reflux into the lower segment ureter and pelvis. Blunting of calyces due to pyelonephritis is evident.

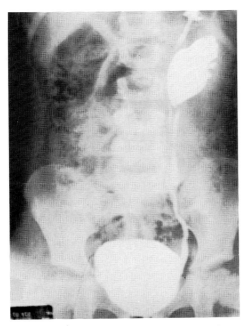

Fig. 2. Five-year-old girl with persistent urinary tract infection. Voiding cystogram shows reflux into both segments of the duplicated left kidney.

Ureteroureteral Reflux. If the duplicated ureters join before entering the bladder, in a Y-shaed configuration, the structure is termed ''incompletely duplicated'' or ''bifid'' ureter. In such a structure, urine may reflux from one limb of the Y to the other. Such flow is called ''ureteroureteral reflux'' (Fig. 4*A*). In children with bifid ureters, Lenaghan in 1962[10] noted that urine flowing toward the bladder down one limb of the Y reversed and flowed back toward the kidney in the other limb; indeed, he demonstrated retrograde peristalsis in the receiving limb. Both the incidence and the magnitude of ureteroureteral reflux increases with the length of the duplicated portion of the ureter. Ureteroureteral reflux is demonstrable by retrograde urography and cineradiography.

Vesicoureteral Reflux. Reflux from the bladder into the ureter commonly occurs in one of two duplicate ureters—most often in that which is attached to the *lower* renal segment. For reasons related to embryologic development, the intramural portion of the lower renal segment ureter is shorter than the intramural portion of the upper renal segment ureter (Fig. 4*B*). In patients with complete ureteral duplication, the common type of reflux is into the upper renal segment ureter when it opens ectopically and into the lower renal segment ureter

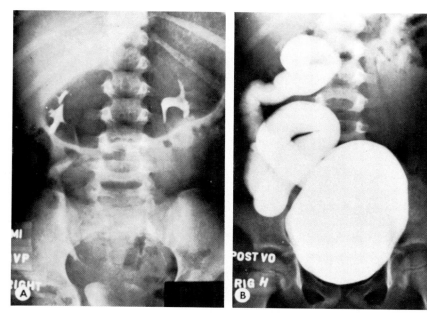

Fig. 3. Four-year-old boy with urinary tract infection had right epididymitis as the presenting symptom. (*A*) Excretory urogram shows lateral displacement and dilation of the right ureter. Duplication is unsuspected. (*B*) Voiding cystogram shows dilated and tortuous ureter belonging to the upper renal segment, which had failed to visualize on excretory urography.

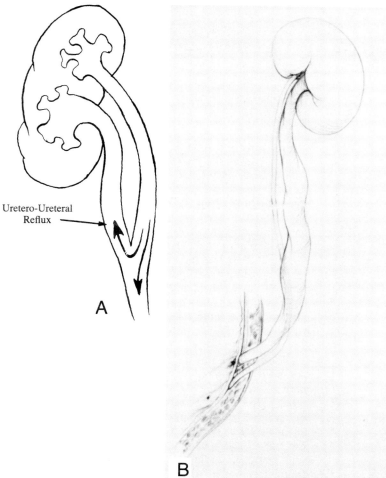

Uretero-Ureteral
Reflux

A

B

Fig. 4. Schematic drawings showing (*A*) ureteroureteral reflux in association with incomplete ureteral duplication and (*B*) left ureteral duplication. The ureter belonging to the lower renal segment has a short intramural portion, increasing the likelihood of reflux in that ureter. The upper segment ureter has an intramural portion of normal length.

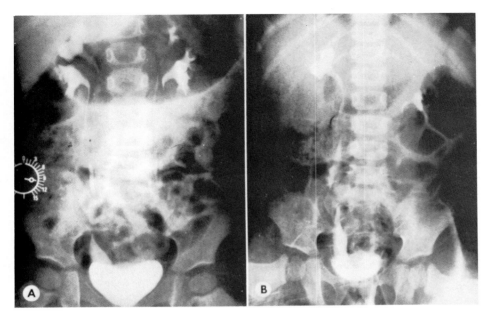

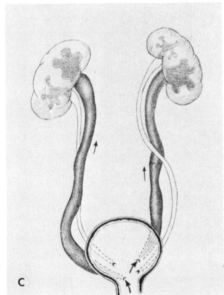

Fig. 5. Four-year-old girl with bilateral ureteral duplication (A) seen on excretory urogram. (B) Voiding cystogram shows reflux into the upper renal segment on the right, which opens ectopically into the bladder neck. Reflux into the lower renal segment on the left. Both ureters open eutopically on this side. (C) Schematic drawing of this classic combination.

when both ureters open ectopically. A classic example of the coexistence of these two forms of reflux in a single patient is seen in Figure 5.

The probability of reflux in the lower segment ureter is increased by the presence of a ureterocele, which frequently develops at the vesical end of the upper segment ureter. In this situation, the orifice of the lower segment ureter, even though it may be otherwise normal, is supported by bladder wall which is weakened by the ureterocele, instead of by firm bladder muscle (Fig. 6A).

In incompletely duplicated ureters, both ureteroureteral and vesicourteral reflux may occur (Fig. 6B).

Urethroureteral Reflux. Reflux from the urethra into the ureter is most likely to occur in ectopic ureters, whose orifice may open into the bladder neck or the urethra. Urethroureteral reflux occurs only during voiding (Fig. 3). Ectopic ureterocele, frequent in children and seen more often in girls than in boys, may be the seat of reflux in addition to causing obstruction of the bladder

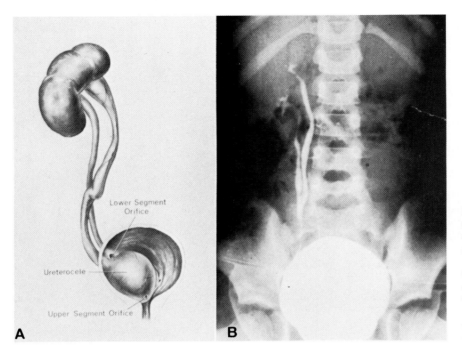

Fig. 6. (*A*) Schematic drawing showing ureterocele at the lower end of the upper segment ureter and the ureteral orifice of the lower segment ureter supported by the wall of the ureterocele, increasing the likelihood of reflux in that orifice. (*B*) Vesicouteral reflux in a child with incomplete ureteral duplication on the right. Junction of the two ureters is evident.

neck and urethra and even of the contralateral ureteral orifice(s). In rare instances, an ectopic ureteral orifice opens into the vagina or vestibule; reflux may occur at this site. Even more unusual is an ectopic ureteral orifice opening into the rectum of either sex; reflux of feces is possible in such cases.

TREATMENT

There is no single method of treating reflux in children with ureteral duplication. One must assess the situation in the individual child. The status of the entire urinary tract must be studied, including both left and right kidneys and ureters, since there may be reflux, duplication, or both, in each. The age of the child may be a decisive factor in selecting methods of management, or in choosing a specific surgical procedure. It is important to allow for future growth and to consider the effect of growth on the anatomy and physiology of the structures affected. Certain of the surgical procedures for correction of reflux are more difficult to perform in a child younger than 2 years, but the urgency of the situation may be such that intervention must be considered to avert grave injury to the salvageable portion of the urinary tract.

In each child, the presence or absence of obstruction to urinary flow in any portion of the tract must be determined. One must ascertain whether there is an associated ureterocele; and whether the ureteral orifices open into the bladder trigone, or into some ectopic site. Other pathologic conditions are frequently associated with ureteral duplication and may contribute to obstruction and persistence of infection: examples are bladder neck obstruction (often caused by ectopic ureterocele), posterior urethral valves in boys, and distal urethral stenosis in girls.

Of paramount importance is the frequency and severity of urinary infection and the degree of obstruction. All reasonable efforts must be made to control infection by chemotherapeutic and antimicrobial agents before any surgical operation is undertaken. Their use may also be necessary in addition to surgical procedures. Where associated pathologic conditions are contributory, their surgical correction is indicated. Surgical correction of the ureteral duplication and associated anomalies becomes necessary when infection persists, or if progression or recurrence is judged likely in the future, in spite of conservative management.

Factors Governing Surgical Procedure Design. All successful surgical procedures for the correction of ureteral duplication have been designed to eliminate reflux and stasis and permit unimpeded urinary flow, while protecting two vital structures: functioning renal parenchyma and the vessels supplying blood to those tissues that are to remain in place.

When partial nephrectomy is planned, the renal and

ureteral structures may offer a selection between removal of the upper or the lower segment. In such a case, the crucial factor governing election is the health of the tissue in the individual renal segment. The segment that is not diseased, or that has superior function, should be left in place. When all factors appear to be equal, the upper segment can usually be spared without much decreasing renal function. The upper segment is rarely the larger, except when the chronic infection that is associated with reflux has caused atrophy of the lower segment.

Procedures Used for Incompletely Duplicated Ureters.

The amount of urinary stasis that is present in incompletely duplicated ureters depends upon the quantity of urine that is engaged in retrograde flow. When the junction of the Y of a bifid ureter is in its superior third, ureteroureteral reflux is minimal. Beyond this point, the lower the junction of the ureteral limbs, the greater the quantity of urine that is likely to reflux and to collect at the junction, there to harbor bacterial growth. Although we have not seen marked ureteral stasis due to ureteroureteral reflux in a child, we have seen vesicoureteral reflux in children with incomplete ureteral duplication. In these children, surgical correction of the vesicoureteral reflux has eliminated urinary infection. Lenaghan[10] has recommended that when frequent, persistent infection cannot be controlled by lesser means in patients with ureteroureteral reflux associated with bifid ureter, one limb of the partially duplicated ureter should be removed. Usually, the renal segment to which it is attached (most often the upper) must also be resected.

Treatment of Reflux in Completely Duplicated Ureters.

Surgical procedures available for treatment of reflux in completely duplicated ureters are: heminephro-ureterectomy, Gibson's operation,[12] ureteral reimplantation, total nephro-ureterectomy of both renal segments and ureters, and removal of the refluxing ureteral stump(s) following previous partial removal of ureter(s).

In 28 children below the age of 14 years, treated surgically for reflux in duplicated ureters, the procedures employed were those shown in Table 1.

Ureteral Reimplantation for Vesicoureteral Reflux. Because any operation for the correction of reflux that entails removal of part or all of a ureter endangers the blood supply of the remaining ureter, it is advantageous to limit the procedure as closely as is feasible. In many children, it is possible to leave both of the duplicated ureters by reimplanting them in a fresh, strong site in the bladder wall, and to augment this by extending the length of the intravesical portion of the ureter. Both ureters are made to pass through the bladder wall and then to traverse a common submucosal tunnel 2–3 cm

TABLE 1. Surgical Procedures Used for Correction of Reflux in Duplicated Ureters, in 28 Children Younger than 14 Years

Procedure		Number of Patients
Ureteral reimplantation		17
Bilateral	11*	
Unilateral	6	
Heminephro-ureterectomy		5
Upper segment	3	
Lower segment	2	
Pyelopylostomy and removal of dilated distal ureter		2
Primary nephro-ureterectomy, both segments		1
Secondary nephro-ureterectomy, previous heminephrectomy		1
Removal of ureteral stump, previous heminephrectomy		2
		28

* In some patients treated by bilateral ureteral reimplantation, ureteral duplication was unilateral; the contralateral single ureter was also reimplanted to correct reflux.

long. Formation of the submucosal tunnel is facilitated by injecting normal saline solution under the bladder mucosa; this elevates the mucosa from the muscular layer, thus avoiding injury to both of these layers.[7] The lower end of each ureter is anchored individually to the upper edge of the trigone with fine chromic catgut at a site medial to the point at which the lower segment ureter formerly opened into the bladder. To avoid injury to the posterior bladder wall, the rectum, or the vasculature in this area, a short stump of each ureter is left in place behind the bladder (Fig. 7A).

For a much dilated ureter and renal segment, reimplantation may have to be preceded or accompanied by nephrostomy of the dilated renal pelvis.

Results of ureteral reimplantation in children have been very gratifying. Reflux has been stopped in 15 of 17 patients in whom we have used this procedure. In one child, the lower end of the duplicated ureter became obstructed; this was corrected by reoperation. In another, the lower renal segment had to be removed 6 months after reimplantation because advanced pyelonephritis and persistent infection did not respond to antibiotic therapy.

Ipsilateral ureteroureteral anastomosis, near the bladder, for vesicoureteral reflux in a patient with duplicated ureter was recently described by Gutierrez, Chang and Nesbit[13] (Fig. 7B).

Gibson's procedure[12] is designed to preserve renal parenchyma in patients with one of two duplicated ureters widely dilated and unsuitable for reimplantation. It is likely to be successful where one of the duplicated ureters has become obstructed after surgical work has been done near the bladder, while urinary flow is unimpeded in the other ureter. Gibson first used this procedure in 1957 in a 17-year-old girl with incontinence caused by ureteral

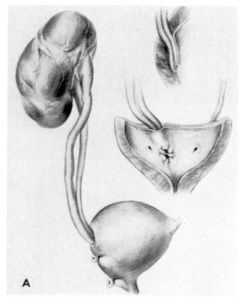

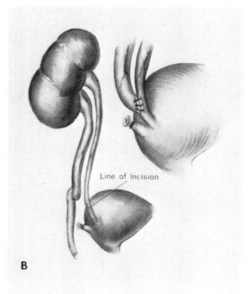

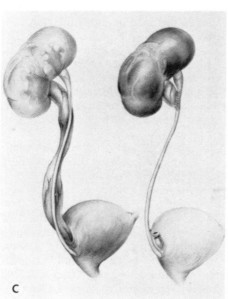

Fig. 7. Techniques: (*A*) Reimplantation of duplicated ureters through a common submucosal tunnel. (*B*) Ureteroureteral anastomosis near the bladder for treatment of reflux in the lower segment ureter. (*C*) Gibson's operation. The dilated lower segment ureter has been excised leaving a small stump near the bladder. The pelvis of the lower segment has been anastomosed to the upper segment pelvis.

ectopia associated with ureteral duplication. As much as possible of the ectopic ureter was removed and the upper renal pelvis was then anastomosed to the lower renal pelvis. If satisfactory results are not obtained, the diseased renal segment can be removed at a later date. Antimicrobial therapy is used postoperatively to eradicate infection in the diseased renal segment and to prevent infection of the previously uninfected renal segment.

We have used Gibson's procedure in 2 children, with good results. In one, most of the refluxing lower segment ureter was excised and its pelvis was anastomosed to the superior segment ureter (Fig. 7*C*). In the other, as much as possible of the ectopic, refluxing upper renal segment ureter was excised, and its pelvis was anastomosed to the normal lower segment pelvis (Fig. 8, insert).

Heminephro-Ureterectomy. Superior segment heminephro-ureterectomy used to be the most commonly performed operation for the correction of ureteral duplication. Figure 8 (center) depicts complete duplication of

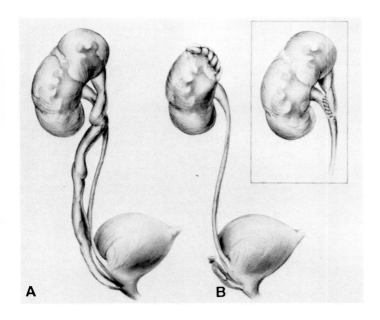

Fig. 8. (A) and (B) Upper segment heminephro-ureterectomy. (*Insert*) Alternative method utilizing Gibson's technique, allowing the upper renal segment to be saved.

the right ureter with the upper segment ureter opening ectopically into the urethra, and shows (center) the lower renal segment remaining after the upper renal segment with its dilated pelvis and calyces has been excised. The lower renal segment is saved, together with its blood supply. In some children, the upper renal segment has been destroyed by progressive dilation, and only a shell of atrophic tissue remains. Such a segment is easily separated from the healthy lower segment parenchyma. The dilated ureter of the upper renal segment is also removed as completely as possible, leaving a small distal stump. Injury to surrounding blood vessels in the deep pelvis, rectum, and bladder is avoided. During this procedure, the ureter belonging to the lower renal segment is particularly vulnerable to injury because it shares the sheath and blood supply of the lower segment ureter. Postoperatively, ureteral obstruction may be produced by fibrosis resulting from inadequacy of the blood supply, by hematoma, leakage of infected urine, or a combination of these factors. Reflux may be *produced* for the first time in the remaining ureter, because the bladder wall may be weakened in the area of the surgical scar. To avoid this complication, one may reimplant the remaining ureter in a new site when excising the diseased ureter. If vesicoureteral reflux causes refractory chronic pyelonephritis in the lower renal segment, this segment may have to be excised together with its ureter—as was necessary in two of our patients.

Excision of Refluxing Ureteral Stump. After heminephro-ureterectomy with or without partial ureterectomy, reflux may persist in the ureteral stump. Such a stump is likely to become a reservoir for chronic or intermittent infection; if it does, it should be removed. Two patients in whom this occurred are included in this report.

Total Nephroureterectomy. In some cases both renal segments and both ureters must be removed, occasionally as the primary procedure (as was necessary in one of our patients). Or heminephro-ureterectomy may be performed initially; the patient is observed closely and if infection or obstruction has not been eradicated, the remaining renal segment may be resected as a secondary procedure.

SUMMARY

Reflux is more common in duplicated than in nonduplicated ureters. Since reflux may cause recurrence or persistence of urinary infection and destruction of renal parenchyma, the surgical treatment of ureteral duplication with reflux may be the most important aspect of management of children with such a pathologic picture. Available surgical procedures include ureteral reimplantation, heminephroureterectomy, pyelopylostomy with removal of dilated distal ureter, primary nephro-ureterectomy of both segments, nephro-ureterectomy secondary to primary heminephrectomy, and removal of refluxing ureteral stump remaining from previous heminephrectomy. In 28 children treated surgically for refluxing duplicated ureters, the most frequently used technique was ureteral reimplantation (17 cases). Excellent results were obtained in the majority of the 28 patients.

REFERENCES

1. Amar, A. D.: Cystoscopic demonstration of vesicoureteral reflux: Evaluation in 250 patients. J Urol 95:776, 1966

2. ———, and Scheer, C. W.: Comparative length of unilateral bifid kidney and its single counterpart. New Engl J Med 273:211, 1965

3. ———: Double dose contrast medium in excretory urography. Surg Gynec Obstet 118:1083, 1964

4. ———: Reflux in duplicated ureters. Brit J Urol 40:385, 1968

5. ———, Chabra, K., and Weber, P. M.: Radioisotopic renal imaging in infants and children. Urol Digest November 1969, p 12

6. ———, and Hutch, J. A.: Anomalies of the ureter. In Alken, E. E., Dix, V. W., Goodwin, W. E., Weyrauch, H. M., and Wildbolz, E. (Eds): Encyclopedia of Urology, Vol VII. Berlin, Heidelberg, and New York, Springer-Verlag, 1968

7. ———, and Weyrauch, H. M.: Submucosal saline injection technique for ureteral reimplantation. Surg Gynec Obstet 126:552, 1968

8. Hutch, J. A.: The Ureterovesical Junction. Berkeley and Los Angeles, University of California Press, 1958, p 17

9. Ambrose, S. S., and Nicolson, W. P.: Ureteral reflux in duplicated ureters. J Urol 92:439, 1964

10. Lenaghan, D.: Bifid ureters in children: an anatomical, physiological and clinical study. J Urol 87:808, 1962

11. Thompson, I. M., and Amar, A. D.: Clinical importance of ureteral duplication and ectopia. JAMA 168:881, 1958

12. Gibson, T. E.: A new operation for ureteral ectopia: Case report. J Urol 77:414, 1957

13. Gutierrez, J., Chang, C.-Y., and Nesbit, R. M.: Ipsilateral ureteroureterostomy for vesicoureteral reflux in duplicated ureter. J Urol 101:36, 1969

Commentary: Progress in Ureteral Duplication

Arjan D. Amar

Surgery of ureteral duplication has come a long way since Young and Davis in 1917 performed upper-pole heminephrectomy in a case of duplex kidney and bifid pelvis.[1] The preceding article, published in 1970, made a comprehensive yet brief statement of the application of advances in this area of urology that occurred in the previous half century. It is now worthwhile to review the statements made in the light of clinical experience since that time. Recent advances in radiographic and ultrasonic imaging, endoscopic lenses and lighting systems, and computed tomography (CT) scanning have increased workers' ability to make accurate preoperative diagnoses and have helped improve the surgical management of urologic disease associated with ureteral duplication.

The preceding article surveys the anatomic and physiologic problems underlying the phenomena associated with reflux and shows why reflux is the major cause of disease associated with ureteral duplication. Summarized is 10 years of experience with 28 children who had reflux in duplicated ureters. A child's age and size may be important factors in the selection of methods of management or the choice of surgical procedure. The effects of a child's future growth on the anatomy and physiology of the structures affected must be considered. Certain operations are more difficult to perform in children under 2 years of age, but surgical intervention may be necessary to save the kidney.

Note that reflux in either or both of a duplicate pair of ureters may be treated by reimplantation of both ureters through a common submucosal tunnel by any standard antireflux operation. The article describes a simplified technique that combines extravesical dissection of ureters with intravesical formation of a submucosal tunnel.[2] Injection of saline under the mucosa facilitates its separation from the underlying muscularis, averting injury to the vesical wall during tunnel formation. Both ureters are firmly attached to the trigone. This operation can be modified to fit any situation that may necessitate reimplantation and allows for auxiliary correction of associated abnormalities of the lower end of the ureter, including ureterocele and ectopia. Reimplantation of both ureters through a common submucosal tunnel has been carried out in 31 patients (25 children and 6 adults) with gratifying results (Fig. 9).

In the treatment of reflux in one of the duplicate ureters and for ureteral ectopia, increasingly frequent use is being made of procedures that preserve renal parenchyma (ureteropyelostomy, ureteroureterostomy) following Gibson's introduction of ipsilateral pyelopyelostomy.[3]

I have recently described a technique of ipsilateral ureteroureterostomy near the bladder to treat single ureteral disease in patients with complete ureteral duplication.[4] This simple procedure, which avoids opening of the bladder and dissection inside it, was employed as an alternative to reimplantation of both ureters in 16 patients during the past 8 years. Reflux in the lower-segment ureter was treated in 13 patients; upper-segment ectopia, or ureterocele, was managed in 3 patients with this operation. This surgical technique is simpler and safer than reimplantation of both ureters into the bladder. The

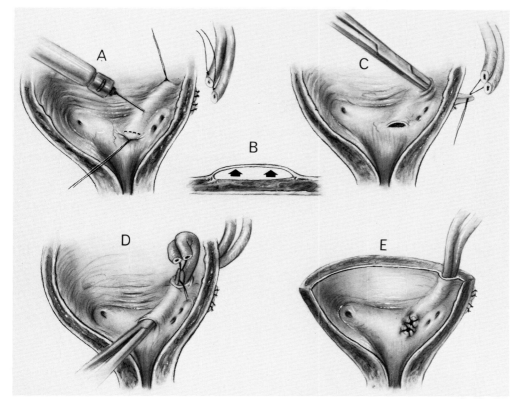

Fig. 9. Schema show technique (*A*) through (*E*) for reimplantation of duplicated ureters.

chances of success in correcting reflux appear better than with reimplantation of both ureters into the bladder. Long-term follow-up study has shown few complications, and no repeat operations were needed. The small stump of diseased ureter left behind near the bladder caused no serious problems (Fig. 10).

It is important to establish preoperatively that the ureter to transport urine from both renal segments to the bladder is free of reflux and obstruction. To ensure adequate patency of the anastomosis, the recipient ureter should have a lumen of adequate caliber. In very small children or in patients with hypoplastic recipient ureter, use an alternative procedure if possible.

The article does not mention congenital hydronephrosis of the lower segment of a duplicated kidney. It may be complicated by the formation of calculus, chronic infection, perinephric abscess, or functional failure of the renal parenchyma. I treated congenital hydronephrosis of the lower renal segment in the duplex kidney in 12 patients during the past 10 years.[5]

Available surgical procedures include side-to-side pyelouteral or end-to-side anastomosis, plastic widening of a narrowed, obstructed site, removal of calculus with relief of obstruction, and heminephrectomy (Figs. 11 and 12).

Since publication of the article, reports have appeared describing additional forms of surgical treatment for ureterouteral reflux, which often occurs in bifid (incompletely duplicated) ureter. Techniques have included longitudinal, side-

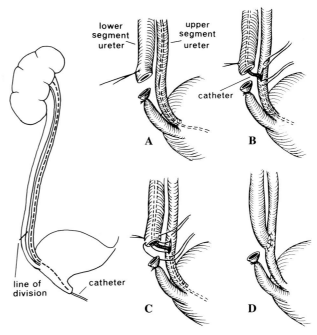

Fig. 10. Schema shows stages (*A*) through (*D*) of operative procedure of ipsilateral ureteroureteroerostomy near bladder to treat reflux in lower segment ureter.

457

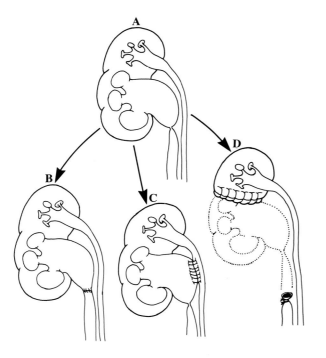

to-side anastomosis and formation of a bladder flap, into which one of the two ureters is reimplanted after having been divided at the junction of the Y.[6] Incomplete ureteral duplication with ureteroureteral reflux can, on rare occasions, lead to parenchymal damage in the related hemikidney when there is chronic infection elsewhere in the urinary tract. An illustrative case was recently reported by Broecker and Johnston.[7] When the junction of the bifid ureters is within 3 cm to 4 cm of the bladder, vesicoureteral and ureteroureteral reflux can be corrected by converting to complete duplication and reimplanting both ureters into the bladder.[8] In this operation, the distal end of both ureters and the common stem are excised (Fig. 13), and the two ureters are reimplanted into the bladder through a common submucosal tunnel with a separate ureteral orifice for each of the two renal segments. I have performed this operation in 8 patients in the last 7 years, correcting vesicoureteral reflux

Fig. 11. (a) Schema of hydronephrosis of lower segment due to obstruction at its ureteropelvic junction. (b) Plastic operation of reteropelvic junction of lower renal segment. (c) Side-to-side pyeloureterostomy. (d) Lower-segment nephrectomy.

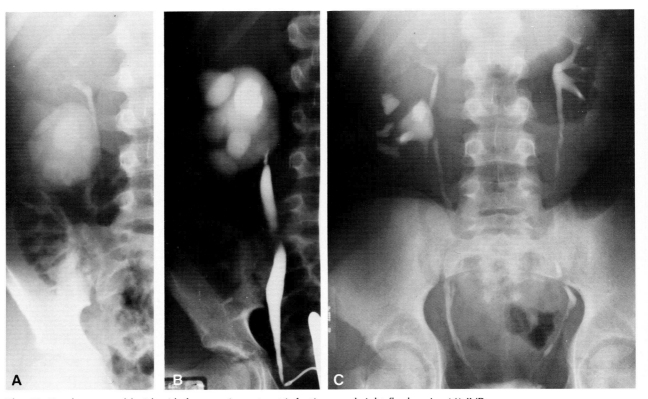

Fig. 12. Twelve-year-old girl with fever, urinary tract infection, and right flank pain. (A) IVP shows marked hydronephrosis of lower calices of right kidney and normal-caliber upper segment ureter. (B) Retrograde ureteropyelogram shows marked obstruction of lower segment ureteropelvic junction. (C) Postoperative result after side-to-side ureteropyelostomy.

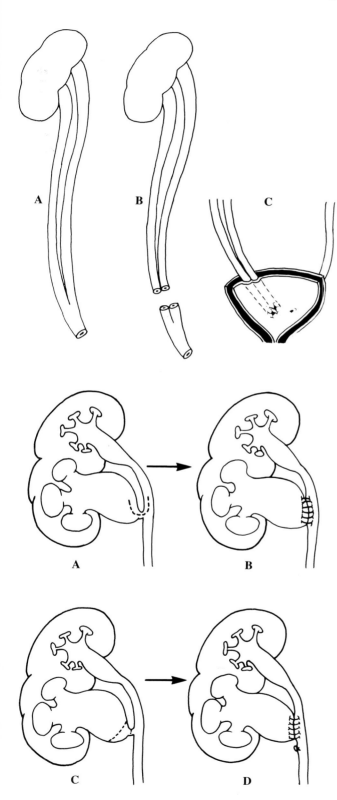

Fig. 13. Schema of conversion procedure. (A) Bifid ureter with junction near bladder. (B) Removal of terminal portions of both ureteral limbs, their point of junction, and part of common ureter converts incomplete duplication to complete duplication. (C) Implantation of newly formed, completely duplicated ureters. Each ureter now has separate opening into bladder. Single left ureter (unoperated) is shown for comparison.

and preventing future ureteroureteral reflux. Review of my experience with the management of urinary calculous disease in association with ureteral duplication (complete and incomplete) was published in 1972.[9] A recent update of the subject was performed.

Urinary calculus disease was found associated with ipsilateral bifid pelvis or ureter in 18 adult patients during the past 20 years. Surgical removal of renal or ureteral calculi was performed in 10 patients. Spontaneous passage of ureteral calculi or transurethral manipulation was successful in 8 patients. Congenital obstruction of the ureteropelvic junction of the lower renal segment in association with incomplete ureteral duplication or bifid pelvis was treated surgically in 6 patients during the last 10 years. Operative procedures included pyeloplasty, ureteropyelostomy, and heminephrectomy (Fig. 14).

The need for heminephrectomy is steadily decreasing as physicians become aware of the importance of earlier diagnosis and as anastomotic procedures that preserve the renal parenchyma are used more frequently. The newer diagnostic imaging techniques and procedures, which are becoming more available, are likely to help physicians make earlier and more accurate assessment of urologic disease associated with ureteral duplication. Innovative studies such as ultrasonography and CT

Fig. 14. (A) Bifid renal pelvis with obstruction of lower pelvis as it joins upper segment ureter. *Dotted line* indicates incision for plastic widening of this narrowed site. (B) Suture line showing completed operation. (C) Narrow segment similar to (A) needing excision. (D) End-to-side anastomosis for correction of obstruction.

scanning and various specific radiographic and radionuclide procedures are emerging and are being applied more often in the diagnosis of complex problems. The article suggests surgical removal of the refluxing ureteral stump after heminephroureterectomy if urinary tract infection persists and cannot be managed with antimicrobial therapy. Only a widely dilated, refluxing, ureteral stump needs excision. Surgical alternatives to excision of the refluxing stump have been fully discussed elsewhere.[10]

For treatment of single ureteral disease in patients with complete ureteral duplication, ipsilateral ureteroureterostomy has been performed in 21 patients during the last 9 years. A small stump of the diseased ureter was left behind near the bladder in each patient. In none of the 16 patients in whom reflux was present preoperatively was any serious problem noted postoperatively, and none of the stumps required surgical removal after the initial ipsilateral ureteroureterostomy.

The specific benefits of indigo carmine cystoscopic tests for detecting reflux in patients with ureteral duplication were recently summarized.[11] In patients with duplicated ureters, cystography may show reflux in the distal segment of a ureter. Which of the two ureters of the duplicated set has reflux may not be evident, because contrast medium does not enter either of the two renal pelves. The indigo carmine cystoscopic test can differentiate the ureteral orifice with reflux from the one without reflux. When ipsilateral ureteroureterostomy is planned for single ureteral disease in a patient with complete ureteral duplication, the indigo carmine cystoscopic test can show preoperatively that the ureter used to transport urine from both renal segments is free of reflux. For this purpose, the indigo carmine test was used preoperatively in all 21 patients in whom ipsilateral ureteroureterostomy was performed during the last 9 years.

In patients with complete ureteral duplication, the upper renal segment and its ureter may remain unvisualized during excretory urography. Detection of the refluxing ureter belonging to the upper renal segment may be the first evidence that ureteral duplication exists. The indigo carmine cystoscopic test provided the first evidence of previously undiagnosed duplication in seven patients. In each of these patients, the upper-segment ureter had an ectopic orifice in the urethra. The problems of ureterocele and ectopia are not reported here in detail, since they are outside the scope of this chapter.

The pioneering era in the treatment of reflux is evidently past. Surgeons will continue to introduce refinements, but treatment is stabilizing. Surgical correction of reflux in single ureters is effective in 95% to 99% of most modern series. This degree of success cannot be accomplished in duplicate ureters because of the anomalies so often associated with ureteral duplication (*e.g.*, ureterocele, ectopia, and obstruction along the course of one or both ureters). These problems will continue to demand physicians' attention.

REFERENCES

1. Young HH, Davis EG: Double ureter and kidney, with calculus pyonephrosis of one half; cure by resection. The embryology and surgery of double ureter and kidney. J Urol 1:17, 1917

2. Amar AD: Reimplantation of completely duplicated ureters. J Urol 107:230, 1972

3. Gibson TE: A new operation for ureteral ectopia: Case report. J Urol 77:414, 1957

4. Amar AD: Ipsilateral ureteroureterostomy for single ureteral disease in patients with ureteral duplication: A review of 8 years of experience with 16 patients. J Urol 119:472, 1978

5. Amar AD: Congenital hydronephrosis of lower segment in duplex kidney. Urology 7:480, 1976

6. Tresidder GC, Blandy JP, Murray RS: Pyelo-pelvic and uretero-ureteric reflux. Br J Urol 42:728, 1970

7. Broecker BH, Johnston JH: Yo-yo ureteric reflux. Soc Pediatr Urol Ns1 2:52, 1979

8. Amar AD: Treatment of reflux in bifid ureters by conversion to complete duplication. J Urol 108:77, 1972

9. Amar AD: The management of urinary calculous disease in patients with duplicated ureters. Br J Urol 44:541, 1972

10. Amar AD: Surgical alternatives to excision of refluxing ureteral stump. Br J Urol 43:297, 1971

11. Amar AD: Fifteen-year progress report on nonradiographic cystoscopic test for the detection of vesicoureteral reflux. Soc Pediatr Urol Ns1 2:10, 1979

ANNOTATED BIBLIOGRAPHY

Gibson TE: A new operation for ureteral ectopia; case report. J Urol 77:414, 1957

This is the first description of anastomosis of the upper renal pelvis to the lower renal pelvis for treatment of ureteral ectopia. It was performed in a girl aged 17 with urinary incontinence. As much as possible of the ectopic ureter below the anastomosis was removed, leaving a short ureteral stump near the bladder.

Swenson O, Ratner IA: Pyeloureterostomy for treatment of symptomatic ureteral duplications in children. J Urol 88:184, 1962

This is a well-documented presentation of the application (in children) of the parenchyma-conserving principle introduced by Gibson. Pyeloureterostomy was performed to conserve kidney tissue and to remove the aperistaltic, widely dilated ureter of the diseased segment, below the anastomosis. Indications for operation and surgical technique are described.

Ambrose SS, Nicolson WP: Ureteral reflux in duplicated ureters. J Urol 92:439, 1964

The authors treated 27 patients with complete ureteral duplication and associated reflux. The renal parenchyma that was drained by the refluxing ureter was pyelonephritic in each patient. The most common site of reflux was the lower-segment ureter. Reflux in this ureter is caused by the short intramural segment that results from embryonic development.

Amar AD: Reflux in duplicated ureters. Br J Urol 40:385, 1968

This monograph shows why reflux is the major cause of persistent urinary disease in patients with ureteral duplication. Improved or new methods of diagnosis include the indigo carmine cystoscopic test, comparison of renal size, urography with an increased amount of contrast medium, cineradiography, and radioisotopic renal scan. If the diagnostic steps suggested in the article are followed, correct diagnosis of urologic disease associated with ureteral duplication can often be achieved. Various surgical methods of treatment are discussed, and their application in 29 patients (children and adults) is described.

Timothy RP, Decker A, Perlmutter AD: Ureteral duplication: clinical findings and therapy in 46 children. J Urol 105:445, 1971

In this retrospective study, the most significant abnormality of the upper renal segment ureter was found to be obstruction caused by a ureterocele or by ectopia of the ureteral orifice. The lower renal segment was the one most often damaged by reflux into the ureter. The authors advise avoiding nephrectomy or partial nephrectomy whenever salvageable renal parenchyma is present.

Johnston JH, Heal MR: Reflux in complete duplicated ureter in children: Management and techniques. J Urol 105:881, 1971

Management of primary vesicoureteral reflux in association with complete ureteral duplication in 11 boys and 30 girls is discussed. In addition, management of iatrogenic reflux following the uncapping of ectopic ureterocele in 37 cases is discussed. Surgical methods employed included removal of the lower hemikidney and its associated refluxing ureter in 9 patients. Reimplantation of the duplicated ureters was carried out in 6 patients. Pyeloureterostomy with ureterectomy of the diseased ureter was performed in 10 patients. Also discussed is management of reflux with ectopic ureterocele. Patients with advanced disease, for whom conservative management is needed alone or in combination with surgical management, are discussed.

Belman AB, Filmer RB, King LR: Surgical management of duplication of collecting system. J Urol 112:316, 1974

Experience with 47 females and 11 males with duplication of the collecting system is described. Vesicoureteral reflux and ureteral obstruction were the common significant problems. Ureteral reimplantation was performed in 15 patients, 27 had partial nephrectomy, and 16 had pyeloureterostomy. Reimplantation was done most often for reflux; partial nephrectomy, for obstruction. Half the pyeloureterostomies were performed for reflux and half for obstruction.

Barrett DM, Malek RS, Kelalis PP: Problems and solutions in surgical treatment of 100 consecutive ureteral duplications in children. J Urol 114:126, 1975

In 63 children, 85 duplicated ureters with reflux required surgical treatment. In 44 patients, ureteroneocystostomy was done by transvesical mobilization of the duplex ureter in a common sheath. Ectopic ureterocele was the primary abnormality in 21 children. In 14 of these patients, upper-segment heminephrectomy and subtotal ureterectomy was performed. Ureteropyelostomy was done in seven patients. Three children with incomplete ureteral duplication who had ureteroureteral reflux required ureteropyelostomy.

Amar AD: Ipsilateral ureteroureterostomy for single ureteral disease in patients with ureteral duplication: A review of 8 years of experience in 16 patients. J Urol 119:472, 1978

Ipsilateral ureteroureterostomy near the bladder was performed in 16 patients during the past 8 years. The operative technique, indications, results, follow-up study, and complications are presented. Reflux in the lower-segment ureter was treated in 13 patients and upper-segment ectopia or ureterocele was managed in 3 patients. This operative technique is simpler and safer than reimplantation of both ureters into the bladder. Long-term follow-up study has shown few complications. The small stump of diseased ureter left behind near the bladder has caused no serious problems.

Overview: Management of Ureteral Duplication

J.H. Johnston

As Dr. Amar states, the management of ureteric duplication in its various forms is stabilizing as the basic pathophysiologic features of the abnormalities have become better understood. My experiences correspond closely with his. However, I would think that his recommended technique of ipsilateral end-to-side ureteroureterostomy close to the bladder has very limited application. The anastomosis of the extremity of a dilated, thickened ureter to the side of an undilated one would be technically difficult and therefore hazardous to the recipient ureter and its related kidney. In any event, the hemikidney

drained by a ureter opening ectopically or into an ectopic ureterocele is generally severely atrophic or even dysplastic. Preservation of such diseased parenchyma contributes little, if anything, to overall renal function, and it could promote persistent infection or induce subsequent development of hypertension. In my view, such patients are best managed by heminephroureterectomy.

Ureterectomy in patients with complete duplication is rendered difficult by the fact that as a rule, the two ureters share a common wall over the lowest 2 cm or 3 cm outside

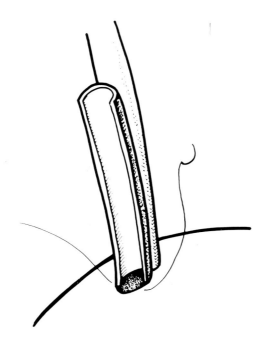

the bladder. Attempts to separate them will almost certainly irretrievably damage the ureter to be retained. Simple ligation and division of the ureter being removed above the point of fusion leaves a stump that, if reflux is present, acts as a vesical diverticulum, allowing continuing infection. The dilemma is best resolved by slitting the stump of the ureter down to the bladder, leaving the common wall undisturbed. Trim off redundant ureteric fringes on each side, and close the small gap in the bladder musculature with one or two catgut sutures; insert these with care to avoid possible occlusion of the twin ureter (Fig. 15). I have not attempted to remove the mucosal strip from the ureteric stump, and, over a follow-up period of many years, this has not had any undesirable consequences, although recent animal experimentation has suggested that secretions from the exposed urothelium may lead to cyst formation.[1]

Fig. 15. Technique of ureterectomy in cases of complete ureteric duplication. Slit the stump of the ureter down to the bladder, leaving the common wall undisturbed. Trim off redundant fringes, and close the hiatus in the bladder musculature with sutures.

REFERENCE

1. Pringle KC: Sequestration of ureteric segments in dogs. Br J Urol (in press)

35

A NEW APPROACH TO INFANTS WITH SEVERE OBSTRUCTIVE UROPATHY: EARLY COMPLETE RECONSTRUCTION

W. Hardy Hendren

From the Children's Service and the General Surgical Service of the Massachusetts General Hospital and the Department of Surgery of the Harvard Medical School, Boston, Mass.

Journal of Pediatric Surgery, Vol. 5, No. 2 (April) 1970

Severe obstructive uropathy with hydronephrosis and hydroureter is one of the most difficult problems facing surgeons who care for infants and children. Born with a sterile urinary tract, and often seemingly quite healthy, these infants usually acquire urinary infection which brings to light their serious problem. The natural course of their disease, even with appropriate antimicrobial therapy, is usually an early death. Curiously, a few children with great hydronephrosis do not develop urinary infection for several years and may escape attention during infancy, but this is uncommon.

Presented before the Surgical Section of the American Academy of Pediatrics, Chicago, Ill., October 18–20, 1969.

W. Hardy Hendren, M.D.: Assistant Clinical Professor of Surgery, Harvard Medical School. Surgical Chairman, Children's Service, and Associate Visiting Surgeon, Massachusetts General Hospital, Boston, Mass.

At birth in some of these cases there has already occurred great loss of renal parenchyma from long standing intrauterine back pressure. In others, even with great dilatation of the ureters and the upper tracts there still remains enough renal parenchyma to sustain life, and even normal renal extretory function, provided excellent drainage, can be achieved and infection can be abolished or prevented.

A variety of methods have been used to provide better drainage for these infants:

1. *Long-term catheter drainage*[1] per urethra or suprapubic cystostomy. Doubtless some urinary tracts will improve by this expedient, but as long as a foreign body is present in the urinary tract, infection will persist. Furthermore, drainage of the bladder in many cases *may not drain dilated, tortuous ureters above*, because there is often obstruction of the lower ureter at the bladder as

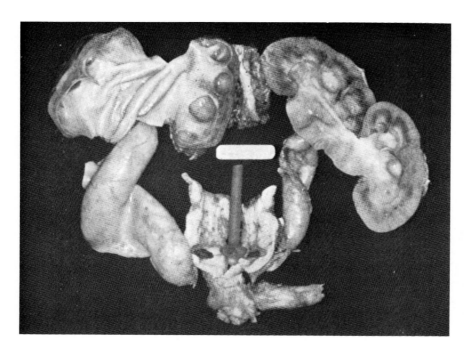

Fig. 1. Urinary tract at autopsy of infant male with urethral valves and hydronephrosis, treated in 1955 by suprapublic cystostomy, but with continuing infection, renal failure and death. Drainage of bladder alone did not suffice. Ample renal parenchyma, especially on left. This child could likely have survived with total reconstruction.

well as urethral obstruction. Figure 1 illustrates this point.

2. *Nephrostomy drainage.* This has a place in the treatment of these children, but as a long-term measure carries the objection of placing a foreign body in the kidney, which is soon followed by persisting low-grade infection, which will gradually reduce renal function. It is, further, an unpleasant burden with which to cope socially. We believe nephrostomy should be used only as a short-term aid in selected cases while pursuing an aggressive restorative program for the entire urinary tract. The concept of long-term nephrostomy drainage to await slow spontaneous improvement of dilatation and tortuosity of the ureters is not sound, for although renal function may be immediately improved, stasis in the ureter below (often amounting to a large volume) perpetuates infection. Many of these children fall by the wayside through the years.

3. *Removal of urethral valves in the male.* Upper-tract pathology varies greatly in boys with urethral valves. Some with low-grade, partial obstruction, have normal upper tracts and ureters. Others with high-grade obstruction have great hypertrophy of the bladder and severe dilatation of the upper tract, often with great ureteral tortuosity. Within this spectrum lie many variations in severity. Removal of valves usually suffices in mild cases, but in our experience it *does not* in severe ones where there is considerable secondary hypertrophy of the bladder neck plus ureteral decompensation. Some of these cases have massive vesicoureteral reflux; others do not, paradoxically, having lower ureteral *obstruction.*

Simple removal of valves in these severe cases does not suffice. To get rid of their infection and to provide optimal upper-tract drainage, one must remove the valves, revise the secondarily hypertrophied and obstructed bladder neck (Fig. 2), and refashion the decompensated ureters in such a way that they drain and do not have reflux.

4. *Exteriorization of the urine flow.* Recognizing the problems associated with long-term indwelling tubes, a number of indirect methods have been employed to provide drainage in these infants.

a. *Cutaneous vesicostomy.*[2,3] This will palliate some children, but leaves the basic problem to be dealt with subsequently, and this may be *more difficult* in a bladder which has been previously operated upon and is contracted from long-term disuse.

b. *Cutaneous vesicostomy plus lateral anastomosis of the ureter to the bladder.* This has been used in those where there is concomitant urethral and ureteral obstruction, which is common in males with valves. Previous palliative treatment by this method, in my experience, makes more difficult a subsequent definitive repair.

c. *Cutaneous ureterostomy*[4–9] either low in the ureter or high near the kidney has been in vogue for the past few years. Our experience with it, although small, has not been entirely satisfactory. Although the children may improve initially, some continue with low-grade infection, possibly causing an insidious increase of ureteral fibrosis, reducing the likelihood of a later direct repair.

All of the above-mentioned techniques are based on the premise that these children need long-term prelimi-

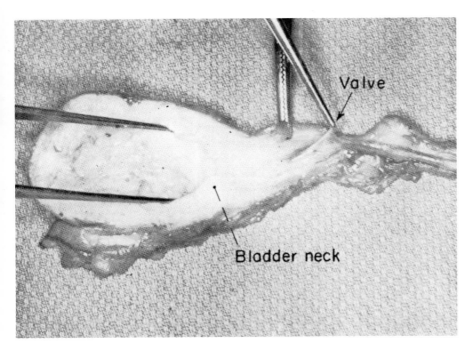

Fig. 2. Bladder and urethra of infant male with posterior urethral valves, treated in 1962 by cutaneous ureterostomy, who subsequently died. Kidneys dysgenetic. Specimen shows urethral valves which can be removed endoscopically, but demonstrates also tremendous hypertrophy of bladder, with remarkable thickening at bladder neck. It is necessary to open bladder neck in front by Y-V plasty, and in some to resect posterior bladder neck also either initially or later.

nary drainage to prepare for a definitive repair later or that definitive repair during infancy cannot be accomplished.

Although there are some congenital malformations in which an initial palliative, temporizing procedure followed by a corrective procedure later may give an increased overall salvage, we have seen little evidence that this is true in infants with urinary anomalies where infection causes further damage while awaiting the definitive repair.

In the past 10 years we have employed an aggressive approach to children with severe decompensation of the urinary tract in the belief that if one corrects all of the levels of obstruction (in some at three levels, the urethra, the lower ureter, and the upper ureter), and reduces the reservoir capacity of the urinary tract, the best possible renal function will ensue for the child. Some of this work as applied to children of all ages has been reported previously.[10,11] In this paper we wish to focus upon a special and most difficult segment of this group of patients, the infant under two years of age. We have found that they are remarkably able to undergo major complete reconstruction with extremely good results if one repairs completely the urinary tract.

CASE MATERIAL

From this series we have excluded many children with basically good urinary tract, who have nonetheless undergone major definitive surgery under age two (children with reflux but reasonably good upper tracts and

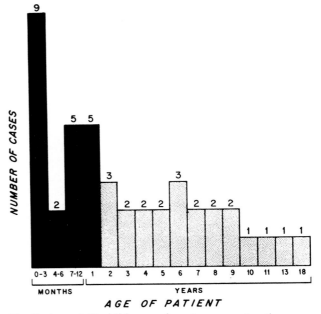

Fig. 3. Age of 43 children undergoing reconstructive surgery for megaureter. Darkly shaded columns represent those under two years of age, 21 cases, which are subject of report.

ureters not requiring tapering, children with ureterocele, with a destroyed renal segment, etc.) Included are only those with severe decompensation requiring ureteral reconstructive surgery. Figure 3 shows by age our overall experience with reconstructive surgery for a megaureter, and illustrates that one half are infants under age two.

Of the 21 children, 14 were males, all with urethral valves, and seven females. (A poor urinary stream had been noted prior to admission only in two of these 14 cases with urethral valves.) Twelve of the children electively, usually having a urinary infection which led to investigation and then referral. Nine entered with a more pressing clinical presentation which included inability to void in one newborn male, and infection complicated by uremia and acidosis in eight cases. In these we pursued a course of *short-term* catheter drainage with intravenous correction of dehydration and acidosis, brief radiographic assessment of urinary pathology and vigorous antibiotic treatment of infection. In each after an initial fall in BUN and improvement of the clinical state of the child a reconstructive procedure was performed.

Preoperative evaluation of these patients included: (1) *Intravenous Pyelogram.* In those with poor function delayed films should be followed for several hours. (2) *Baseline creatinine clearance studies** usually two, 24-hour determinations. These are of value in following renal function after repair. Baseline studies in the uremic children were those obtained after beginning catheter drainage, for it is not justified to delay even a short while for pretreatment creatinine clearance values in an acidotic, ill infant. (3) *Cystography,* preferably cine cystography. Valves can be demonstrated in the infant male by passing a very small urethral catheter, filling the bladder by drip until quite full, after which the bladder will usually force enough dye into the urehtra to make the diagnosis, even with the small catheter in place. Suprapubic compression with a lead-gloved hand under fluoroscopy is occasionally needed. Thirteen patients had massive vesicoureteral reflux; six had lower ureteral obstruction without reflux; two had a refluxing ureter on one side and an obstructive megaureter on the other side. (4) *Bacteriologic cultures* with appropriate antibiotic treatment guided by sensitivity studies. (5) *Cystoscopy.* This was performed preliminary to operative correction under the same anesthesia. When the outline of dilated tortuous ureters is not clear by a preoperative I.V.P. or cystogram films, retrograde pyelogram should be done, for it is of great help to outline clearly the kinks and the turns to guide one in the lower ureteral repair. Retrograde pyelograms should *not* be done until ready to proceed immediately with repair, especially in obstructive megaureter, because passing a ureteral catheter through the orifice can cause edema, total obstruc-

* The values given in this paper are expressed in liters of clearance per square meter of body surface area per day.

tion, and precipitate a crisis requiring preoperative emergency nephrostomy. This occurred in one of these cases.

OPERATIVE TREATMENT

(1) Urethral valves are fulgurated through an infant McCarty panendoscope using a Bugbee fulgurating electrode, with cutting, not coagulating current. In males where the urethra will take a No. 14 sound, this can be done transurethrally. In the particularly small male, whose urethra will not accept a No. 14 sound comfortably, a small perineal urethrostomy incision is made, cutting down upon the tip of a small sound placed in the urethra, and the panendoscope is introduced via the perineum just distal to the external urethral sphincter. This affords visualization of the valves. With experience valves can be removed in a few minutes by this technique. We feel that open resection of valves with cutting of the symphysis pubis, etc., is entirely outmoded today. The perineal urethrotomy wound closes in a day or two spontaneously, if a small plastic catheter is left in the urethra, through the penis, to drain the bladder. In some cases the valve fulguration is done as a separate procedure, waiting a few days to proceed with the major reconstructive operation. In others the major reconstructive procedure is done under the same anesthesia, but this makes for a prolonged operative session.

Steps in the operative correction are shown in Figure 4. Certain of the details have been reported previously.[10] Figures 5–9 illustrate representative cases.

Figure 4A shows the typical pathology with urethral valves just at or distal to the verumontanum, great secondary hypertrophy of the bladder neck, and impressive thickening of the bladder wall. The two principle types of megaureter are shown: refluxing megaureter in which the orifice is usually patulous, and often laterally placed and too far craniad in the trigone; and obstructive megaureter in which the orifice usually appears normal, and the intramular ureter is quite small. The tortuous ureteropelvic junction is sometimes partially obstructed because it is kinked, although it is probe patent.

Figure 4B shows the completed lower repair. Valves have been removed, the bladder neck has been opened anteriorly by a Y-V plasty, the lower ureters have been shortened, tapered and reimplanted. A No. 5 plastic gavage feeding catheter remains in the ureters for about two weeks for temporary decompression. In the male they are brought out through the opposite side of the bladder, for they lie better in this way. These catheters are never removed simultaneously, but instead one is removed, and the patient observed to see if the urethral catheter which has been draining nil begins to put out an amount commensurate with what had been coming from the ureteral catheter, giving assurance that the kidney is draining. Two or three days later, the second ureteral catheter is removed, and output is observed again. If all is well the urethral catheter is removed around the 16th day. Preliminary nephrostomy

(Text continues on p. 470)

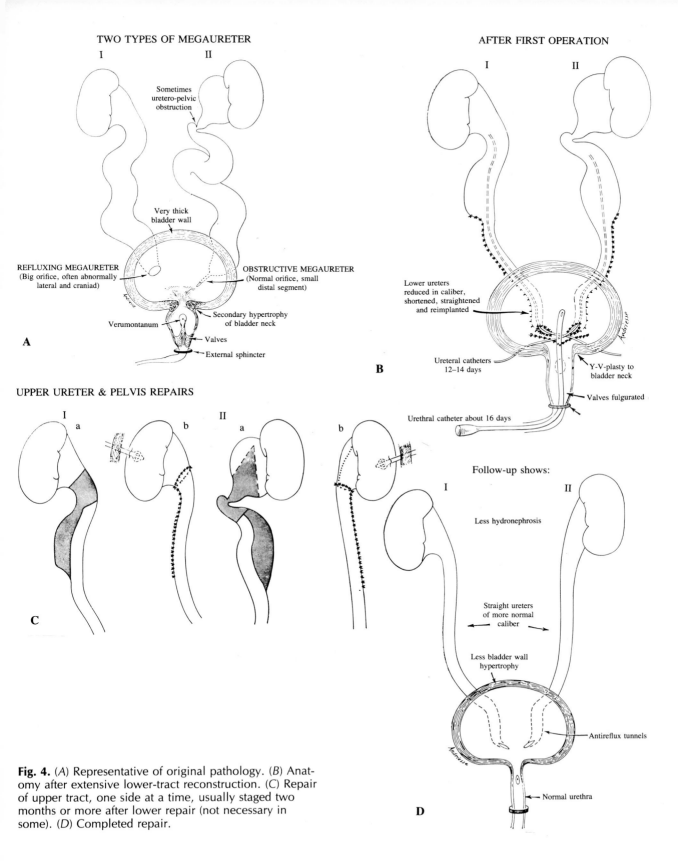

TWO TYPES OF MEGAURETER

I II

Sometimes
uretero-pelvic
obstruction

Very thick
bladder wall

REFLUXING MEGAURETER
(Big orifice, often abnormally
lateral and craniad)

OBSTRUCTIVE MEGAURETER
(Normal orifice, small
distal segment)

Verumontanum

Secondary hypertrophy
of bladder neck

Valves

External sphincter

A

AFTER FIRST OPERATION

I II

Lower ureters
reduced in caliber,
shortened, straightened
and reimplanted

Ureteral catheters
12–14 days

Y-V-plasty to
bladder neck

Valves fulgurated

Urethral catheter about 16 days

B

UPPER URETER & PELVIS REPAIRS

I II
a b a b

C

Follow-up shows:

I II

Less hydronephrosis

Straight ureters
of more normal
caliber

Less bladder wall
hypertrophy

Antireflux tunnels

Normal urethra

D

Fig. 4. (*A*) Representative of original pathology. (*B*) Anatomy after extensive lower-tract reconstruction. (*C*) Repair of upper tract, one side at a time, usually staged two months or more after lower repair (not necessary in some). (*D*) Completed repair.

Fig. 5. Group of infants all under one year of age from this series, who have recently undergone extensive reconstruction.

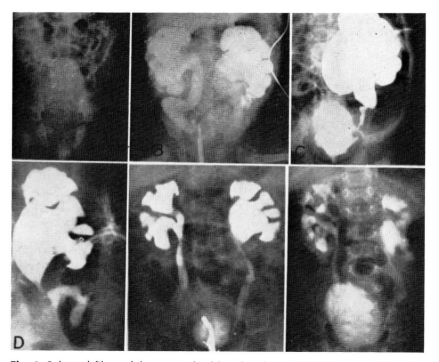

Fig. 6. Selected films of three-month-old male admitted 2/6/69 uremic (Blood Urea Nitrogen 70 mg percent, acidotic (CO_2 nine volumes percent, Creatinine 3.6 mg percent) with urinary infection and temperature of 105 degrees. (A) IVP before referral, showing poor visualization and large bladder. Clinically improved rapidly with four days of bladder drainage through small plastic urethral catheter. Major reconstruction undertaken. (B) Retrograde pyelogram defining ureters and upper tracts at time of definitive lower construction five days after admission. (C) Nephrostogram, left side, three weeks after lower reconstruction. After removal of ureteral catheters, left side did not drain well and nephrostomy tube inserted. This picture at three weeks shows recently cut-down lower ureter partially obstructured by edema, and still very dilated upper ureter and renal pelvis. Upper repair performed, one side at time, two months from admission. (D) Nephrostogram left side two weeks after upper repair, showing extravasation at ureteropelvic junction. Kidney left on drainage for additional week and this disappeared. Nephrostomy tube removed. (E) Retrograde pyelogram five months after lower repair, and three months after upper repair. (F) Intravenous pyelogram during reevaluation admission, age eight months, five months from first admission. BUN 19, CO_2 24, Creatinine 0.4. Original weight below third percentile, now in 20th percentile.

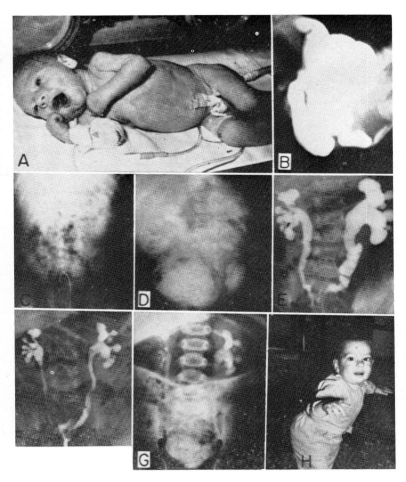

Fig. 7. Films of three-week-old male entered 11/16/68 severely ill with urethral valves and urinary infection. He was grey and lethargic, with BUN 114, Creatinine 2.8, CO_2 6, blood pH 7.15, Potassium 8.6. Treated by immediate drainage of bladder through small plastic catheter per urethra, vigorous supportive therapy with fluid and antibiotics, prepared to perform bilateral nephrostomy shortly if infant did not improve quickly. (A) Photograph 11 days after admission just prior to total lower tract reconstruction at age one month. (B) Cystourethrogram, on admission, showing urethral valves, wide posterior urethra, secondary hypertrophy of bladder neck, and massive reflux bilaterally. (C) IVP prior to admission showing bilaterally poor visualization. (D) IVP one month after lower repair, showing better dye excretion but still considerable hydronephrosis. (E) Retrograde pyelogram six weeks after lower-tract reconstruction. (F) Retrograde pyelogram five months after lower-tract reconstruction. (G) Intravenous pyelogram, five minute film, 10 months after surgery (no upper reconstruction necessary). (H) Photograph of baby, at 11 months of age. He is a well child, BUN 28, Creatinine 0.8, Creatinine clearance risen from 10 to 28 liters. Original weight under third percentile, now in 12th percentile. Urine sterile.

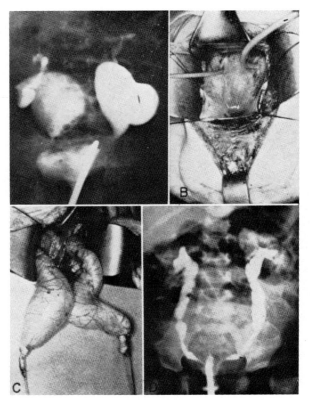

Fig. 8. Eight-week-old male with mild case of "prune belly syndrome." Not ill, referred electively for evaluation, condition having been recognized by referring physician because of wrinkling of abdominal wall skin. (A) Retrograde pyelogram at time of lower reconstruction, consisted of transurethral resection of valves, open revision of bladder neck, extensive resection, shortening and tapering of lower ureters. Note peculiar upper tracts, without hydronephrosis. BUN 33. (B) Interior of bladder at operation. Bladder neck in center of photograph. Ureteral orifices both very patulous (14 Fr. catheter in each) and are located abnormally craniad and lateral in bladder trigone. (C) Ureters mobiles intra- and extravesically, following which several inches excess length resected, then tapering caliber of remaining lower ureters to about level of iliac vessels, then reimplanting them into bladder. (D) Retrograde pyelogram one month later, showing tapered and reimplanted lower ureters. BUN 15.

before repairing lower ureters has been seldom needed. In one patient with extremely little renal function, and in whom a crisis was precipitatd by doing a retrograde pyelogram, a preliminary nephrostomy was employed. In two patients a kidney failed to drain well upon removing the ureteral stent catheter, and when this was evident by elevation of temperature, a palpable flank mass, and poor function by I.V.P., a temporary nephrostomy tube was inserted immediately. (A No. 12 or 14

Malecot catheter placed in a dependent position in the lower pole of the kidney using a small grooved director as a stylet.) In these cases the nephrostomy tube was left in place until after the upper ureter was repaired several weeks later. In the small, thick-walled bladder, it is important not to carry the Y incision too far laterally, for this will interfere with the tunnelling of the ureter into the bladder. When opened, these greatly hypertrophied bladders are contracted and very thick walled, and are not easy to work with. The ureter is mobilized from within the bladder, and then extravesically as well. The obliterated hypogastric ligament is divided which permits easy dissection and mobilization of the ureter upward into the retroperitoneal area. It is best to avoid entering the peritoneal cavity. No attempt is made to straighten the entire ureter all the way to the kidney, for fear of losing its blood supply. Instead, the ureter is mobilized to about the level where the ureter crosses the iliac vessels, being careful not to injure the blood supply of the medial aspect of the ureter. It is then cut down and tapered over a No. 10 or 12 French catheter, using special clamps.* The edges are approximated with fine chromic catgut and the ureter is tunnelled into the bladder. It is desirable usually to move the ureteral orifice location more medially and caudad. After closing the original muscle defect where the ureter entered the bladder, a tunnel is made in the trigone starting at an appropriate point close to the midline and close to the posterior bladder neck, tunnelling directly upward, not laterally, for about 2–3 cm, and then breaking through the bladder wall muscle posteriorly close to where the vagina lies next to the bladder in the female, or the rectum in the male. (If, after reimplantation, a ureter is too far lateral in the bladder, when the bladder fills, it can draw the ureter forward, causing angulation and obstruction. This can be prevented by placing the ureter posteriorly and close to the center of the trigone.)

Figure 4C shows a similar repair of the upper ureter which should be done in the most severe cases in which it is wide and tortuous. In 16 cases in this series an upper repair was required, but not in five. Again, the blood supply should be carefully preserved. The upper repair is performed two months or more after the lower repair, by which time the lower ureter has healed and established new blood supply. In a few cases the upper repair has been sooner, and in some we have waited as long as a year, but in the majority the interval between the lower stage and the upper stage has been about two months. The upper ureter repair has not been standard, but has consisted of whatever resection and tapering is required to have a ureter which is straight and of satisfactory caliber. A stent is not usually left in the ureter nowadays, although we nearly always employ a temporary nephrostomy for about two weeks. At that time dye is gently instilled into the kidney, and if there is free passage down into the bladder the tube is removed. We fill the collecting system with half per cent Neomycin upon pulling the catheter, for this may help prevent bacteremia which can occur upon pulling a nephrostomy tube.

We prefer to do the lower ureter first, because it is by far the more difficult procedure, and risk to blood supply is greater with the lower operation than with the upper. Furthermore, an

* Available from V. Mueller Co., 6600 W. Touhy Ave., Chicago, Ill.

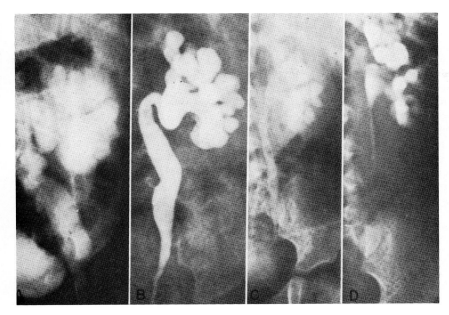

Fig. 9. Representative films of four-month-old infant female referred for evaluation of abdominal mass which proved to be solitary, hydronephrotic left kidney. (*A*) IVP, delayed film, on admission. BUN 16 (!) but Creatinine clearance much reduced, 15 liters. (*B*) Retrograde pyelogram four months later showing still dilated, tortuous, upper ureter. Clearance 44 liters. Upper resection, shortening and tapering performed 10 months after lower repair (in retrospect would now do sooner). (*C*) Intravenous pyelogram 14 months after upper repair. Clearance 90 liters. (*D*) Intravenous pyelogram at almost age four years, with normal Creatinine clearance 104 liters, BUN 11, Creatinine 0.5.

upper ureter repair is sometimes not necessary if the upper ureter is only moderately dilated and is not tortuous. We would, however, fix the upper ureter first if the function of the kidney were doubtful and exploration was required to see if there were a reasonable amount of salvageable parenchyma. We have seen a kidney which showed nonfunction by pyelogram in which there was a lot of renal parenchyma well worth saving, determined by exploring the flank. In such a case the upper ureter and renal pelvis repair can be performed followed by the lower repair several weeks later, leaving a temporary nephrostomy tube in place meanwhile.

After all tubes are removed a maximal effort is made to sterilize the urinary tract, guided by appropriate culture and sensitivity tests. In some cases this has been simple, but in others has required several weeks longer in the hospital. It is nearly always possible to get the urinary tract sterile after satisfactory drainage has been achieved even though there is still hydronephrosis.

Figure 4D shows the end result. There is no longer obstruction of the urethra, less bladder wall hypertrophy, disappearance of pseudodiverticula, satisfactory drainage of the ureters without reflux, and frequently dramatic improvement in hydronephrosis.

POSTOPERATIVE RESULTS

These children must be followed extremely closely, watching cultures and renal function, making certain there is not obstruction or reflux of a ureter, that the bladder is emptying completely and that there is improvement in the upper urinary tract. They are all readmitted to the hospital several months after discharge for creatinine clearance, cystoscopy, retrograde pyelo-

graphy, determination of intraureteral peristaltic pressures, etc. At followup, residual urethral valve tissue was seen in several, and further fulguration was performed. The posterior bladder neck was, additionally, incised with the cutting electrode to correct partial remaining bladder neck obstruction in three of the boys.

Complications: There has been one death, a two-week-old infant with multiple urinary anomalies in association with hypoplasia of the abdominal wall muscles. Although the surgical correction was uneventful, there was cardiac arrest and brain damage, resulting in death from aspiration two months postoperatively; urinary tract function was satisfactory. A suture line leaked twice, once in the lower ureter, which resulted in stenosis requiring reoperation in the first case in the series. In another (Fig. 5), there was leakage after the upper repair noted upon nephrostogram, but this closed spontaneously without sequel by leaving the nephrostomy tube in an additional week.

Antibiotic treatment has been maintained on these children for about one year postoperatively, to let upper-tract dilatation, etc., improve before removing the protective umbrella of drug coverage. In all cases it has been possible to keep these urinary tracts sterile. Of those who have been taken off antibiotic therapy (10 patients), in only one has recurrent bacilluria appeared to date. This came under control quickly with appropriate medication.

On followup, cystogram vesicoureteral reflux was present in one ureter in one child. This was corrected by reoperation.

Details concerning improvement of renal function, and growth and development will be the subject of a subsequent report. At present about half of these patients are too recently operated upon to draw any valid long-term conclusions. The early patients in the series, however, have shown great improvement in renal function. In one child with an original borderline creatinine clearance of 15 liters, the renal function increased to 104 liters, which is normal. (This was a solitary kidney with obstructive megaureter, shown in Fig. 8.) Growth spurts were seen in several of these children. They are usually below the third percentile initially and enter a more normal range when free of urinary infection and when renal function is improved. In two children with extremely low clearances (less than five liters), there has been no improvement in renal function, although they have been clinically better. We do not feel that low creatinine clearance is a reason to exclude children from this anatomic reconstruction, because achieving satisfactory drainage can facilitate sterilization of the urinary tract, possibly preventing further renal loss. Furthermore, in a urinary tract which has been reconstructed but still has borderline function, renal transplantation might be feasible at a later age. This is less likely so if the child has been palliated by urinary diversion. A child with borderline renal function is in a better state of affairs if he can void normally, has no tubes, appliances, etc., as compared to being encumbered with nephrostomy tubes, cutaneous urinary fistulas, etc. In planning the surgical care of children we must think not only of quantitative salvage for these patients, hopefully with the goal of a normal life span, but also we must consider the qualitative aspects of life we are providing for them.

We have been amazed at the return of good renal function in some very badly dilated upper urinary tracts. Conversely, we are not discouraged from proceeding with definitive repair even in the face of very-low creatinine clearance values, because great improvement has been observed postoperatively in some. In normal infants renal functional capacity increases in a curve which levels off at about a year of age. It is our impression, at present, that greatest improvement in renal function has been observed in those infants presenting in the first few months of life, whereas certain of the children over a year of age when first seen have not achieved so great an increase in renal function if borderline before surgery. Possibly those with early definitive repair have great eventual functional capacity if their obstructive uropathy is repaired while the kidney is still maturing. No child in this series has had decreasing urinary function following corrective operation.

Some children had a postobstructive diuresis immediately following surgical repair, with large urinary outputs containing up to 30 mEq of sodium per day.

They were managed with quarter-strength normal saline in five per cent dextrose and water, containing 20–30 mEq/L of sodium bicarbonate, monitoring blood and urine electrolyte values. Renal tubular acidosis was present in two children pre- and postoperatively. Both are currently returning to normal, no longer requiring supplementary oral bicarbonate. They are currently able to handle in satisfactory manner an acid stress load with ammonium chloride.

DISCUSSION

Our experience with direct repair of badly decompensated urinary tracts in small children has led us to the conviction that this is entirely feasible and that preliminary long-term drainage by one method or another is not necessary. Although there have been numerous reports on various techniques of temporarily diverting the urinary tract in these children, often with dramatic initial improvement, there is a paucity of literature describing their subsequent total rehabilitation to the point where renal function is stable or improving, the child has a sterile urinary tract, and voids in a normal fashion. In our experience these children can with an early, aggressive, staged approach reach a very satisfactory state of life in a relatively short time. In contrast to a long-term preliminary drainage, we think that short-term drainage for a few days has great merit to correct acidosis, put infection under control, and prepare for operation. These babies tolerate very prolonged major surgery if it is done skillfully. Several points cannot be overemphasized. This is extremely demanding surgery technically. Compared with correction of many of the other difficult problems in the urinary tract, the chest, etc., I believe that this ranks among the most difficult. Tissues must be handled gently, technique must be very precise, anatomy must be made as close to normal as possible, suture material must be appropriately small, etc. These are long operations, often lasting three hours or more. Surgery of this magnitude requires expert anesthesia, thorough familiarity with fluid and electrolyte management in babies, close collaboration with physicians well versed in the optimal antibiotic management for various organisms, etc. We have been fortunate to have medical colleagues expert in these areas, without whom success would have been impossible in several of these children. This surgery should not be attempted by those not thoroughly accustomed to operating on small infants. For the surgeon not prepared to undertake a totally reconstructive operation, I would think that the second alternative in an ill child with a badly decompensated urinary tract would be a high-loop cutaneous ureterostomy at the ureteropelvic junction through a small flank incision. This will drain the kidney without a tube and is less likely than other types of diversion to interfere with later total reconstruction. This is not a good state of affairs in which to leave a child permanently, however. These are, of course, some infants with dysgenetic kidneys or upper-tract damage so severe that they will die from renal failure despite drainage, antibiotics, etc. During the past five years in which we have treated all these children below age 2 coming under our care by early, complete reconstruction, we have not had an unreconstructable case or one who has subsequently died (except the one brain-damaged infant mentioned above). We do not wish to imply, however, that such cases do not exist.

SUMMARY

Twenty-one infants under age two years were operated upon for severe obstructive uropathy with hydronephrosis and hydroureter, with the goal of early definitive urinary tract repair. Results of this approach are sufficiently good to recommend it in most babies as being preferred to long-term preliminary drainage of the urinary tract which is practiced widely today. We believe that many children are being permanently diverted who could well have a reconstructive procedure instead. Although the results of this surgery have been extremely good, the magnitude of this undertaking should not be underestimated.

REFERENCES

1. Rickham, P. P.: Advanced lower urinary obstruction in childhood. Arch Dis Child 37:122, 1962
2. Paquin, A. J., Howard, R. S., and Gillenwater, J. Y.: Cutaneous vesicostomy: A modification of a technique. J Urol 99:270, 1968
3. Scott, E. V. Z., and Crowe, A. D.: Vesicocutaneous conduit: A method of permanent vesicle urinary diversion. J Urol 100:24, 1968
4. Johnston, J. H.: Temporary cutaneous ureterostomy in the management of advanced congenital urinary obstruction. Arch Dis Child 38:161, 1963
5. Eckstein, H. B.: Cutaneous ureterostomy. Proc Roy Soc Med 56:749, 1963
6. Wasserman, D. H., and Garrett, R. A.: Cutaneous ureterostomy; indications in children. J Urol 94:380, 1965
7. Williams, D. I., and Rabinovitch, H. H.: Cutaneous ureterostomy for the grossly dilated ureter of childhood. Br J Urol 39:696, 1967
8. Perlmutter, A. D., and Tank, E. S.: Loop cutaneous ureterostomy in infancy. J Urol 99:559, 1968
9. Fein, R. L., Young, J. G., and Van-Buskirk, K. E.: The case for loop ureterostomy in the infant with advanced lower urinary tract obstruction. J Urol 101:513, 1969
10. Hendren, W. H.: Operative repair of megaureter in children. J Urol 101:491, 1969
11. Hendren, W. H.: Functional restoration of decompensated ureters in children. Am J Surg 119:477, 1970

Commentary: Surgery of Megaureter

W. Hardy Hendren

In the 10 years since publication of the preceding article, I have become all the more convinced that early repair gives the best results in infants with severe uropathy. This is true not only in those infants with megaureter, but also in infants with other types of uropathies, such as ureteropelvic junction obstruction, massive vesicoureteral reflux, and ureterocele. Some of my views have changed, however, on certain technical aspects in managing these children. In this commentary, I will describe some of these changes. Also, I will provide a long-term follow-up study of the four infants described in the article. Finally, recent experiences reported by other surgeons will be discussed.

Twenty years ago the surgical correction of megaureter was in its infancy.[1-7] Today, it is a well-established procedure done in most centers with generally satisfactory results.[8-20] There is now general agreement that megaureter as an isolated problem in the urinary tract should be corrected. Two principal types occur, as shown in Figure 10. In megaureter with an obstructed terminal segment, it is resected, together with shortening, tapering, and reimplantation of the ureter. In megaureter with massive reflux, an identical procedure is performed, except that there is no obstructed terminal segment of ureter to be resected. My experience to date is summarized in Figure 11.

Considerable controversy exists on male infants with megaureters and urethral valves. Various authors advocate different aproaches.[21-25] They include destroying the urethral valves without any reconstructive procedure, (particularly in patients with massive reflux), performing some type of temporary urinary diversion, such as high ureterostomy, and later reconstructing the lower tract, and resecting valves and proceeding with early total reconstruction in selected patients. It

MEGAURETER

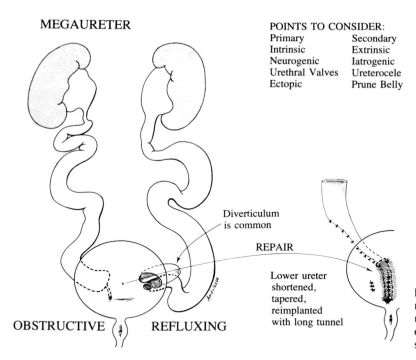

Diverticulum
is common

REPAIR

Lower ureter
shortened,
tapered,
reimplanted
with long tunnel

OBSTRUCTIVE   REFLUXING

Fig. 10. Two principal anatomic types of megaureter and scheme for repair of lower ureter. Enlargement can be caused by several pathologic states, which one must consider in deciding if repair is needed.

MEGAURETER REPAIR 1960–80 (March)

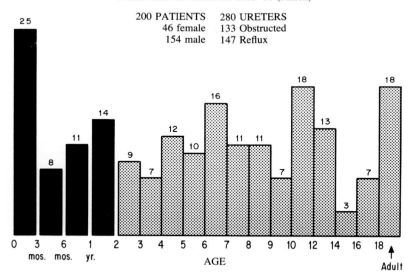

200 PATIENTS   280 URETERS
46 female   133 Obstructed
154 male   147 Reflux

Fig. 11. A 20-year experience with megaureter. Note that 58 patients were under age 2; almost half of those were under 3 months of age.

DIAGNOSIS

Cinefluorography was used in the cases discussed in the article. That technique has been replaced by multiple-spot films, which give better detail and less radiation exposure. Bladder emptying, is likely that controversy will surround management of these difficult cases for many years.

infravesical obstruction from valves, vesicoureteral reflux, and ureteral peristalsis can be recorded with multiple-spot films. Intravenous pyelography (IVP) will often fail to show anatomic detail in grossly dilated and tortuous urinary tracts. If there is vesicoureteral reflux, contrast medium used for cystography will delineate the ureters and upper tracts. If there is no reflux, however, I perform percutaneous antegrade pyelography as described by Goodwin.[26] With the patient prone, insert a small

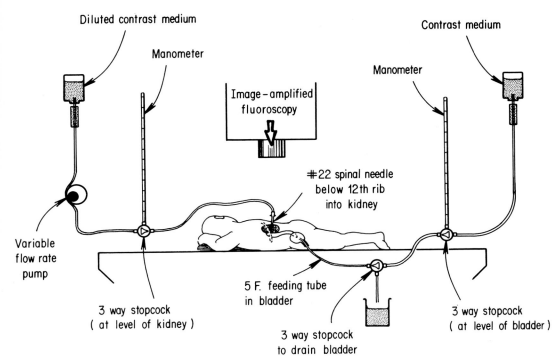

Fig. 12. Schema of antegrade pyelography and pressure perfusion.

needle beneath the 12th rib into the kidney. Infuse contrast medium to outline the renal collecting system and ureter. Constant-pressure recording during antegrade perfusion as described by Whitaker can show whether pressures are significantly higher in the kidney and ureter than in the bladder.[27] A pressure gradient of more than 10 cm of water may indicate obstruction, depending on the rate of flow. The scheme of this method is shown in Figure 12. I seldom use retrograde pyelograms to delineate these dilated ureters.

Cystography is performed by passing a small feeding catheter per urethram, filling gradually until the infant voids. If the small feeding catheter does not pass easily, contrast medium can be instilled through a small bore needle inserted suprapubically into the bladder. I have not encountered complications from percutaneous needle instillation of contrast medium into the bladder or kidneys in infants.

Procedures Valve Destruction. Formerly, the infant Mc-Carthy panendoscope was the smallest instrument available. It was too lage for many babies, however. Frequently, perineal urethrostomy was needed. Today, with the advent of fiberoptic endoscopy, instruments are not only much smaller, but the view is much better. Perineal urethrostomy is rarely needed. For destroying valves in small a infant, I prefer to use a small wire electrode thorugh a no. 8 or 10 Fr. sheath. Never is an open operative attack on valves indicated today (as was previously used through the perineum) or a retropubic, symphysis-splitting approach.

Bladder Neck. In males with great hypertrophy of the bladder neck, I formerly did a YV-plasty of the bladder neck. *I no longer do this.* Some of the infants were made incontinent by the procedure. Furthermore, in many of these boys the greatly hypertrophied bladder neck will recede in time. This is not always true, however. I have treated some infants in whom the bladder neck remained partially obstructive despite removal of the urethral valves. I have seen contracture and persisting hypertrophy of the bladder neck even in some bladders that had been made dysfunctional by supravesical diversion for several years. By means of urodynamic study, including urethral profilometry, objective assessment can be obtained to determine whether the bladder neck is obstructive. If pharmacologic management does not achieve bladder emptying at normal intravesical pressures, I then endoscopically incise the bladder neck with a cutting electrode a little at a time until normal bladder emptying is obtained. Doing too much can cause incontinence or retrograde ejaculation. Some of the early patients made incontinent by a YV-plasty have been corrected with a Young–Dees procedure.[28]

Upper Ureter. A decade or more ago I operated on the upper ureter more often than I do today. Greater experience showed that after correction of a lower ureteral pathologic condition, either obstructive or refluxing, upper ureteral tortuosity and dilatation can frequently disappear. This it not always true, however. These signs can be assessed by serial IVP. Also, physicians now have the very useful method of antegrade

(Text continues on p. 478)

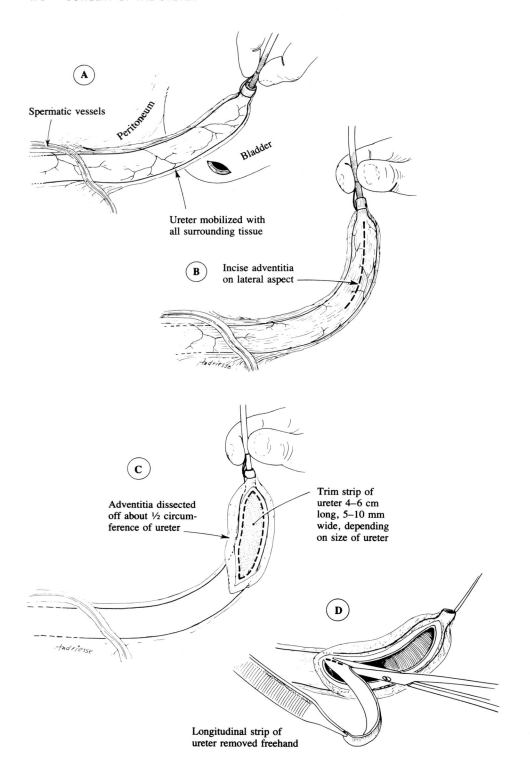

A

Spermatic vessels

Peritoneum

Bladder

Ureter mobilized with
all surrounding tissue

B Incise adventitia
on lateral aspect

C

Adventitia dissected
off about ½ circum-
ference of ureter

Trim strip of
ureter 4–6 cm
long, 5–10 mm
wide, depending
on size of ureter

D

Longitudinal strip of
ureter removed freehand

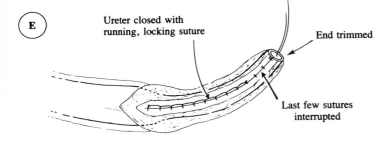

E

Ureter closed with
running, locking suture

End trimmed

Last few sutures
interrupted

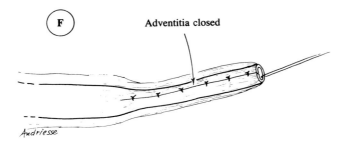

F

Adventitia closed

Andriesse

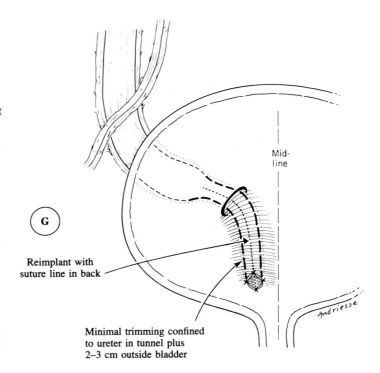

G

Mid-
line

Reimplant with
suture line in back

Minimal trimming confined
to ureter in tunnel plus
2–3 cm outside bladder

Andriesse

Fig. 13. Minimal tapering of a ureter that is not very large or tortuous by excision of strip of ureteral wall. (A) Mobilize ureter intravesically and extravesically, preserving all periureteral adventitia with it for blood supply. (B) Incise adventitia to expose segment to be removed. (C) Mark with skin pencil the segment to be excised while the ureter is distended with saline. (D) Excise lateral strip by free hand technique, using straight, sharp scissors. Megaureter clamps can facilitate trimming an especially big ureter. (E) Close ureteral wall, taking care not to narrow its lumen. (F) Close the adventitia over it. Preservation of that adventitia helps protect against ischemia of the distal ureter and also gives added protection against leakage. (G) Minimal trimming is required in a minimal case. In very wide ureters carry the trimming to the level of the common iliac vessels.

pyelography with pressure perfusion studies. Some authors seldom, if ever, revise the upper ureter. I believe that a large renal pelvis or tortuous ureteropelvic junction is best revised in some patients.

Formerly I occasionally operated first on the upper ureter. These were usually patients in whom I felt there was a reason to perform nephrostomy—either to relieve obstruction or to provide temporary drainage for the purpose of assessing function. *I never operate first on the upper ureter today*; doing so can cause relative ischemia of the lower ureter, which in turn may cause ischemic fibrosis when the lower ureter is tapered. Although animal experiments show that collateral circulation of the ureter is soon re-established after its transection, there seems little doubt that every effort should be made in clinical practice to maintain maximum blood supply of the ureter when it is being tapered and reimplanted.[29] Furthermore, in recent years there is no longer the need for open nephrostomy drainage. If obstruction requires temporary drainage, insert a small Silastic catheter percutaneously, directly into the kidney, through a small trocar. Also, modern radionuclide scanning has improved assessment of renal function, and it helps the physician to decide whether or not a renal unit is worth saving.

Lower End of Megaureter. The technical details of megaureter repair have changed slightly in recent years. As before, mobilize the ureter, first intravesically and then extravesically. Divide the lateral umbilical ligament. This facilitates forward retraction of the perineum to expose the lower ureter. As the ureter is mobilized, preserve its periureteral adventitia to spare all possible collateral blood supply. If the lower ureter is tortuous, straighten it appropriately. In most cases, the length to be sacrificed is short. In some cases, however, especially in the prune-belly syndrome, a great length of redundant ureter may be best resected. In any event, the remaining lower ureter is not tapered radically. I generally taper no higher than the level at which the ureter crosses the common iliac vessels. To go much higher risks loss of blood supply. This gives a more normal caliber to the segment of ureter that will be implanted into its tunnel in the bladder as well as several centimeters extravesically. The ratio of tunnel length to ureter diameter, as in any reimplantation, should be about 5:1 to avoid reflux. Megaureter clamps can be used, but, as shown in Figure 13, tapering can also be performed freehand.

Incise the periureteral adventitia along the lateral aspect of the ureter, and lay it back to expose the segment of wall to be narrowed. Blot dry the ureteral wall with surgical gauze.

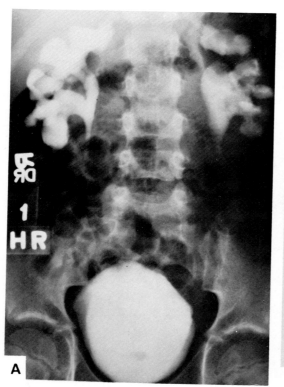

Fig. 14. Long-term follow-up of infant shown in Fig. 6. Patient was first seen as a uremic and acidotic male aged 3 months with urethral valves and massive bilateral reflux. (*A*) IVP at age 9. (*B*) The patient aged 8. Height and weight were both above the 50th percentile at that time. BUN, 16 mg/dl; creatinine, 0.6 mg/dl; CO_2, 26 meq/liter; creatinine clearance, 69 liters absolute, i.e., about 70% of predicted normal for age. The patient is now 11½ years of age and is healthy.

Mark out the segment to be excised with a skin pencil, and remove it with very sharp, straight scissors. Close the ureter with a running, interlocking suture of fine chromic catgut. Interrupt the lower part of the suture line; in that way, the tip can be excised without cutting a running suture if there is excess length. Then close the periureteral adventitia over the suture line for extra protection against leakage.

The most important aspects for success in megaureter repair include carefully maintaining blood supply of the ureter by not skeletonizing it during mobilization, selecting the hiatus in the proper position in the back wall of the bladder, not the side wall or dome of the bladder where it will angulate when the bladder fills, tapering the ureter to an adequate caliber but not making it too narow and obstructed, avoiding radical tapering, which can result in ischemic necrosis of the distal ureter, and obtaining a 5:1 ratio of tunnel length to ureter diameter.

Upper Ureter. The decision whether to operate on the renal pelvis, ureteropelvic junction, and the upper ureter can be made by assessing subsequent IVPs or by antegrade pyelography. Repair should be considered if the renal pelvis remains large, the ureteropelvic junction remains tortuous and appears partially obstructed, or the upper ureter remains wide and empties poorly. If a procedure is done on the upper tract, it is much more individualized than is the lower repair. In some, it consists of only segmental resection of the ureteropelvic junction. In others, the size of the renal pelvis is reduced. In some, the upper ureter is tapered. In any event, just as in a lower repair, preservation of blood supply is vital. I mobilize only that which is to be removed and preserve all periureteral tissue possible. Clamps are not used in tapering an upper ureter. Instead, it is done freehand similar to the method shown in Figure 13.

LONG-TERM FOLLOW-UP STUDY

Figures 14 to 17 show long-term follow-up studies of the four infants presented in detail in the preceding article. I have repeatedly observed the greatest gains in renal function in those

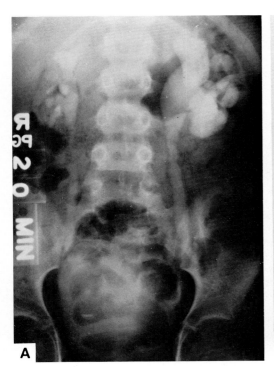
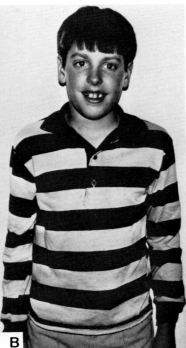

Fig. 15. Long-term follow-up of patient shown in Fig. 7. He was seen when aged 3 weeks, uremic and acidotic from urethral valves, with massive reflux and hydronephrosis. Total lower tract reconstruction was performed 11 days later. (A) IVP at age 8 years. Its appearance has changed very little since examination at age 10 months, showing a relatively small right kidney, but it functions. (B) The patient aged 10½ years. Height and weight are at 50th percentile, BUN, 29 mg/dl; creatinine, 1.2 mg/dl; creatinine clearance, 60 liters/m² of body surface area. The patient had stress urinary incontinence from Y-V plasty to the bladder neck during infancy. Operation to narrow the bladdeer neck at age 10 corrected this problem. The patient is now aged 11½ and in good health.

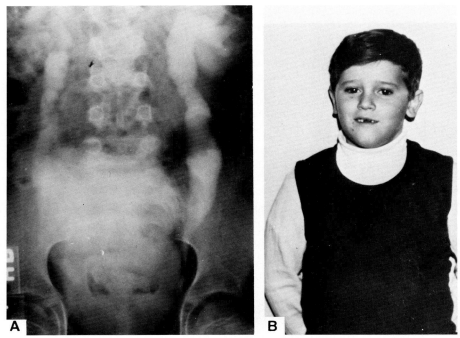

Fig. 16. Long-term follow-up of patient with prune-belly syndrome shown in Fig. 8. This patient underwent total lower tract reconstruction at age 8 weeks. (*A*) IVP at age 9 years. Note large bladder, often seen in prune-belly syndrome. (His upper tracts are less dilated on postvoiding films.) The patient has no reflux. BUN, 25 mg/dl; creatinine, 1 mg/dl; CO^2, 18 meq/liter. (*B*) The patient is now aged 12 and is in good general health. He is at the 60th percentile for height and the 90th percentile for weight for his age.

children whose defects were discovered and corrected early. This is especially significant when one considers that it is the worst cases that present clinically at an early age. Renal function in normal infants at birth starts at relatively low levels and matures gradually to adult values of creatinine clearance per square meter of body surface area by about 1 year.[30] I believe that correcting severe obstructive uropathy during the first year, when renal function should be increasing even in healthy babies, gives greater overall gains for an infant who is relieved of obstructive uropathy. The ultimate function attained is less in those whose operative corrections are done at an older age.

DISCUSSION

Several recent reports have confirmed the feasibility of performing early definitive correction of obstructive uropathy with megaureter. Boehncke and colleagues recently reported a most important series of patients operated on from 1954 to 1974 by Dr. Peter Bischoff at the Elisabeth Children's Hospital in Hamburg, Germany: 101 children with bilateral anomalies operated on by an early and aggressive approach that included tapering of ureters and correction of obstruction or reflux.[31]

Professor Bischoff long believed that early and aggressive reconstruction was preferable to preliminary diversion. Retrospective review by his colleagues of his work supports his long-held views.

Bjordal and colleagues reported on 50 children with 66 megaureters treated by complete surgical reconstruction and reimplantation.[32] They concluded that early reconstruction forms a ureter that is not wide, elongated, or tortuous and is thus better able to transport urine. These authors, who treat nearly all the children with obstructive uropathy in Norway, had previously treated similar patients in their clinic with preliminary long-term drainage. They concluded that direct repair of megaureter was not only feasible but gave better results and that there was less morbidity than in patients treated by other means.

Recently, Parrott and Woodard have described their experience with the correction of obstructive uropathy in the neonate.[33] They concluded that early definitive reconstructive surgery offers the best chance of a good result.

Megaureter in the prune-belly syndrome offers a special challenge. These ureters are often extensively convoluted. Also, the kidneys are often abnormal. Woodard and Parrott described their experience with early definitive reconstruction

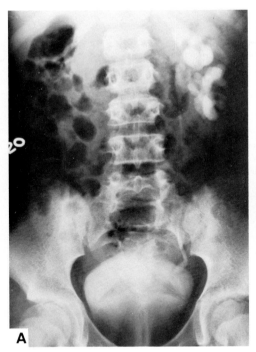

Fig. 17. Long-term follow-up of patient shown in Fig. 9. This girl was seen at age 4 months with a hydronephrotic solitary left kidney, caused by obstructive megaureter. She underwent immediate correction of the lower megaureter; repair of upper ureter occurred 10 months later. (*A*) IVP at age 11 years. Note entirely normal ureter. (*B*) The patient at age 11. She is now 16 and is entirely well. Height and weight are both at the 50th percentile for her age. BUN, 15 mg/dl; creatinine, 0.7 mg/dl; creatinine clearance, 105 liters/m² of body surface area.

in ten patients and concluded that this is the best treatment.[34] On the other hand, Randolph reported an excellent experience in high temporary diversion of these patients, followed by an aggressive total reconstruction at a later age.[35] Rabinowitz and colleagues reported an experience with 25 patients; although some had preliminary diversion and later reconstruction, they concluded that it is best not to jeopardize subsequent surgery by any type of diversion.[36] They noted that often the proximal ureter is functionally and histologically better than the lower ureter.

The current role of temporary ureterostomy deserves comment. Its use in the management of advanced congenital urinary obstruction was reported by Johnston many years ago; however, Johnston has done none of these high diversions in recent years.[37]* To be sure, high cutaneous diversion has a place in the urologic armamentarium, but it has been overused. Various techniques for its performance have been described, including high loop ureterostomy, pyelostomy, ring ureterostomy, and roux-en-Y ureterostomy.[38–40] I have reconstructed 36 young patients who had undergone cutaneous ureterostomies

* Johnston JH: Personal communication.

elsewhere and were referred for a definitive reconstruction.[41] Many were very hard to repair after previous diversion of the urine. I agree with Dwoskin that if temporary diversion is elected, it should be high, and that later reconstruction is usually best done in an single stage that includes closure of the previous cutaneous diversion.[42]

Recently, Johnston reviewed his experience in 66 boys with posterior urethral valves with regard to the management of vesicoureteric reflux.[25] He concluded that reflux that persisted on a long-term basis despite valve ablation was usually associated with a functionless kidney and that it would be pointless to tailor and reimplant the ureter. On the other hand, I see many patients who now have good renal function and whose massively dilated and refluxing ureters were repaired relatively early. In some of them, reflux might have subsided had it been observed sufficiently long; however, as Johnston himself pointed out, reflux that continues after valve ablation may continue to damage the kidney. I have not been willing to risk that in the more severe cases. In lesser degrees of reflux in boys who valves have been removed, I watch the patient while he receives microbial therapy, knowing that reflux will subside in some. If the ureters are massively dilated, or the upper tracts badly damaged, I have been unwilling to permit it to continue. Massive reflux in patients without urethral valves takes its toll of upper tract function, even when the urinary tract is sterile. It is likely that the same holds true for post-valve-ablation patients.

Johnston has noted fewer good results of megaureter repair in refluxing units than in those which are orignally obstructed. I have not, in my own series of megaureters, which are divided almost evenly between refluxing and obstructed units (Figs. 10 and 11), observed any profound difference in the results in the two groups. On the other hand, there are indeed patients in whom, at the outset, massive reflux will be seen with a functionless shell of kidney, whereas the opposite nonrefluxing side has good function. Renal scan or short-term temporary percutaneous nephrostomy can help sort out those patients in whom nephroureterectomy is indicated rather than megaureter repair. I cannot subscribe to a nihilistic, ''do-nothing'' approach to a megaureter with massive reflux and a potentially salvageable kidney. ''Conservative treatment,'' in my view, is that which preserves and conserves function. Often conservative treatment in that light is an operation!

· · ·

The pendulum sometimes swings widely on current surgical management of various conditions. This applies to the surgery of megaureter. In megaureter without other problems, most surgeons today feel that repair is indicated. The main controversy involves infants, especially boys with urethral valves. It is my belief that accurate destruction of the valves should always be done first. In some patients that is all that will be needed; reflux will disappear in many. I am content to let it do so if the child has good upper tracts, good renal function, and no infection and if the anatomy looks fairly normal endoscopically. In those patients with massive reflux and gopher-hole ureters or with demonstrable ureterovesical obstruction, I continue to favor an early reconstructive operation. Although that is a difficult undertaking, I and others have had excellent results from that course of management.[31-33]

REFERENCES

1. Carlson HE: The intrapsoas transplant of megalo-ureter. J Urol 72:172, 1954
2. Swenson O, Fisher JH, Cendron J: Megaloureter, investigation as to the cause and report on the results of new forms of treatment. Surgery 40:223, 1956
3. Stephens FD: Treatment of megaureters by multiple micturition. Aust NZ J Surg 27:130, 1957
4. Bischoff P: Megaureter. Br J Urol 29:416, 1957
5. Wrenn EL Jr: Proposed operation for megaloureter. Surgery 54:950, 1963
6. Hirschhorn RC: The ileal sleeve. I. First case report with clinical evaluation. J Urol 92:113, 1964
7. Bergman H: The Ureter. New York, Harper & Row, 1967
8. Paquin AJ Jr: Considerations for the management of some complex problems for ureterovesical anastomosis. Surg Gynecol Obstet 118:75, 1964
9. Johnston JH: Reconstructive surgery of megaureter in childhood. Br J Urol 39:17, 1967
10. Hendren WH: Ureteral reimplantation in children. J Pediatr Surg 3:649, 1968
11. Flatmark AU, Maurseth K, Knutrud O: Lower ureteric obstruction in children. Br J Urol 42:434, 1970
12. Williams DI, Hulme–Moor I: Primary obstructive megaureter. Br J Urol 42:140, 1970
13. Tanagho EA: Ureteral tailoring. J Urol 106:194, 1971
14. McLaughlin AP, Leadbetter WF, Pfister RC: Reconstructive surgery of primary megaloureter. J Urol 106:186, 1971
15. Pitts WR Jr, Muecke EC: Congenital megaureter. A review of 80 patients. J Urol 111:468, 1974
16. Hendren WH: Complications of megaureter repair in children. J Urol 113:238, 1975
17. Hanna MK, Jeffs RD: Primary obstructive megaureter in children. Urology 6:419, 1975
18. Pfister RC, Hendren WH: Primary megaureter in children and adults. Urology 12:160, 1978
19. Retik AB, McEvoy JP, Bauer SB: Megaureters in children. Urology 11:231, 1978
20. Hendren WH: Megaureter. In Harrison JH, Gittes RF, Perlmutter AD, et al (eds): Campbell's Urology, p 1697. Philadelphia, W B Saunders, 1979
21. Hendren WH: Posterior urethral valves in boys: A broad clinical spectrum. J Urol 106:298, 1971

22. Perlmutter AD: Temporary urinary diversion in the management of the chronically dilated urinary tract in childhood. In Johnston JH, Goodwin WE (eds): Reviews of Paediatric Surgery. Princeton, Excerpta Medica, 1974
23. Duckett JW Jr: Current management of posterior urethral valves. Urol Clin North Am 1:471, 1974
24. Williams DI: Urethral valves: A hundred cases with hydronephrosis. In Bergsma D, Duckett JW (eds): Urinary System Malformations in Children, p 55. New York, Alan R. Liss, 1977
25. Johnston JH: Vesicoureteric reflux with urethral valves. Br J Urol 51:100, 1978
26. Goodwin WE, Casey WC, Woolf W: Percutaneous trocar (needle) nephrostomy in hydronephrosis. JAMA 157:891, 1955
27. Whitaker RH: The ureter in posterior urethral valves. Br J Urol 45:395, 1973
28. Dees JE: Congenital epispadias with incontinence. J Urol 62:513, 1949
29. Saidi F, Osmond JD, Hendren WH: Microangiographic study in experimentally produced megaureter in rabbits. J Pediatr Surg 8:117, 1973
30. McCrory WW, Shibuya M, Leumann E, Karp R: Studies of renal function in children with chronic hydronephrosis. Pediatr Clin North Am 18:445, 1971
31. Boehncke H, Lassrich MA, Clemens P: 20 Jahre Urologie in einem Kinderkrankenhous (1954 bis 1974). Urologe A 18:260, 1979

32. Bjordal R, Eek S, Knutrud O: Early reconstruction of wide ureter in children. Urology 11:326, 1978
33. Parrott TS, Woodard JR: Obstructive uropathy in the neonate: The case for early definitive correction. J Urol 116:508, 1976
34. Woodard JR, Parrott TS: Reconstruction of the urinary tract in prune-belly uropathy. J Urol 119:824, 1978
35. Randolph JG: Total surgical reconstruction for patients with abdominal muscular deficiency (''prune-belly'') syndrome. J Pediatr Surg 12:1033, 1977
36. Rabinowitz R, Barkin M, Schillinger JF, Jeffs RD: Urinary reconstruction in prune belly syndrome. Urology 12:333, 1978
37. Johnston JH: Temporary cutaneous ureterostomy in the management of advanced congenital urinary obstruction. Arch Dis Child 38:161, 1963
38. Perlmutter AD, Tank ES: Loop cutaneous ureterostomy in infancy. J Urol 99:559, 1968

39. Williams DI, Cromie WJ: Ring ureterostomy. Br J Urol 47:789, 1975

40. Sober I: Pelvioureterostomy-en-Y. J Urol 107:473, 1972

41. Hendren WH: Complications of ureterostomy. J Urol 120:269, 1978

42. Dwoskin JY: Management of the massively dilated urinary tract in infants by temporary diversion and single-stage reconstruction. Urol Clin North Am 1:515, 1974

ANNOTATED BIBLIOGRAPHY

Pitts WR Jr, Muecke EC: Congenital megaureter. A review of 80 patients. J Urol 111:468, 1974

In this large experience of dilated ureters in 526 patients at the New York Hospital, 80 patients with 113 true congenital megaureters are reported. Almost 40% of the patients received no therapy. When therapy was required, reimplantation of the tailored ureter into the bladder was the treatment of choice. The results of surgical intervention yielded an overall success rate of 90%.

Hanna MK, Jeffs RD: Primary obstructive megaureter in children. Urology 6:419, 1975

The experience with obstructive megaureter from the Hospital for Sick Children in Toronto stresses that treatment must be planned according to the status of renal and ureteral functions. In selected patients a short period of nephrostomy drainage before remodeling of the lower ureter was useful. The authors stress that the best result in this series resulted from surgical excision of the obstructed segment, reduction of ureteral caliber when indicated, and reimplantation. In addition, they suggest that conservative treatment of children with relatively few symptoms and slight ureteral dilatation is frequently worthwhile.

Retik AB, McEvoy JP, Bauer SB: Megaureters in children. Urology 11:231, 1978

The authors' experience with 40 children undergoing ureteral tailoring and reimplantation at the Children's Hospital, Boston, is reported, emphasizing what excellent results can be expected in cases with normal bladders in contrast with those with very abnormal bladders. They stress that no child in this series required upper ureteral tailoring.

Boehncke H, Lassrich MA, Clemens P: 20 Jahre urologie in inem Kinderkrankenhous (1954 bis 1974). Urologe A 18:260, 1979

A review of Dr. Bischoff's cases of early total reconstruction in cases of megaureter from 1954 to 1974 is presented. This review emphasizes the desirability of that approach and the superior results attained by it as compared to temporizing and to preliminary diversion.

Bjordal R, Eek S, Knutrud O: Early reconstruction of wide ureter in children. Urology 11:326, 1978

This report concerns a large experience of 50 children with 66 megaureters who underwent early complete surgical reconstruction and reimplantation of the ureter, representing most such patients in Norway, from August 1970 to June 1974. The authors have prior experience treating such patients with temporary diversion and concluded that early reconstruction without diversion is preferred.

Williams DI, Hulme–Moir I: Primary obstructive mega-ureter. Br J Urol 42:140, 1970

The experience with megaureter from the Hospital for Sick Children, London, is reported. The authors' experience with 70 patients with obstructive ureter indicated that subgroups of patients exist, with little tendency to progress and with mild or negligible symptoms. This group of patients can be treated well with conservative management. However, the majority of patients require a reflux-preventing reimplantation if active ureteric function remains and only moderate dilatation is present. Excellent results are obtained in this group of patients. However, in those patients with grossly dilated unilateral ureters, the authors consider nephroureterectomy the best method of treatment. In patients with bilateral grossly dilated ureters, the outcome in unsatisfactory.

Randolph JG: Total surgical reconstruction for patients with abdominal muscular deficiency ("prune-belly") syndrome. J Pediatr Surg 12:1033, 1977

The author reports gratifying results in six of seven children treated by high diversion and later extensive reconstruction, including ureteral shortening, tapering and reimplantation, reduction cystoplasty, bilateral orchidopexy, and partial abdominal wall excision.

Overview: Urethral Valves

J.H. Johnston

I agree with Dr. Hendren on the need to tackle the essential pathologic condition when dealing with congenital urinary obstruction in infancy and to avoid preliminary, temporizing, diversionary operations as far as possible. However, perhaps we differ on the extent of the surgical procedures necessary to achieve the desired aim.

In babies with urethral valves, I commonly find that the child is dehydrated, acidemic, and infected. While these aspects are being corrected and controlled by IV and antimicrobial therapy, the bladder, if tensely distended, is drained by a small polyethylene catheter or feeding tube passed per urethram. Rarely should surgical relief of the obstruction be delayed for

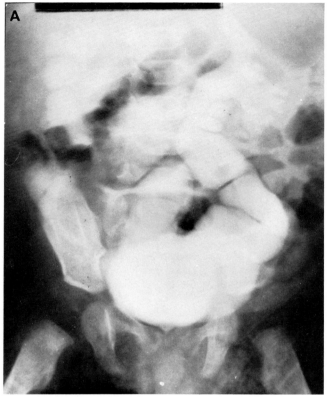

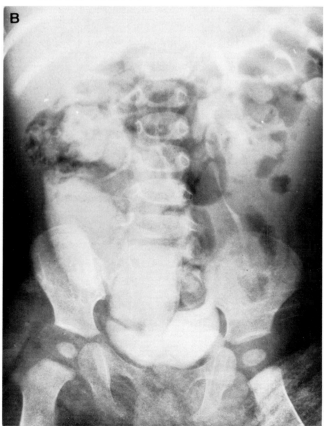

Fig. 18. Boy with urethral valves and obstruction in right intramural ureter. (*A*) IVP at 10 weeks of age, before valve fulguration. Note severe bilateral hydroure-teronephrosis. (*B*) IVP 6 months after valve fulguration. Left side is improved; there is still gross dilatation on right. Right ureter was tailored and reimplanted follow-ing excision of obstructing fibrotic segment. (*C*) IVP shows improved appearance 9 months after right ure-teric reimplantation.

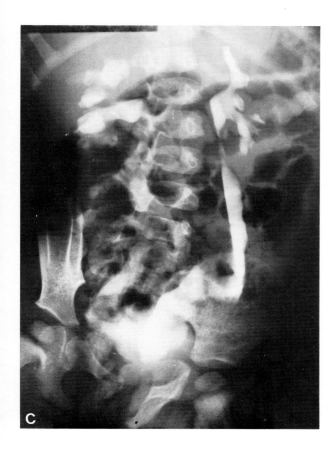

more than a day or two. The valves are destroyed by endoscopic diathermy fulguration. For this purpose, I find the Storz resectoscope more easily controllable than an electrode inserted through a cystoscope. The valves are coagulated in their entirety, including the lowlying anterior commisure. I agree that the bladder neck must not be resected at the time of valve fulguration, since this increases the likelihood of subsequent incomplete urinary control. However, I have had some patients in whom dysuria and incomplete bladder emptying recurred later, in 1 boy 4 years later, due to obstruction by the thickened bladder neck. In such patients, simple endoscopic incision of the hypertrophied tissue in the 6 o-clock position is all that is needed.

After valve destruction the bladder generally empties completely during voiding, but stasis may persist in the dilated, decompensated ureters. This, with complicating infection, may lead to the patient's failing to improve or even to deteriorate clinically and biochemically. In such circumstances one might employ temporary loop cutaneous ureterostomies. This was formerly my practice, but the procedure has not proved to be necessary for many years, mainly, I believe, because of better medical management of affected babies. Physicians now have improved methods of assessing and controlling acid–base disturbances and are aware of the need to compensate for water and salt losses and to avoid a diet consisting of high-protein cow's milk formula. Since the importance of these aspects of treatment has been recognized, the need for temporary ureterostomies has been eliminated.

I have had some experience of Dr. Hendren's recommended procedure of complete reconstruction of the urinary tract after valve fulguration, and undoubtedly the method can give satisfactory results. However, I think it is rarely necessary. Although the ureters in valve cases are generally dilated, they are rarely themselves obstructed, and upper tract improvement, often striking, occurs spontaneously with time simply by relieving the urethral obstruction.[1] Infrequently, however, an obstruction does exist in the intramural ureter. In such instances the upper tract shows no improvement on urography after valve destruction, and the existence of an obstructing lesion can be confirmed by isotope methods under diuresis or by Whitaker's perfusion–pressure studies.[2] Resection of the obstructing portion of ureter followed by limited ureteric tailoring and reimplantation to the bladder are then needed (Fig. 18). Histologically, the musculature of the intramural ureter in such patients is replaced by fibrous tissue, possibly because of its compression and partial devascularization by the hypertrophied detrusor. There is no actual stricture in the sense of severe lumenal narrowing, and presumably the fibrotic segment obstructs by producing a block in the peristaltic continuity.

In my experience, and also in that of Williams, the existence of bilateral reflux in valve cases at the time of presentation carries a graver prognosis than when there is no or only unilateral reflux. Clearly, although urethral obstruction alone can cause severe upper tract and kidney damage, the additional existence of reflux makes the situation worse. However, when the related kidney shows useful function, reflux stops spontaneously after valve fulguration, although it can take some months to do so. Persistent unilateral reflux virtually always means that that kidney is functionless, and in many patients it is seen histologically to be completely dysplastic. The operative cure of reflux in valve cases is therefore either unnecessary or pointless. Whether, after valve destruction, uninfected reflux does harm before its spontaneous cessation is unknown. Dr. Hendren states that it "takes its toll of upper tract function," but neither he, nor, to my knowledge, anyone else, has any proof of this. Massively dilated refluxing ureters are, in my experience, poor surgical material, since their peristaltic function is generally severely impaired, and it is not too difficult, in curing the reflux, to end up with an obstructed system. I would therefore prefer to avoid surgery in such patients and give the reflux a lengthy chance to cure itself.

REFERENCES

1. Johnston JH, Kulatilake AE: The sequelae of posterior urethral valves. Br J Urol 43:743, 1971
2. Whitaker RH: The ureter in posterior urethral valves. Br J Urol 45:395, 1973
3. Johnston JH: Vesicoureteric reflux with urethral valves. Br J Urol 51:100, 1979

4. Williams DI: Urethral valves: A hundred cases with hydronephrosis. In Bergsma D, Duckett JW (eds): Urinary System Malformation in Children, p 55. New York, Alan R. Lass, 1977

36

OMENTAL SLEEVE TO PREVENT RECURRENT RETROPERITONEAL FIBROSIS AROUND THE URETER

G. C. Tresidder, J. P. Blandy and M. Singh

The London Hospital, London

Urol. int. 27:144–148 (1972)

ABSTRACT—(1) After ureterolysis for retroperitoneal fibrosis we recommend wrapping the ureter up in a sheath of great omentum. (2) This technique prevented the return of fibrosis around the ureter in 11 of 12 ureters: in the 12th the fibrous tissue recurred just where the omentum had not been made to cover the ureter.

KEY WORDS
Fibrosis, retroperitoneal
Retroperitoneal fibrosis
Hydronephrosis
Ureter
Omentum
Uropathy, obstructive

Much has been written about idiopathic retroperitoneal fibrosis since ORMOND first described the condition in 1948, but one of the still unsolved problems of the disease remains how to stop it from recurring after ureterolysis. In the past, the usual advice had been to give steroids, or put the ureters into the peritoneal cavity [Hewitt *et al.*, 1969] but our own experience with 4 ureters that were placed in the peritoneal cavity has been

disappointing, and it appears from the literature that rather few cases have been followed up for sufficient time for this or any other method to be recommended with confidence.

Seven years ago, one of us (G.C.T.) was confronted by the development of recurrent obstruction to the ureter in the side opposite to that upon which ureterolysis had been followed by placement of the ureter in the peritoneal cavity, and despite this precaution, the ureter had become obstructed. On this occasion it seemed possible that one might be able to prevent the return of the fibrous tissue

Authors' address: Prof. J. P. BLANDY, The London Hospital, Whitechapel, London, E. I. (England)

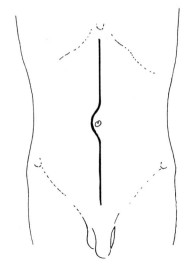

Fig. 1. Incision used for bilateral ureterolysis and omental investment.

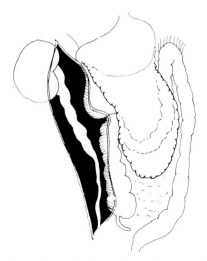

Fig. 3. The whole of the right ureter is exposed.

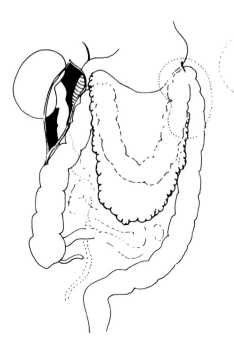

Fig. 2. The right ureter is exposed by mobilising the ascending colon medially, and displacing the duodenum by Kocher's manœuvre.

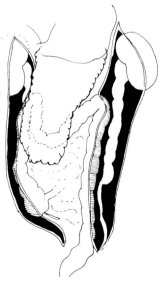

Fig. 4. The left ureter is similarly exposed by displacing the descending colon medially with the splenic flexure.

METHOD

The operative technique is simple. A long midline or paramedian incision is made (Fig. 1). The ureters are exposed by mobilising the colon medially (Figs. 2–4). In performing the ureterolysis it is best to expose the dilated upper part of the ureter first, and trace it down to the plaque of retroperitoneal fibrosis. Then the lower end is found, and traced upwards, and finally the ureter is delivered with great care from the plaque itself. In

by wrapping the ureter in great omentum. This was done, and the patient showed no evidence of recurrent obstruction to the second ureter for a period of 7 years. Since that time, we have used this technique to treat a total of 12 ureters in 7 patients.

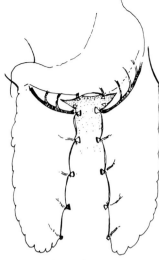

Fig. 5. After separating the omentum from the transverse colon it is divided in the midline, and the gastro-epiploic vessels are divided between ligatures, forming 2 omental pedicles.

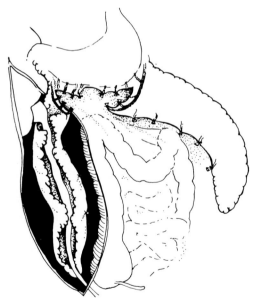

Fig. 6. Each pedicle of omentum is brought lateral to the colon and used to invest the ureter from end to end. The omentum is secured with fine catgut sutures.

dissecting the ureter out of the plaque of fibrous tissue one must take particular care not to injure the aorta or the vena cava, since these are usually hidden behind the dense white fibrous tissue.

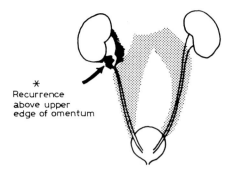

*
Recurrence
above upper
edge of omentum

Fig. 7. Summary of results.

Retroperitoneal Fibrosis, The London Hospital

Treatment	Patients	Ureters	Recurrence
Not operated	2	4	—
Peritonealisation	3	4	4
Omental sleeve	7	12	1*

* Recurrence above upper edge of omentum.

The omentum is then separated from the transverse colon and then divided in the midline. The gastro-epiploic arch is divided into 2, and separated from the greater curvature of the stomach by division of the small vessels between ligatures (Fig. 5). In this way 2 long flaps of omentum are made available, each with its vascular pedicle based on the gastroepiploic arch.

Each pedicle is then brought lateral to the colon on either side, and carefully wrapped round the ureter from top to bottom, and held there with a few sutures of 4–0 plain catgut. The colon is then replaced on either side, and the wound closed in the usual way without drainage. Tension sutures are a wise precaution.

RESULTS

12 ureters have been so treated in 7 patients. The period of follow-up has now extended for from 2 to 7 years. Recurrence of the fibrosis took place in 1 patient, and was limited to a short length of ureter that had not been included in the investment of omentum. The remainder of the ureter was found, at re-operation, to be normal and free from fibrosis (Fig. 7).

These findings are in contrast to our previous experience with 4 ureters operated on in 3 patients: recurrent obstruction by fibrosis took place in every instance, given sufficient time.

DISCUSSION

We freely admit that our experience with 7 patients and only 12 ureters treated by this method is too small a series upon which to base any firm conclusions. Nevertheless, we are encouraged to believe that this technique of omental investment does prevent recurrent fibrosis, not so much because of the 11 successful instances, but because of what we found in the 12th, unsuccessful case.

In this case retroperitoneal fibrosis recurred 1 year after the first, initially successful operation at which omentum had been used to wrap up the right ureter. On this occasion insufficient care had been taken to make sure that the omentum covered the ureter right up as high as the renal pelvis. At the second exploration, although all that part of the ureter which was ensheathed in omentum looked perfectly healthy, the proximal 2 in, and the renal pelvis, which had not been so protected, were densely encased in typical retroperitoneal fibrous tissue.

REFERENCES

ORMOND, J. K.: Bilateral ureteral obstruction due to envelopment and compression by an inflammatory retroperitoneal process. J Urol, Baltimore 59:1072–1079, 1948

ORMOND, J. K.: Idiopathic retroperitoneal fibrosis. An established clinical entity. J Am Med Ass 174:1561–1568, 1960

HEWITT, C. B.; NITZ, G. L.; KISER, W. S.; STRAFFON, R. A., and STEWART, B. H.: Surgical treatment of retroperitoneal fibrosis. Ann Surg 169:610–600, 1969

Commentary: Ureteral Obstruction Caused by Retroperitoneal Fibrosis

Bernard Levine

Ureteral obstruction due to retroperitoneal fibrosis may be a result of malignant or benign disease processes. It was first reported in 1948 by Ormond, who coined the term *retroperitoneal fibrosis*.[1] Since then, a large number of cases have been reported due to idiopathic retroperitoneal fibrosis or to periureteral metastases, primary retroperitoneal tumors, or serotonin production by a carcinoid tumor. Primary sites of metastasis are frequently the breast, prostate, lungs, and kidney. Benign causes of retroperitonel fibrosis are iatrogenic, retroperitoneal injury, hemmorhage, or trauma, spinal abscess, endometriosis, regional enteritis, ruptured diverticulitis, appendicitis, aortic or iliac aneurism, ovarian vein syndrome, urinary extravasation, and radiation therapy. In addition, methysergide ingestion, used in the treatment of migraine headaches, has been invoked as a cause. Rarely, retroperitoneal fibrosis is due to osteomyelitis or to the Weber–Christian syndrome or mesenteric panniculitis.

CLINICAL FEATURES

The clinical features found with retroperitoneal fibrosis are frequently obscure, but, in approximate decreasing order of frequency, they are pain (usually a dull lumbo-sacral backache that is exaggerated by extension and relieved by flexion, which may radiate to the lower abdomen, inguinal region, and testes), bilateral ureteral obstruction, hypertension, weight loss, gastrointestinal (GI) and urinary symptoms, anuria, lower extremity edema (including edema of the scrotum, inguinal areas, ankles, and legs late in the diseae process), and, occasionally, hydrocele. The process may involve the peritesticular tissues, resembling neoplasm of the testicles; azotemia and anemia may be present, and the erythrocyte sedimentation rate is frequently elevated. There are no pathognomonic findings, except that on very rare occasions, a palpable retroperitoneal mass may be noted over the sacral promontory.

DIAGNOSIS

The disease is usually suspected on the excretory urogram, which classically demonstrates the following triad: (1) bilateral ureteral narrowing at L–5, (2) medial deviation of the ureters, and (3) dilatation of the calices, pelvis, and ureter. Other investigations, occasionally of diagnostic significance, are occlusive tip retrograde pyelography and nonocclusive tip retrograde pyelography, which characteristically permit the ureteral catheters to pass the deviated ureters with no appreciable obstruction of the catheter, lymphangiography, inferior veno-cavography, and, more recently, sonography.[2] However, the defintive diagnosis requires surgical exploration and biopsy of the lesion. It is found in twice as many males as females.

TREATMENT

It is generally accepted that the treatment of choice for retroperitoneal fibrosis is ureterolysis to conserve renal tissue and to alleviate obstructive uropathy. Recently, in some occasions when the diagnosis of idiopathic retroperitoneal fibrosis has been established, medical therapy with corticosteroids has replaced or preceded surgical intervention. Improvement of renal function is then monitored by the radioisotope renogram. Acutely ill patients with elevated erythrocyte sedimentation rates and lymphocytosis may be prepared for surgery with steroid therapy, ureteral catheter insertion to drain the kidneys, and, rarely, dialysis, thereby allowing surgery on an elective or semielective basis.

If surgery is elective, the preferred approach is transabdominal, since the disease usually affects both ureters by envelopment or compression. However, in the acutely or seriously ill patient with renal failure, a unilateral retroperitoneal flank approach for ureterolysis with or without nephrostomy is satisfactory for immediate relief of obstruction.

TECHNIQUE

Bowel preparation is advisable. The transabdominal approach requires a midline abdominal incision from the xiphoid to the symphysis pubis. To proceed: incise the parietal peritoneum lateral to the ascending or descending colon, extending to the splenic or the hepatic flexures. The fibrosis may be localized or extend from the kidney to the bladder, which also may be involved. Carry the retroperitoneal dissection down between the duodenum and the inferior mesenteric vein. Create posterior peritoneal flaps, thus exposing both ureters. Identify the ureters in the area of the iliac vessels; dissect them from this point cephalad to the renal pelvis and caudad to the area of the juxtavesical ureter. Take care not to damage the ureteral wall or compromise its blood supply. Routinely take a biopsy of the fibrous tissue for frozen and permanent sections. Recently, I have seen a patient with a periureteral sleeve of "fibrous tissue" reported an anaplastic carcinoma. Ureterolysis is usually accomplished without significant difficulty if the correct plane is entered with blunt dissection and, when necessary, with sharp dissection. After inspecting the ureter for adequate ureteral viability and peristalsis and, perhaps, performing a Whitaker test, fix the mobilized ureter either intraperitoneally or laterally in the retroperitoneal space with several superficial sutures of 3–0 chromic gut.[3] Then reapproximate the posterior peritoneal flaps, isolating the ureter intraperitoneally from the level of the renal pelvis to the area of the ureterovesical junction. It is important to place the mobilized ureter well away from the area of fibrosis. It is generally not necessary to excise the fibrous tissue surrounding the ureter or that surrounding the aorta or the vena cava. Close the peritoneum behind the ureter. A stenting ureteral catheter may be employed during the procedure to help in dissection of the ureter; leave it *in situ* postoperatively to facilitate fixation of the ureter in its new position. Retroperitonel drainage is usually not necessary.

On occasion, it is necessary to incise and anastomose the ureter because of the extensive intrinsic involvement of a small segment of the ureteral wall by the retroperitoneal fibrotic process or because of iatrogenic damage to the ureter during dissection. In this situation, it is wise not to intraperitonealize the ureter but, rather, to place it lateral to the retroperitoneal fibrotic process. If, however, a large segment of the ureteral wall is involved by severe deep involvement of the fibrotic process, replacement of the ureter with ileal substitution, possibly leaving the fibrotic ureter *in situ*, or Boari bladder flap or autotransplantation of the kidney may be required. In recent years it has been advised that omental wrapping of the ureter be carrier out to prevent recurrence of ureteral obstruction.[4] It is extremely important to employ postsurgical surveillance to detect recurrent ureteral obstruction. Postoperative corticosteroid therapy has been employed to prevent recurrent ureteral obstruction. The success rate with ureterolysis and intraperitonealization of the ureter for benign disease is reported to be as high as 90%.

REFERENCES

1. Ormond JK: Bilateral ureteral obstruction by an inflammatory retroperitoneal process. J Urol 59:1072, 1948
2. Jacobsen JE, Redman AC: Ultrasound findings in a case of retroperitoneal fibrosis. Radiology 113:423, 1974
3. Whitaker RH: Urodynamic assessment of ureteral obstruction in Retroperitoneal fibrosis. J Urol 113:26, 1975

4. Tressider GC, Blandy JP, Singh M: Omental sleeve to prevent recurrent retroperitoneal fibrosis around the ureter. Urol Int 27:144, 1972

ANNOTATED BIBLIOGRAPHY

Koep L, Zuidena GE: The clinical significance of retroperitoneal fibrosis. Surgery 81:250, 1977

A study of 281 cases from the literature and 10 patients from the authors' experience are reviewed. They note that most of the patients are men aged 40 to 50 and that poorly localized back pain, flank, and general abdominal pain were the most frequent initial symptoms. Physical examination was usually unremarkable, and laboratory investigations were not of great assistance. Bilateral hydroureteral dilatation was noted in 67.6% of patients on the excretory urogram and was considered the most definitive test for retroperitoneal fibrosis. Unilateral hydroureteral dilatation was noted in 20.3% of patients. In 68% of patients, the etiology of retroperitoneal fibrosis was unknown; 12% had had methysergide administration. At laparotomy, ureteral compression by a condensed rubberlike retroperitoneal mass was noted. Frozen section biopsies revealed chronic inflammation and fibrosis suggestive of retroperitoneal fibrosis. Malignancy was the second most frequently associated finding in patients with retroperitoneal fibrosis. The authors note that patient failure to improve satisfactorily after surgery was an indication for steroid therapy and possibly surgical re-exploration for malignancy.

Waller G: Idiopathic retroperitoneal fibrosis. Scand J Urol Nephrol 9:110, 1975

In this paper, the author stresses the similarity of the symptoms of retroperitoneal fibrosis as seen in its early stages (and compares them) to symptoms similar to those seen in collegen diseases. Interestingly, in two patiients treated with steroids, their symptoms improved markedly, with normalization of their erythrocyte sedimentation rate, in both patients, the correct diagnosis was not made before institution of steroid therapy. In one patient, autopsy indicated the correct diagnosis; in the second patient, surgical exploration was required after 18 months of remission of symptoms. The author carried out serologic and histopathologic investigations, including mixed agglutination tests, to detect immunologic activity. However, no activity was demonstrated. The author believes that in relapse of retroperitoneal fibrosis, detected by an increase in the erythrocyte sedimentation rate, particularly with impairment of the patients general medical condition, corticosteroids should be used as an adjunct to surgery for a few months.

Hochsner MG, Brannan W, Pond HS, Goodlet JS Jr: Medical therapy in idiopathic retroperitoneal fibrosis. J Urol 114, 700, 1975

In this paper, the authors stress the medical approach to therapy for this disease by noting their response in three patients with retroperitoneal fibrosis. In two patients, the surgical ureterolysis of the fibrosis was employed, after which the patients were treated with steroids. In the third patient, steroids alone were employed. They stress that steroid therapy is not employed unless tissue diagnosis has been obtained to confirm the diagnosis of idiopathic retroperitoneal fibrosis. They advocate steroid therapy for idiopathic retroperitoneal fibrosis when the operative risks are high. They stress that after surgical exploration and tissue confirmation of retroperitoneal fibrosis, ureterolysis may be avoided if steroid therapy is instituted. They caution that patients must be carefully followed with renal function studies and excretory urograms.

Nitz GL, Hewett CB, Straffon RA, Kiser WS, Stewart BH: Retroperitoneal malignancy masquerading as benign retroperitoneal fibrosis. J Urol 103:40, 1970

This report summarizes the authors' experience with four cases of malignancy masquerading as retroperitoneal fibrosis. The authors note that preoperative differentiation between malignant retroperitoneal fibrosis and idiopathic retroperitoneal fibrosis may be extremely difficult. They conclude that a history of prior neoplasm should increase the index of suspicion for a malignant etiology of the fibrosis and that the ability to pass ureteral catheters beyond the obstruction does not rule out malignancy. They indicate that deep, generous biopsies should be obtained from all patients whenever possible.

Persky L, Huus JC: Atypical manifestations of retroperitoneal fibrosis. J Urol 111:340, 1974

The authors review their experiences with five patients that demonstrated ureteral obstruction at an unusual level, the absence of medial deviation of the ureters, and the presence of an impermeable obstruction to the passage of the ureteral catheter. They stress that although these findings are atypical, they certainly do not preclude the diagnosis of retroperitoneal fibrosis. In addition, they indicate that an acute illness does not preclude the presence of retroperitoneal fibrosis. All their patients underwent exploratory laparotomy with tissue biopsy to confirm the diagnosis.

Whitaker RH: Urodynamic assessment of ureteral obstruction in retroperitoneal fibrosis. J Urol 113:26, 1975

The author describes the application of the "Whitaker test" to urodynamic assessment of the upper urinary tract during laparotomy in three patients undergoing ureterolysis for retroperitoneal fibrosis. He recommends the use of urodynamic perfusion studies in assessing the extent of lysis whenever ureteral peristalis is in question. In one of the patients, the results of perfusion suggest that greater efforts to free the ureter to a greater extent might be advisable in order to achieve normal perfusion pressures. This would not have been noted if perfusion studies were not employed. Indeed, it was only after a long partial ureterotomy of the muscle coat of the ureter that a high flow rate through the narrowed section could be achieved. Whitaker inserts small nephrostomy tubes into the renal pelvis and wraps the ureters in omentum, removing the nephrostomy tubes after ten days.

Jacobson JB, Redman AC: Ultrasound findings in a case of retroperitoneal fibrosis. Radioilogy 113:423, 1974

The authors believe that ultrasonography has a definite place in the diagnosis of retroperitoneal fibrosis and its follow-up study. In the present case they noted that ultrasonic scanning accurately determined the extent of the mass before surgery, thus aiding the surgical approach. They note that the ultrasonic appearance of retroperitoneal fibrosis is most likely to be confused with a retroperitoneal malignancy, either adenopathy or diffuse sheets of tumor tissue. However, they feel that other investigations, such as lymphography and inferior vena cavography, will help exclude these disease processes. Since ultrasonic scanning is without known hazard and visualizes the mass directly, they believe that it can be repeated periodically in follow-up examinations.

Linke CA, May AG: Autotransplantation in retroperitoneal fibrosis. J Urol 107:196, 1972

This paper reports the authors' experience with renal autotransplantation in a patient aged 59 in whom bilateral ureteral intraperitonealization and ureterolysis were successful on the left side but unsuccessful on the right because of extensive retroperitoneal fibrosis. Indeed, a second attempt to establish drainage of the right kidney by ureteroplasty was unsuccessful. The authors performed autotransplantation of the right kidney rather than nephrectomy because of the uncertain future course of the disease process and the possibility of progressive changes that might involve the solitary left kidney.

Overview: Use of Ureterolysis

Paul C. Peters

Ureterolysis is an operation of continued but limited use to the urologist. It is most successfully employed in nonmalignant processes surrounding the ureter in which there is little or no intrinsic disease of the ureter. Advances in fields related to urology have allowed better selection of patients for surgery and better planning of the operative procedure of choice and will ultimately reduce the number of failures due to ureterolysis through use of alternative procedures that are more likely to be successful in a given patient, such as ileal substitution of ureter, transureteroureterostomy, autotransplantation, uretero-ureterostomy, in-dwelling stenting catheter and steroids, psoas hitch and reimplantation, and omental wrapping of ureters combined with ureterolysis.[1-8]

Gray-scale and real-time sonography are noninvasive techniques that allow preoperative evaluation of the extent of retroperitoneal processes obstructing the ureter.[9] Often, hydronephrosis is advanced by the time clinical manifestations are present. One cannot always pass a ureteral catheter easily, as Persky and Huus have pointed out, even if a nonmalignant inflammatory process is present.[10] Thin (skinny) needle biopsy of retroperitoneal processes with sonographic or CT control may obviate the need for exploration or cause one to consider alternatives to ureterolysis by providing a preoperative diagnosis with minimal discomfort to the patient.

Evaluation of the degrees of obstruction of the ureters and simultaneous evaluation of renal function may be obtained before any surgery by the use of isotope injection (*i.e.,* 30 μCi of ^{131}I-hippuran) and diuresis renography techniques to evaluate the effectiveness of peristalsis and to provide baseline data for comparison with surgical results.[11,12] Defects in ureteral peristalsis may be appreciated with image-intensified fluoroscopy if renal function is adequate, or, if not, adequate contrast material may be introduced by percutaneous puncture to evaluate peristalsis or to determine the level of obstruction and thus provide temporary diversion to get the patient in better shape for surgery if catheters cannot be passed from below.

Simple ureterolysis often fails, particularly when there is considerable intrinsic involvement of the ureter. Intraperitonealization, when used, must be carried out from the renal pelvis to the point of entry of the ureter into the bladder. Even this maneuver has been associated with a 17% to 30% failure rate in nonmalignant retroperitoneal fibrosis.[13] If there is any indication of intrinsic ureteral involvement in those cases of non-malignant-associated retroperitoneal fibrosis, I much prefer omental wrapping of the ureter throughout its course, bilaterally if necessary, as advocated by Tresidder and Blandy and by Turner–Warwick.[6,7] The process of retroperitoneal fibrosis involves both ureters in the majority of patients (75% to 83%).[13]

Use of the in-dwelling ureteral stent often obviates the need for ureterolysis, particularly when a preoperative diagnosis of lymphoma or metastatic carcinoma has been made by thin needle biopsy.[12] It is possible, by the use of sonography and CT, to differentiate lymph node enlargement due to systemic or metastatic disease from the diffuse idiopathic benign process of retroperitoneal fibrosis. Again, skinny needle biopsy or a limited exploration for extraperitoneal biopsy may establish the diagnosis and the need for alternatives to ureterolysis such as systemic chemotherapy or urinary diversion. Those patients known to have ingested ergot alkaloids such as methysergide maleate (Sansert or Desernil) or to have taken hydralazine and to have subsequently developed retroperitoneal fibrosis may be treated by withdrawal of the medication and temporary use of in-dwelling ureteral stents or percutaneous nephrostomy.

In cases with established tissue diagnosis, steroids and an in-dwelling ureteral stent (Cook or Gibbon catheter) may be used as definitive therapy or as preparation for surgery. A definitive response is anticipated in half the cases of benign disease. Best results are seen in patients with early stage and marked cellular response.[5] Initially, 30 mg of prednisone daily, tapering at the rate of 2.5 mg/week when a response is noted to a minimum dosage of 5 mg daily, maintained for 3 months after resolution of hydronephrosis (minimal ureterectasis may persist), is recommended for initial therapy.[5,13] The erythrocyte sedimentation rate, initially high, will usually fall to normal during therapy.

When surgery is necessary, I currently prefer intraperitonealization of the ureter with lateral displacement for minimal involvement (1 cm to 4 cm). If more than 5 cm of ureter is involved, I prefer a bilateral omental sleeve.

I find several technical points to be of benefit. To proceed: place the patient on a clear liquid diet for 3 days before the surgery. Give cleansing enemas the evening before surgery. Place the patient on the operating table in the supine position with slight extension at the lumbosacral junction. Open the abdomen through a midline incision from the epigastrium, as necessary above the umbilicus, to the symphysis. Incise the mesentery lateral to the colon on either side, usually first on the more affected side and as needed on the opposite side. On the left, it is of great help to carry the incision lateral to the colon and superiorly around the splenic pedicle, thus allowing medial retraction of the spleen and pancreas and complete exposure of the left retroperitoneal area. Dissect the ureter out from the renal pelvis to the juxtavesical ureter. If the greater omentum is to be used in conjunction with the ureterolysis, separate it from the transverse colon and then split it into two equal parts in the midline from its tip superiorly through the gastroepiploic vessels. Wrap the two omental pedicles about the collecting system of each kidney from the renal pelvis to the bladder using interrupted fine absorbable sutures for the enclosure; affix the parietal peritoneum over the omental sleeve or tack the sleeve to the peritoneum if coverage is impossible. Use layered abdominal closure with nonabsorbable suture except in patients over age 60, patients with malignant processes, and patients who have had previous radiation; in those patients use retention sutures. Prophylactic antibiotics are not recommended.

As a result of diagnostic advances in urography and nuclear medicine, coupled with more sophisticated biopsy and diversion techniques and the use of indwelling stents, ureterolysis is less frequently indicated. When used in extensive benign retroperitoneal fibrosis, its combination with omental-sleeve techniques is recommended.

REFERENCES

1. McCullough DL, McLaughlin AP, Gittes RF, Kerr WS Jr: Replacement of the damaged or neoplastic ureter by ileum. J Urol 118:375, 1977

2. Sharer W, Grayhack JT, Graham J: Palliative urinary diversion for malignant ureteral obstruction. J Urol 120:162, 1978

3. Linke CA, May AG: Autotransplantation in retroperitoneal fibrosis. J Urol 107:196, 1972

4. Finney RP: Experience with new double J ureteral catheter stent. J Urol 120:678, 1978

5. Cosbie-Ross J, Goldsmith HJ: The combined surgical and medical treatment of retroperitoneal fibrosis. Br J Surg 58:422, 1971

6. Turner–Warwick R, Worth PHL: The psoas bladder hitch procedure for the replacement of the lower third of the ureter. Br J Urol 41:701, 1969

7. Turner–Warwick RT: Retroperitoneal fibrosis use of omental pedical graft. J Urol 116:341, 1976

8. Tresidder GC, Blandy JP, Singh M: Omental sleeve to prevent recurrent retroperitoneal fibrosis around the ureter. Urol Int 27:144, 1972

9. Sanders RC, Duffy T, McLoughlin MG, Walsh PC: Sonography in the diagnosis of retroperitoneal fibrosis. J Urol 118:944, 1977

10. Persky L, Huus JC: Atypical manifestations of retroperitoneal fibrosis. J Urol 111:340, 1974

11. O'Reilly PH, Testa HJ, Lawson RS, Farrar DJ, Charlton–Edwards E: Diuresis renography in equivocal urinary tract obstruction. Br J Urol 50:76, 1978

12. Lupton EW, Testa HJ, Lawson RS, Charlton–Edwards E, Carroll RNP, Barnard RJ: Diuresis renography and the results of pyeloplasty for idiopathic hydronephrosis. Br J Urol 51:449, 1979

13. Peters PC: Surgery of retroperitoneal fibrosis. In Glenn J (ed): Urologic Surgery, 2nd ed, pp 869–873. New York, Harper & Row, 1975

PART SIXTEEN

SURGICAL TREATMENT OF URETERAL CALCULI

37

MANAGEMENT OF URETERIC STONE: A REVIEW OF 292 CASES[1]

By Miles Fox, M.D., Ch.M., F.R.C.S.,
L. N. Pyrah, C.B.E., D.Sc., Ch.M., F.R.C.S.,
and F. P. Raper, F.R.C.S.

Department of Urology, General Infirmary and St. James's Hospital, Leeds

Reprinted from *British Journal of Urology,* Vol. 37, pp. 660–670, 1965. Copyright 1965 by E. & S. Livingston, London.

The management of stone in the ureter is frequently dependent on the combination of a number of factors which include size, position, and shape of the stone, pain, degree of obstruction and infection. In most cases the decision to carry out a certain method of treatment is not difficult, but in some a number of alternative ways of treatment is available, and in these cases considerable variations in the management have been recorded in the past. In the present paper a report has been made of the management of stone in the ureter in patients treated in the Department of Urology at General Infirmary and St. James's Hospital, Leeds, over a five-year period, 1957 to 1962, and follow-up results are given. The main interest in the survey was to follow those cases in which treatment had been varied, to assess recovery of the urinary tract after different periods of obstruction and to correlate the results with the methods and timing of treatment.

[1] Read at the Twenty-first Annual Meeting of the British Association of Urological Surgeons at London, June 1965.

Case Material, Presentation, and Diagnosis. There were 292 patients with ureteric stones in the present series; 216 male and seventy-six female, a distribution of 2.8 to 1. Age and sex incidence according to age are shown in Figure 1. The mean age was 46 years; the youngest patient was 15 and the oldest 71 years. The incidence was almost equal in both ureters, right 148 and left 141. Three patients had bilateral stones.

Stones were most frequently arrested in the lower third of the ureter (Fig. 2); 61 percent (178) were in the lower third, 27 percent (seventy-nine) in the upper third, and 12 percent (thirty-five) in the middle third. Duration of symptoms varies between three hours and five years (Fig. 3); 80.5 percent of patients attended within one month of the onset of symptoms. Thirteen patients gave a history of one year or longer, which was probably attributable to the same stone. Pain was the usual presentation.

Pain	271 cases
Painless hæmaturia	12 cases

Urinary infection   2 cases
Anuria   2 cases
Incidental finding   5 cases

Frank hæmaturia was reported in sixty-five patients and red cells on microscopy were seen in a further forty-two.

Intravenous pyelography was performed while pain was present in 119 patients. When carried out in the acute state, pyelography yielded the most useful results, particularly if delayed films, up to twenty-four hours after injection, were taken. In most cases an outline of the affected collecting system down to the stone was eventually obtained and its position, degree of obstruction, and dilatation of the collecting system ascertained.

The filled ureter often acted as a pointer to an opacity which would otherwise have been difficult to recognise as a stone (Figs. 4 and 5). Films taken after evaluation of the bladder and in the oblique position were useful (Figs. 6 and 7). Cystoscopy and passage of a ureteric catheter were carried out in ninety cases to confirm the diagnosis. Contrast medium was injected in eleven cases in which more information about the upper urinary tract was required or the presence of a radio-translucent stone was suspected.

MANAGEMENT

The methods of management are shown in Figure 8.

Spontaneous Passage. In eighty-nine patients (30.5 percent of all cases) the ureteric stones were passed spontaneously (forty-seven from the left and forty-two from the right ureter). Adequate information was not available in nine cases.

Duration of Passage and Degree of Obstruction. The time interval between onset of pain and passage of the stone is shown in Figure 9. It varied from two days to twelve months. The degree of initial urinary tract obstruction is also shown. The dark lines indicate cases (sixty-four) in which no radiological evidence of obstruction or only ureteric hold-up or mild hydronephrosis was present. The light spaces represent patients (sixteen) who had severe ureteric obstruction at the time of admission, marked by long delay in excretion, nephrogram effect, or considerable dilatation of the collecting system. All the patients with marked obstruction managed to pass their stones within one month. Severe obstruction in

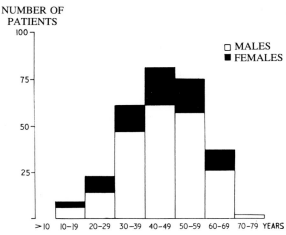

Fig. 1. Age incidence of ureteric stone.

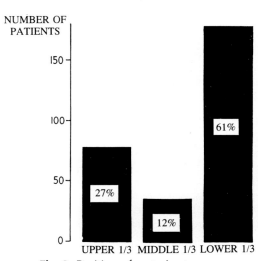

Fig. 2. Position of ureteric stones.

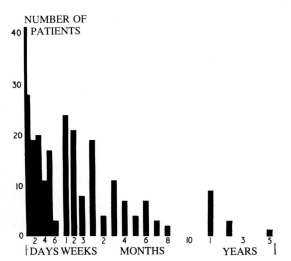

Fig. 3. Duration of symptoms in 292 patients with ureteric stones.

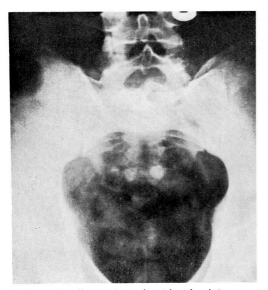

Fig. 4. Plain X-ray. Small opacity right side of pelvis.

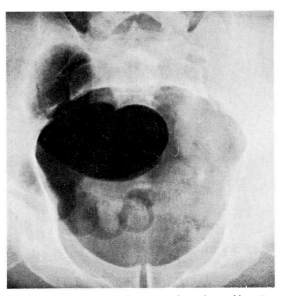

Fig. 6. Intravenous pyelogram. Three-hour film. Two opacities in line of ureter.

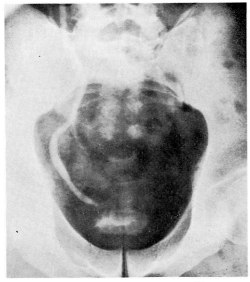

Fig. 5. Intravenous pyelogram, post-evacuation film, 1½ hours after injection of contrast medium.

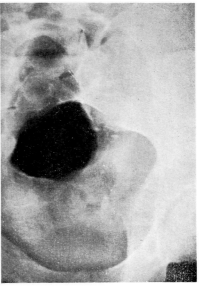

Fig. 7. Intravenous pyelogram. Three-hour film, oblique. The larger opacity is extra-ureteric.

itself, therefore, did not appear to be a contra-indication to spontaneous passage.

Size of Stone. In all but five cases the ureteric stone had one diameter smaller than ⅓ cm. No stone was passed with a diameter greater than ½ cm; 70 percent were in the lower third when first seen, 2 percent in the middle, and 28 percent in the upper third of the ureter. All the stones which passed within one week of the start

of symptoms wer situated in the lower third of the ureter. Thereafter there was no obvious relation between the position in which the stone was found and the length of time it took to pass.

Follow-up pyelography was performed in forty-six cases. Mild hydronephrosis was noted on only one

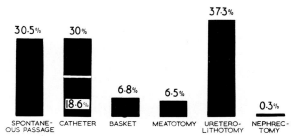

Fig. 8. Management of ureteric stones. Ureteric catheter inserted in 30 percent for diagnostic and for therapeutic purposes. 18.6 percent stones subsequently passed.

occasion in a patient who had passed a stone two weeks previously and who also had a stone in one of the lower renal calyces. No relation was found between the degree of initial upper urinary tract dilatation, duration of passage, and return of the collecting system to normal, provided the stone passed spontaneously. Infection was not present in any of these cases.

Ureteric Catheterisation. In eighty-nine patients a ureteric catheter was passed usually as a diagnostic procedure, and withdrawn one to two hours later after X-rays had been taken. On twenty-four occasions a catheter was inserted beyond the stone and in two it was left in place for one and two days. There was no convincing evidence that this procedure speeded up the process of spontaneous passage. None of the stones passed (18.6 percent) was larger than $\frac{1}{3}$ cm at its narrowest diameter.

Ureteric Basket. In twenty patients an attempt was made to remove a low-lying stone with a ureteric basket. On sixteen occasions the attempt failed, usually as a result of inability to insert the basket past the stone. In twelve of these cases, however, the stone passed within one week afterwards. Extraction was successful on three occasions. The stones which were removed or subsequently passed were again all less than $\frac{1}{3}$ cm in diameter. The Council basket was used mainly in the first part of the survey, while later the Dormia basket was employed. In one case the Dormia basket, with the engaged stone, became impacted and finally broke when attempts were made to free it. Ureterolithotomy was required in the remaining case.

Ureteric Orifice Meatotomy. Ureteric orifice meatotomy was performed on nineteen occasions. In all cases the stone was in the lowermost part of the ureter and the orifice was œdematous, or the stone was just visible at the ureteric orifice. In eighteen patients, the stone was

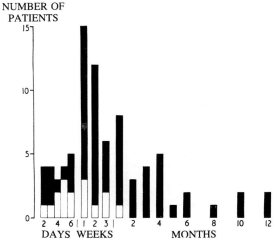

Fig. 9. Duration of spontaneous passage of 80 ureteric stones.

passed within the succeeding seven days. Ureterolithotomy was required in the remaining case.

Ureterolithotomy. Ureterolithotomy was carried out in 109 patients. Distribution was almost equal on both sides (fifty-five on the right and fifty-one on the left). In three cases the stones were bilateral in the lower parts of the ureter. They were removed by a transperitoneal approach at one operation.

Position. Figure 10 shows the distribution of all stones in this series among the three parts of the ureter, and the proportion of cases in which open operation was performed. Operative removal was carries out most frequently when the stone was arrested in the upper third of the ureter—76 percent, 23 percent in the middle third, and 23 percent in the lower third. Out of the whole series only 9 percent of stones which were $\frac{1}{3}$ cm or smaller in diameter were operated on. Ureterolithotomy was required in 77 percent of cases when the stone was $\frac{1}{2}$ cm or larger. All stones with a diameter of $\frac{1}{2}$ cm or more were removed by operation when arrested in the upper third of the ureter.

Degree of Obstruction. The table shows a comparison between the severity of ureteric obstruction and frequency of operative and conservative management. The figures show that the degree of obstruction was not in itself the determining factor in the management.

Size of Stone. No relation was found between the size of the stones and site of impaction in the ureter, except that only the very large calculi (over $\frac{3}{4}$ cm) were stopped in the middle portion. Stones impacted in the upper third of the ureter produced severe obstruction to urine flow twice as often as stones in the lower two-thirds.

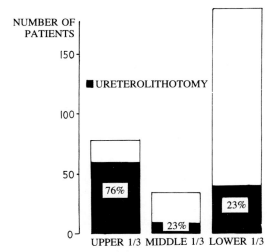

Fig. 10. Frequency of ureterolithotomy.

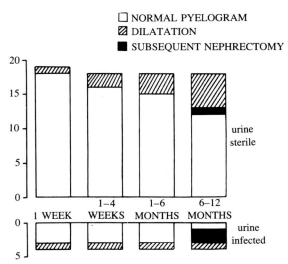

Fig. 11. Postoperative IVP results compared with time between onset of symptoms and ureterolithotomy.

TABLE. Comparison between Degree of Ureteric Obstruction and Method of Treatment

	Total (%)	Uretero-lithotomy (%)	Conservative Management (%)
Ureteric hold-up Mild hydronephrosis Delay in excretion	57.8	34.5	65.5
Marked hydronephrosis Nephrogram effect No excretion	42.2	53.5	46.5

Time of Operation. In twenty-two patients ureterolithotomy was performed within forty-eight hours of diagnosis, in forty-three within two to seven days, in twenty patients within one week to one month, and in twenty-five between one and six months. Surgical intervention was carried out as soon as possible if infection was present and in some cases where marked ureteric obstruction was being produced by a stone of a size unlikely to pass, particularly in the upper third of the ureter.

Results. Post-operative pyelograms were performed in ninety out of the 109 patients, between three months and five years after operation. Results are shown in Figure 11. Findings are grouped according to whether follow-up pyelograms were normal (clear spaces), signs of dilatation were seen (shaded spaces), or subsequent nephrectomy was required (black spaces). In six out of seventeen cases in which the urine had been infected at the time of operation, permanent dilatation remained and in two patients in whom operation had not been carried out till six to twelve months after the onset of symptoms, subsequent nephrectomy was required because of poor

function, hydronephrosis, and continued infection. In the absence of urinary infection dilatation remained in 5.3 percent (one ut of nineteen) when operation was performed within one week of the onset of symptoms. In the group operated on after one and under four weeks, 11.1 percent (two out of eighteen) showed mild residual dilatation, 16.7 percent (three out of eighteen) between one and six months, and 33.3 percent (six out of eighteen) between six and twelve months. One patient in the last group finally required nephrectomy.

Stricture of the ureter occcurred in two patients, mild in one, complete in another, necessitating re-implantation of the ureter into the bladder after three months (without residual dilatation). In another patient the lower third of the ureter became detached while being mobilised. It was re-implanted into the bladder at the same operation. After six months there was no obvious function and nephrectomy was carried out. In one patient a second stone became arrested at the site of the operation two months after ureterolithotomy, and surgical removal was again required.

Adequate records of the length and extent of postoperative urinary leakage through the incision are not available. If leakage did not subside spontaneously in about three weeks, it did so fairly promptly following insertion of a ureteric catheter which was left in place for two to three days.

There was no mortality.

Nephrectomy. Nephrectomy and ureterectomy was carried out in one patient as a primary procedure because of a large stone in the middle third of the ureter which had probably been there for a number of years. The kidney was hydronephrotic and infected. Nephrectomy was performed in two cases after ureterolithotomy because of continuing infection.

Partial nephrectomy, because of stone in the lower pole of the kidney, was carried out in one patient at the same time as removal of a calculus from the upper third of the ureter. The kidney was œdematous but this did not appreciably add to the difficulty of the operation and convalescence was uneventful.

Calculous Anuria. Two patients were admitted with anuria because of a stone obstructing the ureter from the solitary kidney. A ureteric catheter could not be inserted past the stone in either case. Ureterolithotomy was carried out on the day of admission in one patient. The other had a blood urea of 380 mg percent. Hæmodialysis was performed the day he was admitted and the stone was removed two days later.

DISCUSSION

In 1935 Hinman stated that about 10 percent of ureteric stones were missed on urography. Besides non-opaque stones small calculi can easily be overlooked, especially in the middle and lower thirds of the ureter, and about 3 to 5 percent are invisible (Herman, 1938). Although in most cases the history is clear, in some it is atypial and the pain may closely mimic abdominal emergencies. Vague abdominal discomfort or only right iliac fossa pain with vomiting may occur, and in a percentage of cases there is no pain at all. A diagnosis of acute appendicitis with subsequent appendicectomy is a mistake which has been made fairly frequently. In 1930 Bumpus and Thompson reported mistaken appendicectomy in 26.8 percent of 1,001 patients, while as recently as 1945 Dourmashkin recorded 11.8 percent in 910 cases.

Accurate and prompt diagnosis is most important in the management of ureteric stone. It is achieved by the intravenous pyelogram carried out in the acute stage (Hellmer, 1935) and the use of delayed films (Pyrah, 1951). By establishing the site, size, shape and degree of obstruction produced by the stone, it is possible to make an early decision whether conservative, manipulative, or operative treatment should be carried out, and to institute treatment without delay and thus avoid the danger of permanent damage to the urinary tract.

The following factors have to be considered in deciding on a course of management:

1. *Duration and Severity of Symptoms.* In a series of 518 cases reported by Sandegard (1956), 76 percent of the stones were passed spontaneously. Proportions of over 50 percent have been recorded by many other

observers including Boeminghaus (1940), Arnesen (1940), Busch (1943), and Prentiss *et al.* (1952), while a considerably lower percentage (17.1) was reported by Higgins and Straffon (1963). Figures between 24 and 36 percent have been given in other, including recent large series (Chwalla, 1929; Hellström, 1935; Prince and Scardino, 1960; Fetter *et al.*, 1963). In many cases one of the major deciding factors appears to be the waiting period deemed safe and praticable before endoscopic or operative measures are undertaken. In the present series 30.5 percent of stones were passed spontaneously and of these, one-third were passed between one month and one year after the onset of symptoms. A further 18.6 percent passed following insertion of a ureteric catheter, but it is not possible to determine whether this procedure had any significant influence on the passage of the stones.

It is well known (Higgins, 1954) that the longer a stone stays in the ureter the less are its chances of spontaneous passage. A significant number, however, do pass after one month. Sandegard (1956) reported that 11 percent of stones passed only one to eighteen months after diagnosis. In the present series it was shown that a stone could stay in the ureter for up to one year without producing residual damage, provided it was eventually passed spontaneously. Delay in operative treatment, however, if required, did lead to significant irrecoverable damage, even if no infection was present, when the waiting period was longer than one week from the onset of symptoms. A decison should therefore be made within about one week which stone is likely to pass spontaneously and which will not, so as to avoid the risk of permanent damage.

2. *Size of Calculus.* Most observers agree that prognosis is influenced by the size of the stone (Sandegard, 1956), but there is marked divergence of opinion as to the actual dimensions. Joly (1929) advised medical treatment for patients who passed gravel or in whom the X-ray shadow was not larger than 5 to 10 mm in diameter. Stevens and Collings (1930), Engel (1939), Brosig (1948), Davidson (1952), and Nation (1953) believed that spontaneous passage was probable if the stone was not larger than 1 cm. Others (Hellström, 1932; Foley, 1935; Priestley, 1954; Winsbury-White, 1954) have claimed that stones were unlikely to pass if larger than ½ cm, while Braasch (1917) advised against manipulative treatment if the stone was larger than 2 cm. Perlmann (1950) even stated that the size of the stone had no influence on the prospects of passage. However, in many reports it is not clear whether the measurement given refers to the length or width of the stone, and its shape and type of surface are given but rarely.

In the present series 91 percent of stones ½ cm or

smaller at their narrowest diameter passed either spontaneously or with the help of endoscopic procedures. Ureterolithotomy was required in 77 percent of cases when the stone was ½ cm in diameter or larger.

3. *Position.* A large proportion of stones in the upper third of the ureter require removal by open operation. Foley (1935) and Priestley (1954) advised open operation for high stones with a diameter of ½ cm or more, while Sargent (1954) suggested open operation for all high stones independent of size, unless they soon passed down the ureter. Sandegard (1956, 1958) found that about 50 percent of upper stones with a diameter between 4 and 6 mm passed down the ureter, but when larger than 6 mm they rarely moved. Similar findings were reported by Fetter *et al.* (1963).

In the present cases no stones ½ cm or larger in diameter were passed when found in the upper part of the ureter. Some might have done so if left longer, but as obstructive symptoms were present more often and were usually more marked in the upper part of the ureter than elsewhere, early intervention appeared the safer course to follow. Smaller stones were carefully watched and if obstruction was present and the stone did not move soon, open operation was usually advised.

More conservative measures were adopted when the stone was in the lower parts of the ureter. If it was producing obstruction, not moving, and over ½ cm in diameter, early open operation appeared the safest course to follow. From the results obtained it appeared that in these cases the period of waiting should not be longer than one week from the beginning of symptoms.

There has been a marked difference in the literature in the proportion of stones removed by endoscopic procedures. Figures as high as 93.3 percent have been recorded by Dourmashkin (1945) in 1,550 cases. He used metallic dilators for stones in the lower third of the ureter and aimed to dilate the ureter at or below the level of the calculus, to or just above the size of the stone. Alyea (1938) removed 72 percent of 377 ureteric stones, some larger than ¾ mm at their narrowest diameter. Squires (1930) extracted 87.15 percent of stones in a series of 606 patients and Dodson *et al.* (1957) in a collected series of 4,947 found the proportion to be 68.2 percent. More recently, considerably lower figures have been given by Fetter *et al.* (1963), 48.1 percent while in Prince and Scardino's 1960 series of 816 cases, endoscopic manipulation was attempted in only 31 percent and extraction was successful in 65.4 percent of these cases. It was noted, however, that in the unsuccessful cases 63 percent of the stones were passed subsequently.

In the present series endoscopic extraction, using either a Councill or a Dormia basket, was performed

relatively infrequently (6.8 percent). In most cases the attempt was unsuccessful, but in many the stone when ⅓ cm or smaller passed soon afterwards. Manipulation or dilatation of the ureter below the level of the stone probably accelerated its passage. The method has its dangers as pointed out by Rushe and Bacon (1940), Wishard (1943), Councill (1945), and Dodson *et al.* (1957). It should not be used to try to remove stones from the upper or middle thirds of the ureter. When larger stones are present, ureterolithotomy offers a more certain, safer, and frequently more expeditious method of treatment.

4. *Degree of Obstruction.* Some reports have indicated that obstruction of the ureter for even a short period may give rise to permanent renal damage (Kerr, 1954; Widén, 1958), while case histories of patients with complete recovery of renal function after prolonged total obstruction have been recorded (Badenoch, 1963). Prince and Scardino (1960) believed that when a stone completely obstructs the ureter, immediate action should be taken to reinstate drainage by endoscopic or surgical measures.

The present results show that the chances of spontaneous passage are not necessarily related to the degree of obstruction. The smaller stones sometimes produce complete obstruction and they are subsequently passed spontaneously, without leaving residual damage. The size and position of the stone appear to be more important in determining management. However, if repeated X-rays reveal little or no progress in the descent of the stone and a progressively enlarging hydronephrosis, the obstruction should be relieved.

5. *Infection.* In the presence of infection prompt relief of obstruction is required. Pyonephrosis with destruction of renal tissue soon occurs and the prognosis of the affected kidney rapidly deteriorates. Nephrectomy, together with removal of the dilated ureter, should be considered as a primary procedure if infection has been long-standing, and if marked dilatation and destruction of renal tissue are present.

6. *Renal Function.* When a stone becomes impacted in the ureter from a solitary functioning kidney, operative intervention is required as a matter of emergency. If it is not possible to bypass the obstruction with a ureteric catheter when the blood urea is high, haemodialysis will allow an elective operation to be carried out one to two days later.

7. *Associated Renal Stone.* A stone may be washed from the kidney by the increased flow of urine after the relief of ureteric obstruction and may be arrested at the site of the ureterolithotomy. Removal of the renal stone and partial nephrectomy if necessary, at the same time as ureterolithotomy will avoid this complication.

SUMMARY

The management of 292 patients with stone in the ureter treated in the Department of Urology in Leeds between 1957 and 1962 is described.

Indications for conservative and operative procedures are discussed in the light of follow-up results.

REFERENCES

ALYEA, E. P. (1938). J Urol, 40:83

ARNESEN, A. (1940). Z urol. Chir., 45:94

BADENOCH, A. W. (1963). Br J Urol 35:385

BOEMINGHAUS, H. (1940). "Konservative und chirurgische Behandlung des Harnleitersteins." (Leipzig: Georg Thieme Verlag)

BRAASCH, W. F. (1917). Surg Gynec Obstet, 24:8

BROSIG, W. (1948). Beitr Klin. Chir, 177:121

BUMPUS, H. C., and THOMPSON, G. J. (1930). Surg Gynec Obstet, 50:106

BUSCH, F. (1943). Zbl Chir 70:172

CHWALLA, R. (1929). Z Urol Chir, 26:157

COUNCIL, W. A. (1945). J Urol, 53:534

DAVIDSON, G. R. (1952). Med J Aust, 1:840

DODSON, A. I., SIPE, W. R., and LORD, K. H. (1957). J Urol, 78:575

DOURMASHKIN, R. L. (1945). J Urol, 54:245

ENGEL, W. J. (1939). Surg Clin N Am, 19:1275

FETTER, T. R., ZIMSKIND, D. P., GRAHAM, R. H., and BRODIE, D. E. (1963). J Am Med Ass, 186:21

FOLEY, F. E. B. (1935). J Am Med Ass, 104:1314

HELLMER, H. (1935). Acta Radiol (Stockh), 16:51

HELLSTRÖM, J. (1932). Hygiea (Stockh), 94:337

——— (1935). Njur-och uretärsten. Nord Kirurg Fř, Förhandl Köpenhafn

HERMAN, L. (1938). "The Practice of Urology." (Philadelphia: W. B. Saunders Co)

HIGGINS, C. C. (1954). In "Urology," Ed by MF Campbell. (Philadlphia: W. B. Saunders Co)

HIGGINS, C. C. and STRAFFON, R. A. (1963). In "Uorology," p. 746. Edby MF Campbell. (Philadelphia: WB Saunders Co)

HINMAN, F. (1935). "Principles and Practice of Urology." (Philadelphia: W B Saunders Co.)

JOLY, J. S. (1929). "Stone and Calculous Disease of the Urinary Organs." (London: Wm. Heinemann)

KEER, W. S. (1954). J Appl Physiol, 6:762

NATION, E. F. (1953). J Urol, 70:373

PERLMAN, S. (1950). Z Urol, 24:303

PRENTISS, R. J., MULLENIX, R. B., and WHISENAND, J. M. (1952). Calif Med, 7:77

PRIESTLEY, J. T. (1954). Urol Surv, 4:49

PRINCE, C. L., and SCARDINO, P. L. (1960). J Urol, 83:561

PYRAH, L. N. (1951). Proc Roy Soc Med, 44:933

RUSHE, C. F., and BACON, S. F. (1940). J Rol, 44:777

SANDEGARD, E. (1956). Acta Chir Scand, Suppl 219

——— (1958). Acta Chir Scand, 116:44

SARGENT, J. C., (1954). Postgrad Med, 15:238

SQUIRES, C. B. (1930). J Urol, 24:461

STEVENS, A. R., and COLLINGS, C. W. (1930). Am J Surg, 9:484

WIDÉN, T. (1958). Acta Radiol (Stockh), Suppl 162

WINSBURY-WHITE, H. P. (1954). "Stone in the Urinary Tract." (London: Butterworth & Co. Ltd)

WISHARD, W. N. (1943). J Urol, 50:775

DISCUSSION

Mr Turner Warwick (London): Most of us would wish to endorse the value of the emergency intravenous pyelogram in confirming the diagnosis of ureteric colic. Unfortunately many radiodiagnostic departments are overworked and find difficulty in fitting in unbooked intravenous pyelograms without warning; none, however, should find the "Casualty Officer's" modified I.V.P. too burdensome. A straight X-ray alone is of little value in cases of suspected ureteric colic because it may or may not show an opacity which may or may not be in the ureter; while the pain is still present at least one I.V.P. film should be taken in addition. No compression is used and fluid restriction is not essential. In most cases a thirty-minute film demonstrates the ureter distended down to an obstructing calculus which may not itself be visible. If a nephrogram only is defined on the side of the colic, a second post-voiding film is taken after two hours; if this fails to demonstrate the site of the ureteric obstruction, a second injection of contrast is given and a further post-voiding film taken after six to eight hours (timing of additional films according to indications). An additional oblique film is occasionally indicated if, after voiding, a residual bladder shadow obscures a suspected calculus at the lower end of the ureter. The presence of some small opaque and non-opaque ureter stones can best, and sometimes only, be diagnosed by intravenous pyelography during an attack of colic; *per contra*, absence of ureteric obstruction at such a time excludes a diagnosis of ureteric colic. The single thirty-minute pyelogram usually provides all the information that is urgently required; it is, however, not an alternative to a full pyelogram which, if indicated, may be better postponed until the technique is not compromised by colic.

Conservative management of ureteric calculi of critical size is most usefully controlled by a series of single-film post-voiding thirty-minute pyelograms, repeated at suitable intervals or days or weeks. Other things being equal a stone which is not causing obstruction between attacks of colic can be treated conservatively for longer than one which is obstructing; this fact cannot be determined from a straight X-ray and is considerably more important than the actual position of the calculus. The single-film pyelogam is also useful for checking the state of the upper tract before the patient leaves hospital after a urinary tract reconstruction.

Commentary:
The Two-Incision System for Ureterolithotomy

Adrian W. Zorgniotti

The anatomic basis for ureterolithotomy was set forth in 1892 by Cabot, who showed the important relationship of the ureter to the peritoneum, and in 1910 when Gibson wrote a classic article on the retroperitoneal approach to the previously inaccessible lower ureter by a curved incision parallel to and just above Poupart's ligament.[1,2] The advantages of operating outside the peritoneal cavity had already been exploited by the pioneers of nephrectomy. What gave ureterolithotomy impetus was the development of the wax-tipped ureteral catheter (1895) and roentgen examination (1896) for calculi. Readers of the previous volume will note that the same article is again offered, for two reasons. The first has to do with the excellent and enduring qualities of the preceding article. The other reason is that a search failed to discover a later communication on the subject of ureterolithotomy that was better or more comprehensive. Ureterolithotomy is not a subject on which great reputations or great research is made. Indeed, it is probably the most dangerous shoal upon which a surgical ego can founder. I will, *faute de mieux,* proceed with the previous article and the illuminating commentary by Dr. Turner–Warwick.

APPROACHES

It is preferable to perform ureterolithotomy extraperitoneally, whenever possible, even though the ureters are easily accessible through a peritoneal approach through a midline incision. Textbooks of urologic surgery usually show incisions to expose the ureter based on the extraperitoneal approach, giving the impression that a different incision should be chosen depending on which third of the ureter happens to contain the offending calculus. For calculi of the upper third, an incision starting at a point below the tip of the 12th rib, midway to the crest of the ilium, which extends forward and downward to a point medial to the anterior superior spine of the ilium, is thus advised and has the advantage of avoiding injury to important nerves. For calculi of the middle third of the ureter, a modification of the McBurney incision is suggested, while for calculi of the lower third, one of several variations of the Gibson incision are advised. In practice, this is not what many capable operators actually do. For calculi in the ureter from the level of the kidney to the pelvic brim, a standard subcostal incision is very satisfactory and is to be preferred when the calculus is impacted in the uppermost ureter or if the renal pelvis must also be explored. An advantage of such an incision and the more anterior one cited above for upper third calculi is that either permits tracing the ureter to a point below the pelvic brim. Only with accumulated experience will the surgeon

learn what is the smallest possible incision that will give sufficient exposure for easy removal of the calculus.

For calculi at or below the pelvic brim, many surgeons find the midline approach best. After the bladder is emptied, a low paramedian incision is made, and the peritoneum is swept medially with blunt dissection. It is usually necessary to free the perietal peritoneum in the vicinity of the iliac vessels for higher exposure. These vessels are quickly identified, and the ureter found as it crosses them. The incision may be enlarged upward by careful incision of the posterior rectus sheath above the linea semilunaris. The midline has the advantage over the Gibson incision of making the bladder and both ureters easily accessible. I have used the midline incision for lower ureteral stone for over 3 decades, and it has always proved satisfactory.

Exceptions to such a two-incision system are the valuable Foley muscle-splitting incision and vaginal ureterolithotomy. Both require careful selection of patients and reward the operator with excellent results, but failure to adhere to the rules can lead to considerable difficulties. Both can be performed with local infiltration if need be. The Foley incision is limited to upper-third ureteral calculi that the surgeon is reasonably certain are impacted and unlikely to move when palpated with finger dissection, since this is often the only way the stone can be identified. The other requirement is that the patient be neither heavily muscular nor obese. The vaginal approach to the ureter is also often overlooked, and this is unfortunate. The requirements are simple: the calculus must be impacted below the ischial spine and palpable on bimanual examination. Vaginal ureterolithotomy is safe and deserves more widespread use (see annotated bibliography).

FINDING THE URETER

Identification of the ureter at any point in its course can sometimes be particularly vexing. If the surgeon anticipates difficulty, a ureteral catheter can be passed preoperatively as far as it will go. When the ureter is not seen crossing the iliac vessels, or otherwise cannot be found, exploration underneath the retracted peritoneum is necessary. This is particularly likely when working on the lower ureter. Sometimes the ureter can be so dilated as to resemble gut; the operator can always aspirate a suspicious structure with a fine needle in the hope of finding urine. Peristalsis seen in the undilated ureter stimulated by gentle pinching is sure identification. *Most important,* one should not forget that palpation for the calculus is invaluable for identification.

It is always preferable to isolate the ureter just above the calculus; a narrow Penrose drain placed around it allows for traction, steadying the ureter and preventing upward migration of the calculus. Sharp and blunt dissection can then be carried downward to the site of the calculus, separating it as little as possible from its bed. In the upper ureter, take care to avoid the ovarian or spermatic vessels. In the retrovesical area, dissection of the ureter may be impeded by the vas deferens or the blood supply of the uterus or bladder crossing over the ureter. If necessary, these should be severed and tied, permitting visualization right to the insertion of the ureter into the bladder.

A useful trick in finding the distal ureter takes advantage of its relationship to the obliterated hypogastric artery (also called the umbilical artery), which crosses the lower ureter anteriorly. When the obliterated hypogastric artery can be identified, it can be traced laterally to find the ureter.[3]

A final word of caution on calculus in the lower 3 cm to 4 cm of a duplicated ureter. Here the operator should bear in mind the nature of the common sheath; this lessens the possibility of damaging the important blood supply.

REMOVAL OF THE CALCULUS

Once the calculus has been palpated and identified and the ureter immobilized, the ureterotomy is made by incision over the stone in the direction of the longitudinal axis of the ureter. A no. 11 or 12 Bard Parker blade, sharp side up, serves admirably. Take care not to make a spiral incision because of a poorly immobilized ureter. After *all* layers have been severed, the calculus can often be lifted out with the point of the knife, which is far less traumatic than the insertion of a stone forceps. The calculus can then be inspected and compared with its radiographic image. A ureteral or red rubber catheter must be passed up and down the ureter through the incision to test its patency. Gentle irrigation of the catheter with saline serves to wash out any residual small stone particles. The edges of the ureterotomy should be approximated with a few widely spaced 4–0 chromic atraumatic sutures placed in the serosa. A large Penrose drain is left at the ureterotomy site. If the stone appears to be particularly mobile, a Babcock clamp placed above and below the stone is helpful. Transfer of the calculus to an unaffected site by "milking" before opening the ureter is usually not necessary.

A flat plate of the abdomen on the day of surgery can be of inestimable value. If the calculus cannot be found, the surgeon must stop and consider whether the stone has passed into the bladder or has migrated upward, perhaps even into the kidney. Emptying the bladder before operation is important, and cystotomy is permissible if the surgeon suspects the calculus to be in the bladder. Calculi that have migrated upward are a different matter. If a dilated ureter is present, vigorous irrigation with a catheter passed through ureterotomy into the renal pelvis may wash the calculus back into the ureter within reach. Another maneuver is to attach an no. 8 French red rubber catheter to suction. The catheter tip must be cut off squarely, and a small hole cut near the flared end to control the suction within the fingertip. The catheter is passed up the ureter in the hope of engaging the calculus by suction. If this fails, the Dormia stone basket can be tried, for one or two "passes" before extending the incision upward.

CONCLUSIONS

The two-incision system advocated here has the advantage that either incision can be extended, within limits, to explore almost all the ureter if need be. The ureter, if handled gently and intelligently and not stripped any more than necessary, will heal rapidly.

REFERENCES

1. Cabot AT: Observations upon the anatomy and surgery of the ureter. Am J Med Sci 103:43, 1892
2. Gibson CL: The technique of operations of the lower portion of the ureter. Am J Med Sci 139:65, 1910

3. Fishman JL, Weiner I, Wexler N: Relationship of the distal ureter to obliterated hypogastric artery. Urology 8:387, 1976

ANNOTATED BIBLIOGRAPHY

Cabot AT: Observations upon the anatomy and surgery of the ureter. Am J Med Sci 103:43, 1892, and Gibson CL: The technique of operations on the lower portion of the ureter. Amer J Med Sci 139:65, 1910

These two articles would be required reading for the history buff. both are well written, the Cabot article being an excellent exposition of ureteral surgical anatomy. One is amused to learn that silk was used to close the ureterotomy. Gibson's report is about a pioneering operative approach to the lower ureter, previously considered inaccessible. The reader should compare what is now called a Gibson incision with the original illustrations!

Prince CL: Lumbar ureterolithotomy, J Urol 54:368, 1945

This concerns the Foley incision. Because of the fine Didusch illustrations and clear text this is to be preferred to Foley's original (1935) article and most other texts. Prince made several important changes in technique (Foley neither drained the operative site nor passed a catheter or bougie up or down the ureter).

The operation can be completed with local infiltration anesthesia in 20 minutes if all goes well. A small incision over Petit's triangle reveals the transversalis layer, which is incised after the lattissimus dorsi and external oblique layers have been undermined and retracted. Deep retrators are inserted as the posterior surface of Gerota's fascia is dissected off and up from the quadratus lumborum and iliopsoas muscles. The ureter can be seen coursing downward under this posterior surface of Gerota's. Noncrushing clamps are applied above and below the stone, which is then removed. The ureter is closed as are the transversalis layer and skin, leaving a Penrose drain at the ureterotomy site. Placement of the incision directly over the location of the stone is important to success. This article is a must.

Shaw EC: Vaginal ureterolithotomy. J Urol 35:289, 1936.

This article also has superb Didusch drawings and should be consulted. In this procedure the cervix is drawn downward and laterally with a tenaculum. A small horizontal incision is made in the vaginal fornix adjacent to the cervix and a finger inserted to dissect the portion of ureter which can be felt to contain the stone. Assisted by a finger, the operator grasps the ureter with a Babcock clamp above the stone and draws it through the vaginal incision. With the patient in lithotomy position, the direction of the ureter will seem reversed; the direction of the ureter coursing downward and laterally (toward the sacrum) is, in fact, toward the kidney. The calculus is removed in the usual manner, and a Penrose drain is inserted adjacent to the ureterotomy; this is important, since retroperitoneal urinary accumulation can occur. The drain is removed when urinary drainage (if there is any) ceases. The vagina is closed with interrupted 0 chronic catgut sutures.

Barnhouse DH, Johnson SM III, Marshall M Jr, Price SE Jr: Transvesical ureterolithotomy J Urol 109:585, 1973, Landes RR, Gavigan JR, Fehrenbaker LG: Transvesical meatal-sparing ureterolithotomy. J Urol 109:587, 1973, and Maynard JF, Landsteiner EK: Pull-through ueterolithotomy. J Urol 107:365, 1972

These three articles relate to calculi impacted in the intramural or juxtavesical ureter. The pull-through operation suggested by Maynard and Landsteiner requires circumcision of the orifice and dissection of the ureter in Waldeyer's sheath, thus allowing the ureter to be pulled down into the opened bladder to a degree that brings the calculus into view. It is then a simple matter to do a ureterotomy. The anatomic relationships are then restored by closing the ureter and sewing the meatus in place. Similarly,

Barnhouse and Landes in their articles suggest opening the bladder above the orifice over the intramural ureter. The dissection is simple especially if the calculus can be palpated. Closure of the ureter and bladder restores anatomic integrity. Landes feels that Maynard's pull-through operation is preferable when calculus lies in one of duplicate ureters with double orifice. This would also tend to protect the vascular sheath. The transvesical approach is also suitable for juxtavesical calculi if an appropriate extravesical drain is placed.

Gil–Vernet JM: Transverse ureterotomy. J Urol 111:755, 1974, and Maddocks R, Jewell E, Decenzo JN, Leadbetter CW Jr: Management of ureterotomy incision in 100 consecutive ureterolithotomies. J Urol 116:422, 1976

Gil–Vernet reports on 73 transverse ureterotomies for stone that encompass half to two thirds of the ureteral circumference. The author does a careful, watertight, 6–0 chromic catgut closure, which, he feels, avoids extravasation of urine, fistula formation, and postoperative stenosis. There were no complications in 72 cases done this way. U.S. urologists, however, will probably continue to do longitudinal ureterolithotomy. Maddocks compared drainage time and other Morbidity among patients whose ureterotomies were left open or closed loosely with 5–0 or 6–0 chromic catgut either as interrupted or as continuous suture. There were "no striking disparities among three closure methods" except that wound drainage of urine appears to have been shortened by primary closure of the ureterotomy by 1 to 2 days.

Overview: Ureteral Calculi

Arthur T. Evans

NATURAL HISTORY

In order to provide good care for patients with ureteral calculus disease, one must understand the natural history of ureteral calculi. Note that only four problems necessitate ureteral calculus surgery: (1) urosepsis due to infection in the renal unit above the obstructing ureteral calculus, (2) unrelenting pain due to ureteral obstruction, (3) calculus obstruction of a ureter in a patient with a solitary kidney, and (4) progressive deterioration of renal parenchyma due to ureteral calculus obstruction. At times, there is a social or economic need for the removal of a calculus (*i.e.,* so that a patient can reassume business, social or family activities).

The size of any calculus in a ureter is predetermined by the size of the ureteropelvic junction. Sixty percent of ureteral calculi under 4 mm in the upper ureter and 70% of those in the lower ureter will pass spontaneously. Calculi of 5 mm or more in the upper half of the ureter rarely pass spontaneously. Many calculi remain in the ureter for many months without producing significant symptoms or producing changes in the ureter or renal parenchyma above them. The patient who is being considered for surgery for the removal of a ureteral calculus must therefore be evaluated in light of these facts

before surgical removal of the ureteral calculus is undertaken. In addition, note that it is possible, by use of the Evans loop, to manipulate and guide stones out of the upper ureter into the bladder and, by use either of the Evans loop or of one of the stone baskets, to remove calculi from the lower fourth of the ureter.[1] Also, it is essential to consider, before surgical intervention, in the patient who has had a previous calculus, performing a metabolic evaluation to determine the etiology of the calculus.[2]

DIAGNOSIS

Before undertaking surgical removal of ureteral calculus, the proper diagnosis must be made. A plain x-ray film of the abdomen, including both kidneys and the full length of the ureters and the bladder, must be obtained. A calcification in the line of the ureter indicates that a calculus may be present in the ureter. This is especially true in the patient who has severe pain in the costovertebral angle radiating down along the course of the genital femoral nerve into the suprapubic area, the scrotum, the labia, and the uppermost medial aspect of the thigh. Tenderness in the area of the calculus and in the costovertebral angle and flank associated with nausea, vomiting, and ileus and the finding of red blood cells (RBCs) or white blood cells (WBCs) in the urine helps substantiate the diagnosis of a ureteral calculus as a cause of ureteral obstruction. However, in the case of xanthine and uric acid calculi, no calcification need be seen. Therefore, it is important to obtain an excretory urogram to identify the presence, and the position, of the calculus in relationship to the ureter on the symptom-producing side. Also, one must rule out the presence of additional calculi in the upper urine transport system on the symptomatic side and, also important, the presence of calculi in the renal calices, pelvis, or ureter on the asymptomatic side, because stones are at times bilateral but symptomatic only on one side.

The first films of a serial excretory urogram study may demonstrate a column of contrast medium down to the point of the calcification. There may be mild or considerable ureteral dilatation above the point of the calculus. There may be caliectasis and pyelectasis also. However, the simple appearance on the anteroposterior film of a calcification in apposition to the column of contrast medium does not ensure that the calculus is in the ureter. Oblique, and at times even lateral, x-ray studies should be done to demonstrate that the column of contrast medium in the ureter overlies the calcification on the anteroposterior, oblique, and lateral positioned x-ray films. Ensure that the opacity is not extrinsic to the contrast column and, in actuality, is a phlebolith, a calcified node, or a plaque of calcium in a vessel wall. One should never operate just on the basis of the anteroposterior film.

Frequently a calculus will obstruct the ureter to such a degree that the intraureteral and renal pelvis pressure become so great as to delay the passage of contrast medium from the nephrons into the calices, pelvis, and ureter immediately. Delayed films at 1, 2, 3, 6, 12, or 24 hours may be necessary to identify contrast medium in the ureter at a great enough concentration to identify the position of the suspected obstructing calculus. Again, obtain anteroposterior and oblique films. If the calculus is low, it may be necessary to have the patient empty his bladder of the excretory contrast medium in order to identify calculi in the lower ureter.

If in doubt about the existence of a ureteral calculus, pass a ureteral catheter to the point of obstruction and obtain anteroposterior and oblique films. If the calculus can be bypassed by the ureteral catheter, again obtain anteroposterior and oblique films. On all films the calcification must be overlaid by the ureteral catheter. A fine, nonopaque space between the calcification and the ureteral catheter may represent only the width of the ureteral wall; the suspected calcification may be attached to the exterior of the ureteral wall and not be within the lumen.

Ascertain that there are not multiple calculi in the kidney or the ureter before entertaining the idea of surgical removal. Renal tomograms with and without contrast medium may be beneficial. I believe all patients who are to have a calculus removed from the ureter should have plain nephrotomography of the renal unit above the calculus. I consider it imperative to obtain an x-ray film to identify the position of the calculus in the ureter just before the patient is placed on the operating table. CT scans are very helpful. Always obtain a KUB on the way to the operating room.

SURGICAL INCISION

The type of incision used for removal of a calculus depends on the position of the calculus in the ureter. As a rule, the standard incisions, subcostal or Gibson type for exposure of the upper or lower ureter, respectively, are the most dependable for efficient removal of a ureteral calculus. Some workers have advocated other types of incisions for ureterolithotomy. I believe the subcostal incision gives adequate exposure for any calculus in the upper ureter. Resecting a rib or incising through an interspace of the ribs to gain access to a ureteral calculus is not necessary. The most important point in the subcostal incision is to incise the transversalis fascia at the tip of the 12th rib so that the ileohypogastric nerve is below the incision and can be protected and not damaged. I have never seen this nerve course downward from above the tip of the 12th rib. The retroperitoneal space, when entered with an incision at this level, should expose the lower pole of the kidney once Gerota's fascia is opened. Stones a bit lower in the ureter—below the lower pole of the kidney—can be readily palpated, and dissection, eluding the principal portion of Gerota's fascia, can be directed specifically to the calculus. Dissection posteriorly, with removal of fat, will protect one from becoming involved with the main blood supply to the kidney. Use the x-ray films previously taken; place them on the viewbox in the operating room to show where the calculus is positioned in relation to the lower pole of the kidney. Once the calculus is palpated in the ureter, ensure that it does not undergo trauma, which could cause it to slide back up into the renal pelvis. Prevent this by placing a Penrose drain or a hernia tape around the ureter and producing slight traction and angulation of the ureter above the calculus before manipulating it. Place a Babcock clamp around the ureter to prevent a stone from moving back up into the kidney. Once I feel the calculus with my left hand, I at times use my index finger and thumb to continually but lightly compress the ureter just above the stone and, with the aid of my assistants, dissect away the periureteral fat, allowing for complete control of the ureter and calculus during the exposure of the ureter and stone.

Once I have freed the periureteral fat from at least half the ureter, I consider this adequate for performing the ureterolithotomy. Try to avoid devascularization of the ureter any more than necessary. Before incising the ureter, I reassess the position of the calculus on the x-ray film in relationship to the lower pole of the kidney to make certain that the firm object I feel is the calculus. It is an unfortunate situation to incise the ureter and find that no calculus is present in the ureter at the point of the incision. Place a 4–0 chromic catgut suture with a wedged-on needle in the wall of the ureter at the point of the upper end of the intended ureteral incision. This will allow elevation of that ureteral wall and make incision of just the one wall more certain. To guard against such a mishap, I use a no. 12, or curved, blade to make the ureterotomy. I never incise the ureter until I have passed just the tip of the curved blade through the ureteral wall and wiggled the tip to make certain that I feel the gritty resistance of the calculus. I prefer to make the incision in the ureter at the top of the calculus because the ureter is dilated above the calculus. Frequently, a not-too-long incision, one that extends about halfway along the length of the calculus, is sufficient when the incision is begun at the upper extent of the calculus. A frequent error is making the incision through the muscularis but not through the urothelium of the ureter. Stretch the urothelium by the calculus to ensure that it has been cleanly and completely incised. Incomplete incision makes removal of the calculus impossible and increases ureteral wall trauma. With an incision as described, the calculus can often be "milked" up into the incision by pressure on it from below so that the calculus, including the lower portion, can easily be delivered through the ureterotomy incision. Deliver the calculus slowly with smooth tissue forceps, using side-to-side and front-to-back fine movement with only slight pressure. Attempt to make this incision through an avascular area of the ureter; however, this may be difficult to assess because of stretching of the ureteral wall and thinning out of the normally visible vasculature of the ureter.

Once the calculus is removed, place it in a dry specimen bottle and send it for complete analysis. Flush the ureterotomy incision with saline irrigating solution from an Asepto. Carefully palpate the ureter above and below the incision to make certain that no other calculi are present in the ureter in the immediate area. Then pass a no. 5 feeding tube up the ureter into the renal pelvis slowly to investigate for another calculus or an obstruction. The urine thereby obtained should be sent for culture. Thoroughly irrigate the renal pelvis, washing all "sand" from the pelvis and calices. Ensure that the irrigating fluid returns clear. If there is any obstruction in the ureter to the passsage of the feeding tube, explore the ureter and evaluate and correct the abnormalities. Withdraw the feeding tube, introduce it into the ureterotomy, and slowly pass it downward into the bladder. Pass it to the point where the patient can aspirate urine freely from the bladder through the tube with a syringe.

The treatment of the ureterotomy incision, once the stone has been removed and the ureter has been explored by catheter, varies in the hands of different urologists. I seriously question the value and certainly believe there is inherent danger in attempting to close a 3-mm (or less) incision tightly. Before long there will be microsurgical closure of the ureterotomy incision, but will it lead to any significant lasting benefits? The length of the ureterotomy incision is a factor in deciding on the treatment of this incision in the ureter. I prefer to close it loosely with 4–0 chromic catgut sutures, but I do not grasp the ureter wall; I simply grasp the adventitia on each side of the wound and bring the ureteral wall into juxtaposition. Some small incisions probably do not require closure. Some urologists do not close any ureterotomy incisions. Whatever the manner of treatment, thoroughly irrigate the area around the ureter, and, most important, replace the ureter in its normal bed. I believe that too frequently the ureter is angulated during removal of the calculus and afterward not replaced in its normal position in the retroperitoneal space. As a result, many times the angulation produced will be a site of future obstruction. Often, because of the size of the calculus and because of the trauma to the ureter from the calculus or during the ureterolithotomy, the viability of the ureter or the sharpness of the incision will be in question. Because of the availability of new synthetic in-dwelling stents such as the Finney and the Cook memory catheters, it may be wise to place a "double J" Finney multiholed ureteral catheter in the ureter from the kidney to the bladder.[3] This will permit constant diversionary drainage of the kidney for an extended time and will protect the questionable area of the ureter. If in real doubt about ureteral viability, resect the traumatized ureteral segment and then use a spatulated type of reanastomosis of the ureter over a Finney-placed "double J" catheter. Do not use a large-sized stent but, rather, a no. 5 French catheter, 26 cm to 27 cm. Obtain x-ray films at the operating table to ensure proper positioning of the stent. I feel that the availability of this type of stent makes the use of a ureterostomy tube, which has been advocated by some clinicians for unusual situations, a less realistic approach to the problem. Ensure that all the bleeding is controlled in the wound so that there is no possibility of a hematoma. Place Penrose drains in the cavity created by the surgery. Place one Penrose drain at the ureterotomy opening. The one at the ureterostomy should lead directly to the skin wound. All Penrose or cigarette drains should exit through a stab wound rather than through the incision. Close the wound in layers with interrupted 0 chromic catgut. The skin can be closed with staples or silk.

If the calculus "gets away" in the ureter or it cannot be located, intraoperative x-ray films are necessary. Most frequently, the calculus will be lost superiorly. This may require opening up Gerota's fascia of the entire kidney. Deliver the kidney into the wound and use Eastman operative x-ray film to assess the location of the migrant calculus in the kidney. If the subcostal incision does not suffice for delivery into the wound and adequate renal exposure, use the Nagamatsu technique of posterior segments of subperiosteal rib resection to obtain adequate exposure.[4] This is an extremely valuable exposure technique; every urologist should undertand it in order to improve renal and adrenal exposure. Approach the renal pelvis only from the posterior aspect; rotate the lateral border of the kidney anteriorly and medially to enter the renal pelvis and to obtain the stone in the area. Also, this exposure facilitates search of the calices with Randall forceps, if necessary.

The use of a Gibson incision for exposure of the lower end of the ureter gives good visualization. Extending it across the midline in the suprapubic area will permit bladder entrance or displacement away from the low-lying calculus and ureter for better exposure. In the obese patient, a problem exists in that if the calculus is very low in the ureter or just outside the bladder, exposure is very difficult. In such patients, I usually open the bladder and may work from inside and outside it to remove the calculus. The calculus may be brought out through a ureterotomy; sometimes, using an intraoperative stone basket through the ureteral orifice may help removal of the stone from the ureter. The ureter may be difficult to identify, but this is made easier if one identifies the ureter at the point at which it crosses the iliac vessels and then traces it down to the calculus. Placing a catheter in the ureter may facilitate the identification of the lower end of the ureter in the deep pelvis. Once the ureteral calculus is identified and the ureter freed of its adjacent fat, the incision in the ureter and the technique for calculus removal is the same as that for a calculus in the upper ureter, as described above. Do not hesitate, however, to work from within and without the bladder for calculi that are in the lower 1 cm to 2 cm of the ureter. Stenting the ureter has merit, and I suggest the "double J" memory type stents, either the Finney or the Cook type, especially if unusual trauma or excessive urine leakage from the ureter occurs. If there is extensive damage to the ureter at the very lower end, it may be wise to reimplant the ureter in the bladder by an antirefluxing technique.

Occasionally, a patient wil be anuric because obstructive calculi are in both ureters. However, bilateral ureteral calculi may permit normal urine flow around them. Approach such calculi through a transperitoneal midline incision, thereby removing the calculi from each ureter at the same operation. Correlate the immediate preoperative kidney, ureter, and bladder location with palpation to identify the location of the calculi. Incise the peritoneum over the portion of the ureter entrapping the calculus. Expose the ureter, and remove the calculus as described above. Penrose drains should be placed at the ureterotomy site and brought out through the retroperitoneal space to the skin through a stab wound. Close the peritoneum tightly with a 2–0 chromic catgut, locking, running suture.

Other interesting incisions that may be used are the muscle-splitting incision of Foley, in which an incision is made in the skin over Petit's triangle and the calculus removed without any muscles being cut. This is applicable only to calculi below the lower kidney pole and above the iliac crest. I frequently use this incision, and, if I can identify the calculus in the ureter readily and can gain access to the calculus, continue to use it without cutting any muscle. However, if at any time during the ureterolithotomy there is question about the application of this incision, abandon it. Extend the incision by cutting the muscles anteriorly, thus making the ureter visible and accessible.

An incision that may have some use is a posterior incision extending from the lower level of the 12th rib down along the perispinalis muscles, allowing entrance to the retroperitoneal space through the back to identify a ureteral stone. This can be an excellent incision if the calculus can be satisfactorily reached. It can be a disastrous incision if the calculus moves into the kidney pelvis or, especially, into a calix. Movement to a position in the lower half of the ureter would make the incision most inappropriate. I do not find the transperitoneal approach to the ureter or renal pelvis for calculi a wise choice except when bilateral ureteral calculi must be removed. An incision that I have used a few times is a paramedian-type incision directed down to the peritoneum. Upon exposure of this membrane, the peritoneum is dissected free and retracted medially to the midline, thus allowing visualization of the retroperitoneal space. This avoids entering of the peritoneal cavity and affords access to an adequate length of ureter to remove the calculus. This longitudinal extraperitoneal exposure can be used for ureterolithotomy of a calculus at any position in the ureter. Also, it is appropriate for multiple ureteral calculi dispersed in the ureter. This extraperitoneal exposure can be accomplished by a transverse incision at the level of the upper ureteral calculus for a single calculus. The incision has merit for upper ureteral calculi only.

COMPLICATIONS

The two most significant problems of ureterolithotomy are movement of the ureteral calculus after the last x-ray film is taken and severe damage to or interruption of the ureter.

Prepare for the first problem by making the proper initial incision in anticipation of such an event; that is, make an incision that can be extended upward or downward along the course of the ureter to permit exposure of the entire ureter if need be. The subcostal and Gibson incisions meet these requirements.

Anticipate intraoperative interruption or extensive damage to the ureter as a possible consequence of ureterolithotomy, especially if there is infection of that renal unit or if the ureteral calculus has been in place for an extended period and has therefore produced extensive ureteral ischemia. If interruption or extensive ureteral laceration occurs, resect the damaged portions of the ureter. Preferably, carry out a spatulated type of ureteral reanastomosis over a stent or catheter. Today, a Finney or Cook "double J" multiholed memory catheter is the method of choice. However, an alternative approach to the problem might be the placement of a nephrostomy tube to divert the urine and the combined use of a separate tube as a stent for the anastomosis site of the ureter. Unfortunately, significant ureteral damage occurs most frequently in the infected renal unit, and plastic reanastomosis surgery on the ureter in such instances is less likely to be successful.

POSTOPERATIVE CARE

The problems of postoperative care of the patient who has had a ureterolithotomy are, in general, the same as those of any postoperative patient. However, the specific problems are urinary fistula, obstruction of the ureter, uroma, and urosepsis.

Urocutaneous fistula can be prevented from becoming persistent by retracting the Penrose drain from the ureterotomy site after 2 or 3 days. At first, retract it only 1 cm or 2 cm and then withdraw it daily so that it is removed by the 5th postoperative day. If the fistula persists, pass a filiform-tipped no. 6 or 7 French ureteral catheter, by cystoscope, up the ureter and into the renal pelvis, leaving it for 6 to 7 days to divert the urine and to allow periureteral fat to plug the ureterotomy opening. If there is ureteral obstruction below the ureterotomy, the fistula will tend to persist.

Only if the ureter is quite dilated would I introduce a Cook or Finney memory catheter first—a filiform-type catheter should be used for simple bypassing of the ureterostomy. Cinefluoroscopy or x-ray studies used during the passage of the catheter will assist in preventing passage of the catheter into the extraperitoneal space.

Ureteral obstruction due to fibrosis of the ureter at the ureterostomy site, or site of reanastomosis if such was required, usually can be corrected only by open surgery. A nephrostomy in such a case, to divert the urine above the obstruction, is essential and should be used for an extended period before and after surgery to correct the obstruction. The time for re-exploration of the ureter should be immediately, that is, within the first 10 days. I probably would explore the ureter any time after acute sepsis has been corrected for 72 or more hours. It is a difficult, tedious operation at any time to remove or correct the obstruction of such a ureter.

Uroma is not an uncommon occurrence. If the ureter can be catheterized by cystoscopy, the renal pelvis urine diverted through it, further ureteral urine extravasation avoided, the uroma may resolve. If the uroma persists or enlarges, it may have to be drained by surgical incision and the ureteral rent repaired or the urine diverted. The use of a "double J" memory ureteral catheter may be the least traumatic to the kidney, the most convenient to the patient, and the method maintained for the longest acceptable period.

Acute pyelonephritis after ureterolithotomy is common. It may be less likely to occur if a broad-spectrum antibiotic is used preoperatively. Postoperative sepsis may be secondary to a uroma or postoperative ureteral obstruction. The institution of preoperative antibiotics is wise, especially in obstructive ureteral calculus disease.

REFERENCES

1. Evans AT: Manipulation of ureteral calculi. American Urological Association Courses, Vol 1, pp 79–98, Baltimore, Williams and Wilkins, 1979
2. Resnick MI, Rush WH, Boyce WH: Metabolic evaluation of renal stone patient. Urol Digest, August 1978
3. Finney RP: Experience with new double J ureteral catheter stent. J Urol 120:678, 1978
4. Nagamatsu G: Dorso-lumbar approach to the kidney and adrenal with osteoplastic flap. J Urol 63:569, 1950

ADDENDUM

Since this overview was written, time has allowed change. The change has been that of the significant advent of endourology and ureteroscopy with the rigid ureteroscope. Probably by the time this appears in print, the flexible ureteroscope will be available. The changes and advances in equipment for percutaneous nephroscopy and pyelolithotripsy, as well as upper ureteral calculus manipulation and percutaneous nephrostomy, may be great by 1984. At the present rate of development of these procedures, percutaneous upper ureteral calculus removal by lithotripsy or extraction will increase. The changes will make it more acceptable and more persons will be trained to perform such procedures. There will continue to be calculi extracted from the mid, lower, and even upper ureter by loops and baskets, however. There will also be a need for safe ureteral calculus removal by means of incisional ureterolithotomy. Ureteroscopy may permit safe ureterolithotripsy with time or very soon. Today these endoscopic areas are producing the greatest urologic wave of interest, along with extracorporeal shock wave lithotropsy. This area of activity will be interesting to observe and witness through the remainder of the 1980s.

PART SEVENTEEN

RECONSTRUCTIVE SURGERY OF THE URETEROVESICAL JUNCTION

38

THE LICH-GREGOIR ANTIREFLUX PLASTY: EXPERIENCES WITH 371 CHILDREN

Michael Marberger,* Jens E. Altwein, Eberhard Straub, Hans D. Wulff and Rudolf Hohenfellner

From the Departments of Urology and Pediatrics, University of Mainz Medical School, Mainz, West Germany

0022-5347/78/1202-0216$02.00/0
The Journal of Urology
Copyright © 1978 by The Williams & Wilkins Co.
Vol. 120, August
Printed in U.S.A.

ABSTRACT—The Lich-Gregoir antireflux procedure is a simple and safe method for the treatment of primary reflux of all grades if the ureter is not grossly dilated on the excretory urogram. Reflux was cured in 97.7 percent of 429 ureters in 371 children. A stenosis of the terminal ureter requiring reimplantation occurred in 0.5 percent. The over-all rate of reinterventions was 3.7 percent. This low complication rate makes surgical correction of reflux advisable if urinary tract infection and primary reflux cannot be eradicated by continuous antimicrobial therapy within 6 months.

In the treatment of children with vesicoureteral reflux the control of urinary infection is important to preserve renal function. The inability to achieve this is considered the common indication for antireflux operation. The

Accepted for publication September 2, 1977.
* Requests for reprints: Urologische Universitätsklinik, Langenbeckstr. 1, 6500 Mainz, West Germany.

extent of the conservative treatment trial preoperatively, however, is largely debatable, with a strong tendency today towards prolonged antimicrobial therapy. The success and complication rates of antireflux operation also influence this decision.

For the correction of congenital, primary vesicoureteral reflux we use routinely the Lich-Gregoir antireflux

515

plasty.[1,2] Since this technique is only used rarely in Anglo-American countries and differs significantly from the standard procedures of ureteral reimplantation our experiences with this method are presented herein.

CLINICAL MATERIAL AND METHODS

Between 1967 and June 1976, 371 children underwent the Lich-Gregoir antireflux procedure and were followed from 6 months to 8½ years. All children had had at

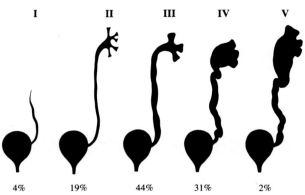

Fig. 1. Grades of reflux of patients subjected to operation. Classification according to cystogram as recommended by Heikkel and Parkkulainen.[3]

least 1 urinary tract infection and had received appropriate antimicrobial therapy for at least 3 months. Cystography was done via a small catheter. Reflux demonstrated with filling of the bladder at rest (low pressure) was graded from I to V, according to Heikkel and Parkkulainen (Fig. 1).[3] Ureters showing gross dilatation and distortion on the excretory urogram (IVP) are not included in this series. These cases are unsuitable for the Lich-Gregoir antireflux plasty.[4] In ureters of a normal caliber on the IVP with reflux the technique is, however, universally applicable, regardless of the extent of reflux (grades I to V) (Fig. 2). Of the operated renoureteral units 34 percent demonstrated radiological signs of pyelonephritis. Cystoscopy was done preoperatively with urethral calibration and evaluation of position and shape of the ureteral orifice. An antireflux operation was not performed when infravesical obstruction was present, in bladders with neurogenic dysfunction or in cases with severe renal insufficiency (renal function < 30 percent of normal).

The surgical technique was essentially as recommended by Gregoir,[5] with slight modifications. The ureter was approached routinely through a suprainguinal incision. In cases of bilateral reflux only 1 side was operated upon at a time. Duplicated ureters were not separated but were treated as a single unit. With the bladder filled the detrusor muscle was severed completely down to the mucosa and over 3 to 5 cm along a line

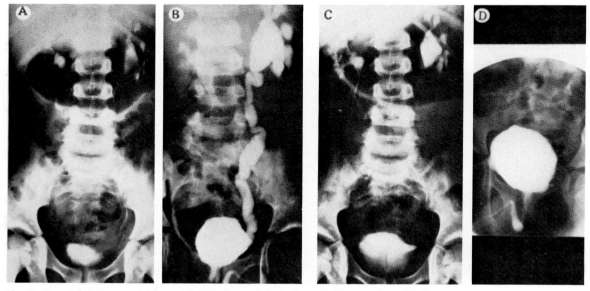

Fig. 2. Case of 6½-year-old boy. (A) IVP shows left pyelonephritic scarring. (B) Cystogram reveals bilateral reflux—grade IV on left side and grade II on right side. IVP (C) and cystogram (D) 6 months after Lich-Gregoir antireflux plasty on left side are negative for reflux. Reflux on right side resolved spontaneously.

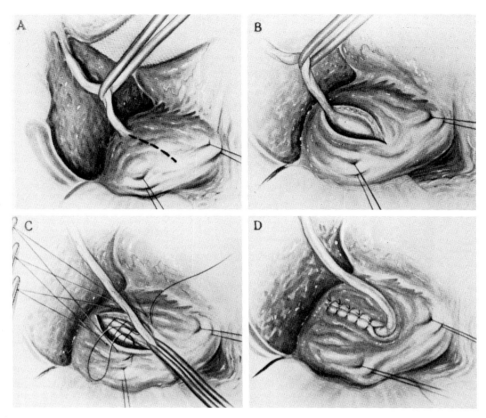

Fig. 3. Surgical technique. (*A*) Line of incision of detrusor muscle. (*B*) Incision completed down to bladder. (*C*) Ureter transposed into furrow in bladder wall and sutures for tunnel closure placed. (*D*) Final situs with musculature closed over ureter.

running vertically from the ureterovesical junction to the bladder dome (Fig. 3, *A* and *B*). Incidental tears in the mucosa were repaired with 4-zero plain catgut. After transposing the ureter in the formed furrow the musculature was closed over it in 1 layer (Fig. 3, *C* and *D*). Postoperatively, a drain was left in the paravesical space for 3 days and a thin Foley catheter was placed in the bladder for 5 days. No stents were used. An IVP 10 days postoperatively (1 exposure at 30 minutes postinjection was done to rule out obstruction. A potent antibiotic was administered immediately postoperatively. After discharge from the hospital all children received a continuous long-term antimicrobial chemotherapy, usually nitrofurantoin or cotrimoxazole. At regular intervals chemotherapy was interrupted for approximately 2 days and a urine culture was made. Significant infections were treated with appropriate antibiotics. If the urine was sterile after 6 months chemotherapy was discontinued. Otherwise it was administered until sterility was obtained in at least 2 cultures 6 to 12 weeks apart. A control

reflux cystogram was done 3 months postoperatively and another IVP after 6 months.

RESULTS

In the 371 children, 279 girls and 92 boys (sex relationship 3:1), 429 Lich-Gregoir procedures were done. The right side was involved in 191 plasties (44.5 percent), the left side in 180 (42 percent) and both sides in 58 (13.5 percent). Of the children 63 percent were between 6 months and 5 years old (Table 1).

The results of the reflux classification are given in Figure 1. Cystoscopically, a golf-hole orifice was encountered in 17 percent of the orifices with reflux. Another 67 percent displayed the sluggish behavior considered characteristic of reflux by Politano.[6] In 12 of 371 patients (3.2 percent) a contralateral reflux was noted on the cystogram 3 months after a unilateral antireflux procedure. However, in 64 of 371 patients (17.3 percent) the contralateral reflux had disappeared or improved

TABLE 1. Age at the Time of Antireflux Operation

Age (yrs)	No. Pts.	(%)
<1	45	(12)
1	33	(9)
2	24	(6)
3	39	(11)
4	46	(12)
5	49	(13)
6	30	(8)
7	32	(9)
8	24	(6)
9	17	(5)
10	15	(4)
11	12	(3)
12	2	(1)
13	3	(1)
Totals	371	100

TABLE 2. Associated Malformations

	Renoureteral Units (429 = 100%)	
	No.	(%)
Ureteral duplication	53	(12.2)
Hutch diverticulum	9	(2.1)
Ureterocele	4	(1.0)
Solitary kidney	2	(0.5)
Urethral stenosis	8	(1.9)
Occult neurogenic bladder	2	(0.5)
Totals	78	18.2

TABLE 3. Surgical Complications of 429 Lich-Gregoir Antireflux Procedures

	Renoureteral Units*	
	No.	(%)
Persistent reflux:	10	(2.3)
Reoperated	7	(1.6)
Managed conservatively	3	(0.7)
Hematoma:	13	(3.0)
Reoperated	6	(1.4)
Managed conservatively	7	(1.6)
Ureteral stenosis:	2	(0.5)
Reimplantation	2	(0.5)
Iatrogenic diverticulum:	14	(3.2)
Reoperated	1	(0.2)
No treatment	13	(3.0)

* Of 39 (9%) complications 16 (3.7%) were treated surgically and 23 (5.3%) were not.

significantly. Among the associated urinary tract malformations ureteral duplication was the most common (Table 2).

There was no operative mortality but in 3.7 percent (16 of 429 operated units) a surgical complication requiring reintervention occurred (Table 3).

Reflux was cured in 97.7 percent after 429 Lich-Gregoir procedures. The 10 instances of recurring reflux were treated conservatively in 2 patients, with Cohen's antireflux plasty[7] in 3, with the Paquin procedure in 2 and with a second Lich-Gregoir plasty in 2. All of these children became free of reflux subsequently. Two cases of stenosis of the terminal ureter were managed successfully by a temporary nephrostomy and subsequent reimplantation, 1 by the Boari flap technique and 1 by the Cohen technique.

Of the 371 children 245 have been followed for more than 3 years. The results of the bacteriological urine followup studies are reported extensively elsewhere.[8] In brief, 18 percent of the patients had positive urine cultures, despite long-term antimicrobial treatment after 6 months, and 12 percent after 1 year. Even after 3 years of chemotherapy 1 percent of the children were infected. After urine sterilization had been achieved and the antimicrobial therapy discontinued 5 percent of the

patients had a reinfection within the first 3 postoperative years, with 2 percent displaying clinical signs of acute pyelonephritis.

DISCUSSION

''The primary goals of antireflux surgery are: preservation of renal function, restoration of the anatomy of the incompetent ureterovesical junction, and elimination of urinary tract infection. The differences in the various antireflux procedures are the manner in which the end-result is achieved, the ease with which surgery is performed, the mortality involved and the surgical cures obtained.''[6]

The Lich-Gregoir operation is a simple and safe method for the treatment of vesicoureteral reflux of all grades except for ureters that appear dilated on the IVP. It is a unique procedure in that it is the only antirefluxing operation done entirely outside of the bladder without severing the ureter. The extravesical approach avoids damage to adjacent viscus as has been described occasionally after transvesical reimplantation.[9]

Lich and associates reported that reflux was cured in 94 percent of 37 patients with moderate ureteral dilation and 5 of 11 patients with dilated ureters.[1] Gregoir and Schulman achieved relief of reflux in 97 percent of 409 ureters,[10] and Moormann and associate reported relief in 96 percent of 116 ureters.[11] Among American urologists, however, this operation has not gained popularity, obviously owing to the poor results achieved with the technique in early reports. Hendren failed to cure reflux with the Lich-Gregoir operation in 58 percent (43 ureters in 23 patients)[12] and Glenn had only 1 positive result out of 8 operations.[13]

A majority of these operative failures was owing to a neglect of important technical details. The tunnel must be fashioned vertically on the posterior bladder wall in a line between the bladder dome and vesicoureteral orifice. If it has a slanting or horizontal position, as shown in a schematic drawing of the technique by Hendren,[12] or is situated on the lateral or anterior bladder wall, ureteral obstruction by kinking will occur frequently. The bladder musculature between the ureter and the bladder mucosa must be severed completely, particularly the transverse fibers near the ureteral hiatus. To prevent reliably reflux the length of the tunnel should be at least 3 cm and in older children preferably 4 to 5 cm long.

In our series reflux was resolved in 419 of 429 ureters (371 children), rendering a 97.7 percent success rate. The percentage of postoperative complications requiring revision was 3.7 percent. These results are comparable to the surgical cure rate of 95 to 97 percent reported for the Politano-Leadbetter technique.[9,12,14] Contralateral reflux, however, occurred in only 3.2 versus 20 percent after reimplantation,[14] apparently because the attachment of the ureter to the trigone is not disturbed by the Lich-Gregoir technique. Furthermore, its application in ureteral duplications with lower pole or upper and lower pole reflux is simple and was successful in all 53 cases.

Admittedly, a number of our patients probably could have been managed conservatively without any harmful effect on renal function. However, pyelonephritic scarring of a previously normal, reflux-exposed kidney cannot be absolutely prevented by precise, intermittent antibiotic therapy. In the series by Lenaghan and associates treated in this manner 21 percent of 76 unscarred kidneys deteriorated.[15] On the other hand, in the Stanford series renal clubbing and scarring were not observed in previously normal renal units after surgical correction of reflux.[16] Continuous prophylactic antimicrobial therapy seems to be superior to intermittent antibiotic treatment in preventing fresh renal scarring.[17] However, the impact of this treatment on the child's life is considerable: continuous drug administration for years, regular doctor visits at short intervals, frequent laboratory and radiological controls, and a strict regimen of toilet habits and also of recreational activities. Aside from possible undue drug effects the psychological problems of this therapy, marking the child chronically ill, are obvious. A large number of patients will be poor attenders and these are especially endangered by recurrent infections and progressive renal scarring.[16,18] Finally, although a detrimental effect of chronic sterile reflux on renal function owing to a water-hammer effect has not been proved definitely there is growing evidence that this will occur.[19–21]

Because of the low complication rate in our series it is our policy to perform an antireflux operation if urinary tract infection and significant reflux are not eradicated after 6 months of continuous conservative treatment.

REFERENCES

1. Lich, R., Jr., Howerton, L. W. and Davis, L. A.: Recurrent urosepsis in children. J Urol, 86:554, 1961
2. Grégoir, W. and Van Regemorter, G. V.: Le reflux vésico-urétéral congénital. Urol Int, 18:122, 1964
3. Heikkel, P. E. and Parkkulainen, K. V.: Vesico-ureteric reflux in children. A classification and results of conservative treatment. Ann Radiol, 9:37, 1966
4. Stockamp, K., Boehm, G., Greinacher, I., Straub, E. and Hohenfellner, R.: Surgical management of the congenital megaureter: results of 72 reimplantations. Acta Urol, in press
5. Gregoir, W.: The Lich-Gregoir antireflux operation. In: Surgical Paediatric Urology. Edited by H. B. Eckstein, R. Hohenfellner and D. I. Williams. Stuttgart: Thieme, p 56, 1977
6. Politano, V. A.: Vesicoureteral reflux. In: Urologic Surgery, 2nd ed. Edited by J. F. Glenn. New York: Harper & Row, Publishers, Inc., p 278, 1975
7. Cohen, S. J.: Ureterocystoneostomie: eine neue Antireflux-technik. Acta Urol, 6:1, 1975
8. Straub, E. and Stockamp, K.: 'Urologisch bedingte' Pyelonephritis: Verlauf unter medikamentöser Therapie nach operativer Behandlung der kongenitalen Harnwegsfehlbildung. Langzeitbeobachtungen an 398 kinderurologischen Fällen aus fünf Jahrjgängen. Monatsschr Kinderheilkd, 124:511, 1976
9. Tocci, P. E., Politano, V. A., Lynne, C. M. and Carrion, H. M.: Unusual complications of transversical ureteral implantation. J Urol, 115:731, 1976
10. Gregoir, W. and Schulman, C. C.: Die extravesikale Antirefluxplastik. Urologe A, 16:124, 1977
11. Moormann, J. G., Burwick, P. and Kemper, K.: Antirefluxoperation: Indikation und Ergebnisse. Urologe A, 9:241, 1970
12. Hendren, W. H.: Reoperation for the failed ureteral reimplantation. J Urol, 111:403, 1974
13. Glenn, J. F.: Panel on Hydronephrosis and Hydroureter: Perspectives in Management. Annual meeting of Society for Pediatric Urology, American Urological Association, Chicago, Illinois, May 16, 1971
14. Warren, M. M., Kelalis, P. P. and Strickler, G. B.: Unilateral ureteroneocystostomy: the fate of the contralateral ureter. J Urol, 107:466, 1972
15. Lenaghan, D., Whitaker, J. G., Jensen, F. and Stephens, F. D.: The natural history of reflux and long-term effects of reflux on the kidney. J Urol, 115:728, 1976
16. Govan, D. E., Fair, W. R., Friedland, G. W. and Filly, R. A.: Management of children with urinary infections: the Stanford experience. Urology, 3:273, 1975
17. Smellie, J., Edwards, D., Hunter, N., Normand, I. C. S. and Prescod, N.: Vesico-ureteric reflux, and renal scarring. Kidney Int, Suppl 4, 8:S65, 1975
18. Tanagho, E.: Personal communication, June 1977
19. Berquist, T. W., Hattery, R. R., Hartman, G. W., Kelalis, P. P. and DeWeerd, J. H.: Vesicoureteral reflux in adults. Am J Roentgen, 125:314, 1975
20. Salvatierra, O., Kountz, S. L. and Belzer, F. O.: Primary

vesicoureteral reflux and end-stage renal disease. JAMA, 226:1454, 1973

21. Helin, I.: Clinical and experimental studies on vesico-ureteric reflux. Scand. J Urol Nephrol, Suppl 28, 1975

22. Hohenfellner, R., Stockamp, K. and Wulff, H. D.: Urologie. In: Operationen im Kindeslater. Edited by H. Kunz. Stuttgart: Georg Thieme Verlag, vol 2, p 327, 1975

EDITORIAL COMMENT

This is a most provocative report. The Lich-Gregoir procedure is considered historical in this country. Although early results may be quite satisfactory, the followup is not so encouraging in regard to recurring reflux (Hendren). The results in this report are for a 6-month followup. Lich believes that his long-term results have held true to the 94 percent reported many years ago and attributes this success to a generous undermining of the mucosa after the muscular furrow is created.

Some interesting statistics should be noted. On an evaluation of the 3-month cystogram after unilateral procedures contralateral reflux was evident in only 3.2 percent of the cases. Contralateral reflux disappeared or improved in 17.5 percent of the patients. Only 13.5 percent required bilateral reimplants. I wonder why the authors elect to repair only 1 side at a time when bilateral reflux is present. *J.W.D.*

REPLY BY AUTHORS

This procedure is widely used in Europe and excellent results have been reported (Gregoir). The high rate of recurring reflux noted in some American reports can be traced obviously to the neglect of decisive technical details, as indicated in our paper. Our patients were followed between 6 months and 9 years. At the examination terminating the 2-year postoperative period of close followup for control of urinary infection late ureteral stenosis or recurring reflux was not noticed in a single case.

Simultaneous, bilateral repair of reflux always has the potential hazard of severe complications of the upper urinary tract. Although it may be uneconomical in light of our low complication rate we prefer staged repairs. The improvement of contralateral reflux observed in 17.5 percent of patients after a unilateral operation further justifies this attitude.

Commentary: The Lich–Gregoir Antireflux Plasty: Indications and Limitations

Michael Marberger

Primary, uncomplicated vesicoureteric reflux resulting from a congenital malformation of the ureterovesical junction can be corrected by a variety of surgical techniques, with success rates exceeding 95%.[1] The small number of complications, however, occasionally turn out to be surgical catastrophes, disabling the patient for life.[2] A single experience of this kind will, in the memory of the managing physician, outweigh many successful operations, in particular when performed for a borderline indication. This partly explains the popularity of conservative treatment regimens and the continuing quest for safer surgical techniques. For over 10 years the Lich–Gregoir antireflux plasty has been our method of choice, mainly because of its technical simplicity and low complication rate. The preceding article was intended to underline this point, and continuing experience with now well over 500 children sub-

mitted to this procedure further substantiates the results reported therein.

LIMITATIONS

However, it is essential that the surgeon be aware of the limitations and potential pitfalls of the technique. First, the method is unsuitable for managing obstructed refluxing ureters, in which excision of the stenosed segment and, very often, ureteral tailoring is necessary for success. In his earlier reports, Gregoir modified his method for these cases by combining ureteral tailoring, ureteroneocystostomy, and formation of a submucosal tunnel exclusively by an extravesical approach. He later abandoned this technique, obviously because of poor results.

The main advantage of the standard extravesical antireflux plasty as described lies in the preservation of ureteral continuity. This is lost with any pathologic condition requiring opening of the bladder or transection of the ureter. It has therefore been our policy to restrict the method to refluxing ureters not dilated on the excretory urogram when the bladder is empty. The ureteral caliber demonstrated at cystography is unimportant for this decision; 77% of the operated ureters presented in the article appeared dilated on the preoperative cystogram, and 37% were tortuous despite a slender appearance on the excretory urogram.

Second, neurogenic dysfunction, contraction or fibrosis of the bladder, and severe infravesical obstruction are clear contraindications for the procedure. Kidneys with less than 30% of the function of a normal kidney in split renal function tests may rapidly deteriorate after any type of antireflux surgery because of their inability to compensate for even the slightest increase of ureteral pressure. These patients should likewise be exempted from corrective surgery.

Third, in bilateral vesicoureteric reflux we routinely stage reconstruction. Dissection of the posterior and lateral bladder wall results in some denervation of the detrusor. In a unilateral procedure this is without functional sequelae, but when performed bilaterally, temporary atonic vesical dysfunction may occur, particularly in children younger than 12 months of age. Since the trigone remains untouched in extravesical antireflux plasty, contralateral reflux into a ureter free of reflux preoperatively is exceedingly rare. In a substantial number of patients with bilateral reflux, contralateral reflux will disappear after a unilateral procedure, rendering surgery of this ureter superfluous.

Finally, the risk of stenosis or recurrent reflux after an extravesical reflux plasty is considerably higher in adults than in children.[3] This is probably due to the bulkier periureteral structures in adults, which require more extensive dissection of the distal ureter and a longer and wider detrusor incision. In adults we therefore now prefer the Cohen technique of transvesical ureteroneocystostomy.[4]

TECHNIQUE

Although simple, the following technical details of the procedure must be adhered to meticulously:

The tunnel must be fashioned vertically on the posterior bladder wall in a line between the ureteral orifice and bladder vertex; if performed on the lateral bladder wall or in a slanting or transverse position, postoperative obstruction will invariably occur in a high number of patients because of kinking of the ureter.

The tunnel must have an adequate length (at least 3 cm to 4 cm), and all detrusor fibers within the tunnel between bladder mucosa and ureter must be completely transected.

Two of my early cases of recurrent reflux resulted from faulty closure of the detrusor muscle over the ureter. Avoid this by preplacing all sutures for closure of the tunnel under sight, grasping plenty of detrusor muscle. The bladder should be half-filled during this phase and emptied before the knots are tied. Follow-up cystograms occasionally demonstrate small diverticula, but in our experience these are usually of no clinical significance, and we do not routinely close the tunnel in the two-layer technique advocated by Gregoir.

Recently one of my patients experienced a ureterocutaneous fistula that subsided spontaneously without subsequent obstruction after temporary ureteral catheter drainage. The complication was obviously due to an excessive use of diathermy, which should therefore be employed judiciously in dissection of the distal ureter.

Scrupulous adherence to these details will help control primary vesicoureteral reflux in this procedure. In Europe, it is one of the most commonly employed methods for the surgical treatment of this clinical entity, and uniformly excellent results have been reported.[5]

DISCUSSION

The role of surgery in the management of primary vesicoureteric reflux has aroused considerable controversy in the last years, and, based on newer experimental and clinical data, a more conservative approach has generally been adopted.[6,7] Conservative management, however, is not without risks. High-grade reflux persists in over 50% and low-grade reflux in over 15% of all patients, even under a most precise and meticulous conservative treatment regimen over years.[7] Follow-up examination can become critical in the adolescent, who outgrows the scope of the pediatrician and may come under medical surveillance only, for example, after a spell of pyelonephritis during pregnancy. Seventy-five percent of 134 ureterorenal units with primary vesicoureteric reflux seen in 87 adults at one hospital during a 10-year period showed radiologic signs of severe pyelonephritic damage, 39% in an end-stage phase.[3] Seventy-one of these patients were women. Many had been treated for recurrent urinary tract infection during childhood, experienced a period of rather few symptoms during early adolescence, and had severe reinfections when they reached the age of sexual activity.

The rate of significant surgical complications in the series presented, namely, ureteral stenosis and persistent reflux, was 3.7%. All the afflicted renoureteral units were salvaged, and corrective surgery proved to be considerably simpler than when performed after a primary transvesical approach, particularly because the problem was unilateral. With the extravesical antireflux plasty, we therefore feel antireflux surgery is even justified in the occasional patient with low grade reflux who does not respond to a conservative treatment trial over 6 to 12 months.

REFERENCES

1. Politano VA: Management of vesicoureteral reflux. In Libertino JA, Zinman L (eds): Reconstructive Urologic Surgery. Baltimore, Williams & Wilkins, 1977

2. Rabinowitz R, Barkin M, Schillinger JF, Jeffs RD: Salvaging the iatrogenic megaureter. J Urol 121:330, 1979
3. Thüroff JW, Altwein JE, Marberger M, Hartmann I, Hohenfellner

R: Der primäre vesico-ureterale Reflux im Erwachsenenalter. Akt Urol 10:328, 1979

4. Cohen SJ: The Cohen technique of ureteroneocystostomy. In Eckstein HB, Hohenfellner R, Williams DI (eds): Surgical Pediatric Urology. Philadelphia, WB Saunders, 1977

5. Sigel A: Harnwegsinfekt und Vesikorenaler Reflux, Diskussion, Springer-Verlag, Berlin, 1977

6. Ransley PG: Vesicoureteric reflux: Continuing surgical dilemma. Urology 12:246, 1978

7. Edwards D, Normand CS, Prescod N, Smellie JM: Disappearance of vesicoureteric reflux during long-term prophylaxis of urinary tract infection in children. Br Med J 2:285, 1977

ANNOTATED BIBLIOGRAPHY

Lich R Jr, Howerton LW, Davis LA: Recurrent urosepsis in children. J Urol 86:554, 1961

The first description of an extravesical antireflux procedure, in which the ureter is intubated with a 4–0 ureteral catheter, dissected from contiguous vesical muscle, and placed in a 3-cm submucosal bed formed by incising the detrusor muscle down to the mucosa and reapproximating it over the ureter. The authors state that they were impressed by the smooth convalescence of these patients, the lack of postoperative obstruction, and the reliable interruption of reflux.

Gregoir W, Van Regemorter G: Le reflux vésico-urétéral congénital. Urol Int 18:122, 1964

A description of an extravesical antireflux plasty that differs from the Lich technique in that the intramural ureter is not freed circumferentially of all muscular fibers, but only in its anterior aspect in the ureterovesical angle, and that neither a ureteral nor a urethral catheter is used. Reflux was successfully corrected in 31 of 35 refluxing ureters; 17 of these were extremely tortuous and dilated, and obviously obstructed, so that in addition to the submucosal tunnel fashioned by the technique described, ureteral tailoring and reimplantation from an exclusively extravesical approach was performed. Of the four failures, three were in this latter group.

Moormann JG, Burwick P, Kemper K: Antirefluxoperation: Indikation und Ergebnisse. Urologe A 9:241, 1970

The authors report a 96% success rate of the Gregoir antireflux plasty in 116 unobstructed ureters with primary reflux of a moderate degree.

Strohmenger P, Mellin P, Olbing H: die Bedeutung der Harnstauung für das Ergebnis von Antirefluxoperationen. Urologe A 10:195, 1971

Based on experience with the Gregoir antireflux plasty in 101 ureters with reflux of all grades with or without obstruction, the authors clearly point out that if the refluxing ureter already

appears dilated on the excretory urogram, the technique should not be used because of a failure rate exceeding 30%. In urographically slender ureters, however, they achieved a success rate of almost 90%, despite extreme tortuosity of some of them in the reflux cystogram. The authors stress the importance of a precise surgical technique, in particular, complete transection of all muscular fibers in the muscle trough fashioned for the ureter.

Hendren WH: ureteral reimplantation in children. J Pediatr Surg 3:649, 1968

In 43 ureters operated on by an extravesical technique similar to the Lich–Gregoir technique, the author observed postoperative obstruction in 7 and recurrent refflux in 18 and therefore rejects the extravesical approach. However, this series, which was mainly responsible for the poor acceptance of extravesical antireflux procedures in Anglo–American countries, contains a considerable number of obstructed megaureters, in which ureteroneocystostomy is clearly indicated. According to the schematic drawings of the technique in the article, the author forms the muscle trough for the ureter in the lateral bladder wall in a horizontal position and obviously does not divide all the muscular fibers at the ureteral hiatus between bladder mucosa and ureter, which would provide a good explanation for his high failure rate.

Gregoir W, Schulman CC: Die extravesikae Antirefluxplastik. Urologe A 16:124, 1977

The authors report the late results of 409 extravesical antireflux plasties performed in 247 patients with primary reflux. The late complication rate attributable to the surgical technique was 5%, which includes 4 cases of ureteral stenosis and 13 cases of recurrent vesicoureteral reflux. The authors now state that they consider serious dilatation of the terminal ureter with lengthening and kinking, which requires reconstructive procedures, as well as any associated pathology requiring opening of the bladder and serious renal failure as contraindications for extravesical antireflux surgery.

39

TECHNICAL CONSIDERATIONS IN DISTAL TUNNEL URETERAL REIMPLANTATION

James F. Glenn* and E. Everett Anderson

From the Division of Urology, Duke University Medical Center, Durham, North Carolina

0022-5347/78/1192-0194$02.00/0
The Journal of Urology
Copyright © 1978 by The Williams & Wilkins Co.
Vol. 119, February
Printed in U.S.A.

ABSTRACT—The advantages of a distal tunnel ureteral reimplantation have been elaborated upon previously. This method offers simplicity of transvesical exposure, rapidity of execution, excellent visibility of the terminal ureteral segments, minimal dissection and trauma in the paravesical space, the opportunity to advance the ureteral orifices to a physiologic position on the trigone and minimal risk of angulation, kinking or obstruction of the terminal ureter. It is now recognized that this method, with the modifications discussed herein, has wide applicability in the management of vesicoureteral reflux of all varieties and etiologies.

The surgical correction of vesicoureteral reflux is now clearly established as necessary and desirable in many cases of this pathological entity.[1] The various etiologic factors in vesicoureteral reflux have been discussed thoroughly[2-5] and are beyond the scope of this presentation.

Accepted for publication April 7, 1977.

* Requests for reprints: Box 3707, Duke University Medical Center, Durham, North Carolina 27710.

Techniques used to correct reflux[6-10] are various but all embrace the principle of a submucosal tunnel, creating a valve-like effect that permits only a unidirectional antegrade flow of urine. In 1964 the modified technique of a distal tunnel (Glenn-Anderson) ureteral reimplantation was first used after experimental study of the method in the laboratory by one of the authors and clinical application by the other. The technique and the results in the first 8 patients were reported.[11]

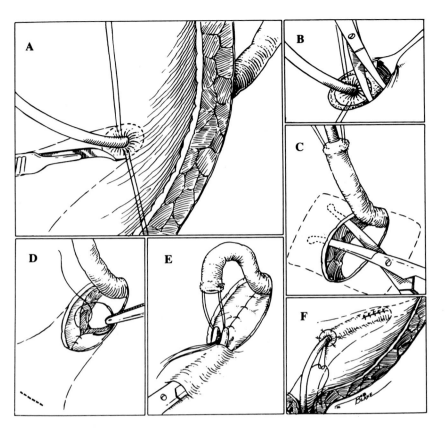

Fig. 1. Technique of distal tunnel ureteral reimplantation. (*A*) Catheter or probe in ureter with reflux, traction sutures taken in orifice are circumferential incision of mucosa. (*B*) Blunt and sharp dissection to mobilize transmural portion of ureter with blunt dissection of terminal ureter for 6 or 8 cm. (*C*) Mucosa lateral to enlarged hiatus mobilized from underlying bladder musculature. (*D*) Distal submucosal tunnel developed down on trigone and transverse incision made in mucosa with subsequent closure of bladder hiatus distally, everting knots and displacing ureter to proximal portion of hiatus. (*E*) Ureter then drawn down through distal submucosal tunnel (*F*) Ureteral orifice sutured to trigone and mucosa with everting 4-zero chromic catgut sutures and mucosa of original hiatus similarly approximated.

During the last 2 decades we have managed more than 800 adults and children with vesicoureteral reflux and attendant complications. During the last 12 years the distal tunnel technique of ureteral reimplantation has emerged as the treatment of choice. Virtually all of the techniques of ureteral reimplantation that have been advocated[3,7,12–19] have been used sporadically and, indeed, a large number of Politano-Leadbetter procedures have been accomplished. However, results of the distal tunnel technique so encouraged us[20,21] that this method had been applied preferentially to a broader segment of patients and is now used for the majority of our patients who require ureteral reimplantation.

As with all surgical procedures experience has brought about alterations in philosophy and technique. Herein we present the modifications of our concepts regarding the distal tunnel ureteral reimplantation and emphasize the operative technique currently used.

APPLICATION

In our original report we stated that the distal tunnel procedure was not universally applicable and was dependent upon size and configuration of the trigone since an adequate length of tunnel was necessary. It was indicated that the technique was usually not feasible in infants and that massively dilated ureters were probably best managed by other methods. We now recognize that neither of these concepts is absolutely correct and the modified technique described herein permits use of a distal tunnel reimplantation in virtually all patients of all ages and also affords ample opportunity for a reconstructive distal ureteroplasty if required.

A third concept originally held was that the technique was not applicable to patients with complete ureteral duplication. We have now used the distal tunnel technique in more than 2 dozen patients with complete duplication, unilaterally and bilaterally, usually reimplanting both ureters of a duplex system as a single unit. However, on 5 occasions we have accomplished a distal tunnel reimplantation of only the ureter with reflux, advancing the orifice to a point on the trigone distal to the orifice without reflux.

Similarly, it was our original impression that the distal tunnel technique could not be used in cases of massive reflux. We have treated successfully a series of patients with grade IV reflux, massive ureteral dilatation and tortuosity by the modified technique, which permits ample and adequate development of the terminal portion of the ureter for amputation, tapering or tailoring.

Finally, we believed that the distal tunnel ureteral reimplantation was a procedure to be used primarily and not in cases requiring reoperation to correct complications of previous procedures.[22,23] On the contrary, we have now used the disdal tunnel technique in a variety of situations requiring secondary or even tertiary reimplantation, usually for correction of persistent reflux but also in cases of ureterovesical junction obstruction.

TECHNIQUE

The procedure originally described embraced mobilization of only the terminal 2 or 3 cm of ureteral length and efforts were made to maintain the ureterovesical hiatus in its original configuration, avoiding enlargement of this hiatus. The principal modification of the technique has been the intentional generous development of a large hiatus, providing visibility of the extravesical and extraperitoneal space, the peritoneum and contiguous structures. Furthermore, the development of this hiatus permits mobilization of at least 6 to 8 cm of distal ureter,

often as much as 15 cm of ureter. Subsequent closure of the enlarged hiatus distal to the point of vesical entry of the ureter constitutes a substantial and significant portion of the tunnel, since mucosa lateral to the hiatus is mobilized for closure over the ureter after its advancement onto the trigone. Finally, creation and use of the hiatus in this manner diminish the necessary submucosal tunnel length distally on the trigone.

With a ureteral catheter or a flexible probe inserted in the ureteral orifice and the terminal portion of the ureter, traction sutures are placed at the orifice and a circumferential incision is made through the mucosa (Fig. 1A). Fine dissecting scissors are used for blunt and sharp techniques and the transmural portion of the ureter is liberated from the bladder wall (Fig. 1B). A vein retractor is placed on the superior aspect of the hiatus created, enlarging the hiatus by traction to permit mobilization of a generous portion of terminal ureter. Most often, the peritoneal reflection on the ureter can be visualized and the peritoneum can be displaced from the ureter bluntly using a bronchial dissector.

The mucosa lateral to the hiatus on either side is developed from underlying musculature to permit sub-

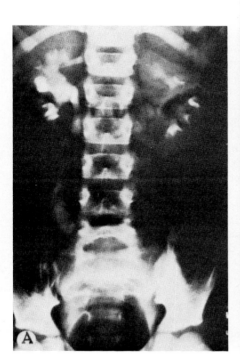
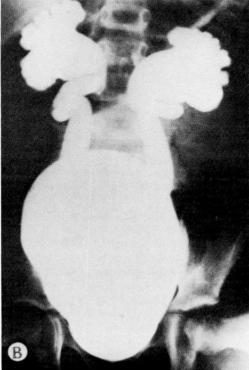

Fig. 2. Grade IV vesicoureteral reflux managed by distal tunnel technique. (A) Preoperative excretory urogram (IVP). (B) Preoperative voiding cystourethrogram.

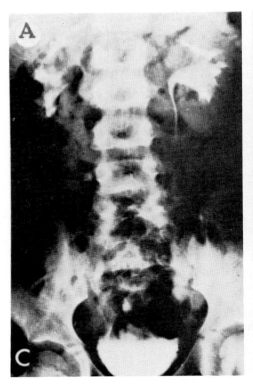

Fig. 3. Grade IV vesicoureteral reflux managed by distal tunnel technique. (*A*) Postoperative IVP. (*B*) Postoperative cystourethrogram.

sequent closure of mucosa over the ureter, which will be anterior to the closed musculature (Fig. 1*C*). The distal submucosal tunnel may then be developed. The bladder musculature of the enlarged hiatus is then closed distal to the point of entry to the ureter, usually using 5 or 6 interrupted sutures of 2-zero chromic catgut, and with the knots everted to the exterior surface of the bladder wall (Fig. 1*D*). Care must be taken not to occlude the ureter by closing the hiatus too snugly and the tip of a tonsil clamp should pass easily through the final hiatus parallel with the ureter.

The mucosa at the distal end of the trigonal submucosal tunnel is then incised transversally, a clamp is passed proximally through this tunnel, the traction sutures are grasped and the ureter is drawn down into the new position on the trigone (Fig. 1*E*). The terminal portion of the ureter, usually quite redundant, may be amputated to appropriate length and the ureter may be spatulated if desired. Anastomosis of the ureter to the trigonal substance and overlying mucosa is accomplished with interrupted sutures of 4-zero chromic catgut, usually using about 6 sutures to evert the ureteral mucosa, although no effort is made to create a nipple. Finally, the mucosa lateral to the hiatus is closed over the ureter to create the proximal portion of the submucosal tunnel,

again using an appropriate number of interrupted 4-zero chromic catgut sutures (Fig. 1*F*).

Stenting ureteral catheters are optional. Since the ureter has been advanced in its original direction there is little chance for angulation. If stents are used they are brought out through the urethra in female subjects or through the opposite anterolateral aspect of the bladder suprapubically in male subjects. A urethral Foley catheter may be used but we now prefer a suprapubic Malecot catheter in most cases, since this seems to diminish the tendency for postoperative bladder spasm and provides more effective urinary drainage.

If stents are used it is usually for 4 to 6 days. The suprapubic or indwelling Foley catheter may be removed after 6 days and patients generally are discharged from the hospital 7 days postoperatively.

RESULTS

A previous report documents the successful application of the distal tunnel technique.[21] In grade I reflux a successful result was achieved in 100 percent of patients operated on by this method. Grades II and III reflux were managed successfully in 97 and 96 percent of the clases, respectivley, failures primarily owing to persistent

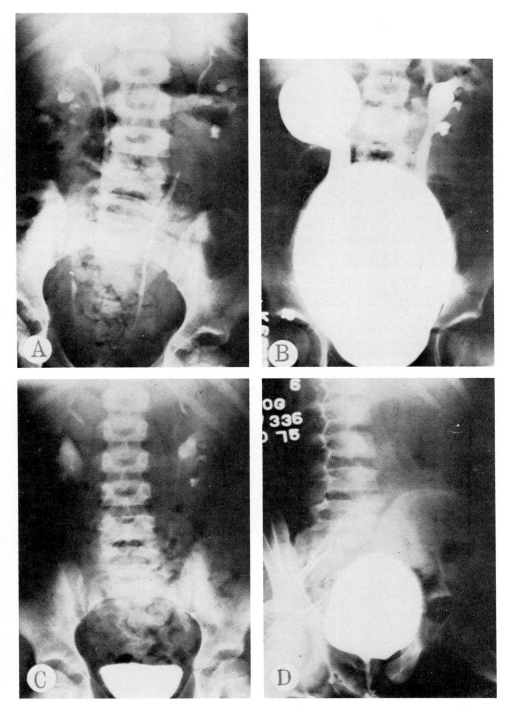

Fig. 4. Bilateral complete ureteral duplication with reflux to 3 of 4 segments managed by bilateral distal tunnel ureteral reimplantation. (*A*) Preoperative IVP. (*B*) Preoperative voiding cystourethrogram. (*C*) Postoperative IVP. (*D*) Postoperative cystogram.

or recurrent reflux, with secondary obstruction rarely encountered. By contrast, totally satisfactory management of grade IV reflux was achieved in only 50 to 60 percent of patients using various submucosal tunnel techniques, experience that parallels that of others.

Previous publications have provided illustrative cases of successful management of reflux by the distal tunnel technique, including all grades of reflux and the management of the single unit of a duplicated system with reflux in which only the ureter with reflux was reimplanted by the distal tunnel method. Figures 2 and 3 document successful use of the distal tunnel method in a 4-year-old girl with grade IV vesicoureteral reflux. Bilateral complete duplication with reflux into 3 of the 4 renal-ureteral units (left lower pole, right upper and lower poles) was managed successfully by simultaneous bilateral double-barreled distal tunnel ureteral reimplantation (Fig. 4).

REFERENCES

1. Leadbetter, W. F.: Discussion. J Urol, 90:700, 1973
2. Hutch, J. A.: The Ureterovesical Junction. Berkeley and Los Angeles: University of California Press, 1958
3. Paquin, A. J., Jr.: Ureterovesical anastomosis: the description and evaluation of a technique. J Urol, 82:573, 1959
4. Ambrose, S. S. and Nicolson, W. P., III: The causes of vesicoureteral reflux in children. J Urol, 87:688, 1962
5. Howerton, L. W. and Lich, R., Jr.: The cause and correction of ureteral reflux. J Urol, 89:672, 1963
6. Grey, D. N., Flynn, P. and Goodwin. W. E.: Experimental methods of ureteroneocystostomy: experiences with the ureteral intussusception to produce a nipple or valve. J Urol, 77:154, 1957
7. Politano, V. A. and Leadbetter, W. F.: An operative technique for the correction of vesicoureteral reflux. J Urol, 79:932, 1958
8. Bischoff, P. F. and Busch, H. G.: Origin, clinical experiences and treatment of urinary obstructions of the lower ureter in childhood. J Urol, 85:739, 1961
9. Ambrose, S. S. and Nicolson, W. P., III: Vesicoureteral reflux secondary to anomalies of the ureterovesical junction: management and results. J Urol, 87:695, 1962
10. Paquin, A. J. Jr.: Ureterovesical anastomosis: a comparison of two principles. J Urol, 87:818, 1962
11. Glenn, J. F. and Anderson, E. E.: Distal tunnel ureteral reimplantation. J Urol 97:623, 1967
12. Williams, D. I., Scott, J. and Turner-Warwick, R. T.: Reflux and recurrent infection. Br J Urol, 33:435, 1961
13. Hutch, J. A.: Ureteric advancement operation: anatomy, technique and early results. J Urol, 89:180, 1963
14. Winter, C. C.: Clinical application of an operation to correct vesicoureteral reflux. Am J Surg, 112:20, 1966
15. Graham, J. M.: A method for correction of vesicoureteral reflux in children. J Urol, 102:510, 1969
16. Glenn, J. F.: Proceedings of a Workshop on Ureteral Reflux in Children. Washington, D.C.: National Academy of Sciences-National Research council, 1967
17. Garrett, R. A. and Switzer, R. W.: Antireflux surgery in children. JAMA, 195:636, 1966
18. Gregoir, W.: Le traitement chirurgical due reflux vèsico-urètéral congénital, Acta Chir Belg, 63:431, 1964
19. Lich, R., Jr., Howerton, L. W. and Davis, L. A.: Recurrent urosepsis in children. J Urol, 86:554, 1961
20. Gonzales, E. T., Glenn, J. F. and Anderson, E. E.: Results of distal tunnel ureteral reimplantation. J Urol, 107:572, 1972
21. Wacksman, J., Anderson, E. E. and Glenn, J. F.: Management of vesicoureteral reflux. J Urol, in press
22. Glenn, J. F. and Anderson, E. E.: Complications of ureteral reimplantation. Urol Surv, 23:243, 1973
23. Anderson, E. E.: Complications of ureteral reimplantation. In: Urologic Surgery, 2nd ed Edited by JF Glenn and WH Boyce: New York, Harper & Row Publishers, Inc., chap 20, 1975

Commentary: Transvesical Ureteral Reimplantation

R. Lawrence Kroovand

The incidence of primary (congenital) vesicoureteral reflux in healthy children is unknown but is thought to occur in 1% to 2% of the general population.[1,2] In children with urinary symptoms, especially urinary tract infection, vesicoureteral reflux may be demonstrated in 30% to 55% when first studied.[3]

The combination of vesicoureteral reflux and urinary tract infection in children may produce segmental renal scarring from pyelonephritis. Renal damage is seen at initial evaluation in up to 54% of refluxing kidneys, progresses in 66% of previously damaged kidneys, or may develop in 21% of initially normal kidneys.[4] On the basis of these data, vesicoureteral reflux should be diagnosed and treated to reduce the likelihood of recurrent infection and consequent renal damage.

MANAGEMENT

Children with urinary tract infection and vesicoureteral reflux may be treated medically or surgically. In selecting a treatment plan for these children, consider the cost of long-term follow-up examination, the consequences of repeated x-ray exposure, anticipated patient or parental compliance, and the relative risks of medical vs surgical therapy. Most children with reflux can be managed by medical means. Effective antibiotic treatment minimizes the likelihood of recurrent infection and progressive renal damage and does not appear to prejudice good results. Spontaneous cessation of reflux may be anticipated in 30% to 60% and is more common in younger children.[5] Resolution is less likely in those children more severe degrees of reflux or a deficient ureterovesical valvular complex.

For children with persistent reflux after an appropriate program of nonoperative management and in those with progressive renal scarring, renal growth arrest, absence of the submucosal ureteral tunnel, breakthrough infections during an appropriate antibacterial regimen, or poor patient or parental compliance, consider an antireflux surgical procedure.

SURGICAL PROCEDURES

Transvesical, extravesical, and combined operative procedures have been used to correct reflux. To be successful, an antireflux operative procedure should sufficiently lengthen the intravesical ureter against a solid detrusor backing to allow its compression against the detrusor in the manner of a check valve and thus prevent reflux.

I prefer a transvesical approach for ureteral reimplantation, since this method is suitable for most refluxing ureters and, if necessary, allows for distal ureteral resection or for ureteral tapering. A transvesical approach also reduces the potential risk of development of paravesical fibrosis and ureteral obstruction and the impairment of bladder innervation, complications occasionally seen after the extensive extravesical dissection necessary for extravesical ureteral reimplantation.[5]

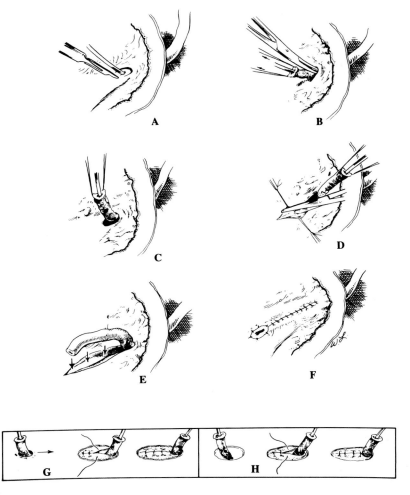

Fig. 5. Operative technique of ureteral advancement. (*A*) and (*B*) Placement of ureteral catheter and traction sutures, circumscription of ureteral orifice, and intravesical mobilization of distal ureter. (*C*) Mobilized distal ureter. (*D*) Development of mucosal flaps in ureteral advancement. (*E*) Advancement of ureter over mucosal defect. (*F*) Ureter sutured to distal trigone, and mucosa reapproximated to create tunnel. (*G*) Alternate method to create additional muscle backing for the ureter: the detrusor muscle is incised cephalad, the ureter is displaced to the apex of the detrusor incision, the incised detrusor is reapproximated below the displaced ureter, and the ureter is then advanced. (*H*) Repair of patulous ureteral hiatus to create additional muscle backing for the ureter.

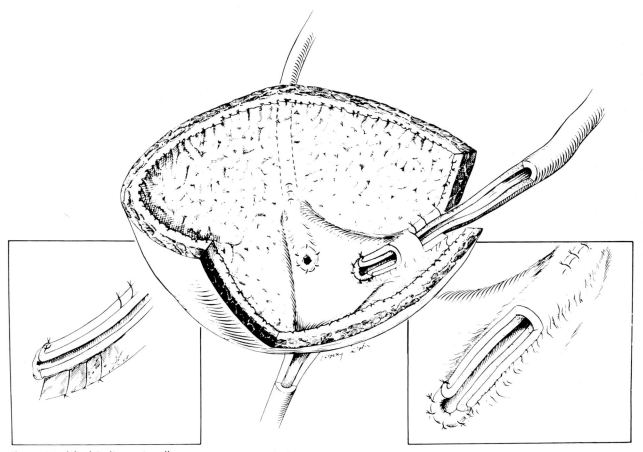

Fig. 6. Modified Politano-Leadbetter ureteroneocystostomy.

The Glenn–Anderson distal tunnel ureteral reimplantation (advancement) procedure is a modification of the advancement technique originally described by Williams in 1961 and by Hutch in 1963.[6,7] The procedure is a simple, rapid, and efficient one involving minimal dissection and trauma to the bladder and paravesical space. Because neocystostomy is not required, angulation, kinking, or obstruction of the ureter is unlikely.

Operative exposure for ureteral reimplantation is best achieved with a curved, lower abdominal skin crease (Pfannenstiel) incision. Open the bladder in the midline with cautery, taking care not to injure the bladder neck; place an absorbable suture in the inferior portion bladder incision to prevent distal tearing and injury to the bladder neck. I use symmetrically placed traction sutures in the cut edges of the bladder, the Denis–Browne retractor, and moist packs in the dome of the bladder to provide operative exposure and to stabilize the bladder and prevent rotational distortion.

In the original description of the Glenn–Anderson advancement, the distal 2 cm to 3 cm of ureter is mobilized and brought through a 1 cm to 1.5 cm submucosal tunnel developed under the trigonal mucosa, distal to the original ureteral orifice,

and toward the bladder neck.[8] The ureteral orifice is then sutured to the trigone in its new position. Drs. Glenn and Anderson emphasized that ureteral advancement was not universally applicable to all refluxing ureters but required sufficient trigonal size and configuration to permit construction of a tunnel of adequate length to prevent reflux, thus making the procedure unfeasible for infants and children with small trigones. Additionally, the procedure probably was not indicated in the management of dilated ureters requiring tapering.

Twelve years of experience with the operation has modified the surgical technique, permitting increased applicability of ureteral advancement in the treatment of vesicoureteral reflux. The authors now feel their technique allows use of distal tunnel ureteral reimplantation (advancement) in most patients requiring operative correction of vesicoureteral reflux, including those with dilated ureters requiring tapering or duplicated ureters, and in reoperations to correct complications of prior ureteral reimplantation. The principal modification in technique is the intentional development of a large ureteral hiatus to permit visualization of the extravesical and extraperitoneal space from within the bladder and additional ureteral mobilization (Fig. 5).

Subsequent closure of the enlarged ureteral hiatus distal to the point of vesical entry of the ureter then provides a major portion of the muscular backing and tunnel for the advanced ureter and reduces the length of submucosal tunnel required distally on the trigone. In closing the detrusor muscle of the enlarged ureteral hiatus, the authors point out that the absorbable sutures used to close the hiatus should be everted outside the bladder and that closure of the hiatus should not be too tight or ureteral obstruction may occur. These precautions should minimize postoperative reaction around the ureter and avoid the major potential complication of ureteral advancement—ureteral obstruction at the ureteral hiatus due to excessive angulation or a narrow hiatus.

For several years I have employed a technique for ureteral advancement similar to that described by Drs. Glenn and Anderson (Fig. 5). The initial surgical exposure and ureteral mobilization are similar to that described; however, I find that after ureteral mobilization, the defect created in the detrusor at the ureteral hiatus is usually large enough to necessitate formal closure and that intentional enlargement of the hiatus is usually unnecessary. With a large hiatus, closure of the inferior margin of the hiatus, distal to the ureter, lessens the defect and provides necessary detrusor backing and tunnel

length for an antireflux procedure (Fig. 5H). Or, if the detrusor backing between the original hiatus and the proposed advancement position of the ureteral orifice is inadequate in length, cephalolateral incision of the muscular ring of the hiatus and closure below, inferior to the ureter, provides additional detrusor backing for ureteral advancement and eventual submucosal tunnel length (Fig. 5G). In doing either of these maneuvers, in addition to avoiding too tight a closure of the hiatus around the ureter, take care not to position the hiatus too far lateral or cephalad on the bladder wall, or ureteral obstruction may occur.

After closing the hiatal defect and creating a solid detrusor backing, I find that sharp incision of the mucosa and mobilization of mucosal flaps medially and laterally avoids difficulties encountered during tunneling under the adherent trigonal mucosa and, additionally, allows easier and more accurate placement of the trigonal anchoring sutures than is possible after elevating a submucosal tunnel and drawing the ureter through it, as described by Drs. Glenn and Anderson (Fig. 5D and E). After the ureter is advanced and sutured to the trigone, anastomose the incised mucosa to the ureteral meatus and close it over the ureter to form the submucosal tunnel (Fig. 5F). After mobilization, the distal portion of the ureter is frequently

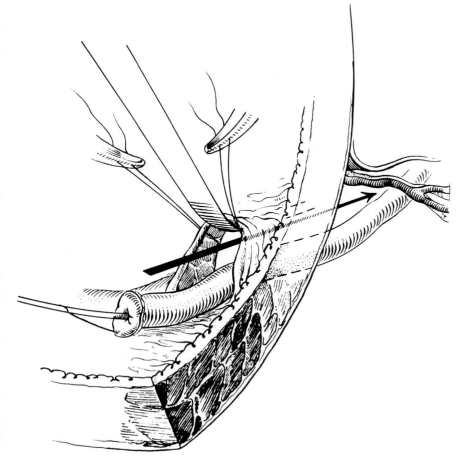

Fig. 7. My preferred method of ureteral reimplantation. Note midline incision of the detrusor, symmetric placement of traction sutures around incisional margins, and placement of the Denis Browne or other suitable retractor. Follow by placement of ureteral catheter secured by traction suture, sharp circumscription of ureteral orifice, and intravesical mobilization of 2–3 cm of distal ureter, taking care not to injure its adventitial blood supply. Traction sutures in upper margin of ureteral hiatus or tiny retractor are used for extravesical visualization.

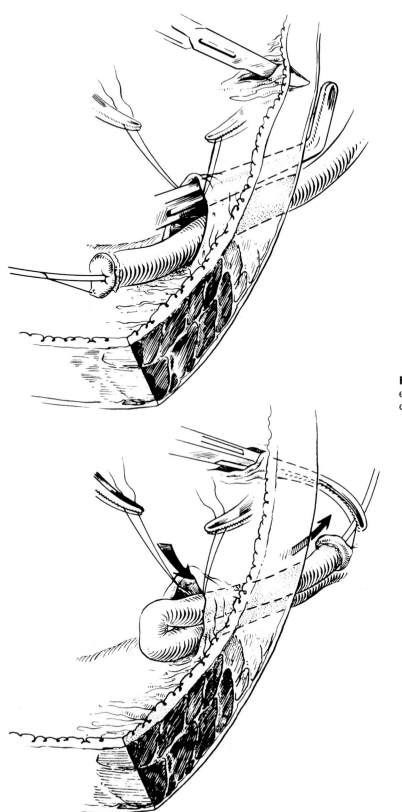

Fig. 8. Pass clamp superiorly through hiatus extravesically; make a sharp incision over the clamp.

Fig. 9. Pass a clamp extravesically through the new into the old hiatus, and draw the ureter through the new hiatus. Alternatively, pass a tape or a Penrose drain through both hiatuses to provide a guide.

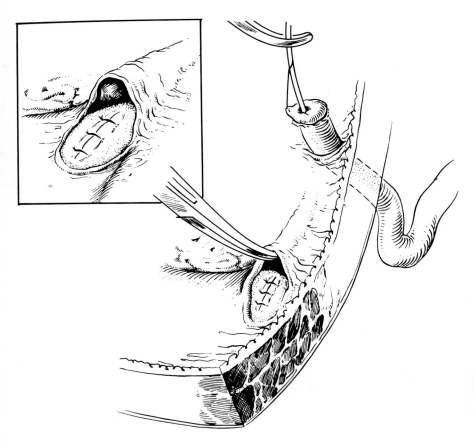

Fig. 10. Close the original ureteral hiatus with absorbable sutures (*insert*). Develop a submucosal tunnel with sharp and blunt dissection.

quite redundant and also may be aperistaltic or hypoplastic because of muscular deficiency, or traumatized or devascularized during mobilization, and usually should be resected. Additionally, the ureter, if of small caliber, may be spatulated for 3 mm to 5 mm.

My results with ureteral advancement in small infants and older children with small trigones, and in infants and small children with dilated ureters, have not been as gratifying as those of Glenn and Anderson, and therefore I have not applied the advancement procedure as extensively as the authors advocate.

In infants and children with small trigones or dilated ureters and in others in whom an advancement procedure does not appear appropriate, I prefer a modified Politano–Leadbetter procedure (Fig. 6).[9] After mobilization of the ureter from its detrusor attachments, extravesical visualization through the ureteral hiatus is assisted by placement of traction sutures in the upper margin of the hiatus or by use of a tiny retractor (Fig. 7). This permits identification of potentially obstructing extravesical structures and allows relocation of the ureter around them. Also, extravesical visualization facilitates dissection of a closely adherent peritoneal reflection from the juxtavesical ureter and posterior surface of the bladder. The ureter should be sufficiently mobilized to permit tension-free anastomosis of the ureter to the trigonal muscle and creation of a 2 cm to 3 cm submucosal tunnel. Ideally, a ratio of at least 3:1, and preferrably 5:1, tunnel length to ureteral diameter should be achieved.[10]

To avoid obstructing bands or peritoneal folds, pass a small right-angle clamp, under vision, through the hiatus extravesically to a position selected for the new ureteral hiatus; make a sharp incision over the clamp (Fig. 8). The location of the new hiatus should not be too far lateral or cephalad in the bladder wall, or kinking or obstruction of the ureter may occur, especially when the bladder is full. When the detrusor muscle is thick, beveling of the inferior margin of the ureteral hiatus creates a trough and prevents angulation of the ureter as it enters the bladder.

Pass a clamp extravesically through the new hiatus into the old hiatus to bring the ureter through the new hiatus (Fig. 9). After drawing the ureter through the new hiatus, close the original muscular defect with absorbable suture material, develop a submucosal tunnel (Fig. 10), and draw the ureter through it (Fig. 11). Carefully anastomose the ureter to the trigonal muscle and mucosa with absorbable suture material (Fig. 12). Elevate the mucosa lateral to the original hiatus from the detrusor muscle to facilitate easier anastomosis of the mucosa to the reimplanted ureter after the ureter has been sutured to the trigone.

In children with laterally placed orifices or a trigonal

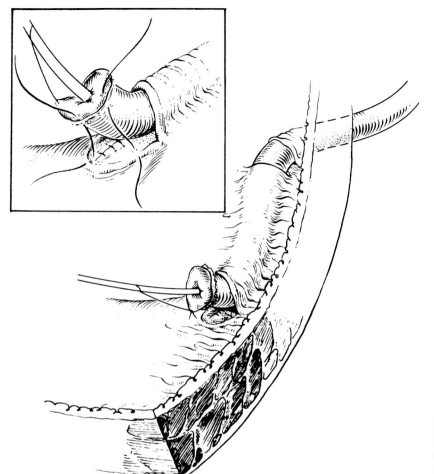

Fig. 11. Draw the ureter through the new submucosal tunnel and anastomose it to the trigonal muscle with fine absorbable suture. Optional resection of distal ureter (when hypoplastic) with spatulation of anterior wall or 2–3 mm before reattachment is not shown.

configuration that will not permit either a ureteral advancement or a Politano–Leadbetter reimplantation, ureteral advancement may be added to the Politano–Leadbetter procedure (Fig. 12, insert) to provide additional intravesical tunnel length and to avoid the hazards of placing the ureter too far cephalad or lateral on the expandable portion of the bladder, possibly producing kinking or obstruction of the ureter, especially when the bladder is distended. Alternately, Cohen's transverse trigonal ureteral advancement allows development of sufficient submucosal tunnel to prevent reflux by bringing each ureter transversely across the trigone to the opposite side; however, potential difficulties with subsequent endoscopic catheterization may negate the advantages of this simple procedure.[12]

At completion of a ureteral advancement or reimplantation, a small ureteral catheter or infant feeding tube should pass easily up the ureter; if it does not, identify and correct the obstruction.

Duplicated ureters may be dealt with either using an advancement technique as described by Glenn and Anderson, by a modified Leadbetter–Politano procedure, or by a combined

technique. Because duplicated ureters usually lie within a single muscular sheath in their distalmost portion and share a common blood supply, both ureters generally should be reimplanted as a common sheath. With incomplete duplication and juxtavesical union of the ureters, employ a modified common sheath procedure, amputating the duplicated segment and reimplanting the two ureters as a common sheath, as for a total duplication (Fig. 13).

The use of stenting catheters postoperatively is optional, although a temporary ureteral catheter may avoid the effect of edema on a small ureter and may protect a damaged and dilated upper tract. When required, I use a no. 3½ or 5 French feeding tube.

A small, straight catheter taped to the thigh in girls or to the penis in boys, or retained by a nylon suture brought out through the incision or drain site and held in place with a sterile button, provides postoperative urinary drainage. I avoid using a balloon retention catheter, since this appears to reduce trigonal irritation and postoperative bladder spasms. Alternately, in boys, a suprapubic Malecot catheter may be used.

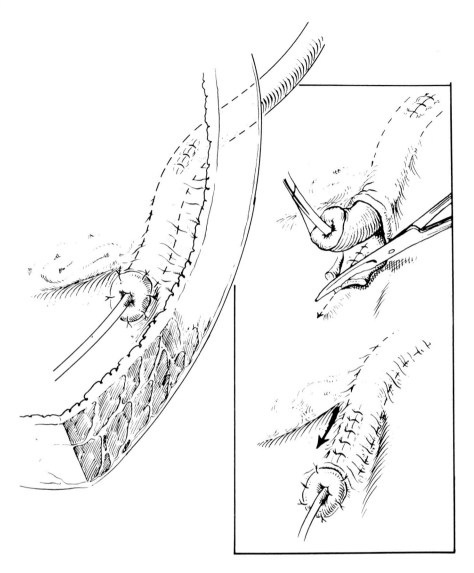

Fig. 12. Completed ureteral reimplantation and closure of mucosal defects. *Insert* shows ureteral advancement to provide additional intravesical tunnel length to the Politano-Leadbetter procedure, if required.

Close the bladder in two layers, using continuous fine absorbable suture. Suturing the dome of the bladder to the rectus muscle and sheath maintains the position of the dome during healing and prevents contraction of the decompressed bladder. A small Penrose drain and ureteral stents, when used, may be brought out through the wound or through a separate suprapubic stab incision. Alternately, in girls, the ureteral stents may be brought out through the urethra. Reconstruct the wound anatomically; subcuticular sutures and Steristrips provide for a cosmetic skin closure.

Generally, remove the tissue drain the morning after surgery and the ureteral catheters, if required, in 2 to 3 days, when declining urinary drainage through them reflects drainage around the tubes. Remove the urethral catheter on the third or fourth postoperative day. The children may then be discharged

from the hospital with prophylactic antibiotic coverage and with antispasmodics, if required.

I obtain a limited intravenous pyelogram (IVP) 4 weeks postoperatively to rule out early asymptomatic obstruction, and I generally discontinue chemotherapy at this time. A follow-up cystogram is done at 4 to 6 months postoperatively, and if the IVP and cystogram are satisfactory, a follow-up pyelogram is obtained yearly for a least 3 years if no postoperative obstruction or upper tract deterioration is found. In the absence of episodes of pyelonephritis, a cystogram need not be repeated. The use of radionuclide imaging greatly reduces radiation exposure and provides an excellent adjunct for postoperative follow-up examination.

Using the transvesical operative techniques described and employing meticulous operative technique, at least 95% of

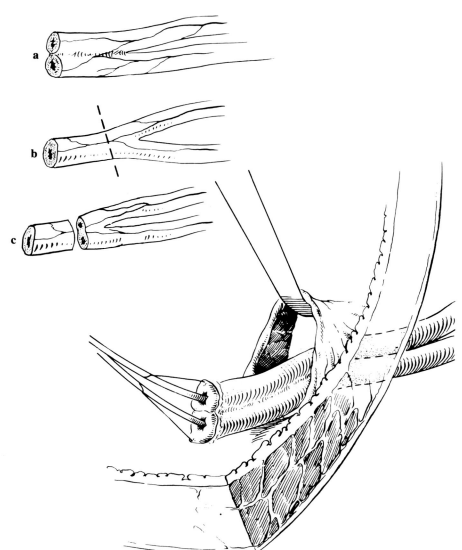

Fig. 13. Completely duplicated ureters lying within a single muscular sleeve in the most distal portion reimplanted as a common sheath. *Insert* shows (a) appearance of complete duplication, (b) low incomplete duplication with juxtavesical union of the ureters, and (c) treatment of low incomplete duplication by resecting common stem to level of double lumen followed by common sheath reimplantation.

children having operative correction of vesicoureteral reflux will be cured. Although clinical pyelonephritis is unusual after successful antireflux surgery, bacteriuria or occasional episodes of cystitis may occur in up to 30%.

REFERENCES

1. Jones BW, Headstream JW: Vesicoureteral reflux in children. J Urol 80:114, 1958

2. Peters PP, Johnson DE, Jackson JH: The incidence of vesicoureteral reflux in the premature child. J Urol 97:259, 1967

3. Kelalis PP: Proper perspective on vesicoureteral reflux. Mayo Clin Proc 46:807, 1971

4. Rolleston GL, Shannon FT, Utley WLF: Relationship of infantile vesicoureteral reflux to renal damage. Br Med J 1:460, 1970

5. Lenaghan D, Whitaker JG, Jensen F, Stephens FD: The natural history of reflux and long-term effects of reflux on the kidney. J Urol 115:728, 1976

6. Gonzales ET, Glenn JF, Anderson EE: Results of distal tunnel ureteral reimplantation. J Urol 107:572, 1972

7. Williams DI, Scott J, Turner–Warwick, RT: Reflux and recurrent infection. Br J Urol 33:435, 1961

8. Hutch JA: Ureteric advancement operation: Anatomy, technique and early results. J Urol 89:180, 1963

9. Glenn JF, Anderson EE: Distal tunnel ureteral reimplantation. Trans Am Assoc Genitourin Surg 58:37, 1966

10. Politano VA, Leadbetter WF: An operative technique for the correction of vesicoureteral reflux. J Urol 79:932, 1958

11. Paquin AJ Jr: Ureterovesical anastomosis: The description and evaluation of a technique. J Urol 82:573, 1959

12. Cohen SJ: Ureterozystoneostomie: Eine neue antirefluxtechnik. Aktuel Urol 6:1, 1975

ANNOTATED BIBLIOGRAPHY

Willscher MK, Bauer SB, Zammuto PJ, Retik AB: Renal growth and urinary infection following antireflux surgery in infants and children. J Urol 115:722, 1976

This is a comprehensive review and analysis of the effects of antireflux surgery on renal growth and the incidence of postoperative urinary tract infection and pyelonephritis, indicating that after successful antireflux surgery, renal growth resumes at a rate equal to or greater than normal and that although urinary tract infection is not uncommon, clinical pyelonephritis is rare.

Ahmed S: Ureteral reimplantation by the transverse advancement technique. J Urol 119:547, 1978

A description of the transverse advancement technique popularized by Cohen together with operative results. The procedure is a simple, reliable, and universally applicable one of low morbidity that appears to be a valuable addition to the urologist's technical armamentarium.

Warren MM, Kelalis PP, Stickler GB: Unilateral ureteroneocystostomy: The fate of the contralateral ureter. J Urol 107:466, 1972

A discussion of the fate of the contralateral nonrefluxing ureter after unilateral ureteral reimplantation, concluding with the recommendation that bilateral ureteral reimplantation be done in the presence of any abnormality of the contralateral nonrefluxing ureterovesical junction.

Broaddus SB, Zickerman PM, Morriseau PM, Leadbetter GW Jr: Incidence of late ureteral obstruction after antireflux surgery in infants and children. Urology 11:139, 1978

A report documenting that most ureteral obstructions after ureteral reimplantation are evident within the first few months after surgery and that late occurrence of ureteral obstruction is unusual. The data suggests that periodic IVPs, more than several years postoperatively, are unnecessary. Other authors disagree with this opinion (see Weiss RM, Schiff M Jr, Lytton B: Late obstruction after ureteroneocystostomy. J Urol 106:144, 1971).

De Sy W, Oosterlinck W: Reintervention for complications after antireflux surgery. Eur Urol 4:21, 1978

An excellent review of the causes and management of the complications of ureteral reimplantation.

Jeffs RD, Jonas P, Schillinger JF: Surgical correction of vesicoureteral reflux in in children with neurogenic bladder. J Urol 115:449, 1976

A documentation that vesicoureteral reflux occuring in the neurogenic bladder can be successfully managed by ureteral reimplantation, provided patients are carefully selected, the operation is meticulously done, and a method of postoperative bladder emptying is provided (e.g., clean intermittent catheterization, prosthetic sphincter).

OVERVIEW: ANTIREFLUX SURGERY

Alan B. Retik

Vesicoureteral reflux is commonly seen in children and is generally discovered in the course of radiologic evaluation of the urinary tract for infection. Reflux has been noted in 30% to 70% of children with urinary tract infection. The incidence of vesicoureteral reflux is 1:1000 population. It is primarily a disorder of whites, rarely being described in blacks, and it is five times more common in females than in males. This figure may be somewhat misleading, however, because the short female urethra predisposes to urinary tract infection and thus to an increased investigation for detection of reflux.

In the past few years, a number of authors have reported reflux to occur in families and have commented on the hereditary aspect of primary or congenital reflux. Evidence suggests that vesicoureteral reflux may be inherited either as an autosomal recessive trait or as an autosomal dominant trait of variable expression.

A number of studies have demonstrated that reflux does not occur in the urinary tract of healthy human beings, although, under high pressure, mild reflux has been demonstrated in babies. A number of factors are responsible for the prevention of reflux in healthy people. In the normal urinary tract, the ureter tunnels obliquely through the bladder wall to insert on a well-developed trigone in such a way that the intravesical portion of the ureter is compressed between the mucosa and bladder musculature. The angle of passage through the bladder wall, the intravesical portion of the ureter, and the competency of the musculature together constitute a valve mechanism that normally does not permit retrograde flow. The prevention of reflux may be due to active muscle contraction or to passive valvular action. Both mechanisms are probably operative. Most authors stress the length of the intravesical portion of the ureter as the most important factor in the prevention of reflux.

A number of circumstances can compromise valvular efficiency and result in reflux. These include infections and anatomic variations. Radiologic evaluation of the child with urinary tract infections should be delayed if at all possible until the urine has been sterile for 4 to 6 weeks to allow reflux secondary to inflammatory changes to disappear. A short intravesical ureter and deficient muscular support of the intravesical ureter have also been implicated as etiologic factors.

Vesicoureteral reflux is usually detected in infants and children with urinary tract infection. Infants may be septic or may fail to thrive. Although reflux may result from inflammatory changes in the bladder, it may also predispose to infection by leading to continuous residual urine in the bladder. Vesicoureteral reflux with infection has been found to be the most common cause of chronic pyelonephritis. In my series of children with radiologic evidence of chronic pyelonephritis, vesicoureteral reflux was demonstrated by voiding cystourethrography in over 90%. In the remaining children, a definite anatomic abnormality of the ureteral orifice was seen cystoscopically, leading to the assumption that reflux had been present in the past and had subsided or that the orifices refluxed intermittently.

It has been shown that the higher the grade of reflux, the more likely a patient is to show progressive renal damage. Development and progression of clubbing and scarring have been reported by a number of authors. It has been demonstrated that infection and reflux appear important in the development of these changes and that it sometimes takes up to 2 years for clubbing and scarring to become maximally evident.

Although it is generally agreed that mild to moderate degrees of reflux without infection do not harm the kidney, mounting evidence suggests that severe sterile reflux may, on occasion, form the basis of renal scarring seen with chronic atrophic pyelonephritis. Several authors have reported impaired renal growth or progressive renal scarring associated with severe reflux in children and in animals. Sterile reflux associated with chronic pyelonephritis has also been observed in hypertensive children.

Rolleston showed "intrarenal reflux" to occur in some children under age 4 years with severe reflux and chronic pyelonephritis, the mechanism appearing to be pyelotubular backflow. Of the kidneys in which intrarenal reflux was observed, 65% showed focal renal damage that corresponded exactly to those parts of the kidney in which intrarenal reflux had been observed.

It has been suggested that renal growth is inhibited in the presence of reflux. In my series of children with reflux, however, preoperative measurements of refluxing kidneys without pyelonephritis did not vary significantly from normal. Although reflux may inhibit renal growth in selected instances, very small kidneys with reflux alone and no pyelonephritic scarring more likely represent maldevelopment of the entire ureteral–renal unit. Faulty development of the ureteral bud may account for an incompetent ureterovesical junction with hypoplasia and dysplasia of the renal parenchyma. It appears, therefore, that for reflux to cause impaired renal growth, it must be associated with infection leading to pyelonephritis.

EVALUATION AND TREATMENT

Although the findings on the excretory urogram may lead one to suspect vesicoureteral reflux, the definitive diagnostic study is the voiding cystogram, done while the patient is awake. Physicians grade reflux on a scale of one to four. More severe grades of reflux are observed in the scarred kidneys of infants and younger children and milder reflux in those of older children, indicating the natural tendency for reflux to improve or cease with time. This is so even among children with renal scarring and with dilatation of the upper urinary tract. However, reflux is more likely to cease in milder grades and when kidneys are unscarred. Contrary to previous statements, the rate of disappearance appears to remain constant throughout childhood—being 20% to 30% within each 2-year period of those ureters in which reflux is still present. In my experience, virtually all grade 1 and approximately 60% to 70% of grade 2 reflux will eventually subside. With greater degrees of reflux, there is less likelihood that this will occur; however, most observers have noted the occasional patient, especially the infant, with ureteral dilatation and moderately severe reflux that subsides over a period of years.

Treatment of vesicoureteral reflux must be individualized; factors such as duration of disease, age, onset, number of infections, and ease with which they are controlled should be considered in deciding whether to perform surgery. As mentioned above, it is generally agreed that reflux in the absence of infection does not cause renal damage in most children. Therefore, if one decides to pursue a nonoperative approach, it is imperative to employ continuous antibiotic therapy as a prophylactic measure against infection as long as reflux persists. Obtain urine cultures at 2-month intervals, and repeat excretory urograms and radionuclide cystograms annually. The indications for antireflux surgery that I have employed are recurrent urinary tract infections despite adequate continuous antibiotics, severe reflux with pyelonephritis, failure of renal growth, reflux persisting into puberty, noncompliance, and persistent reflux with a basic anatomic abnormality at the ureterovesical junction.

Surgery offers a reasonable guarantee of success in children with vesicoureteral reflux. In most large series, the success rate is over 95%. In my recent review of more than 750 children undergoing antireflux surgery, the surgical success rate was greater than 99%. I have employed a modified Politano–Leadbetter procedure in most children, a procedure done very similarly to that described by Dr. Kroovand. Virtually all my ureteral reimplantations are done intravesically, except for some of the reoperations, which I do both intravesically and extravesically. In recent years, I have done more of the intravesical advancement and cross-trigonal procedures without any appreciable complications. In children with bilateral vesicoureteral reflux, I do bilateral surgery at the same operation. In general, I do not perform bilateral antireflux surgery with unilateral reflux unless there is a marked anatomic abnormality of the contralateral ureteral orifice. As far as I am concerned, there is no basis for improvement in contralateral reflux after a unilateral operation, as was noted in Dr. Marberger's series.

POSTOPERATIVE DATA

In 1975, I reviewed a series of 223 children who had antireflux surgery over a 6-year period. Forty-eight boys and 175 girls were followed for 6 months to 7 years after surgery. All children who had other anatomic abnormalities (*e.g.,* posterior urethral valves, ectopic ureteroceles, neurogenic bladder dysfunction) were excluded from this analysis. After surgery, each child received low-dose antibiotic therapy for 4 to 6 months. An excretory urogram was obtained in the early postoperative period (4 to 6 weeks) and repeated, along with a voiding cystourethrogram, at 4 months and then yearly thereafter. Urine cultures were obtained at 2-month intervals during the first postoperative year and periodically thereafter.

After surgery, unilateral obstruction occurred in four children early in this series; this required either nephrostomy drainage (one child) or rereimplantation (three children). Transient postoperative reflux was observed on the operated or ipsilateral side in 10 of 340 ureters (3%) but subsided spontaneously within 1 year in every patient. Seventeen of 104 children undergoing unilateral reimplantation (16%) developed reflux on the nonoperated or contralateral side. Within 1 year, this reflux stopped in all but two children, each of whom had demonstrated transient preoperative reflux. Subsequently, reflux on the contralateral side stopped in another child, and only one child required surgery for postoperative contralateral reflux. This transient reflux postoperatively is probably related to trigonal dissection. Therefore, I believe that bilateral surgery is unnecessary in most instances of unilateral vesicoureteral reflux.

The postoperative urinary tract infection rate has generally been reported to be between 10% and 30%. In my series, the incidence of infection after surgery was 21%. There were only two boys in this group, both of whom clinically had cystitis. The majority of the postoperative urinary infections occurred in girls, but clinically only 3 of them (1.7%) appeared to have pyelonephritis. It is believed that girls are reinfected because of anatomic and physiologic factors peculiar to their lower urinary tract rather than to the presence of old pyelonephritis. Boys rarely develop postoperative infection, the protective effect of the longer male urethra probably accounting for this finding. The incidence of postoperative infection is not related to the preoperative urographic appearance or to the rate of reflux.

Ninety-four children with readily distinguishable renal outlines on the 15-minute supine film had their kidney lengths measured preoperatively and at various periods of time postoperatively. It was found that all refluxing kidneys without radiologic evidence of scarring demonstrated accelerated postoperative growth; the postoperative growth of a unilateral scarred kidney was not greater than normal, while in the case of bilateral scarring, there was accelerated growth in both kidneys postoperatively. Even the smallest kidneys were able to maintain reasonable growth, regardless of whether the contralateral kidney was hypertrophied. It is apparent that renal growth in the child with vesicoureteral reflux depends on a physiologic balance between both kidneys. There is evidence to suggest the existence of a serum factor (renotropin), which could stimulate damaged refluxing renal units to faster-than-normal growth after the removal of the injury stimulus. This would be a recuperative response by the kidney to make up for lost nephrons. The effect would be finite and would last only as long as needed to allow for functional recovery. When the injury stimulus is removed, the minimally damaged kidney may be able to compensate for its own nephron loss by accelerated growth. When unilateral scarring is present, compensation for nephron loss occurs primarily in the opposite kidney. When both kidneys are similarly injured, whether by vesicoureteral reflux alone or in conjunction with scarring, a cooperative counterbalance appears to be present. Regardless of the degree of injury, both kidneys may respond with accelerated growth and improved function.

Even in the very severely scarred kidney, the potential exists for expected normal growth based on initial renal size and is not related to the fact that the contralateral kidney may be hypertrophied. It is my feeling, therefore, that unilateral reimplantation with preservation of renal tissue in the child with severe unilateral scarring and vesicoureteral reflux is more appropriate than nephrectomy, because the recuperative powers of even the smallest kidney may produce a life-sustaining organ in the future. Nephrectomy is indicated only if the involved kidney contributes less than 10% of total renal function.

Hypertension is now recognized as one of the potential complications of reflux nephropathy. The true incidence of hypertension is yet to be determined, but this complication might turn out to be as or more significant than renal scarring.

It is also worthwhile mentioning that in selected instances, I do perform antireflux surgery in children with neurogenic bladder dysfunction. The only children whom I do correct are ones whose reflux is reasonably significant, who develop recurrent infections while receiving adequate antibiotics, and whose bladders can be emptied by Crede or intermittent catheterization. The results of surgery in this group have been similar to those in the nonneurogenic group. The poor results reported in the past are due to surgery performed in bladders that did not empty.

PART EIGHTEEN

SURGICAL TREATMENT OF URETEROCELE

40

SURGICAL CORRECTION OF URETEROCELES IN CHILDHOOD

By W. Hardy Hendren and Gerard J. Monfort

From the Children's Service and the General Surgical Service of the Massachusetts General Hospital and the Department of Surgery of the Harvard Medical School, Boston, Mass.

Journal of Pediatric Surgery
June 1971, Vol. 6, No. 3

Ureterocele is a descriptive term for obstruction of the ureteral orifice with cystic dilatation of the terminal ureter which balloons into the bladder and sometimes into the urethra. Some are small, causing only slight obstruction of the ureter and mild hydronephrosis; these generally present in older children or adults and the involved ureter is usually single. In the majority of cases in childhood, however, ureteroceles present as a large mass within the bladder, sometimes projecting into the bladder neck or urethra, causing obstruction of the outflow of urine. Occasionally they prolapse out through the urethra in the female; this can cause acute urinary retention. The renal collecting system on the side of the ureterocele is usually duplicated; the ureterocele is associated with the ureter which drains the upper pole of the duplex kidney.

Large ureteroceles, often termed "infant type," tend to present early in life because there is high grade

Presented before the Surgical Section of the American Academy of Pediatrics, San Francisco, calif., October 17–19, 1970

W. Hardy Hendren, M.D.: Director, Division of Pediatric Surgery, Associate Visiting Surgeon, Massachusetts General Hospital; Assistant Clinical Professor of Surgery, Harvard Medical School, Boston, Mass. Gerard J. Monfort, M.D.: Assistant in pediatric Surgery Hôpital Nord, Marseille, France; formerly Clinical Assistant in Pediatric Surgery, Massachusetts General Hospital, Boston, Mass.

obstruction of the associated ureter and hydronephrosis. Also there is often reflux or obstruction to the ipsilateral twin ureter or the contralateral ureter, further predisposing to infection and early clinical illness. The term "ectopic ureterocele" has been used by some authors to describe that variety in which the orifice of the ureterocele is located in the bladder neck or posterior urethra, proximal to the external sphincter. In these the ureterocele presents in the urethra and bladder neck rather than in the trigone of the bladder. Ureteroceles are much more common in girls than boys. The majority are unilateral; only in an occasional case are both sides affected. The associated upper pole of the duplex kidney in severe cases is usually badly damaged. In some it is very hydronephrotic (although occasionally worth salvage). In others the upper pole is a small dysgenetic remnant (high grade ureteral obstruction during embryogenesis may favor faulty development of renal parenchyma). Figure 1 shows the principal types of ureteroceles and associated pathology.

DIAGNOSIS

The diagnosis of ureterocele should be fairly straightforward. Nevertheless, as emphasized by Uson et al.[1]

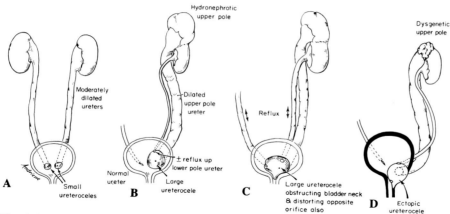

Fig. 1. Types of Ureteroceles. (*A*) Small "adult type" ureteroceles with single ureters, minimal upper tract dilatation, and excellent renal function. (*B*) Large "infant type" ureterocele with the common problem of duplex ureters. There is hydronephrosis of the associated upper pole and often reflux to the ipsilateral lower pole. (*C*) Very large ureterocele extending into the bladder neck and proximal urethra, causing outlet obstruction and encroaching on opposite renal collecting system causing obstruction or reflux. (*D*) Ectopic ureterocele in which the orifice enters the posterior urethra, not the trigone. Upper pole is frequently dysgenetic. If the ureter enters distal to the external sphincter in the terminal urethra or vestibule, it becomes a different problem, ectopic ureter with "incontinence."

in many there is undue delay in diagnosis and proper surgical correction. Most cause urinary infection, and the more severe the pathology, in general, the earlier the clinical presentation. Every child with urinary infection, often heralded by unexplained fever, failure to thrive, or nonspecific lower abdominal symptoms, should have complete urinary investigation. This includes both intravenous pyelography and cystography and should be instigated after the *first* urinary infection, to diagnose early such problems as ureterocele. Success in saving involved kidneys can depend on prompt diagnosis and correction before recurrent pyelonephritis takes its toll. There is still the widespread pernicious practice of permitting children, especially girls, to have more than one infection before instituting screening studies. Although this practice causes no harm in some children, in others it is responsible for their eventual demise.

Figure 2 illustrates some of the typical roentgenographic findings in ureteroceles. A small ureterocele, the so called "adult type" with its usually single kidney, often appears on intravenous pyelography as a rounded density of dye in the bladder with columning of dye in the ureter above. This is sometimes referred to as a "cobra head" deformity (Fig. 2*A*). Larger ureteroceles can cause marked deformity of the entire urinary tract

(Fig. 2*B*, *C*, and *D*). On intravenous pyelography they appear as rounded, radiolucent, filling defects in the bladder because the associated renal segment is usually badly damaged and concentrates dye poorly. Sometimes reflux and/or obstruction of adjacent uninvolved renal segments is severe, so that they are destroyed as well as that associated with the ureterocele (Fig. 2*E*, *F*).

TREATMENT

Surgical management of ureteroceles has changed markedly in recent years. In 1951, Campbell,[2] in reporting a large experience with ureteroceles in children, advocated transurethral or open resection of the ureterocele, and subsequently resection of its renal unit and ureter if necessary. He emphasized that leaving the distal ureter, in effect a diverticulum, can cause stasis and infection. Little mention was made, however, of the important problem of vesicoureteral reflux which perpetuates infection in cases managed this way. Gross and Clatworthy,[3] recognizing that to trade reflux for obstruction is often of no benefit to the patient, advocated open incision of the ureterocele enough to let it drain, but not so much as to create reflux up its ureter. Experience has shown that this is not feasible in most cases. It should be

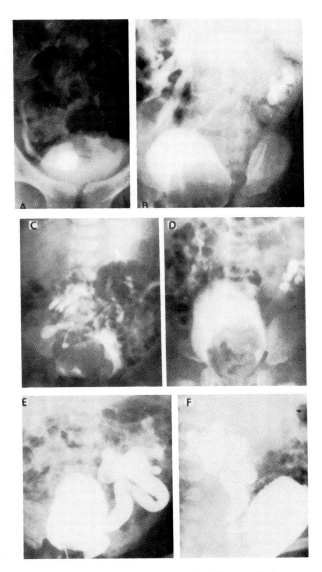

remembered, however, that antireflux surgery was uncommon in those days. In a comprehensive monograph, Ericsson[4] emphasized that nephrectomy or heminephrectomy, leaving the ureterocele is poor treatment, and that transurethral or open incision of ureteroceles is inadequate. They should be completely resected, together with the associated ureter and renal segment in most cases. More recent papers[5–8] have paid greater attention to the fact that the surgeon must deal not only with ureteral obstruction from the ureterocele, but also with the problem of reflux in that ureter, as well as the ipsilateral twin ureter, and sometimes the contralateral ureter.

MATERIAL

In the past 10 years we have had an experience with 25 children with ureteroceles, 18 treated entirely by us, and seven operated upon elsewhere with a variety of initial procedures after which there was need for secondary surgery. From treating this group of 25 we believe that in most children with ureteroceles a sterile urinary tract can be achieved, if appropriate reconstructive surgery is performed. The number of secondary cases we have seen would suggest that considerable confusion exists as to what comprises satisfactory surgical treatment of ureteroceles.

In all but one patient urinary infection was the presenting clinical problem. One infant was referred with a lower abdominal mass (the bladder) and urinary retention caused by a ureterocele obstructing the bladder outlet (Fig. 2E, F).

Fig. 2. (A) Small unilateral ureterocele filling with dye, the "cobra head" defect. Best treated by excision of ureterocele and reimplantation of ureter. (B) Large ureterocele associated with hydronephrotic, nonvisualized upper pole of left kidney. Lower pole of left kidney is displaced, but there is excellent cortex. Obstructive hydronephrosis of right kidney. The entire left kidney was removed elsewhere, unfortunately, together with resection of ureterocele. The right ureter was reimplanted without a tunnel, resulting in massive reflux, for which child was referred. (C) Six-week-old female with huge ureterocele associated with very hydronephrotic, nonvisualized upper pole of right kidney. The ipsilateral lower pole ureter was angulated causing hydronephrosis, and there was massive reflux to the lower pole of duplicated contralateral collecting system. Treated by single-stage operation: open resection of ureterocele, removing its dilated ureter, repairing the defect in bladder wall, reimplanting adjacent ipsilateral lower pole ureter, reimplanting as a "single unit" the two ureters of the upper side. Through a separate flank incision, the destroyed right upper pole was removed. (D) Three-month-old female with large ureterocele associated with nonvisualized upper pole of left kidney which proved to have considerable good renal parenchyma. There was massive reflux to the ipsilateral lower pole. Treated by single-stage open resection of ureterocele. Y-V plasty to bladder neck, resection of dilated ureter draining ureterocele, reimplantation of ipsilateral refluxing ureter, and simple advancement of contralateral ureteral orifice. Through a separate flank incision, pyelopyelostomy spared upper pole. (E) Anteroposterior and (F), lateral cystogram of a 2-day-old female with urinary retention causing "lower abdominal mass." There was a large ectopic ureterocele, associated with the upper pole of the left kidney, which was destroyed. There was massive reflux to the lower pole of that kidney which had destroyed that half of the kidney also. There was severe obstructive hydronephrosis of right side. Eventually left nephectomy was necessary.

TABLE 1. Seven Secondary Cases

Original Surgery Elsewhere	Subsequent Operation
1. Excision prolapsed ureterocele → reflux. Excision of only lower ureter → incontinence. Pyelopyelostomy.	Urethral lengthening to cure incontinence. Removal of ureter. Bilateral reimplantation to stop reflux.
2. Excision of prolapsed ureterocele → reflux. Upper pole heminephrectomy, leaving distal ureter.	Removal refluxing stump and reimplantation of two ureters for reflux.
3. Excision ureterocele → reflux. Upper pole heminephrectomy leaving distal ureter.	Removal of stump of ureter and ipsilateral reimplant, later nephrectomy (did not grow).
4. Total nephrectomy (unnecessary) and resection opposite terminal ureter for obstruction → reflux.	Reimplantation of remaining ureter for reflux.
5. Incision ureterocele → reflux. Upper pole excision, leaving lower ureter.	Removal stump and reimplant ipsilateral refluxing ureter.
6. Transurethral resection of ureterocele → reflux.	Bilateral ureteral reimplantation for reflux.
7. Excision ureterocele → reflux. Excision of upper pole and its ureter → reflux ipsilateral ureter.	Reimplantation for reflux.

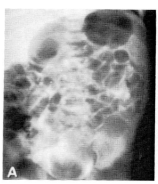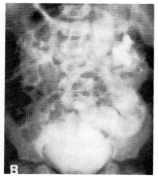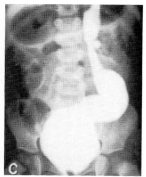

Fig. 3. The consequences of simple uncapping of a ureterocele. (*A*) IVP 2 week old female with large ureterocele, involving left upper pole ureter. Function evident in lower pole of left kidney and in right kidney. Ureterocele was merely uncapped. (*B*) Later IVP showing satisfactory function of right side and left lower pole, and apparent function of very hydronephrotic upper pole. This was in fact dye refluxing up from the bladder. (*C*) Cystogram showing massive reflux up the ureter. The upper pole of the left kidney and its ureter were removed. Patient subsequently had correction of reflux and at age 9 years, is well with excellent function bilaterally.

Age: Eight children were under 6 month of age, the youngest only 1 day old. There were 3 who were 3 years old; 2 from 6 to 12 months of age; two 4 years of age; and 1 each at ages 1, 2, 6, 7, 8, 9 , 10, 11, 15, and 17 years. There were 22 girls and 3 boys. (the boys had small ''adult type'', simple ureteroceles with a single ureter). The ureterocele was on the left in 10 cases, the right in 14 cases, and bilateral in 1. There was a duplicated renal collecting system in 18, and it was single in 7. *Of the 18 duplicated collecting systems there was reflux up the ipsilateral ureter in 15 cases!* There was reflux up the contralateral ureter in 2 cases, obstruction of the contralateral ureter in 2 cases, and obstruction of the ipsilateral ureter in 1. In 7 of these cases there was bladder neck obstruction from the ureterocele.

SURGICAL TREATMENT

Table 1 lists the cases referred for secondary procedures. In *every* case the patient had been left with the problem of vesicoureteral reflux into either a stump of ureter and/ or into one or both of the other ureters (Fig. 3).

Table 2 lists treatment performed in cases treated primarily by us, and Figure 4 illustrates the two varieties of ureteroceles.

In some cases it is impossible to be sure how much damage a renal segment has suffered, and this may be apparent only in time with serial intravenous pyelography. We would prefer to do reconstructive surgery when in doubt, follow the patient, and remove the questionable segment if it becomes atrophic. We have done this in

TABLE 2. Eighteen Primary Cases

Small Ureteroceles	
Seven cases:	Excised and simple ureteral reimplantation. Two had duplication, the two ureters reimplanted as a single unit.
Large Ureteroceles	
Seven cases:	Excision ureterocele, its ureter and associated upper pole, and ipsilateral reimplantation. In one, simultaneous contralateral double reimplantation for reflux. In two, advancement of contralateral ureter.
Two cases:	Excision ureterocele, its ureter and ipsilateral reimplantation and pyelopyelostomy.
One case:	Excision and tapering reimplantation of single large ureter. Later nephrectomy (kidney did not grow).
One case:	(Early in series) Excision of ureterocele, its ureter and partial nephrectomy. Later ileal diversion. Subsequent reconnection to bladder.

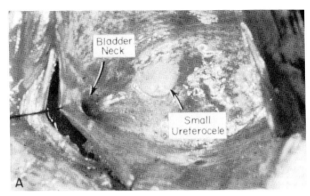

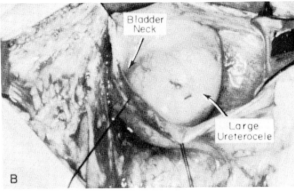

Fig. 4. (*A*) Small ureterocele in a 6 year old boy. (*B*) Large ureterocele in a 6-week-old girl.

one case with an entire kidney, and in two cases with a lower pole originally thought insufficient to salvage. Four of the 25 patients now have only one kidney, which fortunately is healthy in each. One case, early in the series, had excision of a ureterocele, its ureter and partial nephrectomy (Fig. 2*E*, *F*). Because there was extreme hydronephrosis on the right side, and massive destruction on the left from reflux, an ileal diversion was done. The child fared well for 6 years, although the left kidney, previously damaged, became tiny, and was removed. The right kidney was reconnected to the bladder using the ileal segment as midureter with success.

There have been no deaths. All patients in this series are presently free of urinary infection. We believe this results not only from relief of obstruction from their ureteroceles and from stasis in their dilated ureters, but also from correction of their reflux.

Details of operative correction are shown in (Fig. 5). The technique for management of small ureteroceles is not shown, since their unroofing and reimplantation does not pose any formidable technical problem. Reimplantation can be done by the intravesicle technique of Leadbetter and Politano[9] or by alternate means,[10] provided an antireflux tunnel 25–30 mm long is constructed. In reimplanting ureters it is important to place them posteriorly in the trigone, in that part of the bladder which is fixed and where there is good muscle backing for the ureter. A common fault is placement of the ureter in the side wall of the bladder, where it angulates and obstructs as the bladder fills, carrying the ureter forward.

Large ureteroceles, on the other hand, present a formidable technical challenge. The ureterocele is excised, except for its back wall, taking care to remove all flaps of tissue which might prolapse down into the urethra. Its ureter and its twin, duplex ureter, are mobilized upward to the iliac vessels. The two ureters

are then separated taking great care to preserve the blood supply of the smaller ureter, which is then reimplanted with a long antireflux tunnel. We have preferred to perform under the same anesthesia the upper tract reconstruction, usually removing the associated upper pole, but in two cases, preserving it, performing a pyelopyelostomy. It would be perfectly possible to stage this, however, by temporarily bringing the enlarged ureter out as a cutaneous ureterostomy. For a grossly deformed contralateral ureter with massive reflux we would employ simultaneous contralateral ureteral reimplantation. This does, however, add something more to the procedure, and so in a doubtful case, with a small amount of reflux or just a short tunnel, the tip of that ureter can be advanced with the simple maneuver shown, excising mucosa distal to the orifice and bringing it caudad a few millimeters.

We believe that these operative diagrams illustrate the desired end point the surgeon should seek in reconstructing the urinary tract in most of these children. It should be emphasized that judgment must be exercised in viewing the individual case. This must take into account the degree of illness of the baby, the experience

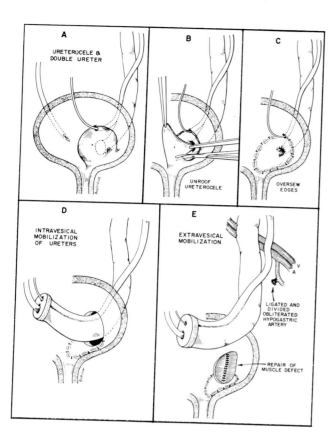

Fig. 5. Principles of operative repair. (*A*) Large uretero-cele with a catheter sewn in adjacent ipsilateral ureter. Operative exposure usually through T-shaped incision, extending barely through bladder neck, to be closed later as a V. (*B*) and (*C*) Unroofing of ureterocele and over-sewing edges. Mucosa of the back wall remains to cover trigone. Certain ectopic ureteroceles extend well down into the urethra. It is important to unroof them com-pletely to avoid leaving a flap valve which can obstruct the urethra. These low ectopic ureteroceles can thin greatly the posterior urethral wall. In these we excise the back wall of the ureterocele, taking great care not to go deeply (lest a urethral-vaginal or a vesico-vaginal fistula be created) and this posterior cleft is repaired in two layers, first the muscle, then mucosa, similar to the method in (*E*). (*D*) Both ureters are mobilized as a single unit, first from within bladder, and then extravesically dividing obliterated hypogastric ligament to facilitate dis-section up to level of iliac vessels. (*E*) Repair of large defect in bladder muscle at site of ureterocele. (*F*) Ends of two ureters lie in a common sheath. The smaller ureter, to be saved, is divided and dissected away from the large, upper pole ureter, to be removed. All of the blood supply is left with the small ureter, staying close to wall of larger ureter in separating them. (*G*) Upper pole ureter ligated, amputated, and pushed upward into posterior gutter, to be dealt with later through a separate flank incision. Or, it can be temporarily brought out as a skin ureterostomy if staging upper repair is desired. (*H*) Good lower pole ureter has been reimplanted with an anti-reflux tunnel. If definite reflux is seen on opposite side, reimplantation of it too may be desired. Since opposite orifice has been displaced upward and laterally, and tunnel is short, which predisposes to reflux, the simple procedure of advancement of the orifice is shown. Dia-mond-shaped piece of mucosa is resected, pulling ureter caudad by suturing it as shown, lengthening its tunnel. Bladder neck is closed as a V. (*I*) Completed lower tract reconstruction. (*J*) and (*K*) Management of upper urinary tract: (*L*) Through a separate flank incision either at same sitting or later (using temporary cutaneous ureterostomy), kidney is explored and decision made whether to remove or save upper pole. In most cases it is best removed. In the occasional case, worth salvage, pyelopyelostomy is performed with temporary nephrostomy decompression if upper repair is done at the same time (postoperative edema of the trigone can cause leakage of upper suture line if kidney is not decompressed).

of the surgeon, the availability of skilled pediatric anesthesia, particularly for the total, one-stage recon-struction, which can be a prolonged undertaking, lasting several hours. Although possibly prepared to cope with a large ureterocele in a duplex kidney in one stage in a 10 year old child who presents in relatively good health electively, the same surgeon might wish to stage the repair in a 3 week old infant with similar anatomy.

Possibly there is a place for simple transurethral resection or open resection of a ureterocele in a very sick baby, provided it is followed soon by appropriate additional reconstructive surgery to reach the intended goal. We prefer a total reconstruction in a single procedure but readily admit that staging is possible.

We are convinced of the following: transurethral or open resection of a ureterocele as the definitive procedure

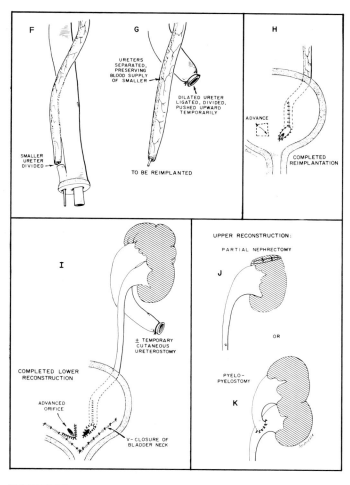

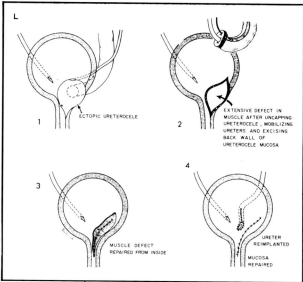

is inadequate; removal of the renal unit associated with a ureterocele is inadequate as definitive treatment; in most ureteroceles with duplex kidney the associated renal segment is destroyed and should be removed, along with its ureter, but in an occasional case it can be salvaged; insufficient attention has been given to the problem of vesicoureteral reflux in these cases, as it should be corrected either at the time of initial reconstructive surgery, or, certainly, soon thereafter.

SUMMARY

Ureteroceles can present complex problems, but appropriate reconstructive surgery can abolish urinary infection in nearly all cases. It does not suffice to resect or unroof a ureterocele, for this creates vesicoureteral reflux. Instead, for small ureteroceles, total resection by open technique should be carried out, together with reimplantation of the ureter. In large ureteroceles, usually with duplex kidney, removal of the ureterocele and its associated ureter, reimplantation of the ipsilateral ureter, and sometimes the contralateral ureter, should be performed. The associated upper pole renal segment should be removed in most instances; occasionally it can be saved, anastomosing it to the adjacent lower pole renal pelvis. Although management of an individual case must vary with anatomy, age of the patient, etc., the fundamental goals remain identical in all cases: relief of obstruction, removal of destroyed renal segments, and surgical correction of vesicoureteral reflux.

REFERENCES

1. Uson, A. C., Lattimer, J. K., Melicow, M. M.: Ureteroceles in infants and children. A report based on 44 cases. Pediatrics 27:971, 1961

2. Campbell, M.: Ureterocele: A study of 94 instances of 80 infants and children. Surg Gynec Obstet 93:705, 1951

3. Gross, R. E., and Clatworthy, H. W., Jr.: Ureterocele in infancy and childhood. Pediatrics 5:68, 1950

4. Ericsson, N. O.: Ectopic ureterocele in infants and children. Acta Chir Scand (Suppl 197), 1954

5. Williams, D. I., and Woodard, J. R.: Problems in the management of ectopic ureteroceles: J Urol 92:635, 1964

6. Johnston, J. H., and Johnson, L. M.: Experiences with ectopic ureteroceles. Br J Urol 41:61, 1969

7. Hutch, J. A., and Chisholm, E. R.: Surgical repair of ureterocele. J Urol 96:445, 1966

8. Mogg, R. A.: Some observations on the ectopic ureter and ureterocele. J Urol 97:1003, 1967

9. Politano, V. A., and Leadbetter, W. F.: An operative technique for the children of vesico-ureteral reflux. J Urol 79:932, 1958

10. Hendren, W. H.: Ureteral reimplantation in children. J Pediat Surg 3:649, 1968

Commentary: Approaches to Ureteroceles in Childhood

David T. Uehling

Since the clinical and anatomic presentation of a ureterocele can vary, no one surgical procedure is adequate to handle all situations. The article by Drs. Hendren and Monfort offers a detailed technical description of the intravesical repair of the trigone and urethra after excision of the large ectopic ureterocele. It is widely quoted in the recent literature and qualifies as a classic reference. Other philosophies and approaches also have been described and need discussion.

Although most ureteroceles appear in infants as urinary tract infections (or bladder outlet obstruction in the more severe cases), eventually the diagnostic evaluation will disclose the upper tract involvement of hydronephrosis or megaureter. The recent classification of megaureter by an international committee is useful in considering the obstructive, nonobstructive, or refluxing component of the megaureter and whether the process is primary or secondary.[1] For instance, the orthotopic ureter in a child with ureterocele and duplication may be dilated from reflux, and the contralateral ureter or ureters may be dilated from bladder outlet obstruction by the large ureterocele. In that situation, the three or four ureters may be dilated because of two or three different causes, and expectations on improvement might thus differ. As also emphasized in the classification schema, ureteroceles themselves may be obstructive for the ureter involved or nonobstructive. In borderline cases, a decision to undertake surgical repair of the simple ureterocele may be based on physiologic information about the degree of obstruction (as obtained from renal pressure–flow studies or diuretic isotope imaging) rather than on the radiographic degree of megaureter.

In obstructed ureteroceles with ipselateral duplication, heminephrectomy is usually indicated and easily accomplished, since the upper segment is severely dysplastic and has a separate blood supply. Uncommonly, the upper segment will have function on intravenous pyelogram (IVP) or isotope imaging, look reasonably healthy at the time of surgery, and be salvageable by pyelopyelostomy. Particularly in infants, most of the dilated ureter can be exposed and removed through the flank incision. Controversy exists in the current literature on whether the remaining ureterocele itself and lower ureteral stump will cause enough problems to warrant simultaneous or staged intravesical ureterocele resection. This is critical, since these children usually are very young and quite sick. When the ureterocele and lower ureteral stump are allowed to remain, estimates on the need to remove them later vary from 10% to 50%. In my experience, heminephrectomy with removal of most of the dilated ureter usually has resulted in a well child.

When excision of the ureterocele is elected, several options exist for the intravesical part of the procedure. These options are well illustrated in the preceding article. Unroofing the ureterocele and suturing the edges of the back wall of the ureteocele to cover the trigone has the disadvantage of not remedying the usual orthotopic ureteral reflux. Preferable is a diamond-shaped mucosal incision including the orthotopic orifice, complete intravesical and extravesical dissection of both ureters, trigonal repair, reimplantation of the orthotopic ureter, and removal of the ureterocele and its ureteral stump. Particularly troublesome are ectopic ureteroceles extending into the urethra, where partial unroofing may leave obstructing flaps. Even ureteroceles with the orifice in the bladder may extend into the urethra, the so-called cecoureterocele. The back wall of the ureterocele is a thin muscular layer, making identification and removal difficult. Also, the posterior urethral wall can be thinned to allow entry into the vagina. The preceding article calls proper attention to the pertinent surgical anatomy and risks. The technical difficulties of the intravesical dissection, particularly in very small infants, have been the main impetus to do a lesser procedure.

Kroovand and Perlmutter have recently described an extravesical approach.[2] To avoid the hazards of intravesical reconstruction, a one-stage, extravesical heminephrectomy and total ureterectomy to the level of the muscular hiatus of the bladder was carried out in 9 of 37 children with ureteroceles. None required a secondary procedure to remove the intravesical ureterocele. In neonates and small infants, the surgery frequently was accomplished through a single incision; in older infants or children, separate subcostal and inguinal incisions were used. Placement of a large catheter in the divided distal end of the obstructed ureter facilitated identification of the distal ureter during the extravesical ureterectomy when a second inguinal incision was used. Division of the dilated ureter as it passes around the normal (lower-pole) ureter helped avoid injury to the good ureter, which was left in its vascular bed. The dissection was kept close to the wall of the diseased ureter. Although a distal common sheath was normally present in duplicated ureters, a typical common sheath was not encountered in this series of large ectopic ureteroceles, although easily dissected muscular bridges were found. If a dense common sheath is encountered, a small muscular strip from the ectopic ureter can be left attached to the orthotopic ureter to avoid injuring it. After extravesical dissection of the ureter and its resection at the level of the detrusor muscle, the muscular hiatus of the bladder fell together passively, and the mucosa forming the ureterocele wall collapsed against the muscular backing. Although the muscular defect remaining in the bladder wall after ureterectomy may be sutured closed when the defect is large and deforming, the authors preferred to let it approximate passively to avoid potential surgical distortion of the vesical neck and upper urethra and injury to the orthotopic ureter, nearby neurovascular bundles, and the vas deferens in males. By amputating the ureter flush with the bladder, there was no ureteral stump remaining into which the ureterocele membrane could prolapse to form a diverticulum, and none of the nine patients had herniation through the unsutured muscular defect.

On the subject of whether intravesical removal of the ureterocele is necessary, opinions, as expressed in the current surgical literature, remain divided. The prudent surgeon will keep abreast of this controversy and apply judgement to each patient.

REFERENCES

1. Smith ME (chm): Report of working party to establish an international nomenclature for the large ureter. In Urinary System Malformations in Children, pp 3–8. New York, Alan R. Liss, 1977

2. Kroovand RL, Perlmutter AD: J Urol 122:367, 1979

ANNOTATED BIBLIOGRAPHY

Barrett DM, Malek RS, Kelalis PP: Problems and solutions in surgical treatment of 100 consecutive ureteral duplications in children. J Urol 114:126, 1975

Of 14 patients undergoing heminephrectomy and subtotal ureterectomy, 4 required a later procedure of ureterocele unroofing and reimplantation of the refluxing units. This gave a 71% success rate for the upper tract procedure alone.

Belman AB, Filmer RB, King LR: Surgical management of duplication of the collecting system. J Urol 112:316, 1974

Through a subcostal incision, heminephrectomy and subtotal ureterectomy to below the iliac vessels were done. Below that point, the duplicated ureters became too intimately joined to risk further dissection. If the ureter in question was obstructed, it was left open and drained. Remaining ureteral stumps did not dilate and become diverticulum. Initial bladder excision of the ureterocele was not recommended because only 10% of patients later needed it and because the potential surgical damage incurred during the bladder dissection outweighs the potential gain.

Brock WA, Kaplan GW: Ectopic ureteroceles in children. J Urol 119:800, 1978

One-stage total heminephroureterectomy, transvesical excision of the ureterocele, and reconstruction of the detrusor gave satisfactory results in eight of nine children so treated. Concomitant orthotopic ureteroneocystotomy was undertaken when there was reflux into the duplicated ureter. In the seriously ill children, a staged approach was used. As a diagnostic aid, injection of the ureterocele with an endoscopic needle localized the side of origin of the ureterocele.

Smith ME (chm): Report of working party to establish an international nomenclature for the large ureter. In Urinary System Malformation in Children, pp 3–8. New York, Alan R. Liss, 1977

After struggling with the definition of wide ureters or megaureters of diverse causes, the following classification scheme was suggested. It has subsequently proved generally useful and has gained qualified acceptance.

Megaureter Classification

A
Reflux megaureter

Primary	Secondary
Primary reflux	Urethral obstruction
Prune-belly syndrome	Neuropathic bladder

B
Obstructed megaureter

Primary	Secondary
Intrinsic obstruction stenosis	Urethral obstruction
Adynamic segment	Neuropathic bladder
	Extrinsic obstruction
	Retroperitoneal tumor

C
Nonrefluxing, nonobstructed megaureter

Primary	Secondary
Prune-belly Syndrome	Infection
	Polyuria
	After relief of obstruction

Tanagho EA: Ureteroceles: Embryogenesis, pathogenesis, and management. Journal of Continuing Education in Urology 18:13, 1979

The ureterocele expansion involves only the submucosal ureter and does not interfere with Waldeyer's sheath, which has already started to leave the ureter and sweep to its side to continue as deep trigone. Ureterocele expansion occurs ventral to the underlying layer of Waldeyer's sheath and supporting detrusor muscle fibers. As the ureterocele expands, the musculature of the submucosal segment alone is subjected to expansion and distention, while the rest of the musculature around this segment is not directly involved in the cystic formation. As the ureterocele expands, the musculature of the submusocal ureter becomes implicated to a varying degree.

Williams DI, Woodard JR: Problems in the management of ectopic ureteroceles. J Urol 92:635, 1964

This is another classic reference, although from a decade past. Sixty-eight cases are described, including many pitfalls, "double-barrel" incontinence, and reasons for surgical failures.

Hendren WH, Mitchell ME: Surgical correction of ureteroceles. J Urol 121:590, 1979

This updating of Hendren's series now includes 73 cases and again espouses one-stage complete reconstruction as the initial procedure in robust children. The article includes excellent illustrations on the surgical technique of separating the duplicated lower ureters while preserving the blood supply of the lower-pole ureter.

Overview: Ureteroceles

Edmond T. Gonzales, Jr.

Surgery for ureteroceles spans a long and interesting chapter in pediatric urology, and still no consensus exists on management. Ureteroceles appear as a broad spectrum: orthotopic or ectopic, in association with single ureters or duplication anomalies, large and small, and with reflux or obstruction in ipsilateral or contralateral ureters. With so many facets to the same diagnosis, one must carefully individualize each case, and considerations must include both the management of the upper renal anomaly (dysplasia, hydronephrosis) and of the distal ureter and ureterocele.

The classification and nomenclature of ureteroceles can be confusing. The terms *orthotopic* and *ectopic* generally refer to the position of the ureteral meatus, but, by convention, also refer to ureteroceles associated with single or double systems (involving the upper segment), respectively. Ureteroceles associated with a single ureter, however, may be positioned ectopically, especially in males; not all ureteroceles associated with the upper segment of duplication anomalies involve the bladder neck and urethra. Cecoureteroceles may have a reasonably normally positioned ureteral meatus but a long "ectopic" extension beneath the trigone and urethra.

In 1961, Uson proposed a classification scheme for ureteroceles that emphasized the vast differences between these lesions, but its complexity has limited its clinical application.[1] For purposes of this discussion, orthotopic ureteroceles will refer to those associated with single ureters and ectopic ones to those associated with the upper segment of completely duplicated systems. Deviations on this classification will be emphasized in the text.

ORTHOTOPIC URETEROCELES

Orthotopic ureteroceles are recognized less often in children than in adults and are generally larger and more destructive of the anatomy of the trigone than they are in adults. These lesions tend to be associated with single ureters, and it is uncommon for them to involve the bladder neck or more distal structures. The embryology of orthotopic ureteroceles is thought to represent persistence of Chwalla's membrane, which is a thin epithelial structure that occludes the stoma of the wolffian duct at the urogenital sinus. Normally, this membrane lyses spontaneously and completely during embryogenesis. If it lyses only partially, ureteral meatal stenosis might result, with the ensuing development of a ureterocele. Hence, these ureteroceles are usually tense and thin-walled and associated with a pinpoint ureteral meatus. There is, though, no embryologic evidence to support this concept, and not all authors agree on the mechanisms of formation of simple ureteroceles.[2] Significant hydroureter and hydronephrotic parenchymal damage may be present, but severe renal dysplasia is uncommon. They may occur bilaterally and have been reported to show a familial tendency.[3,4]

Simple incision or unroofing of the ureterocele will allow for rapid decompression of the upper tract, and this approach has been suggested as appropriate in adults. In children, though, the trigone is usually significantly distorted, and this technique will almost always result in reflux into a massively dilated system. For this reason, the surgical approach to orthotopic ureteroceles in children, when the kidney is salvageable, is most often an open one with excision of the ureterocele, reconstruction of the bladder base, and reimplantation with an antireflux technique—with tailoring—if necessary.[5]

ECTOPIC URETEROCELES

The main controversy in management of ureteroceles involves the management of ectopic ureteroceles. By definition, an ectopic ureterocele is one associated with a ureter whose meatus is placed distal to the normal location on the trigone. However, many variations exist within this concept. In the great majority of patients, ectopic ureteroceles are associated with completely duplicated systems, affect the upper-pole ureter, and occur about six times more frequently in girls than in boys. The meatus may be present at the bladder neck or somewhere along the course of the urethra. However, such ureteroceles may be associated with a single ectopic ureter. This anomaly is seen somewhat more commonly in boys than in girls, and the ureteral meatus is often located in the prostatic urethra. The bladder neck and proximal urethra is often severely distorted, and the kidney is dysplastic and nonfunctional. Other ureteroceles may have a ureteral orifice positioned within the bladder, but with a long extension beneath the bladder neck and urethra— the so-called cecoureterocele. Appropriate management requires a thorough understanding of all these variations and individualization of each case.

Embryology

The embryology of ectopic ureteroceles remains a debated topic. Ericsson originally proposed that ureteral meatal stenosis was responsible for these lesions, but it is obvious that not all ureteroceles have a stenotic meatus, and several authors have questioned obstruction as the primary etiologic factor.[2,6-8] Tanagho has proposed that a longer than normal trigone precursor and excessive widening of the distal portion of the ureteral bud results in incomplete absorption of this structure into the developing urogenital sinus, resulting in persistent dilation of the lower portion, and intravesical segment, of ureter.

The dilated ureter so commonly associated with ureteroceles continues, though, to suggest some component of obstruction; perhaps the bladder neck and proximal urethra contribute some resistance to ureteral flow when the ureteral meatus is distal in the urethra, but Gribetz and Leiter have postulated that the primary defect is in the ureter itself.[9] Supporting this latter concept is the observation that some ureteroceles are associated with multicystic dysplastic kidneys and upper ureteral atresia, but with marked dilation of the lower ureter. In the absence of apparent urine flow or reflux, the dilated lower ureter suggests primary ureteral dysplasia rather than obstruction.

It has long been recognized that renal parenchymal maldevelopment is associated with anomalies of the collecting structures of the urinary tract. For many years, these parenchymal changes were thought to be due to ureteral obstruction. But, as discussed previously, not all ureteroceles appear to be obstructive, and Mackei and Stevens have proposed convincingly that renal dysplasia in anomalies of ectopia is a result of induction of an abnormal segment of primitive metanephrogenic mass by the abnormally positioned ureter.[10] Their theory supposes that the metanephrogenic ridge is rather broad, but that only the central region is able to form normal kidney. A normally positioned ureteral bud will meet this central metanephrogenic tissue and allow for normal renal development. An ectopically positioned ureteral bud, as one would expect in association with ureteroceles, would meet peripherally located tissue and induce abnormal or dysplastic kidney. But whatever the cause of the dysplasia, it is commonly present in association with ectopic ureteroceles, and its severity tends to parallel the more severely ectopic examples of this disorder.

Management

In electing a form of management for the child with an ectopic ureterocele, many options are available, and one must individualize therapy for each child.[11] For discussion purposes, therapy can conveniently be divided into two broad areas: management of the kidney and upper ureter and management of the lower ureter and ureterocele.

The management of the renal parenchymal anomaly depends on recognition, since the dysplastic tissue is best excised and not saved. Lack of function on an IV urogram and, more recently, on radioisotope scanning would tend to support renal dysplasia. In most cases, though, visual inspection of the kidney will be the final determining factor whether there is salvageable tissue there or not. If doubt exists on the quality of parenchyma, I would choose to excise it rather than to save what amounts to a very small percentage of the renal mass. If the upper segment is to be saved, a ureteropyelostomy is the accepted procedure of choice. However, it is not clear that most cases of ectopic ureterocele have associated dysplasia. In fact, Churchill and colleagues have recently reported only 25% incidence of true dysplasia in their series of ureteroceles.* In addition, not all dysplastic tissue must be excised. Bauer and

* Churchill BM: Personal communication.

Retik have proposed at times leaving the small dysplastic cap when the upper ureter is not particularly dilated and proceeding with a simple common-sheath reimplantation and excision of the ureterocele.[12] It has been suggested that in some patients a lower ureteroureterostomy (upper segment ureter to *in situ* lower segment ureter) might be appropriate if there is no reflux into the lower-pole system, but this approach has not gained general favor among urologists interested in this problem.[13] One of the drawbacks with this approach is that the upper segment would not be visualized in order to estimate the degree of dysplasia. In addition, one would be concerned about setting up a situation in which "yoyo" reflux might become a significant factor when such a long ureteral segment was used.

The main controversy, though, involves the amount of surgery necessary on the lower ureter and ureterocele. The considerations included initial endoscopic unroofing of the ureterocele with secondary total reconstruction, or an upper (renal) procedure and one of the following: (1) total reconstruction, (2) subtotal ureterectomy, or (3) total ureterectomy and decompression of the ureterocele extravesically. Each of these concepts can be treated individually and has merit in its own right.

Endoscopic unroofing of a ureterocele (or, occasionally, direct incision when the ureterocele is prolapsed through the urethra) is an easy and quick way to decompress the upper urinary tract in infants. Its main drawback is that a previously "obstructed" system is converted into a massively refluxing one—into a very dilated, atonic, and dysplastic system. Although this procedure has not been looked on favorably in recent years, Tank has recently reported a series of children in whom internal decompression (endoscopic unroofing) of ureteroceles was associated with favorable results.* Although reflux occurred in some, as expected, infection was readily controlled after decompression, and reconstruction was accomplished at a later date in an older child and in a more elective fashion. Of particular interest was the identification of function in the upper segments after decompression when nonvisualization was the rule when the child was first seen. Although uncontrolled, the data suggest that perhaps endoscopic unroofing in the very young infant allows for recovery of renal parenchyma and might promote salvage of more renal tissue than has been practiced in the past. Despite this encouraging early report, one must be cautioned about using this procedure routinely. I believe it should still be reserved for the very young infant with severe sepsis who seems nonresponsive to intensive modern antibiotic therapy.

Total ureterocele excision and reconstruction of the bladder neck is a formidable operation in a baby.[8,14–16] In addition to the fact that bilateral ureteral reimplantations are commonly necessary and may require tailoring, the ureterocele often extends well down into the urethra. If the ureterocele is not totally excised and the bladder mucosa carefully repaired, a flap along the posterior bladder neck may remain and act as a valvular obstruction with voiding.[17] This is a common cause of urinary retention after ureterocele repair. On the other hand, aggressive ureterocele excision may damage the bladder neck

* Tank E: Personal communication.

and continence mechanism or result in damage to the vagina, with the possible development of a vesicovaginal fistula.

Because of these concerns, cautious surgeons have looked for less extensive means of managing these defects, especially in the very young infant. At diagnosis, ureteroceles may be very large and undermine and distort the trigone and bladder neck. They may in themselves be a source of vesical outlet obstruction. But once the upper segment of kidney is detached from the ureterocele, it collapses and becomes no more than a bit of redundant mucosa on the bladder floor. In this fashion, it is not an obstructive lesion any longer, and the child should be able to void normally. In addition, any obstructive component to the ipsilateral or contralateral ureters should be relieved. In some cases, reflux into the other ureters has been seen to resolve.

Some pitfalls do remain, however. Often the detrusor below a ureterocele is thinned and weakened and without repair will form a bladder diverticulum during voiding. In addition, one must always be alert to the possibility of a cecoureterocele where the ureteral orifice, often gaping and patulous, is within the vesical lumen.[7] With voiding, reflux occurs into the diverticulum and down the mucosa-lined extension behind the bladder neck and uretha and in, itself, may act as a valvular defect and cause obstruction. But despite these drawbacks in some children, excision of any infected, nonfunctioning, upper-segment parenchyma and relief of stasis by *decompression of the ureterocele* will often result in a healthy child who may undergo a second-stage reconstruction later without the need for such extensive revision of the lower urinary tract. Two variations on this theme are currently practiced.

Belman and colleagues have proposed *subtotal ureterectomy* through a subcostal or flank incision only.[18] In an infant, nearly all the ureter can be excised in this fashion. In an older child, the dissection usually stops at about the level of the iliac vessels. If the ureter refluxes, it is simply tied off. If there is no reflux, it is left open, and a drain is left in place down to the ureteral stump. In this fashion, the ureterocele will decompress out the ureter. With this approach, anywhere from 10% to 50% of children will require a second procedure to complete the ureterocele excision and reconstruction of the bladder neck.[19] Although some may argue that this justified a total one-stage repair, the second-stage reconstruction is often much easier technically than if it had all been done at one time. Hydroureters may decompress, and, in my experience, the limits of the collapsed ureterocele are more easily defined than when it is tense and distended.

Kroovand and Perlmutter have proposed a somewhat more aggressive, although still limited, approach to this problem.[20] After appropriate management of the parenchymal anomaly, the ureter is excised in total, usually through two separate incisions. Dissection must be careful and stay right on the adventitia of the upper segment ureter lest the common vasular tissue between the two ureters is damaged. In addition, as the ureterocele progresses under the bladder neck, one again runs the risk of damaging the urethra or vagina. But with care and experience, one can identify the ureteral wall and excise the majority of the ureterocele extravesically without opening the bladder mucosa. To date, no second-stage procedures have been required in any of the nine children in whom this procedure was undertaken.

It has been my choice over the past several years to follow the principles outlined by Kroovand and Perlmutter. In the baby with this problem, I do only as much surgery as seems necessary to remove all problems of urinary stasis and maintain a healthy child, even if other abnormalities such as reflux or bladder diverticulum remain. In the majority of situations, infection will be controlled with lesser surgery, and second-stage reconstructions will require less aggressive lower ureteral modeling when they are necessary. The spectrum of ureteroceles is so great and variable that no one approach should ever be rigidly adhered to, however. Careful, thoughtful evaluation of each patient will always be necessary.

REFERENCES

1. Uson AC: A classification of ureteroceles in children. J Urol 85:732, 1961

2. Tanagho EA: Embryogenic basis for lower ureteral anomalies: A hypothesis. Urology 7:451, 1976

3. Rabinowitz R, Barkin M, Schillinger JF, Jeffs RD, Cook GT: Bilateral orthotopic ureteroceles causing massive ureteral dilatation in children. J Urol 119:839, 1978

4. Abrams HJ, Sutton AP, Burkbinder MI: Ureteroceles in siblings. J Urol 124:135, 1980

5. Snyder HM, Johnston JH: Orthotopic ureteroceles in children. J Urol 119:543, 1978

6. Ericsson NO: Ectopic ureterocele in infants and children: a clinical study. Acta Chir Scand 197 (Suppl):1, 1954

7. Stephens D: Caecoureterocele and concepts in the etiology of ureteroceles. Aust NZ J Surg 40:239, 1971

8. Williams DI, Woodard JR: Problems in the management of ectopic ureteroceles. J Urol 92:635, 1964

9. Gribetz ME, Leiter E: Ectopic ureterocele, hydroureter, and renal dysplasia: an embryogenic triad. Urology 11:131, 1978

10. Mackei GG, Stephens FD: Duplex kidneys: A correlation of renai dysplasia with position of the ureteral orifice. J Urol 114:274, 1975

11. Mandell J, Colodny AH, Lebowitz R, Bauer SB, Retik AB: Ureteroceles in infants and children. J Urol 123:921, 1980

12. Bauer SB, Retik AB: The nonobstructive ectopic ureterocele. J Urol 119:804, 1978

13. Amar AD: Ipsilateral ureteroureterostomy for single ureteral disease in patients with ureteral duplication: A review of eight years of experience with sixteen patients. J Urol 119:472, 1978

14. Hendren WH, Monfort GJ: Surgical correction of ureteroceles in childhood. J Pediatr Surg 6:235, 1971

15. Brock WA, Kaplan GW: Ectopic ureteroceles in children. J Urol 119:800, 1978

16. Hendren WH, Mitchell ME: Surgical correction of ureteroceles. J Urol 121:590, 1979

17. Ashkraft KW, Hendren WH: Bladder outlet obstruction after operation for ureterocele. J Pediatr Surg 14:819, 1979

18. Belman AB, Filmer RB, King LR: Surgical management of duplication of the collecting system. J Urol 112:316, 1974

19. Barrett DM, Malek RS, Kelalis PP: Problems and solutions in surgical treatment of 100 consecutive ureteral duplications in children. J Urol 114:126, 1975

20. Kroovand RL, Permutter AD: A one-stage surgical approach to ectopic ureterocele. J Urol 122:367, 1979

PART NINETEEN

SURGERY OF URETERAL TRAUMA

41

MANAGEMENT OF OPERATIVE URETERAL INJURY

Leonard M. Zinman, M.D., John A. Libertino, M.D., Robert A. Roth, M.D.

From the Department of Urology, Lahey Clinic Foundation, Boston, Massachusetts

Urology / September 1978 / Volume XII, Number 3

Although major strides have been achieved in the technical training of pelvic and abdominal surgeons, the reported incidence of operative ureteral trauma continues to increase.[1-3] This may be attributed in part to the increased volume of complex retroperitoneal and vascular surgical procedures and to the increased magnitude of pelvic operations in patients who have undergone prior irradiation. Critical factors, which will determine the successful management of ureteral injury, are careful identification of the location and length of ureteral wall involved, status of the contralateral kidney or ureter, the etiologic surgical procedure, and relative risk to the patient, prior pelvic and abdominal radiation, presence of a fresh vascular prosthesis, retroperitoneal fibrosis from previous operation, retroperitoneal or pelvic abscess, and the presence of a concomitantly produced vesicovaginal fistula. The most decisive factor influencing the ureteral reconstructive technique selected will be the level at which the ureter is injured and the amount of viable ureter available for a tension-free, well-vascularized anastomosis.

MATERIAL AND METHODS

To identify the danger points and to define some of the problems of the injured ureter, we reviewed the records of 67 patients referred to our department from 1965 to 1976 inclusive for the management of surgically induced ureteral trauma. Of our patients, 38 had pelvic ureteral injuries and 29 had abdominal or lumbar ureteral injuries (Tables 1 and 2). Thirty-four patients were referred for primary reconstructive surgery and 33 after at least one previous reparative procedure had been unsuccessful.

Etiology. *Pelvic Ureter.* Pelvic surgical procedures account for the majority of ureteral injuries with the reported incidence varying between 0.4 and 2.5 percent of all gynecologic procedures.[4,5] The ureter enters the pelvis behind the ovarian peritoneal fold on the lateral pelvic wall and crosses the right external iliac or left common iliac artery. It courses medially in women into the lower and medial part of the broad ligament. The uterine artery crosses it at this point and continues medially. At this level the ureter is 1 to 4 cm lateral to the supravaginal portion of the cervix.

It is this close anatomic proximity which puts the ureter at risk in women. Hysterectomy for benign fibroid tumor contributed to the majority of the 38 pelvic ureteral injuries. Most of these occurred paravesically within the lower 5 cm of the ureter where it passes posterior to the uterine artery as a result of blind clamping or application of suture ligatures in an attempt to arrest uncontrolled

TABLE 1. Type of Surgical Procedure Associated with 38 Pelvic Ureteral Injuries (1965 to 1975)

Operation	No. of Patients
Abdominal hysterectomy	
Fibroids	11
Endometriosis	4
Radical for cancer	
With radiation	3
Without radiation	6
Marshall-Marchetti	2
Vaginal hysterectomy	2
Oophorectomy (ovarian mass)	1
Anterior repair	1
Rectal excision	
Lateral ligament level	7
Inferior mesenteric artery level	1
Total	38

TABLE 2. Type of Surgical Procedure Associated with 29 Lumbar Ureteral Injuries (1965 to 1975)

Operation	No. of Patients
Pancreatic cyst	1
Anterior sigmoid resection	3
Right colectomy	2
Duodenal resection	1
Aortic procedures	6
Vena caval ligation	1
Sympathectomy (right)	2
Laminectomy (left)	1
Retroperitoneal fibrosis	3
Retroperitoneal lymphadenectomy	1
Retroperitoneal tumor	2
Ureteral lysis	1
Ureterolithotomy	5
Total	29

bleeding. Some occurred at the pelvic inlet during radical hysterectomy and oophorectomy, approximately 10 to 12 cm from the ureterovesical junction. Eight of the pelvic ureteral injuries were recognized at operation, and the remainder were identified between the third and tenth day. Ureteral stricture with hydronephrosis was present in 32 of the injured pelvic ureters and usually presented with flank pain or fever. Twelve patients presented with incontinence secondary to a ureterovaginal fistula; 4 of these had previously been diverted by nephrostomy tubes to control pelvic and renal sepsis, 3 patients had associated vesicovaginal fistulas, and 1 patient had an associated rectovaginal fistula. Two patients had intraperitoneal and incisional urinary leakage. Pelvic inflammatory disease, endometriosis, and an ovarian tumor adherent to the pelvic wall distorted the ureteral anatomy and rendered it vulnerable to injury during ligation of the infundibulopelvic ligament in 5 patients. Two Marshall-Marchetti urethropubic suspension procedures resulted in ligature obstruction of the ureterovesical junction by proximal, laterally placed sutures.

In men, the pelvic ureter is crossed by the ductus deferens below the hypogastric artery, passes in front of and slightly above the upper end of the seminal vesicles under the lateral bladder ligaments, and enters the bladder at the distal portion of the lateral bladder pedicle. Rectal excision was the procedure most often associated with the injured pelvic ureter in men. These were sustained during division of the lateral rectal ligaments low in the pelvis and were associated with removal of a large, bulky, or adherent rectal tumor. Two patients had extensive Crohn's disease with dense pelvic adhesions.

Upper Ureter. The abdominal or upper ureter extends from the ureteropelvic junction to the common iliac vessels. It is loosely adherent to the posterior peritoneum and is usually reflected ventrally with the gonadal vessels when gaining access to the retroperitoneum. Operative

procedures during which ureteral transection and ligation were encountered were colonic resection, aortic reconstruction, sympathectomy, laminectomy, pancreatic and duodenal resections, and excision of retroperitoneal tumors and lymph nodes (Table 2). In 3 patients, ischemic ureteral strictures developed after ureterolysis from the obstructing fibrous envelope of idiopathic retroperitoneal fibrosis. Five patients had injuries sustained during the course of ureterolithotomy that resulted in extensive upper midureteral strictures. Avulsion of the ureteropelvic junction with subsequent ureteropelvic and upper ureteral stricture accounted for 2 of these cases. In 3 patients extensive strictures of the entire ureter developed after repeat basket extraction of calculi that were lodged in fixed, inflamed ureters.

Clinical Recognition of Ureteral Injury. Only 20 to 30 percent of ureteral injuries are recognized at the time of operation. If ureteral injury is suspected during a difficult pelvic or retroperitoneal procedure, identification may be made by injecting 12.5-Gm bolus of mannitol intravenously followed by 5 cc of indigo carmine dye. If a blue stain is noted in the operative field, the ureter should be dissected out to identify the damage. If the distal ureter cannot be found, a cystotomy should be made and a ureteral catheter placed through the ureteral orifice until it presents in the operative field revealing the transected distal end. When ligation without penetration is suspected, a proximal linear ureterotomy allows antegrade insertion of a ureteral catheter to test ureteral patency and integrity.

Patients undergoing troublesome pelvic operations when major hemorrhage or difficult dissection has been encountered should be selected carefully for intraoperative high-dose infusion excretory urography to rule out a silent ureteral injury. This maneuver is most useful to demonstrate the functional status of the contralateral kidney if an injury is found and nephrectomy is being contemplated. Since this is the most ideal time to repair ureteral trauma, it is critical that the suspicion of a ureteral injury be allayed by compulsive scrutiny of the ureteral wall before the incision is closed.

Flank pain, which may be colicky or may be steady and dull, with tenderness was the most common presenting signal to ureteral injury in the early postoperative period. Of our patients, 15 percent had high fever, and 20 percent presented with urinary leakage through the wound or vagina. Early fistula formation to the abdomen or vagina resulted from unrecognized partial or complete ureteral transection. Delayed fistula formation after ligation or devascularization occurred between seven and twenty-one days, with one fistula developing as late as four weeks. Three patients had concurrent vesicovaginal fistulas; these fistulas are extremely important to identify since management will be affected by their presence.

A cystogram should be obtained to evaluate the presence of reflux as was demonstrated in 1 patient with a right ureteral injury and a ureterovaginal fistula who had reflux of contrast material up the injured ureter, through the fistula, and into the vagina. Cystography will also help to identify bladder capacity and any other vesical disease if ureteral reimplantation is chosen. Excretory urography is adequate to document most ureteral injuries in the postoperative period, but cone-tipped catheter retrograde ureterography will more accurately determine the extent of stricture and the distance between the injury and the bladder. This study will also establish the patency of the ureter proximal and distal to the injured site. Good quality ureterograms in the anteroposterior and oblique positions can help define the extent of a partial ureteral tear and help determine how much ureteral wall is still intact. This was demonstrated in the following case report.

Case Abstract 1. A forty-three-year-old man with a two-year history of chronic left lumbosacral pain and sciatica underwent an uneventful lumbar laminectomy from an L4,5 protruding intervertebral disk. On the third postoperative day the patient experienced progressive ileus, abdominal distention, a temperature of 101°F, and severe pain in the left flank. Excretory urography revealed left retroperitoneal extravasation below the lower pole of the kidney. Retrograde ureterography revealed extravasation of contrast material from left midureter (Fig. 1*A*).

The patient underwent transperitoneal exploration of the left ureter, at which time a large collection of urine was drained from the left retroperitoneal space, and the midureter was carefully mobilized. A transverse defect, 3 mm, was found in the midureter on its posterolateral wall. The edges of the incised ureter were viable and were approximated with three interrupted sutures of 5–0 chromic catgut. The wound was drained through an extraperitoneal site. Postoperative excretory urography revealed a normal left collecting system (Fig. 1*B*). The patient had an uneventful convalescence; findings of follow-up urography one year after operation were normal.

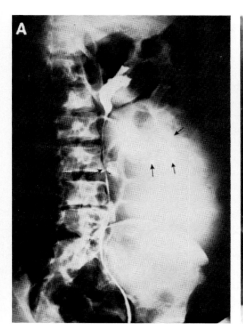
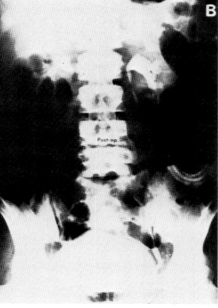

Fig. 1. Case 1. (*A*) Retrograde pyelogram shows extravasation of contrast material from left midureteral partial tear incurred during L-4, L-5 laminectomy. (*B*) Excretory urogram one week after drainage of left retroperitoneal urine collection and limited repair of injured left midureter.

Approach to Management. Repair of a ureteral transection, when injury is recognized immediately, is frequently straightforward and technically uncomplicated, and yields excellent results. Crush injuries from hemostatic clamps, partial tears, and ligatures involving the ureter and periureteral tissues with angulation obstruction may offer a significant challenge to the surgeon. Each problem must be managed individually, but limited repairs, simple intubation, deligation, and intubation, are procedures that should be selected carefully and avoided in most instances since the extent of ureteral trauma is usually underestimated.

When the patient's condition does not permit further extension of operative time and a defintive reparative procedure is not feasible, the most expedient temporary solution is an in situ feeding tube used as a urinary diversion above the injured area. The tube is brought out through a small, watertight linear ureterotomy and is securely anchored to the ureteral wall and retroperitoneal musculature in association with closely placed Penrose drains. Intentional proximal ureteral ligation with expectant renal death in the poor-risk elderly patient or the patient with a limited life span produces a considerable incidence of fistula formation and serious sepsis.[6]

Patients with ureteral trauma identified one to two weeks after operation have frequently undergone preliminary tube nephrostomy.[7,8] A more aggressive approach with immediate operative repair when the problem is initially seen will avoid lengthy hospitalization and staged surgical procedures and result in a favorable outcome with less psychologic trauma.[9,10] An early reparative procedure may be technically more difficult but has not resulted in a higher rate of complications. Preliminary urinary diversion may be a more prudent appropriate course in the patient with sepsis, a concomitant vesicovaginal fistula, and pelvic irradiation and in the patient who has experienced a stormy postoperative course and is a poor surgical risk. Fistulous communication to the skin, peritoneum, or retroperitoneal bed should undergo immediate drainage and repair to avoid delayed wound and retroperitoneal abscess formation. Proximal nephrostomy tube drainage has been inadequate on occasion in preventing or resolving pelvic sepsis and should be complemented by wide pelvic and retroperitoneal drainage.

MANAGEMENT OF LOWER URETER

The transperitoneal route is the preferred approach to the ureter requiring delayed reconstructive procedures. It provides ready access to every part of the ureter, kidney, and bladder and leaves open the option of transureteroureterostomy, ileal substitution, or autotransplantation if the amount of viable ureter is limited. The transperitoneal route permits release of renal adhesions with renal descensus for increased ureteral length and allows the use of omental pedicle wrap in the difficult repair. The ureter is approached retroperitoneally just above the iliac vessels lateral to the colon on the left side and just above and lateral to the cecum on the right side. A narrow Penrose drain is placed around the ureter for gentle traction, and the ureter is dissected distally with careful preservation of the sheet of adventitia that contains the nutrient arterial plexus. Branches from the aorta and iliac arteries must be divided to gain adequate length, since a tension-free anastomosis is a critical factor in healing. The ureter is divided above the site of stricture and the proximal end is debrided until healthy, viable ureter is visible.

Ureteral Reimplantation. Ureteroneocystotomy is the reparative procedure of choice for injures of the pelvic ureter. Strictures and injuries of the paravesical ureter less than 5 cm from the ureterovesical junction are readily reimplanted by mobilizing the lower ureter and ipsilateral bladder wall. We prefer to use the modified submucosal tunnel technique of Politano and Leadbetter[11,12] to achieve an antirefluxing ureteral anastomosis. No attempt is made to bring the ureter down into the trigone. The tunnel is usually made in an upper posterolateral site and varies between 2 and 4 cm in length. The distal ureter is spatulated for 1.5 cm and sutured to the bladder with interrupted 5–0 chromic catgut sutures. The no. 5 feeding tube ureteral stent is brought out alongside a suprapubic cystotomy catheter and is removed in seven days. This technique has achieved a uniformly successful antirefluxing reimplantation.

When the lower ureteral injury is so extensive that the proximal ureter cannot be brought to the bladder without tension, several techniques to reduce the ureterovesical gap are available. The Boari bladder flap tube technique has been the most widely employed for 10 to 15 cm defects with a reported success rate of 50 to 80 percent.[13] This method has the inherent technical difficulties of any vascularized pedicle graft. The critical factors in its construction are the size of the bladder, prior bladder operation, and a visible vascular pedicle from the superior vesical artery.

The procedure has, therefore, been discontinued in favor of the psoas hitch maneuver as our procedure of choice for long lower ureteral defects.[14] The technique is simple to perform and has been successful in restoring an obstructed reflux-free ureterovesical anastomosis. The technique involves a variable amount of vesical mobilization depending upon the length of the gap. The bladder is detached from its superior and inferior vascular pedicle down to the ureterovesical junction and the posterior peritoneum. It is separated from the cervix and proximal vagina or rectum. A very thin bladder wall should have a patch of peritoneum left adherent to provide an adequate area for the anchoring sutures. Three or four 2–0 chromic catgut sutures are used to anchor the bladder securely to the psoas minor tendon, which lies lateral and cephalad to the common iliac artery. This may be congenitally absent in 10 percent of patients and can be replaced by large bites of psoas major muscle. The bladder is opened transversely to give added length, and the upper portion of the bladder is stretched cephalad with traction before the sutures are sited. The submucosal tunnel is created before the hitch sutures are secured. In 26 patients since 1968, no bladder dysfunction has developed after this procedure, and lower ureteral defects as long as 14 cm

have been bridged successfully with minimal postoperative morbidity.

Case Abstract 2. A fifty-year-old man underwent bilateral ureteral lysis for obstructing retroperitoneal fibrosis and incurred a lower right ureteral ischemic injury that resulted in an obstructing lower-third ureteral stricture. Acute obstructive pyelonephritis was resolved by a preliminary diverting nephrostomy tube and parenteral antibiotics. A nephrostogram revealed the upper margin of the stricture to be located above the level of the common iliac artery (Fig. 2A). Cystoscopy and right retrograde pyelography demonstrated the location of the stricture 10 cm from the bladder (Fig. 2B).

Through a midline transabdominal incision, the right ureter was dissected from a fibrous bed lateral to the

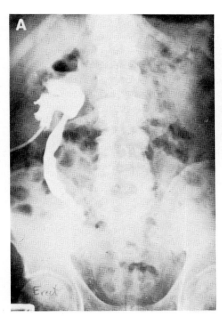

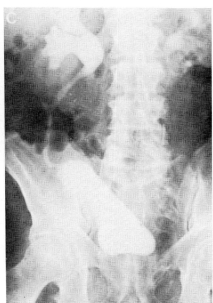

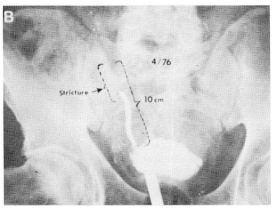

Fig. 2. Case 2. (A) Right nephrostogram reveals lower ureteral stricture that developed after ureterolysis for retroperitoneal fibrosis from ischemic injury. (B) Right retrograde pyelogram demonstrates location of stricture above level of common iliac artery. (C) Excretory urogram six months after ureteral reimplantation and extensive psoas hitch maneuver allowing 3-cm submucosal antirefluxing anastomosis.

right colon. It was mobilized down to its obstructed point and transected just above the right common iliac artery. The distal portion was noted to be markedly fibrotic. The bladder was completely mobilized from its peritoneal attachment and from both vascular pedicles. It was opened transversely and fixed to the right psoas minor tendon with three anchoring 1–0 chromic sutures. A submucosal tunnel, 3 cm, was created before fixation sutures were tied, and the ureter was reimplanted through the tunnel after being spatulated on its mesenteric side. This was accomplished with interrupted 4–0 chromic sutures that picked up bladder muscle in the mucosal stitch for anchoring. The ureter was stented with a no. 8 feeding tube that exited from the bladder next to a no. 20 Malecot catheter.

The stent was removed on the seventh postoperative day, and intravenous pyelography performed six months later revealed a normal right collecting system (Fig. 2C). Urine cultures were sterile, and no bladder dysfunction was found.

Transureteroureterostomy. Transureteroureterostomy may be a valuable option in the repair of the injured or resected ureter. The operation is not new. It was conceived in 1894 by Boari and Casati[15] and was performed on the experimental animal in 1905 by Bernasconi and Colombino[16] and in 1906 by Sharpe[17] in the United States. Higgins[18] first reported the successful use of this procedure when he anastomosed the right ureter to the left in a twenty-five-year-old man with recurrent right pyelonephritis and right unreteral reflux.

The patient was reported to be well thirty-three years later, and results of intravenous pyelography were normal. On theoretical grounds, urologists feared the potential complication of damage to the contralateral recipient ureter and kidney and avoided this procedure until 1963 when Hodges *et al.*[19] rekindled interest with the report of a large, successful series of transureteroureterostomies. In 1975, Smith and Smith[20] assessed the collective experience of British and Irish surgeons with transureteroureterostomy by having them complete a questionnaire to test their preliminary claim that the operation was a sound one and to search for any evidence of damage to the healthy recipient ureter. Of the 141 instances in which this procedure was employed, no damage to an opposite ureter was encountered. Mild, early, and temporary dilatation was noted in the contralateral ureter in many patients, but this was consistently transient. Crossover anastomosis to spare ureters that had been left after contralateral nephrectomy was successful in 10 patients with injury to the ureter of a solitary kidney. The over-all results were excellent, and the procedure was identified as the ideal reparative

technique for patients, who had a distressing postoperative ureteral fistula in a pelvis that had prior irradiation.

Two recent reports of serious injuries to the recipient ureters have given support to our prejudicial attitude in the use of this operation.[21,22] It is a precarious method of repair for injuries of the lumbar ureter and should be limited to use in the upper pelvic ureter. Before this technique is considered, the retroperitoneum should be free of infection, irradiation, idiopathic retroperitoneal fibrosis, and carcinoma. Calculous disease, retroperitoneal fibrosis, tuberculosis, and transitional cell carcinoma in the donor kidney and obstruction in the recipient ureters are absolute contraindications to this operation. Infection in the donor kidney and the size of the donor ureter have not precluded the selective use of this procedure, but attempts should be made to sterilize the urinary tract preoperatively. The optimal indication for transureteroureterostomy is found in the patient who has lost a long segment of lower ureter and in whom other reparative methods have failed and in the patient whose scarred, irradiated, or septic pervesical space precludes a repeat reconstructive pelvic operation.

Transureteroureterostomy is executed ideally through a generous midline transperitoneal incision. The donor ureter is mobilized lateral to the colon after incision of the lateral peritoneal reflection (Fig. 3A). The healthy portion of the ureter is mobilized and transected to permit easy transfer across the midline to the other ureter. An injured ureter should be resected at a point of certain

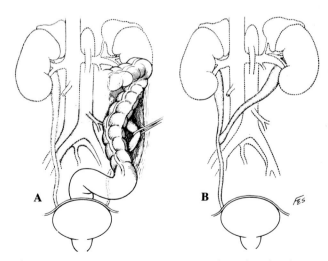

Fig. 3. (A) In transureteroureterostomy funnel is developed by gentle, blunt retroperitoneal dissection after exposure of upper ureter lateral to colon. (B) Ureter is brought across retroperitoneal space above level of inferior mesenteric artery to avoid tension to anastomosis. (From Zinman and Libertino[51])

viability. This may require frozen section biopsy of the proximal end in patients with prior irradiation before the anastomosis is begun. Where the ureter is mobilized for a considerable length, the adventitia must carefully be preserved to protect the intrinsic blood supply. The posterior peritoneum over the aorta and vena cava is elevated extensively to receive the donor ureter, which is delivered medially through a large opening at the base of the mesocolon to prevent acute angulation. The crossing should be made above the inferior mesenteric artery to prevent any anastomotic tension (Fig. 3B). The distal end of the involved ureter is spatulated for 1.5 cm on its medial side avoiding obvious nutrient vessels and sutured to a longitudinal ureterotomy of similar size in the recipient ureter with interrupted 5-0 chronic catgut in a watertight closure. An oblique rather than a perpendicular anastomosis is preferred with the donor ureter lying in a gentle unobstructed course (Fig. 4). The recipient ureter should not be mobilized from its bed

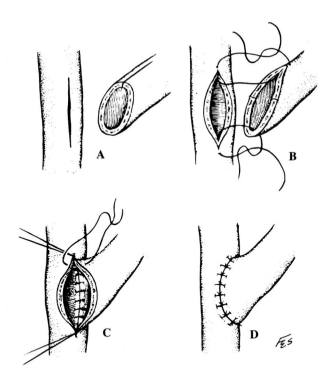

Fig. 4. (A) Distal end of donor ureter is spatulated for 1.5 to 2 cm on its antimesenteric side. Similar sized ureterostomy is created on medial side of recipient midureter. (B) Two fixation sutures of 5-0 catgut are placed at vertex of ureterotomy to initiate end to side anastomosis. (C) Posterior wall is approximated with knots on outside. (D) Anastomosis is completed with closely placed interrupted 5-0 chromic catgut sutures in watertight closure. (From Zinman and Libertino[51])

since wide medial deviation may cause angulation obstruction with disruption.

In the presence of a refractory donor kidney infection and a large, thickened donor ureter with a delicate recipient ureter, a nephrostomy is placed in the donor kidney as a proximal diverting safety valve to reduce intraluminal pressure and decrease leakage of infected urine. The retroperitoneal anastomosis is drained with a large Penrose drain passed under the mesocolon and brought out through a generous lateral stab incision on the side of the injured ureter.

Transureteroureterostomy is an easily performed nonshocking procedure with a low morbidity when selectively applied and properly performed.

Case Abstract 3. A forty-nine-year-old woman, para 3, underwent left oophorectomy for a 5-cm ovarian cyst. During the course of the procedure, uncontrolled hemorrhage developed from the lateral pelvic vessels. Hemostatic sutures to control alarming bleeding resulted in left unreteral ligation at the level of the common iliac artery. This was repaired immediately by ureteroureterostomy and T-tube stent diversion which resulted in ureteral stricture and ureterovaginal fistula. Three weeks later a second attempt to repair the stricture by repeat ureteroureterostomy failed, producing recurrent stricture, extravasation of urine, and retroperitoneal sepsis (Fig. 5A). Four weeks after the second operation the patient underwent transperitoneal exploration with drainage of a left pelvic urinoma and a left to right transureteroureterostomy. The distal ureter was noted to be necrotic. The patient's convalescence was uneventful, and early postoperative excretory urography revealed grade 2 left hydroureteronephrosis. One year later an excretory urogram demonstrated good prompt bilateral function and a normal unobstructed collecting system (Fig. 5B).

MANAGEMENT OF UPPER URETER

Injuries of the midureter and proximal ureter often provide the most challenging problems in reparative surgery of the urinary tract. The distance of the ureter from the kidney and bladder allows for fewer surgical options, and the marginal blood supply makes the lumbar ureter more vulnerable to ischemic damage. Primary repair with end to end ureteroureterostomy is the preferred technique for establishing ureteral continuity of upper ureteral injuries. Ureteral loss of up to 8 cm can be restored by Popesco's[23] renal lowering technique for gaining extraureteral length with a ureteroureterostomy. When longer segments of this ureter have been excised or damaged from ischemic injury and ureteral continuity cannot be accomplished, the more elegant options of ileal segment substitution or autotransplantation should be applied selectively.

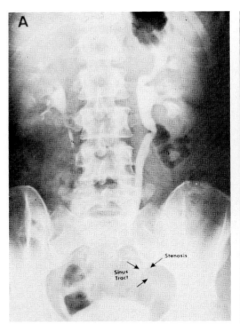

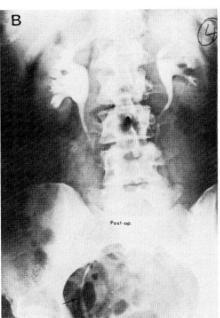

Fig. 5. Case 3. (A) Excretory urogram after failure of ureteroureterostomy repair for transected ureter that developed during left oophorectomy. Extravasation with pelvic abscess and partial ureteral obstruction developed. (B) Excretory urogram one year after drainage of pelvic abscess and left to right transureteroureterostomy.

Patients with extensive ureteral loss who are clearly not candidates for these more formidable reconstructive procedures because of age, surgical risk, underlying terminal disease, or potential failure of planned repair should undergo nephrectomy if function in the contralateral unit is adequate. This latter determination can only be established at times by formal divided renal functional measurements before the status of the remaining kidney can be known with certainty. Patients with calculous disease, advanced tuberculosis, retroperitoneal fibrosis, or other diseases which may potentially affect the contralateral kidney should have all reparative options exhausted before resorting to nechrectomy.

Ureteroureterostomy. End to end ureteroureterostomy was performed in 1886 by Schopf[24] who transected a ureter during removal of a cyst of the broad ligament. However, the side to side technique first proposed by Monari[25] gained more popularity than the end to end method in early years. In 1900 Boari[26] suggested the use of an indwelling stent, and in 1928 Iselin[27] advised urinary diversion proximal to the site of the ureteral anastomosis to minimize the harmful effects of urinary leakage on ureteral healing.

In a classic article on ureteral repair, Bovée, in 1897,[28] contributed the concept of an oblique end to end technique to avoid the potential stricture of circular anastomosis. Since that time, scores of methods and modifications have been described but used with limited success. In 1929 Marion[29] concluded after a review of

84 cases that the operation was hazardous and usually resulted in formation of stricture and hydronephrosis. He believed that transection of the ureter caused the peristalsis in the two segments to become asynchronous and that hydronephrosis would result even if a stricture did not develop because of the physiologic properties of the ureter. Moore, as late as 1954,[30] stated that an anastomosis between the ends of the ureter was probably not a worthwhile procedure since "stricture would be inevitable in the majority of the patients."

Experimental and clinical studies, however, have established the fact that the ureter has great potential for repairing itself without stricture if many of the principles developed in the late nineteenth and early twentieth century are carefully observed. These include adequate debridement of devitalized tissue, avoidance of urinary leakage at the anastomotic site, performance of an oblique anastomosis, approximation of the edges with the minimal amount of fine suture material to create a watertight anastomosis, and elimination of tension at the suture line. In 1957, Hamm and Weinberg[31] demonstrated good results with ureteroureterostomy using a spatulated end to end anastomosis with everting chromic catgut sutures and proximal diverting well-drained linear ureterotomy for diversion. They proposed that a vertical linear ureterotomy of 2.5 cm in length placed 5 cm above the anastomosis would drain urine from the site of healing and make the segment below the ureterotomy and the anastomotic site quiescent; this would allow healing and prevent extravasation of urine around the anastomosis.

Diversion is a critical factor in the repair of a transected ureter. The ureter is a retroperitoneal organ, and urinary extravasation from the anastomotic site is not reabsorbed. The urine may become infected and, if not vented by adequate drainage, will be a source of delayed healing, fibrosis, and stricture. Temporary proximal urinary diversion was advocated by most urologic surgeons, but great unresolved controversy continued for years over the best technique of diversion and the pros and cons of internal stents. In 1957 Hinman[32] stated that a watertight anastomosis and well-drained proximal linear ureterotomy obviated the need for an indwelling stent in most instances. Subsequent clinical experience with injured ureters of normal caliber supported this method of diversion.[33] In contrast, Davis[34] gave an excellent review of the arguments for the use of stents in the ureter, and Küss and Chatelain,[35] on the basis of their large clinical experience, suggested that a loose-fitting internal ureteral stent inserted during the early phase of ureteral repair, when there is atony and temporary retention, would prevent anastomotic leakage.

The most suitable method of diversion employed is not always simple; large indwelling tubes will distend the ureteral wall, cause ischemia, and effect myoelectrical activities. Smaller catheters and nephrostomy tubes do not effectively divert all the urine from the anastomotic site. A loose-fitting multifenestrated Silastic stent between the renal pelvis and the bladder in conjunction with vertical linear ureterotomy above the anastomosis will produce excellent results in most situations. We prefer to use a 6 to 8 F Silastic catheter with a 2-cm diverting ureterotomy approximately 5 cm above the anastomosis. The stenting catheter is secured by a 1-0 Dexon ligature that is passed through the diverting ureterotomy and tied loosely to a sterile button on the skin of the flank (Fig. 6).[36]

The cut ends of the ureter are first debrided to remove all devitalized tissue so that primary healing will be ensured. The ureter or kidney is mobilized as adequately as is needed to bridge the gap comfortably without tension. The ureters are spatulated on opposing sides of each end to achieve on oblique anastomosis and to prevent the stricture potential of a circumferential anastomosis. The edges are then approximated in one layer with interrupted sutures of fine 5-0 chromic catgut on a fine, curved, tapered needle using smooth, noncrushing vascular forceps to grasp the edge of the tissue. Each stitch is placed through the full thickness of unreter, preventing the prolapse of mucosa, and the sutures are tied on the outer aspect of the unreter (Fig. 7). The presence of an intraluminal catheter will aid in the placement of sutures. A running suture line should not be used in any ureteral reconstruction procedure since it

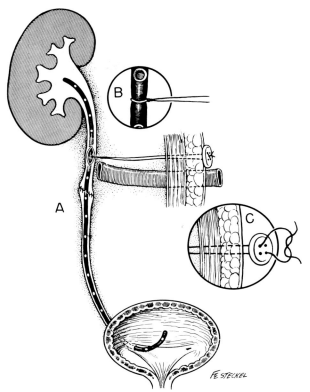

Fig. 6. (*A*) Uncomplicated midureteroureterostomy is diverted by internal loose Silastic stent in conjunction with linear ureterotomy above anastomosis. (*B*) Stenting catheter is secured by 1-0 Dexon ligature that is brought through diverting ureterotomy placed approximately 5 cm above anastomosis. (*C*) Dexon suture is tied loosely to button on skin surface to prevent spontaneous passage of stent by ureteral peristalsis. (From Zinman and Libertino[51])

may interfere with the ureter's already tenuous blood supply.

If a significant disparity exists in the ureteral size with a dilated proximal ureteral lumen and a normal distal one, the dilated end is cut transversely and the distal lumen is spatulated to fit appropriately. One Penrose drain is placed at the site of the diverting ureterotomy and one is positioned at the site of repair to drain any accumulation of blood and urine. The drains are brought out through separate stab wounds. When a ureteral repair is believed to be compromised with the potential for delayed healing, it should be diverted by nephrostomy tube with a small, intraluminal Silastic stent brought out along the side of the nephrostomy tube. Delayed healing should be suspected when the

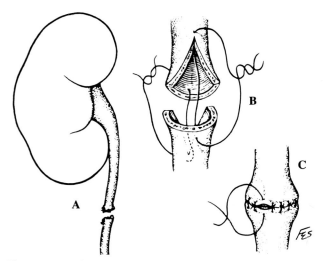

Fig. 7. (A) Ends of injured ureter are carefully debrided to remove devitalized tissue. (B) Ureters are spatulated on opposing sides of each end to achieve oblique anastomosis. (C) Edges are approximated with interrupted fine catgut sutures placed through full thickness of ureteral wall taking care to invert mucosa. (From Zinman and Libertino[51])

anastomosis is under tension or associated with ureteral ischemia, fibrosis, sepsis, pancreatic injury, or prior irradiation.

Ureteral injury incurred during the course of aortic or iliac vascular reconstructive or prosthetic replacement operation presents the special problem of potential sepsis to the arterial suture line or prosthetic graft with the disastrous sequela of mycotic aneurysm. The ureteral anastomosis must be excluded from the graft or the arterial suture line by an omental sleeve procedure and drained from above by nephrostomy and an internal occluding stent. No drains or catheters should be placed near a prosthetic vascular graft.

In the usual uncomplicated ureteral anastomosis in which an indwelling ureteral internal stent and diverting ureterotomy are employed for drainage, the stent is removed on the tenth day, and the drain is removed forty-eight hours after urinary drainage has ceased, If urinary leakage is prolonged from obstructive edema or cellular debris, a catheter is inserted cystoscopically under fluoroscopic guidance for five days. In patients in whom delayed healing is suspected, the internal stent should remain in place for twenty-one days to act as a scaffold to aid ureteral regenerative healing without stricture. This can only be achieved by nephrostomy and transrenal placement of the stent.

Omental Sleeve. Experimental studies have shown that ureteral repair may be interfered with when exposed to retroperitoneal fat and fascia, which can induce metaphlasia and periureteral bone formation.[37,38] Large, experimentally produced defects in the canine ureter when wrapped with an omental pedicle seal promptly without leakage and develop orderly regenerative repair without excessive fibrosis.[39]

The intact omental pedicle has been used since the latter part of the nineteenth century in attempts to increase blood flow to the ischemic heart, to relieve ascites, to drain hymphedema of the extremities, and to repair fistulas of the bladder.[40] Turner-Warwick[41] has recommended the routine use of omentum in all complex reconstructive procedures of the lower and upper urinary tract to prevent fibrosis, to aid in anastomotic healing, and to allow urodynamic mobility by maintaining a supple bed for the ureteral wall. We have consistently used the omental wrap for potentially precarious midureteral anastomoses and for reconstruction of the ureter injured during the course of aortoiliac operations to seal off the site of repair from the Dacron prosthesis and to prevent the disastrous sequela of an infected vascular graft. The possible need for an omental graft should be anticipated before ureteral exploration so that the proper incision can be used for its preparation.

The greater omentum consists of a double layer of peritoneum with a rich blood and lymphatic supply interposed with surrounding fat between the two layers. The blood supply comes from the right and left gastroepiploic arteries, which join along the greater curvature of the stomach to form the gastroepiploic arterial arch. The right gastroepiploic artery is a branch of the gastroduodenal artery and on occasion originates from the superior mesenteric artery. The left gastroepiploic artery originates immediately before the terminal branching of the splenic artery.

Five variations of the omental blood supply can be found, but 85 percent of patients have the pattern demonstrated in Figure 8. Knowledge of this vascular pattern is essential to the proper construction of an omental pedicle of adequate length. The omentum is mobilized by first removing it entirely from the transverse colon and mesocolic edge along its avascular plane. It is then separated from the greater curvature of the stomach by carefully ligating and dividing each of the numerous gastric branches to the gastroepiploic arcade. Critical ligatures are those on the gastroepiploic side of the gastric branches, and these must be placed carefully to avoid injury to the main gastroepiploic arch. The portion of the omentum coming from the antral part of the greater curvature of the stomach is adherent to the anterior surface of the head of the pancreas. This fusion does not occur along the anterior surface of the body and tail

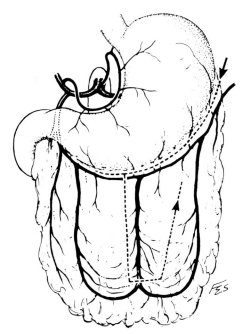

Fig. 8. Blood supply of omental apron. About 85 percent of patients have this pattern of arterial arcade. It is mobilized by first removing it entirely from transverse colon and greater curvature of stomach by ligation and division of gastric branches. Further lengthening of omental flap can be achieved by dividing omental vessels in manner outlined. (From Zinman and Libertino[51])

of the pancreas, so that freeing the omentum is much easier to accomplish when performed from a left to right direction. The gastroepiploic artery is divided after the gastroepiploic arcade is fully mobilized. The right gastroepiploic artery is slightly larger in caliber than the left and is probably a more dependable pedicle, but both should be checked for pulsation before they are divided. If the omental length is not adequate after this degree of mobilization, further lengthening can be achieved without loss of blood supply by division of the omental vessels. The fashioned omental pedicle is delivered to either ureter by mobilizing the respective colonic flexure, retracting it medially, and placing the omentum in the required location in the rotrocolic retroperitoneal space.

Case Abstract 4. A forty-three year-old woman was incapacitated by severe claudication of the right thigh and calf from aortoiliac atherosclerotic obliterative disease. She underwent two unsuccessful endarterectomies on the aortic and right iliac artery in 1969. The right ureter was mobilized extensively and retracted laterally on each occasion. In 1970 a right aortoiliac Dacron bypass graft was inserted, at which time the right ureter

was again dissected out of a fibrous retroperitoneal envelope. The incision became red and edematous, and clear fluid began to drain from the upper end of the wound on the ninth postoperative day. Excretory urography revealed mild right hydroureteronephrosis with lateral deviation of the midureter and gross retroperitoneal extravasation of contrast material from the midureter (Fig. 9A). The patient underwent transperitoneal exploration of the right ureter at which time the kidney and the entire ureter was mobilized. A necrotic and ischemic area, 3 cm, was excised from the right midureter, and ureteral continuity was established by ureteroureterostomy with a Silastic stent and nephrostomy tube diversion. The kidney was displaced downward and fixed to the psoas muscle, and the omentum was mobilized and wrapped around the entire ureter from the renal hilus to the bladder to seal off the site of repair from the Dacron prothesis. Nephrostography on the tenth postoperative day revealed a leak at the anastomosis with a patent lumen (Fig. 9B). The nephrostomy tube and stent were removed five weeks after operation. The patient had a smooth convalescence, and postoperative excretory urography two years later revealed a prompt functioning right kidney with a normal nonobstructed collecting system (Fig. 9C).

Five variations of the omental blood supply can be found, but 85 percent of patients have the pattern demonstrated in Figure 8. Knowledge of this vascular pattern is essential to the proper construction of an omental pedicle of adequate length. The omentum is mobilized by first removing it entirely from the transverse colon and mesocolic edge along its avascular plane. It is then separated from the greater curvature of the stomach by carefully ligating and dividing each of the numerous gastric branches to the gastroepiploic arcade. Critical ligatures are those on the gastroepiploic side of the gastric branches, and these must be placed carefully to avoid injury to the main gastroepiploic arch. The portion of the omentum coming from the antral part of the greater curvature of the stomach is adherent to the anterior surface of the head of the pancreas. This fusion does not occur along the anterior surface of the body and tail of the pancreas, so that freeing the omentum is much easier to accomplish when performed from a left to right direction. The gastroepiploic artery is divided after the gastroepiploic arcade is fully mobilized. The right gastroepiploic artery is slightly larger in caliber than the left and is probably a more dependable pedicle, but both should be checked for pulsation before they are divided. If the omental length is not adequate after this degree of mobilization, further lengthening can be achieved without loss of blood supply by division of the omental vessels. The fashioned omental pedicle is delivered to either ureter by mobilizing the respective colonic flexure,

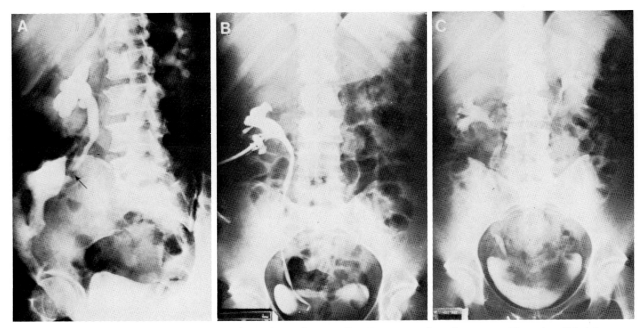

Fig. 9. Case 4. (A) Excretory urogram nine days after right aortoiliac Dacron graft replacement. There is mild right hydronephrosis with extravasation of contrast material into retroperitoneal space and abdominal incision. (B) Right nephrostogram reveals patent lumen with minimal leakage at anastomotic site on tenth postoperative day. (C) Excretory urogram two years after midureteral repair; right ureter is normal with prompt appearance of contrast material and no renal atrophy.

retracting it medially, and placing the omentum in the required location in the retrocolic retroperitoneal space.

Case Abstract 4. A forty-three-year-old woman was incapacitated by severe claudication of the right thigh and calf from aortoiliac atherosclerotic obliterative disease. She underwent two unsuccessful endarterectomies on the aortic and right iliac artery in 1969. The right ureter was mobilized extensively and retracted laterally on each occasion. In 1970 a right aortoiliac Dacron bypass graft was inserted, at which time the right ureter was again dissected out of a fibrous retroperitoneal envelope. The incision became red and edematous, and clear fluid began to drain from the upper end of the wound on the ninth postoperative day. Excretory urography revealed mild right hydroureteronephrosis with lateral deviation of the midureter and gross retroperitoneal extravasation of contrast material from the midureter (Fig. 9A). The patient underwent transperitoneal exploration of the right ureter at which time the kidney and the entire ureter were mobilized. A necrotic and ischemic area, 3 cm, was excised from the right midureter, and ureteral continuity was esatblished by ureteroureterostomy with a Silastic stent and nephrostomy tube diversion. The kidney was displaced downward and fixed to the psoas muscle, and the omentum was mobilized and

wrapped around the entire ureter from the renal hilus to the bladder to seal off the site of repair from the Dacron prosthesis. Nephrostography on the tenth postoperative day revealed a leak at the anastomosis with a patent lumen (Fig. 9B). The nephrostomy tube and stent were removed five weeks after operation. The patient had a smooth convalescence, and postoperative excretory urography two years later revealed a prompt functioning right kidney with a normal nonobstructed collecting system (Fig. 9C).

EXTENSIVE URETERAL LOSS

Fortunately, extensive ureteral loss is an uncommon surgical injury to the ureter, but is has been reported to occur after retroperitoneal vascular operations, anterior spinal fusion, pyeloplasty, multiple ureterolithotomies, basket extractions, and repeat attempts at ureteral repair. The most common cause of massive ureteral injury in our experience has been ischemic insults from ureterolysis for retroperitoneal fibrosis, multiple ureterolithotomies, and extensive stricture formation after failed attempts at primary repair of the transected ureter. The options available for repair of loss of long ureteral segments include nephrectomy, bridging silicone prosthetic conduits, ileal segment substitution, and autotransplantation.

Nephrectomy may be the most conservative approach to the management of extensive ureteral loss in some circumstances, but it is a very difficult treatment choice to select since most of our patients had recurrent calculous disease and idiopathic retroperitoneal fibrosis—two potentially bilateral diseases. When normal contralateral renal function has been established securely, nephrectomy should be the treatment of choice in the extensively destroyed ureter in patients over sixty years of age, patients at poor cardiovascular and pulmonary risk, patients with metastatic cancer, and patients with extensive pyelonephritis with formation of intrarenal and perirenal abscess. If a functioning nephrostomy tube is present, a twenty-four-hour creatinine clearance from the injured renal unit should be obtained. A creatinine clearance of more than 20 cc a minute represents sufficient renal function to justify a reconstructive procedure.

Prosthetic replacement of a ureter by silicone has had extensive experimental trials but only limited clinical use. Technical improvements in the quality of materials employed may in the future overcome calcareous incrustations, fibrous tissue obstruction, and disruption of anastomotic sites now being experienced by some European surgeons. Good initial results seen in 4 of 9 patients recently reported by Dufour and Blondel[42] lasted an average of only six months when silicone polymer conduits were used to bridge ureteral defects created by obstructing retroperitoneal metastatic tumor.

Autotransplantation was a logical extension of the renal allograft experience. One of its first applications was in the management of ureteral injury incurred during an aortoiliac reconstructive procedure.[43] Although extensive ureteral loss constitutes the clearest indication for this operation, relatively few autotransplants had been reported for ureteral injuries. Autotransplantation is a formidable procedure that should not be considered for patients with extensive inflammation of the kidney or renal pedicle.

After long-term nephrostomy tube drainage and active pyelonephritis, kidneys are often extremely difficult to remove without injury to the renal veins and the development of severe vascular spasm with ultimate renal arterial thrombosis. Kidneys with preexisting parenchymal disease demonstrate a low tolerance to ischemia and do not perfuse well during preservation periods. These patients are best treated by other reparative techniques, avoiding autotransplantation. Patients with extensive aortoiliac arterial sclerosis are also poor candidates for this procedure since the pelvic vessels that are often involved early in arteriosclerotic disease may be an inadequate source of renal blood flow. Retroperitoneal fibrosis may be a relative contraindication to autotransplantation if it extends into the pelvis and obstructs the iliac veins, which are the outflow system from the autograft.[44,45]

In general, autotransplantation is most suitable for good-risk patients less than fifty years of age who do not have significant vascular disease when the renal pedicle to the injured kidney is not encased in a fibrous and inflammatory process. Preoperative renal and pelvic angiography should be obtained to determine the vascular pattern and to establish the presencce of a patent pelvic arterial tree. Iliac and inferior venacavography should be used selectively in patients with retroperitoneal fibrosis to ensure patency of the iliac veins. Kidneys with prior reparative attempts or nephrostomy tubes should then be removed through a generous flank or thoracoabdominal incision with adequate exposure for dissection of the pedicle. The artery is perfused at low gravity pressure with a hypothermic, hyperosmolar, hyperkalemic solution of intracellular electrolyte composition (Collins C3) and stored in sterile ice during the closure of the flank incision and dissection of the contralateral iliac vessels. In contrast to the renal allograft, the iliac fossa should be drained adequately for seven to ten days, and the anastomosis at the ureteropelvic junction should be diverted routinely with a nephrostomy tube complemented by a small stenting Silastic catheter. In the proper circumstances, renal atotransplantation may provide the most suitable option for restoring drainage to a normal kidney with an extensively destroyed ureter.

Ileal substitution is our choice for replacement of extensive ureteral injuries and irreparaable damage at the ureteropelvic junction. Interposition of the small bowel in the closed urinary system has not been a widely accepted procedure by most urologists despite early favorable reports by Wells[46] and Goodwin, Winter, and Turner.[47] Concern that vesical ileal reflux would result in recurrent pyelonephritis and nephrolithiasis and that production of mucus would lead to obstruction in male patients by mucous plugs has not been confirmed. Tanagho[48] reported 5 patients in whom serious renal complications developed from ileal-ureteral replacement and warned against the use of this option. Our experience parallels the favorable results reported by Fritzsche et al.[49] and McCullough and associates[50] and does not support Tanagho's pessimism when the ileal segments are selectively used in patients with normal bladder function and a serum creatinine level of less than 2.5 mg/100 ml.

Our technique for this procedure involves complete mobilization of the kidney and skeletonization of the renal pedicle with maximum downward nephropexy. The renal pelvis is prepared by excising any fibrous avascular edges, and the pyelotomy is occasionally extended into the lower infundibulum to ensure good drainage. This may require, on occasion, a limited lower pole resection to obtain good calyceal access if the ureteropelvic junction is extensively destroyed. Attention should then be turned to the bladder, which should be mobilized widely and be detached from peritoneum and both superior vesical pedicles. The bladder should be anchored to the pelvic wall in the manner of a psoas hitch procedure to bring the ileovesical anastomosis as close to the ileorenal anastomosis as possible. This will decrease the length of intestine needed for bridging the defect. It is critical that drainage be accomplished by nephrostomy tube diversion with 9 to 12 F stenting catheters. Vesi-

coileal reflux has been identified in the 6 patients on whom we performed ileal ureter operations for ureteral injury. Renal function has been preserved uniformly in the entire group of four men and two women. Bladder neck revisions were required in two men. The paucity of problems experienced by this group of patients supports our contention that the unobstructed drainage of a refluxing ileal segment is a viable option for repairing the extensively destroyed ureter.

Boston, Massachusetts 02215

(DR. ZINMAN)

REFERENCES

1. Bowen WC: Bladder fistulas and ureteral injuries. J Urol 96:706, 1966
2. Higgins CC: Ureteral injuries during surgery. JAMA 199:82, 1967
3. Ihse I. Arnesjö B, and Jönsson G. Surgical injuries of the ureter. A review of 42 cases. Scand J. Urol Nephrol 9:39, 1975
4. Bright TC and Peters PC. Ureteral injuries secondary to operative procedures. Report of 24 cases. Urology 9:22, 1977
5. Gangai MP, Agee RE, and Spence CR: Surgical injury to ureter, Ibid 8:22, 1976
6. Mehan DJ, and Chehval MJ: Perinephric abscess 19 years after an intentional ureteral ligation, J Urol 118:460, 1977
7. St Martin EC, Trichel BE, Campbell JH, and Locke CM: Ureteral injuries in gynecologic surgery, Ibid 70:51, 1953
8. Burns E. and Peiser I: Treatment of urologic complications in gynecology, Ibid 75:438, 1956
9. Hoch WH, Kursh ED, and Persky L: Early aggressive management of intraoperative ureteral injuries. Ibid, 114:530, 1975
10. Beland G: Early tratment of ureteral injuries found after gynecological surgery. Ibid, 118:25 1977
11. Politano VA, and Leadbetter WF: An operative technique for the correction of vesicoureteral reflux. Ibid, 79:932, 1958
12. Libertino JA, and Zinman L: Technique for ureteroneocystotomy in renal transplantation and reflux. Surg Clin North Am 53:459, 1973
13. Bischoff PF: Boari-plasty and vesicorenal reflux, in whitehead ED, Ed: Current Operative Urology. New York, Harper & Row Publishers, Inc, 1975, pp 708, 723
14. Turner-Warwick R, and Worth PH: the psoas bladder hitch procedure for the replacement of the lower third of the ureter. Br J Urol 41:701, 1969
15. Boari A, and Casati E: Contributo sperimentale alla plastica dell' uretere, Atti Accad. d. sc. med. e. nat. In Ferrar 68:149, 1894
16. Barnasconi F. and Colombino S: Contribution a l'etude du traitement des blessures de l'uretere ucours des interventions chirurgicales. Ann Mal Org Genito-Urin 22:1361, 1905
17. Sharpe NW: Trans-uretero-ureteral anastomosis. Ann Surg 44:687 1906
18. Higgins CC: Transuretero-ureteral anastomosis; report of clinical case. Trans Am Assoc Genitourin Surg 27:279, 1934
19. Hodges CV, et al: Clinical experiences with transureteroureterostomy. J Urol 90:552, 1963
20. Smith IB, and Smith JC: Trans-uretero-ureterostomy: British experience. Br J Urol 47:519, 1975
21. Ehrlich RM, and Skinner DG: Complications of transureteroureterostomy. J Urol 113:467, 1975
22. Sandoz IL, Paull DP, and MacFarlane CA: Complications with transureteroureterostomy. Ibid 117:39, 1977
23. Popesco C: Résection de l'uretère ilio-pelvien pour tumeur pap-

illaire. Restauration de la voie excrétrice par abaissement rénal et élévation vesicale. J Urol Nephrol (Paris) 73:269, 1967
24. Schopf F: Intraligamentäre Ovariencyste Óvariotomie; Durchtrennung des Ureters und Vereinigung durch die Naht. Allg Wien Med Ztg 31:374, 1886
25. Monari W: Ueber Ureter Anastomosen. Beitr Klin chir 15:720, 1896
26. Boari A: Chirurgia dell'ureter, XIV, 8¼, Roma, 2 (1900)
27. Iselin M: Recherches expérimentales sur la suture de l'urèter. Bull et Mem Soc Nat de Chir 54:650, 1928
28. Bovee JW: Uretero-ureteral anastomosis. Ann Surg 25:51, 1897
29. Marion H: Étude critique et expérimentale des plaies transversales de l'urétère. Déductions chirurgicales et therapeutiques. J d'Urol 27:273 and 369, 1929
30. Moore TD: Surgery of the ureter, in Campbell M, Ed: Urology. 1st ed., Philadelphia, W B Saunders Co, 1954, pp 1843–1889
31. Hamm FC, and Weinberg SR: Management of the severed ureter. J Urol 77:407, 1957
32. Hinman F Jr: Ureteral repair and the splint. Ibid 78:376, 1957
33. Carlton CE Jr, Scott R Jr, and Guthrie AG: The initial management of ureteral injuries: a report of 78 cases. Ibid 105:335, 1971
34. Davis DM: The process of ureteral repair; a recapitulation of the splinting question. Ibid 79:215, 1958
35. Kuss R, and Chatelain C: Surgery of the ureter, in Andersson L, Gittes RF, et al., Eds: Handbuch der Urologie/Encyclopedia of Urology, Band 13, Teil 3, Berlin, Springer-Verlag, 1975, p 34
36. Holden S, et al: Gunshot wounds of the ureter: a 15-year review of 63 consecutive cases. J Urol 116:562, 1976
37. Hinman F Jr, and Oppenheimer RO: Ureteral regeneration. IV. Fascial covering compared with fatty connective tissue. Ibid 76:729, 1956
38. Witherington R: Histological evaluation of fatty connective tissues used as an adjuvant in experimental ureteral surgery. Ibid 85:258, 1961
39. Finney HR, and Rinker JR: Live omentum as a substitute for the fatty periureteral sheath: an experimental study. Ibid 102:414, 1969
40. Walters W: Omental flap in transperitoneal repair of recurring vesicovaginal fistulas. Surg Gynecol Obstet 64:74, 1937
41. Turner-Warwick R: The use of the omental pedicle graft in urinary tract reconstruction. J Urol 116:341, 1976
42. Dufour B, and Blondel P: The prosthetic replacement of the ureter: experimental and clinical results. Eur Urol 1:134, 1975
43. Hardy JD: High ureteral injuries. Management by autotransplantation of the kidney. JAMA 184:97, 1963
44. Linke CA, and May AG: Autotransplantation in retroperitoneal fibrosis. J Urol 107:196, 1972

45. Stewart BH, et al: Renal autotransplantation: current perspectives. Ibid 118:363, 1977
46. Wells CA: The use of the intestine in urology, omitting ureterocolic anastomosis. Br J Urol 28:335, 1956
47. Goodwin WE, Winter CC, and Turner RD: Replacement of the ureter by small intestine: clinical application and results of the ileal ureter. J Urol 81:406, 1959
48. Tanagho EA: A case against incorporation of bowel segments into the closed urinary system. Ibid 113:796, 1975
49. Fritzsche P, et al: Long-term radiographic changes of the kidney following the ileal ureter operation. Ibid 114:843, 1975
50. McCullough DL, et al: Replacement of the damaged or neoplastic ureter by ileum. Ibid 118:375, 1977
51. Zinman L, and Libertino JA: Surgery of the midureter, in Libertino JA, and Zinman L, Eds: Reconstructive Urologic Surgery: Pediatric and Adult, Baltimore, Maryland, Williams & Wilkins, 1977, pp 97–117

Commentary: Avoiding Iatrogenic Ureteral Injury

Richard J. Macchia

It is an unfortunate but understandable irony that those countries whose physicians possess the most advanced surgical techniques have the highest rates of iatrogenic ureteral injury. In the United States, iatrogenic injury is, by a wide margin, the most common type of ureteral trauma.

Prudent judgment in selecting a therapeutic plan is the most essential element for successful management. The most elegant procedure, adeptly performed, will fail if used in an inappropriate circumstance.

A review of the literature reveals consistently high cure rates for repair of ureteral injuries. That this does not truly reflect the situation as a whole is indicated in the preceding article. Half the authors' patients were referred to them after an initial attempt at correction had failed. Since the first attempt at repair has the greatest chance of success, each surgeon must judge whether to undertake such surgery or to refer the patient to more experienced hands.

Meticulous preoperative preparation of both the patient and the surgeon is necessary. It seems advisable, both from a legal and from a medical viewpoint, to educate the patient on his condition, the therapeutic options, and the chances of success or failure. The patient's needs must be paramount, not merely the needs of the ureter. For complex cases, the patient should be physically prepared as for any extensive surgery. Selective use of preoperative intravenous (IV) hydration, bowel preparation, perioperative antibiotics, prophylactic antiphlebitis measures, and other such adjuvants may facilitate a successful outcome.

The surgeon must be willing and able to deviate from the operative plan if conditions at surgery so dictate. Familiarity with all therapeutic options will give the surgeon the greatest flexibility in confronting an unexpected situation (Table 3).

An exact preoperative definition of the nature and extent of injury is mandatory. Excretory urography can be combined with retrograde ureterography, voiding cystourethrography, or percutaneous antegrade pyeloureterography to achieve this goal. The preceding article points out that ureteral injury is not necessarily isolated; the clinical suspicion of associated injuries such as vesicovaginal fistula must be high. Failure to be absolutely compulsive about this can lead to surgical mayhem. Documentation of the existence of a normal contralateral renal–ureteral unit is a basic tenet of urologic surgery.

As in most series, the majority of injuries mentioned in the preceding article were the result of gynecologic or general surgical procedures. However, the authors clearly document that both endoscopic and open urologic procedures were responsible for a significant percentage of the injuries.

TABLE 3. Ureteral Injury: Techniques for Management

Passage of antegrade or retrograde ureteral catheter
Debridement, resection, and repair
Deligation and deangulation
Transureteroureterostomy
Ureteroneocystostomy
Autotransplantation
Ureterosigmoidostomy (bilateral injury only)
Ureterocalyceal anastomosis
Flap from renal pelvis or capsule
Nephrectomy
Ureteral substitutes
  Natural
  Synthetic
To lessen gap
  Bladder–psoas hitch
  Renal mobilization
  Boari bladder flap
Adjunctive measures
  Proximal diversion nephrostomy, slash ureterotomy
  Stent
  Omental sleeve
Emergency diversion
  Intubated ureterotomy *in situ*
  Cutaneous ureterostomy

It is universally agreed that the optimal moment to repair iatrogenic ureteral damage is almost always at the time of injury. Drs. Zinman, Libertino, and Roth note that only 20% to 30% of injuries were recognized when they occurred. In addition to the standard methods of intraoperative detection of ureteral injury as outlined in their article, I have occasionally found it convenient to reprepare the patient in a modified lithotomy position and to perform a cystoscopy with retrograde ureteral catheterization. I have not been very successful in obtaining useful intraoperative excretory urograms. Techniques for achieving this, however, have been described in detail.[1]

Under optimal conditions, my choice for immediate repair of the ureter above the pelvic brim is adequate debridement and an oblique end-to-end ureteroureterostomy fashioned with fine, interrupted, absorbable sutures into a watertight anastomosis. Under ideal circumstances I do not use a stent.

If a lower ureteral injury is suspected and the patient is in the lithotomy position, adequate inspection and repair may be difficult, since such a position tilts the symphysis pubis in a posterior and cephalad direction. Simply shifting the patient to a low lithotomy or supine position has occasionally been most beneficial. Under optimal conditions, my choice for immediate repair of the pelvic ureter is a ureteroneocystostomy. I use a modified Paquin technique rather than the Politano–Leadbetter procedure preferred by the authors of the preceding article. I use always a stent. For lessening tension on the anastomosis, if necessary, I perform a psoas–bladder hitch with or without renal mobilization. My experience with the Boari flap encourages me to avoid it if possible; I thus agree with the preceding article. I generally use suprapubic cystostomy drainage in males but large-bore urethral catheter drainage in females.

Theoretically, the most difficult decision is choosing between immediate versus delayed repair in patients whose injury is detected days or weeks after the original surgery.[2] In practice, however, this is usually not as perplexing as might be surmised from the literature. Few absolute rules exist. Assessment of surgical capabilities and experience must be considered. The preceding article gives some guidelines with which I totally agree. The simple procedure of inserting an indwelling ureteral catheter for 10 to 14 days through the cystoscope is not mentioned but is sometimes all that is required to allow a fistula to close.

My selection of a stent depends on the type of repair. For ureteroureterostomy, I use a double-pigtail stent with a cone tip at each end to allow simultaneous antegrade and retrograde passage. For ureteroneocystostomy, I prefer a soft pediatric feeding tube, which I secure to the bladder with a single, fine, absorbable suture.

The use of a linear proximal ureterostomy as an adjunct to water-tight anastomosis was originally popularized by Hamm and colleagues.[3] The recent availability of nontraumatizing, self-retaining stents has decreased my use of this technique.

Whenever ureteral repair is undertaken, it is essential to preserve whatever blood supply remains. Mobilization of the ureter must be adequate to eliminate tension. Avoid excessive mobilization. Whatever mobilization is required, accomplish it at some distance from the ureter to preserve the periureteral fatty tissue, which contains the blood supply. Keep ureteral manipulation, even with nontraumatizing instruments, to a minimum. If possible, I prefer to avoid even gentle ureteral traction such as commonly provided by a narrow rubber drain.

I do not hesitate to use a transureteroureterostomy, but I totally agree with Zinman, Libertino, and Roth's concept of contraindications for this procedure. These authors stress that the crossing should be made cephalad to the inferior mesenteric artery. Others have advocated the caudad crossing. I believe that the donor ureter should be mobilized first and brought to the recipient ureter in whatever way "the ureter wants to go." The most important thing about the route is to provide a smooth curve with no angulation or extrinsic compression from blood vessels. Only after a convenient site for the anastomosis has been chosen should mobilization of the recipient ureter be undertaken. Again, mobilization of the recipient ureter should be as minimal as is consistent with adequate exposure. I do not stent transureteroureterostomies.

The three authors quite correctly acknowledge the contribution of Turner–Warwick in repeatedly reminding physicians of the superiority of the omental pedicle over retroperitoneal fat. The article includes an excellent description of the technique of omental mobilization.

Ileal substitution has been used with great success for bridging lengthy ureteral gaps. Although my experience with this procedure is not extensive, I have sufficient experience to agree heartily with its major advocates, including the authors of the preceding articles, that it can be extremely difficult and time consuming.[4] The transplant service at my institution is a busy one: 125 renal transplants were done in 1982. For patients in whom ileal substitution might be used, I much prefer to take advantage of this considerable transplant experience. A team composed of a transplant surgeon and a urologist is used. In these hands, I feel autotransplantation is much the more conservative approach. The service uses autotransplantation in only a small percentage of patients with ureteral injury as well as in other complex problems. Such patients are selected carefully after alternatives are fully considered. Although the service uses autotransplantation only occasionally, it makes preparations before all complex cases to have it instantly available if the need arises. Twenty-two autotransplants have been performed at the institution for various reasons. One kidney has been lost.

The management of patients with urinary fistulae and strictures by percutaneous antegrade intraureteral manipulation is attractive.[5] This technique may be combined with conventional endoscopic retrograde methods when necessary. My experience to date is insufficient for me to make a final judgment. Initially, I reserve our attempts to those patients I thought would need extremely difficult or hazardous operative repairs. As might be imagined, my failure rate in this group has been high. I am now investigating using this technique in patients whose situation is not as grim.

The surgical circumstances accompanying a gunshot wound to the ureter are considerably different than those of iatrogenic injury. I advocate close cooperation between the trauma surgeon and the urologist, with immediate notification of the latter when documented or suspected ureteral trauma is present. A high index of suspicion and adequate immediate radiologic evaluation will maximize success. I agree with those advocating a more liberal use of stents for gunshot wounds than is suggested for iatrogenic injury.[6]

The general topic of ureteral replacements has been thoroughly reviewed.[7]

REFERENCES

1. Cass AS: Immediate radiological evaluation and early surgical management of genitourinary injuries from external trauma. J Urol 122:772, 1979
2. Mendez R, McGinty DM: The management of delayed recognized ureteral injuries. J Urol 119:192, 1978
3. Hamm FC, Weinberg SR, Waterhouse RK: End-to-end ureteral anastomosis: A simple original technique. J Urol 87:43, 1962
4. Boxer RJ, Fritzsche P, Skinner DG, Kaufman JJ, Belt E, Smith RB, Goodwin WE: Replacement of the ureter by small intestine: Clinical applications and results of the ileal ureter in 89 patients. J Urol 121:728, 1979

5. Lang EK, Lanasa JA, Garrett J, Stripling J, Palomer J: The management of urinary fistulas and strictures with percutaneous ureteral stent catheters. J Urol 122:736, 1979
6. Holden S, Hicks CC, O'Brien DP III, Stone HH, Walker JA, Walton KN: Gunshot wounds of the ureter: A 15-year review of 63 consecutive cases. J Urol 116:562, 1979
7. Baum N, Mobley DF, Carlton CE Jr: Ureteral replacements. Urology 5:162, 1975

ANNOTATED BIBLIOGRAPHY

Cass AS: Immediate radiological evaluation and early surgical management of genitourinary injuries from external trauma. J Urol 122:772, 1979

This article reviews 1389 patients with urologic injuries from external trauma. Eighteen of these patients had ureteral injuries. An excretory urogram and retrograde pyelogram provided an accurate diagnosis and localized the site of injury in all 18. Cass believes that early surgical management prevented urinary extravasation, retroperitoneal infection, and urinary fistula.

Mendez R, McGinty DM: The management of delayed recognized ureteral injuries., J Urol 119:192, 1978

This article reviews 90 patients with ureteral damage from all causes. Forty-six injuries resulted from external trauma, and 44 were surgical injuries. Of those patients with external trauma, 84% were diagnosed immediately, while only 31% of patients with surgical injuries had immediate diagnosis. In both groups those patients whose injury was immediately diagnosed and repaired had a much better rate of successful repair.

Hamm FC, Weinberg SR, Waterhouse RK: End-to-end ureteral anastomosis: A simple original technique. J Urol 87:43, 1962

In this oft-quoted article, nine cases of ureteral injury are reviewed. Five were surgical accidents, one was an external injury, and three were deliberate surgical transections. No attempt was made to secure a watertight anastomosis, although this is now our policy. Also, sufficient emphasis was not placed on isolating the anastomosis from urine exiting from the linear proximal-venting ureterotomy.

Boxer RJ, Fritzsche P, Skinner DG, et al: Replacement of the ureter by small intestine: Clinical application and results of the ileal ureter in 89 patients. J Urol 121:728, 1979

Partial or total ureteral replacement with small intestine was performed 94 times in 92 patients. Indications included recurrent calculi, ureteral stricture, fistula, congenital obstruction of the ureter, and ureteral carcinoma with a solitary kidney. The authors classified 81% of patients as having had a successful outcome.

They admit that the procedure can be extremely difficult and time consuming.

Lang EK, Lanasa JA, Garrett J, et al: The management of urinary fistulas and strictures with percutaneous ureteral stent catheters. J Urol 122:736, 1979

The treatment by percutaneous antegrade introduction of a ureteral stent is reported for four patients with ureteric fistula and one with ureteric stricture. We believe that a longer period of follow-up study is required before the value of this technique can be judged.

Holden S, Hicks CC, O'Brien DP III, et al: A 15-year review of 63 consecutive cases. J Urol 116:562, 1979

This article reviews 63 patients with gunshot wounds of the ureter. No ureteral injuries were missed if an excretory urogram was performed. In 5 of the 19 patients who did not undergo a prelaparotomy excretory urogram, the diagnosis was not established during the initial laparotomy. Watertight reconstruction with internal stenting is emphasized. A nephrostomy is added when the ureteropelvic junction is involved or the major vessels or pancreas injured. The authors prevented migration of internal stents by afixing a nylon suture to the stent, exiting it through the ureteral wall and then attaching it to a button after bringing the suture through the abdomenal wall. We have not used this technique and prefer to use a double-pigtail catheter whenever possible. Fifteen percent of these patients required a second procedure, but all patients available for long term follow-up study had good results.

Baum N, Mobley DF, Carlton CE Jr: Ureteral replacements. Urology 5:162, 1975

Carlton, the senior author, has published extensively on urologic trauma. He and his coauthors reviewed the history and present status of ureteral replacements including nonbiologic substitutes, pedicle grafts, free grafts, and implantation and diversion. The physiology of ureteral repair is also reviewed. An extensive bibliography is included.

Overview: Surgery of Ureteral Trauma

Robert H. Whitaker

An overview easily drifts toward armchair theorizing, which is often of little use to the practicing urologist. To counteract this tendency I will stress some practical aspects of ureteral trauma. For instance, I support the authors' enthusiasm for the *psoas hitch* for its simplicity and, in many patients, its ease. In patients whose bladder is still quite mobile, it can give great length. It is essential to divide the superior vesical pedicle on the opposite side and helpful to remove the peritoneum off the dome of the bladder, at least on the affected side. In children this is easy, but in adults the peritoneum can be quite stuck. The bladder should be opened transversely at its widest point, since by closing this longitudinally several more inches can be obtained. This maneuver, however, can be overdone, since if more than half the circumference is opened the closure gives an hourglass effect. In a patient with tuberculosis and the risk of further fibrosis, this could be a disadvantage. A large bite of psoas is needed to keep the bladder fixed, and polyglycolic acid (Dexon) is preferable to catgut because it probably lasts longer.

Incidentally, this psoas hitch is a most useful adjunct to reimplanting large ureters, refluxing or otherwise, in children after tapering them. It keeps the tunnel the correct length in the immediate postoperative period, when there is usually a tendency for the bladder to contract into a small muscular ball. When the bladder is surrounded by fibrous tissue, or fixed from the effect of longstanding urinary leakage, a *Boari flap* is most useful. The illustrations in many papers on this subject are, however, almost laughable, since they often show an enormous reconstructed tube with the residual bladder the same size as before. This is far from the truth. Not only is the bladder smaller after the procedure, but the Boari flap itself is a cigar-shaped mass of thick muscle and bunched mucosa. The point where the tube joins the residual bladder never looks quite like the drawings. It is often quite narrow, and any reinforcing suturing narrows it only further. However, even with all these reservations, it is undoubtedly a most useful procedure; with a curved incision, a truly remarkable gap can be bridged. Indeed, the bladder capacity usually soon recovers and the late postoperative urogram often looks almost normal. Blandy used a Boari flap to repair 52 of 62 injured ureters, and in 2 the flap was able to reach the pelvoureteric junction.[1] In discussions on this topic I have heard Turner-Warwick make the sensible suggestion that the submucosal tunnel should begin a few centimeters down from the top of the flap so that if problems arise, a second attempt is not fraught with difficulties because of length. In a patient with a tuberculous ureter that had already strictured twice, I have anastomosed the top of the tube to the wide ureter as an end-to-end anastomosis to avoid recurrence. An intraperitoneal approach is perfectly acceptable if an extraperitoneal approach is difficult.[2]

Transureteroureterostomy, although occasionally a useful technique, should probably be reserved for the exceptional patient. Sandoz and colleagues recently reported four instances of serious complications involving the recipient ureter in a series of 23 patients.[3] Urologists have a natural reluctance to involve the opposite system unless there is no alternative. The more normal the recipient ureter, the more difficult the anastomosis.

The paucity of reported cases of ureteral trauma due to attempted endoscopic stone removal does not reflect the incidence accurately. This may be because the problem solves itself with conservative treatment or, perhaps, a natural reluctance to advertise mistakes. The ground rules for basketry are well known. The procedure should be restricted to those small calculi at the lower end that might, or should, pass on their own yet fail to do so; 5 mm is about the largest size that should be tackled. Misguided attempts to pull out bigger and higher stones court disaster. Although the occasional report of complete avulsion or intussusception of the ureter into the bladder is sobering, the majority of ureteral injuries are due to perforation of the lower ureter by the basket during efforts to pass it beyond the stone.

Injury is easily confirmed by ureterography, and these minor perforations often settle well with ureteric catheter drainage. If catheterization is impossible, the stones can simply be removed by open ureterolithotomy and the area drained. A ragged tear is best left unsutured, but a pigtail simple splintage is wise for a week. I have been surprised how well the ureter heals after small or even moderately large pieces of mucosa are pulled down with the basket. If the mucosa is still attached, I push it back and leave a ureteral catheter in for a few days.

This leads to my final comment, in which I would like to add support to the conservative approach to injury by retrograde or antegrade catheterization in selected patients. Ureteral catheterization with a double-pigtail stent can, for instance, be helpful in the management of patients with early ureterovaginal fistula. Spontaneous closure around the catheter may avert a major reconstructive procedure. However, I otherwise agree with Blandy that a 6-wk waiting period before exploration has little advantage, and I tend to explore the situation as soon as the patient is referred.[1] Perhaps there is no other aspect of urology that calls for closer cooperation between the gynecologist, general surgeon, and urologist in the early recognition and prompt management of an iatrogenic ureteral injury.

REFERENCES

1. Flynn JT, Tiptaft RC, Woodhouse CRJ, et al: The early and aggressive repair of iatrogenic ureteric injuries. Br J Urol 51:454, 1979

2. Hendry WF: Injuries to the pelvic ureter. Proc R Soc Med 70:183, 1977

3. Sandoz IL, Paull DP, MacFarlane CA: Complications with trans-ureteroureterostomy. 117:39, 1977

PART TWENTY

ENDOSCOPIC SURGERY OF THE URETER

42

FORCEFUL ENDOSCOPIC EXTRACTION OF URETERAL CALCULI

Hugh Lamensdorf, M.D., Dolphus E. Compere, M.D., Grant F. Begley, M.D.

From the Urology Clinic, Forth Worth, Texas

Urology / April 1973 / Volume I, Number 4

ABSTRACT—Two hundred seventy cases of stone manipulation are reviewed. Manipulation was successful in 68 percent and 9 percent had to have open ureterolithotomy. There were no serious complications. An aggressive approach to the treatment of lower ureteral calculi is recommended. Manipulation is indicated if the patient is incapacitated. If certain rules are followed, the risk of complications should be minimal.

We have developed an aggressive attitude toward the treatment of lower ureteral calculi. It is our impression that our approach is similar to that taken by many other urologists.

Our indications for stone manipulation by endoscopy are subjective. We manipulate stones in all patients who are incapacitated by the presence of calculi. If the patient must be admitted to the hospital because of pain, nausea, vomiting, or fever, we proceed with manipulation after twenty-four or more hours of persistent symptoms. If a patient has recurring pain or nausea of sufficient degree to interfere with his usual activity, admission to the hospital and subsequent manipulation are recommended. This is also done with some patients who probably would pass the calculi with longer trials of conservative therapy.

In patients with pain, it is difficult to clear fecal material from the intestinal tract. Intestinal gas is often present in increased volumes because of ileus secondary to pain or to narcotic therapy. For these reasons, radiographic studies that are less than ideal must often be used. We therefore do not demand that urographic findings be unequivocal. We will occasionally pass a stone basket in a patient with typical renal colic or pain suggestive of calculus disease and with a pyelogram that is suggestive, but not diagnostic, of ureteral calculus. We feel that passing a stone basket up a normal or slightly dilated ureter is a benign procedure and may be another diagnostic help by ruling out the possibility of urinary calculus. The only patients with complications following stone manipulation are those in whom the stones are large or impacted, those with severe infection, or those with diseased ureters. These patients present different problems.

HISTORY

Kelly in 1900[1] and Young in 1902[2] were the first to report successful results with forceful endoscopic extraction of stones. Lewis in 1904[3] introduced instruments especially made for removal of ureteral calculi by cystoscopic manipulation. Several surgeons modified these instruments, but the procedure was still poorly accepted. Crowell in 1921[4] stimulated interest when he reported on a large series of patients with stones successfully treated with the aid of indwelling ureteral catheters and the injection of a lubricant oil and procaine (Novocain) into the ureter.

Bumpus and Thompson in 1930[5] reviewed 1,000 cases of ureteral calculi treated over a period of nine years. They felt that Crowell's method required too much time. Judd,[6] of The Mayo Clinic, had previously reported 400 ureterolithotomies with only one death. They therefore decided that conservative therapy followed by open surgical procedure on the unsuccessful cases was the safest course of treatment.

O'Connor and Dykhuizen in 1937[7] reviewed 192 cases of stones in the lower third of the ureter. They felt that although some success had been obtained with mechanical devices, the trauma that might result offsets the advantage of occasionally succesful immediate extraction. They reported that they had dilated ureters and then had given neostigmine (Prostigmin) in large doses successfully.

Councill in 1945[8] presented an impressive series of cases of stone manipulations in which he used his instrument to remove stones from any area the entire length of the ureter. At that time, he was gradually reaching the conclusion that forcible extraction should be limited to those patients with stones in the lower third of the ureter.

In 1945 Dourmashkin[9] reviewed the literature extensively and carefully. He had introduced metallic dilators (tunneled bougies) for removal of stones in the lower third of the ureter in 1924.[10] In 1926 he had introduced the use of an inflatable rubber bag which was used to progressively dilate the ureter below the stone and allow the stone to follow the dilatation into the bladder.[11] He used this instrument even for stones in the renal pelvis. His results are impressive. Dourmashkin credited Livermore (1922)[12] with inventing the first instrument for forcible removal of ureteral calculi. This consisted of a flexible bougie with a cup at the end.

Johnson's[13] stone basket was developed in 1937. Thompson and Kibler in 1940[14] reviewed a large series

of cases reported by other urologists in which the Councill extractor, the Johnson basket, and the Howard spiral were used. They felt that the success achieved in 96 percent was commendable but were convinced that such results were obtainabale only in the hands of a few urologists who were "gifted with extraordinary skills." They felt that generalized use of forceful extraction would result in many instances of disastrous injury to the ureter.

Rusche and Bacon in 1940[15] reviewed 1,314 cases of stones removed with no ureteral ruptures or deaths and suggested that stone manipulation could be done by an intern without special skill. At that time the procedure was generally in use, and there were strong differences of opinion as to whether or not the Johnson basket was as safe to use as other potentially less traumatic instruments devised by Elik and others. More urologists began to use forceful extraction, and many new instruments were introduced, all with reports of excellent results.

In the past twenty years, few articles have been written on this subject, and we feel that this is probably due to standardization of techniques and lessening controversy.

TECHNIQUE

The patient is always warned that the procedure used to extract the stone may be unsuccessful. He is also informed that an open surgical procedure may be necessary while he is under the anesthetic.

A preoperative scout film is obtained. The bladder is carefully examined. If the stone is present at the orifice, it can often be teased out using a ureteral catheter or milked out with the use of a resectoscope loop. We do not advocate meatotomy or fulgeration of the orifice. In our series, we have used the Johnson stone basket exclusively. We have had no recent experience with other instruments.

The basket is passed above the stone using a 2-inch olive-tipped filiform attached to its end. Care is taken not to advance the basket above the lower third of the ureter. The basket is generally pulled from the ureter using a slow trolling maneuver or a stuttering advancement. If the basket is twisted, this must be done slowly because the basket may collapse or the wires may be bent out of shape. Also, if the basket is rotated, it must be done in a clockwise direction because twisting it counterclockwise may unscrew the filiform from the basket.

When the stone is engaged it should not be necessary to pull hard to extract it. While we have had circumstances in the past when it was impossible to remove the basket without resorting to open surgical procedures, this has not occurred in this series. We feel that these patients would have eventually needed ureterotomy for the removal of the stone; we do not feel that the preliminary attempt at manipulation added to the morbidity rate.

The use of long-term traction on the basket is dangerous. We have never left a basket in place in such situations in hopes of later being able to extract the stone. We would proceed with open surgical intervention at the time the patient is under anesthesia.

The most common place for the basket containing the stone to meet resistance is in the intramural ureter or at the ureteral meatus. In these cases, the basket is left in place, the cystoscope removed, and a resectoscope inserted into the urethra beside the basket. Using the resectoscope loop, the fibers of the ureteral orifice can usually be teased back around the stone and basket in such a way as to allow them to slide past this narrow area. This maneuver helps the surgeon to avoid tearing the orifice during extraction. This maneuver was used in 20 of our patients.

After the stone is extracted, it is irrigated from the bladder and a no. 4 French ureteral catheter is inserted up the ureter to the renal pelvis and left anchored to an indwelling ureteral catheter for twenty-four hours. In 9 patients, we were unable to insert catheters after the stone was extracted. Seven of these were able to leave the hospital the day after the surgical procedure, thus shortening the "routine" hospital stay by twenty-four hours. One of these patients remained an extra day and another four extra days because of pain.

RESULTS

Two hundred seventy manipulations have been carried out on 243 private patients in the five years between 1965 and 1971 (Table 1). There are no patients who have had to undergo surgical procedures because of complications caused by manipulations. Of course, some stones have been inaccessible to endoscopic removal and have had to be removed by open surgical intervention.

TABLE 1. Results of 270 Manipulations in 243 Patients

Cases		Number
Success		198
Routine course with or without minor variations	169	
Stone passed shortly after unsuccessful manipulation	16	
Stone teased out of orifice	8	
Unsuccessful		40
Needed remanipulation	10	
Had ureterolithotomy	28	
Stone pushed into kidney	2	
Manipulations probably unnecessary		37
Stone in bladder at time of cystoscopy	5	
No stone obtained, no further trouble	25	
No stone obtained, no follow-up	7	
Total		270

These patients would have needed open surgical procedures regardless of manipulation. No urinary tract has been permanently damaged as a result of the manipulation.

A total of 119 patients had what we consider completely routine clinical courses. That is, they had stones extracted using the Johnson stone basket; a ureteral catheter was inserted and left in place for twenty-four hours; the patient was allowed to leave the hospital after an additional twenty-four hours of observation. These patients reported no further problems, and results of follow-up urograms were normal.

This routine course was altered slightly in 28 additional patients who had fever during the preoperative or postoperative period, or both, but not long enough to change the duration of their hospitalization. Sixteen patients had ureteral catheters left in for forty-eight hours instead of twenty-four. In seven, persistent pain was the cause, in five, persistent fever, and in four the surgeon felt that the extraction was more traumatic than usual or ureteral catheterization was difficult. Five patients had successful manipulation on the second attempt, and one on the third attempt.

In 16 cases no stones were obtained by manipulation, but in 9 cases the stone was spontaneously passed within three days and in 7 the stone was passed within seven days after manipulation.

In 21 patients the basket went past the stone easily but never engaged it, ureterolithotomy was done in 15 and in 6 ureteral catheters were left in place and remanipulation was attempted. In 5 of these cases manipulation was successful the second time, and in 1 patient it was successful the third time.

In 13 patients the basket would not go past the stone, and of these 6 had ureterolithotomies immediately. It was possible to put a catheter by the stone in 7 patients, 4 of whom had the stone removed later by manipulation and 3 passed the stone shortly after the catheter was removed. In 8 patients the stone was seen at the ureteral orifice and was either teased out with ureteral catheter or milked out with a resectoscope loop. Twelve patients retained stones after unsuccessful manipulation and were discharged from the hospital with no follow up available.

Two patients had the stone pushed back into the renal pelvis at the time of manipulation. One of these patients subsequently passed the stone, and the other patient had the stone successfully removed by manipulation four months later.

COMMENT

The presence of infection or fever is not considered a contraindication to manipulation. Broad-spectrum antibiotic therapy is used after urine has been cultured. Postoperative ureteral catheter drainage is maintained until there has been no fever for twenty-four hours.

Stone manipulation is never performed if the stone is above the junction of the lower and middle one third of the ureter.

Presence of the stone in the same location for a long period of time (months or longer) is not a contraindication to manipulation. These stones are likely to be smoothly embedded into the wall of the ureter, and the basket passes up and down the ureter without engaging the stone. However, one is often pleasantly surprised at the easy extraction in these cases, and manipulation should be tried.

In 26 of our patients the results of excretory urograms were suggestive, but not diagnostic, of ureteral calculus. Twelve of these patients had successful manipulation and are included in the routine cases. In 12 patients no stone was found with the exploring basket, and these patients were discharged without symptoms the day after the surgical procedure. In two patients the exploring basket found no stone, but a stone was subsequently passed in three days by 1 patient and in seven days by the other.

The age range was from sixteen to seventy-four years, and no difference was found in the degree of complication or success between males or females or between the younger or older patients.

The anesthesia time varied from nine to ninety minutes, with a mean of thirty minutes. Operating time averaged fourteen minutes less than anesthesia time. General inhalation anesthesia with sodium pentothal induction was used in all except 6 patients, in whom the anesthesiologist chose to use a low spinal block for various reasons.

Two patients had two stones in the lower ureter, and one patient had three stones. All were successfully extracted and are included in the "routine" cases. One patient had three stones one of which was removed on the first pass of the basket and the other two with the second pass. Another patient with two stones underwent preliminary unsuccessful passes. The two stones were removed on the second attempt.

After reviewing our data we felt we were justified to treat lower ureteral calculi by endoscopic means with a secure optimism that it would reduce the patient's morbidity without causing significant complications.

1415 Pennsylvania Avenue
Forth Worth, Texas 76109

REFERENCES

1. KELLY, H. A.: Ureteral calculus. JAMA 34:515, 1900

2. YOUNG, H. H.: Treatment of calculus of the lower end of the ureter in the male. Am Med 4:209, 1902

3. LEWIS, B.: Review of operative work in the ureter through the author's catheterizing and operative cystoscope. Am J Urol 1:135, 1905

4. CROWELL, A. J.: The removal of ureteral stones by cystoscopy. J Urol 6:243, 1921

5. BUMPUS, H. C., JR., and THOMPSON, G. J.: Stones in the ureter. Surg Gynec & Obst 50:106, 1930

6. JUDD, E. S.: The results of operation for removal of stones from the ureter. Ann Surg 41:128, 1920

7. O'CONNOR, V. J., and DYKHUIZEN, H. D.: Stone in the lower portion of the ureter: A review of 192 cases. Wisc Med J 37:653, 1937

8. COUNCILL, W. A.: The treatment of ureteral calculi. A report of 504 cases in which the Councill stone extractor and dilator was used. J Urol 53:534, 1945

9. DOURMASHKIN, R. L.: Cystoscopic treatment of stones in the ureter with special reference to large calculi, based on the study of 1,550 cases. Ibid. 54:245, 1945

10. IDEM: A new tunneled ureteral bougie for dilatation, catheterization, and irrigation. Urol & Cutan Rev 28:70, 1924

11. IDEM: Dilatation of the ureter with rubber bags and the treatment of ureteral calculi. Presentation of a modified operating cystoscope, a preliminary report. J Urol 15:449, 1926

12. LIVERMORE, G. R.: Presentation of instrument for removal of ureteral calculus. South Med J 15:316, 1922

13. JOHNSON, F. P.: New method of removal of ureteral calculi. J Urol 37:84, 1937

14. THOMPSON, G. J., and KIBLER, J. M.: Treatment of ureteral calculi with particular reference to transurethral manipulation. JAMA 114:6, 1940

15. RUSCHE, C. F., and BACON, S. F.: Injury of the ureter due to cystoscopic intraurethral instrumentation. J Urol 44:777, 1940

Commentary: Techniques of Endoscopic Ureteral Surgery

Leonard R. Dourmashkin and Zafar Khan

Endoscopy was born when Philipp Bozzini succeeded in illuminating the bladder in 1806. The problem of ureteral catheterization was solved when Albarrán invented his lever in 1897. Therefore, retrograde ureteral catheterization was a major diagnostic and therapeutic achievement. Kelly used wax-tipped catheters to diagnose ureteral stones in 1895. This technique enjoyed great popularity in an era when roentgenograms were not yet widely available. Subsequently, many innovative surgeons devoted their skills to endoscopic surgery of the ureter. Dourmashkin popularized the use of diathermy meatotomy in 1922. That same year, Zondek warned of cicatrization following electrocauterization. Recently, enthusiasm for this procedure has waned consideraly because of resultant reflux. Dourmashkin devised many ingenious methods to dilate the ureter and remove ureteral calculi.

Since 1900, attempts have been made to remove ureteral stones endoscopically, sparing the patient a ureterolithotomy. To achieve this aim many ingenious methods have been devised. The experience of many innovative investigators with a variety of different methods has resulted in certain principles to be followed by those who wish to undertake this procedure.

Although special instruments were designed by Lewis in 1904 for endoscopic removal of ureteral stones, the most widely employed technique was insertion of a single or multiple ureteral catheters with injection of lubricants and local anesthetics. This method, while relieving the obstructed kidney, had its own risk of infection. The discovery of sulfa drugs provided a new hope and indeed was heavily relied on. This method remained popular well after 1940, although many other techniques were evolving. The most important was dilation of the ureter below the stone, for which Dourmashkin designed metal ureteral dilators and a hydrostatic balloon catheter, a forerunner of the Fogarty catheter.

Councill designed the multiple expandable wire basket for engagement and active removal of ureteral stones in 1926. He presented an impressive series in 1945. The superiority of this method was established from 1940 to the present, and it has become the most widely used instrument. Many refinements were incorporated into this wire basket method, notably by Johnson in 1937 and Dormia in 1958. The extensive use of wire baskets has been reviewed by many authors and certain principles have evolved for its safe use:

1. Subject only stones in the lower third of the ureter, ideally the distal 5 cm, to this manipulative technique. It is not prudent to exceed this limit because of the danger of seriously injuring the ureter.
2. Avoid repetitive passage of the basket. As a rule, three attempts are sufficient. However, this may depend on the operator's experience. Although it is a relatively safe procedure, it is by no means innocuous in inexperienced hands. Many serious ureteral injuries have been recorded.
3. If more than usual resistance is met when the basket is being withdrawn, consider the possibility of ureteral mucosal entrapment. If considerable traction is applied, mucosa will be stripped, resulting in ureteral stenosis. If the basket is impacted, an immediate ureterolithotomy with delivery of the basket is necessary. Gradual prolonged traction of the basket belongs to the past.
4. In the modern age of antibiotics, urinary tract infection is not a contraindication to the basketing procedure, but appropriate and adequate antibiotic cover should be provided.
5. Finally, the reason for basketing is relief of ureteral obstruction or amelioration of severe symptoms. The natural history of the disease is such that if left alone, the overwhelming majority of stones will pass unaided.

In recent years endoscopic ureteral surgery has begun to encompass other techniques besides ureteral stone manipulation. As scientific knowledge expands in other spheres, it is applied to medicine in due course. In 1953 Mulvaney applied ultrasonic vibration to fragment ureteral calculi. In 1968 he used laser beams to disintegrate ureteral stones. In 1973 Reuter applied the electronic lithotripsy, using the pulse voltage for ureteral stones.

Gill and Thompsen have introduced the technique of retrograde brushing in order to improve the diagnostic accuracy of radiolucent filling defects in the ureter and renal pelvis. This procedure has gained wide acceptance, and initial results are encouraging.

The ureteral obstruction may be bypassed by self-retaining ureteral stents. Gibbon's ureteral catheters have been used in selected patients. Modified angiography catheters in pigtail form appear to be easy to insert and hence are gaining in popularity.

A new vista is being opened up by the invention of the flexible fiberoptic ureteroscope, prototypes of which have recently been tested. This indeed is an important milestone in the 200-yr history of endoscopy.

ANNOTATED BIBLIOGRAPHY

Constantian HM: Management of ureteral calculi: Series of 574 cases with special emphasis on use of Davis loop extractor. J Urol 112:33, 1974

The author has reported a 90% success rate of stone extraction from the lower third of the ureter. The Davis nylon loop extractor is used because of safety, ease of operation, and low cost. The technique is fully described in this article. After stone extraction, no ureteral catheter is left in place. The patient is discharged the day after stone extraction.

Walsh A: An aggressive approach to stones in the lower ureter. Br J Urol 46:11, 1974

An experience with the Dormia basket in a series of 126 patients is described. A success rate of 65% is claimed. Certain technical details are mentioned. The instrument is considered to be potentially dangerous; therefore, proper use is emphasized. The combination of obstruction and acute infection is an absolute contrainidication to basketing. Transurethral ureterolithotomy is advised when a stone is impacted in the intramural ureter.

Pfister RR, Schwartz R: Development of ureteral stone basket. Urology 6:337, 1975

The wire cage design for ureteral stone extraction was first conceived by Councill in 1926. The modification of this design in 1953 appeared in the form of the Dormia basket. Retaining the original concept but using more modern materials, Pfister and Schwartz have improvised on this time-honored instrument. This new basket has six wires made of cobalt-nickel-chromium alloy and a catheter made of polytetrafluoroethylene (Teflon). It can be autoclaved and possesses unsurpassed mechanical characteristics, thanks to "space age" technology.

Dourmashkin RL: Cystoscopic treatment of stones in the ureter with special reference to large calculi; based on the study of 1550 Cases. J Urol 54:245, 1945

This classic publication remains a landmark in the history of endoscopic surgery of the ureter. This monumental work, compiled with sheer dedication, provides great insight into the manipulation of ureteral stones. The brief review of the history of endoscopic methods puts present-day concepts in a proper perspective. Although the method used by Dourmashkin has not been adapted by modern urologists, his observations culminated in certain principles that are current guidelines. The article discusses 780 small ureteral calculi (less than 5 mm) and 741 large calculi (5 mm wide or more). Six cases of calculus anuria are also presented. The stones removed were collected by Dourmashkin for critical examination of physical characteristics. The stone grooves or channels were seen in almost one third of the stones, providing an explanation for the normal drainage of urine in an otherwise impacted stone. A remarkable success rate of stone retrieval was achieved: 99.7% for small stones and 85.9% for large ureteral stones.

Hans Joachim, Reuter and Eberhard Kern: Electronic lithotripsy of ureteral calculi. J Urol 109:110, 1973

The pulverization of a bladder stone by pulse voltage is enjoying greater popularity. Similar ideas have been extended to ureteral stones at all levels. Mechanical difficulties had to be overcome, and hence special instruments were designed. These authors claim that it is a viable technique. Minimum suggested size of the ureteral stone is 3mm to 5 mm. In this initial report of 11 cases, no damage to the ureter occurred.

Gill WB, Thomse S: Retrograde brushing: A new technique for obtaining histologic and cytologic materials from ureteral, renal pelvic and renal calyceal lesions. J Urol 109:573, 1973

Retrograde brushing was developed to enhance the diagnostic accuracy of the radiolucent filling defects of the ureter and renal pelvis. Since cytologic findings of voided urine do not, by themselves, have a high diagnostic accuracy rate, direct brushing of the upper tract tumor was developed. The authors have described a relatively simple technique for inserting the brush and obtaining the specimen. The ureter, renal pelvis, and superior calyx are readily accessible, but the inferior and middle calices will still remain unexplored by this technique. Nevertheless, the technique is useful, albeit limited.

Overview: Surgical Judgment in Treatment of Ureteral Calculi

Peter L. Scardino

There has not been a significant change in the incidence or chemical nature of ureteral calculi in patients in the United States in several decades.[1-5] Perhaps some progress has been made in controlling recurrences of calculi in those patients who adhere to a supervised medical regimen.[2] The opportunity for endoscopic manipulation of ureteral calculi is as great as ever. There has been no decrease during the past 80 yr in the introduction of "new" stone extractors or techniques that address themselves to stone extraction.[6] There has apparently been no change during the passage of this scenario in the attitude of urologists toward surgical, endoscopic, or conservative management of ureteral calculi. The literature is replete with successful reports of manipulations with few complications.[7] No report adequately reviews each case relative factors that determine intervention or observation.

Wizardry at basketry must be tempered by the realities of the natural history of stone disease. More than 90% of all ureteral calculi will pass unaided by urologists if pain can be relieved. Since each devotee of basketry has a favorite extractor, and new extractors are periodically introduced, one can conclude that endoscopic ureteral surgery is a personalized technique that does not lend itself to rigid surgical dogma. It is surgical judgment that is at stake, and judgment is difficult to evaluate. Since Gustav Simon first suggested, in 1865, the use of multiple catheters to facilitate the extraction of calculous bodies, many ingenious devices have been suggested, of which a scant few have withstood the test of time.[6]

Two distinct types of stone extractors are popular in the United States: the rigid metallic and synthetic fiber baskets and the nonrigid loops. The loops may be used as both extractor and dilator. The dilator loop permits urinary drainage as well as spontaneous passage of dilator and calculus. The loop technique is not widely employed.

The following guidelines have been established for the use of a rigid or semirigid extractor:

1. The calculus should not exceed 0.5 cm in diameter and must be in the distal ureter below the brim of the pelvis.
2. Relieve infection. Determine by urine and blood culture and sensitivity tests the antimicrobial agents required.
3. Normalize electrolyte deficiencies.
4. Evaluate contralateral renal status.
5. Determine whether additional calculi exist in ipsilateral system.
6. Perform metabolic studies for hyperuricemia, hyperuricosuria, urinary crystalluria (oxalate, uric acid, urates, or cystine), urinary pH, hypercalcemia, and urinary magnesium.
7. Obtain a detailed history and physical examination with special reference to prior stone disease, family history of stone disease, and cardiovascular, hematologic, metabolic, or oncologic problems.

To proceed, determine the operational status of television monitoring devices. Have the following endoscopic equipment ready: a 24 French panendoscope and a single-fin, direct-vision telescope without deflector. Perform a careful bladder and ureteral inspection. Initially do not pass a ureteral catheter. Choose a favorite extractor, and request an available spare. Attach a 15-cm, No. 4 French straight-tipped filiform to basket, and insert the tip in the ureteral orifice. Allow the filiform to gently strike the calculus until the filiform can be advanced alongside the calculus.

Advance the closed basket. Proper positioning of the basket is determined by a hydronephrotic drip or visualization of its position relative to the stone on the television monitor. Rotate the basket clockwise if desirable. The 6-in filiform provides repeated introduction of the basket past the calculus if engagement fails. The long filiform provides easy introduction of ureteral catheters in extraction failures. Once the catheters are introduced, remove the basket and attach the ureteral catheters to an in-dwelling Foley catheter.

If surgery is required, the catheter is a useful guide or can be used as a stent after ureterolithotomy. Cystoscopic stone extraction without excessive trauma requires no ureteral catheter. If not removed by surgery, a stone can be dislodged by removing multiple ureteral catheters 48 hr after insertion.

Obtain postoperative x-ray films if the calculus has not been recovered endoscopically or surgically. Appropriate antimicrobial agents, fluid replacement, and electrolyte stabilization are mandatory. Finally, the calculus must be analyzed. If a metabolic disorder has not been established, postoperative management is dictated by the analysis of the stone and the history of recurrences.

Endoscopic surgery of the ureter is usually innocuous but should not be taken lightly. The following serious complications may occur:

Ureteral meatal stenosis
Ureteral fibrosis
Ureterovesicle reflux
Urinary extravasation
Instrumental disruption with detachment of extractor or tip or fragmentation of the extractor
Ureteral avulsion
Pyelonephritis (septic shock)
Urethral instrumental scarring
Ureteral performation

Recent urologic innovations include percutaneous nephrostomy, antegrade ureteral catheterization, manipulation of calculi, biopsy of ureteral masses, and ultrasonic disintegration of ureteral stones. Percutaneous antegrade calculus manipulation is rarely preferable to ureterolithotomy. Direct-vision flexible fiberoptic ureterorenoscopes have been marketed for useful identification of ureteral neoplasms and calculi. The urologist must become acquainted with technologic advances in optics and radiology.

REFERENCES

1. Boyce WH, Garvey FK, Strawcutter HE: Incidence of urinary calculi among patients in general hospitals 1948–1952. JAMA 161:1437, 1956
2. Pak CY: Idiopathic renal lithiasis: New Developments in evaluation and treatment. In Urolithiasis Research, p 213. New York, Plenum Publishing, 1976
3. Blacklock NJ: Pattern of urolithiasis in the Royal Navy. In Hodgkinson A, Nordin BE, (eds): Renal Stone Research Symposium, pp 33–47. London, J & A Churchill, 1969
4. Anderson DA: Historical and geographical differences in the pattern of incidence of urinary stones considered in relation to possible etiological factors. In Hodgkinson A, Nordin BE (eds): Renal Stone Research Symposium, pp 7–32. London, J & A Churchill, 1969
5. Stutor DJ: The nature of urinary stones. In Finlayson B et al (eds): Urolithiasis: Physical Aspects, pp 43–60. Washington, DC, National Academy of Sciences, 1972
6. Scardino PL: Endoscopic manipulation of ureteral stones. In Landes RR, Bush RB, Zorgniotti AW (eds): Perspectives in Urology, p 85. Nutley, NJ, Hoffman-LaRoche, 1976
7. Lamensdorf H, Compere DE, Begley GF: Forceful endoscopic extraction of ureteral calculi. Urology 1:301, 1973

PART TWENTY-ONE

NONCONTINENT SUPRAVESICAL DIVERSION AND UNDIVERSION PROCEDURES

43

INSERTION OF GIBBONS URETERAL STENTS USING ENDOUROLOGIC TECHNIQUES

Arthur D. Smith, M.D., Robert P. Miller, M.D., Donovan B. Reinke, M.D., Paul H. Lange, M.D., and Elwin E. Fraley, M.D.

From the Departments of Urology and Diagnostic Radiology, Veterans Administration Hospital, and the Department of Urologic Surgery, University of Minnesota College of Health Sciences, Minneapolis, Minnesota

Urology / October 1979 / Volume XIV, Number 4

ABSTRACT—We describe our technique for the antegrade insertion of the redesigned Gibbons ureteral stent. We have used this technique for 19 kidneys without failures or complications. The advantages of internal drainage and of antegrade stent placement are discussed.

Recently we described a technique for inserting Gibbons ureteral stents in patients in whom retrograde placement of stents is not possible.[1] After percutaneous nephrostomy has been performed, the ureter is catheterized antegrade with an angiogram catheter. The end of this catheter is retrieved from the bladder. A filiform follower, to which a Gibbons stent has been attached with a silk ligature, is attached to the angiogram catheter and pulled retrograde up the ureter until the stent is in place. Although this technique proved highly successful, the stent did not tolerate traction well and often broke at the point where the ligature pulled on it.

The Gibbons ureteral stent was redesigned recently.

The new stent is firmer and has a larger internal diameter; and the wire spring, which occasionally separated from the stent or partially occluded it, has been eliminated. These changes have necessitated several modifications in the procedure for inserting Gibbons ureteral stents.

TECHNIQUE

The first stage of the procedure is a percutaneous nephrostomy, performed under fluoroscopic control. The patients are screened for bleeding tendencies, and before the procedure they are given antibiotics and a narcotic such as fentanyl and droperidol (Innovar). If necessary, diazepam is administered during the procedure. Initially, the patient is placed in the prone position, and the skin overlying the kidney is prepared with povidone-iodine and draped.

We prefer the posterolateral transparenchymal approach to the kidney instead of the direct transpelvic route. First, with the transparenchymal approach, the upper end of the ureter can be catheterized more readily because the angle at which it is entered is less acute. Second, the catheter has a longer course in the kidney, so there is less chance of it slipping out. Third, the renal parenchyma supports the catheter, so there is less chance of it tearing the renal pelvis. Fourth, the patient can lie on his back without bending the catheter, so it is more comfortable. Finally, the catheter can be reached more easily for manipulation by the cystoscopist.

An attempt is made to opacify the collecting system with intravenously administered contrast material (50–100 ml of 50 percent diatrizoate may be required for an adult). It may be necessary to inject the contrast material ten to twelve hours before the nephrostomy if renal function is delayed. If the collecting system is not adequately opacified by intravenous contrast material, direct injection is necessary. A radiograph is taken with the patient in the prone position in mid-breath. The relation of the renal outline to the twelfth rib and the lumbar spine is noted, and the anticipated location of the renal pelvis is marked on the skin.

This site is infiltrated with 5 ml of 1% Lidocaine, and an attempt is made to insert a 22-gauge skinny needle into the renal pelvis under fluoroscopic control while the patient holds his breath. To-and-fro movement of the needle during normal breathing indicates that it is within the kidney. The stylet is withdrawn, and an anesthetic extension tube is attached to the cannula. If urine is aspirated, it is replaced with an equal volume of contrast material, and this is repeated until there is excellent opacification of the renal pelvis and calyces. If no urine is obtained, the needle may have passed through the renal pelvis; the cannula should be withdrawn slowly and aspirated at intervals. Because the skinny needle causes little damage, numerous attempts can be made to enter the renal pelvis provided that all kidney punctures are performed while the patient holds his breath. The needle should not be removed until the end of the procedure, because it may be necessary to inject more contrast material and because withdrawal of the needle may cause extravasation, which would obscure the renal pelvis and ureter.

It is also possible to use ultrasound to perform percutaneous nephrostomy.[2] We have not done this because we usually proceed immediately with antegrade ureteral catheterization, which requires fluoroscopic control. In our hospitals, this would mean moving the patient to another table.

When the renal pelvis is clearly visible under the fluoroscope, the percutaneous nephrostomy is performed. The patient is placed in an oblique position so that the calyces are seen end-on, or, if rotating fluoroscopy is available, the patient remains in the prone position and the image intensifier is rotated so that the calyces are seen end-on. The site of the posterolateral insertion usually is near the postaxillary line; attempts to insert the needle too far anteriorly will result in a transperitoneal route (Fig. 1). An 18-gauge needle with a Teflon sheath is used to enter the renal pelvis transparenchymally,

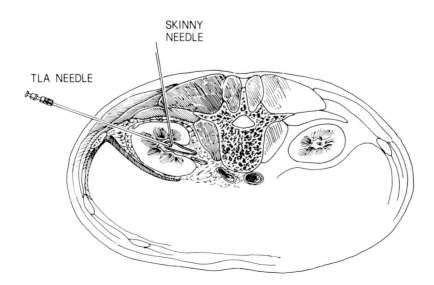

SKINNY NEEDLE

TLA NEEDLE

Fig. 1. Note posterior peritoneal reflection: TLA needle must not be introduced via direct lateral approach.

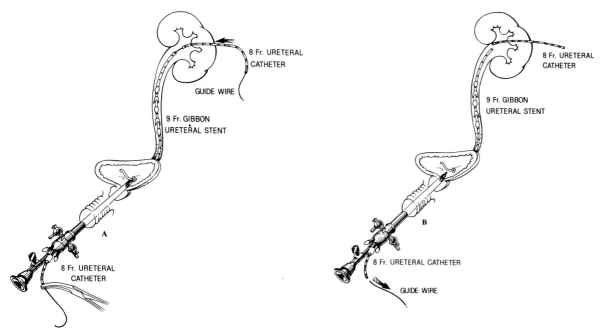

Fig. 5. (*A*) Whistle-tip end of ureteral catheter advanced over guide wire serves as temporary nephrostomy tube. (*B*) Guide wire is removed while Gibbons stent is held in place with ureteral catheter.

Traction on the filiform follower then separates it from the Gibbons stent (Fig. 4*B*), which is left in an ideal position, with the guide wire protruding from the nephrostomy site. If necessary, the ureteral catheter can be passed over the guide wire as a temporary nephrostomy tube (Fig. 5*A*), which separates from the Gibbons stent when the guide wire is removed.

The guide wire is removed transcystoscopically under direct vision so that the flange of the Gibbons stent can be held in position with the cut end of the ureteral catheter until the wire has been removed (Fig. 5*B*). The ureteral catheter is removed when the correct position of the flange of the stent has been assured.

A cystogram is performed to determine whether or not free reflux is occurring. Occasionally it is not, even though adequate drainage is evident on subsequent intravenous urography. This may result either from the lysis of blood clots by urokinase or from raised intrapelvic pressure.[5]

To prevent blockage of the Gibbons stent, a good urinary output is maintained by administering intravenous fluids and, if necessary, diuretics. Antibiotic administration is continued. If the stent becomes obstructed, it can be cleared easily with a 0.038-inch guide wire with a straight flexible tip, passed retrograde through a cystoscope. The flexible tip allows the guide wire to follow the contour of the stent without emerging from the side holes. If the stent becomes obstructed repeatedly, it is advisable to replace it with another Gibbons or other ureteral stent. Retrograde insertion seldom presents a problem, since both the ureteral orifice and the ureter already have been dilated. If the distal end of the stent migrates up into the ureter, it can be retrieved with flexible alligator forceps under fluoroscopic control.[6]

COMMENT

The value of ureteral stents and internal drainage is generally accepted.[6–8] Internal stents were compared with other forms of diversion by Singh, Kim, and Ware,[9] who showed that morbidity and mortality are both lower with stents than with conventional nephrostomy. In a recent review of 500 percutaneous nephrostomies, Stables, Ginsberg, and Johnson[10] stressed the safety of the procedure and the low incidence of failures. We believe that conventional nephrostomy should be used only for patients who require it as part of a definitive operation and those in whom percutaneous nephrostomy has failed. Relative contraindications to conventional nephrostomy include bleeding tendencies, hypertension, and a solitary kidney.

The new Gibbons stent is inserted more easily by

the conventional transcystoscopic retrograde route than was the original version. If a ureteral catheter can be passed retrograde during initial cystoscopy, we persist in our attempt to pass the Gibbons stent retrograde. However, in most of our patients, either the ureteric orifice could not be seen or stenosis was so severe that the orifice could not be negotiated transcystoscopically.

In contrast, antegrade passage of the stent seldom posed a problem. We have performed 90 percutaneous nephrostomies. In 19, we used the technique described in this article, which is essentially a variation of the original one, described by Goodwin, Casey, and Woolf,[11] and is simpler and more controlled than the technique we used to place the original Gibbons stent. With the new technique, we have had no technical problems placing the stent accurately. Two of the nephrostomy sites leaked urine for a few days after the nephrostomy tube was removed, but the leaking stopped after the stents were cleared with guide wires.

Our new technique also can be used to place Finney double-J Silastic ureteral stents[8] if a 0.025-inch guide wire is substituted for the 0.038-inch wire. The double-J Cook catheter also can be placed by this method.[9] However, these two catheters cannot be cleaned if they become blocked.

The advantages of antegrade catheterization of the ureter before the stent is pulled into place are several. First, the operator gains complete control of the stent at all times, which ensures its accurate positioning. Second, only local anesthesia is required for percutaneous nephrostomy and positioning of the stent. Third, the cystoscopic procedure takes less time, because the ureteric orifice and ureter are dilated while the stent is being pulled into position. Fourth, the patient's condition is allowed to stabilize before cystoscopic manipulation takes place. If pyuria is present, the kidney can be drained through the percutaneous nephrostomy until the urine clears, making subsequent blockage of the stent less likely. Fifth, if the kidney has been obstructed for a long time, temporary nephrostomy drainage can indicate how well it is functioning and whether internal drainage is warranted. Finally, this is one of the few techniques for inserting a Gibbons stent in a patient with a ureteroileal diversion.[12]

At the present time, we restrict antecedent percutaneous nephrostomy for the insertion of Gibbons ureteral stents to patients in whom transcystoscopic placement has failed. As our facility with antegrade ureteral catheterization and other endourologic techniques[13] increases, we will rely more on antegrade catheterization, and it may well become the technique of choice in the not-too-distant future.

Box 394, Mayo Building
Minneapolis, Minnesota 55455
(DR. SMITH)

REFERENCES

1. Smith AD, Lange PH, Miller RP, and Reinke DB: Introduction of Gibbons ureteral stents facilitated by antecedent percutaneous nephrostomy. J Urol 120:543, 1978

2. Harris RD, McCullough DL, and Talner LB: Percutaneous nephrostomy. Ibid 115:628, 1976

3. Gross DM: Diagnostic renal cyst puncture and percutaneous nephrostomy. Urol Clin North Am 6:409, 1979

4. Fowler JE Jr, Meares EM Jr, and Goldin AR: Percutaneous nephrostomy: techniques, indications, and results. Urology 6:428, 1975

5. Gibbons RP: In my hands: indwelling ureteral stents. Urol Times, February 1979, p 8

6. Smith AD, and Hekmat K: Retrieval of Gibbons ureteral stents under fluoroscopic control. J Urol 121:133, 1979

7. Camacho MF, et al: Double-ended pigtail ureteral stent: useful modification to single-ended ureteral stent. Urology 12:516, 1979

8. Finney RP: Experience with new double-J ureteral catheter stent. J Urol 120:678, 1978

9. Singh B, Kim H, and Ware SH: Stent versus nephrostomy: is there a choice? Ibid 121:268, 1979

10. Stables DP, Ginsberg NJ, and Johnson ML: Percutaneous nephrostomy: a series and review of the literature. AJR 130:75, 1978

11. Goodwin WE, Casey WC, and Woolf W: Percutaneous trocar (needle) nephrostomy in hydronephrosis. JAMA 157:891, 1955

12. Smith AD, Lange PH, Miller RP, and Reinke DB: Percutaneous dilatation of ureteroileal strictures and insertion of Gibbons ureteral stents. Urology 13:24, 1979

13. Smith AD, Lange PH, and Fraley EE: Applications of percutaneous nephrostomy: new challenges and opportunities in endourology. J Urol 121:382, 1979

Commentary: Indications for Nephrostomy Drainage

Arthur D. Smith

The indications for nephrostomy drainage have been extended as new techniques have evolved, and the procedure is no longer confined to the relief of acute and chronic obstruction. Because the new techniques involve closed, controlled manipulation within the urinary tract, and because they require the skills and instruments of the urologic surgeon, the term *endourology* was proposed to describe this rapidly expanding new disciple.[1]

One common situation in which nephrostomy drainage in some form may be indicated is uremia in a patient with cancer. However, there are medical, ethical, and legal questions involved in many cases, and it may be difficult to decide whether diversion is indicated. After reviewing the complications, survival time, and benefits in 218 patients who had undergone conventional nephrostomy, Holden and colleagues said that the final decision on diversion usually is made by the patient.[2] However, they provided three relative contraindications: intractable pain, previous adequate but unsuccessful trials of all types of treatment so that there is no prospect of further therapy, and emotional or mental deficits that would preclude proper management of the nephrostomy.

I will here review the following procedures:
Open nephrostomy
Changing the nephrostomy tube
Open U-loop nephrostomy
Percutaneous U-loop nephrostomy
Changing the U-loop nephrostomy tube
Other endourologic procedures

OPEN NEPHROSTOMY

The indications for open nephrostomy, with its attendent hazards and complications, have been curtailed sharply by the introduction of percutaneous nephrostomy.[3] Open nephrostomy now is limited to patients in whom it is part of another operation on the kidney and those in whom percutaneous nephrostomy has failed or is contraindicated.

To proceed, expose the kidney through any of the standard incisions and then expose the renal pelvis and lower pole. Place a stay suture of 4–0 chromic catgut on either side of the site (1 cm long and parallel to the long axis of the kidney) selected for the pyelotomy and make the incision.

Insert a Satinsky or other curved clamp through the pyelotomy and direct it into a lower calyx; incise the renal parenchyma over the tip of the instrument. Pull a 22 French to 28 French catheter into the renal pelvis (Fig. 6A). (If Randall stone forceps are used, the catheter must be sutured to the jaws, since these forceps are not strong enough to hold the

catheter while it is being pulled.) Pezzer, Malecot, Robinson, Councill, and Foley catheters are all suitable. However, if a Foley catheter is used, take care that the inflated balloon does not obstruct the other calyces.

After the nephrostomy tube is positioned, close the pyelotomy with 4–0 chromic sutures. Check the position of the tube and the security of the closure by irrigation. The surgeon may wish to mobilize the kidney so that it can be sutured to the lateral abdominal wall. This maneuver will provide a short, straight drainage tract and thus makes it easier to change the nephrostomy tube. Suture the nephrostomy tube to the skin and fix it to a nephrostomy-tube flange (Fig. 6B). Continued bleeding at the nephrostomy site can be controlled by inserting one or two mattress sutures.

CHANGING THE NEPHROSTOMY TUBE

Do not change the tube until the nephrostomy tract is well established. Mark the skin level on the tube with a nylon suture and remove the tube.[4] Also mark the new tube, which must be the same size and type as the first one, with a nylon suture so that the correct depth can be gauged. If the new tube is positioned properly, there should be no difficulty irrigating it. Perform a nephrostogram if in doubt.

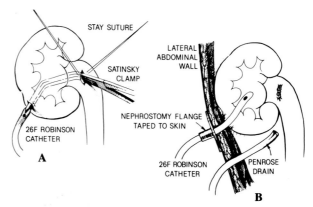

Fig. 6. (*A*) A Satinsky clamp has been passed through the pyelotomy and a lower calix and is grasping the catheter. (*B*) The nephrostomy tube is in place. The kidney has been sutured to the abdominal wall to ensure easy replacement of the tube.

If a Councill catheter is used as a nephrostomy tube, mark it as just described. It may be changed over a filiform catheter.

A nephrostomy tube usually can be inserted through an established tract that has been extubated for more than 12 hr or one that has been traumatized if angiographic techniques and fluoroscopy are used. I have been most successful with the 5 French polyethylene angiogram catheter with an angled tip, as described by Smith and colleagues, but it may be necessary to try a variety of angiogram catheters and guide wires.[5] Connect the catheter with a syringe of contrast medium and manipulate it through the opacified nephrostomy tract into the renal pelvis. Insert a heavy-duty guidewire and dilate the tract to 18 French with polytetrafluoroethylene (Teflon) dilators. Leave the 18 French dilator in the tract and pass a 14 French Malecot catheter and stylet through it into the renal pelvis. Withdraw the dilator and stylet, leaving the Malecot catheter as the nephrostomy tube.[6]

OPEN U-LOOP NEPHROSTOMY

There are three major problems with standard nephrostomy tubes. First, they often fall out. Second, they drain inadequately. Third, they become obstructed easily and therefore must be changed, a hazardous procedure. Because of these problems, U-loop nephrostomy drainage was devised.[7,8]

The technique of open U-loop nephrostomy is similar to that described for open nephrostomy in that a pyelotomy is performed and a 16 French to 17 French Silastic U-loop catheter (Heyer–Schulte) is pulled into the renal pelvis. The catheter is then made to describe a gentle curve through the pelvis and to emerge from an upper calyx (nephronephrostomy; Fig. 7A). Alternatively, the catheter can pass through a calyx and the ureter to form a nephroureterostomy, as shown in Figure 7B. Care must be taken to ensure that the drainage holes of the catheter are in the renal pelvis. The ends of the catheter are then attached to the Y connector, which is connected with a drainage bag.

PERCUTANEOUS U-LOOP NEPHROSTOMY

U-loop drainage can also be installed by percutaneous methods, with the patient requiring only local anesthesia.[5] A well-established nephrostomy tract, obtained by either open or percutaneous techniques, must be available; it should be at least 1 wk old.

Perform a nephrostogram with the patient in a supine position and opacify the renal pelvis and calyces. Then place the patient in a semiprone position. Select a puncture site far enough from the first nephrostomy site that the U-loop catheter will make a gentle wide curve through the renal pelvis and parenchyma; prepare, drape, and infiltrate the area with local anesthetic. Introduce a translumbar aortogram (TLA) needle below the ribs into an upper calyx under fluoroscopic control (Fig. 8A). Thread a small J-shaped guide wire through the TLA needle into the renal pelvis and remove the nephrostomy tube. Pass a J-shaped angiogram catheter over the wire and manipulate the two out through the established nephrostomy tract (Fig. 8B). Alternatively, Randall forceps may be introduced through the nephrostomy tract under fluoroscopic control to retrieve the guide wire.

With the path of the U-loop catheter now marked by the

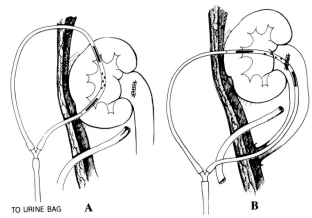

TO URINE BAG **A** **B**

Fig. 7. (*A*) A silicone rubber U-loop catheter has been inserted through a pyelotomy incision. The kidney has been sutured to the abdominal wall. (*B*) The catheter extends from a middle calix of the ureter's amputated end, allowing a wider curve than does the technique shown on the left.

guide wire, dilate the new tract to 18 French with Teflon dilators. I prefer next to replace the guide wire with a 7 French angiogram catheter inserted through the lower nephrostomy tract (Fig. 8C). To do so, suture a filiform catheter into the lumen of the angiogram catheter (Fig. 8D) and attach it to a filiform follower in the usual way. Cut off the other, larger end of the follower and attach a silicone rubber U-loop nephrostomy tube with standard connectors (Fig. 8D).

Pull the angiogram catheter until the side hole of the follower appears at the skin of the lower nephrostomy site. Thread a guide wire through the follower and the U-loop tube as insurance (Fig. 3E) and pull the U-loop tube into the renal pelvis, judging its location by the position of its radiopaque markers (Fig. 8F). Then remove the guide wire. After a nephrostogram has shown that the holes of the U-loop tube are all within the collecting system, attach the ends of the tube to a Y connector, which is in turn attached to a drainage bag.

CHANGING THE U-LOOP TUBE

Usually a U-loop tube can be changed easily; to do so, fasten the new tube to the old one with an adaptor and pull it into position. In the rare instances in which a U-loop drainage tract becomes extubated, the path can be reestablished with angiogram catheters as described. Alternatively, a J-shaped guide wire and a stone basket can be introduced, one into each tract, and manipulated until the loop is reestablished.[10] This may be done under fluoroscopic control.

OTHER ENDOUROLOGIC PROCEDURES

The nephrostomy tract can serve purposes other than drainage. For example, it provides access for urodynamic studies. In patients with severe obstruction of the ureteropelvic junction, studies of the function of the obstructed kidney can indicate whether pyeloplasty or nephrectomy is preferable. It also is

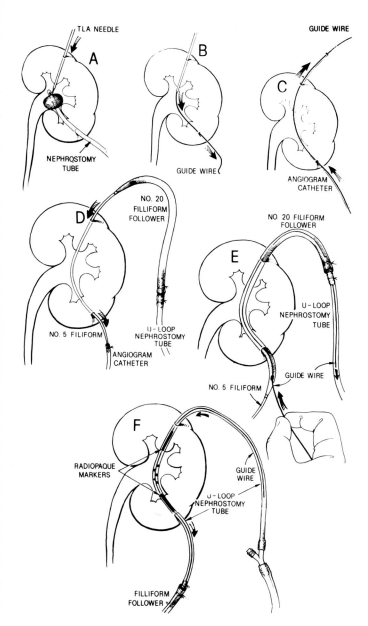

Fig. 8. (*A*) Introduce a TLA needle under fluoroscopic control. (*B*) Manipulate a J-shaped angiogram catheter and guide wire out through the original nephrostomy site, and withdraw the catheter, leaving the guide wire. (*C*) Pass a 7F angiogram catheter over the guide wire from the lower to the upper nephrostomy site, and withdraw the wire. (*D*) Suture a filiform catheter into the angiogram catheter. Attach a 20F filiform follower, and cut off its other end. Fix the U-loop catheter to the follower; traction on the angiogram catheter then draws the assembly through the kidney. (*E*) When the side hole of the follower is visible at the skin of the lower nephrostomy site, thread a guide wire through the follower into the nephrostomy tube as an added safety measure. (*F*) Pull the U-loop tube into the correct position (as judged by the location of its radiopaque markers) in the renal pelvis.

possible to study dilated ureters, including those implanted in ileal or colonic conduits.[11,12]

The nephrostomy tract also provides access to renal and ureteral calculi. Some stones can be dissolved by irrigation: struvite stones can be dissolved with Renacidin or Suby's solution G, urate stones can be dissolved with sodium bicarbonate, and cystine stones can be dissolved with a combination of sodium bicarbonate and acetylcysteine or, possibly, with tromethamine (THAM).[13–15]

Insoluble stones such as those of calcium oxalate must be removed mechanically. If the stones are in the renal pelvis or calyces, the tract is dilated to at least 18 French and allowed

to mature for several days. Instruments then can be introduced. Both irrigation and manipulation may be needed in some patients.

If there are insoluble stones in the ureter, pass an angiogram catheter through the nephrostomy tract into the bladder and retrieve it transcystoscopically with Bumpus or alligator forceps. Attach a stone basket to the catheter and pull it retrograde above the calculus. Capture the stones under fluoroscopy, having both proximal and distal control of the stone basket. This technique is especially suitable for multiple stones or those difficult to basket with conventional methods. Also, it is one of the few closed methods available to retrieve stones at a ureteroileal junction.[16] Ureteral stenting with a silicone rubber catheter is advisable.

A controlled ureteral meatotomy also can be performed through a percutaneous nephrostomy. To proceed, insert an angiogram catheter and recover it from the bladder as described above. Attach a ureteral catheter with an exposed 2-cm length of steel stylet (similar to a Davis stone basket) to the angiogram catheter and pull it retrograde until the stylet is in contact with the ureteral orifice. Apply cutting current. This can be repeated until the area of stenosis is opened completely. Place a silicone rubber catheter to stent and drain the ureter.[17]

. . .

The many uses of the nephrostomy tract encourage regarding it as a conduit to the upper urinary tract in much the same way that the urethra is a conduit to the lower tract. As further endourologic techniques are devised, management of a variety of urologic diseases should be improved.

REFERENCES

1. Smith AD, Lange PH, Fraley EE: Percutaneous nephrostomy: New challenges and opportunities in endo-urology. J Urol 121:382, 1979

2. Holden S, McPhee M, Grabstald H: The rationale of urinary diversion in cancer patients. J Urol 121:19, 1979

3. Hepperlen EW, Mardis HK, Kammendel H: The pigtail ureteral stent in the cancer patient. J Urol 121:17, 1979

4. Karsburg W, Leary FJ: Nephrostomy tube replacement. Urology 13:301, 1979

5. Smith AD, Lange PH, Miller RP et al: Percutaneous U-loop nephrostomy. J Urol 121:355, 1979

6. Levine R: A technique for re-insertion of the displaced nephrostomy tube. J Urol 112:393, 1974

7. Comarr AE: The U tube catheter. J Urol 92:78, 1964

8. Binder C, Bonick P, Ciavarra V: Experience with Silastic U-tube nephrostomy. J Urol 106:499, 1977

9. Bissada NK, Cole AT, Fried FA: Renal diversion with silicone circle catheters. Urology 2:238, 1973

10. Chuang VP: Nonsurgical method of replacing a lost loop nephrostomy tube. Am J Roentgenol 128:699, 1977

11. Whitaker RH: Methods of assessing obstruction in dilated ureters. Br J Urol 45:15, 1973

12. Yoder IC, Pfister RC: Radiology of colon loop diversion: Anatomical and urodynamic studies of the conduit and ureters in children and adults. Radiology 127:85, 1978

13. Smith AD, Reinke DB, Miller RP, et al: Percutaneous nephrostomy in the management of ureteral and renal calculi. Radiology (in press)

14. Dretler SP, Pfister RC, Newhouse JH: Renal-stone dissolution via percutaneous nephrostomy. N Engl J Med 300:341, 1979

15. Crissey MM, Gittes RF: Dissolution of cystine ureteral calculus by irrigation with tromethamine. J Urol 121:811, 1979

16. Smith AD, Lange PH, Miller RP, et al: Extraction of ureteral calculi from patients with ileal loops: A new technique. J Urol 120:623, 1978

17. Smith AD, Lange PH, Miller RP, et al: Controlled ureteral meatotomy. J Urol 121:587, 1979

ANNOTATED BIBLIOGRAPHY

Holden S, McPhee M, Grabstald H: The rationale of urinary diversion in cancer patients. J Urol 121:19, 1979

Gibbons RP, Correa RJ Jr, Cummings KB, et al: Experience with indwelling ureteral stent catheters. J Urol 115:22, 1976

A review of 218 open nephrostomies in uremic cancer patients revealed life-threatening complications in 99 patients (45%) and minor complications in nearly all. The operation was directly responsible for 6 deaths and was a contributing factor in 74. Only half the patients with regional or widespread metastases obtained 2 mo or more of "useful life" as a result of the procedure. Although the final dicision about diversion is usually the patient's, there are relative contraindications: intractable pain, no prospect of further antineoplastic treatment, and emotional or mental problems preventing adequate management of the nephrostomy. The authors state: "While technical refinements . . . promise to make urinary diversion easier . . . it behooves those who treat cancer patients to have a definite rationale to eliminate the personal bias and controversy that often accompany [the uremic cancer patient]."

The authors describe the then-new stent and the technique for inserting it. They used the stent in 22 patients (26 ureters), 17 of whom had ureteral obstruction by cancer. Endoscopic placement had a lower morbidity and mortality than did open procedures, and the stent often could be placed at the time the obstruction was diagnosed. If diversion becomes undesirable because the patient's health deteriorates, the stent can be removed.

Fowler JE Jr, Meares EM Jr, Goldin AR: Percutaneous nephrostomy: Techniques, indications, and results. Urology 6:428, 1975

The authors performed percutaneous nephrostomies on 42 kidneys in 33 patients, aged 2 to 84, one of whom had a solitary kidney. In 28 patients the indication was obstruction; in five it was extravasation or fistula. Two techniques were used: the Pedersen technique, which requires a commercial kit, and the Goldin technique, which requires only the equipment used for visceral arteriography. Both are described in detail, and the advantages of the Goldin technique are outlined.

Adequate drainage was established in 76% of the 50 attempts. Open nephrostomy was necessary in three patients. In two patients, percutaneous nephrostomy drainage in one kidney was adequate, so no further attempts were made to intubate the other. In one patient, a second attempt at percutaneous nephrostomy was successful. One patient underwent pyeloplasty 4 days later without further attempts at diversion. Two patients who were septic lost both tubes within 24 hr, but both improved during the brief period of drainage.

The only postoperative death was from causes unrelated to the procedure. Eight patients had bleeding at the nephrostomy site or hematuria for 1 to 3 days, but there were no serious bleeding episodes. The most common complication was premature dislodgement of the tube (3 to 177 days after nephrostomy), which occurred in 11 patients.

The authors discuss the therapeutic results and note that important diagnositc studies became possible in 29 patients because of the percutaneous nephrostomy. In one patient a struvite calculus was irrigated with 10% hemiacidrin; most of it dissolved, and the remaining portion passed spontaneously.

Stables DP, Ginsberg NJ, Johnson ML: Percutaneous nephrostomy:

A series and review of the literature. Am J Roentgenol 130:75, 1978

The authors performed percutaneous nephrostomies on 53 kidneys in 9 children and 33 adults; they also review 516 published cases. Ultrasound, with or without fluoroscopy, was used in some patients to locate the pelvocalyceal system. The results were satisfactory in 91% of the authors' cases. Major complications (retained blood clot, transient urinary peritonitis, pyelonephritis secondary to catheter obstruction) occurred in four patients; minor complications occurred in eight. In 62% of patients, no further operations were required, so percutaneous nephrostomy is not just a temporizing preoperative procedure. The authors note: "The limited use of the procedure for *permanent* diversion does not reflect deficiencies in the percutaneous method so much as the availability of alternative methods of permanent urinary drainage . . . which are often more desirable." However, they continue: "The ease of percutaneous nephrostomy demands restraint in its application." If there is no prospect of tumor response to further treatment, nephrostomy is not indicated.

Hepperlin TW, Mardis HK, Kammandel H: The pigtail ureteral stent in the cancer patient. J Urol 121:17, 1979

Diversion with the stents was performed for pain as well as for anuria in 20 patients. Seventeen achieved 2 mo or more of "useful life." The internal stent should be considered before nephrostomy, since the morbidity and mortality appear to be lower.

Karsburg W, Leary FJ: Nephrostomy tube replacement. Urology 13:301, 1979

The authors list and illustrate all the materials needed to change a nephrostomy tube and all the steps in the process. Their directions should make "changing the tube a relatively simple procedure" rather than a "time-consuming, frustrating exercise."

Bissada NK, Cole AT, Fried FA: Renal diversion with silicone circle catheters. Urology 2:238, 1973

The authors performed 24 open U-loop nephrostomies in 21 patients. Two patients had delayed hemorrhage, apparently resulting from erosion of the collecting system by the catheter.

One patient died; in the other, bleeding was controlled with transfusions and ε-aminocaproic acid. In a third patient, transient bleeding also was probably the result of erosion of the collecting system. The patient did not report the bleeding when it occurred, and the kidney healed spontaneously. The chances of erosion are reduced if the catheter curves gently through the kidney and is prevented from moving by flanges at the nephrostomy sites. The tubes were changed every 3 to 6 mo, but in one patient who was lost to follow-up study for 9 mo, the tube continued to function. It was not possible to replace tubes that came out, but it usually was easy to install conventional nephrostomy drainage.

Dretler SP, Pfister RC, Newhouse JH: Renal-stone dissolution via percutaneous nephrostomy. New Engl J Med 300:341, 1979

Recurrent renal stones, presumably composed of magnesium, ammonium, and calcium phosphates, were irrigated with hemiacidren in eight kidneys (six patients) through percutaneous nephrostomies. Perfusion rates varied from 30 ml/hr to 120 ml/hr, and perfusion time varied from 7 to 30 days. In six kidneys, the stones were dissolved completely; in two, other methods were used to remove portions that did not dissolve. Antibacterial agents were administered before, during, and for 10 days after treatment. There were no serious complications. Careful attention to the placement and care of the catheters is essential, and patients must be monitored for obstruction, hypermagnesemia, and renal failure. In an accompanying editorial (Guano on the renal pelvis, pp 361–363), Rennie points out that the prolonged hospitalization, constant nursing supervision, and bacteriologic and biochemical monitoring make cost-effectiveness studies of this technique necessary.

Kurth KH, Hohenfellner R, and Altwein JE: Ultrasound litholapaxy of a staghorn calculus. J Urol 117:242, 1977

The authors destroyed a struvite staghorn calculus with an ultrasound lithotriptor inserted through one of the passages of a U-loop nephrostomy. Two 30-min sessions reduced the stone to a fine sand, which was removed by suction. There was no visible damage to the renal pelvic mucosa, and convalescense was uneventful.

Overview: Nephrostomy Drainage: Medical and Philosophical Considerations

William R. Fair

Dr. Smith has provided an excellent review of open and percutaneous nephrostomy to relieve urinary tract obstruction. As he points out, a common indication for nephrostomy drainage is in the patient with ureteral obstruction secondary to advanced malignancy. Whether to divert the urine in a given patient with recurrent abdominal cancer and urinary tract obstruction is more a philosophical than a medical judgment.

Although all physicians are inclined to relieve the obstruction and prolong the patient's life, in my opinion it is, in many circumstances, inappropriate to proceed with nephrostomy drainage. Nephrostomy, although often prolonging life, in some cases condemns the patient to an agonizing death from painful metastatic disease rather than a relatively peaceful death from progressive uremia. The physician must also be aware that the decision to proceed with a nephrostomy is usually irrevocable. The idea that obstruction can be relieved for a short time in the terminal cancer patient does not usually hold up in actual practice. Once the tube is in place, the physician, patient and family become unwilling to remove the tube, causing the patient to lapse into eventually fatal uremia. Thus, due consideration must be given *before* the initial step is made, since the decision to terminate nephrostomy drainage, once it is in place, is many times more difficult than deciding whether to put in a nephrostomy tube in the first place. As pointed out by Holden and colleagues (reference 2 in the preceding commentary), the decision to proceed to nephrostomy drainage in a terminally ill cancer patient is usually made by the patient and the family in consultation with the physician. It is often kinder to allow the patient to die of obstructive uropathy than it is to relieve the obstruction. In no other area of urology is the ancient admonition "to heal sometimes—to comfort always" more appropriate. In many patients with ureteral obstruction in terminal cancer, maximum comfort can be obtained by the least amount of therapeutic intervention.

Although not absolute contraindications to percutaneous nephrostomy, significant bleeding abnormalities or the patient's total inability to manage tube drainage are relative contraindications to use of a nephrostomy tube.

Although the authors did not stress a preference for a particular type of catheter material, in general experience has shown that silicone or silicone-coated catheters are associated with less tissue and catheter reaction than the standard latex tubes and also require less frequent changes. Similarly, the type of tube used to provide percutaneous nephrostomy drainage should be given careful thought. The use of a Foley catheter makes changing the tube very easy. However, the Foley is a very poor draining catheter with a smaller lumen in relation to its external diameter than any catheter that does not require an additional lumen to inflate the balloon. This is a disadvantage. Because of the occasional problems of balloon breakage or gradual loss of fluid from the balloon while it is in the pelvis, the Foley is also less secure than a Malecot catheter in keeping the catheter within the kidney.

As to antimicrobial therapy in patients with nephrostomy tubes, as with bladder catheters, the physician must accept that after a given period, virtually all patients with nephrostomy tubes will have infected urine. However, there is no evidence that freely draining infected urine, at least in the adult kidney, leads to deterioration of renal function. What is important is that all steps be taken to prevent stone formation or the emergence of a bacterial species totally resistant to antimicrobial agents. For this reason, it is my practice not to treat these patients with routine antimicrobial agents. Rather, the urine is cultured frequently and treatment is initiated only when urea-splitting bacteria are recovered on urine culture. Thus, the presence of *Escherichia coli* (which never splits urea) in the culture from a nephrostomy tube in an otherwise asymptomatic patient would *not* be an indication for antimicrobial treatment.

Vigorous attempts to keep the urine sterile with a succession of antimicrobial agents will eventually lead to the development of an infection resistant to most antibiotics. This poses a greater therapeutic challenge and often requires the use of potentially nephrotoxic antimicrobial agents to sterilize the urine, with subsequent greater loss of renal function secondary to antibiotic therapy than due to the original infection. The stones that form in patients with nephrostomy tubes are almost always magnesium ammonium phosphate (struvite) stones, which can be prevented by prompt treatment and eradication of urea-splitting bacteria. Since the most common of these organisms is *Proteus mirabilis,* and since the vast majority of *P. mirabilis* strains are exquisitely sensitive to small doses of oral (PO) penicillin, treatment of these organisms presents no major problems. In summary, however, the routine use of antimicrobial agents in patients with nephrostomy tubes should be discouraged.

The use of relatively nonreactive catheter materials such as silicone has made it possible to consider long-term ureteral stents as an alternative to nephrostomy in patients in whom it is possible to catheterize the ureteral orifice. I believe that, where possible, the internal ureteral stent is far preferable to a nephrostomy, either open or percutaneous, for long-term kidney drainage. Most urologists are more familiar with techniques of ureteral catheterization than they are with percutaneous nephrostomy, and, if ureteral stenting is successful, the absence of an external appliance is a decided advantage for the patient.

As Dr. Smith has noted, adequate visualization of the upper tract is a necessary prerequisite to perform a percutaneous nephrostomy. However, more recently physicians have relied primarily on ultrasonic localization for nephrostomy tube placement. Improved detection devices, which enable the needle to be placed directly through the center of the transducer, have greatly facilitated the ease with which the renal pelvis can be localized and punctured using ultrasound guidance.

Some have advocated the use of computed tomography (CT) scanning to ensure accurate placement of the tube in percutaneous nephrostomy. In my experience this is not necessary. The physical design of CT scanners makes the necessary manipulations difficult, and, compared to ultrasonography, CT scanning involves the risk of radiation exposure and greater expense to the patient. I take exception to Dr. Smith's statement that the nephrostomy tract should be regarded as "a conduit to the upper urinary tract in much the same way that the urethra is a conduit to the lower tract." The potential complications with percutaneous nephrostomy are much greater than those encountered with urethral catheterization. Furthermore, it seems imprudent to use a nephrostomy tract as a method of stone manipulation, ureteral dilatation, or calculus dissolution simply to avoid a "surgical" approach involving cystoscopy.

Aggressive "interventional radiologists" have convinced many internists that a needle through the flank is a safer, quicker, and less expensive modality than transurethral instrumentation. Undoubtedly this stems from the totally irrational, morbid fear of the urethral catheter in some medical professionals. The *New England Journal of Medicine* editorial by Rennie referred to in the preceding annotated bibliography is worth reading. It is not at all clear that the length of hospitalization, close medical and nursing supervision, bacteriologic and biochemical monitoring, and the readily available radiologic expertise required to perform these sophisticated endourologic manipulations is cost effective or justified on the basis of superior patient care.

44

CUTANEOUS PYELOSTOMY

Mark A. Immergut, James J. Jacobson, David A. Culp and Rubin H. Flocks

From the Department of Urology, University of Iowa Hospitals, Iowa City, Iowa

Reprinted from *Journal of Urology,* Vol. 101, pp. 276–279, 1969. Copyright 1969 by The Williams & Wilkins Company, Baltimore.

Bilateral hydronephrosis accompanied by tortuous, dilated, atonic ureters is a potentially life threatening problem most commonly encountered in children (Fig. 1). Urinary drainage with a suprapubic cystostomy or a urethral catheter is usually ineffective in these patients because of poor ureteral peristalsis and ineffecient urinary transport to the bladder. In addition to a poorly performing urinary transport system, these patients often have damaged renal parenchyma and decreased renal function. Ideally, therefore, high urinary diversion should be promptly instituted without inflicting the trauma associated with placement and maintenance of a nephrostomy tube on the already damaged kidney.

The hydro-ureteronephrosis seen in these children may arise from obstruction at the bladder neck or the ureterovesical junction or may be the result of neurologic disease of the bladder or ureter. However, the etiology is of secondary importance when the child enters the hospital. Prompt high urinary diversion should be carried out and, after maximum renal function has been recovered, the origin of the trouble should be investigated.

In the past 3 years, 13 patients with hydronephrosis and hydroureter, who previously would have been candidates for nephrostomy tube drainage, have undergone

Accepted for publication June 15, 1968.

Read at annual meeting of American Urological Association, Miami Beach, Florida, May 13–16, 1968.

cutaneous pyelostomy at the University of Iowa Hospitals. This procedure is a simple method of establishing tubeless urinary drainage from the kidney. It lends itself to the size of the patient and the renal pelvis encountered in children with dilatation of the upper urinary tracts.

SURGICAL PROCEDURE

Technique. the patient is placed on the operating table in the flank position (Fig. 2A). A short skin incision is made just below the 12th rib and carried down through the subcutaneous tissue and the muscles of the flank. Gerota's fascia is entered and the renal pelvis is mobilized, incised and sutured to the posterior corner of the skin incision. The pyelostomy should be performed at a safe distance from the ureteropelvic junction (Fig. 2B). The pelvis should lie in a position so that effective urinary drainage will occur without undue tension on the kidney or the ureteropelvic junction. In the child, because of the paucity of subcutaneous fat, the underdevelopment of the musculature of the flank and the relative mobility of the kidney, it is technically quite simple to bring the dilated renal pelvis to the skin. The remainder of the wound is closed in layers with 3-zero chromic catgut and a small Penrose drain is placed beside the cutaneous pyelostomy, protruding through the suture line (Fig. 2C). A temporary plastic urinary drainage bag is placed over the stoma until wound healing has taken place.

603

Results. Thirteen patients (9 less than 3 years old) have undergone 23 cutaneous pyelostomies. Four children had obstruction at the bladder neck and 9 children had assorted congenital anomalies of the bladder and ureters. Ureteral reflux was present in 11 of the 13 cases and 9 children had demonstrable decreased renal funcion.

The patients were evaluated with a history, physical examination, urinalysis, blood urea nitrogen, serum creatinine, creatinine clearance and urine cultures. Ra-

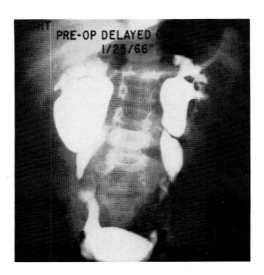

Fig. 1.

diological studies included an excretory urogram, a delayed cystogram with a voiding cystourethrogram and retrograde pyelograms; cinefluoroscopy was done when indicated. If the child was too ill with azotemia and infection to undergo diagnostic studies, the cutaneous pyelostomies were performed as soon as the diagnosis of bilateral hydro-ureteronephrosis was confirmed.

Convalescence was uneventful in all cases. Patients with azotemia showed obvious improvement in a very short time. Peristomal skin irritation in the early postoperative period occasionally occurred and was treated with waterproof ointments or gum karya powder. Several types of collection devices were used. Some children wore 2 sanitary napkins tied together around the flanks (Fig. 3A). Three patients (less than 2 years old) wore only diapers which covered the cutaneous pyelostomy sites. Older children have used the Lapides or the Marlen appliances (Fig. 3B).

In the late postoperative period, renal funcion and radiographic studies were repeated. Antegrade pyelography, performed by using a bulb syringe to inject contrast material into the cutaneous pyelostomy, demonstrated whether the pelvis and the tortuous, atonic ureter had improved. In addition, cine-antegrade pyelograms showed the presence or absence of effective ureteral peristalsis.

Eleven of the 13 patients have been followed from 6 months to 3 years. Two patients died in the later postoperative period of unrelated congenital abnormalities. The remaining 11 patients have done well. Although

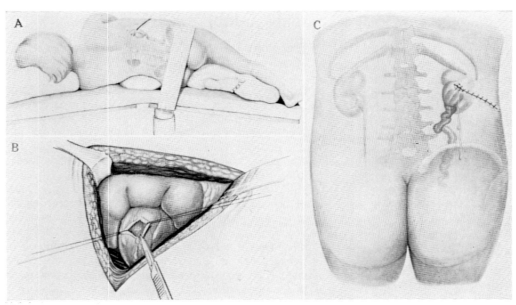

Fig. 2.

all children have bacteriuria, there have been no episodes of clinical acute pyelonephritis. Renal function, measured by creatinine clearance and phenolsulfonphthalein excretion, has improved markedly in 9 patients and slightly in the other two. Postoperative radiographic evaluation has shown either excellent or good improvement in the configuration of the kidneys in 9 of the 11 cases. In addition, ureteral size diminished and peristalsis improved in 9 of the 11 children.

Four patients have undergone closure of the cutaneous pyelostomy. This procedure should be considered after a complete diagnostic re-evaluation of renal function and the radiographic appearance of the urinary tract. If the ureters are smaller in size and show good peristalsis of urine into the bladder, if there is no vesicoureteral reflux and if the bladder functions effectively without residual urine, and if renal function has improved to the point where it is normal or near normal, then closure of the cutaneous pyelostomy may be undertaken.

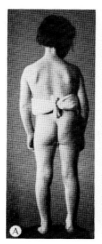

Fig. 3.

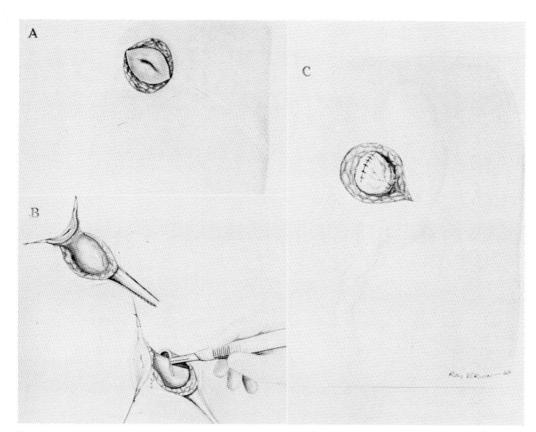

Fig. 4.

CLOSURE OF PYELOSTOMY

Technique. The renal pelvis is circumscribed from the surrounding skin and the neck of the pyelostomy is excised, being careful to notice the relationship of the pyelostomy to the ureteropelvic junction (Fig. 4A). The renal pelvis is closed with 3-zero chromic catgut sutures (Fig. 4B). A small red rubber catheter mauy be left in the corner of the renal pelvis as a safety valve or a Penrose drain may be left outside the suture line (Fig. 4C). The muscle and skin are closed routinely.

Results. In the 3 patients who have had the cutaneous pyelostomies closed, 5 of the 6 kidneys are functioning effectively. One kidney has required a postoperative nephrostomy tube because of persistent hydronephrosis. Seven children remain with semi-permanent or permanent cutaneous pyelostomies (Fig. 5). No evidence of stomal stenosis has occurred. These children have too little renal function and too much kidney and ureteral disease to permit closure of the cutaneous pyelostomies. This type of urinary drainage should provide them with the longest possible longevity.

CONCLUSION

Renal damage in the child or the infant, secondary to hydro-ureteronephrosis, demands prompt high urinary drainage which should be accomplished without a foreign body drainage tube. Cutaneous pyelostomy fulfills these criteria and also offers the urologist an early opportunity to inspect the condition of the renal parenchyma.

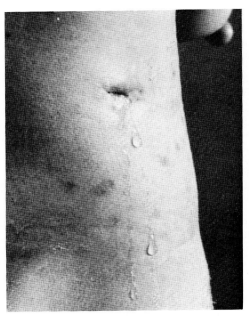

Fig. 5. Cutaneous pyelostomy, one year postoperative.

A cutaneous pyelostomy may be maintained for weeks, months or years and it can always be converted to a closed urinary collection system if and when the hydro-ureteronephrosis and renal function improve sufficiently to permit reconstitution of the urinary transport system.

Commentary: Cutaneous Pyelostomy for Temporary Diversion

Mark A. Immergut

Cutaneous pyelostomy was formulated in an effort to treat children with massive hydronephrosis, hydroureter, and decreased renal function with or without vesicoureteral reflux. When initially encountered, the majority of these children are under the age of 3 yr and are too severely ill to undergo a myriad of diagnostic and therapeutic procedures. The impaired kidney function, azotemia, and negative nitrogen balance dictate relief, in the most expedient manner, of their rapidly deteriorating renal parenchyma or urinary transport system. Recovery and preservation of remaining kidney function should be the primary aim of any initial operative procedure. In my opinion, cutaneous pyelostomy most consistently fulfills that objective. Repair of the hydronephrosis should be attempted only when renal function and ureteral dilatation have maximally improved after a period of decompression.

High loop cutaneous ureterostomy was advocated in 1963

by Perlmutter and Tank.[1] The basic tenets of this procedure are the same as those of cutaneous pyelostomy. Unfortunately, because of the extreme redundancy, and the massive dilatation and serpentine tortuosity of the diseased ureter, it is often difficult to establish drainage at the highest possible point in a loop ureterostomy to ensure that urinary stasis will not persist. It was with this thought in mind that the cutaneous pyelostomy was developed.

The grossly hydronephrotic renal pelvis lends itself readily, first, to cutaneous anastomosis and later to simple resection, if renal function returns sufficiently to justify reconstitution of the entire urinary tract. The surgeon may elect to repair the transport system in one procedure or in stages using the existing cutaneous pyelostomy as a convenient safety valve. The advantages over the more conventional nephrostomy tube drainage are obvious. The revision of a loop ureterostomy may compromise precious periureteral vasculature and, in addition, does not afford the urologist the temporary urinary diversion that may be necessary when complete reconstruction of the transport system is undertaken.

In 1969, Hendren described a procedure for the one-stage primary operative repair of severe megaureter in young children.[2] His approach to the problem has been quite the opposite of mine, and his statistics are quite impressive.[3] Thirty-three megaureters were repaired with extensive resection of the ureter to shorten its length and reduce its caliber. In about half his patients an operation on the lower ureter sufficed; in the rest, upper ureteral repair was performed at a second stage at least 2 mo later. Since his initial report in 1968, in which he studiously avoided any preliminary drainage procedure, he has written more recently: "Occasionally we have used short term preliminary nephrostomy drainage in critically ill babies as a first step towards subsequent reconstructive procedures."[4] This is the philosophy that urologists have been taught and have been teaching for many years. I believe that cutaneous pyelostomy has a place in the management of such cases, therefore obviating the use of a temporary nephrostomy tube and preserving renal parenchyma.

Since the appearance of the foregoing paper, 12 additional cutaneous pyelostomies have been performed in patients with massive hydroureteronephrosis. There have been no mortalities and no significant morbidity in this series of patients, and in all instances renal function and radiographic appearances have improved in the postoperative period.

Stomal problems have been minimal. The dilated renal pelvis, which has an excellent capillary blood supply, forms a capacious stoma. Several children have cutaneous pyelostomies, which, after years, show no evidence of stomal stricture or peristomal inflammation.

In 1973, Schmidt and associates reviewed their experience with cutaneous pyelostomy diversion at the University of Iowa.[5] Forty-one patients underwent the procedure, and general improvement was noted in 83%. The most common complication was peristomal skin irritation. Appliance failure, stomal stenosis, and wound infection were also reported in a small number of patients. In 1974, Frances and Bussey reported a case of a dysplastic kidney that herniated through its own cutaneous pyelostomy.[6] They believe that the complication was caused by an unusually large pyelostomy stoma and increased abdominal pressure secondary to constant straining from severe diarrhea.

Stein and Leiter reported, in May 1978, on a similar complication involving bilateral prolapse of cutaneous pyelostomies in a boy of 4 mo with bilateral congenital hydronephrosis.[7] Again, this event was associated with increased abdominal pressure, since as the child also had recurring pneumoccal pneumonia. Stein and Leiter suggested suturing the renal pelvis to the lumbodorsal fascia in addition to the skin to prevent predisposition to prolapse of the cutaneous pyelostomy.

In summary, cutaneous pyelostomy is a procedure developed to provide temporary high tubeless urinary diversion. Patients suited for this procedure are usually critically ill, with severe renal or urinary transport system damage. The operation has the distinctive advantage of providing a continuous safety valve for the recovery of renal function and for future reparative operative procedures on either the lower or upper ureter or the urinary bladder.

I agree with the concept that the urinary transport system should be repaired as completely and as early as possible in infants with massive hydronephrosis and hydroureter. I feel, however, that the preservation and recovery of renal function are more important than postoperative radiologic evidence of improvement of ureteral configuration. Maximal renal function may be saved and improved, initially, by cutaneous pyelostomy and, subsequently, by staged ureteral and ureterovesical repair.

REFERENCES

1. Perlmutter AD, Tank ES: Loop cutaneous ureterostomy in infancy. J Urol 99:559, 1968
2. Hendren WH: Operative repair of megaureter in children. J Urol 101:491, 1969
3. Hendren WH: The functional restoration of decompensated ureters in children. Am J Surg 119:477, 1970
4. Hendren WH: Posterior urethral valves in boys. J Urol 106:298, 1971

5. Schmidt JD, Hawtrey CE, Culp DA, et al: Experience with cutaneous pyelostomy diversion. J Urol 109:990, 1973
6. Frances DR, Bussey JG: Inside-out kidney: An unusual complication of cutaneous pyelostomy. J Urol 112:514, 1974
7. Stein ML, Leiter E: Bilateral herniation of renal pelvis, a complication of cutaneous pyelostomy. Urology 9:504, 1978

ANNOTATED BIBLIOGRAPHY

Sober I: Pelvioureterostomy-en-Y. J Urol 107:473, 1972

This procedure embodies all the basic concepts of cutaneous pyelostomy in a more complicated and involved operation. The

proximal ureter is diverted to the skin, making a cutaneous ureterostomy. The remaining upper ureter is then anastomosed to the renal pelvis in the manner of a dismembered pyeloplasty.

In my opinion, this procedure has no advantage over a

cutaneous pyelostomy and is more difficult and more time consuming and may lead to early and late postoperative complications. It requires an anastomosis between an atonic renal pelvis and an atonic upper ureter. Urinary extravasation may occur at the site of the new ureteropelvic junction, and scar tissue will likely form and may produce a ureteropelvic junction stricture. This anastomosis is an unnecessary added risk that can easily be eliminated by simply pulling the redundant renal pelvis to the skin.

Lome LG, Howat JM, Williams DI: The temporarily defunctionalized bladder in children. J Urol 107:469, 1972

Thirty patients with temporarily suspended bladder function secondary to cutaneous ureterostomy diversion are reviewed. The defunctionalized bladder in 15 patients showed a markedly reduced capacity. I have not had this complication occur in any patients who have undergone cutaneous pyelostomy. The authors suggest that the total absence of urine in the bladder increases its potential for contracture.

Patients who have undergone cutaneous pyelostomy usually micturate once a day. The urine that does not egress through the cutaneous pyelostomy passes into the urinary bladder. This situation may explain why bladder contracture has not been a problem in my cases.

Leadbetter GW Jr: Skin ureterostomy with subsequent ureteral reconstruction. J Urol 107:462, 1972

In this manuscript, skin ureterostomy with ureteral straightening is advocated for sick, uremic newborns and infants with hydroureteronephrosis. The author favors preliminary drainage rather than primary reconstruction of the hydroureteronephrosis. His preference for urinary diversion is a single-stoma, low cutaneous ureterostomy. His main objection to bilateral cutaneous pyelostomies seems to be that two appliances may be necessary if the urinary tract does not compensate and permanent diversion becomes necessary. This consideration is certainly valid. However, in my opinion, if a permanent form of urinary diversion becomes mandatory, better drainage and fewer stomal stricture problems would be achieved by a high ileal conduit.

Frances DR, Bussey JG: Inside-out kidney: An unusual complication of cutaneous pyelostomy. J Urol 112:515, 1974

This serious complication of cutaneous pyelostomy probably results from a combination of factors. The dysplastic kidney, which was pictured in a photograph in the article, appears to be extremely thin walled with very little renal parenchymal substance. The combination of diarrhea-induced increased intra-abdominal pressure and a large cutaneous pyelostomy stoma also were factors in the result, necessitating a nephrectomy.

Stein ML, Leiter E: Bilateral herniation of renal pelvis, a complication of cutaneous pyelostomy. Urology 9:504, 1978

Stein and Leiter discuss bilateral prolapse of cutaneous pyelostomies, a complication also associated with increased abdominal pressure related to respiratory complications of recurrent pneumoccal pneumonia. The authors suggest suturing the cutaneous pyelostomy first to the lumbodorsal fascia and then to the skin to prevent the prolapse or herniation of the renal pelvis. This modification of the original technique is a useful suggestion.

45

FOLLOWUP OF CUTANEOUS URETEROSTOMY IN CHILDREN

Ronald W. Sadlowski,* A. Barry Belman,† R. Bruce Filmer,‡ Paul Smey and Lowell R. King

From the Department of Urology, McGaw Medical Center of Northwestern University and the Division of Urology, Children's Memorial Hospital, Chicago, Illinois

0022-5347/78/1191-0116$02.00/0
The Journal of Urology
Copyright © 1978 by The Williams & Wilkins Co.
Vol. 119, January
Printed in U.S.A.

ABSTRACT—Thirty-two children with cutaneous ureterostomies are reviewed, of whom 27 were evaluated with an average followup of 3 years 8 months. Of these 27 patients 26 had successful stabilization of the upper tracts as determined by gross radiographic and renal function parameters. The incidence of stomal stenosis and revisions is no worse than the reported rates in cases of ileal conduits followed for a comparable length of time. Proper patient selection and careful long-term followup are mandatory for the successful application of this procedure in children.

Cutaneous ureterostomy has been advocated in the urologic literature for nearly 20 years as a satisfactory alternative for permanent diversion in selected children with ureterectasis.[1-4] In conjunction with transureteroureterostomy the advantages of a single lower quadrant stoma are maintained and only 1 of the ureters need be thickened and dilated significantly.[5-7] Since there are few reports in the literature of larger series of children with cutaneous ureterostomies who have been followed for any length of time, herein we review those patients with cutaneous ureterostomies from the Children's Memorial Hospital in Chicago.

Accepted for publication May 6, 1977.

Read at annual meeting of American Academy of Pediatrics, Section on Urology, Chicago, Illinois, October 16–21, 1976.

* Current address: Department of Surgery, Section of Urology, University of South Florida College of Medicine and Tampa Veterans Administration Hospital, Tampa, Florida 33612.

† Current address: Department of Pediatric Urology, Children's Hospital National Medical Center, Washington, D.C. 20009.

‡ Current address: Royal Alexandra Hospital for Children, Cheltenham, New South Wales, Australia.

MATERIALS AND METHODS

Cutaneous ureterostomy was performed in 32 children from 1968 to 1975. Five patients had no significant followup and are excluded from further data analysis. Two patients are included who were converted to high jejunal conduits early postoperatively because of a disruption of the transureteroureterostomy 1 week postoperatively in 1 and because of recurrent fever, infected urine and poor drainage of the collecting system 9 months after initial diversion in the other. Two other patients presented with end stage dilated upper tracts with serum creatinine more than 4.5. The diversion in these children was a temporizing procedure in preparation for dialysis and ultimate transplantation. Another patient was born with a cloacal exstrophy and bilateral hydronephrosis. Disruption of the transureteroureterostomy with associated infection contributed to death 20 days later when she was 24 years old. As seen in Figure 1 the remaining 27 patients were followed for at least 1 year and for as long as 7 years. The average followup was 3 years 8 months.

Table 1 illustrates the types of diversion performed. Two patients had bilateral (double-barreled) cutaneous ureterostomies with a single stoma in the midline. These were done early in our experience with this type of diversion, according to the technique of Swenson and Smyth.[8]

The age distribution is shown in Figure 2. The patients ranged in age from 4 days to 15 years and 13 were less than 2 years old.

The primary clinical conditions for which diversion became necessary are shown in Table 2. In many of these patients, such as those with vesicoureteral reflux, an attempt had been made to correct the primary problem but had resulted in failure. The gender distribution was equal.

The technique used has been described previously in detail.[9,10] A lower abdominal midline incision is generally used (Fig. 3A).[11] If possible the dissection is maintained entirely extraperitoneally, identifying the ureters and transecting them at the ureterovesical junction. The ureteral stumps are closed with a 3-zero chromic

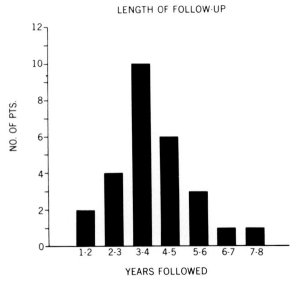

LENGTH OF FOLLOW-UP

Fig. 1. Length of follow-up.

TABLE 1. Types of Diversion

	No. Pts.
Transureteroureterostomy with end cutaneous ureterostomy	23
Unilat. cutaneous ureterostomy	7
Bilat. cutaneous ureterostomy	2
Total	32

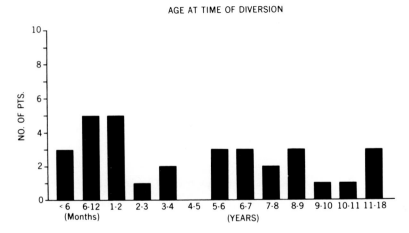

AGE AT TIME OF DIVERSION

Fig. 2. Age at time of diversion.

suture ligature and the ureters are dissected bluntly to the junction of the upper and middle thirds (Fig. 3*B*). Kinks are straightened, avoiding excessive dissection in order not to devascularize the ureter. The ureter to be brought to the skin is chosen on the basis of degree of vascularity, freedom from tension, luminal size and thickness of its wall. A core of full thickness abdominal wall is removed from an appropriate preselected site equal to or slightly smaller than the diameter of the chosen ureter (Fig. 3*C* and *D*). A blunt tunnel, retroperitoneal and anterior to the great vessels, is formed just cephalad to the bifurcation of the aorta through which the contralateral ureter is passed (Fig. 4*A*). An end-to-side tension-free anastomosis is made with interrupted or running 4 or 5-zero chromic catgut sutures (Fig. 4*B*). The end cutaneous ureterostomy can be created first so that the stoma does not change the relationship between the ureters at the site of the anastomosis. The anastomosis is actually oblique, with the length of the incision in the recipient ureter slightly greater than the transected diameter of the transposed ureter. A separate cutaneous stab wound drain is left in place after an appropriate cutaneous anastomosis is completed (Fig. 5).

Retention sutures are used routinely in patients with neurogenic disease.

If ureteral length is a problem or if an appliance cannot be worn in either lower quadrant because of lordosis or scarring a double-barreled side-by-side cutaneous anastomosis may be created, usually in the epigastric region.

RESULTS

The 27 patients eligible for evaluation were reviewed for evidence of radiographic or functional deterioration. Serial reviews of the excretory urograms revealed a stable condition in 13 patients and improvement in 14. None of these 27 patients had evidence of radiographic deterioration of the upper tracts during followup.

Serial evaluation of the blood urea nitrogen and serum creatinine revealed a stable condition in 26 patients and improvement in 1. None of the patients manifested functional deterioration as judged by these 2 parameters. In 22 patients the serum creatinine was less than 1.2 mg percent and stable, while the remaining 5 patients had serum creatinine concentrations between 1.3 and 1.8 mg percent. This group was also stable with an individual variation less than 10 percent.

Six of the 27 patients (22 percent) had 8 revisions, of which 6 were for stenosis as judged by the inability to pass an 8F catheter or for a collecting system residual urine of more than 10 to 15 ml. One stoma was revised because of metaplasia with bleeding and prolapse and another was revised because the stoma was too close to the iliac crest for proper fitting of the appliance. Four stomas were revised early (4 to 6 months postoperatively) and 4 were revised late (2½ to 7 years postoperatively).

TABLE 2. Indications for Cutaneous Ureterostomy

Primary Problem	No. Pts.	Male	Female
Meningomyelocele	11	4	7
Posterior urethral valves	6	6	—
Exstrophy of bladder	5	2	3
Bladder neck obstruction	5	3	2
Vesicoureteral reflux	4	1	3
Congenital urethral atresia	1	—	1
Totals	32	16	16

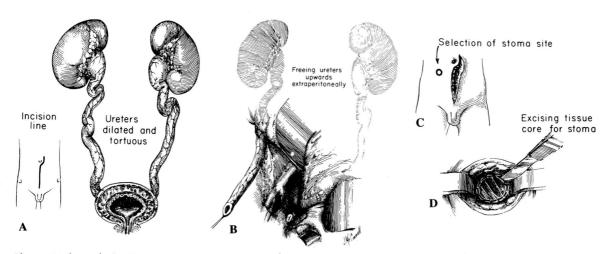

Incision line   Ureters dilated and tortuous   Freeing ureters upwards extraperitoneally   Selection of stoma site   Excising tissue core for stoma

A   B   C   D

Fig. 3. (*A* through *D*) Transureteroureterostomy-end-cutaneous ureterostomy. Reprinted with permission.[11]

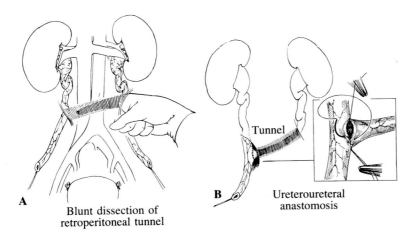

A Blunt dissection of retroperitoneal tunnel

B Tunnel   Ureteroureteral anastomosis

Fig. 4. Transureteroureterostomy-end-cutaneous ureterostomy. Reprinted with permission.[11]

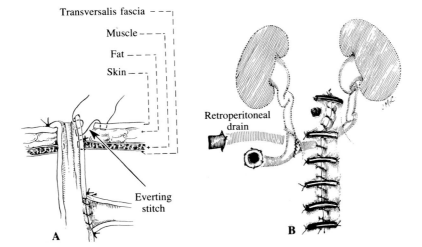

Transversalis fascia

Muscle

Fat

Skin

Everting stitch

A

Retroperitoneal drain

B

Fig. 5. Transureteroureterostomy-end-cutaneous ureterostomy. Reprinted with permission.[11]

The collecting system residual urine had been recorded in 14 cases. In the majority it was less than 10 ml. and 1 patient had 40 ml immediately before a recent stomal revision. Two patients who were free of stone preoperatively had infectious stones 4 years later, an incidence of 7 percent.

The over-all evaluation of our 32 patients reveals that 26 (81 percent) were stabilized or improved with the cutaneous ureterostomy as determined on radiographic appearance and serum creatinine levels. Six patients (19 percent) either deteriorated, died or were converted to a high conduit, including the 5 who were excluded originally plus another patient who was converted to a high conduit 3 years postoperatively because of recurrent fevers associated with back pain. In retrospect, this patient originally should have had a high jejunal conduit. He had marked bilateral pelviectasis and these patients generally have poor drainage of the collecting systems if they are diverted by cutaneous ureterostomy. As noted previously there was a single death in a newborn with cloacal exstrophy for a mortality rate of 3 percent. Four patients were undiverted subsequently.

DISCUSSION

Although many authors have reported on cutaneous ureterostomy long-term followups are few and the fear of upper tract deterioration and an unacceptable rate of stomal stenosis has persisted. Eliminating bowel segments with the potential metabolic complications and increased surgical risk is appealing, especially in poor risk patients such as the 2 in this series with advancing uremia before dialysis and transplantation. This procedure can be performed more rapidly than an ileal conduit and by performing it entirely extraperitoneally the risk of secondary bowel obstruction is eliminated. The low mortality rate should become significantly lower with further experience since the 1 mortality in this series was in a poor risk neonate with a combination of several complex congenital problems. Stricture of the transureteroureterostomy has not been a problem, although there have been 2 serious breakdowns of this anastomosis: one resulting in death of a neonate and the other requiring an immediate conversion to a high conduit. In the first case ischemia of the donor ureter of the transureteroureterostomy was apparent at operation and an alternative form of diversion should have been performed. In the second instance there was angulation of the anastomosis, resulting in torque of the donor ureter and ultimate disruption of the anastomosis owing to tension on the suture line.

As in all forms of cutaneous urinary diversion there is a risk of stomal stenosis. Three series of ileal conduits in children were found in the literature with nearly the same average followup (3.5 to 4 years) as our series.[12-14] The number of patients requiring stomal revision in these 3 ileal conduit series ranged from 12 to 41 percent (Table 3). Cutaneous ureterostomy in properly selected patients does not appear to suffer from comparison to ileal conduit on the basis of incidence of stomal revision required.

The main disadvantage of this procedure is that it is not universally applicable as a form of cutaneous diversion in children, since the prerequisite of having at least 1 chronically dilated and thickened ureter must be adhered to in order to avoid a distal ureteral slough and an unacceptable rate of stomal stenosis. Conversely, if the pelves are too dilated a high jejunal conduit is the preferred form of diversion, since cutaneous ureterostomy will not drain properly and stasis and infection will persist.

Cutaneous ureterostomy does not appear to protect the upper tracts from stone formation, since this complication appeared in 2 of our patients 4 years postoperatively. Prompt elimination of urea-splitting organisms

TABLE 3. Survey of Stomal Revisions

References	Type of Diversion	Av. Follow-up (yrs)	No. Pts.	No. Pts. with Revised Stomas (%)
Retik and associates[13]	Ileal conduit	3.8	81	29 (36)
Ray and De Dominico[14]	Ileal conduit	3.5	66	27 (41)
Livaditis[12]	Ileal conduit	4.0	25	3 (12)
Béland and Laberge[15]	Cutaneous ureterostomy	4.7	16	0 (0)
Present series	Cutaneous ureterostomy	3.7	27	6 (22)

TABLE 4. Results of Cutaneous Ureterostomy in Children

	Present Series	Béland and Laberge[15]
No. pts.	27	16
Av. followup (yrs)	3.8	4.7
No deterioration (%)	26 (96)	15 (94)

from the urine is an important aspect of the long-term followup of these patients.

In a closely comparable series reported recently 16 children with cutaneous ureterostomy were reviewed with an average followup of 4.7 years.[15] Renal function remained stable or improved in 15 patients and the radiographic appearance was stable or improved in all 16 (Table 4). Only 1 of these patients had a stenosis at the skin level. As Béland and Laberge mention, "In all cases the cutaneous ureterostomy consisted of a simple direct anastomosis of the spatulated end of the ureter with the skin."

Our series as well as that of Béland and Laberge establish an encouraging trend of long-term successful results in the use of cutaneous ureterostomy as a means of permanent urinary diversion in approximately 95 percent of properly selected children. Further long-term followup of larger numbers of patients hopefully will confirm the encouraging trend noted in these 2 series.

REFERENCES

1. Obrant, KO: Cutaneous ureterostomy with skin tube and plastic cup appliance together with transuretero-ureteral anastomosis. Br J Urol, 29:135, 1957
2. Wasserman DH and Garrett RA: Cutaneous ureterostomy: indications in children. J Urol, 94:380, 1965
3. Weiss RM, Beland GA and Lattimer JK: Transureteroureterostomy and cutaneous ureterostomy as a form of urinary diversion in children. J Urol, 96:155, 1966
4. Williams DI and Rabinovitch HH: Cutaneous ureterostomy for the grossly dilated ureter of childhood. Br J Urol, 39:696, 1967
5. Flinn RA, King LR, McDonald JH and Clark SS: Cutaneous ureterostomy: an alternative urinary diversion. J Urol, 105:358, 1971

6. Feminella, JG Jr. and Lattimer JK: A retrospective analysis of 70 cases of cutaneous ureterostomy. J Urol, 106:538, 1971
7. Shapiro SR, Peckler MS and Johnston JH: Transureteroureterostomy for urinary diversion in children. Urology, 8:39, 1976
8. Swenson O and Smyth BT: Aperistaltic megalourter: treatment by bilateral cutaneous ureterostomy using a new technique. Preliminary communication. J Urol 82:62, 1959
9. Halpern GN, King LR and Belman AB: Transureteroureterostomy in children. J Urol, 109:504, 1973
10. Belman AB and King LR: Urinary diversion of children. In: reviews in Paediatric Urology. Edited by JH Johnston in WE Goodwin. Amsterdam: Excerpta Medica, p 173, 1974

11. Belman AB and King LR: Permanent urinary diversion. In: Clinical Pediatric Urology. Edited by PP Kelalis, LR King and AB Belman. Philadelphia: WB Saunders, Co. 1976
12. Livaditis A: Cutaneous uretero-ileostomy in children. Acta Paed Scan, 54:131, 1965
13. Retik AB, Perlmutter AD and Gross RE: Cutaneous ureteroileostomy in children. New Engl J Med, 227:217, 1967

14. Ray P and De Dominico I: Intestinal conduit urinary diversion in children. Br J Urol, 44:345, 1972
15. Béland G and Laberge I: Cutaneous transureteroureterostomy in children. J Urol, 114:588, 1975

Commentary: Continuing Role of Cutaneous Ureterostomy

Ronald W. Sadlowski and A. Barry Belman

Recent nonsurgical advances in the care of patients with neurogenic bladders have markedly reduced the need for eventual urinary diversion in this population. Nevertheless, intermittent catheterization and pharmacologic manipulations are not always successful, and certain patients still need upper tract diversion in order to prevent further functional and anatomic renal deterioration. The decision on the type of diversion is as important as its timing, and a thorough knowledge of the advantages and limitations of each type of diversion is essential for the most appropriate selection in any particular clinical setting. Some patients are not good candidates for intestinal types of urinary diversion because of renal insufficiency with attendant electrolyte problems, which may be worsened by such a procedure. One of the main advantages of colon conduits is eliminated if an antireflux reimplantation cannot be performed because the ureter is too dilated. Upper tract drainage with devices such as nephrostomy tubes are usually limited to short-term situations because of the problems associated with chronic infection and foreign body encrustation and the problems inherent in the need for periodic replacement. Permanent urinary diversion by transureteroureterostomy with end cutaneous ureterostomy likewise has specific indications and advantages, disadvantages, and contraindications.

This form of urinary diversion, cutaneous ureterostomy, is restricted by necessity to patients who otherwise need a permanent upper tract diversion and have at least one ureter that is chronically and significantly dilated. An arbitrary but useful guideline requires that the ureter be at least 1 cm in collapsed diameter. The blood supply to the ureter basically comes from the renal artery at the proximal end and the inferior vesical artery at its distal end. This basic blood supply is variably enhanced by branches from the aorta and common iliac and gonadal arteries, which then form a communicating plexus along the ureteral wall and adventitia. If the ureter is chronically dilated, an increased anastomotic plexus of vessels develops in the outer wall of the normally relatively hypovascular midureter. Inflammation adds additional stimulus. Bringing a normal or only acutely dilated ureter to the skin invites slough or rapid stenosis despite the most elaborate skin-flap anastomosis.

Bilateral cutaneous ureterostomy is almost never performed anymore because stoma site selection is severely restricted, usually to a midline location, and effective creation of a more optimal nipplelike stoma is usually not possible. Transureteroureterostomy with end cutaneous ureterostomy offers advantages and flexibility in stoma site selection, allows creation of a more optimal nipplelike stoma, and eliminates the need for use of intestinal segments with their limitations of increased operative time and postoperative bowel complications as well as acid–base and electrolyte problems in patients with renal insufficiency. In some patients end cutaneous ureterostomy with or without transureteroureterostomy can be accomplished entirely extraperitoneally. This offers additional advantages because of easier retraction of the enclosed bowel contents as well as elimination of the risk of postoperative bowel obstruction from internal and parastomal hernias and from adhesions.

Although a chronically dilated ureter with its attendant increased blood supply is necessary to prevent later stenosis of the stoma, a drainage system that is totally decompensated will sometimes drain inadequately, since some degree of peristalsis may be necessary. The short-term postoperative use of in-dwelling ureteral stents may be useful to aid in urinary drainage. However, we have rarely found a stent necessary. Although the use of stents is optional, a poorly placed or nonfunctioning stent is a definite hazard and may lead to complications. Prompt removal of a nonfunctioning stent is required.

Unilateral end cutaneous ureterostomy can also be most useful in the intermediate term, that is, for several months to a few years when a significantly dilated ureter is found to have a markedly thickened wall at reimplantation surgery. Attempted tapering and reimplantation of such a ureter can invite failure from stenosis, particularly in a very young child. Intermediate-term diversion allows for resolution of the hypertrophy and subsequent successful reconstruction and provides time in which to evaluate the function of the ipsilateral kidney.

Contraindications to end cutaneous ureterostomy with or without transureteroureterostomy are found more frequently in adults than in children. They include extensive pelvic irradiation, residual calculus disease in either kidney, and retroperitoneal fibrosis with its attendant poor blood supply. Preexisting infection should be treated aggressively preoperatively with appropriate antibiotics and by itself is not a contraindication.

INDICATIONS

Children with neurogenic bladders secondary to meningomyelocele or sacral agenesis are presently the most common candidates for a permanent form of urinary diversion. In adults, palliative diversion for obstructed ureters from pelvic malignancies and occasionally patients with spinal cord injury have been the most common candidates for diversion.

TECHNIQUE

Proper preoperative selection of the optimal stomal site on the patient's abdominal wall, caution in maintaining ureteral vascularity, and intraoperative creation of the optimal type of stoma, usually a nipple, are among the most important concepts related to the long-term success of this type of urinary diversion. The problem of stomal stenosis has not been entirely eliminated by the use of a significantly dilated ureter. The comparison seen in this article to ileal conduits matched over a similar time reveals that the incidence of stomal stenosis is about the same. Nevertheless, several factors are considered important for the creation of a successful stoma. The selection of an optimal site on the abdominal wall is vital and should be determined before surgery. Particularly troublesome are obese patients, patients with abdominal scars, and those with neuromuscular and spinal cord problems such as spina bifida with severe kyphoscoliosis.

The optimal stoma site should be flat and scar free and lie a sufficient distance from skin creases to allow reasonable room for an average-sized appliance faceplate, usually about 4 in. in both directions. Preoperative evaluation of the patient in the supine, sitting, and standing positions, if possible, is necessary to see how the skin topography changes with position. This responsibility lies with the operating surgeon, since only he knows the full information that careful scrutiny of the patient's urograms, medical history, and body provides. If the type of diversion is in doubt, several sites should be located in order to permit optimal flexibility at surgery. After the appropriate stoma site is selected, a mark with an indelible pencil or a scratch on the skin surface will preserve the location until surgery.

Good techniques for stoma creation are described in this and other papers.[1-3] A full-thickness plug of abdominal wall slightly larger than the size of the ureter coming to the skin must be removed. This defect must be carefully inspected to be sure that a baffle effect of the muscular and fascial components of the abdominal wall is not created. A baffle may impede the emptying of the collecting system at the lowest possible pressure. Muscle should be excised, and no attempt should be made to try to bolster the ureter with a pseudosphincter of muscle. This will only increase the resistance to the outflow of urine from the collecting system. Stasis and residual urine is thereby encouraged, multiplying the difficulties inherent in keeping the upper tracts free of infection.

In suitable wide-caliber ureters, a nipple can be created with everting sutures if the ureteral wall is not too thick. The creation of a nipple is better for a stoma, since it gives the patient a better target for stoma appliance fitting and allows a tighter faceplate-to-skin bond formation. If a nipple cannot easily be formed or if the opening appears too tight after its formation, a skin-flap interposition is indicated. The need for such a maneuver should be anticipated before the stoma site is incised. A U-shaped pedicle flap is then created in the skin instead of the more common circle or button incision.[3] The skin flap is defatted and remains available for interposition into the wall of the spatulated and everted terminal ureter in order to create a nipple stoma about 2 cm long. The flap is merely excised if spatulation is not necessary. An anastomosis flat with the skin is less desirable because the appliance fit is more difficult as the target becomes more obscure and generally allows a shorter total wearing time before a leak occurs. This problem is compounded if the stoma actually becomes concave, seen especially with excessive weight gain.

Although we have found absorbable chromic catgut or polyglycolic acid (Dexon) sutures satisfactory for ureterocutaneous anastomosis, some advocate the use of temporary nonabsorbable sutures. In this case, fine monofilament nylon or prolene should give the least reaction.

Before mobilization of a ureter, careful inspection will reveal the source and direction of its blood supply. Sharp rather than blunt dissection well away from the ureteral adventitia is reconmmended, with careful ligation of all transected blood vessels in order to minimize excessive thrombosis of periureteral blood vessels and thus help preserve an optimal ureteral blood supply. The donor ureter of the transureteroureterostomy should be carefully inspected and positioned so that there is no twisting along its length, since torque in the face of active peristalsis can lead to anastomotic disruption. The donor ureter should lie in a lazy, tensionless path between the posterior peritoneum and the great vessels. Avoid sharp angulation with bowstringing of the ureter brought under the mesosigmoid and inferior mesenteric artery, since this can be a source of early as well as late ureteral obstruction. Make a retroperitoneal tunnel superior to this vessel if there is any suggestion of compromise. Similarly, the ureteroureteral and ureterocutaneous anastomosis should be carefully inspected and observed to be free of any degree of tension.

Other authors have recommended special techniques for ensuring adequate blood supply to the ureters such as including the gonadal vessels with the ureter at dissection and wrapping the ureter with omentum. With the proper choice of candidate these maneuvers are not only unnecessary but suggest that failure is preordained.

The ureterocutaneous anastomosis may be performed first, since the final lay of the recipient ureter will then allow for an optimal site to be chosen for anastomosis with the donor ureter. If the donor ureter is of normal caliber or only minimally dilated, spatulation with an angled Potts scissors will allow for a wider-caliber anastomosis. To proceed, clean the recipient ureter of its adventitia for about 2 cm on its medial aspect and hold it with fine stay sutures. Make an incision with a hooked no. 12 blade and extend it longitudinally with the Potts scissors at a site away from the major blood vessel. Make this incision slightly larger than the flattened diameter of the end of the donor ureter. Removal of a wedge of ureteral wall has never been necessary in our experience and seems inadvisable, since some degree of devascularization will occur. Use two continuous, running, interlocking, full-thickness 4–0 or 5–0 chromic catgut sutures to complete the anastomosis. Use separate sutures on the anterior and posterior walls to avoid a purse-string effect. Nonabsorbable sutures should be strictly avoided even as buttress sutures because of the risk of subsequent stone and fistula formation.

When both anastomoses are completed, inject sterile saline into the stoma to determine that there is no gross leak at the site of the ureteroureterostomy. The use of ureteral stents is optional, but certan clinical situations warrant their use. Stents are recommended if the patient is catabolic for any reason or when poor healing is anticipated. Renal insufficiency, malignancy, and previous full pelvic or abdominal radiation therapy are among the most common clinical situations where stenting may be useful.

At the point where the ureter enters the abdominal wall, carefully place several absorbable sutures to prevent parastomal hernia formation. The technique for preventing internal hernias is well described and illustrated in another article.[1] Briefly, this consists of suturing the lateral margin of the incision in the posterior peritoneum to the lateral margin of the defect in the anterior peritoneum that was made for the stoma. Use absorbable chromic sutures. After fixing the ureter to the skin, suture the medial posterior peritoneal margin to the medial anterior peritoneal margin. Simple closure of any remaining peritoneal defects and any *cul-de-sac* lateral to the ureter effectively retroperitonealizes the ureter and prevents internal bowel herniation lateral to the ureter. Consider placing a temporary Penrose drain retroperitoneally to drain any urine leakage from the ureteroureterostomy, since pooling of the urine around the anastomosis may lead to local retroperitoneal fibrosis and ureteral obstruction.

Abdominal wall closure with retention sutures is strongly advised in all patients with neuromuscular disease such as spina bifida or spinal cord injury and patients with catabolic diseases such as malignancies and chronic liver and renal disease.

Nasogastric suction is recommended in the immediate postoperative period until normal bowel activity returns. Abdominal distention can cause dire consequences, including disruption of either anastomosis.

STOMA PROBLEMS

Peristomal dermatitis can occasionally be troublesome, and several causes can be implicated. A simple scraping and microscopic examination of a potassium hydroxide preparation will enable most yeast infections to be diagnosed. Nystatin (Mycostatin) powder or neomyan sulfate (Mycolog) ointment will effectively resolve these problems.

Alkaline encrustations can become large if neglected for even short periods. Determining urine pH and obtaining an appropriate urine culture will usually identify the source of the problem. A urine pH of 7.5 or greater is nearly always caused by a urea-splitting organism. *Proteus mirabilis* is the most common offender and is effectively treated with ampicillin, in some cases for prolonged periods. With such a finding, obtain a plain x-ray film of the abdomen to rule out the occurrence of struvite stone formation. This is one of the most serious complications associated with urinary diversion, and regular monitoring of urine pH and culture several times a year is necessary for the early detection and irradication of such infections.

Urinary acidification has been recommended by some in order to prevent infections.[2] The value of such regimens as vitamin C, methenamine mandelate (Mandelamine), and methionine remains to be proved. They are contraindicated in the face of renal insufficiency, since this will only worsen the metabolic acidosis and hasten bone demineralization. With normal or near-normal renal function, an acid-ash diet, which basically involves restriction of fruits and vegetables, will maintain a urine pH of 6.5 or less. Drugs and dietary measures are ineffective if the pH is 7.5 or greater in the face of a urea-splitting organism, and only irradication of the infection will lower the pH of the urine into its normal acid range.

Hematuria can be due to multiple causes. The most common etiologies include stomatitis, trauma to the stoma by the faceplate, alkaline encrustations, chronic infection, and stone formation in the collecting system. Simple cauterization of recurrent stoma bleeding from minor trauma with silver nitrate sticks can at times be useful.

The help of an experienced enterostomal therapist (ET) can be invaluable, since stoma sizes change through shrinkage and maturation and the types of collecting devices available are always improving. No more than one 1/8 in of skin should be allowed between the faceplate and the stoma, since further skin exposure leads to pooling of infected urine and creates dermatitis problems.

Stoma revision is indicated if the orifice becomes stenotic, as determined by calibration or as evidenced by progressive increase in the amount of residual urine obtained from catheterization. Revision is sometimes indicated if the stoma becomes depressed or actually concave, making appliance application difficult if not impossible. Stoma revision for alkaline encrustations alone is seldom necessary, since most of these problems can be resolved by aggressive treatment of the infection and by soaking the stoma with 0.25% acetic acid. In the most severe cases, bedrest with the appliance removed and triamcinolone acetonide (Kenalog) ointment applications to the stoma covered by saline-soaked sponges will be useful, along with oral (PO) antibiotic treatment of the urinary infection.

The most worrrisome complication in the early postoperative course is devascularization and distal ureteral infarction. This should become apparent by the color of the stoma, and immediate conversion to a high pyelojejunal conduit should be accomplished.[5,6]

Routine mechanical dilation of the stoma is not generally necessary or recommended. Additional scarring and bleeding can be stimulated, and infection can be introduced as well. If significant stenosis has developed, dilation may delay but usually will not eliminate the need for revision. This may be useful, however, where life expectancy is short, as with progressing malignancy. Continuous intubation with one of the self-retaining ureteral stents may also be useful in this situation, since the urine can still be drained into an appliance bag.

RADIATION THERAPY

Patients who have progressive ureteral obstruction from pelvic malignancy may, in special instances, be candidates for supravesical urinary diversion. Even if the disease is under control or is otherwise treatable, decreased bladder capacity or urinary fistula formation from radiation therapy may preclude the successful use of internal ureteral stents. In the face of previous full-course pelvic radiation therapy, the ureteral blood supply may be significantly compromised despite chronic ureteral dilation. Although end cutaneous ureterostomy with transureteroureterostomy has been successfully used in this situation, this procedure should be approached with caution and reservation under these circumstances. Regional differences in the quality, dose, method of delivery, and type of radiation therapy given make blanket statements about the possibility of successful subsequent surgery virtually impossible.

A full mechanical and antibiotic bowel preparation should be performed beforehand if a colon segment is being considered. The patient should be fully advised of the limitations in this circumstance and of the possible need for alternative procedures. Appropriate preoperative preparation should be made so that a transverse colon conduit or high jejunal segment could be created depending on the operative findings. If the distal ureters appear poorly vascularized at the point necessary for tension-free anastomosis at either the ureter or skin level, then the alternative form of diversion should be pursued. If good judgment determines that the ureters appear free of the effects of radiation, the ureters should be appropriately stented for several weeks postoperatively, with the limitations of stenting already mentioned being observed.

OTHER PROCEDURES

Urinary Tract Infection. The urine should be monitored for infection by regular culture of catheterized specimens obtained from the stoma. Specimens obtained three times a year in most instances will be adequate if there is no intervening illness. Long-term antibacterial prophylaxis, if used, should be limited to antimicrobial agents such as nitrofurantoin, sulfa, or methenamine mandelate. Stronger antibiotics should be limited to short-term use during clinically overt infections. Infections with urea-splitting organisms should be treated and irradicated, since renal damage from subsequent struvite stone formation is a major cause of permanent renal functional deterioration.

Renal Function. Blood urea nitrogen (BUN) and creatinine levels should be obtained yearly and a creatinine clearance determined every year or two to detect any deterioration of renal function.

Radiography. A yearly kidney, ureter, and bladder (KUB) examination will determine if stone formation is developing, especially if the urine is alkaline. Contrast material can be injected through the stoma to obtain pyelograms every 2 to 3 yr if renal function is stable. Drainage films should be obtained to determine if significant stasis or obstruction is present. This also has the advantage of being able to be performed as an outpatient procedure in patients who are allergic to intravenously (IV) administered contrast material.

Undiversion. Four patients in our series were ultimately undiverted. This is usually done by tapering and reimplanting the end cutaneous ureter into the bladder in an antirefluxing fashion. Adequate bladder mobilization can be obtained with the aid of a psoas–muscle hitch or by using a Boari bladder flap.[4] Alternatively, in some patients a cecocystoplasty may be performed. The ileocecal valve can be reinforced to prevent reflux into the terminal ileum. A competent and functioning urinary sphincter mechanism is necessary, of course, and bladder emptying can be spontaneous, sometimes with the aid of phenoxybenzamine hydrochloride (dibenzyline) or diapezam (Valium) to reduce bladder outlet resistance. Intermittent catheterization can be used in those patients in whom the degree of bladder emptying is unacceptable. More skilled selection of patients for initial diversion obviously will reduce the number of potential candidates for later undiversion.

ANNOTATED REFERENCES

1. Straffon RA, Kyle K, Corvalan J: Techniques of cutaneous ureterostomy and results in 51 patients. J Urol 103:138, 1970

   This well-illustrated article discusses in great detail the technique of cutaneous ureterostomy with or without transureterostomy. The technique for retroperitonealizing the ureters is particularly well described and illustrated. Stoma care problems and their solution are discussed in depth.

2. Sweitzer SJ, Kelalis PP: Cutaneous transureteroureterostomy as a form of diversion in children with a compromised urinary tract. J Urol 120:589, 1978

   Nineteen patients were evaluated after this technique was used, and one fifth had no peristalsis preoperatively. Renal function was stable or improved in all patients, and radiographic appearance was stable or improved in all, including those with previously aperistaltic ureters.

3. Mahoney EM, Kearney GP, Prather SC: An improved non-intubated cutaneous ureterostomy technique for the normal and dilated ureter. J Urol 117:279, 1977

   Two types of pedicle skin flaps are discussed. A simple horseshoe-shaped pedicle of skin is raised for the dilated ureter, while a pigtail pedicle skin flap is advocated for the undilated ureter. A nipple protruding 1.5 cm to 2 cm can be created with these flaps. A 3-yr follow-up study of 4 normal and 3 dilated ureters showed no stomal stenosis. The horseshoe-shaped flap may be the procedure of choice for forming a successful stoma if the ureter will not evert easily by itself because of relatively small size or increased wall thickness.

4. Hendren WH: Complications of ureterostomy. J Urol 120:269, 1978

Techniques for undiverting suitable patients are well illustrated. They would apply well to the situation where a single ureter is temporarily brought to the skin to allow resolution of hypertrophy before reimplantation. Errors in initial patient selection are emphasised.

5. Sandoz IL, Paull DP, Macfarlane CA: Complications with Transureteroureterostomy. J Urol 117:39, 1977

Four of 23 patients undergoing transureteroureterostomy developed complications. Solutions included nephrectomy, stricture resection and reanastomosis, and ureteroplasty. Contraindications as well as important technical points of transureteroureterostomy are discussed.

6. Ehrlich RM, Skinner DG: Complications of transureteroureterostomy. J Urol 113:467, 1975

A series of five complications with damage to the recipient, the donor ureter, or both is discussed. Poor blood supply and anastomotic tension were usually implicated as causal factors. In seriously ill patients, especially those with cancer, the value of a nephrectomy in the face of an adequately functioning other kidney can be lifesaving. Errors in patient selection for this procedure are emphasized.

OVERVIEW: CUTANEOUS PYELOSTOMY VERSUS CUTANEOUS URETEROSTOMY

H. B. Eckstein

Cutaneous urinary diversion may be performed without tubes or intestinal conduits using the various available techniques of cutaneous pyelostomy or cutaneous ureterostomy. To be a feasible procedure, at least one side of the upper urinary tract must be grossly dilated, although in clinical practice these procedures are usually employed for severe bilateral dilatation of the ureters and renal pelves. These forms of supravesical diversion are more frequently indicated and performed in the pediatric age group than in adults, and these types of diversion may be intended to be either temporary or permanent. In adults, the most frequent indication for ureterostomy or pyelostomy is the elderly patient with advanced malignant pelvic disease that is obstructing both ureters. In this situation, cutaneous ureterostomy or cutaneous pyelostomy would prolong life, but it will require the patient to wear suitable appliances for the rest of his life. Since reconstruction of the urinary tract is not normally planned in this situation, the exact surgical technique and the siting of the stomas is relatively unimportant. In the pediatric age group, on the other hand, and in infancy in particular, cutaneous diversion is usually the first stage in a series of multiple operative procedures that are done to restore normality to the urinary tract. It is therefore vital that the original ostomy in no way interfere with subsequent reconstruction. Thus, for example, in the patient with refluxing megaureters, a ureteric reimplantation will usually be performed once renal status has improved sufficiently; in this situation, incorrect siting of the stoma would prove disastrous, since it

is technically very difficult to reimplant the terminal ureter once it has been exteriorized on the skin. In this situation, a high cutaneous ureterostomy or pyelostomy is preferable. Equally in the child with a neuropathic bladder and spinal abnormalities, the coexistent kyphoscoliosis must be taken into account in deciding on the site of the final stoma; whenever possible, this should be placed on the convex aspect of the abdominal wall, irrespective of the relative degree of dilatation of the two ureters. Before performing a cutaneous ureterostomy or pyelostomy, the surgeon, and indeed the members of the treatment team, must always consider the following alternative procedures.

Nephrostomy using either a single Malecot catheter or a continuous tube linked to a Y connector is a reasonable alternative form of high diversion. If it is likely that urinary drainage will be required for weeks or months only, then one form or another of nephrostomy is infinitely preferable, since it will not interfere with later surgery to the ureter. Nephrostomy does carry the disadvantage of in-dwelling tubes, the obvious potential complication of infection, and the eternal problem of tube displacement, but with the introduction of Silastic tubes or catheters, the indications for nephrostomy rather than cutaneous diversion have increased considerably, and it is certainly possible to discharge a patient from hospital with a nephrostomy tube *in situ*. One further advantage of nephrostomy is that once the urinary tract has been reconstructed, the nephrostomy will close spontaneously after the tubing is removed, while any form of cutaneous ostomy will require a formal and often difficult surgical procedure.

In children with bilateral megaureter and hydronephrosis (irrespective of cause), the question and possibility of a *primary reconstruction of the urinary tract without preliminary ostomies* must be considered seriously. With the enormous advances in pediatric nephrology and the successful introduction of peritoneal dialysis, it has been my experience that many patients who, 10 yr ago, would have been subjected to a cutaneous ureterostomy as a primary procedure can now be managed medically and improve sufficiently to be able to withstand the major procedure. There is no doubt that the indications for cutaneous ureterostomy or pyelostomy are far fewer today than they were some 10 yr ago, and the advantages and disadvantages of temporary high diversion must be judged in relation to primary reconstruction.

In those patients in whom the urinary diversion is intended to be permanent, it is critical that the patient have only a single stoma, and bilateral cutaneous ureterostomy or pyelostomy should be avoided as a permanent form of urinary diversion. If a single stoma cannot be produced by cutaneous ureterostomy (see below), then an ileal or colonic intestinal conduit must be seriously considered. Cutaneous ureterostomy as a form of permanent diversion has been successful, but I have seen numerous stoma complications from cutaneous ureterostomy if patients are followed for longer than 5 yr. Intestinal stomas appear more stable and less prone to stenosis than ureteric stomas, and revising a conduit stoma is easier and less hazardous than revising a ureterostomy. The disadvantages and problems of intestinal conduits are discussed elsewhere in this volume but these conduits should nevertheless be seriously considered as alternatives if any form of permanent urinary diversion is indicated.

Finally, in patients with a unilateral pathologic condition, it is important to realize that nephroureterectomy may be preferable to temporary diversion and later reconstruction. The advances in recent years in radioisotope scanning techniques of the urinary tract have made it possible to assess accurately the relative function of the two kidneys. If the affected kidney is producing less than 20% of the total urinary output and function, I would now avoid unilateral diversion and choose nephroureterectomy. This situation has tended to leave a scarred and contracted kidney that contributes little to the total clearance of urea and creatinine and may in fact be a permanent source of infection and, in later years, lead to renal hypertension. Obviously nephroureterectomy should never be performed unless the state and function of the contralateral kidney are thoroughly investigated beforehand.

Cutaneous pyelostomy is well described by Dr. Immergut, and I have little to add to the operative technique. Inevitably the patient will be left with two stomas, which may be acceptable in the short term, but in my opinion this operation is much more difficult to perform than a cutaneous ureterostomy, and the final definitive closure of a pyelostomy may damage the blood supply of the kidney. On the other hand, cutaneous pyelostomy offers excellent free drainage of urine and leaves the entire length of the ureter undisturbed for later surgery and reconstruction.

There are a number of different ways in which to perform cutaneous ureterostomy. *Terminal bilateral ureterostomy* is technically simple and eminently suitable for the sick uremic patient. The terminal ureter is divided, mobilized, and exteriorized. The first disadvantage of this procedure is that two separate appliances must be fitted; second, urinary drainage is not all that effective, since the peristaltic activity of the grossly dilated ureter is not very efficient. In my opinion, bilateral terminal ureterostomy is only justifiable in patients with terminal disease who require supravesical diversion.

If both ureters are grossly dilated and tortuous, then extensive mobilization (which should and could be extraperitoneal) will allow one ureter to be brought across extraperitoneally so that both ureters can be sutured together to form a communal stoma. But again, the long dilated ureter is relatively ineffective in draining urine, and a high conduit–type diversion may be a preferable alternative. However, a number of my patients with neuropathic bladder and bilateral megaureter have been treated by *double-barrel ureterostomy* successfully.

If a double-barrel ureterostomy is not possible, then a *terminal ureterostomy* of the more dilated ureter, combined with an anastomosis between the two ureters, is a reasonable alternative and has worked well in a number of my patients. Stricture at the interureteric anastomosis has not been a problem, and the procedure is certainly preferable to an ostomy with two stomas. It is essential to incorporate skin flaps into the stoma of a single ureterostomy to avoid anular scar contracture at the suture line of ureter to skin.

If the urinary diversion is intended to be temporary and if the ureter is grossly dilated and tortuous, it can be mobilized in the loin and exteriorized onto the skin by a *loop or ring ureterostomy*. This type of ureterostomy inevitably requires two stomas but, being situated high up on the ureter, will provide good urinary drainage. On the other hand, it will make the bladder totally nonfunctional if performed bilaterally, and subsequent bladder reconstruction can be difficult in this situation. Also, it is technically difficult and hazardous to close a loop ureterostomy; strictures at the ureterostomy site after closure are not unusual. The modification of this technique by Williams and Crombie using a ring ureterostomy has many advantages.[1] The two limbs of the exteriorized ureter are anastomosed together side to side while the apex of the loop is exteriorized on to the skin so that the bladder is not made totally nonfunctional. The secondary closure of the ring ureterostomy is simple and safe, since the previously fashioned interureteric anastomosis need not be disturbed. The technique is well described and illustrated by Hohenfellner.[2]

The technique of *chimney ureterostomy* using the proximal ureter as a cutaneous stoma was originally described by Sober and is well described in this volume by Sadlowski and Belman (see Chap. 45).[3] The alternative technique of using the distal catheter as the cutaneous stoma has been described.[4] Both types of chimney ureterostomy provide good free drainage of urine and allow for some urine to enter the bladder so as to avoid making the organ nonfunctional, and both types of chimney ureterostomy are easy to close with minimal risk to the blood supply of the kidney or ureter.

Both the loop and the chimney type of cutaneous ureterostomy are useful and simple techniques to provide high cutaneous urinary diversion on a temporary basis. Both allow for subsequent surgery on the distal ureter without previous scar formation, and both are easy to close. In my opinion, these techniques are preferable to cutaneous pyelostomy, which may, however, have a place in the child with a grossly dilated renal pelvis in whom the ureters are not as dilated. Permanent terminal cutaneous ureterostomy is occasionally indicated but must be judged in relation to conduit diversion on the one hand or to primary reconstruction on the other.

REFERENCES

1. Williams DI, Crombie WJ: Ring ureterostomy. Br J Urol 47:789, 1976
2. Hohenfellner R: Temporary supravesical urinary diversion. In Eckstein HB, Hohenfellner R, Williams DI (eds): Surgical Pediatric Urology, p 120. Stuttgart, Georg Thieme Verlag, 1977

3. Sober I: Pelviureterostomy-en-Y. J Urol 107:473, 1972
4. Eckstein HB: Temporary supravesical urinary diversion. In Eckstein HB, Hohenfellner R, Williams DI (eds): Surgical pediatric Urology, p 123. Stuttgart, Georg Thieme Verlag, 1977

46

URETEROSTOMY *IN SITU*[1]

Anthony Walsh, F.R.C.S.I.

Department of Urology, Jervis Street Hospital, Dublin

British Journal of Urology
Vol. 39 (6), Dec. 1967

Despite its disadvantages, nephrostomy has been the accepted method of draining the upper urinary tract for almost a century. The purpose of this communication is to suggest that ureterostomy *in situ* is often a more satisfactory procedure. By ureterostomy *in situ* is meant the open insertion into the ureter of a catheter which is passed up to the renal pelvis. The name is perhaps a little cumbersome, but it serves to distinguish the procedure from other types of ureterostomy, *e.g.* cutaneous.

There is astonishingly little reference in the literature to this simple operation. In a search through many urological textbooks the only relevant passage appears to be that in Campbell's *Urology* (1954). He mentions the operation briefly and suggests that it might be useful but "not for long as the tube may become incrusted and once removed it cannot be replaced" although, as will be seen later, there is no problem when plastic catheters are used.

My attention was first drawn to ureterostomy *in situ* at the 1956 meeting of the British Association of Urological Surgeons. In the discussion on the use of the intestine in urology, Wilfrid Adams advocated ureterostomy *in situ* as an easy and effective procedure.

Technique. The operative technique is very simple. Through a small gridiron incision in the iliac fossa the peritoneum is exposed but not opened. The peritoneum is pushed medially by a large swab which is then held in place by a self-retaining retractor. This manoeuvre is the key to easy exposure of the ureter.

It is best to lead the catheter through a separate stab incision below the medial end of the wound, so that it runs to the ureter in a gentle curve. The ureter is then opened and the catheter passed up to the renal pelvis. The catheter is immediately attached to the skin by a silk stitch so that it does not become dislodged while the wound is being closed.

Catheter. In the usual case where the ureter is dilated, I use the 18F, whistle-tip, sliding-flange modification of the Gibbon catheter (Walsh, 1960). Where the ureter is not dilated I use an ordinary Gibbon catheter of suitable size which is cut to a convenient length so that the tip lies in the renal pelvis when the flange is attached to the skin.

Other catheters may be used, but I think it is important that they should be made of polyvinyl chloride (P.V.C.) to minimise the risk of inflammatory reaction in the ureter through chemical irritation or allergy and also to provide the largest lumen in relation to the external diameter of the catheter.

Yeates has recently (1967) advocated ureterostomy *in situ* in the emergency treatment of a damaged ureter. He favours a T-tube, but I think it is better to use a simple catheter which runs, as described above, in a gentle curve from the skin to the ureter. I prefer this to the T-tube because it is extremely easy to change the

[1] Read at the Twenty-third Annual Meeting of the British Association of Urological Surgeons in London, June 1967.

catheter, and in a large number of personal cases since 1959 I have never regretted not using a T-tube. If the first catheter is left in for two or three weeks, the track becomes well established and the catheter can easily be changed by a nurse. The correct length of the new catheter is determined by comparison with the old one.

When eventually the source of the ureteric obstruction is removed, the catheter is simply withdrawn: provided that no obstruction remains, there is seldom any leakage of urine from the catheter track.

Comparison with Nephrostomy. The advantages of this operation compared with nephrostomy are as follows: Firstly, it is a very simple, easy, and quick procedure which involves little muscle trauma: this may be very important in patients with renal failure in whom muscle trauma and bleeding add a considerable metabolic load to a struggling kidney. Although it is occasionally possible to perform nephrostomy by a stab or trocar method, full exposure of the kidney is often necessary, with accompanying renal damage and bleeding. Secondly, infection seems to be unavoidable with nephrostomy, but is seldom a problem with ureterostomy *in situ*. Thirdly, it is often difficult to change a nephrostomy tube—a problem partly overcome by Tresidder's (1957) ingenious manoeuvre, but this is somewhat complicated. Finally, the ureterostomy catheter emerges at a site which is much more comfortable for the patient than the usual nephrostomy tube.

Indications. The primary indication for this operation is the urgent relief of obstruction in the lower ureter and in this connection it is particularly valuable in the treatment of acute pyonephrosis. It is astonishing how often in cases where the kidney seems merely a bag of pus, the fluid draining from the ureterostomy becomes clear in a matter of days and, as described elsewhere (Walsh, 1964), there is often considerable recovery of function.

I have frequently used ureterostomy *in situ* as a safety device after operations such as pyeloplasty. In most cases, using the Anderson-Hynes operation, no form of drainage is necessary, but it occasionally happens that one is not entirely happy about the immediate result of a pyeloplasty and then, especially when operating on a solitary kidney, it is a simple matter to pass a Gibbon catheter into the ureter below the operation site and up through the anastomosis into the renal pelvis: this gives a great sense of security in doubtful cases. In excising difficult strictures of the ureter it may be helpful to start by performing ureterostomy *in situ* and then completing the anastomosis over the catheter. This is often unnecessary but may be very valuable in some cases, particularly as in a recent personal case of a very difficult stricture in a ureter draining a solitary and heavily infected kidney.

Complications. Only one complication has been encountered in over 150 cases. Bilateral ureterostomy *in situ* was carried out in a young woman with a severe post-irradiation vesico-vaginal fistula and was maintained for some months until repair of the fistula was completed. She subsequently developed a mild stricture of the upper 1 cm of the ureter on both sides, and I have little doubt that this was due to using catheters which were too large.

Ureterostomy *in situ* may be maintained for many months. The longest period in my own series was nine months in a man whose right kidney had been destroyed by tuberculosis and who had a tiny contracted bladder with a large tuberculous prostatic abscess and an impassable stricture of the lower 10 cm of the left ureter. He subsequently had a colocystoplasty.

Conclusion. Ureterostomy *in situ* is very simple and easy to manage and in many cases is preferable to nephrostomy for drainage of an obstructed kidney.

REFERENCES

ADAMS, A. W. (1956). Br J Urol, 28, 414
CAMPBELL, M. (1954). "Urology", Philadelphia: Saunders Vol III, p 1853
TRESIDDER, G. C. (1957). Br J Urol, 29, 130

WALSH, A. (1960). Lancet, 1, 708
——— (1965). XIII Congr Int Soc Urol, London 1964, Vol II, p 243. Edinburgh: Livingstone
YEATES, W. K. (1967). Lancet, 1, 499

Commentary: Revival of Ureterostomy *In Situ*

Anthony Walsh

Ureterostomy *in situ* is an interesting example of an operation that was excellently conceived but fell into disuse because suitable materials were not available. The operation was well known in Europe at the beginning of the century but the only material available for intubating the ureter was red rubber. As is now very well known, many people are allergic to red rubber, and even where there is no allergy rubber causes quite an intense tissue reaction. Rubber tubes draining urine became encrusted with stone, and tissue reaction to the rubber produced a severe ureteritis and often a stricture. The development of modern, biologically inert, plastic materials—in particular, polyvinylchloride (PVC)—made it possible to revive this simple and elegant procedure for the relief of obstruction in the upper urinary tract.

Even when the obstruction is in the upper ureter or at the pelvi-ureteric junction, it is nearly always possible to pass a tube up the ureter and into the pelvis. I have found only three circumstances in which this is not possible:

- Where a large stone is tightly impacted in the pelvi-ureteric junction
- Where there is dense, tuberculous stricture in the upper ureter
- Where there is extensive, infiltrating carcinoma obstructing the upper ureter.

ALTERNATIVE PROCEDURES

Nephrostomy has been the classic method of upper urinary tract diversion for the best part of a century. If the kidney is very large and easily palpable, it is a simple matter to insert a large needle or trocar into the very distended renal pelvis and then to place a PVC tube through the needle or trocar to achieve kidney drainage. In such cases, trocar nephrostomy is an excellent method of temporary upper urinary tract diversion. In most cases, however, the performance of nephrostomy (or pyelostomy) requires full exposure of the kidney, major surgery in an already sick patient. Such major surgery is rarely necessary. Since I began using ureterostomy *in situ* in 1956, I have performed this operation more than 300 times. In the same period I have found it necessary to do nephrostomy (because ureterostomy *in situ* was impossible) on only seven occasions.

In many patients with acute pyonephrosis it is possible to pass a catheter endoscopically, and, if so, this is the procedure of choice. If at all possible, nephrostomy should be avoided in acute pyonephrosis because it tends to compromise subse-

quent renal surgery. The patient with pyonephrosis is usually acutely ill, and the simplest possible procedure that will provide drainage is the best one. In such cases, it is my practice to pass a 6 French catheter endoscopically. If the catheter enters the renal pelvis (and it nearly always will), it is held in place by lashing it to a Foley catheter placed in the bladder. Ordinary ureteral catheters are rather stiff, and it is undesirable to leave them in the ureter for more than a few days for fear of producing pressure sores in the ureter. Hence, a decision must be made within a week. If the patient is then fit for definitive surgery to relieve the obstruction, well and good. If more prolonged drainage is indicated, the ureteral catheter should be replaced by a ureterostomy *in situ*. In such patients it is convenient to leave the ureteral catheter in place to aid in identification while the ureter is being exposed.

CHOICE OF TUBE

In the preceding article I described the use of Gibbon catheters (not to be confused with the Gibbons stent). Gibbon catheters and their variants are no longer available, and I now use PVC infant feeding tubes, or sometimes a small Foley catheter. If a Foley catheter is used it is important to be certain that it is well into the renal pelvis before the bag is distended, and only 2 ml or 3 ml of water should be placed in the bag. The entry of the catheter into the renal pelvis can be verified radiologically, but in practice it is much simpler to rely on the swing test. When the material of the catheter is translucent, the column of urine in it can be seen to swing freely with respiration or in response to pressure over the kidney when the catheter has entered the renal pelvis. If the catheter is not in the renal pelvis, there is no free swing of the urine column. Much more important than the type is the *size* of the catheter. In performing ureterostomy *in situ,* it is very tempting, when a very dilated ureter is exposed, to think that a large catheter should be used. Indeed, in the 1967 article I described the use of an 18 French catheter. I now know that this is a serious mistake. Although the ureter and the renal pelvis may be greatly dilated, the pelvi-ureteric junction does not dilate to anything near the same extent. A large catheter may pass easily into the renal pelvis and yet be too snug in the pelvi-ureteric junction, and in two patients I produced secondary stricture at this point by using too large a catheter. It is not, in fact, necessary to use a tube bigger than 10 French or, at the most, 12 French. Even in patients with very dilated ureters there will be no leak around the catheter unless the catheter is blocked.

CHANGING THE CATHETER

Apart from reviving interest in a forgotten but valuable operation, perhaps the most important contribution of the 1967 article was the demonstration that it should be a simple matter to change the catheter. It is essential that the catheter is brought through a stab wound in the anterior abdominal wall, as low down as possible, so that it runs in a gentle curve to meet the ureter. The catheter should be lying virtually parallel with the ureter at its point of entry into the ureter.

To proceed, make a longitudinal incision in the ureter. This incision should be at least twice the diameter of the catheter, and when the catheter is in place the ureteral incision should not be sutured around it. There is no need to provide additional wound drainage. Leave the catheter in place for 2 or 3 wk before the first change and thereafter change it every 2 wk for as long as necessary to maintain the diversion. When the patient is ambulant, attach the catheter to a standard drainage bag fixed to the thigh.

COMPLICATIONS

The operation has proved delightfully trouble free. Even where the diversion has been maintained for many months, there have been no problems with infection—problems that are such a notorious bugbear with prolonged nephrostomy drainage. Apart from the two patients with secondary stricture at the pelvoureteric junction already mentioned, the only serious complication was in one patient in whom I made the stab wound for entry of the catheter too low and damaged the external iliac artery. Fortunately, the damage was repaired and there were no untoward consequences, either medical or legal. It is obviously important not to pass the catheter through the peritoneal cavity. This is a complication that I have never encountered, but it could occur, with the risk of bowel damage, unless care is taken to sweep the peritoneum away before passing a curved hemostat down through the incision to the point of entry of the catheter.

PERMANENT DIVERSION

I have rarely used this operation as a method of permanent diversion and then only as a palliative procedure in terminal cancer patients distressed by very severe frequency, dysuria, and strangury. If the operation is used for this purpose, the ureters should be ligatured below the point of entry of the catheters so that no urine will bypass the catheters and enter the bladder.

ANNOTATED BIBLIOGRAPHY

Engberg A, Palmlöv A: Ureterostomy in situ. Scand J Urol Nephrol 1:63, 1967

Among other points, this article discusses the use of T-tubes. The authors refer to the fact that in two of 12 patients in whom T-tubes were used, the ureteral peristalsis forced down the proximal arm and obstruction resulted. There is no indication to use T-tubes, but there are two objections. First, the tube cannot be changed; second, it does not reach into the renal pelvis.

Pokorny M, Pontes JE, Pierce JM Jr: Ureterostomy in situ: Technique for temporary urinary diversion. Urology 8:447, 1976

This article is of particular interest because it is the only significant contribution to the subject in recent American literature.

Syme RR: Ureterostomy in situ. Aust NZ J Surg 45:69, 1975

This article reinforces all the points made in the Commentary.

Overview: Ureterostomy *In Situ:* Useful and Quick

Elliot Leiter

Although my experience with ureterostomy *in situ* has been nowhere near as extensive as the more than 300 cases performed by Mr. Walsh, it has been equally satisfactory. I have used procedure primarily in those patients with low ureteral obstruction secondary to neoplasms such as carcinoma of the bladder or prostate. When the bladder and trigone are so distorted as to make ureteral catherization impossible, unilateral or bilateral cutaneous ureterostomies *in situ* can be simple lifesaving procedures that can even be done under local anesthesia in these poor-risk patients.

With recent technical radiologic and sonographic advances that make percutaneous nephrostomy somewhat more simple and reliable, my guess is that there will be fewer instances in which cutaneous ureterostomy *in situ* will be performed. It would still be an appropriate procedure, though, for those patients in whom the contemplated period of drainage will not be prolonged and in whom nephrostomy is not appropriate. As such, it should be a part of every urologist's armamentarium.

Although alluded to by Mr. Walsh, it is most important for the urologist to be certain, if possible, that there is no gross carcinomatous infiltration near the ureter where it will be intubated at the level of the iliac vessels. This may, of course, be impossible to determine preoperatively and has been a minor problem in the one or two patients of mine in whom it occurred.

One technical maneuver that I feel is quite important and that Mr. Walsh did not mention is the use of the Seldinger wire technique for replacing the catheters. This is easily done when a whistle-tip open-end catheter such as a polyethylene feeding tube is used for intubation. However, if the urologist anticipates catheter replacement, he may make the Seldinger wire placement technique equally feasible with a Foley catheter by simply cutting off the tip of the catheter before inserting it into the ureterostomy. I also heartily agree with Dr. Walsh that there is no need to use a catheter larger than 10 French.

The use of intubated ureterostomy *in situ* has been especially gratifying in those men who come in anuric with bilateral ureteral obstruction from carcinoma of the prostate and who have not received any hormonal treatment. Orchidectomy can be done at the same time as the ureteral obstruction is relieved. All this can be accomplished in no more than 30 to 40 min, less time than it would take to do a single nephrostomy. If the prostatic carcinoma responds to orchidectomy, the patient will often begin to drain urine around the ureterostomies into the bladder. At this time the ureterostomies can be removed.

In sum, then, I fully agree with Mr. Walsh's assessment of intubated ureterostomy *in situ*. It is an *extraordinarily* useful, simple, and quick procedure for relieving unilateral or bilateral ureteral obstruction. It has received surprisingly little attention in the urologic literature, but the results in appropriate patients can be most gratifying. Despite most urologists' expectations, replacement of the catheters is virtually foolproof, especially when the guide-wire Seldinger technique is used for such replacement.

47

TRANSURETEROURETEROSTOMY: 25-YEAR EXPERIENCE WITH 100 PATIENTS

Clarence V. Hodges,* John M. Barry, Eugene F. Fuchs, Harper D. Pearse and Edward S. Tank

From the Division of Urology, University of Oregon Health Sciences Center, Portland, Oregon

0022-5347 / 80 / 1236-0834$02.00/0
The Journal of Urology
Copyright © 1980 by The Williams & Wilkins Co.
Vol. 123, June
Printed in U.S.A.

ABSTRACT—During the last 25 years 100 patients have been subjected to transureteroureterostomy. In 2 cases postoperative death was attributable to other pathologic processes. We treated 94 donor units successfully in this manner. An additional 2 units, normal for several years after transureteroureterostomy, had periureteral fibrosis and stricture owing to the inferior mesenteric artery syndrome and required another definitive surgical procedure. Ninety-seven recipient kidneys remained normal after the procedure.

The urological surgeon frequently is faced with a compromised lower ureter. Various procedures are available to divert the urine successfully and to maintain the integrity of the urinary system. None of these procedures is optimal for all cases, since the solution will depend on the causative lesion, the presence or absence of portions of the urinary tract, the condition of the bladder and ureters, the amount of inflammation and sepsis in the perivesical and retroperitoneal area and the breadth and depth of the surgeon's experience. We have used transureteroureterostomy as a method of urinary diversion in 100 patients during the last 25 years.

The majority of these operative procedures were

Accepted for publication July 27, 1979.
Read at annual meeting of American Urological Association, New York, New York, May 13–17, 1979
* Current address: 1380 Lusitana St., #1008, Honolulu, Hawaii 96813.

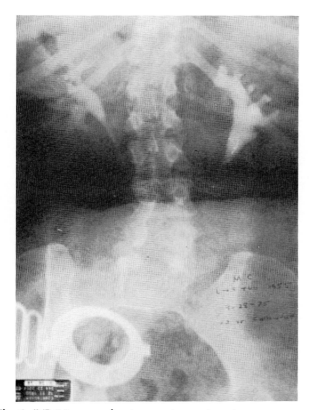

Fig. 1. IVP 24 years after transureteroureterostomy.

TABLE 1. Indications for Transureteroureterostomy in 100 Patients

	No. Pts.
Ureteral strictures:	
After ureteroneocystostomy	22
After radiation therapy	8
Idiopathic	3
After transurethral resection of the prostate	1
After transurethral resection of ureterocele	2
Secondary to periureteral lesion	2
Secondary to pelvic inflammatory disease	1
Ureteral injury during open operation	18
Resection of malignancy involving lower ureter	15
Unilat. reflux	5
Congenital megaloureter	3
Solitary kidney with normal contralateral ureter	3
Reflux after transurethral resection of bladder tumor	2
Ureteral obstruction by aortoiliac graft	1
Ectopic dilated single ureter	1
Bilat. obstruction by bladder lesion (transureteroureterostomy and terminal cut ureterostomy)	13
Total	100

TABLE 2. Complications of Transureteroureterostomy in 100 Patients

	No. Cases
Postop. acute pyelonephritis	5
Prolonged urinary drainage (5 wks)	2
Prolonged postop. ileus	1
Recurrence of pelvic inflammatory disease	1
Oliguria 2 days postop.	1
Tumor blockage at anastomosis	3
Inferior mesenteric artery syndrome	2
Disruption of anastomosis leading to nephrectomy	1
Subsequent reflux of normal ureter	2
Persisting pyelonephritis leading to nephrectomy	2
Stomal stenosis at skin level in transureteroureterostomy with terminal cutaneous ureterostomy	3
Total	23

done by resident physicians under the guidance of the attending staff. The procedure is not difficult but the surgeon must be aware of the contraindications to its use and be thoroughly familiar with the technique before attempting it. We believe strongly that actual experience at the operating table with this method of diversion should be a part of every training program.

MATERIALS AND METHODS

There have been 100 patients who have undergone transureteroureterostomy for ureteral diversion in the last 25 years at our health sciences center or in the practices of staff urologists in the immediate environs. The ages of the patients ranged from 1 to 83 years. All of the patients have been followed for at least 1 year postoperatively, the longest followup being 23 years (Fig. 1). Indications for the procedure are shown in Table 1.

The operative technique has been described by us previously and has not been altered significantly.[1,2] The usual requirements are a normal donor kidney and upper ureter on one side and a normal recipient kidney and ureter (Fig. 2A). In 3 cases the normal kidney and normal ureter were on opposite sides (Fig. 2B). The bladder and infravesical structures must be normal or the terminal end of the recipient ureter must end in an exteriorized bowel segment or cutaneous ureterostomy.

RESULTS

Two patients died within the 30-day postoperative period, 1 of a myocardial infarction and the other of mycotic sepsis.

Complications occurred in 23 patients (Table 2). Many of these complications, particularly infection, tumor and subsequent reflux up the recipient ureter, were sequelae of the preoperative condition. All of the recipient ureters remined normal except in 3 cases in which the tumor was carried along with the end of the abnormal ureter to the anastomotic site, where its subsequent growth blocked both ureters. We have not encountered

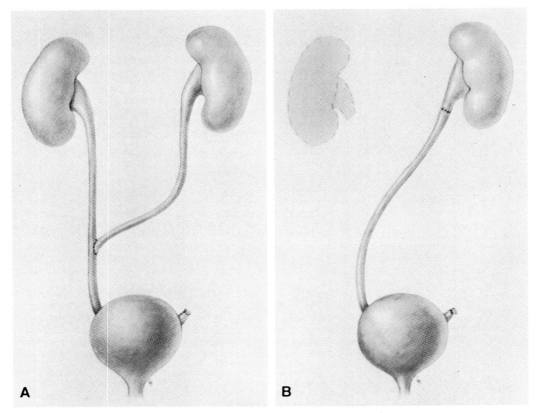

Fig. 2. (*A*) Conventional transureteroureterostomy. (*B*) Transureteropyelostomy or upper ureterostomy. Reprinted with permission.

this complication in such cases since we have started to obtain frozen sections on the cut end of the proximal abnormal ureter before anastomosis.

Two patients had severe pyelonephritis preoperatively and this was not amenable to control by the procedure plus ancillary medical care; nephrectomy of the donor kidney was the ultimate result. None of the recipient kidneys in these patients has become infected as a result of the operative procedure.

A new complication entity has been discovered and not described in previous reports. In 2 patients the donor ureter was brought across the midline with apparently insufficient length to reach the other ureter without the abnormal ureter impinging in the cleft between the aorta and the inferior mesenteric artery. Each of these cases resulted in fibrotic stricturing of the donor ureter where it lay in the V between the 2 arteries (Fig. 3). One of these complications became apparent 7 years after right-to-left transureteroureterostomy for ureteral stricture after open surgical ureterolithotomy. The resulting hydronephrosis was discovered after right costovertebral angle

pain and hematuria developed (Fig. 4A). On exploration the ureter was found to be embedded firmly in a mass of fibrotic tissue at the site of crossing the aorta. The distal donor ureter was of normal size and the anastomosis was not involved. The problem was solved surgically by mobilizing the right kidney and shifting it downward as far as possible. The ureter then was anastomosed to a Boari bladder flap accompanied by a psoas hitch (Fig. 4B).

The second case of mesenteric artery syndrome arose in a 3-year-old boy 11 years after he was seen in 1964 with reflux up 2 markedly dilated ureters, 1 of a duplicated system on the left side and a single ureter on the right side. The left system was treated by ureteroureterostomy and the right ureter was reimplanted (not successfully) into the bladder. In 1966 the right ureter was carried across the midline to be implanted into the left common ureter. The patient showed fairly marked improvement for 9 years until 1975 when, on determining the source of urinary tract infection, it was found that he had marked hydronephrosis on the right side with

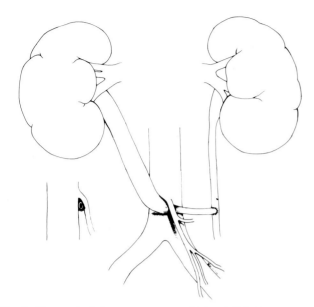

Fig. 3. Concept of donor ureter caught in cleft between aorta and inferior mesenteric artery.

hydroureter down to the point where the ureter crossed the midline. On exploration the ureter was found embedded in scar tissue in the cleft of the aorta and inferior mesenteric artery. The redundancy and tortuosity of the right proximal ureter allowed it to be mobilized out of its scar tissue bed after which ureterotomy and a modified Whitaker test[3] showed that urine traveled readily down the previously obstructed segment. The patient has been clinically well since that time and has not returned to our clinic for followup. However, an excretory urogram (IVP) in February 1978 showed a hydronephrotic right kidney with a markedly dilated ureter that terminates at the pelvic brim; there is prompt function (Fig. 5). The double collecting system on the left side shows the effects of pyelonephritis in the lower system. The upper system shows sharp calices but an incidental caliceal diverticulum.

The donor unit was lost in 6 patients: 3 to tumor, 2 to persisting infection and 1 to disruption of the anastomosis. Two other donor units were at risk owing to hydronephrosis resulting from the inferior mesenteric artery syndrome: 1 was rescued by renal mobilization and Boari tube flap reimplantation and 1 patient under-

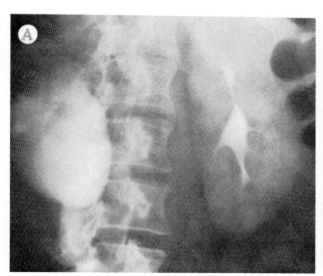

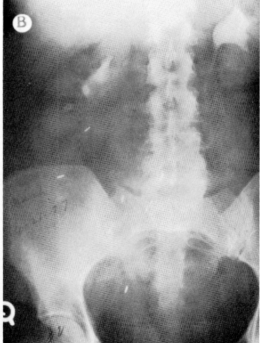

Fig. 4. (*A*) IVP shows right hydronephrosis and hydroureter owing to inferior mesenteric artery compression of donor ureter. (*B*) IVP reveals resolution of right hydronephrosis and hydroureter after Boari flap procedure with psoas hitch.

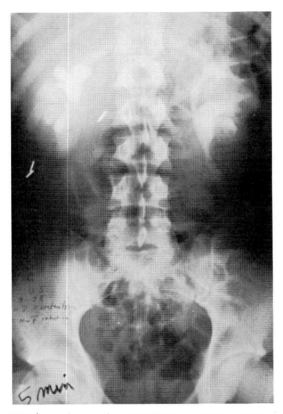

Fig. 5. IVP shows incomplete resolution of right hydronephrosis and hydroureter 3 years after ureterolysis for inferior mesenteric artery compression.

went ureterolysis and has recovered good function but still shows marked hydronephrosis. Thus, 92 percent of the donor units showed satisfactory results after transureteroureterostomy.

Three recipient units were lost to tumor blockade; 97 percent of the recipient units were normal after the procedure. In 2 instances vesicoureteral reflux occurred postoperatively, adversely affecting the entire system and requiring reimplantation in 1 case and cutaneous ureterostomy in another. The latter patient ultimately was undiverted satisfactorily. Neither complication is considered to reflect on the intrinsic merits of transureteroureterostomy.

DISCUSSION

The complication of inferior mesenteric artery syndrome can be prevented by bringing the donor ureter across cephalad to the V between the inferior mesenteric artery and the aorta. If this is difficult to accomplish one might consider sacrificing the inferior mesenteric artery, as is done routinely in bilateral periaortic node dissection for testicular tumor.

This updated series includes a third case in which the normal left kidney with a short upper ureter was saved by diversion to the opposite normal ureter. The right kidney was a non-functioning hydronephrotic mass. The greatly dilated left ureter terminated in a pelvic abscess with a cutaneous fistula (Fig. 6A). The right kidney and the distal left ureter were removed. The upper left ureter, measuring 7 to 8 cm long, was brought across the midline to meet the upper end of the distal right ureter in an end-to-end anastomosis. The postoperative result was excellent (Fig. 6B). Experience and confidence in transureteroureterostomy make this kind of surgical improvisation possible.

Disparity in size between the donor and recipient ureters is not usually a significant consideration. A large donor ureter need not be spatulated before an anastomosis. Small recipient ureters will still accept large donor ureters since the vertical incision in the recipient ureter can be made to any length. In 2 of our patients donor ureters were anastomosed to 1 of 2 completely duplicated, small caliber ureters without change in the proximal ureter or collecting system in either case (Fig. 7).

The disposition of the terminal ureter may introduce problems not associated with the transureteroureterostomy operation itself. Two patients had reflux up the recipient ureter, requiring reimplantation in 1 case and diversion in the other. Of 15 patients in whom transureteroureterostomy was accomplished by terminal cutaneous ureterostomy 3 had stenosis of the cutaneous ureteral stoma that required surgical revision. This method of diversion is attractive in the elderly or poor risk patient requiring cystectomy in that urinary diversion can be done simply and quickly, lessening the operative risk and leaving a stoma that usually is easier to manage than the stoma of an intestinal segment. If one of the ureters is dilated it is preferable to use this as the recipient ureter since dilated ureters usually produce satisfactory stomas.

Complications of transureteroureterostomy have been reported by Ehrlich and Skinner in 5 cases, in 4 of which the recipient unit was damaged, requiring ileal substitution in 2 instances and resulting in hydronephrosis in 1 and ureteral stricture in 1.[4] Sandoz and associates have reported on 4 of 23 patients undergoing transureteroureterostomy who sustained injury to the recipient ureter.[5] These investigators have enumerated 6 requirements for a successful transureteroureterostomy, with which we are in substantial agreement although we have not been reluctant to mobilize the recipient ureter if it was necessary to secure an anastomosis without tension. Sepsis, inadequate blood supply, anastomosis under tension and inadequate provision for urinary drainage

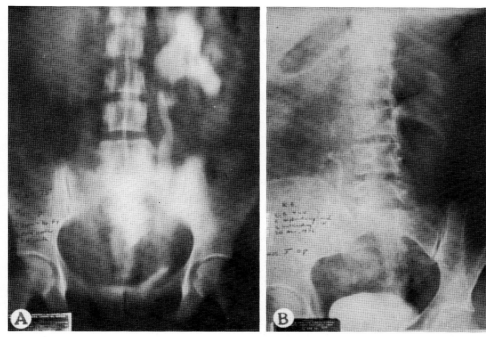

Fig. 6. (A) IVP shows non-functioning right kidney and left hydronephrosis and hydroureter owing to pelvic abscess and cutaneous fistula. (B) IVP 8 months after right nephrectomy, left lower ureterectomy and transureteroureterostomy.

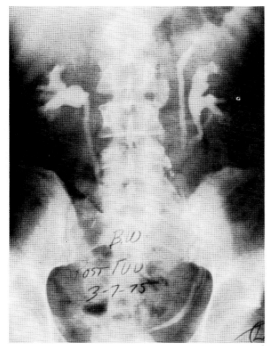

Fig. 7. IVP 5 months after transureteroureterostomy shows right ureter to upper left ureter.

from the anastomotic site during the early postoperative period remain, in our minds, the major causes of complication and failure in the 9 cases reported previously. Although each of these investigators has stressed that they continue to regard transureteroureterostomy as a valuable part of the urologist's armamentarium, this conclusion has been lost sight of in a subjective apprehension regarding the procedure.[6] We were appalled recently to hear that an experienced urologist had removed a good kidney rather than contemplate saving it by transureteroureterostomy since he regarded this procedure too risky. Good results from transureteroureterostomy have been reported in >400 cases.[7-25]

There is no one operation that will satisfactorily provide the remedy for all ureteral problems. Due consideration must be given to ureteroneocystostomy with or without a Boari flap and psoas hitch, replacement of the ureter with intestine, autotransplantation of the kidney or nephrectomy. In our experience transureteroureterostomy has continued to maintain requisites of simplicity, freedom from the undesirable features of bowel substitution, lack of injury to the bladder innervation and excellent results for both kidneys in 92 percent of the cases. The recipient kidney and ureter remained normal in 97 percent of the cases. However, it must not be regarded as fail-safe and deference must be accorded the basic rules governing surgical success that have been mentioned in all of the various reports on this subject.

The well trained urologist will not lack this important part of his surgical repertoire.

REFERENCES

1. Hodges, C. V., Moore, R. J., Lehman, T. H. and Behnam, A. M.: Clinical experiences with transureteroureterostomy. J Urol, 90:552, 1963

2. Udall, D. A., Hodges, C. V., Pearse, H. M. and Burns, A. B.: Transureteroureterostomy: a neglected procedure. J Urol, 109:817, 1973

3. Whitaker, R. H.: Methods of assessing obstruction in dilated ureters. Br J Urol, 45:15, 1973

4. Ehrlich, R. M. and Skinner, D. G.: Complications of transureteroureterostomy. J Urol, 113:467, 1975

5. Sandoz, I. L., Paull, D. P. and MacFarlane, C. A.: Complications with transureteroureterostomy. J Urol, 117:39, 1977

6. Boxer, R. J. and Ehrlich, R. M.: The surgical replacement of the ureter. J C E Urol, 17:10, November 1978

7. Weiss, R. M., Beland, G. A. and Lattimer, J. K.: Transureteroureterostomy and cutaneous ureterostomy as a form of urinary diversion in children. J Urol, 96:155, 1966

8. Young, J. D., Jr. and Aledia, F. T.: Further observations on flank ureterostomy and cutaneous transureteroureterostomy. J Urol, 95:327, 1966

9. Jacobs, D., Politano, V. A. and Harper, J. M.: Experiences with transureteroureterostomy. J Urol, 97:1013, 1967

10. Smith, I: Trans-uretero-ureterostomy. Br J Urol, 41:14, 1969

11. Malament, M.: The ureteral conduit: cutaneous transureteroureterostomy. J Urol, 101:162, 1969

12. Smith, R. B., Harbach, L. B., Kaufman, J. J. and Goodwin, W. E.: Crossed ureteroureterostomy: variation of uses. J Urol, 106:204, 1971

13. Hecker, G. N. and Ocker, J. M., Jr.: Why transureteroureterostomy? J Urol, 108:710, 1972

14. Schmidt, J. D., Flocks, R. H. and Arduino, L.: Transureteroureterostomy in the management of distal ureteral disease. J Urol, 108:240, 1972

15. Halpern, G. N., King, L. R. and Belman, A. B.: Transureteroureterostomy in children. J Urol, 109:504, 1973

16. Zincke, H. and Malek, R. S.: Experience with cutaneous and transureteroureterostomy. J Urol, 111:760, 1974

17. Malkin, R. B., Schellhammer, P. F. and Hackler, R. H.: Experience with transureteroureterostomy in the paraplegic patient with irreversible vesicoureteral reflux. J Urol, 112:181, 1974

18. Brannen, W.: Useful applications of transureteroureterostomy in adults and children. J Urol, 113:460, 1975

19. Béland, G. and Laberge, I.: Cutaneous transureteroureterostomy in children. J Urol 114:588, 1975

20. Hendren, W. H.: Some alternatives to urinary diversion in children. J Urol, 119:652, 1978

21. Sadlowski, R. W., Belman, A. B., Filmer, R. B., Smey, P. and King, L. R.: Followup of cutaneous ureterostomy in children. J Urol, 119:116, 1978

22. Sharer, W., Grayhack, J. T. and Graham, J.: Palliative urinary diversion for malignant ureteral obstruction. J Urol, 120:162, 1978

23. Sweitzer, S. J. and Kelalis, P. P.: Cutaneous transureteroureterostomy as a form of diversion in children with a compromised urinary tract. J Urol, 120:589, 1978

24. Hackler, R. H.: Spinal cord injuries. Urologic care. Urology, 2:13, 1973

25. Shapiro, S. R., Peckler, M. S. and Johnston, J. H.: Transureteroureterostomy for urinary diversion in children. Urology, 8:39, 1976

EDITORIAL COMMENT

Transureteroureterostomy, which has been championed by Hodges and associates for so long, is one of the most important techniques in urologic surgery. As emphasized by the authors it has a wide range of indications in children and adults. Many of the difficult reconstructive cases we have seen were reparable only by including transureteroureterostomy. If the technical points stressed by the authors in this and their previous studies are followed a high success rate will result. As an added safeguard against devascularization of the donor ureter the ipsilateral gonadal vessels can be divided low and mobilized with the ureter to give it extra collateral blood supply. I agree completely that every urologic surgeon should be familiar with this procedure and ready to use it when a suitable case is presented.

W. Hardy Hendren, III
Department of Pediatric Surgery
Massachusetts General Hospitals
Boston, Massachusetts

Dr. J. E. Albrich, Oregon City, Oregon allowed us to include the third case (K. B.).

Commentary: Transureteroureterostomy: Simple but Not Infallible

Harper D. Pearse

Transureteroureterostomy was first described in 1894 by Boari and Casati and by Monari in 1895. Their studies were in dogs, and short-term follow-up examination indicated that the technique was possible although anastomotic disruption and stricture were noted. Transureteroureterostomy was first described in this country by Dr. Norville Wallace Sharpe in St. Louis, who, between 1900 and 1906, described the operation in two dogs and a cadaver.[1] He suggested that the donor ureter could be brought through a tunnel created anterior to the aorta and vena cava and posterior to the peritoneum, making the anastomosis retroperitoneal. His technique was based on limited ureteral mobilization and preservation of the periureteral blood supply to the ureter, which had been recently described by Sampson.

It was not until 1934 that Charles Higgins at The Cleveland Clinic reported the first patient in whom transureteroureterostomy was used.[2] He describes a 25-year-old man who presented with right flank pain, infection, reflux, and progressive hydronephrosis after two previous operations for bladder calculi and a large vesical diverticulum. Ureteroneocystostomy was not possible because of pelvic adhesions and inflammation, and a right-to-left transureteroureterostomy was performed. The patient had an excellent early result, and follow-up examination 30 years later still revealed normal upper tracts.

In 1960, Hodges and associates reported seven successful cases. Their series was updated in 1963 with 32 cases, in 1973 with 76 cases, and in 1980 with 100 cases. Smith has reported good results from England, and Brannan and others have added to the number of cases in the United States.[3,4] Hendren and Hensle recently reiterated that transureteroureterostomy can be used successfully in a variety of ingenious ways in the pediatric population.[5] Their applications in 112 patients included establishment of urinary tract continuity after unsuccessful ureteroneocystostomy, as part of an undiversion procedure, and as an adjunct in conversion of an ileal conduit to a nonrefluxing colon conduit.

Results in over 400 cases in the literature have generally been good; however, Ehrlich and Skinner, and Sandoz and associates, have called attention to failures that include damage to the recipient renal unit.[6,7]

Transureteroureterostomy is, on the whole, an effective method of restoring urinary tract integrity using normal urothelium in patients in whom a long segment of one lower ureter is damaged and restoration is not possible by ureteroneocystostomy with or without a psoas hitch or bladder-flap procedure. Transureteroureterostomy should be successful if (1) The contralateral ureter and ureterovesical mechanism are normal,

(2) the operation is done in a clean, nonirradiated operative field as a planned procedure and not as a "bail-out" endeavor, (3) a watertight anastomosis is done without tension using atraumatic technique with viable donor and recipient ureters, (4) the anastomosis is surrounded with viable fat and not allowed to lie on a rigid surface such as the psoas muscle, (5) the anastomosis is adequately drained, and (6) patients with recurrent urolithiasis and multifocal transitional cell carcinomas are avoided.

In my experience, transureteroureterostomy has been a simple technique, free from the undesirable features of bowel substitution, the technical considerations of autotransplantation, and the loss of renal function attendant to nephrectomy. It has been successful in 92% of patients. However, it is not infallible and certainly is no substitute for lack of attention to surgical principles or poor patient selection.

INDICATIONS

The general indications for transureteroureterostomy may be broadly stated to include a lesion of the lower ureter with a normal ureter on the other side and a normal bladder. As noted previously, in a patient with a compromised lower ureter, several procedures are available for successful diversion and maintenance of the integrity of the urinary system. Due consideration must be given to ureteroneocystostomy with or without a psoas hitch and bladder flap, replacement of the ureter with intestine, autotransplantation of the kidney, drainage and proximal diversion, and nephrectomy. None of these procedures will satisfactorily provide the remedy for all ureteral problems, since the solution will depend on the causative lesion, the presence or absence of portions of the urinary tract, the condition of the bladder and ureters, the amount of inflammation and sepsis in the perivesical and retroperitoneal areas, and the surgeon's experience.

The most common indication for transureteroureterostomy historically has been a compromised lower ureter following unsuccessful ureteral reimplantation. Ureteral injury during a variety of pelvic surgical procedures and malignant involvement of the lower ureter are other common indications for this procedure. Its use as an aid in restoring urinary tract continuity during procedures for undiversion is becoming more common.

TECHNIQUE

The technique of transureteroureterostomy is based on adequate debridement to obtain viable tissue, preservation of blood supply, atraumatic handling of tissue, an anastomosis without tension, adequate drainage, and thoughtful patient selection.

To proceed, after debridement has been carried out, bring the donor ureter to the contralateral side through a retroperitoneal tunnel anterior to the great vessels. Take care not to kink the ureter during this maneuver. Preserve the periureteral blood supply by dissection away from the ureteral wall. The gonadal vessels may be brought with the ureter if extensive mobilization is needed. Limited mobilization of the recipient ureter toward the midline can be accomplished safely but should be avoided if possible because of the risk of interfering with the segmental blood supply of the ureter.

Spatulate the donor ureter on its medial aspect approximately 1.5 cm to correspond to the recipient ureterotomy made on the medial side of the recipient ureter. Make a running, locked, or interrupted anastomosis using 5–0 absorbable suture material. My own experience indicates that atraumatic handling of tissue and a meticulous, watertight, fine suture technique are more important than whether the anastomosis is running or interrupted or what type and size of absorbable suture is used.

Make a conscious effort to avoid grasping the ureteral margins with forceps, since even slight crushing can compromise ureteral blood supply. The anastomosis should be under no tension. Concern about tension means it probably exists. It is helpful to surround the anastomosis with viable fat if easily accessible and adequate, direct drainage is essential. Ureteral stents are not routinely used unless acute infection is present or primary healing is suspect.

RESULTS

Review of the literature suggests that transureteroureterostomy is successful in over 90% of patients; however, all failures probably have not been reported. Major and minor complications occur in 20% to 25% of patients and include ureteral obstruction due to stricture, tumor blockage, ureteral angulation and the inferior mesenteric artery syndrome, anastomotic disruption, acute pyelonephritis, prolonged urinary drainage, ileus, reflux, and stomal stenosis in patients in whom an end ureterostomy is used.

REFERENCES

1. Sharpe NW: Transuretero-ureteral anastomosis. Ann Surg 44:687, 1906
2. Higgins CC: Transuretero-ureteral anastomosis: Report of a clinical case. J Urol 34:349, 1935.
3. Smith I: Transuretero-ureterostomy. Br J Urol 41:14, 1969
4. Brannan W: Useful applications of transureteroureterostomy in adults and children. J Urol 113:460, 1975

5. Hendren WH, Hensle TW: Transureteroureterostomy: Experience with 75 cases. J Urol 123:826, 1980
6. Ehrlich RM, Skinner DG: Complications of transureteroureterostomy. J Urol 113:467, 1975
7. Sandoz IL, Paull DP, Macfarlane CA: Complications with transureteroureterostomy. J Urol 117:39, 1977

ANNOTATED BIBLIOGRAPHY

Sharpe NW: Transuretero-ureteral anastomosis. Ann Surg 44:687, 1906

This excellent paper details the initial efforts in this country with experimental aspects of transureteroureterostomy from 1900 to 1906 by Dr. N. W. Sharpe of St. Louis. Based on knowledge of the development of surgery of the ureter by Simon, Schopf, Poggi, Van Hook, and Bovee and on Sampson's description of the periureteral arterial plexus, the author describes transureteroureterostomy in two dogs and a cadaver. The dogs lived 18 and 48 hr, respectively, and neither had evidence of urinary leakage or hydroureter. The transmesenteric ureteral anastomoses were competent to pressures of 60 mm Hg. Retroperitoneal transureteroureterostomy was carried out in a cadaver using two techniques. In the first, a tunnel was created between the peritoneum and great vessels using finger dissection and the back of a knife handle, and the anastomosis was made anterior to the aorta and vena cava. The alternative method placed the anastomosis posterior to the vessels just anterior to the vertebral column. Sharpe concluded that techniques, based on anatomic and physiologic principles, were available to encourage reconstructive procedures rather than nephrectomy in patients in whom the integrity of the ureter was impaired. The work of Carrel in organ transplantation is noted, and it is suggested that renal autotransplantation might be of benefit in some patients with ureteral injury.

Higgins CC: Transuretero-ureteral anastomosis: Report of a clinical case. J Urol 34:349, 1935

The first clinical application of transureteroureterostomy is presented by Dr. Charles Higgins. The paper was read at the meeting

of the American Association of Genitourinary Surgeons in May 1934 and describes a man aged 25 yr who had had two operations for bladder calculi and a large vesical diverticulum that had ruptured. Right flank pain, reflux, and progressive hydronephrosis prompted a third exploration. Ureteroneocystostomy was not feasible because of adhesions and inflammation in the pelvis, and a right-to-left transureteroureterostomy was performed. Convalescence was uneventful, and the patient was discharged 12 days after the operation. An intravenous urogram taken 1½ yr after operation showed both kidneys to be functioning well with no evidence of obstruction at the site of the ureteral anastomosis. Higgins states: "Although such a procedure may seldom be indicated, it is an anatomic and physiologic possibility and adds another conservative technique to the armamentarium of urologic surgery."

Smith I: Transuretero-ureterostomy. Br J Urol 41:14, 1969

Review of two earlier series from London (58 patients) on the treatment of ureteral injuries indicated that ureteroneocystostomy has been the only procedure associated with a high incidence of good results (85%). The author presents 12 cases in which transureteroureterostomy had been used in restoring urinary tract continuity. Indications were pelvic tumors (colon, uterus, ovary, bladder, and ureter) in nine patients, surgical ureteral injury in two, and idiopathic ureteral stricture in one. Early results were good in all patients; however, one patient developed a ureteral tumor distal to the transureteroureterostomy resulting in progressive hydronephrosis and uremia. Transureteroureterostomy is recommended in any patient in whom the ureter is injured more than 5 cm above the bladder, whether accidentally during pelvic surgery or deliberately for cancer surgery, and provided that ureteral reimplantation is not possible and the recipient system is unobstructed.

Brannan W: Useful applications of transureteroureterostomy in adults and children. J Urol 113:460, 1975

Seventeen patients underwent transureteroureterostomy from 1968 to 1974 for extensive scarring and fibrosis or for tumor involving the lower third of the ureter and an unobstructed kidney and ureter on the opposite side. Thirteen patients are living, one was lost to follow-up study, and three have died of their primary malignancies. All contralateral renal units have remained normal, and all nine compromised upper tracts improved. The author uses a running suture of 5–0 polyglycolic acid and feels that ureteral stents are not needed.

Hendren WH, Hensle TW: Transureteroureterostomy: Experience with 75 cases. J Urol 123:826, 1980

The authors presented their experience with transureteroureterostomy in 75 children and young adults at the American Urological Association Meeting in New York in 1979. Since that time an additional 37 patients have been added to their series, which now totals 112. Common indications were failure of ureteral reimplantation in 35 patients, as part of an undiversion procedure in 23, and as an adjunct in conversion of an ileal conduit to a nonrefluxing colon conduit in 10.

Only three complications were encountered; they were all preventable technical errors. They included (1) positioning the anastomosis on the anterior wall of the recipient ureter instead of its medial aspect, (2) performing the anastomosis just above an unrecognized partial obstruction of the recipient ureter, and (3) draining a small bowel segment across into the opposite ureter, which is less reliable than draining it into the opposite renal pelvis In these three patients the problem was evident on early follow-up x-ray films, and prompt reoperation was corrective.

Technical considerations included an interrupted anasto-

mosis, leaving the gonadal vessels with the ureter if needed for extensive mobilization of the donor ureter, and caution against mobilization of the recipient ureter. The authors stress that many patients with undiversion cases and those with failed ureteral reimplantation can undergo reconstruction only if transureteroureterostomy is used.

Ehrlich RM, Skinner DG: Complications of transureteroureterostomy. J Urol 113:467, 1975

Five cases illustrating serious complications associated with transureteroureterostomy are presented, including the first reported problems with the recipient ureterorenal unit. Poor blood supply, anastomotic tension, and excessive ureteral mobilization were responsible for the failures; safer alternative initial procedures (nephrectomy, vesicopsoas hitch) were available in all five cases. These five cases of anastomotic disruption resulted in nephrectomies in three patients' donor units and damage to four patients' recipient ureters, treated by ileal replacement in two and an extensive vesicopsoas hitch in one. The other patient is being followed conservatively in the hope that progression does not occur.

Sandoz IL, Paull DP, Macfarlane CA: Complications with transureteroureterostomy. J Urol 117:39, 1977

The authors discuss 23 patients who underwent transureteroureterostomy between 1960 and 1975 for stricture (12), reflux (6), or surgical injury (5). Four of these 23 patients sustained injury to the recipient ureter, a complication not prominent in the literature. In two of the four patients transureteroureterostomy was probably not the procedure of choice, and in the other two, there was a marked discrepancy in the size of the two ureters thought to contribute to injury of the recipient ureter Ultimately, three of the four patients had excellent results but not without prolonged morbidity and a series of operations.

The authors feel that transureteroureterostomy is an effective method of diversion, as evidenced by 95% (22 of 23) excellent results in their series; however, complications involving the recipient ureter do occur and should be recognized.

Overview:
The Distinct Advantages of Transureteroureterostomy

Robert K. Rhamy

Transureteroureterostomy has experienced a long and complicated history. The initial attempts were criticized because of the possibility of damage to the recipient unit by the disease process, which afflicted the damaged unit. This concern was great in the preantibiotic era, and it was not until the report of a significant number of cases by Hodges in 1960 that interest was rekindled in this technique and surgeons began to accept it as a replacement for the lower ureter.

It is vital that meticulous surgical technique be carefully followed in order to prevent significant complications. First, the mobilization of the donor ureter must preserve adequate blood supply, which may entail ligation of the gonadal vessels, particularly on the left side, and mobilization of these vessels along with the ureter in an effort to preserve adequate vascularization. Second, the course through the retroperitoneal tunnel must be without angulation of the ureter. Third, the anastomosis should be done without tension. Fourth, discrepancies in the ureteral diameter can be compensated for adequately without threatening the recipient ureter. Fifth, obviously the need for adequate drainage is imperative. Finally, judicious selection of patients is important.

The indications for transureteroureterostomy are many and variable. The most common indications are intrinsic ureteral tumor, extrinsic cancer (rectum, ovary, cervix), segmental bladder resection with distal ureterectomy, radiation-induced stricture, surgical injury, gunshot wound, ureterovaginal fistula, ureterocutaneous fistula, ureteroenteric fistula, ipsilateral reflux, and stricture of failed ureteroneocystoscopy.

When the results of transureteroureterostomy (92% success rate in a large series) are compared with operations other than ureteral reimplantation, the following advantages of transureteroureterostomy become obvious: (1) it obviates the need for nephrectomy, (2) it uses physiologic ureteral drainage, (3) it avoids external appliances, (4) it preserves continence, (5) it avoids distal ureteral dissection in a scarred or irradiated bony pelvis, and (6) it leaves the bladder unaltered.[1] Orkin, in his monograph on ureteral injury, states that 0.3% to 3% of routine and 1% to 10% of radical gynecologic operations injured the ureter.[5] One percent of abdominoperineal resections will result in ureteral injury.[6] In addition, 6% of patients with carcinoma of the uterine cervix who received radiation therapy will develop ureteral strictures.[7] Thus, there is a need to replace the lower ureter in a variety of circumstances.

Only nephrectomy compares more favorably in rate of success than transureteroureterostomy for treatment of ureteral injury. The ureteral complication is solved in this incidence at the sacrifice of the involved ureteral renal tissue.

Ureteral reimplantation with or without the psoas hitch compares well with transureteroureterostomy and should not be the procedure of choice if the ureter can reach the normal bladder (Table 3).[8]

Ureterostomy in the normal-sized ureter is commonly associated with stenosis and usually requires intubation. The rate of success in the dilated ureter is usually higher.

Rejoining the cut ends is successful 65% of the time under ideal experimental conditions, and a similar success rate has been reported clinically.[9-11] This is the procedure of choice only if the ureteral defect is so small that no tension is placed on the oblique suture line. Frequent occurrence of subsequent nephrectomy and even mortality has been reported.[6] This illustrates that a technical error producing even a 1-mm compromise in the diameter of the anastomotic lumen may lead to a poor result.[12]

The Boari flap procedure fails much of the time, even in

TABLE 3. Techniques Available for Ureteral Repair

Procedure	Success Rate (%)	Mortality (%)
Nephrectomy[3]	100	5
Transureteroureterostomy[1,16]	95	0
Reimplantation[5]	85	4
Ileal interposition[13]	81	5
Ureterostomy or nephrostomy[6]	80	15
Rejoining cut ends[7]	65	0
Boari flap[3]	45	5
Ligation of ureter[15]	21	50

the best hands.[3] It is not for the occasional ureteric surgeon, and it requires too much time to allow its use within an operation that has injured a ureter.

Ileal interposition is also time consuming and is associated with 100% electrolyte imbalance.[13] Alimentary morbidity from the enteroenterostomy is an added risk.

The psoas–bladder hitch, popularized by Turner-Warwick and Worth, is a good alternative procedure to keep in mind for a low ureteral defect not quite reimplantable normally.[14] The bladder is freed up ipsilaterally by dividing the superior vesical vessels and contralaterally by lysing peritoneal and pelvic attachments. After the opened bladder is attached to the psoas minor tendon, a ureteral reimplantation is done. This was completely successful in 90% of instances. The technique, however, is not reliable if there has been prior pelvic irradiation or scarring, if the patient is one of the 10% who lacks a psoas minor tendon, or if any bladder dysfunction exists.

Ligation of the ureter is dangerous and wastes renal tissue. One series reported only 21% symptomless atrophy, with 24% fistula formation and up to 50% mortality.[15]

From this data, it seems that any injured ureter that cannot be reimplanted has less than an even chance for a successful outcome with techniques other than transureteroureterostomy, which appears to have two distinct advantages: it is simple, especially when compared with alternative procedures, and it is very safe, with few technical complications. Anastomotic complications have been extremely rare, and temporary leakage has occurred only occasionally. There should be no worry over temporary dilatation of the receiving ureter because this soon disappears. There is, to date, a very low incidence of drainage to the receiving ureter and kidney. In short, transureteroureterostomy appears to conserve kidneys with a consistency unmatched by any other method of ureteral repair.

REFERENCES

1. Hodges CV, Moore RJ, Lehman TH, et al: Clinical experiences of transureteroureterostomy. J Urol 90:552, 1963

2. Jacobs D, Politano VA, Harper JM: Experiences with transureteroureterostomy. J Urol 97:1013, 1067

3. Smith I: Transureteroureterostomy. Br J Urol 41:14, 1969

4. Smith RB, Harbach LB, Kaufman JJ, et al: Crossed ureteroureterostomy: Variations of uses. J Urol 106:204, 1971

5. Orkin LA: Trauma to the Ureter: Pathogenesis and Management. Philadelphia, F A Davis, 1964

6. Graham JW, Coligher JC: The management of accidental injuries and deliberate resections of the ureter during excision of the rectum. Br J Surg 42:151, 1954

7. Rhamy RK, Stauder RW: Post radiation ureteral stricture. Surg Gynecol Obstet 113:615, 1961

8. Landau SJ: Uretero-neocystostomy: A review of 72 cases with comparison of two techniques. J Urol 87:343, 1962

9. Irvine AH, Collins WE, Murphy P, et al: The problem of ureteral anastomosis. Br J Urol 38:44, 1966

10. Prentiss RJ, Mullenix RB: Management of ureteral injuries in pelvic surgery. JAMA 145:1244, 1951

11. Higgins CC: Ureteral injuries. JAMA 185:225, 1962

12. Kosse KH, Suarez EL, Fagan WT, et al: Microsurgery in ureteral reconstruction. J Urol 87:48, 1962

13. Boxer RJ, Fritsche P, Skinner DG, et al: Replacement of the ureter by small intestine: Clinical application and results of ileal ureter in 89 patients. J Urol 121:728, 1979

14. Turner-Warwick R, Worth PHL: The psoas bladder hitch procedure for the replacement of the lower third of the ureter. Br J Urol 41:701, 1969

15. Smith PG, Smith DP: Ureteral injuries and their management. Trans Am Assoc Genitourin Surg 33:175, 1940

16. Hodges CV, Barry JM, Fuchs EF, et al: Transureteroureterostomy: 25-year experience with 100 patients. J Urol 123:834, 1980

48

PYELOILEOCUTANEOUS ANASTOMOSIS

Lowell R. King, M.D. and William Wallace Scott, M.D.

From The James Buchanan Brady Institute of Urology, The Johns Hopkins Hospital, Baltimore.

Reprint from SURGERY, Gynecology & Obstetrics, August, 1964, Vol. 119, 281–292
Copyright, 1964, by The Franklin H. Martin Memorial Foundation

Urinary diversion is often required in patients with severe hydroureteronephrosis. The upper tract dilatation may result from a neurogenic bladder or from bladder outflow obstruction by a contracted bladder neck or urethral valve or by severe urethral stricture. In any case, upper urinary tract damage, usually associated with infection, may be so severe that hydroureteronephrosis progresses or renal function worsens even after the primary obstruction has been removed or cystostomy has been performed. In such instances, urinary diversion may be necessary to preserve and stabilize the remaining renal function. As pointed out by King and Scott, patients in whom grossly dilated and scarred ureters are implanted into an ileal conduit have a poor prognosis, in that the upper tract often becomes more hydronephrotic after implantation, and renal function may deteriorate. This is a common result of ureteroileostomy especially in children, in whom the function of 16 of 31 kidneys involved in hydroureteronephrosis eventually worsened after conventional ureteroileocutaneous anastomosis. A possible reason for these poor results after ureteroileostomy is that the dilated ureter may not undergo normal peristalsis and, thereby may act as a functional obstruction, even

though the ureteroileal anastomosis and ileal stoma are widely patent.

In the 18 patients described, urinary diversion was performed for diverse reasons. Some underwent conventional ureteroileocutaneous anastomosis which resulted in progressive renal damage, and pyeloileocutaneous anastomoses were performed to bypass potentially obstructing ureters (Fig. 1).

This article is presented to report relatively long term follow-up studies on 18 patients treated by pyelo-ileocutaneous anastomosis, and to outline the surgical technique.

REPORTS OF JOHNS HOPKINS HOSPITAL AND BALTIMORE CITY HOSPITALS PATIENTS

Patient 1. This patient, a 29 year old white female, presented with acute left pyelonephritis. She was found to have congenital absence of the right kidney. The left ureter was grossly dilated, and the bladder was atonic. In February 1956, the left ureter was reimplanted into the bladder, but hydro-ureteronephrosis progressed. In June 1957, the ureter was excised, and an ileal ureter running from the renal pelvis to bladder was constructed. Reflux up the ileal ureter occurred.

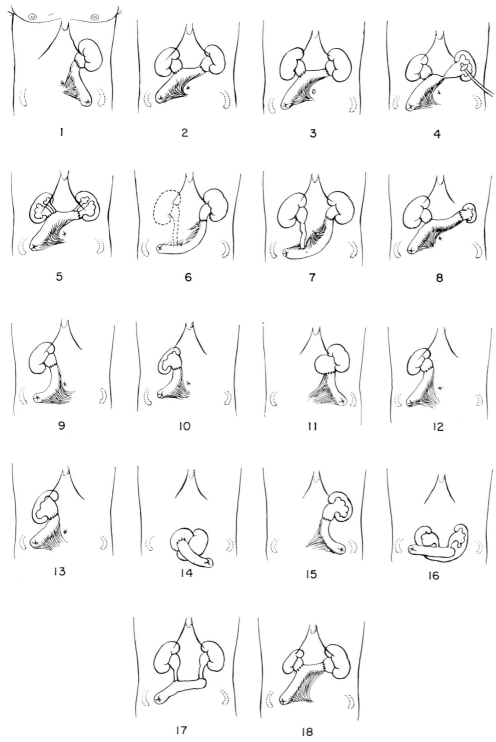

Fig. 1. The techniques used in the 18 patients in this series. The number under each diagram is the same as the number assigned to the patient.

She became hyperchloremic, had several episodes of acute pyelonephritis, and a bladder calculus developed. In August 1958, the distal end of the ileal segment was brought out in the left lower quadrant of the abdomen as an ileostomy. Hyperchloremia disappeared. When last seen in February 1963, the ileostomy was functioning well and intravenous pyelogram showed only a grade 1 caliectasis, which is the least dilatation that this kidney has shown.

Patient 2. A 10 month old male was admitted in June 1958 with azotemia and bilateral hydroureteronephrosis. Bilateral nephrostomies had been performed elsewhere. Diagnostic studies revealed a contracture of the bladder neck, but, because azotemia was present even with nephrostomy drainage, he was judged a poor candidate for plastic revision of the vesical neck, and a conventional ureteroileocutaneous anastomosis was performed in July 1958 to eliminate indwelling nephrostomy catheters. The patient exhibited increased azotemia and ureterocaliectasis subsequent to this procedure, and in November 1958 the ileal loop was anastomosed to the renal pelvis of both kidneys. The patient underwent revision of the ileal stoma in April 1960 because of obstruction at the ileostomy site due to squamous metaplasia of the ileal mucosa. A ventral hernia was repaired in March 1962. Since then the patient has done well. Subsequent to the pyeloileocutaneous anastomosis the serum urea nitrogen returned to normal.

Patient 3. A 13 year old colored male was admitted in August 1958 with hematuria following a fall. He was found to have an elevated serum urea nitrogen and had a severely trabeculated bladder containing 400 cubic centimeters of residual urine. Bilateral vesicoureteral reflux and marked hydroureteronephrosis were present. Diagnostic studies revealed a contracted bladder neck. Plastic revision was carried out, and suprapubic cystostomy drainage was established in August 1958. The upper tracts did not improve, and in December 1958 bilateral pyeloileocutaneous anastomosis was performed.

The serum urea nitrogen remained stable and this patient is now working at a regular job. When last seen in June 1963 the degree of caliectasis was slightly less than on preoperative pyelograms made in 1958.

Patient 4. This 8 year old colored male was seen in February 1958 because of hematuria. He was found to have congenital urethral valves, bilateral hydroureteronephrosis, and vesicoureteral reflux. Resection of the valves did not result in improvement in the upper tracts, although triple micturition was instituted, and suprapubic drainage of the bladder was established in September 1958. The patient then became progressively azotemic with a serum urea nitrogen of 98 milligrams percent due to urinary tract infection. In February 1959, bilateral pyeloileocutaneous anastomosis was performed. Eight days after operation it was apparent that an anastomosis site was leaking and that the patient had urinary ascites. Laparotomy was performed at which time the left pyeloileal anastomosis was found to be widely disrupted. This was repaired, and left nephrostomy was performed. The patient recovered without further incident, but when the nephrostomy tube was clamped 13 days after reexploration, fever developed and unclamping of the tube released a gush of urine. Dye studies, with methylene blue instillations into the ileostomy and nephrostomy tube, and an ileogram demonstrated a stricture of the left pyeloileal anastomosis. The patient was last seen in May 1963 and has remained well. The left nephrostomy tube has been maintained. The right kidney drains well via the ileal segment, and caliectasis has been arrested. The ileal stoma was revised in October 1961, at which time the ileal loop was tacked down intraperitoneally because of a tendency to prolapse slightly.

Patient 5. This white male was noted at birth to have poorly developed abdominal musculature. Urologic investigation revealed bilateral duplication of the ureters, which were dilated and tortuous over their entire length. The bladder neck appeared obstructed, and the testes were cryptorchid. The patient was azotemic.

In April 1959, at 6 weeks of age, pyeloileocutaneous anastomosis was carried out. Because of the double collecting systems only the pelves draining the lower portion of each kidney were anastomosed directly to the ileum; the proximal portions of the ureters draining the upper renal segments were anastomosed to the ileum independently.

After an episode of postoperative pyelonephritis, recovery was satisfactory. Postoperative pyelograms demonstrated satisfactory renal function. This patient died of pneumonia in October 1959.

Patient 6. This white male was born with exstrophy of the urinary bladder and cryptorchidism. Ureterosigmoid anastomosis was performed in 1943 when he was 3 years old. Because of recurrent acute pyelonephritis and moderate bilateral hydroureteronephrosis, the ureters were implanted with a conventional ileal loop in October 1955. Although the hydroureteronephrosis improved initially, the upper tracts began to dilate 1½ years after ureteroileostomy, and renal calculi formed in each kidney. In September 1959, the ileal loop was moved upward and anastomosed to the left ureter 1 inch below the ureteropelvic junction. The ileal segment was left intraperitoneal, and the right ureter, which was not as markedly dilated as the left, was anastomosed to the ileum at the usual site over the sacral promontory. In March 1960, 7 stones were removed from the left kidney, and the caliectasis decreased slightly on that side. The right kidney was removed because of pyonephrosis in May 1960. The patient was working steadily as a theater usher in March 1961 and was doing well clinically, although he required sodium bicarbonate to control a tendency toward acidosis. The patient was living and felt well in June 1963 but refused to return for reevaluation.

Patient 7. This white male was first admitted in October 1958 at the age of 3 years, because of failure to thrive. He was found to have anemia, and pyelography revealed left hydroureteronephrosis. The bladder was large and did not empty, although bladder tone was good. In February 1959, YV-plasty at the bladder neck and segmental resection of the bladder dome were performed. A urinary tract infection continued postoperatively, and the patient had intermittent fever in spite of specific antibiotic therapy. The left hydroureteronephrosis became more pronounced, and in January 1960 urinary diversion was carried out. In this instance, because the left ureter was dilated and appeared atonic at operation, the proximal end of the ileal loop was passed up to the left renal pelvis through a tunnel in the mesosigmoid and anastomosed to the renal pelvis to bypass the left ureter. This was accomplished by using an ileal segment 22 centimeters in length. The more distal portion of the loop then was anastomosed to the right ureter at the conventional level, and ileostomy was established in the right lower quadrant.

This patient had a satisfactory convalescence but continued to have recurrent fever 4 months postoperatively, probably due to the infected bladder. The patient has remained well and was last seen in June 1963.

Patient 8. This patient was born in August 1947 with a meningomyelocele. Frequency of urination was soon apparent, and pyelograms revealed bilateral hydronephrosis. In November 1949, the left ureter was straightened and reimplanted into the bladder, and the bladder neck was enlarged. In addition, the patient subsequently underwent a transurethral resection of the bladder neck. A chronic urinary tract infection persisted, as did overflow incontinence. The left kidney became atrophic. In February 1959 at age 12, conventional ureteroileocutaneous anastomosis was performed. Both collecting systems became much more dilated subsequent to operation, and in January 1960 the ileal loop was moved up to the renal pelvis. Since the left kidney was atrophic, a different technique was tried. The proximal end of the ileal segment was anastomosed to the left renal pelvis, but the ileal loop remained intraperitoneal, passing inferior to the ligament of Treitz and then upward to the right renal pelvis where an end-to-side anastomosis was performed. Ileostomy was then performed in the right upper quadrant.

Since operation, the atrophic left kidney has never visualized on intravenous pyelogram or retrograde ileogram. The calyces on the right had returned to near normal size upon examination in February 1963. The patient has remained well.

Patient 9. This white male was born in July 1949 with exstrophy and epispadias. He underwent a button transplant of trigone to rectum in June 1950. The exstrophic bladder was excised. A pyonephrosis secondary to stone necessitated left nephrectomy in February 1953. Because of increasing right hydroureteronephrosis, the right ureter was implanted into an ileal loop in June 1955. Hydroureteronephrosis diminished initially but then returned, even though the ileal stoma was widely patent. Therefore, in June 1960, the loop was moved up to the right renal pelvis. The degree of hydronephrosis again diminished, and this improvement has persisted. The most recent pyelogram was made in April 1963.

Patient 10. This colored female, aged 45 years, was initially admitted to the Baltimore City Hospitals because of rheumatic heart disease. Embolus of the left femoral artery necessitated amputation of the left leg in September 1955. Apparently because of necrosis secondary to catheter drainage, a urethrovaginal fistula developed. Attempts to repair this were unsuccessful, and chronic urinary tract infection led to a left pyonephrosis necessitating nephrectomy in May 1957. Because of urinary incontinence the right ureter was placed in an isolated ileal loop in July 1957. The patient was temporarily lost to follow-up, and subsequently the ileostomy stoma became obstructed. This resulted in marked lengthening of the ileal conduit, hyperchloremia, and hydroureteronephrosis. Because of the patient's chronic heart disease and uremia, preliminary right nephrostomy was performed in September 1960. This was tolerated well, and the patient's general condition im-

proved. In November 1960, the ileal loop was shortened to 10 centimeters in length and was moved to the right renal pelvis. The ileostomy stoma was moved into the right upper quadrant. The patient survived a cardiac arrest due to digitalis intoxication on the eighth postoperative day and did well, although the right kidney subsequently underwent some atrophy. Hydronephrosis did not recur, but some small stones formed in the renal parenchyma. Status epilepticus developed secondary to diffuse cerebral vascular disease, and she died in October 1962. At post mortem, the right kidney was atrophic, 120 grams, and was the site of chronic infection and calcifying papillitis.

Patient 11. This white male underwent a right nephrectomy for hydronephrosis in October 1953 at the age of 3 months. In March 1958, the patient was seen at the Brady Institute because of inability to empty the bladder. Plastic revision of the bladder neck was carried out. In January 1959, the left ureter was reimplanted into the bladder because of the onset of hydroureteronephrosis. The patient continued to have residual urine, but no demonstrable vesicoureteral reflux. A bilateral pudendal nerve crush did not improve bladder emptying. In September 1960, a left cutaneous ureterostomy and simultaneous nephrostomy were performed. The cutaneous ureterostomy functioned poorly, and in order to allow removal of the nephrostomy tube a left pyeloileocutaneous anastomosis was performed in January 1961. The ileostomy was established in the left upper quadrant. Because of the large size of the renal pelvis the patient wore a Foley catheter inserted via the ileal segment for 4 months. The anastomotic opening between renal pelvis and ileum proved too small to permit prompt drainage without the catheter. Therefore, the pyeloileal anastomosis was enlarged in April 1962. The patient has since been maintained without catheter, and hydronephrosis was diminishing as of April 1963.

Patient 12. This patient, aged 9 years, was admitted with uremia and severe bilateral hydroureteronephrosis secondary to a contracted bladder neck which had been repaired elsewhere. Divided renal function tests revealed that over 90 percent of remaining renal function was due to the right kidney. The left renal cortex was only a few millimeters thick. The urine was chronically infected. In order to establish better urinary outflow and to avoid chronic intubation of the urinary tract, right pyeloileocutaneous anastomosis was performed in October 1961. The right ureter and the left kidney and ureter were removed at the same time. At night on the third postoperative day, the patient suddenly vomited and aspirated gastric contents. Resuscitation was unsuccessful. Postmortem examination revealed that the pyeloileal anastomosis was intact.

Patient 13. This white male, aged 12 years, was found to have a mass in the right upper quadrant on a routine school examination in September 1961. Pyelography and cystoscopy revealed congenital absence of the left kidney. The right kidney was involved in a large hydronephrosis behind a ureteropelvic junction obstruction. Plastic repair was carried out elsewhere and a nephrostomy tube was left in place.

Six months later, in April 1962, urinary drainage was about equally divided between the nephrostomy tube and bladder. Clamping the nephrostomy tube consistently produced fever. The volume of the renal pelvis was 450 cubic centimeters.

In July 1962, the kidney was re-explored. The region of the ureteropelvic junction was involved in scarring. It was thought that a second plastic repair of the ureteropelvic junction would have little chance of success, so excess pelvis was resected and a pyeloileocutaneous anastomosis was performed. Subsequently, the patient has gained 13 pounds and caliectasis is diminishing.

Patient 14. A white female was born in March 1954 with a meningomyelocele. This was repaired at 10 days of age. Subsequently, a chronic urinary tract infection developed, and toilet training was unsuccessful. Urologic investigation at age 3 years revealed an atrophic or hypoplastic right kidney, a left kidney in the bony pelvis, and a large hypotonic bladder. At age 7, the right kidney was no longer visualized by intravenous pyelography. The pelvic kidney showed mild hydroureteronephrosis which disappeared when catheter drainage of the bladder was instituted.

In September 1962, the proximal end of an ileal conduit was anastomosed to the left renal pelvis. The ileal segment then ran behind the descending colon, and ileostomy was established in the left lower quadrant. The normally situated, but nonvisualizing right kidney was excised with its ureter. The patient has done well. No caliectasis has appeared postoperatively.

Patient 15. This white male was seen in June 1960, at 6 months of age, because of failure to thrive. Urologic evaluation revealed a urethral stricture, a contracted bladder neck, and a hypoplastic right kidney which failed to visualize by intravenous pyelography. No vesicoureteral reflux was demonstrated on cystogram. In spite of ureteral dilatations the child became uremic and hydroureteronephrosis progressed. In June 1962, a left nephrostomy was performed to preserve renal function. In November 1962, a left pyeloileocutaneous anastomosis was performed. The hypoplastic right kidney and ureter were removed. The left nephrostomy tube was not removed until January 1963. Subsequently, the patient has done well. Drainage of the renal pelvis was prompt, caliectasis had diminished, and serum urea nitrogen was stable at the postnephrostomy level, 48 to 52 milligrams percent. The patient requires some polycitra or sodium bicarbonate to combat a tendency toward acidosis.

Patient 16. This white female was born in September 1957, with multiple congenital abnormalities including meningomyelocele, absence of 3 ribs on the left side, and talipes equinovarus. The mother noted that the patient voided much more frequently than a normal sibling, and urologic evaluation in February 1960 revealed a urinary tract infection, fusion of the lower poles of the kidneys—horseshoe kidney—and a trabeculated bladder. Specific antibiotic therapy did not result in sterilization of the urine. Attempted toilet training was unsuccessful. Upon re-evaluation in August 1962, vesicoureteral reflux was noted for the first time. Moderate ureterectasis was present. The patient began having episodic chills and fever, so in September 1962 urinary diversion was carried out by anastomosing the uppermost portion of each ureter to an isolated ileal segment. The ureteroileal anastomoses were lower in the bony pelvis than usual, but the ileal segment persued a horizontal course to the skin. One month after operation caliectasis had subsided, and the patient has remained afebrile.

About once a month the patient voids 10 to 20 cubic centimeters of sterile but purulent looking material per urethra. Bladder irrigations with .25 percent silver nitrate or 1 percent neomycin have reduced these episodes in frequency but have not eliminated them. Removal of the flaccid or obstructed bladder, sometimes needed after urinary diversion if infection is present, may become necessary in this patient.

Patient 17. This white man sustained a fractured pelvis and transection of the urethra in an auto wreck in 1941. He was then 15 years old. A very tight urethral stricture developed and the urine was diverted via a ureterosigmoidostomy. Subsequently, in 1943, fever and back pain developed. He had recurrent febrile episodes and required drainage of a pelvic abscess in 1955. Because of recurrent fever and bilateral hydroureteronephrosis, the ureters were implanted into an ileal loop in October 1958. The patient required re-exploration for release of small bowel volvulus in the immediate postoperative period. In April 1960, the patient noted pain in the region of the coccyx, and an abscess involving the perivesical space and bladder was discovered. This was treated by partial cystectomy and marsupilization of the remainder of the bladder. The ileal conduit was densely adherent to the bladder dome. Hydroureteronephrosis gradually progressed, and the patient became azotemic. In January 1963, a left nephrostomy was performed, and the serum urea nitrogen fell to 30 milligrams percent. Subsequently, in February 1963, a new ileal segment was isolated and was anastomosed to the upper portion of each ureter, about 5 centimeters below the ureteropelvic junction. The nephrostomy tube was removed, the serum urea nitrogen fell to 20 to 23 milligrams percent, and as of April 1963 hydroureteronephrosis was diminishing.

Patient 18. This patient, a white male, was noted at birth in December 1961 to have poorly developed abdominal muscles and cryptorchidism. The ureters were easily palpable and were about 4 centimeters in diameter. The right kidney was hypoplastic, and the left pelvis and calyces were markedly dilated. At 2 days of age a suprapubic cystostomy was performed. This drained the left kidney well. To improve the drainage of the right kidney and in the hope of eliminating indwelling catheters, bilateral cutaneous ureterostomies were performed at 3 months of age. The left cutaneous ureterostomy required intubation, and when the catheter came out a fever developed. In April 1963, a bilateral pyeloileocutaneous anastomosis was performed with a left nephrostomy. The patient tolerated the procedure well, and caliectasis was observed to be diminishing on a pyelogram made in June 1963 (Fig. 2b). The nephrostomy tube was removed in the immediate postoperative period.

TECHNIQUE OF BILATERAL PYELOILEOCUTANEOUS ANASTOMOSIS

Patients 2, 3, 4, 5, and 18 underwent bilateral pyeloileocutaneous anastomosis performed by this technique. In each instance, bilateral hydroureteronephrosis was present, and some extrarenal pelvis was available for anastomosis.

The patients are put on a low residue diet for 3 days preoperatively. The intestine is sterilized with appropriate

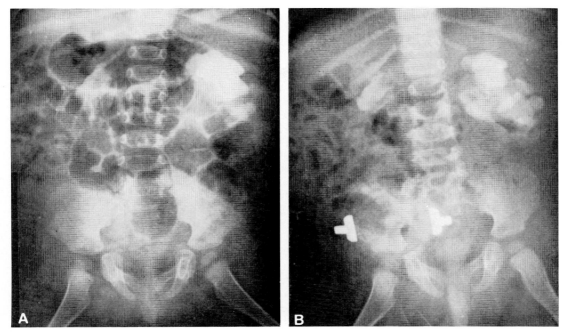

Fig. 2. Patient 18. (*A*) A 60 minute film from an intravenous pyelogram made 3 weeks before bilateral pheloileocutaneous anastomosis. (*B*) Twenty minute film from an intravenous pyelogram made 4 weeks after bilateral pyeloileocutaneous anastomosis.

oral dosage of neomycin started 30 to 48 hours preoperatively. The patient receives enemas until the return is clear on the evening before operation. General anesthesia is given. The entire abdomen is prepared, and the incision is made in the midline starting at the xiphoid and carried down to within 5 to 8 centimeters of the upper border of the pubic symphysis. The umbilicus is skirted away from the side of the projected ileostomy. Subcutaneous tissue, linea alba, and peritoneum are divided in the line of the incision. Exploration of the abdomen is then carried out. Intestinal adhesions are detached, if present. Appendectomy is performed.

Attention is then turned to the isolation of an ileal conduit (Fig. 3). A segment measuring 20 to 25 centimeters in length without stretching is selected. The mesentery must be deep enough to allow the isolated segment to reach the level of the renal pelves, and the segment must be supplied by 2 or 3 pulsating arteries which are palpable or visible in the mesentery. In the obese patient, transillumination of the mesentery may be helpful in defining the arterial supply of the ileal segment. If the mesentery is short, proximal ileum or jejunum may be utilized so that the conduit can reach the renal pelves without any pull on the mesentery. The

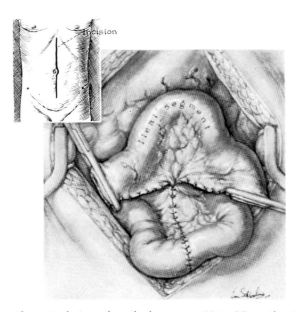

Fig. 3. Isolation of an ileal segment 22 to 25 centimeters in length for use as a pyeloileocutaneous conduit. Note that the isolated loop is turned upward on its mesentery.

loop of small intestine to be utilized having been selected, the mesentery at the ends is incised for a distance of 6 to 8 centimeters to allow maximal mobility of the conduit without sacrificing needed blood supply. The intestine is cleared at the site of transection and is divided between Kocher clamps. The isolated segment is reflected upward on its mesentery and intestinal continuity is restored by end-to-end intestinal anastomosis, usually utilizing an outer layer of silk sutures, and an inner layer of catgut.

The kidneys and renal pelves are identified by palpation. The posterior parietal peritoneum is then incised over the renal pelves, and the peritoneum is dissected away so that the pelves are in full view. A tunnel is then made by blunt and sharp dissection between the renal pelves (Fig. 4). The tunnel is just behind the posterior parietal peritoneum, and is usually just rostral to the pancreas and duodenum and below the superior mesenteric artery. The tunnel, of course, overlies the aorta, vena cava, and renal vessels. Construction of the tunnel requires care to avoid damage to these structures.

It is enlarged by blunt dissection to accommodate the finger or the proximal end of the ileal conduit after tissue crushed by the Kocher clamp has been sharply trimmed away. The proximal end of the ileal segment with trailing mesentery is then led to the region of the exposed right renal pelvis, passing medial and inferior to the hepatic flexure of the colon (Fig. 5). A long clamp is passed through the retroperitoneal tunnel from left to right and is used to grasp the suture in the proximal end of the isolated intestinal segment. By withdrawal of the clamp, the open proximal end of the conduit is drawn over to proximity with the left renal pelvis. Enough pelvis is then excised to produce a stoma approximately equal in caliber to the ileum. End-to-end anastomosis is then carried out, usually with a single layer of No. 4-0 chromic catgut sutures through all layers of intestine and pelvis. These are placed with an atraumatic needle so that the knots are outside the lumen. A drain is left down to the pyeloileal anastomosis and is brought out retroperitoneally through a stab wound in the flank. A left nephrostomy may be performed, as in Patient 18, but the opening is clamped in the immediate postoperative period so that the flow of urine will keep the pyeloileal anastomosis open.

Attention is then turned to the right kidney. It is ascertained that the mesentery of the ileal segment is not taut. If the mesentery appears stretched, the tunnel is widened or the incision in the mesentery is deepened to

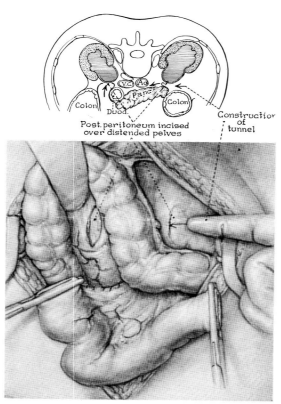

Fig. 4. The renal pelves are exposed by incising the overlying posterior parietal peritoneum or by reflecting the splenic flexure of the colon. A retroperitoneal tunnel is constructed between the renal pelves.

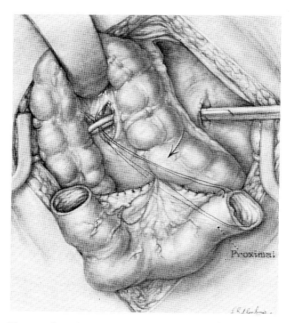

Fig. 5. The proximal end of the isolated ileal segment is led through the retroperitoneal tunnel from right to left.

permit more mobility of the conduit. After this has been done, an incision 2 to 4 centimeters in length is made in the antimesenteric border of the conduit just opposite the right renal pelvis, which is then resected to form a dependent stoma of like caliber which parallels the incision in the ileal segment. Anastomosis is then carried out with a single layer of No. 4-0 chromic catgut. A retroperitoneal drain is inserted through the flank.

The ileostomy is then established in the right upper quadrant. A site is selected which is far enough below the rib cage that the flange of the ileostomy bag will not overlie the ribs. The abdominal wall on the right side is held in the normal position by an Allis forceps grasping the right side of the incision. A "cork bore" type of deficit is then created at the site of ileostomy by circular excision of all layers of the abdominal wall—skin, fat, fascia, muscle, and peritoneum according to the technique of Stamey and Scott. The circular skin incision is made about ¼ inch smaller in diameter than the caliber of the ileal conduit, since such incisions tend to enlarge

slightly. The distal end of the ileal segment is led out of the abdomen through this defect, and if the conduit is redundant it is shortened by trimming the distal end. The conduit should pursue a fairly straight course from right renal pelvis to skin but should not be taut. The ileocutaneous anastomosis is then made with interrupted chromic sutures. Usually, an ileostomy flush with the skin is preferred, but an everted ileostomy bud may be utilized (Fig. 6).

Abdominal contents are replaced, and the pyeloileal anastomoses are checked for leaks by gently filling the ileal conduit with saline by means of a bulb syringe. The ureters may be excised, and defects in the posterior parietal peritoneum are closed. Abdominal contents are replaced, and the abdominal incision is closed. We usually prefer a running stitch of No. 2-0 chromic catgut for the peritoneum and interrupted sutures of medium weight steel wire, for the fascia. Heavy stay sutures may be used in addition. Subcutaneous tissues and skin are closed with silk.

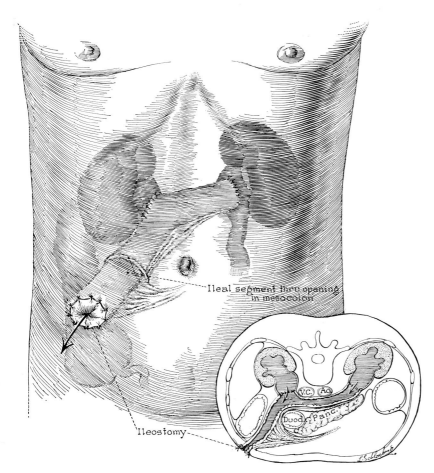

Ileal segment thru opening in mesocolon

Ileostomy

V.C. Ao.

Duod. Panc.

Fig. 6. The ileal conduit in place after bilateral pyeloileal anastomosis. The dilated ureters may be excised.

Postoperatively, the Levin tube is removed after intestinal sounds have returned, or after the first stool. An intravenous pyelogram or retrograde ileogram is obtained before the patient leaves the hospital. If the degree of caliectasis is the same as was present preoperatively, or is improved, the ileal stoma is calibrated by introducing a sterile gloved finger every 3 months to be sure the stoma is widely patent. Pyelograms are obtained at yearly intervals. Urine cultures may be obtained satisfactorily by having the patient assume the knee-chest position, cleaning the ileostomy bud, and then by catching a gush of urine in a sterile container. Should the postoperative pyelograms show increased caliectasis, special attention should be paid to the ileostomy site to rule out significant partial obstruction. If no obstruction is found, pyelograms are made at intervals of 4 to 6 weeks until the caliectasis resolves, or until the underlying obstruction can be found.

UNILATERAL PYELOILEOCUTANEOUS ANASTOMOSIS

Because this form of urinary diversion is often used in patients with severe uropathy or after other operative procedures have failed, many of the patients have only one functioning kidney at the time of operation. Eight of the patients in this series (Patients 1, 9, 10, 11, 12, 13, 14, and 15) fall into this category. The operation is similar to that outlined, but no high retroperitoneal tunnel need be constructed. After an ileal conduit, usually 10 to 14 centimeters in length, is isolated, the renal pelvis is exposed intraperitoneally and resected so that end-to-end anastomosis with the proximal end of the ileal conduit can be performed. On the right side, the conduit passes to the skin below the hepatic flexure of the colon and medial to the ascending colon. Ileostomy is performed in the right upper quadrant.

On the left side, the proximal end of the isolated ileal segment is passed up to the exposed left renal pelvis through a defect created in the mesosigmoid (Fig. 7). This is made large enough to accept the ileal segment and mesentery without compression. Pyeloileostomy is carried out. The distal end of the ileal segment is medial to the sigmoid colon and the ileostomy is placed in the left lower quadrant.

LEFT PYELOILEAL AND RIGHT URETEROILEAL ANASTOMOSIS

Patients 6, 7, and 17 represent special situations in the sense that the left ureter was severely diseased and dilated, but the collecting system on the right side was more normal. In these patients a relatively long ileal segment, 22 to 27 centimeters, was used to conduct urine from the left renal pelvis or upper left ureter to the ileostomy site in the right lower quadrant. The proximal end of the conduit is passed up to the left renal pelvis or upper left ureter through an incision in the mesentery of the sigmoid, and left pyeloileal anastomosis is carried out. The ileal segment is not turned upward on its mesentery (Fig. 8) but was allowed to drop inferiorly, lying just anterior to the sacral promontory. Thus, the right ureter can be picked up and anastomosed to the ileal segment at the conventional level. Adequate outflow from the right kidney was not provided by this method in Patient 6, who eventually needed right nephrectomy because of pyonephrosis.

DISCUSSION

It is hoped that the patients' histories are presented in sufficient detail to allow some evaluation of the procedure. Pyeloileocutaneous anastomosis is not free from severe complications. In Patient 4, for instance, urinary ascites developed postoperatively, and he has since worn a left nephrostomy tube, only the right kidney being drained by the ileal conduit. On the other hand, the postoperative mortality rate of 1 in 18 or 5.6 percent is similar to that reported after conventional ureteroileocutaneous anastomosis by Cordonnier and Nicola and by Creevy and therefore seems acceptable to us. No

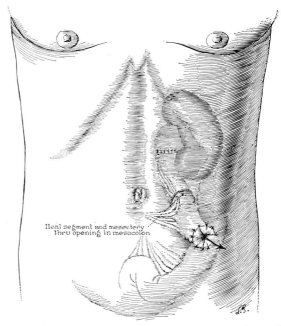

Fig. 7. Left pyeloileocutaneous anastomosis. Note that the proximal portion of the ileal conduit passes under the mesosigmoid.

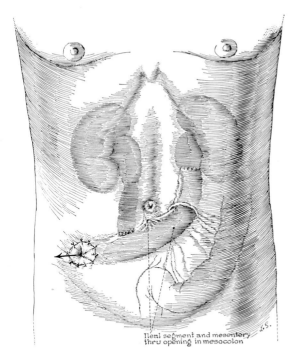

Fig. 8. Left pyeloileal anastomosis. The conduit passes across the sacral promontory, allowing anastomosis of the more normal right ureter to the ileum at the conventional level.

patient has yet experienced intestinal obstruction subsequent to pyeloileocutaneous anastomosis, although this complication must, of course, occasionally be expected. Patient 10 experienced progressive chronic renal disease subsequent to operation, consisting of renal atrophy and calcifying papillitis. This patient had no demonstrable obstruction to urine outflow.

Intravenous or retrograde pyeloileograms subsequent to pyeloileocutaneous anastomosis have invariably shown the same degree of caliectasis as, or less than, was present preoperatively. This is in contradistinction to patients in whom the dilated ureter is implanted into an ileal conduit over the sacral promontory, many of whom exhibit an increase in hydroureteronephrosis and a decrease in renal function after operation. Some patients with pyeloileocutaneous anastomosis have now been observed for 6 years. In general, patients with poor renal function have stabilized, serum urea nitrogen levels have fallen, and caliectasis has diminished subsequent to pyeloileocutaneous anastomosis. Azotemia was present at the time of operation in patients 1, 2, 3, 5, 6, 10, 12, 15, 17, and 18. As pointed out by Butcher, the outcome of operation did not appear to be adversely affected, although Patient 12 accounted for the postoperative death. Compared to elevated preoperative levels, the serum urea fell markedly in 7 of these patients after operation.

In Patient 8, an intraperitoneal ileal segment was anastomosed to both renal pelves, the conduit passing from left to right under the duodenum at the ligament of Treitz. This technique did not result in satisfactory drainage of the left kidney and has been abandoned.

Patients 14 and 16 have anomalies of renal position—pelvic kidneys. Pyeloileocutaneous anastomoses have resulted in satisfactory urinary drainage.

In short, pyeloileocutaneous conduits have proved successful after long term follow-up and have been useful in salvaging kidneys damaged by a variety of causes, most commonly a combination of obstruction and infection. Such conduits are especially helpful in preserving renal function in patients requiring urinary diversion whose ureters are dilated and atonic and who are, therefore, unsuitable for ureteroileocutaneous anastomosis because of the relatively high failure rate after that operation.

SUMMARY

Eighteen patients are presented in whom urinary diversion was performed. In some instances, hydroureteronephrosis or renal function worsened after conventional ureteroileocutaneous anastomosis, and pyeloileocutaneous anastomosis was then performed to bypass the dilated, atonic ureter. In other instances, the ureters were demonstrated to be markedly dilated and to lack the ability to undergo peristalsis prior to operation, and pyeloileocutaneous anastomosis was then believed to be the procedure of choice for urinary diversion.

The operative technique for pyeloileal anastomosis is discussed. Patients' histories are given. The follow-up period has been 3 to 6 years in 9 patients and is less than 3 years in 9 patients. In no instance has hydroureteronephrosis been seen to progress after pyeloileocutaneous anastomosis. Renal function has generally stabilized or improved subsequent to operation. Twelve patients were azotemic at the time of operation.

Pyeloileocutaneous anastomosis has proved feasible and reliable. Long term results show it to be the procedure of choice when urinary diversion is necessary in patients with scarred, dilated, aperistaltic ureters.

REFERENCES

1. BUTCHER, H. R., JR. Utility of ureteroileal urinary diversion in treatment of irreparable ureteral obstructions. Surg Gyn Obst 109:521, 1959

2. CORDONNIER, J. J., and NICOLA, C. H. Evaluation of use of isolated segment of ileum as means of urinary diversion. J Urol, Balt, 83:834, 1960

3. CREEVY, C. B. Renal complications after ileal diversion of urine in nonneoplastic disorders. J Urol, Balt, 83:394, 1960
4. KING, L. R., and SCOTT, W. W. Ileal urinay diversion. J Am M Ass 181:831, 1962

5. STAMEY, T. A., and SCOTT, W. W. Ureteroileal anastomosis. Surg Gyn Obst 104:11, 1957

Commentary: Declining Use of High Ileal Diversions

Roy W. Skoglund, Jr.

The preceding article is the second in a series of four from the Johns Hopkins Hospital on pyeloileocutaneous diversion.[1-3] Although it does not have the advantage of the long follow-up study described in subsequent papers, it is valuable because of its detailed description of surgical technique.[2,3] In addition, it sufficiently details cases to substantiate and illustrate the author's rationale in developing guidelines in the use of the procedure. Even though this publication appeared in 1964, it nevertheless continues to be the definitive article that urologists should refer to for assistance when contemplating creating a high ileal urinary conduit.

The primary indication for high ileal conduit diversion, as Drs. King and Scott state, is to bypass dilated ureters that in themselves are incapable of delivering the urine to the bladder or to a lower-placed ileal segment. However, in bypassing the ureters, it must be borne in mind that a significantly longer segment of ileum is in contact with the urine. This increases the possibility of reabsorption of metabolites from the urine, thus increasing the workload on kidneys that may already be significantly compromised. For that reason, in this type of diversion it is even more important to be alert for stomal or fascial stenosis with subsequent obstruction and urine pooling. In addition, the urologist must be quite ready to revise any redundancy of the segment that may occur. Correction of this redundancy is especially important in the pediatric patient during subsequent growth of the ileal segment.

The selection and creation of the ileal segment for high ileal conduit diversion are more critical than for the usual ureteroileocutaneous segment. The ileal segment must be of generous length; shortening the segment after positioning and anastomosis is far better than compromising a high ureteral or pelvic anastomosis or causing a stomal retraction from tension on a segment that is too short. The terminal segment of ileum is usually used. However, more important than the location of the segment is the availability of mesentery with adequate length to allow anterior reflection and retroperitoneal placement to the left ureter or renal pelvis. In isolating the mesentery to the ileal segment, it must be incised more deeply than for a low ureteroileal anastomosis in order to obtain advantage of the longer mesentery needed. In forming the deep mesenteric separation, preservation of the blood supply becomes even more critical. As Drs. King and Scott have noted, transillumination is valuable in identifying the vessels in the mesentery. I do this routinely in a darkened room, with the operating light shining through the mesentery toward me. This maneuver offers excellent aid in identifying the vessels, and, despite the time required to reposition the lights, speeds this portion of the procedure significantly.

The skin stoma should not be formed before the ileopelvic anastomosis, as other authors have suggested for the standard ureteroileocutaneous diversion. Although it is good advice to pick a stomal site preoperatively on the intact abdomen, in a high ileal conduit the placement of the stoma may vary, and the physician should not commit its final position until the anastomosis has been performed and the conduit placed retroperitoneally.

The kidneys can readily be palpated in their retroperitoneal position. The upper portion of the descending colon must be detached from the posterior lateral abdominal wall. If this in itself does not allow adequate visualization of the left kidney and its pelvis, then the splenic flexure may also need to be taken down. The right kidney may be approached by the authors' method through the colonic mesentery. This requires a rather large opening in the mesentery, and care must be taken to avoid the colonic vessels. The tunnel is bluntly fashioned, with the superior mesentery artery used as a superior boundary, the vena cava and renal veins used posteriorly, and an inferior portion of the pancreas and duodenum used anteriorly. The tunnel may be placed somewhat lower, depending on the size of the pelves and whether the pelvis, a calix, or the proximal ureter is used in anastomosis. In forming the tunnel, if "blind" tunneling is disconcerting to the operator, if the right renal pelvis is not adequately exposed, or if there is a question on exactly where the operator is, I have found that by taking down the ascending colon and hepatic flexure and mobilizing the duodenum, excellent exposure is obtained and confidence gained by visualization of the structure encountered. In any case, the tunnel must be of such caliber that the segment is not compressed and its blood supply is not compromised.

If the anastomosis is to the pelvis, it may include the old ureteropelvic junction if it is located medially and inferiorally. The opening in the pelvis should be the same size as the end of the ileal segment. An interrupted 4–0 chromic suture with an inverting stitch is used in the end-to-end anastomosis. Even if the ureteral pelvic segment is not used in the anastomosis, the ureter should be detached. Experience has shown me that reserving the possibility of returning continuity to the urinary tract in the future by leaving the ureters intact is not realistic and can create significant problems in drainage. The anastomosis of the ileal segment to the right pelvis as described in the preceding article is more easily accomplished with a detached ascending colon and hepatic flexure.

The authors do well to emphasize the propriety of draining the anastomotic site bilaterally and retroperitoneally. A retroperitoneal urinoma after surgery of this magnitude could be devastating.

The decision must be made whether, after the anastomosis to the right proximal ureter or renal pelvis, to bring the segment straight ventrally as described by the authors or to place the distal portion of the segment and its mesentery retroperitoneally behind the ascending colon. This decision depends on the possibility of intestinal obstruction associated with a segment brought as a post through the peritoneal cavity versus the possibility of increased reabsorption from the slightly longer length of ileal segment usually required to retroperitonealize

the segment. If the renal function is good and the length of the segment and its mesentery allow placement behind the colon without tension, this is recommended. If, however, the renal function is significantly compromised, as is often the case, the shorter segment, despite its possible complications, should be employed.

Excretory urograms are best used to evaluate the stabilization or improvement of the pelvic configuration in these patients. The pressure exerted by the retrograde injection in an ileal pyelogram (loopogram) frequently distends the collecting system so much that it interferes with correct assessment. The proper role of the loopogram is to evaluate whether a pelvis or ileal segment is draining properly.

The collected experience of Drs. King and Scott represents one of the largest groups with adequate follow-up study of any published series. This experience, establishment of criteria for use, and introduction of refinements in technique should be familiar to all urologists.

In the 1960s a significant number of articles were published on high ileal diversion. It is somewhat disconcerting that in the 1970s, papers on this subject were rare. It is further disturbing that in the current literature there is a complete absence of long-term follow-up study on those previously reported high ileal diversions. I wonder if the long-term results are such that the procedure has fallen into disfavor or, more likely, if the current use of high jejunal diversions instead of high ileal diversions has been accepted as technically and functionally the procedure of choice.

REFERENCES

1. King LR, Scott WW: Ileal urinary diversion. JAMA 181:831, 1962
2. Holland JM, King LR, Schirmer HKA, et al: High urinary diversion with an ileal conduit in children. Pediatrics 40:816, 1967

3. Holland JM, Schirmer HKA, King LR, et al: Pyeloileal urinary conduit: An 8 year experience in 37 patients. J Urol 99:427, 1968

ANNOTATED BIBLIOGRAPHY

Bard RH: Early high urinary diversion. Urology 3:309, 1974

The major departure from previous reports and the stated contribution of this study concern the decision not to delay high diversion until renal function has begun to deteriorate. Unlike most reports in the literature, which suggest high diversion be performed as a last resort, this article states that once it is evident that surgery on the lower urinary tract will not benefit renal function, high diversion should be considered. The author believes that as soon as renal deterioration is noted, urinary continuity must be sacrificed to achieve renal preservation.

All nine illustrative cases were in the pediatric or adolescent group and were diverted because of dilated functionally obstructed ureters.

Bard stresses that the fundamental concept of high urinary diversion is that the pelves should drain directly into a conduit constructed of jejunum or ileum.

Clark SS: High urinary diversion by retroperitoneal jejunal conduit: Technic and rationale. Rev Surg 30:1, 1973

Clark describes the technique and reasons to use a high jejunal urinary tract diversion, drawing on his experience with 21 patients to support this rationale.

A low ureteroileal conduit may not be available for use because of radiation damage, involvement of the ureters with carcinoma, or ureteral dilation that precludes normal propulsion

of urine. An intraperitoneal conduit may permit an internal hernia, and subsequent abdominal surgery may be compromised. Use of a retroperitoneal jejunal segment anastomosed to the proximal half of the ureters or renal pelvis obviates these problems.

The author discusses the advantages of using high jejunal rather than high ileal conduits, including less angulation of the mesenteric vessels, greater propulsive peristalsis, noncompromised bowel in those patients with pelvic radiation, lack of physiologic objection to using the jejunum, and the relative ease of placing the jejunum retroperitoneally. The operative technique used is well described and illustrated. This article is presented here as an alternative to use of the ileum when high urinary diversion is contemplated.

Skoglund RW Jr, Ansell JS: Pyeloileocutaneous diversion in children. J Urol 100:257, 1968

The authors present their experience with pyeloileocutaneous diversion in seven children with severe renal impairment. A plea is made to find early the patient requiring a high-type diversion. The selective criterion for such a diversion is the presence of dilated aperistaltic ureters, which in themselves are obstructive. Nephrostomy as a method of high diversion has been rejected as unsatisfactory because of the recurrent infection, stone formation, and cumbersomeness of the tubes and collecting devices in children.

It is emphasized and illustrated that these patients all have had multiple operative procedures before pyeloileocutaneous diversion, thus delaying the definitive procedure. Follow-up study ranged from 3 to 7 yr and documents the improvement after diversion in 5 of the patients, stabilization in 1, and progressive renal failure in another (the only mortality). The most frequent complications were recurrent pyelonephritis and bowel obstruction.

The authors suggest that the ureters be left intact to allow possible reconstitution of the urinary tract. (On further follow-up study, this suggestion has not proved to be feasible; it is now felt that the ureters should be interrupted or excised at diversion.)

Holland JM, Schirmer HKA, King LR, et al: Pyeloileal urinary conduit: An eight-year experience in thirty-seven patients. J Urol 99:427, 1968

Thirty-one patients with pyeloileal conduits and 6 patients with very high ureteroileal conduits are presented, along with follow-up evaluations of 3 mo to 8 yr after diversion.

Pyeloileal conduit is favored in those patients with hopelessly damaged upper tracks. A static column of urine in a dilated atonic ureter is an obstruction in itself. This type of urinary tract must receive a definitive procedure; it will not tolerate a failure.

The operative mortality (5%) and complication rate are acceptable, considering that 59% of the patients were azotemic when high diversion was instituted. The renal function stabilized or improved in 83% of the patients surviving the procedure. None of the patients with a normal blood urea nitrogen (BUN) value at diversion subsequently became azotemic or died. Stomal obstruction and calculi formation were the most common late complications.

Excretory urograms or retrograde ileograms are done every 6 wk until the caliectasis resolves or stabilizes. A residual urine in the segment greater than 15 ml to 20 ml should be considered evidence of stomal obstruction. Stone formation or persistent infection may indicate stomal, fascial, or anastomotic stenosis or possible redundancy of the segment.

Renal function should not be expected to improve after pyeloileal conduit if a properly functioning nephrostomy is already in place; however, the infection rate and stone formation make a nephrostomy unacceptable as a form of permanent high diversion.

Sunshine H, Cordonnier JJ, Butcher H: Bilateral pyeloileostomy. J Urol 92:358, 1964

Three children who were treated by three variations of a bilateral pyeloileostomy are discussed. This type of ileostomy is deemed necessary when the ureters are ineffectual, as in megaloureter and with extensive ureteral injury.

The first variation uses a single segment of ileum extending from the left pelvis to the right pelvis, then ventrally to form a stoma. The segment between the pelves was placed intraperitoneally. The other two patients had a segment of ileum divided after it had been selected, and a Y was constructed with the left limb being carried through the mesosigmoid. This again was entirely intraperitoneal.

The recommended procedure consists of the short limb of the Y going to the left kidney and the longer limb going to the right; the stoma was brought out in the right lower quadrant. In one of the patients the large caliber of the ileum allowed passage of multiple large pelvic stones, which were not accessible at surgery.

Campbell WA, Buchel HA: The advantages of the high ileac conduit. J Urol 91:66, 1964

This paper is based on an experience with 33 high ileal conduits, some of which were anastomosed directly to the pelves. Four illustrative cases are presented.

The authors used a transverse incision, indicating that this affords better exposure and allows the passage of the ileal segment through the abdominal wall without danger of angulation. When the segment is isolated, it is distinctively marked so that there is no possibility of twisting the segment on its mesentery during the procedure. The stoma is initially formed before connection is made to the urinary tract so that no stress is placed on the anastomosis once it is fashioned. The ileum is brought through the sigmoid mesentery to the left upper ureter or pelvis. This places the entire segment, except for the anastomoses, intraperitoneally.

The cases presented enforce the authors' contentions that very little if any ureter should be left, the segment should be as short as possible, it should be brought out through the abdominal wall in a carefully selected site without any possible obstruction, and the operation should be done before renal function is irretrievably damaged.

Schwartz GR, Jeffs RD: Ileal conduit urinary diversion in children: Computer analysis of follow-up from 2 to 16 years. J Urol 114:285, 1975

The authors present their experience with 96 ileal conduit urinary diversions in children with follow-up study of 2 to 16 yr. The thrust of the paper is to make the reader aware that by comparing relatively short-term follow-up study (average, 4.5 yr) with longer follow-up study (average, 11.3 yr), there is significantly greater pyelographic and functional deterioration in the children with long-term diversion. The two groups are roughly equal in number, and surgical technique and supervision were controlled. More patients had pyelographic changes than functional deterioration. Whether some of these early changes in the long-term follow-up group can be correlated with failing function has not been shown. Complications early and late affect the long-term results, and some of these complications occur very late. This emphasizes the need for close long-term follow-up study of these patients and care not to rely on short-term apparent success. The point is made to review critically the indications for ileal conduit urinary diversion in children in light of the increased long-term changes.

49

ILEAL CONDUIT URINARY DIVERSION

Ten-Year Review

Richard V. Remigailo, M.D., Ernest L. Lewis, M.D., John R. Woodard, M.D., and Kenneth N. Walton, M.D.

From the Department of Surgery, Division of Urology, Emory University and Affiliated Hospitals, Atlanta, Georgia

Urology / April 1976 / Volume VII, Number 4

ABSTRACT—The experience with ileal conduit urinary diversion at Emory University and Affiliated Hospitals over a ten-year period is presented. Included in this review are patients with benign and malignant disease. The indications, technique, results, and complications of this type of urinary diversion are considered. Some differences between ileal conduit diversion of children and adults are discussed.

The search for an ideal bladder substitute has challenged urologists for many years. The objectives have been to preserve renal function, provide adequate urinary drainage, avoid the presence of foreign body and residual urine, and maintain a manageable form of urine collection. Various types of urinary diversion have been developed to meet a variety of clinical situations. Cutaneous ureterostomy often functions well as a permanent urinary diversion when the ureters are dilated but still capable of peristalsis. The sigmoid conduit allows an antireflux ureteral anastomosis but requires an undilated

Read at the Annual Meeting of Southeastern Section, American Urological Association, Inc., Atlanta, Georgia, April 14, 1975

collecting system which must conform to the formation of a submucosal tunnel. This type of diversion is poorly suited to patients who are obese, have diverticulitis, or a pelvic malignancy which may be irradiated.[1] Ureterosigmoidostomy requires good anal sphincter control, good renal function, and undilated upper urinary tracts with active ureteral peristalsis. In patients having this procedure pyelonephritis, hydronephrosis, and hyperchloremic acidosis are prone to develop. Ureteroileocutaneous diversion (ileal conduit) as described by Seiffert in 1935[1a] and popularized by Bricker in the 1950s[2] has proved to be the most adaptable and widely used permanent supravesical urinary diversion. Peristalsis of

651

the ileal segment avoids residual urine, and isolation from the fecal stream lessens the likelihood of pyelonephritis. The low pressure, isoperistaltic system tends to prevent hydronephrosis and allows a simple ureteroileal anastomosis with less likelihood of stricture and obstruction. Because of the good drainage and low pressure of the system, preoperative hydronephrosis often improves after ileal conduit diversion.

During the past twenty-five years numerous reports have appeared demonstrating that ileal conduit urinary diversion also has significant complications.[3-8] Early operative mortality and late intestinal obstruction are the most distressing. Pyelonephritis and hyperchloremic acidosis occur more frequently when present preoperatively, stomal stenosis and pyocystis are bothersome, but rarely life threatening.

While cutaneous ureterostomy, sigmoid conduit, ureterosigmoidostomy, and ileal conduit are all valuable diversionary procedures in the proper surgical setting, this review focuses on what we believe is the most versatile urinary diversion, the ileal conduit.

MATERIAL

During the period 1965 through 1974, there were 160 ileal conduit diversions performed by the urologic residents and attending staff of Emory University and Affiliated Hospitals. Eight of these patients have been eliminated because of inadequate records. The remaining 152 patients include 69 children and 83 adults with ages ranging from two months to seventy-four years. Ileopyelostomy was performed in 3 cases, and 4 patients had ileal conduit diversion of a solitary kidney. Followup of pediatric patients has been from two months to nine years with the average being two and one-half years. For adults, followup has been from one month to eight years with an average of two years.

INDICATIONS

Ileal conduit diversion was performed for malignant disease in 37 cases and for nonmalignant disease in 115 cases (Table 1). In the pediatric group, only 1 patient suffered from a malignancy (rhabdomyosarcoma of the pelvis). Two thirds of the children underwent diversion because of a congenital neurogenic bladder dysfunction, most commonly myelomeningocele, and one half of the diversions in adults were for neurogenic bladder (acquired type). One patient is included who underwent the creation of an ileal conduit followed by renal homotransplantation.

Urinary diversion is believed to be indicated in those patients with neurogenic bladder in whom unilateral or bilateral vesicoureteral reflux develops with evidence of pyelonephritis or other upper tract changes (namely,

TABLE 1. Indications

	No. of Patients	%
Children		
Neurogenic bladder (congenital)	44	64.0
Neurogenic bladder (acquired)	7	10.0
Exstrophy	8	12.0
Obstructive anomalies	8	12.0
Incontinence	1	1.0
Rhabdomyosarcoma of pelvis	1	1.0
Totals	69	100
Adults		
Transitional cell carcinoma (bladder)	20	24.0
Squamous carcinoma (bladder)	9	11.0
Adenocarcinoma (bladder)	3	3.6
Carcinoma of cervix	2	2.4
Adenomyosarcoma of bladder	1	1.2
Myoblastoma	1	1.2
Neurogenic bladder (acquired)	35	42.0
Neurogenic bladder (congenital)	4	5.0
Urethral stricture	3	3.6
Exstrophy	2	2.4
Incontinence	2	2.4
Interstitial cystitis	1	1.2
Totals	83	100

hydronephrosis or parenchymal atrophy). Diversion is performed with the goal of preserving existing renal tissue and maintaining or even improving renal function. It is this philosophy, coupled with our large population of acquired neurogenic bladders, that has resulted in the great number of diversions done in this series for benign disease. Chronic renal insufficiency, hyperchloremic acidosis and hydroureter, and hydronephrosis were not considered contraindications to ileal conduit diversion.

TECHNIQUE

The creation of an ileal conduit is not a difficult procedure, but demands great attention to detail. We perform the operation essentially as described by Bricker.[2] A button of abdominal wall tissue at the predetermined stomal site is generally excised prior to opening the abdomen. For small children, a stoma at least 0.5 inch in diameter is made, and the bowel splayed when necessary to achieve this size. The conduit is made as short as possible, still allowing it to reach comfortably from retroperitoneum to skin. Ureteroileal anastomosis is accomplished in a single layer. When cystectomy is planned, the conduit is usually created first, since it is the more tedious part of the procedure, demanding maximum concentration.

RESULTS

There was a single postoperative death (0.7 percent) of 152 ileal conduits performed (Table 2). This patient was

TABLE 2. Mortality

	Malignant		Benign	
	No.	%	No.	%
Early	0/37	0	1/115	0.9
Late	17/37	46	5/115	3.3
Total	17/37	46	6/115	4.0

TABLE 3. Early and Late Complications

	Patients	
Complications	No.	%
Early		
Wound infection	11/152	7.2
Dehiscence	5/152	3.3
Ureteral leak	4/152	2.6
Sepsis	4/152	2.6
Azotemia	2/152	1.3
Intestinal obstruction or fistula	1/152	0.7
Ureteral obstruction	1/152	0.7
Loop necrosis	1/152	0.7
Death	1/152	0.7
Late		
Pyocystis	19/107	17.8
Pyocystis (required cystectomy)	6/107	5.6
Stomal stenosis	19/151	12.6
Stomal stenosis (required revision)	11/151	7.3
Hyperchloremic acidosis	16/151	10.6
Intestinal obstruction	16/151	10.6
Intestinal obstruction (required laparotomy)	11/151	7.3
Pyelonephritis	13/151	8.6
Ureteroileal obstruction	6/151	4.0
Calculi	4/151	2.6
Parastomal hernia	4/151	2.6
Uremia	3/151	2.0

a two-month-old child with myelomeningocele and complete sacral agenesis, patent ductus arteriosus, crossed renal ectopia, and vesicoureteral reflux. Wound infection, wound dehiscence, small-bowel fistula, and sepsis developed, and she died on the eighth postoperative day after unsuccessful surgical exploration.

Twenty-two patients (14.6 percent) died after discharge from the hospital. Of these, 5 patients had benign disease and 17 patients had malignant disease. In the benign group, 2 of the 5 died of complications related to their surgery: (1) dehydration and acidosis secondary to chronic renal failure, and (2) gram-negative sepsis secondary to a urinary tract infection. In the malignant group, 16 patients died from the primary tumor, and 1 from sepsis with failure of wound healing after irradiation. Radiation therapy was performed in 43 percent of patients with malignancies in this series. Two adult patients underwent conversion to an ileal conduit, having previously undergone cystectomy and ureterosigmoidostomy for extrophy. In both patients carcinoma of the colon had developed, and 1 of the patients subsequently died of this disease.

Complications have been divided into early and late categories (Table 3). Early complications are those occurring in the first thirty days after surgery, and late complications are all those occurring after that period. Patients with malignant disease were noted to have a higher overall complication rate: 62 percent (23 of 37 cases) malignant versus 50 percent (57 of 115 cases) benign. The malignant group, 13 of 37 cases (35 percent), had a higher incidence of early complications compared with the benign group, 18 of 15 cases (16 percent), while the reverse was true for late complications malignant, 14 of 37 cases (38 percent), and benign, 52 of 115 cases (45 percent).

Wound infection (7.2 percent) was the chief problem in the early period, and wound dehiscence (3.3 percent) was often the result. Two factors contributing to these complications are the long operative time and the transection of bowel during the procedure. Ureteral leak (2.6 percent) and ureteral obstruction (0.7 percent) when they occur, must be appreciated early and repaired, or they can become devastating problems. Two patients in this series suffered distal ureteral slough and urinary leak as late as four weeks after conduit surgery. One patient

experienced loop cyanosis and early necrosis requiring excision and creation of a new ileal conduit. This emphasizes the importance of selecting a good vascular arcade for the loop, and then not compromising it during the remainder of the procedure.

Pyocystis (17.8 percent), which can occur with any type of urinary diversion, was easily our most common late complication. Excluded are 34 patients undergoing cystectomy for malignant disease and 10 patients who underwent the removal of an exstrophied bladder. Two thirds of the patients with pyocystis have not required cystectomy and have been treated successfully with intermittent providone-iodine (Betadine) or neomycin-polymyxin B (Neosporin) bladder irrigation. Cystectomy was believed indicated in the remaining one-third for persistent purulent urethral discharge and fever.

Stomal stenosis (12.6 percent) has also been a significant late problem. Stomal revision was required in 7.3 percent, while 5.3 percent have responded to local care and dilation. Two patients (both children) have undergone repeat stomal revision, and as a group, children clearly have had more stomal problems than adults.

The incidence of hyperchloremic acidosis (10.6 percent) reflects an aggressive approach to urinary diversion in patients, particularly children, who already have impaired renal function. Forty-three percent of adults with hyperchloremic acidosis had preexisting acidosis or renal disease and 78 percent of children with hyperchloremic acidosis suffered from compromised renal function prior to diversion. In the majority of cases the acidosis and hyperchloremia were mild and easily controlled medically. The pediatric patients include 2 with bilateral ileopyelostomies and 1 with a unilateral ileopyelostomy, and 3 children who required loop shortening to relieve persistent acidosis.

Among the cases of intestinal obstruction (10.6 percent) postileal conduit, surgery to relieve the obstruction was necessary in two-thirds, while the other one-third responded to nasogastric decompression. One patient has been explored on two occasions for lysis of intra-abdominal adhesions.

Pyelonephritis (8.6 percent) has occurred in 13 patients including 2 with bilateral ileopyelostomies, 2 with partial ureteral obstruction, and 1 with calculi. Ureteroileal obstruction (4 percent) can precipitate pyelonephritis and even pyonephrosis, or cause a slow, insidious type of renal deterioration. Of the 6 patients with this complication, 2 have undergone revision (1 patient twice), 1 died of carcinoma prior to revision, and 3 are not considered severe enough to repair at this time.

Calculi (2.6 percent) have been surprisingly rare in this series and have not occurred in any pediatric patients. The degree of calculous formation has varied from 1 patient with bilateral staghorn to 3 patients who have passed multiple small calculi. Parastomal hernia (2.6 percent) can be a real problem in maintaining a wellfitting appliance and may contribute to an elevated loop residual urine. The importance of a good peritoneal to serosal (ileal) apposition is emphasized. Three children with chronic renal insufficiency suffered transiently more severe uremia (2 percent) after ileal loop diversion.

Renal status was evaluated by comparison of pre- and postoperative intravenous pyelography. In 72 percent of children (50 of 69) and 80 percent of adults (66 of

83), the pyelogram was unchanged after ileal conduit diversion. However, of those that did change, 26 percent of children (18 of 69) and 8 percent of adults (7 of 83) showed improvement while 2 percent of children (1 of 69) and 12 percent of adults (10 of 83) were seen to deteriorate. Over-all renal status, therefore, was 17 percent improved, 76 percent unchanged, and 7 percent deteriorated.

COMMENT

The results of a study depend greatly on patient population which reflects the surgeon's indications for the operation (Table 4). With the exception of the series by Schmidt el al.[6] most reviews of ileal loop diversion[3-5,7,8] have described a majority of patients treated for malignancies. Several authors[9-11] have limited their discussion to pediatric diversions. In this series 76 percent of the patients suffered from benign disorders and 45 percent of the patients were children. An aggressive approach has been taken with regard to upper tract changes (pyelonephritis, hydronephrosis, or parenchymal atrophy) which are considered secondary to irreversible lower tract disease. Diversion has been performed early enough to preserve renal tissue and function in most cases. However, chronic renal failure, hyperchloremic acidosis and hydroureter, and hydronephrosis have not been considered contraindications to ileal loop diversion.

Operative mortality figures vary considerably, tending to be best for children and worst for patients with cancer. Arnarson and Straffon[10] reported no operative mortality in 55 children who had conduit diversions; Delgado and Muecke[9] had 1.2 percent operative mortality for 80 children, while the figure for this series is comparable at 1.4 percent for 69 children. Our overall operative mortality is 0.9 percent (benign) and 0 percent

TABLE 4. Comparison of Complications (%)

	Mortality		Wound Infec-tion	Wound Dehis-cence	Ureteral Leak	Ureteral Obstruc-tion	Pyelone-phritis	Hyper-chloremic Acidosis	Intes-tinal Obstruc-tion	Stomal Stenosis	Calculi
	Benign	Malig-nant									
Cordonnier and Nicolai (1960)[3]	—	3.7 —	5.2	6.3	2.1	6.8	8.4	—	2.6	12.0	4.7
Creevy (1960)[3]			—	—	—	—	—	16.7	—	—	4.4
Cohen and Persky (1967)[7]	2.2	10.9	6.7	11.6	1.7	7.5	2.5	1.7	10.8	—	1.7
Jaffe, Bricker, and Butcher (1968)[8]	3.1	8.1	7.5	2.6	2.6	—	2.8	—	11.2	—	—
Engle (1969)[5]	—	—	7.6	1.9	3.4	4.3	—	—	6.3	20.7	8.2
Ellis, Udall, and Hodges (1971)[4]	10.0	12.6	8.4	3.6	10.0	5.6	13.2	—	6.8	17.1	6.4
Schmidt et al. (1973)[6]	2.3	6.2	6.2	3.4	2.2	7.9	21.9	9.6	5.1	18.0	10.7
Remigailo et al. (this series)	0.9	0	7.2	3.3	2.6	4.0	8.6	10.6	10.6	12.6	2.6
Bowles and Tall (1967)[11]	15.0		—	—	—	—	—	15.0	—	20.0	24.0
Arnarson and Straffon (1969)[10]	0		—	—	—	5.4	9.1	3.6	—	16.4	3.6
Delgado and Muecke (1973)[9]	1.2		—	—	—	3.7	15.0	—	—	23.7	6.2

(malignant) which compares, favorably with the literature, where figures range from 2 to 10 percent for benign cases[4,12] and from 6.2 to 23 percent for malignant cases.[6,12] Our complication rates for benign (50 percent) and malignant (62 percent) disorders are similar to those of Cohen and Persky:[7] benign (48 percent) and malignant (64 percent). As demonstrated previously by Schmidt and co-workers,[6] the malignant group had more early complications, but late complications were more common for the benign group which had a longer life expectancy.

Wound infection (7.2 percent) and dehiscence (3.3 percent) are a significant problem for this procedure. Other authors have shown the incidence of wound infection to range from 5.2 to 8.4 percent[3,4] and wound dehiscence from 1.9 to 11.6 percent.[5,7] The use of nonabsorbable closure, prolonged nasogastric drainage (four days), and broad-spectrum antibiotic coverage are considered important in avoiding these complications. Postoperative ureteral leak can be a very serious complication which must be diagnosed early and corrected. The importance of preserving ureteral blood supply and creating a watertight anastomosis is emphasized. Prevention of abdominal distention and increased intra-abdominal pressure by nasogastric suction is crucial in avoiding distal ureteral slough. Even small urinary leaks at the site of the anastomosis contribute to periureteral fibrosis and subsequent stenosis. Others reported an incidence of ureteral leak of 2.2 percent,[6] 2.6 percent,[8] 3.4 percent,[5] and 10 percent.[4] In this review the rate was 2.6 percent, and this includes 2 patients in whom ureteral leakage developed three to four weeks after surgery.

In spite of postoperative bladder irrigation with neomycin-polymyxin B sulfate for five days, pyocystis has occurred in a significant number of our patients (17.8 percent), but the percentage requiring cystectomy has been much lower (5.6 percent). Repeat bladder irrigations with neomycin-polymyxin B sulfate and povidone-iodine are often sufficient to prevent further symptoms. Others have reported a varying degree of difficulty with pyocystis (1.8 percent,[10] 11.2 percent,[9] 12.4 percent,[6] 13 percent,[4] and 21.5 percent[5]).

Skin irritation can result from a poorly fitting appliance in the presence of alkaline urine. The removal of a full-thickness button of the abdominal wall is important in creating an adequate stoma and ultimately preventing stenosis. Children are particularly susceptible to stomal stenosis because of the disparity of the initial stomal button with the ultimate size of the ileum. Our incidence of stomal stenosis (12.6 percent) is slightly lower than most: others reporting 16.4 percent,[10] 17.1 percent,[4] 18 percent,[6] 20.7 percent,[5] and 23.7 percent.[9] Stomal revision was required in 7.3 percent of the patients in this series. Pyelonephritis occurred in 8.6 percent of our patients, compared with other reports ranging from 2.5 to 21.9 percent.[6,7] Ureteral obstruction has been noted to occur in from 3.7 to 7.9 percent[6,9] of cases, while this series demonstrated an incidence of 4 percent.

Calculous formation after ileal conduit surgery is related to alkaline urine, urinary stasis, hyperchloremic acidosis,[13] and patient immobilization. An increased incidence of calculi after ileal conduit diversion for myelomeningocele in children has been reported.[14] Our figures do not support this, since there were no calculi formed by children in this series, and the over-all occurrence of 2.6 percent was also low. Schmidt and coworkers[6] reported postconduit stone formation in 10.7 percent of cases, and in a pediatric series Bowles and Tall[11] reported an incidence of 24 percent. The infrequent formation of calculi by our patients is unusual, since hyperchloremic acidosis was present in 10.6 percent of the combined series and in 13.2 percent of the children. Cohen and Persky[7] reported only 1.7 percent of cases with hyperchloremic acidosis while Creevy[15] described an incidence of 16.7 percent. Creevy[15] considers preexisting hyperchloremic acidosis from tubular disease to be a contraindication to ileal loop diversion. Although hyperchloremic acidosis may be aggravated in patients with impaired renal function by the formation of an ileal diversion, renal function in our patients has not deteriorated, and in many cases has improved. The length of the ileum has been kept as short as possible to minimize absorption, and when present, acidosis in most cases has not been difficult to control medically.

Transient postoperative hydronephrosis occurs in 50 percent of patients after ileal loop diversion.[8] In 90 percent of these the hydronephrosis will have resolved by six months and is attributed to anastomotic inflammation and edema.[16] Hydronephrosis secondary to vesicoureteral obstruction or reflux often improves postoperatively, and this is especially true for children. Preexisting hydronephrosis may be aggravated if the conduit is made too long, producing redundancy, poor drainage, and increased conduit pressure. Poor ureteral blood supply and urinary leak with periureteral fibrosis can produce ureteroileal obstruction and hydronephrosis or nonfunction. These changes can progress slowly with the patient remaining asymptomatic. Follow-up intravenous pyelograms are necessary to rule out obstructive changes and a loopogram is useful in diagnosing ureteroileal obstruction in the presence of a nonfunctioning or poorly functioning kidney. Free ileoureteral reflux should be present in an unobstructed conduit.

Postoperative intravenous pyelography in our series showed renal status unchanged (76 percent), improved (17 percent), and deteriorated (7 percent). The percentage improvement in the pediatric group (26 percent) was far greater than in the adult group (8 percent). Other pediatric series reveal an even greater improvement in renal architecture. Delgado and Muecke[9] (38 percent) and Arnarson and Straffon[10] (31 percent), and the combined series by Schmidt et al.[6] (46 percent) reports the best results. Our high percentage of patients with unchanged renal status reflects a willingness to divert early before renal deterioration has occurred.

1365 Clifton Road, N.E.
Atlanta, Georgia 30322
(DR. WALTON)

REFERENCES

1. WILLIAMS, D. I.: Urinary Diversion by Sigmoid Conduit. Current Controversies in Urologic Management, 1st ed, Philadelphia, WB Saunders Company, 1972, p 294

1a. SEIFFERT, L.: Die "Darm-Siphonblase." Arch f Klin Chir 183:569 1935

2. BRICKER, E. M.: Bladder substitution after pelvic evisceration. Surg Clin North Am 30:1511, 1950

3. CORDONNIER, J. J., and NICOLAI, C. H.: An evaluation of the use of an isolated segment of ileum as a means of urinary diversion, J Urol 83:834, 1960

4. ELLIS, L. R., UDALL, D. A. and HODGES, C. V.: Further clinical experience with intestinal segment for urinary diversion, Ibid 105:354, 1971

5. ENGLE, R. M.: Complications of bilateral uretero-ileo cutaneous urinary diversion, Ibid 101:508, 1969

6. SCHMIDT, J. D. HAWTREY, C. E., FLOCKS, R. H., and CULP, D. A.: Complications, results and problems of ileal conduit diversions. Ibid 109:210, 1973

7. COHEN, S. M., and PERSKY, L.: A ten-year experience with ureteroileostomy, Arch Surg 95:278, 1967

8. JAFFE, B. M., BRICKER, E. M., and BUTCHER, H. R., JR.: Surgical complications of ileal segment urinary diversion, Ann Surg 167:367, 1968

9. DELGADO, G. E., and MUECKE, E. C.: Evaluation of 80 cases of ileal conduits in children: indications, complications and results J Urol 109:311, 1973

10. ARNARSON, O., and STRAFFON, R. A.: Clinical experience with the ileal conduit in children. Ibid 102:768, 1969

11. BOWLES, W. T., and TALLI, B. A.: Urinary diversion in children. Ibid 98:597, 1967

12. KERR, W. K., ROBSON, C. J., RUSSELL, J. L. T., and BOURQUE, J. P.: Collective review of urinary tract diversions. Ibid 88:644, 1962

13. DRETLER, S. P.: The pathogenesis of urinary tract calculi occurring after ileal conduit diversion. Ibid 109:204, 1973

14. REGE, P. R., LEVINE, M. S., OPPENHEIMER, S., and EVANS, A. T.: Renal calculi and biochemical abnormalities. Urology 5:12, 1975

15. CREEVY, D. D.: Renal complications after ileac diversion of the urine in non-neoplastic disorders. J Urol 83:394, 1960

16. KOEHLER, P. R., and BOWLES, W. T.: Radiologic evaluation of the upper urinary tract following ileal loop urinary diversion. Radiology 86:227, 1969

17. BUTCHER, H. R., JR., SUGG, W. L., MCAFEE, C. A., and BRICKER, E. M.: Ileal conduit method of ureteral urinary diversion. Ann Surg 156:682, 1962

Commentary: Ileal Conduit Diversion in Adults

Myron S. Roberts*

The cutaneous ureteroileostomy, or ileal conduit, as popularized by Bricker in 1950, remains as the most commonly used method of supravesical urinary diversion in adults.[1] However, over the years the many late complications of this procedure have become increasingly more apparent, raising the question of whether this operation is advisable in patients with an anticipated life expectancy of over 15 to 20 yr.

Fortunately, young adults, who previously would have required a supravesical diversion for nonmalignant disease can often be conservatively managed with appropriate pharmacologic agents, bladder pacemakers, or intermittent catheterization. This has significantly decreased the number of these operations being performed in this age group. In addition, many of these previously "diverted" patients are now being "undiverted," and those young adults who do require urinary diversion do better with a colon conduit with antirefluxing ureterocolic anastomosis.

It is the purpose of this commentary to describe briefly the preoperative management, the surgical technique, and postoperative care of patients who require a cutaneous ureteroileostomy.

* My appreciation to Ms. Yvonne Esposito, ET, for her contribution to this chapter.

PREOPERATIVE CONSIDERATIONS

Perhaps one of the more important aspects of the preoperative management of patients being prepared for ileal conduit diversion is the complete and thorough description of the procedure to the patient so that there will be no surprises regarding the presence and location of the urinary stoma.

The urologist should notify the enterostomal therapist (ET) as soon as the patient is admitted to the hospital to begin preoperative counseling. This preparation is essential, since the period before surgery is anxiety provoking for the patient who will soon have a urinary stoma.

It is often assumed that the patient will not understand the descriptions of such a procedure or will be frightened by too much detail. It has been my experience that patients requiring a urinary stoma approach surgery with totally erroneous ideas. Therefore, precise and factual explanations usually prove to be a relief in comparison to the patient's misconceptions.

Major areas of concern for the patient undergoing ostomy surgery are the pouch, stoma, odor, clothing, sexual activities, diet, and independence. Familiarization with the pouch can be done with a description, diagram, or the appliance itself. Familiarization with the stoma can be accomplished through explanation of its color, approximate size, and location. Reassuring the patient that there will not be a urinary odor and that the pouch will lie flat against the abdomen and will be concealed under clothing is quite comforting.

The prospect of not being able to resume former social, recreational, and vocational activities is another concern; therefore, it should be emphasized that having an ileal conduit does not prevent a person from resuming a job and usual recreational activities.

Most patients are extremely concerned about their sexual capabilities after diversionary surgery. They believe that their sexual activities will be limited and that they will lose their sexual attractiveness. This need not be so if just an ileal conduit is performed, and the patient should be reassured in this regard. However, in the male who is undergoing a total cystectomy in addition to an ileal conduit, impotence is almost certain.

Lastly, many patients assume that the ostomy will be too difficult for them to handle without assistance. Unless handicapped, adult stomates should be taught to be totally independent with their ostomy management.

After consultation with the ET, the patient is placed on a low-residue diet 1 day before surgery. Cleansing enemas are given the night before surgery. Antimicrobial agents are not used preoperatively unless there the large bowel might be entered. If so, 1 g of neomycin is given every hour for 4 doses, followed by 1 g every 4 hr for an additional 5 doses.

SURGICAL TECHNIQUE

The incision to enter the abdomen is either through a left paramedian or a midline approach. To proceed, identify the right ureter medial to the cecum and as it crosses the common iliac artery. Open the posterior peritoneum and mobilize the ureter, taking great care to preserve its adventitial covering. The distal right ureter is usually transected about 4 cm above the right ureterovesical junction. If the procedure is being performed for bladder carcinoma, obtain a frozen section of the distal end of the proximal ureter to be sure the implanted ureter is free of microscopic carcinoma.

Identify the left ureter lateral to the sigmoid colon and as it too crosses the common iliac artery; mobilize it in a similar manner. The proximal segment of the left ureter must be adequately mobilized to allow for easy passage, without angulation, through the mesosigmoid. Place 8 French infant feeding tubes into both proximal ureters and drain them externally while the surgical procedure continues.

The actual surgical technique of isolating the ileal conduit has been described in great detail and will not be repeated.[1-3] However, a short conduit should be created, since it provides better drainage and decreases the incidence of hyperchloremic acidosis.

Suture the ileal conduit to the posterior and lateral parietal peritoneum with nonabsorbable sutures. This prevents postoperative internal herniation. Deliver the proximal end of the conduit through a circular defect in the fascia and a corresponding defect in the skin in a previously selected site. Suture the conduit to the fascia with 3–0 chromic catgut and create a "bud" stoma by suturing the skin, ileal serosa, and then full-thickness of the ileal stoma with 3–0 chromic catgut. I prefer the "bud" stoma over the flush stoma.

My preference for the ureteroileal anastomosis is the Wallace 1 technique, particularly when working with normal-sized, nonradiated ureters. This type of anastomosis has several advantages over the conventional end-to-side Bricker anastomosis:[4]

1. No circumferential suture line exists at the anastomotic site, resulting in a very low incidence of ureteroileal strictures.
2. The Wallace anastomosis, in most instances, can be performed more rapidly than the Bricker anastomosis.

The technique for the Wallace anastomosis includes bringing both ureters out through a central posterior peritoneal incision with the anterior wall of each ureter spatulated for 3 cm. Then suture the ureters along their medial aspect with continuous 4–0 atraumatic chromic catgut, with both ureters coming to lie side by side. Use a single layer of 4–0 atraumatic chromic catgut to anastomose the now-joined ureters to the distal open end of the ileal conduit (Fig. 1). Retroperitonealize the anastomosis; leave 8 French infant feeding tubes in dwelling in each ureter and bring them out through the conduit stoma. The ileal conduit usually becomes aperistaltic after surgery, as does the rest of the bowel. The atonicity of the conduit, together with stomal edema, can produce a large residual urine, which may result in leakage at the ureteroileal anastomosis. It is for this reason that ureteral stents should be left in dwelling for 4 to 5 days.

If urinary leakage does occur, it has been my experience that the fistula will close spontaneously, provided the pelvis has been well drained. Reoperation is rarely necessary unless there has been a complete ureteral separation.

Leave Shirley sump drains in dwelling in the right and left pelvis together with two Penrose drains and bring them out through the lower angle of the incision. Close the wound with no. 28-wire figure-of-8 sutures and reinforce this with vertical mattress nylon retention sutures.

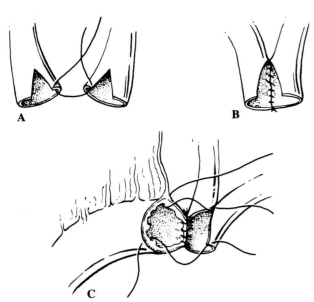

Fig. 1. (*A* through *C*) Ureteroileal anastomosis demonstrating the original Wallace technique.

POSTOPERATIVE CARE

I routinely use postoperative nasogastric drainage and supportive treatment with parenteral antibiotics. Shirley sump drains are usually ineffective after 72 to 96 hr because they plug with fibrin and debris and are then removed. Penrose drains are left *in situ* for at least 7 days or longer if there is evidence of prolonged serous, lymphatic, or urinary drainage.

Immediately after surgery, apply a temporary transparent pouch with an adhesive plate over the stoma. Connect the pouch to a bedside drainage unit to avoid excess accumulation of urine. Change the pouch every 2 days, carefully checking the viability of the stoma and the condition of the peristomal skin.

By the second postoperative week, the patient is ready to help with his own ostomy care. The patient's spouse should be included in some teaching sessions to observe stoma care but not as an active participant.

POSTOPERATIVE COMPLICATIONS

Early. Early postoperative complications of the ileal conduit are often related to one of the following factors: error in surgical technique, the usual problems associated with performing major abdominal surgery, preexisting renal disease, prior pelvic radiation, and a patient's poor preoperative nutritional status.[3]

Some of these complications include wound infection, dehiscence, urinary leakage at the ureteroileal anastomosis, peritonitis, sepsis, azotemia with electrolyte imbalance, intestinal obstruction, ureteral obstruction, ileal fistula, loop necrosis, and stomal necrosis.

Late. Late complications include stomal stenosis, hyperchloremic acidosis, intestinal obstruction, pyelonephritis, ureteral obstruction, renal calculi, parastomal hernia, conduit vasculitis, and a redundant conduit. Careful attention must be paid to the length of the conduit, since a redundant conduit can produce improper drainage, causing upper tract deterioration and metabolic abnormalities.

REFERENCES

1. Bricker EM: Bladder substitute after pelvic exenteration. Surg Clin North Am 30:1511, 1950
2. Butcher H, Sugg WL, McAfee CA, et al: Ileal conduit methods of ureteral urinary diversion. Ann Surg 156:682, 1962
3. Morales P, Whitehead ED: Current Operative Urology. pp 451–456. Hagerstown, Harper & Row, 1975
4. Weiderhorn A, Roberts M: Ureteroileal anastomosis—comparison of Wallace and Bricker techniques. Urology 3:168, 1974

ANOTATED BIBLIOGRAPHY

Jeter K: The flush versus the protruding urinary stoma. 116:424, 1976

Disagreement still exists over the preference for the flush or bud stoma in patients undergoing urinary diversion. Of the 125 patients with urinary stomas that were interviewed, 85 had bud stomas and 40 had flush stomas.

The inability to visualize the stoma when applying the collection device was a unanimous complaint with all patients with a flush stoma and only rarely a complaint in patients with a bud stoma. The average wearing time of the collection apparatus for patients with a flush stoma was 3 days; it was 5 days for those with a bud stoma. The occurrence of diurnal urinary leakage was three times as high in patients with a flush stoma.

Peristomal dermatitis occurred in 75% of patients with a flush stoma and 31% with a bud stoma. This is in part explained by the larger amounts of urine accumulating within the flange and surrounding the stoma and under the faceplate in a flush stoma. Fear of injuring the stoma when changing the appliance was slightly greater in patients with a bud stoma.

The author concludes that a bud stoma is preferred in patients undergoing urinary diversion.

Soloway M, Myers G, Burdick J et al: Ileal conduit cytology in the diagnosis of recurrent cancer. Urol 107:835, 1972

Exfoliative urine cytology is a well-accepted technique for evaluating and diagnosing epithelial tumors of the urinary tract. Ileal loop cytology is more difficult because of the large amount of bacteria, columnar cells, histiocytes, and cellular debris that tends to obscure the neoplastic cells.

The authors reported on four patients with positive ileal conduit urine cytology from the records of the National Institutes of Health between 1960 and 1970. Two of these patients had recurrent transitional cell carcinoma of the urinary tract, and two had metastatic squamous cell carcinoma of the cervix. Gross hematuria from the conduit was the most common complaint in these patients. There were no false-positive cytologic findings.

The authors recommend ileal conduit urine cytology in addition to an intravenous pyelogram (IVP) in those patients presenting with gross hematuria who have undergone diversion for either bladder carcinoma or squamous cell carcinoma of the cervix.

Assadnia A, Lee C, Petre J, et al: Two cases of stone formation in ileal conduits after using staple gun for closure of proximal end of isolated loop. J Urol 108:553, 1972

Autosuture with a stapling instrument was used in five patients undergoing ileal conduit urinary diversion between 1968 and 1970. In two of these patients, struvite calculi developed in the conduit and around the exposed part of the metal clips used to close the proximal end of the conduit 3 to 6 mo after surgery. The authors did not find that using the autosuture decreased operating time, and they believe that the stapling instrument has no place in urologic surgery.

Bagley D, Glazier M, Osias M, et al: Retroperitoneal drainage of ureterointestinal conduits. J Urol 121:271, 1979

Urinary leakage following ureteroileal anastomosis is considered an early and common complication of this operation. The occurrence of urinary leakage is even higher when the diversion is performed after a course of pelvic external radiotherapy. In some series, the morbidity and mortality associated with urinary leakage have been as high as 50%. With the proper use of retroperitoneal and pelvic drains, the overall morbidity associated with this urinary leakage is significantly reduced. Only 5 of 21 patients with urinary leakage in this series of 132 patients with ureterointestinal anastomosis required reoperation, and there were no mortalities.

Redman J: Short ileal conduit: Rationale and description of a technique. J Urol 117:156, 1977

There is growing dissatisfaction with ileal conduits because of the findings of long-term renal deterioration. The author believes that the lack of standardization of the operation, primarily the length of the ileal conduit, is a major etiologic factor in this problem. It has been observed that since the surgeon tends to accept whatever length of ileum he originally isolates and rarely will shorten it, it is wiser to isolate a segment of ileum that almost seems too short.

The technique employs an extended mobilization of the left ureter and additional mobilization of the mesentery of the ileum. The peritoneum of the lateral abdominal wall is then mobilized, allowing the short conduit to be brought out extraperitoneally.

This short conduit will retain a small amount of residual urine, resulting in a lesser degree of bacteriuria and a lower incidence of hyperchloremic acidosis. Long-term studies may indicate a significant decrease in renal deterioration when a short ileal conduit is made.

OVERVIEW: HIGH ILEAL CONDUIT DIVERSION AND ILEAL CONDUIT DIVERSION IN ADULTS

John J. Murphy

As in the case of so many surgical innovations, their introduction is announced with great enthusiasm and received with great acclaim. This is followed either by increasing numbers of reports modifying the original warm reception or by diminishing numbers of comments on the subject. All too seldom, reports of large experience of long duration appear, and the truth or apparent truth of the value of the innovation is revealed. Such is certainly the case in regard to bowel as a urinary conduit. For at least a decade after Bricker's classic description of the use of ileum as a urinary conduit, the literature was crowded with laudatory reports of experience with and modifications of this procedure. During the next 15 yr, there were increasing numbers of reports expressing concern about early and late problems with bowel conduits, and in the past 5 yr, several large series with long-term follow-up studies have apeared. These emphasize the many problems with technique and postoperative management and, in a startling fashion, demonstrate the high incidence of serious complications associated with the use of bowel (of any type) as a urinary conduit. The reviews of Dunn and colleages and of Elder and associates in the *British Journal of Urology* in December 1979 permit comparison of ileal and colonic conduits from long-term experience in children (Table 1).[1,2]

TABLE 1. Comparison of Ileal and Colonic Conduits in Children

	No. of Patients	Follow-up Study (age)	Stomal Problems	Upper Tract Deterioration
Ileal	67	10.2 yrs (mean)	49%	28%
Colonic	41	13.2 yrs (average)	61.5%	48%

Other problems included recurrent severe infection (20% in ileal conduits and 34% in colonic conduits). Stones formed in six patients with colonic conduits and in eight patients with ileal conduits. Most disturbing was the finding of conduit–ureteral reflux in 58% of patients with colonic conduits, in whom special efforts were made at operation to prevent this phenomenon.

Adults fared little better in a report by Renigailo and colleagues.[3] Of 152 patients (including 69 children) followed 1 to 9 yr, they found early complications in 19.8% and later complications in 70.4%. Stomal problems were encountered in 12.6%. It is interesting to note that the incidence of intestinal obstruction was 10.6%, a finding not mentioned in the British reviews.

It is apparent that bowel conduit diversions are not what they were first thought to be, that is, the solution for serious problems in urinary tract dysfunction. Patients managed in this way must be followed carefully, with annual excretory urography and conduitograms.

The use of small bowel as ureteral replacements (pyelo-ileocutaneous diversion) is very well reviewed by Drs. King and Scott in Chapter 48. These procedures are obviously susceptible to the same problems as ordinary conduits, with the additional hazard intrinsic in pyeloenteral anastomosis.

Dr. Roberts has done well to emphasize the importance of the psychological preparation of the patient for cutaneous diversion of urine and the value of the stomal therapist in this as well as in postoperative management of these patients. I am not enthusiastic about the Wallace technique for ureteroenteral anastomosis, however, because any complication in this area then involves both renal units. I implant the ureters individually, with wide spatulation of each ureter.

Experience with bud or flush stoma has convinced most surgeons of the merit of the bud, and I agree that the conduit should be as short as possible. There is apparently no technique available at present that prevents the myriad of problems inherent in the use of bowel as a urinary conduit.

REFERENCES

1. Dunn M, Roberts JBM, Smith PJB, et al: The long term results of ileal conduit diversion in children. Br J Urol 51:458, 1979
2. Elder DD, Moier CV, Rees RWM: A long term follow up of the colonic conduit operation in children. Br J Urol 51:462, 1979

3. Renigailo RV, Lewis EL, Woodard JR, et al: Ileal conduit urinary diversion urology 7:343, 1976

ILEAL CONDUITS IN CHILDREN AT THE MASSACHUSETTS GENERAL HOSPITAL FROM 1955 TO 1970

Anthony W. Middleton, Jr.* and W. Hardy Hendren†

From the Pediatric Surgery and Urology Services, Massachusetts General Hospital and the Department of Surgery, Harvard Medical School, Boston, Massachusetts

The Journal of Urology
Copyright © 1976 by The Williams & Wilkins Co.
Vol. 115, May
Printed in U.S.A.

ABSTRACT—The 45 ileal conduits performed on children at the Massachusetts General Hospital from 1955 to 1963 are reviewed and compared to the 45 ileal conduits performed from 1964 to 1970. Late complications involving the conduits occurred in 60 percent of the early group and in 51 percent of the late group. Of the renal units judged normal pyelographically preoperatively in the early group 77 percent went on to at least some deterioration, while 62 percent of the late group judged normal later deteriorated. Combining all renal units, 34 percent remained unchanged, 26 percent-improved and 41 percent showed some degree of deterioration after ileal conduit urinary diversion. The late complication and renal deterioration rates seem to increase progressively with time.

There was no apparent urinary obstruction in 13 percent of the renal units that deteriorated. Theoretical and experimental considerations indicate the reflux of infected urine as the etiology of the renal deterioration. Because of the late complications and the unacceptably high rate of renal deterioration we no longer perform ileal conduits in children. Instead every effort is made to reconstruct the urinary tract or, if urinary diversion is necessary, a colon conduit with non-refluxing ureterocolonic anastomoses is performed.

Accepted for publication July 18, 1975.

Read at annual meeting of Western Section, American Urological Association, Portland, Oregon, April 13–16, 1975

* Current address: 1060 E. First South, Salt Lake City, Utah 84102.

† Requests for reprints: Massachusetts General Hospital, Boston, Massachusetts 02114

The use of an isolated ileal segment into which both ureters were implanted for urinary diversion was first popularized in 1950 by Bricker who used it in patients who had undergone pelvic evisceration for cancer.[1] In 1954 Bill and associates,[2] and in 1956 Nash[3] reported on the successful use of ileal conduit urinary diversion in children. Since then there have been several series of ileal conduits in children reported.[4-17] Herein we review the experience with ileal conduit urinary diversion in children at the Massachusetts General Hospital between 1955 and 1970.

MATERIALS

Between 1955 and 1970, 90 children underwent ileal conduit urinary diversion at the Massachusetts General Hospital. Patient age at the time of diversion ranged from 1 month to 17 years (Table 1). There were 54 boys and 36 girls in the series.

To determine if the complication rate increased with longer periods of followup, a comparison was made of the conduits performed between 1955 and 1963 with those done between 1964 and 1970. The followup period ranges from 1 to 18 years, with an average of 7 years in the early group and 1 to 10 years, with an average of 3.5 years in the late group. The followup period was shortened because some patients were converted to other forms of urinary diversion, some were undiverted and some were lost to followup.

INDICATIONS

The largest number of ileal conduits was performed for neurogenic bladder, accounting for 37 of 90 children diverted (Table 2). Twenty-one children had exstrophy of the bladder, 16 were diverted after failed ureteral reimplantation, 10 had megaureters secondary to lower urinary tract obstruction and/or reflux, 2 were diverted following pelvic exenteration for tumor and 2 had irreparable surgical trauma to the bladder (Urethral stricture and bladder damage from tuberculosis accounted for 1 each). There is no significant difference in the indications for ileal conduit diversion between the early and late groups.

TABLE 1. Age at Time of Ileal Conduit

Age (yrs)	1953 to 1963	1964 to 1970
1 or less	9	10
2 to 4	5	10
5 to 8	14	10
9 to 12	10	5
13 to 17	7	10

TECHNIQUE

Although a few of the early ileal conduits were constructed with the ileal segment running along the right abdominal cavity side wall, the majority were made with the ureteroileal anastomoses in a mid retroperitoneal location with a short ileal segment passing directly through the peritoneal cavity and through the rectus abdominus muscle to the skin. The ureteroileal anastomosis was retroperitonealized and the ureters were anastomosed separately to the base of the ileal segment. Incidental appendectomy was performed with most of the conduits. All patients had a preoperative mechanical bowel preparation and most had an antimicrobial intestinal preparation as well.

RESULTS

Five children in the series died, only 2 from causes directly associated with the ileal conduit. One child in the early group died of bronchopneumonia in the early postoperative period and another in the early group died following conversion of the conduit into cutaneous ureterostomies because of recurrent pyelonephritis with subsequent increasing azotemia, renal transplantation and death from a perinephric abscess. There were 3 deaths in the late group. One death occurred 1 year after the original operation from a volvulus about the conduit mesentery, 1 resulted in the late postoperative period from an infected V-A shunt in a child with multiple congenital anomalies and 1 child was run over by an automobile.

Early complications are those occurring within 3 weeks of the original operation (Table 3) and late complications are those occurring more than 3 weeks postoperatively (Table 4).

EARLY COMPLICATIONS

In the 1955 to 1963 series 13 early complications occurred in 9 patients (20 percent), while only 3 early compli-

TABLE 2. Indications for Ileal Conduit Urinary Diversion

Disorder	1955 to 1963 No. Pts.	(%)	1964 to 1970 No. Pts.	(%)
Neurogenic bladder	20	(44)	17	(38)
Exstrophy of bladder	9	(20)	12	(27)
Failed ureteroneocystotomy	8	(18)	8	(18)
Megaureters secondary to lower urinary tract obstruction and/or reflux	7	(16)	3	(7)
Tumor	0		2	(4)
Surgical trauma to bladder	1	(2)	1	(2)
Urethral stricture	0		1	(2)
Bladder damage by tuberculosis	0		1	(2)

TABLE 3. Early Complications Occurring Within 3 Weeks of the Initial Operation

	1955 to 1963 No.	1964 to 1970 No.	Totals
Ileal conduit infarction	1	1	2
Gastrointestinal bleeding	2	0	2
Volvulus around adhesions	0	1	1
Ureteroileal anastomosis leak	1	1	2
Postop. hypertension with convulsions	1	0	1
Hypoprothrombinemia with bleeding	1	0	1
Death (from bronchopneumonia)	1	0	1
Convulsions secondary to high fever	1	0	1
Pyelonephritis	1	0	1
Conduit-cutaneous fistula	1	0	1
Stomal stenosis	1	0	1
Subphrenic abscess	1	0	1
Totals	12	3	15

cations were seen in 3 patients (7 percent) in the 1964 to 1970 series.

LATE COMPLICATIONS

In the 1955 to 1963 series 52 late complications occurred in 27 patients (60 percent). In the 1964 to 1970 series 39 late complications occurred in 23 patients (51 percent). Combining the early and late series there were 91 complications in 50 patients, with 55 percent of the children in this study sustaining at least 1 late complication.

Stomal stenosis was the most frequent complication, noted in 25 patients in the 1955 to 1963 series and in 13 patients in the 1964 to 1970 series. In the early series 8 patients required 1 revision of the stoma, 11 required 2 revisions, 1 required 3 revisions, 3 required 4 revisions and 1 required 5 revisions. One patient needed a new conduit because the old one was too short to permit revision. In the 1964 to 1970 series 13 patients required stomal revision, none of them more than once.

Acute pyelonephritis occurred in 10 cases (22 percent) in the early series and 8 cases (18 percent) in the late series. Two patients in the early series had recurrent episodes of acute pyelonephritis for which the ileal conduit was redone with subsequent decrease in the recurrence rate of pyelonephritis in 1. Acute pyelonephritis associated with gross hematuria in 1 of the early cases prompted revision of the diversion to cutaneous ureterostomies. That child subsequently required renal transplantation and later died of complications of the procedure. A nephrectomy was done on 1 child in the early series for recurrent pyelonephritis.

Ureteroileal anastomosis stenosis requiring revision was noted in 4 children in the early series and 5 children

TABLE 4. Late Complications Occurring More than 3 Weeks Postoperatively

	1955 to 1963 No.	(%)	1964 to 1970 No.	(%)	Totals No.	(%)
Stomal stenosis requiring surgical intervention	25	(56)	13	(29)	38	(42)
Pyelonephritis	10	(22)	8	(18)	18	(20)
Ureteroileal anastomosis stenosis	4	(9)	5	(11)	9	(10)
Ureteral obstruction at site other than ureteroileal anastomosis	2	(4)	0		2	(2)
Pyocystis	3	(7)	0		3	(3)
Intestinal obstruction	3	(7)	1	(2)	4	(4)
Calculus	3	(7)	5	(11)	8	(9)
Elongation of conduit requiring shortening or replacement	1	(2)	6	(13)	7	(8)
Replacement of poorly draining conduit of appropriate length and no mechanical obstruction	1	(2)	0		1	(1)
Hypertension secondary to chronic pyelonephritis	0		1	(2)	1	(1)
Totals	52		39		91	

in the late series. Because of recurrence of the stenosis, a second revision of the ureteroileal anastomosis was necessary in 1 case in the early series.

Ureteral obstruction not secondary to ureteroileal anastomosis stenosis was noted in 2 cases in the early series. In 1 case the kidney was severely hydronephrotic and nephrectomy was performed. In the other case the ureter was partially obstructed by a vascular band, which was divided with subsequent relief of the obstruction.

Pyocystis was seen in only 3 children in the early series. This complication was seen less frequently in our study than in other reported series of ileal conduits in children, the reason not being apparent.

Intestinal obstruction secondary to adhesions was noted in 3 cases in the early series. In the late series 1 death resulted from intestinal obstruction secondary to volvulus about the conduit mesentery.

Renal calculus was seen in 3 children in the early series and 5 in the late series. One of the latter patients reformed a stone 3 times and another reformed stones twice. All cases except 1 were associated with moderate to severe ureteropyelocaliectasis. Urine cultures obtained by conduit catheterization in each of these cases demonstrated Proteus in significant numbers, and all of the calculi analyzed were composed of struvite. In 1 case a sliver of calculus-encrusted wood was discovered in the proximal end of the conduit. Urine culture in that case also demonstrated Proteus.

Conduit elongation requiring shortening or replacement of the conduit was seen in 1 case in the early series and 6 in the late series.

TABLE 5. IVP Appearance Before and After Ileal Conduit Urinary Diversion*

Preop. IVP†		Postop. IVP†											
IVP Appearance	Renal Units	Normal	1+	2+	3+	4+	Unchanged No. (%)		Improved No. (%)		Worse No. (%)		
1955 to 1963													
Normal	26	6	9	7	4	0	6	(23)	0	(0)	20	(77)	
1+	8	1	3	4	0	0	3	(37)	1	(12)	4	(50)	
2+	10	1	3	3	1	2	3	(30)	4	(40)	3	(30)	
3+	11	2	0	0	6	3	6	(55)	2	(18)	3	(27)	
4+	23	3	1	8	2	9	5	(22)	14	(61)	4	(17)	
(with 4 deteriorating to non-visualization)													
1964 to 1979													
Normal	37	14	11	8	4	0	14	(38)	0	(0)	23	(62)	
1+	9	4	2	2	1	0	2	(22)	4	(44)	3	(33)	
2+	12	3	3	4	2	0	4	(33)	6	(50)	2	(17)	
3+	2	0	1	0	1	0	1	(50)	1	(50)	0		
4+	17	0	0	3	5	9	8	(47)	8	(47)	1	(6)	
(with 1 deteriorating to non-visualization)													

* Only 155 renal units are included as opposed to 180 renal units possible if all patients had 2 kidneys. The discrepancy occurs because some patients had solitary kidneys and others did not have either the preoperative or postoperative pyelogram available.

† Degree of ureteropyelocaliectasis is classified 1 to 4 plus, with 1 plus being slight calicectasis and 4 plus being severe ureteropyelocaliectasis with delay in visualization.

A poorly draining conduit of appropriate length and no apparent mechanical obstruction was replaced by a new conduit in 1 child in the early series.

Hypertension secondary to chronic pyelonephritis was noted in 1 child in the late series.

ROENTGENOGRAPHIC FINDINGS

We have compared the appearance of the urinary tract on preoperative excretory urography (IVP) with the appearance after ileal conduit diversion (Table 5). In the 1955 to 1963 series 23 renal units (29 percent) were unchanged in long-term postoperative followup, 21 (27 percent) improved and 34 (44 percent) deteriorated in varying degrees. In the 1964 to 1970 series 29 renal units (38 percent) were unchanged postoperatively, 19 (25 percent) improved and 29 (38 percent) deteriorated in varying degrees. Combining the 2 series, 52 renal units (34 percent) remained unchanged postoperatively, 40 (26 percent) improved and 63 (41 percent) deteriorated.

Examination of the cases with normal preoperative IVPs in the 1955 to 1963 series revealed that 6 renal units (23 percent) remained normal postoperatively, while 20 (77 percent) deteriorated in varying degrees. In the 1964 to 1970 series 14 renal units (38 percent) remained unchanged, while 23 (62 percent) deteriorated in varying degrees. Combination of the 2 series shows that of the 63 renal units, which were normal on preoperative IVP, only 20 (32 percent) remained normal postoperatively while 43 (68 percent) deteriorated.

BACTERIOLOGIC FINDINGS

Urine culture following diversion has been obtained at regular intervals. In 47 cases infected urine was noted preoperatively and cultures after diversion continued to show infection. Six patients had sterile urine preoperatively but subsequent postoperative cultures demonstrated infection. Twenty-two patients, most of them with bladder exstrophy, had no preoperative urine culture done and all but 1 had infected urine postoperatively. Only 3 patients had consistently sterile urine postoperatively, 2 of whom had sterile urine preoperatively and 1 suffered accidental death after only 2 postoperative cultures had been taken. In the first 2 cases pyelograms showed bilateral improvement postoperatively in 1, and slight improvement in the appearance of 1 kidney and slight deterioration of the other kidney in 1. Bacteriologic data were not available on the remaining cases. The finding of only 3 cases in the entire series with sterile urine on every culture taken is in close agreement with the findings of Spence and associates, that is that no child's urine is always sterile after ileal conduit diversion.[18]

DISCUSSION

In recent years there have been many series of ileal conduits in children, most reporting relatively high complication rates. We have compared the early ileal conduits in our 1955 to 1963 series to those done between 1964 and 1970 to determine if longer followup would show an increase in complications.

There were 13 early complications in the 1955 to

1963 series as compared to only 3 in the 1964 to 1970 series. It would appear that the greater number of early complications in the early series is at least in part owing to preventable technical problems. With refinement of surgical technique the early complication rate decreased to only 7 percent in the late series.

The reported late complication rates following ileal conduit urinary diversion in children range from 31 percent in the series by Logan and associates[6] with the longest period of followup being 5 years to 70 percent reported by Malek and associates[13] on a series followed for 13 years. In our series late complications occurred in 60 percent of the patients in the 1955 to 1963 group and in 51 percent of those in the 1964 to 1970 group.

The most frequent late complication was stomal stenosis, occurring in 56 percent of the cases in the early series and of these 25 patients 16 required multiple revisions. Stomal stenosis was less of a problem in the late series but still required surgical revision in 42 percent of the patients. Undoubtedly the decrease in stomal stenosis in the late series is partially owing to improvements in stomal care and appliance technology. However, it is also owing to a shorter period of followup in the late group, since we continue to see stomal stenosis occur despite optimal stomal care and appliance management.

The incidence of stomal stenosis reported in the literature ranges from 4 percent in Smith's series[14] followed for 15 years to 52 percent in Rickham's series[5] followed for 10 years. The average incidence of stomal stenosis was 22 percent in the 14 ileal conduit series reviewed.

The next most common late complication was pyelonephritis, occurring in 22 percent of the early series and 18 percent of the late series. The incidence of pyelonephritis reported in the literature ranges from 5[9] to 17 percent.[4,8]

Late ureteroileal anastomosis stenosis occurred in 9 percent of the early series and 11 percent of the late series. Reports of this complication rate in the literature range from 2[14] to 7 percent.[9]

Urinary calculi were noted in 7 percent of the early series and 11 percent of the late series. Calculi occurrence in other series of children with ileal conduits ranges from 2[9] to 24 percent.[8] Most of these calculi were struvite associated with infection. Dretler has implicated excessive conduit length in the formation of urinary calculi in patients with ileal conduits.[19] Twelve percent of our late series and 3 percent of our early series had elongation of the conduit requiring shortening or replacement but only 1 of these cases was associated with stone formation.

In our series the ileal conduit was successful in reversing pre-existing ureteropyelocaliectasis in many cases, with 40 percent of the renal units in the early group and 50 percent of the renal units in the late group improving on IVP. However, in this same group of children with ureteropyelocaliectasis present on the preoperative IVP 27 percent of the renal units in the early series and 15 percent in the late series deteriorated in varying degrees after the creation of the conduit (Table 5). Of the renal units that were normal preoperatively 77 percent in the early series deteriorated to some extent following the creation of the conduit and 62 percent deteriorated in the late series. Others report postoperative renal unit deterioration with normal preoperative pyelograms ranging from 0[8] to 31 percent.[16]

Examination of the 155 renal units in our combined early and late series revealed that 52 (34 percent) remained unchanged on IVP, 40 (26 percent) improved and 63 (41 percent) deteriorated in varying degrees. The deterioration rate is somewhat higher in our series than in other series. Others report postoperative renal deterioration rates ranging from 2[6,8] to 32 percent,[16] with an average rate of 11 percent. We believe that at least part of our higher deterioration rate is owing to a longer period of followup. Furthermore, we suspect that other surgeons will note an increasing incidence of renal deterioration with longer observation of their cases.

In examining the cases that deteriorated radiographically the most common causes were: 1) mechanical obstruction owing to stomal stenosis, 2) failure of the conduit to drain properly owing to excessive length or inadequate peristalsis, 3) ureteroileal anastomosis stenosis and 4) obstruction by calculus. Although the obstructions were corrected surgically, ureteropyelocaliectasis improved only partially in many cases. Of great concern was the finding that 9 renal units (12 percent) in the early series and 11 renal units (14 percent) in the late series deteriorated on IVP with no apparent obstructive cause. Of these 20 renal units 13 were normal radiographically before the ileal conduit was created and the remaining 7 showed ureteropyelocaliectasis preoperatively.

Smith speculated that this deterioration without apparent obstruction can be caused by inapparent stomal or ureteroileal anastomosis stenosis, urinary infection or reflux.[14] Morales and Golimbu recently reported a series of colon conduits in which radiographic deterioration occurred in 12 of 89 (13 percent) renal units wit no apparent mechanical obstruction but with free coloureteral reflux.[20] In contrast, they found no renal deterioration in these colon conduits that had been constructed with a non-refluxing ureterocolonic anastomosis.

Our own experience with non-refluxing colon conduit has shown it to be superior to refluxing ileal loops regarding absence of bacilluria and preservation of the upper tracts.[21] It seems likely that the mechanism of renal damage in freely refluxing colon and ileal conduits must be similar. Dybner and associates showed that the ileal conduit intraluminal resting pressure averages 2 to 5 mm mercury (8 to 13.6 cm water) with the patient in a sitting position.[22] Boyarsky and Labay showed that the ureteral intraluminal resting pressure ranges from 0 to 10 cm water, rising to 20 to 40 cm water at the height of a peristaltic wave.[23] Since ileal conduit pressures can be higher than ureteral resting pressures it is logical to assume that reflux occurs repeatedly in ileal conduits as the bowel peristalses. We believe that the progressive renal deterioration often seen with ileal conduits results from repeated reflux of infected urine from the conduit into the upper urinary tracts. The recent dog experiments by Richie and associates support our view.[24] In dogs undergoing ileal loop to 1 kidney and non-refluxing colon conduit to the other, there was a marked difference in incidence of pyelonephritis on the 2 sides. Pyelonephritis was seen in only 7 percent of the renal units diverted by non-refluxing colon conduit but was present in 83 percent of those diverted by ileal loop with reflux.

CONCLUSION

Because the rate of deterioration of upper tracts after many years of an ileal conduit is high we conclude that this operation should not be performed in children or in fact in any patient with potential longevity.

A variety of alternatives to the ileal conduit are possible today. Many of those patients who have already had ileal loops can be undiverted.[25-27] Seven patients in our conduit series plus an additional 16 patients who had ileal conduits performed elsewhere had the upper tracts undiverted to the bladder. This has proved to be of great value in controlling bacilluria and has improved the quality of life for all. Another promising development is the Scott prosthetic urinary sphincter, which may prove to be of great value in patients with neurogenic bladder or incontinence owing to other causes.[28-29]

If rinary diversion is needed we currently use a non-refluxing colon conduit. Indications for its use include 1) permanent urinary diversion, 2) temporary urinary diversion in bladder exstrophy, later joining the conduit to the colon, accomplishing thereby staged ureterosigmoidostomy, 3) temporary diversion after anterior pelvic exenteration, later joining the loop to the colon if there is no recurrent tumor and 4) a better means for diversion in a patient with an ileal conduit showing deterioration. Although long-term data are not yet available for non-refluxing colon conduits, there is long-term followup on its component parts. Gross reported on the use of colon for a conduit 22 years ago.[30] Mogg also has reported its use.[31,32] The colon segment functions well and stoma problems are rare. The tunneled ureteosigmoidostomy described 20 years ago by Leadbetter and Clarke also has stood the test of time well.[33] We believe that the components in combination, that is non-refluxing colon conduit, will prove superior to what has been the experience with ileal conduits.

In Germany Hohenfellner has performed 30 non-refluxing colon conduits in children since 1962.[34] None required stoma revision and only 6.5 percent of the renal units showed deterioration. Of the ileal conduits in our series 8 have been converted to non-refluxing colon conduits.

REFERENCES

1. Bricker, E. M.: Bladder substitution after pelvic evisceration. Surg Clin N Am, 30:1511, 1950
2. Bill, A. H., Jr., Dillard, D. H., Eggers, H. E. and Jenson, O., Jr.: Urinary and fecal incontinence due to congenital abnormalities in children: management by implantation of the ureters into an isolated ileostomy. Surg Gynec & Obst, 98:575, 1954
3. Nash, D. F. E.: Ileal loop bladder in congenital spinal palsy. Brit. J Urol, 28:387, 1956
4. Staffron, R. A., Turnbull, R. B., Jr. and Mercer, R. D.: The ileal conduit in the management of children with neurogenic lesions of the bladder. J Urol, 89:198, 1963
5. Rickham, P. P.: Permanent urinary diversion in childhood. Ann Roy Coll Sug, 35:84, 1964
6. Logan, C. W., Scott, R., Jr. and Laskowski, T Z.: Ileal loop diversion: evaluation of late results in pediatric urology. J Urol, 94:544, 1965
7. Fonkalsrud, E. W. and Smith, J. P.: Permanent urinary diversion in infancy and childhood. J Urol, 94:132, 1965
8. Bowles, W. T. and Tall, B. A.: Urinary diversion in children. J Urol, 98:597, 1967
9. Retik, A. B., Perlmutter, A. D. and Gross, R. E.: Cutaneous ureteroileostomy in children. New Engl J Med, 277:217, 1967
10. Koehler, P. R., Bowles, W. T. and McAlister, W. H.: Roent-genographic evaluation of late results of ileal loop urinary diversion in infants and children. Am J Roentgen, 100:177, 1967
11. Cook, R. C., Lister, J. and Zachary, R. B.: Operative management of the neurogenic bladder in children: diversion through intestinal conduits. Surgery, 63:825, 1968
12. Arnarson, O. and Staffon, R. A.: Clinical experience with the ileal conduit in children. J Urol, 102:768, 1969
13. Malek, R. S., Burke, E. C. and DeWeerd, J. H.: Ileal conduit urinary diversion in children. J Urol, 105:892, 1971
14. Smith, E. D.: Follow-up studies on 150 ileal conduits in children. J Pediat Surg, 7:1, 1972
15. Kendall, A. R. and Karafin, L.: Urinary diversion in children. J Urol, 109:717, 1973
16. Delgado, G. E. and Muecke, E. C.: Evaluation of 80 cases of ileal conduits in children: indication, complication and results. J Urol, 109:311, 1973.
17. Richie, J. P.: Intestinal loop urinary diversion in children. J Urol, 111:637, 1974
18. Spence, B., Ireland, G. W. and Cass, A. S.: Bacteriuria in intestinal loop urinary diversion in children. J Urol, 106:780, 1971
19. Dretler, S. P.: The pathogenesis of urinary tract calculi occurring after ileal conduit diversion: I. Clinical study. II. Conduit study. III. Prevention. J Urol, 109:204, 1973

20. Morales, P. and Golimbu, M.: Colonic urinary diversion: 10 years of experience. J Urol, 113:302, 1975

21. Hendren, W. H.: Nonrefluxing colon conduit for temporary or permanent urinary diversion in children. J Pediat Surg, 10:381, 1975

22. Dybner, R., Jeter, K. and Lattimer. J. L.: Comparison of intraluminal pressures in ileal and colonic conduits in children. J Urol 108:477, 1972

23. Boyarsky, S. and Labay, P.: Ureteral Dynamics. Baltimore: The Williams & Wilkins Co., p 51, 1972

24. Richie, J. P., Skinner, D. G. and Waisman, J.: The effect of reflux on the development of pyelonephritis in urinary diversion: an experimental study. J Surg Res, 16:256, 1974

25. Dretler, S. P., Hendren, W. H. and Leadbetter, W. F.: Urinary tract reconstruction following ileal conduit diversion. J Urol, 109:217, 1973

26. Hendren, W. H.: Reconstruction of previously diverted urinary tracts in children. J Pediat Surg, 8:135, 1973

27. Hendren, W. H.: Urinary tract refunctionalization after prior diversion in children. Ann Surg 180:494, 1974

28. Scott, F. B., Bradley, W. E. and Timm, G. W.: Treatment of urinary incontinence by an implantable prosthetic urinary sphincter. J Urol, 112:75, 1974

29. Middleton, A. W., Jr.: An unusual case of urinary incontinence successfully treated by urinary prosthetic sphincter. Rocky Mt Med J, 72:160, 1975

30. Gross, R. E.: Urinary and fecal incontinence of neurogenic origin. In: The Surgery of Infancy and Childhood: Its Principles and Techniques. Philadelphia: W B Saunders Co, chapt 56, p 740, 1953

31. Mogg, R. A.: The treatment of urinary incontinence using the colonic conduit. J Urol, 97:684, 1967

32. Mogg, R. A. and Syme, R. R.: The results of urinary diversion using the colonic conduit. Br J Urol, 41:434, 1969

33. Leadbetter, W. F. and Clarke, B. G.: Five years' experience with uretero-enterostomy by the 'combined' technique. J Urol, 73:67, 1955

34. Hohenfellner, R.: Personal communication, March 1975

COMMENT

The discouraging outlook of the long-term results for ileal conduits in children has caused many surgeons to use sigmoid conduits as popularized by Mogg. The advantages appear to be a lesser incidence of stomal stenosis, successful prevention of ureteral reflux and pyelonephritis, and flexibility for later considerations of reconstruction, for example colocystoplasty or sigmoid reanastomosis for rectal urinary control. This paper clearly supports these concepts. *J.W.D.*

Commentary: Will Ileal Conduit Urinary Diversion Stand the Test of Time?

Jerome P. Richie

Urologists have grappled for many decades with the problem of creating an effective alternative pathway for elimination of urine in patients who require urinary diversion. Ureterosigmoidostomy was the procedure of choice from the early 1900s until 1950, when Bricker described the interposition of a segment of small bowel as a cutaneous conduit diversion. This procedure rapidly gained prominence and replaced ureterosigmoidostomy as the procedure of choice for patients who underwent exenteration for malignant disease. The ileal conduit urinary diversion was logically extended to include patients, predominantly pediatric, with severe lower urinary tract disorders in whom primary reconstructive attempts failed. Beginning in the mid-1950s, the principles of cutaneous ileal diversion were applied to ever-increasing numbers of children with a variety of neurogenic and obstructive conditions. This operation seemed to be a panacea for patients with extrophy and irreparable bladders, failed attempts at antireflux correction with deteriorating upper tracts, and urinary incontinence uncontrollable by standard conservative or operative procedures.

The ileal conduit urinary diversion seemed to withstand the early test of time in adult patients. However, many of these patients underwent diversion in conjunction with exenterative procedures for malignancy, and the patient's lifespan was often determined by the primary condition rather than by the effectiveness of the urinary diversion. In children with benign disease, lifespan depends primarily on preservation of remaining renal parenchyma. As more patients with nonmalignant disease have undergone diversion by ileal conduit and have been followed for longer periods, the long-term effects of urinary diversion have become more apparent. Renal deterioration in patients with previously normal upper tracts has been noted in 10% of patients within 5 yr and up to 40% to 50%

of patients within 10 yr after urinary diversion. Calculi formation, rarely apparent less than 5 yr after urinary diversion, is seen more frequently the longer patients are followed after diversion. Episodes of acute pyelonephritis, problems with stomal stenosis, and late malfunction of the ileal conduit are all problems that continue to plague the child with a cutaneous ureteroileostomy.

A better understanding of the etiology and treatment of conditions once thought to necessitate diversion, coupled with improved surgical reconstructive techniques, have resulted in the performance of fewer ileal conduits for patients with non-neoplastic disease. Furthermore, application of newer, more sophisticated techniques and a better understanding of the pathophysiology of neurogenic bladder has postponed the decision for urinary diversion in many children who would have undergone diversion previously. Urodynamic evaluation of the child with neurogenic bladder has increased physicians' understanding of the basic disease process and generated more conservative approaches before urinary diversion is tried. Perhaps the single most important concept to reverse the trend of urinary diversion has been the development of clean intermittent catheterization. With this technique, many patients with large volumes of residual urine and dilated upper urinary tracts have improved with conservative and easily applied measures. The development of artificial urinary sphincters has improved the outlook for patients with urinary incontinence. Newer techniques of reimplantation and augmentation of the bladder with bowel segments, often incorporating antireflux mechanisms, have also brightened the outlook for patients with small-capacity bladders.

Despite the marked advances outlined above, a group still exists in whom urinary diversion is the only satisfactory alternative. Patients with neurogenic bladder secondary to paraplegia may require diversion after conservative measures fail. Patients who have undergone multiple failed operations to correct reflux or incontinence may require urinary diversion as a last-ditch measure. In those patients with benign disease who do require urinary diversion, however, the ileal conduit as a form of urinary diversion has been superceded by other methods incorporating an antireflux mechanism.

As can be seen from Drs. Middleton's and Hendren's article, the long-term results of patients with ileal conduit urinary diversion are poor at best. Sixty-two percent of the ileal conduits judged normal preoperatively had deteriorated in a group of patients followed an average of 8 yr, and 77% followed 15 yr had deteriorated. Stomal stenosis was noted in 42% of their patients, pyelonephritis in 20%, and stenosis at the ureteroileal anastamosis in 10%. Almost 10% of the patients had developed calculi during the follow-up period in their series. Moreover, 13% of the renal units in their series that deteriorated had no apparent cause for urinary obstruction. This group certainly implicates the continued presence of reflux, especially of infected urine, as a probable cause of renal deterioration. It is this finding, together with the lack of stomal problems by the use of large bowel, that has led physicians to abandon the ileal conduit urinary diversion in patients with benign disease.

The ideal urinary diversion has yet to be described. A perfect bladder substitute should maintain continence, empty to completion, protect the upper tracts, shield the body from the osmotic stresses of concentrated urine, maintain sterility, and be socially acceptable. In children, the ileal loop urinary conduit fails on too many counts. The incorporation of antireflux mechanisms, especially with colon conduits, appears to be a preferable procedure, and the colonic or ileocecal conduit is currently the procedure of choice in those pediatric patients who absolutely require urinary diversion. These antireflux forms of diversion must yet stand the test of time. In almost all certainty, newer discoveries will eventually make these operations passé as well.

ANNOTATED BIBLIOGRAPHY

Richie JP: Intestinal loop urinary diversion in children. J Urol 11:687, 1974

This article details the results of 36 children followed an average of 4 yr after ileal conduit urinary diversion and compares them with over 500 patients culled from 8 reports in the literature. The most prominent late complication was stomal stenosis, occurring in 25% of the patients. Calculi were seen in 3% to 5% of patients; pyelonephritis, in 6% to 10%. One of the most important observations from this series was the rate of deterioration of kidneys judged normal before urinary diversion, with 10% to 12% having deteriorated at an average follow-up examination of only 4.5 yr.

Richie JP, Skinner DG: Urinary diversion: The physiological rationale for non-refluxing colonic conduits. Br J Urol 47:269, 1975

This experimental study in the canine model compared the difference between freely refluxing ileal conduits and nonrefluxing colonic conduits in the same animal. A series of 16 dogs each had an ileal conduit created to drain the right kidney and a nonrefluxing colonic conduit to drain the left kidney. The conduits were tested for reflux, rate of emptying, and pressure measurements in open and occluded systems. At 3 mo, all dogs were sacrificed and the kidneys examined for histologic evidence of pyelonephritis. This study clearly shows the dramatic difference in pyelonephritis at 3 mo in the refluxing versus nonrefluxing kidney: 83% of kidneys connected to freely refluxing ileal conduits had pyelonephritis, whereas only 7% of nonrefluxing colonic conduits had pyelonephritis ($P < 0.001$). Furthermore, this study shows that an antireflux mechanism can be created reliably and that ileal and colonic conduits have equal resting pressures and rates of emptying.

Schwarz GR, Jeffs RD: Ileal conduit urinary diversion in children: Computer analysis of followup from two to 16 years. J Urol 114:285, 1975

This article details 96 children with ileal conduit urinary diversion divided into two groups: those with short follow-up study (average, 4.5 yr) and those with longer follow-up study (average, 11.3 yr). Renal deterioration was noted in one fifth of the short follow-up group and 50% of the remote follow-up group. The most frequent complication was stomal stenosis, occurring in 31 of the 96 patients. Almost all instances of calculi formation were in the longer follow-up group, and all patients with calculi had associated urinary tract infection. The incidence of pyelographic deterioration was most prevalent in patients whose preoperative intravenous pyelogram (IVP) had been normal and who were in the longer follow-up group. This suggests that pyelographic deterioration can occur many years after urinary diversion and necessitates routine follow-up study over a long period in all patients with urinary diversion.

Hardy BE, Lebowitz RL, Baez A, et al: Strictures of the ileal loop. J Urol 117:358, 1977

This report concerns 15 patients with obstructing strictures between the proximal end of the ileal conduit and the peritoneal side of the abdominal wall. The strictures were detected radiographically and occurred from 11 mo to 12½ yr after diversion, with a mean interval of 6¼ yr. Fourteen of the 15 patients had had urinary tract infections, but the prolonged periods of infection did not necessarily coincide with discovery of the stricture. Strictures were detected radiologically, usually on routine annual examination in asymptomatic patients.

The strictures were felt not to be ischemic in etiology but rather secondary to inflammatory bowel disease with a local abnormality in host response. Because strictures occur late and are often clinically silent, periodic IVPs are recommended for the patient's entire lifetime.

Kyker J, Gregory JG, Shah J, et al: Comparison of intermittent catheterization and supravesical diversion in children with meningomyelocele. J Urol 118:90, 1977

Comparison is made between children with myelomeningocele treated with intermittent catheterization and those treated with urinary diversion. Twenty-six patients were treated with intermittent catheterization, and 23 have had satisfactory results in terms of continence. Eleven of those patients required pharmacologic agents as well as intermittent catheterization. In this group of patients, 46 renal units were normal at the inception of therapy and only 2 (4%) have shown early changes of deterioration at 2½ yr follow-up study. The surgically diverted group consisted of 26 patients with 52 renal units. Of 31 normal renal units at the time of diversion, 4 (13%) had subsequently deteriorated on the basis of pyelographic determination.

In general, these authors felt that intermittent catheterization, especially when started before the development of upper urinary tract changes, is safe and simple and does not preclude other forms of management. Patient and parenteral acceptance was excellent, and the authors believe that additional follow-up study will continue to show the benefit of intermittent catheterization over supravesical urinary diversion.

Reiner WG, Jeffs RD, Ileal intussusception as an anti-reflux mechanism in urinary diversion for myelomeningocele. J Urol 121:212, 1979

This paper describes the technique and clinical application of ileal intussusception as a mechanism to prevent reflux of ileal urine to the ureters and kidneys in children with meylodysplasia. The authors indicated their distress with long-term pyeographic deterioration in children who had undergone diversion and applied this technique in seven children undergoing conduit revision because of ileal cutaneous stenosis, short conduits, or redundant conduits. The technique described is clear and straightforward. Postoperative follow-up excretory urograms and loopograms demonstrated pyelographic improvement in hydroureteronephrosis and no reflux. Stomal urine cultures and sensitivities disclosed no growth or insignificant colony counts. No episodes of chronic pyelonephritis or obstruction occurred.

This study is an attempt to demonstrate that an antireflux mechanism can be applied to children who have undergone diversion. It suggests that upper-tract deterioration may be prevented and that pyelographic improvement can be documented early. Obviously, long-term data will be necessary to prove the validity of these presumptions.

Overview: Ileal Conduit Urinary Diversion in Children

Casimir F. Firlit

Diversion of the urinary tract at present and "state of the art" is reserved as the last surgical effort, to be employed when all other nonoperative and usual operative modalities have failed to stabilize or improve renal function or urinary drainage. Its use in modern pediatric urologic practice is rare, in contrast to a decade ago.

The use of an ileal segment as a bladder substitute or urinary conduit was introduced in the 1950s in the treatment of patients with pelvic neoplastic disease treated by exenterative surgery. In this context, the ileal conduit still serves an extremely useful role, since the primary disease is still the life- and renal-threatening problem. As a consequence of its early acceptance by the urologic community, appreciation grew. In pediatric urology, it was used to restore or stabilize renal function in situations of multiple failed ureteroneocystomies or in severely obstructed bladders from unrecognized and unknown vesicle sphincteric discoordination. By far its greater appreciation was to "improve" urinary drainage and "continence" in children born with myelodysplasia and its consequent neurogenic bladder. In situations where obstruction and severe infection existed, the immediate and highly proclaimed effects from ileal conduit urinary drainage were dramatic.

However, when the ileal conduit was applied as a method to achieve "social dryness," as was frequent for children with myelodysplasia, it generally failed. In fact, what was achieved was to trade one form of incontinence for another (*i.e.,* appliance leakage or detachment). Culpable with physicians were social and school-district groups, who refused to admit incontinent children into private and public schools. In the effort to achieve "dryness," industry strove to develop the "permanent appliance." This "monster of creation" imparted the notion to the urologist, pediatrician, parents, and child that at all cost this device should remain on for as long as possible. Usually this was from 4 to 6 days. The permanent appliances served to harbor and grow bacteria efficiently (usually coliforms) and, further, to bathe the ileocutaneous stoma with these microorganisms. Since the notion relayed was to wear this appliance for "as long as possible," the continual innoculation of the ileal conduit and eventually the ileal and ureteral lumena occurred. The "lucky" children were those who had severe kyphoscoliosis and distorted abdominal walls. They had extreme difficulty with appliance application and long-term wear. Stomal problems such as hyperkeratosis, fissures, mucosal ulceration, and pseudomembrane formation are all recognized as frequently encountered problems in patients with ileal conduits.

Early description of the operative techniques favored long ileal segment lengths, retroperitoneal positioning, and ileoilealplasty, all in an effort to achieve a reservoir or "pseudobladder" function. Within a short time, it became clear that the static reservoir functions of the ileal conduit facilitated bacterial growth and electrolyte imbalance when extremely large and obstructive segments were used. Shorter segments and transperitoneal positioning facilitated more efficient drainage and decreased residual urine.

As long-term experience became available, it became apparent that children with normal excretory urograms at diversion in time demonstrated pyelographic deterioration, as evidenced by ureterectasis and calculus formation. Ureteral ileal stenosis or obstruction has been reported to occur in 5% to 15% of children who underwent diversion by ileal conduit within 10 yr of diversion. Further, statistically more ureteral and renal parenchymal problems occur on the left side because of technical or compressive effects by midline vascular and vertebral structures. The freely refluxing ileoureteral anastomosis favors free reflux of ileal conduit lumenal contents into the ureters and upper tracts. Bacteria-ladened ileal mucus and urine bathe the ureter, renal pelvis, and calyces and eventually result in renal parenchymal deterioration. Mucus is believed to act as a nidus, facilitating inorganic salt deposition and consequent stone formation.

As the consequences of ileal conduit diversion in children became increasingly alarming, intermittent clean self-catheter-ization was introduced in the early 1970s by Lapides as a method to reduce residual urine volume, infection, and improve continence. This was the single "deathblow" to urinary conduit diversion in children. In addition, and in concert with the introduction and rapid popularity of intermittent catheterization, an increased knowledge of detrusor pharmacologic responsiveness developed. This marriage provided a new and seemingly more effective and safer way to manage the child with urinary incontinence.

The rest is really history. The ileal conduit as a form of urinary drainage is now rarely used in children. When urinary diversion is now needed, for instance, in patients with extrophy or severe nonresponsive neuropathic bladder disease, the colonic conduit is now popular. Its popularity appears justified because of its large stoma, short segmental length, and, above all, ability to create an antirefluxing ureteral colonic anastomosis. Obviously, long-term experience with this technique is lacking, but already reports have surfaced describing ureteral colonic strictures and mid-segment obstructions. Stomal problems are decidedly less and are by virtue of the larger colonic diameter. This form of intestinal urinary diversion has yet to stand "the test of time."

Physicians have learned much from their "friend" the ileal conduit. Although no longer acceptable in children, it is still valuable in adult urology. Physicians have learned that permanent urinary appliances and appliances without baffles or those that allow infected urine to bathe the stoma contribute to stomal problems. Further, the infected urine in these appliances easily innoculates the ileal conduit lumen and colonizes this segment. An antireflux ileal ureteral anastomosis is necessary to prevent the spread of these contaminants into the upper tract, a lesson learned from antireflux ureteral anastomoses in ureteral sigmoidostomy. During the latter half of the 1970s, reports surfaced describing methods of achieving ureteral ileal antireflux anastomoses. These included tunneling, ileal imbrication, and ileoileal intussusception.

These techniques appear valid and appropriate. I believe that if physicians had to "do it again," the new appliances—disposable and baffled—and the antireflux techniques would provide a better perspective on the ileal conduit. It was my intent to present a perspective regarding ileal conduits as applied to children. Physicians clearly see the problems and the long-term causes through the "retrospectiscope." Physicians should not lose sight of this perspective and should hold it true in assessing the colonic conduit. Physicians learned much from the ileal conduit. The colonic conduit should be better if scrutinized likewise.

51

JEJUNAL CONDUITS: TECHNIQUE AND COMPLICATIONS

Mircea Golimbu and Pablo Morales

From the New York University-Bellevue Medical Center and Veterans Administration
Hospital, New York, New York

The Journal of Urology
Copyright © 1975 by The Williams & Wilkins Co.
Vol. 113, June
Printed in U.S.A.

ABSTRACT—Thirty patients underwent jejunal urinary diversion: 27 bilateral cutaneous ureterojejunostomies, 2 cutaneous pyeloureterojejunostomies and 1 bilateral pyelocutaneous jejunostomy. In the majority of the cases this high diversion was indicated for malignant disease with preoperative and postoperative irradiation of the pelvis. Postoperative morbidity in these cases is not different from that in cases of ileal conduit operation, except for a high incidence of reversible hypochloremic acidosis with hyponatremia, hyperkalemia and uremia. This electrolytic syndrome is the consequence of a continuous exchange of ions between the jejunal content and the extracellular fluid with resultant loss of sodium chloride and absorption of potassium and urea. An important link in the pathophysiology of the jejunal syndrome is the hypersecretion of renin-aldosterone, which aggravataes the disturbance. Limited renal function (glomerular filtration rate less than 50 cc per minute), long loop and inadequate salt intake are among contributing factors. The syndrome is correctable by administration of salt. Some patients must be placed on salt supplement indefinitely. The jejunum is not recommended for urinary diversion in patients with limited renal function, those on low salt diet or those in whom a long intestinal loop would be required for diversion.

Accepted for publication August 16, 1974.
Read at annual meeting of American Urological Association, St. Louis, Missouri, May 19–23, 1974.

The ileal conduit has been regarded as the best method of supravesical urinary diversion in adults and children.[1,2] However, it is becoming increasingly apparent that this procedure is not without its limitations and complications.[3-7] Our reasons for using jejunal conduits to divert the urine supravesically were based on the (1) condition of the ureters and terminal ileum as a result of previous pelvic irradiation, (2) planned postoperative irradiation as part of the therapeutic regimen, (3) history of multiple operations on the pelvis, (4) presence of gross malignancy in the ureters, particularly the lower third, in patients with bladder carcinoma and (5) status of ureteral hydrodynamics as a result of obstructive uropathy or neurogenic bladder.[7] We will report our experience with the jejunal conduit in 30 patients and discuss an unusual serum electrolyte disturbance that developed postoperatively in some patients and was characterized by hypochloremic acidosis, hyponatremia, hyperkalemia and azotemia.

MATERIAL AND INDICATIONS

During the last 5 years 30 patients underwent jejunal urinary diversion at our center. Patient age ranged from 3 to 74 years, with the majority being 60 years old or more. The group included 24 male and 6 female patients. In 18 cases the jejunal conduit diversion was done for carcinoma of the bladder (12 cases were performed in conjunction with cystectomy and 6 cases were performed for palliation). Of these 18 patients 7 had preoperative irradiation, 6 had postoperative irradiation and 5 had no irradiation. Of the remaining cases jejunal conduit diversion was done for carcinoma of the prostate in 2, neurogenic bladder in 4, failed ileal conduit diversion in 2 and vesicoureteral reflux and hydronephrosis in 1. Three patients had the diversion for complications of irradiation (Table 1).

SURGICAL TECHNIQUE

A left or right paramedian incision is made, depending on the desired location of the external stoma. The ureters are identified and transected as they cross the iliac vessels. They are bluntly dissected from the retroperitoneal tissue and brought out of the retroperitoneum below the ligament of Treitz. Care is taken to avoid acute angulation in the course of the ureters as they lie in their new beds.

A segment of jejunum is selected about 6 inches from the ligament of Treitz. The proximal portion of the jejunum is used if the external stoma is to be on the left side and the mid portion of the jejunum is used if the stoma is to be on the right side. The length of jejunal segment is determined by the type of conduit required: it is approximately 6 inches long for a bilateral cutaneous

TABLE 1. Indication for Jejunal Urinary Diversion

	No. Cases
Malignant:	
Bladder Ca with pre-diversion pelvic irradiation	7
Bladder Ca with post-diversion pelvic irradiation	6
Bladder Ca with compromised lower third of ureters	
(tumor or dilation)	5
Prostatic Ca	2
Benign:	
Neurogenic bladder	4
Vesicoureteral reflux with hydronephrosis and adynamic ureters	1
Failed ileal conduit	2
Complication of irradiation:	
Vesicovaginal fistula	1
Failed ureterosigmoidostomy	1
Contracted bladder	1

ureterojejunostomy, 8 to 9 inches long for a cutaneous pyeloureterojejunostomy and 10 to 12 inches long for a bilateral cutaneous pyelojejunostomy.

The mesenteric vascular pedicle is prepared with transillumination if necessary, preserving 2 vascular arcades if possible. Jejunojejunostomy is performed in a routine 2-layer fashion.

If a bilateral cutaneous ureterojejunostomy is to be performed, the proximal end of the conduit is closed in 2 layers. The ureters, which have been transected below the ligament of Treitz, are then anastomosed end-to-side to the antimesenteric aspect of the jejunal loop (Fig. 1). The proximal portion of the conduit is then sutured to the posterior peritoneum. If pyeloureterojejunostomy or bilateral pyelojejunostomy is to be performed, the renal pelvis or pelves are exposed by medial reflection of the ascending colon and hepatic flexure and/or descending colon and splenic flexure. A retroperitoneal tunnel is created under the mesocolon and a large end-to-end pyelojejunostomy is performed. The remaining ureter or renal pelvis is anastomosed end-to-side to the loop. The conduit is placed isoperistaltic or antiperistaltic and passes intraperitoneally to the skin. The stoma can be placed on either side of the midline in bilateral ureterojejunostomy. It is placed opposite the side of the renal pelvis draining into the end of the loop in pyeloureterojejunostomy or bilateral pyelojejunostomy (Fig. 1).

RESULTS

We have performed 27 bilateral cutaneous ureterojejunostomies, 2 cutaneous pyeloureterojejunostomies and 1 bilateral pyelojejunostomy. The jejunal stoma was placed on the right side of the abdomen in 12 cases and on the left side in 18 cases.

Of the 5 postoperative deaths 2 patients died of myocardial infarction, 1 of disseminated intravascular coagulation, 1 of gram-negative sepsis and 1 of gastroin-

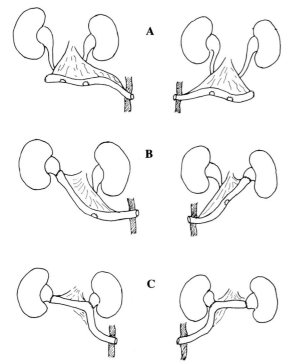

Fig. 1. Types of jejunal urinary diversion. (*A*) Bilateral ureterojejunostomy with isoperistaltic and antiperistaltic loop. (*B*) Pyeloureterojejunostomy with isoperistaltic and antiperistaltic loop. (*C*) Bilateral pyelojejunostomy with isoperistaltic and antiperistaltic loop.

TABLE 2. Urographic Status of 30 Patients with Jejunal Urinary Diversion

Preoperative Pyelogram	Postoperative Pyelogram			
	Un-changed	Im-proved	Deterio-rated	Un-known
Normal	21	15	—	—	6
Mild hydronephrosis	11	4	6	—	1
Moderate hydroneph-rosis	12	2	8	2	—
Severe hydronephrosis	15	4	7	1	3
Totals	59	25	21	3	10

TABLE 3. Postoperative complications following jejunal urinary diversion

	No. Cases
Electrolyte disturbance	11
Stomal problems	2
Partial intestinal obstruction	2
Stricture of ureterojejunal anastomosis	1
Gastrointestinal hemorrhage	1

testinal hemorrhage. The remaining 25 patients have been followed for 1 to 75 months.

The upper tracts of all patients were evaluated with preoperative excretory urograms and postoperative studies were available in the 25 survivors (Table 2). Of 59 renal units (1 patient had a solitary kidney) studied preoperatively, 21 were normal, 11 mildly hydronephrotic, 12 moderately hydronephrotic and 15 severely hydronephrotic. Postoperatively, 25 renal units remained unchanged, 21 improved, 3 deteriorated and 10 did not have followup studies.

Postoperative complications developed in 17 patients (Table 3). An electrolyte disturbance characterized by hypochloremic acidosis, hyponatremia, hyperkalemia and azotemia was present in 11 patients. Two patients had stomal problems (necrosis and intussusception), 1 had stenosis of the ureterojejunal anastomosis, 1 had a gastrointestinal hemorrhage and 2 had a partial intestinal obstruction.

The 2 cases reported herein represent the electrolytic syndrome which occurred postoperatively.

CASE REPORTS

Case 2. B. M., a 56-year-old woman who had previously undergone left nephrectomy for pyonephrosis, underwent cystectomy and jejunal urinary diversion for bladder cancer. Preoperatively, the blood chemistry studies were normal (Table 4) even though the glomerular filtration rate (GFR) was 26 cc per minute. Four weeks post-diversion, while on a regular diet, the patient complained of nausea, vomiting and muscular weakness. The blood chemistry studies showed blood urea nitrogen 89 mg and creatinine 2.8 mg per 100 ml, sodium 121 mEq, chloride 37 mEq, carbon dioxide 20 mEq and potassium 7.2 mEq per 1. Urine collected from the jejunostomy bag showed a higher amount of sodium and chloride and lower potassium and urea than in a concomitantly collected specimen from the ureteral stent (Table 5). The patient was started on 250 mEq intravenous sodium chloride per day and oral sodium polysterne sulfonate (30 gm every 6 hours kayexalate) and her geneal condition and blood chemistry studies improved. Shortly after treatment was discontinued the previously-mentioned complaints and serum electrolyte abnormality returned. The patient was then given 1.5 gm of salt daily besides the regular diet and the blood chemistry studies approached normal values again.

A few weeks later the patient underwent secondary closure of the abdominal wound, which required approximately 12 hours of food and water deprivation. Immediately following the operation the blood chemistry studies indicated hypochloremic acidosis with hyponatremia, hyperkalemia and uremia. This coincided with

TABLE 4. Changes in Electrolytic Composition of the Urine Following Passage Through Jejunal Conduit

Case No.	GFR	Weeks Since Diversion	Serum						Urine*					Treatment
			Na⁻	K⁺	Cl⁻	CO₂	BUN	Cr		Na⁺	K⁺	Cl⁻	Urea	
1	20	1½	114	5.7	79	19	28	2.2	KU	64	24	48	180	Salt
									JU	96	8	72	120	
2	26	4	121	7.2	97	20	98	2.8	KU	32	22	38	100	Salt
									JU	81	13	89	90	
3	30	3	123	6	89	21	33	1.9	KU	51	30	58	325	Salt
									JU	64	24	64	285	
4	35	3	124	6.2	95	20.5	77	2.1	KU	45	28	28	380	Salt
									JU	72	19	52	335	
5†	35	4	139	4.7	100	24.5	19	1.2	KU	27	44	36	300	None
									JU	40	27	59	265	
6	40	2	132	6.1	93	23	38	1.7	KU	32	59	43	235	Salt
									JU	70	45	65	213	
7	40	8	128	5.3	97	22	39	1.5	KU	35	37	42	265	Salt
									JU	48	18	49	230	
8	50	2½	129	6.2	92	21	49	1.5	KU	20	48	32	415	Salt
									JU	39	35	44	355	
9	50	2	135	4.1	96	25	12	0.9	KU	71	42	104	520	None
									JU	87	23	90	415	
10	50	3	142	4.9	103	28	23	1.3	KU	76	40	71	600	None
									JU	88	25	72	360	
11‡	60	3	129	6.8	88	18	42	2.6	KU	21	54	30	525	Salt
									JU	67	18	61	450	
12‡	70	10	133	5.7	95	20	36	1.7	KU	25	48	21	605	Salt
									JU	53	13	49	415	
13	70	2	140	4.5	99	30	12	0.9	KU	110	14	44	680	None
									JU	127	11	57	480	

* KU—kidney urine, JU—same urine after passing through jejunal conduit.
† 10 to 12 cm long loop.
‡ 30 to 35 cm long loop.

TABLE 5. Serum Electrolyte Patterns and Changes in Urine Composition (Kidney Urine versus Jejunal Urine) in Patient with Post-Diversion Electrolyte Imbalance

Case	GFR	Weeks	Serum						Urine*				Treatment
			Na⁺	K⁺	Cl⁻	CO₂	BUN	Cr		Na⁺	K⁺	Cl⁻	
BM	26 cc per min		145	4.8	106	26.5	17	0.9					Diversion
BH 00-49-09		4	121	7.2	97	20	98	2.8	KU	32	22	38	Intravenous NaCl
									JU	81	13	89	and kayexalate
		4½	132	5.5	102	20	49	1.6					Discontinued
		5	129	6.1	99	19.5	59	1.9					Salt, oral 2 gm
			135	5.6	100	20	48	1.5					N.P.O. 12 hrs
			124	5.9	94	17.5	53	1.4					
			140	4.7	105	31.5	8	1	JU	70	10	55	Salt, oral 1 gm plus bicarb. oral 900 mg

* KU—kidney urine, JU—jejunal urine.

an unusually high concentration of sodium chloride in the 24-hour urine collected from the jejunostomy bag. The patient was placed on 1 gm oral salt and 900 mg sodium bicarbonate daily and was discharged from the hospital on this regimen.

Case 11. R. S., a 35-year-old male paraplegic with

neurogenic bladder, underwent a pyeloureterocutaneous jejunostomy that required the use of a 30 to 35 cm segment of intestine. The preoperative blood chemistry studies were normal and the GFR was about 60 cc per minute. Three weeks postoperatively, while on a regular diet, the patient complained of muscular weakness, nausea and loss of appetite. The blood chemistry studies depicted hypochloremic acidosis with hyponatremia, hyperkalemia and uremia, for which he was given an oral supplement of salt. Urine electrolyte determination showed the same pattern of difference between the renal and jejunal samples as encountered in the previous cases (Table 4).

DISCUSSION

Initially, we thought that the electrolytic syndrome was secondary to a salt losing nephropathy because it was manifested in patients with known impairment of renal function. However, these patients were not salt losers prior to the operation and, moreover, we later observed the electrolytic imbalance in other patients who had satisfactory preoperative renal function (patient 11). Therefore, we questioned whether the jejunum itself was responsible.

Consequently, we proceeded to compare the composition of urine before contact with the jejunal loop and after passage through the loop in 13 patients (Table 4). The renal samples were collected through ureteral catheters, nephrostomies or large multi-eyed catheters inserted deeply into the loop adjacent to the ureteral openings. The jejunal samples were collected directly from the stoma. Each sample was obtained over a 2-hour period and analyzed for sodium, potassium, chloride and urea.

In addition, 6 patients had determinations of aldosterone urinary excretion and peripheral renin levels during episodes of serum electrolyte imbalance. Both determinations were done within the same 24-hour period and with the patients on normal salt intake (120 mEq sodium per day). The peripheral renin was obtained after overnight recumbency.

The results indicate that a change in the electrolyte composition of the urine takes place during its passage through the conduit, consisting of an increase in the amount of sodium chloride and a decrease of potassium and urea in the jejunal urine (Fig. 2). The change is more profound in patients with the serum electrolyte disturbance and is associated with increased urinary aldosterone and peripheral renin levels (Fig. 3).

These clinical findings were reproduced in animal experiments and published previously.[8] We created jejunal loops in dogs and compared the changes in composition of urine when perfused through the conduit. The isolated intestinal segments averaged 13 cm long and were located approximately 7 cm from the ligament of Treitz. The proximal end of the loop was closed and the distal end was left open. Urine collected from the bladder of each dog was perfused through the conduit at a rate of 1 ml. per minute. The perfusate collected at the distal end of the jejunal loop was chemically analyzed for content of sodium, potassium, chloride and urea. Other animals had jejunal loops connected to the ureters and bladder for studies in chronicity. The results of the experiment also indicated that during its passage toward the distal end of the loop the amount of sodium chloride increased, and potassium and urea decreased in the perfusate (Fig. 4).

The changes in the urine composition during its passage through the jejunum is the result of normal intestinal physiology. There is a 2-way movement of electrolytes between the extracellular fluid and the intestinal content. The magnitude and direction of this electrolyte movement are related to the differential

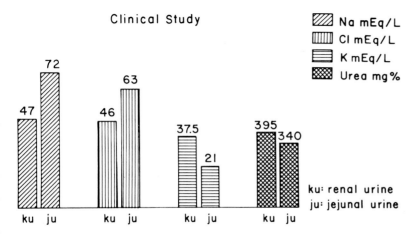

Fig. 2. Changes in electrolyte composition of urine during passage through jejunal conduit (13 patients). Jejunal urine contains more sodium and chloride and less potassium and urea.

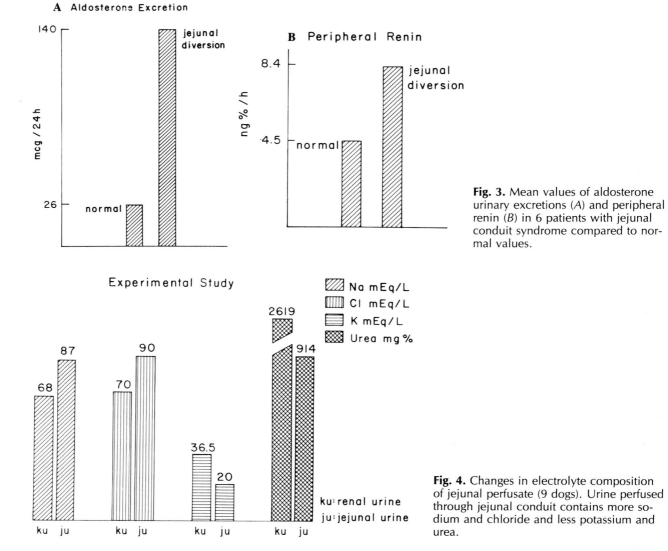

Fig. 3. Mean values of aldosterone urinary excretions (*A*) and peripheral renin (*B*) in 6 patients with jejunal conduit syndrome compared to normal values.

Fig. 4. Changes in electrolyte composition of jejunal perfusate (9 dogs). Urine perfused through jejunal conduit contains more sodium and chloride and less potassium and urea.

concentration on each side of the intestinal mucosa. Sodium, chloride, potassium and urea leave the area of higher concentration and migrate toward the area of lower concentration.[8–11] If the concentration of sodium chloride in the urine entering the loop is lower than in plasma, sodium chloride from plasma will move across the intestinal mucosa into the jejunal urine until isotonicity is achieved and, therefore, the loop will lose salt. If the urinary concentration of potassium and urea is higher than in plasma, the potassium and urea will diffuse across the intestinal membrane toward the extracellular compartment and, therefore, the loop will absorb potassium and urea.

The amounts of sodium chloride lost and potassium

absorbed by the conduit appear to be related to 3 factors: (1) The concentration of electrolytes in the kidney urine prior to jejunal contract: figure 5 depicts the relation of sodium lost and potassium absorbed by the jejunum to their concentration in kidney urine in human subjects. The jejunum lost the largest amount of salt to the urine with lowest concentration of sodium chloride, and absorbed more potassium from the urine with a higher concentration. (2) The degree of renal function: figure 6 shows, in humans, the relation between the amount of sodium lost by the jejunum and the degree of renal function expressed in GFR. The figure indicates that the lower the GFR, the higher the amount of sodium lost by the conduit. (3) The length of the urinary conduit:

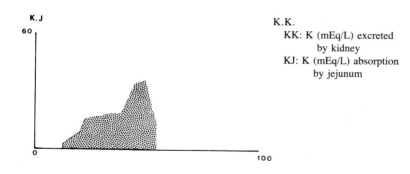

K.K.
    KK: K (mEq/L) excreted
            by kidney
    KJ: K (mEq/L) absorption
            by jejunum

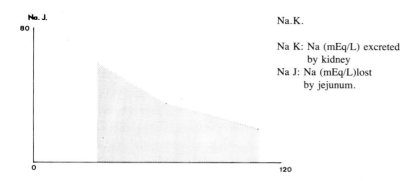

Na.K.

Na K: Na (mEq/L) excreted
        by kidney
Na J: Na (mEq/L)lost
        by jejunum.

Fig. 5. Relation between concentration of potassium and sodium in kidney urine and electrolyte exchange at level of jejunal conduit.

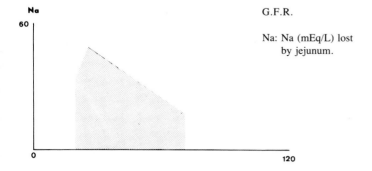

G.F.R.

Na: Na (mEq/L) lost
        by jejunum.

Fig. 6. Relation between amount of sodium lost by jejunum and degree of renal function (13 patients).

patient 11 had a 30 to 35 cm jejunal loop and a GFR of 60 cc per minute, whereas patient 5 had a 10 to 12 cm loop and a GFR of only 35 cc per minute. The comparative study of renal and jejunal urine of both patients indicates a larger loss of salt and absorption of potassium and urea in patient 11, who also had the serum electrolyte imbalance (Table 4).

The length of loop factor was also reproduced experimentally in a dog in which a 30 cm jejunal loop was constructed. The dog died 2 weeks postoperatively of hypochloremic acidosis, hyponatremia, hyperkalemia and azotemia.

As previously mentioned 11 of our 30 patients with jejunal urinary diversion experienced an unusual postoperative serum electrolyte imbalance characterized by hypochloremic acidosis, hyponatremia, hyperkalemia and azotemia. Six patients had severe manifestations requiring intensive therapy with intravenous sodium chloride. The other patients experienced only mild disturbances corrected by supplements of salt to their diets.

The preoperative creatinine clearance in all but 2 patients was between 20 and 50 cc per minute. Two patients with creatinine clearance of 60 and 70 cc per minute had a 30 to 35 cm jejunal loop as a conduit.

Those who manifested the most severe serum electrolyte imbalance had the lowest creatinine clearance and low sodium chloride concentration in urine excreted by the kidneys (Table 4).

There were 5 features in patients with the jejunal conduit syndrome: (1) the syndrome developed when patients were switched from intravenous to oral feeding, (2) the electrolyte composition of renal versus jejunal urine indicates that jejunal conduits lose salt and absorb potassium and urea, (3) the kidney urine had a relatively low sodium chloride concentration, (4) creatinine clearance was less than 50 cc per minute in all except 2 patients in whom a long jejunal conduit was created and (5) the aldosterone urinary excretion and peripheral renin levels were markedly elevated.

The pathophysiology of the electrolyte disturbance exhibited by patients with jejunal urinary diversion is illustrated in Figure 7.

Salt Circle. As the urine with a concentration of sodium chloride lower than plasma enters the loop, there is a free shift of sodium chloride from the extracellular fluid, the degree of transfer being dependent upon the concentration of sodium chloride in the urine, that is the lower the salt in the incoming urine, the higher the amount shifted from the blood. The loss of sodium chloride through jejunal mucosa lowers the serum level

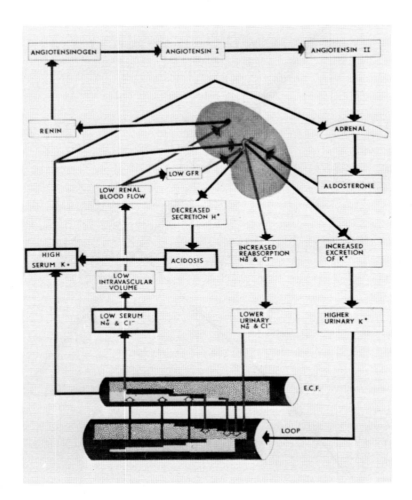

Fig. 7. Pathophysiology of jejunal conduit syndrome. Salt loss and potassium absorption are main vicious circles—hypersecretion of renin–aldosterone system and acidosis aggravate electrolyte disturbance.

of the electrolytes and, consequently, diminishes the entire extracellular fluid volume. The renal blood flow and the GFR are reduced.

The reduction in renal blood flow and serum sodium is sensed by the juxtaglomerular apparatus and results in increased excretion of renin. Renin then acts upon an alpha-2 globulin produced by the liver (angiotensinogen) and liberates a decapeptide called angiotensin I. This is a relatively inactive produce but it is readily converted to angiotensin II, the active element which stimulates the secretion of aldosterone. Aldosterone increases the sodium chloride reabsorption at the level of distal tubule. Its action is enhanced by the reduced GFR and, consequently, reduced volume of fluid going through the distal tubule. Aldosterone also increases the tubular secretion of potassium in exchange for sodium reabsorption. As a result of increased tubular reabsorption of sodium chloride, the amount of salt excreted by the kidneys is reduced. Urine with a lower electrolytic content reaching the jejunum will, subsequently, attract a larger amount of sodium chloride from the extracellular fluid, further decreasing the level of these 2 electrolytes.

Potassium Circle. Potassium concentration in the urine going through the jejunal loop is higher than in plasma and will, consequently, be absorbed by the conduit. Its extracellular fluid level rises. This potassium excess and the high aldosterone will then produce at the level of distal tubule an increase in secretion of potassium and decrease of hydrogen ion (Fig. 7). Therefore, potassium urinary output will become larger, whereas the hydrogen ions accumulate in the extracellular fluid.

It is known that patients with renal disease secondary to obstruction and/or chronic pyelonephritis have an impairment of hydrogen ion secretion mechanism. They are in so-called steady metabolic acidosis, which can easily be converted to manifest metabolic acidosis.[12] Hyperkalemia and the reduced GFR secondary to hyponatremia, will embarrass further the hydrogen ion secretion by the distal tubule and metabolic acidosis ensues. With acidosis, potassium is shifted from the intracellular to the extracellular space, increasing the already abnormally high potassium level. Hyperkalemia by itself is a potent stimulator of the adrenal cortex for aldosterone secretion. This will further aggravate the syndrome by increasing potassium urinary excretion, thereby promoting a larger absorption from the conduit. It is like trying to get rid of the potassium excess but by pumping part of it back into the extracellular fluid.

Thus, in the jejunal conduit syndrome we deal mainly with 2 vicious circles—one of salt loss and the other of potassium absorption. It seems that the salt loss is more important because it triggers the hyperexcretion of renin-aldosterone system which aggravates the electrolyte disturbance. Breaking the first vicious circle by the addition of salt to the regular diet prevents the consequence of salt-losing phenomenon.

With proper management, all patients eventually reach an equilibrium between intake and output of salt and achieve electrolyte balance.

REFERENCES

1. Campbell, M. F. and Harrison, J. H.: Urology, 3rd ed Philadelphia: W B Saunders Co, 1970

2. Retik, A. B., Perlmutter, A. D. and Gross, R. E.: Cutaneous ureteroileostomy in children. New Engl J Med, 227:217, 1967

3. Jaffe, B. M., Bricker, E. M. and Butcher, H. R., Jr.: Surgical complications of ileal segment urinary diversion. Ann Surg, 167:367, 1968

4. Engel, R. M.: Complications of bilateral uretero-ileo cutaneous urinary diversion: a review of 208 cases. J Urol, 101:508, 1969

5. Schmidt, J. D., Hawtrey, C. E., Flocks, R. H. and Culp, D. A.: Complications, results and problems of ileal conduit diversions. J Urol, 109:210, 1973

6. Dretler, S. P.: The pathogenesis of urinary tract calculi occurring after ileal conduit diversion: I. Clinical study. II. Conduit study. III. Prevention. J Urol, 109:204, 1973

7. Morales, P. A. and Whitehead, E. D.: High jejunal conduit for supravesical urinary diversion. Report of 25 cases. Urology, 1:426, 1973

8. Golimbu, M. and Morales, P.: Electrolyte disturbances in jejunal urinary diversion. Urology, 1:432, 1973

9. Visscher, M. B., Fetcher, E. S., Jr., Carr, C. W., Gregor, H. P., Bushey, M. S. and Barker, D. E.: Isotopic tracer studies on the movement of water and ions between intestinal lumen and blood. Am J Physiol, 142:550, 1944

10. Visscher, M. B., Varco, R. H., Carr, C. W., Dean, R. B. and Erickson, D.: Sodium ion movement between the intestinal lumen and the blood. Am J Physiol, 141:488, 1944

11. Phillips, S. F. and Summerskill, W. H.: Water and electrolyte transport during maintenance of isotonicity in human jejunum and ileum. J Lab Clin Med 70:686, 1967

12. Deane, N.: Kidney and Electrolytes. Foundation of Clinical Diagnosis and Physiologic Therapy. Englewood Cliffs, New Jersey: Prentice-Hall, Inc., 1966

Commentary: Technique and Management of Jejunal Conduits

Mircea N. Golimbu

The Bricker procedure, withstanding the test of time since 1950, has become the most accepted method of supravesical urinary diversion. In the initial period of general enthusiasm, numerous patients with benign and malignant conditions of the bladder underwent this type of urinary conduit. However, later on, three series of events gradually changed physicians' concept of using terminal ileum in every patient in favor of a higher intestinal segment such as jejunum or transverse colon. First, the improvement in survival of patients with neurogenic bladder, due in part to the urinary diversion, laid the groundwork for the development and recognition of certain long-term complications of ureteroileostomy (progressive dilation, rigidity of ureters, and deterioration of renal function). Second, the discovery that carcinoma *in situ* also affects the upper tracts in patients with invasive bladder cancer resulted in occasional removal of long segments of ureters at cystectomy, thus making it impossible to use ileum to construct a urinary conduit. Finally, the introduction of radiotherapy as an adjunct to radical cystectomy led to the concept of using intestinal segments located outside the irradiation field to minimize the risk of complications. Such "failures" of ureteroileostomy commended the use of a higher intestinal segment, and since most urologists were not yet prepared to tackle the transverse colon, the jejunum appeared as "the alternative." I should emphasize that certain patients who underwent high urinary diversion in the past, especially those in the pediatric age group, are currently managed by temporary cutaneous ureterostomy.

Surgical technique of ureterojejunostomy is similar to that of ureteroileostomy and has been amply described in the preceding article and in articles noted in the bibliography. I would like to go over some details and emphasize the technique of pyelojejunostomy and the immediate postoperative care of patients with jejunal urinary diversion.

The abdominal incision is midline, although some surgeons may prefer a paramedian incision on the opposite side of the proposed stomal side. A definite advantage in using the upper jejunum is that the conduit can be brought out on either side of the midline without twisting the mesentery or compromising the isoperistaltic flow of urine. To proceed, approach the ureters at the level of iliac vessels, dissect upward, and bring them inside the peritoneal cavity below the ligament of Treitz. If the anticipated diversion is a pyelojejunostomy, approach the ureters at a higher level after mobilizing and reflecting medially the hepatic and splenic flectures of the colon. Trace the ureters up to the ureteropelvic junction and transsect them at that level; the segments below may be removed or left *in situ* after ligation of the proximal end. Then isolate the jejunal

segment. The length of the isolated intestine varies from 10 cm to 15 cm for ureterojejunostomy to 25 cm to 30 cm for pyelojejunostomy. No effort should be spared to use the shortest possible segment, since the patient's future metabolic balance may depend on this. In my experience, patients with the longest jejunal segment developed the most severe electrolyte imbalance for a similar glomerular filtration rate and salt intake.

Two vascular arcades should suffice for blood supply of the conduit. If the patient has a thick abdominal wall, the mesentery should be long enough to transverse the abdominal opening without compression on the vessels; in such cases, use a low jejunal segment.

Reestablish the continuity of the intestinal tract by end-to-end anastomosis in one or two layers of sutures. The operating time may be shortened considerably if autosuturing technique is employed. Close the proximal end of the isolated jejunal segment with double running suture of 3–0 chromic catgut, reinforced by a seromuscular layer of interrupted 3–0 silk stitches. Lay the loop on the posterior perietal peritoneum, with the closed end below the ligament of Treitz, slightly to the right of midline. Orient the loop toward the left or right gutter, depending on the proposed position of stoma, crossing the descending or ascending colon anteriorly; a retroperitoneal–retrocolic position may be preferred by some urologists.

The preferred type of anastomosis is the direct one. Recently there have been numerous attempts to incorporate an antireflux mechanism into the anastomosis; the seromuscular tunnel technique for colon conduits described by Kelalis has been applied to the small intestine with promising results.[1] However, the beneficial effect of an antireflux ureterojejunostomy may be questionable, because 50% of the normal direct anastomoses show no reflux, and, when the reflux is present, it takes place within an open, low-pressure system, which makes it less dangerous than the vesicoureteral reflux.

For pyelojejunostomy, place the interpelvic part of the conduit retroperitoneally above the mesentery of the transverse colon. This is best accomplished by reflecting the transverse colon upward and opening the posterior parietal peritoneum exactly where the base of the mesocolon crosses over the kidneys. By blunt dissection, create a retroperitoneal tunnel from one renal pelvis to the renal pelvis of the opposite kidney. Using a curved clamp, pull the conduit through the retroperitoneal tunnel in such a way that the proximal end and the middle part of the intestinal segment each rest on a renal pelvis, whereas the distal half remains intraperitoneally. During this maneuver, take case not to injure either the superior mesenteric or the middle colic artery. Open each renal pelvis at the most dependent part and anastomose it to the conduit, using 3–0 chromic interrupted stitches.

Some urologists advocate retroperitonialization of urinary conduits to prevent intestinal obstruction or difficulties at future abdominal operations. I place the jejunostomy conduits intraperitoneally and the pyelojejunostomy loops part retroperitoneally and part intraperitoneally. I then carefully suture the conduits to the posterior parietal peritoneum and the serosa of the ascending or descending colon to eliminate potential routes for internal herniation or volvulus.

Stoma is created at a site chosen before surgery. In general, the place is in the left or right upper quadrant, although occasionally it may be created in either of the lower quadrants or umbilicus. Because stomal stenosis develops in up to 25% of small intestinal conduits, incorporation of a triangular skin flap into the intestinal opening or a Z-type jejunostomy may be beneficial.

After surgery, monitor all patients closely for signs of jejunal conduit syndrome. The electrolytic imbalance may first manifest itself between the fifth and seventh postoperative day, when patients are still receiving intravenous (IV) fluids or have just started oral (PO) feeding. Those with low glomular filtration rate (GFR) or long jejunal loop are prone to this development if they do not receive an adequate amount of salt. Daily serum electrolyte readings and every second or third day determination of urinary excretion of sodium chloride and potassium chloride may alert the physician that the patient needs more sodium chloride. However, the most important preventive measure is the proper selection of patients and the elimination from this type of diversion of those unable to handle sudden changes in water and electrolyte balance (such as patients with diabetes mellitus, cardiac problems, hypertension, or poor renal function).

ANNOTATED BIBLIOGRAPHY

Clark SS: Retroperitoneal conduit. Urology 1:420, 1973

The author describes the technique of retroperitoneal ileal and jejunal conduits performed on 42 patients. Surgical complications were not different from other series using intraperitoneal conduits. However, 15 of 21 patients with jejunal urinary diversion showed elevated blood urea nitrogen (BUN) levels postoperatively. This is a consequence of excessive absorption of urinary urea by the long jejunal segment that is required if the conduit has to be retroperitonealized.

Golimbu M, Morales, P: Electrolyte disturbances in jejunal urinary diversion. Urology 1:432, 1973

Diversion of urine through jejunum induces an unusual serum electrolyte imbalance characterized by hypochloremic acidosis with hyponatremia, hyperkalemia, and uremia. Signs of dehydration and hyponatremia such as nausea and intestinal distention are the accompanying clinical manifestations. The disturbance, which the authors call the jejunal conduit syndrome, was found in a third of patients undergoing jejunal urinary diversion. By clinical and experimental studies, the authors determined the causes, the mechanism, and the treatment of this syndrome.

Clark SS: Electrolyte disturbance associated with jejunal conduit. J Urol 112:42, 1974

This is a follow-up report on the group of patients with retroperitoneal jejunal conduits who were included in the article published in Urology 1:432, 1973. Nine of 21 patients developed the serum electrolyte imbalance described by Golimbu and Morales as the Jejunal conduit syndrome. Seven patients survived and fared well on salt maintenance.

Morales P, Whitehead ED: High jejunal conduit for supravesical urinary diversion. Report of 25 cases. Urology 1:426, 1973

This was one of the first papers to report on the use of jejunum for urinary diversion, and the authors present their experience with 25 patients. Primary disease was bladder cancer in 13 patients, neurogenic bladder in 4, failed ileal or sigmoid diversion in 3, complications of pelvic irradiation in 3, and prostatic cancer and vesicoureteral reflux in one each. The majority of patients underwent bilateral ureterojejunostomy with the stoma in the left upper quadrant, a few had isoperistaltic or antiperistaltic pyeloureterojejunostomy, and one had isoperistaltic bilateral pyelojejunostomy. The postoperative period was marked by development of serum electrolyte abnormalities in ten patients. Surgical technique was no more difficult than that of classic ureteroileostomy. Furthermore, half the renal units improved urographically over a period of up to 4 yr, which prompted the authors to recommend the procedure as an alternative to the ileal conduit in patients who either had or would be having irradiation of the pelvis.

Overview: Jejunal Conduit Diversion

Samuel S. Clark

Since 1950, when Bricker revived the ileal conduit urinary diversion procedure to be used predominantly in patients with pelvic malignancies, the procedure became the standard of diversion among modern urologists. The conduit diversion then supplanted the ureterosigmoidostomy, which had the concomitant problems of hyperchloremic acidosis, ascending pyelonephritis, and, more recently, carcinoma of colon associated with the anastomotic site. In 1956 Dr. Stamey discussed the pathogenesis and implications of the electrolyte imbalance in the ureterosigmoidostomy and concluded that "ureterosigmoidostomy was a highly dangerous procedure which should be avoided because of the subtle potassium loss associated with hyperchloremic acidosis." The work of Hindle and Code in 1962 and Rangel in 1969 suggested that there was a bidirectional electrolyte shift in the small bowel, with a net loss of sodium and chloride through the jejunum, and they suggested that the jejunum night not absorb urinary contents as well as the ileum.

In 1969, while trying to find a more suitable diversion procedure and recognizing that no urinary diversion procedure is ideal, I began to look at retroperitoneal jejunal conduits to be used in patients with extensive ureteral disease interfering with peristalsis, when preoperative or postoperative pelvic radiation was given or planned or when ureteral malignancy existed with other pelvic malignancy. I felt that the jejunal segment offered a sound alternative to the use of the ileal conduit in these patients. The surgical technique for the retroperitoneal jejunal conduit was presented in 1971 at the 12th PanAmerican Congress of Urology in Quito, Equador, and at the American Urological Association in 1972 and finally published in 1973. The choice of the retroperitoneal placement of the conduit was to allow adequate access to both upper ureters or to both renal pelves, placing the conduit in a retroperitoneal position so that leakage would not interfere with the abdomen, would allow future abdominal surgery without interference from the conduit, would prevent internal hernia formation, and would prevent the complication of peristomal hernia. I found that it made very little difference whether I placed the conduit in an isoperistalic or antiperistalic position, since the conduit did not undergo significant peristalsis while draining unless stomal stenosis was present. The antiperistaltic conduit does, however, at the time of a conduitogram result in retrograde peristalsis and hyperdilatation of the collecting system under the roentgenogram study conditions of obstructing the stoma with a balloon catheter; this gives a false impression of the degree of the hydroureteronephrosis associated with the conduit. The retroperitoneal placement of the conduit does indeed meet all the criteria, but subsequent experience has taught me that if the conduit must be replaced because of conduit stenosis, the retroperitoneal position makes a secondary procedure much more difficult.

By 1974, I recognized—as did Golimbu and Morales—that there was an electrolyte disturbance associated with a high percentage of jejunal conduits, characterized by hyponatremia, hyperkalemia, and azotemia. Of the 21 retroperitoneal jejunal conduits I performed, 42.9% of patients developed the "jejunal conduit syndrome." In my patients, using the endogenous creatinine clearance as a method of estimating glomerular filtration rate (GFR), we found no significant preoperative and postoperative change in the GFR. But during the syndrome, the creatinine rose with a reduction in the clearance rate, and a return to preoperative levels was noted when salt was administered; however, Golimbu and Morales later demonstrated that the lower the GFR, the more likely the syndrome is to occur. I feel that the experimental data on which this

procedure was based has a basic flaw in that the experimental procedures were all performed on occluded small bowel segments, unlike the continuously flowing clinical conduit. Therefore, the initial impact of allowing urine to flow through small bowel continues without reaching an equilibrated status. The only valid data to be applied to the clinical situation would be the experimental data that occur in the first few minutes of exposing the mucosa to urine.

Looking at the experimental work, as published in the past, I find an outpouring of fluid to the lumen of the jejunum, an outpouring of sodium and chloride, a reabsorption of potassium, and possibly a reabsorption of hydrogen ion, with a net carbonate loss. This situation is the opposite of the syndrome known as hyperchloremic acidosis and results in hyponatremia, hypochloremia, probable increase in total body potassium, intracellular overhydration, hypovolemia, and extracellular hypo-osmolality and azotemia. The clinical picture associated with this syndrome suggests salt-losing nephritis, water intoxication, or adrenal insufficiency. The clinical signs consist of gastrointestinal disturbances (anorexia, nausea, and vomiting with a moist tongue), nervous changes (cramps, various peripheral pains, personality changes, and, occasionally, convulsions or coma), and general changes (extreme asthenia). In the chronic form, it can be confused with anorexia nervosa or renal insufficiency. Golimbu and Morales have demonstrated that there is an activation of the renin–aldosterone mechanism, aggravating the above-described condition.

An interesting feature of this syndrome is that a normal patient with these findings and this degree of hyponatremia would demonstrate a renal failure picture with all the characteristics of salt deficiency—a lower glomerular filtration rate, diminished renal blood flow, and excessive reabsorption of tubular salt and water through the renin-aldosterone mechanism, resulting in oliguria or anuria. But the jejunal conduit patients continue to produce urine from the conduit stoma, usually more than 1 liter/day and often much higher, which is a direct consequence of water loss from the jejunal segment itself.

The subtleness of this syndrome can be found in patients who have a low normal serum sodium and a slightly elevated urinary sodium, who have fatigue, loss of muscle tone, and sometimes unexplained occasional nausea and vomiting. One such patient I saw was reexplored 5 yr after the jejunal conduit and was found to have a small Richter's hernia involving a loop of small bowel in the lower end of the abdominal wound. The patient underwent a small bowel resection with direct reanastomosis. Postoperative bowel sounds, although of poor quality, returned by the fourth postoperative day; however, the patient became immediately distended in the presence of bowel sounds as soon as oral (PO) intake was permitted. After 10 days of nasogastric suction, the patient still was not able to tolerate PO intake. He was reexplored with the thought of possible bowel obstruction, and none was found. After the second exploration, the same result occurred. It was recognized, finally, that the patient had an unrecognized subclinical form of jejunal conduit syndrome. He was given supplemental hypertonic sodium chloride, and bowel activity resumed within 4 hr.

In my institution, physicians now recognize that the jejunal conduit is a highly dangerous conduit for the average patient and have replaced it with colon conduits with (antireflux ureteral anastomosis) when a high urinary diversion becomes necessary because of loss of peristalic function of the ureters, preoperative or postoperative pelvic radiation, and carcinoma of the female genital organs or bladder involving the lower third of the ureters.

In conclusion, the published data suggested that the use of jejunum might prove to be a highly satisfactory alternative urinary diversion in these high-risk patients. I feel that the subtle and potentially dangerous effects of the jejunal conduit syndrome preclude its use for high urinary diversion, except in the rare patient in whom there is no other segment of bowel available. The treatment for the syndrome is to recognize the syndrome, which is often missed in the emergency room when a comatose patient has a high blood urea nitrogen (BUN) level and a high potassium level, to administer sodium chloride intravenously (IV) to reverse the devastating effects of the syndrome, and, finally, to maintain the patient with PO sodium chloride supplements.

BIBLIOGRAPHY

Bricker EM: Bladder substitution after pelvic evisceration. Surg Clin North Am 30:1511, 1950

Clark SS: High urinary diversion by retroperitoneal jejunal conduit: Technique and rationale. Rev Surg 30:1, 1973

Clark SS: Retroperitoneal conduit indications and uses. Urology 1:420, 1973

Clark SS: Electrolyte disturbance associated with jejunal conduit. Amer J Urol 112:42, 1974

Stamey TA: Pathogenesis and implications of electrolyte imbalance in uterosigmoidostomy. Surg Gynecol Obstet 103:736, 1956

52

TRANSVERSE COLON CONDUIT: A PREFERRED METHOD OF URINARY DIVERSION FOR RADIATION-TREATED PELVIC MALIGNANCIES

Joseph D. Schmidt, Charles E. Hawtrey and Herbert J. Buchsbaum

From the Departments of Urology and Obstetrics-Gynecology, University of Iowa Hospitals and Clinics, Iowa City, Iowa

The Journal of Urology
Copyright © 1975 by The Williams & Wilkins Co.
Vol. 113, March
Printed in U.S.A.

Currently the ileal conduit is the most common form of supravesical urinary diversion using intestine. Methods of construction and hazards have been well documented by Bricker and others.[1-7] Patients with pelvic malignancy treated by radiation often require urinary diversion for relief of ureteral obstruction and urinary fistula, or combined with surgical extirpation. Since the field of pelvic radiation necessarily includes the distal ureters, small bowel, sigmoid colon and adjacent structures,

Accepted for publication July 19, 1974.
Read at annual meeting of American Urological Association, St. Louis, Missouri, May 19–23, 1974.
Mr. Paul Ver Vais provided the illustrations.

radiation changes to these areas are unavoidable.[8,9] Use of the ileum as a urinary conduit in such patients often results in poor healing with complications, for example bowel obstruction, fistula formation and peritonitis, as well as urinary fistula, ureteroileal stenosis and hydro-ureteronephrosis.

Theoretically the transverse colon should be an ideal substitute for the ileum or jejunum since this portion of the colon is usually well away from the field of pelvic radiation. Since the transverse colon is ofen redundant a colocolostomy can be performed easily, again using non-irradiated bowel. Bowel continuity can be restored with the fecal stream transmitted to the anus or as an end colostomy, for example total exenteration. Established examples of the use of large bowel for urinary diversion include ureterosigmoidostomy in the treatment of bladder exstrophy or cancer and the sigmoid colon conduit for neurogenic bladder.[10]

Problems of stasis and urine absorption with subsequent electrolyte imbalance and pyelonephritis can occur if a colonic segment is too long, obstructed or not emptied frequently enough. Thus, in the absence of distal obstruction, for example stomal or fascial stenosis, or excessive length (a technical error), an isolated isoperistaltic segment of transverse colon should function suitably as a conduit rather than as a reservoir.

MATERIAL AND METHODS

Since 1970, 8 patients (2 men and 6 women) have been selected for supravesical urinary diversion using an isolated segment of transverse colon. Since 1 patient had had a prior nephrectomy there were 15 ureterorenal units involved. Patients ranged in age from 40 to 68 years, with an average of 51.

Primary diseases included 4 instances each of bladder and cervical carcinoma. Specific indications for the transverse colon conduit diversion are listed in table 1. Note that all patients had been treated with external radiotherapy (4,500 to 6,600 rads). Each patient with cervical cancer received 2 radium applications. One patient was known to be free of tumor yet required urinary diversion because of a radiation-induced vesicovaginal fistula.

The preparation of the patient takes 2 to 4 days. Mechanical cleansing is carried out via mild laxatives, a liquid diet and enemas. Oral antimicrobial usage has varied from none to kanamycin sulfate alone to neomycin sulfate plus non-absorbable sulfonamides. Any existing infection, urinary tract or otherwise, is treated with appropriate systemic antimicrobials. High-calorie-high-protein supplements and multivitamins are administered.

A midline incision has been used since this facilitates the completion of the additional procedures to be performed, for example cystectomy or exenteration. After the pelvic procedure is completed a suitable segment of transverse colon is selected (Fig. 1). Since the length of

colon required to reach from the posterior peritoneum to the anterior abdominal wall and skin is relatively small, a segment 10 to 15 cm in length may suffice. Adequate blood supply to the segment has not been a problem. Transillumination of the mesocolon aids in choosing the segment. The greater omentum is dissected off the superior surface of the transverse colon. Mesenteric incisions are made; the mesenteric vessels are controlled with fine silk or catgut sutures. The more distal mesenteric incision will be the longer of the 2 to supply mobility to the distal end of the conduit to reach the skin. The colon is divided sharply with bowel continuity re-established by a 2-layer colocolostomy superior to the segment (Fig. 2). We have used 3 or 4-zero chromic catgut for the submucosal and mucosal approximation and 4-zero silk Lembert sutures for the seromuscular layer. The mesenteric defect is closed

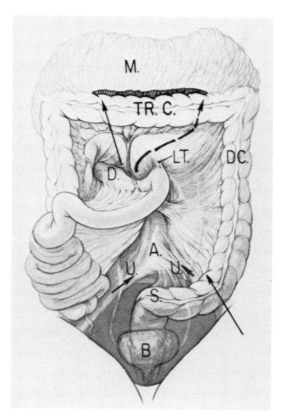

Fig. 1. Technique of transverse colon conduit diversion: selection of segment. *M,* greater omentum. *TR, C,* transverse colon. *D,* duodenum. *LT,* ligament of Treitz. *DC,* descending colon. *A,* aorta. *U,* ureter. *S,* sigmoid colon. *B,* bladder. *Arrows* indicate positions of incisions. *Dotted arrow* indicates longer mesocolic incision to increase conduit mobility.

TABLE 1. Transverse Colon Conduit Diversion (8 Patients)

Primary disease:	
Cervical Ca	4
Bladder Ca	4
Indications for diversion:	
Radiation-induced vesicovaginal fistula	1
Primary bladder Ca (post-radiotherapy)	3
Recurrent cervical Ca (post-radiotherapy)	3
Metastatic bladder Ca (post-radiotherapy)	1

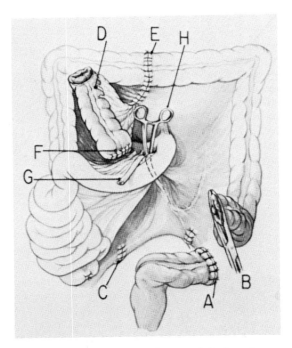

Fig. 2. Technique of transverse colon conduit diversion: *E*, bowel continuity restored. *D* and *F*, segment isolated. *G* and *H*, ureters dissected. *A* and *B*, sigmoidal resection and colostomy are optional. *C*, peritoneal closure.

loosely. Next, the proximal or blind end of the segment is closed in 1 or 2 layers and, most importantly, is fixed to the posterior parietal peritoneum at or near the midline with non-absorbable sutures. This maneuver helps take any tension off the subsequent ureterocolic anastomoses.

The ureters are dissected proximally in the retroperitoneal space and brought into the peritoneal cavity via small stab incisions adjacent to the proximal portion of the colon conduit. Any redundant or ischemic ureter is resected and submitted for surgical pathology examination. Ureterocolic anastomoses are carried out in an end-to-side fashion without any attempt at antireflux procedures (Fig. 3). A normal caliber ureter may require spatulation to ensure a wide anastomosis. Absorbable interrupted sutures (4-zero chromic catgut or polyglycolic acid) are used here with all knots tied on the outside. Retroperitonealization of the anastomoses is accomplished by suturing adjacent parietal peritoneum over the anastomoses to the conduit segment. Ureteral intubation has not been used.

Stomal position is established at this time. Either the right or left upper quadrant is suitable, pending the position and length of the segment and the need for a

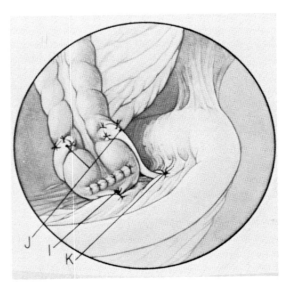

Fig. 3. Technique of transverse colon conduit. *I*, fixation of proximal segment. *J*, ureterocolic anastomosis. *K*, retroperitonealization.

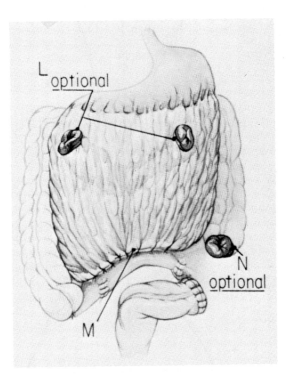

Fig. 4. Technique of transverse colon conduit. *L*, stomal position in either right or left upper quadrants. *N*, optional sigmoid colostomy. *M*, omental covering of viscera.

terminal colostomy (Fig. 4). We prefer to place the 2 stomas at diffent levels and have the patient wear 2 separate belts rather than try to fashion a single belt to hold both appliances. A full-thickness circular core of abdominal wall is removed and the peritoneum is sutured to the anterior fascia with the ends of the sutures left long. These sutures are re-armed and passed through the seromuscular portion of the conduit. Lastly, the skin and subcutaneous tissue are approximated to the distal end of the conduit with either absorbable or non-absorbable sutures. Wound closure and re-peritonealization of the pelvic cavity, if needed, are performed in a routine fashion. A temporary appliance is used for the first 7 to 10 days. Drains have been used only as part of the cystectomy or exenteration procedure.

RESULTS

Additional Procedures. Six patients underwent additional major operations (Table 2). Two patients were treated by transverse colon conduit diversion alone.

Urographic Status. Three patients had normal ex-

TABLE 2. Procedures Performed with Transverse Colon Conduit (8 Patients)

	No. Cases
Cystectomy plus or minus prostatectomy	3
Total pelvic exenteration, sigmoid colostomy	2
Anterior exenteration	1
None	2

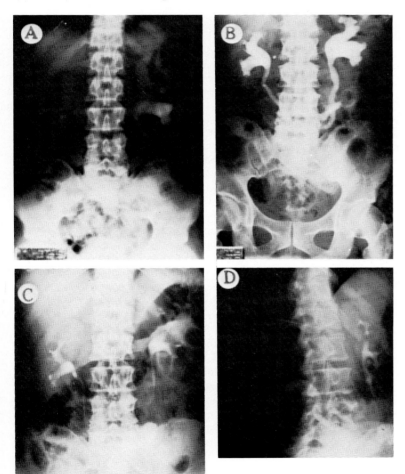

Fig. 5. Patient K. C. (*A* and *B*), IVPs taken preoperatively and 2 weeks after transverse colon conduit. Note improved visualization of right upper tract and fullness of left upper tract at 2 weeks. (*C* and *D*), IVP (anteroposterior and left oblique projections) 7 months after transverse colon conduit. Upper urinary tracts are normal.

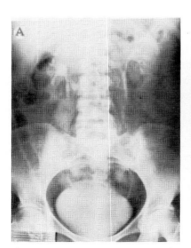
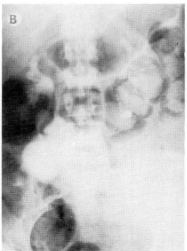
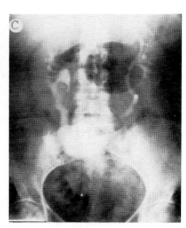

Fig. 6. Patient L. C. (*A*) Normal upper urinary tracts on preoperative IVP. (*B*) Normal upper urinary tracts on IVP 2 weeks after transverse colon conduit. (C) Normal upper urinary tracts on IVP 2 years after transverse colon conduit.

cretory urograms (IVPs) preoperatively. Two remain normal while the third patient had a left hydrouretero-nephrosis 10 weeks later with the formation of a left uretero-recto-vaginal fistula. All 5 patients with bilateral or unilateral hydroureteronephrosis preoperatively demonstrated normal upper urinary tracts on IVPs 4 weeks to 2 years postoperatively (Figs. 5 to 7).

Bacteriology. Preoperative urine cultures were performed in 6 patients and only 1 was positive. All 6 patients had organisms in urine obtained from the colon conduit in the late postoperative period. The array of organisms is depicted in Table 3. Note that multiple organisms were cultured in several patients.

Four patients were studied by culture of their transverse colon segment at the time of the operation. Identified were 2 instances of Candida albicans, 1 of Bacteroides and Candida albicans and 1 of Escherichia coli and Torulopsis glabrata. The latter organism was recovered from the same patient's colon conduit urine 2 months later.

Renal Function. All patients had normal renal function as measured by blood urea nitrogen, serum creatinine and serum electrolytes preoperatively. After urinary diversion all remained normal. No patient demonstrated evidence of urine absorption and hyperchloremic acidosis. Residual urine has been less than 5 ml in all patients.

Complications. Operative mortality was zero. Complications are listed in Table 4. The patient who had a ureterocolic leakage and wound dehiscence required revision of the anastomosis and wound repair as 2

separate operations. The patient who had a uretero-recto-vaginal fistula was treated by loop nephrostomy, ligation of the fistula and revision of the ureterocolic anastomosis. No complications have occurred after the initial 60 days postoperatively.

Patient Survival. Followup of these patients has ranged from 3 to 46 months, with an average of 13. One patient, a 68-year-old man, died of metastatic bladder cancer 3 months after the transverse colon conduit diversion. The remaining 7 patients are well and have had no particular difficulty handling their appliances.

DISCUSSION

Surprisingly, little use of the transverse colon has been mentioned in the literature. Its role in the urinary diversion of gynecological patients treated with radiation to the whole pelvis was described by Nelson in 1969.[11] Catastrophes resulting from the use of standard ileal conduit diversion included breakdown of the end-to-end ileal anastomosis or the ureteroileal anastomoses or both. Nelson chose the transverse colon as an alternative ''to isolate an un-irradiated intestinal segment at a point high enough so that the ureters could be transected above the pelvic brim and still be long enough to perform uretero-intestinal anastomoses''. There were 17 patients initially reported. No patient died as a result of the urinary diversion although 2 died of myocardial infarction and another of hemorrhage. Since his initial report Nelson has treated 70 patients with the transverse colon conduit urinary diversion.[12] Followup has extended up to 8 years

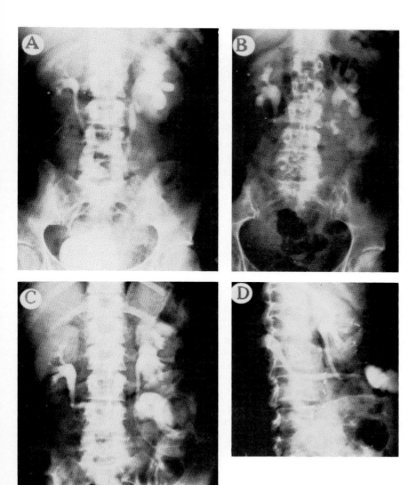

Fig. 7. Patient E. J. (*A*) Preoperative IVP reveals left hydroureteronephrosis. (*B*) Repeat study 1 week following transverse colon conduit demonstrates relief of obstruction. (*C*) and (*D*) Normal upper urinary tracts on IVP (anteroposterior and left oblique projections) 3 months after transverse colon conduit.

TABLE 3. Bacteriology of Transverse Colon Conduit (9 Cultures)

E. coli	4	Citrobacter	1
Candida sp.	3	Pseudomonas	1
Proteus sp.	3	Torulopsis glabrata	1
Klebsiella sp.	2	Strep. faecalis	1

TABLE 4. Complications of Transverse Colon Conduit Plus or Minus Other Procedures (8 Patients)

	No. Cases
None	3
Wound infection	2
Ureterocolic leak and wound dehiscence	1
Small bowel fistula	1
Uretero-recto-vaginal fistua	1

in his series. Three patients (4 percent) have required reoperation for ureteral stricture and hydroureteronephrosis. Also 2 patients, because of a relatively short transverse colon, required mobilization of either the splenic or hepatic flexures. Clark, and Morales and Whitehead have used the jejunum as a source of non-irradiated bowel to furnish a segment functioning as a conduit.[13,14]

Because of our experience with complications related to the use of radiated tissue in ileal conduit diversions, we have performed transverse colon conduits in 8 selected patients during the past 4 years.[15] Primary diseases included carcinoma of the cervix (4 cases) and bladder (4 cases). One patient had a disabling vesicovaginal fistula yet was free of tumor. The technique is relatively simple and can be combined with other procedures, such as cystectomy or exenteration. Preoperative and postoperative IVPs are evidence that in the absence of complications normal upper urinary tracts remain normal and reversal of preoperative hydroureteronephrosis can be achieved. Metabolic acidosis from excessive urine absorption has not occurred. Stomal stenosis is less frequently a problem when dealing with the colon then with the small bowel. Stomal position is generally left upper quadrant but can be adjusted. In this small series

no major complications directly related to the use of the transverse colon rather than the small bowel have resulted. The 2 instances of complications requiring a reparative operation (1 of ureterocolic urinary leakage and 1 of uretero-recto-vaginal fistula) were most likely caused by the use of devascularized or irradiated ureter. Also failure to secure the proximal end of the conduit segment in our first patient contributed to disruption of a ureterocolic anastomosis. Further use of non-irradiated segments of bowel, such as transverse colon, is advocated in the management of patients with pelvic malignancies or complications related to radiation therapy.

SUMMARY

In the management of pelvic malignancies treated by radiation the standard ileal conduit is subject to many hazards related to the use of damaged tissues. The transverse colon affords the use of a short isolated segment of non-irradiated bowel as a urinary conduit. The ureters can be dissected well above the field of pelvic irradiation. Eight patients with bladder or cervical carcinoma treated with high doses of external radiotherapy are presented to demonstrate the usefulness of the transverse colon in supravesical urinary diversions.

REFERENCES

1. Bricker, E. M.: Blader substitution after pelvic evisceration. Surg Clin N Am, 30:1511, 1950
2. Cordonnier, J. J.: Ileal bladder substitution: an analysis of 78 cases. J Urol, 77:714, 1957
3. Parkhurst, E. C. and Leadbetter, W. F.: A report on 93 ileal loop urinary diversions. J Urol, 83:398, 1960
4. Butcher, H. R., Jr., Sugg, W. L., McAfee, C. A. and Bricker, E. M.: Ileal conduit method of ureteral urinary diversion. Ann Surg, 156:682, 1962
5. Jaffe, B. M., Bricker, E. M. and Butcher, H. R., Jr.: Surgical complications of ileal segment urinary diversions. Ann Surg, 167:367, 1968
6. Parkhurst, E. C.: Experience with more than 500 ileal conduit diversions in a 12-year period. J Urol, 99:434, 1968
7. Johnson, D. E., Jackson, L. and Guinn, G. A.: Ileal conduit diversion for carcinoma of the bladder. South Med J, 63:1115, 1970
8. Alfert, H. J. and Gillenwater, J. Y.: The consequences of ureteral irradiation with special reference to subsequent ureteral injury. J Urol, 107:369, 1972

9. Joelsson, I. and Räf, L.: Late injuries of the small intestine following radiotherapy for uterine carcinoma. Acta Chir Scand, 139:194, 1973
10. Mogg, R. A.: Urinary diversion using the colonic conduit. Br J Urol, 39:687, 1967
11. Nelson, J. H.: Atlas of Radical Pelvic Surgery. New York: Appleton-Century-Crofts, pp 181–191, 1969
12. Nelson, J. H.: Personal communication.
13. Clark, S. S.: Retroperitoneal conduit: indications and uses. Urology, 1:420, 1973
14. Morales, P. A. and Whitehead, E. D.: High jejunal conduit for supravesical urinary diversion: report of 25 cases. Urology, 1:426, 1973
15. Schmidt, J. D., Hawtrey, C. E., Flocks, R. H. and Culp, D. A.: Complications, results and problems of ileal conduit diversions. J Urol, 109:210, 1973

Commentary: Colon Conduit Diversion in Adults

Joseph D. Schmidt

Any discussion of supravesical urinary diversion using intestinal segments must focus not only on the relative merits and pitfalls of the procedures available, but also on the status of the host

considered for such procedures. The latter subject includes mention of the primary or underlying disease, presence or absence of malignancy *at the time of diversion,* history of significant pelvic irradiation, general health and performance status, status of the upper urinary tract and overall renal function, and, finally, a history of gastrointestinal disease or surgery. These important factors will be addressed after comments on the procedure of colon conduit diversion itself.

My technique of colon conduit formation has changed, at least regarding ureterocolic anastomoses. My early experience (approximately the first 30 cases of transverse colon conduit) was perhaps somewhat timid in that I used refluxing-type, direct end-to-side ureterocolic anastomoses. This may have been the result of patient selection—for example, patients with marked hydroureteronephrosis or persistent malignancy—or some insecurity in attempting antirefluxing anastomosis in otherwise suitable candidates simultaneously with a fairly new form of intestinal segment diversion. In other words, the departure from the standard ileal conduit was thought to be "radical" enough, not to mention the combination of colon conduit with an antirefluxing ureteral anastomosis (Figs. 8 and 9).

Once I gained sufficient experience using the transverse colon and, occasionally, the descending and sigmoid colon, I incorporated the antirefluxing ureterocolic anastomosis in suitable patients. Over the past 3 yr, particularly with the urging and prodding of an ever-inquiring and vital resident housestaff,

the hospital service has adopted the nonrefluxing ureterocolic anastomotic technique. I incorporated this technique into the procedure with some trepidation at first, as evidenced by the use of stents as well as drains. Currently, with the knowledge that the technique can be done and that stents generally extrude because of active ureteral peristalsis, the nonrefluxing technique is routinely included in suitable candidates, that is, generally those with normal- or near-normal-caliber ureters. Ureteral stents are considered optional and are more likely to be used in patients with solitary kidneys, as is drainage (depending on associated procedures, e.g., cystectomy).

Specifically, the nonrefluxing ureterocolic anastomosis is similar to that used for ureterosigmoidostomy with the intact colon. To proceed, after sufficient mobilization of the proximal ureter and its spatulation, make a longitudinal 2 cm to 3 cm colotomy through the muscularis near the blind stump end of the segment. Such a colotomy need not be performed necessarily in taenia. Enter the colonic lumen distally; suture the full thickness of the ureteral wall to the colonic mucosa and submucosa using interrupted chromic sutures, usually 4–0 or 5–0. Undermine the intramuscular (submucosal) tunnel laterally sufficiently to accommodate the particular ureter. Last, close the colotomy over the submerged ureter using interrupted nonabsorbable sutures, generally 3–0 silk, set in a Lembert

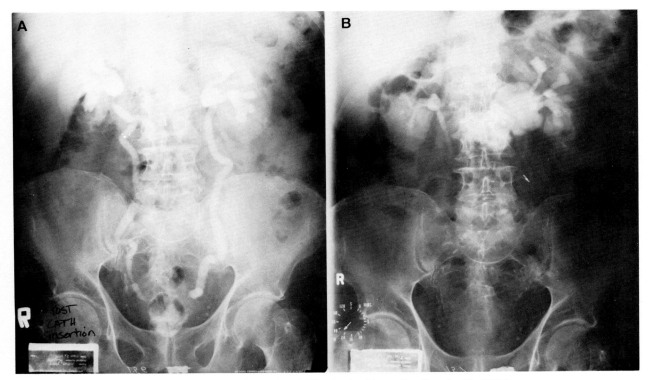

Fig. 8. (A) Preoperative excretory urogram of man aged 73 who had been irradiated with 6000 rads for invasive bladder cancer. Bilateral hydroureteronephrosis and a small bladder are apparent. (B) Excretory urogram 3 months after refluxing transverse colon conduit urinary diversion and radical cystectomy. Note improvement in upper tract dilatation and the conduit's relatively cephalad position.

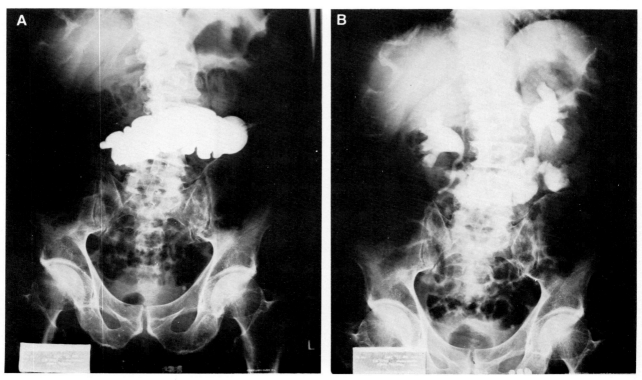

Fig. 9. (*A*) Retrograde loopogram performed 6 months after refluxing transverse colon conduit urinary diversion and radical cystectomy in man aged 65 with bilateral hydroureteronephrosis, severely contracted bladder, and radiation cystitis after 7000 rads of irradiation for infiltrating bladder cancer. No ureteral reflux is seen with maximal conduit distention. (*B*) Excretory urogram performed therafter demonstrates marked improvement in upper tract dilatation. Again, the conduit's cephalad position is apparent.

manner. Should ureteral stenting be desired, direct a 5 French or 8 French polyethylene infant feeding tube through the stomal end of the conduit and across the *partially completed* anastomosis. Fixation of such stents to the colonic mucosa has not prevented early extrusion related to active ureteral peristalsis. Attempt to cover the ureterocolic anastomosis using available posterior parietal peritoneum.

I have been gratified with the results of incorporation of the nonrefluxing anastomosis into the technique for transverse colon urinary diversion. Only one case made me question, at least temporarily, that decision. A woman of 59 yr with infiltrating bladder cancer was treated by preoperative external beam irradiation (4500 rad) followed by early transverse colon conduit diversion and radical cystectomy. Because her upper urinary tracts were normal, nonrefluxing anastomoses were constructed without stents. On postoperative day 4, after an otherwise uneventful course, the patient began to complain of left flank pain but remained afebrile. As the discomfort persisted and local tenderness occurred, an excretory urogram was performed on day 7, revealing moderate left hydroureteronephrosis and backflow extravasation; the right upper tract was normal. Because the patient was otherwise doing well, she

was treated conservatively, and in a few more days her pain and tenderness disappeared. All subsequent urograms have shown bilaterally normal upper urinary tracts. I would presume that early, transient, postoperative edema at the level of the submucosal tunnel and ureterocolic anastomosis were responsible for her clinical and radiographic findings.

The technique otherwise has not been appreciably altered from the form described in the preceding article. I would, however, again emphasize that since the colon segment contracts considerably at surgery, a suitable length of bowel should be chosen to avoid any embarrassing situations wherein the segment is of insufficient length to reach the abdominal wall. Again, a rosebud type of everting stoma is preferable to a flush stoma and is more likely to be achieved if sufficient colonic segment is available.

In general, I favor the increased primary use of colonic segments for supravesical urinary diversion, as opposed to reserving this technique as a "fallback" or "salvage" procedure. Although the colonic conduit, particularly with the transverse or descending colon, is especially useful in patients who have received significant pelvic irradiation (generally more than 4000 rad), it also deserves a place in the management of those patients who have received minimal or no pelvic irradiation. In fact, because of surgeons' ability to incorporate the nonrefluxing anastomosis, the colonic conduit possesses a distinct advantage over the standard ileal conduit technique.

Since the pelvic irradiation field necessarily includes the distal ureters, pelvic viscera, and often the ileum itself, radiation changes to the ileum, distal ureters, and even the sigmoid colon may be unavoidable. In these situations, the use of the isolated ileal segment for conduit diversion may lead to the following complications: (1) poor healing of the ileoileostomy, resulting in bowel obstruction, fistula, and peritonitis, (2) poor healing of the ureteroileal anastomoses, resulting in urinary fistula, ureteroileal stenosis, and subsequent hydroureteronephrosis, and (3) poor blood supply of the ileal segment itself, result in ileal necrosis, fistulae, and peritonitis.

Both theoretically and practically, the transverse and descending colon, because they are not located generally in the field of pelvic irradiation, are ideal substitutes for the ileum or jejunum. The transverse colon particularly is often redundant; thus the colocolostomy can be performed using nonirradiated bowel. Bowel continuity can be restored with the fecal stream transmitted to the anus or with an end colostomy (*e.g.,* in total pelvic exenteration). Alternatively, for total exenteration, the fecal colostomy can be made proximal to the colonic segment chosen for urinary diversion, thus eliminating the need for a bowel anastomosis.

The "battle" between colonic and ileal conduits is far from over. Certainly the longer and greater experience with the ileal conduit (since the early and mid-1950s) has shown that deterioration of previously normal upper tracts occurs in at least 10% of patients so diverted. Admittedly, a similar long and large expereince with colonic conduits will be necessary to determine whether the apparent early advantages of the colon conduits are of long-term benefit to patients.

Over the past several years, reports have been published either comparing the two types of conduits or describing the overall results with one or the other technique. Those pertinent to colonic diversion are listed in the bibliography. In 1979, Pitts and Muecke reported on 242 patients treated with ileal conduits over the past 20 years.[1] Although the authors found only an 11% rate of damage to upper tracts after diversion, they described a progressive risk of renal deterioration with time, related mainly to ureteral obstruction.

Also in 1979, Richie traced the development of the use of intestine for urinary diversion.[2] Free reflux of the direct ureteroileal anastomosis was implicated, at least in part, as a cause of renal deterioration. Richie felt that the use of a 3-cm to 4-cm submucosal tunnel in the taenia was the key in the formation of a nonrefluxing colonic conduit and emphasized that such a procedure was the most satisfactory one presently available for patients with benign disease. The long-term preservation of the upper tracts permitted by the nonrefluxing anastomosis is the key to his conclusion.

Colon conduits were judged superior to ileal conduits by Althausen and associates, who also felt that use of the nonrefluxing colon conduit was indicated in many patients.[3] These authors stated that the procedure, although technically complex, spared the kidney from long-term reflux and was associated with fewer complications than the ileal conduit,

namely, ureterointestinal anastomotic stenosis, clinical pyelonephritis, bacilluria, and stomal problems. Their series included 30 adults and 40 children over a 7 yr period. Over half these patients had previously undergone an ileal loop diversion. Sigmoid conduits were used in 51, descending colon in 12, transverse colon in 6, and the ascending colon in 1 patient. The authors cautioned against over generous tapering of dilated ureters in an attempt to perform a nonrefluxing anastomosis; ureteral obstruction is then more likely. They pointed out that since a greater resorption of potassium occurs in ileal than in colon loops, the latter procedure may really be safer in patients with impaired renal function.

Attention can now be turned to the important matter of the patient, the host for a potential colon conduit. From the prior discussion of the technique, it is obvious that the two are not completely separable. As in all major intra-abdominal procedures, poor patient selection can do as much to undermine the possible usefulness of a procedure as deft hands can do to enhance its chances of success.

Generally, patients originally treated for malignant disease are at a greater risk in undergoing supravesical diversion with intestinal segments than are patients with underlying benign disease. Numerous reviews have identified this dichotomy. Particularly, early mortality and morbidity are enhanced by the disease stage, malnutrition, and advanced age of the former group. Long-term complications are seen more frequently in the benign disease group, primarily because these patients have fewer competing causes of death, (*e.g.,* malignancy) and are alive and thus available for long-term analysis. Hence, a procedure such as the colon conduit, with relatively fewer complications, is in the long run more desirable and safe.

Equally important is the status of the cancer patient at the time of a possible diversion. The patient that is considered NED (no evidence of disease) will more likely be a better risk, albeit having the indication for diversion, for instance, bladder fistula or contracted bladder, than the patient with the identical disease that is persistent, either locally or in distant sites. Again, the use of a colonic conduit, with its lower complication rate, is the better choice over an ileal conduit.

The factor of significant pelvic irradiation was the single most important initial impetus to solution of the problem created by the use of irradiated segments. The host irradiated (often to an average of 6000 + rad) runs a high risk of poor healing at all levels in the irradiated field, from the skin through to the ureterointestinal anastomosis. The use of tissues not suffering radiation changes, for instance, the transverse and descending colon and the proximal ureters, plus the option for the operating surgeon to stay out of the irradiated field, confer a tremendous advantage to the colon conduit over the conventional ileal conduit. Again, patients having had definitive pelvic irradiation, regardless of the current status of their cancer, tend to be of higher risk for major surgery.

Another indicator of overall health and risk for any conduit diversion is that of *performance status*. With a simple five-scale classification, patients can be assessed *vis-à-vis* their general fitness for major surgery as well as have their surgical and medical interventions rationally evaluated. Characteristically, patients in performance status categories 0 and 1 (fully active or ambulatory and capable of light work) fare better after treatments than patients in categories 2 and 3 (in bed less than or more than 50% of the time). Patients in category 4 (bedridden) are generally not even included in results of treatment. The use of such performance status categories would go a long way in assessing the success of many therapeutic and palliative procedures performed for genitourinary disease.

The ideal patient for any conduit diversion is one who has normal upper urinary tracts as shown by excretory urogram and normal renal function as shown by serum creatinine concentration. Such a patient is particularly aided by the colon conduit, wherein an antirefluxing ureterocolic anastomosis is possible and now preferred. Moderately dilated ureters can be tapered for antireflux procedures; those with marked dilatation can still be easily implanted into the colon segment in an end-to-side fashion. Recent data suggest that the absorbing qualities of a colonic segment are less deleterious to patients with impaired renal function.

Last, some assessment of the gastrointestinal tract must be made in the patient considered for conduit diversion. Minimal standards include a detailed gastrointestinal history for medical and surgical disease. Should there be any history of such, a follow-up study requires barium enema and proctosigmoidoscopy and possibly an upper gastrointestinal series with a small bowel follow-through study. Severe diverticulitis involving the majority of the colon might effectively rule out the choice of a colonic conduit. On the other hand, the presence of adhesions from prior intra-abdominal surgery might effectively eliminate the small bowel from consideration as a conduit material.

A history of prior partial colectomy involving the transverse or descending colon will especially dictate which areas of large bowel remain available for use as a conduit. Information of this nature has served me well in a few recent cases. In one, a middle-aged woman who had had an ilea conduit and end-transverse colostomy for cervical cancer treated by pelvic irradiation required yet another operation because of fistulae and abscess formation. In addition to resection of her radiation-destroyed ileal segment, the proximal portion of the defunctionalized left transverse colon was used as the new conduit for urine, and a distal Hartmann's pouch was created from the descending colon.

REFERENCES

1. Pitts WR, Muecke EC: A twenty-year experience with ileal conduits. J Urol 122:154, 1979
2. Richie JP: Nonrefluxing sigmoid conduit for urinary diversion. Urol Clin North Am 6:469, 1979
3. Althausen AF, Hagen-Cook K, Hendren WH III: Non-refluxing colon conduit: Experience with 70 cases. J Urol 120:35, 1978

ANNOTATED BIBLIOGRAPHY

Morley GW, Lindenauer SM, Cerny JC: Pelvic exenterative therapy in recurrent pelvic carcinoma. Am J Obstet Gynecol 109:1175, 1971

Between 1965 and 1970, 37 patients, mainly with cervical carcinoma, underwent pelvic exenteration. The operative mortality was 2.7%. The sigmoid colon conduit was used with a sigmoid fecal colostomy. The authors caution against excessive isolation of sigmoid segments in patients whose vascular supply has been compromised by prior radiation therapy. A one-layer mucosal anastomosis at the antimesocolic border was used. The ileal conduit was considered a second choice for urinary diversion.

Swan RW, Rutledge FN: Urinary conduit in pelvic cancer patients. A report of 16 years' experience. Am J Obstet Gynecol 119:6, 1974

A total of 246 gynecologic patients received urinary conduit diversions. Indications included 189 women treated specifically for pelvic cancer and another 57 who were treated because of urologic complications from earlier cancer therapy (*e.g.*, fistulae, obstruction, and intractable hemorrhagic cystitis). Many of the latter group had no recurrent cancer. Sigmoid–colon conduits were used in a total of 33 patients (30 in group 1 and 3 in group 2), whereas ileal conduits were used in the remaining 213 (159 in group 1 and 54 in group 2). A higher mortality (25%) was noted in those who underwent diversion because of complications related to prior treatment. High-dose radiation therapy was the main factor in morbidity. The authors concluded that the majority of patients do benefit from diversion and that although there are significant complications, they are tolerable when compared to alternatives to urinary diversion. Unfortunately, the authors do not distinguish between the two types of intestinal segments used.

Altwein JE, Hohenfellner R: Use of the colon as a conduit for urinary diversion. Surg Gynecol Obstet 140:33, 1975

Of 42 patients treated with colonic conduits, 8 underwent ''salvage'' procedures. Three patients had gynecologic fistulae that were not surgically repairable, and five had undergone unsuccessful diversions. The colonic conduit was used as an alternative to redoing an existing ileal loop. An antireflux ureterocolic anastomosis is described with the use of ureteral stents for 10 days. Advantages of the colonic conduit included the obviation of reflux and decreased incidence of stomal stenosis.

Morales P, Golimbu M: Colonic urinary diversion: 10 years of experience. J Urol 113:302, 1975

Experience with 46 colonic conduits (tranverse colon in 39 and sigmoid colon in 7) is described. The authors started their series with refluxing anastomoses and then switched to antirefluxing procedures. In general, the advantages of colonic conduits included decreased stomal stenosis, decreased residual urine, decreased electrolyte changes, and applicability of the procedure for either high or low ureteral diversion. Of 26 patients treated because of underlying cancer, the average age was 65 yr. Of 20 patients treated because of benign disease, the average age was only 20 yr.
Variations in the use of transverse and sigmoid segments are described in detail. The authors like to have the sigmoid colon segment medial to the left colon, thus reducing the need for a long right ureter. They also use the ureteral reimplantation of Mogg (intraluminal nipple) but without intubation. Specific early and late complications are listed in detail.

Symmonds RE, Jones IV: Sigmoid conduit urinary diversion after exenteration. In Taymor ML, Green TH (eds): Progress in Gynecology, Vol VI, p 729. New York, Grune & Stratton, 1975

In this series of 42 women undergoing pelvic exenteration and sigmoid colon conduits, subsequent renal deterioration occurred in 9. Upper urinary tracts stayed normal in 12 of 34 patients with preoperatively normal upper urinary tracts. Of 13 patients with preoperatively abnormal upper urinary tracts, all were either unchanced or improved. Hypercalemic acidosis was noted in 17 of the women.

Schmidt JD, Buchsbaum HJ, Jacobo EC: Transverse colon conduit for supravesical urinary tract diversion. Urology 8:542, 1976

In this updated series, 22 patients underwent diversion with transverse colon segment. The average pelvic irradiation exposure was 6300 rad. Indications for the conduit included original treatment planning in six patients, radiation cystitis in seven, vesicovaginal fistulae in seven, and ureteral obstruction in two. All anastomoses were made to reflux freely, and no stents were used. Sixteen percent of patients with preoperatively normal upper urinary tracts became abnormal following surgery. On the other hand, 67% of patients with preoperatively dilated upper urinary tracts improved. Renal function remained normal or stable, and there were minimal stomal problems.

53

URINARY DIVERSION IN CHILDREN BY THE SIGMOID CONDUIT: ITS ADVANTAGES AND LIMITATIONS

Panayotis P. Kelalis

From the Departments of Urology and Pediatrics, Mayo Clinic and Mayo Foundation, Rochester, Minnesota

The Journal of Urology
Copyright © 1974 by The Williams & Wilkins Co.
Vol. 112, November
Printed in U.S.A.

The ideal bladder substitute providing urinary control but without adverse effects to the kidneys remins elusive. In children with a normal bowel and an efficient anal sphincter, the use of the uninterrupted colon for urinary diversion is a practical proposition and should be the first choice—a statement that is supported by Spence's superb results of ureterosigmoidostomy in children.[1] Unfortunately, in most instances permanent supravesical diversion in children is undertaken to alleviate complications of neurogenic bladder and associated anorectal dysfunction is the rule in these patients, preventing any attempt at preservation of the sphincteric mechanism.

Such urinary diversion should be performed before demonstrable changes in the upper urinary tract become

Accepted for publication May 17, 1974.
Read at annual meeting of North Central Section, American Urological Association, Acapulco, Mexico, November 11–18, 1973.
Dr. Floyd Csir performed the intraluminal pressure studies.

evident. Upper tract deterioration prior to urinary diversion frequently predisposes to stone formation.

It is universally agreed that for children with dilated ureters that show reasonably active peristalsis, cutaneous ureterostomy is preferable. When the ureters are normal or minimally dilated it is necessary to interpose a piece of intestinal tract to act as a conduit. To this end the ileum has long been used and, indeed, many authors have reported that this is a satisfactory method of permanent supravesical urinary diversion.[2-7] However, as experience with the procedure accumulates and as long-term results become available it is becoming clear that, at least in children, the ileal conduit has certain inherent risks and disadvantages.[8-12] These may be precluded by the use of the sigmoid colon.[13,14]

The results of supravesical urinary diversion with the sigmoid conduit in 12 children are herein described. The patients comprised 8 girls and 4 boys between 4 and 11 years old at the time of operation. Urinary diversion was performed because of a neurogenic bladder in 10 children and following failure of primary closure of exstrophy of the bladder (rectal prolapse having prevented ureterosigmoidostomy) in 2.

A prolonged followup is necessary to evaluate any procedure relating to permanent supravesical urinary diversion in children, because in children it is in the long-term that the inadequacies and complications become evident. Thus, only children followed for 5 years or more (maximum followup—8 years) are included in this report.

PREOPERATIVE PREPARATION

A 3-day mechanical bowel preparation with rectal washouts and a low residue diet but without antibiotic therapy was used. Saline enemas were given 2 and 3 days preoperatively and a mixture of saline, hydrogen peroxide and glycerol in equal parts was substituted the day before the operation and given until the returns were clear.

During this period the site of the stoma is selected and the collecting device is applied on a trial basis. This is an important test in patients with meningomyelocele and deformity of the spine.

OPERATIVE TECHNIQUE

A midline or right paramedian incision is made. Complete mobilization of the sigmoid colon is achieved by severing the lateral adhesion. Children with myelodysplasia usually have a redundant colon which, together with the absence of mesenteric fat, makes isolation of an adequate length of bowel and subsequent reanastomosis easy. A segment of sigmoid supplied by the inferior mesenteric artery is chosen. Careful selection of the loop of bowel will facilitate isoperistaltic placement, a most important consideration. The length of the loop varies from 10 to 15 cm, depending on the age of the patient and the thickness of the abdominal wall.

Continuity of the bowel is restored and the defect in the mesocolon is closed so that the isolated segment lies almost transversely in the left paracolic gutter (Fig. 1). The proximal end of the conduit is then closed with 2 rows of continuous inverting sutures of fine chromic catgut.

Next, the ureters are ioslated and severed as close to the bladder wall as possible. The right ureter is transposed retroperitoneally beneath the arch of the inferior mesenteric artery and, as with the left ureter, any excessive length is discarded. A 1 cm linear incision is made through all layers of the bowel. Ureterosigmoid anastomosis is carried out between the full thickness of the ureter and mucosa of the bowel. Spatulation of the ureter may be necessary. On each side, 4 or at most 5

chromic 5-zero interrupted sutures are used and the anastomosis is carried over a teflon catheter of appropriate size (usually 8F). Because teflon is non-reactive the catheter must be transfixed in place with a chromic suture through its lumen and tied to the outside of the ureteral wall. Each catheter is brought out via the stoma to drain temporarily into the urinary collecting device (Fig.2A to C). The anastomosis is buried by inverting seromuscular sutures of 4-zero chromic catgut which are continued proximally for 2 to 3 cm so as to create a seromuscular tunnel (sleeve) 2 to 3 cm in length, through which the ureter traverses, thus creating an antireflux type of anastomosis (Fig. 2D to F).

The stoma is constructed next. An inverted V incision is made at the pre-arranged site and subcutaneous fat is removed. Sections of all remaining layers of the abdominal wall are excised in a circular manner and the conduit is brought through the defect to the surface. The external oblique aponeurosis is attached to the seromuscular layer of the conduit with several interrupted chromic catgut sutures. Next, the conduit is spatulated at the inferior border and the skin flap is interposed in the incised defect. In order to keep the skin inverted the edge of the skin flap must be anchored to the aponeurosis (Fig. 3). The stoma is completed by suturing the edges of the conduit to the skin with plain catgut. After the abdominal cavity has been re-entered the leaves of the open retroperitoneum of the left paracolic gutter are used so that

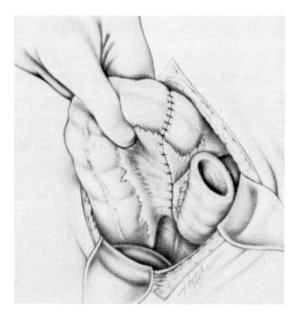

Fig. 1. Restoration of continuity of bowel and closure of defect in mesocolon so that isolated segment lies transversely in left paracolic gutter.

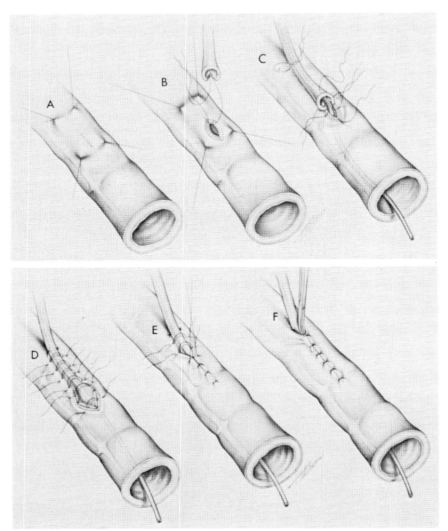

Fig. 2. Details of ureterosigmoid anastomosis. (*A*) to (*C*) Incision, anastomosis and insertion of stent. (*D*) to (*F*) Creation of seromuscular tunnel.

the conduit can be totally extraperitonealized (Fig. 4). A cystectomy is not performed routinely.

POSTOPERATIVE COURSE AND COMPLICATIONS

The first ureteral stent is removed 8 days postoperatively and the other is removed 48 hours later. The average hospital stay has been 14 days.

The only immediate postoperative complication has been the inadvertent removal of 1 stent, necessitating reinsertion in an antegrade fashion via the flank on the first postoperative night.

After the patient is discharged from the hospital suppressive chemotherapy is continued for at least 3 months, at which time urologic evaluation is repeated. Repeat evaluation includes, in addition to electrolyte and renal function studies, excretory urography (IVP) and a sigmoidogram, which is done under fluoroscopic control in order to ascertain the presence or absence of reflux. Vitamin C is given indefinitely (usually 1,000 mg daily) to acidify the urine and to prevent stomal problems related to infection and alkaline urine.

RESULTS OF OPERATION

In 1 patient obstruction at the ureterocolic anastomosis leading to hydronephrosis necessitated revision 4 months later. In retrospect, this patient could have been served best initially by cutaneous ureterostomy because of the

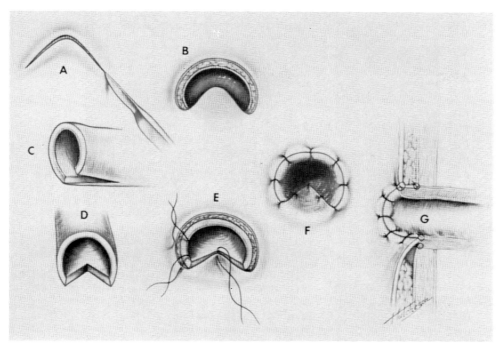

Fig. 3. Steps in creation of stoma.

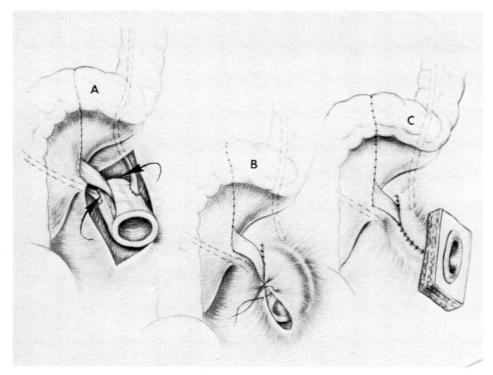

Fig. 4. (*A* through *C*) Extraperitonealization of conduit.

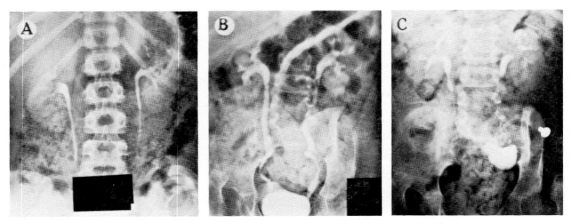

Fig. 5. (A) Postoperative IVP. (B) and (C) Preoperative and postoperative IVP in same patient.

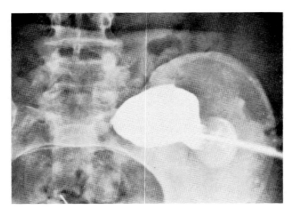

Fig. 6. Sigmoidogram without reflux.

dilated ureter. Six years later, the same patient also has a protruding stoma without elongation of the bowel that will necessitate revision sometime in the future. In another child there was a mild degree of hyperkeratosis around the stoma.

Electrolyte homeostasis and renal function have remained normal, particularly plasma chloride concentrations that remained within the normal range in all patients. The growth rate, as judged by the height and weight, has also remained within normal limits.

There has been no evidence of stenosis of the stoma. Calibration of the stoma has been done routinely at 3-month intervals during the first year and 6-month intervals thereafter.

All 24 renal and ureteral units have remained normal without any evidence of dilatation of the collecting system (Fig. 5). Sigmoidograms[15] are available for all

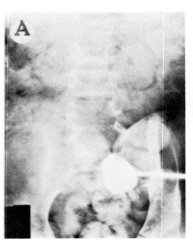
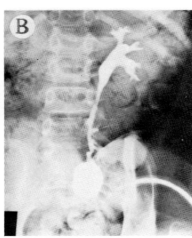

Fig. 7. Sigmoidograms with reflux. (A) Early. (B) Late.

patients and have shown no reflux in 14 units (Fig. 6), immediate reflux of total degree in 4 (in 3 of which there had been no application of the antireflux technique at the anastomosis) and reflux at pressures exceeding 40 cm water in 6 (Fig. 7). Interestingly, 3 of the 4 renal units associated with low pressure reflux have shown minimal retardation of renal growth.

Conduit intraluminal pressures have been measured by small spherical latex balloons (5 mm in diameter) tied over the open end of the polyethylene tube (0.5 mm inside diameter), which was connected to strain gauge pressure transducers (Statham, model P-23De). The balloon, tube and gauge were water-filled and the fluid column conducted intra-balloon pressures to the trans-ducers. Alterations in the output circuit of the strain gauges were recorded photokymographically. Record-ings were obtained for at least 1 hour, with the patients in the supine position and pressures were recorded before, during and after a meal. A typical pattern is noted in Figure 8A. Figure 8B records the response of the large bowel to nearly complete occlusion of the stoma.

DISCUSSION

In this series sigmoid conduit urinary diversion has proved most satisfactory. Admittedly the number of patients is small and, in fairness to the proponents of the ileal conduit, it should be stated that for the 2 forms of urinary diversion, accurate and comprehensive com-parative statistics that directly compete are lacking.

The operation is easy to perform, disturbance of the abdominal contents is minimal and convalescence is surprisingly smooth. Because the conduit is compart-mentalized and extraperitonealized the risk of bowel complication is decidedly small.

Technically, a short segment of bowel suffices and, as a result of this and probably different reabsorptive qualities of the mucosa of the large bowel, electrolyte disturbances are virtually absent. With cutaneous ure-teroileostomy reports on disturbance of homeostasis are at best conflicting and in some series significant.[12]

Stomal problems, one of the most troublesome complications of ileal conduit diversions in children, have been surprisingly few (Fig. 9).[10–12] Such problems are thought to result from differential growth of the scar tissue around the stoma, necessitating repeated revisions during periods of growth. Because of the large lumen of the colon, a certain degree of contraction at the skin level can occur without significant stenosis and, therefore (despite a single report to the contrary),[16] with minimal elevation of intraluminal pressures. Such is not the case in cutaneous ureteroileostomy, in which noticeable in-creases in intraluminal pressure can occur even with minimal degrees of stenosis. Interposition of a skin flap appears to break the continuity of the scar tissue at the skin level and, in this respect, it may be beneficial in preventing stenosis.

Although the early results of ureteroileostomy have been encouraging, there is increasing evidence that this form of urinary diversion causes a significant number of

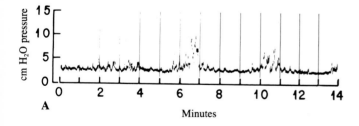

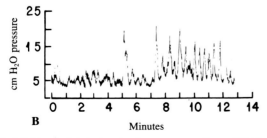

Fig. 8. (*A*) Conduit intraluminal pressure pattern. (*B*) Conduit intraluminal pressure pattern with occlusion at stoma.

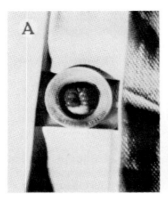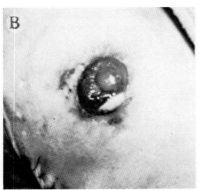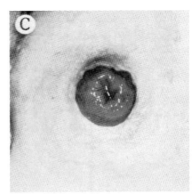

Fig. 9. Examples of sigmoid conduit stomas.

unsatisfactory results when used in children. Critical analysis of results reported in various large series uncovers a significant number of patients (10 to 15 per cent) in whom the condition of the upper urinary tract was normal before operation but deteriorated postoperatively, even in the absence of any evidence of stenosis either at the level of the skin or at the ureteroileal anastomosis.[4,9,12,17] The incidence of such deterioration appears to increase with time. This has been variously attributed to ill-fitting appliances or to occlusion of the lumen by the pressure of underpants, skirts or trousers. However, it is more likely to be related to the prolonged

hydrodynamic effect of reflux, which is universal in the ileal conduit.

In contrast, in the sigmoid conduit an antireflux type of anastomosis between the ureter and the bowel is possible, which protects the kidneys from the ravages of reflux and also prevents access of the infected material of the lumen of the bowel to the kidneys. I believe that this is the singular most important advantage of the procedure.

Acidification of urine with vitamin C appears to have a beneficial effect on the skin around the stoma.

SUMMARY

Permanent supravesical urinary diversion with the sigmoid conduit was performed in 12 children. A minimum followup of 5 years showed that the results of this form of urinary diversion are highly satisfactory. Disturbances in homeostasis are virtually absent and stomal difficulties are minimal. The most important advantage of this technique is facilitation of an effective antireflux mechanism provided by uretero-

colic anastomosis. Thus, in children, there are many advantages of the sigmoid conduit as compared to the ileal conduit. Probably its only limitation is the anorectal dysfunction so frequently present in those children in whom the procedure is necessary, which makes thorough preoperative preparation of the bowel difficult at times.

REFERENCES

1. Spence, H. M.: Ureterosigmoidostomy for exstrophy of the bladder: results in a personal series of thirty-one cases. Br J Urol, 38:36, 1966
2. Ray, P. and De Domenico, I.: Intestinal conduit urinary diversion in children. Br J Urol, 44:345, 1972
3. Livaditis, A.: Cutaneous uretero-ileostomy in children. Acta Paediat Scand, 54:131, 1965
4. Delgado, G. E. and Muecke, E. C.: Evaluation of 80 cases of ileal conduits in children: indication, complication and results. J Urol, 109:311, 1973
5. Retik, A. B., Perlmutter, A. D. and Gross, R. E.: Cutaneous ureteroileostomy in children. New Engl J Med, 277:217, 1967
6. Straffon, R. A., Turnbull, R. B., Jr. and Mercer, R. D.: The ileal conduit in thirty-five children. Cleveland Clin Quart, 30:89, 1963
7. Cordonnier, J. J.: Ileal conduit in children. Urol Int, 23:82, 1968
8. Glenn, J. F., Small, M. P. and Boyarsky, S.: Complications of ileal segment urinary diversion in children. Urol Int, 23:97, 1968
9. Scott, J. E. S.: Urinary diversion in children. Arch Dis Child, 48:199, 1973

10. Rickham, P. P.: Permanent urinary diversion in childhood. Ann Roy Coll Surg, 35:84, 1964
11. Belman, A. B.: Penicillin therapy for metaplasia of the ileal conduit stoma. J Urol, 107:141, 1972
12. Malek, R. S., Burke, E. C. and DeWeerd, J. H.: Ileal conduit urinary diversion in children. J Urol, 105:892, 1971
13. Mogg, R. A.: Urinary diversion using the colonic conduit. Br J Urol, 39:687, 1967
14. Spence, B., Esho, J. and Cass, A.: Comparison of ileac and colonic conduit urinary diversions in dogs. J Urol, 108:712, 1972
15. Nogrady, M. B., Petitclerc, R. and Moir, J. D.: The roentgenologic evaluation of supravesical permanent urinary diversion in childhood (ileal and colonic conduit). J Canad Ass Radiol, 20:75, 1969
16. Dybner, R., Jeter, K. and Lattimer, J. K.: Comparison of intraluminal pressures in ileal and colonic conduits in children. J Urol, 108:477, 1972
17. Smith, E. D.: Follow-up studies on 150 ileal conduits in children. J Pediat Surg, 7:1, 1972

Commentary: Colon Conduit Diversion in Children

Panayotis P. Kelalis

It bears repeating that knowledge of and past experience with other forms of urinary diversion in children have taught physicians the absolute necessity for prolonged follow-up study of these patients, because particular deficiencies of these procedures become evident later. The sigmoid conduit is certainly no exception. It should therefore be both useful and educational to look at the group of children included in the preceding article 6 yr later, at a time when practically all have reached puberty and therefore have passed a period when added growth may have imposed particular stresses on the urinary system and the colonic conduit.

Perhaps as a result of the short segment, the wide unobstructed stoma—allowing free drainage of urine to the outside—and the inherent characteristics of the sigmoid mucosa, biochemical problems have been conspicuously absent. All stomas have functioned satisfactorily, and there has been no tendency to the development of stenosis except for one instance in which the problem was one of hyperkeratosis. Whether this isolated piece of bowel will exhibit the same propensity for the development of tumors as after ureterosigmoidostomy many years later remains to be determined.

When looking at the behavior of the upper urinary tract in these children, however, a different story emerges. In 3 patients (25%), silent unilateral hydroureteronephrosis appeared several years later, as discovered on routine follow-up urographic evaluation. All three patients had undergone initial successful antireflux ureterocolic anastomosis, as proved by excretory urograms and sigmoidograms, which showed neither dilatation of the collecting system nor reflux. At exploration, it was evident that in all patients stenosis of the ureteral segment was present at the proximal end of the tunnel that had been created, and it can safely be assumed that it was directly related to and possibly the result of efforts to create an antireflux mechanism. Correction was successful in all patients. All other renal and ureteral units have remained normal in both urographic appearance and growth. In none of these patients has either idiopathic dilatation of the collecting system or stone formation been identified.

Surprisingly, even in patients in whom ureteral reflux (low or high pressure) was identified at sigmoidography, the renal and ureteral units continued to be normal. This may be directly related to the different dynamics present in the sigmoid colon as compared with the ileum. No doubt the absence of obstruction at the stomal level, allowing free drainage of urine into the bag, is an important factor. This finding is at variance with experimental data available in dogs. Therefore, the logical question that follows is whether, in the presence of a short colonic conduit and a large unobstructed stoma, antireflux ureterosigmoid anastomosis with its attendant risks of complications is necessary. I am inclined to believe that it is.

Last, the psychologic problems attendant on any form of external supravesical urinary diversion are also present in children with colonic conduits. Two girls were "undiverted" and were converted to a permanent ureterosigmoidostomy because of deep psychologic problems.

Fortunately, because of tremendous advances in the field of pediatric urology relating specifically to disease entities for which permanent urinary diversion was the accepted treatment in the recent past—especially neurogenic bladder, exstrophy, tumors of the lower urinary tract, and intractable urinary incontinence—such entities can be treated at present with increasing success by other means. Happily, the indications in children for urinary diversion requiring the interposition of a segment of bowel are now quite uncommon, perhaps even rare. Furthermore, with increasing knowledge of the physiology of the lower urinary tract and improvement in surgical techniques, urinary diversion as a means to relieve the intolerable complications of reconstructive surgery has also, fortunately, become a rare occurrence.

Colonic conduit urinary diversion in children has decided advantages over other forms of permanent urinary diversion in which a piece of bowel is necessary, but this procedure is by no means without complications. Perhaps in the future, further improvement in surgical techniques will eliminate some of these risks. However, just as in all other forms of urinary supravesical diversion with an external appliance, psychologic problems, many of which have hitherto not received proper attention, are present and are likely to continue as long as an external form of urinary diversion is necessary.

ANNOTATED BIBLIOGRAPHY

Mogg RA: The treatment of neurogenic urinary incontinence using the colonic conduit. Br J Urol 37:681 1965

This is a report on the technique of colonic conduit construction. It is the first paper to draw attention to the significance of an antirefluxing ureterocolic anastomosis. Illustrative cases are presented.

Cook RCM, Lister J, Zachary RB: Operative management of the neurogenic bladder in children: Diversion through intestinal conduits. Surgery 63:825, 1968

Groups of myelodysplastic children undergoing refluxing colonic and ileal conduit urinary diversion are compared. A similar percentage of renal and ureteral complications was noted in each group, but a lesser frequency of stomal stenosis was seen in the group with a colonic loop.

Mogg RA, Syme RRA: The results of urinary diversion using the colonic conduit. Br J Urol 41:434, 1969

A series of 40 patients (32 children and 8 adults) are reported on. Half the patients were followed for 3 yr or more, and more than half of these were followed for 5 yr or more. This paper contains a detailed analysis of results, including studies of conduit pressures, stomas, renal units, and conduitography. Complications and difficulties experienced are frankly analyzed, and modifications of techniques that were devised are discussed.

Genster HG: Changes in the composition of the urine in sigmoid loop bladders: A comparison with ileal loops. Scand J Urol Nephrol 5:41, 1971

In five patients with sigmoid loop urinary diversion, the sodium, potassium, and urea concentrations in the urine from the ureters and from the sigmoid loop were compared. Sodium and potassium are treated rather indifferently by the sigmoid segment, but a decrease in urea concentration in the sigmoid loop suggests some transportation into the bloodstream. However, in general, the sigmoid loop showed little tendency toward changes in the urinary composition.

Dybner R, Jeter K, Lattimer JK: Comparison of intraluminal pressures in ileal and colonic conduits in children. J Urol 108:477, 1972

A technique is described for measuring the pressure generated in ileal and colonic conduits and comparing the relative pressures under various conditions. Studies were made in 11 children (7 boys and 4 girls) ranging in age from 2½ to 13 yr. Seven had an ileal and four a sigmoid conduit.

Alpert PF, Tanagho EA: Colonic conduits: Experimental and clinical studies of reflux and ascending infection. Invest Urol 11:336, 1974

Extraperitoneal colonic loop urinary diversion with a nonrefluxing ureterocolic anastomosis was evaluated in six dogs. Results indicate the possibility of maintaining the sterility of the upper tract and of a colonic loop with a minimum of residual urine.

Adequate ureteral drainage was maintained; coloureteral reflux did not occur, even with high intracolonic pressures.

Hendren WH: Nonrefluxing colon conduit for temporary or permanent urinary diversion in children. J Pediatr Surg 10:381, 1975

A technique of operation and the results and complications in 21 children with colonic conduit diversion are described. Illustrative cases are presented. The concept of temporary colonic conduit with a plan for later anastomosis of the conduit to the colon (ureterosigmoidostomy) is presented.

Richie JP, Skinner DG: Urinary diversion: The physiological rationale for nonrefluxing colonic conduits. BR J Urol 47:269, 1975

A freely refluxing ileal conduit and a nonrefluxing colonic conduit were created in the same experimental animal to minimize the number of variables. The most striking findings were noted at autopsy 3 mo after diversion. Histologic evidence of pyelonephritis was present in 83% of kidneys connected to refluxing ileal conduits as compared with 7% of those connected to colonic conduits ($P < 0.001$).

Yoder IC, Pfister RC: Radiology of colon loop diversion: Anatomical and urodynamic studies of the conduit and ureters in children and adults. Radiology 127:85, 1978

Fifty-seven colonic conduits and 107 ureters were studied. No reflux occurred in 67 ureters in which intracolonic loop pressures exceeded 40 cm of water. For evaluation and management of possible ureteral obstruction, percutaneous (antegrade) pyelography was used in 11 kidneys, ureteral perfusion (pressure–flow) studies in 8, and percutaneous catheter nephrostomy in 1.

Althausen AF, Hagen-Cook K, Hendren WH III: Non-refluxing colon conduit: Experience with 70 cases. J Urol 120:35, 1978

This is a report of 70 patients (30 adults and 40 children), more than half of whom underwent conversion from failed ileal loops. In six patients ureterocolic anastomoses developed. The number of significant complications in this series compared favorably with that in an ileal loop series. The follow-up period in the majority of patients was relatively short.

54

ILEOCECAL CONDUIT FOR TEMPORARY AND PERMANENT URINARY DIVERSION

Leonard Zinman and John A. Libertino

From the Department of Urology, Lahey Clinic Foundation, Boston, Massachusetts

The Journal of Urology
Copyright © 1975 by The Williams & Wilkins Co.
Vol. 113, March
Printed in U.S.A.

The ileal conduit has become an established method of urinary diversion since it was popularized by Bricker in 1950.[1] Innovations in a reconstructive operation on the urinary tract during the last 10 years have generated an increasing interest in selectively reversing patients who have diversion with a refluxing ureteroileostomy. Recurrent pyelonephritis and persistent hydronephrosis have not been eliminated completely when the conduit has been converted to an ileocystoplasty.[2] Total exclusion of urine from the bladder by a non-intubated intestinal segment drainage procedure, incorporating a consistently successful antireflux technique, would make planned temporary supravesical diversion a useful preliminary adjunct in many restorative procedures. Patients with insurmountable benign lower urinary tract problems requiring diversion today may be candidates for a future reconstructive procedure if they are not committed to an irreversible form of diversion. Construction of an antirefluxing ureterointestinal anastomosis with the diverting

Accepted for publication July 19, 1974

Read at annual meeting of American Urological Association, St. Louis, Missouri, May 19–23, 1974.

sigmoid and ileal conduits in patients with normal caliber ureters has had variable success and has not been widely accepted.[3,4] We herein report our experience in the diversion of 6 patients with potentially reversible lower tract problems by an ileocecal segment as an antirefluxing conduit enhancing the competence of the ileocecal valve by a cecoileal plication procedure.

OPERATIVE TECHNIQUE

The patients are prepared with a 3-day bowel program, including colonic lavage and orally administered neomycin. The stoma is sited in the right lower quadrant with the patient in the lying, sitting and standing positions to ensure proper location. A generous midline incision is used for good access to the lower and upper parts of the abdomen (Fig. 1A). The right colon and hepatic flexure are mobilized to release the mesentery for inspection and isolation of the appropriate blood supply. The right ureter is easily identified at this time behind the cecum and isolated down to just below the pelvic brim. The ileocolic intestinal segment with its mesentery is isolated, containing the ever constant ileocolic vessels

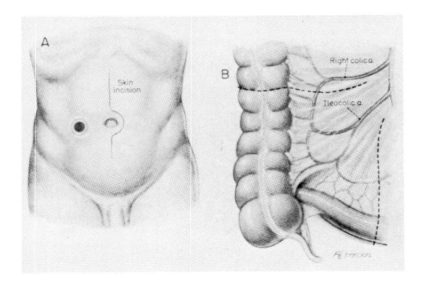

Fig. 1. (A) Generous midline incision is used to mobilize entire right colon and hepatic flexure. (B) Ileocecal segment is isolated with its ileocolic mesentery proximal to right colic artery. Ileum is sectioned 10 to 12 cm proximal to ileocecal junction.

that will be the vascular pedicle to the conduit (Fig. 1B). The ileum is sectioned obliquely 10 cm proximal to the ileocecal valve and will be supplied by the distal ileal branch of the ileocolic artery. The ascending colon is divided proximal to the right colic artery. The paracolic arcade is divided and the mesocolon is incised down to the base of the mesentery parallel to the ileocolic vessels. The isolated segment is irrigated with saline in an antegrade and retrograde fashion. The ileocecal valve was tested by retrograde high pressure irrigations through the colonic opening and found to be incompetent in all patients studied. A No. 30 French whistle-tip catheter is introduced into the proximal end of the ileal portion through the ileocecal valve emerging through the colonic stoma. The antireflux mechanism is obtained by plicating the cecum around the terminal ileum in a collar-like fashion. This procedure is done in a manner similar to the Nissen fundoplication esophagogastric junction operation. The catheter is used as an obturator across the ileocecal junction during the plication to avoid too much narrowing of the distal ileum. The ileum is then intussuscepted into the cecum for 1 cm with 3 seromuscular sutures of 3-zero tevdek (Fig. 2A). The anterior and posterior wall of the cecum is wrapped like a collar around the terminal 4 cm of ileum in a 270-degree encircling fashion with 3 appropriately placed seromuscular non-absorbable sutures incorporating ileum and cecum on either side of the mesentery (Fig. 2B and C). The proximal end of the ileal tail is then closed with an over-and-over 3-zero chromic catgut suture reinforced wtih interrupted seromuscular sutures of 3-zero chromic catgut. The left ureter is isolated and brought behind the sigmoid mesocolon in the usual fashion. The ureteroileal

anastomoses are accomplished by the standard technique of a direct mucosa-to-mucosa technique, with fine interrupted catgut sutures on the inferior antimesenteric border of the proximal ileum (Fig. 2D). The stoma is constructed by excising a 3 to 4 cm circle of skin from the previously designated site in the right lower quadrant. A wide cruciate incision is made in the rectus fascia, the muscle is separated and displaced, and the peritoneum is incised comfortably to allow the transfer of the distal colonic opening through the abdominal wall. The ileocecal intestinal segment with its vascular pedicle has sufficient length and mobility to allow the distal end of the colonic portion to be brought through the right lower quadrant without tension (Fig. 3). A restorative 2-layer end-to-end anastomosis between the spatulated end of the ileum and the ascending colon is a simple procedure, resulting in a wide lumen with well vascularized bowel ends. The mesenteric rent is closed with a continuous chromic catgut suture (Fig. 3). The stoma is constructed with subcuticular sutures of 3-zero chromic catgut, producing an everting nipple-like effect. A temporary appliance is fitted after closure of the abdominal wall and placement of a transperitoneal right lower quadrant drain.

METHODS AND MATERIALS

From January 1969 to the present time 15 patients at this clinic have undergone urinary diversion by the ileocecal intestinal conduit technique with an antireflux modification of the ileocecal valve. Six of these patients with potentially reversible lower tract disorders have been followed from 1 to 5 years (see table). There were 3 male and 3 female subjects. Patient age at the time of

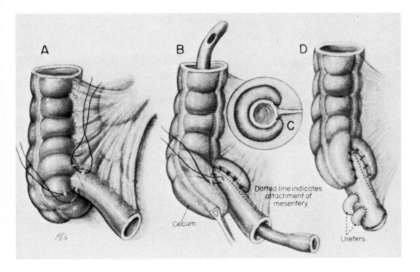

Fig. 2. (*A*) Ileum is intussuscepted into cecum for 1 cm with 3 seromuscular sutures. (*B*) and (*C*) Anterior and posterior wall of cecum is wrapped like collar around terminal 4 cm of ileum in 270-degree encircling fashion with 3 appropriately placed seromuscular non-absorbable sutures on either side of mesentery. (*D*) Completed conduit with plicated ileocecal junction and proximal ureteroileal anastomoses on antimesenteric border.

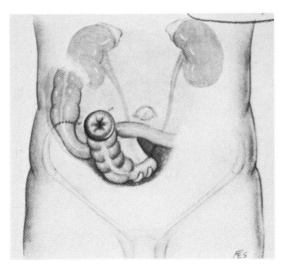

Fig. 3. Colonic stoma is brought out in right lower quadrant and 2-layer end-to-end ileocolonic anastomosis is constructed between spatulated end of ileum and ascending colon.

diversion ranged from 6 to 56 years. Those subjects with less than 1 year followup were excluded from study. Preoperative excretory urography (IVP) revealed hydroureteronephrosis in 3 patients and normal upper tracts in 3. Two patients had acute vesical tuberculosis with persistent bladder outlet obstruction from bladder neck contracture and a posterior urethral stricture. One patient had severe calicectasis and a primary neurogenic bladder with bilateral refluxing megaloureter. A previous antireflux operation in this patient resulted in bilateral ureterovesical junction obstruction and a nonfunctioning

right kidney. One patient had radiation bladder contracture with a large radiation-induced vesicovaginal fistula after therapy of a stage 3 carcinoma of the cervix. No tumor was found in the fistulous margin but a waiting period of 2 to 3 years was planned to rule out recurrence of tumor and to ensure stability of the radiation process.

Preoperative barium enemas revealed incompetent ileocecal valves in 5 of the 6 patients but intraoperative retrograde irrigation in methylene blue-stained saline washes through the colonic end of the conduit revealed an incompetent valve in all 6 patients before the plication procedure. All patients underwent followup studies at 3 to 6-month intervals with IVP, retrograde conduitography, catheter culture of the cecal contents, blood urea nitrogen, serum creatinine and electrolyte determinations. One patient has undergone manometric motility studies of the valve and proximal ileal tail by passing small polyethylene catheters through the stoma with a flexible fiberoptic colonoscope. These studies revealed a high pressure zone in the plicated ileocecal valve area and a simultaneous low pressure zone in the proximal ileal tail. Stomas were inspected periodically and discussed with our enterostomal therapist. No stomal problems were encountered and all stomal measurements decreased in size by a quarter of the original diameter within a 3-month period.

RESULTS

Postoperative IVP revealed marked improvement in the 3 patients with pre-existing hydronephrotic renal units. Of the 3 patients with normal findings on pyelography 2 continued to have normal findings. In 1 patient with normal findings preoperatively a left upper 5 cm periureteral fibrotic stricture developed, requiring lysis and temporary nephrostomy drainage. The stricture has completely resolved and the collecting system is normal at present. Retrograde cecography demonstrated a completely competent ileocecal valve in the entire group at 40 to 60 mm Hg injection pressure observed under fluoroscopy. Five of the 6 patients had infected cecal urine and 1 had infected cecal urine and sterile ileal urine simultaneously obtained at the time of undiversion. Electrolyte disorders were not observed in any of the group. One patient had a preoperative serum creatinine of 2.6 mg per 100 ml, which returned to 1.3 mg per 100 ml 1 month after diversion. Another patient underwent reversal of the conduit diversion with simultaneous cecocystoplasty bladder augmentation and has now been followed for 5 years with no evidence of upper tract deterioration.

CASE REPORT

A 56-year-old white man was seen at this clinic with an 18-month history of 1 hourly frequency, and nocturia, hematuria and terminal dysuria. Transurethral resection of the prostate and bladder neck had been performed twice during the last year with subsequent increase in frequency and strangury. IVP revealed delayed excretion from the right kidney with moderately severe hydroureteronephrosis down to the bladder and delayed emptying up to 140 minutes (Fig. 4A). Voiding cystourethrography revealed a bladder capacity of 90 cc with bilateral ureterovesical reflux, more severe on the right than on the left side (Fig. 4B). Serum creatinine was 1.3 mg per 100 ml. The urine sediment revealed microhematuria and pyuria but a routine culture was sterile. Cystoscopic examination revealed a much inflamed bladder mucosa with a contracted volume, and multiple ulcerations of the trigone and right lateral wall. Both ureteral orifices were deformed and difficult to see. Bladder biopsy demonstrated acute and chronic inflammatory changes throughout the bladder wall with granulomatous lesions consistent with acute vesical tuberculosis. Repeat subsequent cultures for tuberculosis were negative. A barium enema revealed an incompetent ileocecal valve but a normal colon and terminal ileum (Fig. 5). On January 23, 1969, after 4 weeks of antituberculous therapy, the patient underwent urinary diversion by the ileocecal conduit technique with plication of the ileocecal valve. Intraoperative retrograde distension of the cecum revealed a competent valve after cecoileal plication. The distal ureteral stumps were removed. Convalescence was uneventful. IVP 1 year postoperatively revealed normal kidneys and ureters (Fig. 6A). Retrograde cecography revealed no ureteral reflux (Fig. 6B). A repeat bladder biopsy after 1 year of antituberculous therapy (bladder

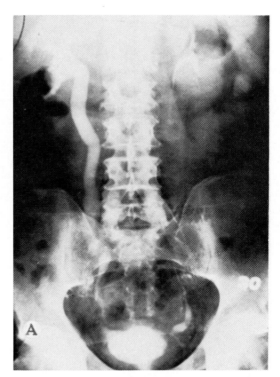

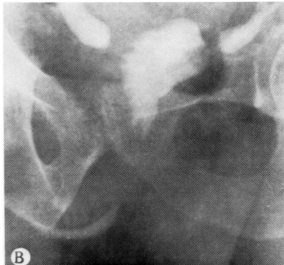

Fig. 4. (A) Preoperative IVP with right hydroureteronephrosis, left lower ureterectases and contracted bladder. (B) Preoperative voiding cystourethrogram with 90 cc capacity and bilateral ureterovesical reflux.

capacity was reduced to 60 cc) revealed a fibrotic bladder wall with no active inflammatory disease. In February 1970 the patient underwent reversal of the diversion with

Clinical Data on 6 Patients with Ileocecal Conduits

Age	Sex	Diagnosis	Preop. IVP	Postop. IVP	Yrs Followup	Comment
56	M	Acute vesical tuberculosis that bilat. refluxing hydroureteronephrosis	Right hydroureteronephrosis and lower left hydroureter, contracted bladder	Normal	5	Reversed to ileocecocystoplasy 1 yr after diversion, sterile urine, normal IVP
51	M	Tuberculous vesical contracture	Normal	Normal	3	Still diverted
26	F	Neurogenic bladder, serum creatinine 2.6	Bilat. grade 3 hydronephrosis, marked decrease in right renal function	Improved with return of right renal function	2.5	Serum creatinine decreased to 1.3
19	F	Painful contracted fibrotic bladder, ? etiology	Normal	Left upper periureteral fibrotic stricture resolved by ureterolysis	1	
40	F	Contracture secondary to radiation cystitis, vesicovaginal fistula	Normal	Normal	1.5	Manometric study reveals low pressure in ileal lumen with high pressure sphincter zone
6	M	Obscure bladder outlet obstruction with megaloureter, preop. serum creatinine 2.0	Bilat. calicectasis grade 4	Improved	3	Postop. serum creatinine 0.9

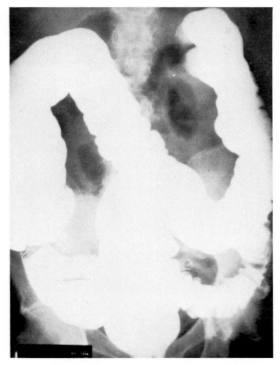

Fig. 5. Preoperative barium enema demonstrates incompetent ileocecal valve with normal colon and terminal ileum.

simultaneous augmentation cecocystoplasty. Postoperative bladder capacity increased to 350 cc. Voiding cystourethrography showed no evidence of reflux with prompt emptying of the bladder and post-void residuum remained at 60 to 90 cc (Fig. 7A). A urine culture has remained consistently sterile, and IVP 5 years after the original diversion and 4 years after cecocystoplasty revealed a normal upper urinary tract (Fig. 7B). Serum creatinine remains at 1.2 mg per 100 ml with a normal electrolyte determination.

DISCUSSION

Long-term followup studies of patients with low pressure ileal conduit diversion are beginning to reveal an increasing incidence of calculi, pyelonephritis and failure to resolve pre-existing hydronephrosis. Stomal obstruction, increased intraluminal pressure, infection and reflux have been questioned as the etiologic basis of these upper urinary tract complications. Deterioration of previously normal upper urinary tracts after construction of an ileal conduit has been found to be considerable in some series.[5,6] There is evidence that ileoureteral reflux of infected urine is a constant phenomenon in this form of diversion and may be exaggerated by the position of the patient, a poorly fitting collection device, stomal or fascial obstruction, excess conduit length and kinking of the bowel, all of which may accentuate the adverse effects of reflux and prevent adequate emptying of the system. The inclusion of an antireflux mechanism in colonic and ileal conduits by a mucosal-tunnel technique with normal caliber ureters has reduced the incidence of reflux to 40 percent.[3,4,7] Whether this mechanism has improved the quality of renal function is still unanswered.

The ileocecal intestinal segment has been used clinically and experimentally as a competent substitute

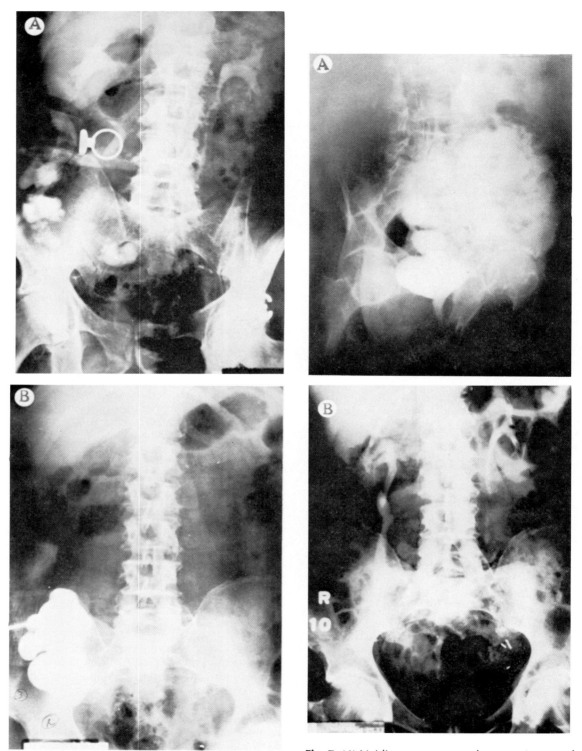

Fig. 6. (*A*) IVP 1 year after ileocecal conduit diversion with resolution of previously noted right hydronephrosis. Conduit in right lower quadrant contains contrast material. (*B*) Retrograde cecogram reveals absence of ileal or ureteral reflux.

Fig. 7. (*A*) Voiding cecocystourethrogram 3 years after cecocystoplasty with no ureteral or ileal reflux and 350 cc capacity with 2 to 3-ounce post-void residuum. (*B*) Postoperative IVP 5 years after original diversion and 4 years after cecocystoplasty reveals normal upper urinary tract.

bladder by Gilchrist and associates since 1950.[8] Gil Vernet first brought attention to the ileocolic valve in the urinary system during the construction of a uretero-ileocecocystoplasty.[9] Experimental attempts to increase the competence of this junction in the dog have not been consistent.[10] The ileocecal junction has been considered as a valve because of its anatomic appearance[11] but manometric and pharmacologic studies demonstrate the characteristics of a true alimentary tract sphincter analogous to the motility patterns of the esophagogastric junction.[12,13] In 1956 Nissen successfully corrected gastroesophageal reflux by completely wrapping the fundus of the stomach 360 degrees around the distal esophagus in a collar-like fashion.[14] Motility studies demonstrated a high pressure sphincter zone and a simultaneous low pressure area in the proximal esophageal lumen. This operation has been used widely with good clinical results, confirming its effectiveness as a non-obstructive antireflux technique. From 1969 to the present time we have adapted this technique to achieve a competent ileocecal sphincter by wrapping the cecum around the distal 4 cm. of terminal ileum in 15 patients undergoing ileocecal intestinal conduit diversion. The enhanced sphincteric mechanism has prevented reflux of contrast material on all retrograde cecograms obtained with injection pressures of 40 to 60 mm Hg. One patient has a competent ileocecal valve mechanism with no reflux at voiding pressures studied 4 years after reversing the conduit to an augmentation cecocystoplasty. The upper tracts are normal with complete resolution of a pre-existing right hydronephrosis.

The ileocolic intestinal segment has certain anatomic advantages as a conduit over the previous traditionally used ileal loop. The ileocolic vessels are constant and easily mobilized providing an abundant blood supply to the bowel. The segment is rarely involved in compromising pathology, such as diverticulitis, and its location under the right lower quadrant makes construction of the proximal ascending colonic stoma easy to accomplish with no undue tension. The cecum requires no refashioning for reversal cecocystoplasty and has been found to be a more efficient emptying unit tolerating voiding pressures more effectively than the ileocystoplasty. Incorporation of a competent sphincter in the conduit has allowed resolution of pre-existing hydronephrotic upper tracts and prevented the deterioration of normal collecting systems in our patients followed for 1 to 5 years. The application of the Nissen fundoplication operation to enhance the sphincteric ability of the ileocecal valve has not produced an obstructive area in the conduit. With the use of a short proximal ileal portion, the churning to and fro peristaltic action, characteristic of small bowel, has not been demonstrated by fluoroscopic study to produce ureteropelvic reflux. Motility studies of one of the conduits revealed a low intraluminal ileal pressure during a period of induced stomal obstruction. The sphincteric mechanism would seem to protect the proximal ileal portion from stomal and fascial stenosis, poorly fitting collection devices and any other phenomena that would induce increased colonic pressure.

SUMMARY

The ileocecal intestinal segment has been used as a diverting conduit with a satisfactory colonic stoma in 6 patients with potentially reversible bladder disorders. Followup has been from 1 to 5 years. The ileocecal valve has been modified successfully by a fundoplication procedure similar to the Nissen esophagogastric junction operation to prevent ileocecal and ureteral reflux. IVP and renal function studies revealed resolution of pre-existing hydronephrosis and preservation of previously normal upper urinary tracts. One patient has undergone reversal of the diversion by cecocystoplasty and simultaneous bladder augmentation, and has been followed for 5 years with sterile urine and normal IVPs. The anatomic and functional advantages of a conduit with an antireflux mechanism that is applicable to the hydronephrotic collecting system are discussed.

REFERENCES

1. Bricker, E. M.: Bladder substitution after pelvic evisceration. Surg Clin N Am, 30:1511, 1950
2. Hodges, C. V., Lawson, R. K. and Seabaugh, D. R.: Temporary urinary diversion by ileal conduit. J Urol, 105:196, 1971
3. Kafetsioulis, A. and Swinney, J: A study of the function of ileal conduits. Br J Urol, 42:33, 1970
4. Mount, B. M., Susset, J. G., Campbell, J. and MacKinnon, K. J.: Ureteral implantation into ileal conduits. J Urol, 100:605, 1968
5. Straffon, R. A., Turnbull, R. B., Jr. and Mercer, R. D.: The ileal conduit in the management of children with neurogenic lesions of the bladder. J Urol, 89:198, 1963
6. Susset, J. G., Taguchi, Y., DeDomenico, I. and MacKinnon, K. J.: Hydronephrosis and hydroureter in ileal conduit urinary diversion. Canad J Surg, 9:141, 1966
7. Mogg, R. A. and Syme, R. R. A.: The results of urinary diversion using the colonic conduit. Br J Urol, 41:434, 1969
8. Gilchrist, R. K., Merricks, J. W., Hamlin, H. H. and Rieger, I.

T.: Construction of a substitute bladder and urethra. Surg Gynec & Obst, 90:752, 1950
9. Gil Vernet, J. M.: Technique for construction of a functioning artificial bladder. J Urol, 83:39, 1960
10. Selvaggi, F. P., Zaini, P. and Battenberg, J. D.: Use of the canine ileocolic valve to prevent reflux. J Urol 107:372, 1972
11. Rendleman, D. F., Anthony, J. E., Davis, C., Jr., Buenger, R. E., Brooks, A. J. and Beattie, E. J., Jr.: Reflux pressure studies on the ileocecal valve of dogs and humans. Surgery, 44:640, 1958
12. Cohen, S., Harris, L. D. and Levitan, R.: Manometric characteristics of the human ileocecal junctional zone. Gastroenterology, 54:72, 1968
13. Bass, D. D., Ustach, T. J. and Schuster, M. M.: In vitro pharmacologic differentiation of sphincteric and non-sphincteric muscle. Johns Hopkins Med J, 127:185, 1970
14. Nissen, R.: Eine einfache Operation zur Beeinflussung der Refluxoesophagitis. Schweiz Med Wchnschr, 86:590, 1956

Commentary: Ileocecal Conduit Diversion

Leonard Zinman

Diversion into intestinal segments has had a long repetitive history of initial enthusiasm for each procedure introduced, followed by a period of complacency and then disappointment. The early promising results of the ileal conduit were not substantiated by comparative long-term follow-up studies.[1] The literature is less muddied now, but many of the collected reviews of refluxing ileal conduits are confusing, with a lack of hard data about their true efficacy. Diversion for benign and malignant disease, children and adults, patients with azotemia, hydronephrotic systems, and prior existing calculus disease have been grouped together in many of these reports. Follow-up information is clouded by such words as *renal deterioration* or *nonobstructive pyelonephritic scarring,* implying reflux-induced disease that is not distinguished from true cicatricial obstructive disease, such as ureteroileal stricture, stomal stenosis, or midloop fibrous contracture. Despite this uncertainty, some facts are irrefutable. A refluxing ileal conduit in a child followed for longer than 10 yr is associated with a significant incidence of stomal obstruction and upper tract complications, making diversion with this system a calculated risk.[1,2] Physicians also know that colon conduit stomas in adults, like fecal colostomies, are more stable and less often plagued with stomal stenosis than the small bowel stoma.[3,4] Despite a large experience and the recommendation of Mogg that diversion should include antirefluxing ureteral anastomoses, the colon conduit was accepted reluctantly by most urologists.[5,6] The sigmoid colon is clearly a more hazardous organ to operate on, with a more precarious blood supply and a greater chance for sepsis. The sigmoid mesentery of obese patients is often short and thickened and makes it more difficult to isolate a secure vascular pedicle. A left colocolostomy has more potential leaks than a small bowel anastomosis and often requires release of the splenic flexure to prevent a tension-induced type of disruption. The Leadbetter combined antirefluxing ureterocolonic anastomosis is a clinically proved concept, but variation in colonic wall anatomy makes the consistent development of an antirefluxing anastomosis unpredictable.

These are some of the factors that directed us to the ileocecal conduit with the ureters directly anastomosed to the ileum and a reinforced ileocecal valve as the main antirefluxing barrier. It appeared to be a technically safer intestinal segment to construct and was particularly suitable for patients with dilated, short, or absent ureters or those patients who might selectively be considered for future undiversion. The use of this segment in the urinary tract was by no means a new concept. It was first used clinically by Gilchrist and co-workers in an attempt to construct a continent substitute bladder.[7] Couvelaire in France first employed the cecum to enlarge the bladder capacity of patients afflicted with tuberculous vesical contracture, and Gil Vernet identified the ileocecal valve in the urinary system as a potential antirefluxing sphincter in patients who required augmentation cecocystoplasty with ureteral reimplantation.[8,9]

Only a few technical modifications have been made since the first report of the antirefluxing ileocecal segment in 1974.[10] The stomal site is established preoperatively in the right lower quadrant in the usual standard fashion. To proceed, open the stoma before the incision to prevent development of staggering abdominal layers. Excise a button of skin (¾ in), retract the subcutaneous fat, and make a cruciate incision in the rectus fascia, preserving the fascial edges. Retract the muscle and open the peritoneum. This opening should be only slightly larger than that used for ileal stomas. Open the abdomen through a very generous midline incision to ensure good access to the right upper quadrant and pelvis in the event that the right colon has adherent lateral attachments in the retroperitoneal position or when a high hepatic flexure requires mobilization. The mesentery of the right colon should be accessible for transillumination to ensure adequate identification of the ileocecal pedicle.

The ileocecal vessels are constant and more dependable than any other colonic vascular arcade. Ninety-five percent of patients have a prominent marginal artery connecting the ileocolic and right colic artery approximately 2 cm to 3 cm from the medial margin of the bowel edge. This blood supply can be identified by palpation alone in obese patients with very thick mesenteries, a considerable advantage over the more tenuous left colon blood supply. The ileocolic pedicle can be isolated with a fairly long mesentery, which creates a mobile segment easily moved to the right or the left lower quadrant, and which is easily converted for a future augmentation procedure.

Obliquely section the ileum approximately 10 cm proximal to the junction and divide the ascending colon transversely just proximal to the right colic artery. A long ascending colonic portion is not necessary when the segment is used exclusively as a conduit, but a longer segment may be advisable for augmentation cecocystoplasty when larger capacity is required. This may be accomplished by resecting the distal colon proximal to the middle colic artery after dividing the right colic artery near its origin. The bowel may be reconstituted by an end-to-end anastomosis of ileum to ascending colon.

Spatulate the ileum on its antimesenteric border to fit the larger lumen of the ascending colon. This is a safe wide anastomosis with a better nutrient blood supply than the left-sided colocolostomy. The ileocolostomy is potentially less disruptive than the left colonic anastomosis where more solid fecal material is present, and ileal length and mobility are always adequate to avoid tension without mobilizing the hepatic flexure.

ANTIREFLUXING ILEOCECAL JUNCTION

Reinforce the ileocecal valve over a 30 French catheter, which acts as an obturator to prevent an excessively tight ileocecal plication during the reinforcement procedure. First intussuscept the ileum into the cecum by placing three or four sutures of nonabsorbable 3–0 polypropylene in equally distant locations, as illustrated in Figure 8A. Then wrap the redundant cecum around to encircle the terminal 6 cm to 8 cm of ileum for about 200 to 270 degrees by a row of 4 to 5 seromuscular sutures of 3–0 Prolene on either side close to the mesenteric border (Fig. 8B to D). A full 360-degree wrapping plication, as in the esophagus, can be achieved if a future augmentation or undiversion cecocystoplasty is planned.

The extent of the wrapping and the length of ileum reinforced by cecum will depend on the amount of cecal redundancy and the amount of fat in the superior and inferior ileocecal recess. The average length of the tunnel is 6 cm to 8 cm with a variable number of seromuscular sutures. Avoid entering the mucosa of the bowel for fear of future formation of calculi on the nonabsorbable material. After the plication procedure, retrograde irrigation of the cecum with blue-stained fluid can help to identify pressures at which reflux occurs. If reflux persists after the first reinforcement, as may occur in children whose ileocecal valve is not quite as well developed, the wrap can be reinforced by another layer of seromuscular sutures placed more lateral to the first layer, creating a consistently effective antireflux procedure.

Bring out the ureters through the posterior parietal opening. Develop a generous tunnel beneath the sigmoid mesocolon where the left ureter exists across the retroperitoneum. If the inferior mesenteric artery is very lowlying, bring the left ureter across above the artery to avoid any obstructive compression.

Construct a Wallace conjoint ureteroureterostomy by careful spatulation of the ureters symmetrically on their medial avascular side. Make ureteral incisions slightly longer than the diameter of the proximal ileal opening. Approximate the posterior ureteral walls with interrupted 5–0 chromic catgut sutures and join the anterior walls proximally with a few interrupted sutures to avoid obstruction of the common ostium by bowel mucosa. Join the conjoint ureters to the proximal ileal lumen by direct anastomosis with interrupted 4–0 chromic catgut sutures over feeding tube stents.

The collected reported experience with this particular anastomosis is very satisfactory, with a low incidence of

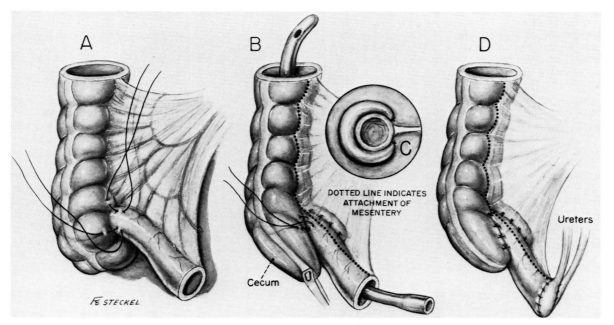

Fig. 8. The ileocecal valve reinforcement. (A) Intussusception of the ileum into the cecum with seromuscular sutures of 3-0 Prolene. (B) and (C) The redundant cecum is then wrapped around the terminal ileum in a 200 to 270 degree encircling fashion over a no. 30 French catheter inserted into the segment. Seromuscular sutures of 3-0 Prolene are placed on either side of the mesentery. (D) Completed antirefluxing ileocecal conduit with plicated ileocecal junction and Wallace conjoint ureteral anastomosis to the proximal end of the ileal portion. (Zinman L, Libertino JA: Ileocecal conduit for temporary and permanent urinary diversion. J Urol 113:319, 1975)

stricture. Contrary to previous speculation, however, ureteroileal stricture can occur on either side, not necessarily involving the entire common opening.

After the ureteral anastomoses is completed, bring out the distal end of the conduit through the previously prepared site in the right lower quadrant for establishment of a stoma. Suture the infant feeding tubes to the stomal margin for 10 to 12 days. Suture the bowel wall to the fascia with a closely placed row of 3–0 chromic catgut sutures and suture the distal edge of the colonic lumen to the skin with subcuticular sutures of 3–0 chromic catgut. Drain the abdomen with a Jackson–Pratt sump drain placed through a right lower quadrant stab incision. Fit patients for permanent collection applicances between the 12th and the 14th postoperative day, monitor the stomas every 12 wk for the first 6 mo.

EARLY AND LONG-TERM RESULTS OF ILEOCECAL CONDUIT DIVERSION

From 1969 to 1978, 62 patients have had antirefluxing ileocecal conduit urinary diversion for both malignant and benign disorders of the bladder. Six of these had subsequent undiversion to cecocystoplasty 1 to 2 yr later, and 15 patients were converted from a troubled ileal conduit to an add-on ileocecal conduit with antirefluxing properties (Fig. 9 *A* and *B*). One patient was returned from a failed augmentation cecocystoplasty back to a conduit diversion because of uncorrectable bladder outlet obstructive disease. Early complications included 4 ureteroileal strictures that developed within the first 6 mo—1 in a Wallace anastomosis and the others in Bricker end-to-side anastomoses. No late strictures at the ureteroileal junction have been encountered. Ureteroileal leak developed in one patient, four had significant anterior abdominal wound infections, and in one patient a pelvic abscess required surgical drainage.

Late complications included 2 small bowel obstructions at 6 mo and 2 yr, stomal prolapse that required operative repair in 3 patients, a parastomal hernia that did not require repair, and a left renal pelvic calculus that developed at 1 yr in a patient with previous calculi and a poorly functioning ileal loop converted to an ileocecal conduit.

Preoperative and postoperative excretory urograms were compared in 60 of the 62 patients followed from 7 mo to 9 yr (average, 6.2 yr with 21 patients followed up 6 to 9 yr). During this period, patients had no episodes of acute nonobstructive pyelonephritis, electrolyte disturbances, or stomal stenosis or the new appearance of renal calculi. Four patients had ureteroileal strictures, which were resolved by surgical

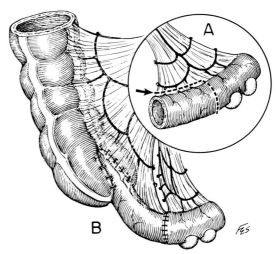

Fig. 9. Add-on ileocecal conduit for salvaging of a malfunctioning ileal loop. (*A*) Resect most of the distal ileal loop, leaving the ureteroileal junctions undisturbed. (*B*) Then anastomose the proximal ileal portion of the plicated antirefluxing ileocecal conduit to the ileal loop. (Zinman L: The use of the colon in urology. In Bonney W (ed): American Urological Association Courses in Urology, Vol 1. Baltimore, Williams & Wilkins 1979)

repair. One patient had a nephrectomy, and one patient with preoperative bilateral hydronephrosis has had no change in the upper tract status. Retrograde cecography in 44 patients revealed a competent ileocecal valve at pressures between 55 cm and 75 cm of water in all but 2 patients. Reflux occurred in 1 patient at 50 cm of water and in 1 at 55 cm of water.

. . .

The successful antireflux mechanism achieved in this conduit establishes this method of diversion as a sound operation that will most likely protect the upper urinary tract in the presence of stomal disorder. It will take another decade, however, before the long-term results can be cataloged properly. The only significant finding at present that points to its efficacy in protecting and preserving renal function is the remarkably low incidence of upper tract calculi observed at the 6 yr to 8 yr point.

REFERENCES

1. Schwartz GR, Jeffs RD: Ileal conduit urinary diversion in children: Computer analysis of followup from 2 to 16 years. J Urol 114:285, 1975

2. Ritchie JP, Skinner DG, Waisman J: The effect of reflux on the development of pyelonephritis in urinary diversion: An experimental study. J Surg Res 16:256, 1974

3. Althausen AF, Hagen-Cook K, Hendren WH: Non-refluxing colon conduits: Experience with 70 cases. J Urol 120:35, 1978

4. Altwein JE, Jonas U, Hohenfellner R: Long-term followup of children with colon conduit urinary diversion and ureterosigmoidostomy. J Urol 118:832, 1977

5. Mogg RA, Syme RR: The results of urinary diversion using the colonic conduit. Br J Urol 41:434, 1969

6. Elder DD, Moisey CU, Rees RW: A long-term follow-up of the colonic conduit operation in children. Br J Urol 51:462, 1979

7. Gilchrist RK, Merricks JW, Hamlin HH, et al: Construction of substitute bladder and urethra. Surg Gynecol Obstet 90:752, 1950

8. Couvelaire, R: La ''petite vessie'' des tuberculeux genito-urinaires;

essai de classification, place et variantes des cysto-intestino-plasties. J Urol 56:381, 1950

9. Gil Vernet, JM: Technique for construction of a functioning artificial bladder. J Urol 83:39, 1960

10. Zinman L, Libertino JA: The ileocecal segment: An antirefluxing colonic conduit form of urinary diversion. Surg Clin North Am 56:733, 1976

ANNOTATED BIBLIOGRAPHY

Schwartz GR, Jeffs RD: Ileal conduit urinary diversion in children: Computer analysis of followup from 2 to 16 years. J Urol 114:285, 1975

In this study, 95 children had diversion by refluxing ileal conduit and were followed for 2 to 16 yr. The group studied for 4.5 yr was described as recent and was compared to a group followed for 11.3 yr and described as remote. The groups were comparable in that they were operated on by the same surgeon with the same surgical techniques. The incidence of postoperative renal deterioration was 56%; 40% required a secondary reparative surgical procedure. The three complications of stomal stenosis, excessive conduit length, and ureteroileal obstruction had the most significant effect on long-term objective results of renal structure and function. Results emphasize the compulsive need to follow patients with ileal loop diversion for life with accurate assessment of renal function and pyelographic status to prevent renal deterioration.

Mogg RA, Syme RR: The results of urinary diversion using the colonic conduit. Br J Urol 41:434, 1969

In this study, 40 patients had diversion by an antirefluxing sigmoid conduit using a nipple and short submucosal ureterocolonic anastomosis and were followed for 6 mo to 10 yr (average, 3 to 4 yr). An antiperistaltic loop was constructed in many patients, and retrograde loopogram performed in 13 patients revealed reflux in 55% of the 24 renal units studied. Renal calculi developed in two patients, and loop calculi developed around silk sutures in two patients. The incidence of stomal stenosis requiring surgical revision was 22%. The incidence of radiologically evidenced pyelonephritis was 17%, with a tendency for this to develop in patients in whom reflux was present.

Elder DD, Moisey CU, Rees RW: A long-term follow-up of the colonic conduit operation in children. Br J Urol 51:462, 1979

This is a longer follow-up study of children who underwent diversion by the Mogg technique with the antirefluxing sigmoid loop. Twenty-six patients followed for 9 to 20 yr (average, 13.2 yr) were assessed. Stomal stenosis requiring surgical revision developed in 61.5%, and ureterocolonic strictures developed in 22%. Renal or ureteral calculi, which developed in 23% (6/26) of the children, were all assciated with reflux, ureterocolic stenosis, or stomal contracture. Reflux was observed in 58% of the renal units (29/50) examined, and only 20% of the refluxing renal units (5/20) remained normal, while 73.3% (11/15) of the nonrefluxing renal units were preserved without any evidence of renal deterioration.

Zinman L, Libertino JA: The ileocecal segment: An antirefluxing colonic conduit form of urinary diversion. Surg Clin North Am 56:733, 1976

The operative technique of ileocecal conduit is demonstrated using a variation of the conjoint ureteroureterostomy of Wallace for the ureteroileal anastomosis. A short follow-up review of 32 patients with both malignant and benign lesions leading to urinary diversion by the antirefluxing ileocecal conduit from 1969 to 1975 is presented. Two of the patients had undergone successful subsequent undiversion by augmentation cecocystoplasty, and two underwent add-on ileocecal conduits for serious stomal stenosis. An antirefluxing ileocecal plication was consistently achieved in the entire group and was documented by retrograde conduitography. Complications revealed two ureteroileal strictures, one stomal prolapse, and and one small bowel obstruction. The pyelographic status of 63 renal units studied revealed renal preservation with no parenchymal atrophy and no renal or ureteral calculi. No stomal stenosis was encountered in this predominantly adult population at this early stage of evaluation.

OVERVIEW: THE USE OF COLON FOR URINARY TRACT DIVERSION AND RECONSTRUCTION

Terry W. Hensle

Since 1950, when Bricker first described the ileal conduit as a means of urinary diversion in cancer patients, this operation has become the standard form of supravesical diversion for patients in almost every age group.[1] Despite very promising early results, over the last few years surgeons have come to realize a high incidence of long-term complications with ileal conduit urinary diversion. A formidable frequency of both stomal stenosis and upper tract deterioration in patients with previously normal kidneys has caused a good deal of consternation, particularly for those clinicians dealing with childhood urinary diversion, where extended follow-up study becomes very important. The classically described ileal conduit allows free reflux from the bowel conduit to the upper tract. Since bactiurea is a consistent phenomenon in patients with ileal conduits, even those with satisfactory drainage, it is not difficult to imagine low-grade infection in combination with free reflux causing upper tract changes, pyelonephritis, stone formation, and gradual deterioration of renal function. This is just as one might see in a child with longstanding vesicoureteral reflux.

The use of colon as a form of supravesical diversion was popularized in the early 1960s by Mogg.[2] Recognizing the importance of reflux in preventing upper tract deterioration, he fashioned a small nipple at the end of the ureter in an attempt to prevent free reflux. Early reports of follow-up study in colon conduits have been encouraging in both the low incidence of stomal stenosis and the long-term protection of renal function. The beautiful experimental model provided by Ritchie and colleagues seems to support this early optimism for the nonrefluxing colon conduit as a form of supravesical diversion, particularly in children.[3] Despite optimism, physicians must continue to look both carefully and critically at the long-term results of colon conduits. Elder and associates feel that there may be little advantage in using colon over ileum as a form of urinary diversion in childhood, since their results show no significant difference in the rate of either stomal stenosis or upper tract deterioration with the colon conduit.[4] Long-term prospective studies are needed to answer questions of this kind.

In looking at the three preceding presentations, all of which involve the use of colon as a form of supravesical diversion, the inherent advantages and disadvantages of colon as a source of bowel conduit must be remembered. Dr. Schmidt's discussion of the use of transverse colon in diverting patients with genitourinary cancer makes several important points on the radiation effect of small bowel versus large bowel. Certainly, the deleterious effect of radiotherapy on small bowel is a well-recognized clinical entity, which in the past has been associated with poor wound healing, small bowel fistula, and small bowel obstruction. The transverse colon is clearly at a lesser risk for radiation damage than terminal small bowel; thus its use seems justified from that standpoint in many patients who have received full-dose radiation for pelvic malignancy. Bear in mind, however, the patient population at hand. For patients in the younger age group with pelvic malignancy, who have a clearly definable chance for long-term survival, a nonrefluxing colon conduit seems preferable to the standard ileal conduit urinary diversion. In the older age group, however, and in patients in whom supravesical diversion is done very much as a palliative procedure, the use of colon seems somewhat excessive. Colon surgery, in general, carries a higher postoperative morbidity than does surgery of the small bowel; this factor, as well as the extra operative time involved in creating a nonrefluxing conduit, makes the use of colon in the older patient, the nutritionally depleted patient, and the patient with extensive malignancy quite a bit more of an operation than is usually necessary.

In turning to the use of sigmoid colon as a form of urinary diversion in children, Dr. Kalalis makes several very good clinical points on the importance of long-term follow-up study of patients undergoing a nonrefluxing conduit. It is important to stress again Dr. Kalalis's point that the tremendous advances in the field of pediatric urology have greatly reduced the number of supravesical diversions done in childhood. The widespread use of clean intermittent catheterization has totally changed surgeons' thinking and concept of the patient with neurogenic vesical dysfunction. Patients with defects in urine storage, and urine emptying, can be effectively dealt with using intermittent catheterization and very infrequently will need any form of supravesical diversion.

My experience with the colon conduit stoma has been much the same as Dr. Kelalis's; however, our incidence of children developing silent hydroureteral nephrosis does not seem at this point to be as high as in the Mayo Clinic series. I take great care to provide a technically adequate spatulated mucosa-to-mucosa anastomosis between colon and ureter. Of equal import is the area at the proximal end of the serosal tunnel where ureter ends the serosal hiatus. Again, I take great care to be sure that this area in no way constricts either ureteral lumen or blood supply. These technical details seem to be very important in avoiding the kind of long-term complications that Dr. Kalalis has described. The patients in whom I have found difficulties with ureteral obstruction after colon conduit diversion are those patients who have preoperatively had dilated ureters and in whom some form of ureteral tapering or remodeling has been carried out at the time of diversion. Three of six patients who have had ureteral tapering in conjunction with the formation of an antirefluxing colon conduit in my series have become obstructed and have required reoperation. Fortunately, each of the patients had a good antireflux procedure on one side, and therefore a simple transureteroureterostomy could be performed to alleviate the obstructed entity.

Perhaps the most intriguing and flexible form of colonic supravesical diversion is that described by Dr. Zinman in his discussion of antirefluxing ileocecal colon conduits. I have found this form of urinary diversion particularly useful in that group of patients with dilated tortuous ureters, in whom ureteral tapering and nonrefluxing sigmoid conduits have given surgeons some degree of difficulty. Dr. Zinman makes some important technical points on the vascular supply of cecum versus sigmoid colon. It is clear that the sigmoid colon is a more difficult area in which to do a precise, well-vascularized anastomosis than is the cecum. It is also clear that the sigmoid mesentery can be very short and often very thickened, making it difficult to bring the conduit through an expansive abdominal wall without a great deal of tension. The stomal durability of conduits created from right colon segments seems to be as good if not better than those created from the sigmoid or transverse colon. In terms of the antireflux aspects of ileocecal conduits, the intussusception of the ileocecal valve, as Dr. Zinman describes it, in both his series and in my hands has been extremely effective in preventing colonic ureteral reflux. I do not routinely use the Wallace conjoint ureteral anastomosis; however, I think this is a minor technical point that has no real impact on the outcome of the operation.

Taking the ileocecal conduit one step further and creating a bladder augmentation with this segment has also been proposed and advocated by Dr. Zinman and by others.[5] I have again found this very useful; however, I find the simple intussusception described by Dr. Zinman not totally adequate for preventing reflux in the higher pressure situation of a bladder augmentation versus an ileocecal conduit. I have made certain modifications, such as removing the mesentery over the area of ileum just adjacent to the cecum to get a better and more technically accurate intussusception. This modification has greatly helped in preventing reflux in the ileocecal bladder augmentations.

In summary, colon is certainly a very adequate and appropriate source for a conduit in supravesical diversions in both adults and children. The choice of a right colon versus transverse colon versus left colon really should be made on the basis of the patient involved and his or her condition and prognosis. The technical advantages to using colon, in my opinion, are clear; however, the long-term aspects of the use of colon in supravesical diversion must still be looked at carefully with long-term controlled prospective studies.

RERERENCES

1. Bricker EM: Bladder substitution after pelvic evisceration. Surg Clin North Am 30:1511, 1950
2. Mogg RA: Urinary diversion using the colonic conduit. Br J Urol 39:687, 1967
3. Ritchie JP, Skinner DG, Waisman J: The effect of reflux on the development of pyelonephritis in urinary diversion: An experimental study. J Surg Res 16:256, 1974
4. Elder DD, Moisey CU, Rees RW: A long-term follow-up of the colonic conduit operation in children. Br J Urol 51:462, 1979
5. Gittes RF: Bladder augmentation procedures. In Libertino JA, Zinman L (eds): Reconstructive Urologic Surgery, pp 216–226. Baltimore, Williams & Wilkins, 1977

55

URINARY TRACT RECONSTRUCTION FOLLOWING ILEAL CONDUIT DIVERSION

Stephen P. Dretler, W. Hardy Hendren and Wyland F. Leadbetter

From the Department of Urology and Division of Pediatric Surgery, Massachusetts General Hospital and Harvard Medical School, Boston, Massachusetts

The Journal of Urology
Copyright © 1973 by The Williams & Wilkins Co.
Vol. 109, January
Printed in U.S.A.

When Bricker popularized the ileal conduit,[1] many of the operative techniques presently in our armamentarium were unheard of, newly developed or poorly performed. Therefore, the use of an ileal conduit became widespread for patients with severe, seemingly unreconstructable, disorders of the lower urinary tract. Fortunately, recent experience with ureteral reimplantation,[2,3] ureteral reconstruction,[4-8] urethral valves,[9] urethral lengthening,[10] creation of a neourethra,[11] vesical augmentation,[12] sphincterotomy[13] and many other techniques has diminished the necessity for the construction of an ileal conduit.

Accepted for publication July 21, 1972.

Read at annual meeting of American Urological Association, Washington, D.C., May 21-25, 1972.

Drs. Ruben Gittes, Guy Leadbetter, Ambrose McLaughlin and Donald Skinner participated in the care of some of these patients.

Therefore, it seemed reasonable that the experience gained with these restorative techniques should be applied not only to new patients but also to selected patients already diverted.

MATERIALS AND METHODS

As a result of periodic examination and reevaluation of patients who had undergone ileal conduit diversion, it became apparent that selected patients were potential candidates for reestablishment of urinary tract continuity. These patients underwent a complete assessment of the functional capacity of the upper and lower urinary tracts. Evaluation included renal function studies, excretory urography (IVP), cystometry, cystourethrography, sphincterometry, observation of voided stream, endoscopic examination and ureteral remnant catheterization. Details of this preoperative evaluation have been reported previously.[14]

Once it was determined that re-establishment of urinary tract continuity was possible and feasible, operative techniques were chosen and modified according to individual circumstances. Techniques included ileal tapering and ileoneocystostomy, ileocecal cystoplasty, sigmoid cystoplasty with ureteral tunneling, creation of neourethra and ileal-ileocecal cystoplasty, ureteroureterostomy, formation of a Boari flap, urethral lengthening and ileocystoplasty.

CASE REPORTS

Case 1. J. R., MGH 124-97-69, a male infant, was unable to void spontaneously at birth. A suprapubic cystostomy was performed. When the boy was 2½ weeks old he was referred to this hospital where massive bilateral vesicoureteral reflux, severe ureteral dilatation and pyelocaliectasis were demonstrated by retrograde cystography (Fig. 1A). Rising creatinine, hyperkalemia and progressive upper urinary tract deterioration prompted the creation of bilateral ureterostomy. However, these provided poor drainage and a high pyeloileal conduit was performed. He then showed marked improvement.

When the child was 6 years old he was evaluated for possible urinary tract reconstruction. Upper urinary tract status was demonstrated by IVP and by retrograde dye study (Fig. 1B). Thorough evaluation of the lower urinary tract showed posterior urethral valves but otherwise normal function.

Posterior urethral valves were fulgurated, refluxing ureteral stumps were removed and the bladder neck was revised. When it was apparent that the bladder would

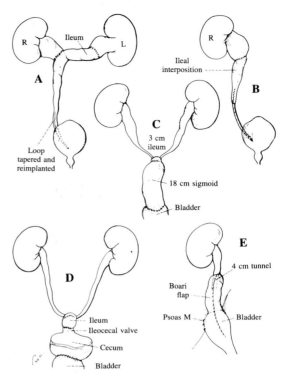

Fig. 2. Procedures for cases 1 to 5.

tolerate redirected urine flow, the conduit was removed from the abdominal wall, tapered to the size of the ureter and implanted in a submucosal intravesical tunnel (Fig. 2A).

He has been followed for 3 years since reconstruction was completed. The urine is sterile, cystography shows no evidence of reflux and a retrograde ureteropyelogram demonstrated a well-tapered ileal segment (Fig. 3). Cine-

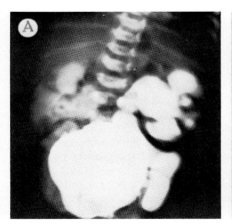
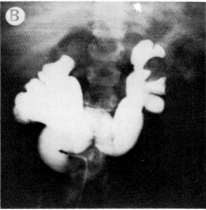

Fig. 1. Case 1. (*A*) Cystogram when child was 2½ weeks old reveals massive bilateral vesicoureteral reflux. (*B*) Loopogram when child was 6 years old demonstrates bilateral pyeloileostomy.

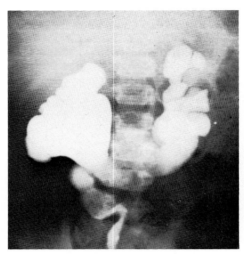

Fig. 3. Case 1. Retrograde ureteropyelogram 2 years after ileal tapering and ileoneocystostomy.

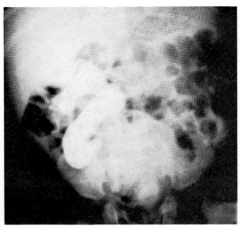

Fig. 4. Case 2. IVP shows non-function of left kidney and right ureterovesical junction obstruction.

IVP shows active ileal peristalsis and prompt emptying of the ileal segment.

Case 2. J. M., MGH 124-14-78, a 1-day-old girl, was admitted to this hospital because of failure to void. Evaluation revealed a left ureterocele obstructing the bladder outlet, massive reflux to the left lower collecting system, right ureterovesical obstruction and a markedly hypertrophied bladder wall. Despite excision of the ureterocele, left heminephrectomy and bladder neck revision, she did poorly with recurrent severe pyelonephritis, progressive right ureteral dilatation and nonfunction of the remainder of the left kidney (Fig. 4). A high pyeloileal conduit was performed.

When the child was 6 years old she was reevaluated for possible urinary tract reconstruction. The bladder, although of small capacity, emptied completely and appeared to be capable of normal function. Vesical hypertrophy had regressed and the right ureterovesical junction appeared normal. IVP did not reveal the left renal remnant. It was thought that an attempt should be made to re-establish urinary tract continuity.

The hypoplastic, non-functioning left renal remnant was removed and the left ureteral stump with reflux was excised. The conduit was removed from the abdominal wall, tapered, shortened and anastomosed to the right lower ureteral remnant. (Fig. 2B).

Since reconstruction, creatinine clearance has remained stable, urine is sterile, bladder capacity has increased, voiding is normal and upper tracts show no evidence of deterioration. Roentgenographic studies show excellent function and prompt emptying of the ileal segment (Fig. 5).

Case 3. A. C., MGH 105-24-07, a 4-month-old white girl, was noted to have a urinary tract infection, severe bilateral vesicoureteral reflux and pyelocaliectasis. Despite bladder neck revision and bilateral ureteroneocystostomy, reflux and infection persisted. Bilateral nephrostomy failed to prevent the accumulation of infected urine in the dilated atonic ureters. When the child was 22 months old an ileal conduit diversion was performed.

Six years later she was re-evaluated for possible urinary tract reconstruction. Bladder function appeared adequate to accept redirected urine flow. Bladder diverticula and lower ureteral remnants were excised. The 3 cm ileal segments (2 stomal revisions had been necessary) was too short to reach the bladder. An ileosigmoid cystoplasty was then performed (Fig. 2C). Postoperatively, severe hyperchloremic acidosis occurred, the result of the long sigmoid segment and poor renal function. This complication necessitated rediversion by ileal conduit. She is now being reevaluated for another attempt at establishing urinary tract continuity.

Case 4. S. C., MGH 95-42-38, a 5½-year-old white girl, was admitted to the hospital with recurrent urinary tract infection, dribbling incontinence and failure to void to completion. Examination revealed marked bladder trabeculation, left vesicoureteral reflux and right ureterovesical junction obstruction (Fig. 6A). Ureteroneocystostomy and bladder neck revision failed to correct reflux (Fig. 6B). Residual urine persisted and hydroureteronephrosis progressed. Ileal conduit diversion was performed.

Four years later, re-evaluation of urinary tract function revealed marked decrease in ureteral dilatation, a bladder capacity of 120 cc and total urinary continence.

Accordingly, the conduit was detached from the abdominal wall, tapered and reimplanted in a vesical submucosal tunnel. Postoperatively, a cystogram showed no vesicoileal reflux and prompt ileal emptying. Unfortunately, reflux and ureteral dilatation recurred 1 year later, necessitating rediversion by ileal conduit.

In July 1970 an ileocecal cystoplasty was performed using the ileocecal valve to prevent reflux (Fig. 2D). Six months later an IVP showed improvement in the appearance of the upper urinary tract (Fig. 7). A cystogram showed no reflux.

Case 5: W. S., MGH 110-23-46, a 6-year-old white boy, was found to have massive bilateral vesicoureteral reflux, right hydroureteronephrosis, non-function of the

left kidney and a bladder that failed to empty. Left nephrectomy and ileal conduit diversion were performed.

Nine years later he underwent evaluation which showed the bladder to be hypertonic and of small capacity but able to empty completely. The upper urinary tract showed prompt function and, although tortuous, the ureter was not considerably dilated. An attempt at reconstruction appeared warranted.

Bladder neck revision and ureteral stump reimplantation were performed as a first stage. Despite reimplantation, reflux persisted in the ureteral stump and the thought of direct ureteral reanastomosis was abandoned. Accordingly, the conduit was removed from the abdominal wall and the tortuous ureter was straightened. Length obtained from ureteral straightening and from mobilization of the bladder to the psoas muscle allowed for direct ureteral reimplantation in a generous submucosal tunnel.

Postoperatively, voiding was normal, a cystogram showed no reflux and an IVP showed prompt function and good drainage (Fig. 8A). However, 6 months later roentgenograms showed progression of ureteral dilatation (Fig. 8B). Reexploration revealed stenosis of the lower ureteral segment. A Boari flap was then fashioned, the stenotic ureter was resected and reimplanted in the Boari flap (Fig. 2E). A cystogram shows no reflux (Fig. 9), the patient voids to completion and renal function remains stable.

Case 6. J. P., MGH 114-84-36, a 3½ year-old white boy, underwent ileal conduit diversion after ureteral reimplantation and bladder neck revision failed to correct severe vesicoureteral reflux and persistent urinary tract infection. When the child was 13 years old he was reevaluated for possible urinary tract reconstruction.

The bladder was hypertonic and of small capacity

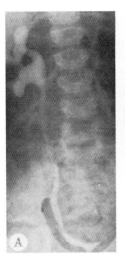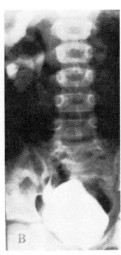

Fig. 5.

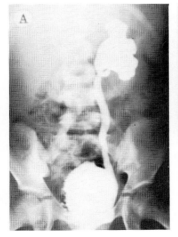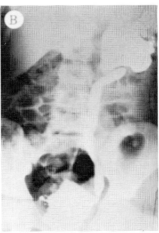

Fig. 6. Case 4. Preoperative (*A*) and postoperative (*B*) cystograms show trabeculated bladder, persistent left vesicoureteral reflux and progressive hydronephrosis.

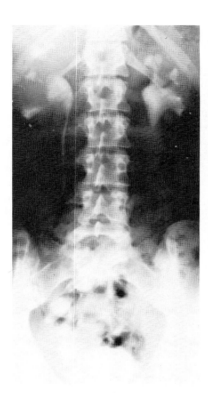

Fig. 7. Case 4. IVP 7 years after urinary diversion and 6 months after ileoceal cystoplasty.

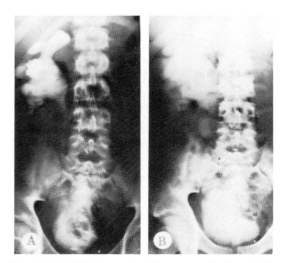

Fig. 8. Case 5. (*A*) IVP 3 months after removal of conduit, ureteral and bladder mobilization and ureteral neocystostomy. (*B*) IVP 3 months later shows progressive hydroureteronephrosis.

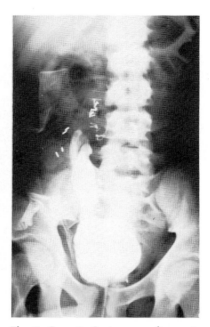

Fig. 9. Case 5. Cystogram after ureteral shortening and implantation in Boari flap demonstrates absence of reflux.

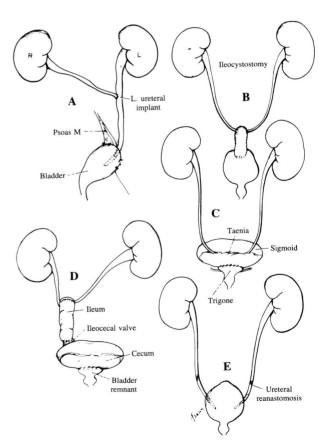

Fig. 10. Procedures for cases 6 to 10.

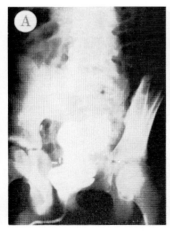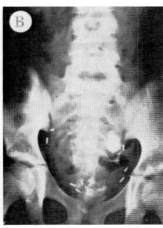

Fig. 11. Case 6. Postoperative cystograms demonstrate prevention of reflux by intussusception of ileum into cecum and excellent emptying of cecum after voiding.

but voiding was complete. Reflux persisted in the lower ureteral stumps. The upper tracts were slightly dilated but had improved since diversion. It was decided that reconstruction should be attempted.

The ureteral stumps were removed, the bladder was mobilized and fixed to the left psoas muscle and dissection of the left ureter provided length sufficient to construct a 3 cm intravesical submucosal tunnel. A right-to-left transureteroureterostomy was performed (Fig. 10A). Although postoperative bladder capacity increased from 50 to 135 ml, vesical pressures remained high. Reflux and subsequent upper tract dilatation occurred, necessitating left nephrostomy drainage.

An ileocecal cystoplasty was then performed, intussuscepting the ileum to prevent reflux. A postoperative cystogram shows no evidence of relux and prompt emptying of the bladder (Fig. 11). IVP demonstrates markedly improved upper tract function.

Case 7. N. A., MGH 144-31-15, underwent an operation for an ectopic ureterocele during infancy. The result was total urinary incontinence. When the child was 12 years old she was referred to this hospital. Examination confirmed that she was totally incontinent and demonstrated severe right vesicoureteral reflux with hydroureteronephrosis. The left kidney was surgically absent. An ileal conduit diversion was performed.

One year later, as the first step towards re-establishing urinary tract continuity, a urethral lengthening procedure was performed and the ureteral remnant with reflux was excised. She was examined a year later and found to be continent. The conduit was then dissected free and implanted in the posterior bladder wall (Fig. 10-B). In the 3 years since reconstruction bladder capacity has increased from 75 to 275 cc, ureteral dilatation has not occurred and renal function is stable.

Case 8. N. I., MGH 13-76-15, a 57-year-old white woman, underwent ileal conduit diversion because of severe interstitial cystitis complicated by bilateral vesicoureteral reflux. The postoperative course was marked by continuous stomal irritation and difficulty wearing an appliance. After 2 years of repeated hospitalizations for stomal care, it was decided to attempt urinary tract reconstruction.

The trigone was preserved but most of the bladder wall was surgically excised. Fear of disturbing trigonal function prevented removal of the ureteral remnants. The conduit was removed and both ureters were tunneled into a segment of sigmoid and a sigmoid cystoplasty was performed (Fig. 10C). The patient has been followed for 5 years; she has suffered no electrolyte abnormalities and has had no deterioration of the upper urinary tract. Although reflux persists in the ureteral remnants the urine has remained uninfected. Reflux does not occur in the ureters implanted in the segment of sigmoid (Fig. 12). Symptoms of interstitial cystitis have not recurred.

Case 9. R. F., MGH 044-29-79, a 28-year-old white man, with spastic diplegia, underwent diversion because of a neurogenic bladder complicated by bilateral ureterovesical reflux and recurrent urinary tract infection. One year later it became apparent that he was unable to care for the stoma and he was considered for urinary tract reconstruction.

The bladder walls were surgically excised, leaving the trigone. Sphincterotomy and ileocecal cystoplasty were performed (Fig. 10D). The patient achieved a bladder capacity of 180 ml and carried only 30 ml residual urine. It is now 4 years since reconstruction was completed. Although bladder neck contractures require periodic transurethral incision and reflux is demonstrated by retrograde cystogram, renal function had remained stable and upper urinary tracts are not dilated (Fig. 13).

Case 10. R. W., MGH 154-94-56, has been pre-

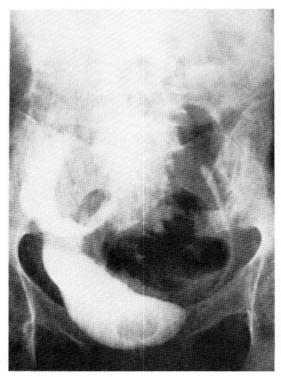

Fig. 12. Case 8. Cystogram after tunneling of ureters into segment of sigmoid and sigmoid cystoplasty. Vesicoureteral reflux persists in left ureteral remnant.

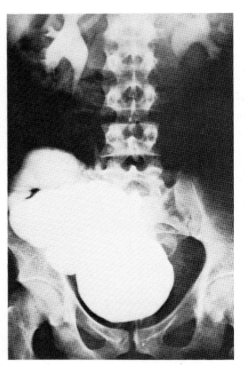

Fig. 13. Case 9. Cystogram 4 years after urinary tract reconstruction by ileocecal cystoplasty. Some reflux is noted.

viously reported.[14] He underwent ileal conduit diversion after a gunshot wound resulted in a prostatic-rectal fistula. Fourteen months after diversion, he was referred to this hospital for evaluation. After studies confirmed that his lower urinary tract was capable of normal function, reconstruction was carried out by transvesical repair of the prostatic fistula, excision of the conduit and direct reanastomosis of the upper and lower ureteral segments (Fig. 10E). The urine is uninfected and upper urinary tracts appear normal (Fig. 14).

Case 11. J. R., MGH 120-17-33, a 6-year-old white girl, underwent transurethral resection of the bladder neck. Following this procedure a urethrovaginal fistula and total urinary incontinence developed. Two attempts at fistula repair failed and an ileal conduit diversion was performed.

When the patient was 17 years old, she was referred to this hospital for evaluation. Bladder capacity was restricted to 50 ml and the urethrovaginal fistula was still present. The upper urinary tract appeared normal. After detailed investigation, it was decided to attempt a staged urinary tract reconstruction, directing attention to the lower urinary tract before disturbing the well-functioning conduit.

Suprapubic exploration showed the bladder and urethra to be encased in scar tissue. The scarred, fistulous urethra was removed and a new urethra was created by the method described by Tanagho.[11] Six months later studies showed the patient to be continent but with a limited bladder capacity. As a second stage, leaving the conduit intact, an ileocecal cystoplasty was performed, intussuscepting the ileocecal valve to prevent reflux. Postoperatively, bladder capacity was 150 ml and she was continent; therefore, as a third procedure, the conduit was removed from the abdominal wall, shortened and anastomosed to the ileal portion of the ileocecal cystoplasty (Fig. 15). She is now continent, bladder capacity has progressively increased and she voids every 3 hours. Renal function has remained stable.

DISCUSSION

To determine whether urinary tract reconstruction is possible requires a total accurate assessment of the functional capacity of the upper and lower urinary tract. A bladder of adequate capacity which had normal

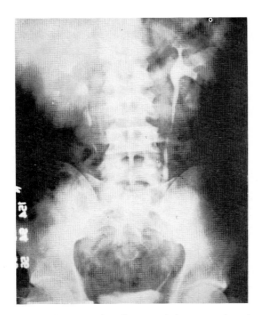

Fig. 14. Case 10. IVP 6 months after conduit removal and ureteral reanastomosis.

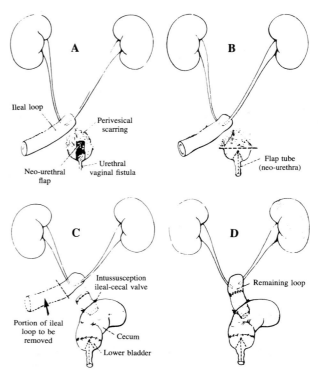

Fig. 15. Case 11. Steps in reconstruction. (*A*) and (*B*) Creation of neourethra. (*C*) Ileocecal cystoplasty with intussusception of ileocecal valve. (*D*) Ileal-ileocecal anastomosis.

functional dynamics prior to diversion will rapidly regain these capabilities after reconstruction is complete. Disuse atrophy does not occur. However, initial evaluation by cystometrics may be misleading. the bladder often appears to be incapable of holding more than 50 to 75 ml fluid and may require repeated filling or distension under anesthesia to provide an accurate indication of capacity.

Patients with significantly depressed renal function who have insufficient renal reserve to tolerate operative failure cannot be considered for reconstruction. Nor should a patient be considered for reconstruction if he is unable to void to completion. It is our experience that the amount of residual fluid present in preoperative studies is an accurate indication of the ability of the bladder to empty following redirection of urine flow.

Once it has been established that reconstruction is feasible and possible, a variety of operative techniques may be considered. Although the method chosen will vary according to individual circumstances, certain basic principles must be followed.

All procedures that require major alterations of the anatomy of the lower urinary tract should be successfully completed before disturbing a well functioning conduit. Minor reparative procedures (transurethral resection of valves, excision of diverticula, removal of ureteral stumps, etc.) do not require staging and may be performed at the time of urinary tract reconstruction.

The inclusion of an antireflux procedure in the technique of reconstrucion is certainly preferable. Meth-

ods of reflux prevention include ileal tapering with neocystostomy, ureterosigmoid tunneling, intussusception of the ileocecal valve, creation of an ileal nipple and tunneling into a Boari flap.

Deficits in ureteral length, caused by disease or conduit construction, may be handled by a variety of means. Upper ureteral mobilization and straightening will allow a few centimeters of length. Bladder mobilization to the pelvic brim will make up 4 to 5 cm ureteral length. Gaps also may be bridged by a bladder (Boari) flap and segments of ileum or large intestine.

This initial experience with reconstruction of the urinary tract following ileal conduit diversion should emphasize the necessity for periodic urinary tract reevaluation in all diverted patients. As newly described operative techniques are perfected, many more patients will become candidates for urinary tract rehabilitation. Unquestionably, the successful re-establishment of urinary tract continuity is preferable to diversion. If a patient is properly selected and carefully studied and if the operative procedure is carefully chosen and properly performed, total urinary tract rehabilitation can be achieved.

SUMMARY

Total urinary tract reconstruction and rehabilitation were carried out in 11 patients from 14 months to 11 years following ileal conduit diversion. Techniques used for reconstruction included ileal tapering with ileoneocystostomy, ileal tapering with ileoureteral anastomosis, ileocecal cystoplasty, sigmoid cystoplasty with ureterosigmoid tunneling, ileoneocystostomy with nipple formation, ureteroureteral reanastomosis and creation of a neourethra with ileocecal cystoplasty. In 10 of the 11 patients reconstruction has been successful; the eleventh patient is currently being re-evaluated for another attempt at establishing urinary tract continuity.

This report stresses the necessity for a thorough preoperative evaluation and consideration of the variety of operative techniques available. Furthermore, it is stressed that all alterations of lower urinary tract anatomy should be completed prior to distubing a well functioning conduit and that these procedures must be properly staged. Finally, it emphasizes the necessity for periodic re-evaluation of every diverted patient to determine whether recent advances have made him a candidate for reconstruction.

REFERENCES

1. Bricker, E. M.: Symposium on clinical surgery bladder substitution after pelvic evisceration. Surg Clin N Am, 30:1511, 1950

2. Politano, V. A. and Leadbetter, W. F.: An operative technique for the correction of vesicoureteral reflux. J Urol, 79:932, 1958

3. Hendren, W. H.: Ureteral reimplantation in children. J Pediat Surg, 3:649, 1968

4. Johnston, J. H.: Reconstructive surgery of megaureter in childhood. Br J Urol, 39:17, 1967

5. Hendren, W. H.: Operative repair of megaureter in children. J Urol, 101:491, 1969

6. Bischoff, P.: Operative treatment of megaureter. J Urol, 79:932, 1958

7. Hendren, W. H.: A new approach to infants with severe obstructive uropathy: early complete reconstruction. J. Pediat Surg, 5:184, 1970

8. Hendren, W. H.: Restoration of function in the severely decompensated ureter. In: Problems in Paediatric Urology. Edited by JH Johnston and RJ Scholtmeijer. Amsterdam: Excerpta Medica, 1972

9. Hendren, W. H.: Posterior urethral valves in boys. A broad clinical spectrum. J Urol, 106:298, 1971

10. Leadbetter, G. W., Jr.: Surgical correction of total urinary incontinence. J Urol, 91:261, 1964

11. Tanagho, E. A., Smith, D. R., Meyers, F. H. and Fisher, R.: Mechanisms of urinary continence. II. Technique for surgical correction of incontinence. J Urol, 101:305, 1969

12. Küss, R., Bitker, M., Camey, M., Chatelain, C. and Lassau, J. P.: Indications and early and late results of intestinocystoplasty: a review of 185 cases. J Urol, 103:53, 1970

13. Ross, J. C., Gibbon, N. O. K. and Damanski, M.: Division of the external urethral sphincter in the treatment of the paraplegic bladder. Br J Urol, 30:204, 1958

14. Dretler, S. P., Skinner, D. G. and Leadbetter, W. F.: Bilateral ureteroureterostomy after ileal conduit diversion. J Urol, 105:365, 1971

Commentary:
Undiversion: Evaluation and
Surgical Techniques

Kiran Kenny Crooks and Stephen P. Dretler

Undiversion has been defined as a surgical procedure that restores urinary tract continuity after previous urinary diversion.[1] Since the form of urinary diversion and the resultant anatomy of each patient will differ, no one procedure can be correct for all patients. Reconstructive options will vary and must be tailored to the patient's anatomy, physiology, and psychological needs. The major goal of undiversion must be the preservation of renal function and a dry, continent patient.

Long term follow-up studies of patients with cutaneous ureterostomies and ileal conduits are now available, and the results are disappointing. Too many patients suffer the problems of chronic infection, stone formation, and a loss of renal function.[2-4] Therefore, every patient forced to live with an external urinary appliance is entitled to periodic meticulous urologic evaluation. The following questions should be asked and answered: What was the reason for diversion? Is that reason still valid? If not, how may a patient be successfully "undiverted"?

In most instances the reason for the initial diversion is readily apparent: uremia and infection secondary to previously uncorrectable urinary anomalies. For these patients, urinary diversion was lifesaving and allowed for the treatment of infection, the stabilization of fluids and electrolytes, and the improvement of renal function. Occasionally the reasons are not obvious, and old records, x-ray films, parents' statements, and previous physicians' records are essential steps in understanding the initial diversion. Many patients were diverted "temporarily" because of a technical failure or incorrect diagnosis and now have "permanent" urinary diversions because of poor follow-up examination.

Once the reason for initial diversion is determined, the physician must ask if it is still valid. If not, the patient becomes a candidate for reconstruction, and a total reevaluation of the urinary tract must be carried out.

The reevaluation of the diverted patient must be done in a well-designed and organized plan. To proceed, assess renal function with a 24-hr creatinine clearance and compare it with previous values (which may have been obtained but not computed). An intravenous pyelogram (IVP) with nephrotomography is essential to determine the relative renal mass, intrarenal anatomy, degree of hydronephrosis, and presence of calculi (lucent or calcified). Calculi should be removed or dissolved before attempted reconstruction, since a calculus dropped into a newly created anastomosis would be disastrous. Determining which kidney is the major contributor to overall renal function is helpful, since this will often be a significant factor in choosing a reconstructive procedure. The differential renal scan may aid in lateralization of function, although split renal function tests, if possible, give a more accurate physiologic parameter. Obstructive hydronephrosis may be relieved by percutaneous drainage. This tube can also be used to document ureteral anatomy by antegrade perfusion and measure the creatinine clearance from that kidney.

A loopogram will reveal the length and quality of the conduit and the proximal ureters. When performed simultaneously with a cystogram, the gap between the upper and lower urinary tract can be determined. When this distance is large, some bridging procedure is necessary for successful restoration of the urinary tract. These procedures include renal autotransplatation, ileal interposition, transureteroureterostomy, Boari flap, and the psoas–bladder hitch.

Evaluation of the lower tract includes cystourethrography, cystometrics, and assessment of ureteral stumps and urinary sphincter competence. A cystogram will reveal the presence of bladder diverticuli and refluxing ureteral stumps, which, if unrecognized, may act as diverticuli when the urine stream is reconstituted. Short refluxing stumps will require excision at the time of reconstruction. Long segments may be useful in certain instances and may be reimplanted at the time of reconstruction. Many stumps will reflux from disuse alone, so the character and caliber of the ureteral orifice must be noted. When the orifice appears normal, many of these stumps will stop refluxing once urine flow is restored.

If one or both of the refluxing ureteral stumps will be used in the undiversion, reimplantation must be done with caution. These ureters are very thin and delicate as a result of disuse, so gentle handling is crucial. Also, the longitudinal blood supply has been lost and the medial pelvic supply is all that remains. This medial adventia should not be disturbed during reimplantation, and all adventia in the lateral retroperitoneal gutter should be swept toward the ureter during mobilization.[5]

Cystourethroscopy and a cystogram identify the anatomy of the bladder and urethra. Urethral valves previously unrecognized or inadequately resected should be resected. If urethral strictures, fistulae, inadequate urethral length, or incompetent sphincters are discovered, the lower urinary tract should be reconstructed initially and then reevaluated before undiversion.[6]

The functional evaluation of the lower urinary tract in diverted patients is both the most difficult and the least precise of the preoperative studies. Bladder capacity, ability to empty, and continence are the main considerations. Cystometrics are performed to assess baseline capacity. Since disuse causes the bladder to contract, the usual finding is that of a small bladder holding 30 ml to 120 ml of fluid with an elevated detrusor tone. If outlet obstruction has been a problem, the bladder may be hypertrophied and scarred.[7] One of the most successful methods to evaluate the functional capacity and control of the bladder involves the percutaneous insertion of a suprapubic catheter. This allows both slow and gentle stretching of the bladder over a few weeks with simultaneous observation of both continence and emptying ability.[8]

Contracted bladders, which are resistant to dilation by hydrostatic pressure, may be manually stretched or augmented by intestine at the time of reconstruction. Augmentation is accomplished by removing the scarred bladder cap and replacing it with a patch of sigmoid, cecum, or ileum.[9,10] There is a potential problem for urea and electrolyte reabsorption in these patients, especially in those with compromised renal function. However, when the bladder empties to completion this complication rarely occurs.

A most difficult and increasingly controversial question is that of undiversion for the patient with a neurogenic bladder or with incontinence from sphincter dysfunction. Intermittent catheterization is an effective means of emptying the flaccid bladder in selected patients.[11] Although children with neurogenic bladders and incontinence have been undiverted successfully with artificial sphincter devices, extreme care must be exercised. Because these devices are "first-generation" machinery, I favor only selected attempts at these procedures by experienced surgeons. When more experience is gained and long-term results are presented or the next "generation" of devices is available, a judgment can be made on the use of these techniques. For the present, however, a neurogenic bladder with incontinence remains a relative contraindication to undiversion.

Once the entire urinary tract has been evaluated, reconstruction may proceed. Patients with cutaneous ureterostomies often afford the chance for the preferred ureteroureterostomy repair. The distal ureter, however, is frequently abnormal with either reflux or obstruction. This obstruction may have been primary, but it is also common in patients with long-term ureterostomies because of poor drainage, infection, and tethering of the ureter from the ureterostomy site.[4]

If careful attention is directed toward preserving blood supply, both ends of the ureter can be operated on simultaneously. To do so, sweep all the adventia toward the ureter. The gonadal vessels may be detached and incorporated into this periureteral adventia.[12] After the ureterostomy is dissected free, perform a spatulated ureteroureterostomy, attaching the kidney caudally, if necessary, for a tension-free anastomosis. If one ureter will reach the bladder but the other will not, a transureteroureterostomy is a safe and effective means of overcoming inadequate ureteral length.[13] The crossing ureter must not be angulated or obstructed by the mesenteric vessels in its retroperitoneal course. Perform the transureteral anastomosis on the medial wall of the recipient ureter. If placed anteriorly, obstruction will ensue. Avoid leaks by doing a watertight tension-free anastomosis using fine, interrupted, absorbable sutures.[14]

If, despite mobilization, ureteral length is insufficient to reach the bladder, a bowel segment may be required.[15] The segment must be placed in an isoperistaltic fashion, and if it joins the upper tracts to the bladder, an antirefluxing mechanism must be used. An ileocecocystoplasty with plication of the ileocecal valve has been successful in preventing reflux and is useful when bladder augmentation is also necessary.[10] An alternative method is the tapered ileal reimplant.[16] The taper along the antimesenteric border of the ileum must be gradual to prevent obstruction. The new hiatus must be generous and is made along the posterior bladder floor. A long submucosal tunnel is created, which may cross the entire length of the trigone toward the opposite bladder wall. The ureteral suture line is placed along the detrusor floor of the tunnel to prevent fistulae.[17] Finally, a psoas–bladder hitch is used, both to stabilize the bladder floor, allowing for a very long submucosal tunnel, and to prevent angulation of the ileum as it enters the new bladder hiatus.[18] The use of the psoas hitch is applicable to many cases of undiversion where lower ureteral loss or inadequate length is a problem, and enough length may often be achieved by mobilizing the bladder to make ileal interposition unnecessary. I prefer its use to a Boari flap, although the latter remains an option if performed with an antirefluxing tunnel.

Renal autotransplantation is another method of overcoming inadequate ureteral length. Although my experience with this technique is limited, others have reported good success and low morbidity with its use.[19] In patients with poor renal reserve, the ischemia associated with renal transplantation may further compromise renal function; in the presence of infected urine a vascular anastomosis is hazardous. With these cautions in mind, it remains an alternative to be considered.

Undiversion is a new and exciting concept. However, failures will occur and the patient and family must be warned that these operations are very difficult and must be regarded as such. Often the failures will still be correctable with repeat or revised approaches. Sometimes they will be irreversible. It is essential that the surgeon protect the patient's future by not undertaking procedures that would make rediversion unnecessarily difficult or impossible. Furthermore, before starting the reconstructive process, a careful assessment must be made of the patient's physiologic and psychological reserve and capacity to withstand a failure.[20]

Some patients diverted in early life have accepted their anatomic anomaly as part of their existence and live with it quite well. Unless these patients have a medical reason, such as loss of renal function or recurrent infections, necessitating reconstruction, they may be best left alone. In these instances, it is the patient rather than the physician who should decide on whether reconstruction is valid.

Patients still require urinary diversion for nonmalignant disease. Consideration should be given now for possible undiversion in the future. Further developments of artificial sphincters, bladder-contracting devices, and drugs that specifically inhibit detrusor hyperreflexia or urinary sphincter hyperactivity will make the patients now being diverted candidates for reconstruction in the future. Every effort must be made to preserve as much structure of the urinary tract as possible and to weigh all the possible implications of diversion procedures done today on possible reconstructive attempts in the future.

REFERENCES

1. Hendren WH: Urinary tract refunctionalization after prior diversion in children. Ann Surg 180:494, 1974

2. Dretler SP: The pathogenesis of urinary tract calculi occurring after ileal conduit diversion. I. Clinical study. II. Conduit study. III. Prevention. J Urol 114:204, 1973

3. Shapiro SR, Lebowitz R, Colodny AH: Fate of 90 children with ileal conduit urinary diversion a decade later: Analysis of complications, pyelography, renal function and bacteriology. J Urol 114:289, 1975

4. Hendren WH: Complications of ureterostomy. J Urol 120:269, 1978

5. Hendren WH: Some alternatives to urinary diversion in children. J Urol 119:652, 1978

6. Richie JP, Sacks SA: Complications of urinary undiversion. J Urol 117:362, 1977

7. Tanagho EA: Congenitally obstructed bladders: Fate after prolonged defunctionalization. J Urol 111:102, 1974

8. Kogan SJ, Levitt SB: Bladder evaluation in pediatric patients before undiversion in previously diverted urinary tracts. J Urol 118:443, 1977

9. Shirley SW, Mirelman S: Experiences with colocystoplasties, cecocystoplasties and ileocstoplasties in urologic surgery: 40 patients. J Urol 120:165, 1978

10. Skinner DG: Secondary urinary reconstruction: use of the ileocecal segment. J Urol 112:48, 1974

11. Lapides J, Diokno AC, Gould FR, et al: Further observations on self-catheterization. J Urol 116:169, 1976

12. Hendren WH: Reconstruction ("undiversion") of the diverted urinary tract. Hosp Prac 11:70, 1976

13. Udall DA, Hodger CU, Pearse HM, et al: Transureteroureterostomy. Urology 2:401, 1973

14. Hendren WH, Hensle TW: Transureteroureterostomy: Experience with 75 cases. J Urol (in press)

15. Goodwin WE, Winter CD, Turner RD: Replacement of the ureter by small intestine: Clinical application and results of the "ileal ureter." J Urol 81:406, 1959

16. Dretler SP, Hendren WH, Leadbetter WR: Urinary tract reconstruction following ileal conduit diversion. J Urol 109:217, 1973

17. Hendren WH: Tapered bowel segment for ureteral replacement. Urol Clin North Am 5:607, 1978

18. Prout GR, Koontz WW Jr: Partial vesical immobilization: An important adjunct to ureteroneocystostomy. J Urol 103:147, 1970

19. Stewart BH, Hewitt CB, Banowsky LHW: Management of extensively destroyed ureter: Special reference to renal autotransplantation. J Urol 115:257, 1976

20. King LR: Undiversion: When and how? J Urol 115:296, 1976

ANNOTATED BIBLIOGRAPHY

Hendren WH: Urinary tract refunctionalization after prior diversion in children. Ann Surg 180:494, 1974

The author describes undiversion procedures in 32 patients; 27 were boys, and in 17 initial obstructive pathologic findings included posterior uretheral valves. The bladder in the majority of these children was small and often fibrotic; however, it stretched up satisfactorily after urine flow and function were restored. Ten children were undiverted after prior ileal loop supravesical diversion. When the ureters were long enough to reach the bladder, the conduit was not used in reconstruction. This occurred uncommonly, however, because of short ureteral length or the small size of the bladder. To overcome the inadequate ureteral length, the better ureter is reimplanted with a transureteroureterostomy or the ileal conduit is reimplanted as a tapered bowel segment. The technique of the tapered bowel segment is described as placing the tapered suture line against the posterior bladder wall, chosing the new hiatus at the bladder base (not on the side wall or dome of the bladder where it can angulate), and making a gradual bowel taper over a 16 to 20 French catheter to prevent stenosis.

The other large group of patients involved those with cutaneous ureterostomies. The author states that these are particularly difficult to undivert, since the upper and lower urinary tract must frequently be operated on at the same sitting to achieve the desired result. In most undiversion cases a large midline incision from xyphoid to pubis is made to give full exposure to the entire urinary tract. Blood supply can be maintained to the ureters if they are mobilized carefully and gently, with all advential tissue swept toward the ureter. The author stresses that these complex, long, and difficult reconstructive procedures require expert pediatric anesthesia and support facilities and should be performed by persons with specific knowledge and training in the area of pediatric urology. Finally, the discussion at the end with comments by noted surgeons is both interesting and informative about the philosophy of pediatric reconstructive urology.

Hendren WH: Some alternatives to urinary diversion in children. J Urol 119:652, 1978

This article is based on the author's experience in undiverting 73 patients. He discusses five techniques that, when used appropriately, may prevent diversions in other children. Case reports for each technique are given. In transureteroureterostomy, no complications were encountered in 45 patients. Technical points involve mobilizing the donor ureter widely so it can be brought across the midline without tension and with a good blood supply. It must not be compressed by mesenteric vessels. A drainage catheter is left in the ureter for about 10 days. In instances where the donor ureter was too short, an interposed bowel segment was used. In one instance this segment became dilated, but when moved more proximally toward the renal pelvis in a second procedure, it drained effectively. The author has found the psoas hitch particularly useful to get extra tunnel length and to prevent angulation of the new reimplanted ureter or bowel segment. The reimplantation is done before anchoring the bladder to the psoas tendon but the location of the hiatus and the psoas bladder hitch must be determined before reimplantation to prevent angulation and compromise of the ureteral segment. In wide mobilization and downward placement of the kidney and ureter, another technique to overcome inadequate ureteral length, the colon is mobilized medially and all advential tissue swept toward the kidney and ureter. This is done medially as well, skeletonizing the mesentery of the colon but taking care not to injure the vessels to the colon. The author warns, however, against disecting

medially below the aortic bifurcation to avoid possible impotence. The kidney is mobilized superiorly, laterally, and posteriorily, being attached only by its renal pedicle. It can then be slipped down several centimeters and fixed in its new location. An interposed bowel segment was used in 29 patients; 22 had had ileal loops and in 7 a bowel loop was prepared at the time of reconstruction. When possible, a ureteral reimplant is preferred. The author describes one patient in whom cecocystoplasty was used. This would seem to be a particularly useful technique when ureteral length is insufficient and bladder size is very small and fibrotic, needing further augmentation.

King LR: Undiversion: When and how? J Urol 115:296, 1976

The author states that "careful consideration must be given to the historical reason for the permanent diversion, the current status of the child judged by many parameters including the psychological," and the strength of the child and parents. He also stresses that preservation of renal function and prolongation of life are the primary considerations in any undiversion attempt. Because of this, he feels that children with very compromised renal function are not candidates for undiversion. We agree with this in most instances; however, in some children with chronic infection and diversions, these techniques should be considered to overcome these problems and allow ultimate renal transplantation in a sterile urinary tract.

Kogan SJ, Levitt SB: Bladder evaluation in pediatric patients before undiversion in previously diverted urinary tract. J Urol 118:443, 1977

This article describes techniques simulating physiologic voiding in the defunctionalized bladder. The bladder is filled through a ureteral catheter, and a silicone suprapubic catheter is placed percutaneously into the bladder. The ureteral catheter is then removed, and normal saline is infused through a three-way stopcock simulating urine production under physiologic conditions. The article notes that "after voiding is simulated residual volumes of 'urine' can be measured." Bladder capacity will increase with this technique, plus urinary continence can be determined. If urine retention or incontinence is the result, a urethral pressure profile is recommended. We agree this is an excellent method of evaluating a defunctionalized bladder. Because of altered supravesical anatomy and scarring from previous procedures, however, we recommend this be done in the operating room under direct vision. This reduces the chance of inadvertent bowel perforation from the percutaneous catheter and ensures a good location in the dome of the bladder. At the same sitting, of course, the uretheral anatomy can be assessed and conditions such as posterior uretheral valves managed.

Richie JP, Sacks SA: Complications of urinary diversion. J Urol 117:443, 1977

The authors describe two case reports involving undiversion attempts: one successful and one a failure. The different result stresses the need for an antirefluxing technique. In the failure an ileal segment was used but was freely refluxing, and 2 yr after the undiversion massive decompensation of the ileal segment and upper tracts was observed. This child required repeat urinary diversion. These reports underscore the need for close follow-up study of all patients, diverted or undiverted. This must include frequent creatinine clearances and monitoring of x-ray films. It is not uncommon for parents to feel that all is well after their child's "bag" has been removed. This false sense of security, however, may be extremely detrimental to the child's overall renal function. Because of this, we cannot allow patient or parent apathy to occur. Patients must be followed closely and frequently by the above parameters.

Overview: Urinary Undiversion

Arnold H. Colodny

The preceding commentary is an excellent review of the topic of undiversion. It lists all the various techniques that have been used for undiversion. It also cautions against the many pitfalls that might ensue if certain basic principles are not followed.

Basically, patients being considered for undiversion should be divided into two main groups: those with previously normal bladders and those with abnormal (neurogenic) bladders. If the bladder functioned normally before the diversionary procedure was carried out, it will almost always regain normal function after the undiversion. This is the easiest group of patients to deal with, since the problem in this group of patients is purely a technical one of connecting their upper tracts to their bladder and correcting the underlying pathophysiology that led to the diversion. However, in those patients who have abnormal bladders, the surgeon must be concerned with the problems of bladder capacity, bladder emptying, and continence.

Recently the dean of a prestigious medical school told the graduating student body that half of what they had been taught would be shown to be untrue in the next 10 yr. ''Unfortunately,'' he continued, ''we don't know which half.'' This observation has certainly been valid in the history of urinary diversion and undiversion. Many patients who had diversionary procedures performed a number of years ago would not have them carried out today. Newer surgical techniques allow surgeons to restore function in patients who previously would have been diverted. Therefore, whenever a patient with a urinary diversion is seen, the surgeon should ask: ''Would this patient, if he presented today with the condition that he had before diversion, be diverted, or would a constructive operation be carried out?'' Even when dealing with patients with neurogenic bladders, physicians have techniques available today that were not used only a few years ago. Urodynamic assessment, pharmacologic manipulation, intermittent catheterization, and artificial sphincters allow surgeons to achieve proper bladder emptying and continence without the necessity for diversionary procedures in most of those patients. Therefore, the same question should be asked when for a patient with a neurogenic bladder who has had a urinary diversion.

A simple office or treatment room study, such as filling the bladder with a known amount and determining how long the patient can retain it and whether the patient can completely empty the bladder on command, may supply as much or more valuable information as a sophisticated urodynamic assessment in the patient with a non-neurogenic bladder.

Another basic principle is that uroepithelium to uroepithelium is preferable to any other undiversion technique using intestinal segments unless bladder capacity has been shown to be permanently reduced and requires augmentation. This is particularly true when dealing with children, who have 50 to 60 yr of life left. This frequently is possible by identifying the distal ureteral stumps that were left attached to the bladder when the urinary stoma was created. These may be used even if they are as short as 6 cm or 7 cm. ''Seek and ye shall find'' should be a guiding light. In my series of over 100 patients, I was able to get uroepithelium to uroepithelium in approximately 60% of patients. It may be possible to get one proximal ureter to one distal ureteral stump and then do a transureteroureterostomy (T-U-U) from the other ureter. Mobilization of the kidney downward may facilitate the anastomosis between the proximal and distal ureters. Occasionally, the proximal ureter will be long enough for a direct reimplantation into the bladder with an antireflux mechanism. This might require the addition of a psoas hitch or even a Boari flap if bladder capacity is sufficient. If the kidneys are reasonably normal and the surgeon cannot get uroepithelium directly to uroepithelium, autotransplantation of one kidney to allow either direct ureteral reimplantation into the bladder or anastomosis with the distal ureteral stump is a possibility. Occasionally, this may be achieved on the right side by descent of the right renal vein only and not a complete autotransplant. If the transplanted kidney is placed on the same side as the remaining kidney, the surgeon usually can do an anastomosis of the remaining ureter to the pelvis of the autotransplantation kidney (T-U-P). Downward nephropexy may be of help in certain cases.

The distal ureteral stumps may be demonstrated by a voiding cystourethrogram preoperatively if there is reflux into the stumps. Otherwise, retrograde ureterograms will be necessary. Reflux may be present because of some underlying anatomic abnormality of the ureterovesical junction or because of disuse. Efflux may prevent reflux in some of these cases. It is unwise to reimplant the ureters either before attempting undiversion or at the time of undiversion. Frequently bladder capacity is small and the reimplantation may have a higher failure rate than in a functioning bladder. If the reflux is only mild or moderate and the anatomy of the ureterovesical junction is reasonable, it is preferable not to do the reimplant at the time of undiversion, since the reflux may diminish or disappear after ureteric peristalsis has been reestablished. Reimplantation in those patients who have persistent, significant reflux after undiversion will be technically easier and more successful after the bladder capacity has been enlarged by the restoration of function.

Children with neurogenic bladder dysfunction present a special problem in evaluation. The most important question is what their bladder function was before they underwent diversion. What was the capacity? Was it a bladder with a reservoir function, or a small-capacity bladder with constant dribbling? These who had overflow incontinence would be managed by intermittent catheterization today. These patients can be undiverted with the expectation that they will become dry if treated with intermittent catheterization. Before undertaking undiversion, surgeons must try intermittent catheterization of the bladder to see if this is an acceptable technique for these patients. Patient selection is vital in this group of children. They should be socially and psychologically mature. They should have stable upper tracts. Their orthopaedic deformities should not be overwhelming. This type of patient can best be evaluated by inserting a suprapubic trocar cystotomy tube at the time of cystoscopy. The bladder function can then be determined on a physiologic basis. This will allow a proper assessment of continence, bladder capacity, ability to empty the bladder either voluntarily or by self-catheterization. Urodynamic evaluation includes monitoring of bladder and rectal pressure with simultaneous external urethral sphincter electromyography. Urethral pressure profiles are recorded at rest and in response to sacral reflexes, bladder filling, attempted voiding by the Credé and Valsalva maneuvers, and voluntary voiding. The status of the external urethral sphincter is probably the most important parameter in predicting postoperative continence. In most myelodysplastic patients, the bladder neck is incompetent and the highest level of urethral resistance has

been noted at the external sphincter region. If after a period of bladder filling, voluntary voiding or self-catheterization with adjunctive drug therapy does not achieve continence, secondary procedures to control continence (such as bladder neck reconstruction, the Stamey procedure, or implantation of an artificial urinary sphincter) should be considered and should be performed before undiversion. It is crucial to demonstrate that these children can be dry and will accept intermittent catheterization, if necessary, before undiversion is attempted.

Although with proper selection urinary undiversion can be accomplished with a high rate of success, occasional failures may ensue. The patient and the parents must understand this before undiversion is undertaken. The magnitude of these operations and the technical expertise required cannot be overstated. Multiple procedures may be required to achieve complete success. If the patient has a well-functioning loop and stoma and the loop is not used in the reconstruction, it should be left in place until it is clear that the undiversion has been a success. It can then be removed by a relatively simple procedure. If rediversion becomes necessary, it would be relatively simple to reconnect the urinary system to the preexisting loop.

PART TWENTY-TWO

CONTINENT SUPRAVESICAL INTESTINAL DIVERSION PROCEDURES

56

URETEROSIGMOIDOSTOMY

Willard E. Goodwin and Peter T. Scardino

From the Division of Urology, Department of Surgery, University of California
Medical Center, Los Angeles, California

The Journal of Urology
Copyright © 1977 by The Williams & Wilkins Co.
Vol. 118, July, Part 2
Printed in U.S.A.

ABSTRACT—Some historical aspects of ureterosigmoidostomy are described, and various techniques are discussed and illustrated. Our own satisfaction with the results when the procedure is done through the open sigmoid colon is expressed. Ureterosigmoidostomy, which has in some surgeons' hands fallen into disuse, will continue to be used and probably should be used more than it is at present.

When ureterosigmoidostomy is done meticulous care is important in producing a long submucosal tunnel with direct anastomosis of the ureter to the bowel. Preoperative bowel preparation is mandatory. Patients who have undergone ureterosigmoidostomy should remain on a low chloride diet indefinitely with an adequate supplement of sodium potassium citrate to diminish the dangers of electrolyte imbalance and hyperchloremic acidosis. Careful postoperative management and followup care are vital to success.

It is a particular honor and pleasure for me (W. E. G.) to participate in Dr. Hugh J. Jewett's Festschrift. He has been one of my most respected teachers, both when I was a medical student and a resident. I am still learning from him and value his many contributions immensely.

Diversion of urine to the large intestine has occupied the attention of many gifted surgeons for almost a century. There are numerous reports of success and failure, replete with triumph and tragedy. The poor results and the complications of this operation are so bad that they are unacceptable.[1] However, the best results are excellent and represent a nearly perfect way to divert the urine when the bladder cannot be used (Fig. 1). Such results have led to continued attempts to achieve the elusive goal of a perfect technique of ureterosigmoidostomy (anastomosis of the ureters to the intact sigmoid colon).

There are numerous excellent reviews of ureterosigmoidostomy.[2-8] In 1947 the International Society of Urology devoted a large part of the program of its Seventh Congress to the subject of ureterosigmoidostomy. Interesting and comprehensive articles are reported in its Proceedings.[9]

735

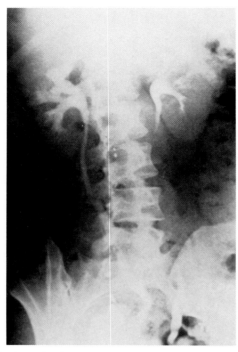

Fig. 1. Excellent result of ureterosigmoidostomy. Excretory urogram 8 years after diversion for neurogenic bladder shows normal kidneys and upper tracts.

HISTORY OF URETEROSIGMOIDOSTOMY

Exstrophy. Perhaps the first ureterointestinal anastomosis was done by Simon in 1852 for exstrophy of the bladder.[10] Since that time many surgeons have turned their attention to the problem of ureterointestinal diversion for patients with exstrophy of the bladder.[8,11,12]

Maydl[13] and Bergenhem[14] used rectal transplantation of the intact or divided trigone for diversion in cases of exstrophy. The operation is appealing because it can be performed entirely extraperitoneally. Maydl had a 15 percent mortality rate with his operation, compared to the 50 percent mortality rate common with other types of ureteroenterostomy performed at that time. The literature on this subject to 1951 was reviewed by Goodwin and Hudson.[15] The Maydl-Bergenhem operations are used rarely now because they do not prevent reflux.

Other ingenious approaches to urinary diversion in cases of exstrophy were devised by Gersuny[16] and by Heitz-Boyer and Hovelacque,[17] who created a blind rectal urinary pouch combined with an anal colostomy. This procedure was revised and described by various investigators.[18–22] Currently, however, the rectal pouch with anal colostomy is used rarely because of the difficulty in achieving satisfactory fecal continence.

Ureterosigmoidostomy itself, even when compared to cutaneous diversion, may still be the best procedure for young children with exstrophy because of the convenience of sphincter control rather than an external appliance for a growing child.[8,12]

First Effective Ureterosigmoidostomy. Probably the first workable and effective ureterosigmoidostomy was described by Tuffier.[23,24] The first American surgeon to describe successful ureterosigmoidostomy was Martin, who reported on a staged procedure—ureterosigmoidostomy followed by a radical pelvic operation for cervical cancer.[25]

PRINCIPLES AND COMPLICATIONS

Reflux and Leakage: Coffey's Contribution. The major defect of the early operations for ureterosigmoidostomy was reflux of fecal material into the upper urinary tracts. Coffey was interested in the dual problem of reflux after anastomosis of the common bile duct to the small intestine and after anastomosis of the ureters to the large intestine. He developed a successful antireflux technique in which he placed the ureter in a submucosal tunnel in the large bowel (Fig. 2).[26] This procedure was called the muscularizing technique by Hinman and Weyrauch.[2] Coffey summarized his experiences in later years[27] and his original paper has been reviewed recently and commented upon.[28]

Coffey's contribution, still important today, was the development of a submucosal tunnel made between the muscular and mucosal layers of the large bowel to prevent reflux into the ureter after ureterosigmoidostomy. Later authors have emphasized the value of an extremely long tunnel to prevent reflux,[29] a principle that remains important.

Obstruction: The Direct Anastomosis. One of the problems associated with Coffey's procedure was a dangling segment of ureter in the intestinal lumen, which sometimes became inflamed and stenotic. The solution was to eliminate the dangling segment by a direct anastomosis of the ureter to the bowel. Independently, Nesbit[30] and Cordonnier[31] described techniques of ureterosigmoidostomy, in which they did a direct mucosa-to-mucosa anastomosis. At that time, the direct anastomosis was considered an important breakthrough, although in fact it was little different from the original technique in use before Coffey. The complications of this direct anastomosis had led Coffey to originate the antirefluxing procedure. Reflux was and continues to be a major problem and some sort of antirefluxing mechanism must be sought. A particularly interesting obser-

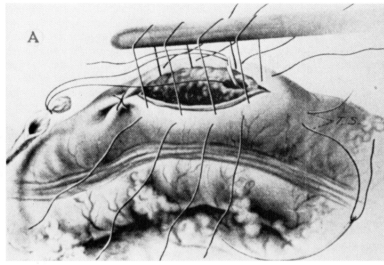

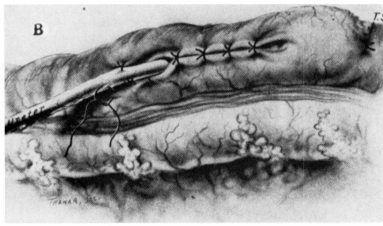

Fig. 2. Muscularizing technique to create submucosal tunnel. (*A*) Tunnel is created by dividing serosal and muscular layers and making small mucosal defect. (*B*) End of ureter is brought into bowel lumen and held in place by single suture (*T.S.*) before tunnel is closed. Reproduced with permission.[26]

vation on this subject was recorded by Whisenand and Moore,[32] who observed a patient with nephrostomy tubes placed after ureterosigmoidostomy who passed fecal material through the nephrostomy tubes.

Infection. With the direct anastomosis, as used before and after Coffey, the problems of pyelonephritis and peritonitis have been the major dangers associated with ureterosigmoidostomy. Before the era of antibiotics considerable effort was made to find an aseptic technique for implantation of the ureters into the large bowel.[33]

Jewett devised a most ingenious technique for 2-stage ureterointestinal anastomosis by a truly aseptic method and won the American Urological Association prize for his contribution.[34] Jewett, who was later to become world renowned for his important contributions concerning the pathology and staging of carcinoma of

the bladder, reported the results of his technique in 33 cases.[35] His work, as well as Hinman's attempts to establish a truly aseptic technique, has fallen a little bit by the wayside with the advent of antibiotics. It is now possible to do ureterosigmoidostomy under almost all conditions with proper preoperative and postoperative antibiotic coverage and proper preparation of the bowel.

Persistent or recurring urinary tract infection after a ureterosigmoidostomy is established continues to be a serious problem. One of the best studies on the frequency of infection is by Harvard and Thompson.[11] They reported long-term observations of patients who had ureterosigmoidostomy for exstrophy. In most of their 144 patients the technique used for the operation was called the Coffey-Mayo nethod. Approximately 50 percent of the hospital deaths were due to pyelonephritis or peritonitis. After the patients left the hospital 65 percent of the deaths were due to pyelonephritis with stones or hydronephrosis. Nevertheless, about a third of the patients seemed to escape clinical symptoms of pyelonephritis altogether and 52 percent of the surviving patients were not troubled by pyelonephritis and rarely had recognizable attacks. Why some patients never have difficulty with pyelonephritis and others seem to have great difficulty needs further investigation.

Electrolyte Imbalance. Many, but not all, patients who have undergone ureterosigmoidostomy have some degree of azotemia and hyperchloremic acidosis. These abnormalities become pronounced in patients with poor renal function and are caused by the intestinal reabsorption of chlorides and ammonia. There is often an additional loss of potassium owing to the obligatory diarrhea. These problems were recognized early but it was not until Ferris and Odel wrote the definitive article describing the pathogenesis of the electrolyte abnormalities after ureterosigmoidostomy that this was more clearly understood.[36] Many authors since that time have written on this subject,[37–41] including Stamey who stated, "Except when a rapid and continuous run-off of urine occurs from a short segment, the operation of ureterosigmoidostomy should probably be abandoned".[42]

Since that time, with better antibiotics to control urinary tract infections and with the clear understanding of the value of a low chloride diet and a sodium potassium citrate supplement, the results of ureterosigmoidostomy generally have become quite acceptable. Stamey has had some second thoughts and recently stated that with the use of trimethoprim and sulfamethoxazole to protect the kidneys he thought ureterosigmoidostomy would have a rebirth as a viable method of urinary diversion.[43]

In our experience a sodium potassium supplement along with a low chloride diet controls the hyperchloremic acidosis. We customarily give a 10 percent sodium potassium citrate solution, 15 to 30 ml twice a day. The formula is 5 gm sodium citrate and 5 cm per 100 ml potassium citrate. The added sodium and potassium make up for the deficiencies of the low chloride diet.

MODERN TECHNIQUES

The Combined Approach: Antirefluxing Tunnel Plus Direct Anastomosis. The problems of obstruction (from ureteral stenosis) with the Coffey technique, and of reflux and leakage (and peritonitis) with the direct anastomosis, led several surgeons almost simultaneously to combine

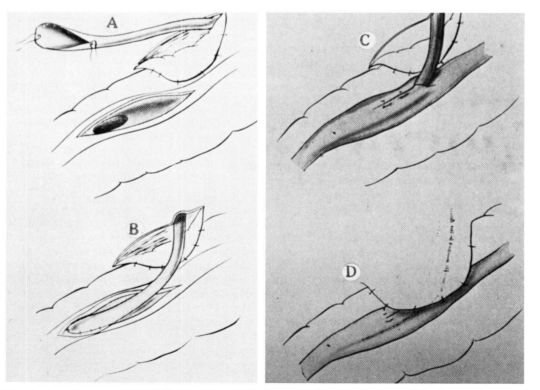

Fig. 3. Combined tunnel and direct anastomosis, incorporating best features of Coffey's and Nesbit's techniques. Reproduced with permission.[44]

the idea of Coffey's tunnel and the direct (mucosa-to-mucosa) anastomosis to create a reliable stoma without reflux.

Leadbetter described a technique of a long tunnel plus direct anastomosis, which is more widely used now than any other method.[44] The tunnel is made as in Coffey's operation from outside the bowel and there is a direct anastomosis of all layers of the ureter to the mucosa of the bowel. This procedure has become more or less standard (Fig. 3).[44]

At the same time, Weyrauch and Young experimented with this technique of a long tunnel plus direct anastomosis in the animal laboratory (Fig. 4).[4]

Operation Through the Open Bowel. In 1948 and 1949 Harris and Goodwin were working in Scott's laboratory at the Brady Urological Institute, experimenting with different types of ureterointestinal anastomosis. We hit upon the idea of doing it from inside the open sigmoid colon with a technique similar to that used for reimplantation of the ureter into the bladder. We had learned the technique of transvesical ureteroneocystostomy with a submucosal tunnel and direct anastomosis from our teacher, Hugh Jewett, and we applied the same technique to ureterosigmoidostomy. A long submucosal tunnel was created and the 2 ureters were brought together, one from each side, retroperitoneally and then sewn together inside the colon with a direct mucosa-to-mucosa anastomosis (Fig. 5). We first used this operation in 1951.

The principle involves use of a long submucosal tunnel as we had learned from Jewett in ureteroneocystostomy. (This is similar to the Politano-Leadbetter operation of ureteroneocystostomy.)[46] The end effect is similar to Leadbetter's combined operation for ureterosigmoidostomy. The difference is that the anastomosis is constructed inside the bowel under direct vision. We have continued to use this technique with satisfaction since that time. Williams and associates described our results with the first 15 years and 51 cases.[47] Harbach and associates reported experiments with transureteroureterostomy associated with ureterosigmoidostomy.[48] The results are as good as those with other methods and there is the added advantage of being able to see the anastomosis from inside. Also, stents may be left in place in the ureters and passed out through the anus if desired. Recently, we made a motion picture demonstrating this technique in a 5-year-old child with exstrophy of the bladder.[49]

Obviously, when the bowel is opened widely and a procedure is done from inside there is a need for careful preoperative bowel preparation with antibacterial drugs. Our regimen for preparation of the bowel is as follows: 8 to 10 days preoperatively (before hospitalization)—begin non-residue, high protein diet; 5 days preopera-

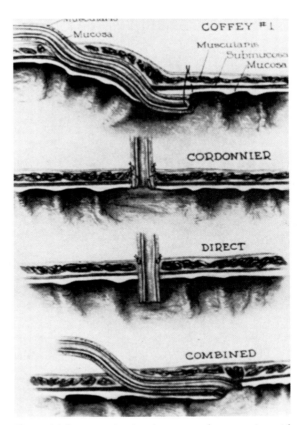

Fig. 4. Major steps in development of ureterosigmoid anastomosis. Reproduced with permission.[4]

tively—laxative, begin sulfathalidine (2 gm every 4 hours), begin soft diet; 4 days preoperatively—enema and begin vitamin supplement; 3 days preoperatively—laxative, begin liquid diet; 2 days preoperatively—enema, begin oral neomycin (1 gm every 6 hours); 1 days preoperatively—in morning Harris flush until clear, nothing by mouth except water, sweetened coffee, tea, clear fruit juices and medications, continue sulfathalidine (2 gm every 4 hours), give neomycin (1 gm every 4 hours), at 6 p.m. begin tincture of opium (10 drops orally every 3 hours for 4 doses), and day of operation—no enema on morning of operation.

In our original article we described this as "a new approach" but later learned that it was not new. Gallo had perfected and reported his technique of ureterosigmoidostomy, which is also a transcolonic method.[50] However, this report was in a Mexican journal and we had not been aware of it. Gallo subsequently has illustrated his technique beautifully.[51] He added the idea of turning up the end of the ureter to make a cuff to prevent reflux, similar to the Mathisen operation for ureterosigmoidostomy and to a technique we had studied experimentally for ureteroneocystostomy.[52]

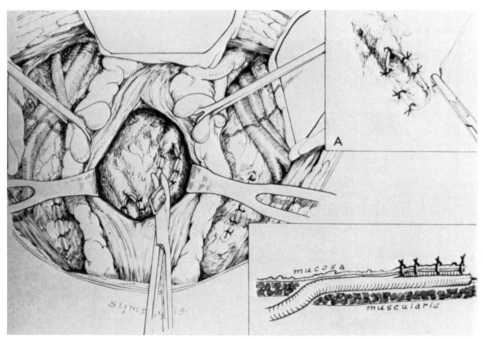

Fig. 5. Technique of open transcolonic ureterosigmoidostomy. Reproduced with permission from: Goodwin, WE: Ureterosigmoidostomy. In: The Craft of Surgery, 2nd ed. Edited by P. Cooper. Boston: Little, Brown and Company, vol. III, p. 1518, 1971.

The same principle of doing ureterosigmoidostomy thorough the open bowel with an antirefluxing nipple was described by Mathisen.[53] In his operation the cuff effect is provided by a small flap of sigmoid colon, which is wrapped around the distal end of the ureter to make an antirefluxing nipple or valve (Fig. 6). His results have been excellent.[7] Bakker and associates also have reported good results with the Mathisen technique.[54]

The Excluded Rectosigmoid Pouch. When Hinman and Smith wrote about total cystectomy for cancer of the bladder in a critical review one of the principles they mentioned was "No. 7, ureters transplanted to excluded bowel".[3] They stated, "Mauclaire, in 1894, first suggested total exclusion of the rectosigmoid by division of the sigmoid loop, sigmoid colostomy and closure of the proximal end of the distal limb with implantation of the ureters into the latter structure. This he performed in dogs.

"Kronig first employed this method in conjunction with cystectomy in 1906. The first stage consisted of exclusion of the rectosigmoid and sigmoid colostomy. Twelve days later the ureters were transplanted into the blind sigmoid and hysterectomy for sarcoma of the uterus was carried out. The patient was alive five years later."

We have used the isolated rectosigmoid as a bladder from time to time and occasionally have created this as a secondary procedure. For example, a patient who cannot tolerate ureterosigmoidostomy because of infection may be converted to a diverting colostomy with a rectosigmoid bladder. Other authors as well have reported satisfactory results with this technique.[55]

The Sigmoid Conduit (with Later Ureterosigmoidostomy). Ureterosigmoidostomy, of course, also has been used when a sigmoid colon is used for cutaneous diversion. In his original article, Bricker reported his use of ureterocolocutaneous diversion before he used the ileum.[56] Goodwin first used it in 1952 and wrote, "There are occasional cases in which the same result may best be achieved by use of an isolated segment of sigmoid colon. I should like to suggest that this always be borne in mind, particularly in patients undergoing pelvic exenteration operation. . . ".[57] The advantage of the colon over small bowel is that a secure antirefluxing tunnel is possible, which can be constructed from either inside or outside the bowel. Satisfaction has been expressed with this type of cutaneous diversion.[58-60]

Hendren has reported his ingenious use of the colonic conduit for temporary or permanent cutaneous urinary

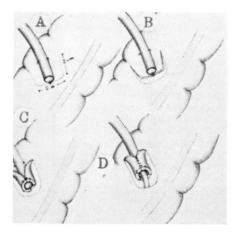 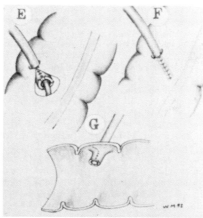

Fig. 6. Concept of antirefluxing nipple, another method of ureterosigmoidostomy done through open bowel. Reproduced with permission.[53]

diversion, particularly in children with exstrophy of the bladder. In selected patients the cutaneous sigmoid conduit was later taken down, once the efficacy of the antirefluxing anastomosis was demonstrated, and the stoma of the conduit was placed end-to-side to the intact sigmoid colon, creating a permanent ureterosigmoidostomy.[12,61,62]

We believe that the operation of ureterosigmoidostomy is due for a renascence.

REFERENCES

1. Goodwin, W. E.: Complications of ureterosigmoidostomy. In: Complications of Urologic Survey, Prevention and Management. Edited by R. B. Smith and D. G. Skinner. Philadelphia, W B Saunders Co, p 229, 1976

2. Hanman, F. and Weyrauch, H. M., Jr.: Critical study of the different principles of surgery which have been used in uretero-intestinal implantation. Trans Am Ass Genito-Urin Surg, 29:15, 1936

3. Hinman, F. and Smith, D.: Total cystectomy for cancer; a critical review. Surgery, 6:851, 1939

4. Weyrauch, H. M. and Young, B. W.: Evaluation of common methods of uretero-intestinal anastomosis: an experimental study. J Urol, 67:880, 1952

5. Weyrauch, H. M.: Landmarks and development of uretero-intestinal anastomosis. Ann Roy Coll Surg Engl 18:343, 1956

6. Nesbit, R. M.: Another hopeful look at ureterosigmoid anastomosis. J Urol 84:691, 1960

7. Mathisen, W.: Clinical and Experimental Studies on Ureterocolic Anastomosis. Oslo, Norway: Oslo University Press, 1969

8. Spence, H. M., Hoffman, W. W. and Pate, V. A.: Exstrophy of the bladder. I. Long-term results in a series of 37 cases treated by ureterosigmoidostomy. J Urol 114:13, 1975

9. Hinman, F.: The technic and late results of transplantation of the ureters. In: Septième Congres de la Societe Internationale d'Urologie, vol 2, p 209, 1947

10. Simon, J.: Ectopia vesicae (absence of the anterior walls of the bladder and pubic abdominal parietes); operation for directing the orifices of the ureters into the rectum: temporary success: subsequent death: autopsy. Lancet, 2:568, 1852

11. Harvard, B. M. and Thompson, G. J.: Congenital exstrophy of the urinary bladder: late results of treatment by the Coffey-Mayo method of uretero-intestinal anastomosis. J Urol, 65:223, 1951

12. Hendren, W. H.: Exstrophy of the bladder—an alternative method of management. J Urol, 115:195, 1976

13. Maydl, K.: Ueber die radikaltherapie der Ectopia vesicae urinae. Wein Med Wchnschr 44:113, 1169, 1209, 1256, 1297, 1894

14. Bergenhem, B.: Ectopic vesicae et adenoma destruens vesicae; exstirpation of blasan; implantation of ureterena i rectum. Eira, 19:268, 1895

15. Goodwin, W. E. and Hudson, P. B.: Exstrophy of bladder treated by rectal transplantation of divided trigone; modification of Maydl-Bergenhem operations. Surg, Gynec & Obst, 93:331, 1951

16. Gersuny, R.: Cited by Foges: Officielles protokll der K. K. geosellschaft der aerzte in Wien. Wien Klin Wschr, 11:989, 1898

17. Heitz-Boyer, M. and Hovelacque, A.: Creation d'une nouvelle vessie et un nouvel urétre. J. d'Urol, 1:237, 1912

18. Lowsley, O. S. and Johnson, T. H.: A new operation for creation of an artificial bladder with voluntary control of urine and feces. J Urol, 73:83, 1955

19. Johnson, T. H.: Further experiences with a new operation for urinary diversion. J Urol, 76:380, 1956

20. Kiefer, J. H. and Linke, C.: Ureterorectostomy and preanal colostomy for bladder exstrophy. Trans Am Ass Genito-Urin Surg, 49:15, 1958

21. Hinman, F., Jr.: The technique of the Gersuny operation (ureterosigmoidostomy with perineal colostomy) in vesical exstrophy. J Urol 81:126, 1959

22. Culp, D. A. and Flocks, R. H.: The diversion of urine by the Heitz-Boyer procedure. J Urol, 95:334, 1966

23. Tuffier, T.: De la derivation par le rectum du cours de l'urine; ureteroenterostomie, cystoenterostomie. Bull Soc Anat, 1:67, 1892

24. Tuffier, T. and Dujarier: De l'extirpation totale de la vessie pour neoplasmes. Rev de Chir, 18:277, 1898

25. Martin, F. H.: Removal of the bladder as a preliminary to or coincidental with hysterectomy for cancer in order to extend the possibilities of surgery for malignant disease of the pelvis. Am J Obst Gynec, 16:395, 1900

26. Coffey, R. C.: Physiologic implantation of the severed ureter or common bile-duct into the intestine. JAMA 56:397, 1911

27. Coffey, R. C.: Production of aseptic ureteroenterostomy. JAMA 94:1748, 1930

28. Goodwin, W. E. and Martin, D. C.: Commentary on article by Coffey, R. C.: Physiologic implantation of the severed ureter or common bile duct into the intestine. In: Classical Articles in Urology. Edited by MA Immergut. Springfield, Illnois: Charles C Thomas, Publisher, p 306, 1967

29. Thompson, I. M. and Smith, J. A.: Double colon sleeve ureterosigmoidostomy. J Urol, 105:205, 1971

30. Nesbit, R. M.: Ureterosigmoid anastomosis by direct elliptical connection: a preliminary report. J Urol, 61:728, 1949

31. Cordonnier, J. J.: Urinary diversion. Arch Surg, 71:818, 1955

32. Whisenand, J. M. and Moore, V.: Hydrodynamics of upper urinary tract after mucosal ureterosigmoidostomy: case report. J Urol, 65:564, 1951

33. Hinman, F.: Ureterointestinal implantation by an aseptic method with a divisible carrier. Tran Am Ass Genito-Urin Surg, 29:157, 1936

34. Jewett, H. J.: Uretero-intestinal implantation: preliminary report. J Urol, 44:223, 1940

35. Jewett, H. J.: Uretero-intestinal anastomosis in two stages for cancer of the bladder: modification of original technique and report of 33 cases. J Urol, 52:536, 1944

36. Ferris, D. O. and Odel, H. M.: Electrolyte pattern of the blood after bilateral ureterosigmoidostomy. JAMA, 142:634, 1950

37. Doroshow, H. S.: Electrolyte imbalance following bilateral ureterosigmoidostomy. J Urol, 65:831, 1951

38. Creevy, C. D.: Facts about ureterosigmoidostomy. JAMA, 151:120, 1953

39. Editorial: Hyperchloremic acidosis after ureterosigmoidostomy. JAMA, 152:334, 1953

40. Rosenberg, M. L.: The physiology of hyperchloremic acidosis following ureterosigmoidostomy: a study of urinary reabsorption with radioactive isotopes. J Urol, 70:569, 1953

41. Parsons, F. M., Pyrah, L. N., Powell, F. J. M., Reed, G. W. and Spiers, F. W.: Chemical imbalance following ureterocolic anastomosis. Br J Urol, 24:317, 1952

42. Stamey, T. A.: Pathogenesis and implications of electrolyte imbalance in ureterosigmoidostomy. Surg, Gynec & Obst, 103:736, 1956

43. Stamey, T. A.: Personal communication, 1975

44. Leadbetter, W. F.: Consideration of problems incident to performance of uretero-enterostomy: report of a technique. J Urol, 65:818, 1951

45. Goodwin, W. E., Harris, A. P., Kaufman, J. J. and Beal, J. M.: Open, transcolonic ureterointestinal anastomosis; a new approach. Surg, Gynec & Obstet, 97:295, 1953

46. Politano, V. A. and Leadbetter, W. F.: An operative technique for the correction of vesicoureteral reflux. J Urol, 79:932, 1958

47. Williams, D. F., Burkholder, G. V. and Goodwin, W. E.: Ureterosigmoidostomy: a 15-year experience. J Urol, 101:168, 1969

48. Harbach, L. B., Kaufman, J. J. and Goodwin, W. E.: Experiments in ureterosigmoidostomy: transureteroureterostomy combined with ureterosigmoidostomy to allow a single ureterocolic anstomosis. J Urol, 104:395, 1970

49. Goodwin, W. E., Dale, G. and Kaufman, J. J.: Open bowel technique: ureterosigmoidostomy for exstrophy of the urinary bladder. (Iliac osteotomy; closure of exstrophy; repair of inguinal hernia; excision of Meckel's diverticulum.) Chicago, Illinois: American College of Surgeons Film, No. ASC 1053, 1974

50. Gallo, D. and Dupont Chacon, J. L.: Tecnia transcolica de utera colostomia. Ginec Obst Mexico, 6:14, 1951

51. Gallo, D.: Urologia Ginecologica Guadalajara, Mexico, 1970

52. Grey, D. N., Flynn, P. and Goodwin, W. E.: Experimental methods of ureteroneocystostomy: experiences with the ureteral intussusception to produce a nipple or valve. J Urol, 77:154, 1957

53. Mathisen, W.: A new method for ureterointestinal anastomosis; preliminary report. Surg, Gynec & Obst, 96:255, 1953

54. Bakker, N. J., Tjabbes, D. and de Voogt, H. J.: Experiences with the ureterocolonic anastomosis after Mathisen. J Urol, 104:824, 1970

55. Dorsey, J. W. and Barnes, R. W.: Urinary diversion through an isolated rectal segment. J Urol, 85:569, 1961

56. Bricker, E. M.: Symposium on clinical surgery; bladder substitution after pelvic evisceration. Surg Clin N Am, 30:1511, 1950

57. Goodwin, W. E.: Discussion of paper by Smith, D. R. and Galante, M.: The use of the Bricker operation in urology. Am J Surg, 96:262, 1958

58. Mogg, R. A.: The treatment of urinary incontinence using the colonic conduit. J Urol, 97:684, 1967

59. Richie, J. P. and Skinner, D. G.: Urinary diversion: the physiological rationale for non-refluxing colonic conduits. Br J Urol, 47:269, 1975

60. Symmonds, R. E. and Gibbs, C. P.: Urinary diversion by way of sigmoid conduit. Surg, Gynec & Obst, 131:687, 1970

61. Hendren, W. H.: Urinary diversion and undiversion in children. Surg Clin N Am, 56:425, 1976

62. Hendren, W. H.: Nonrefluxing colon conduit for temporary or permanent urinary diversion in children. J Pediat Surg, 10:381, 1975

Commentary:
The Value of Ureterosigmoidostomy

Donald F. Williams

Surgeons have long sought an operative procedure that would provide an adequately functioning, uncomplicated, and comfortable substitute for the diseased bladder. Ideally, this method of urinary diversion would combine a readily reproducible and uncomplicated surgical technique with separate sphincteric control of the urine and feces. It would also provide freedom from electrolyte disturbances and recurrent infection.

The first ureterosigmoidostomy was probably performed by Simon more than 115 yr ago.[1] Unfortunately, his operation met with only temporary success, and the patient ultimately died of sepsis. In 1911 Coffey introduced the principle of the submucosal tunnel for anastomosis of the ureter to the colon, which did much to overcome leaking of the anastomosis.[2] However, this procedure also led to a significant incidence of obstruction of the ureter. In 1936 Hinman and Weyrauch presented a comprehensive survey of different procedures used to that date for ureterointestinal anastomoses.[3] In 1949 Nesbit designed a direct, elliptic, mucosa-to-mucosa anastomosis of the ureter to the bowel, and Cordonnier described an end-to-side mucosal anastomosis.[4,5] Both these procedures were designed to obviate ureteral obstruction, but they frequently caused reflux. In 1955 Leadbetter and Clarke reported a 5-yr experience with ureteroenterostomy by a technique that combined the Coffey tunnel and direct mucosal anastomosis.[6] This technique was designed to prevent reflux and formation of strictures. Another operation, an open, transcolonic ureterosigmoidostomy with tunnel and direct mucosal anastomosis, developed by Goodwin and colleagues, was intended to accomplish the same purpose in an easier fashion.[7]

Although this latter technique is reliable, careful attention to preoperative bowel preparation is mandatory to avoid postoperative wound sepsis. Immediate postoperative complications can be held to a minimum by careful attention to technique. Systematic follow-up study is imperative to detect potential urographic, electrolytic, or clinical changes. A low-salt diet, adequate fluid intake, and regular ''by-the-clock'' bowel emptying should be routine advice. Long-term antibiotic coverage has substantially decreased the incidence of pyelonephritis. Major episodes of infection are rare in patients who have neither demonstrable obstruction nor reflux. Impaired pyelograms, although not necessarily associated with serious infection, usually accompany this complication. Significant electrolyte changes seldom occur in the absence of renal damage. Depletion in whole-body potassium can be expected in a patient with ureterocolic anastomosis. This may not be reflected in the plasma concentrations of potassium. Supplements of potassium citrate or carbonate may be advisable from the early postoperative period, but care must be taken if there is impaired renal function. Frequent use of the rectal tube, especially at night, may prove beneficial to the patient with hyperchloremic acidosis.

Unfortunately, the ideal form of diversion has not yet been realized; however, the numerous reports of patients living a cloacal existence with a ureterosigmoidostomy testify that the use of the intact colon as a urinary reservoir is not necessarily inimical to survival. This method of diversion is compatible with good health and long-term survival in selected patients. It has been postulated that the incidence of ureteral reflux and infection is related to existing intraluminal pressure differences between colon and ureter. Although the submucosal tunnel technique was developed to stop the reflux, it has not been universally successful. Pinck reported success with the interposition of an isoperistalic segment of ileum to act as a buffer between the colon and ureters.[8] Daniel and Ram feel that sigmoidomyotomy can be used as a safe and effective method of reducing intracolonic pressures to levels compatible with preservation of renal function.[9] Time will substantiate the value of these techniques.

A word of caution is indicated when attempting to demonstrate reflux following a ureterosigmoidostomy. A suspension of barium has resulted in death when it refluxed from the colon to the kidney. A water-soluble enema is much safer.

If renal deterioration, recurrent infection, or severe electrolyte problems do occur, it may be necessary to separate fecal and urinary streams. Early recognition of the need will prevent further compromise of renal function. The formation of an isolated rectal bladder with a proximal diverting colostomy has proved useful after uretersigmoidostomy has failed. The surgeon may also divert the urine to the skin through ureteroileocutaneous anastomosis.

When urinary diversion is indicated, either following cystectomy or for palliation in inoperable carcinoma, ureterosigmoidostomy may be the procedure of choice. Some patients are unable to take care of external collecting devices because of old age, mental incompetency, crippling arthritis, abdominal wall deformities, or allergy to skin adhesives or rubber. In many parts of the world external collection devices are not available; therefore, a reservoir form of urinary diversion is mandatory. Ureterosigmoidostomy has been used successfully not only following cystectomy for carcinoma but also for urinary diversion for exstrophy of the bladder in children, intractable interstitial cystitis, vesicovaginal fistula, tuberculous bladder contracture, and severe urethral strictures. Caution should be used when diversion is necessary in patients with neurogenic disease of the bladder. Involvement of the anal sphincter is frequently present. Disaster could ensue if this were not recognized and a ureterosigmoidostomy performed. Patients with dilated upper tracts or chronic renal infection are poor candidates for a ureterocolonic anastomosis.

A word of caution on the subsequent development of colonic carcinoma following ureterosigmoidostomy is necessary. The development of a tumor at the site of anastomosis is a rare complication, but the increased risk of cancer development must be taken into consideration, particularly when treating young patients for benign conditions. It is mandatory to look for tumors of the colon, keeping in mind the long latency period, which is approximately 20 yr. Adequate follow-up study should include routine examination for rectal bleeding, ureteral obstruction, and sigmoidoscopy and x-ray examination of the bowel using a water-soluble enema.

Ureterosigmoidostomy is not ideal, but it can be adequate and is sometimes the preferred form of urinary diversion.

REFERENCES

1. Simon J: Ectopia vesicae (absence of the anterior walls of the bladder and pubic abdominal parietes); operation for directing the orifices of the ureters into the rectum; temporary success; subsequent death; autopsy. Lancet 2:568, 1852
2. Coffey RC: Transplantation of the ureters into the large intestine in the absence of a functioning urinary bladder. Surg Gynecol Obstet 32:383, 1921
3. Hinman F, Weyrauch HM Jr: Critical study of the different principles of surgery which have been used in uretero-intestinal implantation. Trans Am Assoc Genitourin Surg 29:15, 1936
4. Nesbit RM: Ureterosigmoid anastomosis by direct elliptical connection: A preliminary report. J Urol 61:728, 1949
5. Cordonnier JJ: Ureterosigmoid anastomosis. J Urol 63:276, 1950
6. Leadbetter WF, Clarke BG: Five years' experience with ureteroenterostomy by the 'combined' technique. J Urol 73:67, 1955
7. Goodwin WE, Harris AP, Kaufman JJ, et al: Open, transcolonic

ureterointestinal anastomosis; a new approach. Surg Gynecol Obstet 97:295, 1953

8. Pinck BD: Ureteroiliosigmoidostomy. J Urol 102:37, 1969

9. Daniel O, Ram RS: The value of sigmoid-myotomy in reducing bowel pressure and thus averting renal damage following uretercolic anastomosis. Br J Urol 37:654, 1965

ANNOTATED BIBLIOGRAPHY

Coffey RC: Physiologic implantation of the severed ureter or common bile-duct into the intestine. JAMA 56:397, 1911

Coffey discovered that direct anastomosis of the bile duct to the intestine resulted in dilatation of the bile duct. He found it possible to avoid the dilatation by developing a submucosal tunnel after spatulating the end of the bile duct and pulling it into the lumen of the bowel with a long traction suture. Retraction of the duct was prevented by fixation sutures between serosa of bowel and duct. This experimental model formed the foundation for future ureterointestinal anastomotic procedures and techniques.

Ferris DO, Odel HM: Electrolyte pattern of the blood after bilateral ureterosigmoidostomy. JAMA 142:634, 1950

The authors describe in detail the alkali deficit that developed in some patients after a ureterosigmoidostomy. They provide a composite definition of the electrolyte disturbance and clinical syndrome of hyperchloremic acidosis. Speculation on the etiology of abnormality is presented. Potentially helpful therapeutic modalities are outlined. Considerable credit on the understanding of electrolyte problems in ureterosigmoidostomy should be give to this work.

Goodwin WE, Harris AP, Kaufman JJ, et al: Open, transcolonic ureterointestinal anastomosis, a new approach. Surg Gynecol Obstet 97:295, 1953

A new approach to ureterocolic surgery is presented. The lower bowel is opened after meticulous bowel preparation with antibacterial drugs. Submucosal tunnels are formed in the manner of a ureteroneocystostomy. A direct mucosal union is accomplished. This technique has the advantage of being simple and direct, and it affords the surgeon an opportunity to view the anastomosis under direct vision.

Spence HM: Ureterosigmoidostomy for exstrophy of the bladder. Br J Urol 38:36, 1966

Ureterosigmoidostomy is presented as the procedure of choice in exstrophy of the bladder. Carefully performed ureterocolic anastomoses yielded good long-term results in two of three patients. Half the patients had no major complications. One patient in three required further surgery (*e.g.*, nephrectomy, removal of stone, or urinary diversionary procedures). Prolonged, careful follow-up study is mandatory.

Harbach LB, Kaufman JJ, Goodwin WE: Experiments in ureterosigmoidostomy: Transureteroureterostomy combined with ureterosigmoidostomy to allow a single ureterocolic anastomosis. J Urol 104:395, 1970

A modification in ureterocolonic technique is presented. Patients with a solitary functioning ureterosigmoid anastomosis seem to fare better (*i.e.*, less clinical pyelonephritis, hydronephrosis, and acidosis). It was postulated that this was secondary to increased flow across the anastomosis. Animal experiments were performed in support of this hypothesis.

Williams DF, Burkholder GV, Goodwin WE: Ureterosigmoidostomy: A 15-year experience. J Urol 101:168, 1969

A long-term experience with the open, transcolonic ureterointestinal anastomosis is presented. Ureterosigmoidostomy can approach an ideal form of urinary diversion when the physician pays careful attention to details of surgical technique and performs close, long-term postoperative monitoring of the patient.

Spence HM, Hoffman WW, Pate VA: Exstrophy of the bladder. I. Long-term results in a series of 37 cases treated by ureterosigmoidostomy. J Urol 114:133, 1975

This further follow-up paper in 1966 strengthens the initial tenet that ureterosigmoid diversion requires continuous, careful, long-term attention to prevent devastating complications.

Rivard J, Bedard A, Dionne L: Colonic neoplasms following ureterosigmoidostomy. J Urol 113:781, 1975

Carcinoma of the colon is a rare but ever ominous threat following ureterosigmoidostomy. The etiology of the cancer has not been adequately elucidated. Long-term careful observation is necessary for its detection.

Overview: Ureterosigmoidostomy: Due for a Renascence?

Willard E. Goodwin and Bernard D. Pinck

The Commentary by Dr. Williams is accurate and to the point. He clearly covers most of the important considerations of ureterosigmoidostomy. I (WEG) should like to refer to my own remarks on the subject: "Our own satisfaction with the results when the procedure is done through the open sigmoid colon is expressed. Ureterosigmoidostomy, which has in some surgeons' hands fallen into disuse, will continue to be used and probably should be used more than it is at present . . . . We believe that the operation of ureterosigmoidostomy is due for a renascence."[1] My feelings have not changed, although I have seen most of the possible complications of ureterosigmoidostomy at one time or another over the past 30 yrs.[2]

The first important complication of this procedure is infection. Between 20% and 50% of patients with ureterosigmoidostomy have pyelonephritis. This can be monitored and, I believe, successfully controlled with long-range antibacterial treatment (*e.g.,* trimethoprim sulfa methoxazole tablets [Bactrim, Septra]) The second important complication is acidosis with hyperchloremia. This can be controlled by a low-chloride diet and an additional supplement of sodium potassium citrate (we use a solution of 5% sodium citrate and 5% potassium citrate). The *potassium* is an important ingredient.

The crucial factor is that the patient have good renal function in order to support a ureterosigmoidostomy. In preoperative evaluation, kidney function should be carefully monitored, and the surgeon should determine that the patient has anal control of liquid stool. This can be done either with an enema of oatmeal or of indigo carmine. This is followed by having the patient walk around the hospital to see if there are any traces of leakage. An adequate and careful bowel preparation with particular attention to low-residue diet and ample cleanout of the lower intestine *is a must* before ureterosigmoidostomy.

As far as technique is concerned, the results seem to be about the same no matter which technique is used as long as attention is paid to a careful antirefluxing procedure. Coffey's original long tunnel with the end of the ureter pulled into the bowel has fallen into disuse because of occasional obstruction of the distal ureter. More modern techniques avoid that complication by direct anastomosis. Whether the procedure is done by Leadbetter's operation from outside the bowel or with the open bowel, as in our technique, by the open transcolonic ureterointestinal anastomosis, or by Mathiesen's technique, which involves creating a nipple to prevent reflux, the important thing is to achieve an anti-reflux procedure. In Leadbetter's and in our operations, this is done by creating a long submucosal tunnel of at least 2 cm to 3 cm with a direct anastomosis of the end of the ureter to the bowel. The procedure is particularly applicable to the very young, as in children born with extrophy or a loss of the mechanism for urinary control, and the very old, who may have difficulty with external collecting devices.

It is well recognized that complications include pyelonephritis and stones, but when compared with various recently reported series of patients who had cutaneous diversion, either with an ileum or colon conduit, the incidence of complications seems no higher in ureterosigmoidostomy. The convenience may certainly justify the procedure, especially in very young and very old patients. If the procedure fails because of recurring infection and renal deterioration, a saving operation is a diverting colostomy to leave a rectal bladder, the so-called Mauclaire operation (see Chap. 57).

In the Urologist's Correspondence Club letter, April 20, 1973, the now-deceased Thomas E. Gibson quoted Dr. Reed Nesbit in a "personal communication" as follows:

My argument is that nature usually behaves in a consistent manner, and if *some individuals can survive* for very long periods of time with

normal pylograms and absolutely no evidence of chemical imbalances in the body economy, then *we should seek* to find the reason why this can occur in some of our patients. Perhaps if we can find the answer to that question, which I feel will eventually be found by the application of new techniques to its performance, then we can hope to see consistently good results rather than good results which occur only rarely.[3]

In an article in *Urology Times,* the following statement appears:

Ureterosigmoidostomy should be considered more frequently as a method of urinary diversion. Drs. Joseph W. Segura and Horst Zincke told the 69th annual meeting of the American Urological Association that they do not mean to imply that urologists should abandon the use of ileal conduit diversion, but they do think that ureterosigmoidostomy does compare favorably with that procedure. The Mayo Clinic and Mayo Foundation urologists noted that the use of ureterosigmoidostomy as the preferred method of urinary diversion was abandoned by many urologists almost 25 years ago after the ileal conduit was first described by Dr. E.M. Bricker. Around the same time, there were reports of complications with ureterosigmoidostomy.

Drs. Segura and Zincke believe that ureterosigmoidostomy has much to recommend it from both the patient's and surgeon's standpoints. For the patient there is the absence of a stoma, with none of the problems of an external collecting device, and a quasinormal form of urinary control. For the surgeon, the operating technique is simpler and is, they stressed, definitely a shorter procedure in terms of operating time. Also, if necessary, conversion to another form of diversion may be accomplished at a later date.

At the AUA session, Dr. Segura reported on 173 patients who underwent ureterosigmoidostomy at the Mayo Clinic over a nine year period.

There is also a place for ureterosigmoidostomy into an isolated segment of colon with the idea of later reestablishing the normal continuity of the bowel. This is well described in the Urologist's Correspondence Club Letter, Dec. 4, 1974, by W. Hardy Hendren of the Massachusetts General Hospital, who related a cure of a boy aged 20 mo with sarcoma of the prostate.[4] Our original first "cure" of this disease is a patient now living more than 20 yr, and happily, with an ureterosigmoidostomy. Hendren has since used this technique rather extensively; Skinner and colleagues have reported favorably on the isolated sigmoid segment as a cutaneous urinary diversion.[5] We have also used it with the idea of following Hendren's path of reestablishing normal continuity at a later date if possible. Bakker and colleagues have followed 13 children after ureterosigmoidostomy and conclude that it had had no effect on their growth. This matter is still open to discussion.[6]

Williams, in his excellent Commentary, cautions against the danger of late malignancy in the bowel. There has been a great deal written about this complication in recent years, and Leadbetter estimated that there was a 500-fold greater chance of bowel malignancy after ureterosigmoidostomy. He calculated this to be a 5% lifetime risk and thought that the development time of these colon cancers varied from 6 to 50 yr after surgery. He recommended follow-up study of stools for blood every 3 mo after 2 yr, an intravenous pyelogram (IVP) yearly after 5 yr, and a colonoscopy every 5 yr. He also recommended a barium enema, which we very much oppose because we have seen one fatality occur from it. If an enema is done, it should be done with one of the water-soluble materials used for cystogrophy and retrograde pyelography.

Sooriyaarachchi and colleagues described a poorly differentiated adenocarcinoma of the rectum in a man aged 43 yr 37 yr after a ureterosigmoidostomy. They stated that the median time interval between the procedure and the diagnosis was 21 yr and that the median age at diagnosis was 33 yr. They thought that lesions occurred at the site of the ureteral anastomosis.[7] In our opinion, *this factor is related to the urine,* which must have some carcinogenic substances in it. Don't blame it on the bowel, blame it on the urine.

Finally, Cromie and Duckett have an excellent chapter on urinary diversion in children. They discuss ureterosigmoidostomy and also the rectal bladder with a separate colostomy.[8] This monograph is well illustrated and informative.

The procedure of ureterosigmoidostomy has a definite usefulness and, in our opinion, is ready to be revived and used much more extensively than it has been in the past 25 years. The technical demands are great. The surgeon should have substantial experience. If he is unable to get such experience with the patient population, he should practice and perfect his technique and expertise in the animal laboratories.

REFERENCES

1. Goodwin WE, Scardino PT: Ureterosigmoidostomy. J Urol 118:169, 1977

2. Goodwin WE: Complications of ureterosigmoidostomy. In Smith RB, Skinner DG (eds). Complications of Urologic Surgery, Prevention and Management, p. 229. Philadelphia, WB Saunders, 1976

3. Nesbit RM: Another hopeful look at ureterosigmoid anastomosis. J Urol 84:691, 1960

4. Hendren WH: Non-refluxing colon conduit with later anastomosis to colon in child with sarcoma of prostate. Presented at the Urologists' Correspondence Club, Dec. 4, 1974

5. Skinner DG, Gottesman JE, Richie JP: The isolated sigmoid segment: Its value in temporary urinary diversion and reconstruction. J Urol 113:614, 1975.

6. Bakker NJ, Van Damme KJ de Voogt HJ: Follow up of 13 children after ureterosigmoidostomy. Arch Dis Child 51: 544, 1976

7. Sooriyaarachchi GS, Johnson RO, Carbone PP: Neoplasms of the large bowel following ureterosigmoidostomy. Arch Surg 112:1174, 1977

8. Cromie WJ, Duckett JW: Urinary diversion in children, past and present. Monogr Urol 1:34, 1980

57

RECTAL BLADDER WITH LEFT ABDOMINAL COLOSTOMY (MAUCLAIRE PROCEDURE)

U. Bracci

Minerva Urologica 31:199–208, Oct–Dec, 1979

The indications for the creation of a rectal bladder according to Mauclaire (Fig. 1) are as a palliative or diversion operation or following cystectomy or cystourethrectomy in patients in poor general condition or older patients (over 70 years of age) and in obese patients on account of the easy onset in these patients of vascular disorders resulting from compression of the sigmoid stump due to thickness of the perineal layer and for the contraindication of using traction on the mesosigmoid, which might be short and thick. In all other cases it is preferable to use the Heitz-Boyer–Hovelaque operation (rectal bladder with intrasphincteric perineal anus in the retrorectal position; Fig. 2), which, compared with the Gersuny technique (rectal bladder with intrasphincteric perineal anus in the retrorectal position; Fig. 3), offers better results in terms of fecal continence and perception of the defecation stimulus. Furthermore, stenosis of the new perineal anus is less frequent with the Heitz-Boyer–Hovelaque operation, probably because the anterior perineum is more rigid and consistent than the posterior perineum.

Conditions needed for the good function of the new bladder are normal anal sphincter and absence of anorectal lesions (fistulae, primary or secondary tumors, cicatricial stenosis, large hemorrhoids, prolapse).

PREPARATION OF THE PATIENT

Antibiotics (preparations containing neomycins) should be given for 3–4 days prior to surgery in order to reduce intestinal bacterial flora, following the usual procedures employed in surgery of the large bowel. Twelve hours before surgery, besides the usual cleansing of the intestines, it is advisable to introduce a Heudel probe with a mercury balloon, which should be radiologically followed beyond the duodenum. This is useful to avoid distention of the small bowel during the postoperative phase. Careful examination of the perineal area and anal sphincters should not be overlooked.

POSITION OF THE PATIENT

The patient is placed in a supine position with the thighs wide apart and the legs left in the stirrups. Preparation and sterilization should include the entire abdominal field.

SURGICAL TECHNIQUE

A median incision of the hypogastric wall is continued for 4–5 cm above the umbilicus (Fig. 4). Good visual-

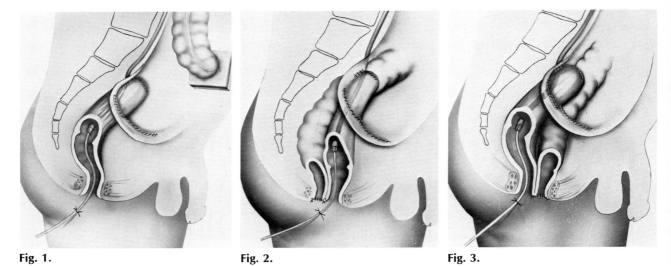

Fig. 1.   Fig. 2.   Fig. 3.

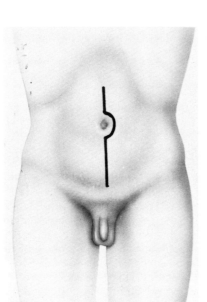   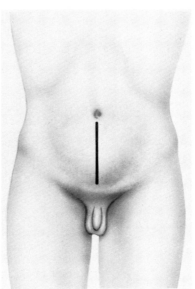

Fig. 4.   Fig. 5.

ization of the perineal cavity is thus obtained, and both lymphadenectomy and mobilization of the sigmoid and descending colon are easier at cystectomy. In the rare event that the left angle must be freed, this is the only way it can be done. In palliative or diversion operations, an incision from the umbilicus to the pubis is usually sufficient (Fig. 5).

Incision of the Peritoneum. In cystectomy the incision follows that of the bladder wall, which is extended over the bladder like an inverted V and varies, so that all the

serosa covering the bladder can be removed (Fig. 6). The tips of the V, joined transversely at the level of the pouch of Douglas, are extended upward on the posterior peritoneum along the common ileac artery until the bifurcation of the aorta is reached. Two peritoneal flaps are thus formed in the shape of wings, which enables, once surgery is completed, reconstruction and closure of the peritoneal cavity.

In palliative or diversion operations, once the peritoneum has been opened and a self-retaining retractor (Fig. 7) has been placed in position, an incision is made

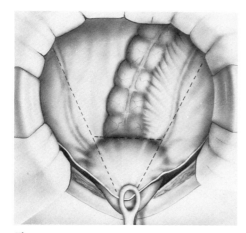

Fig. 6.

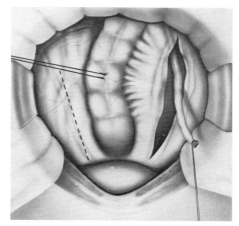

Fig. 8.

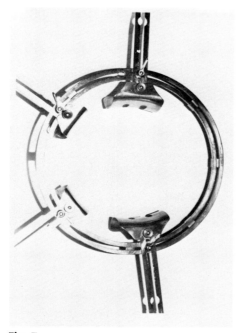

Fig. 7.

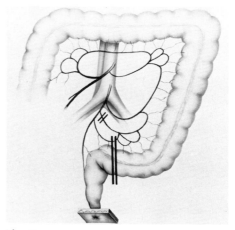

Fig. 9.

to the left of the parietosigmoid peritoneum and to the right, in the posterior perineum below the cecum. This incision should be long enough to free and isolate the ureters and to perform lymphadenectomy if necessary (Fig. 8).

Preparation of the Rectal Bladder. Division of the intestine is made between the transverse portion of the sigmoid and the pelvic colon (Fig. 9) or even higher in the distal third of the sigmoid loop. An incision is made in the serosa of the mesocolon, on both sides, up to its

root (Fig. 10). The sigmoid arcade is sectioned, and the vessels ligated (Fig. 11). The intestine is cut with electric cautery (Fig. 12), and the proximal stump is ligated and protected with a rubber cap (Fig. 13) in order to avoid contamination in the subsequent steps. If necessary, the sigmoid stump is lengthened by cutting and tying some branches of the left colic (Fig. 14). The distal stump is closed in two layers: the first with noninterrupted stitches of 2–0 catgut (Fig. 15); the second, with interrupted seromuscular stitches of 3–0 Trexylene (Fig. 16).

Preparation of the Rectal Bladder. For a better vascularization of the new bladder in dividing the mesosigmoid, the upper hemorrhoidal arteries should be left intact, since the mid-hemorrhoidal arteries may be absent or may be damaged during lymphadenectomy. Division of only the sigmoid arteries usually enables mobilization of the sigmoid colon, which is sufficient to bring it to

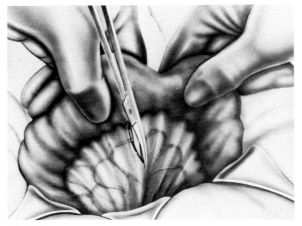

Fig. 10.

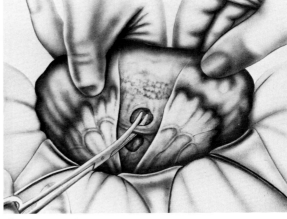

Fig. 11.

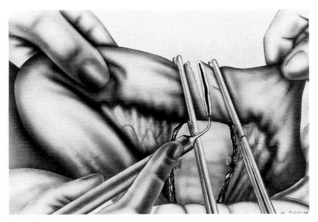

Fig. 12.

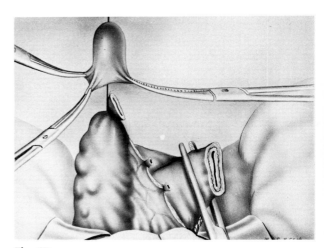

Fig. 13.

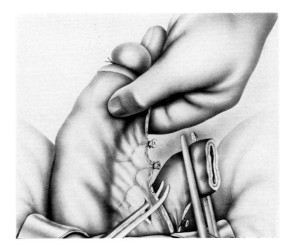

Fig. 14.

Fig. 15.

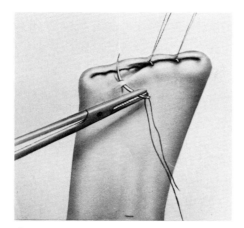

Fig. 16.

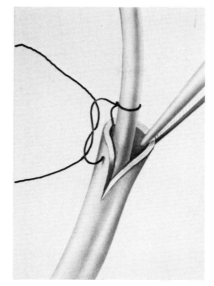

Fig. 17.

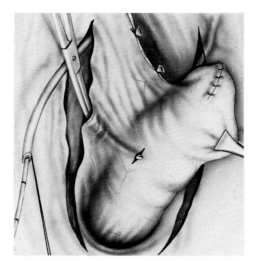

Fig. 18.

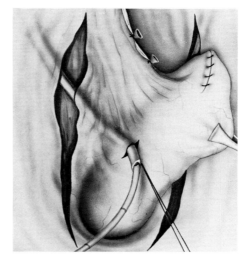

Fig. 19.

the perineal level. Very occasionally it is necessary to cut the left colic artery, but it is preferable to avoid this step, since if the Riolano arch is inadequate (this usually occurs when the artery of the left angle exists), one runs the risk of vascular disorders of the stump and of having to proceed with a permanent iliac colostomy. Mobilization of the left angle is rarely necessary, and I prefer not to do this.

Ureterorectal Anastamosis. This varies depending on the caliber of the ureter. In the presence of the dilated ureter, a polyvinyl catheter (10-12 F) is introduced for 16–18 cm after the stump is divided and an opening of 1 cm made on one side. A suture of 3–0 catgut is then fixed with a knot to the catheter, which is passed through

the wall of the distal aspect of the ureter and used to anchor it to the ureter (Fig. 17). This suture is left long and used to anchor the catheter and ureter to the wall of the rectum 2–3 cm distal to the site of the anastamosis. By blunt dissection a subserosal tunnel is made in the mesosigmoid in order to reach the intestinal wall, through which the intubated ureter is passed (Figs. 18 and 19). An incision is made in the muscular layer, and a tunnel 1–1.5 cm is made between it and the mucosa, which is opened for approximately 1 cm in the more distal aspect. A 20 F Couvelaire catheter is introduced through the

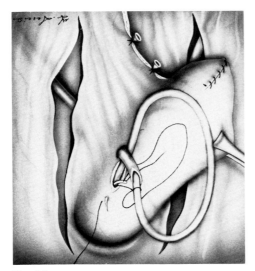

Fig. 20.

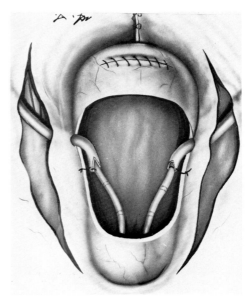

Fig. 21.

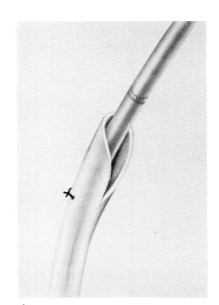

Fig. 22.

anus together with the ureteral catheter introduced into it. The ureter is then anchored to the rectal wall by a suture that fixes it to the catheter (Fig. 20). The small incision in the rectum is sutured and closed onto the ureter with 2 to 4 4–0 Dexon stitches, which catch the wall of the ureter and the serosa and muscle layer of the intestine. The serosa of the mesorectum is closed above with 3–0 Trexylene sutures. Figure 21 schematically illustrates the lateral view of the rectal bladder on completion of this type of anastomosis and may be defined as an *axial implantation*.

In the presence of a thin ureter I prefer to perform anastomosis with an end-to-side mucosa-to-mucosa anastomosis with interrupted stitches. The ureter is prepared in the same way with the exception that, after a narrower catheter (8-10 F) is introduced, the stump is incised for 1–1.5 cm on the posterior wall in order to make it larger by spatulation (Fig. 22).

The suture that fixes the catheter is passed to and knotted on the wall of the ureter about 1 cm above the opening. Passage of the ureter in the subserosal tunnel and passage of the catheter through the rectum is as previously described. Great care should be taken during incision of the intestinal wall to prepare and to detach or separate the mucosa and enable easy suturing of the ureter to the intestinal wall. The anastomosis is performed with two interrupted sutures, one anterior and the other posterior, with 4–0 chromic catgut that is then pushed down with 1 or 2 seromuscular stitches of Trexylene and covered again with the peritoneum of the mesorectum (Figs. 23 and 24).

Another anastomotic technique is that proposed by Goodwin and consists of transintestinal–ureterorectal implantation. I usually employ this technique in cases of dilated ureters.

The ureter is prepared after a catheter is introduced and fixed to its wall, with the tip turned back like a shirt cuff for about 1 cm, carried out with 4 or 5 stitches of 2–0 chromic catgut. This takes the edge of the ureteral mucosa and its adventitia superiorly, without involving the vascular supply. These sutures are left long.

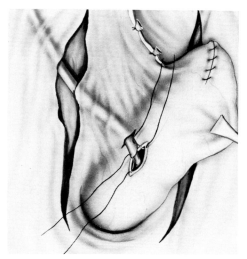

Fig. 23.

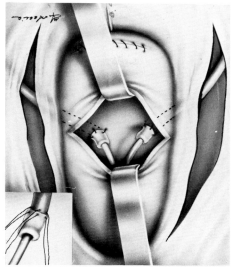

Fig. 25.

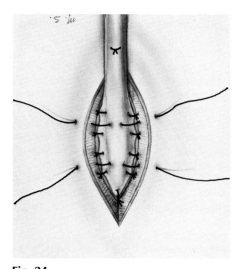

Fig. 24.

A transverse or longitudinal incision is thus made through the entire thickness of the anterior wall of the sigmoid colon for about 3 cm. From within the colon, the ureters are brought to the intestinal lumen by blind dissection or by a small incision in the mucosa and muscular layers. These sutures employed in preparation of the ureter are left long and used to anchor the ureteral ends to the intestinal wall. The everted ureter thus protrudes into the lumen of the intestine for about 1 cm (Fig. 25). The aim is not so much to prevent reflux but to avoid ureteral stenosis. Closure of the intestinal incision in one layer with nonabsorbable inverting suture completes this stage of the anastomosis.

Once anastamosis is completed, the left iliac colostomy can be prepared. A circular incision (2–3 cm) is made between the costal margin and the iliac spine, and the skin and subcutaneous layer is removed up to the muscular wall, which is then opened with a McBurney-type incision. An incision is made in the peritoneum and the sigmoid itself is carefully prepared and its mesentery is brought to the outside and fixed with Trexylene stitches to the peritoneum, to the aponeurosis of the transverse muscle, and to the skin.

Very occasionally the colostomy is constructed by passing the sigmoid stump through the rectus muscle after a longitudinal incision is made in the aponeurosis and the muscular fibers are spread.

Peritonealization. Peritonealization should be as accurate and complete as possible, since intestinal obstruction, usually secondary to strangulation or curvature of the loops of the small bowel in the peritoneal gaps, or in nonperitonealized areas, is the most frequent and the most severe complication in this operation.

In palliative or diversion operations it is necessary to close (1) the two lateral incisions in the posterior peritoneum, which were made to expose the ureters and to enable anastomosis, and (2) the medial opening needed for dissecting the mesosigmoid (Fig. 26). Furthermore, the edge of the mesentery of the sigmoid stump must be carefully sutured to the left parietocolic gutter. The anterior medial incision in the peritoneum is then closed.

In operations after cystectomy, three sutures are necessary—one right above the iliac vessels, one left of the parietocolic gutter, and one medial corresponding to

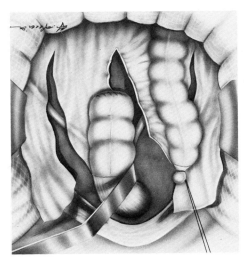

Fig. 26.

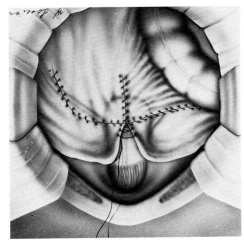

Fig. 28.

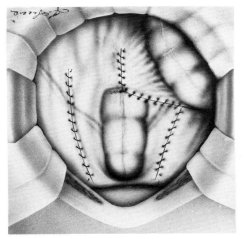

Fig. 27.

the division of the mesosigmoid, which terminates at the level of the proximal stump of the rectal bladder. Suture of the parietocolic gutter is terminated at the point at which the sigmoid is exteriorized to create the colostomy, and the lateral flap is sutured to the edge of the peritoneum of the root of the mesosigmoid and to that of the mesentery of the stump, exteriorized as well to the peritoneum of the iliac cavity, terminating laterally at the coloparietal angle (Figure 27). Subsequently, the lower edge of the two anteriolateral flaps of the peritoneum are sutured, on the left, to the peritoneum of the iliac cavity and to the anterior surface of the mesocolon and, on the right, to the peritoneum of the iliac cavity until the end of the left suture reaches the median line. It is then continued along the medial edges of the above-mentioned flaps (Fig. 28) until it forms the distal beginning of the closure of the anterior peritoneum. Another suture, commencing from above, is brought down to meet the former, to which it is tied.

Commentary:
The Mauclaire Operation

Ulrico Bracci

I have been using the rectal bladder for the last 25 yr, since in my opinion it is the best procedure for urinary diversion from every point of view. The techniques employed are well known, and I will mention only those related to sigmoid stumps, which, like a colostomy, may be brought to the skin

of the left iliac area (Mauclaire procedure) or to the perineum by passing them on the inside of the sphincter, which is employed to ensure continence, in the prerectal position (Gersuny procedure), or in the retrorectal position (Heitz–Boyer–Hovelaque procedure). Of the three surgical techniques, the rectal bladder according to Heitz-Boyer–Hovelaque appears, from a functional viewpoint, to give the best results, with excellent micturation on the one hand and satisfactory and controlled defecation on the other. In patients in whom this procedure is impossible or unwise, I perform a rectal bladder according to Mauclaire, with left iliac colostomy or simple ureterosigmoidostomy.

I consider the Mauclaire operation a simple surgical procedure with limited complications and risks. From a functional point of view, it is the best method as far as urinary diversion is concerned. Complications at the anastomosis or in the upper urinary tract are rare. For many years I almost exclusively employed the rectal bladder according to Mauclaire for diversion in those patients in whom it was impossible to proceed with the Gersuny or Heitz-Boyer–Hovelaque technique because of greater risks or more severe complications (electrolyte disorders, ascending infections) after ureterosigmoidostomy. In fact, I used ureterosigmoidostomy in only 3.1% of patients in 1965, in 1.2% in 1966, in 0% in 1967, and in 7.9% in 1968. Today, I still only use ileal or colonic conduits when it is impossible to employ other procedures and usually only in children requiring external diversion for neurogenic vesical dysfunction or when inoperable tumors make massive radiation treatment of the pelvis advisable. I later modified this tendency; since now, with suitable treatment, it is possible to obviate the majority of complications following ureterosigmoidostomy, I prefer this technique to the rectal bladder according to Mauclaire but not to the Heitz-Boyer–Hovelaque in young patients and in those willing to accept an iliac colostomy, provided the ureters are not dilated or present severe stasis or the kidney is silent.

At present, I perform 50% of rectal bladders according to Heitz-Boyer–Hovelaque, and about 20% according to Mauclaire; in about 25% I perform ureterosigmoidostomy. Of the 769 carried out in 25 yr, I have employed Mauclaire's operation in 360 patients, compared with 409 rectal bladders with intrasphincteric lowering of the sigmoid stump, of which 308 were done according to Heitz-Boyer–Hovelaque and 101 were done according to Gersuny. During that period I performed 121 ureterosigmoidostomies. Indications for Mauclaire's operation are as follows:

With cystectomy: for diversion purposes (inoperable neoplasms in the bladder)	56 patients
With cystectomy: advanced age (over 70 yr)	103 patients
Poor general condition or for technical reason	201 patients

The risk involved in performing rectal bladder according to Mauclaire or Heitz-Boyer–Hovelaque following cystectomy is similar to that encouncered in all major operations inasmuch as the maneuvers related to the construction of the rectal bladder are simple and complications are less frequent than in other types of diversion. Hospital deaths, which in the initial period reached a bare 10%, have dropped in recent years to 2% to 3%. Death following rectal bladder performed merely for diversion purposes may be considered nonexistent. It is worthwhile to stress that I use these operations in patients in poor general condition and in patients over 70 yr (and even 75 yr) of age.

Regarding the more common complications of ureteral fistulae and stenosis, I should point out that fistulae were exceptional, reaching 0.8% to 1%, compared to 5% to 6% observed following ureterosigmoidostomy regardless of the type of anastomosis employed. I believe this is due to the fact that anastomoses are performed in a sterile or little infected field (which does not become reinfected because it is excluded from intestinal contents) in a cavity kept at 0 pressure and with a rectal catheter, which is impossible with ureterosigmoidostomy. In other words, urinary flow continues to occur under conditions not unlike those in the natural bladder. These conditions eliminate or reduce complications arising from anastomosis to a very low percentage. Stenosis and consequent ureterorenal dilatation amount to no more than 7% to 8% of complications.

These dilatations are often only moderate, and kidney function is well preserved. Furthermore, a fairly large percentage of these, observed in the early postoperative stage, are perhaps due to the isolation and mobilization of the ureters, surgical technique, and higher pressure in the rectum than in the natural bladder and decrease or disappear completely with time.

The well-performed ureteral anastomosis has also eliminated any problems with a severely distended urinary tract and even eliminates such problems in cases of trigonal neoplasia. In these cases, anastomoses of the ureters are performed as usual and without difficulty, leading, in a large percentage of patients, to reduced distention and return of normal function, even, surprisingly enough, of silent kidney. Episodes of fever are rare and decrease or disappear in all patients within 2 or 3 mo. Nephrectomy was necessary in only one of these patients. As far as reflux as a cause of ureseptic episodes and dilatation, this is difficult to demonstrate. In fact, a feeling of tension and side pain during micturation was observed in only a few patients (less than 2% or 3%). Chronic pyelonephritis with reduction of parenchyma and renal function, often associated with dilatation of the urinary tract (usually not severe), was observed in 4% to 5% of rectal bladders done according to Mauclaire and 12% to 14% done according to Heitz-Boyer–Hovelaque, but in 30% (at times in the severe form) of patients with ureterosigmoidostomy.

As far as late complications go, with the exception of a few instances of pyelonephritis and a few rare instances of severe renal failure, usually occurring in patients with already severely impaired renal function at the time of surgery, I have observed only one nonfunctioning kidney that required nephrectomy.

In conclusion, Mauclaire's operation is an excellent procedure and the operation of choice, particularly in patients with a poor short-term prognosis. Furthermore, it is unquestionably indicated in patients presenting with dilated ureters or nonfunctioning kidneys. Indications or contraindications may exist, particularly in young patients, on account of the inconvenience of the iliac colostomy. Do not forget however, the typical patients have severe malignant neoplasms; the postoperative period should be short, simple, and uncomplicated. Since these patients' life span is often short, it should be as comfortable as possible and not burdened by unpleasant, severe, and at times dangerous complications.

REFERENCES

1. Barnes RW, Hill MR, Hill JT: Urinary diversion through an isolated rectal bladder with intrasphinteric (anal) colostomy. Dis Colon Rect pp. 485

2. Belt E: Radical perineal prostatectomy in early carcinoma of the prostate. J Urol 48:287, 1942

3. Bisgard JD: Substitution of the urinary bladder with assegment of sigmoid. Ann Surg 117:106, 1943

4. Bracci U: Considerazioni, orientamenti, indicazioni nell'imiego dell'intestino per la sostituzione della vescica. Chir Urol 1:5, 1959

5. Bracci U: L'impiego delle neovescie intestinali dopo cistectomia per indicazioni chirurgiche varie. Boll Soc Toscoumbra Chir 20 (Suppl) 1:911, 1959

6. Bracci U: La vescica rettale. Urologia 19:402, 1962

7. Bracci U: Néovessie rectale. J Urol Nephrol 70:427, 1964

8. Bracci U: I nostri orientamenti nella terapia chirurgica del can cor della vescica. Atti Soc Inter Urol Londra 11:166, 1964

9. Bracci U, Constantini A: II trattamento dei tumori maligni dell'uretra femminile. Chir Urol Fasc 1:27, 1959

10. Bracci U, Constantini A: Sul trattamento chirurgico dei tumo ri maligni dell'uretra femminile. Boll Mem Soc Toscoumbra Chir 20:932, 1959

11. Bracci U, Furbetta A: Considerations on surgical therapy in female urethral tumors. Licentia Medica 4: 1979

12. Bracci U, Giuliani L, Costantini A, et al: La terapia chirurgica del cancro della prostata. Relaz 34 Congr Soc Ital Urol, Roma, 1961

13. Bracci U, Laurenti C, Di Silverio F: On the surgical management of exstrophic bladder: Proceedings of the XX Biennal World Congress of the International College of Surgeons, Vol 1, 1976

14. Bracci U, Tacciuoli M, Giacobini S, et al: Studio urodinamico delle vesciche rettali. Società Italiana di Uro logia, Settembre 1979

15. Bracci U, Tacciuoli M, Lotti T: Rectal bladder, indications, contraindications and advantages. Eur Urol 5:100, 1979

16. Bricker EM, Butcher H, McAfee CA: Late results of bladder substitution with isolated ileal segments. Surg Gynecol Obstet 99:469, 1954

17. Couvelaire R: De la cystectomie totale chez l'homme. J Urol 57:408, 1951

18. Delev N: Substitute bladder made of sigmoid colon. J Urol 79:828, 1958

19. Dorsey JD, Barnes RW: Urinary diversion through an isolated rectal segment. J Urol 85:569, 1961

20. Duhamel B: Exsclusion du rectum avec abaissement rétro-rectal et transanal du côlon. Application et résultats d'une technique nouvelle. Mem Acad Chir 85:192, 1959

21. Giuliani L, Pisani E: Rilievi cistografi e cistomanometrici nelle vesciche intestinali. Chir Urol 1:128, 1959

22. Glodstein AE, Rubin SW, Sachs L, et al: Formation of an artificial urinary bladder in the human: report of 2 cases. Bull. School Med. Maryland 38:2, 1953

23. Levitskj V: Transplantation of ureters into isolated ampulla of the rectum after total cystectomy. Am J Surg 85:91, 1953

24. Lowsley OS, Johnson TH: New Operation for creation of artificial bladder with voluntary control of urine and feces. J Urol 73:83, 1955

25. Nédelec M, Auvigné G, Bouvet M, et al: La neovessie rectale, indications et résultats. Méme Acad Chir 87:921, 1961

26. Nedelec M: La continenza nelle derivazioni urinarie. Min Med 55:829, 1964

27. Nédelec M: La néo-vessie rectale, indications et résultats. Comunic. au congress international d'urologie de Londres, Septembre 1964

28. Nédelec M: La néo-vessie rectale. J Chir 90:281, 1965

29. Schmiedt E: Dunndarm oder dick darm blasen plastik. Urologie 1:155, 1962

30. Tizzoni G, Poggi A: Die wiederherstellung der harnblase. Zentralbl Chir 15:921, 1888

31. Ulm AH: Construction of substitute urinary bladder from ileum and colon. Arch Surg 78:122, 1959

ANNOTATED BIBLIOGRAPHY

Bracci U, Tacciuoli M, Lotti T: Rectal bladder: Indications, contraindications and advantages. Eur Urol 5:100, 1979

An experience with more than 700 patients submitted to rectal bladder over the last 20 yr is reported. The main indications were total cystectomy due to bladder neoplasia and palliative surgery in patients in whom cystectomy was impossible. The rectal bladder, even of the Mauclaire type, is the most useful and best-accepted urinary diversion. Separation of urine from feces avoids serious ascending infections and involvement of renal function. These observations are supported by the long survival of those patients who underwent surgery for nonneoplastic disease.

Ghoneim MA: The rectosigmoid bladder for urinary diversion. Br J Urol 42:49, 1970

Sixty-four patients with carcinoma of the bladder underwent cystectomy with rectal bladder according to Mauclaire. In 40 cases of ureterorectal anastomosis an end-to-end mucosa-to-mucosa anastomosis was performed, while in the others an end-to-side type was used. Stenting was not necessary, but a rectal tube was left in for 10 to 12 days. The mortality is reported at 17.1% (11 of 64 patients). In 17 patients there were 28 postoperative complications (8 urinary fistulae). Manometric studies of the new rectal baldder revealed an emptying pressure of approximately 70 cm of water, for less than that of normal bladder (150 cm of water) or of the rectum during defecation (180 cm of water). Urinary continence was excellent. The author recommends the method and reports that good results can be obtained with it.

Bracci U, Furbetta A: Carcinoma of the female urethra: Surgical techniques. Recenti Med 18, 1979

Two women with urethral tumor observed at 10 yr follow-up examination, are described. Both patients had undergone surgery for urethral tumor invading the vaginal wall. In one patient, cystectomy, hysterectomy and accessory gland removal, and pelvic lymph-adenectomy and associated urethrectomy had been performed, as had resection of the anterior part and the lateral vaginal wall. During surgery a rectal bladder, according to Mauclaire, was constructed. The other patient had undergone hysterectomy and removal of accessory glands with pelvic lymphadenectomy, colpectomy, and removal of the urethra and bladder neck. The latter was sutured and closed on the distal part of the trigone. A suprapubic cystostomy tube was left in the bladder. At 10-yr follow-up examination, both patients were alive and did not have recurrence of metastasis. In fact, they can be considered to be cured.

Nevertheless, while the first patient could resume normal sexual relations, the second patient no longer has a vagina. As far as urinary function is concerned, micturition in the first patient is within normal limits, with urinary frequency four or five times per day and a maximum of one time a night with no nocturnal incontinence. In the second patient, the bladder capacity is reduced to about 120 ml to 140 ml and voiding is necessary every 2 hr. Urinary frequency and dysuria are present. Additionally, the need to replace the suprapubic cystostomy every month has caused the patient some difficulty. The upper urinary tract remains normal with no dilatation or functional changes.

In conclusion, the authors point out that following radical extirpative surgery for urethral tumors invading the vagina, it appears preferable to perform a rectal bladder and colostomy (Mauclaire procedure) in patients in whom it is impossible to perform a Heitz-Boyer–Hovelaque procedure (a rectal bladder with intrasphincteric sigmoid colostomy in a retrorectal position), which should be considered the procedure of choice. In fact, the rectal bladder with colostomy (Mauclaire procedure) should be considered an excellent procedure and preferable to attempting preservation of a normal bladder function, requiring suprapubic cystostomy, because it is better tolerated and permits normal sexual relations in young women.

58

URINARY DIVERSION: URETEROSIGMOIDOSTOMY WITH CONTINENT PRE-ANAL COLOSTOMY

George L. Garske, Lloyd A. Sherman, Joseph E. Twidwell and Robert J. Tenner

431 Marquette Bank Building, Minneapolis 2, Minn.
Current Address
Suite 210 Downtown Professional Building, 822 Marquette Avenue, Minneapolis, Minn 55402

Reprinted from *Journal of Urology*, Vol. 84, pp. 322–333, 1960. Copyright 1960 by The Williams & Wilkins Company, Baltimore.

Diversion of the urinary stream is a palliative or corrective necessity in many clinical conditions. Generally, it is a surgical problem based on many factors, leaving much to be desired in the end result, no matter what procedure is used to divert the urinary stream. Three essential conditions must be satisfied to make urinary diversion an ideal operative procedure: (1) correction of the primary pathological problem or disease, (2) preservation of normal renal function (if present prior to surgery) and (3) continence of the urinary and fecal stream.

Many procedures have been devised since attempts at such surgery first began to satisfy all three conditions, and all have met with inconstant success.

Search for a substitute for the urinary bladder is

centered largely around the use of various portions of the bowel as reservoirs and conduits. Many years of experience involving experimental and clinical trial and error have demonstrated the real difficulties of providing a functional reservoir, and have elicited the factors responsible for dysfunction of the substitutes. Obstruction to urine flow, renal infection, and absorption of urinary constituents (hyperchloremic acidosis) are the main problems. A true substitute for the bladder should protect the kidneys from infection, prevent interference with body fluid and electrolyte balance, permit intermittent evacuation of urine at reasonable intervals under voluntary control (and without the use of catheters or appliances) compatible with a normal social and physiologic existence.

An ideal ureterointestinal anastomosis must be based on the following principles: (1) diversion of the fecal

Read at annual meeting of North Central Section of American Urological Association, Inc., Chicago, Ill., October 7–10, 1959.

stream from the bowel reservoir to prevent ascending infection; (2) elimination of obstruction at the site of anastomosis by a transplantation technique by the direct method; (3) the bowel reservoir receiving the diverted urine should not be too large; (4) the bowel reservoir should be either empty continuously or be emptied frequently, preferably by physiologic rather than mechanical means.

Proximal colostomy and implantation of the ureters into an excluded rectosigmoid pouch, or transplantation of the ureters into an isolated ileal segment or sigmoid loop appear to be the technique with the potential to satisfy these criteria.

Acceptance of colostomy by surgeon and patient alike following radical operations on the rectum is well known. Colostomy should also be accepted as the means of avoiding many of the complications of ureterointestinal anastomosis. One is faced with two alternatives. A patient will have to choose between urinary incontinence from a stoma in the abdominal wall, collecting the urine by catheter or bag, or a colostomy which must be irrigated once a day. Even though feces are more repugnant to the patient than urine, with proper care a colostomy does provide a minimum of discomfort. We are not prepared to decide which arrangement will prove more acceptable and successful clinically, but the rectal bladder with sigmoidostomy offers a more physiological and practical substitute for the normal urinary bladder.

The thinking with regard to an answer which might completely encompass and perhaps solve the problems of ureterointestinal anastomosis lies in the Gersuny operation, diversion of the urine to the isolated rectosigmoid with diversion of the fecal stream to the perineum avoiding abdominal colostomy.[1]

Hinman and Weyrauch[2] in their review of ureterointestinal implantation described Gersuny's original procedure. Using the completely isolated rectum as a urinary reservoir, Gersuny in 1898 devised an operation intended to maintain fecal as well as urinary continence. He first isolated the rectum and implanted the vesical trigone into the divided rectal lumen after Maydl's method.[3] The proximal sigmoid was then drawn through an opening made along the anterior margin of the anus and anchored within the anal sphincter so that this muscle could actively control both the newly-formed bladder and the sigmoid which served as the new rectum.

It was not revived until Lowsley and T. H. Johnson[4-6] reported a case of a 59-year-old man with carcinoma of the urinary bladder upon whom a modified Gersuny type procedure was performed.

In essence, the scheme of the Gersuny-Lowsley-Johnson operation is: (1) anastomosis of the ureters to the isolated rectum through an abdominal incision, (2) dissection of the sigmoid mesentery to liberate and lengthen the sigmoid, (3) through a perineal incision immediately anterior to the anus, a plane of dissection is carried under the external sphincter ani muscle to the rectovesical pouch, (4) the liberated sigmoid is drawn under the external sphincter ani muscle and out the perineum. The final result is two perineal openings—separate but adjacent: the anus of urinary outlet immediately posterior to the perineal sigmoid stoma or new rectum, both orifices encircled by and under the voluntary control of the external sphincter muscle.

The advantages of the technique are: (1) a separate orifice for the urinary stream with voluntary control, (2) a separate orifice for the fecal stream with voluntary control and sensation, (3) possibility of avoiding regurgitation or reflux of urine to the upper urinary tracts, (4) avoiding absorption of metabolites on the basis of the use of the most unresorptive portion of the intestine, (5) avoidance of an abdominal orifice and collecting appliances, (6) a bladder which could be subject to endoscopic examination if necessary.

The Gersuny-Lowsley-Johnson operation potentially will meet the three conditions for an ideal urinary diversion: (1) control of the primary pathological process, (2) preservation of normal renal function, (3) continence of feces and urine, providing the patient with two ''natural'' orifices that do not require collection appliances. Physiologically, approximately a normal voiding pattern with control and holding of the urinary stream is possible and the same situation can conceivably exist with regard to the fecal stream, with a normal filling sensation and emptying reflex.

A modification of the Gersuny-Lowsley-Johnson procedure as used by us in 2 cases of carcinoma of the bladder is reported here.

SURGICAL TECHNIQUE

1. Preoperative Preparation. After a diagnosis of carcinoma of the bladder is made and confirmed by transurethral biopsy of the lesion, and bimanual palpation under anesthesia of the area of the lesion has been done at time of cystoscopy and its fixation or nonfixation determined, a proctoscopic examination and air contrast study of the colon are made. If an excretory urographic series has not been done prior to cystoscopy and biopsy, this is also in order. A survey of the chemical pattern of the serum is obtained (blood urea nitrogen, creatinine, urea clearance, chlorides, sodium, potassium, carbon dioxide combining power and uric acid). A chest film to search for metastasis is made.

Three days prior to surgery, the patient is placed on a low residue diet and the day prior to surgery, bowel sterilization (Poth[7]) is started as follows: At 12:00 noon the day before surgery, 60 cc castor oil, 1.0 gm neomycin with 250,000 units of nystatin and 1.5 gm of phthalylsulfathiazole are prescribed; at 1:00 p.m., 2:00 p.m., and 3:00 p.m., 1.0 gm neomycin with 250,000 units of nystatin and 1.5 gm phthalylsulfathiazole. These medications are prescribed in the same amounts at 4-hour intervals thereafter until the time of surgery, excluding the 4-hour period prior to surgery, in order that the upper gastrointestinal tract may be empty and avoid any danger of vomiting during anesthesia. One hour before surgery, a rectal catheter is placed and 1 quart of 1 percent neomycin is instilled and the indwelling rectal catheter clamped until the time of surgery.

2. Anesthesia. Pentothal sodium with curare is administered intravenously with supplemental nitrous oxide and oxygen via an intratracheal tube.

3. Technique. The technique of the procedure is divided into (a) urologic procedures and (b) the proctologic procedures, the latter consisting of three parts: the abdominal field, perineal field in the first stage, and the revision operation seven to eight days after the first stage operation.

Urologic surgery, first step: Routine urethrocystoscopic examination is first made to determine the status of the urinary bladder as compared with the previous studies, and areas of the biopsy are inspected. The bladder is thoroughly irrigated with a 1:5000 solution of aqueous zepherin solution and size 5 French catheters passed, if possible, to both renal pelves and left indwelling.

These catheters are splinted by an indwelling size 16 French 5 cc Foley bag catheter and again the bladder thoroughly irrigated with 1:5000 aqueous zephirin solution. The urethral catheter is connected to an irrigating unit with the flask of the unit filled with 1:5000 aqueous zephirin solution so the bladder may be filled with fluid if required during the procedure.

The patient is placed supine in low lithotomy position with well-padded knee crutches elevated 10 to 12 inches from the level of the table. All catheters and the patient are prepared with an antiseptic solution. The Trendelenburg position with a sand bag under the hips increases the exposure of the pelvic fossa. A midline incision is made from the symphysis to the mid-hypogastric area circumscribing and removing the navel.

The prevesical and preperitoneal areas are explored and the peritoneum is not opened unless necessary prior to cystectomy.

The ureters are identified and divided including the indwelling catheters within the lumen. The indwelling catheters are removed and size 6 French polyvinyl catheters are inserted and secured by a single suture of size 000 chromic catgut placed at the distal end of the ureter. The catheters are placed to drip outside the operative field. A prostatoseminal vesiculocystectomy is then carried out in the usual manners.

All fatty tissue and lymph nodes in the area are dissected free and stripped down to the great vessels and the anterior surface of the rectum.

After hemostasis has been secured in the entire area, the peritoneum is next opened and the abdominal contents carefully palpated and inspected, in search for metastasis.

Proctologic surgery, first step: The proctologist's contribution to this operation commences with the division of the rectosigmoid at its junction between two large Kocher clamps. The perirectal and pericolic fat is removed from the serosa of both segments of bowel particularly the rectal stump, in preparation for its closure.

Urologic surgery, second step: An open ureteroproctostomy is performed under direct vision. After thoroughly cleansing and irrigating the new urinary bladder with 1 percent neomycin solution, points at which both ureters easily reach the rectum are located and a small longitudinal incision, the size of the ureter, is made through the rectal wall on the posterolateral aspect so that the ureter lies in the sacral curve. Each ureter is transplanted by grasping the previously placed fixation suture and the indwelling ureteral catheter and drawing both into the rectal lumen. The catheter is next passed downward toward the anus through a previously placed rectal tube. The mucosa-to-mucosa approximation of the ureter to rectum is carried out over the catheter with size 000 atraumatic chromic catgut. The ease with which this can be accomplished is amazing because of the widely exposed operative area, but nevertheless it should be done cautiously and precisely. Three or four sutures are placed in the adventitia of each ureter and the adjacent rectum, being careful not to angulate the ureter.

Proctologic surgery, second step: The proximal rectum is closed by approximating the mucosa with an inverting Connell size 00 chromic suture, then Halsted size 3 silk sutures are used to approximate the seromuscular layer, avoiding the mucosal layer.

The sigmoid colon is next mobilized, in preparation for a perineal "pull-through" procedure by incising the lateral peritoneal reflexion up to the splenic flexure. The inferior mesenteric artery and vein are doubly clamped, transected and ligated, just distal to the origin of the left colic artery and vein. This in most cases should provide sufficient mobility, granting a semiredundant sigmoid colon is present, to exteriorize the distal sigmoid colon well beyond the perineum. Particular care is taken to provide adequate vascularity by preserving the marginal artery of Drummond in this procedure. No undue traction should be placed upon the bowel as it is prepared for the new perineal anus.

Perineal phase 1: At this point, the patient, already in stirrups, is elevated to full lithotomy position and the perineal operator makes a semilunar incision along the anterior and anterolateral margins of the external anal sphincter (Fig. 1A). Care is taken to preserve a skin island approximately 3 to 4 cm in width between the former anus and the new anterior anal canal. The tissues of the perineum are carefully spread with a hemostat until the prostatic bed is encountered. Further dissection should be accomplished by blunt finger method. The entire external anal sphincter is exposed around its external periphery to its lateral margins.

The anal sphincter is carefully but forcibly dilated to admit at least three fingers. At this point we consider the division of the external anal sphincter to be an important contribution to the original operation, as proposed by Johnson. The external anal sphincter is divided so the proximal one-half of the sphincter continues to encircle the former anus which is now the outlet of the new urinary bladder. The distal or caudal one-half of the sphincter, that is, the anterior and lateral portion, is carefully and slowly dilated so that it will surround the ''pull-through'' colon which is soon to be introduced into the aperture. Next a large Carmalt hemostat is introduced through the prostatic bed and the abdominal operator introduces the distal sigmoid colon to this clamp. The bowel is carefully threaded through the perineum and through the divided caudal one-half of the external anal sphincter (Fig. 1B). This is perhaps the most important part of the perineal dissection. It must be performed slowly and with considerable caution.

If the colon is surrounded by considerable pericolic fat sufficient to produce marked tension upon the anal sphincter, longitudinal division of the sphincter in its anterior portion must be considered (Fig. 1C). The cut ends of sphincter can be marked with long silk sutures for future recovery. If the tension is great, immediate postoperative strangulation will result. Approximately 6 to 8 cm of ''pull-through'' bowel is exteriorized to compensate and allow for subsequent retraction. A large mushroom catheter is inserted in the ''pull-through'' bowel and secured by a Daniel clamp. A vaseline gauze dressing is applied around the ''pulled-through'' bowel. A sterile rubber glove is placed over the Daniel clamp including the rectal tube in the new rectum. The abdominal wound is then closed by the abdominal operator, establishing drainage from the space of Retzius with no attempt being made to peritonealize the pelvic floor. The ureteral catheters are secured to the perineal skin just distal to their exit from the rectal catheter in the new bladder. Both ureteral catheters and the catheter in the new bladder are connected with a sterile plastic tubing to a urinary drainage bottle (Fig. 1D).

4. Postoperative Care (Early). The patient should be weighed daily. Fluid and electrolyte balance is maintained by daily intravenous fluids based on daily serum chemical pattern determinations. Nasal suction is utilized until bowel activity returns to normal function. Supplementary parenteral vitamins and antibiotics are a must. Careful fluid intake, and output of ureteral and new bladder catheters must be carefully recorded. Ambulation should begin as soon as possible. After the suction has been removed a soft, low salt diet is ordered and parenteral medications are discontinued in favor of the oral route. The ureteral catheters are removed on the seventh day and the bladder catheter is left in place.

5. Protologic Surgery, Perineal Phase 2 (Excision of the Redundant Bowel: Revision Operation). Approximately seven to eight days postoperatively, with spinal anesthesia, the redundant bowel is excised over a Payr clamp. Particular care must be made to free the bowel from the surrounding perineal tissues, and the Payr clamp must be placed at a level corresponding to the cephalad portion of the divided anal sphincter. In case the sphincter muscle has been divided to avoid strangulation of the ''pulled-through'' bowel, it can be reconstructed at this stage of the procedure. Care at this point will ensure against subsequent mucosal prolapse and a bothersome ''wet anus'' due to mucosa extending beyond the anterior portion of the anal sphincter. Next, three or four flaps of perineal skin are developed by undercutting; these are sutured with interrupted 00 chromic catgut sutures to the mucosa and muscularis of the recently excised bowel (Fig. 2A). This is done much as the standard anoplasty for mucosal prolapse of the rectum. Upon its completion, a vaseline gauze dressing is applied.

Postoperatively, hot saline packs are applied to the anal area for several days. As soon as the anal edema has subsided, the patient is instructed in the use of sphincter exercises. The new bladder catheter is removed on the ninth postoperative day (Fig. 2B).

6. Future Followup. The patient is discharged with (1) a low salt diet, (2) antibiotic or chemotherapeutic agent specific for organism found on culture and sensitivity studies of the urine from the new bladder, (3) residual urine is checked at each office visit and the residual is examined microscopically and also cultured; the culture is plated and sensitivity studies run to determine medication of choice, (4) instructions for sphincteric exercises

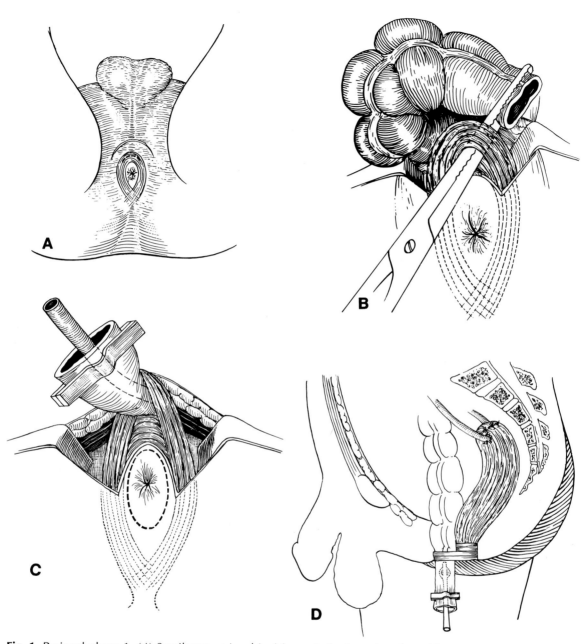

Fig. 1. Perineal phase 1. (*A*) Semilunar perineal incision anterior to rectum for sphincter mobilization. (*B*) Sigmoid colon perianal "pull-through" through caudal half of external anal sphincter. (*C*) Sphincter division with sigmoid colon "pull-through" with Daniel clamp 7 to 8 cm from sphincter securing mushroom catheter in place. (*D*) Sagittal section to diagrammatically show completed first stage and emphasize treatment of external anal sphincter muscle.

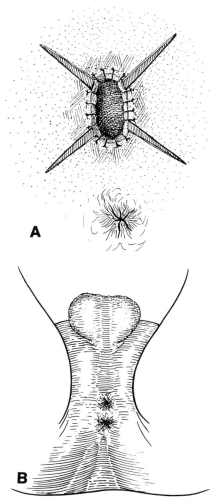

Fig. 2. Perineal phase 2. (*A*) Redundant bowel amputated and sutured to undercut skin flaps to obviate mucosal prolapse. (*B*) Final result.

are given, (5) rectal irrigations daily and/or bulk type laxative as indicated by the bowel movement consistency and pattern.

Serum chemical patterns are done monthly. Excretory urograms are done at 3, 6, 9, and 12 months for the first postoperative year and then as indicated thereafter. A cystoscopic (rectoscopic) examination with chromorectoscopy (indigo carmine intravenously) and retrograde rectograms for reflux are done 3 months postoperatively.

Dextro amphetamine sulfate and decrease in oral fluid intake in the late afternoon will control nocturnal enuresis.

REPORT OF CASES

Case 1. B. R. L. J., aged 36, was admitted February 11, 1958, with a history of sudden onset, 1 week prior to admission, of gross total, painless hematuria with the passage of one large blood clot. The patient had had an episode of ''flu'' and he attributed the urinary bleeding to reaction from an acute infectious process. He noted a similar episode 2 months prior to admission.

Physical examination revealed no definite abnormalities. The prostate was found to be symmetrical and of normal size, shape and consistency without tenderness or induration and no supraprostatic abnormality was noted. The remainder of the rectal examination was normal.

The hemogram was normal. The urine was grossly bloody with a pH of 5.5, specific gravity 1.032, albumin 2 plus, negative for sugar and acetone, and packed fields of red blood cells. The urine culture was negative.

The admission chest film was normal. An excretory urographic series on February 11, 1958, showed no abnormalities on the preliminary film, and the excretion rate of the contrast material was normal bilaterally with no abnormalities noted in either kidney or ureter. Three irregular, overlapping, filling defects, two to three centimeters in diameter, were noted in the right hemisphere of the urinary bladder and the outline of a Foley bag catheter could be seen deflected to the left of the midline (Fig. 3A).

Cystoscopic examination on February 13, 1958 found the bladder filled with grossly bloody urine and several small clots. Situated over and obscuring the right ureteral orifice was a soft, friable, pipillary tumor 1.5 cm in diameter and implanted on a broad base beyond the orifice and extending up the lateral wall of the bladder to the region of the vesical neck. Two similar tumors measuring 1.5 cm in diameter and implanted on broad bases were noted on the roof of the bladder neck. The left ureteral orifice was normal. Two papillary tumors each 3 mm in diameter were seen just beyond the left ureteral orifice. Bimanual examination revealed no evidence of fixation or extension through the bladder wall in any of the areas described. Transurethral resection of the tumors well into the detrusor muscle and beyond the edges of the bases was done.

Microscopic section showed a papillary transitional cell carcinoma of the urinary bladder, grade 2.

The patient's good general physical condition and his age were considered, and coupled with a review of the pathological studies, it was decided that a radical cystectomy with urinary diversion was the procedure of choice. The patient did not wish to have a fecal or urinary orifice on the abdominal wall, and a Gersuny type operation was suggested and accepted.

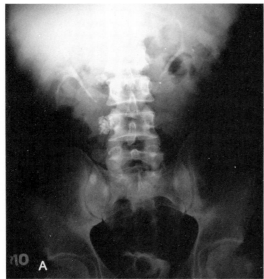

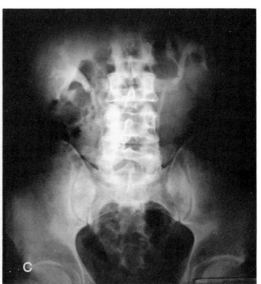

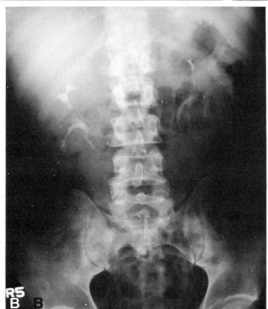

Fig. 3. Case 1. (*A*) Ten minute film of preoperative excretory urographic series, February 11, 1958, shows normal upper urinary tracts and multiple filling defects in urinary bladder produced by tumor, and filling defect of indwelling Foley bag catheter. (*B*) Five minute film of exccretory urographic series fifteenth postoperative day shows normal upper urinary tracts. (*C*) Five minute film of excretory urographic series 2 months postoperatively shows well filled, well outlined normal upper urinary tracts.

The preoperative serum electrolyte pattern was normal. Proctoscopic study and air contrast colon studies were normal.

On February 25, 1958, a prostatoseminal vesiculocystectomy with a Gersuny type disposition of the ureters and colon, as modified by us, was accomplished. The second stage revision operation was done on the ninth postoperative day. The ureteral catheters were removed on the seventh postoperative day and the rectal bladder

catheter was removed on the tenth postoperative day. Diurnal urinary control was excellent. The patient noted sensation of filling in the rectal bladder with an urge to urinate at approximately one hour intervals during the day and every two hours at night. On the fourteenth postoperative day the patient was catheterized for residual urine and approximately 140 cc obtained. An excretory urographic series was done on the fifteenth postoperative day and showed normal upper urinary tracts (Fig. 3*B*). The patient had some difficulty in controlling the fecal stream initially because of diarrhea, but when this was controlled and at the time of his discharge on the twentieth postoperative day, he noticed a normal sensation of filling of the rectum and was able to empty a part of the rectal contents with defecation effort and the remainder by a small tap water enema. Serum patterns of electrolytes determined on the second, eleventh, and nineteenth postoperative days were normal.

The patient was seen on the twenty-seventh postoperative day and stated that the fecal stream control was satisfactory and that the urinary stream control was not as satisfactory as at the time of discharge in that he noted occasional nocturnal enuresis. Residual urine was

45 cc. Moderate leukocyturia was present. Tidal volumes of each voiding were within the normal range, and the pattern of voiding throughout the 24 hour period was similar to that prior to surgery.

Excretory urography on April 24, 1958 showed excellent bilateral function. No evidence of stasis or dilatation of the ureters, pelves, or renal calyces was present and the study was interpreted as normal (Fig. 3C).

On July 6, 1958, an excretory urographic series showed no change from the study done in April 1958. The serum electrolyte pattern was normal. The urinalysis showed 8 to 10 white blood cells per high power field. Examination of the rectal pouch with a size 21F Brown-Buerger cystoscope revealed a normal anal orifice with normal sphincteric control. There was a tortuosity in the lower third of the rectum or new bladder consistent with the usual contour of the rectum. The rectal folds were normal except for minimal hyperemia. The urine itself was grossly clear with some excess mucus within the deep portions of the mucosal folds. The capacity of the new pouch was approximately 10 ounces (Fig. 4A). On either side of the proximal middle lateral wall of the rectum could be seen two elliptical ureteral orifices from which clear urine appeared at regular intervals. Chromocystoscopy with indigo carmine showed vigorous jets of the dye-stained urine from these orifices. A rectogram made after instilling 10 ounces 15 per cent skodan failed to show any evidence of reflux to the upper tracts on initial filling and after defecation effort (Fig. 4B). The serum electrolyte pattern was normal. Subsequent serum chemical patterns on October 10, 1958 and January 18, April 10 and July 7, 1959 were within normal range. Excretory urographic series, rectoscopy, retrograde rectograms and urinalyses showed no change on January 18 and July 7, 1959 when compared with the previous studies. The voiding pattern, tidal volume, capacity and residual urine also showed no change. The patient has excellent control of both the urinary and fecal streams and has returned to his work.

Case 2. J. P., aged 44, was admitted to the hospital on May 16, 1957, with the complaint of coffee colored urine noted intermittently for 3 days, 2 weeks prior to admission. Two similar episodes 6 months and 1 month prior to admission were also noted. Complete review by systems was negative. Physical examination revealed no abnormalities other than bilateral varicosities of the long saphenous veins, with moderate stasis pigmentation over the anterior aspect of the left lower leg. The prostate was found to be symmetrical and of normal size, shape and consistency and without tenderness or induration, and no supraprostatic abnormality was found. The remainder of the rectal examination was normal.

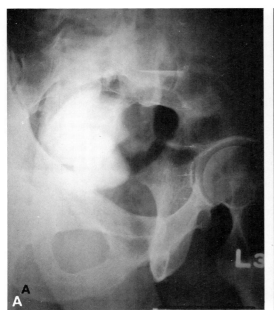
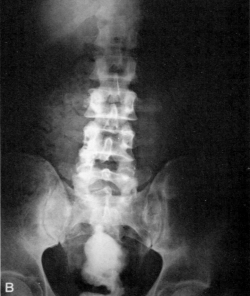

Fig. 4. Case 1. (A) Left oblique cystogram shows rectosigmoid bladder 5 months postoperatively. (B) Retrograde rectogram 5 months postoperatively shows configuration of rectosigmoid bladder and no evidence of reflux to upper urinary tracts.

The hemogram was normal. The urine was grossly clear amber with a pH of 5.5, specific gravity 1.018, 1 plus albumin, negative sugar and acetone, and 25 to 30 leukocytes and 25 to 30 erythrocytes per high power field. The urine culture was negative.

The admission chest film was normal. An excretory urographic series on May 16, 1957, showed no abnormalities on the preliminary film; the excretion rate of the contrast material was normal on both sides with no abnormalities noted in either kidney or ureter. Two filling defects, each approximately 2 cm in diameter, were noted in the urinary bladder, one situated in the left inferior lateral aspect and the second in the left lateral aspect of the bladder (Fig. 5A).

Cystoscopic examination on May 17, 1957 revealed a normal urethra. The bladder urine was clear amber grossly. There was a considerable amount of edematous reaction close to the vesical outlet, particularly on the left bladder floor. It was difficult to determine whether this was a simple inflammatory reaction secondary to the tumor process or extension of the tumor. Both ureteral orifices were normal. A large papillary, friable tumor mass 3 cm in diameter was implanted on a broad base on the postero-superior portion of the bladder wall to the left of the midline surrounded by a number of dilated tortuous veins. A similar tumor was situated on the left wall of the bladder just beyond the left ureteral orifice extending up the left lateral wall of the bladder. Rectal and bimanual examination did not reveal any evidence of fixation or extension through the bladder wall. Transurethral resection of the tumors into the detrusor muscle and beyond the edges of the bases was done.

Microscopic diagnosis was papillary transitional cell carcinoma of the bladder, grade 2.

On September 6, 1957, another cystoscopic study revealed a 2 by 4 by 4 mm nodule of tissue resembling papillary carcinoma near the left ureteral orifice. The scar from the previous transurethral resection could be seen and no recurrence was noted. One area 3 mm in diameter was present in the scar of the left lateral wall of the bladder which was suspicious of recurrent tumor. The areas were resected and microscopic study revealed transitional cell carcinoma, grade 2, similar in all respects to the sections from the first procedure.

Another cystoscopic study on December 6, 1957 revealed a 4 mm papillary tumor lateral to and beyond the right ureteral orifice which was resected and on microscopic study showed a papillary transitional cell carcinoma, grade 1.

On March 16, 1958, another cystoscopic study revealed several new and recurrent papillary carcinomas which were resected transurethrally. Nodules were submitted separately for examination and microscopic study

of the tissues revealed transitional cell carcinoma grade 2 identical with the tissue obtained at the first and second resection. The bladder on bimanual palpation at this time showed no evidence of induration or suggestion of fixation to any of the surrounding structures or to the lateral pelvic walls.

The rapidity with which recurrences and new tumors of the urinary bladder developed suggested that transurethral resection and fulguration were not sufficient to provide control of the process. Our inability to cope with the recurrence of tumors by transurethral means warranted a radical cystectomy with urinary diversion. The patient did not wish to have a fecal or urinary orifice on the abdominal wall and a Gersuny type operation was suggested and accepted.

The preoperative hemogram was normal in all respects. The chest film was normal. A protoscopic study and air contrast colon studies were normal. The serum chemical pattern was normal.

On March 26, 1958, a prostatoseminal vesiculocystectomy with a Gersuny type disposition of the ureters and colon, as modified by us, was accomplished.

The revision operation was done on the seventh postoperative day. Ureteral and rectal bladder catheters were removed on the tenth postoperative day. Diurnal control was excellent, but the patient was enuretic 2 by (sic) 3 times each night. On the twelfth postoperative day he was catheterized for residual urine and approximately 80 cc urine obtained. An excretory urographic series on the twelfth postoperative day showed a moderate dilatation of the right upper urinary tract and a normal left upper urinary tract (Fig. 5B). The patient had some difficulty initially in controlling the fecal stream, but it gradually improved and was complete on discharge, the twenty-fifth postoperative day. Serum patterns of the electrolytes were done on the second, fifth, tenth and twentieth postoperative days and except for a minimal increase in the blood urea nitrogen on the fifth postoperative day, the remainder of the serum pattern was normal.

The patient was seen on the thirtieth postoperative day and stated that the fecal stream control was only fair and the sensation of rectal fulness was not so complete as noted while hospitalized. The urinary stream was in complete control during the day with an occasional episode of nocturnal enuresis, well controlled with dextroamphetamine sulfate. The tidal volumes of each voiding were within normal range. The 24 hour voiding pattern was similar to that prior to surgery. Residual urine was 15 cc with mild leukocyturia; the urine culture was sterile.

On the fifty-sixth postoperative day, the serum electrolyte pattern was normal. The voiding pattern was normal and the bowel control was much improved, with

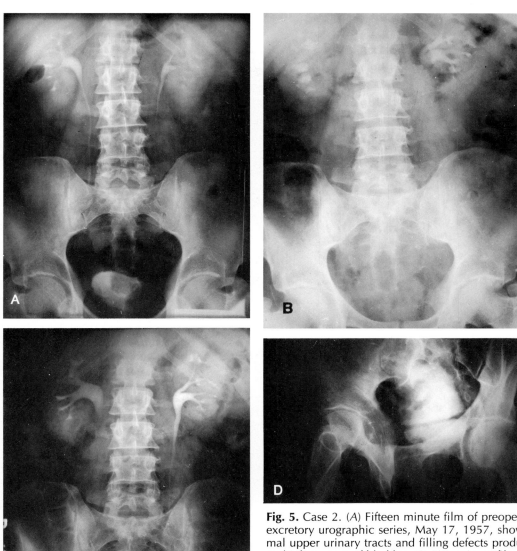

Fig. 5. Case 2. (*A*) Fifteen minute film of preoperative excretory urographic series, May 17, 1957, shows normal upper urinary tracts and filling defects produced by multiple tumors of bladder. (*B*) Five minute film of excretory urographic series twelfth postoperative day shows normal left upper urinary tract and caliectasis and pelviectasis of right kidney. (*B*) Ten minute film of excretory urographic series 66 days postoperatively shows well filled and well outlined upper urinary tracts with some minimal dilatation of right renal pelvis and calyceal systems, and normal left upper urinary tract. (*D*) Right oblique cystogram shows rectosigmoid bladder of sixty-sixth postoperative day.

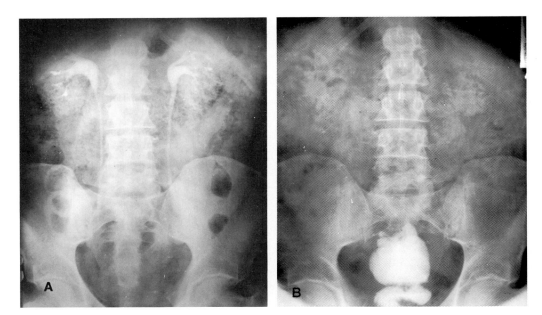

Fig. 6. Case 2. (*A*) Ten minute film of excretory urographic series 5 months postoperatively shows decrease in dilatation of right upper urinary tract. Normal left upper urinary tract showed no change from previous studies. (*B*) Retrograde rectogram 5 months postoperatively shows configuration of rectosigmoid bladder and no evidence of reflux to upper urinary tracts.

intermittent constipation well controlled by daily rectal irrigations.

On May 30, 1958, a serum electrolyte pattern was normal. Excretory urographic series on May 31, 1958, showed no abnormalities on the preliminary film and prompt appearance of the contrast material bilaterally. The left kidney was normal in architecture. Minimal dilatation of the right upper urinary tract was demonstrated (Fig. 5*C* and *D*). Mild leukocyturia was still present. The residual urine was 40 cc and the urine culture was sterile.

On August 28, 1958, the residual urine was 40 cc and 10 to 20 leukocytes were found per high power field. Examination of the rectum with a size 24F McCarthy panendoscope demonstrated minimal hyperemia of the mucosa of the rectum. The pouch capacity was 360 cc. Indigo carmine given intravenously did not demonstrate either orifice clearly but two areas in the proximal lateral folds of the rectal mucosa were visualized from which the dye was seen to appear promptly. An excretory urographic series showed a normal left upper urinary tract and a decrease in dilatation of the right upper urinary tract (Fig. 6*A*). A rectogram made with 300 cc 15 percent skiodan failed to show any evidence of reflux on the initial or defacation effort films (Fig. 6*B*). The serum electrolyte pattern was normal.

Subsequent serum chemical patterns on December 19, 1958, February 4 and June 7, 1959, were within normal ranges. Excretory urographic series, rectoscopy, retrograde rectograms, urinalyses showed no change on February 4 and June 7, 1959, as compared with the studies made in August 1958. The voiding pattern, tidal volumes, capacity and residual urine also showed no change. The patient has returned to his work.

SUMMARY

Three acceptable methods of urinary diversion are available at this time, ileal segment diversion,[8-9] the isolated rectosigmoid with diversion of the fecal stream by abdominal colostomy,[10-12] and the Gersuny-Lowsley-Johnson operation.[13-14] The patient and his physician are faced with the problem of urinary incontinence with stoma in the abdominal wall and collection of the urine by an appliance in the first; the use of a colostomy in the second instance; and in the Gersuny procedure, by a perineal colostomy with voluntary control and the urinary reservoir also with voluntary control with both orifices in a natural anatomical location.

This procedure fulfills the three essential requirements to make urinary diversion an ideal operative procedure: (1) It provides for correction of the primary pathological problem or disease. (2) It provides the mechanism for preservation of normal renal function.[15-16] (3) It provides the patient with continence of the urinary and fecal streams.

Two cases of carcinoma of the urinary bladder treated surgically by the Gersuny-Lowsley-Johnson operation with modification of the proctologic surgical technique are presented. The technique used in the 2 cases as well as the immediate and late postoperative care and course are outlined. The procedure is not intended to supplant common methods of urinary diversion, but its use should be considered particularly when applied to the younger patient requiring vesical exclusion. Advantages over cutaneous ureterostomy, nephrostomy and ureterosigmoidostomy are obvious. Early diagnosis and subsequent early operation by this method of the select patient with carcinoma of the bladder or other surgical condition of the bladder requiring urinary diversion should provide a situation which is economically and socially feasible for comfortable survival.

REFERENCES

1. Gersuny, R. (reported by Foges): Proceedings of K. k. Gesellschaft der Arzte in Wien. Wien Klin Wchnschr, 11:990, 1898; Centralbl f. Chir, 26:497, 1899
2. Hinman, F. and Weyrauch, H. M., Jr.: A clinical study of different principles of surgery which have been used in ureterointestinal implantation. Trans Am A Genito-Urin Surg, 29:15–156, 1936
3. Maydl, K. J.: Ueber die Radikoltherapie der Ectopia Vesicae Urinariae. Wien Med Wchnschr, 44:1169, 1209, 1256, 1297, 1894
4. Lowsley, O.S., Johnson, T. H. and Rueda, A. E.: A new operation for diversion of the urine with voluntary control of feces and urine, preliminary report. J Internat Coll Surg, 20:457, 1953
5. Lowsley, O. S. and Johnson, T. H.: A new operation for creation of an artificial bladder with voluntary control of urine and feces. J Urol, 73:83, 1955
6. Johnson, T. H.: Further experiences with a new operation for urinary diversion. J Urol, 76:380–386, 1956
7. Poth, E. J.: Intestinal antisepsis in surgery. JAMA, 153:1516, 1953
8. Bricker, E.: Substitution for urinary bladder by use of isolated ileal segments. S Clin North Am, 36:1117–1130, 1956
9. Merricks, J. W., Gilchrist, R. K., Hamlin, H. and Rieger, I. T.: Substitute bladder and urethra. J Urol, 65:581–584, 1951
10. Smith, G. I. and Hinman, Frank, Jr.: The rectal bladder, colostomy with ureterosigmoidostomy, experimental and clinical aspects. J Urol, 74:3–354, 1955
11. Kinman, F. M., Sauer, D., Houston, B. T. and Melick, W. F.: Substitution of the excluded rectosigmoid colon for the urinary bladder. AMA Arch Surg, 66:531, 1952
12. Creevy, C. D.: Some observations upon absorption after ureterosigmoidostomy. J Urol, 70:196–202, 1953
13. Kiefer, J. H. and Linke, C.: Ureterorectostomy and pre-anal colostomy for bladder exstrophy. J Urol, 79:242, 1958
14. Stonington, O. G. and Eiseman, B.: Perineal sigmoidostomy in cases of total cystectomy. J Urol, 76:74, 1956
15. Boyce, W. H.: Reabsorption of certain constituents of urine from the large bowel of the experimental animal. J Urol, 65:241, 1951
16. Boyce, W. H. and Best, S. A.: The role of ammonia reabsorption and acid base imbalance following ureterosigmoidostomy. J Urol, 67:169, 1952

Commentary: Ureterosigmoidostomy (Gersuny)

George L. Garske

Since our first report on the modified Gersuny procedure using the technique described in the foregoing article appeared in 1959, only 13 articles in the world literature alluding to, or primarily directed to, this operation have been published.[12-13,15] The operative technique used in the majority of papers is based on that of Lowsley and Johnson.[14] A review of the reports in the English language reveals no significant modification of the original description.

This operation is a useful procedure in the armamentarium for urinary diversion. However, I believe that it should be used only in a selected group of patients. I feel that in the young or middle-aged man who prefers not to have an abdominal urinary collecting appliance and who can accept the perineal neorectum, this could be the procedure of choice. It is essential that there is no anal or rectal pathology that could preclude fecal and urinary control.

Although control of the primary disease process and preservation of renal function are the main concerns of the urologist, the social and economic facets of acceptable alternative methods of urinary diversion must be taken into consideration. The most suitable method of urinary diversion may be any of several methods.[12,13]

The first patient in the foregoing paper, who was operated on on Feb. 27, 1958, was hospitalized for his yearly periodic examination on Dec. 20, 1971. His only complaint, nearly 14 yr after surgery, was that of occasional tenderness of a mild sigmoid mucosal prolapse of the neorectum (Fig. 7). The patient's voiding and defecation pattern was essentially normal. He has normal diurnal and nocturnal urinary and fecal control. However, on rare occasion during heavy sleep, particularly when overly tired, he has fecal soilage. His urinalysis and urine culture have remained normal, as have his complete blood count (CBC) and serum electrolytes. The capacity of the neobladder is 300 ml, and the postevacuation residual is less than 30 ml. Cystoscopic examination of the neobladder clearly reveals the ureteral orifices as elliptic outlets from

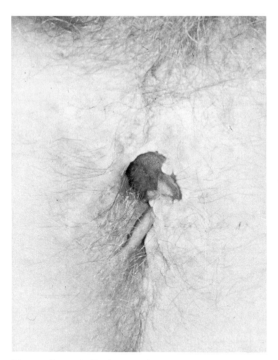

Fig. 7. Case 1. Perineum 14 years postsurgery.

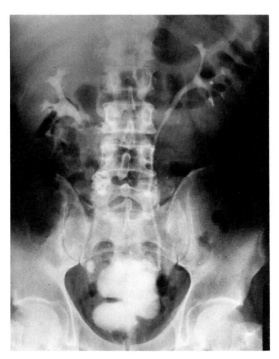

Fig. 9. Case 1. Excretory urographic series 18-minute film, 14 years postsurgery.

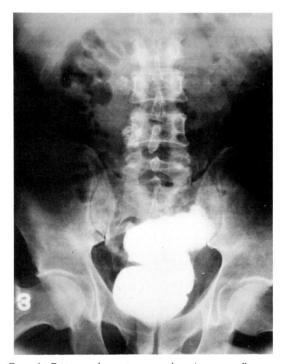

Fig. 8. Case 1. Retrograde rectogram showing no reflux after defecation effort.

which clear urine appears at regular intervals. Intravenous (IV) indigo carmine appears as vigorous jets from these orifices. Retrograde introduction of 300 ml of 40% Skiodan failed to reveal reflux after initial filling or after defecation (Fig. 8). Excretory urographic studies demonstrated bilateral normal upper urinary tracts (Fig. 9).

In summary, the Gersuny procedure provides for correction of the primary pathologic problem. It further provides for preservation of normal renal function and urinary and fecal continence. I believe that the Gersuny procedure should be considered in the young or middle-aged man who finds the other more popular methods of urinary diversion unacceptable.

REFERENCES

1. Garske GL, Sherman LA, Twidwell JE et al: Urinary diversion: Uretero-sigmoidostomy with continent pre-anal colostomy. Minn Med 42:584, 719, 1959

2. Atwill WH, Ensor RD, Secrest AJ et al: The modified Gersuny procedure for urinary diversion. South Med J 63:1377, 1970

3. Ensor RD, Atwill WH, Secrest AJ et al: The modified Gersuny procedure for urinary diversion. J Urol 104:93, 1970

4. Secrest AJ, Ensor RD, Mladick RA et al: Scrotal flap repair of neorectal stenosis following the Gersuny procedure. J Urol 104:557, 1970

5. Hinman F Jr: The technique of the Gersuny operation in vesical exstrophy. J Urol 81:126, 1959

6. Bracci U: The rectal bladder. Urol Int 22:1, 1967

7. Buytendijik FJ, de Vries HR: Results of Gersuny-Lowsley's surgical method in benign and malignant disorders of the urinary bladder. Nederl T Geneesk 107:1250, 1963

8. de Compos Freire JG, de Goes GM: Neo-rectal bladder with anterior intrasphincteric perineal sigmoidostomy. Trans 13th. Congress de la Soc Internat d'Urol 1:175, 1964

9. Socaro AA, Cocchieri G, DiPietrantonio M: Remote results of the Gersuny operation in bladder exstrophy. Policlinico (Chir) 71:222, 1964

10. Rodeck G, van Lessen H: Technique and experience with Gersuny's artificial urinary diversion. Urol Int 23:74, 1968

11. Blandy JP: Methods of urinary diversion and replacement of the bladder. In Riches Modern Trends in Urology. Glasgow, Butterworths, 1970

12. Marchant DJ: Urinary diversion: Historical review. Obstet Gynecol Surv 16:469, 1964

13. McDonald DF: Urinary diversion. Curr Probl Surg Dec. 1968, pp 3–44

14. Lowsley OS, Johnson TH: A new operation for creation of an artificial bladder with voluntary control of urine and feces. J Urol 73:83, 1955

15. Garske GL, Sherman LA, Twidwell JE et al: Urinary diversion: Ureterosigmoidostomy with continent pre-anal colostomy. J Urol 84:322, 1960

ANNOTATED BIBLIOGRAPHY

Atwill WH, Ensor RD, Secrest AJ, South Med J 63:1377, 1380, 1970

The authors experience with eight male patients who underwent the Gersuny procedure following cystectomy for vesical carcinoma is presented. Preoperative evaluation included barium enema, sigmoidoscopy, and the ability to retain a 300-ml enema. Five patients had an uncomplicated postoperative course. Wound dehiscence occurred in two patients. One patient developed necrosis of the perineal colostomy due to excessive exteriorization of the terminal sigmoid colon. This was corrected by interposition of a scrotal skin graft (see reference 2). Mild stomal prolapse occurred in two patients. No patient demonstrated postoperative biochemical or radiographic impairment of renal function, hyperchloremic acidosis, or urinary tract infection. Excellent urinary control was achieved in all patients. Nighttime leakage seldom occurred. The single most common cause of morbidity was fecal incontinence. Some fecal regularity was established after 1 to 3 wk of total incontinence in all except one patient, who required conversion to an abdominal colostomy. The other patients required a pad to prevent fecal soilage of clothing. The authors emphasize that when fecal continence is poor, an abdominal colostomy can be created, which may be easier to manage than a urinary conduit. The authors attribute continence of the rectal bladder to the lack of dissection of the superficial external rectal sphincter muscles. In spite of the relatively short follow-up study, the authors consider their results favorable.

Secrest AJ, Ensor RD, Mladick RA, Urol 104:557, 1970

In one of seven patients who underwent the Gersuny procedure for carcinoma of the lower urinary tract severe stomal stenosis persisted in spite of conservative local measures and subsequent diverting colostomy. An original reconstructive procedure using a scrotal tube flap is described. An excellent result was obtained with fecal and urinary continence after the diverting colostomy was taken down.

Hinman F Jr: The technique of the Gersuny operation in vesical exstrophy. J Urol 81:126, 1959

The Gersuny procedure was used in two patients with vesical exstrophy. The ease of operation due to the wide-open pelvis is

emphasized, and the surgical technique is described and illustrated.

Bracci U: The rectal bladder. Urol Int 22:1, 1967

The author describes a vast experience with the creation of a rectal bladder by the Gersuny method (101 cases), Heitz-Boyer and Hovelacque method (45 cases), and the Mauclaire method (133 cases). (Editor's note: This paper is reproduced in Dr. Bracci's section.)

de Compos Freire JG, de Goes GM: Neo-rectal bladder with anterior intrasphincteric perineal sigmoidostomy. Trans 13th Congress de la Soc Internat d'Urol 1:175, 1964

The authors describe their surgical technique with the Gersuny procedure as performed in 23 cases. The emphasize adequate mobilization of the sigmoid colon, with mobilization of the splenic flexure if necessary; a cruciate perineal incision to receive four triangular flaps of intestine, which they believe reduces the chance of stricture of the perineal stoma; and electrothermometry of the exteriorized perineal intestine to determine if the circulation is adequate in older patients. They believe that the temperature should be 30 degrees or more for good viability of the perineal stump. Metabolic studies were documented in 8 cases. No significant change was noted in the BUN to 4 yr. No significant change was noted in the CO_2 combining power to 1 yr, after which a mild subclinical acidosis occurred. A mild increase in the serum chloride was noted in most patients. There was no significant change in the serum sodium or potassium in the early or late follow-up period. No significant infection occurred in the neorectal bladders. A definite improvement in the radiographic appearance of the kidneys was apparent in the vast majority of patients. No patient showed deterioration of function or morphology. Cystograms demonstrated reflux in most cases that was of no clinical significance. Seven of the eight patients were able to lead a normal social life. They had control of urine and feces during the day even though some leaked gas. When asleep some of them leaked urine. The other patient had slight daytime leakage of urine.

All the above patients had concomitant total cystectomy. The authors conclude that this procedure almost represents the ideal procedure for urinary diversion and that it represents the best method available at the present time.

Constantini H, Lenzi R, Selli C: Rectal bladder with Gersuny procedure after radical cystectomy [motion picture and presentation]. Trans Am Assoc Genitourin Surg 68:97, 1977

The authors are convinced that the rectum is the best substitute for the bladder. In the series of 1029 radical cystectomies for carcinoma done between September 1958 and December 1975, 865 patients had the rectum used for the urinary diversion. In 59.6% the Gersuny procedure was carried out, in 14.7% the Heitz-Boyer–Hoverlacque was used, and in 25.7% the Mauclaire procedure was done. Fecal continence was the prominent problem with the Mauclaire procedure. The Gersuny procedure was used in adults, and the Heitz-Boyer–Hoverlacque procedure was used in children. The mortality was 6%, and the 5-yr survival rate was 29%. The technique of the Gersuny procedure closely follows that modified by Garske and colleagues.[15] Although the postoperative progress was satisfactory, nocturnal urinary incontinence was a problem during the first few months postoperatively; this subsided with time. Fecal soiling was noted occasionally.

59

THE DIVERSION OF URINE BY THE HEITZ-BOYER PROCEDURE*

David A. Culp and Rubin H. Flocks

From the Department of Urology, State University of Iowa Hospitals, Iowa City, Iowa

Transactions of American Association of Genito-Urinary Surgeons, Vol. 57, 1965
Printed in U.S.A.

One of the major concerns of the urological surgeon has been the development of an operative procedure which would provide a patient with an uncomplicated comfortable existence whenever the bladder, because of faulty development or disease, was no longer usable. Two operative procedures have been devised that maintained the separation of the gastrointestinal and urogenital systems and at the same time provided voluntary control of both urine and feces. Each of these procedures, the Gersuny and the Heitz-Boyer, accomplishes these goals be creating an isolated rectal bladder and a perineal sigmoid colostomy. The advantages of the rectal bladder over ureteral anastomosis to the intact colon are reduction in intraluminal pressure, fecal contamination, and area of absorbing surface exposed to urine, which lowers the chance of ureteral reflux, urinary infection and the reabsorption of various urinary components. Therefore, a procedure which would embody all of these advantages, plus urinary and fecal continence would prove to be very useful.

The purpose of this paper is to report our experiences with the Heitz-Boyer technique. A rectal bladder is established by implanting the ureters into the isolated rectum, utilizing a mucosa-to-mucosa anastomosis and an intramural tunnel (Figs. 1 and 2). The sigmoid colon is brought to the surface in the perineum beneath the internal and external rectal sphincters by creating a tunnel posterior to the rectum in the hollow of the sacrum which maintains the normal anatomic position of the 2 systems. Little difficulty is encountered in this phase of the procedure as long as the dissection is confined to the midline behind the rectum. This space is filled with loose connective tissue and the blood vessels to the rectum lie lateral to the area.

The dissection is carried down behind the rectum until the levator ani muscle is encountered. At this point attention is turned to the anal area where an incision is made at the mucocutaneous junction around the posterior third of the anal opening. The mucosal and submucosal areas of the anus and rectum are elevated from the muscular wall by blunt dissection in a cephalad direction until a point just opposite the termination of the dissection behind the rectum is reached. The only structure that obstructs the connection of these 2 tunnels is the muscular layers of the rectal wall. By passing a large, curved hemostat or cystic duct clamp through the lower tunnel and the obstructing partition of rectal wall into the upper tunnel, a continuous channel is created. The sutures closing the sigmoid colon are grasped and pulled through the tunnel until bowel appears at the mucocutaneous junction of the anus (Fig. 3). It is anchored in this position by interrupted catgut sutures at the anal muco-

---

* The authors' technique was illustrated by a motion picture.

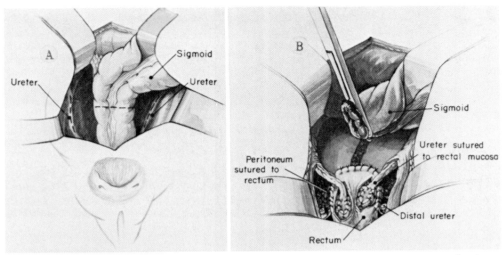

Fig. 1. Heitz-Boyer operative procedure. (A) Abdominal incision exposing rectosigmoid colon and distal ureters beneath posterior parietal peritoneum. Broken lines indicate sites of incisions for exposure of ureters and isolation of rectum from fecal stream. (B) Mucosa-to-mucosa ureterorectal anastomoses within tunnels created in rectal wall. Rectal bladder closed.

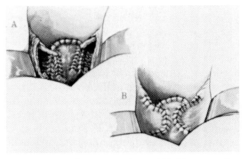

Fig. 2. Heitz-Boyer operative procedure. (A) Closure of rectal wall tunnel over completed ureterorectal anastomoses. (B) Retroperitonealization of ureterorectal anastomosis.

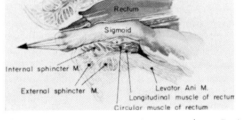

Fig. 3. Heitz-Boyer operative procedure. Perineal sigmoid colostomy in channel posterior to rectum and passing through rectal wall beneath both external and internal rectal sphincters.

cutaneous junction and superiorly to the posterior surface of the rectum. By constructing the perineal colostomy in this manner, in contrast to the Gersuny technique, it is hoped that the proprioceptive impulses initiated by stretching of the internal rectal sphincter will aid in securing more adequate fecal control.

CASE REPORTS

Case 1. Our experience with this method of urinary diversion began in May 1960 when it was utilized in a 24-month-old infant (F. E., hospital No. 60-6682) who had exstrophy of the bladder. Preoperative blood and

urine studies were normal and the excretory urograms revealed normal functioning kidneys (Fig. 4A and B). On May 28, a Heitz-Boyer procedure was performed and 3 days later the splinting catheters were expelled from the ureterorectal anastomosis. The urinary output rapidly diminished and within 24 hours had ceased. The patient had severe bilateral flank pain and a left ureterostomy was established. After 11 days the urine began to flow into the rectal bladder and the ureterostomy drainage was discontinued, following which recovery was prompt and uneventful.

Periodic followup evaluations were obtained during the next 2 years in our clinic. Meanwhile the patient gradually gained control of defecation and urination.

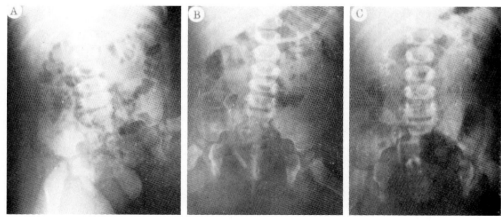

Fig. 4. Excretory urography (F. E., No. 60-6682). (A) Preoperative plain film. (B) Preoperative 5-minute post-injection film demonstrates normal pyelograms bilaterally. (C) Postoperative normal right kidney. Mild caliectasis of left kidney.

Blood chemistry values remained normal and the electrolyte pattern showed no acidosis or hyperchloremia. Excretory urograms demonstrated a normal right kidney and mild left hydronephrosis (Fig. 4C).

Since July 1962 the patient has been followed by a urologist in her home town. He reports that the child has had no progression of the left hydronephrosis, no difficulty with reabsorption of products from the rectal bladder and has been developing normally.

Case 2. A 20-month-old infant (H. L., hospital No. 59-3868) had exstrophy of the bladder (Fig. 5A and B). At the age of 2 months an unsuccessful attempt had been made to close the exstrophied bladder and bury it beneath the reconstructed abdominal wall. On November 3, 1960 an isolated rectal bladder and sigmoid perineal colostomy were established in the manner described previously.

Preoperatively the blood urea nitrogen (BUN) was 11.0 and the creatinine 0.4. The excretory urogram revealed right hydronephrosis and dilatation of the terminal portion of the left ureter (Fig. 5C). The urine collected from the right ureteral orifice contained many white blood cells (WBC) per high power field after centrifugation. The left pyelogram was normal.

The child has been followed for 4½ years with no roentgenographic changes in the upper urinary tract. He continues to have mild dilatation of the right ureter and renal pelvis while the left side remains normal (Fig. 5D). He was found to have hyperchloremic acidosis (CO_2 10.5; chloride 109) 3 months postoperatively which was promptly controlled with 2 teaspoonfuls of 5 percent sodium bicarbonate, 3 times a day. The other electrolytes have remained normal. By the age of 4 years he had

gained control of both urination and defecation and was able to deliver a specimen of urine which was uncontaminated with fecal material and was microscopically normal. There have been no symptoms or signs of urinary tract infection since the urine was diverted.

Case 3. G. S., hospital No. 61-4725, the third patient to undergo this type of urinary diversion, was born on February 9, 1962 with exstrophy of the bladder. Preoperative excretory urograms demonstrated prompt function from normal appearing kidneys (Fig. 6A and B). Blood chemistry and electrolyte studies were normal. On October 1 a Heitz-Boyer diversion of the urine was performed.

Periodic evaluations during the subsequent 2½ years have demonstrated no roentgenographic changes in the upper urinary tract (Fig. 6C and D). There has been no evidence of hyperchloremic acidosis and the child has developed in a normal manner. Within the past year he has achieved continence of both feces and urine and is able to urinate separately from defecation.

Case 4. K. J., hospital No. 63-52452, the only adult patient in our series, was 68 years old when seen on March 14, 1963 (Fig. 7). In 1955 she had gross, total, painless hematuria and a diagnosis of cancer of the bladder was made. Following initial therapy she remained symptom-free until July 1962 when she again noticed hematuria. On urological examination it was found that the neoplasm had recurred around the internal urethral orifice and had extended into the urethra. Radium therapy was administered without beneficial effect. Therefore, on April 9, 1963 the urine was diverted by a Heitz-

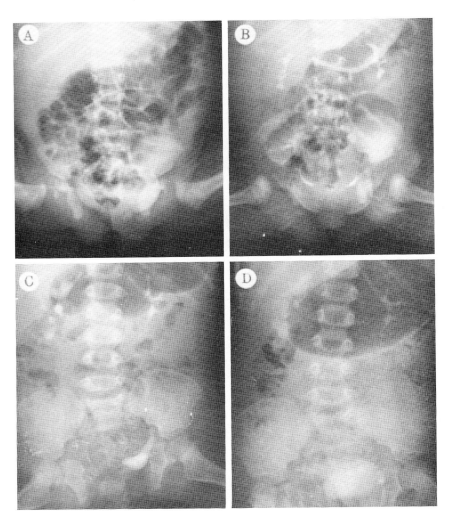

Fig. 5. Excretory urography (H. L., No. 59-3868). (*A*) Preoperative plain film. (*B*) Preoperative 15-minute post-injection film demonstrating normal pyelograms bilaterally and normal distal ureters. (*C*) 10-31-60, film obtained after attempt at construction of intact bladder but before Heitz-Boyer diversion, 15-minute post-injection film shows right caliectasis and left terminal ureterectasis. (*D*) 7-11-62, postoperatively, right caliectasis unchanged. Left ureterectasis improved.

Boyer procedure and a total cystourethrectomy was performed 6 weeks later.

Recovery from each of these procedures was prompt and uncomplicated. The patient had no difficulty controlling the elimination of either urine or feces and postoperative excretory urograms were normal. However, within a year vaginal recurrence of the neoplasm developed. The patient died April 25, 1964. During the entire postoperative period the upper urinary tract remained roentgenographically normal (Fig. 8). There was no evidence of complications associated with the diversionary procedure. She had complete control of both urine and feces and there were no electrolyte disturbances.

Case 5. L. L., hospital No. 63-54147, a 15-year-old girl, had frequency, dysuria, and intermittent sharp suprapubic pain in January 1963. Chemotherapy failed to provide relief and in May a tongue-shaped mass protruding from the floor of the bladder was discovered. A transurethral biopsy of this lesion revealed a myosarcoma (Fig. 9). Excretory urograms demonstrated normal-appearing kidneys with no ureteral obstruction (Fig. 10). The urine was loaded with blood but no WBC were seen. The BUN was 14 and creatinine 0.9.

On May 21, a total cystectomy was performed and the urine was diverted by a Heitz-Boyer procedure. Her immediate recovery was uneventful and by the time of her discharge from the hospital, 3 weeks later, she had gained complete control of urination and defecation.

Since the operative procedure, episodes of chills and fever have occurred at irregular intervals and on November 18, 1964 she had acute pyelonephritis. Her temperature rose to 105 degrees and she had bilateral

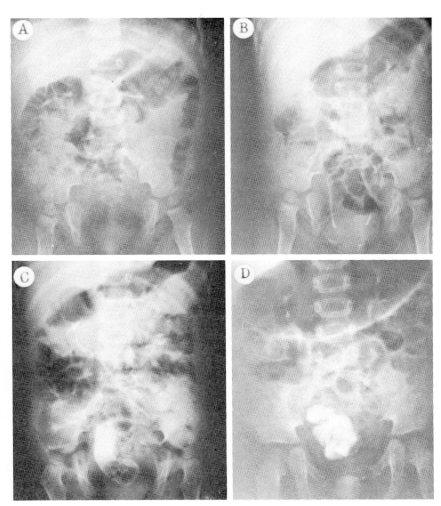

Fig. 6. Excretory urography (G. S., No. 61-4725). (*A*) Preoperative (4-27-62) plain film. (*B*) Preoperative (4-27-62), post-injection film shows normal kidneys and ureters bilaterally. (*C*) Post-injection film 2 months postoperatively demonstrated normal pyelogram bilaterally. Rectal bladder visualized. (*D*) Post-injection film 2 years 10 months postoperatively shows normal pyelograms bilaterally. Good visualization of rectal bladder.

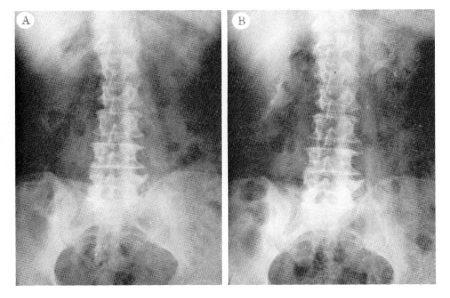

Fig. 7. Preoperative excretory urography (K. J., No. 63-52452). (*A*) Plain film. (*B*) Five-minute post-injection film demonstrates normal pyelograms bilaterally.

777

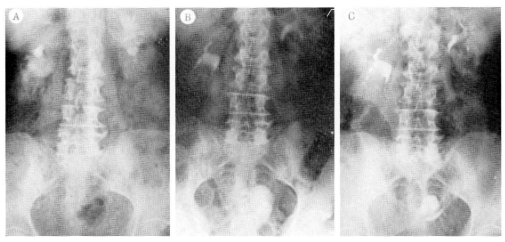

Fig. 8. Postoperative excretory urography (K. J., No. 63-52452). (A) Fifteen-minute post-injection film 1 month postoperatively shows dilatation of both renal pelves and mild caliectasis. (B) Five-minute post-injection film 6 months postoperatively reveals return to normal pyelograms bilaterally. (C) Fifteen-minute post-injection film 11 months postoperatively shows normal pyelograms bilaterally with mild dilatation of terminal left ureter and opaque mateial in rectal bladder.

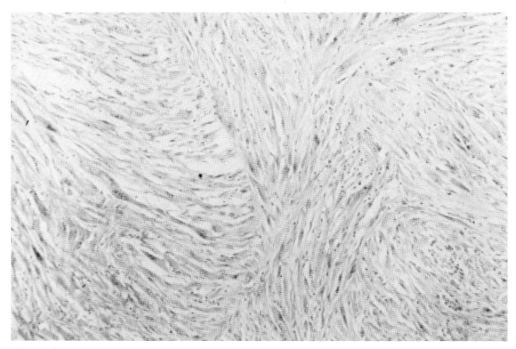

Fig. 9. Photomicrograph of bladder tumor (L. L., No. 54157). Majority of tumor is composed of interlacing bundles of fibrillar cells which resembled smooth muscle cells. Many of bizarre cells are quite large and binucleated. Nuclei are large and bizarre. Atypical mitoses are present but infrequent.

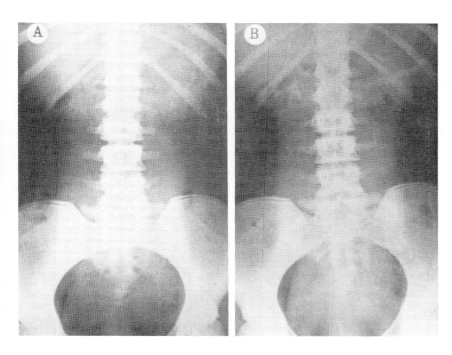

Fig. 10. Preoperative excretory urography (L. L., No. 63-54157). (*A*) Plain film. (*B*) Fifteen-minute post-injection film shows bilateral function with no pelvic or calyceal dilatation. Bladder is large and faintly outlined by opaque material.

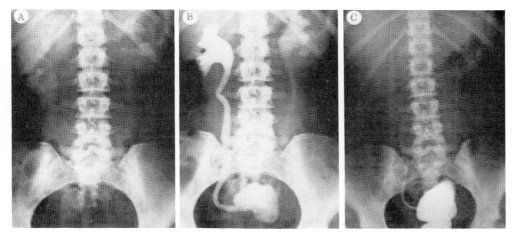

Fig. 11. L. L., No. 63-54157. (*A*) Excretory urogram, 5-minute post-injection film 1 year and 6 months postoperatively shows bilateral hydronephrosis. (*B*) Postoperative excretory urogram, 60-minute delayed film demonstrates bilateral hydroureter and hydronephrosis. Upper portion of rectal bladder well visualized. (*C*) Cystogram, right ureteral reflux.

flank pain and tenderness. Excretory urograms demonstrated bilateral ureteral and pelvic dilatation (Fig. 11*A* and *B*). The terminal portions of each ureter at the site of the rectal anastomosis were narrowed and constricted. Following introduction of radiopaque material in the rectum, right ureteral reflux was noted (Fig. 11*C*). Hyperchloremia (Cl 104) and acidosis (CO_2 16.1) developed shortly after the urinary diversion was completed and have persisted throughout the postoperative period.

Case 6. M. E., hospital No. 63-11581, the final case in our series, was a 15-month-old boy who was born on August 7, 1963 with exstrophy of the bladder. At the age of 2 weeks, multiple biopsies of the bladder wall revealed extensive squamous metaplasia, ulceration and acute cystitis. Excretory urograms demonstrated morphologically normal kidneys with normal function (Fig. 12*A* and *B*).

On November 6, 1964 a Heitz-Boyer procedure was

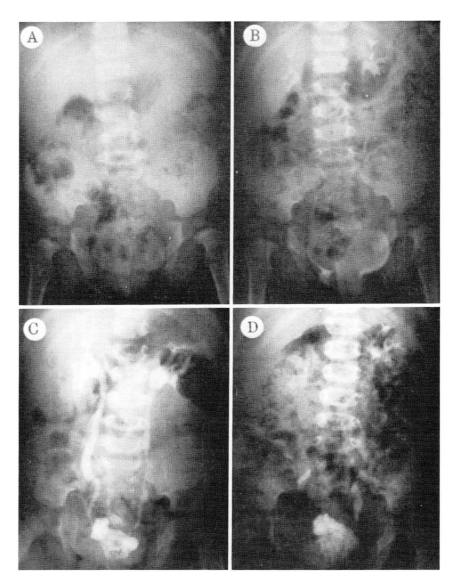

Fig. 12. Excretory urography (M. E., No. 63-11581). (*A*) Preoperative plain film. (*B*) Preoperative 15-minute post-injection film shows normal kidneys bilaterally. (*C*) Fifteen-minute post-injection film 11 days postoperatively demonstrates mild dilatation of both ureters and renal pelves. (*D*) Fifteen-minute post-injection film 3 months postoperatively shows normal functioning kidneys bilaterally, partially obscured by bone shadows. Mild dilatation of ureters.

performed. Recovery from the operation was prompt and without complications. Postoperative excretory urograms (Fig. 12C and D) and the blood chemistry and electrolyte studies remained within normal limits. Urinary or fecal incontinence has not developed.

DISCUSSION

We have followed these 6 patients from 5 to 60 months after the diversion of urine by the Heitz-Boyer technique. Four had exstrophy of the bladder and two had neoplastic disease involving the bladder for which cystectomy was performed. One patient died 1 year following a cystourethrectomy for a recurrent transitional cell carcinoma. Up to 3 weeks prior to death the upper urinary tract was normal and the rectal bladder and sigmoid perineal colostomy were functioning normally with complete continence.

All of the patients obtained voluntary control of both fecal and urinary elimination. All are continent now and the parents did not experience any more difficulty in training these children than with their normally developed siblings. In general, the patient voids 4 to 5 times daily without fecal passage and an additional 2 to 3 times daily with each bowel movement. It is rare that the patient has a bowel movement without the passage of urine.

The external appearance of the patient is unaltered (Fig. 13A). Even in the lithotomy position it is not possible to note a change in the external physical appearance. Only after the buttocks and anus have been retracted is it possible to identify the double-barreled opening (Fig. 13B). Likewise, there is no noticeable difference in the tone of the anal sphincter to palpation. No difficulty has been encountered in entering the desired cavity with either the palpating finger or an instrument. If one desires to enter the rectal bladder the finger or instrument is directed along the anterior wall of the rectum. On the other hand, if entrance into the bowel is desired, the posterior wall is followed.

Catheterization or cystoscopy presents no problem. Visualization of the interior of the rectal bladder was performed on the 15-year-old girl during an attack of acute pyelonephritis. The general location of each ureteral orifice was easily identified following intravenous injection of indigo carmine.

The roentgenographic appearance of the upper urinary tract has remained unchanged in four of the 6 patients. Mild unilateral hydronephrosis which developed immediately after operation in the first patient has shown no progression 5 years after the diversion. The 15-year-old girl with myosarcoma of the bladder has mild bilateral hydroureter and hydronephrosis, which seem to be more pronounced during episodes of acute urinary tract infection. Right ureteral reflux has been demonstrated in this same patient by cystography.

BUN and creatinine determinations have shown no alterations. However, 2 patients have mild hyperchloremia and acidosis which have been readily controlled with sodium bicarbonate.

CONCLUSIONS

Our experience with this operative procedure has been most encouraging. It has provided a method of urinary diversion which maintains the separation of the gastrointestinal and urogenital systems with voluntary control of both urine and feces. Elimination of catheters and external collecting devices has made the diversion more acceptable to the patient. The rectal bladder limits the area of absorbing intestinal mucosa exposed to urine and reduces the intraluminal pressure. Consequently, the incidence of acidosis, pyelonephritis and back pressure effects upon the renal parenchyma has been lowered.

It is our belief that the Heitz-Boyer operative procedure offers the best chance for a longer survival, with fewer complications, and more comfort than any other method of urinary diversion. Furthermore, it is preferable to the Gersuny technique because the position of the sigmoid colostomy permits utilization of both the internal and external rectal spincters. Action of the sphincteric group of muscles is initiated through the proprioceptive stimulus of the internal sphincter by filling of either the rectal bladder or terminal portion of the sigmoid colon. Moreover, it is applicable to both sexes. Considerable difficulty is encountered in establishing the colostomy anterior to the rectum in the female patient because of the interposition of the genital tract. However, when the colon passes posterior to the rectum, no anatomical diferences between male and female patients are encounterered.

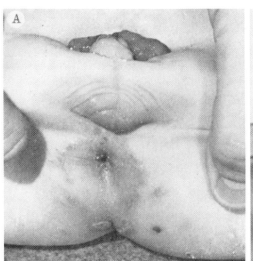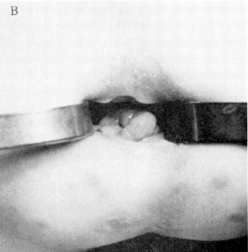

Fig. 13. (A) External view postoperatively. (B) Double barrel opening shows rectal bladder anteriorly and sigmoid stoma posteriorly.

REFERENCES

GERSUNY: In: HINMAN, F. and WEYRAUCH, H. M., JR.: A critical study of the different principles of surgery which have been used in uretero-intestinal implantation. Internat Abstr Surg, 64:313, 1937, and Tr Am A Genito-Urin Surg, 29:15, 1936

HEITZ-BOYER, M. and HOVELACQUE, A.: Creation d'une nouvelle vessie et un nouvel urétre. J d'Urol, 1:237, 1912

HINMAN, F., JR.: The technique of the Gersuny operation in vesical exstrophy. J Urol, 81:126, 1959

JOHNSON, T. H.: Further experiences with a new operation for urinary diversion. J Urol, 76:380, 1956

KIEFER, J. H. and LINKE, C.: Ureterorectostomy and preanal colostomy for bladder exstrophy. Tr Am A Genito-Urin Surg, 49:15, 1958

LOWSLEY, O. S. and JOHNSON, T. H.: A new operation for creation of an artificial bladder with voluntary control of urine and feces. J Urol, 73:83, 1955

Commentary: Heitz-Boyer–Hovelaque Procedure: Not the Procedure of Choice

David A. Culp

When disease renders the bladder an undesirable structure or a malfunctioning segment of the transport system, diversion of the urinary flow with or without cystectomy must be considered. The ideal method for urinary diversion should provide a sphincter-controlled internal reservoir free of encumbrances. Ureterosigmoidostomy meets these requirements in the majority of instances. However, three major complicating problems may be encountered when this procedure is used: colonic–ureteral reflux producing ascending pyelonephritis, intestinal reabsorbtion of urinary-excreted products, and ureterocolonic anastomotic obstruction. An attempt was made to reduce or eliminate the first two complications by constructing a rectal bladder and a perineal sigmoid colostomy, both controlled by the internal and external anal sphincter, a procedure originally described by Heitz-Boyer and Hovelaque in 1912.

In the first edition of *Current Operative Urology,* a Commentary on this procedure discussed the then-current status of the original series of patients. Although the majority of patients were judged on the basis of satisfactory urinary and fecal control, normal electrolyte and blood chemistry profiles, absence of ascending pyelonephritis, and a stable renal pyelographic morphology to have done well, two major complications were encountered. These were perineal fecal and urinary incontinence, which produced an infected, macerated, uncontrollable skin reaction, and retraction of the terminal common septum between the fecal and urinary tracts. This resulted in mixing of the contents with ascending pyelonephritis.

Based on these observations, it was emphasized in the original Commentary that it is essential to determine the electromygraphic (EMG) intactness of the anal sphincter mechanism before performing this procedure. It was also suggested that until the threat of postoperative incontinence had been solved, the Heitz-Boyer procedure should not be employed as a primary method of urinary diversion.

In the ensuing 5-yr interval since the first Commentary, additional observation of these patients has disclosed further breakdown in the anal competency in patients originally capable of controlling both the fecal and urinary streams and an increase in ascending pyelonephritis, forcing conversion to conduit diversion in a number of these patients. Because of this high incidence of fecal and urinary incontinence from a stoma located in an inconvenient anatomic position for application of a collecting device, as well as the other complications associated with ureterointestinal anastomoses, this procedure has not gained favorable acceptance as a supervesical diversionary technique and should be relegated again to one of historical interest.

ANNOTATED BIBLIOGRAPHY

Heitz-Boyer M, Hovelacque A: Creation d'une nouvelle vessie et un nouvel uretre. J Urol Med Chir 1:237, 1912

The original technique of the creation of a rectal bladder with a perineal colostomy using the internal and external and sphincter to maintain urinary and fecal continence is described and illustrated in this paper.

Bracci U: The rectal bladder, Urol Int 22:1, 1967

This paper describes the author's experience with 370 cases in which the rectum was used as a new urinary reservoir. Thirty-seven of these cases underwent the Heitz-Boyer procedure following cystoprostatovesiculectomy or cystohysteroadnexectomy for carcinoma of the bladder, uterus, urethra, and vagina.

A lesser number of patients under the Heitz-Boyer procedure for nonmalignant disease. In the most recent years reviewed the author reports that 41.5% of the rectal bladders were of the Heitz-Boyer type, while only 5.6% were of the Gersuny type. In the earlier years only 8.1% to 11.2% of the rectal bladders were of the Heitz-Boyer type, while 44.4% to 50% were of the Gersuny type. Throughout the study from 44.4% to 53.3% of the rectal bladders were of the Mauclaire type. A very detailed analysis of the technique with modifications, complications, problems, and results is presented. The author concludes that "the use of the rectum represents the best procedure for reconstructing an urinary reservoir which, for its functional characteristics, is the one that is most similar to the normal bladder. As to the important problems of defecation aroused by the rectal bladder, we think that the operation of Gersuny, and mainly that of Heitz-Boyer, Hovelacque are fully satisfying and well accepted by all the patients." (Editor's note: this paper is reproduced in Dr. Bracci's section.)

Rutishauser G, Durig M, Leibundgut B, et al: Rectal bladder with dorsolateral intrasphincteric submucosal pull through of the sigmoid colon in adult bladder cancer patients. Eur Urol 3:57, 1977

The authors review the early and late results of 12 patients with rectal bladders and perineal sigmoid colostomies following total cystectomy for bladder cancer. The immediate course of this group of patients was the subject of a report by two of the authors (Evard and Leibundgut), in which they reported that patients were satisfied with their state of continence, even though they all wore protection, and seven exhibited varying degrees of incontinence of both urine and feces. Late follow-up study of this same group of patients indicated that radiographically recognizable renal damage had occurred in all survivors; of the seven patients who died, six had severe renal infection and terminally septic conditions. The authors' final conclusions were that "the possible advantages of the procedure are at the cost of a poor quality of survival."

OVERVIEW: THE CHOICE BETWEEN URETEROSIGMOIDOSTOMY WITH PERINEAL (GERSUNY, HEITZ-BOYER) OR ABDOMINAL (MAUCLAIRE) COLOSTOMY

Frank Hinman, Jr.

Infants with exstrophy and adults with vesical cancer are the two groups that might profit from intracolonic urinary diversion, free of external appliances: the children are enabled to grow with their peers without altered appearance; the adults can avoid the rituals involved in collection devices. The alternatives are ileal or sigmoid conduits, procedures that are now beginning to show late complications.

Ureterosigmoidostomy may still be the best method of repair for children with exstrophy if they have adequate development of the anal sphincter. They must be followed closely for signs of upper tract deterioration, which makes conversion to colon conduit mandatory.

Ureterosigmoidostomy with perineal colostomy, in which the colon is brought down anteriorly (Gersuny's operation) or posteriorly through the sphincter (Heitz-Boyer–Hovelaque operation) is an alternative.

Between the transsphincteric (Heitz-Boyer) and extrasphincteric (Gersuny) techniques the choice is made mainly on technical grounds. In practice, control by the new transsphincteric anus does not seem to be better than control by the Gersuny anus. Technically, the implantation of the ureters into the sigmoid left in place, as in the Gersuny operation, requires less overall dissection and less ureteral dissection and bridging than their implantation into the anteriorly displaced sigmoid after the colon is moved behind it, as in the Heitz-Boyer procedure.

Although Bracci has had a large and favorable experience with the Heitz-Boyer procedure, which he uses alternatively with ureterosigmoidostomy or ureterosigmoidostomy with abdominal colostomy (Mauclaire's operation), the follow-up period is of necessity brief, since the surgeon often operates on older patients having residual malignancy. As Bracci points out, these operations provide a simple solution for the short term.

Except in elderly patients, diversion through the perineum is not desirable for adults. Ureteroileostomy or anastomosis of the ureters into a colonic segment leading to the skin is preferable. Three reasons underlie this judgment: the greater incidence of complications following diversion to the perineum, adults' poor tolerance for a colostomy in the perineum and for the unavoidable soiling with foul urine, and the problems associated with resorption of electrolytes. Such difficulties are tolerated much better by children because they grow up with them.

My experience, which has included several pediatric patients converted to colon conduits either because of progressive upper tract damage or intolerable rectal incontinence, is in agreement with Culp's—these procedures should be relegated again to those of historical interest.

Ureterosigmoidostomy with abdominal colostomy (Mauclaire's operation), in contrast to procedures involving perineal colostomies, is a rational method of diversion. However, in the United States, the collection of urine on the abdomen is preferable to managing the feces from a colostomy, so that the operation has had little popularity.

In summary, ureterosigmoidostomy without fecal diversion to perineum or abdomen is a reasonable solution for urinary diversion in infants with vesical exstrophy. The ileal or colonic conduit is better tolerated and controlled in the adult than any form of rectal bladder.

PART TWENTY-THREE

VESICAL DIVERSION

60

IMPROVEMENT FOLLOWING TUBELESS SUPRAPUBIC CYSTOSTOMY OF MYELOMENINGOCELE PATIENTS WITH HYDRONEPHROSIS AND RECURRENT ACUTE PYELONEPHRITIS

Alexander J. Michie, Patricia Borns and Mary D. Ames

From the Surgical, Radiologic and Rehabilitative Services of The Children's Hospital of Philadelphia; The Harrison Department of Research Surgery and the Department of Pediatrics, School of Medicine, University of Pennsylvania.
Alexander J. Michie, M.D.: Associate Professor of Pediatric Urology, University of Pennsylvania, and Senior surgeon in Urology, Department of Surgery, Children's Hospital of Philadelphia. Patricia Borns, M.D.: Assistant Professor of Clinical Radiology, University of Pennsylvania. Associate Radiologist, Children's Hospital of Philadelphia. Mary D. Ames, M.D.: Assistant Professor of Clinical Pediatrics, University of Pennsylvania. Coordinator of Rehabilitative Services, Children's Hospital of Philadelphia.

Journal of Pediatric Surgery, Vol. 1, No. 4 (August), 1966

Presented before the meeting of the Surgical Section of the American Academy of Pediatrics, Chicago, October, 1965.

This work was supported in part by U. S. Public Health Service Research Grant AM-2662 from the National institute of Arthritis and Metabolic Diseases; U. S. Public Health Service General Research Support Grant FR-05506-04; the Children's Bureau, Department of Health, Education and Welfare, Washington, D. C.; and the Division of Maternal and Child Health, Pennsylvania Department of Health, Harrisburg, Pennsylvania

The continuous care of the myelomeningocele patient with a distended bladder and overflow incontinence is difficult because of the frequent episodes of acute cystitis and pyelonephritis. Eventually the chronic urinary infection can cause vesicoureteral reflux, redundant hydroureters, and hydronephrosis. While all these complications can be avoided by regular and effective Crede of the bladder, some mothers are untrainable and also, occasionally the pressure of an effective Crede disrupts the meningomyelocele repair. The creation of a tubeless suprapubic cystostomy will correct (Figs. 1 and 2) and if done early, will avoid these troublesome complications.

While Lapides[1] and his co-workers[2] do a more complicated operation resembling a gastrostomy, a simpler procedure seems to work equally well. Since the urine is infected it is important that the area of the dissection be kept as small as possible. Through a 2 cm midline vertical suprapubic incision the underlying fascia is incised and the recti retracted laterally. After pushing away the peritoneum and the perivesical fat, the bladder is grasped, pulled through the wound, opened and evacuated through a 1.5 cm longitudinal incision. About 2 cm cephalad to the bladder and fascial incisions, a stitch is used to fasten the anterior bladder wall to the anterior rectus fascia. The incised margins first of the rectus fascia and then of Scarpa's fascia are sewn to the anterior bladder wall by 4 equally placed stitches which should not cause any infarction of the bladder wall. The rectus fascia is sewn 1.5 cm proximal to, and Scarpa's fascia is sewn 0.5 cm proximal to the incision in the

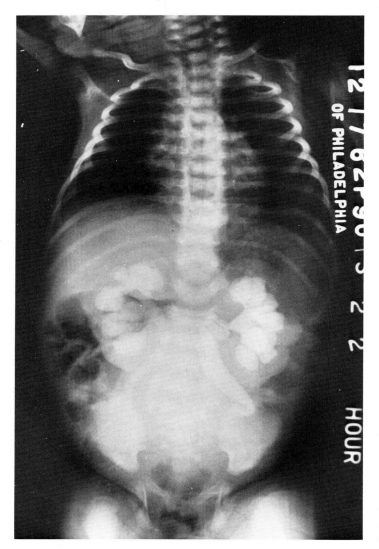

Fig. 1.—Patient #628411 was born on December 4, 1962, with a lumbosacral myelomeningocele associated with perineal anesthesia and partial impairment of voluntary movement of the lower extremities. Following repair of the myelomeningocele, the increasing spinal fluid pressure had to be treated with a ventriculojugular shunt. Then an intravenous urogram done on December 17, 1962, revealed the megalobladder, hydroureters, and bilateral hydronephrosis. Because Crede of the bladder broke the skin of the myelomeningocele repair, a tubeless suprapubic cystostomy was done on December 27, 1962.

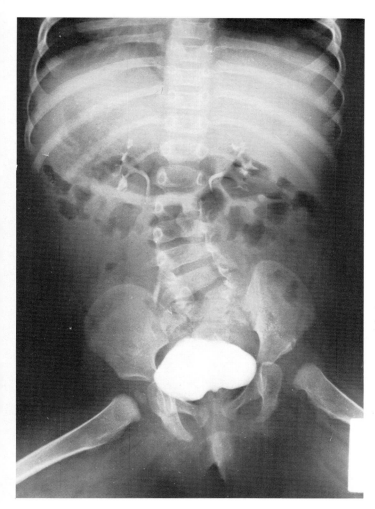

Fig. 2.—Following her tubless cystostomy, patient #628411, was treated with a soluble sulfonamide and has remained completely asymptomatic. Her intravenous urogram of April 15, 1964, revealed that her kidneys and ureters had returned to normal. Following closure of her cystostomy on June 21, 1965, her mother has been Credeing her bladder at 3 hour intervals during the day. One to 2 viable enterococei and B. proteus are present in each ml of urine which contains no albumin or red cells and an occasional white cell. Another intravenous urogram on November 9, 1965, revealed that her kidneys and ureters have remained normal.

bladder. Then the bladder mucosa is fastened to the naterior abdominal wall skin with 10 to 20 stitches of 5–0 nylon. No dressings are necessary. First the nurses and then the mother are instructed to place a small amount of vaseline on that portion of the diaper which comes in contact with the cystostomy. Most of the pericystostomy skin rashes will disappear in 1 to 2 months. A persistent rash will usually disappear after treatment with mycostatin dusting powder. At the time of the cystostomy the antibacterial drug therapy is switched to a soluble sulfonamide. For the duration of the cystostomy we give 50 mg of a soluble sulfonamide/pound of body weight/day in 2 divided doses at 12 hour intervals. If the patient is allergic to sulfonamides, we give one-third to one-half the therapeutic dose of a suitable antibiotic. Within 3 to 6 months of creating the tubeless cystostomy, the bladder urine will contain little

or no pus and a minimal amount, less than 10^6 colonies, of 2 to 4 bacterial species.

Following the establishment of a satisfactory tubeless cystostomy, all 9 of our patients have become asymptomatic, afebrile and have increased their height and weight more rapidly than before the operation. Simultaneously our postoperative x-ray kidney measurements (Fig. 3) showed in all 9 patients a progressive increase in the volume of the renal parenchyma (Table 1), as well as a decrease in the volume of completely formed urine within the kidney.

Measurement of the volume of the renal parenchyma and of the volume of completely formed urine remaining in the kidney is difficult and at best is only an estimate. In making these estimations various parts of the kidney were reduced to regular geometric forms. The bean-shaped kidney was degraded into a rectangular block

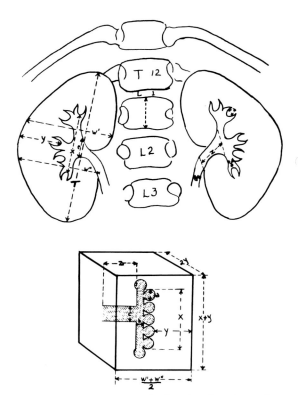

Fig. 3.—Kidney measurements: the height of L1 is used to estimate the size of the patient. Single measurements are made of the length, T; the length of the internal drainage system, X; and the length, Z, of the intrarenal portion of the pelvis. The average of 3 or 4 diameters of the intrarenal portion of the pelvis equals, c. The average width of the kidney is assumed to equal $\frac{W' + W''}{2}$. W' and W'' are measured through the neck of the cephalad and caudad calyx respectively. The average of 7 or more capsule to tip of pyramid measurements equals, Y. The average diameter of 7 or more calyces equals, a. The average of 4 or more measurements of the infundibular diameter equals, b. These measurements are reproducible within 1 mm in consecutive intravenous urograms done on the same patient at weekly intervals.

whose length was the sum of the length of the internal drainage tract plus the cortex to calyx measurement (X + Y). The width (W) of this rectangle was the average width of the kidney at the neck of the cephalad and caudad calyx $\frac{(W' + W'')}{2}$. The thickness of this rectangular block was assumed to equal twice the cortex to calyx measurement (2Y). From this an estimation of the total renal volume can be obtained from W(X + Y)2Y. The volume of the completely formed urine in the

TABLE 1. Percent Renal Dead Space to Functioning Parenchyma

Patient	Pre-cystostomy	Post-cystostomy
Right Kidney		
S. L.	9.2	2.8
M. I.	68.3	1.1
M. Y.	40.3	4.9
B. P.	28.1	16.1
B. C.	181.	16.9
B. B.	25.8	7.9
K. S.	15.0	3.2
H. B.	334.	41.3
K. T.	15.4	2.9
Ave. reduction in dead space 68.8%		
Left Kidney		
S. L.	surgically absent	
M. I.	21.1	1.5
M. Y.	12.1	5.1
B. P.	18.8	2.8
B. C.	411.	35.5
B. B.	20.1	4.6
K. S.	24.2	4.6
H. B.	296.	21.3
K. T.	18.5	3.0
Ave. reduction in dead space 92.9%		

The percent of renal dead space is obtained by multiplying the ratio, volume of renal dead space/volume of functioning parenchyma, by 100. The tubeless cystostomy always caused an increase in parenchymal volume and a decrease in renal dead space.

kidney, the renal dead space, was assumed to equal the sum of the volume of the calyces, of the infundibula and of the intrarenal portion of the renal pelvis. Since we can usually measure the diameter of only 7 calyces in each kidney, the volume of the calyces equals $7 \frac{(\pi a^3)}{6}$ or $3.6652 \, a^3$. The volume of the infundibula was assumed to equal that of a cylinder of diameter (b) and height (X), i.e., $\frac{\pi b^2}{4} X$ or $0.7854 \, b^2 X$. Similarly the volume of the renal pelvis was equated to a cylinder with a diameter (c) equal to the average height of the renal pelvis. Since the intrarenal length of the renal pelvis equalled Z, the volume of the renal pelvis was $0.7854 \, c^2 Z$. The volume of the renal parenchyma equals the volume of the kidney minus the volume of the renal dead space. The 2 important estimates can be related to each other by dividing the volume of the renal parenchyma into 100 times the volume of the renal dead space. Normal values for these parameters are being determined.

Previously the tubeless cystostomy was only used for patients with troublesome chronic infections complicated by vesicoureteral reflux, hydroureters and hydronephrosis. With the tubeless cystostomy, some improvement always occurred in kidney and ureteral function, but often the function did not return to normal. At present, functional and anatomical abnormalities have been avoided in 6 patients in whom the tubeless cystostomy was done early, i.e., as soon as we recognized a persistent residual urine or a chronic infection. The cystostomy is usually closed 6 months prior to the patient's beginning first grade or when the orthopedist needs to use a body brace to ambulate the patient.

The tubeless vesicostomy in the myelomeningocele

patient caused a greater improvement in renal and ureteral function than any other therapeutic procedure we have tried. The damage caused by chronic infection and residual bladder urine can be prevented by doing the tubeless cystostomy early. Usually the social pressure of starting school without diapers forces us to close the cystostomy. At this point the child is carefully trained to empty his own bladder.

SUMMARIO IN INTERLINGUA

Frequente recurrentias de acute cystitis e pyelonephritis causa numerose difficultates in le tractamento del patiente myelomeningocelic. In le curso del tempore, le chronic infection urinari causa refluxo vesico-ureteral, hydroureteres reduntante, e hydronephrosis. Ben que iste complicationes pote esser prevenite per applicar le methodo de

Credé al vesica, a vices isto non pote esser ducite a bon successo. Le creation chiurgic de un non-tubate cystostomia suprapubic, si effectuate precocemente, preveni le mentionate complicationes e, si effectuate plus tarde, corrige multes del acquirite anormalitates del vias urinari.

REFERENCES

1. Lapides, J., Ajemian. E. P., and Lichtwardt, J. R.: Cutaneous vesicostomy. J Urol 84:609, 1960
2. Beland, G. A., and Weiss, R. M.: Cutaneous vesicostomy in children. J Urol 94:128, 1965
3. Hodson, C. J., Drewe, J. A., Karn, M. N., and King, A.: Renal size in normal children. A radiographic study during life. Arch Dis Childhood 37:616, 1962

4. Friedenberg, M. J., Walz, B. J., McAlister, W. H., Locksmith, J. P., and Gallagher, T. L.: Roentgen size of normal kidneys. Radiology 84:1022, 1965
5. Gatewood, O. M. B., Glasser, R. J., and Vanhoutte, J. J.: Roentgen evaluation of renal size in pediatric age groups. Am J Dis Child 110:162, 1965

Commentary: Choosing Between Cystostomy and Vesicostomy

George W. Kaplan

The operative procedures referred to as vesicostomy and a cystostomy are both designed to drain the urinary bladder. The term *vesicostomy* generally refers to a nonintubated procedure. In general usage, the term *cystostomy* usually applies to the operative placement of a catheter of one sort or another. The term *cystotomy*, on the other hand, refers only to opening the bladder and will not be employed in this discussion. Although the general aim of both vesicostomy and cystostomy is identical, the reasons for employing one or the other may vary as clinical circumstances vary.

Suprapubic cystostomy is the older of the procedures employed formally to drain the bladder. It has been used clinically at least since the latter part of the 19th century, following the advent of anesthesia and antisepsis. It is strongly suspected that inadvertent vesicostomies must have resulted from attempts at prostatotomy and lithotomy in even earlier times, but no references verify this bit of conjecture.

Both vesicostomy and cystostomy are employed for either permanent or temporary suprapubic urinary diversion. The advantages that accrue to the use of cystostomy for temporary diversion relate to its reversibility; the tube can be removed without the need for a second operation. Conversely, the theoretic advantage of vesicostomy for permanent diversion revolves around the fact that no foreign body is used and hence urinary sterility can more easily be maintained.

Deferring to historical perspective, let me first consider suprapubic cystostomy. As was stated, it can be employed for either permanent or temporary urinary diversion. Most commonly it is employed temporarily following another surgical procedure in which the surgeon feels it important to drain urine away from the operative site and in which an intraurethral catheter is either not desirable for fear of urethritis (*e.g.,* urethroplasty) or insufficient alone to provide adequate drainage (*e.g.,* suprapubic prostatectomy). Additionally, it can be employed temporarily for the relief of urinary retention or in the spinal shock phase of paraplegia. However, even before the advent of intermittent catheterization, most urologists with experience preferred to avoid suprapubic cystostomy for routine use in paraplegia, since it renders bladder training more difficult. Cystostomy, however, is an excellent alternative in the male paraplegic when urethritis is produced by an in-dwelling urethral catheter and should be promptly employed in this situation to avoid urethral abscesses and fistulas. Cystostomy has also sometimes been employed in paraplegics to prevent epididymitis, but this indication is without rationale because the incidence of epididymitis is no different with intraurethral or suprapubic drainage.

An observation that has been made repeatedly and yet is without satisfactory explanation is that an occasional older man with azotemia and prostatism will not experience improvement in renal function with indwelling urethral cathaterization. In such patients the use of cystostomy drainage may result in improved renal function. Presumably the explanation lies in the position of the tube rather than its caliber, but this is speculative.

It is of interest that infants, for instance, those with posterior urethral valves, do not tolerate suprapubic catheters well. Infants have been noted to lose renal function when such forms of drainage are employed, only to then improve when some other method of drainage is used. Presumably, the cystostomy tube so irritates the bladder that either vesicoureteral reflux and pyelonephritis are produced or further ureterovesical obstruction is promoted.

Cystostomy is also at times employed for permanent urinary diversion. The most common reason for this usage probably occurs in the older man with prostatism who is too infirm to withstand prostatectomy. A less common indication is found with the rare patient with insoluble urethral obstruction usually secondary to traumatic or iatrogenic problems. Another category of patients who occasionally benefit from permanent suprapubic cystostomy are those with neurogenic bladder dysfunction, who do not fare well with clean intermittent catheterization, in-dwelling urethral catheters, or (in men) external catheters. At times it is necessary to surgically close the vesical neck when cystostomy is employed so that the patient will be dry. This can be accomplished relatively easily in women but is quite difficult in men. Fortunately, surgical closure of the vesical neck is required in men very rarely.

The surgical technique of formal suprapubic cystostomy is well described in most urologic textbooks. One such description is listed in the annotated bibliography that follows. In addition to these methods, a tube can be placed in the bladder by less formal means. One such method involves the use of a Lowsley prostatic tractor. The tractor is placed in the bladder per urethra and the hilt depressed so that the tip tents up the suprapubic area. An incision is then made over the tractor tip so that it is exposed. A catheter is then grasped with the tractor and pulled into the bladder, secured in place by balloon or suture, and the tractor is then removed. Another less formal method is to puncture the filled bladder with a trocar. These trocars can be of quite large bore so that a large-caliber catheter can be introduced through them. With all forms of trocar cystostomy, it is important to introduce the catheter quickly before the bladder has a chance to collapse and fall

away from the trocar tip, thereby preventing catheter introduction. A number of kits are now on the market that allow the insertion of a catheter percutaneously (e.g., Cystocath). Last, the surgeon can employ an Angiocath or Intracath for short-term bladder drainage, especially in a patient in urinary retention.

The major complications of suprapubic cystostomy are bleeding or infection. Although bleeding is uncommon, it can be a problem both intraoperatively (in formal cystostomy) or postoperatively (in trocar cystostomy). The reason is similar in both instances, that is, the large friable veins covering the anterior vesical surface. Infection is usually a long-term postoperative problem and occurs because there is a foreign body in situ. Similarly, calculi may form on the cystostomy tube. A rare problem but one that must always be kept in mind is inadvertent placement of the cystostomy through the peritoneum or, even more rarely, through the bowel. Such mishaps are more frequent when trocar cystostomy is employed but can occur with formal open cystostomy. They are prevented by ensuring that the bladder is full before cystostomy placement.

Cutaneous vesicostomy was apparently first described experimentally by Barnes in 1953. In 1957 Blocksam described its use in an elderly man with prostatism. In 1962 Lapides and colleagues reported their experience with vesicostomy and recommended that it be used for permanent diversion of patients with neurogenic bladder dysfunction. Although there was a brief flurry of enthusiasm, the procedure fell into disrepute because of many stomal problems. Despite this, the operation still is of great use in a few selected instances.

The indications for the use of cutaneous vesicostomy are basically similar to those for cystostomy. However, because it requires an operation for its reversal, it is not usually recommended for short-term use for either postoperative states or the relief of obstruction. It is for temporary use that vesicostomy has its greatest use, however. This is true in infants with infravesical obstruction or vesicoureteral reflux in whom immediate reconstruction is not desirable for one reason or another. Even more applicable, however, is its use in the infant with neurogenic vesical dysfunction and hydronephrosis in whom immediate long-term, but temporary, relief is needed.

In adults, major problems are encountered with applying collecting devices to the vesicostomy stoma so that there can be some semblance of continence. In the infant this is not a requirement, since diapers are employed. It is this fact that allows its use in infants and interferes with its use in adults. It is this same fact that virtually mandates conversion of vesicostomy drainage to something else as the infant grows.

Multiple techniques have been used for vesicostomy. For the single indication for which its use is recommended, that is, temporary but long-term drainage of the infant with neurogenic vesical dysfunction or infravesical obstruction, the technique described by Michie (i.e., the Blocksam technique) is excellent. The flaps described by Lapides and others are not necessary for this use and render the procedure unnecessarily complex. They are required in the adult to prevent stomal stenosis, but this is unnecessary in the infant because the bladder is situated so much more cephalad in the infant than in the adult.

Despite many reports decrying the use of vesicostomy (1)

for permanent use, (2) in adults and older children, and (3) because of stomal difficulties, the results obtained in infants have been uniformly gratifying. This is especially true when there is infravesical obstruction, either anatomic or functional, that is, when the bladder is chronically distended and retention or overflow incontinence is present. In this circumstance the surgeon can almost uniformly expect at least partial resolution of hydronephrosis and azotemia and a decrease, if not abolition, of instances of clinical urinary infection. Frequently cultures will be sterile even without suppressive antibacterial agents.

Intraoperative complications are quite uncommon. Postoperative problems include diaper dermatitis, stomal stenosis, and prolapse. Diaper dermatitis occurs because the peristomal area is permanently bathed by urine and becomes inflamed. It has recently been suggested that cutaneous candidiasis may contribute to diaper dermatitis, and this may be a factor in this instance as well. In any event, the prevention of diaper dermatitis if possible by barrier ointments (not creams, as these latter are water soluble), urinary acidification, and topical steroids if necessary is important, since this complication seems to be the single most important factor leading to subsequent stomal stenosis. Presumably, stomal stenosis occurs because of repeated inflammation and scarring of the stoma. Should stomal stenosis occur such that the vesicostomy no longer drains well, that is, residual urine increases, the stoma should be revised.

The converse, vesical prolapse through the vesicostomy stoma, is an infrequent problem. In most instances, even if it occurs it does not interfere with bladder drainage and is of no clinical importance other than cosmesis. However, on rare occasions the bladder may prolapse through the stoma and become incarcerated. Under such circumstances the stoma should be revised. The exact factors leading to prolapse are not well understood, and hence the complete prevention of this problem is difficult. However, placement of the stoma high on the anterior wall of the bladder does seem to offer some protection in this regard.

ANNOTATED BIBLIOGRAPHY

Campbell MF: Surgery of the bladder. In Urology, 2d ed, (ed): pp. 2469–2478. Philadelphia, W B Saunders, 1963

> The descriptions of the operative technique of suprapubic and trocar cystostomy using the Campbell trocar are excellent. Additionally, complications of these procedures are discussed.

Blocksam BH Jr: Bladder pouch for prolonged tubeless cystostomy. J Urol 78:398, 1957

> This was apparently the first clinical report of cutaneous vesicostomy. It was used in a man aged 75 yr with obstructive uropathy.

Lapides J, Koyanagi T, Diokno A: Cutaneous vesicostomy: 10 year survey. J Urol 105:76, 1971

> The authors' experience with 52 patients followed for at least 5 to 10 yr after vesicostomy is reviewed. They conclude that vesicostomy is a good form of vesical diversion, especially in patients with neurogenic bladder dysfunction. They describe a method to close the stoma when it is no longer needed. Admittedly this is a "minority report."

Brady TW, Mebust WK, Valk WL, et al. The cutaneous vesicostomy reappraised. J Urol 105:81, 1971

> The authors reviewed their experience with 34 patients treated by vesicostomy. They concluded that the procedure was suited to short-term use in infants but not to long-term use in adults or children.

Lytton B, Weiss RM: Cutaneous vesicostomy for temporary urinary diversion in infants. J Urol 105:888, 1971

> Vesicostomy was performed in 13 infants with myelomeningocele. Good results were achieved in 10.

Sharpe JR, Ingram JM: Suprapubic cystostomy by trocar catheter. J Urol 110:340, 1973

> Trocar cystostomy was employed in 105 patients aged 4 to 72 yr with uniformly good results and without problems.

Duckett JW Jr: Cutaneous vesicostomy in childhood. The Blocksam technique. Urol Clin North Am 1:485, 1974

> This is an update and expansion of the original report by Michie and colleagues. Of 54 patients with myelomeningocele treated by vesicostomy, 71% achieved improved upper urinary tracts with or without sterile urine. Vesicostomy was also used by Dr. Duckett to treat other problems in infancy such as posterior urethral valves, gross vesicoureteral reflux, imperforate anus, prune-belly syndrome, trauma, ureteroceles, and tumors.

Cohen JS, Harbach LB, Kaplan GW: Cutaneous vesicostomy for temporary urinary diversion in infants with neurologic bladder dysfunction. J Urol 119:120, 1978

> This report reviews the results of vesicostomy in 12 patients with myelomeningocele and hydronephrosis. Pyelographic improvement was noted in all 12. Azotemia was present preoperatively in five and resolved in all five. No clinical urinary tract infections occurred postoperatively, but four patients continued to have positive urine cultures. Complications of the operation included diaper rash, stomal stenosis, and vesical prolapse.

Kroovand RL, Reiner RJ, Perlmutter AD: Trocar cystostomy in pediatric urology. Presented at the American Urological Association, New York, May 16, 1979

> Trocar cystostomy was performed in 101 children using an 8F or 12F Cystocath, 7.9% of the patients had major complications, including perforation of the colon and severe hematuria. Minor complications included transurethral extrusion, kinking, plugging, and premature displacement of the tube.

Overview: Cystostomy and Vesicostomy: Indications and Results

Bernard Lytton

Suprapubic cystostomy became widely used after 1890 and represented a major advance in the treatment of bladder outlet obstruction and as a method of urinary diversion for disease or injury of the lower urinary tract. Preliminary suprapubic drainage of the bladder in patients with prostatic obstruction markedly reduced the mortality and morbidity of subsequent prostatectomy. It provided for correction of azotemia, drainage of infection, and the recovery of detrusor function impaired by prolonged overdistension. The universal adoption of suprapubic cystostomy and drainage of the perivesical space as the primary treatment for injuries of the bladder and urethra during the second World War resulted in a dramatic decrease in mortality from 85% in 1918 to 25% in 1945.[1] It contributed as much to the treatment of these injuries as did the later introduction of antibiotics and better surgical techniques. Recently, there has been renewed interest in suprapubic cystostomy in place of urethral catheter drainage as a method of bladder drainage after gynecologic surgery, since it seems to decrease morbidity and is more comfortable for the patient.

Generally, suprapubic cystostomy remains the more effective method to drain the bladder even though many patients may be successfully managed with a urethral catheter made from nonreactive material. The lumen of the suprapubic tube is nearly twice that of the urethral catheter, and urethritis with its complications of prostatitis and epididymitis are avoided. Bacteriuria occurs with both types of catheter drainage, presumably due to the presence of a foreign body and residual urine. It has been shown that patients with suprapubic catheters have residual urine of between 5 ml and 55 ml, probably due to fixation of the anterior bladder and a consequent inability to contract and empty completely.[2] Intermittent self-catheterization is now the treatment of choice in patients with loss of detrusor function caused by longstanding prostate obstruction. Some elderly men are unable to perform this satisfactorily, and in these cases suprapubic cystostomy is probably the best alternative to allow for recovery of detrusor function, which may take from a few weeks to several months. It remains the only possible procedure when the patient has an impassable urethral stricture.

Suprapubic cystostomy is still the procedure of choice for urethral and bladder injuries. Urethral catheter drainage may be successful treatment in some patients but is generally unsatisfactory because the potential risks of an in-dwelling urethral catheter are considerable. Inadvertent obstruction of the catheter during the first few days after a bladder injury may result in extravasation of infected urine into the surrounding tissues or peritoneal cavity with serious consequences. Inadvertent obstruction of the suprapubic tube occurs less often and is less likely to result in a serious problem because there is still an outlet for urine through the urethra, which is not obstructed with a catheter. Secondary pelvic abscess has been seen in several patiens with ureteral and bladder injuries treated by urethral catheter drainage and occasionally results in osteomyelitis of the fractured pelvic bones. Acute prostatitis not infrequently complicates urethral catheter drainage, and the resultant gram-negative bacteremia may cause metastatic infections in patients with multiple injuries. Chronic bacterial prostatitis may be an unfortunate sequel, with the patient having to take suppressive medication for many years. Morehouse and colleagues have found that suprapubic cystostomy alone, when used as the initial treatment of patients with posterior urethral disruption and followed by a perineal flap urethroplasty after 3 to 6 mo if necessary, gives excellent long-term functional results.[3] They claim that impotence is less frequent with this method than when urethral continuity is reestablished at the time of injury. There is no doubt that suprapubic cystostomy alone is the best form of primary treatment for urethral tears in continuity. When there is total disruption, however, particularly when the two ends of the urethra are widely separated, a strong body of opinion favors immediate reestablishment of urethral continuity over an in-dwelling urethral catheter in addition to suprapubic cystostomy. This may prevent the formation of an impassable stricture, facilitate the subsequent repair, and allow for any stricture that forms to be treated by internal urethrotomy or dilatation rather than by urethroplasty.

The indications for and limitations of suprapubic cystostomy in the management of bladder dysfunction following spinal cord injury now seem fairly well established. It is recommended only as a temporary form of urinary diversion, most applicable in the early phase of management, when clean intermittent catheterization cannot be performed because of limitations of staff or facilities. It does obviate the local complications of urethral catheter drainage, namely, urethritis with the possible formation of a stricture or urethrocutaneous fistula and epididymitis and prostatitis. Long-term use of a suprapubic catheter, however, is associated with significantly higher incidence of chronic pyelonephritis, vesicouretero reflux, and stone disease when compared to patients treated with long-term urethral catheter drainage. Only 39% of 61 renal units in patients receiving suprapubic catheter drainage were normal after an average period of 8 yr, as compared to 51% of 152 renal units that were normal after 20 yr of urethral Foley catheter drainage.[4] This may be due to be fact that suprapubic cystostomy provides less efficient drainage in a bladder that does not contract completely. Moreover, drainage often occurs around the tube in patients with a hypotonic detrusor due to incomplete emptying. Suprapubic catheter drainage, like urethral catheter drainage, leads to progressive bladder contraction with fibrosis of the bladder muscle from the chronic bacteriuria. The incidence of squamous cell carcinoma is also a serious problem after 10 to 20 yr of catheter drainage.[5] Clean intermittent catheterization is the procedure of choice in patients who are continent, and condom catheter drainage is advocated for those who are incontinent. In-dwelling catheters of all types should be reserved only for those patients in whom these methods are impractical or impossible to carry out.

There has been renewed interest over the past 20 yr in the use of suprapubic cystostomy for postoperative bladder drainage in patients undergoing transvaginal gynecologic procedures. A number of studies have compared the incidence of bacteriuria, morbidity, length of hospital stay, and the time taken to reestablish satisfactory voiding postoperatively in patients managed either by suprapubic cystostomy or by urethral catheter drainage. Patients treated by suprapubic cystostomy were found to have less bacteriuria at 5 days (9.3% versus 41% in those managed with a urethral catheters).[6] After 2 or 3 mo, however, bacteriuria was present in only 10% of patients in both groups.[7] This figure is similar to that found among urologic patients who have undergone some form of urethral or bladder instrumentation. Some studies have shown that there is an increase in postoperative infections, an increase in the use of postoperative antibiotics, and a longer hospital stay for patients receiving urethral catheter drainage as compared to those who underwent a suprapubic cystostomy, but others have found no difference in these parameters. The various studies are probably not comparable because some investigators have used historical controls and others have used prospective controls.

Satisfactory voiding seems to be more easily established postoperatively in patients with a suprapubic cystostomy and is certainly more comfortable, since it obviates the need for subsequent repeated catheterization after removal of the urethral catheter. There is a general concensus that the principal advantages of suprapubic cystostomy postoperatively are the significant improvement in patient comfort, greater ease of nursing care, and reduced expense.[8] Most gynecologists advocate percutaneous puncture with some form of trocar or cutting down on a urethral sound pushed up against the anterior bladder wall to establish cystostomy drainage. There have been a number of bowel and peritoneal injuries reported even though ''blind cystostomy'' has been limited to patients who had not undergone an abdominal procedure. This probably occurs as a result of entrapment of a tongue of peritoneum or a loop of bowel between the anterior abdominal wall and the distended bladder.[9] Nevertheless, the use of a trocar or sound to introduce a suprapubic catheter is an acceptable method in a patient who has not had a lower abdominal incision.[10] The possibility of

peritoneal or bowel injury must always be considered, however, in a patient who develops any untoward symptoms after the procedure. Patients who have had abdominal surgery and require cystostomy should have a small vertical suprapubic incision made with direct visualization of the bladder. It is important that the tube be well secured to prevent accidental dislodgment during the first few days, since extravasation of urine in a poor-risk patient, before there is an established tract, can be a serious complication. It has been reported that the mortality of suprapubic cystostomy performed for urinary obstruction in an elderly poor-risk patient is as high as 40%, although this obviously in part reflects these patients' precarious general condition. The bladder should be stitched to the fascia below the tube to close off Retzius' space and to prevent the bladder from retracting away from the tube. The tube should be positioned against the anterior bladder wall to prevent trigonal irritation and brought out at least 3 cm to 4 cm above the symphysis to prevent attachment of the bladder opening to the pubic bone, which may prevent closure of the cystostomy tract when the tube is removed.

Tubeless cystostomy or vesicostomy, as an alternative to an in-dwelling suprapubic catheter, was first introduced by Blocksom in 1956.[11] He also suggested its use as a method of urinary diversion in children with neurogenic bladder. His method consisted of marsupialization of the dome of the bladder midway between the symphysis pubis and umbilicus. Vesicostomy was advocated for long-term bladder drainage in adults by Lapides and associates in 1960.[12] They used a skin flap incorporated into the stoma to help to prevent stomal stenosis. Vesicostomy obviates the use of an in-dwelling foreign body in the bladder and allows for better control of bacteriuria. Its major disadvantage has been the application of a suitable collecting device over the stoma, which is probably the main reason that it did not become a popular method of urinary diversion in adults. Intermittent catheterization has now greatly reduced the indications for both vesicostomy and cystostomy.

Vesicostomy has proved to be most useful as a temporary form of urinary diversion in children when a collecting device is not required, since a diaper is an acceptable method to control the urinary drainage. Duckett has reported the experience at the Children's Hospital in Philadelphia, where over 100 children underwent cutaneous vesicostomy by the Blocksom method as a temporary form of urinary diversion.[13] Over half these children had neurovesical dysfunction secondary to a myelomeningocele, the others having a variety of congenital abnormalities including urethral valves, vesicoureteral reflux, prune-belly syndrome, and imperforate anus. The original Blocksom technique was modified by excising a triangle of rectus fascia to prevent stenosis and fixation of the bladder to the fascia to prevent prolapse. The incised everted bladder dome was sutured to the triangular skin stoma. Lytton and Weiss have found the technique described by Lapides and colleagues, using a skin and bladder flap, very satisfactory in preventing stenosis, and they suture the posterior wall of the bladder to the fascia to prevent prolapse.[14] The abdominal skin is hairless in children, and therefore its incorporation into the stoma does not have the problem of encrustation as it does in the adult. Ross and associates preferred to use a posterior skin flap to prevent prolapse.[15] It seems that all these methods have proved satisfactory and that a vesicostomy performed by any of these methods, if the surgeon bears in mind the potential complications of stomal stenosis and prolapse of the posterior bladder wall, should function effectively in the majority of patients. The irritation caused by urine, producing diaper rash, can generally be controlled by the application of karaya gum powder or vitamin A & D ointment and by soaking the diapers in dilute vinegar to neutralize the ammonia content of the urine.

The main indications for vesicostomy drainage on a temporary basis have been neurovesical dysfunction complicated by persistent infection or upper tract changes, urethral trauma either from accidents or following pull-through procedures for imperforate anus, vesicouretero reflux with ureteral dilatation in young infants, in whom it is more difficult to obtain a satisfactory result by tapering and reimplantation than if the operation is performed at a later age, and in infants with undiagnosed voiding difficulties, in whom some form of diversion is required to allow them to reach an age at which a definitive diagnosis can be established.

The results of vesicostomy drainage have been good; 10 of 54 patients (18%) who had a vesicostomy performed for urologic problems secondary to myelomeningocele failed to have a satisfactory result, either due to deterioration of the upper tracts or a failure to control infection, and have required some other form of diversion. Several other small series have had no failures of vesicostomy drainage in patients with neurogenic problems.[16] Failure of vesicostomy drainage to improve the degree of dilation of the upper tracts has been found principally in patients with bladder outlet obstruction due to urethral valves. About half these patients have been found to have persistent dilatation of the ureters after effective bladder drainage. Whitaker has pointed out that in only a small proportion of patients is this due to an obstruction at the ureterovesical junction and that many of these patients improve over a period of years after the bladder pressure has been restored to normal.[17] A few of these patients with persistent infection or deterioration of renal function will require reconstructive surgery.

Closure of the vesicostomy is easily accomplished when the child is old enough to be reevaluated for any reconstructive procedure to correct urinary obstruction or for management by clean intermittent catheterization rather then by open drainage. One of the major advantages of tubeless vesicostomy is the absence of any bladder contraction, which so often occurs with prolonged catheter drainage.

REFERENCES

1. Clarke BG, Leadbester WF: Management of wounds and injuries of genito-urinary tract. A review of reported experience in World War II. J Urol 67:719, 1952

2. Brushini H, Tanaglio E: Cystostomy drainage: Its efficacy in preventing residual urine and infection. J Urol 118:391, 1977

3. Morehouse DD, Mackinnon KJ: Management of prostato-membraneous urethral dysfunction. 13 years experience. J Urol 123:173, 1980

4. Hackler RA: Suprapubic cystostomy in spinal cord injury patients. J Urol (in press)

5. Kaufman J: Bladder cancer and squamous metaplasia in spinal cord injury patients. J Urol 118:967, 1977

6. Hodgkinson CP, Hodari AA: Trocar suprapubic cystostomy for postoperative bladder drainage in females. Am J Obstet Gynecol 96:773, 1966

7. Hofmeister FT, Martens WE, Strebel RL: Foley catheter or suprapubic tube. Am J Obstet Gynecol 107:767, 1920

8. Frymire LJ: Comparison of suprapubic vs. Foley drains. Obstet Gynecol 38:239, 1971

9. Noller KL, Pratt JH, Symmonds RE: Bowel perforation with suprapubic cystostomy. Obstet Gynecol 48 (Suppl):675, 1976

10. Flock WD, Lituar AS, McRoberts JW: Evaluation of closed suprapubic cystostomy. Urology 11:40, 1978

11. Blocksam BH: Bladder pouch for prolonged tubeless cystostomy. J Urol 78:398, 1957

12. Lapides J, Ajemian EP, Lichtwardt JR: Cutaneous vesicostomy. J Urol 84:609, 1960

13. Duckett JW Jr: Cutaneous vesicostomy in childhood. Urol Clin North Am 1:3, 485, 1974

14. Lytton B, Weiss R: Cutaneous vesicostomy for temporary urinary diversion in infants. J Urol 105:888, 1971

15. Ross G Jr, Michener FR, Brady C Jr: Cutaneous vesicostomy. A review of 36 cases. J Urol 94:402, 1965

16. Bruce RR, Gonzales ET: Cutaneous vesicostomy: A useful form of temporary diversion in children. J Urol 123:927, 1980

17. Whitaker RH: The ureter in posterior urethral valves. Br J Urol 45:395, 1973

PART TWENTY-FOUR

SURGERY OF BLADDER AUGMENTATION AND REPLACEMENT (ENTEROCYSTOPLASTY)

61

AUGMENTATION ENTEROCYSTOPLASTY: A CRITICAL REVIEW

Robert B. Smith,* Paul van Cangh, Donald G. Skinner, Joseph J. Kaufman and Willard E. Goodwin

From the Department of Surgery, Division of Urology, University of California School of Medicine and the Wadsworth Veterans Administration Hospital, Los Angeles, California

The Journal of Urology
Copyright © 1977 by The Williams & Wilkins Co.
Vol. 118, July, Part 1
Printed in U.S.A.

ABSTRACT—An over-all success rate of 58.1 percent has been achieved in 74 patients who have undergone augmentation cystoplasty. Indications for the operation included a contracted bladder secondary to interstitial cystitis in 30 patients, defunctionalized bladder in 12, neurogenic bladder in 11, radiation cystitis in 9, tuberculous cystitis in 7, chemical cystitis in 4 and pericystitis in 1. Male patients did as well as female patients. Specific indications for the operation did not seem to influence success rate, although augmentation cystoplasty used as part of a planned undiversion had a significantly lower success rate (45 percent) than when cystoplasty was used with an intact urinary tract (66.7 percent). The segment of bowel used did not seem to influence results. Patients who underwent associated bladder neck revision seemed to do better, while no benefit was noted in patients who had a supratrigonal excision of the diseased detrusor. Complications were eliminated in 82 percent of the patients, while only 3 patients had progressive uremia. Operative mortality occurred in 2 patients (2.7 percent). Four other deaths have occurred in the entire series, 1½, 2, 5 and 11 years later. Contraindications to the operation include patients with azotemia, vesical neoplasm, neurogenic bladder with spastic pelvic floor and some cases of defunctionalized contracted bladders. The pre-adolescent boy may have difficulty in voiding because of mucus. Patients with a strong psychiatric history should be approached with caution.

Accepted for publication August 6, 1976.
Read at annual meeting of American Urological Association, Las Vegas, Nevada, May 16–20, 1976.

* Requests for reprints: Department of Surgery/Urology, University of California School of Medicine, Los Angeles, California 90024.

Herein we relate a 20-year experience of augmentation cystoplasty in regard to indications, surgical technique and results. Some results have been presented elsewhere.[1,2] Failures are analyzed critically so that similar untoward results can be avoided in the future. We do not intend to review the enterocystoplasty literature, since this has been done previously.[3,4]

MATERIALS AND METHODS

From 1956 to 1975, 74 enterocystoplasties for bladder augmentation have been done. Followup from 3 months to 19 years, mean of 5.1 years, is available in all except 1 patient. An additional 9 cases of enterocystoplasty used primarily as a means of undiversion and not for augmentation of bladder capacity have been excluded from this report.

The indications for the cystoplasties included interstitial cystitis in 30 patients, defunctionalized bladder in 12 (Fig. 1), neurogenic bladder in 11 (Fig. 2), radiation cystitis in 9, tuberculous cystitis in 7, chemical cystitis in 4 and pericystitis in 1. This distribution is strikingly different from that reported in the European literature, in which tuberculous cystitis and vesical neoplasm account for the majority of cases.[5,6]

Female patients represented 77 percent of the cases

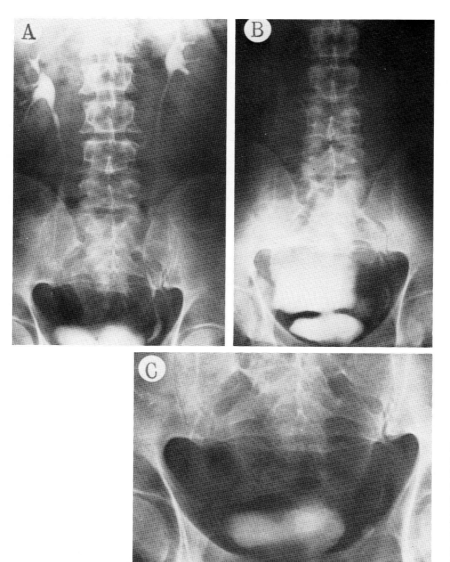

Fig. 1. (*A*), IVP 17 years after ileocystoplasty for contracted defunctionalized bladder secondary to incontinence and related to epispadias. (*B*) A cystogram reveals less-than-ideal hourglass configuration of vesicoenteric anastomosis. However, patient has bladder capacity in excess of 400 cc without residual urine and is asymptomatic. (*C*) Post-void film.

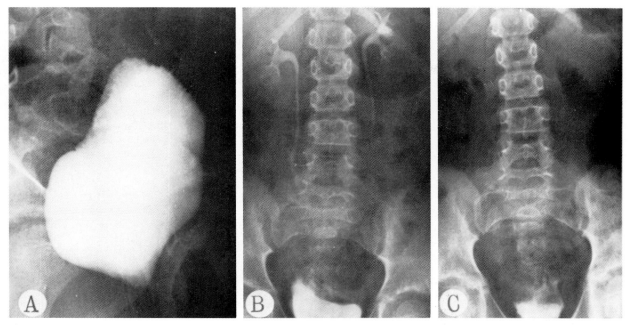

Fig. 2. Patient is asymptomatic 1½ years after ileocystoplasty for neurogenic bladder. Bladder capacity is in excess of 350 cc. (*A*) Cystogram. (*B*) IVP. (*C*) Post-void residual film.

TABLE 1. Results of Enterocystoplasty Related to Primary Diagnosis

	Total No. Pts.	Excellent		Good		Failure		Indeterminate* No. Pts.
		No. Pts.	(%)	No. Pts.	(%)	No. Pts.	(%)	
Interstitial cystitis	30	7	(28.0)	10	(40.0)	8	(32.0)	5
Defunctionalized bladder	12	5	(41.7)	2	(16.6)	5	(41.7)	0
Neurogenic bladder	11	3	(27.2)	4	(36.4)	4	(36.4)	0
Radiation injury	9	1	(11.1)	2	(22.2)	6	(66.7)	0
Tuberculous cystitis	7	3	(42.8)	1	(14.4)	3	(42.8)	0
Chemical cystitis	4	2	(50.0)	2	(50.0)	0	(0)	0

* Indeterminate results have not been included when percentages have been computed.

(17 male and 57 female patients). The patients ranged in age from 5 to 81 years, with a mean of 42.5 years. Six patients younger than 10 years old underwent cystoplasty, with an additional 11 patients between 11 and 20 years old.

Ileocystoplasty as described by Goodwin and associates[7] was by far the most prevalent operative technique used (45 patients), followed by ileocecocystoplasty in 16 cases, sigmoidocystoplasty in 7 and cecocystoplasty in 6. The technique of each procedure has been discussed elsewhere.[7-9]

RESULTS

Excellent results consist of patients who are asymptomatic and represent a cure. Patients in the good category showed marked improvement but still have minimal residual symptoms. In our series 20 patients had excellent results, 23 had good results and 26 were failures. Five patients represent indeterminate results. Of these 5 patients 2 died in the early postoperative period, 1 was without adequate followup and 2 had a disparity in functional and symptomatic results.

Male patients enjoyed equal or superior success when compared to female subjects. There is no significant difference in results of augmentation cystoplasty related to primary diagnosis (Table 1). Patients with radiation cystitis appear to have a worse prognosis than those in the other categories but 2 of the 6 failures in this group are owing to persistent or recurrent vesicovaginal fistulas that were thought to have been repaired. One cannot indict cystoplasty in regard to these failures. The origin of the bowel segment used for augmentation does not influence the outcome of the procedure.

Y-V plasty of the bladder neck or transurethral resection of the prostate was performed on 37 patients. These patients fared better than those who did not have revision of their bladder neck (Table 2). An additional 3 patients who were considered failures after cystoplasty without bladder neck revision were converted to success after subsequent Y-V plasty or transurethral resection. If these 3 patients were included in the initial failure rate of patients who did not have bladder neck resection the failure rate in this group would be 52.9 percent, compared to a failure rate of only 33.3 percent in those patients who underwent bladder neck revision. Excision of the diseased detrusor did not seem to influence the results of the procedure. In fact, a superior success rate was noted in patients who did not have the detrusor removed (63.3 percent), compared to those who did (50 percent). This difference is not significant.

Residual urine ranged from 0 to 175 cc in those patients who were considered to have good or excellent results. Only 2 successful patients had residual urine consistently in excess of 75 cc (125 and 175 cc). Twenty-one patients had less than 15 cc residual urine.

Preoperative bladder capacity was less than 100 cc in 31 of 51 patients in whom this information was available, between 100 and 200 cc in 11 patients and more than 200 cc in 9 patients. Postoperative bladder capacity ranged between 60 and 750 cc. Only 5 of 49 patients with available data had capacities of less than 200 cc postoperatively, 75 percent had a capacity of between 200 and 500 cc and 8 patients had bladder capacities exceeding 500 cc.

Six patients have died up to 11 years after the procedure. In addition, 1 patient with progressive uremia is now on chronic dialysis. Only 2 operative deaths were noted in this series (10 and 40 days postoperatively), an operative mortality rate of 2.7 percent. Three other deaths were directly attributable to the procedure, 2 with progressive uremia 2 and 11 years postoperatively and

another 1½ years after cystoplasty as a result of numerous episodes of small bowel obstruction with subsequent small bowel fistula and sepsis. Both patients with progressive uremia leading to death were uremic when the procedure was performed. The other death occurred 5 years after ileocystoplasty for a tuberculous bladder. The exact cause of death could not be determined. However, it is known that the patient's renal and bladder function were excellent prior to death.

The early and late complications of cystoplasty are listed in table 3. Sixty patients (82 percent) were free of complications, with a hospital stay of between 10 and 16 days.

DISCUSSION

Indications for Cystoplasty. Patients with contracted bladders secondary to interstitial cystitis, tuberculous cystitis, radiation cystitis, and chemical and traumatic cystitis represent ideal indications for this procedure. Cystoplasty also is of value in selected cases of hypertonic neurogenic bladder with incontinence,[10,11] as long as outflow obstruction secondary to a dysfunctional bladder neck or a spastic pelvic floor does not exist or can be modified by pharmacologic[12-14] or surgical means (sphincterotomy[15] or bladder neck revision). However, cystoplasty should be used only after all other methods of controlling the uninhibited contractions have been exhausted. It appears that cystoplasty decreases the magnitude of involuntary pressure spikes, as well as increases the functional capacity of the bladder. Although these goals were accomplished in the early cases in our

TABLE 2. Success Related to Bladder Neck Revision

	No. Pts.	(%)
Bladder neck revision performed* (37 pts.):		
Excellent	12	(32.4)
Good	13	(35.2)
Failure	12	(32.4)
Bladder neck revision never performed (31 pts.):		
Excellent	8	(25.8)
Good	8	(25.8)
Failure	15†	(48.7)

* Performed either preoperatively, intraoperatively or post-cystoplasty.

† Three additional failures were converted to success by subsequent bladder neck revision.

TABLE 3. Complications

	No. Cases
Early:	
Pulmonary embolus	3
Myocardial infarction	2*
Progressive azotemia	1†
Suprapubic fistula	1
Sepsis	1
Contracture of vesicoenteric anastomosis	1
Ischemic fibrosis enteric patch	1
Wound dehiscence	1
Late:	
Bladder calculi	3
Progressive azotemia	2‡
Renal calculi	2
Small bowel obstruction and fistula	1§
Small bowel obstruction (only)	1
Ureteral stricture	1
Osteitis pubis	1

* Both died.

† Preoperative creatinine 4.1 mg percent.

‡ 1 and 11 years later.

§ Died 1½ years later.

series failure occurred because the importance of pelvic floor spasticity was not appreciated.[1,16]

Patients with a significant psychiatric history that may be related to their preoperative symptoms should be approached with caution. Often such patients present with frequency, urgency and suprapubic pain, having been diagnosed as patients with interstitial cystitis. Results in our series on such patients are less than optimal. Only 2 of 10 such patients benefited significantly from cystoplasty. If any question exists in this regard preoperative psychiatric consultation is mandatory.

Chronic renal insufficiency is a contraindication to the procedure. Three patients who were uremic preoperatively progressed significantly after cystoplasty. This experience contradicts the experience of Küss and associates, who state that patients with a creatinine clearance greater than 15 cc per minute are acceptable.[5] However, they noted that 44 percent of patients in their series had a decrease in renal function. Only 4.1 percent of our patients have experienced functional deterioration. We believe that a creatinine clearance of at least 40 cc per minute is mandatory for any procedure in which the bowel is interposed within the intact urinary tract. We have noted no electrolyte aberrations in our series of patients in whom uremia was not present.

We believe that cystoplasty has no place in patients with bladder cancer. Preoccupation with reconstructive procedures is likely to compromise the adequacy of resection. One should not replace an indicated radical cystectomy with a less-than-optimal subtotal bladder resection associated with cystoplasty. In our experience if a malignant bladder lesion is amenable to partial cystectomy augmentation is rarely necessary. The bladder will enlarge to a sufficient capacity within a few months after partial cystectomy. This view is further substantiated by the high morbidity and mortality rates in the series of Küss and associates.[5]

Care also must be exercised in performing cysto-plasty in patients with a defunctionalized bladder.[17] Patients who have had prior diversion because of an obscure bladder dysfunction with residual urine should not be reconstructed unless the original problem has been idenified and corrected. Often, the well meaning urologist will see such a patient with a small contracted bladder that now empties to completion and recommend reconstruction with bladder augmentation. It has been forgotten that the original problem most likely still exists. Such cases in our experience almost invariably result in failure. Of those 20 patients who had augmentation cystoplasty used with undiversion the results were significantly lower (45.0 percent) than in those without undiversion (66.7 percent). Imbalance of micturition was the cause of failure in most of these patients and most likely the imbalance was related to the detrusor dysfunction that necessitated the original diversion.

Surgical Techniques. It is our impression that other factors are more important in regard to success of cystoplasty than which bowel segment was used. This opinion is shared by other investigators.[4,18] Küss and associates express some concern about the fact that septic operative complications may be greater when the colon is used[5] but this is not borne out in our series. In addition, it is our belief and that of others.[4,19] that if the ileum or sigmoid colon is used, a patch cystoplasty is superior to the tubular form.

Y-V plasty or transurethral resection of the bladder neck is thought to be an important addition to cystoplasty in order to decrease voiding resistance (Table 2). With modern urodynamic diagnostic techniques[20] it may be possible to screen patients more accurately preoperatively in this regard. Some failures in our series have been converted to successes by subsequent bladder neck revision (Fig. 3). Urethral pressure profile is an important diagnostic study in all candidates for cystoplasty and is mandatory in those patients with interstitial cystitis. Raz

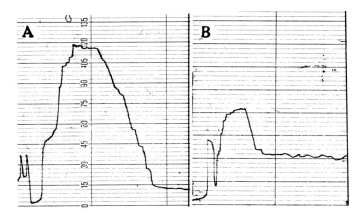

Fig. 3. Urethral pressure profile on patient with interstitial cystitis. (*A*) Before Y-V plasty. (*B*) After Y-V plasty.

has evidence that patients with interstitial cystitis also may have a urethral component to this disease, with resultant increased urethral resistance.[21] However, bladder neck revision is not without risks. Some failures in our series have resulted from incontinence secondary to an overzealous Y-V plasty. Despite multiple attempts to correct this problem surgically, subsequent diversion occasionally has been necessary. The fine line between retention and incontinence in cystoplasty patients is often difficult to achieve. Enuresis has not been a problem.

We have not been able to confirm the experience of some investigators[18,22] who state that resection of the diseased detrusor is essential to achieve success with cystoplasty. Others agree with our observations.[3] Presacral neurectomy was performed in only 7 patients and did not seem to influence results.

Causes of Failure. We have analyzed the cause of failure in each instance. Imbalance of micturition was the cause of failure in 14 patients, 10 of whom were in retention and 4 were incontinent. Modern pharmacologic or surgical therapy may have converted some of these failures to successes. Although the patients in retention are classified as failures many are quite satisfied with the postoperative status, since intermittent self-catheterization is much better tolerated than their preoperative status, of extreme frequency, urgency and, often, incontinence. It is hoped that with improved methods of preoperative evaluation the incidence of this cause of failure will decrease in the future. Persistent symptoms, despite an improvement in anatomic configuration, accounted for 4 additional failures. Three patients in this group had strong psychiatric overlay and some doubt exists retrospectively in our minds whether the correct preoperative diagnosis of interstitial cystitis was made. Four other patients who failed because of retention also had strong psychiatric problems, which may well have contributed to their failure.

Progressive uemia has been a cause of failure in only 2 patients, both of whom were uremic preoperatively and progressed rapidly (1 month and 1 year), requiring supravesical diversion. It is clear that niether patient was a candidate for cystoplasty. An additional patient who died of progressive uremia 11 years later has been considered a good result, since he was asymptomatic throughout this entire period.

Radiographic upper tract deterioration was noted in only 4 patients, whereas 6 patients with preoperative hydronephrosis improved. Twenty-two patients with normal upper tracts remained normal and 5 patients with mild hydronephrosis remained unchanged. The fear that the upper urinary tracts will deteriorate when the intestine is interposed in an intact urinary tract, as expressed by Tanagho,[19] appears to be unfounded if patients are properly selected.

Nine patients with preoperative reflux had improvement in this regard. However, 8 patients without preoperative reflux acquired reflux after cystoplasty. The cause of this is unclear but some of these patients probably had undetected reflux preoperatively. A vesicoenteric suture line near the trigone could be a factor causing reflux. The remaining patients were unchanged. We believe that in many instances the low-pressure system, as seen in enterocystoplasy, protects the upper tract from hydrostatic damage from reflux.

Two patients with radiation cystitis failed because of recurrent or persistent vesicovaginal fistulas. One cannot fault the cystoplasty for these failures but it is certainly clear that adequate time must pass between a fistula repair and cystoplasty to ensure that a successful fistula repair has been achieved.

Technical complications directly related to enterocystoplasty itself were the cause of only 2 failures. A fibrotic enteric patch secondary to ischemia accounted for 1 failure and a contracted, vesicoenteric anastomosis accounted for the other. However, 5 other patients had a less than ideal vesicoenteric anastomosis (hourglass configuration) but nevertheless represent good or excellent results.

In general, patients who were infected preoperatively remained infected postoperatively. As expected, the larger the residual urine the more likely complications related to infections would occur. However, the majority of patients remained asymptomatic on chronic suppressive antibiotics.

The low operative death rate of 2.7 percent is surprising to us, as is the fact that 92 percent of patients are still alive. These statistics attest to the long-term efficacy of this procedure. However, the potential for progressive problems does exist and periodic long-term followup is essential.

SUMMARY

Augmentation cystoplasty appears to offer a successful long-term solution for patients with small contracted bladders of almost any etiology. If proper indications are observed the procedure is well tolerated. With refined urodynamic diagnostic techniques our over-all failure rate of 35 percent can be expected to decrease. Contraindications of the procedure include azotemia (creatinine clearance less than 40 cc per minute), vesical malignancy, neurogenic bladder with spastic pelvic floor (that cannot be modified) and young boys (mucus problems). In addition, patients with a strong psychiatric history should be approached with caution. The non-functional contracted bladder in which the cause of prior diversion is unclear or was performed because of an apparent outflow obstruction that spontaneously has been corrected by rest during the period of supravesical diversion also should be approached with care.

REFERENCES

1. Goodwin, W. E., Turner, R. D. and Winter, C. C.: Results of ileocystoplasty. J Urol, 80:461, 1958

2. Winter, C. C. and Goodwin, W. E.: Results of signoidocystoplasty. J Urol, 80:467, 1958

3. Homsy, Y. L. and Reid, E. C.: Ileocystoplasty. Urology, 4:135, 1974

4. Roblejo, P. G. and Malament, M.: Late results of an ileocystoplasty: a 12-year followup. J Urol, 109:38, 1973

5. Küss, R., Bitker, M., Camey, M., Chatelain, C. and Lassau, J. P.: Indications and early and late results of intestinocystoplasty: a review of 185 cases. J Urol, 103:53, 1970

6. Cukier, J.: Les remplacements de la vessie. Urol Int, 23:436, 1968

7. Goodwin, W. E., Winter, C. C. and Barker, W. F.: "Cup-patch" technique of ileocystoplasty for bladder enlargement or partial substitution. Surg, Gynec & Obst, 108:240, 1959

8. Goodwin, W. E. and Winter, C. C.: Technique of sigmoidocystoplasty. Surg, Gynec & Obst, 108:370, 1959

9. Gil-Vernet, J. M., Jr.: The ileocolic segment in urologic surgery. J Urol, 94:418, 1965

10. Smith, R. B.: Use of ileocystoplasty in the hypertonic neurogenic bladder. J Urol, 113:125, 1975

11. Servadio, C.: Neurogenic bladder treated by subtotal cystectomy and ileocystoplasy: a preliminary report. J Urol, 98:472, 1967

12. Krane, R. J. and Olsson, C. A.: Phenoxybenzamine in neurogenic bladder dysfunction. I. A theory of micturition. J Urol, 110:650, 1973

13. Krane, R. J. and Olsson, C. A.: Phenoxybenzamine in neurogenic bladder dysfunction. II. Clinical considerations. J Urol, 110:653, 1973

14. Raz, S. and Smith, R. B.: External sphincter spasticity syndrome in female patients. J Urol, 115:443, 1976

15. Turner Warwick, R. T. and Ashken, M. H.: The functional results of partial, subtotal and total cystoplasty with special reference to ureterocaecocystoplasty, selective sphincterotomy and cystoplasty. Br J Urol, 39:2, 1967

16. Goodwin, W. E.: Late complications of enterocystoplasty. Acta Urol Belg 37:51, 1969

17. Richie, J. P. and Sachs, S. A.: Complications of urinary tract undiversion. In: Complications of Urologic Surgery: Prevention and Management. Edited by R B Smith and D G Skinner. Philadelphia: W B Saunders Co, p 241, 1976

18. Kerr, W. K., Gale, G. L. and Peteson, K. S. S.: Reconstructive surgery for genitourinary tuberculosis. J Urol, 101:254, 1969

19. Tanagho, E. A.: A case against incorporation of bowel segments into the closed urinary system. J Urol, 113:796, 1975

20. Raz, S. and Kaufman, J. J.: Carbon dioxide urethral pressure profile. J Urol, 115:439, 1976

21. Raz, S.: Personal communication, 1976

22. Gittes, R. F.: Ileocecocystoplasty: clinical and metabolic studies. Read at annual meeting, American Urological Association, Philadelphia, Pennsylavania, May 10–14, 1970

Commentary: Ileocystoplasty

William K. Kerr

The preceding article has been chosen as representing the outstanding long-term experience with cystoplasty in North America by authors who pioneered this field 25 yr ago. Their wide experience in various situations calling for different solutions to fit the case commends this paper to the reader.

Ileocystoplasty as well as colocystoplasty and also cecocystoplasty employed for a wide range of indications have been grouped together by Küss and associates under the title "Intestinocystoplasty." This selected article, which has been commented on by Küss himself, is the most comprehensive review of the subject in recent literature and is based on the largest experience (185 cases) recorded in Western literature. Although my experience is much smaller, I agree with Küss and associates on almost all points and will therefore not criticize it at length but urge the reader to read the original article itself closely.

Although Küss and associates favor colocystoplasty over ileocystoplasty, I will comment on the subject, which I refer to as enterocystoplasty, with particular reference to the use of ileium, with which I have had more experience and which I favor over colocystoplasty, and attempt to delineate the development and very different status of this surgery in North America. Finally, I shall also indicate my experience in the application of cystoplasty after cystectomy for cancer of the bladder.

The early use of ileum in the urinary tract in North America was for replacement of obstructed ureters.[1,2] The use of ileum to enlarge or replace a portion of diseased bladder followed the reports from France and England in the mid-1950s and was at first applied in patients with tuberculous contracture of bladder and vesicoureteral reflux and then also in patients with interstitial cystitis or Hunner's ulcer.[3–9] At this time Bricker became a strong advocate of the ileal conduit to replace the bladder after exenterative surgery for gynecologic cancer and cystectomy for carcinoma of the bladder and rapidly saw wide acceptance of this mode of urinary diversion for many indications, including conditions where ileocystoplasty might have been applied. Refinement in the surgical technique of ileal conduit construction and perfection of ileostomy equipment and their application have confirmed the preeminent position of this mode of urinary diversion for a wide range of indications in North America.

In the meanwhile the incidence of genitourinary tuberculosis has declined so considerably in the United States and

Canada that tuberculous contracture of the bladder is seen very rarely. Occasional cases that still occur are more likely to be treated by an ileal conduit, with which more urologists in North America are familiar.

The next indication for ileocystoplasty is Hunner's ulcer. The results of preservation of trigone and bladder neck with ileocystoplasty for this condition have sometimes been disappointing, again leading urologists to use the ileal conduit with or without cystectomy as the more definitive and certain cure for this condition.

TUBERCULOUS CONTRACTURE AND HUNNER'S ULCER

The first indication for ileocystoplasty and still the best accepted indication is tuberculous vesical contracture with ureteral reflux and hydronephrosis. When tuberculous cystitis has healed by fibrosis rather than resolution, contracture of the bladder gives the patient not only intolerable frequency but is often attended by vesicoureteral reflux and gross hydronephrosis with rapid deterioration of renal function. Before ileocystoplasty is carried out it is necessary to excise the diseased detrusor, and if there is already reflux the ureteral stump and part of the trigone are sacrificed. I have confirmed what pioneers in this surgery demonstrated, namely, that simple enlargement of the bladder without excision of the diseased detrusor does not work. Neither the frequency nor the hydronephrosis is relieved.

The choice of bowel to be used in any enterocystoplasty is, in my opinion, not fundamental. Early experience with ileocystoplasty for tuberculous contracture showed that patients were prone to develop silent residual urine. It was then thought that the sigmoid colon would have better emptying capability and colocystoplasty became the vogue. Experience with this, however, showed that the cystoplasty was still prone to incomplete emptying. Howard Hanley, who has had much experience with cystoplasty for tuberculosis in Britain, has long recognized this and advocates careful supervision to detect development of residual urine and then counter it by transurethral resection of bladder neck and prostate, repeated if necessary until the patient empties satisfactorily. Willard Goodwin, one of the pioneers of ileocystoplasty in the United States and still an advocate of this operation, advises vesical neck plasty at the time of the operation to prevent residual urine.[10] Thus ileum and colon share the same problem of incomplete emptying countered by the same measures. The cecum was advocated by Turner-Warwick and is used frequently by James Gow for tuberculous vesical contracture, leaving a length of ileum into which the ureter is implanted and attaching the cecum to the bladder neck.[11,12] I have tried the cecum a few times but find it a difficult segment of bowel to clean and not as easy to mobilize as the ileum.

I believe that any of the three segments of bowel—ileum, sigmoid colon, or cecum with a tail of ileum—may be used according to the surgeon's personal preference or the circumstances of the cases, an important consideration being the length of mesentery and relative ease of mobilization.

Wesolowski in Poland compares his experience with ileocystoplasty and colocystoplasty and finds in favor of ileocystoplasty.[13] Wehrheim in East Germany favors ileocys-

toplasty.[14,15] On the other hand, in Russia, where considerable reconstructive surgery for tuberculosis of the urinary tract is carried out, colocystoplasty is used most frequently. Mochalova has performed 300 colocystoplasties for tuberculous bladders![16]

There is little doubt that in most areas of the world where tuberculosis in the urinary tract is still common, some form of enterocystoplasty has now replaced nephrostomy, ureterostomy, or ureterosigmoidostomy in tuberculous vesical contracture and is preferred to ileal conduit with a cutaneous stoma. If the rehabilitation of the patient with an ileal conduit is excellent, the rehabilitation of a patient with a successful ileocystoplasty or other enterocystoplasty is superb. I believe that the operation should be used more frequently in North America for both tuberculous contracture and Hunner's ulcer.

CARCINOMA OF THE BLADDER

The article by Küss, Bitker, Camey, Chatelain, and Lassau not only deals with intestinocystoplasty for benign indications but also reports on one of the largest experiences with reconstruction of the urinary tract rather than diversion, after cystectomy for bladder cancer (Table 4).

The remainder of this presentation will describe a personal series of 50 cases of enterocystoplasty after cystectomy for bladder cancer in which the ileum was used in 28, colon in 17, and cecum in 5 cases.[17] The cases selected were almost all male, 45/50, usually young or older men with early invasive carcinoma or widespread papillomatosis.

Cystectomy. The removal of the bladder was usually radical with dissection of iliac, obturator, and perivesical lymphatics (32/50 patients) and also total in that it included all of the bladder seminal vesicles and prostate (44/50). The less than total cystectomy cases include 4 women in whom the urethra was preserved, and 1 man in whom partial cystectomy was performed inadvertently for interstitial cystitis which turned out to be cancer and 1 man who had considerable adhesions after irradiation in whom the seminal vesicles and prostatic capsule were left behind. Both latter cases developed local recurrence. Removal of all bladder and prostate down to the membranous urethra is required to ensure control of local recurrence of carcinoma.

Choice of Bowel and Technique of Cystoplasty. Initially when this surgery was begun in 1955, the ileum was used; then the sigmoid colon was tried, and finally also the cecum.

TABLE 4. Cystoplasty in Bladder Cancer

Author	Journal	Cases
Gregoir:	Urol Int (Basel) 11:628, 1961	
Delibeliosis:	Hellen Iatr 31:1073, 1962	11
Gil-Vernet:	J Urol 94:418, 1965	41
Hradec:	Cesk Radiol 19:116, 1965	60
Charbonneau:	J Urol 97:849, 1967	11
Ong:	Ann Roy Coll Surg 46:320, 1970	28
Küss:	J Urol 103:53, 1970	52
Kerr:	Unpublished, 1971	50
		253

I have reverted to the ileum as easiest to work with; the sigmoid colon is not always easy to mobilize, nor is the cecum, and the latter is moreover difficult to clean. Storage of urine and continence were the same with any of the three segments of bowel. There must be adequate length of mesentery for the bowel to reach the urethral stump without tension and without impairment of blood supply. If this is not possible, an ileal conduit with a cutaneous stoma must be resorted to. The bowel is approximated to the urethral stump with 6 to 8 interrupted 2–0 chromic sutures over a splinting 16 Foley catheter.

Leakage at this suture line is prone to occur due to blockage of the catheter with mucus. Proximal drainage of the bowel segment is therefore carried out as well as drainage down the site of anastomosis in order to avoid the complications of urinary leakage.

Silk must not be used in any layer of anastomosis which is to contain urine lest calculi form. Charbonneau and Bourque reported giant calculi in all of 10 cases of colocystoplasty for bladder cancer (Table 4). In personal communications Charbonneau states that silk sutures were used in the outer layer of closure of the two ends of the sigmoid colon. I have had no calculi in 50 cancer cases, nor in any of the 35 cases of cystoplasty I have done for benign indications, and ascribe this to avoidance of nonabsorbable sutures.

Survival and Cancer Control with Enterocystoplasty. Three of 50 patients died as a result of the surgery. In cases where the bladder, seminal vesicles, and prostate have been removed down to the membranous urethra, the chances of cancer control with reconstitution of the urinary tract with a loop of bowel joined to the patient's own urethra are as good as with any other urinary diversion. The 5-yr survival rate was 66%. One patient died 4 yr postoperatively with perineal urethral recurrence of transitional cell carcinoma (3%). One patient developed carcinoma of the renal pelvis at 7 yr, after removal of which he has survived for 5 yr albeit with intermittent hematuria. There were no ureteral recurrences in any of the 50 patients. Of the four women in the series, two were incontinent and had the cystoplasty converted to an ileal conduit at which time the urethra was removed, and one patient is alive, continent, and free of recurrence at 6 yr. Only exceptionally would this operation be indicated in a woman, balancing the avoidance of a cutaneous stoma against the risk of incontinence and urethral recurrence of cancer.

Preservation of renal function and health was excellent in all but one patient, who died with recurrent carcinoma and pyonephrosis. Three representative pyelograms on patients who have had this operation for up to 20 yr are presented. Renal preservation can be seen to be generally good (Figs. 4, 5, and 6).

Urinary Continence. Is urinary control good enough to accept the additional risk of enterourethral leakage in the postoperative period? Urinary continence has been the major shortcoming, with not all patients being continent in the day and most of the patients being incontinent at night. In women, two out three survivors were incontinent; they probably need conservation of bladder neck to ensure urinary control and so must accept an even greater compromise with cancer control.

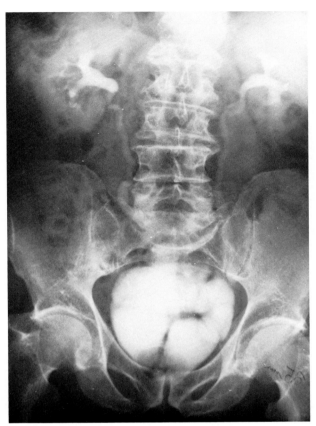

Fig. 4. Patient V.L.: total cystectomy and ileoneocystoplasty, June 10, 1958. Follow-up I.V.P. April 4, 1980.

As far as men with total cystoprostatectomy are concerned, the urinary control with enterocystoplasty was satisfactory both day and night in 23 out of 46 patients voiding every 2 to 4 hr in the daytime and 1 to 2 times at night. In about a quarter there was daytime control but loss of control at night, requiring pads, clamps, or condom apparatus. Finally, in one quarter of the patients there is inadequate control day and night; they may be able to hold urine for a few hours in the morning only. Patients who are completely continent day and night are prone to develop some hydronephrosis, but none has developed renal failure or electrolyte imbalance. Some of the patients with incontinence manage this well and happily, but others would have been better with an ileal conduit. Dr. Camay of Paris presented a series of 100 such patients at the Congress of the International Society of urology in Paris in 1979 with similarly worthwhile results.

In conclusion, I believe, as a result of the experience reported by Drs. Küss and Goodwin and their associates and other authors from abroad as well as my own experience, that enterocystoplasty after cystectomy for bladder cancer has been largely neglected in North America and should be considered more frequently in selected cases.

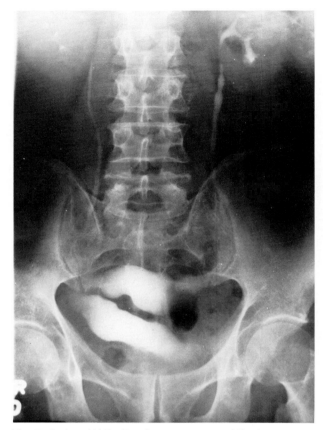

Fig. 5. Patient W.F.: Total cystectomy and ileoneocysto-plasty, June 23, 1960. Follow-up I.V.P. March 23, 1978.

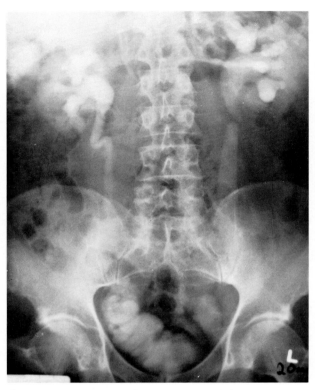

Fig. 6. Patient K.L.: Total cystectomy and ileoneocysto-plasty, March 1, 1962. Follow-up I.V.P. March 19, 1980.

REFERENCES

1. Nesbit RM: Ureterosigmoid anastomosis by direct eliptical connection: Preliminary report. Univ Hosp Bull Ann Arbor 14:45, 1948

2. Goodwin WE, Turner RD, Winter CC: Results of Ileocystoplasty. J Urol 80:461, 1958

3. Couvelaire R: Application de la cysto-entéro-plastie à la core de certains fistulas vésico-vaginales. J Urol 60:623, 1954

4. Kuss R: Sur 21 cas d'ileo-cystoplastie. Mem Acad Chir 82:629, 1956

5. Pyrah LN: The rise of the ileum in urology. Br J Urol 28:363, 1956

6. Riches Sir E: In Modern Trends in Urology, second series. London, Butterworth

7. Yeates WK: Techniques of ileocystoplasty. Br J Urol 28:410, 1956

8. Bourque JP: The indications and techniques of bowel substitution after total cystectomy: Preliminary report on 25 cases. Br J Urol 31:448, 1959

9. Kerr WK: Ileocystoplasty. A. Experimental studies on electrolyte behavior. Canad J Surg 3:35, 1959

10. Goodwin WE: Cup-patch technique of ileocystoplasty for bladder enlargement or partial substitution. Surg Gynecol Obstet 108:240, 1959

11. Turner-Warwick RT: Colonic urinary conduits. Proc R Soc Med 53:1032, 1960

12. Gow J: Partial nephrectomy: A critical study. Lancet 2:759, 1959

13. Wesolowski S: Late results of cystoplasty in chronic tuberculous cystitis. Br J Urol 42:697, 1970; and personal communication

14. Wehrheim W: Die Ileocytoplastik in der Behandlung Blasentuberukulose. Z Urol 52:709, 1964

15. Wehrheim W: Personal communications, 1971

16. Mochalova, Madame: Personal communications, Moscow, 1971

17. Kerr WK: Presented at the Society of Pelvic Surgeons meeting, Newcastle, England, July 1971

ANNOTATED BIBLIOGRAPHY

Abel BJ, Gow JG: Results of caecocystoplasty for tuberculous contracture. Br J Urol 50,511, 1978

This article deals with the specific use of an ileocecal segment in patients with contracture of the bladder due to tuberculosis. Thirty cases between 1963 and 1978 are carefully documented by presenting symptoms and preoperative urographic assessment. Surgical complications and mortality are analyzed. Preoperative and postoperative symptoms and bladder capacity are documented by bladder capacity, urography, renal function, and reflux. In a smaller number of patients pressure studies have been made in symptom-free and obstructed enuretic patients. It appears that "the caecal segment is essentially passive during voiding which is achieved using abdominal straining." Relief of symptoms resulted in over 90% of patients, and renal function was well preserved even when previously impaired.

This is an excellent review of the specific experience with ileocecal segment for the relief of tuberculous contracture of the urinary bladder: much of the experience would apply to other segments of bowel used for bladder augmentation. Very early experience, for instance, showed that if none of the diseased bladder was excised, stenosis between bowel and bladder was prone to occur, and wide excision of the bladder was therefore advocated. These authors have shown that the bladder need not be widely excised as long as a large anastomosis is obtained. This particular feature appears to result in better emptying of the bladder.

Dounis A, Abel BJ, Gow JG: Caecocystoplasty for bladder augmentation. J Urol 123:164, 1980

This is a further review of the same population described in the reference above but with the addition of other diseases, namely, Hunner's ulcer and carcinoma of the bladder. Attention is again drawn to the importance of the antireflux effect of the ileocecal valve. It is also noted that male patients over 45 should have a bladder neck resection or incision and that females may require dilation or urethrotomy in order to empty more completely.

Dounis A, Gow JG: Bladder augmentation—a long-term review. Br J Urol 51:264, 1979

This article, which complements the previous two, includes the authors' experience with colocystoplasty as well as caecocystoplasty, and also a case of ileocystoplasty, for a total experience of 59 enterocystoplasties. The authors conclude that there is very little choice between the cecum and the colon insofar as the functional result is concerned. These authors' experience now extends over 20 yr and so embraces one of the longest and broader experiences analyzed in the English literature.

Leong CH: Use of the stomach for bladder replacement and annals of the royal college of surgeons of england. Urinary Div 60:283, 1978

This article describes a brave pioneering effort of a total of 16 gastrocystoplasties carried out in Hong Kong between 1969 and 1975 for replacement of the bladder after total radical cystectomy

in 9 patients and bladder augmentation in 6. The surgery was performed with a low mortality and morbidity and with highly satisfactory results, particularly as far as metabolic exchange was concerned. This article is included although other surgeons have not yet attempted this form of bladder replacement or augmentation. The procedure might be useful in patients in whom distal bowel is in jeopardy, as in Crohn's disease.

Homsy YL, Reid EC: Ileocystoplasty. Urology 4:136, 1974

Twelve cases of augmentation ileocystoplasty are described (ten female and 2 male patients). Ten of these patients had interstitial cystitis, one tuberculous cystitis, and another cystitis of uncertain origin. The technique was a patch or cup plasty with good results as far as emptying was concerned. This article is of interest in the application of ileocystoplasty to patients with a high incidence of interstitial cystitis. I have been able to control these cases with steroid therapy in recent years following the advice of Mr. Alex Badenodi.

Bruce PT: Colocystoplasty: Bladder replacement after total cystectomy. Aust NZ J Surg 43:270, 1973

This short article describes total replacement of the urinary bladder after total cystoprostatectomy for cancer of the bladder in 10 patients between 1968 and 1973. The author fashioned an isolated segment of sigmoid colon into a pouch after the manner of Ong and finds that renal function is well preserved in spite of reflux. Some patients had a tendency to low serum potassium. Nocturnal incontinence seems to have been frequent in these patients, requiring some to use a Cunningham clamp at night. There was no recurrence of carcinoma in the urethra in these ten patients. This article is of importance in drawing attention to the possible use of enterocystoplasty as replacement of the entire bladder after total cystectomy for cancer, confirming the experience of Ong and of Küss and Kerr.

Camey M: 100 Cases of ileocystoplasty for bladder substitution in cancer. Presented at the 22 Congress Paris, July 1979 (in press)

The technique developed by this author was well illustrated at his presentation. He uses an isolated segment of ileum to form a U-shaped cystoplasty; the ureters are joined to the ileal loop near each end, and the urethra is joined to the middle of the loop of ileum at the antimesenteric border. Half the loop is therefore isoperistaltic, and half is antiperistaltic. The author thinks that this helps to prevent incontinence, which is the chief disability with this operation. His cases are well documented, many showing good preservation of renal function. Experience has enabled him to overcome the immediate postoperative complications, which usually arise from leakage at the enterourethral anastomosis. As both prostate and bladder are removed *in toto,* cancer control is not jeopardized by reconstruction in entirety or compared to urinary diversion. This author has the largest published experience with bladder replacement after total cystoprostatectomy for cancer of the bladder using ileum as a substitute. His technique based on such large experience should be followed by anyone attempting this hazardous surgery.

62

RESULTS OF CAECOCYSTOPLASTY FOR TUBERCULOUS BLADDER CONTRACTURE

B. J. Abel and J. G. Gow

Departments of Urology, Victoria Infirmary, Glasgow and Mossley Hill Hospital, Liverpool

British Journal of Urology (1978), 50, 511-516

SUMMARY—The results of caecocystoplasty for tuberculous bladder contracture in 30 patients over a 15-year period are presented. The operative mortality was 3.3%. Poor renal function was not a contraindication to surgery.

The results indicate that caecocystoplasty provided relief of symptoms in over 90% of patients. Renal function was preserved and associated obstructive uropathy was usually relieved. Efficient cystoplasty emptying was observed in 80% of patients if detrusor resection was kept to the minimum consistent with a wide caecovesical anastomosis.

The caecum was first used in urological surgery as a bladder substitute by Verhoogen in 1908; the technique included the formation of a fistula between the skin and

Read at the 34th Annual Meeting of the British Association of Urological Surgeons in Brighton, June 1978.

B. J. Abel, FRCS, FRCSE, Consultant Urologist, Victoria Infirmary, Glasgow.

J. G. Gow, ChM, MD, FRCS, Consultant Urologist, Mossley Hill Hospital, Liverpool.

the appendix to allow intermittent catheterisation of the caecal reservoir.

Couvelaire was the first to advocate the use of the caecum in bladder reconstruction and published an account of 3 caecocystoplasties in 1950. Gil-Vernet and Adan (1956) and Gil-Vernet (1965) described its use for bladder augmentation and stressed the protection afforded by the ileocaecal valve against reflux into a ureter implanted into the adjacent ileum. Turner-Warwick and Ashken (1967) described their experience and advocated the use of the caecum because it was easily mobilised, required no refashioning and had ample blood supply.

This paper describes the long-term results of caecocystoplasty for tuberculous bladder contracture in 30 patients.

PATIENTS AND PROCEDURES

Thirty patients with tuberculous bladder contracture underwent caecocystoplasty between 1963 and 1978. Thirteen were male and 17 were female. Their ages at presentation, the incidence of presenting symptoms and the pre-operative urographic appearances are shown in Tables 1, 2 and 3.

All the patients received the standard course of therapy in use at that time, following the isolation of *Myco. tuberculosis* from the urine. This regime, combined with excisional surgery when indicated, resulted in the elimination of the organism from the urine in all cases. Bladder symptoms were improved temporarily in 3 patients following the introduction of chemotherapy but in the remaining cases the symptoms were unchanged by both chemotherapy and excisional surgery.

The pre-operative bladder capacities are shown in Table 4. Bladder fibrosis and mucosal vegetations were observed cystoscopically in all patients at presentation and were completely unaffected by excisional surgery and long-term chemotherapy. Endoscopic cauterisation of vegetations and bladder instillations were used over long periods in 4 patients with no improvement.

Surgical Technique. Pre-operative bowel preparation consisted of either oral neomycin or streptomycin 1 g 8-hourly for 48 h before surgery together with colonic washouts using a sulphonamide solution.

Laparotomy was performed through a lower right or left paramedian incision. The caecum was grasped and drawn down into the pelvis to confirm adequate mobility of the ileocolic segment. The caecum, ascending colon and hepatic flexure were then mobilised and, after appendicectomy, the ileocaecal segment was isolated with its mesentery and the ileal stump closed. For bilateral or left-sided ureteric reimplantation into the ileal portion of the segment 30 cm of ileum were included in the segment. With no reimplantation or with right-sided ureteric reimplantation 8 cm of ileum were included. Direct mucosa-to-mucosa implantation was used when the ureter was rigid and dilated; otherwise a cuffed-nipple technique was employed. Intestinal continuity was restored by end-to-side ileocolic anastomosis.

The fundus of the bladder was resected after reflection of overlying peritoneum. The aim of this resection was a wide vesical stoma but as much bladder as possible was conserved.

Ureteric reimplantation, if required, was best performed before caecovesical anastomosis; otherwise technical difficulties were formidable. The caecum was then rotated through 180° and its open end was anastomosed in 2 layers to the bladder remnant using 2/0 chromic catgut sutures. More recently "Dexon" sutures have been preferred. The peritoneal flaps were then sewn to the base of the cystoplasty for further protection of the anastomosis.

The wound was closed in layers with drainage to all anastomoses. A balloon catheter was left *in situ* for 10 days.

TABLE 1. Age at Presentation (30 Patients)

17–30 years	9 patients
30–50 years	14 patients
50–70	7 patients

TABLE 2. Presenting Symptoms (30 Patients)

Increased Frequency	Patients
Diurnal	
¼–1 hourly	14
1–2 hourly	10
2–3 hourly	6
Nocturnal	
4–12 times	19
1–3 times	11
Scalding	19
Haematuria	13
Loin pain	7
Enuresis	3

TABLE 3. Pre-operative Urographic Assessment (30 Patients)

Urographic Appearance	Patients
Poor	
Bilateral severe disease	
Bilateral hydronephrosis	
Severe disease in a solitary kidney	
Hydronephrosis in a solitary kidney	17
Adequate:	
Solitary normal kidney	
Solitary slightly diseased kidney	10
Good:	
One kidney normal, other kidney diseased or hydronephrotic	3

TABLE 4. Pre-operative Bladder Capacities (30 Patients)

Capacity (ml)	Patients
30–100	9
100–200	15
200–300	6

Patient Follow-up. All surviving patients have been reviewed at 6-monthly to yearly intervals to elicit progress of symptoms, renal function, urography, cystoscopic appearance and volume of residual urine. The duration of follow-up is shown in Table 5.

Urodynamic Evaluation. In 23 patients pressure-flow studies have been performed post-operatively using Disa Urodynamic measuring equipment. These studies were combined with synchronous videocystography. Flow curves were obtained after spontaneous diuresis and after filling with Urografin 30%. Residual urine was measured before filling with Urografin 30%. Intravesical (cystoplasty) pressure was recorded via a transurethral 1 mm diameter PTFE catheter. Abdominal (rectal) pressure was recorded via a rectal 2 mm PTFE catheter covered with a finger stall. Methods, definitions and units conform to the standards proposed by the International Continence Society except where specifically noted.

RESULTS

Five patients have died and Table 6 gives the causes of death and times of death following cystoplasty. The operative mortality was 3.3%, representing one early patient who died with a faecal fistula and peritonitis.

Two patients (A.G. and J.C.) died from renal failure 15 months and 2 years after the operation. Cystoplasty provided relief of symptoms in these patients but failed to reverse the progressive deterioration in renal function observed before operation. In retrospect it it clear that cystoplasty outflow obstruction was a significant factor in the deterioration in both patients.

Post-operative complications are shown in Table 7. External urinary fistulae caused most problems but all healed with catheter drainage within 3 weeks. In one patient leakage at a ureteroileal anastomosis required re-exploration and resuture. Three male patients required post-operative transurethral prostatectomy before efficient cystoplasty emptying was achieved. All 3 were over 45 years of age and were the only patients in the series with prostatic calcification on plain X-ray. Two female patients required internal urethrotomy to achieve efficient cystoplasty emptying. One male patient required bladder neck resection. Contraction of the caecovesical anastomosis with delay in caecal pouch emptying has occurred in one patient who is under careful observation.

The progress of symptoms in the 29 patients who left hospital is shown in Table 8. Relief of diurnal frequency was invariable but did not fully develop until 3 to 6 months after operation. Symptomatic improvement correlated with the observed increase in bladder capacity obtained by operation (Table 9).

The progress of urography in the 29 patients who left hospital is shown in Table 10. There has been a

TABLE 5. Duration of Post-operative Follow-up (30 Patients)

Up to 1 year	5 patients
1–5 years	13 patients
5–15 years	12 patients

TABLE 6. Analysis of Mortality

Age of Patient	Cause of Death	Time of Death After Cystoplasty
58	Faecal fistula	4 weeks
64	Ruptured aortic aneurysm	6 weeks
57	Renal failure	15 months
66	Myocardial infarction	2 years
48	Renal failure	5 years

TABLE 7. Post-operative Complications

Faecal fistula	1
External urinary fistula	7
Wound disruption	2
Incisional hernia	4
Intestinal obstruction from adhesions	1
Bladder outflow obstruction	6
Contraction of cystoplasty anastomosis	1
Stenosis of ureteric implant	1
Enuresis	10

TABLE 8. Progress of Symptoms After Caecocystoplasty (29 Patients)

	Pre-operative	Post-operative
Frequency		
¼–1 hour	14	—
1–2 hours	19	—
2–3 hours	5	11
3–4 hours	—	18
Nocturia		
×4–12	19	2
×1–3	10	21
Absent	—	6
Enuresis	3	10
Scalding	19	2
Haematuria	13	—
Loin pain	6	—

TABLE 9. Pre-operative and Post-operative Bladder Capacity (29 Patients)

Capacity (ml)	Pre-operative	Post-operative
30–100	9	—
100–200	14	—
200–300	6	1
300–500	—	24
500–700	—	4

satisfactory improvement in renal function in some cases and renal insufficiency has not proved to be a contraindication to the operation (Table 11).

The incidence of post-operative reflux in 26 of the patients was assessed by cystography (Table 12). The reflux protection offered by a cuffed-nipple ureteroileal anastomosis could, of necessity, only be assessed in the 5 patients with ileocaecal valve incompetence. Free reflux of contrast material to the kidney occurred through 3 out of the 5 nipple anastomoses in these 5 patients.

The 23 patients assessed by videocystography combined with a pressure-flow study were separated on clinical grounds into 3 groups (Table 13).

The results of the pressure-flow studies in the symptom free group are shown in Table 14, in the obstructed group in Table 15 and in the enuretic group in Table 16. Videocystourethrography gave reliable information on the presence of reflux, cystoplasty function and the presence of bladder neck obstruction. Obstruction at the distal urethral segment level was not observed.

TABLE 10. Progress of Urography in the 40 Functioning Kidneys (29 Patients)

	Pre-operative	Post-operative
Normal kidney	16	23
Moderate hydronephrosis	—	9
Gross hydronephrosis	24	8

TABLE 11. Progress of Renal Function (29 Patients)

	Pre-operative	Post-operative
Creatinine clearance:		
More than 100 ml/min	12	16
50–100 ml/min	8	11
Less than 50 ml/min	9	2

TABLE 12. Incidence of Post-operative Reflux (26 Patients Assessed by Cystography)

Caecocystoplasty (ureters left *in situ*)
  12 Patients—vesicoureteric reflux in 3 patients before operation; no change after operation
Ureteroileocaecocystoplasty
  14 Patients — Ileocaecal valve competent (9 patients)
              Ileocaecal valve incompetent (5 patients)

TABLE 13. Patient Groups Assessed Urodynamically (23 Patients)

(A) Symptom-free group	13
Residual urine < 50 ml	
(B) Obstructed group	4
Residual urine > 100 ml	
(C) Enuretic group	6
Residual urine < 50 ml	

DISCUSSION

Surgical Technique. A radical detrusor resection extending to the trigone has been advocated at cystoplasty by many authors (Couvelaire, 1950; Cibert, 1953; Gil-Vernet and Gosalvez, 1957; Turner-Warwick and Ashken, 1967; Charghi *et al.*, 1967). Without such a resection, contraction at the enterovesical anastomosis was judged inevitable, resulting in conversion of the cystoplasty to a non-functioning diverticulum. Hanley (1959) and more recently Smith *et al.* (1977) have challenged this view. The results of this study suggest that as much of the bladder wall as possible should be conserved at operation consistent with an anastomosis of 5 cm or so in diameter. With this approach cystoplasty was technically much easier and the voiding pattern in

TABLE 14. Results of Pressure Studies in the Symptom-Free Patients (13 Patients)

	Mean Value	Range
Residual urine (ml)	30	0–50
First sensation (ml)	250	100–300
Cystoplasty capacity (ml)	400	300–500
Maximum cystoplasty pressure (voiding) (cm H_2O)	17	1–36
Maximum abdominal pressure (voiding) (cm H_2O)	57	17–80
Maximum flow rate (ml/s)	15	10–21
Flow duration (s)	53	10–120

TABLE 15. Results of Pressure Studies in the Obstructed Patients (4 Patients)

	Mean	Range
Residual urine (ml)	210	100–500
First sensation (ml)	400	250–650
Cystoplasty capacity (ml)	600	550–700
Maximum cystoplasty pressure (voiding) (cm H_2O)	15	5–35
Maximum abdominal pressure (voiding) (cm H_2O)	73	60–110
Maximum flow rate (ml/s)	11	6–16
Flow duration (s)	90	30–130

TABLE 16. Results of Pressure Studies in the Enuretic Patients (6 Patients)

	Mean Value	Range
Residual urine (ml)	24	0–50
First sensation (ml)	230	100–400
Cystoplasty capacity (ml)	360	200–600
Maximum cystoplasty pressure (voiding) (cm H_2O)	16	5–24
Maximum abdominal pressure (voiding) (cm H_2O)	68	50–90
Maximum flow rate (ml/s)	14	9–20
Flow duration (s)	46	10–120

the majority of cases was excellent. Contraction of the caecovesical anastomosis occurred in only one case and this was judged to be due to faulty operative technique. The ileocaecal valve prevented retrograde reflux of urine in 64% of cases. However, in order to protect the 36% of cases with ileocaecal valve incompetence a reflux preventing technique of ureteroileal anastomosis is required. In this context a cuffed-nipple anastomosis proved unsatisfactory and it is suggested that a tunnel type anastomosis might be better.

The operative mortality is acceptable although the death should have been prevented. The high incidence of urinary fistulae is unacceptable and has been improved by 2-layer closure with Dexon.. Turner-Warwick and Ashken (1967) reported a relative outflow obstruction in two-thirds of a group of patients who had undergone caecal bladder substitution rather than enlargement. Other authors have reported a lower incidence of outflow obstruction following cystoplasty (Gil-Vernet, 1965; Duff *et al.*, 1970). In our series 6 patients (20%) developed a degree of chronic retention due to obstruction at bladder neck level. Relief was obtained in all cases by endoscopic resection in the male or urethrotomy in the female. If the 3 male patients with prostatic calcification and adenoma formation are excluded, then the incidence of chronic retention in the series as a whole is 10%. This low incidence of impaired emptying is probably related to our deliberate preservation of as much detrusor as possible.

Küss *et al.* (1970) noted a 12% incidence of diurnal incontinence and an 18% incidence of enuresis postoperatively, while Charghi *et al.* (1967) reported enuresis in 27% of their patients post-operatively, but a large number of these were transient. In our series 10 patients noted enuresis during the post-operative period but in no case did diurnal incontinence occur. In 5 the enuresis resolved. Three of the remaining 5 patients had enuresis before cystoplasty.

All the patients had very severe symptoms prior to cystoplasty. Frequency was reduced to 3-hourly or less in all patients and all were delighted with the result.

There have been few well documented reports concerning renal function following enterocystoplasty. Hanley (1959) reviewed renal progress over a 5-year period in 31 ileocystoplasty patients and found no increase in renal damage. Gil-Vernet *et al.* (1962a) found no important disturbance in blood chemistry over a 3-year period in 41 bladder substitute patients. In our series 7 patients with initially poor renal function showed a definite improvement. Our results are at variance with those of Smith *et al.* (1977) who stated that chronic renal insufficiency was a contraindication to caecocystoplasty and that a creatinine clearance of at least 40 ml/min was mandatory for any enterocystoplasty, but con-

firm those of Küss *et al.* (1970) who stated that patients with a creatinine clearance of over 15 ml/min are acceptable.

The urodynamics of enterocystoplasties were studied by Gil-Vernet *et al.* (1962b) who reported peristaltic contractions with raised intrinsic cystoplasty pressure during voiding. These pressures were over and above the abdominal pressures from straining employed during voiding. Turner-Warwick and Ashken (1967) found cystoplasty segments to be relatively weak when compared to a normal detrusor. During filling, typical bowel contractions were noted which diminished during voiding to such an extent that the patient had to complete evacuation using abdominal straining. In all patients urinary flow was slow and intermittent.

The results of pressure-flow videocystography in this series confirm Turner-Warwick and Ashken's (1967) finding that the explusive force during voiding is almost entirely due to abdominal wall contractions. The cystoplasty itself generates only brief low pressure and ineffective contractions.

In several cases at cystography a transfer of contrast medium from the bladder remnant to the caecal segment was observed immediately prior to voiding. This appeared to be due to active bladder remnant contraction and was associated with funnelling of the bladder neck. Abdominal straining was required to initiate and maintain voiding in all cases but bladder remnant contraction, when it occurred, was associated with the most efficient voiding patterns in the group as a whole. Urodynamic evaluation did not reveal any significant difference between the symptom-free and the enuretic cystoplasty patients. The characteristic features of the "obstructed" patients were a large residual urine, a higher total capacity and pronounced caecal peristaltic contractions in total capacity.

This study has shown that caecocystoplasty for tuberculous bladder contracture is a satisfactory procedure producing relief of symptoms in over 90% of patients. Renal function is usually preserved. The ileocaecal valve is important in preventing ileoureteric reflux but a tunnel-type antireflux procedure is recommended when anastomosing the ureters to the ileum. The bladders remnant should be as large as possible and the anastomosis between the caecum and the bladder as wide as can be obtained.

The caecal remnant is essentially passive during voiding which is achieved using abdominal straining.

Cystoplasty function should be assessed regularly to cystourethrography. If emptying is seen to be inadequate transurethral resection in the male or urethral overdilatation or urethrotomy in the female is indicated. The success of any urethral surgery in lowering urethral resistance and eliminating residual urine should be confirmed by post-operative cystourethrography. Routine urodynamic tests, although of interest from the research aspect, are of little practical value in the management of patients treated by caecocystoplasty.

REFERENCES

Charghi, A., Charbonneau, J. and Gauthier, G.-E. (1967). Colocystoplasty for bladder enlargement and bladder substitution: a study of late results in 31 cases. J Urol 97:849–856

Cibert, J. (1953). Bladder enlargement through ileocystoplasty. J Urol 70:600–604

Couvelaire, R. (1950). Le "petite vessie" des tuberculeux génitourinaires; essai de classification, place et variantes des cystointestinoplasties. J d'Urol Médicale et Chirurgicale 56:381–434

Duff, F. A. O'Grady, J. F. and Kelly, D. G. (1970). Colocystoplasty. A review of 10 cases. Br J Urol 42:704–706

Gil-Vernet, J. M. (1965). The ileocolic segment in urologic surgery. J Urol 94:418–426

Gil-Vernet, J. M. and Adan, R. (1956). Etude descriptive d'une nouvelle technique concernant le traitement chirurgical de la petite vessie et de l'urérérite tuberculeuse dans un cas de rein unique. J d'Urol Médicale et Chirurgicale 62:491–495

Gil-Vernet, J. M., Escarpenter, J. M., Perez-Trujillo, G. and Bonet Vic, J. (1962a). A functioning artificial bladder: results of 41 consecutive cases. J Urol 87:825–836

Gil-Vernet, J. M. and Gosalvez, R. (1957). Ileocystoplastie ou colocystoplastie. J d'Urol Médicale et Chirurgicale 63:466–472

Gil-Vernet, S., Gil-Vernet, J. M., Bonet Vic, J. and Escarpenter, J. M. (1962b). Functional results of an artificial bladder. Section II. Y Urol 87:837–843

Hanley, H. G. (1959). Ileocystoplasty: a clinical review. J Urol 82:317–321

Küss, R., Bitker, M., Camey, M., Chatelain, C. and Lassau, J. P. (1970). Indications and early and late results of intestinocystoplasty. A review of 185 cases. J Urol 103:53–63

Smith, R. B., Van Cangh, P., Skinner, D. G., Kaufman, J. and Goodwin, W. E. (1977). Augmentation enterocystoplasty. A critical review. J Urol 118:35–39

Turner-Warwick, R. T. and Ashken, H. M. (1967). The functional results of partial, sub-total and total cystoplasty with special reference to ureterocaecocystoplasty, selective sphincterotomy and cystocystoplasty. Br J Urol 39:3–12

Verhoogen, J. (1908). Néostomie urétéro-caecale; formation d'une nouvelle poche vesicale et d'un nouvel urètre. Assoc Française d'Urol 12:362–365

Commentary: Indications for Cecocystoplasty

Peter H. L. Worth

Of the three types of cystoplasty discussed in this section, the use of the cecum has been the least popular, mainly, I suppose, because it came last on the surgical scene for reasons that are difficult to understand. As mentioned in the Commentary Article, the cecal segment was first used as a bladder substitute in 1908 when the ureters were attached to the cecum and the appendix was brought to the surface, but it was not until the 1950s that its use was again considered. This time the ileal segment was brought to the surface, and it was shown that with the antiperistaltic activity of the ileum and the competence of the ileocecal valve, a continent stoma could be achieved in approximately 94% of patients.

Gil-Vernet popularized the use of the cecum for enlarging the bladder, but in two large series of cystoplasties by Hradec and Küss the former used the cecum in only 6 out of 114 patients and the latter in 8 of 185. Abel and Gow have now described their experience with cecocystoplasty for tuberculosis, which is discussed in the Commentary Article.

INDICATIONS AND TECHNIQUES FOR USE OF THE CECUM

Why use the cecum? There are several advantages in using this portion of bowel. First, provided an adequate portion of cecum and ascending colon is isolated, it can be anastomosed to the bladder without any alteration in shape, and its capacity will not be much less than that of a normal bladder (i.e., 300 ml to 500 ml). Unlike the sigmoid colon, the cecum is only rarely involved in pathologic processes, for instance, diverticular disease. Second, it has a very good and constant blood supply from the ileocolic artery, and mobilization of the bowel with this vessel is relatively easy. Third, the restorative anastomosis between the terminal ileum and the ascending colon is not difficult; a wide lumen can be obtained by spatulating the terminal ileum and using a two-layer closure. In addition, the anastomosis lies well away from the pelvis and the cystoplasty.

There is another very important advantage. If one or both of the ureters must be replaced, this can easily be done by isolating a portion of terminal ileum, with its blood supply derived from the ileocolic vessels and still attached to the cecum. If indicated, the ileal tail can be placed behind the sigmoid mesentery and taken up to the left renal pelvis, and so the whole of the left ureter can be replaced. If the right ureter still has reasonable length, it should be anastomosed at least 10 cm from the ileocecal valve into the ileum. This will make subsequent diversion possible without interfering with the ureteric anastomoses. If both ureters are compromised, the ileal tail can be taken up toward the right renal pelvis and then across to the left. It is probably better to take the tail lateral to the right colon and then to bring it through the mesocolon and across and through the left mesocolon.

There is no doubt that a much better result for ureteric reimplantation is obtained if the ureters are implanted into the ileal tail rather than into the cecum direct. If the ureters are implanted separately, a split-cuff nipple should be used; provided the length of the nipple is twice the diameter of the ureter, no reflux will occur. Sometimes it is easier to join the ureters together and sew them to the end of the ileal tail with the technique described by Wallace and later by Persky. This technique does not prevent reflux *per se*. I do not believe that the surgeon can rely on the ileocaecal valve to provide a competent system, but a technique has been described to make this more certain by inkwelling the ileum into the cecum (Fig. 1). Whether reflux occurs is probably not too relevant, since the pressures generated by the bladder are usually not sustained and are generally quite low.

I do think that it is important to remove a reasonable portion of the bladder whatever the primary pathologic condition. If the cecum is just placed on top of the bladder it is apt to act as a diverticulum during voiding, leading to the problems of infection and residual urine. There are also problems in certain conditions, for instance, interstitial cystitis, when, if too much bladder is left, the symptoms may persist. If the trigone does not need removing it is best to keep about 1 cm above the ureteric orifices because ureteric reflux is then less likely to occur, since the mechanisms that prevent reflux are not disturbed. The problems associated with removing most of the trigone will be discussed later, but cystoplasty can certainly be considered after total cystectomy.

Indications for cecocystoplasty vary very much from country to country and I would certainly disagree with authors who state that there is no place for cystoplasty in bladder cancer.

Interstitial cystitis and chronic cystitis are common indications, once the bladder has contracted down and cystolysis is no longer possible. Everybody has a different definition of interstitial cystitis, and it is not my intention to discuss this now, but I do feel that it is important to do a supratrigonal cystoplasty, removing as much of the bladder above the trigone as possible. It is always interesting to see how the bladder remnant expands postoperatively. When this happens, the symptoms associated with interstitial cystitis may reappear. It is never necessary to reimplant the ureters in these patients, although interstitial cystitis *per se* may produce ureteric reflux, which may resolve postoperatively.

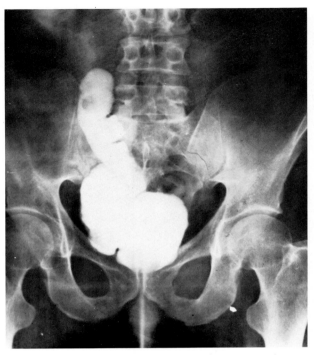

Fig. 1. Static cystogram in a patient with a uretero-ileo-caeco-cystoplasty. Note free reflux into the ileal tail, but not into the ureter. The filling defect in the ileal tail is the nipple of the implanted ureter.

There are really three groups of patients with carcinoma of the bladder that can be considered for cystoplasty. First, there is the patient with multiple recurrent superficial tumors who is not responding to more conventional therapy, for instance, repeated diathermy or intravesical chemotherapy. Provided the trigone is relatively free of disease, a transtrigonal resection can be performed and the ureters implanted into the ileal tail. Careful endoscopic review of the urethra and the remaining bladder epithelium can be continued, and if recurrences do occur they are more easily dealt with than the recurrences previously found in the dome. Second, a patient with a solid invasive tumor in the dome of the bladder can be adequately treated by an extended partial cystectomy and ureteroileocecocystoplasty. None of the patients I have seen treated in this way have had recurrent disease, and indeed one patient died of metastatic disease from a second primary tumor in the cervix 7 yr postoperatively. There is a place for cystoplasty after total cystectomy, but the technical problems of the operation are considerable and continence may well be compromised. The third group are those patients who have had their cancer controlled by radiotherapy but who have severe symptoms from irradiation cystitis. This usually relates to a small bladder capacity but may also be associated with bleeding.

Irradiation cystitis may also be an indication for cystoplasty in patients treated for carcinoma of the cervix, who in addition to a small bladder may also have either a vesicovaginal or a rectovaginal fistula. If the rectum is involved, a preliminary colostomy, preferably in the left iliac fossa, should be performed. A ureteroileocecocystoplasty should be carried out and the fistula repaired at the same time. In order to promote healing, the omentum should be formally mobilized on the right gastroepiloic vessels and brought down behind the hepatic flexure and ileocolic anastomosis and then wrapped round the cystoplasty anastomosis and in between the bladder and vagina, or vagina and rectum, as indicated. If the preliminary colostomy avoided the transverse colon, there should be no difficulty in mobilizing the omentum.

Tuberculosis is the disease par excellence for which cystoplasty was designed. The disease wrecks the urinary tract but tends to spare the sphincter mechanisms, which therefore makes reconstructive techniques possible. There are, in fact, very few indications for diversion in patients with tuberculosis, apart from a temporary need when a patient presents with uremia secondary to obstruction. Indeed, when the surgeon sees a patient who has already been diverted, he should consider converting the diversion to a cystoplasty. Patients have presented with problems related to ureterosigmoidostomy, usually with a solitary kidney, who have subsequently done extremely well following conversion to a cystoplasty. Remember that patients who have had very advanced disease probably only have the one kidney functioning, which is likely to have a damaged ureter, and therefore ureteric replacement will be required (Fig. 2). In men with advanced disease or with previous diversion it is likely that the urethra will also require reconstruction.

I do not recommend cystoplasty in patients with neurologic problems, whatever the etiology. Occasionally a very good result may be obtained, but more often, on account of the uncoordinated detrusor–sphincter mechanism, there are major problems with emptying that cannot be easily resolved without rendering the patient incontinent (such patients probably had a degree of incontinence before the cystoplasty was undertaken). I am certainly not in favor of cecocystoplasty in patients with detrusor instability who have nocturnal enuresis. It is difficult to get a functioning unit, and more often the cystoplasty acts as a diverticulum that fills every time the detrusor contracts. This may keep the patient dry, but in the long term is apt to cause renal damage. The question always arises whether, with the small chance of success, a cystoplasty is justified. It is certainly wise to reimplant the ureters into the ileal tail, since it is easier to convert to a surface diversion because the surgeon has only to separate the ileum from the cecum and bring it to the surface without having to revise the ureteric anastomosis, provided they are satisfactory. In this situation it is wise to remove the cecum as well, since otherwise the patient will be left with a troublesome mucus discharge and pyocystis.

POSTOPERATIVE ASSESSMENT

There is a very good chance that if the upper tracts were dilated preoperatively, they will improve following reimplantation, but undoubtedly better results occur from reimplanting into the ileal tail rather than into the cecum. If deterioration occurs, the ureteric anastomosis must be revised.

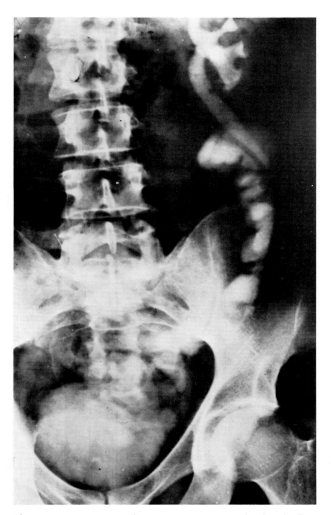

Fig. 2. Intravenous pyelogram in a patient who has had a uretero-ileo-caecocystoplasty for tuberculosis. Note that the ureter has been sewn into the side of the ileum, leaving some spare ileum above it in case a local problem develops.

Cystoplasty is a potentially dangerous procedure in the presence of compromised renal function, but provided that the creatinine clearance is at least 40 ml/min, problems should not arise. However, patients with compromised renal function and those who empty their cystoplasty inefficiently may develop hyperchloremic acidosis, which can be improved by encouraging voiding on a regular basis, improving bladder emptying by surgical means, and, in addition, giving sodium and potassium bicarbonate supplements on a regular basis to those at risk.

Patients with a cystoplasty do not have to have infected urine. They will always pass mucus, but this will only become a problem in the presence of inefficient emptying—first, because the mucus is difficult to get rid of, and second, because obstruction will encourage the production of more mucus and in this situation the chances of developing a stone in the bladder are very high. Likewise, infection is a sign of poor emptying and may be helped by the appropriate surgery. Certainly at least 50% of patients can expect to have sterile urine without resorting to long-term antibiotics.

URODYNAMICS OF CECOCYSTOPLASTY

The important aim in any cecocystoplasty is to have a unit that will empty as efficiently as possible. The bowel muscle, which is replacing the bladder detrusor, is inefficient. When full, the cecum can generate a pressure of about 70 cm of water. This is not, however, capable of opening the bladder neck, which can only be done by the remaining bladder muscle. Once emptying commences, the cecal pressure falls and the process is continued by abdominal straining. Despite this, very satisfactory flow rates can be obtained (Fig. 3).

Provided that the base of the bladder is intact, bladder sensation should be satisfactory. Patients should know when they want to pass urine in the day and at night. With impaired or no sensation, as will occur after subtotal or total cystectomy, voiding at regular intervals in the day should be encouraged, since this will probably keep the patient dry, but it is likely to produce incontinence at night.

It is necessary, therefore, to do a cystogram cystourethogram; pressures are not absolutely necessary, because they are predictable. The surgeon needs to see if the bladder neck is being adequately opened and kept open and if there is any evidence of obstruction in the region of the distal sphincteric mechanism.

In men it is likely that some surgical procedure will be necessary, although I have operated on two men who have not yet required any further surgery. It is usually the bladder neck that fails to open satisfactorily, and therefore either a bladder neck resection or incision will be required. Rarely will an internal urethrotomy be necessary after bladder neck surgery. By this I mean using an Otis urethrotome, which will only cut the smooth muscle component of the distal sphincteric mechanism and leave the striated component intact.

About one third of women require no surgery. Relatively few require bladder neck surgery, but approximately 50% have relative obstruction of the distal sphincteric mechanism and need either a urethral dilatation or an internal urethrotomy. Provided this is done in carefully graduated steps, incontinence is unlikely, but the amount of dilatation may be considerable—up to 75 French in one patient!

In some patients it unfortunately proves impossible to achieve satisfactory emptying without producing incontinence. The surgeon must decide whether infection associated with incomplete emptying or troublesome frequency can be treated adequately with drugs. Also, where drug treatment has failed, can the surgeon accept the situation without compromising the upper tracts? If satisfactory continence cannot be achieved, a

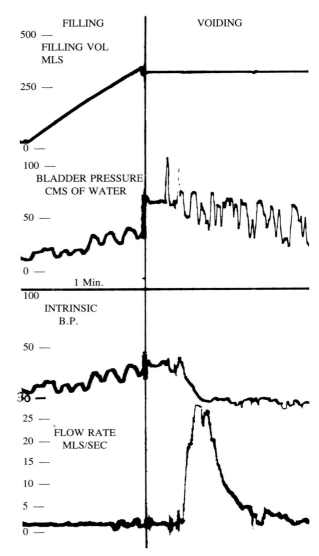

Fig. 3. Cystometrogram in a patient with a caecocystoplasty. Note the bowel contraction in the filling phase. The intrinsic pressure is low, and voiding, which is very adequate with a flow rate of just over 25 ml per second, is maintained by raising intra-abdominal pressure.

diversion must be considered. The ileal tail should be used when previous ureteric reimplantation has been performed. Alternatively, the cecum can be detached from the bladder base and used as a conduit with the ureters implanted into the base of it. Attempting to lift the cecum and bladder base up together with the ureters undisturbed is a difficult alternative.

ANNOTATED BIBLIOGRAPHY

Dounis A, Gow JG: Bladder augmentation—a long-term review. Br J Urol 51:264, 1979

Fifty-nine patients are reviewed; 51 with tuberculosis. The cecum was used in 42, and excellent results were obtained in 78%. The authors found that patients with enuresis failed to improve postoperatively, although no urodynamic abnormality could be detected. They differentiate between bladder augmentation, when only a small part of the bladder is removed, and bladder replacement, which is reserved for patients with severe diffuse disease. They also feel that there is a place for cystoplasty in patients with bladder cancer, although they only reported on one case, which had a good result.

Gil-Vernet JM: The ileocolic segment in urologic surgery. J Urol 94:418, 1965

This paper describes in detail the technique of ileocecal cystoplasty and illustrates the various ways that the bowel segment can be anastomosed to the bladder.

Gleason DM, Gittes RF, Bottaccini MR, et al: Energy balance of voiding after cecalcystoplasty. J Urol 108:259, 1972

The concept of energy loss in six patients is discussed. These patients had good flow rates (27 ml/sec at best), but a number had a large residual urine. They showed that energy loss was 90% in both sexes, whereas normally males lose 70% and females 50%. The results were not related to the quantity of bladder removed. Although all the females had had urethral dilatations to 45 French ± urethrotomy performed empirically, it is possible that some had residual obstruction.

Hradec EA: Bladder substitution. Indications and results in 114 operations. J Urol 94:406, 1965

The ileocecal segment was used only six times. The majority of cases had bladder cancer or radiation damage. The overall results were good. The presence of ureteric reflux was thought to be unimportant, and renal function did not alter. Ten percent of patients had bladder stones.

Kuss R, Bitker M, Camey M, et al: Indications and early and late results of intestino-cystoplasty. A Review of 185 Cases. J Urol 103:53, 1970

The cecum was used only eight times. The authors make two interesting statements. First, they have never favored systematic bladder neck resection at intestinocystoplasty because of the risk of incontinence. Only 16 patients subsequently had a bladder neck resection. One cannot pretend to sterilize the urine of all patients after intestinocystoplasty inasmuch as the infection is usually chronic and resistant to antibiotics. Only 23 patients were sterile. Better results, I think, would have been obtained if attempts to improve emptying were undertaken.

Maddocks RA, Mindell HJ: Ileocecocystoplasty: Some radiological observations. Am J Roentgenol 128:81, 1977

The postoperative radiologic appearances of eight patients are discussed.

Shirley SW, Mirelman S: Experiences with colocystoplasties, ceco-cystoplasties and ileocystoplasties in urologic surgery. 40 patients. J Urol 120:165, 1978

Cecocystoplasty was used in 16 patients—10 with tuberculosis, 4 with interstitial cystitis, and 2 with irradiation; good results were obtained in 15.

Skinner DG: Secondary urinary reconstruction: Use of ileocecal segment. J Urol 112:48, 1974

Two patients had reconstructive surgery. Both had good results.

Smith RB, Van Cangh P, Skinner DG, et al: Augmentation entero-cystoplasty: A critical review. J Urol 118:35, 1977

In a group of 74 patients, the cecum and ileocecal segment was used in 22 patients. Approximately half these patients had interstitial cystitis. Bladder cancer was excluded. Patients who had had previous diversion did less well (45% compared with 66%). The indication for surgery on the outlet was based on carbon dioxide urethral pressure profiles, and the authors claim that patients who had bladder neck surgery did better and tended to have residues of less than 75 ml. The commonest cause of failure was imbalance of micturition; there was retention in ten and incontinence in four.

Turner-Warwick RT, Handley-Ashken M: The functional results of partial, subtotal and total cystoplasty with special reference to ureterocaecocystoplasty, selective sphincterotomy and cystocystoplasty. Br J Urol 39:3, 1967

This article sets out the rationale for treatment of voiding disturbances after various cystoplasties. These are discussed in the Commentary.

Wallack HI, Lome LG, Presman D: Management of interstitital cystitis with ileocecocystoplasty. Urology 3:51, 1975

Two patients with interstitial cystitis are described in detail. One patient was unecessarily explored at 14 days because a urinary leak was present. This was not found at operation, and it subsequently healed spontaneously. Provided the bladder is adequately drained, a urinary fistula will close.

Worth PHL, Turner-Warwick RT: The treatment of interstitial cystitis by cystolysis with observations of cystoplasty. Br J Urol 45:65, 1973

The rationale for sensory denervation is discussed, and its use is suggested in those patients who have a bladder that distends to a reasonable capacity under anesthetic. The results of 40 cysto-plasties—24 colocystoplasties and 16 using the cecum—are described. All had satisfactory results.

63

INDICATIONS AND EARLY AND LATE RESULTS OF INTESTINO-CYSTOPLASTY: A REVIEW OF 185 CASES

R. Küss, M. Bitker, M. Camey, C. Chatelain and J.P. Lassau

From the Departments of Urology, Hôpital Saint-Louis (Paris) and Hôpital Foch (Suresnes) France

Reprinted from *Journal of Urology*, Vol. 103, pp. 53–63, 1970. Copyright 1970 by The Williams & Wilkins Company, Baltimore.

Between 1951 and 1967, 185 intestino-cystoplasties (ICP) have been done by our group. All operations have been performed by a small group of experienced surgeons who used the same operative indications, surgical technique and postoperative care. Data obtained after long-term evaluation will be presented concerning renal consequences of ICP.

Lesions which necessitated ICP are listed in Table 1. Changes in diagnostic indications throughout the study are not evident in this tabulation but should be mentioned. Most patients with vesical tuberculosis underwent the procedure before 1960. Early diagnosis and efficient antibiotic therapy have made this lesion exceptional. Most patients with bilharziasis were treated after 1963,

Accepted for publication January 15, 1969.

Dr. Marcel Legrain, a nephrologist, has contributed to this work since 1951.

when a growing number of workers from African countries had come to France.

Reconstruction of the bladder after radical cystectomy for cancer deserves special consideration. Although one of our group (M. C.) experienced a rather low mortality rate (3 deaths following 25 operations) we have been discouraged by results of the procedure because of high mortality and morbidity rates. We hope that chemotherapy will improve the results.

We believe that in the future tuberculosis and cancer will offer limited indications for ICP but that intestinal segments will become more and more useful in bilharziasis, at least for a limited time, and in traumatic or neurogenic bladder.

The different intestinal segments used in ICP are listed in Table 2. The colon was chosen in 70 percent of the cases.[1] Our reasons will be explained later.

TABLE 1. Etiology

	No. Cases	%
Tuberculosis	97	52.5
Cancer	52	28.0
Multiple papillomas	5	2.7
Bilharziasis	11	6.0
Traumatic, surgical or obstetrical lesions	8	4.3
Bladder gangrene	2	1.1
Neurogenic bladder	7	3.8
Interstitial cystitis	3	1.6
Total	185	100.0

TABLE 2. Types of Intestino-Cystoplasties

Type of Intestinal Segment	Etiology			
	Tuber-culosis	Cancer	Benign Lesions (Nontuber-culous)	Total
Ileum	32	13	10	55
Sigmoid	63	35	24	122
Ascending colon	2	4	2	8
Total	97	52	36	815

POSTOPERATIVE MORTALITY

There have been 16 deaths in 185 cases (8.7 percent). This rate is much lower than the figures in the literature. The role of etiology is a major one. Half of these deaths[2] were due to ICP for cancer; in such cases the mortality rate reaches 17 percent. In 97 ICP for tuberculosis there were only 7 deaths (7.2 percent). This figure would be lower except that many of these operations were performed early in our experience. No deaths have occurred in the 36 cases in which ICP was done for benign, non-tuberculous lesions (bilharziasis, traumatic or neurogenic bladder).

Despite these satisfactory results we do not pretend that ICP is a benign operation even when performed by experienced surgeons for non-tuberculous and non-cancerous lesions. Nevertheless we believe that ICP should be encouraged in preference to other methods of high urinary diversion in those cases where up to now the procedure was still under discussion.

TABLE 3. Postoperative Complications (185 Cases)

Intestinal obstruction	16
Urinary fistula	32
Fecal fistula	18
Urinary-fecal fistula	5
Major infectious complications	11
Venous thrombosis (with pulmonary embolism)	13
Sepsis of the wound	7
Secondary hemorrhage	1
Renal insufficiency	1

Three points should be mentioned in connection with mortality:

1. The high proportion of septicemia and venous thrombosis that was responsible for 8 deaths, equally divided between tuberculosis and cancer, and more frequent following coloplasty than ileoplasty, probably because of greater septicity of the colonic content and pelvic localization of the sigmoid.

2. The rise of preoperative irradiation (more than 3,500 rads) before cystectomy and ICP, responsible in our series for 2 fistulas that were followed by cachexia and death.

3. The actual risk of acute intestinal obstruction (3 patients died, two of them from pulmonary embolism after re-operation).

Acute postoperative renal insufficiency is a slight risk. Even those patients with definite renal insufficiency, but who have a Cl_{Cr} of more than 15 ml per minute, are considered suitable for operation.

POSTOPERATIVE MORBIDITY

Many patients who undergo ICP have an uncomplicated convalescence: ileocystoplasty, 64 percent; colocystoplasty, 58 percent, a slight but statistically significant difference. The complications are listed in Table 3.

Acute intestinal obstruction is analyzed in Table 4. It occurs twice as frequently after ileoplasty (13 percent) as after coloplasty (7 percent). Moreover, re-operation has been necessary more often following ileoplasty (a ratio of 2/1).

Obstruction that requires surgical intervention after ileoplasty is usually mechanical (intestinal strangulation,

TABLE 4. Postoperative Intestinal Obstructions

	No. Operations	No. Intestinal Obstructions	%	Cured by Duodenal Suction	Secondary Operation	Death
Ileum	55	7	13	1	6	1
Sigmoid	122	9	7.4	3	6	2 (embolisms)
Ascending colon	8	0	0			
Total	185	16	8.7	4	12	3

internal hernia). Obstruction has not been caused by paralytic ileus, even when it was associated with electrolyte imbalance, which is often aggravated by previous renal insufficiency but is, in fact, the result of intestinal obstruction and not the reason for it.

Fistula is undoubtedly the most frequent complication (cutaneous urinary and/or fecal).

Urinary fistula: If a fistula is defined as drainage lasting more than 3 weeks, there are 32 in our series (17.3 percent). There were 22 fistulas following coloplasty (122 patients, 18 percent), 7 fistulas following ileoplasty (55 patients, 12.7 percent), 17 fistulas following ICP for tuberculosis (97 patients, 17.7 percent) and 12 fistulas following ICP for cancer (52 patients, 23 percent).

One should not be surprised by difficulties associated with prostato-intestinal or urethrointestinal anastomosis, by comparison to the security of a suture between the trigone and the bowel. This fact explains the higher rate of fistulas after bladder cancer oprations and perhaps for the higher rate (18 percent) in coloplasty versus ileoplasty (12 percent). Sigmoid loops, used more often than ileum, and preoperative radiotherapy, although limited to 3,500 rads, might explain the difference.

The sigmoid is more exposed when the bladder is submitted to x-ray or cobalt therapy and could be a reason for preferring the ileum after radical cystectomy for cancer.

All but 2 fistulas—1 perineal and 1 vesicovaginal—were hypogastric, related to the lower suture of the loop (to the bladder neck, the prostate or the urethra). Closure was obtained in some cases by prolonged drainage with a urethral catheter.

Of 12 secondary operations, the exact site of the fistula could be localized in 11 cases. Ten of these patients were treated by simple trimming and suture, and concomitant transurethral prostatic resection in one.

Ureteral anastomosis to the loop—constant in cancer operations and exceptional in tuberculosis—is an unusual site of fistula. We have no such cases that we can be sure of unless we set apart 1 patient in whom an undissectable mass was found at operation but treatment by prolonged double drainage—urethral and ureteral—was finally successful. Failure of the ends of the loop to close has never been observed.

Fecal fistula, 18 cases: There were 12 fistulas after sigmoidoplasty and only three after ileoplasty. The last 3 fecal fistulas have occurred following cecocystoplasty, but because of our limited experience in this last operation, discussion seems untimely.

Of the remaining 15 fistulas 5 closed spontaneously. Ten fistulas, including 8 following sigmoidoplasty, required colostomy with secondary closure a few months later.

TABLE 5. Mortality of Patients Followed 0 to 16 Years*

Time Elapsed (Yrs)	No. Patients	No. Dead Patients
0 to 2	49	20
3 to 10	52	8
11 to 16	20	0
Total	121	28

* Total cases, 185–16 postoperative mortalities, 48 cases not traced.

Three patients who had been treated for bladder cancer died—one from gram-negative septicemia, the other two from progressive cachexia despite external colostomy. However, in none of these cases had preoperative irradiation exceeded 3,500 rads.

Internal urinary-fecal fistulas are infrequent. Five (27 percent) occurred in our series, all following colocystoplasty. The first symptom may be either fecaluria or emission of urine through the anus. Spontaneous closure by prolonged bladder drainage was obtained twice. In the other 3 patients, intestinal diversion by external colostomy and a direct approach to the fistula were necessary. Sigmoido-prostatic or urethral anastomosis appeared to be the source of the fistula in every case.

LONG-TERM EVALUATION

Sixteen years have elapsed since we performed our first ICP. Of 185 patients, 169 survived the operation. We have been unable to follow 48 of these patients to 1967. Some have not been heard from since they left the hospital, others have been followed as long as 10 years while 121 patients have been following regularly.

During the first 2 years 28 patients died and 8 more died during the following 8 years (Table 5). In other words, we have had no deaths after 10 postoperative years. The first 2 years appear to be the most critical whatever the cause of death (advanced malignant disease, severe infection, severe preoperative renal insufficiency). After this 2-year period, life expectancy seems to increase and might, after 10 years, equal that of normal individuals of the same age group.

Of our first 25 patients 16 are alive, 3 are dead and 6 have been lost to followup. Most surviving patients have good renal function and, although we have not been able to trace some patients to 1967, their renal function when last seen would indicate a good long-term prognosis.

EVALUATION OF RENAL FUNCTION

Renal function has been studied in 89 patients from 2 to 16 years following bladder reconstruction.[3,4] They have been classified according to their glomerular filtration rate (Table 6).

Figure 1 shows the evolution of renal function in these 89 patients. The number with fair function has increased but only slightly. After a 2 to 6-year control, i.e. on an average 8-year followup, 56 percent of the patients have improved or maintained their preoperative function; 44 percent have reduced function.

If renal function is plotted against time, the loss of function is a slow process, represented by an almost horizontal line, and this result is the same whether the ileum or colon was used (Fig. 2).

As far as renal function is concerned, ICP gives a patient an almost normal life expectancy.

Comparable and favorable results are obtained with non-neoplastic lesions (Fig. 3). Surgical improvement of preoperative renal insufficiency explains the ascending slope of the upper line. On the contrary, if renal function in bladder cancer deteriorates somewhat faster, it does so slowly enough not to interfere with the prognosis of the lesion within the limits of therapeutic means. Therefore ICP is comparible with good renal function.

Deterioration of renal function must be considered a complication and may be caused by (1) urinary infection, (2) renal lithiasis, (3) vesicoureteral reflux and (4) mechanical factors, i.e. stenosis of uretero-intestinal anastomosis or prostato-cervical obstruction.

Urinary infection: Most patients had urinary infection and chronic or subacute pyelonephritis before the operation. Urinary infection was often permanent, with numerous organisms (Escherichia coli, Proteus vulgaris, Staphyloccus (sic) aureus, Pseudomonas aeruginosa, etc. However, in 23 cases the urine was sterile and renal function was excellent even a long time after intestinal plasty, except in 4 patients whose renal function was impaired before operation.

One cannot pretend to sterilize the urine of all patients following ICP inasmuch as the infection is usually chronic and resistant to most antibiotics. Some of these drugs may produce nephrotoxicity that precludes long-term usage.

Renal lithiasis is next to infection as a major cause of renal deterioration. There were 21 cases (11.4 percent) of calculi—12 pelvic or calyceal and 9 vesical. Five patients were known to have a stone before ICP but it

TABLE 6. Glomerular Filtration Rate

C_{Cr}		C_{Ur}
>90 ml	Excellent	>40 ml
60–90 ml	Good	25–40 ml
30–60 ml	Fair	15–25 ml
<30 ml	Poor	<15 ml

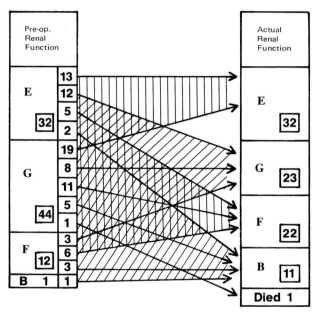

Fig. 1. Renal function in 89 cases followed from 2 to 16 years.

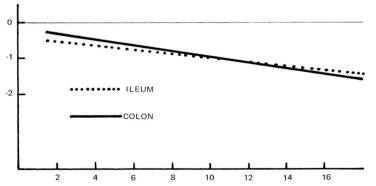

Fig. 2. Postoperative changes in renal function in 89 cases.

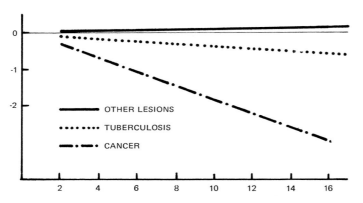

Fig. 3. Postoperative changes in renal function in 89 cases.

seems likely that mucus acts as an organic matrix for calcium-phosphate stones. Treatment has been pyelo-nephrolithotomy, cystotomy of the intestinal bladder or sometimes litholapaxy. In all except 2 of these patients renal function was fair or bad in spite of being excellent or good at the beginning.

Vesicoureteral reflux: Contrary to the opinion of many authors, this factor does not seem to us to be of major importance in renal deterioration. Reflux is quite frequent after direct ureterointestinal anastomosis. We prefer the risk of reflux to the risk of stenosis, the latter being favored by any oblique or tunnellike implantation of the ureter.[5,6]

Forty-six patients have been explored and reflux has been found in 82 percent of cases of uretero-ileal anastomosis, in 67 percent of uretero-sigmoidal anasto-mosis and in 14 percent of uretero-cecal anastomosis. There is a slight but no significant difference between sigmoid and ileum. If reflux is less frequent following cecoplasty, it is due to implantation of the ureter in the ileal stump above the ileocecal valve or in the appendix.

In 75 patients in whom the ureters have not been re-implanted, pre-existing reflux has persisted in 77 percent of the sigmoidoplasties and in 89 percent of the ileoplasties.

Though frequent, reflux does no appear harmful for kidney function as long as the pressure remains low in the intestinal bladder. A comparative study between patients with or without reflux has not disclosed any significant difference in the evolution of renal clearances insofar as the lower urinary tract remains normal.

Mechanical complications, either at the site of ureteral anastomosis or at the prostato-cervical level, have a serious and rapid effect upon the involved kidney. They must be diagnosed and treated as early as possible.

There were 5 late stenoses of the uretero-intestinal anastomosis. In those cases rapid deterioration of renal function developed and required operative correction of the stenosis.[7] This is a late complication and in 2 instances

developed more than 7 years after ICP. Careful followup evaluation of the patient is justified with, if possible, a yearly excretory urogram.

Bladder neck and prostatic obstruction, especially when associated with vesicoureteral reflux, must be recognized and treated early. Since we have never been in favor of systematic bladder neck resection at the time of ICP because of the risk of incontinence, great attention has been directed to emptying of the intestinal bladder, inasmuch as some cases, mostly tuberculous, are prone to secondary lesions—bladder neck sclerosis, prostatitis, urethral stenosis.

We have done 16 transurethral prostatic resections, 4 within a few months after ICP and 12 from 1 to 13 years postoperatively. The primary lesion was tubercu-losis in 10 patients, cancer in 6.

FUNCTION OF THE INTESTINAL BLADDER

We have considered 3 points to be the most representative parameters of intestinal bladder function: (1) interval between 2 micturitions during the daytime, (2) impor-tance of nocturia (3) continence. The results, given in tables 7 and 8, are grossly comparable for ileum and sigmoid. They might be better with cecum, but our experience is too limited. Continence does not depend upon the type of intestinal segment but upon the condition of the vesicourethral junction, i.e. downward extension of cystectomy, depending on preservation of the trigone, of the bladder neck, level of prostatic section. The sex of the patients and the nature of the primary lesion play a major role. Complete incontinence has not occurred but in 3 groups continence is not perfect: (1) in radical cystectomy for cancer when the greater part of the posterior urethra is removed with the bladder neck and the prostate and when the external sphincter might be severely injured; (2) in neurogenic bladder in which improvement of the continence cannot be complete in every case; (3) in traumatic lesions of the bladder and

TABLE 7. Late Results in Micturition According to Type of Intestinal Segment Used

	No. Cases	Cases Studied	Interval Between Micturitions (Day)					No. Micturitions (Night)			
			1 Hr or Less	2 Hrs	3 Hrs	4 Hrs or More	Av.	1 or 2	3 to 5	>5	Av.
Ileum	55	40	13	17	6	4	2 hrs	7	20	13	4
Sigmoid	122	82	20	33	23	6	2⅙ hrs	33	37	12	2
Ascending colon	8	5	0	0	2	3	3½ hrs	4	1	0	1

TABLE 8. Continence

	No. Cases	Cases Studied	Day			Night		
			Complete	Incomplete	% Incomplete	Complete	Incomplete	% Incomplete
Tuberculosis	97	74	65	9	12.0	61	13	17.6
Cancer: Transprostatic cystectomy	34	22	8	14	64.0	2	20	91.0
Subtotal cystectomy	18	10	9	1	10.0	7	3	30.0
Bilharziasis	11	5	5	0	0	5	0	0
Traumatic, surgical or obstetrical lesions	8	6	2	4	66.0	4	2	33.0
Neurogenic bladder	7	5	1	4	80.0	2	3	40.0
Other lesions	10	7	5	2	28.5	5	2	28.5

unrethra in women (following operation or injury of childbirth). Extensive damage to these structures requires another type of correction.

WHAT IS THE BEST INTESTINAL SEGMENT TO USE AS A BLADDER?

Fifty-five ileoplasties (30 percent) versus 122 coloplasties (66 percent) clearly indicate our preference. Our initial experience was the ileum[8] but difficulties with peritonization, frequency of postoperative obstruction (5 cases including 1 death in our first 35 ileoplasties), the opportunity offered by the sigmoid to exclude the pelvis by means of a coloparietal suture and the capacity and contractility of the sigmoid loop impelled us as early as 1956–57 to develop a technique of colocystoplasty that we have since followed.[9] We have been surprised to notice that mortality and morbidity seemed higher following coloplasty than ileoplasty. As we have stated, more frequent use of the colon following radical cystectomy for cancer explains the higher mortality rate in cases of coloplasty.

Septicity of the colonic content favors infection and venous thrombosis, especially after a long and difficult dissection of the pelvis. But there were no deaths following 35 cases of ICP in benign, non-tuberculous lesions whatever intestinal loop was used. That is why the choice of the bowel segment cannot be based upon respective postoperative complications only but upon the function of this segment as a bladder.

Renal function is, of course, of primary importance to appreciate the long-term results of the operation but we have already shown that there was no variation in that respect between the different segments used.

As far as micturition is concerned, the sigmoid seems to give better results than ileum. The amount of residual urine is smaller and frequency is reduced. One of the (R. K.) had already demonstrated this fact in 1956–57 by means of cine radiography.[10]

Evacuation is obtained by abdominal straining and true contraction of the bowel. Two of us (M. C. and C. C.) have analyzed 24 patients by radiomanometry of the intestinal bladder. These classifications are the result of our analysis:

Long intraperitoneal ileoplasty (Fig. 4): Good capacity, incomplete evacuation, normal pressure.

Short extraperitoneal ileoplasty (Fig. 5): Smaller capacity but better evacuation of the urine results in comparable function.

Long extraperitoneal ileoplasty (Fig. 6): Not as good as long intraperitoneal ileoplasty or short extraperitoneal ileoplasty. The ileal loop cannot distend in that limited space. Capacity is smaller, pressure is higher, reflux more frequent. It is the least satisfactory segment.

Sigmoidocystoplasty (Fig. 7): Greater capacity, better evacuation, without higher pressure seems to make the best bladder.

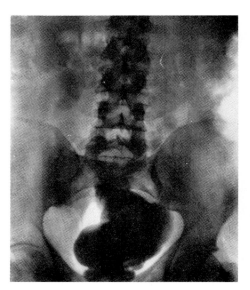

Fig. 4. Long intraperitoneal ileoplasty (average results). Capacity, 325 ml; residual urine, 125 ml; pressure during micturition, 35 cm (water). Reflux: capacity, 300 ml; pressure, 20 cm.

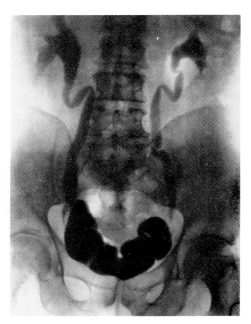

Fig. 6. Long extraperitoneal ileoplasty (average results). Capacity, 175 ml; residual urine, 60 ml; pressure during micturition, 50 cm. Reflux: capacity, 75 ml; pressure, 23 cm.

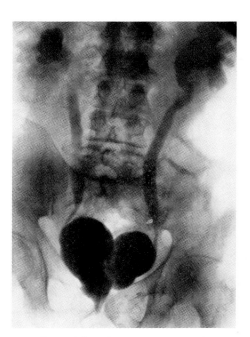

Fig. 5. Short extraperitoneal ileoplasty (average results). Capacity, 290 ml; residual urine, 80 ml; pressure during micturition, 35 cm. Reflux: capacity, 175 ml; pressure, 20 cm.

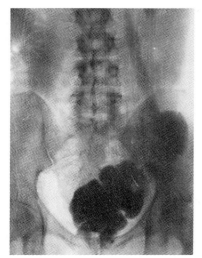

Fig. 7. Sigmoidocystoplasty (average results). Capacity, 315 ml; residual urine, 40 ml; pressure during micturition, 35 cm. Reflux: capacity, 185 ml; pressure, 18 cm.

Ceco-coloplasty (Fig. 8): Only 3 cases have been explored but they have the largest capacity, good evacuation and, as aforementioned,, reflux is less frequent than in other types of ICP. We have preferred sigmoidoplasty but if our early successes with cecocystoplasty are confirmed, we might switch to this form of bladder reconstruction.

VALUE OF ICP: INDICATIONS IN VARIOUS BLADDER LESIONS[2,11]

Urogenital Tuberculosis. Enlargement of the bladder by means of ICP is the treatment of choice of the

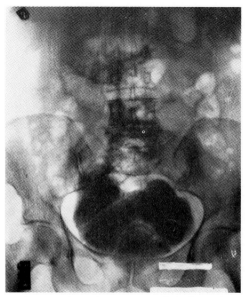

Fig. 8. Caeco-colocystoplasty (average results). Capacity, 425 ml; residual urine, 25 ml; pressure during micturition, 40 cm. Reflux: capacity, 250 ml; pressure, 10 cm.

contracted, tuberculous bladder. The patient is relieved of frequency that may have made life intolerable. He recovers normal micturition. At operation a segment of the ureter can be replaced at the same time or a cutaneous ureterostomy can be suppressed that would have been definitive otherwise (Fig. 9).

As far as micturition is concerned, results are usually excellent when the lower urinary tract is normal.

Associated lesions such as prostatitis, bladder neck sclerosis and urethral stenosis may interfere with the quality of the micturition and require complementary treatment.

Results are also good in regard to renal function. However, the future of such patients who often have only 1 diseased kidney depends upon renal function at the time of ICP. Some patients with advanced renal insufficiency died within a few years of operation in spite of ICP but others have an almost normal life expectancy (Fig. 10).

Bladder Cancer. One of us (R. K.) has always been opposed to radical cystectomy and ICP as a 1-stage procedure, which increases the mortality rate of an operation that is already formidable. One may lose a patient who might have been cured of cancer at the cost of cutaneous ureterostomy or a Coffey procedure. It is true nevertheless that a patient who is offered ICP as a 2-stage operation is more prone to accept radical cystectomy.

A different opinion is held by one of us (M. C.) who has treated 24 patients by a combination of radical cystectomy, ICP and cobalt with surprisingly good results. Three patients died, 2 are incontinent but 19 have survived an average of 3 years or longer and have recovered normal micturition with more or less incontinence (Fig. 11).

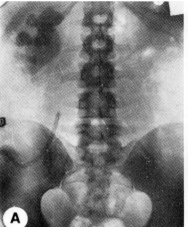
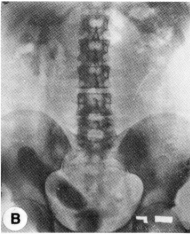

Fig. 9. Boy aged 13 years with tuberculosis. 1949—left nephrectomy. 1950—because of smaller bladder with massive ureteral reflux, right cutaneous ureterostomy was performed (A). 1953—ileouretero-cystoplasty. 1967—patient leads normal life in spite of persistent frequency and nocturia. Continence is excellent. Renal function remains satisfactory: creatinine clearance—68 ml/mn, urea clearance—35 ml/mn, IVP, 90 minutes, shows pyeloureteral dilatation no longer progresses. Good evacuation of long ileal loop (B).

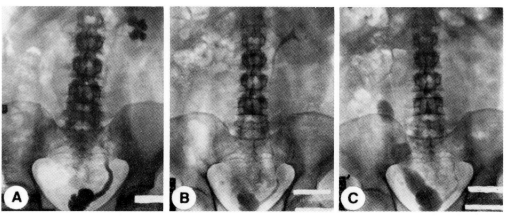

Fig. 10. Man aged 35 years with tuberculosis. 1953—right nephrectomy. 1954—ileo-cysto-plasty for contracted bladder with severe vesicoureteral reflux and dilatation of kidney (*A*). 1967—patient's general condition is excellent, urine is sterile. Renal function is normal: creatine clearance—102 ml/mn, urea clearance—54 ml/mn, PSP—60 percent. Continence is excellent. IVP, 15 minutes, shows excellent secretion, no dilation (*B*). IVP, 60 minutes, shows ileal bladder is well visualized (*C*).

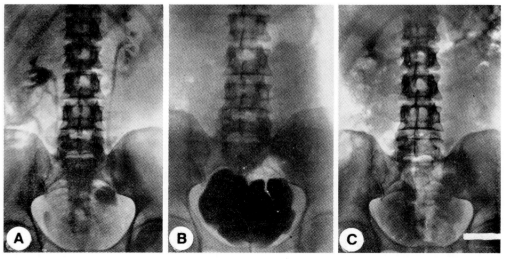

Fig. 11. Man aged 34 years with infiltrating anaplastic bladder carcinoma. 1965—patient was treated by telecobalt and 1-stage radical cystectomy and caeco-cystoplasty. 1967—patient is all right. No recurrence. Perfect continence, 4 hours during day and 1 micturition at night. Creatinine clearance and urea clearance are normal. (*A*) Fifteen-minute IVP. (*B*) Cystography, no reflux. (*C*) After micturition, complete evacuation of caecal bladder.

Urogenital Bilharziasis will represent, in the future, one of the most frequent indications for ICP.[12] The lesions are comparable to those of tuberculosis and, in that respect, one can expect the results to be similar in both diseases (Fig. 12).

A contracted bladder is a clear indication for ICP but in our practice intestinoplasty has more often been necessary for lesions of the pelvic ureter (9 of 11 cases). Moreover, the extensiveness of ureteral lesions and

sclerosis of the bladder make impossible the utilization of a bladder flap to reconstruct the lower ureter.

Since we have had no mortality and few postoperative complications, ICP seems to be the most effective means of preserving renal function in young patients.

Neurogenic Bladder. The place of ICP in neurogenic bladder could become more important and needs to be discussed in detail.[13,14] The urologic factors are the same

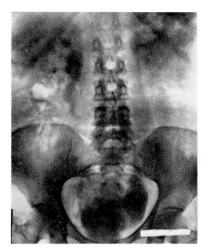

Fig. 12. Woman aged 54 years. 1957—colocystoplasty for bilharziasis. 1967—patient has excellent continence, 3 hours during day and 2 micturitions during night. Renal clearances have not varied: creatinine clearance—83 ml/mn, urea clearance—39 ml/mn IVP is at 90 minutes.

as those in tuberculosis or bilharziasis: (1) a permanently contracted bladder accompanied by increasing and intractable incontinence and harmful vesicoureteral reflux and (2) failure of a previous antireflux operation, the results of which are so disappointing in neurogenic bladder that an intestinal plasty appears to us preferable whenever the bladder wall is thickened.

As far as neuro-urology is concerned, one should consider complete traumatic lesions of the cord above the vesico-spinal center, i.e. upper motor neuron lesions, because they leave a tonic or sometimes spastic perineum and external sphincter capable of maintaining continence. On the contrary, patients with complete autonomous bladders due to lower cord or cauda equina lesions are unsatisfactory candidates for ICP (large bladder, atonic perineum). Cogenital lesions of the cord, i.e. myelomeningocele, may be improved by ICP in cases of incomplete autonomous bladder, hypertrophy and sclerosis of the bladder wall, unilateral or bilateral vesicoureteral reflux. All these conditions are necessary but they are not sufficient. The following requirements must also be fulfilled: failure of bladder training (preferably carried out in a special unit), permanent bladder retraction proved by failure of epidural or pudendal nerve anesthesia, integrity of upper limbs (ICP would be unreasonable in a quadriplegic), integrity of the bladder neck

and posterior urethra (a funnel-shaped urethra or a prior large bladder neck resection might impair the expected continence) and satisfactory renal function (we could not advise ICP in a paraplegic if GFR is more than 50 percent reduced; a Bricker ileal bladder is safer).

While exceptionally necessary in traumatic paraplegia, intestinal plasties might on the contrary be used more often in complete spina bifida.

Multiple Vesical Papilloma. Cure may be obtained by radical cystectomy. If the bladder neck and urethra are free of papillomas or if they can be destroyed, good continence might be secured after reconstruction of the bladder with an intestinal segment and a perfect functional result obtained. However, recurrences may occur not only in that small area of bladder mucosa but also in the upper urinary tract.

Traumatic, surgical or obstetrical lesions with extensive destruction of the bladder and sometimes of the lower ureter that would have in the past required cutaneous or intestinal diversion of the urine can also be cured by ICP. While results as far as renal function is concerned are good, the effect on micturition depends on the condition of the bladder neck.

The foregoing statement is true too in *bladder gangrene* when secondary reconstruction of the bladder does not produce a perfect result.

Interstitial Cystitis, exceptional in France, has not been successfully treated by ICP by us. Despite the large capacity of the loop these patients continued to have a high degree of urinary frequency.

CONCLUSION

ICP has offered to many patients the possibility of alleviating troublesome infirmities and at the same time it has improved renal function and life expectancy. Nevertheless one should not expect from ICP more than it can offer. Good function of the bladder means a good capacity reservoir as well as a normally functioning sphincter system.

ICP provides a satisfactory method of enlarging or replacing the reservoir. However, if sphincter action is altered (i.e. some large vesicovaginal fistulas), absent (i.e. bladder exstrophy) or destroyed during operation (i.e. radical prostato-cystectomy) continence will never be restored and there will still be a place for old methods of urinary diversion.

SUMMARY

The results of 185 intestino-cystoplasties have been evaluated. A 16-year followup was available in some cases. Postoperative mortality and morbidity rates are reviewed. The results are encouraging. ICP

seems to respect renal function fully. Late prognosis depends essentially on the condition of the kidneys at the time of operation.

Possible factors of renal deterioration are analyzed: urinary infection, renal lithiasis, vesicoureteral reflux and stenosis of various anastomoses.

Micturition after ICP is discussed in relation to the type of intestinal segment that has been used, i.e. ileum versus sigmoid or cecum.

A radiometric study of various "bladders" is presented with reference to their respective intraperitoneal or extraperitoneal location. "Colic" bladders seem to have better function than "ileal" bladders.

The value of ICP is also discussed in relation to the primary lesion that required the procedure.

Results are excellent in contracted, tuberculous bladders, promising in bilharziasis, encouraging in some neurogenic bladders and, so far, often disappointing in bladder carcinoma.

Hospital Saint-Louis, 40 Rue Bichat, Paris X^e, France (R. K.)

REFERENCES

1. Küss, R.: Colo-cystoplasty rather than ileocystoplasty. J Urol 82:587, 1959

2. Küss, R.: Intestinal transplants in urology. Acta Chir Belg 59:690, 1960

3. Küss, R., Legrain, M., Bitker, M. and Perrin, C.: Étude du retentissement sur la fonction rénale des plasties intestinales de la voie excrétrice urinaire (à propos de 42 observations). J d'Urol 64:187, 1958

4. Küss, R., Legrain, M. and Chatelain, C.: Insuffisance rénale et pronostic lointain des plasties intestinales de la voie excrétrice urinaire. In: XIII Congress of the International Society of Urology. London: E. & S. Livingstone Ltd., vol. 2, pp. 256–260, 1965

5. Bitker, M. P.: L'urétéro-iléo-plastie. (Technique chirurgicale.) J Chir 91:199, 1966

6. Küss, R.: Discussion sur la technique de l'ileocystoplastie. In: Cinquante-et-Unième Congrès Français d'Urologie. Paris: G. Doin & Cie, p. 554, 1957

7. Küss, R. and Chatelain, C.: Les sténoses tardives des implantations urétérales dans les entéro-cystoplasties. J Urol Nephrol, 72:238, 1966

8. Küss, R.: Sur 21 cas d'iléo-cystoplastie. Mém Acad Chir 82:629, 1956

9. Küss, R., de Tourris, H. and Genon, M.: Une technique de colo-cystoplastie. J Chir, 77:423, 1959

10. Küss, R. and Noix, M.: Radiocinématographie de la vessie iléale. Mém Acad Chir, 82:642, 1956

11. Küss, R. and Legrain, M.: L'utilisation du greffon intestinal en urologie. In: XI Congrès de la Société Internationale d'Urologie. Stockholm: Almqvist & Wiksells, vol. 2, pp. 46–50, 1958

12. Chatelain, C. and Camey, M.: Indications des plasties intestinales de la voie excrétrice dans la bilharziose uro-génitale. J Urol Nephrol, 73 (suppl.):410, 1967

13. Bitker, M. P.: L'iléo-cysto-plastie dans les troubles vesicaux d'origine neurologique. J d'Urol, 63:809, 1957

14. Bitker, M. P.: Colocystoplastie et spinabifida. J Urol Nephrol, 72:789, 1966

Commentary: Colocystoplasty

René Küss and Alain Jardin

For more than 15 yr we have preferred to use sigmoid colon and, less often, ascending colon to enlarge or replace the diseased bladder. To date we have performed 130 sigmoidocystoplasties, 12 cecocystoplasties, and 69 ileocystoplasties.

Since 1918 there have been several isolated attempts at colocystoplasties, including the successes of Strassman in 1924.[1] In the 1950s, ileocystoplasty was in vogue. However, more recently several authors, including J. M. Gil-Vernet, recognized the advantages of colocystoplasty over ileocystoplasty.[2-8] Statistics supporting the advantages of cecocystoplasty over sigmoidocystoplasty are not presently available.

CHOICE OF THE COLON AS A BLADDER SUBSTITUTE

The natural reservoir function of the colon and its larger capacity make the required length of intestine less with colon than ileum. The colon has a higher intraluminal pressure and less mucus secretion than the ileum. The pH and mucosal

resorption of urine are less in the colon than in the ileum. Cineradiographic studies have shown us that during micturation there is more complete emptying of the neobladder after colocystoplasty than after ileocystoplasty. Of greatest importance is the anatomic location of the sigmoid colon and its mesosigmoid. The pelvic location of these organs allows the limitation of the operation to the pelvis, which we believe contributes to the lower incidence of postoperative obstruction than that experienced after ileocystoplasty.

The greatest objection to colocystoplasty has been the development of fecal fistula as a result of the colonic anastomosis. Recent advances in colonic surgery make the validity of this objection open to question. Another objection to the use of colon rather than ileum has been the higher pressure with subsequent renal changes reported with the former graft. We have not noted the very high figures reported by some authors.[9,10] A significant objection to colocystoplasty after total cystectomy is the difficulty encountered in making the colo-trigonal anastomosis or especially the colourethral anastomosis because of the incomplete mobility of the sigmoid colon. We recognize this difficulty and do not advise the use of this segment of colon when a short and fat mesosigmoid is encountered. In such cases we use another intestinal segment.

TECHNIQUE OF SIGMOIDOCYSTOPLASTY

This technique has previously been described by us and does not differ greatly from that described by others[11–14] Our technique is as follows:

A midline infraumbilical incision is made. The abdominal cavity is entered and inspected. A 15-cm segment of sigmoid colon is chosen so that the distal end is able to extend without tension to the pouch of Douglas (Fig. 13). Incision of the coloparietal peritoneum or high division of a sigmoidal artery facilitates mobilization of the segment. The continuity of the colon is then reestablished by end-to-end anastomosis after the isolated segment is placed laterally with the mesenteric vascular supply to the graft passing through a hole left in the mesentery beneath the colonic anastomosis. A midline incision is made in the peritoneum over the bladder, and this is retracted laterally. The cystectomy is then performed. The colovesical anastomosis involves coaptation of the incised antimesenteric colon and previously incised distal end of the colonic segment (Figs. 14 and 15). Zero chromic catgut is used. Careful and complete reperitonealization of the neobladder isolates it and its mesentery from the peritoneal cavity. As an added precaution the reconstituted colon is placed above this suture line (Fig. 16). If the ureters have been divided they are anastomosed by an end-to-end anastomosis to each end of the graft (Fig. 17); 2–0 chromic catgut is used. In women over the age of 45, an associated hysterectomy makes the procedure easier and facilitates drainage through the vagina (Fig. 18). In the younger woman who has not undergone a hysterectomy the graft may be passed through the left broad ligament after division of the round ligament (Fig. 19). We have done this 37 times. Occasionally, after this maneuver expansion of the neobladder may be interfered with and urinary frequency may ensue.

Variations in surgical approach are (1) the use of a closed colonic segment or the use of an opened colonic segment as a flap, (2) the use of a predominantly extraperitoneal approach or an intraperitoneal approach, (3) the use of a decompression cecostomy proximal to the colonic anastomosis, (4) the type of colovesical or colourethral anastomosis, as end-to-end, median end-to-side, or distal end-to-side, (5) the location and type of end-to-side ureterocolonic anastomosis, with or without an antireflux mechanisms, and (6) the necessity of draining the neobladder with a large catheter to permit evacuation of mucus or the use of ureteral drainage.[6,7,11,12,15,16,18–20] The latter has few supporters.[16]

TECHNIQUE OF CECOCYSTOPLASTY

The use of ascending instead of sigmoid colon requires more operative time and more careful reperitonealization. Thus it has been claimed that surgical and postoperative risk is greater when the former intestinal segment is used in colocystoplasty. However, the natural qualities and capacity of this colonic segment make it quite desirable as a bladder substitute in selected patients.

The ascending colon and distal ileum are isolated and excluded from the intestinal tract. Restoration of intestinal

(*Text continues on page 834*)

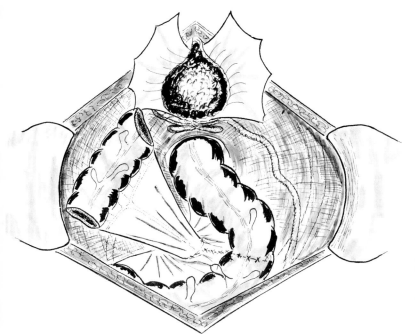

Fig. 13. Isolation of colon and extraperitonealization of the bladder. First, a segment of large bowel is isolated from the sigmoid colon, the continuity of which is restored by end-to-end anastomosis in one layer. Then the bladder is extraperitonealized by midline incision over the fundus, which left two flaps for reperitonealization.

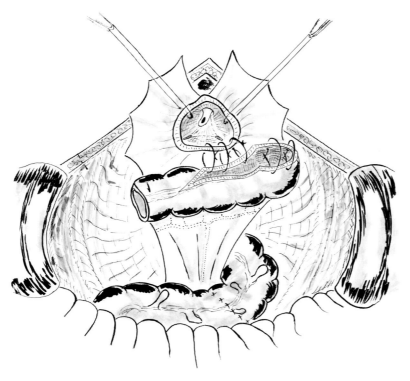

Fig. 14. Colovesical anastomosis. Resection of the bladder excluding the trigone. Urethral sound and ureteral orifices are visualized. Holding sutures are placed in the remaining bladder. The colonic segment is opened along the antimesenteric border inferiorly as required. Starting with the posterior layer, bowel is joined to the bladder in a racket-shaped closure with inverting sutures.

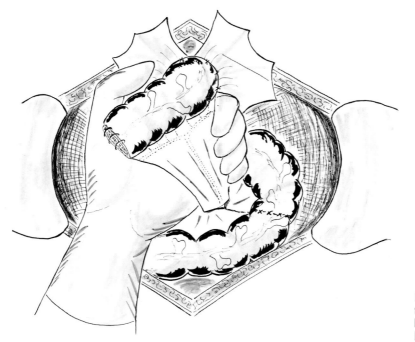

Fig. 15. Termination of colovesical anastomosis. The proximal free end of the bowel segment is closed with one or two layers of catgut.

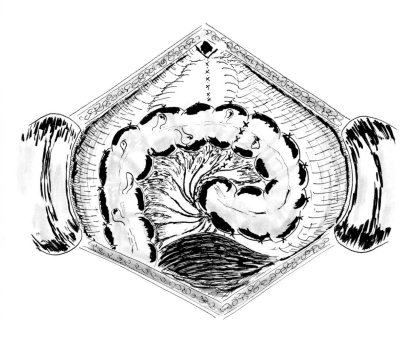

Fig. 16. Reperitonealization. The sigmoid colon is laid over the new bladder and its anastomoses to exclude the true pelvis from the peritoneal cavity.

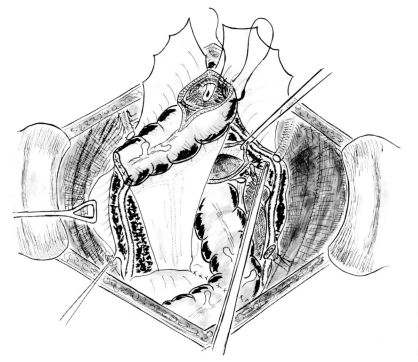

Fig. 17. The two ureters are anastomosed to the colonic segment anterior to the colovesical anastomosis. The opening into the vagina in front of the rectum is repaired separately.

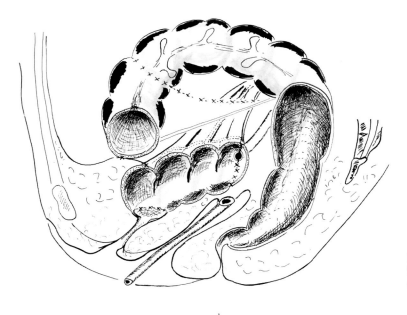

Fig. 18. Sagittal section indicates isolation from the general peritoneal cavity and drainage of the pelvis by way of the vagina.

Fig. 19. The isolated segment of colon is passed through the broad ligament on the left side after division of the round ligament.

continuity is made by ileotransverse colostomy. Incision of the coloparietal peritoneum allows mobilization of the graft to the pelvis. The cecum is well suited to a colovesical anastomosis. We usually anastomose the ureters to the cecum, but on occasion use the distal ileum or appendicular stump (end-to-end) when an appendectomy has not previously been performed. This permits the valve of Bauhin to function as an antireflux mechanism and, therefore, aids in protecting the renal units from high-pressure reflux, as can be demonstrated manometrically. We have used this technique in 11 patients since 1954 with satisfactory results.

RESULTS OF COLOCYSTOPLASTY

It is very difficult to compare the results of the same operation when it is used in such different clinical settings as young "cured" tuberculosis patients and also patients with infiltrative vesical carcinomas. The functional efficacy of the graft can best be determined after complete vesical substitution, since no original detrusor muscle remains to possibly regain functional capacity. Results of total and partial vesical replacement by colocystoplasty have previously been reported by us and others.[3,8,13,20,21]

MORTALITY

After vesical enlargment a mortality of 0% to 9% has been reported.[13,21] After replacement of the bladder for vesical carcinoma a 12% to 25% mortality has been reported.[8,13] Preoperative pelvic irradiation accounts in part for the higher mortality. An improved survival appears to be related to the urologist's experience with intestinal surgery.

IMMEDIATE POSTOPERATIVE COMPLICATIONS

Intestinal Obstruction. Intestinal obstruction occurs two times more frequently after ileocystoplasty than after colocystoplasty. We have noted this complication in 7% of our colocystoplasty patients, in most cases due to mechanical obstruction.

Urinary Fistula. Urinary fistula occurs in 10% to 20% of patients and almost always originates from the colovesical anastomosis or from the colourethral anastomosis. This complication rarely requires reoperation, since 70% to 80% of these patients stop draining after urethral catheter drainage is instituted. This sometimes requires several weeks of expectant observation.

Fecal Fistula. Fecal fistula occurs in 5% to 10% of patients and is always serious and sometimes fatal. This complication is noted particularly in patients who have received prior pelvic irradiation.

Urointestinal Fistula. Urointestinal fistula is rarely noted.

Gram-Negative Septicemia. Better antibiotics and other measures have decreased the frequency and mortality from gram-negative septicemia.

Thromboembolism. Thromboembolism occurs infrequently but justifies the fairly wide use of prophylactic anticoagulants.

EFFECT OF COLOCYSTOPLASTY ON RENAL FUNCTION

A well-functioning colocystoplasty should not jeopardize renal function. However, regular follow-up of these patients by urographic, serum electrolyte, and creatinine clearance studies is mandatory. The following conditions can cause deterioration in renal function.

Urinary Tract Infection. Seventy percent to 90% of patients demonstrate urinary tract infection, frequently with *Proteus* organisms. Optimal renal function is correlated with sterile urine.

Colovesical Stenosis. Correct surgical technique of the colovesical anastomosis will generally preclude colovesical stenosis.

Ureterocolonic Stenosis. Ureterocolonic stenosis is noted in 3% to 15% of patients at a late date. It occurred in a patient 7 yr after colocystoplasty. This potential complication justifies lifetime follow-up study of these patients.

Bladder Neck Obstruction. Such obstruction may require endoscopic treatment.

Association of Infection, Obstruction, and Mucus. This unfortunate combination of problems probably accounts for the development of lithiasis in or proximal to the graft in 5% to 10% of patients.

Neovesicoureteral Reflux. Reflux occurs in at least 70% of colocystoplasties. We do not believe that this itself is very deleterious to the patient. It occurs somewhat less frequently after cecocystoplasty.

Hyperchloremic Acidosis. Acidosis is absent or minor concern, requiring only alkalinization of the urine. This complication is noted most frequently in patients with severe renal disease.

ADVANTAGES OF ENTEROCYSTOPLASTY FOR URINARY DIVERSION

Complete continence of urine is to be expected after any form of enterocystoplasty when a normal sphincter mechanism is present before operation. However, although this is generally true after bladder enlargement procedures, the same is not true after bladder replacement procedures. After colocystoplasty for vesical replacement, nocturnal incontinence is frequent but daytime incontinence is less frequent. Reeducation plays an important role in the latter instance. Urinary frequency may be of great concern to the patient. Voiding at 2- to 3-hr intervals is usual. Longer intervals are more often seen after cecocystoplasty. However, we have never been asked to divert the urinary stream for this problem.

INDICATIONS FOR COLOCYSTOPLASTY

We recognize the following indications for colocystoplasty: (1) the destruction of the bladder with preservation of urethrovesical continence due to trauma, infection, parasite infestation, toxins, or radiotherapy, specifically, in cases of tuberculosis with associated vesical sclerosis and reflux the use of colocystoplasty avoids the morbidity caused by cutaneous urinary diversion, and (2) vesical carcinoma of the diffuse papillomatous type and noninfiltrating vesical carcinoma.

We do not advise enterocystoplasty where urethrovesical continence is abnormal, as in vesical exstrophy or neurogenic bladder.

CONTRAINDICATIONS FOR COLOCYSTOPLASTY

We recognize the following contraindications for colocystoplasty: (1) the absence of a suitable length of colon, approximately 15 cm, that is well vascularized, and free of diverticula, sigmoiditis, tumor, and other pathological entities, and (2) the presence of prior pelvic irradiation, which probably more adversely affects the colon than the ileum.

CHOICE OF SIGMOID COLON, ASCENDING COLON, OR ILEUM AS A BLADDER SUBSTITUTE

We cannot be too dogmatic on the choice of intestinal segment, since none appears to be greatly superior to the others. However, we still prefer the sigmoid colon or ascending colon but do not make a final decision until laparotomy.

REFERENCES

1. Strassmann P: Ersatz einer schrumpfblase durch transposition des Sigmoidum Romanum. Z Urol 19:583, 1925

2. Bourque JP: Les divers segments intestinaux en urologie. Technique personnelle de la colocystoplastie d'agrandissement et de substitution vesicale. Un Med Canada 88:1503, 1959

3. Winter CC, Goodwin WE: Results of sigmoidocystoplasty. J Urol 80:467, 1958

4. Gregoir W: Le transplant intestinal en chirurgie urinaire. Acta Chir Belg (Suppl) 1:123, 1960

5. Küss R: Colocystoplastie plutot qu'ileocystoplastie. Mem Acad Chir 84:331, 1958

6. Morales PA, Ong G, Askari S, et al: Sigmoidocystoplasty for the contracted bladder. J Urol 80:455, 1958

7. Gil-Vernet JM: Colocystoplasty. Technique chirurgicale de la sigmoido-cystoplastie laterolaterale. J Urol Nephrol 64:301, 1958

8. Gil-Vernet JM, Escarpenter JM, Perez-Trujillo G, et al: A functioning artificial bladder: Results of 41 consecutive cases. J Urol 87:825, 1962

9. Küss R: Remarques sur l'entero-cysto-plastie a propos de 185 observations (1951–1967). Ann Chir 22:693, 1968

10. L'utilisation du greffon intestinal en urologie. Xleme congres de la SIU Rapport: Tome 1, 1–67. Discussion: Tome 2, 29–191, Stockholm, 1958

11. Küss R, Tourris H de, Genon M: Une technique de colocystoplastie. J Chir 77:324, 1959

12. Brenez J: La colocystoplastie. Acta Urol Belg 28:441, 1960

13. Cukier J: Rapport au 61eme congres de l'association francaise d'urologie, 1966. J Urol Nephrol 73:147, 150, 1967

14. Riches E: Colocystoplasty. Proc R Soc Med 53:1029, 1960

15. Bourque JP: Colocystoplasty for enlargement and substitution of bladder: Preliminary report of 25 cases. J Urol 84:527, 1960

16. Gil-Vernet JM: Technique for construction of a functioning artificial bladder. J Urol 83:39, 1960

17. Goodwin WE, Winter CC: Technique of sigmoidocystoplasty. Surg Gynecol Obstet 108:370, 1959

18. Mathisen W: Open loop sigmoidocystoplasty. Acta Chir Scand 110:227, 1955

19. Bourque JP: La substitution vesicale par colocystoplastie. J Urol Nephrol 67:122, 1961

20. Hradec EA: Bladder substitution: Indications and results in 114 operations. J Urol 94:406, 1965

21. Gil-Vernet JM, Perez-Truillo G, Escarpenter J, et al: Resultats obtenus avec la colocystoplastie (d'apres 34 observations). J Urol Nephrol 66:775, 1960

ANNOTATED BIBLIOGRAPHY

Lambert D, Allergre JP, Guillou ML, et al: Late problems arising from intestinal plasties of the excretory system. Semin Nephrol 2:10, 1976

The authors studied 50 cases of colocystoplasty with follow-up study of between 5 and 25 yr. These patients were studied together with 21 patients with ileocystoplasty with the same follow-up time. Renal function became impaired in 30% of patients. Factors involved in the etiology of this renal failure were infection, lithiasis, reflux, stenosis at the site of ureteric implants, and lesions of the lower urinary tract. Good function of a graft, when obtained during the first few years, persisted (*e.g.,* continence). In 30% of patients, cervicourethroprostatic lesions developed but could be treated easily. In conclusion, the authors advise against the use of an intestinal graft in the presence of marked renal failure (creatinine clearance less than 20 ml/min) or in the presence of severe cervicourethroprostatic lesions. Apart from these two contraindications, colocystoplasty remains an operation of choice if the patient can be adequately followed.

Seddon JM, Best L, Bruce AW: Intestinocystoplasty in treatment of interstitial cystitis Urology 10:431, 1977

Interstitial cystitis remains a fairly poorly defined entity that nevertheless leads to problems requiring major surgical solutions such as intestinoplasty. The authors performed eight colocystoplasties and one patch ileocystoplasty in women with interstitial cystitis. Seven good results encouraged them to continue in this direction.

Shirley SW, Mirelman S: Experiences with colocystoplasties, cecocystoplasties and ileocystoplasties in urologic surgery: 40 patients J Urol 120:165, 1978

Twenty-six colocystoplasties (including 16 cecocystoplasties and 10 sigmoidocystoplasties) were performed in patients with interstitial cystitis. The results were excellent and similar to those obtained in the enlargement of tuberculous small bladders. The authors suggest using the colon rather than the ileum when bladder capacity is so reduced that the bladder must really be replaced. When bladder capacity, under anaesthesia, is greater than 200 ml, they prefer the ileum.

Smith AM: Enterocystoplasty and pregnancy Am J Obstet Gynecol 117:915, 1973

The author reports two cases of pregnancy in women who several years previously had undergone an ileocystoplasty and a colocystoplasty. They point out that cesarian section after colocystoplasty may be performed inadvertently through the mesocolon.

Rao MS, Bapna DC, Bhat VN, et al: Blow out of a colocystoplasty loop owing to bladder neck obstruction. J Urol 117:667, 1977

This article emphasizes the possibility of rupturing an intestinal graft because of proximal cervicourethral obstruction and hence the necessity, mentioned elsewhere, of watching of this region in patients who have undergone colocystoplasty.

OVERVIEW: CAUTION NEEDED IN CYSTOPLASTY

Chester C. Winter

It has been some 8 yr since my first overview of this subject in the first edition of *Current Operative Urology*. It is of interest that intestinal cystoplasty (or enterocystoplasty) continues to be applied infrequently in the United States. Although I have been interested in the operation for 25 yr, along with most urologists I use it only very sparingly. This may be due to several factors. First, few patients in the United States have contracted bladders due to tuberculosis. Second, the experience with treating interstitial cystitis with this operation has been too unrewarding. Third, the modifications of the Bricker procedure (use of colon, antireflux techniques, more satisfactory drainage bags and equipment) have continued to make it a popular method of upper urinary system diversion.

Enterocystoplasty is a tedious, time-consuming operation, and the proper anastomosis of the new bladder to the membranous urethra in the man after prostatectomy is somewhat difficult to achieve. Advocates of enterocystoplasty tend to gloss over the postoperative complications (*e.g.*, intestinal and abdominal sequelae). They also tend to minimize the urinary problems, of which several are profound. In my experience, elderly patients do not tolerate the operation well because of incontinence, which is almost always present at night. Residual urine is often significant, and vesicoureteral reflux almost invariably occurs unless an antireflux procedure has been performed during the enterocystoplasty. The latter is difficult when ileum is used but more easily accomplished with the colonic conduit.

Compromised renal function should act as a deterrent to the performance of complete enterocystoplasty because of the residual problem, the reflux phenomenon, the propensity to form stones in the new bladder, and the probability of electrolyte imbalance.

When this operation is performed the general practitioner or family physician should be warned that pyuria is the rule, since the bowel sloughs off white cells and this can be mistaken for infection. The latter would have to be proved by culture. Too often this is not done, and the asymptomatic patient is commenced on antibiotic therapy when the physician receives a report of pyuria.

Interstitial cystitis continues to be an indication for bladder enlargment or complete replacement of the detrusor. I agree with the reviewers that the detrusor should be completely removed if this operation is to be performed. If not, the symptoms will undoubtedly persist. In my experience only about half the patients with interstitial cytitis are relieved of their symptoms sufficiently for both patient and physician satisfaction after enterocystoplasty.

The performance of complete bladder replacement with bowel also is controversial when bladder cancer is the indication for surgery. Perhaps this is a moot point, but recurrence of carcinoma in the pelvic region will certainly compromise a new bladder and may require surgical intervention where it would not if higher diversion were used.

Incontinence after enterocystoplasty is a greater problem in the woman, who will require an in-dwelling catheter or higher urinary diversion to control this while the man can wear a condom catheter for control.

I agree that enterocystoplasty or complete bladder replacement with bowel is not indicated for a contracted neurogenic bladder or in an attempt to alleviate bladder dysfunction. There has been at least one advocate of doing this in order to faciliate intermittent catheterization.

If my overview of this area seems reserved or pessimistic, it is because after 25 yr I have been unable to develop much enthusiasm for intestinal cystoplasty. Yet I think it should be pursued in large, research-oriented medical centers in an effort to improve and modify its application rather than abandoning it completely in favor of the Bricker procedure. It still holds out the prospect of allowing the patient to urinate normally without having to wear an appliance, a goal to be sought.

PART TWENTY-FIVE

SURGICAL TREATMENT OF CARCINOMA OF THE BLADDER

64

RADICAL CYSTECTOMY WITH OR WITHOUT PRIOR IRRADIATION IN THE TREATMENT OF BLADDER CANCER

W. F. Whitmore, Jr., M. A. Batata, M. A. Ghoneim, H. Grabstald and A. Unal

From the Urologist Service, Department of Surgery and the Department of Radiation Therapy, Memorial Sloan-Kettering Cancer Center, New York, New York

The Journal of Urology
Copyright © 1977 by The Williams & Wilkins Co.
Vol. 118, July, Part 2
Printed in U.S.A.

ABSTRACT—This is a summary presentation on certain aspects of an experience with the use of radical cystectomy with or without prior irradiation in the treatment of selected patients with bladder cancer at the Memorial Sloan-Kettering Cancer Center.

Any modern student of the subject must recognize the fundamental, meticulous and perceptive nature of the observations of Dr. Hugh J. Jewett and his associates relative to the clinical staging and pathologic characterization of bladder cancer. The importance of these contributions virtually assures their principal author of urologic immortality.

MATERIALS AND METHODS

Between 1949 and 1971, 451 patients with bladder cancer were treated by radical cystectomy at the Memorial Sloan-Kettering Cancer Center. Patients who were explored with the intent of radical cystectomy but in whom the operation was not actually accomplished have been excluded. Indications for cystectomy were (1) low stage tumors (O, A and B_1) judged unsuitable for conservative treatment because of 1 or more of the following (a) too many for conservative treatment (multiple judged (b) rapid development of new lesions (multiple over a short time), (c) repeated development of new lesions (multiple over a long time) and (d) initial presence or subsequent development of high grade lesions, and (2) high stage tumors judged unsuitable for segmental resection because of 1 or more of the following (a) multicentricity in space, (b) multicentricity in time and (c) proximity to the bladder neck. During the last 30 years the indications for cystectomy have remained unchanged, although there is obviously room for variations in clinical judgment in selecting patients within the framework of the specified indications.

Virtually all patients had radical cystectomy.[1] In the vast majority of patients bilateral pelvic lymph node dissection, beginning midway on the common iliac arteries, was performed but in a few patients pelvic lymph node dissection was more limited or was omitted entirely. During the 20 years encompassed by this experience the following changes in operative technique have been recognized (1) the use of abdominal drainage was abandoned about 15 years ago; a Foley catheter placed via the urethra is sometimes used to obtain hemostasis in the area of the urogenital diaphragm in male patients; (2) early experience demonstrated the futility of efforts at surgical cure of massive lymph node metastases within the pelvis proper or of recognized metastases above the level of the common iliac artery bifurcations and, accordingly, the extent of lymph node dissection routinely used has been modified as previously specified and (3) prophylactic urethrectomy in the male patient has been used increasingly in the last 10 years.

The methods of clinical and pathological staging and of tumor grading have not changed during the 20 years covered by this study. An analysis of the various treatment groups relative to the age and sex of the patients and to the histologic type, histologic grade, clinical stage and pathologic stage of the tumors has revealed no significant differences among the various treatment groups. Patients with only papilloma (considered grade I carcinoma in the classifications of many) are not included in this series.

The 451 patients may be divided into 4 distinct treatment groups: group 1—137 patients who had radical cystectomy alone, group 2—109 patients who received definitive megavoltage irradiation to the bladder of approximately 6,000 rads during approximately 6 weeks and who were subjected to radical cystectomy plus or minus 1 year following the completion of radiation therapy because of persistent (?), recurrent (?) or new lesions (?), group 3—119 patients who received 4,000 rads to the bladder and true pelvis in 4 weeks with megavoltage as deliberate preoperative irradiation and who were subjected to radical cystectomy approximately 6 weeks later and group 4—86 patients who received 2,000 rads to the bladder and true pelvis in 1 week with megavoltage as deliberate preoperative irradiation and who were subjected to radical cystectomy within 1 week thereafter.

The experience with group 1 was largely accumulated between 1949 and 1958, the experience with group 3 between 1959 and 1966, and the experience with group 4 between 1966 and 1970. Experience with group 2 was distributed over the entire 20-year interval, since most patients in this group received definitive irradiation elsewhere and came to Memorial Sloan-Kettering Cancer Center as treatment failures for radical cystectomy.

RESULTS AND DISCUSSION

Analyses of the pathologic versus clinical stage in each of the groups are shown in Tables 1 to 4. Clinical staging for all patients was based upon bimanual examination

TABLE 1. Pathological Versus Clinical State in Group 1

Clinical Stage		Pathological Stage						
		O	A	B_1	B_2	C	D_1	D_2
					Understaging			
O	7	7	—	—	—	—	—	—
A	17	—	15	2	—	—	—	—
B_1	42	—	—	28	9	1	3	1
B_2	39	—	—	—	16	8	6	9
C	26	—	—	—	6	11	4	5
D_1	6	—	—	—	—	—	3	3
				Stage Reduction				
Totals	137	7	15	30	31	20	16	18

TABLE 2. Pathological Versus Clinical Stage in Group 2

Clinical Stage		No Tumor	O	A	B_1	B_2	C	D_1	D_2
						Understaging			
O	1	—	[1]	—	—	—	—	—	—
A	9	2	1	[5]	1	—	—	—	—
B_1	37	7	5	13	[4]	1	—	4	3
B_2	41	4	2	2	8	[12]	4	4	5
C	17	2	—	—	1	—	[8]	3	3
D_1	4	—	—	—	—	—	—	[1]	3
				Stage Reduction					
Totals	109	15	9	20	14	13	12	12	14

TABLE 3. Pathological Versus Clinical Stage in Group 3

Clinical Stage		No Tumor	O	A	B_1	B_2	C	D_1	D_2	D_3
						Understaging				
O	9	3	[4]	1	1	—	—	—	—	—
A	13	4	—	[7]	—	1	—	—	1	—
B_1	36	4	7	6	[7]	3	1	2	6	—
B_2	35	6	—	10	—	[12]	3	1	2	1
C	15	1	—	2	1	2	[3]	2	3	1
D_1	11	1	—	—	—	—	1	[4]	4	1
				Stage Reduction						
Totals	119	19	11	26	9	18	8	9	16	3

TABLE 4. Pathological Versus Clinical Stage in Group 4

Clinical Stage		No Tumor	O	A	B_1	B_2	C	D_1	D_2
						Understaging			
O	1	—	[1]	—	—	—	—	—	—
A	6	1	—	[3]	—	—	1	1	—
B_1	22	2	3	2	[6]	2	1	—	6
B_2	43	1	2	—	8	[12]	5	9	6
C	9	—	—	—	1	—	[4]	1	3
D_1	5	—	—	1	1	—	1	[1]	1
				Stage Reduction					
Totals	86	4	6	6	16	14	12	12	16

under anesthesia, cystoendoscopy with appropriate transurethral biopsy and excretory urograms. Routine history, physical examination, posteroanterior and lateral films of the chest, and hematologic and blood chemical studies were done in all cases. Such staging procedures as lymphangiograms, lung tomograms, bone scans and liver scans were not used. Clinical staging was recorded immediately prior to cystectomy in group 1 and immediately prior to irradiation in groups 2, 3 and 4. The major staging errors are (1) in understaging clinical B_1 tumors [33 percent (14 of 42) for group 1, 22 percent (8 of 37) for group 2, 33 percent (12 of 36) for group 3 and 41 percent (9 of 22) for group 4] and (2) in understaging clinical B_2 and C lesions—failure to recognize stage D lesions [37 percent (24 of 65) for group 1, 26 percent (15 of 58) for group 2, 20 percent (10 of 50) for group 3 and 37 percent (19 of 52) for group 4]. Failure to distinguish clinically between pathologic O and A lesions or between pathologic B_2 and C lesions is not currently recognized to be of great importance since such distinctions do not dictate differences in management. The difficulty in clinically distinguishing between pathologic stage B_1 and B_2 lesions has been recognized since the inception of clinical staging, although the prognostic significance of this distinction seems less certain now than it did then. Furthermore, there is increasing uncertainty regarding the therapeutic relevance of this distinction as far as the surgical treatment of bladder cancer is concerned.

In the clinical staging of group 1 any influence of irradiation on staging errors is categorically excluded. In group 2 there was a tendency for tumor overstaging, which was not evident in group 1. This is a probable consequence of the expectedly large error involved in attempts to clinically stage patients retrospectively on the basis of information submitted from outside of the institution that was often incomplete and a possible consequence of tumor downstaging secondary to the administered irradiation. In group 3 there is also evidence of tumor overstaging, which is in part a consequence of true stage reduction from the preoperative irradiation—clinical staging was based on evaluation prior to administration of 4,000 rads in 4 weeks and postoperative staging on evaluation of the cystectomy specimen at an average of 6 plus weeks after the completion of irradiation. In group 4 the total interval among preoperative clinical staging, preoperative irradiation and cystectomy with pathologic staging was less than 2 weeks and true stage reduction due to a rapid radiobiological effect of high fractional radiation doses and/or pure clinical staging error are potentially responsible factors.

The multiple discrepancies between clinical and pathologic staging clearly define the limitations of clinical staging, at least as practiced in this experience. On the other hand, it has practical value in distinguishing low stage tumors (O, A and B_1) from deeply infiltrating or metastatic stage tumors (B_2, C and D), wherein its accuracy was 79 percent (52 of 66) for group 1, 83 percent (39 of 47) for group 2, 76 percent (44 of 58) for group 3 and 62 percent (18 of 29) for group 4. In sum, the principal value of clinical staging is in generally distinguishing the very favorable from the very unfavorable lesions. Its practical limitations are most evident in distinguishing the muscle infiltrating tumors (pathologic stages B_1 versus B_2), which make up the mid portion of the staging spectrum and in distinguishing the deeply infiltrating (pathologic stages B_2 and C) from the metastatic (pathologic stage D) lesions. Obviously, efforts to improve the accuracy of clinical staging should continue.

The present status of all patients in the 4 groups is shown in Table 5. The proportion of patients dying within 5 years of causes other than cancer is quite similar in the various groups. The proportion of patients dying of causes other than bladder cancer more than 5 years postoperatively is understandably highest in group 1, since these patients have had the longest followup. The proportion of patients dying of bladder cancer within 5 years of cystectomy is highest in patients having cystectomy alone and is rather similar in the other 3 groups. A source of potential selection bias in group 2 should be pointed out. Patients in this group represent radiation failures, in general referred from outside Memorial Sloan-Kettering Cancer Center with persistent (?), recurrent

TABLE 5. Over-all Results

Present Status of All Patients	Group 1 137 Cases		Group 2 109 Cases		Group 3 119 Cases		Group 4 86 Cases	
	No.	(%)	No.	(%)	No.	(%)	No.	(%)
Alive and no evidence of disease 5 or more years	14	(10)	31	(28)	32	(27)	33	(38)
Dead with no evidence of disease less than 5 years*	25	(18)	27	(25)	22	(18)	15	(18)
Dead with no evidence of disease more than 5 years	30	(22)	8	(7)	13	(11)	2	(2)
Dead of disease less than 5 years	66	(48)	35	(32)	46	(39)	35	(41)
Dead of disease more than 5 years	1	(1)	3	(3)	6	(5)	1	(1)
Lost to followup less than 5 years	1	(1)	5	(5)	0		0	

* Postoperative or later complications in 19 patients in group 1 (14 percent), 22 in group 2 (20 percent), 13 in group 3 (11 percent) and 8 in group 4 (19 percent).

(?), or new (?) bladder tumors. Patients who had a good result from irradiation and those who died of pelvic and/ or extrapelvic recurrences after irradiation represent an undefined segment of the radically radiated population from which group 2 was derived.

The 5-year survival rate according to clinical stage is shown in Table 6. For superficially infiltrating tumors there is no significant difference in survival among the 4 groups. For deeply infiltrating tumors survival is approximately double in groups 2, 3 and 4 compared to group 1. Patients clinically staged as having metastatic tumors fared poorly in all groups. Within each group the correlation between clinical stage and survival reaffirms the usefulness of clinical staging.

Table 7 shows 5-year survival rates relative to pathologic stage. A source of potential bias is the fact that in group 3 tumor downstaging as a consequence of preoperative irradiation shifts some originally deeply infiltrating tumors to the superficially infiltrating category. The precise number is not accurately definable because of the previously described limitations in clinical staging. The precise impact of this event on survival results is uncertain but one might logically expect that removal of favorably responding patients from the deeply infiltrating category might adversely effect survival rates in the latter group and that their deposition in the superficially infiltrating category might have indetermi-

nate effects on the results in the latter group. Some conception of the bias from radiation-induced tumor downstaging is derived from the circumstantial evidence provided by a comparison of the survival rates in the clinically stage B_2 and C categories of group 3 (34 percent) and group 4 (40 percent) to the pathologically staged B_2 and C categories of the 2 groups, 38 percent and 58 percent, respectively. The difference in the latter figures may logically be considered an "artifact" of tumor downstaging.

An advantage of radical cystectomy with pelvic lymph node dissection is the added dimension provided for pathologic staging. In this analysis D_1 tumors are those in which involvement of adjacent organs but without lymph node metastases was demonstrated, D_2 lesions are those in which lymph node metastases below the level of the common iliac artery bifurcation(s) occur (with or without adjacent organ invasion) and D_3 lesions are those in which lymph node metastases beyond the limits of surgical excision or other metastases were evident. Limited as these data are they, nevertheless, underscore the potential for at least occasional contro¹ of bladder cancers that actually have invaded the prostate or vagina or metastasized to regional lymph nodes.

The clinically deep tumor category (Table 6) contains a proportion of patients who have been overstaged [none in group 1, 33 percent (19 of 58) in group 2, 40 percent

TABLE 6. Five-Year Survival According to Clinical Stage

Clinical Stage		Five-Year Survival							
		Group 1		Group 2		Group 3		Group 4	
Sup.*	O	5/7		1/1		8/9		1/1	
	A	11/17	53%	7/9	55%	8/13	59%	4/6	54%
	B_1	19/42		18/37		18/36		10/22	
Deep	B_2	6/38	16%	12/38	30%	12/35	34%	18/43	40%
	C	4/26		4/15		5/15		3/9	
Met.†	D_1	0/6		0/4		0/11		0/5	

* Sup.—superficial.
† Met.—metastasis.

TABLE 7. Five-Year Survival According to Pathological Stage

Pathological Stage		Five-Year Survival							
		Group 1		Group 2		Group 3		Group 4	
Sup.*	No tumor	—		10/15		10/19		2/4	
	O	5/7		5/9		9/11		3/6	
	A	10/15	63%	13/19	60%	15/26	58%	4/6	56%
	B_1	18/30		6/14		4/9		8/16	
Deep	B_2	8/31	20%	4/12	27%	8/18	38%	9/14	58%
	C	2/19		2/10		2/9		6/12	
Met.†	D_1	2/16		1/11		2/9		3/12	
	D_2	0/18	6%	1/14	8%	1/16	11%	1/16	14%
	D_3	—		—		0/3		—	

* Sup.—superficial.
† Met.—metastasis.

(20 of 50) in group 3 and 23 percent (12 of 52) in group 4] and a proportion of patients who have been understaged (vide supra). These more or less systematic errors, to some extent, tend to offset one another. Moreover, since a major source of staging error is in distinguishing B_1 from B_2 tumors and since the data in Table 7 show no significant survival differences between B_1 and B_2 tumors in any of the irradiated patients (groups 2, 3 and 4), this particular staging error may be of little, if any, clinical significance in the radically treated patient.

For patients with superficially infiltrating tumors survival rates are similar in all groups. Within the superficial tumor category the various substages, although the numbers are small, demonstrate no significant intragroup or intergroup differences, although it is noteworthy that the B_1 tumors in each group had the worst prognosis and that, paradoxically, the B_1 tumors in all of the irradiated patients did less well than in group 1 (Table 7). In groups 2, 3 and 4 the failure to identify tumor in the surgical specimen did not signify cure: in group 3 tumor downstaging from irradiation was the principal basis for the failure to find residual bladder tumor and in group 2 intractable radiation cystitis with or without hemorrhage, with or without radiation necrosis and with or without a positive urinary cytology provided the indication for cystectomy in the "tumor free" cases.

For patients with pathologically staged deeply infiltrating tumors survival rates are better in groups 3 and 4 than in groups 1 and 2. In each of the groups patients with stage B_2 lesions survived better than patients with stage C lesions but the difference was least evident in group 4. It is of interest that B_2 lesions have about the same survival rate in groups 2, 3 and 4 as do B_1 lesions

in the respective groups. Patients in group 4 with high stage tumors survived better than patients in group 3 but the downstaging bias previously referred to easily explains this difference.

An analysis of survival relative to tumor grade is presented in Table 8. These data demonstrate the significance of tumor grade to prognosis, although the precise contribution of tumor grade versus tumor stage is obscured by the established facts that low grade tumors are usually of low stage and that high grade tumors are usually of deep or metastatic stage.

The data in Table 9 demonstrate the diminished frequency of pelvic recurrences in all irradiated patients (groups 2, 3 and 4), although the role of selection bias in group 2 is uncertain (vide supra). These data further demonstrate that most therapeutic failures are associated with distant metastases (Table 10). One may conclude that radiation therapy reduces the local pelvic recurrences following cystectomy.

Since precise details of radiation therapy often were not known in group 2 patients no discussion of the specific role of the irradiation in the local recurrences and survival in this group seems warranted other than to point out that "salvage" cystectomy in radiation failures is well worthwhile. Furthermore, the survival rates for the various stages of tumors so managed are quite consistent with the possibility that full course irradiation (plus or minus 6,000 rads in 6 weeks) might be a legitimate alternative to preoperative irradiation plus cystectomy were it possible, by some yet undefined technique, to identify the radiation failures early enough in the post-treatment interval to permit salvage cystectomy without appreciable reduction in survival prospects.

TABLE 8. Five-Year Survival According to Histological Grade

Histologic Grade		Five-Year Survival							
		Group 1		Group 2		Group 3		Group 4	
Low	0	5/7		1/1		6/7		1/1	
	I	6/7	46%	5/5	51%	3/4	56%	6/6	49%
	II	20/53		25/55		21/43		17/42	
High	III	14/65	20%	11/43	26%	21/61	32%	12/34	32%
	IV	0/4		—		0/4		0/3	

TABLE 9. Site of Recurrence

Recurrence	Group 1 136 Cases		Group 2 104 Cases		Group 3 119 Cases		Group 4 86 Cases	
	No.	(%)	No.	(%)	No.	(%)	No.	(%)
Pelvic only	38	(28)	15	(15)	19	(16)	12	(14)
Extrapelvic plus or minus pelvic	22	(16)	21	(20)	31	(26)	22	(26)
Undetermined	7	(5)	2	(2)	3	(3)	2	(2)
Totals	67	(49)	38	(37)	53	(45)	36	(42)

TABLE 10. Extrapelvic Sites of Tumor Involvement Outside the Urinry Tract

Extrapelvic Site*	Group 1	Group 2	Group 3	Group 4
Bone	8	4	14	12
Lung	10	6	10	10
Liver	4	2	8	9
Para-aortic nodes	3	1	3	4
Inguinal nodes	3	1	3	2
Neck nodes	1	1	4	2
Bowel	2	0	2	3
Mesenteric nodes	1	0	3	1
Peritoneum	2	1	1	1
Brain	1	2	1	1
Pleura	2	1	3	0
Chest wall	0	0	2	1
Axillary nodes	0	0	2	0
Adrenal	0	1	1	0
Heart	0	2	0	0
Spleen	0	0	1	0

* Patients usually had more than 1 site involved.

The operative mortality and complication rates within the different treatment groups will be the subject of a future report. The hospital mortality rate was 14 percent for group 1, 16 percent for group 2, 11 percent for group 3 and 9 percent for group 4. The complication rates within the 4 groups were quite similar and tended to negate, especially in groups 3 and 4, conceptions of a major adverse impact of prior irradiation on the complications of cystectomy.

FINAL COMMENT

Although the data of this experience were not assembled through the mechanism of a controlled, randomized, prospective study, over-all similarities in the clinical material, methods of staging, surgical treatment methods and physicians responsible for the treatment support the conviction that the results are meaningful relative to the role of preoperative irradiation as an adjunct to cystectomy in the treatment of selected patients with bladder cancer.

Limitations in clinical and pathologic staging are amply illustrated by the data presented. Nevertheless, the over-all usefulness of both techniques is affirmed, and the effort should be not to discourage the use of such staging techniques but to improve their accuracies.

Survival results in patients with clinically staged tumors are a function of the treatment received and of the clinical staging error. Survival results in patients with pathologically staged tumors are a function of the treatment and of the downstaging bias from preoperative irradiation.

For patients with low stage tumors or with metastatic stage tumors, whether clinically or pathologically staged, no survival advantage from prior irradiation is evident. The possible explanations for these observations will be the subject of a future report. For patients with high stage tumors, whether clinically or pathologically staged, survival rates are materially improved by prior irradiation, although the significance of such improvement must be interpreted in the light of various sources of potential bias (vide supra).

Prior irradiation materially reduced the incidence of pelvic recurrences in groups 2, 3 and 4. In doing so, it especially exposes the high risk of distant metastases (with or without pelvic recurrence) as the principal cause of treatment failure. Furthermore, that the risk of such metastases is high in patients with B_1 and B_2 tumors tends to reduce the importance of discriminating between such tumors and to imply that muscle invasion opens the door to distant dissemination quite apart from the question of regional lymph node metastases.

The generally improved local control by combinations of preoperative irradiation and cystectomy coupled with the demonstration of distant metastases as the principal cause of treatment failure provides a basis for earlier radical treatment of appropriately selected patients on the one hand and for the development of effective adjunct chemotherapy and/or immunotherapy on the other. It must be emphasized that, although current evidence indicates improved results from preoperative irradiation combined with cystectomy, it would be presumptuous to conclude that the optimal program of such combination treatment has yet been defined.

REFERENCE

1. Whitmore, W. F., Jr.: Total cystectomy. In: The Biology and Managment of Bladder Cancer. Edited by E H Cooper and R E Williams. London: Blackwell Scientific Publications, Chap 9, pp 193–227, 1975

Commentary: Radical Cystectomy: Necessary, If Not Sufficient

Peter T. Scardino and Donald G. Skinner

Radical cystectomy has now become established as the necessary, if not sufficient, treatment for most patients with invasive bladder cancer. Several recently reported series attest to the low operative mortality, in the range of 1% to 5%, now being achieved in many major medical centers.[1-4] The duration of hospitalization and the short- and long-term complication rates, even among this elderly population, seem acceptable in light of the lethal natural history of the disease.[1,2]

There is now general agreement that radical cystectomy is indicated in the presence of high-grade deeply invasive bladder cancers (Jewett–Strong stages B_2 and C, UICC stage T_3).[5-7] Moreover, recent appreciation of the significance of carcinoma *in situ* (CIS) and severe atypia of the urothelium has diminished the role of partial cystectomy and transurethral resection in most high-grade or superficially invasive (B_1 or T_2) lesions.[8,9] Severe epithelial atypia or CIS has been reported in association with overt bladder tumors in more than half of cystectomy specimens.[9] The conscientious urologic surgeon must perform cold cup biopsies of the bladder adjacent to and remote from any overt tumor before electing conservative therapy. Transitional cell carcinoma of the bladder is clearly a "field defect."[10] Intraepithelial malignancy can be found in the urethra and in the distal ureters in 12.5% to 33% of cystectomy specimens.[9,11,12] CIS alone may be an indication for radical cystectomy if the lesion is diffuse, severely symptomatic, or fails to respond to fulguration and intravesical chemotherapy.[13]

Simultaneous urethrectomy need not be done routinely in the male patient, but it is certainly advisable when the primary tumor is high-grade, multifocal, or found in the prostatic urethra (whether invasive or *in situ*).[12,11] A urethrectomy should be performed at a later stage if the patient develops pain, bloody urethral discharge, or positive cytologic findings from urethral washings. The procedure is best performed as described by Whitmore and Mount in the preceding article. It is simple, safe, and not disfiguring. Even when done at the time of cystectomy, it adds only little to the morbidity or duration of the procedure.

Metastases to pelvic lymph nodes occur in 10% to 50% of patients, the frequency increasing with increasing stage of the primary tumor.[1] Some 18% to 33% of patients with microscopic metastases to the pelvic nodes will survive for 5 yr after radical cystectomy and pelvic lymphadenectomy.[4,14-16] It would appear from Johnson's series at M.D. Anderson Hospital that full-field preoperative pelvic radiotherapy (5000 rad/25 fractions/5 wk) can also control microscopic metastases to the pelvic nodes.[17] Nevertheless, we prefer to perform the pelvic lymph node dissection as an integral part of the radical cystectomy, since we do not employ high-dose preoperative radiotherapy. The lymphadenectomy aids in defining the vascular pedicles of the bladder, adds little to the operating time or the morbidity of the procedure, and provides staging information of use in planning adjuvant therapy.

Radical cystectomy has been performed as primary therapy for bladder cancer, as a salvage procedure for radiotherapy failures, or in combination with planned preoperative radiotherapy (see the annotated bibliography). There seems to be little place for a two-stage surgical procedure, which has not been shown to accomplish the intended result with a lower morbidity or mortality and which has the disadvantage of increased cost and prolonged hospitalization.[18]

Two prospective controlled randomized clinical trials have conclusively demonstrated that radiotherapy alone is inferior to combined therapy with preoperative irradiation and radical cystectomy. Miller and Johnson reported a 46% 5-yr survival rate for patients treated with preoperative radiotherapy plus cystectomy compared to a 16% 5-yr survival rate for patients treated with definitive radiotherapy alone.[19] In 1976 Wallace and Bloom reported the experience of the British Clinical Trials Groups: 189 patients with deeply invasive bladder cancer (T_3) were randomized to receive either definitive radiotherapy (6000 rad in 6 wk) or preoperative radiotherapy (4000 rad in 4 wk) followed by radical cystectomy with pelvic lymphadenectomy 4 wk later. The 5-yr survival rate was 21% in patients who received radiotherapy alone and 33% for those who recieved radiotherapy plus radical cystectomy ($P = 0.077$). Based on these two controlled trials, it is fair to say that radiotherapy alone as primary treatment for bladder cancer is only indicated when the tumor is inoperable or the patient is a prohibitive operative risk because of severe mental or physical incompetency or severe cardiac, pulmonary, renal, or hepatic disease. Nevertheless, radiotherapy can render the bladder free of tumor in 30% to 40% of patients.[17,20-22] Hence, its role as a preoperative adjuvant to cystectomy continues to attract wide attention.

The evidence is not as strong to support the superiority of combined therapy (radiotherapy plus cystectomy) over cystectomy alone. The only controlled clinical trial that has addressed this question is that of the National Surgical Adjuvant Bladder Project, which compared radical cystectomy alone to preoperative radiotherapy plus radical cystectomy.[21] The results of this study have been somewhat confused by the number of treatment arms (six) and the large numbers of patients who failed to complete the protocol. The enormous amount of data generated by the study has tended to obscure the central compelling fact that, among those who did not receive adjuvant chemotherapy, preoperative irradiation plus definitive surgery was statistically significantly superior to definitive surgery alone.[21] If one compares the 5-yr survival results of patients with clinical stage B_1, B_2, and C (T_2, T_3) cancer, 37.4% of those who received combined therapy survived 5 yr, versus 29.4% of those who received definitive surgery only.[23]

The paper by Whitmore and associates reprinted in this chapter provides additional, albeit circumstantial, evidence that preoperative irradiation plus cystectomy is superior to cystectomy alone for patients with invasive bladder cancer (B_2C, T_3). Additional uncontrolled but carefully performed studies of combined therapy also tend to support this conclusion: 5-yr survivals have been reported as 35%, 43%, 50%, and 55%.[17,22,24,25]

One difficulty in accepting this conclusion has been the scarcity of current reports on the results of radical cystectomy *alone*. Within the past decade there has been an appreciable drop in the operative mortality and an improvement in the accuracy of staging (bone scans, lung tomograms, computed tomography [CT] scans), so there is reason to expect that earlier reports of 15% to 20% 5-yr survival rates for patients with stage B_2C (T_3) bladder cancer treated with cystectomy alone are inappropriately low. McCarron and Marshall found that only 18% of patients treated before 1952 survived 5 yr, compared to 28% of patients treated between 1960 and 1971.[26]

One further area of controversy concerns the dosage of preoperative radiotherapy. Most patients have received 4000 to 5000 rads/4 to 5 wk, but Whitmore and Skinner and Kaufman have reported comparable results with short-course, high-dose fractionation, using either 1600 rad/4 days or 2000 rad/5 days followed by immediate radical cystectomy.[1,25] A pelvic lymphadenectomy must be done when this fractionation is used, since there is no evidence that short-course, high-dose radiotherapy can control microscopic metastasis to the pelvic nodes.

In any event, the results of therapy for invasive bladder cancer are poor in the best of circumstances. At least 40% of patients develop recurrent disease, two thirds of which occurs in distant sites with or without local recurrence in the pelvis.[5] Consequently, no treatment program directed solely at the pelvis can hope to substantially improve cure rates unless therapy is instituted earlier in the course of the disease before muscle is invaded or unless the therapeutic regimen incorporates effective systemic chemotherapy (or immunotherapy). Several recent studies indicate that the natural history of superficial bladder tumors can be predicted and those that will become invasive and potentially lethal identified. Patients with superficial papillary tumors associated with severe epithelial atypia or CIS elsewhere in the bladder have an 83% risk of developing invasive bladder cancer within 5 yr.[8] Utz and colleagues reported that diffuse CIS, especially in the symptomatic patient, heralds the development of invasive carcinoma in 50% of patients within 5 yr.[27] Experimental data on the presence or absence of ABO antigens on the surface of bladder cancer cells suggests that a given tumor, from its inception, either retains or loses these antigens and is therefore destined either to become invasive or not.[28a] If indeed these characterizations are confirmed, then cystectomy would seem justified for superficial papillary lesions that have lost their ABO antigens or that are associated with CIS elsewhere in the bladder.

Chemotherapy, with *cis*-platin alone or in combination with other drugs, yields a 37% to 71% objective response rate for patients with metastatic bladder cancer.[29,30] These agents are now being incorporated in clinical trials of adjuvant therapy following radical cystectomy with or without preoperative radiotherapy for carcinoma of the bladder.[31] The results of these trials are eagerly awaited; urologists are urged to enter their patients in such treatment programs whenever available.

The modern surgical technique for radical cystectomy with *en bloc* pelvic lymphadenectomy is based on the work of Leadbetter and of Marshall.[32,33] The technique we use has recently been published.[33a] Patients are prepared for the operation with a clear liquid diet for 24 hr, a heavy laxative (Neoloid, 60 ml) on the morning of the first preoperative day, followed by oral neomycin, 1 g and erythromycin base, 1 g.[34] On the preceeding night, the stoma site is marked in the right lower quadrant, over the lateral aspect of the rectus muscle, on a line between the umbilicus and the anterior superior iliac spine. The patient is placed supine on the operating table and hyperextended at the pubis with the table in a Trendelenburg position. A Foley catheter is inserted, the bladder is drained, and 30 ml of 10% formalin is instilled into the bladder by gravity. The catheter is clamped for 10 min, then released. Make an incision in the midline at the pubic symphysis and carry it to the left paramedian area some 5 cm above the umbilicus. After a thorough manual exploration of the abdomen, mobilize the bladder from the anterior abdominal wall. Leave the uracus and umbilical ligaments attached to the bladder. Mobilize the cecum and small bowel mesentery until the right ureter and the bifurcation of the aorta are identified. Follow the ureter into the pelvis, occlude it with hemoclips, and divide it several centimeters below the iliac artery. Begin the right pelvic lymphadenectomy at the bifurcation of the aorta. Dissect the presacral, common iliac, external iliac, hypogastric, and obturator nodes *en bloc* and leave them attached to the lateral wall of the bladder.[35] Mobilize the sigmoid colon medially, identify and divide the left ureter, and complete the left pelvic lymphadenectomy. Once the lymphadenectomy has been performed, the lateral vascular pedicles of the bladder are easily identified. Insert the middle finger medial to the vascular pedicle as it branches from the hypogastric artery. By blunt dissection isolate the narrow lateral pedicle from the hypogastric artery to the endopelvic fascia. Ligate this artery just distal to its first posterior branch (the superior gluteal artery). Quickly divide the lateral vascular pedicle between metallic hemoclips. Divide the left lateral pedicle similarly.

Sharply incise the peritoneum in the pouch of Douglas. Turn the hand supine and gently dissect the rectum away from the base of the bladder and prostate distally to the urethra, where the Foley catheter can be palpated. The posterior pedicle of the bladder is now easily identified as the bridge of tissue on each side between the bladder and the pelvic wall just lateral to the rectum. Bluntly divide the endopelvic fascia on each side, mobilizing the prostate, and divide the posterior pedicle between hemoclips. Long curved Finochietto scissors and long right-angle clip appliers facilitate this part of the dissection. Finally, leave the bladder attached only by the puboprostatic ligaments and the urethra. Divide the ligaments anteriorly between hemoclips. Mobilize the membranous urethra bluntly so that a large curved pedicle clamp can be placed on the urethra well beyond the apex of the prostate. Divide the urethra distal to the clamp to avoid spillage of bladder contents. Pass the specimen off the operating field. Take figure-of-8 2–0 chromic sutures in the levator muscles and genitourinary diaphragm to oversew the inevitable bleeding from the area of the urethra and the dorsal vein of the penis. No drains or catheters are left in the pelvis. Accomplish urinary diversion with a standard ileal conduit as described by Bricker, using bilateral end-to-side ureteroileal anastomoses. We prefer the Turnbull everted ileocutaneous stoma, suturing the serosa of the bowel to the fascia.[36] Recently, however, a continent urinary diversion using the Kock pouch has been enthusiastically received by our patients.[37]

Excellent reviews of the current management of bladder cancer have recently been published and are well recommended.[5–7]

REFERENCES

1. Skinner DG: Experience with high-dose, short course preoperative radiotherapy and immediate radical cystectomy for bladder cancer: Preliminary report. Trans Am Assoc Genitourin Surg 20:113, 1978

2. Johnson DE, Lamy SM: Complications of single-stage radical cystectomy and ileal conduit diversion: Review of 124 cases. J Urol 117:171, 1977

3. DeWeerd JH, Colby NY Jr: Bladder carcinoma treated by irradiation and surgery: Interval report. J Urol 109:409, 1973

4. Dretler SP, Ragsdale BD, Leadbetter WF: The value of pelvic lymphadenectomy in the surgical treatment of bladder cancer. J Urol 109:414, 1973

5. Whitmore WF Jr: Management of bladder cancer. Curr Probl Cancer 4:1, 1979

6. Prout GR Jr: The role of surgery in the potentially curative treatment of bladder cancer. Cancer Res 37:2764, 1977

7. Skinner DG: Current perspectives in the management of high-grade invasive bladder cancer. Cancer 45:1866, 1980

8. Althausen AF, Prout GR Jr, Daly JJ: Non-invasive papillary carcinoma of the bladder associated with carcinoma in situ. J Urol 116:575, 1976

9. Skinner DG, Richie JP, Cooper PH, et al: The clinical significance of carcinoma in situ of the urinary bladder and its association with overt carcinoma. J Urol 112:68, 1974

10. Koss LG, Tiamson EM, Robbins MA: Mapping cancerous and precancerous bladder changes. JAMA 227:281, 1974

11. Richie JP, Skinner DG: Carcinoma in situ of the urethra associated with bladder carcinoma: The role of urethrectomy. J Urol 119:80, 1978

12. Schellhammer PF, Whitmore WF Jr: Transitional cell carcinoma of the urethra in men having cystectomy for bladder cancer. J Urol 115:56, 1976

13. Farrow GM, Utz DC, Rife CC, et al: Clinical observations on 69 cases of *in situ* carcinoma of the urinary bladder. Cancer Res 37:2794, 1977

14. Long RTL, Grummon RA, Spratt JS, et al: Carcinoma of the urinary bladder (comparison with radical, simple, and partial cystectomy and intravesical formalin). Cancer 29:98, 1972

15. Pearse HD, Reed RR, Hodges CV: Radical cystectomy for bladder cancer. J Urol 119:216, 1978

16. Richie JP, Skinner DG, Kaufman JJ: Radical cystectomy for carcinoma of the bladder: Sixteen years' experience. J Urol 113:186, 1975

17. Chan RF, Johnson D: Integrated therapy for invasive bladder cancer. Urology 12:549, 1978

18. Bredin HC, Prout GR Jr: One-stage radical cystectomy for bladder carcinoma: Operative mortality, cost/benefit analysis. J Urol 117:447, 1977

19. Miller LS: Bladder cancer: Superiority of preoperative irradiation and cystectomy in clinical stages B_2 and C. Cancer 39:973, 1977

20. Wallace DM, Bloom HJG: The management of deeply infiltrating (T_3) bladder carcinoma: Controlled trial of radical radiotherapy versus preoperative radiotherapy and radical cystectomy (first report). Br J Urol 48:587, 1976

21. Slack NH, Bross ID, Prout GR Jr: Five-year follow-up results of a collaborative study of therapies for carcinoma of the bladder. J Surg Oncol 9:393, 1977

22. van der Werf-Messing B: Carcinoma of the bladder $T_3N_xM_o$ treated by preoperative irradiation therapy followed by cystectomy. Cancer 36:718, 1975

23. Prout GR Jr: The surgical managment of bladder carcinoma. Urol Clin North Am 3:149, 1976

24. Reid EC, Oliver JA, Fishman IJ: Preoperative irradiation and cystectomy in 135 cases of bladder cancer. Urology 8:247, 1976

25. Whitmore WF Jr, Batata MA, Hilaris BS, et al: A comparative study of two preoperative radiation regimens with bladder cancer. Cancer 40:1077, 1977

26. McCarron JP, Marshall VF: The survival of patients with bladder tumors treated by surgery: Comparative results of an old and a recent series. J Urol 112:322, 1979

26a. Mathur VK, Krahn HP, Ramsey EW: Total cystectomy for bladder cancer. J Urol 125:784, 1981

27. Utz DC, Hanash KA, Farrow GM: The plight of the patient with carcinoma in situ of the bladder. J Urol 103:160, 1970

28. Johnson JD, Lamm DL: Prediction of bladder tumor invasion with the mixed cell agglutination test. J Urol 123:75, 1980

28a. Newman AJ Jr, Carlton CE Jr, Johnson S: Cell surface A, B or O(H) blood group antigens as an indicator of malignant potential in stage A bladder carcinoma. J Urol 124:27, 1980

29. Samuels ML, Moran ME, Johnson DE, et al: CISCA combination chemotherapy for metastatic bladder cancer. In Johnson DE, Samuels ML (eds): Cancer of the Genitourinary Tract, pp 101–106. New York, Raven Press, 1979

30. Yagoda A: Phase II trials in bladder cancer at Memorial Sloane-Kettering Cancer Center, 1975–1978. In Johnson DE, Samuels ML (eds): Cancer of the Genitourinary Tract, pp 107–119. New York, Raven Press, 1979

31. Cummings KB, Shipley WV, Einstein AB, Cutler SJ: Current concepts in the management of patients with deeply invasive bladder cancer. Semin Oncol 6:220, 1979

32. Leadbetter WF, Cooper JF: Regional gland dissection for carcinoma of the bladder: A technique for one-stage cystectomy, gland dissection, and bilateral ureteroenterostomy. J Urol 63:242, 1950

33. Paquin AJ Jr, Marshall VF: Technique for radical cystectomy. Cancer 9:585, 1956

33a. Skinner DG: Technique of radical cystectomy. Urol Clin North Am 8:353, 1981

34. Scardino PT: Modern methods of antibiotic bowel preparation. In Kaufman JJ (ed): Current Urologic Therapy, Philadelphia, WB Saunders (in press)

35. Skinner DG: Pelvic lymphadenectomy. In Glenn JF (ed): Urologic Surgery, 2d ed, pp 589–595. Hagerstown, Harper & Row, 1975

36. Weakley FL, Turnbull RG Jr: Creation of ileal stoma. In Stewart BH (ed): Operative Urology, pp 337–345. Baltimore, Williams & Wilkins, 1975

37. Kock NG, Nilson AE, Nilsson LO, Norlen LJ, Philipson BM: Urinary diversion via a continent ileal reservoir: Clinical results in 12 patients. J Urol 128:469, 1982

ANNOTATED BIBLIOGRAPHY

Dretler SP, Ragsdale BD, Leadbetter WF: The value of pelvic lymphadenectomy in the surgical treatment of bladder cancer. J Urol 109:414, 1973

Among all patients who underwent radical cystectomy and pelvic lymphadenectomy for bladder cancer at the Massachusetts General Hospital between 1955 and 1967, 35 had metastases to the pelvic lymph nodes only. Of 12 patients with 1 or 2 positive nodes, 4 (33%) survived 5 yr. Of 23 patients with more than 2 positive nodes, 2 (8.7%) survived 5 yr. The operative mortality rate was 2.8%. No complications were attributable to the pelvic lymphadenectomy itself. The patients who have the most to gain from a node dissection are those with limited microscopic metastases. Hence, the absence of palpable nodes at operation should induce the surgeon to proceed with lymphadenectomy wherever cystectomy is indicated.

Skinner DG, Richie JP, Cooper PH, et al: The clinical significance of carcinoma in situ of the bladder and its association with overt carcinoma. J Urol 112:68, 1974

Histologic section from 59 radical cystectomy specimens were reexamined to document the presence and location of incidental carcinoma *in situ* (CIS) of the urothelium. The cell type, grade, and stage of the primary tumor were recorded. Grossly uninvolved epithelium from the bladder adjacent to and remote from the tumor, the mid-prostatic urethra, and the ureteral and urethral margins was examined for CIS. None of the six patients with squamous cell carcinoma had CIS. Of the 53 patients with transitional cell carcinoma, 36 (68%) had CIS. Of the 42 patients with overt transitional cell carcinoma present in the cystectomy specimen, CIS was present in 27 (64%). The bladder epithelium adjacent to the tumor showed CIS in 57% of the specimens, yet 44% had CIS in areas remote from the overt tumor. The ureteral epithelium showed changes of CIS in 24% and the urethra in 22%. There was no correlation of *in situ* changes with the stage of the overt tumor, but CIS was much more frequent when a high-grade tumor was present. When the distal ureter contained CIS, 23% of the patients later developed an upper tract tumor requiring nephroureterectomy. This report provides additional evidence that overt transitional cell carcinoma of the bladder is the manifestation of a field defect.

Schellhammer PF, Whitmore WF Jr: Transitional cell carcinoma of the urethra in men having cystectomy for bladder cancer. J Urol 115:56, 1976

Over a 12-yr period 461 men underwent radical cystectomy for bladder cancer. The *anterior* urethra was removed *en bloc* prophylactically in 110 patients who did not have any recognizable urethral abnormality. Carcinoma *in situ* was found in 4.5% and severe epithelial atypia in 8% of these specimens. Nearly 7% of the patients who did not have prophylactic urethrectomy later developed an anterior urethral tumor, requiring therapeutic urethrectomy. Twelve of these patients had invasive lesions; tumor emboli were found in the vessels of the corpora in each case. Only 4 of the 27 patients (15%) who had therapeutic urethrectomy were alive at the time of the report. Subtotal urethrectomy, leaving the fossa navicularis and meatus in place, resulted in a 25% risk of later development of tumor in the retained urethral segment. The risk of metastases to the inguinal nodes and perineum was much greater if an overt urethral tumor developed. Nearly 27% of patients found to have a urethral tumor later developed a tumor of the ureter or renal pelvis—ample evidence of the "neoplastic diathesis" that affects the entire transitional epithelium.

Miller LS: Bladder cancer: Superiority of preoperative irradiation and cystectomy in clinical stages B$_2$ and C. Cancer 39:973, 1977

This comprehensive review of the experience at M.D. Anderson Hospital and Tumor Institute is an update of earlier reports by Miller and Johnson (Seventh Natl. Cancer Conf. Proc. 771-782, 1973). Sixty-eight patients with clinical stage B$_2$C (T$_3$) bladder cancer were randomly allocated o recieve either definite radiotherapy alone (7000 rad/35 fractions/7 wk) or preoperative radiotherapy (5000 rad/25 fractions/5 wk) followed 6 wk later by total cystectomy without pelvic lymphadenectomy. Only 16% of the 32 patients treated with radiotherapy survived 5 yr. However, 46% of the 35 patients allocated to the combined therapy survived 5 years ($P < 0.01$). For radiotherapy alone, 5-yr survival figures were inadequate. Attrition between the fifth and tenth years after radiation was a stunning 50%! Definitive radiotherapy failed to control the local disease in 45% of the patients, partially because new tumors developed in the retained bladder. When radical cystectomy followed radiotherapy the local failure rate was only 16%. Among patients who received preoperative radiotherapy, 29% of the cystectomy specimens contained no tumor. These patients had a 54% 5-yr survival, compared to 25% if tumor could be identified in the specimen ($P < 0.01$). The mortality for definitive radiotherapy was 5%, while that for combined radiotherapy plus cystectomy was only 3.3%. The combined therapy is clearly superior to definitive radiotherapy for invasive bladder cancer.

Slack NH, Bross IDJ, Prout GR Jr: Five-year follow-up results of a collaborative study of therapies for carcinoma of the bladder. J Surg Oncol 9:393, 1977

The National Surgical Adjuvant Bladder Project completed a prospective randomized trial of adjuvant therapy for invasive bladder cancer. This is the only controlled clinical trial yet reported that compares standard therapy in the United States (definitive surgery) to combined regimens incorporating preoperative radiotherapy or postoperative chemotherapy or both. This cooperative trial involved 13 separate institutions. A variety of problems, including incomplete therapy and patient ineligibility, made 51% of the patients unable to be evaluated when the results were tabulated. Nevertheless, the study firmly established several crucial facts. Preoperative radiotherapy increased the incidence of surgical specimens containing no tumor from 9% to 34%. The group with no tumor in the surgical specimen had a 55% chance of surviving 5 yr, as opposed to a 32% chance for those where radiotherapy failed to eradicate the tumor ($P = 0.06$). For the patients who had partial cystectomy as the definitive surgical procedure, radiotherapy offered no protection against and may have stimulated local recurrence (38% of the irradiated and 19% of the nonirradiated patients developed a recurrent bladder tumor). Postoperative chemotherapy with 5-fluorouracil was of no benefit. When the patients who received postoperative chemotherapy are excluded, there was a small but statistically significant improvement in the 5-yr survival for those who were irradiated preoperatively.

Johnson DE, Lamy S, Bracken RB: Salvage cystectomy after radiation failure in patients with bladder carcinoma. South Med J 70:1279, 1977

An admirable series demonstrating that radical cystectomy for radiation failure (salvage cystectomy) is safe and efficatious. Thirty-two patients underwent a single stage cystectomy for bladder cancer that persisted or recurred after definitive radiotherapy (30 patients received 5000 to 7560 rads). There were no postoperative deaths. Only three patients developed complications that required reoperation. The average operating time was 5 hr, the average patient received 4 U of blood, and the average hospital stay was 22 days. These results are similar, in the authors' experience, to those for nonirradiated patients. Only 3 patients (9%) showed definitive evidence of local pelvic recurrence, but in 4 others (13%) it was suspected. Fourteen patients (44%) remain alive and free of disease 11 to 75 mo after the operation. The clinical stage was the best indicator of prognosis. All 14 patients who died had at least stage T_3 (B_2C) tumors, although six others with T_3 lesions did survive. None of the patients with T_{IS} or T_1 tumors died. Salvage cystectomy is indicated when bladder cancer persists or recurs after definitive radiotherapy.

65

TOTAL CYSTECTOMY FOR CARCINOMA OF THE BLADDER

William T. Bowles and Justin J. Cordonnier

From the Department of Surgery, Division of Urology, Washington University School of Medicine, St. Louis, Mo.

Reprinted from *Journal of Urology*, Vol. 90, pp. 731–735, 1963. Copyright 1963 by The Williams & Wilkins Company, Baltimore.

Since 1953, when we became interested in the use of ileal segment urinary diversion, total cystectomy for cancer of the bladder together with prostato-seminal-vesiculectomy in male patients has been performed in conjunction with ileal segment diversion in 146 patients. The diagnosis of transitional cell carcinoma of the bladder was made in 140 of these patients. Three patients had epidermoid carcinoma; 2 patients had adenocarcinoma and one, sarcoma. Seventy-three of these patients had their operations performed before February 1, 1958, and are available for the determination of 5-year survival statistics. Only 3 patients have been lost to followup study and will be presumed dead following our last contact with them.

It is felt that it would be useful to review our accumulated experience with this procedure and to determine its effectiveness in the management of vesical neoplasms.

PATIENT SELECTION

The selection of patients for total cystectomy was based on certain pathological criteria correlated with roentgenologic and physical findings. All patients with demonstrable metastatic disease in any location outside of the pelvis were treated by palliative radiation and/or urinary diversion only. Cystectomy was not carried out in 43 patients in whom positive evidence of extravesical spread of tumor was obtained by biopsy or gross inspection. All patients had had previous transurethral biopsies of their tumors either in this hospital or elsewhere. Cystectomy was chosen as the mode of therapy in most patients whose biopsy specimens demonstrated lesions of high grade cellular malignancy (Broders' grade 3 and 4, and epidermoid carcinoma). Pathological evidence of muscle invasion was the basis of case selection in many patients, some of whom had grade 2 tumors. In some cases cystectomy was employed because of the rapid recurrence of tumors of increasing cellular malignancy. Cystectomy was also carried out in a few patients who were found to have generalized involvement of the bladder mucosa by tumor.

OPERATIVE PROCEDURE

In male patients, total cystectomy and prostato-seminal-vesiculectomy are performed. In female patients the

Accepted for publication June 28, 1963.

Read at annual meeting of American Urological Association, Inc., St. Louis, Mo., May 13–16, 1963.

This work was supported in part by Public Health Grant CS 9673, National Institutes of Health.

853

urethra is removed together with the bladder and the internal genital organs. No attempt is made to include all the pelvic lymph nodes in the dissection.

The urinary flow is then diverted into an isolated segment of ileum as previously described by Bricker.[1] Recently, because of a significant rate of urethral recurrence in male patients,[2] a total urethrectomy has been performed. The technique of this procedure will be described in a subsequent report. We have also been using intravenous injections of mannitol, as described by Nesbit,[3] during the closing minutes of the operation. This substance promotes rapid diuresis and results in prompt flow of urine into the collecting apparatus in the recovery room. Mannitol may offer some as yet unexplained protection against postoperative renal insufficiency associated with operative hypotension.

POSTOPERATIVE MORBIDITY AND MORTALITY

Total cystectomy and ileal segment diversion were employed in 146 patients, seven of whom died before leaving the hospital, an operative mortality of 5.4 percent. The causes of operative deaths are summarized in Table 1. The series comprises 125 male patients and 21 female patients. The average age at the time of operation was 61 years. There wre 52 complications noted in 42 patients, a rate of 31.5 percent. There were 19 secondary operations for various complications in 17 patients, a rate of 11.6 percent. Table 2 summarizes the postoperative complications. The late complications of ileal loop diversion have previously been described.[4] Of the 146 patients, 73 are dead or lost to followup study. The causes of death are summarized in Table 3.

SURVIVAL RESULTS

Seventy-three patients were operated upon prior to February 1, 1958. Of these, 30 have survived 5 years or more and have no evidence of recurrent tumor. The over-all survival rate is 41.2 percent. The pathological type of tumor and the extent of penetration of the bladder wall were determined in each case.

There was only one patient in the group of those operated upon prior to 1958, whose tumor was classified as Broders' grade 1. In this case transitional cell carcinoma of the kidney developed 3 years following surgery and the patient died of generalized carcinoma 5 months following nephrectomy. Eight patients (37 percent) of 21 patients with Broders' grade 2 tumors have survived 5 years. There were 33 patients whose tumors were classified grade 3, and 15 or 45 percent have survived 5 years or more. Eight of 15 patients (53 percent) with grade 4 tumors are alive 5 years later. These figures support Jewett's[5] original impression that cytological grading alone has limited prognostic importance in vesical carcinoma.

There were 40 patients in Jewett's stages O, A, and B_1 (Table 4). Twenty-one or 52 percent survived 5 years or more. Ten out of 20 patients with tumor penetrating to stage B_2 survived 5 years. Four out of 20 patients with stage C lesions were alive five or more years following their operations. It is interesting that three of these 4 patients had Broders' grade 4 tumors and the other, a grade 3 tumor. No patients with tumors in stages D_1 or D_2, as described by Whitmore and Marshal.[6] have

TABLE 2. Postoperative Complications Encountered in 17 Patients

Complications directly attributed to surgery	
1. Wound infection	8
2. Anastomotic leak (ureteroileal anastomosis)	7
3. Intestinal obstruction	6
4. Wound dehiscence	6
5. Wound hematoma	2
6. Ileostomy stenosis	2
7. Pelvic abscess	1
8. Fecal fistula	1
9. Infarction ileal segment	1
Secondary complications	
1. Pneumonia	3
2. Thrombophlebitis	3
3. Acute cholecystitis	2
4. Pulmonary embolism	2
5. Epididymitis	2
6. Staphylococcal enteritis	1
7. Cerebral vascular accident	1
8. Acute parotitis	1
9. Adrenal failure	1

TABLE 1. Causes of Operative Death, 7 Patients

M. E. A.	11 days	Pulmonary embolism
T. S.	4 days	Bronchopneumonia
J. T.	12 days	Peritonitis. Right ureter pulled off segment. Reexplored 24 hours before death
J. R.	4 days	Thrombosis renal artery in solitary kidney
L. R.	32 days	Ureteroileal leak. Peritonitis. Pneumonia
A. F.	15 days	Anastomotic leak ileum. Peritonitis. Pneumonia
B. S.	6 days	Diabetes. Pneumonia

TABLE 3. Causes of Death, 73 Patients

	No. of Cases	%
1. Operative	7	9.6
2. Carcinoma	47	64.4
3. Unknown	10	13.7
4. Uremia*	2	2.7
5. Extraneous causes (intercurrent disease)	4	5.5
6. Lost to followup study	3	4.4
	73	100

* J. B.: Progressive hydronephrosis and loss of renal function.
C. McC.: Progressive hydronephrosis; staghorn calculus, left kidney.

survived longer than 2 years. The 74 patients followed 5 years or more are shown in the dual classification of Marshall[7] in Tables 5 and 6.

In the reporting of cancer statistics, the arbitrary 5-year survival as a point of separating supposed cures from failures of therapy has long been used. This method of reporting data necessarily eliminates the inclusion of any recent case in a series. The life table, a tool long used by statisticians in other fields of investigation, shows the average yearly survival rate and permits the calculation of the accumulative survival rate. This method of presentation is both more informative and more accurate as it is based on a larger case experience. In our series, 73 patients or one half of the total cases have been operated upon since February 1, 1958. For this reason we have included life tables (Tables 7–9) constructed from all the available data. These tables show the yearly expectation of death and survival for each stage of Jewett's classification.

The tables are constructed for each year following operation. All patients dying in a given year are matched with those patients alive at the beginning of the year,

and the average yearly survival is computed. Those patients alive but not followed into the next year are dropped from the number of patients "at risk" for the subsequent year. The accumulated survival is computed by multiplying the average yearly survival by the accumulative survival for the previous year. In this manner, by the end of 5 years, an accumulative survival figure is achieved which should correspond with the over-all 5-year survival if the case experience is large enough to be statistically significant.

Some interesting observations can be made from the life tables. Table 8 shows the yearly survival for tumors in stage A following cystectomy. For the first 5 years following surgery, the yearly survival rate has been essentially the same. A theoretical 5-year survival rate based on the accumulative survival is 59 percent, which

TABLE 4. Five-Year Survival by Stage of Tumor

Stage	Operated	Survival	%
O, A, B_1	40	21	52
B_2	10	5	50
C	20	4	20
D_1, D_2	3	0	0

TABLE 5. Grade and Stage of Cancers in Patients Surviving 5 Years or More: Operation Before February 1, 1958

	Stage						
Grade	O	A	B_1	B_2	C	D_1	D_2
1							
2		4	2	1			
3		5	7	3	1		
4		1	2	1	3		
Squamous							
Adenocarcinoma							
Sarcoma							

TABLE 6. Grade and Stage of Tumor of Those Patients Not Surviving 5 Years or More: Operation Before February 1, 1958

	Stage						
Grade	O	A	B_1	B_2	C	D_1	D_2
1		1					
2		9			3	1	
3		3	4	2	8		1
4			2	2	3	1	
Squamous				1	1		
Adenocarcinoma					1		
Sarcoma							

TABLE 7. Life Table Showing Course of Patients with Jewett Stage A Tumors

Year	At Risk	Dead	% Survival	Accumulated Survival
0–1	48	3	94	94
1–2	45	4	91	86
2–3	38	4	89	77
3–4	27	3	89	68
4–5	17	2	88	59
5–6	11	0	100	59
6–7	4	1	75	44

TABLE 8. Life Table Showing Yearly Course of Patients with Jewett Stage B_1 Tumors

Year	At Risk	Dead	% Survival	Accumulated Survival
0–1	29	4	86	86
1–2	21	4	81	71
2–3	16	2	88	63
3–4	13	0	100	63
4–5	11	0	100	63
5–6	10	0	100	63
6–7	7	0	100	63
7–8	6	0	100	63

TABLE 9. Life Table Showing Yearly Course of Patients with Jewett Stage B_2 Tumors

Year	At Risk	Dead	% Survival	Accumulated Survival
0–1	20	4	80	80
1–2	13	3	77	62
2–3	9	1	89	55
3–4	5	1	80	44
4–5	4	0	100	44
5–6	4	0	100	44
6–7	2	0	100	44

TABLE 10. Life Table Showing Yearly Course of Patients with Jewett Stage C Tumors

Year	At Risk	Dead	% Survival	Accumulated Survival
0–1	42	14	67	67
1–2	25	8	68	46
2–3	16	4	75	34
3–4	9	0	100	34
4–5	8	1	87	29
5–6	4	0	100	29
6–7	2	0	100	29

TABLE 11. Life Table Showing Yearly Course of Patients with Stage D (Marshall) Tumors

Year	At Risk	Dead	% Survival	Accumulated Survival
0–1	7	3	57	57
1–2	2	1	50	28
2–3	0	0	0	0

is probably more accurate than the true 5-year rate of 31.5 percent for stage A lesions. The latter figure is based on only 19 cases while the former reflects the yearly experience with a group of 48 patients.

The 29 patients with stage B_1 lesions are represented by Table 8. The theoretical 5-year survival rate of 63 percent closely approximates the 65 percent rate based on the 17 patients actually followed 5 years. In Table 9, the course of 20 patients with stage B_2 lesions is recorded. Based on 20 patients, the theoretical 5-year survival rate is 44 percent as compared to the acutal rate of 50 percent, deduced from only 10 cases followed 5 years or more. In stage C lesions, Table 10 shows a theoretical 5-year survival rate of 29 percent, which compares to the actual rate of 20 percent. It is interesting that the patients who died with stage B_1, and B_2 and C tumors succumbed mainly in the first 3 years following surgery. Few deaths were noted in this group of patients who have been followed longer than 3 years. Table 11 shows the yearly experience with patients whose tumors penetrated beyond the bladder wall (stage D). No patient survived longer than 2 years.

CONCLUSION

Since the development of the ileal segment, cystectomy has enjoyed renewed popularity for the treatment of vesical neoplasms. Many observers have considered the procedure to be worthless in those patients who have extravesical spread of their tumors. Our experience supports this impression. In our opinion, the radical forms of therapy such as total pelvic evisceration or radical iliac node dissection are rarely indicated. Indeed, the occasional patient salvaged by such therapy hardly justifies the increased operative mortality and morbidity which may result from such extensive surgical procedures.

Since the anatomical extent of the disease rather than the morphological characteristics of the tumor cells is the most important single criterion in estimating future survival, it would seem that the goal of urologists should be the early diagnosis of vesical neoplasia and the employment of total cystectomy before the tumor growth extends beyond the confines of the bladder wall. Repeated transurethral resections of recurrent tumors involving the muscular layers of the bladder wall are to be condemned if only because such treatment will delay extirpative therapy until the patient's cancer has become either inoperable or has extended deep into the bladder wall, making cure less likely.

The fact that 3 patients who had grade 4, stage C tumors are still alive and without evident recurrence of their tumor five or more years following surgery is indeed encouraging. We feel that the low operative mortality rate and the acceptable survival statistics indicate that total cystectomy has proven its place in the management of bladder cancer.

SUMMARY

One hundred forty-six patients have undergone total cystectomy and ileal segment urinary diversion since 1953. Of these, 73 are available for 5-year evaluation. The results of surgery as well as the mortality and morbidity figures are presented. It is our feeling that cystectomy has a definite place in the management of vesical neoplasms, and that its earlier employment would result in the cure of many more patients.

REFERENCES

1. Bricker, E. M.: Bladder substitution after pelvic evisceration. S Clin North Amer, 30:1511–1521, 1950
2. Cordonnier, J. J. and Spjut, H. J.: Urethral occurrence of bladder carcinoma following cystectomy. J Urol, 87:398–403, 1962
3. Nesbit, R. M., Cerny, J. C., Heetderks, D. R. and Kendall, A. R.: Acute renal failure. J Urol, 88:331–336, 1962
4. Cordonnier, J. J. and Nicolai, C. H.: An evaluation of the use of an isolated segment of ileum as a means of urinary diversion. J Urol, 83:834–838, 1960
5. Jewett, H. J. and Strong, G. H.: Infiltrating carcinoma of the bladder: Relation of depth of penetration of the bladder wall to incidence of local extension and metastases. J Urol, 55:366–372, 1946
6. Whitmore, W. F. Jr. and Marshall, V. F.: Radical total cystectomy for cancer of the bladder: 230 consecutive cases, five years later. J Urol, 87:853–868, 1962
7. Marshall, V. F.: Current clinical problems regarding bladder tumors. Cancer 9:543, 1956

Commentary: Simple Cystectomy

William T. Bowles

The term *simple cystectomy* denotes total cystectomy with prostatoseminal vesiculectomy, with or without urethrectomy. When *en bloc* removal of the pelvic lymphatic tissue accompanies simple cystectomy, the operation is termed *radical cystectomy* or *anterior pelvic exenteration*. Although simple cystectomy is technically less difficult than the radical procedure, in recent years, with continued improvement in anesthetic techniques and postoperative care, morbidity and mortality have become similar for both procedures. In the 1960s, a radical cystectomy was rarely performed at our medical center, while since 1970, simple cystectomy has only been used in a few selected patients.

At the time the initial analysis of our results with simple cystectomy was published (1963), we had been performing total cystectomy and ileal segment diversion since 1953, when Bricker showed us the advantage of this method of urinary diversion. All patients who were not judged suitable for transurethral resection of their tumors underwent simple cystectomy if they agreed to the procedure and it was thought that their tumors were limited to the bladder wall. For several years we performed ileal segment diversion without cystectomy on patients who were thought to be inoperable at the time of surgery; however, analysis of the subsequent course of these unfortunate patients has shown that there was little, if any, palliation of their disease.[1] After the first few years' experience with this procedure, an analysis of the surgical results indicated that we were salvaging approximately 40% of the patients (5-yr survival rates) and losing approximately 5% because of operative mortality. Eighteen months before our analysis was published, Whitmore and Marshall had thoroughly discussed their operative experience with 230 consecutive patients subjected to radical cystectomy.[2] Except for the reported 5-yr survival of 4 patients with tumors having progressed to stage D_1, their 5-yr survival figures were not thought to be significantly higher than ours. We noted that their operative mortality was approximately 14% for radical cystectomy and 22% for total pelvic exenteration, and we initially felt that the higher mortality meant that we would lose more patients in the postoperative period than we would be able to save by extending the scope of the operation. Perhaps this belief was unwarranted. There have been recent reports from other surgeons employing radical cystectomy as a procedure of choice in the treatment of nonelectroresectable bladder cancer that show a continuous decline in the reported operative mortality. Stone and Hodges gave us an analysis of 35 radical cystectomies in which their initial operative mortality of 13.5% had dropped to 5.4% in their later cases—an operative mortality identical with that we have encountered with simple cystectomy.[3] In their series of 35 patients, there was a single 5-yr survival of a patient with a stage D_1 tumor. This patient would not have been operated upon by our group, since we had considered any patients with carcinoma in a single pelvic lymph node to be incurable by a surgical procedure.

Higher grade tumors and tumors penetrating to stage B_2 or beyond will most likely benefit from a more radical procedure. The additional salvage rate is small, but any patient saved by such a radical operation is a worthwhile effort if the increased resultant mortality is not unacceptable.

Higher survival rates for lower stage tumors were also noted by Wajsman and associates, who described their results in a series of 92 patients undergoing simple cystectomy.[4]

Another instance in which a simple cystectomy may be preferable to the more radical procedure is in the treatment of the elderly patient. Kursh and associates used this operation in a group of 25 patients over 70 yr of age with no operative deaths.[5]

The question of adding total urethrectomy in men to simple or radical cystectomy has been debated at our center since Cordonnier and Spjut first noted the distressing incidence of urethral recurrence of bladder cancer following cystectomy.[6] Long and his group have recently been performing total urethrectomy in the man in association with simple and radical cystectomy and, since employing this additional procedure, have noted a decrease in the pelvic recurrence of cancer from 43% to 11%. It therefore seems that the entire urethra should be removed in continuity with the bladder specimen at cystectomy to avoid the possibility of persistent urethral tumor or tumor spillage in the pelvis when the urethra is transected.

Removal of the female urethra is very simple and can be performed without perineal exposure. Removal of the male urethra necessitates a perineal exposure but adds less than 30 min to the total operating time.

Our most recent analysis of our long-term results with simple cystectomy are shown below.[7] The survival results for those patients are listed in Table 12. (The B_2 survivals in the original paper were all Veterans Hospital patients and are not included in these later figures.)

In summary, simple cystectomy, although a proven treatment modality in the approach to bladder cancer, should probably be reserved for high-risk patients and those in which the tumor is shown to manifest only superficial invasion of the bladder wall.

With the decreasing morbidity following radical anterior pelvic exenteration, the indication for radical surgical treatment seems to be clear. To be able to say how many more patients are saved by including removal of the pelvic lymphatic tissue awaits the future analysis of present endeavors.

Bladder cancer, at best, is a discouraging disease to treat when it has progressed to an advanced stage. The only way physicians will increase the salvage rate with present knowledge is to stress the importance of immediate investigation of all cases of unexplained hematuria so that the proper treatment can be instituted at the earliest possible moment in the course of the disease.

TABLE 12. Total Cystectomy and Ileal Segment Diversion (5-Year Survival by Stage and Grade)
(Alive 5 Years/Total Patients)

Grade	O	A	B_1	B_2	C	D_1	D_2	?	Total	% 5-Year Survival
I		1/2							2	50
II	0/2	11/17	4/4	0/2	0/1	0/1			27	54
III	1/1	9/14	5/8	0/3	1/11	0/1		0/1	39	41
IV		3/5	2/6	0/6	4/13	0/8	0/2	0/1	41	22
Squamous cell carcinoma		1/1			2/4	0/1		0/1	7	43
Adenocarcinoma			0/1		1/3				4	25
Unknown								1/2	2	50
Total	3	39	19	11	32	11	2	5	122	
% Alive 5 years	33	64	63	0	28	0	0	20		

REFERENCES

1. Silber I, Bowles WT, Cordonnier JJ: Palliative treatment of carcinoma of the urinary bladder. Cancer 23:586, 1969
2. Whitmore WF Jr, Marshall VF: Radical total cystectomy for cancer of the bladder: 230 consecutive cases five years later. J Urol 87:853, 1962
3. Stone JH, Hodges CV: Radical cystectomy for invasive bladder cancer. J Urol 96:207, 1966
4. Wajsman Z, Merrin C, Moore R, et al: Current results from treatment of bladder tumors with total cystectomy at Roswell Park Memorial Institute. J Urol 113:806, 1975
5. Kursh ED, Rabin R, Persky L: Is cystectomy a safe procedure in elderly patients with carcinoma of the bladder? J Urol 118:40, 1977
6. Cordonnier JJ, Spjut HF: Urethral occurrence of bladder carcinoma following cystectomy. J Urol 87:398, 1962
7. Bowles WT, Silber I: Carcinoma of the bladder—a computer analysis of a large series (516) of patients. J Urol 107:245, 1972

ANNOTATED BIBLIOGRAPHY

Bowles WT, Cordonnier JJ: Total Cystectomy for Carcinoma of the Bladder. J Urol 90:731, 1963

This paper is the classic article on total cystectomy for carcinoma of the bladder, reporting the results at the Washington University on 146 patients undergoing total cystectomy and ileal segment urinary diversion from 1953 to the date of reporting.

Silber I, Bowles WT, Cordonnier JJ: Palliative treatment of carcinoma of the urinary bladder. Cancer 23:586, 1969

The ultimate survival of patients with inoperable bladder cancer was not shown to be influenced by urinary diversion or radiation therapy; indeed, the longest survivals were noted in the group receiving only supportive therapy.

Whitmore WF Jr, Marshall VF: Radical total cystectomy for cancer of the bladder: 230 consecutive cases five years later. J Urol 87:853, 1962

In a series of 650 newly examined patients, Whitmore and Marshall found 230 patients who were suitable candidates for radical total cystectomy. In this article, they propose a dual classification that is now currently employed in most bladder cancer statistics. They felt that patients with more than a few metastases in the pelvic nodes close to the bladder or with any metastases beyond the pelvis had such a poor prognosis that radical cystectomy was useless for cure. They noted a 47% survival rate in patients whose carcinomas were of low degree of penetration of the bladder wall. Deeply infiltrating tumors showed a 14% 5-yr survival rate.

Stone JH, Hodges CV: Radical cystectomy for invasive bladder cancer. J Urol 96:207, 1966

In this report, 35 patients were studied who underwent radical cystectomy together with 2 patients who had total cystectomy and urinary diversion before April 1960. The overall survival rate was 48.6%, and the operative mortality was 13.5%. With superficially infiltrating tumors, B_1 or less, the survival rate was 80%. With tumors penetrating to stage B_2 or greater, the survival rate was reduced to 27%. There was one survival of seven patients with Stage C, and one survival of eight patients with stage D. The authors noted that the operative mortality decreased to 5.4% in the later cases in the series.

Wajsman Z, Merrin C, Moore, et al: Current results from treatment of bladder tumors with total cystectomy at Roswell Park Memorial Institute. J Urol 113:806, 1975

Of 365 patients treated for bladder cancer at Roswell Park Memorial Institute between 1968 and 1972, 92 underwent simple cystectomy. The authors note acceptable results for superficially infiltrating tumors. The group included high-risk patients with various severe medical problems. The overall mortality was 8.6%.

Kursh ED, Rabin R, Persky L: Is cystectomy a safe procedure in elderly patients with carcinoma of the bladder? J Urol 118:40, 1977

A series of 25 elderly, high-risk patients were subjected to simple cystectomy at the University Hospitals in Cleveland. Although many of the patients had severe medical problems, there was no operative mortality in this small series.

Cordonnier JJ, Spjut HF: Urethral occurrence of bladder carcinoma following cystectomy. J Urol 87:398, 1962

Four percent of patients undergoing cystectomy for the treatment of bladder cancer were eventually noted to have urethral persistence of their tumors.

Bowles WT, Silber I: Carcinoma of the bladder—a computer analysis of a large series (516) of patients. J Urol 107:245, 1972

An overall review of all patients with bladder cancer treated at Barnes Hospital, St. Louis, Missouri, since 1942.

66

SALVAGE CYSTECTOMY AFTER RADIATION FAILURE IN PATIENTS WITH BLADDER CARCINOMA*

Douglas E. Johnson, M.D., S. Lamy, M.D., and R. B. Bracken, M.D. †

Southern Medical Journal, Vol. 70, No. 11, November 1977

ABSTRACT—Thirty-two patients with cancer of the bladder definitively treated with irradiation had radical cystectomy without lymphadenectomy for treatment of recurrent or persistent tumor. Preoperative clinical staging was accurate in distinguishing between superficial and deeply invasive disease in 94% of patients, while in 44% clinical and pathologic stage were identical. There were no postoperative deaths. Fourteen patients have no evidence of disease 11 to 75 months postoperatively, 14 developed recurrent disease two to 20 months after surgery, and four died of other causes after satisfactory recovery from surgery. Assessment of clinical stage offers the best prognostic indication of survival, as all patients whose tumor was TIS (carcinoma in situ) or T_1 survived without developing recurrence whereas only six patients with stage T_3 or greater are alive without recurrent disease. Cystectomy can thus be recommended for selected patients with bladder cancer who have failed definitive irradiation therapy.

Preoperative irradiation with cystectomy has gained increasing acceptance as the treatment of choice for

* Read before the Section on Urology, Southern Medical Association, 70th Annual Scientific Assembly, New Orleans, La., Nov 7–10, 1976.

† From the University of Texas System Cancer Center M. D. Anderson Hospital and Tumor Institute, Houston, Tex 77030.

Reprint requests to Dr. Johnson at the above address.

infiltrating bladder carcinoma,[1-6] but radiotherapy alone is still widely used as definitive treatment for these tumors throughout this country.[7,8] Unfortunately, radiotherapy fails to keep the irradiated tissues permanently free of malignant disease in at least 44% of patients,[9] and surgery is subsequently required to salvage these cases. Since there is little information in the literature on the results of salvage cystectomy, we herein report our experience with 32 patients who had single-stage cystectomy and ileal conduit diversion when previous definitive irradiation failed to control local vesical malignant disease.

MATERIAL AND METHODS

Two hundred fourteen patients with primary carcinoma of the bladder had single-stage cystectomy and ileal conduit urinary diversion at The University of Texas System Cancer Center, M. D. Anderson Hospital and Tumor Institute (Houston) between Jan 1, 1969 and Dec 30, 1975. Of these patients, 32 (15%) had cystectomy and ileal conduit urinary diversion after persistence or recurrence of bladder carcinoma three or more months after a definitive course of radiation therapy, which we have arbitrarily defined as "radiation failure." In all except three cases the irradiation had been delivered before referral of the patient to Anderson Hospital. The radiation doses varied; one patient received 3,200 rads, one received 4,600 rads, and all other patients received between 5,000 and 7,560 rads. Portal size and arrangement, number of treatments, type and energy of delivered radiation, and duration of therapy varied considerably.

Radical cystectomy without pelvic lymphadenectomy as described by Whitmore[10] was used in all cases. The extent of the vesical malignant disease was assessed by physical examination, chest roentgenogram, skeletal survey, endoscopic findings, and bimanual palpatory examinations in all patients. An "equivalent" clinical stage was then recorded according to Marshall's modification of the Jewett and Strong[11] classification and according to the TNM system proposed by the American Joint Committee on Cancer Staging and End Results Reporting.[12] Stage assignment was considered "equivalent" since all patients had received previous definitive treatment for malignant disease of the bladder. The term "stage equivalent" therefore refers to restaging after radiotherapy and immediately before cystectomy. Pathologic stage was determined by examination of the excised bladder and by pathologic examination of biopsy specimens of suggestive lymph nodes or other issues as deemed clinically appropriate during operation.

RESULTS

Clinical Findings. Subjects included 24 men and eight women ranging in age from 51 to 79, with an average age for men of 62.3 years and for women of 59.5 years. Thirty patients were white, one was black, and one was of Latin-American descent. Twenty-eight patients had transitional cell carcinoma, three had squamous carcinoma, and one had adenocarcinoma. All had cystectomy as described. Three had concomitant urethrectomy.

TABLE 1. Relation of Preoperative Clinical Stage to Pathologic Stage

Pathologic Stage	Clinical Stage (Equivalent*)							
	O	A	B₁	B₂	C	D₁	D₂	Total
Stage O	3							3
Stage A		3	3					6
Stage B₁		3	1	1				5
Stage B₂				3	3			6
Stage C				2	3			5
Stage D₁				2	1	1		4
Stage D₂								0
No residual tumor		1	1		1			3
Total	3	7	5	8	8	1	0	32

* See text

Staging. Comparison between clinical stage equivalent and pathologic stage (Table 1) demonstrates the difficulty which may be encountered in staging the heavily irradiated bladder. There were errors both in understaging and overstaging. Only 14 of 32 patients were accurately staged preoperatively. Three patients had all evidence of tumor removed by precystectomy transurethral resection of the bladder tumor.

Surgical Complications. Although there were no postoperative deaths among the 32 patients, 11 patients had 12 early postoperative complications which occurred before discharge from the hospital. Of the early complications, two ureteroileal anastomotic leaks and one wound dehiscence required reoperation. The other nine early complications were managed conservatively. Nine patients developed 13 late complications, eight of which required operative intervention (Table 2).

Operating time varied from less than four hours to over seven hours, with an average of five hours. Blood loss varied from 1 to 9 units per case; a mean blood loss of 3 units occurred per cystectomy. Postoperative blood replacement ranged from 0 to 9 units and averaged 1

TABLE 2. Summary of Surgical Complications

Early		Late	
Wound infection	5	Intestinal urethral fistula*	4
Ureteroileal anastomatic break*	2	Pelvic abscess	2
Wound dehiscence*	1	Ventral hernia*	1
Intestinal obstruction	1	Stomal stenosis*	1
Stress ulcer	1	Radiation proctitis*	1
Hepatitis	1	Wound dehiscence*	1
Pulmonary emboli	1	Spontaneous rectal perforation	1
		Heal conduit regional enteritis	1
		Pyelonephritis	1
	12		13

* Required surgical intervention

unit per patient. Length of postoperative hospitalization ranged from 15 to 99 days, with a median of 22 days.

Survival. The five-year survival rate for the entire group determined from the time the first bladder malignant disease was diagnosed was 51.5%. The time interval between the initial diagnosis of bladder cancer and the time of cystectomy ranged from 5 months to 12 years, and the median duration was only 17 months. Presently, 14 patients are alive without evidence of disease (Table 3); two patients are alive with metastatic disease (lung, one case; pelvic lymph node, one case); 12 patients have died for either proven or suspected recurrent pelvic carcinoma (Table 4); and four patients have died of intercurrent disease, without clinical evidence of metastases.

Survival after cystectomy correlated best with the stage equivalent of the patient's tumor. Of the 14 patients alive after cystectomy with no evidence of disease, eight had either TIS (carcinoma in situ) or T_1 and only six had T_3; whereas the 14 patients with proven or suspected recurrent bladder cancer had T_3 or higher lesions. The causes of death in the four patients who died without evidence of metastases were: myocardial infarction four months after cystectomy; diabetes and heart disease two months after cystectomy; a postoperative death following surgical correction of an intestinal fistula five months after cystectomy; and a pelvic abscess secondary to radiation-induced rectal perforation 38 months after cystectomy. Three of these patients had T_3 lesions and one was a TOM_1 (abdominal wall tumor implantation).

Treatment Failure. Proven metastatic disease was demonstrated after cystectomy in nine patients (28%) and became clinically evident within two to 20 months. Seven of these patients have died from their malignant disease three to 28 months following cystectomy (median—12 months) and two patients are currently receiving chemotherapy. Pelvic recurrence was clinically evident in three of these nine patients, but in only one was it the sole evidence of malignancy at death. The other eight of the nine patients developed widespread metastases (Table 4). Pelvic recurrence was suspected but not proved in four additional patients (Table 4); one of these developed a colourethral fistula with a pelvic mass and the other three had severe pelvic pain without clinically demonstrable recurrent tumor before death.

DISCUSSION

Earlier reports had suggested an increase in complications in patients who, prior to cystectomy and ileal conduit diversion, had received definitive irradiation for management of their vesical malignant disease.[13] However, our more recent studies[14] have failed to substantiate this finding. Surgery may appear to be more difficult without distinct tissue planes and may result in an increase in small vessel bleeding; however, as we reported previously,[14] we found no differences in operating time, blood loss, postoperative complications, and length of in-hospital convalescent periods between irradiated patients and nonirradiated patients. It is noteworthy that there were no operative deaths in the present series.

TABLE 3. Patients Alive Without Evidence of Disease After Salvage Cystectomy

Patient	Sex	Initial Diagnosis	Date XRT Started	Amount of XRT (rads)	Date of Cystectomy	Pathologic Stage	Postoperative Survival (mo)	Complications Early	Complications Late
1	M	1957	1/68	6,000	6/69	TIS	75	—	Regional ileitis conduit, late pelvic abscess pyelonephritis
2	M	6/70	7/70	5,500	5/71	TIS	64	Ureteroileal anastomotic leak	—
3	M	4/63	4/63	5,000	4/70	T3	77	—	—
4	M	1/70	4/71	5,000	5/72	T1	52	Wound infection	—
5	F	7/72	8/72	5,700	6/73	TIS	39	—	Late wound dehiscence
6	M	7/74	8/74	6,000	9/75	T3	12	Wound dehiscence, wound infection	—
7	F	3/75	3/75	5,000	10/75	T1	11	—	—
8	F	9/74	10/74	5,000	6/75	T3	15	—	—
9	F	7/73	7/73	5,000	11/74	T3	22	—	—
10	F	5/73	9/73	6,000†	8/75	T1	13	—	—
11	M	1968	12/73	5,000	5/75	T3	16	—	Pelvic abscess
12	F	11/71	12/71	5,000	4/73	T1	41	—	—
13	M	3/71	4/71	5,600	6/72	T1	51	—	—
14	M	3/75	3/75	6,000	10/75	T3*	11	Stress ulcer	—

* Squamous cell carcinoma
† Irradiated at M. D. Anderson Hospital

TABLE 4. Patients With Biopsy-Proven or Clinically Suspected Tumor Recurrence

Patient	Sex	Initial Diagnosis	Date XRT Started	Amount of XRT (rads)	Date of Cystectomy	Pathologic Stage	Status	Months Cystectomy to Recurrence	Months Cystectomy to Death	Complications Early	Complications Late	Recurrence
Proven Recurrences												
1	F	8/72	9/72	6,000	8/73	T3	Alive	12	†	—	—	Lung
2	M	1/75	2/75	7,560	8/75	T3	Alive	10	‡	—	—	Lymph nodes
3	M	9/73	9/73	5,200	9/74	T3	Dead	5	14	—	—	Lung
4	M	12/64	6/74	6,000	6/75	T3*	Dead	6	8	—	Urethral fistula	Pelvis
5	M	3/70	4/70	5,800	11/72	T3	Dead	20	28	Intestinal obstruction	Stomal stenosis, rectourethral fistula	Pelvis, urethra, lung
6	M	10/63	11/72	4,000 6,000	4/73	T3	Dead	2	3	Pulmonary emboli	—	Lung, bone
7	M	8/71	8/71	5,000	3/72	T3	Dead	12	14	—	—	Pelvis, liver, bone
8	M	4/69	9/69	6,000	7/70	T3	Dead	3	16	Wound infection	—	Left supraclavicular node
9	M	9/73	10/73	7,200	12/75	T3	Dead	2	3	—	—	Bone marrow
Suspected Recurrences												
10	M	12/66	1/67	7,000	6/69	T3*	Dead	?	16	—	Colourethral fistula	Pelvis
11	M	12/69	2/70	6,000	8/73	T3	Dead	?	22	—	—	Pelvis
12	M	9/71	9/71	6,500	2/72	T3	Dead	?	39	—	XRT Proctitis requiring colostomy	Pelvis
13	M	8/72	9/72	6,300	9/73	T3	Dead	?	18	—	—	Liver
14	M	5/70	6/70	6,000	9/73	T4	Dead	?	24	Wound infection	Ventral hernia	Pelvis

* Squamous cell carcinoma
† Alive 22 months after cystectomy, on chemotherapy ten months
‡ Alive 11 months after cystectomy, on chemotherapy one month

Prognosis for patients undergoing salvage cystectomy appears directly related to the clinical stage of the disease at cystectomy. No patient whose tumor was either TIS or T_1 has developed recurrent cancer, whereas in all patients manifesting recurrent disease the clinical stage was T_3 or higher. However, high-stage tumor is not inevitably fatal since six patients with T_3 lesions (32%) are alive without evidence of disease 11 to 77 months after cystectomy and four patients with high-stage tumor have died without evidence of disease.

Accurate assessment of the clinical stage relative to whether the malignant process had invaded the muscle layer greater than halfway was correct in 30 of the 32 patients (94%), but deviation of clinical stage from the pathologic stage was frequent. Eight (25%) tumors were pathologically in a stage higher than by clinical appraisal (underestimated); ten (31%) were pathologically in a stage lower than that determined by clinical appraisal (overestimated); and 14 (44%) were found to have the same pathologic stage as that estimated preoperatively.

The high degree of accuracy noted in this series is thought to be directly related to the amount of attention given jointly by members of the urologic and radiotherapy team in assessing the clinical stage in these patients preoperatively. Although fixation may be confused with postirradiation failure by the inexperienced, adequate endoscopic biopsies may offer aid in distinguishing between high and low clinical stages. In some cases, however, operability can only be assessed at the time of laparotomy.

In conclusion, our results strongly support the premise that cystectomy and ileal conduit diversion can be safely used for treatment of recurrent or persistent carcinoma of the bladder in patients who have received previous definitive radiotherapy, without fear of increased mortality or morbidity. Prognosis closely parellels the clincal stage, which can be accurately assessed by the judicious use of physical, endoscopic, and radiologic findings.

REFERENCES

1. Miller LS, Johnson DE: Megavoltage irradiation for bladder cancer: alone, postoperative or preoperative? Seventh National Cancer Congress. Philadelphia, JB Lippincott Co, 1973, pp 771–782

2. Whitmore WF: Preoperative irradiation with cystectomy in the management of bladder cancer. Frontiers of Radiation Therapy and Oncology. Baltimore, University Park Press, Vol 5, 1970, p. 231

3. Deweerd JH, Colby MY Jr: Invasive carcinoma treatment by preoperative radiotherapy and operation. J Urol 99:593, 1968

4. van der Werf-Messing BHP: Carcinoma of the bladder $T_3N_xM_0$ treated by preoperative irradiation followed by cystectomy: Third report of the Rotterdam Radiotherapy Institute. Cancer 36:718—722, 1975

5. Richie JP, Skinner DG, Kaufman JJ: Radical cystectomy for carcinoma of the bladder: 16 years of experience. J Urol 113:186–189, 1975

6. Powel-Smith CJ, Reid EC: Preoperative irradiation and radical cystectomy in carcinoma of the bladder. Cancer 23:781–786, 1970

7. Goffinet DR, Schneider MJ, Glatstein EJ, et al: Bladder cancer: results of radiation therapy in 384 patients. Radiology 117:149–153, 1975

8. Green N. George FW III: Radiotherapy of advanced localized bladder cancer. J Urol 111:611–612, 1974

9. Miller LS, Crigler CM, Guinn GA: Supervoltage irradiation for carcinoma of the urinary bladder. Radiology 82:779–785, 1964

10. Whitmore WF: Total cystectomy. The Biology and Clinical Management of Bladder Cancer. Edited by EH Cooper, RE Williams. London, Blackwell Scientific Publications, 1975, pp 193–227

11. Jewett HJ, Strong GH: Infiltrating carcinoma of the bladder: relation of depth of penetration of the bladder wall to incidence of local extension and metastases. J Urol 55:366–372, 1947

12. Clinical staging system for carcinoma of the urinary bladder. Chicago, American Joint Committee on Cancer Staging and End Results Reporting, 1967

13. Johnson DE, Jackson I, Guinn GA: Ileal conduit diversion for carcinoma of the bladder. South Med J 63:1115–1118, 1970

14. Johnson DE, Lamy SM: Complications of single-stage radical cystectomy and ileal conduit diversion: review of 214 cases. J Urol 117:171–173, 1977

Commentary:
Postradiation Salvage Cystectomy

Paul F. Schellhammer

Salvage cystectomy in the following discussion is defined as a surgical procedure undertaken to rescue the patient in whom definitive radiation therapy has failed to eliminate the original tumor or in whom new tumors have subsequently appeared after control of the original neoplasm. Also included in the definition of salvage cystectomy is surgery primarily performed for severe radiation complications including fibrosis, bleeding, and pain where microscopic tumor is found on subsequent histologic examination of the removed specimen. If no neoplasm is found, the cystectomy should be considered as a radiation complication and not as salvage for radiation failure. Frequently reports use the term *salvage cystectomy* without qualifying the procedure as simple, radical, or with or without adenectomy or urethrectomy.

A discussion of salvage cystectomy must address two issues. The first deals with the technical difficulties encountered intraoperatively and complications encountered postoperatively after a definitive dose of radiation therapy (5500 to 7000 rad in 5 to 7 wk) has been delivered. How do mortality and morbidity associated with cystectomy after definitive radiation compare with mortality and morbidity after cystectomy alone or cystectomy following a lower dose (4000 to 4500 rad in 4 wk) of integrated preoperative radiation? The second and much more difficult issue to resolve centers about the survival increment that salvage cystectomy can add to the anticipated 20% to 25% 5-yr survival possible by delivery of definitive radiation alone. Assuming that salvage cystectomy can be performed with acceptable mortality and morbidity, can it then

be applied with sufficient success among patients failing definitive radiation such that the aggregate survival of patients so treated approaches that of integrated preoperative radiation followed by cystectomy? If so, the advantage of such an approach is significant in that it will preserve survival and in addition, for a certain number of patients, preserve as well vesical and sexual function.

The first question concerning acceptable postoperative morbidity and mortality can be answered in the affirmative. If certain precautions are observed, salvage cystectomy can be done with relative safety.

The surgical technique of salvage cystectomy does not differ appreciably from that employed with cystectomy alone. Increased difficulty in dissection may be encountered secondary to fibrosis and thickening of the perivesical tissues. Retroperitoneal fibrosis may render identification and mobilization of the ureters more tedious and time consuming, and, if lymph node biopsy or dissection is undertaken, the pliable fibroareolar tissue that normally surrounds the vessels will often be found to be replaced by a dense layer of fibrosis.

Definitive bladder radiation usually covers a pelvic field (14 cm × 15 cm) whose upper border is defined as the top or bottom of the L5 vertebra. Of major importance is the care that must be exercised to select a bowel segment outside this field for conduit formation and enteroenterostomy. Selection of heavily radiated bowel in the pelvis will, in the minimum, result in fibrosis and possible stricture of the conduit and enteroenterostomy but more likely will result in progressive ischemia with necrosis and fistulization of these anastomoses. The visible footprints of radiation damage include thickening and shortening of the bowel mesentery and thickening and pallor of the bowel wall together with relative loss of peristaltic action. In general, the distal ilium, which is relatively fixed, is subject to a greater degree of radiation changes than the more mobile proximal ilium and distal jejunum. Fixation due to adhesions from prior surgery may result in spotty areas of irradiation damage along the entire bowel length. The distal ureters are included in the radiation field. Enough ureter should be removed, usually to above the common iliac bifurcation, so that an unirradiated portion is used for ureteroenterostomy. The microscopic changes associated with radiation effects have been well characterized. Initially, acute injury results in edema and capillary congestion in the submucosal layer and denudation of the mucosa secondary to direct irradiation injury. With replication and replacement of directly injured cells, acute changes will usually resolve gradually with restoration of normal bowel function. However, a delayed or chronic response to injury may occur. This is characterized by swelling of the endothelium of the arterial and capillary vessels with subsequent narrowing causing ischemia and eventually fibrosis, stenosis, and fistulization. Even though the mucosa is able to recover from the direct effect of radiation injury, the extrinsic reduction of blood supply may be sufficient to interfere with usual regeneration and intestinal function. These same factors seriously impair wound healing after surgery. Although the degree of radiation damage depends on the external source of radiation, the volume of tissue radiated, and the total dose and fractionation, the severity of injury may not be uniform. Other factors more difficult to identify include fixation of intestinal loops secondary to prior surgery, the volume of tumor in the area and its attendant necrosis, and the patency of the mesenteric vasculature. Preexisting arteriosclerotic vascular disease and diabetes are very important but less well appreciated factors in determining the degree of early and late radiation injury. In fact it may only be with the progression of cardiovascular disease many years after radiation that injury becomes manifest.[1] In order to identify the microscopic changes of severe radiation injury and avoid these areas for anastomoses, a frozen section of the distal ureters and the bowel edges may be useful. The need for careful selection of bowel and ureter for anastomosis is emphasized by the prohibitive complication and mortality reported by those who initially faced the problem of cystectomy following definite radiation therapy. In a series 66% of patients undergoing cystectomy after radiation developed ureteral or intestinal fistulization and sepsis or both; 50% of these patients (33% of the series) died.[2] In another series, although the mortality was an acceptable 17%, 32% of patients had complications of intestinal or ureteral anastomosis in the first postoperative month and 28% had either intestinal or ureteral fistula during long-term follow-up study.[3] At times ureterosigmoidoscopy was employed as the method of diversion, indicating that heavily irradiated ureter and rectum provided the sites for anastomosis.

If the precautions outlined above are followed, anastomotic morbidity and attendent mortality can be minimized (Table 5). Operative mortality in the table ranges from 0% to 16% and very closely approximates the mortality encountered when

TABLE 5. Salvage Cystectomy: Post-Operative Mortality and 5-Yr Survival Rate

Series	No. of Patients	Mortality (%)	Stage and Survival (%)
Whitmore and colleagues (1968)[11] (1977)[7]	99	15	O, A, B$_1$, 60* B$_2$, C, 27* D$_1$, D$_2$, 8*
Poole-Wilson (1971)[12]	88	15	Overall, 30*
Edsmyr and colleagues (1971)[3]	35	17	T$_1$S, 53† T$_2$ OR, 6†
Wallace and Bloom (1976)[9]	18	11	T$_3$, 52*
Johnson and colleagues (1979)[10]	32	0	T$_1$S, T$_1$, 100‡ T$_3$, 21‡

* 5 Year survival
† Survival with 6 months–5 years follow
‡ Survival with 1–6 years follow

cystectomy is performed alone or following planned preoperative radiation in these same series. A higher incidence of superficial wound infection and separation of the irradiated lower abdominal wall has been reported in most series dealing with postradiation cystectomy.

The second issue to be analyzed deals with the success rate of salvage cystectomy to cure patients in whom tumor persists or recurs after radiation. To do this one must not only tabulate the absolute cure rate of the procedure but also the success of appropriate and timely identification of radiation failures so that surgical rescue still remains a viable option.

There is an inherent difficulty in reviewing reported series of salvage cystectomies with regard to successful identification and rescue of radiation failures. Those patients presenting for cystectomy after radiation failure include neither the best results of radiation, namely, those patients cured, nor the poorest results, namely, those patients already deceased or with metastatic disease. The total group or pool of patients from which the radiation failures are derived is often unavailable, making accurate analysis difficult.

There is a tendency toward complacency after definitive treatment by radiation therapy on part of both physician and patient. There is no evidence that radiation delivered for the treatment of bladder tumor will prevent development of subsequent tumors in the bladder. Therefore, interval cystoscopy must be carried out on a periodic basis, just as in pretreatment follow-up study. After radiation therapy cystoscopic identification of recurrent tumor is made difficult by the similar appearance of radiation-induced edema, ulceration, and recurrent neoplasm. Furthermore, a normal mucosal appearance at cystoscopy does not ensure a tumor-free state.[4] Frequent biopsies therefore are necessary to distinguish mucosal changes and to identify submucosal and muscle tumor nests under normal-appearing mucosa. The necessity of periodic cystoscopy and biopsy is strongly supported by Miller's report of a 50% attrition rate secondary to fatal bladder cancer between the 5- and 10-yr interval after definitive radiation. The patient continues at risk for fatal tumor recurrences even after a 5-yr radiation cure from the initial tumor has been achieved.[5]

The first issue of this two-part problem is the curative potential of salvage cystectomy. Although an occasional series with discouraging surgical rescue after failed definitive radiation therapy has been reported, the majority of recent series in the literature report satisfactory survival from salvage cystectomy.[6] In some reports survival is superior to that anticipated from cystectomy alone and approaches that anticipated for combined preoperative radiation and cystectomy (Table 5). Indeed, Whitmore states that

The survival rates for various stages of tumors so managed by salvage cystectomy are quite consistent with the possibility that full course irradiation (plus or minus 6,000 rads in 6 weeks) might be a legitimate alternative to pre-operative radiation plus cystectomy [he then goes on to state the second issue] were it possible, by some yet undefined technique, to identify the radiation failures early enough in the post-treatment interval to permit salvage cystectomy without appreciable reduction in survival prospects.[7]

Reference has already been made to the difficulty of investigating the bladder with regard to cystoscopic appearances (see above). Cytologic accuracy may also be altered by radiation effect. Where information is available concerning the percentage of patients undergoing definitive radiation judged at a later date on recurrence to be suitable for cystectomy, it is clear that this number is extremely small (Table 6). In Goffinet and associate's report of 348 patients treated with definitive radiotherapy, 176 were found to fall initially in the bladder (local failure), and yet only 16% (30 patients) underwent subsequent cystectomy.[8] Miller reported 533 patients treated with definitive radiotherapy; 45% (240) failed locally and only 13% (32 patients) came to salvage cystectomy.[5] Edsmyr and associates reported 450 patients treated with definitive radiation, and less than 10% (35 patients) were selected for subsequent salvage cystectomy.[3] In these three series the patients were primarily treated with radiation, and it may be presumed that a number of them undoubtedly had contraindications to cystectomy or had refused cystectomy as an initial form of treatment. Therefore, the low number of patients coming to subsequent surgery may be in part explained by these factors. However, in one series from Miller and in another from Wallace and Bloom patients were randomized, and these series therefore give a more accurate reflection of the success in identifying radiation failures for salvage cystectomy.[5,9] Since patients were randomized, all were initially deemed suitable candidates for radical surgery. Thus, those who failed the radiation arm of the protocol would be suitable operative candidates for salvage cystectomy. In Miller's series, 32 patients underwent definitive radiation; 84% (27) failed and only 2 subsequently underwent salvage cystectomy.[5] In Wallace's and Bloom's series, 85 patients underwent definitive radiation, 85% (72) failed, and only 18 subsequently underwent salvage cystectomy.[9] The highest rate of identification of radiation failures and highest percentage survival for salvage cystectomy are found in Wallace and Bloom's series. This is in part attributable to the very prompt diagnosis of recurrent or persistent neoplasm, since all salvage cystectomies but 1 were performed within 18 mo of completion of therapy. Where information is available from other series concerning the radiation–salvage cystectomy interval, the duration of this interval was longer.

A summary of the conclusions that are drawn from reviewing these series dealing with salvage cystectomy is as follows. First, a relatively low percentage of patients who received definitive radiation and failed subsequently underwent cystectomy. This is attributable to a number of factors, including patient refusal of surgery, medical contraindications to surgery, and the clinical appearance of metastases simultaneous with or preceding local radiation failure due in part to the delay and difficulty in early identification of the local failure. Second, if the surgeon uses extreme care in handling irradiated tissue and in selecting appropriate sections of bowel for ureteral intestinal anastomoses and enteroenterostomy, postoperative mortality will not significantly exceed that of cystectomy following peroperative radiation in lesser doses or cystectomy alone. Third, a 30% to 50% 5-yr survival for patients undergoing salvage cystectomy can be anticipated. Fourth, in the randomized series of both Wallace and Bloom and Johnson and colleagues, the patients undergoing integrated preoperative radiation followed by cystectomy demonstrate a survival advantage over those patients undergoing definitive radiation even when those patients cured by salvage cystectomy after definite radiation failure are added to the 5-yr survival rate.[9,10] Newer diagnostic methods, for instance, antigen, chromosomal, and biochemical markers, may contribute toward the earlier identification of residual or recurrent neoplasm and therefore narrow this advantage. In support of this is the superior 5-yr survival rescue from salvage cystectomy attained in Wallace and Bloom's series where early identification of failure was made.

TABLE 6. Postradiation Failures Undergoing Salvage Cystectomy and Rescue

Series	No. of Patients	No. of Local Failures (%)		No. of Local Failures Treated with Salvage Cystectomy (%)		No. of Local Failures Rescued (%)*
Edsmyr and colleagues (1971)[3]	450	202	45*	35	17	4‡
Goffinet and colleagues (1975)[8]	384	176	46	30	17	8‡
Wallace and Bloom (1976)[9]	85	38	45*	18	47	23 (5-yr survival)
Miller (1977)[5]	531	239	45	32	13	3 (5-yr survival)
Miller (1977)[5]	34	15	45*	2	16	16‡

* Based on 45% of total number of patients treated
† Percentage of *total local failures* subsequently rescued by Salvage cystectomy
‡ Variable follow-up study

REFERENCES

1. DeCosse JJ, Rhodes RS, Wentz WB, et al: The natural history and management of radiation induced injury of the gastrointestinal tract. Ann Surg 170:369, 1969

2. Higgins PM, Hamilton RW, Hope-Stone HF: The hazards of total cystectomy after supervoltage irradiation of the bladder. Br J Urol 38:311, 1966

3. Edsmyr F, Moberger G, Wadstrom L: Carcinoma of the bladder. Scand J Urol Nephrol 5:215, 1971

4. Engel RM, Urtasun RC, Jewett HJ, et al: Treatment of infiltrating bladder cancer by cobalt[60] radiation: recurrence of tumor in bladder after initial disappearance. J Urol 101:859, 1969

5. Miller, LS: Bladder cancer. Cancer 39:973, 1977

6. Nerstrom B, Hansen RI, Jorgensen SW: Total cystectomy and cutaneous uretero-ileostomy following supervoltage radiotherapy for bladder carcinoma. Acta Chir Scand 472:77, 1976

7. Whitmore WF Jr, Batata MA, Ghoneim MA, et al: Radical cystectomy with or without prior irradiation in the treatment of bladder cancer. J Urol 118:184, 1977

8. Goffinet DR, Schneider MJ, Glatstein EJ, et al: Bladder cancer: Results of radiation therapy in 384 patients. Radiology 117:149, 1975

9. Wallace DM, Bloom HJG: The management of deeply infiltrating (T_3) bladder carcinoma: Controlled trial of radical radiotherapy versus preoperative radiotherapy and radical cystectomy (first report). Br J Urol 48:587, 1976

10. Johnson DE, Lamy S, Bracken RB: Salvage cystectomy after radiation failure in patients with bladder carcinoma. South Med J 70:1279, 1977

11. Whitmore WF Jr, Grabstald H, MacKenzie A, et al: Preoperative irradiation with cystectomy in the management of bladder cancer. Am J Roentgenol 102:570, 1968

12. Poole-Wilson DS, Barnard RJ: Total cystectomy for bladder tumors. Br J Urol 43:16, 1971

ANNOTATED BIBLIOGRAPHY

Edsmyr F, Mosberger G, Wadstrom L: Carcinoma of the bladder Scand J Urol Nephrol 5:215, 1971

This report from the Karolinska Institute deals with 35 patients undergoing cystectomy after failure of definitive radiation for carcinoma of the bladder. Of specific note is the high degree of anastomotic complications, both of the ureteroileal anastomosis and the enteroenterostomy. The survival rate in patients whose tumor was found to be penetrating muscle was poor.

Whitmore, WF, Jr, Grabstald H, MacKenzie A, et al: Preoperative irradiation with cystectomy in the management of bladder cancer. Am J Roentgenol 102:570, 1968

Both an early report in 1968 and a follow-up report in 1977 of a large group of patients provide information on the acceptable mortality and 5-yr survival rate for salvage cystectomy.

Wallace DM, Bloom HJG: The management of deeply infiltrating (T_3) bladder carcinoma: Controlled trial of radical radiotherapy versus preoperative radiotherapy and radical cystectomy (first report). Br J Urol 48:587, 1976

This large randomized series clarifies some questions on the advantages of preoperative radiation followed by cystectomy versus radiation therapy alone. Excellent survival in patients treated with salvage cystectomy after failure of definitive radiation is probably in part accounted for by the prompt recognition of persistent or recurrent tumor and prompt intervention. It is of extreme interest that the 5-yr survival rate in the salvage cystectomy group exceeds the 5-yr survival attained by those who received definitive radiation alone and was essentially similar to that achieved in patients who underwent planned integrated preoperative radiation followed by cystectomy.

DeCosse JJ, Rhodes RS, Wentz WB, et al: The natural history and management of radiation induced injury of the gastrointestinal tract. Ann Surg 170:369, 1969

A thorough review of radiation complications that emphasizes the importance of ischemia in producing the delayed radiation effects of stenosis, ulceration, and perforation. The degree of radiation injury is correlated with the presence of diabetes, arteriosclerotic vascular disease, hypertension, and congestive failure. Also noted is the significant complication rate encountered when operating on radiation injured bowel. Methods of minimizing complications include wide excision, microscopic examination of tissue intended for anastomotic sites, meticulous management of cardiac status so as to maintain optimal splanchnic profusion, and employment of intravenous hyperalimentation.

67

TRANSURETHRAL RESECTION FOR THE ASSESSMENT AND TREATMENT OF VESICAL NEOPLASMS

A Review of 840 Consecutive Cases

J.D. O'Flynn, J.M. Smith and J.S. Hanson

Urological Department, Meath Hospital, and Department of Surgery,
Trinity College, Dublin

Eur. Urol 1:38 40(1975)

ABSTRACT—Non-infiltrating (T1), and superficially infiltrating (T2), vesical neoplasms can be treated satisfactorily by transurethral resection. Some T3 neoplasms can also be treated this way, but most will require radiotherapy. The assessment and treatment of 840 cases are presented. Survival rates of 62% in T1 cases, 59% in T2 cases, and 20% in T3 cases are reported in 465 cases followed up for 5 years.

Key Words
Vesical neoplasm
Assessment
Transurethral resection
Staging and grading

To establish a basis for the satisfactory treatment of vesical neoplasm it is essential that at the initial assess-

Dr. J.D. O'Flynn, Urological Department, Meath Hospital, Heytesbury Street, Dublin 8 (Ireland)

ment the histological characteristics and the extent of muscle infiltration should be accurately determined. Bimanual rectal or vaginal examination under anaesthesia, and transurethral resection of the neoplasm affords the best means of deciding the degree of muscle invasion, but to do this correctly it is essential that the neoplasm be resected deeply into muscle (even to the extent of exposing the perivesical fat), to achieve two main objects: (1) the radical extirpation of the neoplasm, and (2) to determine the correct staging of the neoplasm.

Bimanual rectal or vaginal examination under anaesthesia is helpful when the tumour is palpable, but may be inconclusive when the patient is very obese and the neoplasm is small. Pyelography is of limited value in determining the stage, but obstruction of the kidney on the same side as the neoplasm almost always indicates deep muscle involvement.

The technique of transurethral resection is well established, but it is essential that the operation be done carefully and accurately, and that when the procedure is completed it should be possible to determine either that: (1) all macroscopic neoplastic tissue has been removed and that only smooth vesical muscle is visible at the site of the neoplasm, or (2) the resection is incomplete, and that deep infiltration of the vesical muscle is present, and the extravesical tissues may be invaded.

It has been shown (Barnes et al., 1967), that 80% of all vesical neoplasms can be treated by transurethral methods with good results; and it has also been demonstrated that some high grade infiltrating neoplasms can be dealt with in this way. When complete transurethral excision is impossible (as occurs in stage T3 and T4 neoplams), some alternative treatment is necessary, and it has been our practice to prescribe radiotherapy in preference to total cystectomy—the latter procedure being reserved for squamous cell carcinoma and carci-noma in situ. In cases where the neoplasm is of high grade and is extending outside the bladder (Broders grade IV, stage T4), no adequate therapy is available, but many of our cases in this group have been treated by radio-therapy.

During the 10 years, 1961–1970 inclusive, 840 new

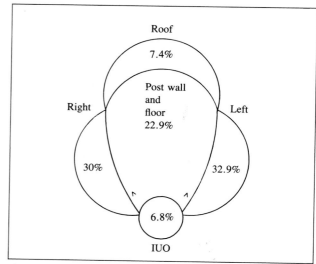

Fig. 2. Site distribution (total 840).

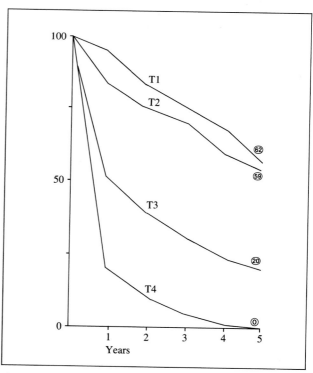

Fig. 3. 5-Year survival (465 cases).

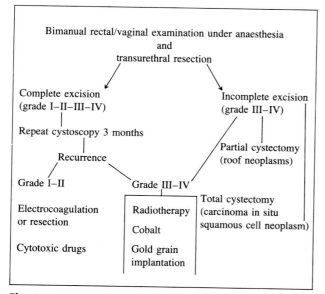

Fig. 1. Management plan.

TABLE 1. Age and Sex Percentage Incidence in 840 Cases

	Age, Years							
	0–19	20–29	30–39	40–49	50–59	60–69	70–79	80 +
Males, %	0.2	0.5	1.5	5.7	16.1	25.9	20.6	6.0	76.7
Females, %	0	0.4	0.7	2.1	4.0	7.1	6.7	2.0	23.3

TABLE 2. Multiplicity Figures (Total 810)

	n	%
Single neoplasms	580	70
Multiple neoplasms	230	30

TABLE 3. Intravenous Urography (Total 805)

	%
Unobstructed upper urinary tract	80.2
Obstructed upper urinary tract	19.8

TABLE 4. Grade and Stage of Neoplasms at the First Assessment (Total 840)

Stage	Grade				%
	1	2	3	4	
1	11.9	20.3	3.7	0.6	36.6
2	1.5	21.9	6.3	1.5	31.3
3		1.8	12.6	5.8	20.3
4			4.1	7.5	11.6

TABLE 5. Treatment in the 840 Cases

	n	%
Transurethral resection	631	75
Transurethral electrocoagulation	42	5
Cystectomy total	8	1
Cystectomy partial	5	0.6
Radiotherapy	304	36
DXT	125	15
Cobalt	174	20
Radon	4	0.5
Gold grains	1	0.1

TABLE 6. 5-Year Survival (Total 465)

	Years											
	1		2		3		4		5		Total	
Grade	n	%	n	%	n	%	n	%	n	%	n	%
T1	113	90	103	82	89	71	84	67	78	62	126	27
T2	156	87	134	75	122	20	107	60	101	59	181	40
T3	56	51	46	43	33	31	26	25	21	20	109	23
T4	11	22	5	12	4	8	2	4	0	0	49	10

cases of vesical neoplasm arising from the uro-epithelium were investigated and treated at the Urological Department, Meath Hospital, and the results of this retrospective study are presented here.

In most cases (except for a small group where electrocoagulation was carried out), the initial approach was an endeavour to resect the tumour completely by endoscopic means; the histological material was graded according to Broder's classification, and the staging (on the T and M system), decided on the basis of the presence of muscle infiltration in the histological sections, and on the bimanual rectal or vaginal examination.

Many of the treated cases were lost to follow-up, but in 465 cases a 5-year post-treatment survey was possible, and the survival figures are presented in table 6 and Figure 3.

It is evident that stage T1 and T2 cases can be treated satisfactorily by transurethral methods, and that stage T4 cases respond very badly to any form of treatment. The biggest problem in therapy arises in the stage T3 cases. Some of these have been treated by transurethral resection only, but others need supplementary treatment, such as radiotherapy or total cystectomy. In this group of cases radiotherapy has been largely employed, and, as can be seen, a 20% 5-year survival rate has resulted. While this figure is comparable to that in other series, it cannot be regarded as satisfactory. Total cystectomy for this group does not appear to offer a better alternative.

It is evident from this study that histological grading and staging do not always provide sufficient information to assess prognosis; what will cure one neoplasm fails to affect a similar neoplasm, and this is because we have no definite information on the biological characteristics of any particular tumour, and therefore cannot show how it will behave. It is apparent that some accessory means must be found to help us to detect what the likely performance of a given vesical neoplasm may be.

REFERENCE

Barnes, R.W.; Bergman, R.T.; Hadley, H.L.; Love, D.: Control of bladder tumors by endoscopic surgery. J Urol 97:864–868, 1967

Commentary: Transurethral Resection and Fulguration of Bladder Tumors

E. Douglas Whitehead

When compared to other treatment modalities for bladder tumors, transurethral resection has a well-defined place.[1] Approximately 80% of all patients with bladder tumors can be treated with good results using transurethral resection, transurethral fulguration, or both.[1,2] Tumors amenable to this form of therapy are those that are papillary or superficial of low stage (stages 0/TIS and A/T1) and low grade (grades 1,2) with no muscle infiltration. Some low-grade (grades 1,2) tumors with superficial muscle infiltration (stage B1/T2) and a few superficial tumors (stages 0/TIS and A/T1) that are high grade (grades 3,4) are also amenable to transurethral resection. However, if superficial infiltration of the bladder wall (stage B1/T2) or deep infiltration of the bladder wall (stage B2/T3) with moderate or poor differentiation (grades 3,4) has already taken place, the probability is that additional therapy is required and that the transurethral resection was of diagnostic and assessment value only.

Patients with initially low-grade, low-stage bladder tumors that subsequently develop recurrent tumors with muscle invasion, multiplicity of tumors, rapid recurrences of tumors of a progressively increasing stage or grade are not candidates for therapeutic transurethral resection of the tumors. In these situations, consideration should be given to adjunctive therapy with thiotepa or other chemotherapeutic agents, or possibly segmental, total, or radical cystectomy with or without radiation therapy.[3-6]

The reasons for employing transurethral resection of bladder tumors are fourfold: (1) to obtain histologic diagnosis of bladder tumor, (2) for staging assessment (degree of bladder wall penetration), (3) for grading assessment (degree of histologic differentiation), and (4) for management of bladder tumors, be it therapeutic or palliative. Naturally, this form of therapy is useful only in tumors that are accessible to the resectoscope and to tumors that are of limited size.

Before transurethral management of bladder tumors, all patients should have excretory urography, bimanual rectal or vaginal examination with the bladder empty under anesthesia to access the stage of the tumor, and careful direct visualization of the bladder and urethra by cystoscopy–panendoscopy. In patients with sessile tumors or positive findings on bimanual examination, suggestive of deeply infiltrative carcinoma (stage B2,C/T3), a computed tomography (CT) scan should be performed before transurethral resection to assist in determining the correct stage of the tumor.[7]

There are four methods of transurethrally managing bladder tumors: (1) resection with the cold knife (punch resectoscope) popularized at the Mayo Clinic, (2) avulsion of the tumor by grasping the tumor between the resectoscope loop and beak, (3) fulguration of the tumor (if it is less than ½ cm in diameter), and, most commonly, (4) transurethral resection using a resectoscope.[8]

TECHNIQUE OF TRANSURETHRAL RESECTION OF BLADDER TUMORS

A high-intensity cutting current to aid precision of resection in conjunction with a coagulating current to prevent dissemination of tumor cells is employed. The Iglesias continuous irrigation resectoscope is mainly preferred in order to keep intravesical volume and pressure low. Distilled water is the preferred irrigating medium because of its good optical qualities and its possible cytotoxic effects on free tumor cells.

For pedunculated tumors, it is theoretically ideal to initially resect the intramural portions starting about 1 cm lateral to the base of the tumor in the hopes of preventing tumor dissemination through lymphatic, vascular, or perineural pathways. These pieces of tissue are sent to the pathology department in separately labeled containers for histologic study. For larger, more bulky tumors it is advisable to employ systematic resection from the posterior peripheral or superior peripheral aspect of the intravesical portion of the bladder tumor in a steplike fashion to the inferior and medial aspect of the bladder in a progressive manner until the stalk of the tumor and bladder muscle is exposed.

Suprapubic or rectal counterpressure is used as needed, and a wide variety of cutting motions, including antigrade, retrograde, oblique, and scooping bites, are frequently necessary. All these bites with the loop of the resectoscope must follow the contour of the bladder to prevent perforation. It is extremely important to use a slow infusion and low volume of bladder filling in order to prevent stretching and thinning of the bladder wall and thereby increasing the chance of inadvertent bladder perforation. Volumes in excess of 100 ml are not generally necessary in order to move the adjacent bladder wall away from the area of resection. This is particularly important during the resection of the base of the tumor when the bladder muscle is being exposed. After the muscle fibers have been exposed over the entire base of the bladder tumor, several deep pieces of tissue of the intramural portion of the tumor may be obtained and sent to the pathology department in separately labeled containers for histologic study. Similarly, additional pieces of tissue from the periphery of the apparently completely resected base, for a distance of 1 cm, may also be sent separately for study. In most cases, it is advisable to fulgurate lightly the entire exposed base of the bladder wall as well as the margins of the resected area. After completing the resection, multiple random quadrantic cold cup biopsies may often be obtained in order to determine whether a "field change" is present, implying a generalized or multifocal cellular instability that would preclude adequate transurethral therapy of the patient's neoplasm. The presence of carcinoma *in situ* presents an ominous prognosis.[9,10]

If the bladder wall is perforated and shiny and glistening fat is noted, the procedure should be rapidly stopped, obtaining complete hemostasis with very minimal distention of the bladder and a very low irrigating fluid pressure. In this situation it is quite possible that the stage of the tumor has been increased due to perivesical implantation of tumor cells. If during resection it appears that the tumor extends through the deep muscle, the resection should be stopped before intentional bladder wall perforation unless therapeutic alternatives have been considered and decided against and the tumor is believed to be not greater than stage C(T3). Hemostasis should be obtained as the procedure progresses. When multiple bladder tumors are present, one tumor should be resected completely before proceeding to resect others in order to obtain complete hemostasis and to determine that a complete resection of the first tumor has been performed.

If a bladder tumor is located adjacent to, on, or in a ureteral orifice, it may be resected with impunity. However, the cutting current only should be used in this situation in order to prevent ureteral stenosis. Postoperatively, consideration should be given to a high fluid intake and antibiotic treatment. When treating tumors in this location, preresection ureteral stenting might be of assistance, after which the ureteral catheter can be left *in situ* for 48 to 72 hr to prevent obstruction due to postoperative edema. Vesicoureteric reflux frequently follows resection of the ureteral orifice.[11,12]

Occasionally, with very bulky tumors, transurethral resection must be performed in two stages; the second stage may be performed 5 to 7 days after the first resection.

At the completion of the resection, one should carefully palpate the bladder and abdomen to rule out abdominal distention or tenderness secondary to bladder perforation and extravasation. In addition, a bimanual examination should be performed at this time to determine if any persistent movable mass is present, signifying residual unresected tumor (stage B2, C/T3) or if a fixed mass or induration is present, signifying extension of the tumor (stage D/T4). In the latter circumstance the transurethral resection would have been performed for palliative reasons only, and additional adjunctive therapy would then be considered.

MANEUVERS TO INCREASE ACCESSIBILITY OF BLADDER TUMORS IN VARIOUS LOCATIONS

Theoretically, all areas of the bladder are accessible to the resectoscope. Approximately two thirds of bladder tumors are located at the base of the bladder or in the trigonal area and pose no difficulty in resection. However, tumors located in the so-called inaccessible areas, that is, the dome (air bubble), lateral walls, cephalad (vertex) aspect, and bladder neck areas, require considerable technical skill to resect completely.

Resection of tumors on the dome of the bladder can frequently be performed with ease if suprapubic pressure is applied by either the resectionist or an assistant. Additionally, tumors in this location close to the anterior bladder neck can be resected completely if the patient and table are tilted in the Trendelenberg position, sometimes to a severe degree.

For tumors located on the lateral walls and on the cephalad (vertex) aspect of the bladder, resection at times is difficult and is considerably aided by placing the patient in a severe Trendelenberg position. The bladder is thus elevated, and the resectionist might find it helpful to resect while standing. Rectal or vaginal counterpressure may be of assistance for tumors in these locations.

Resection of tumors in the area of the posterior bladder neck is frequently aided if the patient and table are tilted in an exaggerated reverse Trendelenberg position with the feet low. Although the usual position of the patient on the cystoscope table is that of lithotomy, it is occasionally of value to place the patient prone on the table for resection of tumors of the anterior bladder wall from the dome to the bladder neck. This is particularly suitable in women, but in men a perineal urethrostomy must be peformed.[13]

TREATMENT OF COMPLICATIONS

Treatment of various complications is discussed below.[14]

Bleeding and Hemorrhage. For moderate bleeding, frequent hand irrigations usually suffice. If this is not successful, then suprapubic cystostomy with evacuation of clots and fulguration of the base of the tumor and edges of the resected area is required. Rarely will additional treatment, such as ligation or embolization of the hypogastric arteries, be necessary. Through and through continuous irrigations are not advised.

Perforation. *Perivesical (Extraperitoneal) Perforation.* A perivesical perforation is usually not a serious complication. However, if the amount of extravasated fluid is large, such that there is a palpable abdominal mass, then Penrose drains must be inserted in the perivesical space. It may be advisable to perform a suprapubic cystostomy. Foley catheter drainage for 5 to 7 days is necessary. Antibiotic coverage is required.

Intraperitoneal Perforation. An intraperitoneal perforation is a much more serious complication, with potentially life-threatening sequelae. Suprapubic cystostomy is required immediately, and residual tumor may be resected by excision of the bladder wall with wide margins if tumor is still thought to be present. If no tumor is present, the perforation is closed with sutures and the extravasated fluid is drained. Foley catheter drainage for 5 to 7 days is necessary. Antibiotic coverage is necessary.

Obturator Nerve Reflex. Obturator nerve reflex is occasionally noted during resection of tumors located on the inferior, posterior, and base of the bladder. The obturator reflex, a violent contraction of the thigh, is frequently complicated by bladder perforation. If continued resection is necessary and no perforation has occurred, it is highly advisable to use only a low-cutting current, taking particular care that the bladder is only minimally filled. This reflex may be prevented by employing a muscle relaxant if the patient is under general anesthesia. Infiltrative local anesthesia around the obturator nerve has been used to prevent this reflex.[15]

Pyelonephritis. Pyelonephritis is usually due to ureteal obstruction due to resection of the ureteral orifice. Treatment consists of increased fluid intake, antibiotic therapy, and observation.

POSTOPERATIVE MANAGEMENT

After resection of a bladder tumor, usually a 22 or a 24 French Foley catheter is connected to straight drainage and left in for at least 48 hr. If the bladder tumor is less than 1 cm the patient might be left without a Foley catheter. If perivesical fat has been exposed during the resection the catheter is left in place for 5 to 7 days. If bleeding is present postoperatively, frequent hand irrigation of the Foley catheter is necessary. It is not advisable to use through and through continuous bladder irrigation because unnoticed obstruction of the catheter lumen by a blood clot might occur, resulting in severe bladder distention and inadvertent postoperative perforation of the bladder. Antibiotics are usually prescribed.

FOLLOW-UP SURVEILLANCE

Approximately 60% of patients having transurethral resection have recurrence of bladder tumors. Therefore, diligent surveillance and monitoring of these patients is necessary.[1] Cystoscopy–panendoscopy is necessary every 3 mo for at least 3 to 5 yr. If no recurrences occur during this time, interval cystoscopy–panendoscopy is advisable every 6 mo for at least 3 to 5 yr and then semiannually or annually for the remainder of the patient's life.[1,2,4,14,16] Limited or complete excretory urography is advisable every 6 to 12 mo for at least 3 to 5 yr because of the unstable uroepithelium of the upper urinary tract and the propensity for patients with a history of bladder tumors to develop papillary transitional carcinoma.[17] After 5 yr, annual limited excretory urograms should be obtained. In addition, periodic urinary cytologic examination between cystoscopic–panendoscopic examinations is strongly advised.[18,19]

SURVIVAL

Almost all urologists believe that tumors of stage 0(TIS) and stage A(T-1) can be treated satisfactorily with transurethral

resection and fulguration. In support of this belief, survival figures indicate that 62% to 82% of patients survive 5 years after transurethral resection for such tumors.[1,2,20,21,22] Many urologists believe stage B-1(T2) tumors can be managed satisfactorily with transurethral resection and fulguration. In support of this viewpoint, 5-year survival figures of 47% to 59% are noted.[2,14,20] Patients with lower-grade lesions generally have a higher 5-year survival rate than those with higher-grade lesions, and patients with small tumors generally have a higher 5-year survival rate than patients with larger tumors.[1]

However, in patients with deeply infiltrative tumors (stage B-2,C/T-3), transurethral resection and fulguration is not the recommended treatment in view of 5-year survival figures of only 15% to 40% (stage B-2/T-3) and 7% (stage C/T-3).[1,2,20,22] In other words, with stage C tumors (T-3), the role of transurethral resection is generally, at most, palliative, and certainly, in patients with stage D(T-4) tumors, transurethral resection is only palliative. In these stages adjunctive radiation therapy is usually employed after such transurethral "resection."

Therapeutic alternatives for deeply infiltrative tumors (stage B-2,C/T-3) are partial, simple, or total cystectomy, with or without adjunctive radiation therapy after staging/grading by transurethral "resection."

CONCLUSION

Transurethral resection of bladder tumors or transurethral fulguration of bladder tumors is adequate therapy for approximately 80% of all bladder tumors, comprising, in general, patients with superficial tumors, low-grade/low-stage patients with bladder tumors that manifest no increase in frequency of recurrence or increase in grade or stage, and patients with no "field change" on random quadrantic bladder biopsies. Complete removal of the tumor, if possible, and diligent follow-up surveillance are essential. The postoperative period is short, and complications and mortality are unusual. This technique of therapy preserves bladder function, allows the patient a good quality of life, and provides acceptable survival statistics in patients with low-grade and low-stage tumors.

REFERENCES

1. Whitehead ED; Management of bladder carcinoma. NY State J Med 81:201, 1981.

1a. Barnes RW, Bergman RT, Hadley HL, et al: Control of bladder tumors by endoscopic surgery. J Urol 97:864, 1967

2. O'Flynn JD, Smith JM, Hanson JS: Transurethral resection for the assessment and treatment of vesical neoplasms: A review of 840 consecutive cases. Eur Urol 1:38, 1975

3. Veenema RJ, Romas NA, Fingerhut A: Chemotherapy for bladder carcinoma. Urology 3:135, 1974

4. Whitmore WF: The treatment of bladder tumors. Surg Clin North Am 49:349, 1969

5. Prout GR Jr: The surgical management of bladder carcinoma. Urol Clin North Am 3:1, 1976

6. Grossman HB: Current therapy of bladder carcinoma. J Urol 121:1, 1979

7. Hodson NJ, Husband JE, MacDonald JS: The role of computed tomography in the staging of bladder cancer. Clin Radiol 30:389, 1979

8. Utz DC: Transurethral surgery by cold punch technique. In Glenn JF, Boyce WH (eds): Urologic Surgery, p 473. New York, Harper & Row, 1969

9. Gittes RF: Tumors of the bladder. In Harrison JH, Gittes RF, Perlmutter AD, et al (eds): Urology, 4th ed., p 1059. Philadelphia, WB Saunders, 1979

10. Aethansen AF, Prout GR Jr, Daly JJ: Non-invasive papillary carcinoma of the bladder associated with carcinoma in situ. J Urol 110:575, 1976

11. Rees RWM: The effect of transurethral resection of the infravesical ureter during removal of bladder tumors. Br J Urol 41:2, 1969

12. Gottfries A, Nilsson S, Sundin T, et al: Late effects of transurethral resection of bladder tumors at the ureteric orifice. Scand J Urol Nephrol 9:32, 1975

13. Girgis AS: Position for cystoscopic surgery of anterior bladder wall. Urology 2:199, 1973

14. Milner WA: Transurethral resection of bladder tumors. In Glenn JF (ed): Urologic Surgery, 2d ed, pp 355–356. Hagerstown, Harper & Row, 1975

15. Creevy CD: Preventing stimulation of the obturator nerve during transurethral resection. Trans Am Assoc Genitourin Surg 60:90, 1968

16. Marberger H, Marberger M Jr, Decristoforo A: The current status of transurethral resection in the diagnosis and therapy of carcinoma of the urinary bladder. Int Urol Nephrol 4:35, 1972

17. Sherwood T: Upper urinary tract tumours following on bladder carcinoma: Natural history of urothelial neoplastic disease. Br J Radiol 44:137, 1971

18. Geisse LJ, Tweddale DN: Pre-clinical cytological diagnosis of bladder cancer. J Urol 120:51, 1978

19. Flanagan MJ, Miller A III: Evaluation of bladder washing cytology for bladder cancer surveillance. J Urol 119:42, 1981

20. Milner WA: The role of conservative surgery in the treatment of bladder tumors. Br J Urol 26:275, 1954

21. Flocks RH: Treatment of patients with carcinoma of the bladder. JAMA 145:29, 1951

22. Nichols JA, Marshall JF: The treatment of bladder carcinoma by local excision and fulgruation. Cancer 9:559, 1956

ANNOTATED BIBLIOGRAPHY

Barnes RW, Bergman T, Hadley HL, et al: Control of bladder tumors by endoscopic surgery. J Urol 97:864, 1967

In this classic paper on transurethral management of bladder tumors the authors report their 5-, 10-, and 15-yr results in terms of survival, grade, stage, size of the original tumor, number of endoscopic procedures performed on each patient, recurrence of bladder tumors after transurethral removal, and recurrence of tumors in relation to size during a 5-yr follow-up study.

This report relates to 505 patients followed 5 yr or longer, 410 patients (81%) of whom were treated by transurethral resection of their bladder tumors. The 5-yr gross survival rate of all grades and depths of invasion treated by transurethral resection was 53%; 22% of the 410 patients died of carcinoma within 5 yr, and 25% died of other causes.

The authors note that patients with grade 1 tumors have an 80% 5-yr survival rate; grade 2 tumors, a 39% 5-yr survival rate; and grade 3 and 4 tumors, a 19% 5-yr survival. Patients with tumors infiltrating only the mucosa and submucosa have a 63% 5-yr survival rate, and those with tumors infiltrating into the muscle have a 40% 5-yr survival rate; those with tumors extending through the muscle have a 5% 5-yr survival rate. Patients with demonstrable metastasis also have a 5-yr survival rate of 5%. They note that patients with tumors less than 1 cm have an 80% 5-yr survival rate; between 1 cm and 3 cm, a 59% 5-yr survival rate; between 3 cm and 6 cm, a 44% 5-yr survival rate; and greater than 6 cm, a 31% 5-yr survival rate. Only 41% of all patients required only 1 transurethral resection, while 26% required 2 transurethral resections and 15% required 3 transurethral resections. Six percent of patients required more than six transurethral resections. In other words, nearly 60% of patients had 1 or more repeated transurethral resections for removal of recurrent tumor. Sixty-five percent of tumors 1 cm or less did not recur in 5 yr.

The authors conclude that 80% of bladder tumors can be controlled better by adequate endoscopic surgery and persistent follow-up study than by any other method and that there is a significant correlation between survival rate and three factors: grade of malignancy, depth of invasion, and size of tumor. Patients with tumors of low-grade malignancy, shallow invasion, and small size have longer survival rates than those with tumors of large size, high grade of malignancy, or deep invasion. They stress that removal of all tumor, including the bladder wall 1 cm beyond the tumor, and follow-up cystoscopy at 3-mo to 1-yr intervals are the chief factors in control of bladder tumors by endoscopic surgery.

Creevy CD: Preventing stimulation of the obturator nerve during transurethral resection. Trans Am Assoc Genitourin Surg 60:90, 1968

In this paper numerous methods of preventing the obturator nerve reflex are reviewed, including reversing the polarity of the power supply, substituting another unit, and myoneural blockage with D-tubocuraraine or succinylcholine chloride. Other methods of preventing this reflex consist of transprostatic and transvesical injection of a local anesthetic agent.

The author describes his preferred method, employing an O'Conor sheath and a spinal puncture needle that is long enough to reach beneath the trigone and adjacent lateral walls and thick enough to be palpable through the rectal wall. The needle is guided by a finger in the rectum and infiltrates the tissues around the posterior three quarters of the prostate and the trigone and contiguous bladder with 0.5% lidocaine (Xylocaine) containing 1:100,000 epinephrine (60 ml will usually be adequate). Resumption of resection can be commenced within a few moments.

The author concludes that periprostatic and subvesical infiltration with lidocaine and epinephrine abolishes muscular contractions resulting from inadevertent stimulation of the obturator nerve during transurethral resection.

Gottfries A, Nilsson S, Sundin T, et al: Late effects of transurethral resection of bladder tumors at the ureteric orifice. Scand J Urol Nephrol 9:32, 1975

The authors report their experience of transurethral resection of bladder tumor involving resection of low-grade tumors at or near the ureteric orifice. The mean follow-up time was 12 mo and included excretory urography, voiding cystourography, and creatinine determination. The excretory urograms indicated that the ureters on the operated side were significantly wider than those on the control side. Vesicoureteric reflux was found in 9 patients (48%). Ureteral catheterization with a 5 French catheter revealed that all patients could accommodate this catheter and thus no severe stenosis was found in any patients. Four patients had positive urine cultures postoperatively, three of whom had vesicoureteric reflux.

The authors call attention to the possibility that in patients with reflux and recurrence of bladder tumors, there is a risk that the tumor cells might be refluxed into the ureter and renal pelvis with possible implantation of tumor. They conclude that use of tube-cutting current with minimum coagulation carries a small risk of stenosis and therefore recommend that tube-cutting current with minimum coagulation be used during resection and coagulation in the areas of the ureteric orifices.

Jewett HJ: Conservative treatment vs. radical surgery for superficial cancer of the bladder. JAMA 206:2720, 1968

In this paper the author notes that there are at least five general contraindications to transurethral resection as definitive treatment of bladder tumors: (1) lack of complete and easy accessibility of the tumor to the resectoscope, (2) poorly differentiated cancer, especially with lymphatic permeation, (3) evidence of deep invasion of the muscularis with tumor cells, probably beyond the region of the loop, (4) rapid recurrences of multiple, extensive tumors with cells becoming less differentiated, and (5) invasion of the stroma of the prostate gland. The author stresses that the transurethral resection must include at least part of the tumor, with some of the underlying vesical wall for biospy purposes.

Green LF, Yalowitz PA: The advisability of concomitant transurethral excision of vesical neoplasms and prostatic hyperplasia. J Urol 107:445, 1972

This report concerns a study of two groups of patients: the first group containing 100 men who had undergone simultaneous transurethral resection of vesical tumors and transurethral resection of the prostate, and the second group contained 100 men, used as control patients, who underwent transurethral resection of the bladder tumor only.

In both groups the bladder tumors were predominantly low-grade transitional cell tumors. Results indicate that the incidence of recurrent vesical tumor, irrespective of the site of recurrence for both groups, was 54% in each group. The authors believe that patients in each group who had a tendency to form recurrent tumors in the bladder were more likely to have recurrences in the prostatic urethra. They believe that the recurrence of the tumor in the prostatic urethra is a manifestation of a propensity of certain epithelial membranes, vesical or prostatic, to develop neoplastic changes and not the result of implantation of tumor cells on a raw prostatic bed.

Staehler G, Hofstetter A: Transurethral laser irradiation of urinary bladder tumors. Eur Urol 5:64, 1979

The authors report their experience using the Neodym-YAG laser in 39 patients with bladder tumors. In this patient population, 83 tumors were treated. Most of the patients had papillomas, grade 0, and transitional epithelial carcinoma, grade 1. There were 8 patients with grade 2 transitional cell tumors and 6 patients with grade 3 tumors. Spinal or general anesthesia was used in all cases. The authors indicate that in contrast with transurethral resection of bladder tumors, transurethral laser irradiation does not require maximum relaxation, and 4 days after laser irradiation the necrotic tumors had either fallen off or could be stroked off instrumentally.

They believe that laser irradiation will obtain a secure place in the transurethral treatment of bladder tumors and indicate that a combination of transurethral resection and irradiation of the tumor bed for destruction of urethral tumor cell nests appears especially useful. They stress that laser therapy cannot replace transurethral resection but can complement it, inasmuch as laser irradiation therapy leads to lack of bleeding and deep necrotizing of the bladder wall without danger of perforation and allows for the insertion of an in-dwelling catheter for only a short time with a lower danger of nosocomial infection.

England HR, Anderson JD, Minasian H, et al: The therapeutic application of hyperthermia in the bladder. Br J Urol 47:849, 1976

The authors report on ten patients treated with hyperthermia. In all patients urinary diversion by ileal conduit was performed. Three patients had hyperthermic treatment for T-4 tumor palliation using the Helmstein balloon technique. Four patients had hyper-thermic treatment for intractable hemorrhage and T-1 tumor using an irrigation system, and two patients had hyperthermic treatment for contracted bladder and T-1 tumor after having received between 5500 and 6000 rad. The temperature ranged between 50°C and 80°C to 90°C, and the time ranged between a few to 5 min and 120 min. The system of hyperthermic bladder irrigation employs the use of saline, a pump, a heater, a thermocouple from the bladder, and monitor.

The authors stress that this technique is not regarded as a substitute for cystectomy in the usual patient but indicate that it seems to offer great advantages for certain groups of patients: (1) where more conservative methods have failed, it appears to be a safer method of controlling hemorrhage than cystectomy, (2) when patients refuse cystectomy, irrigation with hot saline may provide a way of destroying their tumor without interfering with potency, and (3) in selected T-4 patients in the hopes of achieving palliation. The authors have not noted any visceral damage, although one patient developed thermal injury to the urethra.

The authors conclude by noting that their experience suggests that irrigation with saline at 80°C for 10 min will stop the bleeding and destroy epithelial and muscle layers without causing cell injury or systemic disturbance. Furthermore, they indicate that this technique may be preferable to cystectomy in certain poor-risk patients or in those who refuse cystectomy for fear of impotence.

Hirose K, Seto T, Takayasu H: Re-evaluation of hydrostatic pressure treatment for malignant bladder lesions. J Urol 118:762, 1977

In this paper the authors review their experience with 50 cases of bladder cancer treated with the hydrostatic pressure technique (Helmstein procedure). These patients were divided into three groups: Group 1—12 patients in whom a dramatic response was noted, wherein the tumors disappeared completely within 1 mo of treatment and no recurrent lesions were noted throughout the follow-up period; Group 2—20 patients in whom a response was satisfactory, characterized by marked regression and partial necrosis of tumor nests immediately after treatment (subsequent transurethral resection of the tumor achieved a tumor-free status); Group 3—18 patients with fairly good response, in whom only slight regression of the tumors were noted but clinical size and symptoms improved markedly. Radical cystectomy followed the hydrostatic pressure treatment in seven of these patients.

The authors note that serious complications were not encountered but indicate that in 50 patients treated a total of 70 times 23 fissures were observed in the bladder walls. They note that tumors around the ureteral orifices showed a marked resistance to therapy and that tumors on the anterior bladder wall were also less responsive but indicate that most of these patients had prior open operations. They studied the results of tuberculin skin tests in patients with bladder cancer and the preoperative reaction of tuberculin skin tests versus effects of hydrostatic pressure treatment. In addition, they studied lymphocyte counts of peripheral blood in the preoperative phase and carefully analyzed histo-pathologic findings of transurethral resection.

The authors summarize their findings by indicating that this technique is encouraging when (1) single or multiple papillary tumors were not located around the ureteral orifice, with a presumed depth of tumor infiltration within T-2, (2) there was no history of open operation, (3) there was observed activity of immunologic surveillance, for example, a positive reaction to a tuberculin test, and (4) management of anesthesia was satisfactory. They stress that hydrostatic pressure therapy is not palliative for far-advanced tumors but should be considered the first choice for new patients beyond the scope of transurethral operation and when indications in tumor and host condition appear satisfied.

68

CURRENT STATE OF CLASSIFICATION AND STAGING OF BLADDER CANCER*

Donald G. Skinner

Division of Urology, UCLA School of Medicine, Los Angeles, California 90024

Cancer Research 37, 2838-2842, August 1977

SUMMARY—The most important determinant for treatment as well as prognosis is the presence or absence of muscle invasion as determined by the histopathological material obtained by a properly performed biopsy. Histological grade of the tumor is also important inasmuch as high-grade tumors are usually always associated with invasion, whereas low-grade tumors are usually superficial. The presence or absence of carcinoma *in situ* is also an important histological feature and may be diagnosed with increasing accuracy by improved cytopathological techniques.

The TNM system, although useful in the accurate staging of definitive cystectomy specimens, offers little to clinical management. The inherent and significant problems of clinical staging and difficulties in attempting to correlate presenting pathology with correct management planning persist. What is needed, in my opinion, is simplification of clinical staging, elimination of stages that cannot be accurately determined by existing methods, and better identification of criteria for treatment planning.

In 1922, Broders[2] noted that malignant tumors of the bladder epithelium varied in behavior and prognosis according to their cellular activity, and he subsequently formulated a method of grading based on the percentage of undifferentiated epithelium. Since Broders' initial observation, a considerable volume of information and knowledge has accumulated concerning various histological features and their relationship to prognosis. Nevertheless, there has been little effort to formulate a clinical plan of management on the basis of these histological features in attempting to alter the natural history of bladder cancer.

Various histological criteria such as cell types, patterns, and grades have been well described in previous studies.[4,6,13,17] Jewett and Strong[9] were the first to

* Presented at the National Bladder Cancer Conference, November 28 to December 1, 1976, Miami Beach, Fla.

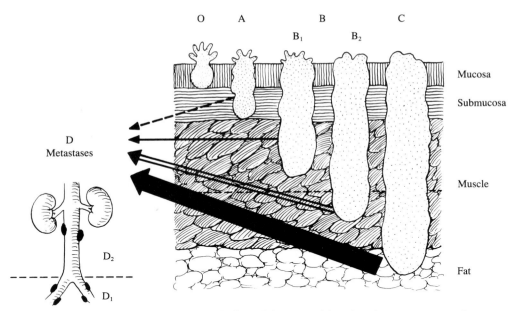

Fig. 1. Schematic illustration of the Marshall modification of the classification system of Jewett and Strong. *Arrows*, propensity for metastases with increasing depth of invasion.

emphasize the significance of pathological stage relating to prognosis. From an autopsy study they noted that, when tumors of the bladder were confined to the mucosa (Stage A), there was little likelihood of concomitant lymph node or disseminated blood-borne metastatic disease. However, 74% of bladder tumors that had penetrated the muscularis (Stage C) were associated with lymph node or disseminated blood-borne metastases. In the group of tumors infiltrating but confined to the muscularis (Stage B), metastases were present in 12%.[9] In a later publication, based on 80 cases, Jewett[8] suggested the clinical segregation of the Stage B category into superficial (Stage B_1) and deep (Stage B_2), stating that "regardless of histologic pattern and degree of malignancy, [tumors] which have infiltrated less than half way through the muscularis usually are still confined to the bladder wall and tumors which have infiltrated more deeply usually have spread beyond."[8] This basic premise has resulted in a division of the initial staging system of Jewett and Strong, further modified by Marshall in 1952 to include Stage 0, indicating those tumors not infiltrating the lamina propria as well as including *in situ* or intraepithelial carcinoma. In addition, Marshall included "those cancers in which, although there [had] been biopsy proof of the existence of the tumor within 30 days of surgical removal of the definitive specimen, no tumor can be found microscopically in that specimen."[10] Figure 1 illustrates the current version of the Marshall modification on the staging system used exten-

sively in the United States, that of Jewett and Strong. Although the initial staging system was based on pathological material, its main use is in clinical staging with its relation to prognosis and indication for treatment alternatives.

In 1950, the Union Internationale Contre le Cancer (UICC) appointed a Committee on Tumor Nomenclature and Statistics to develop general definitions of local extension of malignant tumors and, in 1954, established a special Committee on Clinical Stage Classification and Applied Statistics under the chairmanship of Dr. P. Denoix of France. The charge of this committee was to "pursue studies in the field and to extend the general techniques of classification to cancer at all sites."[24] Between 1954 and 1967 this committee developed and outlined the general rules of the TNM system and proposed a classification system of cancer at 23 sites, none involving the genitourinary system. The TNM system is based on the assessment of: (*a*) the extent of the primary tumor (T), (*b*) the condition of the regional nodes (N), and (*c*) the absence or presence of distant metastases (M).

The stated objectives are to: (*a*) aid the clinician in the planning of treatment, (*b*) give more indication of prognosis, (*c*) assist in an evaluation of treatment results, (*d*) facilitate the exchange of information between treatment centers, and (*d*) contribute to the continuing investigation of human cancer.[24] Essentially, it is a universal system designed to provide a method of conveying

1946 Jewett-Strong	1952 Jewett	1952 Marshall		1974 Clinical	TNM Patho-logical
		O	No tumor definitive specimen	T_0	P_0
			Carcinoma-in-situ	TIS	PIS
A	A		Papillary tumor's invasion	T_1	P_1
		A	Invasion lamina propria		
B	B_1	B_1	Superficial	T_2	P_2
			Muscle invasion		
	B_2	B_2	Deep		
C	C	C	Invasion perivesical fat	T_{3A} T_{3B}	P_3
		D_1	Invasion continuous viscera	T_{4A}	P_4
			Pelvic nodes	N_{1-3}	
		D_2	Distant metastases	M_1	
			Nodes above aortic bifurcation	N_4	

Fig. 2. Illustration comparing the original classification of Jewett and Strong with modifications by Jewett and Marshall and with the TNM system.

one's experience to others without ambiguity. In 1974, the UICC and its committee on TNM Classification, chaired by Dr. Bridget Van derWerf-Messing of the Netherlands, classified cancer of the bladder, prostate, kidney, and testis according to the TNM system.[24] As in other sites, this classification proposal will be subjected to a trial of 5 years, 1975 to 1979. Therefore, the classifications of these tumors of urological sites are not definitive and may be adjusted by further experience and input by groups of urological oncologists acting through the United States representative to the UICC, Dr. F. K. Mostofi. Nevertheless, the classification represents the 1st potentially workable classification of cancer of the various genitourinary sites acceptable to an international group (see "Appendix").

Figure 2 compares the original system of Jewett and Strong with Marshall's modification and the TNM system. Several obvious advantages of this TNM system are apparent. (a) Clinical (T) and histopathological (P) criteria use different letter symbols for comparable stages, thus avoiding confusion in interpretation of results of therapy. (b) TIS has been introduced as a specific entity for carcinoma *in situ,* and it defines the lesion as "anaplasia of surface epithelium without the formation of papillary structures and without infiltration."[24] This definition and classification is an important contribution to bladder staging and should help alleviate much of the current confusion over definition of this lesion.

In Marshall's modification, carcinoma *in situ* was grouped with papillary tumors that did not involve the lamina propria as well as the definitive surgical specimen in which there was no microscopic tumor, even though there had been biopsy-proven tissue present during the previous 30 days.[10,11] (c) Stage T_1 or histopathological stage P_1 represents all papillary tumors not involving muscle, thus relegating the Stages O and P_0 to no microscopic evidence of tumor in the definitive specimen

and T_0, being a clinical stage, to no residual tumor on biopsy.

The TNM system also adds N and M groups for classification of those tumors associated with metastases, to either regional nodes (N) or distant sites (M). These distinctions are of little practical importance because of serious limitations in our ability to detect early metastases as well as our inability to influence prognosis once gross metastases are apparent.

The disadvantages of the TNM system are that it perpetuates the apparent bad features of the Marshall modification of the Jewett-Strong classification, simply substitutes different letters for similar stages, and does not meet its 1st stated objective, to "aid the clinician in the planning of treatment." The primary weakness of the Marshall-Jewett-Strong system was Jewett's segregation of muscle invasion into superficial (less than half way) (B_1), and deep (more than half way) (B_2). This modification, recommended by Jewett in 1952, was based on 80 patients and has been adopted by others, including the TNM system.[9] In the 1956 Symposium on Bladder Cancer, Whitmore and Marshall[23] attempted to further group patients into superficial (OAB_1) and deep (B_2C) in an effort to improve accuracy of staging, initiation of treatment, and prevention of progression.

This grouping was based on Jewett's report in 1952 that superficial and deep tumors could be segregated by means of a properly performed bimanual pelvic examination and biopsy specimen.[9] A palpable mass or induration with histological evidence of tumor in the muscle almost always indicated deep penetration unless the induration disappeared following transurethral resection of the tumor growth. If no induration could be felt, it was most probable that the tumor was superficial. Subsequent reports by Marshall,[11] Marshall and Whitmore,[12] and Whitmore and Marshall[23] demonstrated that the preoperative estimation for this 1 criterion was 81%

accurate by this method. The simple consideration of these observations was the ability to determine whether or not the tumor was deeply infiltrating, and these investigators demonstrated a direct relation to prognosis, inasmuch as approximately 50% of patients with superficial tumors survived 5 years after cystectomy compared to a 5-year survival of only 15% for those with deeply infiltrating tumors. Marshall further demonstrated a clinical relationship between the histological grade of the malignancy and its depth of invasion.[10] He noted that, in general, low-grade tumors were encountered in superficial stages and high-grade tumors were associated with deep invasion, and that deviation from this observation was observed in only 7 of 104 consecutive cystectomy specimens.[10] Thus the grade of the tumor became an important consideration in the classification of bladder carcinoma according to stage.

On the other hand, has the test of time borne out the importance of distinguishing between superficial muscle invasion and deep invasion, or has this segregation increased the clinical or histopathological staging error? In 1975, Richie et al.[21] pointed out in a group of 140 patients that any degree of muscle infiltration significantly influenced survival compared to tumors without muscle infiltration or those penetrating into the perivesical fat (Table 1). Similar findings can be found in the published reports of other investigators (Table 2). The

depth of muscle infiltration thus becomes far less important than the significance of any degree of muscle infiltration, and the latter can be determined with far greater accuracy than our efforts to assess depth. If the major goals of a classification system are to aid the clinician in the planning of treatment as well as to give indication of prognosis, current evidence would support the contention that a properly performed biopsy indicating the presence or absence of muscle invasion as well as the grade of the tumor remains the most important determinant of clinical staging, and that further efforts to assess depth of penetration or extension of the primary tumor have resulted in increasing error and confusion over management.

For example, any classification system is only as good as the existing methodology in determining extent of the local tumor. Numerous techniques, including i.v. pyelography, pelvic arteriography, triple-contrast cystography, and ultrasound, have been used to assess clinical stage before therapy. Results of the National Cooperative Bladder Cancer Study, however, indicate that accuracy of clinical staging according to the Marshall modification of the Jewett-Strong system approaches only 50% and that the main error was in assessing depth of infiltration (Table 3). It is unlikely that computerized axial tomography will significantly alter this error, although it may improve our ability to detect early soft tissue metastases.

Recently, considerable enthusiasm has been expressed for the use of bilateral pedal lymphangiography in detecting the early presence of pelvic or retroperitoneal nodal metastases from bladder and prostatic cancer. Unfortunately, even under the best of circumstances this examination has such a margin of error that its use has only increased the error of clinical staging vis-à-vis pathological staging and further confused the clinician attempting to plan management. J. Schmidt (personal communication) has recently reported a prospective study of 40 consecutive patients undergoing bilateral pedal lymphangiography followed by surgical staging and has

TABLE 1. Pathological Stage and 5-Year Survival for 140 Patients Treated by Cystectomy

Stage	5-Year Survival (%)	
O–A	78.6	
B$_1$	39.9 All B, 40.0	$p < 0.01$
B$_2$	40.4	
C	19.7	
D	6.2	

Note the nearly identical survival for Stage B$_1$ and Stage B$_2$ and the statistical significance between survival of those patients with tumor confined to the mucosa compared to those with muscle invasion ($p < 0.01$) [Data from Richie et al. (21)].

TABLE 2. Recorded 5-Year Survival (Percentage) According to Stage

Treatment	Series	Year of Series	Stage				
			O–A	B$_1$	B$_2$	All B	C
Transurethral resection	Flocks (7)	1951	130/168 (77)			68/142 (47)	
Transurethral resection	Barnes (1)	1967	146/233 (63)			46/114 (40)	3/57 (5)
Segmental resection	Riches (20)	1960	7/12 (58)			16/44 (36)	0/6 (0)
Radiotherapy	Miller (16)	1971		10/39 (26)	12/40 (30)	22/79 (28)	5/32 (16)
Cystectomy	Cordonnier (3)	1974	31/67 (46)	24/46 (52)	12/30 (40)	36/76 (47)	11/36 (31)
Cystectomy	Richie et al. (21)	1975	43/54 (79)	14/36 (40)	9/22 (40)	23/58 (40)	4/21 (20)
Cystectomy	Pearse et al. (17)	1975		7/14 (50)	5/12 (42)	12/26 (42)	2/15 (13)
Cystectomy	Prout (19)	1976		16/51 (31)	19/61 (31)	35/112 (31)	5/24 (21)
Total			357/534 (67)	71/186 (38)	57/165 (35)	258/651 (40)	30/191 (16)

Note the similarity in survival between Stages B$_1$ and B$_2$, both substantially different from Stage O–A and C.

TABLE 3. Bladder Cancer Staging Error (Percentage): Clinical (T) versus Pathological (P)

Preoperative Stage	Understage T < P		Overstage T > P	
	Surgery Only	Preoperative Radiotherapy	Surgery Only	Preoperative Radiotherapy
B$_1$	44	35	23	49
B$_2$	48	26	18	51
All B	46	31	20	50
C	20	0	24	74
B$_2$-C	40	18	20	58
Total error	42	26	21	54

documented a 50% error in the ability of lymphangiography to predict either the presence or absence of nodal metastases in patients with prostatic carcinoma. It would appear, therefore, that this test should be relegated to history in the management of bladder cancer, and patients should be spared the burden of the expense associated with its use.

Therefore the TNM system, although clarifying some of the ambiguous portions of the Jewett-Strong system, perpetuates the problems. Basically, except for TIS and T$_1$, the TNM system defines stage according to the A, B, C, D method of Jewett and Strong, simply changing the letters and clearly identifying the clinical from the histopathological staging.

Although accurate pathological staging is important in assessing the results of therapy, the accuracy of clinical staging is probably not as important to the patient as the ability of the clinician to group those tumors requiring aggressive therapy *vis-à-vis* those satisfactorily managed by more conservative methods. In this area there has been progress, and we hope the cytopathologist will offer further advances.

The presence and natural history of carcinoma *in situ* have become an extremely important contribution to our understanding of bladder cancer.[14,15,22,25] Current evidence suggests that the presence of carcinoma *in situ* in association with overt bladder cancer is ominous and should encourage the clinician to aggressive therapy. Carcinoma *in situ* is usually associated with a high-grade overt tumor or may precede high-grade bladder cancer, and evidence suggests that any degree of invasion associated with a high-grade tumor signifies an ominous prognosis unless aggressive therapy is initiated.[22]

Thus it would appear that the clinician needs simplification of staging rather than further confusion and fragmentation as offered by the TNM system. The original proposal of Jewett and Strong for an A, B, C system combined with histological grade and the presence or absence of carcinoma *in situ* would increase the accuracy of staging, offer definite criteria for treatment, and closely correlate with prognosis.

The important points that should be emphasized include the following. Staging of localized bladder cancer should depend primarily on the histopathological material obtained by biopsy. Important observations are grade, presence or absence of muscle invasion, and presence or absence of carcinoma *in situ*. Carcinoma *in situ* is determined by random biopsies as well as by assessment of the mucosa immediately adjacent to the primary tumor. If muscle invasion is obvious at the time of biopsy, on the basis of endoscopic appearance and/or bimanual examination, sufficient biopsy to document invasion and determine grade may be all that is required to indicate aggressive therapy, and complete resection is not necessary and may be detrimental. Dretler *et al.*[4] reported that survival of those patients with extensive localized lesions was better if only a biopsy was made for diagnosis rather than an attempt at resection, suggesting that resection may play a detrimental role by causing tumor dissemination.

Once the diagnosis of a high-grade or muscle-invading tumor has been established, efforts should be made to rule out metastatic disease. Appropriate studies should include chest X-ray, bone scan with correlated bone X-rays of any suspicious areas, and biochemical liver function studies with radioisotope liver scan performed only if the liver function studies are abnormal. If there is no evidence of metastatic disease, definitive therapy should be entertained. Other diagnostic efforts to stage the localized primary tumor, including pelvic arteriography, bilateral pedal lymphangiography, and triple-contrast cystography, offer little in the way of significant changes in treatment plan and burden the patient with expensive tests of primarily academic interest.

In conclusion, the most important determinant for treatment as well as prognosis is the presence or absence of muscle invasion as determined by the histopathological material obtained by a properly performed biopsy. Histological grade of the tumor is also important, inasmuch as high-grade tumors are usually always associated with invasion, whereas low-grade tumors are usually superficial. The presence or absence of carcinoma *in situ* is also an important histological feature and may be diagnosed with increased accuracy by improved cytopathological techniques.

The TNM system, although useful in the accurate staging of definitive cystectomy specimens, offers little to clinical management. The inherent and significant problems of clinical staging and difficulties in attempting to correlate presenting pathology with correct management planning persist. What is needed, in my opinion, is simplification of clinical staging, elimination of stages that cannot be accurately determined by existing methods, and better identification of criteria for treatment planning.

APPENDIX

The TNM System for classification of bladder cancer follows (24).

1. The classification applies only to epithelial tumors. Papilloma is excluded, but such cases may be listed under the category G_0.
2. There must be histological or cytological verification of the disease.
3. The following are the minimum requirements for assessment of the T. N. and M categories.

T categories: Clinical examination, urography, cystoscopy, bimanual examination under adequate anesthesia and biopsy or transurethral resection of the tumor (if indicated) before definitive treatment.

N categories: Clinical examination, lymphography, and urography.

M categories: Clinical examination, chest radiography, and biochemical testing. In the more advanced primary tumors or when clinical suspicion warrants, radiographic or isotope studies should be done.

If these requirements cannot be met the symbols T_x, N_x, or M_x will be used.

TNM CLASSIFICATION

T = *Primary tumor.*
The suffix (m) may be added to the appropriate T category to indicate multiple tumors, thus: $T_{2(m)}$.

TIS   Carcinoma *in situ*. Definite anaplasia of surface epithelium without the formation of papillary structures and without infiltration.

T_x The minimum requirements to assess fully the extent of the primary tumor cannot be met.

T_0 No evidence of primary tumor.

T_1 On bimanual examination a freely mobile mass may be felt. This should not be felt after complete transurethral resection of the lesion and/or, microscopically, the tumor does not extend beyond the lamina propria.

T_2 On bimanual examination the indurated bladder wall is mobile. There is no residual induration after complete transurethral resection of the lesion and/or there is microscopic invasion of superficial muscle.

T_3 On bimanual examination induration or a nodular mobile mass is palpable in the bladder wall that persists after transurethral resection of the exophytic portion of the lesion and/or there is microscopic invasion of deep muscle or extension through the bladder wall.
T_{3a} Invasion of deep muscle.
T_{3b} Extension through the bladder wall.

T_4 Tumor fixed or invading neighboring structures and/or there is microscopic evidence of such involvement.
T_{4a} Tumor invading prostate, uterus, or vagina.
T_{4b} Tumor fixed to the pelvic wall and/or infiltrating abdominal wall.

N = *Regional and juxtaregional lymph nodes.*
The regional lymph nodes are the pelvic nodes below the bifurcation of the common iliac arteries. The juxtaregional lymph nodes are the inguinal nodes, the common iliac, and para-aortic nodes.

N_x The minimum requirements to assess the regional lymph nodes cannot be met.

N_0 No evidence of involvement of regional lymph nodes.

N_1 Involvement of a single homolateral regional lymph node.

N_2 Involvement of contralateral or bilateral or multiple regional lymph nodes.

N_3 There is a fixed mass on the pelvic wall with a free space between this and the tumor.

N_4 Involvement of juxtaregional lymph nodes.

Subsequent information regarding the histological assessment of the regional lymph nodes may be added to the clinical N category by means of negative and positive signs, thus: $N-$ for nodes with no microscopic evidence of metastasis, or $N+$ for nodes with microscopic evidence of metastases (*e.g.,* $N_{1-}N_{0+}$).

M = *Distant metastases.*

M_x The minimum requirements to assess the presence of distant metastases cannot be met.

M_0 No evidence of distant metastases.

M_1 Distant metastases present.

M_{1a} Evidence of occult metastases based on biochemical and/or other tests.

M_{1b} Single metastasis in a single-organ site.

M_{1c} Multiple metastases in a single-organ site.

M_{1d} Metastases in multiple-organ sites.

Note: The location of metastases should be specified. The lymph nodes beyond the regional and juxtaregional nodes and bone are regarded as single-organ sites.

P = *Histopathological categories.*
Assessment of the P categories is based on evidence derived from surgical operation and histopathology; that is, where tissue other than biopsy is available for examination. The suffix (m) may be added to the appropriate P category to indicate multiple tumors, thus $P_{2(m)}$.

PIS   Preinvasive carcinoma (carcinoma *in situ*).

P_x The extent of invasion cannot be assessed.

P_0 No tumor found on examination of specimen.

P_1 Tumor not extending beyond the lamina propria.

P$_2$ Tumor with infiltration of superficial muscle (not more than half way through muscle coat) or infiltration of perivesical tissue.

P$_3$ Tumor with infiltration of deep muscle (more than half way through the muscle coat) or infiltration of perivesical tissue.

P$_4$ Tumor with infiltration of prostate or other extravesical structures.

G = *Histopathological grading*.

G$_x$ Grade cannot be assessed.

G$_0$ No evidence of anaplasia (*i.e.,* papilloma).

G$_1$ Low-grade malignancy.

G$_2$ Medium-grade malignancy.

G$_3$ High-grade malignancy.

L = *Invasion of lymphatics*.

L$_x$ Lymphatic invasion cannot be assessed.

L$_0$ No lymphatic invasion.

L$_1$ Superficial lymphatics invaded.

L$_2$ Deep lymphatics invaded.

Note: The histopathological categories and grading conform to the recommendations of WHO. (See Histological Typing of Urinary Bladder Tumors, Geneva, WHO, 1973.)

Stage grouping

No stage grouping is at present recommended.

REFERENCES

1. Barnes, R. W. Endoscopic Surgical Treatment of Bladder Tumors. Urol Digest 6:13–15, 1967

2. Broders, A. C. Epithelioma of the Genitourinary Organs. Ann Surg 75:574–580, 1922

3. Cordonnier, J. J. Simple Cystectomy in the Management of Bladder Carcinoma. Arch Surg 108:190–191, 1974

4. Dretler, S. P., Ragsdale, B. D., and Leadbetter, W. F. The Value of Pelvic Lymphadenectomy in the Surgical Treatment of Bladder Cancer. J Urol 109:414–416, 1973

5. Dukes, C. E. The Institute of Urology Scheme for the Histological Classification of Epithelial Tumos of the Bladder. In: Wallace (ed.), Neoplastic Disease at Various Sites: Tumors of the Bladder, Vol 2, pp 105–115. Edinburgh: Livingstone, 1959

6. Eposti, P. L., and Zajicek, J. Grading of Transitional Cell Neoplasms of the Urinary Bladder from Smears of Bladder Washings: A Critical Review of 326 Tumors. Intern Acad Cytol 16:529–537, 1972

7. Flocks, R. H. Treatment of Patients with Carcinoma of the Bladder. J Am Med Assoc 145:295–301, 1951

8. Jewett, H. J. Carcinoma of the Bladder: Influence of Depth of Infiltration on the 5-Year Results Following Complete Extirpation of the Primary Growth. J Urol 67:672–676, 1952

9. Jewett, H. J., and Strong, G. H. Infiltrating Carcinoma of the Bladder: Relation of Depth of Penetration of the Bladder Wall to Incidence of Local Extension and Metastases. J Urol 55:366–372, 1946

10. Marshall, V. F. The Relation of the Preoperative Estimate to the Pathologic Demonstration of the Extent of Vesical Neoplasms. J Urol 68:714–723, 1952

11. Marshall, V. F. Symposium on Bladder Tumors: Current Clinical Problems Regarding Bladder Tumors. Cancer 9:543–550, 1956

12. Marshall, V. F., and Whitmore, W. F., Jr. The Surgical Treatment of Cancers of the Urinary Bladder. Cancer 9:609–619, 1956

13. McGovern, V. J. The Histological Classification of Bladder Tumors. Pathology 1:255–264, 1969

14. Melicow, M. M. Histological Study of Vesical Urothelium Intervening between Gross Neoplasms in Total Cystectomy. J Urol 68:261–269, 1952

15. Melicow, M. M., and Hollowell, J. W. Intra-urothelial Cancer Carcinoma *In-Situ,* Bowen's Disease of the Urinary System: Discussion of Thirty Cases. J Urol 68:763–769, 1952

16. Miller, L. S. Clinical Evaluation and Therapy for Urinary Bladder: Radiotherapy. In: Diagnosis and Management of Cancer: Specific Sites, pp 283–290. Chicago: Yearbook Medical Publishers, 1971

17. Pearse, H. O., Pappas, J. T., and Hodges, C. V. Radical Cystectomy for Bladder Cancer: 10-Year Survival. J Urol (in press)

18. Pomerance, A. A Prognostic Index for Carcinoma of Bladder Based on Histopathological Findings in Cystectomy Material. Br J Urol 44:451–458, 1972

19. Prout, G. R., Jr. The Surgical Management of Bladder Carcinoma. Urol Clin North Am 3:149–175, 1976

20. Riches, E. Choice of Treatment in Carcinoma of the Bladder. J Urol 84:472–480, 1960

21. Richie, J. P., Skinner, D. G., and Kaufman, J. J. Radical Cystectomy for Carcinoma of the Bladder: 16 Years Experience. J Urol 113:186–189, 1975

22. Skinner, D. G., Richie, J. P., Cooper, P. H., Waisman, J., and Kaufman, J. J. The Clinical Significance of Carcinoma *In-Situ* of the Urinary Bladder and Its Association with Overt Carcinoma. J Urol 112:68–71, 1974

23. Whitmore, W. F., Jr., and Marshall, V. F. Radical Surgery for Carcinoma of the Urinary Bladder: One Hundred Consecutive Cases Four Years Later. Cancer 9:596–608, 1956

24. Union Internationale Contre le Cancer. TMN Classification of Malignant Tumors. Geneva: Imprimerie G. de Buren S. A., 1974

25. Utz, D. C., Hansah, K. A., and Farrow, G. M. The Plight of the Patient with Carcinoma *In-Situ* of the Bladder. J Urol 103:160–164, 1970

Commentary: Bladder Biopsy in Staging of Carcinoma of the Bladder

Sam D. Graham, Jr. and David F. Paulson

Although Jewett's original description of the clinical staging of transitional cell carcinoma of the bladder has undergone several modifications, it remains the basis for treatment selection. The subsequent modification of Marshall enhances the Jewett classification as a powerful predictor of disease progression and prognosis, directly establishing the relationship between the stage of the disease and the prospective clinical course.

In brief, the classification advocated by Marshall reflects the biologic potential for invasion and extension. Stage A tumors are those carcinomas that do not extend into the muscularis. Stage B_1 tumors are those tumors extending superficially into the muscle. Stage B_2 tumors extend through the muscle but do not invade the perivesical fat, and stage C tumors extend through the perivesical fat. Stage D tumors are distantly metastatic.[1]

Current technology permits the clinician to assess the local anatomic extent and the biologic potential for aggressive behavior of any single transitional cell carcinoma. The traditional value of transurethral staging has been to assist the clinician in assigning a clinical stage for selection of treatment. In vesical carcinoma, as in other tumor systems, regional nodal involvement adversely selected for survival. The inherent value of the Marshall classification is that it reflects the tendency for tumors with a progressive character to be associated with a higher incidence of microscopic regional nodal and distant spread. This classification system, in defining the absence or presence and depth of muscle penetration, predicts the probability of disease outside the margins of a reasonable surgical dissection. The accuracy of clinical staging by transurethral resection is limited by the skill and thoroughness of the clinician. Before transurethral resection of the bladder, a bimanual examination should be done under anesthesia with attention to any induration of the bladder wall. The resection then is begun. To proceed, first resect the tumor flush with the bladder wall. Next, remove the bladder muscle from beneath the tumor. Submit the two specimens separately. The first specimen will assess the grade of the tumor, and the second will determine the depth of penetration into the muscle. Following the resection of all visible tumor, perform a repeat bimanual examination. If there was no induration on the preresection bimanual examination, then the tumor probably is stage A or possibly early stage B_1. If induration was present initially but disappeared following the transurethral resection, the tumor is clinically a Stage B_1. If, however, the induration persists following resection of the tumor, then suspect either a clinical stage B_2 or possibly a stage C tumor.[2,3] Recent studies have questioned whether there are true survival differences between superficially invasive and deeply invasive disease, a query that may be obscured by inaccuracies in determining the depth of invasion.[4] However, as postmortem studies have shown a higher incidence of distant spread with deep muscle invasion; the clinician should consider the deeply invasive tumors to have a poorer prognosis.

The value of transurethral resection in assessing the absence or presence and depth of muscle invasion is not so much to direct the surgeon to select conservative or radical surgery, but to permit him to predict the outcome of treatment intervention selected to achieve local disease control.

Recently, the role of transurethral resection in assessing the biologic hazard of low-stage transitional cell carcinoma has been enhanced with recognition of the adverse impact of associated carcinoma in situ, loss of blood group antigens from the tumor cells, or the appearance of chromosomal abnormalities in the tumor cells themselves. Effective treatment decisions require that the surgeon be able to evaluate the potential for the tumor to recur or invade. It is now recommended that biopsies of mucosa be taken both adjacent to and distant from the primary tumor. The demonstration of carcinoma in situ adjacent to a low-stage, low-grade transitional cell carcinoma predicts recurrence with invasion in over 70% of patients so identified.[5-8] Whether these patients should be subjected to early radical cystectomy remains a point of considerable debate. Lange and others have shown that patients whose low-grade tumors retain their blood group antigens will experience future invasion only 5% of the time.[9-11] Conversely, patients whose tumors have lost the blood antigens will develop invasion 80% of the time. Chromosomal analysis of cells of the resected tumor can predict recurrence or invasion. If the tumor has a normal diploid chromosomal pattern, there tends to be no invasion. However, if the tumor should tetraploid or polyploid nuclear chromatin, ring, or other chromosomes, the recurrence frequency will be 90%. The impact of these biologic predictors of tumor aggression remains in debate. Associated carcinoma in situ does not demand a cystectomy but should urge segregation of that patient into a high-risk category. Carcinoma in situ adjacent to a tumor selected for partial cystectomy is a contraindication to segmental cystectomy, and carcinoma in situ at the bladder neck and prostatic urethra at the time of selection for radical cystectomy urges a simultaneous urethrectomy. Other than in those specific instances, the necessity of extended surgical intervention when the biologic predictors are indicative of future recurrence and invasion is not absolute.

The clinical staging of transitional cell tumor by transurethral resection aids in treatment selection by permitting the surgeon to assess preoperatively the potential salvage value of his assigned treatment and to weigh the potential adverse impact of treatment assignment against those survival benefits. The Marshall classification, with its segregation of depth of penetration of the tumor, reflects the intrinsic aggressive nature of any given tumor and its propensity for metastatic spread.

Transurethral resection does have a place in the clinical staging of carcinoma of the bladder and remains the cornerstone of treatment selection in patients with transitional cell carcinoma of the bladder.

ANNOTATED BIBLIOGRAPHY

Marshall VF: The relation of the preoperative estimate to the pathologic demonstration of the extent of vesical neoplasms. J Urol 68:714, 1952

This is the classic article relating the stage of the disease to the ultimate prognosis of the patient. This proposed staging system has formed the basis for subsequent reports relating stage of disease to prognosis.

Skinner DG: Current state of classification in staging of bladder cancer. Cancer Res 37:2838, 1977

This article is a more recent update of the article by Marshall. In review of 140 patients at the UCLA School of Medicine, the single most powerful predictor of ultimate prognosis and patient survival was the invasion of muscle. The determination of muscle invasion was performed on biopsy material. A second finding in this paper is that the histologic grade of the tumor is also important, since high-grade tumors were usually associated with invasion and low-grade tumors were usually superficial. Carcinoma in situ was found to be an important histologic feature in this series. The author concludes that the Marshall modification of the Jewett system of staging tumors is perhaps better than the TNM system in that it is simpler and eliminates stages that could not be "accurately determined by existing methods."

Schmidt JD, Weinstein SH: Pitfalls in clinical staging of bladder tumors. Urol Clin North Am 3:107, 1976

The authors discuss the various methods of clinical staging and the history of clinical staging of bladder cancer. Several articles are reviewed, as is their own experience in the accuracy of clinical staging. A significant number of patients are upstaged pathologically. The percentage of upstaging ranges from 34% to 50% and the inaccuracy increases with the higher clinical stages. Methods of clinical staging are discussed; the most significant method is fractionated transurethral biopsy and bimanual examination. The authors favor the TNM system because it is more exact and allows standardization of the staging systems in the world literature.

Bowles WT, Cordonnier JJ: Total cystectomy for carcinoma of the bladder. J Urol 90:731, 1963

The authors review 73 patients who have undergone total cystectomy and ileal conduit diversion for carcinoma of the bladder. The overall survival rate is 41.2%, and it is directly correlated to the stage. The authors conclude that cystectomy is indeed a worthwhile procedure, but it should not be considered in those patients with advanced disease.

Althausen AF, Prout GR, Daly JJ: Non-invasive papillary carcinoma of the bladder associated with carcinoma in situ. J Urol 116:575, 1976.

This article reviews 129 patients with low-grade and low-stage transitional cell carcinoma of the bladder. All patients were followed for at least 5 yr. Patients were observed for various indicators, and in 12 patients carcinoma in situ was found incidentally. Of these 12 patients, 10 developed invasive disease.

Those patients who had atypia likewise had a high incidence of invasive disease. The authors conclude that patients with low-grade, low-stage tumors associated with carcinoma in situ are at a much higher risk and should be aggressively managed.

Anderson CK: Current topics in pathology of bladder cancer. Proc R Soc Med 66:283, 1973

This paper from the University of Leeds discusses grading and staging of bladder tumors. A postmortem study of 149 patients dying with the diagnosis of bladder cancer showed 15% of the patients to have died with no evidence of recurrence. The majority of patients showed only local disease confined to the pelvis and lower abdominal cavity, and only 12 % of the patients exhibited metastatic spread. Investigation of predicting factors such as histologic appearance, multiple tumors, and carcinoma in situ shows that of the 15 patients with carcinoma in situ, only 3 did not develop invasive disease within 3 yr. Change in histologic appearance was found in only a small number of patients, and multifocal disease was found in approximately 40% of the patients.

Farrow G.M, Utz DC, Rife CC, et al: Clinical observations on sixty-nine cases of in situ carcinoma of the urinary bladder. Cancer Res 37:794, 1977

One hundred and six patients were found at the Mayo Clinic to have abnormal cytology. Of these, 69 had biopsy-proven carcinoma in situ and were treated in a variety of fashions ranging from no therapy to total cystectomy. Those patients who underwent immediate total cystectomy were found to have 80% of the bladder mucosa replaced by carcinoma in situ. No patient died of carcinoma. Late cystectomy was performed in 14 patients all having symptoms ranging from 4 to 96 mo. None of these patients died of uroethelial cancer. Of the 38 patients treated without cystectomy, 9 were lost to follow-up studies and 3 developed invasive cancer. Duration of symptoms before invasive disease developed ranged from 23 to 58 mo (average 40.7 mo). The authors point to the possibility of two forms of carcinoma in situ, one being focal and the other extensive.

Melamed MR, Voutsa NG, Grabstald H: Natural history and clinical behavior of in situ carcinoma of the human bladder. Cancer 17:1533, 1964

Twenty-five patients with carcinoma in situ were followed. All but one had had previous bladder tumors. Eight patients underwent radical cystectomy, all being free of cancer. Seven more patients not treated by cystectomy remain free of disease in periods ranging from 1 mo to 5 yr. Invasive cancer developed in eight patients at intervals ranging from 8 to 67 mo. In no patient was there spontaneous regression to the tumor. Twenty-three of the 25 patients were discovered on cytology to have carcinoma in situ.

Bergman S, Javadpour N: The self-surface antigen A, B, or O (H), as an indicator of malignant potential in stage A bladder carcinoma: Preliminary report." J Urol 119:49, 1978

The authors use the specific red cell adherence reaction using a sandwich-type antigen antibody reaction to determine the presence or absence of self-surface antigens. This test was originally described by Davidsohn. Fourteen patients with stage O or A bladder cancer were followed and studied with this test. Five patients had no recurrence of the disease, and three of these had positive red cell adherence tests indicating antigens present. Two patients from this group had lost their red cell antigens. Nine patients had recurrence, and these patients showed 0 or low degree of self-surface antigens. The authors conclude that the loss of the glycoproteins, which the self-surface antigens represent, is a powerful predictor of future invasive disease.

Lange PH, Limas C, Franley EE: Tissue blood-group antigens and prognosis in low-stage transitional cell carcinoma of the bladder. J Urol 119:52, 1978

This study is of 37 patients who initially had low-stage transitional cell carcinoma of the bladder. Sixteen patients were red cell antigen positive on initial biopsies, and 2 later developed invasive disease (13%). Twenty-one patients were red cell negative, and 16 (76%) developed invasive disease. The correlation with grades showed that most grade 3 tumors were red cell negative and most grade 1 and 2 tumors were equally divided between red cell positive and negative lesions. Thirty-four patients with recurrent bladder tumors were also followed with the red cell antigen test, and of 11 tumors that were red cell antigen positive, 1 became invasive. Of 18 tumors that were red cell antigen negative, 16 became invasive. If the lesion had been red cell antigen positive at least once, then there was little chance of invasion. As in the first group, grade correlated with the absence or presence of antigen. The authors conclude that this is a good predictor of disease progression.

Decenzo JM Howard P, Irish CE: Antigenic deletion and prognosis of patients with stage A transitional cell bladder carcinoma. J Urol 114:874, 1975

Twenty-two patients with stage A transitional cell carcinoma of the bladder were followed with the mixed cell agglutination reaction for 5 to 14 yr. Of the nine patients who had negative mixed cell agglutination reaction, all but one developed at least stage B disease, and one patient died of metastatic disease. Patients who had a positive mix cell agglutination reaction showed no tendency to develop invasive or metastatic disease.

Richie JP, Blute RD, Waisman J: Immunologic indicators of prognosis in bladder cancer: The importance of self-surface antigen. J Urol 123:22, 1980

Eighty-nine patients were studied retrospectively for self-surface antigens by the sandwich technique. Ninety-seven percent of the patients with negative red cell antigen test had invasion. Of the seven patients with stage A disease and negative red cell antigen markers, 71% developed invasive disease. Nine patients with stage A tumors and positive specific red cell inheritance were followed, and none developed invasive disease.

Sandberg AA: Chromosome markers in progression in bladder cancer. Cancer Res 37:2950, 1977

The author examines 137 patients with transitional cell carcinoma of the bladder. Twelve benign papillary tumors were found to be diploid. Of the remaining 50 papillary cancers, the modal chromosome number was also diploid, but the karyotypic picture differed. Thirty-two of the 50 tumors had marker chromosomes. Of the 12 papillary tumors that recurred, only 1 did not have a marker. Invasive transitional cell tumors were associated with a large number of marker chromosomes, complicated karyotypic pictures, and a high modal number of chromosomes. He felt that the presence of marker chromosomes indicated the likely recurrence or progression of the disease.

OVERVIEW: CARCINOMA OF THE BLADDER

David M. Wallace

For anyone attempting to assess the efficacy of the multitudinous methods of therapy for bladder tumors, the difficulties are formidable.

In the first place, the natural history of this disease is so pleomorphic, so uncertain that errors of evaluation will arise purely because of reporting treatment series based on different forms of the disease. Can it be that the lesions physicians are considering are not primarily bladder tumors but represent a disease of the whole urinary collecting system and that the bladder is more frequently involved because it represents the storage function of the collecting system? The numbers of papers appearing in both American and European urologic literature suggest that carcinoma *in situ* may exist at many areas in the bladder away from the first tumor site much more frequently than was previously supposed.[1,2] Multiple cup biopsies are now recommended to establish whether, in the presence of a primary tumor, areas of *in situ* carcinoma exist in other parts of the bladder.

Is the disease always multifocal, and can it be that so-called recurrences after conservative endoscopic surgery are not recurrences in the sense that they are related to any previous tumor but new tumors developing on an "unstable" mucosa, "potential tumors" that at the time of the first treatment were unrecognized?

Papers on urethrectomy, urethral tumors, and the incidence of emboli in the corpora suggest that some of the failures of surgery have been due to persistence of neoplastic change in the urethra, that surgical failure was due to inadequate appreciation of the extent of the neoplastic change.[3] Similarly, papers are beginning to appear on tumors developing in the upper urinary tract either before or after cystectomy.[4]

If the idea of a widespread field change is accepted, it is surprising that so few papers are appearing on biochemical changes in the urine in association with an unstable urothelium.

The possibility that biochemical changes in the urine could be produced by industrial environmental factors, smoking, additives in the diet, or even the general pollution of civilization has yet to be fully explored. How many clinics nowadays collect information related to patients' environmental exposure as well as the usual details of stage, grade, and financial status?

It is only in the last 20 yr, since Gowing in England and Cordonnier and Spjut in the United States began reporting urethral pathology, that urethrectomy in both men and women has become a recognized part of a cystectomy. Surgical fashions change, even during the lifetime of one clinician, so that reports based on lifetime experience may represent many differing facts and changes in treatments.

Immunologists have recently begun to take a practical interest in bladder tumors, although one of the major challenges in urology has always been what factor after many years of noninvasive growth decides whether a tumor remains confined to the urothelium or whether it becomes highly invasive. Is it a loss of an immunologic barrier, a change in the character of the chromosomes, or the result of a surgical breakthrough of some protective layer?[7]

Interest in chromosomal behavior is a relatively new field of research. Abnormal chromosomal patterns are associated with high-grade tumors and invasion. But which is the hen and which is the egg? Tetraploidy, an excess of chromosomes, is more frequent with invasive tumors, but is this abnormality the cause of the invasion or is it merely coincidental association, both due to some third factor?[8,9]

For the statistician the difficulties are even greater, since, when numbers are dealt with, it is often the numbers that are excluded that may be of the greatest importance. How many patients have been excluded from a series because of incomplete documentation, because they were unfit, or because they were lost to follow-up study? How many were other people's failures and, therefore, further along the road of the tumors' natural history? How many patients elected for personal or financial reasons to accept one form of treatment in preference to another? What is the age structure of any patient series; will a series with an average age of 55 yr have a better survival rate than a series with an average age of 70 or more?

The division of clinical material by clinical as well as pathologic stage has helped to reduce confusion, but as Skinner points out, to be useful a clinical stage must be simple. Not all centers have sophisticated diagnostic equipment or the personnel able to interpret the results, so that clinical staging must be based on a clinical examination by an experienced clinician, without invoking such accessory aids as computed tomography (CT) scanning, ultrasound, or possibly lymphography. When discussing clinical staging, especially when comparing clinical with pathologic staging, how rarely is it stated who made the original examination. Accuracy of staging increases with experience, but any series based on staging by the relative newcomer to urology cannot be expected to have great value.

The field becomes more difficult when one considers clinical trials, especially when a large number of centers are involved. Exclusion of patients after randomization in a blind controlled trial invalidates the conclusions. Often a smaller trial, where "like" is compared with "like," where the choice of treatment arms is minimal with as few exclusions as possible, is possibly of greater value even when the figures fail to satisfy a statistician.

The current habit of increasing the numbers of patients in a reported series by going back in time is to be deprecated. Certainly the conditions for treatment have changed over the years; operative mortality has decreased, radiotherapy has become more accurate and more sophisticated, and postoperative care and anesthesia have improved immensely. Even such details as endoscopic equipment have, with the advent of fiberoptics, been revolutionized.

There is a minimal period of effective follow-up study. Too short and the conclusions are valueless, too long and too many patients will be lost to follow-up study. Five years appears to be the optimum time, but Miller has shown that there is a considerable attrition rate between 5 and 10 yr of follow-up study. The accuracy of follow-up information about the late group between 5 and 10 yr is vital: how many patients were known definitely to be tumor free? How many died from unrelated intercurrent disease? how many died from their original tumor? How many died as a result of the treatment they received? It is fallacious to compare two series, one from each of two separate centers. The expertise at one might not be available at the other; the methods of selection may differ, the type of patient excluded may differ, and the quality of follow-up study and pathology may also vary. The clinician's ethics may also influence selection, or the patient may elect one form of treatment in preference to another. All that even a well-documented series of patients can prove is that, within the terms of selection for treatment, with the expertise available,

a limited percentage, which will vary with extent of spread and degree of malignancy, may survive tumor free.

The recent popularity of multicenter clinical trials has cast an aura of respectability on the reporting of clinical material, but when too much is attempted the results can be misleading. Massive clinical trials may result in massive statistics but little real clinical evidence. The failure of clinical trials in general is due to the difficulty of matching similar patients. The factors of age, status, and general fitness must all be matched. Even with the most meticulous examination, errors in clinical assessment will inevitably arise, but where the patient has been randomized as suitable for inclusion in a trial, preferably with only two arms of treatment, the errors intrinsic in the clinical examination should be similar in each group. Overstaging or understaging would apply equally; errors in biopsy reporting or errors of radiologic interpretation would appear equally in each group.

The greatest errors creep in when patients are subsequently excluded from the trial. When patients develop metastases before planned surgery these patients should not be excluded but counted as planned treatment failures even when they have failed to complete the planned treatment. Likewise, a patient receiving planned radiotherapy may develop metastases during the course of treatment. Even when the treatment is changed such a patient becomes a failure of planned treatment.

The use of chemotherapy as an adjunct to surgery or irradiation makes evaluation even more complicated. Unlike penicillin, where no trial was necessary, and unlike streptomycin, where a controlled trial yielded a clear-cut answer, chemotherapy for malignancy has not yet produced a drug that is all effective and nontoxic. Combination of drugs makes assessment even more confusing. Furthermore, not merely are a large number of drugs being used in combination, but the dosage and timing also vary.

As with testicular tumors, the gradual experience of clinical practice will, in time, indicate which drugs have ever produced significant regression and which have been valueless. Here the vital factor is not the number of publications but critical clinical evaluation of the evidence.

The attempt to describe changes in clinical practice over the last 20 yr, to sift out the really worthwhile reports for the benefit of the practicing urologist, is not an easy task. There is still a place, and a very important place, for conservative endoscopic surgery, but recurrences must not be regarded as evidence of inadequate treatment; they may merely represent evidence of a more widespread neoplastic process. Intracavitary chemotherapy has a well-defined role in patients whose bladders have multiple or rapidly reforming tumors or where areas of carcinoma *in situ* have been proved. Here some patients do well; they become tumor free and remain tumor free. Others have persistent symptoms and persistent tumors, and in this group early removal gives the best chance of cure.[10] Like radiotherapy, intracavitary chemotherapy is successful in a limited number of patients only. Success with this method lies both in securing a cure but also in recognizing those patients whose lesions will not respond so that an alternative therapy can be used while the lesion is still confined to the bladder.

The major controversy, however, lies in the treatment of the deeply invasive tumor. Let it be said here that this lesion represents the penultimate phase of the disease, the end of the road, where effective medicine has failed, early diagnosis has failed, and conservative therapy is now too late. As with breast cancer, early diagnosis may at present be the most effective way to reduce mortality. Self-examination of the breast is now routine practice, but how effective is the investigation of urinary dysfunction or hematuria?

The invasive tumor, when the neoplastic process has spread to the deeper muscle layers, has a high incidence of lymph node metastases, but radical surgery can only be curative when one or two nodes only are involved. More than this is rarely helped by surgery. Radiotherapy may be effective in controlling lymph nodes but, almost by definition, radiotherapy cannot be used on histologically proved nodes, and enlarged nodes without histologic confirmation can be inflammatory.

There is growing evidence that radiotherapy can, with benefit, be combined with surgery. Several series have reported an increased survival rate by combined therapy: a short sharp course of therapy followed rapidly by radical excision; a planned preoperative course of therapy to a restricted dose followed by planned radical excision or even a full course of radiotherapy, followed by salvage surgery within a year, for those patients whose tumor has not disappeared but who are still technically operable.

It has been argued that radiotherapy can preserve normal micturition and, it is claimed, normal sexual function. When it fails, salvage surgery may still be possible, but the numbers of patients submitted to salvage surgery is still very low. There appears to be only a slightly increased morbidity or mortality in salvage surgery, but the decision may well rest with the patient, since the elderly may not take kindly to radical surgery.

The largest centers have a responsibility in that careful clinical evaluation by experienced clinicians and the meticulous carrying out of small clinical trials within these centers may indicate a possible effective cure rate, but to a patient a survival rate is merely an indication, not a guarantee, of what might be achieved. The smaller centers have an even more significant role: to detect local environmental risks and to couple these with early diagnosis while the disease is still in the noninvasive stage. There is no cure rate for tumors that have been prevented by prophylactic measures, and the cure rate for noninvasive tumors is still surprisingly good.

Two major questions remain unsolved: what is the cause of widespread mucosal disease—the maladie de mucose of the older French urlogists—and what factors precipitate invasion in a previously benign condition?

REFERENCES

1. Schade RO, Swinney T: Per-cancerous changes in bladder epithelium. Lancet 2:943, 1968

2. Heney NM, Daly J, Prout GR, et al: Biopsy of apparently normal urothelium in patients with bladder carcinoma. J Urol 120:559, 1978

3. Hendry WF, Gowing NFC, Wallace DM: Surgical treatment of urethral tumors associated with bladder cancer. Proc R Soc Med 67:304, 1974

4. Schade RO, Turingen Serck Hanssen A: Morphological changes in the ureter in cases of bladder cancer. Cancer 27:1267, 1971

5. Cordonnier JJ, Spjut HJ: Urethral occurrence of bladder carcinoma following cystectomy. J Urol 87:398, 1962

6. Gowing NFC: Urethral carcinoma associated with cancer of the bladder. Br J Urol 32:428, 1960

7. Kay, HEM, Wallace DM: Alpha and beta antigens of tumors arising from urinary epithelium. J Nat Cancer Inst 26:1349, 1961

8. Lamb D: Correlation of chromosome counts with histological appearances and prognosis in transitional cell carcinoma of bladder. Br Med J 1:273, 1967

9. Spooner ME, Cooper WE: Chromosome constituents of transitional cell carcinoma of the bladder. Cancer 29:1401, 1972

10. Fitzpatrick JM, Khan O, Oliver RTD, et al: Long-term follow-up in patients treated with intravesical Epodyl. Br J Urol 51:545, 1979

69

SEGMENTAL RESECTION IN THE MANAGEMENT OF BLADDER CARCINOMA

K. B. Cummings,* J. T. Mason, R. J. Correa, Jr. and R. P. Gibbons

From the Department of Surgery/Urology, Virginia Mason Medical Center, Seattle, Washington

0022–5347/78/1191–0056$02.00/0
The Journal of Urology
Copyright © 1978 by The Williams & Wilkins Co.
Vol. 119, January
Printed in U.S.A.

ABSTRACT—Segmental resection for bladder carcinoma was performed on 144 patients at our medical center between 1945 and 1971. Of these 144 cases 101 had sufficient documentation to provide meaningful data for a retrospective study. The 5-year survival rates for patients with invasive bladder carcinoma, expressed as a function of the stage of disease, were stage A—79 percent, stage B1—80 percent, stage B2—45 percent and stage C—6 percent. The combined survival rates for patients with stages O, A and B1 tumors and for those with B2 and C disease were 83 and 27 percent, respectively. A significant observation was that of the patients with stages O, A and B1 disease only 7 percent had a history of antecedent tumor. In contrast, 59 percent of the patients with stage B2 and C disease had antecedent tumor.

Accepted for publication May 20, 1977.
Read at annual meetings of Western Section, American Urological Association, San Francisco, California, March 13–17, 1977 and the American Urological Association, Chicago, Illinois, April 24–28, 1977.
* Requests for reprints: The Mason Clinic, 1100 Ninth Ave., Seattle, Washington 98101.

Segmental resection appears to be an efficacious procedure in patients who present with the first high grade tumor in a mobile portion of the bladder or in patients in whom a more aggressive surgical approach is not prudent because of medical contraindications. Contraindications to this procedure include (1) high grade-high stage tumor involving the trigone and/or ureteral orifice, (2) invasive transitional cell carcinoma involving the bladder neck in the female patient and (3) field change in the bladder (carcinoma in situ or severe mucosal atypia). Segmental resection is an attractive surgical procedure in the management of carcinoma of the bladder in that it spares bladder function and it does not jeopardize the patient with extension of the disease when used appropriately. The procedure has fallen into disrepute in certain circles because of failure in its appropriate clinical application. Jewett and Strong, reflecting on postmortem studies in patients with bladder carcinoma, revealed that of the patients with stage C disease 41 percent (37 of 89) of the autopsy studies failed to reveal evidence of nodal or distant metastatic disease, indicating that there is a finite period in the natural history of this disease when a less aggressive surgical procedure is suitable and indicated.[1]

MATERIALS AND METHODS

Between 1945 and 1971, 144 patients underwent segmental resection for carcinoma of the bladder at our medical center. Of these 144 patients 101 had sufficient documentation in their records to permit a significant retrospective study. Segmental resection was the first surgical procedure performed in 73 of these 101 patients, 84 percent of whom were men (85 of 101) and 16 percent of whom were women (16 of 101). The mean age of the patients was 62 years, with a range of 38 to 82 years. The cases were classified according to stage and grade of disease (Tables 1 and 2). Segmental resection was performed as a definitive procedure (1) for stage O disease which, because of size or location, was not

amenable to complete endoscopic resection, (2) as a definitive surgical procedure for invasive carcinoma of the bladder deemed curable by segmental resection and (3) in those patients who because of medical contraindications were not considered candidates for a more aggressive surgical procedure (8 of 101 patients).

RESULTS

The 5-year survival rates for these patients, calculated from the time of segmental resection and related to the stage of disease as classified according to the method of Jewett and Strong, are given in Table 3.[1] Because of the minor differences in pathologic grading during the period of study it was elected to segregate grades I and II tumors into low grade disease and grades III and IV tumors into high grade disease and to correlate this with stage. There was a significant correlation between high grade and high stage disease. Survival rates at 5 years, expressed as a function of the grade of disease, are shown in Table 4. Survival is diminished with increasing tumor grade. Of the 101 patients 28 had antecedent tumors before the segmental resection and 12 of these 28 patients experienced multiple antecedent tumors. Subsequent to segmental resection, which was considered to have been a definitive procedure, recurrence was noted in 49 percent of the patients and, of these, 77 percent had multiple recurrences (Table 5). Fifty percent of the recurrences (24 of 49) were within the first year after segmental resection. Increased tumor grade was witnessed in 40 percent of those patients who suffered multiple recurrences (Table 6). The location of the tumor as it relates to survival must be considered in association

TABLE 1. Breakdown of Cases According to Stage of Tumor

	No. Pts.
O	9
A	29
B1	21
B2	22
C	17
Diverticulum	3
Total	101

TABLE 2. Breakdown of Cases According to Grade of Tumor

	No. Pts.
I	8
II	28
III	42
IV	23
Total	101

TABLE 3. 5-Year Survival Rates According to Stage of Tumor

	No. Pts. (%)		Grade	
			I–II	III–IV
O	9/9	(100)	9/9	0/9
A	23/29	(79)	23/29	6/29
B1	17/21	(80)	2/21	19/21
B2	10/22	(45)	0/22	22/22
C	1/17	(6)	0/17	17/17
Diverticulum	1/3	(33)	1/3	2/3
Totals	61/101	(60)	35/101	66/101

TABLE 4. 5-Year Survival Rates According to Grade of Tumor

	No. Pts. (%)	
I	8/8	(100)
II	26/27	(96)
III	20/41	(48)
IV	7/25	(28)
Totals	61/101	(60)

TABLE 5. Recurrent Tumor

	No. Pts. (%)	No. Multiple Recurrences (%)
O	4/9 (44)	3/4 (75)
A	19/29 (66)	15/19 (79)
B1	10/21 (48)	8/10 (80)
B2	10/22 (45)	8/10 (80)
C	4/17 (24)	3/4 (75)
Diverticulum	2/3 (66)	1/2 (50)
Totals	49/101 (49)	38/49 (77)

TABLE 6. Increasing Grade with Tumor Recurrence

	No. Pts. (%)	No. Multiple Recurrences (%)	↑ Grade (%)
I	5/8 (62)	3/5 (60)	2/5 (40)
II	18/27 (66)	17/18 (94)	11/18 (61)
III	17/41 (41)	13/17 (76)	3/17 (17)
IV	9/25 (40)	5/9 (55)	—
Totals	49/101 (49)	38/49 (77)	16/40 (40)

TABLE 7. Survival (Stage and Location)

		Location		
	No. Pts. (%)	Fixed No. (%)	Ureteral Reimplant No. (%)	Mobile No. (%)
O	9/9 (100)	7/9 (78)	3/9 (33)	2/9 (22)
A	23/29 (79)	10/29 (34)	5/29 (17)	19/29 (66)
B1	17/21 (80)	4/21 (19)	3/21 (14)	17/21 (81)
B2	10/22 (45)	6/22 (27)*	3/22 (14)‡	16/22 (73)
C	1/17 (6)	9/17 (53)†	7/17 (41)§	8/17 (47)
Totals	60/98 (61)	36/98 (37)	21/98 (21)	62/98 (63)

* 4 of 6 patients dead at 5 years.
† 3 of 3 patients dead at 5 years.
‡ 9 of 9 patients dead at 5 years.
§ 6 of 7 patients dead at 5 years.

TABLE 8. 5-Year Survival of Patients Who Received Adjuvant Radiation Therapy

	Radiation Therapy >5,000 Rads No. (%)
I	—
II	3/11 (27)
III	6/22 (27)
IV	3/9 (33)
Totals	12/34 (35)

TABLE 9. Correlation of 5-Year Survival with Antecedent Tumor

	5-Year Survival No. (%)	Antecedent Tumor No. (%)
O, A, B1	49/59 (83)	4/59 (7)
B2, C	11/39 (28)	23/39 (59)

with the depth of invasion (Table 7). The fixed portion of the bladder included the trigone and bladder base in contrast to the mobile portion, which included the dome and bladder walls. Survival was significantly compromised in patients with high stage disease who had involvement of the bladder base. Furthermore, survival appeared further compromised in this group (stages B2 and C) when tumor location necessitated ureteral reimplantation as exhibited by the 90 percent of the patients dead at 5 years (9 of 13).

Radiation therapy in excess of 5,000 rads was used in cases in which it was considered that surgical excision alone (absence of tumor-free margin or depth of invasion) would not constitute definitive therapy to ensure survival. The 5-year survival rates in the population who received radiation therapy are given in Table 8. Of the 34 patients who were candidates for radiation therapy nearly a third of the patients with grades II, III and IV disease appeared to benefit, suggesting that the 5-year survival rates were not dependent only upon grade of disease.

There were no operative deaths in this series. However, there were 5 complications: (1) 3 vesicocutaneous fistulas, (2) 1 recurrent tumor in the suprapubic tube tract and (3) 1 colovesical fistula. Bladder function was compromised significantly in 18 percent of the patients in this series (19 of 101). Nineteen patients had significant diminution in capacity, 12 had significant irritative symptoms and 5 required a palliative diversion because of bladder dysfunction. Cystectomy was resorted to in 9 percent of the patients (9 of 101 cases). The interval from segmental resection to cystectomy was less than 5 years in 8 of the 9 patients. Six of 9 patients were classified ''salvage cystectomies'' and occurred

after radiation therapy and the failure of this modality in association with segmental resection to control the disease. Three of 9 patients had cystectomy performed because of increased stage of tumor after recurrence.

A most significant observation was the correlation of antecedent tumor with the 5-year survival rates (Table 9). Patients with stages O, A and B1 disease had a combined survival of 83 percent and only 7 percent of these patients had antecedent tumor. In contrast, patients with stages B2 and C disease had a combined survival of 28 percent and exhibited antecedent tumors in 59 percent (23 of 39).

DISCUSSION

There is reasonable agreement that the patient who presents with a first high grade invasive tumor in the mobile portion of the bladder is a suitable candidate for segmental resection.[2] The timing of this procedure in the natural history of the disease is critical.[1]

The surgical procedure has been described amply

by other authors but includes the common dictum of an ample surgical margin free of tumor.[2,3] Regional lymphadenectomy has been advocated by Coetzee.[4] Lymphadenectomy was not used consistently in this series and, therefore, no statement regarding its efficacy can be made. Lymph gland dissection would be desirable in selected patients because of the (1) greater accuracy in surgical staging, (2) identification of the patients who might benefit from adjuvant therapy and (3) improved understanding of the biology of this disease. It was evident in this series that patients with antecedent tumors, particularly those who had multiple recurrent antecedent tumors, fared poorly when segmental resection was performed as a definitive procedure for cure. This observation is consistent with that of Cooper and associates, reflecting on the field change of the bladder mucosa in patients with bladder carcinoma in whom the mucosa appears normal on endoscopy but has been demonstrated to reflect frank carcinoma in situ on a random cold cup biopsy.[5] This series suggests additionally that in those patients in whom segmental resection is performed for high stage disease (in which the fixed portion of the bladder—base, trigone or neck—is involved and especially in those instances in which ureteral reimplantation is required) that survival would appear to have been improved with the use of a more radical surgical procedure. In this series there were 21 ureteral reimplantations performed and survival was compromised only in those with high stage disease (42 percent or 9 of 21 patients did not survive 5 years). In those patients in whom radiation therapy was used as an adjuvant to segmental resection the indications were largely depth of infiltration or absence of tumor-free margins. An interesting observation was that survival in this group, related to grade of disease, failed to distinguish radiation sensitivity by grade and indicated that approximately a third of those patients in whom this modality was used, regardless of grade, might anticipate a beneficial response. A further observation is that in only 1 percent of patients subjected to this procedure was there recurrence of tumor in the wound. The recurrence was in the patient who was found within the

first year postoperatively to have a mass in the site of the suprapubic tube tract and who after surgical excision of this mass experienced a survival of greater than 5 years. This finding is consistent with the review of Utz and associates, in which the incidence of tumor recurrence in the wound was slightly greater than 1 percent (3 of 193).[6] Compromise in bladder function was witnessed most consistently in patients with multiple prior surgical procedures and associated radiation therapy. The choice of this procedure must be weighed against our observation that 49 percent of the patients in this series subsequently had recurrent tumor (50 percent during the first year after segmental resection) and, of these 49 percent of patients, 77 percent have experienced multiple recurrences. Furthermore, of the 77 percent with multiple recurrences 40 percent exhibited increased grade of malignancy. The consideration of a bladder-sparing procedure by the performance of segmental resection is a paramount concern or urologists. However, the observation that 9 percent of the patients in this series ultimately required cystectomy and that 8 of these 9 patients required this procedure within the first 5 years after a presumed definitive surgical procedure by segmental resection would raise a question regarding patient selection.

CONCLUSION

Segmental resection appears to be an appropriate procedure for patients with a first high grade tumor that is in a mobile portion of the bladder, reflecting particularly on the timing of this procedure in the natural history of the disease. If further has its application in patients with medical contraindications to more aggressive therapy and in those in whom complete endoscopic resection cannot be performed because of the location of the tumor. It would appear that contraindications to this procedure would include (1) high grade and high stage tumors that involve the trigone and/or ureteral orifice, (2) invasive carcinoma involving the bladder neck in female patients in whom incontinence would be the consequence of segmental resection and (3) the observation that transi-

TABLE 10. Comparative 5-Year Survival Segmental Resection

References	O No. (%)	A No. (%)	B1 No. (%)	B2 No. (%)	C No. (%)	D No. (%)
Flocks[7]			5/13 (38)			
Marshall and associates[8]		40/64 (62.5)		11/50 (22)		
Jewett and associates[9]		16/23 (70.0)		4/48 (8)		
Riches[10]		7/12 (58)		16/44 (36)	0/6 (0)	
Magri[3]		8/10 (80)		10/26 (38)	5/19 (26)	
Resnick and O'Conor[11]	3/4 (75)	17/24 (70.7)	10/13 (77)	3/16 (18)	2/24 (12.5)	1/5 (20)
Utz and associates[6]		17/25 (68)	18/38 (47)	14/35 (40)	11/38 (29)	0
Current series	9/9 (100)	23/29 (79)	17/21 (80)	10/22 (45)	1/17 (6)	

tional cell carcinoma appears to be a field change mucosal disease and that while a visible tumor might appear amenable to segmental resection co-existent mucosal changes not evidenced on endoscopy would dictate a more radical procedure.

A comparative 5-year survival for segmental resection is illustrated in table 10 and would indicate that for low stage disease survival appears to be excellent with this procedure.[3,6-11] However, for high stage disease (B2 and C) the survival statistics are quite poor and alternative forms of therapy (aggressive surgery and adjuvant therapy) might be expected to effectuate increased survival rates.

REFERENCES

1. Jewett, H. J. and Strong, G. H.: Infiltrating carcinoma of the bladder: relation of depth of penetration of the bladder wall to incidence of local extension and metastases. J Urol 55:366, 1946

2. Whitmore, W. F., Jr.: The treatment of bladder tumors. Surg Clin N Amer 49:349, 1969

3. Magri, J.: Partial cystectomy: a review of 104 cases. Br J Urol 34:74, 1962

4. Coetzee, T.: Radical partial cystectomy. S Afr J Surg 4:1, 1966

5. Cooper, T. P., Wheelis, R. F., Correa, R. J., Jr., Gibbons, R. P., Mason , J. T. and Cummings, K. B.: Random mucosal biopsies in the evalution of patients with carcinoma of the bladder. J Urol 117:46, 1977

6. Utz, D. C., Schmitz, S. E., Fugelso, P. D. and Farrow, G. M.: Proceedings: a clinicopathologic evaluation of partial cystectomy for carcinoma of the urinary bladder. Cancer 32:1075, 1973

7. Flocks, R. H.: Treatment of patients with carcinoma of bladder. JAMA, 145:295, 1951

8. Marshall, V. F., Holden, J. and Ma, K. T.: Symposium on bladder tumors; survival of patients with bladder carcinoma treated by simple segmental resection; 123 consecutive cases 5 years later. Cancer 9:568, 1956

9. Jewett, H. J., King, L. R. and Shelley, W. M.: A study of 365 cases of infiltrating bladder cancer: relation of certain pathological characteristics to prognosis after extirpation. J Urol 92:668, 1964

10. Riches, E.: Choice of treatment in carcinoma of the bladder. J Urol 84:472, 1960

11. Resnick, M. I. and O'Conor, V. J., Jr.: Segmental resection for carcinoma of the bladder: review of 102 patients. J Urol 109:1007, 1973

COMMENT

It has never seemed logical to me to include stage O cases with stages A and B1. Stage O tumors cannot metastasize and the more patients with stage O tumors in the series the better will be the survivorship. This opinion is confirmed by the authors' Table 3. *H.J.J.*

Commentary: Segmental Cystectomy

Irving M. Bush, Nader Sadoughi, Patrick D. Guinan, and Richard J. Ablin

"As surprising as it may be, partial cystectomy provides results comparable with other operative procedures and radiation therapy alone for similar stages and grades of bladder tumors."[1] This statement, made in the 1975 edition of *Current Operative Urology,* still holds true. If the urologist is careful, the undesirable aspects of bladder removal can be avoided in "selected patients" without any decrease in 5-yr survival with less morbidity and initial mortality and with preservation of the patient's sexual function.

In the foregoing article, just as in the original paper by Marshall and colleagues (published in the first edition of this book), the authors stress that the key to success is careful patient selection.[2,3] Each author of these and other recent reviews of the subject, however, disagrees, in part, on the criteria for patient selection. Cummings and colleagues and Brannan and associates recommend its use in primary cases, while others such as Resnick and O'Conor, and Evans and Texter used the procedure with success in patients with recurrent lesions.[2,4-6] Novick and Stewart, Brannan and colleagues, and Resnick and O'Conor all perform segmental resection in cases of bladder diverticulum and, like others, think nothing of resecting the ureteral orifice, while Olsson and deVere White and Cummings and colleagues indicate that involvement of the trigone contraindicates the segmental approach, even though they have performed the procedure in the past.[2,4-11]

It is of interest to us that no matter what criteria differences

TABLE 11. Stage of Carcinoma (% Survival)

Reference	No. of Patients	O	A	B₁	B₂	C	D	5 Yr
Flocks	13				38			38
Marshall and associates[3]	114		62.5			22		44.7
Jewett and associates[13]	71		70.0			8		28.4
Riches[15]	62	58			36		0	35.7
Magri[26]	55	80			38	26		41.8
Resnick and O'Conor[5]	86	75	70.7	76.9	18.7	12.5	20	41.9
Utz and associates[17]	153		68	47	40	29		43.3
Evans and Texter[6]	47		69.2	42.9	14.3	0		59.5
Novick and Stewart[7]	50	67			53	17	25	50
Cummings and associates[2]	98	100	79	80	45	6		61
Brannan and associates[4]	45	100	68.8	54.5	62.5	33.3		57.7
Schoberg and associates[10]	44	69		29	50	12	100	38.6
Merrell and associates[8]	54		100	67	37.5	25	0	48
Faysal and Freiha[24]	93	75	58	29	32	7	0	40

there may be, the survival figures (Table 11) are basically similar and may reflect intrinsic tumor biology.

Stage and grade of the bladder tumor still seem to be the most significant survival factors. In Marshall and colleagues 1936 to 1949 study of 123 patients treated by simple segmental resection, patients with low-stage lesions had a 63% 5-yr survival rate, and those with high-stage lesions had a 22% survival rate.[3] In Cummings and colleagues 1945 to 1971 study of 101 evaluable patients, the equivalent figures were 83% and 27%, which may reflect better general medical care, earlier diagnosis of the initial and subsequent lesions, and increased use of more radical procedures (salvage cystectomy) when significant tumor recurs.[2,12] Table 11 seems to bear this concept out. The more recent reviews certainly report better survival figures.[2,4,6,7]

In both series similar results were seen when lesion grade was considered. In the New York Hospital series, patients with low-grade tumors had a 64% 5-yr survival rate, as compared to 35% in those with high-grade lesions.[3] Interestingly, the 25 patients with high-grade, low-stage lesions had a 56% survival rate, a favorable indication for segmental resection also highlighted by the Virginia Mason Medical Center review.[2] Their 5-yr survival rates according to grade were grade I, 100%; II, 96%; III, 48%; and IV, 28%.

These figures compare favorably with those of Jewett and colleagues, who found a 58% 5-yr survival rate for low-grade lesions and a 16% 5-yr survival rate for high-grade lesions in nonselected patients treated by segmental resection. Similar studies from England tend to corroborate this impression.[14–16]. In Utz and colleagues 1973 study of 64 5-yr survivors with transitional cell cancer treated by segmental resection, a similar trend was seen: grade I, 100%; II, 48%; III, 47%; and IV, 21%.

There seems to be no common agreement about what size lesion should be approached by segmental resection.[4,8] Jewett interdicted the procedure where the tumor was so large that the resultant bladder size would be markedly compromised.[18] Masina observed that the lesion should be "single, solid, sharply defined, protuberant, and less than a 6 cm spheroid."[16] Whitmore also recommended that segmental resction be employed in the patient with a solitary lesion if it were at least 2 cm from the bladder neck with no antecedent history of

tumor elsewhere in the bladder and if the tumor were so localized to permit removal of a minimum border of 2 cm of apparently healthy bladder wall. Since patients with smaller noninfiltrative (T₁ and T₂) lesions are managed by transurethral excisional biopsy and have good survival rates, they are usually excluded as possible candidates for partial cystectomy.[20,21] The most suitable patients are therefore those with single, localized T₃ (B₂ and C) lesions of several centimeters located in the movable portion of the bladder. Patients with bulky T₂ (B₁) lesions that cannot be adequately resected because of size or position or that recur (not new lesions) should also be considered for partial cystectomy.

The procedure, described by Baker and colleagues and adopted in part by Jose, advocates the use of transurethral resection and fulguration intially to decrease chances of seeding viable tumor cells.[22,23] At surgery 4 to 7 days later, the pelvic nodes can be evaluated, and, if they are positive, the procedure terminated. If the nodes are negative, a "subtotal" cystectomy is recommended. In many instances this consists of removing a large portion of the bladder (a 4-cm margin) and reimplanting one or both ureteral orifices. The remaining bladder may at times only be adequate to close around the Foley balloon. There may not even be enough tissue to close, in which case the bladder is left open, with ureters attached, to await regeneration.

Segmental resection came into disrepute in the past decade because of the high failure rate due to the natural history of bladder cancer, poor patient selection, and improper surgical technique, often manifested by tumor growing up through the suprapubic incision.[19,24,25] However, in recent studies these ocurrences have been reduced by the application of proper surgical care.[2,4,7] Various authors have suggested the use of preoperative or postoperative radiation, 1% silver nitrate, 95% alcohol, thiotepa, 10% alcohol lavage and a change of gloves and instruments, phenol alcohol, radon seeds, and perivesical excision of contiguous tissue, viscera, and nodes to enhance the results to this operation and prevent tumor spillage into the wound.[2,3,5,8,10,11,14,26–32] We are still impressed that careful desiccation (cutting current and roller electrode) of the surrounding area at the time of resection decreases recurrence and tumor spillage.

Brannan and colleagues presented an excellent review of

the indications, contraindications, and principles of technique for partial cystectomy.[4] These appear in tables 12, 13, and 14. Our suggested modifications to this tabular presentation are italicized.

Partial cystectomy is rarely recommended in teaching programs or erudite discussions but is often performed in selected patients by private practioners in this country and abroad. Its reputation has been tarnished over the past 30 yr by its performance in an inexact manner without benefit of adequate predictive methods of tumor extent spread and aggressiveness. The latter is a problem inherent in any bladder cancer therapy. The former is perhaps an indication of not giving enough attention to the "lessons of past."

In the future it may be possible to proceed as follows:
- Clinically stage bladder lesions accurately
- Delineate the specific lateral lymphatic spread and occurrence of concomitant mucosal changes
- Routinely evaluate ureteral (renal pelvis) involvement[60]
- Determine the biologic potential of the tumor by immunologic, histologic, and enzymatic tests
- Establish the casual agents or factors that produce bladder tumors so as to predict new or continuing carcinogenic activity
- Use improved intracavitary agents such as retinoids, chemotherapeutic drugs, immunotherapeutic measures such as OK-432, bacille Camille Guérin (BCG), or oral medications, thereby reducing the recurrance rate and allowing for the proper selection of patients for segmental resection[63,64]

A good method to prevent tumor spillage in addition to obtaining a wide margin around the tumor was described by Novick and Stewart.[7] Our modifications are italicized:
- *First wash bladder with sterile water,* then empty
- Isolate bladder from rest of surgical field with packs
- *Isolate wound edges with plastic drapes*
- *Perform cystostomy away from tumor*

TABLE 12. Indications for Partial Cystectomy

Solitary lesion
Primary *or residual of primary* lesion
Invasive tumor—stages B_2 to C with residual tumor on rebiopsy 8 to 12 wk later
High-grade tumor—grades II to IV
Inaccessibility to adequate transurethral resection
Tumor in a vesical diverticulum
Moderate-risk patients with B_2 or C (T_3) lesion

TABLE 13. Contraindications to Partial Cystectomy

Prior irradiation *above 2000 rad to bladder area*
Recurrent or multiple tumors
Inability to obtain adequate margins
Involvement of the vesical neck in women
Invasion of the prostatic urethra
Carcinoma *in situ*
Low-grade and noninvasive tumors
Evidence of extravesical extension of tumor
Poor-risk patients
Inability to maintain adequate vesical volume (third of normal) *if no bladder enlargement procedure is contemplated*

- *Perform enblock* removal of the tumor with perivesical fat and overlying peritoneum (dome)
- Freeze sections at edges of bladder resection
- Irrigate entire wound with distilled water

Though "everyone" agrees that segmental resection is a "poor cancer operation," the 5-yr survival figures with this procedure are consistent with the other treatment modalities available for bladder cancer. In a recent review of five series of cystectomy alone by Olsson and deVere White, patients with B_2C tumors had a 5-yr survival rate of only 18%, while the results of those with B_1 lesions varied between 50% and 63%.[11] The operative mortality was 5.4% to 19%. In a similar compilation, preoperative radiation improved cystectomy results to 42% in patients with B_2C lesions and 56% in those with B_1 tumors. However, the operative mortality was still 7.8% to 13%. External radiation therapy by itself has really not improved since Crigler and colleagues report, and therefore most centers have abandoned it because of the inability to stage the lesion properly.[34] Although there may be some advantage to the neutron beam, cooperative studies with it are not yet completed. Van Der Wolf-Messing's investigation on using radium implantation alone (A, 50%; B, 80%; B_2C, 12.5%) and with 1050 rad preoperatively (A, 91%, B_1, 67%, and B_2C, 47%) or 1500 rad postoperatively (A, 91%; B_1, 55%; and B_2C, 47%) indicate that preoperative irradiation with 1000 rad or the use of concomitant ^{125}I seed implants might improve partial cystectomy results sufficient to encourage its increased use.[35]

To date, the use of preoperative external radiation therapy, implantation of radiation seeds at surgery or endoscopically before partial cystectomy, has not been used continuously.[3,10] However, several authors are firmly convinced that the clinical stage reduction seen with total cystectomy and radiation should

TABLE 14. Principles of Technique

Plan preoperative procedures carefully
Use all predictive modes possible (random biopsies, ABH typing)
Excise transurethrally *and desiccate carefully* as much tumor as possible before open resection
  Since this delineates *the* margins, *be careful not to desiccate or coagulate indiscriminately*
  It may decrease potential for wound implantation
Perform as much extravesical dissection, including perivesical fat and peritoneum, as possible before beginning vesical dissection; *palpate and obtain nodal tissue for frozen section if possible*
Suprapubic catheter drainage is suggested *by some,* unless only the dome is involved; *try to avoid cystotomy if possible** *or* perform cystotomy well away from the tumor
Avoid placement of suprapubic catheter close to the pubis
Obtain frozen sections of margins
If distal ureterectomy is performed, resect as far proximally as possible, maintaining adequate length for ureteroneocystostomy (antireflux procedure is not mandatory)
Endoscope all lower ureteral segments at surgery with rigid instruments if preoperative fiberoptic ureteroscopy is not available
Provide *adequate* extravesical drainage; *ureteral stents may be required if suture lines are in proximity to orifices or to reimplantation sites or may be used in conjunction with Foley catheter drainage*
Bladder closure may be one or *preferably* two layers
Continue suprapubic drainage *(vented)* until extravesical drainage has ceased

* In large bladder with dome lesions, where more than two thirds of the bladder is removed, or where a multiple-hole catheter is used.

apply to partial cystectomy.[3,28] Postoperative radiation was used by several authors with some success.[2,3,11,17,24,27] The use of lymph node biopsy or dissection as suggested by Cummings and colleagues should be helpful in evaluating patients undergoing segmental resection because of the inherent value in an accurage pathologic staging and to predict tumor biology (spread) and the need for further therapeutic measures, including radiation.[2,10] The specific value of the removal of submicroscopic lesions with lymph node dissection without prior radiation is still controversial.

Understanding the basic nature of bladder cancer would, of course, be of great value in selecting patients for segmental resection. However, as each newly heralded discovery is tested with the "tincture of time," few potentially helpful, clinically applicable biologic predictors remain.[37]

Lactic dehydrogenease (LDH) isozymes, lysozyme, and muramidase seem to be little more than responses to inflammation.[38,39] The widespread use of ABH antigens, chromosomal analysis, immunologic testing, urinary polyamines, creatine phosphokinase and β-glucuronidase, adenosine deaminase, and microtoxicity assays for cell mediated immunity as predictors of tumor potential or tumor and host relationships are yet to be confirmed.[11,37,40–48] The reliability of elevations of carcinoembrionic antigen (CEA) or α_2-globulins in the blood to indicate tumor spread or aggressiveness is at best undependable.[11,49,50] Whether a composite computer analysis of all the factors would be of help is only a possibility.

There is still no substitute for careful cystoscopy with adequate nondistorting biopsies of the lesion and surrounding muscosa and repeated urine cytologic study with and without brushing or by the washout technique.[51–53] Careful preoperative bimanual examination and clinical staging, proper transurethral surgical technique, and reporting of findings definitely aid in evaluating every suitable patient for segmental resection as well as other procedures. The use of random biopsies has been a great advance.[54] Where ultraviolet cystoscopy with tetracycline and acridine orange is available, such as in our institutions,

it is helpful in determining multicentricity even though the tumors or muscosal changes are not yet visible by normal cystoscopy.[55] In the presented paper, the authors emphasize that bladder cancer must be considered a field disease and therefore that segmental resection should not be performed where random biopsies indicate coexistent mucosal changes or where the bladder washings show a higher grade than the tumor to be removed.[2,11,56,*]

Computed tomography (CT) scan, arteriography, and lymphangiography do delineate advanced cancer.[57,58] However, detailed studies of their beneficial use to evaluate patients undergoing segmental resection are not as yet available. A cost–benefit ratio might preclude such a study; however, a failed segmental approach to be followed by secondary procedures with concomitant poorer results certainly is expensive to the involved patient and health insurance provider. Selection of appropriate diagnostic techniques for each situation, although unsuitable for study purposes, should benefit each patient.

In our institutions, we now attempt to improve our results in partial cystectomy by increased use of ABH testing, immunologic screening, careful delination of the single tumor at resection, CT scanning, wide removal of the bladder with augmentation cystoplasty using temporary Silastic sheeting, television endoscopic recording of bladder tumors to determine recurrence, and preoperative or operative endoscopic evaluation of the ureters and renal pelvis.[59,60] Several patients have received bleomycin instillation or 2000 rad with and without radiation potentiators such as penicillamine, 1 wk preoperatively with initial good results.[61] Mitomycin-C instillation therapy is theoretically better than bleomycin.[11] Recently, lymph node staging, as orginally described by Coetzee and lately suggested by Cummings and colleagues, and peritoneoscopy where indicated have been added to our protocol.[2,62] Arteriography and lymphagiography have not been used routinely but are considered with each patient.

* Cummings KB: Personal communication, 1979.

REFERENCES

1. Bush IM, Garlovsky IS, Guinan PD, et al: Segmental cystectomy—commentary. In Whitehead ED (ed): Current Operative Urology, p. 646. Hagerstown, Harper & Row, 1975

2. Cummings KB, Mason JT, Correa RJ, et al: Segmental resection in the management of bladder carcinoma. J Urol 119:56, 1978

3. Marshall WF, Holden J, Ma KT: Survival of patients with bladder carcinoma treated by simple segmental resection. Cancer 9:568, 1956

4. Brannan W, Ochsner MG, Fuselier HA, et al: Partial cystectomy in the treatment of transitional cell carcinoma of the bladder. J Urol 119:213, 1978

5. Resnick MI, O'Conor VJ: Segmental resection for carcinoma of the bladder: Review of 102 patients. J Urol 109:1007, 1973

6. Evans RA, Texter JH: Partial cystectomy in the treatment of bladder cancer. J Urol 114:391, 1975

7. Novick AC, Stewart BH: Partial cystectomy in the treatment of primary and secondary carcinoma of the bladder. J Urol 116:570, 1976

8. Merrell RW, Brown HE, Rose JF: Bladder carcinoma treated by partial cystectomy: A review of 54 cases. J Urol 122:471, 1979

9. Jewett HJ: Tumors of the bladder. In Campbell MF, Harrison JH (eds): Urology, 3rd ed, p 1025. Philadelphia, 1970

10. Schoborg TW, Sapolsky JL, Lewis CW: Carcinoma of the bladder treated by segmental resection. J Urol 122:473, 1979

11. Olsson CA, deVere White RW: Cancer of the bladder. In Javadpour N (ed): Principles And Management Of Urologic Cancer, p 337. Baltimore, William & Wilkins, 1979

12. McCarron JP, Marshall VF: The survival of patients with bladder tumors treated by surgery: Comparative results of an old and a recent series. J Urol 122:322, 1979

13. Jewett HJ, King LR, Shelley WM: A study of 365 cases of infiltrating bladder cancer: Relation of certain pathological characteristics to prognosis after extirpation. J Urol 92:668, 1964

14. Wallace DM: Tumors of the bladder. Edinburgh, E & S Livingston, 1959

15. Riches E: Choice of treatment in carcinoma of the bladder. J Urol 84:472, 1960

16. Masina F: Segmental resection for tumor of the urinary bladder: Ten-year follow-up. Br J Surg 52:279, 1965

17. Utz D, Schmitz SE, Fugelso PD, et al: A clinicopathologic evaluation of partial cystectomy for carcinoma of the urinary bladder. Cancer 32:1075, 1973

18. Jewett HJ: Tumors of the bladder. In Campbell W (ed): Urology, vol 2, 2d ed, p 1090. Philadelphia, WB Saunders, 1963

19. Whitmore WF: The treatment of bladder tumors. Surg Clin North Am 49:349, 1969

20. Barnes RW, Bergman HL, Hadley HL, et al: Control of bladder tumors by endoscopic surgery. J Urol 97:864, 1967

21. Schmidt JD, Anwar H: Transurethral resection of vesical neoplasms. In Green LF, Segura JW (eds): Transurethral Surgery p 256. Philadelphia, 1979

22. Baker R, Kelly T, Tehan T, et al: Subtotal cystectomy and total bladder regeneration in treatment of bladder cancer. JAMA 168:1178, 1958

23. Jose JS: Extended partial cystectomy in the management of bladder carcinoma: Technique and results. Br J Urol 44:120, 1972

24. Fsysal MH, Freiha FS: Evaluation of partial cystectomy for carcinoma of bladder. J Urol 14:352, 1979

25. Gilbert HA, Logan JL, Kagan AR, et al: The natural history of papillary transitional cell carcinoma of the bladder and its treatment in an unselected population on the basis of histologic grading. J Urol 119:488, 1978

26. Magri J: Partial cystectomy: A review of 104 cases. Br J Urol 34:74, 1962

27. Donovan H: A consideration of the operation of partial cystectomy for bladder neoplasms. Br J Urol 31:95, 1959

29. Bonnin NJ: Extended partial cystectomy in the management of bladder carcinoma: Rationale and case selection. Br J Urol 44:120, 1972

30. Browne HS: Bladder tumors and grain alcohol: A clinical observation. J Urol 88:405, 1962

31. Arduino LJ: Chemotherapy of carcinoma of the bladder. In Benign And Malignant Tumors Of The Urinary Bladder. Flushing, NY, Medical Examination Publishing Co., 1971

32. Dean AL, Mostofi FK, Thomson RV, et al: A restudy of the first fourteen hundred tumors in the bladder tumor registry, Armed Forces Institute of Pathology, J Urol 71:571, 1954

33. Gonick P, Berlet EJ, Roswit B: Stage B carcinoma of the bladder: Treatment and results in 71 cases. J Urol 99:728, 1968

34. Crigler CM, Miller LS, Guinn GA, et al: Radiotherapy for carcinoma of the bladder. J Urol 96:55, 1966

35. Van Der Werf-Messing B: Carcinoma of the bladder treated by suprapubic radium implants. Eur J Cancer 5:277, 1969

36. Whitmore WF: Summary of all phases of bladder carcinoma. J Urol 119:77, 1978

37. Lessing JA: Bladder cancer: Early diagnosis and evaluation of biologic potential: A review of newer methods. J Urol 120:1, 1978

38. Schmidt JD: Significance of total urinary lactic dehydrogenase actively in urinary tract disease. J Urol 96:950, 1966

39. Kovanyi G, Letnansky K: Urine and blood serum muramidase (lysozyme) in patients with urogenital tumors. Eur J Cancer 7:25, 1971

40. Sadoughi N, Rubenstone A, Mlsna J, et al: The cell surface antigens of bladder washing specimens in patients with bladder tumors, a new approach. J Urol (in press)

41. Alroy J, Teramura K, Miller AW, et al: Isoantigens A, B and H in urinary bladder carcinomas following radiotherapy. Cancer 41:1739, 1978

42. Falor WH, Ward RM: Prognosis in early carcinoma of the bladder based on chromosomal analysis. J Urol 119:44, 1978

43. O'Toole C, Perlmann P, Unsgaard B, et al: Cellular immunity to human urinary bladder carcinoma. I. Correlation to clinical stage and radiotherapy. Int J Cancer 10:77, 1972

44. Sanford EJ, Drago JR, Rohner TJ, et al: Preliminary evaluation of urinary polyamines in the diagnosis of genitourinary tract malignancy. J Urol 113:218, 1975

45. Block NL, Jaksy J, Tessler AN: Carcinoma of urinary tract: Clinical significance of urinary phosphokinase activity in diagnosis. Urology 4:174, 1974

46. Senda H: Studies on beta-glucuronidase and DNA synthesis activities in the bladder tumors. Nagoya J Med Sci 33:203, 1971

47. Sufrin G, Tritsch GL, Mittelman A, et al: Adenosine deaminase activity in patients with carcinoma of the bladder. J Urol 119:343, 1978

48. Vilien M, Wolf H: The specificity of the microcytotoxicity assay for cell-mediated immunity in human bladder cancer. J Urol 119:338, 1978

49. Orjasaeter H, Fossa SD, Schjolseth SA, et al: Carcinoembryonic antigen (CEA) in plasma of patients with carcinoma of the bladder/urethra. Cancer 42:287, 1978

50. Guinan PD, Dubin A, Bush IM, et al: The CEA test in urologic cancer: An evaluation and a review. Oncology 32:158, 1975

51. Bush IM, Sadoughi N, Barakat H: A modified insulated cauterizing deep bladder biopsy ferceps. Read before the 46th annual meeting, North Central Section, American Urological Association, Chicago, September 1972

52. Rife CC, Farrow GM, Utz DC: Urine cytology of transitional cell neoplasms. Urol Clin North Am 6:599, 1979

53. Flanagan MJ, Miller A: Evaluation of bladder washing cytology for bladder cancer Surveillance. J Urol 119:42, 1978

54. Soloway MS, Murphy W, Rao MK, et al: Serial multiple-site biopsies in patients with bladder cancer. J Urol 120:57, 1978

55. Bush IM, Whitmore WF Jr: Occult cancer of the bladder: Its detection by ultraviolet tetracycline cystoscopy. J Med Soc New Jersey 64:56, 1967

56. Brannan W: Editorial comment. J Urol 122:472, 1979

57. Seidelmann FE, Cohen WN, Bryan PJ, et al: Accuracy of CT staging of bladder neoplasms using the gas-filled method: Report of 21 patients with surgical confirmation. J Urol 130:735, 1978

58. Winterberger AR, Wajsman Z, Merrin C, et al: Eight years of experience with preoperative angiographic and lymphographic staging of bladder cancer. J Urol 119:208, 1978

59. Bush IM, Bush RB: The use of T.V. endoscopy in urology. Scientific Exhibit, American Urological Association Annual Meeting, Chicago 1977

60. Bush IM, Goldberg E, Javadpour N, et al: Ureteroscopy and renoscopy: A preliminary report. Chicago Med School Quart 30:46, 1970

61. Guinan P, Bush IM: The effect of oral penicillamine on rat bladder mucosa undergoing radiation (ongoing animal research).

62. Coetzee T: Radical partial cystectomy. S Afr J Surg 4:1, 1966

63. Kagawa S, Ogura K, Kurokawa K, et al: Immunological evaluation of a streptococcal preparation (OK-432) in treatment of bladder carcinoma. J Urol 122:467, 1979

64. Morales A, Eidinger D, Bruce AW: Intracavitary bacillus Calmette-Guerin in the treatment of superficial bladder tumors. J Urol 116:180, 1976

ANNOTATED BIBLIOGRAPHY

Whitmore WF Jr: Summary of all phases of bladder carcinoma. J Urol 119:77, 1978

This is a concise article on the problems inherent in the rational treatment of bladder tumors. The author reviews the significant previous studies in a logical and incisive manner and compares them with his own extensive findings: A careful reading indicates that the primary deterrant of survival in the patient with bladder cancer is not the method of treatment but the nature of the tumor.

Marshall WF, Holden J, Ma KT: Survival of patients with bladder carcinoma treated by simple segmental resection. Cancer 9:568–571, 1956

This is the classic paper on segmental resection. These authors emphasize that the single most significant factor affecting survival is the stage (and grade) of the lesions. Sixty-four patients with low-stage lesions had a 63% 5-yr survival rate, 50 patients with high-stage lesions had a 22% 5-yr survival rate. The results of this study may be more significant today when patients see urologists earlier in the course of their disease. If the figures are analyzed from the outset of symptoms, the 5-yr survival figures increase to 72% for low-stage lesions and 30% for high-stage lesions.

Masina F: Segmental resection for tumors of the urinary bladder: Ten-year follow-up. Br J Surg 52:279, 1965

A report embodying a 10-year follow-up study of 72 patients who had partial cystectomy for bladder tumors. The "critical factor" in case selection is that "there should be almost an abrupt change from tumor to normal mucosa and no mucosal changes in the rest of the bladder." The author concludes that "ill-chosen treatment is harmful even in . . . lower grade tumors and that it can be worse than no treatment" at all.

Donovan H: A consideration of the operation of partial cystectomy for bladder neoplasms. Br J Urol 31:95, 1959

A report on 136 nonselected patients with partial cystectomy with a 5-yr survival rate of 55.8% that demonstrates some of the difficulties in evaluating retrospective studies. Recurrence rates, postoperative complications, and involvement of the internal urinary meatus are considered. The 29 patients who received preoperative or postoperative radiation therapy had a survival rate of 41.3%.

Sarma KP: Partial cystectomy or segmental resection. In Tumors Of The Urinary Bladder. New York, Appleton-Century-Crofts, 1969

An extensive 20-page review of the subject detailing the indications, operative technique, and results of the procedure. A section on methods of bladder enlargement is well done. The author concludes that there is much confusion with this mode of treatment of bladder cancer in view of the differing criteria for the selection of patients.

Baker R, Kelly T, Tehan T, et al: Subtotal cystectomy and total bladder regeneration in treatment of bladder cancer. JAMA 168:1178, 1958

A general review of the operative treatment of bladder tumors, highlighting bladder regeneration techniques after subtotal cystectomy. The use of complete transurethral resection before open exploration is stressed. The author points out that "the subtotal operation is preferred even in patients with cancer so far advanced that the operation must be regarded simply as palliative, for it removes a mass that is a source of pain and hemorrhage," but does not prove this point with personal results.

Resnick MI, O'Conor VJ: Segmental resection for carcinoma of the bladder: Review of 102 patients. J Urol 109:1007, 1973

A detailed review of 102 patients who underwent segmental resection for malignant disease between 1955 and 1965 in all stages. Eight percent had postoperative occurrance of superficial tumor. The authors emphasize that many of the recurrences suggesting that wider resection might have prevented recurrence and enhanced survival. In their series, 36% of patients had undergone previous treatment for bladder tumors.

Novick AC, Stewart BH: Partial cystectomy in the treatment of primary and secondary carcinoma of the bladder. J Urol 116:570, 1976

This is a review of 50 patients who underwent partial cystectomy for primary cancer of the bladder. Survival was improved for patients with tumors on the posterior bladder wall. Patients with free margins of resection attained longer survival periods. A concise description of the operative technique to reduce tumor spillage is included. Of patients who had partial cystectomy for adjacent carcinomas secondarily invading the bladder, 7% 12 survived 3 mo and 1 survived 5 yr.

Brannan W, Ochsner MG, Fuselier HA, et al: Partial cystectomy in the treatment of transitional cell carcinoma of the bladder. J Urol 119:213, 1978

This is an enlightened review of aggressive partial cystectomy for selected patients with bladder cancer. The authors report a 57.7% 5-yr survival rate and a 32.4% 10-yr rate. Some patients received postoperative irradiation to the bladder and/or subsequent metastatic lesions. During the procedure a significant number of ureters were reimplanted and prostates enucleated; 62.5% of patients with B2 lesions and 33% of those with C lesions survived 5 yr. The procedure was "an effective mode of therapy when performed on carefully selected patients."

Faysal MH, Freiha FS: Evaluation of partial cystectomy for carcinoma of bladder. Urology 14:352, 1979

This is a review of recurrence rates and therapy of recurrences in a group of 117 patients undergoing partial cystectomy. This negative paper highlights a recurrence rate of 78% and details recurrence by stage, grade, and post partial cystectomy treatment. No detail of patient selection or operative technique is included.

Schoborg TW, Sapolsky JL, Lewis CW: Carcinoma of the bladder treated by segmental resection. J Urol 122:473, 1979

Survey of 45 patients treated between 1955 and 1976 demonstrates that a favorable 5-yr survival rate can be obtained even in patients necessitating ureteroneocystotomy. Patients with high-grade stage A lesions had a 100% recurrence rate (40% survived 5 yr) while those with low-grade stage A lesions had a 28% recurrent rate (86% survived 5 yr).

Merrell RW, Brown HE, Rose JF: Bladder carcinoma treated by partial cystectomy: A review of 54 cases. J Urol 112:471, 1979

Report emphasizes low morbidity and mortality in 54 "very select" patients undergoing partial cystectomy. Recurrence rate in this series was low (30%), and no tumor was found postoperatively in the wound. The recurrence rate may reflect careful patient selection and might have been even further improved by the use of random biopsies.

Overview: Indications and Contraindications for Segmental Cystectomy

William Brannan

Dr. Bush and associates have provided an excellent discussion of the indications for segmental cystectomy for carcinoma of the bladder and an exhaustive review of the literature with appropriate comments from the pertinent articles. I can therefore comment advisedly to the reader to pay particular attention to the indications and contraindications for segmental cystectomy contained in their discussion. Table 12 lists the indications that should be strictly adhered to.

Dr. Bush has indicated that one of the requisites for consideration of partial cystectomy is a primary or "residual of primary" lesion. My approach to these tumors is to resect as much of the primary tumor as is possible at the initial sitting, including tissue from the base of the tumor, which would represent muscle. Should early invasion be seen, it is then my practice to rebiopsy the lesion or the scar 2 to 3 mo later and then decide on the need for open surgery. If residual neoplasm is found, I perform segmental resection. This, of course, amounts to treatment of the primary lesion and not of a recurrent one. I also feel strongly that, whenever possible, resection of all visible tumor at the initial sitting transurethrally minimizes the chance of any seeding of the tumor at any subsequent operation. I feel that such tumor should be given the benefit of preoperative irradiation before elective segmental resection and the pelvic nodes should be sampled before resection, just as in performing a radical cystectomy.

Dr. Bush's modification of my original indications to include "moderate risk patients with B2 or C lesions" needs some clarification. I believe that, in all likelihood, if a patient can withstand a segmental resection, he can probably also undergo a radical cystectomy, since the mortality and morbidity from the latter have so decreased in the last 10 yr that the operation really is hardly more traumatic than segmental cystectomy. My recent experience with one-stage cystectomy has provided a mortality of not over 3% in those patients whose only indication is carcinoma of the bladder without concomitant lymphomatous neoplasms (*i.e.,* "Cytoxan tumors").

I would have no further comment on the contraindications to partial cystectomy listed in Table 13, but currently I prefer to do a total cystectomy rather than depend on some type of augmentation procedure to provide the patient with a functioning bladder. A patient with a lesion so widespread as to necessitate augmentation probably is not a good candidate for a more conservative approach.

There are two primary reasons why partial cystectomy will fail in the control of a bladder neoplasm. One is that all the tumor has not been removed, either from the bladder or because metastases are already present. Second, as has been previously noted, bladder carcinoma is frequently a field change disease and recurrences are likely to occur. Using all the modalities mentioned by Dr. Bush and associates, physicians are still unable to predict accurately which patients will have a recurrence and which will not. To avoid failures because of the first factor, the surgeon must rely strongly on clinical judgment and assessment of various laboratory modalities, including random biopsies of normal-appearing bladder close to and remote from the lesion in question as well as urine cytologic studies after removal of the primary lesion. Should marked focal atypia be present in the random biopsies, or should cytology remain positive following eradication of the initial lesion, partial cystectomy either should not be contemplated or should be followed by repeated biopsies and probably eventual cystectomy. Such a conservative approach need not necessarily exclude the patient from a curative procedure later should the need arise. Evidence of lymphatic invasion at the margins of the resected tissues should immediately alert the surgeon to the fact that partial cystectomy has not been curative; postoperative irradiation or cystectomy should then be considered. On the other hand, subsequent low-grade, superficial, recurrent tumors can still be managed by more conservative methods.

Partial cystectomy has very limited application in the treatment of patients with urethelial neoplasms of the bladder, but in a selected few patients it can offer as much as a more radical approach. It is certainly not indicated for epidermoid tumors or adenocarcinomas, which, I believe, should be treated by radical cystectomy as soon as the diagnosis is made.

PART TWENTY-SIX

SURGICAL TREATMENT OF VESICAL DIVERTICULUM

70

THE TREATMENT OF DIVERTICULUM OF THE BLADDER

Panayotis P. Kelalis and Peter McLean

From the Mayo Clinic and Mayo Foundation, Section of Urology and the Mayo Graduate School of Medicine, University of Minnesota, Rochester, Minnesota

The Journal of Urology
Copyright © 1967 by The Williams & Wilkins Co.
Vol. 98, Sept.
Printed in U.S.A.

Even though diverticulectomy was first described toward the end of the last century, enthusiasm for the procedure has been only sporadic. This is understandable since seldom is the diverticulum incriminated as the principal cause of the urinary difficulties. When it is responsible for urinary retention and infection, everyone agrees that diverticulectomy is indicated but few would otherwise recommend the procedure. Yet within its confines, carcinoma develops at a disturbing frequency[1] and, when discovered, it is usually beyond the stage of cure, irrespective of the type of treatment used.[2,3]

This paper discusses the incidence and prognostic significance of such malignant lesions within the urinary diverticulum and attempts to reach valid conclusions regarding their management.

Accepted for publication October 27, 1966.
Read at annual meeting of North Central Section, American Urological Association, Inc., Chicago, Illinois, September 28–October 1, 1966.

MATERIAL

From 1955 to 1964, 285 cases of bladder diverticulum were seen at the Mayo Clinic. In all cases undisputed urographic and, in most cases, cystoscopic evidence was present to fulfill the definition of a vesical diverticulum, namely a herniation of bladder mucosa through the musculature joined by a constricted neck to the bladder cavity proper. Pseudo-diverticula, large cellules and diverticula found in female patients were excluded. In 19 cases a neoplasm had arisen in the diverticulum. This does not include 6 cases in which the extensive nature of the neoplasm precluded any attempt at detemining its origin or in which it was apparent that the tumor had grown from the bladder into the diverticulum.

This report therefore deals with the 19 cases in which review of the clinical and diagnostic features, operative records and surgical specimens definitely and indisputably indicated that the neoplasm arose within the diverticulum.

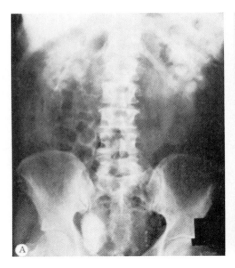 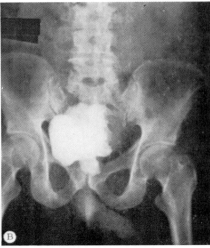

Fig. 1. (A) Left hydronephrosis and incomplete filling of bladder due to tumor in bladder diverticulum. (B) Retrograde cystogram shows tumor in vesical diverticulum.

CLINICAL FEATURES

All patients in this study were men; their ages ranged from 44 to 84 years with an average of 64.3 years. Gross painless hematuria was the initial and only complaint in 15 of 19 cases (79 percent). In 2 cases the presenting symptoms were suggestive of severe lower urinary tract infection, 1 patient had rectal and perineal discomfort and in 1 man prostatism had been present for many years and was complicated by recent hematuria. The interval between the onset of symptoms and the institution of definitive treatment was less than 1 month in 10 cases and less than 3 months in 15 of the 19 cases. Varying degrees of micro-hematuria and pyuria were found in all, but in only 2 of 15 cases in which the residual urine was measured did it exceed 100 ml.

On excretory urography, hydronephrosis was found in 3 cases and absence of function on the same side as the diverticulum in another 3 cases (Fig. 1A); the upper part of the urinary tract in the remaining 13 cases was normal. The excretory cystogram was generally indeterminate because of incomplete filling (Fig. 1A) and marked displacement (Fig. 2). Retrograde cystograms, obtained in 8 instances, revealed the diagnosis in four (Fig. 1B).

The lesion was diagnosed cystoscopically in 15 cases. In two, pus exuding from the diverticular orifice led to a mistaken diagnosis of perivesical abscess communicating with the bladder. In another the initial impression was one of extravesical mass but the correct diagnosis was made by retrograde cystography. In the remaining case the cystoscopic findings were indeterminate; the diagnosis was made at laparotomy.

Two diverticula were present in 3 cases. Despite obvious difficulties in establishing the accurate size, the diverticulum containing the neoplasm was large in 3, small in 3 (Fig. 3) and medium in 13 cases.

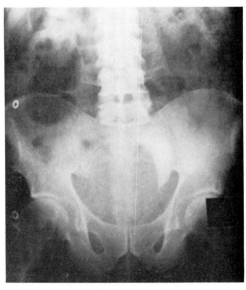

Fig. 2. Marked displacement of bladder from tumor in vesical diverticulum.

TUMOR IN THE DIVERTICULUM

A malignant lesion was present in 19 of the 285 consecutive cases of vesical diverticulum (6.7 percent). Nearly all were of the non-papillary infiltrating type, which had penetrated barely through the diverticular wall. There were 12 transitional and 6 squamous carcinomas. By the histologic grading of Broders, 5 were grade 4, 10 grade 3, 1 grade 2 and 2 grade 1. One was a leiomyosarcoma. In no instance was an associated tumor found in the bladder cavity proper.

Elective diverticulectomy for other than malignant

lesions was performed in 31 cases; in 26 cases the excised mucosa showed changes varying from chronic inflammation, cellular infiltration and mucosal ulceration to squamous metaplasia and leukoplakia (84 percent).

TREATMENT

In 4 cases transurethral prostatic resection with removal of the posterior lip of the orifice leading to the diverticulum had been performed before development of the tumor in an apparently successful effort to improve drainage. In 3 cases, only transurethral prostatic resection had been performed; the diverticulum was left intact (Fig. 4). In 1 case, multiple stones had been removed transurethrally. The interval between these procedures and the ultimate discovery of the tumor ranged from 1.5 to 16 years with an average of 7.5 years.

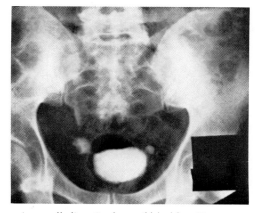

Fig. 3. Tumor in small diverticulum of bladder. Treatment by partial cystectomy and cobalt therapy (longest survival was 4 years).

In the treatment of the malignant lesions themselves, partial cystectomy was done in 9 cases; in six of these, varying doses of radiotherapy were also given. Total cystectomy supplemented with cobalt treatment was performed in 3 cases. In 3 cases a combination of transurethral excision and a full course of cobalt therapy was done. In the remaining 4 cases a hopelessly inoperable lesion was found and palliative treatment was given after suprapubic biopsy.

FOLLOWUP INFORMATION

Thirteen of the 19 patients died within the first year of the onset of symptoms and another 3 patients died during the second year. The average survival period was 11 months.

Only 3 of the 19 patients are alive. Two of these, for whom a diverticulum containing a grade 1 non-infiltrating transitional cell carcinoma was removed by partial cystectomy, are alive without evidence of recurrence after 1 and 2 years, respectively. In the third patient, total cystectomy became necessary 3 years later for recurrence of a grade 3 superficially infiltrating transitional cell epithelioma, despite initial treatment with partial cystectomy and cobalt therapy. This patient has no evidence of recurrence nearly 4 years after the discovery of the tumor.

DISCUSSION

Bladder diverticula, unless they are large and responsible for retention and infection of urine, are usually not regarded as requiring treatment. Their propensity to undergo malignant change has received little attention (while a similar problem, but in our opinion one of less

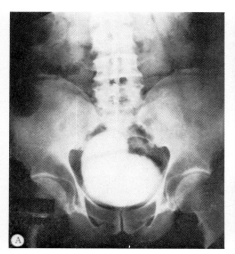

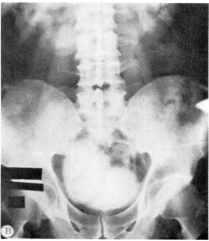

Fig. 4. (*A*) Diverticulum seen at transurethral prostatic resection, no evidence of tumor. (*B*) Diverticulum with tumor 1.5 years later.

significance, namely the problem of malignant change in the undescended testicle, has received considerable attention).

Despite the stringent criteria applied in the selection of our cases, nearly 7 percent of the urinary diverticula studied were associated with tumor within their cavities; furthermore, 84 percent of the diverticula that were excised electively showed changes in their lining secondary to stasis and infection, which at times could be considered frankly premalignant. This high incidence of carcinoma in vesical diverticula becomes of even greater significance when the dismal results of treatment are taken into consideration. Sixteen patients survived less than 1 year after the onset of symptoms (84 percent). Neither prompt diagnosis nor the use of various forms of treatment (alone or in combination) affected the final outcome. The reason for this is that the lesion had already been far advanced when the symptoms appeared, as a result both of the pathologic features of the tumor and of its anatomic location.[4] Thus, the predominantly high-grade, infiltrating nature of the tumor in 80 percent of the cases together with the thinness of the diverticular wall (which is composed only of mucosa and a scanty layer of muscle fibers) was responsible for the penetration of the tumor to the peri-diverticular tissues either simultaneously with, or a short time after, invasion of the wall, which created conditions that nearly always precluded successful operative procedures.

To avert the fatal consequences of such lesions, it is apparent that a more aggressive attitude should be adopted toward removing uncomplicated diverticula.[5] Presently, excision of bladder diverticula is usually undertaken only in instances in which retention of urine exists, resulting in repeated infections or upper urinary tract obstruction. Yet it is the disturbing incidence of malignant change, with its associated uniformly dismal prognosis, that should be the primary consideration in their treatment and, in our opinion, justifies their prophylactic excision. If in 8 of the 19 cases the presence of the diverticulum had not led only to treatment of the prostatic or vesical disease alone, and if instead excision had been undertaken, the development of carcinoma years later could have been forestalled and, in all likelihood, a fatal outcome averted.

It may be argued that the risk associated with such prophylactic excision of bladder diverticula outweighs the advantages. However, on critical review of the procedure this hardly proves to be the case. From the available reports in the literature, the mortality seldom exceeds 2.5 percent.[6] Significant complications are related to technical difficulties due to the size of the diverticulum and the associated inflammatory reaction; this is the group of cases in which elective diverticulectomy is usually necessary. Prophylactic excision of the uncomplicated diverticulum of the bladder should mitigate such technical difficulties and complications. The risk inherent in the propensity of the vesical diverticulum to undergo malignant change would seem by itself to be greater than the risk of its prophylactic excision, and this does not even take into consideration the possible complications resulting from its abnormal anatomic and physiologic features.

We therefore unhesitatingly recommend prophylactic excision of all true diverticula, irrespective of their size, in all patients less than 70 years old unless compelling medical contraindications exist. Such treatment may appear radical, but in our opinion it is fully justified. Those who prefer to treat diverticula of the bladder otherwise must take on themselves the full responsibility of the hazards that may thereby arise.

SUMMARY

Of 285 patients with bladder diverticula, 19 were found to have an associated malignant tumor. Because of the predominantly nonpapillary infiltrating nature of the lesion and the thinness of the diverticular wall, allowing early penetration through it, the lesion was, in most cases, already beyond the possibility of successful removal when discovered. Sixteen of the 19 patients who died survived an average period of 11 months.

This association of tumor and diverticulum should be a primary consideration in their treatment. The high incidence of malignant change and the poor results of subsequent treatment justify prophylactic excision of vesical diverticula.

REFERENCES

1. Knappenberger, S. T., Uson, A. C. and Meyer, M. M.: Primary neoplasms occurring in vesical diverticula: A report of 18 cases. J Urol 83:153–159, 1960
2. Boylan, R. N., Greene, L. F. and McDonald, J. R.: Epithelial neoplasms arising in diverticula of the urinary bladder. J Urol 65:1041–1049, 1951
3. Abeshouse, B. S. and Goldstein, A. E.: Primary carcinoma in a diverticulum of the bladder: A report of our cases and a review of the literature. J Urol 49:534–557, 1943

4. Badenoch, A. W.: Prostatic obstruction: Indications for prostatectomy. Proc Roy Soc Med 55:741–742, 1962
5. Judd, E. S. and Scholl, A. J.: Diverticulum of the urinary bladder. Surg Gynec & Obst 38:14–26, 1924
6. Fox, M., Power, R. F. and Bruce, A. W.: Diverticulum of the bladder—presentation and evaluation of treatment of 115 cases. Br J Urol 34:286–298, 1962

Commentary:
Vesical Diverticulectomy

Ector LeDuc

My experiences with diverticulum of the bladder led me some years ago to agree with the thesis of Kelalis and McLean, as indicated in the selected article, and the recent recommendation of Gittes in the fourth edition of *Campbell's Urology* that prophylactic diverticulectomy is often a highly recommended and justifiable procedure.[1,2]

In reviewing my records of a series of 47 patients with vesical diverticula, 8 had developed malignant tumors in the diverticulum. In seven of these patients an inexorable and rapid downhill course ensued because of intraperitoneal extension, distant metastasis, or both. In the other patient, removal of the diverticulum near the dome, which contained a grade I papillary tumor, was followed by multiple recurrences of low-grade tumors in the bladder.

In this connection, one of the most tragic cases in my series was that of Dr. A., a radiologist and friend, who consulted me within an hour of the onset of hematuria. His history indicated that at age 20 he had had a cystoscopy for urinary symptoms. A bladder diverticulum was discovered, but because the patient developed no further symptoms he failed to return for observation. Subsequently, at age 50 he was found to have two papillary tumors in the orifice of the diverticulum on the floor of the bladder, slightly to right of the middline at the border of the trigone. Transurethral resection of the tumors was performed. The pathology report indicated grade 3 transitional cell carcinoma invading through the muscle (stage C). This report belied the innocent appearance of these tumors as viewed on cystoscopy. The patient underwent vesical diverticulectomy and intraperitoneal exploration. The diverticulum presented below the trigone to the left of the bladder neck and was removed in its entirety with a surrounding collar of bladder measuring 3 cm × 4 cm. The procedure required bisection of the bladder down to the level of the diverticulum. The tissue removed showed no evidence of tumor. However, with 6 mo, cystoscopy demonstrated papillary tumors of the bladder neck, which were resected transurethrally. Shortly thereafter the prostate showed massive induration. The patient refused further investigations; his condition rapidly deteriorated, with metastasis demonstrable in the right ischium. At autopsy widespread metastases to the lung, liver, right kidney, left adrenal gland, visceral nodes, prostate, and seminal vesicals were found. In this case, I believe that prophylactic diverticulectomy following the original diagnosis of diverticulum would have prevented this outcome.

Another patient with whom I was acquainted, also a physician, underwent prostatectomy elsewhere without recommendation for surgical removal of a relatively small diverticulum and later developed a chronic urinary tract infection resistant to therapy, gross hematuria, and metastatic nodules in the corpora cavernosum. Upon urologic investigation, the diverticulum was noted to be the site of a squamous cell carcinoma. Attempted therapy with penectomy, lymph node dissection, and removal of the vesical diverticulum was performed. However, peritoneal metastases caused his death within 2 mo. Again, I believe that prophylactic diverticulectomy at the time of open prostatectomy would have prevented squamous cell carcinoma.

The following information delineates the unfortunate experiences that I have had with tumor formation in patients with vesical diverticula. Four of my patients were under observation for several years, two of whom had been strongly advised to undergo diverticulectomy. One was a woman in her 70s who had had a nephrectomy in the 1920s and who had refused the advice of Dr. Frank Hinman Sr. to have her bladder operated on. For 50 yr she tolerated extreme difficulty in voiding, foul-smelling urine, and residual volumes of urine up to 1000 ml due to a contracture of the bladder neck and multiple large diverticula. Finally, after hematuria developed, squamous cell carcinoma in the largest diverticulum was diagnosed. Her remaining ureter, which was obstructed, was drained by a catheter ureterostomy. Later she underwent abdominal exploration, which demonstrated perineal extension of carcinoma. She died shortly thereafter.

In 1974, while I was preparing my report for the 1974 meeting of the Western Section of the American Urological Association, Drs. Piconi, Henry, and Walsh, at the U.S. Naval Hospital in San Diego, where I was a consultant in urology, had a patient who refused diverticulectomy for chronic infection.[1] The patient returned in 4 mo with a filling defect in his diverticulum. He then submitted to an extensive procedure to remove both it and the contained squamous cell carcinoma.[3]

In studies of the epithelial lining of removed diverticula, not only have Kelalis and McLean shown premalignant changes, but other authors agree with these findings. Peterson and associates confirmed this finding and also have shown that squamous metaplasia can develop in a *noninfected* diverticulum.[4] Most authors agree that stasis of urine enhances and prolongs the contact of carcinogens with the vesical epithelium. This effect is regarded as applicable both to vesical neck obstruction and to poorly draining diverticula, supporting the recommendation that obstruction should be dealt with and poorly draining diverticula removed. The apparent preponderance of squamous cell carcinoma in patients with vesical diverticula appears to be correlated with the frequent reports of squamous cell metaplasia noted in pathologic study of excised diverticula. It has recently been stressed by Pfister that when a tumor occurs in a diverticulum it is immediately a stage C tumor because there is little or no muscle beneath the tumor.[5] Thus, the thin wall of the diverticulum allows early penetration with local and distant metastases. That vesical diverticulectomy is mandatory in patients with secondary stone formation within diverticula and in patients with chronic urinary tract infection secondary to poorly draining diverticula should be no less evident than that diverticulectomy can prevent tumor formation, at least within the vesical diverticulum.

That there are pitfalls in the diagnosis of carcinoma in a diverticulum is universally agreed. In a patient lacking hematuria and with poor filling and drainage of a diverticulum whose orifice is too small to permit cystoscopic observation, the diagnosis can be missed. However, with hematuria, if no other source can be found, diverticula can sometimes be explored with a ureteral catheter and study of the aspirated contents, possibly combined with isotonic bladder washings.[6] These investigations, together with better radiologic studies such as double-contrast cystography (*i.e.*, a "diverticulogram"), should increase diagnostic accuracy.[7]

Fellows is the only author who takes issue with prophylactic diverticulectomy.[8] He compared men with obstruction and tumors to those with obstruction but no tumors. However, a careful reading of his report shows contradictory evidence, inasmuch as 3 of the 12 patients with obstruction and tumor had their tumors arise within a diverticulum. Whitehead emphasizes that if prophylactic diverticulectomy is not performed, the patient should be managed with periodic cystography, endoscopy, and urinary cytology.[9]

The surgical treatment of vesical diverticula varies with the size, location, number of diverticula, and presence or absence of concurrent tumor within the diverticulum. Young's technique, as reported in 1906, and modifications of his intravesical removal of the urethelial lining with closure of the muscular wall, are very satisfactory techniques for small and moderate diverticula.[10,11] The extravesical technique of Ashton Miller, described in the first edition of this text, appears to have great merit, particularly with a large infected sac that cannot safely be removed *in toto* without jeopardizing neighboring structures.[12] In this case, partial or complete removal of the lining is followed by external drainage, and, if desired, phenol can be applied to destroy any residual epithelial lining. More recently, two very satisfactory methods of removing vesical diverticula have been described by Goldman and by Colodny.[13,14] Goldman stresses that the surgeon should not remove more than the true diverticulum, which is a single layer of outpouching.[13] He makes an incision directly into the superior lateral wall of the diverticulum, removing only the true diverticulum and working through the interior of the diverticulum itself, leaving behind the displaced perivesical and endopelvic fascia. His technique is both rapid and safe. Colodny's intravesical technique is extremely easy to perform.[14] He employs a Fogarty catheter secured in the orifice of the diverticulum and a small feeding tube placed in the ureteric orifice. The diverticulum is removed with a circumscribing incision. In this manner the entire intact diverticulum can be removed. This technique lessens the chance of injury to the ureter or vas deferens or innervation of the bladder. The surgical technique presently advised for patients with a diverticulum containing a tumor is aggressive and generally requires surgical exploration and staging with pelvic lymphadenectomy and wide excision of the bladder wall with the contained diverticulum, with possible reimplantation of the ureter or transureteroureterostomy or cystectomy.[3,15] Redman and colleagues stress that if total cystectomy is not chosen, all other diverticula should be excised.[15]

It is reasonable to assume that the previously documented mortality of 2.6% to 4% in patients undergoing diverticulectomy with or without relief of bladder outlet obstruction, frequently in the presence of urinary tract infection or stone disease, no longer applies to patients undergoing uncomplicated, that is, prophylactic, diverticulectomy because of (1) the absence of urinary tract infection or stone disease at surgery, (2) improved methods of preoperative and postoperative management of these elderly patients (3), modern methods of anesthesia, and (4) improved surgical techniques such as those described by Goldman and Colodny.[11-17]

In summary, I agree with Kelalis and McLean that the patient with a diverticulum of the bladder who is under age 70, in reasonable health, and facing the risk of chronic urinary tract infection, stone formation, or tumor development should undergo prophylactic diverticulectomy irrespective of the size of the diverticulum or the presence or absence of residual urine in the diverticulum because no type of treatment yields good results in patients with tumor development in vesical diverticula. This viewpoint is supported by Piconi and associates, who note that it is impractical to perform frequent cystoscopies to detect malignant transformation before invasion occurs and who suggest that "surgical excision of the diverticula of the bladder in the healthy patient appears warranted" and by Gittes, who states that "the presence of a diverticulum in addition to benign prostatic obstruction is often sufficient to indicate the use of open prostatic surgery with coincident diverticulectomy as a prophylactic maneuver to avoid both subsequent tumor and chronic infection."[2,3]

REFERENCES

1. LeDuc E, Piconi JR: Carcinoma in diverticulum of the bladder. Trans American Urological Association meeting, 1974

2. Gittes RF: Tumors of the bladder. In Harrison JH, Gittes RF, Perlmutter AD, et al (eds): Campbell's Urology, Vol 2, 4th ed, p 1061. Philadelphia, WB Saunders, 1979

3. Piconi JR, Henry SC, Walsh PC: Rapid development of carcinoma in diverticulum of the bladder. Urology 2:676, 1973

4. Peterson LJ, Paulson DF, Glenn JF: The histopathology of vesical diverticula. J Urol 110:62, 1973

5. Pfister RR: Endoscopy and the detection of genitourinary carcinoma. Cancer (Suppl) 37:471, 1976

6. Montague DK, Boltuch RL: Primary neoplasms in vesical diverticula: Report of X cases. J Urol 116:41, 1976 (comment by J.D. Young)

7. Shawdon HH, Doyle FH, Shackman R: Double contrast cystography applied to the diagnosis of tumours in the bladder diverticula. Br J Urol 36:536, 1965

8. Fellows GJ: The association between vesical carcinoma and diverticulum of the bladder. Eur Urol 4:185, 1978

9. Whitehead ED: Letter to the editor: Management of bladder diverticula by transurethral resection: Re-evaluation of an old technique. J Urol 124:162, 1980

10. Young HH: The operative treatment of vesical diverticulum with report of 4 cases. Johns Hopkins Hosp Rep 13:411, 1906
11. Wesselhoeft CW Jr, Perlmutter AD, Berg S, et al: Pathogenesis and surgical treatment of diverticulum of the urinary bladder. Surg Gynecol Obstet 116:719, 1963
12. Miller A: The aetiology and treatment of diverticulum of the bladder. Br J Urol 30:43, 1958
13. Goldman HJ: A rapid safe technique for removal of a large vesical diverticulum. J Urol 106:380, 1971
14. Colodny AH: An improved surgical technique for intra-vesical resection of the bladder diverticulum. Br J Urol 47:399, 1975
15. Redman JF, McGinnis TD, Bissada NK: Management of neoplasms in vesical diverticula. Urology 67:492, 1976
16. Fox M, Power RF, Bruce AW: Diverticulum of the bladder—presentation and evaluation of treatment of 115 cases. Br J Urol 34:286, 1962
17. McLean P, Kelalis PP: Bladder diverticulum in the male. Br J Urol 40:321, 1968

ANNOTATED BIBLIOGRAPHY

Bruziere J, Jablonski JM, Bianchi M: Diverticula of bladder in children. Report of 20 cases. J Urol Nephrol 78:914, 1972

The authors cite various theories of diverticulum formation. In the light of clinical and surgical experience, one type is due to obstruction, such as valves and bladder neck contracture. The other types are congenital. The largest eight diverticula in this series correspond to those without obstruction. All 20 patients were men, but 6 had no infravesical obstruction.

Cendron J, Alain JJ: Vesical diverticula in the child without obstruction of the lower urinary tract. J Urol Nephrol 78:793, 1972

In reporting 43 cases, the authors state that the cause, without doubt, is a localized defect in bladder musculature and predominates at the juxtaureteral orifices; 39 of their cases were of this type. Various renal and ureteral anomalies are listed in association with some of the diverticula. Urinary tract infection is an almost constant finding. They speculate that, in intrauterine life, there may be transient obstruction to the outflow of urine, because of accumulations of desquamated epithelial masses, which are eventually passed in the urine.

Fellows GJ: The association between vesical carcinoma and diverticulum of the bladder. Eur Urol 4:185, 1978

Men with obstruction and tumor were compared with a group with obstruction but without tumor. Incidence of diverticula was not significantly higher in the group with carcinoma of the bladder. However, of 12 patients with cancer and diverticula, the tumor arose in the diverticulum in 3. In the discussion, Fellows' opinion is that there is an association between outflow obstruction and vesical carcinoma but that the present study indicates that prophylactic diverticulectomy is unjustified.

Le Duc E, Piconi JR: Carcinoma in diverticulum of the bladder. American Urological Association meeting, 1974

In a study of 47 patients with diverticulum of the bladder, 8 were found to have carcinoma arising within a diverticulum. Of those, four patients were under the observation of the authors for some years before the malignancy developed, two of these having refused to consider diverticulectomy. Four patients appeared with tumor already present in a diverticulum, one a man of 50 known to have had a diverticulum at age 20. Another was in a man whose diverticulum was not removed at the time of open prostatectomy. Of five women with diverticula, 1 with at least a 50-year history of infection and multiple diverticula died of an invasive squamous cell carcinoma in the largest diverticulum.

Murdgieff AT, Boziloff UV: Malignant formations in diverticulum of the bladder. Khirurgiia 24:219, 1971

The authors stage that more than 260 persons with cancer in a diverticulum, plus 6 with sarcoma, have been reported in the literature. They report one patient, 80 yr of age, with undifferentiated transitional cell carcinoma in a diverticulum and another, 69 yr of age, with a leiomyosarcoma within a diverticulum. The histopathology is illustrated.

Peterson LJ, Paulson DF, Glenn JF: The histopathology of vesical diverticula. J Urol 110:62, 1973

The authors studied records of 119 patients, 22 of whom were women. As a result of 41 diverticulectomies performed, 20 diverticula demonstrated chronic inflammatory infiltrates, 3 with squamous metaplasia and 1 with squamous metaplasia without inflammation; 3.6% of 2053 patients with diverticula had intradiverticular malignancy. The authors recommend careful and periodic evaluation of patients with diverticula.

Piconi JR, Henry SC, Walsh PC: Rapid development of carcinoma in diverticulum of bladder: a pitfall in conservative treatment. Urology 2:676, 1973

A man aged 52 refused diverticulectomy when cystoscopy and urography showed no tumor, but on repeat study for chronic infection a urogram showed a filling defect in the dome of the diverticulum. A hemicystectomy, pelvic lymphadenectomy, and left to right transureteral ureterostomy were performed. The tumor was grade I squamous cell with negative nodes. The authors recommend that early surgical excision of diverticulum of the bladder in healthy patients be performed.

Redman JF, McGinnis TD, Bissada NK: Management of neoplasm in vesical diverticula. Urology 67:492, 1976

The authors report two cases of neoplasm in diverticula in men. They recommend pelvic lymphadenectomy with extensive segmental resection of the diverticulum and surrounding bladder wall, after open staging, and if total cystectomy is not chosen, they remove other bladder diverticula.

Siegel WH: Neoplasms in vesical diverticula. Urology 4:411, 1974

The author reports on four cases of neoplasm in patients with diverticula. He indicates that some elderly patients are best treated with repeated cystoscopy and cold loop transurethral resections.

Sugaya K, Masuda F, Minami T: Acta Urol Jpn 17:243, 1971

The author reports on four cases of neoplasm in patients with diverticula. He indicates that some elderly patients are best treated with repeated cystoscopy and cold loop transurethral resections.

Viville C, Meyer P: Diverticula of the bladder in children without bladder neck obstruction. Ann Chir Infant 13:201, 1972

The authors report seven cases of diverticulum of the bladder in children, with obscure origin. The usual location of the diverticulum in the neighborhood of the ureteral orifices is thought to be due, as per Williams and Hutch, to a weak area in this location.

Whitehead ED: Letter to the editor: Management of bladder diverticula by transurethral resection: Re-evaluation of an old technique. J Urol 124:162, 1980

The author has recently compared the reported incidence of carcinoma developing in vesical diverticula (2.9%–6.7%) to the case rate of carcinoma of the prostate, and has noted the alarming fact that if the indices are correct, more men who have bladder diverticula will suffer carcinoma in the diverticulum than those who suffer carcinoma of the prostate in the general population of persons ⩾ 50 years old. He recommends that if prophylactic diverticulectomy is not performed, the patient should be managed with periodic cystography, endoscopy, and urinary cytology.

OVERVIEW: BLADDER DIVERTICULA

Arthur N. Tessler

The diagnosis and techniques of surgical management of bladder diverticula are generally well known at present. The etiology, with the exception of the relatively uncommon congenital bladder diverticula, is also widely recognized as obstruction, whether anatomic or neurogenic. Less certain are the factors permitting diverticulum formation at a given part of the bladder or why some bladders seem more prone to diverticulum formation than others. There is also general agreement that diverticula associated with retention of urine, and particularly those with chronic inflammation and stone formation, should be excised and the bladder defect repaired. The technique for diverticulectomy varies with the size and location of the diverticulum, but in any event, removal of the associated and anatomic obstruction is the mandatory part of bladder diverticulum repair. In the past, the question of staged procedures and the choice of surgical approach were more important. Improvements in anesthesia, preoperative and postoperative care, and the availability of antibiotics and blood for replacement have drastically altered the problems of surgery, permitting the surgeon a choice of techniques depending on the size, number, and location of the diverticula and the surgeon's preference and past experience.

Unresolved are the indications for diverticulectomy for the asymptomatic single or multiple diverticula unassociated with significant retention or inflammation. Most urologists agree that diverticulectomy is desirable, particularly if but one or two large diverticula are present and an open surgical procedure is contemplated to correct the obstruction, but there remains a large reservoir of patients with asymptomatic diverticula whose bladder outlet obstruction is now treated by transurethral surgery, and I believe the risk of subsequent tumor development in bladder diverticula may be overstated. The poorer prognosis of the patient developing tumors within the bladder diverticula is well known. The higher grade malignancies tend to be more invasive earlier, since the absence of the investing detrusor around the diverticulum wall permits earlier penetration into the perivesical tissues. By definition, this represents a more advanced stage and probably, at present, a poorer prognosis. In the figures presented by Kelalis and McLean, the incidence of tumor seen in bladder diverticula is reported as 6.7% but has been reported as lower in other series. In the 19 patients discussed in the Kelalis and McLean paper, 15 presented with gross, painless hematuria, 2 with severe lower urinary tract infection, and another with rectal and perineal discomfort and recent hematuria. The finding of a bladder neoplasm was clinically anticipated. The finding of a bladder neoplasm in men studied for prostatism, but without the presence of a bladder diverticulum, is not rare, but I am unaware of any specific figures to compare with the incidence seen in the series with diverticula. Although the specific etiology of bladder tumor formation is not fully understood, the reservoir function of the bladder has been recognized as a contributing factor in the development of urothelial tumors within the bladder, and stasis and chronic inflammation have also been identified as contributory and are, of course, associated with bladder diverticula disease. Therefore, the physician must not ascribe a causal relationship of bladder diverticulum to bladder tumor formation. Indeed, they may be concomitant rather than causally related. In the Kelalis and McLean series of 285 patients, the 19 patients with tumor were treated, as were 31 treated with elective diverticulectomy. In 235 patients the underlying obstruction was corrected but the diverticula were untreated. Personal communication with Dr. Kelalis reveals that three of these patients subsequently presented with bladder tumor formation, but only one definitely arose within a diverticulum. If there were a causal relationship, one would anticipate a much higher incidence of subsequent tumor development. It is the absence that leads me to believe that the risk of tumor development in bladder diverticula may be overstated. I do not profess to have a definitive answer, and whenever possible I favor diverticulectomy as part of therapy, particularly if there is stasis, chronic infection, and stone formation within the diverticulum. Well documented is the higher grade and advanced stage as well as the poorer prognosis of tumors found within bladder diverticulum. Less certain is the incidence of tumor development in the asymptomatic, uninfected, freely draining diverticulum following correction of the bladder outlet obstruction. The advantages of transurethral surgery are well recognized, and I therefore continue to favor this approach whenever applicable.

PART TWENTY-SEVEN

RECONSTRUCTIVE SURGERY OF THE BLADDER NECK

71

PLASTIC RECONSTRUCTION OF THE BLADDER NECK AND PROSTATECTOMY

An Operation Suitable for All Types of Non-Malignant Bladder Neck Obstruction

By N. J. Bonnin

Adelaide

Reprinted from *The Australian and New Zealand Journal of Surgery*, February, 1958, Vol. 27, No. 3

Before describing operative procedures, it is necessary to consider the mode of healing of the prostatic fossa and of the bladder neck.

It has been shown by Flocks (1938) and by Berry (1946) that provided a layer of prostatic tissue is left lining the true capsule, rapid healing occurs. Epithelium creeps out from innumerable open prostatic ducts, undergoes metaplasia to transitional epithelium and covers the surface completely within three to four weeks. Healing is thus closely similar to the healing of skin after a split skin graft has been taken from it and as the underlying tissues are provided with early epithelial covering, little scarring and contraction occurs. These observations are of fundamental importance and explain why the prostatic fossa remains open after prostatectomy.

The result of removal of the false capsule can be seen when dealing with the post-operative strictures of the prostatic fossa by endoscopic resection. I have observed repeatedly that in the region of the stricture a ring of dense fibrous tissue has been covered by a thin epithelium only, while in that part of the prostatic cavity which had remained open, there has been a layer of prostatic tissue beneath the covering epithelium. The only reasonable explanation is that loss of the false capsule at the original operation had resulted in exposed fibrous tissue behaving as exposed fibrous tissue always does behave; it had ulcerated, scarred and contracted.

Furthermore, post-operative panendoscopic examinations carried out personally in a number of cases have shown that a trigonal flap sutured down over the "false capsule" does not stay in place. The false capsule epithelializes beneath it. On the other hand, when a flap of trigone is fixed down to a bed devoid of prostatic tissue, then the flap has stayed in place and the smooth surface of trigonal mucosa has been seen to have united nicely edge to edge with the epithelialized false capsule. The false capsule thus behaves as if it were a mucosa, albeit a damaged one, and it should be handled by the surgeon as such.

At the bladder neck the situation is fundamentally different. Prostatic tissue here is a pathological intrusion and when it is stripped away a raw surface of the fibro-muscular tissue is exposed. Healing is delayed and the granulating surface is slowly covered by epithelium, which creeps over it from the edge of bladder mucosa above and from the false capsule below.

It is characteristic of this type of healing that scarring and contraction inevitably follow and the degree of scarring and contraction will depend on the time taken for the raw surface to acquire a complete epithelial covering. The most important factor affecting the healing time will be the width of the raw surface, but infection and diathermy burns will both delay healing and thus increase scarring.

It may be reasonably concluded that in the prostatic fossa, scarring can be prevented by leaving a layer of prostatic tissue lining the true capsule, but the only way in which scarring at the bladder neck may be prevented will be by eliminating the raw surface here, either by excising it or by providing immediate epithelial covering for it.

When urinary obstruction is due to a contracted bladder neck, the essential feature to be dealt with is a ring of fibro-muscular tissue beneath the epithelium in this region. It has seemed reasonable to assume that satisfactory and permanent widening of the bladder neck will be attained only by the application to this situation of established surgical principles for the management of subepithelial bands and scars. A review of such principles here would be out of place and it will suffice to say that to sever a band lying beneath a mucosal surface and leave a gaping wound to heal by granulation, as is done when a wedge is taken from the bladder neck, is not in accord with these principles.

With these ideas in mind, the following operative procedures have been evolved.

The operation is described as it is applied to a case of congenital bladder neck dysfunction or to a small fibrous prostate. Modifications of the procedure entailed by the presence of an adenomatous prostate will be mentioned later.

THE APPROACH

The retropubic approach to the prostate as described by Millin (1947) is employed and no detailed description is

necessary. Unless a hernia is to be dealt with at the same time, a midline incision is preferred. Veins in the retropubic fat are dealt with by diathermy coagulation. A gauze pack is inserted on each side of the prostatic capsule.

THE ANTERIOR BLADDER NECK AND ANTERIOR PROSTATIC CAPSULE

The object of the procedure here is to cut the ring of fibro-muscular tissue at the bladder neck and insert a flap of bladder into the interval between the cut ends.

At first this was done by a simple Y-plasty. This operation was kindly published under the author's name by Reed Nesbit in 1955. The illustrations, Figs. 1 and 2, should make the procedure clear.

The bladder flap however did not always fit nicely into the acute angle in the lower end of the incision in the thick prostatic capsule.

This was suspected to be the cause of a temporary urinary fistula which occurred in one case and the incision has been modified.

The capsular incision now employed is illustrated in Fig. 3. A suture is first placed across the apex of the prostate as far down as possible, catching the upper portion of the pubo-prostatic ligaments. This suture underruns the dorsal veins of the penis and also acts as a stay suture. If capsular veins are seen lying lateral to this stitch, they are separately under-run and ligated near the prostatic apex. A second stay suture is placed through the bladder wall in the midline just above the bladder neck. (This stitch is not shown in the illustrations.)

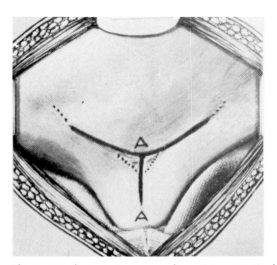

Fig. 1. YV-plasty (not now used). Incision: Vertical limb of incision cuts bladder neck. Lateral limbs extend out into bladder wall.

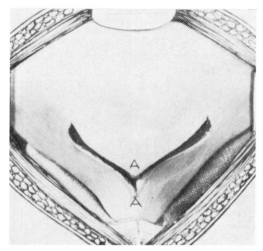

Fig. 2. YV-plasty. Closure: The apex of bladder flap may not fit nicely into acute angle in rigid capsular tissue near apex of prostate.

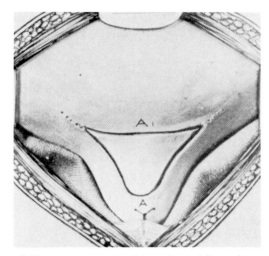

Fig. 3. Small fibrous prostate. Incision: Dotted lines show how incision may be extended. Stay suture at prostatic apex. Rounded lower end allows nice approximation of bladder flap (see Fig. 15).

Cutting deeply with a scalpel, the curved lower part of this incision is made first. It is placed as near the apex of the prostate as is practicable, care being taken to leave sufficient capsule below to provide a secure hold for sutures later. The proximal ends of the incision extend up and laterally through the bladder neck. The flap thus outlined is picked up and cut away by a transverse incision through the bladder wall just above the bladder neck. A portion of the anterior prostatic capsule, together

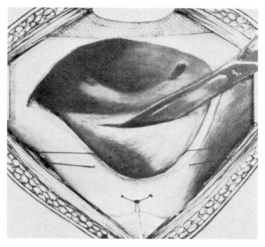

Fig. 4. Small fibrous prostate. Anterior capsule and sphincter have been removed and bladder neck spreader (not shown) inserted. Incision is made along elevated bladder neck. Lateral stay sutures inserted where shown are tied to the Millin retractor and hold up the cut edges of the capsule, thus increasing exposure and decreasing bleeding.

with a wide segment of the anterior sphincter muscle are thus excised, and there is a rounded lower end to the capsular incision.

If the bladder mucosa has not already been opened it will be seen bulging like a balloon into the upper part of the incision. It is picked up and incised. The opening thus made into the bladder should admit two fingers comfortably and if desired it may be enlarged as indicated by the dotted line in Fig. 3.

Stay sutures on each side of the prostatic capsule are tied to the arms of the Millin retractor. These increase exposure and diminish bleeding from the capsular edge. A Millin bladder neck spreader is inserted. The ureteric orifices are identified. With a scalpel a deep incision is made along the crest of the ridge of the raised posterior neck of the bladder (Fig. 4). Above the blade of the scalpel will lie the distal portion of the trigone with a good thick layer of fibro-muscular tissue including the upper fibres of the sphincter, supporting the mucosa. (It is most important not to leave the fragile mucosa unsupported.) Below the scalpel blade lies the bulk of the posterior sphincter. Into this incision one blade of a Denis Browne forceps is thrust with the other blade in the prostatic urethra, so that between the blades the posterior sphincter is gripped and held up (Fig. 5). With a pair of curved scissors, the trigone is cleared away further from the upper aspect of the sphincter (Fig. 5) and then a wide and deep wedge or U-shaped piece of

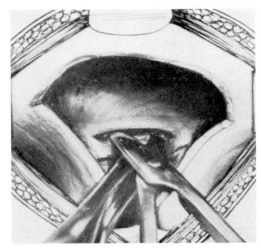

Fig. 5. Small fibrous prostate. Trigone (with thick layer of tissue supporting the mucosa) is undermined by blunt scissor dissection.

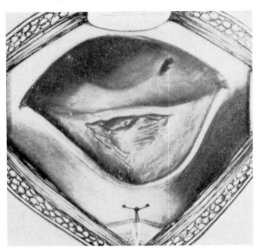

Fig. 7. Small fibrous prostate. Appearance after wedge of posterior sphincter has been removed.

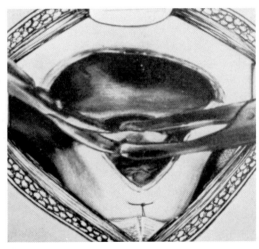

Fig. 6. Small fibrous prostate. The posterior sphincter below the trigone is picked up and a deep wedge removed.

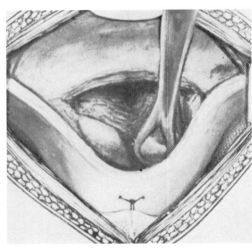

Fig. 8. Small lateral lobes are present (enucleation with finger is not feasible). Trigone has been undermined and sphincter cut away from beneath it (Figs. 4 to 7). Tops of lateral lobes are now clearly visible. Lobes are bitten away piece by piece with Denis Browne forceps, leaving a layer of prostatic tissue still lining the capsule.

the sphincter is removed from beneath the trigone (Fig. 6 and 7). Sometimes this wedge is cut so deeply that the vesicles are exposed. No harm results as the defect is later securely covered.

In a congenital dysfunction of the bladder neck, or where the prostate is atrophic, lateral lobes are not disturbed.

If lateral lobes are not atrophic, the upper end of each lobe will now show up distinctly. Each lobe, together with its covering mucosa, is bitten away piece by piece (Fig. 8) with Denis Browne tonsil holding

forceps (Fig. 9). This instrument is well suited to the purpose for its dull edges are sharp enough to bite away prostatic tissue without risk of perforating the capsule. Moreover, since one blade is larger than the other, it is hardly possible to avoid leaving the necessary thin layer of prostatic tissue lining the fibrous capsule. This piece-meal removal is carried out under control of vision and touch and through this incision and with this instrument there is no difficulty in removing each lobe down to its

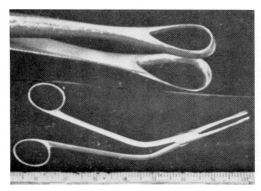

Fig. 9. Denis Browne forceps. Note that one ring is larger than the other.

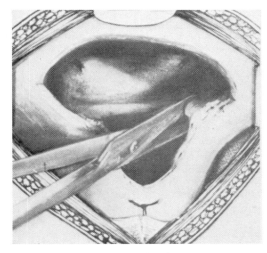

Fig. 10. Small fibrous prostate. The bladder mucosa, together with remaining upper portion of sphincter beneath it, is cut on each side, lateral to the trigone, so that the distal trigone becomes a free flap.

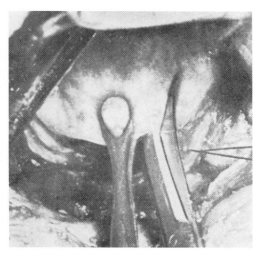

Fig. 11. Photograph taken at operation showing trigonal flap being freed. The left ureteric orifice can be seen medial to the tip of the scissors.

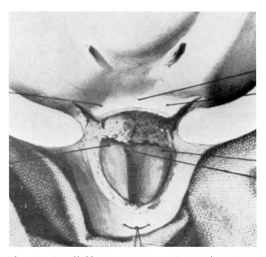

Fig. 12. Small fibrous prostate. Coronal section of model to show the position of postero-lateral incisions which free the trigonal flap. The three sutures which will fix the flap down are shown in place.

apex. If desired a finger in the rectum can be used to press the prostatic tissue into the bite of the forceps, but this is rarely necessary.

Whether lateral lobes are removed or not, the next step is to free the trigonal flap. The flap is drawn down with Denis Browne forceps which allow a secure hold without mucosal damage. With one blade of the scissors in the prostatic fossa and the other blade in the bladder, a short incision is now made lateral to the trigone on each side. Each incision is directed upwards and outwards, parallel to the lateral edge of the trigone, and well clear of it (Figs. 10, 11 and 12). The incision cuts through bladder mucosa for not more than half an inch, but it does cut through a thick layer of the upper portion of the sphincter muscle, which has been left supporting the trigone and as these incisions are made the bladder neck will be seen to widen considerably. The distal trigone with a strip of bladder mucosa on each side of it will now fall to lie covering the defect left by removal of the wedge of sphincter posteriorly (Fig. 12 and Fig. 14).

The flap is fixed in this position. Usually three interrupted sutures are used and these must get a firm

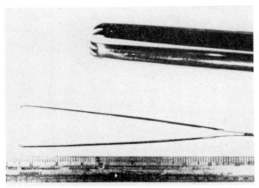

Fig. 13. Long forceps wtih catsclaw teeth help in picking up true capsule to insert sutures.

Fig. 15. Small fibrous prostate. Photograph at operation showing flap sutured down. Note exposure of prostatic fossa from which prostate has been bitten away piecemeal.

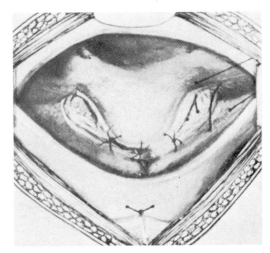

Fig. 14. Small fibrous prostate. Trigonal flap has been fixed down with three interrupted sutures. These sutures are all placed before any are tied. One postero-lateral suture has been placed. This will close the defect made by the postero-lateral incision and also control arterial bleeding. An over-and-over stitch is inserted and so deeply that it reaches or penetrates the external surface of bladder and prostatic capsule, comprising the branches of the prostatic artery.

bite of the posterior capsule. This is not always easy and a long pair of dissecting forceps with fine sharp teeth (Fig. 13) help to pick up the posterior capsule, so that a curved needle can be thrust through it. All three sutures are placed before any are tied.

There is still a raw surface on each side in the region of the postero-lateral incisions which freed the trigone (Fig. 14). The bladder here is mobile and a suture placed on each side draws the mucosa forward to cover the raw surface. These sutures are placed from bladder through

to prostatic fossa taking a very deep bite, and an over-and-over stitch is used, for it is in this region that the prostatic arteries enter the bladder neck. After these sutures are tied, if they have been properly placed, arterial bleeding ceases. The suture thus serves the purpose of the Harris (1928) haemostatic stitch as well as covering the defect made by the postero-lateral incisions. If bleeding is profuse these sutures are inserted before the trigonal flap is sutured down.

CLOSURE OF THE ANTERIOR INCISION

A stitch of No. 1 chromic catgut is first placed in the midline anteriorly (Fig. 16) taking a secure bite of capsule and of bladder wall. This suture is held and is not tied until the closure is completed.

Each half of the anterior incision is now closed by a running catgut suture which begins laterally and progresses towards the midline. Care is taken that the bladder mucosa is caught with each stitch. Finally, the ends of the two running sutures are tied together and further support is provided by tying the two stay sutures together.

It will be found that the anterior bladder wall will move readily down into the defect in the prostatic capsule and although it would appear that a short edge of bladder wall has to be approximated to a longer incision in the capsule, this is not in fact the case. The prostatic capsule is fibrous and does not stretch, but the free bladder edge does stretch and so much that sometimes a longer upper edge has to be sewn to a shorter lower one.

When closed it will be found that the incision in the prostatic capsule has opened from a U-shape to almost

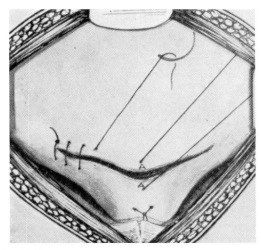

Fig. 16. Small fibrous prostate. Closure of anterior incision. Note central suture. A continuous suture begins on each side and progresses towards centre where two ends are tied. Bladder mucosa is caught with every stitch.

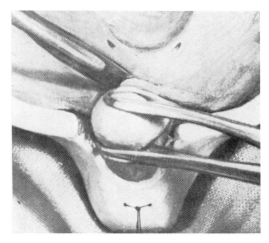

Fig. 17. A middle lobe is present. Coronal section of model to show middle lobe held forward. Incision at junction of lobe and trigone.

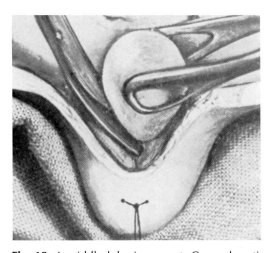

Fig. 18. A middle lobe is present. Coronal section of model. Middle lobe has been dissected free posteriorly and laterally until only remaining attachment is urethra. This is cut with scissors. Posterior sphincter and trigone are then dealt with as described before.

a straight line, so that the bladder neck is widened and the dense fibrous tissue of bladder neck is replaced by a pliable bladder wall. Tissues appear to lie nicely in place without tension and the mucosa of the bladder is applied directly to the mucosa of the prostatic urethra, or to false capsule if the prostate has been removed. (Any tension on the suture line could be completely relieved by freeing peritoneum and urachus from the superior surface of the bladder, but this has not been found necessary except in a case of post-operative bladder neck stricture.)

Before closure is completed the prostatic cavity and bladder are sucked clear of clot and a catheter is inserted. If the trigonal flap has been fixed down properly, the catheter will run smoothly into the bladder. In the occasional case where persistent oozing of venous type occurs, a Foley balloon catheter is employed. Traction is necessary as the bladder neck is now so wide that the balloon will not otherwise stay in the prostatic fossa.

WOUND CLOSURE

The lateral packs are removed and the suture line inspected. Any remaining bleeding point is under-run with fine catgut. A drain is inserted to the retropubic space. The rectus sheath is closed with interrupted sutures of gauge 30 stainless steel wire.

REMOVAL OF A SMALL MIDDLE LOBE

The anterior capsular incision is made as has been described. If a middle lobe is present it will be seen protruding into this incision and it is removed as the next step in the operation.

The lobe is drawn forward (Fig. 17). An incision is made at the junction of the lobe and trigone and the trigonal flap is elevated as before. The ends of the dissecting scissors are now turned against the back of the middle lobe and the plane of the adenoma is found. A snip with scissors on each side frees the lobe laterally. Blunt dissection then progresses distally, until the prostatic urethra is the only attachment. This is severed and the lobe is removed (Fig. 18). Removal of the lobe from

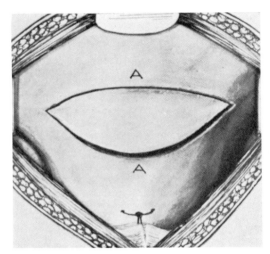

Fig. 19. The large adenoma. Incision: Note that lower incision is curved more strongly than upper because bladder stretches and capsule does not stretch. Incision gives good exposure and excises anterior segment of internal sphincter.

Fig. 20. The large adenoma. Sagittal section of model to show method of enucleation. Space "A" was opened first by blunt scissor dissection then with finger. Space "B" was broken into by finger curled round the lobe. Apex is still attached by strip of prostatic urethra.

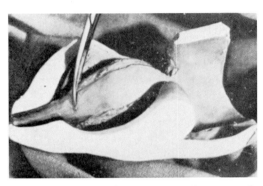

Fig. 21. The large adenoma (sagittal section of model). If the apex does not come away readily no force is used. The apex is cut off with scissors and later removed piecemeal with Denis Browne forceps. Gentleness at the apex is essential. Nothing can compensate for damage to the external sphincter.

above down in this way avoids damage to the ejaculatory ducts. The posterior sphincter which lay beneath the lobe is now in view. This is seized and cut away as shown in Fig. 6. It is important that no prostatic tissue be left beneath the trigonal flap, and any retrotrigonal adenoma is removed with the sphincter at this stage.

Postero-lateral incisions in the bladder neck now follow and the operation proceeds as before (Figs. 6 to 16).

LARGE ADENOMATA

For large glands, the incision approaches the shape of an ellipse (Fig. 19). The anterior bladder neck and upper part of the anterior prostatic capsule are excised. The incision gives excellent exposure and when it is closed, bladder mucosa is applied edge to edge with false capsule. The distal part of the incision has cut deeply into prostatic adenoma so as to show up the line of cleavage between adenoma and false capsule. This plane is opened up all round by blunt dissection with scissors.

The lateral lobes are removed separately by combined intra and extra urethral dissection in a manner somewhat similar to that employed by Millin. A finger is inserted into the prostatic urethra and brought forward through the anterior raphe so that the two lobes are separated in front. On each side the plane between adenoma and false capsule, which has already been opened up by scissor dissection, is extended further with a finger. Now from within the urethra firm pressure is made laterally just behind the bulge of each lobe and

the prostatic urethra splits longitudinally (Fig. 20) and by working first inside the urethra and then outside the adenoma, the apex of each lobe is freed. If the urethra near the apex does not tear across easily, it is cut across with scissors. If the apex or one or other side does not come free easily, no force is used, but the lobe itself is cut across as far down as possible with scissors (Fig. 21) and remaining apical tissue is later removed piecemeal with Denis Browne forceps. Gentleness at the apex of the gland is essential in order to avoid damage to the external sphincter, the worst accident in prostatic surgery. Having been freed, the apex of each lateral lobe is seized and lifted up through the capsular incision. By applying traction and with a finger beneath it, it is dissected out and delivered. Its attachment at the bladder neck is finally cut with scissors. At this stage a Millin bladder

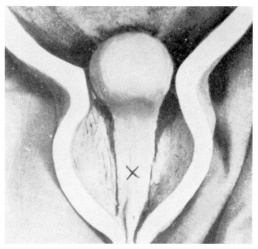

Fig. 22. The large adenoma (coronal section of model). Section of model showing appearance after removal of lateral lobes. Middle lobe and a strip of urethra remain. Middle lobe will not be removed from above down as shown in Figs. 16 and 17 and prostatic urethra will be cut across somewhere about "X," the proximal portion being removed with underlying middle lobe. The remainder of the operation then follows the plan already described.

neck spreader is inserted and there is seen a central ribbon of urethra in the prostatic fossa spreading out proximally to cover the bladder neck or middle lobe (Fig. 22).

A middle lobe will next be removed from above down, the prostatic urethra being finally cut across at about the point "X" in Fig. 22.

The rest of the procedure then follows the lines already described, and differs only in such details as are imposed by distorted anatomy. In a very large gland with retrotrigonal extension for instance, a formal trigonal flap may be redundant.

NOTES ON TECHNIQUE

Diathermy is used to control bleeding only until the prostatic capsule is exposed. For control of bleeding within the prostatic cavity, transfixion ligatures are used. Diathermy burns in this region are not only liable to be followed by later secondary haemorrhage, but will also delay epithelialization.

A two-needle holder technique with a curved round bodied needle is preferred and presents no great difficulties. Boomerang needles have cutting edges and those available here do too much damage and are liable to cause bleeding.

Operating time has been about one hour.

POST-OPERATIVE CARE

The wound drain is removed forty-eight hours after operation. As a routine the catheter is removed within forty-eight hours, unless clots are present in the urine, and in a very few cases has it remained in place for more than four days. Patients are usually out of bed on the third or fourth day. Antibiotics are given in all cases until twenty-four hours after the catheter has been removed. Penicillin and streptomycin are used except when culture of the urine has demonstrated the presence of an organism sensitive to some other antibiotic.

COMMENTS

In general the operation described does not appear to have increased risk in terms of either morbidity or mortality.

In particular excision of the anterior bladder neck has not once in 160 consecutive cases been followed by urinary leakage, in spite of early removal of the catheter.

A low mortality in a small series such as this means little; and the operation is only one of many factors which affect the patient's safety. A brief digression on management outside the operating theatre seems pertinent here.

Pre-operative intravenous pyelography is carried out as a routine and cystoscopy has been performed a day or two before operation. Cystoscopy on the table immediately before surgery can give rise to an embarrassing situation if a diverticulum or a carcinoma is discovered.

In this series not one case has been operated upon as an emergency. For retention of urine an inlying Foley catheter has been used and catheter drainage continued for as long as the patient's general condition could be improved by waiting. For overflow retention gravity decompression was employed. Repeated urinary cultures with sensitivity tests to antibiotics were carried out whenever an inlying catheter was in place to enable immediate effective therapy of any pyrexial episode.

A large minority of patients requiring prostatectomy are suffering from another serious disease and it is the discovery and care of this other condition which often decides the outcome. For instance, even in the presence of acute retention, patients in congestive cardiac failure are not operated upon until oedema has been eliminated with mercurial diuretics, together with other appropriate treatment, chronic bronchitics are taught to breathe and to cough by a physiotherapist, and all patients with a history of peptic ulcer have a Ryles tube passed into their stomach before operation and a milk and "Amphogel" drip is continued until they can again take food orally. These examples are only three among the many serious co-existing diseases frequently encountered in this age group.

After operation any tenderness in the calf of the leg is regarded as due to venous thrombosis and the patient is treated with "Dindevan" at once. Prostatectomy is no contraindication to the use of anticoagulants. With prothrombin levels ranging between 15 percent and 25 percent, risk of bleeding appears to be slight and it is rarely that the treatment has had to be discontinued because of haemorrhage.

One of the objects of this procedure has been to prevent post-operative stricture. The fibro-muscular ring of the bladder neck is severed in several places and partially excised. The prostatic cavity and bladder neck are converted into a wide open epithelialized funnel and round the rim of this funnel the suture line is not circular, but is staggered. Late post-operative stenosis should not occur but many years must pass before it can be known whether this complication has been prevented.

TREATMENT OF POST-OPERATIVE STRICTURES OF THE BLADDER NECK AND PROSTATIC CAVITY

Two cases only of late post-prostatectomy obstruction are listed in the table as having been treated by open operation and two more cases have been operated upon since June, 1957. Other cases have been treated by transurethral resection.

The tentative opinion held at present is that these strictures fall into three groups. Firstly, cases in which the prostatic cavity is wide open and there is a short or diaphragm-like stricture at the neck of the bladder. In such cases the resectoscope can give a very wide bladder neck with a narrow raw surface. The procedure is quick and easy and in most cases subsequent scarring will probably not be sufficient to again cause obstruction and even should this occur, open surgery is still feasible.

There is a second type in which the lower part of the prostatic cavity is open, but there is a long and dense stricture at the neck of the bladder. Transurethral resection can only cause another and probably even denser scar, since it leaves a wide burned raw surface. It is in four cases of this type that the operative procedure described has been employed. Immediate results seem satisfactory, but exposure and access are difficult, especially if a retropubic approach has been used for the first operation and the operation is not one to be lightly undertaken.

In a third type of case stricturing involves the whole prostatic cavity and the external sphincter may also have been damaged. (At the original operation the prostate had presumably been removed against the plane of the true capsule.) Section of the scar postero-laterally on each side with the resectoscope and then intermittent dilatation is an unsatisfactory but safe solution. It would probably be possible to bring down bladder wall to membranous urethra in front, if the pubo-prostatic ligaments were sectioned, but this has not been tried, as it seems likely to carry some risk of incontinence.

In all cases careful assessment with a panendoscope is essential before considering surgery.

CONCLUSION

In the case of the large adenomata many operations in current use give good results and indeed the procedure described does not differ greatly from that employed by many surgeons. However, excision of the anterior bladder neck does give better exposure than does a transverse capsular incision. The postero-lateral incisions which free the trigonal flap facilitate placement of sutures which do control arterial bleeding, and it is believed that elimination of the raw surface in the region of the bladder neck has paid dividends in the form of a smoother and more rapid convalescence; but this latter is an impression and the impressions of a surgeon concerning his own cases are notoriously unreliable.

For cases of contracted or spastic bladder neck, and for small glands which will not enucleate, there has not been available any really satisfactory operative procedure.

In this group of cases the operation described is technically pleasing to do since tissues can be handled gently under full vision and results so far have been good. The requirements of a satisfactory operative procedure appear to have been met.

SUMMARY

The mode of healing of the post-operative prostatic cavity and of the bladder neck have been considered. It is noted that the "false capsule" of the prostate behaves as if it were an abraded mucosa.

It is concluded that to obtain rapid healing and to prevent later scar contraction, it is necessary in the prostatic fossa to leave a layer of prostatic tissue lining the true capsule; at the bladder neck it is necessary to eliminate the raw surface either by excising it or by providing immediate epithelial covering for it.

It is suggested that a contracted bladder neck can be permanently widened only by the application of old established principles of plastic surgery.

An open operative technique is described suitable for the management of all types of bladder neck obstruction, including the small fibrous prostate and the congenital bladder neck dysfunction.

In brief the operation entails excision of the upper portion of the anterior prostatic capsule together with the anterior sphincteric tissue at the bladder neck. At the end of the operation the excised tissue is replaced by pliable bladder wall, together with its covering mucosa.

The incision provides what is probably the best possible exposure of the prostate and prostatic cavity and also results in widening of the bladder neck with the elimination of any raw surface in this region.

Posteriorly the internal sphincter is cut away beneath and below the trigone and the raw surface is then covered by a trigonal flap.

Postero-lateral incisions which free the flap at the same time widen the bladder neck still further, and also allow placement of sutures, which stop arterial bleeding.

The prostate is removed by finger enucleation if it is adenomatous. If it is of small fibrous type it is removed piecemeal with Denis Browne tonsil holding forceps. The exposure allows this to be done readily with full control by vision and touch.

The final result is the conversion of the prostatic cavity into a wide open epithelialized funnel. One hundred and sixty consecutive cases are reported with three deaths. No case of post-operative urinary leakage occurred in these series.

REFERENCES

BERRY, N. E. and MILLER, J. (1946), J Urol (Baltimore), vol 56, page 223

FLOCKS, R. H. (1938), J Urol (Baltimore), vol 40, page 209

HARRIS, S. H. (1928), J Coll Surg Aust, vol 1, page 65

MILLIN, T. (1947), "Retropubic Urinary Surgery." Edinburgh, E. & S. Livingstone Ltd

NESBIT, R. M. and CRANSHAW, W. B. (1955), J Urol (Baltimore), vol 78, page 516

Commentary: Vesical Neck Reconstruction

Noel J. Bonnin and John S. Jose

Although the selected article on bladder neck reconstruction was published in 1958, the procedures described have stood the test of time. Many variations have been tried over the years, but there has been no major change in the technique of the operation on the bladder neck itself. A helpful preliminary procedure, however, has been suture ligation of the prostatic arteries before incision of the prostatic capsule or bladder neck. Originally suggested by Pearson,* it was first used by us in 1963, although priority for publication of preliminary arterial ligation belongs to Gregoire.[1] Blood loss has been considerably reduced. Other changes have been the use of a transverse abdominal incision, closed suction drainage of the retropubic space, and light traction on a Foley catheter as a routine part of postoperative care.

THE ABDOMINAL INCISION

The vertical midline incision described in the article is no longer used. To proceed, make a transverse incision about 2 cm above the pubis. Cut the rectus sheath transversely at the same level, free it up and down, and separate the recti. A short vertical incision in the lower part of the rectus sheath down to the pubis improves access (Fig. 23.)[1] This presents no difficulty in closure, and no wound weakness in the region has ever been detected as a sequel.

SUTURE LIGATION OF THE PROSTATIC ARTERIES

To proceed, place a stay suture at the apex of the prostate to catch both puboprostatic ligaments and deeply enough to underrun the dorsal vein of the penis. Place another stay suture

* Pearson HH: Personal communication.

in the bladder wall in the midline just above the bladder neck. Any veins that would be cut by the incision in the prostatic capsule are either underrun or coagulated by diathermy.

The next step is the suture ligation of the prostatic arteries.

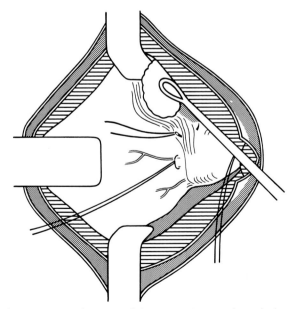

Fig. 23. Suture ligation of the prostatic vessels and placing of the haemostatic suture. The lower flap of the rectus sheath has a short vertical incision centrally to improve access.

These branches of the inferior vesical arteries run forward, medially, and a little downward to enter the region of the bladder neck laterally and posteriorly, although not quite so far back as some anatomic illustrations suggest. There may be a single vessel, or, in the perivesical fat, it may have broken into its three or four branches.

Attempt to locate the vessel by palpation. Push a finger gently down beside the upper prostate and press the pulp of the finger medially and a little upward against the region of the bladder neck. As often as not the pulsating vessel can be plainly felt. When it cannot be palpated, probably because it has already broken up into its several branches, its position may still be indicated by a large companion vein. When the artery cannot be located, pass the needle carrying the ligature to encircle the tissue through which the vessel usually runs; in most patients this is effective.

With a tampon held in a sponge forceps, push the fatty tissue lateral to the prostate gently down and back out of the way (Fig. 23). Pass a round-bodied Mayo needle from above down to encircle the vessel, moving through bladder neck tissue and the upper prostatic capsule. The point of the needle emerges far back on the lateral aspect of the upper prostate, where the needle is seized with another needle holder and drawn out along its circular track.

Any attempt to ligate the artery by passing a ligature carrier around it in what would seem the obvious place, just before it enters the dense tissue of the bladder neck, is apt to tear the veins of the venous plexus in this region and cause most troublesome bleeding.

The welcome absence of arterial bleeding later when the posterior bladder neck is dealt with, and when the prostate is removed, is evidence of the success of this maneuver, but just occasionally on one side or the other a spurting vessel shows that a branch of the artery has been missed by the blind ligation. With increasing experience this has become quite uncommon. In addition to decreasing the loss of blood, there is improved vision in the drier field.

The remainder of the operation is carried out as described in the article except that the retrigonizing sutures are tied as placed, in the midline first and then on each side.

SUCTION DRAINAGE OF THE RETROPUBIC SPACE

Provided closure of the defect in the anterior prostatic capsule is carried out carefully as described, urinary leakage does not occur. An open tube drain to the retropubic space is no longer used. Closed suction drainage through a small plastic tube (Redivac) is all that is needed and decreases the risk of introducing infection as well as makes the patient more comfortable.

LIGHT TRACTION ON A FOLEY BALLOON CATHETER

A Foley balloon catheter through the urethra is used for bladder drainage. Usually a 22 French catheter with a 30-ml balloon is employed. Pass the catheter before the anterior capsule is closed, pushing the empty balloon well into the bladder, out of the way of the point of the needle until closure is completed. Distend the balloon a little and draw it down into the prostatic

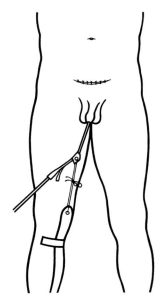

Fig. 24. Light traction applied to a Foley catheter after operation.

cavity, continuing inflation until it is felt to fill the prostatic cavity completely and comfortably. There is no standard size for a prostatic cavity, and a 30-ml balloon of a well-made catheter will hold up to 3 times this amount if required to do so. It is important to select a catheter with a long tip that will project well beyond an overdistended balloon. Apply light traction and wash out the bladder. Maintain traction by clipping the catheter to the drapes until the operation is completed; continue light traction by tape and strapping attached to the inner thigh, as shown in Figure 24. The aim is to apply light pressure to the raw surface to check venous and capillary oozing. This is no more than the standard first aid procedure for an oozing abrasion on the body surface. It is not effective for the control of arterial bleeding and should not be used for this purpose. Arterial bleeding must be stopped before the capsule is closed.

COMMENTS WITH SPECIAL REFERENCE TO TRANSURETHRAL PROCEDURES

John S. Jose

The great advantage of Bonnin's method of bladder neck reconstruction is that it can be applied to all varieties of bladder neck stenosis in the male, including the reconstruction of the bladder neck associated with retropubic prostatectomy, whether the hypertrophied gland is large or small. This versatility makes it unnecessary to define precisely before operation the nature of the bladder outflow obstruction, be it bladder neck stenosis or prostatic hypertrophy, since both lesions can be managed by the same operative technique once an open procedure has been decided on.

In practice, in recent years retropubic prostatectomy has

come to be confined to those patients in whom prostatic hypertrophy is complicated by another condition that requires an open operative approach, such as a large vesical calculus, a significant bladder diverticulum or an inguinal hernia, and, in our hands, where the prostatic hypertrophy is estimated to approach 70 g or greater. The majority of cases of bladder outflow obstruction, including most cases of prostatic hypertrophy, are therefore dealt with by a transurethral endoscopic technique.

Primary bladder neck obstruction in the young adult male (without significant prostatic hypertrophy) is now most commonly corrected with the resectoscope by deep bladder neck incision using a Colling's knife. The incision may be made posterolaterally on either side, extending from the lateral margin of the trigone through the bladder neck medial to the lateral lobes of the prostate into the floor of the prostatic urethra, or the incision may be made in the midline, posteriorly splitting the trigone. In depth, these incisions must be carried through the detrusor muscle at the bladder neck to the point where fatty tissue can be seen glistening between the separating muscle fibers if the bladder neck is to be opened sufficiently for long-term relief of obstruction. In many patients treated in this way, normal ejaculatory function can be retained, although the more radical the incision, the greater the liklihood of retrograde ejaculation.

This technique of linear bladder neck incision, in contrast to a formal circumferential transurethral resection of the narrowed bladder neck, accords with Bonnin's concept of the mechanism of preventing postoperative scarring at this site by preserving intact the mucosa overlying the greater part of the bladder neck musculature, exposing only the muscle fibers in the depths of the incisions. Rapid reepithelialization from the bridging mucosal strips alongside the incisions can then occur, thus minimizing secondary cicatricial stenosis. However, if such contracture should occur, it is inadvisable to persevere with repeated attempts at endoscopic incision, each attempt leading to additional fibrosis and scarring, since an excellent result can be achieved in these patients with Bonnin's reconstruction operation.

The same endoscopic method can be used in those patients in whom a secondary bladder neck stenosis has followed open retropubic or suprapubic prostatectomy. In such patients a second operative approach to the anterior bladder neck region through the retropubic space is fraught with difficulty because dense adhesion between the bladder and the pubis as a result of the initial procedure frequently eliminates the route of access, making sharp dissection mandatory with risk of inadvertent damage to the bladder wall. In our view, in this situation a transurethral procedure is preferable. A single posterior midline incision with a Colling's knife usually suffices because the margins of the fibrotic bladder neck commonly spring apart as the circumferential scar tissue is divided, making further interference unnecessary.

Recently, with the aim of minimizing the resultant scar tissue at the bladder neck, diathermy incision with a Colling's knife has been replaced by a similar incision of the prostatic bladder neck using a Sachse's urethrotomy knife blade, held in the inverted position. The avoidance of diathermy coagulation leads to more rapid epithelialization and has given excellent results in the short term.

RETROGRADE EJACULATION

If the operation is carried out in full, including removal of the prostate, then retrograde ejaculation will occur; it is wise to inform the patient of this. If normal ejaculation is to be retained and it is considered that surgery to the prostate is not required, the operative procedure should be limited to reconstruction of the bladder neck. Gute and associates report uniformly normal ejaculation after this procedure, with bladder outlet obstruction completely relieved.[2] Their observations and ours taken together tend to confirm the view that the whole length of the prostatic urethra has a sphincteric function.

REFERENCES

1. Gregoire W: Hemostatic adenomectomy. Urol Int 24:426, 1969
2. Gute DB, Chute R, Baron JA: Bladder neck revision for obstruction in men: A clinical study reporting normal ejaculation post operatively. J Urol 99:744, 1968

ANNOTATED BIBLIOGRAPHY

Berry NE, Miller J: Regeneration of epithelium of prostatic urethra following resection. J Urol 56:223, 1946; Flocks RH: Local repair following transurethral prostatic resection. Its role in clinical events associated with this operation. J Urol 40:208, 1938

These articles are reports of careful and detailed studies of the process of healing of the prostatic cavity and bladder neck. These works are of fundamental importance, and search of the literature since has confirmed their validity.

Nesbit RM, Crenshaw WB: Treatment of bladder neck contracture by plastic operation. J Urol 73:516, 1955

The authors allude to the difficulty in treating a man with bladder neck contracture and note the bad results that sometimes follow transurethral resection. They report good results following use of an open Heineke–Mikulicz procedure to the anterior bladder neck. They also publish a personal communication from Bonnin with a sketch, describying the Y-V plasty procedure.

Gute DB, Chute R, Baron JA Jr: Bladder neck revision for obstruction in men: A clinical study reporting normal ejaculation postoperatively. J Urol 99:744, 1968

A series of 49 men with bladder neck obstruction were treated by open plastic revision of their bladder necks. A modified Y-V plasty was used in front, and in many of the men a submucosal excision of a raised posterior bar at the bladder neck with closure of the defect was done. The procedures used were basically similar to those described, but the prostate was not removed. Results were consistently good, and there was normal ejaculation. This important observation contrasts with our patients, in whom the prostate was removed and retrograde ejaculation uniformly occurred.

Gregoir W: Hemostatic adenomectomy. Urol Int 24:426, 1969

This paper begins with a clear and detailed description of the anatomy of the blood supply of the prostate and bladder neck. This information is then applied to a technique of preliminary ligation of the arterial supply and final complete control of arterial bleeding after prostatectomy. Arteries and veins are ligated *en bloc* outside the bladder neck using carefully placed curved scissors to guard a ligature carrier. Gregoir states that the procedure is somewhat difficult and requires practice. He warns that attempts to isolate arteries by open dissection only result in laceration of veins. If Gregoir's technique is attempted, this article should be consulted and his technique carefully followed. However, the transfixation ligature we have described gives good control of arterial bleeding in most cases, is technically easy, and does not risk venous damage.

Overview: Vesical Neck Reconstruction

Jesse I. Abrahams

The reconstruction of the bladder neck is undertaken for three distinct reasons: to prevent cicatrical stenosis of the bladder neck at initial prostatectomy, for operative relief of bladder outlet obstruction (*i.e.,* to relieve bladder neck contracture following prostatectomy), and, more recently, to reverse retrograde ejaculation in patients who have had Y-V plasty bladder neck reconstruction.

RECONSTRUCTION OF THE BLADDER NECK AT PROSTATECTOMY

My own preference for open prostatectomy is the retropubic approach as described by Millin, employing a Pfannenstiel incision and separating the recti muscles.[1] Occasionally the anterior rectus sheath is incised on each side at its insertion into the pubis to obtain greater exposure to the retropubic space. This approach is reserved for glands estimated to be over 60 g. I have not routinely employed ligation of the prostatic arteries before incising the capsule. However, it is routine to ligate these arteries at the 5 and 7 o'clock positions on the bladder neck with deep sutures following enucleation of the adenoma. This is followed by trigonization of the posterior bladder neck by suturing a flap of bladder mucosa down to the posterior prostatic capsule. Three points of mucosa are brought into the posterior capsule—in the midline and at both lateral extremities of this wound.[1,2] Sutures of 2–0 chromic catgut on swedged rounded needles are used. Epithelialization of the posterior portion of the bladder neck prevents cicatrization. Careful hemostasis in the remainder of the prostatic fossa is achieved by suture ligation of any arteries visualized under direct vision with the aid of a sterile Cameron light. Cautery is rarely used, so that tissue destruction and scar formation is reduced to a minimum. Light traction is placed on an inflated catheter balloon placed in the bladder for 1 to 2 hr postoperatively. A watertight closure of the anterior capsule is achieved with interrupted sutures of 0 chromic catgut. Retzius' space is drained with two Penrose drains brought out through the lateral angles of the wound. The catheter is removed in 48 hr and the drain 24 hr later. Only rarely has this routine been altered because of urinary leakage or secondary bleeding.

RECONSTRUCTION OF THE BLADDER NECK FOR BLADDER NECK CONTRACTURE

Bladder neck contracture secondary to cicatrical stenosis frequently follows transurethral prostatectomy and is more commonly noted following resection of small glands and vigorous resection of the bladder neck. This complication may also follow open prostatectomy where a raw surface is left following enucleation and no effort made to epithelialize the posterior bladder neck. It is sometimes very disconcerting to observe a tight bladder neck contracture occurring a few short weeks after the removal of a huge prostate with a wide-open bladder neck noted at the initial surgical procedure. The preferable approach toward correcting this condition is transurethral. To proceed, make linear incisions from the interior of the bladder through the entire stricture and into the prostatic fossa at the 3 and 9 o'clock positions. These incisions cause the scar to spring apart, allowing adequate access to the bladder. The previously used Colling's knife and diathermy have been replaced by cold incisions using the Optical Urethrotome. The absence of cautery results in a finer incision and less destruction of tissue so that the epithelialization of the recent incisions may occur. Another noticeable advantage of the Optical Urethrotome is the ability to pass a ureteral catheter through the pin hole opening under direct vision so that this eccentrically situated opening can be incised with precision, guided by the ureteral catheter. Transureteral resection of bladder neck contractures, although initially widening the contracted bladder neck, frequently results in rescarring and is not the preferred procedure. Should recontracture occur following incision of the originally contracted bladder neck, open exposure and mobilization of the trigone as described by Bonnin in the reproduced article, although a more difficult secondary procedure, will result in cure.

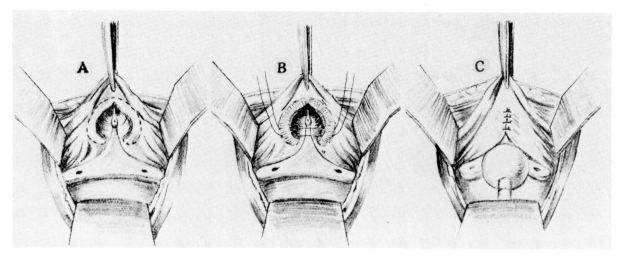

Fig. 25. (*A*) View of the urethrovesical junction within the bladder reveals the limits of incision. (*B*) Exposed muscle of the bladder neck illustrates placement of sutures to reconstruct internal vesical sphincter. (*C*) Appearance of the reconstructed internal vesical sphincter with No. 16 Foley catheter in place. (Abrahams JI, Solish GI, Boorjian P et al: The surgical correction of retrograde ejaculation. J Urol 114:888, 1975. By permission of the Williams & Wilkens Co, Baltimore)

RECONSTRUCTION OF THE BLADDER NECK FOR RETROGRADE EJACULATION

More recently I have devised a procedure to reconstruct the bladder neck in young men who have suffered retrograde ejaculation as a result of Y-V plasty and who had bladder outlet obstruction as children. Evaluation of these patients confirmed the patulous bladder neck through panendoscopic examination and the presence of contrast material within the prostatic fossa on cystography. The operative procedure is performed transvesically. Use inspection and palpation to confirm a patulous internal vesical sphincter. Expose the anterior portion of the bladder neck muscle by an inverted U incision from the 4 to 8 o'clock position. Excise the mucosa and scar and approximate the exposed muscle by encircling sutures of 0 chromic catgut, uniting the bundle in the midline.

Four sutures are all that are necessary. Calibrate the size of the opening to fit snugly around a 16 French catheter, which is left in place for 21 days to allow healing of the bladder incision and secure adherence of the approximated muscle bundles (Fig. 25). This procedure has been performed for sterility secondary to retrograde ejaculation and has resulted in antegrade ejaculation in six of seven patients. The concept employed here is to excise the mucosa and scar so that the underlying muscle bundles are closely approximated. Follow-up study for as long as 1 yr after surgery confirmed the presence of an intact vesical sphincter. The presence of a bridge of intact epithelium on the posterior bladder neck prevents cicatrization and bladder neck contracture, confirming the principles of the procedure described by Bonnin.

REFERENCES

1. Millin T: Retropubic Urinary Surgery. Edinburgh, E&S Livingston, 1947
2. Harris SH: Prostatectomy with complete closure. J Coll Surg. Aust 1:65, 1928

3. Abrahams JI, Solish GI, Boorjian P, et al: The surgical correction of retrograde ejaculation. J Urol 114:888, 1975

PART TWENTY-EIGHT

SURGERY OF VESICAL TRAUMA

72

DIAGNOSIS AND MANAGEMENT OF BLADDER TRAUMA

Stanley A. Brosman, M.D., and Raymond Fay, M.D.

From the Department of Surgery (Urology), UCLA School of Medicine, and the Department of Surgery (Urology), Harbor General Hospital, Torrance, California

The Journal of Trauma
Copyright © 1973 by The Williams & Wilkins Co.
Vol. 13, No. 8
Printed in U.S.A.

Damage to the bladder may be caused by either nonpenetrating or penetrating trauma, but most prevalent are those injuries that occur as a result of blunt abdominal trauma. Ninety patients with bladder injuries seen at the Harbor General and UCLA Hospitals during the past 12 years were reviewed for this study. Injury resulted from nonpenetrating trauma in 78 (86%) and from penetrating trauma in 12 (14%) (Table 1). Waterhouse and Gross,[8] in a report on 38 patients with bladder injury, found a similar distribution of injury.

Blunt trauma to the bladder frequently is associated with pelvic fracture.[3] Seventy-two percent of our patients had sustained a fracture of the pelvis. Conversely, Levine and Crampton[6] found that bladder injuries occurred in 14% of patients with fractured pelves.

For purposes of discussion and therapy, bladder injuries may be classified as follows:

1. *Contusion.* An ecchymosis of the intact bladder wall with microscopic or gross hematuria.
2. *Extraperitoneal rupture.* Laceration of the bladder below the pelvic peritoneum. Cystography demonstrates extravasation of medium perivesically and outside of the peritoneal cavity.
3. *Intraperitoneal rupture.* Rupture of the bladder into the peritoneal cavity. Cystography demonstrates extravasation of medium into the peritoneal cavity.
4. *Combined extraperitoneal and intraperitoneal ruptures.* Characterized by cystographic findings of extravasation into the peritoneum as well as the perivesical tissues.

TABLE 1. Patients with Bladder Injuries

	Blunt	Penetrating
Contusion	35	
Extraperitoneal	22	2
Intraperitoneal	10	4
Combined	11	6
	78	12

Address for reprints: Stanley A. Brosman, M.D., Department of Surgery, Harbor General Hospital, 1000 West Carson, Torrance, California 90509.

TABLE 2. Cystographic Findings in Bladder Injuries

Contustion	Extraperitoneal Rupture	Intraperitoneal Rupture
a. Teardrop-shaped bladder b. Elevation of bladder c. Obliteration of the soft tissue planes in the pelvis by hematoma d. Deviation of the bladder laterally e. Absence of extravasation of contrast materials	a. Ranges from small lines or streaks to a large stellate or sunburst pattern of extravasated dye b. Base of the bladder obscured by dye	a. Hour-glass pattern when the extravasated contrast medium layer is in the dependent portion of the peritoneal cavity b. Gas-containing small bowel loops are surrounded by opaque contrast material c. Colon is outlined by the contrast medium in an irregular fashion, resulting in a scalloped appearance d. Opaque linear bands along the peritoneal reflections of the paracolic recesses e. Contrast medium may outline portions of the diaphragm, liver, and spleen

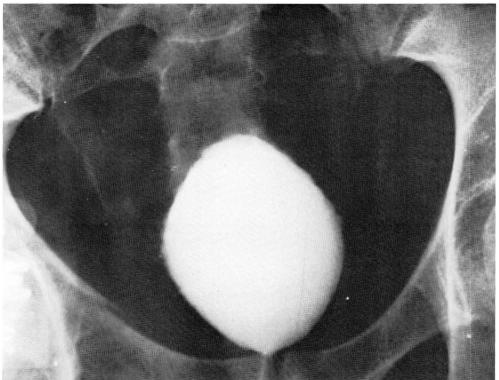

Fig. 1. Retrograde cystogram demonstrating a "teardrop" bladder due to perivesical hematoma. Right superior and inferior rami pelvic fractures, without bony displacement.

Nonpenetrating and penetrating trauma to the lower abdomen or pelvis associated with hematuria require a thorough urologic evaluation. Hematuria does not localize the site or delineate the type of urinary tract injury. Although the diagnosis may be suspected from the history and physical findings, confirmation is obtained with radiologic studies, i.e., cystograms and retrograde cystourethrograms in the male, followed by excretory urography. The retrograde cystourethrogram, performed because of the association of bladder and urethral injuries, outlines the continuity of the urethra before advancing the catheter into the bladder. When laceration of the urethra is present, no attempt is made to pass the catheter into the bladder. If the urethra is intact, the catheter is introduced, and 150 to 200 ml of a 10% water-soluble contrast medium are introduced by gravity technique in preference to forceful filling, since a diseased or contused bladder may be ruptured by forceful injection.[4] The catheter is clamped, and anteroposterior (AP) films are obtained. If the patient can be moved, oblique X-ray exposures may be helpful. If no extravasation is demonstrated, an additional amount of dye sufficient to produce subjective distention is added, and the AP view X-ray film is repeated. The contrast medium then is evacuated from the bladder, and a final film is taken to determine whether any extravasation is hidden behind the shadow of the full bladder.

A double-dose or infusion excretory urogram (IVP) is performed to assess the upper urinary tract, and may demonstrate bladder injury. Holland, Hurwitz, and Nice,[4] however, found that only 11% of their patients with proved rupture demonstrated extravasation by this method. In our series, only 15% could be diagnosed by IVP. The most accurate diagnosis is made by retrograde cystography. Although Rieser[7] reported that retrograde cystography did not demonstrate existing perforation in four of 57 patients, these four had sustained their bladder lacerations by penetrating missiles. In our series, the retrograde cystogram was diagnostic in every case.

BLADDER CONTUSION

This is the most common type of bladder injury, and is manifested by hematuria, either microscopic or gross. It usually is caused by blunt trauma, and produces an ecchymosis in the bladder wall.

Diagnosis. The cystographic appearance is that of an intact bladder deformed by pelvic hematoma (Table 2). The bladder may assume a teardrop appearance, and may be elevated or deviated to one side of the pelvis (Fig. 1). The hematoma may obscure local tissue planes.

Treatment. Observation is the only treatment necessary in most of these patients. Those who are immobilized and unable to void while lying in bed will need catheter drainage (Table 3).

EXTRAPERITONEAL RUPTURE OF THE BLADDER

Eighty percent of extraperitoneal ruptures of the bladder are associated with fracture of the pelvis.[5] The most probable mechanism of injury is a direct puncture of the bladder by the pelvic bony edges, generally the pubic rami, with avulsion of the ligamentous moorings of the bladder. The bladder tears occur most frequently on the anterolateral surfaces near the bladder neck.

Symptoms and Signs. Diagnosis of the ruptured bladder may be complicated by the fact that symptoms and signs

of injury are similar to those of the fractured pelvis.[3] Frequently, the pain from the fractured pelvis is so severe that bladder injury may be completely overlooked. The pelvic fracture may be of such severity that extensive blood loss results in hypovolemic shock. The possibility of injury to the iliac vessels should also be considered. Pelvic angiography has been of value in assessing these lesions.

Diagnosis. An extraperitoneal bladder laceration may not be revealed by clinical examination alone. Retrograde cystourethrography is used to establish the diagnosis. The radiographic appearance of the extravasated contrast medium depends upon the size and location of the bladder laceration, the amount of perivesical hemorrhage, and the time lapse between the injection of the contrast medium and the exposure of the X-ray film (Table 3). With perivesical hematoma, the bladder will assume a teardrop form. The appearance of the extravasated medium may vary from a small, feathery streak to the large stellate or "sunburst" pattern often seen with more extensive tears (Fig. 2). Postevacuation X-ray films are best used to demonstrate residual dye in the pelvis. The

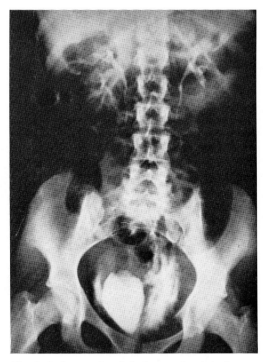

Fig. 2. Left superior–inferior rami pelvic fractures with severe dislocation. An intravenous urogram demonstrates a "teardrop" bladder deviated to the right and a large stellate extension of contrast medium into the left perivesical area. Small, feathery streaks of extravasated contrast medium are noted in the right pelvis.

TABLE 3. Treatment of Bladder Injuries

Contusion	No treatment or urethral catheter drainage
Extraperitoneal laceration	Perivesical drainage
	Repair of laceration
	Bladder drainage
Intraperitoneal laceration	Exploration of the peritoneal cavity
	Closure of the bladder laceration
	Perivesical drainage
	Bladder drainage
Combined injuries	As above

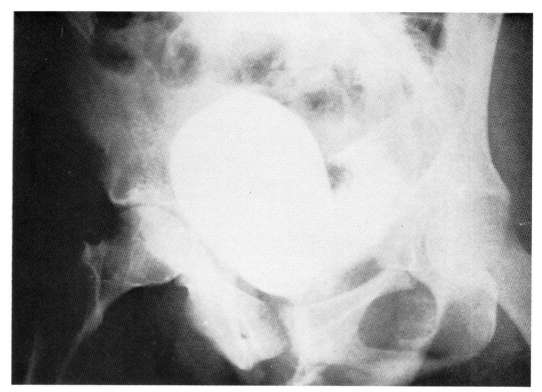

Fig. 3. An oblique cystogram shows posterior extravasation of contrast material which was partially hidden by the full bladder outline on the AP X-ray film.

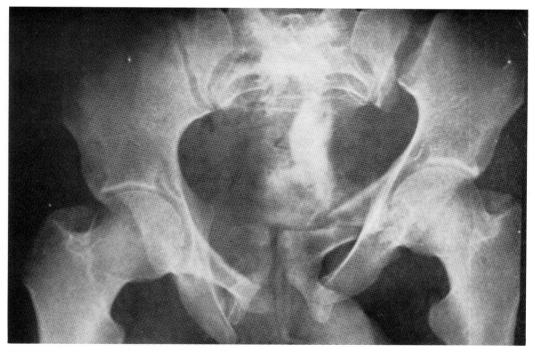

Fig. 4. Postevacuation cystogram demonstrates extravasated dye in the pelvis.

base of the bladder frequently will be obscured by the contrast medium that extends between lacerated muscle bundles or into the perivesical and perirectal spaces[4] (Figs. 3, 4).

Treatment. After the patient's clinical condition has stabilized, early operative intervention has been employed to establish adequate bladder drainage and to drain the perivesical and prevesical spaces.[1] Closure of the bladder laceration usually is accomplished with sutures. Whereas urethral catheter drainage alone may suffice in some situations, suprapubic drainage is more reliable (Table 3). The perivesical drain is removed gradually after 7 days, followed by removal of the cystostomy tube a few days thereafter. When a urethral catheter also is used, it is left for an additional 2 to 3 days until the suprapubic incision heals. All patients in the present series received appropriate antibiotic therapy when indicated.

In some patients with limited bladder injury and small amounts of extravasation, we have used urethral catheter drainage alone. Eight patients in this series were successfully treated in this manner. One advantage of this approach is that a closed pelvic fracture is not converted to an open fracture. We would not, however,

consider this therapy for a patient with extensive bladder trauma.

INTRAPERITONEAL RUPTURE OF THE BLADDER

Intraperitoneal rupture of the bladder most commonly follows a blow to the lower abdomen with the bladder fully distended. The distal and lateral surfaces of an empty bladder are well protected by bony and muscular structures; thus, in the distended bladder, the peritoneal surface becomes most susceptible to injury. Other causes of intraperitoneal rupture of the bladder are missile injury, iatrogenic instrumentation, and fractured pelvis.

Symptoms and Signs. Despite urinary leakage into the peritoneal cavity, the initial signs of peritoneal irritation may be minimal or absent. Uninfected urine may remain intraperitoneally for several hours without causing peritonitis. Ileus may be the initial manifestation of impending early peritonitis.

Patients with extensive intraperitoneal rupture have no desire to void, and often are unable to do so. Catheterization will yield small amounts of bloody urine. Complete recovery of irrigant fluid may be misleading. If the catheter has been placed in the peritoneal cavity,

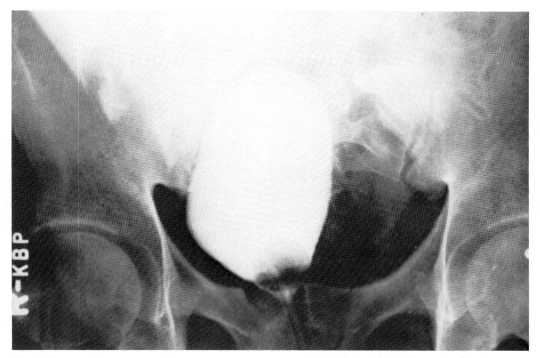

Fig. 5. Retrograde cystogram demonstrates contrast material outlining the peritoneal reflections and deviation of the bladder from an intraperitoneal bladder laceration. The large and small bowels are coated with contrast material.

the volume of irrigant recovered may be equal to or exceed the volume instilled into the bladder.

Diagnosis. Retrograde cystography will demonstrate layering of extravasated medium in the dependent portion of the pelvic peritoneum, producing an hour-glass radiographic configuration. The superior aspects of the bladder will be obscured by the extravasated medium. The large and small bowel may be coated with opaque medium. If the contrast material is allowed time to layer out, linear bands will form along the peritoneal reflections of the paracolic recesses (Figs. 5, 6). Portions of the diaphragm, liver, and spleen also may be outlined (Table 2).

Treatment. Early surgical intervention is important. The peritoneal cavity should be explored, the urine removed, and the peritoneal aspect of the bladder rupture closed (Table 3). The bladder may be drained with a suprapubic or urethral catheter after the intravesical portion of the bladder has been repaired. With missile injuries, perforation of either small or large bowel, or both, is quite frequent. Rectal injuries are often difficult to detect, and must be carefully excluded.

COMBINED EXTRAPERITONEAL AND INTRAPERITONEAL RUPTURES

Penetrating missile injury is a common cause of combined rupture of the bladder. However, a full bladder may be

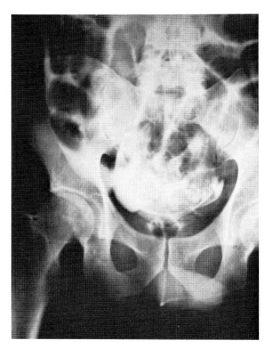

Fig. 6. The bladder is obscured by extravasted contrast material. Dye is layered out along the reflections of the paracolic recesses.

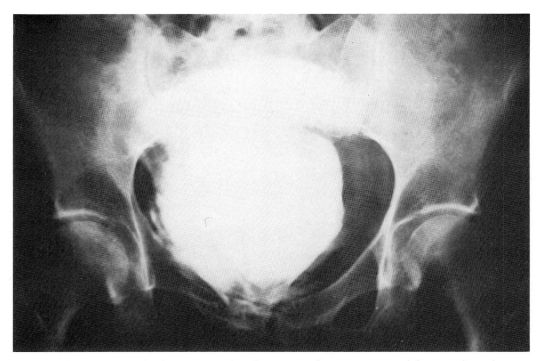

Fig. 7. Right superior and inferior rami pelvic fractures with extravasation of dye into the right perivesical area and an hour-glass bladder configuration.

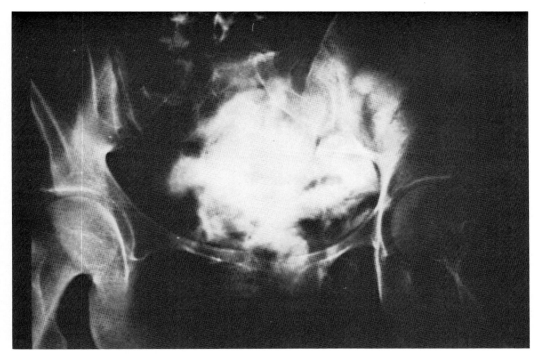

Fig. 8. Gunshot wound of the right lower abdomen. Postevacuation cystogram demonstrates extensive extraperitoneal extravasation.

ruptured both intra- and extraperitoneally by a bony spicule from a fractured pelvis. Cystographic findings will demonstrate both intraperitoneal and extraperitoneal extravasation (Fig. 7). An excretory urogram is imperative to disclose concomitant ureteral injuries (Fig. 8). Treatment is essentially the same as that for intraperitoneal bladder laceration (Table 3).

COMMENT

Prior to 1900 the mortality resulting from a ruptured bladder was almost 100%, but Evans and Fowler[2] demonstrated in 1905 that surgical repair was possible.

In Campbell's series of 45 patients (20 with extra-peritoneal and 25 with intraperitoneal ruptured bladders) treated with suprapubic drainage, primary closure of the bladder laceration, and perivesical drainage, the operative mortality was 40% for the extraperitoneal and 68% for the intraperitoneal bladder laceration.[1] Of interest was the fact that two patients died of acute pelvic osteomyelitis. With antibiotic therapy, mortality rates have decreased. Waterhouse and Gross[8] reported, in 1969, a 21% mortality in 38 cases. None of the deaths was related to bladder injury. There were no deaths in our series of 90 patients directly related to the urologic injury, and the only urologic complications were four instances of acute bacterial cystitis due to prolonged catheter drainage.

SUMMARY

Ninety patients with traumatic bladder injuries were classified according to type of injury: contusion, extraperitoneal rupture, intraperitoneal rupture, and combined injuries. Seventy-eight (86%) of these patients had sustained blunt injury, and 12 (14%) had penetrating injuries. The diagnosis was made by cystography. In patients with blunt trauma, contusions were found in 45%, extraperitoneal lacerations in 28%, intraperitoneal lacerations in 13%, and combined injuries in 14%. Eighty percent of the patients had associated pelvic fractures.

Contusions were treated by observation or catheter drainage; the other injuries were treated with surgical exploration, closure of the bladder laceration, and suprapubic drainage.

Early diagnosis and therapy are necessary to reduce the morbidity and mortality. Every patient with pelvic fracture should be suspected of having a bladder injury, and should be studied accordingly.

REFERENCES

1. CAMPBELL MF: Rupture of the bladder. Surg Gynec Obstet 49:540–546, 1929

2. EVANS E, FOWLER HA: Punctured wounds of the bladder. Ann Surg 42:215–241, 1905

3. FLAHERTY JJ, KELLEY R, BURNETT B, et al: Relationship of pelvic bone fracture patterns to injuries of urethra and bladder. J Urol 99:297–300, 1968

4. HOLLAND ME, HURWITZ LM, NICE CM JR: Traumatic lesions of the urinary tract. Radiol Clin North Am 4:433–450, 1966

5. KAISER TF, FARROW FC: Injury of the bladder and prostatomembranous urethra associated with fracture of the bony pelvis. Surg Gynec Obstet 120:99–112, 1965

6. LEVINE JI, CRAMPTON RS: Major abdominal injuries associated with pelvic fractures. Surg Gynec Obstet 116:223–226, 1963

7. RIESER C: Diagnostic evaluation of suspected genitourinary tract injury. JAMA 199:714–719, 1967

8. WATERHOUSE K, GROSS M: Trauma to the genitourinary tract: a 5-year experience with 251 cases. J Urol 101:241–246, 1969

Commentary: Surgery of Vesical Trauma

Douglas D. Morehouse

In the excellent article reproduced here, the authors have clearly outlined the methods of diagnosis and management of bladder injuries. They stress the need for a "stress cystogram" as well as a postevacuation film to rule out definitely the presence of a bladder rupture during cystography. They describe in detail the cystographic findings with contusion, extraperitoneal rupture, and intraperitoneal rupture. In 90 patients with bladder injuries, 86% of injuries resulted from nonpenetrating trauma and 14% from penetrating trauma. This distribution is similar to my experience.

The authors stress the high incidence of false-negative findings on intravenous (IV) urographic studies. In their series, only 15% could be diagnosed by intravenous pyelograms (IVPs). They also stress the need to perform a retrograde urethrogram before introducing a urethral catheter in patients who have associated fractures of the pelvis. I believe this is an important point to stress because the introduction of a catheter may convert an incomplete rupture of the prostatomembranous urethra to a complete one. If this should occur, it greatly exaggerates the difficulties in management of the ruptured urethra and potentially increases the complications. Many patients with incomplete ruptures of the prostatomembranous urethra will heal spontaneously without reconstructive urethral surgery.

The majority of patients with significant bladder injury present with a fractured pelvis, and consequently there is generally no difficulty in recognizing the possibility of bladder rupture. Patients without associated fractures may present with only lower abdominal pain and hematuria. If there has been a delay in seeking medical treatment, acute abdominal trauma may be present and the patient may be extremely ill. It seems prudent to suspect the possibility of bladder injury in any patient with lower abdominal or pelvic trauma and to proceed with the stress cystogram as soon as the patient is stable.

In patients who have sustained a rupture of the bladder in association with fractures of the bony pelvis, approximately 80% will have extraperitoneal ruptures and 20% will have intraperitoneal ruptures. The majority of intraperitoneal ruptures result from a blow to the lower abdomen when the bladder is distended with urine. Occasionally I encounter both intraperitoneal and extraperitoneal ruptures in association with fractures of the pelvis; however, these combined ruptures are more common with penetrating injuries.

It is important to remember that some patients, particularly alcoholics, may sustain trauma to the abdomen and not remember the injury. When they appear with evidence of acute abdominal trauma, a ruptured bladder should be considered.

Penetrating injuries to the bladder can be very serious and not infrequently fatal. This fatality rate is not the result of the bladder injury but of the high incidence of associated injuries to the bowel and particularly to the rectum. These associated injuries must be suspected and, if present, appropriately managed.

The principles in the management of the patient with a ruptured bladder are adequate urinary diversion from the area of injury, prompt adequate drainage of the perivesical area or other areas of extravasation, and closure of the defect in the bladder wall if possible. In the patient with penetrating trauma, exploration should always be promptly performed, not only to evaluate and treat the bladder injury but also to assess the integrity of surrounding abdominal viscera and vasculature.

I believe that all penetrating bladder injuries should be explored because of the possibility of associated injuries to the rectum or other viscera that could prove fatal if unattended. I also explore all patients with intraperitoneal lacerations. Some of these patients have had omentum or small bowel protruding into the bladder defect. I do not explore all patients with extraperitoneal lacerations. A number of these patients have been managed by urethral catheter drainage alone. This conservative approach has usually been reserved for those patients with multiple injuries who are in critical condition. These patients are selected on the basis of severity of bladder injury and clinical status. If the patient is going to have abdominal exploration, I repair the bladder laceration and drain the pelvis.

This conservative approach is also occasionally used if a small bladder perforation is made during transurethral surgery and immediately identified. If there is excessive extravasation of irrigating fluid, I prefer to also place a Penrose drain in the retropubic space. Although the majority of patients with bladder rupture will require exploration, closure, and drainage, in selected patients the nonoperative treatment may be the treatment of choice. However, there must be proof of bladder rupture and the patient must not be a candidate for surgical exploration because of some other complicating injury. The diagnosis must be made shortly after injury, and there should be no history of active urinary tract infection or complicating genitourinary disease. These patients must be in the hospital and very carefully observed to be certain that there is free urinary drainage from the catheter. Should the patient's condition deteriorate, surgical intervention should be instituted immediately.

Multiple injuries in the trauma patient, including lower urinary tract trauma, are associated with significant mortality. Although the associated injuries are mainly responsible for this mortality, immediate diagnosis and treatment of the ruptured bladder are important in an effort to reduce the death rate.

ANNOTATED BIBLIOGRAPHY

Reiser C: Diagnostic evaluation of suspected genitourinary tract injury. JAMA 199:714, 1967

The author stresses the unreliability of excretory cystography in diagnosing bladder rupture. He also points out that a bladder rupture can be missed on retrograde cystography and emphasizes the necessity of distending the bladder to capacity, especially when dealing with penetrating injuries. After the bladder is filled to capacity, anterio-posterior and bilateral oblique x-ray exposures are made. The contrast medium is then completely evacuated from the bladder and a final film taken, which may reveal extravasation hidden posterior to the shadow of a full bladder. The typical radiologic features of both intraperitoneal and extraperitoneal bladder ruptures are described. I agree that it is very important to do a postevacuation x-ray film during cystography to rule out small perforations or even larger intraperitoneal ruptures that have been occluded with a loop of bowel or piece of omentum. However, this is only necessary if the distended bladder appears to be intact on cystography.

Moy HH: Lower urinary tract injuries. Br J Urol 42:739, 1970

In this paper the author stresses the need for careful urologic investigation in all patients with fractures of the bony pelvis to rule out injuries to the urinary bladder and urethra. This has been my approach over the past several years. Approximately 10% of patients with fractures of the pelvis will have rupture of the bladder or urethra.

Harrow BR: Conservative and surgical management of bladder injuries following pelvic operations. Obstet Gynecol 33:852, June 1969

The author states that many vesico vaginal fistulas that result from nonradical gynecologic operations could be cured by conservative measures if detected early and treated promptly. Of 21 fistulas diagnosed over a 10-yr period, 9 healed without requiring surgical repair. He feels that the fistula will usually heal spontaneously if the vaginal leakage can be prevented by catheter drainage. The need for an IV urogram to rule out ureteral obstruction or fistula is also stressed. I agree that a conservative approach should be tried initially because it is frequently successful, avoiding the need for more extensive surgery.

Robards VL Jr, Haglund RV, Lubin EN, et al: Treatment of rupture of the bladder. J Urol 116:178, 1976

In this paper the authors describe their indications and technique of nonoperative management of ruptured bladders. Many patients with ruptured bladders have multiple injuries, and even limited procedures can threaten their lives. They state that "patients considered for conservative management must be evaluated as completely and promptly as possible with close attention being placed on general and supportive management as well as on the condition of the urinary tract." I agree that the conservative approach is indicated in selected situations, but the urologist must be aware of the potential risks and the indications for prompt surgical intervention.

Brosman SA, Paul JG: Trauma of the bladder. Surg Gynecol Obstet 143:605, 1976

The authors classify bladder trauma and describe the mechanism of injury. Fifteen percent of their patients with pelvic fractures had a significant injury to the bladder. They stress the need to perform a retrograde urethrogram before passing a catheter because of the frequent association of rupture of the prostato-membranous urethra in patients with fractures of the pelvis. It is important to do a retrograde urethrogram before passing a catheter to avoid converting a partial urethral rupture into a complete one. Also, incomplete ruptures may be missed if a retrograde urethrogram is not performed.

Flaherty JJ, Kelley R, Burnett B, et al: Relationship of pelvic bone fracture patterns to injuries of urethra and bladder. J Urol 99:297, 1968

This paper stresses the need for retrograde urethrography and cystography in all patients with certain types of pelvic fractures. In a review of 425 cases of pelvic fractures, the authors found that fractures involving the pubic arch adjacent to or involving the symphysis proved to be the usual finding when signs of urinary tract injury were present. The severity of displacement and comminution was in direct proportion to the severity of injury to the bladder or urethra. They also stress the need for using aqueous contrast media for the radiologic studies because this may enter the pelvic veins. My experience is similar to the authors'. Most injuries to the bladder and urethra in association with pelvic fractures occur with fractures or displacement of the anterior portion of the pelvic ring. I also stress the need for an aqueous contrast medium (IV urographic contrast medium) during urographic investigation of the lower urinary tract in the acutely injured patient.

Richardson JR Jr, Leadbetter GW Jr: Non-operative treatment of the ruptured bladder. J Urol 114:213, 1975

Nonoperative management of ruptured bladder is described in this paper. The authors state that if this method of therapy is elected, various points must be kept in mind. The patient must have proven bladder rupture and not be a candidate for surgical exploration because of some other complicating injury. The diagnosis must be made early, probably in less than 12 hr.

There should be no history of active urinary tract infection or complicating genitourinary disease. Prophylactic broad-spectrum antibiotics are recommended routinely for 2 wk. There should be no difficulty in passing a large-bore catheter. All patients must be admitted to the hospital for observation to ensure adequate control of hemorrhage and extravasation and to be certain that there is free urinary drainage. Should the patient's condition deteriorate or should there be evidence that the treatment is for any reason inadequate, surgical exploration and open drainage is immediately instituted. The conservative approach may be used in selected situations if the above points are carefully followed. However, the urologist must accept the increased responsibility of very close monitoring.

Montie J: Bladder injuries. Urol Clin North Am 4: 1977

This article classifies bladder injury with respect to etiology. It describes prevention and treatment of these injuries during obstetric, gynecologic, and urologic surgery, including transurethral techniques. The author stresses the need for surgical exploration in the majority of patients with penetrating injuries to rule out concomitant abdominal visceral injury. The danger of "spontaneous rupture" is stressed. The mortality may be as high as 50% because of delay in diagnosis. He points out the need for careful genitourinary history in patients with acute abdominal symptoms. When the history is positive and no cause for the acute abdominal symptoms is immediately apparent, a cystogram must be performed immediately. I agree with the author that all penetrating bladder ruptures should be explored because of the danger of associated visceral or vascular injuries.

Oliver JA, Taguchi Y: Rupture of the full bladder. Br J Urol 36:524, 1964

In this paper the authors describe the mechanism of bladder rupture during overdistension. A series of cadaver bladders were distended *in situ* and another group after removal from the cadaver. The *in situ* bladders all ruptured in the posterior peritonealized portion of the bladder. In all cases where the bladders were removed from the body, the tears occurred without a site of predilection. They concluded that the supports determine the site of rupture in the full bladder and that developmental factors need not be implicated. The authors have confirmed in the cadaver what physicians see in the clinical situation. Rupture of the distended bladder occurs in the area least supported by adjacent structures, that is, the peritoneal surface.

Overview: Diagnostic Approach Crucial in Suspected Vesical Trauma

C. Eugene Carlton, Jr.

The diagnostic approach to a patient with suspected vesical trauma cannot be overemphasized. Any patient with lower abdominal trauma, particularly in association with a fractured pelvis or following a period of inebriation, should be suspected of having a rupture of the bladder, and this should be ruled out by a carefully performed stress cystogram, as emphasized in the Commentary. Of particular importance is the preoperative diagnostic evaluation of patients with penetrating injuries of the bladder. As indicated by Dr. Morehouse, the consequences of overlooking a rectal injury can be disastrous and fatal, as was reported in the Vietnamese war experience. It is imperative that any patient with a penetrating wound of the bladder have a thorough proctosigmoidoscopic examination before surgical exploration. Unless injury to the rectum can be conclusively excluded, a diverting colostomy should be performed. It is extremely difficult to mobilize the rectum at the time of surgical exploration sufficient to exclude rectal injury. Therefore, it is my practice to perform diverting colostomy in those patients who have not had proctosigmoidoscopy before surgery or in whom I suspect such an injury. The consequences of a missed rectal injury cannot be overemphasized.

Standard accepted treatment of lacerations of the bladder includes adequate and thorough debridement and multilayer watertight closure of the bladder, as shown in Figure 9. If

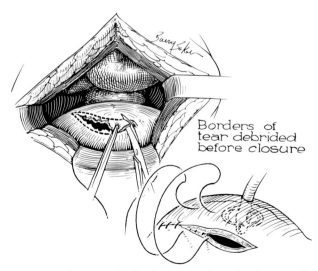

Borders of tear debrided before closure

Fig. 9. Technique of debridement and repair of ruptured bladder.

adequate debridement is achieved so that healthy tissues can be reapproximated, the mucosa can be approximated with 4–0 running chromic catgut suture and the muscularis closed with running 4–0 or 3–0 chromic catgut sutures in a watertight fashion. The bladder can then be drained with a Foley catheter, which can be removed on the first or second postoperative day to allow for spontaneous voiding without the complications of long-term indwelling catheter drainage. If, in the man, mitigating factors such as an extensively fractured pelvis might prevent early voiding, then suprapubic cystostomy should be carried out.

The role of nonsurgical management of bladder injuries is not clear at this point and, in my institution, is reserved for the woman with a small extraperitoneal laceration without significant clinical symptomatology and for the patient with extraperitoneal laceration of the bladder whose other injuries make him a poor surgical candidate. The precautions outlined in the article by Richardson and Leadbetter should be carefully followed.

PART
TWENTY-NINE

ENDOSCOPIC SURGERY
OF BLADDER
CALCULI

73

EXPERIENCE WITH THE ELECTROHYDRAULIC DISINTEGRATOR

Michael E. Mitchell and Walter S. Kerr, Jr.

From the Massachusetts General Hospital, Boston, Massachusetts

The Journal of Urology
Copyright © 1977 by The Williams & Wilkins Co.
Vol. 117, February
Printed in U.S.A.

ABSTRACT—Experience with the electrohydraulic lithotrite in treating 14 cases of bladder calculi is reported. This revolutionary lithotrite is applicable to most bladder stones and is associated with few complications.

Removal of bladder calculi is a problem that has challenged the ingenuity of physicians for centuries.[1] The Egyptians devised a method to abstract vesical stones that required wide dilatation of the urethra with wooden probes. The transurethral approach in later centuries was abandoned for open surgical procedures. However, in the late 18th century interest rekindled in the transurethral approach to bladder stones. Civiale developed the first functional lithotrite early in the 19th century. This instrument was improved upon subsequently, until 1878 when Bigelow combined, under general anesthesia at one sitting, the procedures of stone fractionation and evacuation of fragments. Bigelow used a lithotrite of his own design and named the procedure litholapaxy. Unfortunately, even with the new improved endoscopic control litho apaxy frequently has been associated with significant complications, including excessive hemorrhage, urethral or prostatic trauma often necessitating prostatectomy and bladder injury or perforation.

In the late 1950s 2 Russians, Yutkin and Goligoswky, developed a lithotrite of a completely new and different principle, the electrohydraulic lithotrite.[2] We believe that this lithotrite is a major technologic advance in the treatment of bladder calculi.

Various experiences with the electrohydraulic lithotrite (URAT-1) have been reported (Table 1).[3-7] In general, the lithotrite has been found to be applicable to

Accepted for publication June 18, 1976.

Read at annual meeting of American Urological Association, Las Vegas, Nevada, May 16–20, 1976.

TABLE 1. World Experience with the Electrohydraulic Lithotrite, as Reported in the English Literature

Reference	No. Cases	Comments
Reuter[3]	50	URAT-1, 2 cases stones too hard, 22 cases combined with transurethral resection of prostrate, operative time—<10 min
Rouvalis[4]	100	URAT-1, 50 percent urate stones, 60 percent cases treated with topical analgesia as outpatients
Albrecht and associates[5]	64	URAT-1, 2 failures, 1 death, average operative time—60 min
Angeloff[6]	100	URAT-1, 70 patients done with local anesthesia, 50 patients treated as outpatients, complications minimal
Alfthan and Murtomas[7]	23	URAT-1, 16 cases lithotripsy alone, 1 case perforation of bladder

TABLE 2. United States Experience with the Electrohydraulic Lithotrite

Reference	No. Cases	Comments
Eaton and associates[8]	9	URAT-1, 6 cases followed by transurethral resection of prostate, 3 cases topical analgesia as outpatients
Tessler and Kossow[9]	30	T.B.F. stone disintegrator SD₂, no complications
Raney[10]	37	SD-1 Northgate Research Corp., no significant complications

most stones (only 7 failures reported), virtually as atraumatic as simple cystoscopy (many procedures were done on outpatients under local anesthesia) and associated with few significant complications (1 bladder perforation and no cases of significant hemorrhage). Presumably because of the late appearance of a commercially available device in the United States experience with the electrohydraulic lithotrite has been limited to several recent reports (Table 2).[8-10] The results of the series have been satisfactory and the conclusions similar to those stated previously.

The instrument consists of a generator unit, a foot pedal control and a flexible 8 to 10F stone probe.* The generator unit converts currents of 120 volts, 60 hertz units to low frequency (50 per 100 seconds) high impulse discharges that, when released at the stone probe tip, generate hydraulic shock waves in the irrigating solution. These shock waves are of sufficient energy to disrupt

* T.B.F. Stone Disintegrator, T.B.F. Instruments, New York, New York.

TABLE 3. Massachusetts General Hospital Summary of Experience with the Electrohydraulic Stone Disintegrator

Number cases	14
Patient age (years):	
Range	18–88
Mean	54
Diagnosis:	
Neurogenic bladder	6
Benign prostatic hypertrophy	7
Ca prostate	1
Stone composition:	
Magnesium ammonium phosphate	9
Uric acid	2
Calcium oxalate	2
Calcium phosphate	1
Procedure:	
Removal of stone	10
Transurethral resection of prostate and removal of stone	4
Failure	1

stones of any composition, including harder stones of uric acid or calcium oxalate. With this device electrical energy is converted directly to hydraulic (mechanical) energy. Therefore, it differs significantly from ultrasound devices that operate at a much higher frequency (20,000 to 100,000 hertz units) and that convert electrical energy to crystal vibrations, which in turn propagate through a liquid medium.

The technique required for the use of the electrohydraulic lithotrite is similar to that used in the fulguration of a small bladder tumor. The bladder is filled with 150 to 200 cc irrigation solution. The flexible stone probe, adaptable to any endoscopic equipment, is then directed perpendicularly to the surface of the stone at a distance of approximately 3 to 5 mm. Care must be taken not to let the probe come in contact with the bladder wall nor to direct the probe at the light source. Several short bursts lasting 1 to 5 seconds are usually sufficient to disrupt most calculi. Larger and harder stones require higher and longer discharge periods as determined by the appropriate setting on the generator unit. As these larger stones are fragmented the settings may be reduced and discharged periods are shortened. Once fractionated stone fragments are irrigated free from the bladder with ease, using a standard 24 to 28F resection sheath and an evacuator.

CLINICAL EXPERIENCE

Since January 1975, 14 cases of bladder calculi have been treated with the electrohydraulic lithotrite (Table 3). The patients range in age from 18 to 88 years, with a mean of 54. Seven patients had bladder outlet obstruction secondary to benign prostatic hypertrophy, 1 had carcinoma of the prostate and 6 had neurogenic bladders. Nine patients had struvite stones that were associated with chronic infection, 2 had pure uric acid stones, 2 had calcium oxalate stones and 1 had calcium phosphate.

In 10 patients litholapaxy was performed alone. However, 3 patients also underwent transurethral resection of the prostate to relieve bladder outlet obstruction after litholapaxy. In 1 patient a large prostatic calculus was dislodged from the prostatic fossa and washed into the bladder during resection of the prostate. Because of its size the stone was fractionated with the electrohydraulic lithotrite and then evacuated with the prostatic chips at the conclusion of the resection.

Complications and failures were minimal. In no case was significant hemorrhage or bladder injury noted. In fact, postoperative catheterization was not found necessary for a simple litholapaxy. The only failure to disrupt a stone using the lithotrite was encountered when the tip of the probe became worn. With loss of the insulation between the axial and co-axial electrodes in the probe tip the efficiency of the probe was reduced markedly. Unfortunately, a replacement probe was not available and the lithotripsy was completed with a standard mechanical lithotrite. In another case the tip of the probe fell apart and was left in the bladder. It was passed per urethram subsequently. In a third patient some stone fragments could not be irrigated free. A fourth patient suffered aspiration pneumonitis postoperatively, necessitating an extra 2 days of hospitalization.

It has been our experience, and that of others, that excessive wear of the probe tip can be prevented by avoiding direct contact with the calculi and by restricting discharges to short bursts to prevent overheating and subsequent loss of critical structure of the probe tip. The probe tip must be checked frequently and changed with early signs of wear.

DISCUSSION

The principle of the electrohydraulic lithotrite is such that energy shock waves generated at the tip of the flexible stone probe are effective in the fragmentation of most bladder calculi without causing damage to the bladder. Because of the small caliber of the probe the device is adaptable to standard endoscopic equipment. Electrohydraulic litholapaxy is done under precise visual control and results in minimal injury.

Limitations to the use of the device are few and are similar to those that would be anticipated for any transurethral procedure. A pediatric probe is not available and, therefore, the instrument cannot be used in the urethra that does not accommodate a cystoscope sheath large enough to take the 10F probe, that is boys less than 13 years old or cases of urethral strictures or bladder neck obstruction. Litholapaxy is contraindicated in patients with sepsis. A bladder that cannot contain enough irrigating solution to conduct the shock waves generated from the probe tip will not be suited for electrohydraulic lithotripsy. Electrohydraulic litholapaxy has been performed in patients with cardiac pacemakers without ill effect.[9]

Although some authors have reported success in the disruption of stones in ureteroceles[3,9] little clinical experience supports the use of the present device in the treatment of ureteral calculi. Significant ureteral damage has resulted experimentally.[4,7] However, there may be a place for electrohydraulic lithotripsy in the treatment of calculi in the renal pelvis.

CONCLUSION

The electrohydraulic lithotrite is effective in the treatment of bladder calculi. Its use has not been associated with significant complication, minimizing trauma to the bladder and urethra. Our experience is consistent with that reported by other authors who have had access to the device for more than 9 years.

REFERENCES

1. Riches, E.: The history of lithotomy and lithotripsy. Ann Roy Coll Surg 43:185, 1968
2. Yutkin, L. A.: Electrohydraulic effect. Published Union of Soviet Socialist Republics, 1955. English Translations United States Department of Commerce Office of Technical Services Document, 62-15184, MCL, 1207/1-2
3. Reuter, H. J.: Electronic lithotripsy: transurethral treatment of bladder stones in 50 cases. J Urol 104:834, 1970
4. Rouvalis, P.: Electronic lithotripsy for vesicle calculus with "URAT-1". An experience of 100 cases and an experimental application of the method to stones in the upper urinary tract. Br J Urol 42:486, 1970
5. Albrecht, D., Nagel, R. and Kölln, C. P.: Electrohydraulic waves (URAT I) for the treatment of vesical calculi. Int Urol Nephrol 4:45, 1972
6. Angeloff, A.: Hydroelectrolithotripsy. J Urol 108:867, 1972
7. Alfthan, O. and Murtomaa, M.: Experiences with the clinical and experimental use of URAT-1 lithotriptor. Scand J Urol Nephrol 6:23, 1972
8. Eaton, J. M., Jr., Malin, J. M., Jr and Glenn, J. F.: Electrohydraulic lithotripsy. J Urol 108:865, 1972
9. Tessler, A. N. and Kossow, J.: Electrohydraulic stone disintegration. Urology 5:470, 1975
10. Raney, A. M.: Electrohydraulic cystolithotripsy. Urology 8:379, 1976

Commentary: Endoscopic Surgery of Bladder Calculi

Walter S. Kerr, Jr.

Before the invention of the electrohydraulic lithotrite by the Russians in the late 1950s, bladder stones too large to wash out were either crushed using a visual lithotrite or the Bigelow lithotrite or removed through a cystotomy. The visual lithotrite had the disadvantage of being able to crush only small soft stones. The Bigelow lithotrite had the disadvantage of being a blind procedure; also, its manipulation caused so much edema and swelling of the prostate that frequently patients had to have a prostatectomy after stones were removed.

Since 1975 the electrohydraulic lithotrite has been used in a large number of patients by a large number of residents with a minimal number of complications and failures. The technique used with the electrohydraulic lithotrite is very simple to teach and to master. The bladder is filled with 150 ml of irrigation fluid. The flexible stone probe fits through any of the endoscopic equipment. It is directed against the surface of the stone at a distance of a few millimeters. The current is delivered in short bursts lasting a few seconds. The stones usually bounce away when the current is turned on; inexperi- enced physicians tend to try to corner the stone between the end of the probe and the bladder wall. This should be avoided, since the stone will pop away and the probe will rest against the bladder wall and injure it. It is essential to look at the probe before and during use, especially if the stones do not seem to break apart in the expected time interval. If there is a defect in the end of the probe, replacing it will usually result in quick disruption of the stone.

I try to use the equipment in a 24 French sheath, since this allows for irrigating the stone fragments with ease and avoids changing of the sheaths, which is desirable. Excessive wear of the probe tip can be prevented by restricting the discharges to short bursts to prevent overheating and subsequent loss of the typical structure of the probe tip.

All the members of the urological staff at the Massachusetts General Hospital have used the electrohydraulic lithotrite over the past 5 yr and are still enthusiastic about its effectiveness in the treatment of bladder calculi.

ANNOTATED BIBLIOGRAPHY

Eaton JM Jr, Malin JM Jr, Glenn JF: Electrohydraulic lithotripsy. J Urol 108:865, 1972

In this report the authors describe their experience using the Russian-designed Ypat I portable lithotriptor. After the authors used this instrument in mongrel dogs, they treated nine patients with this instrument. Six of these patients also had concomitant transurethral resection of the prostate. They had spinal anesthesia. The average operating time was 1½ hr. The lithotripsy followed the transurethral resection of the prostate, and in no patient was bleeding sufficient from the lithotripsy to cause difficulty with the transurethral resection of the prostate. Hospital stay was no longer than that for transurethral resection of the prostate, and no complications ensued from electrohydraulic lithotripsy. Three of their patients underwent the lithotripsy under topical analgesia as outpatients.

Tessler AN, Kossow J: Electrohydraulic stone disintegration. Urology 5:470, 1975

The authors describe their experience using electrohydraulic stone disintegration in 30 patients with innumerable calculi of varying compositions without any complications. The stone disintegrator they have employed is the PBF Stone Disintegrator Model SD2. The authors note that they were able to disintegrate one calculus in a wide-mouth diverticulum without disrupting the diverticulum wall, and on two occasions they used the electrohydraulic stone disintegrator in patients with cardiac pacemakers. They noted no changes in cardiac rate or pacemaker dysfunction. They conclude that this method of stone disintegration is the best available method for rapid, safe fragmentation of bladder calculi.

Raney AM: Electrohydraulic lithotripsy: Experimental study and case reports with the stone disintegrator. J Urol 113:345, 1975

In this paper the author discusses his experimental findings in laboratory animals and in 19 patients using the SD-1 stone disintegrator produced by the Northgate Research Corporation. He concludes that the procedure is safe and superior to conven- tional methods of lithotripsy. No morbidity or mortality was seen in any of these patients.

Angaloff A: Hydro electrolithotripsy. J Urol 108:867, 1972

In this report from Bulgaria, the author reports a large experience with 100 patients, 71 men and 29 women, who underwent electrohydraulic lithotripsy with the Urat-1 apparatus. Local anesthesia was used in 70 patients and general anesthesia in 30. In three patients the electrohydraulic lithotripsy was unsuccessful. In one of them it was unsuccessful because of the exceedingly small bladder capacity, precluding irrigation and creation of an electrohydrohynamic impulse. The size of the stones ranged from 1 cm to 4 cm. In 15 patients there were multiple stones of varying sizes. The length of the procedure was about 15 min in half the patients, approximately 30 min in 25% of the patients, and more than 30 min in the rest. Half the patients were treated as outpatients; the remainder were hospitalized for a maximum of 7 days. Included in this experience were oxylate, phosphate, urate, uric acid, and mixed stones. There were no complications from the operative procedure when it was carried out properly. However, the author noted minor transient hematuria in 12 patients. Seven patients developed fever, and two patients passed gravel. In another three patients, fragments of the crushed stone became embedded in the pendulus urethra, where they were

extracted endoscopically. The author notes the following contraindications to electrohydraulic lithotripsy: urethral stricture, pronounced obstruction of the bladder neck (large prostatic adenoma), small-capacity bladder, sepsis, or severe renal failure. The author concludes that when patients are selected properly, the operative procedure is safer than mechanical lithotripsy.

Overview: Endoscopic Surgery of Bladder Calculi

Hubert G. W. Frohmüller

In the past two decades there have been several major steps forward in the technique of transurethral removal of bladder stones. The first improvement over the time-honored blind and visual lithotrites, which used mechanical energy to crush the calculi, was the development of electrohydraulic lithotripsy in 1969. Around 1971 ultrasound was introduced as a destructive force for bladder stones. In 1975 I designed a punch lithotriptor* that uses the same principle as punch prostatectomy—fragmenting calculi by engaging them in the fenestra of the sheath. (A similar stone punch was developed independently by Mauermayer at about the same time.) The latest evolution is the disintegration of stones by extracorporeally produced shock waves without direct body contact.[1] After extensive experimental studies this newest method has so far been used only in a limited number of patients with renal calculi at the urology department of the University of Munich, Germany, but technically it is conceivable that it could also be applied in patients with bladder stones.

Following its introduction, ultrasonic lithotripsy was first hailed as far superior to electrohydraulic lithotripsy because its probe cannot harm the muscle or mucosa of the bladder and because there is no risk of stone fragments being driven into the vesical wall, since the destruction of the calculus is effected by vibration rather than explosion. The procedure of ultrasonic lithotripsy is rather time consuming, however, particularly when large stones are encountered, and its equipment is quite expensive as compared with the armamentarium used with other methods. Because up to the present this procedure appears not as thoroughly tested clinically as other methods, lithotripsy by ultrasound is in use in only a small number of institutions.

The destructive effect of electrohydraulic shock waves was discovered in 1950 by the Russian engineer L. A. Yutkin.[2] After the first device using this method had been built by the

engineer L. Rose in Riga (Latvian Republic, USSR), the urologist V. V. Goldberg first performed a transurethral electrohydraulic lithotripsy on May 7, 1959, in Riga.[3] He reported this operation at the meeting of the Latvian Urological Society on May 13, 1959.

Soon after its introduction in Germany in 1968 I began using electrohydraulic lithotripsy at my institution. Before long I realized that the available endoscopic equipment was not up to the requirements of this procedure. I therefore constructed a cystoscope that permitted both electrohydraulic lithotripsy and removal of crushed stone fragments by aspiration under direct vision control.[4] This way, damage to the expensive telescope was avoided and total evacuation of the fragments could be ensured.

Since then I have further improved the entire armamentarium used in electrohydraulic lithotripsy (in collaboration with Richard Wolf Company, Knittlingen, West Germany). A new impulse generator (RIWOLITH) (manufactured by Richard Wolf Company) that produces a maximum discharge voltage of 8 kV forms the electrohydraulic shock waves. The impulses can be regulated in three power levels, the frequency can be modified in an ungraded range of 1 to 70/sec, and the duration of the impulses can be adjusted between 1 and 5 sec. A foot switch is used to trigger the impulses. The energy is transmitted through a Teflonisolated probe, size 9 French, that is mounted in a guide element that prevents the operating telescope from being damaged. I generally use a 24 French continuous irrigation resectoscope sheath, which can also be fitted with a punch lithotrite, a direct vision aspiration attachment, and an electroresection element (*i.e.*, the sheath of the instrument can remain in place throughout the entire procedure) (Fig. 1).

The technique I use with the electrohydraulic lithotriptor is essentially the same as so classically described by Kerr. Once the stone fragments have been broken down sufficiently to be removed through the instrument sheath, the guide element carrying the lithotrite probe and the observation telescope is removed and replaced by a direct vision attachment that allows

---

* in collaboration with Richard Wolf Company, Knittlingen, West Germany.

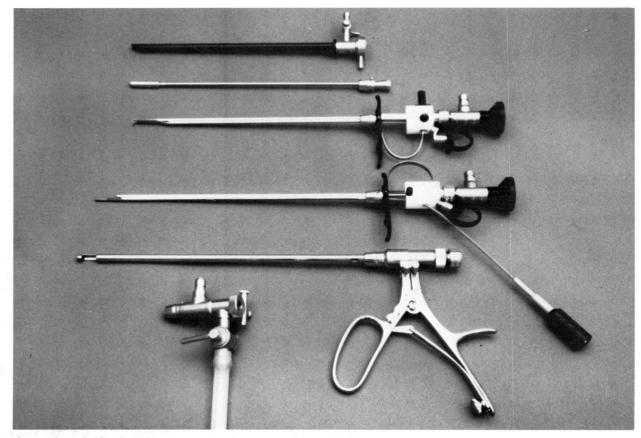

Fig. 1. Electrohydraulic lithotriptor in combination with punch lithotrite. From top: F 24 cystoscope sheath; obturator; electroresection element; F 9 electroprobe element for electrohydraulic lithotripsy; punch lithotrite; aspiration attachment with direct vision observation window. (Bülow H, Frohmüller HGW: Electrohydraulic lithotripsy with aspiration of the fragments under vision—304 consecutive cases. J Urol 126:454, 1981)

observation of the aspiration procedure. By dispensing with the observation telescope at this stage of the operation, the entire lumen of the instrument sheath can be used to remove the stone fragments. Aspiration itself is performed with the aid of a vacuum pump in a closed system. The fragments of the calculi are collected in an interposed strainer.

Urologists who are experienced with electrohydraulic lithotripsy know that the simplest part of the procedure is the beginning of the fragmentation, when the stone is still large. The smaller the fragments get, the more difficult it becomes to corner the particicles with the probe. As pointed out by Kerr, there is the danger of injuring the bladder at this stage of the operation if the probe slips off the stone and touches the bladder wall. This is regarded as a main disadvantage of electrohydraulic lithotripsy as compared, for instance, with ultrasonic lithotripsy. In order to avoid this drawback I combine electrohydraulic lithotripsy with punch lithotripsy. As soon as the stone has been fragmented into pieces the size of a cherry

or a pea by electrohydraulic waves, I exchange the probe element for the punch lithotrite without changing the sheath of the instrument. By engaging the stone fragments in the fenestra of the punch lithotriptor, which has an opening of 1.5 cm × 0.5 cm, they can be nibbled down easily and very rapidly to smaller sizes (Figs. 2 and 3), which then can be aspirated conveniently with the suction attachment under visual control.

Within the last few years I have become quite enthusiastic about punch lithotripsy because it is even simpler to teach and to master than electrohydraulic lithotripsy. Therefore, when I am faced with vesical calculi not larger than a cherry, I forgo electrohydraulic lithotripsy entirely and perform a punch lithotripsy exclusively. Especially with uric acid stones, which because of their firmness are difficult to disintegrate by electrohydraulic shock waves, punch lithotripsy offers the additional advantage of rapid fragmentation. Electrohydraulic lithotripsy as well as punch lithotripsy can easily be combined

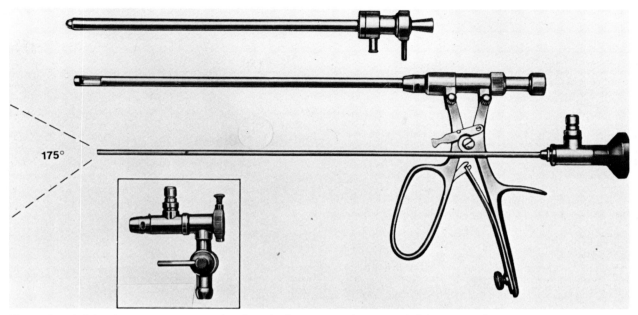

Fig. 2. Punch lithotrite. From top: F 24 sheath with obturator in place; punch lithotrite, with characteristic fenestra at distal end; and telescope. *Insert:* aspiration attachment with direct vision observation window.

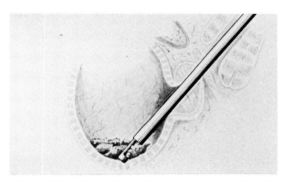

Fig. 3. Punch lithotripsy. Stone fragment to be crushed is engaged in the fenestra of the instrument.

TABLE 4. Age and Sex Distribution of 304 Patients in Whom Electrohydraulic Lithotripsy was Performed

Sex	No.	%	Age (yr)
Males	281	92.4	68.5 (14–102)
Females	23	7.6	63.9 (30–65)
	304	100	

(Bülow H, Frohmüller HGW: Electrohydraulic lithotripsy with aspiration of the fragments under vision—304 consecutive cases. J Urol 126:454, 1981)

with transurethral prostatectomy or resection of bladder tumors in the same session.

A word of caution on the method of electrohydraulic lithotripsy was introduced by Tidd and colleagues, who demonstrated in animals that the bladder can be perforated easily and the gas-filled small intestine can even be ruptured by this type of electrical discharge.[5] Although it is well known that damage and even perforation of the bladder wall can occur when the lithotrite probe is brought in direct contact with it, disruption of the small intestine by this procedure has not been reported in humans so far.

I recently reviewed the cases of electrohydraulic lithotripsy performed between July 1969 and September 1979 at Bülow's and my institution.[6] During this time the procedure was carried out in 304 patients. A further group of 41 patients was treated alone or by a combination of punch and electrohydraulic lithotripsy. The age and sex distribution of those 304 patients is shown in Table 4. The oldest patient was 102 yr of age, and the removed stone fragments in this case weighed 50 g. There were no operative or postoperative deaths attributable to electrohydraulic lithotripsy as a solitary procedure.

Two hundred and sixty six (87.5%) of the operations were performed under spinal anesthesia, 35 (11.5%) under general anesthesia, and 3 (1%) under local anesthesia of the urethral mucosa. Solitary (56.3%) and multiple (43.7%) vesical calculi were about equal in distribution. The operative risk was increased in 117 (38.5%) of the 304 patients because of preexisting cardiac, pulmonary, neurologic, or other pertinent diseases. In 245 (80.5%) of the men infravesical obstructive disease was present (Table 5). The removed calculi had an average weight of 11 (1 to 135) g. Electrohydraulic disintegration of the stones, including aspiration of the fragments,

TABLE 5. Types of Infravesical Obstruction in 245 Men in Whom Electrohydraulic Lithotripsy was Performed

Diagnosis	No.	%
Prostatic adenoma	176	71.8
Prostatic carcinoma	21	8.6
Vesical neck stenosis	9	3.7
Urethral stricture	7	2.8
Several of the above	32	13.1
	245	100

(Bülow H, Frohmüller HGW: Electrohydraulic lithotripsy with aspiration of the fragments under vision—304 consecutive cases. J Urol 126:454, 1981)

was completed in an average of 26.1 (2–122) min, and 53.5% of the stones consisted or uric acid or urates.

A subsequent transurethral procedure in addition to lithotripsy was performed under the same anesthesia in 238 (84.6%) of the male patients. In 198 (83.2%) a transurethral prostatic resection was carried out.

As an intraoperative complication of electrohydraulic lithotripsy, deep lesions of the vesical wall occurred six times. A laparotomy was necessary only once, however, when a resident perforated the bladder wall with the probe during his first attempt with the electrohydraulic lithotriptor. The remaining patients had a smooth postoperative recovery with a Foley catheter in place for several days. No intravesical bleeding occurred that would have required electrocoagulation.

Both electrohydraulic and punch lithotripsy are well established and efficient methods for transurethral removal of bladder stones. Both procedures are easy to learn and safe, and they can be applied in very old and in high-risk patients. The intraoperative complication rate is very low, and postoperative complications are practically nonexistent.

REFERENCES

1. Eisenberger F, Schmiedt E, Chaussy C, et al: Berührungsfreie Harnsteinzertrümmerung. Dtsch Arztebl 74:1145, 1977
2. Trapeznikova MF, Borodulin GG: Electrohydraulic impulse lithotripsy of bladder stones with Urat-1. Endoscopy 9:6, 1977
3. Goldberg V: Eine neue Methode der Harnsteinzertrümmerung—electrohydraulische Lithotripsie. Urologe 19:23, 1979
4. Frohmüller H: Elektro-hydraulische Lithotripsie mit Direktsicht-Aspiration der Konkrementtrümmer. Urologe 10:64, 1971
5. Tidd MJ, Wright HC, Oliver Y, et al: Hazards to bladder and intestinal tissues from intravesical underwater electrical discharges from a surgical electronic lithoclast. Urol Res 4:49, 1976
6. Bülow H, Frohmüller HGW: Electrohydraulic lithotripsy with aspiration of the fragments under vision—304 consecutive cases. J Urol 126:454, 1981

PART THIRTY

SURGERY OF NEUROGENIC BLADDER

74

THE CONTINENT VESICOSTOMY: CLINICAL EXPERIENCES IN THE ADULT

Keith M. Schneider, Roberto E. Reid and Bernard Fruchtman

From the Departments of Surgery and Urology, The Albert Einstein College of Medicine and Montefiore Hospital and Medical Center, Bronx, New York

The Journal of Urology
Copyright © 1977 by The Williams & Wilkins Co.
Vol. 117, May
Printed in U.S.A.

ABSTRACT—During a 2-year period continent vesicostomy has been attempted in 17 adults and a continent stoma has been achieved in all but 4 patients. Operative morbidity is low and there has been no operative mortality. Definition of precise indications and contraindications must await further experience but this operative procedure seems to be a useful alternative in the management of neurogenic bladder and incontinence.

In 1974 we reported on a new operative procedure for urinary diversion.[1] The continent vesicostomy involves a valve-like intussusception from an anterior wall bladder flap, which communicates with a stoma on the anterior abdominal wall. Findings in the experimental animal were encouraging enough to undertake a clinical evaluation. Continent vesicostomies now have been performed on 17 adults. Herein we evaluate our clinical experience during the last 2 years.

Accepted for publication September 10, 1976.

CLINICAL MATERIAL

Nineteen procedures have been performed on 17 patients. The 11 women and 6 men ranged in age from 19 to 84 years. Followup has been from 2 to 26 months, with a mean of 13.5 months. No patient has been lost to followup. Indications for the operation were neurogenic bladders in 15 cases and a decompensated bladder secondary to advanced prostatism and post-prostatectomy incontinence in 2. Seven patients had traumatic paraplegia, 2 of whom were considered to have lower motor

TABLE 1. Diagnosis in 17 Patients Undergoing Continent
Vesicostomy

	No. Patients
Neurogenic bladder:	15
Spastic bladder (paraplegia), 5	
Lower motor region (paraplegia), 2	
Multiple sclerosis, 4	
Pernicious anemia, 1	
Diabetes, 1	
Unknown, 2	
Decompensated bladder secondary to advanced prostatism and post-prostatectomy incontinence	2
Total	17

neuron lesions. Four women had multiple sclerosis.
Pernicious anemia and diabetes were the etiologies in 1
patient each. In 2 patients the cause of the neurogenic
bladder was undetermined but resulted in a large capacity
hypotonic bladder (Table 1).

TECHNIQUE

The surgical technique has undergone essential modifications, which have improved our clinical results.[2] A
major factor in constructing a continent valve is the
maintenance of an intussusception of adequate length
against the hydrostatic pressure of the bladder. A technical error in early patients was the use of absorbable
sutures, coating the muscle in the wall of the intussusception. Early dissolution of these sutures allowed dehiscence and/or reduction of the intussusception before
fibrosis had secured the intussusception in place sufficiently. We now use non-absorbable sutures for this
critical step in the operative procedure (Fig. 1).

Two factors not sufficiently appreciated during the
initial operations were the importance of the length of
the intussusception and the need for prolonged catheter
diversion. The intussusception now is constructed so
that it is at least 3.0 or, preferably, 4.0 cm in length.
Suprapubic and stomal catheter diversion is maintained
for 6 weeks to avoid hydrostatic pressure reduction of
the intussusception until healing has taken place (Fig.
2).

A bladder capacity of 200 cc or more is required.
In those individuals with low bladder outlet resistance a
technique for closure of the bladder neck was required
to prevent urethral leakage. This additional step was
required in 5 patients.

Patients are discharged from the hospital in 2 weeks
and are readmitted 4 weeks later. The suprapubic tube
is removed, followed in 2 or 3 days by removal of the
stomal tube. Intermittent stomal catheterization is started
at 2-hour intervals and gradually increased to 6-hour
periods.

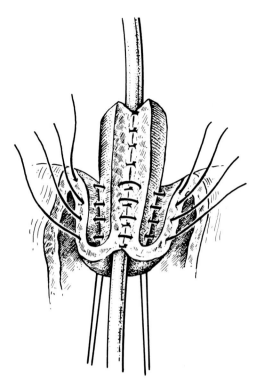

Fig. 1. Reprinted with permission[2]

RESULTS

A successful continent vesicostomy has been constructed
in 13 patients. These 13 patients included all 4 with
multiple sclerosis and 4 of 7 with traumatic paraplegia.
Patients catheterize themselves in the sitting or supine
position with 14 to 18F catheters. Catheterization intervals range from 3 to 8 hours. Some leakage through the
stoma occurred in most patients for 1 or 2 weeks after
the catheter is withdrawn. We are uncertain as to the
cause of this temporary leakage. The presence of a
catheter in the stoma for 6 weeks may compromise
temporarily the contractility of the intussusception. Cystoscopy in patients in whom the bladder neck had not
been closed revealed a well formed nipple within the
bladder lumen (Fig. 3). The longest followup is 26
months. The nipple persists and still is functioning in
this patient. Bladder neck closure has been successful
in 4 of 5 cases. There have been 4 failures to achieve a
continent vesicostomy. However, 2 cases in the successful group required a second procedure, necessitated
by reduction of the intussusception after the initial
operation. In these patients absorbable sutures were used
for the initial operation and non-absorbable sutures were
used for the second and successful operation (Table 2).

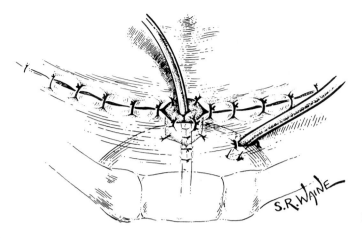

Fig. 2. Reprinted with permission[2]

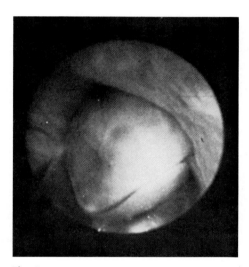

Fig. 3.

TABLE 2. Results of Continent Vesicostomy in 17 Patients

	No. Patients
Good	13
Failure*	4

* Failures were caused by wound infection and disruption in 2 cases, and because of absorbable sutures in 2.

In 2 patients, 1 with diabetes and 1 with traumatic quadriplegia, failure was associated with necrotizing fasciitis. Two other failures, both in paraplegics, were the result of reduction of the intussusception. In all 4 patients intermittent stomal catheterization was suspended and the stoma was closed spontaneously.

Bladder calculi developed in 2 patients, while stomal stenosis was noted in 2 others. The bladder calculi were secondary to extruded non-absorbable sutures and were removed transurethrally. The stomal stenosis has responded to intermittent dilatation.

One patient had reflux in 1 ureter during a bout of cystitis but the upper tract has remained normal. Another 39-year-old paraplegic had a staghorn calculus that required an operation 2 years after the continent vesicostomy. All other patients have normal upper tracts without reflux, including 1 patient with reflux who had unilateral ureteral reimplantation at the time of the continent vesicostomy. Bacteriuria has been present intermittently in all but 2 patients. However, clinical cystitis has occurred in only 3 of our cases.

DISCUSSION

Current techniques for urinary diversion are less than ideal. Complications range in severity from embarrassing appliance leakage to upper tract deterioration. The continent vesicostomy preserves the capacity of the bladder to function as a reservoir, maintains the intact ureterovesical junctions and requires no external appliance. The procedure offers the patient and physician an alternative to ileal or sigmoid loops and to intermittent urethral catheterization. A large number of patients and longer followup are necessary before the ultimate value of the continent vesicostomy can be determined.

We believe that we are justified in proposing this operation to patients in whom intermittent urethral catheterization has failed or has been refused, making them candidates for upper tract diversion. In addition, the procedure seems to be indicated for unmanageable incontinence, particularly in the female patient for whom a suitable external appliance has not been devised. Intermittent catheterization through an abdominal stoma, instead of per urethram, may be more compatible with the prospects of returning the patient to an active and involved social life.

More precise indications and contraindications for the continent vesicostomy must await further experience. However, it would seem that the patient with a large capacity neurogenic bladder who is unable to empty it well is the ideal candidate. The decompensated or hypotonic bladder does not require bladder neck closure, which offers the advantage of a totally reversible pro-

cedure. If continence is not achieved the stoma will close when catheterization is stopped.

CONCLUSION

The continent vesicostomy seems to be a useful alternative procedure to the usual urinary diversion and intermittent urethral catheterization. While the ultimate role of this procedure awaits further clinical experience initial results indicate its usefulness in selected patients.

REFERENCES

1. Schneider, K. M., Ewing, R. S. and Signer, R. D.: Continent vesicostomy. Urology 3:654, 1974

2. Schneider, K. M., Ried, R. E., Fruchtman, B. and Ewing, R. S: Continent vesicostomy—surgical technique. Urology 6:741, 1975

Commentary: The Continent Vesicostomy

Edward J. McGuire

The final applicability of the continent vesicostomy is, as noted in the preceding article, still not defined. I have found it extremely useful in some circumstances. It is a good operation for women with areflexic vesical dysfunction, and is useful in some men with similar lesions without a functional urethral continence mechanism in whom the urethra must be deliberately closed.[1]

However, only a limited number of surgical procedures are useful in patients with a neurogenic bladder. These include external sphincterotomy or transurethral resection of the bladder neck or proximal urethra and, rarely, augmentation cystoplasty or ureteral reimplantation.[2-4]

Improving vesical function by decreasing urethral resistance surgically is not useful in women, and not all men tolerate condom catheter drainage with equanimity. Spinal-cord-injured women, even those with C5–C6 lesions, can, however, intermittently catheterize a vesicostomy stoma. Wider applicability of this operative technique, which is basically sound, depends in patients with reflex detrusor activity on control of the reflex response. This is often impossible with pharmacologic therapy alone, and the entire matter of limited, selective, or complete sacral neurectomy should be reexamined in view of the fact that a good technique to create a continent lower abdominal stoma has been described and enables easy self- (or attendant) intermittent catheterization, even in those patients with very high lesions.[5-8] Moreover, even women paraplegics who have been managed with intermittent self-catheterization through the urethra may occasionally have difficulty with this. The

technique requires that special clothing be worn and that easy wheelchair access to toilet facilities be ensured. Although special clothing can certainly be designed, wheelchair accessibility in all circumstances to toilet facilities is obviously impossible to guarantee.

The continent vesicostomy has, for the present, only a limited applicability in neurogenic vesical dysfunction. However, if this technique is kept in mind and an ideal neurolytic procedure is evolved, a much wider potential applicability is possible; with it, urologists might achieve the solution to one of the most vexing problems in neurogenic vesical dysfunction—female incontinence related to suprasacral neural lesions.

I feel that the ideal neurectomy is a selective procedure on the dorsal root or dorsal root ganglion by resection or coagulation. This sensory denervation should produce a bladder that functions like that seen in a diabetic or tabetic—a low-pressure areflexic bladder that tolerates filling and does not contract. In contrast, a preganglionic motor transection leads to a bladder that resists filling with an intrinsic muscular response that is greater than normal. This is often associated with the development of trabeculation and, not infrequently, the development of vesicoureteral reflux and upper urinary tract deterioration. Basic research in this area would provide information that would be extremely useful and might well enable urologists to use the continent vesicostomy to supplant a number of other management techniques that are presently less than satisfactory.

REFERENCES

1. Woodside J, McGuire EJ: Urethral hypotonicity following spinal cord injury. J Urol (in press)
2. O'Flynn JD: Early and late management of the neuropathic bladder in spinal cord injury patients. J Urol 120:726, 1978
3. Hirsch S, Carrion H, Gordon J, et al: Ureteroneocystotomy in the treatment of reflux in neurogenic bladders. J Urol 120:552, 1978
4. Smith RB, VanCaugh P, Skinner DG, et al: Augmentation enterocystoplasty: A critical review. J Urol 118:35, 1977
5. McGuire EJ, Diddle G, Wagner F: Balanced bladder function in spinal cord injury patients. J Urol 118:626, 1977

6. McGuie EJ, Wagner F: The effects of sacral denervation on bladder and urethral function. Surg Gynecol Obstet 144:343, 1977
7. Diokno AC, Vinson RK, McGillicuddy J: Treatment of severe uninhibited neurogenic bladder by selective sacral rhizotomy. J Urol 118:299, 1977
8. Mulcahy JJ, Young AB: Percutaneous radiofrequency sacral rhizotomy in the treatment of the hyperreflexic bladder. J Urol 120:557, 1978

ANNOTATED BIBLIOGRAPHY

McGuire EJ: Urethral sphincter mechanisms. Urol Clin North Am 6:39, 1979

The author reviews current concepts regarding urethral function as a sphincter and as a compliant conduit during voiding. The active components of urethral resistance include smooth and skeletal musculature innervated by sympathetic and somatic motor nerves. Loss of smooth muscular function is associated with severe incontinence, but loss of skeletal muscle function is not. One of the passive components of urethral resistance is the position of the proximal urethra closed by smooth musculature within the intra-abdominal cavity, where it is subjected to the same changes in intra-abdominal pressure as is the bladder.

Normally, both active components of urethral resistance relax with detrusor activity. Dyssynergia occurs when the reciprocal relationship between the detrusor and its spincter is disturbed. The author identifies three types of detrusor external sphincter dyssynergia that ocur in neurogenic conditions. In the most common, the bladder contracts strongly against the contracting sphincter. In the second, the sphincter contracts but the bladder does not, and in the lest common both sphincter and detrusor contract and relax without urinary flow. Treatment is based on urodynamic identification of which type is present. If detrusor reflexes are present, even if the patient is not voiding, some kind of sphincter ablative procedure in men or a method to decrease reflex detrusor responses in women is mandatory. If detrusor reflexes are not present, intermittent catheterization is practical and safe for protracted periods.

Schillhaus PF, Hackler RH, Bunts RC: External sphincterotomy: An evaluation of 150 patients with neurogenic bladder. J Urol 110:199, 1973

The authors discuss results of external sphincterotomy by knife electrode in 150 patients. They use incisions at the 3 o'clock and 9 o'clock positions in the sphincter. (At present the better location for sphincterotomy incision is 12 o'clock, since this appears to largely avoid problems with impotence noted after the lateral bilateral incisions.) Seventy four percent of patients achieved balanced bladder function. Those who did not showed an arreflexic bladder or collapse of tissue in the prostatic urethra that was obstructive. In 21 patients who failed an initial operation, a repeat sphincterotomy resulted in achievement of balanced bladder function. Bladder neck hypertrophy was not found to be a significant cause of obstruction to voiding in this patient group. Rather, it appeared that in patients with arreflexic bladders, the bladder neck simply did not open as a result of the loss of the detrusor reflex.

O'Flynn JD: Neurogenic bladder in spinal cord injury. Urol Clin North Am 1:155, 1974

The author notes that vesical outlet obstruction is a major contributing feature to the decline in renal function in patients with spinal cord injury. He reviews his experience with 378 patients at the National Rehabilitation Center in Dublin. After a period of intermittent catheterization or continuous catheterization (usually 3 mo), a trial at voiding is given. If this is unsatisfactory, a surgical procedure on the external or internal sphincter or both is performed. Generally, those patients with higher lesions require external sphincterotomy and those with lower lesions internal sphincterotomy or transurethral resection of the bladder neck. The author describes his technique of external sphincterotomy using a knife electrode, which involves several incisions through the external sphincter. He found operative procedures necessary in 31% of 378 patients, but he calls attention to the difficulty with incontinence in women treated for outlet obstruction in this manner.

Khanna OP: Disorders of micturition: Urologic basis and results of drug treatment. Urology 8:316, 1976

The author describes newer concepts of the neurophysiology of the bladder and urethra and their application clinically. These structures are innervated by both divisions of the autonomic nervous system, and both are richly supplied with cholinergic and both alpha- and beta-adrenergic receptor sites. Interaction between the cholinergic and adrenergic nervous systems occurs centrally and peripherally. The author reviews recent findings regarding the predominance of alpha-adrenergic receptors in the bladder base and urethra, which principally subserve continence function, and beta-adrenergic receptors predominant in the bladder fundus, which apparently results in relaxation of the bladder during filling. During filling, sympathetic activity relaxes the fundus by an action on the beta receptors and contracts the base and urethra by differential reaction on alpha receptors. The parasympathetic nervous system is inhibited during this phase. During voiding, parasympathetic discharge occurs, which inhibits sympathetic tonus and which in turn is associated with urethral relaxation. Clinically, poor micturition can be treated by a combination of cholinergic and alpha-blocking agents. Stress incontinence may respond to alpha-adrenergic agents, as may postprostatectomy incontinence.

McGuire EJ, Wagner FC: The effects of sacral denervation on bladder and urethral function. Surg Gynecol Obstet 144:343, 1977

The authors report their experience with complete S1 to S4 intradural sacral rhizotomy in the treatment of neurogenic vesical dysfunction resulting from a transverse suprasacral spinal cord injury. The procedure resulted in a mildly hypertonic but arreflexic bladder with preservation of urethral smooth but not skeletal muscular closing function and cure of autonomic dysreflexia. These findings indicate that an arreflexic bladder is not necessarily flaccid without a superimposed muscular injury, usually overdistention, and that urethral smooth muscular function persists after total sacral denervation. Patients were managed by intermittent catheterization and anticholinergic agents, which controlled vesical hypertonicity and resulted in good urinary continence between intermittent catheterizations. These findings have important implications about the dual innervation of the lower urinary tract and indicate that complete sacral neurectomy can interrupt detrusor reflex function, and, provided hypertonic vesical responses to filling are controlled with anticholinergic agents, patients can be managed safely for protracted periods on intermittent self-catheterization.

Torrens M, Hald T: Bladder denervation procedure. Urol Clin North Am 6:283, 1979

The authors discuss the indications for bladder denervation procedures, which are limited to intractable, uncontrollable bladder hyperactivity or pain. Alternative therapy would be diversion or augmentation cystoplasty. Denervation may be central or peripheral. The latter is more selective but less reliable. Selective blockade of the S2 and S3 roots using alcohol or phenol under x-ray control is described. This procedure may increase vesical capacity and may impair voluntary sphincteric activity, but the latter is not usually clinically significant. The authors report that deliberate vesical overdistention has been used by other workers to induce detrusor denervation as well as the technique of bladder transection. Neither of these techniques has achieved widespread clinical applicability. The authors describe their own results in a small number of patients treated by selective sacral neurectomy (cutting or crushing the S2 or S3 roots). The procedure resulted in improvement without major side-effects, but the improvement was less than hoped for and somewhat transient. The authors then used radical selective neurectomy in which all S3 and S4 fibers of fascicles carrying motor fibers to the detrusor identified intraoperatively by stimulation were transected. Results were again disappointing except in patients with clear neurogenic conditions, since the detrusor reflex usually returned. The authors review the published results of other series of denervation procedures, which in general report only a 50% improvement rate.

Overview: Surgical Management of Neurogenic Urinary Dysfunction

Jacques G. Susset and Paul Hochsztein

The role of surgery in the management of neurogenic urinary dysfunction is relatively limited. The use of pharmacologic agents, intermittent catheterization, and various types of rehabilitation constitute the most commonly used approach in the management of these problems. Whatever the contemplated management is, it must be realistic, more so than in the management of other conditions. What is the point of making a patient void when he will be physically incapable of undressing himself or sitting on a toilet? Multiple factors must be considered in formulating a plan of management, including the progress of the neurologic disease, the coexistence of superimposed complications that may alter the clinical appearance, completely patient reliability and intelligence, social environment, financial resources, and outside assistance.

The elaboration of such a plan must encompass a careful analysis of the many factors responsible for the urinary imbalance between the bladder's forces of expulsion and forces of retention, between detrusor activity and urethral resistance. The expulsive forces are represented by the quality of the detrusor contract and the patient's inherent ability to raise his intra-abdominal pressure to compensate for a deficient detrusor. The retention forces include the forces of resistance involving the dynamics of the vesical neck and posterior urethral smooth muscle and the extrinsic striated external sphincter.

Former classifications by Bors and Comarr and later by Lapides and Baum, trying to associate anatomic level of lesions to neurovesical dysfunction, proved unrewarding and impractical.[1-3] The level and degree of lesion is often difficult to ascertain when the lesion is complete, presenting even a greater challenge in the incomplete variety. Furthermore, secondary occurrence of common complications such as overdistension or infection may further obscure the clinical presentation and thereby require modification of the plan of management. The importance of individualization of therapeutic intervention rather than preoccupation with self-limiting classification and labeling cannot be overemphasized. A physiologic approach in the evaluation of imbalance between detrusor activity and urethral resistance must be maintained. It begins with a detailed case history and physical. It is reinforced by further investigation such as voiding cystourethrogram and urodynamics and electromyographic (EMG) assessment. The plan of management will be apparent from the understanding of the interplay of these factors, and the quality of treatment will be directly proportional to the accuracy of this assessment. When planning management, the surgeon must differentiate between factors involving the vital prognosis, that is, renal function, and the functional prognosis that is urinary continence. The first objective is directly related to urinary retention, infection, presence of vesicoureteral reflux, and hydronephrosis. Incontinence, on the other hand, depends on both the degree of detrusor activity and sphincter competence. The functional prognosis is also related to the motivation, that is, manual dexterity effecting intermittent self-catheterization as well as a psychosocial environment, that is, accessibility of bathroom facilities, availability of family assistance or visiting nurses, and financial feasibility. Preferably, the combined supervision of the pyschiatrist, psychologist, and social worker should be sought to help define these aforementioned factors before a definite plan of treatment is implemented.

Basically, surgical management should be specifically directed toward reestablishing as normal a urinary balance as possible. Management of dysfunction should be considered separately for expulsive forces and retentive forces. In other words, the two questions to ask are, ''What can be done for detrusor hypoactivity or hyperactivity? What can be done for diminished or exaggerated urethral resistance?''

DETRUSOR HYPOACTIVITY

Definition. Detrusor hypoactivity is defined by the association of dysuria, (difficulty voiding), residual urine, a flat cystometric curve with delayed sensation, increased bladder capacity, and decreased maximum voiding and maximum isometric pressures.

Bladder acontractility may be reversible. It is known that detrusor contraction may return after several days or sometimes weeks of catheter drainage, which has the advantage of placing the detrusor at rest and allowing contractility to return. However, acontractility may remain irreversible. Despite the fact that the patient has an acontractile bladder, he may still be able to empty his bladder satisfactorily provided the intra-abdominal pressure is adequate, the vesical neck is patent, and

abdominal straining does not result in changes in the position of bladder and vesical neck, inducing dynamic obstruction. Most patients with complete lesions below T10 are able to substantially increase their intra-abdominal and intravesical pressure by straining or using Crede's maneuver to urinate satisfactorily. When the lesion is higher, it might be more difficult to reeducate abdominal pressure, since less muscles are available. However, we observed a patient with a T7 complete lesion able to develop 80 cm of water with intra-abdominal pressure. When the bladder fails to contract, the vesical neck is not drawn open. A transurethral resection may be indicated. If, in spite of adequate abdominal straining and an open vesical neck, the bladder still cannot empty, look for bladder or urethral displacement exaggerated by straining. This is a common problem when denervation has resulted in atrophy of the perineal floor with loss of posterior bladder support. This results in bladder descent with kinking of the vesical neck and the urethra at the level of the prostatic apex.[4] (Fig. 4). In addition, we observed posterior displacement of the vesical neck resulting in a closure of the anterior vesicourethral angle that straining will only exaggerate. In obese patients principally, we reported a complete ''division'' of the bladder, which is displaced over the symphysis pubis, resulting in the formation of an anterior pseudodiverticulum that fails to empty completely. A voiding cystourethrogram in the lateral position both at rest and on straining, with and without catheter, is the most important test, since it will allow visualization of these abnormalities.

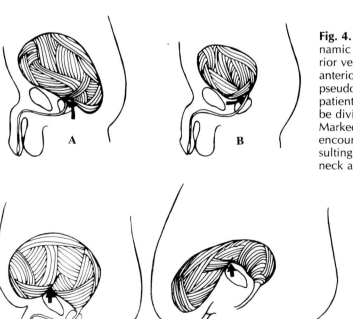

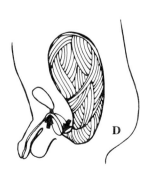

Fig. 4. Four abnormalities resulting in dynamic obstruction. (A) Closure of the posterior vesicourethral angle. (B) Closure of the anterior vesicourethral angle. (C) Anterior pseudodiverticulum of the bladder; when the patient strains, the bladder has a tendency to be divided over the symphysis pubis. (D) Marked descent of the bladder and prostate encountered in flaccid paraplegia with resulting narrowings at the levels of the vesical neck and prostatic apex.

Management. *Intermittent self-catheterization.* Intermittent self-catheterization is widely used and represents the most striking progress in this field.[5-10] A clean unsterile technique is easier to handle and can be employed by most patients when this type of management is undertaken. Intermittent catheterization is impractical when the patient is incontinent between catheterizations. In such instances, the use of anticholinergic drugs and alpha-stimulating agents and reduced fluid intake may help patients to remain dry between catheterizations. A perineal urethrostomy is sometimes advisable to make catheterization easier, particularly in boys.

Making the patient void. If enough intravesical pressure can be developed, it should be possible to reestablish satisfactory micturition.[11] The patient's ability to strain can be reeducated through biofeedback methods, whereupon the patient is provided the opportunity to observe on a cystometric graph the amount of intravesical pressure that can be generated. The sessions may be repeated with physiotherapy to increase abdominal muscle capability thereby allowing the patient to reach an intravesical pressure of 60 cm to 80 cm of water, sufficient for effective bladder evacuation. When this goal is achieved, the vesical neck may not open satisfactorily as observed on cystourethrography. In such a case, the patient should undergo a *resection of the vesical neck.* Before performing a resection, however, the surgeon should be aware of the possibility of incontinence, since the external sphincter may be completely or only partially denervated. Incontinence in men may be the treatment of choice if the patient is willing to wear an external collecting device. In other instances, incontinence is not the desired result. In case of partial lesion, it remains almost impossible to predict whether the patient will be incontinent following resection of the vesical neck.

As previously mentioned, if intra-abdominal pressure is sufficient and the vesical neck is patent, the patient should be able to empty the bladder unless straining results in dynamic obstruction as carefully analyzed on lateral voiding cystourethrogram. According to results, several surgical treatments may be contemplated. The principle is to prevent posterior bladder descent and vesical neck or urethral kinking by fixing or *supporting the bladder posteriorly* either through the use of the sigmoid colon or through a hammock made of nonresorbable sutures (Figs. 5 and 6).

In some instances, straining may result in obstruction of the anterior vesical urethral angle. *An anterior fixation of the prostate and vesical neck* similar to a Marshall–Marchetti or a Burch operative procedure may then be performed in conjunction with a posterior fixation. Finally, psuedodiverticulum in the large bladders often seen in obese people should be treated with partial cystectomy, preferably in conjunction with a posterior cystopexy, which should reduce the rate of recurrence observed after partial cystectomy alone.

None of these surgical interventions will restore the

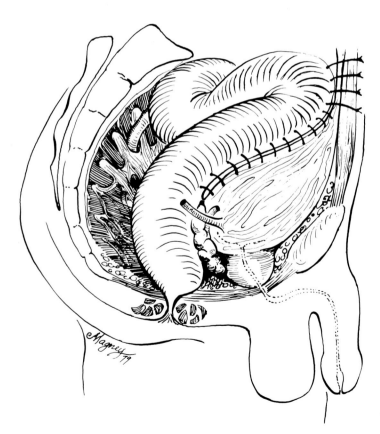

Fig. 5. Posterior cystopexy, with supporting fixation to the sigmoid colon.

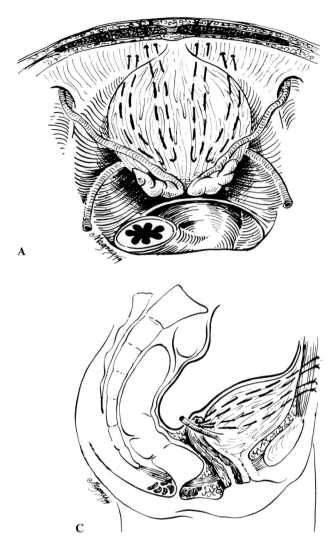

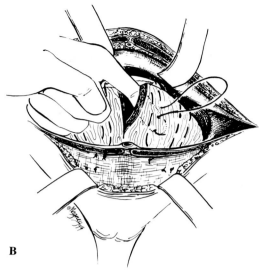

Fig. 6. (*A*) Posterior cystopexy, hammock technique, using four heavy nonresorbable sutures in the vesical wall from above the trigone in men and the vaginal dome in women with hysterectomy; sutures are attached anteriorly as high as possible to the rectus fascia. (*B*) The bladder is open to facilitate positioning of the sutures and to prevent perforation of the mucosa. (*C*) Four sutures form the hammock keeping the bladder in the anterior and superior position.

detrusor contractility when it has been lost forever. The aforementioned surgical approaches, however, have the distinct advantage of placing the bladder in a position of function where intra-abdominal pressure may achieve complete evacuation. Obviously, patients undergoing these types of operations should be followed at intervals by repeated residual urine determinations. They should also be encouraged to continue their effort of achieving effective abdominal straining. Finally, if necessary, they should be allowed to observe, through biofeedback methods, the effect of their efforts in evacuating their bladders.

The use of bethanechol chloride remains limited to the patients in whom degeneration of bladder muscle has not deteriorated to the stage beyond the usefulness of this medication. Aging, obstruction, and, most important, denervations and atrophy will promote collagen growth and interposition within the bladder wall. The ratio of muscle to collagen becomes markedly reduced.[12] Furthermore, collagen deposits occur in the intracellular spaces with disappearance of the closed junctions, making impossible the depolarization to progress from one cell to the other.[13–14] Only the effect of the abdominal musculature and increased pressure on straining can promote bladder emptying. Although bethanechol chloride may often be of little help in these cases, it remains possible that alpha-blocking agents such as phenoxybenzamine may be used in combination, providing urethral relaxation.

Implantable electrical stimulators. Implantable electrical stimulators provide another method of making the patient void through direct detrusor stimulation.[15–22] In our opinion, this technique is excellent but of limited indications. The surgeon may use electrodes of alternate polarities implanted on the upper part of the detrusor (physicomedical system) (Fig. 7) or

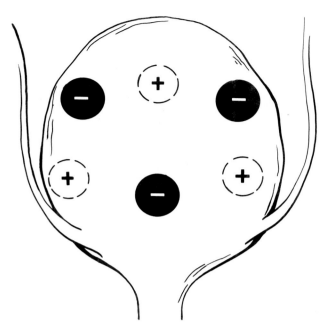

Fig. 7. Position of disc electrodes in the bladder wall.

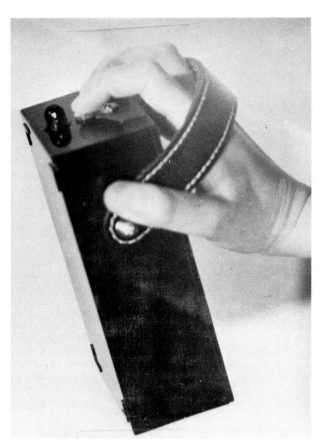

Fig. 9. Rechargeable transmitter for bladder stimulation.

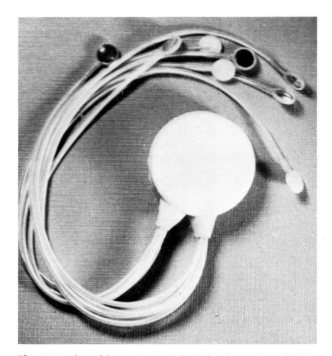

Fig. 8. Implantable receiver with eight electrodes of different polarity.

platinum wire electrodes implanted into the lower part of the bladder and trigone (Mentor). In all instances, bladder layers are imbricated (Fig. 8) in order to reduce the dissipation of current through tissues. A receiver is placed underneath the skin, and a rechargable transmitter (Fig. 9) is used on the average of four times a day to trigger bladder contraction. There are two major inconveniences to this technique. If the external sphincter is normally or partially innervated, it will contract earlier than the bladder and prevent evacuation. The second drawback is the pain resulting from stimulation. In spite of these limitations, the stimulators are being implanted with some success in various types of lesions. In upper motor neuron lesions with spastic sphincter, the external sphincter may become rapidly fatigued during stimulation. When the pressure builds sufficiently in the bladder, the evacuation preceeds while the sphincter is unable to contract. In case of complete motor neuron lesion, however, massive lower extremity spasms and erection are observed. The pain may also be sufficiently severe, especially in case of incomplete lesion below T10, that the patient will refuse to stimulate himself on a regular basis.[11] The same inconvenience exists with the use of the spinal cord stimulator. A direct detrusor stimulation is, however, recommended when there is a complete lesion above

T10 that is flaccid. The indication for detrusor stimulation is in lesions T10 or below, since patients are usually able to strain enough to empty their bladder (in lesions above T10, patients are usually spastic). The rare cases where this mode of treatment was definitely successful were cases with a high level of lesion accompanied with flaccidity, which can only occur when there is a complete necrosis of the cord as observed in the lesions affecting the anterior spinal artery or in case of transverse myelitis or, finally, when there are two levels of lesion (*i.e.*, simultaneous fracture of cervical and lumbar spine). The indications for spinal cord stimulator implantation appear to us even more rare, since it would mostly be applied to lower motor neuron lesions often accompanied by nerve degeneration, making it impossible for the current to reach the bladder.

DETRUSOR HYPERACTIVITY

Definition. Bladder hyperactivity is defined by the presence of urgency and urgency incontinence and uninhibited detrusor contraction on cystometrogram. Detrusor hyperactivity with poorly controllable or totally uncontrollable bladder contractions may be due to a cortical or subcortical lesion of the inhibitory center of urination or an interruption of the upper motor neuron anywhere between the cortex and the bladder cord synapse. A very limited lesion simply affecting one of the six sacral nerves commanding detrusor contraction may cause severe detrusor spasticity (Fig. 10). As a corollary, the interruption of the peripheral neuron corresponding to the damaged upper motor neuron may completely improve the situation.

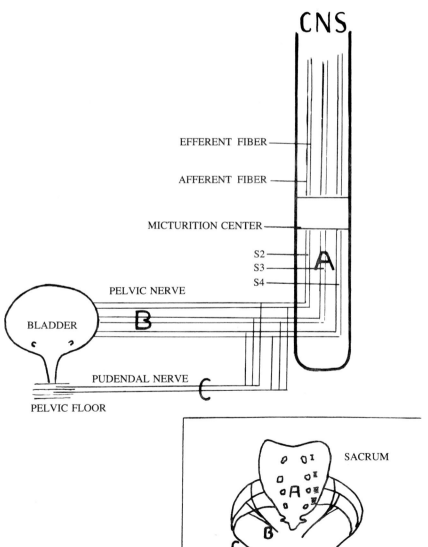

Fig. 10. Sacral innervation of detrusor and sphincter.

This allows the patient to void normally through the control of the remaining intact sacral nerves. This observation forms the basis of management of bladder and sphincter spasm by *selective sacral neurotomy*. Other causes of bladder spasticity that may be associated with neurologic etiologies are cystitis and lower urinary tract obstruction. The management of bladder hyperactivity in neurologic lesion is initially conservative. The use of anticholinergic drugs such as propantheline or oxybutynin is recommended.[23,24] Be aware that the use of these drugs may increase the amount of residual urine present and that some action is often warranted, aimed at lowering urethral resistance by using alpha-blocking agents or sphincterotomy. If this treatment fails, we proceed to *sacral anesthetic blocks* in order to determine the exact pathways of the detrusor spasticity. In incomplete lesions, blocks may have to be repeated several times at intervals of several days in order to determine the root(s) responsible for spasms.[25–29]

Technique of Sacral Blocks. Sacral blocks are better performed either in a radiology department or in the operating room using an image intensifier. A C-arm is particularly helpful, allowing lateral visualization of the sacrum. The patient is placed in the prone position. A Foley catheter is left in the bladder and a cystometrogram is performed initially in order to ascertain the capacity at which the bladder spasms occur. After preparation of the sacral area, 23-gauge, 8.9-cm needles are inserted under x-ray control into the posterior sacral foraminae. When a radio frequency apparatus is not being used, it is better to use needles covered with epoxy down to their very tip, which will allow stimulation of the sacral root. The tip of the needles should be located in the sacral canal, projecting into the lateral view within the sacral bone. The root is medial in relationship to the anterior foramen, and the tip of the needle should ideally be directed medially in order to get as close as possible to the nerve. One milliliter of opaque media may be used to localize the tip of the needle and ascertain the diffusion of the anesthetic solution. Six needles are usually positioned in S2, S3, and S4 bilaterally. Sometimes, however, the need for selected block allows for implantation of only a limited number of needles. One milliliter of 2% lidocaine is injected in one or two foraminae. After 15 min the cystometrogram is repeated in order to see whether the bladder capacity has increased and the contraction is reduced. If there is no effect, a similar amount of anesthetic solution can be injected through needles at other sites and the cystometrogram repeated after 15 min.

It is difficult to follow a definite pattern in the sequence of anesthetic infiltration, since it will be essentially defined by the type of existing lesion. If there is a hemiplegic distribution, blocks will preferably be done unilaterally. If there is a sacral sensory deficit involving S2 or S3, distribution of the injection will begin in the most likely roots. At the end of this examination, it is possible to ascertain the role played by a particular root(s), since anesthesia of this root(s) has resulted in bladder relaxation. Take advantage of the position of these needles by injecting 1 ml of 60% alcohol to the root or use radio frequency neurolysis if available.

Localization of roots will be helped by *electrical stimulation*. The same amount of water is left in the bladder while the pressure is recorded. A significant rise in pressure indicates that the needle is adjacent to or within the root itself. In some instances, results are confusing and the test must be repeated until the responsible roots have been isolated. This test, however, should not be repeated more than twice a week. The indications for a definitive neurolysis are variable. Consider the following: A woman who has a complete spinal cord section, whether she receives intermittent self-catheterization or in-dwelling catheter drainage, may complain of spontaneous incontinence due to detrusor spasticity. In such a case, lyse S2 and S3 on both sides. This is better done with a *radiofrequency apparatus*. For such purpose, a no. 14 needle is inserted under fluoroscopic guidance, along the no. 23 needle in order to minimize unnecessary trauma. The coagulation probe is placed inside the no. 14 needle. The stimulation current is initially used to determine the proximity of the probe to the nerve. The lytic current is then applied to the roots at 70C for 2 min. A temporary lesion can be achieved by using only 45C. In men, a series of anesthetic blocks should be performed, aiming at only one or two sacral roots in order to preserve erections when present. We observed in one instance that a bilateral S3 open neurotomy was not followed by a loss of erection or bladder dysfunction. However, the metamerization is variable, and no definite pattern can be established. We are reasonably certain that if the neurolysis only encompasses one or two roots, the chance of losing erection is remote.

When the lesion is unilateral, particularly in cortical lesions with hemiplegia, proceed with a *section of pelvic nerves* on the side of the paralysis (Fig. 11). This is better achieved through a sacrococcygeal approach with the patient in the prone position. The incision is carried out along the edge of the sacrum and coccyx and extended into the buttock. The gluteus maximus is easily disinserted with cautery, and the sacrotuberous ligament is severed. The sacrorectal space is opened, and the rectum is retracted forward. Nervi erigentes can be easily located arising from the anterior sacral foraminae and coursing along the rectal wall. They are transected between clips, resulting in the separation of its sacral attachments. This operation has the advantage of suppressing the bladder spasm and still allowing normal urination through a normal unilateral innervation that is sufficient to complete bladder emptying.

Indications for a bilateral section of nervi erigentes can also be sought when spasms are so severe that they preclude any type of in-dwelling catheterization or cystostomy. If, for some reason, a bilateral neurolysis of the second and third sacral roots is contraindicated, particularly when skin sensation is intact, we believe that pelvic nerves should be severed bilaterally through a lateral approach as previously described. In such case, a right or a left incision may be indiscriminately chosen.

Although radiofrequency neurolysis appears to us preferable and simpler, a *selective neurotomy* under vision may be performed by a neurosurgeon. In some instances it might be preferable to cut the motor root only and spare the sensory supply. This will constitute another indication for open surgery. As to the permanence of results, we are able to report that a single alcohol injection may achieve permanent results for 9 mo, provided the injection has been done within the root itself,

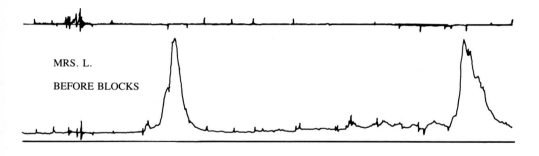

MRS. L.

BEFORE BLOCKS

AFTER BLOCK OF S$_2$L, S$_3$L, S$_4$L

FIRST CONTRACTION - 300 cc

300 cc

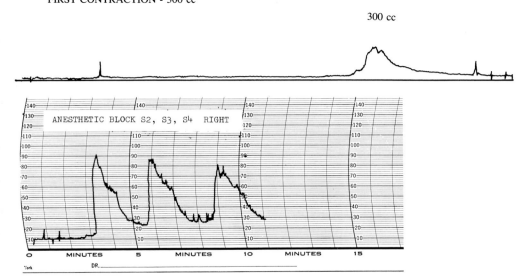

ANESTHETIC BLOCK S2, S3, S4 RIGHT

Fig. 11. Results of unilateral sacral blocks in a left hemiplegic patient. Only left-sided blocks stop the spasm—indication for a unilateral parasympathetic denervation.

which often is difficult to ascertain. This was the case in Figure 12. In some instances, it will not last more than 1 or 2 mo. The advantage remains, however, the demonstration of the level at which the neurotomy should be performed. A unilateral pelvic neurotomy done for detrusor spasms associated with hemiplegia gave us an excellent result for 18 mo. A bilateral pelvic neurotomy done for a spastic bladder due to multiple sclerosis gave us a good result, which was followed for 3½ yr in which the patient was able to urinate by herself without bladder spasms. The risk of recurrence after this operation exists, since the pathways of pelvic nerves have not been completely ascertained. Some parasympathetic fibers may run along vessels. Moreover, the extent of vesical denervation obtained with this method has never been demonstrated. This approach is rewarding, however, in the treatment of difficult bladder spasticity. Minimal complications may occur. Alco-

holization should be done with 60% alcohol and not more than 2 ml at a time. A larger amount of solution and especially a higher concentration could predispose to severe radiculitis, which is usually rare with the dose proposed here.

Hindmarsh and associates reported the results of *vesical transection* in 45 patients with hyperactive detrusor.[30] Twenty-four of 45 were reported having excellent results over a 1-yr period. Parsons and colleagues cured 11 of 17 enuretic patients with the same method.[31] Freiha and colleagues report good results by *supratrigonal cystolysis* in six patients presenting intactable interstitial cystitis and in four patients with an uninhibited neurogenic bladder.[32] Note, however, that the latter technique involved a section of the inferior vesical vessels. Nervi erigentes are known to enter the bladder wall alongside these vessels. It is possible that some results could be obtained without dividing the bladder. Actually, Ingelman-Sundberg

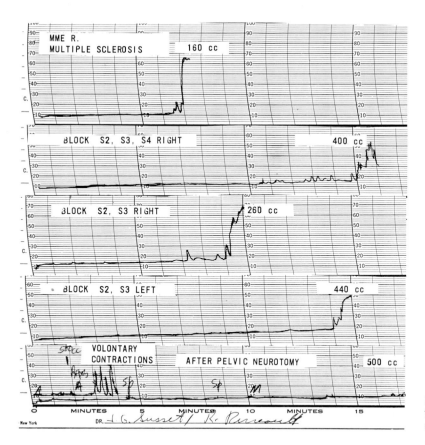

Fig. 12. In multiple sclerosis, spasms arise from both sides. A bilateral pelvic neurotomy results in relief of these spasms.

performed a *transvaginal denervation* on one or both sides in 66 patients with prolonged good results, comparable to the one obtained by cystolysis or pelvic neurotomy in the sacrorectal space.[33] The advantages of this approach were confirmed by Warrell and by Hodgkinson and Drukker.[34,35] *Hyperbaric distension* as proposed by Dunn does not appear to have prolonged good results.[36,37]

ABNORMAL URETHRAL RESISTANCE: HOW TO REDUCE IT

Obviously the resection of benign obstructive prostatic hypertrophy or of porstatic cancer may be part of the surgical treatment of neurogenic urinary dysfunction. A resection that may not be needed under ordinary circumstances may become mandatory when the bladder is weak as a result of Parkinson's disease, diabetic neuropathy, or multiple sclerosis. The reestablishment of urinary balance is more critical than the absolute value of urethral resistance. The same degree of obstruction may be well compensated in one patient and require surgery in another. Some treatments aim at reducing resistance at the level of urethral smooth muscle, while others are directed at the level of the striated external sphincter.

The reduction of smooth muscle tone can be obtained by the use of alpha-blocking agents such as phenoxybenzamine.[38,39]

Beta-stimulating drugs act in a similar fashion, although they have not yet been found practical.[40] A *transurethral resection or a Y-V plasty of the vesical neck* may become indicated when voiding cystourethrogram has demonstrated insufficient vesical neck opening in spite of satisfactory bladder contraction. Future direct measurement of vesical neck compliance, providing accurate insight into the role played by fibrous tissue at this level, will certainly assist in the indication of resection in such cases.

At the external sphincter level, relaxation may be obtained by using diazepam or dantrolene sodium, which provides a direct relaxing action on the periurethral striated muscle and may be indicated particularly in patients with supraspinal cord lesions.[41] In the management of detrusor–sphincter dysynergia, there is a role for *local anesthetic blocks* as suggested by Bors.[1] A. Leriche has also shown that *repeated ice water tests* daily for 1 or 2 wk can achieve sphincter relaxation during detrusor contraction.* If these conservative methods fail, there is the choice between performing a spincterotomy or a sacral neurolysis or neurotomy. The external sphincter in paraplegics may become fibrous as a result of degeneration. In such a case, a *sphincterotomy* is the only way to provide complete bladder evacuation. However, it usually results in incontinence.

---

* Larische A: Personal communication

For this reason, the surgeon may choose intermittent catheterization rather than sphincterotomy. Most patients are indeed able to catheterize themselves. In some instances, however, there is no sphincter fibrosis and the treatment of choice in such a case of a sphincter spasticity may not be a sphincterotomy but rather unilateral or bilateral *alcoholization or neurotomy of the fourth sacral roots* to neutralize spasticity. In order to choose between sphincterotomy and direct action on S4, it is important to repeat voiding cystourethrogram before and after bilateral pudendal nerve blocks. When sensation is absent, the quality of the pudendal block can be evaluated on the relaxation of the anal sphincter and the reduction or disappearance of electromyographic (EMG) potentials. When a constricted membranous urethra appears on voiding films and is due to fibrosis, pudendal nerve blocks will have no effect. On the contrary, if pudendal nerve blocks achieve good evacuation through a wide open sphincter, it is better to perform a block of S4. The same information can be achieved by retrograde urethrogram following epidural anesthesia. A similar technique as reported above for bladder hyperactivity is used, but the needles are placed only in the S4 posterior foraminae. One milliliter of 60% alcohol is injected, usually on both sides, resulting in the relaxation of the external sphincter appreciated by uroflow-

metric technique (Fig. 13). The effect may last for several months. On several occasions, spasticity did not return. Bedoiseau, using this method, has reported 55% success in 18 patients presenting with spinal cord lesions.[42] Obviously, neurotomy of S4 or, preferably, radiofrequency neurolysis may achieve better and more prolonged results. The indication of sphincterotomy therefore becomes restricted to patients in whom incontinence is preferred to self-catheterization or where sphincter fibrosis is severe enough to prevent the releasing action of sacral neurolysis. Note that S4 alcoholization has not appeared thus far to be followed by sexual impotence. If sphincterotomy is performed, it should be done at the 12 o'clock position.[43–44] In our opinion, any surgical action to reduce urethral resistance such as sphincterotomy should be based on stronger criteria than the ones currently used. Most of the information necessary for choosing a procedure can be provided by the systematic use of the voiding cystourethrogram.

ABNORMAL URETHRAL RESISTANCE: HOW TO INCREASE IT

Pharmacologic agents such as alpha-stimulant ephedrine or beta blockers such as propanolol may be used to increase

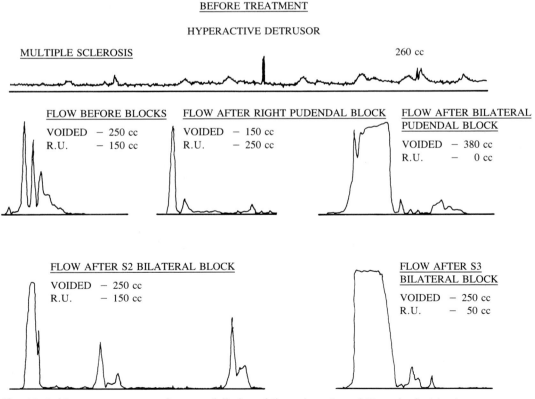

Fig. 13. Sphincter spasm treated successfully by a bilateral section of S3 on both sides in a 21-year-old man with multiple sclerosis. S4 blocks alone did not control the spasms.

urethral resistance.[40,45–48] Surgical techniques aiming at increasing urethral resistance are not recommended when detrusor spasticity is present. In such instance, bladder distension and vesicoureteral reflux may develop.

Some techniques use the anal sphincter and are of little benefit in patients with neurogenic vesical dysfunction, since the anal sphincter is incompetent. They include the use of the *Mathiesen procedure* or of the *Duhamel operation,* using the rectum as a new bladder by implanting the ureters and threading the proximal sigmoid colon within the anal sphincter.[48,49] *The use of a prosthesis such as described by Kaufman, Rosen, Scott, and Cook and colleagues may be contemplated.*[50–53] Such a procedure however, is not foolproof. Patients must be carefully selected and mentally able and reliable enough to handle the prosthesis satisfactorily. Many of these patients have no sensation, and thus the risk of erosion or perforation through the urethra would be increased when the prosthesis is used. Such a patient could easily forget to deflate the device. Such limitations prevent to some extent the universal application of these techniques.

Injection of polytetrafluoroethylene (Teflon), paste into the female urethra gave 70% good results to Politano.[54] Tanagho and colleagues have reported successful results in increasing urethral resistance by *lengthening the proximal urethra* using a bladder flap.[55] Hendren provided five girls with continence by lengthening the *distal urethra* by using the vaginal wall and a perineal flap. In most instances the detrusor is of limited competence and may be unable to cope with increased resistance. This type of technique may be used when the final goal is self-catheterization, which cannot be achieved as a result of incontinence.

Electrical sphincter stimulation remains a reasonable alternative. It is indicated when the denervation is partial, since a complete denervation will lead to atrophy and muscular fibrosis, precluding the use of such a procedure. A deficient urethral sphincter due to partial denervation, for example, in meningomyelocele can be reinforced by systematic electrotherapy of the sphincter. Such a conservative approach should be employed more often than it is at present. The indication for permanent implantation of an electrical stimulator in partially denervated sphincters does exist, provided a proper stimulator can be developed. Sphincter stimulators used by Caldwell, Alexander and Rowan, DeBacker, and ourselves in the past used a continuous current that resulted in muscular fatigue, making the stimulation inefficient within several minutes.[6,15,57,58,60] If such a sphincter stimulator is developed, it is necessary to give the muscle a resting period as a function of the time of stimulation.[61] This has not been technically realized, but there is no good reason why it cannot be achieved in the future.

URINARY DIVERSION

Among the procedures currently available, a suprapubic cystostomy may still be the best solution. This is particularly true in cases of quadriplegia when the patient is essentially dependent on external help. We have seen patients doing very well for many years with an in-dwelling Foley cathether or with a suprapubic cystostomy. The latter is preferable in men in view of the increased incidence of periurethral abscess secondary to an in-dwelling catheter. We have seen patients after 20 yr being perfectly content with a cystostomy.[62] A *cutaneous vesicostomy,* later modified, has been proposed.[64,65] Schneider and colleagues have reported 17 cases of continent vesicostomy.[65] Although results are generally satisfactory, failure may occur on several accounts. An acontractile bladder may not drain satisfactorily, since the vesicostomy increases outlet resistance, which contributes to incomplete evacuation. Furthermore, incontinence may still persist, necessitating a vesical neck closure, which may be followed by loss of erection. Furthermore, the midline suprapubic area is not a favorite location to apply an external collecting device, which is more prone to leak in this position. Although an increased incidence of carcinoma has been reported with an in-dwelling catheter in the bladder, we are reluctant to use the vesicostomy as a routine procedure in view of the aforementioned limitations. Furthermore, bladder carcinoma occured in 2 of 40 patients.[64] In summary, we are not convinced that vesicostomy is better than an ordinary cystostomy as the procedure of choice unless complications related to in-dwelling tube arise.

We performed a transureteroureterostomy in three cases of unilateral vesicoureteral reflux in paraplegics with excellent long-term results, also reported by Malkin and associates.[66] If unilateral reflux develops, there will always be time to perform a total diversion. The treatment of vesicoureteral reflux can be conservatively aimed at reducing the pressure reaching the kidneys. Urethral resistance should be reduced through either catheter drainage, cystostomy, sphincterotomy, or even sacral neurolysis. Ureteral reimplantation in neurogenic bladders has been rather disappointing, although Jeffs and colleagues have reported 33 successful reimplantations of 37 ureters in children.[67] Poor results were obtained when massive hydronephrosis was present.[68]

A time comes when the lower urinary tract cannot be easily managed, and the upper tracts decompensate as a result of vesicoureteral reflux or fibrosis. It is then time to perform an ileal conduit diversion without waiting for any further renal deterioration. We would like to insist that such a diversion should not be undertaken when the upper tracts are normal, since long-term complications are more frequent than initially thought.[69,70]

REFERENCES

1. Bors E: Neurogenic bladder. Urol Surv 7:177, 1957

2. Bors E, Comarr AE: Neurological urology. Basel, S. Karger, 1971

3. Lapides MD: Symposium on neurogenic bladder. Urol Clin North Am 1:181, 1974

4. Susset JG, Smith SJ: Dynamics of obstruction in acontractile bladder: Attempt at management. Urology 15:240, 1980

5. Guttman L: Spinal cord injuries: Discussion of the treatment and prognosis of traumatic paraplegia. Proc R Soc Med 40:219, 1949

6. Guttman L, Frankel HL: The value of intermittent catheterization in the early management of traumatic paraplegia and tetraplegia. Paraplegia 4:63, 1966

7. Comarr AE: Intermittent catheterization for the traumatic cord bladder patient. J Urol 108:79, 1972

8. Frankel HL: Intermittent catheterization. Urol Clin North Am 1:115, 1974

9. Lapides J, Diokno AC, Lowe BS, et al: Follow-up on unsterile, intermittent self-catheterization. J Urol 3:184, 1974

10. Wein AJ, Raezer DM, Benson GS, et al: At-home intermittent self-catheterization in the treatment of patients with neuromuscular bladder dysfunction. Proc Kimbrough Urol Sem 8:41, 1974

11. Rabinovitch HH: Bladder evacuation in child with meningomyelocele. Urology 3:425, 1974

12. Susset JG, Servot-Viquier D, Lamy F et al: Collagen in 155 human bladders. Invest Urol 16:204, 1978

13. Clermont A: Etude ultrasmecturale du muscle vesical chez l'humee. Thesis, Nice, France, 1976

14. Gosling JA, Dixon JS: The structure and denervation of trabeculated detrusor smooth muscle. Annals of Sixth Congress of the International Continent Society, Rome, Italy, September 1979

15. Susset JG: The electrical drive of the urinary bladder and sphincter, neural organization and its relevance to prosthetics. New York, Intercontinental Medical Book Corporation, 1973

16. Bradley WE, Timm GW, Chou SN: A decade of experience with electronic stimulation of the micturition reflex. Urol Int 26:283, 1971

17. Merrill DC, Conway CJ: Clinical experience with the Mentor bladder stimulator. I. Patients with upper motor neuron lesions. J Urol 112:52, 1974

18. Merrill DC: Clinical experience with the Mentor bladder stimulator. II. Meningomyelocele patients. J Urol 112:823, 1974

19. Merrill DC: Clinical experience with the Mentor bladder stimulator. III. Patients with urinary vesical hypotonia. J Urol 113:335, 1975

20. Halverstadt DP, Parry WL: Electronic stimulation of the human bladder: 9 years later. J Urol 113:341, 1975

21. Grimes JH, Nashold BS, Currie DP: Chronic electrical stimulation of the paraplegic bladder. J Urol 109:242, 1973

22. Grimes JH, Nashold BS, Anderson EE: Clinical application of electronic bladder stimulation in paraplegics. J Urol 113:338, 1975

23. Benson GS, Sarshile SA, Raezer DM, et al: Bladder muscle contractility: Comparative effects and mechanism of action of atropine, propantheline, flavoxate and imipramine. Urology 9:31, 1977

24. Diokno AC, Hyndman CW, Hardy DA, et al: Comparison of action of imipramine (Tofranil) and propantheline (Probanthine) on detrusor contraction. J Urol 107:42, 1972

25. Rockswold GL, Bradley WE, Chous SN: Differential sacral rhizotomy in the treatment of neurogenic bladder dysfunction. Preliminary report of six cases. J Neurosurg 38:748, 1973

26. Susset JG, Zinner N, Archimbaud JP: Differential sacral blocks and selective neurotomies in the treatment of incomplete upper motor neuro lesion. Urol Int 29:236, 1974

27. Toczek S, McCullough DC, Gargour GW, et al: Selective sacral rootlet rhizotomy for hypertonic neurogenic bladder. J. Neurosurg 42:567, 1975

28. Torrens MJ, Griffith HB: Management of the uninhibited bladder by selective sacral neurectomy. J Neurosurg 44:176, 1976

29. Mulcahy JJ, Young AB, Lexington KY: Percutaneous ratio frequency sacral rhizotomy in the treatment of hyperreflexic bladder. Presented at the 73rd Annual Meeting of the American Urological Association, Washington DC, May 23, 1978

30. Hindmarsh JR, Essenhigh DM, Yeates WK: Bladder transection for adult enuresis. Br J Urol 49:515, 1977

31. Parsons KF, O'Boyle PJ, Gibbon NOK: A further assessment of bladder transection in the management of adult enuresis and allied conditions. Br J Urol 49:509, 1977

32. Frehia FS, Stamey TA: Cystolysis: A procedure for the selective denervation of the bladder. J Urol 123:360, 1980

33. Ingelman-Sundberg A: Urge incontinence in women. Acta Obstet Gynecol Scand 54:153, 1975

34. Warrell DW: Vaginal denervation at the bladder nerve supply. Urol Int 32:114, 1977

35. Hodgkinson P, Drukker BK: Transvaginal denervation of the bladder. Acta Obstet Gynecol Scand 56:401, 1977

36. Dunn M, Smith JC, Ardan GM: Prolonged bladder distension as a treatment for urgency and urge incontinence of urine. Br J Urol 46:645, 1974

37. Ramsden PD, Smith JC, Dunn M, et al: Distension therapy for the unstable bladder: later results including an assessment of repeat distensions. Br J Urol 48:623, 1976

38. Krane RJ, Olsson CA: Phenoxybenzamine in neurogenic bladder dysfunction: Clinical considerations. J Urol 110:653, 1973

39. Stockamp K, Schreiter F: Alpha-adrenolytic treatment in congenital neuropathic bladder. Urol Int 30:33, 1975

40. Ghoneim MA, Fretin JA, Gagnon DJ, et al: The influence of vesical distension on urethral resistance to flow: The expulsion phase. Br J Urol 47:663, 1975

41. Murdock M, Sax D, Krane RJ: Use of dantroline sodium in external sphincter spasm. Urology 8:133, 1976

42. Bedoiseau M: Sixth International Congress of Physical Medicine and Rehabilitation, Barcelona, Spain, July, 1972

43. Madersbacher H, Scott FB: Twelve o'clock sphincterotomy: Technique indications, results. Urol Int 30:75, 1975

44. Carrion HM, Brown BT, Politano VA: External sphincterotomy at the 12 o'clock position. J Urol 121:462, 1979

45. Awad SA, Downie JW, Kiruluta HC: Alpha-adrenergic agents in urinary disorders of the proximal urethra. Br J Urol 50:332, 1978

46. Steward BH, Banowsky LHW, Montague DKK: Stress incontinence: Conservative therapy with sympathomimetic drugs. J Urol 115:558, 1976

47. Diokno AC, Taub M: Ephedrine in treatment of urinary incontinence. Urology 5:624, 1975

48. Mathisen W: A new operation for urinary incontinence. Surg Gynecol Obstet 130:606, 1970

49. Campos-Freire JG: The rectal bladder. In Glenn J (ed): Urologic Surgery, p 841. New York, Harper & Row, 1975

50. Kaufman JJ: The Silicone-gel prosthesis for the treatment of male urinary incontinence. Urol Clin North Am 5:393, 1978

51. Rosen M: The Rosen inflatable incontinence prosthesis. Urol Clin North Am 5:405, 1978

52. Scott FB: The artificial sphincter in the management of incontinence in the male. Urol Clin North Am 5:375, 1978

53. Cook WA, Swenson OS, King LR: Incontinence in children. Urol Clin North Am 5:353, 1978

54. Politano VA: Periurethral Teflon injection for urinary incontinence. Urol Clin North Am 5:415, 1978

55. Tanagho EA, Smith DR, Meyers FH, et al: Mechanism of urinary incontinence. II. Technique for surgical correction of incontinence. J Urol 101:305, 1969

56. Hendren WH: Construction of female urethra from vaginal wall and a perineal flap. J Urol 123:657, 1980

57. Caldwell KP: The treatment of incontinence by electronic implants (Hunterial Lecture delivered at the Royal College of Surgeons of England, Dec. 8, 1966). Ann R Coll Surg Eng 41:447, 1967

58. Alexander S, Rowan D: Closure of the urinary sphincter mechanism in anaesthetized dogs by means of electrical stimulation of the perineal muscles. Br J Surg 53:1053, 1966

59. DeBacker E, Archimbaud JP: Emploi ees stimulateurs electroniques en urologie. Encycl Med Chir 41350:1–12, 1968

60. Susset JG: Implantation de stimulateurs sphincteriers au cours des myelomeningoceles. Presented at the Sixth International Congress of Physical Medicine and Rehabilitation, Barcelona, Spain, July 1972

61. Rottembourg JL, Ghoneim MA, Fretin J, et al: Study on the efficiency of electric stimulation of the pelvic floor. Inv Urol 13:354, 1976

62. Blocksom BH, Jr: Bladder pouch for prolonged tubeless cystostomy. J Urol 78:398, 1957

63. Lapides J, Koyaragi T, Diokno A: Cutaneous vesicostomy: Ten year survey. J Urol 105:76, 1971

64. Sonda LP, Soloman MH: Twenty-year outcome of cutaneous vesicostomy. J Urol 124:326, 1980

65. Schneider KM, Reid RE, Fruchtman B: The continent vesicostomy: Clinical experiences in the adult. J Urol 117:571, 1977

66. Malkin RB, Schellhammer PF, Hackler RH: Experience with transureteroureterostomy in the paraplegic patient with irreversible vesicoureteral reflux. J Urol 112:181, 1974

67. Jeffs RD, Jonas P, Schillinger JF: Surgical correction of vesi- coureteral reflux in children with neurogenic bladder. J Urol 115:449, 1976

68. Rabinowitz R, Barken M, Schillinger JT, et al: Surgical manage- ment of massive neurogenic hydronephrosis. J Urol 122:64, 1979

69. Susset JG, Taguchi Y, De Domenico F, et al: Hydronephrosis on ileal conduit urinary diversion. Can J Surg 9:141, 1966

70. Schwarz GR, Jeffs RD: Ileal conduit diversion in children: Computer analysis of follow up from two to sixteen years. J Urol 114:285, 1975

PART THIRTY-ONE

SURGERY OF URINARY FISTULA

75

TRANSVAGINAL REPAIR OF VESICOVAGINAL FISTULAS

Roger Barnes, M.D., Henry Hadley, M.D., and Oliver Johnston, M.D.

From the Section of Urology, School of Medicine, Loma Linda University, Loma Linda, California

Urology / September 1977 / Volume X, Number 3

The position of the patient and the technique of closure of the fistulas are vital to the success of this operation. The inverted lithotomy position is used (Fig. 1).* The patient is placed face down on the operating table; the thighs are flexed over the end of the table and are abducted and held in place with a sheet passed around the thighs and knees and fastened with towel clips around a Bierhoff crutch on each side of the table. The advantages of this position are: (1) the field of operation is on the floor, and (2) the perineum is much more retractable than the pubis, giving better exposure of the field of operation.

A right angle blade retractor 4 to 6 cm wide is placed in the vagina and the perineum retracted dorsally and caudad (Fig. 2). The best retractor for this is the posterior retractor used for perineal prostatectomy. A Gelpi retractor separates the labia. If the fistula is located high in the vagina, the vaginal mucosa can be grasped with Babcock forceps and pulled down to give better access to the fistula. An incision through the dorsolateral vaginal orifice, similar to an episiotomy, may be done if the vagina is small. A longitudinal incision is made through the anterior vaginal mucosa beginning 1.5 to 2 cm above the fistula and extending it down into the upper edge of the fistula. This is then continued around the edge of the fistula at junction of vaginal mucosa with the bladder mucosa. This junction can be easily identified in a large fistula because the bladder mucosa is of a darker red color than the vaginal mucosa. The longitudinal incision through the vaginal mucosa is extended for 1.5 to 2 cm below the fistula. The vaginal mucosa is separated from the bladder for 1.5 to 2 cm on all sides of the fistula (Fig. 3). Sharp dissection is used and care is taken to avoid buttonholing the vaginal mucosa and/or cutting or tearing into the bladder. A Foley catheter is passed through the urethra and left in the bladder.

The wound is closed in five layers with a 3-0 chromic catgut or 3-0 polyglycolic acid sutures swedged on a ⅝ circle needle. Each layer is continuous. The first layer inverts the bladder mucosa (Fig. 3). Each subsequent layer covers the previous layer and approximates the tissues above, below, and lateral to the previous layer. The second layer approximates the under surface of the bladder wall; the third approximates the lateral angles of the dissected area; the fourth approximates the under surface of the vaginal mucosa, and the fifth layer is submucous to the vaginal mucosa. The tissues are firmly approximated, obliterating all dead spaces, thus con-

---

* St. George J: Factors in the prediction of successful vaginal repair of vesicovaginal fistula, Obstet. Gynecol. Br. Cwlth. 76:741 (1969).

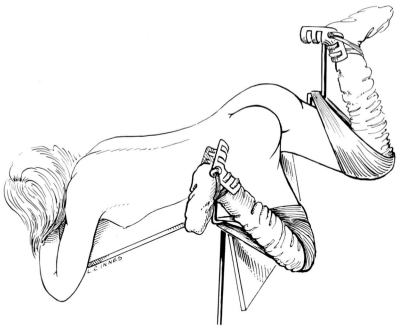

Fig. 1. Inverted lithotomy position. Patient is prone. Thighs are flexed over lower edge of table and are abducted and held in position by sheet passed around thighs and knees and fastened to uprights on side of table.

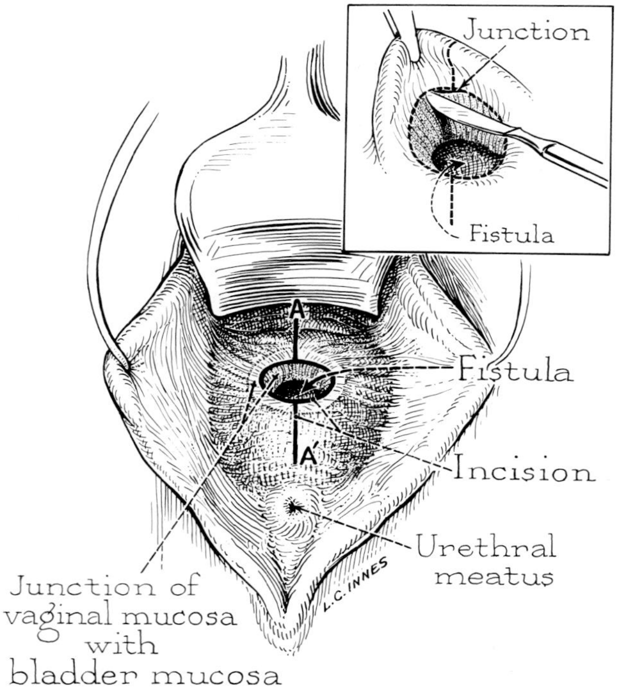

Fig. 2. Posterior retractor used for perineal prostatectomy retracts perineum dorsally and caudad. Gelpi retractor separates labia. Incision through anterior vaginal wall extending 1.5 to 2 cm both above and below fistula. At fistula, incision is at junction of vaginal mucosa with bladder mucosa.

structing a firm layer of tissue 2 to 3 cm thick between the bladder and vagina. For the first and last layers 5-0 suture may be used. If there is excessive tension on the vaginal mucosa, a longitudinal relaxing incision is made through the vaginal mucosa on each side 3 or 4 cm lateral to the midline. The vagina is then packed with a 2 inch gauze upon which beta lactose powder is dusted.

We employ a similar multiple layer closure after excision of a urethral diverticulum and for closure of a urethrovaginal fistula. It is usually not necessary, however, to put the patient in the inverted lithotomy position for these procedures on the urethra because their location is not deep in the vagina.

POSTOPERATIVE CARE

Free drainage through the catheter is maintained at all times. No bladder irrigations are given unless for some unusual reason the catheter becomes plugged. The vaginal pack is removed in twenty-four hours. When we first used this technique for closing vesicovaginal fistulas, we left the catheter in for twelve days. We have gradually reduced the time for removing the catheter; in the last few cases the catheter has been removed on the third postoperative day and the patient has left the hospital the next day. No fistula has recurred because of early removal of the catheter. There is no other postoperative care. Antibacterial medication is not given routinely.

Loma Linda, California 92354
(DR. BARNES)

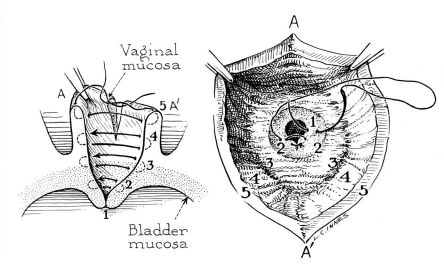

Fig. 3. Vaginal mucosa is separated from bladder for 1.5 to 2 cm on all sides of fistula. Fistula is closed in five layers by: (1) inverting bladder mucosa; (2) approximating under surface of bladder wall, then (3) lateral angles of dissected area, and (4) under surface of vaginal mucosa and (5) submucosal approximation of edges of vaginal mucosa. Each layer is continuous and covers layer below it.

Commentary: Transvaginal Repair of Urinary Vaginal Fistula: Indications and Technique

Roger Barnes

The transvaginal approach to repair vesicovaginal fistulae is simpler and less disturbing to the patient and requires less hospitalization than other approaches. It cannot, however, be used to treat all urinary vaginal fistulae.

Indications for using the transvaginal approach are as follows:

Small or medium size fistulae, less than 5 cm in diameter
Tissues pliable
No previous extensive radiation therapy
Not complicated by ureterovaginal fistula
Vaginal size normal or larger than normal
No carcinoma in the tissues involved
When the surgeon has knowledge of and skill in using the proper techniques for successful closure

The technique used by different authors varies in minor detail but the basic principles are similar. The repair should not be attempted less than 2 mo following the formation of the fistula. Sims placed the patient in the knee–chest position.[1] The inverted lithotomy position, which is similar to the knee–chest position, gives better exposure of the ventral vaginal wall than the conventional lithotomy position.[2] Most surgeons, however, use the conventional lithotomy position.[3,4] Sims used silver wire for the suture.[1] Absorbable suture is satisfactory if a wide approximation of raw surfaces is accomplished.[2,3] Nonabsorbable suture may be used if the suture does not extend near or into the bladder mucosa.

All authors recommend wide separation of the vagina and bladder, permitting a multi-layered closure without tension. Transfer of normal tissue, either vaginal mucosa or fat from the labia, has been used with successful results.[5] The use of a Foley catheter inserted through the fistula has been recommended to pull the operative field closer to the surgeon.[6]

The technique that I have found to be most successful is explained in the preceding article. One variation of the technique is to use nonabsorbable suture such as polytetrafluoroethylene (Teflon) in the middle three layers and absorbable suture in the first and last layers. This will result in a more successful repair in patients who have had a limited amount of radiation therapy. Those who have had extensive radiation therapy will nearly always have breakdown after closure through the transvaginal approach.

Urethrovaginal fistulae are repaired by the same technique as vesicovaginal fistulae. It is not necessary, however, to put the patient in the inverted lithotomy position for closure of urethrovaginal fistula because the position of the fistula is close enough to the vaginal orifice to be reached with the patient in the conventional lithotomy position. Marsupializing the fistula by making an incision through the floor of the urethra into the vagina from the meatus to the fistula has been reported.[7]

Lamensdorf and colleagues state that three patients were not incontinent following this procedure and one was still partially incontinent.

A very small fistula will sometimes close after electro-coagulation through the bladder or vagina using a Bugbee electrode. A very small fistulous tract may also be curetted by rotating a wood screw into it through the vagina, then pulling it out. To facilitate this maneuver the head of the screw is first flattened from side to side by filing the opposite sides of the head.[8]

REFERENCES

1. Sims JM: The treatment of vesicovaginal fistula. Am J Med Sci 23:59, 1852
2. Barnes R, Hadley H, Johnston O: Transvaginal repair of vesico-vaginal fistulas. Urology 10:258, 1977
3. Keettel W, Sehring F, Deprosse C, et al: Surgical management of urethrovaginal and vesicovaginal fistulas. Am J Obstet Gynecol 131:425, 1978
4. Pers M: The closure of urinary-vaginal fistulas. Scand J Plast Reconstr Surg 11:147, 1977
5. Birkhoff J, Wechsler M, Romas N: Urinary fistulas: Vaginal repair using a labial fat pad. J Urol 117:595, 1977
6. Belt E: Nueva tecnica para el tratamiento de las fistulas vesicova-ginales por via vaginal. Rev Esp Obstet Ginecol 7:45, 1948
7. Lamensdorf H, Compere D, Begley G: Simple correction of urethrovaginal fistula. Urology 10:152, 1977
8. Aycinema J: Small vesicovaginal fistula. Urology 9:543, 1977

ANNOTATED BIBLIOGRAPHY

Keettel W, Sehring F, Deprosse C, et al: Surgical management of urethrovaginal and vesicovaginal fistulas. Am J Obstet Gynecol 131:425, 1978

The authors report the management of 157 vesico vaginal and 24 urethrovaginal fistulas during 50 yr. Ninety six percent were repaired vaginally by multiple layers. The abdominal approach was used for complicated fistulas. For urethrovaginal fistulas, a bulbocavernous fat pad from the inner aspect of the labia majora was used to reinforce the repair. Final cure rate was 94.3% for vesicovaginal fistulas and 87.5% for urethrovaginal fistulas. I have not found urethrovaginal fistulae to be more difficult to repair in multiple layers except where there is almost complete destruction of the urethra; then it is necessary to reconstruct the urethra with a tube from a bladder flap.

Pers M: The closure of urinary-vaginal fistulas. Scand J Plast Reconstr Surg 11:147, 1977

The author reports an 85% successful primary closure rate through the vagina. He stresses the importance of wide separation of the vagina from the bladder and the approximation of broad raw surfaces. The vaginal approach is preferable in most cases, and the plastic surgeon should be engaged in the management of urinary vaginal fistulae. A plastic surgeon may be helpful if pedicle flaps of skin or mucosa are used to close the fistula.

Birkhoff J, Wechsler M, Romas N: Urinary fistulas: Vaginal repair using a labial fat pad. J Urol 117:595, 1977

The authors describe using a fat pad obtained from the labia majora on one side to interpose between the bladder or urethra and the vagina. First the vagina is separated from the bladder or urethra. One end of the fat pad is left attached, and the free end is tunneled under the mucosa of the vestibule to the site of the fistula. They report successful primary closure of all patients: six with vesicovaginal and three with urethrovaginal fistulas.

Lamensdorf H, Compere D, Begley G: Simple correction of urethro-vaginal fistula. Urology 10:152, 1977

The authors incise the urethrovaginal septum from the meatus to the fistula and suture the urethral mucosa to the vaginal mucosa. They report on three patients who were cured of urinary incontinence and one who improved but still had some incontinence. It is probable that urinary incontinence will be troublesome following this procedure, whereas after closure of the fistula with multiple layers incontinence is very rare.

Aycinema J: Small vesicovaginal fistula. Urology 9:543, 1977

The author files two sides of the head of a common metal screw larger than the estimated size of the fistula. The head of the screw is grasped at right angles with a needle holder and forced through the fistula from the vaginal side, and a cystoscope is used to visualize the tip of the screw in the bladder. The screw is then pulled out, thus curetting the fistula. Two 3–0 chromic sutures are placed through the vaginal mucosa, and the catheter is left in 3 wk. He reports successful primary closure of seven cases of small fistulae but failure with larger ones. This is a very simple method of treatment, but it would be discouraging to find that the fistula was too large to be closed by this method after leaving the catheter in for 3 wk.

76

MANAGEMENT OF VESICOVAGINAL FISTULAS WITH PERITONEAL FLAP INTERPOSITION

M. Eisen, K. Jurkovic, J.-E. Altwein, F. Schreiter and R. Hohenfellner

From the Department of Urology, University of Mainz Medical School, Mainz, West Germany

The Journal of Urology
Copyright © 1974 by The Williams & Wilkins Co.
Vol. 112, August
Printed in U.S.A.

Vesicovaginal fistulas can be surgically repaired via the vaginal route or the transvesical extraperitoneal or intraperitoneal technique. The vaginal approach is used for the majority of closures. The rate of failure with this technique is close to 10 percent.[1-5] The vaginal method has certain advantages in cases of small, anteriorly located vesicovaginal fistulas. It is a minor procedure, well tolerated and results in an uneventful recovery. However, this route is unfavorable in cases of large fistulas (more than 25 mm) and those with a high opening, fistulas involving the ureteral ostium, vesicocervical fistulas, extensive radiological fistulas and fistulas in patients who have undergone a previous operation.

Since there are various causes and locations of vesicovaginal fistulas and because of the aforementioned

Accepted for publication November 9, 1973.

disadvantages of the vaginal route, several closure techniques have been described. Some techniques are complicated.[6-8] while others are not applicable in young patients[9] or are limited to certain types of fistulas.[10] Failures do occur more frequently in patients previously operated upon or irradiated.

The suprapubic approaches provide a better operative view in women with large fistulas or those who have undergone a previous operation or irradiation. Thus, it is necessary for gynecological and urological surgeons to select the appropriate procedure for fistula repair. However, fistulas with cloacal formation and severe radiation damage, fistulas with decreasing bladder capacity or fistulas associated with tumor recurrence are beyond the scope of this report. These patients need to be treated by supravesical urinary diversion.

The technique of the peritoneal flap interposition by

means of the transperitoneal, transvesical approach is simple. It is applicable for fistulas of any type or location and provides a secure closure. It has been effective even in patients who have undergone a previous operation. The peritoneal flap interposition was first described in 1900 by Bardescu[11] and was modified in 1920 by Solms.[12] Use of the procedure was resumed just recently.[13–15]

Indications for interposition include fistulas involving the ureters, fistulas with scar formation and impaired supply owing to an unsuccessful prior operation, post-radiation fistulas and high fistulas, particularly vesico-cervical.

Good timing is a prerequisite for a successful operation. In addition, a smooth epithelial outline of the fistulous area is needed. In general a smooth epithelial outline is not observed in less than 3 months after the occurrence of a fistula, allowing time for all mucosal irritations to heal.[2,16] In contrast, Collins and associates recommend an early fistula repair if a fast consolidation of mucosal conditions can be achieved through high dose corticosteroid treatment.[17] Radiological ulcers and fistulas noted as late as several months up to 25 years

hamper good timing for a corrective operation. If extensive encrustation is encountered at the site of the fistula, eventual preoperative curettage is necessary. Since it is a rather characteristic behavior of fistulas to enlarge after rejection of necrotic marginal tissue, the importance of waiting enough time is accentuated. Thus, it is necessary to control repeatedly the local findings, to maintain antimicrobial therapy for relief of inflammatory changes of the bladder mucosa, to exclude preoperatively an additional uretero-vesicovaginal fistula which might cause an operative failure if overlooked in case of a nearby ureteral ostium and to administer estrogens in postmenopausal patients for improved healing in the vagina.[2]

METHOD

Preoperatively, the finding is controlled cystoscopically and a Foley catheter is inserted. Lower median laparotomy and incision of the bladder are done approximately 4 to 5 cm above the fistula. The incision is made toward the fistula and a flap with a pedicle of appropriate length is dissected from the lateral parietal pelvic peritoneum.

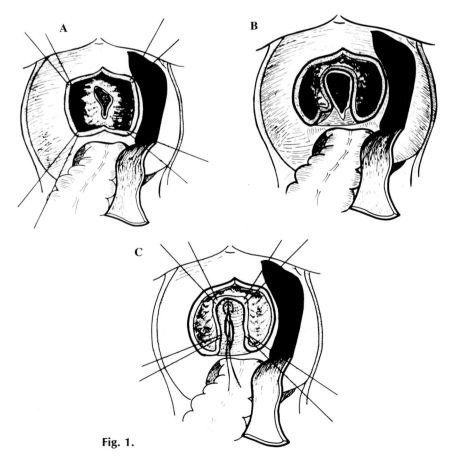

Fig. 1.

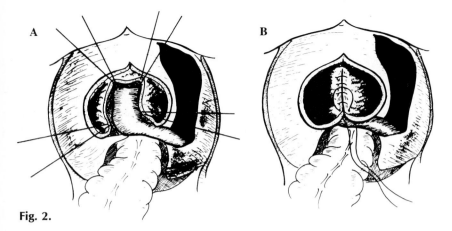

Fig. 2.

This flap is attached paravesically (Fig. 1A). The edges of the fistula are circumcised and severed from the vaginal wall. Stents are used if the fistula is adjacent to the ureteral meatus. If the ureters are involved in the area of repair, reimplantation is done according to the Politano-Leadbetter method. With sharp dissection the edges of the bladder incision are mobilized up to 1 cm and the anterior vaginal wall is separated from the bladder floor extending 1 cm around the fistula (Fig. 1B). The vagina is closed with interrupted sutures of 3-zero catgut everting toward the vagina itself (Fig. 1C). Subsequently, the peritoneal flap is placed between the bladder and the vagina, and attached with chromic catgut interrupted sutures (Fig. 2A). Careful adaptation of the single tissue layers is mandatory. The bladder defect is closed with interrupted chromic catgut sutures tied on the outside (Fig. 2B). The peritoneal edges of the area from which the flap has been taken are sewn together with interrupted chromic catgut sutures.

The urine is diverted through a cystostomy at the bladder dome for 7 to 10 days. A silastic drain is placed intraperitoneally and another drain remains prevesical extraperitoneally. A Foley catheter is left indwelling for 14 days to avoid even slight urine retention. The patient is given antibiotics and the vagina is loosely packed with bacitracin ointment gauze for 3 to 5 days postoperatively.

Interposition of the omentum is indicated in cases involving large defects and those in which the peritoneum is not appropriate owing to scarring, adherence or attenuation, particularly in patients with prior irradiation and extensive fibrotic changes.[18,19]

RESULTS

The peritoneal flap method has been used between 1967 and February 1973 on 29 patients with vesicovaginal fistulas. Prior unsuccessful operations had been done once in 4 patients, twice in 2 and 3 times in 2. One patient each had 4, 5 and 6 previous operations. In 6 patients the fistulas were radiogenic owing to irradiation of a gynecological tumor.

A Politano-Leadbetter reimplantation of the ureter was done in 4 cases, a non-functioning kidney was removed in 1 case and a large intraligamentar cyst was excised at the time of repair in 1 case.

Complications. In 1 case cystostomy drainage was not used and an obstructed catheter caused the fistula to recur. In another case, a 49-year-old patient, there was a 4 by 7 cm defect at the bladder floor owing to an electric conization attempt of the portio. This vesicovaginal fistula reached to the vicinity of the internal vesical sphincter. The anterior vaginal wall had almost completely disappeared and the portio uteri extended into the bladder lumen. In this case 3 sessions were required for complete closure. A second laparotomy was inevitable in 2 patients with postoperative adhesions which had to be released but further healing was uneventful. In 1 patient a pea size abscess was noted 4 months postoperatively within the lower abdominal scar which perforated spontaneously. Subsequently, a vesicocutaneous fistula developed but was closed with conservative means.

DISCUSSION

Recurrence of a corrected vesicovaginal fistula has been observed predominantly in cases of scarring owing to prior surgical repair of fibrosis after irradiation with impaired blood supply and healing. According to Füth-Mayo and Sims-Simon, attempts to close these fistulas transvaginally are charged with a high rate of failures. Although the colpocleisis of Latzko is a safe method to close fistulas after an unsuccessful operation, it is not applicable in young women since the vagina does obliterate partially.[9] In our opinion it is a kind of ultima ratio. Besides, because of the establishment of vaginal dead space it bears a high risk for infection and, thus, even fistula recurrence.[6,20]

The transperitoneal, transvesical fistula repair has several advantages over the vaginal and exclusively transvesical approaches.[7,8,20] The defect is covered with intact viable tissue which guarantees through its adherence a safe operative closure. Besides, since the peritoneum sticks quickly to the anterior vaginal wall the infiltration or leakage of urine following the stitches into the space between bladder and vagina is obviated. The technique of repair is rather simple and applicable in fistulas of any size and at any location. There is no need for modifications according to the type of fistula encountered. Even vesicocervical fistulas can be managed readily through the transvesical route.

In agreement with Schmiedt and Carl,[20] and Szemesi[21] it is our belief that the size of a defect is not as important in deciding the success or failure of a fistula operation as the local tissue conditions and vascularization. Peritoneal interposition is a valuable method particularly in patients who have undergone a previous operation or those who have a radiogenic fistula within large poorly vascularized scars.

SUMMARY

The vaginal approach to repair vesicovaginal fistulas provided good results in more than 90 percent of the cases. However, with this technique there is a high risk of recurrence of large fistulas involving the ureters, recurrent fistulas and radiogenic fistulas. In cases of radiogenic fistulas the suprapubic procedure is technically simpler and more reliable than the vaginal procedure. As a standard repair the transvesical peritoneal flap interposition is recommended. Since the interposed flap quickly adheres to the anterior vaginal wall it is the operation of choice in the presence of large fistulas, operations for recurrence and in the prognostically bleak radiogenic fistulas. We herein report on 29 women with vesicovaginal fistulas, 11 of whom had undergone a previous operation and 6 of whom had radiogenic fistulas. In 93 percent of the cases the repair was successful at the first attempt. Two of 29 patients required a second operation.

REFERENCES

1. Counseller, V. S. and Haigler, F. H., Jr.: Management of urinary-vaginal fistula in 253 cases. Am J Obst Gynec 72:367, 1956
2. Massee, J. S., Welch, J. S., Pratt, J. H. and Symmonds, R. E.: Management of urinary-vaginal fistula: ten-year survey. JAMA 190:902, 1964
3. Bakowski, E.: Urological fistulae in Berlin Universität Frauenklinik from 1941 to 1955. Zbl Gynäk 79:401, 1957
4. Moir, J. C.: Personal experiences in the treatment of vesicovaginal fistulas. Am J Obst Gynec 71:476, 1956
5. Anselmino, K. J., Oppelt, H. G. and Stockhammer, H.: Ergebnisse der operativen Behandlung von 108 Blassen- und Harnröhren-Scheiden-Fisteln. Geburtsh Frauenheilk 27:15, 1967
6. Michalowski, E., Modelski, W. and Klesky, B.: Die operative Behandlung der nach Uterusexstirpation entstandenen Blasenscheidenfisteln. Z Urol 61:805, 1968
7. Su, C. T.: A flap technique for repair of vesicovaginal fistula. J Urol 102:56, 1969
8. Quartey, J. K. M.: Bladder rotation flap for repair of difficult vesicovaginal fistulas. J Urol 107:60, 1972
9. Latzko, W.: Karzinom der Bartholin schen Druse. Zbl Gynäk 38:906, 1914
10. Laibe, J. E. F.: A simple technique for the closure of vesicovaginal fistula. Surg Gynec & Obst 120:353, 1965
11. Bardescu, N.: Ein neues Verfahren für die Operation der tiefen Blasen-Uterus-Scheidenfisteln. Centralbl f Gynäk 24:170, 1900
12. Solms, E.: Blasenfisteloperation mittels uterovaginaler Interposition der Plica. Zbl. Gynäk. 44:1022, 1920
13. Pecherstorfer, M.: Peritoneal-Fettlappenplastik zum Verschluss der Blasenscheidenfistel. Geburtsh Frauenheilk 24:1079, 1964
14. Hohenfellner, R.: Die urologischen Komplikationen des Collum-Carcinoms. Berlin: Springer-Verlag, 1965
15. Zingg, E. and Kurth, K.: Operative Behandlung einer grossen urethrorektalen Fistel nach Prostatektomie. Acta Urol 2:185, 1971
16. Weyrauch, H. M. and Rous, S. N.: Transvaginal-transvesical approach for surgical repair of vesicovaginal fistula. Surg Gynec & Obst 123:121, 1966
17. Collins, C. G., Collins, J. H., Harrison, B. R., Nicholls, R. A., Hoffman, E. S. and Krupp, P. J.: Early repair of vesicovaginal fistula. Am J Obst Gynec 111:524, 1971
18. Kiricuta, I. and Goldstein, A. M. B.: The repair of extensive vesicovaginal fistulas with pedicled omentum: a review of 27 cases. J Urol 108:724, 1972
19. Turner-Warwick, R. T., Wynne, E. J. C. and Handley-Ashken, M.: The use of the omental pedicle graft in the repair and reconstruction of the urinary tract. Br J Surg 54:849, 1967
20. Schmiedt, E. and Carl, P.: Transvesicaler Verschluss von Blasenscheidenfisteln mittels Verschiebelappenplastik. Urologe 11:309, 1972
21. Szemesi, J.: Die Behandlung erfolglos operierter Blasen-Scheidenfisteln. Zbl Gynäk 88:1332, 1966

Commentary: Management of Vesicovaginal Fistula

Rudolf Hohenfellner

Since my original article was written, the urologic and gynecologic literature has become replete with a large number of scientific papers demonstrating that the controversy regarding the methodology of urinary–vaginal fistula repair and the eventual benefit of interposing autologous, homologous, or alloplastic material between the pathologically communicating organs remains unsettled.

FIRST ATTEMPT AT REPAIR

Beyond all argument, however, the first operator attacking the fistula should realize his pivotal position in the optimal situation for successful closure. Whether this is the gynecologist's responsibility, as pointed out by Robertson, is of lesser significance than the experience of the surgeon who takes the first opportunity for closure.[1] This requirement is supported by the observations conveyed from most of the published series that deal predominantly with referred patients: Carl and colleagues reported 18% (from 65 patients); Massee and colleagues, 35% (from 262 patients); Steg and colleagues, 55% (from 40 patients); and Moir, 75% (from 100 patients who had undergone prior repair attempts *elsewhere*).[2-5]

Updating my experience gives a figure of 33% in 54 patients with a total of 44 previous procedures (Table 1), virtually all of which were carried out at the institution where the fistula was created. Thus one is forced to question Robertson's statement that the operator who caused the fistula should repair it, since it has been shown repeatedly that the chances for successful closure decrease with each repair attempt.[1,3,6,7]

FACTORS ADVERSELY AFFECTING CORRECTION

At any rate, besides the number of previous operations, etiologic anatomic, and technical factors account for the rate of first-attempt failures occurring even in the hands of surgeons familiar with the problem. It is difficult to select the most appropriate approach. The more recent results in closure of the vesicovaginal fistula in *one single operation* (Table 2) give no clue, since they are influenced by factors other than pure technical ones. In Massoudnia's series all fistulas were of obstetric origin without prior surgery, whereas in Steg's experience, 55% had prior surgical intervention elsewhere.[4,9] Cancer surgery that had been preceded or followed by irradiation accounted for only 4% of the fistulas in Keettel's patients but for 80% in Kirichuta's.[7,9]

TABLE 1. Prior Attempts at Repair of Urinary–Vaginal Fistulas at Other Hospitals

Attempts	No. of Patients: 1967–1973	No. of Patients: 1973–1979
None	18	18
One	4	3
Two	2	3
Three	2	
Four	1	
Five	1	
Six	1	
Total	29	25

TABLE 2. Successful First-Attempt Closures of Vesicovaginal Fistulas According to Technique

Technique	Closure (%)	N	Author
Vaginal route			
Füth-Mayo	76	34	Lange and colleagues, 1977[18]
Sims	94	157	Keettel and colleagues, 1978[7]
Döderlein	96	29	Massoudia, 1974[8]
Latzko	92	38	Käser, 1977[19]
Moir	70	40	Steg and colleagues, 1977[4]
Abdominal route			
Bladder ration flap	87	56	Carl and colleagues, 1974[2]
Omental pedicle graft	100	27	Kirichuta and colleagues, 1972[9]
Suprapubic	75	20	O'Conor and colleagues, 1973[20]
Legueu-O'Conor	78	19	Akkilic and colleagues, 1974[21]
	73	15	Louis and colleagues, 1975[16]
Peritoneal flap	90	54	Present study

TABLE 3. Etiology of Fistulas

	No. of Patients
Vesicovaginal fistula	
Uterine operation	37
Radical hysterectomy and irradiation	9
Vaginal wall cautery	1
Vesicovaginorectal fistula	
Radical hysterectomy and irradiation	2
Miles procedure	1
Vesicocervical fistula	4
Total	54
Peritoneal flap interposition	51
Omental pedicle graft	3

Of my patients, 20% were previously irradiated, and, in addition, 33% had prior unsuccessful repair attempts in outside hospitals (tables 1 and 3), including 9 of the 54 patients who had prior previous transabdominal corrective surgery. Another ten patients had undergone abdominal gynecologic surgery in addition to the intervention creating the fistula. Thus, 35% of my patients had their third transabdominal operation at the time of repair.

LIMITATIONS OF VAGINAL PROCEDURES

At this point it appears that, in considering etiology, prior surgery, and anatomic features, the vaginal route has distinct disadvantages in the following situations:

    Large fistulas (more than 2 cm)
    Fistulas located in the apex of the vaginal vault
    Multiple fistulas
    Fistulas involving the uterine cervix
    Prior unsuccessful repair attempts
    Prior abdominal surgery in addition to the operation
       causing the fistula
    Prior radiotherapy

As a matter of fact, under the above-listed circumstances, the vesicovaginal fistual correction constitutes a major problem of urologic surgery, which is tackled more easily and safely through the suprapubic route. Furthermore, certain vaginal procedures are not applicable in sexually active women, particularly the Latzko and Döderlein techniques, which result in foreshortening of the vagina.[8]

TRANSABDOMINAL FISTULA REPAIR: TECHNICAL CONSIDERATIONS (FIGS. 3–8)

To proceed, using an incision to excise the previous laparotomy scar, cut adhesions of the small or large bowel and expose the bladder transperitoneally. Incise it along the posterior aspect between several stay sutures in a sagittal plane, allowing the vesical edges to be elevated toward the anterior abdominal wall. I share O'Conor's view that bisection of the bladder is the key to successful closure.[10]

The communications incorporated in Table 2 generally stress the repair of vesicovaginal fistula, but it is my conviction that it is more important to excise the fistulous tract, leaving only normal tissue that is meticulously approximated. Failure

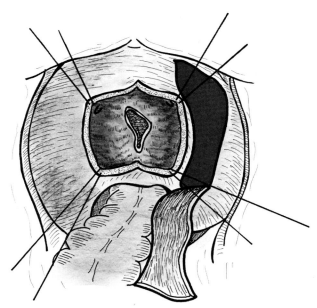

Fig. 3. Median incision of the bladder and preparation of a pedicled peritoneal flap.

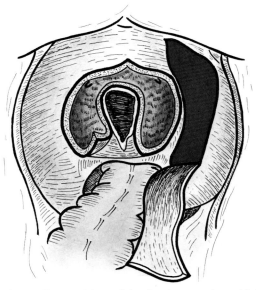

Fig. 4. Circumcision of the fistular margins with liberation of the anterior vaginal wall.

to excise the tract is a major factor in failure of reconstruction despite adequate technique. The removed tissue of the fistulous tract consists of bladder mucosa, bladder wall, intervening fibrous tissue, vaginal wall, and vaginal mucosa. If at all possible, only pliable tissue of the bladder floor and vaginal

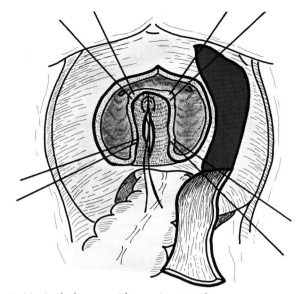

Fig. 5. Vaginal closure with running 3-0 dexon.

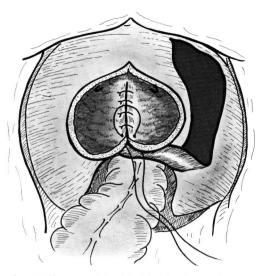

Fig. 7. Closure of the bladder fundus with interrupted 3-0 chromic.

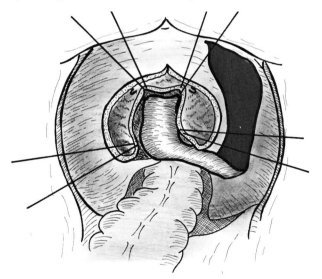

Fig. 6. Placement of the prepared peritoneal flap between vagina and bladder.

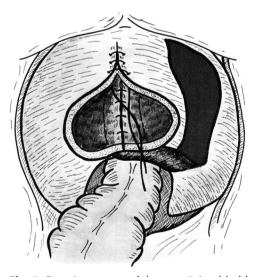

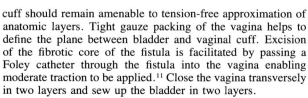

Fig. 8. Running suture of the remaining bladder defect.

cuff should remain amenable to tension-free approximation of anatomic layers. Tight gauze packing of the vagina helps to define the plane between bladder and vaginal cuff. Excision of the fibrotic core of the fistula is facilitated by passing a Foley catheter through the fistula into the vagina enabling moderate traction to be applied.[11] Close the vagina transversely in two layers and sew up the bladder in two layers.

The interposition of tissue secures the suture lines, prevents the accumulation of urine between the two separated organs, reduces the dead space, and acts as an nonpermeable membrane.

Peritoneum has advantages in comparison to other tissues or materials (Table 4). It is readily available, tends to adhere rapidly to the suture lines, and heals over firmly. Its usefulness has been nicely demonstrated by Wandschneider, who sewed the peritoneal flap over the defect remaining after dissecting off the vaginal cuff.[12] The meticulous closure of the bladder, as stressed by many authors (*e.g.,* Gonzales and colleagues), proved to be unnecessary because of the sealing effect of the peritoneum.[13] Peritoneum may be used as a free patch instead of a pedicled flap. The latter has been proven successful in

TABLE 4. Material Used for Interposition in Urinary–Vaginal Fistula

Type	Author	Year
Peritoneal flap	Bardescu[22]	1900
Omental pedicle graft	Walters[28]	1937
Uterus	Solms[26]	1960
Muscle (gracilis, rectus pubococcygis)	Ingelmann-Sundberg[23]	1948
Vaginal flap	Döderlein[24]	1955
Gold leaf	Malin[25]	1967
Lyophilized dura	Thiel[29]	1974
Fetal bladder	Tözüm[27]	1975

TABLE 5. Additional Procedures at the Time of Corrective Surgery

Procedure	Number
Ureteral reimplantation (Paguin type)	
Unilateral	6
Bilateral	1
Nephrectomy	2
Boari flap	
Unilateral	1
Bilateral	1
Parametrial cyst resection	1
Total	12

our hands in repairing vesicorectal or urethrorectal fistulas in the man.

Omentum was only employed in dealing with radiogenic vesicovagino-rectal fistulas or large postirradiation defects when separation of the communicating organs was not feasible. The omental graft firmly seals the fistula when sewn to it. There is no need to revitalize the edges of the bladder defect.[9,14] Admittedly, however, applying a peritoneal flap is considerably easier. Furthermore, in using a pedicled omental flap there is potential danger of bowel obstruction.[12]

Before completing the vesical closure, withdraw the ureteral stents except in those patients with ureteral reimplantation (Table 5). Always insert a suprapubic tube. Steg and colleagues admit that 3 of their 12 failures were due to an obstructed catheter.[4]

TIMING OF REPAIR

Virtually all authors emphasize the need to individualize the timing of surgery. It may take 3 to 5 mo for edema and inflammatory changes to subside. During that time incrustation disappears, with occasional enlargement of the fistula; upon cystoscopic follow-up study epithelization of the tract is visible. Collins and coauthors recommend a high-dose cortisone regimen to permit early closure.[15] The average time interval was

TABLE 6. Postoperative Complications of Urinary–Vaginal Fistula Repair

Type	No. of Patients
Mortality	0
Persisting fistula	5
Bowel obstruction	2
Stress incontinence	2
Creatinine rise	1
Pelvic abscess	1
Total	11

4.3 wk in their 38 patients, but they had 28% first-attempt failures.

Preoperative care includes helping afflicted women to lessen psychologic impact, advice to drink adequate amounts of fluid to avoid irritation or excoriation of the vulva, long-term antimicrobial treatment, estrogen administration for menopausal patients, and repeated control of local findings. Careful search for additional ureteral fistulas is necessary.

RESULTS AND COMPLICATIONS

As pointed out, the results after the various repair methods do not tell the whole story. The success rates of first-attempt closures are given in Table 2. I achieved primary closure in 90% of patients operated on (Table 6).

In analyzing the causes of failure it became evident that in one patient a second fistula was overlooked. Closure required reoperation by the same technique. Two patients suffered from severe diabetes; one had had pelvic irradiation and the other had had two laparotomies because of bowel obstruction. In both patients severe wound infection ensued as encountered in one of Louis's patients.[16]

In one patient cystostomy drainage was not used, and because of a plugged catheter the fistula recurred as reported by Steg and colleagues in 3 patients.[4] Spontaneous closure ensued after prolonged in-dwelling catheter drainage. In another case, a patient of 49 yr had a 4 cm × 7 cm defect at the bladder floor from an electric conization attempt. The vesicovaginal fistula encompassed the internal sphincter. Since the anterior vaginal wall had almost vanished, the uterine cervix protruded into the lumen of the bladder. In this case three operative sessions were required for closure. Eventually, in 96% of my 54 patients the fistulas were cured.

Two patients already included in the original report needed reintervention for bowel obstruction due to adhesion. Since that time this complication has not been encountered. Mild stress incontinence occurred twice (3%) in the 54 patients (Table 2) but resolved within 6 mo following corrective surgery. This complication is more frequently encountered after vaginal fistula repair, ranging from 16% to 27.5%.[17]

REFERENCES

1. Robertson JR: Vesicovaginal fistula. The gynecologists' responsibility. Obstet Gynecol 42:611, 1973
2. Carl P, Praetorius M: Der transvesikale Verschluß von Blasenscheidenfisteln. Geburtshilfe Frauenheilkd 34:699, 1974

3. Masse JS, Welch JS, Pratt JH, et al: Management of urinary-vaginal fistula. JAMA 190:124, 1964
4. Steg A, Vialatte P, Olier C: Le traitement des fistueles vésico-vaginales par la technique de Chassar-Moir. Ann Urol 11:103, 1977

5. Moir JC: Personal experiences in the treatment of vesico-vaginal fistulas. Am J Obstet Gynecol 71:476, 1956

6. Ingelman-Sundberg A: Surgical treatment of urinary fistulae. Zentralbl Gynäekol. 100:1281, 1978

7. Keettel WC, Sehring FG, DeProsse CA et al: Surgical management of urethrovaginal and vesicovaginal fistulas. Am J Obstet Gynecol 131:425, 1978

8. Massoudnia N: Ein Beitrag zur "Einrollplastik" nach G. Döderlein zur operativen Behandlung großer Blasen- und Harnröhren-Scheidenfisteln. Zentralbl Gynäekol 96:624, 1974

9. Kirichuta I, Goldstein AMB: The repair of extensive vesicovaginal fistulas with pedicled omentum: A review of 27 cases. J Urol 108:724, 1972

10. O'Conor VJ: Female urinary incontinence and vesico-vaginal fistula. In Glenn JF (ed): Urologic Surgery pp 767–782. Hagerstown Harper & Row, 1975

11. Glenn JF, Stevens PS: Simplified vesicovaginal fistulectomy. J Urol 110:521, 1973

12. Wandschneider G: Peritoneallappenplastik zur Behandlung vesikovaginaler Defekte. Z Urol 969:49, 1976

13. Gonzalez R, Fraley EE: Surgical repair of post-hysterectomy vesico-vaginal fistulas. J Urol 115:660, 1976

14. Helmbrecht LJ, Goldstein AMB, Morrow JW: The use of pedicled omentum in the repair of large vesicovaginal fistulas. Invest Urol 13:104, 1975

15. Collins CG, Collins JH, Harrison BR, et al: Early repair of vesicovaginal fistula. Am J Obstet Gynecol 111:524, 1971

16. Louis JF, Grasset D, Navratil H: L'abord transpéritonéo-vésical dans la cure des fistulas vésico-génitales. J Urol Nephrol 82:669, 1975

17. Hassim AM, Lucas C: Reduction in the incidence of stress incontinence complicating fistula repair. Br J Surg 61:461, 1974

18. Lange J, Hardt W: Ergebnisse bei der Behandlung von Fisteln und Stenosen der unteren Harnwege in Gynäkologie und Geburtshilfe. Geburtshilfe Frauenheilkd 37:322, 1977

19. Käser O: The Latzko operation for vesico-vaginal fistulae. Acta Obstet Gynecol Scand 56:427, 1977

20. O'Conor VJ, Sokol JK, Bulkley GJ, et al: Suprapubic closure of vesico-vaginal fistulas. J Urol 109:51, 1973

21. Akkilic M, Solok V, Büyüksalvarci K: Die suprapubische transvesikale operative Behandlung von Blasenscheidenfisteln. Z Urol 67:653, 1974

22. Bardescu N: Ein neues Verfahren für die Operation der tiefen Blasen-Uterus-Scheidenfisteln Zentralbl Gynäekol 6:170, 1900

23. Ingelmann-Sundberg A: Utero-vesical fistula following therapeutic abortion; a new operation. Gynecologica 126:274, 1948

24. Döderlein G: Die "Einrollplastik" zum Verschluß großer Blasendefekte am blinden Ende der Scheide. Gynäekologie 77:93, 1955

25. Malin JM, Quiambao VR, Evans AT: Gold leaf in the treatment of urinary fistulas. Invest Urol 4:346, 1967

26. Solms E: Blasenfisteloperation mittels uretero-vaginaler Interposition der Plica. Zentralbl Gynäekol. 37:1022, 1920

27. Tözüm R, Atasü T, Aksu F: A new approach for treatment of vesicovaginal fistula. Obstet Gynecol 45:687, 1975

28. Walters W: Omental flap in the transperitoneal repair of recurring vesicovaginal fistulas. Surg Gynecol Obstet 64:74, 1937

29. Thiel KH, Braun HP: Verschlub einer Vesico-Vaginal-Fistel mit lyoplülisierter menschlicher Dura. Z Urol 67:657, 1976

ANNOTATED BIBLIOGRAPHY

Masse JS, Welch JS, Pratt JH, et al: Management of urinary vaginal fistula. Ten-Year survey. JAMA 190:124, 1964

There were 262 patients with urinary–vaginal fistulas operated on at the Mayo Clinic from 1951 through 1960. As review of these cases indicates that complete investigation of the urinary tract should precede repair, since these abnormal communications appear in many varieties and may be multiple. Anatomic as well as etiologic considerations are important in diagnosis. The abdominal hysterectomy immediately preceded formation of fistula in 153 patients. Preventive measures are discussed. After complete preoperative evaluation of the patient, repair may be effected using two major principles: preservation of blood supply and accurate tissue approximation. Unobstructed postoperative urinary catheter drainage is of primary importance. In the present series, successful surgical correction of vaginal–urinary fistula was effected at first attempt in 88.2% of cases; after reoperations on some patients the eventual success was 95%.

Kirichuta I, Goldstein AMB: The repair of extensive vesicovaginal fistulas with pedicled omentum: A review of 27 cases. J Urol 108:724, 1972

The authors review 27 patients with large vesicovaginal fistulas, 80% of which appeared following a Wertheim operation and irradiation for cancer of the cervix. After bivalve dissection of the bladder, the edges of the fistula are separated, which is accomplished by detaching the wall from the vaginal cuff. If at all possible, the vagina is closed with interrupted sutures. An omental graft is prepared, occasionally with the gastroepiploic artery included. The bladder defect is covered with this omental patch, which is attached with several chromic catgut mattress sutures. The authors stress that the omental patch will become part of the bladder wall and eventually be covered by transitional epithelium and may also contain some bundles of smooth muscle

fibers.[14] All 27 patients were followed from 1 to 3 yr without recurrence. Urinary tract infections subsided 2 mo postoperatively. The bladder capacity progressively increased to normal.

Massoudnia N: Ein Beitrag zur "Einrollplastik" nach G. Döderlein zur operativen Behandlung großber Blasen- und Harnröhren-Scheidenfisteln. Zentralbl. Gynakol 96:624, 1974

At the Department of Gynecology and Obstetrics, University of Tabriz (Iran), during a 6-yr period 612 patients with vesicovaginal fistulas were operated on; 570 were of obstetric origin, 28 were the result of trauma, and only 14 occurred postoperatively. The author focuses on the Döderlein vaginal flap plasty in 29 women with postobstetrical fistulas of at least 2 yr persistence; 28 were successfully repaired, but 16 patients experienced pain during intercourse because of narrowing of the vagina.

Carl P, Praetorius M: Der transvesikale Verschluß von Blasenscheidenfisteln. Geburtshilfe Frauenheilkd 34:699, 1974

A method for the transvesical operation of vesicovaginal fistulas is reported. After closure of the fistula in two layers, a flap is placed over the fistula through the open bladder. In 64 women, 69 operations were performed. The success rate is just short of 95%. The operation of fistulas following radiotherapy is unsatisfactory. The advantage of transvesical operations compared to vaginal operations for vesicovaginal fistulas is that large defects and recurrencies can be covered without tension. The ureteric orifices can be constantly seen during the operation and indications for implantation of the ureter can readily be made.

Ingelman-Sundberg A: Surgical treatment of urinary fistulae. Zentralbl Gynakol 100:1281, 1978

A survey is presented, based on 225 patients with urinary fistulas; 173 of which were postoperative or obstetric fistulas, and 52 of which appeared after radiotherapy. The author's method for preparing the region of the fistula from a transverse incision under the external urethral orifice and his grafting techniques are presented using flaps from one or both pubococcygeus muscles, the rectus abdominis muscle, or the gracilis muscle. For vesicovaginal fistulas lying high in the vaginal vault a graft from the omentum or an appendix epiploicum is used. They are usually grasped from below after opening the periotneum. In case of postirradiation damage to the ureters the damaged portion was resected and the ureters implanted into an ileum segment anastomosed to the fistula in the bladder. The 173 patients without prior irradiation were, with a few exceptions, cured in one operation. Of the remaining 52 patients 46 were treated by vaginal surgery, creating a functioning bladder. In two patients an ileum segment was formed, two were inoperable, and two had recurrences after vaginal repair attempts.

Keettel WC, Sehring FG, DeProsse CA, et al: Surgical Management of Urethrovaginal and Vesicovaginal fistulas. Am J Obstet Gynecol 131:425, 1978

This report reviews a 50-yr period during which 157 vesicovaginal and 24 urethrovaginal fistuals were managed. Although the etiologic factors have changed, there has not been a dramatic decrease in the incidence of this complication. In the last 17 yr the author noted an increased number of both types of fistula, primarily related to the increased frequency of gynecologic operative procedures. Only 11 (6%) of the fistulas reported in this series resulted from surgical procedures performed in their department. In this series 96% were repaired vaginally, but the abdominal approach was used for certain complicated fistulas. The author initial cure rate was 89%, and the final success rate in 157 vesicovaginal fistulas was 94.3%. The urethrovaginal fistulas represent a special problem because of the location, scarring, and lack of sufficient fascia for a second-layer closure. In such instances the authors have successfully used bulbocavernous fat pad. The success rate for 24 patients with this type of fistula was 87.5%.

OVERVIEW: MANAGEMENT OF VESICOVAGINAL FISTULA: A CONTINUING CONTROVERSY

Vincent J. O'Conor, Jr.

The controversy goes on. Who should do the original operation, and should it be vaginal or abdominal? There are strong advocates on both sides, and good results are obtained by both routes. The technique described by Barnes is perfectly straightforward and emphasizes several points: the wide mobilization of vaginal mucosa with closure of both bladder and vagina under *no* tension obliterating all dead space. A five-layer closure is a bit unusual but cannot be criticized if it works. A similar method has been described by Marshall with an 85% initial success rate.[1] A unique method is that currently performed at the University of California Los Angeles, where no attempt is made to close the bladder. The vagina is mobilized and brought together without tension over the bladder opening, which apparently closes.* I find this hard to accept from a surgical view point, since the edges of the fistula are generally fibrotic and should not reepithelialize readily. Excision of this scar with approximation of fresh, well-vascularized tissue seems preferable. As so often stated, the surgeon should create a fresh injury to obtain the best result in closing vesicovaginal fistulas.

The use of the Latzko operation as a routine method for closure of uncomplicated fistulas seems illogical to me because the loss of vaginal length is a significant impediment to the patient, and this complication is unnecessary.[2] The argument

presented by gynecologists that "this is a relatively small sacrifice when compared to incontinence" just does not hold water when physicians consider alternative methods of closure that have an equally impressive cure rate.[3]

As mentioned in the Commentary, the use of the fibrolabial fat pad as described by Martius (which has been used by competent gynecologic surgeons for over 50 yr and finally described in the urologic literature by Berkhoff) is an excellent supplement to protect the closure, and its use should probably be routine when vaginal repair is chosen.[4]

Finally, the use of electrocoagulation or curettage with a wood screw should be tried for very small fistulas because this often obviates more extensive surgery. Electrocoagulation was described by O'Conor in 1938, and in my recent review of experience with vesicovaginal fistula, 6 patients healed following coagulation and catheter drainage only.[5]

Dr. Hohenfellner makes several excellent points regarding who should do the surgery and which approach should be used. In my practice I see very few of the small, lowlying fistulas in nonirradiated patients that are amenable to vaginal repair. Most of my patients (42 in the recent review) have been previously operated on and have fistulas larger than 2 cm; these are located high in the vagina well above the trigone and are most suited to the transabdominal repair described by Dr. Hohenfellner. I have used peritoneum as described but much prefer the use of pedicled omentum because this provides a

* Raz J: Personal communication, 1980.

987

bulky well-vascularized material to buttress the suture lines. I have not had a failure when omentum has been used. It is gratifying to find the reference to Dr. Waltman Walters' original description of this technique in 1937, one that is often overlooked in the literature.

The timing of the operation has recently come under question by Persky, who suggests an earlier attempt, reasoning that if failure occurs little is lost.[6] In reviewing the old literature to find the origin of the 3-mo waiting period, I found numerous references to failure resulting from early closure. In my experience early cystoscopy reveals infected, indurated tissues, often with sutures visible. It is my strong opinion (which coincides with that of the late Dr. Meredith Campbell) that "surgery should be postponed at least 3 to 4 months to allow absorption of inflamatory infiltrate, softening and healing of tissues. Especially in vesicovaginal fistula, suturing of indurated friable infected tissue is certain to fail."[7] A recent report from Philadelphia describing results with the supravesical technique includes two failures felt to result from too-early closure after diagnosis.[8]

Finally, for completeness, mention should be made of recent publications describing techniques for repair of fistulas associated with urethral loss, a most difficult situation. The vaginal approach is well described by Symmonds with good results and suprapubic reconstruction of the urethra from a bladder flap is described by O'Conor.[9,10] Whichever method is used for urethral reconstruction, urinary continence is achieved only when vesicourethral suspension is added to the procedure.

REFERENCES

1. Marshall VF: Vesicovaginal fistulas on one urologic service. J Urol 121:125, 1979

2. Latzko W: Postoperative vesicovaginal fistulas. Am J Surg 58:221, 1942

3. Mattingly RF: Operative Gynecology, p 608. Philadelphia, JB Lippincott, 1970

4. Martius H: Gynecologic Operations: With Emphasis on Topographic Anatomy. Boston, Little, Brown & Co, 1957

5. O'Conor VJ Jr: Review of experience with vesicovaginal fistula repair. Trans Am Assoc Genitourin Surg 71:120, 1979

6. Persky L, Herman G, Guerrier K: Non delay in vesicovaginal fistula repair. Urology 11:273, 1979

7. Campbell MF: Urology. Baltimore, Williams & Wilkins, 1954

8. Wein JJ et al: Repair of vesicovaginal fistula by a suprapubic transvesical approach. Surg Gynecol Obstet 150:57, 1980

9. Symmonds RE, Hill LM: Loss of the urethra: A report on 50 patients. Am J Obstet Gynecol 130:130, 1978

10. O'Conor VJ Jr: Repair of vesicovaginal fistula with associated urethral loss. Surg. Gynecol Obstet 146:250, 1978

77

MANAGEMENT OF PROSTATIC FISTULAS

Carl A. Olsson, Max K. Willscher, Robert J. Krane and George Austen, Jr.

From the Boston Veterans Administration Hospital and Boston University Medical Center, Boston, Massachusetts

Urological Survey
Copyright © 1976 by The Williams & Wilkins Co.
Vol. 25, October
Printed in U.S.A.

ABSTRACT—Prostatic fistulas communicating with the rectum or perineal skin are unusual complications of a prostatic operation, pelvic trauma, prostatic abscess or other iatrogenic injury. A third of these fistulas may close spontaneously with proper urinary drainage and avoidance of fecal soilage. The many operative procedures described for the repair of these fistulas indicate that no ideal method of repair can be applied to every case. Operative management should be mandated by the size, location and duration of the fistula as well as by the surgeon's experience with the various anatomic approaches.

Fistulas from the prostate to the rectum or perineal skin are vexing problems for patient and surgeon. More than 15 different surgical procedures have been described for treatment of these conditions, attesting to a lack of unanimity in management. Weyrauch reviewed more than 150 cases of such fistulas and concluded that most of the literature contained information about patients and management insufficient to allow development of a cohesive therapeutic plan.[1] We herein review our experience with these conditions and selected articles from the literature, hoping to resolve controversies regarding the pathogenesis and management.

PATIENT DATA

Present Series. During the last 15 years we have treated 9 patients with prostatorectal or prostatocutaneous fistulas (Table 1). There were 5 examples of each type of fistula, 1 patient having a branched fistulous tract leading to the rectum and the perineal skin. Two cases each resulted from rectal injury incurred at the time of a simple perineal prostatectomy, spontaneous rupture of prostatic abscess and pelvic fracture with associated injury to prostatic urethra and rectum. In 3 patients prostatocutaneous fistulas developed after an extensive abdominoperineal

TABLE 1. Prostatorectal and Prostatoperineal Fistulas

Patient	Fistula	Etiology	Surgical Repair	Colostomy	Result
1	Prostatorectal	Simple perineal prostatectomy	Transrectal	Yes	Healed
2	Prostatorectal	Suprapubic prostatectomy	Young-Stone	Yes	Healed
3	Prostatorectal	Prostatic abscess	Perineal	Yes	Healed
4	Prostatorectal	Prostatic abscess	Perineal	No	Healed*
5	Prostatorectal, prostatoperineal	Trauma	Perineal	Yes	Healed*
6	Prostatoperineal	Trauma	Perineal	No	Healed
7	Prostatoperineal	Miles resection	None	Yes	Healed
8	Prostatoperioneal	Miles resection	Abdominoperineal omentopexy	Yes	Healed
9	Prostatoperineal	Miles resection	Perineal (bulbocavernosus flap)	Yes	Healed

* Required curettage and fulguration for prostatoperineal drainage.

TABLE 2. Review of Literature

Reference	No. Patients	Etiology Pro-static Surgery	Trauma	Abscess	Other	Failed Prior Treatment No. Operations	No. Patients	Colostomy	Spontaneous Cure	Surgical Repair	Success Rate (%)
Young and Stone[3]	3	3				8	3	0	0	3 Young-Stone	100
Wilhelm[4]	13*	6		2	5	2	2	4	5	2 perineal / 2 Young-Stone	100
Lewis[7]	13		13			12	5	13	0	13 Young-Stone	100
Vose[2]	4	4				0	0	0	0	4 transrectal	100
Weyrauch[1]	4	4				0	0	0	0	4 perineal	100
Erlik[8]	1		1			3	1	1	0	1 rectal flap	100
Goodwin and associates[4]	21	21				Not listed		7	9	9 perineal / 1 transrectal	100
Kilpatrick and Thompson[9]	6	6				2	2	6	0	6 paracoccygeal	100
Culp and Calhoun[10]	20	8	4	1	7	22	7	6	3	14 perineal / 1 Young-Stone	86 / 100
Turner-Warwick and associates[5]	2		2			2	1	2	0	2 A-P omentopexy	100
Limbert[11]	1				1	0	0	1	0	1 paracoccygeal	100
Talarico and Fernandes[12]	1	1				1	1	1	0	1 transrectal	100
Kilpatrick and Mason[13]	7†		Not listed			9	9	16	0	7 paracoccygeal / 9 York Mason	92 / 100
Mason and Kilpatrick[14]	9										
Beneventi and Cassebaum[15]	1	1				2	1	1	0	1 York Mason with flap	100
Smith and Veenema[16]	4	4				Not listed		2	2	2 perineal	100
Dahl and associates[17]	5	5				0	0	5	2	3 York Mason	100
Morgan[18]	1	1				2	1	1	0	1 paracoccygeal (with skin graft)	100
Present series	9	2	2	2	3	5	1	7	1	6 perineal / 1 transrectal / 1 Young-Stone / 1 A-P omentopexy	100

* Five cases excluded: autopsy findings only.

† Six cases previously reported.

resection (2 for inflammatory bowel disease and 1 for previously irradiated rectal carcinoma), an etiology not previously stressed.

In the 2 patients with rectal tears sustained during prostatectomy primary closure was attempted without success. Also, in the 3 patients whose fistulas developed after abdominoperineal resection, the prostatic injury was repaired at the time of the initial operation, again without success.

Many of our patients were referred from other institutions and none had undergone formal surgical repair prior to a 6-week interval. One patient had undergone 5 separate attempts at surgical repair (all via the perineal route) prior to referral to our hospital.

There was 1 instance of spontaneous closure of prostatoperineal fistula in our series, the other 8 patients requiring operative intervention. Four of the 5 patients with prostatorectal fistulas had undergone colostomy. Three patients with prostatoperineal fistulas already had colostomies created during abdominoperineal resection. Complete healing of the prostatorectal or prostatoperineal fistula was accomplished with a single operation in 6 of the 8 patients operated. Two patients had residual prostatoperineal drainage tracts that required additional fulguration and/or curettage. Ultimately, total healing was accomplished in all cases.

The surgical management in each case varied widely. One patient with a prostatorectal fistula was repaired by the transrectal route suggested by Vose.[2] Another patient with the same condition was treated by the Young-Stone procedure.[3] Five patients with fistulas were repaired by the perineal route.[4] In one of these patients in whom the fistula was large a flap of bulbocavernosus muscle was interposed between the prostatic and cutaneous openings. One patient was treated by the combined abdominoperineal omental graft technique of Turner-Warwick and associates.[5]

Literature Survey. We reviewed 18 reports in which there was sufficient information regarding pathogenesis and management to allow derivation of meaningful data (Table 2).[1-18] We omitted from review cases that were discovered only at autopsy.[6] When the cases in our series were added to those in the literature survey there were 125 available for review.

The etiology of the prostatorectal or prostatoperineal fistula was discussed in 109 instances.[1-12,15-19] Complications of a prostatic operation accounted for 66 fistulas. As might be expected the perineal prostatic operation was most often implicated, accounting for 43 fistulas. Of interest was the fact that only 13 of these 43

cases were examples of total prostatectomy and the majority (30 cases) represented simple prostatectomy or open perineal prostatic biopsy.[1-4,6,9,10,12,17-19] Twelve fistulas developed after retropubic prostatectomy, 8 following total prostatectomy.[4,9,15,16] Seven fistulas developed after transurethral resection of the prostate and 4 fistulas occurred after suprapubic prostatectomy.[4,6,9,10,17] Six fistulas resulted from a prostatic abscess with spontaneous perforation into the rectum.[3,6,10,19] Four fistulas were caused by assorted inflammatory disorders, primarily tuberculosis of the prostate.[6,10,11] An additional 6 fistulas resulted from various iatrogenic injuries (3 from abdominoperineal resection and 3 from catheters, urethral sounds and so forth).[6,10,19] One patient had a prostatorectal fistula secondary to extensive urethral carcinoma.[10]

The incidence of spontaneous healing of fistulas could be reviewed in only some series. Many published reports dealt exclusively with fistulas requiring surgical repair. Of the 72 cases reviewed in reports in which spontaneous healing was mentioned, 22 fistulas resolved without direct surgical intervention.[4,6,10,16,17,19] Although many patients had been treated with colostomy and/or suprapubic bladder drainage, no precise figures were obtained on the contributions of fecal or urinary drainage to spontaneous fistula closures.

The most common operative technique used in those patients requiring an operation for fistula closure was the perineal repair.[1,4,6,10,16,19] Thirty-seven perineal repairs were done and 35 fistulas were successfully closed with this technique (Fig. 1). Twenty patients underwent fistula repair via the Young-Stone maneuver and all patients were treated successfully with this technique (Fig. 2).[3,6,7,10,19] Fifteen patients were treated via a paracoccygeal approach to the fistula and 14 were cured (Fig. 3).[9,11,13,18] Thirteen patients were treated with the York Mason repair and all 13 were cured (Fig. 4).[14,15,17] Eight fistulas were treated by a transrectal approach and

PERINEAL REPAIR

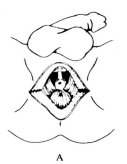 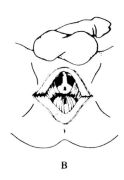 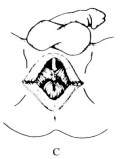

A   B   C

Fig. 1. (*A*) Transected fistula. (*B*) Layered closure of prostatic and rectal opening. (*C*) Levator ani muscle interposed between prostatic and rectal opening.

YOUNG-STONE PULL THROUGH OPERATION

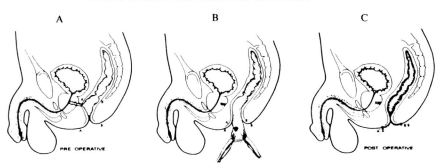

Fig. 2. (*A*) Preoperative prostatorectal fistula. (*B*) Rectum mobilized and fistulous opening drawn beyond anal verge. Prostatic opening is closed. (*C*) Rectal cuff reanastomosed to perineal skin.

TRANSCOCCYGEAL REPAIR

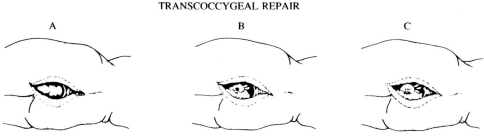

Fig. 3. Patient is in lateral position—head to right. (*A*) Oblique incision in buttock, rectum identified and coccyx removed. (*B*) Rectum rotated laterally and fistula exposed. (*C*) Layered closure of prostatic and rectal openings.

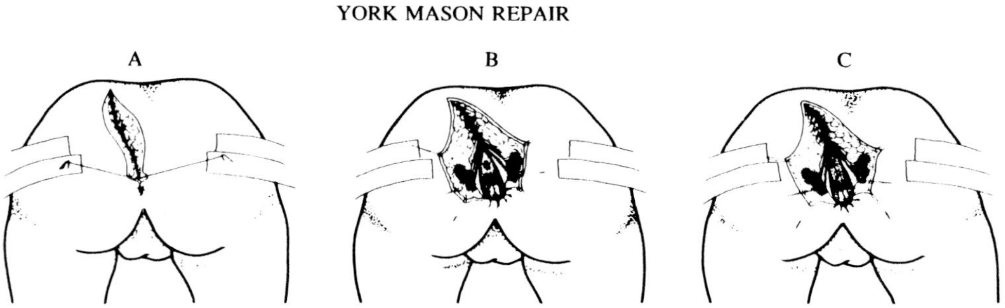

YORK MASON REPAIR

Fig. 4. (*A*) Incision down to rectum. Prior to rectal incision anal sphincter is identified (with silk suture) for later reanastomosis. (*B*) Anal sphincter and rectum divided. Fistula identified and excised. (*C*) Layered closure of prostatic urethra and anterior rectal wall.

successful closure of the fistula was achieved in all such patients (Fig. 5).[2,4,8,12,19] Finally, 3 successful fistula closures were accomplished by the abdominoperineal omentopexy technique (Fig. 6).[5,19]

The contribution of fecal diversion to a successful fistula operation could not be determined accurately. Seventy-three of the 125 patients available for review (58 percent) had undergone colostomy at some time.[4–19]

Stated in the reverse 51 patients (42 percent) did not require colostomy for the successful management of the fistulas.

Most of the operations performed for the repair of prostatorectal or prostatoperineal fistulas were done months to years after the onset of the fistula. The only procedure that seemed applicable to early operative intervention was the transrectal approach suggested by Vose.[2] In

TRANSRECTAL APPROACH

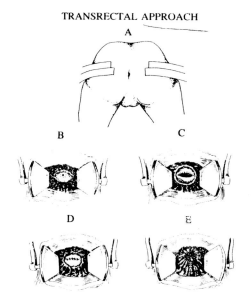

Fig. 5. (*A*) Patient in Buie position. (*B*) Anus dilated. Fistula visualized. (*C*) Fistula excised. (*D*) Prostatic capsule closed. (*E*) Anterior wall of rectum closed.

TURNER-WARWICK OMENTAL REPAIR

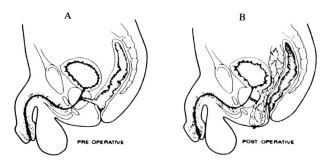

Fig. 6. (*A*) Preoperative prostatorectal fistula. (*B*) Omentum interposed between rectum and prostate.

Vose's experience patients could be operated upon during the first month after the diagnosis of the fistula.

CASE REPORTS

Case 1. BVAH 022401777, a 74-year-old man underwent simple perineal prostatectomy for benign prostatic hypertrophy at another institution. During the operation the rectum was inadvertently entered and repaired in a layer fashion. Removal of the Foley catheter 5 days postoperatively resulted in continuous drainage of urine from the rectum. A transverse colostomy was performed

subsequently. When the patient was referred to our institution 3 months later a fistulous tract from the prostate to the rectum was documented. A transrectal repair of the fistula was done. After 6 weeks of urethral catheter drainage a voiding cystourethrogram showed that the fistulous tract had healed completely and the patient was discharged from the hospital.

Case 2. U-34287, a 61-year-old man underwent suprapubic prostatectomy for benign prostatic hypertrophy at another institution. No rectal injury was noted during the operation but postoperative onset of fecaluria led to the discovery of a prostatorectal fistula. The fistula persisted despite a diverting colostomy and suprapubic urinary drainage. A Young-Stone procedure resulted in a successful repair of the prostatorectal fistula 3 months after the initial operation. After removal of the suprapubic tube and the colostomy closure urinary and fecal continence remain intact.

Case 3. BVAH 012684397, a 67-year-old man had a prostatic abscess that drained spontaneously into the rectum. A persistent prostatorectal fistula developed. A colostomy was created and a suprapubic tube was placed. The fistula persisted despite 3 months of conservative management. A perineal repair of the prostatorectal fistula was done with careful layer closure of the defects. The suprapubic tube was removed and the colostomy was closed 1 month postoperatively. The fistula was cured, and fecal and urinary control were normal.

Case 4. BVAH 250013846, a 55-year-old man had a chief complaint of passing air through the urethra. He was evaluated and found to have a prostatorectal fistula. He gave a history of prostatis with fever and chills. We, therefore, thought that this fistula probably represented another example of spontaneous drainage of a prostatic abscess into the rectum. After adequate bowel preparation the patient underwent primary closure of the fistula through a perineal approach. After removal of the urethral catheter studies showed closure of the prostatorectal fistula, although there was intermittent perineal drainage of urine. The small prostatoperineal fistula was treated by curettage and the drainage ceased. Final studies showed that all urinary leakage was repaired.

Case 5. BVAH 723141887, a 39-year-old man sustained a pelvic fracture with rectal laceration and prostatic urethral transection in an automobile accident. Four months after insertion of a urethral catheter and fecal diversion by loop colostomy the patient was referred to us for treatment of persistent prostatorectal and prostatoperineal fistulas (Fig. 7A). Suprapubic tube drainage was instituted and the colostomy was converted to an

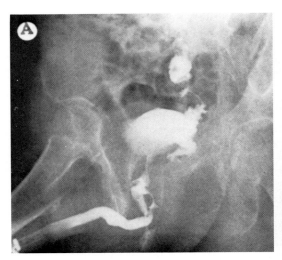
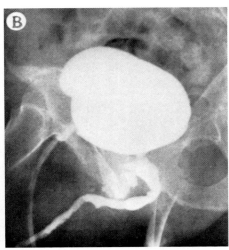

Fig. 7. (*A*) Preoperative retrograde urethrogram demonstrates prostatorectal and prostatoperineal fistulas. (*B*) Postoperative voiding cystourethrogram; fistulas healed.

end colostomy. The fistulas persisted and the patient underwent perineal repair of the prostatic and rectal defects. A small prostatoperineal fistula persisted, requiring curettage and drainage. The fistulas then remained closed and voiding cystourethrography demonstrated only a small prostatic sinus tract (Fig. 7*B*). The colostomy was closed and the suprapubic tube was removed. The patient has only occasional stress urinary incontinence.

Case 6. BVAH 010038303, a 59-year-old man sustained a pelvic fracture with prostatic urethral transection 2 years prior to referral to us. The injury was initially treated by suprapubic tube diversion. However, a prostatoperineal fistula developed in addition to a membranous urethral stricture (Fig. 8*A* and *B*). Excision of the stricture and repair of the fistula were done via the perineal approach and end-to-end reanastomosis. The procedure resulted in complete resolution of the stricture and perineal fistula (Fig. 8*C*). The patient remains continent and requires no dilatations.

Case 7. BVAH 153301886, a 55-year-old man with a 12-year history of Crohn's disease involving the small bowel and colon required multiple abdominal operations. Because of enterorectal fistulas a transverse colostomy was created, and the anus and rectum were removed. With the intense perirectal inflammation and fibrosis the prostate was inadvertently injured. The injury resulted in a "watering pot" perineum. A suprapubic tube was inserted and the perineum was drained, and the prostatic fistula healed spontaneously within 4 weeks.

Case 8. BVAH 025050878, a 59-year-old man with extensive rectal carcinoma was treated with 4,500R of radiotherapy prior to abdominoperineal resection. Because of dense perirectal inflammation the prostate was entered accidently. A urethral catheter was passed and the prostatic urethra was closed in 2 layers. When the urethral catheter was removed a persistent prostatoperineal fistula developed. The patient underwent simultaneous abdominoperineal repair of the fistula, using an omental graft interposition between prostatic and cutaneous defects 6 months postoperatively. Suprapubic urinary diversion was maintained for 6 weeks. When the suprapubic tube was removed the patient was continent of urine and no further perineal leakage ensued.

Case 9. UH 539240, a 37-year-old man with ulcerative colitis underwent total colectomy and diverting ileostomy at another institution. A prostatic injury at the time of the operation resulted in a persistent prostatoperineal fistula. Five separate attempts were made to close the fistulas (all through a perineal approach) without success. When the patient was examined at our institution the prostatic opening was closely apposed to the perineal wound, such that a finger placed in the perineum could be seen in the prostatic urethra on urethroscopy. Since the colon had been entirely removed no omentum was available to buttress the fistula repair. Through a combined suprapubic and perineal approach the complete bladder and prostate were mobilized and pexed anteriorly. A bulbocavernosus flap was developed to lie over the prostatic urethra defect, which was closed in a layer

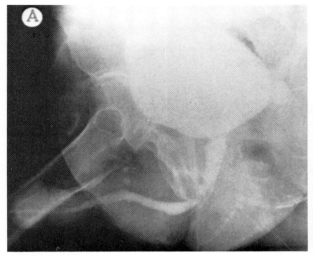

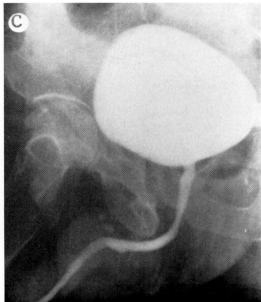

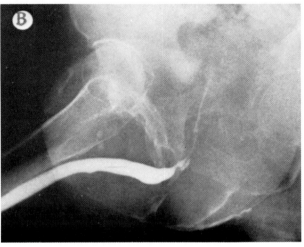

Fig. 8. (*A* and *B*) Preoperative voiding cystourethrogram and retrograde urethrogram; prostatoperineal fistula and bulbous urethral stricture demonstrated. (*C*) Normal postoperative voiding cystourethrogram.

fashion. Postoperatively, there was temporary drainage of serosanguineous material from the large, newly-created presacral space. Urine leakage was entirely absent and the suprapubic tube was removed after 8 weeks. The fistula was totally healed and the patient voids fairly well with mild stress urinary incontinence (Fig. 9).

SURGICAL TECHNIQUES

As mentioned previously more than 15 operations have been described for the management of prostatic fistulas. The more commonly used procedures will be reviewed in this section, along with the description of a variation in operative technique developed by the authors.

The perineal repair was first described by Frankel in 1876.[1] Since that time various authors have contributed slight variations in technique to the procedure. The method consists of a perineal approach to the fistula and resection of the fistulous tract (Fig. 1). The resultant openings in the prostate and rectum are then closed in a layer fashion. Some workers stress that non-absorbable suture material be used in at least the seromuscular closure of the rectum.[10,16] All workers stress that dissection should be carried well above the fistulous site in order to expose completely and repair comfortably the openings in the prostate and rectum.[1,4,6,10,16] Most authors suggest interposition of levator ani muscle, approximated in the midline, to buttress the prostatic defect.[1,4,10,16] Some authors make a point to rotate the rectal repair site away from the midline or else free the rectum sufficiently to allow the rectal repair site to lie at a lower position than the opening in the prostate.[4,16] Goodwin

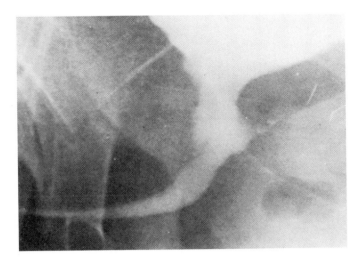

Fig. 9. Postoperative voiding cystourethrogram; prostatoperineal fistula healed.

Resection End to End Reanastomosis

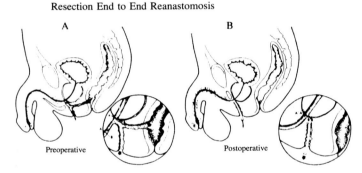

Preoperative   Postoperative

Fig. 10. (*A*) Prostatorectal and prostatoperineal fistulas. (*B*) End-to-end anastomosis of urethra; perineal drain present.

and associates suggest that the linearly closed defects in the prostate and rectum be oriented at right angles to one another (vertical closure of prostate and horizontal closure of rectum).[4]

Two variations in the perineal technique are worthy of mention. One is useful in the patient with a severed prostatic urethra resulting from pelvic trauma. In such cases the membranous urethra is often densely strictured. After excision of the fistulous tract the fibrotic membranous urethra can be resected and an end-to-end anastomosis of bulbous urethra with prostate can be accomplished (Fig. 10). A final variation of the perineal approach is useful in patients with prostatoperineal fistulas after abdominoperineal resection. This technique will be described (Fig. 11).

The Young-Stone technique was actually developed by Tedenat in 1903 and popularized by Young and Stone in 1917.[1,3] The procedure is a variation of the Whitehead operation for hemorrhoidal disease. The rectum is freed from the anal sphincter and, after dividing the prostatorectal fistula, the portion of rectum containing the fistula is drawn outside of the body and excised (Fig.

2). The resultant cuff of rectal mucosa is reanastomosed to perineal skin after the defect in the prostatic capsule is closed in layers. This operation is probably most useful for low-lying rectourethral or prostatorectal fistulas.

The paracoccygeal approach to prostatorectal fistulas was described first by Kilpatrick and Thompson in 1962.[9] The patient is in the lateral position and an oblique incision is made in the buttock, paralleling the sacral notch (Fig. 3). The tip of the sacrum and entire coccyx are removed and, after dividing the fascia propria, the rectum is exposed and rotated, allowing access to the fistula. The fistula is resected and the tissues of prostate and rectum are repaired in a layer fashion. The rectal closure is rotated so as to leave normal rectal wall in apposition to the prostatic or urethral repair site. A variation of the paracoccygeal technique traverses the rectum instead of rotating the rectum to gain access to the fistulous tract. With large defects free full-thickness skin grafts can be used to close the prostatourethral opening.[18]

The York Mason technique was first described by

Bulbocavernosus Flap Interposition

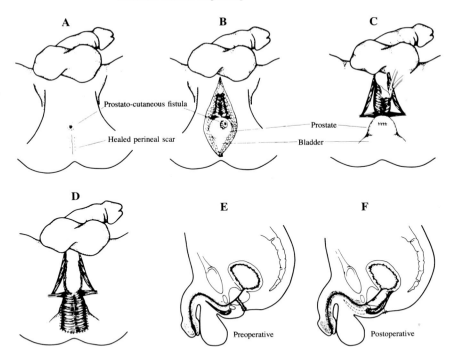

Fig. 11. (*A*) Rectum removed; prostatocutaneous fistula visible. (*B*) Prostatic fistula and urethra identified. (*C*) Prostatic fistula closed and bulbocavernosus muscle mobilized. (*D*) Bulbocavernosus muscle swung as flap over prostatic fistula. (*E*) Lateral view of prostatocutaneous fistula. (*F*) Lateral view of completed repair.

that author in 1969.[13] This operation is essentially a transrectal approach, which provides greater exposure by simply dividing the anal sphincter and rectum in the midline posteriorly (Fig. 4). York Mason developed this technique because of lack of exposure achieved with the usual transrectal approach. After the anal canal is divided posteriorly the fistula is widely exposed and can be excised with resultant prostatic and anterior rectal defects closed in a layer fashion. The posterior anal canal and lower rectum are then repaired, taking great care to reapproximate the anal sphincter. One variation of the York Mason approach has been developed by Beneventi.[15] An elliptical incision is made around the anterior rectal fistulous site and the mucosa from the ellipse is denuded. The seromuscular rectal flap of the ellipse is closed in a sandwich fashion and the resultant elliptical rectal wall defect is closed linearly. This variation is advantageous in that the neural and vascular structures surrounding the prostate and responsible for potency are not damaged.

Simple transrectal repair of fistulas was first described by Nott and Emmett in 1870 and popularized by Vose in 1949.[1,2] This procedure involves dilating the anal sphincter sufficiently to gain access to the fistulous tract and then carrying out excision of the tract with layer closure (Fig. 5).

The abdominoperineal omentopexy was described

by Turner-Warwick and associated in 1967.[5] For very large fistulas the omentum is freed from the gastric margin and fashioned into an apron that can be passed down between the openings in the rectum and prostate and fastened to perineal skin (Fig. 6). Little or no attempt to close defects in either prostate or rectum is necessary. The interposed, well-vascularized omentum acts as a buttress on which neoepithelialization can occur.

In treating prostatoperineal fistulas resulting from abdominoperineal resection some additional surgical points must be stressed. With abdominoperineal resection the bladder and prostate fall backward to fill the void in the presacral space after excision of the rectum. This causes the prostatic defect to be in close apposition with the perineal skin opening. During repairs of prostatic fistulas following abdominoperineal resection, the bladder and prostate must be thoroughly freed and relocated anteriorly with suprapubic variations of the Marshall-Marchetti-Krantz technique. Since it is difficult to interpose normal tissues over the fistulous closure in the prostate, omentopexy is of great value in the management of such cases.

An alternate variation we have used in the treatment of prostatoperineal fistula following abdominoperineal resection can be used when omentopexy is not possible. Again, because of the proximity of the prostatic opening with the skin, it is a good idea to interpose normal tissues between the prostatic opening and the cutaneous incision. In a patient who has undergone total colectomy, however, the omentum is not available for use in this fashion. One of our patients suffered a prostatic injury at the time of total colectomy performed for ulcerative colitis. This patient underwent treatment via a combined perineal and suprapubic approach (Fig. 11). The bladder and prostate were freed from the perineal skin and elevated anteriorly out of the sacral fossa. The large prostatic defect was closed in a layer fashion, and to interpose normal tissue between the prostatic opening and the skin margin, bulbocavernosus muscle was excised from its attachments to the crura of the penis and swung backward in a "trap door" fashion and sutured to the posterior wall of the bladder. This simple maneuver completely covered the prostatic closure and prevented its contact with the perineal skin opening.

DISCUSSION

Pathogenesis of Prostatic Fistulas. The figures presented herein regarding etiology of prostatorectal and prostatoperineal fistulas require no special interpretation. However, a few points should be emphasized. Problems encountered during the course of a prostatic operation are responsible for 60 percent of such fistulas.[1–4,6,9,10,12,17–19] The majority of these problems occurs after perineal prostatic operations. However, only 30 percent of these are of the radical extirpative sort. The other 70 percent represent simple enucleation operations or even more suprisingly, simple open prostatic biopsies.[4,10,18] When a simple retropubic or suprapubic prostatic operation precedes the development of prostatic fistulas there is often unsuspected carcinoma in the gland or else a small fibrous prostate has been injudiciously selected for open enucleation. Open surgery in such prostate glands is prone to easy capsular tears and rectal injury.[4] Over-aggressive transurethral resection of the prostate accounts for slightly more than 10 percent of prostatic surgery-related fistulas.[4,6,10,17]

A point not previously stressed is the relationship of abdominoperineal resection to the subsequent development of prostatoperineal fistula. In large reviews of abdominoperineal resection complications, prostatic fistula is mentioned only twice in 485 patients.[20,21] Three of our patients sustained prostatic injuries during the course of abdominoperineal resection. In each case the dissection of the anus and rectum was quite difficult, leading to the prostatic injury. In 2 cases the difficult dissection was caused by the presence of inflammatory bowel disease (ulcerative colitis and regional enteritis). In the third case a large rectal cancer was removed after extensive pelvic irradiation.

Spontaneous Healing of Prostatic Fistulas. It should be emphasized that 31 percent of prostatic fistulas may be expected to heal with conservative therapy alone. Such conservative therapy usually consisted of diversion of the urinary stream by either urethral catheterization or suprapubic tube drainage. The influence of fecal diversion on spontaneous healing could not be ascertained in our review.

Surgical Techniques. In all literature reports it is striking to the reader that success rates of 90 to 100 percent are reported for each surgical technique used in managing prostatic fistulas. In this regard, however, it is of interest that many reports contain information about failures of prior surgical therapy. Of 100 such cases available for review, 34 patients had undergone 70 separate operations prior to their definitive repairs.[3,5–10,12,13–15,18,19] In many instances these previous operations represented surgical techniques reported by other authors as resulting in 100 percent success rates. For example, 15 patients underwent 28 prior perineal repairs that resulted in failure.[5–10,12,15–18,19]

Timing of Surgical Repair. Most authors suggest an interval of weeks to months from the time a prostatic fistula is established to the time operative repair should be attempted. The acute fistula is often accompanied by urinary infection, fecal or urinary extravasation into perineal tissues and resultant inflammation and edema of the structures requiring repair. Perhaps the single exception to this principle of delay in formal operative therapy is the transrectal repair popularized by Vose. In the early, small fistulous tract, simple transrectal suturing of the defect may obviate the need for subsequent, more extensive, formal surgical repair.[2,4]

Fecal Diversion. Obviously, fecal diversion is not required in treating prostatoperineal fistulas. The role of colostomy in the management of the patient with prostatorectal fistula is unclear. As mentioned previously 42 percent of patients with prostatic fistulas were managed without the aid of colostomy fecal diversion. Opinion is divided among authors in the recent as well as the historical literature. Some authors state that colostomy is required in all such patients.[13,14,17] Others state unequivocally that colostomy is not needed, as long as fecal soilage is diminished by the use of preoperative catharsis and/or bowel antibiotics and the postoperative administration of constipating agents. Six different workers proposed the opinion that colostomy was definitely not necessary in the management of prostatic fistulas. However, a review of their 54 operated cases demonstrates that 31 patients (57 percent) had undergone colostomy.[4,7,10,16]

Suggested Management. The initial management of a patient with prostatoperineal or prostatorectal fistula is diversion of the urinary stream by either suprapubic tube drainage or urethral catheter, along with drainage of infection or extravasated urine and débridement of necrotic perineal tissues. If a urethral catheter is used some consideration should be given to the use of a multi-fenestrated catheter, allowing proper discharge of urethral secretions to avoid subsequent stricture formation and epididymitis. Whether colostomy assumes a prominent role at this point of the patient's management is unclear. Certainly, in prostatoperineal fistulas colostomy is not needed. In patients with large rectal defects or in those in whom fecal soilage seems to be the source of continued perineal infection and inflammation colostomy should be considered. With this initial therapy alone approximately a third of the patients will undergo spontaneous resolution of their fistulas.

If surgical repair is anticipated during the initial weeks following the onset of a prostatorectal fistula, the only procedure that should be used during this early period is the transrectal repair. More formal operations are likely to fail owing to edema and inflammation of the involved tissues. However, it should be recalled that this operation affords only limited exposure of the fistulous site and should be reserved for fistulas that are small and close to the anal verge.

After failure of conservative therapy or failure of initial rectal repair there are few guide lines to direct the urologist in his choice of a subsequent operation. Formal surgical approaches should not be used for at least a month, if not 3 to 6 months after the onset of fistula, so as to allow resolution of all perineal inflammation. If a colostomy has not been established by this point preoperative preparation of the patient with catharsis and bowel antibiotics is certainly necessary and postoperative use of constipating agents should be anticipated. To further prevent fecal soilage while providing the patient with sufficient nutrient postoperatively, one of the various elemental diets should be administered in the postoperative period instead of the restitution of a normal dietary patern.[16]

One's choice of operative technique should certainly be dictated by his previous experience. Again, if a small fistula persists close to the anal margin a further attempt at more formal rectal repair and layer closure may be all that is necessary. When the fistula is higher in the rectum or when exposure is poor the anal sphincter and posterior wall of the lower rectum may be transected. Although we have had no personal experience with this procedure as described by York Mason, it appears to give excellent exposure and the reported incidence of anal incontinence is nil. The paracoccygeal approach to repair of prostatorectal fistulas should be used only by surgeons who are familiar with the retrorectal anatomy. Anatomic guide lines are difficult to distinguish in this approach until the rectum is actually exposed.

Most urologists would have greatest familiarity with the perineal approach to fistula repair. This approach has the additional advantage that panendoscopic monitoring of the prostatic repair can be done. When this technique is used complete dissection of the rectum from the prostate and bladder is mandatory and the surgeon should not fear enlarging the fistulous openings in order to accomplish this.[4] After layer closure the freed rectum may then be brought downward so that the repairs in the prostate and rectum do not lie in apposition with one another. In the paracoccygeal or perineal repair it is always a good idea to interpose normal tissues between the recal and prostatic repair sites. Usually, this tissue would consist of levator ani musculature brought together in the midline. If the defect in the prostatic capsule is large it might be closed with the use of a free full-thickness skin graft.[18]

The rectal advancement procedure popularized by Young and Stone may be a reasonable alternative in the management of postatorectal fistulas, particularly if the fistula is low-lying and of relatively large size. In this procedure the rectum must be freed extensively and the middle hemorrhoidal vessels are usually ligated to achieve adequate mobilization to advance the portion of rectum containing the fistulous opening outside of the perineum. In high-lying fistulas, such a degree of mobilization may be impossible. Problems with the Young-Stone repair include mucosal irritation and fecal soiling. The exteriorized rectal mucosa continues to secrete mucous and is quite fragile. A small, though definite, incidence (20 percent) of patients treated with the Young-Stone maneuver do have the problem of fecal soiling.[7]

Although the majority of fistulas can be repaired with the aforementioned operations large fistulas or those associated with severe chronic infection or occurring in irradiated tissues may require additional forms of therapy. In such patients and in patients with fistulas after abdominoperineal resection the usual tissue barriers have either been destroyed or are ineffective to provide adequate support for fistula repair. The use of the omental pedicle graft, as described by Turner-Warwick, is of special value in these instances. The well vascularized omental pedicle can be freed from the gastric margin and brought down into the perineum, being interposed between the prostatic and rectal or cutaneous portions of the fistula. Margins of a large fistulous opening can be sewn to the omental pedicle without the need for formal closure of the defects. It should be emphasized that, after total colectomy, omentum is not available for future prostatic fistula repair and alternative means of interposing normal tissues might include the procedure described in this series (bulbocavernosus flap interposition).

After abdominoperineal resection, an additional surgical challenge exists, because in each case the bladder and prostate are retroflexed so that the prostatic fistula is quite close to the perineal incision site. In these cases the bladder and prostate should be freed and relocated anteriorly by a modification of the Marshall-Marchetti-Krantz technique.

REFERENCES

1. Weyrauch, H. M.: A critical study of surgical principles used in repair of urethrorectal fistula. Stanford Med Bull 9:2, 1951
2. Vose, S. N.: A technique for the repair of recto-urethral fistula. J Urol 61:790, 1949
3. Young, H. H. and Stone, H. B.: The opertive treatment of urethrorectal fistula. Presentation of a method of radical cure. J Urol 1:289, 1917
4. Goodwin, W. E., Turner, R. D. and Winter C. C.: Rectourinary fistula: principles of management and a technique of surgical closure. J Urol 80:246, 1958
5. Turner-Warwick, R. T., Wynne, E. J. and Handley-Askhen, M.: The use of the omental pedicle graft in the repair and reconstruction of the urinary tract. Br J Surg 54:849, 1967
6. Wilhelm, S. F.: Treatmnt of recto-urethral and recto-vesical fistula. J Urol 53:719, 1945
7. Lewis, L. G.: Repair of recto-urethral fistulas. J Urol 57:1173, 1947
8. Erlik, D.: Use of rectal wall flap for reconstruction of posterior urethra. J Urol 80:40, 1958
9. Kilpatrick, F. R. and Thompson, H. R.: Post-operative recto-prostatic fistula and closure by Kraske's approach. Br J Urol 34:470, 1962
10. Culp, O. S. and Calhoun, H. W.: A variety of rectourethral fistulas: experiences with 20 cases. J Urol 91:560, 1964
11. Limbert, D. J.: Transcoccygeal repair of prostatorectal fistula. J Urol 100:666, 1968
12. Talarico, R. D. and Fernandes, M.: Transrectal closure of urethrorectal fistula: a case report. J Urol 101:332, 1969
13. Kilpatrick, F. R. and Mason, A. Y.: Post-operative recto-prostatic fistula. Br J Urol 41:649, 1969
14. Mason, A. Y. and Kilpatrick, F. R.: Rectoprostatic and recto-urethral fistulae. Proc Roy Soc Med 66:245, 1973
15. Beneventi, F. A. and Cassebaum, W. H.: Rectal flap repair of prostatorectal fistula. Surg Gynec & Obst 133:489, 1971
16. Smith, A. M. and Veenema, R. J.: Management of rectal injury and rectourethral fistulas following radical retropubic prostatectomy. J Urol 108:778, 1972
17. Dahl, D. S., Howard, P. M. and Middleton, R. G.: The surgical management of rectourinary fistulas resulting from a prostatic operation: a report of 5 cases. J Urol 111:514, 1974
18. Morgan, C.: Dorsal rectotomy and full thickness skin graft for repair of prostatic urethrorectal fistula. J. Urol., 113:207, 1975
19. Olsson, C. A., Willscher, M. K., Krane, R. J. and Austen, G., Jr.: Present series
20. Tank, E. S., Ernst, C. B., Woolson, S. T. and Lapides, J.: Urinary tract complications of anorectal surgery. Am J Surg 123:118, 1972
21. Ward, J. N. and Nay, H. R.: Immediate and delayed urologic complications associated with abdominoperineal resection. Am J Surg 123:642, 1972

Commentary: Urinary Enteric Fistulas

Carl A. Olsson and Ralph deVere White

Although the accompanying article reviews prostatorectal and urethrorectal fistulas, it serves as an appropriate introduction to the discussion of urinary enteric fistulas affecting other structures because of similarities in management principles. These management principles have been born of years of trial and error and are worthy of emphasis in this Commentary. Before outlining the surgeon's task in the treatment of fistulous connections between the urinary tract and bowel, however, it would be reasonable to summarize the clinicopathologic features of these variously located fistulas.

Fistulous connections between the upper urinary tract and intestinal tract primarily involve the kidney and large bowel (renocolic). The ascending and descending colon are equally involved. Less frequently, renoduodenal and renogastric fistulas may occur. Finally, renoenteric fistulas involving the small bowel have been reported, occasionally because of ectopic positioning of the kidney.[1]

The etiology of renoalimentary fistulas is perinephritis and perinephric abcess. Heretofore, tuberculosis of the urinary tract was a prominent etiologic consideration; the most common diagnostic consideration today is perinephric abcess, usually secondary to calculous disease with pyonephrosis or pyocalyx.

The diagnosis of renoalimentary fistulas can be accomplished with intravenous pyelography (IVP), provided the kidney is still functioning. Often, however, the kidney will not demonstrate function because of the degree of inflammatory or calculous involvement. In these instances, retrograde pyelography establishes the diagnosis dependably. The treatment of renoalimentary fistulas is straightforward. Medical management alone is rarely successful. The nature of surgery should be dictated by the underlying pathologic condition. If renal function is damaged to an extensive degree, simple nephrectomy and closure of the bowel will be the optimum therapy. When there is sufficient renal function to warrant kidney-conserving surgery, stone removal, nephrostomy drainage, and closure of the defect with segmental colectomy is preferred.[1]

Vesicointestinal fistulas can be separated into three categories: appendicovesical, ileovesical, and the common colovesical fistula. Appendicovesical fistulas are predominantly due to perforated appendicitis with abcess formation. Ileovesical fistulas are primarily due to regional enteritis (Crohn's disease). Occasional examples of ileovesical fistula can be found due to tuberculosis of the small bowel.

Colovesical fistulas are the most common of all abnormal connections between the urinary tract and bowel. Men are affected more frequently than women by a ratio of approximately 3:1. The most common disease underlying the development of a colovesical fistula is diverticulitis, occuring in 50% to 75% of cases. Malignancy accounts for an additional 10% to 20% of cases. Adenocarcinoma of the colon is most frequently implicated in malignant causes of colovesical fistulas; an occasional example will follow the development of perforation through a bladder cancer.

Urinary symptoms are the predominant clue to the diagnosis of colovesical fistula. The majority of patients will have urinary tract infection. Most patients will have microscopic hematuria and pyuria. Irritative urinary symptoms are common. Pneumaturia may be found in at least two thirds of patients. As an aside, we should mention that pneumaturia is not pathognomonic of a connection between the bowel and the urinary tract. Pneumaturia may also result from fermentation of diabetic urine, gas-producing organism infection, or urinary tract instrumentation or catheterization. Fecaluria, on the other hand, is pathognomonic of a connection between the bowel and the urinary tract. Unfortunately, this finding occurs in only 20% to 50% of patients with colovesical fistulas.

Regarding the symptomatic presentation of patients with colovesical fistula, it should be recalled that although two thirds of patients may present with urinary symptoms, abdominal pain, and fever, nearly a third of patients will have *no* symptoms or else the symptoms will be overlooked by the physician.[2] Furthermore, many patients with diverticulitis underlying the colovesical fistula will have demonstrated no bowel symptoms before the onset of fistula.[3] Finally, more than a third of patients will have no physical findings on examination.[2] The absence of symptoms and signs combined with oversight on the part of the physician results in a delay of the diagnosis of colovesical fistula in numerous instances. The average duration of fistula is more than a year in most series, and extends to as long as 17 yr in some of the literature references.[2]

Therefore, a high index of suspicion of fistula is essential to the physician's diagnostic armamentarium. Armed with this suspicion, he must institute a series of investigations. Sigmoidoscopy will be helpful in only 10% to 15% of cases.[2,4] Cystoscopy is the most useful diagnostic test, confirming the diagnosis in at least two thirds of patients.[2-4] The findings on cystoscopy will vary. An actual fistulous connection or the presence of feces in the bladder can be discerned in more than a third of patients. A "herald" patch of local inflammatory infiltration or a localized area of bullous edema, usually situated on the posterolateral surface of the bladder (usually high) is a common finding. In these latter instances, abdominal compression may allow the visualization of colon gas bubbles emanating from the area of inflammation, even when the actual fistulous tract cannot be demonstrated.

Radiologic studies are also helpful in delineating colovesical fistulas, although not nearly so helpful as cystoscopy. Rarely, an upright flat film of the abdomen will show air fluid levels in the urinary tract. IVP may demonstrate bladder distortion, but demonstration of a fistulous connection should be expected in less than 20% of cases. Barium studies of the lower bowel are diagnostic for those patients with colon cancer with associated fistula. Actual demonstration of the fistula should be expected in 25% to 50% of patients at best.[2-4] One technique that may be employed to improve the diagnostic ability of barium enema is to perform radiography of the urinary sediment after barium study. Small quantities of barium may be detected in this fashion, confirmatory of a fistulous connection. Cystography is the most accurate of radiologic procedures in the delineation of colovesical fistula, resulting in demonstration of the fistula in at least one third of cases.

The diagnosis of colovesical fistula is usually established after a number of radiologic and endoscopic procedures. None should be omitted. For example, despite the low yield of sigmoidoscopy and barium enema, knowledge of the condition of the bowel is obviously essential in the management of the patient.

A final diagnostic maneuver should be discussed. Many workers suggest that oral or rectal administration of dyes may be employed to demonstrate a fistulous connection between the bowel and urinary tract. If the material administered is charcoal, the finding of charcoal in the urine would indeed confirm the presence of a fistulous tract. Similarly, IV injection of indigo carmine may be employed to look for colored feces. The use of methylene blue requires a caveat.[5] It is well known that methylene blue is absorbed by the intestine, so that the appearance of blue urine after either oral or rectal installation of this dye is meaningless. If methylene blue is employed, the only dependable test is to look for colored feces following intravesical installation of the dye.

As mentioned previously, the accompanying article on prostatorectal and urethrorectal fistulas serves as a reasonable introduction to the discussion of urinary enteric fistulas in general. There are only two real differences to be borne in mind. First, since the etiology of prostatorectal fistula is usually iatrogenic, the diagnosis is often made early in the course of the disease, in contradistinction to other urinary enteric fistulas. The second difference relates to success of conservative management. Spontaneous closure of prostatorectal fistulas may be anticipated in one third of cases. Spontaneous closure of other urinary enteric fistulas is rare indeed.

The rest of this Commentary will serve to emphasize the surgical principles to be followed in the management of any fistulous connection between the bowel and the lower urinary tract. It is mandatory that the tissues surrounding the fistulous tract be free of active infection at the time of surgical repair. For this reason, a chronic fistula, surrounded by clean fibrosis, may be managed with a single operative procedure.

In the case of a chronic uninflamed colovesical fistula, bowel resection and bladder closure may be performed without a diverting colostomy. If a colovesical fistula is found with a small amount of active inflammation surrounding it, the surgeon would be wise to carry out bowel resection, bladder closure, and temporary diverting colostomy. If an active abcess is discovered surrounding the colovesical fistula, conservative management would dictate that a diverting colostomy be employed alone initially, pending the resolution of the active sepsis with antibiotic care.[3,4] Diverting colostomy in itself is not a preventive against the development of a colovesical fistula.[3] Therefore, the surgeon should not depend on a colostomy alone to resolve the infection. Vigorous antibiotic therapy or abcess drainage or both will also be required.

In the case of adjacent organs (prostate and rectum), it is mandatory to carry out a wide operative dissection. This wide dissection will allow the surgeon to expose the normal, healthy tissues at the periphery of the fistulous tract. If the surgeon makes the unanticipated discovery of continued inflammation surrounding the fistulous tract, all the inflamed tissue should be resected so that reanastomosis or closure can be accomplished by the juxtaposition of normal tissues.

In the case of anatomically contiguous structures, the surgeon should position the suture line closing each structure so that they do not lie in apposition to one another. In the case of the prostate and rectum, this may be managed by adherence to the wide dissection technique, such that sufficient mobility of the structures is accomplished. When it is impossible to separate the two closures, they should be made at right angles to one another (horizontal prostate closure and vertical rectal closure). This particular principle is most applicable in dealing with prostatorectal fistulas repaired through a transrectal route, a York–Mason repair, or a transcoccygeal operation.

It is preferable to interpose normal tissues between the two structures to be closed. With perineal approaches to prostatorectal fistulas, this can be accomplished by closing the edges of levator ani between the prostate and rectum or else by carrying out a Young–Stone pull-through operation. Some workers feel that rectal pull-through operations result in an uncomfortable degree of neoanal irritation and mucus discharge. Other options for interposition of normal tissues between the two elements of a prostatorectal fistulous tract are the use of pedicle of omentum or a sling of gracilis muscle.

In the case of colovesical fistulas, the task of separating the organs is not nearly as difficult. It is unlikely that the area of colon anastomosis will necessarily lie in juxtaposition with the bladder closure. This separation of organs may explain the attitude of some workers who feel that resection of the bladder portion of the fistula is unnecessary, provided the contributing bowel pathology has been removed.[4] Our personal preference is to resect the edges of the bladder portion of the fistula in all cases. Certainly, in the case of a malignancy contributing to the fistula, this is an essential move. Even when dealing with inflammatory fistulae, the surgeon should remove the small amount of tissue surrounding the fistula, which may contain organisms that would potentially lead to a fistula recurrence. In the postirradiated pelvis, the wise surgeon will bear in mind the usefulness of an omental pedicle in separating the two structures definitively.

Some details of operative principles should be emphasized. A good bowel preparation is mandatory in all cases. Although fecal diversion is not necessary to the success of either prostatorectal or colovesical fistula repair, urinary drainage *is* essential. There does not seem to be any advantage in using suprapubic tube drainage compared to urethral catheter drainage in the case of colovesical fistula repair. In prostatorectal or urethrorectal fistulas, we prefer a suprapubic urinary tube, and when a urethral tube is employed, we use a fenestrated catheter to ensure drainage of all urethral secretions.

The suture material employed in the management of urinary fistulas is a matter of choice. Certainly absorbable material is adequate. Some workers advocate that the outer layer of closure of the two structures be carried out with nonabsorbable suture material. In fact, we prefer to employ nonabsorbable material in this fashion. However, other workers have had excellent operative results using absorbable material exclusively.

The use of drains and postoperative antibiotics demands comment. In the case of repairs between juxtaposed organs (prostate and rectum), liberal wound drainage is mandatory. This is easily accomplished through drains set dependently through a perineal incision. In the case of higher operative sites, it is not as easy to accomplish dependent drainage. However, it is still wise to insert a drain to the bowel anastomotic site, exiting through the lower quadrant. All these patients are contaminated and many are actually infected at the time of surgery. Our practice is to initiate antibiotic therapy a full 24 hr before surgery and maintain this therapy for 7 days. Our choice of antibiotic is dictated by the findings on urinary culture as well as by the operative findings. Ordinarily we employ an antibiotic known to be effective against the organism in the urine. If a mixed urinary tract infection is present, a battery of two or three antibiotics may be necessary. If there is active inflammatory reaction surrounding the fistula at the time of operation, we may alter antibiotic therapy so as to employ more potent agents as well as adding an agent known to be effective against microaerophilic organisms (*e.g.*, clindamycin).

A succinct statement of operative technique cannot be made for the management of these various fistulas. Attention to the above principles and a knowledge of the disease process is essential. Inventiveness on the part of surgeon may be necessary in many instances, however. Whenever possible, resection of the diseased bowel should be carried out in addition to removal of the fistula. If there is a choice between a conservative staged approach and a single operation, choose the former whenever there is doubt that the condition is not a simple chronic fistula. Finally, the nutritional status of the patient should be monitored carefully, as emphasized by Shatila and Ackerman.[3] Elemental diet feedings or parenteral hyperalimentation should be employed both preoperatively and postoperatively whenever there is a questionable nutritional status, particularly in patients with diseases known to be associated with cachexia (Crohn's disease and malignancy).

REFERENCES

1. Bissada NK, Cole AT, Freed FA: Renal alimentary fistula: An unusual urologic problem. J Urol 110:273, 1973
2. Carson CC, Malek RS, Remine WH: Urologic aspects of vesicoenteric fistulas. J Urol 119:744, 1978
3. Shatila AH, Ackerman NB: Diagnosis and management of colovesical fistulas. Surg Gynecol Obstet 143:71, 1976

4. Ray JE, Hughes JP, Gathright JB: Surgical treatment of colovesical fistula: The value of a one stage procedure. South Med J 69:40, 1976
5. Deshmukh AS, Bansal NK, Kropp KA: Use of methylene blue in suspected colovesical fistula. J Urol 118:819, 1977

ANNOTATED BIBLIOGRAPHY

Bissada NK, Cole AT, Freed FA: Renal alimentary fistula: An unusual urologic problem. J Urol 110:273, 1973

This article reports 4 cases of renal alimentary fistula and reviews an additional 92 cases from the literature. The most common lesion found was a renocolic fistula (59 cases). Other fistulas found were renoduodenal (22 cases), renogastric (7 cases), renoenteric (5 cases), renoappendiceal (2 cases), and renorectal (1 case). The authors state that indigo carmine and charcoal could be used to confirm the presence of fistulas, but these methods did not allow for demonstration of the anatomic site of involvement. Upper gastrointestinal series or barium enema studies are useful. Intravenous pyelography is also diagnostic when kidney function has not been impaired by the inflammatory process that usually leads to the fistulous tract. Retrograde pyelography was the most dependable study, however. Bowel disease was etiologic in the fistulous process in only four cases. The majority of renoalimentary fistulas resulted from renal infection. Before 1945 fulminant infections were the cause of fistula in over 80% of cases. In the antibiotic era (after 1945), infection still accounted for 41% of renoalimentary fistulas, most commonly involving a kidney that contained a staghorn calculus. In the postantibiotic era, the incidence of fistulas secondary to primary obstructive lesions (even without infection) and secondary to trauma (including iatrogenic) has risen to 24% and 35%, respectively.

Carson CC, Malek RS, Remine WH: Urologic aspects of vesicoenteric fistulas. J Urol 119:744, 1978

The authors review 100 consecutive cases of vesicoenteric fistula at the Mayo Clinic. Men predominated (male:female ratio, 2:1). The estimated duration of disease was 1 day to 17 yr, with a 14-mo average. A comment was made on the delay in diagnosis, resulting from absence of symptoms and signs or oversight by the physician in investigating patients promptly. Pneumaturia was present in two thirds of cases, fecaluria in a third. Urinary tract infection was present in 95% of cases, but less than a third of these had the anticipated mixed bacterial flora. The predominant cause of urinary tract infection was *Escherichia coli*. More than a third of patients had no findings on physical examination. Radiologic studies suggested a fistula in 18% to 35% of patients; sigmoidoscopy was diagnostic in 14%. The most successful diagnostic technique was cystoscopy (79%), demonstrating either the fistulous tract or feces in the bladder or else a localized area of inflammation and bullous edema. Diverticulitis of the colon accounted for 51% of cases. Colon cancer accounted for 16%, and bladder cancer for another 5%. Since this survey included small bowel fistulas, Crohn's disease was mentioned as the underlying disease process in 12% of patients. The management of these patients was also reviewed. Two thirds of patients underwent a one stage bowel resection and closure of the fistula. Twenty-seven percent had a two-stage procedure (bowel resection and diverting colostomy, followed by restoration of bowel continuity). A few patients had only fecal diversion. Patients with malignancy were more likely to undergo staged operations.

This group did not find that the presence of a malignancy underlying vesicoenteric fistula connoted a dismal prognosis. Forty-five percent of patients with such fistulas were alive after 3 yr. Although the operative experience was not detailed in this report, morbidity and mortality statistics were recounted. An operative mortality of 7% and a major operative complication rate of 9% were reported. Recurrent fistula developed in 6.5% of cases; patients with fistula recurrence suffered from Crohn's disease or malignancy.

Shatila AH, Ackerman NB: Diagnosis and management of colovesical fistulas. Surg Gynecol Obstet 143:71, 1976

This report summarizes the authors' experience with 27 patients suffering from colovesical fistula. Males predominated by a factor of 5 because of the contribution to the series from a Veterans Administration Hospital. There were 20 patients with diverticulitis and 5 with malignant causes for the colovesical fistula (4 colon cancer, 1 bladder cancer). Abdominal pain and pneumaturia were each present in two thirds of patients. Fecaluria, hematuria, and symptoms of urinary tract infection were each present in 50% of patients. No bowel symptoms prior to the onset of fistula were present in nearly half the patients with diverticulitis. These authors' experience also speaks to the delay in diagnosis of colovesical fistulas. The estimated duration of fistula ranged from 3 days to 3 yr. The diagnostic test most useful in detection of the fistula was cystoscopy (two thirds accurate). Cystography was diagnostic in 40% of cases; other radiographic studies were less efficient. With regard to management, the authors state that malignancy underlying a colovesical fistula is an ominous sign; no patient with malignancy was treated satisfactorily in their experience. With regard to colovesical fistulas of inflammatory origin, the authors decried the use of colostomy alone. In fact, three of their reported cases had undergone transverse colostomy for other complications of diverticulitis before the onset of urinary fistula. Fistulas occurred in these three patients despite the protective transverse colostomy. Patients with inflammatory causes of colovesical fistula were managed by single-staged approach predominantly. Complications were experienced only when this technique was employed in the presence of active inflammation. The authors present five criteria necessary for the selection of a single-staged approach to the treatment of colovesical fistula: (1) no abscess present, (2) no severe inflammatory change in the surrounding tissues, (3) no colon obstruction, (4) no involvement of a third organ, and (5) good nutritional status. If a patient satisfied these five criteria, the authors preferred a single operative procedure for the management of colovesical fistula.

Ray JE, Hughes JP, Gathright JB: Surgical treatment of colovesical fistula: The value of a one stage procedure. South Med J 69:40, 1976

The authors review 43 cases of colovesical fistula. Males predominated by a factor of 3.3. Symptoms related to the urinary tract predominantly. Pneumaturia was present in 79% of patients, fecaluria in 21%. In more than 50% of patients the symptoms had been present for more than 6 mo. Cystography was diagnostic in only one third of patients; barium enema was diagnostic in 44%. When the fistula was due to diverticulitis, however, the radiographic features of diverticulitis were present in only one third of cases; the other two thirds of cases showed radiographic evidence for diverticulosis alone. Sigmoidoscopy was diagnostic in less than 10% of cases. Cystoscopy, on the other hand, was diagnostic in over 80% of cases. In one third of patients the actual fistulous tract was detected on cystoscopy; other patients showed the typical "herald" patch of localized inflammation and edema. Diverticulitis accounted for 77% of cases; cancer accounted for 12%. Thirty-five patients underwent fistula repair. Twenty-two patients had the operation carried out in a single stage; 13 patients underwent a two- or three-stage repair. There was one operative death, and the complications resulting from the single-staged approach were much less than those experienced after the multistaged operations. Part of the improved morbidity with one-stage repair can be explained by patient selection. The single-staged approach was reserved for those patients with a chronic fistula, without any inflammatory mass or active abcess. If a small inflammatory mass was present, a two-stage approach was employed; if there was an active abcess, diverting colostomy was carried out initially, followed by an additional two operations. This article discusses the evolution of staged to single-staged operations for the management of colovesical fistula. Initially, because of the morbidity, mortality, and high fistula recurrence rate associated with the single operative technique, staged procedures became the treatment of choice. When it was recognized that chronic fistulas without active inflammation of abcess could be managed with a single operation associated with low morbidity and fistula recurrence, the repeated hospitalization, lengthy disability, and additional expense seemed unwarranted in the majority of patients.

Deshmukh AS, Bansal NK, Kropp KA: Use of methylene blue in suspected colovesical fistula. J Urol 118:819, 1977

This article emphasizes the bowel absorption of methylene blue. Previous workers had demonstrated that oral administration of methylene blue leaves 75% of the dye excreted in the urine. It has been suggested that rectal instillation of methylene blue can be used to demonstrate a colovesical fistula. These workers studied the rectal absorption of methylene blue instilled into the rectum (50 mg) in volunteer patients requiring in-dwelling urinary catheter drainage for outlet obstruction. All patients had normal renal function; no patient had bowel disease. In each instance methylene blue could be detected in the urine. It is clear, then, that methylene blue cannot be used to confirm a suspected diagnosis of colovesical fistula when administered either orally or by enema. Its use should be limited to bladder instillation followed by observation of the feces for blue.

Overview: Management of Prostatic Fistulas

Willy Mathisen

A fistulous communication between the rectum and the male urethra may be *congenital* or *acquired,* usually as a postprostatectomy complication or after trauma to the perineum. In rare cases a rectourethral fistula may develop in connection with a prostatic abscess or a rectal carcinoma.

Many methods are described for repairing rectourethral fistulas, and no set rule applies in all cases. I agree with the well-known principle: fit the operation to the patient and not the patient to the operation. A thorough knowledge of the anatomy and physiology of the rectal outlet and structure adjacent to it is necessary.

Congenital rectourethral fistula results from failure of the urogenital septum to separate completely the rectum from the posterior urethral segment. The fistulous connections are at the level of the verumontanum or in the membranous urethra. These fistulas are usually in connection with a high type of imperforate anus. The rectal stump is above the pelvic floor. A more infrequent type is the so-called H-type fistula in which the urine passes preferentially into the otherwise normal rectum at the pectinate line.

Treatment of congenital rectourethral fistula should start with a transverse colostomy. The distal intestinal segment should be irrigated and cleared. The repair of the fistula is postponed for some weeks.

Reconstruction of an imperforate rectum is best done through a sacrococcygal approach. The operation is performed with the child in a prone position with the pelvis elevated by a sandbag. To proceed, introduce a catheter through the urethra to the bladder. Make the incision in the midline over the sacrum down to the anal region. Divide the median raphe of the diaphragmatic part of the levator to give entrance to the supralevator space. Sufficient mobilization is usually possible through this approach to bring the end of the rectum through the puborectal sling down to the perineum. Ligate and divide the fistula and mobilize the rectum proximally by finger dissection. Extend the dissection as high as possible. Open the rectum and bring it out through the anal ring and suture it to the skin. Close the operative area with a cigarette drain to the perirectal fossa. Drain the bladder through a suprapubic catheter for 3 wk, and close the colostomy 2 mo later. If the rectal pouch ends more than 2 cm from the external anal sphincter, perform an abdominal mobilization of the sigmoid colon.

In *adults* the perineal repair is most commonly used. From the literature it appears that there is a 50% recurrence rate after perineal repair. Why is this so high? Some general principles apply to repairing of fistulous connections between two hollow organs. Besides preparing a good exposure in all directions around the fistula, all scar tissues must be removed and the fistulous openings closed by inverted sutures. Most important is to separate the two suture lines by interposing living tissue. A transverse colostomy should be done some weeks before repairing the fistula; this will diminish the fecal loading of the fistulous region and reduce the risk of infection.

After failure of initial perineal repair of a rectourethral fistula, the next step depends on the size of the remaining fistula. A minor fistulous leakage may heal spontaneously and may be treated conservatively by a in-dwelling urethral catheter. If the fistula still persists after 2 to 3 mo, I think more sophisticated surgical techniques are required. In my experience the best way to treat difficult rectourethral fistulas is by an abdominoperineal pull-through operation.

I always perform a transverse colostomy weeks before the main operation. Clear and irrigate the distal intestinal segment. Treat the urinary tract infection adequately.

Perform the operation with the patient in a lithotomy position. Introduce a catheter through the urethra to the bladder. Start the operation in the perineum with a transverse curved incision 2 cm anterior to the anus. Approach the fistula from either side, and carry out the dissection above the prostate. Divide the fistula and freshen and close the opening in the prostatic urethra by inverted sutures in two layers using absorbable suture material. Continue the dissection up to the peritoneum. Carry on the mobilization of the rectum posteriorly well above the insertion of the levator ani muscles.

Continue the operation through a midline incision in the abdomen. Incise the posterior peritoneum vertically to both sides of the sigmoid colon and the rectum, giving access to the vasculature of the mesocolon. Intestinal vessels may be secured if necessary to permit mobilization of the sigmoid. Take care to preserve the marginal arcade. It is usually not necessary to mobilize the splenic flexure.

Divide the rectum distally to the fistulous opening and remove the mucosa from the remaining rectal stump. Pull out the rectum with the fistulous opening through the anal ring, excise it, and suture it to the skin. Introduce a suction drain through a stab incision in the iliac fossa and take it to the pelvis alongside the intestinal wall. Close the abdominal and perineal wounds. The bladder is drained through a suprapubic tube for 3 wk. The colostomy is closed a couple of months later.

I have used this method in five patients with rectourethral fistulas of different causes. All patients had been operated on several times without success. A youth of 15 had been operated on 12 times before he was admitted to our service. Complete healing of the fistulas was accomplished in all patients with a single operation.

Different *complications* are reported after a pull-through operation for rectal carcinoma. Necrosis of the distal intestinal stump may occur, but that should not happen in an operation for rectourethral fistulas because the mobilization of the sigmoid colon does not need to be very extensive.

Bladder denervation and retrograde ejaculation have also occured after rectal amputation. I have not seen any of these complications.

The most common abnormality is stricture at the site of anastomosis. This happened in a man of 52, who required dilatation for some time.

Some degree of mucosal prolaps with mucus secretion and skin irritation occurred in one patient with a weak anal sphincter. He was completely cured after one-side gracilis plasty.

Many rectourethral fistulas may heal after perineal repair, but if the first attempt has been unsuccessful, I don't think the surgeon should try the same operation again. In such cases an abdominoperineal pull-through procedure should be the method of choice. The advantages are removal of all damaged rectal tissue and its replacment with completely normal tissue at the site of the fistulous tract. The complications are few and easy to manage.

PART THIRTY-TWO

SURGERY OF VESICAL EXSTROPHY, EPISPADIAS, AND PENILE LENGTHENING

78

EXSTROPHY AND CLOACAL EXSTROPHY

Robert D. Jeffs, M.D.

Professor of Pediatric Urology, The James Buchanan Brady Urological Institute and
The Johns Hopkins University School of Medicine, Baltimore, Maryland.

Urologic Clinics of North America—Vol. 5, No. 1, February 1978
Symposium on Gongential Anomalies of the Lower Genitourinary Tract

EMBRYOLOGY

Classic exstrophy and cloacal exstrophy are developmental abnormalities resulting from perforation of the abnormal cloacal membrane. Normally, ingrowth of mesenchyme between the ectodermal and endodermal layers of the cloacal membrane allows completion of the pubic arch and development of midline fusion of the infraumbilical structures of the abdominal wall. Simultaneous down-growth of the urorectal septum divides the cloaca into the anterior bladder and posterior rectal portions and meets the clocal membrane in the perineum before perforation, dividing the subsequent perforation into anal and urogenital openings. The paired genital tubercules migrate medially and fuse in the midline cephalad to the cloacal membrane before perforation.

The abnormal development of the cloacal membrane results in a spectrum of conditions that vary in severity from glandular epispadias, pubic diastrasis without exstrophy, and superior vesical fissure, to cloacal exstrophy, which is the most severe form of the defect. Classically, bladder exstrophy accounts for more than 50 percent of the patients in the spectrum.

Department of Pediatric Urology
The James Buchanan Brady Urological Institute
Baltimore, Maryland 21201

The high incidence of classic exstrophy,[16] the absence of the exstrophy stage in normal embryologic development, and the rare occurrence of exstrophy in other mammals[19] are facts that require inclusion in any explanation of the pathologic development of this complex.

Two main theories of embryologic maldevelopment require mention. Patton and Barry[21] theorize that caudal displacement of the paired primordia of the genital tubercle is the basic abnormality that permits persistence of the cloacal membrane cephalad to the fused phallus. Depending on the degree of caudal displacement and the timing of rupture of the membrane, conditions of varying severity would develop, from glandular epispadias to cloacal exstrophy. Epispadias might be expected to occur most frequently, as this would result from minimal or mild phallic displacement. Furthermore, severe displacement would be expected to cause dislocations of the penis from the inferior ramus of the pubis, a condition that rarely occurs.

Marshall and Muecke[4,17,19] believe that the basic defect in the complex of conditions is an abnormal overdevelopment of the cloacal membrane, preventing migration of the mesenchyme tissue between its endodermal and ectodermal layers. Rupture of this abnormal membrane creates a larger defect than the usual anal and urogenital orifices, thus exposing the urethra and bladder to the extent that the infraumbilical abdominal wall is deficient. Central perforation of the cloacal membrane would account for the high incidence of incontinent epispadias and classic exstrophy, and superior and inferior perforation for the less frequent penile epispadias and superior vesical fissure. Early perforation before descent of the urorectal septum would result in cloacal exstrophy.

Pohlman's[22] observation of an abnormal embryo in which the cloacal membrane was unusually large lends support to the Marshall-Muecke theory of overdevelopment. Further support is seen in the experimental production of cloacal exstrophy in the chick embryo. Muecke[19] inserted a plastic disc in the tail bud region of the developing embryo, preventing normal cloacal membrane regression and resulting in exstrophy of the cloaca.

In mammals other than man, the exstrophy complex is rare. This may be explained by the close association of the cloacal membrane to the allantois, which is a vital structure in obtaining nutriment from the uterine wall in animals but is unimportant in man. Abnormalities of the cloacal membrane would be expected to interfere with the allantois and to cause early demise in animal embryos, whereas the unimportance of the allantois in man permits survival despite the abnormal development of the cloacal membrane.

CLASSIC EXSTROPHY

Anatomy. The urinary tract is open and everted from the urinary meatus to the umbilicus, with fusion of the bladder and urethral mucosa to the surrounding skin and with foreshortening of the urethra and bladder as measured from glans penis to umbilicus. The ureters end in short tunnels on a wide trigone, and will reflux almost invariably if the bladder is closed. The pubic bones are separated at the symphysis by 3 to 10 cm, with accompanying lateral rotations of the acetabulum and femur. The crural attachment of the penis to the inferior ramus of the pubis and the short urethral groove produce a short stubby penis with dorsal chordee. The scrotum is broad, and the testicles are usually palpable, but may be retractile. Orchiopexy is seldom necessary to correct nondescent.

There is wide separation of the rectus muscles even above the umbilicus, where the linea alba is widely spread. Umbilical and inguinal hernias are common but may not be apparent at birth. The bladder mucosa is usually smooth with intact transitional epithelium at birth, but ulceration and inflammatory changes quickly occur from trauma and contaminations. Gross and mi-

croscopic intestinal tissue, polyps, and mucosal cysts may be present at birth and influence the choice of treatment. The anal canal may be patulous and anteriorly displaced; prolapse is common. Covered anus with perineal fistula may occur in the male, and rectovaginal fistulas may occur in the female. In the female, the clitoral halves and labia are widely separated, exposing the vaginal orifice at the end of the urethral groove. The müllerian tract may show varying degrees of duplication. Unrelated anomalies in other systems occur, but there is no pattern to their occurrence. Renal and ureteral anomalies such as hydronephrosis, dysgenesis, agenesis, and horseshoe kidney occur in a small percentage of the patients.

Investigation and Care at Birth. The initial care of exstrophy in the newborn should begin in the delivery room. The diagnosis is obvious, but all too often no thought is given to the protection and eventual management of the delicate exposed bladder. When the umbilical cord is divided, heavy clamps that can scrape and scuff the exposed normal transitional epithelium should be avoided. Sutures should be used to tie the cord, and the stump prevented from lying on the bladder. The child should be placed undressed in an isolette and the bladder periodically moistened with warm saline. Saline mist may be directed at the bladder to prevent drying during the early hours after delivery. If transportation to a distant center requires that the baby be clothed and the bladder covered, a moist sheet of silastic membrane or smooth plastic film should cover the bladder area to protect it from the diaper and clothing. Drying and excoriation caused by bladder coverings frequently denude the delicate bladder mucosa. Only when a decision is made not to close the bladder should Vaseline dressing be applied and diapering be started. Contact with a dressing, diaper, and clothing causes the mucosa to become thick and edematous and promotes bacterial invasion, producing a panmural cystitis and later chronic changes of squamous metaplasia and cystitis cystica. Stimulation of the bladder by foreign material causes detrusor contraction, pain, tenesmus, and unnecessary straining that can promote rectal prolapse, to which these babies are prone.

The baby should be examined by a pediatrician and immediate consultation sought by a urologist who is familiar with the treatment possibilities in exstrophy so that the infant's general health can be assessed, coexisting anomalies detected, and the anatomy of the exstrophy condition appreciated. Assessment will be made of the cardiopulmonary status, central nervous system, and spinal column as well as special anomalies of the anal canal, penis, ureteral orifices, bladder, and abdominal wall. As the child approaches 48 hours of age, renal output and function can be assessed and kidney and ureteral architecture determined by intravenous pyelogram.

TREATMENT ALTERNATIVES

Three alternatives exist in the treatment of classic exstrophy: dressing and diapering, urinary diversion, and functional closure. The first, although compatible with health and longevity in some, is socially and psychologically unacceptable in modern society. When early attempts to cover or close the bladder failed to provide satisfactory continence, urinary diversion and bladder excision became the treatment of choice. Anorectal imperfections, acidosis, and stomal difficulties prevent this alternative from being ideal in many patients, yet it is the best alternative in some patients not suitable for functional closure. Functional closure, frequently attempted unsuccessfully in the past, can now be approached with a better prospect of success. Johnston and Kagan[10] have reviewed the published results of closure and generously ascribe a 20 percent success rate overall. Staged reconstruction, however, in their collected results indicate success in 40 percent of the patients. The mode of treatment should be selected after study of the anatomy of the defect, choosing the treatment that is most likely to succeed in rehabilitating the child for a comfortable, healthy, and productive life.

Functional Closure. The staged approach to functional closure appears to offer a good prospect of rehabilitation with continence.[8] We have selected 53 patients for closure from 72 cases of classic exstrophy and have completed treatment in 39 of them. Sixty percent are continent, 20 percent have partial control and are expected to improve, and 20 percent have failed and have required other management. The approach to treatment has been to select closure for those patients who have a distensible functioning detrusor muscle of a size that is expected to increase in volume and in whom genital rectal and upper tract anomalies will not unduly complicate the staged reconstruction. Patients with severe hydronephrosis, small fibrotic bladder patch, penile duplication, and rectovaginal fistula may not be suitable for bladder and urethral reconstruction. Detrusor function may be tested in the newborn by stimulating the bladder surface with cold saline or the gloved finger and observing the resulting muscular contraction.

The plan of treatment for those patients selected for closure begins by converting exstrophy to incontinent epispadias early in life. Incontinence and reflux are treated by bladder neck and urethral reconstruction at three or four years of age, and closure of the epispadiac penis follows in the fourth or fifth year. One-stage total repair of the bladder, the continence mechanism, the reflux, and the epispadias depends on success in all aspects of the procedure to achieve a good result, and failure may prevent subsequent successful revision of the bladder neck, ureteral vesical junction, and penis.

In staged reconstruction, initial closure is best performed in the neonatal period.[2] When the child can be evaluated by the pediatric, surgical, and anesthesiology teams at birth, closure should be carried out within the first 48 hours when the pelvis is easily molded to allow pubic closure. Osteotomy appears to be necessary to provide firm pubic apposition when the child is more than a few days of age. While the bladder can be closed and covered in the older child with facial flaps, a firm fibrous closure of the pelvic ring in front of the bladder neck and urethra appears to contribute to the eventual success in producing a continent reconstruction of the bladder neck and urethra.* Later bladder closure can also be successful, but progressive changes in bladder epithelium and detrusor muscle make this less desirable.

Initial Closure (Figs. 1, 2, and 3). In the first stage, a 2 cm wide strip of bladder neck and urethral tissues, distal to the ureteral orifices, is selected to form the bladder neck and posterior urethra. The mucosa is closed in the midline, and muscular closure is buttressed anteriorly by approaching tissues of the urogenital diaphragm, which are detached from the body of the pubis on each side. The bladder is closed above, draining the ureters by stenting catheters and the bladder by a Malecot catheter. The three catheters emerge suprapubically through the abdomen at a point that corresponds to the normal position of the umbilicus, and the resulting scar will have the appearance of an umbilicus above the linear midline closure. The pubic arch is approximated by a horizontal mattress suture of number two nylon that passes through the body of the pubic on each side and is tied anteriorly.

The dorsal urethral groove of the epispadiac penis is short and the penis is dorsally recurved. The glans and verumontanum of the prostate may be closely apposed. Diversion of the urethral strip and dissection of the corpora to free the suspensory ligament of the penis and its anterior attachment to the inferior ramus of the pubis provides penile length and corrects dorsal chordee (see the article by John W. Duckett in this symposium, p. 107).[10] Pink transitional skin adjacent to the prostate or urethra is moved distally to elongate the urethral groove after joining the mobilized corpora in the midline. Thus, additional penile length is obtained by using three maneuvers: release of suspensory ligaments, release of crural attachment, and crural approximation that occurs with closure of the pelvic ring. No

---

* Toguri, A., Churchill, B., and Schillinger, J.: personal communication.

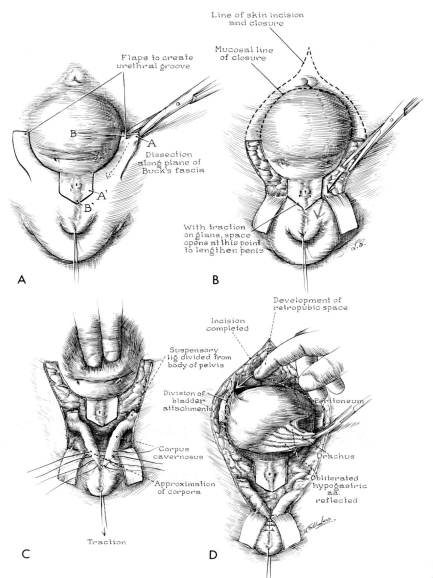

Fig. 1. Urethral lengthening and bladder mobilization.

attempt is made to complete the epispadias repair at this age. The mucosal strip of the bladder neck and urethra are not stented, to avoid pressure injury and infection. Nonreactive sutures are used throughout. Broad spectrum antibiotics are used to convert a contaminated field to a clean surgical wound.

The Incontinent Interval. Suprapubic drainage and leg suspension in Bryant's traction is maintained for three to four weeks to ensure firm fibrous healing of the pubic ring and soft tissues. The urethra should be calibrated before removing the suprapubic catheter to ensure free drainage for the bladder and refluxing ureters. Regular examination by urine cultures, residual urine studies, and intravenous pyelograms is required to ensure that the kidneys are not damaged by back pressure, reflux, or infection, Urethral dilatation may be required to improve drainage, or, if bladder neck closure is unexpectedly continent, early ureteral reimplantation to correct reflux may be necessary.

Bladder Neck Reconstruction. At three or four years of age, when the uninfected bladder is noted to have a smooth thin mucosa and a capacity of 40 to 50 ml,

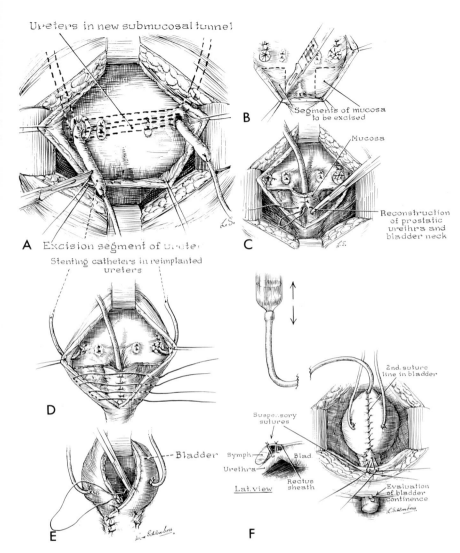

Ureters in new submucosal tunnel

A Excision segment of ureter

B Segments of mucosa to be excised

C Mucosa

Reconstruction of prostatic urethra and bladder neck

Stenting catheters in reimplanted ureters

D

E Bladder

Suspensory sutures

Symph — Urethra — Blad.

Rectus sheath

Lat. view

F 2nd. suture line in bladder

Evaluation of bladder continence

Fig. 4. Note the transtrigonal advancement to correct reflux, bladder neck and urethral reconstruction, and bladder neck suspension. Drawings by Leon Schlossberg reprinted by permission from Jeffs, R. D.: Exstrophy. *In* Campbell's Urology, Philadelphia, WB Saunders Co., 1978, in press.

otomy, but cosmetic appearance and genital reconstruction are definitely improved by this procedure.

A well coordinated surgical team can perform osteotomy, colon conduit drainage, cystectomy, and genital reconstruction during a single administration of anesthesia. However, initial colon conduit diversion followed later by osteotomy, cystectomy and genital reconstruction may be advisable because of the duration of the effects of the anesthetic and the small size of the child.

Diversion should be performed when the patient is between six months and one year of age, and cystectomy with genital reconstruction performed three to six months later. Final epispadias repair of the lengthened urethral groove is accomplished when the patient is three to four years of age.

CLOACAL EXSTROPHY

Cloacal exstrophy is the most severe defect associated with perforation of the abnormal cloacal membrane. Perforation occurs at an early stage before complete descent of the urorectal septum, allowing eversion of both the bladder and the hindgut. The defect may be associated with many other anomalies, including meningomyelocele and paralysis, omphalocele, short small intestine, duplication of the appendix, and a very short phallus. The child's condition may be critical at birth, and attempts to support life may be futile or morally and ethically unwise. The more robust infant without serious spinal defects will survive, and reparative surgery must be undertaken. The cecum protrudes between the two lateral bladder halves, and the ileum may prolapse through the ileocecal valve. Distally a small blind rudimentary hindgut opens on the cecum near the perineum. The ureter on each side enters the distal bladder halves.

Fluid and electrolyte loss from the short small intestine can be lifethreatening. Fluid replacement and dietary management of this problem is difficult and may prove insurmountable.

At birth, rapid and complete assessment should be made of the child and its chances of survival. The severity of spinal anomalies with associated paralysis and hydrocephalus, the size of the omphalocele, the associated cardiopulmonary status, the length of absorptive bowel, and the renal status will indicate whether sustained life is possible and whether management and reconstruction are likely to be successful. Penile length will suggest whether the surviving male child is likely to function sexually or whether sex reassignment is advisable.[25]

Ileostomy or colostomy, depending on the length of usable colon, is first performed. The midline defect can then be closed by excising the omphalocele and joining medial edge of the two bladder halves. Consideration can also be given to the bladder and abdominal wall closure without osteotomy at the time of ileostomy or at a later stage. The child's early treatment will focus on management of the ileostomy, fluid and electrolyte balance, and nutrition. The management of urinary incontience from the incontinent urethra of the closed bladder halves is deferred until satisfactory growth and development are established.

Five patients whom we have managed underwent early colostomy or ileostomy and subsequent bladder closure, leaving them incontinent through the reconstructed urethra. This course of action allowed time for their intestinal absorption problems to settle before the most advantageous type of urinary control was decided upon. One patient subsequently had an ileal conduit, one had a trouble free suprapubic catheter, and one eventually developed urethral continence. In two patients the incontinence has not yet been handled. The possibility of using an artificial sphincter is being considered.

Sex reassignment was carried out in two male patients due to a very short penile length, and two other males might have been better managed in the same way. The adequacy of eventual penile reconstruction must be considered in all males with cloacal exstrophy and in some patients with classic exstrophy. The testicles in reassigned males are removed at the time of bladder closure and genital reconstruction.

When these children show promise that they will survive, sex reassignment, bladder closure, and genital reconstruction should be carried out early to establish proper parental attitudes toward the child's potential and its sex of rearing.

MALIGNANCY

Untreated exstrophy has a tendency to develop adenocarcinoma in later years.[6] It is not known whether this condition arises from developmental rests or metaplasia of normal epithelial structures.[7] In patients with closed exstrophy, four cases of malignant transformation have developed, two with rhabdomyosarcoma and two with epithelial malignant disease.[10] Early closure may help to prevent malignant change in epithelium, but probably has little bearing on the development of rhabdomyosarcoma. Epithelium that is invaginated in prostatic closure after cystectomy in patients who have undergone urinary diversion is also potentially at risk.

Carcinoma of the colon has been reported to occur at the site of the ureterointestinal anastomosis, and it may be expected to appear in patients with colon conduits and ureterocolosigmoidostomy.[20]

Long term follow-up and repeated investigation of patients who have undergone urinary diversion and closure of exstrophy are required. A searching history and physical examination to detect bleeding or discharge, and an intravenous pyelogram to assess ureteral architecture and drainage are advised. Patients with closed exstrophy over the age of 20 years should have cystoscopy performed at yearly intervals to allow early detection of mucosal change. Long term experience in bladder closure is rare, but a pathology examination of the entire bladder and prostate of a 17 year old patient who died accidentally showed no evidence of malignant or premalignant change in his exstrophied bladder, which was closed at birth.

SUMMARY

Classic bladder exstrophy and cloacal exstrophy are grotesque anomalies in the eyes of young parents. An immediate evaluation by an experienced team is required to assess the variations in the condition and to devise a plan of treatment that can reassure the parents as to eventual prognosis and rehabilitation. This plan of treatment must include provisions for renal preservation, urinary control, cosmetic appearance, and sexual function.

The newborn is usually normal in respect to nutrition and its cardiopulmonary state, and will tolerate surgery well. Passive parental immunity provides better resistance to intercurrent illness at this time than will be present in the later months of infancy. When applicable, the initial stages of surgery should be undertaken at birth when the pelvic ring can be approximated without osteotomy and the bladder mucosa has not deteriorated from inflammatory changes.

Parental attitudes toward the child as well as successful reconstruction may both be best served by immediate surgery to begin reconstruction and reduce the visible defect.

REFERENCES

1. Ambrose, S. S., and O'Brien, D. P.: Surgical embryology of the exstrophy epispadias complex. Surg Clin North Am 54:1379, 1974
2. Ansell, J. S.: Vesical exstrophy. In Glenn, J. F. (Editor): Urologic Surgery. Hagerstown, Harper and Row, 1975, 316
3. Bennett, A. H.: Exstrophy of the bladder treated by ureterosigmoidostomies: long-term evaluation. Urology 2:156, 1973
4. Cohen, S. J.: Ureterozysloneostomie. Eine neue Antirefluxtechnik. Aktuelle Urologie 6:24, 1975
5. Culp, D. A. The histology of the exstrophied bladder, J Urol 191:538, 1964
6. Dees, J. E.: Congenital epispadias with incontinence. J Urol 62:513, 1949
7. Hendren, W. H.: Exstrophy of the bladder—an alternative method of managment. J Urol 115:195, 1976
8. Jeffs, R. D., Charrois, R., Many, M., and Juriansz, A. R.: Primary closure of the exstrophied bladder. In Scott, R. (Editor): Current Controversies in Urologic Management. Philadelphia, W. B. Saunders Company, 1972, 235
9. Jeffs, R. D., and Schwarz, G. R.: Ileal conduit urinary diversion in children: computer analysis followup from 2 to 16 years. J Urol 114:285, 1975
10. Johnston, J. H., and Kogan, S. J.: Problems in surgery. June, 1974
11. King, L. R., and Wendel, E. F.: Primary cystectomy and permanent urinary diversion in the treatment of exstrophy of the urinary bladder. In Scott, R. (Editor): Current Controversies in Urologic Management. Philadelphia, W. B. Saunders Company, 1972, 244
12. Kozak, J. A., Watkins, W. E., and Jewell, W. R.: Neoplastic stoma obstruction: a complication of ureterosigmoidostomy. J Urol 96:891, 1966
13. Leadbetter, G. W.: Surgical correction of total urinary incontinence. J Urol 91:261, 1964
14. Leadbetter, W. F.: Consideration of problems incident to performance to ureteroenterostomy: report of a technique. J Urol 73:67, 1955
15. Marshall, V. F., Marchetti, A. A., and Krantz, K. E.: The correction of stress incontinence by simple vesicourethral suspension. Surg Gynecol Obstet 88:509, 1949
16. Marshall, V. F., and Muecke, E. C.: Variations in exstrophy of the bladder. J Urol 88:766, 1962
17. Marshall, V. F., and Muecke, E. C.: Congenital abnormalities of the bladder malformations. In Alken, C. E., Dix, V. W., and Goodwin, W. E.: Handbuch der Urologie, New York, Springer-Verlag, 1968, 192
18. McIntosh, J. F., and Worley, G., Jr.: Adenocarcinoma arising in exstrophy of the bladder. Report of two cases and review of the literature. J Urol 73:820, 1955
19. Muecke, E. C.: The role of the cloacal membrane in exstrophy: the first successful experimental study. J Urol 92:659, 1964
20. Oetjen, L. H., Jr., Campbell, J. L., Thomley, M. W., and Pausons, R. L.: Carcinoma of the colon following ureterosigmoidostomies: report of a case. J Urol, 104:536,1970
21. Patton, J. F., and Barry, A.: The genesis of exstrophy of the bladder and epispadias. Am. J. Anat., 90:35, 1952.
22. Pohlman, A. G.: The development of the cloaca in human embryos. Am J Anat, 12:1, 1911
23. Scott, F. B., Bradley, W. E., and Timms, G. W.: Treatment of urinary incontinence by an implantable prostatic urinary sphincter. J Urol, 112:75, 1974
24. Shapiro, S. R., Lebowitz, R., and Colodny, A. H.: Fate of 90 children with ileal conduit urinary diversion a decade later: analyses of complications, pyelography, renal function, and bacteriology. J Urol, 114:289, 1975
25. Spence, H. M., Hoffman, W. W., and Pate, V. A.: Exstrophy of the bladder. I. Long term results in a series of 37 cases treated by ureterosigmoidostomy. J Urol, 114:133, 1974
26. Tank, E. S., and Lidenauer, S. M.: Principles of management of exstrophy of the cloaca. Am J Surg., 119:95, 1970
27. Welch, K. J.: Cloacal exstrophy. In Mustard, S., et al. (Editors): Pediatric Surgery. Ed. 2. Chicago, Year Book Medical Publishers, Inc., 1961, Vol. 2, 1233
28. Young, H. H.: An operation for cure of incontinence associated with epispadias. J Urol, 7:1, 1922

Commentary: Functional Closure: A Practical Goal

Edward C. Muecke

Ten years ago we reported on the then-accumulated clinical experience with functional closure of typical exstrophy of the bladder and concluded that surgical restoration to normalcy of bladder exstrophy should be regarded as an investigational program unless the surgeon could achieve a success rate of 50% or better.[1] The staged surgical procedures, as described by Jeffs in the foregoing article, promise attainment of this goal, and functional closure again deserves serious attention as a possible and practical therapeutic goal in management of these unfortunate infants.

Both patient selection and the timing of initial closure are crucial to eventual success. We erred in the past in delaying closure until after the age of 6 mo, thereby allowing the exposed bladder to become increasingly more fibrotic and inelastic. Ansell has advocated immediate closure after birth, at which time pelvic osteotomies may not be necessary.[2] Most of the time, however, we do not see the child until 4 to 6 wk after birth, at which time closure should be undertaken at once. For the child born with a small exstrophied bladder patch, closure can still be achieved with the first stage, followed at a later age with genital reconstruction and urinary diversion. The possibility of ureterosigmoidostomies deserves attention, provided the anal sphincter tone is adequate, since long-term studies of ileal conduits show increasing impairment with time of the renal units at risk.[3,4]

The child selected for functional closure by staged reconstruction will undergo five stages of management: (1) osteotomy and closure, (2) interim management of incontinence, reflux, and possible infections, (3) correction of incontinence and reflux, (4) epispadias repair and penile lengthening, and (5) lifelong review regarding urinary infections, renal function, malignant potential, and psychosocial adjustment.[5]

In the first stage of surgical repair, exstrophy is converted into epispadias. To proceed, close the abdominal wall defect by means of midline apposition of recti muscles and skin. The infant will be totally incontinent, and some attention will have to be given to postoperative care to minimize the inevitable skin rash associated with constantly damp or wet diapers. Address the problems of dorsal chordee and "short penis" in this first stage of repair. The "short penis" is mainly due to

the separation of the anterior pelvic ring; mere approximation of the anterior pubic tubercles is accompanied by a downward tilting of the front of the pelvis with increased lateral displacement of the inferior pubo-ischial rami. Thus, the penis may become even less prominent than before.[6] Partial detachment of the crura from the bony rami allows some element of lengthening to take place and improves the overall cosmetic result. Since the epispadiac urethra must be divided to allow for this lengthening, Duckett describes an ingenious way of using strips of paraexstrophy skin to cover the resultant gap between the prostatic urethra, which remains attached to the exstrophied bladder outlet, and the urethra of the distal epispadiac penis and glans.[7] Further correction of the dorsal chordee can be attained by excising one or more transverse ellipses of tunica albuginea from the ventrum of the penis and resuturing the edges. The more radical operation for penile lengthening described by Kelley and Eraklis has not met with general acceptance for fear of loss of a portion or all of the penis because of ischemic necrosis.[8]

Finally, a word on orthopaedic management. We have used with universally good result the iliac compression hoop or ring described by Heiple.[9] It has obviated the need for plaster casts and suspension traction, has allowed for easier nursing care, and has provided more mobility to the youngster whose pelvic girdle must be stabilized following pelvic osteotomies and exstrophy closure.

REFERENCES

1. Marshall VF, Muecke EC: Functional closure of typical exstrophy of the bladder. J Urol 104:205, 1970
2. Ansell JS: Vesical exstrophy. In Glenn JF (ed): Urologic Surgery, 2d ed, p 317. Hagerstown, Harper & Rowe, 1975
3. Spence HM, Hoffman WW, Pate VA: Exstrophy of the bladder. I. Long-term results in a series of 37 cases treated by ureterosigmoidostomies. J Urol 114:133, 1975
4. Pitts WR, Jr and Muecke EC: "A 20-year experience with ileal conduits: The fate of the kidneys". J Urol 122:154, 1979
5. Jeffs RD: Exstrophy. In Harrison JH, Gittes RF, Pearlmutter AD,

et al (eds): Campbell's Urology, p 1681. Philadelphia, WB Saunders, 1979
6. Johnson JH: The genital aspects of exstrophy. J Urol 113:701, 1975
7. Duckett JW: Epispadias. Urol Clin North Am 5:107, 1978
8. Kelley JH, Eraklis AJ: A procedure for lengthening of the phallus in boys with exstrophy of the bladder. J Pediatr Surg 6:645, 1971
9. Heiple, KG: The pelvic compression hoop in the management of exstrophy of the bladder. Cleveland, University Orthopaedic Associates, (in press)

ANNOTATED BIBLIOGRAPHY

Muecke EC: Exstrophy, epispadias and other anomalies of the bladder. In Harrison, Gittes, Pearlmutter, et al (eds): Campbell's Urology, pp 1443–1468. Philadelphia, WB Saunders, 1979

In this chapter the author shows the interrelationship between epispadias and the various forms of exstrophy based on embryology and clinical observations. It provides an informative background to the reader interested in this group of congenital anomalies.

Duckett JW Jr: Epispadias. Urol Clin North Am 5:107, 1978

In the description of the surgical management of epispadias, the author describes in some detail the use of paraexstrophy skin to allow lengthening of the penile urethra. This article complements Jeff's article well.

Johnston JH: Epispadias. In Harrison, Gittes, Pearlmutter, et al (eds): Campbell's Urology, pp 1663–1671. Philadelphia, WB Saunders, 1979

This is an excellent summary of the principles of penile lengthening with good illustrations.

Jeffs RD: Exstrophy. In Harrison, Gittes, Pearlmutter, et al (eds): Campbell's Urology, pp 1672–1696. Philadelphia, WB Saunders, 1979

This is an enlarged version of the article chosen for reproduction in this textbook. Jeffs includes follow-up statistics on the 23 good results he achieved by the described surgical procedures.

Toguri AG, Churchill BM, Schillinger JF, et al: Continence in cases of bladder exstrophy. J Urol 119:538, 1978

The relationship among the onset of continence, staged surgical procedures, and continence length is reported for 21 patients who underwent successful functional exstrophy closure. Continence occurred within a year of operation in 13 patients. Ten of these 13 patients had a Marshall-Marchetti suspension in addition to the Young–Dees urethroplasty.

Lattimer, JK, Beck L, Yeaw S, et al: Long-term follow-up after exstrophy closure: Late improvement and good quality of life. J Urol 119: 664, 1978

This positive overview of patients who have undergone functional closure of bladder exstrophy shows long-term improvement and good psychological adjustment. The authors stress the need for continued care: the fifth step in the current program of staged reconstruction, interim and long-term care of the child born with exstrophy, as described in the foregoing article.

Boyce WH, Vest SA: A new concept concerning the treatment of exstrophy of the bladder. J Urol 67:503, 1952; Boyce WH: A new concept concerning the treatment of exstrophy of the bladder: 20 years later. J Urol 107: 476, 1972

In these two articles Boyce describes an alternate means to supravesical urinary diversion in children not selected for functional reconstruction. A permanent vesicorectal fistula is established, the rectal pouch is closed, and the fecal stream is diverted by a permanent colostomy. If the anal sphincter tone is good, this method deserves serious consideration, since the care of a colostomy is less complicated than that of an ileal or colon conduit. This is important in areas of the world where lack of ready availability of urinary drainage bags may be a serious handicap in the care of children with conduit urinary diversion.

79

EXSTROPHY OF THE BLADDER. I. LONG-TERM RESULTS IN A SERIES OF 37 CASES TREATED BY URETEROSIGMOIDOSTOMY

Harry M. Spence, William W. Hoffman and Virgil A. Pate

From the Department of Urology, The Dallas Medical and Surgical Clinic and the University of Texas Southwestern Medical School, Dallas, Texas

The Journal of Urology
Copyright © 1975 by The Williams & Wilkins Co.
Vol. 114, July
Printed in U.S.A.

ABSTRACT—Of the 37 patients with exstrophy of the bladder in whom ureterosigmoidostomy was selected as the mainstay of treatment 4 died of causes related to the procedure. Faulty judgment and poor followup accounted for these deaths, which might well be preventable today. In 18 survivors, or approximately half of the entire series, the operation has held up well for many years, with no further surgical procedure being required for complications. In 12 patients, or approximately a third of the group, remedial operations for complications attributable to the ureterosigmoidostomy have been required but it was elected to retain this form of diversion. The long-term end result in these patients also remains acceptable. Combining these 2 groups 30 of 37 patients with ureterosigmoidostomy may be considered to have been eventually successful. However, in 7 of 37 patients the method was a frank failure, in that 4 patients died and 3 required substitution of another form of diversion.

While all forms of treatment for exstrophy of the bladder leave much to be desired, results obtainable in today's setting lead us to recommend ureterosigmoidostomy as first choice in the management of this disorder. This recommendation is

Accepted for publication October 25, 1974.

accompanied by the admoniton that systematic followup is imperative so that if things do go badly from the clinical, laboratory or urographic viewpoint corrective measures can be done before renal deterioration occurs. The measures required may range from simple correction of elecrolytes to conversion to an ileal loop.

For many years we have practiced simultaneous bilateral ureterosigmoidostomy as the preferred basic approach in the treatment of exstrophy except when obvious incompetence of the anal sphincter precluded use of the large bowel as a reservoir for the urine.* Clearly whenever any form of urinary diversion is done some disposition of the bladder must be made and the external genitalia must be reconstructed. Specialized techniques for cystectomy and for correction of the genitalia that we have found useful are described elsewhere.[1,2] We herein update and extend our previous report[3] by analyzing the long-term results achieved in 37 patients with exstrophy in whom it was chosen to divert the urine into the intact sigmoid by ureterocolic anastomosis. All living patients have been followed for a minimum of 5 years and most much longer. How have our patients fared early and late? Has the operation held up over the years? Answers to be found in the laboratory, urographic and clinical data on this group may provide helpful information for improving future results when this form of diversion is chosen as well as affording a base line for comparison with series of patients treated by methods other than ureterosigmoidostomy.

MATERIAL STUDIED

One of us (H. M. S.) has been responsible for either all or a significant portion of the surgical care in each of the 37 patients (Table 1). In 35 cases the ureterocolic anastomosis was done by the senior author personally, under his direct supervision or by close associates. One patient when seen originally had already suffered the surgical loss of a kidney but the remaining kidney and exstrophic bladder were untouched. Two patients had had bilateral ureterosigmoidostomy done elsewhere (in 1921 and 1934) but came under our care for major complications requiring operation and still remain under our supervision. Thus, we have available for review 73 renal units in 37 patients. Recent data are available on all patients so that the final outcome or current status is known at the time of this report (September 1, 1974).

Previous Operations for Exstrophy. In 5 patients 1 or more attempts at anatomic closure had been carried out

---

* It is elementary that in all discussions involving urinary diversion and bowel one must distinguish between the bowel as conduit and the bowel as urinary reservoir.

before the patient was seen by us. Two were acceptable cosmetically but all were complete failures with respect to urinary control. Furthermore, in the 2 patients whose bladders had been turned in successfully significant bilateral reflux was persistent. One girl was made particularly miserable by erosion into the vagina of wire sutures used to approximate the pubes.

Age Factors. We had the opportunity of seeing many of these patients as newborns and the majority within the first few months of life. Aside from those instances in which ureterosigmoidostomy or anatomic closure had been performed elsewhere all patients were seen within the first 4 years of life except for a 13-year-old girl from a remote depressed rural area. The individuals who had undergone attempts at functional closure came to ureterosigmoidostomy 2, 3, 8 and 10 years after the original procedure had proved unsatisfactory. All patients seen early in life had completely normal upper tracts by urography and none had suffered overt urinary infection. Indeed, to our surprise only 1 instance of preoperative major upper tract damage was encountered in the entire group.

As our early favorable experiences with ureterocolic anastomosis grew our standard approach evolved of recommending 1-stage bilateral ureterosigmoidostomy in any robust infant more than 3 months old with exstrophy if the tone of the anal sphincter seemed good on digital examination.

TABLE 1. Material Studied: Ureterosigmoidostomy Basic Treatment in 37 Patients

	No. Cases
Sex:	
Male	27
Female	10
Age at operation:	
3 months or less	14
4 to 9 months	9
1 to 4 years	9
More than 4 years	5
Technique:	
Coffey I method	5
Mucosa-to-mucosa plus tunnel or nipple antireflex component	32
Bowel preparation after effective bowel sterilizing agents available	35
Cystectomy and genital reconstruction	35
Previously reconstructed bladder left in situ	2
One or more prior attempts at functional closure	5

Operative Technique. Five cases were done by the Coffey I technique, making a submucosal tunnel but permitting the distal raw end of the ureter to dangle within the bowel lumen. In 32 cases a mucosa-to-mucosa anastomosis of the ureter and bowel was combined with some antireflux measure, either tunnel (Leadbetter) or nipple (modified Cordonnier). Interrupted fine catgut sutures are preferred for the inner mucosal layer with swedged on 5-zero arterial silk suture material for the serosa to adventitia approximation. Ureteral stents are regarded as unnecessary and undesirable. Only 2 cases were done before the availability of effective bowel sterilizing drugs and antimicrobial agents.

RESULTS

Meticulous followup studies are essential in the evaluation of any form of management of exstrophy. In our series emphasis has been placed on the performance of excretory urograms (IVPs) and blood urea nitrogen (BUN), creatinine and electrolyte determinations every 3 to 6 months in the first postoperative year or until stability appears assured and annually thereafter. A cystokon enema is useful to make sure reflux is not present, as is a close look at the film of the kidneys, ureter and bladder for pneumopyelogram. In assessing the long-term results our 37 patients have been divided into 4 groups composed respectively of (1) deaths, (2) original ureterosigmoidostomy maintained unaltered, (3) subsequent surgical intervention required for complications but the initial type of diversion retained and (4) substitution of a different form of diversion necessary (Table 2).

Deaths. No hospital deaths occurred but 5 patients have died from 18 months to 19 years postoperatively, 4 of urologic causes and 1 of a traffic mishap (Table 3).

Death 1: J. C., a 6-month-old female infant, had undergone bilateral Coffey I transplant in 1945. About 9 years later recurrent urinary tract infections and pyelographic deterioration from obstruction at the anastomotic site developed. Anastomotic revision in the presence of chronically dilated ureters proved unavailing and

the girl died a few months later of an unrecognized acute electrolyte imbalance. Autopsy showed badly damaged kidneys.

Death 2: K. C., a miserable 9-year-old girl with massively dilated upper tracts, had undergone several unsuccessful attempts at primary reconstruction and finally underwent bilateral cutaneous ureterostomy in 1948. Management of the ureterostomies was a problem and we decided to perform an end-to-side bilateral ureterosigmoidoscopy in 1949. As should have been anticipated subsequent roentgenograms showed reflux of gas to the already severely damaged kidneys. A diversion colostomy was eventually performed but had been too long delayed and the patient died a year later when she was 18 years old of renal failure. Postmortem examination showed both kidneys to be mere shells filled with stones.

Death 3: M. F., a 15-year-old boy with exstrophy, had suffered the surgical loss of a kidney elsewhere. In 1950 a ureterosigmoidostomy was chosen to divert the normal left kidney. He did well thereafter, undergoing cystectomy and genital reconstruction uneventfully in addition to the diversion. A pyelogram after 6 months was satisfactory but a significantly elevated BUN and decreased carbon dixode were worrisome. The patient returned to his home in a remote rural area and was lost to followup. Eventually it was learned that he died suddenly of kidney infection 18 months postoperatively, probably in electrolyte crisis.

Death 4: A. C., after several unsuccessful attempts to reconstruct the bladder in the newborn period, underwent ureterosigmoidostomy in 1956 when he was 2 years old. Convalescence was smooth but he was not seen again until 3 years later when his pediatrician admitted him to a hospital moribund from intractable vomiting and dehydration secondary to respiratory and urinary infections. Autopsy showed pyelonephritis, stones and hydronephrosis.

Original Ureterosigmoidostomy Unaltered. The ureterosigmoidostomy was unaltered in 20 individuals, embracing 39 renal units. Two of these patients died of

TABLE 2. Duration of Followup and Current Status Regarding Original Ureterosigmoidostomy in 33 Surviving Patients

	No. Patients
Duration:	
20 years or more	15
10 to 19 years	13
5 to 10 years	5
Bilateral ureterosigmoidostomy retained	27
Unilateral ureterosigmoidostomy retained	3
Another form of diversion necessary	3

TABLE 3. Deaths

	No. Cases
Attributable ureterosigmoidostomy:	4
10 years postoperation	
9 years postoperation	
3 years postoperation	
1½ years postoperation	
Poor choice of operation	2
Inadequate followup	2
Unrelated to ureterosigmoidostomy	1*

* Death from traffic accident 19 years after successful unilateral ureterosigmoidostomy.

causes unquestionably related to the procedure. In the remaining 18 survivors the clinical state and quality of life remain good. Mild hyperchloremic acidosis is the rule but this is controlled readily by oral administration of Shohl's solution when the carbon dioxide combining power decreases to less than 20 mEq. Several patients have had minor infections responsive to ambulatory treatment but only 3 have required hospitalization for urinary tract infection. In none has infection been of significant magnitude to make us consider conversion to an ileal loop. The urograms in the majority of this group maintain a consistently normal appearance from 5 to 25 years after the original procedure. Only 1 kidney causes concern now and in this patient since the urographic changes have remained stationary for several years nothing further is contemplated.

Operation Required for Complications but Ureterosigmoidostomy (Unilateral or Bilateral) Has Been Retained (Table 4). Of the 37 patients 13 or just more than a third have required subsequent operative procedures because of complications or failure of the original ureterosigmoidostomy on either one or both sides. Nevertheless, in these patients it has been possible to retain this form of diversion after a corrective operation. In 5 patients revision of the initial anastomosis was done. Ureterolithotomy with or without such revision has been necessary in 4 instances, pyelolithotomy and segmental resection in 2 and nephrectomy in 3. What has been the outcome over the years in these patients in whom it was elected to continue with ureterosigmoidostomy after corrective operations for complications have been performed? One patient has died (death 1), 1 continues to have stone problems and 2 have significant permanent unilateral renal damage. Nevertheless, the 17 remaining renal units in 12 patients remain normal or nearly so on urography and all of the 12 individuals enjoy good health from 5 to 53 years after the original ureterocolic anastomosis. The interval between the original ureterosigmoidostomy and the time that operation for complications was actually performed ranged from 6 months to 10 years.

TABLE 4. Operations for Complications Subsequent to Ureterosigmoidostomy in 17 Patients (22 Procedures)*

	No. Cases
Nephrectomy	4
Ureterolithotomy	5
Nephrolithotomy and resection lower pole	2
Revision and/or reanastomosis	7
Conversion to ileal loop	2
Cutaneous ureterostomy	1
Diversion colostomy	1

* Calculi played a significant role either primary or secondary in 8 of the 17 patients requiring operation for complications.

Substitution of a Different Form of Diversion Necessary. Recurrent urinary tract infection associated with urographic deterioration in 3 patients prompted conversion to an ileal loop in 2 and cutaneous ureterostomy in 1 with a single kidney (Table 4). A diversion colostomy was done in another patient but had been delayed far too long and was ineffective (death 2). Clinical responses have been gratifying in the 3 patients who were formally converted from ureterosigmoidostomy and the urographic results show that progressive damage has been halted.

The findings on IVP after ureterosigmoidostomy are tabulated in Table 5. The examinations are done without preparation other than nothing by mouth for 6 hours prior to the test.

The Incidence of Infection After Ureterosigmoidostomy. Major infection occurred at some time after the original operation in almost half (17 of 37) of the entire series (Table 6). Minor infections were less frequent (9

TABLE 5

	No. Patients
Postoperative urography after initial ureterosigmoidostomy in 36 patients prior to operations for complications:	
Both sides good	17
Solitary kidney good	1
One side good/opposite side poor	13
Both sides poor	5

	No. Units
Urographic findings by individual:	
No. kidneys	71
Good urographically	48
Poor	23

	No. Units
X-ray findings after secondary operation for complications but with ureterosigmoidostomy retained:	
No. kidneys	12
Good*	7
Poor†	5

* No or minimal dilation of collecting system, prompt excretion in adequate concentration of urographic medium and no stones.

† Abnormal collecting system, calculi and inadequate function as judged by appearance, time and concentration of radiographic medium.

TABLE 6. Infection Problem

	Major*	Minor†	None‡
37 patients after original ureterosigmoidostomy	17	9	11
17 patients after corrective operations for complications	8		9

* Average of 2 or more attacks per year and acutely ill often requiring hospitalization.

† Less than 2 attacks per year, mildly ill and no hospitalization.

‡ No history of loin pain, fever, malaise or unexpected symptoms.

TABLE 7. Blood Chemical Findings 6 Years or More Postoperatively in 29 Living Patients with Ureterosigmoidostomy

	No. Cases
BUN determinations in 29 patients (normal range 10 to 20 mg %):	
20 mg % and less	15
21 to 32 mg %	14
Creatinine values in 23 patients (normal range 0.5 to 1.2 mg %):	
1.2 mg % or less	21
1.5 and 1.9 mg %	2
Carbon dioxide combining power in 29 patients (normal range 24 to 32 mEq per liter):	
24 mEq per liter or more	17
19 to 23 mEq per liter	10
Less than 19 mEq per liter	2
Blood chloride determinations in 28 patients (normal range 99 to 108 mEq per liter):	
100 to 108 mEq per liter	18
109 to 114 mEq per liter	9
117 mEq per liter	1

TABLE 8. Over-all Appraisal of 37 Patients Treated with Ureterosigmoidostomy*

	No. Cases
Acceptable result†:	30
Original anastomosis intact, 17	
Required secondary operation, 13	
Failure (including 4 deaths)‡	7

* Clinical status. IVPs and labortory data.

† No regret on part of patient or doctor; doubtful if patient would have fared better with another approach.

‡ Ureterosigmoidostomy abandoned or death related to procedure.

DISCUSSION

Three methods of treatment are in general use for the management of exstrophy of the bladder: (1) anatomic closure, (2) ileal loop diversion and (3) ureterosigmoidostomy. The first procedure retains a potentially dangerous epithelium, is prone to upper tract deterioration and yields disappointing results in the percentage of patients who achieve true urinary control.[4,5] The ileal conduit which has become justifiably popular as an effective form of permanent upper tract diversion is by no means free of complications, major or minor, and carries the obvious drawback of requiring an external device. However, when the loop was introduced a number of our patients were doing so well with ureterosigmoidostomy that we elected to continue its use.

In retrospect this choice seems warranted in our series and is supported by the long-term evaluations of others which are now appearing in the literature.[6,7] From a review of these it is apparent that a combination of factors accounts for the improved outlook in a patient with ureterocolic anastomosis that is obtainable today as compared to former times. First, techniques combining mucosa-to-mucosa approximation between ureter and bowel with an antireflux component added are clearly superior. Conversely, implantation of dilated ureters into intact colon either initially or as a salvage effort is questionable and the hazard increases with the degree of ureterectasis. Under such circumstances the ileal loop is our choice now. However, frequent IVPs may detect beginning dilation early enough to permit successful anastomotic revision.

Within the last 2 decades along with improved techniques the development of effective antimicrobials and an understanding of electrolyte physiology have changed the picture immearsurably for the better after ureterosigmoidostomy. Although half of our patients have at no time exhibited evidence of significant clinical or urographic pyelonephritis it definitely remains a potential threat. It is here that aggressive antimicrobial and rational parenteral fluid therapy of infection in the acute phase followed by long-term suppressive medication has lessened dramatically the occurrence of renal

of 37), yet it is noteworthy that in a third no demonstrable infection was encountered.

Electrolyte and Blood Chemical Disturbances. Evaluation of the laboratory data in our long-term survivors confirms our previous findings that a tendency toward slight lowering of the carbon dioxide combining power along with an elevation of the blood chloride level may be anticipated although this is by no means invariable (Table 7). From the clinical viewpoint these findings are surprisingly asymptomatic. However, if the carbon dioxide is less than 20 mEq or the chloride level is more than 110 mEq, correction by the judicious use of an oral alkalizing agent is indicated. Likewise a modest elevation of the BUN is a frequent finding but usually the accompanying normal serum creatinine level is reassuring in regard to renal function. Potassium and sodium levels are rarely abnormal as are the calcium and phosphorus concentrations.

Other Parameters in the Over-All Clinical Appraisal. Other parameters include growth and development, rectal control and the psychological status (Table 8). We have no firm figures on the growth rate, although our impression is that the patients with ureterosigmoidostomy may be somewhat smaller than their contemporaries. We have relied preoperatively on simple digital examination of the anal sphincter to predict its competence. Acceptable control has been present in all but 1 girl who requires protective padding. Frequent diaper change in infancy with emphasis on good perineal hygiene thereafter is obviously necessary.

Finally the psychological status of patient and parents has impressed us as being superior to that noted with other forms of diversion. This status is particularly true if the ureterosigmoidostomy is performed early in life.

damage, especially when the kidneys are urographically normal. We have found it ill-advised to rely on such conservative measures when obstruction or stones complicate the picture. Here appropriate early surgical intervention is indicated. A mild degree of hyperchloremic acidosis is encountered frequently and appears innocuous. Nonetheless, the clinician must be alert to sudden and marked alterations associated with renal, respiratory or gastrointestinal infectious episodes. Severe acidosis and hypokalemia will be lethal unless effective electrolyte reconstitution is undertaken promptly. These facts must be impressed upon primary physicians and patients (or parents) who are often unaware of the unique and insidious hazards which ureterosigmodostomy presents.

Ranking in importance with all of the foregoing in achieving successful long-term results after ureterosigmoidostomy is a systematic followup program. Inherent hazards peculiar to this form of diversion make monitoring of electrolytes and close surveillance of urograms imperative.

The IVP unquestionably has furnished the most valuable information in our postoperative followup protocol. In general prompt excretion of the contrast medium by unobstructed kidneys presages a good over-all result while hydronephrosis, ureterectasis, calculi and poor drainage go hand in hand with clinical infection and metabolic disturbances. An important point is whether on serial examinations minimal changes are stationary or progressively worsening. Systematic reappraisals in the light of our current knowledge will disclose insidious renal deterioration sufficiently early to permit medical and surgical corrective measures.

REFERENCES

1. Spence, H. M.: A simplified technique for cystectomy and repair of the abdominal defect in exstrophy of the bladder. J Urol 77:428, 1957
2. Hoffman, W. W. and Spence, H. M.: Management of exstrophy of the bladder. South Med J 58:436, 1965
3. Spence, H. M.: Ureterosigmoidostomy for exstrophy of the bladder. Results in a personal series of thirty-one cases. Br J Urol 38:36, 1966
4. Marshall, V. F. and Muecke, E. C.: Functional closure of typical exstrophy of the bladder. J Urol 104:205, 1970
5. Megalli, M. and Lattimer, J. K.: Review of the management of 140 cases of exstrophy of the bladder. J Urol 109:246, 1973
6. Wear, J. B. and Barquin, O. P.: Ureterosigmoidostomy: long-term results. Urology 1:192, 1973
7. Bennett, A. H.: Exstrophy of bladder treated by ureterosigmoidostomies: long-term evaluation. Urology 2:165, 1973

Commentary: Ureterosigmoidostomy in Vesical Exstrophy

William W. Hoffman

Over the years, despite advances in surgical techniques and therapeutic modalities and in physicians' understanding of the physiologic bases of concomitant homeostatic alterations, one fact stands immutably true in the management of exstrophy: there is no universal or ideal therapeutic procedure to apply to all cases of exstrophy of the urinary bladder. At present, three therapeutic avenues remain: (1) primary reconstruction with "functional closure" of the exstrophic bladder, (2) primary diversion by ureterosigmoidostomy, and (3) urinary diversion by either the ileal loop or colonic conduit. The second two alternatives incorporate excision of the bladder remnant and subsequent genital reconstructive procedures that are now fairly standard.

It would be incorrect and, in effect, the perpetuation of a disservice to the urologic profession to convey the impression that those physicians long identified with ureterosigmoidostomy in the treatment of exstrophy close their minds to other therapeutic approaches. Indeed, when the anatomic configuration seems to warrant it, there is no question that primary closure should be considered in each case. The personal series of one of us (WWH) includes a case of functional closure with excellent continence and a totally benign clinical course for over 12 yr. The greater number of patients, however, present with extremely small vesical rosettes and, unless viewed with unrealistic optimism, cannot in fact be considered candidates for a successful or functionally useful primary reconstructive procedure. This fact is eminently supported by Marshall and Muecke's report of a collected series of 349 functional closures of the exstrophic bladder that documents only 5% "good," 14% "fair," and 81% unsatisfactory results. Still, a recent report noting the somewhat more favorable clinical results achieved by the "staged primary closure" technique elaborated by Jeffs in his series of 39 selected patients certainly commands attention and should provide hope and encouragement for continuing efforts with this mix of time-honored techniques. Jeffs is able to report that 60% of his patients have had a "good" result with "night and day control." To quote Victor Marshall, "the technical challenge to surgeons has been enhanced. Imaginative efforts must be made or the ideal solution will remain inaccessible forever."

At present, however, ureterosigmoidostomy remains the most viable therapeutic approach for the greatest number of cases of exstrophy. My own series and those of Wear and Barquin, Bennett, Aaronson, and Morgan bear this out. As these series and my own indicate, ureterosigmoidostomy, done by a technique that uses a mucosa-to-mucosa anastomosis with an antireflux component in relatively normal renal units, is not inevitably followed by urinary tract infections, renal functional and anatomic deterioration, or electrolyte problems. In this context, however, it is with a certain uneasiness that I am impelled to bring to urologists' attention a late complication of ureterosigmoidostomy that has only recently surfaced in my series of cases and those of others. This is the problem of colonic malignancy that appears at the site of the original ureterocolic anastomosis. I have now documented two such occurrences in my own series and have been able to tabulate data from 55 other cases reported in the literature to 1979. A complete review of these cases is being prepared; however, summary findings indicate that including my two cases, 37 of the 55 reported cases occurred in patients in whom the ureterosigmoidostomy was established as the definitive therapy for exstrophy. The average time interval between the estab-

lishment of the ureterosigmoidostomy and the diagnosis of the colonic neoplasm was 25 yr, with two thirds of the cases being found in the second to fourth decade after the original procedure. The time interval, however, varied from 4 to 30 yr. The predominant lesion is a colonic adenocarcinoma, although in one fourth of the cases the lesions were considered to be adenomas or benign polyps. The lesion in one of my patients and in others described in the literature can even develop in the ureterocolic anastomotic remnant many years after the ureterosigmoidostomy has been terminated and another form of urinary diversion instituted. In my case, conversion of the ureterosigmoidostomy to a ureteroileocutaneous conduit had been performed 14 yr previously, leaving the distal ureteral remnant in its submucosal colonic tunnel. The diagnosis was made after the patient passed a bloody stool.

It is now apparent that in addition to the classic systematic follow-up study that includes monitoring the patient with a ureterosigmostomy for evidence of infection, electrolyte imbalance, and deleterious changes in the radiographic representation of the kidneys and ureters, a schedule of proctoscopic or fiberoptic colonoscopic examinations of the ureterocolic anastomoses should be instituted.

In summary, ureterosigmoidostomy remains one of the viable alternatives in choosing the therapeutic solution for the profound problems presented by the patient born with exstrophy of the urinary bladder. It obviates the social stigma that accompanies incontinence and avoids the problems attendant upon the presence of any stoma and its necessary collecting devices. Furthermore, it allows for essentially normal growth and development with minimal negative influence on the expected *good* human "quality of life" and permits the achievement of a reasonably normal lifestyle.

ANNOTATED BIBLIOGRAPHY

Aaronson IA, Morgan TC: Ureterosigmoidostomy in childhood: The quality of life. J Pediatr Surg 14:74, 1979

Thirty-one patients in whom ureterosigmoidostomy had been performed 3 to 22 yr previously are reviewed. Despite the fact that a variety of techniques were used in the ureterocolic anastomoses, 19 children (61.3%) retained their ureterosigmoidostomy. All were normotensive and growing normally. Plasma sodium, potassium, and creatinine levels were normal. A water-soluble contrast enema failed to demonstrate reflux in any case. The authors conclude that their findings show that in the great majority of patients, the quality of life during childhood, adolescence, and into adulthood is very satisfactory, with little effect on schoolwork or social activities and requiring only slight modification of routine. In general, patients felt no different from their peers. The quality of life for the child who retains a normal upper urinary tract and good bowel habits surpasses anything that can be achieved by conduit diversion.

Bennett AH: Exstrophy of bladder treated by ureterosigmoidostomies: Long-term evaluation. Urology 2:165, 1973

The author presents the Children's Hospital experience from Peter Bent Brigham Hospital and the Harvard Medical School. In the series are 94 children with exstrophy of the bladder treated by ureterosigmoidostomies 5 to 35 yr before the report; 39 patients were followed 20 or more yr, and 87% were alive at the end of the study period. Of the 34 children treated surgically since 1954, when the submucosal tunnel was corporated into the

procedure, 33 are alive, 28 are functioning with ureterosigmoidostomies, and 5 have had conversions to ileal conduit. Intravenous urograms are normal in 25 of these 28 patients; 64 patients are over 20 yr of age, 26 are married, and 9 are the parents of 13 children. Most are well adjusted, productive persons.

Wear JB, Barquin OP: Ureterosigmoidostomy. Long-term results. Urology 1:192, 1973

The authors report on long-term follow-up study of 103 patients operated on between 1928 and 1963 at the University of Wisconsin Medical Center. Thirty-two patients had the procedure done as definitive therapy of exstrophy of the urinary bladder. Of the 32 procedures, 12 were done by the combined mucosa-to-mucosa Leadbetter technique. In this group, comparison of pyelograms postoperatively indicates that only 17% of patients manifest any evidence of deleterious changes in their renal units on pyelography. This compares very favorably with the usually reported 10% to 20% incidence of some abnormality on intravenous pyelogram noted after "ileal loop" diversion. In the same group of patients, the incidence of pyelonephritis has been reduced to less than 25% by close follow-up study and vigilance in the correction of even minor abnormalities as they are noted.

Mogg RA: The treatment of urinary incontinence using the colonic conduit. Trans Am Assoc Genitourin Surg 58:90, 1966

This classic paper on the use of the colonic conduit in pediatric urology should be read by all workers in the field. In my own center, the colonic conduit is rapidly approaching the ileal conduit in frequency of usage as the chosen method of urinary diversion. Most of the surgeons, however, add the submucosal tunnel, as in the classic Leadbetter ureterocolic anastomosis, to the technique described by Mr. Mogg.

Schwarz GR, Jeffs RD: Ileal conduit urinary diversion in children: Computer analysis of followup from 2 to 16 years. J Urol 114:285, 1975

A follow-up study of 96 ileal conduit urinary diversions in children is presented, 17 of whom had diversion performed for exstrophy of the bladder. Emphasis is placed on the assessment of renal structure and function in the long-term survivors. Preoperative pyelonephritis was associated with a significant (15%) percentage of patients who progressed to poor renal function. Three preventable and correctable late complications—stomal stenosis, excessive conduit length, and ureteroileal obstruction—were associated with significant long-term deterioration (53%, 44%, and 60%, respectively) in either function or pyelographic appearance. Overall, if all pyelographic evidence of deterioration is considered to be significant, then patients with normal preoperative pyelograms are at risk in up to 50% of the cases when studied to 10 to 16 yr postoperatively.

Shapiro SR, Lebowitz R, Colodny AH: Fate of 90 children with ileal conduit urinary diversion, a decade later; analysis of complications, pyelography, renal function and bacteriology. J Urol 114:289, 1975

A review of the long-term results (10 to 16 yr) of ileal conduit urinary diversion for nonmalignant diseases in 75 children is presented. Over the years, complications relating to the renal units or conduit were not infrequent, and loop revisions especially were often required on more than one occasion. Of 144 renal units, 76% improved or remained stable and 69.3% of normal kidneys remained normal after more than a decade of urinary diversion. Creatinine clearance remained in the normal range after 10 yr, if the excretory urogram remained normal. Analysis of factors leading to renal deterioration in 26 renal units showed that causes for renal deterioration were apparent in nearly every case. The authors stressed the need for close lifetime follow-up study and aggressive management of problems as they occur.

Marshall VF, Muecke EC: Functional closure of typical exstrophy of the bladder. J Urol 104:205, 1970

Surgical restoration of the typical classic exstrophy of the urinary bladder (functional closure) is still an investigative program. Satisfactory results, in spite of many efforts, are rare. Urinary diversion with covering of the exstrophy proper is a worthy compromise, yet functional closure is obviously the ideal solution. The experimental production of exstrophy indicates that the entire urethrovesicle sphincter mechanism, or the major portion of it, is not necessarily missing. This fact has enhanced the technical challenge to surgeons to continue to attempt functional closure. The authors provide a description of their ''turn in procedure'' used in their series of 20 patients between the years 1954 to 1968. Each step is described in detail, including alternative techniques and the virtues and the pitfalls associated with each of them. Each step identifies the ideal result and documents what is achievable at the time of the report. The authors emphasize that only 5 of their 20 patients had relatively large and elastic bladders. The others had small, fibrotic, contracted remnants with many mucosal alterations. These were extreme in four cases. All the vesicle walls were at least somewhat deficient.

Only one patient in the series has achieved ''socially acceptable though not ideal continence'' after 10 yr. Among the rest of the patients in the series, 20 are considered to have a ''fair'' result, which is considered to be ''argumentitively'' as good as a patient treated by standard programs, 60% were unsatisfactory, and 40% had to be secondarily diverted. The paper includes a report on 329 cases selected from the literature.

Jeffs RD: Functional closure of bladder exstrophy. Birth Defects 13:171, 1977

This contribution describes Jeffs' staged approach to functional closure of bladder exstrophy, which he considers a major breakthrough in the surgical treatment of the condition. The newborn with a suitable bladder undergoes closure within the first week or two of life. Iliac osteotomies are an essential part of the procedure. At 2½ to 4 yr of age, the Young–Dees–Leadbetter bladder neck revision for continence is done with correction of reflux, if present. A retropubic suspension of the bladder neck and urethra (Marshall–Marchetti) complements this stage. A Young epispadias repair completes the final stage before the child achieves school age. Of 53 patients from a series of 72 patients so treated over a period of 18 yr, 39 are available for assessment; 60% have had a ''good'' result with ''day and night control,'' 20% had an ''imperfect'' result, and 20% were completely incontinent or required diversion. The factors that augur for success in these cases appear to be the selection of suitable patients and a staged approach, iliac osteotomy, a second-stage incontinence procedure with bladder neck suspension, and the liberal use of antibiotics to ensure primary wound healing.

Lasser A, Acosta AE: Colonic neoplasms complicating ureterosigmoidostomy. Cancer 35:1218, 1975

The authors report two benign reactive polyps with submucosal mucinous cysts in the stalk occurring at a 4-yr interval at each ureteral orifice in a patient with bilateral ureterosigmoidostomy for exstrophy of the bladder. The first polyp occurred 23 yr and the second polyp 27 yr after the diversion. These submucosal cysts resembled colitis cystica profunda, except that they were confined to the pedunculated polyps. A complete review of the literature of neoplasms complicating ureterosigmoidostomy is presented. It is concluded that a benign or a malignant colonic tumor may develop at the site of the ureterocolic anastomosis many years later. Therefore, patients who undergo this operation should be followed for the rest of their lives.

Sooriyaarachchi GS, Johnson RO, Carbone PP: Neoplasms of the large bowel following ureterosigmoidostomy. Arch Surg 112:1174, 1977

The authors report a case of adenocarcinoma of the rectum developing 37 yr after ureterosigmoidostomy in a patient with epispadias. The paper, however, is most valuable for the excellent discussion and review of the literature regarding this pathologic condition.

Whitaker RH, Pugh RCB, Dow D: Colonic tumors following ureterosigmoidostomy. Br J Urol 43:562, 1971

This paper reports three cases of carcinoma complicating ureterosigmoidostomy and presents the finest review of the literature on the pathology, summary of recorded cases, possible etiologic factors, and varieties of treatment employed. A tabular presentation of details on all the recorded cases before publication of this article is presented.

OVERVIEW: THE CONTINUUM OF EPISPADIAS, EXSTROPHY OF THE BLADDER, AND EXSTROPHY OF THE CLOACA

P. Mollard

EMBRYOLOGY

Epispadias, exstrophy of the bladder, and exstrophy of the cloaca are aspects of the same congenital defect that exists as a continuum. Whatever the degree of malformation, except perhaps for glandular epispadias, the pubic bones are widely separated and there is a wide triangular diastasis between the recti muscles, even above the umbilicus. The basic developmental fault in all forms of the complex is a failure of the mesenchyme of the infraumbilical wall. This results from abnormal size, position, or time of rupture of the urogenital membrane.

Patten and Barry theorize that caudal displacement of the paired primordia of the genital tubercle is the basic defect that permits persistence of the cloacal membrane cephalad to the fused penoclitoris. A dislocation of the crura from the inferior ramus of the pubis would be expected in the severe form of the abnormality, but it very rarely occurs. Marshall and Muecke believe that the basic abnormality is an overdevelopment of the membrane, preventing migration of the mesenchymal tissue between its endodermal and ectodermal layers, but this does not explain the abnormal position of the urogenital membrane cephalad to a subnormal genital tubercle. However, the theory of Solere may easily explain the site and the abnormal extension of the membrane. He has noted that an endoblastic formation

of the rat embryo grows in the cloacal tubercle, later to become the genital tubercle. It lies between the endoblastic anterior wall of the cloaca to the top of the tubercle and extends to the front of the endoblast of the cloacal membrane (Fig. 1).

At the same time, the urorectal septum divides the cloaca and joins the anterior edge of the cloacal membrane and the posterior edge of the endoblastic formation in the cloacal tubercle. The endoblastic formation hollows to form the lower part of the urogenital sinus, closed underneath by the urogenital membrane. Behind the urorectal septum, the cloaca has become the anal canal closed by the anal membrane. Contrary to the classic theories, the cloacal membrane forms only the anal membrane.

The abnormal extension, to different degrees, of the endoblastic formation in the genital tubercle or in the infraumbilical wall may explain all types of the abnormal urogenital membrane and hence all degrees of exstrophy and epispadias, even the most complex. Indeed, this sounds like fiction, but it is logical.

CLASSIC EXSTROPHY

Half the patients presenting with the epispadias–exstrophy complex have classic bladder exstrophy, but this is a rare

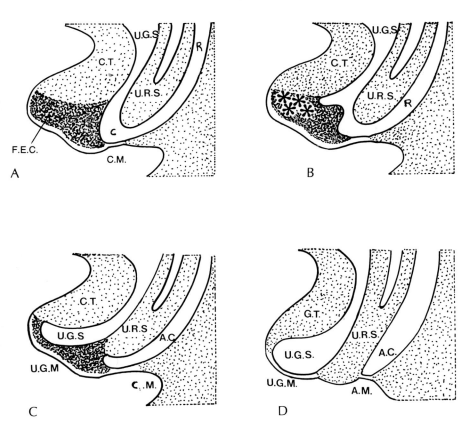

Fig. 1. (*A*) An endoblastic formation (F.E.C.) grows in the cloacal tubercle. (*B*) The endoblastic formation hollows to form the lower part of the urogenital sinus (U.G.S.), closed inferiorly by the urogenital membrane (U.G.M.). (*C*) The urorectal septum (U.R.S.) joins the anterior edge of the cloacal membrane (C.M.) and the posterior edge of the endoblastic formation in the cloacal tubercle (C.T.). (*D*) Behind the urorectal septum, the cloacal membrane becomes the anal canal (A.C.) closed by the anal membrane (A.M.). Contrary to the classic theories, the cloacal membrane forms only the anal membrane. (Adapted from Solere M: Atlas embryologie humaine. Maloine Editeur [Paris] 1:97, 1976)

malformation—1:30,000 or 50,000 births with a male:female ratio of 3:1. Thus, it is difficult for any one surgeon to acquire experience in treating this very complex malformation. Such patients should therefore be referred to centers specializing in this condition.

The bladder is incomplete, and the portion that exists is often abnormal. The trigone always exists, but the vesical neck is abnormally shaped, hypoplastic, and invaded by fibrosis. The posterior part of the external sphincter exists in the interpubic band but is incomplete, variable, and embedded in fibrosis. Most important, a significant part of the detrusor is lacking. The bladder may be very small, reduced only to the trigone. Often it is sufficiently developed to allow its invagination to create a vesical cavity, albeit a small one. The size of the bladder is the essential criterion in deciding on functional closure. The portion that exists is abnormal. The bladder mucosa is edematous and inflamed with metaplasia and pseu-

dopolyps. Mucosal cysts and intestinal tissue are frequent. Muscularis is thick and rigid, with fibrosis disorganization of the muscular bundles. Some of these abnormalities exist at birth, but often, initially, the bladder is supple with a smooth mucosa and an intact transitional epithelium. However, ulceration and inflammatory changes quickly occur from trauma. The umbilical clamp, diapers, and drying irritate the epithelium and promote bacterial invasion, cystitis, and, later, metaplasia and cystitis cystica. As Jeffs reports, ''Initial care should begin in the delivery room; the child should be placed undressed in an isolette and the bladder periodically moistened with saline.''

After closure, the bladder lesions can regress, as has been demonstrated by surgery or endoscopy, but it is better to prevent subsequent problems by immediate neonatal closure.

The kidneys and ureters are generally normal and, during the first years of life, renal function and drainage are almost always normal. However, the ureters end in a very short tunnel on a rigid trigone, the meatus is patulous, and reflux is almost certain after closure of the bladder.

All the other abnormalities result from the separation of the pubic bones, which are spread apart anteriorly at the symphysis by 5 cm to 10 cm. Lateral rotation of the acetabulum and femur is constant but does not cause any real orthopaedic problem. The wide separation of the recti muscles create a challenging parietal defect. The anterior insertions of puborectalis sling are spread apart with the pubic bones, and the anal canal may be patulous and anteriorly displaced. Anal prolapse is common, and some degree of anal incontinence can affect the results of ureterosigmoidostomy. The separation of the pubic bones affects the appearance of the external genitalia. In the female, the clitoris is split and the labia are widely separated, exposing the urethral groove and the vaginal orifice. In the male, the crural attachments of the penis to the inferior rami of the pubis are widely spread apart, resulting in a short stubby penis. The short urethral groove and adherence of the corpora cavernosa to the interpubic band create a very important dorsal chordee. The length of each corpus cavernosum is normal or nearly normal, but much of it is wasted between the penile body and the puboischial attachment. In the female, the müllerian tract may show some degree of duplication but is often basically normal.

In conclusion, if the bladder is sufficiently developed, all the structures necessary for surgical reconstruction are present and functional closure should be possible.

Treatment

Dressing and diapering are socially and psychologically unacceptable and probably reduce the patient's longevity.

Urinary diversion and bladder excision can reasonably be reserved for cases where reconstruction fails or is not feasible (small bladders and those associated with unusual renal, genital, or rectal anomalies).

Functional closure, frequently attempted unsuccessfully in the past, although not universally accepted because of the complexity of the malformation, can now be considered with good prospects of success if performed by a well-trained pediatric urology team. The problem of patient selection for reconstruction remains. Failures are certain because of the poor quality of the bladder, which is small, fibrous, and not contractile. My experience, consisting of 40 patients selected and 7 rejected, was less strict than that of Williams and Keeton (17 rejections of 36) or Jeffs (19 rejections of 72). Bladder closure is always justified if technically feasible. In male patients it is necessary to reconstruct the bladder wall, lengthen the penis, and close the urethra. It might be expected that the bladder will grow once it is closed, but it may be necessary to be more selective at the time of sphincter reconstruction by evaluating patients according to bladder capacity, suppleness, and contractility.

At the time of operation with the child under anesthesia, examine the bladder to determine if it is large and smooth enough to be invaginated and to form a cavity, even if only a small one (pad of a forefinger). Sometimes the bladder can be enlarged by excising polyps, dividing the fibrous superior edge of the bladder, and stretching the detrusor.

In past years closure of the bladder was usually performed when the patient was 1 yr, but some children were not seen until they were 4 or 6 yr. At present, initial closure is best performed during the neonatal period or as soon as the patient is seen. As both Jeffs and Ansell reported, the closure of the lower abdominal wall and pelvic ring is easier. Early closure prevents subsequent development of bladder abnormalities, and the child can go home with a more normal appearance. The postoperative course is relatively uncomplicated.

Success depends very much on the operative technique. Performed simultaneously, repair of the bladder, reflux, continence mechanism, and epispadias is too ambitious. A multistaged operative program seems more reasonable and may be performed as follows:

1st Stage

The goal of *initial closure* is to create a complete incontinent epispadias. Continence is not a goal at this stage, but in male patients the penis is lengthened at this time. According to both Jeffs and Ansell, a posterior iliac osteotomy is usually unnecessary in the newborn, but I always perform it in the hope of obtaining a better and easier approximation of the pubic bones and of the recti muscles. No wound or hip complications have been observed. Proximally, separate the bladder and the peritoneum without entering the latter. Laterally, it is not necessary to free the bladder wall extensively. Spare the largest blood vessels. In this dissection it is essential to follow the medial border of the rectus downward. In this manner continue dissection to the pubic bone exactly at the attachment of the interpubic band, which may be cut right along the pubic bone. Continue dissection deeply along the inferior surface of the pubic bone. This will free the anterior border of the urogenital diaphragm.

In the male patient, correct the dorsal chordee and lengthen the penis. Extend the incision along the urethral groove anteriorly up to the tip of the penis, and lift up and free the urethral band until the intercrural space is reached. A mass of erectile tissue located under the urethral band, representing the vestigial corpus spongiosum, is then visible. Stop dissection at the veru montanum to avoid injuring the genital tract. Retract the urethral band attached to the bladder upward and backward. Subsequently, remove all the fibrous tissue on the surface of the corpora cavernosa. Theoretically, the penis is lengthened by approximating the pubic bones after osteotomy. However, this causes retraction of the penis and is often only a temporary solution. Eventually, the corpora cavernosa are freed from their attachment on the pubic arch. Once freed, the corpora cavernosa will turn inward and downward, as stated by Allen and Johnston, and it is then possible to increase the length of their fused portion by approximating the crura. Tubularize the urethral band and reinsert it on the origin of the penis, which is covered with skin. The divided prepuce can be used, but now it seems better to create two pedicle grafts of the shiny periexstrophy skin, according to Duckett. A more radical penile lengthening procedure was introduced by Kelley and Eraklis with complete disruption of the crura from their attachment to the pubic ramus. However, the risk of ischemic necrosis seems too great, and the procedure has not met with general acceptance.

Close the bladder and urethra with two rows of absorbable polyglycolic acid sutures. On the anterior aspect of the bladder neck, reinforce the muscle layer by suturing the wings of the urogenital diaphragm, which is already detached from the pubic bones. Close the abdominal wall by approximation and suture of the rectus sheaths while an assistant approximates the pubic bone by squeezing the greater trochanters. If it is possible to pull the pubic bones completely together, approximate the pubic arch by a horizontal mattress suture. This is frequently possible in the neonate; but if it is impossible to pull the pubic bones completely together, I prefer to remove the suture as soon as the rectus approximation is finished. The "bladder neck" and the urethra are projected anteriorly, between the pubic bones, and can be damaged by the large approximating thread. The pubic bones will separate again when the stitch cuts through them and is eliminated. Therefore, if the pubis does not come together easily, only the muscles and sheath are sutured as far down as possible. A triangular defect usually persists, but it is small (about 10 mm to 15 mm on each side) because of the posterior iliac osteotomy, which permits easier abdominal wall closure and avoids fascial and skin plasties. These plasties are difficult to perform; they do not properly reconstruct the abdominal wall, and they disturb hair distribution.

Finally, close the skin and suture the urethral opening to the distal part of the wound. Two catheters are left in the ureters and brought out through the urethral orifice. No catheter is left in the bladder, and the legs are approximated and pulled vertically with traction until 20 days postoperatively. This decreases the tension on the abdominal wall and keeps the osteotomy immobilized. For older patients, the orthopaedic surgeon likes to use external fixation.

A small plastic cast wrapping the pelvis for 2 or 3 mo may mold the pelvis into a normal configuraiton. According to Jeffs, a solid fibrous ring in front of the bladder neck and urethra is important for continence acquisition.

After initial closure regular examination by urine culture, residual urine studies, and excretory urography is required to ensure that the kidneys are not damaged by back pressure or reflux with infection. Urethral dilatation, excision of polyps, or early ureteral antireflux procedures may be necessary.

Reflux is always present after closure of the bladder. Since the surgeon aims to obtain continence at a latter stage, it is imperative to perform an antireflux procedure. Orifices are moved upward to allow lengthening of the urethra by using part of the trigone. It is difficult to create a good submucous tunnel because of the small size of the bladder, and, despite the normal ureters, reimplantation is difficult and yields uncertain results because of the detrusor fibrosis and small size of the bladder. If bladder closure is unexpectedly continent, early ureteral reimplantation to correct reflux may be necessary.

Generally, reflux is well tolerated after closure of the bladder because of the complete incontinence. It is possible to perform ureteral reimplantation as a separate procedure before bladder neck reconstruction. In this way no tension is put on the reimplantation before complete healing occurs. However, this requires an additional opening of the bladder, and the success of the reimplantation is not certain until bladder neck reconstruction is performed. At present, ureteral reimplantation and bladder neck reconstruction are done simultaneously.

2nd Stage

Bladder neck reconstruction is performed when the child is 4 to 6 yr old. The basic technique is the Young–Dees–Leadbetter procedure; that is, the urethra is lengthened and a new bladder neck is reconstructed using part of the trigone musculature. After suprapubic incision, open the bladder and urethra in a vertical plane without opening the urethral orifice. Isolate a urethral mucosal band wide enough to be tubularized on a 10 French stent. Avoid narrowing the urethra. Peel off the mucosa of the two triangles laterally. The muscular plasty has been modified. On one side, cut the trigone in the transverse direction at the level of the new bladder neck. On the other side, cut the trigone parallel to the urethra, thus leaving the triangle attached to the bladder by its base (Fig. 2). Tubularize the mucosa on a 10 French stent with interrupted 6–0 polyglycolic acid sutures. Place a second row of interrupted sutures on the muscular layer of the urethra using a smaller 8 French stent. The muscular triangle still attached to the urethra is turned inward and sutured with mattress stitches to the other side of the urethra. The muscular triangle on the other side, attached to the bladder, is pulled upward in front of the new bladder neck and the lowest part of the detrusor. This will reconstitute a muscular loop in front of the new bladder neck and a distinct urethrovesical angle. Unlike Jeffs, I do not measure bladder neck suspension because such measuring is not accurate because

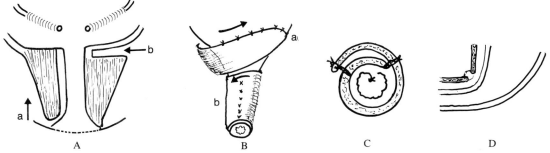

Fig. 2. Modification of the Young–Dees–Leadbetter plasty aims to create an anteriorly increased vesico-urethral angle and an anterior muscular loop that correspond to Heiss' loop.

of mucosal edema. Drain the urine suprapubically by two ureteral catheters. Leave a large nylon thread as a guide passing through the new urethra and bladder neck and bring it out suprapubically. Bladder secretion will run along it, and it will serve as a guide to introduce a urethral catheter 15 days postoperatively. Remove the catheter 20 days postoperatively, since the child should begin to void spontaneously. This period is facilitated greatly by the monitoring of a physiotherapist. Discharge the patient only when it is certain that there is no large postvoiding residual in the bladder. Approximately 25% of my patients suffered from urinary retention with dysuria, fever, and lumbar pain. Dilatations of the new bladder neck resulted in relief.

According to Jeffs, the *broad spadelike penis* is best closed after bladder neck revision to prevent damage to the urethra, should dilatation or cystoscopy be required in the postoperative period.

Results

Incontinence

The success rate after functional closure varies among authors: 30%, (Fischer–Ansell); 50%, (Cendron); 60 to 70% (Jeffs–Mollard). These patients can retain urine for 3 hr during the day and live normally. The oldest can remain dry during the night. They have a good stream without residual. Urodynamic evaluation shows normal bladder contraction or inactive detrusor. In the latter instance, the bladder is emptied by abdominal pressure. Excretory urography is normal or almost normal, without reflux or urinary tract infection or asymptomatic bacteriuria. It is necessary to be patient regarding improvement. Usually continence is acquired 6 to 24 mo after the surgical procedure, and improvement can continue until puberty.

Failure may result from chronic urinary retention with urethral dilatation, reflux, and renal impairment. In these patients the anterior edge of the new bladder neck is prominent and fibrous. Resection of this edge causes complete urinary incontinence with immediate improvement of the kidneys and ureters. Incontinence can improve gradually or another attempt can be made to restore continence, but if the bladder is small with rigid detrusor inactive at manometry, urinary diversion may be the alternative.

Failure due to incontinence in the face of normal kidneys and ureters may be treated by a new trial of cervicocystoplasty after a delay of 1 or more years. The Scott artificial sphincter can be considered as a possible alternative. Colocystoplasty was not used to enlarge the bladder, since Williams and Keeton reported no success and Cendron reported one success and one failure.

Arap presented an *alternative to diversion* for the small bladder. This reconstruction begins with the creation of a sigmoid conduit with antireflux implantation of the ureters. Protected by this diversion, urethrovesical tubularization is accomplished. All the bladder muscle is used to construct a 5-cm to 6-cm muscular tube, which must provide continence. After 3 mo the sigmoid conduit is anastomosed to the cranial extremity of this detrusor tube and the intestinal stoma is closed, allowing voiding. Arap's results are astonishingly good. The percentage of success is 75%. The continent patients

void every 1 to 3 hr. This procedure was described by Couvelaire, but he failed to achieve success. The technique, however, is perhaps worth further study.

Patients not selected for closure and those in whom functional closure is unsuccessful are treated by urinary diversion.

External diversion by ileal conduit has been disappointing in many patients, and the colon conduit with an antireflux procedure appears to be better. However, external diversion and the necessary appliance is not well accepted, especially among teenagers and young adults, who sometimes threaten suicide.

Internal diversion is more classic and more widely used in ureterosigmoidostomy and was first performed for bladder exstrophy by Simon in 1851. After the pioneer work of Coffey in 1932, ureterosigmoidostomy was widely used, but after 1950 this procedure acquired a bad reputation, namely, reflux, stenosis, lithiasis, renal impairment, and metabolic disorders appeared very frequently (Harvard and Thompson, Kendall and Karafin, Megalli and Lattimer). However, this reputation has recently been reversed since the adoption of the modern procedure. Many studies (Barcat, Bettex, Chatelain, Petit in Europe or Spence and Hoffman and colleagues in the United States) have shown in numerous cases that ureterosigmoidostomy may, during very long follow-up study (20 to 40 yr), ensure a normal active life free of the burden of an external appliance, normal renal function, and good psychological acceptance. However, certain conditions appear absolutely indispensable. Rectoanal function must be adequate to retain liquids. It seems desirable to wait 6 to 8 yr before performing the procedure. The anal sphincteric apparatus should be carefully investigated with manometric and electromyographic study. The kidneys and ureters must be normal. Ureterosigmoidostomy is absolutely contraindicated in patients with pyelonephritis or ureterohydronephrosis. The technical procedure of implantation must be perfect; a mucosa–mucosal anastomosis should be combined with an antireflux procedure (Leadbetter, Goodwin, Mathiesen). Metabolic disorders must be prevented by urinary alkalinization and by the use of frequent voiding. Sometimes the use of a rectal probe during the night may be necessary. Infection must be checked and treated systemically. It is imperative that a systematic follow-up program be instituted. Patients must be followed for their entire life and observed for lithiasis, stenosis, reflux, and pyelonephritis. These are inherent and insidious hazards peculiar to this form of diversion. It makes monitoring of electrolytes and close surveillance of urograms imperative. When any complication appears, revision of the ureteral implantation is hazardous and an external transcolonic diversion must be undertaken.

Other kinds of intestinal urinary diversion are less frequently used, for instance, the anastomosis of the bladder (Singer–Boyce–Hays) or of the trigone (Maydl) to the rectum or the isolated rectal bladder (Gersuny–Hovelacque–Duhamel). Another alternative is a staged ureterocolosigmoidostomy as advocated by Cendron and Hendren. A sigmoid loop with an antireflux implantation is done. This procedure is feasible even in the case of dilated ureters by tailoring the ureters. Postoperatively, if the upper urinary tract remains or becomes normal with good drainage and absence of reflux and if the anal sphincter is functioning well, the abdominal stoma can be turned into the sigmoid after the age of 7. In any case, regardless of the diversionary procedure chosen cystectomy, reconstruction of the abdominal wall and reconstruction of the genitalia are indispensable.

Genital Function

In the female, duplication of the clitoris can be corrected by Allen's technique. A cut-back type of vaginoplasty or perineotomy is often necessary to permit coitus. Krisiloff had observed 5 women with successful deliveries. The most common and major problem seen was cervical and uterine prolapse. In the male "the acquisition of a penis which will look alright during boyhood and which will function satisfactorily in adult life is generally the prime consideration of the patient and his parents" (J.H. Johnston). After lengthening of the penis all patients achieve good erections and orgasm, but ejaculation can be impaired by damage to the veru montanum or obstruction of the urethra, especially after urinary diversion or repeated reconstructive attempts (Hanna and Williams). The potential for fertility is not impaired by the deformity itself but may be affected by the correction of the deformity.

Malignancy

Untreated exstrophic bladders have a tendency to develop adenocarcinoma. In reconstructed bladders two cases of rhabdomyosarcoma and two of epithelioma have been reported. Carcinoma has also been reported as occuring at the site of ureteral implantation after ureterosigmoidostomy. It is probably a tumor of the ureter irritated by the fecal stream (Rabinovitch). There have not been any reports of carcinoma after diversion into an isolated colonic conduit.

Conclusion

Without a doubt, functional closure of bladder exstrophy must now be accepted as the primary goal. Success depends very much on a complete understanding of all aspects of the defect and on the operative technique using a multistaged program.

Only patients not selected for closure and those in whom functional closure is unsuccessful are treated by urinary diversion. The best method of diversion seems to be ureterosigmoidostomy. In the future, better techniques will have to be devised to ensure a stable anterior closure of the pelvic ring to select patients for implantation with the artificial urinary sphincter and to reconstruct the very small bladder.

CLOACAL EXSTROPHY

Cloacal exstrophy is the most severe form of the exstrophic defect. This rare anomaly occurs once in every 200 to 250,000 births. Rupture of the abnormal cloacal membrane occurs at an early stage, before the urorectal septum divides the cloaca. There is a very large defect of the abdominal wall and pelvis that includes an omphalocele of variable size and a duplication of the genitalia.

Although anatomic details differ in different cases, the exstrophic zone show the same basic pathology, for example, an exstrophic hemibladder with a ureteric orifice lying on each side of a median exstrophic bowel. The exstrophic bowel is the ileocaecal segment, with an upper opening being the terminal ileum and a lower opening leading to a short length of large intestine that ends blindly in the pelvis. The anus is absent. The external anomaly itself is not incompatible with survival. It is, however, frequently associated with a shortened bowel and severe malabsorption. This problem may prove insurmountable.

Coexistent anomalies in other systems are frequent. These include myelomeningocele (more than 50%), and major abnormalities of the upper urinary tract (50%). Both internal and external genitalia are frequently absent. As quoted by Jeffs, in some circumstances attempts to support life may be futile, besides being morally and ethically unwise. However, the more robust infants without other serious anomalies will survive, and reparative surgery must be undertaken.

In the first stage, a fecal diversion is performed. The midline defect is closed by excising the omphalocele and suturing the two bladder halves. In a second stage, the urinary problem may be solved by a urinary diversion or by closure of the bladder and the urethra. In all probability, continence will be rarely obtained, but Jeffs considers the possibility of using an artificial sphincter. Reconstruction of the abdominal wall and genitalia may necessitate an osteotomy. In the male, the phalli are generally duplex and rudimentary, and sex reassignment may be necessary. In all cases, surgical reconstruction is formidable and may not be justified. The expected quality of life for the patient and the emotional perturbation of the family must be considered before such treatment.

VARIANTS OF THE EXSTROPHY

These variants of the exstrophy represent stages in the continuum of abnormal embryologic development that are less severe than those associated with classic exstrophy. These entities have been designated "the split symphysis variant" by D.I. Williams. It is rarer than exstrophy (10 times) and occurs most commonly in females.

All patients with split symphysis variants have a widely separated symphysis pubic with divergent recti muscles. The abdominal wall defects vary. The most common are low umbilicus and various types of hernia. The bladder, or one of the bladders, if the bladder is duplicated (30%), is closed and covered by skin. Bladder epithelial covering may be complete (ectopia vesicae) and may also include a patch of ectopic vesical mucosa (duplicate exstrophy) or vesicocutaneous fistula. Genital anomalies are found in a high proportion of patients. In the female, duplication of the clitoris is almost constant; double vagina and uterus are frequent. All male patients have a small, short penis, and all require surgery for penile revision. The penis may be duplicate. The most prevalent gastrointestinal tract anomaly seems to be an anterior anus that is often incontinent. The severity of the abdominal wall defect does not seem to be related to the ultimate continence of the patient. Complete coverage of the bladder does not yield a better prognosis for continence either, but patients with the exstrophy variants do seem to have a better prognosis for surgically produced continence. Some are spontaneously continent. Some become continent after closure of a vesicocutaneous fistula. Some with double bladders become continent after cystocystostomy. Other patients must undergo a cervicoplasty procedure (Young–Dees–Leadbetter–Mollard). Very few patients have been diverted, but some have reflux with pyelonephritis and scarring, and early antireflux diagnosis and management seems to be indicated.

EPISPADIAS

Epispadias is an extremely rare malformation that occurs more frequently in males (1:120,000 births in males and in 4:500,000 in females).

In the male there are two types of epispadias; (1) anterior (glanular or penile), characterized by normal continence, and (2) posterior (penopubic and subsymphyseal), associated with an incompetent bladder neck and constant dribbling of urine. Sometimes the degree of incontinence is difficult to assess at birth. In the female, the clitoris is duplicate and the cleft extending along the entire urethra usually involves the bladder neck and causes incontinence. Degree of incontinence varies from stress incontinence to total incontinence with permanent dribbling. The pubis symphysis is generally separated in these patients, with the degree of separation dependent on how proximal the defect is. It is not, however, as wide as in cases of exstrophy. The primary objectives in the treatment of epispadias are to restore continence, reconstruct the urethra, and reconstruct the genitalia.

Most patients with epispadias will have *severe urinary incontinence*, which remains a major problem. The detrusor is thin; the trigone may be poorly developed with incompetence of the ureterovesical junction. Reflux is not constant but exists in 75% of patients. Most epispadias patients require ureteral reimplantation. The bladder neck is wide open, patulous, and without a posterior edge. Notwithstanding this, all parts of the bladder exist and surgical restoration of continence is universally accepted. Urinary diversion is reserved for failures. Posterior iliac osteotomy is generally unnecessary. The Young–Dees–Leadbetter operation with antirefluxing reimplantation is the standard procedure for epispadias incontinence in most reports. My own modification of the Young–Dees cervicoplasty gives me very good results and seems to be most effective. Operation is easier than for exstrophy, but postoperative complications of dysuria and retention are exactly the same. Urethroplasty must be postponed.

Reconstruction of the urethra and bladder neck using a tube from the anterior bladder wall was first described by Barnes and Wilson. The procedure was developed for varying reasons by Flocks and Culp, and Tanagho, and its success in the management of female epispadias patients with total urinary incontinence has been documented by several authors. Alternative means of achieving continence in female epispadic patients include suspension of the bladder neck and transvaginal plication of the urethra. The Scott prosthetic urinary incontinence device may prove to be a valuable procedure after others have failed. The results of incontinence surgery are better than for bladder exstrophy and exceed 70%. A well-developed bladder with good capacity and musculature, bladder training, and considerable patience are the keys to success. After failure, a cervicoplasty can be successful. It is preferable to wait for the final decision concerning urinary diversion until after puberty.

Urethral and Genitalia Reconstruction

In the female, the urethra can be tubularized at the time of cervicoplasty. In another stage the medial halves of the duplicate clitoris are denuded and brought together in the dorsal midline to the meatus. The cosmetic appearance of the depression in the mons veneris and the hair distribution may be corrected by using rotational skin flaps of the lateral inguinal tissue.

In the male, the penis must be straightened and possibly lengthened before urethroplasty. The short urethral groove, the shortage of skin on the dorsum of the penis, and the adherences of the corpora cavernosa to the interpubic area create a very important dorsal chordee. There may also be intrinsic deformities of the corpora cavernosa themselves, and, in addition, bands of fibrous tissue similar to those causing chordee associated with hypospadias may be present. In the posterior epispadias, as in exstrophy, the crural attachments of the corpora to the inferior ramus of the pubis are spread widely apart and result in a short stubby penis. Shortening and dorsal tethering are lesser in anterior epispadias but most epispadias patients require straightening and often lengthening.

When the patient is incontinent, it is possible to combine the penile procedure with the cervicoplasty. The incision along the urethral groove is extended anteriorly up to the extremity of the penis. The urethral band is lifted up and freed completely until the intercrurae space is reached. A mass of erectile tissue located under the urethral band, representing the vestigial corpus spongiosum, is then seen. Dissection is stopped at the veru montanum to avoid injuring the genital tract. This allows the urethral band, the proximal urethra, and also the bladder neck to retract further back into the pelvis and allows a better vesicourethral angle and perhaps a better chance for continence. Subsequently, the corpora cavernosa are freed completely of their cutaneous coat and all the fibrous tissue on their surface is removed. All fibers of the chordee are then removed. But, according to Devine and Horton, in some cases the dorsal portion of the corporal bodies should be lengthened by incising the tunica and inserting a dermal graft into the defect. In the most severe form of epispadias the penile body must be lengthened. The corpora cavernosa are freed from their attachments on the pubic arch. Once freed, the corpora will turn inward and downward (Allen–Johnston), and it is then possible to increase the length of their fused portion by approximating the crura. The urethral band is then tubularized and reinserted on the origin of the penis, which is covered with skin. In the majority of cases penile skin and the redundant ventral prepuce may be used. When its two layers have been separated, the additional skin obtained may allow the penile skin to be sutured longitudinally on the dorsum using a Z-plasty. Alternatively, bilateral rotation flaps formed from the prepuce may be swung to the dorsum. If there is insufficient penile skin for either of these methods, the shaft may be buried under a bridge of scrotal skin or a free, thick, split-skin graft may be used. The use of penile skin is preferable whenever possible. In many cases skin contracture of the lower abdominal skin may appear after healing. If this occurs, a Z-plasty scar release or rotational inguinal skin grafts may solve the problem.

Urethroplasty

Various significant procedures have been advanced over the years for reconstruction of the urethra. Cantwell's method was modified and popularized by Young and further by Gross and Cresson. The penile urethra is constructed 1 yr after the penis is lengthened. When, as often occurs, there is skin redundancy on the dorsum of the penis, excision of part of the length of the skin strip may be needed in order to prevent the neourethra from having tortuosities of valvular folds. This is very important. The glans may be reconstructed into a quite normal-appearing structure. Cantwell's and Young's procedure may give excellent results.

Additional ingenious techniques have been proposed without attempting to bury the neourethra between the corpora using the principle of hypospadias surgery. Others have converted cases of epispadias into hypospadias by tubing the urethral strip and passing it ventrally between the two corpora.

This staged procedure seems complex and without real benefit. Devine and Horton, and Hendren, demonstrated a method using mobilized urethral mucosa and full-thickness skin grafts for urethral reconstruction. For epispadias patients without incontinence, penile straightening and urethral reconstruction can be done in a single stage with gratifying results. Skin coverage of the dorsum of the penis is accomplished by using the undisturbed penile and preputial skin.

Conclusions

Epispadias surgery is difficult and time consuming. Fistula or stricture may occur. But with training, the overall complication rate is low. As in exstrophy, the genital cosmetic result is paramount. During early childhood, the surgeon tends to concentrate on the urinary aspects of the epispadias, although in fact the appearance and functional capacity of the genitals is often the main concern of teenagers and young adults. According to Hanna and Williams, erection, ejaculation, and semen analysis are often normal after correction. There is very much less danger of damage to the veru montanum or of obstruction to the newly formed urethra than in exstrophy.

PART THIRTY-THREE

SURGICAL TREATMENT OF BENIGN PROSTATIC HYPERTROPHY

80

COMPARISON OF PILCHER BAG TECHNIQUE WITH STANDARD SUPRAPUBIC PROSTATECTOMY

Dhanvant M. Rathod, M.D., Natver K. Pareek, M.D., John W. Coleman, M.D., and John H. McGovern, M.D.

From the Department of Surgery, Division of Urology, Lenox Hill Hospital, New York, New York

Urology / April 1980 / Volume XV, Number 4

ABSTRACT—A total of 930 cases of open prostatectomies done at Lenox Hill Hospital from 1965 to 1974 are reviewed. The Pilcher bag technique utilized in 830 cases is compared with 100 cases of suprapubic prostatectomy with suturing of the bladder neck. Operating time, intra- and postoperative blood transfusions, hospital stay, and complications are compared. Operative time and intra- and postoperative blood loss are significantly less with the Pilcher bag technique.

The first open prostatectomy was described by Belfield in the United States in 1887[1] and later by McGill in England in 1888.[2] Since then, surgeons have utilized a variety of methods to achieve hemostasis.[3,4] Harris,[5] in Australia, popularized the suprapubic prostatectomy with hemostasis achieved by suturing the bladder neck under direct vision. An alternate technique, using hemostatic bags, was described by Pilcher[4] in 1914. This method has not gained popularity, but was used extensively by Slaughter, former director of urology, at The Lenox Hill Hospital. While it was recognized that his technique enabled him to remove prostates rapidly via a suprapubic approach, no definite statistics on his technique were available.

To evaluate the Pilcher bag technique, we compared it with suprapubic prostatectomies done by other staff members using the Pilcher bag technique, as well as suprapubic prostatectomies where bleeding was controlled by direct suturing of the bladder neck. The procedures were compared with regard to operating time, duration of postoperative hospitalization, postoperative complications, and the need for intra- and postoperative transfusions.

TECHNIQUE

Through a small midline incision the bladder is opened just enough to permit enucleation of the gland by using counter pressure with a gloved finger in the rectum. Once the prostate is removed, a metal sound is passed through the urethra into the bladder. The long arm of the Pilcher bag is then threaded onto the sound, and the sound is drawn through the urethra (Fig. 1). This pulls the arm of the Pilcher bag down into the prostatic urethra. The bag is inflated with 100 to 300 cc of water, depending on the size of the prostatic fossa. The urethral end of the tubing and the pear-shaped bag are drawn snugly into the prostatic fossa and against the bladder neck. The traction is increased until hemostasis is adequate and is maintained by strapping the tube to the thigh. The bladder is then closed loosely to permit removal of the Pilcher bag suprapubically. The abdominal wall muscles are closed with through and through retention sutures. Traction on the bag is maintained for six or more hours. The next day the bag is deflated and removed while patient is under heavy sedation or light general anesthesia. A multi-eyed Robinson catheter is then passed through the urethra and into the bladder and is taped in place. This is connected to straight drainage and is left indwelling for five to seven days.

RESULTS

Of 930 patients who underwent open prostatectomies at Lenox Hill Hospital between 1965 and 1974, the Pilcher bag was utilized in 830 cases. A total of 542 of these were done by Slaughter, and 288 were performed by other staff members. A standard suprapubic prostatectomy with suturing of the bladder neck for hemostasis was performed in 100 cases, most of them since 1969. At first the two techniques of open prostatectomy were compared as to operative time, postoperative stay, sig-

nificant complications, and mortality. The average operative time was appreciably less in those cases where the Pilcher bag technique was used. Slaughter's technique averaged thirty-two minutes and in several instances was less than fifteen minutes. The same technique done by other surgeons averaged fifty-four minutes, and the standard suprapubic prostatectomy averaged one hundred eight minutes.

The postoperative hospital stay was approximately the same in all groups: fifteen days with the Pilcher bag technique and sixteen days with the standard suprapubic prostatectomy. The postoperative urologic complications included urinary incontinence and urethral strictures. Using the standard suprapubic approach, there was no incidence of incontinence, while in Slaughter's group there was an 0.3 percent incidence. This same technique performed by other members caused incontinence in 2.5 percent of their patients. While 18 percent of Slaughter's patients required dilatation of urethral strictures, only 3, less than 1 percent, required this as a long-term measure. None required urethroplasties. Twenty percent of the patients undergoing suprapubic prostatectomy with suturing of the bladder neck required dilatation of urethral strictures. Again, none required multiple dilatations or urethroplasties.

In general, postoperative complications were comparable in all three groups. The over-all mortality after open prostatectomy was 2.4 percent. Slaughter's mortality rate was 1.6 percent. The same technique utilized by other members of the staff resulted in a 3.8 percent mortality. The standard suprapubic prostatectomy yielded a 2 percent mortality. Twenty patients who died as a result of the prostatectomy had preexisting medical diseases. Two patients in Slaughter's series had no

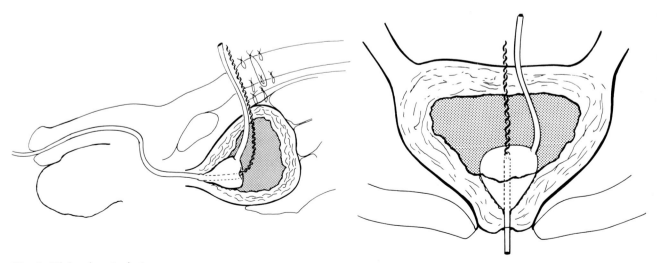

Fig. 1. Pilcher bag technique.

TABLE 1. Comparison of Intra- and Postoperative Transfusions

Technique	Number of Intra- and Postoperative Transfusions		Percentage Requiring Transfusions		
	Patients	Units of Blood	Intraoperative	Postoperative	Combined
Pilcher bag					
Slaughter	75/542	199	0.7	13.4	13.9
Others	56/288	155	1.4	19.1	19.5
Suprapubic prostatectomy with bladder neck suture	74/100	190	45.0	55.0	74.0

preexisting medical problems; both died of postoperative myocardial infarctions.

The Pilcher bag technique was then compared with the standard suprapubic prostatectomy in terms of operative and postoperative blood loss. Only 4 of 542 of Slaughter's patients required intraoperative blood transfusions, and, indeed, only 1 of these was due to the nature of the prostatectomy. This patient had a gland weighing 690 Gm which required 4 units of blood during the operation. A second patient with a prior history of gastrointestinal bleeding underwent surgery with a hematocrit of 31, for which he required transfusions. The third and fourth patients bled from bladder tumors which were removed at the same time as the prostate. Most of the bleeding was thought to be from the bladder tumors and not the prostate. While the decision to perform an open resection of the bladder tumor combined with a transvesical prostatectomy may be open to criticism, and the wisdom of beginning surgery with a hematocrit of 31 may be likewise criticized, the fact remains that only 1 of 542 patients required transfusions during prostatectomy because of bleeding from the prostatic bed. In Slaughter's series, only 9 units of blood were given during the operation, while with the standard technique of suprapubic prostatectomy and suturing of the bladder neck, 45 of 100 patients required intraoperative transfusions (total of 82 units).

Of Slaughter's 542 patients, 17 (13.4 percent) required postoperative transfusions. Of the 288 patients who also underwent the Pilcher bag technique, 55 (19

percent) required postoperative transfusions, while of the 100 prostatectomies done by the suprapubic approach with suturing of the bladder neck, 45 (55 percent) were given transfusions postoperatively. When these three groups were examined from the point of view of both intra- and postoperative transfusions, the statistics were even more impressive (Table 1). Seventy-five of the 542 patients in Slaughter's group required transfusions, for a total of 202 units. Fifty-five of the 288 patients operated on by other staff members using the Pilcher bag technique received a total of 155 units; whereas 74 of the 100 patients in the standard suprapubic prostatectomy group required transfusions.

CONCLUSION

The Pilcher bag technique compared favorably with the standard method in terms of total hospital stay, complications, and mortality. It provides a significantly faster method of prostatectomy. The need for intra- and postoperative transfusions were also significantly reduced using this method. While not advocated for general use, it is a safe, proved method for hemostasis in the patient with uncontrollable intraoperative hemorrhage. In the poor-risk patient with a prostate beyond transurethral size, it offers the advantage of a quick, relatively blood-free procedure with no greater risk of complications.

932 Fifth Avenue
New York, New York 10021
(DR. RATHOD)

REFERENCES

1. Belfield WT: Prostatic myoma: a so-called middle lobe of the hypertrophied prostate removed by suprapubic prostatectomies, JAMA 8:303, 1887
2. McGill AG: Hypertrophy of the prostate and its relief by operation, Lancet 1:215, 1888
3. Lydston G: Surgical Diseases of the G.U. Tract, Philadelphia, I. A. David, 1902
4. Pilcher PM: Technique of transvesical prostatectomy, Surg Gynecol Obstet 24:162, 1917
5. Harris S: Prostatectomy with closure, five years' experience, Br J Surg 21:434, 1934
6. Herman JR, and Castro L: Suprapubic prostatectomy, some early methods of hemostasis, Urology 16:612, 1973

Commentary: Suprapubic Prostatectomy

John W. Draper and W. Reid Pitts, Jr.

Suprapubic prostatectomy (or transvesicle prostatectomy) is one of the oldest and most frequently done operations for the open removal of obstructing prostatic tissue. The wide acceptance of this operation attests to its versatility, success, and safety. Indeed, all other prostatectomies are judged against the standards of suprapubic prostatectomy.

The versatility of the procedure is one of its strongest points. Although suprapubic prostatectomy is usually done for benign prostates not suited for transurethral resection, it can be used for all but the smallest fibrous prostates. In selected circumstances the procedure can be combined with such bladder procedures as diverticulectomy, segmental resection, cystolithotomy, anterior or posterior bladder neck revision, excision of papillomas, or removal of a calculus in the intramural ureter. No special equipment or assistance is required. As evidenced by the preceding article on the use of the Pilcher bag, the procedure can be done blindly by a solo operator if necessary. In fact, we have had some experience using the Pilcher bag after removal of very large prostates (over 200 g) with good results. This versatility and ease make suprapubic prostatectomy such a widely accepted procedure.

The long and large experience with suprapubic prostatectomy has resulted in very few articles on the subject in the last 10 yr. Each modification of the basic technique of digital enucleation of the prostatic tissue through the bladder has been designed to improve hemostasis. Some suggestions for better hemostasis have included the use of various types of absorbable or removable bladder neck or prostatic fossa stitches, direct suturing or fulguration of the prostatic fossa, packing, various catheters used for tamponode, or the use of thrombotic agents in the prostatic fossa. The urologist should be familiar with each of these techniques for special circumstances but should routinely use the technique with which he has the most confidence and success.

The mortality of suprapubic prostatectomy has continued to fall in current series (often less than 3%). This improvement reflects better medical and anesthetic management rather than improved surgical technique. Modern antibiotics, cardiopulmonary care, dialysis, blood banking, coagulation studies, and the like have dramatically lowered mortality figures. There is still occasional use for two-stage suprapubic prostatectomy, usually in the management of benign hypertrophy with acute infection or uremia from chronic obstruction.

Suprapubic prostatectomy is a very successful procedure for the relief of bladder outlet obstruction due to enlargement of the prostate. Complications such as hemorrhage, incontinence, impotence, infection, and azotemia are no more frequent after this procedure than after any other type of prostatectomy. The long popularity of this form of open prostatectomy attests to its success and low complication rate.

Our personal preference for suprapubic prostatectomy involves the following points:

1. A lower abdominal midline incision is used to allow good exposure and maximum versatility.

2. The bladder is opened in the midline from 2 cm from the dome to 2 cm from the bladder neck. This cystotomy allows excellent exposure and can be easily adapted for anterior Y-V plasty or extension into the anterior prostatic capsule. We rarely incise the anterior bladder neck or prostatic capsule.

3. After careful inspection of the bladder, the prostate is enucleated in the usual fashion using the counterpressure of a shielded finger in the rectum. Care is taken not to stretch or damage the membranous urethra–external sphincter mechanism. Gentle manipulation of the apex between thumb and forefinger or sharp division at the apex helps to avoid damaging the sphincter.

4. Indigo carmine is used to identify the orifices and is given as the rectus fascia is opened.

5. Hemostasis is achieved by figure-of-eight stitches of 0 plain catgut in the prostatic capsule at the 5, 6, and 7 o'clock position. Exposure can be improved by grasping the prostatic capsule with long-toothed forceps or Allis clamps. Often a red rubber catheter is passed through the urethra into the prostatic fossa and attached to a second suction apparatus to improve visualization of the prostatic capsule. A fiberoptic light source attached to a narrow Deaver retractor placed just inside the anterior bladder neck gives excellent illumination. A temporary pack in the prostatic fossa can be of help if care is taken not to catch the packing with the hemostatic sutures.

6. Bleeders in the prostatic fossa are directly sutured with 2–0 plain catgut or fulgurated.

7. The anterior bladder neck is *not* routinely closed about a transurethral 24 French Foley catheter. The Foley catheter is inflated until the balloon will not drop into the prostatic fossa with light traction. If the prostatic fossa is unusually large and the Foley balloon pops into the prostatic fossa easily, the anterior bladder neck is closed about the transurethral Foley with two or three simple transverse stitches of 2-0 plain catgut. If the anterior bladder neck is closed, a no. 2 nylon retention stitch is tied to the tip of the Foley and brought out through the bladder to aid in the replacement of the Foley should it come out in the early postoperative period before adequate hemostasis has been achieved.

8. The posterior bladder neck between the ureteral orifices is *not* excised unless the posterior bladder neck is high riding and makes it difficult to pass a transurethral catheter directly to the bladder.

9. A 28 French cystotomy tube and suprapubic drains are routinely used. The cystotomy tube is brought out the superior end of the cystotomy incision and is placed oblique through the abdominal muscle at the superior end of the incision. The drains are brought out through the inferior portion of the midline skin incision.

10. Traction is usually used on the transurethral Foley for the first 6 to 36 hr. Through and through continuous irrigation into the Foley and out the cystotomy is used until the drainage is clear. Normal saline or 3% glycine is used as irrigating fluid. Water should not be used. The rate of flow should prevent blood from clotting.

11. When the tube drainage is clear, we remove the transurethral Foley first and leave the cystotomy in place for urinary diversion. If the bladder neck has been closed, we leave the nylon stitch from the Foley in place. This nylon stitch is taped to the thigh as it exits from the urethral meatus and is secured to the anterior abdominal wall as it exits from the midline incision. Should a transurethral Foley need to be replaced for hemostasis, the new Foley can be tied to the nylon stitch and gently guided into the bladder through the narrow bladder neck.

12. The drains are removed when there is no more drainage. The suprapubic tube is left in place until the seventh to tenth day after surgery when the drainage is clear. The tube is then clamped for a voiding trail after the bladder has been filled by gravity with normal saline. After a 24-hr voiding trial, the postvoiding residual is checked by opening the cystotomy tube. The cystotomy tube is removed if voiding has been adequate and the postvoiding residuals have been small (less than 50 ml).

13. Suprapubic urinary fistulas are rare because the cystotomy tube is brought out obliquely through the rectus fascia and musculature. Urethral strictures and septic urethritis are minimized by using the transurethral Foley for as short a time as possible. The suprapubic cystotomy can be maintained indefinitely should complications arise (*i.e.,* secondary hemorrhage, failure to void, myocardial infarction, pulmorary emboli, pneumonia, cerebral vascular accidents).

14. Should a suprapubic urinary fistula occur, a short period of transurethral Foley catheter drainage will usually close the fistula.

15. Although hospitalization is slightly longer with this management of the suprapubic tube, we feel the flexibility and safety of the suprapubic cystotomy drainage warrants this extra time in the postoperative period.

ANNOTATED BIBLIOGRAPHY

Smiley LV: Modified suprapubic transvesical prostatectomy followed by voiding after second day. J Urol 84:493, 1960

This article follows the usual procedures for transvesical prostatectomy and emphasizes the importance of excising the ridge at the bladder neck so that a catheter can be passed freely from the urethral meatus into the bladder. He also emphasizes the importance of suture ligature of the bleeding points which can be visualized in the prostatic fossa, particularly at five and seven o'clock. In short, he uses the combination hemostatic sutures and traction on a Foley bag to control bleeding. He employs a suprapubic tube and advises a continuous drip of 1:10,000 silver nitrate during the first 24 hr after surgery. I would personally question the wisdom of the silver nitrate irrigation because of the well-known risk of absorption from the open vessels in the prostatic fossa.

Of the 50 patients operated on by this procedure, 2 required packing because of excessive bleeding. Forty-five patients voided voluntarily when the urethral catheter was removed on the second day, and checking the residual urine through the suprapubic tube revealed complete emptying and absence of residual urine. Three patients were unable to void after removal of the urethral catheter. The catheters were then replaced.

In our practice we also usually remove the urethral catheter before removing the cystostomy tube but as a rule not until about the fourth day. We have not experimented with clamping the cystostomy tube until after about the tenth day, and we think it wise to irrigate the bladder and fill it with saline before the patient attempts to void. This reduces the bacterial population in the voided urine, which has obvious value, and also we are assured before we leave the room that the patient will be able to void.

Hutch JA: Combined prostatectomy. J Urol 83:67, 1960

In this paper Hutch proposes to enucleate the prostate in the usual manner from above and then have the operating surgeon move to the lower end of the table with the patient in modified lithotomy position and secure hemostasis with a resectoscope. While he is controlling the bleeding his assistant closes the bladder and abdominal incision. He uses a 28 Malecot suprapubic tube for drainage, and this, of course, will allow a large quantity of irrigating fluid to flow through the prostatic fossa.

Hutch reports on 80 consecutive patients with an overall mortality rate of 1.25% and the average amount of blood used during surgery was 200 ml. This compares favorably with the 465 ml used during surgery for conventional prostatectomy, by the same surgical team and at a similar time.

A. R. Stevens many years ago proposed to me the use of this combined procedure, and probably because of our lack of familiarity at that time with the resectoscope, we found it difficult to obtain hemostasis and abandoned this in favor of conventional procedure. We just might be persuaded to try it again.

Malament M: Maximal hemostasis in suprapubic prostatectomy. Surg Gynecol Obstet 120:1307, 1965

Malament has developed an ingenius procedure. Following conventional suprapubic prostatectomy figure-of-eight sutures are placed at five and seven o'clock and then a purse-string suture of 2 Dermalon is passed around the bladder neck. The ends of the suture are brought out through the abdominal wall. A urethral catheter is passed through the urethra and the suture is snugged up so that it completely obliterates the space around the catheter. The bladder is closed without use of suprapubic tube, and the nonabsorbable suture is left in place for 24 to 48 hr. After the hemostatic suture has been removed the urethral catheter is not irrigated unless it appears obstructed, and it is removed on the fifth postoperative day. In his article Malament reports satisfactory results with 70 patients.

We have tried this surgical procedure only once, and that one patient developed a contracture of the bladder neck requiring subsequent transurethral resection.

Beck AD, Gaudin HJ: The Hryntschak prostatectomy. I. A review of 1,346 cases. J Urol 103:637, 1970

The surgical technique used by these authors was similar to that described by Hryntschak, the salient points being that the prostate was enucleated suprapubically in the usual manner. The prostatic fossa, however, was closed with interrupted sutures around an in-dwelling catheter to make a watertight and bloodtight closure. The suprapubic incision was then closed completely without a cystostomy tube.

The mortality of this large group of 1346 patients was 4.8%. Beck and Gaudin conclude from their study that the Hryntschak technique offers a simple and reliable solution to postoperative hemorrhage, and they feel that the morbidity and mortality are at least equal and possibly superior to those of other comparable series.

Beck AD: The Hyrntschak prostatectomy. II. A late review of 179 cases. J Urol 103:778, 1970

Each of these patients was asked to describe the result of the operation. Some 78.8% thought it was excellent. Seventeen patients, or 9.5% described the operation as fair only, and 2 were frankly dissatisfied with the result. Of the 179 patients, 9.5% admitted to varying degrees of urinary leakage. However, only two patients wore a protecting pad and one was totally incontinent. Eleven percent of these patients were impotent. Forty-one patients, or 23% developed a urethral stricture. In 23 of these the stricture was at the bladder neck.

Beck concludes his paper as follows, "Therefore a satisfactory late result cannot be relied upon to follow Hryntschak's technique of suprapubic prostatectomy."

We also have been disappointed in this procedure because of the high incidence of post-operative stenosis of the bladder neck.

Beck AD, Gaudin HJ: The Hryntschak prostatectomy. III. A modified technique of closing the vesical neck and prostatic cavity. J Urol 104:739, 1970

In this article it is noted that the late results of the Hryntschak procedure are marred by obstruction in the prostatic urethra in 29.2% of the patients treated.

In this present technique a wire loop is fashioned in the catheter, which is to be placed in the urethra so that the figure-of-eight suture that is used to close the bladder neck can be passed through the loop. The free end of the wire is passed through the catheter and emerges beyond the tip of the penis. At any time desired by the surgeon postoperatively the figure-of-eight suture used to obliterate the prostatic fossa can be cut and the closure of the bladder neck relieved. Beck concludes that the late results of the modified operation were superior to those following the classical Hryntschak technique of suprapubic prostatectomy.

We have had no personal experience with this procedure.

Zorgniotti AW, Narins DJ, Dell'Aria SL: Anesthesia, hemorrhage and prostatectomy. J Urol 103:774, 1970.

These authors emphasize the significant improvement they have found in using epidural anesthesia for prostatectomy over other forms of anesthesia. They note that in their series 52.4% were transfused when given general anesthesia, 24.4% with spinal or subarachnoid anesthesia, and 17.3% with epidural anesthesia.

We feel this article makes a great contribution to our management of prostatectomy. We have used epidural anesthesia whenever possible during the past 10 yr for prostatic surgery and are very impressed with the increased comfort of the patient and the decreased blood loss.

Wines RD, Lane V, O'Flynn JD: Post prostatectomy bleeding: Active management by early endoscopic hemostasis and packing in a series of 3219 prostatectomies. Aust NZ J Surg 43:274, 1973

These authors report the management of severe postprostatectomy bleeding in 136 patients. The bleeding occurred after suprapubic and transurethral prostatectomy. If irrigation and catheter tamponade was not successful, transurethral fulguration was undertaken. This controlled the bleeding after suprapubic prostatectomy in 34 of 44 patients. Open packing was used for bleeding not controlled by transurethral fulguration. The packing was removed within 4 days and was succcessful in all 26 patients treated by packing. There were no deaths in the group treated by packing, but seven patients died of hemorrhage with transurethral fulguration alone. None of the patients treated with packing was incontinent.

We have had the same success with packing. Unsuspected coagulation defects should be excluded, but usually the bleeding is related to the surgery. Some urologists use packing routinely after all suprapubic prostatectomies and have the same results as those who use sutures for hemostasis.

Krahn H, Morales P, Hotchkiss R: A Comparison of suprapubic prostatectomy with and without vesicle neck closure. J Urol 96:83, 1966

In this article the efficacy of closing the bladder neck to control hemorrhage after suprapubic prostatectomy is documented. The authors comment on the difficulty in replacing a transurethral Foley if the bladder neck has been closed. In addition, they also notice some increase in the bladder neck contracture. We have noted the above complications and therefore do not routinely close the bladder neck. Should the bladder neck be closed, a nylon stitch in the Foley catheter will allow its replacement.

O'Conor BJ, Bulkey GJ, Sokol JK: Low suprapubic prostatectomy: Comparison of results with the standard operation in two comparable groups of 142 patients. J Urol 90:301, 1963

This excellent article outlines a technique very similar to one that we use. In it the authors demonstrate the superiority of their technique of direct suturing of the prostatic bladder neck. A good description of their procedure is contained in this article.

81

RETROPUBIC PROSTATECTOMY, 1947–1960: A CRITICAL EVALUATION

David B. Stearns

From the Department of Urology of the Massachusetts Memorial Hospitals and
Boston University School of Medicine, Boston, Mass.

The Journal of Urology
Vol. 85, No. 3, March, 1961
Copyright © 1961 by The Williams & Wilkins Co.
Printed in U.S.A.

When Terence Millin[1] invaded the shores of this country in 1947 and dazzled his audiences not only at the American Urological Association meeting in Buffalo but also in a number of other urological centers with his brilliant description and superb technical demonstrations of the retropubic prostatectomy, we, like many others, were enchanted.

Here was the "perfect" operation for the elderly man suffering from prostatism. No more the aftermath of prostatic surgery as we knew it; the more than occasional incontinence following the perineal route, the stricture formation following the much heralded transurethral resection, and those horrible spasms with long, wet convalescences following the suprapubic operation; and of course hemorrhage, the post-operative hemorrhage which nearly all denied but for which we were all finding devices or maneuvers to control. The Millin operation, as he described and performed it, was simple, rapid, bloodless, and with a convalescence which was brief and almost pleasurable.

Read at annual meeting of American Urological Association, Inc., Chicago, Ill., May 16–19, 1960.

It looked as if the suprapubic operation would soon be but a historical procedure and the perineal route would be used only where carcinoma was suspected and a biopsy desired.

It was not long before reports began to appear from all parts of the land. Bacon[2], Lowsley and Gentile[3], Moore[4], Lich[5], Owsley Grant[6], Presman[7], Toulson[8] and others were enthusiastic but nearly all were troubled by osteitis pubis. In some reports it ran as high as 17 percent. Blood loss of consequence was reported only by the foreign authors and S. K. Bacon[9] (six out of 102 in the first series).

All were agreed upon the smoothness and benignancy of the convalescence. There was surprisingly little pain and the postoperative hospital confinement was amazingly short to the patients—since so many of them knew of the long hospital stay associated with the two stage and even one stage suprapubic[10] operations experienced by their fathers and friends.

The operation gained adherents very rapidly, but there was a gradual return to the one stage transvesical prostatectomy. Why, then, the change? What encourages the search for a better operation?—the "combined prostatectomy'' of Hutch[11] or the ''combined prostatectomy'' of Leadbetter and associates[12] or the transvesico-capsular approach of Bourque[13]?

It is my belief that the reasons are multiple; first, the retropubic operation is technically a longer and more difficult procedure; also, it is not the bloodless operation[14–16] as first thought; finally, the fear of osteitis pubis[17] drove many away from the operation.

TECHNIQUE

In our hands the technique of Millin remains unchanged in its major features. Suture ligatures are used to control bleeding, rarely coagulation. The lateral fossae are not packed; therefore, we have not seen obturator neuritis. No retractors are used against the pubis. The fatty and areolar tissue overlying the prostatic capsule is wiped from the center to right and left, and toward the pubis; it is not cut or picked away. This, we believe, may be a factor in the absence of osteitis pubis in this series. With more than just wedge tissue excision from the floor of the bladder neck there has been no instance of bladder neck contracture after the first 50 cases. The capsule is incised and sutured transversely, either by interrupted or continuous suture. In general, the retropubic prostatectomy is, for us, more difficult and more time-consuming than the transvesical approach. Those who watched Millin in 1947 went away with the idea that here was a short, truly surgical operation, nearly everything under vision, made to seem easy by a superb technician. This is no operation for the weak-backed or lazy; it is easy on the patient but hard on the surgeon.

CHOICE OF OPERATION

Like most urologists[15] it is our belief that one should fit the operation to the pathological process at hand. During the course of a year all the techniques are used: approximately 50 percent retropubic, 25 percent transvesical, 25 percent transurethral and the occasional perineal. The decision to do a retropubic operation is based on the conclusion that an enucleation procedure is indicated unless the concomitant bladder disease prohibits it. We have found the retropubic approach of special value in large subtrigonal adenomatous enlargements where, because enucleation is carried out under vision, the ureteral orifices can be noted and guarded.

PREPARATION OF PATIENTS

Preparation of patients in this series has included all the blood, urinary and x-ray studies which are necessary with special emphasis on the cardiac status. Operation is not carried out unless approval is given by the internist. In case of a sharp urinary tract infection we believe in a prolonged (3–4 weeks) wait on constant drainage (14F–16F Foley). We believe that we have avoided acute postoperative bacteremias by this practice.

ACUTE RETENTION

Acute urinary retention was the complaint in 178 patients or 35.6 percent. Residual urine varied in amount to 2700 cc. Preoperative catheter drainage lasted from 2 to 8 days, except in those patients who were sent home, as mentioned previously.

AGE OF PATIENTS

In this series the youngest was 51 and the oldest 96, average 67. This does not differ much from the age groups reported by others in the literature (Table 1). The age[18] of the patient did not enter as a criterion for the choice of this operation. A 96-year-old patient went home in 8 days after an uneventful convalescence.

CONDITION OF PATIENT

Previous to the use of this operation, the medical consultant has at times almost insisted that any patient with a cardiac history or any other poor risk patient should be done transurethrally. The impression was that the transurethral route was a minor procedure. Physicians remembered with apprehension the tedious convalescence of the suprapubic route with the extensive bleeding, marked drops in blood pressure and, worst of all, the spasms. They soon found that known cardiacs could tolerate the retropubic procedure quite well. Impaired renal function has not contraindicated this method of surgery. The patients did well with a progressive postoperative drop in the blood urea nitrogen.

TEMPERAMENT OF THE PATIENT

I have noted that the temperament of the patient plays a very important role in his convalescence. This is true

TABLE 1. Age Groups

Reference	Age	
	Span	Average
Retropubic Prostatectomy		
Stearns	51–96	67
Blue and Campbell	48–93	69.9
Moore	50–86	69.5
Toulson, Mays and Hawkins	50–86	69.4
Suprapubic Prostatectomy and Transurethral Prostatectomy		
John E. Byrne	35–89	67.8
Johnson and Gundersen	42–89	70½

regardless of the operative approach. The patients who are nervous, introspective, and emotional will have a rougher course. They will often have a labile hypertension; they bleed more readily, have a tendency to bowel distension, and will have nausea for 2–3 days.

OBESITY

The man with the obese abdomen presents a technical problem at this operation, not only because of the heavy layers of fat obstructing vision and limiting manipulations, but because these patients do poorly under anesthesia due to wretching and straining. To the one who does the occasional retropubic operation we recommend transvesical enucleation in the obese patient.

ASSOCIATED DISEASES

The aging group will of necessity have the deterioration inherent to this period of life and the patients in my series had it in good measure. One hundred and thirtynine, almost 28 percent, had various types of cardiovascular disease of whom 80 (16 percent) had coronary heart disease and seven, a history of myocardial infarction (Table 2). Forty-two had hypertension. Forty-one had diabetes, a disease which should always put one on the alert, but following retropubic prostatectomy the patients do well since the tissues are not suffused with urine. A variety of other diseases found peroperatively are listed in table 2. Gross hematuria was the chief complaint in 46 patients (9.2 percent).

ASSOCIATED GENITOURINARY DISEASE

As Prather[19] has indicated, the incidence of other genitourinary diseases associated with prostatism can run high (approximately 13 percent). See Table 3. In this

TABLE 2. Associated Diseases

Cardiovascular diseases			
History of previous heart attacks		80	(16%)
Coronary	73		
Myocardial infarct	7		
Hypertension		42	(8.4%)
Thrombophlebitis		6	
Arteriosclerosis (severe)		5	
Cardiovascular accident		5	
Aortic aneurysm		1	
Total		139	(27.8%)
Anemia		6	
Azootemia		8	
Pulmonary disease		27	
Diabetes		41	
Gastrointestinal disease		23	
Hemorrhoids		6	
Hernias		19*	

* Two large scrotal.

TABLE 3. Concomitant Urinry Tract Disease (13.0%)

Bladder calculi	25 operated
Ureteral calculus	1 operated
Diverticulum	4 operated
Prostatic calculi	13 operated
Bladder neoplasm	7 operated
Hydrocele	9 operated
Epididymitis, chronic	1 operated
Renal cyst	2 later operated
Malignant renal tumor	1 operated 1 week later
Functionless kidney	1
Renal calculus	3
Lone kidney	1
Gross hematuria	46 (9.2%)

TABLE 4. Operations Done at Same Time (11.4%)

Removal of bladder calculi	25
Removal of diverticulum	4
Hydrocelectomy	9
Epididymectomy	1
Repair of scrotal hernia	1
Removal of bladder tumor	7
Removal of ureteral calculus	1
Orchiectomy	9
Total	57

series 61 patients had a variety of pathological entities, to which we must add two large scrotal hernias, which necessitated repair, thus making a total of 12 percent. Consequently, 57 additional procedures, some major, some minor, were done at the time of prostatectomy (Table 4).

POSTOPERATIVE COURSE

All who have tried this operation, whether or not they have persisted in its use, have remarked on the smoothness of the postoperative course from the point of view of the patient's comfort and well being. This has been true in this series except for one patient who had paralytic ileus for a period of 2 days.

POSTOPERATIVE COMPLICATIONS

Bleeding. In this series troublesome bleeding occurred in one of every 17 patients. At first, we must have had beginner's luck because the blood loss in the first 25 cases coincided with our preconceived thoughts about the operation; the bleeding was minimal. Nevertheless, we have come to the conclusion, from a careful perusal of the critical reports in the literature (Table 5), that patients will bleed following every type of prostatic surgery,[14,15,20–22] only some will bleed more than others. It is true in this operation.

In this series 8 patients (1.6 percent) had severe primary hemorrhage and 21 had secondary hemorrhage:

TABLE 5. Reports of Bleeding in Literature

	Primary	Secondary
Lich, Grant and Maurer	0	2
Presman and Rolnick	1 (died)	5
Moore (1951) 116	0	7 (8.9%)
Blue and Campbell	7 (packed)	7 (T.U.R.)
Lowsley and Gentile (28)	2	
Bulkley and Kearns		
Suprapubic, 142	5 (2 died)	6 bloody
		15 pink
T.U.R., 724	41 (11 cystotomy, 30 T.U. coag.)	13 clear 1 st day
		9
Birdsall and associates, 1 suprapubic	4%	6%
Johnson and Gundersen, transurethral (100 cases)	8 (8%) operation, 0; irrigation, 8	6 (6%) 4 requiring operation, 2 catheter irrigations

TABLE 6. Postoperative Complications

Hemorrhage			5.8%
Primary		8	1.6%
Packed (3 units)	1		
Cystotomy and 3-way catheter (5 units)	1		
Strong traction and irrigations			
(2–3 units)	6		
Secondary			
Mild		14	2.8%
Use of catheter			
Cleaning of small clots	4		
3–10 days post-discharge	10		
Severe		7	1.4%
Resectoscope			
Coagulated	3		
Ellik evacuation (1 unit)	4		
Total		29	

(Of 178 cases in acute retention, 6 or 3.3% bled and 3 (1.6%) needed resectoscope and Ellik instrument.)

Myocardial infarct	4 (2 died)
Thrombophlebitis	2 (recovered)
Fibrillation	2
Cerebrovascular accident	1 (facial, recovered)
Pulmonary infarct	2 (1 recovered, 1 died)

seven, severe; fourteen, mild (Table 6). In each case sufficient units of blood were given as were believed necessary to prevent hypotension. In the entire series one transfusion was given to nearly every patient who underwent operation; four units were used in the one who was packed; five units to the physician in whom a cystotomy was done; the others were given two or three units. The patients were followed closely and no surgical shock ensued. No death occurred from hemorrhage.

No cases of *osteitis pubis* occurred in this series. The 2 cases reported by Abrams, Sedletzky and myself[23] in 1949 were in service patients done by the resident and visiting man on the service at the time. Among the serious complications, 2 patients had pulmonary infarcts, one of whom died; and four had myocardial infarcts, two of whom died.

Fistula Formation. One desirable advantage of the retropubic operation is the absence of prolonged suprapubic urinary leakage[24] There was slight leakage in 5 cases (1 percent); three resulted from clamps placed erroneously on the catheters by nurses for convenience of the patient in moving about and then forgetting to take them off; and two after discharge, cause unknown. All five were relieved promptly by unobstructed catheter drainage; no leakage for more than one day.

Infection. It has been interesting to observe that whenever infection followed this operation, the patient seemed oblivious of it. Pyelonephritis occurred in 1 patient resulting in a delay in hospital confinement. Epididymitis continues to be a troublesome though not serious complication, 1.4 percent in this series (Moore[4] 19 percent and 6.8 percent,[17] Cooper[18] 10.4 percent, Toulson 7 percent.[8]) Two cases of epididymitis necessitated readmission. The different types of infection are listed in Table 7.

Contracture Necessitating Reoperation. In 8 patients (1.6 percent) contracture of the bladder neck developed. All contractures occurred in the first 50 patients. Three of these required subsequent transurethral section, followed by good results. The other five were amenable to dilatation by sounds.

URINARY CONTROL

Two of the patients (0.4 percent) in this series have incontinence (Table 8); neither loses urine when in bed or asleep, only when active; the leakage is easily controlled by a clamp. Both patients had neuropsychiatric stigmata.

URINARY FUNCTION

One of the pleasant advantages of this operation has been early return to practically normal urinary function (Table 8). In 301 cases nocturia has been reported as none or once toward early morning; 225 reported day

TABLE 7. Postoperative Complications: Infections

Low grade fever: 99–100	11	
Temperature 101–102	8	{6 in hospital, 2 post-discharge} 5 of these vesiculitis
Epididymitis (orchitis-1)	7	{4 occurred when vasectomy was not done in a group of 20 cases, 2 of these required operations; one, 1 month later; one, 2 months later}
Pyelonephritis	1	
Wound infection		{3 (involved fascial)—no incision necessary, 1 stitch abscess}
Vasitis (funiculitis)		4 (one 30 days later) no fever; all stopped short of epididymitis

TABLE 8. Postoperative Urinary Function

301 cases (60%) with nocturia 0–1, diuria 3–5×
225 cases (45%) reported D—3×, N—0
40 cases (8%) reported diuria 6–9×

Force of stream: good, except in 8 cases of bladder neck contracture.
Five had strictures of urethra or meatus with strong but fine stream;
   helped by dilatations.

Incontinence
   2 cases (0.4%) on activity; do not wet at rest
      1 case now 2 years p.o.
      1 case now 1 year p.o.
   4 cases:—mild, stress,—lasted 1 to 4 weeks.
   Contracture of vesical neck: 8 (1.6%)
      3 required transurethral resection
      5 treated with dilatations

TABLE 9. Mortality Rate

Suprapubic Prostatectomy	
Stearns	3 deaths (0.6%)
Blue and Campbell	24 deaths (2.4%)
Moore (1951)	2 deaths (1.7%)
Toulson, Mays and Hawkins	5 deaths (4.7%)
Suprapubic Prostatectomy and T.U.R.	
Bulkley and Kearns, 866 operations	
T.U.R., 724	11 deaths (1.4%)
One stage suprapubic, 142	12 deaths (8.5%)
Birdsall, Poore, Barron and Lang, one stage suprapubic	2 deaths (7.4%)
Johnson and Gundersen, T.U.R.	1.0%

frequency from three to five times, with nocturia not at all. In all but eight, the stream has been reported as strong (these eight have been previously described). Five had strictures of the meatus which were easily dilated.

POTENCY

Out of this series 280 patients answered the interrogation regarding potency. Two hundred and twenty-eight (81.4 percent) claimed ability to have sexual relations; of these, some claimed improved ability. Fifty-two (17 percent) stated that they were impotent following the operation. Many were averse to give answers; some were widowers and others regarded this question as too personal.

MORTALITY

There were 3 deaths in this series (0.6 percent). See Table 9. One patient, aged 59, eight days postoperatively, dressed to go home, died suddenly of a pulmonary infarct. He had no calf pain or tenderness during his postoperative course. Another patient, a dentist, aged 63, a known cardiac with a history of a myocardial infarct 3 years previously, died on the seventh postoperative day. He was due to go home the next day. An electrocardiogram demonstrated a myocardial infarct. The third and latest patient, an 81-year-old man, also a known cardiac, died on his third postoperative day while walking in the corridor with his nurse. Careful review

of this case showed that death might have been avoided if there had been a less optimistic appraisal of the electrocardiogram taken previous to operation.

PATHOLOGY OF TISSUE REMOVED

In this series one leiomyofibroma weighed 41 gm; two leiomyomas, one 280 and the other, 63 gm. In 15 cases adenocarcinoma was reported by the pathologist; the remainder (482) were cases of benign prostatic hypertrophy. It might be stated that in these 15 cases of carcinoma, a malignant process was not suspected before or at operation; there was no difficulty at enucleation. These can be regarded, then, as the group which Freiman[25] reports as not originating in the posterior lobe. The size of the glands varied from 32 gm to 280 gm (average 57.2 gm).

POSTOPERATIVE HOSPITAL DAYS

In these days of truly frightening hospital costs, it is not just enough to cure a patient of his disease. The staggering bill he receives may leave him a financial cripple if he is not adequately protected by one of the better health insurance contracts. No patient in this group was discharged until well enough to go home. The number of postoperative days ran from six to twenty. The median was 8.4 days; 408 (81 percent) stayed from 7 to 10 days. One patient who had a postoperative myocardial infarct stayed 20 days. The patient who was confined 19 days had uremia, coronary disease, Buerger's disease and hypertension. For the most part then, length of hospital stay and medical costs, because of smooth convalescence, were considerably diminished (Table 10).

FEELING OF NORMALCY AND BACK TO WORK

The concept *was* that the 'old fellow' who went through this operation was lucky to be alive. No longer can one be satisfied with that idea. Therefore we have tried to determine how well we have done in restoring these patients to a normal, useful life. Because of the large number of retired men in our group an accurate evaluation was not possible. However, 264 (52.8 percent) did answer interrogations on this subject and it was found that 89 percent returned to work or normal activities in from three to eight weeks after the first visit following discharge from the hospital.

Early feeling of well-being and return to normalcy have been two of the great advantages of this operation.

SUMMARY

A critical evaluation of the retropubic operation for the relief of prostatic obstruction in a large number of patients resulted in the following conclusions:

It is an operation which should be considered for the larger enucleable gland. It has added value in the large subtrigonal lobe.

The presence of additional bladder disease need not deter from its use.

From the point of view of pre-existing medical disease, the indications for operation can be just as flexible as for transurethral resection.

Age was no deterrent to the operation.

It was noted that obesity must be taken into consideration in this operation.

Technically, the operation is more difficult and longer than the transvesical.

Because it is an extravesical operation, the patient has a feeling of well-being postoperatively.

Operative bleeding remains a problem here, too. There is no excuse for surgical shock or mortality from hemorrhage. There should be no hestitation in using transfusions.

TABLE 10. Postoperative Hospital Days

	Total Average Hospital Stay	Pre-operative	Post-operative
Stearns	10.9	2.5	8.4
Cooper:			
T.U.R.	14.0		
Suprapubic	22.		
Perineal	30.		
Retropubic	16.4		
John Byrne			
T.U.R.	24		14.2
one stage suprapubic	25		21.
two stage suprapubic	52		34.2
Harrison and Poutasse:			
suprapubic	16		
retropubic	16		
T.U.R.	14		
Perineal	18		
Johnson and Gundersen, T.U.R.	11	2½	8½

Cardiovascular disease continues to be the disease most feared in this, as in other methods.

The mortality rate was low: 3 deaths in 500 cases (0.6 percent).

Postoperative infection was not a major concern. Osteitis pubis can be avoided.

The postoperative hospital stay is shorter. Only 26 patients, 5.2 percent, remained from 13 to 20 days.

Early return to useful life and normal physiology of voiding and sexual ability occur in a high percentage of patients.

CONCLUSIONS

In a large series of cases subjected to retropubic prostatectomy, the patients had a comfortable recovery with early return to "normal" urinary function and daily usefulness. Mortality and serious morbidity are definitely low, but troublesome postoperative bleeding still persists. Short postoperative hospital confinement and the benignity of the convalescence help control soaring hospital costs. Though not the perfect operation, retropubic prostatectomy has taken its place as one to be considered in the relief of the benign obstructing prostate.

416 Marlboro St., Boston 15, Mass.

REFERENCES

1. Millin, T.: Retropubic prostatectomy. J Urol 59:207, 1948

2. Bacon, S. K.: Retropubic prostatectomy: An extravesical technique. J Urol 59:376, 1948

3. Lowsley, O. S. and Gentile, A.: Retropubic prostatectomy. J Urol 59:281, 1948

4. Moore, T. D.: Experiences with retropubic prostatectomy. J Urol 61:46, 1949

5. Lich, R., Jr., Grant, O. and Maurer, J. E.: Extravesical prostatectomy. J Urol 61:930, 1949

6. Lich, R., Jr.: Retropubic prostatectomy: A review of 678 patients. J Urol 72:434, 1954

7. Presman, D. and Rolnick, H. C.: Retropubic prostatectomy. J Urol 61:59, 1949

8. Toulson, W. H., Mays, H. B. and Hawkins, C. W.: Experiences with retropubic prostatectomy. J Urol 65:874, 1951

9. Bacon, S. K.: Retropubic prostatectomy. J Urol 61:75, 1949

10. Byrne, J. C.: Mortality of prostatectomy. J Urol 67:121, 1952

11. Hutch, J. A.: Combined prostatectomy. J Urol 83:67, 1960

12. Leadbetter, G. W., Jr., Duxbury, J. H. and Leadbetter, W. F.: Can prostatectomy be improved? J Urol 82:610, 1959

13. Bourque, J. P.: Transvesico-capsular prostatic adenomectomy (transcommissural). Preliminary report on 80 cases. J Urol 72:918, 1954

14. Taylor, W. N., Kaylor, W. N. and Taylor, J. N.: Retropubic and suprapubic prostatectomy: Comparative clinical study. J Urol 74:129, 1955

15. Harrison, J. H. and Poutasse, E. F.: Choice of operative approach for prostatectomy. J Urol 63:132, 1950

16. Goodyear, W. E. and Beard, D. E.: Blood loss in prostatectomy. J Urol 62:849, 1949

17. Moore, T. D.: Retropubic prostatectomy. J Urol 65:865, 1951

18. Cooper, H. G.: Retropubic prostatectomy. J Urol 77:297, 1957

19. Prather, G. C. and Reich, M.: Associated pathological conditions of the bladder in cases of prostatic obstruction. J Urol 41:498, 1939

20. Bulkley, G. and Kearns, J. W.: Results of prostatic surgery in 866 cases, J Urol 68:724, 1952

21. Blue, G. D. and Campbell, J. M.: Clinical review of 1000 cases of retropubic prostatectomy. J Urol 80:257, 1958

22. Johnson, M. A. and Gundersen. A. H.: Transmethral prostatic resection: A comparison of two series of cases. J Urol 63:147, 1959

23. Abrams, M., Sedletzky, I, and Stearns, D. B.: Osteitis pubis. New Eng J Med 240:637, 1949

24. Klinger, M. E.: Retropubic prostatectomy. Am J Surg 91:749, 1956

25. AMA Arch Path 68:243, 1959

ADDITIONAL REFERENCES

BIRDSALL, J. C., POORE, G. C., BURROS, H. M. and LEARY, D. S.: Progress in suprapubic prostatectomy. J Urol 68:729, 1952

BOYD, M. L.: Suprapubic or retropubic prostatectomy? J Urol 76:625, 1956

BUTLER, J., BRAUNSTEIN, H., FREIMAN, D. G., and GALL, E.: Incidence, distribution and enzyme activity of carcinoma of prostate gland. AMA Arch Path 68:243, 1959

FINDLAY, H. V. and RIPARETTI, P. P.: Retropubic prostatectomy and diverticulectomy as one stage procedure. J Urol 72:429, 1954

GOLDSTEIN, A. E., GOLDEN, M. C. and SILBERSTEIN, H.: Retropubic blood loss in prostatectomy. J Urol 71:63, 1954

HAND, J. R. and SULLIVAN, A. W.: Retropubic prostatectomy. Analysis of 100 cases. JAMA 145:1313, 1951

MACDONALD, S. A.: Prostatectomy, mortality and morbidity. J Urol 72:439, 1954

SCHEINMAN, L. J.: Experiences with retropubic prostatectomy. Northwest Med 51:118, 1952

SLOTKIN, G. E.: Retropubic prostatectomy: Survey of indication and results of 119 cases. NY State J Med 52:220, 1952

THURMANN, R. C., JR. and STUMP, G. D.: Suprapubic, transvesical prostatectomy with primary closure. J Urol 67:95, 1952

ZIMMERMAN, I. J.: Art of prostatectomy in age of automation. J Urol 76:776, 1956

Commentary: Retropubic Prostatectomy

Mendley A. Wulfsohn

The selected article analyzed and evaluated a large series of patients some 20 yr ago over a 13-yr period. Although there have been numerous contributions to the literature on the technique of retropubic prostatectomy since that time, the basic operation has remained unaltered. The main changes that have taken place have been in preoperative and postoperative care as well as major improvements in anesthesia. As a result, many patients at that time considered unfit for surgery now fall into the realm of operative therapy. Stearns reported a 35.6% incidence of acute urinary retention in his series. Allan and Coorey in 1965 reported a 69% incidence of acute retention in a series of a 1000 patients undergoing retropubic prostatectomy and claimed that this unusually high incidence of retention adversely effected mortality.[1] In more recent times more liberal indications for prostatectomy have resulted in a higher incidence of prostatism as an indication for surgery and a lower incidence

of acute urinary retention. The decision to operate on patients with prostatism is based on the presumption that the results of surgery will be improved if prostatectomy is carried out before complications such as urinary retention, urinary tract infection, diverticulum, hydronephrosis, and renal failure occur. The patient's age, general condition, and medical condition must be taken into consideration. A high degree of clinical acumen is required. Probably the least important factor is the size of the prostate gland. More important are the patient's urinary symptoms. In particular, weakness of the stream, hesitancy, and intermittency are important symptoms suggesting detrusor failure. Overflow incontinence suggests severe chronic retention. Objective measurement of the stream itself using uroflowmetry is also an important investigation in modern urology. A maximum flow rate of less than 10 ml/sec is a strong indication that prostatectomy will be required soon. In doubtful cases serial measurements of flow can be obtained and compared to see if any deterioration occurs. Intravenous (IV) urography remains an important tool in the investigation of prostatism. Large intravesical intrusions of the prostate, bladder saculations, and large amounts of residual urine favor early operation. Any dilatation of the ureters resulting from the bladder outlet obstruction is an indication for surgery.

Bladder instrumentation before prostatectomy should be avoided if at all possible, and cystoscopy should not be performed unless disease other than the prostatic enlargement is strongly suspected. Cystoscopy should be carried out routinely immediately preoperatively and should be performed in the operating room under the same anesthetic as administered for the prostatectomy. Prior insertion of catheters for cystography, measurement of residual urine, or cystometrogram should be avoided unless specifically indicated. Instrumentation can readily precipitate urinary retention, infection, or bleeding, all of which add to morbidity and mortality.

Preoperative bladder drainage, however, will be required for acute urinary retention or severe chronic retention, particularly if there is infected urine or hydronephrosis with renal failure. The latter group of patients as well as patients who have developed urinary retention related to intercurrent medical conditions such as myocardial infarction or cor pulmonale will require more prolonged periods of bladder decompression. Although some urologists prefer suprapubic cystostomy, many are satisfied to use prolonged urethral catheter drainage and claim minimal complications. If suprapubic cystostomy is elected, trochar cystostomy is preferred to an open procedure. Some of the newer plastic trochar catheters, which include a retention balloon, are very suitable for this purpose.

Since the operation of retropubic prostatectomy, as known today, was introduced by Millin in 1947, the procedure has gathered popularity amongst urologists worldwide.[2] Regular reports appears in the literature suggesting technical improvement in the operation and instruments used.[3-5] The operation was originally described using a special set of instruments, but the procedure can very satisfactorily be performed, if necessary, with any ordinary set.

Stearns in his paper mentions that the operation is "easy on the patient but hard on the surgeon," which indicates that the retropubic approach may be difficult to learn. Once mastered, however, it has the advantage of being applicable to all types of prostatic obstruction, and there are virtually no contraindications to its use. Obesity, which is disadvantageous in all forms of open surgery, is certainly no absolute contraindication. Small fibrous and malignant glands are more suitably treated by transurethral resection but can also be very safely managed by the retropubic approach, where the obstructing tissue can be totally excised under direct vision. A preexisting suprapubic cystostomy tract is also not a contraindication to retropubic prostatectomy, although clearance of the retropubic space requires more dissection to release adhesions.

Hemorrhage is a problem in all forms of prostatic surgery, including retropubic prostatectomy. Some advantage is gained in this approach because it allows more adequate suture–ligature and cautery of bleeding points. Special suturing techniques to minimize bleeding during and after prostatectomy have been suggested by Bensimon and by Gregoir but are not in general use.[6,7]

Postoperative bladder neck contracture, a common complication in the early days of retropubic prostatectomy, has been minimized by various techniques. Millin himself in 1953 proposed wedge resection of the bladder neck.[8] Since then, there have been further improvements, including wide excision of the whole posterior rim of the bladder neck and subsequent covering of the raw area with trigonal mucosa (trigonization).[9] Excision of the anterior lip of the bladder neck and a Y-V type of closure has also been suggested.[10] More recently, excision of the posterior lip of the bladder neck has been extended inferiorly to include removal of the whole posterior lamella of the prostate. This step has been advocated as a routine step in prostatectomy and was originally described for prophylactic removal of the main cancer-bearing portion of the gland.[11,12] It is particularly important in cases of chronic prostatitis where a residual thickened, infected posterior capsule is likely to result in persistent postoperative symptoms.

Operative Technique. The patient is in the supine position with a moderate amount of Trendelenberg. The pelvis is elevated either by flexing the table or elevating the bridge. A modified Pfannenstiel incision is used. The linea alba is divided transversely immediately above the symphysis pubis and the incision extended laterally and upward on either side through the anterior rectus sheath and external and internal oblique aponeuroses in the shape of a V. The upper flap of rectus sheath is freed from the underlying muscle and the small amount of remaining linea alba below the incision is divided down to the symphysis pubis. The medial half of the insertion of the rectus abdominus muscle on each side may be separated from the pubis as well at this stage if extra exposure appears necessary. The inferior skin flap is retracted downward using a temporary suture that attaches it to the fascia overlying the pubic symphysis. The pyramidalis muscles and recti are separated in the midline and the pre-peritonal fat and peritoneum are wiped upward off the anterior surface of the prostate and bladder.

The vas deferens is identified on either side as it crosses the pelvic brim. The vas is picked up with an Allis forcep, crushed with a hemostat and ligated, or clipped. The Millin self-retaining retractor is then inserted to expose the region of the anterior prostatic capsule. The long- or short-bladed Millin retractor can be employed depending on the size of the patient. One or more veins are identified within the preprostatic fatty tissue. These veins should be carefully suture-ligated or cauterized in continuity and then divided. Immediately after these vessels are divided the fatty tissue may be swept laterally on either side to allow the anterior capsule of the prostate to be seen. The vesical neck is easily identified by palpation and by the appearance of decussating fibers in the capsule. Two traction sutures are placed in the prostatic capsule above and below the contemplated line of incision using a boomerang or Mayo needle. The capsulotomy incision is usually placed approximately 1 cm. below the bladder neck but its location will vary, depending on the prostatic size and height of the gland. It should not be made too low because this may make final closure difficult. The incision is made transversely (Fig. 1), using the cutting cautery and the capsular bleeders are coagulated as they appear. The length of the incision will depend on the size of the prostate gland but it should extend

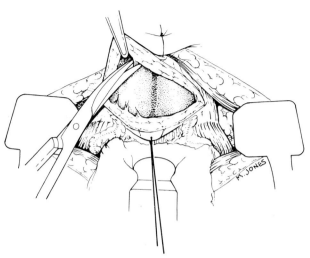

Fig. 2. The incision has been deepened and the prostatic urethra has been entered. The plane of cleavage between the false capsule of the prostate and adenoma is being developed with scissors.

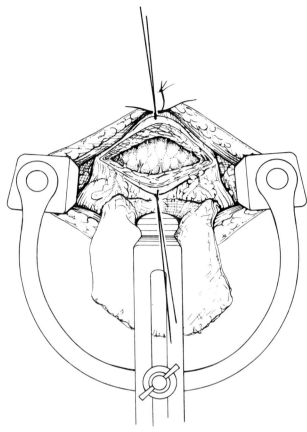

Fig. 1. The transverse capsulotomy incision has been completed following insertion of traction sutures above and below the line of incision. The adenoma is visible in the depths of the incision. Note that the superifical pre-prostatic veins have been ligated and divided separately.

to the lateral borders of the capsule to afford maximum exposure of the prostatic fossa later in the operation. At the lateral edges large prostatic vessels are frequently divided, and require coagulation. Care should be taken when making the incision to have the cutting instrument at right angles to the prostatic capsule so as not to undercut the inferior edge. The incision is deepened well into the adenoma so that the prostatic urethra is entered. This affords ready visualization of the plane of cleavage between the false capsule and the adenoma. This plane is developed for a short distance (Fig. 2) using curved scissors and the urethral mucosa on either side of the anterior commissure is divided.

At this stage of dissection one of two methods of removal of the prostate can be adopted depending on the type of gland, size of enlargement, and choice and experience of the operator. A particularly safe method suitable for large adenomas is digital enucleation along the plane of cleavage already established. Removal of the superior blade of the self-retaining retractor is usually required. The apical portions of the lateral lobes should be dissected free early in the enucleation because this will obviate traction on, and possible damage to, the distal sphincter mechanism. As the dissection precedes upward from this point and the lateral lobes become delivered through the capsulotomy, a strip of urethral mucosa consisting of the posterior and lateral walls of the urethra remains intact. The verumontanun can be readily identified in most patients but the surgeon should appreciate that this structure appears much smaller when seen with a naked eye then when viewed cystoscopically. Division of the urethra is performed under vision with the scissors immediately above the verumontanum (Fig. 3). Enucleation of the adenoma now proceeds upward as far as the bladder neck. The attachment to the bladder neck is divided by sharp dissection. The second method of prostate removal is more suitable for small adherent glands but may also be used for large adenomas if preferred. Complete removal of the gland is accomplished by sharp dissection under direct vision. In both methods the keystone for preventing postoperative incontinence is the early approach to apical parts and visual division of the urethra.

After the adenoma has been removed, the Millin bladder neck spreader or other suitable retractor is inserted into the bladder through the bladder neck. Upward traction facilitates exposure of the depth of the prostatic fossa and enables removal of any residual tags or small separate adenomas. Attention is now directed to the bladder neck itself. Excision of the posterior lip of the bladder neck is carried out in all cases to prevent the development of postoperative contracture. The trigone and ureteral orifices must be positively identified before any resection is carried out. It is not uncommon for the orifices to be extremely close to the area of resection and the surgeon must be sure to identify both and if necessary to protect them by insertion of ureteral catheters. A wide ellipse of bladder neck tissue is resected from the 4 o'clock to the 8 o'clock position

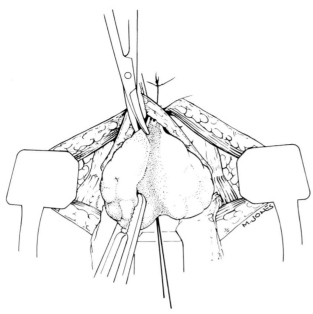

Fig. 3. The lateral lobes have been enucleated and delivered out of the prostatic fossa. The verumontanum is identified in the depths of the opened prostatic urethra. The urethra is divided sharply above the verumontanum.

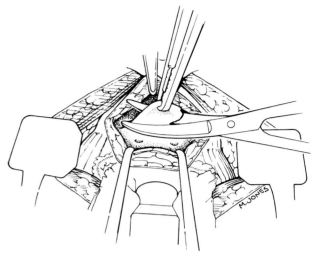

Fig. 4. The posterior lip of the bladder neck is excised. A thick ellipse of tissue is removed from the 4 o'clock to 8 o'clock positions. The ureteral orifices are clearly identified and preserved.

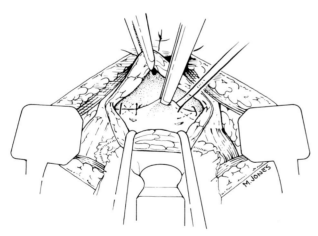

Fig. 5. Figure-of-eight posterolateral hemostatic sutures are inserted. These sutures are placed through the lateral extremities of the cut bladder neck and distally pick up generous bites of the posterolateral recesses of the prostatic capsule.

(Fig. 4). A small wedge resection of the bladder neck is not sufficient.[9]

Hemostatic figure-of-eight 0 dexon sutures are placed in the bladder neck area at the 4 and 8 o'clock positions using a round-bodied Mayo needle (Fig. 5). These sutures are placed

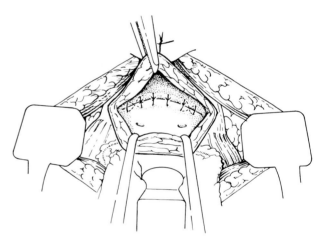

Fig. 6. Trigonisation has been completed. Interrupted sutures tack the cut edge of the trigone down to the posterior capsule.

in such a way as to draw the trigonal mucosa down into the prostatic fossa. If correctly placed they control the posterolateral vascular supply. Further interrupted sutures are placed to tack the free edges of trigone down to the posterior capsule; these sutures have a further hemostatic effect (Fig. 6). This procedure of trigonization covers the posterior raw surface of the bladder neck and adjacent capsule and has the advantage of preventing fibrosis and encouraging more rapid postoperative epithelialization of the prostatic fossa. It also allows easier catheter introduction into the bladder. Residual bleeding points in the prostatic fossa may now be fulgurated, but mild venous oozing,

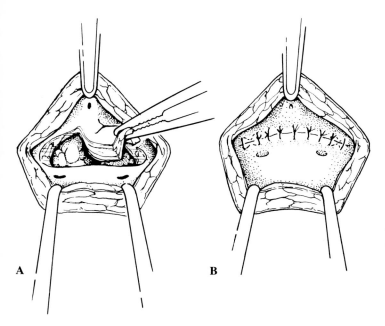

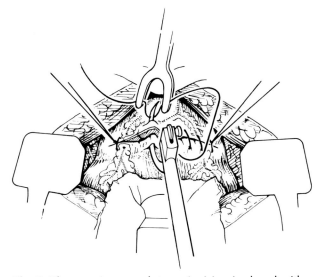

Fig. 7. (*A*) Excision of the posterior capsule. A transverse incision is made below the ureteral orifices. A triangular wedge of posterior capsule is being removed. The seminal vesicles and ampullae are seen posteriorly. (*B*) The posterior capsule is reestablished with interrupted sutures. Hemostatic figure-of-eight sutures are placed at the corners of the incision.

particularly from the deeper portion of the fossa, is best left alone because of the danger of damaging the distal sphincter mechanism.

If the surgeon elects to carry out posterior capsulectomy, this is performed before trigonization. A transverse posterior incision is made immediately proximal to the bladder neck and is deepened until the seminal vesicles are identified. The plane between the posterior capsule and seminal vesicles is developed and followed distally, where it reenters the prostatic fossa a short distance above the level of the verumontanum. The lateral borders of the posterior capsule are also divided along with this dissection, and this portion of the gland is then removed (Fig. 7A). If seminal vesiculectomy is required, it can be done through the opening produced in the posterior capsule. It should be remembered, however, that the removal of the seminal vesicles is more likely to result in postoperative impotence. If there is evidence of chronic vesiculitis, the vesicle on either side should preferably be incised so that postoperative fistulization with the prostatic fossa occurs, allowing free drainage. Apposition of the divided trigonal edge to the cut edge of the posterior capsule is easily accomplished with interrupted 0 dexon sutures (Fig. 7B).

Bladder calculi may be removed through the bladder neck, and, if necessary, diverticulectomy can also be performed. The incision may be extended vertically into the bladder if required or a separate cystotomy incision may be used. A #22 Foley catheter with a 30-ml balloon is inserted and the balloon is distended in the bladder. If there is any narrowing of the external urethral meatus, this should be dealt with at this stage by a plastic meatotomy.

The anterior prostatic capsule is now closed using a single layer of continuous heavy chromic catgut suture (Fig. 8). At each end of the wound the corner sutures should be placed deeply, providing a further hemostatic effect. The boomerang

Fig. 8. The anterior capsulotomy incision is closed with a continuous suture using the boomerang needle. The corner sutures are placed first, and deep bites are taken on either side to increase hemostasis. All the bites should pick up the full thickness of both cut edges of the incision. In the case of the upper edge, the bladder mucosa should be included in the sutures.

needle is preferred for the placement of these sutures. Some surgeons prefer to use a Mayo needle, and this technique is very suitable for large glands where the suture line is high. There is no substitute, however, for the boomerang needle when suturing a lowlying capsulotomy incision. The urologist in training is therefore well advised to use the boomerang needle in all cases in order to become familiar with this instrument. Whatever needle is used, care should be taken that the periosteum of the pubic bone is not damaged. Damage to the periosteum may be instrumental in producing osteitis pubis, but this is a complication that is extremely rarely seen today.

The urethral catheter is irrigated to make sure that the sutures are watertight, but no attempt should be made to close small leaks. A 0.25-inch suction drain is placed in the space of Retzius and brought out through the lower wound flap.

Usually hemostasis is adequate with this operation, and straight catheter drainage can be used postoperatively. An IV injection of a diuretic, for example, 20 mg of furosemide,

should be given during closure of the wound and the patient should be given adequate amounts of IV fluid. This produces sufficient diuresis to obviate the necessity for postoperative catheter irrigation in most cases. If bleeding appears excessive, a three-way cathether may be employed instead, with continuous bladder irrigation immediately after the operation. When continuous irrigation is used, this should be done with chlorhexidine 1:5000 in water, since irrigation with saline has been reported to increase the incidence of postoperative infection.[13]

The wound drain is usually removed on the fourth day, and the catheter can be removed from the third day onward once the urine becomes completely clear of blood.

REFERENCES

1. Allan WR, Coorey GJ: Retropubic prostatectomy. Br J Urol 37:569, 1965

2. Millin T: Retropubic prostatectomy: A new extravesical technique: Report on 20 cases. Lancet 2:693, 1945

3. Michell TD: Retropubic dissecting forceps. Br J Urol 39:64, 1967

4. Reid RE: Self retaining bladder neck spreader for retropubic prostatectomy. J Urol 103:452, 1970

5. Abreu LM, Abelson L: New forceps for retropubic prostatectomy. J Urol 107:626, 1972

6. Bensimon H: Hemostatic retropubic prostatectomy. J Urol 108:326, 1973

7. Gregoir W: Haemostatic prostatic adenomectomy. Eur Urol 4:1, 1978

8. Millin T: In Riches Sir E (ed): Modern trends in urology, p 285. Scarborough, Ont, Butterworth & Co, 1953

9. Caine M, Pfau A: The prevention of post-prostatectomy bladder neck stenosis. Br J Urol 35:173, 1963

10. Salvatierra O Jr, Rigdon WO, Malley JA: Modified retropubic prostatectomy: A new technique. J Urol 108:126, 1972

11. Turner-Warwick R, Whiteside CG, Worth PHC, et al: A urodynamic view of clinical problems associated with bladder neck dysfunction and its treatment by endoscopic incision and trans trigonal posterior prostatectomy. Br J Urol 45:44, 1973

12. Riches E: Posterior capsulectomy in routine retropubic prostatectomy. J Urol 85:965, 1961

13. Bastable JRA, Peel RN, Birch DM, et al: Continuous irrigation of the bladder after prostatectomy: Its effect on post-prostatectomy infection. Br J Urol 49:689, 1977

ANNOTATED BIBLIOGRAPHY

Abrahams PH: Prostatism and prostatectomy: The value of urine flow rate measurement in the preoperative assessment for operation. J Urol 117:70, 1977

Fifty-three patients were assessed preoperatively and postoperatively using maximum urine flow measurement; 20 of the patients underwent prostatectomy, and the remaining 33 underwent transurethral resection. Mean maximum flow rates of the patients operated on for prostatism was 8 ml/sec compared with a mean maximum of 17 ml/sec noted in a control group. Flow rate in the patient group did not correlate well with preoperative symptoms and prostatic sizes. Postoperatively, patients who had unimproved symptoms were found to have had a higher preoperative mean urine flow rate. The author recommends routine urine flow rate measurement in the preoperative assessment of patients with prostatism, which will allow the isolation of a group of patients with symptoms of prostatism but without bladder outflow obstruction who are unlikely to benefit from prostatectomy.

Bensimon H: Hemostatic retropubic prostatectomy. J Urol 108:326, 1973

A technique for minimizing hemorrhage during retropubic prostatectomy is described. This consists of placing deep suture–ligatures around the line of capsular incision. The main vesicoprostatic pedicles are suture–ligated on either side. Following this, sutures are placed in the prostatic capsule above and below the bladder neck as well as at the vesicostatic junction. Finally, a suture is placed across the capsule at the level of the apex. After enucleation of the prostate, sutures are placed around the

main posterolateral bleeders. The needle pierces the lateral wall of the fossa, and the suture is tied outside after going through the full thickness of the capsule. The final hemostatic sutures attach the cut edge of the trigone to the floor of the prostatic cavity.

Salvatierra OR Jr, Rigdon WD, Malley JA: Modified retropubic prostatectomy: A new technique. J Urol 108:126, 1972

In addition to a wide posterior wedge resection of the bladder neck, the authors remove a rectangle of anterior bladder neck as well to prevent bladder neck stenosis. This also affords better exposure to the prostatic fossa. Only 1 bladder neck stenosis occurred postoperatively in 157 patients.

Hickinbotham P, Turner WD, Sarma KP: Retropubic no catheter prostatectomy: A review of 106 cases. J Urol 97:899, 1967

Retropubic prostatectomy was performed in 106 cases with hypertensive anesthesia using hexamethonium bromide and the head-down position of the patient. Systolic blood pressure was maintained between 70 and 80 mm Hg. As a result of the bloodless operative field, excellent hemostasis was obtained using diathermy and inserting sutures between the trigonal cut edge and posterior capsule. Normally the patient passed heavily blood-stained urine within 12 hr. The indication for postoperative catheterization was a painful distended bladder. Catheter insertion is facilitated by the accurate trigonization that had been employed. Four patients required catheterization at operation because of a doubtful capsular suture line. Eight required postoperative catheterization for suprapubic leakage. Six further patients were catheterized when they developed retention or inadequate voiding. There were four deaths in the series, three of which were related to infection. The remaining 88 patients did well and passed urine spontaneously. Some passed large clots. Blood transfusion was reduced and was required by only four patients. Patient comfort was increased, and postoperative care was less demanding for the nursing staff. Seventy-eight patients left the hospital before 11 days and 44 from 6 to 8 days.

Bastable JRG, Peel RN, Birch DM et al: Continuous irrigation of the bladder after prostatectomy: Its effect on post prostatectomy infection. Br J Urol 49:689, 1977

This study showed that postoperative irrigation with normal saline led to an increased incidence of postoperative urinary tract infection. Irrigation with chlorhexidine 1:5000 water led to the same incidence of infection as occurred with straight urinary drainage. The conclusion was that if irrigation was required, chlorhexidine should be added to the irrigating fluid.

Whitaker RH: The fate of the prostatic cavity after retropubic prostatectomy. Br J Urol 43:722, 1971

Twenty-three patients were studied following retropubic prostatectomy, nine of whom consisted of a prospective study. Cystograms were carried out to demonstrate the appearance of the residual prostatic cavity. The size of the cavity 10 days postoperatively correlated with the weight of the tissue removed. However, there is little or no relationship between the size of adenoma removed at prostatectomy and the final size of the cavity. The minimal size is generally reached by the third month, although there may be a little shrinkage up to 1 yr. The cavities of the nine patients in the prospective study reduced in size to 9% to 86% of the original size. The bladder neck was found to be incompetent at rest in all the patients, which confirms that continence after prostatectomy depends on the distal sphincter mechanism.

82

A NEW ANATOMIC APPROACH IN PERINEAL PROSTATECTOMY[1]

Elmer Belt, Carl E. Ebert and Alva C. Surber, Jr.

Reprinted from The Journal of Urology
Vol. 41, No. 4, April, 1939

Because of the precision of approach, accuracy of hemostasis, visual control at all stages, ready adaptation to individual anatomic variations, large reduction in shock, rapidity of healing and shortness of hospitalization, perineal prostatectomy has rapidly become the method of choice in the surgical removal of selected prostatic hypertrophies.

The logical outgrowth of the ancient procedure of perineal lithotomy—even the usual incision dates from Celsus—the historical development of modern perineal prostatectomy has been a story of constant controversy. The debatable differences between the suprapubic, transurethral and perineal schools are hotly argued to this day.

But the most significant developmental trend of all is traceable to the early perinealists themselves and the overthrow of the blind "closed" operation, offspring of external urethrotomy, by the visual "open" procedure based upon accurate anatomic dissection of the individual perineum.

The anatomists were already firmly entrenched in Germany. Billroth had performed the fist definitely planned perineal prostatectomy in 1867 when he enucleated a malignancy of the entire gland through a median perineal incision. Leisrink (1882) using the curved perineal incision of Celsus also removed a carcinomatous prostate and reconstructed the urethra. Zuckerkandl (1889) further developed the approach by painstaking dissection of the perineum. Proust and Albaran (1901) devised a perineal prostatic tractor, described the median capsular incision, individual lobar enucleation and developed a perineal "frame" or table.

Goodfellow of San Francisco (1891) was the leading exponent of the "closed" operation and was remarkably successful without any real attempt at hemostasis. This method had great vogue and consisted simply and effectively enough of an external urethrotomy over a "staff" following which the gland was forced down with suprapubic pressure, blindly enucleated, grasped and forcibly avulsed from its pelvic moorings.

The "big dissecting operation" of Leisrink and Zuckerkandl so ably perfected by Young was viewed with alarm by these men and properly provoked Dr. Young's prophetic rebuke in 1903:

"Why these gentlemen prefer darkness to light and object to a technique carried out under full visual control is incomprehensible. In my opinion, the near future will see the surgery of the prostate on the same rational basis of careful technique under visual inspection as that of other parts of the body."

Young accordingly developed his "conservative perineal prostatectomy" effecting enucleation of the individual lobes and preserving the integrity of the ejaculatory ducts.

More recently, Hinman has repeatedly stressed the necessity of proper anatomic approach and adequate training in the various perineal procedures.

---

[1] Read before the annual meeting of the American Urological Association, Quebec, Canada, June 29, 1938.

Gibson of San Francisco (1928) employing the essential Young technique emphasized the importance of eliminating packs and bags to control hemorrhage and suggested the simple use of a retained urethral catheter and complete closure by suture.

Anatomy. The new anatomic approach described here uses the cleavage plane present between the longitudinal muscle fibers of the rectum and the external sphincter ani muscle. By using this route, the capsule of the prostate can be exposed bloodlessly and without cutting a nerve. Other factors developed in this new surgical technique are: Complete hemostasis obtained by suturing the bleeders present in the neck of the bladder and complete closure of the perineal wound except for a Penrose drain from the capsule to the skin. This drain is usually removed within twenty-four hours. In visualizing this new anatomic approach it is important first to review the anatomy of the male perineum involved in this procedure.

Figure 1 is a drawing from a dissection in which all superficial and deep fascia has been removed and the Fascia of Colles can be seen covering the deep sutures lateral to the ischio-cavernosus muscles. The nerves and arteries are left intact on the right side. The rectum is distended with cotton. The median raphé is shown from the scrotum to the anus. The continuity of the bulbo-cavernosus muscles, the superficial transverse perineal and the external anal sphincter is demonstrated. All these

muscle fibers seem to converge to a point which the anatomists have described as the central tendinous point of the perineum. In reality this is not a point but is two planes, one extending transversely and the other extending in an antero-posterior direction.

Figure 2A is a lateral view. It demonstrates the superficial transverse perineal muscle lying deeply in relation to the bulbo-cavernosus muscles. Some of the fibers of the bulbo-cavernosus muscles converge toward the central tendinous plane of the perineum, helping to form this plane. In the insert (Fig. 2B) a drawing of the surgical route is presented. On close scrutiny, one observes why it is very easy to elevate the external sphincter ani from the rectum since there is no intrinsic attachment of the external sphincter fibers to the longitudinal fibers of the rectal wall. In the operative procedure herein described, neither the superficial transverse perineal muscle nor the deep transverse perineal muscle is seen since they lie above the external sphincter ani muscle and are, therefore, hidden by its fibers when the plane between the longitudinal fibers of the rectal wall and this external sphincter muscle is followed. The location of the transverse perineal muscles above the external spincter muscle is shown in Figure 2B.

The dissection presented in this drawing shows the pubo-coccygeal fibers of the levator ani muscles. The medial bundles of these muscles sometimes become fibrous in character. They converge to form part of the central tendinous plane of the perineum and are some-

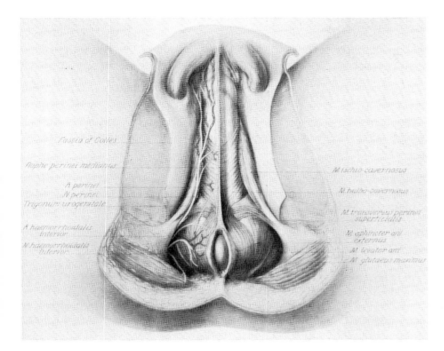

Fig. 1. Dissection of male perineum showing superficial musculature and main trunks of arteries and nerves.

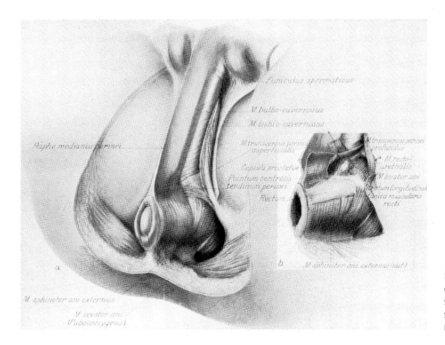

Fig. 2. Oblique view demonstrating location of central tendinous plane, showing insertion of muscles. Inset shows anatomic dissection of operative route with muscles cut for clarity.

times spoken of as the recto-urethralis muscle. They are shown in this drawing as covering the posterior surface of the capsule of the prostate. Inferiorly they merge with the longitudinal fibers of the rectum and superiorly they diverge and pass to the pubic arch on each side of the urethra. In this dissection, the external sphincter muscle has been cut and laid open in order to give free vision of the operative route along the cleavage plane which follows the longitudinal muscle fibers of the rectum to the central tendinous plane. The recto-urethralis muscle has been split in the mid-line and each edge is pushed laterally exposing the capsule of the prostate at the apex of the gland.

Figure 3 is a drawing of a dissection which demonstrates the location of the bladder in relation to the ischial tuberosities. It shows the course of the internal pudendal vessels and nerves as they emerge underneath the pubic ramus to supply the penis. They are thus demonstrably outside this operative field and remain untouched and uninjured in this operative procedure. The pubo-coccygeal fibers of the levator ani muscles are shown as they dip down and hold the rectum in a sling continuing with some of the fibers of the opposite side and adhering to the coccyx by a fibrous attachment.

Operation. A description of the operative procedure follows in which reference is made only to those anatomic structures actually encountered.

A spinal anesthetic is given. The patient is placed on a perineal table so constructed that an extreme lithotomy position is attained. In this position, the thighs are well flexed and separated, the buttocks are elevated and the upward tilted perineum comes to be parallel to the floor. The operative field, external genitalia and inside of both thighs are well scrubbed with green soap, with water, and then with 1:10,000 bichloride. With the aid of a syringe pressed against the external urinary meatus, about 200 cc of ½ percent solution of meroxyl is allowed to traverse the urethra and flow into the bladder. This is done to effect a sterilization of the bladder contents. The skin of the perineum, peri-anal region, inside of both thighs, scrotum and pubis is painted with 1-1000 tincture of merthiolate. The perineum is then draped with towels wet with 1:10,000 bichloride of mercury, leaving the operative site and external genitalia exposed. A rubber dam is fastened to the perineum with skin clips in a manner which walls off the external anal aperture in order to prevent contamination. A towel is fastened to the skin at the base of the scrotum with skin clips and then folded upward over the scrotum and penis to leave only the external urinary meatus exposed (Fig. 4).

The special instruments necessary to the operation are shown in Figure 5.

The incision through the skin is semicircular and placed on a radius about 1½ cm from the anal mucosa running in effect from one ischial tuberosity to the other. The flap of skin thus released is depressed backward with the aid of a dry gauze sponge held against it beneath the fingers of the left hand (Fig. 6).

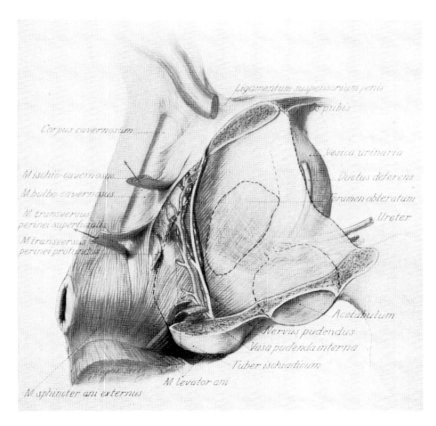

Fig. 3. Lateral oblique view showing superficial and deep layers of perineal muscles with course of deep pudendal vessles toward trigonum urethralis.

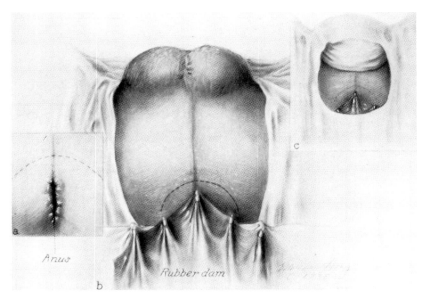

Fig. 4. (A) Incision line 1½ cm from the rectal mucosa. (B) Rubber dam covering the rectum. (C) Final draping.

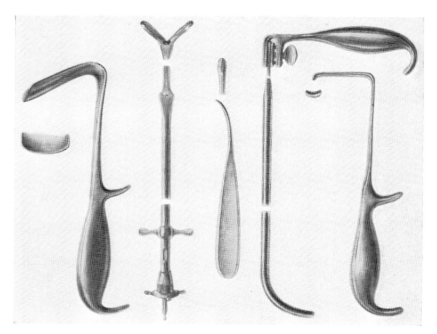

Fig. 5.

Fig. 6. Skin incision. Superifical skin flap pulled down stretching fibers of median raphe before they are cut.

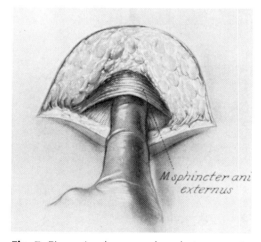

Fig. 7. Finger in cleavage plane between external sphincter ani muscle and rectum.

The tension thus created causes the delicate fibers of the median raphe to stand out. These are cut. Their release permits the handle of the knife to obtain an entrance by means of blunt dissection below the muscle fibers of the external anal sphincter (Fig. 7).

These muscle fibers can be seen close to the skin of the lower flap. The fibers of the external anal sphincter separate very easily from the longitudinal fibers of the rectum, opening up a cleavage plane which is readily followed along the longitudinal fibers to the apex of the prostate. Here the free anterior borders of the levator ani muscles run within a few millimeters of one another ("recto-urethralis" muscle). The handle of the knife may be pressed between these borders. With the left forefinger, the anal canal can be depressed (Fig. 8).

Lateral pressure is exerted against the borders of the levator ani muscles separating them widely. This movement exposes the tough fascia covering the posterior surface of the prostate (Fig. 9).

A number 24 French sound is passed through the external urinary meatus traversing the prostatic urethra

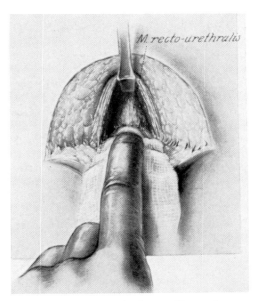

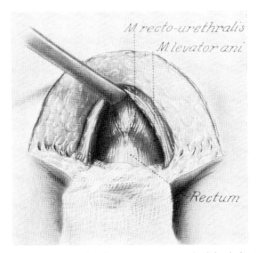

Fig. 9. External sphincter ani muscle lifted disclosing part of central tendinous plane of perineum; central fibers of recto-urethralis muscle divided longitudinally in mid-line.

Fig. 8. Finger depressing rectum disclosing fibers of recto-urethralis muscle.

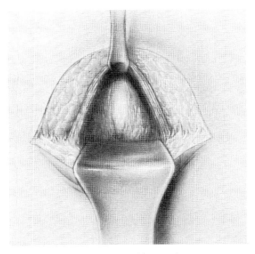

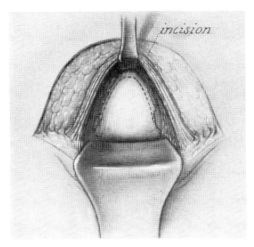

Fig. 11. Levator ani muscles pushed laterally; rectum eased backward. Posterior surface of prostate exposed. Dotted line marks incision through capsule.

Fig. 10. Posterior retractor in place; fibers of recto-urethralis and levator ani muscles split by blunt dissection to disclose posterior layer of fascia of Denonvilliers.

and passing into the bladder. Forward and downward pressure against the handle of this sound helps to present the prostatic capsule into the wound and permits the posterior surface of the prostate to be more completely exposed. A posterior retractor placed over the rectum holds it down away from the operative field (Fig. 10).

The prostatic capsule is entered through an inverted U-shaped incision, the transverse part of which is care-fully placed in a point peripheral to the verumontanum (Fig. 11).

This point is recognized as a soft spot which can be felt with the tip of the finger just proximal to the membranous urethra in the prostatic capsule. A flap thus formed is pressed backward carrying with it the verumontanum and the ducts leading from the seminal vesicles into the verumontanum. The ducts remain in the flap close to the prostatic capsule. A small triangle of urethra containing the verumontanum goes backward with the flap exposing the sound in the urethra. The adenomatous nodules can be seen bulging into the prostatic urethra against the sound. At their upper margins, within the apex of the gland, the urethra can be seen leaving the surface of the adenomatous lobes and passing toward the membranous urethra. This posterior (dorsal) aspect of the membranous urethra is carefully isolated and cut off with scissors (Fig. 12).

The adenomatous nodules are bluntly dissected from the compression capsule of the prostate with a sweeping motion of the finger which carefully keeps to the cleavage plane between adenoma and capsule (Fig. 13).

The sound in then withdrawn, a number 24F urethral catheter introduced through this urethral opening and the bladder contents (admixture of urine and meroxyl) evacuated, following which the catheter is discarded.

The remaining (anterior or ventral) portion of the membranous urethra is then divided thus severing the urethra completely. Care is taken to leave as long a cuff of urethra as possible to facilitate its reconstruction later in the operation.

The freeing motion is aided by means of a Markley prostatic tractor passed through the prostatic urethra into the bladder where it is opened to allow traction (Fig. 14A), and, as the lobes are mobilized, by thyroid clamps which pull the adenomatous nodules toward the operator. With them comes a cone of bladder neck which is stripped backward by blunt dissection, carefully preserving the circular muscle fibers of the bladder neck which can be clearly seen. A cylinder of mucosa is finally reached which passes from the inner surfaces of the adenomatous masses to become continuous with the bladder mucosa. This tube is cut off with scissors. The first snick is made in the anterior portion and the bladder edge is at once grasped with an Allis clamp to keep it from retracting upward out of sight. Then the cut is extended around the entire circumference of the tube of urethra and the entire prostate thus freed and removed (Fig. 14B). Often a large middle lobe necessitates carrying the cut high up transversely across the base of the trigone. Allis clamps are applied to each side of the bladder neck (Fig. 14C). The cone of bladder mucosa thus held in two Allis clamps carries a rich blood supply coming down to it from the bladder. Often large spurting vessels can be seen within it. These arteries are sutured with number 2 chromic hemostatic ligatures passing through the bladder neck (Fig. 15A).

At times spurting vessels can be seen farther up on the side of the bladder inside the capsule. These are similarly controlled. When one is assured that there is no more bleeding from the bladder neck and inside the capsule, the neck of the bladder is examined to make sure that there are no remnants of adenomata or tags of tissue. If any are present, they are carefully trimmed away. Following this a two-hole urethral catheter, F number 24 in size, is introduced into the urethra through the penis and caused to emerge from the cut end of the urethra inside the capsule. It is then pulled out of the wound and held in an elevated position by a narrow anterior retractor, revealing the cut end of the urethra (Fig. 15B). A number 2 chromic stitch is then taken through this anterior (ventral) border of the urethra, carried through the anterior (ventral) border of the bladder neck, tied and cut (Fig. 15B). After this procedure the free tip of the catheter is introduced into the bladder

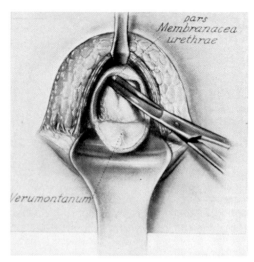

Fig. 12. Scissors cutting membranous urethra off at junction with prostatic urethra.

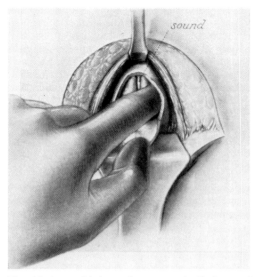

Fig. 13. Lateral lobes of prostate shelled out of capsule.

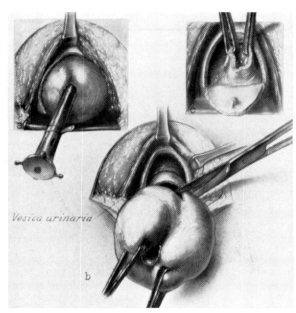

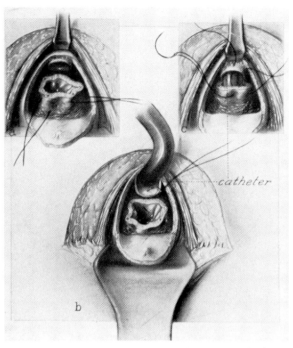

Fig. 14. (a) Prostatic tractor inserted. (b) Prostate being cut from bladder neck. (c) Prostate removed; bleeding from bladder neck controlled by Allis forceps.

Fig. 15. (a) Bleeders in bladder neck are ligated. (b) Rubber catheter inserted into urethra and retracted outward to facilitate placing first suture uniting anterior wall of urethra and bladder neck. (c) Catheter then inserted into bladder and lateral and posterior walls of urethra are sutured to bladder neck.

thus splinting the cut ends of anastomosis (Fig. 15C). A chromic stitch is taken on each side and one medially, completing the reconstruction of the urethra by its approximation to the bladder neck (Fig. 15C).

The closure of the prostatic capsule is the next step (Fig. 16). In this procedure an attempt is made to close the dead space between the bladder and the capsule. This is done by taking a stitch at each lower corner of the capsule, which includes some bladder tissue and emerges through the central flap (Fig. 16A). Five number 2 chromic sutures are usually necessary to approximate the flap and close the capsule (Fig. 16B). Thus the structures are brought back to their original anatomic position (Fig. 16C).

DISCUSSION

Dr. Oswald S. Lowsley (New York City): Dr. Van Duzen's sections were most instructive. At one time I made a study of the prostate at each decade. The lack of capsule at the base of the prostate was recognized by us very early in our studies of the prostate, and Dr. Van Duzen has shown it beautifully.

Dr. Belt has modified Dr. Young's operation in an ingenious manner. The technique which he has demonstrated is a real masterpiece in surgical demonstration. One cannot look at such beautiful work without contem-

plating the recent trend in prostatic surgery. It seems to me impossible for a surgeon to carelessly toss aside a beautiful operation, open and bloodless, for a blind, apple-coring procedure on big prostates, because if there is bleeding, one can handle the bleeding under perfect vision.

When my resident urologist, Dr. Hunt, studied our cases, I was amazed to find that we were doing 62 percent vesical neck resections, but we also found that that statement had to be modified, because a lot of those patients on whom we did vesical neck resections, were patients that in former years we wouldn't have operated upon at all; we would have treated these by dilatation and massage.

The modern methods have increased Dr. Young's original punch operation, increased the incidence of it in our hands about 600 percent. We intend to do perineal prostatectomy, suprapubic prostatectomy, when we have tremendous intrusion into the bladder, and vesical neck resection on suitable cases, but when in doubt, we do perineal prostatectomy.

Dr. Prather has given us a very splendid study of

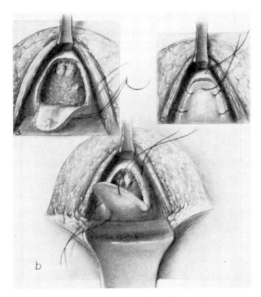

Fig. 16. (a) Membranous urethra and bladder neck united; sutures through capsule into bladder musculature to obliterate all dead spaces. (b) Capsule being closed with interrupted sutures. (c) Completion of closure.

the various complications or accessory findings in a series of 404 cases of prostatectomy.

Dr. Thomas E. Gibson (San Francisco): There are 2 points I would like to speak about briefly: I think all of us who do perineal prostatectomy will readily admit that the most difficult part of the operation is the approach to the prostate. After that, the rest is easy.

Dr. Belt and I are neighbors. In the last 3 or 4 years he has been showing me pictures of his new approach to the prostate. It didn't sound good to me, so I remained skeptical. However, about 6 weeks ago I had the privilege of seeing and assisting Dr. Belt in Los Angeles at 2 of these operations. I was thoroughly surprised with the ease of this exposure.

The second point I wish to speak about is primary closure. I began to do primary closures in 1926, and in 1928 published a report on it. I have continued to follow this procedure. In close to one-half of the cases, primary closure will result in primary healing, and the patient will be able to leave the hospital completely healed in 12 to 14 days postoperative.

One objection to primary closure is that it increases the likelihood of postoperative sepsis and embolism. A piece of rubber dam bound to the prostatic capsule avoids this danger and readily permits drainage, if drainage is going to occur.

Dr. Hugh H. Young (Baltimore, Md.): Dr. Van Duzen has presented an interesting and instructive paper, but as my time is limited, I wish to pass on to the paper by Dr. Elmer Belt, which was accompanied by most beautiful motion picture of an operation I have ever seen. Dr. Belt has demonstrated his new modifications of perineal technique graphically. Many urologists say that one of the reasons why they do not do perineal prostatectomy is the fear of injuring the rectum, but here comes Dr. Belt who shows how little fear he has of the rectum by carrying out his operation within the external sphincter of the rectum. By lifting up this sphincter and retracting it widely he simply follows the longitudinal fibers of the rectum to the prostate. He tells me he divides the rectourethralis muscle longitudinally and pulls it aside with the levator ani on each side. Whether this is preferable to dividing the rectourethralis transversely close to the membranous urethra and obtaining the freedom which this gives, to push the posterior layer of Denonvilliers' fascia back with the rectum is a moot point. I agree that one should dispense with an incision into the membranous urethra and open the urethra directly through the anterior part of the prostate either transversely or longitudinally, depending on whether one carries out the operations in an inverted "U" capsular incision such as many of us have used for years, and which Dr. Belt prefers, or through an oblique incision through one of the lateral lobes followed by separate enucleation of the lateral and median lobes and complete preservation of the floor of the urethra, verumontanum and ejaculatory ducts. In Dr. Belt's operation after pushing the verumontanum backward, the prostatic urethra is divided transversely, the lateral lobes with the anterior commissure are enucleated and cut off from the vesical neck, and then removed in one piece with the median lobe. This is followed by approximation of the vesical mucosa with the urethra anteriorly, a method which we and others have employed from time to time. The operation which he has shown has the advantage of great thoroughness, complete visability, arrest of hemorrhage with sutures and approximation of mucous surfaces, and the avoidance of perineal drainage, an inlying catheter supplying exit for drainage. We described a similar method of complete closure without perineal drainage, but after employing it in about 100 cases, we decided that it was safer to insert through the perineum a small rubber drain which was removed the following day, the inlying catheter being kept in place for about a week. Some members of our staff still prefer this method and have in fact modified the suture technique in various ways. I myself am inclined to be a little less radical in the prostatic enucleation and often enucleate the lateral and median lobes separately, preserving the roof of the urethra and the anterior commissure which generally has no hypertrophied lobules in it. In cases where anterior lobes are present they are removed with the laterals. The problem presented is so varied that one should be prepared to modify his technique accordingly. In young men with excellent sexual powers a very conservative operation with bilateral capsular incisions with preservation of the floor of urethra, verumontanum and ejaculatory ducts and the roof of the urethra and anterior commissure is certainly desirable. In older men, who have lost their sexual powers, and in cases of markedly enlarged prostates with involvement of the anterior commissure with adenomatous lobules, the more radical enucleation of most of the posterior urethra and anterior commissure is preferable because of the greater ease with which such a technique can be employed. Where speed is desirable and if arrest of hemorrhage is difficult, the Davis bag offers great advantages. The arrest of hemorrhage is immediate, good drainage is afforded and the vesical neck drawn down in approximation with the urethral mucosa.

Whatever method is employed little difficulty should be encountered in carrying out a safe, thorough, comparatively bloodless operation through the perineum, and in leaving a wound that should heal kindly. What a marked contrast there is between the splendid wound condition left by Dr. Belt after approximation of the vesical and urethral mucosa and the great necrotic ragged infected would left after transurethral resection in cases of marked enlargement of the prostate! Instead of primary healing they are confronted with weeks of sluggish convalescence during which the dead tissue has to come away and the vesical mucosa struggle to cover the great defect left by extensive resection. Dr. Belt's demonstration of the simplicity with which the prostate can be exposed without danger of injuring the rectum, even when he goes within the external sphincter, the clean enucleation of the hypertrophied masses within the normal prostate which is left behind and the excellent conditions for healing of the wound which are obtained by plastic obliteration of the operative wound in the prostate in his anastomosis of mucous surfaces is a splendid argument for the supremacy of the perineal prostatectomy in the treatment of the markedly enlarged prostate. Our several publications of cases in which prostatectomy was necessary after from one to four transurethral resections confirms Dr. Belt's stand in favor of perineal prostatectomy, but the fact that by perineal exposure many early cases of carcinoma of the prostate may be discovered and cured radically is, I believe, the supreme argument for the wider usage of perineal prostatectomy.

Three number 2 chromic stitches are taken in the fibers of the rectourethralis and the medial portion of the pubo-coccygeal fibers of the levator ani muscles

(Fig. 17A). A Penrose drain is placed in the space between the rectum and the capsule. The edge of the external sphincter ani muscle is approximated to the longitudinal fibers of the rectum with a purse-string stitch, number 2 chromic (Fig. 17B). Several interrupted plain catgut stitches close the superficial fascia. A continuous subcuticular running stitch closes the skin, (plain catgut) (Fig. 17C)

The wound is dressed with moist compresses (hexylresorcinal, "S.T. 37"), the bladder irrigated, all clots removed and the catheter is strapped in place. The patient is sent back to his room.

The Penrose drain is removed after 24 hours. Five percent glucose in normal saline is given intravenously twice daily for 2 days, the catheter is irrigated frequently. These patients are afebrile on the third post-operative day. At this time they are allowed to stand at the side of the bed for a few minutes, several times a day. A non-residue diet is given for 1 week. The bowels are moved (oil retention enema) about the sixth or eighth post-operative day. The catheter is removed the eighth to twelfth post-operative day. Per primam healing is expected in 40 percent of the cases. Persistent sinuses are unknown. The length of hospitalization is from 10 to 21 days. Most patients leave on the sixteenth post-operative day.

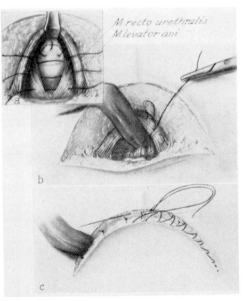

Fig. 17. (a) Interrupted sutures bringing together rectourethralis and levator ani muscles. (b) Purse-string in sphincter ani externus, Penrose drain in space between capsule and rectum. (c) Superficial fat and fascia brought together by continuous subcuticular stitch.

SUMMARY

Some salient historical factors in the development of perineal prostatectomy are outlined.

A pertinent review of the essential anatomy of the male perineum from original dissections is given.

A new anatomic approach in perineal prostatectomy is presented: A curving transverse perineal incision 1½ cm. from the anal mucosa exposes the delicate fibers of the median raphe. These are cut revealing the arching fibers of the median raphe. These are cut revealing the arching fibers of the external rectal sphincter which are raised to disclose the glistening longitudinal muscle layer of the rectum. The anal canal and rectum are depressed and pushed backward defining the central tendinous plane of the perineum. The areolar tissue and tendinous protion of the recto-urethralis muscle joining the rectum to the base of the perineal membrane are snipped through revealing the anterior free borders of the levatores ani and the flat sheath of the recto-urethralis. The recto-urethralis is split medially and retracted laterally with the levatores ani exposing the tough, white, shining fascia of Denonvilliers covering the posterior surface of the prostatic capsule. By using the cleavage plane present between the external sphincter ani and the longitudinal muscle fibers of the rectum, therefore, the capsule of the prostate is exposed bloodlessly and without cutting a nerve.

A technique for perineal prostatectomy is presented with illustrations and general operative results.

1983 Wilshire Blvd., Los Angeles, Calif.

REFERENCES

GIBSON, T. E.: Improvement in perineal prostatectomy. Surg Gynec and Obstet 47:531–539, 1928

GOODFELLOW, G.: Median perineal prostatectomy. J Am Med Assoc 43:194, 1448, 1904

HINMAN, F.: Perineal prostatectomy. Surg Gynec and Obstet 49:669–681, 1929

LEISRINK, H.: Tumor prostate; Totale exstirpation der prostata. Arch F klin Chir Berlin 28:578–580, 1882

PROUST, R.: Manuel de la Prostatectomie Perineale pour Hypertrophie. Paris, 1903

WATSON, F. S.: The operative treatment of the hypertrophied prostate. Ann Surg 39:833, 1904

YOUNG, H. H.: Conservative perineal prostatectomy. JAMA 41:999–1009, 1903 Also discussion Dr. Goodfellow's paper. JAMA 43:1448, 1904

ZUCKERKANDL, O.: Ueber die perineale blosslegung der prostata und der hinteren blasenwand. Wien Med, Presse 30:857; 902, 1889

Commentary: Perineal Prostatectomy

Otto M. Lilien

There must be a word between *tragic* and *sad* that applies to the fact that most urologists are not trained to do perineal surgery. In terms of craftsmanship, it is sad to be lacking in a skill that is specific to the discipline. From the patient's point of view, the unavailability of this approach could be the difference between a good and a morbid outcome. The tragedy lies in the potential decline of this craft, whose benefits extend beyond the issue of how to enucleate a prostate.

Perineal surgery is a unique surgical art whose mastery guarantees the urologist a high level of competence and knowledge when dealing with genitourinary pathologic conditions below the bladder neck. It involves a singular level of surgical dexterity that is intermediate between microscopic and gross. It requires a precise knowledge of exquisite anatomic relationships in a potentially hazardous arena. It is urologic surgery at its best. Why then, is perineal surgery approaching the status of an "endangered species"? Probably because it is difficult to learn, is taught in a relatively limited number of centers, and is obviously not essential in the vast majority of urologic problems. The most devastating blow to the craft of perineal surgery, however, arises as a consequence of current controversies regarding the management of prostatic carcinoma. By the time the smoke has settled, and if it becomes generally recognized that localized (B_1) carcinoma of the prostate is indeed best treated by radical perineal prostatectomy, ancient treatises may have to be researched to rediscover this art.[1]

In the interim, let us consider the case for simple perineal prostatectomy. The surgical advantages of simple perineal enucleation are based on several anatomic, physiologic, and biologic conditions. Given a patient who requires open prostatic surgery, the perineal route permits an exposure that does not compromise the anterior abdominal wall. Avoidance of a suprapubic incision has certain pulmonary physiologic advantages that become significant in the elderly or respiratory-compromised patient. This conclusion derives from the fact that ventilatory exchange in the older patient relies entirely on diaphragmatic movement. An abdominal incision in such a patient results in abdominal wall splinting, decreased diaphragmatic excursion, pneumonia, and so on. In addition, Giesecke and associates, studying the effects of the exaggerated lithotomy position in 18 patients with pulmonary disease, manifested by decreased forced vital capacity and forced expiratory volume, observed a paradoxic improvement in forced expiratory volume during surgery, presumably due to the mechanical effects of the viscera, resulting in improved end exhalation position of the diaphragm and added force to the maximum expiratory effort.[2]

Postoperative immobilization, with its associated peripheral vascular complications, is reduced when perineal as opposed to a transabdominal approach is used. Patients ambulate the first postoperative day, pain requiring narcotics is less than with transabdominal surgery, ileus is reduced, and normal feedings replace intravenous (IV) fluids earlier. In general, the overall physical and psychologic trauma of a surgical onslaught is kept to a minimum. Thus, perineal surgery is the safest open surgical approach for patients with cardiac disease, pulmonary dysfunction, ileal loops, colostomies, and large hernias.

In terms of hemostasis, there is probably little significant difference between the actual blood loss associated with a properly performed retropubic prostatectomy as opposed to a perineal enucleation. Note, however, that the perineal approach provides the most direct and easiest access to the inferior hypogastric vascular wing. This difference in accessibility becomes very significant when radical prostatic surgery is indicated as well as in patients who have hematologic disorders but require open prostatic exposure. Thus, direct access to the vascular pedicle provides a margin of safety not otherwise available. It is the approach of choice in the treatment of prostatic hyperplasia complicated by multiple prostatic calculi, suppurative prostatitis, and prostatic abscess. Perineal prostatectomy is the easiest enucleation procedure in patients who are undergoing or have undergone abdominoperineal resection for rectal carcinoma.

Finally, the biologic quirk responsible for the localization of early carcinoma to the posterior lamella of the prostate precludes any approach, other than perineal, for open biopsy.

Consideration of prostatic malignancy underscores the value of the perineal approach. This opinion is based on the following considerations:

- An analysis of all relevant studies reporting the incidence of prostatic carcinoma (Rich, 1935; Moore, 1935; Gaynor, 1938; Baron and colleagues, 1941; Franks, 1954; Halpert and colleagues, 1966; Lilien and colleagues, 1968; and Rullis and colleagues, 1975) leads to the conclusion that the incidence of prostatic carcinoma is at least 30% in the age group 60 to 79, 41% in the age group 70 to 79; and 67% in the age group 80 to 89.[1]
- Most carcinomas begin in the outer prostate, posteriorly. Thus, if one is committed to establishing a preprostatectomy diagnosis of prostatic carcinoma, and this diagnosis depends on biopsy of the posterior lamella of the prostate, there are two alternatives: needle biopsy of the prostate and open perineal prostatic biopsy.

It can be argued that open perineal prostatic biopsy is the procedure of choice, specifically in the case of the B_1 lesion (a nodule confined to one lobe of the prostate surrounded by nonindurated tissue) in a patient who is a potential candidate for radical prostatectomy: that is, his age and medical history predict an actuarial life expectancy of greater than 10 yr and preoperative evaluation fails to reveal evidence of metastatic disease. (It would be inappropriate in this Commentary to debate the virtues of different methodologies for acid phosphatase determination, the pros and cons of lymphangiography, the usefulness of computed tomography (CT), or the indication for diagnostic lymphadenectomy except to emphasize that the probability of lymph node involvement in our hypothetical B_1 patient is less than 10%).[3]

The conclusion that open biopsy is preferrable to needle biopsy, in such an instance, is based on two principles: radical prostatectomy is the procedure of choice for B_1 carcinoma and a negative needle biopsy does not, because of sampling error, rule out the existence of a carcinoma. Therefore, if open surgery will follow positive and negative needle biopsy results (radical prostatectomy if positive; open biopsy if negative), and the surgical approach is identical for both procedures, needle biopsy can be avoided. An exception will be the patient in whom the risk of impotence, which may be associated with open biopsy, outweighs the risk of missing an early carcinoma.

In 1968 I reported a study in which I compared the relative merits of suprapubic (50 cases) versus a perineal approach (150 cases) in the surgical treatment of prostatic enlargement.[4] Patients requiring prostatectomy for benign prostatic hyperplasia were divided into 2 groups: those with no clinical suspicion of malignancy and those with localized induration or nodularity suggestive of carcinoma confined to the prostate. Group 1 patients were subjected to either open perineal frozen section biopsy of the posterior surgical capsule followed by perineal prostatectomy (Hudson's modification of Belt's procedure) or suprapubic prostatectomy. (More debilitated patients were operated on perineally, while patients in whom potency was a strong issue were operated on suprapubically.) Group 2 patients were all subjected to the perineal approach. Patients found to have carcinoma in frozen section biopsies underwent radical prostatectomy if, on preoperative assessment, an actuarial life expectancy of more than 10 yr was predicted.

The following clinical data were obtained:

- The median age of patients who had a perineal prostatectomy was 70.5 yr, while the median age of patients undergoing suprapubic prostatectomy was 67 yr.
- The overall incidence of malignant disease confined to the prostate in 150 perineal prostatectomies was 31.3%.
- The probability of an unsuspected carcinoma was twice as great in glands weighing more than 55 g than in smaller glands.
- The error in preoperative clinical diagnosis of benign and malignant disease confined to the prostate was as follows:

  In 115 patients diagnosed as benign preoperatively, 24% had unsuspected carcinoma.

  In a similar group of 50 patients operated on suprapubically, only 4 instances (8%) of unsuspected malignancy could be documented. It was concluded, therefore, that any form of prostatic enucleation that does not sample the posterior surgical capsule will miss the diagnosis of up to two thirds of unsuspected malignancies.

In 35 patients preoperatively diagnosed as having malignancy confined to the prostate, slightly less than half proved to be benign.

With regard to postoperative retention of sexual potency, approximately a third of those potent before perineal surgery retained their potency, in contrast to two thirds of those who underwent suprapubic prostatectomy. However, as these patients were not randomized, that is, debilitated patients were selected for perineal surgery, the actual difference in retained potency in the two approaches must be significantly less than indicated in this study.

Although the history of perineal surgery can be traced back to before the Christian era (the earliest perineal lithotomy is attributed to Ammonius, 460 to 357 bc), the evolution of modern perineal surgery is a relatively recent event.

In a paper read by Hugh Young before the American Association of GenitoUrinary Surgeons in Washington, June 12, 1903, entitled "Conservative Perineal Prostatectomy. A Presentation of New Instruments and Technic," he described his surgical approach and reported his experience with 15 patients.[5] He concluded, regarding the operation of prostatectomy, that

where before it was (with me—perhaps not with others) an operation done somewhat haphazard, depending largely on the sense of touch, and in the dark; now the entire operation is performed in a shallow wound, accurately under visual control, proper regard being paid to the urethra and to the ejaculatory ducts, so that they are preserved to continue their pleasant duties.[5]

It must be admitted, however, that like politics, perineal surgery catalyzes controversy. Parker Syms wrote that the

French operation described by Albarran, Proust and others, and which has been presented to us by Young of Baltimore, involves an unnecessarily elaborate dissection of the perineum which requires an unnecessary amount of time and entails an unnecessary amount of hemorrage. Every hypertrophied prostate can be removed through a simple straight median incision of the perineum, the cut can be made by practically one sweep of the knife down to the membranous urethra, which should be opened on the lithotomy staff; the rest of the operation is done by simply stretching and pushing the tissues with the finger, and enucleation of the prostate may be rapidly and easily accomplished by the single finger of the operator. Goodfellow of San Francisco accomplished this with the greatest success without the aid of any retractor.[6]

To which Young responded at the 55th Annual Session of the American Medical Association, 1904:

Drs. Syms and Goodfellow pretended to have holy fear of "the big dissecting operation" which they say I do. . . . No more injury, (and perhaps less) is done than in those blind operations done by touch alone. Why these gentlemen should prefer darkness to light and object to a technic carried out under full visual control is uncomprehensible. . . . The much vaunted difference in time counsumed in our methods of prostatectomy does not count for much in view of the absence of mortality in my 50 cases and its presence in theirs. In fact, one can easily employ careful, intelligent technic, seeing what he is doing and still not consume more than 10 or 12 minutes exposing and removing

the prostatic lobes; and when the operation is finished he has the satisfaction of feeling that he has done no unecessary mutilation.[7]

Young prevailed. With publication of his classic *Practice of Urology* in 1926, the Hopkins' school of perineal surgery was firmly established, a vast experience had been achieved, and his students in turn were to carry this craft to other centers.

The anatomic basis for Young's operation is based on an approach in which "the entire exposure of the prostate is by incising the skin and dividing the central tendon and the insignificant rectourethralis muscle beneath it in the median line. . . . The levator ani muscles and other important structures are merely separated and held apart by retractors."[7] Having exposed the posterior surface of the prostate, Young devised elaborate enucleation procedures with the objective of preserving the continuity of the urethra and ejaculatory ducts in an attempt "to do nothing to injure [the patient's] manly vigor."[7]

In 1938, Belt and colleagues' paper, read before the annual meeting of the American Urological Association, described "A New Anatomic Approach in Perineal Prostatectomy" which proved an exquisite refinement of Young's procedure. In this approach a bloodless cleavage plane between the longitudinal muscle fibers of the rectum and the external spincter ani muscle is used to expose the capsule of the prostate bloodlessly" and without cutting a nerve". Using an inverted U-shaped incision in the prostatic capsule, a flap of posterior lamella was developed in an attempt to preserve the verumontanum and the ducts from the seminal vesicles. They described, in fine detail, the placing of hemostatic sutures based on precise knowledge of vascular anatomy as well as a meticulous closure over a urethral catheter (as opposed to Young's perineal prostatotomy drainage technique). Using the concepts of Young and the surgical refinement of Belt's group, subsequent workers modified, expanded and simplified perineal surgery. To date, the definitive treatise on perineal surgery remains the work of Perry B. Hudson. With publication of Hudson and Stout's *An Atlas of Prostatic Surgery* in 1962, as well as Hudson's chapter on perineal surgery in *Urology*, perineal surgery is *au courant*.[9,10] No serious student of perineal surgery cannot but be enriched by a careful study of these works.

Hudson's approach is closer to Belt's than to Young's. Unlike both, he makes no attempt to preserve the veru or ejaculatory ducts; instead, he gains access to the inner prostate through a "window" cut in the posterior lamella. Removal of this tissue has the advantage, not emphasized by his predecessors, of making available a biopsy specimen that, on frozen section, demonstrates malignancy in over one quarter of those requiring prostatectomy for benign disease.[4] Depending on one's philosophy, the options for enucleation prostatectomy, radical prostatectomy, or enlightened observation can be exercised.

In any event, the properly trained urologist should aspire to a working familiarity with this unique approach. The confidence that derives from a surgical knowledge of this region, whether for a challenging urethroplasty, genital reconstruction, or prostatic pathologic condition, outweighs the investment necessary to acquire such competence.

REFERENCES

1. Lilien OM: Radical perineal prostatectomy. Spring-Mills E, Hafez, (eds): in Male Accessory Sex Glands. Amsterdam, ESE, Elsevier North Holland Biomedical Press, 1980

2. Giesecke AH Jr, Cole JO, Jenkins MT: The prostate, ventilation and anesthesia. JAMA 203:389, 1968

3. Nicholson TC, Richie JP: Pelvic lymphadenectomy for Stage B_1 adenocarcinoma of the prostate: Justified or not? J Urol 117:199, 1977

4. Lilien OM, Schaefer JA, Kilejian V, et al: The case for perineal prostatectomy. J Urol 99:79, 1968

5. Young HH: Conservative perineal prostatectomy. A presentation of new instruments and technic. JAMA 41:999, 1903

6. Syms P: Prostatic obstruction to urination, when to operate and how to operate. JAMA 43:1378, 1904

7. Young HH: Discussion on prostatectomy. JAMA 43: 243, 1904

8. Young HH, Davis DM: Young's Practice of Urology. Philadelphia, WB Saunders, 1926

9. Hudson PB, Stout AP: An Atlas of Prostatic Surgery. Philadelphia, WB Saunders, 1962

10. Hudson PB: Perineal prostatectomy. In Harrison JH, Gittes RF, Perlmutter AD, et al (eds): Urology. Philadelphia, WB Saunders, 1979

ANNOTATED BIBLIOGRAPHY

Lilien OM: Radical perineal prostatectomy. In Male Accessory Sex Glands. Spring-Mills E, Hafez ESE (eds): Amsterdam, Elsevier North Holland Biomedical Press, 1980

This paper presents an overview of the case for radical prostatic surgery. It contains an analysis of published figures on the incidence of prostatic carcinoma, making the point that the apparent discrepancy in published data, which ranges from an incidence of 14% to 67%, can be resolved by correcting for age and technical variables (i.e., single section versus step sections). The paper summarizes the prognostic significance of grading and staging, proposes a more exact staging schema, reviews the published survival and morbidity data with current modalities of therapy for each stage, and reconciles published data of lymphatic metastases with the observed clinical course for each stage. The role of radical surgery is discussed.

Nicholson TC, Richie JP: Pelvic lymphadenectomy for B_1 adenocarcinoma of the prostate: Justified or not? J Urol 117:199, 1977

There are relatively few studies that subgroup stage B lesions into stages B_1 and B_2. This paper reports findings on 47 consecutive patients who had undergone staging pelvic lymphadenectomy for clinically localized (stage B) adenocarcinoma of the prostate. Of these, 26 had clinical stage B_1 disease. Only 2 of these patients (8%) had positive pelvic nodes. Because of the low of incidence of lymphatic spread, the potential complications of a properly executed lymphadenectomy, and the unresolved role of regional lymphatics in generating an immunologic defense, the authors put the challenging question: is pelvic lymphadenectomy for stage B_1 adenocarcinoma justified? The authors do not think so. I agree.

Young HH: Conservative perineal prostatectomy. A presentation of new instruments and technic. JAMA 41:999, 1903

In this classic presentation, Young reviews the circumstances leading to his design of his "new instruments" and the evolution of the open perineal surgical approach to the prostate. Despite some turn of the century misconceptions of physiology (e.g., the importance of not disrupting the continuity of the ejaculatory ducts in the preservation of the "sexual powers of vigorous men"), Young's presentation is a model of anatomic investigation and surgical insight. Several step illustrations, not found in his subsequent descriptions of perineal prostatectomy, make this historical paper worthy of contemporary attention.

Hudson PB: Perineal prostatectomy. In Harrison, Gittes, Perlmutter, et al: Urology. Philadelphia, WB Saunders, 1979

Publication of Hudson and Stout's Atlas of Prostatic Surgery in 1962 and subsequent inclusion of the section on perineal prostatectomy in Campbell's Urology completes the trilogy of perineal surgery: Young–Belt–Hudson. This last contribution to the craft of perineal surgery is the most complete treatise to date, reviewing the history of the perineal approach, indications for surgery (biopsy, enucleation prostatectomy, subtotal prostatectomy, and radical prostatectomy), and surgical techniques. It contains a rich collection of lucid stepwise illustrations that are invaluable to the student of perineal surgery. Postoperative care is presented in detail, as is the realistic consideration of complications and their management. Hudson's dissertation brings perineal surgery into the "historical present."

OVERVIEW: OPEN PROSTATECTOMY

E. Darracott Vaughan, Jr.

An overview of the series of articles concerning open prostatectomy would be lacking without an introductory comment on patient evaluation, indications for prostatic adenomectomy, and selection of the operative technique in patients with adenomatous hyperplasia of the prostate. Subsequently, I will comment on each specific technique.

Essentially all elderly men will exhibit some enlargement of the prostate accompanied by variable symptoms of outlet obstruction. I cannot condone the concept of "early" or "prophylactic" adenomectomy to avoid the development of bladder decompensation. At present, despite the development of sophisticated urodynamic techniques, urologists cannot predict which patient with early symptoms of outlet obstruction will eventually warrant an adenomectomy. Certainly many patients thrive for years on conservative management without operative intervention. My "hard" indications for adenomectomy include anatomic changes of the upper tract secondary to obstruction, obstructive nephropathy, antibiotic-resistant infection, and severe bladder decompensation. Acute urinary retention is not an absolute indication for surgical intervention. Frequently, a precipitating event can be identified: ingestion of alcohol, antihistamines, alpha-adrenergic drugs, anticholenergics, bladder overexpansion, "trauma" often related to long periods of travel, or infection. Hence, following temporary bladder drainage, a voiding trial is often successful and the patient can be managed expectantly. Finally, symptoms alone are only rarely an indication for adenomectomy, and I often let the patient be the judge of the need for intervention. Thus, if the patient's daily activities are being disrupted by his symptoms in the absence of other indications, I feel relief of obstruction is indicated.

My selection of a patient for adenomectomy is based on the history, the urinalysis, the intravenous (IV) urogram, and the blood urea nitrogen (BUN) and creatinine levels. I strongly agree with Dr. Wulfsohn that bladder instrumentation before prostatectomy should be avoided if at all possible and cystoscopy not be performed unless disease other than prostatic enlargement is strongly suspected. In fact, I also eschew the passage of catheters to measure residual urine or perform urodynamic studies unless there are other indications. In contrast, catheter drainage is mandatory before operation in the azotemic patient with both renal damage and salt and water retention. This patient is likely to excrete large volumes of urine, the postobstructive phenomenon, most commonly as a physiologic release of retained urea, sodium, and water. Less commonly there is true nephrogenic diabetes insipidus or salt-losing nephropathy due to obstructive renal injury. The patient should be allowed to return to an optimal state of renal function before adenomectomy. Occasionally a patient with severe renal impairment should be maintained on suprapubic urinary drainage for several months to ensure maximum renal repair before intervention is contemplated. Since I routinely avoid catherization, I rely heavily on the critical information concerning both the upper and lower urinary tract obtained from the IV urogram and therefore disagree with those who would abandon it as a part of the evaluation of patients with outlet obstruction.

Once the decision has been made ascertaining the need for adenomectomy, the next question concerns the operative approach. The decision primarily is based on the size of the adenoma. At The New York Hospital the ratio of transuretheral resections for adenomatous hyperplasia to open suprapubic or retropubic adenomectomies is approximately 50:1. A urologist should be capable of resecting a 50-g adenoma, and many feel that only adenomas greater than 100 g, or situations that require coincident bladder surgery, warrant open adenomectomy. Drs. Draper and Pitts have reviewed the variety of combined procedures. I would add the combination of open adenomectomy and properitoneal inquinal hernia repair. Open cystolithotomy, even for multiple bladder calculi, is much less commonly employed in my institution since the development of the electronic lithotripe, which can be used immediately before a transuretheral resection of the prostate.

The three alternative procedures for prostatic adenomectomy are concisely reviewed in the article and the adjoining Commentaries. As stated by Drs. Draper and Pitts, the open suprapubic approach is time honored and commonly performed. I find the approach easier than the retropubic one when the patient has a deep pelvis and it is difficult to approach the anterior surface of the prostate. However, I prefer the retropubic approach, which I perform almost exactly as described by Dr. Wulfsohn. In essence, the urologist must be a master of both techniques, and perhaps the best time to decide which is proper is on exposure of the retropubic space.

The suprapubic technique requires little additional comment. The idea of the retained nylon stitch as described by Drs. Draper and Pitts is a clever one, supporting the old urologic dictum "Never give up an advantage." I do not routinely close the bladder neck but have found the use of a "pursestring" suture exiting through the abdominal wall useful in the face of troublesome bleeding. Capsular hemostasis is aided by the use of a fiberoptic light and controlled withdrawal of vaginal packing, which I place in the fossa immediately after the adenoma is removed. I have had no experience with the use of the Pilcher bag.

I personally find the retropubic approach more anatomically pleasing in terms of both visual transection of the urethera and obtaining better hemostasis. At the onset, before capsulotomy I place 0 chromic sutures at each lateral extent of the proposed incision. If these are not placed the incision is often traumatically extended and may be troublesome to close. I would like to reemphasize Dr. Wulfsohn's comment about the care required to make the capsulotomy at a right angle and not to bevel the incision into the distal capsule. I feel that this is the most common mistake in performing the procedure and leads to difficulty in establishing the true plane between capsule and adenoma. Excellent hemostasis can usually be obtained following retropubic adenomectomy. However, if there is any concern and through and through irrigation is contemplated, there should be no hesitation in placing a suprapubic tube.

I felt considerable empathy with Dr. Lilien as he eloquently related the rise and demise of the perineal approach to the prostate. I too feel that the unique art of perineal surgery is not being passed down to trainees. However, except for the rare case, simple perineal adenomectomy for adenomatous hyperplasia is of historical interest alone. There are few contraindications to an abdominal approach, and the incidence of impotence weighs heavy if the patient is potent. The idea of posterior capsulectomy, proposed years ago by Drs. Young and Vest, is intriguing but unstudied and also feasible through a retropubic approach. Simple (total) prostatectomy for chronic infection or calculi remains a part of the current armentarium. It is beyond the scope of this Overview to enter the morass concerning the management of prostatic carcinoma. It is sufficient to say I agree with Dr. Lilien; the evidence to date has not convinced me to abandon radical perineal prostatectomy as the best treatment for localized carcinoma of the prostate.

83

CRYOSURGERY IN BENIGN AND MALIGNANT DISEASES OF THE PROSTATE*

Ward A. Soanes, M.D., F.A.C.S., and
Maurice J. Gonder, M.D., F.A.C.S.

Kenmore, New York

Cryosurgery
Edited by John G. Bellows, M.D., Ph.D.
(Reprinted from International Surgery, Vol. 51, No. 2, February, 1969)

Cryosurgery is the art and skill of inducing sub-zero temperatures in tissue for the selective destruction of diseased areas. The merits of tissue destruction by freezing have been recognized for some time, however, only during the past decade has the controlled freezing destruction of living tissue become a practical surgical tool. This has been made possible by the design and development of specialized cryosurgical equipment along with a greater understanding of the processes of tissue temperature reduction by the clinician.[5] In the field of urology, our main interest was to perfect an instrument capable of applying sub-zero temperatures to prostate tissue. A cryoprobe resulted for urethral insertion and subsequent cryothermic destruction of obstructive prostatic tissue. Histologic evaluation confirming controlled cell destruction was made immediately following cryosurgery and at predetermined time intervals thereafter. When it became obvious, from extensive animal studies, that this technique was both safe and effective, the existing equipment was modified for human use.[8] To date, we have documented 350 cryosurgical prostatectomies. An attempt is made here to review cryosurgical application and compare this new modality with standard methods as transurethral resection and suprapubic removal. The cases selected for treatment of both benign and malignant disease of the prostate will be discussed.

TISSUE TEMPERATURE REDUCTION

Tissue temperature reduction occurs by transfer of heat from the tissue more rapidly than it can be replaced by its surroundings. The primary factor required to attain cell death by freezing is the production and application of controlled sub-zero temperatures via a heat sink (Fig. 1). A heat sink is anything that will absorb tissue heat. For our purposes, this heat sink must remove sufficient amounts of heat to cause subzero temperatures in large

* Presented at the XVIth Biennial Congress of the International College of Surgeons, Japan, October 23, 1968.

Supported by The John A. Hartford Foundation, Inc., New York, New York.

Cryosurgical equipment manufactured by Linde Division, Union Carbide Corporation, New York, New York.

Accepted for publication October 23, 1968.

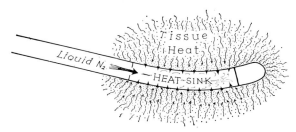

Fig. 1. Heat sink removing from surrounding tissue.

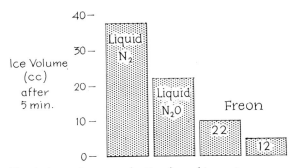

Fig. 2. Ice volume production by refrigerants.

masses of tissue. Various refrigerants are capable of reducing heat sink temperatures to tissue destruction levels. These include pressurized as well as liquefied gases. The most commonly used liquefied gases are nitrogen and Freon. Temperature reduction employing the foregoing is accomplished by decreasing refrigerant pressure within a heat sink chamber. This allows heat absorption to occur from surrounding tissue. Liquid nitrogen is the most practical for generating very low, sub-zero heat sink temperatures (Fig. 2). The vaporization of this gas at atmospheric pressure produces heat sink temperatures near its atmospheric boiling point of $-196°C$. Other refrigerants, including Freon, nitrous oxide and carbon dioxide, are not capable of providing equally low sub-zero temperatures even under optimal conditions. Although there are cryosurgical applications for refrigerants other than liquid nitrogen, only this gas will satisfy heat load cryosurgery. High cryosurgical heat loads are caused by the prostate, bladder, cervix and certain tumors due to their location, size and vascularity. Effective destruction of these structures can be achieved only by very low heat sink temperatures.

The equipment which we have developed and employed for our cryosurgical procedures in urology utilize liquid nitrogen as the refrigerant. The liquefied gas is stored in a vacuum insulated container. The pressure within the container forces the refrigerant through a tube to a heat sink (probe freezing surface) which is in contact with the tissue target area. At the heat sink, the liquid nitrogen vaporizes, absorbing sufficient tissue heat to produce lethal sub-zero temperatures. The nitrogen is then conducted through a concentric tube and exhausted to the atmosphere. These concentric tubes are also vacuum insulated thereby limiting heat exchange to the heat sink and tempertures may be controlled between $40°C$ and $-196°C$. Changing heat sink temperatures are sensed by a thermocouple and shown by a temperature indicator. Ambient temperatures are attained by an integral electrical heater.

For the purposes of cryosurgical prostatectomy, the heat sink takes the form of a copper cannula, $1\frac{1}{3}$ inches long and 25 F in diameter. There is a projection $\frac{1}{2}$ inch

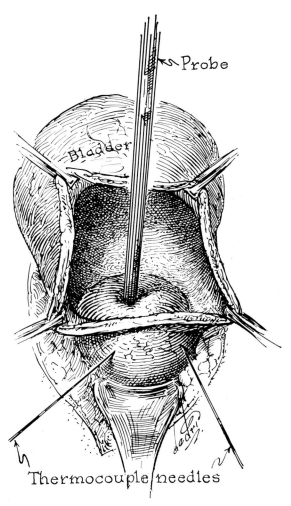

Fig. 3. Canine prostate frozen through a cystostomy incision.

proximal to the cannula which is palpated rectally to properly situate the heat sink within the prostatic urethra.

EXPERIMENTAL CRYOSURGERY IN ANIMALS

Experiments were designed to study the effects of freezing canine prostates. A cryoprobe was inserted in the prostatic urethra through a cystotomy incision. Thermocouple needles placed in specific areas determined the depth of tissue freezing (Fig. 3). The bladder was drained and radiopaque material injected through a cystostomy catheter. Marked edema of the prostate was noted immediately following freezing (Fig. 4A). Seven days later, cystography showed the bladder filled and the prostate reduced to a spongy, necrotic mass which absorbed the dye (Fig. 4B). Prostatic biopsies taken at various intervals illustrated typical changes that occurred. A core biopsy immediately upon thawing noted a clean line of demarcation between the frozen and unfrozen portions (Fig. 5A). Seven days following, a repeat biopsy revealed complete tissue destruction with marked intraacinar hemorrhage and minimal inflammation (Fig. 5B). Further biopsies taken from the periphery of the prostate, 40 days post-freezing, noted acinar regrowth (Fig. 5C).[4]

This regeneration has an appearance which has been termed by some as a malignant change occurring after freezing.[2] However, this alteration is simply a healing phenomenon rather than a new growth. If the change induced by freezing of tissue did, in fact, produce neoplastic alteration, evidence should be available from other sources, e.g., tissue regeneration following frostbite, which would support this speculation. To our knowledge, such evidence does not exist. Another variation, squamous metaplasia, results from prostatic infarction caused by freezing injury (Fig. 5D).

Our studies of the changes produced by freezing of prostate tissue have been extended to the subcellular level by using electron microscopy.[6] An electron photomicrograph of unfrozen prostate tissue is shown in Figure 6A. Note the nuclei (N) and lumen (L) which are easily distinguishable landmarks. The points of interest are closely opposed cell margins indicated by arrows. There is a high degree of organization of structures such as mitochondria and ribosomal aggregates. An area at lower magnification biopsied from the same prostate immediately after freezing and thawing is shown in Figure 6B. The obvious change is in the intercellular spaces which we interpret to be the sites of ice crystal formation. There are no intercellular spaces similar to those in unfrozen tissue. A higher magnification of the same specimen demonstrates these intercellular spaces and the general disruption of cytoplasmic organization with clumping of the nuclear chromatin material (Fig. 6C).

Evidence such as the above provides further proof that the cause of cell death by cryosurgery is due to dehydration of the cells rather than by physical disruption. The studies clearly demonstrated that prostate tissue, sufficiently frozen, could be destroyed with subsequent reduction in the total mass of the gland. As a result of these findings, the technique was refined and applied to humans.

CRYOSURGICAL TECHNIQUE FOR PROSTATECTOMY

The patient is placed in the usual lithotomy position and given local, regional or general anesthesia. The bladder

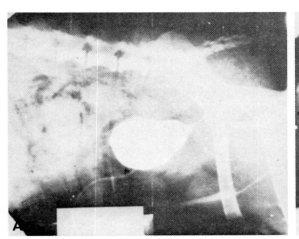
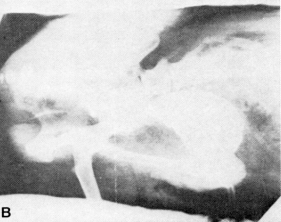

Fig. 4. (A) Cystogram through a cystotomy catheter after freezing. (B) Cystogram through a cystotomy catheter—seven days postfreeze.

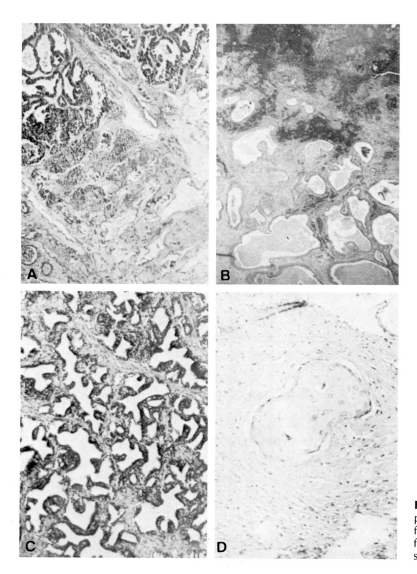

Fig. 5. (*A*) Core biopsy after freezing canine prostate. (*B*) Core biopsy seven days post-freeze. (*C*) Core biopsy forty days post-freeze, periphery of gland. (*D*) Area of squamous metaplasia.

is drained of all fluid and filled with approximately 400 cc of air. Care is taken while preparing to insert the prostate cryoprobe to maintain this air within the bladder. An assistant holds the distal urethra so that none can escape. The probe is then well lubricated and inserted into the urethra (Fig. 7). By palpating the button on the shaft of the probe, the freezing surface or heat sink is placed in contact with the prostatic enlargement. The entire probe must remain stationary with the handle depressed so that the distal tip is actually pointed toward the patient's chin. This assures the operator that the intravesical part of the freezing surface is away from the bladder wall and ureteral orifices. The probe shaft must remain parallel with the table. The positioning button

should be one centimeter from the prostatic apex. At this point, the temperature of the probe is set at −10°C to fix the freezing chamber to the surrounding tissue. Palpation of the prostate through the rectum senses probe fixation. This prevents improper positioning. Thermocouples are inserted into the capsule and prostate to give the operator additional tissue temperature determinations. Once satisfied that placement is correct, the temperature control point is set at −180°C. This causes further flow of the refrigerant to the heat sink and deep freezing begins. The most vital area of concern is the rectal wall where the temperature must be kept above 0°C. Constant palpation is carried out to assure that the rectal mucosa is always movable over the prostatic capsule. If fixation

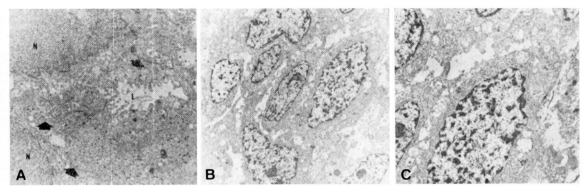

Fig. 6. (A) Electron micrograph of human carcinoma of the prostate before cryosurgery. Easily distinguishable features are nuclei (N) and acinar lumen (L). The arrows indicate the cell margins which approach each other very closely ($\times$24,000). (B) Low power electron micrography of tissue immediately after freezing and thawing. The most striking features are the large, intercellular spaces which are probably the site of ice crystal formation ($\times$13,000). (C) Higher power view. In addition to the intercellular spaces, other signs of disruption can be seen. These are the clumped chromatin material in the nuclei, the exploded mitochondria and the disorganized aggregates of ribosomes ($\times$25,000).

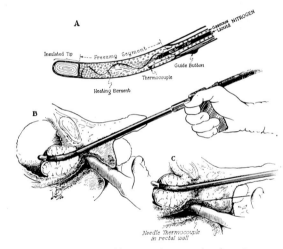

Fig. 7. (A) Cross section of heat sink or probe freezing cannula. (B) Positioning of the probe and button in air filled bladder by rectal palpation. (C) Positioning of thermocouples at apex of prostate in rectal wall.

of the rectum should occur or if the thermocouple temperature of the rectal wall at the apex reaches 0°C, freezing is terminated and the heater is engaged. The heating element is an added safety factor incorporated to permit quick warming and withdrawal if the need arises. In large prostates, where there is a disparity in the size of the lobes, gentle pressure applied to the prostatic pedicles will cut down on the blood supply (heat source), allowing more rapid freezing of the tissue.

In other words, avascularization occurs from the pressure applied and permits freezing to the capsule. Care is taken not to palpate rectally above the prostate during the procedure to prevent the protruding probe freezing surface from adhering to the trigone. Cold cannot distinguish normal from abnormal tissue. However, rectal palpation easily notes when the prostate is nearly frozen. The end point of freezing is reached when the temperature of the periphery of the prostate reaches −20°C to −30°C. The gland should then be frozen adequately. The second end point is attained when the rectal wall temperature registers 10°C. If there is no further reduction in temperature at the periphery of the prostate, it can be assumed that an equilibrium has been effected between the heat sink and surrounding tissue. It must be noted that digital detection of the frozen gland varies with each operator and is not a reliable method in itself of determining the end point of freezing. Also, because all prostates vary in size and vascularity, total time of freezing is not a factor and should never be used to ascertain the end point.

When the above requirements are met, flow of the liquid nitrogen is stopped and the heating element is engaged to warm the probe. After the probe is freely movable, it is withdrawn. Since the heater is distal to the positioning button, the last area to thaw is the bladder neck. Any hasty attempt to withdraw the probe before proper thawing occurs could cause troublesome bleeding by tearing of the delicate prostatic lining.

A Foley catheter is inserted. If it does not pass easily through the frozen prostatic urethra, it is desirable to wait until further thawing takes place. This will prevent possible urethral or bladder neck injury. The bladder is emptied of air and irrigation begun. Usually, the urine at this point is slightly blood tinged due to the acute hyperemia caused by thawing and manipulation. The urine generally clears in four to six hours. Routine postoperative management is observed.

VARIATIONS IN CRYOSURGICAL TECHNIQUE

Should the patient have a severe urethral stricture, a simple perineal urethrotomy can be performed and the above technique followed. A cystotomy should be done and the prostate frozen under direct vision when the conditions of: ureteral reflux, large middle lobe, large bladder calculi or resectable diverticuli exist and for inexperienced operators to better visualize the extent of freezing. Prostates with small calculi are never frozen.

In carcinomas of the prostate, the following variations in technique can be employed:

1. Open perineal exposure of the prostate tumor deflecting the rectum and allowing freezing under direct vision.
2. Cystotomy with retrograde freezing when the tumor involves the bladder neck and the cryoprobe cannot be passed transurethrally.
3. A combination of cystotomy and perineal exposure can be used where large infiltrating tumors are present.

Transurethral resection immediately following the prostate freezing offers a fairly bloodless field for tissue removal.[7] Subsequent transurethral resection of sloughed tissue, if necessary, is an uncomplicated procedure.[1]

Discussion. Cryosurgical prostatectomy is a highly technical innovation and demands the utmost skill of the operator. He must be knowledgeable in an entirely new field of cryogenics and must also have mastered the technique of present day transurethral surgery.

From the patient's standpoint, standard cryosurgical prostatectomy provides distinct advantages and has eliminated many complications associated with accepted methods of prostate surgery.[3] Some of these advantages are:

1. Minimal surgical trauma.
2. Less anesthesia required (may be done under local anesthesia if necessary).
3. Immediate postoperative hemorrhage eliminated.
4. Delayed postoperative hemorrhage rarely noted.
5. Operative time shortened.
6. No obturator nerve stimulation.
7. No hyponatremia or hypervolemia.
8. Possibility of immediate septicemia eliminated.
9. Blood dyscrasias with bleeding tendencies are operable.
10. Anticoagulants can be used immediately following cryosurgery.
11. Pacemaker patients are operable without danger of electrical stimuli.

The disadvantages of standard cryosurgical prostatectomy are caused mainly by poor technique on the part of the operator in failing to adhere to the basic principles described. The few complications that have been noted are:

1. Catheter requirements may be extended.
2. Necrotic tissue slough may cause urinary blockage and necessitate removal. Local instillation of enzymes has been ineffective in solving this problem to date.
3. Infection from necrotic tissue requires postoperative antibacterial therapy.

CASE REVIEWS AND PRESENTATIONS

To evaluate the operative risk, patients were classified on the basis of accumulative systemic diseases. They could be divided into four groups. As example, Group I had no other existing diseases, past or present, except prostatic obstruction requiring surgery. Group II included patients who had an accumulation of diagnosable diseases which did not require treatment. Group III included an accumulation of diseases requiring therapy, e.g., a diabetic patient on oral treatment or a cardiac patient on digitalis. Group IV had diseases that imperiled life and required treatment every day, e.g., emphysema associated with congestive failure or a severe diabetic requiring insulin.

Two hundred of our standard cryosurgical cases were evaluated and classified as well as 200 transurethral resections and 200 suprapubic prostatectomies performed by competent urologists. These were all consecutive cases. The results show that candidates for cryosurgery were poorer risks than those subjected to conventional procedures. (Fig. 8)

The amount of blood administered in the postoperative period to these 600 cases is shown in Figure 9.

Comments. A review of our mortality rate in the 200 cryosurgical prostatectomies noted ten deaths in the first *100 postoperative days*. Of these, six deaths were possibly related to the surgery. Three cases expired of acute coronary thrombosis on the 16th to the 30th day postoperative. One died of a bronchopneumonia complicating a severe emphysema on the 17th day. One died of diabetic coma with associated uremia at 81 days and one of secondary coronary thrombosis (first attack occurred two days after the procedure) on the 98th day. The remaining four deaths were unrelated to the proce-

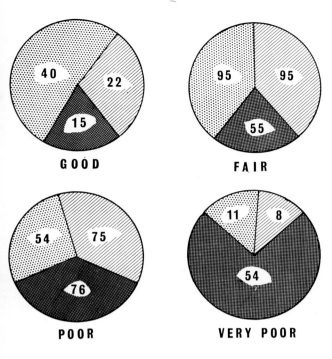

GOOD   FAIR

POOR   VERY POOR

Fig. 8. Two hundred cases (consecutive) of cryosurgical, suprapubic and transurethral prostatectomies classified by preoperative medical risk status.

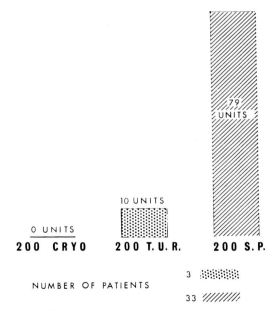

Fig. 9. Postoperative blood requirements.

dure. No postoperative mortality studies of the transurethral resections or suprapubic cases were reported. The cryosurgical mortalities were all in the poor to very poor categories.

CARCINOMA OF THE PROSTATE

Based on the successful destruction of benign tumors of the prostate, 75 cases of malignant tumors were treated. All of these patients had obstructive tumor growth. Their preoperative surgical risk status was determined as in the benign series of cryoprostatectomies. In addition, they were individually classified according to the stage of their carcinomas. These stages were divided into four groups.

Stage 0—nonpalpable tumor within the prostate.
Stage 1—palpable tumor within the capsule of the prostate.
Stage 2—palpable tumor with local invasion outside the prostatic capsule.
Stage 3—palpable tumor with metastasis and elevated acid phosphatase.

We did not treat any Stage 0 patients in our series of 75 cases presented (Tables 1-3).

Results. The results of cryosurgery in 75 patients with carcinoma of the prostate are shown in Tables 1–3.

TABLE 1. Living Cancer Patients—44 Cases

Postop Time (years)	1	2	3	4
Good 7 cases	0	4-CA2	2-CA3	1-CA2
Fair 16 cases	3-CA1 2-CA2 1-CA3 1-CA1	3-CA2	1-CA1 3-CA2 2-CA3	1-CA2
Poor 15 cases	6-CA2 1-CA3 1-CA1	2-CA2 3-CA3	0	1-CA2 1-CA3
Very poor 6 cases	1-CA2 1-CA3	2-CA2 1-CA3	0	0

TABLE 2. Cancer Patients—Death from Cancer—17 Cases

Postop Survival Time (years)	1	2	>2
Good 3 cases	2-CA3	1-CA1	0
Fair 4 cases	2-CA3	1-CA2 1-CA3	0
Poor 7 cases	2-CA2 3-CA3	2-CA2	0
Very poor 3 cases	1-CA2 1-CA3	1-CA3	0

TABLE 3. Cancer Patients—Death from Other Causes—14 Cases

Postop Survival Time (years)	1	2	3	4
Good				
1 case	1-CA3	0	0	0
Fair				
2 cases	1-CA3	0	0	1-CA2
Poor	2-CA1			
4 cases	1-CA3	1-CA3	0	0
Very poor	3-CA2			
7 cases	3-CA3	1-CA1	0	0

There are 44 patients still alive with various stages of malignancy up to four years. Seventeen died as a direct result of their malignancy, e.g., uremia from local tumor extension and ureteral obstruction. Fourteen died of other causes, e.g., acute coronary thrombosis.

Of the 44 patients alive, 12 have lived for three to four years and 90% of these had Stage 2-3 carcinoma. Thirty-two patients have survived one to two years and 87% of these had Stage 2-3 carcinoma. Of the 17 patients who died of their malignancies, 94% were in the Stage 2-3 carcinoma category. Of the deaths due to unrelated causes, 64% occurred during the first year. These patients were classified in the poor to very poor status.

CASE HISTORIES

1. A 73-year old patient was diagnosed as having Stage 1 carcinoma of the prostate. A needle biopsy noted a typical carcinoma (Fig. 10A). A transurethral cryosurgical prostatectomy was performed. The patient suddenly expired from an acute coronary 11 months later. Multiple sections taken in the postmortem study revealed no active carcinoma in the prostate. There was typical squamous metaplasia with lymphocytic infiltration throughout the remaining tissue (Fig. 10B).

2. An infiltrating, Stage 2 tumor of the prostate and bladder neck (Fig. 11A) was diagnosed in a 76-year-old patient. Cryosurgery was performed to relieve this obstruction. Six weeks postoperatively, the prostatic urethra and bladder neck were widely patent (Fig. 11B).

3. This 66-year-old patient had a Stage 3 cancer of the prostate with both local and chest metastases (Fig. 12A). Cryosurgery was performed to alleviate his local symptoms. Approximately two years later, the metastasis and local disease had regressed (Fig. 12B).

4. A Stage 3 carcinoma of the prostate was diagnosed in a 68-year-old patient. He had severe cervical pain, immobility of the neck and paresthesias of the right arm and hand (Fig. 13A). Roentgenograms of the cervical spine noted mixed lytic and blastic changes at C_4 involving mainly the vertebral body and right pedicle with compression of C_4. Cryosurgery was performed and the prostatic tumor frozen only partially. He obtained no clinical relief following this initial partial freezing. One month later, further cryosurgery was performed and the remainder of the local tumor was frozen. Within two weeks, the cervical pain and paresthesias disappeared. Mobility of the neck gradually returned. Four months following the second freezing, a cervical roentgenogram was taken (Fig. 13B). There were changes consistent with regeneration of bone both in the vertebral body and right pedicle. Acid phosphatase determinations had also diminished 50% but were still elevated.

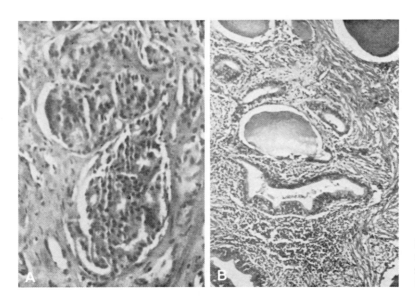

Fig. 10. (A) Needle biopsy—typical carcinoma of prostate. (B) Postmortem section—squamous metaplasia, marked lymphocytic infiltration.

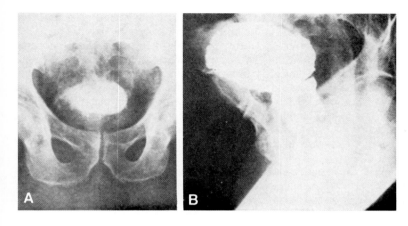

Fig. 11. (A) Post-voided cystogram, marked elevation of base, obstruction of bladder neck with residual. (B) Injected cystogram six weeks postcryosurgery.

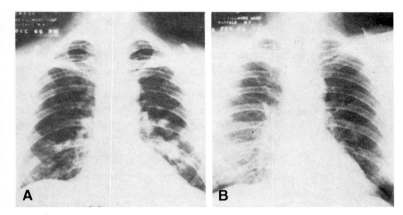

Fig. 12. (A) Chest roentgenogram of prostate carcinoma patient shows metastasis to both lungs. (B) Chest roentgenogram 26 months following cryosurgery.

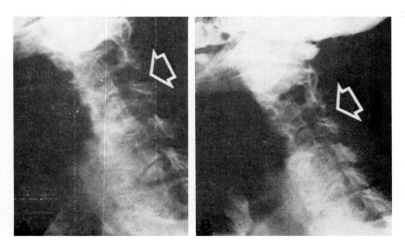

Fig. 13. (A) Cervical spine—arrow points to area C, osteolytic and osteoblastic metastasis from carcinoma of the prostate. (B) Cervical spine 120 days later; arrow pointing to same area shows remission of lesion with new bone formation.

Discussion. In carcinomas of the prostate that are localized, it is possible to completely destroy the tumor as demonstrated in Case 1.[9] Dissemination of tumor cells is not likely because of the avascularization incurred by freezing of the malignant site and subsequent killing of the cells in situ. Relief of large malignant obstructions at the bladder neck can be accomplished where surgical removal is impractical or difficult. This was demonstrated in Case 2.

Of further interest are the possible immunologic effects produced by cryothermic destruction of tissues. Studies initiated in our laboratory in June, 1965 demonstrated that freezing two glands of the rabbit prostatic accessory gland complex (seminal vesicle and coagulating gland) in situ elicited the production of relatively low levels of autoantibodies detectable approximately tour to seven days following freezing.[12,13]

Clinical observations during the past four years on patients undergoing cryosurgery have revealed partial remission of tumors occurring beyond the freeze site. Such findings are suggestive of factors causing cell destruction other than freezing (see Cases 2 and 3).

It is a well-founded principle of immunology that a second inoculation of the same antigen, often referred to as a "booster," at a moderate interval following the initial inoculation usually elicits a more rapid rise in antibody titer than the first inoculation. The peak attained is greater and antibody persists for a longer period. This is well documented by the immune response observed in man to inoculation with tetanus toxiod.

In lieu of the possible therapeutic implications of this principle with reference to the relatively low level of antibody produced by a *single* freezing, the rabbit's prostatic accessory gland complex was frozen in situ twice at intervals of 30 days. In what may be termed an "antibody booster" phenomenon, increased circulating antibodies to prostatic tissue were detectable seven to twenty days following the *second* freezing of the prostate accessory gland complex.[11] Interpretation of this experimental data led us to the conclusion that this phenomenon occurring following a *second* freezing might be of more therapeutic value in man than a *single* freezing.

In keeping with this hypothesis, we initiated the new procedure on an individual with a Stage 3 carcinoma (see Case 4). The possibility of an "immuno-cryothermic response" created by the freezing of the local tumor in situ twice at an interval of 30 days was noted in this patient by remission of metastatic lesions. It is suggested that the four-year survival rates in tumors Stages 2 and 3 may be due to an "immuno-cryothermic response."[10]

At the present time, as a result of our research, all patients with clinical Stage 2 and 3 carcinomas of the prostate are frozen only partially in an effort to elicit an initial immunologic response. After 30 days, the tumor site is refrozen to boost the production of prostatic tumor antibodies.

SUMMARY

The adaptation of cryothermic destruction to urology has produced an effective alternative to standard methods of prostate surgery. Understanding of the basic principles of tissue freezing along with extensive histologic evaluation enabled us to treat both benign and malignant prostatic obstructions in man. The equipment and technique designed specifically for this use has resulted in a relatively uncomplicated procedure.

The observation of immunologic response to freezing and refreezing carcinomas of the prostate offers an entirely new concept to the already successful treatment by cryosurgical prostatectomy.

BIBLIOGRAPHY

1. Backer, O. G., and Lund, F.: Kryoptostatektomi. Saetryk Nord Med 77:532, 1967
2. Calams, J. A.; Flanagan, M. J., and McDonald, J. H.: Rapid Freezing of the Prostate: An Experimental Study. J Urol 96:512, 1966
3. Creevy, C. D.: Complications of Transurethral Resection: Urol Rep 2:6, 1965
4. Gonder, M. J.; Soanes, W. A., and Smith, V.: Chemical and Morphologic Changes in the Prostate Following Extreme Cooling. Proc NY Acad Sci 125:716, 1965
5. Jagodzinski, R. V.; Gonder, M. J., and Soanes, W. A.: Experimental Cryosurgery and Temperature Measurement (Abstract). J Cryobiology 2:295, 1966
6. Maser, M. D.; Soanes, W. A., and Gonder, M. J.: Fine Structure of Carcinomatous Human Prostate Treated by Cryosurgery: Changes Immediately After Thawing (Abstract). J Cryobiology 4:273, 1968

7. Ortved, W. E.; O'Kelly, F. M.; Todd, I.; Maxwell, J. B., and Sutton, M. R.: Cryosurgical Prostatectomy. Br J Urol 39:5, 1967
8. Soanes, W. A., and Gonder, M. J.: Apparatus and Technique for Cryosurgery of the Prostate. J Urol 96:508, 1966
9. Idem: Cryosurgery for Prostatic Cancer. J Urol 99:793, 1968
10. Soanes, W. A.; Gonder, M. J.; Witebsky, E., and Ablin, R. J.: Immuno-Cryopthermic Response (Abstract). J Cryosurg (In Press)
11. Witebsky, E., and Ablin, R. J.: Personal communication
12. Yantorno C.; Gonder, M. J.; Soanes, W. A., and Shulman, S.: The Freezing of Tissue During Surgery and the Production of Antibodies (Abstract). Fed Proc 25:3052, 1966
13. Yantorno, C.; Soanes, W. A.; Gonder, M. J., and Shulman, S.: Studies in Cryo-Immunology I: Production of Antibodies to Urogenital Tissue in Consequence of Freezing Teatment. Immunology 12:395, 1967

Commentary: Technique Of and Indications For Cryosurgery

Maurice J. Gonder

It has been demonstrated that prostate obstructions due to benign or malignant enlargements can be relieved by necrosis of tissue resulting from freezing. The technique involved is deceptively simple and should only be attempted by a physician expert in endoscopic evaluation who spends sufficient time to learn the pathology of freezing. In addition, he must understand heat conduction in relationship to surrounding organs. As a result of this type of background, he can then learn the advantages and disadvantages of the clinical application of freezing. Without this type of preparation, the results can be as disastrous as the injudicious application of radiation, cautery, laser, and ultrasound. For example, no one would permit a transurethral resection to be performed by a physician not trained in that technique. I believe the biggest problem in exploiting cryosurgery is education and training.

TECHNIQUE

The operator must be able to draw a mental image of the space relationships of the probe *in situ*. Direct visualization (open technique), as described by Reuter, may be helpful to some.[1]

The freezing surface of the probe should be in contact with the prostate and no other tissue. For example, after proper positioning of the probe, do not push the bladder against the freezing surface by digital pressure rectally. The moist bladder wall will stick to the supercold probe. A difficult anesthetic procedure or a moving patient might result in the same thing. Operative injuries to the adjacent organs could result. If the anatomy of the prostatic urethra is such that the probe cannot be so placed, the procedure should be abandoned (*e.g.*, in the presence of a lone intravesical middle lobe).

The probe, likewise, must be kept stationary during freezing. Air must be maintained in the bladder during the operation and cannot be permitted to escape along the probe before this area is sealed by the freezing process. Obviously, a bladder incapable of distention is a contraindication to the closed technique.

The extent of freezing must be calculated by rectal examination and, if necessry, by direct measurement of the tissue temperature by the use of thermocouples.

PATIENT SELECTION

The prostate should be a certain size to provide some margin of safety in its own right, for example, 30 g or greater. The enlargement should be primarily intraurethral; for example, a patient with hypertrophy of the middle lobe intravesically only would be a poor candidate.

The selective early freezing of the prostate is in part due to tissue pressure occlusion of the blood supply at its point of origin. Tissue pressure is produced by expansion of the water in its frozen state against a strong prostatic capsule. Once the prostate is avascularized by this mechanism, the freezing proceeds rapidly. When the freezing front reaches an organ supplied by a different source, equilibrium between the heat provided by the blood and cold provided by the probe rapidly occurs. This provides a considerable margin of safety in skilled hands. The idea that a symmetric plug of tissue from the center of the prostate can be destroyed will be discarded when this principle is understood.

The good-risk patient with a benign gland can be well handled by conventional methods. The poor-risk patient with a small prostate can be resected safely in a few moments. Patients with bulky cancers, in whom reduction in tumor mass is important, are probably ideal candidates. Patients in whom bleeding may be a serious problem should be considered. Pulmonary or cardiac cripples might be better able to tolerate this procedure than other methods of prostatectomy. Patients belonging to religious orders precluding transfusion would be candidates to consider. The advantages are less anesthesia requirement and less blood loss than conventional operations.

I do not believe that there is anything peculiar to freezing that contributes to lack of bleeding. Actually, the histologic study of freezing reveals hemorrhage. The reason that bleeding is not a problem is probably that the vasculature is interrupted at the periphery of the prostate, and after thawing the ruptured vessels allow hemorrhage into the tissues. The destroyed tissue acts as a maze that controls the bleeding. This is somewhat in the fashion that Gelfoam works as a hemostatic agent.

DISADVANTAGES

There are problems with all types of prostatectomies that occur from time to time, but the problems of cryosurgical prostatectomy are totally different. This makes them harder to accept because physicians do not ordinarily encounter them in their practices. What is strange or out of the ordinary is understandably met with concern.

The major disadvantages are longer catheter time, pyuria, and secondary procedures that are required to remove necrotic tissue and permit voiding. If the necrotic tissue accumulates in the bladder, it must be removed. All prostate operations occasionally require secondary procedures for one reason or another, but not necessarily for these reasons.

Complete sloughing time varies from days to months and depends on the histologic makeup of the gland and the competence of the bladder. When the prostate is primarily glandular, sloughing may occur quickly. If fibromatous, it takes longer. When the bladder is competent and empties itself completely, it does not allow the intracystic accumulation of necrotic debris.

Cryosurgery of the prostate began in 1963 at the Veterans Administration Hospital in Buffalo, NY, subsequent to the development of vacuum-insulated equipment by the Linde Corporation and Dr. Irving Cooper. This permitted the conduction of liquid nitrogen to the interior of the brain under delicate control for the treatment of Parkinson's disease.

The development of a transurethral probe for intraurethral application of freezing followed. The technique was modified by Lund and Backer to include TUR of some of the prostate while frozen.[2]

Jordan and associates pointed out that it could be performed with minimal anesthesia.[3] Reuter added suprapubic visualization of freezing through cystotomy.[1] Other variations, such as preoperative cystotomy drainage, suggested by Dowd and associates, seemed to preclude the accumulation of necrotic material in the bladder during the sloughing process.[4]

Recently, Dr. A. J. Keller has presented a large series of patients who were treated with ingenious equipment that could first freeze and then heat the prostate with the same probe.*

* Keller AJ: Personal communication, 1979.

The probe permits good tissue freezing, and, by a simple flip of a switch, the nitrogen is stopped and heat generated. This creates temperatures of +200 C in the probe adjacent to the prostate. Also, this adds to denaturization of tissue. He demonstrates good hemostasis, short catheter requirements, and safety to patients. In addition, he demonstrates 85% long-term satisfactory results.

Serious controversies ensued during the course of this early development. The whole idea was repugnant to meticulous endoscopic surgeons. The mystery of freezing and its anti-surgical characteristics were a concern to all. Those who had labored hard to learn or to develop other standard techniques were understandably concerned over what they felt was a retrogression.

It was pointed out at the outset, without much justification, that the healing cryolesion resembled cancer. This was an extremely serious charge in view of the relationship of unsuspected cancer in the clinically benign prostate. The absence of complete histologic study at the time of surgery made subsequent developments difficult to evaluate. The passage of time would make it appear that this change was without merit.

I think if a serious genetic change were to be associated with freezing, it would have been demonstrated in the frozen sperm program. Frozen sperm has been extensively used in animal husbandry for many years and, more recently, in clinical application in humans.

REFERENCES

1. Reuter HJ: Endoscopic cryosurgery of prostate and bladder tumors. J Urol 107:389, 1972
2. Lund F, Backer O: Cryotherapy applied to prostatic disease. Bull Millard Fillmore Hosp 14:131, 1967
3. Jordan W, Walker D, Miller G, et al: Cryotherapy of prostatic disease. J Cryosurg 1:130, 1968

4. Dowd B, Flint D, Zinman LN, et al: Experiences with cryosurgery of the prostate in the poor-risk patient. Surg Clin North Am 48:627, 1968

ANNOTATED BIBLIOGRAPHY

Jordan W, Walker D, Miller G, et al: Cryotherapy of prostatic diseases. J Crysurg 1:130, 1968; Cryotherapy of benign and malignant diseases. Surg Gynecol Obstet 125:1265, 1967

These authors describe their experience in treating 70 patients with cryosurgery. In 35% of the patients, they performed the treatment without general or regional anesthesia. The average blood loss in the urine was found to average 20 ml in 16 of their patients. They felt that the procedure was indicated in the poor-risk patient or the one with relapsing carcinoma of the prostate. They indicate that the postoperative catheter requirement is increased as compared with other methods and report a 10% failure rate by reason of incomplete dissolution of prostate tissue or secondary to bladder decompensation that existed before cryosurgery.

Lund F, Backer O: Cryotherapy applied to prostatic disease. Bull Millard Fillmore Hosp 14:131, 1967

These authors point out that the postoperative catheter requirement can be reduced by a partial resection of the prostate while still

frozen in the immediate postfreezing period. This can be accomplished without increasing the morbidity of the procedure.

Dowd JB, Flint DL, Zinman LN, et al: Experience with cryosurgery of the prostate in the poor-risk patient. Surg Clin North Am 48:627, 1968

Dowd and colleagues emphasize the importance of heat conduction in relationship to freezing and describe how they overcome some of the complications:
1. A preliminary ligation of the vas was performed.
2. A cystoscopy was performed to confirm the diagnosis of surgical obstruction and to rule out unsuspected significant coincident bladder disease, especially bladder tumor.
3. A needle biopsy of the prostate was performed for a pathologic diagnosis.
4. A cystotomy was performed. This was useful in the postoperative period and apparently was maintained until satisfactory voiding was obtained. A patient was placed in a Trendelenburg position to assist in keeping intraabdominal contents away

from the intravesical freezing probe. They described their end points of freezing as follows:

a. When rectal thermometer approached + 10°C.
b. When the prostate was palpably frozen.
c. If the adjacent rectal mucosa began to lose its resilience.

They describe their contraindications as follows:

1. A patient without a rectum.
2. A patient with curable carcinoma of the prostate who could tolerate a radical prostatectomy.
3. An undistendible bladder.
4. Other diseases present that required open operation.
5. They were unable to perform this operation on a patient in whom they could not properly position or instrument the urethra.

They reserved the procedure for the following:

1. The poor-risk patient with a large gland who must have either a prostatectomy or live with a catheter.
2. The patient with obstructing incurable carcinoma of the prostate.
3. The patient with a blood dyscrasia.

Reuter HJ: Endoscopic cryosurgery of prostate and bladder tumors. J Urol 107:389, 1972

Reuter describes an enormous experience with cryosurgery. He delineates his indications and contraindications and his results in a favorable light. Beyond this, he makes a basic contribution in the description of an ingenious technique of observing endoscopically, by cystotomy, the freezing process. He uses an air cystoscope through a punch or trocar cystotomy, permitting observation of the progression of the freezing and preventing freezing of the ureteral orifices and bladder wall; residual urine on the floor can be aspirated through the cystoscope, and the cryoprobe can be placed precisely. In addition, he describes the freezing of bladder tumors with generally good results with a similar technique. He generally extends the indications for cryosurgery in prostate disease.

Gonder MJ, Soanes WA, Smith V: Experimental cryosurgery. Invest Urol 1:610, 1964

The authors describe the healing process secondary to cryoinjury. In addition, they clearly demonstrate that freezing would destroy prostate tissue if the tissue was reduced to a lethal temperture.

Keller AJ: Personal communication, 1979

Keller describes equipment permitting freezing followed by desiccation of the prostate. There has been an 85% success rate in poor-risk patients with decompensated bladders with his procedure.

Overview: Cryosurgery of the Prostate

Joseph B. Dowd

Cryosurgery of the prostate remains a useful and ingenious technique that is only rarely applicable. Its performance must be confined to those centers with a demonstrated interest and skill.

Having enthusiastically undertaken this procedure almost 15 yr ago, impressed by Gonder's results and sincerity, I modified his procedure and limited the indications.

The preliminary placement of a suprapubic Foley catheter (20 French with a 5-ml bag) by trocar cystostomy added the certainty of intraoperative distention of the bladder with air to prevent the cryoprobe tip from damaging the bladder wall. In addition, the liquefaction of the frozen necrotizing prostate was not complicated by intermittent bouts of urinary retention from slough occluding the urethral channel or bladder outlet. Simple unplugging of the suprapubic tube permitted evacuation of the urine and passable necrotic material. Bidaily irrigations of the suprapubic tube hastened removal of the slough. The early and continued effort at normal urethral voiding seemed to hasten demarcation of the abnormal prostatic adenoma by freezing from the unfrozen remnant adenoma and capsule. This later was remarkably free of scar or sequelae. The hospital stay was shortened to less than a week, including patient or family training. The patients tolerated the procedure uneventfully in most instances. The suprapublic tube was removed in

the office about 4 wk later, aided by a pressure dressing over the trocar site for 48 hr.

The procedure was limited to poor-risk patients having a bulky intraurethral obstructing prostate in whom a conventional operation was imprudent or contraindicated. Less often, bulky, obstructing, surgically incurable prostatic malignancies were similarly treated, including two sarcomas. Least often, patients with a dyscrasia or on anticoagulants with similar intraurethral bulky obstructions were included in a series of 92 patients in the first 7 yr. Over the ensuing 7½ yr, however, only 20 cyrosurgical procedures on the prostate were undertaken. These were primarily done on those with incurable obstructing malignancy (16 patients), immense benign obstruction in patients refusing any possibility of transfusion (2 patients), a bleeding tendency secondary to mercury-induced cirrhosis (1 patient), and a severe cardiac patient receiving anticoagulants.

Why this turnabout? Obviously, many reasons, including the lack of predictably uniform good results, the improvement in resectoscopes with the advent of constant flow techniques, and acceptance by staff and patients of intermittent catheterization. Pharmacologic resort to the alpha-receptor blocking agent phenoxybenzamine and improved deliverance of radiation to bulky stage C & D obstructing malignancies with and without hormonal manipulations further deterred my original enthusiasm for cryosurgical techniques. Equipment failures and frustration with prohibitive faulty repairs curtailed my interest, so that no cryosurgery whatsoever has been done on my urologic service for over a year. I do own the world's most expensive swizel stick, but could be persuaded to part with it for a fair trade, such as a cracked bat and at least one taped ball.

At no time have I recognized any demonstrable immunologic advantage in patients with prostatic malignancy undergoing cryosurgery. Others have similar conclusions.[1]

The addition of heat to the procedure has reportedly augmented the degree and depth of tissue destruction and hastened the evacuation of slough and curtailed the period of postoperative infection. The short duration of freeze and its depth unmonitored, however, suggests that this was primarily a heat-induced destruction of adenoma rather than a meaningful cyrosurgical result.[2]

Had cryosurgery preceded the development of the resectoscope, it has been conjectured that the latter would never have been needed. True, it is that most urologists have never taken cryosurgery seriously enough to learn of its proven ability to debulk by controlled tissue destruction. Unappreciated as it is, cryosurgery awaits physicians' finding more imperative uses for its definite potential.

REFERENCES

1. Milleman LA, Weissman WD, Culp DA: Serum protein, enzyme and immunologic response following perineal cryosurgery for carcinoma of the prostate. J Urol 123:710, 1980

2. Keller AJ, Völter D, Schubert GE: Cryocautery of prostate. Urology 15:548, 1980

84

NEW IGLESIAS RESECTOSCOPE WITH CONTINUOUS IRRIGATION, SIMULTANEOUS SUCTION AND LOW INTRAVESICAL PRESSURE

Jose J. Iglesias, Andrew Sporer, Alexander C. Gellman and Joseph J. Seebode*

From the Department of Surgery, Division of Urology, College of Medicine and Dentistry of New Jersey and Affiliated Hospitals, New Jersey Medical School, Newark, New Jersey

The Journal of Urology
Copyright © 1975 by The Williams & Wilkins Co.
Vol. 114, December
Printed in U.S.A.

ASTRACT—The new Iglesias resectoscope that allows simultaneous suction, continuous irrigation and low intravesical pressure is described. Advantages of this instrument include no interruption, better endoscopic vision by a continuous clear inflow of more than 600 ml. per minute, a low intravesical pressure less than 10 mm Hg during the transurethral resection, shorter operating time, less bleeding, easier teaching and no more wet floor and wet surgeon. Since the entire amount of irrigating fluid is collected blood loss can be calculated and the amount of absorption can be determined.

Accepted for publication May 2, 1975
* Requests for reprints: Martland Hospital, 65 Bergen St., Newark, New Jersey 07107.

Transurethral resection of the prostate and of bladder tumors has been performed for the last 40 years with several different instruments. During this time there has been a constant attempt to improve the instruments to simplify the operation and the difficulty involved in teaching its performance. Major advances have included the intense fiberoptic light systems, the Hopkins lens and transistorized electrosurgical units. It only remained to improve the irrigating system and to lower the intravesical pressure, thereby preventing absorption. The instrument described herein was designed with the hope of solving these 2 problems.

DESCRIPTION OF THE INSTRUMENT

A resectoscope has been designed to avoid the present inconvenience of periodically interrupting resection to evacuate the accumulation of bloody fluid from the bladder and maintain the intravesical pressure constantly at less than 10 mm Hg. Using isotopes in 1973 Madsen established 30 mm Hg as the initial intravesical pressure for irrigant absorption during transurethral resection of the prostate.[1-3] The new resectoscope has 2 conduits— 1 for the inflow of clear fluid and the other for the outflow of bloody fluid. Both conduits are completely separate and have their distal opening at different sites in the beak of the resectoscope sheath. The volumetric capacity of the outflow conduit is smaller than the inflow conduit. To maintain the bladder adequately distended suction is applied to the outflow, establishing an equal rate of flow in both conduits. Clear fluid is constantly flowing in front of the lens to irrigate the operative field before being evacuated via the outflow conduit. The bladder and prostatic urethra must be moderately distended to allow exact visualization of the pathologic changes at the prostatic urethra. The intravesical hydrostatic pressure should be less than 10 mm Hg to avoid the absorption of electrolyte-free irrigant. At the inflow pressure venous bleeding is decreased and uninterrupted resection is possible. To maintain the bladder and prostatic cavity adequately distended at all times with an inflow of more than 400 ml. fluid per minute, it is necessary to regulate the suction. We have learned in our research while measuring the intravesical pressure that the bladder can be adequately distended at pressures less than 10 mm Hg or 13.6 cm water. At these levels of pressure the resectionist is able to see the posterior wall of the bladder while the resectoscope is in the prostatic fossa.

The 2 conduits are established by a fine metallic inner tube, which encompasses the entire length of the telescope together with the stem and arms of the cutting loop. This tube is smaller than the sheath in cross section. Its distal end closes the space between the inner tube and sheath. The proximal end is attached either to the working element or to the sheath. This space is the outflow conduit. The inflow conduit is within the inner

metallic tube as is the free space surrounding the telescope, loop, stem and arms. It ends in front and below the distal end of the telescope. At the beak the pressure of the inflowing irrigant pushes the resected pieces of tissue to the bottom of the bladder. Bloody irrigant from the bladder enters the outflow conduit by way of multiple vents around the distal part of the sheath, preventing resected pieces from blocking the outflow entrance. At the upper proximal end of the sheath socket the inflow conduit communicates with an external tube connection through which clear irrigating fluid flows to the operative field. The outflow conduit communicates at the lower part of the socket with an external tube to which suction is applied (Figs. 1 to 3).

Both external tubes are supplied with stopcocks. Just proximal to the outflow stopcock there is a filter device which prevents the suction tube from becoming plugged. The metallic tube stabilizes the cutting loop and also deflects the arms of the loop upward and out of the field of vision. By operative monitoring of intravesical hydrostatic pressure and observation of serum chemistry studies, preoperative and postoperative weights, and volume of irrigants used we have found that there is minimal absorption of irrigant at an intravesical pressure less than 10 mm Hg.[4] A typical patient record is seen in the table. Above this critical pressure absorption of irrigant rapidly increases. During our research with the new resectoscope a fine suprapubic catheter connected to a Lewis cystometer or to a water manometer allowed continuous monitoring of the intravesical pressure which was maintained at less than the critical 10 mm Hg. A typical tracing is seen using the conventional resectoscope and the new suction resectoscope in Figure 4.

The handling of this resectoscope is simple. The entrance of air at the irrigating flask should be at 70 cm. or more above the level of the operating table. The suction is applied to the outflow conduit only after the posterior wall of the bladder is completely separated from the bladder neck while the bladder is filling. Suction is regulated from 10 to 15 inches Hg vacuum to maintain the posterior bladder wall away from the bladder neck. Maximum visibility and minimal bleeding are realized with undisturbed hemodynamics and undetectable irrigant absorption if the periprostatic sinuses are not opened. The performance and teaching of transurethral surgery are made easier. The attending surgeon is allowed to appreciate the amount of bleeding through the transparent tube of the suction.

Explosive gases produced during the resection are removed from the bladder, thus avoiding possible explosion which has been reported with the use of the suprapublic trocar suction. The vacuum pump must be adjustable between 10 and 50 cm Hg vacuum. The loop must be in the corrrect position prior to beginning the

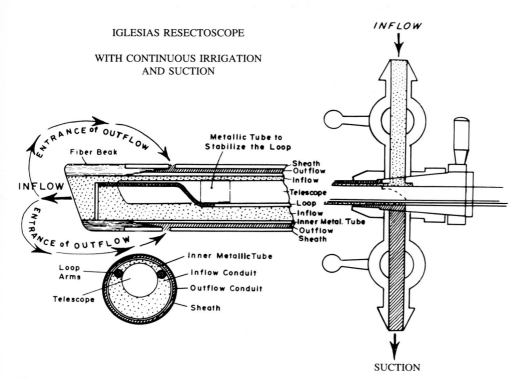

IGLESIAS RESECTOSCOPE

WITH CONTINUOUS IRRIGATION
AND SUCTION

Fig. 1.

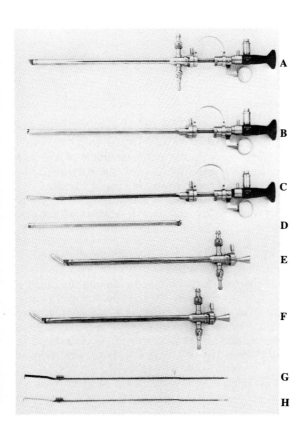

Typical Protocol Form Demonstrates Preoperative and Postoperative Findings While Using the New Iglesias Resectoscope with Simultaneous Irrigation, Suction and Low Intravesical Pressure

	Preop.	Postop.
Blood pressure	149/90	135/90
Weight (pounds)	145	145
Serum osmolality (mOsm)	289	287
Serum tree hemoglobin (mg %)	2.4	2.3
Serum sodium (mEq %)	138	142
Serum chloride (mEq %)	104	102
Serum potassium (mEq %)	3.2	3.2
Hematocrit (%)	39	40

Name—A.G.

Age—64 years

Diagnosis—BPH

Operative time—35 minutes

Adenoma weight—45 gm

Irrigant used—24.1 H_2O

Bloody fluid sucked—23.5 liters

◀ **Fig. 2.** (*A*) Resectoscope No. 28 sheath. (*B*) Resectoscope No. 28 with sheath removed. (*C*) Resectoscope No. 25 after removal of inner metallic tube. (*D*) Inner metallic tube of No. 25F. (*E*) No. 28F sheath with obturator. (*F*) Sheath No. 25 with obturator. (*G*) Loop for No. 28, black. (*H*) Loop for No. 25, yellow.

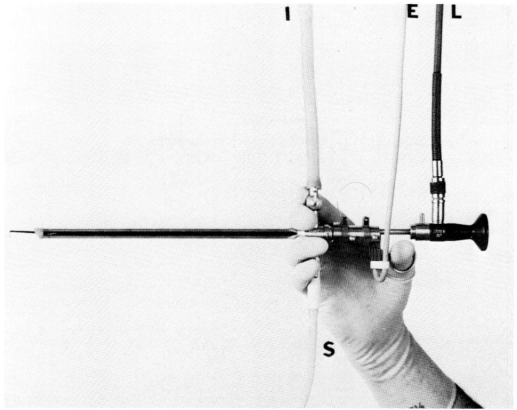

Fig. 3. (*I*) Irrigation tube. (*E*) High frequency electrical current. (*L*) Light bundle cord. (*S*) Suction tube.

operation. This is achieved when the loop is situated inside of the sheath while viewing through the telescope. When evacuating pieces of tissue from the bladder, the outflow stopcock must be closed to ensure that it will not become blocked.

ADVANTAGES

(1) Periodic interruptions in the resection in order to evacuate the bladder are eliminated. Therefore, the resectionist can concentrate on the field of resection without the previous frequent reorientation and the operative time is shortened.

(2) The ability to control the amount of distension of the bladder and prostatic fossa at a constant hydrostatic intravesical pressure of less than 10 mm Hg decreases the likelihood of extravasation and/or absorption of the irrigant.

(3) A superior endoscopic vision is maintained at all times by the continuous flow of clear fluid and the decreased venous bleeding owing to the intravesical

pressure less than 10 mm Hg. It is easier to visualize the exact amount of obstructing tissue to be resected, thus avoiding injury to the muscular fibers of the true prostatic capsule and the internal and external sphincters, and the opening of the periprostatic venous sinuses.

(4) Less operative time is required for hemostasis with most time being used for resection. Blood and blood clots do not accumulate in the bladder. Less irrigating fluid is used.

(5) The possibility of explosion of accumulated gases in the bladder is avoided.

(6) During resection of bladder tumors the bladder is maintained at the same distension, allowing easy resection, good vision and excellent hemostasis.

(7) The transurethral resection syndromes are eliminated because the intravesical pressure is maintained at less than 10 mm Hg. the critical pressure for irrigant absorption.

(8) Operative time is reduced by an average of 50 percent.

(9) It permits transurethral resection of larger glands.

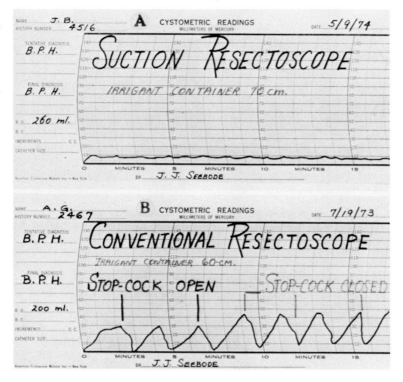

Fig. 4. Continuous intravesical pressure recording by Lewis cystometer via suprapubic cystocath during transurethral resections using conventional resectoscope and new suction resectoscope.

It allows removal of resected chips from the bladder when they are too large to be evacuated by suction, by means of grasping the tissue between the loop and the inner tube.

(10) The simple measurement of irrigant inflow and outflow allows calculation of irrigant absorption. The level of hemoglobin in the irrigating fluid can be converted to blood loss.

(11) No more wet floor and wet surgeon.

(12) Plain sterile water can be used safely even though hemolysis and plasmolysis may occur if the periprostatic sinuses are opened. There is a potential hazard with inexperienced resectionists if venous sinuses are opened during the operation. The use of a non-hemolytic solution in no way interferes with the advantages found with this instrument.

The resectoscope has 2 sheaths—the 25F accommodates a yellow loop No. 26 and the 28F uses a black loop larger than the blue No. 28. The 25F sheath can be used for most cases.

REFERENCES

1. Madsen, P. O. and Naber, K. G.: The importance of the pressure in the prostatic fossa and absorption of irrigating fluid during transurethral resection of the prostate. J Urol 109:446, 1973
2. Wakim, K. G.: The pathophysiologic basis for the clinical manifestation and complications of transurethral prostatic resection. J Urol 106:719, 1971
3. Ganong, W. F.: Review of medical physiology. Los Altos, California: Lange Medical Publications, P. 468, 1967
4. Reuter, HJ. J. and Jones. L. W.: Physiologic low pressure irrigation for transurethral resection: suprapubic trocar drainage. J Urol 111:210., 1974

Commentary: Transurethral Prostatectomy

Winston K. Mebust

Transurethral prostatectomy has become the most accepted method of relieving bladder outlet obstruction in patients with benign and malignant prostatic disease. With the wide-angle Hopkins' lens system, fiberoptic light source, and solid state electrosurgical units, the urologist can quickly and effectively relieve bladder outlet obstruction. Iglesias and associates have further refined the resectoscope so it can be used with continuous irrigation and simultaneous suction. This permits the surgery to be done without interruption and reduces operating time. Water spillage is reduced as compared to the more conventional resectoscopes, which require intermittent filling and emptying of the bladder. The constant flow, as compared to the standard resectoscope, is a more closed system and the risk of intra-operatively induced infection should be reduced. The low intravesical pressure should also be associated with a lower incidence of fluid and electrolyte changes that can occur during a transurethral prostatectomy, particularly the TUR syndrome or hyponatremia.

To obtain adequate vision with the new Iglesias resectoscope, a high flow rate must be obtained. Even so, in patients with large adenomas, I have occasionally noted vision to be obscured from bleeding. This is presumably secondary to the relatively short distance of the inflow to outflow fluid arc. Under such circumstances, the surgeon may quickly convert the constant flow resectoscope to a standard scope and extend the length of water flow from the tip of the scope directly through the fossa and into the bladder. Adequate vision is obtained and the bleeding points controlled, and then the instrument may be returned to the constant flow technique.

With modern instrumentation and recognition of the fluid and electrolyte changes that may occur during prostatectomy, death from electrolyte imbalance or hemorrhage is exceedingly rare. The most common cause of death remains cardiovascular complications. With modern monitoring techniques, the patient's cardiovascular status can be evaluated not only preoperatively, but in the operating room during surgery. With all of the aforementioned, the mortality following a transurethral prostatectomy is less than 4%.

The complications of transurethral prostatectomy continue to be modest problems in the immediate and long-term period. In reviewing my results in over 2000 patients, I noted that 312 (14%) had 1 complication and 44 had 2 or more complications in the immediate postoperative period. The overall nonfatal complication rate was 17%, with complications being divided into the following categories: bleeding, 6%; infection, 6%; technical problems, 5%; cardiac, 1%; gastrointestinal, 1%; and general medical, 3%. Complications were noted to be directly correlated with an increase in age with 3.5% of those aged 80 or greater having complications in the immediate

postoperative period, as compared to 0.7 in the 60 to 69 age group. The length of surgical time also correlated with the incidence of immediate postoperative complications. Those requiring greater than 150 min of operative time had a complication rate of 5%, as compared to an overall complication rate of 1.3%. When the adenoma resected was greater than 60 g, the complication rate was 3.1%, as compared to 1% if it was less than 60 g. Renal function was also a factor, with those having a creatinine level greater than 1.5 mg/ml having a complication rate of 4.1%, as compared to 0.7% in those with normal renal function.

Long-term or delayed complications must also be considered in evaluating transurethral prostatectomy. These include postoperative urethral strictures, continuing infection, impotence, and urinary incontinence. Postoperative urethral strictures are particularly annoying to both the surgeon and the patient. After a technically adequate surgical procedure with initially satisfactory relief of bladder outlet obstructive symptoms, the patient returns at a later date with the same symptoms that brought him to the urologist initially. The incidence of postoperative urethral strictures is approximately 6% and is unquestionably due to the trauma of the resectoscope on the urethra. Emmett and colleagues pointed out that 20% of men have a urethra that calibrates less than 28 French. The urologist should therefore calibrate the urethra immediately preoperatively with a bougie a boule, and if there is any restriction to a 28 French bougie, I recommend that a perineal urethrostomy be done so that the resection can be carried out through the more commodious bulbous urethra. The incidence of postoperative urethral stricture at the site of the urethrostomy or the distal urethra is less than 1%, and the postoperative complications are minimal. If the patient has a narrow, distal urethra secondary to a preexisting urethral stricture, the incidence of additional stricture formation is increased threefold if the resection is done through the dilated stricture. Therefore, I prefer the perineal urethrostomy when there is an inadequate urethra for the size of the resectoscope I wish to use or if the patient has preexisting urethral strictures.

I have previously described the technique of perineal urethrostomy (Fig. 5). To proceed, insert a grooved, no. 24 Van Buren sound into the urethra. Tent up the perineum by the grooved sound and stabilize it by a Conger clamp. Make a midline incision, identify the urethra, and secure it by stay sutures. The stay sutures facilitate insertion of the resectoscope. Following the resection, I usually bring the catheter out through the perineal incision, eliminating trauma to the distal urethra by the catheter. Should the surgeon wish to bring the catheter out through the full length of the urethra, the bulbospongiosus and subcutaneous tissue may be loosely approximated with

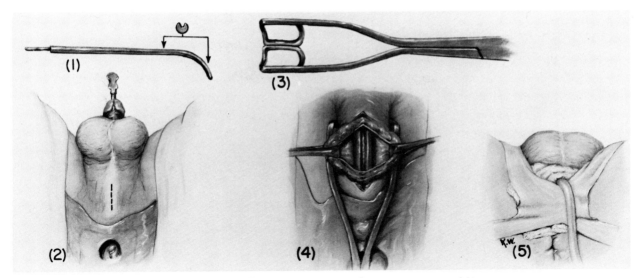

Fig. 5. Technique of perineal urethrostomy. The perineum is tented up over a grooved Van Buren sound and the incision made in the midline. The urethra mucosa is secured by Allis clamps or stay sutures to facilitate insertion of the resectoscope. At the completion of the procedure, the catheter is brought out through the perineal urethrostomy, which is allowed to heal by secondary intention. (After Mebust WK: In Hinman F Jr: Benign Prostatic Hypertrophy. New York, Springer-Verlag, 1983)

absorable suture. A watertight closure including the skin can be difficult to achieve and, if not accomplished, may lead to extravasation of urine and abscess formation.

An internal urethrotomy done at the 12 o'clock position with an Otis urethrotome can also be done when the urethra is inadequate. Although this is a relatively safe procedure, there is a 2% incidence of postoperative chordee, and bleeding from the internal urethrotomy can be troublesome. The surgeon may use a smaller resectoscope if the urethra is normal but less than 28 French. However, the amount of tissue removed in each stroke of the cutting loop is less with a 24 or 26 French resectoscope, and therefore the operating time is increased. The water flow is somewhat compromised as compared to the 28 French sheath, and thus visibility is impaired. Therefore, if the gland is estimated to be 40 g or greater, a perineal urethrostomy should be done and a larger resectoscope used. The surgeon may also avoid trauma to the urethra by adequately lubricating the resectoscope sheath and the urethra. Many have suggested coating the resectoscope sheath with a sterile, water-insoluble petroleum jelly and then instilling directly into the urethra a water-soluble jelly. The water-insoluble petroleum jelly poses a theoretic problem of possible embolization, but this apparently has not been a clinically significant problem. A perineal urethrostomy, an internal urethrotomy, a reduced-size resectoscope, and adequate lubrication should dramatically reduce the incidence of urethral stricture.

Surgical technique is important in reducing immediate and delayed complications following a transurethral prostatectomy. The operation should be a carefully planned procedure done in a basically routine manner that will expeditiously remove the adenoma. The surgical technique may vary with the type of pathologic condition and the surgeon's training. I prefer the method described by Nesbit.

To begin, start the resection at the bladder neck at the 12 o'clock position and carry it circumferentially around the bladder neck. The depth of the resection is just sufficient to expose the circular fibers of the bladder neck (Fig. 6). Overresection of the bladder neck may lead to a vesical neck contracture. The mid-fossa is then resected starting again at the 12 o'clock position and removing the adenoma in quadrants (Fig. 7). I prefer to resect the upper or anterior quadrants, allowing the bulk of the lateral lobe tissue to drop down into the fossa. The lateral lobe tissue is thus more easily resected, and then the resection is carried across the posterior lobe. Finally, the apex is cleared of adenoma (Fig. 8). Although the experienced resectionist does not need the verumontanum as a landmark, it is the most reliable point to delineate apex from the external sphincter. I prefer to start the resection immediately adjacent to the veru on one side of the apex, continuing to the 12 o'clock position, and then repeating the procedure on the other side of the verumontanum. All adenoma must be removed but the smooth muscle and elastic tissue preserved. Loss of this component of the external sphincter mechanism may result in stress incontinence. With completion of the resection, the surgeon should be able to place the resectoscope distal to the veru and have an unobstructed view into the bladder. The surgeon must be cognizant of the landmarks encountered during the resection. The adenoma has a crystalline, snowlike appearance as compared to the striated appearance of the prostatic surgical capsule. The recognition of venous sinuses or peri-prostatic fat indicates too deep a resection (Fig. 9). The type of resectoscope, whether it requires the use of two hands or

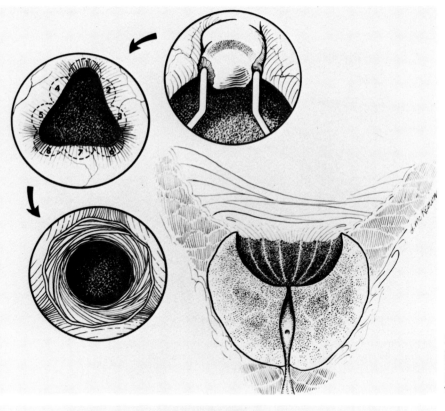

Fig. 6. First stage of a transurethral prostatectomy. (After Mebust WK: In Hinman F Jr: Benign Prostatic Hypertrophy. New York, Springer-Verlag, 1983)

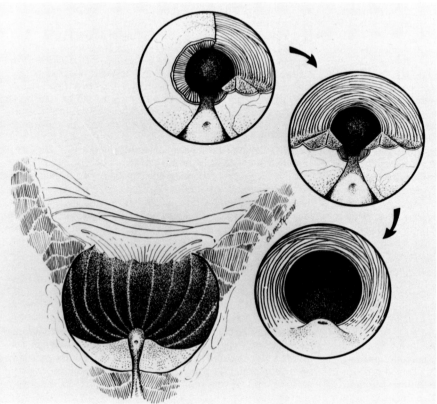

Fig. 7. Second stage of transurethral prostatectomy. (After Mebust WK: In Hinman F Jr: Benign Prostatic Hypertrophy. New York, Springer-Verlag, 1983)

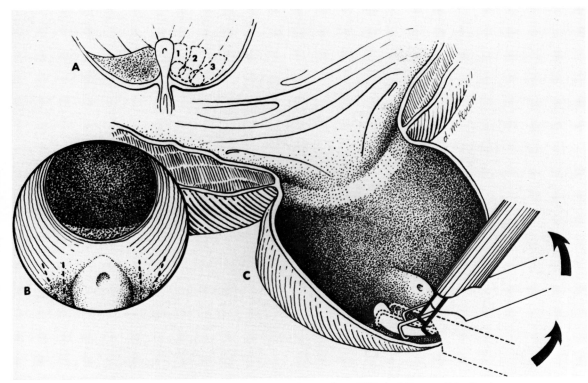

Fig. 8. Third stage of a transurethral prostatectomy. (After Mebust WK: In Hinman F Jr: Benign Prostatic Hypertrophy. New York, Springer-Verlag, 1983)

Fig. 9. Landmarks noted during the resection are (A) residual adenoma; (B) prostatic capsule; (C) arterial bleeding point; (D) periprostatic fat protruding through capsule; and (E) venous bleeding. (After Mebust WK: In Hinman F Jr: Benign Prostatic Hypertrophy. New York, Springer-Verlag, 1983)

one, is not important as long as the surgeon uses that particular scope repetitively and becomes exceedingly familiar with the instrument. I prefer the Iglesias modification of the Nesbit resectoscope used with one hand, which permits the surgeon to insert a finger into the rectum through an O'Connor rectal shield. This allows digital manipulation of the gland during the resection and facilitates the procedure.

The use of antibiotics in transurethral prostatectomy remains controversial. Approximately 60% of patients in whom the prostate tissue has been cultured after prostatectomy have been found to be infected. There is no question that those patients with positive urine cultures should be treated with specific antibiotics preoperatively. The incidence of positive blood cultures is 10% in those patients being treated with a specific antibiotic, whereas in those with infected urine and not receiving specific antibiotics, the incidence of positive blood cultures is 50%. The patient with a positive urine culture should be treated vigorously preoperatively and in the immediate postoperative period with specific antibiotics. However, the use of prophylactic antibiotics in the uninfected patient has been questioned. The studies of Gibbons and colleagues failed to show any benefit from prophylactic antibiotics in reducing postoperative infection or protecting high-risk patients such as the diabetic. In a similar study, Morris and colleagues also failed to find any effect on reducing bacteremia or fever when antibiotics were used on a prophylactic basis but did notice a reduction in the incidence of postoperative positive urine cultures. However, the clinical significance of the positive urine cultures was not clear. Many patients resolve their infection with their own natural defense mechanisms once the bladder outlet obstruction has been removed and the patient can effectively empty the bladder. Therefore, in the patient with uninfected urine preoperatively, there appears to be little advantage to prophylactic antibiotics. Rather, in the postoperative period, those patients who are symptomatic, such as with frequency and dysuria, or have persistent pyuria should then have appropriate cultures and be treated with specific antibiotics.

The incidence of epididymitis is approximately 2% to 7%. This can be reduced by treating those with infected urine with specific antibiotics preoperatively and in the immediate postoperative period. However, the role of surgical interruption of the vas deferens in those with uninfected urine remains uncertain. Undoubtedly, bladder spasms in the postoperative period may force urine down the vas deferens into the epididymis, resulting in a chemical epididymitis. Whether this occurs frequently enough to warrant the routine use of vasectomy is problematic. In those patients who have a preexisting infection that may not be well controlled, such as the patient with an in-dwelling catheter, I suggest a percutaneous vasal interruption with 3–0 chromic catgut to help avoid postoperative epididymitis. This is a relatively simple technique and is equally effective in controlling epididymitis as compared to a formal vasectomy.

Impotence is of concern to both the patient and the urologist when considering the sequela of a prostatectomy. Finkle reported that 67% of men were potent at the time of prostatectomy. He noted that 84% retained their potency, but that this was directly related to the patient's preoperative sexual ability and a willing sexual partner. Hargreave noted that 57% of men at an average age of 66.5 yr were potent before transurethral prostatectomy. The incidence of impotency in those who were totally potent preoperatively was 4%, but in those patients with failing potency preoperatively, 10% became impotent and 22% worse. The incidence of impotency following a transurethral prostatectomy as compared to other types of prostatectomy appears to be somewhat less. Windle and colleagues, in reviewing impotency following prostatectomy, compared their patients to a control group of similar age undergoing intraperitoneal or inguinal scrotal surgery. They found the incidence of postoperative impotence was 6% in the control group. Therefore, the risks of any surgery in the elderly patient may be associated with subsequent impotency. Zohar and colleagues have noted that impotency is related to the patient's level of anxiety and whether the patient had been counseled preoperatively. Approximately one third to two thirds of patients will have retrograde ejaculation, and the patient may confuse this with decreasing sexual ability. It appears, therefore, that the incidence of impotence after transurethral prostatectomy is 4% to 6%, depending on the patient's general sexual ability and satisfaction with his sexual life. I suggest that the patient be counseled preoperatively. The risk of postoperative TUR impotency is not great and should not be confused with the problem of retrograde ejaculation. Obviously, many factors are involved in postprostatectomy impotence and include the patient's prior sexual activity, a willing partner, and reassurance preoperatively.

Incontinence following a transurethral resection occurs in 1% to 4% of patients. Many patients will have urgency incontinence immediately postoperatively, which will improve as the prostatic fossa heals and the edema around the external sphincter resolves. During a transurethral prostatectomy, the internal sphincter mechanism around the bladder neck and proximal urethra is essentially removed with the resection of the adenoma. However, great care should be taken to preserve the external sphincter, which includes not only the striated muscle, but the smooth muscle and elastic tissue around the distal urethra. Overresection of the prostatic capsule, particularly at the apex, can result in permanent stress incontinence. If the striated muscle of the external sphincter is resected or injured in addition to removal of the internal sphincter, gravity incontinence may result. It has been my policy to follow those patients with mild stress incontinence for at least a year before considering surgical correction. Those patients who fail to resolve on conservative measures as well as those with gravity incontinence should be considered for surgical correction of their incontinence with the use of the Kaufman perineal pad or the Scott inflatable prosthesis.

The mortality following a transurethral prostatectomy as noted is quite low. However, the leading cause of death in my experience following a transurethral prostatectomy was secondary to cardiovascular complications. In those patients who had a recent myocardial infarction, I recommend waiting 2 to 6 mo if at all possible.

Sinclair and colleagues, using the ^{125}I fibrinogen technique, found that patients undergoing open pelvic surgery had a 68% incidence of deep vein thrombosis. This was in contrast to 33% of those undergoing a transurethral prostatectomy. The incidence of clinically apparent thrombophlebitis was only 30% in those with deep vein thrombosis. In avoiding the problem of deep vein thrombosis and pulmonary emboli, which, in my experience, occurred in 0.2% of patients, I have relied primarily on early ambulation of the patient. Giving the patient a small dose of heparin preoperatively has been used in other areas of surgery to prevent this complication. However, the fear of intraoperative and postoperative hemorrhage remains a deterrent to most urologists in considering this modality with transurethral prostatectomy.

BIBLIOGRAPHY

Emmett EL, Rous SN, Greene LF et al: Preliminary internal urethrotomy in 1036 cases to prevent urethral stricture following transurethral resection: Caliber of normal male urethra. J Urol 89:829–836, 1963

Nesbit RM: Transurethral Prostatectomy. Springfield, Illinois, Charles C Thomas, 1943.

Melchior J, Valk WL, Foret JD, et al: Transurethral prostatectomy: Computerized analysis of 2223 consecutive cases. J Urol 112:634, 1974

Gibbons RP, Stark RA, Correa RJ, et al: The prophylactic use or misuse of antibiotics in transurethral prostatectomy. J Urol 119:381, 1978

Morris JJ, Golovsky D, Guinness MDG, et al: The value of prophylactic antibiotics in transurethral prostatic resection: A controlled trial with observations on the origin of postoperative infection. Br J Urol 48:479, 1976

Finkle AL, Prian DV: Sexual potency in elderly men before and after prostatectomy. JAMA 196:125, 1966

Hargreave TB, Stephenson TP: Potency and prostatectomy. Br J Urol 49:683, 1977

Flachenecker G, Fastenmeier K: High frequency current effects during transurethral resection. J Urol 122:336, 1979

Sinclair J, Forbes CD, Prentice CRM, et al: The incidence of deep vein thrombosis in prostatectomized patients following the administration of the fibrinolytic inhibitor, aminocaproic acid (EACA). Urol Res 4:129, 1976

Windle R, Roberts JBM: Ejaculatory function after prostatectomy. Proc R Soc Med 67:1160, 1974

Melchior J, Valk WL, Foret JD, et al: Transurethral resection of the prostate via perineal urethrostomy: Complete analysis of 7 years of experience. J Urol 111:640, 1974

ANNOTATED BIBLIOGRAPHY

Mommsen S, Genster HG, Moller J: Changes in the serum concentrations of sodium, potassium, and free haemoglobin during transurethral resection of the prostate—parts of the TUR syndrome? Urol Res 5:201, 1977

In 133 patients undergoing transurethral prostatectomy using sterile water, all patients were found to have elevated free hemoglobin postoperatively. Although serum elevations of the free hemoglobin were minimal in the majority of patients and none had clinical symptoms, the use of hemolytic solutions continues to pose a potential threat to the patient undergoing transurethral prostatectomy. The use of a nonhemolytic solution such as 1.5% glycine is recommended.

Oester A, Madsen PO: Determination of absorption of irrigating fluid during transurethral resection of the prostate by means of radioisotopes. J Urol 102:714, 1969

The authors, using a double isotope technique, demonstrated convincingly that 29% of the fluid used for irrigation during a transurethral prostatectomy is absorbed intravenously. The majority of the fluid is absorbed toward the end of the resection. Fluid absorbed directly through the venous sinuses may result in hyponatremia and the transurethral resection syndrome.

Andersen JT, Bourne RB, Bradley WE: Combined electromyography and gas urethral pressure profilometry before and after transurethral resection of the prostate. J Urol 116:622, 1976

This is one of many current articles where patients have been studied with modern urodynamic techniques before and after a transurethral prostatectomy. Not only can the degree of response from the removal of the bladder outlet obstruction be quantitated, but perhaps those patients whose symptoms are secondary to a disease other than benign prostatic hypertrophy can be noted and not subjected to transurethral prostatectomy with a subsequent poor clinical result.

Abrams PH: Prostatism and prostatectomy: The value of urine flow rate measurement in the preoperative assessment for operation. J Urol 117:70, 1977

Not all patients undergoing a transurethral prostatectomy for bladder outlet obstructive symptoms need to undergo a complete urodynamic evaluation. Perhaps the best single test is the urinary flow rates. Urinary flow rate is related to the volume voided. The reader is also referred to other reports by Olsson and Susset.

Lentz HC Jr, Mebust WK, Foret JD, et al: Urethral strictures following transurethral prostatectomy: Review of 2223 resections. J Urol 117:194, 1977

The authors have reviewed an extensive experience with transurethral prostatectomy in reference to postoperative urethral stricture. The primary factor appears to be trauma of the resectoscope within the urethra.

Flachenecker G, Fastenmeier K: High frequency current effects during transurethral resection. J Urol 122:336, 1979

Even with modern electrosurgical units, intraoperative accidents may still occur and present a problem not only to the patient but to the surgeon. The authors superbly illustrate the electrical current pattern occurring in a patient during a transurethral prostatectomy. They clearly point out the risks of an inadvertent electrical contact between the loop and an uninsulated sheath causing heat and secondary injury to the urethra. Sheaths that are insulated may also be dangerous if the area of insulation becomes worn. Careful review of this article is imperative for the transurethral surgeon if the complications associated with the electrosurgical current are to be reduced.

Melchior J, Valk WL, Foret JD, et al: Transurethral resection of the prostate via perineal urethrostomy: Complete analysis of seven years of experience. J Urol 111:640, 1974

In this report the experience of the University of Kansas Medical Center and the Kansas City Missouri Veterans Administration Hospital from 1965 to 1971 are reported. Thirty-two percent of the patients underwent transurethral resection of the prostate through a perineal urethrostomy. The most frequent indication for perineal urethrostomy was a prostate over 40 g, which was present in 44.2% of the patients. No mortality and little morbidity were noted in this series.

Overview:
Transurethral Prostatectomy: Most Accepted Method to Relieve Bladder Outlet Obstruction

William B. Garlick

There is no question that transurethral prostatectomy has become the most accepted method for relieving bladder outlet obstruction in patients with benign and malignant prostatic disease. This has come about with the overall improvement of equipment, such as the wide-angle lens, the fiberoptic photolight source, and the new electrosurgical units. I have been disappointed in the solid state electrosurgical units because of their poor coagulating ability, and so I have returned to the original Bovie unit with settings on spark gap no. 2 and cutting and coagulating at 55.

As to the type of resectoscope, it does not matter as long as the surgeon is adept with the instrument. It depends largely on how he has been trained. The irrigating fluid should be safe and cheap and give the best possible visualization. The constant flow system is a good addition, but it really does not add a great deal. In large glands it is almost impossible to use because of poor visualization. This may be due to the short inflow and outflow arc and may also be due to lower vesical pressure, which, even though desirable, may allow more bleeding to occur.

With modern equipment, increased speed of resections, and early recognition of complications, death from electrolytic changes, hemorrhage, and perforation is very rare. Cardiovascular problems are the most common cause of death, but this has largely been averted with proper preoperative evaluation and careful monitoring at surgery.

Complications, as a rule, have been reduced to a modest rate. There is no question that they occur more frequently in patients with large glands, which require over an hour of operating time, and in elderly patients. There is a place for a planned two-stage procedure if the patient requires more than an hour, since both morbidity and mortality rise rather sharply after an hour.

Hemorrhage is probably the most common complication, and this, of course, leads to further problems such as perforation and damage to the external sphincter. The bleeding may be arterial or venous or both. It is important to recognize the type of hemorrhage because arterial bleeding can be controlled with fulguration, while venous bleeding requires pressure. Uncontrollable bleeding usually comes about because of an incomplete resection or from jumping from one area to another without adequate control. Large venous sinuses may be a contributing factor. It is important to resect each area completely, control the bleeding, and then proceed. If a large venous sinus is encountered early in the procedure, it is wise to stop resecting, put in a Foley balloon catheter, and operate at a later date. Small sinuses will do little harm provided the surgeon lowers the irrigating fluid pressure and increases the speed of resection, thus preventing excessive hypervolemia. In arterial bleeding it is important to remember that a cross-firing of vessels can occur from one wall to the other. Spot coagulation of arteries is far superior to splattering current over a wide area. In troublesome bleeders that are difficult to locate, the retrograde lens is of great benefit in spotting these and thus allowing coagulation. This is particularly true of bleeders at the vesical neck, which shoot directly at the lens.

Perforations usually occur because of poor visualization in uncontrollable hemorrhage. These can be located in the bladder, vesical neck, or prostatic fossa. The treatment depends on location and severity. In perforations of the bladder and vesical neck, if small and extraperitoneal, usually an in-dwelling catheter and antibiotics will suffice. In patients in whom pain is suddenly encountered, signaling intraperitoneal involvement, suprapubic intervention with proper repair and drainage is mandatory. Perforations of the prostatic capsule are not as important, and usually the resection can continue. Here, also, the surgeon should resect more quickly and lower the irrigating fluid pressure because a venous sinus is often involved.

Postoperative urethral strictures remain a painful and annoying complication. Fortunately, they are not too common, occurring in only 4% of my patients. Calibration of the urethra is important and used routinely. An adequate meatotomy must be done when indicated. Lubrication of the urethra with water-soluble lubricant is essential. In patients with preoperative strictures, several courses are open. The smaller (24 or 26 French) sheaths and resectoscopes work well in smaller glands. In larger glands, where the 28 French sheath and resectoscope are required, if the urethra can be dilated to 30 French without too much problem, the surgeon can proceed. If, after dilatation, the surgeon is unable to pass the sheath, sometimes a filiform with a follow-up one may be passed and a sheath passed over the follow-up filiform. Direct visualization of the urethra may also be helpful in passing the sheath. If all these methods fail, one alternative is to put in an in-dwelling Foley catheter, discontinue the procedure, and allow the patient to drain for a few days. This will dilate the strictures so that a later procedure can be carried out. A very satisfactory alternative, of course, is to do a perineal urethrostomy and proceed in that manner.

In anterior urethral strictures, internal urethrotomy may be used. In all preoperative strictures, the surgeon must inform the patient of their existence because of the great possibility that they will remain postoperatively. However, it has been my experience that posterior urethral strictures are no worse postoperatively, and, in fact, some disappear. Anterior urethral strictures are troublesome, but many will respond to internal urethrotomy.

The surgical technique will vary with the surgeons' training. It matters little where the resection is started. The most important point is to develop a carefully planned procedure and never vary from this set routine. It can be likened to a game plan. When one strays, complications occur.

I have no quarrel with the method described by Nesbit many years ago. However, I believe it is more difficult for the resident and new resectionist to learn this technique, since the lateral lobes, which drop into the fossa, obscure the landmarks. Also, the floor tends to become bloody and harder to resect because of this.

For many years I have used a different technique that has been very satisfactory, not only in results, but in the ease of teaching many residents and new resectionists. In the teaching of residents, many and varied teaching attachment scopes have been tried. These are very cumbersome and do not add a geat deal. I have found that the best way to start a resident is first to establish and demonstrate landmarks and to teach recognition of tissue. This orients them and seems to make it easier. I make it a practice to start the resection and complete the right side of the gland, showing the resident the tissue and the landmarks. I then let the resident proceed on the left side. As he becomes more adept, I increase his operating time and eventually let him start and establish his own landmarks. I never leave the resident alone and do not allow him to operate over 1 hr. This is not only important for the patient, but also for the resident.

In describing technique, it is first essential to learn all about the equipment used and to be very familiar with it. It does not matter whether the resectoscope is one handed or two handed, but the surgeon must become adept with whichever instrument is used and never change.

The management of preoperative strictures has been previously discussed.

Since speed is important, particularly in large glands, "time savers" should be employed. These consist of a no. 12-gauge wire loop for quicker and sharper cutting, a movable stool, pulley, and weight arrangement for the cords, a fan to keep the lens clear of fog, an automatic table, and spinal anesthesia when feasible.

Before attempting passage of the sheath, introduce about 60 ml of irrigating fluid into the bladder with an asepto syringe to prevent possible rupture of the bladder by passage of the sheath and obturator. Lubricate the urethra with water-soluble lubricant before careful calibration. Perform a urethral meatotomy when indicated. After passing the resectoscope, carefully inspect the bladder. Occasionally, a lobe of prostate has been split off inadvertently by passing the sheath. This should not deter the procedure; resect in normal fashion, since this lobe will be eliminated when all the prostate has been removed.

Next, assess the prostate as to size, shape, and position (middle lobe). It is very important to stay within one's capability. If the prostate is too large to resect in 1 hr, a two-stage resection or open procedure may be safer and give better overall results. It is important to recognize tissue—the whitish granular prostate versus the fibrous surgical capsule, and the bluish gray true capsule versus a perforation exposing fat. Venous sinuses are important to recognize. Equally important are the landmarks—circular fibers of the vesical neck, the smooth muscle and elastic tissue of the external sphincter, the verumontanum versus the urethral ridge.

Begin the resection at the 9 o'clock position at the vesical neck, well above the ureteral orifice. For the beginner, this prevents damage to the orifice. Expose the circular fibers of the vesical neck at this point and make a groove out to the external sphincter. This groove extends down to the surgical capsule and is widened. All bleeding is controlled in this area. Once the vesical neck is established, stay in this same vertical plane, neither extending into the bladder or distally into the prostatic fossa. Widen the groove up to the 12 o'clock and down to the 6 o'clock positions, removing all the prostate down to the surgical capsule. Bleeding is controlled in this whole area. At this stage, pull out the resectoscope to the level of the verumontanum or external sphincter and make sure there are no apical lobes falling in on the right side. Complete the floor, removing all the tissue adjacent to the verumontanum. The surgeon must recognize the external sphincter at the level of the verum, because this smooth muscle and elastic tissue must be preserved in order to have continence postoperatively.

Widen the groove down to the surgical capsule, completing the floor and up to the 3 o'clock position. This area, again, is completely resected, and the bleeding controlled. Then, switch to the roof, where it is essential to resect quickly or the adenoma will tend to slide into the bladder and make it very difficult to resect. Resect the left side down to the completed area at the 3 o'clock position. Remove the apical lobe, which falls in after orientation with the vesical neck. Control all bleeders. Do not attempt to fulgurate any venous sinuses. It is extremely important to control the bleeding in order and not jump from one area to the other. Completing the resection down to the capsule helps to control bleeding. Also, at capsule level, the surgeon is fulgurating the trunk of the tree rather than its branches. At the completion of the resection, place the resectoscope distal to the verum and obtain an unobstructed view directly into the bladder, showing that all lobes have been removed. Carefully inspect the resected area for bleeders and retained tissue. Insert the retrograde lens system, which gives a view of the vesical neck and of possible lobes that may have slipped into the bladder and been missed with the foroblique system. Also, with this lens, some difficult bleeders can be located and later fulgurated. This will also show how completely the vesical neck has been resected.

Carefully insert a 22 or 24 French Foley catheter with a 30-ml balloon. Pass the catheter with a guide to prevent possible perforation under trigone, since if the resection is complete, the vesical neck will be undermined. Inflate the Foley catheter balloon to about 10 ml to 15 ml, ensuring that it is snugged down and filled with about the same amount of fluid as grams removed (45 ml–45 g).

It is best to try to get clear drainage at this point. If the drainage is not clear, add more to the balloon or adjust the catheter to another position. This sometimes will control gross bleeding, particularly in venous sinuses. If there is gross bleeding at this stage, remove the catheter, reintroduce the resectoscope sheath, remove all clots, and fulgurate the bleeders. Do this at the end of the resection, since there is no more optimal time to check the bleeding then while the patient still has anesthesia and is on the resectoscope table.

In larger glands, give 20 mg of furosemide (Lasix) intravenously in the recovery room and repeat if necessary. This seems to cut down the amount of postoperative hemorrhage, most likely due to diuresis.

Use this same technique in carcinoma of the prostate, but be extremely careful of the external sphincter. These patients are more prone to incontinence, particularly if they have some infiltration of the sphincter with carcinoma. If the landmarks are rather obscure because the carcinoma, resect very conservatively.

In delayed postoperative hemorrhage, it is essential to remove all clots before attempting any fulguration. Many times, after all the clots have been removed, there is no further bleeding.

The routine use of antibiotics in transurethral prostatectomies is very controversial. Over half the glands resected are infected. It is my practice not to treat patients with preoperative sterile urine but only to treat those with a positive preoperative culture. This tends to reduce the incidence of positive blood cultures postoperatively.

Epididymitis is relatively rare. Vasectomy is not done routinely and is reserved for the patient who has some indication for the procedure.

As far as impotency is concerned following transurethral prostatectomy, the most important thing is counseling. Advise the patient that if he is potent before surgery, he will most likely be potent after surgery. Also discuss retrograde ejaculation and sterility. A frank discussion with the patient and his wife is important.

Incontinence, of course, is a most distressing complication. Fortunately, complete incontinence is very rare. Stress incontinence may exist for a time but usually corrects itself with proper exercise and counseling. If incontinence persists, recystoscope the patient to make sure there is no retained prostate. This will occasionally act to inhibit control by the external sphincter. Also, a large residual with overflow should be ruled out. In carcinoma of the prostate, a patient can occasionally get incontinency because of invasion of the external sphincter mechanism. This is distressing and very difficult to overcome.

In grave incontinence, the surgeon should wait at least 1 yr before resorting to incontinence devices. This is only after other things, such as exercise and medication, have been used. Consider the newer modalities, such as the Rosen, Kaufman, and Scott prostheses.

Fortunately, thrombophlebitis and pulmonary emboli are very rare in transurethral surgery. Low-dose heparin is available but not widely used because, as a rule, it is not necessary.

PART
THIRTY-FOUR

SURGERY OF
CARCINOMA OF THE
PROSTATE

85

TOTAL PROSTATOVESICULECTOMY— RETROPUBIC APPROACH

Joseph Memmelaar

From the Urological Service, Eastern Maine General Hospital, Bangor, Maine

The Journal of Urology
Vol. 62, No. 3, September 1949
Printed in U.S.A.

The perineal operation for total removal of the prostate is unpopular. Relatively few surgeons have been trained to use this approach and therefore this approach has often been avoided. Attributable to this fact many early carcinomas of the prostate must have progressed to the incurable state. There is only one cure for carcinoma of the prostate, and that is early complete prostatectomy. It seems likely that if a more familiar approach could be used which would accomplish Young's concept of a total prostatectomy, the mortality statistics would be influenced favorably. I believe the retropubic approach offers a relatively facile and more definitive method of performing a total prostatovesiculectomy and removing malignant metastases related to the pelvic vessels.

From the observations and experiences gained in the radical treatment of carcinoma of the bladder in which a total prostatectomy, seminal vesiculectomy, cystectomy, and ureteroenterostomy were done in that order it seemed apparent that a total prostatectomy could be performed in much the same manner, by concluding the operation following the vesiculectomy and then performing an anastomosis of the bladder neck and urethra. The feasibility of this procedure was more apparent after the experiences of Millin and Souttar. Souttar reported an instance in which he inadvertently accomplished the removal of the prostate with its capsule while in the process of a retropubic enucleation.

The retropubic approach permits the removal of metastatic glands along the great vessels of the pelvis. Leadbetter et al. have suggested this additional maneuver, in order to complete an operation for carcinoma of the bladder and the prostate. We have to date no generally accepted urological procedure for the radical treatment of carcinoma of the bladder or prostate which approaches the Wertheim operation for carcinoma of the cervix. Present indications are that the retropubic approach may be exploited to this end.

TECHNIQUE

The technique is illustrated in Figures 1, 2, 3, 4.

A midline retropubic or a transverse incision is made and carried through the abdominal muscles and trasversalis fascia. The bladder is emptied, per catheter, and the catheter permitted to remain in place. The retropubic pad of fat is bluntly dissected from the anterior surface

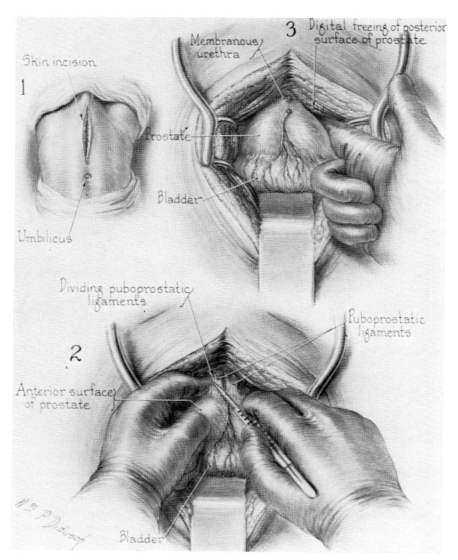

Fig. 1.

of prostatic capsule. The puboprostatic ligaments may or may not be seen at this point. With the index finger as a guide, these ligaments may be palpated and then cut, and beginning at the apex, the prostate is digitally freed posteriorly from its surrounding attachments. The urethra is then partially cut and this becomes evident when the catheter becomes visible. An O chromic suture is then placed in the anterior lip of the urethra to be used as a guide and also to later assist in the anastomosis of bladder neck and urethra. The transection of urethra is then accomplished expeditiously and sponges are placed in the prostatic bed and held in situ with a small

Deaver retractor to control bleeding from Santorini's plexus and other vessels. The seminal vesicles are individually freed and each vas ligated and transected and the bladder neck is then transected. Ureteral catheters may be placed in the ureters through the open bladder neck if the operator desires comfort while transecting the trigone. Hemostasis is carefully secured and the pelvis may be explored for metastatic glands at this point. The retropubic pack is now removed and any obvious bleeding vessels are secured and ligated or fulgurated. The O chromic suture placed in the urethra is now placed through the bladder neck, with additional

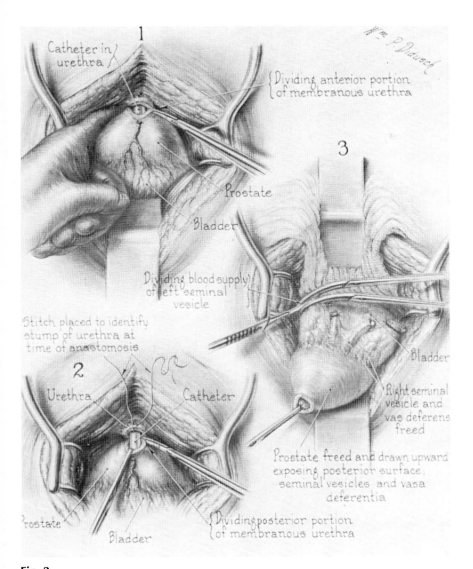

Fig. 2.

sutures to effect an anastomosis. Sutures may be placed in the anterior portion of bladder neck to effect a smaller bladder outlet and facilitate approximation to the membranous urethra. Approximately 4 interrupted sutures are placed loosely in the urethra and bladder outlet. A Foley catheter is placed through the penile urethra and guided into the cavity of the bladder and then the balloon is inflated. Traction on the catheter pulls the bladder toward the urethra and the chromic sutures are then tied. Gelfoam sponges are placed anterior and lateral to the anastomotic line to ensure hemostasis. A cigarette drain and sulfanilamide powder are placed in the pericystic area. The

wound is closed in the usual manner. The Foley catheter is removed in 10 days.

The indications which are currently used for the procedure are: (1) carcinoma of the prostate or suspicion of carcinoma; this is true except when the prostate is obviously "frozen" to the surrounding structures; (2) the "irritative prostate"; (3) it has been suggested that a total prostatectomy be done in patients who are suffering from obstructive prostates, who are in generally good physical condition, who are between the arbitrary ages of 50 to 70 and are sexually indifferent. This would preclude the recurrence of obstruction and decrease the

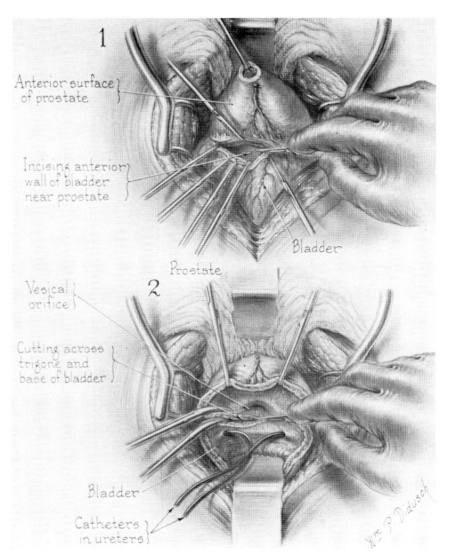

Fig. 3.

incidence of clinical carcinoma by removing the occult.[1] This seems to the writer to be justified in view of the fact that the morbidity of total perineal prostatectomies as reported by the Johns Hopkins group has compared very favorably with enucleative procedures. This has also thus far proved to be true in the small number treated by the retropubic route.

The comparison of this procedure with enucleative operations is very favorable. Hemorrhage has not oc-

curred postoperatively. In all but one instance bleeding from the area of Santorini's plexus has been insignificant. If the operation proceeds expeditiously up to and including the transection of the urethra, the operative bleeding is not more than that observed in enucleation procedures. All patients receive blood prophylactically when the operation starts. The incidence of infection is less, probably because the reservoirs of infection are removed, namely the prostate and seminal vesicles. Morbidity as observed in the few patients thus far treated has been minimal. Patients have been ambulatory beginning the second or third day. Catheters have been removed on the tenth day. Following this there has been

[1] The incidence of occult carcinoma has been given as 46 percent in 50 consecutive prostates examined completely by Baron and Angrist in men over 50 years of age.

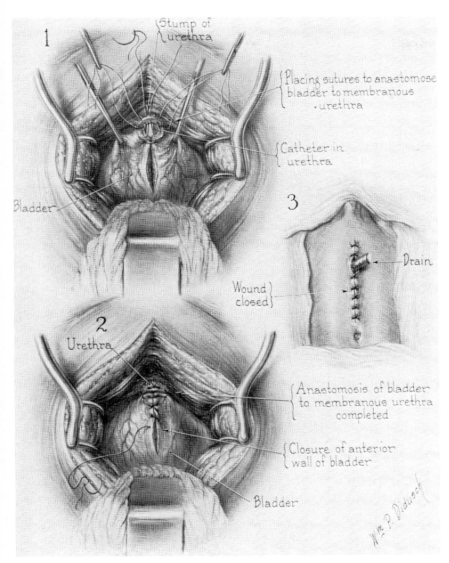

Fig. 4.

some stress incontinence in one-half of the patients which lasted from 1 to 2 weeks. There has been no suprapubic drainage after the tenth day. Wounds have healed readily. The operating time varied directly with the familiarity of the procedure from 2½ hours initially to 1½ hours for the last three. In one instance 1 hour sufficed. In the first 3 patients the seminal vesicles were not removed. The operator wished to become more familiar with the prostatectomy before proceeding to do the vesiculectomy. However, the writer believes careful attention should be given to the vesiculectomy and ligation of the vasa. In one instance, 3 weeks following his operation, a patient returned for his checkup examination and at this time he was found to have small bilateral scrotal abscesses at the distal end of the vasa. Following incision of the abscesses he had a small persistent drainage which resembled urine. The drainage eventually ceased after 10 days and has not recurred since. No cases of osteitis pubis have occurred to date.

CASE REPORTS

Mr. H., aged 70, had a diagnosis made of obstructive carcinoma of the prostate by digital examination, after he gave a history of prostatism and a residual urine of 4 ounces. Operation: Total prostatectomy using retropubic approach; refused orchiectomy. Placed on stilbestrol mg. 6 per diem. Foley catheter remained in place 10 days. Wound healed 10 days postoperatively. Discharged with good urinary control, 17 days postoperatively. No sutures were used in approximating bladder neck and urethra. The Foley bag was used to effect the approximation. Pathological report: Carcinoma of prostate, grade 3. Five months check-up revealed patient with minimal complaints. He had gained weight. Appetite was good. Urethra dilated to 26 F, without difficulty. Ten month check-up revealed sustained good urinary control without stress incontinence. Moderate bladder neck contracture.

Mr. H., aged 76, had a diagnosis made of obstructive carcinoma of the prostate by digital examination together with a history of prostatism and a residual urine of 6 ounces. Operation: Total retropubic prostatectomy. Foley catheter was removed on the tenth day. Wound closed on the eighth day. Patient had been ambulatory since the third postoperative day. Patient suddenly expired on the twelfth postoperative day, presumably from pulmonary infarct or coronary thrombosis. No autopsy could be obtained. pathological report: Marked fibrosis and hyperplasia of prostate; no evidence of malignancy.

Mr. C. S. was aged 71. The pathological diagnosis of carcinoma of prostate was made after the patient had been subjected to a transurethral prostatectomy for a clinically benign obstructive prostate. Operation: Total prostatectomy. Wound healed on the ninth day. Discharged with stress incontinence on fourteenth postoperative day. Three weeks check-up revealed good control, nocturia 9. Had small, bilateral scrotal abscesses at distal ends of vasa. Urine clear. Three month check-up revealed no complaints. Urethra dilated to 26 F sound without difficulty. Gained weight. Good appetite. This patient had stress incontinence for 2 weeks following discharge from hospital. At end of 6 months patient had sustained continence. Pathological report: Carcinoma of the prostate, grade 2–3.

Mr. R. was aged 69. The diagnosis of obstructive carcinoma of the prostate was made by digital examination, with history or prostatism and residual urine of 15 ounces. Prostate suggested malignant nodule. Total retropubic prostatovesiculectomy was done; refused orchiectomy. Postoperative course was excellent; no bleeding. Pathological report: Adenocarcinoma, grade 2. One month check-up revealed good sphincter control; nocturia 9. Patient is taking stilbestrol. There was sustained good sphincter control 8 months postoperatively.

Mr. B., aged 25, had a diagnosis made of irritative prostate. He had been subjected to a transurethral pros-

tatectomy 1 year previously, but his irritative symptoms persisted. A total retropubic prostatovesiculectomy was performed. In 10 days the Foley catheter was removed and the patient was discharged 2 days later with good sphincter control, feeling very happy with the results of the operation. Pathological report: Benign hyperplasia of prostate. Five months postoperatively the patient had sustained good urinary control.

Mr. R. was aged 60. Diagnosis:? Carcinoma of prostate by digital examination. Operation: Total retropubic prostatovesiculectomy. Foley catheter was removed in 10 days. Wound healed on the fourteenth postoperative day. The patient had moderate stress incontinence which was aggravated by chronic cough and bronchial asthma. He was discharged on his eighteenth postoperative day with an incontinence bag. Pathological report: Adenocarcinoma of prostate, grade 2. Seven month check-up revealed satisfactory urinary control. Patient "leaks a few drops on certain days", and only if he strains or coughs excessively.

Mr. C, was aged 58. Diagnosis: Chronic prostatovesiculitis; obstructive benign prostate, producing a persistent low grade pyuria. Pyeloureterograms normal. Operation: Total prostatovesiculectomy. Pathological report: Chronic infection of prostate and vesicles with many depositions of lymphocytes and polymorhonuclears; some hyperplasia of prostate. Monthly check-ups for 5 months revealed good urinary control.

Mr. J. B. was aged 73. Diagnosis: Carcinoma of prostate, by digital examination. Operation: Total prostatovesiculectomy; refused orchiectomy. During the operation brisk hemorrhage occurred while operator was in the process of freeing prostate from its surrounding fascia preparatory to transecting the urethra. Foley catheter was removed in 10 days. There was moderate stress incontinence. An anterior urethral stricture had to be dilated following operation. In 3 weeks patient had good urinary control and had no complaints. Suprapubic wound was completely healed 12 days postoperatively. Patient was discharged on his twenty-first postoperative day. Pathological report: Carcinoma of prostate, grade 3. Two month check-up revealed clear urine and good urinary control. At eighth month check-up patient had sustained good urinary control.

Mr. M. was aged 58. Diagnosis:? Cancer of prostate. The patient had had a bladder papillary carcinoma fulgurated 1 year previously. Operation: Total prostatectomy; cystectomy; bilateral ureteroenterostomy. On opening the bladder to place ureteral catheters, there were recurrences of papillomata found near the bladder neck on the anterior bladder wall, which appeared to be papillary carcinoma, and which were not evident on cystoscopy. At this time a change in plan seemed advisable; the operation was extended, and cystectomy and bilateral uretero-enterostomy were performed. Pathological report: Carcinoma of prostate and transitional cell carcinoma of bladder. The patient was discharged on the twenty-eighth postoperative day.

Mr. O. T. was aged 76. Diagnosis: Carcinoma of prostate, clinically. Operation: Total prostatovesiculectomy. Catheter removed in 12 days. Wound healed in 12 days. He was discharged on his fourteenth postoperative day in good condition, with good urinary control. Pathological report: Benign hyperplasia of prostate with many areas of chronic inflammation and fibrosis. A 6 month checkup revealed good urinary control.

Mr. J. A. was aged 67. Diagnosis: Carcinoma of prostate by digital examination. Operation: Total prostatovesiculectomy. Patient was sexually indifferent. Suprapubic wound healed in 10 days. Mild stress incontinence for 5 days after removal of Foley catheter. He was discharged on sixteenth postoperative day. Pathological report: Benign hyperplasia of prostate with areas of fibrosis and chronic inflammation. Four month checkup revealed good urinary control.

SUMMARY

In summary, there is evidence to support the contention that total prostatectomies may be done successfully using the retropubic approach. It is a desirable approach because it is more familiar to the average urological surgeon than the perineal route. It permits a relatively facile and more definitive method of treating carcinoma of the prostate. The morbidity compares favorably with other prostatic surgery. Although stress incontinence occurs in certain patients it has disappeared in all after a relatively short period. The suggestion is made that total prostatectomies be done in patients who are sexually indifferent and who are in the younger prostatic age group even though at the time the gland is apparently benign. There is some indication that a certain proportion of patients develop a moderate degree of bladder neck contracture, but thus far have responded without difficulty to the usual dilations. Whether this group will contain a greater number of contractures than enucleative procedures must be determined later. In the first case where definite bladder neck contracture occurred, no sutures had been used to approximate the urethra and bladder neck.

ADDENDUM

Since my initial experience with this approach in November of 1947, approximately 30 similar cases have been subjected to this operation. To date all patients are living. There has been 1 case of postoperative hemorrhage that was controlled satisfactorily without a secondary procedure. I believe one patient suffered from a mild osteitis pubis 4 months postoperatively. There were 4 instances of bladder neck contracture in which spasm seemed to play a role. The cases in which spasm predominated had been castrated and the question is posed whether this may not be a "withdrawal" symptom.

11 Ohio St., Bangor, Maine.

REFERENCES

BARON, E. AND ANGRIST, A.: Incidence of occult adenocarcinoma of prostate after 50 years of age. Arch Path 32:787–793, 1941

LEADBETTER, W. F.: Personal communication

SOUTTAR, H. S.: Complete removal of the prostate. Br Med J 1:917–918, 1947

VOSE, S. N.: Personal communication

Commentary:
Radical Retropubic Prostatectomy

Ralph J. Veenema and Michael Wechsler

At present there are two accepted surgical procedures for radical excision of the prostate. We believe that the retropubic approach is more applicable than the perineal for several reasons. Regional selective lymph node biopsy may be performed, and, if positive, the operation can be terminated. Direct superior extension can be more readily assessed, and the seminal vesicles and surrounding fascia are easily removed.

To proceed, place the patient in a modified Trendelenburg position with the sacrum elevated. Wrap the legs with Ace bandages to mid-thigh. Insert a no. 22 Foley catheter and attach it to gravity drainage to keep the bladder empty and to facilitate dissection and indentification of the urethra.

As shown in the article by Memmelar, a lower midline extraperitoneal incision is made. We do not perform a radical lymphadenectomy but selectively biopsy any suspicious nodes. At present, there is no evidence to indicate any increase in survival with lymphadenectomy. We have seen several patients referred to us with debilitating lymphedema of the scrotum after pelvic lymphadenectomy.

Pierce described removing the symphysis to gain adequate exposure.[1] We have not found it necessary, but it can easily be performed with a Gigli saw. Bone wax should be applied to the cut edges. It is also important to remain medial to the obturator fossa to avoid undue bleeding. Postoperatively, patients experience moderate pain but no instability after excision of the symphysis pubis.

Campbell advocated early ligation of the prostatic blood supply and removal of the prostate and seminal vesicles starting from the vesicoprostatic junction.[2] Theoretically, this may be a good cancer operation, and it is particularly useful when the apex of the gland cannot be easily separated from the anterior rectal wall.

Attention should be turned first to the puboprostatic ligaments. Reiner and Walsh recently described an anatomic approach to the management of the dorsal vein and Santorini's plexus.[3] The dorsal vein leaves the penis under Buck's fascia and penetrates the urogenital diaphragm. At this point, it divides into three branches. The superficial branch goes between the leaves of the puboprostatic ligaments. This can be easily ligated first. The puboprostatic ligaments can be incised sharply without fear of bleeding. They are completely avascular structures. The incision of the endopelvic fascia should be performed laterally to the apex of the prostate to void the two lateral branches of the superficial vein. At this point, at the apex of the prostate, tissue is approximately 1 cm thick. This contains the dorsal vein and can be ligated quite easily by direct vision.

The urethra is easily identified after the puboprostatic ligaments have been divided. We do not leave any apical prostatic tissue. As the urethra is severed, place four sutures of 0 chromic in the urethral stump. Use color-coded clamps to identify right, left, anterior, and posterior sutures. Use a pack to compress the venous bleeding and leave the Foley catheter in the prostate and bladder. This is used for traction. Dissection continues outside Denonvilliers' fascia. Both vasa are ligated with 0 chromic sutures.

As seen in Figure 3 in Memmelaar's article, the bladder neck is preserved to maintain continence. After the anterior vesical neck is incised, pass ureteral catheters bilaterally. Incise the posterior bladder neck and grasp it with no. 2 Allis clamps. Develop the plane between the bladder and seminal vesicles. If a great deal of bleeding occurs, it is important to check the landmarks to ensure that dissection is not occurring between the plane of the bladder musculature. At the tips of both seminal vesicles is a vascular pedicle that must be ligated. After removing the specimen, carefully inspect for bleeding, especially laterally to the rectum.

At this point, attend to closure of the bladder and the vesicourethral anastomosis. Pass a no. 20 or 22 Foley catheter

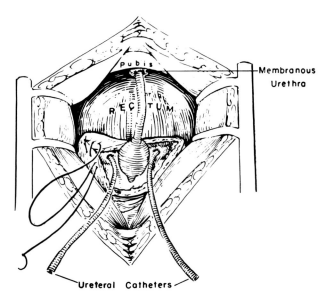

Fig. 5. The bladder is closed in the form of an inverted Y, and the Foley is brought out at the upper end.

with a 5-ml balloon into the urethra. In Figure 4 (in Memmelar's article) the anastomosis is completed first and then the anterior wall of the bladder is closed. We prefer to close the bladder before the anastomosis. The bladder closure is also performed in a horizontal fashion, starting lateral to each orifice. The bladder is closed in an inverted Y, whereby the orifices are recessed back from the neourethra (see Fig. 5). The tip of the Foley and Foley bag is then placed in the bladder, and the previously placed four sutures are passed through the bladder, with the knots being tied on the outside. After the anastomosis is complete, the Foley balloon is then inflated. In this way, the balloon is not inadvertently punctured.

Occasionally a suprapubic tube may be used. If there is excess bleeding or the continuity of the anastomosis is in question, temporary suprapubic drainage is an excellent safety valve. Penrose drains are placed on either side of the bladder and brought out through a separate stab wound. The Foley catheter is left in place for 10 days and then removed.

Radical retropubic prostatectomy has been our treatment of choice for cancer of the prostate since 1951. We have peformed over 200 radical operations since that time. In reviewing our 20-year experience, the overall crude survival was 84% at 5 yr, 52% at 10 yr, and 45% at 15 yr.[4] Upon reviewing the deaths of 40 of 170 patients, 9 of these died of disseminated prostate cancer; the others died of unrelated causes. These radical operations were performed for stages A and B, and the diagnosis was always confirmed histologically. Whenever a decision is made not to treat a patient with prostate cancer after simple prostatectomy, we usually advise follow-up cystoscopy and endoscopic biopsies of the prostatic urethra in 4 mo.

Our complications following radical retropubic prostatectomy are listed below:

Complication	No. of Patients	% of Patients
Postoperative death	4	2.5
Pulmonary emboli	6	3.7
Stricture	29	17
Incontinence	20	12.5
Rectal injury	13	7
Fecal fistula	3	2.5
Osteitis pubis	1	0.6

Stricture at the anastomotic site can be troublesome. At 6 wk we rouinely pass a small rubber catheter. With the advent of the optical urethrotome these early strictures can be incised and treated readily. The incontinence can be kept to a minimum by avoidance of the Vest technique and accurate placement of the sutures. However, there will of necessity be a small number of incontinent patients. Our management of rectal injury has been previously reported.[5] However, we prefer that all our patients undergo at least a mechanical bowel preparation before surgery. If a rectal injury is performed early in the procedue, the safest choice is to repair the injury and terminate the procedure. Occasionally, depending on the surgeon's judgment, the operation may proceed.

Radical retropubic prostatectomy permits wide exposure of the operative area and the ability to assess both nodal and extraprostatic extension before extensive dissection and transection of the urethra. As staging becomes more accurate, the cure rates may become higher. An excellent example is the newer, more specific immunoassay of acid phosphatase and its application to bone acid phosphatase.

In the past our failures were probably the result of understaging the disease.

We agree that prostate cancer is slow growing, but it seems unwise to practice therapeutic nihilism or rely on hormonal control if the patient has a life expectancy of 10 yr. In general, if a patient lives long enough, he will probably die of his disease if the physician relies only on hormonal control.

REFERENCES

1. Pierce JM: Exposure of the membranous and prostatic urethra by total pubectomy. J Urol 85:256, 1962

2. Campbell EW: Total prostatectomy with preliminary ligation of the vascular pedicles. J Urol 81:464, 1959

3. Reiner WG, Walsh PC: An anatomical approach to the surgical management of the dorsal vein and santorimi's plexus during radical retropubic surgery. J Urol 121:198, 1978

4. Veenema RJ: Radical retropubic prostatectomy for cancer: A 20 years experience. J Urol 117:330, 1977

5. Smith AM, Veenema RJ: Management of rectal injury and recto-urethral fistulas following radical retropubic prostatectomy. J Urol 108:778, 1972

ANNOTATED BIBLIOGRAPHY

Hodges CV: Radical prostatectomy for carcinoma: 30-year experience and 15-year survivals. J Urol 122:180, 1979

This article presents a series of cases performed at university, Veterans, and community hospitals. Over 90% of the operations were performed perineally; 196 patients were the basis for this report. The 15-yr survival rate at the university hospital was 15%, compared to 61% at the community hospital. No high-grade lesion allowed the patient to survive 15 yr. The 15-year survival rate compares favorably to those already published. A 15-yr rate survival for other modalities, such as radiation, chemotherapy, and immunotherapy, is necessary before any meaningful comparison can be made.

Freiha FS: Pelvic lymphadenectomy for staging prostatic carcinoma: Is it always necessary? J Urol 122:176, 1979

One-hundred patients were staged surgically to evaluate the extent of lymph node involvement. The authors attempt to correlate the incidence of lymph node metastasis with the level of acid phosphatase and stage and grade of the primary tumor. Their data suggest that nodal disease could produce an elevated acid phosphatase. The authors have begun to establish a rational means by which certain patients can avoid the financial and surgical risks of a lymphadenectomy.

Fowler JE, Barzell W, Hilaris B, et al. Complications of [125]iodine implantation and pelvic lymphadenectomy in the treatment of prostatic cancer. J Urol 121:447, 1979

The operative, postoperative, and late complications experienced by 300 consecutive patients are analyzed; 6% had operative complications, 23% had postoperative complications, and 28% had late complications. The authors state that the therapeutic value of pelvic lymphadenectomy is of undetermined value but no doubt has prognostic significance. The morbidity is roughly compared to radical surgery and external radiation. However, it remains to be seen whether this procedure will cure prostate cancer.

Lytton B, Collins JT, Weiss RD, Schiff D Jr, McGuire EJ, Lilvolsi V: Results of biopsy after early stage prostate cancer treatment by implantation of ^{125}I seeds. J Urol 121:306, 1979

Seventy-seven patients were treated with implantation and pelvic lymphadenectomy. The morbidity compares favorably with other series. However, 22 patients had needle biopsy after treatment, and persistent tumor was seen in 11. Considering that a needle biopsy is only 70% accurate, the figure could be much higher. The histologic appearance is distinctly different, but biologic activity could not be assessed. The authors conclude that they have controlled disease for 5 yr despite what appears to be a high incidence of persistent tumor in biopsies 1 to 3 yr after treatment.

Correa RJ Jr, Gibbons RP, Cummings KB, Mason JT: Total prostatectomy for stage B carcinoma of the prostate. J Urol 117:328, 1977

Sixty-seven cases of radical prostatectomy were evaluated. Most of these procedures were performed through the perineal route. No deaths were recorded. The complications were that of impotence and incontinence. The findings confirm the poorer prognosis for higher grade and larger lesions. This has led the authors to recommend postoperative radiation for pathologic C lesions. The survival rates of 92% at 5 yr, 79% at 10 yr, and 62% at 15 yr suggest that this is the preferred mode of therapy.

86

THE PRESENT STATUS OF RADICAL PROSTATECTOMY FOR STAGES A AND B PROSTATIC CANCER

Hugh J. Jewett, M.D.

Professor Emeritus of Urology, Johns Hopkins University School of Medicine, and Urologist, Johns Hopkins Hospital, Baltimore

Urologic Clinics of North America—Vol. 2, No. 1, February 1975
Symposium on The Prostate

It should be obvious to everybody that one cannot determine the value of a single method of treatment of this disease unless one knows what one has been treating. Furthermore one should know what would probably have happened without treatment, or with some other single treatment, under the same circumstances. To establish a firm pathologic base as well as control of other variables which may exert an influence over tumor behavior, statisticians have laid down rules—most of which seem complicated to the clinician. The language of these technical men, though unintelligible at times to most practicing urologists, nevertheless emphasizes principles that are scientifically sound.

Studies regarding therapy should be controlled if the data are to be conclusive, and the Veterans' Administration Cooperative Urological Research Group is in the process of doing this. In practice, however, randomizing is difficult because of the relatively small number of cases treated in any single institution, and because the conscientious urologist who believes in the superiority of one method is not likely to deny his patient what he thinks is best. Since most clinical urologists lack the mathematic formulas and techniques of the trained biostatisticians, the author feels constrained to present the published facts as he sees them. The pathologic base is perhaps not always solid but is nearly so, variables are controlled as well as clinically possible, and comparisons with results of other treatments are made on these bases.

ORIGIN OF PROSTATIC CANCER

There now is ample evidence to show that prostatic cancer usually arises peripherally and is often multifocal. Of 96 localized tumors studied by Kahler,[36] 8 were multicentric and he believed metastases went first to the nodes, then lung followed by peritoneum, and lastly bones. Kahler's prostatic findings have been confirmed by others, and Byar and associates[8] reported 177 of 208 cases to be multifocal. They also stated that a palpable prostatic nodule does not indicate the amount of tumor present and should not suggest that there are not other foci of cancer in that prostate. McNeal,[40] however, raises the point that apparent multicentricity may actually represent intragland metastases or extensions from a single lesion.

NATURAL HISTORY

Franks[24] discussed at length latency versus active prostatic cancer, without specific correlation with stage or grade. He stated that latency is not a peculiar characteristic of prostatic cancer because it has been noted in other organs, that the latent tumor is morphologically indistinguishable from active cancer, that it does not metastasize, but that it may infiltrate blood vessels and lymphatics locally. He also stated that latent tumors may be large or small, well differentiated or anaplastic—a declaration that should be confirmed by further follow-up in living patients.

To the clinician it seems that a cancer which infiltrates blood vessels, lymphatics, and laminated capsule indicates one with a greater degree of biologic activity than evidenced by one which does none of these things. In the former instance one might consider the tumor cells poised, awaiting a triggering mechanism, a lowering of host resistance, or merely the passage of sufficient time, for wide dissemination. Franks[24] summed up his thesis by suggesting that the only method of determining latency of a tumor is the observation of its behavior in the host. Although this statement may be true at the present time, the average clinician may not wish to procrastinate. The risk to a patient of an incorrect assumption of latency with consequent neglect may be disastrous.

Further pursuit of this matter of latency versus aggressiveness led first to greater emphasis on the histologic grade of the tumor as introduced by Broders in 1922,[6] and later modified somewhat. Objections raised by some pathologists on the grounds that different parts of the same tumor showed different grades of malignancy have been largely overcome by presenting them with larger or multiple sections. There is no question that patients with high grade tumors have a poorer outlook. But such grading did not provide the sole pathologic base upon which longevity could be predicted or method of treatment selected. Another factor equally important was the extent of the tumor, or its stage.

In 1969 McNeal[40] made a detailed autopsy study of 45 cases of prostatic cancer. Evidence found by him led him to conclude that there are not two types of cancer with different biologic potential, but rather a single species having a slow growth rate with a logarithmic curve. He believed that a gradual increase in malignant potential was clearly related to tumor size. A gross

confirmation of this hypothesis was indicated by us in 1970. In 99 cases of advanced disease collected in 1965 by Schirmer and associates[46] 70 percent of the patients had a high grade cancer; in 92 smaller cases radically excised only 4 percent were high grade. McNeal stated that the capacity for dissemination is probably limited to tumors over 1 cubic centimeter in volume. In this connection it should be recalled that in a random series of 100 cases radically excised at the Johns Hopkins Hospital for palpable nodules 1 cm to 1.5 cm in diameter, there was widespread microscopic invasion of the prostate in 77 percent, and seminal vesicle involvement in 26 percent.

PATHWAYS OF SPREAD

Cancer of the prostate may not stay long confined to the gland. The less active variety usually follows the path of least resistance and moves toward the urethra or the center of the gland, whereas the more active variety invades the laminated capsule and the perivesicular tissue from which it metastasizes rapidly. But there is histologic evidence that it can metastasize while still microscopically confined to the prostate.

Microscopic sections through the prostate show an abundance of blood capillaries. In recent years there has been doubt concerning the presence of lymphatics within its substance. Connolly and associates[13] showed what appeared to be intraprostatic lymphatics containing particulate matter after injecting the prostates of living dogs with India ink and with imferon through the opened bladder. Recently Peters[43] injected 0.5 cc of India ink into the prostate of a man 48 hours before death from a terminal illness unrelated to the prostate. At autopsy the gland was carefully sectioned. Figure 1A shows an accumulation of India ink particles in endothelial-lined spaces grouped around an artery. None of these spaces contained blood cells. Figure 1B represents a higher power view of a space full of India ink near an acinus, lined by endothelium but again containing no blood cells. This study demonstrated clearly the presence of intraprostatic lymphatics in man. Peters[43] reports that there was no tracking of the ink outward along the puncture path, no accumulation outside the capsule, and that the obturator nodes and nodes along the internal iliac vessels were clogged with the particles.

These careful histologic studies indicate that lymphatics coexist with blood capillaries within the prostate, but appear to be less numerous. The opportunity for a cancer to permeate a blood capillary therefore is greater, but this does not necessarily mean that metastases are more often blood borne, although they may be. Factors incompletely understood may play a role. The greater velocity of the plasma stream in the blood capillary may

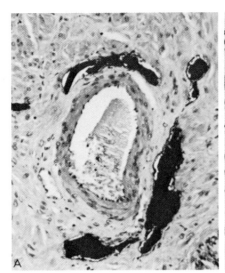
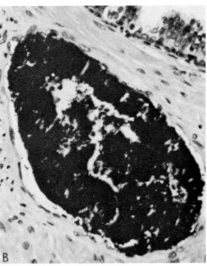

Fig. 1. (A) Lymphatics containing Inda ink but no blood cells, clustered about an artery inside the prostate (×240). (B) Lymphatic containing India ink but no blood cells, lined by conspicuous endothelium, near an acinus within the prostate (×370). (Courtesy of Dr. Paul C. Peters.)

interfere with the clumping and cohesion of cancer cells which seem necessary for the establishment of metastatic tumor deposits. On the other hand, Catalona[11] has stated that host response is slower in the blood, and immune surveillance in the regional nodes occurs early.

At any rate, pathways for cancer dissemination to bones and regional nodes exist within the substance of the prostate, and the greater the volume of the tumor the greater is the opportunity for vascular and lymphatic permeation. According to Franks[24] even latent tumors will permeate these endothelial walls.

STAGING OF PROSTATIC CANCER

For a long time the need for staging prostatic cancer seemed apparent and in 1949 this was brought vividly to our attention after a first report that radical perineal prostatectomy achieved a much better five-year success rate when the tumors in 78 cases had seemed on rectal palpation to be confined to the prostate gland.[31] The survivorship was poor in 54 cases when there had been evidence of local extraprostatic extension, and this indicated the futility in subjecting such patients to the operation. A later study of 127 cases[32] showed that 12.5 percent of 48 patients with locally extensive cancer lived 10 years after radical perineal prostatectomy without cure, and 37 percent of 79 patients with clinically confined cancer lived 10 years after the operation without evidence of disease. Microscopic examination of these 79 surgical specimens, however, showed that only half those believed to have been clinically localized were actually localized, and 49 percent of those patients with localized cancer lived 10 years or longer without recurrence.

Whitmore introduced his system of staging in 1956[49] separating all cases into four categories: A, B, C and D. Stage A represents a tumor not clinically manifest but found microscopically within the surgically removed obstructing tissue; stage B, clinically manifest without metastasis but palpably localized to the prostate, stage C, locally extensive beyond the prostate but without metastasis; and stage D, metastases.

In 1959 the American Joint Committee for Cancer Staging and End Results Reporting appointed a task force to stage urogenital tumors. This smaller committee recommended a system much like that of Whitmore but advised the use of the Roman numerals I, II, III and IV instead of letters, to make it consistent with TNM (tumor, nodes, metastases) classifications of other tumors. That is why one sees in the literature numerals in one report and letters in another—all signifying the same four recognized stages.

Stage A Cancer. It now seems evident that clinical stage A (or I) cancer is self-contradictory because it is not possible to make the diagnosis of localized prostatic cancer that is not clinically manifest, without pathologic help. But we can proceed to discuss stage A if we bear that point in mind.

In 1960 Bauer, McGavran and Carlin[4] published their findings in 55 consecutive stage A cases found on microscopic study of the enucleated obstructing tissue. Of these, 23 patients had small tumors and 14 of them had a favorable outcome; 29 had large tumors and only 9 of these did well over the long term. Therefore the volume or size of the tumor mass within stage A has a bearing on survivorship. Of 52 graded cancers 28 were well differentiated, and the 10-year survival rate was 47 percent. Of 24 patients with moderately to poorly differentiated cancers, the 10-year survivorship was 14 percent. Grade, therefore, is another factor in prognosis even in stage A. There was no evidence that antiandrogenic teatment influenced survival since half of their patients with a favorable outcome had neither orchiectomy nor estrogens.

Hanash and associates[27] in 1972 analyzed by stage and grade a large group of patients with prostatic cancer treated only by transurethral resection. There were 50 patients with stage A tumors, and 39 of these (78 percent) had well differentiated cancers. The 15-year survivorship of these 39 patients equaled that of the general population of the same age when no treatment was provided other than transurethral resection for relief of obstruction (Fig. 2). The remaining 22 percent with high grade tumors did as well as the expected survivorship for 10 years but none lived 15 years. They did not state how many of these stage A tumors were focal and how many diffuse.

Byar and the Veteran's Administration Cooperative Urological Research Group (VACURG)[7] in 1972 reported a study of 148 patients in Stage A (I) with focal cancer treated conservatively or not at all. Over a rather short period of follow-up only 6.8 percent of the cases showed progression of the disease, probably because of less well differentiated cancer. From the literature since 1951 they collected 262 cases of stage A (I) cancer in which death from cancer occurred in only 5 (1.9 percent). Their exhaustive randomized comparisons led to the conclusion that prostatic cancer in this stage is peculiarly nonaggressive and ordinarily does not require heroic treatment.

In 1974 Correa and associates[15] made a detailed study of 47 cases in stage A. In 39 the tumor was focal (present in not more than ''several'' microscopic foci) and all were well differentiated, in 8 it was diffuse, and in 5 of these the patient had died either of cancer or with cancer present. Three of these diffuse cancers were poorly differentiated. Therefore in 62 percent of the 8 patients with diffuse stage A cancer the tumor had progressed without response to estrogen, whereas in only 3 patients of 39 in the focal category had it progressed.

The published accounts of longevity among patients with stage A cancer, untreated except for removal of obstruction, indicate clearly that the great majority of these tumors are either latent in the true sense or have a low biologic potential. Lacking aggressiveness they may grow away from the capsule and seminal vesicles along the lines of least resistance toward the urethra. The two exceptions which are relatively infrequent among all the stage A tumors encountered are high grade and diffuseness (large size or volume of the tumor mass) and these usually have not responded to endocrine treatment. Therefore it seems appropriate to divide these cancers

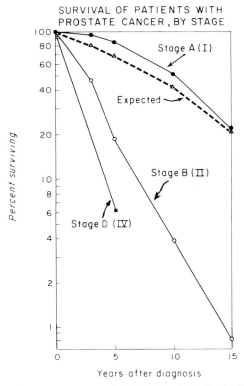

Fig. 2. (From Hanash, KA, Utz, DC, Cook, EN, et al: Carcinoma of the prostate: A 15-year follow-up. J Urol., 107:450, 1972. With permission.)

into stages A$_1$ (focal) and A$_2$ (diffuse), and record the grade. Stage A$_2$ and high grade tumors progress and require additional treatment.

Radical excision has been advocated for these diffuse and high grade tumors in stage A, but the present author does not recommend it, for the following reasons: (1) Under the best of circumstances radical perineal prostatectomy for a localized nodule of high grade cancer in an intact prostate has not provided a cancer-free 15-year survivorship in our series of cases. (2) A secondary radical prostatectomy is difficult and can rarely if ever be made classical. The idea of trying to do so is not appealing. (3) No one has reported longterm survivals after secondary radical excision in such cases. (4) Megavoltage radiation may have a special usefulness in cases of this sort where high grade tumors are likely to show a more rapid response, and a gross shrinkage of the local growth has been almost universally noted.

Stage B Cancer. Belief in the superiority of radical prostatectomy over other single methods of treatment of this type of disease rests on two propositions: (1) If all the cancer cells resided in the tissue to be excised, and excision is properly accomplished, cure is assured. (2) In such a case there is no alternative treatment of equal efficacy. There is sufficient evidence, some factual and some theoretical on both sides of the double proposition, to generate honest and sincere differences of opinion, but one must constantly be on guard against bias.

Radical excision by the perineal route began in 1866 by Küchler[38] in Germany. The case was far advanced and the procedure did not gain popularity. In 1904 H. H. Young[51] modified and improved the operation and made it more anatomic and practicable. His first radical perineal prostatectomy was done at Johns Hopkins in March of that year.

From 1904 to June 1974, 503 radical perineal prostatectomies have been done at the Johns Hopkins Hospital, and much has been learned about the advantages and limitations of the operation. Aside from technical improvements, probably the most important fact that eventually emerged was that the operation was not a cure-all, but its success in eradicating the cancer obviously depended on the confinement of the tumor to the prostate, and therefore on the clinical steps in the diagnosis that are necessary to make one fairly certain of this. These steps entail a thorough search for local or distant spread so that the surgeon can be satisfied that he is dealing with a tumor in stage B. The identification of a stage B tumor and its clinical significance evolved slowly over a period of about 50 years.

Until January 1, 1951, 182 traced patients with clinical stage B cancer without prostatic obstruction underwent radical perineal prostatectomy at the Johns Hopkins Hospital. After 15 years of careful follow-up of this closed series there was no evidence of recurrence among the 42 who were living and well (23 percent). Of these 182 patients, one lobe or more was palpably involved in 79, and among these there was no known recurrence in 14 (18 percent). Of the same group of 182 cases 103 apparently had a discrete nodule of cancer involving less than one lobe. Of these, whose average age was 61.9 years, 28 patients (27 percent) lived 15 to 32 years without recurrence and without adjunctive treatment (Fig. 3). In stage B the difference between the 15-year survivorship without cancer of 18 percent with palpable involvement of one lobe or more, and 27 percent with involvement of less than one lobe, indicates the

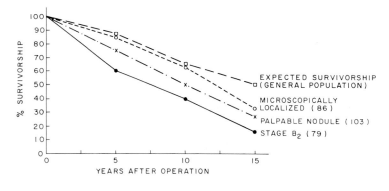

Fig. 3. Results of radical perineal prostatectomy in stage B according to subgroups.

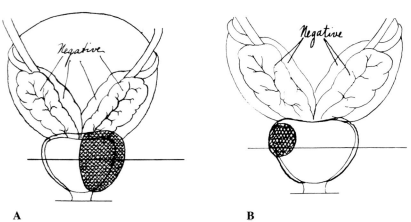

A   **B**

Fig. 4. (*A*) Stage B$_2$ cancer, 1 lobe or more, 50 percent or more microscopically stage C. (*B*) Stage B$_1$ cancer, less than 1 lobe, includes the palpable nodule, less than 10 percent microscopically stage C.

desirability of separating stage B into stages B_2 (one lobe or more) (Fig. 4A) and B_1 (less than one lobe). Stage B_1 naturally includes the discrete palpable nodule (less than 1.5 cm in diameter) (Fig. 4B).

Microscopic examination of the specimen is more accurate than rectal palpation. The tumor actually was limited to the prostate in 86 cases of the discrete palpable nodule and 28 (33 percent) of these patients were living without cancer 15 to 32 years after operation (Table 1). Clinical stage B, therefore, taken as a whole includes many cases that microscopically have penetrated the laminated capsule or invaded the perivesicular tissue (stage C), and often reached the retroperitoneal nodes (stage D). In 1962 Arduino and Glucksman[1] reported that of 71 patients with "early" prostatic cancer the seminal vesicles had been invaded in 17, and of these 17 patients the nodes were involved in 84.2 percent. This report emphasized the significance of seminal vesicle involvement, and in 1968 we reported that none of our patients with seminal vesicle involvement lived 15 years cancer-free after radical perineal prostatectomy. Figure 4A represents a stage B_2 tumor which grossly occupies one lobe or more, with 50 percent microscopically in stage C. Castellino and associates[10] have shown that in fully developed clinical stage B cases positive lymphangiograms were obtained in 4 of 9, and according to McCullough and associates[39] pedal lymphangiograms do not reveal the earliest involved pelvic nodes such as the obturator nodes and those along the internal iliac vessels.

On the other hand, stage B_1, involving less than 1 lobe, and of course including the discrete locally palpable nodule (Fig. 4B) is much less likely to have metastasized. When the palpable nodule is appreciably less than 1 cm in diameter the operation usually is deferred and the patient is re-examined at regular intervals unless the needle biopsy reveals undisputed cancer.

Although the palpable size of the nodule is not an infallible guide to the amount of tumor present in the gland,[8,33] the smaller the nodule the less likely the tumor has extended microscopically beyond the prostate. Of 79 of our patients with clinical stage B_2 cancer only 40 (approximately 50 percent) were microscopically limited to the prostate, whereas of 103 patients with nodule cancer ranging in gross size from 1 cm to somewhat less than one lobe (stage B_1) 86 (84 percent) were microscopically localized. Berlin and associates,[5] and Culp[16] have reported a slightly better 15-year survivorship after radical perineal prostatectomy (Table 2), but Berlin does not say how many patients were cancer-free.

An important key to surgical success therefore appears to be the microscopic confinement of the tumor to the prostate. If it is confined and the prostate is properly removed cure is assured. Every effort naturally should be made to exclude distant spread and local extension. To do this the following basic conditions must be fulfilled: (1) no indication of extensive malignancy by the history of weight loss, pain or frequency not otherwise explained; (2) no evidence of metastases by x-rays of chest, spine, pelvis and upper femurs, by bone scan, by the level of the prostatic fraction of the serum

TABLE 1. Results After Radical Perineal Prostatectomy in 86 Patients with Histologic Stage B Cancer, Johns Hopkins Hospital

Grade	Well 15 to 32 Years Postoperatively	Living 15 Years With Cancer	Died With Cancer Within 15 Years	Died Without Cancer; Years of Survival
1	7	3	2	26 (1 to 9 years)
2	14	4	8	2 (10 years)
3	0	0	3	2 (11 years)
Not graded	7	0	1	1 (12 years)
				3 (13 years)
				3 (14 years)
Total	28 (33%)	7 (8%)	14 (16%)	37 (43%)

TABLE 2. Cancer-Free Survivorship 15 Years or Longer after Radical Perineal Prostatectomy

Author	Clinical Stage	Pathologic State	Number of Patients	Number Surviving	Percent Surviving
Berlin (1968)		B	116		38.6*
Jewett (1968)		B	103	28	27
	B_1		86	28	33
Culp (1973)					
(1974)	B_1		74	25	34

* No statement regarding proportion of cancer-free survivals.

acid phosphatase, and possibly the bone marrow acid phosphatase, or by enlarged positive inguinal or cervical nodes; (3) the presence of a discrete nodule of proved and differentiated cancer (acini present) palpably confined to the prostate, occupying less than one lobe, and surrounded by prostatic tissue of normal consistency; (4) a movable prostate of fairly normal size with a smooth capsule without fixation, or edema of the anterior rectal wall; and (5) soft seminal vesicles without induration around, between, or lateral to them.

An indication of how accurate a skillful rectal palpation of the prostate can be made is shown by a retrospective examination of the rectal findings in 17 of 103 patients with a palpable, discrete nodule previously discussed who, on microscopic examination, had involvement of a seminal vesicle.[35] On first rectal examination these patients were all thought to have stage B cancer with no involvement of the vesicles, but a careful review of the rectal findings showed that the surgeon's enthusiasm had overcome caution and that in 11 of these 17 patients extension to the vesicles was clinically evident (stage C). In these 11 instances there was induration of the extreme base of the prostate contiguous with a vesicle in 3 patients; induration of the vesicles themselves in 5 patients; and induration along the lateral edge of a vesicle with fixation in 3 patients. If these 11 patients had been removed from the total group fo 103 there would be 92 patients fulfilling all criteria for grossly localized (clinical stage B_1) cancer, and of these 92 patients 28 (30 percent) were surgical successes without reappearance of tumor from 15 to 32 years after radical perineal prostatectomy.

Therefore a skillful digital assessment of a nodule by an expert should cause underestimation of its extent in no more than 6.5 percent of the cases. If these details are strictly and expertly observed the chance of microscopic spread beyond the prostate will be less than 1 in 10 unless the cancer is undifferentiated. In our series of cancerous nodules only 4 percent were anaplastic.

Among the 86 patients with microscopic confinement of the cancer to the prostate gland there were 21 failures after radical perineal prostatectomy.[35] Seven of these patients had metastases discovered up to 11 years after operation which probably had been present and unrecognized at the time of operation. This series was closed in January 1951 and certain valuable tests now available had not been developed then. Of the 21 failures 14 patients had local recurrence of tumor at the site of vesicourethral anastomosis from 6 months to 11 years after operation, which possibly could have been avoided by giving the prostate gland a wider berth during the perineal dissection. There was only 1 postoperative death among the 103 radical perineal prostatectomies in this series and this occurred in 1916 as a result of sepsis long before antibacterial therapy was available.

But even a suitable case with cancer confined to the prostate may not be cured by radical perineal prostatectomy if the dissection is carried too close to the prostate. We pointed out[35] that the so-called posterior layer of Denonvilliers' fascia did not exist, at least as a membrane of any surgical importance and that a filmy membrane covering the back of the seminal vesicles and attaching to the laminated capsule of the prostate might represent the true Denonvilliers' fascia (Fig. 5). If the surgical exposure of the back of the prostate results in stripping off this delicate membrane or some of the capsule itself, tumor cells within the layers of the capsule will be left behind. Figure 6 shows even more clearly that Denonvilliers' fascia, apparently of peritoneal origin, is a single-layered membrane adherent to the prostate and should be left there. Figure 7, from a fixed autopsy specimen, shows closeness of rectum, slightly caudad to Figure 6.

It seems quite possible, therefore, by ensuring confinement of the tumor to the prostate, and by giving the latter a wider berth in the dissection, the 15-year survival rate will rise from 33 percent. It probably will never or rarely exceed 50 percent, because in the general population only 50 percent of men 62 years old have a life expectancy of 15 years.

RADICAL RETROPUBIC PROSTATECTOMY

Because of unfamiliarity with the male perineum and increasing experience with pelvic surgery, many urologists (Millin, Memmelaar, Hand and Sullivan, Lattimer and associates, Chute, Flocks, Kopecky and associates, Salvatierra and associates, and Hudson and Howland, and others) have turned to the retropubic method for radical removal of prostatic cancer, and many of them have become highly skilled with this technique. Their position is bolstered by the fact that involved lymph nodes can be recognized, and either removed, or the operation terminated, but in stage B cases Flocks[20] has reported that the nodes are involved in only about 7 percent. He further believes [19] the incidence is less in nodule cases. It is possible that larger primary cancers can be ablated by this method but there are no 15-year figures to prove it. The belief that removal of involved nodes is beneficial also awaits confirmation by the passage of time. However there is no apparent reason to believe that the retropubic operation is less effective than the perineal. It may be somewhat longer and perhaps bloodier with a longer convalescence, but in the long run may be better. However there are no longterm figures now to show that it is.

Both types of operation cause impotence, which follows the perineal operation in 85 to 90 percent of the cases. Some authors, each with a very small series, claim avoidance of incontinence with the retropubic

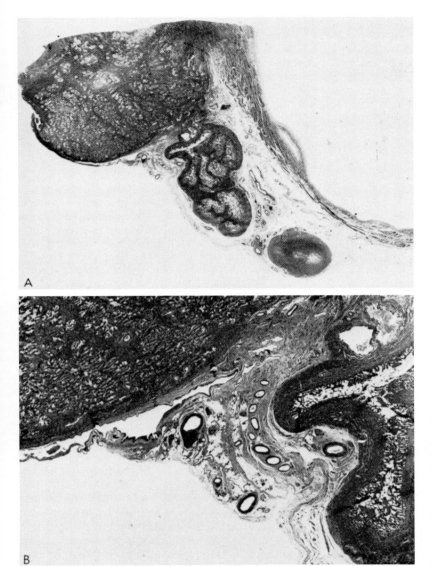

Fig. 5. (*A*) Photomicrograph of prostate, vesicle and bladder wall. Note loose areolar tissue around vesicle extending downward to lie against prostatic capsule. Rectum has been removed. H & E, reduced from ×2.5. (*B*) Higher power view of part *A*. Note areolar tissue behind seminal vesicle containing vessels. Prostate to left, vesicle to right. H & E, reduced from ×12. (From Jewett, HJ, Eggleston, JC, and Yawn, DH: Radical prostatectomy in the management of carcinoma of the prostate: Probably causes of some therapeutic failures. J Urol, 107:1034, 1972. With Permission.)

procedure, and a few recommend leaving some prostatic apical tissue to prevent it and to make the closure easier. Byar and Mostofi[8] deplore this because they found cancer at the prostatic apex in about 75 percent of 208 total prostates removed for early carcinoma. The easier, more visible, and accurate water-tight closure made possible perineally has provided perfect and prompt control in 112 of 116 personal cases, and minimal stress incontinence in 4, insufficient to require a protective device or pad.

Complications. Of the 116 radical perineal operations performed by the author, there have been no significant complications other than rectal injury in five instances.

All but one were closed effectively and completely at the time of operation and remained healed. The fifth injury broke down after closure, necessitating a colostomy. These injuries occurred during a surgical dissection now abandoned, which was designed to encompass the prostate and its coverings very widely. Similar injuries have followed radical retropubic prostatectomy. There have been no deaths in this personal series.

In the beginning of the discussion of stage B cancer it was stated that the superiority of excision over other single methods of treatment depended on two propositions. The first was complete localization of the cells to the prostate so that the entire cancer could be excised. It now seems evident that in a small, carefully selected

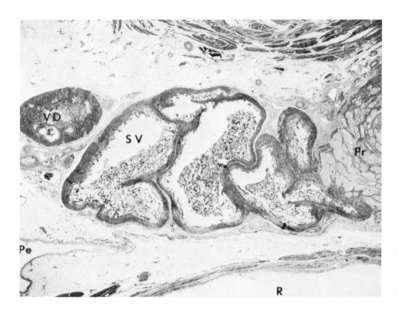

Fig. 6. Section from a fixed autopsy case, showing filmy connective tissue extending from peritoneum in rectovesical pouch to cover the back of the vesicles and to fuse with the prostatic capsule. No comparable fascia on rectum (×4).

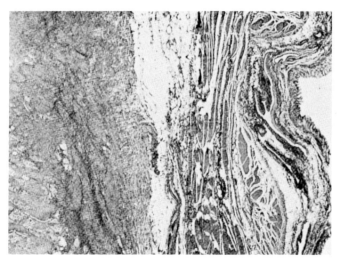

Fig. 7. Photomicrograph of section through anterior rectal wall and prostate caudad to Fig. 6 showing closest approximation of rectum to prostate. No fascia on rectum. H & E, reduced from ×21. (From same source as Fig. 5. With permission.)

group of patients such localization can usually be recognized clinically, making complete ablation possible.

The second proposition concerned the necessity for radical excision in order to provide longterm control of the disease. This involves a close scrutiny of the results of other single treatments for similar cases, so that the patient can be properly apprised of the options that are available to him, and their respective efficacy. Whitmore in his exhaustive study on the natural history of prostatic cancer[50] has emphasized that the life expectancy of a patient having prostatic cancer is necessarily short because of the age at which the disease is evident; that other methods of treatment are effective in many in-

stances; and finally that the natural history of the disease indicates that it is slow growing and may never overtake the patient. The first option therefore is no treatment at all.

No Treatment. What would have happened to the 96 percent of our patients with nodule cancer that was differentiated if they had been left untreated? Not many healthy men aged 62 would relish the pronouncement that their life expectancy is so short they should not worry about a little thing like prostatic cancer. Cook stated that after 10 years only 24 percent of similar patients in his series that were not treated were still alive, as compared with our 49 percent without cancer after radical excision.

We know that 96 percent of discrete nodules of cancer are differentiated (make acini), and have growth rates varying from very slow (the majority) to very fast. We also know that the rates are not predictable by routine histologic techniques, and that a stage B_1 cancer can move rapidly (within months) or almost imperceptibly to stage B_2, C, or D (Fig. 8). Therefore the policy of "wait and see what happens to a discrete nodule of cancer in a 62 year old man with a nonobstructing prostate" sounds somewhat like a game of Russian roulette. The implication that most stage B tumors remain stage B and are inactive may or may not be true. It may be true that the patient will outlive his tumor, but the probability that it is not true is suggested by Figure 2, showing that of 129 patients in stage B only 1 lived 15 years. Of this group receiving transurethral resection only, 19 were merely discrete nodules.

The assumption that a biologically active and clinically manifest cancer never, or almost never, occurs in a surgically curable stage is hard to believe (Figs. 4, *A* and *B*, and 8). If it were true, the prostate would be unique among cancer-bearing organs in man. To prove that radical excision of a nodule of proved cancer is neither necessary nor desirable one must be able to show that similar patients not treated at all, or with other treatments, would do just as well over the 15-year follow-up term. Cook's patients were not followed beyond the 10-year limit so we have no figures for a 15-year study of these untreated cases. At the present time, therefore, it is impossible to prove that the patients surviving 15 years after radical perineal prostatectomy had latent unimportant cancer and would have done just as well without operation. Gleason and associates[26] believe that they have found a way to predict the prognosis for prostatic cancer. They have combined histologic grading, patterns, clinical staging and numerous categories, but have followed their 1032 cases only five years. For this system to be practicable for the radical surgeon the information must be obtainable from needle biopsies and based on longterm experience for proof of accuracy. At the present time, therefore, the policy of nonintervention seems rather dangerous and one must conclude that ablation by radical excision is not only possible but, when properly done, is also an effective method of treatment for a selected group of patients.

ENDOCRINE TREATMENT

Most conservative therapists withhold endocrine treatment until progression of the disease is evident, or symptoms appear, because there is little if any evidence that such treatment actually lengthens the life span of

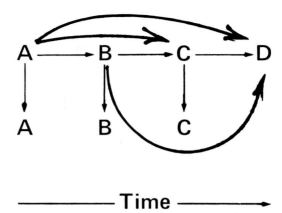

Fig. 8. Stage progression of prostatic cancer. (From Whitmore, WF Jr: The natural history of prostatic cancer. Cancer 32:1104, 1973. With permission.)

the patient. When the clinician finally prescribes this treatment he has no idea how great the response will be. Barnes[3] has reported a 15-year survivorship of 33 percent among 108 patients with stage A and nodule cancers and 21 percent were presumably cancer-free at the end of the period. His patients differed from ours, however, in several respects: our patients averaged 62 years of age and had no prostatic symptoms. His were older (68 years of age); they presented with prostatic obstructive symptoms with cancer cells in the hyperplastic mass; and there was no pathologic proof that cancer was microscopically absent from the prostate in those reported clinically to be cancer-free. The extraordinary thing about his series of 108 cases was that in that particular sample 33 percent of the patients actually did live 15 years, and 75 percent of these survivors apparently remained in good health. Most if not all of his patients must have had latent cancer. His figures for survival should be confirmed by other similar studies on patients under 65 with a discrete nodule of cancer without obstructive symptoms, and the longterm results reported by independent observers.

From Barnes' report one can say that some patients with prostatic obstruction together with a discrete palpable nodule of prostatic cancer will live 15 years without excision. In the Mayo Clinic series apparently only 1 of 19 patients with nodule cancer not receiving endocrine treatment lived 15 years (Fig. 2).[27]

Culp,[16] however, reported that 15 patients in his series of 74 having radical excision had cancer 15 to 19 years later (20 percent), but Barnes' patients were predominantly in stage A. Any conclusion that all or even most patients with a nodule of cancer without prostatic obstruction will do so represents what is known as an inductive leap. The suggestion that our cancer-free survivors had similar latent cancer and our 24 percent failure rate indicated aggressive cancer is impossible to prove. Our patients were younger (averaging 62 years) and Rosenberg[44] from a study of 500 autopsy cases has shown that at this age patients with prostatic cancer are more likely to die of this disease than older patients who he found usually had died with prostatic cancer coincidentally present.

Hauschka[29] showed that tumors were really cell populations in which individual cells varied in responsiveness to chemical and physical agents. Franks[22] also showed that hormone sensitivity was not a property of the tumor as a whole but varied in different parts of the same tumor. Tavares[48] has attempted to show that susceptibility, or lack of it, was related to ploidy. Geneticists from the Roswell Park Memorial Institute do not deny this but criticize the method Tavares used and state that it can be determined only by the painstaking method of chromosomal analysis. At any rate the genetic distinction between tumors cannot be recognized by standard histologic techniques. Furthermore there is no solid evidence today to show that their genetic peculiarities may underlie the rate of tumor growth and aggressiveness (latency and biologic activity).

Franks[23] reported that 20 percent of patients with active cancer fail to regress after castration-estrogen treatment, and 70 percent of all patients die within three years. If untreated, 85 percent of the patients die within three years, a margin of only 15 percent. Since large, uncontrollable tumors probably start as small asymptomatic and localized tumors, recommendation for radical excision of the localized cancer seems reasonable.

RADIATION

Prior to World War II radiation of prostatic cancer by conventional units or by implanted radium needles had little to offer. Later, Flocks, Kerr, and associates[21] obtained some striking results from local injections of radioactive colloidal gold. In 1958 del Regato[18] began using cobalt-60 teletherapy but postponed a published report until 1967. George and associates,[25] Bagshaw and associates,[2] and many others have followed suit and have collected large series of cases. It will not be long before 15-year survival figures for prostatic cancer in stage B_1 and in the nodule stage will be forthcoming to compare with the success rates after radical prostatectomy. At present the emphasis seems to be on cases representing fully developed clinical stages B and C cancer.

The appeal of this treatment to most urologists is strong. It relieves them of the necessity for precise clinical staging, and of the burden of radical excision. The question is, does the treatment result in cure or merely palliation. Some patients undoubtedly are cured, but Sewell and associates[47] remain pessimistic. Of 17 of their patients with stage A or B cancer radiated with the 6 MEV linear accelerator, only 6 (35 percent) became tumor-free; but of 8 patients living five years or longer after treatment, 6 (75 percent) were tumor-free. Of the total series, 47 percent became permanently impotent and 12 percent had lymphedema of legs or penis.

Carlton and associates[9] believe a combination of radon implantation and external radiation is better than either alone. They implant the tumor with seeds amounting to 2500 to 4500 rads, and follow this with 4000 to 4500 rads by external beam therapy. At the time of this report they had treated 225 patients, but by April 1974 the series had grown to more than 400. In their original group 20 patients had clinical stage B cancer, and serial postradiation prostatic biopsies showed that 6 (30 percent) still had cancer 12 to more than 30 months later, whereas 14 (70 percent) were cancer-free. Survival data beyond six years have not been provided.

Radiation in one form or another for operable stage B cancer may be promising, and should be used now for cancer in stage B_2 in which there is high microscopic incidence of local extension. For stage B_1 cancers, total excision seems to be a surer and quicker method of ablation.

The second proposition concerned the absence of an alternative treatment that is at least as effective as radical prostatectomy for stage B cancer. To date there are no longterm figures showing that conservative treatments for strictly comparable stage B_1 cancers are as effective as radical prostatectomy.

SUMMARY

The natural history of prostatic cancer is incompletely understood. Small cancers may have a very slow or rapid growth rate, and the majority are differentiated. Cells may leave the prostate by blood or lymph without penetrating capsule or invading the seminal vesicles. The prediction of latency or of biologic activity in any given case is impossible.

Stage A cancer should be separated into A_1 (focal) and A_2 (diffuse). Stage A_1 cancer that is low grade is best left alone. Stage A_2 cancer and high grade cancer probably should be treated by megavoltage radiation.

Stage B includes many cancers that are microscopically stage C. If this stage is separated into clinical stage B_1 (tumors grossly involving less than one lobe), and B_2 (tumors involving one lobe or more) the underestimation of microscopic extent in B_1 will be less than in 10 percent of the cases. In clinical stage B_2 cancer, 50 percent are microscopically stage C.

Radical prostatectomy for cure should be limited to clinical B_1 cases without distant spread. It is not a cure-all, but it provides the best 15-year survival rate more completely, more quickly, less expensively, and with fewer discomforts than other methods. The alternative options are no treatment, endocrine treatment, and radiation. The first is risky in many instances and may allow an active cancer to get out of control. The second rarely destroys all of the cells in the total cell population and gives one a false sense of security. The last should be reserved for cases well beyond stage B_1, but without distant metastases, where its usefulness exceeds that of radical excision.

1201 North Calvert Street
Baltimore, Maryland 21202

REFERENCES

1. Arduino, L. J., and Glucksman, M. A.: Lymph node metastases in early carcinoma of the prostate. J Urol 88:91, 1962
2. Bagshaw, M. A., Kaplan, H. S., and Sagerman, R. H.: Linear accelerator supervoltage radiotherapy: VII. Carcinoma of the prostate. Radiology 85:121, 1965
3. Barnes, R. W., and Ninan, C. A.: Carcinoma of the prostate: Biopsy and conservative therapy. J Urol 108:897, 1972
4. Bauer, W. C., McGavran, M. H., and Carlin, M. R.: Unsuspected carcinoma of the prostate in suprapubic prostatectomy specimens: A clinicopathological study of 55 consecutive cases. Cancer 13:370, 1960
5. Berlin, B. B., Cornwell, P. M., Connelly, R. R., and Eisenberg, H.: Radical perineal prostatectomy for carcinoma of the prostate: Survival in 143 cases treated from 1935 to 1958. J Urol 99:97, 1968
6. Broders, A. C.: Epithelioma of genito-urinary organs. Ann Surg 75:574, 1922
7. Byar, D. P., and Veterans Administration Cooperative Urological Research Group. Survival of patients with incidentally found microscopic cancer of the prostate: Results of a clinical trial of conservative treatment. J Urol 108:908, 1972
8. Byar, D. P., Mostofi, F. K., and Veterans Administration Cooperative Urological Research Group. Carcinoma of the prostate: Prognostic evaluation of certain pathologic features in 208 radical prostatectomies. Cancer 30:5, 1972
9. Carlton, C. E., Jr., Dawoud, F., Hudgins, P., and Scott, R., Jr.:' Irradiation treatment of carcinoma of the prostate: A preliminary report based on 8 years of experience. J Urol 108:924, 1972
10. Castellino, R. A., Ray, G., Blank, N., Govan, D., and Bagshaw, M.: Lymphangiography in prostatic carcinoma: Preliminary observations. JAMA 223:877, 1973
11. Catalona, W. J.: Personal communication, 1974
12. Chute, R.: Radical retropubic prostatectomy for cancer. J Urol 71:347, 1954
13. Connolly, J. J., Thomson, A., Jewett, M.A.S., Hartman, N., and Webber, M.: Intraprostatic lymphatics. Invest Urol 5:371, 1968
14. Cook, G. B.: Personal communication, 1967
15. Correa, R. J., Jr., Anderson, R. G., Gibbons, R. P., and Mason, J. T.: Latent carcinoma of the prostate—why the controversy? J Urol 111:644, 1974
16. Culp, O. S.: Personal communication, 1974
17. Culp, O. S., and Meyer, J. J. Radical prostatectomy in the treatment of prostatic cancer. Cancer 32:1113, 1973
18. del Regato, J. A.: Radiotherapy in the conservative treatment of operable and locally inoperable carcinoma of the prostate. Radiology 88:761, 1967
19. Flocks, R. H.: Personal communication, 1974
20. Flocks, R. H.: Present status of interstitial irradiation in managing prostatic cancer. JAMA 210:328, 1969
21. Flocks, R. H., Kerr, H. D., Elkins, H. B., and Culp, D.: Treatment of carcinoma of the prostate by interstitial radiation with radio-active gold (Au198): A preliminary report. J Urol 68:510, 1952
22. Franks, L. M.: Estrogen-treated prostatic cancer: The variation in responsiveness of tumor cells. Cancer 13:490, 1960
23. Franks, L. M.: Some comments on the long-term results of endocrine treatment of prostatic cancer. Br J Urol 30:383, 1958
24. Franks, L. M.: The natural history of prostatic cancer. Lancet 2:1037, 1956
25. George, F. W., Carlton, C. E., Dykhuizen, R. F., and Dillon, J. R.: Cobalt 60 teletherapy in definitive treatment of carcinoma of the prostate: A preliminary report. J Urol 93:102, 1965
26. Gleason, D. F., Mellinger, G. T., and Veterans Administration Cooperative Urological Research Group: Prediction of prognosis for prostatic adenocarcinoma by combined histological grading and clinical staging. J Urol 111:58, 1974
27. Hanash, K. A., Utz, D. C., Cook, E. N., Taylor, W. F., and Titus, J. L.: Carcinoma of the prostate: A 15-year followup. J Urol 107:450, 1972
28. Hand, J. R., and Sullivan, A. W.: Retropubic prostatectomy— Analysis of one hundred cases. JAMA 145:1313, 1951
29. Hauschka, T.: Tissue genetics in relation to cancer. Proceedings of the New York State Association of Public Health Laboratories, 36(2):42, 1956
30. Hudson, H. C., and Howland, R. L., Jr.: Radical retropubic prostatectomy for cancer of the prostate. J Urol 108:944, 1972
31. Jewett, H. J.: Radical perineal prostatectomy for cancer of the prostate: An analysis of 190 cases. J Urol 61:277, 1949
32. Jewett, H. J.: Radical perineal prostatectomy for carcinoma: Analysis of cases at Johns Hopkins Hospital, 1904–1954. JAMA 156:1039, 1954
33. Jewett, H. J.: The case for radical perineal prostatectomy. J Urol 103:195, 1970
34. Jewett, H. J., Bridge, R. W., Gray, G. F., Jr., and Shelley, W. M.: The palpable nodule of prostatic cancer. Results 15 years after radical excision. JAMA 203:403, 1968
35. Jewett, H. J., Eggleston, J. C., and Yawn, D. H.: Radical prostatectomy in the management of carcinoma of the prostate: Probable causes of some therapeutic failures. J Urol 107:1034, 1972
36. Kahler, J. E.: Carcinoma of the prostate gland: A pathologic study. J Urol 41:557, 1939
37. Kopecky, A. A., Loskowski, T. Z., and Scott, R., Jr.: Radical retropubic prostatectomy in the treatment of prostatic carcinoma. J Urol 103:641, 1970
38. Küchler, H.: Uber Prostatavergrosserungen. Deutsch Klin 18:458, 1866
39. McCullough, D. L., Prout, G. R., Jr., and Daly, J. J.: Carcinoma of the prostate and lymphatic metastases. J Urol 111:65, 1974
40. McNeal, J. E.: Origin and development of carcinoma in the prostate. Cancer 23:24, 1969
41. Memmelaar, J.: Total prostatovesiculectomy—retropubic approach. J Urol 62:340, 1949
42. Millin, T.: Retropubic Urinary Surgery. Baltimore, Williams and Wilkins Co., 1947
43. Peters, P. C.: Personal communication, 1974
44. Rosenberg, S. E.: Is carcinoma of the prostate less serious in older men? J Am Geriat Soc 13:791, 1965
45. Salvatierra, O., Jr., Rigdon, W. O., and Malley, J. A.: Modified retropubic prostatectomy: A new technique. J Urol 108:126, 1972
46. Schirmer, H. K. A., Murphy, G. P., and Scott, W. W.: A correlation between histologic differentiation of prostatic cancer and the clinical course of the disease. Urol Dig 4:15, 1965

47. Sewell, R. A., Braren, V., Wilson, S. K., and Rhamy, R. K.: Extended biopsy followup after full course radiation for resectable prostatic carcinoma. J Urol, accepted for publication.
48. Tavares, A. S., Costa, J., and Costa Maia, J.: Correlation between ploidy and prognosis in prostatic carcinoma. J Urol 109:676, 1973
49. Whitmore, W. F., Jr.: Symposium on hormones and cancer therapy; Hormone therapy in prostatic cancer. Am J Med 21:697, 1956

50. Whitmore, W. F., Jr.: The natural history of prostatic cancer. Cancer 32:1104, 1973
51. Young, H. H.: The early diagnosis and radical cure of carcinoma of the prostate. Being a study of 40 cases and presentation of a radical operation which was carried out in 4 cases. Bull. Johns Hopkins Hosp 16:315, 1905

Commentary:
Radical Perineal Prostatectomy

Hugh J. Jewett

From 1909 to 1963, allowing for a 15-yr follow-up study, 447 procedures have been done at The Johns Hopkins Hospital for what was thought to be clinical stage B cancer. A detailed study of 79 patients within this group considered to be in stage B2 showed that 40 (50%) were histologic stage B and that 39 were stage C or D. Since the operation must be restricted to cases in histologic stage B in order to provide a reasonable 15-yr success rate, I focused attention on clinical B_1 cases, in which more than 90% are now known to be histologic stage B.

Obviously not all of this latter group can be cured by surgical excision, since a small number will always have metastasized from within the prostate by lymphatic and vascular channels coexisting therein. The presence of cancer in a pelvic lymph node therefore does not exclude minimal hematogenous metastasis as well, despite a negative report of a modern sophisticated serum or bone marrow assay or a skeletal scan. The only proof that a micrometastasis in a node is a single manifestation of spread awaits a 15-yr cancer-free survival following radical excision and without adjunctive treatment. At present, pelvic lymphadenectomy is useful for staging only and may be replaced later by noninvasive techniques. However, the incidence of metastases is directly proportional to the size of the local mass.

The foregoing article represents the record from 1909 to 1951, comprising a total of 238 cases. Of these, 103 traced patients were staged clinical B_1 and 86 of them were microscopically staged B. Of the remaining patients, 127 were in clinical B_2 and were not followed.

The curve representing survivorship among the 86 histologic stage B patients receiving no adjunctive treatment deviated considerably from that of the general male population of comparable age between the tenth and fifteenth year (Fig. 3 in the preceding article). Table 1 indicates that there were three patients graded III, none of whom survived free of cancer for 15 yr. If these are included, 21 histologic stage B cases were surgical failures. A later study showed that seven of these patients without local recurrence died of metastases that must have been present and undetected before operation. The

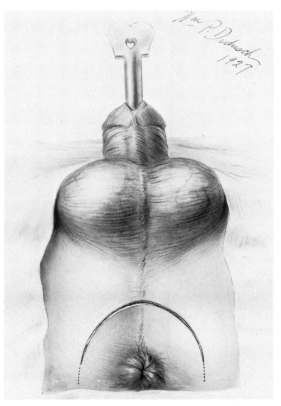

Fig. 9. Modifications now are a curved Lowsley tractor in the urethra, and a more crescentic incision beginning one finger breadth anterior to the anal mucocutaneous margin. (Young HH: The cure of cancer of the prostate by radical perineal prostatectomy [prostato-seminal vesiculectomy]: History, literature, and statistics of Young's operation. J Urol 53:188, 1945. Reprinted with permission.)

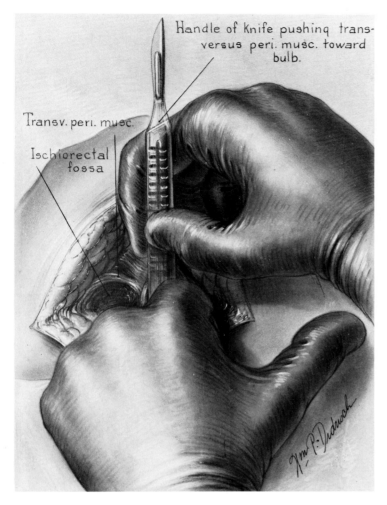

Fig. 10. Development of ischiorectal fossa on each side of the central tendon. (Young HH: The cure of cancer of the prostate by radical perineal prostatectomy [prostato-seminal vesiculectomy]: History, literature, and statistics of Young's operation. J Urol 53:188, 1945. Reprinted with permission.)

remaining 14 died of local recurrence with or without metastasis. Of these 21 failures, 6 showed no capsular invasion, 9 showed partial, and 6 showed complete penetration. All cases of surgical failure had demonstrable recurrence within 11 yr, although a few of these patients may have lived longer. These were the only patients who received endocrine supplementation.

The classic perineal operation developed by Young is depicted in Figures 9 to 16.[1] Because of a fairly high incidence of postoperative incontinence following Young's original operation, the vesicourethral anastomosis has been modified by a number of perineal surgeons beginning with Vest in 1940. The most satisfactory of all, however, is the procedure I have used for over 25 yr; it consists of a careful end-to-end anastomosis over a 22 French catheter using not more than four sutures of 2–0 chromic catgut on an atraumatic needle. The needle avoids the external sphincter, and the suture provides a watertight approximation (Fig. 17).[2] With this method I have had only 3 instances of minimal incontinence among 119 patients, and these have required no protective device. Hodges

reports slight stress incontinence in one patient among more than 200 procedures.[2]

The second series extended from 1951 to 1963 and comprised 70 clinical stage B_1 cases. Thirteen could not be traced. Of 57 traced patients, 29 (51%) were alive and free of cancer after 15 yr without postoperative adjunctive treatment. Ten died of recurrent cancer, and 18 died within the 15-yr period without cancer. When compared with the life table for men with the same age distribution, the survivorship in the general population was 51%. The biostatistical significance of these results is obvious.

Among 3711 patients with prostatic cancer diagnosed at The Johns Hopkins Hospital to 1967, 475 (12.8%) underwent the operation, but only 292 (8% of all prostatic cancers) were in clinical stage B_1. This low figure of operability among the unscreened population is almost insignificant. But if nearly all these large inoperable prostatic cancers seen in a general hospital or urologic clinic must begin earlier as small operable

(*Text continues on p. 1132.*)

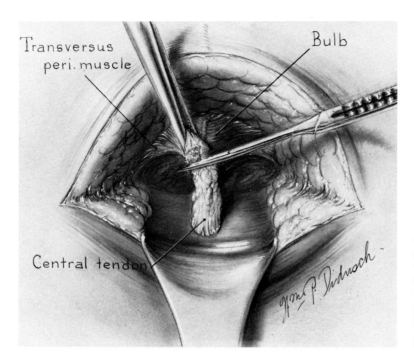

Fig. 11. After tension is put on the central tendon by a posterior bifid retractor, a finger usually is passed around the tendon in front of the rectum, and the tendon is sharply divided. (Young HH: The cure of cancer of the prostate by radical perineal prostatectomy [prostato-seminal vesiculectomy]: History, literature, and statistics of Young's operation. J Urol 53:188, 1945. Reprinted with permission.)

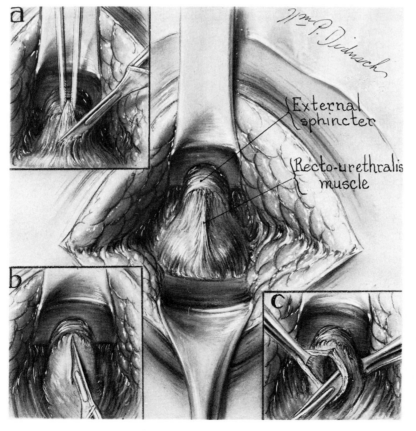

Fig. 12. Modification consists in substitution of an anterolateral thyroid retractor on each side behind the triangular ligament instead of a bulb retractor, which might damage the sphincter. (a) The recto-urethralis muscle is gently elevated from the prostatic apex with the handle of a knife and cut transversely without entering the rectum, and the fascia is stripped backwards from the prostate with a knife handle. Urethrotomy is not done as depicted in insert b, but a gooseneck clamp is passed around the urethra at the apex of the prostate, the Lowsley tractor is removed, the clamp is opened, and the urethra on slight stretch is transsected close to the prostatic apex (c). (Young HH: The cure of cancer of the prostate by radical perineal prostatectomy [prostato-seminal vesiculectomy]: History, literature, and statistics of Young's operation. J Urol 53:188, 1945. Reprinted with permission.)

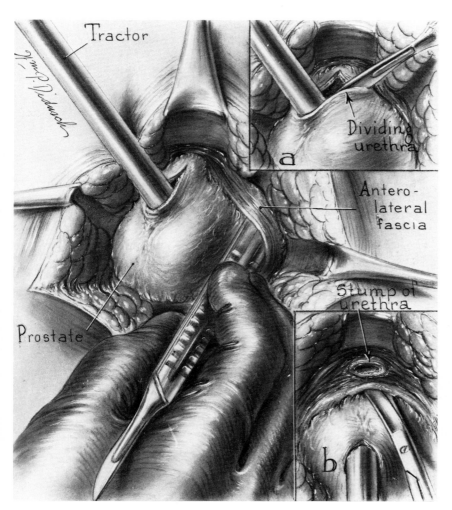

Fig. 13. A straight Lowsley tractor is introduced through the transsected urethra at the prostatic apex, eliminating the technique shown in insert a. Instead of sharp dissection, as shown in insert b, the anterior prostate is exposed by gentle finger dissection proceeding under the puboprostatic ligaments. (Young HH: The cure of cancer of the prostate by radical perineal prostatectomy [prostato-seminal vesiculectomy]: History, literature, and statistics of Young's operation. J Urol 53:188, 1945. Reprinted with permission.)

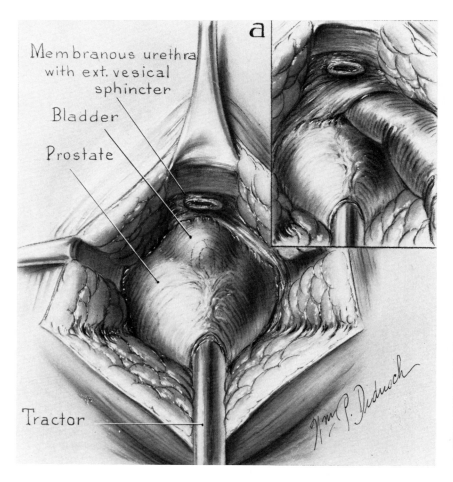

Fig. 14. The blade of the tractor elevates the anterior wall of the bladder. A transverse incision in made through it. (Young HH: The cure of cancer of the prostate by radical perineal prostatectomy [prostato-seminal vesiculectomy]: History, literature, and statistics of Young's operation. J Urol 53:188, 1945. Reprinted with permission.)

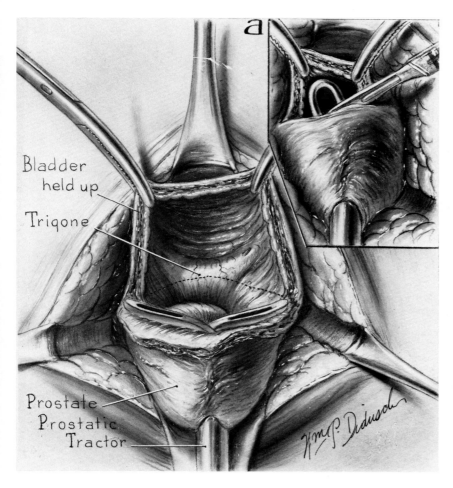

Fig. 15. Narrow Deaver retractors are inserted. With traction upward and outward, and downward with the tractor, the index finger is placed in the bladder and held downward against the prostate. The bladder wall is then cut away with curved scissors close to the prostate as far around as the posterolateral quadrants. (Young HH: The cure of cancer of the prostate by radical perineal prostatectomy [prostato-seminal vesiculectomy]: History, literature, and statistics of Young's operation. J Urol 53:188, 1945. Reprinted with permission.)

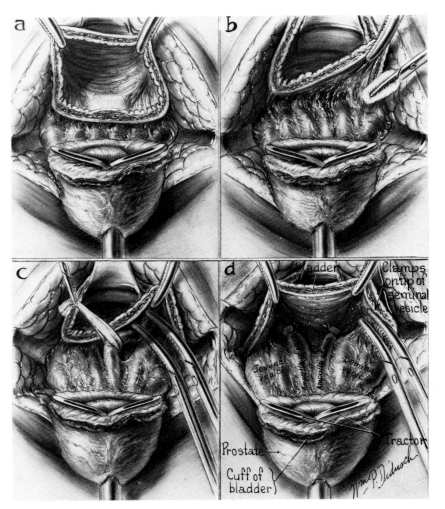

Fig. 16. Care is taken not to cut too close to the ureters (1 cm or more away), and not to cut into fibrous investments of seminal vesicles, which are always left intact. Vesicles within fasciae are exposed to their tips by placing a Deaver beneath the elevated bladder base and gently lifting upward with help of a long knife handle. Similar dissection is carried out behind the prostate and vesicles, and the whole specimen is removed in one piece. Bleeding vessels are fulgurated. A 6F whistle-tip catheter may be passed up each ureter to identify them during closure. (Young HH: The cure of cancer of the prostate by radical perineal prostatectomy [prostato-seminal vesiculectomy]: History, literature, and statistics of Young's operation. J Urol 53:188, 1945. Reprinted with permission.)

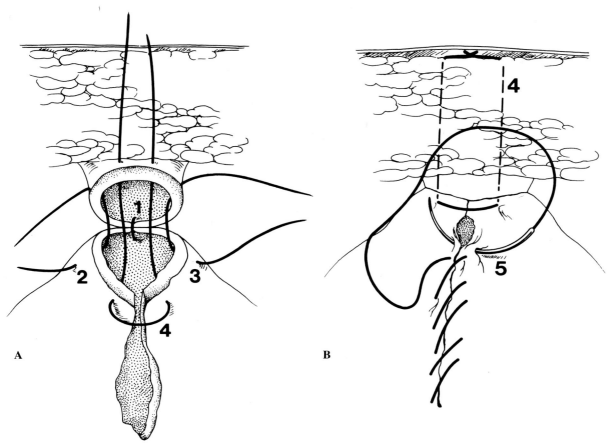

A

B

Fig. 17. (*A*) As illustrated by Hodges, the vesico-urethral anastomosis is accomplished first by simple suture of 2-0 chromic catgut on an atraumatic needle at 12, 3, and 9 o'clock. A mattress suture of the same material is placed posteriorly and passed posterior to the triangular ligament. All sutures avoid the urethral sphincter. But to take tension off the anastomosis, the posterior suture, often figure-of-eight, makes a good bite in the superficial transverse perineal muscle. (*B*) When all sutures are placed and tied, closure should be watertight without strangulation. Usually a 22F, 5 cc Foley catheter is left indwelling and strapped to the penis so that the balloon does not press on the suture line. (Hodges CV: Vesicourethral anastomosis after radical perineal prostatectomy: Experience with the Jewett modification. J Urol 118:209, 1977. Reprinted with permission.)

cancers, why do they elude detection in that early curable stage? They do so because men over 50, without symptoms, object to the annoyance of a seemingly unnecessary rectal examination, and many times the physician, if consulted, agrees. Yet to date that is the only way a stage B_1 cancer can be found. These B_1 cancers are not dormant but progress by cell division at a variable rate. All my surviving B_1 patients, grade I or II, had tumors that had invaded the laminated capsule, indicating biologic aggressiveness rather than dormancy.

It therefore seems reasonable to predict that the current annual death rate from large and presently incurable cancers can be reduced by first eliminating a greater proportion of the small cancers from which they spring. The complications of the properly performed perineal operation are minimal and temporary, aside from impotence occurring in 85% to 90% of patients. It is possible that clinical B_1 cases can be treated successfully by implantation of ^{125}I into the prostate without losing sexual function, but since 77% of clinically discrete nodules 1 cm to 1.5 cm are microscopically diffuse within the prostate, great care must be taken to distribute the radiation adequately. Remember that seminal vesicle involvement occurred microscopically in 49% of my clinical stage B_2 cases and led to death from cancer in 95% of this group. To place ^{125}I seeds suprapubically into this seminal vesicle area at the time of prostatic implantation if at all possible would require extraordinary ingenuity and dexterity. However, 50% of my clinical B_2 cases were microscopically stage B. If these probably operable cases could be identified among the greater number of clinical stage B_2 cancers seen in practice, the figure for operability possibly could be increased.

REFERENCES

1. Young HH: The cure of cancer of the prostate by radical perineal prostatectomy (prostato-seminal vesiculectomy): History, literature and statistics of Young's operation. J Urol 53:188, 1945

2. Hodges CV: Vesicourethral anastomosis after radical perineal prostatectomy: Experience with the Jewett modification. J Urol 118:209, 1977

ANNOTATED BIBLIOGRAPHY

Berlin BB, Cornwell PM, Connelly RR, et al: Radical perineal prostatectomy for carcinoma of the prostate: Survival in 143 cases treated from 1935 to 1958. J Urol 99:97, 1968

Ater operation the survival curve at 15 yr was only about 6% less than the expected curve for men of the same age in the general population, a remarkable achievement. The authors referring to this, however, do not say how many of their total group of 143 patients had stages A and B cancer, how many were cancer free at 15 yr, and how many had hormonal supplementation. In their summary they do state that 33% of their patients survived 15 yr.

Scott WW, Boyd HL: Combined hormone control therapy and radical prostatectomy in the treatment of selected cases of advanced carcinoma of the prostate: A retrospective study based upon 25 years of experience. J Urol 101:86, 1969

Forty-four patients with clinical stage C disease regressed markedly after hormonal manipulation. After radical perineal prostatectomy in this carefully selected group, 29% lived 15 yr. Since most clinical stage C cases have nodal or other evidence of metastases, the good results must be attributed to very marked responsiveness to hormonal treatment, unless it can be shown in a control series that surgical ''debulking'' was contributory.

Culp OS, Meyer JJ: Radical prostatectomy in the treatment of prostate cancer. Cancer 32:1113, 1973

From 1950 through 1972, 264 patients at The Mayo Clinic had a radical prostatectomy. Of these, 74 qualified for a 15-yr survival study. Forty of these 74 patients (54%) lived 15 yr or longer, but 20, or half the group, had supplemental endocrine treatment. Three patients with grade 3 cancer and 3 others with seminal vesicle involvement lived 15 yr, but it is unclear whether they were among the 20 who received endocrine support.

Bruce AW, O'Cleireachain F, Morales A, et al: Carcinoma of the prostate: A critical look at staging. J Urol 117:319, 1977

The authors have made an exhaustive study on 75 patients with microscopically proved cancer. They conclude that the bone marrow acid phosphatase estimation is the most sensitive test yet devised to detect blood-borne metastases in the earliest stage. They were not impressed with the value of serum acid phosphatase levels in very early dissemination. Bone scanning was more accurate than x-ray surveys but was nonspecific. Lymph node involvement was best determined by pelvic lymphadenectomy, but all nodes were negative in their three cases of stage A and six cases of stage B_1 cancer. In 13 B_2 cases the nodes were positive in 5 (38.4%); they were positive in 75% of stage C cases. These figures, although based on small numbers, suggest that the perineal operation is usually adequate if the primary tumor is in clinical stage B_1.

Correa R J Jr, Gibbons R P, Cummings K B, et al: Total prostatectomy for stage B carcinoma of the prostate. J Urol 117:328, 1977

Thirteen of 67 stage B patients qualified for a 15-yr survival study; of these, 5 (38%) survived 15 yr without cancer. Of the 67 patients thought to be stage B before operation, 53 were pathologic stage B and 14 were stage C. It would be interesting to know how many of the patients with pathologic stage B cancer lived 15 yr cancer free without supplemental treatment.

OVERVIEW: DEFINING SUITABLE PATIENTS: KEY IN CHOOSING TREATMENT MODE

Elliot Leiter

Both Drs. Jewett and Veenema have a virtually unparalleled experience with the operative procedures that they describe. Each is a master of technique, and any disagreement must therefore necessarily be conceptual rather than technical. Thus, for example, I take issue with Drs. Veenema and Wexler when they state that they do not perform a radical lymphadenectomy but, rather, selectively biopsy any suspicious nodes. This bias does not stem from a feeling that radical lymphadenectomy yields an increase in survival as claimed by some, but rather from a conviction that micrometastases are so common that understaging must necessarily result unless a complete lymphadenectomy is performed.[1] In fact, a standard lymphadenectomy may result in significant understaging unless the presacral and presciatic lymph nodes are removed.[2] Consequently, if the surgeon is to use the advantage of retropubic prostatectomy maximally, namely, the ability to perform lymphadenectomy, the lymphadenectomy should be complete rather than selective.

On the other hand, I fully agree with and support their contention that a radical prostatectomy can be performed in patients with only occasional incontinence, in addition to an acceptable incidence of stress incontinence. There has been a tendency on the part of some urologists to leave a portion of the prostatic apex in order to avoid incontinence. There is no doubt that this results in a less satisfactory cancer resection in some, and perhaps many, patients. Both Drs. Jewett and Veenema demonstrate conclusively that in their series this maneuver has not been necessary and that continence has been preserved.

Almost more important, though, than the choice of procedure or the surgical maneuvers employed is the choice of patient for whom a radical prostatectomy is appropriate treatment. If one accepts the fact that the presence of lymph node metastases militates against a cure, no matter which surgical procedure is employed, then ideally radical prostatectomy should be reserved for patients who have localized disease. Identification of the patient with truly localized disease, however, has continued to present some problems. The difficulty, of course, lies in the fact that an appreciable number of patients with localized disease (stage B and C) will, in truth, have nodal metastases. In fact, the reported incidence of pelvic lymph node metastases for stage B tumors ranges between 7% and 45%; for stage C tumors, between 33% and 85%.[3] Although simply limiting radical prostatectomy to stage B_1 tumors

decreases the likelihood that radical prostatectomy would be inappropriately performed in the face of metastases, it will remove many potentially curable patients from consideration for extirpative surgery.

In an attempt to improve the predictive accuracy of whether nodal metastases are present, various other clinical and histologic criteria have been advanced. The most successful, of course, has been the use of histologic grading as advocated by Gleason and Mellinger.[4] By combining both clinical stage, as well as histologic grade, the probability of whether nodal metastases are likely to be found is more accurately predicted.[5] In fact, in one series, pelvic lymphadenectomy was unrewarding for staging purposes both in patients with early, localized, low-grade disease as well as in patients with clinically advanced, poorly differentiated disease.[6] In the first group, none of the patients had nodal metastases, while in the second group, all patients had pelvic lymph node metastasis. Unfortunately, though, there is some controversy among pathologists on the reliability and reproducibility of histologic grading. Consequently, the routine grading of prostatic neoplasms has not become a widespread practice.

Aside from simple palpatory and histologic evaluation, and before surgical staging lymphadenectomy, more accurate clinical staging is certainly possible with the variety of radiographic, radioisotopic, and manipulative procedures presently available. It is perhaps redundant to point out that before even considering radical prostatectomy, the urologist must perform all such pertinent staging investigations. As a minimum this should include an excretory urogram, serum acid and alkaline phosphatase, and a radioisotope bone scan. There is, as yet, insufficient data available on the computed tomography (CT) scan and whether it will improve preoperative clinical staging. Similarly, pelvic lymphangiography, with or without skinny needle biopsy of suspicious lymph nodes, has yielded variable results.

There is general agreement that, in the final analysis, truly accurate staging is accomplished only with pelvic lymphadenectomy. This ability to perform staging pelvic lymphadenectomy is generally felt to be the major technical advantage inherent in radical retropubic prostatectomy. This is certainly true in those patients who have large, palpable lymph nodes that prove to be positive on biopsy and in whom an unnecessary radical prostatectomy is thereby avoided. The question, of course, is whether such patients can be identified with reasonable accuracy, without surgery, by the use of CT scan, lymphangiography, and selective lymph node biopsy. If so, then many of the advantages of the radical retropubic prostatectomy would be lost.

In fact, the results of staging lymphadenectomy are rarely known to the surgeon until several days after he has completed the radical prostatectomy. Therein lies the flaw of staging pelvic lymphadectomy when performed at the time of radical prostatectomy. The presence of micrometastases are not determined until permanent sections are obtained, and, of course, by that time the patient is several days postoperative. One might get around this dilemma, obviously, by getting frozen sections at the time of lymphadenectomy. Generally, though, it is impractical to expect the pathologist to do a frozen section on all nodes removed at the time of lymphadenectomy, nor could this be accomplished in a reasonable time. Therefore, it is common practice to perform a lymphadenectomy and to follow this with radical retropubic prostatectomy before the results of the staging lymphadenectomy are known. There is no doubt, therefore, that a certain number of patients will have undergone radical surgery but do *not* have localized disease.

It would seem more logical, therefore, that in patients in whom, statistically, the only certain way to rule out lymph node metastases is by staging lymphadenectomy that the results of such a lymphadenectomy should be available before a decision is made on the suitability of radical prostatectomy. There are obviously logistical disadvantages to this approach,

since it would require subjecting the patient to two surgical procedures, and, if the pathologic results of the pelvic lymphadenectomy were known before a radical prostatectomy, then the most commonly claimed advantage of the radical retropubic prostatectomy would become invalid, since two surgical procedures are necessary in any case. Parenthetically, I might add that the same conceptual difficulty arises in subjecting patients to "staging" lymphadenectomy and the insertion of ^{125}I seeds.

Thus far in this discussion I have purposely avoided entering into the controversy on whether radical prostatectomy is ever suitable treatment for prostatic carcinoma or whether radiation, for example, provides equivalent results with fewer complications. Although some feel that there is no evidence that survival is improved by local radical surgery, most series suggest that in appropriately chosen patients, the 15-yr tumor-free survival of patients who undergo radical prostatectomy ranges from 38% to 54%.[7-9] In fact, when Walsh and Jewett compared the 15-yr survivorship for patients with clinical stage B_1 disease and undergoing radical prostatectomy with United States 1950 life tables, the observed survival did not differ significantly from the expected survival of the general population.[10] Therefore, at the moment, it seems that radical prostatectomy still offers the best chance for cure in appropriately selected patients. Whether such surgery is performed retropubically or perineally is probably a matter of personal training and choice. What is more important is that urologists develop the ability to define more accurately exactly which patients are appropriate candidates.

REFERENCES

1. Barzell W, Bean MA, Hilaris BS et al: Total perinal prostatectomy for carcinoma of the prostate. J Urol 118:278, 1977

2. Golimbu M, Morales P, Al-Askari S, et al: Extended pelvic lymphadenectomy for prostatic cancer. J Urol 121:617, 1979

3. Whitehead ED, Leiter E: Prostatic carcinoma: Clinical and surgical staging. NY State J Med 81:184, 1981

4. Gleason DF, Mellinger GT, and The Veterans Administration Cooperative Urological Research Group: Prediction of prognosis for prostatic adenocarcinoma by combined histological grading and clinical staging. J Urol 111:64, 1977

5. McCullough DL, Prout GR Jr, Daly JJ: Carcinoma of the prostate and lymphatic metastases. J Urol 111:65, 1977

6. Whitehead ED, Huh SH, Garcia RL, et al: Interstitial irradiation of carcinoma of prostate with ^{125}I iodine and simultaneous extraperitoneal pelvic lymphadenectomy in 32 patients. J Urol 126:366, 1981

7. Byar DP, Corle DK: Vacurg randomized trial of radical prostatectomy for stages I and II prostate cancer. Urology (Suppl) 17:7, 1981

8. Catalona WJ, Scott WW: Carcinoma of the prostate: A review. J Urol 119:1, 1978

9. Correa RJ Jr, Gibbons RP, Cummings KB, et al: Total prostatectomy for stage B carcinoma of the prostate. J Urol 117:328, 1977

10. Walsh PC, Jewett HJ: Radical surgery for prostatic cancer. Cancer 45 (Suppl):1906, 1980

87

RETROPUBIC IMPLANTATION OF I^{125} IN THE TREATMENT OF PROSTATIC CANCER

Willet F. Whitmore, Jr., M.D.

Memorial Sloan Kettering Cancer Center, 425 East 67th Street, New York, N.Y. 10021

Prostatic Disease 6:223–233, © 1976, Alan R. Liss, Inc., New York

Three features of prostatic cancer have confused and confounded efforts to define its optimal management:

(1) Occurrence in an age group wherein the risks of death from a variety of causes other than prostatic cancer are high and increasing. This is not to question that prostatic cancer contributes importantly to mortality nor to disagree with the generalization that the higher the grade and stage of the prostatic cancer and the younger the patient, the greater the probability of death from prostatic cancer. Nevertheless, an analysis of causes of death in patients with various stages of prostatic cancer indicates that deaths from causes other than cancer are common, even when the prostatic cancer therapy has been conservative.

(2) Incomplete definition of the natural history of the cancer both in terms of rate of progression and pattern of progression. The theoretical possibilities for pattern of progression are expressed for the broad categories of the four clinical stages in Figure 1. There is unequivocal evidence that each of these anticipated possibilities does in fact occur but the frequency of each event and the factors determining a particular event are unknown. Furthermore, the frequency and significance of various possible patterns of dissemination (lymphatic, skeletal, visceral, etc.) remain to be defined.

(3) The variety of available treatments—surgical, radiation, endocrine, either individually or in various combinations. The fundamental objective of any therapy of any condition is to lessen the adverse impact of that condition on the quantity and quality of life. Justifiable therapy presupposes adverse effects on the quantity and quality of life from that condition and either no, or at least justifiable, adverse effects on the quantity or quality of life from the treatment per se. In the case/of stage D and most stage C prostatic cancers adverse effects are both direct and immediate; indeed most patients with such conditions have symptoms referable to the cancer. In the case of patients with stage A and stage B cancers direct and immediate effects from the cancer are absent and therapy is necessarily predicated upon existing conceptions regarding the natural history of such cancers. Since the latter conceptions are presently based upon inadequate data, there is understandably a wide spectrum of opinion regarding what constitutes optimal therapy. Such therapy need not necessarily make cancer cure its objective, however worthy that objective per se may be.

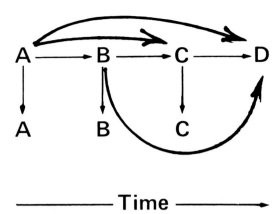

Fig. 1. Stage progression of prostatic cancer.

In the face of a relatively high risk of host death from causes other than prostatic cancer, an array of unquantitated and unpredictable patterns of tumor progression, and a variety of selectively applied, inadequately controlled treatments associated with more or less similar survival rates for comparable stages of cancer, it is not surprising that there are no data unequivocally establishing a favorable, let alone a superior, impact of any specific treatment on the survival of patients with any stage of prostatic cancer. This generalization is negatively phrased. It does not specify that no treatment favorably affects the survival of the patient with prostatic cancer, nor deny the life prolonging potential of such procedures as nephrostomy, blood transfusion, antibiotic administration, etc. (treatment of the host). Rather, it emphasizes the lack of data unequivocally establishing a favorable effect of treatment on patient survival, ascribable to an effect on the natural history of the cancer, per se.

Retropubic implantation of I¹²⁵ in the management of patients with prostatic cancer has been utilized in a pilot study of selected patients with carcinoma of the prostate. Evaluation of the end results of this treatment is subject to the same limitations encountered in evaluating other forms of treatment.

METHODS

Case Selection. Patients in reasonably good health with an estimated life expectancy of five or more years and with clinically stage B or stage C prostatic cancer have been selected for this procedure. Evaluation has included history, physical examination, serum acid and alkaline phosphatase determinations, intravenous urogram, skeletal survey, bone scan, cystoendoscopy and, more recently, lymphangiography. The results of lymphangiography have not been utilized in current clinical staging,

in part because not all patients have had this examination, in part because the reliability of this technique in this disease remains to be fully defined. Clinically stage B lesions are those in which the neoplasm is apparently confined within the prostatic capsule. Such lesions have ranged from isolated nodules less than 1 cm in diameter to lesions which palpably occupy most of the substance of the gland. Clinically stage C lesions are those in which there is palpable evidence of neoplasm beyond the prostatic capsule but in which distant metastases are apparently absent. Extremely bulky stage C lessions or those in which the margins of extension on digital rectal examination fade into the lateral pelvic walls, the urogenital diaphragm, or the bladder base have been electively excluded since the technique of interstitial implantation more or less demands palpably well-defined margins of tumor extension. Thus, some patients with stage C carcinoma suitable for external irradiation are not suitable for interstitial implantation. Cystoendoscopy is a critical examination in case selection since tumors which grossly infiltrate the trigone or extend onto the lateral or anterior bladder wall are considered unsuitable for the implantation technique. Tumor grade has not been utilized in selecting patients. Further clinical experience will undoubtedly alter present guidelines for the selection.

Patients who present with symptomatic or endoscopic evidence of significant prostatic obstruction, due either to neoplasm or to coincidental benign prostatic enlargement are a special problem. Although interstitial implantation in such patients may be expected to produce an ultimate decrease in the size of the gland, initial prostatic swelling following the procedure may produce more or less complete obstruction. In such a situation the alternatives of some form of temporary catheter drainage or of trans-urethral resection are each undesirable, the former because of the associated inconvenience, discomfort, and uncertainty regarding the degree and onset of response, and the latter because transurethral resection will disturb the geometry of the implantation and the interstitial irradiation will delay healing. Accordingly, in patients with significant obstruction, it is present policy to perform a "conservative" transurethral resection (a complete transurethral prostatectomy leaves insufficient tissue to support an implant) and to wait six to eight weeks to permit complete healing and resolution of infection before the implantation is carried out. The latter solution is by no means ideal since incomplete resections do not invariably produce satisfactory relief of obstruction and because the morbidity from incomplete resection is quite unpredictable.

Operative Exposure and Lymph Node Dissection. Operation is performed with the patient in a modified lithotomy position with the thighs flexed approximately

30 to 45 degrees on the trunk and abducted approximately 30 to 45 degrees from the central axis. A #20 F. Foley catheter is inserted under sterile precautions and connected to a closed drainage system. An O'Connor drape is utilized to facilitate digital rectal examination during the procedure. A midline incision is made from the umbilicus to the symphysis although a transverse incision could alternatively be utilized. Incision is carried into the prevesical space but the peritoneum is not opened. The bladder is bluntly mobilized posteriorly from the symphysis and from the superior pubic rami on either side out to the area of the femoral canal. The peritoneal envelope is retracted superiorly and medially from the area of the internal inguinal ring on either side, a maneuver which is facilitated by isolating and dividing the vas near the internal ring, separating the peritoneum from the spermatic vessels at this point, and then bluntly dissecting the peritoneal envelope from the iliac vessels and psoas muscles almost to the level of the aortic bifurcation. The ureter will be observed at the medial aspect of the dissection on either side, adherent to the underside of the peritoneum. This exposure permits facile dissection of the pelvic lymph nodes and, indeed, has been utilized routinely by the author for some years in the iliac phase of radical ilio-inguinal lymph node dissection. Lymph node dissection is commonly begun along the distal portion of the common iliac artery, continued distally along the external iliac vessels to Poupart's ligament, and then centripetally along the inferomedial aspect of the external iliac vein to the origin of the internal iliac artery. The contents of the obturator fossa are mobilized, preserving the obturator nerve but removing the obturator vessels and lymph nodes. With progressive dissection of the posterior pelvic wall the ramifications of the internal iliac vessels become apparent. The fat, areolar tissues, and lymph nodes are mobilized from the lateral aspects of the hypogastric vessels and their anterior ramifications, but most of the vessels are left intact, preventing dissection medial to these vessels. In early experience, the superior vesical arteries were frequently sacrificed but this did not materially improve the quality of the dissection and this practice has been abandoned. With completion of the pelvic lymph node dissection bilaterally, the endopelvic fascia is incised on either side of the prostate to permit exposure of the lateral aspects of the gland but no attempt is made to mobilize the prostate from the rectum nor are the puboprostatic ligaments divided.

Implantation. A Millin retractor is utilized to expose the prostate for implantation. Hollow, stainless steel needles, 17 gauge and 15 cm long are inserted into the prostate in a more or less anterior-posterior direction parallel to one another and approximately 1 cm apart, starting from the superior margin of the gland and proceeding inferiorly. Keeping an index finger inside the rectum against the prostate during insertion of the needles permits the tip of the needle to be sensed prior to perforation of the rectal wall. Since the implanted seeds are 4.5 mm in length, it is important to withdraw the sensed needle aproximately ½ cm so that subsequent implantation of the seeds will not result in rectal wall perforation. Although it seems inevitable that prostatic urethra and/or bladder are traversed by one or more of the needles, this has not created a recognized problem. Penetration of periprostatic veins during implantation inevitably occurs.

The dimensions of the volume to be implanted are estimated from the vertical and horizontal distances between the most peripheral needles and from the anterior posterior diameter of the gland indicated by the average actual depth to which the needles have been inserted. The average of these three dimensions multiplied by an empirically derived factor of five has been found to indicate the number of millicuries of Iodine^{125} required to deliver the planned dose within the implanted volume. This minimum effective dose is in the range of 16,000 rads in one year to 8,000 rads in two months or an equivalent single dose (ESD) of approximately 5,300 rads, calculated by the Shuttleworth and Fowler nomogram. The indicated number of millicuries divided by the average activity of the I^{125} seeds available yields the actual number of seeds required. A semi-automatic inserter is utilized to deposit the seeds at 0.5 to 1 cm intervals as each needle is successively withdrawn. When the implantation has been completed, the wound is thoroughly irrigated with water and drained through its lower angle with a single Penrose drain split at one end to permit one aspect of the drain to be directed into either obturator fossa. The wound is then closed.

The Radionuclide. The iodine^{125} has practical and theoretical advantages as the radiation source. A half life of 60 days means that loss of activity with brief periods of storage is not a practical problem. There is also the theoretical possibility that the protracted irradiation resulting from a 60 day half-life may be advantageous in the treatment of a generally slow growing neoplasm with a relatively long doubling time. The pure gamma irradiation from I^{125} reduces problems of dosimetry and provides irradiation of established therapeutic efficiency. The relatively low energy gamma irradiation (27 KEV) reduces the problems of radiation protection for personnel and also reduces the undesired irradiation outside of the implanted volume. This is epitomized by half value layers of 0.025 mm in lead and 2 cm in tissue for the irradiation for the I^{125}. The implanted seeds consist of I^{125} absorbed on two portions of ion exchange resin, separated by a gold marker (to obtain radio-opacity), and incorporated in a titanium container 4.5

mm in length and 0.75 mm in diameter, capable of being implanted through a 17 gauge needle.

Endocrine Therapy and External Irradiation. Endocrine therapy (usually estrogen) has generally been withheld until the development of symptomatic metastases although it has been transiently utilized in a few patients in an effort to reduce postoperative obstructive symptoms. The concept of combining endocrine therapy at some point with implantation has been entertained on the basis of the possibility that such endocrine therapy might progressively shrink the prostate and increase the effectiveness of the exponentially decreasing irradiation by bringing the I^{125} seeds closer together. On the other hand, the possibility has not been eliminated that such endocrine therapy might adversely influence the impact of irradiation by reducing the metabolic activity of the cancer.

The increased risk of distant metastases experienced by patients with positive lymph nodes has resulted in a trial of postoperative external irradiation through opposing Y fields extending from the diaphragm to the inguinal regions and delivering a dose of 4500 rads in about 4½ weeks with a six MEV linear accelerator. In the small group of patients treated to date no evident benefit has accrued from such treatment.

RESULTS

The Operation. The operation has been generally well tolerated and without major technical mishap. Inadvertent openings of the peritoneal cavity during mobilization of the peritoneal envelope have occurred, especially in patients who have had prior lower abdominal or inguinal incisions but have created no special morbidity.

Intraoperative blood loss has ranged from as little as 50 cc to as much as 2000 cc with a median of about 750 mls. Although bleeding may result from a lacerated obturator vessel during the course of the lymph node dissection the principal cause has been the more or less unavoidable needle damage to the retropubic venous plexus of the prostate during the course of the implantation itself. Such bleeding commonly ceases spontaneously once the needles have been removed and operative manipulation terminated.

Surgical Morbidity. Approximately two-thirds of the patients have no complications. Postoperative hospitalization has ranged from four to nineteen days and has averaged eight days. The most common surgical complication has been suprapubic wound infection, generally mild, without systemic manifestations, and not prolonging hospitalization. The drain is usually removed on the third to fifth postoperative day.

An incompletely quantitated complication has been pelvic vein thrombosis. Its pathogenesis probably rests with vascular damage to the periprostatic venous plexus associated with the implantation per se. Possibly the mild genital and pubic edema noted in many patients postoperatively is related to this event. Consideration is being given to some form of routine postoperative prophylaxis, such as low dose heparin therapy. The single hospital death encountered in an experience of over 160 patients has been from pulmonary embolism (documented by autopsy) but non fatal pulmonary embolus has probably occurred in about five percent of patients, suggesting that this may prove to be the single most important surgical complication. More significant complications such as pelvic wound infections requiring drainage, ischiorectal fossa abscess, secondary bleeding requiring reexploration and prolonged retropubic drainage have occurred in isolated instances usually explicable by some break in technique.

Almost all patients experience symptoms of urinary irritation when the urethral catheter is first removed, usually on the first postoperative day. Digital rectal examination at this time and over the next two to four months may reveal the prostate to be larger and more indurated than preoperatively, a consequence, it is believed, more of the mechanical trauma (? prostatitis) of the implantation procedure per se than of the associated irradiation. Irritative urinary symptoms are generally not severe, not associated with systemic manifestations (although urinary tract infection is often present), and generally progressively subside within three or four months of the operation.

Radiation Morbidity. Except in the few patients who have had prior full course external irradiation to the prostate, early or late symptoms clearly attributable to irradiation have been absent. No cystitis, proctitis, urethral stricture or sexual malfunction ascribable to irradiation has been documented. An occasional patient has experienced unusual prolongation of urinary irritative symptoms but never to a degree to constitute a major complaint. Although proximity of implanted seeds to the posterior urethra is a suggested explanation, this remains to be documented. Late bladder outlet obstruction resulting from bladder neck contracture and relieved by transurethral resection has occurred in a few patients but its pathogenesis, and specifically, its relation to the prior implantation is uncertain.

Clinico-pathologic Correlations. Disregarding the findings from lymphangiography approximately one fourth of patients with clinically stage B lesions and 60 percent of patients with clinically stage C lesions have lymph node metastases revealed by surgical staging. Correlations between primary tumor size or grade and such metastases have not yet been quantitated but it is clear that each correlates directly with the incidence of such metastases. Obturator lymph nodes have been the earliest and most common site of lymph node metastasis with external iliac, hypogastric, and common iliac nodes involved sequentially thereafter, but the limited nature of the lymph node dissection performed may be prejudicial to these observations.

Lymphangiograms have correlated reasonably well with the pathologic findings. Six of 55 clinically stage B lesions had a positive lymphangiogram, whereas 13 of 55 had a positive histology; 12 of 31 clinically stage C lesions had a positive lymphangiogram whereas 17 of 31 had a positive histology. The greater reliability of lymphangiography in detecting lymph node metastases in clinically stage C than in clinically stage B patients is in part a consequence of the generally more extensive metastases in the former patients and of the uncertainty of obturator lymph node filling with pedal lymphangiography.

Information on response of the primary tumor to irradiation is based primarily upon serial rectal examinations since few of the patients have had systematic biopsies. Reduction in the size and/or induration of the palpable tumor has been regarded as a favorable sign. Favorable responses were observed in more than half of the patients by the end of the first year following implantation and in 80 percent by the end of the second year. In some patients palpable prostate has virtually disappeared; in others the gland has become normal to palpation; in still others reduction in size and/or induration of the initial tumor has occurred but the gland then demonstrates no further palpable change.

Distant metastases have developed to date only in patients with high grade tumors or lymph node metastases or both. Approximately 20 percent of patients with histologically negative nodes and 60 percent of patients with histologically positive nodes have developed evidence of distant metastases within three years of implantation.

Survival data are almost meaningless in this small, selected and recent experience but amongst the 160 patients treated by this technique since February 1970, 10 of 12 who are at risk for 5 or more years are alive, with or without clinical evidence of neoplasm.

DISCUSSION

There is unequivocal evidence of the capacity of external irradiation or of interstitial irradiation to locally eradicate prostatic cancer. The frequency with which such occurs and the precise circumstances in which such an event may be anticipated are undefined, however.

Retropubic implantation of I^{125} has been employed in a relatively small and selected group of patients in the reent past and generalizations regarding its ultimate place in the therapeutic armamentarium are not currently justified. The technique permits a more or less precise concentration of irradiation in the target, minimizing undesirable side effects both inside and outside of the implanted volume as verified by the generally low surgical and radiation morbidity. Pelvic lymph node dissection has helped to define the limits of clinical staging and has provided information regarding relationships between the primary tumor grade and size, regional lymph node spread, and the development of more distant metastasis. A legitimate criticism in this experience has been the lack of systematic needle biopsy to attempt pathologic evaluation of the effects of irradiation. Quite apart from the morbidity of such biopsy and questions regarding the significance of a negative, or even of a positive biopsy, a primary concern for the quality as well as the quantity of life in the individual patient has superceded cancer cure as the end point.

Whatever may be the long term effect on the course of the prostatic cancer, this technique of I^{125} implantation has as few or fewer adverse effects on the quality of life of the prostatic cancer patient as any currently extant method of treatment.

BIBLIOGRAPHY

1. Bagshaw, M.A., Kaplan, H.S., and Sagerman, R.H.: Linear accelerator supervoltage radiotherapy. VII. Carcinoma of the prostate. Radiology 85:121–129, 1965

2. Bennett, J.E.: Treatment of carcinoma of the prostate by cobalt beam therapy. Radiology 90:532–535, 1968

3. del Regato, J. A.: Radiotherapy in the conservative treatment of operable and locally inoperable carcinoma of the prostate. Radiology 88:761–766, 1967

4. Flocks, R.H., Kerr, H.D., Elkins, H.B., and Culp D.: Treatment of carcinoma of prostate by interstitial radiation with radioactive gold: preliminary report. J Urol 68:510–522, 1952

5. George, F.W., Carlton, C.E., Dykhuizen, R.F., and Dillon, J.R.: Cobalt 60 teletherapy in definitive treatment of carcinoma of the prostate; a preliminary report. J Urol 93:102–109, 1965

6. Hilaris, Basil S., Whitmore, Willet F., Jr., Batata, Mosafa A. and Grabstald, H.: Radiation therapy and pelvic node dissection in the management of cancer of the prostate. Am J Roentgenology, Radium Therapy and Nuclear Med 121:832–838, 1974

7. Hilaris, Basil, Whitmore, W.F., Grabstald, Harry and O'Kelly, P.J.: Radical radiation therapy of cancer of the prostate: A new approach using interstitial and external sources. Clin. Bull. Memorial Sloan-Kettering Cancer Center 2:94–99, 1972

8. Shuttleworth, E., and Fowler, J.F.: Nomograms for radiobiologically equivalent fractionated x-ray doses. Br J Radiol 39:154–157, 1966

9. Whitmore, W.F., Hilaris, B. and Grabstald, H.: Retropubic implantation of iodine 125 in the treatment of prostatic cancer. J Urol 108:918–920, 1972

10. Whitmore, W.F., Hilaris, Basil, Grabstald, Harry and Batata, Mostafa: Implantation of ^{125}I in prostatic cancer. Surg Clin NA 54:887–895, 1974

11. Whitmore, Willet F., Jr.: The natural history of prostatic cancer. Cancer 32:1104–1112, Nov. 1973

Commentary:
Interstitial Irradiation for Prostatic Carcinoma

Harry W. Herr

Evidence of favorable therapeutic effects from irradiation, limitation in the applicability of surgical treatment, and possible functional advantages of irradiation over radical surgery or endocrine therapy have encouraged explorations of radiation techniques for the control of prostatic cancer. External irradiation, interstitial irradiation, or a combination of both can locally eradicate prostatic cancer. Megavoltage (>1 MeV) external irradiation may be delivered uniformly to the prostate from a cobalt 60 source or a linear accelerator. Interstitial irradiation employs radioactive sources implanted surgically within the prostate gland. In the past few years interstitial therapy has enjoyed a renaissance because of the development and availability of encapsulated radionuclides for permanent implantation. Although a number of radionuclides have been evaluated for the treatment of prostatic cancer, at present only radioactive iodine (^{125}I) and gold ([198]Au) are being used to a significant extent.

Interstitial therapy offers the opportunity to combine some of the most advantgeous aspects of surgery and irradiation in the management of selected patients with localized prostatic cancer. The foregoing article is an excellent example and describes in detail pelvic lymph node dissection and implantation of radioactive iodine seeds. This discussion will expand on the important theoretical and practical aspects of implantation techniques in general as well as update the current results of this form of therapy. I have also drawn heavily on my own experience in preparing this Commentary.

The rationale for embarking on an alternative modality of therapy for prostatic cancer is based on the collective experience (admittedly uncontrolled) of similar 10- and 15-yr survival rates for comparable stages of cancer after radical prostatectomy, megavoltage external irradiation, and hormonal manipulation. Since complications and side-effects as well as functional impairments as a result of treatment are common, the choice between these therapeutic modalities may be based on considerations of least morbidity. The major adverse effect of radical prostatectomy is almost universal impotence, and 10% to 20% of patients suffer some degree of urinary incontinence. With radical radiation therapy impotence occurs in at least 41% of patients. Although a respectable 7% develop severe bowel or urinary complications (ulceration, stenosis, fistula, or persistant incontinence) after local prostatic irradiation, the complication rate may increase dramatically to as high as 28% when both the prostate and the pelvic lymph nodes are irradiated. A primary goal of interstitial implantation techniques is to minimize the complication rate and side-effects of the therapy as well as attempt adequate local and regional control of the prostatic neoplasm.

Prostatic implantation with ^{125}I seeds or [198]Au grains seems to achieve similar local control rates (80% to 90%), and a legitimate question pertains to the relative merits of a suitable radionuclide. Several considerations enter into the choice of a radioisotope for permanent implantation. Some are practical, such as cost and availability. From the biologic point of view, however, the most important considerations are the half-life and the energy of a radionuclide. The half-life determines, together with the total activity, the dose rate and hence not only the treatment time but also the biologic effect. The energy determines the dose distribution and the protection necessary for exposed personnel. Radioisotopes may be divided into two groups, those with short half-lives, such as [198]Au (2.7 days), and those with long half-lives, such as [125]I (60 days). A long half-life radionuclide has practical and theoretic advantages as a radiation source for implantation of the prostate.

Iodine 125 seeds are widely available and are produced at a relatively low cost, and ^{125}I has a low (27 KeV) gamma energy. This provides a half-value layer in tissue of 2 cm, making ^{125}I useful for irradiation of small volumes and reducing the hazards of undesired side-effects outside the implanted volume. The rapid attenuation of irradiation within normal surrounding tissues accounts for the virtual absence of radiation symptoms in the urinary tract or rectum. The low-energy gamma radiation allows the dose to be accurately and safely adapted to an irregular tumor size and shape. The 60 day half-life of ^{125}I is theoretically attractive for irradiation of a relatively slow growing tumor with a long doubling time such as prostatic cancer.

The half-value layer in lead for ^{125}I is 0.025 mm. Thus, a 0.1-mm lead foil will reduce the irradiation from ^{125}I to less than 1%, facilitating radiation protection for personnel, the patient, and the family. The long half-life and low energy of the iodine seeds reduces problems of supply, protection, and use. The seeds may be stored for up to 1 mo without significant decrease in their activity, whereas the activity of [198]Au grains, because of a short half-life, decreases so rapidly that they must be ordered for a specific day and usually must be discarded if not used within a few days thereafter. This fact more or less limits permanent implants with [125]I Au to tumors that can be measured accurately before implantation and requires a specific order for each implant. In the future, transrectal gray-scale ultrasonography may allow accurate preoperative assessment of prostatic volume; however, it is doubtful whether this will prove more accurate than intraoperative determination of the extent of a given tumor.

Gold 198 has a high (0.41 MeV) gamma energy and a half-value layer of 2.5 mm in lead and 6 cm in tissue. These properties increase the hazards of radiation exposure of hospital personnel and, most important, limit the number of [198]Au grains implanted to less than the number required to achieve a full therapeutic dose to the prostate. Significant bladder and rectal complications, such as fistula formation, may be anticipated if a sufficient tumor dose were attempted with gold grains alone because of an unacceptable level of irradiation absorbed by normal tissues outside the implanted volume. Therefore, use of radioactive gold grains requires supplemental external irradiation. The predominant tumor nodule is implanted first with gold grains to achieve an approximate tumor dose of 2500 to 4000 rad. After a 2 to 3-wk recovery period from surgery, external beam irradiation is initiated to deliver another 4000 to 5000 rad to the prostate and immediate periprostatic area over a 30-day period to bring the total tumor dose up to 6500 to 8000 rad. A lesser dose is unlikely to eradicate prostatic cancer locally. Morbidity from this approach may be then anticipated to result from both the surgical procedure and the external irradiation. Treatment time is also prolonged. An additional disadvantage is the uncertain dosimetry achieved by a gold grain implant, whereas the dose delivered from a ^{125}I implant may be determined accurately and approaches the dose delivered from an "ideal" implant, which assumes uniform spatial distribution of the implanted iodine sources. A theoretic advantage of the combined approach is that definition of the prostatic tumor does not have to be so precisely determined or implanted with gold grains, since the supplemental external megavoltage irradiation ensures a homogeneous dose to the prostate.

The rapid falloff in radiation dose from ^{125}I outside the implanted volume has important implications for case selection. The prostatic neoplasm must be palpably distinct, well defined, and not more than 6 cm in greatest diameter or 30 cm[3] in volume. Large or poorly defined tumors are excluded because accurate and effective distribution of the ^{125}I seeds is not feasible and because of the limitation imposed by the fact that the radius of activity of ^{125}I is too small for large volumes. Patients with latent (stage A) carcinomas also are excluded because of poor geometric distribution of the seeds and subsequent inadequate dose after a complete transurethral resection. Neoplasms that cannot be appreciated clinically are difficult, if not impossible, to implant effectively, and often there is insufficient tissue remaining after surgery for presumed

benign prostatic disease to support a subsequent implant. These patients are preferably treated with megavoltage radiation therapy. Patients who present with significant symptoms of prostatic obstruction, usually a sign of more advanced disease, generally require a preliminary "conservative" transurethral resection and are implanted after a healing interval of 6 to 8 wk. However, this approach has proved less than ideal, since such patients seem to have more difficulty after an implant from irritative or obstructive urinary symptoms. For this reason, these patients are not ideal candidates for intestitial implantation and perhaps should be considered for external therapy. More recently, selected patients with locally recurrent carcinoma after megavoltge external irradiation therapy have been retreated with iodine seed or gold grain implants. Residual carcinoma may be implanted retropubically or perineally, although whether a second application of irradiation to the prostate will achieve local control remains to be seen.

The pelvic lymphadenectomy is accomplished extraperitoneally as described and emphasizes complete excision of all the obturator lymph nodes. Available data suggest that micro-metastatic deposits in several of these primary draining nodes may not have an adverse impact on subsequent distant metastases or prognosis. Experience has shown also the futility of dissecting lymph nodes above the bifurcation of the common iliac vessels. Modifications in the extent of the lymphadenectomy may be anticipated as more information of the staging value and therapeutic effectiveness becomes available.

The ^{125}I implant is preferably performed by a radiation oncologist who is trained in this technique. A medical physicist is desirable to ensure accurate dosimetry. Symmetric placement of the needles into the prostate is the most critical part of the entire procedure. Insertion of the needles not more than 1 cm apart facilitates optimal spacing of the ^{125}I seeds throughout the entire prostate and ensures a homogeneous tumor–dose distribution. A rectal finger is used to guide the depth and penetration of the needles (Fig. 2) Approximately 8 to 10 needles are placed into each lobe, a total of 15 to 20 in each prostate. The needles are placed into the seminal vesicals through the bladder neck and laterally at the prostatovesical junction. A variety of applicators used to deposit the ^{125}I seeds through the needles are commercially available. The choice of an inserter depends to some extent on the operator's skill and experience. Two to four seeds are inserted in each needle. An average of 40 to 50 seeds with an average activity of 0.5 to 0.6 mCi/seed is generally required. The number of millicuries of ^{125}I required to deliver an optimal and safe dose within the prostate is determined by the "average dimension" method as described in the preceding article. A recent modification of this method has produced a 20% increase in the minimum effective dose delivered to the margins of the tumor in an effort to improve the local control rate. Additional complications have not been encountered from this higher dose. Postoperatively, orthogonal or stereographic x-ray films of the pelvis are obtained for localization of the seeds to permit computer calculation of isodose distribution curves. Calculation of radiation dose is based on the number of seeds visualized on the film, although because of loss in the urine or tissues this is often several less than the actual number implanted. The minimum effective dose delivered to the margins of the

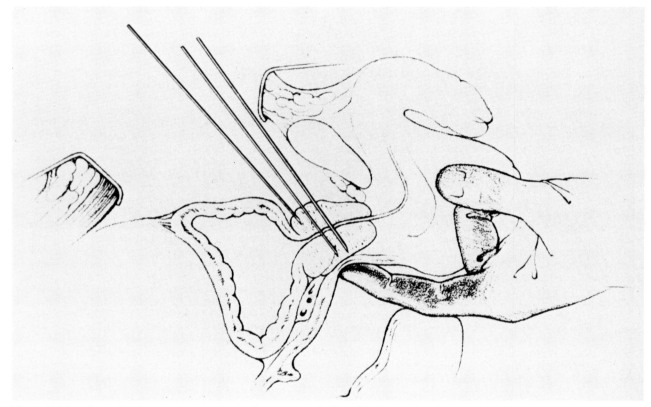

Fig. 2. With a finger in the rectum to palpate the prostate, hollow blunt-nosed 17-gauge needles are introduced retropubically through the entire substance of the gland until sensed by the palpating finger. Needles placed range from 15–20 per prostate.

prostate gland and tumor is in the range of 16,000 to 20,000 rad over 1 yr (the life of the isotope) or 8,000 to 10,000 rad in 2 mo. Larger central portions of the prostate often receive a dose equal to or greater than 32,000 rad. (Fig. 3). Local regression of the size and induration of the prostate as determined by digital rectal examination is recorded for each patient at 2- to 4-mo intervals.

The operation is generally well tolerated by the majority of patients. Hospital stay averages 5 or 6 days. Complications have generally been related to the operative procedure rather than due to the implanted irradiation *per se*. Pelvic complications include abscess, hematoma, and cellulitis and are the most common causes of postoperative morbidity. Lymphoceles and prolonged lymph drainage are generally preventable by meticulous control of lymphatic channels, especially those within the femoral canal. Many patients experience frequency and burning on urination when the catheter is first removed, which spontaneously resolves within several weeks. Prolonged rectal, vesical, and urethral sequelae have been negligible, and particularly noteworthy is the almost complete absence of proctitis. An incompletely quantitated and potentially the most serious complication has been pelvic vein thrombosis and pulmonary embolus, which probably results from penetration

of the periprostatic veins by the needles rather than as a result of the lymph node dissection. Although documented infrequently in less than 5% of patients, pulmonary emboli have been responsible for the only hospital deaths (3) reported so far in over 500 treated patients. Prophylactic anticoagulation with low-dose heparin has been employed to reduce thromboembolic phenomena; however, its protective benefit remains to be seen. Nonfatal pulmonary emboli have occurred in patients treated prophylactically with heparin. My policy is to use thigh-length support stockings, begin ambulation on the day of operation, and reserve low-dose heparin for those patients who have a history of thrombophlebitis or exhibit prominent varicose veins. About 20% of patients develop mild prepubic or genital edema, which generally resolves in 1 to 3 mo. A few patients (5%) have experienced prolonged lower extremity lymphedema, often associated with a pelvic complication. Urinary or fecal fistula formation has not been encountered. Sexual potency after ^{125}I implantation is retained in the majority (96%) of patients who were potent preoperatively. An occasional patient develops loss of ejaculation, presumably as a result of fibrosis of the ejaculatory ducts. The major complication rate after ^{125}I implantation is in the range of 2%. Similar low morbidity also has been documented after

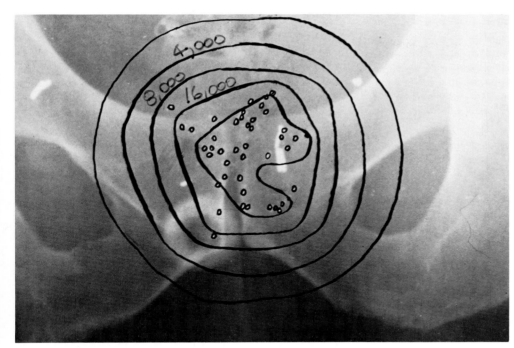

Fig. 3. Isodose curves calculated by computer. Seed distribution within the gland can be visualized and is adapted to the size and shape of the tumor. A minimum effective dose of 16,000 rads is delivered to the margins of the tumor over a 1-year period. The majority of the tumor receives up to 32,000 rads as indicated by the central isodose curve surrounding the majority of the seeds. The radiation dose falls off rapidly and the adjacent rectum absorbs approximately 30% of the minimum effective tumor dose (4800 rads over 1 year), which is well within tolerable limits.

radioactive gold grain implantation and external megavoltage irradiation, with the notable exceptions of a higher incidence of proctitis (30%) and impotence (25%).

Regional lymph node dissection has provided important information on the natural history of the disease. Lymph node metastases have been found in 10% of patients with prostatic nodules (B$_1$), 25% in those with more extensive intracapsular disease (Stage B$_2$), and 50% to 60% of patients with stage C disease. The consequences of regional metastases are well documented. Subsequent distant metastases, usually detected first in the bone, have developed to date only in patients with high-grade tumors, pelvic lymph node metastases, or both. In patients with positive nodes, bone metastases have developed in 60% within 3 yr and in 75% within 5 yr. Thus, the probability of being free of disease at 5 yr appears to be about 75% in patients with negative nodes and only about 25% in patients with positive nodes. However, the extent of regional spread is important. If patients are segregated by the amount of nodal disease, the probability of being free of cancer at 5 yr with minimal lymph node deposits is similar to that of patients with negative pelvic nodes. Minimal nodal disease is defined as a metastatic deposit less than 3 ml in volume or micrometastatic involvement of 1 to 3 lymph nodes, usually limited to the obturator area.

Response of the primary tumor to the implanted irradiation is based primarily on careful serial digital rectal examination. Reduction in the size and induration of the palpable tumor is a favorable prognostic sign. This seems to occur within 6 mo to 1 yr in 94% of patients with stage B and in 80% with stage C neoplasms. Complete regression of the palpable cancer has been noted in 50% of patients by 20 mo. Local failures, usually in those with bulky tumors, have occurred in a few (10%) patients. Local failure is judged by failure of local regression or subsequent local progression and is related to radiation dose and tumor volume. Local regrowth of carcinoma generally has been found to lie outside the implanted volume. This fact indicates improper patient selection or faulty implantation technique or both. Digital rectal examination is admittedly a crude parameter on which to measure a response, and whether local control is actually achieved by interstitial irradiation in patients with palpably regressing tumors is weakened somewhat by the lack of systemmatic postimplant prostatic biopsies. Although up to 50% of the few patients who have been biopsied at 1 yr after implant may reveal glandular elements consistent with residual carcinoma, they are often of a lesser grade and extent compared with the original pretreatment biopsy. Furthermore, biopsies in some of these same patients at 2 yr often reveal fibrosis and almost complete loss of glandular structures, which appear to be in various stages of involution. Nonetheless, any semblance of persistent carcinoma, despite its uncertain viability and biologic potential, is disturbing. Similar findings have been documented after megavoltage radiation therapy or gold grain implants, and final evaluation of the significance of these early prostatic biopsies relative to the ultimate course of a patient's disease requires longer follow-up study.

Although excellent local control may be achieved, the long-term therapeutic effects of ^{125}I implantation on the course of prostatic cancer are at present preliminary. Since the foregoing article was published, significant 5-yr survival data have become available from the Memorial Sloan-Kettering Cancer Center. However, it is important to emphasize that judgments on response and freedom from disease are based on clinical rather than pathologic criteria, and 5 yr is a relatively short follow-up period for prostatic cancer. The determinant 5-yr survival for all patients is 83% (58% tumor free). Determinant survival at 5 yr is 90% (69% tumor free) for stage B patients and 74% for stage C patients (46% tumor free). Meaningful comparison of these data with results obtained from other modalities of treatment is hazardous because of differences in patient selection.

ANNOTATED BIBLIOGRAPHY

Whitmore WF, Hilaris B, Grabstald H: Retropubic implantation of iodine 125 in the treatment of prostatic cancer. J Urol 108:918, 1972

This is the initial report of implantation of ^{125}I seeds in 26 patients with localized prostatic cancer. Staging, case selection, operative technique, implantation, and early results with this technique are described in detail. Minimal morbidity, preservation of sexual function, and an encouraging degree of local prostatic regression was noted during the brief period of follow-up study (3 to 24 mo).

Barzell W, Bean MA, Hilaris BS, et al: Prostatic adenocarcinoma: Relationship of grade and local extent to the pattern of metastases. J Urol 118:278, 1977

This report correlates clinical and pathologic tumor variables in 100 prostatic cancer patients treated by pelvic lymphadenectomy and interstitial ^{125}I implantation. The relationship of tumor size, grade, and stage was evaluated relative to the incidence and sites of metastases and the response of the primary tumor to radiation therapy. Advanced stage, large size, and poor histologic differentiation were related to a high probability of pelvic lymph node metastases. Subsequent to ^{125}I implantation, important indications of future metastases were large primary tumors, poor histologic grade, seminal vesical invasion, absence of local prostatic response to irradiation, and large volume of lymph node metastases.

Hilaris BS, Whitmore WF, Batada M, et al: Behavioral patterns of prostate adenocarcinoma following an ^{125}I implant and pelvic node dissection. Int J Radiat Oncol Biol Phys 2:631, 1977

This very important paper describes the behavioral patterns after ^{125}I implantation in 208 patients with prostatic cancer treated between February 1970 and September 1976. Age, tumor extent, size, location, and grade were correlated with mode of initial nodal involvement, subsequent recurrence, and corresponding survival patterns. A high overall frequency of lymph node metastases was documented with increasing size and extent of the primary tumor. The association of the initial lymph node status with the subsequent development of distant metastases allowed identification of three major groups of patients in terms of survival and probability of distant cancer spread. The first group consisted of patients with disease limited to the prostate gland and having negative regional nodes. The prospect of disease-free survival in this group of patients was 100% at 5 yr. The second group consisted of patients having either extraprostatic extension with negative nodes or smaller prostatic tumors with positive nodes. This group had a 90% prospect of 5-yr survival, although distant metastases developed in about 30%. The third and highest risk group included those patients with large prostatic tumors with or without extraprostatic extension and positive nodes. This group had only a 70% chance of survival at 5 yr and a much higher (50%) probability of distant metastases. This study identifies treatment failure as the result of regional metastases rather than inability to control the primary tumor. Local tumor regression proved an extremely important prognostic parameter, although this was extremely slow (up to several years). Failures documented by biopsy were observed within the first 2 yr after implantation in 8 of 111 patients (7%). Most important, the percentage of local failure rate was inversely proportional to the minimum tumor dose delivered to the gland. No failures were observed when a minimum tumor dose of 30,000 rad was delivered; a failure rate of about 10% was observed with a minimum tumor dose of about 18,000 rad; and a failure rate of over 30% was seen with a dose of less than 10,000 to 14,000 rad.

Carlton CE, Hudgins PT, Guerriero WG, et al: Radiotherapy in the management of stage C carcinoma of the prostate. J Urol 116:206, 1976

Pelvic lymphadenectomy, interstitial implantation with radioactive ^{198}Au grains, and external beam radiation therapy were employed in 109 patients with stage C prostatic cancer. Of 39 patients followed for more than 5 yr, 15 are alive without evidence of disease and 17 are alive with tumor. Seven patients died, six with tumor. Complications included proctitis (mild in 26% and severe in 4%), cystitis (mild in 34% and severe in 2%), and impotency (25%).

Overview: Interstitial Irradiation: Limitations and Concerns Remain

Gerald P. Murphy

As Dr. Whitmore has frequently said, "The silent partner in all good therapeutic results is frequently case selection." Such remains the issue today in his viewpoint and that of others in reviewing results, particularly from ^{125}I interstitial irradiation for prostatic carcinoma. Surgical techniques using this approach have been well described in concert with lymph node dissection and other considerations. It is acknowledged that the impetus for this approach was based on the anticipated and realized expectation that such therapy could be achieved with a significant reduction in impotence, incontinence, and bowel problems and the maintenance of patient satisfaction relevant to the decrease in side-effects and secondary complications. Case selection, however, usually infers that the lesion in question is within the prostate gland, has not metastasized, and is indeed a localized, circumscribed tumor nodule or volume. Diffuse lesions, as Dr. Whitmore points out, are not readily accessible to treatment by [125]I. Moreover, large-volume tumors are not appropriately treated by this technique. One can, however, point out that with a combination of external therapy and radioactive gold, perhaps some C lesions not treatable by ^{125}I may be successfully treated using the so-called Baylor technique. A valid comparison between this technique and external radiotherapy seems not to be in the context of this chapter, however. The fact that localized tumors of small volume and nondiffuse histologic patterns are the sole beneficiaries of this interstitial treatment will doubtless limit the number of patients who are eligible. Failure to appreciate this fact contributes to the lack of satisfaction with this technique in certain clinical sectors of urologic therapy throughout the United States today. Interstitial therapy without question was well used in Europe at the beginning of this century and continues to be applied with different techniques there today. There are, however, a number of factors still worthy of consideration in reviewing the success or failure of treatment with this technique. Whit-more, in the review of the Memorial experience, generally prefers not to subject patients, who have had a prior transurethral resection to selection for interstitial therapy. The fact that interstitial treatment generally precludes a posttreatment transurethral resection is perhaps self-evident and need not be commented on further. These preliminary results to the experience of carefully selected cases also must be scrutinized. Whitmore's experience has acknowledged a near 29% early complication rate and perhaps a 33% estimated late complication rate. These are not inconsequential figures but must be viewed in the context of being associated with an extensive pelvic lymph node dissection and other significant factors. That this treatment can result in significant complications is not necessarily appreciated by all and should be considered both in patient selection and in perhaps encouraging individual patient therapy. It is this area of complication that merits further follow-up study and review. Despite claims to the contrary in the text, a significant number of patients with 5-yr at-risk results are not yet available for study even in the summer of 1980. They will, however, be available shortly and to the extent that prostate cancer results for localized tumors can be discussed in a 5-yr context, surgeons will have an opportunity to compare the results from interstitial therapy at one center with that of other forms of therapy of other groups and at other centers. It will likely be some time before further comments in terms of therapeutic efficacy are available (*i.e.,* 10- and 15-yr results). These limitations should perhaps be kept in mind before unbridled acceptance of this technique and its indiscriminate application is considered. Unquestionably qualified and interested urologists are exploring its potential. That patients have been benefited currently has been documented. These limitations and concerns, however, remain before urologists and can only be resolved by careful follow-up study and review.

88

CRYOSURGERY IN PROSTATIC CANCER: ELIMINATION OF THE LOCAL LESION

William W. Bonney, M.D., Bernard Fallon, M.D., Walter L. Gerber, M.D., Charles E. Hawtrey, M.D., Stefan A. Loening, M.D., Ambati S. Narayana, M.D., Charles E. Platz, M.D., Earl F. Rose, M.D., John C. Sall, M.D., Joseph D. Schmidt, M.D., and David A. Culp, M.D.

From the Departments of Urology and Pathology, the University of Iowa and Veterans Administration Hospitals, Iowa City, Iowa.

Reprinted from Urology, Volume 22, July 1983.

ABSTRACT—From 1969 through 1976 we performed cryosurgery in 229 cases of prostatic cancer. Most of these patients had bulky, locally extensive primary tumors, and one-half had disseminated disease. Through the open perineal approach, which gives exposure for an adequate freeze, cryosurgery has been well tolerated. The primary surgical goal has been to reduce or eliminate the local lesion in order to minimize subsequent cancer-related local urinary tract problems and to cure those patients with truly localized disease. In every case cryosurgery produced dramatic shrinkage of the local lesion. After four to eight weeks a local recurrence was suspected in 13 per cent, and 41 per cent eventually had some evidence of a recurrent cancer nodule or persistent cancer in the bladder neck. In a series of statistical analyses we have related these recurrences to other clinical factors. Cryosurgery has been a safe, effective way to reduce or eliminate the primary prostatic cancer, even in patients with very large local lesions.

Many prostatic cancer patients survive long enough to experience lower urinary tract problems from the tumor. Since 1969 we have treated large stage C and other primary prostatic cancers by open perineal cryosurgery to prevent these lower urinary tract problems and to eliminate the local cancer permanently if possible. This treatment has benefitted the large majority of patients but has not always prevented local cancer recurrences.

From 1969 through 1976 at the University of Iowa and Iowa City Veterans Administration Hospitals cryosurgery was performed in 229 cases of prostatic cancer. The average patient age was 66 years. Forty-nine per cent had recognized cancer dissemination (stage D_1 or D_2 disease) at cryosurgery. Most of the stage C and many of the stage D patients had bulky primary cancers with lateral spread or extension behind the bladder to involve seminal vesicles.

This article reviews our cryosurgical technique and complications, the results of local cancer elimination, and factors associated with local recurrence.*

SURGICAL TECHNIQUE

We use a standard perineal incision and wide exposure of the gland as previously described.[2,3,4] Because cancer may infiltrate through Denonvillier's fascia to involve the rectal wall in these large local tumors, it is occasionally necessary to separate rectum from prostate by sharp dissection. Rarely, buttons of tumor remain on the anterior rectal wall. One of us (W.W.B.) has frozen these buttons without ill effect. All posterior and lateral periprostatic tissues are dissected away to expose the entire prostate and seminal vesicles to distribute a lethal freeze widely throughout the involved area.

The heat exchanger tip of the cryoprobe is inserted a few millimeters into prostatic tissue through small posterior capsular incisions or is covered by a heat conductive cap to create a broad, flat surface for topical application to the prostatic surface (Fig. 1). The ice ball then spreads across the back surface of the prostate and through its depth to the anterior side (Fig. 2). Depending upon the size and extent of the tumor, multiple overlapping freezes may be required on alternating sides and at other points in order to freeze all of the prostate and all of the local tumor (Fig. 3). Behind the bladder neck and in the seminal vesicles, tumor is frozen by surface application or by superficial incision at each site.

One of us (Bonney) has frozen remaining buttons of tumor on the anterior rectal wall without ill effect.

* A previous article[1] (based on a different but closely related data set) describes our selection of patients for cryosurgery in comparison to other treatment modalities and presents survival in relation to stage, histologic grade and therapy.

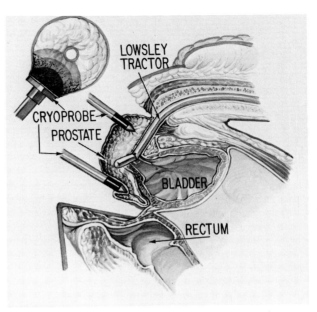

Fig. 1. Open perineal cryosurgery, sagittal view. This incision exposes the posterior capsule and seminal vesicles, where most of the cancer lies. Rounded or pointed cryoprobe inserts a few millimeters into tissue through a small capsular incision, or broad probe is applied to surface.

Digital palpation has proved a useful way to monitor the extent and control the duration of freeze (Fig. 4). The bladder wall, the distal urethra, and the external sphincter all usually remain safely outside of the freezing influence. To treat cancer infiltration at the bladder neck we continue to freeze at the prostatic base until the ice ball becomes palpable anteriorly. Freeze durations, as documented in 115 cases, have been one to nine minutes (average 3.1) for each site and two to eighteen minutes (average 6.9) total freeze.

We do not monitor or control the thaw. The cryoprobe heating element is used to free the instrument for immediate use at the next site, and tissue thawing progresses at a rate determined in part by the proximity of other ice balls. The sites overlap for complete coverage, and so some areas freeze more than once. However, systematic freeze-thaw-freeze of the same tissue was done in a few cases only. After all of the target tissues have been frozen, the Lowsley retractor is replaced with a standard catheter, and the incision is closed over one or two Penrose drains. Incisional drainage, usually enough to require three or four gauze pads a day, continues for seven to ten days.

Fig. 2. Open perineal cryosurgery. Photograph of ice ball spreading across the posterior prostatic surface after insertion of cryoprobe.

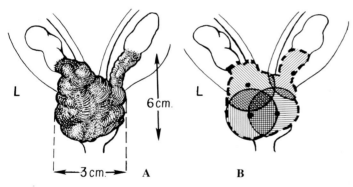

Fig. 3. (A) Locally extensive primary tumor typical of many in this series. (B) Placement of the cryoprobe in several locations for sequential, overlapping freezes to cover entire prostate and all of local tumor.

MATERIALS AND METHODS

In view of our attention to the local control of cancer, we chose the eight-year period 1969–1976 (cases done more than 2½ years prior to this review) because three quarters of the local cancer recurrences have appeared within two years of cryosurgery. Data collection involved a retrospective chart review of the 229 cryosurgery patients in both hospitals. Eleven patients were then omitted because they died in the early postoperative period from cancer-related debility (4 patients), had transitional carcinoma in the postcryosurgical prostatic biopsy (2 patients), or were not studied because the relevant records were unavailable (5 patients). The remaining 218 cases were studied with all available information (including postoperative reports from referring physicians in 22 cases) for statistically significant relationships between local cryosurgical results and various other treatment or disease-related factors in a series of 2 × 2 tables with chi-square analysis. Each table included only cases in which relevant data were available.

Data Analyses. *Histologic grade.* In most cases histologic grade was based on the initial TUR specimen or prostatic needle biopsy. Where multiple biopsies were available, however, the highest grade prevailed. For this analysis our descriptive grading system has been simplified into two categories, well and poorly differentiated.

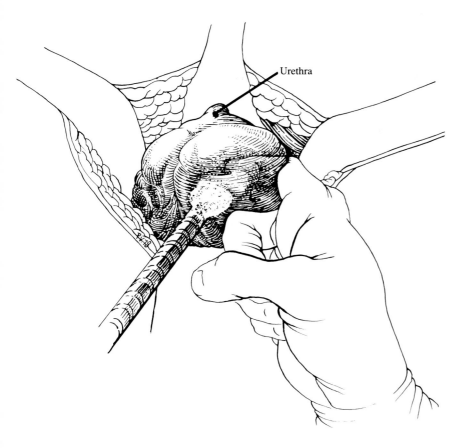

Urethra

Fig. 4. With this exposure surgeon can palpate ice ball as it approaches anterior capsule, urethra, or bladder neck and in this way can monitor extent of freeze.

Tumor Stage. In this study of local cryosurgery effects, primary tumor spread to adjacent tissues has been described in anatomic terms (locally extensive, seminal vesicle involvement, etc.). The classical stages A to D have been used for degree of dissemination.

Local Cancer Recurrence. This term implies persistence of the original primary cancer, incompletely killed by cryosurgery. We have seen two types: (1) postoperative bladder neck obstruction with cancer in the surgical specimen, and (2) early persistent or late recurrent palpable nodule.

Voiding symptoms or urinary retention prompted each postcryosurgical TUR, with the diagnosis of bladder neck recurrence if the chips were positive. (We recognize that obstruction was often due to associated periurethral and vesical neck hyperplasia, but wish nonetheless to report every case of persistent cancer in the post cryosurgical tissues.) Some specimens contained no cancer. Our report has included positive TUR specimens taken any time after cryosurgery, although they have questionable significance before one month.[6]

Each palpable, progressive nodule was regarded as cancer and considered biopsy-proven if positive tissue was obtained by either needle biopsy or concurrent TURP. In fact, among 39 needle biopsies of such nodules, 38 were positive while one contained only scar tissue. In summary, tissue was always obtained on clinical indication, never as a "routine" biopsy.

Size of Primary Mass. Traditionally we have recorded prostatic size on a 0–4 + scale, zero being an essentially normal prostate and 4 + an enormous mass with rectal encroachment or pelvic wall fixation. For analysis purposes each patient has been assigned to either of two categories: smaller tumors 0–1 + and larger tumors 2–3 + . There were no 4 + tumors in this series.

Ureteral Obstruction. This diagnosis was based on intravenous urogram (IVP) done immediately before cryosurgery and at variable intervals after surgery. This allowed us to detect postoperative obstruction from any cause and to judge its presence before surgery.

RESULTS

At the four- to eight-week examination cryosurgery had eliminated all palpable prostatic tissue and local cancer in 144 patients (66%). Despite a dramatic reduction in size there was a persistent nodule or suspect induration in 28 patients (13%) and insufficient information in another 46 (21%). During the subsequent follow-up period 103 patients (47%) remained free of local cancer, 89 (41%) eventually had some form of local recurrence (bladder neck or palpable nodule), and there was insufficient information in another 26 (12%).

The Persistent Nodule. At four to eight weeks the rectal examination was a good predictor of whether the patient would have subsequent palpable tumor regrowth (Table 1) but did not correlate with cancer in the postcryosurgical TUR bladder neck specimens. We found a positive correlation between large size of the original primary tumor and persistence of palpable tissue at the four- to eight-week examination. However, the persistent nodule did not correlate with duration of freeze or histologic grade.

The Recurrent Cancer Nodule. Of 192 patients evaluable beyond eight weeks there were biopsy-proved recurrent cancer nodules in 42 (22%), unconfirmed nodules (assumed to be cancer) in 16 (8%), and freedom from palpable local cancer in 134 (70%). There was no correlation between the recurrent nodule and histologic grade. Nodule appearance times were scattered throughout the follow-up period with similar distribution in both histologic grades. There was also no correlation between the recurrent nodule and the size of the primary tumor or the duration of freeze.

Postoperative Bladder Neck Obstruction With Cancer in TUR Specimen. Of 192 evaluable patients 114 (59%) voided without difficulty after cryosurgery while seventy-nine (41%) had voiding symptoms. The latter group included 54 with positive TUR tissue two months or more after cryosurgery, 6 with positive tissue at less than one month, 12 with BPH or inflammatory tissue only, and 6 treated with catheter only. In summary, of these 192 patients 62 (32%) had biopsy-proved cancer in the bladder neck and prostatic urethra after cryosurgery. One of us (C.E.H.) has observed that the positive TUR chips usually come from the anterior bladder neck.

In contrast to the palpable nodule, recurrent bladder neck cancer did correlate with poorly differentiated histology (Table 2). The time of recurrence, however, was similar with both histologic types.

Postoperative bladder neck cancer did not correlate with the size of the primary tumor or with the duration of freeze. In 1 patient a squamous carcinoma was found in the postoperative bladder neck. We draw no conclusions from this case but note that squamous metaplasia has been seen following cryosurgery.[6]

TABLE 1. Early Persistent Nodule vs. Late Recurrent Cancer Nodule[a]

Late Recurrent Cancer Nodule[b]	Prostatic Fossa at 4–8 Weeks	
	Persistent Nodule	Empty Fossa
Yes	20 (67%)	35 (26%)
No	10 (33%)	102 (74%)
	30 (100%)	137 (100%)

[a] Total evaluable patients 167.
[b] X^2 significant at 1% level for positive correlation between persistent early nodule and palpable late recurrent cancer nodule.

TABLE 2. Postoperative Bladder Neck Recurrence vs. Histological Grade[a]

Bladder Neck Recurrence[b]	Histological Pattern	
	Well or Mod. Well Differentiated	Poorly Differentiated or Undifferentiated
Yes	20 (25%)	37 (47%)
No[c]	61 (75%)	42 (53%)
	81 (100%)	79 (100%)

[a] Total evaluable patients 160.
[b] X^2 significant at 5% level for positive correlation between poorly differentiated pattern and bladder neck recurrence.
[c] Includes 11 patients with benign tissue only in TUR specimen.

Hormone treatment. Bilateral orchiectomy and/or estrogen therapy were used at some point in 168 cryosurgery cases (Table 3). In 57 cases it was possible to evaluate the local prostatic effect of cryosurgery alone because hormone treatment was withheld entirely or until a local recurrence had been detected; of these, 35 (61%) did eventually have a local recurrence. The remaining 135 evaluable cases received hormone treatment before, with, or soon after cryosurgery; 54 (40%) had a local recurrence. There is a significant difference between the two groups at the 1-per cent level.

Postoperative ureteral obstruction. Of 116 evaluable patients, 28 (24%) had postoperative ureteral obstruction. As one might expect, there was a strong correlation between postoperative obstruction and preoperative obstruction (by cancer). There was, however, no correlation with hormone treatment, histologic grade, the size of the primary tumor mass, or duration of freeze.

Surgical complications. Thirty-four patients had postoperative incontinence, usually mild (Table 4). There were 3 cryosurgery patients with stress incontinence after subsequent TUR and 1 with temporary stress incontinence associated with a temporary perineal fistula. Two patients had initial good control but noted subsequent spontaneous onset of stress incontinence and other voiding symptoms, respectively, two years and four years after cryosurgery.

TABLE 3. Timing of Hormone Treatment in Relation to Cryosurgery (CS) and Local Recurrence*

Local Cancer Recur.	Before CS	With CS‡	Hormone Treatment† 1 Mo to 2 yr After CS		Hormone Treatment >2 Yr After CS (After Recur.)	No Hormone Treatment
			Before Recur.	After Recur.		
Palpable nodule	8	6	2	4	2	5
Bladder neck	7	9	0	8	1	6
Both types	14	7	1	4	3	2
Total local recur. (%)	29 (41)	22 (39)	3 (38)	16 (100)	6 (100)	13 (37)
None§	42	34	5	. .	. .	22
Totals	71	56	8	16	6	35
No info.‖	7	3	1	. .	0	1

 * Total patients: evaluable 192, displayed 218.
 † Orhiectomy and/or estrogens.
 ‡ During cryosurgery or within a month.
 § Includes postcryosurgery TUR negative for cancer.
 ‖ Includes postcryosurgery obstruction treated by catheter only, 6 patients. No postcryosurgery treatment information available in 14 patients.

Both cases had local cancer recurrence. Twenty-eight additional patients (13% of the total series) had immediate incontinence related to cryosurgery. One patient needed a permanent collecting device and another upper tract diversion; all the others had mild, often temporary stress or urge incontinence that required no treatment. Taken altogether, this incontinence did correlate with preoperative TURP. There was no correlation with histologic grade, size of the primary tumor, duration of freeze, or recurrent local cancer.

Other complications included early death from cancer-related debility in 2 cases. Urinary fistula formation was usually attributed to tissue cryodestruction, but other recognized factors included penetration of the urinary tract with a biopsy knife, a pointed cryoprobe, or the wing of a Lowsley retractor in at least 3 cases. Two of the urinary fistulas were vesicocutaneous, the remainder urethrocutaneous. In addition to the postoperative rectal fistulas there were 2 more patients in whom rectal incision was recognized and closed primarily without adverse sequelae. Fecal incontinence of moderate degree was associated with early postoperative perineal abscess in 2 cases. Incisional abscess often heralded the appearance of a fistula but was otherwise seen in 3 cases, due at least once to failure to replace Penrose drains lost before incisional drainage had stopped.

COMMENT

Our department has traditionally been aggressive in the surgical management of the primary prostatic cancer, as illustrated by the treatment selected for patients of various stages.[1] With cryosurgery we have extended safe, effec-

TABLE 4. Operative Complications of Cryosurgery

Complications and Treatment	No. of Patients	
	Subtotal	Total
Urinary incontinence		34
Mild stress incontinence no treatment	32	
Permanent collecting device	1	
Upper tract diversion	1	
Death 7 and 30 days, from cancer		2
Urinary fistula		17
Catheter only, 30 days or less	11	
Catheter only, 5 weeks to 9 months	4	
Fistula excision or curettage	2	
Rectal fistula		2
Colostomy (cutaneous fecal fistula)	1	
Spontaneous closure (urethrorectal fistula)	1	
Fecal incontinence		5
Colostomy	1	
Temporary, with urinary incontinence	1	
Moderate, permanent	3	
Incisional abscess without fistula		3
Urethral stricture		3
Epididymitis		2
Thrombophlebitis		2
Acute myocardial infarction		1

tive treatment to additional patients otherwise excluded from surgery by virtue of large local lesions or suboptimal medical condition.

The open perineal approach suits these purposes well. It is tolerated even by elderly patients, who generally ambulate and resume a normal diet within 24–48 hours. By direct exposure of the posterior capsule and seminal vesicles we concentrate the greatest freezing intensity onto the usual cancer sites. With the prostate isolated we can freeze the entire gland through to the anterior surface. By direct visualization and palpation we can limit the ice ball to protect the urethra and urogenital diaphram. These tissues also enjoy a certain degree of intrinsic protection because of their rich blood supply and consequent source of heat. The low incidence of surgically induced ureteral compromise suggests that the trigone is usually spared for similar reasons.

We found more local recurrence in delayed hormone treatment than in concurrent or prior-continuous treatment (Table 3 and related text). Early hormone treatment may actually prevent or postpone local recurrence, being perhaps effective against the rapid regeneration of tumor after a nonlethal freeze. From our experience in patients with hormone treatment delayed or withheld, however, it is clear that cryosurgery alone can shrink effectively even the largest local lesion and the prostate down to nothing or to a tiny fraction of its pretreatment volume. This dramatic immediate postoperative effect is not attributable to hormone treatment.

In our data there is no single factor that might account for an incomplete freeze and consequent failure to eliminate the local tumor. There is no correlation with preoperative size of the primary tumor or with duration of freeze. Patients with recurrence are about equally divided among palpable nodule, bladder neck obstruction, and both. Within a given gland there might easily be multiple sites spared a lethal freezing condition. At the same time, since we apply the greatest freezing intensity to the posterior surface, we might have expected fewer palpable nodules and more bladder neck recurrences. All of this probably means that the local tissue conditions needed for a lethal freeze are determined by many factors.

For comparative local recurrence data it is difficult to find a series of radical prostatectomy patients comparable to our cryosurgery experience. We selected patients in part on the basis of bulky, locally extensive primary tumors; whereas in many prostatectomy series the histologic Stage C cancers were originally chosen for surgery as clinical Stage B lesions. For comparative purposes, however, we have collected some data from the literature (Table 5). Schroeder and Belt[7] and Tomlinson, Currie, and Boyce[8] included clinical Stage C patients, but the patients all had surgically resectable glands. Flocks[9] used partial or total prostatectomy with extensive cautery and adjuvant interstitial radiation in clinical Stage C patients who had failed hormone therapy. Many of these patients were not surgically resectable by usual standards and may provide a comparable albeit historic control series done years ago.

As another comparative treatment, external radiation therapy resembles cryosurgery in several regards. Both are cytodestructive physical modalities locally applied to the cancer and the adjacent normal tissue, which remain in situ to undergo subsequent necrosis and reorganization. At the periphery of the field in both modalities there lies a zone of intermediate or marginal effectiveness, which must be considered in setting the radiation field[10,11] or deciding where to stop the progress of the ice ball. In cryosurgery, early experimental investigation[12] described normal dog prostate regeneration from ducts and glands at the margin of the cryolesion. Again for comparative purposes we have collected data from the literature (Table 5). Bagshaw et al.[13] followed their large series of patients with rectal examination while Nachtsheim et al.[14] performed routine serial prostatic biopsies, withholding estrogen treatment in all cases until a positive biopsy had been obtained. In many patients there appeared to be continued tumor necrosis with reversion of biopsies from positive to negative until eighteen months after treatment. With routine biopsies

TABLE 5. Local Recurrence Rate after Various Treatment Modalities

Reference	Clinical Stage	Treatment		Local Recurrence %
		Primary	Hormone	
Schroeder and Belt[7]	B	Radial prostatectomy	No	6.8
	C	Radial prostatectomy	Yes	12.7
Tomlinson et al.[8]	C	Radical prostatectomy	Yes (43%)	4.3
	C	(No surgery)	Yes (90%)	75.0
Flocks[9]	C	Radical prostatectomy with cautery and interstitial radiation	Yes	4.3
Bagshaw et al.[13]	B, C	External radiation	Unknown	11.0
Nachtsheim et al.[14]	B, C	External radiation	No	45.0
Cosgrove and Kaempf[15]	—	(No radiation)	Yes	64.0
		External radiation	No	56.0
		External radiation	Yes	29.0
Bonney et al.[a]	B, C, D	Cryosurgery	Yes (82%)	41.0

[a] Distribution of cases by classical stage: B (5%), C (46%), D (49%).

performed on small patient groups Cosgrove and Kaempf[15] reported recurrence rates at one year or earlier. They emphasized the discrepancies between biopsy results and findings on rectal examination.

Still another potential control group might be patients treated conservatively with endocrine therapy and TUR. Unfortunately, these reports seldom include detailed information about local tumor progression and related complications. Finally, the most obvious source of potential comparative information might be previous reports of cryosurgery for prostatic cancer. Unfortunately, these reports have contained little detailed, statistically evaluable data about local recurrence.

Among patients with ureteral obstruction noted for the first time after cryosurgery, only 2 appeared to be early surgical complications while the remaining 13 appeared late in association with recurrent cancer. In 11 additional patients there was unmistakable preoperative cancer-related ureteral obstruction persisting after cryosurgery.

To reduce local recurrence rate some modifications should be considered in cryosurgical technique. Regardless of site, each recurrence presumably represents cancer which was inadequately frozen or perhaps never included in the ice ball. Particularly in the posterior capsule and the seminal vesicles, so well exposed by our approach, it may be possible to apply the freezing influence in a more uniform way by the use of thermistor monitors similar to those used in cryosurgery of skin cancer.[16] Some of the palpable nodules arise lateral to the urethra or behind the pubis and therefore possibly represent cancer originally in the periprostatic tissues, swept away from the prostate during its exposure and not included in the freeze. Perhaps these areas could be searched and spot-frozen more thoroughly. In regard to the bladder neck recurrences, perhaps routine cystoscopy at the time of cryosurgery would clarify the tumor distribution in cases with anterior bladder neck infiltration. The freezing influence might better penetrate the bladder neck with replacement of the metal Lowsley retractor by a less heat-conductive catheter, replacement of bladder urine by air for the same reason, and possibly consideration of a concurrent transurethral freeze (a consideration to be approached very cautiously because of the multiple additional factors it might bring).

CONCLUSION

In this series of patients, many with locally extensive prostatic cancer, cryosurgery effectively and safely has reduced or elminated the primary tumor in all cases with subsequent freedom from cancer-related lower urinary tract problems in the majority. However, despite the combined efforts of cryosurgery and hormone treatment, recurrent local cancer required further treatment in many cases. We have suggested modifications of the cryosurgical technique, which might help to reduce this incidence. As cryobiology advances there will be better ways to monitor and control the tumoricidal effects of cryosurgery. Hopefully, there will be more information about local cancer elimination in future reports, particularly those that concern cryosurgery.

Department of Urology
University of Iowa Hospitals
Iowa City, Iowa 52240
(DR. BONNEY)

Acknowledgment. To Mr. Stan Johnson for help in hospital chart review, Dr. William Clarke for review of the statistical methods, Mrs. Mary McBride for manuscript preparation, and Mr. Paul VerVais for original illustrations.

REFERENCES

1. Bonney WW, *et al*: Cryosurgery in prostatic cancer: survival, Urology 19:37 (1982)
2. Flocks RH, Nelson CMK, and Boatman DL: Perineal cryosurgery for prostatic carcinoma, J Urol 108:933 (1972).
3. Schmidt JD: Cryosurgical prostatectomy, Cancer 32:1141 (1973).
4. O'Donoghue EPN, *et al*: Cryosurgery for carcinoma of prostate, Urology 5:308 (1975).
5. Whitemore WF, Jr.: Symposium on hormones and cancer therapy: hormone therapy in prostatic cancer. Am J Med 21:697, 1956
6. Peterson DS, *et al*: Biopsy and clinical course after cryosurgery for prostatic cancer, J Urol 120:308 (1978).
7. Schroeder FH, and Belt E: Carcinoma of the prostate: a study of 213 patients with Stage C tumors treated by total perineal prostatectomy, *ibid* 114:257 (1975)

8. Tomlinson RL, Currie DP, and Boyce WH: Radical prostatectomy: palliation for Stage C carcinoma of the prostate, *ibid* 117:85 (1977).
9. Flocks RH: The treatament of Stage C prostatic cancer with special reference to combined surgical and radiation therapy, *ibid* 109:461 (1973).
10. Jones H, and Cunningham J: Physics of Radiology, 3rd Ed. Charles C Thomas, Springfield, Illinois, 1969, pp. 122–4, 350, 357–8, 438–40.
11. Hendee W: Medical Radiation Physics, Yearbook Medical Publishers, Chicago, Illinois, 1973, pp 106–8.
12. Gonder MJ, Soanes WA, and Smith V: Experimental prostate cryosurgery, Invest Urol 1:610 (1964).
13. Bagshaw MA, *et al*: External beam radiation therapy of primary carcinoma of the prostate, Cancer 36:723 (1975).

14. Nachtsheim DA Jr, McAninch JW, Stutzman RE, and Goebel JL: Latent residual tumor following external radiotherapy for prostate adenocarcinoma, J Urol 120:312 (1978).
15. Cosgrove MD, and Kaempf MJ: Prostatic cancer revisited, *ibid* 115:79 (1976).

16. Zacarian SA; Cryosurgical Advances in Dermatology and Tumors of the Head and Neck, Springfield, Illinois, Charles C Thomas, 1977, chap I.

Commentary: Cryosurgery for Prostatic Carcinoma

William W. Bonney

Cryosurgery is a promising and interesting physical modality, similar in some ways to radiation therapy in its application to cancer. Its only proven therapeutic effect involves reduction or elimination of the local cancer mass under treatment.

LOCAL TISSUE EFFECTS

Early experiments showed clearly the destruction of normal prostatic tissue, with healing by fibrosis and regeneration of prostatic ducts in adjacent, partially frozen tissue.[1] In cases of cryosurgery for benign prostatic hypertrophy, postoperative bladder neck biopsies have shown early liquefaction necrosis with gradual appearance of granulation tissue and ultimate healing by fibrosis a month or so later.[2]

In cryosurgery of cancer, the local tissue events are perhaps less well understood. Freezing has a dual effect, killing some cells while preserving the viability of others.[3] Controlled animal experiments have shown a better local cancer cure rate with colder probe temperatures and with repeated freezing.[4] After open perineal cryosurgery for prostatic cancer, postoperative bladder neck biopsies have suggested that the local cancer gradually disappears as the cryolesion evolves and heals.[5]

RATIONALE

In cryosurgery of prostatic cancer there are two desired results: (1) the local reduction or elimination of cancer, with subsequent freedom from the problems caused by progressive local cancer growth, and (2) possible improvement in survival.

Local Cancer Reduction. Cryosurgery can help patients with locally extensive cancer (local stage C, with or without disseminated disease). Prostatic cancer often grows progressively in the urethra and bladder neck area to cause urinary obstruction, hematuria with clot retention, and occasional rectal compromise. Cryosurgery can alleviate these problems and minimize or prevent their subsequent appearance in the majority of patients.

Survival Effects. In localized disease (stage A_2, B, or C) successful local cancer elimination also means cure. For good surgical candidates a total prostatectomy would be the preferable surgical treatment because the cure rate is predictable in accurately staged patients.[6,7] For less robust operative candidates, however, cryosurgery may offer a chance for cure through a well-tolerated operation with minimal risk of fistula or incontinence.

The University of Iowa and Iowa City Veterans Administration cryosurgery series has been analyzed for postoperative survival.[8] As might be expected, survival had an inverse relationship to tumor stage at the time of cryosurgery (Table 6).

In a large subseries of the same patients,[8] survival was analyzed by tumor stage at diagnosis in a comparison of cryosurgery, radical prostatectomy, and other (nonsurgical) treatment modalities (Fig. 5). In all treatment groups most patients had prior transurethral resection of the prostate, generally before referral to our center. Tumor stage had progressed by the time cryosurgery was considered in many patients. The predominant trend was to manage localized tumors by radical prostatectomy and more advanced tumors by cryosurgery, with conservative measures used as solitary treatment whenever surgery was not a reasonable consideration.

TABLE 6. Survival versus Stage*,†

Patient Status	Classic Tumor Stage			
	B, No. (%)	C, No. (%)	D_1, No. (%)	D_2, No. (%)
Dead of Cancer‡				
1 mo–2 yr		13 (14)	6 (28)	25 (33)
2–5 yr		11 (12)		15 (20)
Dead of other causes	3 (30)	16 (18)	2 (10)	19 (26)
Alive 2 to 8 yr	7 (70)	50 (56)	13 (62)	16 (21)
Total	10 (100)	90 (100)	21 (100)	75 (100)

* Total evaluable patients, 196. Chart review data from University of Iowa and Veterans Administration Hospitals.
† From Bonney and colleagues.[9]
‡ X² significant at 1% level for positive correlation between B and C stages and survival 2 to 8 yr and between D stages and cancer death.
(Bonney WW, Fallon B, Gerber WL et al: Cryosurgery in prostatic cancer: Survival. Urology 19:37, 1982)

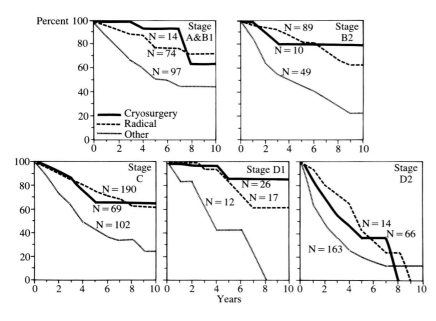

Fig. 5. Probability of survival (%) by years after surgery (cryosurgery or radical prostatectomy) or years after referral to the medical center (other). (Bonney WW, Fallon B. Gerber WL et al: Cryosurgery in prostatic cancer: Survival. Urology 19:37, 1982)

In the graphic presentation of survival data (Fig. 5) the cryosurgery patients have a probability of survival equal to that seen in the total prostatectomy patients of each stage. This appears to represent a true treatment effect. In every stage the cryosurgery and total prostatectomy groups are similar in regard to the percentage dying of prostatic cancer of other causes. Furthermore, the survival similarity is not due to selection of similar patients. We have always recommended cryosurgery to patients with more advanced stage of disease and to patients with larger local lesions within each clinical stage. The cryosurgery patients were generally 2 to 5 yr older than those in the total prostatectomy group. In addition, the similarity is not likely to be due to orchiectomy or estrogen, since we applied hormone therapy equally among the treatment groups in each stage. Altogether, cryosurgery and radical prostatectomy patients have similar postoperative survival despite an apparently poorer prognosis in the cryosurgery group (although a 5-yr average follow-up period in insufficient for firm conclusions).

SURGICAL APPROACHES

Prostatic cancer characteristically begins under the posterior capsule. From this point it spreads locally in all directions and may form a plaque behind the bladder neck or invade the seminal vesicles before it erodes into the urethra. Cryosurgery basically employs two approaches to this cancer.

Transurethral cryosurgery was first applied in cases of benign prostatic hypertrophy, an abnormality of the periurethral glands. In order to control the extent of ice ball formation the surgeon positions the active freezing element carefully within the prostatic urethra and distends the bladder with air to eliminate heat-conductive urine and allow the trigone to fall away from the probe. By rectal palpation he can then monitor the ice ball and decide when to stop. The transurethral approach brings certain advantages. Even the elderly or critically ill patient can tolerate the procedure well. It requires no incision, and the surgeon can even use local anesthesia. For the local elimination of cancer, however, the disadvantages include the lack of prostatic thermal isolation. It may prove difficult to freeze the capsule because surrounding tissues bring in heat and because the posterior capsule may lie some distance from the urethral cryoprobe if the patient also has a benign adenoma. For similar reasons the ice ball may not reach cancer behind the bladder or within the seminal vesicles. The present literature has little information about successful cancer eradication or local recurrence rate with cryosurgery by this route.

In *open perineal cryosurgery* the cryoprobe is applied directly to the posterior capsule and to any other local cancer in the area (cryosurgery by this route would therefore theoretically not be applicable to benign prostatic hypertrophy). The surgeon monitors the extent of freeze and controls its duration by direct observation and palpation of the ice ball. The major advantage of this approach is the wide, direct exposure. The prostate is thermally isolated except for its urethral and bladder neck attachments and its anterior surface. The cryoprobe can apply its greatest intensity directly on the tumor and can reach all the local cancer extension. The average patient tolerates this operation very well, ambulates within 1 or 2 days of surgery, and soon resumes micturition with very little risk of incontinence. However, the anesthesia and the extreme lithotomy position prove too much for some fragile patients who could otherwise tolerate cryosurgery by the transurethral route. The local cancer recurrence rate has been documented after cryosurgery by this route.[9] Obstructive postoperative bladder neck cancer presumably reflects inadequate penetration of cold to the periurethral area, a problem that may respond to proposed surgical modification.

In order to combine the best features of each approach, a

percutaneous trochar cryoprobe has been used.[10] Follow-up clinical results were not available at this writing, but theoretic advantages include avoidance of an incision, the ability to use local anesthesia, and a direct approach to the posterior prostatic capsule. Theoretic disadvantages include the inability to stage the local lesion accurately, to isolate the prostate thermally, to observe the extent of the ice ball directly, and to provide a free route of egress for the sloughing tissue (see below).

SURGICAL COMPLICATIONS

Obviously, cryosurgery causes *in situ* tissue necrosis. The body may resorb some of this, but a certain amount of drainage and tissue slough clearly might be expected. After transurethral cryosurgery the frozen tissue may bleed or drain into the urine for some time or separate into the bladder as a chunk that requires extraction. In open perineal cryosurgery the incisional drainage may continue for 7 to 14 days, and removal of the Penrose drain before the cessation of drainage may result in a wound abscess.

Another inherent potential problem is the uncontrolled or undetected spread of the freezing influence to harm adjacent normal structures by either surgical approach. The external urethral sphincter may sustain damage if the transurethral cooling element should lie in the membranous urethra during the freeze. A readily palpable button makes it easy to position the cryoprobe safely beyond the external sphincter, but it may be more difficult to judge the extent of the bladder neck freeze and stop before trigone involvement. In order to monitor these events more closely, Reuter has introduced a trochar cystoscope by the closed or "punch" suprapubic technique.[11]

A urethral fistula may develop after a thorough prostatic freeze, particularly in the open perineal approach, becaue of the surgical exposure and the shallow capsular incisions frequently used for biopsy or probe placement. In addition, certain complications are unique to each type of surgical approach (*e.g.*, stricture after urethral manipulation, impotence and, rarely, permanent urinary or fecal incontinence after perineal exposure).

IMMUNOLOGIC AUGMENTATION

Several early clinical reports noted the apparent spontaneous regression of prostatic cancer metastasis following cryosurgery of the primary tumor.[12] Subsequent experience has not confirmed the observation. In experiments with a highly antigenic animal tumor, cryosurgery has induced *in vitro* cell-mediated immunity against the tumor cells.[13] However, there is no present evidence to show that human prostatic cancer has similar antigenic properties. Furthermore, there is conflicting evidence about the degree of underlying immunologic impairment seen in patients with disseminated prostatic cancer. For the present I must withhold judgment about this aspect of cryosurgery.

CONCLUSIONS AND PROSPECTS

Cryosurgery offers much to the prosatic cancer patient as a well-tolerated way to eliminate the local lesion or to control its complications. It can effectively serve patients with stage B, C, or D cancer. The major benefit stems from its ability to kill the local cancer cells. Further technical refinements should improve the reliability of complete local cancer elimination:[9] At that point cryosurgery may well compete favorably with total prostatectomy as a way to cure the cancer with less risk of incontinence and anastomotic fistulae in the stage A or B patient.

These technical refinements will depend in part on an improved basic understanding of the physical parameters needed to maximize cell killing in cryosurgery. Preliminary work has been done by systematic tissue temperature measurements in experimental tumors, skin tumors, and prostate, and by the use of double simultaneous cryoprobes in cryosurgery for prostatic cancer.[4,14,15,*] Even in deep tissues such as prostate, impedance may prove superior to thermocouple measurements.[16] Another promising development involves "cryocautery," with incorporation of an augmented heating element in the cryoprobe for intensive, cyclic tissue freezing and warming.[17]

* Bonney WW: Unpublished data.

REFERENCES

1. Gonder MJ, Soanes WA, Smith V: Experimental prostatic cryosurgery. Invest Urol 1:610, 1964

2. Hansen RI, Wanstrup J: Cryoprostatectomy: Histological changes elucidated by serial biopsies. Scand J Urol Nephrol 7:100, 1973

3. Farrant J: Cryobiology: The basis for cryosurgery. In Von Leden H, Cahan WG (eds): Cryogenics in Surgery, pp 15–41. Garden City, NY, Medical Examination Publishing Company, 1971

4. Neel HB III, Ketcham AS, Hammond WG: Requisites for successful cryogenic surgery of cancer. Arch Surg 102:45, 1971

5. Petersen DS, Milleman LA, Rose EF, et al: Biopsy and clinical course after cryosurgery for prostatic cancer. J Urol 120:308, 1978

6. Jewett HJ: The present status of radical prostatectomy for stages A and B prostatic cancer. Urol Clin North Am 2:105, 1975

7. Schroeder FH, Belt E: Carcinoma of the prostate: A study of 213 patients with stage C tumors treated by total perineal prostatectomy. J Urol 114:257, 1975

8. Bonney WW, Fallon B, Gerber WL, et al: Cryosurgery in prostatic cancer: Survival. Urology 19:37, 1982

9. Bonney WW, Fallon B, Gerber WL, et al: Cryosurgery in prostatic cancer: Elimination of the local lesion. Urology, July/August 1983

10. Megalli MR, Gursel EO, Veenema RJ: Closed perineal cryosurgery in prostatic cancer. Urology 4:220, 1974

11. Reuter HJ: Cryosurgery in urology. In Von Leden H, Cahan WG (eds): Cryogenics in Surgery, pp 411–470. Garden City, NY, Medical Examination Publishing Company, 1971

12. Jones LW: Cryosurgery for prostatic carcinoma. Urology 4:499, 1974

13. Bagley DH, Faraci RP, Marrone JC, et al: Lymphocyte mediated cytotoxicity after cryosurgery of a murine sarcoma. J Surg Res 17:404, 1974

14. Zacarian S: Cryosurgical techniques. Presented at the American College of Cryosurgery, June 15, 1979

15. Bonney WW: Tissue temperature in cryosurgery of prostatic cancer. (in preparation)

16. Le Pivert PJ, Binder P, Ougier T: Measurement of intratissue bioelectrical low frequency impedance: A new method to predict peroperatively the destructive effect of cryosurgery. Cryobiology 14:245, 1977

17. Keller AJ: Cryocautery of the prostate. Presented at the American College of Cryosurgery, June 16, 1979

ANNOTATED BIBLIOGRAPHY

Gonder MJ, Soanes WA, Smith V: Experimental prostate cryosurgery. Invest Urol 1:610, 1964

Early cryosurgery experiments on normal dog prostate are discussed. Resulting tissue necrosis with subsequent healing by scar formation and regeneration of prostatic glands from adjacent, partially frozen tissue are described.

Hansen RI, Wanstrup J: Cryoprostatectomy. Histological changes elucidated by serial biopsies. Scand J Urol Nephrol 7:100, 1973

Evolution of the cryolesion through liquifaction necrosis to healing by fibrosis after cryosurgery in benign prostate hypertrophy is discussed.

Petersen DS, Milleman LA, Rose EF, et al: Biopsy and clinical course after cryosurgery for prostatic cancer. J Urol 120:308, 1978

Residual cancer cells and evolving histological change after cryosurgical destruction of the primary prostatic cancer are discussed.

Farrant J: Cryobiology: The basis for cryosurgery. In Von Leden J, Cahan WG (eds): Cryogenics in Surgery, pp 15–41, Garden City, NY, Medical Examination Publishing Company, 1971

A very clear statement of the fundamental cryobiology with which living mammalian cells can be either killed or preserved in a viable state by the use of cold temperatures.

Fraser J: Cryosurgery. Prog Surg 14:136, 1975

A more recent review of cryobiology, particularly as it pertains to cryosurgery of solid tissues and tumors.

Neel HB III, Ketcham AS, Hammond WG: Requisites for successful cryogenic surgery of cancer. Arch Surg 102:45, 1971

A demonstration that colder probe temperature and repeated freezing both contributed to local elimination of an animal tumor.

Soanes WA, Gonder MJ, Ablin RJ: A possible immuno-cryothermic response in prostatic cancer. Clin Radiol 21:253, 1970

The clinical suggestion that cryosurgery of the primary prostatic cancer might induce an antitumor immune response is presented.

Jones LW: Cryosurgery for prostatic carcinoma. Urology 4:499, 1974

This is a review of evidence that cancer cryodestruction stimulates a specific antitumor immune response.

Bagley DH, Faraci RP, Marrone JC, et al: Lymphocyte mediated cytotoxicity after cryosurgery of a murine sarcoma. J Surg Res 17:404, 1974

In vitro evidence of immunity following cryodestruction of a transplanted animal tumor is provided.

Javadpour M, Bagley DH, Zbar B: Failure of cryosurgical treatment of experimental intradermal tumors to eradicate microscopic lymph node metastases in guinea pigs. JNCI 62:1479, 1979

Progresive growth of lymph node metastases after cryodestruction of a transplanted animal tumor is documented.

Soanes WA, Gonder MJ: Use of cryosurgery in prostatic cancer. J Urol 99:793, 1968

This is an early clinical experience in cryosurgery for cancer.

Reuter HJ: Cryosurgery in urology. In Von Leden J, Cahan WG (eds): Cryogenics in Surgery, pp 411–470. Garden City, NY, Medical Examination Publishing Company, 1971

This is an early and thorough discussion of urologic endoscopic cryosurgery, with introduction of the trochar cystoscope to monitor the bladder neck ice ball.

Bonney WW, Fallon B, Gerber WL, et al: Cryosurgery in prostatic cancer: Elimination of the local lesion. Urology, July/August 1983

Surgical technique for open perineal cryosurgery and local tumor recurrence rate with discussion of possible causes are included.

Bonney WW, Fallon B, Gerber WL, et al: Cryosurgery in prostatic cancer: Survival. Urology 19:37, 1982

Survival after cryosurgery in comparison to radical prostatectomy and other forms of treatment is discussed.

Overview:
Cryosurgery: More Data Needed

Gerald P. Murphy

The University of Iowa, without question in the United States and perhaps internationally, has the broadest experience in the use of cryosurgical treatment of prostatic carcinoma for attemptive curative interventions. Moreover, its staff has over the years collectively addressed itself to important issues involving the correlation of patients' preoperative staging postoperative results, and survival. The bibliography from this experience enumerates this fact and covers this field in a broad and most comprehensive manner. Questions that remain unanswered from the current review are doubtless matters that

will be considered in the future. Very likely this technique will continue to be used under close evaluation at the Iowa Center for some time. Thus, both in a retrospective and prospective manner, all students of prostatic cancer may benefit from careful scrutiny of this comprehensive review, and, at the same time, perhaps consider questions that in the future may be answered.

The foregoing article deals primarily with the importance of elimination of the local lesion. Very early in their experience, the Iowa group found that perineal open cryosurgical treatment of prostate cancer was far preferable to transurethral approaches for a number of obvious reasons—dealing with the rate of freezing, control of unnecessary secondary complications, and direct visual inspection. Unfortunately, in some European centers this preliminary knowledge has not yet been realized. Thus, comparison of reports of the benefit of cryosurgical techniques in some European centers at the very outset is not applicable to that technique employed by the University of Iowa group. One always, in the evaluation of a lesion treated by a variety of techniques, wishes to inspect the effectiveness of the treatment in regard to the elimination of the local lesion. The authors correctly point out that a number of their patients are D_1, D_2, or C; in fact, a predominant number. Thus, the anticipation of a total success for elimination of the local lesion, even with this technique, is obviously limited.

Whether an *elimination* or *recurrence* or *persistence* is the proper term for such lesions, I cannot truly answer. At any rate, the authors have found that three fourths of their recurrences occur within 2 yr of the cryosurgical treatment. The rate of local recurrence has, unfortunately, varied from 14% early to up to as high as 41%. These figures mentioned in the text are not directly applicable to all the tables. A resolution, however, is not important because it only involves a few small percentage points. What is important is the assessment of these patients. Very likely few as described underwent a true anatomic staging of the status of their pelvic lymph nodes. Therefore, perhaps for the entire series, a clinical staging should not be entirely accepted. By this, I mean a number of the so-called localized lesions may well have not been based on concurrent assessment of the lymph node status.

Perhaps of more concern is the fact that a number of the patients received hormonal therapy either before or during the cryosurgical treatment, 22% in one part of the series. In addition, as was described in one table, 48% received it afterward. Thus, describing a failure or success of the cryosurgical treatment either in terms of survival or in terms of the primary treatment to cryosurgical therapy alone for a majority of the patients seems to be of doubtful value. I am unable to certify particularly hormonal effects versus other effects, although the biopsies of the recurrent tumors do not suggest, from descriptive terms, the presence of a perceptible effect of estrogens or, at least, androgen ablation. Not all patients, understandably, for a number of appropriate reasons, have confirming histology in terms of recurrence. This was achieved

in several instances by subsequent transurethral resection. The use of transurethral resection in each case was doubtless necessary to relieve persistent obstruction and other secondary problems. It is, however, almost impossible in view of the significant number of such patients treated to ascribe subsequent incontinence or other secondary problems to the cryosurgical treatment and not necessarily to the persistence of tumor at the vesical neck or perhaps to the resulting secondary effects of the transurethral resection. Regardless of what one ascribes these results to, the incidence of incontinence is remarkably low considering the degree and severity of therapy. What is important in all cases, of course, is the knowledge of the ultimate cause of death. I hope that this was certified in most cases by an autopsy result. However, this was not necessarily so.

Urologists are probably more interested in how many patients died from their prostate cancer as well as other causes, in terms of those with so-called C and D lesions. This has been described by the authors with a reasonable survival rate in terms of this difficult problem. What is uncertain and doubtless will be addressed in the future is what effect adjuvant therapy, be it hormonal or nonhormonal, might have on such patients. The use of a controlled, randomized clinical trial will be of benefit. In part, the authors, by participating in the National Prostatic Cancer Project, may provide some answer on a limited basis to this issue. Surgeons have, of course, for some time been aware of the potential immunologic benefits of cryosurgical treatment. Regretfully, despite considerable effort, demonstration of this effect remains illusory or, at least, undocumentable. In animal models further studies are underway, and perhaps these may result in demonstrations to support this theory. Based on the results mixed with the hormonal treatment, however, it is difficult to expect to identify a precise immunologic effect, one at least related to survival or local tumor control. There seem to be far too many factors offered in each of these patients to resolve such a tenuous issue. Cryosurgical treatment for prostatic cancer is thus an area of considerable interest. Patients and physicians alike are fortunate that a group experienced in this area continues to address the importance of such treatment. However, at present it does not appear to be a treatment that should be recommended for widespread application or implementation. Rather, however, it is a field that should be watched and followed for continuing reports from this most qualified center.

89

LYMPHATIC SPREAD FROM PROSTATIC CANCER

R. H. Flocks, David Culp and Richard Porto

From the Department of Urology, The State University of Iowa, Iowa City, Iowa

The Journal of Urology
Vol. 81, No. 1, January 1959
Printed in U.S.A.

Herbut,[1] Kahler,[2] Lowsely and Kirwin,[3] and Arnheim[4] state that lymphatic spread from carcinoma of the prostate occurs frequently and that involvement of the lymphatic vessels occurs early. Herbut believes that the lymph nodes involved are, in decreasing order of frequency, pelvic nodes, lumbar nodes, thoracic nodes and supra-clavicular nodes. Arnheim, in a postmortem study of late cases, found an apparently higher incidence in the lumbar nodes as contrasted to the pelvic nodes.

This mode of spread is considered important from the point of view of prognosis and therapy in carcinoma generally. What is its place in prostatic cancer? Are there patients with primary lesions limited to the prostate itself or to the genital fascial envelope who do have lymph node involvement without evidence of spread to the bone marrow? Are there patients with local spread beyond the genital fascial envelope without evidence of local lymph node involvement and without evidence of bone marrow involvement? Are there patients with evidence of local spread and local lymph node involvement who have no bone marrow involvement or evidence of more distant spread?

The purpose of this report is to describe the findings

with regard to regional lymph node involvement in a consecutive series of 411 patients with histologically proven prostatic cancer explored retropubically during the period of March 1951 to June 1957. From the point of view of the clinical and pathological study of the prostate and seminal vesicles these patients could be divided as follows:

GROUP 1

Lesions limited to prostate, bone x-rays negative; condition good; phosphatases normal; 29 patients.

GROUP 2

Lesion locally inoperable but no evidence of distant metastasis, bone x-rays negative; condition fair to good; phosphatases normal; 382 patients.

It is to be emphasized therefore that this is a series of patients with relatively "early" lesions. Of interest in this regard is a previously reported study in this clinic of 57 cases in which bone marrow aspirations were performed routinely.[5] This showed that in the absence of orchiectomy or estrogen therapy, negative bone x-rays and normal serum phosphatases would make reasonably sure the absence of blood borne spread.

Read at annual meeting of Southeastern Section of American Urological Association, Inc., Hollywood, Fla., January 12–16, 1958.

These patients were all explored through a wide transverse suprapubic incision and careful study made of the areas about the lower portion of the aorta, the common iliacs, the external iliacs, the hypogastrics and the obturators. Unless careful dissection is carried out in these areas, even grossly involved nodes will be missed. Moreover, hyperplastic nodes are not infrequent and the gross impression must be histologically substantiated.

The results of the study are as follows:

Metastatic involvement was found most frequently in the hypogastric and obturator groups of nodes. The next most common was the iliac group. The involvement of these three groups was far more common than the involvement of the aortic groups. These were involved in only two instances and this was associated with pelvic node involvement. In general, the findings confirmed the lymphatic drainage of the prostate as described by Testut[6] (Fig. 1A).

Table 1 shows the incidence of pelvic lymph node involvement as related to the clinical findings. The incidence of proven involvement of the pelvic nodes in this series was 35 percent. This surprisingly high involvement without a large incidence of gross involvement of the abdominal nodes and without evidence of bone metastases or elevation of the serum acid phosphatases

is to be emphasized. It would seem that this is an important stage in the life history of prostatic cancer.

It is to be noted that in the 29 cases which locally were considered operable, both clinically and pathologically, there was a 7 percent pelvic lymph node involvement. As soon as invasion of the seminal vesicles and genital fascial envelope occurred, the incidence of pelvic node involvement rose rapidly. However, it is also to be noted that a significant number of patients with marked local extension had no pelvic lymph node involvement.

DISCUSSION

During this period a total of 911 new patients were examined with a clinical division into: Group 1, 3 percent (7 percent positive nodes); group 2, 56 percent (38 percent positive nodes); group 3, 41 percent, evidence of disseminated cancer. It would seem upon the basis of these studies that removal of the pelvic lymph nodes would add approximately 7 percent to the "cure" rate of radical prostatectomy in so-called operable patients and if node removal is combined with some satisfactory technique for the destruction of periprostatic and perivesicular spread, a significant addition to the salvage percentage would occur. In this regard, it is of interest

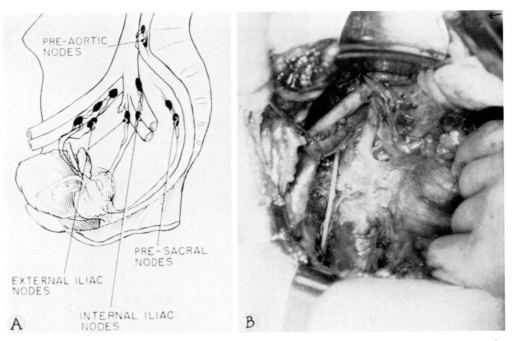

Fig. 1. (A) Diagram of pelvic lymph node drainage from prostate. (After Testut) (B) Exposure of pelvic node area with iliac, obturator and hypogastric nodes being removed. Note obturator nerve completely cleaned off.

TABLE 1

Size of Local Involved Area	No. of Cases	No. with Positive Nodes	Percent with Positive Nodes
Operable	29	2	7
Under 35 gm	130	24	18
35 to 80 gm	185	81	44
80 to 150 gm	55	28	51
Larger than 150 gm	12	11	92
Totals	411	146	35

All 411 patients had no evidence of distant metastases. Bones and phosphatases were normal. Of the 382 considered locally inoperable, 144 (38 percent) had positive regional lymph nodes.

to note that 32 patients of this series have been followed over five years. These received interstitial injection of colloidal Au_{198} into the locally inoperable lesion and into the involved regional lymph nodes. Four of these (12 percent) are alive and well at this time. Improved techniques of therapy should give improved results. Since 1954 lympyh node resection of the entire pelvic node area with instillation of Au_{198} along the lymphatic

passageway in addition to total prostatoseminal vesiculectomy and instillation of Au_{198} into the perioprostatic tissues has been carried out.[7] Over 60 such procedures have thus far been performed. Of 12 with positive nodes done over three years ago eight are alive and well, one died of other causes with no recurrence five months postoperatively, two died of metastases eight months and two and one-half years respectively, and one is alive with local recurrence. When removal of the prostate was not feasible, intensive interstitial radiation in multiple sittings was done. The complications, mortality and morbidity have thus far been very low. The early results have been promising.

In summary then, a study of the regional lymph nodes in early prostatic cancer shows a significant pelvic node involvement in conjunction with relatively small local prostatic lesions without evidence of distant metastases. It also shows a considerable number of patients with large local lesions without local pelvic lymphatic involvement. The clinical significance of these findings is discussed. It would seem that local lymph node involvement is of great significance in prostatic cancer.

REFERENCES

1. Herbut, P. A.: Urological Pathology. Philadelphia: Lea & Febiger, 1952, p. 947
2. Kahler, J. E.: Carcinoma of the prostate gland. J Urol 41:557, 1939
3. Lowsley, O. S. and Kirwin, T. J.: Clinical Urology. Baltimore: Williams and Wilkins Co., 1956, p. 405
4. Arnheim, F. K.: Carcinoma of the prostate. J Urol 60:599, 1948
5. Clifton, J. A., Philipp, R. J. and Fowler, W. M.: Bone marrow and carcinoma of the prostate. Am J Med Sc 224:121–130, 1952
6. Testut, Leo: Traité d'anatomie Humaine. Paris: Doin, 1928, p. 267
7. Flocks, R. H., Elkins, H. B. and Culp. D.: Treatment of cancer of prostate by interstitial injection of Au_{198} Studies in the problem of distribution. J Urol 77:505, 1957

Commentary: Pelvic Lymphadenectomy in Staging of Carcinoma of the Prostate

Richard G. Middleton

Twenty-five years later, I would agree wholeheartedly with Flocks, Culp, and Porto, who stated in their article that "a study of the regional lymph nodes in early prostatic cancer shows a significant pelvic node involvement in conjunction with relatively small local prostatic lesions without evidence of distant metastases." Furthermore, according to these authors, "It would seem that local lymph node involvement is of great significance in prostatic cancer." The great majority of their patients had what is called clinical stage C, that is, tumor

extension beyond the prostatic capsule locally without evidence of distant disease in bones or elsewhere.

My major interest has been in assessing the state of the pelvic lymph nodes in clinical stages A and B prostatic carcinoma, those cancers which seem clinically to be localized to the prostate without extension beyond the capsule.[1-4] Current ability to detect subtle bone metastases has been greatly enhanced by the routine use of radioisotope bone scanning. Still, there is a major concern in the clinical evaluation and the planning of therapy for the patient who has what seems to be localized prostatic carcinoma. The tumor may have spread beyond the prostate to the seminal vesicles, the pelvic lymph nodes, or both.

In either the case of microscopic tumor extension to the seminal vesicles or with tumor spread to the pelvic lymph nodes, the likelihood of cure by radical prostatectomy is slim.[5-7] Yet early involvement of the seminal vesicles and lymphatics is virtually impossible to detect by standard clinical, laboratory, and radiologic methods. Interestingly, there is good evidence from my own experience and from that of others that tumor extension to the seminal vesicles and pelvic lymphatics generally occurs at roughly the same time.[4,7] When pelvic nodes contain metastatic prostatic cancer, the incidence of seminal vesicle involvement by tumor is very high; in the presence of proven negative pelvic nodes, microscopic invasion of the seminal vesicles is unlikely but can occur on occasion. I therefore assume that the state of the lymph nodes pretty much reflects the state of the seminal vesicles.

Lymphangiography seems to be the appropriate study to determine whether there is tumor in the pelvic lymphatics. My own and my associates' experience, and reports of others, however, have shown that lymphangiography is simply not reliable, at least when the surgeon is dealing with the small foci of tumor commonly seen in association with a relatively small primary prostatic carcinoma.[4,8,11] In the case of a large prostatic cancer with extensive spread to the pelvic nodes, lymphangiography can display the nodal involvement impressively. However, with relatively small prostatic cancers and the possibility of early and subtle tumor spread to the nodes, lymphangiography is simply not competitive with pelvic lymphadenectomy for accuracy of staging. Accurate staging, I believe, is necessary for making rational and appropriate therapeutic decisions.

The possibility that lymphadenectomy might be therapeutic is interesting but seems unlikely. My own interest in pelvic lymphadenectomy has been as a staging procedure, as an aid in the careful selection of patients who might benefit and be cured by radical prostatectomy. Patients who seem to have clinical stages A and B prostatic carcinoma are evaluated by the standard tests for possible metastases: skeletal x-rays studies, radioisotope bone scanning, excretory urography (IVP), and serum acid phosphatase determination. If these tests show no evidence of distant metastases, and if the patient is considered a good candidate for radical prostatectomy, I then proceed, with pelvic lymphadenectomy usually as an independent staging manuever.[1]

I prefer to begin by making an oblique, muscle-splitting lower-abdominal incision on the side to which the primary prostatic tumor lateralizes if it is a stage B lesion. If I am dealing with a stage A prostatic carcinoma, I begin on either side; there is no way to know which side on which to begin. The dissection is carried out extraperitoneally. The peritoneum, peritoneal contents, and ureter are retracted medially. A thorough lymphadenectomy is then performed unilaterally from the level of the mid-common iliac vessels down along the external iliac vessels to the inguinal ligament. All lymph nodes and associated fibrofatty tissue are removed. A thorough, skeletonizing type of dissection is accomplished. The hypo-

gastric vessels are then dissected for their proximal 3 cm. Finally, the obturator space is dissected to remove all nodes and associated fat. Suspicious lymph nodes are examined histologically by frozen section. If tumor is detected in any nodes, a contralateral procedure is not performed. The patient is considered not to be an appropriate candidate for radical prostatectomy. If all the lymph nodes are normal, or seem so, a similar lower-abdominal muscle-splitting incision is made on the opposite side, and a similar pelvic lymphadenectomy is performed on the second side. The wounds are usually drained for 2 to 3 days following surgery.

I favor radical perineal prostatectomy in appropriate patients with proven negative pelvic lymph nodes. The radical perineal prostatectomy is usually performed 4 to 5 days after the pelvic lymphadenectomy—providing ample time for review of the permanent histologic sections of the lymph node material.

From 1970 through 1981, my associates and I performed pelvic lymphadenectomy in 452 patients, mostly for the staging of those who had clinical stages A and B prostatic carcinoma. We classify prostatic carcinoma as clinical stage A-1 if five or fewer foci of microscopic tumor are found in prostatic tissue removed for presumed benign hypertrophy. When there is more extensive microscopic carcinoma, the patient is considered clinical stage A-2. Clinical B-1 prostatic carcinoma is defined as a tumor nodule confined to the prostate and judged to be 1.5 cm or smaller in greatest dimension. Stage B-2 prostatic carcinoma is a nodule 2 cm in diameter or larger yet still localized to the prostate. Some patients with clinical stage C prostatic carcinoma have also been subjected to pelvic lymphadenectomy. These were generally patients with rather small C lesions, and lymphadenectomy was carried out at the time of interstitial radiation or to stage the patient prior to treatment with external radiation.

The results of pelvic lymphadenectomy in the various clinical stages of prostatic carcinoma are seen in Table 2. Most stage A-1 prostatic cancers are low-grade lesions. From our experience, my co-workers and I have found no positive pelvic lymph nodes in 41 lymphadenectomies in stage A-1 tumors.[12] On this basis, we no longer perform lymphadenectomy in stage A-1 lesions. The yield is zero or, at least, negligible. Also, we consider radical prostatectomy inappropriate and overly aggressive in patients with stage A-1 (minimal focal microscopic) prostatic cancer.

Stage A-2 prostatic carcinoma is a different matter.[12] Thus

TABLE 2. Pelvic Lymphadenectomy in Patients with Apparently Localized Prostatic Carcinoma (1970–1981): Incidence of Pelvic Node Metastasis by Histologic Grade and Clinical Stage

| Stage | Grade | | | Total |
	Well Differentiated	Moderately Differentiated	Poorly Differentiated	
A₁	0/28	0/12	0/1	0/41
A₂	0/27	5/19 (26%)	2/7 (43%)	8/33 (24%)
B₁	2/53 (4%)	13/94 (14%)	3/9 (33%)	18/156 (12%)
B₂	5/27 (18%)	29/106 (27%)	9/21 (43%)	43/154 (28%)
C	5/10 (50%)	18/44 (41%)	13/14 (93%)	36/68 (53%)
Total	12/125 (10%)	65/275 (24%)	28/52 (54%)	105/452 (23%)

far, we have seen no positive nodes in seven patients with low-grade A-2 prostatic carcinoma, but 26% with moderately differentiated tumors and 43% with high-grade lesions had positive pelvic lymph nodes. The incidence of positive lymphadenectomy in stage B-1 and stage B-2 prostatic cancer can be seen in Table 2. The size of the lesion and the degree of histologic tumor differentiation are definitely important factors in the incidence of positive pelvic lymph nodes. Metastasis to pelvic lymph nodes is a common feature in stage C lesions as noted in Table 2.

In our experience with pelvic lymphadenectomy there has been no death. Nine percent of operations resulted in complications, and the most common complications were wound hematoma, thrombophlebitis, lymphocele, and pulmonary embolus. I cannot see that this rate of thrombo-embolic complications was affected by the use of mini-dose heparin. Postoperative lymphoceles and two ureteral injuries required repeat operations.

The patient with a small localized carcinomatous nodule (clinical stage B-1) has traditionally been considered the best candidate for radical prostatectomy. The possibility of total eradication of the cancer is good. In a patient who has stage B-1 tumor that is well differentiated (Gleason grade 2 to 4), I would now avoid the staging pelvic lymphadenectomy. The incidence of positive nodes is so low (4% in our experience) that I would ignore the nodes and proceed with radical perineal prostatectomy. With medium- and high-grade B-1 lesions, staging pelvic lymph node dissection is important. Those who have positive nodes will not benefit by radical prostatectomy; the operation should be avoided in these cases. Those with negative nodes are likely candidates for surgery with curative intent.

Walsh and Jewett have warned against the employment of radical prostatectomy for stages A-2 and B-2 prostatic cancer because of the high incidence of seminal vesicle invasion found in the radical prostatectomy specimens.[13,14] The incidence of positive nodes in stage A-2 and B-2 lesions is significant and relates to tumor grade. When nodes are free of tumor, however, the likelihood is high that the tumor remains localized and has

TABLE 3. Radical Prostatectomy in Patients with Stage A2 Prostatic Cancer and Negative Pelvic Lymphadenectomy

Histologic Findings	Number of Patients
No tumor	3 (11.5%)
Focal residual tumor (<5% of specimen)	6 (23%)
*Diffuse residual tumor	17 (65.5%)
Total	26 (100%)

*Five had microscopic invasion of capsule, one had microscopic invasion of seminal vesicles.

TABLE 4. Patients with Stage B₂ Prostatic Cancer and Negative Pelvic Lymph Nodes, Treated by Radical Prostatectomy: Pathologic Findings

Number of Patients	Seminal Vesicle Invasion	Capsular Invasion	Tumor Confined to Prostate
50	2 (4%)*	6 (12%)	43 (86%)

* One patient had capsular *and* seminal vesicle invasion.

not yet extended to the seminal vesicles. Tables 3 and 4 review the results of examination of the radical prostatectomy specimens in our patients who have had proven negative pelvic lymph nodes and have undergone radical prostatectomy.[15,16] This experience suggests to me that radical prostatectomy is an appropriate treatment, and likely the best current treatment, for patients with stage A-2 and B prostatic cancer, when pelvic lymph nodes are known to be free of tumor.

I have carefully avoided radical prostatectomy in patients with stage C lesions, that is, with tumor extending beyond the prostatic capsule. Pelvic lymphadenectomy in stage C cancer may have value in the staging of patients prior to external radiation, and it seems reasonable to accomplish a pelvic lymph node dissection at the time of interstitial radiation. The therapeutic value of node dissection seems negligible at this point, and the value of any type of radiation treatment in the presence of positive pelvic lymph nodes seems meager.

REFERENCES

1. Dahl DS, Wilson CS, Middleton RG, et al: Pelvic lymphadenectomy for staging localized prostatic cancer. J Urol 112:245, 1974

2. Dahl DS, Wilson CS, Middleton RG: Staging of localized prostatic carcinoma by pelvic lymphadenectomy: Technique using sequential, unilateral extraperitoneal incisions. Urology 5:805, 1975

3. Wilson CS, Dahl DS, Middleton RG: Pelvic lymphadenectomy for the staging of apparently localized prostatic cancer. J Urol 117:197, 1977

4. Middleton RG, Cutler CL, Dahl DS: Further experience with pelvic lymphadenectomy for the staging of apparently localized prostatic cancer-experience with 203 patients. AUA Courses, Vol 1, p 25. Baltimore, Williams & Wilkins, 1979

5. Arudino LJ, Glucksman MA: Lymph node metastases in early carcinoma of the prostate. J Urol 88:91, 1962

6. Jewett HJ: The case for radical perineal prostatectomy. J Urol 103:195, 1970

7. Byar DP, Mostofi FK: Carcinoma of the prostate: Prognostic evaluation of certain pathologic features in 208 radical prostatectomies. Examined by the step-section technique. Cancer 30:5, 1972

8. Bruce AW, O'Cleireacham F, Morales A, et al: Carcinoma of the prostate: A critical look at staging. J Urol 319, 1977

9. McLaughlin AP, Saltzstein SL, McCullough DL, et al: Prostatic carcinoma: Incidence and location of unsuspected lymphatic metastases. J Urol 115:89, 1967

10. O'Donoghue EPN, Shridhar P, Sherwood T et al: Lymphography and pelvic lymphadenectomy in carcinoma of the prostate. Br J Urol 48:689, 1976

11. Ray GR, Pistenma DS, Castellino RA, et al: Operative staging of apparently localized adenocarcinoma of the prostate: Results in fifty unselected patients. Cancer 38:73, 1976

12. Smith JA Jr, Seaman JP, Gleidman JB, Middleton RG: Pelvic lymph node metastasis from prostatic cancer: Influence of tumor grade and stage in 452 consecutive patients. J Urol (in press, to be published May, 1983)

13. Walsh PC: Radical prostatectomy for the treatment of localized prostatic carcinoma. Urol Clin North Am 7:583, 1980

14. Walsh PC, Jewett HJ: Radical surgery for prostatic cancer. Cancer 45:1906, 1980

15. Parfitt HE Jr, Smith JA Jr, Seaman JP, Middleton RG: Surgical treatment of stage A-2 prostatic carcinoma: Significance of tumor grade and extent. J Urol 129:763, 1983

16. Middleton RG, Smith JA Jr: Radical prostatectomy for stage B-2 prostatic cancer. J Urol 127:702, 1982.

ANNOTATED BIBLIOGRAPHY

Dahl DS, Wilson CS, Middleton RG: Staging of localized prostatic carcinoma by pelvic lymphadenectomy: technique using sequential, unilateral extraperitoneal incisions. Urology 5:805. 1975

This article describes a technique for staging apparently localized prostatic carcinoma using sequential, unilateral, extraperitoneal, lower-abdominal, muscle-splitting incisions. If the lesion is a localized nodule, stage B, a thorough unilateral pelvic lymphadenectomy is accomplished on the side on which the prostatic tumor nodule lateralizes. If tumor-bearing nodes are found, no procedure is done on the second side. If the nodes are free of tumor, or seem so, the same operation is performed on the second side. The authors believe that extraperitoneal pelvic lymphadenectomies are likely to result in less morbidity than would occur with a transperitoneal approach. The purpose of the procedure is accurate staging for the selection of appropriate treatment-radical prostatectomy or radiation therapy.

Middleton RG, Cutler CL, Dahl DS: Further experience with pelvic lymphadenectomy for the staging of apparently localized prostatic cancer—experience with 203 patients. AUA Courses, Vol 1, p 25. Baltimore, Williams & Wilkins, 1979

This is an earlier review of experience with pelvic lymphadenectomy as an aid in the selection of patients who are likely to be appropriate candidates for radical prostatectomy. Those patients with negative pelvic lymph nodes who are subjected to radical prostatectomy have a low rate of seminal vesicle invasion in the radical prostatectomy specimens. Excluding patients with positive nodes results in an apparent improvement in the selection of patients for radical prostatectomy.

Smith, JA Jr, Seaman JP, Gleidman JB, Middleton RG: Pelvic lymph node metastasis from prostatic cancer: Influence of tumor grade and stage in 452 consecutive patients. J Urol (in press, to be published May, 1983)

This article reviews the experience over a decade at the University of Utah with staging pelvic lymphadenectomy for presumably localized prostatic cancer. Four hundred fifty-two patients underwent pelvic lymphadenectomy. The incidence of positive nodes clearly relates to stage and tumor grade. Overall, no patient with stage A-1 prostatic cancer had positive pelvic lymph nodes. The incidence with stage A-2 was 24%, with B-1 12%, and with B-2 28%. Fifty-three percent of patients with stage C prostatic carcinoma had positive pelvic lymph nodes. On the basis of this experience, we would no longer consider pelvic lymphadenectomy in stage A-1 prostatic cancer. The incidence of positive pelvic lymph nodes is so low in well-differentiated stage B-1 lesions that lymphadenectomy can be bypassed. The incidence of positive nodes in poorly differentiated stage C lesions is extremely high.

Arduino LJ, Glucksman MA: Lymph nodes metastases in early carcinoma of the prostate. J Urol 88:91, 1962

The authors point out that radical or total perineal prostatectomy has a serious deficiency, that is, that the pelvic lymph nodes cannot be examined or removed through the perineum. These authors favor the radical retropubic operation, permitting exposure and removal of the pelvic nodes. They also believe that removal of the prostate and seminal vesicles is accomplished more easily by the retropubic route. A 5-yr experience with 71 radical retropubic prostatectomies is reported. In each case the tumor was judged on rectal examination to be confined to the prostate. Each patient had a normal serum acid phosphatase and no evidence of metastases to bones. Nineteen patients (27%) had tumor involvement of pelvic nodes; microscopic invasion of the seminal vesicles was found in 17 (24%). A "surprising finding," according to the authors, was the relationship between seminal vesicle involvement and pelvic node metastases. With microscopic extension of tumor into the seminal vesicles, 82% had pelvic lymph node metastases. Of those without tumor involvement of the seminal vesicles, only 7% had positive pelvic lymph nodes. The authors wondered about the prognostic significance of finding positive nodes, and they wondered about the possible benefits of removal of these nodes. But clearly, nodal involvement was extremely common with microscopic tumor invasion into the seminal vesicles, a situation that they regarded as ominous. Finally, it was suggested that by combining pelvic lymphadenectomy with the retropubic approach, or by combining node dissection with the radical perineal prostatectomy as a two-stage procedure, the survival or cure rate might be improved.

Byar DP, Mostofi FK: Carcinoma of the prostate: Prognostic evaluation of certain pathologic features in 208 radical prostatectomies. Examined by the step-section technique. Cancer 30:5, 1972

Step-sections were taken from radical prostatectomy specimens obtained from the V.A. Co-operative Urological Research Group. The study protocol specified that only patients with localized carcinoma should have had radical prostatectomy, but of the entire group there were some who had tumor extending beyond the capsule and a few with distant metastases. More than half the patients had had hormonal treatment—orchiectomy, estrogens, or both. Of 175 patients who had no evidence of seminal vesicle involvement clinically, 30 (17%) had microscopic tumor extension into the seminal vesicles in the radical prostatectomy specimen. The urologist occasionally overestimated the extent of tumor as well, reporting tumor beyond the capsule or involving the seminal vesicles in cases in which this could not be confirmed histologically. In more than 80% of prostatectomy specimens in which a single nodule was detected clinically, multiple areas of tumor were found microscopically. Eight-five percent of tumors were found to be multifocal, and 80% were bilateral. Although the nodule is the earliest clinically detectable stage of the disease, it does not reflect the amount of tumor present. It is of great significance that 97% of tumors were located either in the peripheral portion of the prostate or were in both peripheral and central locations. It was very unusual to find a tumor that was just central in the prostate and not located peripherally as well. Opportunity to study large transverse sections of radical prostatectomy specimens impressed the authors with the large variety of histologic patterns evident in a single case or even on a single microscopic slide. Because of these variations, grading was very difficult, frustrating, and not reproducible.

Jewett HJ: The case for radical perineal prostatectomy. J Urol 103:195, 1970

Jewett sees little to be gained by radical perineal prostatectomy in occult, latent, or stage A prostatic carcinoma, although the reports that he cites show that some of the patients with this stage prostatic carcinoma ultimately do die of the disease. He would limit this procedure, radical perineal prostatectomy, to patients under 70 yr of age, in good health, with stage B–type lesions. Of 490 radical prostatectomies at the Johns Hopkins Hospital, 307 were done for a solitary prostatic nodule. Of 79 earlier patients with large stage B lesions, 39 (49%) had microscopic invasion of the seminal vesicles, and only 2 lived 15 yr free of tumor. In the other 40 without involvement of the seminal vesicles, 12 patients (30%) lived 15 yr without recurrence and without other treatment. In a later study of radical perineal prostatectomy in 103 patients with a palpable discrete nodule, the seminal vesicles were involved microscopically in 17 (15.5%) All these patients with seminal vesicle invasion had tumor recurrences. There were 86 patients without microscopic invasion of the seminal vesicles. Thirty-three percent of these lived 15 or more yrs free of tumor recurrence. No patients with undifferentiated carcinoma lived 15 yr.

90

NEEDLE ASPIRATION OF THE PROSTATE

F. Peter Kohler, David M. Kelsey, Charles C. MacKinney and Tilde S. Kline

From the Departments of Urology and Pathology, Lankenau Hospital, Philadelphia, Pennsylvania

The Journal of Urology
Copyright © 1977 by the Williams & Wilkins Co.
Vol. 118, December
Printed in U.S.A.

ABSTRACT—Prostatic needle aspiration is rapid, safe and accurate. It should be used without fear of complication as a routine screening procedure in the office and should be considered a primary tool in the diagnosis of carcinoma of the prostate.

We have presented previously our preliminary results with needle aspiration of the prostate compared to other biopsy methods.[1] Needle aspiration has been used extensively in Scandinavia but has not found wide acceptance in the United States.[2–4]

We report herein our results with prostatic needle aspiration in 110 patients. The method used to obtain the aspirate has been described. Briefly, an 18-gauge spinal needle is introduced with the rectal finger and advanced in the rectal lumen to the prostatic lesion and a transrectal insertion of the needle into the prostatic tissue is performed. Because of the flexibility of the spinal needle small lesions can be reached without

Accepted for publication April 1, 1977.
Read at annual meeting of American Urological Association, Chicago, Illinois, April 24–28, 1977.

difficulty. A 10 cc disposable syringe is then attached and, using rotation of the needle and suction with the syringe, an aspirate is obtained. The specimen is ejected immediately onto a prepared albuminized slide and fixed in 95 percent alcohol. We usually perform 2 aspirations on each patient. Because of the paucity of pain fibers in the rectum beyond the rectal sphincter no anesthesia is required under ordinary circumstances and the procedure can be performed in the office.

RESULTS

Of the 110 patients 61 aspirations were reported as myomatous and glandular hyperplasia of the prostate and 43 were diagnosed as carcinoma of the prostate. One aspirate was unsatisfactory and 5 were suspicious.

There were no falsely positive lesions but 6 originally benign aspirates resulted in a diagnosis of carcinoma of the prostate with further wide bore needle biopsy or transurethral resection tissue. Thus, the accuracy of the method is 93 per cent.

DISCUSSION

This method of prostatic biopsy is simple, quick and safe. We have not encountered any adverse effects. Neither have Ekman and associates with 100 patients[3] nor Esposti with 1,100 biopsies.[4] The method offers the chance of a definite treatment plan for a patient during the first office visit. Because of an exceedingly interested and cooperative cytopathologist at our institution results of the aspirations are reported within 30 minutes. The technicians come to the cystoscopy room or to the physician's office upon call.

Because of the flexibility of the needle we diagnosed carcinoma of the prostate in 2 instances in small nodules not readily accessible to a Vim Silverman needle, leading to radical prostatectomies without the need for open biopsy and saving prolonged operating time. Needle aspiration of the prostate should be advantageous in institutions where frozen section diagnosis is not readily available.

We have performed several prostatic needle aspirations on patients with carcinoma of the prostate who had undergone orchiectomy and/or estrogen therapy for several years. Aspirates from these patients were reported routinely as benign in appearance because the cells had lost their malignant characteristics. It might be inferred that needle aspiration could be a simple way to determine whether estrogen therapy and/or orchiectomy or radiation therapy will result in a satisfactory tumor response in a given patient.

REFERENCES

1. Kelsey, D. M., Kohler, F. P., Mackinney, C. C. and Kline T. S.: Outpatient needle aspiration biopsy of the prostate. J Urol 116:327, 1976
2. Alfthan, O., Klintrup, H.-E., Koivuniemi, A. and Taskinen, E.: Cytological aspiration biopsy and Vim-Silverman biopsy in the diagnosis of prostatic carcinoma. Ann Chir Gynec Fenn 59:226, 1970
3. Ekman, H., Hedberg, K. and Persson, P. S.: Cytological versus histological examination of needle biopsy specimens in the diagnosis of prostatic cancer. Br J Urol 39:544, 1967
4. Esposti, P. L.: Cytologic diagnosis of prostatic tumors with the aid of transrectal aspiration biopsy. A critical review of 1,110 cases and a report of morphologic and cytochemical studies. Acta Cytol 10:182, 1966

Commentary: Prostatic Needle Biopsy or Aspiration?

F. Peter Kohler

Transrectal fine needle biopsy of the prostate in the office has been free of any complications in my experience. Thin needle aspiration specimens require some experience in interpretation. At some institutions the pathologists may not offer the ready enthusiasm to which this biopsy method should be entitled. The problem with this method, as indeed with any biopsy, occurs when a negative report results and the clinical impression indicates otherwise. I then proceed with hospitalization and perform either a large bore needle biopsy with the Tru-Cut instrument or open perineal biopsy. The Tru-Cut instrument results in significant morbidity if used transrectally. It is wise to give the patient antibiotics and perhaps use overnight catheter drainage. The transperineal approach eliminates rectal contamination but can cause hemorrhage and edema, resulting in urinary retention. Nevertheless, needle biopsy by either route is the most commonly used method at this time, resulting in about 90% accuracy. It allows free choice of surgical approach and can be repeated at any time.

Transurethral biopsy can be misleading, since it will not reach small capsular lesions, and open perineal biopsy, if positive, means a total radical perineal prostatectomy. It depends on the proper interpretation of a frozen section.

ANNOTATED BIBLIOGRAPHY

Ferguson RS: Prostatic neoplasms: Their diagnosis by needle puncture and aspiration. Am J Surg 9:507, 1930

>This paper gives an early description of transperineal needle aspiration of the prostate using an 18-gauge needle and syringe. The author had been disappointed with other closed biopsy methods and states "we have yet to see any ill effects in a series of very carefully observed cases."

Silverman I: A new biopsy needle. Am J Surg 40:671, 1938

>Because the author became disillusioned with the results of aspiration biopsies of the prostate, he now reports on a new method of wide-bore needle biopsy, resulting in a cylinder of tissue and still widely used today in the Vim–Silverman modification.

Veenema RJ: A simplified prostatic perineal biopsy punch. J Urol 69:320, 1953

>The fusiform cup like biopsy instrument described in this paper is used transperineally, requiring a small skin incision, and delivers small buttons of tissue.

Franzen S, Giertz G, Zajicek J: Cytological diagnosis of prostatic tumours by transrectal aspiration biopsy. A preliminary report. Br J Urol 32:193, 1960

>This author performed 100 needle aspirations of the prostate in his office without complications, using a flexible 22-gauge needle with a special attachment for the guiding rectal finger. He was led to this approach because other needle biopsy methods resulted in false-negative reports from 25% to 40%.

Esposti PL: Cytologic diagnosis of prostatic tumors with the aid of transrectal aspiration biopsy: A clinical review of 1,110 cases and a report of morphological and cytotechnical studies. Acta Cytol 10:182, 1966

>This study from Stockholm reports on the results of 1430 transrectal needle aspirations done on 1110 patients using a 22-gauge needle. In 30% of the patients carcinoma was found. No false-positive but 10% false-negative reports were issued. No complications were encountered. This is the first large-scale report from Scandinavia.

Eckman H, Hedberg K, Persson PS: Cytological versus histological examination of needle biopsy specimen in the diagnosis of prostatic cancer. Br J Urol 39:544, 1967

>The authors compared 96 specimen obtained by fine needle aspiration with punch biopsy specimen obtained in 99 patients and found diagnostic agreement in 76% of cases. There were no complications from the needle aspirations, but the lower than hoped for yield of the cytologic examination cautioned them to a more aggressive biopsy method in cases of uncertainty or suspicion.

Alfthan O, Klintrup HE, Koivuniemi A, et al: Cytological aspiration biopsy and Vim-Silverman biopsy in the diagnosis of prostatic carcinoma. Ann Chir Gynaecol 59:226, 1970

>Of 220 patients biopsied by both methods, 82 were found to have carcinoma. Of these, 69 (84%) were detected by needle aspiration and 72 (88%) by Vim–Silverman needle, but the Vim–Silverman biopsy failed more often (12%) compared to thin needle aspiration (5%). Thin needle aspiration is considered almost equal to Vim–Silverman biopsy in reliability. The authors stress that thin needle aspiration is easier to perform and less uncomfortable for the patient; there have been no complications.

OVERVIEW: PELVIC LYMPH NODE INVOLVEMENT IN CLINICAL STAGING

John T. Grayhack

The concept that evaluation of pelvic lymph node involvement is important to ensure adequate assessment and proper treatment of patients with carcinoma of the prostate has gradually gained widespread although not total acceptance in the past decade. Dr. Middleton[14] has appropriately singled out the contribution of Dr. Rubin Flocks in persistently presenting data that indicated that disseminated carcinoma of the prostate will be unrecognized unless clinical staging procedures include a study of the pelvic lymph nodes. I was impressed by Dr. Flocks's work and began subjecting selected patients with cancer of the prostate to pelvic exploration and lymph node excision in the late 1960s. Our group, along with several others, gradually accepted the essential role of this procedure, just as Dr. Middleton, Dr. Dahl, and their associates in Salt Lake City have. Attempts to employ pelvic marrow histology and enzyme studies to decrease the pool of patients with unrecognized disseminated carcinoma of the prostate have not succeeded in reducing the number of patients in whom pelvic lymph node metastases are the only recognizable evidence of disseminated disease.[13] With current staging procedures about 40% to 60% of patients with disease otherwise designated as C, about 25% to 35% of patients with disease designated as B_2 or A_2, about 15% to 20% of patients with disease designated as B_1, and a very unusual patient with disease designated as A_1 had tumor demonstrable in the excised lymph nodes on histologic examination.[3,10] Although the percentages vary somewhat, these observations seem basically reproducible from series to series. The concept that disseminated carcinoma will be unrecognized clinically unless pelvic lymph nodes are evaluated seems irrefutable and should be accepted. This acceptance does not preclude varying decisions regarding evaluation of patients with carcinoma of the prostate. Recommendations regarding staging and treatment require individual risk–reward assessment. The patient's local and general status and the quality of life he finds acceptable should play a prominent role in these recommendations.

Since disseminated carcinoma of the prostate can be identified in a large number of patients only by lymph node assessment, my prejudice is to use the most accurate safe procedure for this evaluation in patients in whom recognition of disseminated disease is essential for proper treatment. I agree with Dr. Middleton that surgical excision of the pelvic lymph nodes is sufficiently safe and more accurate than indirect evaluation of nodes, such as that provided by lymphangiography, to make it the procedure of choice. I also agree that this procedure is currently not indicated in patients with stage A_1 prostatic carcinoma, since these patients do not seem to require treatment and the lymph nodes are involved very infrequently.[3] Paulson and colleagues[12] have reported that all patients with Gleason's grade 9 and 10 tumors had metastases to the pelvic nodes, whereas 86% of the patients with a Gleason grade of 5 or less had negative nodes. Current evidence does not support the use of the grade of the primary tumor alone to predict the presence of pelvic lymph node metastases accurately. Eventually, dissemination of carcinoma to lymph nodes should be recognizable by using appropriate tumor markers or a combination of pharmacologic manipulations and markers. The goal should be to develop a noninvasive, safe, highly accurate means of identifying patients with metastases to the pelvic lymph nodes.

Discussion of pelvic lymphadenectomy in carcinoma of the prostate should not exclude the possibility of a therapeutic effect from this procedure. The natural history of carcinoma of the prostate with regard to node involvement is not clear. Although patients with advanced local disease have a high incidence of positive nodes, appreciable data indicating the incidence in patients with recognizable dissemination to bone is not available. If all or almost all of these patients had demonstrable carcinoma in the nodes, the probability that nodal spread usually antedated rather than occurred coincidental with or followed bone spread would be a reasonable consideration. If, in the natural history of carcinoma of the prostate, initial metastases are commonly to the pelvic lymph nodes, then removal of these nodes may constitute an acceptable therapeutic endeavor in selected patients. This possibility warrants continued critical evaluation.

Currently, histologic study of a satisfactory tissue sample is the only technique available to establish the diagnosis of carcinoma of the prostate. Failure to confirm the diagnosis when carcinoma is present can result from a failure to sample the malignant tissue or from an inability to interpret the tissue sample properly. Except for those patients in whom tissue removal for a presumed benign condition has disclosed malignancy or in whom a characteristic disseminated neoplasm has

raised the question of a prostatic malignancy, recognition of the risk of carcinoma of the prostate depends on the presence of induration or irregularity of the prostate on rectal examination.[6,11] Studies of prostatic fluid composition and the effort to develop highly specific, sensitive immune assays for acid phosphatase may eventually also be shown to identify a group of men with a high risk of cancer of the prostate.[7] The nature of the abnormality identifying the increased risk of prostatic malignancy is critical to the biopsy effort. Sampling efforts are clearly directed in patients who have a palpable abnormality of the prostate but become random in patients in whom high risk of malignancy is identified by other than the presence of palpable prostatic changes.

In considering prostatic biopsy procedures, physicians must keep in mind a number of considerations: (1) a large percentage of indurated areas in the prostate in the biopsy series reported have been due to benign, not malignant, disease, (2) the accuracy with which a suspicious area can be biopsied and provide diagnostic material varies with the technique employed; (3) a negative finding on biopsy is far from an unequivocal finding, and (4) biopsy procedures have a recognized morbidity varying from life-threatening situations to changes interfering with the quality of life. The unreliability of the rectal finger in differentiating prostatic malignancy from other causes of prostatic induration and irregularity was brought into focus by Jewett, who noted that only about 50% of men with a nodule thought to represent carcinoma of the prostate were found to have the disease on open biopsy.[8] Since then, a number of authors have reported confirmation of a suspicion of malignancy resulting from rectal findings in 26% to 63% of patients biopsied. The accuracy of prediction of malignancy based on rectal findings varies with the extent of prostatic abnormality, but even extensive changes cannot preclude the possibility of a benign condition such as granulomatous prostatitis or tuberculosis.

The accuracy of a biopsy procedure varies with the ability to sample an identified site and the adequacy of the tissue specimen obtained. Although controlled observations are not available, it seems highly probable that open perineal biopsy provides the best opportunity to obtain adequate tissue from a suspicious site. Transrectal needle procedures probably rank next in permitting sampling of a given area.[15] Adequacy of tissue samples obtained by this approach varies. Biopsy needles such as the Franklin–Silverman or the Travenol disposable needle provide specimens that are evaluable by most pathologists; aspiration provides a sample that requires an especially skilled person to achieve a reliable evaluation. Perineal needle procedures are probably less accurate in sampling a suspicious area than transrectal techniques;[5,9] the amount of tissue obtained for analysis by biopsy or aspiration would be comparable in the two approaches. Transurethral biopsy techniques on a random basis have been thought to be the least reliable method to obtain appropriate tissue to establish the diagnosis of carcinoma of the prostate. Transurethral biopsy of an identified suspicious area has theoretic disadvantages but has not been adequately explored to allow assessment of its potential value.

In addition to emphasizing the potential reward of an accurate assessable tissue sample, the risk of the various biopsy procedures warrant consideration in selecting an appropriate approach for a given patient. Bleeding, local and systemic infection, and interference with voiding and sexual activity are the major potential complications recognized as being associated with biopsy procedures. As with the assessment of diagnostic accuracy of the procedures, a meaningful comparative evaluation of the risk of the various biopsy procedures is not available. My assessment is that procedures using a needle to obtain tissue have the highest risk of infection and bleeding. Of these, those carried out by the transrectal route would carry the greatest risk of infection;[2,4] this is probably lessened by the use of prebiopsy broad-spectrum antibiotics, as is the custom in some institutions. Impotence has been associated with the open perineal biopsy procedure. Although this may occur, it should be possible to minimize its occurrence by limiting exposure and tissue sampling of the prostate to the area identified on examination as questionable.

No ideal procedure for procuring a tissue sample to establish the diagnosis in a patient suspected of having a prostatic malignancy exists. Studies that increase the likelihood of malignancy of a suspicious lesion such as analysis of prostatic fluid composition or possibly serum marker studies may prove invaluable in guiding attempts to establish the suspected diagnosis. Both the type and persistence of biopsy effort should be suited to the patient's clinical status and the perceived risk of the presence of carcinoma of the prostate.

REFERENCES

1. Barzell W, Bean MA, Hilaris BS, et al: Prostatic adenocarcinoma: Relationship of grade and local extent to pattern of metastases. J Urol 118:278, 1977

2. Bissada NK, Rountree GA, Sulieman JS: Factors affecting accuracy and morbidity in transrectal biopsy of the prostate. Surg Gynecol Obstet 145:869, 1977

3. Donohue RE, Pfister RR, Weigel WW, et al: Pelvic lymphadenectomy in stage A prostatic cancer. Urology 9:1977

4. Dowlen W Jr, Block L, Politano A: Complications of transrectal biopsy examination of the prostate. South Med J 67:1453, 1974

5. Fortunoff S: Needle biopsy of the prostate: A review of 346 biopsies. J Urol 87:159, 1964

6. Grayhack JT, Wendel EF: Carcinoma of the prostate. In Karafin L, Kendall AR (eds): Lewis' Practice of Surgery, Vol 2. Hagerstown, Harper & Row, 1977

7. Grayhack JT, Lee C, Kolbusz W, et al: Detection of carcinoma of the prostate utilizing biochemical observations. Cancer 45:1896, 1980

8. Jewett HS: Significance of palpable prostatic nodule. JAMA 160:838, 1956

9. Kaufman JJ, Schultz JI: Needle biopsy of the prostate: A reevaluation. J Urol 87:1641, 1962

10. McCullough DW, Prout GR, Daly JJ: Carcinoma of the prostate and lymphatic metastases. J Urol 111:65, 1974

11. Murphy GP: The diagnosis of prostatic cancer. Cancer 37:589, 1976

12. Paulson DF, Piserchia PV, Gardner W: Predictors of lymphatic spread in prostatic adenocarcinoma: Uro-oncology Research Group Study. J Urol 123:697, 1980

13. Sadlowski RW: Early stage prostatic cancer investigated by pelvic lymph node biopsy and bone marrow acid phosphatase. J Urol 119:89, 1978

14. Wilson CS, Dahl DS, Middleton RG: Pelvic lymphadenectomy for staging of apparently localized prostatic cancer. J Urol 117:197, 1977

15. Zincke H, Campbell JT, Utz DC, et al: Confidence in the negative transrectal needle biopsy. Surg Gynecol Obstet 136:78, 1973

PART THIRTY-FIVE

SURGICAL TREATMENT OF CARCINOMA OF THE PENIS

91

SQUAMOUS CELL CARCINOMA OF THE PENIS

Harold J. Hoppmann and Elwin E. Fraley

From the Department of Urologic Surgery, University of Minnesota College of Health Sciences, Minneapolis, Minnesota

The Journal of Urology
Copyright © 1978 by The Williams & Wilkins Co.
Vol. 120, October
Printed in U.S.A.

Although cancer of the penis accounts for less than 1 percent of malignancies in male patients in the United States these neoplasms are a significant world health problem. Between 1964 and 1968 carcinoma of the penis accounted for 12 percent of all cancers in Ugandan male patients, a crude incidence of 2.2 cases per 100,000 men per year.[1] However, the high incidence is not limited to Uganda. Cancer of the penis has been reported to constitute 10 percent or more of all cancers in men in Mexico, China, Burma, Vietnam, Ceylon, some parts of India and the United States Commonwealth of Puerto Rico.[1]

PATHOGENESIS

Cancer of the penis nearly always affects uncircumcised men and often is associated with poor penile hygiene and phimosis. The ability of early circumcision and, by implication, a lifetime of good penile hygiene to curtail the rate of occurrence of squamous cell carcinoma of the penis is well documented. Only 6 cases have been reported in Jews known to have been ritually circumcised and 1 of these tumors developed on the penile shaft and another in a scar.[2-7] Only 3 cases have been reported in non-Jewish white men circumcised in infancy and 2 of these tumors occurred at sites of longstanding, chronic inflammation.[8-10] The Gisu tribe, the only Ugandan tribe to practice ritual circumcision, has a low incidence of cancer of the penis.[11]

PATHOLOGY

Almost all skin lesions of the penis demand histologic examination. The tumor-like lesions encountered most often are leukoplakia (acanthosis with dysplasia, nonspecific[12]), balanitis xerotica obliterans, erythroplasia of Queyrat, Bowen's disease, the Buschke-Löwenstein tumor and anogenital Paget's disease. However, it is important to remember that only 7.6 percent of the patients with penile carcinoma in 1 large series (511 men) had a history of 1 of these conditions.[13] The malignant lesions of the penis include basal cell carcinoma, melanoma, mesenchymal tumors, metastatic tumors and, most commonly, squamous cell carcinoma, including its variant, verrucose carcinoma.

Only 10 basal cell carcinomas of the penis[14] and 50 malignant melanomas[15] have been reported. The connective tissues of the penis also may give rise to tumors, about half of which are malignant. Any histologic type may be encountered, with sarcomatous tumors, especially fibrosarcoma and Kaposi's sarcoma, being the most common. Leiomyosarcoma, the malignant neural tumors and the malignant hemangioendotheliomas are among the other common types. The malignant tumors are found more often on the shaft; the benign tumors are more common on the glans.[16]

More than 200 cases of tumors metastatic to the penis have been reported, the majority of which originated in the bladder or the prostate.[17] Cancers of the rectum, rectosigmoid, lung, kidney, ureter and pancreas also have metastasized to the penis.

Verrucose carcinoma is a variant of squamous cell carcinoma. Kraus and Perez-Mesa reported on 105 cases of verrucose carcinoma.[18] Eight of the 10 lesions on the male genitalia involved the glans and prepuce. Radiation therapy failed to control this form of epidermoid carcinoma in all 17 patients in whom it was tried and appeared to have promoted anaplastic dedifferentiation of the tumor and metastases in 4 cancers of the oral cavity.

CLINICAL PRESENTATION

In most large series of patients with cancer of the penis the men ranged in age from 20 to 90 years old, with most between 40 and 70 years old. The mean age at the time of diagnosis was 58 years.[19-21] It is uncommon in this country to see a patient with squamous cell carcinoma of the penis who is younger than 40. The complaint at the time of admission to the hospital is, in decreasing order of frequency, a penile mass, an ulcerating lesion, penile pain or discharge, although a few patients will complain of swelling of the penis or of lymphadenopathy.[22] Squamous cell carcinoma usually originates on the glans, with the next most common sites being the prepuce and the shaft.[19,23,24]

Staging. Although other systems have been proposed[25,26] most American urologists use Jackson's staging system for carcinoma of the penis: stage I—tumor confined to the glans, prepuce or both, state II—tumor involving the penile shaft, stage III—operable inguinal node metastases and stage IV—tumor extending beyond the penile shaft, inoperable inguinal node metastates or distant metastases.[27] All staging systems are straightforward but they are difficult to use clinically. Often, the clinical stage and the stage of the disease as shown by the histologic findings are not the same. For example, deKernion and associates emphasized that the clinical assessment of the groin nodes in patients with stages I and II disease was misleading.[28] Only 62 percent of their 26 patients with palpable nodes had tumor in the groin and 5 patients

harbored cancer in nodes that were clinically free of tumor. Other physicians also have found that the staging of carcinoma of the penis by physical examination is unreliable. Hardner and associates reported on 82 patients who were staged clinically and then underwent either inguinal node biopsy or lymphadenectomy.[29] Of the 45 patients with clinical state I or II disease 7 proved to have stage III disease. Of the 37 patients with clinical stage III disease 15 had nodes free of tumor histologically. Thus, there was a discrepancy between the clinical and histologic stages of the disease in 27 percent of the patients. Kossow and associates found metastases in the inguinal lymph nodes of 2 of 8 patients whose nodes were clinically free of tumor but not in the nodes of 17 of 28 patients with palpable inguinal nodes.[19] Kuruvilla and associates found metastatic cancer in the groins of 17 of 108 patients who had been thought to have inguinal lymph nodes free of tumor.[30] In our series 13 of 70 patients (18.5 percent) with lymph nodes free of tumor clinically later had tumor in the groin.

TREATMENT

Treatment of squamous cell carcinoma of the penis must be tailored to fit the physical and psychological status of the patient as well as the site of the tumor.

Primary Lesion. Treatment of the primary lesion is selected after clinical assessment of the extent of the cancer. Small, invasive lesions on the distal penis can be treated by partial penectomy. A scrotal skin recession phalloplasty may be done in certain cases to give more penile length.[31] deKernion and associates performed a partial penectomy on 45 patients without complications or recurrence.[28] However, Hardner and associates reported recurrences in the stump in 2 of their 100 patients.[29]

In 2 reports the penile function remaining to patients who had a partial penectomy is described. Of the 16 patients in 1 series 9 could urinate standing without wetting their clothing[32] but in another series a quarter of the patients had difficulty directing the urinary stream.[13] Of the 16 patients in the first series 4 had been having sexual intercourse regularly before the operation but none was able to have satisfactory intercourse afterwards. It is our experience also that few patients can have satisfactory intercourse after a partial penectomy. However, in Jensen's series,[13] of the patients with 4 to 6 cm of corpus cavernosum remaining after partial penectomy 45 percent could have sexual intercourse, as could 25 percent of those with 2 to 4 cm of penis remaining. Nevertheless, the likelihood of long-term adverse psychological effects in this series was the same regardless of whether the patient had had a partial or a total amputation. From a practical standpoint, then, the main advantage of a partial penectomy is that afterwards the patient usually can void standing.

Other operations used to treat small tumors include local excision, circumcision and fulguration. For example, a superficial lesion on the foreskin of a young man might be managed by local excision or circumcision. However, the patient must be followed carefully, since in 1 series 40 percent of the patients who had had a local excision of a tumor on the glans had a recurrence.[22]

In this country total penectomy often is necessary because of the extent of the tumor. Any patient who has a large, fungating tumor or a tumor that involves the shaft of the penis extensively should have a total penectomy.

Radiation has been proposed as therapy for superficial lesions, especially in young men. Kelley and associates treated 10 patients who had small, low grade tumors using a betatron with a single electron-beam portal.[33] All 10 men were free of cancer from 1 to 6 years later. The most serious complication was urethral stricture (in 3 patients) but sexual function was maintained in all 10 men. Duncan and Jackson reported a 90 percent local cure rate in 20 patients with megavoltage radiation.[34] Pierquin and associates, who used iridium-192 implants, also reported excellent control of the primary lesions in all 35 of their patients, although only 7 patients had been followed for 3 years or longer.[35] Dańczak-Ginalska, who also used interstitial iridium, reported recurrences in 2 of 18 patients.[36] Thus, although radiation can be used to treat some patients with small, superficial lesions its advantage over excision has not been demonstrated.

Chemotherapy also have been recommended as treatment for the primary lesion. Ichikawa and associates, the first to report treating squamous cell carcinoma of the penis and scrotum with bleomycin, said that most tumors regressed considerably and several patients were cured.[37] Kyalwazi and associates reported that bleomycin administration was followed by complete regression of the tumor in 7 or 15 Ugandan patients, none of whom had received more than 750 mg (equals 750 units) of the drug.[38] More than half of the patients suffered minor side effects but not as a single case of pulmonary fibrosis was reported. In contrast, the use of bleomyin by other investigators had not produced such remarkable results.[39] The response rate in 67 patients was 73 percent but only 15 percent of the patients had a complete response. Studies of cultured animal-tumor cells led to the prediction that bleomycin plus vincristine would be more effective than either agent alone but this has not been true in penile cancer.[40] Ichikawa reported recently that bleomycin in combination with radiation is effective with lower doses of both agents than usually are used.[41]

Pulmonary fibrosis is the most serious adverse effect of bleomycin;[42,43] approximately 1 percent of the patients given this drug have died of pulmonary fibrosis. Persons more than 70 years old and those who have received more than 400 units all of the drug or who receive other antineoplastic agents at the same time are more susceptible to bleomycin-induced pulmonary toxicity. However, young patients also may suffer pulmonary toxicity from bleomycin, as did a 32-year-old patient of ours who received 405 mg of the drug for embryonal carcinoma of the testicle and as little as 50 mg. has caused pulmonary toxicity. In our experience bleomycin has proved to be exceedingly dangerous drug of little value against squamous cell carcinoma of the penis.

Regional Lymphatic Drainage. The best treatment for the inguinal lymphatics in patients with cancer of the penis is a subject of controversy. Treatment can consist of lymphadenectomy, radiation therapy, chemotherapy of some combination of these. Urologists in the United States generally advocate operation, whereas Europeans generally favor irradiation.

In a series of patients treated exclusively by operation Skinner and associates reported a 5-year survival rate of 59 percent, or 20 of 34 patients, which is the highest recorded for a group treated by operation along.[44] (Since 6 patients died within 5 years of other causes the cure rate might have been as high as 76 percent.) In this series patients with palpable nodes or with lesions that had invaded the corpora cavernosa or urethra were treated with bilateral ilio-inguinal lymphadenectomies. Patients believed to have nodes free of tumor were followed and bilateral dissections were done if the nodes became palpable.

In a series reported by Hardner and associates there was a 5-year survival rate of 48 percent.[29] Of their 100 patients 87 underwent inguinal node biopsy and, thus, could be accurately staged histologically. The survival of patients with metastases to the inguinal nodes (stage C) was best after ilio-inguinal node dissection, the mean survival time being 9.1 years. In contrast, the mean survival time of the patients with stage C disease who were treated with only inguinal node dissections was 5.0 years. Hardner and associates recommended inguinal node dissections for all patients, with iliac node dissections reserved for those with tumorous inguinal nodes.[29]

One of the early published series also is of interest. Hudson and associates treated 70 consecutive cases of penile cancer with penectomy and removal of the inguinal, femoral and dorsal lymphatics bilaterally.[45] They found metastases in the surgical specimens of 47 percent of the patients, some of whom had had biopsies interpreted as free of tumor. Hudson and associates believed that their figure was probably an underestimate and said that half of all patients with cancer of the penis can be assumed to have metastases. Some patients died of widespread metastases even when no tumor was found in the lymph nodes. Of the 46 patients followed for at least 5 years 21 survived, 19 of these having had lymph node metastases.

Ekström and Edsmyr reported a 69 percent 5-year survival rate free of disease in 177 patients, 10 of whom presented with inoperable metastases.[46] The patients who had palpable inguinal nodes had a unilateral or bilateral groin dissection at the time of penectomy or within 3 months thereafter (primary dissection). Patients whose nodes were not palpable received 3,000 to 4,000 rads to the groins and a unilateral or bilateral secondary dissection if the nodes later became palpable. Of the 37 patients who had primary dissections 12 (32 percent) were cured. Of the 130 patients thought initially to be free of metastases 18 had tumorous nodes removed during a secondary dissection (with 9 cures) and 11 others had metastases but did not have a lymphadenectomy. Thus, 22 percent of the men who received prophylactic groin irradiation later had inguinal metastases. Murrel and Williams had a similar experience: 3 of their 11 patients who received radiotherapy to groins without palpable nodes later had proved inguinal metastases.[47] Approximately 20 percent of the patients in a large series who do not receive irradiation to groins with nodes free of tumor clinically can be expected to have inguinal metastases. Because it is more difficult to detect metastases clinically in irradiated groins[46] and because lymphadenectomies in such groins have distressingly high complication rates we believe that the results reported by Ekström and Edsmyr raise a serious question about the propriety of using radiation to try to eradicate possible micrometastases.

Staubitz and associates reported on patients with documented metastatic disease in the inguinal lymph nodes.[23] Some of these patients were treated only with partial penectomy and none lived 5 years. Of 10 patients treated with partial penectomy and inguinal radiation 4 lived for 5 years. Partial amputation and inguinal dissection provided a 5-year survival rate of 50 percent (8 of 16) in those patients with proved metastatic disease.

Newaishy and Deeley advocated irradiating the primary lesion and groins with palpable nodes.[48] With their radiation technique the 5-year control rate was 80 percent in 11 patients with stage I tumors and 37 percent in 12 patients with palpable nodes. Murrel and Williams used radiation as the first treatment for the primary lesion and the palpable inguinal nodes.[47] Eighteen of the 29 patients with palpable nodes completed the course of treatment: 7 had persistent disease and 1 had recurrent disease. Six of these 8 had inguinal node dissections and tumor was found in 5 patients. Eleven patients with

stage I disease received groin irradiation and 3 had recurrences in the groin. Engelstad, who used irradiation for the penile lesion and the inguinal nodes regardless of their clinical status, reported a 67 percent 5-year survival rate in 57 patients.[49] In the American literature Gursel and associates reported that 2 of 15 patients with metastases to the inguinal lymph nodes survived 5 years or longer after receiving radiotherapy.[50]

In summary, based on the literature, we believe, as do others,[51] that although lymph node involvement may be controlled in some patients by irradiation this treatment cannot control metastases to the lymph nodes as reliably as can an operation.

The role of chemotherapy is the face of metastatic disease to the groin is limited. Many drugs and drug combinations have been used, including bleomycin, bleomycin plus vincristine, methotrexate and bleomycin plus doxorubicin hydrochloride, but most responses have been short-lived. However, from our experience we would agree with Baker and associates that any patient who has 2 or more tumor-bearing inguinal lymph nodes should be considered for systemic therapy.[52]

Review of Operative Therapy. The use of the inguinal node dissection in the treatment of cancer of the penis dates back to 1886, when MacCormac reported treating 5 patients with radical penectomy and bilaterial inguinal lymphadenectomy.[35] In 1907 Young recommended bilateral lymphadenectomies for neoplasms of the penis and he suggested doing both procedures together.[54] However, these operations fell into disfavor because of the unacceptably high morbidity and mortality rates of radical groin dissections. Even after enthusiasm for radical groin dissection revived surgeons continued to report serious wound and vascular complications in 40 to 60 percent of their patients.[19,55,56]

Despite the well known complications of extended groin dissection it is now established that the operation increases the survival of those patients with inguinal metastases. Recent reports suggest that 40 to 50 percent of patients with nodes containing tumor can be cured by extended ilio-inguinal dissection, whereas death of metastatic disease usually occurs within 2 to 3 years in untreated patients.[29,44]

The primary lesion need not be deeply invasive to produce metastases; if it has penetrated the basement membrane it is invasive cancer and the tumor cells have access to the extensive lymphatic plexus. This fact supports the approach of Hardner[29] and Hudson[45] and their associates, who advocated inguinal dissections for all patients with penile cancer. There are several other facts that support this position. First, as documented earlier, an accurate clinical assessment of the lymph nodes is difficult. Second, if one waits for inguinal metastases to become obvious clinically the patient often is incurable. Uehling emphasized that this occurs despite all attempts to have the patient make regular followup visits.[57] Further weight is given to the argument by Johnson and associates, who reported that 52 of 125 patients (41.6 percent) with lymph nodes initially free of tumor clinically were thought to have died as a result of the malignant disease.[21] A third reason for treating these patients with extended operation is that with improved surgical techniques inguinal dissections can be done with acceptable morbidity and mortality rates.

Recently, Cabanas has postulated the existence of sentinel lymph nodes in the inguinal region as the first filters along the lymphatic drainage pathways of the penis.[58] He suggested doing biopsies of both sentinel nodes in patients with squamous cell carcinoma of the penis. If these nodes are free of tumor no further surgical therapy is said to be indicated immediately. However, if the sentinel node(s) contains tumor ilio-inguinal dissection should be done. In all 15 patients in his series who had metastases the sentinel lymph node was found to contain tumor. In 12 cases the sentinel nodes were the only ones involved. However, although the sentinel nodes were free of tumor in 31 patients the 5-year survival rate was only 90 percent. Cabanas did not specify whether the 3 patients died of or with penile cancer. If they did then it means that this approach is only slightly better than staging by palpation, which has a 20 percent understaging rate. In addition, other authors have performed a biopsy of suspicious inguinal lymph nodes, although it is possible that lymph nodes other than the sentinel node were biopsied because some patients who were considered free of tumor later had metastases.

The timing of the lymphadenectomy is disputed. The advocates of delayed lymphadenectomy contend that survival statistics are no poorer if the operation is performed only after groin metastases become obvious. Beggs and Spratt described 2 of 5 patients surviving after delayed lymphadenectomy[59] and Ekström and Edsmyr reported that 9 of 18 patients were cured by delayed lymphadenectomies.[46] More recently, Baker and associates reported on 122 cases diagnosed between 1940 and 1974 with 100 percent followup.[52] The cumulative 5-year survival rate, measured from first examination, was 59 ± 10 percent for persons having early inguinal node dissections and 62 ± 14 percent for the patients having delayed, therapeutic dissections. Consequently, Baker and associates concluded that the 5-year survival rates failed to confirm the value of prophylactic groin dissections.

There also is considerable debate among those who advocate regional lymphadenectomy for cancer of the penis about how extensive the dissection should be.

Unfortunately, there are no adequate data to support the various points of view. Hardner and associates showed a large difference between the results of superficial and radical node dissections; the mean survival of patients who had ilio-inguinal lymphadenectomies, as compared with those who had inguinal dissections, was 9.1 years versus 5.0 years.[29] No one else has reported on a large series of cases from which the results of these techniques can be compared.

Even though the data needed to resolve these disputes are not available we agree with those who advocate immediate ilio-inguinal lymphadenectomy for almost all patients who are reasonable candidates for operation. There are 5 reasons for this opinion. (1) The morbidity and mortality rates of this operation have been reduced by improved surgical techniques. (2) Ilio-inguinal lymphadenectomy gives the best surgical margin, especially since metastases may skip the inguinal lymph nodes and go directly to the iliac nodes. (3) If the patient has tumorous nodes extended operation appears to offer the most effective means of controlling the disease. (4) One of the most common causes of treatment failure in penile cancer is the development of inoperable lymph node metastases after penectomy while the patient is being followed. (5) There is no reliable method, short of total extirpation of all ilio-inguinal lymph nodes, of staging the tumors.

Hemipelvectomy has been said to offer a reasonable chance to cure patients in whom metastases to the inguinal nodes have become fixed to bones or vessels, precluding a standard lymphadenectomy. Block and associates reported long-term survival in 3 of 7 patients on whom a hemipelvectomy was performed.[60]

SURGICAL TECHNIQUES

The first task of the urologic surgeon is to control the primary lesion but certain steps shold be taken before the penectomy. First, the tumor should be cultured because it usually will be suppurative and, therefore, the regional lymphatics will be chronically infected. It may be that sepsis has contributed to the reported high incidence of wound complications, especially in the groin. Accordingly, antibiotic therapy should be started when the patient is first seen and continued until the lymnphadenectomy incisions have healed. Second, the stage of the disease should be determined as accurately as possible using physical examination and standard radiographic techniques. We do not do lymphangiography because we believe that this procedure may contribute to the postoperative lymphedema. Third, before deciding how extensive the penile surgery should be the extent of the lesion in the penis must be assessed carefully.

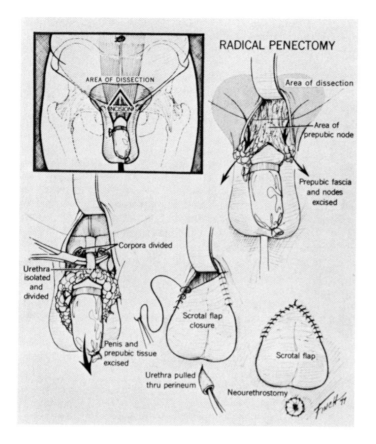

Fig. 1. Technique of total penectomy, including resection of lymphatic tissue at base of penis. Note that tumor is covered to prevent it from seeding wound.

Occasionally, corpus cavernosography may help determine whether the corpora are invaded by tumor.

We favor partial penectomy whenever possible, at least initially. If the surgical margins contain tumor or if the lesion appears histologically to be more aggressive than it was thought to be on clinical examination, the remainder of the penis can be amputated. To ensure an adequate surgical margin the amputation should be 2 cm proximal to the primary lesion. The urethra should be divided and spatulated 5 to 8 mm more distally to ensure an adequate orifice and to help prevent strictures.

The technique of total penectomy calls for comment. As when doing any type of penectomy the lesion should be covered completely to prevent the tumor from seeding the wound. We use either a rubber glove or a condom for this purpose. In a total penectomy we believe that it is important to include all of the lymphatic tissue at the base of the penis in the specimen (Fig. 1). Furthermore, the corpora should be removed as quickly as possible. Finally, the proximal margin of the urethra should be submitted for examination by frozen section before the perineal urethrostomy is performed. The urethra is spatulated to help prevent stricture formation.

With our technique for inguinal lymphadenectomy no incision is made across the groin crease. We have modified our skin bridge procedure and now, for the most part, use 3 incisions (Fig. 2).[61] The midline incision exposes the iliac vessels well and the same midline incision can be used both times if the 2 groins are done in separate operations. However, except for this change in the number of incisions used we do the operation in the way we have described elsewhere.[61] To summarize our experience we have done ilio-inguinal dissections in 9 patients for cancer of the penis. There have been no major vascular complications and the postoperative leg edema has been minimal. One patient who did not receive a low dose of heparin preoperatively had thrombophlebitis and 1 patient had delayed skin slough in the mid portion of the inguinal region that required a small skin graft.

Surgical Rehabilitation of Patients After Total Penectomy. Total penectomy is a debilitating operation physically and psychologically, yet little has been written about the possible surgical rehabilitation of these patients. Recent experience with female-to-male transsexuals shows

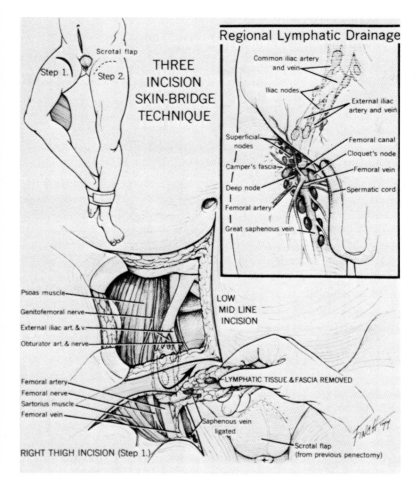

Fig. 2 labels:
Scrotal flap
Step 1.
Step 2.
THREE INCISION SKIN-BRIDGE TECHNIQUE

Regional Lymphatic Drainage
Common iliac artery and vein
Iliac nodes
External iliac artery and vein
Superficial nodes
Femoral canal
Cloquet's node
Camper's fascia
Femoral vein
Deep node
Spermatic cord
Femoral artery
Great saphenous vein

LOW MID LINE INCISION

Psoas muscle
Genitofemoral nerve
External iliac art. & v.
Obturator art. & nerve
Femoral artery
Femoral nerve
Sartorius muscle
Femoral vein
LYMPHATIC TISSUE & FASCIA REMOVED
Saphenous vein ligated
Scrotal flap (from previous penectomy)
RIGHT THIGH INCISION (Step 1.)

Fig. 2. Three-incision approach to inguinal and iliac lymph nodes provides excellent exposure. Skin bridge across groin crease helps prevent some postoperative complications attending certain other lymphadenectomy techniques.

that a neophallus can be created from the anterior abdominal wall. However, this technique has not yet been used extensively in patients who have had radical operations for cancer of the penis.

SUMMARY

All squamous cell cancers of the penis are potentially lethal. Failure to cure these tumors almost always results from lack of control locally. Few patients die of distant metastases without extensive disease in the ilio-inguinal regions. In a sense, then, these tumors clinically resemble epidermoid cancers of the head and neck.

Sometimes the primary lesion can be handled by local excision or by radiation therapy alone but usually the patient will require at least a partial penectomy. When partial penectomy has been adequate there have been remarkably few recurrences in the penile stump. Total penectomy should be reserved for large lesions with extensive involvement of the organ.

Most urologists now believe that radiation therapy alone is not a satisfactory way to treat patients with large primary lesions and suspected inguinal metastases because the statistics suggest that such patients are more likely to be cured by extended operation.

The staging of these patients by any means other than histologic examination of the nodes often is inaccurate. One approach to the treatment of the regional lymphatics is to make a biopsy of both sentinel lymph nodes, as advocated by Cabanas.[58] No immediate treatment is given if the nodes on both sides are free of tumor. An ilio-inguinal lymphadenectomy is performed on the side of a tumor-bearing sentinel node. More experience with this approach is required before it can be evaluated fully.

Some physicians advocate delaying a lymphadenectomy until there is definite evidence of inguinal metastases. To date, there are no data to prove that this is not satisfactory therapy. However, when lymphadenectomy is delayed the patient may be followed inadequately or lost to followup or inoperable disease may develop even while the patient is being watched. The controversy over whether operative treatment of the lymphatics should be limited to superficial groin dissections or whether ilio-inguinal lymphadenectomy should be done in every case is not resolved. We advocate a staged, bilateral, ilio-inguinal lymphadenectomy in almost all cases, using either the skin bridge technique or the 3-incision approach.

REFERENCES

1. Persky, L.: Epidemiology of cancer of the penis. Recent Results Cancer Res 60:97, 1977

2. Dean, A. L., Jr.: Epithelioma of the penis in a Jew who was circumcised in early infancy. Trans Am Ass Genito-Urin Surg 29:493, 1936

3. Marshall, V. F.: Typical carcinoma of the penis in a male circumcised in infancy. Cancer 6:1044, 1953

4. Reitman, P. H.: An unusual case of penile carcinoma. J Urol 69:547, 1953

5. Paquin, A. J., Jr. and Pearce, J. M.: Carcinoma of the penis in a man circumcised in infancy. J Urol 74:626, 1955

6. Melmed, E. P. and Pyne, J. R.: Carcinoma of the penis in a Jew circumcised in infancy. Br J Surg 54:729, 1967

7. Leiter, E. and Lefkovitis, A. M.: Circumcision and penile carcinoma. NY State J Med 75:1520, 1975

8. Amelar, R. D.: Carcinoma of the penis due to trauma occurring in a male patient circumcised at birth. J Urol 75:728, 1956

9. Ledlie, R. C. B. and Smithers, D. W.: Carcinoma of the penis in a man circumcised in infancy. J Urol 76:756, 1956

10. Kaufman, J. J. and Sternberg, T. H.: Carcinoma of the penis in a circumcised man. J Urol 90:449, 1963

11. Dodge, O. G. and Lindsell, C. A.: Carcinoma of the penis in Uganda and Kenya Africans. Cancer 16:1255, 1963

12. Mostofi, F. K. and Price, R. B., Jr.: Tumors and tumor-like lesions of the penis. In: Tumors of the Male Genital System. Washington, D. C.: Armed Forces Institute of Pathology, pp 277–294, 1973

13. Jensen, M. S.: Cancer of the penis in Denmark 1942 to 1962 (511 cases). Danish Med Bull 24:66, 1977

14. Fegen, J. P., Beebe, D. and Persky, L.: Basal cell carcinoma of the penis. J Urol 104:864, 1970

15. Bracken, R. B. and Diokno, A. C.: Melanoma of the penis and the urethra: 2 case reports and review of the literature. J Urol 111:198, 1974

16. Dehner, L. P. and Smith, B. H.: Soft tissue tumors of the penis. A clinicopathologic study of 46 cases. Cancer, 25:1431, 1970

Commentary: Problems and Management of Squamous Cell Carcinoma of the Penis

Lester Persky

The article by Fraley and Hoppmann is an excellent starting point for discussion of the disease entity squamous cell carcinoma of the penis and the problems attending its management. The infrequency of its occurrence in the temperate climates in the civilized world is well documented and needs little amplification.[1] However, it is worthy to note that the incidence in certain backward tribes with poor hygiene and inadequate personal attention exceeds the occurrence rate of every other neoplasm in these underdeveloped areas. These statistics and figures afford a glimpse that the urologic surgeon in these areas and in these communities can personally collect series greater than that seen in whole nations of peoples in the more advanced hemispheres. The occurrence rate of over 10% of all malignancies in large segments of several large countries with citizens of diverse backgrounds heightens the significance of this disease even further.[2]

The notes on the influence of various factors leading to a higher recurrence rate lead one automatically to consider and discuss circumcision. There is much heat engendered when various authors present opposite views and their own intrinsic feelings, hostilities, and beliefs. A host of inciting titles such as "Rape of the Phallus" have only served to further ignite passions in this ongoing continuous debate and discussion.[3] A perusal of the world statistics, however, points out the value of this procedure done at a very early age before there is any opportunity for malignant change to occur. Many observations have been made on the influence of smegma and constant irritation on the development of the predominantly seen penile squamous cell carcinoma.[4] There is an increasing suggestion on the part of a new generation of pediatricians and pediatric surgeons, however, that circumcisions need not be done and that the procedure can cause complications or irreparable harm. They feel there is a risk of anesthesia accidents, bleeding that can occur, meatal stenoses that will later require revision, and that inadequate circumcisions frequently lead to distortion and disfigurement. They have veritably a whole list of objections. As a urologist, having viewed the vagaries of cancer of the penis and the sequelae of the overlooked lesions of the phallus and the hidden changes underneath an adherent prepuce, I feel that there can be no denying the intrinsic worth of prophylactic circumcision.[5] My own belief is that this is the greatest prophylactic operation in the history of mankind. The infrequency of cancer of the penis in Jewish men cannot be refuted. The failure of circumcision at a later date to provide adequate protection is a commentary also worthy of note and heightens the significance of circumcision done early to prevent neoplasia.

Whenever there is a rare case reported of cancer of the penis in a Jewish man, usually it has been one of an unusual situation where there has been an inadequate circumcision or where there has been irritation beneath an adherent area where an incipient precursory change has been overlooked.

As a corollary of this and as an interesting sidelight of all these observations on the value of circumcision and how it prevents penile cancer, there is cervical carcinoma in the woman.[6] Usually it has been said that circumcision prevents the development of cancer of the cervix, and for a long time physicians felt there was a correlation between cervical cancer and the lack of circumcision or the presence of a foreskin. Although these case reports are few and far between, nevertheless there is an increasing incidence of cancer in Jewish women. Probably, however, the original observations are true, and it is certainly a less frequently seen tumor in women of Jewish background. This is not irrefutable evidence of the possible carcinogenic effect of smegma and retained preputial secretion, but this does give some credence to the suggestion that smegma is a true carcinogen. There can be no argument about the ease of maintaining cleanliness when there is no foreskin. The benefits of ready self-inspection are also apparent. These arguments and these observations are part and parcel of the worthwhileness of circumcision.

The further discussion concerning premalignant lesions must also be commented on.[7] The management of balanitis xerotica obliterans still poses a challenge to the physician who has responsibility of the patient with glandular or penile change. All efforts, including repeated biopsies of the readily exposed lesion, have been unavailing in giving any real clue on what is the most worthwhile method of management of these early changes. Local steroids have been of little or no help.[8] Radiation to the area of balanitis has unfortunately been attended by stricture formation, painful erections, fibrosis, and changes concomitant with progression of the disease.[9] Partial penectomy has always seemed like radical therapy for these lesions, which may not progress and may become relatively quiescent. As Hoppmann and Fraley point out in their discussion of these entities, only a small portion of them develop into true neoplastic growths. Nevertheless, continued suspicion of each elevation, ulceration, or crust must be built into the physician's makeup and must be an essential element of his attitude. He must be constantly aware of the need to inspect, to biopsy, to culture, to examine again. This is especially true when there is a biopsy of a mass of seemingly benign condylomata (*e.g.,* in the so-called Buschke–Lowenstein tumor).[10] I have repeatedly seen this tumor develop into true cancer despite what appeared to be benign preputial biopsies. In more than several instances, early amputation of the glans may well have saved the patient from more extensive surgery, more destructive changes, and probably extensive spread of the disease. Every application of topical chemotherapeutic agents has been fruitless in these tumors, and systemic therapy has similarly been seemingly of little use.

The vagaries of penile neoplasm and premalignant lesions have been discussed repeatedly by a variety of authors. It is important, however, to reemphasize that metastatic metastases do occur to the penis and that other primary tumors are encountered.[11] It is imperative that constant search be made if the lesion itself is not well understood. Varieties of every histologic tumor can be encountered, and at times the management of the disease and the structure requires a blend of imagination, conservatism, and occasionally consultation, guessing, and a blend of opinions.

The staging of these tumors has been relatively standardized by the general adoption of the classification of Jackson.[12] Again, as Hoppmann and Fraley emphasize, the difficulty is not in the staging system but rather in the clinical application of these classifications. As in other neoplasms of the genitourinary system, it is harder to stage the tumor adequately. Many are more extensive than appreciated initially, and many are more advanced than suspected at first view. The tumor may be harbored in nodes not felt at all, and on the other hand a vast majority of palpable nodes will be inflammatory. The "wait and see" attitude of most authorities is a position that I find hard to support. This idea of waiting and watching with nonintervention in the case of these lymph nodes, especially in penile cancer, is not an attitude that would be shared for other tumors with areas of lymphatic spread. Physicians do not adopt this reasoning in tumors of the bladder, in tumors of the testes, or in renal tumors. Often surgical disciplinarians share this aversion to watching a lesion grow. I have always believed and always been taught that to sit back and await developments of a mass gives great opportunity for neoplastic spread and for unsuspected ongrowth of the malignancy. The justification for this delay with penile cancer is a statistical one; nevertheless, it is hard to compare series, it is hard to compare cases, and it is hard to standardize peoples' attitudes. I personally prefer to do early lymphadenectomy rather than late.[13] When there is spread to the corpora, I feel that one should explore the nodes whether they are palpable or not. Perhaps this more aggressive approach would afford more exact information and will also permit more rational subsequent treatment profiles to ensue. The use of radiation has been recently advocated by Blandy and associates in England.[14] This modality of therapy has had various advocates throughout the years. Blandy cites high salvage rates with the use of radiation using accurately developed and positioned molds about the penile shaft. Circumcision is first closed, and the area is allowed to heal. The mold is self-applicable and done on an ambulatory basis by the patient himself. The statistics cited are excellent, but I wonder about the true ease of application and whether this highly specialized, selected group will afford the type of results that can be anticipated for the public at large. I have to worry about misapplication, errors of estimation and determination of total dosage, and a variety of other possible sources of error. A similar disparity in results are seen with the results of patients treated with chemotherapy, such as bleomycin as the Japanese advocate and the results seen with surgery.[15] The outstandingly successful results seen in Japan with bleomycin have not been duplicated here. The regression and disappearance of the tumor with chemotherapy is rarely seen, and physicians must, perhaps, contemplate the possibility of different tumors, perhaps different forms of application, perhaps a more personal bias and dedication to the use of this agent. The exact role of chemotherapy in penile cancer is therefore still unknown. It may well be that in conjunction with radiation and other contributions of chemotherapeutic agents, physicians will have the true value of this treatment. It may very well be reserved for those patients in whom surgical extirpation fails or is impossible or where for medical reasons, surgical techniques can not be applied.

I cannot leave the discussion of cancer of the penis without considering the recently advocated diagnostic test, "the sentinel node."[16] This sentinel node is one that has had little general application throughout this country until recently. Perhaps it will have great worth, as the original author underlines. However, various anatomic studies suggest that lessions of the glans may well skip the area of inguinal nodes. It is possible that even in the presence of a negative sentinel node, there will be tumor elsewhere. It is hard for me to believe that one node would always be the seat of metastatic foci and that by simple application of a local node dissection in this one area, the physician can determine the exact extent of the disease. I feel that this is an overly optimistic and an overly simplistic view. I believe it is going to be a long time before there is general adoption of this, although it may be that it will be necessary for controlled studies to be carried out before it can be universally adopted. My feeling is, moreover, that there will be complications attending this so-called brief, simple, surgical exercise, and urologists will need to familiarize themselves with it before they can adopt it unreservedly.

Cancer or the penis fortunately remains an infrequently encountered entity. It is only by pooling observations and experiences and sharing statistical results that physicians can come to valid conclusions. Epidemiologic studies reveal that the incidence of cancer of the penis in America is less than 1:100,000, and I feel that it is going to be a long time before physicians have a standardized rigid protocol for management. Perhaps this is a good thing, and perhaps the infrequency of the lesion will engender this sharing of attitudes and sentiments with a more rapid evolution of appropriate management.

REFERENCES

1. Persky L: Epidemiology of cancer of the penis. Recent results. Cancer Res 60:97, 1977
2. Dodge OG, Linsell CA: Carcinoma of the penis in Uganda and Kenya Africans. Cancer 16:1255, 1963
3. Morgan WK: Rape of the phallus. JAMA 194:310, 1965
4. Licklider S: Jewish penile carcinoma. J Urol 86:98, 1961
5. Garvin EH, Persky L: Circumcision: Is it justified in infancy. J Natl Med Assoc 58:733, 1966
6. Kaplan, II: Cancer of the cervix in Jews and non Jews. JAMA 141:574, 1949
7. McAninch JW, Moore CA: Precancerous penile lesions in young men. J Urol 104:287, 1970
8. Poipiter JH, Levy JB: Balanitis xerotica obliterans: Effective treatment with topical and sublesional corticosteroids. Br J Urol 39:420, 1967
9. Mantell BS, Morgan WY: Queyrat's erythroplasia of the penis treated by beta particle eradiation. Br J Radiol 42:855, 1969
10. Rhatigan RM, Jiminez S, Chopskie EJ: Condyloma accuminnation and carcinoma of the penis. South Med J 65:403, 1972
11. Tuttle JP, Rous S, Kinzel RC: Bladder epithelial neoplasms metastatic to glans penis. Urology 8:80, 1976
12. Jackson SM: The treatment of carcinoma of the penis. Br J Surg 53:33, 1966
13. de Kernion JB, Tynberg P, Persky L, et al: Carcinoma of the penis. Cancer 32:1256, 1973
14. Salaverria JC et al: Conservative treatment of carcinoma of penis. Br J Urol 51:32, 1979
15. Yagoda A, Mukherg B, Yang C, et al: Bleomycin: An antitumor antibiotic. Clinical experience in 274 patients. Ann Intern Med 77:861, 1972
16. Cabanas RM: An approach for the treatment of penile carcinoma. Cancer 39:456, 1977

ANNOTATED BIBLIOGRAPHY

Persky L: Epidemiology of cancer of the penis. Recent results. Cancer Res 60:97, 1977

These studies show amazingly low occurrences of penile cancer in civilized countries. Israel was the lowest in the world, with a reported incidence of 0.1:100,000. This is a remarkable contribution to health and a testimonial to early circumcision.

Dodge OG, Linsell CA: Carcinoma of the penis in Uganda and Kenya Africans. Cancer 16:1255, 1963

The high occurrence rate in these areas is indicative of what poor hygiene and a lack of familiarity with routine circumcision will do. No matter how skillful the area surgeons become, penectomy is not an operation one wishes to become too conversant with.

Morgan WK: Rape of the phallus. JAMA 194:310, 1965

The author describes the assault committed on an unsuspecting populace. His description of the beneficial effect of the present foreskin did not permit a consideration of glandular adhesions, sepsis due to retained smegma, and the occasional disaster from paraphimosis. This is a nonobjective diatribe against the procedure.

Licklider S: Jewish penile carcinoma. J Urol 86:98, 1961

The infrequency of penile carcinoma in Jewish men is well known. The occasional reported case reflects an incomplete surgical job or a poorly executed procedure. The occurrence of cancer is greater when circumcision occurs at a later date but still is very low. There is no known effect on sequal function or adequacy. In some native populations female consorts prefer a circumcised partner.

Garvin EH, Persky L: Circumcision: Is it justified in infancy. J Natl Med Assoc 58:733, 1966

In this publication we consider our experience with cancer of the penis, discuss the pros and cons of circumcision, and render support to the concept of early circumcision. There have been no men seen in Cleveland with penile cancer and a prior circumcision.

Kaplan II: Cancer of the cervix in Jews and non Jews. JAMA 141:574, 1949

Kaplan discusses the low incidence of cancer of the cervix in the rigidly reared Jewish family, where promiscuity plays no part at all. The relationship of smegma to cervical cancer is disputed by some authorities, but his statistics lend credence to the possible etiologic role of smegma. Current literature cites a low but present incidence of cervical carcinoma in women of Jewish extraction.

McAninch JW, Moore CA: Precancerous penile lesions in young men. J Urol 104:287, 1970

The precancerous lesions as discussed here represent erythroplasia of Queyrat's. Local excision was carried out successfully by these authors. Usually physicians have been unable to preclude recurrence and extension with such therapy. The current best treatment seems a combination of local steriods, circumcisions, and dilation.

Poipiter JH, Levy JB: Balanitis xerotica obliterans: Effective treatment with topical and sublesional corticosteriods. Br J Urol 39:420, 1967

The use of steriods is illustrated and exactly detailed by these authors. In their hands it has had great effect. In my own hands it has been of relatively little use in preventing recurrence or obviating the development of meatal stenosis.

Mantell BS, Morgan WY: Queyrat's erythroplasia of the penis treated by beta particle eradiation. Br J Radiol 42:855, 1969

The complications of radiation are often of greater discomfort and source of difficulty than the disability and the psychic trauma of amputation. Useful sexual function is rarely preserved, and although the authors' experience may be more salutory than most, mine has been fraught with continued problems.

Rhatigan RM, Jiminez S, Chopskie EJ: Condyloma accumination and carcinoma of the penis. South Med J 65:403, 1972

The authors depict this experience with so-called benign condylomata accuminata. Their experience with associated cancer and overlooked lesions parallels my own. The apparently innocuous-looking tumor may well harbor true neoplasm at its base and should be an area regarded always with *great* suspicion.

Tuttle JP, Rous S, Kinzel RC: Bladder epithelial neoplasms metastatic to glans penis. Urology 8:80, 1976

The metastatic tendencies of bladder neoplasm to extend to the penis are well documented. I have recently treated such a patient who was initially misdiagnosed as a true penile cancer, only to have the true diagnosis emerge with further microscopic and clinical study.

Jackson SM: The treatment of carcinoma of the penis. Br J Surg 53:33, 1966

This classification of carcinoma of the penis lends itself well to clinical use and interpretation. It is direct, reasonable, and easily understood by all workers. It has been generally adopted by all workers in the field and affords a starting point for discussion and comparison of results.

deKernion JB, Tynberg P, Persky L, et al: Carcinoma of the penis. Cancer 32:1256, 1973

Our results have been extended to include greater numbers of patients. We still advocate surgery and node excision when there is invasion of the corpora. We have also, since this report, had one patient with recurrence of carcinoma *in situ* after partial penectomy.

Salaverria JC, et al: Conservative treatment of carcinoma of penis. Br J Urol 51:32, 1979

The excellent result that these authors have achieved with the tailormade applicators and self-manipulation on the part of the patient makes advocates of more radical surgery somewhat less rigid in their attitudes. The statistics strongly support their contentions that external radiotherapy and radiation in general is still a viable tool in their hands. It is a view that perhaps should be reconsidered by other surgeons.

Yagoda A, Mukherg B, Yang C, et al: Bleomycin: An antitumor antibiotic. Clinical experience in 274 patients. Ann Intern Med 77:861, 1972

The superlative results reported by these authors with bleomycin have not been duplicated by other clinicians. There is still a high incidence of complications (*i.e.,* pulmonary, mucosal, and hematologic). This documentation of results, however, lends credence to their statistics and makes further investigation of this tool mandatory by all workers.

Cabanas RM: An approach for the treatment of penile carcinoma. Cancer 39:456, 1977

The author's series of 90 cases shows beautiful correlation with sentinel node findings and survival statistics. This point of view may well be supported by other observers, and I will await further data.

Overview: Cancer of the Penis

Robert S. Hotchkiss

Although cancer of the penis is one of the oldest known neoplasms, there remains considerable controversy as to proper management. Celsus, Sapota, and Hildanus and other ancient writers described tumors of the penis and operations employed to treat such disorders. During the past 30 yr, however, considerable progress has been made in elucidating metastatic pathways and the application of radical surgery to deal with the primary and secondary neoplasms. The excellent review

TABLE 1

Reporter	Years Involved	Cases
1. Hanash et al. (1970)	1945–1965	169
2. Colon (1952)	1941–1952	145
3. Hardner and Woodruff (1967)	1944–1964	135
4. Jackson (1966)	1942–1957	130
5. Dean (1935)	1915–1935	120
6. Buddington et al. (1963)	1928–1963	104
7. Spratt et al. (1965)	1940–1961	88
8. Furlong and Uhle (1953)	1921–1946	88
9. Basset (1952)	no specific years	78
10. Young (1931) and Lewis (1931)	1916–1931	70
11. Horn and Nesbit (1934)		37
12. Fegan and Persky (1969)	1955–1967	35
13. Dean and Dean (1935)	1947–1950	29
14. Sanjurjo and Flores (1960)	1946–1959	24
15. Harlin (1952)	10 years	21
16. Melicow and Ganem (1946)	1928–1944	19

by Hoppmann and Fraley updates the more recent literature and assists the reader in resolving some of the uncertainties relative to rationales for treatment.

One conspicuous reason for confusion is the rarity of the disorder in America. An estimate has been advanced that its incidence is 1:100,000, although this is fallacious if women are included in the calculation. The advice of Jonathan Hutchinson given in 1889, however, is most pertinent. He wrote, "It is such rare afflictions which are worthy of study because of their rarity which leads to mistakes in diagnoses which might be effective." The report of Furlong and Uhle substantiates the foregoing statement, since they found that 11% of the men in their series of 88 patients were denied early treatment because of errors in diagnoses.[1]

Another factor in permitting the disorder to advance to metastatic stages is the procrastinations of the patients themselves. This negligence is difficult to comprehend, since the organ is exposed and handled several times a day for urination. Furlong and Uhle found that 26% of the afflicted men allowed 1 yr or more to elapse between onset of signs and symptoms before seeking treatment. Buddington and colleagues also tabulated the duration of symptoms before initial treatment and found that 44 of 104 men had lesions for over a year before consulting physicians.[2] The tragedy of this inattention is magnified by the high curability of early lesions compared to the advanced stages of the disease. Perhaps this delay can be explained by its concurrence with the underprivileged and less well-educated members of our society. My experience supports that of others, that advanced carcinoma of the penis is almost, but not exclusively, a disease of the poor.

The rarity of genital carcinoma in Occidental areas of the world accounts for the considerable debate and disagreements on procedures. This is particularly true in relation to the selection of therapy, such as regional lymphadenectomy, chemotherapy, and irradiation. Good documentation suffers because the available literature is necessarily composed of reports based on a limited number of patients. This prohibits detailed statistical analyses on one type of treatment as compared to another. Furthermore, the larger series extend over a period of 15 to 20 yr, implying that several persons were involved in management and policymaking. It is probable that therapeutic principles may have varied according to the convictions of several surgeons. This circumstance has been summarized in Table 1.

Hoppman and Fraley fully realize this dilemma and state, "Unfortunately there is no adequate data to support the various points of view" in regard to how extensive the dissection of the lymph nodes should be. There is an incumbency placed on each surgeon, however, to proceed with a policy of treatment based upon his evaluation and interpretation of the existing information. Hoppman and Fraley have done precisely that, giving five reasons for their current attitudes for lymphadenectomy.

My current policy for the treatment of carcinoma of the penis is in close agreement with Hoppmann and Fraley. A review of 100 patients with penile cancer encountered over a period of 23 yr at New York University Medical Center was published in 1973.[4] The following is a brief summary of that experience, which has established my policy of therapy:

1. The choices of treatment are often predicated by the condition of the patient. His age, the stage and extent of the primary and secondary lesions, and his estimated ability to survive surgical procedures of considerable magnitude are primary considerations. Should the patient qualify as a reasonably good candidate for comprehensive care, I proceed as follows:

   a. Small lesions (less than 2 cm) localized to the prepuce are treated by circumcision if the glans or shaft are not involved.

   b. Small lesions on the distal penis are treated by partial penectomy (stage I).

   c. Lesions in the shaft of the penis are treated by total penectomy and lymphadenectomy (stages II & III).

   d. Total emasculation is required for extensive destructive lesions involving the scrotum.

   e. The management of inguinal nodes is based on the premise that tumor cells allowed to remain in the inguinal lymphatics does not constitute a cure. Antibiotics are given to all patients promptly to modify the common occurrence of secondary infection. Following penectomy, the antibiotic therapy is continued for 4 wk because inflammatory lymphadenitis is a usual concurrent finding; 32% to 60% of patients will have metastatic tumor in their regional nodes if the nodes are clinically palpable. Furthermore, 12% to 20% will have tumor in nodes not enlarged. Therefore, bilateral inguinal lymphadenectomy seems appropriate following penectomy, and 4 wk of antibiotic therapy provided there is no distant metastasis. Only one patient had distant metastasis to his lung found before surgery in my series.

2. I have been impressed with the reports of the short survival of patients who had iliac node metastases and have not elected to add the abdominal approach to inguinal surgery, which in my series had a 34% morbidity, although there were no surgical deaths.

I cannot leave the subject of penile carcinoma without some reflections on the rational of neonatal circumcision. There is overwhelming evidence that early circumcision prevents carcinoma of the penis. The ''cost–benefit'' equation has been advanced, nevertheless, by some pragmatists citing that the removal of several thousand prepuces is hardly justified to control a disorder that involves only 1:100,000. Those who have dealt with the consequences of the dreadful malady of penile cancer cannot but contemplate that early circumcision would have prevented this catastrophy as well as provided to others better penile hygiene even if malignancy were not to occur.

References

1. Furlong RR, Uhle CA: Cancer of the penis—a report of 88 cases. J Urol 69:550, 1953

2. Buddington WT, Kickham CJ, Smith WE: An assessment of malignant disease of the penis. J Urol 89:442, 1963

3. Andrade R, Gumport SL, Popkin GL, et al: Cancer of the skin. Biology—diagnosis and management. Philadelphia, W B Saunders, 1976

4. Kossow JH, Hotchkiss RS, Morales P: Carcinoma of penis treated surgically. Analyses of 100 cases. Urology 2:169, 1973

5. Spratt JS, Shieber WS, Dillard BM: Anatomy and surgical technique of groin dissection. St. Louis, C V Mosby, 1965

6. Hardner GJ, Woodruff MV: Operative management of carcinoma of penis. J Urol 98:487, 1967

7. Whitmore WF Jr: Tumors of the penis, urethra, scrotum and testis. In Campbell MF, Harrison JS (eds): Urology, vol 2, p 1190. Philadelphia, W B Saunders, 1970

PART THIRTY-SIX

SURGERY OF THE GENITALIA

92

THE FATE OF THE FORESKIN
A Study of Circumcision

Douglas Gairdner, D.M., M.R.C.P.

Consultant Paediatrician, United Cambridge Hospitals

British Medical Journal, Vol. 2, p. 1433
Published by British Medical Association
Tavistock Square London WC149JR
December 24, 1949

It is a curious fact that one of the operations most commonly performed in this country is also accorded the least critical consideration. In order to decide whether a child's foreskin should be ablated the normal anatomy and function of the structure at different ages should be understood; the danger of conserving the foreskin must then be weighed against the hazards of the operation, the mortality and after-effects of which must be known. Though tens of thousands of infants are circumcised each year in this country, nowhere are these essential data assembled. The intention of this paper is to marshal the facts required by those concerned with deciding the fate of the child's foreskin.

ORIGINS OF CIRCUMCISION

Male circumcision, often associated with analogous sexual mutilations of the female such as clitoric circumcision and infibulation, is practised over a wide area of the world by some one-sixth of its population. Over the Near East, patchily throughout tribal Africa, amongst the Moslem peoples of India and of South-East Asia, and amongst the Australasian aborigines circumcision has been regularly practised for as long as we can tell.

Many of the natives that Columbus found inhabiting the American continent were circumcised. The earliest Egyptian mummies (2300 B.C.) were circumcised, and wall paintings to be seen in Egypt show that it was customary several thousand years earlier still.

According to Elliot Smith circumcision is one of the characteristic features of a "heliolithic" culture which, some 15,000 years ago, spread out over much of the world; others believe that the practice must have arisen independently among different peoples. In spite of the enormous literature on the subject (well summarized in Hastings's *Encyclopaedia of Religion and Ethics*), we remain profoundly ignorant of the origins and significance of this presumably sacrificial rite. The age at which boys are circumcised varies widely in different races, from the Mosaic practice of circumcising at about the eighth day, to the custom in many African tribes of making circumcision part of an initiation ceremony near the age of puberty. Circumcision was introduced into Roman Europe with Christianity; little is known about its status in mediaeval Europe, but it was probably customary only amongst adherents of the Jewish faith until, with the rise of modern surgery in the nineteenth century, its status changed from a religious rite to that of a common surgical procedure.

DEVELOPMENT OF THE PREPUCE

The prepuce appears in the foetus at eight weeks as a ring of thickened epidermis (Fig. 1A) which grows forwards over the base of the glans penis (Fig. 1B). It grows more rapidly on the upper surface than the lower, and so leaves the inferior aspect of the preputial ring deficient (Hunter, 1935). At 12 weeks the urethra still opens on the inferior aspect of the shaft of the penis and the terminal part of the urethra has yet to be constructed. Arrest at this stage produces the glandular type of hypospadias, with the "hooded" prepuce only partially covering the glans.

From the inferior aspect of the glans a pair of outgrowths are pushed out and meet (the sulcus on the under aspect of the glans marks their fusion), so enclosing a tube which, becoming continuous with the existing urethra, advances the meatus to its final site. These outgrowths from the glans carry with them the prepuce on each side (Fig. 1C), thus completing the prepuce inferiorly and forming the frenulum.

By 16 weeks the prepuce has grown forwards to the tip of the glans. At this stage (Fig. 1D) the epidermis of the deep surface of the prepuce is continuous with the epidermis covering the glans, both consisting of squamous epithelium. By a process of desquamation the preputial space is now formed in the following manner (Deibert, 1933). In places the squamous cells arrange themselves in whorls, forming epithelial cell nests. The centres of these degenerate, so forming a series of spaces (Fig. 1E); these, as they increase in size, link up until finally a continuous preputial space is formed.

The stage of development which has been reached by the time the child is born varies greatly. Figs. 2, 3, and 4 show sections of the penis in three full-term newborn infants; in Fig. 2 separation of the prepuce has not yet begun; in Fig. 3 separation is partial; in Fig. 4 separation is complete, though this, as will be shown, is uncommon at birth.

ANATOMY OF THE PREPUCE

The Younger Child. The prepuce is still in the course of developing at the time of birth, and the fact that its separation is usually still incomplete renders the normal prepuce of the newborn non-retractable. (It will be seen that preputial "adhesions" is an inapposite term to apply to the incompletely separated prepuce, suggesting as it does that the prepuce and glans were formerly separate structures.) The age at which complete separation of the prepuce with full retractability spontaneously occurs is shown in Fig. 5, which has been constructed from observations of the prepuce in a series of 100 newborns and about 200 boys of varying ages up to 5 years. Of the newborns, 4% had a fully retractable prepuce, in 54% the glans could be uncovered enough to reveal the external meatus, and in the remaining 42% even the tip of the glans could not be uncovered. Of the older group 10% had been circumcised and a few had at some time had their prepuce "stretched"; the figures from which the diagram is constructed are therefore not precise, but they indicate with sufficient accuracy that the prepuce is *non-retractable* in four out of five normal males of 6 months and in half of normal males of 1 year. By 2 years about 20% and by 3 years about 10% of boys still have a non-retractable prepuce.

The fact that at these ages non-retractability depends upon incomplete separation of the prepuce can be easily demonstrated by running a probe round the preputial

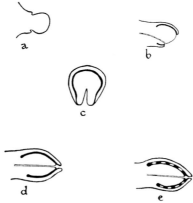

Fig. 1. Development of prepuce. (A) Eight weeks; (B) sagittal section and (C) coronal section, 12 weeks; (D) 16 weeks; (E at about term. Compare Fig. 3.

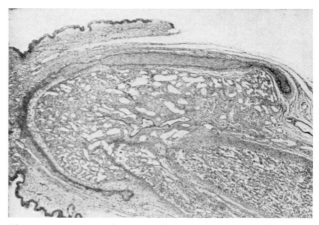

Fig. 2. Separation of prepuce has not begun and there is as yet no preputial space.

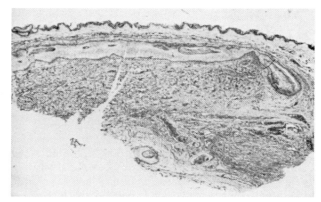

Fig. 3. Foci of desquamation leading to partial separation of prepuce.

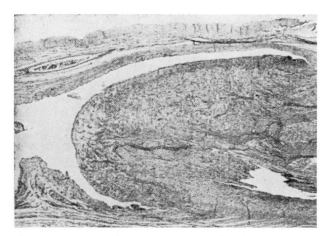

Fig. 4. Separation of prepuce completed to form fully developed preputial space.

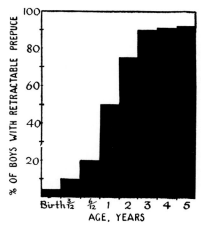

Fig. 5. Proportion of boys of varying ages from birth to 5 years, in whom the prepuce has spontaneously become retractable. Note that it is uncommon for this to occur in the first six months.

space, gently completing its continuity. It will then be found that, although the prepuce is often somewhat tighter than in the adult, it is not tight enough to prevent retraction. This test was applied to a series of 54 boys aged from 2 months to 3 years who had been referred to hospital for circumcision, generally with a diagnosis of phimosis. In 53 of the 54 the prepuce became easily retractable by this simple manipulation; in one 5-month-old infant this manœuvre failed because preputial separation had not advanced far enough to enable manipulation to complete the process. Although in this way the prepuce of nearly every infant can be rendered retractable, the procedure, necessarily involving the tearing apart of two as yet incompletely separated surfaces, causes some bleeding and opens the way to possible infection. For these reasons it is inadvisable as a routine procedure.

Prepuce of the Older Child. Of 200 uncircumcised boys aged 5–13 years from three different schools, 6% had a non-retractable prepuce; in a further 14% the prepuce could be only partially retracted. In the majority of boys in this age group non-retractability depends upon the persistence of a few strands of tissue between prepuce and glans, so that minimal force is required to achieve retractability. In this age group, however, retraction of a hitherto unretracted prepuce discovers inspissated smegma, which, in contrast to that found in the younger child, is in some cases malodorous. This, together with the facts discussed under penile cancer, indicates that a different view ought to be taken of the non-retractable prepuce in the child over about 5 years, and that, whereas a nonretractable prepuce in the young child should be accepted with equanimity as normal, after about 3 years of age steps should be taken to render the prepuce of all boys retractable and capable of being kept clean.

FUNCTION OF THE PREPUCE

It is often stated that the prepuce is a vestigial structure devoid of function. However, it seems to be no accident that during the years when the child is incontinent the glans is completely clothed by the prepuce, for, deprived of this protection, the glans becomes susceptible to injury from contact with sodden clothes or napkin. Meatal ulcer is almost confined to circumcised male infants, and is only occasionally seen in the uncircumcised child when the prepuce happens to be unusually lax and the glans consequently exposed (Freud, 1947).

INCIDENCE OF CIRCUMCISION

Amongst the Western nations the circumcision of infants is a common practice only with the English-speaking peoples. It is, for the most part, not the custom in continental Europe or Scandinavia, or in South America. In England the collected data of various colleagues* who have kindly made observations on infants, school-children, and university students reveal wide variations as between different districts and between different social classes. For instance, in Newcastle-upon-Tyne 12% of 500 male infants aged 12 months were circumcised; in Cambridge the comparable figure was 31% of 89 male infants aged 6 to 12 months. Boys coming from the upper classes are more often circumcised, 67% of 81 13-year-old boys entering a public school had been circumcised, whereas only 50% of 154 boys aged 5 to 14 in primary and secondary schools in the rural districts of Cambridgeshire, and 30% of 141 boys aged 5 to 11 in primary schools in the town of Cambridge, had been circumcised. The influence of social class is shown also by some figures analysed by Sir Alan Rook from a group of university students. Whereas 84% of 73 students coming from the best-known public schools had been circumcised, this was so of only 50% of 174 coming from grammar or secondary schools. Either the boys of well-to-do parents are suffering circumcision much too often, or those of poorer parents not often enough.

In view of the wide difference in the incidence of circumcised males in different parts of the country, it is difficult to give an average figure for the whole country. A conservative estimate of 20%, which is above the rate for Newcastle-upon-Tyne but well below that for all the other groups quoted, would mean that the number of circumcisions performed on children in England and Wales is of the order of 90,000 annually.

MORTALITY AND SEQUELAE OF CIRCUMCISION

Circumcision, like any other operation, is subject to the risks of haemorrhage and sepsis, and, where a general anaesthetic is employed, to the risk of anaesthetic death. The number of deaths presumed to be due to these causes is shown in the accompanying Table. The Registrar-General groups circumcision and phimosis together, but in view of the fact that "phimosis," as the term is commonly applied to infants, is physiological (see below)

* Dr. H. P. Broda, assistant school M.O., Cambridge; Dr. Eileen Brereton, assistant school M.O., Cambridgeshire; Drs. F. J. W. Miller and S. D. Court, Child Health Department, King's College, Newcastle-upon-Tyne; Dr. Margaret Patterson, assistant M.O.H., Cambridge; Sir Alan Rook, senior health officer, Cambridge University; Dr. R. E. Smith, medical officer to Rugby School. It is a pleasure to record my thanks to all these colleagues for their ready co-operation and many painstaking observations, and for generously allowing me to quote their findings.

it is probable that the great majority of these deaths were attributable to operation rather than to any pathological condition necessitating operation.

About 16 deaths in children under 5 years occur each year from circumcision. In most of the fatalities which have come to my notice death has occurred for no apparent reason under anaesthesia, but haemorrhage and infection have sometimes proved fatal.

Haemorrhage is not uncommon after circumcision. F. J. W. Miller and S. D. Court (1949, personal communication), who followed 1,000 infants in Newcastle-upon-Tyne for their first year, found that 58 were circumcised, and two of these bled sufficiently to require blood transfusion. In my own experience about two out of every 100 children circumcised as hospital out-patients will be admitted on account of haemorrhage or other untoward event. Blood losses in the first year are particularly apt to lead to anaemia, and several infants have been seen with severe iron-deficiency anaemia following haemorrhages after circumcision.

Reference has already been made to meatal ulcer, which, in so far as it is so much more frequent in circumcised male infants, should be counted a sequel of the operation.

PATHOLOGICAL CONDITIONS OF PREPUCE FOR WHICH CIRCUMCISION IS PERFORMED

The surprising variety of reasons why different doctors advise circumcision and other operations and manipulations on the prepuce can be found described in the long correspondence on the subject which ran in the *British Medical Journal* from August to November, 1935. Circumcision is sometimes undertaken in order to cure existing pathological conditions, sometimes in order to prevent various diseases from occurring at a much later date.

Phimosis

Since in the newborn infant the prepuce is nearly always non-retractable, remaining so generally for much of the first year at least, and since this normal non-retractability is not due to tightness of the prepuce relative to the glans but to incomplete separation of these two structures, it follows that phimosis

Table Showing Deaths in Children Attributed to Circumcision or Phimosis in England and Wales

	Under 1 Year	1–4 Years	Total, Under 5 Years
1942	12	4	16
1943	10	7	17
1944	10	6	16
1945	15	2	17
1946	16	3	19
1947	9	1	10

(which implies a pathological constriction of the prepuce) cannot properly be applied to the infant. Further, the commonly performed manipulation known as "stretching the foreskin" by forcibly opening sinus forceps inserted in the preputial orifice cannot be justified on anatomical grounds, besides being painful and traumatizing. In spite of the fact that the preputial orifice often appears minute—the so-called pin-hole meatus— its effective lumen, when tested by noting whether or not a good stream of urine is passed, is almost invariably found to be adequate.

Infants with umbilical or inguinal hernia are particularly liable to suffer circumcision on account of "phimosis," but if this simple test is applied, rarely will any obstruction to the urinary flow be found present. Occasionally the preputial orifice is imperfectly related to the external meatus, so that the urinary stream balloons out the subpreputial space; this can be easily remedied by gently separating the prepuce from the glans in the region of the meatus by means of a probe. True phimosis causing urinary obstruction has been described (Campbell, 1948), but must be exceedingly rare: in the cases I have seen in which this diagnosis has been made, simple separation of the prepuce has shown that there was no constriction of the preputial orifice.

Through ignorance of the anatomy of the prepuce in infancy, mothers and nurses are often instructed to draw the child's foreskin back regularly, on the supposition that stretch- ing of the foreskin is what is required. I have on three occasions seen young boys with a paraphimosis caused by mothers or nurses who have obediently carried out such instructions; for, although the size of the prepuce does allow the glans to be delivered, the fit is often a close one and slight swelling of the glans, such as may result from forceful efforts at retraction, may make its reduction difficult.

Balanitis and Posthitis

Inflammation of the glans is uncommon in childhood when the prepuce is performing its protective function. Posthitis— inflammation of the prepuce—is commoner, and it occurs in two forms. One form is a cellulitis of the prepuce; this responds well to chemotherapy and does not seem to have any tendency to recur; hence it is questionable whether circumcision is indicated. More often inflammation of the prepuce is part of an ammonia dermatitis affecting the napkin area. The nature of this condition was firmly established by Cooke in 1921, but is still not universally known. The urea-splitting *Bact. am- moniagenes* (derived from faecal flora) acts upon the urea in the urine and liberates ammonia. This irritates the skin, which becomes peculiarly thickened, while superficial desquamation produces a silvery sheen on the skin as if it were covered with a film of tissue paper. Such appearances are diagnostic of ammonia dermatitis, and inquiry will confirm that the napkins, particularly those left on through the longer night interval, smell powerfully of ammonia. Treatment consists in impreg- nating the napkins with a mild antiseptic inhibiting the growth of the urea-splitting organisms. For this purpose boric acid powder sprinkled over the napkins, or a rinse of 1 in 4,000 mercuric chloride or of the recently introduced non-toxic substance "diaparene" (Benson *et al.*, 1949), are gratifyingly effective.

When involved in an ammonia dermatitis the prepuce shows the characteristic thickening of the skin, and this is often labelled a "redundant prepuce"—another misnomer which may serve as a reason for circumcision. The importance of recognizing ammonia dermatitis lies in the danger that if circumcision is performed the delicate glans, deprived of its proper protection, is particularly apt to share in the inflammation and to develop a meatal ulcer. Once formed, a meatal ulcer is often most difficult to cure.

Enuresis

A number of symptoms of obscure cause, such as enuresis, masturbation, habit spasm, night terrors, or even convulsions, have from time to time been attributed to phimosis, and circumcision has been advised. No evidence exists that a prepuce whose only fault is that it has not yet developed retractability can cause such symptoms.

It may be apposite at this stage to quote the reasons given by the mother for desiring her child's circumcision in a series of 54 infants referred to hospital by a doctor. In 39 infants the reason was a symptomless "phimosis," found on routine inspection by doctor, nurse, mother, or neighbour. In nine cases it was said that "he cries when he wets": five of these proved to be due to ammonia dermatitis; closer questioning of the others revealed either no connexion between when the baby cried and when he urinated, or merely that crying often started micturition. In three cases the foreskin was judged to be too long or redundant, and in a further three the reason was even more frankly cosmetic ("it looks funny") or was intangible ("we believe in it"). As has been stated earlier, in all except one of his group of 54 infants, phimosis was disproved, in so far as gentle manipulation enabled the prepuce to be retracted.

CONDITIONS PREVENTED BY CIRCUMCISION

Universal circumcision of male infants has been urged as a means of preventing the later development of a variety of conditions—paraphimosis, venereal diseases, penile cancer, and cervical cancer of women.

Paraphimosis

Some idea of the importance of paraphimosis can be gained from figures from the Royal Victoria Infirmary, Newcastle- upon-Tyne, a hospital serving a large population in which, as has been mentioned, infants are circumcised less often than in the country generally. In the children's wards paraphimosis accounts for about seven out of a total of 800 male child admissions each year (0.9%): an appreciable number of these are found to be the result of the mother's obeying misguided instructions to retract her infant's prepuce forcibly. In the adult wards it accounts for about 10 out of a total of 5,000 male surgical admissions (0.1%), so that paraphimosis scarcely constitutes an important hazard to the uncircumcised male.

Venereal Disease

Although there is a common belief that the circumcised man runs a lessened risk of venereal infection, particularly syphilitic, there are few figures to support this. Lloyd and Lloyd (1934), who reviewed the published evidence and analysed their own figures, concluded that circumcision did not diminish the chance of a syphilitic chancre. Schrek and Lenowitz (1947) found that hospital patients gave a history of venereal disease equally often whether circumcised or not. Wilson (1947) has published figures showing that, of the men attending a Canadian Army venereal disease centre, the proportion of uncircumcised soldiers (77%) was higher than in the Canadian Army generally (52%), and concluded that the uncircumcised soldier is more prone to venereal infection. It may be, however, that since circumcision of infants is *de rigueur* in Canada, the uncircumcised man will tend to come from a lower social grade and thus to be more likely to expose himself to infection. The evidence seems scarcely to warrant universal circumcision as a prophylactic against venereal infection.

Penile Cancer

This subject merits careful appraisal, for it alone of the medical reasons commonly advanced for the universal circumcision of infants is capable of withstanding critical scrutiny. In England and Wales deaths from penile cancer number about 150 a year. The relation between this disease and antecedent circumcision has recently been reviewed by Kennaway (1947). All observers agree that circumcision in the first five years of life protects absolutely from penile cancer, and this applies not only to one group such as the Jewish but equally to the mixed races of the U.S.A. The reason for this preventive effect of early circumcision is not known: it is not due to removal of the cancer-bearing area, since the usual site of penile cancer, the sulcus behind the glans, is retained. If it is due to retained smegma or its decomposition products being carcinogenic, this effect must be of startling potency, since circumcision after the fifth year fails to prevent cancer occurring several decades later.

A clue to the problem may lie in the exceptionally low hygienic standards of patients with penile cancer, which has struck several observers. Dean (1935), reviewing 120 cases, writes: "Men with penis cancers gave the impression of being less intelligent, as a class, than other cancer patients. Not only had the majority ignored for long periods the precancerous state of physical annoyance, filth, and odoriferous discharges, but also it was not unusual for many to delay seeking advice until a large part of the penis had become affected with an ulcerating growth." The unusual frequency with which patients with penile cancer have had venereal disease has been demonstrated by Dean (1935) and by Schrek and Lenowitz (1947), these authors have come to the conclusion that this fact indicates again the significantly low standard of social hygiene of these patients. A further factor frequently present in patients with penile cancer is phimosis; although this is often the result of the growth, in many patients the prepuce has never been retractable (Lewis, 1931).

With these facts it may reasonably be contended that, if the uncircumcised male has a prepuce which he can retract and which he keeps clean, he is likely to enjoy the same immunity from penile cancer as his circumcised brother.

Cervical Cancer in Women

The low incidence of cervical cancer among Jewesses has led Handley (1947) to the conclusion that this disease is mainly caused by the introduction of irritant material by the uncircumcised husband during coitus. It should be a simple matter to put this theory to the test by noting whether the husbands of women with cervical cancer are more frequently uncircumcised than others. Meanwhile the evidence seems insufficient to warrant universal circumcision or preputiotomy, such as Handley advocates.

Minor Advantages of Circumcision

There remain a number of more or less trivial factors which are sometimes mentioned as reasons why infant circumcision is desirable: difficulties in keeping the uncircumcised parts clean, or the supposed aesthetic or erotic superiority of the shorn member. In order to fulfil the intention of this paper an inquiry on these points should have been made amongst a group of uncircumcised men. This was not attempted, although with regard to the last two of the factors mentioned it should be stated that whenever the subject has been broached in male company those still in possession of their foreskin have been forward in their insistence that any differences which may exist in such matters operate emphatically to their own advantage.

Moreover, if there were sensible disadvantages in being uncircumcised, one would expect that the fathers of candidates for circumcision would sometimes register their feelings in the matter. Yet in interviewing the parents of several hundred infants referred for circumcision I have met but one father who wished his son circumcised because of his own disagreeable experience of the uncircumcised state. The rest of the fathers were equally indifferent about the matter whether they themselves had been circumcised or not. Indeed, so little did the father's personal experience seem important that one-quarter of the mothers did not even know whether their husbands were or were not circumcised. These facts provide some evidence that few uncircumcised men have cause to regret their state.

CONCLUSIONS

It has been shown that, since during the first few years of life the prepuce is still in process of developing, it is impossible at this period to determine in which infants the prepuce will attain normal retractability. In fact, only about 10% will fail to attain this by the age of 3 years. Of this 10% of 3-year-old boys, in most it will be found a simple matter to render the prepuce retractable by completing its separation from the glans by gentle manipulation. In a very few this may prove impossible and circumcision might then be considered a justifiable precaution. Higgins (1949), with long experience of paediatric urology, also concludes that circumcision should not be considered until "after the age of, say, 2 to 3 years."

The prepuce of the young infant should therefore be left in its natural state. As soon as it becomes retractable, which will generally occur some time between 9 months and 3 years, its toilet should be included in the routine of bath time, and soap and water applied to it in the same fashion as to other structures, such as the ears, which are customarily treated with special assiduousness on account of their propensity to retain dirt. As the boy grows up he should be taught to keep his prepuce clean himself, just as he is taught to wash his ears. If such a procedure became customary the circumcision of children would become an uncommon operation. This would result in the saving of about 16 children's lives lost from circumcision each year in this country, besides saving much parental anxiety and an appreciable amount of the time of doctors and nurses.

SUMMARY

The development of the prepuce is incomplete in the newborn male child, and separation from the glans, rendering it retractable, does not usually occur until some time between 9 months and 3 years. True phimosis is extremely rare in infancy.

During the first year or two of life, when the infant is incontinent, the prepuce fulfils an essential function in protecting the glans. Its removal predisposes to meatal ulceration.

The many and varied reasons commonly advanced for circumcising infants are critically examined. None are convincing.

Though early circumcision will prevent penile cancer, there is reason to suppose that keeping the prepuce clean would have a like effect in preventing this disease.

In the light of these facts a conservative attitude towards the prepuce is proposed, and a routine for its hygiene is suggested. If adopted this would eliminate the vast majority of the tens of thousands of circumcision operations performed annually in this country, along with their yearly toll of some 16 child deaths.

My thanks are due to Dr. A. M. Barrett for pathological facilities.

REFERENCES

Benson, R. A., Slobody, L. B., Lillick, L., Maffia, A., and Sullivan, N. (1949). J Pediat 34, 49

Campbell, M. F. (1948). In Brennemann's Practice of Pediatrics, vol. 3, chap. 30, p. 34. Hagerstown

Cooke, J. V. (1921). Am J Dis Child 22, 481

Dean, A. L. (1935). J Urol 33, 252

Deibert, G. A. (1933). Anat Rec 57, 387

Freud, P. (1947). J Pediat 31, 131

Handley, W. S. (1947). Br Med J 2, 841

Higgins, T. T. (1949). In Garrod, Batten, and Thursfield's Diseases of Children, 2, 462. London

Hunter, R. H. (1935). J Anat 70, 68

Kennaway, E. L. (1947). Br J Cancer 1, 335

Lewis, L. G. (1931). J Urol 26, 295

Lloyd, V. E., and Lloyd, N. L. (1934). Br Med J 1, 144

Schrek, R., and Lenowitz, H. (1947). Cancer Res 7, 180

Wilson, R. A. (1947). Canad Med Ass J 56, 54

Commentary: Circumcision

Kenneth I. Glassberg

According to scripture, all Jewish males are to be circumcized on the eighth day of life. However, the method by which the foreskin is to be excised is not defined. Many methods of circumcision have evolved over the ages: without clamps, with clamps. In reviewing modern medical literature, it is difficult to document a classic article recommending a specific procedure. Perhaps the reason for this is that circumcision can be accomplished with almost equal ease and equal results with any procedure. The clamp methods certainly leave a smooth and even incision line. The results nonetheless may not differ from a freehand technique even if the skin edges were ragged initially. More attention instead has been paid to the pros and cons of circumcision. Some of the articles written reveal the authors' prejudices just by their titles alone, such as "The Fate of the Foreskin" and "The Rape of the Phallus".[1]

Why not circumcision? Opponents of circumcision often quote the cost–benefit disadvantages of the procedure. In 1977 Americans spent more than 50 million dollars to circumcise new borns.[2] Complications that have been reported include Fournier's gangrene, skin bridging, excessive bleeding, urinary retention, meatal stenosis, inclusion cysts, urethrocutaneous fistulae, removing too much skin, removing too little skin, necrosis of the glans penis, and excision of the glans penis.[3–10]

The initial reports that carcinoma of the cervix has a lower incidence among wives of Jewish and Moslem men as compared to groups where circumcision is not widely practiced has been used to support the argument in favor of prophylactic circumcision.[11] However, more recent reports seem to refute this claim.[12]

There is certainly a higher incidence of carcinoma of the penis developing in uncircumcized males as compared to circumcized males. However, the statistics suggest that carcinoma of the penis is seen more often in areas of the world where poor hygienic practices exist. Therefore, educating people in good hygiene theoretically may be as effective in preventing carcinoma of the penis as is circumcision.

Since circumcision can be easily accomplished in the newborn, and since there is evidence of a reasonable incidence of phimosis existing beyond the age of 3 yr (10% according to Gairdner), I feel that the pros and cons of circumcision in the newborn are weighted equally. However, prophylactic circumcision in the older child should be discouraged when possible.

In my experience, the major reason for non-Jews requesting that their child be circumcized is based on their belief that circumcision is cleaner for the males and healthier for their future wives. Parents often state that they prefer circumcision because they do not want their son to look different from their father or stand out among his peers. In a country where more than 69% of the males are circumcized, I can understand their feelings.[13]

When there is no medical indication for circumcision in the older child, I try to convince the parents that circumcision is a habit somewhat indigenous to the United States and often quote statistics on the low percentage of males that are circumcized in Western Europe (*e.g.*, 24% in the United Kingdom).[13] However, even after discouraging a mother from having her son circumcized, I often feel the mother leaves me understanding what I have said, yet only reluctantly accepting my advice.

The physician can easily argue against elective circumcision in the older child because of the need for anesthesia and perhaps on the basis of psychological trauma. However, because of the rarity of complications following the procedure, it still is hard to discourage a mother who wants to have her child circumcized even when only for cultural reasons.

In neonates, sutures usually are not needed, especially when one of the clamp methods is used. Even in the case of ritual circumcision, where a clamp method frequently is not used for prevention of bleeding, bleeding is rarely a problem. This is largely because the coagulation mechanism has matured by 8 days of life, when the ritual circumcision is performed, and the vessels are small enough at that age to constrict enough so that hemorrhage does not occur.

In the older child, I have preferred to excise the foreskin by first performing a dorsal slit over the cross-hatch marks made by a straight crushing clamp (Fig. 6A). The dorsal slit should extend to a mark previously made on the outer skin just proximal to the corona and on the inner layer to a point approximately 0.5 cm to 1 cm from the coronal edge. I place hemostats on either side of the dorsal slit, making sure to grab both the inner and outer edges. Then, with a curved tissue scissor, I extend the incision circumferentially around both of these clamps, staying approximately 0.5 cm proximal to the corona (Fig. 6B) until the foreskin is excised (Fig. 6C). Bleeding points are managed with electrocautery. A U-type mattress suture, usually of 4–0 chromic catgut, is used at the frenulum to bring the skin edges together and to control bleeding. Simple sutures close the remainder of the wound (Fig. 6D). A small dressing with petroleum jelly gauze is applied.

In the postoperative period, I have the parents bathe the child on the third day. Especially in infants, more attention must be paid to the meatus than to the suture line. In the

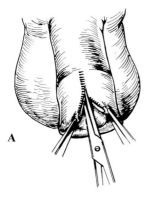

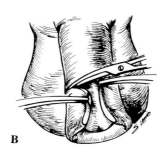

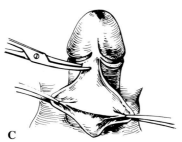

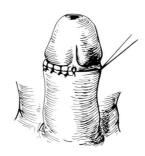

Fig. 6. (*A*) A dorsal slit is made in the midline over the impressions made by a previously applied crushing clamp. (*B* and *C*) The incision is extended circumferentially around the corona. Bleeders are cauterized, with care being taken not to injure the tissues adjacent to the urethra. (*D*) The skin edges are closed with interrupted chromic catgut sutures.

uncircumcized child the meatus is protected from diaper rash. In fact, I have never seen meatal stenosis in an uncircumcized child. In the circumcized child, especially immediately following circumcision, the meatus may crust with blood from the circumcision or become inflamed from contact with wet diapers. I therefore instruct the parents to keep the meatus clean, apply an antibiotic ointment to the meatus the first few days following circumcision, and occasionally spread the meatus at diaper changes in the first few months following circumcision. Following this course, I believe the high incidence of meatal stenosis following circumcision could be lowered drastically.

REFERENCES

1. Morgan WKC: The rape of the phallus. JAMA 193:123, 1965
2. Homan WE: How necessary is circumcision. Editorial comment. Mothers Manual, p 43, May–June, 1978
3. Sussman SJ, Schiller RP, Shashikumar VL: Fournier's syndrome: Report of three cases and review of the literature. Am J Dis Child 132:1189, 1978
4. Klauber GT, Boyle J: Preputial skin-bridging complication of circumcision. Urology 3:722, 1974
5. Patel H: The problem of routine circumcision. Can Med Assoc J 95:576, 1966
6. Horowitz J, Schussheim A, Scalettar HE: Abdominal distention following ritual circumcision. Pediatrics 57:576, 1976
7. Shulman J, Ben-Hur N, Neuman Z: Surgical complications of circumcision. Am J Dis Child 107:149, 1964
8. Byars LT, Trier WC: Some complications of circumcision and their surgical repair. Arch Surg 76:477, 1958
9. Rosefsky JB: Glans necrosis as a complication of circumcision. Pediatrics 39:774, 1967
10. Kaplan GW: Circumcision: An overview. Curr Probl Pediat 7(5):1–33, 1977
11. Aitken-Swan, J, Baird D: Circumcision and carcinoma of the cervix. Br J Cancer 19:219, 1965
12. Terris M, Wilson F, Nelson JH Jr: Relation of circumcision to cancer of the cervix. Am J Obstet Gynecol 117:1056, 1973
13. Leitch IOW: Circumcision; a continuing enigma. Aust Paediatr J 6:59, 1970

ANNOTATED BIBLIOGRAPHY

Gee WF, Ansell JS: Neonatal circumcision: A ten-year overview: With comparison of the Gomco clamp and the Plastibell device. Pediatrics 58:824, 1976

The authors found a 0.2% incidence of complications following circumcision in 5882 newborn males with either the Gomco clamp or Plastibell device. The incidence of complications using either device was approximately equal and included infection, hemorrhage, and trauma. There were no deaths and no transfusions were required. In their discussion, the authors do not recommend routine circumcision but do suggest that the procedure might be advisable in the tropics, where cancer of the penis is more likely to occur, and in desert areas, where balanitis is more likely to occur.

Grimes DA: Routine circumcision of the newborn infant: A reappraisal. Am J Obstet Gynecol 130:125, 1978

The author advises against routine circumcision because he feels that the procedure disregards the infant's stress response to pain, the procedure usually is performed by the mother's physician rather than by the child's physician, and an enormous outlay of money, more than a half billion dollars in the past decade, has been used to trim foreskins for only dubious objectives.

Cleary TG, Kohl H: Overwhelming infection with group B beta-hemolytic streptococcus associated with circumcision. Pediatrics 64:301, 1979

A case of group B beta-hemolytic streptococcal sepsis and eventual death is reported in a male of 6 wk, 24 hr after circumcision. The authors suggest that in this case and in many cases of neonatal sepsis, the sepsis may arise secondary to circumcision. However, previous reports have not bothered to indicate the incidence of septic newborn males having been previously circumcised. The authors attempt to hold circumcision accountable for the 100% higher incidence of neonatal sepsis in males as compared to females on the basis that circumcision opens an additional portal of entry for bacteria.

King LR: The pros and cons of neonatal circumcision. Surg Rounds 2:29, 1979

The author feels that previous arguments supporting routine circumcision based on a higher risk of venereal disease in uncircumcised males and a higher risk of carcinoma of the cervix in the wives of uncircumcized males are unproved. As well, good hygiene may be as effective as circumcision in preventing carcinoma of the penis. The author points out that there is a probable incidence of one serious complication in every 5,000 to 10,000 circumcisions. He at the same time does not deny that there is a significant number of infants who will require circumcision when they are older. Therefore, the author suggests that prospective studies be set up to determine which foreskins are likely to become phimotic and, therefore, which patients should be circumcized.

Overview: Circumcision: Rationale and Complications

Julian S. Ansell

This overview is divided into two parts. The first part attempts to examine the rationale for neonatal circumcision using a cost–benefit analysis. The second part discusses the management of complications of the procedure.

The emotional arguments for and against neonatal circumcisions depend, at least in part, on the conflict between what I will call tropical and temperate zone "tribal memories." In this regard I cite the paper by O.G. Doge on "Carcinoma of the Penis in East Africans" because it shows the difference in incidence of cancer of the penis between adjacent circumcising (2:100,000) and noncircumcising (40:100,000) tropical tribes at the headwaters of the Nile. Oettle believes local hygiene is not a factor.[2] It seems reasonable to assume that this difference does depend on circumcision, and the custom spread to those ancient cultures further east in Ethiopia and north in the Sudan and Egypt. The Semites probably introduced circumcision into the temperate zone, where the incidence of cancer of the penis in uncircumcised males, 2:100,000/yr, is similar to that of those circumcised in the tropics.

The question then arises does the *cost* of circumcision to a society equal or exceed the benefits (*i.e.*, prevention of the *cost* to that society of cancer of the penis). First, let me calculate the cost of a single case of cancer of the penis leaving out assessment of intangibles such as emotional distress and pain, in the chart below.[3]

COST OF SINGLE CASE OF CANCER OF THE PENIS IN US $ IN 1980

Surgical excision and node dissection	$	2000
Average of 20 days in hospital @ $300/day		6000
Radiation therapy		$3000
Work loss attendant to initial therapy, 45 days @ 12,000/yr		1500
Initial Costs		$ 12,500
Overwhelming majority (estimate of 70%) died of disease within 5 yr resulting in a productive work loss of 20 yr to society.		
20 × @ 12,000/yr = $240,000 × 70%		$168,000
Total initial and long-term cost		$180,500
Discounted (amount that would have been earned if invested otherwise for 20-yr period in question) over 20 yr @ 6%		$368,000

The average case of cancer of the penis in the tropics occurs 40 years after the neonatal circumcision.[1] Thus, if we discount the cost to society of the penile cancer case back to 40 yr earlier when it could have been prevented by doing a circumcision and multiply that cost by the number of circumcisions necessary to prevent a cancer of the penis, we should come up with a "break-even" figure.

Discounting at 6% the single cancer of the penis cost of $368,000 back 40 yr, we come up with an initial cost of $35,778. This amount, if invested 40 yr earlier at 6%, would grow to $368,000 40 yr later. In the tropics, where the incidence of penile cancer is over 40:100,000, we would need to perform 2500 circumcisions to prevent one cancer. Thus, we could allow $35,778 for the 2500 circumcisions and "break even."

What do 2500 neonatal circumcisions cost?

COST OF 2500 CIRCUMCISIONS IN US $ IN 1980

In neontal delivery unit		
Obstetrical package fee $10 × 2500		$25,000
Circumcision tray $8 × 2500		20,000
Complications[5]		
1. Meatotomy for meatal stenosis 2:100 in circumcised 2:100 × 2,500 @ $30 each		150
2. 2:100 minor complications @ $5 × 2500		250
3. 1:5000 serious complications @ $5000 each × 2500		2,500
Subtotal		$46,400
4. Subtract cost of circumcision required later in uncircumcised for phimosis, etc.[6] 3:1,000 × 2500 × $300		−750
		$45,650
Cost of circumcision done by (physicians assistant or) ritual circumciser		
Fee @ $15 × 2500		$37,500
Clamp (multiuse) $50		50
Subtotal		$37,550
Subtract 3:1000 circumcisions done as above		−750
		$36,800

The cost of 2500 circumcisions to prevent a single cancer of the penis done under ritual conditions very nearly equals the societal cost of a penil carcinoma. Therefore, circumcision becomes a practical prophylactic measure in the tropics, and the tropical "tribal memory" should be heeded.

When we multiply the 2500 circumcisions by 20 to bring the number up to the 50,000 circumcisions necessary to prevent one penile cancer in the temperate zone, the cost is 20 times the benefit and therefore not worthwhile in the temperate zone. We can see why the European Temperate zone "tribal memory" rebels against neonatal circumcision as a prophylactic against cancer of the penis, since it appears uneconomical to that society.

What to recommend? Clearly, for those males destined to spend a significant part of their lives in the tropics, circumcision would be advisable, but for those who will live mainly in temperate climates, circumcision is a luxury perhaps only affordable in an affluent society.

Since we *are* an affluent society, circumcision will be demanded. Therefore, physicians should be prepared to treat the occasional complication when it arises. The most common complications in recent years, as described by Gee and Ansell, are hemorrhage and infection followed by a variety of other problems, mostly minor.

Most hemorrhages are minor and easily controlled by topical application of 1:1000 epinephrine, local pressure, or, occasionally, a mattress suture. If bleeding persists in spite of these measures, look for a bleeding diathesis (in Gee's series Factor VIII deficiency), and treat accordingly.

In the absence of gross pus locally or systemic signs, *infection* is difficult to diagnose because the local healing reaction is similar in appearance to infection. In circumcised neonates with fever, lethargy, and poor feeding plus local erythema that spreads into skin of shaft and scrotum, culture of the afffected area followed by broad-spectrum antibiotics is indicated, since a variety of organisms including *Proteus, Klebsiella, Staphylococcus, Streptococcus,* and coliforms have been cultured. Recently, we cultured *Clostridium* from one patient. Although there was no death from any cause in Gee's 5521 patients, several attributed to sepsis are described in the literature and one is almost surely related to infection, so this is potentially a very serious problem.[7]

Circumcision of the hypospadiac patient can only be avoided by education of those likely to be involved. Those who desire ritual circumcision may be relieved to hear that in these cases ritual is satisfied if a drop of blood is obtained by merely pricking the precious foreskin. It need not be removed.

Dehiscence is easily corrected by suturing with fine gut.

Denudation of the penile shaft is usually only partial and self-correcting. Rarely plastic revision will be required.

A new complication since the advent of the Plastibell is the selection of too small a "bell," with edema and cyanosis developing within 24 hr.[5] Removal of the constricting ring by cutting it away from the skin relieves the condition. Prolonged retention of the Plastibell for weeks has been reported with resulting edema. Again, the cure is removal.

One penile slough due to electrodissection over a Gomeo clamp has been described. Perhaps the electrocoagulation unit should be left turned off until the clamp has been removed.

REFERENCES

1. Doge OG: Carcinoma of the penis in East Africans. Br J Urol 37:223, 1965
2. Oettle AG: Cancer in Africa, especially in regions south of the Sahara. J Natl Cancer Inst 33:383, 1964
3. Weinstein MC, Stason WB: Foundations of cost effectiveness analysis for health and medical practices. N Engl J Med 296:716, 1978
4. Schellhammer PF, Grabstald H: Tumors of the penis and urethra. In Harrison JH, Gittes RF, Perlmutter AD, et al (eds): Campbell's Urology, Vol. 2, 4th ed, p 1171. Philadelphia, W B Saunders, 1979

5. Gee WT, Ansell JS: Neonatal circumcision: A 10 year review. Pediatrics 58:824, 1976
6. Wirth JL: Statistics on circumcision in Canada and Australia. Am J Obstet Gynecol 130:236, 1978
7. Cleary TG, Kohl H: Overwhelming infection with group B beta hemolytic streptococcus associated with circumcision. Pediatrics 64:301, 1979

93

GENITAL RECONSTRUCTION IN THE FEMALE WITH THE ADRENOGENITAL SYNDROME[1]

Harry M. Spence and Terry D. Allen

Division of Urology, The University of Texas Southwestern Medical School, and Children's Medical Center, Dallas, Texas

British Journal of Urology (1973), 45, 126–130

In the infant with ambiguous external genitalia secondary to adrenocortical hyperplasia, after the sex has been established unequivocally as female, and after appropriate substitution therapy has controlled the electrolyte and hormonal aberrations, the problem of revision of the external genitalia arises. The dual objectives are a satisfactory cosmetic appearance and future functional capability. To these ends the urogenital sinus must be converted into a normal vaginal outlet and the hypertrophied clitoris must be disposed of in some fashion.

In the past we were content simply to do an amputation of the clitoris flush with the symphysis, along with a midline posterior episiotomy, to make the vaginal outlet. The appearance of the external genitalia in girls so treated was improved but left much to be desired, and more importantly the vaginal orifice had a great tendency to show cicatricial contraction requiring repeated digital dilations for prolonged periods of time.

We have achieved distinctly improved results using the techniques described herein. In essence, the urogenital sinus is converted into an appropriate vaginal orifice utilising the VY-plasty principle and a subcutaneous amputation of the shaft and crura of the clitoris is performed, retaining the glans. It is helpful to demonstrate this interrelationship of urethra, vagina and urogenital sinus both by voiding cystourethrography and by panendoscopy prior to operation.

INTROITOPLASTY

Under general anaesthesia with the patient in the exaggerated lithotomy position, an inverted V incision is made with the apex of the V at the posterior aspect of the opening of the urogenital sinus (Fig. 1A). This point is referred to as *a*. Each limb of the V extends backward to a point midway between ischial tuberosity and anus, much as in a perineal prostatectomy. The flap proper is dissected backward to its base and the lateral margins of the incision are undermined widely.

An incision is then made along the floor of the urogenital sinus from the initial point *a* proximally until the separate orifices of the urethra and vagina are seen clearly (Fig. 1B and C). This incision, which is often several centimetres in length, may be regarded as the stem of a Y whose proximal point is designated *a'*. The

[1] Read at the Twenty-eighth Annual Meeting of the British Association of Urological Surgeons in Newcastle upon Tyne, July 1972.

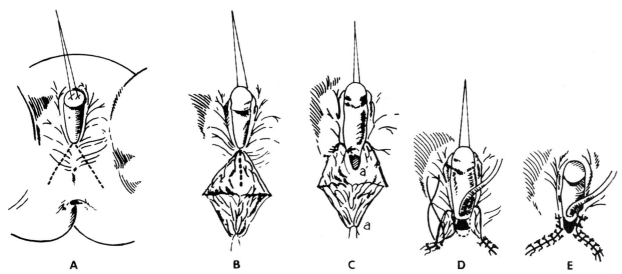

Fig. 1. Technique of vaginoplasty. (*A*) Outline of skin flap. (*B*) Incision of urogenital sinus. (*C*) Urethral and vaginal orifices exposed. (*D*) Skin flap sutured into depth of urogenital sinus. (*E*) Final result.

overlying tissues, including the perineal body, are likewise incised making in effect a midline episiotomy. A Foley catheter is now passed through the urethra to the bladder.

The V flap is next positioned in the midline episiotomy as an inlay and its apex *a* is sutured to *a'* with fine catgut sutures (Fig. 1*D*). Careful approximation of skin to mucosal surface, avoiding raw edges which could give rise to granulations and adhesions, is critical if subsequent stricture is to be avoided. The adjacent margins of the wound are then closed as indicated in the drawings (Fig. 1*E*).

CLITORIPLASTY

Clitoriplasty may be done at the same time as the vaginoplasty or as a separate procedure. The principle utilised is a subcutaneous amputation of the shaft of the clitoris, including the crura, but sparing the glans. Initially, we approached the shaft through a ventral longitudinal incision (Fig. 2*A*), mobilising it down to its attachments to the inner aspect of the pubic arch and up to the base of the glans (Fig. 2*B*). The entire shaft was then excised (Fig. 2*C*), and heamostasis of the stumps secured by means of suture ligature, leaving the glans attached to its hooded prepuce. The base of the glans was sutured to the lower edge of the pubic symphysis (Fig. 2*D* and *E*) following which the mucosal incision was closed (Fig. 2*F*).

This approach proved to be technically satisfactory but there still remained considerable redundancy of the

foreskin and recently the operation has been modified with some improvement cosmetically. The shaft is now approached posteriorly after first wedging out the redundant foreskin (Fig. 3*A* and *B*). As before, the entire shaft, exclusive of the glans, is excised (Fig. 3*C*) and the base of the glans is once more sutured to the inferior edge of the pubic symphysis (Fig. 3*D*, *E* and *F*).

With either approach, the primary blood supply to the glans is interrupted and it must now depend upon soft-tissue collaterals for survival. To date, this has proved adequate since none has sloughed but admittedly the glans is somewhat dusky in colour for several days after the procedure. An unexpected dividend from this state of transient ischaemia, however, has been some degree of atrophy and shrinkage, reducing the glans to a size more consistent with that of the normal female clitoris.

DISCUSSION

The presence of ambiguous genitalia in a child is a continuing source of anxiety to the family even after the sex of the child has been established firmly. Hence it is incumbent upon the attending physician to resolve this issue as soon as practicable. We agree with Money and the Hampsons (1955) that early definitive correction prior to the age of permanent memory is most desirable for the child, while promoting a healthy parental attitude as well. The actual age at which operation is undertaken obviously is dependent upon a stable metabolic and hormonal state in the infant, but it is usually safe to

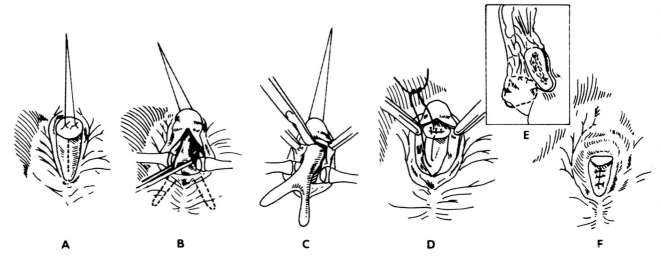

Fig. 2. Technique of clitoriplasty. (A) Outline of incision on ventral surface of shaft. (B) Mobilizing shaft of clitoris. (C) Excision of clitoral shaft, preserving glans. (D) Suturing stump of glans to undersurface of pubis. (E) Final result, side view. (F) Final result, frontal view.

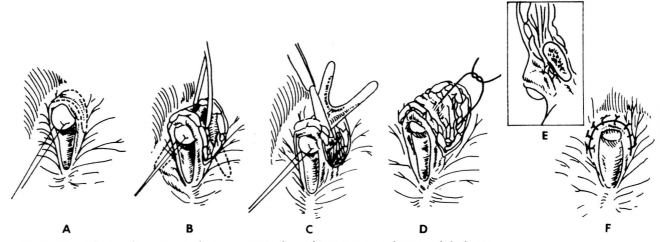

Fig. 3. Clitoriplasty, alternative technique. (A) Outline of incision over dorsum of shaft. (B) Mobilization of shaft. (C) Excision of shaft. (D) Suturing stump of glans to undersurface of pubis. (E) Final result, side view. (F) Final result, frontal view.

proceed with reconstruction at 1 year of age and probably sooner.

Definitive reconstruction is less urgent perhaps as far as the urogenital sinus is concerned since this aspect of the deformity is less apparent to the casual observer than is that of the enlarged phallus. There is, in fact, some justification for postponing the vaginoplasty until the child is older in the hope of lessening the possibility of stricture at the repair site. In this regard the sliding-flap principle introduced by Fortunoff *et al.* (1964) and employed by us to reconstruct the urogenital sinus has proved superior to simple midline incision. It is adequate cosmetically and functionally except perhaps for those rare completely masculinised individuals with a penile urethra and high vaginal termination who may require a more elaborate approach such as that described by Hendren and Crawford (1969).

There seems, however, little to be gained by undue

delay in performing the clitoriplasty. We have never personally observed regression in size of this structure even under good medical management. On the contrary, it has been the experience of most observers that the size of the clitoris parallels the growth of the child. It seems, therefore, that if the size, appearance, projection and erectile tendency of the organ constantly challenge the assigned sex at every diaper change, specific treatment is in order. Possession of a clitoris is not essential for orgasm in the female (Randolph and Hung, 1970) and one need not hesitate unduly to remove it if a useful purpose is thereby served. The objective thus becomes one of selection of the technique which results in an appearance most closely approximating the normal. Until recently the procedure most commonly employed was that of total amputation (Gross, Randolph and Crigler,

1966), although Lattimer (1961) and Randolph and Hung (1970) described relocation and recession of the clitoris as an alternative. This latter procedure may successfully hide the organ from view, but we cannot help but feel that the sheer bulk of the tissue involved with its retained sensitivity and tendency to engorgement may be a serious shortcoming of this approach.

We have now carried out genital reconstruction as described above in two infants and one 19-year-old girl with the adrenogenital syndrome. In all, the appearance of the external genitalia following vaginoplasty and clitoriplasty has closely approximated the normal. The experience of Goodwin (1969) confirms the favourable outcome which may be expected when appropriate surgical procedures are applied to this distressing problem.

SUMMARY

Operative procedures for the correction of ambiguous external genitalia in girls with the adrenogenital syndrome are described. Reconstruction of the vaginal aperture utilises the VY principle, while the hypertrophied clitoris is managed by amputation of its shaft and crura in a subcutaneous manner preserving the glans. Results in 3 cases have been satisfactory, leading us to recommend these methods for further trial.

REFERENCES

FORTUNOFF, S., LATTIMER, J. K. and EDSON, M. (1964). Vaginoplasty technique for female pseudohermaphrodites. Surg Gynecol Obstet 118, 545–548

GOODWIN, W. E. (1969). Anomalies of the genitourinary tract. *In* de la Camp, H. B., Linder, F. and Trede, M. (Eds.): American College of Surgeons and Deutsche Gesellschaft für Chirurgie. Joint Meeting, p. 256. New York: Springer-Verlag

GROSS, R. E., RANDOLPH, J. and CRIGLER, J. F. Jr. (1966). Clitorectomy for sexual abnormalities: indications and technique. Surgery 59, 300–308

HENDREN, W. H. and CRAWFORD, J. D. (1969). Adrenogenital syndrome: The anatomy of the anomaly and its repair. Some new concepts. J Ped Surg 4, 49–58

JONES, H. W. Jr. and SCOTT, W. W. (1958). Hermaphroditism, Genital Anomalies and related Endocrine Disorders. Baltimore: Williams and Wilkins

JONES, H. W. Jr. and VERKAUL, B. S. (1970). Surgical treatment in congenital adrenal hyperplasia: Age at operation and other prognostic factors. Obstet Gynecol 36, 1–10

LATTIMER, J. K. (1961). Relocation and recession of the enlarged clitoris with preservation of the glans: an alternative to amputation. J Urol 86, 113–116

MONEY, J., HAMPSON, J. G. and HAMPSON, J. L. (1955). Hermaphroditism: recommendations concerning assignment of sex, change of sex, and psychologic management. Bulletin of the Johns Hopkins Hospital, 97, 284–300

RANDOLPH, J. G. and HUNG, W. (1970). Reduction clitoroplasty in females with hypertrophied clitoris. J Ped Surg 5, 224–231

WILKINS, L. (1965). The Diagnosis and Treatment of Endocrine Disorders in Childhood and Adolescence, 3rd ed. Springfield, Ill.: C. C. Thomas

The Authors

Harry M. Spence, MD, FACS, Clinical Professor of Urology.
Terry D. Allen, MD, FACS.

Commentary: Surgery in the Intersex States

David T. Mininberg

The biochemistry, endocrinology, and genetics of the adrenogenital syndrome have been satisfactorily delineated to allow prompt diagnosis and the rapid institution of adequate replace-

ment therapy.[1] Once a stable status has been achieved with a regimen of adequate replacement therapy, attention should be turned to the necessary reconstructive surgery. Drs. Spence and Allen clearly present the surgical approach that I personally have found the most satisfactory. They begin their discussion by properly emphasizing the need for a thorough evaluation of the anatomy. In the commonly encountered 21- and 11-hydroxylase enzyme deficiencies, surgical therapy is restricted to girls. The precise location of the vaginal orifice in relation to the urethra and the common urogenital sinus must be established. This can be done by either a voiding cystourethrogram or a genitogram, placing an occlusive tip catheter at the common urogenital sinus meatus and in a retrograde fashion filling the urethra and vagina. A negative radiographic examination does not exclude the presence of a vagina. Endoscopy is an additional aid to precise localization of the vagina. This latter procedure is easily and safely accomplished in these young girls, as long as adequate precautions are taken to supplement their replacement therapy.

If the vagina is quite close to the external meatus, which is to say there is a short urogenital sinus, then a simple "cutback" of the inferior lip will suffice nicely.[2-4] The most commonly performed vaginoplasty requires that a flap of perineal skin be raised and brought down to form part of the floor of the vaginal canal. This manuever permits repair of the vagina when the urogenital sinus is longer than can be repaired by the "cutback" procedure. The flap technique is easy enough to perform and yields good cosmetic and functional results. The procedure can be undertaken in early childhood, at the time of clitoroplasty. If this is done, there is rarely a need for later revision. This is the method found most useful by the author and others.[1,2,5]

In the rare instances where the vagina is deeply recessed, that is, a long urogenital sinus, it is necessary to perform a pull-through vaginoplasty. This more extensive dissection requires mobilization of the deeply recessed vagina with particular care being taken in the area of the bladder neck and internal sphincter mechanism. Skin flaps are developed in the perineum as well as superiorly and at each lateral aspect in order to provide adequate length of the vaginal canal. This procedure, although arduous and tedious, can be undertaken between ages 1 and 2 yr.[2]

Historically, clitorectomy has been the treatment offered for the enlarged clitoris of the adrenogenital syndrome.[6] In my opinion, the aim of surgical repair should be to remove the redundant erectile tissue, preserve the sexually sensitive glans clitoris, and provide an exteriorized vagina that will function adequately for menstruation and intromission. The preservation of the glans clitoris is believed to be important to allow full physical enjoyment of normal sexual activity. From the psychosexual point of view, patients who have had clitorectomy demonstrate an ambivalence toward sexual activity and have sexual inhibition.[7,8] It is conceivable to encounter girls in whom the clitoris is so large as to make clitorectomy a desirable solution. To date, I have not encountered any such children.

A proposed alternative is clitoral recession, which is advocated for those girls with a small clitoris. This operation buries the erectile tissue of the clitoris at the mons pubis, leaving the glans clitoris exposed to function as a sexual organ.[2,9] My only experience with the procedure has been the subsequent need to revise two clitoral recessions that were excrutiatingly painful with erection during normal sexual excitation. There is a visible prominence at the mons pubis, producing compromised cosmetics. In a similar manner, clitoral plication has been proposed.[10] This is an apparent attempt to avoid the pubic bulging that is cosmetically unattractive.

The method of dealing with the enlarged clitoris of the adrenogenital syndrome that has yielded the best functional and cosmetic results has been corporal resection, described in the foregoing article.[11-13] As can be seen, in this procedure the erectile tissue of the clitoris is removed, but the glans is preserved. Along with the glans, a strip of ventral skin with a blood supply is preserved, and, when possible, the dorsal neurovascular bundle is retained as well. In those patients in whom the glans is large, the corners of the glans can be trimmed off, leaving a functionally intact and cosmetically satisfactory result. The skin over the glans will often partially or completely slough in 7 to 10 days. However, the glans will reepithelize and be quite satisfactory after a short time. Two of my patients, operated on by this method, were, respectively, aged 17 and 20 yr and had been sexually active before surgery. They reported similar pleasant sensations postoperatively, without the obviously embarrassing clitoral erection.

REFERENCES

1. Mininberg DT, Levine LS, New MI: Current concepts in congenital adrenal hyperplasia. Invest Urol 17:169, 1979

2. Hendren WH, Crawford JD: Adrenogenital syndrome: The anatomy of the anomaly and its repair. Some new concepts. J Pediatr Surg 4:49, 1969

3. Jones HW Jr: Revision of the urogenital sinus. Fertil Steril 11:157, 1960

4. Jones HW Jr., Verkauf BS: Surgical treatment in congenital adrenal hyperplasia. Age at operation and other prognostic factors. Obstet Gynecol 36:1, 1970

5. Fortunoff S, Lattimer JK, Edson M: Vaginoplasty—technique for female pseudohermophrodites. Surg Gynecol Obstet 118:545, 1964

6. Gross RE, Randolph J, Crigler JF Jr: Clitorectomy for sexual abnormalities: Indications and technique. Surgery 59:300, 1966

7. Money J, Schwartz M: Dating, somatic friendships, and sexuality in 17 early treated adrenogenital females, aged 15–25. In Lee PA, Plotnick JP, Kowarski PV, et al (eds): Congenital Adrenal Hyperplasia. Baltimore, University Park Press, 1972

8. Money J, Ehrhardt AA: Man and woman, boy and girl. Differentiation and Dimorphism of Gender Identify from Conception to Maturity. Baltimore, Johns Hopkins University Press, 1972

9. Lattimer JK: Relocation and recession of the enlarged clitoris with preservation of the glans: An alternative to amputation. J Urol 86:113, 1961

10. Stefan H: Surgical reconstruction of the external genitalia in female pseudohermaphrodites. Br J Urol 39:347, 1967

11. Spence HW, Allen TD: Genital reconstruction in the female with the adrenogenital syndrome. Br J Urol 45:126, 1973

12. Barinka L, Stauratjero M, Toman M: Plastic adjustment of female genitals in adrenogenital syndrome. Acta Chir Plast 10:99, 1968

13. Kumar H, Kiefer JH, Rosenthal IE, et al: Clitoroplasty experience during a 19 year period. J Urol 111:81, 1974

14. Mininberg DT: Phalloplasty in congenital adrenal hyperplasia. J Urol 128:355, 1982

ANNOTATED BIBLIOGRAPHY

Hendren WH, Crawford JD: Adrenogenital syndrome: The anatomy of the anomaly and its repair. Some new concepts. J Pediatr Surg 4:49, 1969

This is a comprehensive review of the adrenogenital syndrome from a surgical point of view. The illustrations are superb.

Jones HW Jr: Revision of the urogenital sinus. Fertil Steril 11:157, 1960

This is a clear exposition of the "cutback" procedure. The authors find that there is no need for later revision, even if the operation is done early.

Fortunoff S, Lattimer JK, Edson M: Vaginoplasty—technique for female pseudohermophrodites. Surg Gynecol Obstet 118:545, 1964

The authors favor their technique over the midline incision. Long term results highlight the frequent necessity for revisions.

Gross RE, Randolph J, Crigler JF Jr: Clitorectomy for sexual abnormalities: Indications and techniques. Surgery 59:300, 1966

A large series of 47 patients with whom the authors state had satisfactory results is discussed. The authors question the need of the clitoris for sexual satisfaction.

Lattimer JK: Relocation and recession of the enlarged clitoris with preservation of the glans: An alternative to amputation. J Urol 86:113, 1961

As stated, the author proposes an alternative to clitorectomy in a series of 11 patients. The author states the need to trim the glans to a size commensurate with neighboring structures.

Stefan H: Surgical reconstruction of the external genitalia in female pseudohermaphrodites. Br J Urol 39:347, 1967

This is a thorough description of corporal plication. The follow-up data includes two patients with satisfactory sexual activity after surgery.

Barinka L, Stauratjero M, Toman M: Plastic adjustment of female genitals in adrenogenital syndrome. Acta Chir Plast 10:99, 1968

Additional satisfactory experiences with corporal resection are presented.

Kumar H, Kiefer JH, Rosenthal IE, et al: Clitoroplasty experience during a 19 year period. J Urol 111:81, 1974

Additional satisfactory experiences with corporal resection are presented.

94

SURGICAL CORRECTION OF INCOMPLETE PENOSCROTAL TRANSPOSITION

James F. Glenn and E. Everett Anderson

From the Department of Surgery, Division of Urology, Duke University Medical Center, Durham, North Carolina

The Journal of Urology
Copyright © 1973 by The Williams & Wilkins Co.
Vol. 110, November
Printed in U.S.A.

Anatomical transposition of the penis and scrotum is a normal occurrence in marsupials[1] but rare in primates. This transposition may be partial or complete and may be associated with hypospadias and chordee or more lethal anomalies. At 9 to 10 weeks of gestation the urethral folds close over the urogenital sinus with formation of the tubular urethra.[2] At this stage the lateral labioscrotal swellings which are anterior to the genital tubercle begin their caudal migration with subsequent midline fusion and development of the scrotum. When the labioscrotal swellings do not migrate or are not displaced caudad to the penis, the event results in the development of the scrotum anterior to the penis. In 1972 Miller published a comprehensive review of 23 cases of complete penoscrotal transposition.[3] Of the 23 cases, 3 occurred in stillbirths and 5 were accompanied by other anomalies incompatible with life. In 21 patients

other urogenital anomalies were present, predominantly hypospadias, chordee and agenesis of one or both upper urinary tracts and 7 patients had gastrointestinal anomalies, predominantly imperforate anus.

Surgical procedures to correct penoscrotal transposition have involved bisecting the scrotum and suturing the 2 halves beneath the penis,[4,5] placing the penis through a subcutaneous tunnel on the anterior scrotal wall[6] and moving the scrotal sacs posteriorly by means of bilateral V-Y plasty.[7]

Incomplete or partial penoscrotal transposition is not as severe a deformity as complete penoscrotal transposition but it is associated with multiple urogenital and other anomalies (Fig. 1). The sexual function of the individual so afflicted will be seriously compromised unless effective reconstruction is accomplished. Surgical correction of complete or partial penoscrotal transposition is neither difficult nor traumatic and it is recommended that the procedure be accomplished during the first few weeks or months of life.

Accepted for publication June 29, 1973.

Read at annual meeting of American Urological Association, New York, New York, May 13–17, 1973.

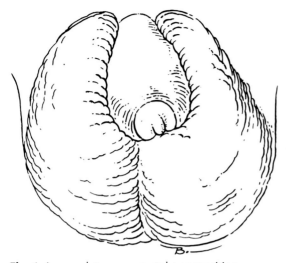

Fig. 1. Incomplete penoscrotal transposition.

TECHNIQUE

The technique for repair of incomplete penoscrotal transposition consists of complete mobilization of the 2 halves of the scrotum as rotational advancement flaps with relocation of the scrotal compartment in a normal dependent position. This technique is applicable to all but the most severe degrees of penoscrotal transposition. In cases of associated hypospadias with chordee, release of chordee is effected simultaneously with repositioning of the urethral meatus appropriately. Secondary urethroplasty is accomplished at a later time, usually with a modified Thiersch-Duplay technique although modifications of other types of urethroplasty may also be used.

General anesthesia is administered and the patient is placed on spreader bars. The abdomen and external genitalia are cleansed and draped in the routine manner. A Foley catheter is inserted through the urethral meatus and passed into the bladder. A curvilinear transverse incision is made above the superior scrotal folds (Fig. 2A) and continued around the base of the phallus on both sides (Fig. 2B). These incisions are joined caudally in the midline for a vertical incision down the raphe with subsequent complete mobilization of lateral scrotal flaps. On the ventral shaft of the penis all fibrous tissue is excised (Fig. 3A). The lateral scrotal flaps are brought together beneath the phallus (Fig. 3B) and the incisions are closed in 2 layers with interrupted sutures of 3-zero absorbable suture to the subcutaneous tissue and similar 4-zero suture for the skin (Fig. 3C). A furacinimpregnated dressing is applied, followed by a dry sterile compression dressing.

CASE REPORTS

Case 1. A 3-month-old boy was hospitalized for evaluation of multiple genital anomalies (J6 2745). His father had agenesis of 1 kidney. Excretory urography (IVP) at birth was normal. Physical examination showed partial penoscrotal transposition with chordee and penoscrotal hypospadias. A right inguinal hernia was repaired and the penoscrotal transposition was corrected with release of chordee. Six months later there was an excellent cosmetic and functional result. The penoscrotal hypospadias will be repaired at a future date.

Case 2. A 3-month-old boy was found at birth to have ambiguous genitalia (Fig. 4A) and a heart murmur (H5 0423). There was a bifid scrotum containing well-

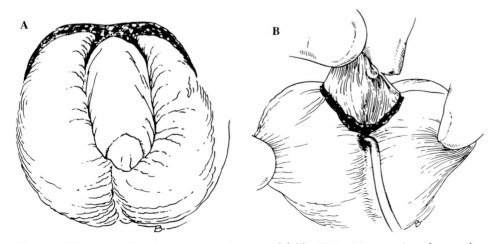

Fig. 2. (A) Transverse incision over superior scrotal folds. (B) Incision continued around entire base of penis and down median raphe.

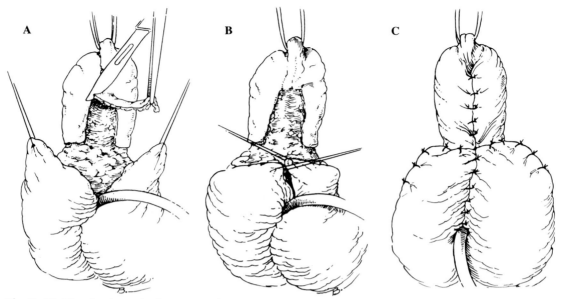

Fig. 3. (*A*) Chordee is excised. (*B*) Lateral scrotal flaps are brought beneath penis. (*C*) Closure in 2 layers.

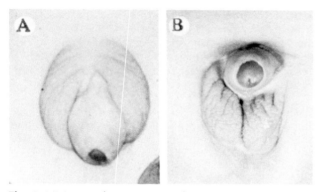

Fig. 4. (*A*) Incomplete penoscrotal transposition without hypospadias. (*B*) Postoperative result—scrotum dependent.

developed testicles and incomplete penoscrotal transposition. Subsequent endocrine studies revealed a chromosomal karyotype of XXXXY compatible with the diagnosis of male Turner's syndrome. IVP was normal. A patent ductus arteriosus was ligated. Penoscrotal transposition was corrected and 9 months later there was a satisfactory cosmetic result (Fig. 4*B*).

Case 3. A newborn, product of a full-term, normal gestation and uncomplicated delivery, had ambiguous genitalia (J1 5975). A phallus was located beneath fused labioscrotal folds containing no gonads. Beneath and

separate from the phallus was a urogenital sinus. The anus was normal. Respiratory distress responded to needle aspiration of a right pneumothorax. Azotemia present at birth increased and IVP revealed no visualization of the upper urinary tracts. The umbilical artery was catheterized and an abdominal aortogram could not delineate the renal arteries. Renal insufficiency progressed and the infant died when he was 13 days old. Autopsy showed congenital atelectasis, hyaline membrane disease, bilateral pneumonia, bilateral small unfused pelvic kidneys containing multiple cysts and supplied by hypoplastic renal arteries, fused labia, hypertrophied clitoris and urogenital sinus. Adrenal glands, ureters, bladder, uterus and ovaries were normal.

Comment. The analogous situation can occur in female subjects. Meyer reported a 7-month female stillborn with transposition of the clitoris and labia minora posterior to the labia majora.[8]

Case 4. A 13-year-old boy was hospitalized for correction of incomplete penoscrotal transposition (E8 9785). When he was 18 and 24 months old he had undergone correction of chordee. When he was a year old he underwent a Cecil urethroplasty. Microphallus and partial penoscrotal transposition were present. Endocrine studies were normal. A cystourethrogram and IVP were not remarkable. Correction of penoscrotal transposition was effected with a good cosmetic and functional result.

SUMMARY

Correction of incomplete penoscrotal transposition is described. The technique consists of complete mobilization of the 2 halves of the scrotum as rotational advancement flaps with relocation of the scrotal compartment in a normal dependent position. This technique is applicable to all but the most severe degrees of penoscrotal transpo- sition. Three patients with partial penoscrotal transposition are described on whom this operation produced a good cosmetic and functional result. A fourth case of complete transposition of the external genitalia, the second case reported in a female subject, is presented.

REFERENCES

1. Francis, C. C.: A case of pre-penile scrotum associated with absence of urinary system. Anat Rec 76:303, 1940
2. Spaulding, M. H.: The development of the external genitalia in the human embryo. Contrib Embryol 61:67, 1921
3. Miller, S. F.: Transposition of the external genitalia associated with the syndrome of caudal regression. J Urol 108:818, 1972
4. Campbell, M. F. and Harrison, J. H.: Urology, 3rd ed. Philadelphia: W. B. Saunders Co., pp. 1576–1577, 1970
5. Forshall, I. and Rickham, P. P.: Transposition of penis and scrotum. Br J Urol 28:250, 1956
6. McIlvoy, D. B. and Harris, H. S.: Transposition of the penis and scrotum: case report. J Urol 73:540, 1955
7. Datta, N. S., Singh, S. M., Reddy, A. V. S. and Chakravarty, A. K.: Transposition of penis and scrotum in 2 brothers, J Urol 105:739, 1971
8. Meyer, R.: Dislocation of phallus, penis and clitoris following pelvic malformations in human fetus. Anat Rec 79:231, 1941

Commentary:
Surgery of Penoscrotal Transposition and Penile Torsion

E. Everett Anderson

PENOSCROTAL TRANSPOSITION

Penoscrotal transposition occurs in varying degrees. Partial penoscrotal transposition is much more common than complete transposition. Other urogenital anomalies are often present, predominantly hypospadias, chordee, and agenesis of one or both upper urinary tracts. Associated gastrointestinal anomalies are not uncommon, predominantly imperforate anus. Patients with more severe forms of transposition have a higher incidence of other urogenital and gastrointestinal anomalies.

Surgical correction is not difficult and should be accom- plished during the first few months of life. Reconstruction can be performed by bringing the scrotum beneath the penis or by bringing the penis above the scrotum through a subcutaneous tunnel.[1-5] The scrotum can be brought beneath the penis by three surgical techniques. Forshall and Rickham, and Campbell and Harrison, split the scrotum and suture it beneath the phallus.[1,2] Datta and colleagues made inverted V incisions over the roots of each scrotal sac and by V-Y scrotoplasty the scrotum was brought beneath the penis.[3] Glenn and Anderson described the technique in the preceding article of complete mobilization of the scrotal skin around the phallus and the use of rotational advancement flaps to relocate the scrotum in a normal dependent position.[4]

Chordee and hypospadias are frequently associated with penoscrotal transposition. Release of chordee should always be performed at time of transposition surgery. We prefer to correct hypospadias at a later operation.

PENILE TORSION

Penile torsion is the result of a disproportion between penile skin and the shaft of the penis that produces a rotation of the penis on its longitudinal axis. Surgical correction involves mobilizing penile skin from the shaft of the penis and resuturing the skin edges to a new position. The condition is different from corporal disproportion, where one corpus cavernosum is longer than the other. In the latter anomaly, surgical correction involves shortening of the longer corpus cavernosum by dorsal elliptic windows in the tunica albuginea of the corpus caver- nosum.[6] The degree of torsion is usually 90 degrees or less and occurs to the left side in 80% of afflicted patients. The median raphe, urethra, and corpora cavernosa are included in the spiral rotation. Minor degrees of torsion do not preclude satisfactory sexual activity and do not warrant surgical correc- tions. Chordee and hypospadias are frequent associated anom- alies, occurring in 35% and 37.5% respectively, of reported patients.[7] The hypospadiac orifice is often balanitic or coronal in position.

Torsion may occur with or without chordee and may or may not be associated with hypospadias. Surgical correction involves mobilization of penile skin from the shaft of the penis and reapproximation of the skin after straightening of the penis. Culp described a circumferential incision at the penoscrotal junction and recommended urethroplasty at a later operation.[8] Reale and Benvenuti described a Z-plasty for correction of the malrotation.[9] Allen and Spence described a technique to correct torsion and coronal hypospadias simultaneously.[10] The penile skin was mobilized from the shaft through a circumferential incision behind the glans penis. This allowed the penis to rotate, bringing the urethral meatus to its normal ventral position. The redundant hood was then brought to the opposite side of the penis using the "buttonhole" technique. This method does not advance the urethral meatus but corrects simultaneously the dorsal hood deformity and torsion. Hodgson has recommended complete shaft skin sleeve mobilization using the Byars procedure to close the skin defect.[11,12] Klauber described a one-stage modification of the Allen and Spence method to correct more severe degrees of hypospadias and chordee associated with torsion.[13] A circumferential incision is made around the penile shaft proximal to the urethral meatus. The dorsal aspect of this initial skin incision is constructed, leaving a V of shaft skin left attached to the dorsal glans penis. When there is deficiency of skin overlying the distal urethra, the initial ventral incision across the urethra is made more proximal to avoid a fistula. The ventral penile skin is mobilized

proximally, releasing the chordee. If the chordee persists following skin mobilization, periurethral tissue and fascia are divided, and, if necessary, the dissection is continued around the urethra. Rarely, the distal urethra is composed only of mucosa with the corpus spongiosum divided as part of the hypospadiac defect. In these patients the corpus spongiosum is incised laterally on both sides of the urethra. The ventral skin defect is covered by mobilization of preputial skin from the dorsum of the penis. Instead of buttonholing the skin and pulling it over the glans, the prepuce is brought around the glans as described by Byars.[12] The dorsal penile skin adjacent to the glans is incised at the midline, proximally converting the V into a Y. The proximal end of the long limb of the Y is advanced to convert the Y into a V, thus creating two lateral skin flaps that are closed in the midline ventrally. For distal penile hypospadias with chordee and torsion, Klauber recommends the same initial circumferential skin incision.[13] The skin is dissected from the shaft with reduction of torsion and release of chordee. The ventral skin strip with attached urethra is mobilized by dissecting the urethra from the corpora cavernosa. A strip of preputial skin is isolated with a vascular pedicle, which is inverted and sutured to the ventral skin strip, producing a tube graft from the urethral meatus to the most distal portion of the ventral skin strip. Lateral V-shaped flaps of glans penis are constructed and approximated in a Z-plasty over the glandular portion of the newly constructed urethral tube. Residual preputial skin is rotated to cover the ventral and lateral penile shaft.

REFERENCES

1. Forshall I, Rickham PP: Transposition of penis and scrotum. Br J Urol 28:250, 1956

2. Campbell MF, Harrison JH: Urology, 3rd ed, pp 1576–1577. Philadelphia, WB Saunders, 1970

3. Datta NS, Singh SM, Reddy AVS, et al: Transposition of penis and scrotum in 2 brothers. J Urol 105:739, 1971

4. Glenn JF, Anderson EE: Surgical correction of incomplete penoscrotal transposition. J Urol 110:603, 1973

5. McIlvoy DB, Harris HS: Transposition of the penis and scrotum: Case report. J Urol 73:540, 1955

6. Pancoast, cited in Gross SD: The Diseases, Injuries and Malformations of the Urinary Bladder, Prostate Gland and Urethra, 2d ed. Philadelphia, Blanchard & Lea, 1855

7. Mobley JE: Congenital torsion of the penis. J Urol 109:517, 1973

8. Culp OS: Struggles and triumphs with hypospadias and associated anomalies: Review of 400 cases. J Urol 96:339, 1966

9. Reale L, Benvenuti M: Note sul trattamento correttivo della torsione congenita del pene. La osservazione. Osped Ital Chir 15:149, 1966

10. Allen TD, Spence HM: The surgical treatment of coronal hypospadias and related problems. J Urol 100:504, 1968

11. Harrison JH, Gittes RF, Perlmutter AD, et al: Urology, 4th ed, pp 1571–1575. Philadelphia, WB Saunders, 1979

12. Byars LT: A technique for consistently satisfactory repair of hypospadias. Surg Gynecol Obstet 100:184, 1955

13. Klauber GT: Distal hypospadias, chordee and torsion: The Allen–Spence procedure and new modifications. J Urol 114:765, 1975

ANNOTATED BIBLIOGRAPHY

Miller SF: Transposition of the external genitalia associated with the syndrome of caudal regression. J Urol 108:818, 1972

The author reviews 21 previously reported patients with penoscrotal transposition and adds 1 of his own patients in whom penoscrotal transposition was associated with the syndrome of caudal regression. In addition to transposition of the external genitalia, the child had malsegmentation of the lumbosacral spine, agenesis of the kidneys and bladder, high imperforate anus, calcaneovalgus foot deformities, patent ductus arteriosus and foramen ovale, and lack of gonadal differentiation. The anatomic proximity of the developing structures and the embryo-logic events and their time sequence were thought to explain the occurrence of these associated defects.

Wilson MC, Wilson CL, Thicksten JN: Transposition of the external genitalia. J Urol 94:600, 1965

The authors review 15 previously reported patients with penoscrotal transposition and add one of their own patients, a man of 28 yr who had complete transposition of external genitalia associated with chordee and hypospadias. This patient was able to void and copulate by manually lifting the scrotum above the penis. (These 16 patients with penoscrotal transposition were included in the review by Miller in 1972.)

Adair EL, Lewis EL: Ectopic scrotum and diphallia: Report of a case. J Urol 84:115, 1960

> The authors report unilateral transposition of the right hemiscrotum associated with diphallia and their surgical reconstruction. Both scrotal sacs contained testes. There was agenesis of the right kidney.

Flanagan MJ, McDonald JH, Kiefer JH: Unilateral transposition of the scrotum. J Urol 86:273, 1961

> The authors report a second case of unilateral transposition. The left hemiscrotum was ectopic. Both scrotal sacs contained testes, and the phallus was normal. There was agenesis of the left kidney.

Meyer R: Dislocation of phallus, penis and clitoris following pelvic malformation in human fetus. Anat Rec 79:231, 1941

> The Author reports an analogous condition in a stillborn female fetus of 7 mo. The clitoris and labia minora were located at the posterior end of the labia majora.

Sakamoto K, Kuroki Y, Fujisawa Y et al: XX/XY chromosomal mosaicism presenting a chordee without hypospadias associated with scrotal transposition. J Urol 119:841, 1978

> This is the first case report of XX/XY mosaicism with chordee and scrotal transposition. Hypospadias was not present.

Glenn JF, Boyce WH: Urologic Surgery, 2d ed, p 618. New York, Harper & Row, 1975

> Good illustrations are presented for correction of corporal disproportion using the Pancoast technique popularized by Nesbit. This involves excision of elliptic windows in the tunica albuginea of the corpora cavernosa. Good illustrations are also presented for management of coronal hypospadias with torsion using the method of Allen and Spence.

Paxson CL Jr, Corriere JN, Jr, Morriss FH, Jr, et al: Congenital torsion of the penis in father–son pairs. J Urol 118:881, 1977

> Congenital torsion of the penis was observed in five newborns, three of whom had fathers with torsion of the penis. The authors believe that this common benign condition may be transmitted as an autosomal dominant trait.

OVERVIEW: MANAGEMENT OF GENITAL ANOMALIES

Terry D. Allen

Any discussion of the management of genital anomalies such as those described in the foregoing two chapters invites two major questions, the first of which relates to the nature of the defect and its probable cause, and the second to the actual technical considerations in correcting it. The latter can be answered in a fairly leisurely manner after careful evaluation of the various options available, but the former is an urgent matter requiring considerable insight into the pathophysiology involved in such disorders.

One of the first questions to be asked in making this preliminary evaluation is whether the genital defect seen is the consequence of a systemic intersex disorder in which the genital findings are really the local manifestations of an underlying endocrinopathy or whether the genital abnormality is purely a local event without general systemic implications. Usually the two can be distinguished without difficulty. The genitalia of the true intersex, for example, always lies along a spectrum that courses from normal female to normal male, while local genital malformations, on the other hand, include a wide variety of seemingly nonsensical, even grotesque, defects that clearly do not fit along the spectrum described.

The significance of these deliberations is that they are instrumental in making the single most important decision in the life of the child, that of sex assignment. In most instances where the genital defect appears to be a local malformation without systemic implications (*e.g.,* penoscrotal transposition and penile torsion) the assigned sex and the true sex of the child will be the same, since subsequent development and function, even fertility, will probably be normal. In other instances, however, such as the case of the child with congenital absence of the penis, formation of the genitalia in a manner concordant with genetic sex is beyond the current capabilities of reconstructive surgery and such a child should be sex converted to female.

In the case of the intersex patient the concept of true sex is often inappropriate, since the concordance that usually exists between genetic, gonadal, and genital sex is often lost. Inasmuch as fertility is seldom a consideration, except in the female pseudohermaphrodite, the decision regarding sex assignment more often rests on the patient's potential to perform sexually in his or her assigned role in the coming years. In this regard the extent to which the genitalia can be reconstructed to fulfill this role is of extreme importance, and since it is far easier to construct the passive genitalia of the female than the active ones of the male, the tendency to lean toward female sex assignment in these cases is understandable. There is no tragedy quite like that of a sex-assigned male attempting to go through life with genitalia inadequate for the task.

Once the sex has been established, plans for the reconstruction of the genitalia may be laid out. Ordinarily surgical intervention in these cases is not an urgent undertaking, and frequently matters are facilitated if the surgeon waits until the child is older and the genital structures are larger and easier to work with. These considerations, however, must be tempered with the realization that genitalia inappropriate to the assigned sex of the child is exceedingly distressing to the family, and often it is advantageous to proceed early with any simple measure that might improve the general appearance of the genitalia without compromising subsequent reconstructive efforts. The sex-assigned female, for example, might be benefited by early clitoral reduction along with removal of inappropriate gonads even though the vaginal reconstruction might be deferred until puberty. Similarly, the first stage of a two-stage hypospadias repair might provide some comfort to the family by allowing the penis to project from the perineum even though the urethral reconstruction might be deferred for several years.

My current policy in the sex-assigned female, except for those with the adrenogenital syndrome, is to do the clitoriplasty in the neonatal period. I approach the phallic shaft through a dorsal incision and remove both corpora cavernosa while preserving the glans, dorsal neurovascular bundle, and ventral urethral strip. The glans is recessed, and a portion of the attached phallic skin is used to create a small hood covering its base. Similar surgery is done in the child with the adrenogenital syndrome but not until she is judged completely stable by pediatric endocrinologists. This usually comes about between 8 mo and 1 yr of age. The vaginoplasty is deferred until puberty, since there has been an unacceptably high incidence of strictures among those who have had their surgery in infancy and early childhood.

Penile torsion is often complicated by the associated distal hypospadias and chordee, but the correction is rendered easier by the knowledge that it is not the penis itself but the overlying skin that is responsible for the bulk of the defect. Once the skin has been stripped back off the shaft of the penis, the penis can easily be rotated to a neutral position. The skin is then replaced by any of several techniques without retorting the penis in the process.

Correction of a penoscrotal transposition can be deceptively difficult. Not only is hypospadias commonly present, but the normal suspensory ligament of the penis is not developed and the penis projects from a more caudal position than usual. Relocation of the scrotal flaps should be accompanied by efforts to bring supporting tissue under the penis at the penoscrotal angle to elevate it as the scrotum descends.

95

SURGICAL TREATMENT OF PEYRONIE'S DISEASE WITH A DERMAL GRAFT

Charles J. Devine, Jr. and Charles E. Horton

The Journal of Urology
Copyright © 1974 by The Williams & Wilkins Co.
Vol. 111, January
Printed in U.S.A.

Peyronie's disease, a condition of unknown etiology in which there is hyalinization of the elastic connective tissue of the tunica albuginea of the corpus cavernosum of the penis (Fig. 1), was first described in 1743.[1] The hyalinized area is a discrete indurated plaque, firm to hard in consistency, located on the dorsum of the penis near the glans, involving both corpora and sometimes the septum between them. Rarely a dorsal plaque may extend onto the ventral aspect of the corpus but involvement of the corpus spongiosum has not been described. Microscopically the plaques show hyalinization of collagen fibers with occasional fibroblasts and a few elastic fibrils in the tunica albuginea (Fig. 2).[2] Buck's fascia over the plaque is not involved but there is obliteration of the areolar space between the plaque and the erectile body beneath it and bone may develop in this space in some patients. Malignant changes have never been found in this lesion. The plaque has a slow and limited growth, occasionally disappearing spontaneously.[3,4]

Accepted for publication July 20, 1973.
Read at annual meeting of American Urological Association, New York, New York, May 13–17, 1973.

Our review of 50 cases agrees statistically with the descriptions of others. Peyronie's disease occurs most frequently in subjects between 40 and 60 years old. With erection there is painful curvature toward the inelastic plaque. Generally, the patient will consult a physician immediately but 12 of our patients waited for more than 6 months and 2 for 1½ years. Impotence is occasionally seen as a result of discouragement associated with disturbed erection. Four of our 50 patients had Dupuytren's palmar contracture.

TREATMENT

Whatever conservative treatment is instituted, it is most effective when the lesion has been present only a short time. Since most patients are quite anxious when first seen, reassurance is an extremely important part of therapy. The patient must be told that he does not have a cancer, that he has not brought this upon himself by his sex practices and that there is an excellent chance it can be cured.

Thirty of the 50 patients surveyed have received

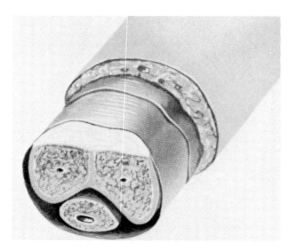

Fig. 1. Diagram of penis with thick Peyronie's plaque on dorsum in tunica albuginea of corpora cavernosa. Buck's fascia overlies plaque and erectile tissue is compressed beneath it.

vitamin E as the primary treatment.[5] We do not anticipate relief for 3 to 6 months. Pain is the first symptom to disappear, then the bend straightens and lastly the knot departs. In 6 patients (20 percent) the lesion disappeared while in 10 (33 percent) there was marked improvement, that is the penis was straight and there was no pain but a softer nodule could be palpated. In 4 patients (13 percent) there was improvement in that there was no pain and, although the penis was bent, it was serviceable. In 6 patients (20 percent) there was no change. Four patients (13 percent) did not return after their first visit. If these were to be dropped from the total the percentage of cure would rise but they remain an enigma and must be considered in further studies of the disease.

There are a number of patients in whom the lesion and the symptoms do not respond to conservative therapy but these patients are benefited by an operation. Simple excision of a small plaque may be successful but as larger segments of the tunica are excised dense scar occurs in the area of resection, causing pain and persistence of the angulation. Poutasse removes enough scar tissue to lengthen the dorsum of the penis, resulting in a useful pain-free erection without necessarily completely straightening the penis.[6] Lowsley placed a free-fat graft into the defect.[7] Lowsley and Boyce as well as Fogh-Andersen reported continuous success with this technique.[8,9]

INVESTIGATION

We thought that we could find a more suitable substitute for the tunica albuginea than the previously used fat grafts which do not have sufficient tensile strength to withstand the engorgement of the corpora during erection. Fascia, artery, vein and dermis were evaluated.[10]

Defects in the tunica albuginea of the corpus cavernosum of dogs were repaired with autogenous grafts. All grafts except the dermis contracted and scarred. The dermal graft retained its integrity and was difficult to distinguish from adjacent tunica. Additional grafts were placed in the tunica and intercavernous septum. All dermal grafts grew and were pliable and soft. The adnexal glands and hair follicles atrophied; no cysts were formed. There was no scarring of the internal structures of the corpora nor of the skin over the graft. Dermis appeared to be an ideal replacement for the tunica albuginea of the corpus cavernosum.

CLINICAL TRIAL

We have operated upon 7 patients, telling each of the experimental nature of the operation. Each patient had disease refractory to other therapy and eagerly accepted this opportunity to control the disease.

We make a circumcising type of incision, just proximal to the corona, freeing the penile skin to the extent necessary to explore the lesion (Fig. 3A). After the dorsal nerves and vessels are retracted to preserve them, the extent of the plaque is easily determined by inspection and palpation. We cut through the tunica and excise all the severely sclerotic and calcified tissue. The plaque, although adherent to the erectile tissue below, is easily separated by gentle blunt and sharp dissection (Fig. 3B and C). The erectile tissue remains contained within the depth of the defect (Fig. 4A). Bleeding is not a problem even though no tourniquet is used.

We then obtain an autogenous dermal graft from the abdominal wall to repair the defect. After the pattern of the defect is outlined on the skin, a section of epidermis 12/1,000 of an inch in thickness is removed with a dermatome, after which the underlying dermis is removed sharply with a knife. Some but not all of the fat is removed from the undersurface of the graft which is then placed in the defect with the fat surface inside (Fig. 4B) and secured with multiple non-absorbable sutures (Fig. 4C). The penile skin is repaired with interrupted 5-zero gut sutures. An elastic pressure dressing is applied and removed 3 days postoperatively. The patient is allowed to void; a catheter is not necessary. Erotic stimulation is kept at a minimum. No attempt is made to prevent erections other than sedation and the use of amyl nitrite pearls in the immediate postoperative period. Sexual intercourse is banned for at least 6 weeks postoperatively. Each patient has been continued on 100 mg vitamin E 3 times a day for 6 months to a year.

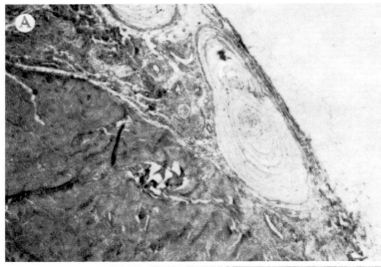

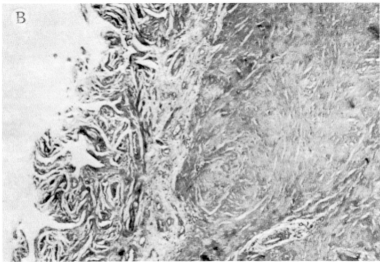

Fig. 2. Microscopic appearance of Peyronie's disease. (*A*) Hyalinized plaque is on left. Uninvolved Buck's fascia is on right with nerve endings. H & E stain. (*B*) Plaque on right, erectile tissue on left. Areolar layer described by Smith is obliterated but there is no continuity of fibers from one tissue to other. Trichrome stain.

CASE REPORTS

Case 1. T. H., a 65-year-old man, was first seen in April 1966. He was treated with vitamin E and the curvature straightened somewhat but pain persisted. In February 1968 potaba was given with little improvement. The operation was done in October 1969. The defect created measured 7 by 2 cm. Erections were markedly straight in February 1970 with a narrow area of fibrosis at the base. When last seen in January 1973 the patient reported adequate sexual function.

Case 2. C. M., a 52-year-old man, was first seen in 1963 with bilateral Dupuytren's contracture. In 1967 a plaque developed in the penis. Despite vitamin E therapy

the disease progressed, the lesion became harder and a second plaque developed near the base causing considerable distortion with erection. The operation was done in September 1970. The plaque was on the dorsum and left side of the shaft of the penis and extended around, involving the tunica deep to the urethra on the undersurface. A month later the graft could still be palpated. Two months later there was a slight curvature on erection with firmness in the graft and some loss of sensation on the left side of the penis. A year later the penis was straight with normal erections. In June 1973 there was no induration and only the sutures could be palpated.

Case 3. D. D., a 55-year-old man, was treated with vitamin E without effect for 6 months prior to being

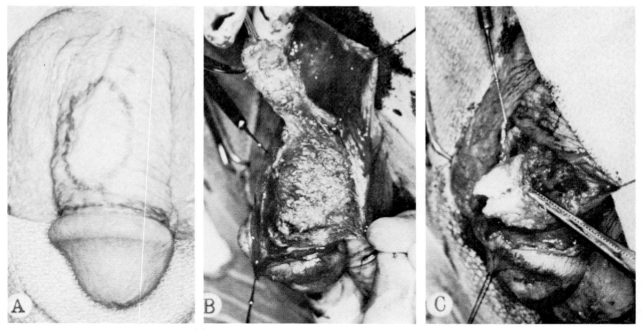

Fig. 3. (A) Penis prepped and draped. Marks outline plaque and circumcising type incision. (B) Plaque has been dissected free from underlying erectile tissue and is about to be excised. Normal edges of tunica albuginea are retracted with hooks. Bleeding is slight. (C) Excised plaque. Note thickness. Tip of spicule of bone can be seen just above tip of clamp.

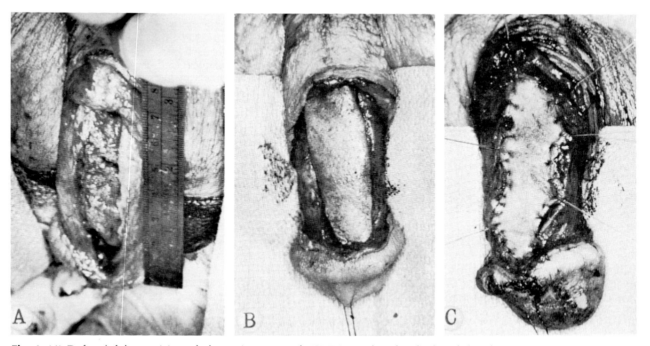

Fig. 4. (A) Defect left by excision of plaque is measured. (B) Trimmed graft is laid in defect fat side down. (C) Graft has been sutured in place with interrupted sutures.

seen by us. At operation in October 1971 the plaque was located in the septum between the corpora. Post-operatively the patient had persistence of the curvature with erection and more plaque could be palpated proximal to the site of the original resection. In April 1972 a Z-plasty skin incision was made over the plaque, which was resected and replaced with another dermal graft. In November 1972 the penis was straight and healing well.

Case 4. H. G., a 59-year-old man, was seen in December 1971 with a rather marked dorsal bend and impotence. Vitamin E caused no resolution. The operation was done in April 1972.[11] The plaque was just behind the glans and involved both corpora but not the septum. A bone spicule was present in the plaque. Two months later there was slight curvature with erection and the graft could be palpated. A year postoperatively the patient was having good erections with only slight curvature and was no longer impotent.

Case 5. L. W., a 48-year-old man, noted deviation with erection in August 1971 with a plaque 1 by 2 cm on the dorsum in the distal half of the penis. Vitamin E was ineffective. The operation was done in May 1972. A month later the curvature was gone. Two months later the graft could be palpated thicker than we had noted in other cases. The patient was having difficulty maintaining an erection in January 1973 with only a gentle curve but the penis was only half the size it had been. Fibrosis could still be palpated in the graft. The patient was given 20 mg prednisone daily, with reduction in dose to no drug in 6 weeks; 8 weeks later he had good strong erection with a very slight bend.

Case 6. G. S., a 69-year-old man, had Peyronie's disease of long duration without response to vitamin E. He had inability to sustain an erection. The operation was done in June 1972. A month later the penis was still curved and tender with segmental anesthesia of the glans. Two months later there was better sensation and less curvature and androgen therapy was started. A year later the patient continued to have difficulty in sustaining an erection but there was no pain and erection was satisfactory when present.

Case 7. C. R., a 47-year-old man, was seen in September 1972 with a tender and freely movable plaque on the dorsal shaft of the penis involving both corpora. No treatment was given and the lesion increased in size. Vitamin E was used without results. X-ray showed calcification in the plaque. The operation was done in February 1973. Six weeks later there was still induration in the graft but the penis was considerably straightened.

DISCUSSION

Each patient in our series had severe disease with pain and curvature of the penis and each was greatly helped by the operation. It is important to resect the entire Peyronie's plaque and to construct the dermal patch the exact size of the defect created by this removal. In 1 patient a secondary procedure was necessary because of inadequate resection of the lesion. In another patient this may be necessary, although he has a useful erection at the present time.

The longest followup is 3½ years. There have been no complications caused by the dermal graft which softens after 3 months and soon is indistinguishable from normal tunica albuginea. One patient required a short course of prednisone to help soften the graft. Pain has been relieved and bending corrected to the degree that intercourse has been possible for all patients, and no further progression of the disease has been seen in any case. One 69-year-old patient has had difficulty sustaining an erection for adequate sexual performance but when he does attain an erection, it is satisfactory. One patient's impotence preoperatively was ameliorated by the relief of the defect in his penis. Impotence or other sexual problems should be thoroughly investigated prior to the operation. We have operated upon 2 other patients since the completion of our study. In one the plaque involved only the left corpus cavernosum but extended in a 3 cm band from the dorsum to the ventral midline where there was much calcification. The other patient had a small lesion on the lateral aspect of the left corpus refractory to treatment. The immediate results are good.

SUMMARY

Peyronie's disease is difficult to treat. The etiologic factor is still unknown and the occasional spontaneous disappearance of the lesions makes assessment of therapy all the more difficult. Many treatment modalities have been recommended and each seems to work in a portion of the patients treated. However, there are a number of patients who require more radical therapy. Our operation has been successful in relieving curvature and penile pain. We resect the hyalinized plaque and repair the defect in the tunica albuginea with a patch graft of dermis from the abdomen. We now recommend that all severe and disabling cases which do not respond to conservative therapy be considered for this treatment.

At the present time we treat all new cases of Peyronie's disease with 100 mg vitamin E 3 times daily. If resolution does not occur in 3 to 6 months we attempt other forms of treatment. If the disease then progresses or does not respond, excision of the lesion and replacement with a dermal graft are offered.

CONCLUSIONS

Many methods of conservative therapy have been proposed for Peyronie's disease. Some are more useful than others, while none work all the time. We have excised the lesion in 9 patients with Peyronie's disease and repaired the defect in the corpus cavernosum of the penis with a patch graft of dermis obtained from the abdomen. The results of our initial series encourage us to recommend that this operation be offered to patients with disabling disease unresponsive to conservative treatment.

REFERENCES

1. Peyronie, F., de la: Sur quelques obstacles qui s'opposent à l'ejaculation naturelle de la semence. Mem de l'acad. roy. de chir., p. 425, 1743
2. Smith, B. H.: Peyronie's disease. Am J Clin Path 45:670, 1965
3. Ashworth, A.: Peyronie's disease. Proc Roy Soc Med 53:692, 1960
4. Williams, J. L. and Thomas, G. G.: The natural history of Peyronie's disease. J Urol 103:75, 1970
5. Scardino, P. L. and Scott, W. W.: The use of tocopherols in the treatment of Peyronie's disease. Ann New York Acad Sci 52:390, 1949
6. Poutasse, E. F.: Peyronie's disease. J Urol 107:419, 1972
7. Lowsley, O.S.: Surgical treatment of plastic induration of the penis (Peyronie's disease). New York State J Med 43:2273, 1943
8. Lowsley, O. S. and Boyce, W. H.: Further experiences with an operation for the care of Peyronie's disease. J Urol 63:888, 1950
9. Fogh-Andersen, P.: Surgical treatment of plastic induration of penis (Peyronie's disease). Acta Chir Scand 113:45, 1957
10. Horton, C. E. and Devine, C. J., Jr.: Peyronie's disease. J Plast Reconst Surg (in press)
11. Devine, C. J., Jr. and Horton, C. E.: Motion picture: Surgical treatment of Peyronie's disease with a dermal graft. Eaton Medical Film Library, Norwich, New York. Presented at annual meeting of American Urological Association, New York, New York, May 13–17, 1973

Commentary: Peyronie's Disease

Charles J. Devine, Jr. and Charles E. Horton

In Peyronie's disease fibrotic changes in the elastic tissue of the tunica albuginea of the corpora cavernosa cause distortion with erection that may occur acutely, the patient having a straight penis with one erection and a bent one with the next, or gradually with progression. Occasionally the disease may first be noticed by a vague pain or discomfort or an asymptomatic lump or plaque in the penis. About 10% of patients with Peyronie's disease have Dupuytren's contracture of the palmar fascia. Familial associations of patients with Dupuytren's contracture are well known. Recently we reported a familial association in Peyronie's disease.[1] To date we have seen 20 men with Peyronie's disease or Dupuytren's contracture in their immediate family. The cause is unknown; there has not been any common thread of etiology in the more than 700 patients we have evaluated.

The plaque is a localized area in which a hyalinized or fibrous scar replaces the normally elastic connective tissue of the tunica albuginea of the corpora cavernosa, possibly extending into strands of the septum between the two corpora cavernosa. There is an inflammatory reaction in the plane between Buck's fascia and the plaque and in the areolar tissue space that lies between the tunica and the erectile tissue, but the fibrous scar does not involve Buck's fascia or the erectile tissue of the penis deep to the plaque. Later the areolar tissue space may become obliterated, and in the more chronic form of the disease the plaque may become calcified, with occasional bone formation deep to the plaque.[2]

Impotence is not caused by Peyronie's disease itself. When a patient with Peyronie's disease complains of impotence, he should have a full-scale investigation to determine the cause. There may be an increased incidence of diabetes in patients with Peyronie's disease, and impotence can be a feature, sometimes even the first symptom, of diabetes. Hypertension and coronary artery disease are also relatively frequent in the patients we have seen for surgery, and many of these men are taking antihypertensive or antidepressive medications that can cause impotence. When the chief complaint is "bent penis and painful erection," the patient is certainly not impotent. However, when there is considerable pain, the patient soon loses interest in maintaining his erection, and this distorted erection can generate psychologic impotence. A patient with Peyronie's disease may be difficult to deal with because this disease of his penis threatens his manhood. The physician prescribing the therapy must not disregard the patient's concern or let the patient's anxiety sway him from a conservative course of treatment.

Surgical treatment should not be undertaken unless the patient has had the disease for a sufficient time to determine whether it is going to resolve spontaneously or if it is going to respond to treatment. If he is sexually incapacitated by the mechanical deformity, surgery is indicated. We recommend observation and treatment for at least 1 yr and probably 1½ yr; however, if calcification is found on an x-ray film of the penis, conservative therapy is not likely to be beneficial. We excise the plaque and cover the defect with a dermal skin graft.

We expose the area of the plaque by making a curvilinear incision directly over it, extending for about half the length of the penis and freeing up the dartos fascia (Fig. 5). We then do an artificial erection to identify the extent of the inelastic tissue. In most cases the plaque is on the dorsal side, and we must dissect beneath Buck's fascia to reach it, preserving the vascular and nerve structures on the dorsum of the penis. We make a longitudinal incision through Buck's fascia on the lateral aspect of the corpora, electrocoagulating and dividing the encircling vessels. Using blunt-tipped strabismus scissors,* we dissect beneath the dorsal layer of Buck's fascia until a broad flap has been elevated, containing the structures to be preserved. This dissection is difficult in the area over the plaque because of the inflammatory reaction but proceeds with ease proximal and distal to it. We dissect enough of the normal plane so that we have easy access to the entire plaque. When the plaque is located on the ventral surface we dissect beneath the urethra, freeing it up in this same fashion to expose the plaque.

The plaque is easily identified by its firm consistency. We outline it with a marking solution and incise around its circumference with a knife, cutting through the tunica albuginea but preserving the erectile tissue. There will be a rush of blood at the start of the incision, but, because this is a venous space, bleeding is easily controlled with pressure. We do not use a

* Parke, Davis & Company, Snowden-Pencer Instruments, Deseret O.R. Division, Greenwood, SC 29646.

tourniquet. A tourniquet left on the penis during the 1½ to 2 hr necessary to do this operation can damage the vascular structures and nerves it is compressing. We elevate the edge of the plaque and sharply dissect it off the erectile tissue (Fig. 6). When the disease involves the septum, we remove the involved strands but do not attempt to place any tissue in this gap.

When the plaque has been excised, the edges of the tunica should be soft and elastic. If the edges feel gritty we excise more tissue. We then make tension on the glans penis, note any restriction, and make releasing incisions extending deep into these areas (Figs. 7 and 8). The resultant defect in the tunica will be one and a half times to twice as large as the plaque. We measure the defect, stretching the penis transversely and longitudinally to determine the size of the dermal graft that will be necessary.

We obtain the dermal graft from the skin of the abdomen below the bathing suit line. We measure and mark the skin, tapering the ends so that a primary closure can be done. The epidermis may be removed with a dermatome but with practice this can be done freehand with a scalpel. This tissue is discarded. We have seen patients in whom the epidermis has been put back as a split-thickness graft to cover the defect. This results in an unsightly scar. After excising the dermis, we trim most of the fat off of its undersurface and tack it in the defect with interrupted sutures of 5–0 polypropylene, then approximate the edges with running sutures of 5–0 Vicryl. We feel that a 1-mm graft heals the most satisfactorily; if the graft is too thick or too thin, it does not work as well and tends to become fibrotic as it heals. The fat side should be placed down because this leaves the fatty layer between the dermal graft and the erectile tissue of the penis.

To close the donor site we undermine the edges of the skin and pull them together with 2–0 black silk sutures to

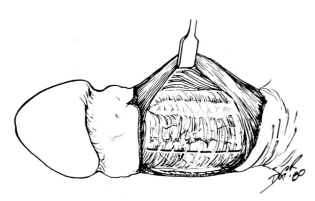

Fig. 5. Exposure of the plaque. A dorsal incision is made, and the skin and dartos fascia layer are retracted. An incision on one side through Buck's fascia will allow reflection of that fascia layer, disturbing only one set of encircling vessels.

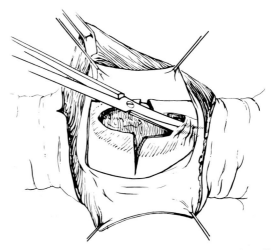

Fig. 6. Buck's fascia with the neurovascular bundle is reflected and the plaque is excised. Lateral incisions will allow greater expansion of the tunica with erection. The erectile tissue is dissected free from the underside of the tunica, relieving another possible restriction.

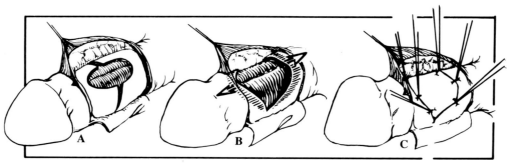

Fig. 7. (A) The plaque is excised, incisions are made into the normal tunica, and the erectile tissue is freed from its underside. (B) Tension on the penis will expand this defect, and a dermal graft this size is placed in the defect. (C) The graft is tacked in place with interrupted Proline sutures. The gaps will be closed with running Vicryl sutures.

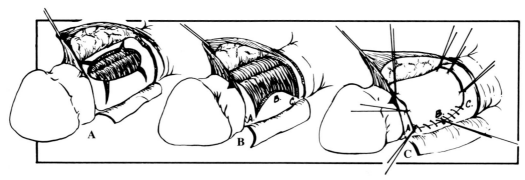

Fig. 8 (A) When the plaque is long, it may be necessary to make two sets of incisions into the normal tissue to release the contracture completely. (B) Stretching the penis produces a more or less square defect. (C) With the Proline stay sutures in place, anastomosis of the graft to the tunica with running sutures is begun.

relieve tension from the closure. We then place sutures of 4–0 Vicryl in the dermal layers, approximating the edges. The black silk sutures are then removed. We complete the skin closure with interrupted and running sutures of 5–0 nylon, removing them on about the tenth day.

After the dermal grafting has been completed, we do another artificial erection to look for leaks in the suture line and to show that we have straightened the penis. If the penis is not straight, we will cut further into the restricting tissue and place an additional dermal graft sewing it to the previous one. When the penis is straight there will be a noticeable bulge of the graft, but approximating Buck's fascia with interrupted sutures of 4–0 chromic gut or Vicryl will contain the bulge of the graft. We place a 16-gauge Minivac drain* and approximate

* The Minivac has been a valuable adjunct. We cut the luer hub off a 16-gauge butterfly needle and cut holes in the side of the tube so that blood and serum will drain, leaving the plastic tube long enough so that the needle end will reach the abdominal wall from the wound. The tip of this tube with the side holes is left in the wound. Plugging the needle at the other end into a sterilized Hemovac blood collection tube provides suction drainage.

the skin with sub-Q Vicryl and cutaneous 4–0 chromic sutures. We apply a pressure dressing for 2 hr, after which we begin a routine of cold saline soaks.

In the postoperative period there is no way to eliminate erections completely, but we discourage them by sedating the patient with diazepam. If the penis becomes erect, the patient is instructed to break an amyl nitrite pearl and inhale the vapors. Two weeks after discharge we encourage him to have erections and then to engage in lovemaking without intercourse during the next month and engage in sexual activity after 6 wk. It is not unusual for a patient, after having a straight penis for several weeks following his surgery, to have a return of some curvature by 3 mo as maturation of the graft proceeds. We ask him to continue to take vitamin E, 200 mg three times a day, during this period. It may take from 6 to 14 mo for the penis to straighten again. The penis will be somewhat shorter than before the patient developed Peyronie's disease, but if there is no pain and the penis is straight enough for intercourse, the surgery has been successful.

Seventy percent of 50 consecutive patients who were operated on more than a year before a recent survey were cured.[1] In a review of 35 more patients, these statistics have held up.[3] Dissection has been more difficult in patients who have had radiation therapy or injection with steroid hormones because there was considerably more inflammation above and below the plaque than in patients who have not had either of these treatments. In the 30% who had less than satisfactory results from our surgery, there was an inordinate percentage of patients who had had these prior treatments.

A small percentage of our patients have developed impotence postoperatively. A case-by-case investigation of these patients shows no direct relationship of the impotence to the surgery.[4] Some patients have organic causes such as diabetes and antihypertensive medication; most are definitely psychogenic. Some patients who claimed to be impotent have demonstrated impressive erections during nocturnal penile tumescence studies. Because most of our patients do well after surgery, we recommend against placing an erectile device at the time of primary surgery except in men with proven impotence after a complete work-up, which should include evaluation by a good sex therapy team, nocturnal penile tumescence studies, and a search for an organic cause for the impotence. There have been several reports of small series of cases in which all or nearly all the patients were impotent postoperatively.[5-7] We do not understand these results because several other authors have reported results similar to ours.[8-10]

We discuss the possibilities and results with each patient and his wife before surgery, and each knows that should he become impotent he might need another operation for a prosthesis. Implantation of an erectile device after a patient has had a dermal graft repair of Peyronie's disease should not differ from implantation in an otherwise impotent man. There may be additional fibrosis in the region of the dermal graft, but the corporal space should be open. If not, the area should be explored to be sure that the implant remains within the corporal body.

Because of these figures and the possibility that patients may be worse after surgery, we do not operate on men just because they have a crooked penis, but only on patients who are sexually incapacitated and only after very careful explanation of what we intend to do and the possible results. Prospective evaluation by our sex therapy team has been a valuable addition to overall care of these unfortunate couples, enhancing their understanding of the condition and helping to guide them to satisfactory post-operative sexual function.

When organic impotence is present and the decision has been made to place an erectile device, we vary the procedure according to the type of prosthesis employed. When the solid rod type is to be inserted, we prefer the Flexirod.* The operation for the excision of the plaque proceeds in the fashion already described. After excising the plaque and demonstrating that there is no longer any restriction of the penis, we measure the length of the corpora from the defect to the tip beneath the cap of the glans and the proximal ends to the tips of the crura with a 16 French Hegar dilator. Selecting the correct size of prosthesis, we cut the tails to fit and manipulate the prosthesis into position, one on each side.

We then cover the defect in the tunica albuginea with a dermal graft trimmed to fit the defect and secured with tacking sutures of 4–0 prolene and running 4–0 Vicryl. Buck's fascia and the skin are closed as described above with a Minivac drain. In the postoperative period we use prophylactic bactericidal medication at a therapeutic level.

The inflatable prosthesis cannot be installed in this manner because of the difficulty in inserting the proximal ends into the crus. When this prosthesis is used, we insert it in the usual fashion through a subsymphyseal incision. Inflating the prosthesis will now reveal the deformity. We then incise the tunica, using electrocautery because a knife might injure the device. Furlow says that if a small area of the device is revealed by this process, he leaves it uncovered, but a larger segment would bulge so he uses a dermal graft to cover the defect.[11]

* Surgitek Flexirod Penile Implant, Medical Engineering Corporation, 3037 Mount Pleasant Street, Racine, WI 53403.

REFERENCES

1. Wild RM, Devine CJ Jr, Horton CE: Dermal graft repair of Peyronie's diseases: Survey of 50 patients. J Urol 121:47, 1979
2. Smith BH: Peyronie's disease. Am J Clin Pathol, 45:670, 1966
3. Horton CE, Devine CJ Jr, Calabretta A: Peyronie's disease. Presented at the American Association of Plastic Surgeons Meeting, Scottsdale, AZ May 1980
4. Jones WJ, Horton, CE, Devine CJ Jr: Evaluation of surgical failures after operation for Peyronie's disease: Development of a prospective study. Presented at the 75th Annual Meeting of the American Urological Association, San Francisco, May 1980
5. Raz S, Dekernion JB, Kaufman JK: Surgical treatment of Peyronie's disease: A new approach. J Urol 117:598, 1977
6. Melman A, Holland TF: Evaluation of the dermal graft inlay technique for the surgical treatment of Peyronie's disease. J. Urol 120:421, 1978

7. Bruskewitz R, Raz S: Surgical considerations in the treatment of Peyronie's disease. Urology 15:134, 1980
8. Bystrom J, Johanson B, Edsmyr F, et al: Induratio penis plastica (Peyronie's disease). Scand J Urol Nephrol 6:1, 1972
9. Hicks CC, O'Brien DP III, Bostwick J III, et al: Experience with the Horton-Devine dermal graft in the treatment of Peyronie's disease. J Urol 119:504, 1978
10. Green, R, Martin, DC: Treatment of Peyronie's disease by dermal grafting. Plast Reconstr Surg 64:208, 1979
11. Furlow WL: The surgical management of Peyronie's disease: Penile straightening with use of the inflatable penile prosthesis. Motion picture. Mayo Clinic, Rochester, MN, 1978

ANNOTATED BIBLIOGRAPHY

Lowsley OS: Surgical treatment of plastic induration of the penis (Peyronie's disease). NY State Med J 43:2273, 1943

Dr. Lowsley's concept of the disease places it as beginning in the septum between the corpora and extending into Buck's fascia but rarely into the erectile tissue. He reviews extensively the possible etiology of the disease, pointing out that then, as now, it is unknown. After discussing various not-so-successful forms of conservative therapy—some still current—he describes his operative treatment of early patients in whom the disease is "confined to the septum between the corpora cavernosa." These would · be dorsal midline lesions because the dissection he describes never got him into the septum. He incises the tunica of the corpora and sharply excises parts of the thickened layer of the plaque, taking care "to avoid entering the corpora cavernosa more than necessary to remove the offending fibrotic tissue." Small pads of fat are applied to cover the inadvertent breaks in what he termed *Buck's fascia,* which in reality is the tunica albugineas of the corpora. He describes seven patients with only one failure, which he ascribes to the extensive lesion present in that patient.

Smith BH: Peyronie's disease. Am J Clin Pathol 45:670, 1966

Smith reviews previous descriptions of Peyronie's disease and finds that most authors have only speculated about its cause and pathogenesis because of the limited number of tissue specimens that had been examined histologically. He found 26 cases in the Armed Forces Institute of Pathology and compares them with 30 normal penises obtained at autopsy, deriving the first accurate description of the histology of the normal and the diseased penis. He describes the vascular, loose, areolar connective tissue sleeve that separates the corpus cavernosum from the tunica albuginea. We have since referred to this layer as the space of Smith and feel that it is important because it affords the elastic tunica mobility as it stretches during erection. He was not able to delineate Buck's fascia in his sections, but in surgical procedures we have found it to be a definite tissue layer in which run the dorsal vein, arteries, and nerves and which, with care, can be dissected free, separating these critical structures from the lesion in the tunica.

Of the 26 patients whose tissues he examined, 5 were black. In over 700 patients we have examined here, only 4 have been black. He found, as others had and as we have, that about 10% of these patients had Dupuytren's contracture, and he also notes, as have we, no common etiologic factor. In early lesions (less than 3 mo) he found a predominance of an inflammatory cellular infiltrate. Since we have not operated on anyone with disease of that short duration, we have not seen specimens of this sort but agree that in those of longer duration there is much fibrosis and little inflammation. We have, however, found calcification and even ossification earlier than he noted in this series. We also have found organized bone to lie in the areolar space between the corpus cavernosum and the tunica but have also found spicules of bone within the plaque in the tunica albuginea and running in the strands of the septum between the corpora cavernosa.

In his discussion Smith states that Peyronie's disease has been one of the enigmas of medicine and despite the light he has shed on it Peyronie's disease remains that 17 yr later. He is able to rule out venereal disease, arteriosclerosis, and noninflammatory plastic fibrosis as causative agents but feels that repetitive trauma may play a part because he is otherwise unable to account for the inflammation he had found in the early cases. His description stands, but the cause of the disease is still unknown. The association of Dupuytren's contracture and our finding of a familial association in some patients makes us believe that the disease is not simply a fibrotic reaction to trauma or inflammation.

Poutasse EF: Peyronie's disease. Trans Am Assoc Genetourin Surg 63:97, 1977

The author correctly describes the penile anatomy and the pathology of Peyronie's disease, and, because of the difficulty of dissecting the plaque off the underlying erectile tissue, he supports Smith's conclusion that the disease begins as a vasculitis in the areolar space, which Smith describes.

He also notes that the inflammation involves tissues superficial to the plaque, stating that frequently a fibrotic, inelastic dorsal vein of the penis must be removed to allow maximum correction of the chordee. He describes the effects of Peyronie's disease and points out that during examination the penis must be stretched to appreciate fully the effect of the plaque and notes the opposing effects of multiple plaques might leave the penis straight.

He reviews later reports of Lowsley's procedure and reviews his own experience with an operation intended to remove a section of the fibrous plaque, allowing the penis to be straightened from a disabling to a usable degree of curvature and defines his criteria for selection of patients for operations.

He makes a transverse incision over the plaque and dissects through Buck's fascia, avoiding the dorsal arteries and nerves but removing a section from the dorsal vein if it is inelastic. He then incises the plaque opening the cavernous tissue layer and cuts away the fibrous tissue until 2 cm to 3 cm of cavernous tissue is exposed and the penis can be stretched. He closes Buck's fascia, the dartos fascia, and the skin and leaves on a pressure dressing for 3 days.

He points out the fact that it is not necessary to remove all the plaque to straighten the penis. Our own procedure is based in part on his experience. We do prefer to fill the defect with a patch to prevent further scarring as healing takes place, allowing us to attempt surgical correction on patients with more extensive lesions who, according to his criteria, would not be candidates for this surgery. A closed blood space also gives us the opportunity to test the straightness of the penis with an artificial erection to be sure we have done all we need to do at surgery.

Horton CE, Devine CJ Jr: Peyronie's disease. Plast Reconstr Surg 52:503, 1973

This is a companion piece to our article reproduced in this text. It discusses the history of the disease and its treatment and describes the experimental aspects of the work leading to our surgical procedure. We were unable to produce the lesion of Peyronie's disease in the tunical albuginea of the corpus cavernosum of a dog with various types of trauma. We tried various tissues to patch a defect of the tunica in dogs and found dermis to be the most suitable of these. Various other tissues and prosthetic materials have been tried by others with no real improvement in results. Early clinical results reported in the reprinted paper are summarized here.

Billig R, Baker R, Immergut M et al: Peyronie's disease. Urology 6:409, 1975

This is a well-done review article with 40 references that gives a summary of most of what is known about the disease to date. It would be impossible to abstract it here, but it should be read by anyone with an interest in this disease. The authors' discussion of the cause of this condition points out the many directions in which study has been carried out without discovery of the etiology and the reasoning responsible for the multiple empirically derived forms of treatment. Because the cause is not known the therapy is nonspecific, and perhaps it is, as has been said, that here medicine is what the physician uses to amuse the patient while nature cures the disease. Recent descriptions of the presence of similar cells described as myofibroblasts in the lesions of Peyronie's disease and Dupuytren's contracture and of our own successful growth in tissue culture of these myofibroblasts from the plaques of Peyronie's disease and the lesions of Dupuytren's contracture point out the unusual nature of these lesions. The authors point out McRoberts' suggestion that a common etiologic factor that ordinarily causes no trouble might, in susceptible men, lead to the formation of a Peyronie's disease plaque.

They discuss surgical treatment, outlining the reported results of various procedures. The psychological effects of Peyronie's disease have not been well studied, and little mention is made of this here. We have found psychological problems to be overwhelming in many of our patients and perhaps the most difficult aspect of the disease to treat.

Wild RM, Devine CJ Jr, Horton CE: Dermal graft repair of Peyronie's disease: Survey of 50 patients. J Urol 121:47, 1979

This is a later survey of the results of our surgery by our resident, Bob Wild. He was able to obtain a detailed follow-up study from 50 of 52 consecutive patients who had been operated on at least 1 yr before. In all, 89 patients charts were reviewed and 2 of them had a familial relationship with either Peyronie's disease or Dupuytren's contracture. This has now been increased to 20 patients of the over 700 we have seen. Selection for the surgical procedure and the operative technique are detailed. Selection remains about the same now, but changes in the operative technique initiated by the results obtained in this study are described above. We would like to point out two important details. It is not necessary to use a tourniquet on the penis while doing this operation, and we feel that use of the tourniquet for the length of time necessary to do the operation may harm the tissues of the penis. Also, the skin of the donor site should be closed as described above because replacement of the epidermis as a split-thickness graft leaves an ugly scar.

Seventy percent of our patients had subjective relief of their problem. Painful erections, significant curvature, or impotence accounted for the 30% who had a poor result. Impotence associated with Peyronie's disease before surgery and after is not a simple matter, and in most patients it definitely can be defined as psychosomatic. Nevertheless, it is real and must be prevented or treated. We have underway a study of this problem with our sex therapy colleagues and hope by prospective studies to be able to outline a plan of therapy that will bring a man and his wife through the trauma of this disease as a functioning couple. This may be difficult because some men approach surgery, despite detailed descriptions of what can and cannot be done, having acquired the idea that the surgeon might work some sort of magic so that the penis will become as large, hard, and straight as he remembers it to have been before having developed the Peyronie's disease and that erections will be instant and automatic so that he will be able to satisfy the most demanding and recalcitrant woman without the bother of loveplay. When this is not the case during the first attempt at intercourse, then he, or the surgery, or the surgeon has failed the test and from then on things get worse. Fortunately few men are just like this but all have some of these characteristics to some degree. Proper care and counseling during the "conservative" treatment of the condition, a good process of evaluation and selection of patients for the surgery, meticulous surgical technique with sparing of as much of the normal tissue of the penis as possible, and careful guiding of the patient in the postoperative period will go a long way to ensuring the surgeon, the patient, and the patient's wife of a satisfactory ultimate outcome.

Evaluation of another 35 patients has been undertaken, but the results have not been reported. Of these patients, 83% have had subjective relief of their problem, 18% have residual penile deformity interfering with intercourse, and 11% are impotent. These results still leave room for improvement.

Overview: Peyronie's Disease

Robert A. Garrett

Peyronie's disease is characterized by penile pain, curvature deformity, and hyaline plaque formation. Impotence may result from embarrassment owing to the deformity or from mechanical factors related to the disease. Impotence for reasons unrelated to Peyronie's disease must also be considered. A category of patients with this disease display spontaneous resolution, or arrest short of functional disability. Pain on erection or intercourse tends to undergo spontaneous resolution; plaque formation and deformity do not. There is no convincing evidence that any form of medical management is objectively beneficial. Orthovoltage radiation therapy, enjoying popularity in the past, has been shown to be ineffective in a careful retrospective study by Furlow. Indeed, radiation may make plaque dissection more difficult.

For those patients who progress to sexual disability or persistent pain, surgical management provides a useful, often problem-solving approach. Criteria for operative approach should include an adequate period of observation from onset to significant disability. Pain alone is not regularly an indication for surgery and is seldom eliminated by surgery. Mature gross deformity coupled with unacceptable sexual dysfunction appears to warrant operative intervention. Controversy arises over which method of surgical manipulation is appropriate.

Impotence occurring with Peyronie's plaque formation has frequently failed to yield to plaque excision and dermal grafting. Indeed, Devine and Horton, our Commentary authors, have categorically stated that excision and grafting is not indicated in cases of impotence, though some of their cited cases were admittedly thus managed. Psychological evaluation of impotence prior to surgery is mandatory so that a realistic prognosis can be offered. Reported experiences with impotence following excision-grafting in cases in which the complaint was not present presurgically have frustrated a consensus in its favor. Raz and our group have found a high rate of impotence postoperatively, and hence have recommended prosthesis insertion with or without plaque excision for curvature correction. Furlow suggests the inflatable prosthesis in preference to the Small-Carrion because it makes curvature control by variable inflation possible.

An acceptable plan of management, when potency is not in question, is to use the Devine-Horton excision-grafting procedure, and to follow with prosthetic insertion at a later date if impotence ensues. For those patients with unacceptable consequences of plaque formation and psychogenic impotence, prosthesis insertion with plaque incision as one procedure is justifiable.

96

PRIAPISM CURED BY CREATION OF FISTULAS BETWEEN GLANS PENIS AND CORPORA CAVERNOSA

Chester C. Winter

From the Division of Urology, Ohio State University Medical Center, Columbus, Ohio

The Journal of Urology
Copyright © 1978 by The Williams & Wilkins Co.
Vol. 119, February
Printed in U.S.A.

ABSTRACT—A simplified method to drain the corpora cavernosa into the spongiosum in cases of priapism is discussed and the advantages are listed.

In adults priapism usually is idiopathic in origin, although evidence is accumulating that a number of drugs, especially the psychotropic variety, are responsible. In children sickle cell disorders and leukemia account for most cases. In a few instances neoplasm, trauma, inflammatory diseases and neurogenic disorders produce the condition. The disease usually results in impotence unless prompt treatment effects complete remission quickly. Although most medical measures fall short of relief notable success has followed aspiration, irrigation, intermittent compression or one of several vascular operations. I previously reported a new method to create fistulas between the glans penis and the paired corpora cavernosa with uniform success.[1] The technical aspects will be reviewed.

TECHNIQUE

With the use of sedation and local anesthesia (lidocaine) the corpora are aspirated with an 18 gauge needle through the tip of the glans penis. The needle is then used for irrigation with saline; dilute heparin may be added. A biopsy needle* is introduced in closed position through

Accepted for publication April 22, 1977.
* Tru-cut, code 2N2704, Travenol Laboratories, Inc., Deerfield, Illinois.

the glans to the coronal septum, care being taken to avoid the urethra (see figure). The biopsy needle is opened by extending the obturator blade through the septum and the needle is closed by pushing the sheath over the fenestrated tip, twisted and removed. Tissue consisting of fibrous septum and cavernosum contents should be seen. The maneuver is repeated through the same site so that 1 or 2 fistulas are created between the glans and each corpus cavernosum body. The penis will detumesce and remain so. Brisk bleeding from the glans puncture site is controlled by a figure-of-8 absorbable suture. Pressure dressings are not necessary. An indwelling catheter is not used even though the corpus spongiosum is fuller than normal and makes the penis look slightly larger than usual. Antibiotic coverage is optional but I advise it. The local anesthesia may be supplemented with methoxyflurane inhalation through a Duke inhalor. The patient may go home after recovering from anesthesia since no portal of bleeding is present. Laboratory blood tests can be postponed until after the procedure, or at least one need not await prior drawn test results before creating the fistulas.

DISCUSSION

Each of my 2 patients had priapism for 3 days before this management and they had undergone several conservative medical measures. One of the patients, a 24-year-old white man, had ingested methaqualone and alcohol and smoked marihuana prior to onset. These agents are believed responsible for the disease. The 49-year-old black patient had a history of hypertension treated with ismelin and was already impotent from this drug. It is believed that this drug caused the priapism since the patient did not have sickle cell disorder. Both patients were impotent after the procedure. Although patients are forwarned that the disease and not the treatment makes them impotent they are prone to believe the reverse.

Since Grayhack and associates reported successful detumescence of priapism by a saphenous vein-corpus cavernosum shunt in 1964,[2] several other types of vascular procedures have been tried with success, including (1) corpus cavernosum-saphenous vein shunt, (2) corpora cavernosa-spongiosum shunt, (3) ligation of internal pudendal artery, (4) creation of fistula between the glans penis and corpus cavernosum and (5) corpus cavernosum-penile dorsal vein shunt (superficial or deep). The most popular shunt has been the corpora spongiosa to cavernosum. Since the 2 corpora cavernosa communicate only one need be drained. Unbeknown to the author Ebbehoj reported in 1975 a procedure similar to the one described, in which he incised the corona with

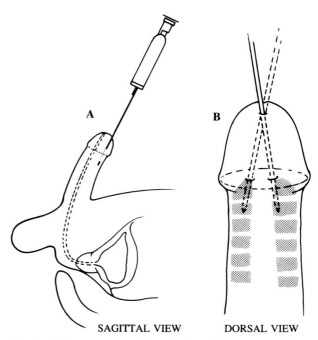

Fig. 1. (A) Sagittal view of genitalia, with biopsy needle entering mid dorsal tip of penis and inserted through septum between glans and corpora cavernosa. Urethral injury is to be avoided. (B) Dorsal view of penis shows sites of fistulas between glans and each corpus cavernosum.

a scalpel and twisted a hole through the coronal septum to drain the cavernosa into the spongiosum.[3] More recently, priapism has been relieved successfully by anastomosis of the penile dorsal veins to a corpus cavernosum. I believe that the use of the biopsy needle to create fistulas between the glans penis and corpora cavernosa has merit and advantages over other shunting methods because of the (1) simplicity of the technique, (2) ease of performance, (3) rapidity of procedure, (4) fact that no special or prolonged preparation of the patient is done, (5) use of a local anesthetic, (6) preservation of the saphenous vein and (7) prediction that this can be an outpatient procedure with marked reduction in hospital and surgical costs.

ADDENDUM

Since submission of this article 3 additional patients have been operated upon with this procedure. Two were done as outpatients. One patient with sickle cell disease subsequently required corpus cavernosum-to-spongiosum shunt.

REFERENCES

1. Winter, C. C.: Cure of idiopathic priapism. New procedure for creating fistula between glans penis and corpora cavernosa. Urology 8:389, 1976

2. Grayhack, J. T., McCullough, W., O'Conor, V. J., Jr. and Trippel, O.: Venous bypass to control priapism. Invest Urol 1:509, 1964

3. Ebbehoj, J.: A new operation for priapism. Scand J Plast Reconstr Surg 8:241, 1975

Commentary: Surgical Treatment of Priapism

Anton J. Bueschen

Priapism is a painful, persistent penile erection unaccompanied by sexual desire. The treatment of priapism has improved considerably during the past 15 yr but remains very frustrating to many physicians because it is a disorder that is seen infrequently, and often irreversible changes have occurred that prohibit successful treatment with current methods of management. This Commentary discusses the following aspects of priapism: etiology, pathogenesis, surgical treatment, and complications.

ETIOLOGY

Priapism is classified as primary (idiopathic) or secondary. The causes of secondary priapism are hematologic (20% of all cases), neurogenic, trauma, inflammations and infections, chemicals and drugs and toxins, carcinoma, and congenital diseases. The hematologic causes of priapism are sickle cell disease or trait, leukemia, and heparin therapy. Priapism occurs in sickle cell disease by the red blood cells (RBCs) in the corpora sickling because of increased oxygen consumption during physiologic erection. The increased blood viscosity may consequently occlude small vessels. Priapism can occur in the presence of leukemia by leukemic infiltration or mechanical obstruction of the corpora cavernosa and dorsal veins of the penis or leukemic infiltrates, irritating the sacral nerve roots. One of the largest series of priapism is a recent report of 48 patients treated during a 22-yr period that showed that idiopathic priapism and sickle cell disease accounted for 81% of all the patients.[1] There were 37 adults and 11 children. Idiopathic priapism occurred in 26 (70%) of the adults, and sickle cell disease occurred in 7 (63.3%) of the children. Other etiologic factors in the adults were sickle cell disease (four), solid tumors (four), trauma (two), and leukemia (one). Other etiologic factors in the children were leukemia (two) and idiopathic (two).

PATHOGENESIS

Normal human penile erection depends on integration of afferent signals in the thoracolumbar or sacral erection centers, intact autonomic nerves to the penis, normal erectile tissues, and an adequate blood supply to the penis.[2] Polsters (valvelike structures) are present in vessels and control the flow of blood through the corpora cavernosa. The polsters are controlled by parasympathetic fibers (S2–S4) and sympathetic fibers (thoracolumbar). The sacral erection center is activated by either psychic or local reflexogenic stimuli, and the thoracolumbar erection center is activated only by psychic stimuli.

Hinman studied the histologic changes that occurred in seven patients with idiopathic priapism, demonstrating evidence of edematous septae and subsequent fibrosis.[3] It was postulated that the basic reasons for failure of the various nonsurgical treatments are that they do not restore venous drainage and that they do not eliminate progressive damage to the local erectile mechanisms.

TREATMENT

The treatment of priapism has undergone significant changes during the past 15 yr, but still remains suboptimal because of the development of fibrosis, which prevents subsequent erection. Before the initial report of a corporosaphenous shunt, many nonoperative forms of treatment were used. The nonoperative treatment was helpful occasionally but not often, as suggested by the multiple methods of observation, oxygen, exercise, catheterization, analgesics, sedatives, prostatic massage, hot or cold compresses or enemas, pressure dressings, steroids, estrogens, fibrinolysin, dextran, anticoagulants, enzymes, antispasmodics, anesthesia (epidural, spinal, or general), sympathetic blockage, succinylcholine, and procaine.

Grayhack and associates, based on the pathophysiology described by Hinman, initiated the surgical treatment of priapism with their report of successful treatment with a cavernosaphenous shunt following unsuccessful nonoperative treatment in the same patient.[3–5] A cavernospongiosum shunt was described almost simultaneously, apparently without knowledge of Grayhack's operative report.[6] Recent reports have described the percutaneous creation of a fistula between the glans penis and the corpus cavernosum, and one of those operations described by Winter has developed popularity.[7–11]

Other recently described procedures that have not been widely used are ligation of the internal pudendal artery, creation of a shunt between the corpus cavernosum and dorsal vein of the penis, and injection of autologous clot into the internal pudendal artery.[12,13]

Currently most patients with priapism are treated initially with surgical procedures. However, surgical treatment is not helpful for the patient with priapism due to direct infiltration with malignant disease. Sickle cell disease management remains controversial regarding nonoperative or operative treatment. Results have been very gratifying following shunt procedures, but nonoperative treatment with hydration, alkalization, analgesics, and transfusions has provided satisfactory results, especially in children, who tend to have a high incidence of recurrence of priapism.[14,15]

Percutaneous creation of a fistula for the treatment of priapism seems to be the easiest satisfactory form of surgical treatment.[10] Winter's technique is easy and rapid and preserves the saphenous vein. It is less expensive than other operative procedures, since it is not necessary to perform it in the operating room. However, it is recommended that the patient enter the hospital for observation, since some patients develop persistent firmness, which can be treated with intermittent pressure with a pediatric blood pressure cuff or a T binder.[16] A pressure dressing should never be used because it can lead to necrosis of the edematous skin.[17,18] If the patient continues to have severe firmness, another shunt procedure can be performed, preferably a cavernospongiosum shunt. However, the more formal development of a shunt has been necessary very infrequently in my experience since the use of the percutaneous technique.

A cavernospongiosum shunt was first described in Belgium in 1964, and an excellent English description of the operation was reported in 1972.[6,19] I prefer a midline perineal incision over a penile incision because there seems to be less chance of a urethral injury during the operation when it is performed through a perineal incision. The bulbocavernosus muscle is incised longitudinally in the midline and dissected laterally, exposing the corpus spongiosum and corpora cavernosa. One corpus cavernosum is sutured to the corpus spongiosum at the level of the bulbous urethra with two separate continuous 2–0 chromic catgut sutures, one going distally 1 cm and the other going proximally 1 cm. An ellipse of tunica albuginea is excised from the corpus cavernosum lateral to the suture. Dark sludged blood is evacuated from the corpus cavernosum until a brisk flow of bright blood is obtained. The corpus cavernosum is irrigated with normal saline, and then an incision is made

in the corpus spongiosum just medial to the previously placed suture line. A fistula is then created by continuing with the running chromic catgut sutures, anastomosing the lateral portion of the incision in the corpus cavernosum to the medial portion of the incision in the corpus spongiosum. Even though the penis becomes flaccid after a unilateral procedure has been performed, I generally perform the same procedure on the contralateral side to provide optimal shunting. Brisk bleeding occurs after the corpus cavernosum has been incised, but there is no evidence of bleeding after completion of the anastomosis with the catgut sutures. The perineal incision is closed without a drain, and a light perineal dressing is applied with no dressing applied to the penis.

The cavernosaphenous shunt is an important landmark in the evolution of surgical treatment of priapism.[4] However, it is used very seldom now because it is a slightly longer operation than the others, eliminates the possible use of the saphenous vein for other bypass procedures that might become necessary, and has a greater risk of embolism.

RESULTS AND COMPLICATIONS

Eventual potency is the major concern in evaluating results of priapism treatment. The incidence of potency is difficult to assess because of the infrequency of priapism and the natural tendency of authors to report their experience only when they have had successful results. Cosgrove and LaRocque, in a literature review, found that 61% of 75 patients were potent and there was very little difference between cavernospongiosum and cavernosaphenous shunts.[20] The shunt operations for priapism due to sickle cell disease produced a potency rate of 77% in 17 patients. Initial experience with the percutaneous fistula seems to be associated with satisfactory postoperative potency, but more experience is needed for adequate evaluation.

Complications of the open shunt operations occur in about 15% of patients. Complications are urethrocutaneous fistula, urethrocavernous fistula, and a painful spongiosum on erection following cavernospongiosum shunt; the major complication is pulmonary embolus following cavernosaphenous shunt. Complications following either procedure are gangrene or necrosis of the distal penis, penile skin necrosis, hematoma, wound infection or abscess, erectile deviation, and wound sinus.[17,18,20,21] Penile skin necrosis tends to occur following application of a pressure dressing; therefore, a pressure dressing should never be used following any of the therapeutic procedures.

REFERENCES

1. Nelson JH III, Winter CC: Priapism: Evolution of management in 48 patients in a 22-year series. J Urol 117:455, 1977

2. Weiss HD: The physiology of human penile erection. Ann Intern Med 76:793, 1972

3. Hinman F Jr: Priapism; reasons for failure of therapy. J Urol 83:420, 1960

4. Grayhack JT, McCullough W, O'Conor VJ Jr, et al: Venous bypass to control priapism. Invest Urol 1:509, 1964

5. Garrett RA, Rhamy DE: Priapism: Management with corpus–saphenous shunt. J Urol 95:65, 1966

6. Quackles R: Cure d'un cas de priapism par anastomose caverno-spongieuse. Acta Urol 32:5, 1964

7. Tarasuk AP, Schneider IM: Management of priapism by caver-noglandular shunt. Urology 8:141, 1976

8. Ebbehog J: A new operation for priapism. Scand J Plast Reconstr Surg 8:241, 1975

9. Winter CC: New procedure for creating fistula between glans penis and corpora cavernosa. Urology 8:389, 1976

10. Winter CC: Priapism cured by creation of fistulas between glans penis and corpora cavernosa. J Urol 119:227, 1978

11. Winter CC: Priapism treated by modification of creation of fistulas between glans penis and corpora cavernosa. J Urol 121:743, 1979

12. Barry JM: Priapism: Treatment with corpus cavernosum to dorsal vein of penis shunts. J Urol 116:754, 1976

13. Wear JB Jr, Crummy AB, Munson BO: A new approach to the treatment of priapism. J Urol 117:252, 1977

14. Kinney TR, Harris MB, Russell MO, et al: Priapism in association with sickle hemoglobinopathies in children. J Pediatr 86:241, 1975

15. Baron M, Leiter E: The management of priapism in sickle cell anemia. J Urol 119:610, 1978

16. Harrow BR: Simple technique for treating priapism. J Urol 101:71, 1969

17. Fortuno RR, Carrillo R: Gangrene of the penis following cavernospongiosum shunt in a case of priapism. J Urol 108:752, 1972

18. Weiss JM, Ferguson D: Priapism: The danger of treatment with compression. J Urol 112:616, 1974

19. Sacher EC, Sayegh E, Frensilli F, et al: Cavernospongiosum shunt in the treatment of priapism. J Urol 108:97, 1972

20. Cosgrove MD, LaRocque MA: Shunt surgery for priapism. Review of results. Urology 4:1, 1974

21. Klugo RC, Olsson CA: Urethrocavernous fistula: Complication of cavernospongiosal shunt. J Urol 108:750, 1972

ANNOTATED BIBLIOGRAPHY

Hinman F Jr: Priapism: Reasons for failure of therapy. J Urol 83:420, 1960

Seven patients with idiopathic priapism showing histologic evidence of edematous septae and subsequent fibrosis were studied. Idiopathic priapism results from prolonged erection accompanied by venous stasis, which increases the viscosity of the blood, producing relative local venous occlusion. Fibrosis in the trabeculae combined with disruption of the arteriovenous supply mechanism makes adequate erections impossible. The basic reasons for failure of the various non-surgical treatments are that they do not restore venous drainage and that they do not eliminate progressive damage to the local erectile mechanism.

Grayhack JT, McCullough W, O'Conor VJ Jr, et al: Venous bypass to control priapism. Invest Urol 1:509, 1964

The first report of successful venous drainage from the corpus cavernosum to the saphenous vein involved a patient who had not responded to many nonoperative forms of therapy over a 7-day period. The operative technique is described.

Cosgrove MD, LaRocque MA: Shunt surgery for priapism. Review of results. Urology 4:119, 1974

The literature was reviewed to determine the results of shunting procedures in 68 patients who had cavernosaphenous shunts and in 32 patients who had cavernospongiosum shunts. The postoperative potency rate was 61%, and there seemed to be very little difference between the two types of operations. The potency rate was 77% in the 17 patients who had sickle cell disease, and only 1 of 6 patients who had heparin-induced priapism had potency during the follow-up period. Those patients with cavernosaphenous vein shunts had a higher rate of potency when the procedure was unilateral than when it was bilateral. There was insufficient data to support the concept that a delay in surgery produces an increased incidence of impotence.

Nelson JH III, Winter CC: Priapism: Evolution of management in 48 patients in a 22-year series. J Urol 117:455, 1977

A review of 48 patients treated during a 22-yr period showed that idiopathic priapism and sickle cell disease accounted for 81% of the patients. There were 37 adults and 11 children. Idiopathic priapism occurred in 26 (70%) of the adults, and sickle cell disease occurred in 7 (63.3%) of the children. Other etiologic factors in the adults were sickle cell disease (four), solid tumors (four), trauma (two), and leukemia (one). Other etiologic factors in the children were leukemia (two) and idiopathic (two). The evolution of treatment is presented.

Quackles R: Cure of a case of priapism by anastomosis of the cavernosum to the spongiosum. Acta Urol 32:5, 1964

This is the first report of a successful corpus cavernosum–spongiosum shunt for the treatment of priapism that resulted in partial preservation of potency. The operative technique is described with accompanying illustrations.

Sacher EC, Sayegh E, Frensilli F, et al: Cavernospongiosum shunt in the treatment of priapism. J Urol 108:97, 1972

Twelve cases of priapism treated by a perineal cavernospongiosum shunt from 70 hr to 18 days after the onset of priapism resulted in a 100% reduction of the priapism and 75% of partial or complete return of sexual function. The operative technique is described with accompanying illustrations. The authors favor a bilateral procedure even though there is cross-circulation in the septum between the cavernosa.

Overview: Management of Priapism

Robert A. Garrett

New methods of management and observations of etiologic background have evolved since I provided commentary on the treatment of priapism in the first edition of this text 9 yr ago.

Recent reports have associated methaqualone and the phenothiazines, especially Mellaril, with priapism. Neonatal priapism may accompany hypoxia and usually responds promptly to its alleviation. Hematologic disorders aside from sickle cell disease and leukemia have been incriminated. At my institution a pediatric patient suffering an enzymatic deficiency of glucose phosphate isomerase activity leading to spherocytosis and anemia had persistent priapism resistant to hematologic treatment. A cavernospongiosum shunt was resorted to.[1] The preference for cavernospongiosum over cavernosaphenous shunt became established in the mid-1970s based on its greater simplicity and lack of embolic complications. Impotence rates following these procedures seem to be about the same after either type of shunt. Ebbehog and Winters independently have further simplified the shunting concept by methods herein described on which Dr. Bueschen comments. Detumescence by aspiration and irrigation followed by tight folding of the catheterized penis onto the perineum by T-binder has been advocated by Harrow. This maneuver, if used, must be followed hour by hour to avoid penile integumental necrosis. Conservative nonsurgical management for several days is appropriate in patients with hematologic disease. Attention is directed toward correcting metabolic abnormalities as well as blood cellular dyscrasias in hematologic disorders. The simplicity and usual effectiveness of the corporoglandular shunt makes early intervention in all other types advisable. The corporospongiosum shunt by perineal approach is reserved for failures of the corporoglandular shunting maneuver. Patients with malignant infiltrations are not candidates for the shunting maneuvers. Grayhack's original concept of shunting from the tumescent cavernosus bodies remains the foundation for current surgical management.

REFERENCE

1. Goulding FJ: Priapism caused by glucose phosphate isomerase deficiency. J Urol 116:819, 1976

97

A ONE-STAGE HYPOSPADIAS REPAIR

Norman B. Hodgson

From the Division of Surgery, Department of Urology, Marquette School of Medicine, Milwaukee, Wisconsin

The Journal of Urology
Copyright © 1970 by The Williams & Wilkins Co.
Vol. 104, Aug.
Printed in U.S.A.

Male hypospadias is one of the more common congenital defects. The abnormal meatus may open on the ventral or undersurface of the penis anywhere between the glans and the perineum. Repair should allow for a directable urinary stream, ease of coitus and cosmetic satisfaction. Many operative procedures have been devised to accomplish the repair. These procedures usually involve 2 or 3 stages unless complications are encountered. Complications are failure of correction of chordee, fistula formation and poor meatal size.

Herein is reported a 1-stage hypospadias repair which has been used in 51 cases. The procedure provides for correction of chordee and construction of a new urethra in 1 operation. It has been used for hypospadias beyond the penoscrotal junction. Complications have included 4 urethrocutaneous fistulas and 3 meatal stenoses which have been corrected at a second operation.

A 2-zero silk suture on a round point needle is placed through the glans penis. The excision of the chordee should allow a collar of tissue to remain around the existing urethral meatus (Fig. 1, *1*). The urethra is mobilized from the corpora cavernosa if necessary to complete chordee correction. Inherent in the success of the procedure is the complete correction of chordee (Fig. 1, *2*). Occasionally there is no chordee so the epithelial continuity between the meatus and the glans can remain intact.

The incision is continued around the shaft of the penis at the corona and the shaft skin is mobilized. Hemostasis has been achieved with 5-zero plain catgut ties and 6-zero chromic catgut suture ligature. The vessels of the dorsal hood can be seen with transillumination and avoided with displacement at the time a buttonhole is created (Fig. 2, *1*). The dorsal hood is transferred to the ventrum by this technique. Either a Y or a cross has been used for the buttonhole. The surgeon should avoid stretching either the penis or the shaft skin when choosing the site for the buttonhole.

With the dorsal hood on the ventrum there are 2 epithelial surfaces with which to work. One can be used as a new urethra and one for the covering. The epithelial surfaces have a common blood supply which has remained intact. Thus the hood can be turned down on the shaft or used in an unrotated position. For ease of identification the external surface of the dorsal hood is labeled *A* and the internal surface is labeled *B* (Fig. 2,

Accepted for publication September 5, 1969.

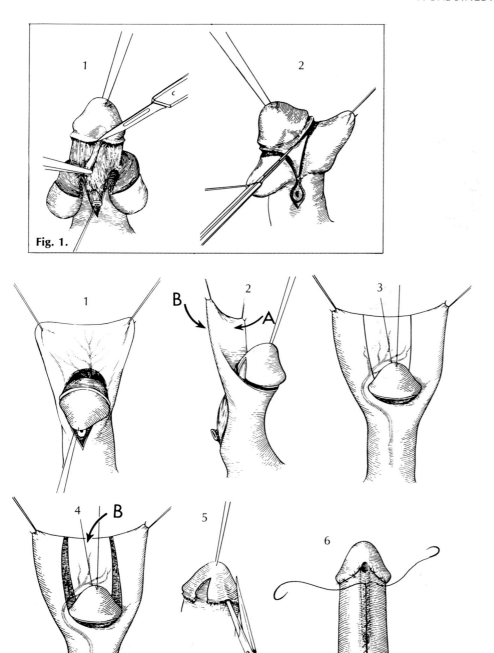

Fig. 1.

Fig. 2.

2). Delicate incisions, through the cutis only, allow isolation of an epithelial remnant which can be rolled into a tube and anastomosed to the existing urethral meatus and then advanced to the chosen site on the glans for the new meatus (Fig. 2, *3*).

Surface *A* will lay against the shaft after the glans has been passed through the buttonhole. Lateral isolating incisions for the new urethra are made and the incision is spread (Fig. 2, *4*). The tissues are so loose that this is easy to do. The isolated remnant is now rolled into a

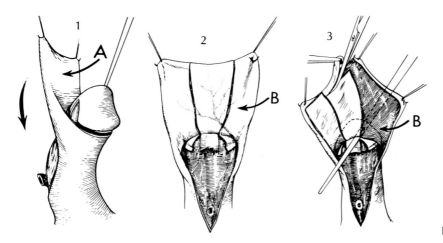

Fig. 3.

tube with continuous 5-zero chromic catgut. The proximal anastomosis is achieved with interrupted or running 6-zero chromic catgut sutures with knots placed intraluminally. Thus when the suture is absorbed the knot will be voided. Hopefully this reduces the inflammatory effect of the material.

At the glans, raw edges are established on either side of the fossa navicularis (Fig. 2, 5). The meatus is constructed with the distal end of the tube. The defect is now closed by suturing at the corona and by vertical closure on the ventrum. Excessive residual epithelium is excised leaving the subcutaneous layer intact. The defect is closed with a subcutaneous and subcuticular layer of 5-zero monofilament nylon (Fig. 2, 6).

This first technique is used for hypospadias occurring in the distal third of the penile shaft. This particular technique has been used for 22 repairs. There has been 1 case of meatal stenosis and no other complications.

When the meatus is further down the shaft a second version of the same concept is used. The dorsal hood is transferred to the ventrum and then inverted down the shaft. Surface *B* will lay against the shaft and provide the epithelium for construction of the tube. The excess skin is removed from both of the surfaces and a vertical closure of surface *A* is used to cover the defect (Fig. 3).

This particular technique was the initial procedure and has been used on 24 occasions. Two fistulas have developed at the proximal anastomosis and have been repaired in a subsequent operation. There have been 2 meatal stenoses which have required a minor procedure.

A third technique has been used to treat penoscrotal hypospadias on 5 occasions. The dorsal hood is transferred to the ventrum through lateral rotation around the shaft of the penis (Fig. 4). This involves a 90-degree shift in the orientation of the prepuce.

Again surface *B* is used to form an epithelial tube

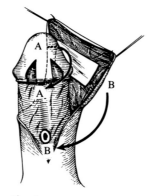

Fig. 4.

and surface *A* is used for covering. To facilitate the transfer of the dorsal hood some freeing of the cut margin is necessary. This procedure has been used on 5 occasions and 2 fistulas have developed which have been subsequently closed.

Diversion has been by perineal urethrostomy or transurethrally with rubber or silastic catheter. Recently a 9.4F silastic catheter was placed transurethrally with the tapered end in the bulbous urethra. Two side holes are created in the catheter. The child then voids intermittently through the catheter. This has been used 7 times with some delay in initial voiding but over-all good acceptance. Obstruction of the catheter has not been a problem. As a functioning stent it has allowed discharge 4 days postoperatively. Subsequent suture and catheter removal can be done in the outpatient department. Tissues have been handled with skin hooks. A compression dressing of Owen's gauze and elastoplast is used. The catheters are removed 8 to 10 days postoperatively.

Thus, 51 hypospadias repairs have been done in 1 stage, using a comparable principle in 3 different techniques. The concept is that of an attached epithelial remnant rolled into a tube to bridge the distance between the existing urethral meatus and the glans penis. The remaining epithelium is used to cover the surgical defect. The results have been cosmetically pleasing and functionally satisfactory. Four fistulas have been repaired at a second procedure. Meatal stenosis has appeared and responded appropriately to simple meatotomy.

Commentary:
Review of Hypospadias Repair

Norman B. Hodgson

The preceding article was the first publication of the work I have been doing. As I reread it, I found that it was written with some innocence and ignorance. A little bit of history seems worthwhile. During my residency and early practice years, I had performed Cecil urethroplasties, Denis–Browne urethroplasties, and Duplay urethroplasties.[1-3] All these were strongly influenced by my teachers' committment to successful release of chordee, demanding a staged repair. I could not be sure that chordee had indeed been released before the initial operation had healed and an erection had been observed by either the mother or the physician. The fibrous elements of the dysplasia of the corpus spongiosum must be excised, and therefore the thin epithelium and distal fibrosis were skimmed off and tissue transposed between the urethral meatus and the fossa navicularis. The Heinecke–Mikulicz approach to this was not popular because of inadequate placement for second-stage repairs as well as some incomplete suburethral dissection of the fibrous elements. When the meatus was subcoronal, there was often little space to cover, so bunching of the tissues did occur, creating a problem in the ultimate cosmetic result of the second stage. Although I aimed for circumcision and shaft skin mobilization, particularly with torsion, it shortly became apparent that some chordee was cutaneous in character and could be released by shaft skin mobilization.

Early on then, I was committed to excision of chordee with none of the guarantees now available through artificial erection. Parental, physician, or operating room observation was the criterion for establishing straightness. Based on that, the surgeon had to make an educated guess on the finality of dissection. Things are dramatically better now, with the contribution of Reuben Gittes creating an artificial erection with the use of a tourniquet at the base or by corporal compression techniques.[4] This ensures that the fibrous elements continuing to the glans have been successfully removed or are not significantly present. Also in recent years, the concept of glandular tilt and that of dissection beyond the corpora, but beneath the glans, have contributed immensely to ultimate straightening. The first, glandular tilt, may need the ventral dissection beneath the glans but beyond the corpora to allow dorsal glandular fixation beneath the corona to Buck's fascia.

However, the ventral correction without dorsal fixation was achieved over many years by the efforts of Devine and Horton in their flip-flap and tube graft techniques.[5] They gave the medical profession a better knowledge of blood supply of the glans and a willingness to carry our that final dissective step beyond the corpora and beneath the glans that may or may not require a sacrifice of epithelial continuity between the existing urethral meatus and the fossa navicularis. The blood supply of the glans penis is derived through the deep dorsal vessels of the penis, through the skin, and through the corpus spongiosum, as well as through transcorporal feeders. The dominant supply is through the deep dorsal vessels, which must be preserved.

In any event, in bygone years these frustrations were part of the concern of all the surgeons working in this area, which committed them almost inexorably to the multistage technique. The observation that chordee was cutaneous or that, following fibrous resection, an abundant dorsal hood was still available opened the avenues that lead to these one-stage repairs. The Nesbit overflap was well known and had been used originally by Beck.[6] In the patient with an abundant prepuce, circumcision dissection at the coronal margin and on the external layer had demonstrated a mobility and versatility of these tissues. It seemed a natural step then to isolate and handle an innerface epithelial island, sewing it into a tube, passing it to the ventrum through a buttonhole, and flipping it down so that the meatus could be advanced and a defect bridged by this new tube. That was the original concept and the first operative effort. It ended with a proximal stenosis and a small fistula plus lateral dog ears that were cosmetically unsatisfactory. The vascular pedicles of the dorsal hood were carefully preserved, but I felt no sense of freedom in sacrificing the dog ears because I was intimidated by those vascular pedicles.

Gradually, the procedure was changed. An ample proximal elliptic anastomosis was achieved by tacking the collar of skin around the meatus back to the corporal bodies. Intraluminal knots were used to avoid retention of excessive chromic material. The overlying skin closure was approximated with subcutaneous and intracuticular monofilament nylon to reduce reaction and offset the suture line. The excessive epithelium of the dog ears was gradually reduced by superficial excision and ultimately overcome by a diamond-shaped central incision to allow for vertical closure with preservation of the pedicles. Distally, the imperfection lay in the limited excision of paranavicular Denis–Browne wedges on the glans, which allowed for occasional retraction from the glans, ensuring only a coronal or mid-fossa navicularis meatus. Meatal stenosis at this point had largely been avoided.

After 11 such procedures, a paper was presented to the *Journal of Urology* for consideration and turned down by their consultant, Dr. Ormond Culp.[7] He felt that one-stage procedures should not be done because the ultimate results would be unsatisfactory for the patient.

The work was put in movie form and presented at the American College of Surgeons on a platform with Dr. Charlie Devine in 1965, which was the first time I had met him. The obvious thing was that one-stage procedures could be done, and people began to be aware of the possibility. As visiting professor in 1968, Dr. William W. Scott was invited to review some of my patients and carried away some enthusiasm for that approach. This stimulated the representation of the material with its expanded case load. Nonetheless, by this time the procedure had taken other forms, all of which were those of a vascularized island flap. It is only recently that these have begun to be numbered and assigned other names, but the most prominent consideration has been the adaptation of the available tissues to the patient's presenting problem. In looking over the original article, I find that the third sentence says that "repair should allow for a directable urinary stream, ease of coitus and cosmetic satisfaction." The first elements seemed easy to achieve, but the last is always a challenge. The second paragraph says that "herein is reported a one-stage hypospadias repair which has been used in 51 cases." In reality, four repairs are shown, which now get the numbers 1, 2, 3 and 5. Five is better known as the Asapo technique, published in 1971.[8] In trying to translate the operation into drawings, I went through three artists. I since have been through two more before encountering Jean McConnell, who has done such an excellent job of drawings presented later. It was difficult to convey then and remains to some extent now.

The 2–0 silk glandular suture has remained unchanged, although Devine and Horton use a 4–0 silk suture with a single knot to stifle glandular ooze during the course of the procedure. Figure 1 emphasizes correction of chordee but note that glandular tilt is not shown, nor is the dissection beneath the glans distal to the corpora, because I really was unwilling to tread in those waters at that time. Cutaneous chordee is mentioned but was then a fallen thought that had been rebuffed, and so it ws snuck in without definition. Perhaps I was unwilling to state it (*i.e.*, cutaneous chordee) because of the influence of past authors and their emphasis on fibrosis.[9]

Shaft skin mobilization became quite aggressive and was carried out in the loose areolar tissue, tunica dartos (the superficial subcutaneous tissue), of the skin. The deep subcutaneous tissue is Buck's fascia and contains the deep dorsal neurovascular bundles. This mobilization maintains the superficial blood supply of the shaft skin. Transillumination continues to be a valuable adjunct to guide the transposition of the hood and preserve the vessels. The careful selection of the site of the buttonhole ensures adequate shaft skin and guides the cosmetic result.

It is easy for me to criticize the article. I had presented it a number of times to local people and, of course, to my wife, it is quite apparent that the concept of an isolated epithelial island on either the inner or outer epithelial surfaces had to be presented as two different operative approaches. The selection of which surface would be chosen for the island was then, and is now, determined by the child's presenting problem.

Thus, if the foreskin is abundant, there is a raw defect to be bridged, and the undersurface is ample, then a type I procedure can be used. This is not a common selection any longer. The tissues do not commonly present themselves with sufficient innerface abundance to allow ready application of that approach. The drawings did not show the tubing or the anastomosis, so the ideas were not carried to their conclusion. Instead, the text attempted to cover the concept with words. A thousand words did not replace appropriate pictures. Type I, then, is shown in Figure 7(*I*), in which the inner epithelial surface is being isolated before rolling into a tube with the Denis Browne lateral denudation of the glans for the distal anastomosis and the collared urethral meatus for the proximal spatulated anastomosis.

Figure 2 leads to types II and III, in which the epithelial strip is isolated on the external epithelial surface, transferred to the ventrum, and used without flipping against the ventrum of the penile shaft. If an epithelial strip is maintained between the meatus and fossa navicularis, the dorsal preputial strip (island) is added and a tube is formed. The procedure is then completed (type II). If this cannot be maintained, then a tube is rolled of the external epithelial strip and anastomosed proximally and distally to bridge the gap (type III). The preservation of the epithelium in the fossa navicularis is essential to avoid meatal stenosis and to allow for satisfactory anastomosis of the transposed epithelial strip or tube.

Thus, too many different ideas were crammed into too few pictures, and it was difficult for other innovators to readily accept these approaches.

Far more difficult has been the conveyance of the application of the various one-stage procedures and the selection of patients for the ultimate finest result. This is an experience-based approach determined by the meatal location, the abundance of prepuce, and the size of the penis. The basic principles can be readily explored through manipulation at the time of elective circumcision, but cosmetic satisfaction is derived through experience.

During the last 9 yr, several hundred more of these 5 procedures have been done, along with the King urethropalsty, the Broadbent urethroplasty, and the Devine–Horton procedure.[10–12] A recent superb addition is the Duckett, which is a mobilized innerface tube with transglandular advancement. It is an extension of the no. 5 on the text. Transglandular meatal advancement by dissection and excision will avoid stenosis. In the last 2 yr this has been a mainstay. In a recent conversation with Drs. Devine and Horton, the question was raised on how many procedures would be necessary to correct 100 patients with hyposapdias in the usual glandular to perineal distribution. I thought about 115, since in my hands some procedures would be three stages, some two, and the majority one-stage approaches. Fistulae would be few and easily corrected. I do not rely on any single approach but continue to choose from among the available armamentarium based on the presenting problem and the established criteria for satisfactory repair. I will now attempt to compare the original article drawings with the subsequent drawings to enhance the reader's understanding of this presentation.

The original incision, Figure 1 (1), was depicted to emphasize the coronal release, isolation of the ventral dysplastic epithelium, and circummeatal extension to allow a cuff of tissue for sewing purposes. The shown hood is not particularly abundant. Figure 5 emphasizes the fibrous elements of chordee associated with corpus spongiosum dysplasia; Fig. 5A overemphasizes the bulk of the fibrous tissue and Fig. 5D overemphasizes the defect created. Figure 1 (2) attempted to demonstrate the fibrous dysplasia extending over the ventral surface of the corpora cavernosum but missed the spongiosum separation. Meatal mobilization has, likewise, been overemphasized. The depicted No. 11 blade should be a No. 15.

Figure 2 (1) was chosen to emphasize transillumination of the dorsal hood and maintenance of blood supply to the transposed double pedicle flap. Up to that time (1970), no serious consideration had been given to the superficial shaft skin vessels. The meatal advancement technique (Fig. 2[5]) was extracted from Denis Browne through Ormond Culp. Figure 2 (2) was chosen to show the new location of the dorsal hood. Considerable controversy and discussion occurred before granting names to the separate epithelial surfaces of the prepuce. I encountered considerable resistance in accepting the "tumble flap" concept and "innerface island," and so, in an attempt

to grant understanding, the letters A and B were used for designation. These have since been replaced by the terms *innerface* and *outerface*.

Figure 3 (1) was chosen to demonstrate the preputial inversion or tumble flap rotation. The proximal meatus is tacked to the corpora cavernosum to avoid secondary contraction. An arbor of vessels proceeds from the coronal margin to join the superficial shaft skin and provide a network for the two faces of the prepuce. The coronal vessels are interrupted by the mobilization but still fill from the superficial skin vessels. Figures 3 (2) and 6E and F emphasize the vascular pedicle and isolation of the epithelial island. It was only after a considerable period that the isolated epithelial remnant could be successfully called an island. A wide variety of other names were tried, but this has prevailed. The delicate incisions do not transect vessels but merely denude the face around the island, providing a raw surface for healing.

Figure 3 (3) was selected to emphasize the process of isolation of the island and the epithelial remnant at the fossa navicularis for the new glans meatus. Initially, the strip was not rolled into a tube, and so the procedure was called "the Denis Browne Upside Down." I enjoyed that, but neither the idea nor the name held. As depicted in Figure 7, tubes were subsequently used exclusively when a new urethra was needed. Figure 7 emphasizes the progressive development of the tube and its new location on the ventrum with preservation of the pedicles. Figure 2 (6) shows ventral vertical closure following construction of a new urethra using two-layer intracuticular monofilament nylon. There are a variety of possibilities depending on skin availability in the area.

Figure 8 deals with the further search for cosmetic

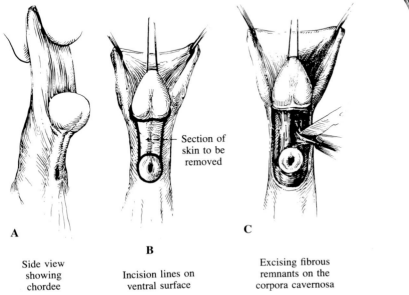
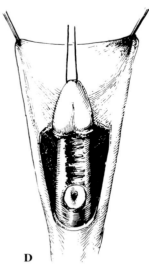

A
Side view
showing
chordee

B
Incision lines on
ventral surface

Section of
skin to be
removed

C
Excising fibrous
remnants on the
corpora cavernosa

D
Skin mobilized
around shaft

Fig. 5. Excision of chordee and shaft skin mobilization.

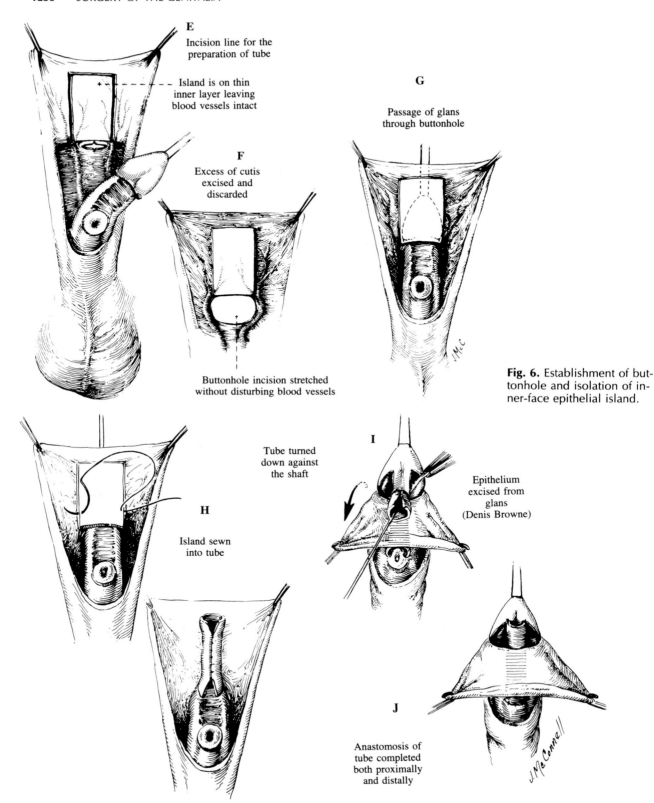

E

Incision line for the
preparation of tube

Island is on thin
inner layer leaving
blood vessels intact

F

Excess of cutis
excised and
discarded

Buttonhole incision stretched
without disturbing blood vessels

G

Passage of glans
through buttonhole

Fig. 6. Establishment of buttonhole and isolation of inner-face epithelial island.

Tube turned
down against
the shaft

H

Island sewn
into tube

I

Epithelium
excised from
glans
(Denis Browne)

J

Anastomosis of
tube completed
both proximally
and distally

Fig. 7. Creation of inner-face tube and anastomoses for advancement.

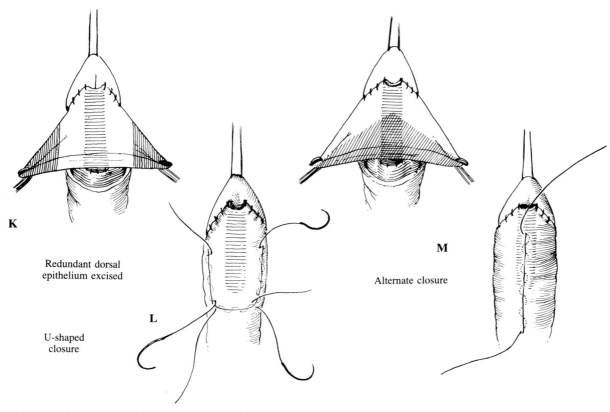

Fig. 8. Options for ventral closure with pedicle preservation.

enhancement with sacrifice of the dog-ears and U-shaped closure. A later development gave vertical intracuticular closure. Subsequent to the development of type 1, it seemed appropriate to proceed with an external surface incision and an isolated island on the dorsum. Figure 97-2(3) subsequently came to be called type 2 and had a natural place when an epithelial strip could remain between the existing urethral meatus and the fossa navicularis. The real question was whether partial denudation of the external face would allow satisfactory wound healing (Fig. 97-2[4]). It has indeed, and this is one of the most complication-free types of repair. The main challenge then is to attain maximum cosmetic benefit, since the procedure is free of proximal stricture disease or meatal stenosis.

Figure 9 is a more satisfactory depiction because it shows the transposition and progressive development of a urethra through the combination of two epithelial strips. This is similar to sewing two sides to a sleeve. Figure 10 shows that the innerface is discarded and the lateral epithelial redundancy of the outerface is joined with intracuticular suture for ventral cover. This has been the most common expression of this, although variations are available depending on the quality and the distribution of skin.

The next development in the repairs was the use of an external surface tube (Fig. 11), which is, of course, limited by the skin resources. That was not thought of in 1970, which shows the natural growth of the procedure. This particular procedure is still not widely used and is limited by the skin shortage in younger children. As the child gets older, the skin becomes more abundant, which makes type III more readily available. Figure 12 (*E,F,G,* and *H*) shows this closure. The next step was a lateral rotation of an innerface tube (see Fig. 4). Figure 13 more effectively shows the 90-degree rotation of the tube on its own pedicle. The cut edges of the outerface are joined for skin coverage. It has been a most satisfactory approach, but recently it has been significantly advanced through Dr. John Duckett's innovations.[13] This contribution consists of mobilization of that innerface tube on its own pedicle to allow free association on the ventrum, unrestricted by the external epithelial surface.[13] Transglandular meatal advancement is now routine and is the accepted goal of the 1980s.

The 1980s have seen a significant advance of the urethral meatus through the glans, which was abandoned as unfruitful decades ago. Currently, the glans-tunneling procedure involves excision of a glans channel and on many occasions the incorporation of a V-flap that has been debulked to avoid the

(*Text continues on page 1241*)

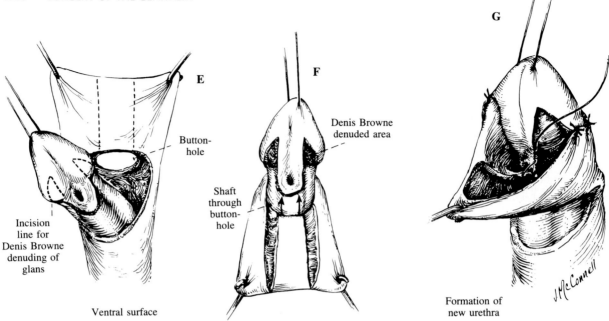

E

Button-hole

Incision line for Denis Browne denuding of glans

Ventral surface

F

Denis Browne denuded area

Shaft through button-hole

G

Formation of new urethra

J McConnell

Fig. 9. Progressive steps in Hodgson Type II, allowing selection of outer-face island (*E*), transposition of ventrum (*F*), and initial construction of urethral tube (*G*).

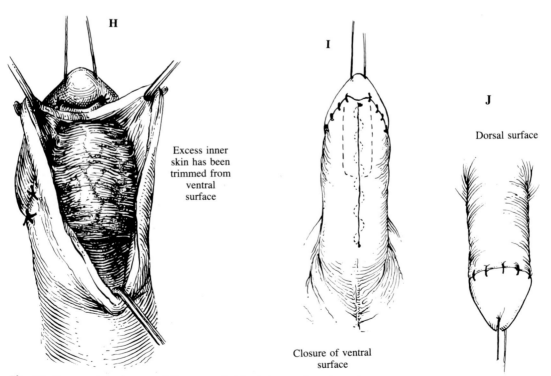

H

Excess inner skin has been trimmed from ventral surface

I

Closure of ventral surface

J

Dorsal surface

Fig. 10. Progressive closure of the ventral skin defect and end result.

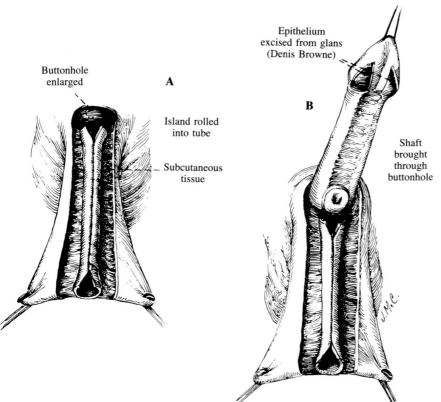

Buttonhole
enlarged

A

Island rolled
into tube

Subcutaneous
tissue

Epithelium
excised from glans
(Denis Browne)

B

Shaft
brought
through
buttonhole

Fig. 11. Hodgson Type III: creation
of external surface tube.

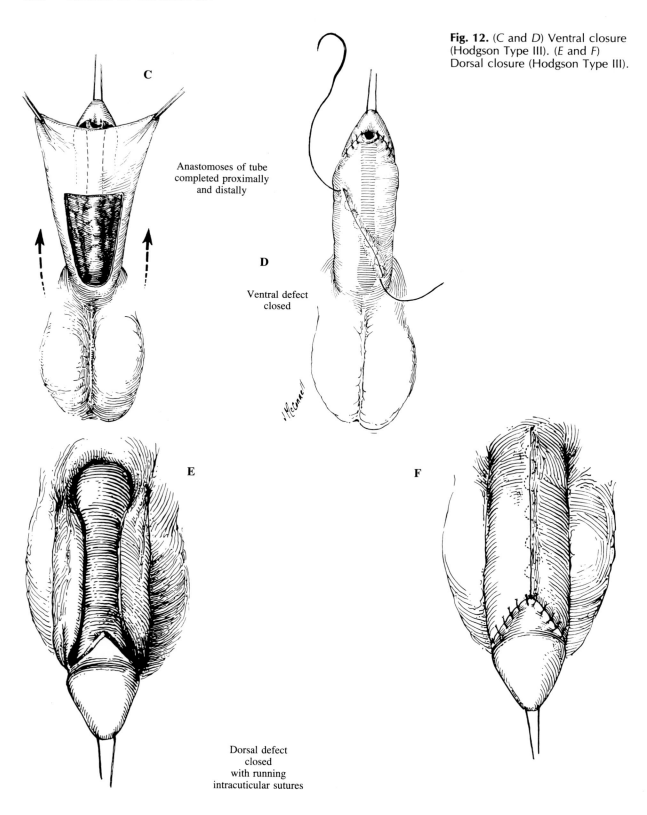

C

Fig. 12. (*C* and *D*) Ventral closure (Hodgson Type III). (*E* and *F*) Dorsal closure (Hodgson Type III).

Anastomoses of tube completed proximally and distally

D

Ventral defect closed

E

F

Dorsal defect closed with running intracuticular sutures

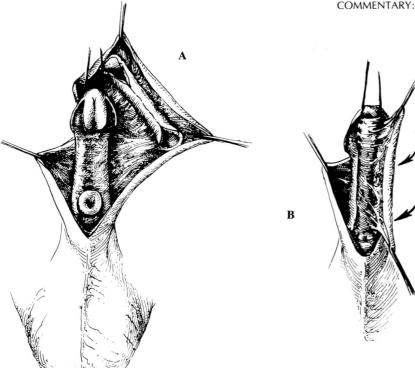

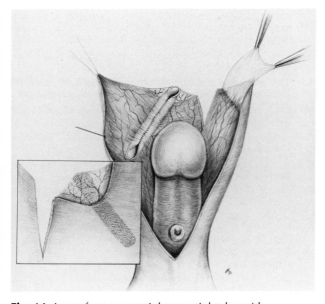

Fig. 13. Hodgson-Asapo inner-face tube with lateral rotation.

Fig. 14. Inner face tangential preputial tube with Byars flaps. The tube's vascular pedicle is not mobilized. It differs from the Asapo in alignment, Byars incision, and external face denudation for transglandular meatal construction (see insert). It also differs from Duckett's mobilized transverse inner face preputial island tube, which functions separately from the external face.

ongoing problem of stenosis. This is a prominent problem and has been handled by family dilatation with a variety of tools. The most recent addition to this has been a short, blunt sound, which is easily used by the parent to achieve the desired calibration.

A mobilized inner face transverse preputial island is used, ala Duckett, and some of the limitations of that procedure are encountered. Sometimes the quality of the vascular pedicle is suspect or the mobilized tips of the tissue are flimsy. For vascular preservation and stability, the newest evolution is a tangential island formed into a tube with spatulated ends. In order to avoid mobilization, a Byars incision is used on the dorsum with an external face, partial epithelial denudation (avoiding vascular injury) to allow for easy transference of the flap to the ventrum and the transglandular advancement. This allows preservation of the undisturbed subcutaneous vessel while achieving tube length of up to 4 cm. The procedure is simply a variation on a theme, but minimizes the risk of vascular depletion carried by mobilization. Figure 14 shows an inner face tangential tube with a denuded outer face to allow for transglandular advancement. The completed procedure is similar to those previously described. Final closure is accomplished currently with an intracuticular monofilament suture and support by the use of adhesive membrane (Tegaderm). The combination of this with the transglandular techniques described above, or enjoined with glans triangularization (Devine-Horton), has produced results previously unavailable.

REFERENCES

1. Cecil AB: Modern treatment of hypospadias. J Urol 67:1006, 1952

2. Browne D: An operation for hypospadias. Proc R Soc Med 42:466, 1949

3. Duplay S: Sur le traitement chirurgical de l'hypospadias et de l'epispadias. Arch Genet Med 145:257, 1880

4. Gittes RF, McLaughlin AP III: Injection technique to induce penile erection. Urology 4:473, 1974

5. Devine CJ Jr, Horton CE: A one stage hypospadias repair. J Urol 85:166, 1961

6. Beck C: Hypospadias and its treatment. Surg Gynecol Obstet 24:511, 1917

7. Culp OS: Struggles and triumphs with hypospadias and associated abnormalities: A review of 400 cases. J Urol 96:339, 1966

8. Asapo HS, Elhence IP, Atri SP, et al: One-stage correction of penile hypospadias using a foreskin tube. Int Surg 55:435, 1971

9. Allen TD, Spence HM: The surgical treatment of coronal hypospadias and related problems. J Urol 100:504, 1968

10. King LR: Hypospadias: A one stage repair without skin graft based on new principle. Chordee is sometimes produced by the skin alone. J Urol 103:660, 1970

11. Broadbent TR, Woolf RM: Hypospadias: One-stage repair. Br J Plast Surg 18:406, 1965

12. Horton CE (ed): Plastic and Reconstructive Surgery of the Genital Area. Boston, Little, Brown & Co, 1973

13. Duckett J: Transverse preputial island flap technique for repair of severe hypospadias. Urol Clin North Am 7:432, 1980

ANNOTATED BIBLIOGRAPHY

Cecil AB: Modern treatment of hypospadias. J Urol 67:1006, 1952

This is a classic discussion of hypospadias repair using the Cecil technique, which is invaluable in today's armamentarium.

Browne D: An operation for hypospadias. Proc R Soc Med 42:466, 1949

This is a classic description of the Denis–Browne procedure, which of course was earlier described by Duplay and Marion. The literature surrounding this is fascinating, since Denis–Browne protected it zealously and won the right to leave his name in the literature. The most disastrous spect of the procedure was the use of wire and shot, which guarantees a significant number of urethrocutaneous fistulae and has largely been discarded in favor of subcuticular and intracuticular suture techniques.

Duplay S: Sur le traitment chirurgical de l'hypospadias et de l'epispadias. Arch Genet Med 145:257, 1880

This is the original classic article by Simon Duplay, which is where it all started.

Gittes RF, McLaughlin AP III: Injection technique to induce penile erection, Urol., 4:473:1974

This is a classic thought that has become as essential part of corrective hypospadias surgery.

Devine CJ Jr, Horton CE: A one stage hypospadias repair. J Urol 85:166, 1961

The initial description of the free graft technique has now been applied by the authors for over 20 yr, with a gradually reduced complication rate from 40% to 18%, showing their dedication and skill.

Beck C: Hypospadias and its treatment. Surg Gynecol Obstet 24:511, 1917

This is an article from days gone by. Many years later, the ideas in this article were reintroduced by Dr. Nesbitt and accredited to his name.

Culp OS: Struggles and triumphs with hypospadias and associated abnormalities: A review of 400 cases. J Urol 96:339, 1966

A self-explanatory article that deserves to be read by any student of the field because it reviews the material as indicated in the title.

Asapo HS, Elhence IP, Atri SP, et al: One-stage correction of penile hypospadias using a foreskin tube. Int Surg 55:435, 1971

I encountered this article while reviewing the literature for a different publication. It shows that people throughout the world were identifying similar solutions to a problem at the same time, unknown to each other.

Allen TD, Spence HM: The surgical treatment of coronal hypospadias and related problems. J Urol 100:504, 1968

The benefit of this publication was the release of cutaneous chordee and the acceptance of that as a true state rather than coexistence with fibrous chordee.

King LR: Hypospadias: A one stage repair without skin graft based on a new principle. Chordee is sometimes produced by the skin alone. J Urol 103:660, 1970

This is a classic example of attaching one name to the combination of two principles, since the King repair is a Duplay tube with a Bayer's flap and is most applicable to those patients in whom the preputial tissue aligns itself alongside the fossa navicularis.

Broadbent TR, Woolf RM: Hypospadias: One-stage repair. Br J Plast Surg 18:406, 1965

This description of a long pedicle graft is applicable in unique situations and has been stretched too broadly in its application.

Horton CE (ed): Plastic and Reconstructive Surgery of the Genital Area. Boston, Little, Brown and Co, 1973

A compendium of the material at hand, this book is important to the student of the art.

Hodgson NB: One-stage hypospadias repair. In Urologic Procedures. Morris Plains, NJ, Warner-Chilcott, 1972

This pictorial essay is used to attempt to convey the thoughts in mind and acts as a format for teaching.

Hodgson NB: In defense of the one-stage hypospadias repair. In Scott R Jr. (ed): Current Controversies in Urologic Management. Philadelphia, WB Saunders, 1972; Hodgson NB: Hypospadias. In Glenn JF (Ed): Urologic Surgery, 2d ed, p. 656. New York, Harper & Row, 1975

These two chapters complement previous articles and show extension of the thought process.

Hodgson NB: Hypospadias and Urethral Duplications. In Campbell's Urology, Vol 2, pp 1566–1595. Philadelphia, WB Saunders, 1979

This is a description of most but not all available by hypospadias repairs.

Duckett J: Transverse preputial island flap technique for repair of severe hypospadias. Urol technique for repair of severe hypospadias. Urol Clin North Am 7:432, 1980

This is a new addition to the armamentarium.

98

THE CORRECTION OF HYPOSPADIAS

Jacques C. H. van der Meulen, M.D.

Rotterdam, The Netherlands

Plastic and Reconstructive Surgery, Vol. 59, pp. 206–215, February 1977

The treatment of hypospadias is a problem which has long challenged the ingenuity of the surgeon. The construction of a canal which at all times may be exposed to high intraluminal pressure never ceases to be a challenge and, considering the circumstances, it is not surprising that complications occur in a high percentage of cases. To prevent these complications a multitude of techniques have been proposed in the past.

Some advocate straightening the penis in all cases; others are more conservative.

Some use only one session for simultaneously straightening the penis and reconstructing the urethra; others prefer separate sessions.

Some use penile skin flaps to construct the urethra; others use a skin graft.

Some divert the urine *via* a catheter; others do not.

Although many of these techniques have withstood the test of time, I have felt that the results could be improved by (1) a better understanding of the morphology; (2) more insight into the causes of complications; and (3) better employment of technical principles.

MORPHOLOGY

It is difficult to simply yet accurately describe the deformity, because of its widely varying manifestations.

However, one can create some order by concentrating on each of these varying features. From a practical point of view, one can make a distinction between features which are always present and those which are not always present.

Features Which Are Always Present. Typical of the deformity, of course, is the dystopic meatus. The urinary canal ends abruptly with its floor tapering out into a V-shaped area, "the urethral delta."

There is a shortage of skin on the ventral aspect of the penis, which is in extreme contrast to the redundance on the dorsal aspect (Fig. 1, *above*). This surplus of skin, also called a "dorsal hood," is characterized by two dog-ears (eyes), each located a short distance from the midline.

On the lateral aspects of the penis, there are obliquely running raphes. These raphes originate in the vicinity of the meatus and lose themselves in the whirls of the dog-ears (Fig. 1, *below*).

Until recently these features could not be explained. However, Glenister[5] has shown that the formation of the urethra in the urethral plate and the closure of the skin over the urethra are independent processes, and Burns[1,2] demonstrated that

From the Department of Plastic and Reconstructive Surgery of Academisch Ziekenhuis Dijkzigt.

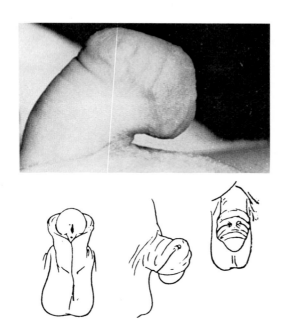

Fig. 1. (*Above*) A great suplus of dorsal skin. (*Below*) Dog-ears and oblique raphes.

growth of the urethral plate is stimulated by male hormones. It follows that growth arrest of the urethral plate is not necessarily associated with a growth arrest of the skin. With this information, Van der Meulen's[7] hypothesis was formulated—that hypospadias is caused by a discrepancy in growth of the urethral plate and the skin of the penis.

The development of the urethral plate is disturbed at a certain moment but the skin continues to grow. As it cannot grow in a longitudinal direction, it folds upon itself and becomes plicated. With this plication most of the skin is shifted toward the dorsal aspect, where the dog-ears are formed. The oblique raphes mark the fusion of the edges of the plication. This discrepancy in growth can also explain why a negligible hypoplasia of the urethra may be associated with a considerable shortage of skin, and *vice versa*. It explains the difference between hypospadias, where fusion of the skin borders of the urethral groove has not taken place, and *cryptospadias,* where complete or partial fusion (fistula) is found (van der Meulen[7,9]).

Features Which Are Not Always Present. There seems to be a widespread belief that hypospadias is always associated with chordee. Few surgeons have criticized this view, but Smith and Blackfield[11] did, writing: "First of all, we find it necessary to explode the myth about the presence of a "bowstringing" of the rudimentary *corpus spongiosum* extending distal to the abnormally placed orifice, as the cause of chorda."

What is chordee and what do we mean when we say "this patient has chordee"? Do we mean that we have found a cordlike structure which is supposed to prevent adequate erection? Cordlike structures are only rarely found and, in those cases, resection of the cord alone would not adequately straighten the penis—because the cord is always part of a hypoplastic layer covering the *corpus cavernosum* and is associated with an extreme shortage of skin. Then what does it refer to precisely? The answer must be, "to the fibrous layer which represents the hypoplastic urethral plate in which the urethra was to develop, and also partly to the other hypoplastic structures which were to develop into the dartos fascia or *tunica albuginea.*"

Whether this layer is always present is irrelevant. Our data show that erection is inadequate in less than 20 percent of all hypospadias cases. These are the patients in whom the *corpus cavernosum* should be freed by retropositioning the meatus and is urethral delta. Frequently, however, an apparent curvature is seen which is caused by the ever-present shortage of skin on the urethral aspect of the penis. The curvature will disappear when the shortage of skin is corrected by mobilization and redistribution of the skin alone. In these cases the urethral delta can be left *in situ* and reconstruction of the urethra, by the creation of a buried skin strip, can follow immediately.

Based on the morphology described, and with the technical implications in mind, two types of the deformity can be distinguished. Type I are cases in which the urethra can be reconstructed without a preliminary straightening procedure. In Type II the *corpora cavernosa* are to be released before reconstructing the urethra.

COMPLICATIONS

One of the keys to success in the treatment of hypospadias is the ability of the surgeon to prevent complications. He will first need to know what causes these complications, and then the choosing of a procedure which allows him to cope with them follows automatically. There are two types of complications: (1) early complications, which result in a defect of the neo-urethra (fistula) or even its complete dehiscence; (2) late complications, such as shortness of the urethra, strictures, pouches, stones, and infection.

CAUSES OF EARLY COMPLICATIONS

Insufficient Redistribution of Skin. Inadequate correction of the shortage of skin on the ventral aspect will be associated with tension on the wound edges. Postoperatively this tension increases as edema occurs. The vascularization of the wound edges will then diminish and dehiscence may result. Overcorrecting the shortage can prevent this complication. Complete transposition of the skin surplus on the dorsum to the ventral surface (accepting a circumcised appearance) is necessary, and one must aim for an even distribution of the transposed skin over the urethral aspect. Attempts to preserve the prepuce and procedures which do not realize an even distribution should be avoided, in my opinion.

Insufficient Vascularization of Skin. Circulatory problems may follow the redistribution of skin. The disasters which occur when a flap is too long or too thin, or even when it has a scarred base, are well known. Two causes of insufficient vascularization, however, have not received the attention they deserve.

One is the tourniquet effect which may result from an uneven distribution of skin or from a circular bandage. The other originates in the anatomy of the penis in general and in the anatomy of hypospadias in particular. Blood reaches the prepuce *via* the dorsal artery, which runs in the midline. Division of the dorsal skin into two flaps may separate one flap from its main source of supply, increasing the danger of necrosis. In hypospadias where plication has resulted in the formation of two oblique raphes, this circulation is even more dependent on the midline artery. Procedures which advocate longitudinal division of the hood should, therefore, be avoided.

Insufficient Wound Closure. Fistulae are formed when epithelium from the wound edges is allowed to grow inward and fuse with epithelium from the edges of the buried urethral strip. Contact between two epithelial strands is all that is needed. One way to prevent this is to close the wound with interrupted subcutaneous stitches. By this technique the wound edges are everted and no epithelial tracts are formed along transcutaneous sutures. Another way to prevent the formation of a fistula is to increase the distance between the skin suture line and the urethral strip. When one avoids superimpositioning the skin suture line on the urethral strip, a urethral canal will form before epithelium from the strip can come into contact with epithelium from the skin wound edges.

Insufficient Drainage. The use of catheters does not guarantee adequate drainage, because they may block or lead to straining and leakage round the catheter. When this happens, or when the urine cannot escape *via* the neo-urethra or *via* drainage incisions, or when the penis on some occasions is also dressed with a circular bandage, even the best wound closure technique will be insufficient and the results may be disastrous.

Perfect drainage can be obtained when the patient is allowed to pass urine *via* the neo-urethra alone when it is not too long (Type I)—or *via* the neo-urethra and one or two drainage incisions when the length of the urethral canal indicates this (Type II). In this way the patient cleans his own wound of debris and blood clots. The drainage incisions are made at a safe distance from the urethra, allowing the urthral canal to form before epithelization of the drainage tract takes place. There is no danger of stasis and no wound infection can occur. I have used these methods since 1964 in more than 300 cases of hypospadias; no catheters or circular dressings have ever been used. All this does not imply that a perineal urethrostomy is to be avoided at all costs. But the method described is reasonably reliable as long as no circular bandage is used and as long as it is used in combination with drainage incisions.

CAUSES OF LATE COMPLICATIONS

Insufficient Length of the Urethra. Persistent chordee, caused by shortness of the urethra, may be found in Type II hypospadias when retropositioning of the meatus has been inadequate.

Insufficient Width of the Urethra. A stricture of the urethra may occur at 3 different levels:

(a) Stenosis of the dystopic meatus may be found after transection of the urethra with release of the *corpora cavernosa* as a goal. This complication can be avoided by retropositioning the meatus in continuity with the urethral delta.

(b) Strictures of the neo-urethra may occur when the surgeon relies to much on the elasticity of the skin, or on the potential of scar tissue, to increase the diameter of the urethra. Because of this, the urethral strip should probably be made a little broader than seems necessary.

(c) Stenosis of the glandular meatus may appear when contraction results from the use of improper techniques.

Insufficient Quality of the Urethra. This may result when the lining is scarred and the possibility of expansion is evenly distributed. In this event pouch formation can occur. How deformed a urethra may gradually become after its reconstruction was recently shown by Townsend[13] (1975), who made silicone rubber casts in a number of these patients. Finally the presence of hairs should be avoided, because they may lead to the formation of stones.

PRINCIPLES OF TECHNIQUE

Following the analyses of the different causes of complications, a number of criteria can be formulated which must be fulfilled if a technique is to be effective in all cases of hypospadias.

(1) The redistributing of skin must be adequate. The shortage of skin on the urethral aspect should be overcorrected to avoid tension.

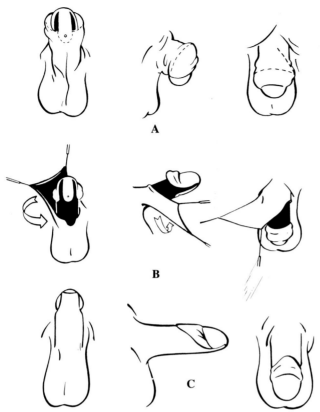

Fig. 2. (A) The circumferential incision and back cut. (B) The skin strip outlined, and the triangular excisions in the glans. (C) The fixation of rotated skin in the desired position.

(2) The vascularization of the skin cover must not be endangered.

(3) Wound closure is to be effected at a safe distance from the urethral strip and consist of interrupted subcutaneous sutures (*e.g.* Dexon).

(4) The drainage of blood and urine should be adequate at all times.

(5) The urethral strip must be sufficiently long.

(6) The urethral strip is to be sufficiently wide.

(7) The urethral lining should be smooth, hairless, and without transverse scarring. The transition between urethra and neo-urethra should be gradual.

TECHNIQUE

During the past 10 years two procedures were developed which fulfilled the criteria described above: (1) a one-stage operation for the correction of Type I hypospadias, in which a preliminary straightening procedure is not necessary; (2) a two-stage operation for the correction of Type II hypospadia, which needs a straightening procedure.

Correction of Type I Hypospadias (Fig. 2). A circumferential incision is made through the penile skin, leaving the meatus distal to the incision. Next, the penile skin is thoroughly undermined over the length of the shaft so that a cylinder of skin is freed. Two small triangles of skin are then excised from the ventral surface of the glans on either side of the meatus, outlining a strip of skin centrally which remains in continuity with the meatus. (This strip will eventually tube itself and thus form the distal urethra.) The strip is covered by rotating ventrally the penile skin after an oblique back cut has been made on the dorsum, thus allowing the best use to be made of the excess dorsal skin. Two or 3 subcutaneous 4-0 Dexon sutures are inserted on either side to attach the skin flap to the two raw triangular areas; the remaining skin margins are approximated with 4-0 Dexon subcutaneous sutures.

The back cut permits easier ventral rotation of the penile skin, but it leaves a defect on the dorsum of the penis—which is now closed with the preputial skin lying distal to the original circumferential incision. This preputial skin will require freeing and some trimming before it is sutured in place.

No catheter is used. A simple gauze dressing is applied, which is changed each time the child passes urine.

Correction of Type II Hypospadias (Fig. 3). When hypospadias is associated with a curvature of the *corpora cavernosa*, reconstruction should be preceded by a retropositioning of the dystopic meatus. Some surgeons attempt to achieve these aims in two stages. Others (Horton and Devine,[6] 1971) prefer a one-stage operation with the greater risks involved.

Our reasons for a two-stage operation in this category are as follows:

(1) A one-stage operation is associated with a relatively high percentage of early and late complications. The development, presence, and treatment of fistulae and strictures may be accompanied by long periods of anxiety, pain, morbidity, and hospitalization.

(2) A two-stage operation allows for a critical judgment of the result of the first operation—and any remaining curvature of the penis or stenosis of the meatus may be corrected before the definitive construction of the urethra is done.

First Stage (Fig. 4). A circumferential incision is made in the coronal sulcus, leaving the meatus proximal to the incision. The *corpora cavernosa* are freed by multiple incisions of the integument, using the diathermy cutting

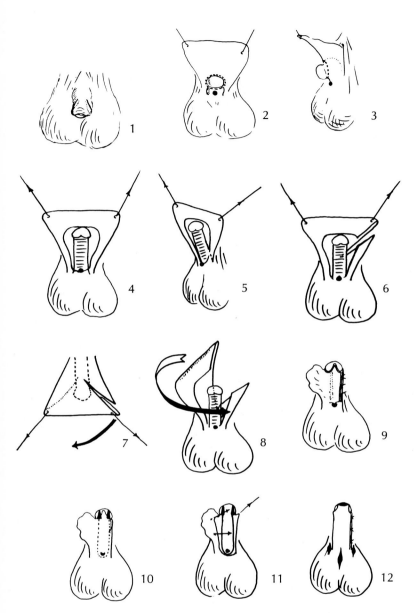

Fig. 3. (*1, 2, 3*) The oblique raphes on the dorsal aspect and the circumferential coronal incision. (*4, 5, 6*) The complete mobilization of the prepuce and the back cut in the oblique raphe. (*7, 8, 9*) The rotation of the prepuce after freeing the *corpora cavernosa,* and closure of the created defect with the inner lining of the prepuce. (*10, 11, 12*) The urethral strip outlined, and closure by transportation of the remaining preputial skin. Parapenile and/or scrotal drainage incisions are made at a safe distance from the urethral strip.

knife. The meatus and the urethral delta are now retropositioned. The penile skin is then thoroughly undermined over the length of the shaft so that a cylinder of skin is freed. A back cut along one of the oblique raphes permits adequate rotation. The defect on the urethral aspect is closed with the inner lining of the prepuce. To bring the meatus as close to the tip as possible, the ventral surface of the glans can be split (Cloutier,[3] 1962) and the transposed skin is sutured into the defect.

Second Stage (Fig. 5). A urethral strip is formed. This strip is now covered by rotation of the surplus skin which was stored on one lateral aspect in the previous session. This well-vascularized flap is anchored to the *corpora cavernosa* at some distance from the urethral strip. Superimpositioning of the skin wound on the urethra is avoided, as the suture line lies lateral to the buried strip. Interrupted, subcutaneous Dexon sutures are used. Drainage incisions are added for extra safety.

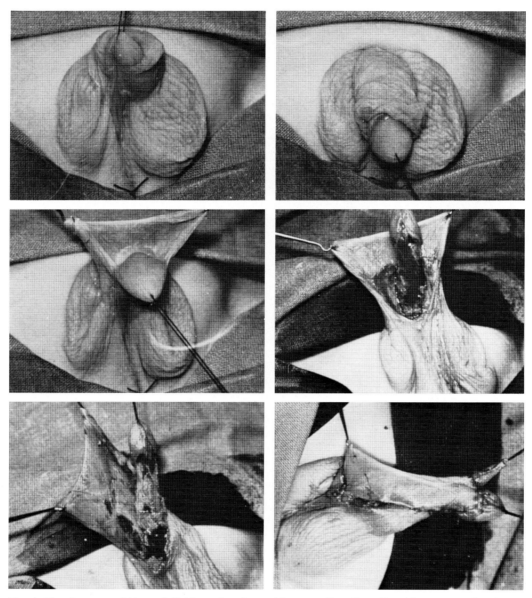

Fig. 4. The first stage (*Above left*) Ventral surface of hypospadias. Type II, with extreme chordee and scrotal meatus. (*Above right*) The dorsal surface, showing penoscrotal transposition. (*Center left*) The inner lining of the prepuce, which will provide sufficient skin for the urethra. (*Center right*) Release of the *corpora cavernosa* by mobilization of the urethral delta, via a circumferential coronal incision. (*Below left*) Transposition of the preputial lining to the ventral surface, following mobilization of the penile skin and a back cut along the oblique raphe. (*Below right*) Preputial lining sutured in place on the ventral surface.

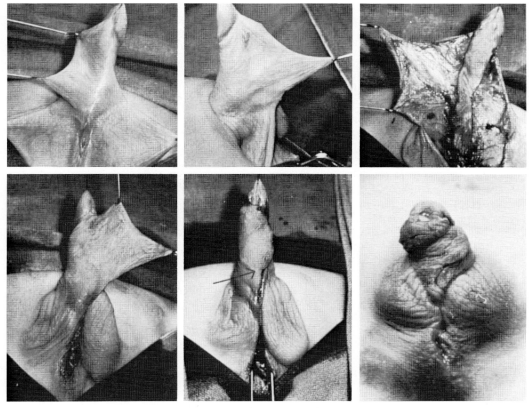

Fig. 5. The second stage. (*Above left*) The result some months after correction of the chordee. (*Above center*) Lateral view of the penis, showing redundance of the skin on the ventral surface. (*Above right*) Creation of the urethral strip, and mobilization of the skin surplus. (*Below left*) The surplus skin is rotated over the buried urethral strip. (*Below center*) The skin and drainage incision, in continuity with the buried strip. The *arrow* indicates the position of the covered urethral meatus. (*Below right*) On the seventh postoperative day, there is little swelling and the drainage incisions are virtually closed. Urine is visible at the site of the new meatus.

DIFFERENTIATION

When differentiation between Type I and Type II is difficult, a simple test (Horton) can eliminate any doubt. Drainage of blood from the penis is controlled with a tourniquet and the *corpus cavernosum* is injected with saline to simulate an erection. If a curvature becomes apparent, it may be solely due to the shortage of skin on the ventral aspect. In those cases the curvature will disappear following a transverse incision which allows one to undermine and release the skin over this aspect. This incision leaves the meatus distal. When as a result of this procedure the curvature disappears, one can safely continue with the procedure used to correct a Type I hypospadias. If, on the contrary, the curvature remains, release of the *corpus cavernosum* (Type II) is imperative.

RESULTS

Correction of Type I. This procedure was used in 200 consecutive cases, and there were two early complications. In one case marginal necrosis of the rotated skin flap developed. The resulting partial dehiscence was corrected easily at a second operation. In the second case a complete breakdown of the wound occurred on the day of discharge, when the boy slid down a tree! In contradistinction to nearly every other series where the incidence of fistula formation is disturbingly high, there were no fistulae whatsoever.

The late complications have been described by Tolhurst and Gorter[12] in their independent follow-up of the series. I will therefore confine myself to a short summary.

(1) Meatal stenosis may occur when: (a) a previously

existing stenosis did not receive adequate treatment; (b) the glandular strip is made too narrow.

(2) Retraction of the meatus may be caused by insufficient rotation of the dorsal skin.

(3) Rotation of the penis, sometimes present before operation, may be caused or aggravated by the design of the asymmetrical skin flap. It can be prevented by more extensive freeing of the skin cylinder, followed by a thorough backcut. (In other patients, however, a preexisting rotation of the penis was corrected by the same procedure.)

(4) Slight curvature of the penis following operation may be due to an incorrect differentiation between Type I and Type II. When doubt exists, it is always safer to release the *corpus cavernosum* first. In our 12 years of experience with this procedure we have not had to reoperate because of shortness of the urethra after its reconstruction. However, it is too early to say whether the percentages cited in this article are entirely correct because the injection test, which gives us more information on the state of the penis in erection, was not used until after the series was completed. The figures given for the relation between Type I and Type II may, therefore, be subject to some change in the future.

Correction of Type II. This procedure has been used

in 20 patients. In this small series there were no complications, which is not surprising because all the necessary technical criteria mentioned before were fulfilled.

DISCUSSION

The procedure designed for the correction of Type I was first described in 1964, and since then it has been used in 200 consecutive patients. The average operating time is 20 to 25 minutes. No catheter or circular dressing was ever used. Our complications were minor, and no fistula formation occurred. The boys were ambulant on the first postoperative day and left the hospital on the 8th postoperative day. There was no need for removal of sutures.

The two-stage procedure designed for the correction of Type II hypospadias has all the advantages of the Type I operation. The drainage incisions which make the operation possible without a perineal urethrostomy usually close by the 8th postoperative day. This procedure was used in 20 patients. Again there were no fistulae.

Jacques C. H. van der Meulen, M.D.
Academisch Ziekenhuis Rotterdam-Dijkzigt
Rotterdam, The Netherlands

SUMMARY

Hypospadias can be divided into Type I deformities, in which only construction of the disal urethra is necessary, and Type II deformities, where the penis must first be straightened.

In 200 consecutive repairs of Type I hypospadias and 20 consecutive repairs of Type II hypospadias there were no fistulae.

REFERENCES

1. Burns, R. K.: Hormones and the growth of the parts of the urogenital apparatus in mammalian embryos. Cold Spring Harbor Symp Quant Biol 10:27, 1942

2. Burns, R. K.: Hormones and experimental modification of sex in the opossum. Biol Symp 9:125, 1942

3. Cloutier, A. M.: A method of hypospadias repair. Plast & Reconstr Surg 30:368, 1962

4. Glenister, T. W.: The origin and fate of the urethral plate in man. J Anat 88:413, 1954

5. Glenister, T. W.: A consideration of the process involved in the development of the prepuce in man. Br J Urol 28:243, 1956

6. Horton, C. E., and Devine, C. J.: Hypospadias. In *Plastic Surgery in Infancy and Childhood*, Edited by J. C. Mustardé. E. & S. Livingstone, Edinburgh, 1971

7. van der Meulen, J. C.: *Hypospadias*. Charles C Thomas, Springfield, Ill., 1964

8. van der Meulen, J. C.: Reconstructive surgery of the anterior urethra. Br J Plast Surg 23:291, 1970

9. van der Meulen, J. C. Hypospadias and cryptospadias. Br J Plast Surg 24:101, 1971

10. Smith, D. R., and Blackfield, H. M.: A modification of Blair's procedure for the repair of hypospadias. J Urol 59:404, 1948

11. Smith, D. R., and Blackfield, H. M.: A critique on the repair of hypospadias. Surgery 31:885, 1952

12. Tolhurst, D. E., and Gorter, H.: A review of 102 cases of hypospadias by the van der Meulen procedure. Br J Plast Surg (in press).

13. Townsend, P. L. G.: Silicone rubber casts of the distal urethra in studying fistula formation and other hypospadias problems. Br. J Plast Surg 28:320, 1975

Commentary: Multiple-Stage Repair of Hypospadias

E. Durham Smith

It is generally conceded by advocates of one-stage repair of hypospadias that the technique is inapplicable to the more severe types of proximal penile or perineal orifices associated with significant chordee. Van der Muelen's paper in which he advocates a single-stage technique for distal hypospadias with minimal chordee due to skin deficiency only but a two-stage technique for more severe degrees, is an example. This paper was chosen because of the remarkable results of no fistulae in 220 patients; not only is this fact alone a tribute to an excellent technique and an excellent surgeon, but the paper includes a careful and critical rationale to substantiate the technique. Admittedly only 20 of the 220 repairs were of the two-stage type, but certain essential principles applicable to multiple-staged repair are included in his single-stage technique. The objectives of operative procedures, as achieved or not achieved by the van der Meulen technique, are as discussed below.

STRAIGHT PENIS IN ERECTION FOR INTERCOURSE

A straight penis through very adequate chordee correction is a *sine qua non* of success and is more important than a terminal orifice. Van der Muelen's thesis is that in most patients with distal hypospadias, the chordee is due to skin shortening only, and his single-stage repair is reserved for such patients in whom skin repositioning only is required, a view supported by King.[1] In "less than 20% of all hypospadias cases," other elements predominant, principally "the fibrous layer which represents the hypoplastic urethral plate . . . and also partly the other hypoplastic structures which were to develop into the dartos fascia or tunica albuginea." In this group, van der Meulen releases the urethral meatus from its attachment and divides the fibrous tissue over the corpora cavernosa, as a preliminary first stage. I would like to make the point that this view of chordee is too simplistic. Some writers constantly stressed that the chordee was due to a rudimentary and fibrous corpus spongiosum and that this band can always be found at operation.[2] Others, like van der Meulen, seldom find such a structure and attribute the chordee to either deficiency of the skin alone or to adherency of skin to the underlying fascia and corpora in the absence of dartos muscle.[1,3–5] The deep fascia (Buck's fascia) may also be thickened or arranged as lateral fibrous bands.[6,7] The urethra itself may be short and tethered and is a further factor.

Further, these same factors may be present *proximal* to the urethral meatus, the extreme example obviously being the condition of chordee without hypospadias. The importance of these proximal factors is also stressed by Marshall and col-

leagues, whose histological sections showed dense collagen tissue beneath the proximal skin and tethering of penile and scrotal skin well proximal to the orifice.[8] They also noted ventral deficiency of the corpus spongiosum proximal to the orifice, so that the urethra and skin were in contact. Devine and Horton, in patients with chordee without hypospadias, similarly describe the varying abnormalities proximal to the orifice, from simple loss of dartos to gross loss or abnormality of spongiosum and fascia over the urethra, so that the urethra is almost transparently thin just beneath the skin.[9] All these features may be found proximal to hypospadias orifices as well.

These varying findings are not contradictory. In truth, the chordee deformity can be due to any or all of these structures, and the relative contribution of each varies among patients. Further, and this is relevant to the argument of one-stage versus multistaged repair, any or all of these factors (and not just skin shortening) may be present *even in distal hypospadias*. The surgeon must recognize at operation *any* degree of hypospadias and each of the possible causes and simply look for them systematically (*e.g.*, tethering of urethra, short skin, skin tethering, lateral fibrous tissue, central fibrous band). Failure to appreciate this in some one-stage procedures with a too-simplistic notion of skin shortening only results in the difficult surgical problem of persistent chordee after urethroplasty. One-stage techniques compel the completion of urethroplasty at the same time as chordee release, since there is no way of knowing if the latter is fully corrected until later. Since I find chordee to be so often multifactorial, even for subglandular hypospadias, I like to be assured of chordee correction by a preliminary stage operation; this is one reason I advocate a two-staged repair for all degrees of hypospadias.

TERMINAL ORIFICE ON TIP OF GLANS

A terminal orifice on the tip of the glans from which to void in the long axis of the penis in the standing position and from which to inseminate well into the vagina is desirable. Controversy surrounds the necessity of a truly terminal orifice on the tip of the glans. Authorities such as Creevy and many since have consistently maintained that an orifice in the coronal groove is functionally adequate; many established procedures are specifically designed to bring the orifice to that point only, with workers believing that attempts to produce a glandular urethra are fraught with undue complications.[2] Many procedures designed otherwise finish with an orifice in the coronal groove in any case! Indeed, the traditional view has for long been that "glandular and subglandular hypospadias only require mea-totomy and hemi-circumcision," the orifice being accepted as adequate at the coronal site. The last decade has seen a reversal of this policy. Although a wide coronal orifice provides little inconvenience to voiding and no interference to intercourse, the expectations of both patient and surgeon demand a better result. Cosmetically, an orifice 2.5 cm from the end of the penis in adult life can be embarrassing in today's society; although the available techniques a decade ago carried high risks of fistuli, stricture, and stenosis in that last inch, the risks were unacceptable. But this is no longer so, and consistently good results with terminal orifices can now be achieved.

I have long advocated the rule: "An orifice on the *distal* half of the glans only needs meatotomy and hemi-circumcision; everything proximal to this requires a urethral reconstruction through to the tip." Truly glandular orifices only 2 mm or 3 mm from the tip, made to join the blind groove by simple meatotomy, certainly look and function normally and continue to stay on the tip as the glans grows. But orifices on the proximal half of the glans after meatotomy only stay at the base of the glans.

In Van der Meulen's technique, a terminal orifice is achieved (in both single-stage and two-stage repairs) by grafting preputial skin onto a denuded surface of the glans; in his two-stage repair, skin is applied onto a split glans, as described by Cloutier.[10] However, it is significant that in the follow-up study of Van der Meulen's patients, in 28 of 102 patients the orifice retracted away from the tip, thus partly defeating the objective of a terminal orifice.[11] I would explain this failure as due to van der Meulen's advocacy of the "buried strip" technique. No actual "tube" is created, except by subsequent epithelial-ization, and the terminal orifice is created ventrally by a single layer of skin only, depending for its integrity on the "take" of the skin on the bare narrow strip of glans at a time while urine passes through it. In contrast, in my technique, the grafted skin is put there by a preliminary stage, its viability is ensured, and the orifice is a full-thickness skin tube.

SOLID INTACT URETHRA WITHOUT FISTULA

Van der Meulen stresses the major factors in causation of fistulae: too little mobilization of skin, producing tension; poor vascularity by too long or too thin a flap by the tourniquet effect of unevenly placed skin or by circular dressings; allowing epithelium to grow between skin and urethra by inverted or superimposed suture lines; poor drainage of urine or blood. His technique avoids all these errors, and every point should be noted. However, I have added two further safeguards. One is the construction of a full-thickness, intact, complete skin tube of single-type epithelium in continuity, without an anas-tomotic suture line or a change of epithelium from one section to another. The "buried strip" technique (as well as free grafts, pedicle tubes for part of the length only, and tubing procedures necessitating a change of epithelium from penile skin to glans epithelium) transgresses this principle. The preliminary grafting of skin well forward to the tip of the glans (in the first stage) ensures a urethral tube of uniform and continuous epithelium throughout its whole length. Further, the tube is full thickness and completely circumferential for 360 degrees, in contrast to

the necessary break in continuity between the edge of the buried strip and the overlying skin flap.

The second safeguard is a multilayer closure. In the buried strip technique only one layer completes the ventral surface of the repair, namely, the preputial flaps. In my technique there are four layers—the urethral skin tube, the overlying fascia, and two layers of overlapping skin grafted together by the strong union of raw flap to raw flap rather than edge to edge. The skin closures are not superimposed over the urethral closure.

The fistula problem cannot be overemphasized. Some surgeons play it down, but nothing is further from the truth. Fistula closure has a legendary reputation for failure, and many a single-stage or a two-stage primary urethroplasty has become a three-, four-, or five-stage marathon. Fistula prevention depends entirely on technique.

URETHRA OF UNIFORM CALIBER

A urethra of uniform caliber, without stricture or sacculation, is desirable. Again, the buried strip technique, with the uncertainty of how the edges will epithelialize, is less pre-dictable than a complete skin tube, a fact substantiated in many papers since the original report by Browne, in which both strictures and diverticuli were recognized complications.[12]

COSMETIC APPEARANCE

The cosmetic appearance should not be minimized as an objective, and the challenge is especially so for the common subglandular varieties, where the principle reason for surgery is cosmesis, it being conceded that voiding and intercourse are not functionally greatly disturbed. Careful planning of the use of skin can generally avoid secondary trimming operations of untidy skin tags. The reported retraction of the orifice is a weakness of the van der Meulen technique.

Bearing the above points in mind, I may summarize my position as follows. There is an obvious advantage in completing the correction in one stage in one hospital admission, one anesthetic, and one stressful period instead of two, and this is a persuasive argument and a highly desirable objective. Further, in the best series, usually by the original authors, there is a low incidence of fistulae, and, when the procedure is performed well, the cosmetic appearance is excellent.[8,9,13–17]

On the other hand, in some one-stage series, there is an unacceptably high morbidity from fistulae, urethral strictures, and especially retraction of the meatus away from the tip.[11] Further, when chordee is present, the one-stage techniques compel the completion of the urethroplasty at the same time as chordee release, but there is no way of knowing that the chordee is fully corrected until later. Persistent chordee after urethroplasty is a difficult surgical problem. If one adds up the additional procedures required because of complications, and if that complication rate is high, it can hardly be claimed as "one stage." A fistula is not by any means confidently closed by just one more operation. Further, although often not mentioned, many one-stage protagonists actually do a mea-totomy (most hypospadiac orifices are stenotic) on a prior occasion, requiring a short hospital admission and anaesthetic, but for some reason this is not considered a "stage." Finally, with the exception of the procedures of Hodgson and of Devine and Horton, the one-stage techniques generally apply only to mid- and distal hypospadiac orifices, so that the surgeon must learn multiple techniques for different situations.[13–15]

Multiple-stage repairs have, again as a generality, fewer complications and more consistent results, but at the price of two procedures. The important technical advantages of the two-stage repairs are that the chordee can be corrected before the urethroplasty is done, an orifice can be consistently obtained at the tip of the glans by a first-stage transfer of skin to that site, and by the same transfer the urethral tube can be fashioned from a uniform and continuous epithelium throughout its whole length, thus reducing the risk of fistuli and strictures. Not all multiple-stage repairs achieve these objectives, however, so that without them one cannot claim an advantage over one-stage repairs.

The repair I describe in the following section does satisfy the objectives, has a low morbidity, and has the added advantage of applying to all degrees of hypospadias, so that only one technique must be learned. Its design requires a two-stage technique.

TECHNIQUE

In 1970 I first developed this technique, described in 1973.[18] By February 1983, 435 repairs had been performed with this technique with 14 fistulae; 3 of these fistuli were in 13 patients with broken-down repairs done elsewhere. Thus, of 422 patients, there were 11 fistulae (2.6%). The results are of a circumcised appearance with a terminal orifice (Figs. 6–9). It is a two-staged repair.

Stage 1 (Fig. 10). As in the Byars technique the prepuce is divided dorsally (Fig. 11A) to create two flaps; the incision on the dorsal surface extends 0.75 cm proximal to the coronal groove (Fig. 11 D). The flaps are denuded of their inner layers (Fig. 11 B and C) and transferred to a denuded strip of ventral glans on either side of the blind groove (Fig. 11 E, F, and G).[19] This maneuver has two purposes; by grafting skin *beyond* the tip of the glans, the urethral orifice can be made truly terminal in the second stage, and the tube from

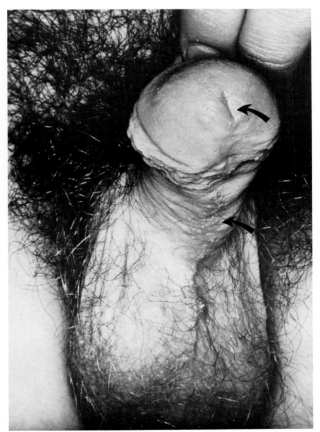

Fig. 7. Postoperative result. The upper arrow indicates the new urethral orifice on the tip of the glans, produced by folding in the lateral masses of the glans over the urethral tube. The lower arrow indicates the suture line on the ventral shaft.

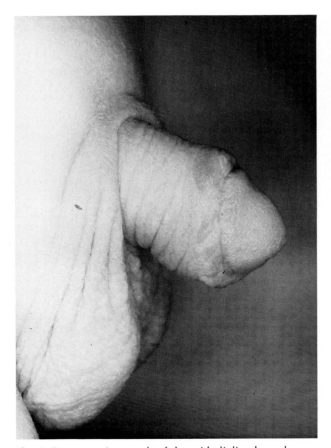

Fig. 6. Postoperative result of de-epithelialized overlap flap technique (previously midpenile orifice).

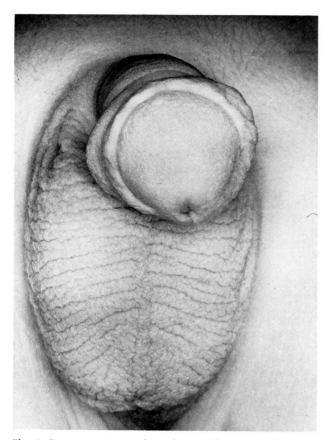

Fig. 8. Postoperative result to show orifice on tip of glans.

Fig. 9. Postoperative voiding from glans. Arrow indicates original site of orifice.

which the urethra is subsequently made can be made of continuous skin in its entire length without change of epithelium. The blind groove on the glans is preserved to ensure a smooth floor to the skin tube to be subsequently buried deeply in the glans. Before actually completing the suture of the flaps to the glans (as in Fig. 11 *G*) the chordee is corrected. This is commenced by incising the ventral skin of the penis transversely (Fig. 12 *A*), thus completing a 360° incision around the penis. With distal urethral orifices this incision is best done just proximal to the orifice and the skin dissected off the urethra. This plane is less vascular than an incision distal to the orifice. However, in proximal orifices, the incision is obviously distal to the orifice. In either case it may be necessary to dissect the urethra from its bed to release it, should such tethering be a factor in chordee. The entire circumference of the skin is then opened up and dissected free both distally and proximally to the orifice (Fig. 12 *B*), right to the base of the penis, even with coronal orifices. All elements of chordee are released (see above; these are, in varying degrees, skin shortening and tethering, fascial bands and Buck's fascia, urethral shortening, and strands of degenerated corpus spongiosum). A generous meatotomy is added (Fig. 12 *C*) to ensure a wide orifice, which will eventually be incorporated in the skin tube of Stage II.

After release of chordee structures, the preputial and penile flaps are then sutured ventrally, partly to cover the ventral defect on the shaft caused by release of ventral skin, and partly onto the denuded glans to provide adequate skin to the tip of the penis for the second stage (Fig. 11 *D* and Fig. 12 *D* and *E*). No catheter or drainage is necessary. A dressing of petroleum jelly or, if preferred, a dressing of Dermahesive with a hole for the urethral orifice (Fig. 12 *F*) can be used. The child goes home on the third day.

Stage II. A U-shaped tube from proximal to the meatus to the tip of the glans is turned in (Figs. 13 and 14*A*); it can be applied to the shortest subglandular or the longest perineal hypospadias (Fig. 15*A*). This is done with a continuous subcuticular 4–0 nylon suture over a 10 or 12 French catheter. The catheter is removed at the end of the operation, but its presence ensures a uniform lumen tube without sacculations or strictures. Interrupted catgut (5–0) sutures then bring further subcutaneous tissue over the tube, sealing off this tube more completely (Fig. 14*B*). At the glandular level a deep lateral cut is made on either side halfway through the glans; in closing the outer skin the lateral glandular masses are brought together over the urethral tube, thus projecting the buried skin tube into the substance of the glans. Thus, the orifice opens right at the tip of the glans. Two further skin layers are then possible. In most techniques the suturing of skin involves edge-to-edge apposition—a potentially weak junction. The principle contribution of this repair is that skin closure is achieved by the apposition of two flat raw surfaces together, produced by shaving of skin from one side, and then overlapping of the flaps like a double-breasted suit (Fig. 14*C* to *G*). Tissue adherence followed by granulation tissue repair is very rapid

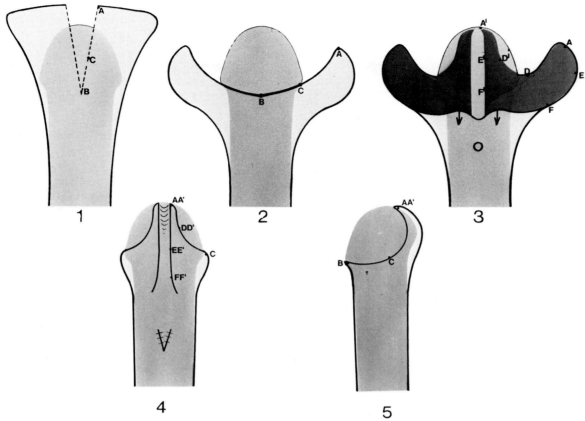

Fig. 10. Diagrammatic steps in Stage 1 (commentator's technique). (*1*) The dorsal prepuce is cut longitudinally to the coronal groove. (*2*) The preputial flaps are rotated from the dorsal to the ventral side (after denuding the inner surface of the flaps), and sutured dorsally and laterally (*B* and *C*) into the coronal groove. (*3*) The ventral surface of the preputial flaps, and of the glans, denuded of epithelium (*dark area*) but preserving the central blind groove. The two raw areas are joined with a transverse incision distal to the orifice, thus completely releasing the penile skin for chordee correction. (*4*) The prepurtial flaps are applied ventrally to the glans and sutured right to the tip of the penis distally, *A to A'*, E to E', *etc.* Proximally, the skin flaps join in the midline to make up any deficiency of skin after chordee correction. The meatotomy is liberal (*5*) Extent of the mobilized and sutured prepuce. (Smith ED: A de-epithelialized overlap flap technique in the repair of hypospadias. Br J Plast Surg 26:106–114, 1973. Reproduced by permission of the editor.)

and solid. Further, the flat plate of overlapping skin has two laterally placed suture lines so that suture lines are not superimposed. All these factors mitigate against fistula breakdown (Fig. 15).

A "Bonanno" suprapubic stab cystotomy drain is inserted; if there is only moderate swelling, I usually do not put a dressing on the penis (these are painful to remove and may produce pressure necrosis if much bleeding and infection), but I have no hesitation in dressing a very difficult or vascular one or one in a nervous child using Dermahesive as illustrated in Fig. 14 *H*.

Postoperative measures are as follows:

1. The catheter must be firmly strapped to the abdomen (not the thigh, which causes movement to the catheter), and this strapping should not be disturbed (Fig. 14 *I*).
2. Low-pressure suction (3 cm to 5 cm of water) is continuously applied to the catheter, and no bladder washouts are necessary (or desirable, because a washout is the surest way for the junior nurse to disturb the dressings and the position of the catheter, especially a perineal urethrostomy).
3. The urine is acified by vitamin C.
4. A urinary antiseptic is administered orally (trimethoprim and sulfa).

(*Text continues on page 1264*)

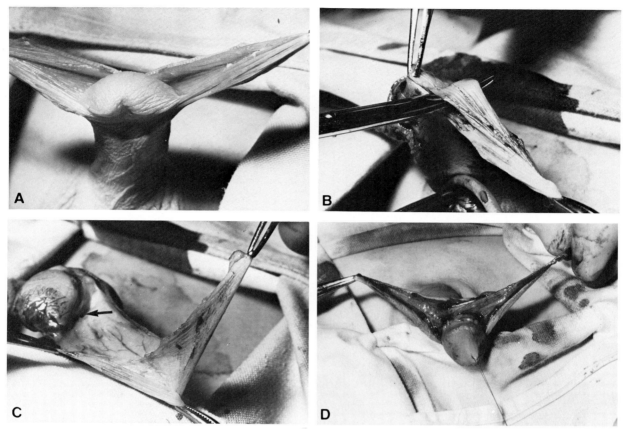

Fig. 11. Operative steps in Stage I: Skin transfer. (*A*) A longitudinal incision of the dorsal prepuce is made to produce two flaps. (*B*) The two layers of the prepuce are separated. (*C*) The inner layer is incised along the doronal groove (*arrow*) and peeled off. I generally excise this inner layer and discard it, but it can be preserved if there is gross skin deficiency. (*D*) The denuded flaps as seen dorsally. The incision in the midline of these flaps extends for 0.75 cm proximal to the coronal groove onto the shaft. (*E*) The ventral glans is denuded of epithelium on either side of the central blind groove. The *arrows* indicate that this denuding extends distally just beyond the tip of the glans, and is broad enough to give a firm attachment to the preputial flaps. (*F*) Note the extent of the glans denuding (*black arrow*) and the continuation of the raw surface with the base of the preputial flap (*white arrow*). Note also the tourniquet with a rubber catheter, which is optional. (*G*) The preputial flaps are now advanced, and the raw surface of the prepuce is applied to the coronal groove and to the denuded glans.

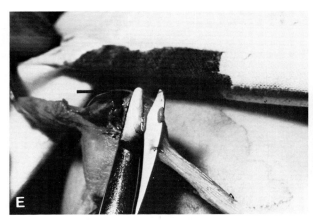

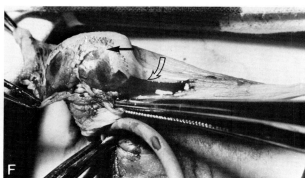

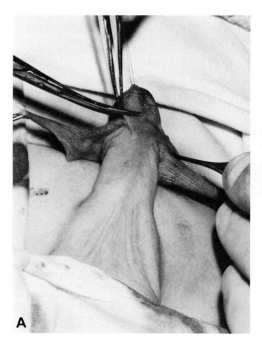 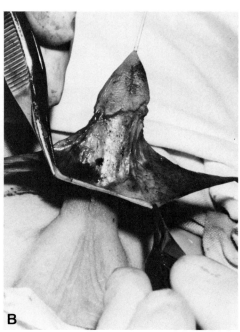

Fig. 12. Operative steps in Stage I: Chordee correction. These steps are done concurrently with those of Fig. 11 if there is chordee to be corrected. (*A*) Transverse incision ventrally across the penile skin joining up with the mobilized preputial flaps. It can be done either proximal or distal to the urethral orifice, depending on the site of the latter. The skin is thus freed for 360°. (*B*) The whole of the penile shaft skin is released from adherency to fascia, corpora, and urethra, down to the base of the penis, no matter where the urethral orifice lies. After release of skin, all other elements of chordee are dissected if present (division of Buck's fascia laterally, release of urethra, and excision of any central fibrous material from corona to or proximal to the urethral orifice). (*C*) A generous meatotomy. (*D*) The dorsal surface at the end of Stage I. The *arrow* indicates how far distally the preputial flaps are advanced to the ventral surface of the glans. (*E*) The ventral surface at the end of Stage I. The *black arrow* shows the prepuce to the tip of the glans; the remainder of the preputial flaps are joined together to make up the skin deficiency after chordee correction. The *white arrow* indicates the meatus after meatotomy. There is now continuous skin to the tip of the glans. (*F*) Usually a dressing of Dermahesive is applied with a hole for the urethral orifice; alternatively the penis can be left exposed apart from a petroleum jelly dressing.

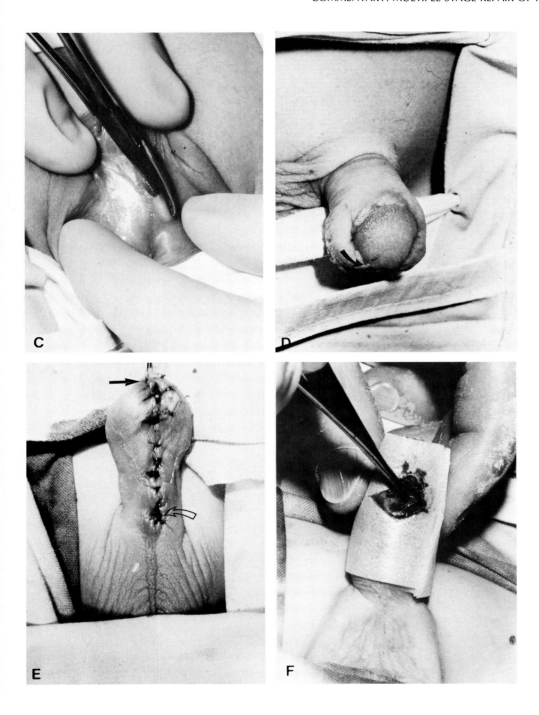

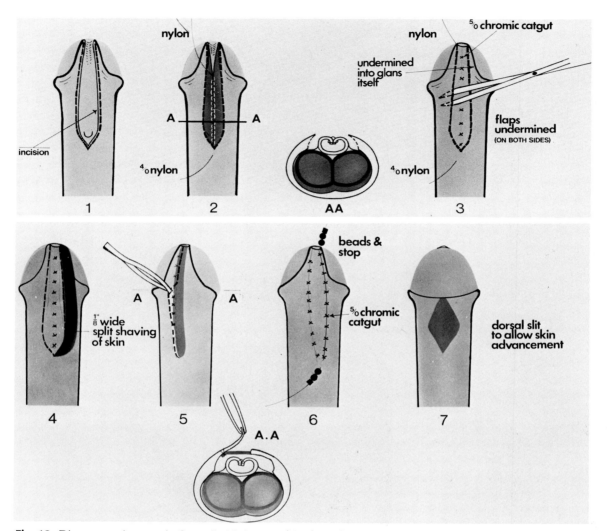

Fig. 13. Diagrammatic steps in Stage II. (*1*) A ventral U-shaped incision is made from orifice to tip. (*2*) A complete skin tube is fashioned by inverting the raw edges together (A–A) by a continuous 4/0 nylon suture over a temporary catheter. (*3*) Further support is given to this tube by interrupted 5/0 chromic catgut sutures drawing fascial tissues over the primary suture line. The lateral skin flaps are undermined. A deep cut is made on either side of the tube halfway through the glans. (*4*) Skin is shaved from one lateral flap 3 mm wide (*dark area*) to provide a raw area. (*5*) The medial edge of the shaved skin is sutured beneath the opposite flap, this suture line not being superimposed on the primary suture of the skin tube, which is now completely covered by the skin flap. (*6*) The opposite flap is swung over the raw area and sutured (A–A). Beads and stops can be used to hold the nylon suture. The glans tissue is brought together in this closure to project the skin tube (into the substance of the glans). (*7*) A dorsal relieving incision is made if there is tension. (Smith ED: A de-epithelialized overlap flap technique in the repair of hypospadias. Br J Plast Surg 26:106–114, 1973. Reproduced by permission of the editor.)

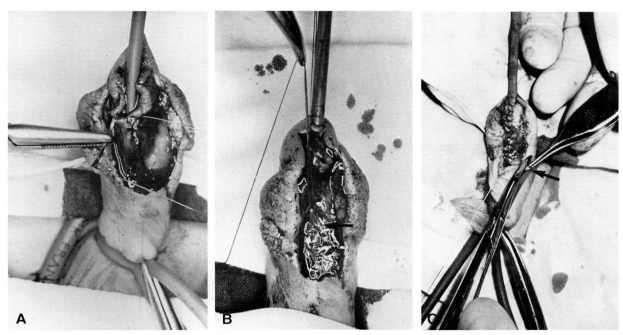

Fig. 14. Operative steps in Stage II. (*A*) The primary skin tube is fashioned by a continuous inverting suture of 4/0 nylon. The needle does not penetrate through the skin but picks up the subcutaneous tissue only. A catheter ensures uniform lumen. A tourniquet aids dissection. (*B*) The skin tube is complete through to the tip, made possible by grafting skin to this area in Stage 1. Fascial tissues are brought together over the primary suture line with interrupted 5/0 chromic catgut. (*C*) Skin is shaved from one lateral flap. A small strip is commenced proximally (*arrow*) with a flat scissors, *not* on the medial edge. (*D*) The skin strip (*upper arrow*) is excised and discarded. The *lower arrow* shows the raw surface of the first strip; two or three additional strips are then excised until the full width of raw area is obtained. (*E*) The shaved lateral flap (the artery forceps were only used to obtain the photograph). (*F*) The medial edge of the shaved skin is sutured (using 5/0 chromic catgut) beneath opposite lateral flap. (*G*) The outer lateral flap is drawn across the shaved raw area and sutured to the lateral border of the shaved strip, thus completely covering the primary skin tube with two skin layers, allowing union by tissue adherence of flat surfaces (rather than edge-to-edge), and with nonsuperimposed suture lines. (*H*) Dermahesive dressing has proved a great advantage. It has a little elasticity that allows some swelling to occur but prevents gross edema. It seals the area completely. The nylon suture (of the primary skin tube) is now not held by beads and stops, but simply overlapped beneath a second piece of Dermahesive. (*I*) The "Bonanno" suprapubic catheter is held in place by adhesives on the abdomen only, not the thigh. The child can sit out of bed or walk with this arrangement. (*A, B, E, F,* and *G* from Smith ED: A de-epithelialized overlap flap technique in the repair of hypospadias. Br J Plast Surg 26:106–114, 1973. Reproduced by permission of the editor.)

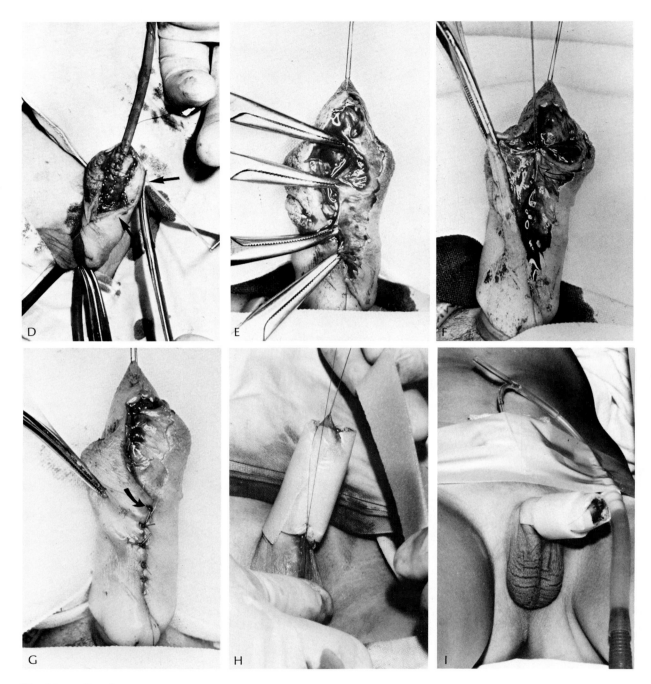

Fig. 14, continued

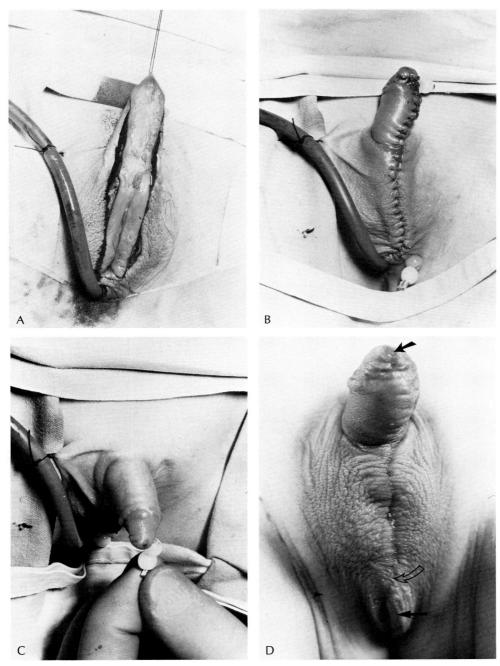

Fig. 15. The same technique can be applied to the most extensive types of hypospadias. (*A*) Incision in perineal hypospadias, prior to tubing. (Perineal urethrostomy is now replaced by suprapubic stab cystotomy; see text). (*B*) Completion of repair (beads and stops on nylon suture). (*C*) Completion of repair, dorsal surface. (*D*) The same patient 2½ weeks later. The *upper black arrow* indicates the orifice on the tip of the glans; the *lower black arrow* indicates the site of perineal urethrostomy, which closed spontaneously; the *white arrow* shows the site of the original hypospadias orifice.

5. A laxative is given from the day of operation, because straining at stool often forces urine past the catheter. With these measures I have had very little catheter blockage.
6. On the ninth day any penile dressings and the nylon suture are removed; the latter slides out easily at this stage, and no anaesthetic is required. All other sutures dissolve.
7. The catheter is removed on the 12th day, and the child goes home on the 13th day.

My results to February 1983 in 422 patients seen are as follows:

422 urethroplasties—11 fistula (2.6%)*
　　　　　　　　　—1 urethral stricture (0.2%)
　　　　　　　　　—21 meatal stenosis (4.9%)
　　　　　　　　　—4 inadequate chordee correction (1%)

* In addition, there were 3 fistuli in 13 patients treated after previous extensive procedures done elsewhere, an incidence of 3.2% in 435 patients.

REFERENCES

1. King LR: Hypospadias: A one-stage repair without skin graft based on a new principle: Chordee is sometimes produced by the skin alone. J Urol 103:660, 1970.
2. Creevy CD: The correction of hypospadias: A review. Urol Surv 8:2, 1958
3. Gross M, Fein R, Waterhouse K: Single stage correction of chordee without hypospadias and coronal hypospadias. J Urol 102: 70, 1969
4. Persky L, Hoffman A, Des Prez J: The repair of chordee without hypospadias. J Urol 98:216, 1967
5. Smith DR: Repair of hypospadias in the pre-school child: A report of 150 cases. J Urol 97:723, 1967
6. Hoffman WW, Hall WV: A modification of Spence's hood for a one-stage surgical correction of distal shaft penile hypospadias. J Urol 109:1017, 1973
7. Jones HW Jr, Scott NW: Hermophroditism, Genital Anomalies, and Related Endocrine Disorders, 2d ed, pp 376–405. Baltimore, Williams & Wilkins, 1971
8. Marshall M Jr, Beh WP, Johnson S III, et al: Etiological considerations in penoscrotal hypospadias repair. J Urol 120:229, 1978
9. Devine CJ Jr, Horton CE: Chordee without hypospadias. J Urol 110:264, 1973

10. Cloutier AM: Method for hypospadias repair. Plast Reconstr Surg 30:368, 1962
11. Tolhurst DE, Gorter H: A review of 102 cases of hypospadias treated by the van der Meulen procedure. Br J Plast Surg 29:361, 1976
12. Browne D: An operation for hypospadias. Proc R Soc Med 41:466, 1949
13. Devine CJ Jr, Horton CE: Hypospadias repair. J Urol 118:188, 1977
14. Hodgson NB: A one-stage hypospadias repair. J Urol 104:281, 1970
15. Hodgson NB: One-stage repair. In Urological Procedures, Vol 1. Warner–Chilcott, Morris Plains, NJ, 1972
16. Hodgson NB: In defence of the one-stage hypospadias repair. In Scott R Jr, Gordon HL, Scott FB, et al (eds): Current Controversies in Urological Management. Philadelphia, WB Saunders, 1972
17. Sadlowski RW, Belman AB, King LR: Further experience with one-stage hypospadias repair. J Urol 112:677, 1974
18. Smith ED: A de-epitheliaslized overlap flap technique in the repair of hypospadias. Br J Plast Surg 26:106, 1973
19. Byars LT: A technique for consistently satisfactory repair of hypospadias. Surg Gynecol Obstet 100:184, 1955

ANNOTATED BIBLIOGRAPHY

Byars LT: A technique for consistently satisfactory repair of hypospadias. Surg Gynecol Obstet 100:184, 1955

This is a classic paper and still the basis for many operative repairs. It underlines the full use of the prepuce in preparation for the main urethral construction and describes in detail the fashioning of a complete skin tube rather than a buried strip. The results were based on 89 consecutive unselected patients. The repair was usually done in two stages. In the first stage, Byars stressed the complete correction of chordee by total freeing of the prepuce and penile skin to provide access; the dorsal prepuce is divided into two flaps, which are laid on to a denuded ventral surface of the glans to provide skin for the subsequent urethral tube. In the second stage, a complete urethral tube is fashioned using perineal urethrostomy diversion as well; if there is no diversion, the new urethra is created only up to the hypospadias orifice, the gap being closed by a third-stage procedure. In the first 60 patients, excluding 8 patients with complications from previous surgery, 12 of 52 patients developed fistuli; in 29 more patients, a single fistula developed in 25 patients previously unoperated on. There were no strictures. The importance of the paper is in its emphasis on the first stage in stressing complete chordee correction and providing preputial skin well forward onto the ventral glans.

Devine CJ Jr, Franz JP, Horton CE: Evaluation and treatment of patients with failed hypospadias repair. J Urol 119:223, 1978

The vast experience of these established authors is brought to bear on an analysis of causes of failure of hypospadias repair. Of 500 patients treated over 22 yr, 13% developed "fistula and/or meatal stenosis." The paper concentrates on 70 failed cases, 9 of their own and 61 of other surgeons. Their analysis suggests the following errors:
　　Errors in preoperative evaluation: unrecognized intersex problem, too young, clotting disorder, associated urinary anomalies
　　Errors in design: inadequate chordee correction, inadequate surgical exposure or hemostasis, use of hair-bearing skin, skin graft from improper site, too small a lumen
　　Errors in technique: eversion of urethral epithelium with inversion of skin, apposing suture lines, ischaemic flaps, tension on flaps, wrong sutures
　　Errors postoperatively: dressings too tight or left on too long, meatal encrustation, urine drainage into wound (bladder spasm, catheter obstruction, constipation), infection, attempted immediate resuture of fistula
　　Uncorrected erections or edema.
Uncorrected chordee and fistulae constituted the main problems.

Farina R: Surgical treatment of hypospadias: Experience in the treatment of 400 consecutive cases using Leveuf's technique. Br J Plast Surg 25:180, 1972

This well-illustrated paper draws attention to the method commonly used in France (Leveuf's) and that of Cecil, in the use of scrotal skin. The first stage is essentially that of Byars, with correction of chordee, but it is noted that the preputial flaps only extend to the coronal groove, not the tip of the glans. The second stage (Leveuf's) tubes a ventral penile strip, and the whole is then buried in scrotum. After 3 mo the penis is released from the scrotum (third stage). Operative correction is not commenced till after 4 yr of age. The technique has not been applied to patients with scrotal or perineal hypospadias, except by a preliminary procedure of reconstructing the proximal urethra up to the penoscrotal junction. There was a rather high incidence of complications (fistulae in 41 of 400 patients; dehiscence of suture line at first stage in 90 of 400, and stricture in 9 of 400), but there was only one patient with hair in the new urethra.

Kaplan GW, Lamm DL: Embryogenesis of chordee. J Urol 114:769, 1975, Marshall M Jr, Beh WP, Johnson SH III, et al: Etiologic considerations in peno-scrotal hypospadias repair. J Urol 120:229, 1978

These two papers are complementary and make important contributions to the understanding of chordee. Few studies of embryos exist, and this is the substance of Kaplan and Lamm's paper. Forty-six aborted male specimens were studied (60-mm to 180-mm crown–rump length, 12–22 wk), of which 89% had ventral curvature, suggesting that chordee is a normal stage of development. No areas of fibrosis or atrophy were seen, and the curvature involved all layers. In 3 stillborn premature babies and 13 living premature ones, chordee was present in 5 patients; in 1 infant the chordee was observed to disappear spontaneously.

In the paper by Marshall and colleagues, the simplistic concept that chordee is due to a "chordee band" is similarly dismissed; rather, chordee is a phenomenon of several layers, especially adherence of skin to the urethra. In hypospadias there is some increase in collagen in the fascial layers, decrease in subcutaneous areolar connective tissue, and splaying out of the poorly developed corpus spongiosum laterally, resulting in adherence and anchoring of skin. Further, this adherence extends for some distance proximal to the urethral meatus, and operative repairs must free this area in the correction of chordee.

Smith PJB, Townsend PLG, Hiles JRW, et al: Hypospadias—problems of post-operative fistuli formation and a modified 2-stage procedure to reduce these. Br J Urol 48:703, 1976

This paper describes a study in which silicone casts were made of the urethra in patients with fistuli. It demonstrates the weak areas in repairs. A common finding was an overhanging pouch of urethra at the junction between the new and old urethra, and many fistulae occurred there, especially with the Denis Browne repair. The casts also showed a high frequency of distal stenosis or intervening skin bridges. The Mustardè repair showed constriction of the tube in the glans; the Broadbent repair showed the neourethra to be oblique and coiled. No figures are provided on the results of the authors' operations.

Woodard JR, Green BG: A technique for the correction of bifid scrotum in patients with hypospadias. J Urol 117:516, 1977

This is a small but quite significant additional technique to facilitate the repair of the difficult penoscrotal type. The technique adds length to the penis and directs the erect penis away from the scrotum. The penis is extensively dissected out of the scrotum at the second-stage operation, leaving a defect in the midline of the scrotum that is subsequently closed longitudinally up to the base of the penis, thus elongating this area. It is similar to a technique described by Glenn and Anderson (J Urol 110:603, 1973) for incomplete penoscrotal transposition.

OVERVIEW: HYPOSPADIAS REPAIR

Lowell R. King

The commentators on single-stage and multistage hypospadias repair have set forth the indications for the techniques that they espouse in extremely lucid fashion. Although many types of single-stage and multistage procedures are in current use, the approaches themselves are complementary. Planned single-stage repairs are most often applicable when the meatus lies on the penile shaft. To be sure, a one-stage operation can be elected for penoscrotal hypospadias, or even for perineal hypospadias, using the Horton–Devine free graft technique. However, an enormous amount of foreskin is required if two 12-mm strips of prepuce are detached and used for the neourethra, the distal portion of which must be covered by the remaining transferred foreskin. Few urologists have chosen to

use thin, non-hair-bearing skin from the neck for the urethral graft as an alternative to a staged technique, although this option is clearly available and may be an excellent solution when a previous repair must be excised and the urethra replaced in a patient with only scarred and deficient local skin remaining.

It would be fair, I think, to argue that in general one-stage repairs are readily feasible and have a low complication rate in the correction of the most common varieties of hypospadias, in which the meatus lies on the penile shaft. In this circumstance, the chordee is usually caused by the skin alone, and release can be demonstrated by intraoperative erection, as Dr. Hodgson emphasizes, after the penile shaft has been denuded. When this is the case, the simplest repair, to my mind, is to tubularize a strip of ventral midline skin that has been preserved distal to the hypospadias meatus to bring the new meatus to the tip of the glands. It is important, as Mr. Smith so eloquently points out, not to have a preconception of what one will encounter. If the chordee is not corrected by freeing the shaft skin lateral and proximal to the meatus, the surgeon must of course excise the skin strip distal to the meatus and the underlying tissue causing the chordee. The surgeon can then still sometimes elect to continue a one-stage repair using one of the Hodgson or Devine techniques or can revert to a multistage procedure.

Staged repairs are generally most satisfactory when the meatus is at, or proximal to, the penoscrotal junction, since buried tissue causing penile chordee is almost invariably present and must be carefully and completely excised. The resultant increase in penile length is often so great that the entire unrolled dorsal hood is needed to make good the resulting skin defect on the ventral surface of the penile shaft. Put another way, in this circumstance there is enough foreskin to make the neourethra or to cover the exposed ventral shaft, but not to do both. If the neourethra is formed, the penis is dropped into the scrotum to heal without tension, requiring release at a later time. If staged repair is elected, it is equally feasible to split the glans, bringing the transposed foreskin to the tip so that the meatus can be more reliably established there at the next stage, as in Mr. Smith's technique. Many techniques and variations have staunch supporters who have demonstrated the feasibility and reliability of each procedure. What follows is essentially my own ''recipe'' for deciding which procedure to employ.

But first, a word about preoperative evaluation. Hypospadias is generally an isolated anomaly. A routine intravenous pyelogram (IVP) is unnecessary in this situation, since the incidence of associated upper tract abnormalities is less than 2%—little, if any, greater than in the population at large. The incidence of an otherwise unsuspected lesion of the urinary tract that requires surgical correction is much less—0.5% to 0.8%. If another congenital anomaly is present, however, the incidence of renal anomalies increases, and a screening IVP should be performed.

Hypospadias plus a hernia or cryptorchidism suggests intersexuality. A buccal smear at least should be done, and ultrasound of the abdomen can be considered to rule out internal müllerian duct derivatives where doubt exists. Hypospadias, especially severe hypospadias, and an empty scrotum suggests the adrenogenital syndrome, especially if the gonads are not palpable.

Many genetic males with hypospadias have dilatation and elongation of the utricle, the analogue of the vagina, due to incomplete suppressions of müllerian duct differentiation. A urethrogram or a cystoscopy is necessary to delineate this, but these procedures are generally not warranted, since the utricle usually does not cause illness or symptoms in childhood or in later life.

GLANDULAR AND CORONAL HYPOSPADIAS

Glandular and coronal hypospadias is usually primarily a cosmetic problem, although the degree of associated chordee is occasionally marked. If this is the case, cutaneous lysis of the skin on the distal half of the penile shaft almost always corrects the chordee, except for a ventral glandular tilt. A dorsal meatotomy, connecting the meatus with the dimple on the inferior aspect of the glands, allows the stream to be cast in a more horizontal fashion and improves the appearance of the penis. The glandular tilt may be corrected by developing the potential space between the dorsal vein, arteries, and nerves on the dorsum of the penis just behind the glands, exposing the corpora cavernosa. With a tourniquet around the base of the penis, a transverse wedge of corpora cavernosa is excised just behind the glans, and Buck's fascia is then closed with interrupted absorbable suture. All the chordee is thereby eliminated, as proved by intraoperative erection.

When the meatus lies on the glans or at the corona, and only slight or moderate chordee is present, several treatment options are available. From a medical point of view, as opposed to a cosmetic one, no treatment is needed. The child will be able to learn to direct the urinary stream and will not have problems with intercourse in later life. Thus, no treatment is a viable option. I do not recommend a formal hypospadias repair with construction of neourethra in such instances to place the meatus at the tip of the glands, although I agree this should be the objective in modern hypospadias repair if new urethra is to be formed. Obviously, this can be accomplished if the surgeon feels the procedure is warranted. In that circumstance, I prefer an Ombredanne–Belt–Fuqua approach, forming a tube from a flap of skin taken from the ventral midline proximal to the meatus. A wide meatotomy is first performed by spreading the small meatus with the tip of a clamp. The flap, 12-mm wide and about 20% longer than the distance between the hypospadiac meatus and the tip of the straightened penis, is tubularized. A tunnel is developed through the glans to the tip of the penis using blunt dissection. Enough of the thick fibrous tissue of the glans is excised as the tunnel is developed to prevent compression of the tubed flap, which is then transposed through the tunnel to bring the meatus to the tip. As in other types of hypospadias repair in which a neourethra is formed, the urine is diverted by urethral catheter, perineal urethrostomy, or suprapubic cystostomy for 8 to 10 days to permit the flap to become watertight. In young children and in infants I prefer cystostomy drainage with small belladonna and opium suppositories given every 4 hr, when the patient is awake, to prevent bladder spasms. I also employ a light pressure dressing for 2 to 5 days to minimize edema. The external dressing also immobilizes the penis, making the immediate postoperative period more comfortable. The dressing should be removed if it becomes wet, or skin maceration will result.

The options most commonly employed in coronal hypospadias, which I more enthusiastically recommend, include dorsal meatotomy with removal of the dorsal hood when little or no chordee is present, or dorsal meatotomy with partial transposition of the unrolled dorsal hood, using the Allen–Spence technique, when chordee is moderate. If an Allen–Spence procedure is elected, I usually keep a catheter in overnight in order to use a pressure dressing for 24 hr to minimize edema. The preputial flaps are transposed using the Byars methods, since this gives a nice tailored and pleasing cosmetic result immediately.

DISTAL SHAFT HYPOSPADIAS

Distal shaft hypospadias is the most common form of hypospadias, in which a neourethra must be constructed to allow the boy to direct the urinary stream adequately. My original technique was very similar to that of Allen and Spence, described above (Fig. 1). A circumcision type of incision is made, except that the incision passes behind the meatus and a strip of ventral midline skin, 12 mm wide, is left intact between the meatus and the glans. Chordee is eradicated by extensive lysis of the skin on the ventral and lateral aspects of the penile shaft. If residual chordee remains, all agree that the strip of skin and buried tissue between the meatus and the glans must be excised to the corpora cavernosa to completely straighten the penis and another procedure elected. In most instances, however, the penis does straihten completely except for a ventral tilt in the glans. The strip of skin distal to the meatus is then tubularized, bringing the meatus to the corona, and the neourethra is covered by the unrolled dorsal hood, transferred by the Nesbit or Byars technique. The bulky pedicles of the Nesbit flap give a less satisfactory appearance immediately, but the skin eventually smooths out as the boy's penis grows.

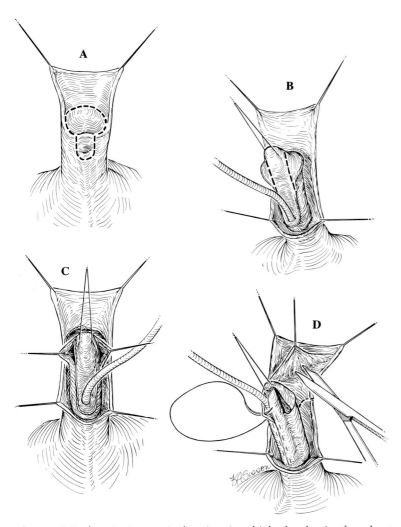

Fig. 1. (*A*) Deformity in a typical patient in which chordee is often due to the skin alone. The meatus lies on the distal penile shaft. Incisions preserve a strip of ventral midline skin to be used for neourethra if the chordee straightens completely with skin lysis. (*B*) If, using intraoperative erection, the penile shaft is straight, the ventral incisions are extended onto the glands to bring the meatus to the tip. (*C*) Glandular flaps are developed to close over the distal neourethra. (*D*) The strip of ventral skin is tubularized, and the dorsal hood is unrolled.

The advantage of the Nesbit transposition over the Byars is that no skin closure overlays the neourethra, so fistula are probably less likely. Even with a Byars transposition, where the interdigitated foreskin flaps come together over the neourethra, fistulae are relatively uncommon and have been as low as 7% in my experience.

In the past few years this procedure has been modified in three important ways. First, as described above, I usually excise a dorsal wedge of corpora cavernosa from behind the glans to straighten glandular tilt. Second, I place a tourniquet around the base of the glans and extend the incisions from the strip of skin ending at the corona out to the tip of the penis. These incisions are carried deep into glandular tissue, allowing me to tubularize the glanular strip to bring the meatus to the tip. The lateral glan flaps so formed are closed over the buried glandular urethra. Alternately, the tubed glanular skin can be covered with transposed foreskin. Third, I transpose the unrolled foreskin by the Nesbit technique or by Van der Meulen's method, bringing the unrolled dorsal hood around one side of the penis. This also prevents overlapping suture lines. When the foreskin is completely unrolled, with blood supply and venous drainage preserved, as described by Dr. Hodgson, a very pleasing cosmetic result is usually achieved without the asymmetry one would expect when the dorsal hood is swung only around one side of the glans (Fig. 2).

This manner reduces the fistula rate still further. I have not been able to employ Mr. Smith's offset two-layer skin closure in patients undergoing one-stage repairs. The prepuce is simply too thin and lacking in cutis to allow deepithelialization of the skin edge. This technique is very useful at a second stage, however, because the dermis is then thickened enough to define and to hold a separate suture layer.

With this modernized technique, the main risk of failure is necrosis of the unrolled foreskin flap. The pressure dressing must be applied to compress the flap, not the base of the penis, since pressure there may impede venous outflow and promote flap edema. When the dressing is removed, rebound edema may occur and compromise the vascularity of the flap. This should be treated aggressively by pricking the flap in many places with a 25-gauge needle to permit edema fluid to escape. This is surprisingly not very painful and can be done with the child awake or under mild sedation.

Catheter drainage is continued for 8 to 10 days to allow the neourethra to seal before voiding begins. I agree with Mr. Smith and Dr. Hodgson that a tubularized neourethra seals faster than a buried skin strip, and I see no advantage in allowing the neourethra to encyst itself. I have seldom encountered problems with urethral saccularization or stricture when this operation was employed, and, of course, no potentially hair-bearing skin is incorporated into the urethra. Meatitis and resultant meatal stenosis are prevented by suturing the skin edges of the new meatus to the edges of adjacent glanular skin so that granulations do not occur on exposed subcutaneous tissue. It is noteworthy that I have not seen any patient repaired by this technique with residual or recurrent chordee. I hope, of course, that this will continue to be the case, but I feel confident enough now, after employing the repair described above for over 12 yr, to be certain that skin lysis alone does in fact correct all but glandular tilt in the great majority of boys with a distal shaft meatus.

Parenthetically, I have had to correct recurrent chordee in some of my own patients initially repaired by staged techniques. My own theory, or explanation, of why this is recurrent rather than persistent chordee is that in doing the first operation and expecting to find a buried "chord," I resected Buck's fascia and the ventral aspect of the fascia of the corpora cavernosa. As this healed, and the scar tissue contracted, the chordee recurred long after the urethroplasty had been completed. This complication necessitates further straightening with insertion of a tubed island flap of penile skin to lengthen the urethra.

MID-SHAFT, PROXIMAL PENILE, AND PENOSCROTAL JUNCTION HYPOSPADIAS

Several different one-stage techniques can be used in mid-shaft, proximal penile, and penoscrotal junction hypospadias, and, of course, a staged repair can also be elected. The operation of choice among the planned one-stage procedures depends mostly on the degree of chordee and the length of the dorsal hood. If chordee is mild, it may only be cutaneous, in which case it is readily possible to employ the operation just described. More commonly, especially when the meatus is nearer to the penoscrotal junction than to the mid-penile shaft, some of the chordee will be caused by buried tissue between the meatus and the glands. This should be excised down to the fascia of the corpora cavernosa. Residual glandular tilt may also be corrected by removing a dorsal wedge from the distal corpora. If the unrolled dorsal hood is long enough, an island flap of skin from the distal prepuce may be tubed and transposed to the ventrum of the penis—one of Dr. Hodgson's operations. Alternately, especially when a little more urethral length is needed, the distal prepuce may be used as a free graft—the Horton–Devine procedure. Satisfactory cosmetic results are usually achievable with all these procedures, and postoperative fistulae become less and less frequent as experience is gained. The management and prevention of postoperative complications is discussed more fully toward the end of this paper.

When one-stage repairs were introduced by the Devines, the fistula rate, to use this common complication as an example, was probably no higher than the fistula rate from the two-stage repairs then in use. If the surgeon wished to minimize the risk of fistula, a Cecil repair was then clearly the most reliable operation. A third stage is required to release the penis from the scrotum, but covering skin could be tailored, and the meatus advanced, at this stage without additional morbidity, and a pleasing cosmetic result could be achieved without the presence of skin ears or bulky folds of tissue near the corona, which might require some time to smooth out after a one-stage procedure. These folds, of course, contain the vascular pedicles of the foreskin flaps, which are, to a degree, unavoidable if a good blood supply to the transposed prepuce is to be maintained.

Proponents of staged repairs—generally two-stage repairs—have perfected the technique of these operations to the degree that a strong case can be made for a planned two-stage repair when buried tissue is the cause of chordee. The experiences of Smith and Van der Meulen, detailed above, are good cases in point. At the time of chordee release, skin can be placed out to the tip of the glans, which is split ventrally

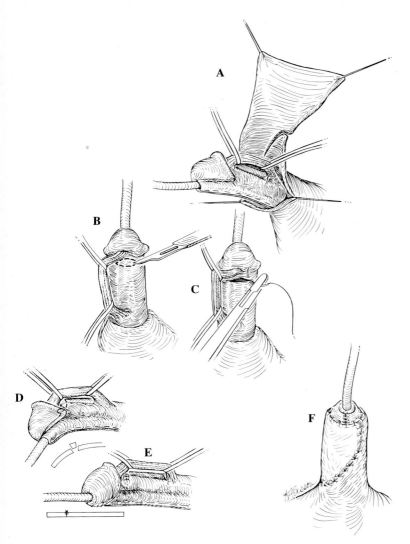

Fig. 2. Newer advances and modifications in this type of hypospadias repair. (*A*) The dorsal penile nerves and vessels are mobilized to expose the underlying corpora cavernosa. (*B* and *C*) A distal transverse ellipse of corpora is excised to straighten residual glandular tilt. (*D* and *E*) Lateral before and after views. The result is again confirmed by intraoperative erection. (*F*) The unrolled foreskin is incised eccentrically as in *A*, preserving major arteries and veins. The foreskin is then transposed in asymmetrical fashion so that suture lines do not overlap.

(Smith). At a second stage the tubed neourethra is brought to the end of the glans and covered with reapproximated glanular tissue or adjacent mobilized foreskin. The suture line in the neourethra is covered by a flap without overlapping suture lines (Van der Meulen, Walsh) or by foreskin with a deepithelialized edge to permit an extra layer of closing suture (Smith). A nice tailored appearance is immediately achieved, and these procedures now carry a lower fistula rate than can be consistently achieved in one-stage repairs in this situation. On the other hand, proponents of one-stage operations would argue, and do, that it is usually simpler and less traumatic to

close a fistula, particularly a small fistula, than to perform a planned two-stage repair. Each urologist must be guided by experience in deciding which approach is likely to be most satisfactory. In either instance, nuances of technique are important, as is postoperative care, which is discussed in more detail below.

PERINEAL HYPOSPADIAS WITH BIFID SCROTUM

It is especially important to screen children with perineal hypospadias for genetic sex, particularly if a hernia is present or if one or both testes are undescended. Also, in this group—even in the true males—are those with the greatest risk of developing müllerian duct structures internally, most commonly a dilated urticle that seldom requires treatment, but sometimes a utertus and fallopian tubes that should be removed. Ultrasonic imaging of these structures has become a useful aid in detection and minimizes the need for exploratory laparotomy or intraperitoneal inspection at the time of insertion of a cystostomy.

Generally speaking, the chordee associated with perineal hypospadias is severe and is associated with buried tissue as well as a shortage of skin on the ventral and lateral aspects of the penile shaft. After chordee is completely released, the length of neourethra needed is more than can be obtained from a strip of foreskin, so a staged repair is most often needed. All the foreskin that can be transposed to the ventral shaft is saved. The surgeon attempts to smooth the skin in the ventral midline, since this will become the neourethra. The technique described by Smith is very applicable in this situation. After healing is complete, usually in about 6 mo, the neourethra is formed and tubed as he describes, carrying the meatus to the tip of the glands. The lateral skin is closed in layers with deepithilialization of one skin edge to provide an extra layer for closure—one suture line is in the dermis with an offset layer in the overlying epidermis.

POSTOPERATIVE CARE

The blood supply of the genitalia is excellent, and postoperative wound infections are unusual. When they occur, they should be treated by meticulous local cleaning with soaks or whirlpool. Urinary diversion can be maintained until it is certain that a fistula has occurred. At times, the deep urethral suture layer will remain intact, and a superficial skin separation does not necessarily result in a fistula.

The most common problem in the postoperative period is wound edema. This may result in progressive engorgement of the skin flaps overlying the neourethra. Untreated, venous drainage of the flap is impeded, resulting in further swelling and eventually in arteriolar embarrassment and necrosis. Swelling can be minimized by applying a pressure dressing following surgery. One way to do this is to coat the penis with an antibacterial jelly, such as Bacitracin or Betadine, and gauze to prevent clotted blood from holding the dressing sponges to the penis. After a sponge is wrapped over the gauze, an Elastoplast dressing is applied. The pressure should be exerted on the glands and penile shaft, not at the penoscrotal junction, and the whole incorporated in a large bulky dressing for comfort. This acts as a splint and prevents most postoperative pain. If the dressing stays dry, I usually leave it in place for several days.

When the dressing is removed, rebound edema can still occur. If the skin flaps become tense, they are pricked several times with a 25-gauge needle. Light pressure is then applied to express the edema fluid. This does not seem to hurt much, but sedation is generally employed. The procedure may be repeated if necessary. An ice bag to the exposed penis also probably helps to prevent potential swelling.

I usually employ a suprapubic Pezzar or Malecot catheter for urinary diversion in boys to about age 6 yr, and a Foley, inserted through a perineal urethrostomy, in older boys. An urethral catheter serving to stent the neourethra, and exiting at the new meatus on the glands, is increasingly employed at my hospital and seems not to result in an increased risk of wound infection. No matter which form of diversion is used, infants and young boys especially tend to have bladder spasms. When these occur, they are painful and may result in the passage of urine through the neourethra despite the presence of a patient diverting catheter. Spasms are best prevented by giving infants half a belladonna and opium suppository every 4 hr when they are awake without waiting for the spasms to occur.

In older boys, erections are painful in the postoperative period and may usually be aborted by keeping amyl nitrite ampules at the bedside. Inhalation of this vasodilator usually terminates the erection.

Medium-term complications include meatal stenosis and, more rarely, stricute. Meatal stenosis is best prevented by making the meatus at least 10 to 12 French in caliber. The surgeon can still achieve a nozzle effect by tapering the skin strip that will become the new urethra slightly at the apex of the glands. The meatus is "matured" by meticulously suturing the edges of the new meatus to adjacent glandular skin so that no raw areas that might granulate and stenose are left exposes. When meatal stenosis does occur before healing is complete, meatotomy alone is all too likely to provide only temporary relief, since under these circumstances the stenosis has a marked tendency to recur. It is best to perform the meatotomy and insert a short piece of Silastic tubing, which is held in the urethra by a suture placed through the glands. This tube should be snug enough to fill the urethra, but not tight. The boy voids through this stent for 10 to 14 days while the meatus has a chance to heal.

Deep strictures, if detected in the postoperative period, are soft and are easily ruptured by urethral dilatation. This may be all the treatment that is required. If the stricture recurs and becomes fibrous, therapy depends on the length and location of the stricture.

When short, mature strictures can sometimes be incised transurethrally with the cold knife, three or four cuts are made, as in the technique of Kirchheim. Catheter drainage is employed for several days postoperatively. If the stricture is more than 1 cm long, or is not eradicated by this maneuver, a formal open urethroplasty is required. The Johanson procedure in two stages is the classic solution to this problem. However, it is often possible to use an island flap of penile or scrotal skin to enlarge the strictured area. In this one-stage procedure, the length and location of the stricture is first delineated by combined antegrade and retrograde urethrogram. An offset skin incision is then made parallel to the strictured area so that a strip of mid-line skin—15 mm wide and 2 cm wide and 2 cm longer than the stricture—can be outlined and detached from the skin and then turned in with vascular pedicle intact to become the ventral portion of the urethra in the strictured area. The stricture should be mature and not acutely inflamed at surgery. The surgeon opens the stricture longitudinally in the ventral midline, carrying the incision 5 mm to 10 mm into healthy urethra at either end of the stricture. The island flap of the skin is then rotated down against the opened urethra, and the flap edges are approximated to the urethra. Care is taken to approximate the epithelial edges accurately, especially at the ends of the urethral incision. The wound is then closed in as many layers as possible without compromising the vascular pedicle to the island flap. Proximal urinary diversion is established and maintained for 7 to 10 days.

Diverticula of the neourethra are always present to some degree, as demonstrated by the urethral casts described above. The best known means of preventing such diverticula is to form the neourethra from a uniform strip of skin that is tubularized and not left to encyst itself. This closure should be buttressed by approximating as many layers as are available over the newly formed urethra.

A small diverticulum, or "step," is almost always present where the neourethra joins the original meatus. This is seldom symptomatic but may make subsequent catheterization with a soft catheter difficult. When a sizable diverticulum results in postoperative dribbling, the patient may be taught to empty the diverticulum by expressing the overlying skin. When such dribbling persists, there is little the urologist can do but excise the diverticulum to restore the urethra to a more normal uniform caliber.

Hair eventually grows in the urethra whenever scrotal skin is incorporated in the neourethra during the hypospadias repair. It is usually an incidental finding at cystoscopy in adulthood. Rarely, calculi form on the hairs or the hairs grow out of the meatus. Hair may be avulsed through the cystoscope using small grasping forceps. Rarely, the problem is so troublesome that the urethra must be opened to permit staged total dipilliation or replacement by non-hair-bearing skin.

99

RECONSTRUCTION OF MALE EXTERNAL GENITALIA WITH ELEPHANTIASIS

Charles M. Holman, Jr., M.D., Phillip G. Arnold, M.D.,
Maurice J. Jurkiewicz, M.D., and
Kenneth N. Walton, M.D.

From the Divisions of Urology and Plastic Surgery, Joseph B. Whitehead Department
of Surgery, Emory University and Affiliated Hospitals, Atlanta, Georgia

Urology / December 1977 / Volume X, Number 6

ABSTRACT—The surgical rehabilitation of a patient with severely deformed and functionally disabled genitalia due to long-standing lymphedema and infection is described and illustrated. The term "elephantiasis" has been applied to such gross lesions. Appropriate surgery to the penis, scrotum, and perineum has yielded a gratifying result. The principles and techniques of the surgical approach in such an undertaking are presented and discussed.

Massive elephantiasis of the genital region is an entity rarely seen in the United States. When such cases have been reported, lymphogranuloma venereum, hidradenitis suppurativa, and tuberculosis have been the most common causes.[1] Repeated or persistent inflammation leads to lymphatic obstruction in the cutis and subcutis. When the lymphatic channels become damaged, stasis and accumulation of lymph results. Regional nodes and larger lymphatic channels are secondarily affected leading to increased lymphedema of the cutis. The end result is the fibrosis which is clinically recognized as elephantiasis.

Herein we report our experience with radical excision of the involved skin and subcutaneous tissue in a case of genital elephantiasis secondary to hidradenitis suppurativa, and reconstruction with split-thickness skin grafting.

CASE REPORT

A forty-nine-year-old black male was admitted because of massive elephantiasis of the penis, scrotum, and perineum. He had been hospitalized five years previously

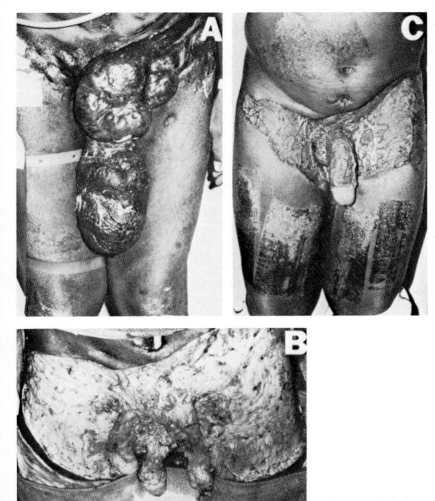

Fig. 1. Genital elephantiasis of seven years' duration (A) Preoperative appearance. (B) After radical excision. (C) Postoperative appearance.

with slightly less extensive disease and a suprapubic catheter had been inserted because of difficult urination. Etiologic evaluation including tuberculin and fungal skin tests, cultures, lymph node biopsy, and Frei tests was inconclusive. He had been managed conservatively during the interval period with no improvement. Indeed, he was completely disabled and had become a social outcast.

On physical examination the patient had involvement of the penis, scrotum, perineum, inguinal areas, and left axilla with woody, inflamed, indurated lymphademateous skin riddled with multiple draining sinuses (Fig. 1A). Laboratory evaluation disclosed a moderate anemia (hemoglobin 7.9, hematocrit 27) and hypoalbuminemia but normal renal function and liver enzymes.

Following admission, the patient was placed on a high caloric, low-residue diet. His anemia with ameliorated by transfusions. Frequent whirlpool baths and preoperative broad-spectrum antibiotics brought his superficial infection under control.

Ten days after admission, he underwent radical excision of the skin and subcutaneous tissue in the involved areas under hypotensive anesthesia. The penis, spermatic cords, and testicles were preserved (Fig. 1B), and the entire area of excision was covered with fine mesh gauze impregnated with silver sulfadiazene.

He was returned to the operating room forty-eight hours later where inspection disclosed a clean wound, suitable for grafting. His penis was then covered with thick, split-thickness skin grafts taken from the upper abdominal wall. The testicles and spermatic cords were also covered with grafts which were meshed 1.5:1 with the Tanner mesher to conform with the scrotal contour.

The remainder of the open areas was covered with meshed grafts five days later with silver sulfadiazene having been used to protect the recipient site in the interval period. Within five days the patient was started on whirlpool therapy for debridement and the topical antibiotic was applied after each treatment to retard bacterial colonization of the grafts.

Physical therapy was instituted soon thereafter, and the patient was ambulatory three weeks after original surgery. At present the suprapubic catheter has been removed, and the patient is voiding normally with minimal residual (Fig. 1C). He has gained 20 pounds, anemia has vanished, and he is socially active. Gone is the stench and the stigma which had essentially forced him into seclusion for the previous seven years.

COMMENT

Although genital elephantiasis is infrequently seen, the physical and psychologic morbidity associated with the lesion is significant. Treatment may also be delayed or avoided because of the surgeon's reluctance to undertake such an extensive reconstruction. This case illustrates that a satisfactory functional and cosmetic result can be obtained by the use of basic principles of reconstructive surgery.

Careful preoperative preparation is essential and may substantially reduce postoperative morbidity. As noted, anemia is often present and may be multifactorial.[2] When this has been evaluated, transfusion to near normal levels is often indicated prior to surgery. In addition, clotting abnormalities should be sought for and corrected. Superficial infection can be improved by frequent whirlpool therapy and judicious use of antibiotics.

Nutritional and vitamin deficiency states can be improved by appropriate dietary supplementation. A short bowel preparation period has been suggested by some to minimize postoperative fecal contamination of grafts.[3] We found that the use of an elemental diet (Vivonex) for several days preoperatively was helpful while maintaining an anabolic state.

During the operative procedure, hypotensive anesthesia is valuable in reducing blood loss. Meticulous hemostasis is necessary for early grafting and reduced bacterial colonization. Because oozing can be a problem, the delayed primary closure by skin grafting used in this case appeared to be appropriate.

Peripherally the excision should include a margin of uninvolved skin and is carried down to the deep fascia to encompass all sinus tracts. As noted by many au-thors,[1,4,5] the pathology is limited to the cutis and subcutis and can be completely excised in this manner. Once the proper plane of dissection is reached, one can proceed centrally by sharp dissection.

The spermatic cords should be identified at the external rings and their surrounding fascia preserved. Special care is necessary in the area of the fossa ovale to avoid injury to the femoral vessels. The superficial saphenous vein should be ligated and divided at this point.

Considerable difficulty may be encountered in iden-tification of the penis because the weight of the genitalia may have stretched the suspensory ligaments and drawn a portion of the lower abdominal skin and fascia beneath the pubis. Once the shaft of the penis has been identified, the dorsal neurovascular bundle must be carefully pre-served. Most frequently, the preputial skin is uninvolved because of its anatomically different lymphatic supply. It should be preserved as it is useful in supporting the penis after grafting.

As noted by Conway et al.[4] early grafting is both feasible and desirable. While immediate grafting might have been successful, the delayed primary technique will permit inspection for hematoma or wound sepsis.

The penis was covered with thick split-thickness skin graft (0.018 inch) taken from the upper abdominal wall with a Reese dermatome to ensure uniform thick-ness. The grafts were sutured in place with absorbable sutures, and the suture lines were interdigitated ventrally to eliminate late ventral curvature. A nonadherent dress-ing was placed on the grafts followed by a bulky compression dressing. By using an indwelling Foley catheter and supporting sutures placed through the pre-putial skin, the penis was suspended in overhead traction to avoid kinking.

The testicles were positioned anatomically and su-tured together. They were then covered with thin split-thickness skin grafts (0.012 inch) which were meshed 1.5:1 with the Tanner mesher. Meshed grafts offer the advantages of superior conformity in irregular areas, adequate escape routes for serosanguineous exudates and pus, and, when expanded, more efficient coverage of large recipient sites.

Silver sulfadiazene is a very effective topical anti-biotic, widely used in patients with thermal injuries. It can be applied without disruption of the grafts and does not impede their growth. Bacterial destruction of the grafts did not occur in this man in significant quantity and in those small areas where it did occur, epitheliali-zation from the surrounding viable grafts filled the void.

Early utilization of whirlpool therapy (four days postgrafting) allowed for gentle mechanical debridement of bacteria, serosanguineous exudate, nonviable graft, and residual topical antibiotic. In addition, it afforded an opportunity to examine the recipient bed daily under optimal conditions.

Pooling of secretions in the groin creases did constitute a problem. With the patient supine, all secretions tended to accumulate there and threatened to ruin the grafts overlying the femoral vessels. This was dealt with by fashioning an orthopedic splint to rotate the hips externally and allow for adequate drainage.[4]

Altanta, Georgia 30322
(DR. WALTON)

REFERENCES

1. Wood AM, and Kerr WJ, Jr: Elephantiasis of the penis and scrotum, in Horton CE, Ed.: Plastic and Reconstructive Surgery of the Genital Area, Boston, Little, Brown, and Company. 1973, p. 507
2. Tennant F, Bergeron JR, Stone OJ, and Mullins JF: Anemia associated with hidradenitis suppurativa, Arch Dermatol 98:138, 1968

3. Mladick RA, Horton CE, Adamson JE, and Carraway, JR: Hidradenitis suppurativa of the perineum, p. 515, op cit[2]
4. Conway H, et al: The surgical treatment of chronic hidradenitis suppurativa, Surg Gynecol Obstet 95:455, 1952
5. Bulkley GJ: Scrotal and penile lymphedema, J Urol 87:422, 1962

Commentary: Management of Male External Genitalia with Elephantiasis

Thomas Zaydon, Jr., Charles Cardany, Charles Devine, Jr., and Charles E. Horton

Elephantiasis in a clinical term describing the gross lesions that result from chronic lymphedema. The disease is characterized by hard, brawny edema with rough, thickened skin. Elephantiasis represents an irreversible state for which surgical management is the only definitive remedy. This Commentary will review the surgical approach to elephantiasis of the scrotum and penis.

Lymphedema, regardless of etiology, begins with obstruction of the lymphatic channels. The valvular function of the channels is disrupted, and accumulation of lymph occurs. This stagnant lymph becomes a fertile ground for inflammation and a fibroproliferative response. In time, the lymphatic channels become sclerosed, with the skin becoming hard and wrinkled. The result is a fibrosis that is clinically recognized as elephantiasis.

The exact physical chemistry that leads to the fibroproliferative response is unknown. It has been shown *in vitro* that fibroblasts will form connective tissue under proper conditions. The high concentration of albumin in stagnant lymph fluid, as well as the increased tendency toward fibroplasia in dark-skinned persons, are contributory factors. Subclinical anomalous variations of lymphatic drainage might explain why elephantiasis affects some people more than others.

Elephantiasis of the penis and scrotum may be due to primary or secondary etiologic factors. The essential defect in primary elephantiasis is aplasia or hypoplasia of the lymphatics. The lower extremities are usually involved, and genital manifestations are uncommon. Milroy's disease is an example of primary lymphedema. Secondary etiologic factors are the most frequent cause of genital elephantiasis. The majority of these cases are due to either tuberculosis or repeated nonspecific bacterial infections. Filariasis accounts for a small percentage of cases in North America.

The noninfectious causes of elephantiasis are all mechanical. Scars in the groin, radiation therapy, and cancer surgery are etiologic factors. Strategically placed tumors have the potential to obstruct lymphatic drainage. Lymphedema of the scrotum and penis may be the first sign of an internal malignancy; therefore, occult neoplasm must be ruled out where the etiology is unclear.

Historically, surgical therapy has been directed toward either draining lymph by diverting it to normal channels (lymphangioplasty) or excising the elephantoid areas followed by primary closure or grafting (lymphangiectomy).[1-6] Lymphangioplasty includes the use of a variety of methods to bridge the involved tissue with the uninvolved tissue. Livermore[7] described unsuccessful attempts at improving lymphatic drainage by the use of pedicle flaps from the scrotum to the thigh. McDonald and Huggins[8] were more successful in using a procedure in which surgically created lateral scrotal skin defects were sutured to corresponding thigh defects. Lymphangioplasty has only been useful in treating mild degrees of lymphedema and not in elephantiasis.

Lymphangiectomy has been the most successful approach

for elephantiasis. Since elephantiasis is a disease of the superficial lymphatic system, excision of the skin and subcutaneous tissue leaves behind uninvolved fascia. The coverage of this remaining tissue can be dealt with in many ways. Standard textbooks of tropical medicine[9] describe burying the testicles in the thigh and covering the penile shaft with skin grafts. Muller and Jordan[10] observed that in the majority of cases, uninvolved posterior scrotal skin can be spared in the excision to provide testicular cover. By this approach, a functional scrotum may be reconstructed in an anatomically correct position. We have successfully treated genital elephantiasis by the method of Muller and Jordan.

SCROTAL LYMPHEDEMA

Scrotal elephantiasis is usually seen in conjunction with a similar process in the penis but may occur without penile involvement. Attention is initially turned to the involved scrotum before any procedure on the penis. The primary goal is to obtain relief from the weight and bulk of excessive scrotal tissue. Since the disease is benign and slowly progressive, radical surgery is not necessary. Testicular function should be preserved, and an asthetically acceptable scrotum should be reconstructed. Excision of the thickened and involved tissue must be complete to prevent recurrence. Most failures occur where the removal is not radical enough. However, the posterolateral scrotal skin near the perineum is but little affected and, if normal, should be preserved for scrotal reconstruction.

Care must be exercised to avoid injury to the penis, which may be hidden in the enlarged scrotum. By careful manipulation it may be possible to deliver the penis to the scrotal surface. Usually a long tunnel of preputial skin forms a channel from the external urinary meatus to the scrotal surface. There is rarely obstruction to the flow of urine.

If the penis is visible, the incision is started at its base. When the penis is hidden, the incision is started at the middle of the pubic symphysis. Massively edematous dorsal penile skin may be hardly identifiable. Many grossly dilated veins are encountered along with the marked interstitial edema of the skin and subcutaneous tissue.

Once the penis is clearly identified and placed out of the way, the upper scrotum is widely bivalved. The dissection is continued down until the cords are identified bilaterally and then extended to identify the testicles. Both testicles are divided from the gubernacular attachments, wrapped in a moist sponge, and placed on the abdomen. Periareolar tissue around the spermatic cords should be preserved.

The scrotal dissection is extended downward and posteriorly, with the intent of leaving a U-shaped, posteriorly based, uninvolved perineal flap for reconstruction of the new scrotum. Following resection of the disease tissue, attention is then turned toward correcting hydrocoeles, if present. The hydrocoele is excised by opening the tunica vaginalis and everting it back on itself, in the classically described fashion. The testicles are then sutured together.

The posteriorly based perineal flap is brought up over the testicles, and, in a T-shaped revision, a new scrotum is fashioned. Although the remaining scrotal tissue may appear to be under great tension, it has the phenomenal capacity to stretch out markedly. Three Penrose drains are placed in the corners of the "Ts". If sufficient scrotal skin is not present to reconstruct testicular cover, we feel that the best option is to use split-thickness skin grafts in conjunction with the spared posterior wall. The two testes are sutured together and to Colles' fascia. Meshing of the skin grafts allows for better conformity in the irregular areas. Excellent survival of these grafts is expected, and a reasonably normal looking scrotum is formed. Some authors have reported difficulty in securing the grafts to the recipient bed. Deep quilting sutures and a bolster-type tie over dressing ensure successful skin grafting.

The testes may be implanted in the subcutaneous tissue of the medial thighs. We do not favor this method, but it is popular and therefore discussed. An oblique incision is made in the medial aspect of the upper thigh, as far posteriorly as the length of the spermatic cords will allow. In a more anterior position, the spermatic cords would be under tension when the thighs were spread apart. The testicles should be staggered at different levels so that they will not directly oppose each other. Since this procedure is expedient, it is a feasible choice for those debilitated patients who would not endure extensive reconstructive procedures.

Disagreement exists on the future function of testicles buried in subcutaneous thigh pockets. Although the temperature may be approximately the same, the normal thermoregulatory process is lost. In addition, thigh implantation does not satisfy the asthetic need to reconstruct a scrotum where nature intended it to be, in a separate sac below the abdomen.

Minor degrees of lymphedema that have not progressed to elephantiasis may be treated by support of the penis in an upright position against the abdomen, diuretics, and prompt treatment of the lymphangitis. However, once the disease has progressed to a brawny edema of extensive proportions, excision of the involved tissue is indicated. As in the scrotum, the surgical correction involves the superficial lymphatic system.

PENILE LYMPHEDEMA

The procedure to address penile lymphedema begins with the insertion of a urinary catheter. Some authors use a tourniquet around the base of the penis to provide a drier surgical field. We do not feel this aids the surgical dissection. The margins of excision are marked at the beginning of the procedure which resects all involved tissue. A circular incision is made at the base of the penis. The incision is then extended along the lateral aspect of the shaft to the tip of the prepuce. A second circular incision is made 2 mm proximal to the glans. Dissection is then extended through the hypertrophied skin and edematous subcutaneous tissue down to the fascia. The diseased tissue between the two circular incisions is literally peeled away from the underlying fascia. Accumulation of lymphatic fluid at this junction provides a plane for sharp dissection.

The glans is usually uninvolved. No more than 2 mm of tissue is preserved proximal to the glans. This distal cuff may later develop into an edematous ring, which may cause difficulty during coitus.

The areolar tissue around Buck's fascia serves as an excellent graft bed. A 0.015-in to 0.017-in split-thickness skin graft is obtained. Its width should be approximately 2 cm greater than the circumference of the penis. The graft is then tailored around the shaft of the penis to fit between the base and distal cuff.

The location of the suture line is controversial. A ventral suture line will simulate the median raphe; however, a dorsal suture line may be preferred, since the contracted skin graft will then accentuate the normal curvature of the penis in erection. The suture line should be interdigitated to give more length to the penis in erection. We prefer the ventral interdigitated suture line.

An adequate pressure dressing is needed. One method is to secure a fine mesh xeroform dressing with fluffed gauze to stent the dressings with previously placed sutures. A second method is to build a cylindric fence around the penis, which acts to compress the gauze. In either method, the previously placed urethral catheter is suspended by overhead traction to avoid kinking.

Follow-up study on surgical correction of genital elephantiasis is limited. Immediate results are gratifying, since the troublesome bulky tissue is now absent. Patients resume social interaction for the first time since the disease became severe. Although some impairment of sensation is reported, most patients can resume sexual relations. No recurrence of genital elephantiasis is reported in skin grafted areas in long-term follow-up periods. Adjacent tissue previously uninvolved may become edematous and require further reconstruction in time.

REFERENCES

1. Berger JC: The surgical treatment of elephantiasis of the scrotum. Plast Reconstr Surg 19:67, 1957

2. Bulkley GJ: Scrotal and penile lymphedema. J Urol 87:422, 1962

3. Holman CM, Arnold PG, Jurkiewicz MJ et al: Reconstruction of male external genitalia with elephantiasis. Urology 9:576, 1977

4. Khanna NN: Surgical treatment of elephantiasis of male genitalia. Plast Reconstr Surg 46:481, 1970

5. McKay HA, Meehan WL, Jackson AC et al: Surgical treatment of male genital lymphedema. Urology 9:284, 1977

6. Morales PA: Surgical treatment of severe lymphedema of the penis. J Urol 72:880, 1954

7. Livermore GR: Pseudo elephantiasis of the scrotum. J Urol 51:170, 1944

8. MacDonald DF, Huggins C: Surgical treatment of elephantiasis. J Urol 63:187, 1950

9. Wood AM, Kerr WJ Jr: Elephantiasis of the penis and scrotum. Horton CE (ed): Plastic and Reconstructive Surgery of the Genital Area, pp 507–513. Boston, Little, Brown Co, 1973

10. Muller GP, Jordan CG: Elephantiasis nostra. Am Surg 97:226, 1933

ANNOTATED BIBLIOGRAPHY

Berger JC: The surgical treatment of elephantiasis of the scrotum. Plast Reconstr Surg 19:67, 1957

The surgical treatment of elephantiasis of the scrotum is outlined by a detailed case report. The author states that retaining uninvolved posterior scrotal skin allows the surgeon to construct a new and smaller scrotum. This technique excises diseased tissue yet allows an asthetic and functional scrotum to be reconstructed.

Bulkley GJ: Scrotal and penile lymphedema. J Urol 87:422, 1962

Four patients with penile and scrotal lymphedema were treated by excision of diseased tissue with satisfactory results. The removal of such tissue must be complete to prevent subsequent procedures. Construction of a new scrotum was by adjacent skin of the perineum or thigh. Free grafts were rarely needed to provide coverage. Excision offers the quickest and most direct approach. Surgical procedures for the restoration of lymphatic drainage lead to a high percentage of failure.

Muller GP, Jordan CG: Elephantiasis nostra. Am Surg 97:226, 1933

This article is one of the classic works on the subject of elephantiasis. Medical management is briefly reviewed, and several surgical methods are presented. Modifications of the Kondoleon procedure are the basis for our current approach to scrotal and penile elephantiasis.

Wood AM, Kerr WJ Jr: Elephantiasis of the Penis and Scrotum. pp 507–513. In Horton CE (ed): Plastic and Reconstructive Surgery of the Genital Area. Boston, Little, Brown & Co., 1973

This chapter presents an overview of elephantiasis of the penis and scrotum. The lesion is described, and clinical features are reviewed. Preoperative management is given special emphasis.

Overview: Lymphedema

John Marquis Converse

The reading of the paper by Holman, Arnold, Jurkiewicz, and Walton and the Commentary leaves me puzzled. My own experience has been mostly confined to upper and lower extremity lymphedema. What seems to be missing is a rigorous follow-up study on the patients treated by a technique that appears to be successful.

The resection of the lymphedematous tissue, including the subcutaneous tissue and the deep fascia down to muscle, has been a technique used for the treatment of lymphedema of the lower extremity. Cutaneous resurfacing is achieved by split-thickness skin grafting. The results of these operations have not been permanent. It would be of great value if long-term reports could be obtained after the treatment of lymphedema of the male external genitalia by the technique described.

In upper extremity lymphedema, some degree of success has been achieved by a microsurgical lymphatic–venous bypass in lymphedema following radical mastectomy. Microsurgical lymphatic anastomoses are being attempted. When the testes are exposed, burying them in subcutaneous thigh pockets with the plan to replace them in a reconstructed pendulous scrotum appears to be the best procedure.

GENITAL INJURIES: ETIOLOGY AND INITIAL MANAGEMENT

David A. Culp. M.D.

Department of Urology, University of Iowa Hospitals and Clinics, Iowa City, Iowa

Urologic Clinics of North America—Vol. 4, No. 1, February 1977
Symposium on Genitourinary Trauma

The incidence of genital trauma in civilian life compared to other body areas is relatively low. Protection from ordinary injuries is afforded by the relative mobility of the genitalia. Objects traveling at high rates of speed are responsible for the greater portion of genital injuries and, as would be expected, occur most frequently during times of armed combat. While the conditions in our mechanized and industrialized civilian society may be nonetheless hazardous, genital wounds are not seen with the same frequency since fragmentation devices, the major cause of combat injuries to the genitalia, are seldom encountered. Most civilian genital injuries occur in industrial, farm, or automobile accidents, athletic contests, or attempts at self-mutilation or malicious assault.

Genital injuries are classified in much the same manner as injuries to other portions of the human body: nonpenetrating wounds (contusions), penetrating wounds (incisions, lacerations, or punctures), avulsions (partial or complete), thermal, chemical and electrical burns, and irradiation injury.

NONPENETRATING INJURIES

Nonpenetrating genital wounds result from a crushing or bruising force that does not break the surface epithelium, but produces extensive damage to the underlying tissues. More extensive devitalization of tissue may accompany contusions than lacerations or perforations. Blood vessels rupture and considerable exudation develops in response to tissue damage. Because of the elastic nature of tissue in this area, hemorrhage and edema are not limited by mounting tissue pressure. The scrotal sac and penile coverings may enlarge several times normal size and extravasated blood may discolor the area completely, extending into the perineum and abdominal regions. Initially, tissue damage and increased tissue tension are responsible for pain, but as inflammation develops about the devitalized tissue and blood clots, it too becomes a contributing factor.

During the acute phase treatment is aimed at relief of pain, prevention and control of additional hemorrhage and exudation, and immobilization to promote healing of the injured tissues. Immediately after the injury the scrotum should be elevated and ice bags applied to the area of the injury. Rest and elevation diminishes the pain and facilitates venous and lymphatic drainage. Cold helps to reduce the pain, hemorrhage, and edema. Furthermore, it reduces the subsequent inflammatory reaction. Pressure dressings may be applied for the control of hemorrhage and edema when the aforementioned measures fail to provide adequate control. Persistent hemorrhage requires an exploratory operative procedure to secure the open vessels and provide adequate drainage.

Suspected associated trauma to the deep structures is an indication for immediate surgical exploration. Crushing injuries from blunt objects that impinge the testis between the force and the bone frequently produce rupture of the tunica albuginea with hemorrhage and extravasation of intracapsular contents. The tough tunica albuginea, covering the testis and corporal penile bodies, provides an excellent layer of tissue for repair of these injuries. Bleeding from the corporal tissue subsides when the fascial coverings have been approximated with interrupted longitudinal mattress sutures. In the severely disrupted testis it may be necessary to excise some of the extravasated seminiferous and interstitial testicular tissue, but as long as the multiple fragments appear to be viable, an attempt should be made to return as much of the intracapsular substance as possible beneath the reconstructed tunica. When the bleeding is confined by an intact tunica vaginalis a hematocele develops and should be drained. The use of oral medication for control of pain and prophylaxis against infection is advisable.

Unless complicated by uncontrollable hemorrhage the acute cellular reaction to a contusion subsides within 3 to 4 days. At this point changes in therapy should be instituted, primarily aimed at encouraging the reduction of the edema. The cold applications should be changed to heat, which accelerates fluid absorption by increasing blood flow through the injured area. Likewise, subcutaneous injections of 300 turpidity reducing units of hyaluronidase into the edematous area facilitates reduction of the extravasated fluid. Unresolved edema or intrascrotal collections of fluid and blood frequently require late incision and drainage, particularly should they become secondarily infected.

PENETRATING INJURIES

Wounds that penetrate the skin of the genitalia are of three types: incised, lacerated, or punctured. All penetrating wounds, regardless of their type, have the common problem of introduction of foreign material and bacteria into the wound. Based on this common property, of at least potential infection, the principles of management are the same. They consist of lavage, debridement, and removal of foreign bodies, hemostasis, inspection and repair of the underlying structures, adequate drainage, repair and closure of the wound, systemic antibiotics, and postrepair wound care.

Every penetrating wound contains some bacteria and foreign material. Initially, the microorganisms simply lie on the surface of the wound. Approximately 6 to 8 hours are required for the organisms to become acclimated to their environment and to begin proliferation and invasion. During this time the wound is contaminated but not infected, and proper lavage administered during this interval provides a more favorable climate for the normal healing process. In addition, superficially located foreign bodies such as soil, dust, grease, and bits of clothing can be removed by copious lavage. Generous quantities of cleansing agents and water are used to cleanse the area about the wound as well as the wound itself. Every portion of the wound should be reached and where necessary, an irrigating syringe should be utilized. After the wound has been thoroughly scrubbed large quantities of nonirritating solution should be flushed through the wound. The main advantage of lavage is mechanical washing of the wound. Sterile normal saline in a copious quantity is capable of rendering the wound free of contaminating microorganisms and superficially imbedded foreign materials. Antimicrobial or antiseptic agents may be used, but generally in the immediate period of wound care, they have little to offer since they are not permitted to remain in the vicinity of the organisms long enough to exert a beneficial action. They are, however, useful in the care of a secondarily infected wound.

Nonviable tissue is a hindrance to normal reparative processes and should be removed. The criteria indicative of tissue injured beyond repair are deep, bluish-black discolorations and absence of bleeding from the cut edges of the tissue. If there is the slightest doubt of the viability of tissue, it should be excised, and since the tissue in this area has elastic properties, large quantities of devitalized tissue can be removed without compromising primary repair. Likewise, foreign bodies driven or carried into the deeper areas of the wound should be sought and removed. This is particularly true of the puncture type of wound where deep-seated, contaminated foreign bodies do not have ready access to the surface and subsequently produce abscesses that require drainage. Unless the puncture wound is known to have been produced by a relatively clean instrument, it should be incised to the point of puncture and the depths exposed, cleansed, and drained. Probing from the surface only introduces more contamination and aggravates hemorrhage.

Extravasated blood delays wound healing by interposing a foreign body between healing surfaces, producing tension within the wound and providing an excellent cultural media for implanted bacteria. Therefore, blood within the wound should be washed away and the bleeding vessels securely ligated with incorporation of as little surrounding tissue as possible. Large stumps of ligated tissue act as a foreign body and further delay wound healing. Diligent search and control of bleeding vessels within the wound is eventually rewarding since the spontaneous cessation of blood flow from an open vessel in this area is less likely than in other areas of the body because of the elastic properties of the tissue.

After the wound has been thoroughly cleansed, hemostasis achieved, and devitalized tissue removed, repair of the injured tissue should be undertaken. The object is to restore the tissue to as normal a relationship as possible so that the healing process will proceed with a minimum of fibrous tissue replacement. When the wound is carried into the depths of the scrotum, the testes and their associated structures should be thoroughly inspected for bleeding and viability. Repair of the ruptured or lacerated testis and corpora cavernosa is performed as described in the nonpenetrating injuries section. Having reestablished the intactness and soundness of these structures, they should be returned to their normal position and tissue drains inserted to provide an avenue of escape for unwanted collections of serum, blood, and infection.

Primary closure should be accomplished unless there is gross contamination of the wound. Under these circumstances, it is advisable to dress the wound without closure and delay the approximation of the wound edges until the infection has been eradicated. Anaerobic gangrenous infections with vibrial, spirochetotic, anaerobic streptococci, staphylococci, and other gas forming organisms may result in complete loss of genital skin. When primary closure is possible, the tissue should be accurately approximated without tension with absorbable suture material. Wide spectrum systemic antibiotics to combat mixed infection, commonly encountered, should be initiated promptly and continued until satisfactory wound healing is evident.

Application of a dressing to this portion of the body is somewhat difficult to maintain. Where satisfactory hemostasis has been achieved, a loose, sterile dressing held in place with a scrotal support is adequate. Occasionally, a pressure dressing is helpful in minimizing the postrepair oozing and edema. Should such a dressing be necessary, it should be removed immediately if pain, tenderness, or elevated temperature develops, and certainly within 48 hours to provide inspection of the wound. Otherwise, dressings should be disturbed as little as possible. Drains are removed when the wound drainage diminishes and infection has failed to develop.

AVULSIONS

Avulsions of the genital skin occur when the patient's clothing becomes entangled in a revolving machine and is ripped from his body, carring with it the enmeshed skin of the penis and scrotum (Fig. 1). Pain is not a major problem with this type of injury. Patients complain more of back and leg pain than discomfort from the denuded area. Presumably this is due to the patient's resisting the force drawing him into the machine. In addition, the appearance of the genitalia creates great

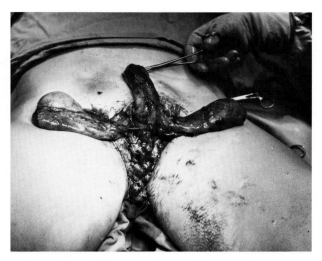

Fig. 1. Avulsion injury of male genitalia. Skin coverings of penile shaft and scrotum have been completely avulsed. Extension of tear extends into the perineum. Note abrasions of left thigh eliminating this area as a source for a skin graft.

anxiety for the patient so that mind analgesics and sedatives are required to provide comfort for the patient until more definitive therapy can be employed. Since the skin separation occurs along relatively bloodless planes, superficial to Buck's fascia in the penile shaft and just beneath the dartos fascia of the scrotum, bleeding is rarely severe. Furthermore, the mobility of the skin coverings over the penile shaft and scrotum generally provides protection for the corporal bodies and testes. However, cases have been encountered in which the glans penis and/or testes have been ripped away with avulsed skin (Fig. 2). Emergency treatment usually consists of analgesics to relieve pain, application of warm, sterile, moist saline packs, broad spectrum antibiotics, tetanus and gas gangrene antitoxin, and transportation to a hospital for prompt definitive repair.

Repair of traumatic avulsion is an emergency procedure and should be performed within 8 to 12 hours after the injury before wound sepsis develops. Conservative therapy is contraindicated when there is a clean demarcation between viable and nonviable tissue.

The best covering for the denuded penile shaft is a split-thickness skin graft (Fig. 3). Pedicle flap grafts have been mobilized from the adjacent abdomen or thigh, but usually produce an objectionable result because of the large, hairy grotesque appearance of the skin covering and the soft flabby nature of the organ, even during erection (Fig. 4). Occasionally, the general condition of the patient may not warrant an immediate repair or the

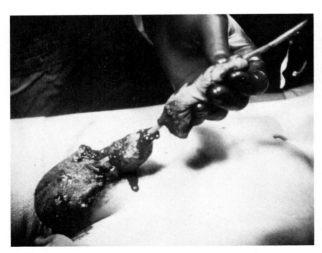

Fig. 2. Avulsion injury of male genitalia with separation of glans penis and attached penile skin.

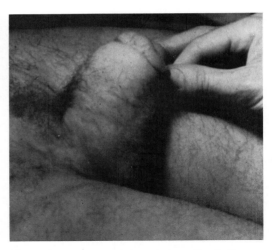

Fig. 4. Appearance of denuded penile shaft covered with pedicle flap grafts from adjacent area.

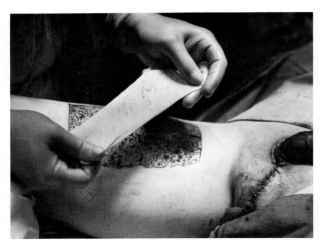

Fig. 3. Split-thickness graft from adjacent thigh for covering of denuded penile.

available skin has been depleted, and under these circumstances, the penile shaft may be buried in a subcutaneous tunnel in the abdominal wall, allowing the glans to protrude through a buttonhole incision until a more favorable time for a definitive grafting occurs.

A long hood of skin may remain attached to the corona in an uncircumcised victim, but this should not be used to cover the penile shaft, even though it may reach all the way to the base of the penis. Marked edema of long duration has been observed when this partially avulsed skin has been used. Generally, it is advisable to excise this skin, leaving only a small cuff at the corona to which the skin graft can be anchored.

Completely avulsed skin should not be reapplied for it invariably becomes necrotic and infected and must be subsequently removed, leaving an unacceptable base for grafting (Fig. 5). Additional time is then required to prepare the area to accept the graft (Fig. 6). Successful results are much more likely to be achieved with primary graft than one applied to a secondarily infected bed, even after weeks of debridement and antibiotic therapy.

Prior to the application of the split thickness graft, the denuded area should be cleansed with saline, fragments of hair, clothing and dirt removed, hematomas incised and drained, and bleeding areas completely controlled. Scrubbing with cleansing agents should be comfined to the surrounding, intact skin. A donor site that will yield a split-thickness skin graft of 10 × 20 cm is selected, and unless the adjacent inner thigh skin has been abraded by the twisting clothing, this area is usually the most convenient. The thickness of the graft is dependent upon the bed to which it will be applied. When it is clean and uninfected, a relatively thick graft (0.020–0.024 inch) may be employed. If the bed has been secondarily infected and has required preparatory treatment, a thinner graft (0.012–0.016) should be used.

A 10 × 20 cm graft is more than adequate in the majority of cases. Even though the penis is in a semierect state immediately following the injury, the 10 cm width encircles the shaft without undue tension. In fact, the semirigidity of the penis contributes to the survival of the graft, helping to maintain contact with all portions of the graft and insuring better graft survival.

A basting suture is inserted through the intact skin at the base of the penis to hold the graft in place while the graft edges are approximated along the dorsum of the shaft with a continuous mattress suture of 4-0 silk.

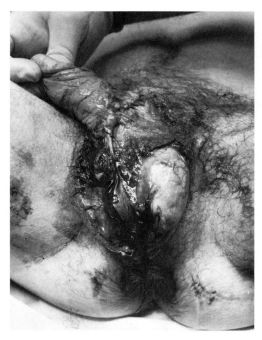

Fig. 5. Results of applying completely denuded skin. Necrosis and secondary infection delays covering with skin graft.

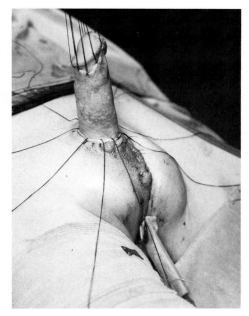

Fig. 7. Split-thickness skin graft applied to denuded penile shaft. Seam placed on dorsal penile surface. Graft anchored at the base and coronal areas. Insufficient scrotal skin to permit housing of both testes. Left testis placed in thigh pocket.

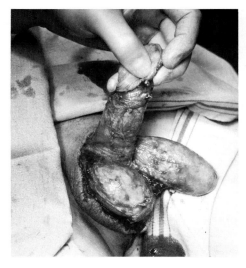

Fig. 6. Denuded area of patient in Fig. 5 after 2 weeks of debridement and local therapy.

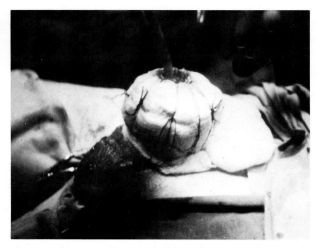

Fig. 8. Bolus stent dressing held in place by utilizing tails of coronal and base anchoring sutures.

Longitudinal contracture of the suture line rarely occurs but it is placed on the dorsum to prophylactically prevent a hypospadic chordee should it develop.

Additional sutures are placed at the base of the penis and corona, anchoring the graft firmly (Fig. 7). These sutures should be long enough to be tied over a bolus dressing in a longitudinal direction and should be strong enough to resist breaking when tied with enough tension to hold the dressing firmly against the penile shaft. The bolus dressing should be thickest at midshaft so that an even pressure is created on the graft (Fig. 8). The bolus

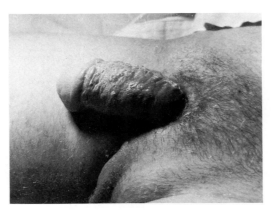

Fig. 9. Immediate postoperative appearance of split-thickness skin graft on penile shaft.

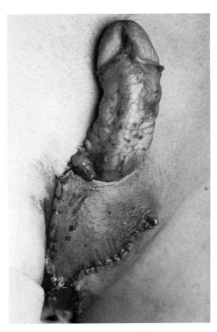

Fig. 10. Primary closure of scrotum.

dressing is then converted to a conical one and strapped firmly to the abdominal wall to prevent shifting of the graft on its bed.

An indwelling urethral catheter is inserted to prevent urinary soilage of the dressing. Prophylactic antimicrobial therapy is continued and the patient is kept immobilized in bed for several days to prevent displacement of the graft. The glans penis should be visible at the top of the dressing and repeatedly inspected for discoloration. Occasionally, an ecchymotic appearance of the glans occurs from blood extravasated at the time of the injury. If there is any suspicion that the circular dressings have compromised the circulation in the corpora, they should be removed. Otherwise, they should remain intact 10 to 14 days.

At the end of 2 weeks the graft no longer requires protection, but when it is exposed to the air, small crusts may form on tiny points not completely covered by epithelium (Fig. 9). These are usually very superficial and due only to the loss of graft epidermis. Application of a nonirritating, water-soluble ointment softens these crusts and permits healing without contractile scars. In 3 to 4 weeks the graft is well enough established to withstand friction from clothing, but the patient should be advised to abstain from sexual intercourse for another 3 to 4 weeks. While there is a decreased sensitivity to the penis, none of the patients complains of sexual impairment. Several have noted that a greater stimulus is required to produce an ejaculation, but this has not been detracting to either the patient or his partner.

With the loss of scrotal skin, the question of testicular housing arises. If sufficient scrotal skin remains, it is the covering of choice, even though initially it may appear to be under considerable tension (Fig. 10). Usually within a few months the scrotum will have returned to a more nearly normal size, permitting normal testicular mobility.

When insufficient skin prevents primary repair, other measures for housing the testes must be made. The main function for the scrotum is to provide an area outside the body cavity where the temperature is ideal for spermatogenesis and free mobility prevents trauma from normal activity.

Pedicle skin grafts from the adjacent thighs have been utilized to construct a new scrotum. However, thigh pockets offer the simplest covering available, but have been condemned by some as being too warm for testicular function. In order to determine the advisability of burying the exposed testes in subcutaneously constructed thigh pockets, simultaneous temperatures were recorded in a series of patients with iron constantine thermocouples situated in the abdominal cavity, scrotum, and thigh, both superficial and deep to the subcutaneous fat. The scrotal readings were considered to be the desired temperature while the abnormal readings presented conditions under which testicular function would be most likely to degenerate. The thigh recordings showed that the thermocouples placed beneath the subcutaneous fat paralleled those of the abdominal cavity and those superficial to the subcutaneous fat paralleled those of the scrotum. These findings indicated that testes implanted immediately beneath the skin of the thigh would be housed in an environment sufficiently cool to permit normal spermatogenesis. The patients treated in this manner have normal sperm counts so that superficial thigh implantation allows ample mobility and offers

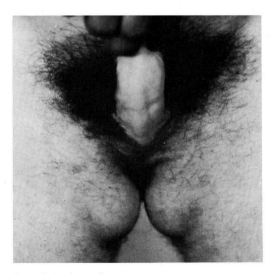

Fig. 11. Bilateral thigh pockets.

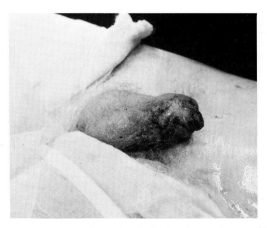

Fig. 12. Charred penile shaft skin from electrical burn.

suitable temperature environment for the denuded testis (Fig. 11). Initially, the testes are restricted in motion, but after several weeks, the testis establishes the right of domicile and moves about freely within the expanded thigh pocket. They should be implanted as far posteriorly as possible in the thigh to prevent stretching of the spermatic cord when the thighs are abduced and at different levels to allow crossing of the thighs without discomfort.

BURNS

Secondary, partial or complete loss of tissue may occur with thermal, chemical, or electrical burns (Fig. 12). In most instances, genital involvement is only a small facet of the patient's burn problem, and is therefore treated in the course of managment of the overall problem. Initially, the degree of damage inflicted by the burns should be evaluated to ascertain its extent and degree of damage. The immediate therapy consists of relief of pain, evaluation and treatment of concomitant injuries, particularly those of vital structures, administration of oxygen, fluid therapy to prevent or correct shock, and control of infection. Local or direct therapy of the burned area should not take precedence over systemic and supportive therapy. However, both may be undertaken simultaneously.

Anoxia and hypoxia demand first attention. The airways should be unobstructed and oxygen should be administered when there is dyspnea, cyanosis, and a cherry red discoloration of carbon monoxide hemoglobinemia burns about the face or 50 percent or more involvement of the body surface. An intravenous polyethylene catheter should be inserted, by cutdown if

necessary, to provide ready access for the administration of plasma, plasma expanders, electrolyte solution, and glucose and water. Prophylactic tetanus therapy with booster doses of 1 cm of toxoid should be given where applicable and 5000 units or more of tetanus antitoxin in patients who have not been previously immunized. Systemic antibiotic therapy should be administered daily.

Local therapy consists of initially removing gross dirt in adherent clothing under aseptic precautions prior to the application of multiple layers of sterile gauze soaked with 0.5 percent silver nitrate solution. The dressing is kept moist by wetting the external layers with additional silver nitrate solution. Dressings are changed as needed for debridement of the burn. Extensive debridement or excision of burn tissue is employed only where the total extent of the burn is small and the line of demarcation between viable and devitalized tissue is obvious. Generally, within 10 days to 2 weeks the burn eschar will separate from the underlying granulation tissue, and if the granulations are clean and uninfected, the area is ready for skin grafting.

Chemical burns should be treated with copious flushing. Generally, sterile water or saline is adequate to dilute and remove the chemical which has not been fixed by the tissue. If the type of chemical is known, specific neutralizing fluids may be used, although care should be taken not to injure further the already damaged tissue. In the case of acid burns, sodium bicarbonate solution may be used; for alkaline burns, a dilute acetic acid solution. Should these not be available, extensive flushing with water is usually satisfactory in terminating the chemical. At this point the management is essentially the same as for thermal burns.

The severity of electical burns may not be appreciated immediately. In contrast to chemical burns, the dissemination of electrical current through the tissue produces an extensive coagulation necrosis for considerable distance beyond the limits of the obvious burn. Because of this extensive, unrecognized involvement there is a poor line of demarcation for several days. Furthermore, the electrical current passes through the body from the point of contact to the point of grounded exit and burns occur in both areas. Since the limits of the burns cannot be accurately assessed until a sharp line of demarcation is established, the immediate therapy is conservative management aimed at preventing secondary infection in the injured tissues. After demarcation has been accurately established, therapy consists of excision of the devitalized tissue with immediate skin grafting or continued local therapy until the dry eschar separates, exposing the healthy granulation tissue which can then be safely grafted.

RADIATION INJURY

The cause of radiation injury to the genitalia is exposure to forms of ionizing radiation. The acute cutaneous manifestations are loss of hair, pigmentation, and erythema with vesiculation. The skin swells and becomes scaly and excoriated with weeping, denuded areas that may proceed to gangrene. The more delayed effects consist of telangiectasia, atrophy, brawny edema, verrucal formations, and cutaneous neoplastic changes. Isolated genital involvement with radiation injury is rare, but may occur when insufficient protection is provided during the administration of radiation therapy to lesions in the area of the genitalia. Generally, no therapy is indicated for correction of the cosmetic appearance in this area, and when extensive radiation has produced cutaneous changes, the healing capacity of the local tissue has been so severely impaired that excision and grafting is rarely advisable.

Department of Urology
University of Iowa Hospital and Clinics
Iowa City, Iowa 52240

Commentary: Genital Injuries

Charles E. Hawtrey

Culp's review of genital injuries provides an excellent overview for practitioners. Using the general outline of Culp's article, additional information, obtained from the literature, will assist in patient care.

Avulsion of genital skin, electrical burns, wounds from high-velocity missiles, and grossly contaminated wounds represent special circumstances for delayed primary coverage of genital wounds. Topical solutions or agents, 0.5% silver nitrate, scarlet red (5%), and biologic dressings provide temporary surface coverage while underlying tissue planes demarcate. Hawtrey and colleagues used irradiated pigskin xenografts to cover large, irregular surfaces over the perineum and phallus.[1] The xenografts, which are replaced every 3 days, stimulate a clean bed of granulation tissue before autodermic graft placement. The authors recommend vents in the xenograft and loose bolster dressings to avoid loculation of purulent material under the graft.

Peters and Bright suggest another important principle involved in managing avulsion injuries. Reporting on the complications of trauma surgery, these authors report disfiguring lymphedema when preputial mucosa is retracted and sutured to cover the raw penile shaft.[2,3] The appropriate management includes excision of preputial mucosa to the coronal sulcus and full- or split-thickness skin grafting of the shaft, using the established techniques outlined by Culp.

LOSS OF THE SHAFT OF THE PENIS

Recent advances in microvascular surgery have produced gratifying results following traumatic amputation of the penis. Tuerk and Weir and others replanted the glans penis after traumatic amputation.[4,5] Usually a corporal segment was excised, allowing vascular and neural anastomoses without these techniques. The operating microscope facilitates a meticulous reanastomosis of the dorsal penile vein or other large venous branch from the distal stump of the amputated penile segment. Five 6–0 or 7–0 microsurgical sutures close the splayed vein in an elliptic anastomosis. Perfusion of the corpus cavernosa is not difficult, and anastomosis of the central corporal artery is not required. The tunica albuginea is approximated, and the corpus spongiosum is closed with 6–0 chromic catgut sutures, with the knots placed within the urethral lumen. This technical detail, advocated by Devine and Horton, leaves no chromic catgut suture knots in the healing corporal space.[6] A second outer fascial tunic layer completes the urethral repair, and suprapubic cystostomy drainage avoids the need for an indwelling urethral catheter as a source of infection from the presence of the foreign body. The small nerve bundles accompanying the dorsal vein are repaired with 10–0 Prolene sutures, and skin closure completes the surgical repair (Fig. 13).

URETHRAL INJURY

Urethral stricture therapy is refined by adding the patch graft technique outlined by Devine and colleagues.[7–9] Several technical details ensure an excellent surgical result. As the authors suggest, careful fashioning a round tip of the elliptic graft avoids problems of terminal necrosis of the graft (Fig. 14).

The preputial skin graft provides an excellent elastic, non-hair-bearing source of the skin. Careful removal of the loose areolar dermal connective tissue is a requirement. Helpful tools for the defatting process include fine Church scissors and 10 × loupe glasses. The gossamer connective tissue fibers are elevated with forceps and incised with the Church scissors held parallel to the skin surface. If a colored towel is placed under the skin, the graft becomes progressively translucent as

loose areolar connective tissue is removed. As the tissue plane is established, the connective tissue rolls off the underlying tissue, providing a full-thickness graft. Saline irrigations keep the epithelial surface viable and help to identify the remaining dermal connective tissue, which swells when irrigated.

After the graft is defatted, careful suturing technique with 4–0 or 6–0 chromic sutures (depending on the patient's age) completes the patch graft. The surgical square knot should remain within the urethral lumen and avoid exposing the healing subcutaneous tissue to reaction from the suture material. The graft should be large enough to accommodate the maximum caliber of the urethra, which is anticipated postoperatively (*i.e.,* 22 French in an adult male). The stenting urethral catheter, which maintains the graft's position against its vascular base, should have a slightly smaller caliber (18 to 20 French). Since the small catheter distends the urethral lumen adequately, pressure necrosis of the graft is obviated and urethral secretions drain around the catheter.

Subcutaneous tissues require special attention, including wide mobilization to allow closure without tension. Whenever

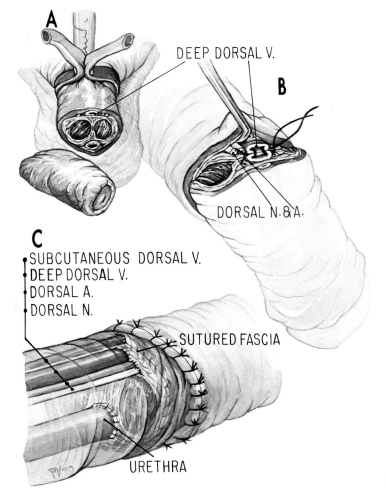

A

DEEP DORSAL V.

B

DORSAL N. & A.

C

SUBCUTANEOUS DORSAL V.
DEEP DORSAL V.
DORSAL A.
DORSAL N.

SUTURED FASCIA

URETHRA

Fig. 13.

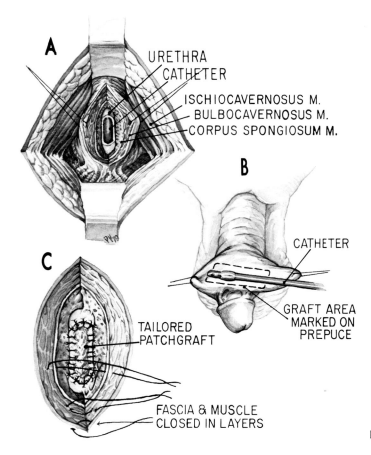

A

URETHRA
CATHETER
ISCHIOCAVERNOSUS M.
BULBOCAVERNOSUS M.
CORPUS SPONGIOSUM M.

B

CATHETER
GRAFT AREA
MARKED ON
PREPUCE

C

TAILORED
PATCHGRAFT

FASCIA & MUSCLE
CLOSED IN LAYERS

Fig. 14.

possible, fresh muscle tissue such as the bulbocavernosus muscle should be mobilized to cover the graft, thus ensuring adequate vascularization of the graft. Again, the sutures should be placed so that the knots are away from the graft. Subcutaneous tissue and skin closure should eliminate dead space and accurately oppose the skin edges.

External trauma in women becomes more common as motorcycling and snowmobile sports speed persons toward immobile objects. Straddle injuries produce extensive crush injury and displacement of perineal structures. The principles of adequate debridement and cleansing of the wound permit primary closure if the patient is seen within 6 to 8 hr of the time of injury.

Injuries of the female urethra have been classified by Symmonds, who divided urethral injuries into four groups.[10] Type I injuries preserved some bladder neck function, while Type IV were so severe that bladder neck and trigonal function might be lost. Symmonds's reparative technique included wide mobilization of the anterior contractile urethra to form a urethra of 10 to 12 French caliber. The lateral vaginal tissues or a labial flap were used to cover the urethra, and in some situations a urethral suspension was used as a secondary procedure.

REFERENCES

1. Hawtrey CE, Culp DA, Hartford CE: The management of severe inflammation and traumatic injuries to the genital skin. J Urol 108:431, 1972

2. Peters PC: Complications of penile surgery. In Smith RB, Skinner, DG (eds). Complications of Urologic Surgery: Prevention and Management, p 420. Philadelphia, WB Saunders, 1976

3. Bright TC III, Peters PC: Injuries of the external genitalia. In Harrison JH, Gittes RF, Perlmutter A, et al (eds): Urology, pp 933–935. Philadelphia, WB Saunders, 1978

4. Tuerk M, Weir WH Jr: Successful replantation of a traumatically amputated glans penis. Plast Reconstr Surg 48:499, 1971

5. Shulman ML: Re-anastomosis of the amputated penis. J Urol 109:432, 1973

6. Devine CJ Jr, Horton CE: One-stage repair–III. In Horton CE (ed): Plastic and Reconstructive Surgery of the Genital Area, pp 273–281. Boston, Little, Brown & Co, 1973

7. Devine PC, Horton CE, Devine CJ, et al: Use of full-thickness skin grafts in repair of urethral strictures. J Urol 90:67, 1963

8. Devine PC, Sakati IA, Poutasse EF, et al: One-stage urethroplasty: Repair of urethral strictures with free full-thickness patch of skin. J Urol 99:191, 1968

9. Devine PC, Devine CJ, Horton CE: Anterior urethral injuries: Secondary reconstruction. Urol Clin North Am 4:157, 1977

10. Symmonds RE: Loss of the urethral floor with total urinary incontinence. Am J Obstet Gynecol 103:665, 1969

ANNOTATED BIBLIOGRAPHY

Hawtrey CE, Culp DA, Hartford CE: The management of severe inflammation and traumatic injuries to the genital skin. J Urol 108:431, 1972

Twenty-seven patients were evaluated and treated for injuries involving the genital integument. Traumatic avulsion and infection caused most of the skin loss. Temporary surface covering was accomplished by sterile, irradiated porcine zenografts. The authors shortened hospital stays and improved wound care with the "biological dressing."

Peters PC: Complications of penile surgery. In Smith RB, Skinner DG (eds): Complications of Urologic Surgery: Prevention and Management, p 420. Philadelphia, WB Saunders, 1976

Peters calls on his extensive surgical experience to describe complications of circumcision, urethral reconstruction, amputation injury, priapism treatment, and skin avulsion. Safe, effective surgical techniques are described and provide a means for avoiding surgical complications.

Bright TC III, Peters PC: Injuries of the external genitalia. In Harrison, Gittes, Perlmutter, et al: (eds): Urology, pp 933–935. Philadelphia, WB Saunders, 1978

Expanding on their experiences outlined in *Complications of Penile Surgery,* the authors outline surgical plans for scrotal and testicular injuries. Principles for electrical burns and their delayed debridement are also outlined.

Tuerk M, Weir WH Jr: Successful replantation of a traumatically amputated glans penis. Plast Reconstr Surg 48:499, 1971

The authors describe the reanastomosis of the distal corpus cavernosa, urethra, and glans penis without special attention to the central arteries or neural bundles. The 1-yr follow-up result was associated with an 85% take and intact sensation during sexual activity.

Shulman ML: Re-anastomosis of the amputated penis. J Urol 109:432, 1973

The author reports the eighth incident of penile amputation. The repair of urethra and corporal bodies did not include dorsal venous or central artery repairs. Immediately postoperatively the patient experienced lymphedematous swelling of the penis. One year postoperatively sensation was confined to a zone supplied by the intact penile skin. Intromission and ejaculation were possible 1 yr postoperatively.

Devine CJ Jr, Horton CE: One-stage repair–III. In Horton CE (ed): Plastic and Reconstructive Surgery of the Genital Area, pp 273–281. Boston, Little, Brown & Co, 1973

Although the techniques described by Dr. Devine are used for hypospadias repair, the use of prepucial "free" grafts can be used to replace lost segments of the urethra. The techniques of "defatting" the free graft and suture techniques represent important plastic surgical principles for urethral repair.

Devine PC, Horton CE, Devine CJ, et al: Use of full thickness skin grafts in repair of urethral strictures. J Urol 90:67, 1963

Dr. Devine outlines his technique for free graft urethroplasties in adults with urethral strictures, which varies slightly from the hypospadias techniques. He also reports his first six patients; four patients experienced complete relief of stricture symptoms.

Devine PC, Sakati IA, Poutasse EF, et al: One stage urethroplasty: Repair of urethral strictures with free full-thickness patch of skin. J Urol 99:191, 1968

The authors report twenty-six repairs in twenty-three patients who had good surgical results. A good result was characterized by free urinary flow and no postoperative dilations over 1-yr follow-up study. Most patients required single patch graft repairs, while occasional patients received more than one graft.

Devine PC, Devine CJ Jr, Horton CE: Anterior urethral injuries: Secondary reconstruction. Urol Clin North Am 4:157, 1977

Replacement of anterior urethral strictures by full-thickness grafts requires special suturing techniques and principles that evolve from the authors' discussion. The authors use suprapubic cystostomy, "deflated" full-thickness grafts from prepucial skin, stenting catheters, and fine suture techniques to provide excellent surgical results.

Overview: Male Genitalia After Trauma

John Marquis Converse

Avulsion of scrotal skin of the shaft of the penis usually occurs in a relatively bloodless plane superficial to Buck's fascia, just beneath the dartos layer. As a result of the cremasteric reflex, the skin is easily torn off of the scrotum; the plane of cleavage is superficial to the cremaster through a layer of loose areolar tissue. The amount of avulsed skin varies.

Wartime wounds of the external genitalia are more extensive, involving the urethra and partial or even total loss of the penis and testicles. In the Vietnam conflict, because of the extensive use of land mines, injuries to the male genitalia accounted for 41.6% of all urogenital trauma.[1]

Such injuries are best treated by the collaborative efforts of urologic and plastic surgeons as well as the surgical and orthopaedic team required to stabilize a patient in shock with multiple injuries, the most frequent being fracture of the pelvis and the head of the femur and extensive surrounding soft tissue damage.

To resurface the shaft of the penis, scrotal skin has been used.[2,3] Scrotal skin has the advantages of being extensile; this characteristic facilitates penile erection. It also permits removal of a considerable amount of skin, and the resulting defect can be closed by direct approximation. However, tension should be avoided because, in addition to necrosis of the skin and infection, tension can be fatal for the normal function of the testes.

Partially avulsed skin can often be replaced, even if it remains attached by a relatively narrow pedicle, unless it is badly contused or excoriated. If the flap of partly avulsed skin appears to be insufficiently vascularized by the pedicle, it can be completely detached, treated, and applied as a full-thickness graft.

When split-thickness skin grafting is required, for example, in a case of total avulsion of penile skin, a single graft is wrapped around the shaft and sutured on the ventral aspect. To avoid postoperative linear contracture, a Z-plasty procedure is done at the midway point of the ventral suture line. A similar procedure is done at the proximal end of the skin graft to avoid circular contracture. During the grafting the penis is maintained extended. One of the best dressings appears to be a polyurethane sponge, which is wrapped around the shaft; its edges are sutured on the ventral aspect as advocated by Arneri.[4] The polyurethane exerts moderate pressure, is slightly extensile, and maintains the penis in an extended position.

Arneri has mentioned that in the rare situation where skin grafting is not feasible, the denuded penis can be temporarily buried in a subcutaneous tunnel in the pubic or inguinal region, allowing the glans to protrude through the buttonhole incision. A Foley catheter is inserted. Delayed skin grafting is then performed when conditions are favorable.

Skin grafting after avulsion of scrotal skin is feasible if the testicles are not denuded. The meshed split-thickness skin graft, as mentioned in the Commentary, is preferable as a technique for cutaneous resurfacing because this type of skin graft adapts well to the recipient site. The surgeon must remember that the scrotal skin retracts. As a result, the scrotal defect is an apparent, not a true, defect. The retracted scrotal skin should be mobilized to diminish the size of the defect before skin grafting.

When the penis is irredeemably destroyed, reconstruction by the technique of Arneri is the preferred one. This technique uses an abdominal skin tube. The urethra is reconstructed by the technique of Denis Browne. Rigidity is provided by a costal cartilage graft or a penile prosthesis.

REFERENCES

1. Salvatierra O, Bucklew WB, Morrow JW: Penetrating ureteral injuries. Surg Gynecol Obstet 128:591, 1969

2. Banham AR: Total denudation of the penis. Br J Surg 36:268, 1948

3. Casson PR, Bonnano PC, Converse JM: Penile skin replacement: Indications and techniques. In Hueston (ed): Transactions of the Fifth International Congress of Plastic and Reconstructive Surgery. Scarborough, Ont, Butterworth & Co, 1971

4. Arneri V: Reconstruction of the male genitalia. In Converse JM (ed): Reconstructive Plastic Surgery, Vol 7, 2d ed, p 3902. Philadelphia, WB Saunders, 1977

PART THIRTY-SEVEN

TRANSSEXUAL SURGERY

PENILE RECONSTRUCTION IN IRRADIATED PATIENT

Richard J. Boxer, M.D. and Timothy A. Miller, M.D.

From the Urology and Plastic Surgery Section, Surgical Service, Veterans Administration Wadsworth Hospital Center, and University of California School of Medicine at Los Angeles, California

Urology / April 1976 / Volume VII, Number 4

ABSTRACT—Reconstruction of a penis using a modified Gillies technique was performed on a forty-one-year-old man who had a total penectomy, inguinal node dissection, and 6,000 rads of cobalt-60 irradiation for carcinoma of the penis. The three different surgical techniques for reconstructing the penis are discussed in detail. It is our belief that reconstruction of a urethra and placement of a baculum in penile reconstruction after radiation therapy have more disadvantages than advantages. The literature is reviewed.

The patient who has had an accidental or surgical penectomy undergoes tremendous psychologic trauma and presents an enormous challenge to genitourinary and reconstructive surgeons. Because of the important considerations of urinary drainage, close contact must be maintained between the two services. Psychiatric consultation is also helpful.

The case to be presented is a forty-one-year-old man who had a penectomy, bilateral inguinal node dissection, and 6,000 rads of cobalt-60 therapy for squamous cell carcinoma of the penis. The fact that this man had been irradiated made this case unusual and uniquely challenging. The skin of the thighs and lower abdomen could not be utilized for local reconstructive methods, and therefore the thoracoepigastric area was employed. A thoracoepigastric tubed pedical flap was constructed and

then transposed to the penile stump using the contralateral forearm as a carrier.

The patient understood that the reconstruction of his penis would involve a number of procedures over an extended period of time. He also understood that the penis would lack sensation and that there would be extensive scarring from the reconstructive procedure. The patient nevertheless felt strongly about proceeding. His single-mindedness and determination were an undeniable factor in the eventual successful outcome.

CASE REPORT

A forty-one-year-old black male was admitted to a private hospital in Los Angeles, in September, 1972, for excision of a fungating lesion of the glans penis. The patient had

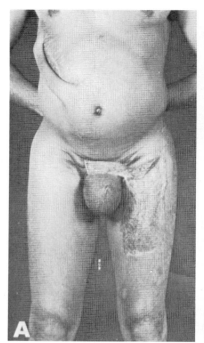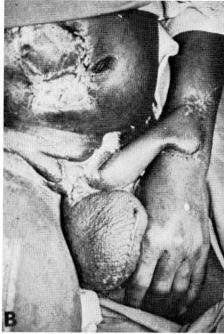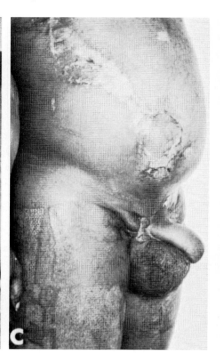

Fig. 1. (A) Thoracoepigastric tubed pedicle has been developed; previous unsuccessful attempt at resurfacing irradiated indurated pubic tissue by means of left groin flap can be seen. (B) Using contralateral forearm as carrier, bipedicle tube is transposed to penile stump. (C) Six months after completion of reconstruction.

a twenty-year history of condyloma acuminata, treated with podophyllin and surgical excisions. Pathologic report noted moderately well-differentiated squamous cell carcinoma in the specimen. a partial amputation of the penis was done on September 29, 1972, along with superficial bilateral inguinal node dissection. No tumor was found in the inguinal nodes, but well-differentiated squamous cell carcinoma of the penis was noted to extend along the corpus spongiosum in the lymphatics, and was present in the line of excision.

On October 24, 1972, total penectomy was performed. No residual tumor was found. Although considerable lymphedema of the scrotum developed, the patient had an uneventful recovery. Between November, 1972, and January, 1973, he received 6,000 rads cobalt-60 modality to the anterior and posterior pelvis to include deep pelvic lymph nodes. His perineal urethrostomy subsequently required several dilations.

The patient entered the Veterans Administration Wadsworth Hospital Center on July 23, 1973, for reconstruction of a penis. Excretory urogram (intravenous pyelogram) cystoscopy, femoral arteriogram, technetium bone scan, liver-spleen scan, chest roentgenogram, SMA-6, SMA-12, and complete blood cell count were all within normal limits. It was impossible to utilize any local tissue in the irradiated, indurated pubic area. On September 6, 1973, a right thoracoepigastric tubed bipedicle flap was constructed (Fig. 1A). The inset of the proximal portion of the tube was placed into the left forearm on February 21, 1974. The detachment of the distal pedicle and transposition of it to the pubic area utilizing the forearm as a carrier was done on June 24, 1974 (Fig. 1B). The final procedure of releasing the proximal pedicle from the forearm was done on July 29, 1974, after two delay procedures. Subsequently he required a split-thickness skin graft on the distal end of the new phallus (Fig. 1C).

The patient is satisfied with the reconstructed penis. In spite of the fact that he has no sensation in the phallus, he obtains satisfaction from sexual intercourse.

COMMENT

There are presently three basic surgical procedures for reconstructing the penis.[1] These methods have evolved over the past one hundred years of surgical experience.

In 1948, Gillies and Harrison[2] developed a three-stage procedure which utilized lower abdominal tissue to create a penis. An abdominal tubed pedicle is developed within a surrounding abdominal tube (Fig. 2). This

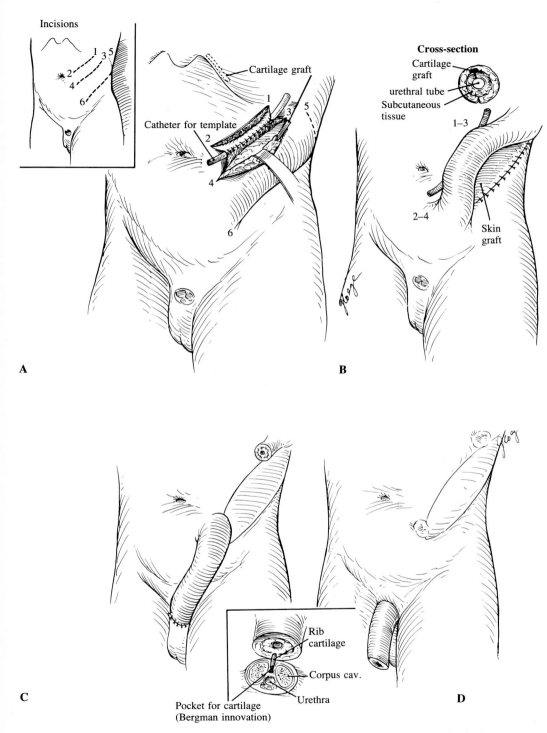

Fig. 2. Gillies procedure. (*A*) Stage 1: Urethra is formed, cartilage inserted, and split-thickness skin graft applied. (*B*) Stage 2: Four weeks later tube is elevated and skin graft applied (Stages 1 and 2 can be done at same time). (*C*) Stage 3: Six weeks later double pedicle tube is transferred to penile stump; cartilage is inserted between corpora cavernosum (Bergman innovation[16]). (*D*) Stage 4: Eight weeks later distal end of graft is freed.

is done by three parallel incisions made in the abdominal wall to form a urethral tube within the penile tube. The first incision (most lateral) is the lateral border of the abdominal tube. The second (middle) incision is the medial border of the abdominal tube, as well as the lateral border of the urethra. The third and smallest incision is the medial border of the urethra. An autologenous rib cartilage is placed in the subcutaneous tissue as a baculum. The inferior portion of the pedicle is based on the superficial inferior epigastric artery, and the venous return through the thoracoepigastric vein. The pedicle is then rotated down and the epithelial tube is anastomosed to the existing urethra.

The Goodwin-Scott technique utilizes the scrotum for the phalloplasty.[3] The urethra is formed tubing the ventral midline scrotal skin. The new meatus lies at the bottom of the scrotum. The next stage is the second stage of the Cecil hypospadias procedure. Parallel or zigzag incisions are extended from the base of the penis down to the bottom of the scrotum to the new urethral meatus. The incisions on either side of the new urethra are extended through the subcutaneous tissue to include some of the dartos. This tissue is lifted upward and sutured on its vental surface to form the new penis, with the new urethra within (Fig. 3).

An alternate technique developed in 1971 by Kaplan

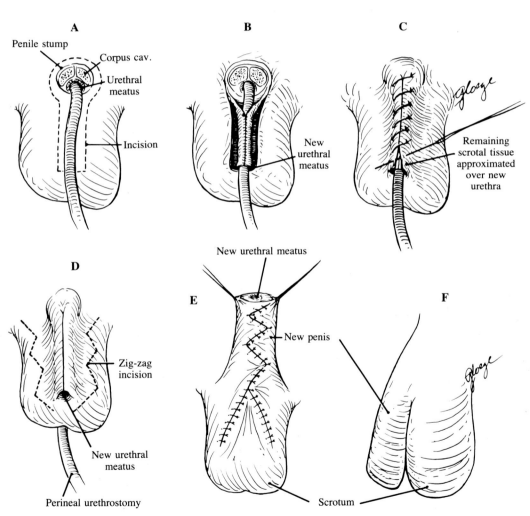

Fig. 3. Goodwin–Scott procedure. First stage: (*A, B, C*) New urethra is constructed from midline scrotal skin. Second stage: (*D*) Eight weeks later incisions are made on each side of new urethra to form new phallus; (*E*) new phallus and urethra are elevated; and (*F*) side view of new phallus.

and Wesser[4] uses the scrotum for urethra as in the Goodwin-Scott procedure. However, a medial thigh flap based on the inguinal ligament is utilized simultaneously to reconstruct the dorsal aspect of the new penis. In the second and final stage this flap is elevated and sutured on the ventral surface, thus forming the penis. The femoral branches of the genitofemoral nerve are left intact, providing the reconstructed penis with sensation (Fig. 4).

In 1959, Gelb, Malament, and Lo Verme[5] reported a case in which squamous cell carcinoma of the glans penis developed in a forty-year-old man after thirteen years of chronic balanitis. This patient had a bilateral inguinal node dissection and subsequent necrosis of the inguinal region negating the possibility of local flap reconstruction of the penis. However, the patient had not had radiation therapy. Gelb used the forearm as a carrier of an abdominal wall skin flap.[5] In our case local

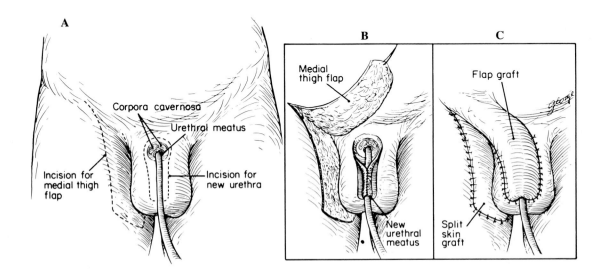

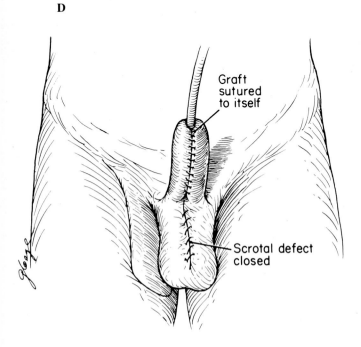

Fig. 4. Kaplan–Wesser procedure. Stage 1: (*A*) Racquet-shaped incision is made in scrotum around penile stump, forming new urethra; (*B*) medial thigh flap based on inguinal ligament is brought over to cover new urethra; and (*C*) flap is sutured to scrotum and defect is covered with split-thickness skin graft. Stage 2: (*D*) Two weeks later incision is reopened and the flap is raised from scrotum together with new urethra; flap is curled under and sutured to itself.

tissue pedicles could not be used because of the profound irradiation changes. Distant tissue was required.

In the follow-up period, our patient reported that his reconstructed penis was capable of penetrating into a vagina. This brings up an important point: does the phalloplasty require a baculum? Costal cartilage,[5–8] acrylic,[3,9,10] Silastic,[11] and periosteal tibial bone with steel mesh[12] have all been used to give permanent substance to the phallus. There are many significant problems in placing foreign bodies into poorly vascularized tissue. These must be surmounted. In addition, a permanently erect penis runs the additional risk of frequent trauma. Some authors believe that scar tissue gives enough firmness for intromission.[13,14] In transsexual female to male surgery, Noe, Birdsell, and Laub[15] never place a baculum, but use a removable prosthetic support.

Should a urethra be reconstructed? In reconstruction of a penis by the Gillies, Goodwin-Scott, or Kaplan-Wesser procedure, a urethra is an integral part of the procedure. However, in these procedures, patients had had traumatic amputations and no irradiation to the pelvis. The potential severe complications inherent in urethral reconstruction in a patient such as the one presented herein, outweighed the potential advantages. It is usual practice in transsexual surgery not to reconstruct the urethra, principally because of the additional complications inherent in this portion of the reconstruction.[15]

Division of Urology
Department of Surgery
Center for Health Sciences
Los Angeles, California 90024
(DR. BOXER)

Acknowledgment: Dr. Clifford N. Edwards, Kaiser Hospitals, for referring this patient to us, and Gwynn Gloege for the medical illustrations.

REFERENCES

1. BOXER, R. J.: Reconstruction of the male external genitalia. Surg Gynecol Obstet 141:939, 1975
2. GILLIES, H. D., and HARRISON, R. J.: Congenital absence of the penis with embryological considerations. Br J Plast Surg 1:8, 1948
3. GOODWIN, W. E., and SCOTT, W. W.: Phalloplasty. J Urol 68:903, 1952
4. KAPLAN, I., and WESSER, D.: A rapid method for constructing a functional sensitive penis. Br J Plast Surg 24:342, 1971
5. GELB, J., MALAMENT, M., and LoVERME, A.: Total reconstruction of the penis. Plast Reconstr Surg 24:62, 1959
6. ARNERI, V.: A new method of phalloplasty; a film presentation, Second International Congress of Plastic Surgery. London, 1959
7. BORGORAS, N.: Über die volle Plastiche Wieden herstellung eines Zum Koitess Fahigen Penis (Peniplastica Totalis). Zentralbl Chir 63:1271, 1936
8. FRUMKIN, A. P.: Reconstruction of male genitalia. Am Rev Soviet Med 2:14, 1944
9. LOEFFLER, R. A., and SAYEGH, E. S.: Perforated acrylic implants in the management of organic impotence, J Urol 84:559, 1960

10. MORALES, P. A., O'CONNOR, J. T., and HOTCHKISS, R. S.: Plastic reconstructive surgery after total loss of the penis. Am J Surg 92:403, 1956
11. PEARMAN, R. O.: Treatment of organic impotence by implantation of penile prosthesis. J Urol 97:716, 1967
12. MUNAWAR, A.: Surgical treatment of male genitalia. J Internat Coll Surg 27:352, 1957
13. FARINA, R., and FREIRE, G. DE C.: Total reconstruction of the penis (phalloplasty). Plast Reconstr Surg 14:351, 1954
14. JULIAN, R., KLEIN, M. H., and HUBBARD, H.: Management of a thermal burn with amputation and reconstruction of the penis. J Urol 107:580, 1969
15. NOE, J. M., BIRDSELL D., and LAUB, A. R.: The surgical construction of male genitalia for the female-to-male transsexual. Plast Reconstr Surg 53:511, 1974
16. BERGMAN, R. T., HOWARD, A. H., and BARNES, R. W.: Plastic reconstruction of the penis. J Urol 59:1174, 1948

Commentary:
Female Transsexual Surgery

Richard J. Boxer and Harvey A. Zarem

The ideal in female-to-male transsexual surgery is to create totally functional and aesthetically pleasing male external genitalia; however, the present state of the art and the realistic goals of most females seeking male genitalia mandate only an organ that is aesthetic to prevent "discovery" and secondarily capable of accomplishing successful intercourse. The "fear of discovery" by others with whom the transsexual works or socializes is the primary goal, with sexual gratification of the

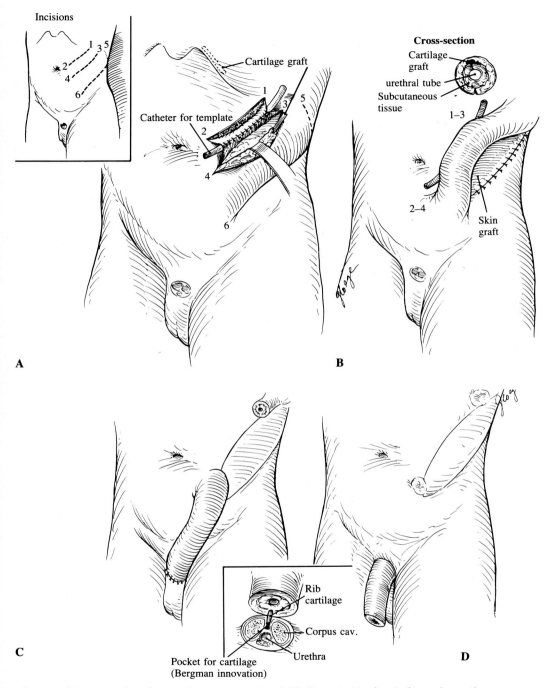

Fig. 5. Gillies procedure for penile reconstruction.[5] (A) *Stage 1*: Urethra is formed, cartilage inserted, and split-thickness skin graft applied. (B) *Stage 2*: Four weeks later, tube is elevated and skin graft applied (stages 1 and 2 can be done at the same time). (C) *Stage 3*: Six weeks later, double pedicle tube is transferred to perineum; silastic rod can be inserted where rib cartilage is illustrated.[11] (D) *Stage 4*: Eight weeks later, distal end of graft is freed. (Boxer RJ, Miller TA: Penile reconstruction in irradiated patient. Urology 7[4]: 403–408, 1976. Used with permission.)

person or consort being a second priority; thus, using the constructed penis as a conduit for urine is not nearly as important. Because the vast majority of complications stem from constructing the urethra, many authors do not recommend it. The anatomic location of the female urethra is more posterior and inferior than the normal male urethra. Thus, creating a urethra within a penis requires a major anatomic change in position as well as length. This advancement of the urethra exposes the patient to stricture and fistula. Millard's illustration of a functional penis including a urethra in a female transsexual indicates that the procedure is possible.[1] However, variation

in the configuration of perineums accounts for this difficulty, which we encountered in carrying out a transsexual operation.

The psychological aspects of a patient seeking sexual reassignment must never be underestimated. However, the female-to-male transsexuals as a group are not as hysterical and have a greater sense of reality than the male-to-female transsexuals.[2] The etiology of the condition of transsexualism is not defined. The two theories include the theory of postnatal social environment etiology versus the theory of prenatal endocrine environment of the developing thalamus.[3,4] The basic requirements for consideration for transsexual surgery is the

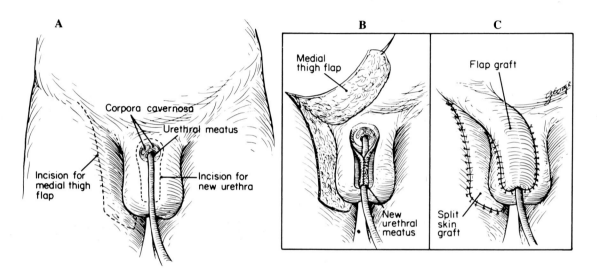

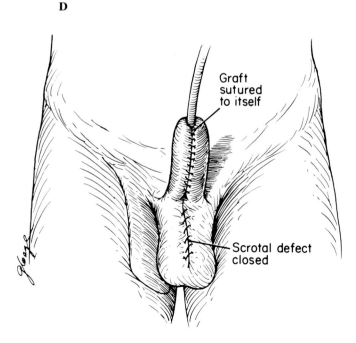

Fig. 6. Kaplan–Wesser procedure.[6] *Stage 1:* (A) A racquet-shaped incision is made in the scrotum around the penile stump, forming a new urethra. In transsexual surgery the labia minora are used to create the urethra. (B) The medial thigh flap based on the inguinal ligament is brought over to cover the new urethra. (C) the flap is sutured to the scrotum (labia) and the defect is covered with split-thickness skin graft. *Stage 2:* (D) Two weeks later the incision is reopened and the flap is raised from the scrotum (labia) together with the new urethra; the flap is curled under and sutured to itself. (Boxer RJ, Miller TA: Penile reconstruction in irradiated patient. Urology 7[4]: 403–408, 1976. Used with permission.)

patient must have lived in the male role in work and socially for at least 1 yr before requesting surgery. Furthermore, intensive psychiatric evaluations must conclusively and without reservation state that the patient needs the surgery. Patients receive testosterone during their 1 yr of evaluation.

Reduction mammoplasties are the first operations. The hysterectomy and bilateral salpingo-oophorectomy may be done at the time of the first stage of phallus construction or may be done as a separate procedure. This depends on the method of phallus creation. We presently use the thigh flap method as a combination of the Gillies and Harrison technique (Fig. 5) and that of Kaplan and Wesser (Fig. 6).[5,6]

The techniques used in transsexual surgery were derived from experience in the reconstruction of the male external genitalia.[7] The tubed groin flap used by Puckett and Montie in the previous article was first described by McGregor and Jackson.[8] The vascular supply and (theoretic) sensation by the ileoinguinal make it ideal. However, the midline tubed abdominal wall flap also has a rich blood supply. By either maintaining the clitoris in its normal position or splitting it and transposing it more anteriorly, the patient can have the pudendal nerve sensation to reach orgasm. Many patients have stated that they can reach orgasm without the pudendal stimulation just by the act of satisfying their partner.

The use of the Scott prosthesis manages the problem of erection but increases the complications of infection and poor vascularity in the flap.[9] Even in a normal penis, the Scott prosthesis has the problem of infection and mechanical failure. We have not tried this method yet and anxiously await further follow-up study. Fibrosis is often enough to allow intromission, although the penis is not erect. Uninflatable prostheses have been successfully used but still are complicated by infection and necrosis. Construction of a scrotum with placement of a Silastic prosthesis is of secondary importance.

Several surgical procedures can give a satisfactory result. Gillies creates a scrotum by using a transverse lower abdominal bipedicle flap incorporating the pubic hair. This was placed beneath the constructed phallus; however, the abnormal escutcheon provided a poor aesthetic result.[12] The use of medial thigh flaps increases the size and provides sensation to the scrotum. The labia majora would seem to provide the perfect tissue, yet there is not enough tissue to provide sufficient bulk

to construct an adequate scrotum. Millard describes a technique using bilateral inguinal pedicle flaps based inferiorly and slightly posterior to the base of the phallus. However, if the inguinal area is the base of the phallus construction (Kaplan–Wesser method), then this method of scrotal construction cannot be used. We prefer not to construct a scrotum, but the medial thigh plus labia majora tissue may give satisfactory results.

The complications of all the procedures are significant. Skin graft loss requiring regrafting, dehiscence of the tubes, wound infection, distal necrosis, and hematomas give an overall complication rate of 30%.[13] This does not include complications involving the mastectomies, hysterectomies with salpingo-oophorectomies, scrotal construction, and construction of a urethra. Thus, there is a very substantial morbidity to these procedures. Finally, although the patient population is carefully screened, the complication rate does not include psychological failures. This is the reason why many groups around the country have discontinued transsexual surgery. The government has become very reluctant to spend thousands of dollars in public funds for this surgery, and the private sector (insurance companies and consumers) is equally reluctant. Thus, there is a decline in the number of cases performed, although the state of the art is slowly advancing.

Although the total experience for any one group in the construction and reconstruction of the penis is limited, it appears feasible to create a penis and scrotum in the patient who is properly motivated. The undertaking of such a task must consider the patients' background and psychological make-up and the presence of preexisting scars, tumor, or irradiation. The restoration or creation of a urethral channel creates operative complications of stenosis and fistula. The young patient who has an intact urinary tract without infection presents further concern in that subsequent operative procedures to create a urethral channel may result in recurrent urinary tract infections in long-term follow-up study. However, if a patient is adamant in the need for a penile urethra, it has been demonstrated that this is technically feasible. The status of construction and reconstruction of the male external genitalia has advanced significantly over the past 40 yr, but there remains a great deal to be learned with more experience and refinement in techniques.

REFERENCES

1. Millard DR Jr: Scrotal construction and reconstruction. Plast Reconstr Surg 33:10, 1966

2. Hoopes E: Surgical construction of the male external genitalia. Clin Plast Surg 1:325, 1974

3. Hampson JL: Determinants of psychosexual orientation. In Beach FA (ed): Sex and Behavior, pp 108–132. New York, John Wiley & Sons, 1965

4. Baker HJ, Stoller RJ: Can a biological force contribute to gender identity? Am J Psychiatry 124:1653, 1968

5. Gillies H, Harrison RJ: Congenital absence of the penis. Br J Plast Surg 1:8, 1948

6. Kaplan I, Wesser D: A rapid method for constructing a functional sensitive penis. Br J Plast Surg 24:342, 1971

7. Boxer RJ: Reconstruction of the male external genitalia. Surg Gynecol Obstet 141:939, 1975

8. McGregor IA, Jackson IT: The groin flap. Br J Plast Surg 25:3, 1972

9. Scott FB, Bradley WE, Timm GW: Management of erectile impotence—use of implantable inflatable prosthesis. Urology 2:80, 1973

10. Boxer RJ, Miller TA: Penile reconstruction in irradiated patient. Urology 7:403, 1976

11. Bergman RT, Howard AT, Barnes RW: Plastic reconstruction of the penis. J Urol 59:1174, 1948

12. Gillies HD, Millard DR: Principles and art of plastic surgery, pp 368–388. Boston, Little, Brown, & Co, 1957

13. Dubin BJ, Sato RM, Laub DR: Results of phalloplasty. Plast Reconstr Surg 64:163, 1979

ANNOTATED BIBLIOGRAPHY

Millard DR Jr: Scrotal construction and reconstruction. Plast Reconstr Surg 33:10, 1966

A complete discussion of the different situations and different methods where construction and reconstruction of the scrotum is presented. The use of split-thickness skin grafts for penile skin avulsions is the therapy of choice. Although skin grafts for scrotal skin avulsions can be done, the thigh pocket method of permanently burying the testicles remains most frequently used. To create a more aesthetic scrotal reconstruction, thigh flaps shaped as ping-pong paddles are quite useful. These methods are of value for female-to-male transsexual surgery. A case is presented. Flaps using the labia major do not offer enough thickness, and thus bilateral inguinal flaps were used.

Kaplan I, Wesser D: A rapid method for constructing a functional sensitive penis. Br J Plast Surg 24:342, 1971

A method for creating a urethra and a functional sensitive penis is presented with a case photographic report. The urethra is created from the hairless portion of scrotal skin sutured around a catheter. Median thigh flaps based on the inguinal ligament are raised and brought over to cover the new urethra and the scrotal defect by the use of scrotal skin to create the urethra. This flap is innervated by the genitofemoral nerve; thus, the dorsal surface of the new penis is sensitive. Split-skin grafts cover the donor sites of the thigh flaps. Two weeks later, the thigh flap is again raised, with the new urethra curled under and sutured on the ventral surface. The scrotum is closed. Silicon rods may be inserted into the penis at a later date. In constructing the sensitive penis in transsexual surgery, the labia minora are used for the new urethra, and the remainder of the operation is the same.

Hoopes E: Surgical construction of the male external genitalia. Clin Plast Surg 1:325,1974

The discussion begins with a description of the differences between the hysterical male and more stoic female transsexuals. The experience of the Johns Hopkins Gender Identity Clinic is presented. After 1 yr of complete social/occupational functioning in the male role using testosterone, the patient is considered for surgery. The testosterone enlarges the clitoris, deepens the voice, increases hirsutism, and masculinizes the musculoskeletal system. The first surgical step is breast amputation. The Webster technique (Ann Surg 124:557, 1946), using a circumareolar incision, is recommended and discussed. The second surgical step is a hysterectomy and oophorectomy.

The "fear of discovery" or being "unmasked" is the motivation for construction of external genitalia. Sexuality is of lesser importance than gender to the transsexual patient. The Gillies technique (see below) is used to form a tube within a tube. This makes a satisfactory functional penis that can later have a prosthesis for rigidity if intromission is not possible. The author has found that scrotal construction with obliteration of the vagina is not necessary. Furthermore, the creation of the urethra is a vexing problem with tremendous complications, and usually he tries to avoid it.

Dubin BJ, Sato RM, Laup DR: Results of phalloplasty. Plast Reconstr Surg 64:163, 1979

A description of the reconstructive techniques of female-to-male transsexual surgery in 48 patients is presented. Fifty-eight percent of the patients had complications, including skin graft loss, dehiscence of the Gillies tube within a tube penile construction, infection, and distal necrosis. The surgical technique used at Stanford is a midline tube technique described by Gillies. The scrotum is formed from the labia with testicular prostheses placed between the transposed hair-bearing labial flaps. Rigidity is gained by using a Teflon baculum, which is inserted by the patient into the inner skin-lined tube within the neophallus. The urethra is not created, and thus no urinary function is attempted.

Laub DR, Fisk N: A rehabilitation program for gender dysphoria syndrome by surgical sex change. Plast Reconstr Surg 53:388, 1974

A complete analysis of the patients at the Stanford Gender Identity Clinic is discussed. The history, etiology, differential diagnosis, definition of gender dysphoria, psychotherapy including behavioral modification, and the operations and complications are presented. All aspects of the syndrome are critically analyzed.

Gillies H, Harrison RJ: Congenital absence of the penis. Br J Plast Surg 1:8, 1948

In this classic article, Gillies describes the construction of a phallus in patients with congenital absence of the penis and penis amputation. He attributes many of the principles to Frumkin and Maltz. His article is the basis of the subsequent literature on the total construction of the penis. The principles of the detailed description by Gillies have been applied by numerous other authors to construct the penis in cases of total traumatic avulsion of the penis and in patients undergoing penectomy for carcinoma of the penis. In recent years the same principles have been applied to female transsexual patients who want male external genitalia.

Gelb J, Malament M, LaVerne S: Total reconstruction of the penis: A review of the literature and report of a case. Plast Reconstr Surg 24:62, 1959

The authors review the literature of reports of 25 reconstructions of the penis. There is a detailed account, including photographs, of one case of total reconstruction of the penis and urethra using a modification of the Gillies technique. A composite tubed pedicle from the abdomen was migrated to the penile stump with the forearm as a carrier, a variation of the Gillies method employed because of scarring in the inguinal regions secondary to bilateral groin dissections for metastatic carcinoma of the penis. Although extensive scarring of the abdomen resulted from the operative procedure, and although the appearance of the constructed penis was unnatural, the patient was able to acccomplish urination, coitus, and ejaculation successfully.

Overview:
State of the Art of Female
Transsexual Surgery

Milton T. Edgerton

Drs. Boxer and Zarem have offered an interesting commentary on the status of female-to-male transsexual surgery. They correctly point out that the present state of the art has resulted in many patients with postoperative complications, and multiple stages of surgery have been required to reconstruct the male external genitalia and urethra. This, of course, reflects the still rather early stage of evolution of this type of surgery. I have little doubt that over the next 10 yr increasingly efficient and successful methods of reconstruction of the male genitalia will become well established and widely used throughout the world. In the 1980s, it will be the responsibility and the task of plastic and urologic surgeons to evaluate properly the current methods that have been advocated and to find ways of improving and simplifying the execution of these programs.

Drs. Boxer and Zarem suggest that the obtainment of sexual gratification is a second priority in the surgical treatment of the female transsexual. They further suggest that it is even less important that the patient be able to stand to void following penile reconstruction. Although at first blush this might seem resonable to the surgeons doing genital constructions, it has not, in fact, reflected the findings of physicians in our Virginia Gender Clinic. In interviewing patients both before and after surgery for reconstruction of the male genitalia, many of the patients point out that the use of public rest rooms makes it important for them to be able to stand to void. Without this capacity, they feel physically unacceptable in the male role. This goal ranks equal to that of being able to satisfy a female partner in intercourse in our female transsexual population. The authors suggest that there may be a decrease in the number of patients recently seeking surgery for female transsexualism. I would suggest that the evidence for this is very slim. A large number of new teams of surgeons have undertaken to construct the male genitalia in recent years. As a result, many of the patients who formerly applied to only the two or three centers willing to undertake such surgery are now being seen and treated by an unknown, but steadily increasing, number of surgeons throughout the country. In some instances, gender change surgery is not accompanied by proper work-up. This should always include searching psychiatric evaluation and proper team management of any surgical reconstruction. When this is not done, such patients may appear later for treatment of surgical complications at one of the major University Gender Identity Clinics. The number of such persons may be increasing and suggests to me that the overall number of *female transsexuals seeking surgical care may actually have increased in recent years*.

Drs. Boxer and Zarem raised the philosophical question of whether complex surgery of this type should ever be undertaken for a non-life-threatening disorder. It is true that the operations are expensive and that the total cost of hospitalization and professional care for six or eight operations may have significant repercussions on the cost of health care for citizens as a whole. At the present time, only a few third-party health insurance carriers in the United States consistently provide financial help for transsexual patients undergoing surgery. Despite this fact, transsexual patients consistently find a way to earn and save money so that they may be able to purchase this medical and surgical care which they feel they need so desperately. In our Gender Identity Clinic, the late follow-up results of both male and female transsexual patients indicate that they continue to be gratified with the results of this surgery and pleased that they made the original decision to embark on it. I have had such follow-up experience now in some patients for periods between 15 and 20 yr following surgery. Physicians' most pressing need is to develop even better surgical techniques. Patients feel that we ''have not gone far enough.'' Only some skeptical lay persons and physicians believe gender surgery has ''gone too far.'' It seems evident that unless a way is found to prevent the development of the condition known as transsexualism, surgeons will continue to need operations that will provide this rather dramatic relief to such patients.

I agree with Drs. Boxer and Zarem that it is still too early to determine whether the use of the Scott prosthesis is sufficiently reliable to be used routinely in the female transsexual patient. I have learned to avoid placing a rigid prosthesis with a highly polished or smooth external surface within an abdominal tube flap. Such a prosthesis, over time, as the result of the sliding movements between its surface and the fat of the surrounding pedicle flap, will tend to gradually necessitate or extrude. Firm intramural tissue fixation of any penile prosthesis at multiple points is needed to avoid this gradual shifting over time.

I have found that a number of patients with penile construction developed sufficient fibrous tissue thickening within the flap so that no implant was required to provide intromission. These patients have reported such satisfactory results over a period of years that I wonder if it might not be possible to provide such fibrosis in a deliberate method by a scarification agent. Such an approach might eliminate some of the danger of late extrusion of a penile prosthesis. Boxer and Zarem are accurate when they point out that construction and reconstruction of male external genitalia has advanced greatly over the past 40 yr, but there remains much more to be learned.

102

SURGICAL APPROACH TO MALE TRANSSEXUALISM

Roberto C. Granato, M.D., F.R.C.S.

From the Columbia University College of Physicians and Surgeons, New York,
New York

Urology / June 1974 / Volume III, Number 6

The word transsexualism was used for the first time by Cauldwell[1] almost a quarter of a century ago; Wolf *et al.*[2] define the transsexual syndrome as the "complete identification of a person with thoughts, feelings, and especially the sense of gender identity of a member of the opposite sex." More commonly, transsexuals have been characterized as men who sincerely believe that they are women born into a man's body (or vice versa). The technique of sex reassignment surgery is described.

TECHNIQUE

Preoperative Period. It is required that all patients undergo psychiatric and endocrinologic evaluation for a period of no less than one year, preferably two or more, before being considered a suitable candidate for the procedure. A large percentage of our patients had received estrogen and progesterone therapy for several years and had developed female-type breasts. Others had surgical implants of silastic and a few, augmentation by silicone injections; we do not utilize the latter. As a result of prolonged hormonal treatment the beard becomes scanty, and many patients find that shaving is no longer necessary or is required less frequently; the prostate becomes smaller and the testicles atrophic. It is interesting that about two thirds of the patients had been castrated by the time of the first interview. Others have had cosmetic surgery to the face and breasts. An important requirement is that the patient has cross-dressed for at least one year prior to the surgical procedure.

Because of the possibility of rectal injury during the surgical procedure, the patient is placed on a low-residue diet for at least three days prior to surgery. The night before the operative procedure the patient receives soap suds enemas until clear returns are obtained.

Most procedures are done under general anesthesia; however, when this is not possible due to recent cosmetic surgery of the nose, epidural anesthesia is used.

Surgical Procedure. The patient is in an exaggerated lithotomy position. The perineum, abdomen, thighs, and posterior aspect of the gluteal area are prepared and draped. A Thompson rectal sheet is applied with the upper border sutured to the perineum about 1 cm above the anal margin and a VI-Drape instant vaginal bib with pouch is applied (Fig. 1). A 20 F Foley catheter is introduced into the bladder and the balloon inflated with 20 ml of water.

A midline incision is made from the scrotum to about 2 cm above the upper border of the anal margin. The incision is deepened through subcutaneous tissue and superficial fascia, and dissected laterally. The edges of the incision are sutured to the inner aspect of the thighs to provide ample exposure of the underlying corpora cavernosa and corpus spongiosum covered by the ischiocavernosus and bulbocavernosus muscles, respectively. At this time the perineal arteries and veins are suture-ligated and transected. They are readily identified at the medial aspect of the ischiocavernosus muscles. Attention is then directed to the insertion of the left corpus cavernosus into the pubic ramus. Suture

ligature with 0 chromic catgut is applied at the lowermost part of the root of the corpus; a heavy clamp is applied 0.5 cm above the ligature, and the corpus is transected from its insertion on the bone. It is desirable to remove this erectile tissue completely since, if a stump of corpus cavernosus remains, it might cause complications due to its painful protrusion during sexual excitement. By sharp dissection the entire crus of the corpus is freed. A similar procedure is done on the right side (Fig. 2).

After the two roots of the corpora cavernosa are separated from the bone, attention is directed to the septum between the urethra and the corpora cavernosa. By sharp dissection, the urethra is separated from the latter. The dissection is carried out toward the glans penis underneath the skin in such a way that the penile skin together with the skin of the glans are separated, in toto, from the underlying corpora cavernosa and urethra (Fig. 3). The suspensory ligament of the penis is suture-ligated and transected. The disengagement of the corpora cavernosa from the pubic symphysis is then completed, and suture ligatures are applied to the branches of the dorsal arteries and veins of the penis. We cannot overemphasize how important it is to obtain precise hemostasis at this site.

A Deaver retractor is applied to the upper angle of the incision. Dissection of the hypogastrium from the underlying fascia of the external oblique muscle is carried out to the level of the umbilicus (Fig. 4). This maneuver is intended to advance the skin of the root of the penis downward to a more posterior site in the perineum, where it will become the entrance to the newly formed vagina. In those who have not been castrated previously, the spermatic cords are sectioned at the level of the

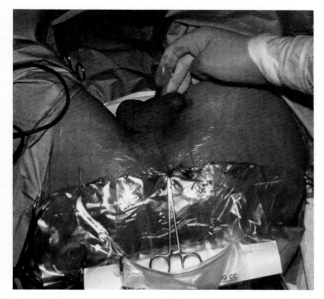

Fig. 1. Patient in exaggerated lithotomy position with rectal sheet in place. Incision made from scrotum to within 2 cm. of anus.

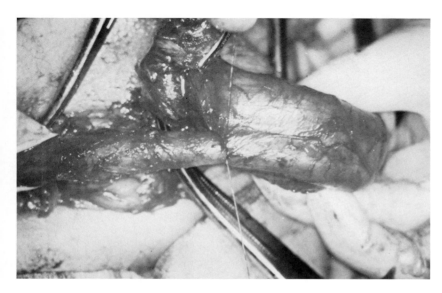

Fig. 2. Corpus cavernosum and crus separated from rami of pubis, and tie placed around urethra.

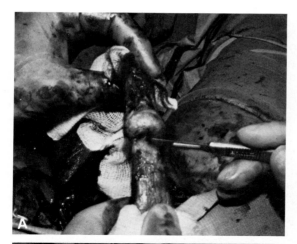

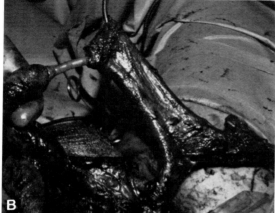

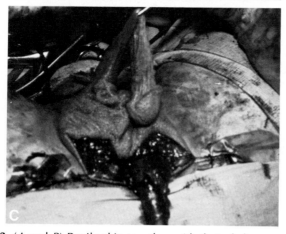

Fig. 3. (A and B) Penile skin together with that of glans are separated from corpora cavernosa and urethra. (C) Completed dissection: Penile skin and glans hang limply without any erectile tissue; at lower end of incision urethra with its Foley catheter hands downward; testes removed.

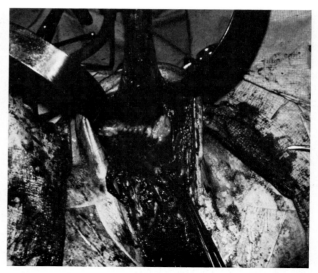

Fig. 4. Dissection of hypogastrium which permits advancement of penis (new vagina) to position more posteriorly; maneuver is essential to proper placement of new vaginal orifice.

external inguinal rings and suture ligatures are applied to their stumps. The testes together with their spermatic cords are then removed, and the inguinal rings closed with interrupted 0 chromic catgut sutures. Two or three dry lap pads are placed into this space in the lower part of the abdominal wall for hemostasis.

The next step consists of the excision of the subcutaneous tissue from the inverted penile skin; the plastic case of a 50-ml syringe is introduced into the inverted penile skin; a circular incision of the subcutaneous tissue and superficial fascia is performed at the base of the penis. The incision reaches the deepest part of the penile skin without actually cutting it. A vertical incision is then made from the base down to the tip of the inverted penis (Fig. 5A). By careful, sharp dissection the superficial fascia and fatty tissue are stripped off, leaving only a very thin layer of skin (Fig. 5B). This enables us to increase both the length and width of penile skin, thus permitting more lining material facilitating the creation of a larger vagina. This is important since many patients have a small penis following estrogen therapy, and we prefer to avoid the utilization of free-skin grafts which are often followed by vaginal stricture. It has been our experience that a denuded penile skin will ''take'' faster than one on which this subcutaneous tissue has been preserved.

Attention is then directed to the perineum. The bulbospongiosus muscle is excised completely; thus the bulge which sometimes occurs at the anterior aspect of

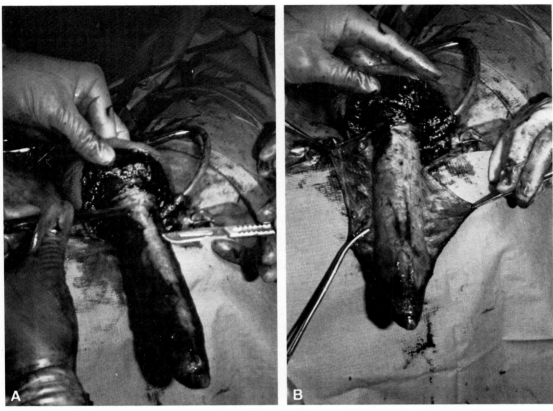

Fig. 5. (*A*) Plastic case of 50-ml. syringe is placed inside invaginated penis. Penile skin will become new vagina and glans new cervix. (*B*) Superficial fascia and fatty material are dissected off leaving very thin layer of skin; by denuding penile skin, larger vagina can be obtained. Note urethra on side.

the vulva is minimized. Retractors are applied to the lower part of the incision. The central tendon of the perineum is transected and the rectourethralis muscle sectioned transversly.

With the aid of the left index inserted in the rectum and traction to the Foley catheter, the posterior aspect of the apex of the prostate is readily exposed. A transverse incision is made in Denonvilliers fascia. The plane of cleavage thus created is essential since it is an almost avascular space and facilitates the dissection between the posterior aspect of the bladder and prostate and the anterior wall of the rectum up to the uper part of the posterior vesical wall. Figure 6 demonstrates the shiny appearance of the posterior aspect of the anterior layer of the Denonvilliers fascia. It is important to cut the medial part of the levator ani muscles to secure a wide vaginal entrance, otherwise stricture can occur. The opening of the new vaginal cavity should be not less than three fingerbreadths in width. A gauze leg-roll is temporarily inserted into this cavity for hemostasis.

Fig. 6. Rectum dissected off prostate to make room for new vagina in this space.

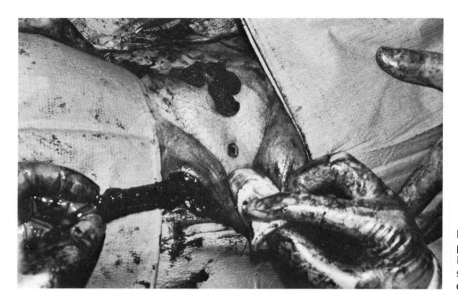

Fig. 7. New vagina has been placed and new meatus created. Note sponges which act as bolsters for wire sutures which hold down advanced hypogastrium

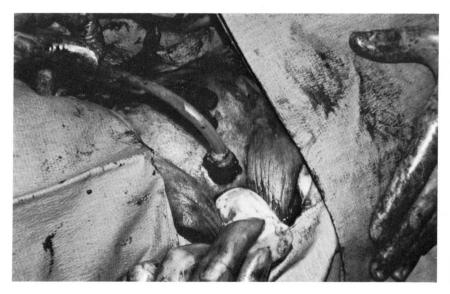

Fig. 8. Urethra brought out through new meatal opening.

Attention is then directed to the upper part of the incision. The laparotomy pads from the subcutaneous cavity previously developed in the lower part of the abdomen are removed. The skin of the hypogastrium is brought down by gentle traction, and two wire retention sutures are placed from the base of the flap down into the periosteum of the pubis to secure the flap. They are tied over a pad of gauze so they will not cut through the skin. This prevents the retraction of the "flap" in the lower part of the abdomen and eliminates tension on the invaginated penile skin.

A small circular incision is then made at the proper location in the new "vestibule" in the upper part of the base of the new vaginal entrance through which the urethra is passed. The urethra is then trimmed to about 1.5 cm beyond the skin level, and the free edge is sutured to the surrounding skin with interrupted sutures of 3-0 chromic catgut. The urethra is not transected at the skin level because when the anchoring wire sutures are removed a minor upward retraction of the flap may occur, and this could result in a short "buried" urethral meatus (Figs. 7 and 8).

The gauze roll from the vaginal cavity is then removed and, with the aid of the aforementioned plastic

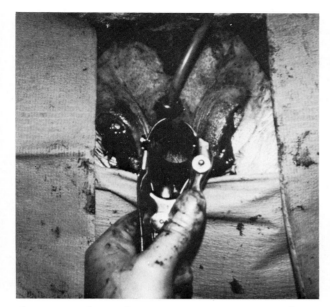

Fig. 9. Vaginal speculum in new vagina prior to packing.

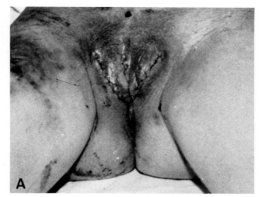

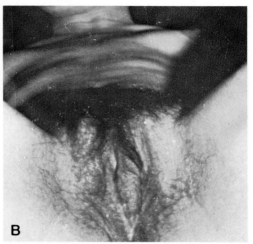

Fig. 11. Postoperative: (*A*) One week, packing and Foley catheter removed, and (*B*) six to eight weeks.

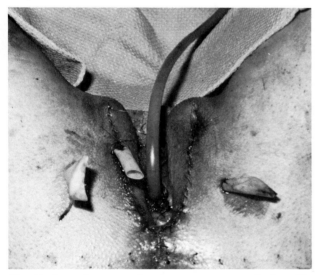

Fig. 10. Procedure completed: excess scrotum "tailored" to produce labia.

syringe case, the inverted penile skin is pushed into the new vaginal cavity (Fig. 9). No attempt is made to suture it to the adjacent structures. A packing consisting of a rubber glove which contains a leg-roll soaked with antibacterial agents is then placed into the new vagina. It is important to introduce enough of this packing to secure adequate coaptation of the raw aspect of the penile skin to its surrounding tissues to facilitate a prompt "take." Loose packing might result in hematoma formation between the inverted skin and the bladder or rectum or both, and this might be followed by necrosis of the new vaginal lining.

The excess scrotal skin is removed and tailored to give the appearance of labia majora. A Penrose drain is then inserted into the perineal cavity on each side and are brought out through separate stab-wound incisions. The subcutaneous tissue is approximated with 3-0 chromic catgut interrupted sutures, and the skin is approximated with 4-0 nylon continuous sutures (Fig. 10).

Postoperative Period. The patient is given broad-spectrum antibiotic therapy and intravenous feeding for two to three days. A clear-fluid diet is started on the third day followed by a nonresidue diet between the fourth and seventh days. Rectal treatments (enemas, taking of temperature, and others) are contraindicated during the first three weeks. Forty-eight to seventy-two hours after the operative procedure, the wire sutures in the pubic area are removed, and the patient is started on sitz baths twice a day.

On the seventh postoperative day, the vaginal packing and the urethral Foley catheter are removed (Fig. 11A). The patient is instructed on hygiene of the new vagina and the use of a vaginal form (obturator* made

* No . 382 Medical Grade Elastomer, The Dow Chemical Company, Corning, New York.

of silastic) which is provided. The patient is advised to use the obturator for no less than three hours twice a day for several months. Periodic follow-up examinations ae made (Fig. 11B). Usually, coitus is permitted six to eight weeks after the surgical procedure.

Elmhurst, New York 11373

Acknowledgment. Advisers: Ralph J. Veenema, M.D., John K. Lattimer, M.D., and Stanford Pulrang, M.D., Department of Urology, Columbia University, College of Physicians and Surgeons, New York, New York.

REFERENCES

1. WOLF, S. R., *et al.*: Psychiatric aspects of transsexual surgery management, J Nerv Ment Dis 147:525, 1968

2. CAULDWELL, D. O.: Psychopathis transsexualis, Sexology 16:274, 1949

Commentary: Updated Technique in Male Transsexual Surgery

Roberto C. Granato and Eduardo S. Granato

Since the writing of the preceding article, minor modifications have been made in our surgical technique in order to increase both the functional effectiveness of the vaginoplasty and its cosmetic aspect. However, since there are an increasing number of surgeons are interested in the area of sex change operations, I believe it is necessary to familiarize the young and inexperienced surgeon with aspects other than those strictly surgical.

DEFINITIONS AND ETIOLOGY

Sexual identity refers to the anatomic distinction of being biologically male or female. *Gender* is a psychological rather than biologic concept that implies masculinity or feminity. Stollers's definition of *gender identity* connotes awareness or belief that one belongs to one sex rather than the opposite one.[1] The phrase clearly refers to one's self-image as belonging to a specific sex. *Core gender identity* is the earliest basic and nonconflictually originated sense of belonging to one's sex. *Gender role* refers to the public or social expression of one's gender identity.

Stoller concluded that core gender identity is produced by the following factors: the anatomy and physiology of the external genitalia, parental attitudes toward the child, and biologic force that he cannot clearly explain. A person's core gender identity is crystalized at about the age of 1½ to 2 yr and irreversibly established before the age of 5.

In the male, the sense of maleness is permanently fixed long before the Oedipal phase (3 to 5 yr). This unalterable core gender identity must be distinguished from the related but different belief, "I am manly (or masculine)." The penis is not essential to this sense of maleness (as demonstrated by R. Stoller in his studies of male children with congenital defects).[2] In the woman, the core gender identity, is also fixed in early life. Stoller emphasizes that feminity develops regardless of chromosomal state or anatomy of the genitalia as long as the parents have no doubts their infant is a female.[3]

The origin of transsexualism is subject to numerous theories and controversies. Organic etiology, even though not discarded, has not been proved (and I am not referring to people with endocrinologic, genetic, or intersexed conditions.)

Helene Stourzh-Anderle, a Viennese physician, in her book *Sexual Constitution,* favors a biologic approach to the etiology of transsexualism.[4] She minimizes the psychological influences and considers transsexuals as having inborn chromosomal disturbances or some other biologic preconditioning. She feels that transsexuals are a kind of intersex and should be so classified. She thinks that limiting the term *intersex* to biologically visible defects is incomplete and also should include the gender-reversed patient.[4]

Schlegel has mentioned in his book that transsexualism is an intersexed condition. Based on the examination of thousands of patients spanning a wide variety of medical

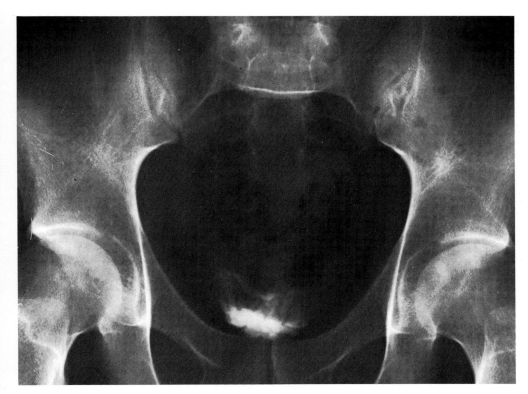

Fig. 12.

conditions related to sex or gender, he has found differences from the normal in pelvic outlet measurements. This, he says, indicates a biologic involvement in transsexualism rather than a psychological one.[5] Incidentally, I have observed gynecoid pelvis in some male-to-female transsexual patients (Fig. 12).

It is conceivable that the continuous research of H-Y antigen described by Wachtel and others will eventually enlighten physicians on the possibility of a biologic explanation for these patients' behavior.[6] The H-Y antigen is a surface component of all male mammalian cells. At the fifth World Congress of Sexology held in Jerusalem in June 1981, Wolf Eicher and colleagues presented their very interesting findings in their evaluation of the H-Y Antigen in 71 transsexuals. It was found that of 40 44-XY-male-to-female transsexuals, 32 were H-Y antigen negative, 6 were H-Y positive, and the remaining 2 were intermediate. They also found that of 31 44-XX-female-to-male transsexuals, 27 were H-Y antigen positive, 3 were H-Y antigen negative, and the remaining 1 was intermediate. That is to say, in 85% of the cases of transsexualism, there was an H-Y antigen discordance. On the other hand, Brzostovski believes that a psychological cause for transsexualism seems to offer a more logical explanation on its origin.* Stoller's research in male transsexuals led him to postulate the following psychodynamics: The mothers of the male transsexual show a specific personality characterized by

* Brzostovski M: Personal communication.

unconscious bisexuality; they do not clearly accept their femininity. They are mildly and chronically depressed and feel "empty," and sexual relations are infrequent and not gratifying. They usually were tomboyish in their latency years, preferred the company of boys, and were very sports minded. The ones in treatment openly stated that as a child they looked and acted as boys and wanted to become males. This behavior was relinquished at the onset of puberty. These mothers select, unconsciously, *one* male child to establish an intense, long-lasting, overgratifying type of relationship in which "skin to skin" contact takes place between mother and infant. This body contact begins at birth and continues into early latency. In this way, the mother finds fulfillment for her emptiness and amelioration of her depression, since her wish for a penis is answered by this boy who becomes an extension of her fantasized phallus. This close symbiotic relationship psychologically blurs the outlines of their respective bodies, creating in the little boy a faulty body ego representation. In addition, this special mother–child relationship leads to early, massive, overpowering identification in the boy with his mother, which eventually leads to his entrenched desire to be a woman and to the establishment of a core gender identity that is acquired as a conflict-free learning, nearly imprinting experience that does not correspond to his sexual anatomy. These mothers unconsciously encourage and consciously do not discourage the boy's early cross-dressing attempts.

The fathers of transsexual boys are either physically or

emotionally absent. They do not participate in a family triangular relationship, and therefore they do not interfere with the mother–child symbiotic diad. In addition, they do not participate and are not instrumental in helping the child traverse the separation-individuation phase of development, a role that many workers, Abelin among them, have demonstrated to be crucial for the child at this stage. Greenson, for instance, feels that the boy at this point in development must go through a process of disidentification from his mother, by which he relinquishes, in great part, his feminine identification, and the presence of the father serves as a model for masculine counteridentification.[8] The self-object differentiation phase of the developmental line of object relationships parallels the preoedipal phase of the psychosexual line of development, in which the little boy identifies with his phallic, pre-Oedipal mother. In the transsexual, this reinforced identification establishes the child's core gender identity and precludes the normal unfolding of the Oedipal conflict as it develops in an "average child,"—the boy who has already successfully negotiated the separation-individuation phase of Mahler and who already feels himself as masculine as revealed by his behavior, attitude, and play, and who proceeds to identify with the parent of the same sex and takes the parent of the opposite sex as a love object.[9,10]

The future transsexual male child does not give up the early massive, nonconflictual feminine identification. A sense of maleness does not develop. He seeks out the father as the love object not in a homosexual sense, since he does not perceive himself as a male, but rather in a heterosexual way. Because he does not see himself as a male, the little boy has not cathected his phallus; consequently, he treats his penis as if it were not part of himself. Nothing can happen to something that does not exist. In addition, since he is not in competition with father for mother as a love object, he does not suffer from castration anxiety. The child does not want mother, but he wants to be *like* mother, so there is no conflict, no anxiety, and no guilt for Oedipal transgression.

DIAGNOSIS

This syndrome is characterized by the crucial paradox in which a person's conscious and mental self-representation is the opposite one of his actual anatomic sex. This particular syndrome shares with other syndromes, such as transvestism, effeminated homosexuality, butch lesbianism, and some psychotic states, the wish for sex change. In fact the person, in consulting a physician, does so not for diagnostic purpose but rather to search for surgical treatment. In recent years and through the work of many scientists in this field, common criteria for the diagnosis of this disturbance in the male were outlined:

Lifelong conscious and unconscious pursuit of characteristics of the opposite sex

Very feminine physical appearance, mannerisms, and gestures

History of cross-dressing, usually beginning around age 3 or 4 yr

Fantasies and dreams where the patient sees himself as a female, whether in pursuit of sexual gratification or otherwise

No history of dating or romantic interest (females are sought out for friendship)

Early disavowal of genitals, which is accompanied by a sense of shame; genital pleasure rare, particularly in regard to cross-dressing

Cross-gender behavior is the common denominator that underlies conditions such as transsexualism, transvestism, effeminate homosexuality in the man or butch lesbianism in the woman, intersexed states, and psychotic states. The preceding considerations lead us to the unquestionable deduction that the psychiatrist's role in the management of the transsexual patient is of paramount importance.

TREATMENT

A multidisciplinary team represented by a psychiatrist, psychologist, urologist, endocrinologist, and plastic surgeon completes the evaluation of the patient requesting a "sex change" procedure. The diagnosis of transsexualism is made, based on a clinical picture that must include screening of the patient's conscious and unconscious fantasies, dreams, motivation, extent of female identification in the male and male identification in the female, careful study of body image and self-representation, and a developmental history and consultation with close relatives (parents, siblings). The next step is to consider the treatment modality.

The adult transsexual is unshakeable in his conviction and does not experience conflict over it; therefore, he or she would not be amenable to psychotherapy or psychoanalysis. Supportive psychotherapy and counseling should be provided to help the patient confront the obstacles ahead, including clarification and educational aspects concerning the surgery and its possible complications (physical as well as psychological).

The treatment of transsexuals is carried out in stages. First, the patient must live as a woman if a man, or vice versa, full time. This includes passing as a member of the opposite sex at work and socially for a minimum of 1 yr. Some teams require a minimum of 2 yr as a transition period before undertaking the irreversible surgical step. Simultaneously in the male transsexual, electrolysis to remove facial hair is advised. Both female and male require voice and speech retraining. Hormone therapy is begun; estrogen compounds in the male and androgen compounds in the female transsexual are given to modify the secondary sexual characteristics and development of an opposite gender phenotype.

The hormonal treatment in the male results in a redistribution of the subcutaneous fat, decreased muscle strength, decreased libido (which probably accounts for the lessening of anxiety), decreased erection and ejaculation, and increased breast tissue. The administration of testosterone to the female transsexual results in decreased menstruation, deepened voice, and increased body hair growth and libido.

Throughout this period, counseling and supportive psychotherapy must be maintained. In some instances, cosmetic surgery is useful to improve external appearance, particularly in the male-to-female transsexual. This procedure consists of rhinoplasty, breast augmentation, and laryngoplasty. Finally, surgical castration is carried out. In the male, penectomy and orchiectomy are followed by construction of a vagina. In the female, after a first stage in which bilateral mastectomy is performed, a hysterectomy and bilateral salpingo-oophorectomy follow. The final stage consists of phalloplastia and testicular prosthesis.

For true transsexuals, as mentioned above, psychoanalysis or behavioral therapies offer negative results. Rather, since gender identity is firmly established in childhood, efforts should be made to spot the future transsexual during those formative years. In addition, cross-gender disturbances in childhood are the source of other psychological difficulties during adolescence and adulthood. Among them are social maladjustment, depressive reactions, suicidal tendencies, and self-mutilation. Early diagnosis and treatment are the best preventive measures. Several workers in this field reported good results in treating these children with psychoanalysis or dynamic psychotherapy.[11–13] Behavioral therapy is also reported to be effective in some patients.[13,14] Of extreme importance is to engage the parents of these children into therapy.

Crucial to the transsexual adolescent is the emergence of puberal changes. Since these changes are a product of the biologic development push, the secondary sex characteristics become more pronounced, to the dismay of the youngster who psychologically rejects his or her body and feels in conflict with the environment that expects conformity to a biologically assigned role.

The early diagnosis of adolescent transsexualism is a challenge to the clinician, since a treatment program that will help these patients pass through adolescence in reasonable psychological comfort is immediately needed. In the absence of such help, these youngsters feel ostracized, isolated, and withdrawn or tend to act destructively. They are at odds with themselves, their families, school, and society at large.

Patients for whom surgery is not recommended include the following:

Patients who look grotesque passing for a member of the opposite sex (*i.e.,* men who look very masculine and women who look very feminine)

Patients who are psychotic or have had psychotic episodes or depressive episodes

Patients who experience genital pleasure (*e.g.,* homosexuals and transvestites, who are requesting a "sex change")

Unstable, immature persons with difficult social adjustments

Drug- or alcohol-addicted patients

Habitual criminal offenders.

PROGNOSIS

One of the most frustrating aspects in the research work with transsexual patients who undergo surgical sex reassignment is the scarcity of follow-up studies, both short and long range. Once the surgeon discharges the patient, the transsexual tends to move away or go underground so as to leave his or her past behind, which makes it difficult if not impossible to trace the person. Transsexuals are not willing, for the most part, to participate in a longitudinal follow-up study. An important factor that contributes to this problem is that transsexuals come from all over the nation, making the economic aspect of

traveling to the clinic an obstacle. As a consequence, no precise methodology and research strategies have been developed to allow for a systematic scientific validation and rating of results. The lack of follow-up data makes it difficult to predict which patient seeking surgical reassignment would be helped by this procedure.

In general, the small statistics available that deal with the postoperative adjustment of transsexuals reveal that the majority of them report having achieved a more satisfactory lifestyle.[16–19] They had adjusted better to their environment and experienced a considerable diminution of anxiety and depression. They achieved more stable object relations and more permanent working positions.

People who had considerable psychopathology before surgery remained troubled by it after surgery and probably fall into the category of patients for whom surgery was not indicated. Sex reassignment is not a solution for psychiatric problems. Some patients committed suicide after surgery. Others became very depressed when confronted with the irreversibility of the procedure. We believe that these tragedies could have been avoided by proper psychiatric evaluation and counseling for not less than 1 yr. For the carefully selected few, surgical reassignment produces a stabilization of a previously chaotic life and with subjective and objective improvements in feelings of well-being and satisfaction in the new gender role. Such persons retain their capacity for sexual gratification; in some cases this is enhanced. As a result of this careful selection of patients, in our series less than 15% of those requesting the operation reached the operating table.

Obviously, such dramatic surgery cannot escape controversy and it lends itself for discussion and scrutiny not only from the scientific point of view but also from the ethical, moral, religious and legal aspects, which are beyond the scope of this discussion.

INFORMED CONSENT

As in any other major operation, we obtain a very detailed informed consent from the patient. The text of this consent is explained very carefully to the patient. It reads as follows:

CONSENT TO OPERATION, ANESTHESIA, SPECIAL TREATMENTS OR PROCEDURES

Patient's Name	Date

1. The undersigned hereby authorizes Robert C. Granato, M.D., and such associates and assistants as may be designated by him, to treat the condition or conditions which appear indicated by the psychiatric, psychological, and physiological studies already performed in connection with the above patient.

2. The nature and purpose of the operation and/or diagnostic procedures necessary to treat the above patient's condition has been explained to the undersigned by the above physician and the undersigned understands the nature of these to be: sex reassignment surgery involving the removal of the testicles and the erectile part of the penis and creation of a vagina.

3. The undersigned has been made aware of certain risks, hazards, complications and consequences that are associated with the above operation, anesthesia, treatment(s) and procedures and the undersigned understand them to be:

The operation is irreversible and permanent. Due to the anatomical site of the operation, there is the possibility of a fistula formation (abnormal opening between two organs) between the rectum and the new vagina or the bladder and the new vagina. To correct such complications, further surgery, including a colostomy (exteriorization of the bowel to the skin), would be necessary. Other possible complications which may occur and may require further surgery are urinary tract infection, urethral stricture (narrowing) at different levels, gangrene of the surgical area and any other complication inherent to any major surgical procedure such as this one.

4. The undersigned has also been informed that there are other risks such as severe loss of blood, infection, cardiac arrest, etc., that may occur in the performance of any surgical procedure. The undersigned understands the need for this operation and/or procedure and acknowledges that no guarantee or assurance has been given the undersigned by anyone as to its result. The undersigned is fully aware of the risks and possible complications, and the undersigned is willing to assume any and all such risks and complications. The undersigned hereby release and agree to hold harmless Dr. Granato, his associates and assistants, the hospital, his nurses and other employees.

5. It has been explained to the undersigned that during the course of an operation unforeseen conditions may be revealed that necessitate an extension of the original procedure(s) or different Procedure(s) than those set forth in Paragraph 2 such as the possibilities of the formation of vaginal and/or vulvar stricture necessitating further surgery including skin graft. The undersigned therefore authorizes and requests that the above-named physician, his associates and/or assistants perform such surgical procedures as are necessary and desirable in the exercise of their professional judgement. The authority granted under this paragraph shall extend to treating all conditions that require treatment and are not known to the above physician at the time the operation is commenced.

6. The undersigned consents to the administration of such anesthesia as may be considered necessary or advisable by the physician responsible for this service, with the exception of none.

7. The undersigned consents to the photographing or televising of the procedure(s) of the operation(s) to be performed, including appropriate portions of the patient's body, for medical, scientific or educational purposes, provided the patient's identity is not revealed by the pictures or by descriptive texts accompanying them.

8. The undersigned consents to disposal by hospital authorities, in accordance with its accustomed practice, of any member, tissues or parts which may be removed.

9. The undersigned certifies that his/her marital status is _____.

Dated: _____

_____   _____
Witness   Patient's Signature

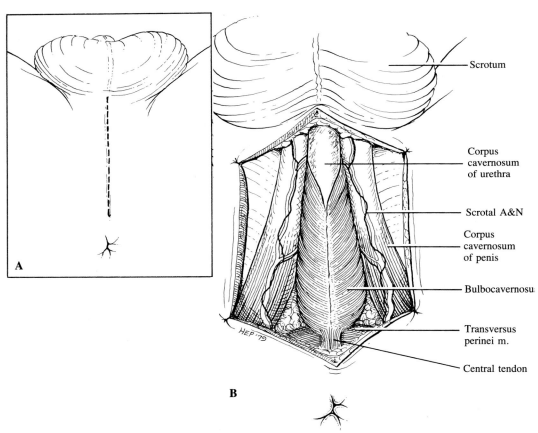

Scrotum

Corpus cavernosum of urethra

Scrotal A&N

Corpus cavernosum of penis

Bulbocavernosu

Transversus perinei m.

Central tendon

Fig. 13. (*A*) A midline perineal incision is made from the base of the scrotum to 1.5 cm from the anal margin. (*B*) The edges of the incision are sutured to the inner aspects of the thighs. The urethra and the two corpora cavernosa are widely exposed.

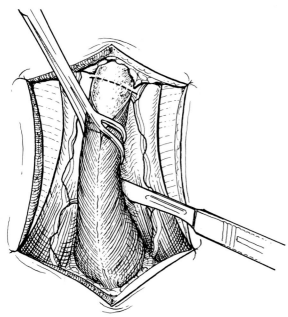

Fig. 14. Sharp dissection between the corpora cavernosa and the corpora spongiosa urethrae.

TECHNIQUE

Our technique has undergone several minor modifications.

Following the original vertical incision of the perineum and the suturing of the resulting edges (Fig. 13) to the inner aspect of the thigh to provide a proper exposure, we proceed by transecting the urethra at about 7 cm to 8 cm distal to the triangular ligament and by sharp dissection detach it from the anterior aspect of the corpora cavernosa (Figs. 14 and 15). In this manner the excision of the roots of the corpora is facilitated (Figs. 16 and 17). With the urethral stump out of the way, the separation of the penile skin from the underlying corpora cavernosa as well as the separation of the subcutaneous vascular layer from the penile skin are facilitated (Figs. 18 and 19).

As in the original technique, we continue with the bilateral orchiectomy and dissection of the hypogastrium from the underlying fascia of the external oblique muscles up to the level of the umbilicus (Fig. 20). At this point in our original technique, removal of the bulbospongiosus muscles was carried out; nowadays we preserve them temporarily because this allows the application of an Allis clamp to them to achieve

(*Text continues on p 1319*)

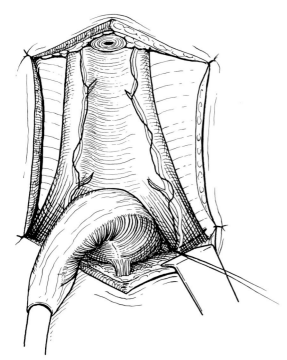

Fig. 15. The urethra is transsected at about 6 to 7 cm from the external urethral sphincter and brought downward in order to expose the base of the corpora cavernosa.

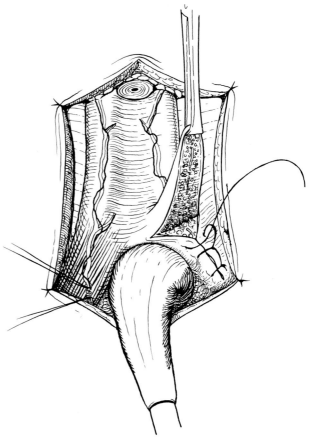

Fig. 16. The left corpora cavernosa is dissected off the left pubic ramus. A continuous locking suture with No. 1 chromic catgut is applied to the stump.

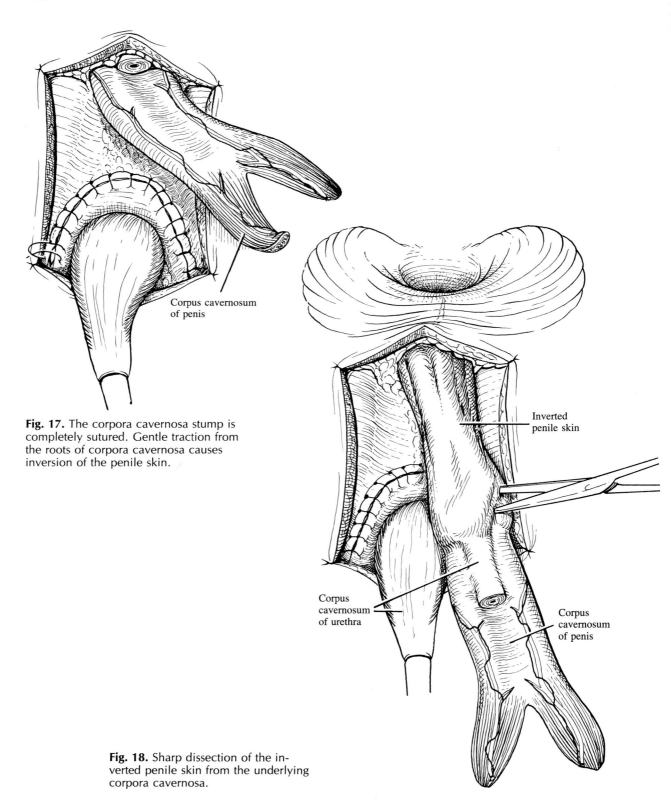

Fig. 17. The corpora cavernosa stump is completely sutured. Gentle traction from the roots of corpora cavernosa causes inversion of the penile skin.

Corpus cavernosum of penis

Inverted penile skin

Corpus cavernosum of urethra

Corpus cavernosum of penis

Fig. 18. Sharp dissection of the inverted penile skin from the underlying corpora cavernosa.

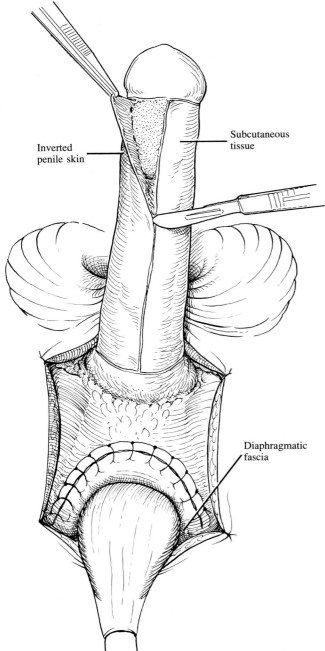

Inverted
penile skin

Subcutaneous
tissue

Diaphragmatic
fascia

Fig. 19. A circular incision is performed over the subcutaneous fat layer of the base of the penis. A vertical incision is then performed in this layer, from the glans penis to the base of the penis. By sharp dissection the fat layer is dissected from the penile skin. This maneuver facilitates "taking" of this graft and also increases the elasticity of the penile skin otherwise limited by the presence of the subcutaneous layer.

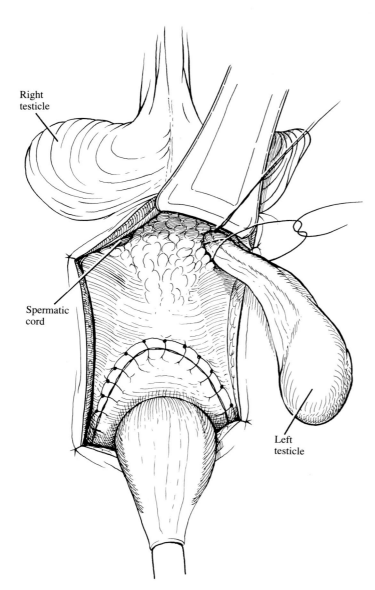

Right
testicle

Spermatic
cord

Left
testicle

Fig. 20. Orchiectomy performed by double suture ligature of the spermatic cord at the external inguinal orifice.

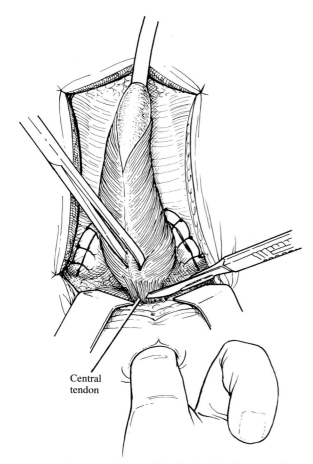

Fig. 21. With the guidance of the left index finger in the rectum and minor traction applied from the midline of the bulbospongiosus muscles, the central tendon of the perineum is transsected.

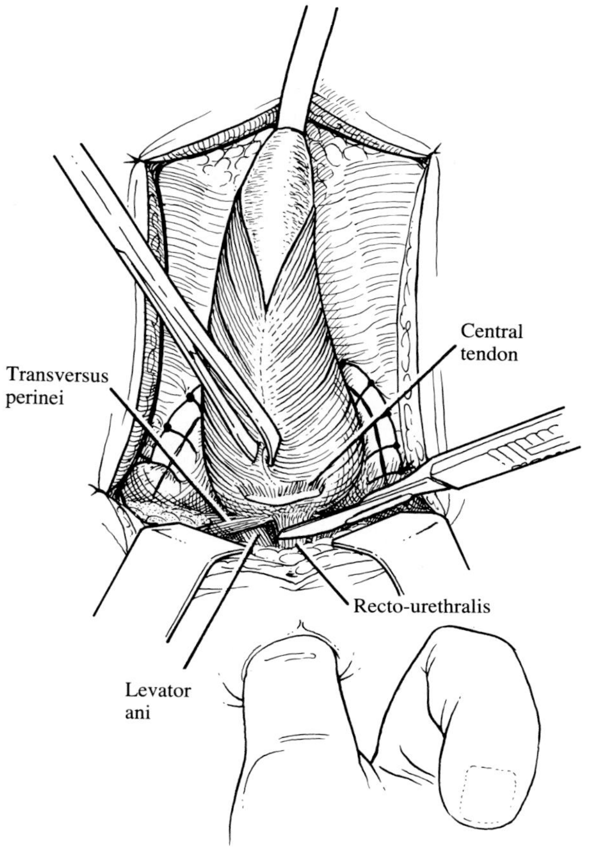

Fig. 22. The transversus perineous muscles is widely exposed. Upward traction is applied from the distal stump of the central tendon exposing the recto-urethralis muscle; the latter is transsected.

upward traction and facilitates sectioning the central tendon and the rectourethralis muscles (Figs. 21 and 22). Once the fascia of Denonvilliers' is opened, an avascular plane of cleavage is encountered (Fig. 23). However, taking into consideration that following this procedure in many patients the vagina shrinks, it is well to start off with a rather large cavity to allow for some decrease in size resulting from perivaginal fibrosis. In order to make the vaginal cavity larger and not limit it to the level of the upper end of the two layers of Denonvilliers' fascia, we now perform a transverse incision at the upper part of the anterior layer of Denonvilliers' fascia and carry it up to between the superior posterior angle of the bladder and the anterior aspect of the peritoneum of the cul de sac of Douglas (Fig. 24).

Our final modification involves the creation of a clitoris. As seen in Figure 25, a flap of corpora spongiosum urethra is made to pass underneath a bridge of skin at about 1 cm above the external urethral meatus and exteriorized through a 1-cm

circular incision and sutured to the skin edge. A sagittal view of the resulting operation is seen in Figure 26.

In those patients having a small penis, a skin graft is obtained and fashioned into a sac (Fig. 27). This is sutured to the patient's own penile stump. In these cases, obviously, the glans skin is excised.

COMPLICATIONS

The surgeon who embarks on this kind of operation must be ready to deal with several possible serious complications. These can be very distressing both to patient and surgeon. Table 1 lists the immediate complications.

A rectovaginal fistula (3% of cases) is the most frustrating complication. Before surgery we clearly explain to the patient the possibility of a temporary colostomy in the event that an opening is made in the rectum during the operation. The patient

(*Text continues on p 1324*)

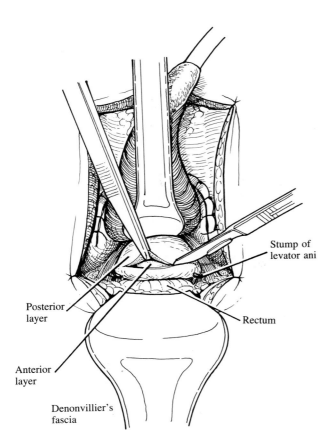

Posterior layer

Anterior layer

Denonvillier's fascia

Stump of levator ani

Rectum

Fig. 23. The levator anal muscles are separated sideways, exposing the posterior layer of the Denonvilliers' fascia. A transverse incision is performed and dissection is continued upward by gentle blunt maneuver with the index finger until the junction of the anterior and posterior layers of the Denonvilliers' fascia meet.

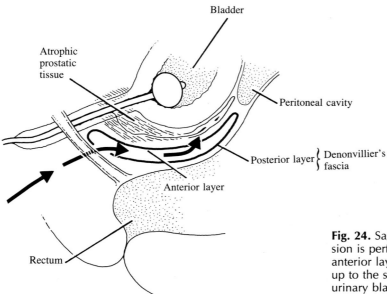

Bladder

Atrophic prostatic tissue

Peritoneal cavity

Posterior layer } Denonvillier's fascia

Anterior layer

Rectum

Fig. 24. Sagittal view. A transverse incision is performed at the upper part of the anterior layer of the Denonvilliers' fascia up to the superior–posterior angle of the urinary bladder. At this time visualization of the seminal vesical is clearly obtained.

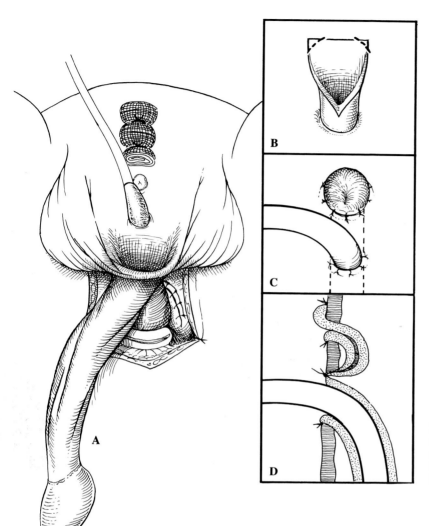

Fig. 25. Clitoroplasty. (*A*) A circular opening is performed above the urethral meatus. The spatulated urethra (*B*) is made to exit through the upper orifice and sutured to its edge (*C* and *D*).

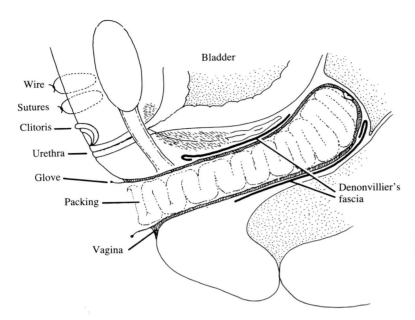

Wire

Sutures

Clitoris

Urethra

Glove

Packing

Vagina

Bladder

Denonvillier's fascia

Fig. 26. A No. 8½ glove is introduced into the invaginated penile skin and a Betadine leg roll soaked with jelly is packed into the glove. This provides the best coadaptation of the inverted penile skin to the adjacent pelvic structure.

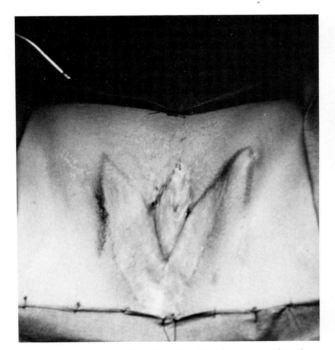

Fig. 27. Divergent labia. A vertical Z-plasty is outlined on the skin of the external genitalia bilaterally.

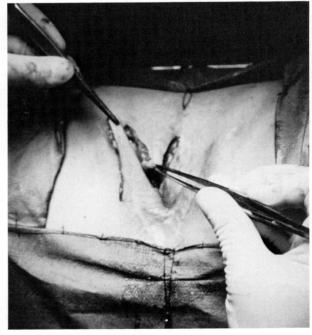

Fig. 28. An upper (medial) and a lower (lateral) flap are developed.

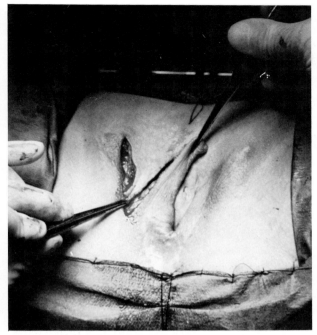

Fig. 29. The lateral and middle flaps are now inverted.

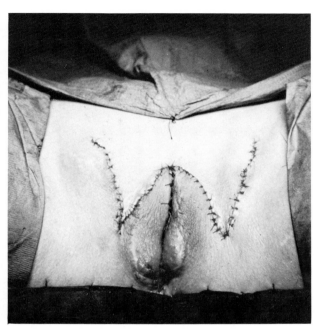

Fig. 31. Skin is approximated with interrupted sutures of 4-0 Dermalon.

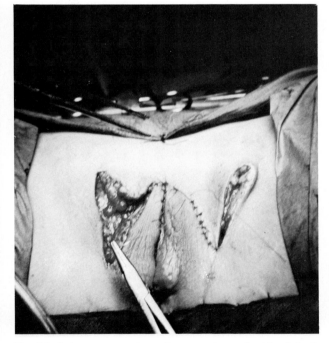

Fig. 30. Subcutaneous tissue is approximated with triple-0 Dexon.

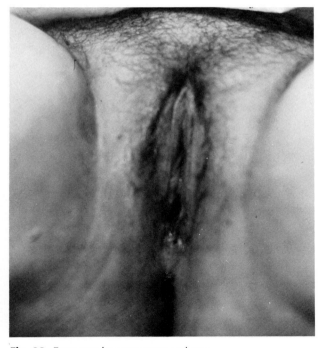

Fig. 32. Four weeks post crown plasty.

TABLE 1. Immediate Complications (305 Cases in 11 Yr)

Rectovaginal fistula	8
Retrovaginal hematoma	2
Cellulitis of vulva or vagina with necrosis	1
Dehiscence of lower part of suture line	14
Hematoma of labia	10
Pressure necrosis of labia	2

TABLE 2. Late Complications (305 Cases in 11 Yr)

Strictures	
Urethra	7
Vulva	4
Vagina	9
Vulvovaginitis (traumatic)	5
"Divergent" labia	28

signs a separate consent to this effect. In our opinion, it is unrealistic to expect that the simple repair of the fistulous tract alone would lead to adequate results; a concomitant bowel diversion (transverse colostomy) is indicated. The colostomy is closed from 2 to 6 wk after the original operation. On the other hand, if the opening of the rectum was not noticed during the sex change procedure, and a rectovaginal fistual occurs, a transverse colostomy is readily done. Four to six weeks later the rectovaginal fistula is closed transvaginally, and finally 4 to 6 wk later the colostomy is closed.

Among late complications (see Table 2), the most distressing is the vaginal stricture.

This has occurred in 3% of our cases. Hard, tenacious fibrous tissue forms around the vaginal lining, which constricts in such a way that dilatation is absolutely impossible. In these cases excision of vaginal lining and surrounding fibrous tissue is done, followed by the application of skin graft to the new cavity. Obviously, the chance is higher of inadvertently surgically penetrating the bladder anteriorly or, more likely, the rectum posteriorly.

Divergent labia is a rather common complication. The new "labia majora" appear in the shape of a V with a separation at the upper end. In order to correct this aesthetic deformity, we have "reinvented" the double Z-plasty, which was called "crown plasty" because of its shape (Figs. 28 to 31). The final result is quite acceptable (Fig. 32).

REFERENCES

1. Stoller RJ: A Contribution to the Study of gender identity. Int J Psychoanal 45:220, 1964
2. Stoller RJ: The sense of maleness. Psychoanal Q 34:207, 1965
3. Stoller RJ: The sense of femaleness. Psychoanal Q 37:42, 1968
4. Stourzh-Anderle H: Sexuelle Konstitution. Wien-Bonn, Verlag F. Medizinisehe Wissenschaften, 1955
5. Schlegel WS: Die Sexualinstinkte des Menschen. Hamburg, Ruetten an loening Verlag, 1962
6. Wachtel SS et al: Serologic detection of a Y-linked gene in XX males and XX true hermaphrodites. N Engl J Med 750, 1976
7. Wolf E et al: Abstracts of the fifth World Congress of Sexology, Jerusalem, June 1981
8. Greenson RR: Dis-identifying from mother: Its special importance for the boy. Read at the 25th International Psychoanalytic Congress, Copenhagen, July 1967
9. Mahler M, La Pierriere K: Mother–child interaction during separation–individuation. Psychoanal Q 34:483, 1965
10. Mahler M: On two crucial phases of integration of the sense of identity: Separation–individuation and bisexual identity (abstr). J Am Psychoanal Assoc 6:131, 1958

11. Stoller R: Sex and gender. In Problems in Treatment, Vol 11, pp 272–280. New York Jason Aronson, 1976
12. Newman LE: Transsexualism in adolescence. Arch Gen Psychiatry 23:112, 1970
13. Greenson R: A transvestite boy and a hypothesis. Int Psychoanal 47:396, 1966
14. Rekers G, Lovaas I: Behavioral treatment of deviant sex role behaviors in a male child. J Appl Behav Anal 7:173, 1974
15. Rekers G, Lovaas I: Psychotherapy: Child gender disturbances: A clinical rational for intervention. J Appl Behav Anal 14:2, 1977
16. Pauly, I: The current status of the change of sex operations. J Nerv Ment Dis 147:460, 1968
17. Money J: Prefatory remarks on outcome of sex reassignment in twenty four cases of transsexualism. Arch Sexual Behav 1:163, 1971
18. Benjamin H: Newer aspects of the transsexual phenomenon. J Sex Res 5:125, 1969
19. Walinder J: Report to the International Gender Dysphoria Symposium. Clin Psychiatr News 5:30, 1977

ANNOTATED BIBLIOGRAPHY

Money J: Sexual dimorphism in the psychology of female transsexuals. J Nerv Ment Dis 147:487, 1968.

This report presented data on components of gender identity in six female transsexuals. They scored very low on femininity and fairly high on masculinity on the Guilford–Zimmerman M-F scale. In childhood they had no girlish interests. They were tomboys and prone to fight, usually with boys. Sensory and perceptual erotic arousal thresholds in adulthood conformed more to those of the female than the male, But the imagery of arousal and erotic performance was masculine. There was no fetishistic dependence on clothing for erotic arousal. The six patients were at various stages of hormonal and surgical reassignment treatment. Five were living as males. A universal presenting symptom was hatred of the breasts. There was no evidence suggestive of phantom breast or womb in those who had received mastectomy or hysterectomy. Parental feeling toward infants and children, insofar as it could be estimated, was fatherly rather than motherly. None of the patients wanted anything to do with pregnancy and motherhood.

Hoopes JE, Knorr NJ, Wolf SR.: Transsexualism: Considerations regarding sexual reassignment. J Nerv Ment Dis 147:510, 1968

This paper reviewed some of the historial aspects of transsexualism, explored possible reasons for previous neglect of this major problem, and attempted characterization of the transsexual patient on the basis of information contained in correspondence from individuals seeking evaluation and treatment. The authors stated that the primary deterrent to physician involvement in the transsexual problem is a self-protective one, namely, fear of censure and considerations regarding reputation.

Berger JC, Green R, Laub DR et al: Standards of care—the hormonal and surgical sex reassignment of gender dysphoric persons. Janus Information Facility of The University of Texas Medical Branch.

This pamphlet presents in a very precise and clear manner the standards of care of transsexual patients. It defines hormonal reassignment, surgical reassignment, and gender dysphoria in a very comprehensive way. Among the standards of care, it emphasizes that the psychiatrist or psychologist making the recommendation in favor of hormonal and nonsurgical sex reassignment must have known the patient in the therapeutic relationship for at least 3 mo before making said recommendation and that the psychiatrist or psychologist making the recommendation in favor of genital (surgical) sex reassignment must have known the patient for at least 6 mo before making said recommendation. Genital sex reassignment should be preceded by at least 12 mo during which the patient lives full time in the social role of the genetically other sex.

Feinbloom DH, Sherwood M: Counseling issues with transsexuals. Human Sexuality, pp 33–37, Jan–Feb 1977

The authors present the general principles considered in setting up a gender identity clinic. They have a working classification of patients with different sexual derangements: chromosomal sex, somatotype, gender identity, preferred gender role, preferred sexual object choice, and preferred pattern of sexual arousal.

Blandau RJ, Bergsma D: Morphogenesis and malformation of the genital system. The National Foundation, March of Dimes, Birth Defects: Original Article Series, Vol XIII, no. 2. New York, Alan R. Liss, 1977

This booklet presents a modern synthesis of knowledge of the intricacies and complexities of the morphogenesis and malformations of the genital system. We believe this booklet is a must in the reading list of those interested in plastic surgery of the genital organs.

Veit-Sherwin R: Legal aspects of male transsexualism, transsexualism and sex reassignment, Green and Money pp 417–430. Baltimore, The Johns Hopkins University Press, 1969

Although it is impossible to cover all legal contingencies facing the transsexual starting a new everyday life, the author attempts to cover at least some of the major areas of legal endeavor immediately after medical and surgical sex reassignment. The beginning period in the legal life of the transsxual is crucial. Almost no legal precedent is available, and inappropriate precedents should be avoided wherever possible while new and appropriate precedents are being created. In the meantime, transsexuals must also remember to avoid litigation wherever possible, even if it means temporarily forfeiting some legal rights that would be unquestionable if the person were not a transsexual.

Overview: Dynamics of Surgery in Male Transsexualism

Milton T. Edgerton

In this paper and in their follow-up comments, the Drs. Granato have described the surgical approaches they are using to reconstruct the vagina and labia in patients with male transsexualism. They report operating on a series of 271 patients over a 10-yr period. This is a sizeable experience.

A word about the basic surgical procedure: The Granato technique is one that combines aspects of various other procedures previously described. The details of the operation are described in their excellent article of June 1974 in *Urology*. Although the procedure superficially resembles the use of a true pedicle flap technique that uses the penile skin for vaginal lining, it is in fact a free skin graft method. The removal of the subcutaneous fat and fascia from the deep surface of the penile flap in combination with the strong traction that is placed on the pedicle of the flap in order to move it back into the vaginal position greatly reduces the perfusion of blood through the penile skin. In addition, the deliberate ligation of the perineal arteries absolutely ensures that there will be no chance

of survival of the penile skin except as a *free skin graft*. This is not necessarily bad. It is true that a vascularized pedicle flap of penile skin provides the most supple and expansile lining for the neovagina in the surgical treatment of the male transsexual. When a true flap is used, the patient will ordinarily not need to use a vaginal form or dilator in the months following surgery. When free skin grafts are employed to line the wall of the neovagina, dilatation and stenting of the lumen are always necessary for a prolonged period. I have had the occasion a number of times to use penile skin as a free full-thickness skin graft, and it is evident that the quality of this elastic penile skin is much superior to a free skin graft (either split or full thickness) taken from nongenital portions of the body. Such a skin graft of penile skin may be left attached anteriorly to the tissues in the pubic region, or the penile skin may be cut free entirely and fitted into the vaginal pocket (without the strain and stretch required to pull the pubic tissue downward and backward, as in the procedure described by Dr.

Granato). Either method, properly applied, will produce a very satisfactory vagina.

Although Dr. Granato's surgical procedure is described as though it were a one-stage procedure, it is apparent that the initial operation will always leave the patient with a wide separation of the labia in the region of the fornix. Dr. Granato points out that he regularly uses a second operation to bring the divergent labia to the midline by a "crown plasty." In fact, almost all so-called one-stage operations for construction of the female vagina and labia are carried out in two or more steps.

Dr. Granato lends special emphasis to the importance of obtaining very precise hemostasis at the time of removal of the corpora cavernosa from the pubic symphysis. He also stresses the necessity of removing all the erectile tissues around the urethra and in the region of the pubic rami if the patient is to experience pain-free intercourse postoperatively. I entirely agree with these admonitions and have had a similar experience. The importance of dissecting the vaginal pocket to a greater depth than might seem necessary for the final dimensions of the vagina should also be stressed. In this connection, the use of a sharp incision through the upper part of Denonvilliers' fascia is needed in order to enter the plane that will allow dissection of the deepest part of the vaginal pocket up to the peritoneal reflection of the sac of Douglas.

The follow-up article by Drs. Granato, an excellent and sensible discussion, gives the authors' theories on the etiology of transsexualism. I am forced to admit that acceptance of the psychodynamic mechanisms described by Dr. Stoller is tempting as explanation of a possible mechanism for the cause of this unusual disorder. Unfortunately, my attempts and those of others, first at The Johns Hopkins Hospital Gender Identity Clinic in the 1960s and over the subsequent decade at the University of Virginia Gender Identity Clinic, to confirm this interesting theory have been unsuccessful. My reviews of the family histories of parental behavior or attitudes in transsexual patients has only rarely supported Dr. Stoller's hypothesis. It has been, in fact, quite uncommon for the psychiatrists and psychologists on our team to be able to identify parental influences as causative factors that would have led to the development of transsexualism in patients.

At present I am forced to lean toward the ideas expressed by Helene Stourzh-Anderle in suspecting that transsexualism may have a biologic origin. Although physicians have not been able to identify consistent chromosome abnormalities, the very early age of onset of this condition and the essentially 100% "nonreversibility" of the disorder by psychological treatment suggests that physicians should continue the search for an as yet undetected organic or physiologic abnormality as the cause of transsexualism. If this is indeed a psychologic disorder from the standpoint of etiology, then the lack of response to psychotherapy makes it quite unlike most other psychogenic disorders known to medicine. The rather uniform, long-term, subjective satisfaction of these patients following surgery also suggests a biologic origin. It is rare to find a patient who wishes to return to the original gender.

I agree with the common sense criteria for the selection of patients as described by the Drs. Granato. It does appear that they are unduly pessimistic about the percentage of patients seeking this surgery who are appropriate candidates. They refer to a patient selection system that finds only 15% of those presenting to be suitable candidates for surgery. I have found in the patient population at Virginia that at least 40% of those seeking surgery have proved to be suitable candidates. This figure may be partly related to the fact that my patients may be somewhat selected, since most of them are physician referred—many from psychiatrists who have worked with the patients for some years.

I also disagree with the Drs. Granato about the importance of the gender physical features of the candidate in selecting those appropriate for transsexual surgery. I have looked hard at those patients seeking feminization who have indeed been unusually tall or heavy or masculine in their features or voice. In follow-up visits, when such patients have received surgery, they have seemed every bit as subjectively satisfied with the changes and have used the operation as effectively in their social lives as those who, on the surface, appear to be better adapted physically for the feminine role. I have tended to pay less attention to basic physical shape, size, or form in making the decision for surgery in recent years.

I would like to compliment the Drs. Granato on their frank reporting of the significant complications they have encountered. Most large gender identity clinics will encounter occasional patients who develop a rectovaginal fistula after surgery. This is a troublesome complication, and, indeed, the need for a colostomy and additional surgery is a factor that must be anticipated by the patient in a candid discussion before surgery is undertaken. I believe that the operative permit should indeed include a separate consent to perform a colostomy at the time of reconstruction, should a perforation into the rectum be encountered. However, although complications are relatively common in surgery of this type, patients, at least in my experience, have been uncommonly tolerant of these difficulties and have continued to be very cooperative. Indeed, the motivation of these patients for gender reassignment surgery is so strong that they usually will bend over backward in helping the surgeon obtain a good result.

Finally, I support the contention of the Drs. Granato that the psychiatric member of the gender identity team is the essential, and central, person in the evaluation of patients for surgery. Like the Drs. Granato, I have found that psychoanalysis is a virtually useless technique for the treatment of transsexualism. "Supportive" psychotherapy, (*i.e.*, support for the patient's choice of gender), by contrast, has proved effective if the psychiatrist is genuinely willing to accept the patient's gender choice. Any intellectual refusal by the psychiatrist to deal with the patient in the chosen gender has met with a 100% therapeutic failure in my experience.

Physicians still need to know much more about the dynamics of surgery in the treatment of transsexualism, but, at present, it is much the best (if not *only*) treatment for many of these patients, and continued follow-up study after surgery should offer valuable information on the nature of gender in general.

PART THIRTY-EIGHT

SURGICAL TREATMENT OF ERECTILE IMPOTENCE

103

THE SMALL-CARRION PENILE PROTHESIS

Michael P. Small, M.D.

Clinical Professor of Urology, University of Miami School of Medicine, Miami, Florida

Urologic Clinics of North America — Vol. 5. No. 3., October 1978

The surgical management of impotence by the use of prosthetic devices is not new. Operative procedures involving the use of internal penile splinting date back to 1936. The history of the surgical management of impotence has previously been described.[16]

The majority of earlier penile prostheses were unsatisfactory because of the high rate of extrusion through the urethra or the skin of the dorsal shaft, lymphatic edema, irritation of the glans penis, breakage of the prosthesis, and slippage of the glans over the prosthesis. The last complication had been relatively common, making vaginal penetration either very painful or difficult, and occasionally resulting in erosion of the prosthesis through the penis.

Recently, two prostheses were developed at approximately the same time and have rejuvenated the urologists' interest in the field of surgical management of impotence. This has also renewed the interest of other individuals dealing in the area of sexuality, such as psychiatrists, sexual counselors, and the family physicians and internists.

In 1973, Scott, Bradley, and Timm reported their initial experience using an inflatable prosthesis.[12] The hydraulic system as well as the inflation and deflation pump bulbs of this prosthesis has been subsequently revised. Several other modifications in the penile cylinders have also been made. The idea of an implantable hydraulic fluid transfer system by which the corpora are inflated and deflated at will in an attempt to more closely approximate the normal physiolgic erectile state has excellent potential. The idea is ingenious, but as of this time, the drawbacks frequently outweigh the advantages because of the extensive surgery required, the long length of hospitalization, and the high incidence of hydraulic and mechanical failures that have required reoperation.

Furlow reported that the inflatable prosthesis and the pump mechanism allow the patient to select a state of flaccidity or of turgidity at his own discretion. He felt that acceptance by the patient and partner was ideal; however, he also felt that modification of the engineering of the device as well as its material was necessary to minimize existing mechanical problems.[3] In 15 patients, Ambrose has reported a mechanical failure rate ranging from 25 to 35 percent with the inflatable prosthetic device.[1]

SMALL-CARRION PENILE PROSTHESIS

From February 1973 to January 1975, the Small-Carrion penile prosthesis was implanted in 41 patients.[15] As of November 1975, the prosthesis had been implanted in 75 patients.[13] As the interest of the physician and patient in the Small-Carrion penile prosthesis has increased around the country, so have the number of surgical

TABLE 1. Patients Receiving The Small-Carrion Penile Prosthesis

Diagnosis	Number of Patients*	Results	Comments
Postprostatectomy: cystectomy; abdominal-perineal resection	21	Excellent	
Aortobifermoral bypass	1	Excellent	
Postpriapism	4	Excellent (3); Poor (1)	Unable to implant prosthesis
Psychogenic	40	Excellent	One patient had prolonged discomfort in glans
Pelvic fractures	13	Excellent (12); Good (1)	Lost one prosthesis secondary to infection
Peyronie's disease	11	Excellent (10); Good (1)	Plaque not incised
Arteriosclerosis or venous insufficiency	84	Excellent	
Spinal cord injury	17	Excellent (16); Good (1)	Lost one prosthesis secondary to infection
Post electrical burn	1	Excellent	Required urethroplasty
Diabetes mellitus	65	Excellent (63); Poor (2)	Infection and septicemia with loss of both prostheses
Epispadias and extrophy	1	Good	Small phallus
Hypogonadism	1	Excellent	
Scleroderma	1	Good	Lost one prosthesis secondary to surgical perforation of glans

* Total—260; Excellent—251; Good—5; Poor—4.

implantations. By December 1977, my series of patients had increased to 260.

Table 1 summarizes the etiology of the impotence, the number of patients operated, and results and complications in this group.

Sizes. Figure 1 shows several sizes of the Small-Carrion penile prosthesis. Prostheses are now available in eight standard lengths. Two diameters for sizes up to 17.0 cm lengths, and, at this point, a third and wider diameter, 1.3 cm, are available. Construction of the prosthesis has not changed from that originally described.[16]

One of the criticisms of the Small-Carrion prosthesis is that too many sizes are available. This feature is definitely not a handicap except perhaps in the initial purchase price of a complete set. On the contrary, with greater availability of sizes, it is much easier to provide a proper fit at the time of surgery and therefore a good surgical result.

Table 2 shows the various lengths and diameters that have been used in the 260 patients reported. Initially, the prostheses were only available and only used in patients who required 18 cm or less. As more patients have been evaluated and operated upon, there has been an increased demand for larger prostheses. The sizes required and used have followed the typical ''bell-shaped curve'' pattern.

My personal experience has been that a broad selection of sizes is not only desirable but mandatory in order to prevent or avoid a number of potential problems, which I shall describe.

First, it is extremely difficult to determine the proper size of prosthesis prior to the time of surgery. It is, in my opinion, impossible. At the time of surgery I frequently have to try two or three different lengths and diameters to achieve the optimum fit for the particular patient. If the prosthesis is too long, the patient may suffer severe and unnecessary pain in the area of the glans as well as in the area of the ischial tuberosities. There may even be buckling of the prosthesis in the midportion of the penis. If the prosthesis is too short, flexion of the glans penis over the prosthesis will occur, making vaginal penetration quite difficult, painful, or

Fig. 1. The Small–Carrion penile prosthesis is available in eight different lengths and three diameters.

TABLE 2. Size of Prosthesis Used in 260 Patients

Length (cm)	Diameter (cm)	Number of Patients*
12.0	0.9	1
12.0	1.1	1
13.3	0.9	3
13.3	1.1	14
14.5	0.9	18
14.5	1.1	30
15.8	0.9	17
15.8	1.1	46
17.0	0.9	4
17.0	1.1	63
17.0	1.3	3
18.0	1.1	22
18.0	1.3 with a 1.1 cm Tip	18
19.0	1.3 with a 1.1 cm Tip	13
20.0	1.3 with a 1.1 cm Tip	11
21.0	1.3 with a 1.1 cm Tip	4

* Figures total more than 260 because eight patients have returned for insertion of a larger prosthesis.

impossible, and may lead to the so called "SST deformity." An implanted prosthesis that is as little as 0.5 cm too short will make a marked difference in the surgical result, and the patient may be quite distressed by it.

It must also be kept in mind that there are certain patients who may have a different length corpora and crus on one side than on the other. The etiology of this may be congenital, inflammatory, or secondary to pelvic fracture. It is in this group of patients that the surgeon should be prepared to implant a different length prosthesis on each side, so that the prostheses actually implanted will set evenly under the glans although there is a disparity in the posterior placement. While the absolute necessity of a proper surgical fit has been duly emphasized, it would be well to note that the area of the glans penis is the most important area into and under which the prosthesis must fit perfectly.

Medical-legal considerations are also a good reason to have many sizes of prosthesis available. While it is possible to shorten an implant that is slightly too long, it is much more desirable for all concerned to have the proper length available in the operating suite. This saves time and effort, and obviously, the factory-finished product would be superior. In the event that shortening is necessary, it is best accomplished by trimming a small portion from the tail. Occasionally a small portion may be removed from the distal tip of the prosthesis. If this is done, plastic surgical sandpaper must be used to smooth the revised area so that it is left in a completely non-irritating end underneath the glans. Of course, after the sanding has been accomplished to satisfaction, the prosthesis must be washed thoroughly in an antibiotic irrigating solution.

If a surgeon implants a prosthesis of the improper

size because the selection available to him at the time of surgery is incomplete or inadequate, complaints from the patient are almost inevitable.

SURGICAL TECHNIQUE

The basic surgical procedure has not deviated from that which was described in 1975.[16] The perineal approach is still preferred, since it leaves the patient with no penile scar. It is also much easier to identify the urethra as well as the crus and the corpora with this approach. The use of Incise Drape* has been helpful in isolating the rectum from the sterile field, thereby maintaining a very low incidence of infection. For the same reason, the preoperative, intraoperative, and postoperative antibiotic regime, which has previously been described, is highly desirable and should be followed in all patients.[14] A urethral catheter is inserted prior to making the perineal incision. It is usually removed after the bladder is emptied at the conclusion of the operative procedure but may be left in overnight.

In all patients who have borderline symptoms of prostatism or diabetes mellitus and who do not wish to have bladder neck or prostatic surgery, a 12 French catheter is left in the urethra for one or two nights postoperatively. With this small catheter, any periurethral secretions will easily exude from around the catheter and will not build up and allow development of periurethritis or periurethral abscess formation.

The prostheses are soaked in a solution of polymyxin B sulfate and neomycin sulfate solution and the wound is copiously irrigated with the same solution before and after implantation.

Figure 2 shows the patient in the lithotomy position after a midline perineal incision has been performed. The patient had been prepared with a 15 minute scrub and the rectum was draped from the sterile field. The incision here is carried through the subcutaneous tissues and to the bulbocavernosus muscle. At this point, the urethral catheter should be palpated within this muscle and more specifically within the corpus spongiosum and urethra.

THE SMALL-CARRION PENILE PROSTHESIS

In Figure 3 the urethra with the bulbocavernosus muscle is being retracted to one side. The ischiocavernosus muscle overlying the crus of the penis and a portion of the corpus cavernosum are freed and opened vertically. In this area there are usually multiple small veins that have to be carefully cauterized.

The urethra should be kept retracted or in view at

* Johnson and Johnson, New Brunswick, New Jersey

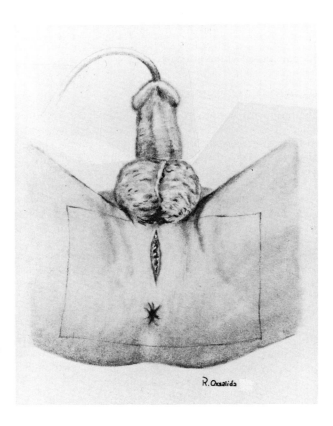

Fig. 2. A midline perineal incision has been performed.

all times. Once the corpora and the crus have been opened, dilation is started proximally, as shown in Figure 4, with a No. 7 Hegar dilator; care must be taken not to perforate the crus in this area. The dilator will not go too far posteriorly and will come close to the ischial tuberosity. No further dilation is needed in this area since the prostheses are narrow posteriorly. Excessive dilation may allow the tail of the prosthesis to bend upon itself and will not give the tail the support it needs. Dilation is then carried out distally, putting the corpora on stretch so that perforation does not occur if the penis or corpora ''accordion.'' That is shown in Figure 5. Dilation should be carried out underneath the glans penis to prepare proper implantation of the prosthesis. The Hegar dilators should face laterally and not medially, as there is a greater chance of perforating the urethra if the tip of the Hegar dilator angles toward the urethra.

With the smaller Hegar dilators, dilation is accomplished underneath the glans, but with appropriate caution. As the dilators progress to size No. 10, 11, 12, or even 13, it is usually quite easy to dilate under the glans

by simply rotating the Hegar dilator, without applying to much pressure to the glans. If the patient has had priapism, scleroderma, or some other condition that has left the area in a scarred condition, extra care and more vigorous dilation will usually be indicated.

As has been mentioned earlier, it is impossible to determine which size prosthesis will be required for the patient prior to the time of surgery. This must be determined with the corpora opened. Several lengths and diameters may be tried before the ideal implant has been selected. When the proper size is determined and the fit into the glans penis is snug, smooth, and reveals no buckling or twisting of the prosthesis, the corpora is again irrigated and closed with multiple interrupted sutures of 0 chromic catgut. The same procedure is carried out on the contralateral side.

Figure 6 schematically shows the prosthesis in place prior to closing the crus. It also demonstrates the relationship to the ischial tuberosities posteriorly, to the urethra and the bulbocavernosus muscle in the midline, and, most importantly, to the undersurface of the glans penis distally. With all this accomplished to the surgeon's satisfaction, the subcutaneous tissues and skin are closed in a routine manner.

A decision must be made as to whether the catheter should be left indwelling overnight. This depends upon the patient's symptomatology, as well as his previous response to spinal anesthesia. Drains are not used and the patients are usually discharged one and one-half days after surgery. During this time they remain on antibiotic therapy and are discharged from the hospital with antibiotics. The patients are asked to remain in town for four to five days postoperatively and are seen at least once to be sure that no complications are developing. At that time, questions can be answered regarding how to best wear the penis inconspicuously, what type of underwear is best for their particular size prosthesis, and when they can resume intercourse.

INDICATIONS FOR A PENILE PROSTHESIS

The many etiologies of impotence have been tabulated in Table 1. These, in general, are considered excellent indications for implantation of a penile prosthesis. There is some difference of opinion among physicians as to whether psychogenic impotence should be treated surgically. Some feel that the treatment of such patients would best be left to therapy by psychiatrists or sexual counselors. It has been my experience that there are certain patients with psychogenic impotence who would definitely benefit from a penile prosthesis. This particular category of patients includes those who have undergone sexual counseling, psychiatric therapy without response, and/or even an empiric course of androgen therapy

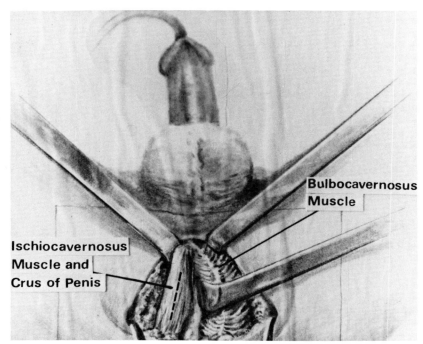

Bulbocavernosus Muscle

Ischiocavernosus Muscle and Crus of Penis

Fig. 3. The urethra with the bulbocavernosus muscle is being retracted to one side. The ischiocavernosus muscle overlying the crus of the penis and a portion of the corpus cavernosum are freed and opened vertically.

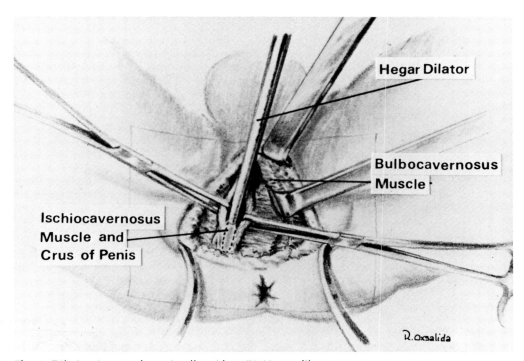

Hegar Dilator

Bulbocavernosus Muscle

Ischiocavernosus Muscle and Crus of Penis

R. Oxsalida

Fig. 4. Dilation is started proximally with a #7 Hegar dilator.

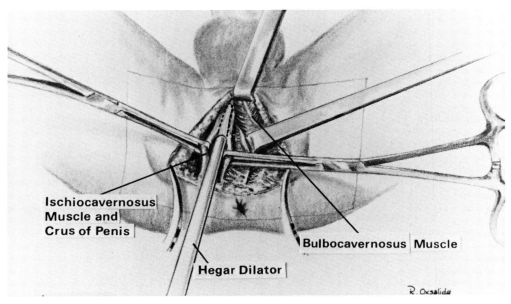

Ischiocavernosus
Muscle and
Crus of Penis

Bulbocavernosus Muscle

Hegar Dilator

R. Oxsalida

Fig. 5. Dilation is carried out distally to a size compatible with the diameter of the prosthesis to be inserted.

without improvement, but are still quite distressed regarding their sexual disability. When impotence has reached the point that it is adversely and significantly affecting the life of a patient, and after more conventional methods of treatment have failed, I feel that surgical correction of the problem by implantation of a penile prosthesis is indicated.

In this group of patients and certain patients with organic impotence, I routinely studied rapid eye movement (REM) tumescence with the nocturnal penile tumescence monitor as advocated by Karacan et al.[6] and Fisher.[2]

Osborne,[9] using the Minnesota multiphasic personality inventory, feels that he can be of some help in identifying emotional factors in impotent patients prior to corrective surgery for impotence. He evaluates both husband and wife.

A previously unreported benefit of the use of the penile prosthesis is in the management of the impotent male who has a normal semenogram but is unable to produce children because of his inability to penetrate the vagina. In the younger individual this is not an uncommon problem and use of a prosthesis will reverse the "infertility."

COMPLICATIONS OF PENILE PROSTHESIS

Complications with the inflatable penile prosthesis are somewhat more common. The major complications have

been mechanical failure secondary to kinking of the tubing, fluid leakage, or failure of the system to properly inflate or deflate. With the Small-Carrion prosthesis, with the proper antibiotic coverage, the rate of infection has been minimal, with a reported incidence of less than 0.5 percent.

With the Small-Carrion penile prosthesis, the incidence of serious complications in the first 20 patients, prior to the routine use of antibiotic therapy, revealed a complication rate of 15 percent. Since antibiotic therapy has been routinely administered preoperatively, intraoperatively, and postoperatively, the incidence of infection has decreased to less than 0.5 percent. These infections were in two diabetic patients who subsequently required removal of the prostheses.

Other complications include the inability to insert the prosthesis because of extensive scarring in the corpora after priapism, urinary retention in one diabetic patient, paraphimosis (treated with a dorsal relaxing incision), and surgical perforation of the glans penis in one patient who had severe scarring in the corpora secondary to scleroderma. Including infection, serious complications have been less than 1 percent.

ADVANTAGES AND DISADVANTAGES OF THE SMALL-CARRION PROSTHESIS

As with any implantable device, whether it is for the management of impotence, urinary incontinence, or it is

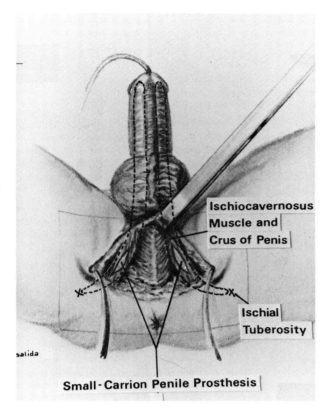

Ischiocavernosus
Muscle and
Crus of Penis

Ischial
Tuberosity

salida

Small - Carrion Penile Prosthesis

Fig. 6. The prosthesis is in place prior to closing the crus. Note the relationship to the ischial tuberosities posteriorly, the urethra and bulbocavernosus in the midline, and, most importantly, the undersurface of the glans penis distally.

for non-urologic prosthetics, such as hip and knee replacements, potential problems and disadvantages are a reality. With the Small-Carrion penile prosthesis, the patient is left with an erect or a semierect penis. The patient must be made fully aware of this fact well in advance of surgery. My only comment regarding this particular "disadvantage" is that of the more than 260 patients in whom I have personally implanted the Small-Carrion penile prosthesis, no one has requested removal of the prosthesis because of this factor. Various types of under and outer clothing can make the penis completely inconspicuous.

Performance of cystoscopy may be difficult or impossible depending upon the length of the prosthesis implanted. Cystoscopy and transurethral resection of the prostate may require a perineal urethrostomy. If the prostate gland needs to be removed through a suprapubic approach, catheterization should also be maintained postoperatively through this area. If long-term catheter

drainage is necessary with a large diameter catheter, it should be done suprapubically.

In patients who have neurogenic bladder or who are rendered incontinent after an internal sphincterotomy to allow bladder emptying, the Small-Carrion prosthesis gives excellent support to an external or condom type catheter.

Partner satisfaction has been excellent. Many patients have reported that certain partners are not even aware that they have a prosthesis, as it is not palpable under the additional blood flow that many patients receive around the prosthesis after the capsule has formed. This additional blood flow around the prosthesis was unexpected and gives many patients an additional degree of erection. In addition, the increased blood flow through the corpus spongiosum and into the glans penis provides an extra cushion effect over the tip of the prosthesis during intercourse. It is normal for the glans to be hypersensitive for the first few vaginal penetrations, but this additional blood flow to the glans minimizes this discomfort.

The Small-Carrion prostheses are readily sterilized and completely nonreactive. There have been no reports of breakage. The patients may begin sexual activity usually within two to three weeks when a perineal incision has been used. A few patients have reported pain for as long as six weeks postoperatively.

Because of its simplicity of design, complete absence of moving parts, and relative ease and simplicity of the recommended method of surgical implantation, the cost of the implantation of the Small-Carrion prosthesis is only a fraction of that required for the inflatable prosthesis.

PRECAUTIONS

As with any operative procedure, certain precautions should be taken. The surgeon should be sure that the patient definitely is impotent. If it is psychogenic impotence, it should be so noted and documented in the patient's record.

Prostatism. In general, the prospective patient should exhibit little or no evidence of prostatism. If the symptoms are moderate to marked, the patient will almost certainly develop urinary retention postoperatively, which may or may not subside after several days of catheter drainage with a small size Foley catheter. If obstructive symptoms are significant, I recommend to the patient that he first undergo a prostatectomy.

Neurogenic Bladder. Special consideration should be given to patients with neurogenic bladder, such as the diabetic who has an increased residual urine. With the prosthesis, his residual urine may increase even further, resulting in accelerated deterioration of the bladder. In this group of patients it is extremely important to resolve all bladder, prostatic, or external sphincter problems prior to implantation of a prosthesis.

Peyronie's Disease. Certain patients with Peyronie's disease also require special consideration. If the Peyronie's disease is so severe that there is marked chordee after implantation of the prosthesis, then I feel that the technique described by Raz and Kaufman[10] should be performed. A 1- to 2-inch vertical incision can be made in the dorsum of the penis, which is carried down to the corpora bilaterally. The dissection is quite easy and the neurovascular bundle has never been damaged through this small incision. Dissection is then carried proximally to the base of the penis if necessary. A transverse incision is then made across the plaque in the corpora on one side and then the other if necessary. These transverse incisions can be multiple, can start at the base of the penis and be carried out to the corona, and can cut through the corpora down to the implanted prosthesis.

The only complication has been penile edema. This usually resolves within two weeks and the patient is left with a small vertical penile scar on the dorsal midline and an almost perfectly straightened penis.

In the usual patient with Peyronie's disease, there is every little that has to be done other than insertion of the Small-Carrion penile prosthesis.[14] Occasionally if there is a tendency for the penis to bend to one side or the other, a longer prosthesis can be inserted in the concave side so that the penis will be straight. Most impotent patients with Peyronie's disease can be handled with one of these techniques.

Dilation. When dilating the corpora, care should be taken that perforation does not occur. If this occurs in the crus posteriorly, the prosthesis will migrate posteriorly. If dilation is done too vigorously distally, perforation may occur through the glans; therefore, care should be taken during the dilation, although it can be performed slightly more vigorously under the glans than back toward the crus. In addition, if theHegar dilators are not carefully guided through the corpora and the corpora "accordians" during the dilation process, perforation may occur along the course of the corpora. Dilation of the corpora should not be performed toward the midline, but the tip of the Hegar dilator should be directed more laterally, so that perforation of the urethra does not occur.

To determine the diameter of the prosthesis to be used, the largest diameter that will fit adequately and comfortably under the glans penis is selected. It must not protrude laterally, since it may subsequently cause painful intercourse and possible erosion.

SUMMARY

A normal state of erection can be achieved by bilateral, intracorporal implantation of the Small-Carrion penile prosthesis. This prosthesis gives adequate length and, more importantly for normal intercourse, normal width to the penis. Although the prosthesis is firm, it is flexible enough to keep the phallus inconspicuous under various types of undershorts, either in the normal position or against the abdominal wall. The fact that the patient will have a permanent erection has not been a deterrent. Furthermore, there have been no complaints about this postoperatively. Raz and Kaufman,[11] Goodwin,[4] Melman,[7] Nellens et al.,[8] and others have reported excellent results with the use of the Small-Carrion prosthesis.

REFERENCES

1. Ambrose, Robert. Miami, Florida. Personal Communication, February, 1978

2. Fisher, C: Conference on Penile Prosthesis. N.Y. Academy of Medicine, October 1976

3. Furlow, W. L.: Surgical management of impotence using the inflatable penile prosthesis: experience with 36 patients. Mayo Clin Proc 51:325, 1976

4. Goodwin, W. E.: Complication of perineal prostatectomy. In Smith, R. B., and Skinner, D. C. (eds.): Complications of Urologic Surgery. Philadelphia, W. B. Saunders Co., 1976, p. 261

5. Gottesman, J. E., Kosters, S., Das, S., et al.: The Small-Carrion prosthesis for male impotency. J Urol 117:289, 1977

6. Karacan, I., Williams, R. L., Thornberry, J. J., et al.: Sleep-related penile tumescence as a function of age. Am J Psychiatry 132:9, 1976

7. Melman, A.: Experience with implantation of the Small-Carrion penile implant for organic impotence, J Urol 116:49, 1976

8. Nellans, R. E., Naftel, W., and Stein, J.: Experience with the Small-Carrion penile prosthesis. J Urol 115:280, 1976

9. Osborne, D: Psychologic evaluation of impotent men. Mayo Clin Proc 51:363, 1976

10. Raz, S., DeKernion, J. B., and Kaufman, J. J.: Surgical treatment of Peyronie's disease: A new approach. J Urol 117:598, 1977

11. Raz, S., and Kaufman, J. J.: Small-Carrion operation for impotence. Urology 7:68, 1976

12. Scott, E. B., Bradley, W. D., and Timm, G. W.: Management of erectile impotence. Urology 2:80, 1973

13. Small, M. P.: Small-Carrion penile prosthesis: a new implant for management of impotence, Mayo Clin Proc 51:3–36, 1976

14. Small, M. O.: Small-Carrion penile prosthesis: a report on 160 cases and review of the literature. J Urol 119:365, 1978

15. Small, M. P., and Carrion, H. M.: Penile prosthesis: new implant for management of impotence. J Fla Med Assoc 62:21, 1975

16. Small, M. P., Carrion, H. M., and Gordon, J. A.: Small-Carrion penile prosthesis. Urology, 5:479, 1975

7414 Miami Lakes Drive
Miami Lakes, Florida 33014

EDITORIAL COMMENTS

Dr. Small's extensive, well-documented experience with his prosthesis has clearly demonstrated the value of the surgical treatment of impotence. He provides us with several surgical tips based on his experience. Those include the value of the use of sizers, the trend toward a larger prosthesis, and the detailed description of the technique of dilation of the corpus cavernosum.

An alternative to Dr. Small's prosthesis is the hydraulic prosthesis popularized by Dr. Brantley Scott. Although rather extensive surgery was required for the hydraulic prosthesis in the beginning, Dr. Scott states that the current procedure is accomplished either through a one-inch incision at the base of the penis or else a one-inch incision at the junction of the penis and scrotum. He now slips the reservoir into the prevesicle space by means of the inguinal canal and implants the cylinders into the penis directly, along with the scrotal pump. Scott further states that, although mechanical failure was of great import at the inception of use of the hydraulic prosthesis, he has had only one leak in his last 198 cylinder implantations. Also, in a recent series, he found four infected prostheses out of 270 (1.5 percent). Lastly, Dr. Scott feels that his prosthesis allows periprosthetic tumescence following implantation. However, he makes a point of the fact that the patient should not be informed that this is an added bonus of prosthetic placement and should be totally dependent on the prosthesis for full erectile support (Dr. Scott, personal communication, 1978).

It is the opinion of the editors that both these prostheses, i.e., the Small–Carrion and the hydraulic device of Brantley Scott, have their individual merit and the needs of the patient and the experience of the surgeon must be considered in selecting the proper prosthesis. Certainly, the price differential is significant between the two devices, yet each is unique in its design and method of implantation. It must be emphasized that when describing either of these prostheses to a patient, one should describe both prostheses and let the patient make the choice of which he feels to be most appropriate for his needs.

Commentary: Value of Penile Prostheses

Michael P. Small

Until fairly recently, improvements in the surgical management of impotence have been conspicuous by their absence. Although the operative use of internal splinting dates back to the mid 1930s, refinements in the surgical correction of impotence have been quite late in developing.

As Dr. Pearman pointed out in the first edition of *Current Operative Urology*, impotence as a medical problem has historically either been ignored completely or relegated to insignificant spots on medical programs and back pages in the literature. Dr. Pearman's work is all the more outstanding because it called attention to a long neglected but very real need for surgical alternatives in the treatment of impotence.

The first use of intracorporeal penile implants in the United States was reported by Whitehead in 1972.[1] This implant was a leader in penile implant surgery but because of the rigidity of the polyethylene material, complications such as extrusion and pain occurred; therefore this implant was abandoned.

In 1973 the Small–Carrion penile prosthesis was introduced. The device itself, along with the technique recommended for implantation, has helped eliminate many of the complications and side-effects that had plagued recipients of earlier prosthetic devices.

The concept of this method of treatment is remarkable in its simplicity. Two semirigid silocone bodies are implanted intracorporally and secured so as to minimize slippage, pressure points, and unnecessary stress. Nature is duplicated closely and disturbed as little as possible. The use of a perineal approach to accomplish the surgery reduces the length of time required for healing and avoids scarring of the penis.

The results in my series of 900 patients indicate to me that the Small–Carrion penile prosthesis has stood the test of time. The overall results remain as reported in the foregoing article. The complication rate, including infection, erosion, and surgical trauma, remains approximately 5%. Patient and partner satisfaction is good to excellent in over 95% of those interviewed. Many patients have reported having a supplemental erection when sexually aroused—apparently the result of increased blood flow through the cavernous bodies. Interestingly, there has been a small group of patients with mild degrees of urinary incontinence, usually after prostatectomy, who have attained complete control of their urine from the increase in resistance along the course of the urethra.

A number of semirigid penile prostheses other than the Small–Carrion are available and have been reported. One of these is the hinged silicone penile prosthesis developed by Dr. Roy Finney and reported in the *Journal of Urology* in October 1977. The benefit of the Finney semirigid prosthesis is reported to be the manner in which the hinge allows the penis to be inconspicuous when not in use. The Jonas implant, reported in 1980, is similar to the Small–Carrion but has a coiled silver wire rather than a silicone sponge inside. The silver wire gives the implant more malleability and therefore it is less conspicuous. In comparison, Figure 7 shows schematically the Small–Carrion prosthesis in a postoperative patient with the penis in an erect state. Figure 8 demonstrates that the penis is firm yet flexible enough to be inconspicuous under the proper type of under clothing but without a hinge. Although most patients inquire about how obvious the penis will be postoperatively, the fact that it will be semirigid has not deterred them from having the surgery nor proved to be a significant problem.

A significant number of patients with Peyronie's disease who require surgery can be managed by incision of the Peyronie's band or plaque without any other surgery. On the other hand, some patients with Peyronie's disease have varying degrees of impotence and would be better managed with the use of a semirigid prosthetic device. After the surgical implantation of the prosthesis and appropriate closure, the penis should be evaluated for the degree of bend. If the patient still has a significant curvature, a dorsal incision may be made in the penis and the Peyronie's area incised for proper straightening.

Numerous and varied surgical approaches and techniques have been reported in the urologic literature for use in implanting various prosthetic devices. I have continued to use the perineal approach and the same techinque initially described and illustrated when the Small–Carrion penile prosthesis was introduced. With this approach there is easy access to the corpora and crus, and dilation of the corpora is possible with better control. Elimination of a penile incision reduces healing time and allows the patient to resume normal sexual activity within 2 to 3 wk. Avoidance of an obvious scar is also an advantage.

Obviously, prevention of infection is always a chief concern when implanting a prosthetic device so close to a contaminated area. The rectum is always draped from the surgical field with one of the various adhesive barrier drapes when the surgical approach that I recomend is used. Incorporating the antibiotic regimen that has previously been described into my surgical routine has been instrumental in keeping my incidence of infection for this particular procedure to less than 0.5%. Regardless of which antibiotic regimen is selected, it is most essential that one be used along with strict aseptic technique and antibiotic wound irrigation at the time of surgery.

Suffice it to say that no amount of skill or effort can produce satisfactory results if the prosthetic device used is not fitted perfectly and correctly into the patient at the time of surgery. Both sides of the prosthesis must set firmly in the crus posteriorly and under the glans distally if the fit, and therefore the function, are to be optimum.

Most semirigid prostheses are produced in a variety of widths and lengths, and it is imperative that an adequate assortment be available at the time of surgery so the proper

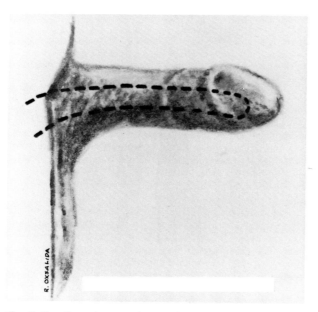

Fig. 7. Small-carrion penile prosthesis with the penis in an erect state.

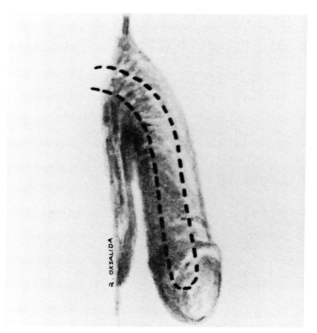

Fig. 8. The small-carrion penile prosthesis is flexible enough, without a hinge, to be inconspicuous under the proper clothing.

selection can be made. An implanted prosthesis that is as little as 0.5 cm too long or too short will adversely affect the surgical result. A sizer set may be helpful in determining the proper size to use. Also, in certain patients it will be necessary to implant a different length of prosthesis in each side of the penis in order to achieve a desirable result. This may occur in patients who have congenital shortening of one corpora or in those patients who have had a pelvic fracture with subsequent distortion of one or both corpora.

REFERENCE

1. Whitehead ED: Penile implant for erectile impotence. Presented at the annual meeting of the American Urological Association, Washington, D.C., 1972

ANNOTATED BIBLIOGRAPHY

Osborne D: Psychologic evaluation of impotent men. Mayo Clin Proc 51:363, 1976

The author describes goals in his evaluation of patients: to differentiate organic from psychogenic impotence, to identify the factors that have caused the erectile difficulty, to evaluate the patient's motivation for surgery, and to prepare the patient and his wife for postsurgical adjustment. Interestingly, one of the goals is to identify patients in whom surgery might precipitate emotional problems. The patient is evaluated by an intensive interview and many times the wife is included. Psychological testing such as the Minnesota Multiphasic Personality Inventory Profile is used to help evaluate the goals. The author points out the importance of nonsurgical treatment whenever possible. His technique is described, but he points out that if this does not alleviate the patient's impotence, then surgical correction should be reconsidered.

Furlow WL: Surgical management of impotence using the inflatable penile prosthesis: Experience with 36 patients. Mayo Clin Proc 51:325, 1976

The author summarizes his experience with the inflatable penile prosthesis in 36 patients with organic impotence treated from October 1974 through September 1975. He also comments on an additional 15 patients who underwent successful implantation of the inflatable prosthesis. All patients underwent extensive preoperative evaluation, including psychologic testing and the Minnesota Multiphasic Personality Inventory. The author points out that the description and demonstration of the prosthetic device preoperatively, as well as showing its advantages and potential risks, are extremely important features of any interview. Surgical guidelines were established in an effort to standardize the surgical technique originally described by Scott and associates. The author reports major complications occurring in 7 of 36 patients, with the majority of these being mechanical failures that were all corrected by a secondary surgical procedure. Infection was an infrequent complication. Patient–partner acceptance was excellent, and orgasm and ejaculation were unaffected. To evaluate mechanical problems associated with the use of the inflatable device, a radiopaque contrast material is placed into the system for postoperative evaluation. It is pointed out that further developments in device engineering and material modification should minimize mechanical problems.

Finney RP: New hinged silicone penile implant. J Urol 118:585, 1977

The author presents his experience with a soft silicone elastomer that has an inner distal rigid silicone rod to produce penile shaft stiffness. He reports that the shaft hinge permits the penis to hang down more normally but does provide stability for coitus. The proximal or tail end is cylindric and may be trimmed to the proper length during surgery. It is reported that the prosthesis comes in one diameter but with various lengths to fit each patient. He further points out that the length is determined preoperatively and only that size need be available in the operating suite. The proper size is determined by measuring the distance from the pubic bone to the approximate mid-glans dorsally. The implant incision and dilation of the corpora are performed in the identical manner as with the Small–Carrion penile prosthesis. The author reports his experience in 39 patients and states that no patient has reported any problem with the hinge buckling or any reported lack of stability during coitus. He also states that the partners seem to prefer the more normal dependent appearance of the hinged implant during day-to-day contact. He further states that some partners report better performance from their consorts than when they were fully potent.

Cramer SA, Anderson EE, Bredael JJ, et al: Complications of Small–Carrion penile prosthesis. Urology 13:49, 1979

The authors present the etiology of impotence and their results with complications in 76 patients. Complications in 20 patients ran the gamet from superficial wound infection through urethral erosion, inappropriate size, prolonged pain, and nonurologic complications such as hypoglycemia and atelectasis. Seven of the 20 patients required removal of their prosthesis if they had not already extruded it spontaneously. Urethral erosion occurred in three patients. Thirteen complications were considered minor and resolved with sitz baths and antibiotics for superficial wound infection, lidocaine injections for prolonged pain, and temporary Foley catheter drainage for acute urinary retention. The authors summarize the complications reported in the literature and found that most reported series include wound infection as the most common complication. They point out that this occurred in earlier series, when antibiotic regimens were not uniform. This complication was more common in diabetics. Also emphasized is meticulous preparation of the patient, including appropriate transurethral surgery when necessary, careful skin preparation, and systemic antibiotic coverage. The proper size prosthesis is critical and must be determined intraoperatively. It is stated that problems with concealment were reported in earlier series, but most patients accommodate well to that inconvenience with appropriate underwear. In summary, 96% of this group of patients had good functional and cosmetic results following insertion of the penile prosthesis.

Karacan I, Ilaria RL: Nocturnal penile tumescence (NPT): The phenomenon and its role in the diagnosis of impotence. Sexual Disabil 1:260, 1978

It is pointed out that the differential diagnosis of impotence has rested on questionable clinical grounds. Erectile impotence (impotence) is defined and the separation of impotence into primary and secondary is clarified. The importance of an accurate history in the diagnosis of impotence is emphasized but the authors pointed out that the history has its limitations and that the penis must be examined in its flaccid and erectile states to get an accurate evaluation of erection. Interviews with a sexual partner help to a degree but do not necessarily clarify whether the impotence is organic or psychogenic. The authors and others have documented that in young adult men, at least 80% of REM sleep is associated with nocturnal penile tumescence. They point out that NPT is a common phenomenon that undergoes changes with increasing age. The authors describe the use of the nocturnal penile tumescence monitor and in studies on normal subjects describe how erections occur and change throughout advancing age. The first work done on organic impotence was done in diabetics. While evaluating this group of patients, it was felt that NPT could serve as an objective method of indicating organic involvement in, at least, some types of impotence. Through the mercury strain gauges, penile circumference is evaluated on three consecutive nights, and since disturbed sleep may alter REM sleep, the examination must be evaluated against the context of the patient's sleep. It is, the authors point out, the function of the monitor and the changes that occur on the polygraph tracing through changes in penile circumference that allow one to make the diagnosis of impotence or to diagnose erections of varying degrees. They point out that in certain men there is a variation in the capacity of the penis to expand. In some men, a sufficiently rigid penis will be attained with a smaller tip circumference than usual, while in others a large-tip circumference will not even reflect an adequate degree of rigidity. It is pointed out by the authors that in cases such as these, relying solely on the NPT data would result in incorrect conclusions. A separate device to measure penile rigidity has been developed by the authors. In 375 patients with the diagnosis of impotence, the authors report that approximately 60% were found to have abnormal or completely absent NPT (the great bulk of these patients had a clinically important organic basis for their diagnosis of impotence). Conventional figures usually attribute organic basis as the etiology of impotence in about 10%, and the figure of 60% (even in a biased setting because of their referral center) reveals a number of extreme clinical importance when considering treatment. The authors summarize various errors that can occur in NPT interpretation and are unsure of its final clinical role in the evaluation and treatment of impotence. For the present though, the authors do recommend NPT monitoring as an essential screening procedure in the assessment of impotence.

Furlow WL: The current status of the inflatable penile prosthesis in the management of impotence. Mayo Clinic experience updated. J Urol 119:363, 1978

It is stated that 500 inflatable prosthesis were implanted worldwide by the date of publication. The author reports the Mayo Clinic experience in 63 consecutive patients over a 24-mo period. He adds that an additional 37 patients underwent implantation during the 5-mo period before the manuscript was written and increased

the experience to 100 patients. Patient selection and the cause of impotence are reviewed. Mechanical complications occurred in 27% of the patients reported, but the author states that all mechanical complications were correctable. The majority of these problems were in the cylinders, and new ones have been developed to prevent problems in this area. It is further emphasized that most of the cylinder problems occurred during the first year of implantation, and in the last year there was a significant decrease in complications to approximately 10%. Criteria for evaluating functional postoperative results are listed. Of 63 patients, 60 had satisfactory erections and, therefore, satisfactory functioning devices. Fifty-nine of the 60 patients experienced satisfactory intercourse using the inflatable prosthesis. The author stresses advantages to the inflatable penile prosthesis such as near physiologic mechanical response, efficient return from penile rigidity to flaccidity and visa versa, mutual satisfaction to patient and partner, and uniform success is achieving preoperative goals. Disadvantages included infection and the fact that the prosthesis is a mechanical device and therefore requires a certain physician dependence. The author stresses that the expandable prosthesis has the advantage of maintaining a near-normal physiologic state that will allow cystoscopy and possible bladder neck surgery in patients with neurogenic bladder, such as the diabetic patient.

Jonas U, Jacobi GH: Silicone-silver penile prosthesis: Description, operative approach and results. J Urol 123:865, 1980

The authors report on their development of and experience with a penile implant made of silicone rubber but with the internal architecture containing twisted 999.7-per-ml. silver wires. They report that this implant has the characteristics of not fatiguing but yet allowing the penis to be down for urination and straightened for intercourse. In addition to the implant, a distal penile surgical approach is described. Long-term follow-up is lacking, but the early and late complications appear to be low and comparable to other semi-flexible penile implants. The main advantage of this implant appears to be the ability to voluntarily move the penis in any direction or position.

Whitehead ED, Leiter E: New frontiers in alloplastic genitourinary prostheses: The surgical management of erectile impotence. NY State J Med 82:1806, 1982

The history of impotence is reviewed and surgical treatment using penile implants is discussed by the authors. Procedures for evaluating patients with erectile dysfunction are covered, and indications for surgery are discussed. The authors report that complications have occurred in approximately 1% of patients with semirigid and adjustable types of implants. They also report that the long-term success rate after implantation of the Small–Carrion, Finney, and Jonas implants approximates 95%. Furthermore, after implantation of the inflatable penile implant they report a long-term success rate, including possible surgical revision, in terms of patient–partner satisfaction in approximately 90% to 95% of patients.

Overview: Semi-Rigid Penile Prosthesis

Arnold Melman

The introduction of silicon rubber to medicine revolutionized the opportunity for reconstructive surgery. Robert Pearman was the first to recognize the potential value of silicone to urology by developing a device that simulated the os penis of other mammalian species.[1] Earlier, Goodwin had introduced the use of an artificial synthetic baculum in man.[2] However, those splints were composed of acrylic plastic, a nonreactive but rigid substance. Pearman's prosthesis was a distinct advance over unyielding acrylic devices, which caused either pain or eventual erosion through the tissues. Despite the initial success described by Pearman, after several years of use many of the devices were reported to fracture and the product was removed from the market. Advances in the technique of manufacturing silicone rubber have led to the development of other, more reliable silicone penile prostheses, which have not been reported to develop that problem with prolonged use. In 1973, Small and Carrion introduced a silicone rubber modification of an acrylic prosthesis used in Egypt by Beheri.[3,4] That device carefully followed the natural anatomy of the penile crura and has proved to be eminently successful in thousands of patients.

SURGICAL TECHNIQUE

Pearman's original operative technique allowed placement of the prosthesis through a dorsal midline incision, which allowed dissection of the corporal septum in the pendulous portion of the penis. Beheri inserted his paired polyethylene rods in a similar manner in approximately 700 patients. The perineal approach to prosthetic rod placement was advocated initially by Small and Carrion. The major advantage of that incision is that the incision itself is inconspicuous, and the patient may have intercourse within 2 to 3 wk of surgery. However, the incision does have many disadvantages. The proximity to the anus allows an increased potential for bacterial contamination at the time of implantation. Many urologists who use that approach must use potentially nephrotoxic prophylactic antibacterial agents. In older patients or in those with diabetic nephropathy, there is an increased potential risk of renal complications. As greater numbers of centers perform this operation, increasing numbers of complications have been reported.[5]

The dorsal penile incision has several distinct advantages for the surgeon with less experience with the implantation of the prosthesis, the most important of which is ease and safety to corporal dilatation. Dilatation of the corpora can be difficult when performed through an incision in the crus of the corpora. The distance to the glans penis from the incision may be as much as 23 cm to 25 cm. The distal control of the rigid dilating instrument is difficult, and the possiblity of a urethral perforation is increased. It is both far simpler and safer to dilate the corpora from the mid-penile shaft where the dilating distance is halved. Thus, control over the dilating instrument is maximal and the chance of accidental urethral perforation is minimized. A single penile incision in the skin can be made, and gentle retraction of the skin and the underlying Colles' fascia allows ample exposure of the area to the tunica albuginea to be incised. The longitudinal nerves coursing beneath Buck's fascia can easily be avoided. Closure of the incision in separate fascial layers with 5–0 chromic catgut will separate the skin incision from the tunica incisions so that they are not in that position, thereby further minimizing infection. The surgeon must be especially meticulous when placing a penile prosthesis in patients with paraplegia. These patients have a thinned tunica albuginea, and aggressive corporal dilatation may result in urethral perforation with minimal effort. Few patients require Foley catheterization postoperatively; therefore, a urethral catheter need not be inserted at the time of surgery, further minimizing potential rate of infection.

Scarring in the penile skin is minimal when a 5–0 chromic catgut suture is used to close the skin. Polyglycolic sutures should be avoided because they tend to remain undissolved for too long a time and may result in a secondary skin infection. With wound healing, fine, nonabsorbable sutures are difficult to remove from the penile skin. The advantage of early intercourse advocated with a perineal incision seems inconsequential in a patient who has been impotent for many months to years before surgery.

PREOPERATIVE EVALUATION

The most satisfactory results from the surgical implantation of penile prosthesis occurs in men who are impotent over extended periods as a result of a disease or prior radical surgery. In those men with stable marriages, both husband and wife have been reported to show postoperative satisfaction in more than 90% of interviewed cases.[6] However, there have been no published reports of objective testing of both the husband and sexual partner before and after surgery. Does it matter if the prosthesis is placed in all patients desiring its insertion? No objective data have been published with results of such an implantation into a man who is impotent on a psychologic basis alone. It has been my experience that when a patient in whom the implant is placed is impotent for psychologic reasons, postoperatively he is not content. Frequently the reason for the discontent was not the inability to effect vaginal penetration but rather an interpersonal conflict with his sexual partner that was not resolved by the ability to have coitus. At a time when physicians are beginning to realize that there is an increasing number of organic causes of impotence it is imperative that they clearly identify the etiology of the impotence.[7] Many surgeons have attempted to do just that by using nocturnal penile tumescence monitoring. That device has been reported as a means of separating those patients with organic from psychogenic impotence.[8] However, caution must be exercised in the interpretation of those results as well. Many sleep laboratories study patients for three successive nights under carefully controlled conditions.[9] Even those normal controls may exhibit inhibition of nocturnal erection under the conditions of study. Moreover, changes in penile circumference alone may not accurately indicate the degree of tumescence of the penile shaft necessary for vaginal penetration. A 10-mm deviation may be a maximal erection for one man and only a partial erection for another. These differences will not be detected on a patient-to-patient basis by the penile tumescence monitor. Moreover, motion during sleep can cause artefactual changes on the polygraph tracing on the monitor. These aberrations increase the difficulty of interpretation of data, particularly if the tracing is obtained without inspection and confirmation of the erection and direct confirmation of the erection.

Several reports have advocated the use of the Minnesota Multiplasic Personality Inventory as a means of screening patients for prosthetic implantation.[10] However, although the test may be satisfactory for distinguishing personality disorders, Staples and associates have recently been unable to support the earlier claim that the test could differentiate between organic and psychogenic impotence at a rate significantly greater than chance alone.[11]

REFERENCES

1. Pearman RO: Treatment of organic impotence by implantation of a penile prosthesis. J Urol 97:716, 1967

2. Goodwin WE, Scott WW: Phallo-plasty. J Urol 68:903, 1952

3. Small MP, Carrion HM, Gordon JA: Small Carrion penile prosthesis: A new implant for management of impotence. Urology 5:479, 1975

4. Beheri GE: Surgical treatment of impotence. Plast Reconstr Surg 38:92 1966

5. Kramer SA, Anderson EE, Bredael JJ, et al: Complications of Small–Carrion penile prosthesis. Urology 13:49, 1979

6. Smith AD, Large PH, Fraley EE: Comparison of Small–Carrion and Scott–Brodley penile prosthesis. J Urol 121:587, 1979

7. Spark RF, White RA, Connolley PB: Impotence is not always psychogenic. JAMA 243:750, 1976

8. Karacon I, Ilaria RL: Nocturnal penile tumescence (NPT): The phenomenon and its role in the diagnosis of impotence, sexuality and disability. Sexual Disabil 1:260, 1978 1:260–271, 1978

9. Fisher C, Schiavi RC, Edwards A, et al: Evaluation of nocturnal penile tumescence in the differential diagnosis of sexual impotence. Arch Gen Psychiatr 36:431, 1979

10. Beutler LE, Scott FB, Karacan I: Psychological screening of impotent men. J Urol 116:193, 1976

11. Staples RB, Fisher IV, Shapiro M, et al: A re-evaluation of MMPI discriminators of biogenic and psychogenic impotence. J Consult Clin Psycho (in press)

104

INFLATABLE PENILE PROSTHESIS: MAYO CLINIC EXPERIENCE WITH 175 PATIENTS

William L. Furlow, M.D.

From the Mayo Clinic and Mayo Foundation, Rochester, Minnesota

Urology / February 1979 / Volume XIII, Number 2

ABSTRACT— Sex prosthetics have become an established alternative of therapy for both the organically and the psychogenically impotent male patient. Functional success with the implantation of the inflatable penile prosthesis can be anticipated in 90 to 95 percent of the patients. Both mechanical and pathologic complications occur, but with relatively low frequency. There have been no reported operative or postoperative deaths associated with the implantation of more than 6,000 devices. The availability of penile prostheses to impotent patients should be limited only by the patient's ability to meet the rigid criteria for selection of patients. When these criteria are fulfilled and the patient's expectations are in harmony with the known results that can be provided by implantation, uniformly successful results can be expected.

As urologists, we have long been aware of our inability to manage surgically the problem of failure of erection in men. The various new sex therapy techniques known to be effective in the treatment of psychogenic impotence are rarely applicable to those patients whose impotence is the result of organic disease. Scardino[1] first recognized

the needs of these patients and realistically endeavored to reestablish a functionally erect penis by using a centrally placed acrylic rod beneath Buck's fascia on the dorsum of the penis. The result was a flaccid penis reinforced against buckling of the shaft, which thereby provided for adequate vaginal penetration.

Goodwin and Scott,[2] Lash, Zimmerman, and Loeffler,[3] Loeffler and Sayegh,[4] and Pearman[5] were among the early pioneers in the surgical correction of failure of

Presented at the meeting of the American Urological Association, Washington, D.C., May 21, 1978.

erection with use of the semirigid rod prosthesis. Even though results with these various devices were reported as satisfactory, a review of the literature does not suggest widespread use of these early prostheses.

Centrally placed single semirigid rod prosthetic devices were soon replaced by paired semirigid rods implanted within the corpora cavernosa of the penis. Beheri,[6] Small, Carrion, and Gordon,[7] and, more recently, Finney[8] have applied their techniques to this problem in a further effort to provide a more nearly normal erectile state suitable for vaginal penetration and satisfactory intercourse. In this regard, these prosthetic devices have been reported to be highly satisfactory.

The hydraulically inflatable penile prosthesis, devised by Scott, Bradley, and Timm,[9] was first introduced in 1973 for the surgical correction of organic impotence. This device has undergone considerable modification and simplification. In its present form, the device consists of four separate parts: an inflate-deflate pump, a storage reservoir, and paired inflatable cylinders (all composed of medical-grade silicone elastomer) (Fig. 1). Long-term results with the inflatable penile prosthesis have been excellent and are comparable to those reported with use of paired semirigid rods.[10-14]

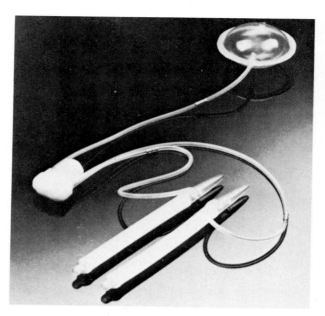

Fig. 1. Inflatable penile prosthesis. (From Furlow WL: Surgical treatment of erectile impotence using the inflatable penile prosthesis. Sexuality Disability 1: Winter 1978. By permission of Human Sciences Press.)

MATERIAL AND METHODS

At the Mayo Clinic, the inflatable penile prosthesis has been in use for surgical correction of male impotence for the past three and one-half years. Since the inception of our implant program in October, 1974, 249 patients have undergone implantation of an inflatable penile prosthesis. This report summarizes our experience with the first 175 consecutive patients, who now have been followed up for a period of six months or more.

Selection of Patients. In this series, impotence was presumed to follow as a recognized complication of certain disease states (Table 1). To distinguish organic from psychogenic impotence in a clinical setting, we rely on the history, the Minnesota Multiphasic Personality Inventory (MMPI), psychologic consultation, and lengthy discussion with the patient and with his spouse if he is married—and, in some instances, with the patient's fiancée if permission has been granted. Early in our experience, we excluded as surgical candidates those patients with functional or psychogenic impotence; however, we have found that there are patients with psychogenic impotence who are refractory to new sex therapy but who are, in fact, excellent candidates for implantation of a prosthetic device. Twenty-two of 175 patients in this series have undergone implantation of the inflatable penile prosthesis after having been diagnosed as being functionally or psychogenically impotent.

We also consider it essential to be certain of the patient's motivation to undergo implantation. To this end, an important feature of the interview has been the description and demonstration of the prosthetic device, including its advantages and the potential complications and risks involved. At this point, we have found it important to establish a clear understanding of the patient's expectations in order that these expectations do not exceed what can be achieved by means of implantation. To aid in this discussion, we use a model of the male torso with the prosthesis in place (Fig. 2).

TABLE 1. Etiologic Factors (175 Patients)

Cause	No of Patients
Organic	141
Diabetes mellitus	57
Radical prostatectomy	20
Postperineal trauma	18
Neurologic disorders	16
Radical cystectomy	9
Aortoiliac disease	6
Peyronie disease	6
Coronary artery disease	3
Proctocolectomy	2
Aortic aneurysmectomy	1
Estrogen therapy	1
Perineal adenectomy	1
Postradiation	1
Psychogenic	22
Physiologic	12

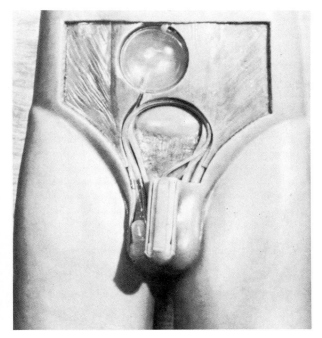

Fig. 2. Model of male torso with inflatable prosthesis in place. (By permission of the Mayo Clinic [Mayo Foundation].[12])

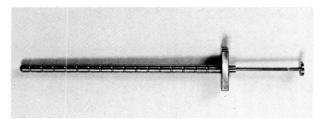

Fig. 3. Furlow tool for cylinder insertion.

inserted by means of the newly designed Furlow insertion tool (Fig. 3). This tool ensures accurate determination of cylinder size and rapid, accurate, and atraumatic positioning of the distal ends of the cylinder beneath the glans penis. The technique of implantation also has been modified to include rerouting of the tubing from each cylinder subcutaneously into the area of the right external inguinal ring. The inflate-deflate pump is then positioned well down in the dependent portion of the right hemiscrotum, lateral to the right testicle. The reservoir is placed beneath the right rectus muscle, and the tubing is brought out through the external inguinal ring. All connections involving the pump, cylinders, and reservoirs are then made in the subcutaneous region near the right external inguinal ring. With this new technique, the tubing no longer needs to be routed through the left and right inguinal canals, as described by Scott *et al*.[9] Kinks in the tubing are avoided by using right-angle, stainless steel connectors to join the cylinder tubing to the pump tubing.

SURGICAL RESULTS

Complications have occured in 47 of 175 patients. Complications associated with this surgical procedure can be divided into two categories, pathologic (Table 3) and mechanical (Table 4).

The pathologic complications included infections of the prosthesis, scrotal hematoma, and scrotal erosion. The two instances of postoperative phimosis occurred early in our series. Concomitant circumcision is now done when indicated. Infection of the prosthesis is the

Age Distribution.

Age Distribution. The youngest patient in this series was a twenty-two-year-old man with an imperforate anus, neurogenic bladder dysfunction, and lifelong impotence. The oldest man in the series was eighty-one years of age (Table 2). In the absence of a chronic and debilitating disease state, age alone should not be a factor in selection of patients.

Surgical Technique. The operative technique used is a modification of that originally described by Scott and associates.[9]

The entire implant can be inserted through a small transverse suprapubic incision made approximately 1 cm. above the upper border of the symphysis pubis. Through this incision, the corpora cavernosa can be exposed infrapubically and the paired cylinders can be

TABLE 2. Age Distribution (175 Patients)

Age (Yr.)	No. of Patients
20–29	14
30–39	22
40–49	38
50–59	43
60–69	51
70–79	6
80–89	1

TABLE 3. Pathologic Complications (175 Patients)

Complication	No. of Patients	Disposition
Infection	6	Removed
Scrotal hematoma	3	Drained
Scrotal erosion	1	Repositioned
Phimosis	2	Circumcision
Wound erosion	1	Removed
Total	13	

TABLE 4. Mechanical Complications (175 Patients)

Complication	No. of Patients	Disposition
Buckling of cylinder	5	Replaced
Ballooning of cylinder	9	Replaced
Rupture of cylinder	1	Replaced
Leak in cylinder	2	Replaced
Inadequate cylinder length	2	Replaced
Kink in tubing	8	Corrected
Loss of fluid	6	New prosthesis
Inadequate fluid volume	1	Fluid added
Defect in pump	1	Replaced
Malposition of pump	2	Repositioned
Total	37*	

* Three patients had two mechanical complications each.

TABLE 5. Number of Patients with Mechanical Complications

Group*	Complications No.	Complications %	Cumulative Incidence No.	Cumulative Incidence %
I (36)	4	11	4/36	11
II (27)	13†	48	17/63	27
III (40)	10	25	27/103	26
IV (72)	7 (4)‡	10 (6%)	34/175	19

* Figures in parentheses represent total number of patients.
† Three of these patients had two complications each.
‡ Omitting those with kinks in tubing.

most serious complication because it necessitates total removal of the prosthesis to permit eradication of the infection. Fortunately, the incidence of infection remains low, having occurred in only 6 of 175 patients (3 percent).

Mechanical complications with this device have occurred in 34 patients. Several of these problems that occurred early in the series are now readily avoided by strict adherence to specific surgical guidelines. All of these mechanical complications were correctable, although secondary and occasionally tertiary surgical procedures were required.

Results of implantation with the inflatable penile prosthesis in our first 175 patients have been extremely satisfactory. Of these 175 patients, 168 have normally functioning prosthesis. Six of the failures resulted from infection involving some portion of the prosthetic device. In each instance, it was necessary to remove the entire device to eradicate the infection. One patient had the device removed because recurrent transitional cell carcinoma of the urethra developed two years after he had had a radical cystectomy for bladder carcinoma.

COMMENT

Implantation of the inflatable penile prosthesis has thus far proved to be a highly satisfactory method of treating both organic and psychogenic impotence. Our experience originally was limited to patients considered to have organic impotence. We have extended our guidelines for selection of patients to include those with functional or psychogenic impotence considered refractory to current forms of sex therapy. Through careful screening of patients and the cooperative efforts of a clinical psychologist or psychiatrist who is expressly interested in the problems of human sexual behavior, we have avoided implanting the device in patients who, because of deep-seated emotional problems, would not benefit from implantation. This decision is often difficult when such emotional problems exist in an organically impotent man. We believe that use of the MMPI and psychiatric consultation are essential for good selection of patients.

The urologist must be prepared to accept and manage the possible consequences of the strong dependence on the physican that may occur as a result of implantation of any prosthetic device in an otherwise emotionally stable patient. In the case of patients with psychogenic impotence, transfer of this dependence from the psychiatrist to the urologist, if it occurs, may be premature and unsettling for both the physician and the patient.

The patient/partner acceptance has been excellent. If orgasmic sensation was present before the onset of the impotence, it is preserved. Ejaculation usually is not affected. Pain has not been a problem after the first six weeks unless associated with some form of complication. Long-standing low-grade pain that moves from one poriton of the prosthesis to another suggests infection within the spaces surrounding the implanted material. From our experience with the genitourinary sphincter, we found that infection may be present for months and cause only low-grade pain, finally becoming evident clinically after reaching the skin surface in a dependent portion of the prosthesis—either in the scrotal pouch or in the distal end of the corpus cavernosum.

Mechanical problems encountered initially have been minimized appreciably with further experience in the surgical technique of implantation.[13] These mechanical problems can be recognized easily if the physican understands the function of the device. A 12 percent diatrizoate (Hypaque) solution used to fill the system permits reliable roentgenographic visualization of the device. In our experience mechanical complications always have been correctable, but only by surgical intervention.

A recent review of our results has shown a decrease in mechanical complication from 48 percent to 10 percent (Table 5; group IV). Strictly speaking, kinks in the tubing are not the result of device malfunction; if these complications are not included, the rate of mechanical complications has been reduced to 6 percent. We firmly believe that all of the mechanical complications associated with kinking of the silicone tubing could be prevented by strict adherence to the principles of surgical implantation. In addition, specific guidelines for post-operative care should be followed to ensure the success of this surgical procedure.[13]

Implantation of the inflatable penile prosthesis is a highly acceptable method of treating organic impotence. The principal advantage of this device is the nearly physiologic function. When the prosthesis has been implanted, the patient is able to have an erection when desired and also can maintain an inconspicuous flaccid penis at other times. The penile shaft attains a rigidity that is nearly normal to palpation, and patient/partner acceptance has been excellent. In this series, the over-all functional success rate with the inflatable prosthesis has been 96 percent; of the 175 patients, 168 have satisfactory function and 7 had poor results.

The main disadvantage of this device is that it is a mechanical prosthesis and therefore is susceptible to the complications experienced with most artificially im-planted devices. The mechanical nature of this device has caused some degree of physcan dependency by the patient. In our experience, these disadvantages have not been important deterrents for most patients.

As our clinical experience has increased, it has become evident that there are specific indications for the implantation of an inflatable prosthetic device in those patients who probably will require subsequent cysto-scopic manipulation—in the form of a transurethral surgical procedure, follow-up examination for a bladder tumor, or periodic evaluation in the case of neurogenic bladder dysfunction. This is especially true with the large population of patients with diabetes who are now seeking correction of their organically induced impo-tence; it has been estimated that neurogenic bladder dysfunction will develop in at least 50 to 70 percent of these patients.[15] Cystoscopic manipulation and exami-nation can be performed easily in the presence of an inflatable penile prosthesis when the penis is in the flaccid state. Several patients in this series have returned at a later date with symptoms of progressive obstruction caused by benign prostatic hyperplasia and have suc-cessfully undergone transurethral prostatic resection without the need for perineal urethrostomy, as is required in patients with the semirigid prostheses.

Section of Publications
Mayo Clinic
Rochester, Minnesota 55901

REFERENCES

1. Scardino PL: Cited by Goodwin, WE, and Scott WW.[2]

2. Goodwin WE, and Scott WW: Phalloplasty. J Urol 68:903, 1952

3. Lash H, Zimmerman DC, and Loeffler RA: Silicone implantation: inlay method. Plast Reconstr Surg 34:75, 1964

4. Loeffler RA, and Sayegh ES: Perforated acrylic implants in management of organic impotence. J Urol 84:559, 1960

5. Pearman RO: Treatment of organic impotence by implantation of a penile prosthesis. Ibid. 97:716, 1967

6. Beheri GE: Surgical treatment of impotence. Plast Reconstr Surg 38:92, 1966

7. Small MP, Carrion HM, and Gordon JA: Small-Carrion penile prosthesis: new implant for the management of impotence. Urology 5:479, 1975

8. Finney RP: New hinged silicone penile implant. J Urol 118:585, 1977

9. Scott FB, Bradley WE, and Timm GW: Management of erectile impotence: use of implantable inflatable prosthesis. Urology 2:80, 1973

10. Ambrose RB: Treatment of organic erectile impotence: experiences with the Scott procedure. J Med Soc NJ 72:805, 1975

11. Malloy TR, and Voneschenbach AC: Surgical treatment of erectile impotence with inflatable penile prosthesis. J Urol 118:49, 1977

12. Furlow WL: Surgical management of impotence using the inflatable penile prosthesis: experience with 36 patients. Mayo Clin Proc 51:325, 1976

13. IDEM: The current status of the inflatable penile prosthesis in the management of impotence: Mayo Clinic experience updated. J Urol 119:363, 1978

14. IDEM: Surgical management of impotence using the inflatable penile prosthesis: experience with 103 patients. Br J Urol 50:114, 1978

15. Ellenberg M: Impotence in diabetes: the neurologic factor. Ann Intern Med 75:213, 1971

Commentary:
The Inflatable Penile Prosthesis

William L. Furlow

The development of implantable products for the surgical management of male erectile failure has brought about a renewed interest among urologists in the field of male sexual dysfunction. The arbitrary differentiation of organic impotence from psychogenic impotence is no longer suitable as the principal criterion for the selection of either conservative or surgical treatment. The major emphasis today is on the development of both subjective and objective documentation of a patient's erectile dysfunction, which will enable the physician to differentiate accurately between these two causes of sexual dysfunction. The well-recognized value of the general medical history and the urologic history has now been supplemented by the equally important sexual history. Physicians who elect to become involved in the diagnosis and management of patients with male erectile failure recognize the importance of developing an expertise in this highly specific area of history taking. As but a single example of the worth of the sexual history is the patient who is referred to the urologist with a diagnosis of impotence as determined by the fact that following 20 min of vaginal penetration with adequate penile tumescence the patient is unable to sustain the erection and is thus unable to reach orgasm and ejaculation. Additional questioning may soon reveal that the patient is able to achieve adequate penile tumescence with orgasm and ejaculation through masturbation. Clearly this is not a cause of organic impotence. This was subsequently confirmed by psychological investigation. This patient is suffering from psychogenic sexual dysfunction, fully amenable to conservative behavioral therapy.

Objective documentation of organic impotence may include the use of Doppler penile blood pressure recordings, penile pulse volume recordings, nocturnal penile tumescence monitoring, sacral reflex latency tests, and, in special instances, cystometry and sphincter electromyography. Apart from nocturnal penile tumescence monitoring, I believe it is fair to say that these studies must still be considered, as investigational or only supportive of the physician's clinical impression, rather than diagnostic. The value of nocturnal penile tumescence monitoring has been extensively studied and has recognized value in differentiating organic from psychogenic impotence when performed in the proper clinical setting. It should be recognized, however, that even the NPT study is as yet only a qualitative measurement of erectile capacity. Objective criteria for determining whether nocturnal erections as currently monitored are within the normal limits for a given patient have not yet been determined. Techniques for volumetric determination of the patient's nighttime sleep erections have been investigated. The basic problem in such determination is physicians' lack of knowledge of the patient's maximal penile circumference before the onset of these symptoms. In this regard, the only useful tool currently available is to awaken the patient when an erection occurs during sleep monitoring so that he may assess the degree of his tumescence.

At the Mayo Clinic all patients who undergo evaluation of their erectile dysfunction are seen in consultation by a psychiatrist or clinical psychologist. Psychological evaluation of the patient with erectile dysfunction not only allows the physician to differentiate organic from psychogenic impotence but also provides invaluable information on the suitability of the patient for implantation of an inflatable penile prosthesis. In addition, this form of psychological assessment allows physicians to determine the need for psychological support postoperatively in terms of sexual readjustment for both the patient and his partner.

A final important consideration in patients considered for implantation of the inflatable penile prosthesis is a discussion with the patient about his postoperative expectations. The patient should be made aware that the implantation of a penile prosthesis will provide him with an erection suitable for vaginal penetration and sexual intercourse. Penile prostheses cannot be expected to enlarge the penis in the erect state beyond that attained when the patient was potent. Nor can a penile implant, of itself, be expected to save or revive a failing marriage. In my experience, failures in patient–partner satisfaction after implantation, when they occurred, have uniformly been the result of unrealistic preoperative expectations.

The operative technique for implantation of the inflatable penile prosthesis has been modified and significantly simplified. A short 6-cm transverse suprapubic incision is made at the upper edge of the symphysis pubis. The incision is carried down through the subcutaneous tissue to the rectus fascia. The rectus sheath is incised transversely immediately above the insertion of the rectus muscles to expose the midline. The midline is opened, and blunt finger dissection develops a space beneath the posterior belly of the right rectus muscle in the right paravesical space. The right external inguinal ring is then identified in the region of the pubic tubercle, and a long curved clamp is introduced through Hesselbach's triangle into the prevesical space using the index finger of the opposite hand to guide penetration of the clamp through the thin transversalis fascia. The clamp is passed medially beneath the belly of the right rectus to the midline. The tubing of the spherical dip-coated reservoir is introduced between the jaws of the clamp, and the clamp along with the end of the tubing is drawn back through Hesselbach's triangle into the subcutaneous tissue of the right external inguinal ring, bringing the reservoir into position in the right paravesical space snugly against the floor of Hesselbach's triangle. The spherical reservoir is filled with 65 ml of 11.7% sterile Cysto-Conray II solution. The rectus sheath is then closed with running O prolene suture.

Subcutaneous dissection is carried out over the symphisis

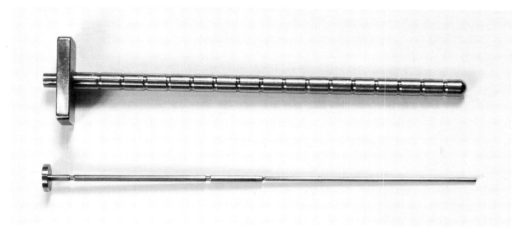

Fig. 4. Furlow cylinder insertion tool. The obturator has been removed from the barrel of the insertion tool. Centimeter markings correspond to the individual ribbed sections of the outer barrel.

pubis into the infrapubic area to expose the corpora cavernosa at the base of the penis. A small 1½-cm to 2-cm incision is then made in the tunica albuginea of the corpus cavernosum to expose the erectile tissue of the corpus. Sutures of 2–0 prolene are then placed along the opposite edges of the incised tunica albuginea for later closure of the tunica albuginea. The corpus cavernosum is then prepared for the insertion of the inflatable cylinders. To accommodate introduction of the Furlow Cylinder Insertion Tool (Fig. 4), the proximal and distal segments of the corpus cavernosum is dilated up to 12 mm using Hegar dilators. The cylinder insertion tool is then introduced into the incision and advanced to the distal end of the tunica albuginea of the corpus cavernosa. The distal length is determined from the markings on the tool. The insertion tool is then advanced proximally through the incision into the crus. Preparation of the proximal crural tunnel must extend down to a point near the insertion of the crus into the ischial tuberosity. The measured proximal length is added to the measured distal length to give the total length of the prosthesis required for implantation.

The removal suture of the prepared cylinder is threaded on to a 5-cm (2-in) Keith needle, and the needle is loaded into the Furlow tool. The insertion tool is then introduced into the corpus cavernosum and advanced distally to the distal limits of the corpus beneath the glans penis. The obturator of the insertion tool is then advanced; the needle is advanced through the glans penis, where it is grasped and removed along with the two ends of the removable suture. The insertion tool is removed, and the prepared cylinder is pulled into the distal portion of the corpus cavernosum and advanced to the distal end of the corpus by gentle traction on the two ends of the suture. With the distal end of the cylinder positioned beneath the corona, the proximal end of the cylinder is inserted into the proximal portion of the corpus cavernosum and down into the crus. The defect in the tunica albuginea is then closed using the previously placed interupted 2–0 prolene sutures.

Cylinder insertion in the opposite corpus cavernosum is accomplished in a similar fashion.

The inflate–deflate pump is then positioned subcutaneously in the most dependent portion of the right hemiscrotum. The tubing from each cylinder is then tailored to length and positioned subcutaneously to permit connection with the tailored cylinder tubing from the inflate–deflate pump. A right-angle stainless steel connector is used to connect the cylinder tubing from the pump to the tubing from each cylinder, thus avoiding any possibility of a cylinder tubing kink. Reservoir tubing is also tailored to length to permit its connection to the reservoir tubing from the pump. This connection is usually made in the region of the right external inguinal ring using a straight stainless steel connector. Once all connections are made, the system is tested by activating both the inflate and deflate portions of the pump. Two layers of subcutaneous tissue are then closed over all tubing and tubing connectors with 3–0 plain catgut, and the skin is then closed using interrupted stainless steel clips or a running subcuticular 4–0 Vicryl suture. The penile cylinders are usually left only very slightly inflated. A 12 French Silastic Foley catheter is passed through the urethra into the bladder and is left in dwelling with 5 ml of sterile saline in the balloon. The penile shaft is then lightly wrapped with a comparison dressing.

Postoperatively the compression dressing and the urethral catheter are removed on the day after surgery. Postoperative hospital convalescence varies from 5 to 8 days. During the patient's hospitalization he is fully instructed in the inflation and deflation of the prosthetic device. At the time of his dismissal he is given a set of printed instructions on the day-by-day activation of his device for the next 4 weeks before beginning sexual activity (Fig. 5).

I have now implanted more than 500 inflatable penile prosthesis in patients with erectile failure. Ninety-one percent of these patients suffer from well-established organic impotence. The remaining patients who were diagnosed as having

INSTRUCTIONS FOR THE USE OF THE INFLATABLE PENILE PROSTHESIS FOLLOWING HOSPITAL DISMISSAL

Week 1:

Inflate the device and then deflate immediately once a day.

Week 2:

Inflate the device and then deflate device twice a day.

Week 3:

Inflate the device and then deflate once a day. Also once a day, firmly inflate and keep inflated for 30 minutes; then deflate.

Week 4:

Inflate firmly twice a day for 30 minutes; then deflate.

NOTE: The device need only be deflated to that point where penis is soft. Do not attempt to completely empty cylinders by squeezing the penis.

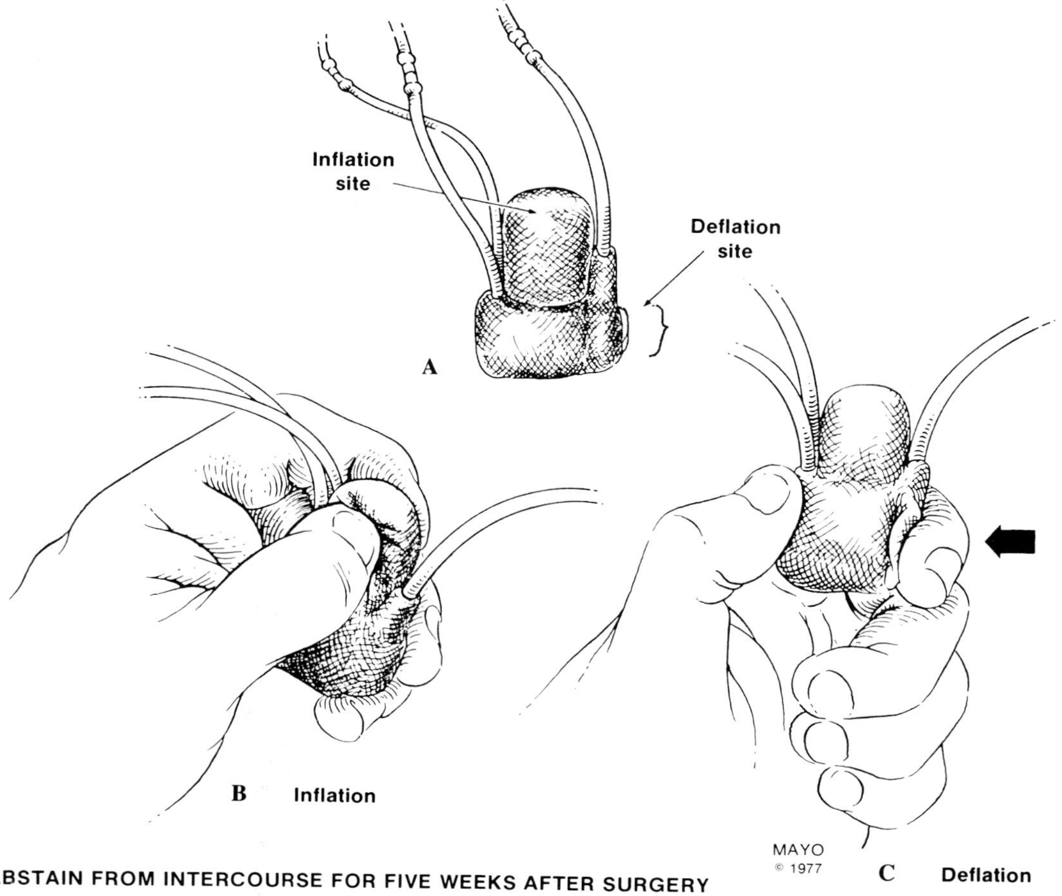

ABSTAIN FROM INTERCOURSE FOR FIVE WEEKS AFTER SURGERY

MAYO © 1977

MC 642/R579

Fig. 5. Postoperative instruction sheet. This instruction guide is given to the patient at the time of hospital dismissal as a guideline in post-operative management of the inflatable penile prosthesis.

psychogenic impotence were offered implantation only after careful psychological and psychiatric assessment and sex therapy, as were those who failed to respond to conservative measures in the management of their erectile dysfunction and who have been considered therefore refractory to further conservative treatment. The operative technique has been refined whereby the average implant time is 40 min. There have been no surgical deaths. Current statistics indicate that the patient has a 98% chance of undergoing a successful surgical procedures free of immediate postoperative complications and with a normally functioning device. Mechanical complications associated with device failure are not to be anticipated for at least 1 yr following surgery, and then my experience indicates that this only occurs in approximately 8% of patients. The most common mechanical complication encountered has been fluid loss as a result of a cylinder leak, which may occur from 1 to 3 yr after implantation. Current studies relative to the cause of cylinder leaks in this small group of patients suggest that this mechanical complication can be significantly reduced through an alteration in surgical implantation. Application of this new surgical technique is currently under investigation.

Long-term postoperative patient–partner satisfaction rates relative to the implantation of an inflatable penile prosthesis have been investigated in both retrospective and prospective studies. It is now apparent that the overall patient–partner satisfaction rates for the patient who receives the inflatable penile prosthesis approximate 90% or better, and, as stated previously, dissatisfaction has usually been the result of inappropriate preoperative expectations and dissatisfaction associated with device malfunction. An important observation, I feel, is that those patients and their partners who have continued to maintain a good sexual relationship despite the patient's impotence can be expected to achieve the greatest benefit from the implantation of an inflatable penile prosthesis.

Implantation of the inflatable penile prosthesis continues to be a highly satisfactory means of correcting organic erectile dysfunction. The device provides the patient with a nearly physiologic type of controllable erection suitable for vaginal penetration and sexual intercourse. It is my opinion that further reports pertaining to the statistical justification for the successful implantation of an inflatable penile prosthesis will probably be redundant. It is now well documented that the inflatable penile prosthesis can be implanted with a high expectation for surgical success. It can also be anticipated that newer devices of even more sophisticated, simplified design will soon be introduced for consideration. In this regard, it will therefore be incumbent on those participating in the field of implantation to carefully reassess guidelines for patient selection and device selection. The ultimate goal should continue to be to establish a high level of patient and partner satisfaction.

Author's Comment. Since this article was written, the AMS Inflatable Penile Prosthesis (Fig. 6) has undergone significant

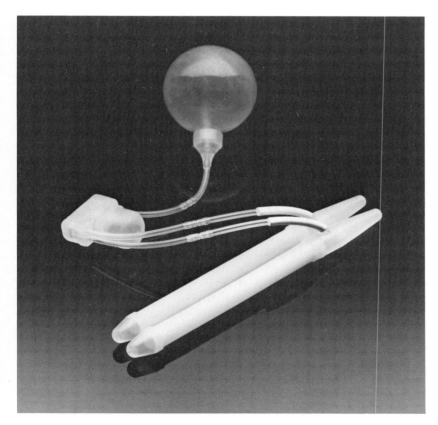

Fig. 6. The new AMS Inflatable Penile Prosthesis 700. The device is wholly constructed of silicone rubber elastomer and consists of two inflatable cylinders, an inflate–deflate pump, and a spherical reservoir. Components are connected through the use of stainless steel connectors.

design changes that further improve device reliability. The surgical technique described remains essentially the same except for the use of rear tip extenders and the methods needed to determine rear tip extender size.

ANNOTATED BIBLIOGRAPHY

Osborne D: Psychologic evaluation of impotent men. Mayo Clin Proc 51:363, 1976

The author describes five goals that he includes in his evaluation of patients: to differentiate organic from psychogenic impotence, to identify the factors that have caused the erectile difficulty, to evaluate the patient's motivation for surgery, and to prepare the patient and his wife for postsurgical adjustment. Interestingly, one of the goals is to identify patients in whom surgery might precipitate emotional problems. The patient is evaluated by an intensive interview, and many times the wife is included. Psychological testing such as the Minnesota Multiphasic Personality Inventory profile is used to help evaluate the five goals. The author points out the importance of nonsurgical treatment whenever possible. His technique is described, but he points out that if this does not alleviate the patient's impotence, then surgical correction should be reconsidered.

Furlow WL: Surgical management of impotence using the inflatable penile prosthesis: Experience with 36 patients. Mayo Clin Proc 51:325, 1976

The author summarizes his experience with the inflatable penile prosthesis in 36 patients with organic impotence treated from October 1974 through September 1975. He also comments on an additional 15 patients who underwent successful implantation of the inflatable penile prosthesis. All patients underwent extensive preoperative evaluation including psychologic testing and the Minnesota Multiphasic Personality Inventory. The author points out that the description and demonstration of the prosthestic device preoperatively, as well as showing its advantages and potential risks, is an extremely important feature of any interview. Surgical guidelines were established in an effort to standardize the surgical technique originally described by Scott and associates. The authors reports major complications occurring in 7 of 36 patients, with the majority of these being mechanical failures, which were all corrected by a secondary surgical procedure. Infection was an infrequent complication. Patient–patient partner acceptance was excellent, and orgasm and ejaculation were unaffected. To evaluate mechanical problems associated with the use of the inflatable device, a radiopaque contrast material is placed into the system for postoperative evaluation. It is pointed out that further developments in device engineering and material modification should minimize mechanical problems.

Furlow WL: Inflatable penile prosthesis: New device for cylinder insertion. Urology 12:447, 1978

The author describes a new instrument that significantly aids in the surgical technique for implantation of the inflatable penile prosthesis. The Furlow Cylinder Insertion Tool, as designed by the author, provides for a safe, simplified, and accurate method of positioning the inflatable cylinders within the corpora cavernosa. Inherent in its design is the capability of the instrument to deliver the two free ends of a removable suture attached to the distal end of the inflatable cylinder through the glans penis, thus enabling the operator to pull the inflatable cylinder accurately into the distal end of the corpus cavernosum using gentle traction. The author then points out that while gentle traction is held on the suture, the proximal end of the inflatable cylinder is readily positioned in the proximal crus. Once cylinder insertion is complete and the tunica albuginea is sutured closed, one limb of the removable suture is cut adjacent to the glans and the opposite limb removed through the glans penis. A further feature pointed out by the author is the reliability of this insertion tool to measure accurately the required cylinder length to be implanted through the designation of centimeter markings along the barrel of the instrument.

Gerstenberger DL, Osborne D, Furlow WL: Inflatable penile prosthesis: Follow-up study of patient–partner satisfaction. Urology 14:583, 1979

The authors point out that the surgical success rate using implantable penile prostheses, although well established, has not necessarily been substantiated through follow-up study on the functional success with respect to patient–partner satisfaction. The authors have followed 175 patients who underwent implantation of an inflatable penile prosthesis. Patients and their partners were evaluated as to patient–partner satisfaction, levels of satisfaction, cause of dissatisfaction, frequency of intercourse, and overall acceptance of the device by the patient and partner. The authors report that this study represents the first attempt to delineate the causes of dissatisfaction and to examine the postoperative sexual function of the patient who has undergone implantation of the inflatable penile prosthesis. From their investigation, the authors determined that 79% of the patients were satisfied with their implant. Of the 21% who reported some type of dissatisfaction with their inflatable penile prosthesis, it was pointed out that dissatisfaction could not be correlated with age, diagnosis, or number of reoperations to correct a complication. Dissatisfaction appeared to be related to existing uncorrected mechanical problems and to discomfort. Patients with mechanical failures, when corrected, enabled reestablishment of normal artificial erectile function and satisfactory intercourse. Another major cause of dissatisfaction pointed out by the authors was a lack of understanding of device function. These findings served to reinforce the authors' feeling that it is essential to determine the patient's preoperative expectations. In this regard the authors emphasize the need to point out to the patient that the subjective quality of the erection may not be identical to previous erections. Overall, it is the authors' impression that the inflatable penile prosthesis has been well accepted by the large majority of patients (89%). A final point emphasized by the authors is the recognition that patient who are dissatisfied for psychologic reason may be more likely to notice discomfort or mechanical difficulties and use these as a nidus for their dissatisfaction.

Furlow WL: Evaluation of impotence. In Siroky MB, Krane RJ (eds): Clinical Neuro-Urology, pp. 135–142. Boston, Little, Brown & Co, 1979

In this chapter the author details the essential steps to be taken in the clinical evaluation of the impotent man. For the purposes of this chapter the author defines impotence as the patient's ability to either obtain or sustain an erection for vaginal penetration and sexual intercourse. Within the contents of this chapter are described the essentials of general history taking with emphasis on sexual history, the physical examination, and laboratory investigation. Special studies including nocturnal penile tumescence monitoring, Doppler penile blood pressure measurements, and penile pulse volume recordings are discussed as to their relative merits in the objective documentation of the patient's impotence. The procedural steps in the differentiation of organic from psychogenic impotence are discussed in detail, emphasizing the value of the Minnesota Multiphasic Personality Inventory and psychological evaluation. Commentary is also provided on several of the newer investigational methods for the diagnosis of organic impotence.

Furlow WL: Therapy of impotence. In Siroky MB, Krane RJ (eds): Clinical Neuro-Urology, pp 213–228. Boston, Little, Brown & Co, 1979

In this chapter the author provides an indepth review of the current status of medical therapy in the treatment of erectile dysfunction as well as a broad overview of the management of psychogenic impotence and surgical management of erectile failure. Within the framework of this chapter is an indepth review of the prosthetic device previously as well as currently employed in the treatment of male erectile failure. The author divides the currently available prosthestic devices into two categories: semirigid rod prostheses and the inflatable penile prosthesis. Currently available devices are described as to their design function, technique of surgical implantation, and reported results.

Scott FB, Bradley WE, Timm GW: Management of erectile impotence: Use of implantable inflatable prosthesis. Urology 2:80, 1973

In this article the authors describe for the first time a completely implantable erectile prosthesis designed for the treatment of erectile organic impotence. In this report the five patients who have undergone successful surgical implantation of this device are described. The prosthesis, surgical technique of implantation, and patient selection are briefly described.

Overview: Inflatable Penile Prosthesis: State of the Art

Terrence R. Malloy

The diagnosis and treatment of erectile impotence as described by Dr. Furlow gives a broad assessment of the "state of the art" as it presently exists. However, many facets of sexual dysfunction therapy require emphasis or further clarification.

No surgeon should decide to be a casual "dabbler" in treating erectile impotence. If he anticipates doing only three or four cases a year he will probably experience unacceptable surgical complications. Although Dr. Furlow's operative technique is clearly stated and succinct, experience is required in obtaining proper positioning of the various components and tubing to obtain optimum results from the prosthesis. If a urologist does not have a patient population that will provide a minimum of 6 or 8 cases a year, he probably would be well advised to refer patients wishing the inflatable prosthesis to a center specializing in genitourinary prosthetics.

A sexual questionnarie (Fig. 7) completed by the patient before his initial visit will expedite clarifying the major areas of sexual dysfunction. This will save the physician's time and allow him to concentrate on major problem areas with the patient. Interviewing the sexual partner should be strongly emphasized so that neither the patient nor the partner has an erroneous conception of what the prosthesis will accomplish.

Diagnostic tests, as previously mentioned, are important in distinguishing organic from psychogenic impotence. These studies are important not only from a medical view but for socioeconomic reasons. Many insurance carriers, government agencies, and other third party carriers request documentation of the etiology of sexual dysfunction. Their determinations of organic pathologic conditions establish financial eligibility in many instances. The nocturnal penile tumescence study, as mentioned by Dr. Furlow, may not be 100% precise. However, at present, it is probably the most accurate study available to prove organic sexual dysfunction. For any patients involved in litigation, this study should be mandatory to protect the patient's interest as well as the physician's. Surgeons contemplating implanting any type of penile prosthesis should have access to nocturnal penile tumescence studies.

The chances of mechanical failures were well discussed by Dr. Furlow. Patients should understand the advantages and disadvantages of the inflatable prosthesis versus the semirigid rod prosthesis. A thorough understanding is essential for proper prosthetic selection and postoperative satisfaction.

The operative technique described by Dr. Furlow is excellent and provides outstanding results. I have used this technique extensively and found it to be as reliable as Dr. Furlow's series would indicate. A midline lower abdominal incision may also provide essentially the same exposure and results.

Another operative approach of merit has been developed by Dr. Brantley Scott. This is a scrotal approach to implant the inflatable prosthesis. A midline incision is made in the scrotum at the perineal junction. The incision is extended into the subcutaneous tissue to delineate both corpora cavernosa. A 1½-cm to 2-cm incision is made in each tunica albuginea on the lateral aspect. A lateral tunnel is dissected to the glans penis distally and proximally to the crus. This tunnel is dilated with Hegar dilators up to 10 mm to 12 mm. The Furlow inserter tool measures the tunnel length both distally and proximally. An appropriate inflatable cylinder is inserted with the Furlow inserter tool as described in Dr. Furlow's technique.

SEXUAL FUNCTION QUESTIONNAIRE

Please answer the following questions to the best of your ability and bring with you at the time of your appointment.

1. Please describe in your own words your past sexual history and include in this description your current problem. How does this affect your life?

2. Describe your social and educational background (parents, marriage, children, social environment).

3. Do you have any erections at all?
   (a) Can you make a vaginal penetration?
   yes_____ no_____ rarely_____ occasionally_____
   (b) Do you awaken with a.m. erection?
   If so describe:
   full_____ partial_____ poor_____
   (c) Does the quality of erection improve occasionally?
   yes_____ no_____

4. Do you have orgasms?
   (a) If so, how is it achieved?
   intercourse_____ masturbation_____ oral sex_____ others_____
   (b) Can you masturbate to organsm but not achieve it with intercourse?

5. Are you concerned with the size of your penis? If so, what is the problem?

6. How strong is your desire for sexual intercourse?
   slight_____ poor_____ fair_____ strong_____ very strong_____

7. How strong is the desire of your wife or sexual partner for sexual intercourse?
   slight_____ poor_____ fair_____ strong_____ very strong_____

8. What is your partner's attitude about surgery to correct impotence?

9. Have you seen other physicians for this condition? If so, when and what therapy was given?

10. Have you consulted a psychiatrist for this problem? If so, please describe results and name of doctor.

11. Are you on any medications?

12. Have you had any major surgery? If so, what surgery and describe results.

13. Have you had a serious major illness or accident?

14. Is there any further information you feel is important to your problem?

Fig. 7.

After the cylinder is inserted, the tunica albuginea is closed with 3–0 or 2–0 proline sutures. The region of the external inguinal ring is exposed, and the ring is dilated with a nasal speculum. With blunt and sharp dissection over Cooper's ligament, the floor of the inguinal canal is opened. Using a specifically developed inserter tool, Dr. Scott places the empty spherical reservoir in the perivesical space. This is filled with 65 ml of a dilute radiopaque solution. The inflate–deflate mechanism is placed in a subcutaneous pouch in the scrotum. The entrance tubing is measured, cut, and attached with a straight stainless steel connector to the tubing from the reservoir. Right-angle stainless steel connectors are used to connect the exit tubings from the pump to the tubes from the cylinders. The device is then activated and deflated several times to ensure proper function and location. The midline scrotal incision is closed with a continuous subcutaneous chromic suture and a subcuticular Vicryl suture. A perineal ring-type retractor specifically developed by Dr. Scott facilitates this operative technique immeasurably.

Dr. Scott believes that the scrotal technique was efficient and has obtained excellent results using it in a large series of patients. This approach allows the surgeon to operate with only one or no assistants.

The scrotal approach should be considered in patients with previous radical abdominal surgery who have complicated scars, fistulas, stomas, or colostomies. The possibility of contamination and injury to bowel will be lessened with the scrotal approach.

Postoperative care is essential for a successful result. As stated by Dr. Furlow, the patient should have an in-dwelling Foley catheter for 18 hr. In my series, I have also found it advantageous to place ice on the scrotum and penis for 18 hr. Additionally, the patients are placed in a true Trendelenburg position (pelvis higher than chest) until the morning following surgery. These measures appreciably decrease the incidence of scrotal edema and fluid collection, which make pump operations difficult. Antibiotics are administered during surgery and in the postoperative period. Patients receive antibiotics for 2 wk after discharge. With this antibiotic regimen plus strict aseptic technique in the operating room, I have not had to remove a prosthesis for infection in a primary implant in more than 200 patients.

Patient education in the use of the prosthesis is essential. Although Dr. Furlow likes to train the patients while they are in the hospital, I have found that scrotal and penile tenderness in the immediate postoperative period precludes good patient education. I wait until the first postoperative visit to instruct the patients in detail. At that time tenderness in the scrotum and penis have abated appreciably. The patient can be taught more quickly with less chance of error. A printed instruction sheet is essential, as illustrated by Dr. Furlow. Patients are seen periodically to make sure the prosthesis continues to work properly. In many instances patients appear to understand the proper function of the prosthesis but on subsequent visits are still unable to use the device properly. Long-term follow-up study should be stressed with all patients.

Future improvements in the materials and design of the inflatable penile prosthesis should decrease postoperative complications. Design efforts are being made to decrease the inflatable portion of the cylinder and increase the solid proximal base. This should decrease the incidence of cylinder leakage that Dr. Furlow cited. The ''dip-coated'' spherical reservoir has eliminated the leakage that plagued the original ''sandwich'' type of reservoir. The inflate–deflate mechanism has been perfected to the point where, in my series, there has not been a malfunction in more than 3 yr.

Dr. Furlow cited the need for all surgeons to reassess continually their results with all types of prostheses. This cannot be emphasized too strongly. Only in this manner will the truly ideal prosthetic device be developed.

105

PHALLOARTERIOGRAPHY IN THE DIAGNOSIS OF ERECTILE IMPOTENCE

V. Michal, C.Sc. and J. Pospíchal, C.Sc.

Cardiovascular Research Center, Institute for Clinical and Experimental Medicine, Prague, Czechoslovakia

World J. Surg., 2, 239–248, 1978

ABSTRACT—An angiographic method has been developed for x-ray visualization of the arteries supplying the cavernous bodies of the penis, namely, the internal iliac, internal pudendal, and penile artery and its branches (dorsal, deep, and bulbocavernous arteries). Under normal conditions the technique makes pulsations in both dorsal penile arteries palpable, and the flow rate of fluid into the cavernous bodies necessary to produce and maintain erection can be determined. The principle of the method involves artificial passive erection or semierection, during which we perform selective or semiselective arteriography of the bed supplied by the internal iliac artery, or retrograde arteriography by puncture of the dorsal artery of the penis.

Thirty males complaining of more than 1 year of impotence (including 12 diabetics) were investigated, 29 by our standard technique and 1 by translumbar pelvic arteriography with retrograde arteriography of the dorsal penile artery. All patients showed severe stenosis or obliteration of the vessels supplying the cavernous bodies. There was agreement between absence of pulsation in the dorsal penile arteries and the angiographic findings. Flow rates necessary to produce erection varied from 45 to 160 ml/min, with a mean of 90 ml/min. For controls, angiographic studies were performed in 4 men with clearly psychogenic impotence, all of whom were found to have normal-appearing arteries supplying the cavernous bodies.

On the basis of these findings and previously reported histological investigations, we believe that most impotence is the symptomatic and functional result of arterial disease. The arteriographic technique described allows a precise anatomical diagnosis to be made, and can indicate surgical and microsurgical correction.

As a corollary of the development of techniques for direct arterial anastomoses with the cavernous bodies of the penis, the hypothesis was put forth in 1973 that impotence can result from a loss of the capacity to develop full arterial inflow to this site [1–4]. Two further directions of research have been undertaken to determine the incidence of organic changes in the arterial bed supplying the cavernous bodies. First, the arteries of the penis have been examined histologically in organs of 30 males who died at various ages. This investigation showed in all cases over 38 years of age various degrees of pathological change, such as replacement of smooth muscles in the Ebner pads by collagen connective tissue, calcification of the pads and arterial walls, and arterial stenoses and occlusions. The degree and extent of these changes were correlated with age and the presence of diabetes mellitus [5, 6]. Secondly, we have worked out an arteriographic technique for visualizing the internal pudendal artery and penile artery and its branches (dorsal penile, deep penile, and bulbourethral arteries) [7]. The results are the subject of this communication.

MATERIAL AND METHODS

Patient Material. Thirty males ranging in age from 20 to 56 years (mean of 45 years) complaining of impotence lasting more than 1 year (mean duration, 4.8 years) were investigated. Impotence was defined as the inability to achieve a degree of erection permitting coitus.

Twelve patients had diabetes mellitus (mean duration, 7.9 years). Two patients had essential hypertension, but blood pressure levels were normal at the time of investigation due to drug therapy. One patient had suffered bilateral pelvic fractures and one patient had fractured the left cavernous body of the penis. In 14 patients there was no other associated disease. Two patients had mild ischemic heart disease; all of the others were free of signs of vascular disease involving any vascular bed. Sixteen patients (52.3%) reported that they had neither morning nor evening erections, while 10 (33.3%) reported weak morning erections which occurred at longer than weekly intervals. The remaining 4 patients (13.3%) reported more frequent morning erections than once weekly, of reasonable turgidity but short duration. Fourteen of the patients (46.4%) reported having nocturnal emissions.

For controls, 4 patients ranging in age from 28–38 years (mean of 34 years) with obvious psychogenic impotence were included in the study. Three of these men were not capable of coitus with new female ac-

Reprint requests: MUDr. V. Michal, C.Sc., Cardiovascular Research Center, Institute for Clinical and Experimental Medicine, Budějovická 800, 146 22 Praha 4-Krč, Czechoslovakia.

quaintances to whom they felt emotionally attached. The other man was 32 years of age and had his first sexual experience at age 29 under stressful conditions. All 4 patients had regular morning erections and erections at various times of the day but were unable to achieve erection in connection with sexual intercourse.

Phalloarteriography. Under general anesthesia a plastic cannula (Brunülle No. 1) was introduced dorsally into the cavernous body through the preputial insertion just behind the corona of the glans. The cannula was connected to a rotary pump and heparinized saline was infused initially at a rate of 30 ml/min. The infusion rate was increased every 30 sec. by 15 ml/min until erection was achieved. Pulsation in both dorsal penile arteries could be easily palpated under normal conditions; if no pulsation was felt, it indicated organic obstruction of the arteries or of the infusion into the arteries. The infusion rate was then decreased to determine the threshold value which would maintain erection.

Seldinger catheters were introduced into the roots of the internal iliac arteries from the femoral arteries on both sides under fluoroscopic control. Thirty milliliters of contrast material was injected at a rate of 2 ml/sec. Seriographic pictures were taken in an oblique projection first on one side and then on the other. In the last 5 patients 1 mg of acetylcholine in 20 ml saline was injected into the catheter before injection of contrast material. (In these cases the amount of contrast medium was increased to 40 ml and the flow rate to 5 ml/sec).

In one patient the twisted course of the external iliac arteries made the investigation impossible and pelvic arteriography through translumbar aortic puncture was made. The investigation was completed by retrograde arteriography through puncture of the left dorsal penile artery during passive artifical semierection (the right dorsal penile artery was not palpable).

RESULTS

Erection was attained at infusion rates ranging from 45 to 160 ml/min, depending on the size of the penis, with a mean of 90 ml/min. After attaining erection, the maintenance infusion rate was about 60% of the initial erectile rate. During erection dorsal penile artery pulsation was felt bilaterally in 5 patients and unilaterally in 18. In 7 patients pulsation was lacking. In 7 patients (23.3%) during artificial erection, the state of induratio penis plastica (Peyronie's disease) was observed.

Analysis of the arteriographic results showed that no patient presented a normal picture of the penile vasculature bilaterally. In 2 patients a normal picture was seen on one side (Fig. 1). In all patients there were various degrees of narrowing and obliteration of either

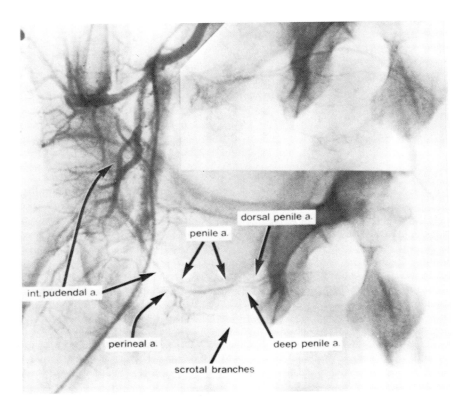

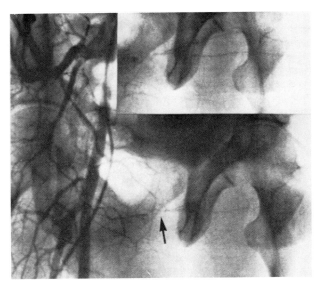

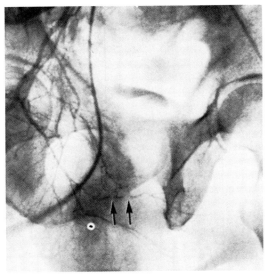

Fig. 1. Normal phalloarteriogram in the right side in a 54-year-old nondiabetic patient: initial phase; in the right upper corner: late phase, dorsal penile artery and branching of the deep penile artery.

Fig. 2. Occlusion of right penile artery bypassed partially by homocollaterals and heterocollaterals from the area of internal obturator artery. In the late phase, filling of dorsal and deep penile arteries is seen (diabetic, age 45).

Fig. 3. Double occlusion of right penile artery bypassed partially by homocollaterals and heterocollaterals from the area of internal obturator artery (nondiabetic, age 55).

the pudendal or penile arteries or their branches, the deep and dorsal penile arteries. Obliteration or stenosis of the internal pudendal and penile arteries was partially bypassed by homo- (originating from the proximal stump of the same artery) or heterocollateral vessels, most frequently from the region of the internal obturator or caudal vesical arteries. No communications between the left and right sides were observed at this level. The types of stenosis and occlusion of the internal pudendal, penile, and dorsal and deep penile arteries are shown in Figs. 2–7. The phalloarteriographic results agreed with the observations on pulsation in the dorsal penile artery during erection.

All 4 control subjects had readily palpable pulsations of both dorsal penile arteries at the time of artificial erection. The flow required to produce erection averaged 95 ml/min (range 90–105 ml/min), and to maintain erection averaged 62 ml/min (range 55–65 ml/min). Arteriography showed normal arteries in all 4 control subjects (Fig. 8).

DISCUSSION

In 1971 Gaskell reported a decrease of the penile systolic pressure in patients with impotence and little other evidence of peripheral vascular disease. He suspected obstruction to blood flow in the main vessels supplying the penis [8]. Our previous histological investigation of the arterial bed of the penis showed pathological changes related to age and the presence of diabetes mellitus [5, 6]. Although these findings suggested impairment of the capacity to increase blood flow to produce erection, the study provided no information on the sexual history and competence of the subjects antemortem. Also, we did not study the incidence of changes in the internal pudendal and penile arteries.

The technique of phalloarteriography, which allows visualization of the branches of the penile artery of males complaining of impotence, complements our original histologic study of the vascular basis of the syndrome. With passive artificial erection or semierection, we have at least some approximation of the condition that occurs during normal erection. The arterial bed of the penis is elongated, the tortuous course of the arteries is straightened, and the Ebner pads are extended. This provides the conditions for good filling of these arteries with contrast material and adequate visualization by x-ray. The regional vasodilating effect of acetylcholine improves the picture.

Determinations of flow rates required for artificial erection provide useful basic information for direct arterial anastomosis to the cavernous body during surgery [1–4]. At present, they are the only quantitative data that approximate the actual values of the natural arterial flow rate needed for erection, thereby contributing to our knowledge of its physiology.

Severe stenosis and obliteration of the arteries of the penis in both diabetics and nondiabetics is not a chance finding, but is directly related to the history of impotence. The character of the stenosis and occlusion, the development of collaterals, the variations in site, and agreement with the absence of pulsation on the dorsal penile artery mitigate against interpretation of these changes as artefacts or anatomical variations. They can only be interpreted as pathological changes in the vessels. In 2 patients, a unilaterally normal angiogram, and in 4 control patients, normal-appearing arteries bilaterally, were used as a basis for comparison. The relatively high incidence of "wet dreams" indicates that there was not a generalized depression of sexual function and that there was probably not an endocrine basis for impotence.

At first approximation there is some discrepancy between the appearance of morning erections reported in 4 patients and organic impotence on a vascular basis. It should be kept in mind that impotence is a symptom like intermittent claudications or angina pectoris. Just as occlusion of the femoral or crural arteries need not imply inability to walk, occlusion of the arterial bed supplying the cavernous bodies does not necessarily mean complete inability of erection. Limited capacity to increase arterial input shortens the interval of claudication, but prolongs the time needed for erection (given continued erotogenic stimuli). The time needed for erection increases more than with the square of age [9]. In nocturnal and morning erections, erotogenic stimuli induced by dreams [10] and arising locally from the bladder area [11] are present for a prolonged time period and may bring on erection even if the capacity to increase arterial input is barely of a threshold value.

The reasons for the localization of pathological changes are probably related to the particular character of this bed and its functional and morphological peculiarities as opposed to other beds. Histologically there is some similarity to the coronary arterial bed, particularly in terms of the thickness of the intima. The Ebner pads, which represent a marked intimal thickening, changes of blood flow in this bed, its distension and expansion during erection, mechanical stress during coitus, and the natural changes of aging are all factors that can contribute to the pathology found. The importance of loss of the ability of Ebner pads to free up arterial inflow to the cavernous bodies, and their gradual transformation into occlusive blocks protruding into the lumen, has been discussed elsewhere [3, 5]. There is no doubt that diabetes mellitus and nicotine play a role in the pathology.

Two patients of the present series had closure of the arterial supply vessels to the cavernous bodies as a result

(Text continues on p 1364)

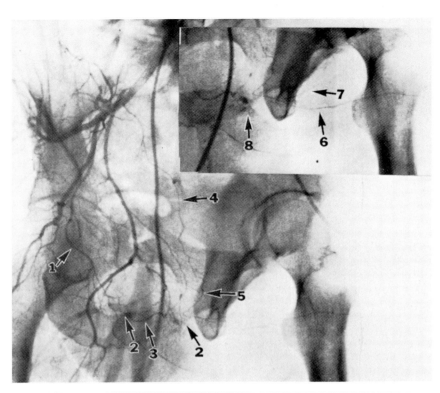

Fig. 4. Diabetic age 45 years with occlusion of the right penile artery bypassed by a collateral (*arrow 5*) from the superior vesical artery (*arrow 4*). The dorsal penile artery (*arrow 7*) is occluded (pulse not palpable during erection). Reference numbers are: (*1*) internal pudendal artery; (*2*) occlusions of penile artery; (*3*) segment of penile artery filled by heterocollateral from internal obturator artery. From this segment originate bulbourethral artery filling the bulbus urethrae (*8*); (*4*) superior vesical artery; (*5*) heterocollateral filling periphery of penile artery; (*6*) deep penile artery; (*7*) occlusion of dorsal penile artery; (*8*) bulbus urethrae.

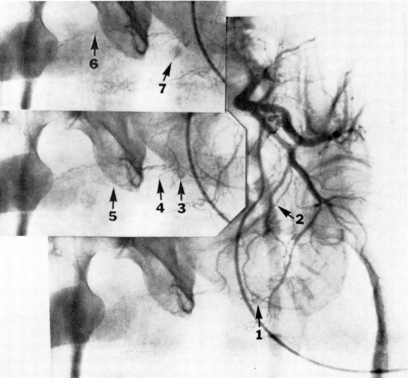

Fig. 5. Nondiabetic age 55 years with occlusion of the left penile (*1*), dorsal and deep (*4*) penile arteries. The stump of penile and deep arteries (*4*) is filled by a branch (*3*) of the caudal vesical artery (*2*), which is sclerotic and stenosed in the middle part (*arrow*). The second branch of this artery communicates with the periphery of the deep penile artery (*5*). A branch from the stump of the original deep penile artery (*4*) rises to the surface of the cavernous body and communicates with a superficial tortuous branch (*6*). No pulse was felt during erection in the dorsal penile artery. In the late phase, filling of the bulbourethral artery and partial filling of the bulbus urethrae (*7*) are seen.

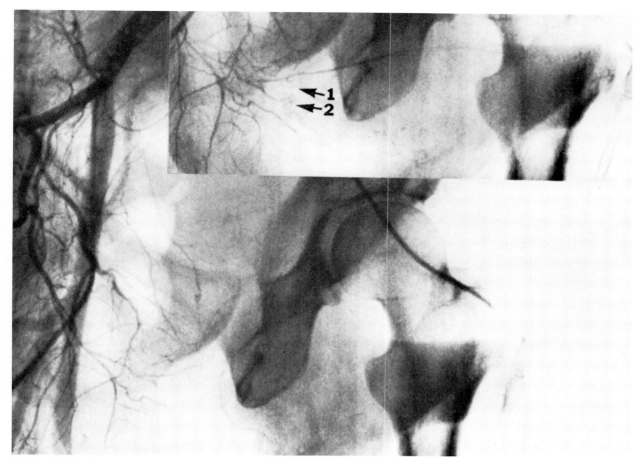

Fig. 6. Diabetic, age 49 years, with occlusion of the deep penile artery (*1*). Filling of the dorsal penile (with palpable pulse) and bulbourethral arteries is seen with partial filling of bulbus urethrae (*2*).

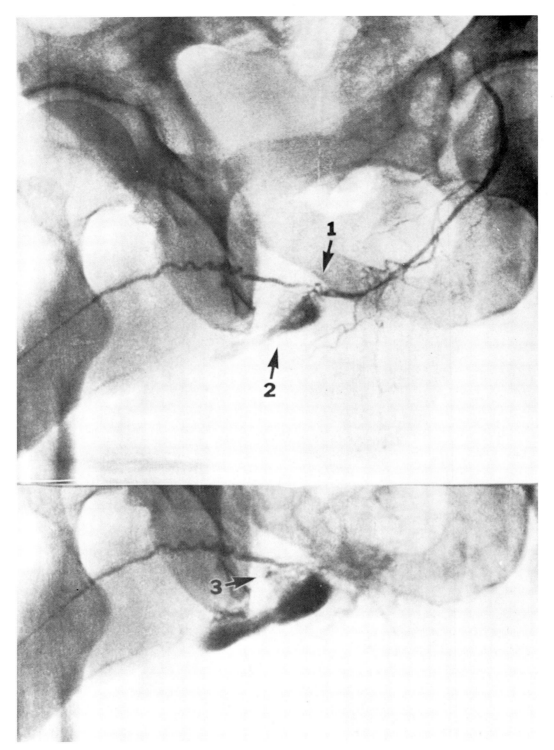

Fig. 7. Retrograde phalloarteriography by puncture of dorsal penile artery in a 49-year-old nondiabetic. Filling of dorsal penile, penile and internal pudendal arteries is seen, as is filling of the bulbourethral artery and bulbus urethrae (*2*). There is severe stenosis of the origin of the dorsal penile artery (*1*). No filling of the deep penile artery is seen. In the late phase, partial filling of the left crus of the cavernous body and of the stump of the deep penile artery is seen (*3*).

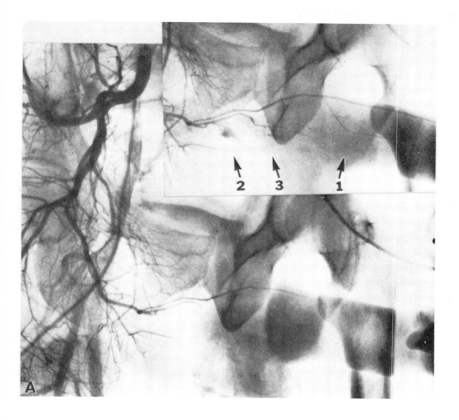

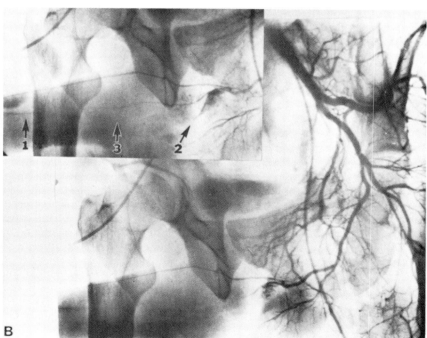

Fig. 8 (*A*) Right-sided normal phalloarteriogram of a 38-year-old man in the control group. Accessory deep penile artery is seen originating from dorsal penile artery (*1*), urethral bulbus (*2*). (*B*). Left-sided normal phalloarteriogram from the same man in the control group. Accessory deep penile artery is seen originating from the dorsal penile artery. (*1*), urethral bulbus (*2*), deep penile artery (*3*).

of trauma. In one of these, there had been fracture of the left cavernous body and obliteration of the deep penile artery on the same side (induratio penis plastica was present at the site of healed fracture). The second patient had pelvic fractures and the internal pudendal artery could be followed to the site of the previous fracture of the pubic bone on the right side, where there was partial bypassing with collaterals. On the left side the pudendal artery was afflicted in its middle third. In this patient, both dorsal penile arteries had changed into stiff connective tissue strands and formed during artificial erection a deformation of the penis of the nature of induratio penis plastica. In one further case, the same

findings was present only on the left side with deformation of the penis during erection (its rotation and deviation). In the remaining 4 patients with induratio penis plastica the relation to observed changes in the penile vasculature was not as clear. The question can be raised, however, whether induratio penis plastica does not also have a vascular basis (including ischemia).

The previous histological and present arteriographic data suggest that a high percentage of impotence is related to artertial disease. The angiographic technique makes it possible to obtain a precise anatomical diagnosis of organic impotence and to suggest surgical and microsurgical correction.

REFERENCES

1. Michal, V., Kramář, R., Pospíchal, J., Hejhal, L.: Direct arterial anastomosis to the cavernous body in the treatment of erectile impotence (In Czech). Rozhl Chir 52:587, 1973

2. Michal, V., Kramář, R., Pospíchal, J.: Femoropudendal bypass, internal iliac thromboendarterectomy and direct arterial anastomosis to the cavernous body in the treatment of erectile impotence. Bull Soc Int Chir 33:343, 1974

3. Michal, V., Kramář, R., Pospíchal, J., Hejhal, L.: Gefässchirurgie der impotenz. Sexualmedizin 5:15, 1976

4. Michal, V., Kramář, R., Pospíchal, J., Hejhal, L.: Arterial epigastricocavernous anastomosis for the treatment of sexual impotence. World J Surg 1:515, 1977

5. Ruzbarský, V., Michal, V.: Morphological changes in the arterial bed of the penis with aging: relationship to the pathogenesis of impotence. Invest Urol 15:194, 1977

6. Michal, V., Kramář, R., Pospíchal, J., Ružbarský, V., Hejhal,

L.: Vascular pathogenesis and surgical treatment of erectile impotence. Almanach of the XXVth Congress of the European Association for Cardiovascular Surgery (in press)

7. Michal, V., Pospíchal, J., Lachman, M.: Penile arteries occlusions in erectile impotence. A new type of angiography—phalloarteriography. (preliminary report in Czech, Engl. summary). Cas Lek Ces 115:1245, 1976

8. Gaskell, P.: The importance of penile blood pressure in cases of impotence. Can med Assoc J 105:1047, 1971

9. Masters, W.H., Johnson, V.E.: Human Sexual Response, 1st edition. Boston, Little, Brown & Co., 1966

10. Jovanović, U.J.: The periodicity of erection during sleep in healthy man. Electroencephalogr. Clin Neurophysiol. 27:626, 1969

11. Bors, E., Comarr, A.E.: Neurological distrubances of sexual function with special reference to 529 patients with spinal cord injury. Urol Survey 10:191, 1960

INVITED COMMENTARY

Adrian W. Zorgniotti, M.D. Department of Urology, Cabrini Medical Center, New York, New York, U.S.A. Michal can be credited as the pioneer of revascularization of the corpus cavernosum for impotence. In this article he brings forth several interesting and provocative points. Michal has shown that infusing heparinized saline produces erection. This was first reported by Newman et al. [1] who produced erections in cadavers and normal volunteers at flow rates of 20–50 ml/min and maintenance rates of 12 ml/min. Newman et al. did not concern themselves with impotent males. Our efforts to repeat their work in impotent males were not successful and we reasoned at that time that the impotence problem might have been due to failure of the corporal shunts to close rather than to decreased inflow as suspected.

We have been doing pudendal arteriography using the techniques outlined by Ginestié and Romieu [2]. This work at our institution has been done by Dr. Guido Padula. We have done angiography on 8 patients with impotence. We have been classifying our patients into 3 groups: (a) complete loss of erection; (b) erection too

soft to penetrate, usually able to ejaculate; and (c) loss of erection after intromission. In all patients we have been able to demonstrate some form of obstruction of the artery or arteries to the penis, although we have not been able to demonstrate the dysplasia noted by Ginestié in his book.

Although the authors do not deal with corpus cavernosum revascularization in their article, the operative procedure for the relief of impotence is the first concern of the clinician interested in this vexing problem. Michal and his coworkers have devised a procedure whereby the inferior epigastric artery is anastomosed to the corpus cavernosum. We have done 8 such procedures with some variations. The surgery was performed by Dr. Giuseppe Rossi. Thus far, following initial success in 5, all but 2 have reverted to the original impotent state (*manuscript in preparation*).

Michal's article is most valuable and points to the need for more research in this interesting area. One clearcut result of this work is the finding of arterial disease in impotent males in their 40's, and 50's, and 60's. This observation can only lead to the necessity for psychiatrists and serologists to begin a reconsideration of their views of the psychiatric and behavioral nature of impotence. After all, a man who is normal in all ways who suddenly cannot erect could just as likely be suffering from pudendal artery insufficiency as from coronary artery insufficiency. Indeed, there are great similarities between these two vessels.

REFERENCES

1. Newman, H., Northup, J.D., Devlin, J.: Mechanism of human penile erection. Invest Urol 1:350, 1964

2. Ginestié, J., Romieu, A.: L'exploration Radiologique de L'impuissance. Paris, Maloine, 1977

Commentary: Penile Revascularization

V. Michal

Thus far, no article in the literature summarizes the current possibilities of revascularization of the penis. Therefore, I selected a paper concerned with angiography on account of its pivotal importance in the detection and demonstration of vasculogenic impotence. The indication for and the type of revascularization depend on a precise anatomic diagnosis of the lesions in the vascular system. The term *revascularization of the penis,* just as *vasculogenic* (ethymologically better would be *angiogenic*) *impotence*, emerged in recent years and reflects certain changes in the view on etiology and pathogenesis of impotence in a large proportion of patients.

Erection is a vascular phenomenon caused by blood congestion in the lacunae of cavernous bodies where the blood pressure approaches and in some animals highly exceeds the level in the aorta.[1,2] Erectile impotence is the inability of the organism to increase arterial input to the cavernous bodies sufficiently and damp down venous runoff in response to sensory, imaginary, and memory erotogenic stimuli.

Neurogenic and psychogenic impotence results from the inability to transmit to the vascular system impulses necessary to induce erection (neurogenic, any time; psychogenic, at a proper moment). Vasculogenic impotence is a failure of the mechanism of erection due either to organic insufficiency of the arterial bed supplying the cavernous bodies or to their pathologic venous drainage.

ARTERIAL INSUFFICIENCY

The arterial bed supplying the cavernous bodies (Fig. 9) can be divided into two parts. The proximal part is common to the arterial supply of the lower extremities (the aortoiliac area). The distal part—the hypogastricocavernous system—comprises the hypogastric, internal pudendal, penile, bulbourethral, dorsal, and deep penile arteries and its branches up to the helicoid arteries, terminating in the lacunae of cavernous bodies. The common denominator of insufficiency of both parts is impairment of erection and impotence. (Erection makes extremely great demands on increase of blood flow to the cavernous bodies. In experiments on dogs, Dorr and Brody showed that stimulation of the nervi erigentes increases the rate of blood flow across the penile vasculature about 16-fold–20-fold. The luminal changes of the internal pudendal and penile arteries that we observed in young patients during artificial erection correspond to these flow changes.[4])

HYPOGASTRICOCAVERNOUS SYSTEM

Arterial insufficiency of the hypogastricocavernous system (HCS) in some patients with impotence, assumed by Gaskell and others, was documented by arteriography in 1976 in two independent studies done at two different centers.[5–8] Ginestie, Ginestie and Romieu were the first to report stenoses, occlusions, and dysplasia of this arterial bed, established by selective arteriography of the hypogastric and internal pudendal arteries.[9,10] My technique of phalloarteriography and the results achieved in the first 25 patients were published in the same year.[11] The preceding paper deals with these results supplemented by a control group. The technique of phalloarteriography remains essentially the same.

My experience in over 200 patients has proved the combination of artificial erection with selective arteriography of hypogastric arteries to be very useful.

A comparative study of five arteriographies in the same patients both without and with artificial erection showed that artificial erection induces selective dilatation of the internal pudendal and penile arteries (Fig. 10), which double their diameter in young patients.[4] (According to Poiseuille's law a twofold increase in diameter brings a 16-fold increase in flow rate.) At present, I no longer administer acetylcholine into the origin of the internal iliac arteries. Acetylcholine probably dilates the muscle bed and, to some extent, acts against selective dilatation of the HCS. Epidural anesthesia seems to produce a similar effect.

High flow rates needed for achieving and maintaining

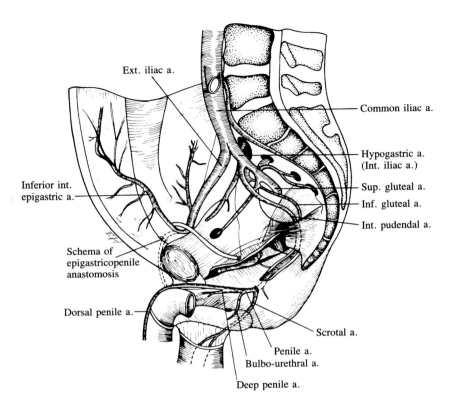

Ext. iliac a.

Common iliac a.

Hypogastric a.
(Int. iliac a.)

Sup. gluteal a.

Inf. gluteal a.

Int. pudendal a.

Inferior int.
epigastric a.

Schema of
epigastricopenile
anastomosis

Dorsal penile a.

Scrotal a.

Penile a.

Bulbo-urethral a.

Deep penile a.

Fig. 9. Anatomy of the arterial bed supplying the cavernous bodies. (Michal V: Role of Vascular Disease in Impotence. Springfield, Illinois, Charles C Thomas [in press])

erection in some patients suggested the presence of pathologic venous drainage, confirmed in some by cavernosography or surgery. Finally, about 20% of patients reported a distinct improvement of erectivity lasting several weeks to months following phalloarteriography. I attribute it to distention of the arterial bed of the penis or activation of a potential blocking mechanism. Whatever the cause, 21 patients had artificial erection under local anesthesia at intervals of 2 to 9 mo.

The high number of occlusions and stenoses in the group of the first 30 patients (100%) can be attributed to the selection of patients. All were referred to me by the Charles University Institute of Sexology after unsuccessful medical treatment as possible subjects for stenoses and occlusions in this area. All but those with sustained pelvic fracture were older than 40 yr and comprised a high percentage of diabetics (40%). To date over 200 men, including younger ones, have been examined. The percentage of pathologic findings in the latter 100 patients of this still selective group oscillated in the neighborhood of 60%.

Phalloarteriography demonstrated two types of abnormalities of the hypogastricocavernous system, that is, occlusions and stenoses in men with acquired impotence, and dysplasia in those with primary impotence (*i.e.,* men who have never achieved a full erection).

Trauma-related lesions were demonstrated in cases of impotence following pelvic fractures and were present in all patients with posttraumatic impotence lasting more than a year. Occlusions and stenoses were commonly localized at the site of a previous fracture of the pubic bone. Three men with a history of penile fracture exhibited homolateral occlusion of the deep penile artery. High flow rates needed for achieving and maintaining erection in one of them suggested the presence of a cavernosospongeous fistula, later confirmed by cavernosography.

Stenoses and occlusions, probably of sclerotic origin, occur in diabetics, hypertensives, and men older than 38 yr. In essence these entities have the following pattern: (1) isolated stenoses and occlusions of hypogastric and the origin of internal pudendal arteries (6% to 10%) (Fig. 11), (2) diffuse changes of the internal pudendal and penile arteries, and (3) involvement of the distal third of the internal pudendal artery and the penile artery and its branches (the most common type).

Unilateral severe hypoplasia to aplasia (Fig. 12) of the deep penile artery, usually combined with contralateral hypertrophy, was observed in 12 of 20 patients with primary impotence. Primary impotence has been attributed to psychic trauma in childhood and adolescence, religious bigotry, Oedipus complex, and other psychogenic factors. Unilateral hypoplasia to aplasia of the deep penile artery is always associated with some degree of erectile malfunction.[10]

REVASCULARIZATION PROCEDURES

In principle, the indication for revascularization is determined by the type and location of the arterial lesion and accessibility of the HCS.

The hypogastricocavernous axis can be reached at the level of hypogastric arteries and their branching, in the

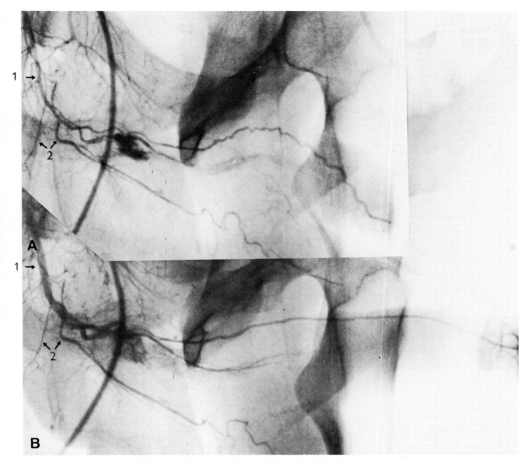

Fig. 10 Arteriography of the penile bed without (*A*) and with (*B*) artificial erection. Note selective dilatation of the pudendal artery (*arrow 1*) and its branches supplying the cavernous bodies during artificial erection. The remaining branches (*i.e.,* scrotal and perineal arteries, *arrow 2*) have a uniform diameter. (Michal V, Pospichal J, Blažková J: Arteriography of the internal pudendal arteries and passive erection. In Zorgniotti AW, Rossi G [eds]: Vasculogenic Impotence. Springfield, IL, Charles C Thomas, 1980. Used with permission.)

ischiorectal fossa, on the dorsal penile artery, and at the level of the cavernous bodies.

Reconstruction of the Hypogastric Artery. Stenoses and occlusions of the hypogastric arteries, combined with similar lesions involving the external and common iliac arteries, are very frequent findings in patients with aortoiliac occlusive disease (60% to 80%). Isolated stenoses and occlusions of the hypogastric arteries made up about 8% of all pathologic phalloarteriographic findings.

Reconstruction of these isolated lesions was carried out in eight patients; four also had stenoses and occlusions of the penile arteries. Five of the patients were able to resume a normal sexual life.

For bilateral procedures use the extraperitoneal approach by midline incision, and for the unilateral, the extraperitoneal approach by pararectal incision or the same approach as employed for renal transplantation. The type of reconstruction depends on local findings and discretion of the surgeon (Fig. 13). The iliacohypogastric bypass from the common or external iliac arteries and open endarterectomy are alternative procedures if the branches of the hypogastric artery are patent and not severely stenosed. However, in the presence of severe stenoses of their roots, endarterectomy by squeezing out the endarterium is one other possibility. A soft arterial clamp is placed at the borders of the changes on the peripheral soft part. Then, applying relatively high pressure, I place thin hemostatic forceps (mosquito clamp) proximal to the arterial clamp, thus separating the indurate parts of proximal endarterium and the soft peripheral part held by the arterial clamp.

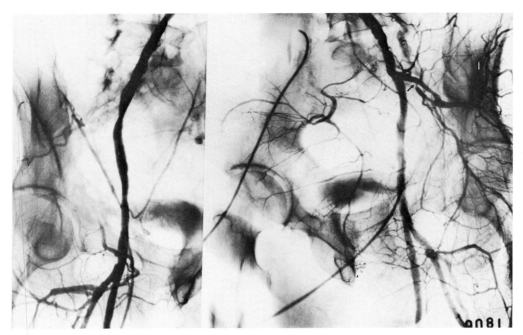

Fig. 11. (*A*) Bilateral phalloarteriography in a 51-year-old man (2 years' history of impotence) with no signs of leg ischemia, and well palpable pulse over all arteries but the dorsal penile artery. Note the occlusion of the right hypogastric artery, and collateral filling of its branching from the area of the inferior mesenteric artery and the pelvic bottom by way of the right internal pudendal artery. (*B*) There is severe stenosis of the origin of the common trunk of the left pudendal artery and inferior gluteal artery (*arrow 1*). (Michal V: Role of Vascular Disease in Impotence. Springfield, Illinois, Charles C Thomas [in press])

A second and third hard forceps are successively placed in proximal direction, and the endarterium is separated from the wall in the appropriate layer. In this manner I proceed up to the site of arteriotomy. The endarterectomized artery is repeatedly and carefully flushed by saline and blood from the periphery to remove all potential fragments. This procedure does not permit visual control to ascertain whether the peripheral part of the endarterium firmly adheres to the wall, but in some cases it can be the only way to restore patency of a near-occluded branching of the hypogastric artery. I employ this type of endarterectomy often as part of reconstruction of the aortoiliac area; it is quick and, with some experience, gives good results.

Femoropudendal Bypass. The internal pudendal artery in the ischiorectal fossa is reached by perineal incision. The venous bypass is brought through a subcutaneous tunnel into the scrotal and inguinal regions and anastomosed to the common femoral artery. The procedure is indicated if the bypass flow rate can be expected to exceed 70 ml/min, which is a rate needed for ensuring long-term vein graft patency. It follows that in addition to the periphery of the internal pudendal artery, the bypass must also supply a relatively large portion of the pelvic and gluteal regions. Thus far, I have used this procedure in three patients, of which one procedure was successful.

Epigastricopenile Anastomosis. Epigastricopenile anastomosis joins the inferior epigastric artery with the dorsal penile artery (Fig. 9).[13] It is a comparatively new type of procedure developed in my institute and relies on phalloarteriographic findings.

I used the epigastricopenile anastomosis in patients with occlusions or severe stenoses of the internal pudendal or penile arteries but having a patent segment of the dorsal penile artery communicating with the deep penile artery (Fig. 14).

The procedure includes *mobilization and relocation of the inferior epigastric artery* and its anastomosis to the dorsal penile artery. The epigastric artery is approached by pararectal incision and isolated, together with concomitant veins, preperitoneally. The arterial and venous branches are ligated together and divided (Ligaclip accelerates this part of the procedure). Leaving the concomitant veins in the pedicle facilitates orientation and prevents its torsion during subsequent handling. The pedicle is transsected at the level of the umbilicus, and a small cannula is placed in the central stump of the inferior epigastric artery (to provide for its dilatation and filling by heparinized blood).

The pedicle can be brought to the dorsal penile artery either through an opening excised in the aponeurotic part of the abdominal wall (Fig. 9) or is shifted below and behind the inguinal ligament (Fig. 18). For this type of relocation the

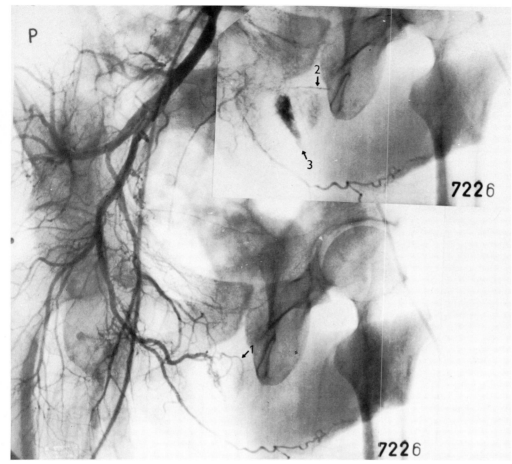

Fig. 12. Severe hypoplasia of the right deep penile artery (*arrow 1*) and dorsal penile artery (*arrow 2*). With the exception of the urethral bulb (*arrow 3*), in the late stage only a small part of the cavernous body is filled. (Normal phalloarteriogram on the left.) Dysplasia according to J.F. Ginestie and A. Romieu. (Michal V: Role of Vascular Disease in Impotence. Springfield, Illinois, Charles C Thomas [in press])

pararectal skin incision is extended to the symphysis. The inguinal ligament and the common femoral artery are reached from this incision subcutaneously.

During the operation the penis remains in the operative field and an indwelling catheter is placed in the bladder. A plastic needle is inserted into the cavernous body to induce artificial erection (for details, see the preceding article).

The dorsal penile artery is reached by a small skin incision at the lower margin of the symphysis. During artificial erection a weak pulse may be palpable over the artery if the pudendal or penile arteries are only stenosed. The artery straightens, and its lumen dilates. Arteriotomy (after systemic heparinization) should be performed either on the previously straight part or on the convexity of the former bow (the concave part is usually thickened—Ebbner's pad?) (Fig. 15).

The anastomosis is constructed end-to-side of the dorsal penile artery as close as possible to the symphysis to prevent its dislocation during erection. (In one of my patients the anastomosis tore during the first coitus.) I use continuous 8-0 to 10-0 sutures.

After unclamping, the pulse over the dorsal penile artery can be easily palpated. Using a magnetic flowmeter, I recorded a flow rate between 4 and 30 ml/min. Even lower flow rates need not necessarily imply a technically defective anastomosis. More important is a well-palpable pulse over the periphery of the dorsal penile artery.

Intravenous infusions of low molecular weight dextran are administered perioperatively. During the preoperative and postoperative periods the patients receive acetylsalicylic acid (0.5 g 3 times a day) and dipyridamole (Persantin) (75 mg 3 times a day), combined from the third postoperative day with subcutaneous heparin (5000 U 2 to 3 times a day).

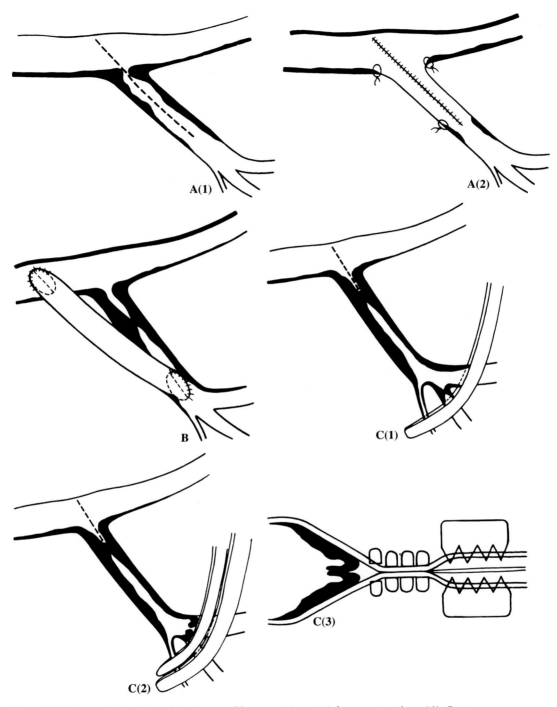

Fig. 13. Schematic drawing of the types of hypogastric arterial reconstruction. (A) Open endarterectomy. (B) Ilicohypogastric bypass. (C) Endarterectomy of the branching of the hypogastric artery by squeezing out the endarterium. (Michal V: Role of Vascular Disease in Impotence. Springfield, Illinois, Charles C Thomas [in press])

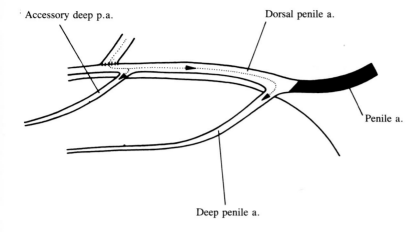

Accessory deep p.a.

Dorsal penile a.

Penile a.

Deep penile a.

Fig. 14. Schematic drawing of the supply of the deep and accessory deep penile arteries by an epigastricopenile anastomosis. (Michal V: Role of Vascular Disease in Impotence. Springfield, Illinois, Charles C Thomas [in press])

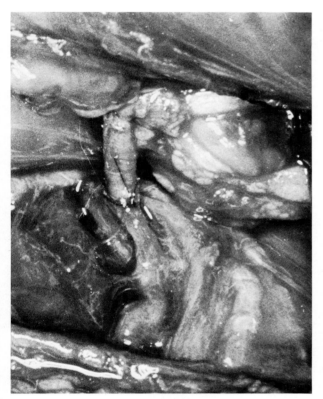

Fig. 15. Epigastricopenile anastomosis (perioperative picture). Magnification × 3.5. (Michal V: Role of Vascular Disease in Impotence. Springfield, Illinois, Charles C Thomas [in press])

From August 1977 through June 1979 the epigastricopenile anastomosis was performed in 25 patients. In 5 patients the anastomosis became occluded within the first week, and in another 5 patients it became occluded later. At present the anastomosis is still patent in 15 patients. All but two of them reported improvement and resumption of normal sexual activity. In the latter three the improvement (including sexual life) lasted only for 3 postoperative mo despite angiographic evidence of patent anastomosis (one angiography showed diffuse narrowing of the afferent epigastric artery; the other showed occlusion of the proximal part of the dorsal penile artery). See Figure 16.

Epigastricocavernous Anastomosis. The epigastricocavernous anastomosis connects the inferior epigastric artery directly to the cavernous body.[6,15] Its objective is to increase basal penile blood flow to a level just below that necessary to maintain an effective erection. A limited capacity to increase blood flow or activation of a potential blocking mechanism in response to an erotic stimulus could than suffice to produce erection.

In the past 3 yr I have carried out this anastomosis in patients with occlusions and stenoses of the hypogastricocavernous axis that did not permit construction of an arterioarterial bypass (occlusion and hypoplasia of the deep penile artery) and in those with a flow rate needed for maintaining artificial erection under local anesthesia exceeding 50 ml/min.

The inferior epigastric artery is isolated and mobilized in the same way as for an epigastricopenile anastomosis. After systemic heparinization, the body of the penis is occluded by two tourniquets applied subfascially above and below the site of the intended cavernostomy. Injection of heparinized saline into the cavernous body (between the tourniquets) dilates larger and deeper lacunae. The cavernostomy is performed under a dissecting microscope in an oblique direction to the circular and longitudinal fibers of the tunica albuginae or by its excision. Connecting several deeper lacunae creates a space to which the epigastric artery is connected by an end-to-side anastomosis. I use a continuous suture (9–0). The suture is placed so that there is direct contact between the intimae of the epigastric artery and the lacunae. The suture passes on the side of the cavernous body through the superficial lacunae and the tunica albuginae. See Figure 17.

Among the 39 epigastricocavernous anastomoses thus far performed I have recorded 6 permanent erections and 13 occlusions during the first 3 postoperative wk. In two cases

(Text continues on p 1374)

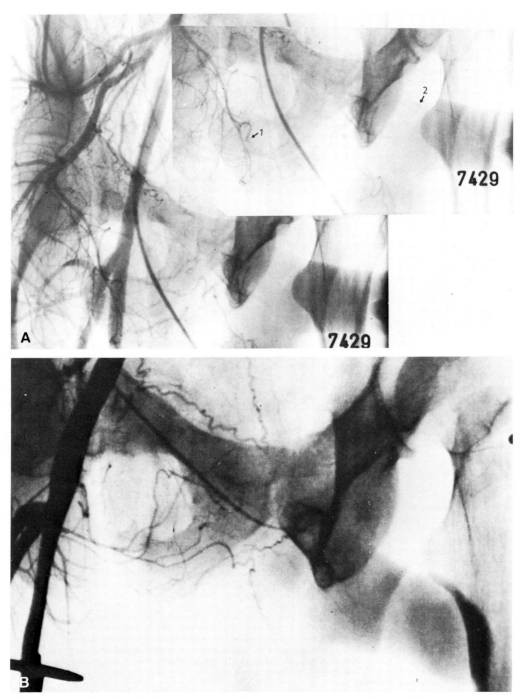

Fig. 16. (A) Right-sided phalloarteriogram of a patient with a 2-year history of impotence after bilateral pelvic fracture. In the late stage (inset) note occlusion of the penile artery (arrow 1) at the site of fracture of the pubic bone. Dorsal, penile (arrow 2), and partially deep penile arteries fill by way of collaterals. (B) Control arteriography of the same patient 11 months after epigastricopenile anastomosis. Early stage: filling of the epigastric artery and

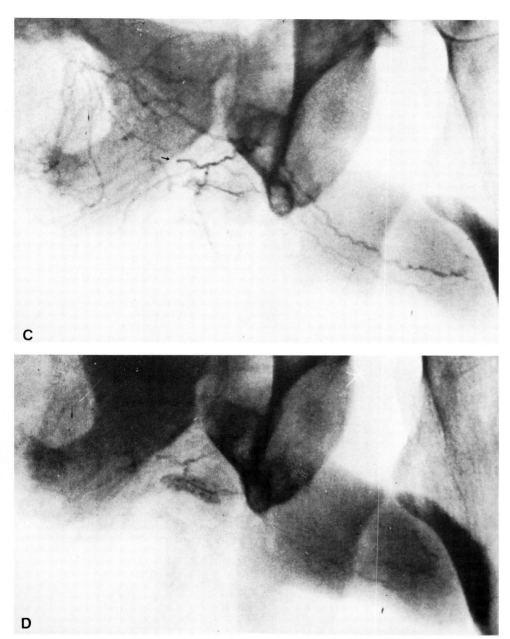

anastomosis. (C) Middle stage: filling of the anastomosis and dorsal penile artery, and retrograde filling of the bifurcation of the penile artery (*arrow 1*), accessory deep penile artery, and deep penile artery. (D) Late stage: partial filling of the cavernous bodies. (Michal V, Kramář, R, Hajhal L: Revascularization procedures of the cavernous bodies. In Zorgniotti AW, Rossi G [eds]: Vasculogenic Impotence. Springfield, IL, Charles C Thomas, 1980. Used with permission.)

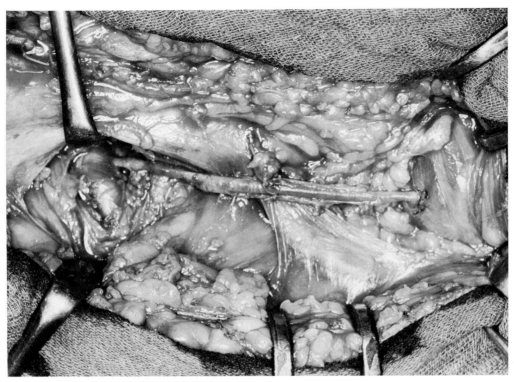

Fig. 17. Perioperative picture of an epigastricocavernous anastomosis. *Left*: common femoral artery with the origin of the inferior artery from it. *Right*: anastomosis of the mobilized epigastric artery to the cavernous body. (Michal V: Role of Vascular Disease in Impotence. Springfield, Illinois, Charles C Thomas [in press])

we abolished the permanent erection by a venous shunt after Grayhack; in four we had to ligate the anastomosis.[16] None of the patients showed signs of thrombosis of the cavernous bodies. Of the 20 patients with a patent anastomosis, 2 reported a distinct improvement of erection and 15 a resumption of normal sexual life. Follow-up studies showed a tendency to late anastomosis occlusions, but in 10 the occlusion did not affect continued improvement of erection. See Figure 18.

The outcome of this procedure depends, in my opinion, on an appropriate adjustment of anastomosis flow. Higher flow rates carry the risk of priapism, while lower flow rates are associated with the danger of anastomosis occlusion, the more so as a small-caliber artery is anastomosed to the cavernous body and not to a vessel.

Ginestie and Romieu, who report most satisfactory results in 60% to 70% of their patients with epigastricocavernous anastomosis, stress, in addition to the operative technique, the importance of subcutaneous administration of heparin for 2 mo postoperatively.[7]

AORTOILIAC OCCLUSIVE DISEASE

In 1940 Leriche described a syndrome characterized by ischemia of the lower extremities and erectile impotence.[17] The patho-logic basis of the syndrome was occlusion of the aortic bifurcation. Thus, Leriche was the first to demonstrate that arterial occlusion can result in failure of the penis to achieve erection. In 1958 O'Conor reported a successful management of this syndrome by endarterectomy of aortic bifurcation.[18]

The incidence of erectile malfunctions in aortoiliac occlu-sive disease varies from author to author, depending on their definition of impotence and impairment of erection and selection of patient groups. (May and colleagues report 70% of impaired erection; Scheer, 90% of occlusions of aortic bifurcation and 70% of common iliac arteries; Herman, total impotence in 36% of patients with arteriosclerotic disease without and, in 56%, with diabetes.[19,20,22] According to my observations, aortoiliac occlusive disease is associated with impaired erection or impotence in 40% to 50% and 25% to 30% of patients, respectively, manifesting itself in the initial stage by a lower coitus frequency and a decreased ability to achieve and maintain erection.[7,14,21] Sexual complaints may develop several years before or coincide with the onset of claudications; the devel-opment of sexual disorders is delayed in about a third of patients.

Analysis of aortographic findings in a group of 112 patients with aortoiliac occlusive disease (nondiabetics younger than 55 years without rest pain or gangrene and with opportunity

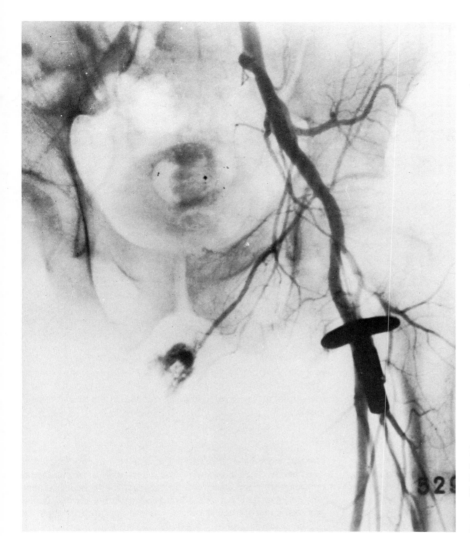

Fig. 18. Control arteriography of an epigastricocavernous anastomosis performed 6 weeks after surgery. (Michal V: Role of Vascular Disease in Impotence. Springfield, Illinois, Charles C Thomas [in press])

for leading a normal sexual life) showed bilateral limitation of arterial flow to the branches of hypogastric arteries due to severe stenoses or occlusions of aortic bifurcation and common iliac arteries, specifically of the roots of hypogastric arteries, in about 80% of patients with sexual complaints.[21]

The objective of reconstruction of this group was to improve the arterial supply of the legs and pelvic bottom. The operation included endarterectomy of stenosed and occluded internal iliac arteries and restoration of full blood input to the common iliac artery bifurcation. Of the 80 patients with impaired erection or impotence, 64% reported a distinct improvement for a period of more than a year and 17% for less than a year; 19% reported no improvement.[21]

Two types of postoperative disorders are described after reconstruction of the aortoiliac area: erectile malfunction and dry emission. Some authors attribute both to damage of hypogastric plexus during dissection of aortic bifurcation.

Inferring from my operative results and from the observations of May and colleagues, injury of the plexus is a major causal factor in the development of ejaculation disorders but does not play any important role in the development of erectile disorders.[20] In my opinion, postoperative erectile malfunction is caused, to a large degree, by the routine use of aortofemoral bypasses, which tend to divert the bloodstream from the internal iliac arteries, especially if the aortic anastomosis is end to end and the external iliac arteries are occluded or stenosed. Stagnation of blood flow results often in further occlusions and thrombosis, as evidenced by control angiographies.

Analysis of aortographic findings has recently raised doubts about the prognosis of reconstruction of the hypogastric arteries because of the observed narrowings of the internal pudendal arteries, which impede the improvement of blood input to the cavernous bodies.[22] This finding does not concur with my operative results. Just as renewal of blood flow to the common femoral artery improves ischemia in legs with occluded superficial femoral arteries, removal of proximal obstruction improves blood flow through pudendal arteries and collateral arterial bed.

PATHOLOGIC VENOUS DRAINAGE

Excessive venous drainage of the cavernous bodies was considered a causal factor of impotence as early as the beginning of this century, and ligation of the dorsal penile vein seems to have been the first vascular procedure designed to restore erectivity.[26]

However, abnormal venous drainage has been documented only recently, initially as persistent patent shunts following operation for priapism.[27,28]

It was only in 1979 that Ebbehoj and Wagner described a fistula between the high-pressure system of cavernous bodies and the low-pressure system of the spongeous body of the urethra in two patients and pathologic venous drainage of cavernous bodies across the veins originating from a hemoangioma localized in the tunica albuginea in one patient.[28] One of the cavernosospongeous, most likely congenital, fistulas was demonstrated in a young man who has never achieved sufficient erection. All were demonstrated by infusion cavernosography.

This gave the impetus to my cavernosographic studies of patients with relatively high flow rates necessary to achieve and maintain erection, which led to the detection of cavernosospongeous fistulas in two patients. One was a young man with primary impotence and a normal phalloarteriographic finding, and the other a man with a history of penile fracture and subsequent urethral bleeding.

One more case of pathologic venous drainage was established perioperatively and involved a young man with insufficient erection who was initially indicated for epigastricocavernous anastomosis. On dissection of the cavernous bodies I found, aside from a normally appearing dorsal penile vein, a large and tortuous vein with several branches perforating the tunica albuginae. Instead of constructing an anastomosis, the vein and all perforating branches were ligated and the openings in the tunica albuginea sutured. The operation resulted in a full restoration of erection, and for the past 6 mo the patient has enjoyed a normal sexual life.

The surgical treatment of patients with cavernospongeous fistulas consists of separation of the spongeous and cavernous bodies at the site of the fistula and closure of the opening in tunica albuginea with a few stitches.[27] Injection of saline dyed with methylene blue is helpful in locating the fistula. Thus far I have no results to report other than those in the aforementioned young man.

Four years have elapsed since different centers have reported angiographic evidence of occlusions and stenoses of the arteries supplying the cavernous bodies in impotent males. Understandably enough, vascular surgery of impotence suffers from all the infant diseases associated with all new procedures, such as uncertainty regarding indication and lack of experience, not to mention that the operation is performed on small arteries in a bed that has many peculiarities. However, with growing experience improved results can be reasonably expected because revascularization of the penis is a causal therapy of angiogenic impotence.

SUPPLEMENT

The commentary on penile revascularization was written in the early spring of 1980. In new and rapidly developing disciplines, 4 years is a relatively long time. This is obviously also true for the areas of angiogenic or arteriogenic impotence and revascularization procedures of the arterial bed supplying the cavernous bodies. I consider it, therefore, appropriate to supplement my commentary with new information gained since 1980.

ARTIFICIAL ERECTION

The field of artificial erection has developed a functional examination of cavernous bodies, which sheds light on the physical principles governing the hemodynamics of erection and on its anomalies.

Technique of Examination. Introduction of a second needle into the cavernous body, connected by a second line to an electrical manometer coupled by feedback to a rotary pump, enabled me not only to monitor the intracavernous pressure but also to stabilize it at chosen levels. Circumferential changes (measured by a calibrated strain gauge or induction ring), intracavernous pressures, and infusion rates, all registered by a polygraph during artificial erection, together with recorded degrees of erection, allowed me to gain an understanding of their interrelations and the function of the cavernous bodies.[29,30]

Hemodynamics of Erection. Erection is a process characterized by a change of two physical variables: volume and pressure.[29,30] The basic volume change (i.e., the difference between a completely flaccid and a completely erected penis) represents the minimal volume of blood that must be supplied by the arterial system, to fill the cavernous bodies (erectile blood volume, or EBV).

Using the data of Kinsey (cited by Wagner and Green[31]), I calculated the EBV for a medium-sized penis (the crura and urethral bulb included) as 140 ml. Intracavernous pressure (ICP) increases from 15 mm Hg at the flaccid state to values between diastolic and mean arterial pressure at semierection. These volumes and pressures must be delivered by the arterial system and can be classified as critical or threshold values. If they are not achieved, full erection is impossible.

The process can be subdivided into three phases:
1. Filling of the cavernous bodies: 90% of EBV can be delivered at subdiastolic ICP.
2. Ten percent of EBV must be supplied at supradiastolic ICP during its rapid rise. Semierection appears at ICP approximating values of mean arterial pressure.
3. Full erection is achieved at systolic and suprasystolic ICP. Contraction of ischiocavernous compresses the crura in osteomuscular channels, presses blood into the bodies, and raises ICP to suprasystolic values (mean increment 100 mm Hg, peaks often exzceeding 300–400 mm Hg). During

contraction the cavernous bodies must function as a closed (hydraulic) system. Suprasystolic ICP can be maintained until the end of tonic contraction (in the absence of major leakage into the venous system) In between contractions of ischiocavernous muscles, the cavernous bodies must be quickly refilled at supradiastolic values of ICP.

Functional Examination of Cavernous Bodies. In addition to the above values, artificial erection enables one to examine the capability to raise pressure in the cavernous bodies, the function of ischiocavernous muscles, and leakage from the cavernous bodies into the venous drainage at the time of suprasystolic values during tonic contraction, and enables one to establish the volumes needed for filling the cavernous bodies, and pressures inducing and maintaining erection.

Decrease of Blood Pressure in Penile Arteries. At the end of the 1970s measurement of systolic blood pressure (BP) in the penile arteries became a routine examination of vasculogenic impotence, due to the studies of Karacan and co-workers, Engel and co-workers, Queral and co-workers, and Kempczinski.[32-35] A small pressure cuff is placed around the base of the penis, filled to suprasystolic values, and gradually deflated. Appearance of the first systolic peaks is detected over the glans by a sensitive plethysmograph (*e.g.*, a relex photoplethymograph) or over the dorsal penile arteries by an ultrasonic device based on the Doppler principle (10 MHz). The obtained values are compared with systolic pressure in the arm and most commonly expressed as the penile brachial pressure index (PBPI = penile systolic BP/brachial systolic BP).

Most authors interpret PBPI below 0.6 indicative of arteriogenic impotence, values between 0.6–0.75 as suspect, and values above 0.75 as normal. Measurement of systolic pressure in the penile arteries has been considered a simple, noninvasive differential diagnostic and screening method capable of distinguishing arteriogenic impotence.

It should be noted that the above criteria were evolved mainly in groups of men with aortoiliac lesions and hold for them. Application of the hemodynamic principles to the bed supplying cavernous bodies shows that only aortoiliac lesions that are associated with a pressure gradient and a decrease of peripheral pressure below the critical values interfere with the hemodynamics of erection. However, many peripheral stenoses and occlusions of the HCS underlying impotence need not manifest themselves by a decrease of systolic pressure in penile arteries at very low resting flow rates in the flaccid penis; they become hemodynamically significant only at the time of loading of this bed by erection when they substantially decrease the volume and pressure delivery to the cavernous bodies.[29]

We compared PBPI and the arteriographic findings in 60 men with aortoiliac lesions or stenoses and occlusions of the peripheral HCS. PBPI averaged as follows: 0.73 ± 0.13 in aortoiliac disease without erectile disorders; 0.56 ± 0.16 in aortoiliac disease with erectile disorders; 0.92 ± 0.08 in erectile disorders without significant phalloarteriographic finding (three cases); and 0.79 ± 0.16 in erectile disorders with bilateral severe peripheral stenoses or occlusions of HCS. According the PBPI, only 11% of the last group (3 of 28 cases) fall in the area of evident arteriogenic impotence, and 61% would be considered normal values.

Therefore, PBPI can confirm but not exclude arteriogenic impotence; it is not and, in its present form, cannot be a reliable screening method and, even less, a differential diagnostic criterion of arteriogenic and other types of impotence. On the other hand, it provides useful information about the pressure gradient between penile and systemic arteries, which influences the future resting flow through the reconstructions. Postoperatively, PBPI can also often confirm the patency or occlusion of reconstructions, and the improvement or deterioration of penile circulation.

Currently, it is unfortunately only phalloarteriography that is capable of detecting, with reasonably accuracy, stenoses and occlusions of the internal pudendal and penile arteries.

PHALLOARTERIOGRAPHY

For inducing erection we now use intracavernous injection of 40 mg—80 mg papaverine in a 20-ml–40-ml water solution. This injection induces semi-erection to full erection within 10 to 15 minutes. However, in some cases it must be combined with intracavernous infusion.

Examination of 280 men carried out in recent years confirmed the earlier findings and showed a close relationship between HCS lesions and other arterial diseases (*e.g.*, ischemic heart disease [IHD], myocardial infarction [MI], peripheral arteriosclerosis) and their high-risk factors (diabetes mellitus, hypertension). Stenoses and occlusions of HCS are the most common causes of organic impotence and the impotence in middle and older age groups, which would be routinely classified as phychogenic.

CONSERVATIVE THERAPY

Arteriosclerotic lesions of HCS are a sign of a more or less generalized arterial disease, and conservative therapy should minimize a further progress of arteriosclerosis to prevent its even more serious complications (IHD, MI, cerebrovascular disease and stroke, intermittent claudication, and gangrene). Therefore, prohibition of smoking, antisclerotic diet, and regular control and therapy of diabetes and hypertension are the most important therapeutic measures. They should be taken no matter whether and how impotence will be treated.

NEW REVASCULARIZATION PROCEDURES

New types of reconstruction of the HCS were reported at the Second International Conference on Penile Revascularization in Monaco, 1980.

Reconstruction of the Proximal Part of the Internal Pudendal Artery. For *gluteo-, hypogastrico-,* and *iliacopudendal bypass* I started to use the gluteal approach to the midsegment of the internal pudendal and gluteal arteries described in old anatomical textbooks. At the site, at which the internal pudendal and inferior gluteal arteries leave the small pelvis through the infrapyriform foramen, both arteries are covered only by fasciculi of the gluteus maximus muscle and can be reached by incision in the direction of muscle fibers in the inferior Farabeuf's line. The type of procedure depends on the phalloarteriographic finding. Interposition of the autovenous graft

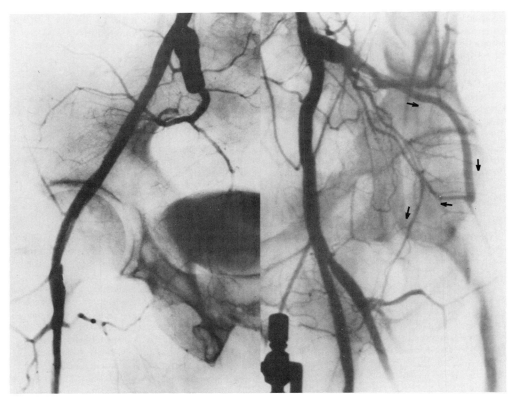

Fig. 19. Bilateral control arteriography performed 6 months after iliacohypogastric autovenous bypass on the right and inferior iliacogluteal antovenous bypass on the left. Filling of left internal pudendal and penile arteries from the bypass by way of the inferior gluteal artery and the common trunk (*arrows*). The patient reported complete restoration of potency, and coitus frequency over 100 per year. (Michal V: Role of Vascular Disease in Impotence. Springfield, Illinois, Charles C Thomas [in press])

between the pudendal and inferior gluteal arteries can be used only in isolated stenoses and occlusions of the origin of the internal pudendal artery. If there common trunk or the more central arteries are afflicted, only a peripheral anastomosis is constructed, either to the internal pudendal or to the inferior gluteal artery, according to the patency of the bifurcation of their common trunk (Fig. 19). The graft, filled with heparinized saline and clamped by microbulldogs, is then tunnelized through the suprapyriform foramen into the retroperitoneal space of the small pelvis. After insertion of a vacuum drain the wound is closed. The proximal end of the bypass is anastomosed to the hypogastric, common, or external iliac artery through the extraperitoneal approach by pararectal or oblique incision.

Deep Epigastricopenile Anastomosis. *Deep epigastricopenile anastomosis* was first reported by MacGregor and Konnak at the 1980 conference.[37] The procedure is indicated in the following cases:

- Lesions of the origin of the deep penile artery
- More proximal lesions where an anastomosis to the dorsal penile artery could not be performed (*e.g.*, occlusion,

hypoplasia) or would not improve flow to the cavernous bodies.

The deep penile artery is approached through longitudinal cavernosotomy, circumvented (together with erectile tissue), elevated on a rubber strip, and isolated. The mobilized stump of the epigastric artery is sutured, end to side, under dissecting microscope. The epigastric artery should pass freely, without bending and compression, between the stitches closing the cavernosotomy.

MacGregor and Konnak reported one successful case. Our experience is still limited but promising (two good results out of three procedures).

Femoropenile Bypass. Femoropenile bypass, either to the dorsal or deep penile artery, or to both, on one or both sides was reported at the above mentioned conference, by Crespo and co-workers.[38] For this type of reconstruction the authors use the dorsal vein of the foot. In bifurcated and trifurcated sequential bypasses the additional branches are sutured to the original vein, end to side.

For isolation and elevation of the deep penile artery the

authors recommend a special instrument called Lyddia's hook. The procedure seems to be a complete revascularization and the reported results are favorable (78% of 22 cases). In the opinion of my co-workers and me, the venous bypasses should be performed only after a thorough bilateral arteriographic examination of the HCS. The probability of long-term patency of the venous graft depends largely on the flow rate through the reconstruction (see Femoropudendal Bypass). The resting flow through the penile arterial bed is relatively very small (about 7 ml/min through both cavernous bodies) and increases substantially only at the time of erection. Therefore, the venous graft is indicated only in cases where it supplies also a larger part of the pelvic area by retrograde flow. Preoperative arteriography of the penile bed can also suggest restriction of the procedure to only one artery, which is essential to the supply of the cavernous bodies and retrograde flow.

Arterialization of the Deep Dorsal Vein.
Arterialization of the deep dorsal vein is a further procedure for excessive venous drainage. Venous bypass connecting the femoral artery with the deep dorsal vein end to side was described by Le Veen and Diaz in 1978 at the First International Conference on Penile Revascularization.[39] The aim of the procedure is to increase pressure in the penile venous system and improve blockage of venous outflow during erection. The procedure and its variations were used in 29 patients and reported at the Second Conference by Virag.[40]

The variations involved include the following:
- Alternative use of the epigastric artery for the shunt
- Distraction of the competent venous valves in the direction of the glans, resulting in its retrograde filling by arterialized blood
- Proximal ligature of the deep dorsal vein at the symphysis, further increasing venous pressure and run of the arterialized blood into the glans, and through the spongenous body and urethral bulb into the venous system
- Peripheral anastomosis of the shunt end to the peripheral end of the transsected deep dorsal vein, with similar results

The procedures were indicated by the author in patients with unsustained erection and flow rates needed for achieving and maintaining artificial erection in excess of 120 ml/min.

The reported results were "good in 39%, fair in 48%, and bad in 13%." Complications of arterialization include tumescence and pulsation of the glans, which, if uncorrected, can result in its erosion. Corrective operation involves ligature of the branches of the deep dorsal vein at the corona of the glans, or ligature of the shunt.

Combined Procedures.
Combination of the previous a–v shunt with anastomosis to the cavernous body was reported also by Virag.[40] The procedures involve anastomosis of the arterialized deep dorsal vein with the cavernous body (side-to-side or the proximal end of the arterialized vein to fenestration in the cavernous body). Indication was unsustained erections with high flow rates at artificial erection, combined with peripheral lesions of HCS. Such procedures, according to the author, yielded good results in 42%, fair in 33%, and bad in 25%. Long-term patency of this type of arteriocavernous shunt has not been reported yet, but should not differ from the epigastricocavernous anastomosis, that is, an average of 3 to 6 months. The patency of the a-v shunt will be probably longer.

Revascularization of the penis now includes a wide range of procedures. Some of them may be procedures of trial and error, but the increase of arterial flow to the cavernous bodies through the reconstructed natural arterial channels without bypassing the regulating mechanism of the branches of the penile arteries seems to be physiologic, and according to our experience should be preferred. Just as aortocoronary bypasses replaced the Vineberg's operation, the epigastricocavernous anastomosis and femorocavernous bypass are replaced, at least in our institute, by epigastricopenile anastomosis, femoropenile bypasses, and reconstructions of the pudendal arteries (not to mention the hypogastric arteries). They have better long-term patency without the danger of further complications. Restoration of arterial flow to the erectile bodies improves not only the quality but also the duration of natural erection, without the need for additional procedures. Improvement of the blood flow in the penile arteries seems to improve also the blocking of the outflow during erection. Only good visualization of lesions and patency of different HCS arteries can indicate an appropriate surgical procedure. Reconstruction of the different arteries of HCS has been performed in 170 patients.[36] Restoration and long-lasting improvement of natural erection were recorded in 75% (80%–90% of the reconstructions of the hypogastric and proximal internal pudendal and 65% of reconstructions of the distal pudendal and penile arteries).

REFERENCES

1. Beckett SD, et al: Blood pressures and penile muscle activity in the stallion during coitus. Am J Physiol 225:1072, 1973

2. Beckett SD, Hudson RS, Walker DF, et al: Corpus cavernosum penis pressure and external penile muscle activity during erection in the goat. Biol Reprod 7:359, 1972

3. Dorr LD, Brody MJ: Haemodynamic mechanism of erection in the canine penis. Am J Physiol 213:1526, 1967

4. Michal V, Pospíchal J, Blažková J: Arteriography of the internal pudendal arteries and passive erection. In Zorgniotti AW, Rossi G [eds]: Vasculogenic Impotence. Springfield, IL, Charles C Thomas, 1980

5. Gaskell P: Importance of penile blood pressure in cases of impotence. Canadian Medical Association Journal 105:1047, 1971

6. Michal V, Kramář R, Pospíchal J, et al: Direct arterial anastomosis to the cavernous bodies. Rozhl Chir 52:587, 1973

7. Michal V, Kramář R, Pospíchal J: Femoro-pudendal by-pass, internal iliac thromboendarterectomy and direct arterial anastomosis to the cavernous body in the treatment of erectile impotence. Bull Soc Int Chir 33:343, 1974

8. Michal V, Kramář R, Pospíchal J, et al: Gefässchirurgie der Impotenz. Sexualmedizin 5:15, 1976

9. Ginestié J, Romieu A: Traitement des impuissances d'origine vasculaire La revascularisation des corps caverneux. J Urol Nephrol 82:853, 1976

10. Ginestié JF, Romieu A: L'exploration radiologique de l'impuissance. The Hague, Martinus & Nijhoff Medical Division, 1978

11. Michal V, Pospíchal J, Lachman M: Penile arteries occlusions in erectile impotence. A new type of angiography—phalloarteriography. Cas Lek Ces 115:1245, 1976

12. Michal V, Kramár R, Barták V: Femoro-pudendal by-pass in the treatment of sexual impotence. J Cardiovasc Surg 15:156, 1974

13. Michal V, Kramár R, Hejhal L: Revascularization procedures of the cavernous bodies. In Zorgniotti AW, Rossi G [eds]: Vasculogenic Impotence. Springfield, IL, Charles C Thomas, 1980

14. Michal V, Kramár, Hejhal L, et al: The tactics of reconstruction in the aortoiliac area with respect to erectile disorders in men. Rozhl Chir 52:591, 1973

15. Michal V, Kramár R, Pospíchal J: Epigastricocavernous anastomosis. World J Surg 2:239, 1978

16. Grayhack JT, et al: Venous bypass to control priapism. Invest Urol 1:509, 1964

17. Leriche R: De la résection du carrefour aortico avec double sympatectomie lombaire pour thrombose artéritique. Le syndrome de l'obliteration termino-aortique par artérite. Presse Med 48:601, 1940

18. O'Conor VJ Jr: Impotence and the Leriche syndrome: An early diagnostic sign; consideration of mechanism; relief by endarterectomy. J Urol 80:195, 1958

19. Scheer R: Die Impotenz als Symptom der arteriellen Durchblutungsstörungen im Beckenbereich. Munch Med Wochenschr 102:1713, 1960

20. May AG, DeWeese JA, Rob CG: Changes in sexual function following operations of the abdominal aorta. Surgery 65:41, 1969

21. Michal V, Kramár R, Hejhal L, et al: Aorto-iliac occlusive disease. In Vasculogenic Impotence. Springfield, IL, Charles C Thomas (in press)

22. Herman A, Adar R, Rubinstein Z: Vascular lesions associated with impotence in diabetic and nondiabetic arterial occlusive disease. Diabetes 27:975, 1978

23. Machleder HI, Weinstein M: Sexual dysfunction following surgical therapy for aorto-iliac disease. Vasc Surg 9:283, 1975

24. Weinstein M, Machleder HI: Sexual function after aorto-iliac surgery. Ann Surg 181:787, 1974

25. Spiro M, Cotton L: Aorto-iliac thromboendarterectomy. Br J Surg 57:161, 1970

26. Gee WF: A history of surgical treatment of impotence. Urology 5:401, 1975

27. Moloney PJ, Elliott GB, Johnson HW: Experiences with priapism. J Urol 114:72, 1975

28. Ebbehoj J, Wagner G: Insufficient penile erection due to abnormal drainage of cavernous bodies. Urology 13:507, 1979

29. Michal V: Arterial disease as a cause of impotence. In Clinics in Endocrinology and Metabolism, pp. 725–748. London, Sannders Company, 1982

30. Michal V, Šimána J, Řehàk J et al.: Haemodynamics of erection in man. Physiologia Bohemoslovaca (in press)

31. Wagner G, Green R: Impotence: Physiological, Psychological, Surgical: Diagnosis and Treatment, p. 182. New York, Plenum Press

32. Karacan J, Catesby JW, Dervent B et al.: Impotence and blood pressure in the flaccid penis: Relationship to nocturnal penile tumescence. Sleep 1:125–132, 1978

33. Engel G, Burnham SJ, Carter MF: Penile blood pressure in the evaluation of erectile impotence. Fertility and Sterility 30:687–690, 1978

34. Queral LA, Whitehouse WM, Flinn WR et al: Pelvic hemodynamics after aortoiliac reconstruction. Surgery 86:799–809, 1979

35. Kempczinski RF: Role of the vascular diagnostic laboratory in the evaluation of male impotence. Am J Surg 138:278–282, 1979

36. Michal V: Revascularization of the hypogastricocavernous system in arteriogenic impotence. Intern Angiol (in press)

37. MacGregor RJ, Konnak JW: Treatment of vasculogenic erectile dysfunction by direct anastomosis of the inferior epigastric artery to the central artery to the corpus cavernosum. J Urol 127:136–139, 1982

38. Crespo E, Soltanik E, Bove D et al.: Treatment of vasculogenic sexualimpotence by revascularization of cavernous and/or dorsal arteries using microvascular techniques. Urology 20:271–275, 1982

39. LeVeen HH, Diaz C: Treatment by corpus cavernosum revascularization. In Zorgniotti AW, Rossi G (eds): Vasculogenic Impotence, pp 217–233. Springfield, Illinois, Charles C Thomas, 1980

40. Virag R: Syndrome d'erection instable par insuffisance veineuse. Diagnostie et correction chirurgicale. A propos de 10 cas avec un recul moyen de 12 mois. J Urol Vasc 6:121–124, 1981

ANNOTATED BIBLIOGRAPHY

Gaskell P: The importance of penile blood pressure in cases of impotence. Canadian Medical Association Journal 105:1047, 1971

The author recorded penile blood pressure in normal young men, patients with vascular diseases, and diabetics with and without impotence by the spectroscopic method. The values of systolic pressure in the dorsal penile artery exceeded those of the mean pressure in the arm in all potent men. He found distinctly lower pressure values in the dorsal penile artery in almost all impotent males, which he attributes to occlusions and stenoses of the afferent arteries. "On this basis, obstruction to blood flow was identified as a cause of impotence in patients with little other evidence of peripheral vascular disease."

Ginestié J, Romieu A: Traitement des impuissances d'origin vasculaire. La revascularization des corps caverneux. J Urol Nephrol 82:853, 1976

The authors discuss vasculogenic impotence and group it as Lériche syndrome and isolated lesions of the internal pudendal arteries. They classify pathologic findings in the internal pudendal arteries as stenoses and occlusions, and dysplasia, documenting the types arteriographically. In the annotated paper they distinguish three types of dysplasia: aplasia, fibromuscular dysplasia, and luminal asymmetry. Listed under indications for operation are occlusions and stenoses of the internal pudendal arteries and dysplasia. Epigastricocavernous anastomosis, which they used in 30 males, yielded good results in 60% (renewal of erection permitting resumption of sexual activity). The authors stress the use of microsurgical techniques and administration of anticoagulants before, during, and for 6 wk after operation. They express the view that partner cooperation plays an important role in the renewal of sexual activity.

Ginestié JF, Romieu A: Radiologic exploration of impotence. The Hague, Martinus & Nijhoff Medical Division, 1978

The monograph deals with the technique of arteriography of the internal pudendal arteries and that of cavernosography, serving at the same time as an atlas of angiographic findings. The authors list the indications for internal pudendal arteriography and, from a comparison of the degree of erectile malfunction and angiographic findings, infer that a unilateral occlusion or aplasia of the deep penile artery is invariably associated with reduced erection, while bilateral occlusions cause impotence. The authors show that a major portion of erectile disorders are due to stenoses and occlusions, and dysplasia, of the arteries supplying the cavernous bodies.

May AG, DeWeese JA, Rob CG: Changes in sexual function following operation on the abdominal aorta. Surgery 65:41, 1969

The authors examined sexual function in 70 males 6 to 9 mo following operation on the abdominal aorta (44 for aortic occlusive disease and 26 for aneurysm). Impaired erection was present preoperatively in 70% of patients with aortoiliac occlusive disease and in 8% of those operated on for aneurysm. Of the men with a normal sexual function preoperatively, 21% of the aneurysmectomized and 34% of those operated for aortoiliac occlusive disease developed erectile disorders; 32% of the patients with aortoiliac occlusive disease and preexisting impairment of erection improved after surgery, but none improved after aneurysmectomy. Abnormalities of ejaculation (dry emission) occurred after operation for aortoiliac obstruction and after aneurysmectomy in 49 and 63% of patients, respectively. The authors attribute erectile disorders to the reduction or failure to improve pelvic blood flow and ejaculation disorders to the destruction of portions of the vegetative nervous plexus secondary to dissection of aortic bifurcation. Since at this age patients tolerate ejaculation disorders better than erectile disorders, they recommend thromboendarterectomy or resection and graft replacement with revascularization proximal to the hypogastric artery to preserve or renew blood flow to these arteries.

Michal V, Kramář R, Hejhal L, et al: The tactics of reconstruction in the aortoiliac area with respect to erectile disorders in men. Rozhl Chir 52:591, 1973

The authors discuss the possibility of restoration or preservation of erectile potency in males indicated for reconstruction of the aortoiliac bed. In a group of 54 men under 55 yr, 37 (68%) had evidence of reduced erectile potency or impotence in addition to signs of ischemia of the lower limbs. In 30 of these patients (81%), stenoses or occlusions of the internal iliac arteries were demonstrated angiographically, in 3 perioperatively. Endarterectomy of the bed supplying the lower limbs was combined with endarterectomy of the internal iliac arteries in all of them. In men without evidence of impotence or reduced erectivity, endarterectomy of the common and external iliac arteries, combined with fixation of the intima at the origin of the internal iliac artery, was performed. Postoperatively, erectile potency was preserved or restored in all but one patient.

Michal V, Kramář R, Pospíchal J: External iliac "steal syndrome." J Cardiovasc Surg 19:355, 1978

A steal syndrome in the external iliac artery characterized by distinct clinical signs and reversal of blood flow in the internal iliac artery secondary to the closure of the common iliac artery is described. The patient reported a marked decrease in sexual activity and impaired erection, combined with intermittent claudication of the corresponding lower extremity. He achieved and maintained erection only at absolute rest. Coital movements led to disappearance of erection and pain in the gluteal region. Endarterectomy of the common, external and internal iliac arteries resulted in disappearance of claudication and impotence. A similar observation was reported by P. Metz and F. R. Mathiesen (External iliac steal syndrome leading to a defect in penile erection and impotence: A case report. Vasc Surg 13:70, 1979).

Herman A, Adar R, Rubinstein Z: Vascular lesions associated with impotence in diabetic and non-diabetic arterial occlusive disease. Diabetes 27:975, 1978

The authors evaluated the degree of affection of the common iliac artery, internal iliac artery, and internal pudendal artery on the basis of aortographies in 91 men with arterial occlusive disease and classified them in five degrees. They examined patients with respect to sexual life and determined patients with impotence, which they defined as a complete inability to achieve erection in all circumstances, including a complete disappearance of spontaneous morning erection. They divided the patients into 4 groups: nondiabetics and diabetics with and without impotence. They established impotence in 36% of the nondiabetics and in 58.6% of the diabetics. Statistical analysis showed a higher degree of mean stenosis of all evaluated arteries in all impotent patients than in the remaining ones. Findings in the left internal iliac artery and internal pudendal arteries showed statistically significant and highly significant differences, respectively. Their observations indicate that vascular lesions play an important role in the pathogenesis of impotence both in diabetics and non-diabetics.

Overview: Management of Vascular Impotence

Harry H. LeVeen

It is interesting that identical concepts come simultaneously to the awareness of different people in different parts of the world. Vascular surgeons have long been aware that patients with peripheral vascular disease often have associated impotence. The advent of angiography allowed the surgeons to assess visually the patency of pelvic vessels. The hypogastric artery is frequently associated in the arteriosclerotic process, and occlusion of this vessel is common. This type of vascular occlusion, or occlusion of the terminal aorta, was known to

bring on impotence. In some cases, restoration of patency of the terminal aorta brought renewed sexual vigor.

In my hands, angiography has been less valuable in diagnosing vascular impotence than the penile blood pressure. Pressures in the erect penis have been measured by needles introduced into the corpora. Pressures in the corpora are near the systolic blood pressure during erection. Therefore, low pressures in the penile artery make it impossible to support an erection. Noninvasive methods of blood pressure measurement makes the diagnosis of vascular impotence relatively easy. The simplest technique involves the use of an infant pediatric blood pressure monitor. This instrument uses a small disposable plastic cuff that is inflated about the base of the penis. Flow is detected by Doppler sound. The cuff is inflated until flow ceases. Hence, a simple method existed to detect those patients with impotence due to vascular insufficiency, but there remained the problem of the remedial surgery for those patients who did not have correctable lesions in the large vessels of the pelvis. My initial endeavor was to create a bypass from the femoral artery to the internal pudendal artery, but this involves small vascular anastomoses, and the flow through the pudendal artery is minimal except during those times of erection. When the literature on this topic was searched, I found Dr. Michal's article on the treatment of a patient who had impotence following a pelvic fracture and who was successfully treated by a femoral to pudendal artery bypass.[1] Since I was more concerned with the arteriosclerotic group, it did not seem logical to use this approach for my patients.

In 1976, I presented a paper before the International Cardiovascular Society in Albuquerque on the treatment of impotence using a direct anastomoses of the inferior epigastric artery to the base of the corpus cavernosum. There was an excellent return of sexual function in these patients. Five or six months lapsed between the presentation of the paper and the time for publication in *Archives of Surgery*. In the interim, several of these patients had undergone occlusion of the bypass grafts, and the results were less promising than were anticipated in the initial report. Therefore, I withdrew the manuscript. My first efforts were made with a bypass graft from the femoral artery to the base of the corupus cavernosum using the saphenous vein. Several such patients were operated on, but they all developed priapism and required ligation of the shunt.

After the first case, I decided to narrow the venous bypass graft by taking several sutures along its lateral side. This did not prove to be satisfactory, and thrombosis occurred at the area of narrowing. Therefore, after several operations of this type, I decided to make a bypass directly between the inferior epigastric artery and the corpus cavernosum. This was suc-cessful, and the patient had returned sexual function. This procedure entailed two vascular anastomoses: one at the corpora cavernosum and another to the inferior epigastric artery. This operation was abandoned in favor of direct anastomoses of the inferior epigastric artery from the external iliac artery to a point almost at the umbilicus. The inferior epigastric artery runs in the very lateral portion of the rectus sheath and can easily be isolated and identified by making an incision at the lateral border of the rectus sheath. Although almost all these patients had an early return of sexual function, the bypass graft soon occluded, with the return of impotence. Because of the successful nature of the initial operation, most of these patients underwent a second operation. In a series of 36 operations, only 3 had patency longer than 2 yr. These patients were young men who had a fractured pelvis with traumatic laceration of the inferior pudendal artery. There were four such patients, and three have maintained their sexual function over an extended period. All the patients in the arteriosclerotic group had a return of impotence in 2 yr or less. It was for this reason that direct revascularization of the penis is not advised for patients in the arteriosclerotic group and should be limited strictly to younger men in whom impotence is of vascular etiology caused by trauma. Subsequently, Dr. Michal published his data, but the long-term follow-up study on direct revascularization of the penis remains discouraging. I believe this approach has thrown considerable light on the mechanism of erection but has failed as yet to yield good therapeutic results. Because the results have been so universally poor in the arteriosclerotic group and because it seemed unlikely that some small technical detail would improve these results, the operation has been totally abandoned.

I have less enthusiasm than Dr. Michal for invasive radiographic methods, especially since the radiography does not delineate a group that will benefit from penile vasculari-zation. Restoration of flow through large-caliber vessels, such as the aorta or hypogastric arteries, is the only vascular procedure that will restore function in the occlusive vascular group. Small-vessel surgery for the penis has a much lower duration of patency than small-vessel surgery in the legs.

REFERENCE

1. Michal V, Kramer R, Bartak V: Femeropudendal bypass in the treatment of sexual impotency. J Cardiovasc Surg 15:165, 1974

PART THIRTY-NINE

INFRAVESICAL DIVERSION

106

TRANSPERINEAL URETHRAL RESECTION OF THE PROSTATE

Malachi J. Flanagan

From the Rush Medical College and Presbyterian-St. Luke's Hospital, Chicago,
Illinois

The Journal of Urology
Copyright © 1972 by The Williams & Wilkins Co.
Vol. 107, June
Printed In U.S.A.

Postoperative stricture of the anterior urethra after endoscopic resection of the prostate is a significant, potentially disabling and common occurrence. To reduce or eliminate the occurrence of posttransurethral resection (TUR) stricture, in 1966 I initiated routine perineal urethrostomy when an endoscopic operation on the prostate was performed. This method, described as transperineal urethral resection (TPUR) of the prostate, has been done on more than 300 patients and is the basis of this report.

PROBLEM OF STRICTURE

Several factors contribute to urethral injury and subsequent stricture formation after TUR. The anatomically narrowest and least distensible portions of the urethra, the urethral meatus and pendulous urethra, are subject to the presence of a large resectoscope for an extended period. This effect is heightened when more time for resection is required and by the in-and-out movement

Accepted for publication October 8, 1971.
Read at annual meeting of American Urological Association, Chicago, Illinois, May 16–20, 1971.

often necessary to operate the resectoscope optimally. Pre-existing urethral inflammation and/or narrowing are contributing factors. Significant narrowing at various points along the urethra has been observed in 24 percent of all cases in which TUR was considered.[1] Urethral mucosal ischemia, laceration and exudation may be prolonged by use of a large indwelling catheter several days postoperatively. Catheter traction for tamponade of postoperative hemorrhage may also aggravate urethral injury, particularly at certain pressure points along the urethra. Urethral inflammatory response in certain instances may occur with hypersensitivity to catheter material.

The problem of post-TUR stricture has been recognized for many years. Nesbit called attention to urethral injury and stricture particularly with use of large instruments in pathologically small or anatomically ill-suited urethras.[2] Thompson estimated that urethral stricture occurrence following endoscopic operation is as high as 25 percent and believed it to be greatly underestimated and underemphasized.[3] Valk observed a 29 percent incidence of post-TUR stricture in endoscopic resection of larger prostates without benefit of perineal urethrostomy.[4] Orr described the occurrence of stricture following

16 percent of all TURs, noting that it often developed when least expected.[5] Landes cited the occurrence of post-TUR urethral stricture to be 20 percent, in spite of liberal urethral meatotomy.[6] Hess noted that post-TUR urethral stricture may completely nullify the effects of prostatic resection.[7]

Perineal urethrostomy in conjunction with TUR is not a new practice. The perineal urethra is larger and more elastic than the penile and terminal urethra, accepting more easily the large instruments necessary for resection. Nesbit states that perineal urethrostomy may be indicated when difficulty is encountered in the passage of a calibrating sound or when any hindrance to free maneuverability of the instrument within the urethra

exists. He reports the practice of perineal urethrostomy in 20 percent of all his resections.[8] Valk reports this practice in 33 percent of his resections, and Isaac in 53 percent of his.[9,10] Conger has stated perineal urethrostomy contributes much to the safety and ease of the TUR and its freedom from postoperative complications.[11] Two minutes spent in carrying out this procedure, according to Conger, may save the patient 2 years of postoperative dilations.

Nevertheless, it has been stated that perineal urethrostomy with TUR is seldom performed, even when demonstrable tightness of the urethra to the resectoscope is apparent.[1] Among objections have been that the procedure is difficult and that exposure and suture of the

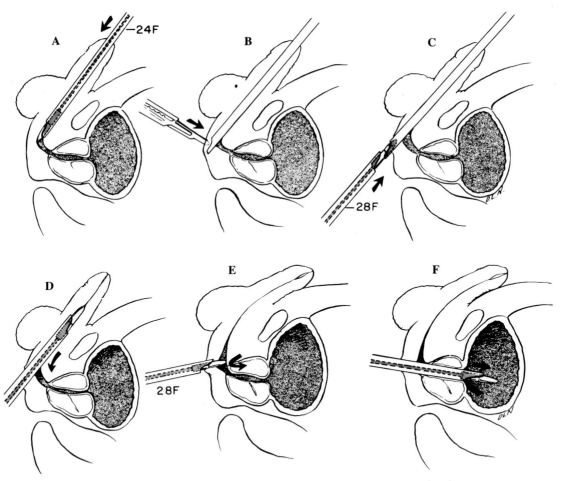

Fig. 1. (*A*) 24F sheath and obturator are placed in perineal urethra. (*B*) Obturator has been removed, incision is made in grooved portion of 24F sheath and sheath end "popped" out of perineum. (*C*), 28F sheath and obturator are locked into 24F sheath. (*D*) 28F sheath and obturator have been delivered into pendulous urethra. (*E* and *F*) Sheath and obturator's direction is reversed and instrument is passed into bladder.

urethral edges are time-consuming and tedious. There is also fear of a chronic urethroperineal fistula.[11]

METHOD

Between 1966 and 1970, 301 male patients underwent transperineal urethral resection of the prostate, irrespective of demonstrable tightness of the urethra to the resectoscope. Except in special instances—patient objection, inability to carry out perineal urethrotomy or histologically established preopeative carcinoma of the prostate—all patients requiring an endoscopic operation on the prostate were resected by the transperineal approach. Perineal urethrostomy was the sole method of urethral operation used in this series, except when pre-established urethral stricture was present. Urethral meatotomy and internal urethrotomy were not used.

The operative method used is a modification of the O'Heeron technique.[12]

In addition to standard resection instruments, a scalpel, a Mandarin stylet and an extra 24F resectoscope sheath and obturator are required. Surgical assistants, sometimes required for direct exposure of the urethra with the standard perineal urethrotomy, are not necessary.

After calibration of the urethra with a 25 or 26F sound, perineal urethral insertion of the resectoscope is carried out (Fig. 1). Endoscopic resection of the prostate is then carried out (Fig. 2A). With all anterior urethral resistance to resectoscope movement eliminated, greater mobility of the instrument is experienced and a reduction in operative time is accomplished in many cases.

Upon completion of the resection, a large caliber Foley catheter (usually a 26 or 28F) is directed into the bladder (Fig. 2B and C) and left indwelling in the perineal urethra for 3 to 5 days. Recalibration of the urethra is not done unless urinary sepsis, retention or bleeding occurs.

In the early phase of the study calibration of the anterior and posterior urethra with 22 or 24F sounds was done 3 weeks postopeatively, except when pre-existing urethral stricture necessitated treatment sooner, to determine the effectiveness of the method in preventing stricture. After the first 110 cases, when the occurrence of anterior urethral stricture has been observed rarely, urethral sounding was done only when the clinical syndrome of urethral stricture was suspected or a pre-existing urethral stricture was present. In all instances the urethral meatus was inspected carefully for narrowing and the meatal area and distal urethra were palpated for induration. All patients were followed for a minimum of 6 months.

RESULTS

Transperineal urethral resection was attempted in 318 cases but in 17 cases the method was not followed: in 9 cases because the sheath and obturator could not be negotiated in reverse fashion in the pendulous urethra back into the bladder, in 6 cases because the catheter could not be negotiated into the bladder although the initial resectoscope insertion was successful and in 2 cases vesical stones were found which required either endoscopic removal by way of the entire urethra or suprapubic cystotomy.

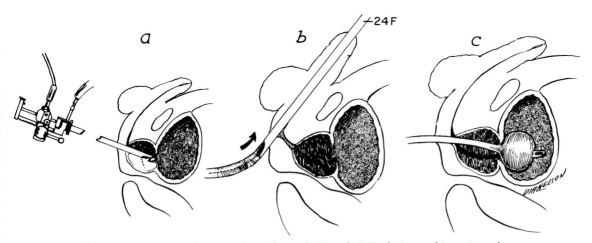

Fig. 2. (A) endoscopic resection of prostate is performed. (B and C) Technique of insertion of catheter. Perineal urethrotomy opening is re-identified by reinsertion of 24F sheath and obturator and catheter supported by stylet is delivered into pendulous urethra, reversed and passed into bladder.

Fifteen patients were lost to followup, including 2 patients who died postoperatively, leaving a total of 286 cases in which followup data were available.

Complications were minimal. Hemorrhage of significance occurred in 3 cases: once with bleeding severe enough to produce a large scrotal hematoma and in 2 cases copious enough to require packing with iodoform gauze around the emerging catheter. No blood transfusions were necessary. Minor degrees of ecchymoses of the inferior portion of the scrotum often occurred.

No perineal infections or abscesses occurred. Postoperative epididymitis developed in 3 cases. Chordee was not observed postoperatively.

TPUR was not carried out when it was known that carcinoma of the prostate was present. However, in 11 cases in which unsuspected carcinoma was found, no perineal tumor seeding was observed to develop.

No permanent urethroperineal fistulas occurred. Persistent perineal drainage for 18 days occurred in 1 patient who had a pre-existing urethral stricture. In 202 cases (70 percent) complete voiding was experienced by way of the urethral meatus within 48 hours after removal of the perineal catheter and 269 patients (94 percent) were voiding by the normal route within 4 days. Closure of the perineal urethrostomy in the remaining 16 patients occurred within 8 days of removal of the catheter. Facilitation of closure of the fistula often could be aided by a cooperative patient who was encouraged to exert pressure on the edges of the perineal opening upon voiding.

The total incidence of urethral stricture was 2.79 percent (8 of 286 cases). However, when use of an indwelling catheter along the entire urethral length could be avoided, before and after TPUR, the incidence was 1.12 percent (2 of 178 cases). In cases in which a preoperative indwelling catheter was required along the entire urethral length, the incidence of stricture rose to 5.4 percent (4 of 74 cases) and a similarly higher incidence of stricture, 9.55 percent (2 of 21 cases) was noted when postoperative reinsertion of the catheter (for bleeding, retention or sepsis) became necessary.

DISCUSSION

Transperineal urethral resection requires neither direct exposure of the urethra nor placement of sutures along the urethral edges. Once familiarity with the procedure is acquired, perineal urethrostomy seldom requires more than 1 or 2 minutes. A reduction in total operative time often occurs owing to greater mobility of the resectoscope. Prolongation of hospitalization time while awaiting closure of the urethroperineal opening was infrequent. No permanent or chronic fistula developed in any patient.

Certain impressions about TPUR have been gained. The precise execution and finesse that are the hallmark of endoscopic prostatic resections seem to be even further enhanced. With all anterior urethral resistance to resectoscope movement eliminated, greater instrument mobility occurs. Such advantage is particularly helpful in instances of progressive urethral tightness on the instrument during the operation and when a tight suspensory ligament, high-riding prostate, markedly elongated prostatic urethra, large middle lobe or a markedly elongated anterior urethra is encountered.

Because of the capacious proximal urethra, larger caliber catheters (usually 26 or 28F) can be used with safety. Larger caliber catheters are particularly useful when more bleeding than usual is encountered postoperatively. If traction is necessary, a more direct tamponade of the bladder neck and urethra is effected by emerging catheter via the perineal urethra rather than the urethral meatus, minimizing further urethral trauma along various points of the urethra which catheter traction can produce.

Routine use of a large caliber catheter in the perineal urethra postoperatively is associated with less pain and discomfort than is the case when a catheter is used emerging from the urethral meatus. Free drainage of urethral secretions occurs and crusting of secretions is rarely seen along the edges of the emerging catheter.

The low incidence of postoperative urethral stricture compares favorably with the reported incidence of stricture with standard transurethral resection.

The projected benefits to the patient, therefore, are considerable: significantly reduced need for postoperative dilations and much avoidance of pain and discomfort.

CONCLUSION

Transperineal urethral resection is an acceptable and highly desirable alternative to transurethral resection when an endoscopic operation is performed on the prostate.

REFERENCES

1. Emmett, J. L., Rous, S. N., Greene, L. F., DeWeerd, J. H. and Utz, D. C.: Preliminary internal urethrotomy in 1036 cases to prevent urethral stricture following transurethral resection; caliber of normal adult male urethra. J Urol 89:829, 1963

2. Nesbit, R. M.: Transurethral Prostatectomy. Springfield, Illinois: Charles C Thomas, Publisher, pp 94–98, 1943

3. Thompson, I. M.: Transurethral surgery. In: Urologic Surgery. Edited by J. F. Glenn and W. H. Boyce. New York: Harper & Row, Publishers, p 415, 1969

4. Holtgrewe, H. L. and Valk, W. L.: Late results of transurethral prostatectomy. J Urol 92:51, 1964

5. Hayward, J. C., Glanton, J. B. and Orr, L. M.: Common causes

for unsatisfactory results in endoscopic prostatic resection. J Urol 64:114, 1950

6. Landes, R. R.: Painless dilatation of urethral meatal strictures following transurethral prostatic resection. J Urol 70:626, 1953

7. Hess, E., Roth, R. B. and Kaminsky, A. F.: The aftermath of prostatectomy. J Urol 67:977, 1952

8. Nesbit, R. M.: The advantages of perineal urethrotomy in prostatic resection. South Surg 7:501, 1938

9. Valk, W. L.: Personal communication, 1971

10. Isaac, C. A.: Use of perineal urethrotomy to prevent urethral strictures after transurethral prostatectomy. J Urol 82:120, 1959

11. Conger, K. B.: Transurethral Prostatic Surgery. Baltimore: The Williams & Wilkins Co., p 136, 1963

12. O'Heeron, M. K.: External perineal urethrotomy. Motion picture presented at annual meeting of American Urological Association, Chicago, Illinois, May 30–June 2, 1966

Commentary: Perineal Urethrostomy

David I. Millstein

Perineal urethrostomy is an extraordinarily useful method of gaining access to the urethra. It can be particularly helpful when used for a transurethral resection of the prostate (TURP) or for temporary or permanent diversion of the urine, such as in hypospadias or stricture repair. Despite its potentially wide applications, perineal urethrostomy is relatively infrequently used.

Perineal urethrostomy was used successfully first by Bigelow about 100 yr ago when he performed cystolitholapaxies.[1] He noted that when urethral strictures were present, the large lithotrites caused more postoperative scarring when manipulation was through the penile urethra than when through a perineal urethrostomy. This observation led the way to further use of perineal urethrostomy in problems with the penile urethra.

Normal urethras vary in size. The fossa navicularis or meatus calibrates to 26 to 30 French in about 75% of normal males and below 24 French in 15%. The bulbous urethra is about 34 French and the prostatic urethra about 45 French. Therefore, even though strictures are not present, the urethra may be traumatized by a large instrument.

In 1937, Thompson reported that Cabot suggested that when a 30 French resectoscope was difficult to introduce through the urethra, a perineal urethrostomy, like Bigelow's, might reduce the incidence of postoperative stricture.[2] He also performed the first TURP through a perineal urethrostomy. Thompson's work was noted by Nesbit, who performed 31 of his next 240 TURPs through a perineal urethrostomy.[1] His rationale in these patients was that their urethras were smaller than the resectoscope used. He felt that the incidence of postoperative strictures in this selected group of patients was significantly reduced. Studies published since then have reinforced this observation.[3–7]

From the mechanical point of view, urologists should be aware of the fact that with perineal urethrostomy, the resectoscope tends to move more freely while resecting anteriorly or medially because the suspensory ligament does not limit its motion. This may require some accommodation for the urologist unfamiliar with this procedure. As a result, however, resections tend to go more quickly than when done through the penis.

In general, there are two accepted techniques for creating a urethrostomy for TURPs. In Nesbit's approach, a 20 French grooved Van Buren sound is introduced into the urethra, a perineal incision is made down to the sound, stay sutures are used to hold the urethral incision open, the sound is withdrawn, and the resectoscope and obturator are introduced into the prostatic urethra through the urethrostomy. Often an assistant proves helpful because the surgeon must manipulate a sound, a scalpel, sutures and a resectoscope. Conger has modified this approach by inventing a clamp to hold the perineal tissues tightly around the sound in an attempt to reduce some of the manipulation necessary for the urethrostomy.[8]

In the article reproduced, Flanagan reduces the manipulations even further, thus making it easy to do the procedure unassisted.

Overall, then, perineal urethrostomy for TURP is a straightforward relatively simple procedure that yields good results.

Perineal urethrostomy also can be used to drain the bladder in a temporary or permanent fashion. Certainly with perineal diversion in preference to cystostomy, the less obvious scar yields a cosmetically better result. Most controversy nevertheless centers on whether a suprapubic cystostomy or a perineal urethrostomy will better divert the urine from the neourethra in hypospadias repairs. The small-size Foley catheter that may be used in a child will have such a small intraluminal diameter that drainage may be slow. A larger lumen can be obtained with the same external diameter if a Robinson or Malecot catheter is used and sutured to the skin to maintain it in position. Hodgson and Culp both advocate the use of the perineal urethrostomy catheter in this fashion. On the other hand, King and Smith prefer a suprapubic systostomy for drainage because they feel that the Foley balloon is less likely to irritate the trigone. Hence, they feel there is less bladder spasm. The suprapubic catheter, however, does not occlude the urethra, and urine may still pass down the urethra should such spasms occur.

Insertion of a temporary perineal catheter can be accomplished by any one of several described methods. A formal urethrostomy can be done with a sound in the urethra, an incision over the sound, stay sutures, and finally insertion of a Foley catheter. In some urethras this may be difficult to do because the tissue is delicate and easily torn by clamps and sutures.

Flanagan's method causes minimal trauma and uses nothing that will tear or injure the urethra such as Allis clamps or sutures. However, one difficulty may be the inability to rotate the resectoscope 180 degrees while keeping the tip of the obturator in the urethra. Although unlikely, the obturator may slip from the urethra and the surgeon can accidentally create a false passage.

Regardless of the method employed, there may be problems associated with perineal urethrostomies. Chief among them is delayed closure of the urethrostomy. Most will, of course, close spontaneously, but in up to 10%, closure may be delayed for 2 wk or more.[3,5] On occasion, therefore, it may be necessary to use a 16 or 18 French Foley catheter through the urethra to allow the urethrostomy to close. Less commonly, the urethrostomy can bleed. Because of the sliding layers of tissue and of vessel retraction, finding the bleeding vessel may be difficult. Usually, compression of the bleeding area will stop the blood flow if the bleeder cannot be located and sutured.

As a result of several cases of prostatic carcinoma that were reported to have grown out the needle tract of perineal prostatic needle biopsies, there has been some theoretic concern that resection of prostatic carcinoma through a perineal urethrostomy might allow cancer to spread out the urethrostomy, as has been reported in the cases of needle biopsy.[9,10] The possibility remains theoretic, however, since there have been no reports of this type of carcinomatous extension. In fact, although Melchior and colleagues found prostatic carcinoma in 11.4% of their perineal TURPs (26% of these were poorly differentiated), there was no evidence of such extension.[3]

In pediatric cases, Johnson described a simpler method of inserting a Foley catheter.[13] This method is similar to that described in *Campbell's Urology*, except that Johnson is able to use a Foley while Campbell's describes using a Malecot.[14] Because a standard mandarin will not fit into a pediatric Foley catheter, he fashions one from a Kirschner wire. The wire should fit the catheter easily and be bent to conform to the normal shape of the proximal urethra. He then cuts off the self-sealing arm for filling the balloon so that the catheter is straight. He inserts the stylet into the catheter an inserts the catheter into the bladder through the penis. Leaving the catheter tip in the bladder, the stylet is withdrawn so that the tip of the stylet is in the perineum. The stylet is rotated 180 degrees so that it causes a bulge in the perineum. An incision is made over the bulge, and the penile end of the catheter is pulled through the distal urethra and out the perineum. Because the wing and valve used to inflate the balloon have been removed, the balloon lumen is occluded with a needle and the balloon inflated. The balloon lumen is then tied off with silk.

In carcinoma of the penis requiring a penectomy, a permanent perineal urethrostomy is needed. Diverting the urine through the perineum has a tremendous psychological impact because the man can no longer direct his stream or void while standing. The basic perineal urethrostomy for these situations was described by Lovelace and Thompson in 1938 when they performed experimental urethrostomies in dogs in order to practice TURPs.[17] They freed the urethra from the bulbocavernosum and corpus spongiosum, brought the urethra out through a buttonhole proximal to the incision, and left it dangling. In several days this projecting urethra sloughed.

Because this method was likely to result in some scarring and stricture, Caffery and Witherington performed a similar procedure, except that they removed a wedge of subcutaneous fat and sutured the urethra directly to the skin with interrupted chromic sutures.[18] They reported little difficulty with strictures and felt that removal of the fat was responsible. The usual etiology of meatal strictures in perineal urethrostomy is retraction of the urethra into the perineum and stenosis of the buttonhole in the perineum.

Sawhney has devised a postpenectomy urethrostomy that can be constructed so that the patient can direct his stream while standing to void.[19] Three flaps are created from scrotal skin and used to support the urethra. Because the flaps are sutured directly to the urethral mucosa and no buttonhole is used with this method, not only can the stream be directed but there is less meatal stenosis and less chance of retraction of the urethra.

In summary, there are two primary indications for perineal urethrostomy. One is for access to the prostate for TURPs, and the other is for diversion of urine on a temporary or permanent basis. It is a procedure that can be done relatively easily and should be available in every urologist's armanentarium.

REFERENCES

1. Nesbit RM: The advantages of perineal urethrostomy in prostatic resection. South Surg 7:501, 1938

2. Thompson GJ: Perineal prostatic resection. Proc Mayo Clin 12:360, 1937

3. Melchior J, Valk W, Foret J, et al: Transurethral resection of the prostate via perineal urethrostomy: Complete analysis of 7 years of experience. J Urol 3:640, 1974

4. Holtgreiwe L, Valk W: Late results of transurethral prostatectomy. J Urol 92:51, 1964

5. Isaac C: Use of perineal urethrostomy to prevent urethral strictures after transurethral prostatectomy. J Urol 82:120, 1959

6. Bissada N, Redman J, Welch L: Transurethral resection of prostate via perineal urethrostomy. Urology 7:70, 1976

7. Falk W, Mebust W, Melchion J, et al: Transurethral resection for benign prostatic hypertrophy. Urol Clin North Am 2:85, 1975

8. Conger K: A new clamp for use in perineal urethrostomy. J Urol 90:242, 1963

9. Clarke B, Leadbetter W, Campbell J: Implantation of carcinoma of the prostate in site of perineal needle biopsy: Report of a case. J Urol 70:937, 1953

10. Blackard C, Soucheray J, Gleason D: Prostatic needle biopsy with perineal extension of adenocarcinoma. J Urol 106:401, 1971

11. Hopkins R, Campbell W: A one-stage hypospadias repair: Modification of the broadbent procedure. J Urol 112: 674, 1974

12. Sadlowski R, Belman B, King L: Further experience with one-stage hypospadias repair. J Urol 112:677, 1974

13. Johnson H: Perineal urethrostomy made simple. Plast Reconstr Surg 59:923, 1977

14. Campbell M, Harrison J: Urology 3rd ed, 2546. Philadelphia, WB Saunders, 1970

15. Tolhurst D: Catheter introduction in perineal urethrostomies. Urology 10:57, 1977

16. Elsahy N: Ideas and innovations. The use of the foley catheter in perineal urethrostomy. ACTA Chirurgiae Plasticae 15:131, 1973

17. Lovelace W, Thompson G, Mann F: External urethrostomy. An experimental study. J Urol 39:186, 1938

18. Caffery E, Witherington R: Permanent Perineal urethrostomy. J Urol 83:682, 1960

19. Sawhney, C: Management of the urethra following total amputation of the penis. Br J Urol 39:405, 1967

ANNOTATED BIBLIOGRAPHY

Holtgrewe HL, Valk WL: Late results of transurethral prostatectomy. J Urol 92:51, 1964

This study of 2015 prostatectomies reinforces the idea of using perineal urethrostomy to reduce postoperative strictures. The two factors that exerted the most influence on stricture formation were gland size and use of perineal urethrostomy. Large glands, when resected through a urethrostomy, had fewer postoperative strictures.

Melchior J, Valk WJ, Foret JD et al: Transurethral resection of the prostate via perineal nephrostomy: Complete analysis of 7 years experience. J Urol 3:640, 1974

In this review, 2223 TURPs were reviewed; 676 (30.5%) were done through a perineal urethrostomy, with an incidence of stricture of only 0.6%. The authors reiterate their feelings, expressed in 1964, that perineal urethrostomy should be used more frequently, particularly in the resection of large glands.

Conger J: A new clamp for use in perineal urethrostomy. J Urol 90:242, 1963

This article shows the clamp Conger designed and its use. The clamp may be preferred by some urologists who wish to do the more classic perineal urethrostomy and are uncomfortable using Flanagan's method.

Johnson H: Perineal urethrostomy made simple. Plast Reconstr Surg 59:923, 1977

The photographs and drawings in this innovative article make the temporary perineal urethrostomy a much easier procedure.

Elsahy NI: Ideas and innovations. The uses of Foley catheter in perineal urethrostomy. ACTA Chir Plast 15:131, 1973

Elsahy's method is similar to the one described by Johnson on creating a temporary perineal urethrostomy, and for some this may be easier to do. The article has good descriptions and is very straightforward.

Sawhney C: Management of the urethra following total amputation of the penis. Br J Urol 39:405, 1967

Sawhney describes his method of creating a perineal urethrostomy with succinct detailed drawings. Surgeons should be familiar with his method because it offers males a chance to direct their stream after a total penectomy.

Overview: Diminishing Indications for Perineal Urethrostomy

Robert S. Waldbaum

Perineal urethrostomy is a procedure whose indications continue to diminish. However, it is still the procedure of choice for permanent diversion following penectomy for carcinoma. Its major complication is stricture at the urethrocutaneous anastomosis. This can be obviated by mobilizing enough proximal urethra to form an anastomosis without tension. Moreover, removing the subcutaneous fat around the urethra, creating perineal skin flaps to cover the portion of urethra above the skin level, or forming an Y-V plasty of perineal skin into a V-shaped incision in the wall of the perineal urethra will help reduce stenosis of perineal urethral stoma.

The use of perineal urethrostomy as a temporary diversion after operation for stricture or hypospadias repair is more controversial. In adolescents and adults there is probably little difference between suprapubic cystostomy or perineal ureth-rostomy, and the choice usually depends on the surgeon's preference. In children, in whom most diversions are performed following hypospadias repair, suprapubic cystostomy seems to have several theoretic advantages over perineal urethrostomy.

A properly placed suprapubic catheter at the dome of the bladder causes less bladder spasm then a perineal catheter, which usually rests on the trigone. Furthermore, a smaller catheter must be used in the perineal urethra, increasing the risks of catheter obstruction. Finally, a perineal urethrostomy is technically more difficult in small children, increases the risk of injury to delicate urethral tissue, and occasionally leads to complications such as fistula formation, stricture, or bleeding.

The development of a percutaneous suprapubic catheter has decreased the use of perineal urethrostomies. This procedure can be used as a temporary method of urinary diversion in all but the very young and in those patients in whom the chance of clot formation may obstruct these small multieyed catheters. Soft, flexible Silastic Foley catheters inserted transurethrally with a larger internal diameter are also being used with increasing frequency. These catheters can be used in the repair of distal penile hypospadias, urethral fistula, and urethral stricture. In urethral repairs where free or pedicle grafts are used to bridge large defects, I continue to use a Silastic splint with multiple holes along with a suprapubic cystostomy.

A perineal urethrostomy before a transurethral prostatectomy is rarely indicated. In my series of 803 transurethral resections, all performed without the use of a urethrostomy, only 12 (1.5%) patients developed a deep urethral stricture requiring two or more dilations. Meatal stenosis was more common, occurring in 22 (2.7%) of patients. Preliminary evaluation of the urethra, prostate, and bladder is performed using a no. 17 panendoscope. Then, if necessary, a meatotomy can be performed, a smaller resectoscope can be used, or, if a localized stricture is found, a cold knife urethrotomy can be performed. The few strictures that are seen postoperatively can also be handled quite adequately with cold knife urethrotomy if they do not respond to urethral dilation. The only real indication for perineal urethrostomy before a transurethral resection of the prostate is a patient with a long narrow urethral stricture or a small scarred urethra following previous hypospadia or urethral stricture repair. (In these cases it would be quite difficult to use the double sheath method of urethrostomy.)

The proper placement of stay sutures will facilitate the creation of a perineal urethrostomy. A sound is introduced into the urethra, and pressure is placed on it, causing a bulge in the perineum. The sound is then trapped between the thumb and index finger, and an incision is made in the perineal skin. The urethra is then opened on the sound, and stay sutures of 4–0 chromic are placed through urethral and periurethral tissue. The final suture is placed in a similar fashion at the proximal opening in the urethra. Traction on these sutures will facilitate the passage of a catheter through the urethrostomy and into the bladder. In a patient with a small urethra I never test the balloon before insertion, since it will never reduce to its original shape. The balloon is tested after insertion by simply pulling it back until it settles against the prostatic urethra. I then push the Foley into the bladder again so the balloon does not rest on the trigone. All stay sutures are removed, and the skin is closed around the catheter with two nylon sutures, one of which is tied to the catheter to help maintain its position in the bladder.

Perineal urethrostomy is a procedure whose time has passed. However, specific indications still remain. Although suprapubic cystostomy has several theoretic advantages, a perineal urethrostomy still remains the procedure of choice for temporary urethral diversions for some urologic surgeons.

PART FORTY

SURGICAL TREATMENT OF URETHRAL STRICTURES IN THE MALE

107

THE ROLE OF SELECTIVE INTERNAL URETHROTOMY IN THE MANAGEMENT OF URETHRAL STRICTURE: A MULTI-CENTRE EVALUATION

C. G. C. Gaches, M. H. Ashken, M. Dunn, J. C. Hammonds, I. L. Jenkins, and P. J. B. Smith

British Journal of Urology 51:579, 1979

C. G. C. Gaches, MB, BS, FRCS, Consultant Urological Surgeon, Norfolk and Norwich Hospital (name and address for reprints)
M. H. Ashken, MS, FRCS, Consultant Urological Surgeon, Norfolk and Norwich Hospital
M. Dunn, ChM, FRCS, Senior Urological Registrar, Bristol Royal Infirmary; currently, Consultant Urologic Surgeon, Nottingham General Hospital
J. C. Hammonds, MA, FRCS, Consultant Urological Surgeon, Plymouth General Hospital
I. L. Jenkins, MB, BCh, FRCS, Surgeon Lieutenant Commander, Royal Naval Hospital, Haslar
P. J. B. Smith, ChM, FRCS, Consultant Urological Surgeon, St. Martin's Hospital, Bath

ABSTRACT—The advent of selective internal urethrotomy under direct vision has enabled precision endoscopic surgery to be undertaken on a wide range of urethral strictures. A multi-centre survey of 197 cases involving 322 urethrotomy procedures from 5 Urological Departments in England is reported. The overall results after a follow-up of up to 4 years suggest that there is no indication for further procedures currently existing in 160 (81%) of those cases subjected to selective internal urethrotomy. The additional injection of Triamcinalone Acetate into the strictured area prior to urethrotomy is recommended in resistant cases.

The procedure of selective internal urethrotomy is, in our opinion, the best primary method for the treatment of urethral stricture, and it is hoped this will reduce the indications for anastomotic or substitution urethroplasty.

The treatment of strictures of the urethra is one of the oldest problems facing the urological surgeon, and attempts to enlarge a stricture by internal urethrotomy have been made for at least 420 years. The names of Paré, 1560; Physick, 1795; Amussat, and Reybard, 1818; Civiale, 1844; Maisonneuve, 1853 and Otis, 1872, are all associated with blind urethrotomy and their work has been well reviewed by Murphy (1972). The last 25 years have seen a resurgence and refinement of these traditional methods using either the Otis urethrotome alone (Katz and Waterhouse, 1971; Wise et al, 1972; Carlton et al, 1974), or observing the effects before and after Otis urethrotomy (Helmstein, 1964) or as now, operating in a precise manner under direct vision using the recently developed optical urethrotome (Keitzer et al, 1961; Sachse, 1974, 1977; Lipsky and Hubmer, 1977; Matouschek, 1978; Smith et al, 1978; Kirchheim et al, 1978; Kinder and Rous, 1979).

The early British experience using the Sachse optical urethrotome has already been the subject of a communication by one of the authors (Smith, 1978) and this paper records the overall experience of 5 English centres (Bath, Bristol, Norwich, Plymouth and Portsmouth) in selective internal urethrotomy. The objective throughout has been to keep the urethral trauma to a minimum and where necessary to try and modify the inevitable ensuing inflammatory response and prevent cicatricial scarring.

The use of direct vision urethrotomy will be considerable, if long term results confirm a stable stricture, relieving bladder outflow obstructive symptoms and reducing the indications for anastomotic or substitution urethroplasty.

METHOD

Pre-operative evaluation of the patients has included excretion urography, ascending urethrography, measurement of urinary flow rate and urine culture. The operative procedures have variably been undertaken under general, regional or local anaesthesia. In all cases, the procedure as suggested by Sachse (1974) has been adopted, using the Storz urethrotome with 0° (direct vision) telescope and the full range of urethrotome knives.

The operative procedure has been further modified in two centres. In Plymouth Depo-medrone has been injected into the site of the urethrotomy and the patient maintained on oral prednisolone for two weeks post-operatively, whilst in Norwich Triamcinolone acetate has been injected into the strictured area before incision *only* in those cases which have failed to respond to two previous urethrotomies. Following the visualisation of the stricture face, the strictured channel has invariably been cannulated using a 3F calibrated retrograde ureteric catheter to avoid creating a false passage with the urethrotomy knife. Incision into the strictured urethra, with a *sharp* blade, has been confined to the 12 o'clock position with the cutting blade extended and moving the whole instrument en bloc in an upward and outward direction. This very importantly has extended not only through the full thickness of the maximally strictured segment but also both proximally and distally into macroscopically normal urethral tissue. Bleeding points have occasionally been diathermised, exchanging the knife blade for a standard diathermy electrode.

Following urethrotomy, an 18F self-retaining catheter on an introducer has been inserted into the bladder and left in situ for 1–7 days. Antibiotic cover has not been used unless there has been a history of previous proven urinary infection, the urine appears infected at the time of operation, or the stricture has followed a urethroplasty. Post-operative hydraulic dilatation of the urethra (Marshall et al 1971) has been advised at two centres (Norwich and Portsmouth) to try and minimise bridging across the healing area within the urethra.

PATIENTS AND RESULTS

Selective internal urethrotomy has been performed on 197 patients involving 322 procedures with a follow-up of up to four years (Table 1). The age distribution of the patients prior to their first urethrotomy is shown in Figure 1 with 75% of the cases over the age of 50 years. The aetiology of the strictures is given in Table 2: 10 (5.1%) had a congenital basis, 30 (15.2%) were due to infective causes, 16 (8.1%) followed attempts at urethroplasty correction and 21 (10.4%) were of uncertain aetiology. A very large proportion, however, were of traumatic origin (120 cases, 61.2%), and of these 105 (53.5%) were due to previous urethral manipulation. The site occupied by the stricture within the urethra (A) is shown in Table 3 together with the overall number of urethrotomies performed (B) at each particular site. The ratio B:A gives a true indication of the responsiveness of a stricture to urethrotomy.

An attempt has also been made to demonstrate as precisely as possible, the stricture site within the bulbous urethra and this was done by four centres (Table 4). The

TABLE 1. Source of Cases Evaluated

	No. of Patients	Duration of Study (Months)
Bath	51	48
Bristol	12	18
Norwich	82	30
Plymouth	41	18
Portsmouth	11	26
	197	

majority of those cases occurring within the *mid* bulbous urethra were related to previous urethral trauma by either instruments or catheters. The level of complication following selective internal urethrotomy has been 8.4%, the problems being of a transient rather than a long standing nature (Table 5). There have been no instances of impotence, incontinence or the development of chordee in this series to date. The patients have been reviewed regularly at 3 to 4 monthly intervals, using outpatient evaluation, endoscopy and urinary flow rates. A flow rate of greater than 15 mls/sec has been accepted as satisfactory evidence of a reasonable urethral calibre. Repeat urethrographic studies have not been done routinely as previous workers have not necessarily demonstrated a good correlation between the urethrogram and the actual extent of the diseased urethra (Lapides and Stone, 1968; Shaver et al, 1975). The duration of follow-up in this series of patients as of May, 1979 is given in Figure 2. The effectiveness of the treatment is indicated by the rate of discharge from further operative procedures of any type to either the outpatient department or to general practitioner follow-up. (Table 6).

There has been no obvious benefit in relation to either patient numbers or stricture siting from the use of Depo-medrone when the rates of discharge of the patient from further procedures are compared with those of the other 4 centres. The use of Triamcinolone in Norwich has been useful in modifying and preventing recurrent stricture formation in those patients who have not responded to two initial urethrotomy operations.

DISCUSSION

The principle that lies behind selective internal urethrotomy is to minimise tissue trauma in zones where there is already excessive scar tissue formation. This is in great contrast to the repetitive and often unvisualised trauma that takes place with frequent urethral dilation or

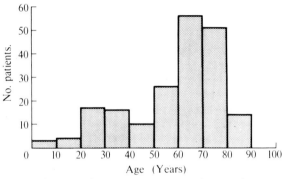

Fig. 1. Distribution of patient age prior to first urethrotomy.

TABLE 2. Stricture Aetiology

	No. of Patients		
Congenital			10 (5.1%)
Inflammatory			30 (15.2%)
Traumatic:			
1. Ruptured urethra		15	
2. Instrumentation alone	19		120 (61.2%)
RPP/TVP	32	105	
TUR	54		
Post urethroplasty			16 (8.1%)
Unknown			21 (10.4%)
			197

TABLE 4. Stricture Site Within The Bulbous Urethra (Bath, Bristol, Norwich and Portsmouth Only)

	Bulbous Urethra		
	Proximal	Mid	Distal
A. No. of cases per site	24	47	21
B. Overall No. of urethrotomies performed at each site	27	64	34
Ratio B:A	1.12	1.36	1.62

TABLE 5. Complications Following Urethrotomy (322 Procedures)

	No. Cases
Penile oedema	5
Haemorrhage (2 patients transfused)	10
Bacteraemia/Septicaemia	12
Epididymitis	9
	27 (8.4%)

TABLE 3. Stricture Site Within the Urethra

	Navicular Fossa	Ant. (Penile) Urethra	Mixed Ant. and Bulbous Urethra	Bulbous Urethra	Membranous Urethra	Bladder Neck
A. No of cases per site	1	28	23	111	31	18
B. Overall No. of urethrotomies performed at each site	1	48	43	161	51	18
Ratio B:A	1.0	1.71	1.87	1.45	1.64	1.0

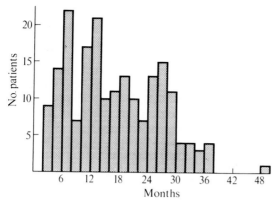

Fig. 2. Duration of follow-up as of May, 1979.

TABLE 6. Patient Discharge Rate (Urinary Flow Rate Greater than 15 mls/sec)

Urethrotomy Number	1	2	3	4	5
No. of cases discharged from further procedures (i.e. to O.P. or G.P. followup)	102	40	13	3	2

"calibration." The results in this series to date would suggest that this operation (160 (81%) out of 197 cases already discharged from further operative procedures) has a wide application and should, as many authors have already suggested, (Sachse, 1974; Matouschek, 1978; Kidner, 1979) be employed as the primary treatment of choice for urethral stricture. This technique may be applied to nearly all forms of urethral stricture be they of short or long standing and the truly impassable stricture which inevitably needs alternative therapy is in our opinion a rare event. It is worthwhile progressing beyond the second or third urethrotomy as there are 18 cases in this series which have subsequently responded with a stable scar.

This has been confirmed endoscopically, for it is appreciated that considerable narrowing of the urethra may occur, to about 10F, before significant reduction in urinary flow rate can be demonstrated with urodynamic studies.

Of those strictures within the bulbous urethra (Table 4) more than half were situated within the *middle third* of that structure and the aetiological factor in most cases was that of previous manipulation, either by catheter or instrument within the urethra. Our evidence would suggest that this may well be the long term consequence of pressure on the delicate submucosal vascular network within the bulbous urethra in particular and we would as a preventive measure also recommend preliminary internal urethrotomy before per urethral surgery (Emmett et al, 1963; Bailey and Shearer, 1979). Six cases have progressed from repetitive urethrotomy to either inlay urethroplasty (usually with extensive stricture disease) or less regular and easier out patient urethral dilatation in the less fit case.

In an attempt to further reduce stricture formation, Sachse (1978) has recommended the self instillation of Terracortril-Gel into the urethra. Particularly in the resistant case, two of us (JCH and CGCG) have been using intra-urethral steroid injections at the time of urethrotomy. Triamcinolone has previously been used to prevent hypertrophic scar, keloid and contracture development in plastic surgery (Ketchum et al, 1966) and has recently found application in the treatment of vesical neck contracture (Farah et al, 1979). Immediately preceding urethrotomy, 2–4 mls of 5 mg/ml Triamcinolone acetonide has been injected into the strictured area circumferentially. It is felt that this is of undoubted benefit in the more resistant case and particularly where the stricture is of primary inflammatory origin and the pathology is still in the active phase.

REFERENCES

Bailey, M. J. and Shearer, R. J. (1979). The role of internal urethrotomy in the prevention of urethral stricture following transurethral resection of prostate. Br J Urol 51, 28–31

Carlton, F. E., Scardino, P. L. and Quattlebaum, R. B. (1974). Treatment of urethral strictures with internal urethrotomy and six weeks of silastic catheter drainage. J Urol 111, 191–193

Emmett, J. L., Rous, S. N., Greene, L. F., DeWeerd, J. H. and Utz, D. C. (1963). Preliminary internal urethrotomy in 1036 cases to prevent urethral stricture following transurethral resection; caliber of normal adult male urethra. J Urol 89, 829–835

Farah, R. N., DiLoreto, R. R. and Cerny, J. C. (1979). Transurethral resection combined with steroid injection in treatment of recurrent vesical neck contractures. Urology 13, 395–397

Helmstein, K. (1964). Internal urethrotomy modifications in the operative technique. Urethroscopic control for evaluation of both the primary results of operation and of long term healing. A discussion of 68 cases. Acta Chirurgica Scandinavica, Supp 340, 1–80

Katz, A. S. and Waterhouse, K. (1971). Treatment of urethral strictures in men by internal urethrotomy. A study of 61 patients. J Urol 105, 807–808

Keitzer, W. A., Cervantes, L., Demaculangan, A. and Cruz, B. (1961). Transurethral incision of bladder neck for contracture. J Urol 86, 242–246

Ketchum, L. D., Smith, J., Robinson, D. W. and Masters, F. W. (1966). The treatment of hypertrophic scar, keloid and scar contracture by Triamcinolone Acetonide. Plastic and Reconstructive Surgery 38, 209–218

Kinder, P. W. and Rous, S.N. (1979). The treatment of urethral stricture disease by internal urethrotomy: a clinical review. J Urol 121, 45–46

Kirchheim, D., Tremann, J. A. and Ansell, J. S. (1978). Transurethral urethrotomy under vision. J Urol 119, 496–499

Lapides, J. and Stone, T. E. (1968). The usefullness of retrograde urethrography in diagnosing strictures of the anterior urethra. J Urol 100, 747–750

Lipsky, H. and Hubmer, G. (1977). Direct vision urethrotomy in the management of urethral strictures. Br J Urol 49, 725–728

Marshall, S., Lyon, R. P., Olsen, S. (1971). Internal urethrotomy with hydraulic urethral dilatations. J Urol 106, 553–556

Matouschek, E. (1978). Internal urethrotomy of urethral stricture under vision—a five year report. Urol Res 6, 147–150

Murphy, L. G. (1972). The history of urology. Charles C. Thomas, Springfield, Illinois, p. 432

Sachse, H. (1974). Zur behandlung der harnröhrenstriktur. Die transurethrale schlitzung uter sicht mit scharfem schnitt. Fortschritte der Medizin 92, 12–15

Sachse, H. (1977). Die transurethrale scharfe schlitzung der harnröhrenstriktur unter sicht. Alpenlandisches Urologisches Symposium Innsbruk

Sachse, H. (1978). Die Sichturethrotomie mit scharfem Schnitt. Indikation–Technik–Ergebnisse. Urologe (A), 17, 177–181

Shaver, W. A., Richter, P. H. and Orandi, A. (1975). Changes in the male urethra produced by instrumentation for transurethral resection of the prostate. Radiology 116, 623–626

Smith, P., Dunn, M. and Dounis, A (1978). Sachse optical urethrotome in the management of urethral stricture in the male: preliminary communication. J Roy Soc Med 71, 596–599

Wise, H. A., Engel, R. E. M. and Whitaker, R. H. (1972). Treatment of urethral strictures. J Urol 107, 269–272

Commentary: Endoscopic Surgery of Urethral Strictures Using The Optical Urethrotome (Regeneration Urethroplasty)

Michael Handley Ashken

The foregoing article was selected because it represents the latest available results of the largest published series of urethrotomy under direct vision reported by urologists in England. Great credit must be given to Sachse for his pioneer work in introducing direct vision urethrotomy in the management of urethral strictures.[1] This is a considerable technical advance over blind urethrotomy, as introduced by Maisonneuve in 1854 and Otis in 1872, allowing more precision and deeper cutting of strictures at selected sites. Since Sachse first reported an 80% success rate using the Storz optical urethrotome, many urologists throughout the world have a comparable 2 to 4 yr of experience with this instrument with uniformly encouraging results.

The last 20 yr have seen an enthusiasm for urethroplasty, whether of the staged scrotal inlay, anastomotic, or patch graft design.[8–12] Although the results of anastomotic urethroplasty, particularly for posttraumatic strictures, remain good, there is a discouraging incidence of recurrent strictures following scrotal inlay urethroplasty. Blandy and colleagues and Brannan reported recently that ''the optical urethrotome has almost replaced patch urethroplasty and considers anterior urethroplasty a now rare operation.''[13,14]

There is currently an enthusiasm for selective internal urethrotomy under direct vision. The practical dilemma is whether the long-term results of this regeneration urethroplasty, by reepithelialization following urethrotomy, will reduce the indications for substitution or anastomotic urethroplasty. The former is much simpler for both the patient and the urologist.

Sachse has the largest personal experience in the use of the optical urethrotome, and at the International Society of Urology Meeting in Paris in 1979 he reported on 813 urethrotomies performed on 697 patients between 1970 and 1978.[15] The recurrence rate was only 12%, and in many cases the urethrotomy was done under local anesthetic on an outpatient basis.

The aim of a urethrotomy is to achieve a stable stricture of adequate caliber so that the patient remains free of urinary symptoms and has a peak urinary flow rate of over 15 ml/sec.

In the selected paper, the 20 French Storz urethrotome was used, but both ACMI and Storz have now produced an 11 French child's urethrotomy sheath, which may also be useful for cutting anterior urethral strictures in the adult.

The results from the English urological centers are similar to those of Sachse, with 160 (81%) of the 197 patients having been discharged to nonoperative outpatient follow-up study. Two, three, or four urethrotomies may be necessary to achieve a stable scar, and urodynamics alone cannot be used as a reliable guide of a stable stricture of good caliber.

Endoscopic calibration 3 to 4 mo after urethrotomy is considered the most reliable method of follow-up study, with serial color photography of the stricture site a useful record of the findings. In the present series, the results have been best in strictures of the bulbar urethra and less good in strictures of the anterior urethra. The findings concur with those of Lipsky and Hubmer, Smith and associates, and Sacknoff and Kerr that urethrotomy is likely to fail in strictures over 3 cm.[3,5,6]

There is universal agreement that the urethrotomy incision should be in the 12 o'clock position, and the article emphasizes the importance of passing a 3 or 4 French ureteric catheter through the stricture site, as a guide, to minimize the risk of creating a false passage with the urethrotomy knife and subsequent extravasation of irrigating fluid or urine (Figs. 3 to 6).

Lipsky and Hubmer replace the endoscopic sheath after the ureteric catheter reaches the bladder to ''increase the mobility of the cutting manoevre'' and to reduce the risk of cutting the guiding catheter with the urethrotomy knife.[3] Storz has recently introduced an improved selection of urethrotomy knives, including one with an off-center step, to avoid damaging the ureteric catheter during the *en bloc* cutting movement of the whole instrument in an upward and outward direction.

It is worrying to note in the selected paper that 105 of the 197 patients had iatrogenic postcatheter or postinstrumental strictures. Fifty four of these patients had previously undergone transurethral surgery, and that complication supports both the routine use of Otis urethrotomy at the onset of prostatic resections and the introduction of endoscopes under direct vision, rather than using resectoscope sheaths, which can only be introduced blindly with an obturator *in situ*.[16]

The authors have used the Storz optical urethrotome regardless of the etiology or site of the stricture. This includes 51 urethrotomies in 31 patients with strictures of the membranous urethra. No incontinence has developed after these urethrotomies, but care must be taken in postprostatectomy patients in whom there is an ablated incompetent bladder neck, since there is a possibility that fibrosis following urethrotomy could compromise the delicate intrinsic urethral sphincter mechanism; and Waterhouse and Selli have warned that internal urethrotomy may risk incontinence in postprostatectomy strictures.[17]

It is, however, reassuring that Smith and colleagues found such urethrotomy most effective in the 12 of their 39 patients with strictures in the membranous urethra.[6] The optical urethrotome is likely to remain the instrument of choice in postprostatectomy strictures, even if only to make later long-term dilatation with metal sounds easier and less frequent.

In only 3 of the 197 cases discussed in the article has it been necessary to return to a substitution urethroplasty. In two, the strictures recurred 6 yr after scrotal inlay urethroplasties and were not responding well to repeated urethrotomies, while in the third patient there was extravasation of the irrigating fluid during urethrotomy.

In only one new patient, with a long postgonococcal bulbar stricture, was it found technically impossible to pass either the guiding ureteric catheter or urethrotome under direct vision. A one-stage substitution urethroplasty was therefore performed. In a small number of patients with a tight stricture that is impossible to negotiate completely, either with blind filiform bougies or the guiding ureteric catheter with the optical urethrotome, the advantages of the latter over the Otis ure-

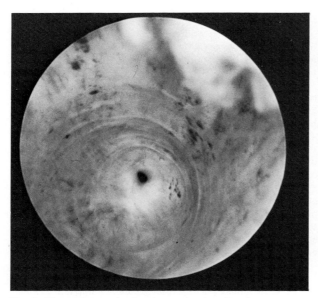

Fig. 3. The tight urethral stricture is visualized.

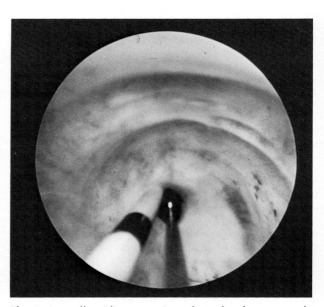

Fig. 4. A small guiding ureteric catheter has been passed through the stricture and the urethrotomy knife positioned alongside the catheter.

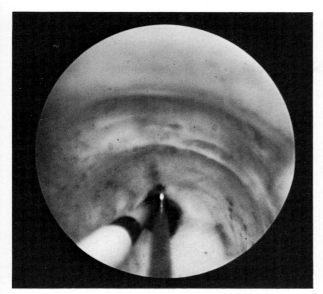

Fig. 5. Using an *en bloc* outward and upward movement of the whole instrument, the urethrotomy cut is started in the 12 o'clock position.

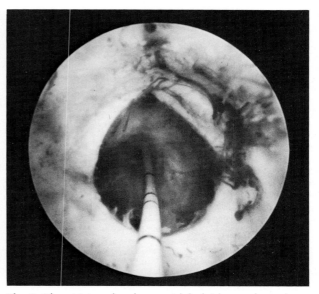

Fig. 6. The stricture has been widely laid open by a deep urethrotomy incision, showing the ureteric catheter disappearing from view through the bladder neck.

throtome are clearly emphasized. Urethrotomy under direct vision can still be done by a gentle staged introduction of the ureteric catheter into the stricture, followed by incision of the stricture millimeter by millimeter until the guiding catheter is passed through the length of the whole stricture. It is in such a stricture that the blind passage of dilators followed by a blind internal Otis urethrotomy could produce false passages and damage the urethral sphincter methanism.

It is still too early to know whether fibrosis following optical urethrotomy will make any subsequent urethroplasty more difficult. Lipsky reported no significant difficulty in such cases, while Turner-Warwick has noted increased fibrosis in the roof of the urethra following a temporarily effective deep dorsal urethrotomy incision, making anastomotic urethroplasty a little more difficult.[18,19] Sachse has emphasised the importance of postoperative management to try and maintain a good urethral calibre and minimize bridging across the raw area in the roof of the urethra.[20] Should these techniques prove too complicated or long lasting, they will detract from the simplicity of the operative technique and will represent urethral dilatations in disguise.

These techniques include simple hydraulic self-dilatations for 3 to 6 mos, the weekly installation of steroid jelly into the urethra, and dilatation by two to four weekly "calibration" of the urethra for 3 mo using a 16 French urethral catheter, as advocated by Kircheim and colleagues.[21] Weaver and Schulte have shown that the urethra will regenerate in 6 to 8 wk if a strip of mucosa remains.[22] The introduction of a thick split-skin graft into the stricture area, combined with a urethrotomy, may prove useful in the resistant stricture recurring after repeated urethrotomies.[23,24]

The optimum time for urethral catheter drainage after urethrotomy remains uncertain, but about 3 days is a commonly used empiric time. Sacknoff and Kerr have used a 22 French silicone catheter for 1 to 2 days to help tamponade urethral bleeding.[5] Sachse has reported a number of cases done under local anaesthetic as an office procedure without any catheter, while Carlton and colleagues favor a 24 French silicone catheter for 6 wk after Otis urethrotomy.[20,25] If a urethral catheter is used for more than 3 days, it should be fenestrated as explained by Sachse to allow free drainage of periurethral exudates.[1] This is a principle also stressed by Turner-Warwick.[26]

The recommended size of urethral catheter varies between 16 and 22 French, and the prophylactic use of antibiotics is not universal but should be used in patients with a known urinary tract infection or with posturethroplasty strictures where hair-bearing inlaid scrotal skin may predispose to septicemia following urethrotomy.

Complications following urethrotomy are rare. Significant *hemorrhage* requiring readmission to hospital occurs in about 1% of patients, usually about 5 to 7 days after urethrotomy. Coagulation of arterial bleeding with a small flexible electrode at urethrotomy should be restricted to minimize tissue necrosis and fibrosis.

Extravasation and penile edema occur in about 5% of patients, but this incidence should fall with increasing experience with the optical urethrotome and the regular passage of a guiding ureteric catheter under direct vision immediately before the urethrotomy incision. If extravasation occurs and urethral catheterization fails, a temporary suprapubic catheter should be inserted into a distended bladder.

Bacteremia and septicemia have been surprisingly rare following urethrotomy, and no epididymoorchitis was recorded in the English series.

REFERENCES

1. Sachse, H: Zur Behandlung der Harnrohrenstricktur. Die transurethrale Schlitzung unter Sicht mit scharfem Schnitt. Fortschr Med 92:12, 1974

2. Michaelis WE, Matouschek E: Über die transurethrale Schlitzung von Harnrohren-strikturen unter endoskopischer Kontrolle. Urol Int 30:266, 1975

3. Lipsky H, Hubmer G: Direct vision urethrotomy in the management of urethral strictures. Br J Urol 49:725, 1977

4. Kirchheim D, Tremann JA, Ansell JS: Transurethral urethrotomy under vision. J Urol 119:496, 1978

5. Sacknoff EJ, Kerr WS: Direct vision cold knife urethrotomy. New York, American Urological Association Meeting, 1979

6. Smith PJB, Dunn M, Donnis A: The early results of treatment of stricture of the male urethra using the Sachse optical urethrotome. Br J Urol 51:224, 1979

7. Waterhouse K: Internal urethrotomy. New York, American Urological Association Meeting, 1979

8. Turner-Warwick, RT: A technique for posterior urethroplasty. J Urol 83:416, 1960

9. Blandy JP, Singh M, Tressider GC: Urethroplasty by scrotal flap for long urethral strictures. Br J Urol 40:261, 1968

10. Turner-Warwick RT: A personal view of the management of traumatic posterior urethral strictures. Urol Clin North Am 4:111, 1977

11. Devine PC, Fallon B, Devine CJ: Free full thickness skin graft urethroplasty. J Urol 116:444, 1976

12. Brannan W, Ochsner MG, Fuselier HA, et al: Free full thickness skin graft urethroplasty for urethral stricture: Experience with 66 patients. J Urol 115:677, 1976

13. Blandy JP, Wadhura S, Singh M, et al: Urethroplasty in context. Br J Urol 48:697, 1976

14. Brannan W: Discussion on the management of urethral stricture disease. New York, American Urological Association Meeting, 1979

15. Sachse H: Transurethral cold knife urethrotomy under vision. Indication—technique—results. Paris. Society of International Urology, 1979

16. Bailey MJ, Shearer RJ: The role of internal urethrotomy in the prevention of urethral stricture following transurethral resection of prostate. Br J Urol 51:28, 1979

17. Waterhouse K, Selli C: Technique of optical internal urethrotomy. Urology 11:407, 1978

18. Lipsky H: Discussion on the role of selective internal urethrotomy in the management of urethral stricture. Bristol, British Association of Urological Surgeons Meeting, 1979

19. Turner-Warwick RT: Discussion on the role of selective internal urethrotomy in the management of urethral stricture. Bristol, British Association of Urological Surgeons Meeting, 1979

20. Sachse H: Die Sichturethrotomie mit scharfem Schnitt. Indikation-Technik-Ergebnisse. Urologe 17:177, 1978

21. Kirchheim D, Tremann JA: Transurethral urethrotomy under vision for urethral strictures and vesical neck contracture. New York, American Urological Association Meeting, 1979

22. Weaver RG, Schulte JW: Experimental and clinical studies of urethral regeneration. Surg Gynecol Obstet 115:729, 1962

23. Pettersson S, Asklin B, Bratt CC: Endourethral urethroplasty. A simple method for treatment of urethral strictures by internal urethrotomy and primary split skin grafting. Br J Urol 50:257, 1978

24. Rosin RD, Edwards L: Endourethral urethroplasty. Bristol, British Association of Urological Surgeons Meeting, 1979

25. Carlton FE, Scardino PL, Quattlebaum RB: Treatment of urethral strictures with internal urethrotomy and six weeks of Silastic catheter drainage. J Urol 111:191, 1974

26. Turner-Warwick RT: Observations on the treatment of traumatic urethral injuries and the value of the fenestrated urethral catheter. Br J Surg 60:775, 1973

ANNOTATED BIBLIOGRAPHY

Sachse H: Zur Behandlung der Harnrohrenstriktur Die transurethrale Schlitzung unter Sicht mit scharfem Schnitt. Fortschr Med 92:12, 1974

The author introduces urethrotomy under direct vision as being safer than blind bouginage or blind internal urethrotomy and reports on the use of transurethral diathermy of urethral strictures, with restricturing in some patients because of tissue necrosis following the diathermy. The new optical urethrotome was developed in collaboration with the firm of Storz to incise strictures under direct vision. He recommends preoperative urethrography and urine flow rates and a guiding ureteric catheter through the stricture to facilitate cutting the stricture along the correct route. Following urethrotomy, a fenestrated 24 French urethral catheter is left in place for 3 wk. Terracortril gel is used both as a catheter lubricant and for the patient to instill into his urethra after urination for 2 wk following removal of the catheter. Hydraulic "self-bouginage" is recommended for a further 8 wk. The author concludes that scalpel incision of strictures is preferable to the formerly used cutting diathermy and that urethroplasty operations are no longer necessary.

Lipsky H, Hubmer G: Direct vision urethrotomy in the management of urethral strictures. Br J Urol 49: 725, 1977

The authors report their experience with direct vision urethrotomy in 32 cases and recommend replacing the panandoscope sheath after passing the ureteric catheter into the bladder to increase the mobility of the cutting maneuver. They use a 22 French silicone urethral catheter for 5 to 14 days and advise hydraulic self-dilatation for 6 mo. In their 32 patients, the results were good in 20, improved in 5, and bad in 5, with 2 operative failures. They consider the technique easy and safe but likely to fail if the stricture length is over 3 cm. All their recurrent strictures occurred within 3 mo of urethrotomy. In 10 patients steroid jelly was installed weekly.

Kirchheim D, Tremann JA, Ansell JS: Transurethral urethrotomy under vision. J Urol 119:496, 1978

This enthusiastic report emphasizes the advantages of transurethral urethrotomy under vision over the previously used blind internal urethrotomy in 36 patients with a follow-up study of over 6 mo. It gives a clear description of the operative technique, using a 20 French Sachse cold knife urethrotome and isosmotic irrigating fluid in case of extravasation. A 24 French silicone Foley catheter was inserted for 1 to 3 days because the authors believed that longer catheterization would do more harm by promoting infection. Hydraulic urethral distension was advised, and urethral dilatation was done under local anesthetic if the urinary stream or flow rate deteriorated. Of the 36 patients, 20 had urethral strictures and 16 bladder neck contractives. Sixteen (80%) of those with urethral strictures had a good result, only 3 cases having a second urethrotomy, and there was only 1 failure. The authors believe that urethrotomy under direct vision is a further improvement in the management of urethral strictures.

Waterhouse K, Selli C: Technique of optical internal urethrotomy. Urology 11:407, 1978

A clear description is given of the introduction of the Sachse urethrotome under vision, with the passage of a 5 French ureteric catheter through the stricture before the whole instrument is moved upward and outward. They emphasize that the movement of the instrument is different from the in-and-out motion associated with a transurethral resection of the prostate. The authors use a 16 or 18 French urethral catheter for 2 to 5 days and do not use any regular postoperative calibration and dilatation. They repeat the optical internal urethrotomy at intervals if necessary to achieve stability.

Matouschek E: Internal urethrotomy of urethral stricture under vision—a five year report. Urol Res 6:147, 1978

This is a report on urethrotomy under vision in 547 patients, involving 602 internal urethrotomies between 1972 and 1977. Follow-up study shows good results in 79.3% of patients. Initial operations were done under general anesthetic but now are mostly done under local anesthetic. Gel containing cortisone and antibiotic is instilled into the urethra, and an 18 French catheter is retained for 3 days. Hydraulic self-dilatation is avoided because of the risk of extravasation of infected urine, leading to recurrence of the stricture. The most frequent mistake is failure to cut deeply enough through the stricture. The author advocates optical urethrotomy as the method of choice for the treatment of urethral strictures.

Sachse H: Die Sichturethrotomie mit scharfem Schnitt. Indikation—Technik—Ergebnisse. Urologe 17:177, 1978

The author describes the use of local anesthetic instilled 5 min before the urethrotomy and details of the operative technique. He emphasizes the importance of using a sharp knife to produce a smooth incision and irrigation with an isotonic solution. He considers that the results depend on good cooperation from the patient during postoperative care. This includes hydraulic dilatation for 6 months, combined with occlusion of the distal urethra using a special tape and the urethral instillation of Terracartil gel. Sachse reports a recurrence rate of only 12% and considers that restricturing occurs in patients who have neglected their postoperative management.

Overview: Endoscopic Surgery of Urethral Stricture

John H. McGovern

The availability of instruments to permit incising a stricture under direct vision has been a great improvement over the blind use of previously available urethrotomes. These instruments are also a marked improvement for treating urethral stricture as has been practiced in the past, that is, urethral dilatation with metal sounds or whips and followers. Internal urethrotomy also seems to be superior to other forms of surgical procedures except in the hands of a few experts. Also, a patient with a failed internal urethrotomy can still be a candidate for an open surgical revision.

This procedure is the frequent procedure of choice because it is easy to perform, the complication rate is low (8.5%), and it can be repeated when necessary. The success rate, as noted in the article by Gaches and colleagues is 81%.

Whether catheters are left indwelling for various intervals of time does not appear to affect the surgical result. Also, the use of steroids either locally or systemically has not been proved beneficial except in rare cases. However, as with open surgical revisions of strictures, longer follow-up study is necessary. I have seen open surgical revisions of urethral stricture recur and become symptomatic as long as 10 yr after the original surgical procedure.

108

MEATAL RECONSTRUCTION

George E. Brannen

From the Urology Service, the Madigan Army Medical Center, Tacoma, Washington

The Journal of Urology
Copyright © 1976 by The Williams & Wilkins Co.
Vol. 116. September
Printed in U.S.A.

ABSTRACT—A technique for repair of fossa navicularis and distal pendulous urethral strictures includes elevation of a ventral flap of penile skin, which is inverted and interposed into a distal urethrotomy. Epithelial strips created on the ventral penile skin and on the glans penis are sutured face-to-face, permitting a directable urinary stream and cosmetically fine result. Results of a personal series of 7 patients are uniformly good.

Frequently urethral dilatations are unsatisfactory for long-term management of fossa navicularis and distal pendulous urethral strictures. Although techniques to repair distal urethral strictures have been reported[1-5] the one described herein provides a simple method to repair fossa navicularis and distal pendulous urethral strictures, and to reconstruct a meatus capable of directing the urinary stream. Since the simplicity of the technique suggests that it may have been developed previously no claim is made for its originality.

SURGICAL TECHNIQUE

With the patient supine a silk holding suture is placed through the glans penis. Intraurethral injection of methylene blue to stain the urethral mucosa may facilitate its identification.

Accepted for publication January 16, 1976.
Read at annual meeting of Western Section, American Urological Association, Coronado, California, February 22–26, 1976.

Repair of Strictured Urethra. Patterned after the technique described by Blandy and Tresidder, a ventral subcoronal incision is made to the depth of Buck's fascia (Fig. 1A).[3] After elevation of the ventral flap of penile skin (Fig. 1B), an external urethrotomy is made to include all layers except the elevated ventral flap (Fig. 2A). The urethrotomy is extended from the meatus at least 1 cm into non-diseased urethra.

The distal mid point of the ventral penile skin flap is inverted into the apex of the urethrotomy and secured with 4-zero chromic catgut suture (Fig. 2B). This inverted ventral cutaneous flap is interposed into the urethrotomy, using interrupted sutures of 4-zero chromic catgut with intraluminal knots (Fig. 3).

Reconstruction of Meatus. To facilitate directability of the urinary stream and to eliminate hypospadias resulting from the reconstruction of the distal pendulous urethral strictures, further reconstruction may bring the meatus onto the glans penis. An epithelial strip is created on the glans penis by denuding skin on either side of

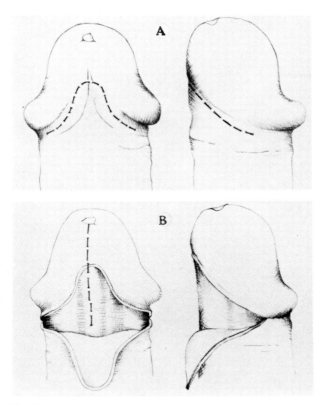

Fig. 1.

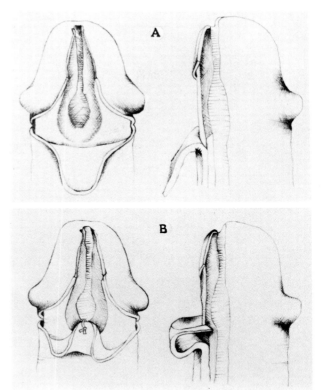

Fig. 2.

the midline,[1] and an epithelial strip is created on the ventral penile skin by cutaneous incision on either side of the midline (Fig. 4A). The epithelial strip on the ventral skin is sutured face-to-face with the strip on the glans, permitting a directable urinary stream and a cosmetically acceptable result (Fig. 4B and C).[6] Lateral margins of the denuded ventral tissue are sutured to the lateral margins of the denuded glans and to the margins of the subcoronal incision as they are most easily opposed (Fig. 4C and D).

A dorsal slit is performed frequently to eliminate the possibility of tension on the ventral repair. Generally, the procedure may be performed in less than 30 minutes and under local anesthesia. A No. 16 silastic Foley catheter placed per urethram is left indwelling for 3 days.

RESULTS

This technique has been applied to 7 patients with either fossa navicularis or distal pendulous urethral strictures. All results were acceptable (see table). The first 2 patients had mild splaying of the urinary stream. As the technique improved all patients had a single directable urinary

stream. None of the patients has required dilatations after the reconstruction—the shortest interval being 6 months postoperatively. Satisfaction with the cosmetic appearance seems uniform.

DISCUSSION

This technique seems uniformly successful for reconstruction of the penile meatus as well as definitive repair

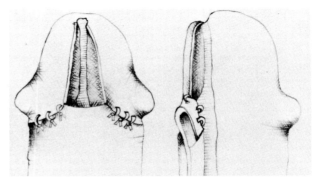

Fig. 3.

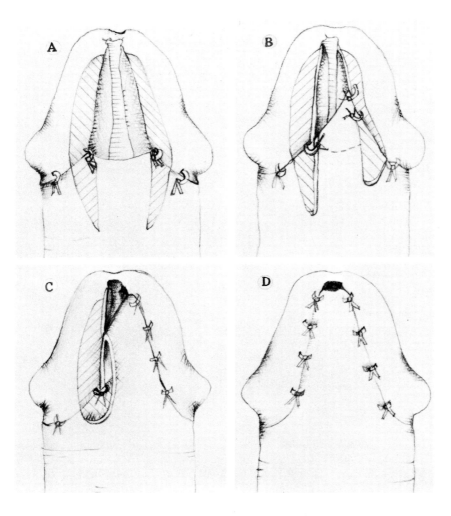

Fig. 4.

Postoperative Data on Patients Undergoing Meatal Reconstruction

Pt.	Diagnosis	Mos. Postop.	Postop. Dilatations	Directability of Urinary Stream	Obstructive Symptoms	Pt. Satisfaction with Cosmetic Result
CB	Fossa navicularis stricture	18	None	Fair	Resolved	Very good
WF	Distal pendulous urethral stricture	18	None	Fair	Resolved	Very good
HH	Fossa navicularis stricture	17	None	Perfect	Resolved	Excellent
EM	Burn injury to glans penis	12	None	Very good	Resolved	Very good
JB	Distal pendulous urethral stricture	10	None	Perfect	Resolved	Excellent
AJ	Fossa navicularis stricture	7	None	Perfect	Resolved	Excellent
EH	Fossa navicularis stricture	6	None	Perfect	Resolved	Excellent

Information obtained frm confidential patient questionnaires.

of fossa navicularis and distal pendulous urethral strictures. The advantages of this procedure over the more conventional techniques are 3-fold: (1) strictures more proximal to the fossa navicularis may be repaired, (2) the new meatus permits a directable urinary stream and (3) a cosmetically fine result is provided.

REFERENCES

1. Browne, D.: An operation for hypospadias. Proc Roy Soc Med 42:466, 1949
2. Cohney, B. C.: A penile flap procedure for the relief of meatal stricture. Br J Urol 35:182, 1963
3. Blandy, J. P. and Tresidder, G. C.: Meatoplasty. Br J Urol 39:633, 1967
4. Turner-Warwick, R.: The repair of urethral strictures in the region of the membranous urethra. J Urol 100:303, 1968

5. Kahn, S., Simon B. E. and Hoffman, S.: Advancement of retracted urethral meatus following Cecil urethroplasty for hypospadias. J Urol 108:808, 1972
6. Hodgson, N. B.: A one-stage hypospadias repair. J Urol 104:281, 1970

COMMENT

This author has shown us a good technique for using ventral penile skin to enlarge the caliber of the distal urethra in the cure of a fossa navicularis stricture. For distal strictures involving only the meatus I would choose to interpose a distally based flap of glans tissue into a dorsal urethral incision to advance the meatus with the meatotomy.[1] For strictures proximal to the fossa navicularis, which do not involve it. I would prefer to use our patch graft.[2] However, for this type of stricture I would use this procedure and I think that we should give the author credit for originality.

Charles J. Devine, Jr.
801 Medical Tower
Norfolk, Virginia

1. Devine, P. C., Sakati, I. A., Poutasse, E. F. and Devine, C. J., Jr.: One stage urethroplasty: repair of urethral strictures with a free full thickness patch of skin. J Urol 99:191, 1968
2. Horton, C. E. and Devine, C. J., Jr.: Hypospadias and epispadias. Ciba Clinical Symposia, vol 24, no 3, 1972

Commentary: Surgery of Meatal Stenosis

Henry A. Wise II and Paul Marsidi

PEDIATRIC AGE GROUP

Meatitis, an inflammation of the meatus caused by ammoniacal diaper irritation, has been cited as the underlying cause of secondary meatal stenosis. This has been noted more often in the circumcised male, most probably because of the lack of protection by the foreskin. The formation of a ventral membranous web is characteristic of acquired meatal stenosis. Meatitis or perimeatal balanitis due to diaper rash is often found in the history. Characteristic for this condition is a forceful, fine stream with a great casting distance and dorsal deflection of urinary flow.

The embryologic basis for congenital neonatal meatal stenosis is thought to be a failure of the urethral membrane to canalize completely. Partial canalization results in stenosis, while complete failure to canalize results in distal urethral obstruction and possibly a stillborn fetus.

Incidence. Allen and Summers evaluated 1800 boys between the ages of 6 and 10 yr and found 578 (32%) to have a pinpoint-size meatus. In a previous study they calibrated 200 consecutive newborn boys and found an incidence of congenital meatal stenosis of 10%. By subtracting the 10% incidence of congenital stenosis, they concluded that the incidence of acquired stenosis is 22%. These studies were done by visual inspection.

The study of the 200 neonates by meatal calibration showed that 9% of these neonates had meati that calibrated at 4 French and 10% had meati of 6 French. Seventy-five percent had meati that calibrated at 8 or 9 French.[1]

Allen and associates concluded that a urethral meatus of 4 or 6 French represented urethral meatal stenosis, those of 6 French being classified as questionable stenosis.[2]

Diagnosis. Visual evaluation of the urethral meatus in male neonates is highly unreliable and should be documented by bougie à boule calibration. Litvak and coauthors noted that the size of the meatus corresponds generally with age and recognized three distinct groups:

In boys 6 wk to 3 yr of age, 85% had meati that were calibrated to be more than 10 French, while 15% were less than 8 French.

Between 4 and 10 yr, 73% measured 12 French, while only 7% were tight to 8 French.

Between 11 and 12 yr, 4% had a tight meatus at 10 French, while 75% were calibrated at 12 French.[3]

As noted earlier, a significant number of patients can be labeled as having meatal stenosis; however, only a fraction of them will eventually need surgical intervention. The clinical status of the patient and not the appearance of the meatus must be the deciding factor. Symptoms may range from mucosal glandular fissuring, bleeding from fresh fissures, or meatal ulceration to proximal urethral dilatation and proximal bulbous urethritis due to stasis and infection.

Selection of Operation. *Ventral Meatotomy.* The ventral portion of the meatus is infiltrated with a 1% lidocaine solution using a 25-gauge hypodermic needle. This area is crushed, using a hemostat at the midline. After a few minutes, the crushed area can be incised without much bleeding, and if bleeding is encountered, a suture of 4–0 chromic catgut may be applied on both sides for additional hemostasis. These sutures additionally serve to prevent the two sides from adhering to each other, but whether or not they are placed, parents should be instructed to pull the meatus apart at least once a day. Another method of maintaining patency is to use an ophthalmic ointment tube, applying the ointment as a lubricant and using the tip of the tube as a dilator.

Meatoplasty. In cases of dense strictures obliterating the fossa navicularis, as is often the case in balanitis xerotica obliterans, a meatoplasty as described by Cohney and by Blandy and Tresidder can be performed.[4,5] However, this procedure tends to produce a mild hypospadias, which may be a detriment in pediatric patients. It has been suggested that a wedge be removed from the meatus and both sublesional triamcinolone injections into the involved glandular and periurethral tissue and a topical application of 0.25% triamcinolone acetate be used postoperatively.

ADULT AGE GROUP

Strictures of the fossa navicularis and external meatus in the adult are sometimes seen, especially after a period of indwelling catheter drainage or transurethral surgery. These strictures usually can be managed with a meatal dilator, but in a few patients dense scar tissue develops, making dilatation very difficult. This can be resolved by simple meatotomy, creating a hypospadiac meatus. A pedicle of coronal skin, as described by Cohney, can be turned inward to ensure patency of the new meatus.[4] Splaying of the urinary stream postoperatively is common.

Meatoplasty in cases of glanular hypospadias is accomplished easily and effectively by advancing a V flap of glans epithelium into the meatus dorsally, as described by Horton and Devine.[6] Another type of reconstruction of the distal urethra can be performed with the two-stage Turner-Warwick procedure. In this the distal urethra is created by forming a tube graft of the ventral penile skin, the defect being closed with a preplaced penoscrotal graft.[7]

COMMENT

The technique of meatal reconstruction described by Brannen appears to be a very satisfactory procedure for strictures located in the fossa navicularis and distal pendulous urethra. Although no long-term follow-up study of his initial seven patients has been reported, the immediate results in terms of obstructive symptoms, directability of urinary stream, and cosmetic results seem to be encouraging, especially if it is taken into consideration that the procedure can be performed in less than 30 min and under local anesthesia.

In strictures involving only the meatus, we would prefer doing a simple ventral meatotomy as described earlier. If this procedure fails to give a permanent result and the patient develops recurrent stenosis requiring dilatation, a flap of glans tissue can be interposed.

REFERENCES

1. Allen JS, Summers JL, Wilkerson JE: Meatal calibration in newborn males. J Urol 107:498, 1972

2. Allen JS, Summers JL: Meatal stenosis in children. J Urol 112:526, 1974

3. Litvak AS, Morris JA, McRoberts JW: Normal size of the urethral meatus in male children. J Urol 115:736, 1976

4. Cohney BC: A penile flap procedure for the relief of meatal stricture. Br J Urol 35:182, 1963

5. Blandy JP, Tresidder GC: Meatoplasty. Br J Urol 39:633, 1967

6. Horton CE, Devine CJ Jr: Hypospadias and epispadias. Clin Symp 24(3):2–27, 1972

7. Turner-Warwick R: Complications of Urologic Surgery, p 365. Philadelphia, WB Saunders, 1976

ANNOTATED BIBLIOGRAPHY

Cohney BC: A penile flap procedure for the relief of meatal stenosis. 35:182, 1963

This technique of foreskin transposition employs a flap to resurface the ventral aspect of the fossa navicularis after meatotomy. It is quite easy to perform and yields superior results.

Nesbit RM, McKinney CC, Dingman RO: Z-plasty for correction of meatal urethral stricture following hypospadias repair. J Urol 72:681, 1954

This technique for release of meatal strictures by a modified Z-plasty of the meatus is useful in limited strictures. The authors have employed the techniques in correcting meatal urethral stricture following hypospadias repair.

109

THE TECHNIQUE AND RESULTS OF ONE-STAGE ISLAND PATCH URETHROPLASTY

J. P. Blandy and Manmeet Singh

Department of Urology, The London Hospital, and St. Peter's Hospital, London

British Journal of Urology (1975), 47, 83–87

Over the last 10 years we have performed 205 urethroplasties of various types for strictures which were not amenable to conventional treatment by intermittent dilatation, or which were complicated by fistulae or post-dilatation bacteraemia. Most of these strictures have involved the posterior urethra (Table 1) so that most of our experience has been with the ∩-shaped scrotal flap urethroplasty, or one of its several modifications (Blandy et al. 1968, 1971, 1972, 1974; Symes and Blandy 1973). One of the principal drawbacks of this type of urethroplasty is that the patient must undergo two operations separated by an interval of several months between first and second stages.

Leadbetter and Leadbetter (1962) referred to a method of letting in an island of skin based on a pedicle of dartos muscle as a means of treating penile strictures in children in one stage. This technique received little attention until it was described again by Orandi (1968, 1972). Following Orandi's publication, we tried this method for a few anterior urethral strictures and were pleased with its simplicity and its good results. Unfortunately anterior strictures were seldom encountered

which could not be dealt with perfectly well by intermittent dilatation, and our major clinical problem continued to be the difficult high posterior bulbar and membranous urethral strictures. Orandi's pedicled island of skin could not be made to reach high up into the posterior urethra.

By now our experience with the ∩-shaped scrotal flap had made us confident of its excellent blood supply and ready adaptability. Perhaps, it seemed, we could make an island on a pedicle of the dartos obtained from the tip of the scrotal flap. Our first patient presented 3 years ago: since then we have come to employ this one-stage technique increasingly often.

METHOD

The operation begins by forming a ∩-shaped scrotal flap which is based upon a wide base, and is carried well posteriorly so that the edge of each incision almost reaches the ischial tuberosities. Unless the flap is carried well back, it is difficult to get a clear view of the deeper part of the urethra (Fig. 1).

At first the flap is carried through the full thickness of skin and dartos and allowed to fall back. This allows the surgeon to keep open the option of making a one-

Read at the 30th Annual Meeting of the British Association of Urological Surgeons in Torquay, June 1974.

1409

TABLE 1. 205 Urethroplasties. Site of Stricture

		%
Meatus	21	10·2
Penile	15	7·3
Posterior	130 } 169	82·5
Full length	39	
	205	100·0

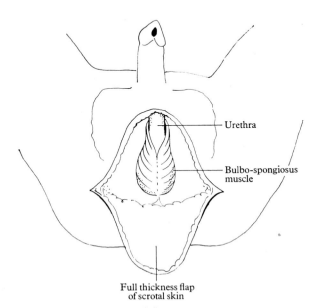

Fig. 1. The ∩-shaped scrotal flap.

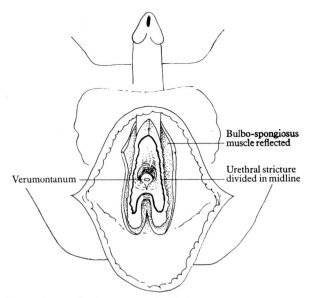

Fig. 2. The urethral structure divided.

or a two-stage operation according to the findings in the urethra. If, for example, he encounters many false passages or fistulae, he may think it better to perform the procedure in the standard 2 stages.

After reflecting the bulbospongiosus muscle, the urethra is slit open along its ventral midline, and this incision is carried right through the full length of the stricture. Not only must the narrow segment of the corpus spongiosum be laid open, but any periurethral fibrous bands must also be severed completely. At the end of this step in the operation one must be able to feel the verumontanum easily, and feel no bands or ridges of fibrous tissue behind the urethra (Fig. 2).

Now the decision must be taken whether or not to try to complete the urethroplasty in one stage. If it is not a very complicated stricture, then nowadays we prefer to go ahead with a one-stage patch. The island of skin is formed by taking an ellipse from the tip of the scrotal flap. The knife divides the dermis down to, but not through, the dartos. The plane of cleavage between the dermis and the dartos is then opened up with curved scissors (Fig. 3) until the island patch has been provided with a sufficiently long and supply pedicle to allow it to be placed in the urethra without the least tension.

Trimming off the sharp ends of the ellipse of skin, one end is now sewn into the apex of the incision in the floor of the urethra. This is the only difficult part of the operation (Fig. 4). We find it most convenient to use 3-0 chromic catgut on a small half-circle atraumatic needle. With a little practice it is not difficult to manipulate the needle in the posterior urethra, and once the suture has been placed and tied, the insertion of the remaining stitches becomes progressively more easy, since it is now possible to pull down the edge of the urethra by traction on the suture.

The patch is sewn in with one layer of continuous catgut. As the incision in the urethra is patched, it becomes necessary to trim away surplus skin, for we have found it almost impossible to judge precisely in advance just how large to cut the skin patch in the first place (Fig. 5).

Before the patch is completely closed, a 12 Fr. latex Foley catheter is left indwelling or, in selected cases, a suprapubic catheter inserted.

The bulbospongiosus muscle is loosely approximated over the muscular pedicle of dartos supplying the patch, and the skin is closed with interrupted Nylon with two Penrose drains in either corner of the incision. As a precaution against postoperative haematoma formation a pad of "Reston" © sterile foam is applied over the perineum, and firmly secured with a T-bandage (Fig. 6).

Antibiotics are withheld unless there is any evidence of wound infection or urinary infection, except in the

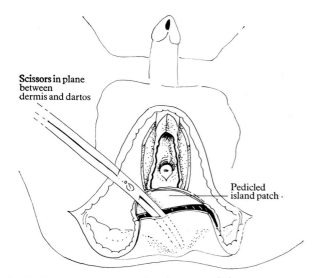

Fig. 3. The plane between the dermis and dartos.

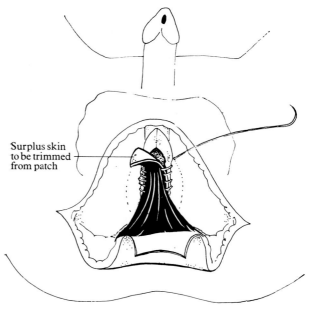

Fig. 5. Trimming away surplus skin.

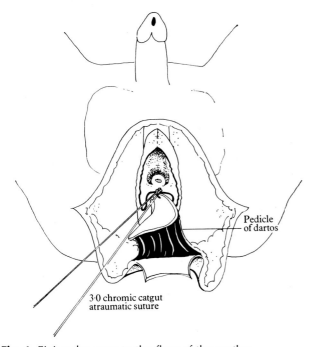

Fig. 4. Fixing the apex to the flow of the urethra.

TABLE 2. 205 Urethroplasties: Methods Used

		%
Meatoplasty	22	10·7
Marion	1	0·5
Swinney 2 stage	8	3·9
Scrotal flap 2 stage	138	67·3
Tubed pull through	9	4·4
One-stage patch	27	13·2
	205	100·0

TABLE 3. 27 Island Patch Urethroplasties: Complications

Temporary fistula	1
Re-stenosis	1
Pulmonary embolism	1
Too large a patch	3
	6

RESULTS

27 one-stage patch urethroplasties have so far been performed: 20 involved the posterior urethra—one of these with a second patch to the anterior urethra in the standard Orandi method—6 were single anterior patches, and a 7th had two patches put in one behind the other.

The longest follow-up is 3 years. One patient (to date) has undergone a re-stenosis, the narrowing being at the anterior end of the patch, probably because the stricture was opened out insufficiently. He is awaiting a

elderly patient, when we have been giving a suitable dose of crystalline penicillin in view of the theoretical danger of clostridial infection from a perineal incision.

The catheter is removed after 14 days, the sutures on the 10th postoperative day.

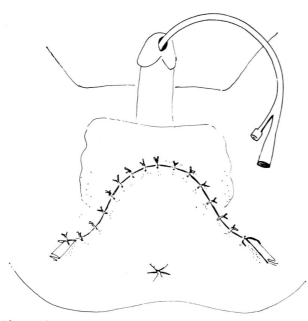

Fig. 6. The completed operation.

as time goes by we may see hair-ball formation in the redundant pouch of urethra, and it may be necessary to trim away some of the surplus pouch at a second revision operation.

One symptom may be worth recording: some of these men have complained of a feeling of "wetness" in the scrotum: this is not incontinence, nor is it related to pooling of urine in the surplus urethra, but it seems to be related to preservation of the sensory nerve supply of the patch of scrotal skin which, lying in the lumen of the urethra, is kept moist.

CONCLUSIONS

Early experience with island flap modifications of well-tried methods of urethroplasty suggests that this is an excellent and reliable technique which can be recommended for straightforward strictures which are not unduly complicated by infection, false passages or fistulae. As with any method of urethroplasty, it is necessary to follow these patients for a long period of time before one can state with any certainty that re-stenosis will not occur: the natural history of urethral stricture is measured in decades, not in months.

SUMMARY

27 one-stage island patch urethroplasties have been performed with the longest follow-up of 3 years.

The method seems to have most of the advantages of standard 2-stage scrotal flap urethroplasty, and is suited to all but the most difficult and complicated strictures at any site in the urethra.

THE AUTHORS

J. P. Blandy, DM, MCh, FRCS, Professor of Urology.
Manmeet Singh, FRCS, Senior Lecturer in Urology.

second operation. The others have not had any more instrumentation.

One patient developed a pulmonary embolism on the 8th postoperative day which responded to anticoagulants.

The main postoperative problem has arisen from failure to make the patch the right size for the urethra: in 3 patients the pouch has been too big and baggy; curiously enough only one of these patients has complained of pooling of urine in the pouch, but our experience with two-stage urethroplasties suggests that

REFERENCES

Blandy, J. P. and Singh, M. (1972). Fistulae involving the adult male urethra. Br J Urol 44:632–643
——— (1974). Einzeitige Lappen-Harn-Röhren-Plastik bei Harn-Röhrenstrikturen. Aktuelle Urologie vol 5, pp 1–6
Blandy, J. P., Singh, M. and Tresidder, G. C. (1968). Urethroplasty by scrotal flap for long urethral strictures. Br J Urol 40:261–267
Blandy, J. P., Singh, M., Notley, R. G. and Tresidder, G. C. (1971). Results and complications of scrotal flap urethroplasty for stricture. Br J Urol 43:52–57

Leadbetter, G. W. and Leadbetter, W. F. (1962). Urethral strictures in male children. J Urol 87:409–415
Orandi, A. (1968). One-stage urethroplasty. Br J Urol 40:717–719
——— (1972). One stage urethroplasty: 4 year follow up. J Urol 107:977–980
Symes, J. M. and Blandy, J. P. (1973). Tuberculosis of the male urethra. Br J Urol 45:432–436

Commentary: One-Stage Urethroplasty

Manmeet Singh

Urethroplasty for stricture of the urethra has undoubtedly come of age. Without putting too fine a point on it, this new and bold attack on a condition so long regarded as hopeless is a little short of a revolution. It is therefore a pity that the total clinical pool that could have benefited from these procedures has diminished with decreased instance of postinflammatory urethral stricture. Urethral strictures today are relatively uncommon. Consequently, apart from a handful of practitioners, most urologists lack ongoing experience with various operative techniques available today. Appraisals thus appear in literature on a limited experience with relatively short follow-up study and the techniques tend to be viewed exclusively when really they complement one another. There can be little doubt that reconstructive surgery of the urethra is a specialized field in urology. It needs extensive training, wide experience, and, above all, an aptitude for this form of surgery. No stricture today is intractable, but to get a lasting cure a surgeon needs the judgement and ability to select and undertake the technique most suited to each problem. When dealing with particularly complicated stricture, the urologist must know how to adopt or adapt techniques. Simple run-of-the-mill problems are today likely to respond equally well to adequate internal urethrotomy performed under vision as to a standard urethroplasty, but success or failure, and morbidity or lack of it, on the whole depends on very careful selection of patients, techniques, and, above all, surgical ability of the operator.[1-3] Increased awareness of the pathology and nature of strictures has additionally contributed to management of the problem.[4]

It is churlish to claim that operations are devoid of complications, and certainly none is exclusive. Multistaged skin inlay urethroplasty has had its problems besides the obvious consequence for the patient in that the treatment is prolonged, and yet it has served me well ever since Johanson and Swiney introduced the concept of viable buried skin strips.[4a,4b] The surgical ideal of one-stage urethroplasty for longer strictures was inevitable, and this can today be achieved by a variety of techniques such as pedicled skin graft, free skin grafts, and even an excision and end-to-end anastomosis of urethra. However, none of these operations has been available for long enough for a surgeon to claim that any of them will provide a permanent solution to a pathological condition whose natural history should be measured in decades. Urologists therefore must wait for another generation of surgeons to judge the procedure that has stood the test of time.

I have selected as a basis for commentary the one-stage urethroplasty using an isolated island of skin on a vascular pedicle. In doing so it does not decry the authors and other protagonists of the technique using a free full-thickness patch graft of skin.[5,6] I view the island patch urethroplasty as a logical extension of both the Devine and the multistage procedures. Island patch urethroplasty, although inspired by Leadbetter and by Orandi, is based on undoubted success over a quarter of a century of either a viable buried strip of skin used by Denis-Browne–Johanson–Swiney or pedicle scrotal skin inlay flaps in the multistage procedures of Turner–Warwick–Blandy.[7-9] It is not unreasonable therefore to expect an equally good outcome when using pedicle skin graft for one-stage procedures. The operation described in the article is quite versatile, and almost any defect in the urethra can be bridged. It can be used to treat multiple strictures and ones complicated by simple fistulas or excess periurethral fibrosis. Besides, anybody exposed to stricture work very soon realizes how nortoriously difficult it is at times to judge the extent of diseased urethra until it has been laid open. The urethral defects in such cases may do better with a two-stage procedure. Island patch urethroplasty does keep the option open, and, with more posteriorly sited strictures, it is reassuring to have this option.

Experience with the technique has demonstrated that the ultimate of complications, that is, recurrent stricture formation, can be minimized to an acceptable level by meticulous care in technique and, in particular, by making certain that the urethral stricture is divided well into healthy urethra on either side.[2] Technically it is always possible to trim down to size a generous isolated "island patch," thus preventing the postrepair sacculation in the urethra. An inert urethral catheter left *in situ* for at least 10 to 14 days reduces the incidence of cross-bridging. I have in this respect personally found little advantage in using polyglycolic suture material over collagen. The operation provides for a short period of hospitalization.

The major criticism of the technique has been leveled at the use of hair-bearing skin as opposed to non-hair-bearing skin used in free graft urethroplasty. Experience, however, in both one- and two-stage urethroplasty does not vary the quantity of risk and morbidity attributed to hair. On the contrary, safety and satisfaction of knowing that the skin used has its own blood supply and does not depend on subsequent vascularization far outweighs the risk attendant on using hair-bearing skin, particularly if the immediate postoperative period is marred by formation of a hematoma or infection.

The free grafts of skin have a good success rate in appropriate cases.[10] For strictures in the penile urethra this operation is easier to comprehend, but it can be equally daunting with deep bulbar on membraneous urethra, as has been suggested by Devine and colleagues.[6] It has enjoyed well deserved success, but unless carried out correctly it is not devoid of complications, and postoperative sacs in the urethra and the attendant problems are not unknown. It seems to me that complications and failures have resulted by employing this procedure in inappropriate circumstances when another procedure may have served better. The long-term survival of a free skin graft *in situ* is an assumption that evades proof. The incidence of graft survival or its persistence may well be less than the overall success rate of the operation. Uncomplicated strictures of the bulbar and penile urethra do well, but a critical analysis of its long-term success in complicated situations where there is extensive fibrosis and infection is lacking.

Clearly, single-stage urethroplasty using a pedicled or free skin graft has no place in the treatment of dismembered urethra following fracture of the pelvic girdle. In these cases the transpubic approach to the bladder neck and the posterior urethra and an end-to-end anastomosis has been most elegantly demonstrated by Waterhouse and associates, and, in appropriate circumstances, the use of omentum on a vascular pedicle advocated by Richard Turner-Warwick adds to the success rate enjoyed by this procedure.[11] Long-term results are still awaited in order to evaluate this technique critically. It would be only fair to caution that one-stage transpubic repair of the posterior urethra is to be accorded due respect unless the surgeon has been well initiated and trained to undertake such procedures. A failed transpubic operation is a formidable challenge to anyone.

Today, short and uncomplicated strictures of the anterior urethra are likely to respond to adequate internal urethrotomy. The visual urethrotome or a trailing Collin's knife in a resectoscope enables the surgeon to divide the stricture completely, and there is every indication that the outcome is likely to be much better than earlier and similar attempt with an Otis urethrotome. The surgeon should not overlook the role of the urethral dilator, either on its own, or in conjunction with internal urethrotomy.

One-stage substitution urethroplasty is theoretically open to complications of both the stages of a two-stage procedure, but in practice the incidence of complications is not any greater. Whether there is also an incidence of graft failure can only be a conjecture. Successful cases do not need and should not need to be endoscoped. The cosmetic outline of a reconstructed urethra is only significant if there is gross sacculation, since this will promote problems from hair nests in the scrotal skin flap. Otherwise, a functional result achieved by a single operation should be the objective, and patients like the operation. With time and experience, longer and deeper strictures are being treated by one-stage procedures just as short and more difficult strictures are being divided transurethrally under vision. Excision and end-to-end anastomosis of stricture in the distal urethra can be undertaken for strictures that are a bit too long or too gross for endoscopic incision and not long enough to prevent a tension-free anastomosis or cause a chordee. In the immediate long-term period such repairs do well, but most series include cases where such a repair in the past has led to restricturing. A one-stage substitution urethroplasty is at the moment more promising. Having stated this, there are limitations. Acute traumatic urethral injuries should be treated by two-stage procedures and, in particular, if there is accompanying extravasation of urine and infection. Similarly, a proximal urethral stricture where an isolated graft cannot be sited accurately without a struggle will undoubtedly do better with a two-stage procedure. It is imprudent to stretch the indication of a one-stage procedure purely on grounds of preference. Radiographic preoperative assessment of a urethral stricture may belie the true extent of urethral involvement.

Peer and Paddock as early as 1939 and Butcher were able to demonstrate that sebaceous glands and hair follicles did not survive higher temperatures than is natural for them.[12,13] Although a few straggly hairs may be seen on endoscopy following a plastic repair, substituted skin, if it ever has to be excised, in my experience has shown distinct paucity of hair follicles on histologic examination. Certainly hair follicles should not deter the surgeon from using a one-stage island patch urethroplasty.

I see little objection to this successful procedure if used within the defined limits. The ultimate assessment will be made in another decade.

REFERENCES

1. Smith PJB, Roberts JBM, Dunn M: Late results of skin inlay urethroplasty. Br J Urol 50:570, 1978

2. Olson LA, Krane RJ: The controversy of single versus multistaged urethroplasty. J Urol 120:414, 1978

3. Patil UB: Selection of an operation in the management of 155 cases of urethral strictures in male subjects. J Urol 119:605, 1978

4. Singh M, Blandy JP: The pathology of urethral stricture. J Urol 115:673, 1976

4a. Johanson B: Reconstruction of male urethra in strictures. Acta Chir Scand (Suppl 176), 1953

4b. Swiney J: Urethroplasty in treatment of strictures. Proceedings of the Royal Society of Medicine 47:395, 1954

5. Devine PC, Sakati IA, Poutasse EF, et al: One stage urethroplasty repair of urethral strictures with a free full thickness patch of skin. J Urol 99:191, 1969

6. Devine PC, Wendelken JR, Devine CJ Jr: Free full thickness skin graft urethroplasty: Current technique. J Urol 121:282, 1979

7. Leadbetter GW, Leadbetter WF: Urethral strictures in male children. J Urol 87:409, 1962

8. Orandi A: One stage urethroplasty. Br J Urol 40:717, 1968

9. Orandi A: One stage urethroplasty: Four year follow up. Urol 107:977, 1972

10. Pressman D, Greenfield D: Reconstruction of perineal urethra with free full thickness skin graft. J Urol 69:677, 1953

11. Waterhouse K, Abrahams JI, Gruber H, et al: Transpubic approach to lower urinary tract. J Urol 102:486, 1969

12. Peer LA, Paddock R: Histological studies on deeply implanted dermal grafts. Arch Surg 34:269, 1934

13. Butcher EC: Hair growths and sebaceous glands in skin transplanted under the skin and into the peritoneal cavity in the rat. Anat Rec 91:101, 1946

ANNOTATED BIBLIOGRAPHY

Devine PC, Wendelken JR, Devine CJ Jr: Free full thickness skin graft urethroplasty: Current technique. J Urol 121:282, 1979

This attractive and widely used operation has been updated. A point is made of not dilating the urethra for 6 wk preceding the operation, presumably to permit accurate identification of the diseased areas of the urethra. The operation would not enjoy such uniform appeal unless it were assessed as worthwhile. I feel that a tubed free graft replacement in the prostatomembraneous area needs evaluation, since in this area of the anatomy postoperative complications such as hematoma and infection are more likely to occur and hinder vascularization of the free patch of skin. The innate ability of the urethra to heal itself (Weaver RG, Shulte JW: Clinical aspects of urethral regeneration. J Urol 93:247, 1965) could also be a significant factor contributing to the success of the procedure.

Orandi A: One stage urethroplasty: Four year follow up. Urol 107:977, 1972

The author has once again outlined an elegant operation. His reasoning is sound and his deductions unnecessarily modest. The operation is recommended for moderate to severe urethral strictures. He has reported a small series followed up to 4 yr. The morbidity is minimal, and a significant follow-up study will, I trust, flatter the author.

Waterhouse K, Abrahams JI, Caponegro P, et al: Transpubic repair of membraneous urethral strictures. J Urol 111:188, 1974

The authors have achieved a one-stage repair of membraneous and supramembraneous urethra by resecting the symphysis pubis. They have described this approach previously. The operation has the appeal of the Badenoch procedure, but with a better view of the anatomy an accurate end-to-end anastomosis of the two ends of the urethra is possible and is less likely to run the postoperative problems associated with the pull-through operation. The follow-up study is necessarily short, but an analysis over the next 10 yr is vital. The initial results are encouraging. With time, this procedure could prove to be a significant step forward in the management of one of the most difficult urologic problems.

110

URETHROPLASTY BY SCROTAL FLAP FOR LONG URETHRAL STRICTURES

By J. P. Blandy, D.M., M.Ch., F.R.C.S., M. Singh, F.R.C.S., and G. C. Tresidder, F.R.C.S.

From the Department of Urology, The London Hospital

British Journal of Urology 40:261, 1968

The great majority of urethral strictures are best managed by regular and gentle dilatation. With time and patience it is usual for the dilatations to become progressively less painful and the intervals progressively longer, and for strictures which respond to this management there is of course no question of urethroplasty.

A minority of strictures fail to respond to these traditional measures, however skilfully applied. Sometimes there are complications such as fistulæ, or false passages: in some the dilatations are excessively difficult or painful and in others dilatation is followed by bacteræmia: here urethroplasty is a solution to the problem.

Simple excision and end-to-end anastomosis of the urethra is useful when the stricture is short and situated in the anterior urethra. Where there is a longer stricture of the anterior urethra, it can be corrected by methods which make use of the buried skin-strip principle of Denis Browne (Swinney, 1952, 1954, 1957). In the posterior urethra, if the stricture is short, the pull-through operation of Badenoch (1950) gives excellent results, with the important advantage that it is completed in one stage.

Unfortunately there remain a large number of stric-tures which fall into none of these categories. For example, Swinney's operation cannot be used when the stricture extends round the curve of the bulb towards the membranous urethra, because the taut skin of the peri-neum cannot be brought up to the edges of this part of the urethra without tension. Again, pull-through opera-tions apply only when the gap can be overcome by mobilisation of the healthy urethra distal to the stricture. In practice it may be difficult to determine just how far a stricture extends proximally, particularly when the distal part of the stricture is so tight that only a small amount of contrast medium can be injected past it: here a technique is needed which is so flexible that it can be adapted to the operative findings.

Going some way to meet these requirements are methods described by Bengt-Johansen (1953), Turner-Warwick (1960) and Gil-Vernet (1966), which make use of an inlay graft of scrotal skin. None of these operations is technically easy, principally because it is always difficult to place the sutures accurately high up in the prostatic urethra. A further stricture will develop if the edge of the skin is not accurately apposed to the urethra, or if it is sutured under tension.

When stricture occurs after these procedures, it can be corrected by a simple Y-V advancement. This makes use of an inverted U-shaped flap, which is essentially derived from scrotal skin. Experience with this revision operation led us to believe that a urethroplasty making use of this kind of flap could be used as a primary procedure. In the event we found not only that the operative technique was rendered much easier, but the end-results fully justified the change of approach.

The design of the flap is such that it cannot be placed under tension and the most difficult step of the operation—namely placing the sutures high in the prostatic urethra—is carried out before the skin inlay is put into position, at the stage when access to the prostatic urethra is best.

Fundamentally this technique is a much exaggerated version of the method originated by Leadbetter (1960) and developed by Wells (1966), but there is one rather important difference. The flap recommended here is derived from the pliable skin of the scrotum and not from the inelastic skin of the perineum.

The operation is carried out in two stages on lines already laid down by Johansen.

Stage I. In the first stage it is important to keep the operative field as bloodless as possible. The general anæsthetic may be combined with controlled hypotension and it is advantageous to infiltrate the tissues with adrenaline in saline. If necessary, the operation can be done under spinal or epidural anæthesia. The patient is put in the lithotomy position for both first and second stages.

The incision is in the form of an inverted Y (Fig. 1). The scrotal flap is defined, raised and dissected well back so as to expose the bulb. The flap is then allowed to hand down freely. The anterior limb of the incision is carried forward along the shaft of the penis.

To locate the lumen of the urethra it is convenient to cut down on to an anterior straight bougie. Once the urethral lumen is entered, it is held open with stay sutures and the edge of the urethra sutured piecemeal to the edge of the skin as the operation progresses, so as to keep the field tidy and control hæmorrhage. (These sutures have been omitted in the accompanying illustrations for the sake of clarity) (Fig. 2).

The lumen of the urethra is opened progressively backwards, laying open the stricture. This incision is extended round the bulbar urethra and carried right up to the level of the verumontanum. It is essential that this landmark should be easily visible at the end of the first stage of the operation. If one cannot easily insert a finger right up into the prostatic urethra after laying open a posterior stricture, then it is certain that the stricture and its surrounding fibrous tissue have not been adequately divided, a point previously emphasised by Turner-Warwick.

The next step is to insert the flap of scrotal skin into the gap which has been made by slitting open the urethra. The sutures are first passed into the proximal cut edge of the urethra, if necessary into the verumontanum itself, using a fine Reverdin needle and 5·0 nylon sutures. We have found it convenient to insert four or five of these sutures into the prostatic urethra first, and then to pass the free ends of each suture through the apex of scrotal

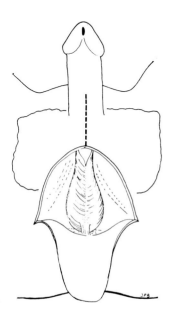
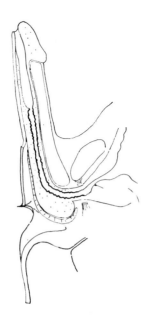

Fig. 1.

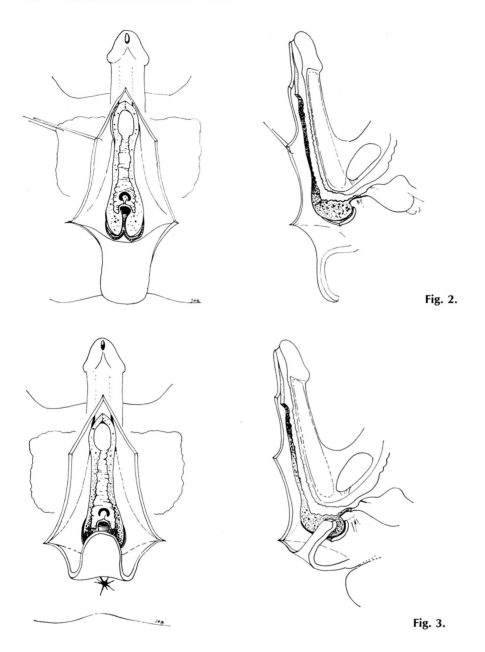

Fig. 2.

Fig. 3.

skin before tying any of them. In this way the most difficult part of the operation is done whilst the surgeon has an unimpeded view of the deepest part of the wound (Fig. 3). The sutures are now tied and drawn up whilst at the same time the flap is tucked into the gap in the floor of the prostatic urethra (Fig. 4). The remaining nylon sutures are now easily inserted using a small curved cutting needle on a small needle-holder.

No drain is inserted. A small 12 Ch. latex Foley catheter is left indwelling for the first three or four days after the operation. Antibiotics are not given unless the patient's urine has previously been infected.

The catheter is removed on the third or fourth day. The patient then has twice daily saline baths, with additional baths after defæcation.

The sutures are removed under a second general anæsthetic on the fourteenth post-operative day and the patient goes home a day or two later.

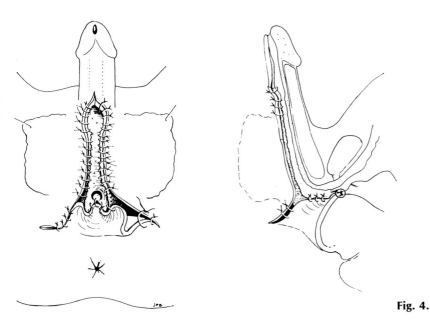

Fig. 4.

In the course of the next few months the patient is seen at regular intervals to ensure that the opening of the urethra has not undergone re-stenosis. At these visits the opportunity may be taken to remove hairs by electrolysis or to excise any granulations or redundant tags of skin.

Stage II. The second stage is undertaken three months after the first. Before beginning it is necessary to make sure that the index finger can easily be inserted into the prostatic urethra. An incision is now made into the skin at a convenient distance all around the previously opened strip of urethra (Fig. 5). The incised skin is now mobilised so as to form a new tube for the urethra. The success or failure of the entire operation depends on how precisely this tube is reconstructed. It must not be too large, or else pockets will form, whilst on the other hand it must not be too narrow, or there will be a new stricture. It has been found convenient in practice to free one side of the skin first and adjust it for size over a bougie held in position by an assistant. If the skin flap on the first side has been cut too generously, that on the second can be trimmed appropriately. The skin is now formed into a tube by suturing it with continuous plain atraumatic 4·0 catgut, whose bites take only subcutaneous tissue and avoid the lumen (Fig. 6). Once the suture has been started, the bougie is removed and a No. 12 Ch. silicone rubber tube passed into the bladder to serve as a convenient means of urinary diversion. A preliminary suprapubic catheter may be used for diversion, but in recent cases has been avoided without ill-effect.

After reforming the skin tube, the connective tissue on each side of the new urethra is brought together with interrupted plain catgut atraumatic sutures. It is often impossible to identify the bulbo-spongiosus muscle, but

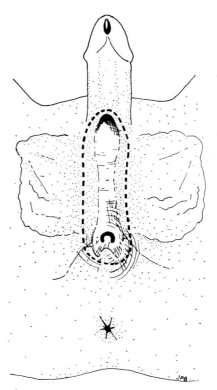

Fig. 5.

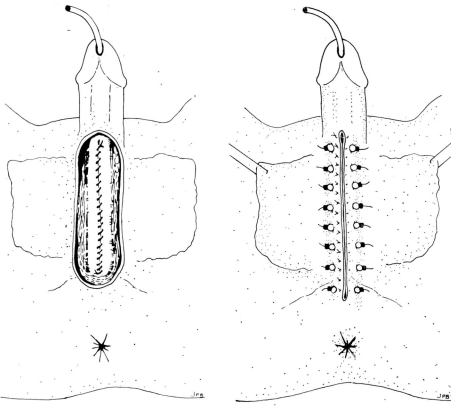

Fig. 6.   **Fig. 7.**

where this is possible it may be carefully approximated over the urethra. The skin is then brought together, either with Denis Browne sutures (Fig. 7), or straightforward mattress sutures of nylon; the latter being easier to place and just as effective.

Following the second stage, the catheter is withdrawn 10 days after operation. The patient then voids normally. The stitches are removed 14 days after the operation.

Results. So far the operation has been completed in 17 patients, whose ages range from one child aged 7 who had a congenital urethral diverticulum, to a patient aged 88 who came in with multiple strictures, sinuses and diverticula of the urethra. In all the adult patients the stricture of the posterior urethra had been of very long standing. In 11 cases there had been previous internal urethrotomies and we gained the impression that the worst strictures of all followed this procedure. In addition to these 17 cases which have been completed, four others have not had the second stage done yet. One of these died of a carcinoma of the lung about six months after the first stage. Another patient has had repeated operations for vesical calculi, which have formed proximal to

his long-standing post-traumatic stricture. Following the first stage urethroplasty, it has been possible to deal with these stones by means of a lithotrite and the patient is unwilling to have the urethra converted back to the normal situation in case litholapaxy will then not be possible.

Difficulties must be expected with any relatively new procedure. One mentally strange patient could not be persuaded not to meddle with his catheter after the second stage had been completed and now has a minute fistula in the shaft of the penis, but is otherwise well. He is waiting to have this revised. A second patient developed two episodes of acute retention, which were considered to be due to re-stenosis. Eventually it was realised that the patient had severe endogenous depression, and after psychiatric treatment, both depression and attacks of retention have been relieved. He is the only patient in this series in whom a bougie is still being passed after the urethroplasty. The instrumentation is extremely easy and it is debatable whether we are treating the surgeon or the patient. The instrumentation is carried out at intervals of six months.

Post-operative urethrograms have been performed

in all 17 patients. The films are not all equally satisfactory. In some of the reconstructed urethras there has been a slight tendency for a little dilatation of the urethra at its most proximal end, a common finding after urethroplasty by any technique. It has not given rise to any trouble in any of these patients. If previously normal, sexual function has been satisfactory in all these patients and indeed one of them has already acquired a second attack of gonorrhœa.

This approach to the posterior urethra, which makes use of an inverted U-shaped flap of scrotal skin, has been of value not only in the surgery of strictures, but also in closing low-level fistulæ between rectum and prostatic urethra. We have used it in two such cases with success.

Conclusions. Each year sees a new technique for the surgery of urethral stricture and there is no doubt that methods will continue to improve in the future. The present technique has been found easy and adaptable. The follow-up now extends in 10 patients for more than one year and in three for more than two years. Bearing in mind Johansen's experience with the late complications which followed early success with his technique, this report must be regarded as a preliminary communication, and only time and experience will show whether these early promising results are maintained over the next 10 years.

SUMMARY

Seventeen patients have been treated by a new type of urethroplasty, which embodies an inverted U-shaped flap of scrotal skin. It has certain practical advantages. It is technically easy to perform and can be used to deal with a stricture of any length from one end to the other of the urethra.

REFERENCES

BADENOCH, A. W. (1950). Br J Urol 22:404
GIL-VERNET, J. M. (1966). J Urol Nephrol 72:97
JOHANSEN, B. (1953). Acta Chir Scand Suppl 176
LEADBETTER, G. W. (1960). J Urol 83:54
SWINNEY, J. (1952). Br J Urol 24:229

——— (1954). Proc Roy Soc Med 47:395
——— (1957). Br J Urol 29:293
TURNER-WARWICK, R. T. (1960). J Urol 83:416
WELLS, C. (1966). Br J Urol 38:93

Commentary: Two-Stage Urethroplasty

Manuel Fernandes

During the past 16 yr I have devoted considerable effort to improving the two-stage urethroplasty with the objective of obtaining better long-term results with fewer complications. I have continued to use the two-stage urethroplasty because of disappointing results with the one-stage urethroplasty and other more conservative surgical techniques for the treatment of urethral strictures in men.

In 1953, Johanson first described an effective surgical procedure for the repair of both anterior and posterior urethral strictures based on knowledge of the underlying pathologic condition. The Johanson surgical technique required that the strictured area be completely opened into the normal urethra on either end of the strictured area and that the edges of the urethral canal then be marsupialized to the skin in the first stage.

The second stage of the urethroplasty consists of reconstruction of the urethra to a normal caliber, which is carried out 3 or more mo later when the tissues are uninfected and well healed. This is done by the Denis Browne technique of using and burying a strip of skin. A suprapubic urinary diversion is maintained for both stages of this procedure. However, Johanson's first-stage button-hole scrotal inlay flap for strictures of the deeper portions of the urethra was considered technically difficult, and it also had a higher rate of complications, mainly stomal strictures. Hence, multiple modifications have since been described by Lapides, Turner-Warwick, Steward, Leadbetter, Gil-Vernet, Blandy and colleagues, and Fernandes and Draper.[3-10]

The technique using the inverted U-shaped perineal or scrotal skin flap gives a much wider exposure to the perineal anatomy and permits incision of strictures and suturing of the skin flaps much higher in the membranous urethra without the necessity of special instruments. All these modifications of the original Johanson procedure have the same basic surgical concept and differ only in the type of skin used and the way the skin is fashioned and sutured around the opened urethra.

From 1961 to 1967, I used the original Johanson first-stage operation for strictures involving the anterior urethra (27 patients) but have employed the Leadbetter modification (inverted U-shaped perineal skin flap) for strictures of the posterior urethra (91 patients). This latter technique, which uses an inelastic, thick perineal skin flap, does not easily reach strictures either of the proximal bulb or the membranous urethra. The tension resulting on the suture line is unavoidable and resulted in a high incidence of proximal stomal strictures (20%) that were difficult to revise.

From 1967 to the present I have been using a technique similar to the one advocated by Blandy and colleagues.[9] However, the inverted U-shaped scrotoperineal skin flap is somewhat shorter; the scrotum is never split entirely, and another V-shaped flap is developed that can be sutured to the distal stoma.

TECHNIQUE

To proceed (Fig. 8), outline an adequate inverted U-shaped scrotoperineal flap with the apex on the scrotal raphe, 2.5 cm from the perineal scrotal junction. Divide the strictured area and extend the urethrotomy proximally and distally for more than 1 cm into the normal urethra. Excise all scar tissue with abscesses or fistulous tracts, and, when possible, accomplish continuity of the roof of the urethra by end-to-end suturing. Anchor the scrotoperineal flap to the proximal end of the urethrotomy. Make a midline incision along the scrotal raphe, depending on the length of the area to be marsupialized. This incision establishes two large scrotal skin flaps laterally, which are then mobilized. Suture the edges of these lateral scrotal flaps to the urethral edges. Another small scrotal flap is developed and sutured to the distal stoma. In the completed procedure, the skin surrounding the entire marsupialized urethra is pliable, elastic, fat-free scrotal skin, made by joining the four scrotal flaps previously described.

In patients in whom the proximal bulbous urethra was completely excised because of necrosis, fibrosis, or abscesses, this scrotoperineal skin flap was made into a tube by suturing the lateral edges together. With the combined suprapubic approach, this tube was brought up and easily sutured to the vesical neck (four patients).

In patients with strictures involving the anterior and posterior urethra, I have used a combination of Johanson and the scrotoperineal skin flap techniques (Fig. 9). This resulted in complete bridging, rather than splitting, of the scrotum.

In all the techniques described, I have used no drains. All sutures consisted of fine absorbable material. An 18 French Foley catheter was left indwelling for 3 to 4 days postoperatively. A pressure dressing was applied for 48 hr.

Second-stage closure is postponed for several months, until the inflammatory reaction has subsided and all tissues are well healed and stomas are calibrated to 26 or 28 Fr. Cysto-panendoscopy is performed in all patients to exclude vesical outlet obstruction or other pathologic conditions (tumors, calculi). Transurethral surgery, when indicated, should precede the second stage by at least 4 wk. Fifty percent of my patients had to have transurethral prostatectomies between the first- and second-stage urethroplasties because of enlarged prostates.

Most of my patients (209) had a single-layer closure that is a simple modification of the Denis Browne procedure.[11] In this procedure, an elliptic incision is made on the skin around the marsupialized urethra. Two thick lateral flaps are developed and brought over a wide strip of skin and urethral mucosa. They are approximated with a single continuous 0 monofilament nylon suture (Fig. 10). In those patients who had a posterior urethroplasty, the bulbocavernosus muscles are also included in these lateral flaps. Either end of the suture is tied over rolled Penrose drains (Fig. 11). I emphasize that in the adult patient, the buried strip of skin and mucosa should be 2½ cm (26 French) wide in the anterior urethra and 3 cm (30 French) wide in the bulb. Urinary drainage is accomplished by a 16 or 18 French Foley catheter through the new urethra for 10 to 12 days. The monofilament nylon suture is removed 1 day after the catheter is removed.

RESULTS AND COMPLICATIONS

The two-stage urethroplasty has been performed in 260 patients who had severe and complicated strictures. These strictures involved the bulbomembraneous urethra in 180 patients, the bulbous and penoscrotal urethra in 46, and only the penoscrotal urethra in 34. Gonorrheal infection was responsible for 60% of the strictures; 20% were secondary to urethral instrumentation (transurethral resection of the prostate, endoscopy, or in dwelling catheters); 6% were traumatic (3 ruptured membranous urethras); in 10% the etiology was unknown. The remaining 4% (11 patients) included 7 patients with previous urethral repairs, 2 patients with congenital strictures, 1 with a congenital diverticulum, and another with multiple venereal warts.

Ages ranged from 2 to 88 yr, but most patients were between 50 and 79 yr of age. Approximately 62% of my patients were black.

Although urinary diversion was not carried out as a routine procedure, 20 patients had suprapubic cystostomy before the first stage and 3 other patients presented with permanent cystostomy diversion.

In 34 patients who had Johanson's first-stage urethroplasty, stomal strictures occurred in 10 and in 17 of 91 patients who had Leadbetter's modification or the combined Leadbetter–Johanson procedure, respectively. In the latter group, nine strictures were at the proximal stoma and were revised by my lateral perineal scrotal flap technique (Fig. 12). In 135 patients (10%) who had the scrotoperineal flap technique alone or in combination with the Johanson operation, only 13 had stomal strictures. Three strictures were at the proximal stomas but were easily revised by lifting the flap, incising the stricture, and resuturing it in place. Two patients had disruption of their wound, either secondary to infection or to a large hematoma. All 42 patients with the aforementioned complications required another operation for revision, and 2 patients required 2 revisions each.

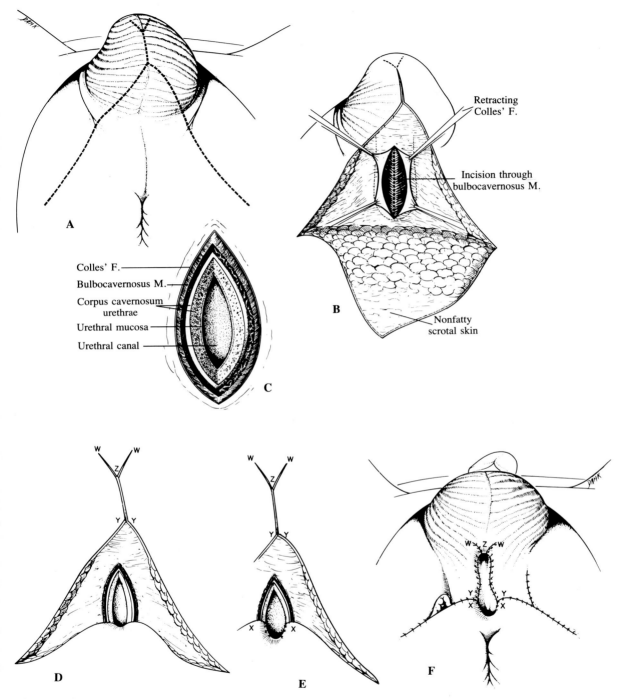

Fig. 8. Technique for bulbomembranous strictures. (*A*) Scrotal perineal flap, lateral scrotal flaps, and small distal flap are outlined. (*B*) Scrotal perineal flap is raised, and incision of Colles' fascia and bulbocavernosus muscle is made. (*C*) Strictured area is incised. (*D*) Scrotal perineal flap is sutured. (*E*) Flap is sutured in place, and lateral scrotal flaps and small distal V flap are raised. (*F*) Entire marsupialization of urethra is completed.

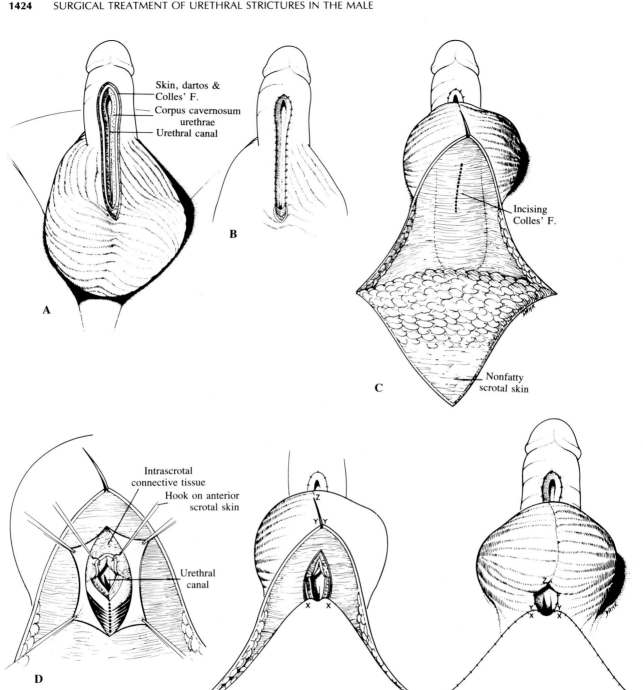

Fig. 9. Technique for multiple urethral strictures that involve penile and bulbous urethra. (*A*) Incision of pendulous stricture. (*B*) Marsupialization of urethra with sutures approximating urethral mucosal edges to skin edges. (*C*) Scrotal perineal flaps are raised. (*D*) Incision of bulbous stricture and anterior scrotal skin brought underneath scrotum. (*E*) Suture of scrotal perineal flaps into proximal gap of urethrotomy. (*F*) Completed procedure showing both anterior and posterior marsupialization of urethra with scrotal bridge.

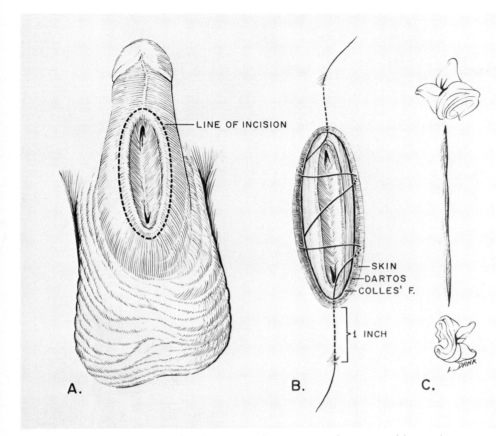

Fig. 10. (*A*) Appearance of healed first stage Johanson procedure. Dotted line indicates incision for second stage. (*B*) Mobilization of thick lateral flaps and continuous nylon one-layer suture in place. (*C*) Layers are closed with nylon suture; ends are secured to sponge rubber.

In 226 patients who had the second-stage operation, 209 of whom had single-layer closure, 10 patients developed early complications within 6 mo. Five of these developed urethrocutaneous fistulae (2.4%; 2 penile and 3 perineal) that required surgical closure. Three patients developed large urethral diverticulae (1.4%; 2 penile and one perineal), and one required excision of the diverticulum. Two patients (1%) developed recurrent strictures (one penile and one perineal), necessitating another two-stage operation.

Considerable urinary leakage occurred in 10 patients but healed spontaneously before hospital discharge without the need for catheter drainage. Two patients died of unrelated causes.

Ninety-eight patients had short term follow-up study (between 1 and 3 yr). Of these patients, 75 were at St. Luke's Hospital, and 6 of them have since died of unrelated causes. One developed recurrent strictures following a transurethral resection for benign prostatic hypertrophy, which was reoperated on by a two-stage procedure. Marked chordee was seen in one patient with penile urethroplasty but improved with Z-plasty.

A recent review of patients with long-term follow-up study of 3 to 12 yr was undertaken, and it was found that 6 patients have died of unrelated causes, 26 patients were lost to follow-up study, and 100 patients were available for careful study and evaluation. From 3 to 5 yr, 40 of the 100 patients were followed, and 60 of these patients were followed from 6 to 12 yr. The strictures were previously located at the bulbous and membranous urethra in 68 patients, the bulbous and penile urethra in 21, and the penile urethra in 11.

Ten of these 100 patients had transurethral resection of the prostate 3 or more years after completion of their urethroplasties. Of these ten patients, five developed recurrent strictures and two of them also formed hairball stones. All were reoperated on with the two-stage urethroplasty. Three other patient (no transurethral surgery) also developed urethral strictures, and one of them who had had 8 yr of follow-up study developed hairball stones. Of this latter group, one patient was reoperated on with the two-stage procedure and the other had the stones removed endoscopically. The remaining patient who developed strictures was dilated once under anesthesia.

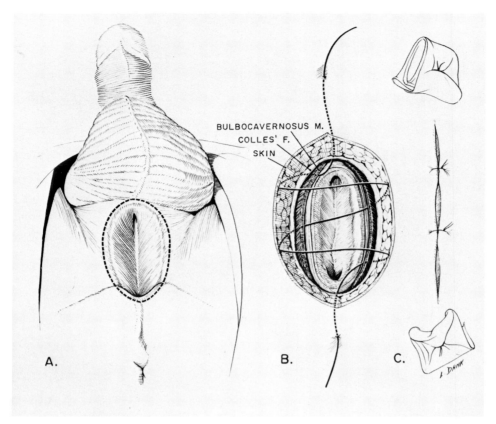

Fig. 11. (A) Appearance of healed first stage Leadbetter modification. Dotted line indicates skin incision for second stage. (B) Mobilization of thick lateral flaps that includes bulbocavernosus muscle. Continuous nylon suture is in place, incorporating all layers. (C) Skin closure: sutures tied over sponge rubber pads.

Lately, two patients who had urethroplasty more than 12 yr ago presented with prostatism symptoms and were reevaluated. Both had developed recurrent strictures but were managed conservatively. Urinary incontinence developed in one patient following transurethral resection of the prostate for residual tissue 8 yr after completion of urethroplasty. No cases of impotence were encountered in my census, and the urinary stream was good in more than 95% of 226 patients. Pyuria with an occasional urinary tract infection occurred in 20% of these patients.

Cystopanendoscopy every 2 yr is routine part of follow-up study. Voiding or retrograde urethrograms are performed once a year in the majority of patients. Although numerous complications were encountered, the final long-term results remain encouraging.

DISCUSSION

The two-stage urethroplasty offers the most advantageous surgical treatment of severe, complicated strictures with ab-

scesses, fistulae, or extravasation because it allows drainage. It is safer for the patient because any tendency to restricture will become apparent before the operation is over. It also permits transurethral endoscopy or surgery to be performed between the two stages.

Blandy and associates advocated the creation of a new epithelial tube for the second stage, without suprapubic urinary diversion.[9] I prefer the buried strip technique with a single-layer closure for the second stage. This allows free drainage, avoids formation of dead spaces, and also minimizes trapping of bacteria with infection and resulting fistulous formation. I make no attempts to epilate the buried strip of skin because I feel that as long as the urine does not stagnate in the new urethra, no trouble should ensue.

The urologist can now expect a better than 94% long-term success rate even when dealing with the most discouragingly difficult and complicated strictures.[12,13] Success depends on strict adherence to the basic principles of the operation.

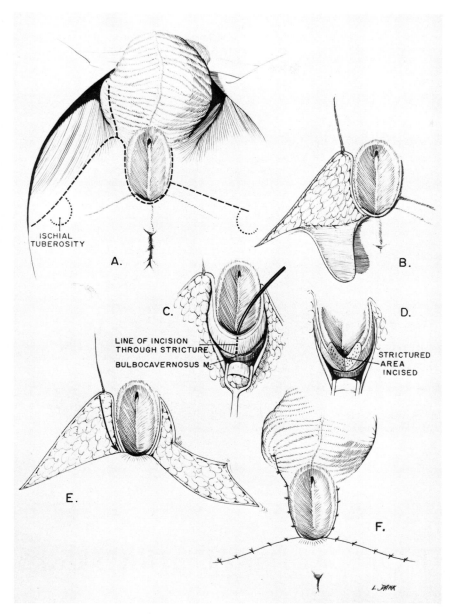

ISCHIAL
TUBEROSITY

A.

B.

C.

D.

LINE OF INCISION
THROUGH STRICTURE

BULBOCAVERNOSUS M.

STRICTURED
AREA
INCISED

E.

F.

L. JAYNE

Fig. 12. Revision of recurrent strictures at proximal stoma (Leadbetter first stage). (*A*) Dotted line indicates position of skin incision. (*B*) Development of skin flap. (*C*) Mobilization of bulbous urethra with strictured stoma. (*D*) Incised strictured area. (*E*) Skin flap (demonstrated in (*B*) being sutured to proximal edges of urethrotomy and mobilization of sliding scrotal flap to close bare area. (*F*) Revision completed.

REFERENCES

1. Johanson B: Reconstruction of the male urethra in strictures. Acta Chir Scand (Suppl) 176:3, 1953

2. Browne D: An operation for hypospadias. Proc Soc Med 42:466, 1949

3. Lapides J: Simplified modification of Johanson urethroplasty for strictures of deep bulbous urethra. J Urol 82:115, 1959

4. Turner-Warwick RT: A technique for posterior urethroplasty. J Urol 83:416, 1960

5. Turner-Warwick R: The repair of urethral strictures in the region of the membranous urethra. J Urol 100:303, 1968

6. Stewart HH: Reconstruction of the urethra for the treatment of severe urethral strictures. Br J Urol 32:1, 1960

7. Leadbetter GW Jr: A simplified urethroplasty for strictures of the bulbous urethra. J Urol 83:54, 1960

8. Gil-Vernet JM: Un traitement des stenoses traumatiques et inflammatoires de l'uretre posterieur. Nouvelle methode d'urethroplastie. J Urol Nephrol 72:97, 1966

9. Blandy JP, Singh M, Tresidder GC: Urethroplasty by scrotal flap for long urethral strictures. Br J Urol 40:261, 1968

10. Fernandes M, Draper J: Two stage urethroplasty improved method for treating bulbomembranous strictures. Urology 6:568, 1975

11. Fernandes M, Orandi A, Draper JW: Urethroplasty. New method of closure. J Urol 96:779, 1966

12. Blandy JP, Singh M, Notley RG, et al: Results and complications of scrotal-flap urethroplasty stricture. Br J Urol 43:52, 1971

13. Blandy J: Urethroplasty in males. In Hendry W (ed): Recent Advances in Urology, no. 2, pp 208–231. New York, Churchill–Livingstone, 1976

ANNOTATED BIBLIOGRAPHY

Blandy JP, Singh M, Notley RG, et al: results and complications of scrotal flap urethroplasty for strictures. Br J Urol 43:52, 1971

The scrotal flap urethroplasty has been used in 70 patients, 51 of whom have had both first and second (closure) stages of the operation and 21 of whom have been followed for more than 3 yr. There have been no operative mortality, recurrence of stricture, incontinence of urine, impotence, or problems arising from growth of hair on the scrotal flap. Meticulous care is necessary to preserve the viability of the scrotal flap. Sloughing of the tip of the flap occurred in 8 of the 70 patients. If part of the tip of the flap becomes necrotic, it should be excised and resutured to prevent stenosis and revisions. Bridging was a minor problem, and it was easily treated with dilatations. Fistulae occurred in 3 patients and were excised. Modifications in the technique were recommended: no infiltration of saline and epinephrine to raise the flap; broad-based flap to preserve the blood supply; if the perineum is grossly scarred, adopt the lateral based flap; and double stop sutures are no longer used (instead, the skin is apposed with vertical mattress sutures of 3–0 nylon).

Blandy JP, Wadhwa S, Singh M, et al: Urethroplasty in context. Br J Urol 48:697, 1976

This article reports the complications of intermittent dilatation of strictures versus complications and results of urethroplasties. The advantages and disadvantages of the urethroplasty are also reviewed. Seventy-three (57%) patients on routine dilatations had no complications, but 43% of the patients had gross complications, and the others with more serious difficulties were selected for urethroplasty. Thirty-two complications (14%) were noted in 228 patients undergoing urethroplasty. In addition, of 146 patients undergoing two-stage urethroplasties, 29 (19.9%) had to have one or more adjustments made to the flap after the first stage and before the second stage. The major complications were as follows: 14(6.2%) patients had restenosed and 11 of them had either one or two-stage urethroplasties performed again. Fistulae occurred in 7 (3.1%), and hairball calculi occurred in 4 (1.8%). There was no incontinence or impotence related to the procedure. The outcome of this decade of experience with urethroplasty shows it to have a failure rate of about 6%. The authors suggest that the urethroplasty should be offered sooner, since it is safer in many cases than a lifetime of dilatations.

Wein AJ, Leoni JV, Sansone TC, et al: Two-stage urethroplasty for urethral stricture disease. J Urol 118:392, 1977

Of 97 patients who underwent first-stage urethroplasty, 23% required at least one revision. Sixty-seven patients had a completed urethroplasty with a 90% success rate. The various factors that influenced the results of the two-stage operation are critically analyzed.

OVERVIEW:
TREATMENT OF URETHRAL STRICTURES
Patrick C. Devine

The treatment of urethral strictures starts with simple dilatation. When infrequent uncomplicated dilatation maintains the urethra at adequate caliber, that is the treatment of choice.

When dilatation fails in short, uncomplicated urethral strictures, precise visual internal urethrotomy, producing a buried strip of urethra allowed to regenerate, is often effective. The more complicated structures require all of physicians' surgical skill and ingenuity. The procedures recommended range from multiple-staged procedures moving flaps of scrotal or perineal skin through the one-stage island patch urethroplasty and the one-stage free full-thickness skin graft urethroplasty to the incision and primary anastomosis.

Drs. H. A. Wise and P. Marsidi describe accurately the surgery of meatal stenosis. The first line of treatment of urethral meatal stricture in the boy is dilatation. Most of the patients not relieved by dilatation can be treated by simple ventral meatotomy without significant distortion of the glans penis. When this ventral incision would produce a coronal hypospadias, the dorsal meatotomy described by Ochsner and Warren is effective.[1] When the meatal stricture is so severe

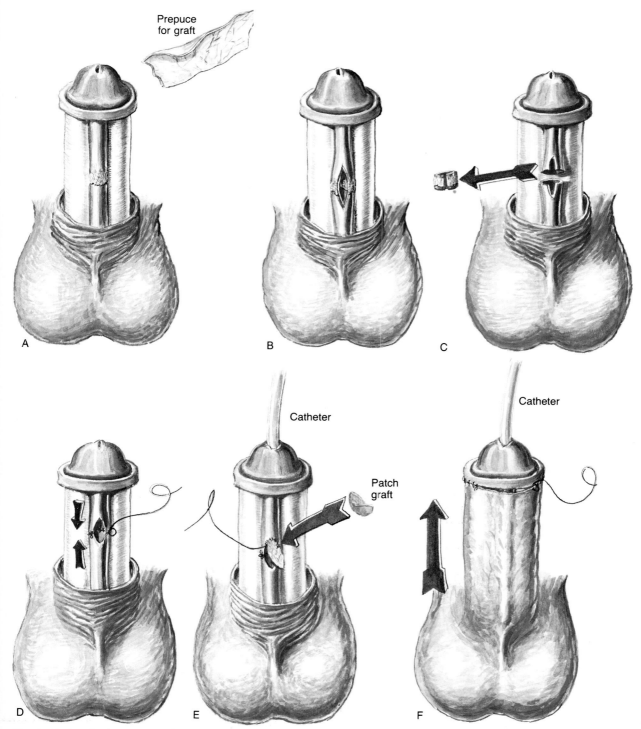

Fig. 1. (*A*) Penile skin retracted and portion of prepuce isolated for graft. (*B*) Urethra incised through stricture. (*C*) Stricture resected. (*D*) Urethra reapproximated dorsally. (*E*) Patch graft applied ventrally. (*F*) Completion.

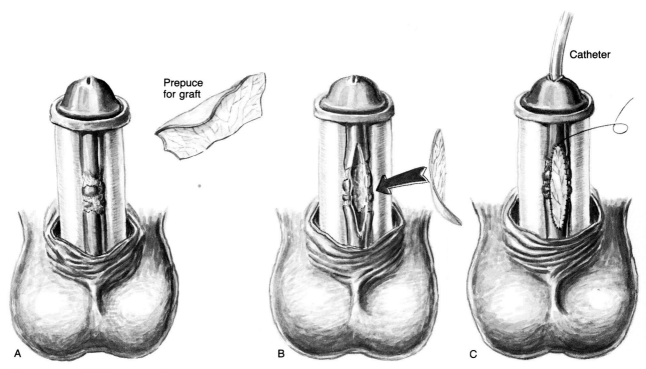

Fig. 2. (*A*) Penile skin retracted exposing stricture graft isolated. (*B*) Urethra incised including stricture. (*C*) Patch graft applied.

that treatment by ventral or dorsal meatotomy would cause severe distortion of the glans, the V-flap meatoplasty described by Devine and Horton places a normal-appearing urethral meatus of adequate caliber at the tip of the glans.[2]

For strictures of the urethral meatus that extend back to the fossa navicularis, the operation described by Brannen, which is exactly like the original work of Blandy and Tressider even to the drawings, is a quick and simple procedure that has the advantage of bringing the urethral meatus to the glans penis and the disadvantage of leaving its ventral lip surrounded by penile skin rather than by glans tissue.[3,4]

The staged operations described by Dr. M. Fernandes have the advantage of allowing drainage of abscesses and excision of sinus tracts at the initial procedure with repair of the urethra with a vascularized flap of viable tissue following at the second stage. These procedures have the disadvantages of requiring multiple operations and of placing hair-bearing skin in the urethra. Although the presence of hair in the urethra is not always a severe disadvantage, it is certainly never an asset.

The one-stage island patch urethroplasty described by Dr. M. Singh is an ingenious technique that has the advantages of being a single operation and of using vascularized tissue for the repair. However, the placement of the island is limited by the length of its pedicle, and the skin still grows hair.

Since 1961 we have treated urethral strictures with the same full-thickness skin graft techniques that we have used successfully for hypospadias repair since 1955.[5–12]

The stricture in most cases can be adequately exposed through the penis, scrotum, or perineum. Even the most proximal prostatomembranous urethral strictures, with displacement of the prostate, can usually be adequately exposed through the perineum if the patient is placed in the exaggerated perineal position. Skin used for repair or replacement of the urethra must be full-thickness skin, which will not contract and will grow with the patient even if the surgery is carried out in childhood.

After adequate exposure, one of three techniques can be employed:

When the stricture is short, it can be excised. The urethra is approximated dorsally and then incised ventrally. A free full-thickness patch graft is approximated with its epithelial surface toward the lumen of the urethra (Fig. 1).

When long segments of the urethra are strictured, all the strictures can be incised and single or multiple patch grafts applied (Fig. 2). There is no limit to the length of urethra that can be repaired in this manner.

When the strictured urethra has been completely destroyed, it can be excised and a free full-thickness tube graft of hairless skin can be applied to replace it (Fig. 3).

Any of these same techniques can be employed in the

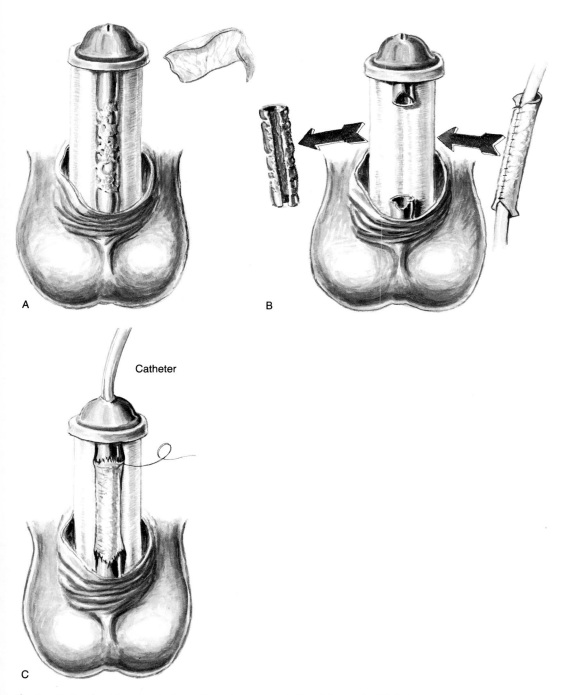

Fig. 3. (*A*) Penile skin retracted, portion of prepuce isolated for graft. (*B*) Stricture excised and tube graft prepared. (*C*) Tube graft in place.

perineum to repair or replace damaged urethra back to and including the prostatomembranous urethra.

The free full-thicknes skin graft technique has the advantage of a single operation and of allowing replacement of diseased urethra without limitation by its length. This technique requires a sterile, stable, vascularized bed free of hematoma or other complications that might prevent revascularization by separation of the graft from its bed. In 20 yr of experience with the single-stage urethroplasty with free full-thickness skin grafts, I have found that those patients who have good results after 1 yr have not had later recurrences of the strictures.

The surgeon who undertakes the correction of severe urethral deformities must handle tissues gently and must be familiar with all the techniques available.

REFERENCES

1. Ochsner MG, Warren H: Routine internal dorsal urethrotomy. J Urol 84:630, 1960

2. Devine CJ Jr, Horton CE: Hypospadias and epispadias. Clin Symp 24:1–28, 1972

3. Brannen GE: Meatal reconstruction. J Urol 116:319, 1976

4. Blandy JP, Tresidder GC: Meatoplasty. Br J Urol 39:633, 1967

5. Devine CJ Jr, Horton CE: A one stage hypospadias repair. J Urol 85:166, 1961

6. Devine PC, Horton CE, Devine CJ Jr, et al: Use of full thickness skin grafts in repair of urethral strictures. J Urol 90:67, 1963

7. Devine PC, Sakati IA, Poutasse EF, et al: One stage urethroplasty: Repair of urethral strictures with a free full thickness patch of skin. J Urol 99:191, 1968

8. Devine PC, Fallon B, Devine CJ Jr: Free full thickness skin graft urethroplasty. J Urol 116:444, 1976

9. Devine PC, Devine CJ Jr, Horton CE: Anterior urethral injuries: secondary reconstruction. Urol Clin North Am 4:157, 1977

10. Devine PC: Strictures of the male urethra. In Devine CJ Jr, Stecker JF Jr (eds): Urology in Practice, p 909. Boston, Little, Brown & Co, 1978

11. Devine PC, Wendelken JR, Devine CJ Jr: Free full thickness skin graft urethroplasty: Current technique. J Urol 121:282, 1979

12. Devine PC, Devine CJ Jr: Surgical treatment of strictures of the male urethra. In Ehrlich R (ed): Modern Technics in Surgery. Mount Kisco, NY, Futura Publishing Co, 1980

PART
FORTY-ONE

SURGERY OF URETHRAL TRAUMA

111

URETHRAL INJURY AND FRACTURED PELVIS

R. E. Glass, J. T. Flynn, J. B. King and J. P. Blandy

Departments of Urology and Orthopaedics, London Hospital and St Peter's Hospitals,
London

British Journal of Urology (1978), 50, 578–582

SUMMARY—In 333 consecutive cases of fractures of the pelvis admitted as emergencies to one hospital 53% were in males, of whom 34 had suspicious clinical signs of urethral or vesical injury.

In 15 patients catheterisation was performed uneventfully and in no case did this make the injury worse; in 8 an attempt at primary realignment was performed, resulting in 4 cases without any stricture, and 2 who needed annual dilatation only. In 4 additional cases associated laceration of the bladder was repaired of which one had no stricture and 2 needed infrequent dilatations. In a further 41 cases a catheter was used and led to no strictures.

Among 67 males with post-traumatic urethral injuries caused by pelvic fracture the best results were seen when the 2 ends were approximated. In 4 cases a stricture was prevented entirely, and in 17 others it led to an easy urethroplasty. Difficult strictures occurred in severe injuries with uncorrected displacement of the soft parts. Where feasible, early surgical repair appears to give the best chance of minimising the severity of subsequent urethral stricture.

When injury to the urethra is suspected in a patient with a fractured pelvis, there is still some uncertainty as to how best the case should be managed so as to avoid, or at least minimise, subsequent urethral stricture. Authorities argue that the passage of a catheter may turn an incomplete urethral rupture into a complete one, and a

Read at the 34th Annual Meeting of the British Association of Urological Surgeons in Brighton, June 1978.

Requests for reprints to: J. P. Blandy, Department of Urology, London Hospital, Turner Street, London E1 2AD.

simple pelvic fracture into a compound one; that the torn ends of the urethra will come together as the haematoma resolves and the consequent stricture may be cured by means of a urethroplasty, which will avoid impotence (Morehouse *et al.*, 1972; Mitchell, 1975; Coffield and Weems, 1977). Against this are the views of those who believe that the torn ends of the urethra should, whenever possible, be brought together so that the resulting stricture should be as short as possible, and sometimes avoided altogether (Jackson and Williams, 1974; Blandy, 1975;

Malek *et al.*, 1977). According to these investigators little harm arises in cases of doubt by the gentle passage of a narrow soft catheter.

We have examined a series of patients with fractured pelvis and another series of patients treated for urethral stricture in order to see how the early management of the injury has affected the subsequent stricture. In both series we were particularly interested to see what harm catheterisation had caused and whether early attempted surgical repair of the ruptured urethra had made things worse.

PATIENTS

Cases of Fractured Pelvis. A consecutive series of 333 emergency admissions for fractured pelvis to the London Hospital from 1950 to 1978 was studied; 176 were male and 157 were female. Although injury to the urinary tract was present in a proportion of these females, they present different problems which will be discussed in a separate communication. Of the 176 males 101 had no urological problem; in 34 there was blood at the external meatus or haematuria, so raising the suspicion of urethral or vesical injury. In 16 cases there was retention of urine, and in a further 25 massive associated injuries required intensive efforts at resuscitation.

Of the 101 cases in which there was no urological problem, 2 developed impotence; in neither of these men had a catheter been passed.

In 34 men haematuria or the presence of blood at the meatus raised the suspicion of associated urethral injury (Table 1). In 15 of these a soft narrow rubber catheter was passed. In one man (who was subsequently found to have positive serological tests for syphilis) an old and presumably gonococcal stricture was noted as the catheter was introduced; in another a bougie was passed at decreasing intervals after he left hospital for the purposes of diagnosis rather than treatment, and a third patient returned 6 years later with a urethral stricture, possibly caused by the catheter.

In 10 patients the gentle attempt to pass a soft rubber catheter failed: in 8 of them the retropubic space was explored and an attempt made to mobilise the prostate and bring the torn ends of the urethra together over a narrow splinting catheter. Of these cases 4 recovered with no detectable stricture 5 years later; 2 still attend for annual dilatation (though it is questionable whether by now this is still necessary); 2 developed a stricture which needed urethroplasty. In 2 of the patients in whom the gentle passage of a narrow soft catheter failed, the general condition of the patient forbade exploration of the pelvis: both had a suprapubic cystostomy tube inserted, and both developed a stricture.

TABLE 1. Fractured Pelvis: 34 Males with Haematuria or Blood at the Meatus

Catheter passed easily			
Previous GC stricture		1	
Follow-up bouginage ×3		1	15
Stricture 6 years later		1	
No problems		12	
Catheter failed to pass easily			
Explored and repaired		8	
No stricture	4		
Annual bougie	2		10
Urethroplasty	2		
Unfit for operation, suprapubic only (both strictured)		2	
Catheter not attempted			
Died in resuscitation		1	
Microscopic haematuria		2	5
Solitary renal stone		1	
Torn prepuce		1	
Laparotomy for associated rupture of bladder			
Died of head injury		1	
Stricture, annual bougie		2	4
No stricture		1	
Total			34

A further 5 patients had blood at the meatus or haematuria, but a catheter was not passed: in one it was because massive internal haemorrhage from associated injuries led to his death in the resuscitation room: in 2 the haematuria was disregarded because it was found only on microscopy and the patients were able to void without difficulty; in one patient the emergency IVU disclosed a calculus in a solitary kidney which was dealt with later on. In one patient the blood was obviously coming from a lacerated prepuce.

Laparotomy was indicated in 11 of the 176 men with fractured pelvis. In 4 patients with haematuria, a lacerated bladder was found in association with an injury to the membranous urethra: one of these died of his head injury, 2 attend for annual dilatation, and in one no stricture can be detected 4 years later.

In a further 41 patients a catheter was required for other reasons: in 16 it was because they developed retention of urine on being confined to bed with the fractured pelvis: none developed a subsequent stricture. In 25 a catheter was passed in the intensive care unit in order to monitor urine output as part of the treatment of the depleted blood volume: of these 2 were dialysed for anuria secondary to shock, 9 died of associated multiple injuries, but none of the survivors developed a stricture.

Urethral Strictures. This series consisted of 470 patients treated for urethral stricture from 1964 to 1978 at the London Hospital and by one firm at St Peter's Hospital.

Inevitably this series must be unrepresentative for 302 of the 470 cases underwent urethroplasty, often

TABLE 2. Urethral Strictures: All Cases with Traumatic Aetiology

Iatrogenic	Dilatation 70	Urethroplasty 61	Total 131
Accidental			
Perineal, fall astride	6	21	27
Fractured pelvis	10	52	62
Penile injury	0	4	4
Total	86	138	224

having been specially referred for that procedure. Of the entire series, 224 had a history of trauma (Table 2), but for the purpose of the present enquiry we have disregarded the 131 cases in whom the trauma was post-surgical, the 27 fall-astride perineal injuries not associated with a fractured pelvis, and the 4 men with urethral injuries caused by a variety of bizarre accidents to the penis. This leaves 62 males with urethral strictures caused by the fractured pelvis, to whom are added 5 patients whose urethral injury healed without a detectable stricture. We have attempted to see how the initial management of these 67 patients affected the end-result, with particular concern as to the possible evil effects of initial diagnostic catheterisation and early surgical repair.

From the viewpoint of the patient post-traumatic strictures fall, we believe, into 2 groups—"good" and "bad". In the "good" group are those who have no stricture at all, or one that requires them only to attend at very infrequent intervals for the painless passage of a bougie. To these should be added those in whom the approximated ends of the urethra, though not completely aligned, are nevertheless separated (Fig. 1) by such a thin shelf or membrane that it can be successfully divided by an endoscopic knife or electrode (Fig. 2). In the past, before we recognised this as a regular entity, a number of 1- and 2-stage urethroplasties were performed whereas today they would be found unnecessary. If the shelf separating the 2 ends of the urethra is too thick to be cut with safety endoscopically, the shortness of the stricture still permits an easy one-stage urethroplasty using a dartos-pedicled pouch in the technique described by Gardiner et al. (1978). In many of these patients the anteroposterior radiograph shows little apparent bony deformity, but the lateral view (Fig. 3) shows that the symphysis has been displaced backwards, giving a characteristic S-shaped malalignment of the prostatic and membranous urethrae.

In the "bad" strictures which follow fractured pelvis, there is nearly always gross displacement of the pelvic fragments (Fig. 4). If the ends of the urethra have not been mobilised and brought into proximity, they heal with a gap, filled with dense and difficult scar tissue. To cross this gap is a problem which taxes surgical ingenuity at the time of urethroplasty. In some cases a very high 2-stage scrotal flap urethroplasty has been used with success: in others a tubed-flap modification allows the scrotal skin to be brought up to the prostatic urethra: more recently the transpubic operation of Waterhouse et

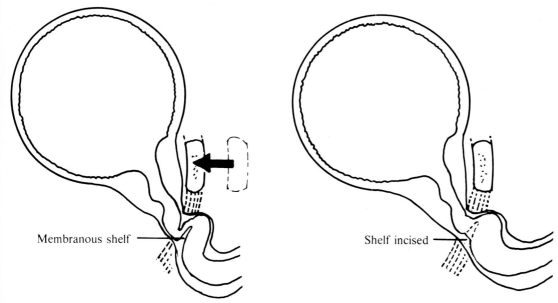

Fig. 1. An "easy" post-traumatic stricture is formed when the prostatic urethra comes to lie behind the membranous urethra, separated from it by a thin "shelf" which may be cut perurethrally, so avoiding the need for urethroplasty.

al. (1974) has been preferred by us as the procedure of choice for these difficult strictures.

When we looked at the method by which our patients with post-traumatic strictures had been treated in the first instance (Table 3), we were unable to get complete details in 20 of the 67 cases, and in a further 3 patients so many previous attempts at repair had been made elsewhere that it was unclear whether the stricture we were faced with was caused by the injury or the previous surgical intervention.

It is therefore not possible to state with conviction that one or other method of management is superior:

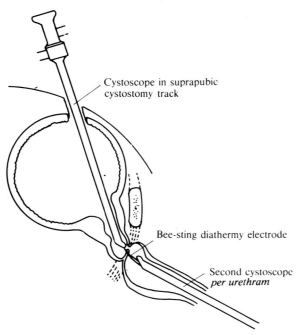

Fig. 2. If the "shelf" is completely closed off, the light of a cystoscope introduced through the suprapubic cystostomy may reveal it to the second cystoscope passed *per urethram,* and the shelf may still be cut with the cold urethrotome or the bee-sting electrode.

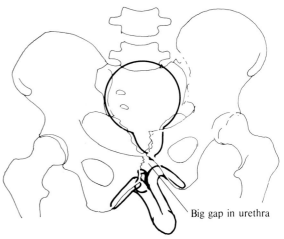

Fig. 4. "Difficult" strictures occur when there is gross bony displacement and the prostate has not been mobilised to bring the torn ends of the urethra into apposition.

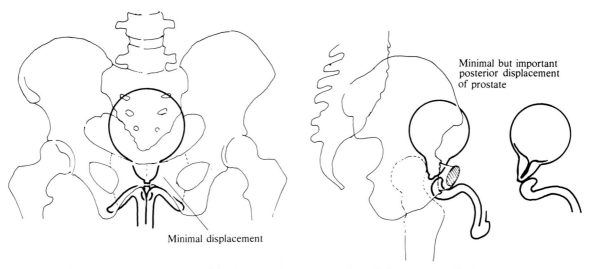

Fig. 3. (*A*) The anteroposterior X-ray of the fractured pelvis may show little apparent displacement, but this may fail to reveal an important posterior displacement, (*B*) which results in a typical "easy" post-traumatic stricture.

TABLE 3. Initial Management of Ruptured Urethra

End-Result	Early Surgical Repair	Supra-pubic Cyst-ostomy Alone	Details Not Avail-able	Total
Good				
No stricture	5			5
Dilatation	5			5
Shelf cut	5			5
Pedicled island patch	2	2	5	9
Easy scrotal flap	5	1	7	13
Bad				
Difficult scrotal flap	2	6	2	10
Tubed scrotal flap	3	2	7	12
Waterhouse	—	6	2	8
Total	27	17	23	67

TABLE 4. Fractured Pelvis, Urethral Injury and Potency

	Potent	Impo-tent	Under 12	No Data
No urological problem	99	2	—	—
Urethral injury	23	13	5	24

where we have complete details, and there was a "good" stricture or none at all, an early attempt at surgical repair had been performed in 22 of 25 cases (88%). Where the result was "bad" a suprapubic cystostomy alone had been done in 7 of 19 cases (37%). However, when only a suprapubic cystostomy had been done it was usually because the patients had very severe multiple injuries, and similarly when the stricture called for a very difficult urethroplasty it was nearly always because there was a long gap and severe persisting bony deformity.

The same difficulty in obtaining accurate information beset our enquiry into potency (Table 4). In 24 patients the men were too old or could not be properly questioned; 5 were too young. Data were available in only 36—but of these 23 (64%) claimed to be potent. All of those who were impotent had had severe urethral injuries and crush injuries of the pelvis, usually with residual bony displacement.

DISCUSSION

Advances in the technique of urethroplasty have defined a distinct group of patients with post-traumatic membranous urethral stricture in whom the 2 ends of the urethra come to lie separated by a relatively narrow shelf or membrane. If this can be identified it may be cut endoscopically and the patient spared the need for any form of urethroplasty. In other cases, if the ends of the divided urethra can be brought near to each other, even if the shelf of tissue separating them is not so thin that it can be safely cut perurethrally, it poses an easy problem for urethroplasty at which a one-stage pedicled patch can be used or, if a 2-stage operation is to be done, the first stage is relatively easy.

Study of this material suggests that the major factor leading to a "bad" and difficult urethral stricture is uncorrected displacement of the pelvic bones, and that the advantage of an early surgical repair is that the prostate can be mobilised and brought into apposition with the membranous urethra from which it has been avulsed. In those who are most fortunate, early surgical repair may be followed either by no stricture at all, or by a stricture which is easily and safely dealt with without the need for a urethroplasty at any stage. Our data regarding impotence permit no rigid conclusions to be drawn, but it appears to be a complication of a severe fracture and related to the soft tissue injuries rather than to any particular technique used in managing the disrupted urethra.

THE AUTHORS

R. E. Glass, MB, BS, FRCS, Surgical Registrar, London Hospital.

J. T. Flynn, MB, BS, FRCS, Senior Urological Registrar, London Hospital.

J. B. King, MB, BS, FRCS, Senior Lecturer and Consultant Orthopaedic Surgeon, London Hospital.

J. P. Blandy, DM, MCh, FRCS, Professor of Urology, London Hospital; Consultant Surgeon, St Peter's Hospital.

REFERENCES

Blandy, J. P. (1975). Injuries of the urethra in the male. Injury 7:77–83

Coffield, K. S. and Weems, W. L. (1977). Experience with management of posterior urethral injury associated with pelvic fracture. J Urol 117:722–724

Gardiner, R. A., Flynn, J. T., Paris, A. M. I. and Blandy, J. P. (1978). The one-stage island patch urethroplasty. Br J Urol 50:575–577

Jackson, D. H. and Williams, J. L. (1974). Urethral injury: a retrospective study. Br J Urol 46:665–676

Malek, R. S., O'Dea, M. J. and Kelalis, P. P. (1977). Management of ruptured posterior urethra in childhood. J Urol 117:105–109

Mitchell, J. P. (1975). Trauma to the urethra. Injury 7:84–88

Morehouse, D. D., Belitsky, P. and MacKinnon, K. (1972). Rupture of the posterior urethra. J Urol 107:255–258

Waterhouse, K. Abrahams, J. I., Caponegro, P., Hackett, R. E., Patil, U. B. and Peng, B. K. (1974). The transpubic repair of membranous urethral strictures. J Urol 111:188–190

Commentary: Management of Urethral Injuries

Norman Slade

The management of urethral injuries is as provocative a subject as that of the different techniques of prostatectomy and invariably generates endless and heated argument whenever discussed. Those readers familiar with the first edition of this publication may wonder why I have chosen Glass and colleagues paper, which apparently advocates the opposite approach to the management recommended by J.P. Mitchell, (Br J Urol 40:646, 1968), my choice of paper in the first edition of this publication. On closer examination, however, the differences in management advocated by the authors of the two papers may be more apparent than real. If one takes, for example, the incidence of lower urinary tract injury in reported series of pelvic fractures, Mitchell's figure of 5% is the lowest of all previously quoted series (9.8% to 25%). In Glass and colleagues' series, 18% of 176 males with pelvic fracture were considered to have had urethral or bladder injury. It is tempting to suggest that the severity of cases of fractured pelvis and therefore the incidence of what Glass and colleagues describe as "bad" posttraumatic strictures varied greatly in the different series. Certainly no other author has reported such a high incidence of incomplete (i.e., "good") traumatic ruptures as Mitchell.

In the less severe case of fractured pelvis it is more likely that an incomplete urethral rupture has occurred even though the symptoms of hematuria, blood at the external meatus, or acute retention may be no less obvious. If the radiologic appearances suggest this, and if on rectal examination the prostate is normally situated, that is, not displaced upward or "floating," it would seem to indicate that the urethral injury, if present, is more likely to be of the "good" variety and possibly incomplete. In this case there is the choice of management between passage of a soft rubber catheter as described by Glass and associates or a suprapubic cystotomy and panendoscopy by a trained urologist 10 days later as recommended by Mitchell. Both techniques should lead to good results, since surely a gentle attempt at passage of a soft rubber catheter (supposing, of course, that this commodity is still available!) cannot do much harm, that is, is unlikely to make an incomplete rupture complete. A great deal of course depends on the skill and gentleness of the surgeon, a point underlined by Mitchell.

In my view the danger lies in neglecting to diagnose the "bad" injuries. In almost all of these not only is there gross bony displacement on radiology, which should include good lateral views, but on rectal examination the prostate is "floating." The resulting separation of the urethra ends is so great that serious problems arise if healing is allowed to take place before approximation has been attempted, and herein lies the danger of overall management of urethral injuries by immediate suprapubic catheterization followed by endoscopy, especially since the surgeon may now be tempted to use the modern disposable fine bore catheter, which certainly precludes the digital exploration of the bladder cavity to exclude associated bladder rupture and to confirm that the prostate is normally situated, as advised by Mitchell.

In neither series apparently was diagnostic urethrography considered at the initial stage. I have little recent personal experience of this procedure, but I have no doubt that with improvement in radiographic techniques a combination of ascending urethrography with a simultaneous cystogram obtained through a fine suprapubic catheter may clearly delineate the extent of the urethral injury especially with lateral and oblique views. The risks of introducing infection can be obviated by using disinfective fluid into the bladder (100 ml of 1:2000 chlorhexidine) and similar preparations combined with a local anesthetic jelly into the urethra. Ageous contrast medium should be used for the urethrogram.

If there is any evidence that a more serious urethral rupture exists it is essential to carry out retropubic exploration and approximation of the urethra ends either by primary anastomosis or at least catheterization of the urethra by a combination of retrograde and prograde bouginage.* Subsequent urethroscopy may then reveal either a short (anular) stricture or one of the shelf ("S bend") variety, both of which can be dealt with endoscopically and especially easily with the Sachs urethrotome. At the worst, as Glass and colleagues point out, this type of stricture can be dealt with by urethroplasty.

I think the paper by Glass and colleagues could possibly be criticized on the grounds that meaningful conclusions should not be made on the results of management of the retrospective series of 470 patients because of the inevitable incomplete information of their initial management. However, this criticism applies to other series, including Mitchell's.

The success or failure in management of urethral injuries still rests to a great extent on expert assessment and investigation in the acute phase, and this is one emergency situation that should not be left to a newly qualified resident or intern.

---

* It would seem that massive suprapubic exploration of the suprapubic space and evacuation of blood clots often results in a high incidence of postoperative incontinence and should be avoided. Postoperative splintage should be by traction on the prostate rather than by traction on the in-dwelling catheter.

ANNOTATED BIBLIOGRAPHY

Jackson DH, Williams JL: Urethral injury: A retrospective study. Br J Urol 46:665, 1974

> A retrospective study of 63 patients showed that 50% treated by railroading technique did well, whereas all those with complete membranous rupture treated by suprapubic cystotomy did badly.

Janknegt RA: Management of complete disruption of the posterior urethra. Br J Urol 47:305, 1975

> In management of complete disruption of the posterior urethra, this author advocates simple realignment without traction to the catheter but with traction on the prostate.

Morehouse DD, McKinnon KJ: Symposium on genito-urinary trauma. Urol Clin North Am 4:69, 1977

> The authors reiterate their belief in the Johansen technique in the initial management of posterior urethral injuries, avoiding the use of the diagnostic catheter by suprapubic cystotomy. Investigation is by excretion urography and urethrography, and they claim that complications such as serious stricture, impotence, and incontinence that result from the immediate realignment technique are avoided. In their hands only 1 patient was incontinent in 41 treated by the Johansen technique and only a very few complained of impotence, whereas in 54 patients treated by urethroplasty following conventional realignment, 24 were incontinent and 23 impotent. De-Weerd (p 75) advocates immediate realignment where complete disruption of the urethra has taken place and claims that rectal examination should make diagnosis certain confirmed by urethrography. He says that most patients are well qualified for this approach, which involves antegrade and retrograde interlocking sounds followed by an in-dwelling balloon catheter with continuous postoperative traction. Turner-Warwick (p 81) considers that the best treatment of all but the most severe urethral injuries is by suprapubic catheter without local exploration. Where immediate realignment is indicated, free drainage of exudates from fracture site and urethral injury is by fenestrated urethral catheter and traction on the apex of the prostate and not by the catheter.

Hanna A: Repair of the prostatomembranetous urethra: A new technique for primary repair. Urol Surv 27:157, 1977; Earlam M: Anterior and posterior ruptures of the urethra; simplified methods of immediate surgical management. Aus NZ J Surg 48:207, 1978

> Both authors describe similar techniques for immediate realignment using interlocking sounds or pull-through technique. They deprecate extensive exploration or evacuation of blood clots from the fracture site, which in their view leads to a high incidence of postoperative impotence.

Crassweller PO, Farrow GA, Robson CJ et al: Traumatic rupture supramembranous urethra. J Urol 118:770, 1977

> Traumatic rupture of the supramembranous urethra is discussed, and the approaches of Johansen, Morehouse, and Mitchell are compared with that of immediate exploration and alignment. The authors consider that the good results and low incidence of impotence following their technique of immediate exploration is due to avoidance of massive exploration of suprapubic space and evacuation of hematoma.

Pokorny M, Pontes JE, Pierce JM Jr: Urological injuries associated with pelvic trauma. J Urol 121:455, 1979

> The authors discuss the etiology and mechanism only of urethral injury in relation to the bony injury.

Overview: Trauma to the Urinary Tract

J. P. Mitchell

At the meeting of the International Society of Urology in Johannesburg in 1976, trauma to the urinary tract was one of the main topics of discussion. It was interesting to note that neither on the round table, nor from the floor, did anyone support the use of the diagnostic catheter. It is therefore surprising to see in the article by Glass and colleagues that this means of diagnosing damage to the urethra is once again being advocated.

DANGERS OF THE DIAGNOSTIC CATHETER

The objections that have been voiced over the years to the use of a catheter to determine whether there has been injury to the urethra are twofold: it may aggravate the damage and it can give a false diagnosis. As regards the aggravation of the urethral trauma, this may be first by the introduction of infection to an area of broken bones, blood clot, and possibly some extravasated urine, all of which together can make a perfect nidus where organisms could multiply; second, the tip of the catheter may impale a contused area of urethral mucosa and convert this from a simple contusion into a tear through the full thickness of the urethral wall.

Today, with aseptic and antiseptic techniques of catheterization, it should be possible to prevent the introduction of organisms. Yet, even with the use of urethral antiseptics, a child of 9 yr admitted to the Bristol Royal Infirmary with a fractured pelvis and ruptured developed pelvic cellulitis from a *Klebsiella* species resistant to all known antibiotics at the time. Therefore, the complications due to infection from the introduction of a catheter can still occur, even though they are relatively uncommon with modern techniques.

TABLE 5

Author	%
Vermooten (1946)	25
Kisner (1958)	12.4
Kusmierski and Tobik (1965)	10
Peacock and Hain (1926)	9.8
McCague and Semans (1944)	16.7
Graham (1967)	9.5
Wakeley (1929)	6
Holdsworth (1963)	5
Mitchell (1968)	4.7

REDUCED INCIDENCE OF LOWER TRACT INJURY ASSOCIATED WITH FRACTURED PELVIS

It has been noticeable over the years that the incidence of damage to the posterior urethra in association with fractures of the pelvis has undergone a marked reduction, from 25% to less than 5% (Table 5).[1-9] Such a reduction could perhaps be attributed to different types of injury today, when road traffic accidents are responsible for a much higher proportion than the crush injuries of mining accidents or falling masonry, which were the major causes of fractured pelves half a century ago. Road traffic accidents are more likely to give impact injuries with a "sprung" pelvis; in other words, the bones are grossly deformed at the moment of accident but partially return to their normal position, and there may be, as a result, an appearance of less bony distortion following the impact injury in the emergency room. This, however, seems a much less likely explanation than the fact that the diagnostic catheter has, over the last 30 yr, been steadily condemned as the aggravating factor in lower urinary tract damage.

URINARY EXTRAVASATION IN RUPTURED URETHRA AND RUPTURED BLADDER

In textbooks on the management of ruptured urethra it will often be read that patients should be discouraged from attempting to pass urine for fear of extravasation. In fact, extravasation of sterile urine is unlikely to cause more than a mild local irritation, very different from the extravasation of urine that may accidentally occur in the management of stricture of the urethra by simple urethral dilatation, when a false passage may occur as a result of a bougie being passed with undue force. Here the urine is often infected, and extravasation would then result in a pelvic cellulitis. For this reason, the modern management of a suspected rupture of the urethra is actively to encourage the victim to try to pass urine.

SIMPLE CONTUSION OF THE MUCOSA OF THE URETHRA WITH URETHRAL BLEEDING

If the patient passes urine successfully, then there is presumably only a contusion of the mucosa of the urethral wall without a full-thickness breach of all layers. Such a patient would be managed conservatively, although it is known that even contusion can give rise to subsequent stricture of the urethra.

A man of 23 yr was admitted to the Bristol Royal Infirmary with urethral bleeding in association with a fracture of the pelvis. However, he succeeded in passing urine and no attempt was made to divert the urine by suprapubic drainage or by passing a urethral catheter. Endoscopy 3 wk later confirmed mucosal damage to the urethral wall extending round more than two thirds the circumference of the lumen. Conservative management was continued, but 15 mo later he presented with a urethral stricture. Although it must be relatively uncommon for simple contusion of the urethral wall to give rise to subsequent stricture, nevertheless, if this patient had been managed by suprapubic cystostomy and diverting of urine, he may have avoided the severe degree of stricture he subsequently developed. On the other hand, had the urethral catheter been used on this patient, the simple contusion would almost certainly have been converted into a full-thickness tear, since the catheter would have impaled the area of damage and probably passed completely through the urethral wall. How often has this happened in the past, and does it explain the apparent increased incidence of urethral injury in association with a fractured pelvis in the past?

ERRORS OF DIAGNOSIS FOLLOWING THE PASSING OF A CATHETER

The fallacies of diagnosis from the passage of the diagnostic catheter fall into two categories: those patients in whom urine is withdrawn and those who have a dry tap. In the patient in whom the young surgeon passes a diagnostic catheter and withdraws 50 ml or more of urine, is the surgeon really safe in assuming that there is no damage to the lower urinary tract? In extraperitoneal rupture of the bladder, the wound of the anterior wall may be only a puncture hole from a spicule of bone, probably projecting from the pubic ramus. Such an injury can often leave as much as 200 ml of urine in the bladder, usually faintly tinged with blood; however, the simple passage of a catheter is not infrequently associated with a faint tinge of blood.

Several instances are recorded in the literature of patients on whom catheters were passed, urine withdrawn, the patient failed to micturate, and a subsequent catheter was left in. Either at open operation or at subsequent postmortem examination it was found that there was no continuity between the prostatic and membraneous urethra. The only explanation of such an occurrence is that the urethra must have necrosed from infection or have been damaged by the presence of the catheter. It was inconceivable that a catheter could have passed across a total rupture of the urethra, and, on the assumption of there being only a partial rupture in many of these patients, a prospective study was carried out in Bristol. In this study it was found that over 90% of patients with ruptures of the posterior urethra had some remaining bridge of tissue, even though the wall was partially torn. Therefore, the passage of a catheter does not necessarily exclude either a rupture of the bladder or the rupture of the urethra.

If, on the other hand, a catheter fails to draw any urine, is the young surgeon correct in making the observation that this is a ruptured urethra? The bladder may have been empty at the time of injury, the patient may have anuria, there may be an extensive rupture of the bladder with total extravasation of urine such as occurs in an intraperitoneal injury of the bladder, or, finally, the tip of the catheter may simply have impaled the urethral mucosa where there had been nothing more than a simple contusion.

CONDEMNATION OF THE DIAGNOSTIC CATHETER

Therefore, for these reasons, the diagnostic catheter was finally condemned at the Johannesburg meeting of the International Society of Urology in 1976 because of further damage that may be caused by the catheter, for instance, infection and iatrogenic trauma, and because of the fallacies in diagnostic accuracy either when urine is withdrawn or when there is a dry tap.

Glass and colleagues state that authorities argue that the passage of a catheter may turn an incomplete urethral rupture into a complete one. This would appear to be a slight misinterpretation in that it implies that a partial tear might be converted into a total transection. This, as far as can be seen from the literature, would appear to occur only in the event of the introduction of infection that necroses the remaining part of the urethra, bridging the gap between the torn ends. On the other hand, a contusion can certainly be converted into a full-thickness breach of the urethral wall by the inadvertent passage of a catheter. This in fact is only too common, even in the healthy urethra, let alone the urethra that has sustained some damage to its mucosal lining.

Finally, on the subject of the diagnostic catheter, it must be conceded to Glass and colleagues that there is, as Slade has quite rightly commented, all the difference in the world between the gentle passage of a soft catheter by an experienced urologist and the passage of any catheter by the resident on duty in the emergency department of a large hospital.

URETHROGRAPHY

Surely if confirmation of urethral trauma is necessary and cannot be made on clinical grounds alone, then a urethrogram, preferably under screened control, will immediately identify the exact site of the tear of the urethral wall without the risk of iatrogenic trauma to a contused area of urethral mucosa.

TIMING THE DEFINITIVE REPAIR

The other feature that came out clearly at the meeting of the International Society of Urology in Johannesburg was the total disagreement on when these various injuries should be explored once the diagnosis had been confirmed. Marberger of Innsbruck, Austria, claimed the best results with immediate exploration and realignment of the urethra; Rocchi of Buenos Aires claimed equally good results with exploration at 6 to 8 days, the time appropriate for delayed primary suture, when viable tissue can

be distinguished much more clearly from tissue that is no longer viable and the surgeon can achieve a much clearer view of the area of damage without the persistent oozing of blood from torn vessels.[10,11] The majority of opinion appeared to be in favor of exploration at about 3 wk, but participants agree that already a certain amount of organized fibrous tissue will have formed, making approach rather more difficult. The speakers from Canada and from New Zealand advocated delays up to 3 mo before exploring the urethra and claimed that by this longer delay the prostate was much more likely to return to a more normal position when the induration consequent upon the trauma had all subsided.[12,13] Glass and colleagues, in their series, adhere to the immediate approach, although it is clear from their paper that the figures of the London Hospital do not provide more than eight cases, even on a retrospective study. Postponing any definitive repair to 3 wk after injury, it was shown in the Bristol series that the urethra could be negotiated with an endoscope in two thirds of the ruptures of posterior urethra. This high proportion of ruptures, negotiable by endoscopy at 3 wk, would, in the hands of those who advocate immediate repair, have been subjected to an extensive open operative procedure.

COMPLETE TRANSECTION

In those patients with complete transection of the urethra, Mitchell advocates immediate repair with a catheter splint in order to realign the torn ends of urethra.[14] Complete transection is diagnosed when the bladder and prostate are found floating high in the abdomen with no chance of any bridge of urethral wall remaining between the two ends, but, in his prospective study, he found that fewer than 10% of patients had complete transection.

PROSPECTIVE VERSUS RETROSPECTIVE STUDY

It is important when assessing the comments by Glass and colleagues to appreciate that theirs was a retrospective study, implying the usual problems of interpretation of past hospital records, as compared with the Bristol study, which was a prospective study starting in 1951.

ASSESSMENT OF THE PROSTATE

The rectal examination can be very fallacious when used to assess displacement of the prostate, since surrounding edema, blood, and extravasated urine can mask the outline of the gland to the extent that in several instances the prostate could not be felt through the rectum, yet at formal suprapubic cystostomy the gland was almost in its normal position.

REFERENCES

1. Vermooten V: Rupture of the urethra. A new diagnostic sign. J Urol 56:228, 1946

2. Kisner CD: Injuries of the urethra with special reference to those occurring in fracture of the pelvis. S Afr Med J 32:1105, 1958

3. Kusmkerski S, Tobik S: Surgical management of ruptured urethra in fractured pelvis. J Urol 93:604, 1965

4. Peacock AH, Hain RS: Injuries of urethra and bladder. J Urol 15:563, 1926

5. McCague EJ, Semans JH: Management of ruptured urethra and bladder complications of fracture of the pelvis. J Urol 52:36, 1944

6. Graham WH: Injuries to the urinary tract. Proc R Soc Med 61:477, 1967

7. Wakeley CPG: Fractures of the pelvis: Analysis of 100 cases. Br J Surg 17:22, 1929

8. Holdsworth FW: Injury to the genito-urinary tract associated with fractures of the pelvis. Proc R Soc Med 56:1044, 1963

9. Mitchell JP: Injuries to the urethra. Br J Urol 40:649, 1968

10. Marberger H: Round table on urethral injuries, International Society of Urology Meeting, Johannesburg, read by W Gregoir

11. Rocchi A: Round table on urethral injuires, International Society of Urology Meeting, Johannesburg

12. Morehouse BD, Belitsky P, MacKinnon K: Rupture of the posterior urethra. J Urol 107:255, 1972

13. Macky W: Round table on urethral injuries, International Society of Urology Meeting, Johannesburg

14. Mitchell JP: Injuries to the urethra from operative surgery. In Rob, Smith (eds): Urology, p 307. London, Butterworth & Co, 1977

PART FORTY-TWO

ENDOSCOPIC SURGERY OF THE URETHRA IN CHILDREN

112

URETHRAL VALVES[1]

D. Innes Williams, R. H. Whitaker, T. M. Barratt and J. E. Keeton

The Hospital for Sick Children, Great Ormond Street and St Peter's Hospitals, London

British Journal of Urology (1973), 45, 200–210

The primary lesion of posterior urethral valves is a simple one which might be expected to respond readily to simple transurethral resection. Nevertheless, the total care of a boy with urethral valves can be a most complicated undertaking. The object of this paper is to describe a new method of valve ablation and to identify and discuss the factors leading to failure of recovery and to persistent urinary infection.

PATIENTS

From 1951 up to October 1972, 206 boys with posterior urethral valves have been treated by the senior author; of these, 172 presenting before the end of 1970 are available for statistical analysis.

CLINICAL FEATURES

Presentation. Table 1 shows the age distribution indicating that just over half the boys presented under 1 year of age, one-third of them being under 3 months. The mean age of all cases was 2½ years. Table 2 shows how the symptomatology varies with the age of presentation:

[1] This paper formed the basis for the Robert V. Day Lecture delivered by D. Innes Williams to the Western Section of the American Urological Association in Vancouver, 1972.

most children have a combination of the symptoms and signs listed. In the older boys infection and incontinence were common; the younger children had more frequently general signs of renal failure. At all ages infection was important and at times seemed to have had a value in drawing the attention of the doctor to the presence of a serious lesion of the urinary tract which might otherwise have escaped notice for some years.

Certain misleading presentations may be remarked upon: a number of children had abdominal enlargement apparently due to intestinal distension; in these there was a great deal of oedema of the posterior abdominal wall around infected dilated ureters. Some children had a remarkably good urinary stream, and in them it appeared that massive hypertrophy of the bladder was able to compensate for the obstruction at the expense of very considerable upper tract damage, so that paradoxically some of the children with a good stream had the most serious renal destruction. At other times renal enlargement rather than bladder distension was the prominent feature, and with infection there was sometimes a pyonephrosis.

Diagnosis. The diagnosis was made in almost all cases by the findings in intravenous pyelography and micturition or expression cysto-urethrography. Any difficulties which arose were in older enuretic children with doubt-

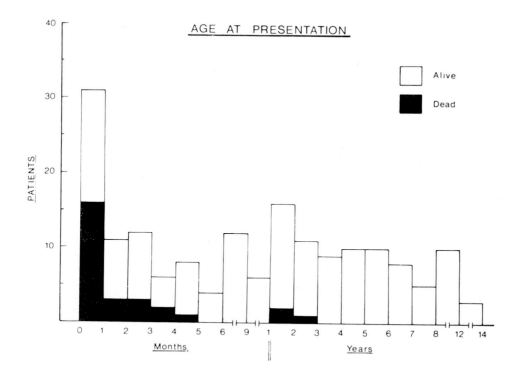

TABLE 2

Symptoms and Signs	<3m %	3m − 1y %	1y − 5y %	>5y %	All %
Distended bladder	62	62	64	43	56
Poor stream or difficulty	12	15	23	32	20
Failure to thrive or vomiting	35	44	50	5	29
Urinary infection	18	24	41	39	29
Haematuria	8	6	14	2	6
Incontinence or dribbling	20	24	23	48	30
Acute retention	7	3	5	7	6
Other	12	6	0	7	9
Numbers	54	36	26	56	172

fully obstructive valves in the posterior urethra, but such cases have been excluded from this series. We are here concerned with unquestionable obstruction. Thus, of 144 boys who survived there were 124 whose pre-operative pyelograms were available for assessment and of these only 22 had normal upper urinary tracts. The remainder had varying degrees of dilatation, and in 31 one or both kidneys failed to opacify on the initial urogram. In the earlier years an intravenous pyelogram was not performed as a routine on uraemic cases so that the figures given minimise the number of cases with upper tract dilatation.

Management of the Infant Emergency. The uraemic infant constitutes the most difficult problem in the management of urethral valves. The mean blood urea of all cases on admission was 102 mg percent, but a number of the older children had a normal upper urinary tract, uraemia being largely a feature of the neonates.

The initial examination demands a clinical assessment of the general condition, particularly the state of hydration and the degree of distension of the bladder or kidneys. Immediate urinary microscopy to detect the presence of pyuria is required pending the results of urine culture studies. Estimation of blood urea, electrolytes and haemoglobin are obviously essential, but studies of blood gases, of plasma pH, of serum calcium and magnesium have also proved of value recently. Intravenous pyelography is carried out routinely when the blood urea is high, but no attempt should be made to dehydrate an infant in these circumstances.

The programme of medical management, emergency drainage and definitive surgery must be carefully integrated, since the chances of survival from any operation are greatly enhanced if the biochemical state is first corrected. Our present routine is as follows:

If the child's condition on admission is good, the blood urea less than 100 mg percent and hydration adequate, early ablation of the valves is planned. If the bladder is very tense it is drained by an indwelling urethral catheter in the meantime.

If the child's condition is poor, management depends upon an estimate of the capacity for improvement under medical treatment and the sterility or otherwise of the urine.

Sterile Cases. A dehydrated baby with acidosis but with sterile urine can be treated by catheterisation and rehydration. Where, however, the blood urea remains high despite drainage, rehydration and a low protein milk diet, it is clear that severe renal damage is present and that upper urinary tract drainage is likely to be required. A child whose condition is poor, who is already overhydrated or has severe electrolyte disturbance but sterile urine, may best be treated by peritoneal dialysis.

Infected Cases. In any child the presence of a urinary infection will influence us in favour of early operative intervention, but immediate antibiotic therapy is instituted, usually with gentamicin, pending the results of urine culture and sensitivity tests. A severe infection with renal enlargement is best treated by emergency nephrostomies.

In the earlier part of the series *pre-operative catheterisation* was used as little as possible, but with the manufacture of better plastic catheters drainage by this route is safer and can be employed for a few days. We now ordinarily use an 8 F polythene infant feeding tube.

Bilateral nephrostomy has been performed with a 14 F malecot catheter: it is a simple operation and efficient for short periods, but long-term nephrostomy has been little used as we have encountered troubles with infection around the tube and great difficulty in replacing a tube which fell out prematurely. Temporary diversion was performed in 74 out of the 172 cases, and of these bilateral nephrostomy was the method employed in 38. *Ureterostomy-in-situ* has been used in some cases referred to us, but it did not appear to be a very satisfactory form of drainage because of the tortuous nature of the ureter. *Cutaneous ureterostomy* has been employed in a number of boys and the results are discussed below.

OPERATION FOR URETHRAL VALVE ABLATION

In the series analysed the valves were approached suprapubically in 5, and endoscopically in the remainder. In 92 boys in the younger age group, perineal urethrostomy was essential although it will become less so with the development of better instruments. In approximately a quarter of the cases the valves were destroyed with a simple diathermy electrode; in the remainder a resectoscope loop was employed. In 11 percent a second operative procedure was necessary, reflecting our reluctance to perform a deep resection because of the danger of subsequent incontinence.

During the past year experiments have been made with other forms of valve ablation. Any form of endoscopic treatment requires the introduction of a relatively large instrument to carry the light and the telescope, but the obstructive valve is much more easily seen by radiological screening. This consistently shows that the important element of the valve is the membrane attached anteriorly to the urethral wall (Fig. 1), whereas endoscopy allows easier visualisation of the ridges which constitute the margin of the opening in the valve posteriorly. Endoscopic resection is therefore apt to cut the posterolateral ridges rather than the more obstructive anterior membrane. It was perhaps the practice of demonstrating valves at post-mortem by splitting the urethra longitudinally through an anterior midline incision, which led to the belief emphasised in Young's classification that there are two lateral valves rather than an anterior curtain with a posterior opening.

In the endeavour to avoid the introduction of an endoscope in a neonatal case a trial was made of rupturing

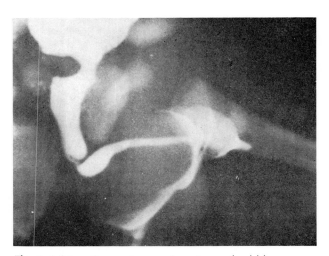

Fig. 1. Micturating cystogram in a 3-month-old boy showing urethral obstruction due to valve with clearly defined anterior curtain-like membrane.

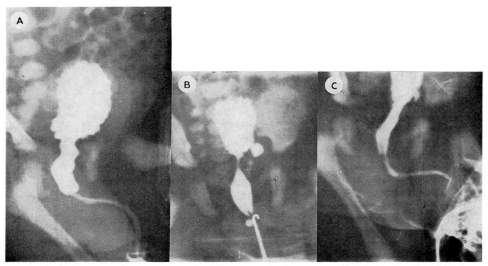

Fig. 2. Cystography and urethral valve ablation with diathermy hook. (*A*) Expression cysto-urethrogram with clear cut valvular obstruction. (*B*) The diathermy hook engaged in the valve prior to ablation. (*C*) Expression cystogram immediately after ablation showing free passage of opaque medium into anterior urethra.

the valve by the sharp withdrawal of a Fogarty catheter under X-ray control: this was effective in 3 very young infants, but more recently ablation of the valve has been achieved by the introduction of an insulated diathermy hook, as shown in Figure 2. Under radiological control the hook is pressed against the ventral wall of the posterior urethra and drawn downwards until it engages in the valve. This engagement can be felt as well as seen on the television screen. By applying the diathermy cutting current while the valve is engaged the obstructing membrane is ruptured and the completeness of relief of obstruction can be immediately verified by the freedom with which the opaque medium passes into the anterior urethra. This method entirely avoids the necessity for a perineal opening in neonates with corresponding less-ening of the infection problem. A urethral catheter has been left in for 2 days only and its withdrawal has been followed by normal micturition in the 3 cases on which it has been employed.[1]

42 boys (24 percent) had a procedure to widen the bladder neck by Y-V plasty or endoscopic resection: it was felt in earlier years that a secondary bladder neck obstruction might complicate urethral valves, but recently we have found little evidence of obstruction at this level and since there is a high risk of incontinence following

[1] A total of 7 neonatal cases have now been treated by the diathermy hook: in all the obstruction has been satisfactorily removed but 1 required perineal urethrostomy drainage for 5 days because of a slight extravasation from the bulb of the urethra.

bladder neck revision (Whitaker *et al.*, 1972) our incli-nation has been to avoid surgery at this level.

EARLY POST-OPERATIVE MANAGEMENT

In the series as a whole postoperative infections have been common and there has been a number of biochemical disturbances, some of them serious. In infants with a very acute type of obstruction, often evidenced by a nephrogram in the pre-operative I.V.P., there has been a tendency to diuresis with sodium loss, but these children have ultimately a good prognosis and often the first postoperative I.V.P. shows an amazing improvement (Fig. 3). Other cases with less acute obstruction may have less easily reversible changes in the urinary passages and more long-lasting disturbance of renal function. Sometimes these problems have been readily controlled by antibiotics, parenteral fluids and a low protein diet, but sometimes persistent infection and failure to improve renal function have necessitated further surgery.

MANAGEMENT OF THE UPPER URINARY TRACT

The Functionless Kidney. If the kidney on one side has ceased to function there is obviously little point in preserving it, particularly as it may well be the major focus of infection. In all, 24 out of 172 boys had a kidney removed. In 15 of these the pre-operative pye-lograms showed no opacification. There was gross hy-

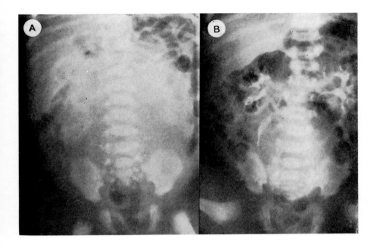

Fig. 3. Intravenous pyelography 2 days before and 3 days after urethral valve ablation. (*A*) Bilateral hydronephrosis. (*B*) Return to normal calyceal pattern.

TABLE 3. Vesico-Ureteric Reflux

63 boys had pre-operative reflux (44 percent). A total of 86 pre-operative refluxing ureters were analysed as follows:	
Stopped spontaneously	22
Cured by surgery	12
Dried	8
Permanent diversion	2
Persistent reflux (no surgery)	20
No postoperative M.C.U.	13
Primary nephrectomy	9
	86

11 ureters previously non-refluxing developed reflux postoperatively.

dronephrosis in 6, but reflux may have been responsible for outlining some of these kidneys. The failure of function was usually demonstrated by cutaneous ureterostomy. It is remarkable that the upper tract damage in urethral valve cases is usually asymmetrical, one side being much more severely damaged than the other, and while unilateral reflux may often be the factor involved it did not appear to be so in all.

Reflux. Overall, reflux was present in 44 percent of children in whom adequate pre-operative data were available for review. In 16 percent it was bilateral, in 28 percent unilateral. It ceased spontaneously after valve resection in 17 out of the 63 children analysed, and the fate of the remainder is set out in Table 3.

Reflux may occur with or without a para-ureteric saccule: when a saccule is present there may be an element of obstruction to downflow as well as reflux backflow (Fig. 4).

In reviewing the figures we have been surprised to find that reflux is not such a serious complication of urethral valves as had been anticipated, and the difference between the children with and without reflux was not so remarkable. The mortality was, in fact, lower in the

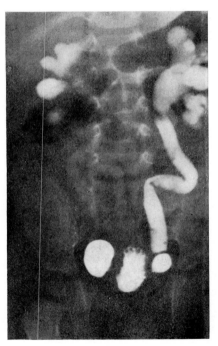

Fig. 4. Micturating cystogram showing bilateral para-ureteric saccules with normally emptying bladder after urethral valve ablation.

refluxing group (9·5 percent against 12·5 percent), but the pre-operative infection rate was somewhat higher (56 percent against 45 percent). The incidence of nephrectomy for functionless kidney was also higher when there was reflux; in the nephrectomy cases reflux was present in 61 percent of children, whereas the overall incidence of reflux was 44 percent. Judged by the blood urea levels the renal function did not differ significantly in the two groups.

Persistent Ureteric Dilatation without Reflux.

Dilatation of the ureter persisting after restoration of bladder function can be due to a failure of ureteric peristalsis or to the presence of a uretero-vesical obstruction. There is a further possibility that the extremely hypertrophied bladder present in these cases may, even after relief of obstruction, retain normal volumes of urine at abnormally high pressures and thus prevent free drainage from the ureters. The differentiation of these various factors is at present being studied by pressure/flow measurements, as described by Whitaker (1973), and a later paper will give details of the results.

In the retrospective series the distinction between an intrinsic ureteric failure and a ureteric obstruction was not clearly made, but the figures available emphasise the fact that it is not simply reflux which causes persistent upper tract disturbance. Thus, of non-refluxing ureters preoperatively 67 percent showed gross dilatation or non-function; post-operatively 48·5 percent had still to be put in this category. In the earlier part of the series an expectant attitude was always adopted towards such persistent dilatation, and in many instances this was rewarded by slow but steady improvement in the radiological appearance of the ureters together with improvement of renal function. It is clear that provided the urine can be maintained free from infection such an expectant attitude is justifiable. In a small number of cases the ureter became more dilated in the postoperative period and in these the involvement of the lower end of the ureter with a para-ureteric saccule was the usual finding, more often with obstruction than with reflux.

Operations on the Ureter.

In a total of 25 boys, *cutaneous ureterostomy* was performed on the hypothesis that such free drainage would allow control of infection, improvement of renal function and recovery of ureteric peristalsis with some reduction in calibre. The operations were initially performed in the expectation that this recovery would allow restitution of the ureter at a later stage, perhaps after some months. In 8 boys, however, permanent diversion was necessary because of chronic renal failure and persistent infection, often with the additional problem of incontinence. One of the kidneys was found to be functionless in 10 cases and nephrectomy was performed on that side.

Loop Ureterostomy. Most of the ureterostomies were performed by the loop method, in which a length of ureter is brought to the surface and opened laterally, but not cut across. The abdominal muscles, and sometimes the skin, were brought together behind the loop. This proved in most cases to be a simple procedure, although in some there was difficulty in preventing obstruction from kinking of the ureters, and in others there was bleeding from the cut edge of the ureter in the postoperative phase.

Terminal Ureterostomy. A smaller number of cases had terminal ureterostomies, the ureter being divided at the bladder level and brought directly on to the surface. This procedure was undertaken in refluxing cases with the idea that re-implantation at a later stage would both close the ureterostomy and prevent reflux at a single procedure.

Restoration of Continuity in Cutaneous Ureterostomy. The results of these procedures were reported by Lome and Williams (1972); 16 bilateral *loop* cutaneous ureterostomies were analysed in valve cases, 24 ureters being reconstructed by excision of the exteriorised portion and anastomosis of the ends. Four ureters developed complications secondary to closure of the loop, which ultimately responded to a second operation. The effects of some months of external drainage in these cases was some improvement in renal function, some diminution in calibre and slight restoration of peristaltic activity. The general health of the child improved considerably, but the local effect was perhaps less than had been hoped. Restoration of continuity gave satisfactory function if reflux was absent, but was followed by deterioration if reflux was present. In later cases a reflux prevention operation of the Gregoir type was performed at the same time as closure of the loop.

Terminal ureterostomy was less satisfactory in that drainage from the cutaneous stoma was not so reliable, perhaps due to kinking of the long length of ureter above, perhaps due to greater tendency to stenosis of a terminal stoma; and after restoration of continuity by re-implantation of the ureter into the bladder several late stenoses occurred.

Lome, Howat and Williams (1972) also analysed the effects of defunctioning the bladder by cutaneous ureterostomy: in 21 defunctioned bladders in association with urethral valves 6 became seriously contracted. They were mostly cases who had had considerable inflammation of the bladder wall; 3 of them required permanent diversion, but 3 subsequently enlarged after restoration of the ureteric continuity on one side.

With a view to obtaining the benefits of free drainage by cutaneous ureterostomy without completely defunctioning the bladder the *Y type of ureterostomy* suggested by Sober (1972) was employed in a few cases, many of them after the close of the analysed series. While this system has given good results in older children with grossly dilated ureters, in the uraemic neonate the cutaneous limb of the Y, which has a terminal stoma on the skin, has tended to stenose and retract so that free drainage was not obtained.

Although it is difficult to substantiate from a statistical analysis we have the impression that loop ureterostomy was of considerable value in a number of uraemic infected children and that by this method their kidneys were preserved.

There is no doubt that in some cases ureterostomy was performed unnecessarily and improvement could have been seen with simpler methods, but a place remains for ureterostomy drainage in the infected case with renal failure.

Remodelling and Re-implantation of the Ureter into the Bladder. The alternative operative approach to the persistently dilated ureter has been re-modelling and re-implantation into the bladder. Although because of the diversity of the material and varying methods of treatment the series analysed does not give any useful numerical assessment of the value of this procedure, re-implantation has been strikingly successful in clear-cut cases of obstruction due to involvement in a saccule (Fig 5); re-implantation with re-modelling has also been of value in children over the age of a year with a chronically dilated ureter which was incapable of obliterating its lumen and so of propelling the urine forwards.

In order to test the hypothesis that it was the ureteric failure rather than the obstruction which maintained the dilatation, re-modelling was performed on one side and re-modelling together with re-implantation on the other

in 3 children. There did not appear to be any very important differences in the 2 sides at follow-up. Nevertheless it is usually hard to avoid the impression of a uretero-vesical obstruction in these cases and simple remodelling can seldom be justifiable. Even so, in several chronic cases there have been disappointing results from re-implantation and even some deterioration after operation; it is never easy to obtain a reflux-preventing but unobstructed junction between a grossly dilated ureter and a massively sacculated and trabeculated bladder.

We have not undertaken the immediate reconstruction of the urinary tract in neonatal cases as advised by Hendren (1971), but in the extensive re-modelling done in early infancy since the close of the statistically analysed series our results have been disappointing compared with the improvement obtained by cutaneous ureterostomy. Re-modelling can give a ureter of lesser calibre and perhaps with better function, but where the kidney substance has already been excavated by long-standing obstruction this excavation remains. Moreover, the appearances after re-modelling are somewhat misleading in that there may be an obstruction at the lower end of a ureter which appears to be of more or less normal calibre. From our own experience and from cases referred to us from other centres we believe that there are considerable hazards to extensive re-modelling and re-implantation in the neonatal period.

MORTALITY

28 out of 172 boys (16.2 percent) died. All but 3 of the 28 presented under the age of 1 year, and it is clear that

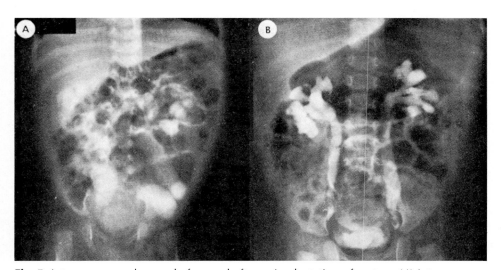

Fig. 5. Intravenous pyelogram before and after re-implantation of ureters. (*A*) Intravenous pyelogram after valve ablation and restoration of fully emptying bladder accompanied by persistent non-refluxing dilatation of ureters. (*B*) Intravenous pyelogram after re-implantation of ureters showing a degree of recovery.

a very early presentation is unfavourable. Of the 54 children presenting under the age of 3 months 22 (40.6 percent) died. In retrospect it is not possible to be certain of the cause of death, but amongst the causes quoted in autopsy reports were: renal infarct, subdural and cerebral haemorrhage, peritonitis, urinary ascites, pyonephrosis, peri-nephric abscess, perforated duodenal ulcer, patent ductus arteriosus and dysplastic kidneys. There is evidence that the 28 boys who died were the more seriously ill at the time of admission: their mean blood urea was 155 mg per 100 ml as opposed to 92 mg per 100 ml for survivors. Nevertheless, over the years the mortality has fallen, and while it is clear that a few babies will be born with inadequate renal tissue for survival, the proper medical and surgical management should carry the great majority through, at least into adolescence. Thus, from 1956 to 1960, 36 percent of infants treated under the age of 1 year were dead before their first birthday. In the period 1961–65 the corresponding figure was 20 percent and in 1966–70 it was 15 percent (refer to Table 4). In the last 2½ years of the survey period, and since that time, there have been no deaths amongst 21 boys, 9 of whom presented under the age of a year. There have been no obvious changes in the referral pattern during this period.

LATE FOLLOW-UP

The 144 boys who survived have been followed for a mean period of 5 years, 7 months; the longest period being 15 years. The mean age at the end of 1970 was 8 years, 6 months; the oldest patient was 25 years.

Features of the follow-up requiring comment are renal function, urinary infection and continence. With regard to *renal function* the mean blood urea level decreased postoperatively in surviving cases from 92 mg to 43 mg, per 100 ml whilst in the boys who died there was a mean blood urea on admission of 155 mg, which rose to higher figures prior to death. There was only 1 boy among 144 survivors whose postoperative blood urea level at 91 mg was higher than the pre-operative level of 60 mg. Nevertheless, in 17 survivors high blood urea levels remained. All had had extreme dilatation of the upper tract with unilateral functionless kidneys in 5; it would seem likely that there will be some increase in the late mortality of this group when the follow-up is carried further.

Information regarding *urinary tract infection* was available for pre-operative and postoperative periods in 102 boys; 50 had no infection before or after surgery;

28 of these had pre-operative infections but were sterile afterwards. "Persistent" infection was defined as more than 1 attack of urinary infection more than 1 year after surgery: 26, who had had infection before surgery, had persistent infection afterwards. All the boys who died had persistent urinary infection.

Postoperative incontinence in this group has been analysed in a previous paper (Whitaker *et al.*, 1972). Overall results show that of 112 patients, 33 were fully continent, 42 had some stress incontinence and 37 were continuously wet. However, careful investigation of this group showed that the young infants were much more liable to incontinence than were children treated in later years, and that there was a definite trend toward spontaneous improvement, particularly about the time of puberty. Since the conclusion of this review the increased use of imipramine in incontinent patients has led to a surprising improvement in the situation. This presumably indicates that we are dealing not only with a simple sphincter weakness but with some abnormality of bladder function as well. In a few cases implanted stimulators have been used with occasional success in some, but with disappointing results in more.

SUMMARY

Our experience with 206 cases of posterior urethral valves in boys has been reviewed with statistical analysis of 172 cases followed up for at least 2 years.

A new method of valve ablation has been described.

The mortality in the disease has been confined almost to infants presenting in the first year of life with uraemia, and the results have improved enormously with better integration of medical and surgical corrective measures.

Later mortality is a comparatively uncommon event, but considerable morbidity occurs with recurrent infection, persistent dilatation of the ureter being the most important cause of this complication. Temporary diversion and re-implantation as alternative methods of treatment are discussed, but we have been impressed by the value of the conservative approach in many cases.

THE AUTHORS

D. Innes Williams, MD, MCh, FRCS, Consultant Urologist, The Hospital for Sick Children, Great Ormond Street, and St Peter's Hospitals, London.

R. H. Whitaker, FRCS, Senior Registrar, St Peter's Hospitals, London (now Consultant Urologist, Addenbrooke's Hospital, Cambridge).

T. M. Barratt, MRCP, Consultant Nephrologist, The Hospital for Sick Children and St Peter's Hospitals, London.

J. E. Keeton, MD, Research Assistant to the Hospital for Sick Children (now Urologist, U.S. Navy).

REFERENCES

HENDREN, W. H. (1971). Posterior urethral valves in boys, broad clinical spectrum. J Urol 106:298–307

LOME, L. G., HOWAT, J. M., and WILLIAMS, D. I. (1972). The temporarily defunctionalized bladder in children. J Urol 107:469–472

LOME, L. G. and WILLIAMS, D. I. (1972). Urinary reconstruction following temporary cutaneous ureterostomy diversion in childhood. J Urol 108:162–164

SOBER, I. (1972). Pelviureterostomy-En-Y. J Urol 107:473–475

WHITAKER, R. H. (1973). Methods of diagnosing obstruction in ureters. Br J Urol. Awaiting Publication

WHITAKER, R. H., KEETON, J. E. and WILLIAMS, D. I. (1972). Posterior urethral valves: a study of urinary control after operation. J Urol 108:167–171

Commentary: Accepted Methods for Valve Ablation

Richards P. Lyon

The report by D. I. Williams and his group from Great Ormond Street and St. Peter's Hospitals in London was published in 1973 primarily to present a new mode for valve ablation, namely the use of a hook. The report represents the largest experience to date with this problem and also is the most complete in the literature, covering both methodology and the effects of ablation. Although the anatomy and serious obstructive effects of the urethral valve have been recognized since Young and colleagues first described the anomaly in 1919, it would seem that time stood still for 40 yr before a major attack was first directed at this problem.[1] Reports on this entity are still not numerous, presumably because of its rarity, coupled with relatively short and inadequate follow-up periods—10 to 15 yr at most—to provide the critical data on a lesion that, when first discovered, has frequently seriously damaged renal function.

Reports of experience with valves to date are remarkably consistent in their recommendations regarding diagnostic criteria and specific modes of therapy. The intravenous pyelogram (IVP) and the voiding cystourethrogram give definitive information. Similarly, after suitable correction of systemic fluid and electrolyte imbalances and prompt decompression by catheter, early ablation of the valve is recommended. Direct upper tract decompression simultaneously, or before valvotomy, is required if sepsis is not easily controlled or if fluid electrolyte problems are not resolved with urethral catheter drainage alone.

At present, the two accepted methods for valve ablation are fulguration and transurethral resection of the valve cusps as they take origin at the base of the verumontanum; the frequency of each method depends on the caliber of the child's urethra and the urologic instruments available. Williams recommends the use of the hook for the infant, placed under x-ray control, and causing simple rupture. However, this method was used in only 3% of his patients. In the tiny infant, the perineal urethrostomy is often still advisable. However, as instruments become refined to the point where the resectoscope and the fulgurating electrode can be used in the very smallest of urethras, the perineal approach may no longer be required. Williams feels that the suprapubic approach has passed into the discard, and with this view most agree.

Williams regards the valve as a continuous curtain with a small posterior opening. This is surely its effect, severely stretching the posterior urethra and external sphincter in the form of the familiar spinnaker sail. When the surgeon introduces a filiform through the tiny opening and follows this with a sound, the membrane splits in the midline. It has been my experience that when the split is complete, I see lateral cusps arising as cristae from the base of the veru, extending diagonally through the length of the external sphincter, and meeting above as an arch at the bulbar margin of the sphincter itself. It has seemed logical to me that the single physical splitting of the membrane throughout its length should eliminate all but the most obstructive effects. Therefore, I have used a third method—simple dilatation for valve ablation.

I have been strongly motivated by the same fears mentioned in the preceding article of causing sphincteric damage that would initially lead to incontinence and later, perhaps, to functional damage that would manifest itself in adult life, to be recognized only as follow-up studies become long enough. The use of electrical current in this sensitive area is most suspect. Therefore, the valves in 24 boys have been ablated by simple dilatation. This has been accomplished in the infant through a perineal urethrostomy, using filiforms and followers and finally the endoscope itself. In the older child the manipulation of the endoscope beak under direct vision to split the membrane vertically has been most feasible. Often the initial catheterization has already begun the split. Success has been determined under anesthesia at the time of valve rupture by observation of urinary flow as suprapubic pressure is applied. I have considered as diagnostic of adequate ablation the combination of a normal to a very high flow coupled with cystourethrographic evidence of a smaller posterior urethra.

Two clinical problems tend to occur following what looks to be a successful ablation procedure. The first is continuation of what seems to be obstructed voiding patterns. The second is urinary incontinence. In regard to the first, reports by Agusta and Howards, Cans and Stephens, and Waldbaum and Marshall corroborate that of Williams, and this too has been my experience, that in 10% to 20% of the youngsters reinstrumentation and further attempts at valve ablation have seemed necessary.[2-4] However, when a full stream is mechanically produced under anesthesia and the endoscope discloses the midline split in the valve as complete, even though valve remnants are present, I suspect that a functional problem exists. That this may very likely be the case is documented by the report of McGuire and Weiss, who showed that the use of a phenoxybenzamine, through alpha-sympatholytic action, made possible normal voiding and eliminated second and third attacks on the valve.[5] It surprised me to see a single oral does in the youngster under the age of 1 yr, seeming still to be obstructed, lead to an immediate large and full urinary stream. This successful voiding pattern has subsequently been maintained, suggesting that valvular remnants do not need to be meticulously removed with the resectoscope in order to achieve adequate removal of voiding resistance.

The second and most resistant problem is that of urinary incontinence. This is usually reported to be a problem with 10% to 20% of the children. Williams notes problems with incontinence in 70% of his patients. This too has been my experience, and after dilatation alone. Thus, it seems that the use of electrical current in judiciously fulgurating and cutting is not the agent of incontinence. As suggested in an earlier report, Whitaker and colleagues believe that the damage to the external sphincter, presumably through high tension before the valve has been destroyed, is a major contributor to incontinence and is finally reversed during puberty by the increased resistance in the posterior urethra as the adult prostate develops.[6] A recent study of the external sphincter in a limited number of valves suggests that there is no neurologic deficit and that the muscle works effectively in these children. These investigators suggest that the problem lies within the bladder itself and that this dysynergetic function should be tested. I can add to this from my own experience the single case of continued incontinence up to the age of 8 yr, reversed completely by discovery and removal of a gradually expanding diverticulum, taking origin just proximal to the interureteric ridge on one side and presumably enlarging enough at times to interfere with the continual function of the bladder neck.

A third modality should be considered when assessing the problems of incontinence, namely, the excessive fluid requirements of these children with seriously damaged urinary tracts. With renal damage to the degree here the kidney rarely produces a density above 1.008, and an immense water load is acquired. This is made obvious by the degree of thirst. Thus, moderate limitations on continence certainly become more manifest when one recognizes that 2- to 3-hr voiding frequencies are required, both night and day. Thus, if one accepts the concept of a voiding reflux being excited through introduction of urine into the posterior urethra—these urethras of course being immense—these children will almost constantly be subject to such stimuli during play, and it is here that theoretically the pubertal enlargement of the prostate with its increasing posterior urethral resistance as an agent of continence is attractive.

I too have had help from imipramine (Tofranil) but have learned also to be on guard against the child who on this regimen places himself in chronic subacute retention. He is suddenly dry but at the same time has increased the obstructive effects at the ureterovesical junctions. The continually full bladder in any of these youngsters must be constantly guarded against.

The subject suggested for review was described as endoscopic surgery in children. Ablation of the uretheral valve is the only surgical procedure I approve of in children. However, this is more than a surgical procedure, since no description of a treatment would be complete without considering, at least briefly, the effects of the valve on renal functional mechanisms. Physicians are just beginning to observe the long-term effects of the original valve and attempts at therapy. If there is any criticism to be levied in reports on urethral valves to date, it is the lack of sufficient emphasis on the careful measurements of renal function in attempting to anticipate the eventual renal reserve that must be maintained if renal transplantation is to be averted. I contend that in youngsters with obviously marginal renal function (usually manifested by thirst) upper tract decompression continued into the teens, with total continence maintained by ostomy appliances, should be given greater consideration for valve ablation. Thus, early undiversion should be limited to those children where renal damage can be measured as normal to minimal.

REFERENCES

1. Young HH, Frontz WA, Baldwin JC: Congenital obstruction of the posterior urethra. J Urol 3:289, 1919
2. Agusta VE, Howards SS: Posterior urethral valves. J Urol 112:280, 1974
3. Cass AS, Stephens FD: Posterior urethral valves: Diagnosis and management. J Urol 112:519, 1974
4. Waldbaum RS, Marshall VF: Posterior urethral valves: Evaluation and surgical management. J Urol 103:801, 1970

5. McGuire EJ, Weiss RM: Secondary bladder neck obstruction in patients with uretheral valves. Urology 5:756, 1975
6. Whitaker RH, Keeton JE, Williams DI: Posterior urethral valves: A study of urinary control after operation. J Urol 108:167, 1972
7. Bauer SB, Dieppa RA, Labib KL, et al: The bladder in boys with posterior urethral valves: A urodynamic assessment. J Urol 121:769, 1979

ANNOTATED BIBLIOGRAPHY

Waldbaum RS, Marshall VF: Posterior urethral valves: Evaluation of surgical management. J Urol 103:801, 1970

This is a thoughtful review of 28 patients, with primary attention to the upper tracts and recognition of the serious damage present in at least two thirds of patients at the time of valve ablation. Emphasis on measurements of renal function is great, with the recognition that only one third of the patients have minimal secondary upper tract changes not requiring surgical attention. The authors feel that one third of children with damage serious enough to require renal transplantation eventually should be given as much time as possible with continued urinary diversion. They reserve reconstructive procedures for these patients in the middle one third but only after extensive evaluation in terms of renal potential.

My experience mirrors this report in that of one third of my group of eight, with marked upper tract damage, three have already required renal transplantation. In contrast, two others who initially appeared to have a similar limited potential for adequate renal function were left diverted until ages of 11 and 14 yr, during which time they maintained their percentiles of growth; they will not require transplantation. Thus, it is in this group that I contend that greater attention should be given to the desirability of prolonged diversion through ureterostomy until renal growth is complete. Finer tests of renal potential in the pubertal years are obviously necessary.

Hendren WH: Posterior urethral valves: A broad clinical spectrum. J Urol 106:298, 1971

This author presents a much broader projection of urethral valve possibilities, in that 69% of the 182 boys on discovery had normal upper tracts in contrast to 30% in the other reported series. Only time will tell whether this early and extensive correction of severe upper tract abnormalities are an advantage.

The description of valvular anomoly and the technique of valve fulguration are particularly well done. The advisability in certain cases of incising the bladder neck also will be tested only by time. I agree with him that suprapubic cystostomy can be disastrous as a preliminary procedure where the bladder is small or goes immediately into spasm.

Whitaker RH, Keeton JE, Williams DI: Posterior urethral valves: A study of urinary control. J Urol 108:167, 1972

The authors' report on 112 cases is well followed with details on incontinence following valve ablation. No difference in frequency of incontinence could be found in comparing resection and fulguration. No patient was continent immediately after operation. Fifty were under the age of 1 yr, and 14 over the age of 8 yr. The average follow-up time was 6½ yr. In this time, 29% became continent with rare enuresis, 38% had stress incontinence, and 33% were continuously wet. (My experience is almost identical, although with a much smaller group). Imipramine is mentioned as a therapeutic agent, and puberty is given primary credit for late attainment of continence.

Cass AS, Stephens FD: Posterior urethral valves: Diagnosis and management. J Urol. 112:519, 1974

This report from Melbourne, Australia, is similar in clinical recommendations to that of Williams and his group. One hundred and thirteen boys (68% uremic at discovery) were treated primarily by decompression and fluid and electrolyte control followed by endoscopic valve and ablation. The authors resist any early surgical invasion of the bladder neck with either the endoscopic or open operation. Of particular interest is their low (17%) incontinence rate in patients followed an average of 5.4 yr, despite aggressive incision and fulguration of the valvular cuffs. This article like Williams's, should be studied as source material.

Overview: Endoscopic Surgery of the Urethra in Children

John W. Duckett

Dr. Lyon states that ablation of urethral valves in boys is the only truly surgical procedure performed endoscopically in children, and I must agree. However, urologists should probably expand their definition of surgery to include other endoscopic manipulations in children. In this regard I will discuss other uses of endoscopic instruments beyond that of observation endoscopy.

BIOPSY OF BLADDER OR URETHRAL LESION

The most common malignant bladder tumor in children is rhabdomyosarcoma. It characteristically grows in two gross configurations, sessile and polypoid.[1] Either lesion is best biopsied by use of the pinch forceps through the endoscope. Storz has such an attachment for use with its resectoscope assembly. Bimanual manipulation is sometimes helpful with a finger in the rectum to elevate the lesion and offers resistance for the forceps to grasp the tissue. Bleeding is generally not a problem when obtaining these specimens. Occasionally, fulgerations may be helpful to gain hemostasis.

When the lesion is a sarcoma botryoides variant of the embryonal rhabdomyosarcoma, the grapelike protrusions may sometimes be grasped within the resectoscope loop and the beak without using a cutting current, avulsing the specimen.

Use of the small infant resectoscope loop with the cutting current will not provide a satisfactory biopsy because of the damage to the tissue by the current. Bladder tumors in children should not have a transvesical exploration for excisional biopsy if possible. My treatment of rhabdomyosarcoma of the genitourinary system has been dramatically enhanced recently with newer chemotherapy protocols, so that radical surgery is a secondary treatment consideration.

Biopsy of the more solid prostatic rhabdomyosarcomas by the transurethral route is also possible at times. There is usually a filling defect on the voiding cystourethrogram when this is possible. Otherwise, a transperineal needle biopsy is used to obtain a prostatic specimen in the solid tumors.

RETRIEVAL OF FOREIGN BODIES

Endoscopic manipulation using the biopsy forceps or resectoscope loop as a pincher without the current is also effective in removing catheter fragments, sutures, stones, or other extraneous items inappropriately within the bladder. Care must be taken in grasping gently with biopsy forceps, since a catheter fragment will be easily cut into additional pieces by the cutting edge. Removal of the entire resectoscope element once the item is trapped against the beak is more effective than pulling the item through the sheath.

CATHETERIZATION OF A TRANSVERSELY PLACED URETER

Since the Cohen ureteral reimplantation has met with enthusiasm recently, situations will surely arise more often for passing catheters in a right-angle plane to the endoscope. This may be accomplished by first placing a percutaneous transvesical Seldinger needle and threading the wire up the ureter using a grasping forceps through the resectoscope. Retrieval of a broken catheter within the ureter may be accomplished using the Dormier or Pfister stone basket.

RESECTION OF URETHRAL POLYP

Fibromatous polyps based on the verumontanum are occasionally seen in children as benign growths that may cause obstructive symptoms.[2] The stalk may be divided endoscopically with a current or with the biopsy forceps and the polyp retrieved from the bladder or urethra.

RESECTION OF ANTERIOR URETHRAL VALVES

The distal lip of a diverticulum situated in the anterior urethra becomes an obstruction to varying degrees when the diverticulum fills with urine. Careful resection of the distal lip or ''valve'' may sometimes relieve this obstruction in mild cases. More often a urethroplasty will be necessary for such a diverticulum.

This obstructing lesion should not be confused with the cystic dilations of Cowper's ducts, which course toward the bladder and are not obstructing. Endoscopic treatment is not usually needed for these lesions.

ABLATION OF POSTERIOR URETHRAL VALVES

It was previously thought that two folds or valves were present as obstructing lesions in the rather common congenital anomaly, ablation of posterior urethral valves. However, Robertson and Hayes clearly showed the folds to be an oblique diaphragm fused anteriorly.[3] Ablation of the obstruction may then be accomplished by dividing the connection on both sides at the base where the folds join the crista urethralis (5 and 7 o'clock positions through the endoscope) or by splinting the anterior fusion (12 o'clock position).

To accomplish this, several methods may be successful. As Lyons suggests, some may be split anteriorly by just passing a sound (or filiform and follower) through a perineal urethrostomy. There is certainly no objection to this provided endoscopic confirmation is used at the time and a cystogram shows no further obstruction. Passing a relatively large sound through the pedulous urethra is likely to lead to stricture in an infant and is contraindicated.

Avulsion of the obstructing valve has been reported when a Fogarty catheter is blown up in the posterior urethra and pulled distally. I have tried this technique without success.

Hendren has described the method of fulgerating the valve base at the 5 and 7 o'clock positions using a Bugbee electrode passed through the 10 French panendoscope through the penile urethra. In this way the valve is pushed away from the sphincter area, avoiding injury.

The valve may be hooked with the electrodes attached to the infant resectoscope. The loops are not as effective as the hooked wires. The valve edge is engaged with the wire, and the cutting current is applied, making a clean cut at the 5 and 7 o'clock positions. I prefer to make the cut at the 12 o'clock position, disrupting the fusion anteriorly. This method of valve resection was first performed in 1952 by Ericsson and colleagues, advocated by Parkkulainen, and has proved effective in my hands for the past 8 yr.[4–6]

Williams's report of using an insulated crochet hook to engage the valve under x-ray control was premature. The complications were considerable, and the technique has been abandoned.

Another technique that should be condemned is the use of increasing sizes of Foley catheters through the urethra. Destruction of the valve was due to urethritis from the catheter. Urethral stricture was not an uncommon complication.

The transurethral approach for the ablation of valves is generally successful even in the newborn provided the anterior urethra is given great respect. The urethra should not be dilated in order to pass an instrument. Gentle stretching of the meatus or a meatotomy is permissible, but not of the urethra itself. A perineal urethrostomy should be the alternate approach if a proper size (10 French panendoscope or 11.5 French resectoscope) cannot be passed with ease.

An alternative to valve resection in a small baby is a vesicostomy.[7] Since the bladder is an abdominal organ lying just under the lower abdominal wall, the bladder dome may be fixed to the fascia and skin very effectively to decompress the urinary tract proximal to the obstruction. Even dilated, tortuous ureters will decompress with this method of temporary diversion. When the baby is larger, resection of the valves is easier and the vesicostomy may be closed.

CONTINENCE AFTER VALVE ABLATION

Damage to the external sphincter using electrofulgaration is a potential complication of valve resection. However, incontinence with valves is probably a result of the overstretching of the intrinsic continence mechanism of the distal prostatic urethra due to the obstruction itself. This tends to improve with time, especially after puberty when the prostate enlarges. Another cause for incontinence is polyuria from poor renal concentration and overflow from a bladder with diminished sensation.

No data has supported transurethral bladder neck resection or Y-V plasty to relieve secondary bladder neck obstruction associated with valves. This procedure may contribute to the incontinence problem or to retrograde ejaculation later.

URETEROCELE DIAGNOSTIC MANEUVERS

Although endoscopic resection of a ureterocele for relief of obstruction was common therapy in the past, it has very little place today, since further reconstructive surgery is nearly always required. "Unroofing" of a ureterocele will lead to vesicoureteral reflux into the upper pole segment and potential infection.

Diagnostic studies of a ureterocele may be done by injecting contrast material into an intravesical ureterocele through a long needle guided with endoscopic control. An alternative method is using a 22-gauge needle, breaking off the hub and wedging the blunt end of the needle into a 3 French ureteral catheter with the tip cut off. This catheter needle may be passed through the panendoscope and the ureterocele to be injected.

REFERENCES

1. Ghazali S: Embryonic rhabdomyosarcoma of the urogenital tract. Br J Surg 60:124, 1973
2. Downes RA: Congenital polyps of the prostatic urethra: A review of the literature and report of two cases. Br J Urol 42:76, 1970
3. Robertson WB, Hayes JS: Congenital diaphragmatic obstruction of the male posterior urethra. Br J Urol 41:592, 1969
4. Kjellberg RS, Ericsson NO, Rudhe U: The lower urinary tract in childhood. Stockholm, Almqvist & Wiksell, 1957
5. Parkkulainen KV: Cine-uethroscopy in the diagnosis of posterior urethral valves. Color film presented at the XVIth Congress of the International Society of Urology, Amsterdam, 1973
6. Carpiniello V, Duckett JW, Filmer RB: Posterior urethral valves with a review of 57 cases. Kimbrough Urol Semin 11:282, 1977
7. Duckett JW: Cutaneous vesicostomy in childhood—the Brocksom technique. Urol Clin North Am 1:485, 1974

PART FORTY-THREE

SURGERY OF URINARY INCONTINENCE

113

PUBOVAGINAL SLING PROCEDURE FOR STRESS INCONTINENCE

Edward J. McGuire and Bernard Lytton

From the Department of Surgery, Section of Urology, Yale University School of Medicine, New Haven, Connecticut

The Journal of Urology
Copyright © 1978 by The Williams & Wilkins Co.
Vol. 119, January
Printed in U.S.A.

ABSTRACT—Urinary stress incontinence associated with poor urethral sphincter function and indicated by a urethral pressure of less than 10 cm water was treated in 52 cases with a pubovaginal autogenous fascial sling. No urethral sphincter function could be measured in 7 patients. Of these 52 patients 42 had undergone a previous operation for stress incontinence.

The uninhibited detrusor dysfunction that accompanied the stress incontinence in 29 cases ceased after operation in 20 but persisted in 9. Postoperative urethral pressure measurements indicated that while the sling increased urethral pressure it did not cause an obstruction during voiding, since there was a measurable decrease in urethral pressure during a detrusor contraction.

Urodynamic determinations were useful in patient selection, in the adjustment of sling tension at operation and in the assessment of reasons for failure. A satisfactory result with good urinary control was obtained in 50 cases and the procedure was a failure in 2.

Most patients with stress incontinence can be treated successfully, either with an anterior colporrhaphy or with an anterior urethropexy. These procedures have

Accepted for publication May 20, 1977.

resulted in the correction of the hypermobility of the posterior urethra and maintenance of its correct anatomical location above the pelvic diaphragm, so that sudden changes in intra-abdominal pressure are transmitted equally to the bladder and proximal urethra.[1] The choice of procedure depends upon the degree of mobility of the posterior urethra and the resultant anatomical deformity.[2] Most patients have a normal urethral closing pressure and, as a rule, have shown no significant changes in urethral pressure after a successful corrective operation, further emphasizing the overriding importance of the position of the proximal urethra within the abdominal cavity.[2,3] However, there remains a small group of patients in whom stress incontinence persists despite adequate anatomical correction of the position of the urethra and hypermobility, and most of these patients have a low urethral closing pressure exerted over a short distance. Many have undergone a previous operation for stress incontinence so that mobilization, elevation and fixation of the urethra may be difficult because of scarring and rigidity of the periurethral tissues. Insertion of a pubovaginal sling in these cases usually has been successful in correcting the incontinence and a significant increase was found postoperatively in the posterior urethral pressure. It was concluded that patients with stress incontinence and a low urethral closing pressure, and/or scarring and fixation of the urethra because of a previous operation are best treated with a pubovaginal sling, which corrects the urethral position and increases the intraurethral pressure. The results in 52 of 560 patients evaluated for stress incontinence and in whom a pubovaginal fascial sling was used to correct the condition are described.

PATIENT POPULATION

Of the 52 patients 42 had had a prior operation for urinary stress incontinence and 6 had had more than 1 procedure. The urodynamic methodology, which has been reported in detail previously, included the recording of simultaneous bladder and urethral pressure during stress, urethral pressure profile measurements and fluoroscopic determination of alterations in the anatomical position of the urethra and bladder.[1]

Mean peak urethral profile pressures were significantly lower (10 cm water) than those observed in a previous series of 125 patients with urinary stress incontinence (32 cm water). No urethral sphincter function was measurable in 7 patients, all of whom had undergone a previous operation for incontinence.

Uninhibited detrusor dysfunction, in addition to stress incontinence, occurred in 29 patients. This condition was defined as an involuntary detrusor contraction provoked by an increase in intra-abdominal pressure, bladder filling or on assuming the upright position.

OPERATIVE PROCEDURE

A combined abdominal vaginal approach was used. A low transverse abdominal incision was made and the rectus sheath was divided in the line of the incision, care being taken to ensure that the inferior fascial flap was at least 4 to 5 cm above the symphysis. The fascia was reflected off the rectus muscles and these were separated in the midline to expose the retropubic space. The bladder neck was defined and dissected free on each side to make room for the fascial sling. A 1 cm wide by 12 cm long strip of rectus and external oblique fascia was cut from the lower margin of the fascial incision and was fashioned so that it hinged on 1 side, about 2 cm from the midline (Fig. 1). The free end of the sling was detached as far laterally as possible and then passed through the body of the rectus muscle beneath its attachment to the fascia.

A median incision was made in the anterior vaginal wall and the vaginal mucosa was reflected laterally off the posterior urethra and bladder neck. A tunnel was established by blunt and sharp dissection on either side of the bladder neck, between the retropubic space and the vaginal incision. The bladder was opened to ensure that it was not injured during this part of the dissection. The free end of the sling was placed around the urethrovesical junction, into the retropubic space on the contralateral side and then through the other rectus muscle, to be attached to the inferior fascial flap 2 to 3 cm from the midline. Sling tension was adjusted by the intra-operative determination of urethral pressures, so that there was an increase of at least 10 cm water in urethral pressure, in the region of the sling. The sling was secured to the rectus fascia with 2-zero sutures and the bladder was drained by a suprapubic cystotomy tube.

RESULTS

Patients have been followed for 10 months to 6 years, with a mean followup of 2.3 years (see table).

The stress incontinence was cured in 50 cases. Postoperative urodynamic studies showed an increase in the urethral profile pressure, anatomic fixation of the urethra with stress and equal transmission of intra-abdominal pressure to the bladder and urethra during straining (Fig. 1). Two patients had persistently high residual urine volumes and required a second procedure to decrease the sling tension.

There were 29 patients who exhibited uninhibited detrusor dysfunction preoperatively. In 20 of these patients uninhibited detrusor contractions could not be provoked postoperatively. The remaining 9 patients were treated with anticholinergic drugs and 3 of these had persistent incontinence owing to detrusor dysfunction despite medication but none showed evidence of stress incontinence on postoperative urodynamic evaluation.

Seven patients had no measurable urethral pressure preoperatively but 6 recovered complete urinary control postoperatively, even though urethral pressures were

PRE OPERATIVE   POST OPERATIVE

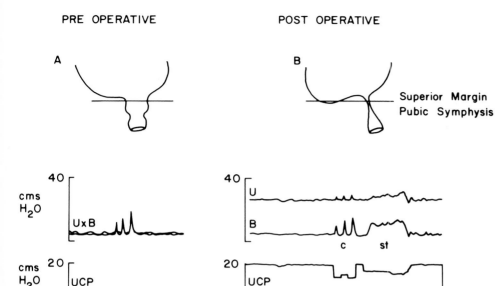

Fig. 1. (*A*) Preoperative tracing of straining lateral cystogram shows patulous urethra with bladder (B) and urethral (U) pressures and calculated urethral closing pressure (UCP) showing no positive urethral pressure. Both areas are virtually isobaric. (*B*) postoperative tracing and straining cystogram and simultaneous recording of urethral (U) bladder (B) and urethral closing pressure (UCP) during coughing (c) and straining (st) shows preservation of urethral pressure advantage.

Results of Operation and Medical Therapy for Detrusor Instability in 52 Patients

	No. Pts.	(%)
Cured:		
Operation alone	41	(80)
Operation and medication	6	(11)
Total	47	(91)
Failed:		
Persistent stress incontinence	2	(4)
Persistent detrusor dysfunction	3	(5)
Total	5	(9)

considerably lower than normal. One patient had persistent incontinence despite an increase in resting urethral closing pressure owing to autonomous bladder dysfunction. Neither stress incontinence nor uninhibited detrusor contractions were seen on urodynamic investigation. The response of the bladder to filling was a gradual increase in pressure with no corresponding rise in urethral pressure. While the urethra resisted stress at low volumes, bladder and urethral pressures were equal and urinary leakage occurred at a volume of 300 cc Cystograms showed satisfactory urethral closure after operation with stress (Fig. 2).

Urodynamic evaluation during voluntary voiding after successful control of incontinence with a fascial sling operation showed a decrease in urethral closing

pressure prior to the onset of a detrusor contraction, indicating that the sling was not a significant cause of obstruction unless the patient attempted to void entirely by straining (Fig. 3).

DISCUSSION

The use of a pubovaginal sling procedure for recurrent stress incontinence has been advocated by others.[4-6] Problems with the procedure have included persistent postoperative urinary retention, injury to the bladder or urethra during the operation, erosion of the sling into the urethra or bladder as a late complication and difficulty in judging sling tension to ensure a satisfactory result.[7,8] The procedure usually has been reserved for patients who have had failures from previous operations, particularly Marshall-Marchetti-Krantz procedures or vaginal operations that were followed by scarring and rigidity of the urethra or periurethral tissue. The application of this technique to patients with marginal urethral smooth muscle closing function, as determined by urodynamic evaluation in an effort to correct an anatomical deformity and low urethral closing pressure, necessitates intraoperative urethral pressure profile determinations to quantitate precisely the increase in urethral pressure effected by the sling. This procedure did not eliminate voiding difficulty in the immediate postoperative period

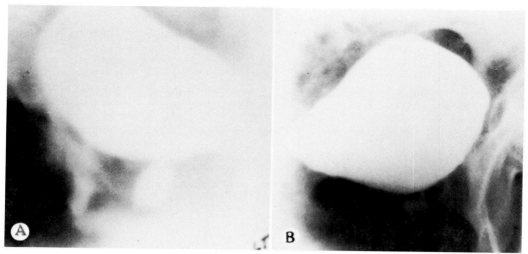

Fig. 2. (A) Preoperative lateral resting cystogram shows patulous urethra with free urinary loss. (B) Postoperative lateral stress cystogram shows urethral closure and elevation of urethrovesical junction. Note patulous urethra distal to sling.

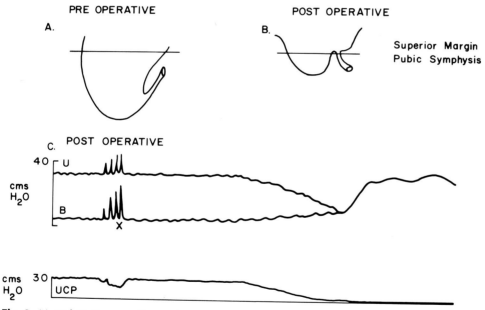

Fig. 3. (A and B) Preoperative and postoperative tracings of stress cystograms show elevation and fixation of urethra after sling procedure. (C) Bladder (B) and urethral pressure (U) with calculated urethral closing pressure (UCP) after sling procedure; no loss of urethral pressure advantage with coughing (X), but note loss of urethral pressure that precedes detrusor pressure rise with voiding.

but only 2 patients in this series failed to achieve satisfactory bladder emptying by 6 weeks postoperatively. A pressure increase of 10 to 20 cm water in the area of the sling has proved satisfactory.

The association of uninhibited vesical dysfunction with urinary stress incontinence has been described previously.[9] In this series two-thirds of the patients with such dysfunction no longer had evidence of the disability postoperatively, while in one-third it persisted. It was found previously that uninhibited detrusor dysfunction associated with stress incontinence usually ceased after surgical correction of the stress incontinence by colporrhaphy or urethropexy. Thus, this diagnosis established preoperatively is not in itself a contraindication to an operation. The incidence of uninhibited detrusor dysfunction in this group of patients is higher than in the larger group of patients with stress incontinence previously reported and may contribute to the difficulty in achieving a perfectly continent patient postoperatively. However, of the 9 patients who continued to manifest detrusor instability postoperatively 6 responded satisfactorily to anticholinergic medication.

The establishment of normal voiding postoperatively takes longer in some patients than in others. It is apparent from the urodynamic studies that urethral relaxation manifested by a decrease in urethral pressure precedes detrusor contraction despite the sling. However, during stress, the sling exerts a considerable increase in pressure on the urethra, even in patients who had poor or absent urethral smooth muscle function preoperatively. Straining to void postoperatively will not result in urinary loss if the sling is effective. This fact may be a source of considerable difficulty in patients who have been voiding in this way for protracted periods preoperatively and they must be encouraged to resume voiding by detrusor contraction. The period of relearning may be facilitated with intermittent catheterization.

REFERENCES

1. McGuire, E. J., Lytton, B., Pepe, V. and Kohorn, E. I.: Stress urinary incontinence. Obst Gynec 47:255, 1976
2. Tanagho, E. A.: Colpocystourethropexy: the way we do it. J Urol 116:751, 1976
3. Green, T. H., Jr.: Development of a plan for the diagnosis and treatment of urinary stress incontinence. Am J Obst Gynec 83:632, 1962
4. Goebell, R.: Zur operativen besetrigung der angeborenen incontinentia vesicae. Z. f. Gynäk 2:187, 1910
5. Aldridge, A. H.: Transplantation of fascia for relief of urinary stress incontinence. Am J Obst Gynec 44:398, 1942
6. McLaren, A. C.: Later results from sling operations. J Obst Gynec 75:10, 1968
7. Merrill, D. C.: Surgical treatment of urinary incontinenence. In: Urinary Incontinence. Edited by K. P. S. Caldwell. London: Grune and Stratton, Inc., 1975
8. Zacharin, R. F.: Stress Incontinence of Urine. New York: Harper and Row, Publishers, Inc., 1972
9. Bates, C. P., Loose, H. and Stanton, S. L. R.: The objective study of incontinence after repair operations. Surg Gynec & Obst 136:17, 1973

Commentary: Surgery of Female Urinary Incontinence

John Libertino

Urinary incontinence is a symptom that is much more frequently encountered in females. It varies in degree from the involuntary escape of a few drops of urine to the continuous uncontrolled flow of the entire urinary output.

The etiology of urinary incontinence in the female may be divided into three major categories: congenital defects of the urinary tract, incontinence resulting from trauma or diseases of the urinary system, and lesions of the nervous system involving control of micturition.

The more common congenital defects that cause urinary incontinence in females are hypospadias, epispadias, exstrophy of the bladder, and anomalous ectopic opening of a ureter outside of the bladder. Incontinence resulting from trauma or diseases of the urinary system such as partial or complete destruction of the urethra, urethral, vesical, or ureteral fistulae, and urge incontinence and stress incontinence are also common causes of urinary incontinence in the female. The final category, lesions of the nervous system involving nerve control of micturition, includes congenital lesions such as spina bifida occulta or acquired lesions such as tabes, multiple sclerosis, spinal cord tumors, transverse myelitis, and traumatic injuries to the spinal cord. A miscellaneous category of enuresis would complete the classification of the etiology of urinary incontinence in females.

The surgical management of the neurogenic bladder and the management of urinary fistulae are well covered elsewhere in this textbook. I have selected the article entitled "Pubovaginal Sling Procedure for Stress Incontinence" by Drs. Edward J. McGuire and Bernard Lytton because I feel this article presents a rational approach to the management of patients suffering from urinary stress incontinence who have had previous failed surgical procedures. Since this problem is frequently encountered in clinical practice, I believe that the information contained in this article in terms of the preoperative and intraoperative management of these patients is an important contribution which the practicing urologist should be aware of.[2]

Hodgkinson, in his elegant review of stress urinary incontinence, defined it as the involuntary loss of urine through the intact urethra as a result of a sudden increase in intra-abdominal pressure. Stress incontinence is usually worse when the patient is erect, is aggrevated by any action or disease that increases abdominal pressure, and, most important, is never caused by contraction of the detrusor muscle.

Clinically, residual urine is never present, and its absence should always be confirmed. This is done obviously to eliminate patients who have atonic bladders with large residual urines who can present with a clinical history similar to patients suffering from stress urinary incontinence. Needless to say, if these patients are operated on, they will obviously not benefit from surgery. In stress urinary incontinence, urine is not lost as a result of detrusor contraction and the imminency of the urine loss is not usually preceded by a sensation of urinary urgency. In patients who have urgency incontinence, the surgeon must consider detrusor dyssynergia as the cause of the patient's urgency incontinence. At any rate detrusor dyssynergia and urgency incontinence must be carefully ruled out in the female with urinary incontinence before surgery for stress urinary incontinence is contemplated.

The most important part of the physical examination other than noting the absence of pelvic masses is the visual demonstration of involuntary loss of urine during coughing or straining. After residual urine is measured, the patient's bladder is filled until she has a comfortable sensation of fullness. The patient is then asked to cough, both in the lithotomy position and in the upright position. If the patient does not demonstrate stress incontinence in either the lithotomy or the upright position with her legs spread, then the surgeon must consider other causes of urinary incontinence.

The Bonney test or the Marshall–Marchetti test is a useful diagnostic maneuver and is positive in patients suffering from stress urinary incontinence. It is also very important, especially in patients who have had previous operative failures, to judge the mobility of the tissues on either side of the urethra and the bladder neck. The difficulties of surgery will be proportional to the degree of fixation of these tissues. The degree of pelvic relaxation should be observed with a vaginal speculum. Asymptomatic cystoceles obviously do not require repair at the time of correction of the urinary incontinence. The unfortunate practice of referring patients with stress urinary incontinence and asymptomatic pelvic relaxation for hysterectomy should be stopped. Stress urinary incontinence has nothing whatsoever to do with pelvic relaxation. This was demonstrated by Hodgkinson in an analysis of 3400 patients suffering from urinary incontinence.[2]

In addition to a routine general examination and gynecologic examination, several urologic examinations should be carried out. Measurement of the residual urine, as previously mentioned, is important to exclude overflow incontinence. Cystourethroscopy is, of course, essential to exclude relevant and incidental abnormalities of the urinary bladder such as vesicovaginal fistulae, urethrovaginal fistulae, and urethral diverticula. A cystometrogram in the supine and then erect position is occasionally carried out to unmask the patients with unstable bladders. Voiding cystourethrograms and chain cystourethrograms have been of little importance in my clinical practice. Useful information, however, can be gotten if preoperative cystourethrograms are compared to postoperative x-ray films. This will reveal the quality of the previous surgical repair. The radiologic hallmark of a successful operation for stress urinary incontinence is elevation of the urethrovesical junction above the lowest bladder level. If the urologist is interested in documenting this, the chain cystourethrogram can clearly delineate the preoperative and postoperative anatomy.

Much has been recently written about the urodynamic evaluation and synchronous video pressure flow cystourethrography in the evaluation of patients who have stress urinary incontinence.[3] In addition, urethral pressure profiles and electromyographic (EMG) studies have been used to assess urethral and sphincter function. The value of many urodynamic investigations fundamentally depends on the experience of the operator and the interpretor; unfortunately, the simpliest are open to overinterpretation. For these reasons, I do not feel that urodynamic evaluation should be routinely carried out in patients who have clinically straightforward urinary stress incontinence and normal cystometrograms. Urodynamic evaluation should be used selectively, for example, in those patients who have had several previous operative failures. Because urodynamic evaluation is expensive, and occasionally its cost approaches that of the operative procedure, I urge that its use not be abused. The clinical urologist must ask himself whether the investigative means presently available for the study of stress urinary incontinence justify the additional time, effort, expense, and inconvenience to the patient.

SURGICAL MANAGEMENT

In my view, there are three operations the urologist should have in his surgical armamentarium for this problem: the Marshall–Marchetti operation, the endoscopic suspension of the vesical neck, and the Millin fascial sling.

The Marshall–Marchetti operation, described in 1949, has changed little since its original description.[4] The only change made has been the placement of the periurethral sutures adjacent to but not into the urethra. In my view, the Marshall–Marchetti operation is the standard to which all other operations for urinary stress incontinence should be compared. The technique that I employ is to place the patient in a supine frog-legged position. The vagina is prepared with Betadine, and a no. 18 5-ml Foley catheter is inserted into the bladder. The Foley balloon will subsequently be used to identify the bladder neck region. Next the anterior abdominal wall and perineum are prepared with Betadine solution, and the patient is draped. A Pfannensteil or vertical incision is made. The rectus muscles are divided in the midline, and a Smith ring retractor is used to maintain exposure. The retropubic space of Retzius is entered, and the vesical neck, urethra, and anterior vaginal wall are exposed. The anterior surface of the vagina and urethra are then freed from the pubic symphysis down to the level of the external urethral meatus. At this point the assistant places two fingers in the vagina in a periurethral fashion and elevates the anterior vaginal wall. A total of six 2-0 chromic catgut sutures are placed periurethrally into the anterior vaginal wall as illustrated (Fig. 4). Next, two more sutures are placed on either side of the vesical neck, which has been defined by the Foley balloon. (Fig. 5) The assistant then elevates the anterior vaginal wall digitally, and the sutures are passed into the cartilage of the pubic symphysis. I prefer to place these sutures in pairs and tie them as I proceed up toward the bladder neck. I believe this allows more accurate placement of the sutures in the cartilaginous portion of the pubic symphysis. If the upper edge of the pubic symphysis is below the location required for placement of the perivesical sutures at the bladder neck, these sutures can be inserted into the lower most portion of the fibrous insertions of the rectus muscle.

Two technical points should be stressed. The suspending sutures should be tied with support from the assistant's fingers in the vagina. This will take tension off the individual sutures. Secondly, the surgeon should not overcorrect cystoceles at the time of Marshall–Marchetti repair. Overcorrection of the cystocele alters the urethrovesical junction and its function and may cause persistence of urinary stress incontinence.

The Foley catheter is left in place for 5 days. Occasionally during the early postoperative course a mild degree of urinary retention is seen. This is usually resolved by 1 to 2 wk of Foley catheter drainage.

In properly selected patients the surgeon can expect to achieve an excellent result in 90% of operations. If stress incontinence recurs, the suprapubic vesicourethral suspension can be repeated if the stress test is positive. Marshall and Segaul in 1968 reported on 16 patients who had repeat suprapubic vesicourethral suspensions from above with an 80% success rate.[5]

Endoscopic suspension of the vesical neck for urinary incontinence is being reported with greater frequency in the urologic literature. Its long-term results will ultimately need to be compared to the Marshall–Marchetti operation. The operative technique for this procedure was described by Dr. Stamey in 1973 and is a modification of the Pereyra technique.[6,7]

In this procedure the patient is placed on a cystoscopy table. After the induction of anesthesia, the legs are placed in a low lithotomy of Edebohl's position in order to keep the inguinal and suprapubic areas as flat as possible. The vagina and suprapubic areas are prepared with Betadine, and a half towel is sutured in place to cover the rectum. The labia are then sutured to the skin with 2–0 silk ligatures.

Two 2.5 cm transverse incisions are made 2 to 4 cm from the midline just above the upper margin of the pubic symphysis. The fascia of the anterior rectus muscle is exposed. A Foley catheter is placed in the bladder, and the urine is evacuated. Slight tension is placed on the catheter so that the Foley balloon rests against the vesical neck. A weighted posterior vaginal retractor is placed in the vagina. A transverse incision is made

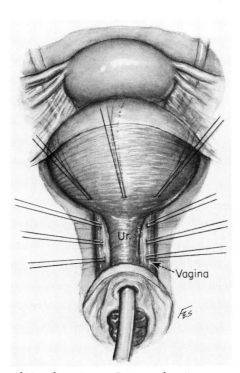

Fig. 4. Diagram of sites for sutures. *Dots* are for sites along urethra and vesical neck. *Crosses* are for sites in lower bladder and vagina. Other sutures are often taken, as explained in text.

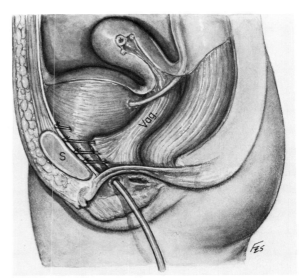

Fig. 5. Sutures tied (diagrammatic; actually, less space remains between origin and insertion of sutures).

below the urethra as illustrated (Fig. 6A). The anterior vaginal wall is separated from the underlying urethra and the distal trigone. It is best to free the entire vaginal wall by sharp dissection through the transverse incision before the anterior vaginal wall is incised in the midline, as illustrated (Fig. 6B). After the midline incision is extended to the bladder neck region, there must be enough room in the area of the dots (Fig. 6C) to accommodate a 1-cm Dacron tube. Therefore, some lateral separation of the vaginal wall from the area of the internal vesical neck is occasionally needed for placement of the Dacron buttress.

The weighted posterior vaginal retractor is then removed to free the urethra and the bladder neck from undue tension. Special needles (Fig. 7) are passed from the medial or lateral edge of the suprapubic incision and outside of the internal vesical neck into the vaginal incision. A needle is passed vertically through the anterior rectus fascia, near the upper border of the symphysis pubic, and stops abruptly just below the fascia. The handle of the needle is depressed toward the abdominal wall so that the cephalad edge of the symphysis pubis can be probed with the point of the needle. The needle is then passed 1 cm parallel to the undersurface of the symphysis pubis. It is important to realize that this 1-cm passage of the needle beneath the parallel to the symphysis pubis is the only blind part of the entire procedure. The remainder of the needle is passed under bimanual control with one hand on the needle and the other in the vagina.

As illustrated (Fig. 7), the index finger locates the tip of the needle 1 cm below the upper border of the symphysis pubis. The location of the needle point is facilitated by bouncing the needle suprapubically without advancing it. As soon as the needle point is firmly located on the tip of the index finger, the needle is straightened to a more vertical position and passed down into the vagina alongside the Foley balloon. The needle should exit well back into the vagina at the urethrovesical junction. Next, the Foley catheter is removed and the patient cystoscoped. The bladder is examined for evidence that the needle has entered it. A word of caution—the bladder must be filled with a large volume of fluid in order to rule out the possibility of needle penetration of the bladder. Although cystoscopy is important in detecting perforation of the bladder by the needle or even in locating a submucosal passage, its critical purpose is making sure that the needle has passed the bladder and the urethra exactly at the urethrovesical junction. This is readily determined by moving the needle in a vertical or transverse direction, as illustrated, while holding the right-angle lens of the cystoscope exactly at the urethrovesical junction.

Once the needle is determined with the cystoscope to be in a good position outside the bladder at the urethrovesical junction, the cystoscope is removed, the posterior vaginal speculum is replaced, and a no. 12 monofilament nylon is threaded through the eye of the needle, which is then withdrawn suprapubically. A hemostat is placed on the end of the nylon suture at both the suprapubic and vaginal ends. The Foley catheter is reintroduced. The bladder is emptied, the vaginal

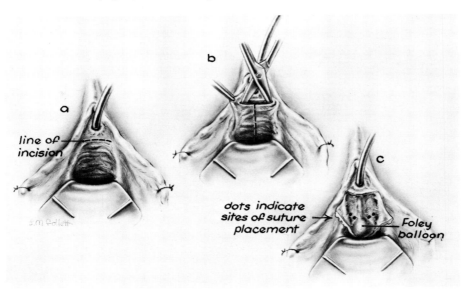

Fig. 6. (A) A transverse incision is made below the urethral meatus at the level of the vaginal wall. (B) With the use of Metzenbaum scissors, the vaginal wall is separated by blunt dissection from the urethra and trigone. (C) The Foley balloon should be palpable within the incision. The two dots on either side of the urethrovesical junction indicate the sites of suture placement. Dissection, blunt or sharp, of the fascia between the vaginal wall and the overlying urethra and trigone is avoided; this pubovesicocervical fascia is the primary source of support for suspension of the vesical neck. (Stamey TA: Endoscopic suspension of the vesical neck for urinary incontinence. Surg Gynecol Obstet 136:547–554, 1973. By permission of Surgery, Gynecology, & Obstetrics.)

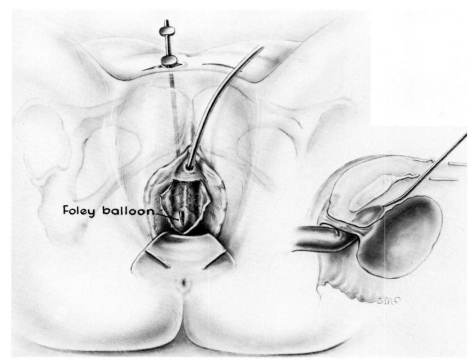

Fig. 7. The 15° angle needle is passed through the right anterior rectal fascia; immediately turned toward the undersurface of the symphysis pubis to avoid perforating small intestine that may be adhered to the top of the bladder in patients who have undergone previous operation; and then guided vertically by the vaginal finger alongside the urethrovesical junction (*insert at right*). The needle should exit in the vaginal incision immediately in front of the Foley balloon and to the right lateral side of the vesical neck. (Stamey TA: Endoscopic suspension of the vesical neck for urinary incontinence. Surg Gynecol Obstet 136:547–554, 1973. By permission of Surgery, Gynecology, & Obstetrics.)

speculum is removed, and the needle is passed a second time on the same side. Double-pronged needles are currently available to eliminate this step, as originally described by Stamey. All that is necessary with a double-pronged needle is one passage of the needle into the anterior vaginal wall. The vaginal end of the nylon suture is passed through the lumen of a 1-cm tube of 5-mm knitted Dacron used to buttress the vaginal loop.

One side of the operation is now complete, and certain quantitative measurements are made at this point. Endoscopy of the bladder neck is carried out to determine the nature of the bladder neck closure by the previously placed suture. The opposite side of the vesical neck is suspended using the same technique. Again, panendoscopy should demonstrate good symmetry between the two sides when each loop is manipulated individually. At this point, Dr. Stamey fills the bladder to capacity and inserts a suprapubic catheter. The vaginal incision is closed with a continuous 3–0 chromic suture. The vaginal closure must be done before the suspending loops are tied. The vaginal pack is inserted and left in place for 24 hr. Note that a urethral catheter is not used.

After the vaginal closure, gloves are changed. The incisions are then irrigated with 80 mg of gentamycin and 100 ml of saline. Then panendoscopy is again carried out. The assistant observes the vesical neck with a panendoscope and tells the surgeon when tension is adequate to allow closure of the vesical neck. The nylon sutures are tied. The subcutaneous tissue of the suprapubic incisions are closed with 3–0 chromic and the skin with 4–0 nylon.

The procedure described here has two major limitations as I see it. The first is the blind passage of a needle in the retropubic space in patients who have had previous abdominal surgery. In this circumstance it would be easy to injure a loop of small bowel inadvertently. Second, the endoscopic manipulation required to determine the placement of the bladder neck suture as well as to detect needles that have inadvertently passed into the urethra or bladder is very time consuming. However, I am sure that as one uses this operation more frequently, facility is easily achieved. The long-term results of this operation will have to be carefully compared to the Marshall–Marchetti–Krantz operation.

The final operation that urologists should have in their armamentarium for dealing with stress incontinence is the Millin sling procedure.[8] Presently, I prefer to use the Millin sling procedure in those patients who have had several operations for the management of urinary stress incontinence that have failed.

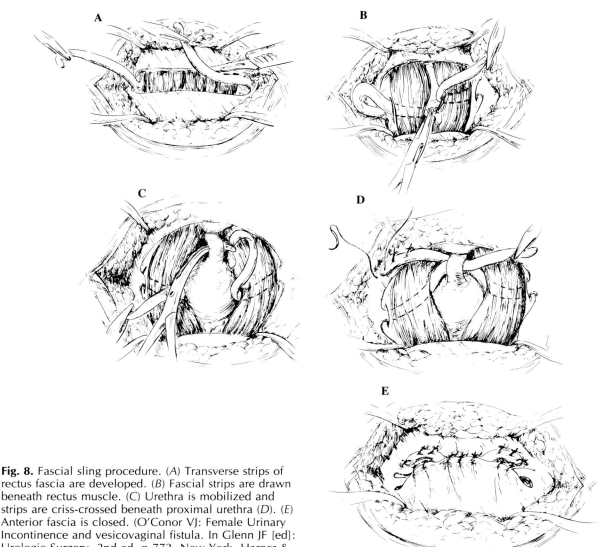

Fig. 8. Fascial sling procedure. (*A*) Transverse strips of rectus fascia are developed. (*B*) Fascial strips are drawn beneath rectus muscle. (*C*) Urethra is mobilized and strips are criss-crossed beneath proximal urethra (*D*). (*E*) Anterior fascia is closed. (O'Conor VJ: Female Urinary Incontinence and vesicovaginal fistula. In Glenn JF [ed]: Urologic Surgery, 2nd ed, p 772. New York, Harper & Row, 1975.)

With a Foley catheter in the bladder and the bladder distended with 200 ml of sterile saline, the patient is placed in a slight Trendelenburg position. A Pfannenstiel incision is made. The underlying rectus sheath is dissected as little as possible to maintain adequate blood supply. Two flaps of rectus fascia are isolated, measuring at least 1 cm wide and somewhat wider at their origins (Fig. 8*A*). The fascial flaps are made as long as possible. Next, the rectus muscle bellies are separated in the midline, and the retropubic space of Retzius is entered. The bladder neck region is dissected and the urethra is separated from the anterior vaginal wall. Care is exercised at this point not to injure the urethra or the anterior vaginal wall so as to create a urethrovaginal or vesicovaginal fistula.

Under direct vision, a right-angle or a curved pedicle clamp is placed beneath the urethra, and both fascial straps are brought to lie around the urethra as illustrated (Fig. 8*C*). The straps are brought up superiorward through the rectus muscle bellies and then sutured to each other using 0 silk or prolene on either side of the bladder neck (Fig. 8*D*). They are finally sutured again to themselves as part of the closure of the remaining rectus sheath (Fig. 8*E*). The retropubic space is drained, and the overlying rectus fascia is approximated with figure-of-eight interrupted 0 chromic catgut. A Foley catheter is left in place for 5 days.

In my experience many of the patients develop urinary retention after removal of the Foley catheter and require several weeks of catheter drainage before voiding spontaneously. The Millin technique has been very useful in those patients who have had previous failures following other types of operations for stress urinary incontinence. The success rate using the Millin sling in this category of patients approximates 80%.

Careful selection and meticulous employment of the surgical techniques as outlined in the Marshall–Marchetti, Pereyra, Millin, and Leadbetter operations will yield gratifying results in patients suffering from urinary incontinence.

REFERENCES

1. Leadbetter GN: Urinary incontinence. In Libertino JA, Zinman L (eds): Textbook of Reconstructive Urologic Surgery. Baltimore, Williams & Wilkins, 1977
2. Hodgkinson CP: Stress urinary incontinence—1970. Am J Obstet Gynecol 108:1141, 1970
3. Turner-Warwick RT, Brown AG: A urodynamic evaluation of urinary incontinence in the female and its treatment. Urol Clin North Am 6(1):203–216, 1977
4. Marshall VF, Marchetti AA, Krantz KE: The correction of stress incontinence by simple vesicourethral suspension. Surg Gynecol Obstet 88:590, 1949

5. Marshall VF, Segaul RM: Experiences with suprapubic vesicourethral suspension after previous failures to correct stress incontinence in women. J Urol 100:647, 1968
6. Stamey TA: Endoscopic suspension of the vesicle neck for urinary incontinence. Surg Gynecol Obstet 136:547, 1973
7. Pereyra JJ, Lebhertz TB: Combined urethrovesicle suspension and vaginourethroplasty for correction of urinary stress incontinence. Obstet Gynecol 30:537, 1967
8. Millin T: Discussion of stress incontinence in micturition. Proc R Soc Med 40:364, 1947

ANNOTATED BIBLIOGRAPHY

Leadbetter GE: Urinary incontinence. In Libertino JA, Zinman L (eds): Textbook of Reconstructive Urologic Surgery. Baltimore, Williams & Wilkins, 1977

This chapter deals with urinary incontinence, both male and female. The major focus, however, is the management of total urinary incontinence by the Leadbetter technique of trigonal tubularization. The surgical technique of tubularizing the urethra and allowing the trigone to become, in essence, the bladder neck with bilateral ureteroneocystotomy is very well illustrated. In addition, the indications used to manage total urinary incontinence in 31 children and 9 adults are outlined. The reasons for failure in 15 patients are also presented.

Hodgkinson CP: Stress urinary incontinence—1970: Am J Obstet Gynecol 108:1141, 1970

Doctor Hodgkinson reviews his experience with 3400 patients suffering from urinary stress incontinence. The proper method for evaluating these patients, ruling out an unstable bladder, is underscored. Asymptomatic cystoceles should not be repaired, and cystoceles in general should not be surgically overcorrected. The concomitant use of hysterectomy for asymptomatic pelvic relaxation is an unfortunate practice that should be abandoned.

Turner-Warwick RT, Brown AG: A urodynamic evaluation of urinary incontinence in the female and its treatment. Urol Clin North Am 1979

A physiologic basis for female urinary incontinence and incontinence in general is discussed. These observations of the functional characteristics and morphology of both the proximal and distal female urethra are discussed. There is an effort to relate the urethral pressure profile, EMG, continuous monitoring, and urodynamic evaluation to the management of stress urinary incontinence. The surgical approach to the management of urinary incontinence is touched on, as is the management of the unstable bladder.

Marshall VF, Marchetti AA, Krantz KE: The correction of stress incontinence by simple vesicourethral suspension. Surg Gynecol Obstet 88:509, 1949

This article describes the original procedure of simple vesicourethral suspension for the correction of stress urinary incontinence in 50 patients. Of 44 suitable cases, excellent results were obtained in 82%, significant improvement in 7%, and no improvement in 11%. The causes of failure are discussed. The technical aspects of the operation as presented in the original article have changed very little and are clearly illustrated.

Marshall VF, Segaul RM: Experiences with suprapubic vesicourethral suspension after previous failures to correct stress incontinence in women. J Urol 100:647, 1968

Thirty-seven patients were reoperated on between 1945 and 1967 following various types of surgical manuevers to control urinary stress incontinence without achieving success. The operative technique is similar to the original procedure described by Marshall, Marchetti, and Krantz in 1949. This experience indicated that with careful selection and extended surgical technique, a repeat vesicourethral suspension has a 75% to 80% chance of correcting postoperative recurrent stress incontinence in females.

Stamey TA: Endoscopic suspension of vesical neck for urinary incontinence. Surg Gynecol Obstet 136:547, 1973

The results of 16 patients operated on by this method are presented. Nine patients were cured, two were improved substantially, and five had no improvement and were considered failures. The technical aspects of the procedure are detailed in a step-by-step fashion and are very well illustrated. Anyone intending to use this procedure would do well to read this article.

Pereyra AJ: A simplified surgical procedure for the correction of stress incontinence in women. West J Surg 67:223, 1959

This is the original description of the technique described by Pereyra, which demonstrated the feasibility of suspending the pubocervical fascia by the simple passage of a suture through a special needle from the abdominal wall to the vagina.

Millin T: Discussion of stress incontinence in micturition. Proc R Soc Med 40:364, 1947

The Millin technique is a modification of the technique described originally in 1945. This procedure combined a plication of the pubocervical fascia beneath the urethra and vesical neck through a vaginal approach with the construction of a sling from two straps of fascia taken from the aponeurosis of the external oblique muscles on each side. The straps of fascia were brought down through the rectus muscle about 3 cm above their attachment to the symphysis pubis and sutured beneath the plicated urethra. The Millin modification of this technique eliminates the vaginal portion of the operation, making this a purely suprapubic approach. This article discusses Dr. Millin's experience with over 67 patients treated by his procedure, which controlled urinary incontinence in approximately 80% of the patients.

Overview: Diagnosis and Treatment of Stress Urinary Incontinence

Guy W. Leadbetter, Jr.

Libertino has adequately discussed many aspects of the diagnosis and treatment of stress urinary incontinence in the foregoing commentary. For knowledge and research purposes, measurements of pressure, flow, electromyography (EMG), and cinefluorography are excellent tools. Practically speaking, however, I agree with the author that a simple cystometrogram performed with a water manometer to determine if there is a spastic or atonic neurogenic element in the bladder and the "Marshall" test, that is, elevation of the vesicourethral angle with a finger on either side of the urethra, are all that is needed to make a decision for surgery. In my experience, the classic Marshall–Marchetti–Kranz procedure is successful in almost all but the unusual stress incontinence problems. These unusual problems have been adequately discussed.

The effectiveness of vesicourethral suspension of Marshall depends partly on the return of the vesicourethral angle to normal, reestablishment of normal urethral length, and, most important, fixation of the urethra and bladder neck area. Without proper and normal fixation of these areas, the normal physiologic action of the muscles cannot function efficiently. The tissues are loose, and there is no fixed point for them to work against. Surgery restores the anatomy and eliminates relaxation. Fixation by surgery creates an area for the muscular sphincter to work against, allowing proper and efficient function with resultant urinary control.

There may be urinary retention after repair for stress incontinence. Rather than burden the patient with an in-dwelling urethral or suprapubic catheter as the author suggests, I prefer intermittent catheterization. This technique is accepted well by the patients and works very satisfactorily.

In the poor-risk patient, for whatever reason, a trial of Ornade twice a day may control stress incontinence very well. I have used this successfully in 50% to 60% of such patients.

In some patients residual urine may be unexpectedly found and may be the cause of stress incontinence. For such patients, intermittent catheterization may solve the problem.

Before I discuss total urinary incontinence, the patient with the ectopic ureter with wetting should be mentioned. Characteristically, these are children or young adults who void normally but seem to be constantly damp or wet. This abnormality is simply corrected by resection of the ureter and vesicoureteral reimplantation if the kidney has good function or by resection of the portion of the kidney that the ectopic ureter drains if renal tissue is inadequate.

The female with total urinary incontinence or complete lack of urinary control has not been discussed. Fortunately, this is not too common an occurrence, but when present it is a very difficult problem for the urologist and patient alike. Since 1961 I have successfully used a surgical procedure to correct total urinary incontinence and believe that it is *apropos* to discuss this here.

TOTAL URINARY INCONTINENCE AND THE PROCEDURE FOR URETHRAL RECONSTRUCTION

The various types and degrees of stress incontinence are relatively easy to correct. Total urinary incontinence, whether mild or severe, makes social fraternization of persons so afflicted difficult, to say the least. The causes of total urinary incontinence include congenital and anatomic defects of the urethral sphincter and bladder neck, exemplified by epispadias with incontinence, bladder exstrophy, absence of the urethra or urethral sphincter, a congenital deficiency of innervation to the sphincter (often associated with myelomeningocele or absence of the sacrum), division or loss of the bladder neck and urethra from external trauma to the pelvis, and surgically induced injury to the bladder neck (internal sphincter) and external sphincter during transurethral or open bladder neck revision or excision of congenital posterior urethral valves. Current therapeutic alternatives are external collecting devices, in-dwelling urethral catheters, urinary diversion, or corrective surgical reconstruction. In general, urinary incontinence calls for surgical treatment, because permanent use of external collecting devices is unsatisfactory. Treatment, however, must not be instituted in any case until the patient is thoroughly studied and consideration given to the functional status of the upper and lower urinary tract, neurologic and orthopedic problems, general condition, and long-range complications in view of life expectancy.

The first successful surgical correction was reported by H. H. Young in 1908. Young achieved continence by narrowing the urethral and bladder neck lumens to the size of a silver probe. Since that time, many surgical techniques have been proposed and tried. These include plication of the urethra and vesical neck, slings, creation of a sphincter with musuclar graft, formation of new urethras with bladder muscle, vaginal flaps or denervated ileum.[1-8] Some success has been reported with these techniques, but in general, patients treated for total urinary incontinence are no better or have moderate to marked loss of urine on stress.

I have used the technique described below for the past 18 yr on 49 patients.[9,10] Others have also used the procedure successfully.

TECHNIQUE

The patient is placed supine with the pelvis elevated to allow better exposure deep in the retroperitoneal space. Transverse suprapubic incision is used unless a previous vertical incision exists. Exposure of the bladder neck and urethra is accomplished by dissection of prevesical fat and fascia, and when previous surgery has been performed, scar tissue must often be removed with sharp dissection. The posterior aspect of the bladder base and urethra is not mobilized, because disruption or injury of the nerve and blood supply to this segment may cause eventual failure of the operative procedure due to slough or to deficient innervation.

The bladder is entered in the midline, and the incision is carried distally into the urethra almost to the triangular ligament and sometimes the meatus (Fig. 9). If exposure in this area seems inadequate at this time or later during reconstruction, the symphyseal band should be divided and the symphysis spread 3 cm to 4 cm. This maneuver causes no problems

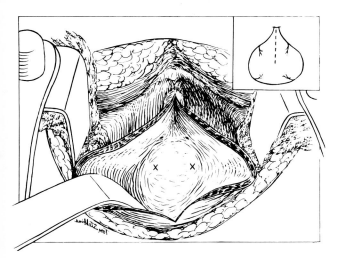

Fig. 9. Bladder incision.

postoperatively and may greatly enhance exposure and surgical technique.

The ureteral orifices are identified and reimplanted 3 cm to 4 cm more superiorly in the bladder, using a tunnel technique similar to that described by Politano and Leadbetter[14] (Fig. 10).[11] The *ureter must always be reimplanted, because it is the tubularized trigonal muscle that, when reconstructed into the new bladder neck, is responsible for continence.*

After the ureters are mobilized, they should be transposed from under the uterine vessels and ligaments to a position superior to these structures. If this is not done, a hooking of the ureters will result after reimplantation high in the bladder. To accomplish this, the surgeon must first work inside the bladder to free the ureters and then outside the bladder to transpose them superior to the uterine structures. The ureters should follow a smooth curve into the bladder; they must not be hooked or angled. Following reimplantation of the ureters, the junction between urethra, bladder neck, and vagina should be mobilized slightly. This will allow tissues to be approximated without tension during the reconstruction. Longitudinal lateral incisions are then made on each side of the urethra and bladder wall as the first step. The incisions are begun at the apex of the urethral incision and include the entire thickness of the bladder wall. The incisions are extended longitudinally and posteriorly through the base of the bladder, through the sites where ureteral orifices were originally inserted, and to a point 1 cm to 2 cm beyond this. These incisions are 3 cm to 5 cm long, so that the newly constructed urethra will measure 3 cm to 5 cm.

When both lateral incisions have been completed, the residual posterior urethral bladder strip should be 2.5 cm to 3 cm wide. The triangular flaps, or "dog ears," produced by these incisions should *not* be excised (Fig. 10). If they are, bladder capacity may be significantly decreased, causing the procedure to fail. Reconstruction of the urethra and contiguous bladder tissue to form an elongated muscular urethra must be meticulous. No attempt is made to constrict the urethral or bladder neck lumen, as has previously been described by H. H. Young. To the contrary, a no. 10 to 14 catheter is used as a stent, and closure made loosely over this. Reconstruction of the new urethra is in two layers: mucosa and muscle. The

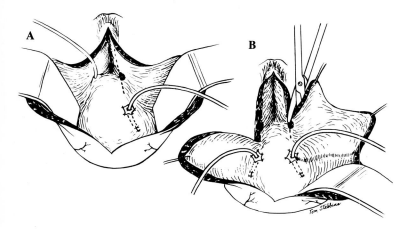

Fig. 10. (*A*) Reimplantation of ureters superiorly. (*B*) Incision in urethra and bladder, and through trigone.

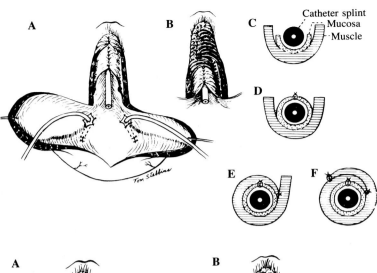

Fig. 11. Reconstruction of urethra.

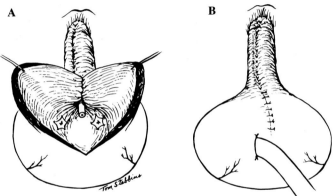

Fig. 12. Closure of the bladder.

mucosa is closed with fine chromic catgut sutures (6–0) up to the area of the bladder neck. The muscle is closed by imbricating it on each side; that is, chromic catgut sutures (4–0 or 3–0) are placed into one muscle edge and then placed on the underside of the opposite muscle away from this edge (Fig. 11). These sutures are continued as far as possible without tension. When the imbrication is complete, the remaining edge is sewed to the opposite side as an overlap. In the area of the newly formed bladder neck, imbrication is not possible, and the remaining closure is completed in three layers: mucosa, muscle, and serosa (Fig. 12). Ureteral stenting catheters, suprapubic tube, and urethral catheter are used for drainage purposes. The wound area is drained, and the wound is closed in layers. Ureteral stents are placed and left in for 7 to 10 days to create as dry a field as possible within the bladder and new urethra to aid healing. The urethral catheter and suprapubic tube are removed in 2 to 3 wk, depending on reaction about the operative areas.

Continence has not been complete in any of the patients except for one immediately after removing the catheter. Time required for regaining continence has varied from 3 to 12 wk. Reasons for this delay are probably bladder spasm, return of muscle tone in the newly constructed urethra, and tissue edema.

Agents such as belladonna are useful, but recently I have used amitriptyline (Elavil) and imipramine (Tofranil). These drugs aid in controlling hyperactivity of the bladder and thus help with urinary control.

DISCUSSION

Results have been gratifying. Initially, during the developmental phase of the technique, both errors in technique and errors in proper selection of patients were made. For example, the "dog ears" were removed on one patient and the procedure failed because of decreased bladder capacity. Another failure resulted when urethral reconstruction was made on a patient with a neurogenic dysfunction. Patients such as these are eliminated from the results. There have been 31 successes in 42 patients, or about a 75% success rate. These patients so treated have been followed for 3 to 15 yr, have no infection, and have no leakage on stress.

The explanation for good results seems to be the fact that when the striated trigonal muscle is tubularized, it is able to act as a sphincter. The actual length of the newly constructed urethra seems to play no part in continence (as originally thought). The sphincter action of the trigone developed by this procedure differs from the Young or Young–Dees procedure, both of which seem to depend on narrowing of the urethra, which causes some obstruction rather than a muscular sphincteric action.[1,12]

Lapides and colleagues first described a "continent" urethra made of bladder muscle of a specified length in diameter.[13] I could not make this work when creating a new urethra. Tanagho and associates have reported the use of an anterior bladder tube for reconstruction of the urethra to create continence.[14] My experience with this technique has been unsuccessful. Such tubes must be, to a degree, deficient in nerve and blood supply, as contrasted to the above-described new urethra.

This operation is simple in conception but rather tedious to perform. Requirements for success are normal bladder function and capacity. Particular note must be made of the muscular tone in the area of the base of the bladder trigone. There are borderline situations, of course (*i.e.,* in patients who have had several operations and some thinning of the vesicovaginal septum). However, if the patient is willing, I will do the procedure in an attempt to avoid urinary diversion.

The patient must be totally incontinent. If only severe stress incontinence is present and the usual stress incontinence procedures have not been used, they should be.

Any neurogenic bladder or contracted scarred bladder is a contraindication to surgery. Patients who have had eight to ten procedures are poor candidates. Children with exstrophy should have an attempt to recreate continence. Dr. Jeffs has had an excellent success rate of approximately 75% in creating continence in these children.[15]

The use of an artificial sphincter is being used with some success, but I have no experience with this.

REFERENCES

1. Young HH: An operation for the cure of incontinence of urine. Surg. Gynecol Obstet 28:84, 1919

2. Kelly HA: Incontinence of urine in women. Urol Cutan Rev 17:291, 1913

3. Strong GH, Van Buskirk KE: Operation for the cure of incontinence in the male. J Urol 66:586, 1951

4. Uhle CAW, Bradley RH Jr: The use of rectus fascia and fascia lata in sling operation for urinary incontinence in the male. J Urol 80:132, 1958

5. Deming CL: Transplantation of the gracilis muscle for incontinence of urine. JAMA 86:822, 1926

6. Tsuji I, Kuroda K, Ishida H: A new method for reconstruction of the urinary tract, bladder flap tube. J Urol 81:282, 1959

7. Kimura C, Harada N, Tatsumi W: Antipubic vesico-ileal-neo-urethrostomy. J Urol 77:227, 1957

8. Torbey K: Urinary continence and normal micturition provided by urethral and sphincter substitution with special seromuscular segment of ileum in male and female dogs. J Urol 84:717, 1960

9. Leadbetter GW Jr: Surgical correction of total urinary incontinence. J Urol 91: 1964

10. Leadbetter GW Jr, Fraley EE: Surgical correction for total urinary incontinence: 5 years after. J Urol 97:1967

11. Politano VA, Leadbetter WF: An operative technique for the correction of vesicoureteral reflux. J Urol 79:932, 1958

12. Dees JE: Congenital epispadias with incontinence. J Urol 62:513, 1949

13. Lapides J, Ajemian EP, Stewart BH, et al: Further observation on the kinetics of the urethrovesical sphincter. J Urol 84:86, 1960

14. Tanagho EA, Smith DR, Meyers FH, et al: Mechanism of urinary incontinence. II. Technique for surgical repair of incontinence. J Urol 101:305, 1969

15. Jeffs RD: Exstrophy of bladder. In Campbell MH (ed): Urology, pp 1688–1692, Philadelphia, WB Saunders, 1979

114

THE ARTIFICIAL SPHINCTER IN THE MANAGEMENT OF INCONTINENCE IN THE MALE

F. Brantley Scott, M.D.

Professor, Division of Urology, Roy and Lillie Cullen Department of Urologic Research, Baylor College of Medicine and St. Luke's Episcopal Hospital, Houston, Texas

Urologic Clinics of North America—Vol. 5, No. 2, June 1978
Symposium on Male Incontinence

Though the artificial sphincter was developed for primary application to patients with neurogenic bladder dysfunction,[1-4] it has had effective application in the male who has suffered urinary incontinence secondary to urethral injury. The data presented in this paper concentrate on those males who have suffered injury to the continence mechanism as the result of radical prostatectomy, transurethral prostatectomy, posterior urethral surgery, or accidental trauma resulting in pelvic fractures and disruption of the urethra.

The following are the objectives imperative for the development and application of this prosthesis for urinary incontinence:

1. A prosthesis that could be used in both males and females.
2. A prosthesis that would produce urethral occlusion effective for urinary control, but which could so open as to allow free voiding with no interference of flow.
3. A prosthesis that would open automatically should unphysiologic bladder pressures develop owing to detrusor contraction, but that would automatically increase its occlusion should stress occur.
4. The occlusive mechanism and the pressures applied should be automatic and inherent within the design of the prothesis itself.
5. Should the prothesis fail, the patient should be no worse off than before.
6. Its implantation should not require extensive alteration of the urinary tract.
7. It should allow subsequent repeated endoscopic procedures if necessary.
8. It should not interfere with sexual function in either the male or the female.
9. It should be dependable for the life of the patient.

THE GENITOURINARY PROSTHETIC SPHINCTER

The artificial sphincter that will be described in this article includes two different types. Though the first type, which I initially implanted in June 1972, has

Roy and Lillie Cullen Department of Urologic Research
Division of Urology
Baylor College of Medicine
Houston, Texas 77030

undergone many improvements and modifications in its construction and in the techniques used for its fabrication, it remains essentially unchanged from its original concept. This artificial sphincter has been manufactured by American Medical Systems in Minneapolis, Minnesota, and has been given the code number AS721.

The AMS AS721 Artificial Sphincter. The AS721 (Fig. 1) consists of four main parts:

1. An occlusive cuff, which encircles the urethra.
2. A reservoir, which contains the fluid used to activate the device.
3. An inflating mechanism.
4. A deflating mechanism.

The deflating and inflating mechanisms each contain two valves; these valves control the direction of flow of the fluid as the patient squeezes the device. The number 4 valve on the deflating side also controls the pressure that is applied to the urethra. This valve bleeds off excessive pressure regardless of how many times the patient squeezes the pumps, which are placed in either the scrotum or the labia for easy accessibility and manipulation by the patient. The pressure generated by

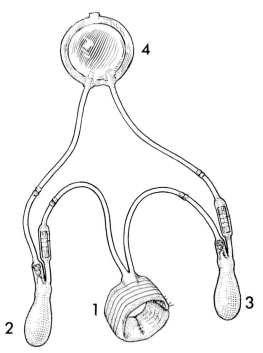

Fig. 1. The AMS AS721 artificial sphincter consists of (*1*) cuff that encloses the urethra, (*2*) inflating pump, (*3*) deflating pump, and (*4*) reservoir that houses fluid and serves to equalize pressures of stress. The valves control direction of flow and the occlusive pressure.

the number 4 valve is that pressure sufficient for occlusion but less than the patient's diastolic blood pressure, allowing perfusion of blood into the tissues contained and occluded by the cuff.

To operate this device the patient squeezes the pump, which has been placed in the scrotum or labia. Squeezing the pump, which lies in a subcutaneous position, transfers fluid from the reservoir into the cuff. The number of squeezes is not critical since excessive squeezing merely forces fluid on through the deflating pumping mechanism and back into the reservoir. The number 4 valve maintains occlusive pressure against the urethra until the patient is ready to urinate. Then the patient squeezes the pump in the left side of the scrotum or labia. This transfers fluid from the cuff into the reservoir and creates a vacuum inside the cuff, thus removing all occlusive pressure from the urethra. Once urination has been completed, the patient then repeats this process. Because of the intra-abdominal placement of the reservoir, the pressures of stress generated against the bladder are offset by the same pressures generated against the reservoir. This arrangement is necessary to permit a temporary transient increase in pressure in the cuff exactly equal to those pressures created by stress. The ideal location is achieved by attaching the reservoir to the posterior rectus sheath, placing the reservoir between the rectus muscles and the peritoneum.

The AMS AS742 Artificial Sphincter. The AS742 (Fig. 2) appears to be a much simpler prosthesis and apparently more reliable than the AS721. It consists of the following parts:

1. A cuff that encircles and occludes the urethra.
2. A balloon that delivers to the cuff sufficient pressure to close the urethra, but insufficient pressure to strangulate the blood supply within the urethra. The balloon, which is implanted inside the abdominal muscular cavity, also equalizes intravesical and intracuff pressure during stress, so as to prevent stress incontinence.
3. A pump, which when squeezed in its intrascrotal or intralabial position activates the control assembly causing the cuff to open.
4. The control assembly, which has three functions:
   a. It transfers fluid from the cuff to the balloon in response to squeezing the pump, thus releasing pressure against the urethra to allow voiding.
   b. It slowly allows the fluid in the balloon to then return to the cuff for repressurization, giving the patient sufficient time to void before repressurization and automatic closure.
   c. It releases pressure from the cuff in response to high unphysiologic bladder pressures produced only by detrusor contractions.

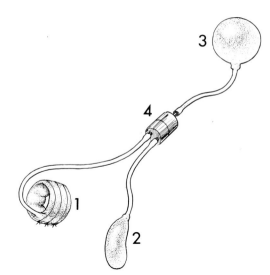

Fig. 2. The AMS AS742 artificial sphincter consists of (1) cuff, (2) pump, (3) balloon, which controls pressures at a level safe for arterial circulation, yet provides occlusion, and which also senses changes of pressures owing to stress, and (4) a control assembly that opens the cuff in response to pumping and closes the cuff automatically.

To operate the AS742, the patient simply squeezes the pump several times, causing a transfer of all the fluid from the cuff and pump into the balloon. This, of course, opens the cuff, allowing urination. The control assembly contains a resistor that allows the fluid to slowly return from the balloon back into the cuff and pump for automatic closure.

Basically, both of these prostheses are produced with silicone rubber. The production process avoids all vulcanized seams whenever possible, and the integrity of the device is checked by both pressurization and electrical detection, as part of the quality control procedures. It is important for the surgeon to take great care in avoiding any scratching of the surface of the prosthesis, which can weaken it; this is particularly true of the balloon.

While the automatic closure feature of the AS742 represents one of its primary benefits, this also can be its only disadvantage. Because of this feature, it cannot be left in the ''open'' position, and since the pressures applied automatically are greater than venous pressure, this prosthesis cannot be used around the urethra coincident with urethral reconstruction, since in such cases impairment of venous drainage could result in poor healing. This device is particularly suited, however, for that group of patients presented in this article.

PATIENTS TREATED

Etiology of Sphincter Injury. Forty-one patients have received one or the other of the artificial sphincters described. Eleven patients had total urinary incontinence as a result of radical prostatectomy. Seventeen patients had incontinence as a result of sphincter injury created by transurethral prostatectomy. Ten patients were incontinent as a result of pelvic fracture causing disruption of the membranous urethra. Three patients received injury to the sphincter as a result of urethral surgery: (1) a 30-year-old man who had injury to the posterior urethral valve resected during infancy, (2) an 11-year-old boy who received injury to the sphincteric mechanism as a result of a Y-V plasty, and (3) a 37-year-old man who received injury to the sphincteric mechanism caused by multiple transurethral procedures performed in an effort to eradicate prostatitis.

Previous Procedures. There were 14 patients who had undergone previous operative procedures in an effort to cure their urinary incontinence. The procedures that had been performed on these patients included transfer of the gracilis muscle around the urethra, the transcrural procedure described by Kaufman, the implantation of the Berry prosthesis, the implantation of the silicone pillow prostheses (Kauman prosthesis), the placement of a fascial sling around the urethra, the Tanagho procedure, the spiral Flock's flap procedure, as well as the injection of teflon paste around the urethra and the reduction urethroplasty procedure described by Leadbetter. All these procedures had, of course, contributed to the difficulty of applying the artificial sphincter because of the previous surgical dissection and fibrosis.

Preliminary Treatment. A number of procedures were necessary in order to prepare the patient so that he would be a suitable candidate for the inflatable artificial sphincter. Several patients who had post radical prostatectomy incontinence also had obstruction owing to fibrosis in the area of the membranous urethra. In order to improve the urodynamics of their voiding, these patients underwent transurethral resection of a segment of this fibrotic stricture until an excellent flow rate was obtained, before implanting the artificial sphincter. Two patients underwent urethral diverticulectomy to eliminate the stagnating infected urine puddling in a large diverticulum. Two patients required removal of the silicone-gel prosthesis before they were suitable candidates for the artificial sphincter because of an infected eroding prosthesis, and because of the obstructive, yet incontinent, effect of the prosthesis. Several patients previously had, and continue to have, chronic urinary tract infections resistant to treatment. One of these persists in its infection because of multiple prostatic calculi, and another because of prostatic urethral diverticula. All patients were treated for their infection, and in those who had no infections, prophylactic antibiotics were administered. Garamycin as well as Staphcillin are administered to achieve a satisfactory blood level prior to the operation. Parenteral administration at least three hours prior to the surgery, during the surgery, and for 24 hours following the surgery was sufficient. Those patients who had chronically infected urinary tracts were treated for a minimum of seven days prior to the operative procedures, and no operative procedures were performed until two urine cultures disclosed no evidence of bacteria.

EVALUATION

Urodynamic Evaluation. All patients had uroflowmetry in order to ascertain whether or not there was obstruction to the outflow of urine. The great majority of these patients were totally incontinent and, therefore, temporary occlusion of the urethra by a clamp allowed filling of the bladder in order to obtain the urinary flow rate. The post-voiding residual was determined either by direct catheterization, or in some cases, by the post-voiding film on the intravenous pyelogram. Routine cystometry was performed to detect any evidence of bladder instability.

Urethral pressure profilometry was performed in the majority of patients in an effort to detect points of obstruction along the course of the urethra and to assess the severity of the injury to the continence mechanism, though the occlusive effect of the profile catheter gives false high pressures in the area of the sphincter in some patients. In a very few patients, pressure-flow studies were obtained to rule out evidence of obstruction. By obtaining pressure and flow, resistance defined by P/F^2 was calculated. If this figure was greater than 1.0, some surgical procedure was required to treat the obstruction.

Cinefluorography. A voiding cine cystogram was obtained in all cases to detect abnormalities created by urethral diverticula, strictures, and reflux, as well as to aid in the selection of the appropriate site for placement of the occlusive cuff.

Bacteriologic Studies. Of course, all patients had a careful urinalysis, but in addition, serial urine cultures were obtained to detect any evidence of infection. Sensitivity studies were done to aid in selecting the antibiotic of choice in those cases with infection.

Endoscopy. Panendoscopy was done in all cases, not only to evaluate the urinary tract for incidental pathology, but also to aid in the selection of the appropriate site for placement of the occlusive cuff. Panendoscopic evaluation of the post-operative result was performed in some cases, though this is not required as a general follow up procedure.

SURGICAL TECHNIQUE FOR IMPLANTATION

Placement of the Cuff. *Placement Around Bladder Neck.* Most of the males who have received injury to the continence mechanism should have the cuff placed around the bulbous urethra. Placement of the cuff around the bulbous urethra is technically easy in comparison to placement of the cuff around the bladder neck. However, if the bladder neck has not been traumatized, and if the patient is anxious to maintain his fertility, placement of the cuff around the bladder neck will separate the urine from semen, preserving fertility. I have found that if one encounters significant difficulties in dissecting around the bladder neck, that the bladder should be open for direct visualization of the bladder neck during the dissection. However, in most cases, unless there has been extensive trauma and fibrosis in the area of the bladder neck, dissection around the bladder neck can be achieved by the following technique:

A large Foley catheter is placed in the bladder for palpation of the balloon at the bladder neck. The endopelvic fascia adjacent to the bladder neck is opened to allow the introduction of the thumb and the index finger of the left hand. With the thumb and the index finger one can palpate the catheter, the trigone, and, posteriorly, each vas deferens. The trigone can be pinched anteriorly, separating it from the vas deferens. Right angle dissecting scissors can be used to dissect against the fingers, which contain the catheter and the trigone in an anterior position. This then allows dissection precisely between the bladder neck and the ejaculatory mechanism. Dissection in this location will not disturb the ejaculatory or erectile sexual function. Once dissection around the bladder neck has been accomplished, retraction of the bladder neck by means of surgical tape and the introduction of a vein retractor exposes and allows suture ligation of the venous bleeding that usually results from this dissection. The distance around the bladder neck is then measured and a cuff of appropriate length is selected and passed into position. The cuff is secured by means of the sutures lying in its back, thus creating an encircling cuff.

Placement Around Bulbous Urethra. The placement of the cuff around the bulbous urethra is easier (Fig. 3). A perineal incision is preferable and is placed over the posterior bulbous urethra, palpable by means of a urethral balloon created by cutting the finger from a rubber glove and securing this finger to a Robinson catheter (Fig. 3

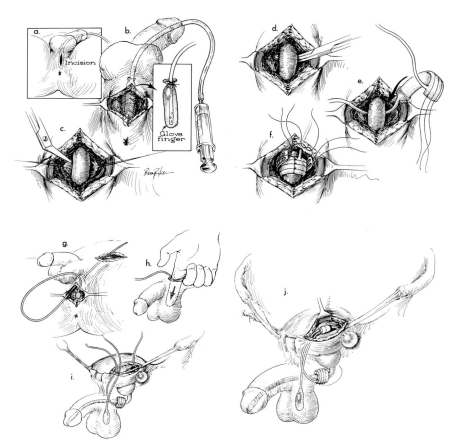

Fig. 3. (a) A perineal incision is placed over the posterior bulbous urethra. (b) The urethra is inflated to facilitate palpation and (c) dissection. (d) The space around the urethra is enlarged sufficiently to allow (e) passage of the cuff, which is tied and then (f) enclosed by a metal sheath for protection. (g) A special needle carries tubing through subcutaneous tissues for proper position in an inguinal wound. (h) Blunt dissection creates a space for the pump. (i) The balloon is placed in the prevesical space between the bladder and the pubic ramus. (j) The control assembly is attached after excess tubing is trimmed. The prosthesis is then tested to prove continence and appropriate function.

A and B). Inflation of the urethra by means of air contained within this balloon allows ready palpation of the posterior bulbous urethra and facilitates dissection. In addition, this technique of inflating the urethra helps to define precisely the plane of dissection between the urethra and the adjacent pelvic fascia (Fig. 3 C). The bulbo cavernosus muscles are divided in the mid line and retracted laterally, exposing the urethra and its enclosing spongiosum. Dissection laterally exposes the pelvic fascia immediately adjacent to the urethra. Traction on a stay suture placed on each side of the urethra in this fascia delivers the urethra into the wound. Tension created by traction on this fascia also helps to define the cleavage plane of dissection that needs to be followed by delicate dissection between the urethra and this adjacent fascia (Fig. 3 C).

The 12 o'clock position of the urethra in this area is quite friable and thin. It should be treated with care and delicate dissection. Upon completion of dissection around the urethra, the urethra is inflated with fluid (after removing the glove finger balloon) to check to be sure that there has been no inadvertent injury to the urethra.

The space around the urethra needs to be enlarged until it will readily accept the cuff (Fig. 3D). A cuff of appropriate length is pulled into position and secured by tying the sutures lying in its back (Fig. 3E). In addition to enclosing the urethra with the inflatable cuff, a malleable stainless steel strip of metal enclosed in silicone rubber is also secured around the cuff, also by tying sutures lying within its back (Fig. 3F). This metal enclosure serves to protect the cuff, so that upon sitting the patient does not compress the cuff, causing the artificial sphincter to open.

The tubing of the cuff is secured to the end of a tubing needle (Fig. 3G), and the tubing needle is used to carry the silicone rubber tubing of the cuff through a subcutaneous position anterior to the pubis into a left inguinal incision. The left inguinal incision also allows blunt dissection into the left side of the scrotum for placement of the pump (Fig. 3H). The inguinal canal is opened, as well as the floor of the inguinal canal, to allow the introduction of the dissecting finger to create a space between the bladder and the pubic ramus for the introduction of the pressure controlling balloon (Fig.

3*J*). After closure of the inguinal canal, the excess tubing coming from the balloon, the cuff, and the pump is trimmed and then connected to the appropriate three connectors that extend from the metal control assembly (Fig. 3*J*). The tubing is secured to these connectors by ligation with triple zero prolene suture. Before making these connections, however, the appropriate volume of fluid is placed inside the prosthesis according to the directions of the manufacturer. Throughout the dissection the wound is sprayed with an antibiotic solution of 50,000 units of bacitracin and 1 gm of Kantrex dissolved in 300 cc of physiologic saline. The wound is closed in layers. No drains should be used and the skin should be closed with a running subcuticular technique.

TESTING THE PROSTHESIS AND THE RESULTS OF THE SURGERY

Intraoperative testing should be done by filling the patient's bladder with fluid. Once the bladder is full, pressure is applied to the lower abdomen in such a manner as to create as much pressure over the patient's bladder as is applied over the area of the balloon. This is accomplished by placing multiple towels stacked on the patient's abdomen, so that the pressure applied to the abdomen is distributed over a wide area. There should be no leakage, regardless of the pressure applied, and while applying continuous pressure, the pump should be squeezed to open the device to then appreciate the immediate flow of urine from the bladder. Another method of testing the prosthesis intraoperatively is to do direct sphincterometry by inflating the distal urethra. The artificial sphincter should hold fluid distal to the cuff until the pressure in the urethra exceeds the pressure in the balloon, which will range from 60 to 90 cm of water pressure. If equipment and facilities are available for intraoperative urethral pressure profilometry using sterile techniques, urethral pressure profilometry will show the occlusion of the urethra with a pressure ranging from 60 to 90 cm.

RESULTS

Although the first AS721 prosthesis was implanted in June 1972, the earliest successful implantation in this particular group was in February 1973. The most recently implanted prosthesis in this series was placed in November 1977. The patient who received the implantation in February 1973 continues to do well five years following his implant.

The definition of success is that the patient should be sufficiently dry that he does not require a pad. He must be continent even with stress, and he must be able to urinate easily with a good urinary stream. Using these criteria, the results to date show 10 successful patients out of those 17 patients who received the AS721 (59 percent success) (Table 1). Twenty-two of 24 patients who received the AS742 are successful (92 percent) (Table 2). The combined overall results of both prostheses showed a 78 percent success rate (Tables 3, 4, 5, and 6). According to etiology, the patients who were incontinent as a result of urethral surgery or following a radical prostatectomy have achieved a 100 percent success result. The poorest success was achieved in those patients with pelvic fractures causing disruption of the membranous urethra, in which only a 50 percent success rate was achieved. Four of the five failed implantations in those patients with pelvic fractures were initially successful, but infection of the prosthesis became apparent and required its removal. There were six patients in the entire series who required removal of the prosthesis as the result of surgical contamination and infection. It is significant that all these had had chronic urinary tract infections that were resistant to therapy. In these cases the infection cleared upon use of antibiotics only for the surgery, but immediately upon withdrawal of antibiotics, the urines resumed their previously infected state with the same previous bacteria. These patients are, therefore, particularly vulnerable to infection.

There were a total of nine failures (Table 7). Six of these were because of an infection. Two of the patients had urinary leakage as a result of a fibrotic urethra that resisted the occlusive effect of the cuff. One of these was a patient whose bladder neck was fibrotic because of previous transurethral resection of the prostate, and the other had fibrosis caused by extensive pelvic fracture and injury. It is highly probable that both of these patients could be made continent by revision of the sphincter and

TABLE 1. Results of AS721 Prosthesis

Etiology	Total No.	No. Successful	Percentage
Radical Prostatectomy	3	3	100%
TUR	8	4	50%
Pelvic Fracture	5	2	40%
Urethral Surgery	1	1	100%
Overall	17	10	59%

TABLE 2. Results of AS742 Prosthesis

Etiology	Total No.	No. Successful	Percentage
Radical Prostatectomy	8	8	100%
TUR	9	9	100%
Pelvic Fracture	5	3	60%
Urethral Surgery	2	2	100%
Overall	24	22	92%

TABLE 3. Prosthesis Results for Incontinence Caused by Transurethral Prostatectomy

| Patient | Prior Surgical Procedures | Artificial Sphincter Implanted | Flow Rate | | Implant Result |
			Preop	Postop	
O.W.	None	2/20/73	None	Good	F
L.S.	None	2/27/73	Good	Good	S
M.B.	None	3/15/73	Good	Good	S
R.H.	None	4/19/73	Good	Good	F
M.J.	Berry Prosthesis Muscle Sling Procedure Muscle Sling Procedure Silicone Gel Implant Silicone Gel Implant	1/28/74	Good	Good	S
R.F.	Reduction Urethroplasty Ischial Fascial Flap Flock's Spiral Flap	2/26/74	Good	Good	S
C.C.	Transcrural Procedure Kaufman Prosthesis Tanagho Procedure	11/22/74	Good	Good	S
G.F.	None	11/25/74	Poor	Poor	F
J.U.	None	11/12/75	Good	Good	S
R.H.	None	1/30/76	Good	Good	S
G.G.	None	2/19/76	Poor	Poor	S
V.F.	Kaufman Prosthesis	4/14/76	Good	Good	S
O.K.	Transcrural Procedure Kaufman Prosthesis	6/2/76	Good	Good	S
A.D.	None	6/11/76	Good	None	S
M.R.	Kaufman Prosthesis	7/23/76	Good	None	F
L.S.	None	5/19/77	Good	None	S
H.L.	None	11/8/77	Good	Good	S

TABLE 4. Prosthesis Results for Incontinence Caused by Radical Prostatectomy

| Patient | Prior Operative Attempts | Artificial Sphincter Implanted | Flow Rate | | Implant Result |
			Preop	Postop	
T.S.	None	2/15/74	Poor	None	S
V.S.	Kaufman Prosthesis Kaufman Prosthesis Kaufman Prosthesis	3/5/75	Good	Good	S
W.S.	None	8/20/75	Good	Good	S
L.W.	Kaufman Prosthesis	3/12/76	Good	Good	S
J.S.	None	11/10/76	Good	None	S
F.B.	None	12/7/76	Good	Good	S
A.B.	Kaufman Prosthesis	3/15/77	Good	Good	S
R.B.	Perineal Plication of Muscle Kaufman Prosthesis Kaufman Prosthesis	4/29/77	Good	None	S
E.G.	None	5/12/77	Good	Good	S
C.O.	Kaufman Prosthesis	9/27/77	Good	Good	S
E.G.	None	10/6/77	Good	Good	S

by placing the cuff around the bulbous urethra rather than the bladder neck. Another patient had failure because of an instrumental injury that lacerated the urethra and exposed the artificial sphincter, which had been placed around the bulbous urethra. This injury occurred in another institution where the patient was being treated for cardiac problems. The injury to the urethra was created by a catheter guide used by an individual who was not aware of the artificial sphincter.

CASE REPORT

F.B. is a 51-year-old man who underwent radical retropubic prostatectomy in October 1975 for adenocarcinoma of the prostate. Subsequently, this patient was totally incontinent, as well as impotent. Cystometry was normal. Uroflowmetry revealed no evidence of significant obstruction, though the peak flow was slightly less than normal (Fig. 4). Cystoscopic findings disclosed the presence of fibrosis in the area of the membranous urethra, which did not close completely at this point. There was no evidence of obstruction and the bladder

TABLE 5. Prosthesis Results for Incontinence Caused by Pelvic Fracture Injury

Patient	Prior Surgical Procedures	Artificial Sphincter Implanted	Flow Rate		Implant Result
			Preop	Postop	
R.S.	None	5/24/74	Good	Good	F
R.P.	None	2/27/75	Good	Good	F
S.H.	Perineal Procedure	8/15/75	Poor	Poor	S
B.H.	None	11/26/75	Good	Good	F
J.D.	None	12/23/75	Good	Good	F
G.S.	Teflon Injections	2/4/76	Good	Poor	F
J.W.	None	8/9/76	Good	Good	S
R.S.	None	12/22/76	Poor	Poor	S
J.C.	None	7/5/77	Good	Poor	S
G.F.	Bladder Neck Plication	9/27/77	Good	Good	S

TABLE 6. Prosthesis Results for Incontinence Caused by Urethral Surgery

Patient	Prior Surgical Procedures	Artificial Sphincter Implanted	Flow Rate		Implant Result
			Preop	Postop	
R.T.	None	9/15/75	Good	Good	S
B.M.	None	7/15/76	Good	None	S
J.M.	Perineal Procedure	5/17/77	Poor	Poor	S

TABLE 7. Causes of Failure

Infected Prosthesis	6
Fibrotic Urethra	2
Instrument Injury to Urethra	1

was essentially normal in appearance. There was no evidence of recurrence or persistence of his carcinoma.

The AS742 was implanted on December 7, 1976, using the technique described in this article. After the skin was completely closed from the implantation of the artificial sphincter, and the patient had been tested for his continence, an incision was then made in the mid line and an inflatable erectile prosthesis was implanted for the treatment of his impotence. The patient has subsequently had excellent urinary control and has resumed sexual function. His post-operative follow up evaluation in March 1977 disclosed normal urethral mucosa upon panendoscopic examination. The urethra closed in a sphincteric manner. Upon opening of the artificial sphincter, there was complete opening of the urethra. Post-operative uroflowmetry was considerably better than that which had been recorded before implantation, thus proving that the artificial sphincter is not interfering with urinary flow (Fig. 5). Urethral pressure profilometry with the artificial sphincter in the open, and then closed, positions (Fig. 6) discloses the location of the artificial sphincter and shows that the maximum pressure being exerted against the urethra is at a safe level, allowing blood perfusion of the occluded urethral tissues. The patient has continued to do well sexually and has complete urinary control.

DISCUSSION

Both of the artificial sphincters are manufactured by American Medical Systems. The AS721 and the AS742 have proved to be effective in the control of urinary incontinence. The AS742, however, is proving to be more effective and more reliable for this particular type of urinary incontinence. Based on my experience in the use of these two prosthetic devices in 243 other patients with urinary incontinence, it appears that the AS742 is generally more effective and more reliable in other

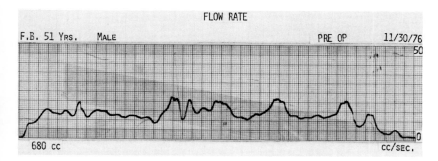

Fig. 4. Preoperative flow rate shows no obstruction.

groups of patients as well. The most noteworthy exception is that group of patients who must, during a period of recovery, keep the artificial sphincter in an open position; this can be accomplished only with the AS271.

Infection. The most significant complication is infection in the area of the prosthesis. The patient who has resistant urinary tract infection requiring the continuous administration of antibiotics is more prone to develop an infection. To achieve a higher percentage of success, it is obvious that this group of patients should be eliminated. However, we have been successful in achieving continence in a number of patients who have had, and still have, chronic urinary tract infections. Therefore, at this time it would appear that such unfortunate patients still

deserve a chance to at least be continent. However, preparatory procedures to eliminate obstructive uropathy as well as other conditions, such as strictures and diverticula, should be done in an attempt to eliminate chronic infections. The patients in this series in whom this could not be accomplished were generally those who had severe injuries leading to various distortions of the urethra caused by pelvic fracture injury.

The manifestations of an infection associated with the prosthesis have been different than what one might expect from infections elsewhere related to surgical procedures. In the presence of a prosthetic device, the body can very often handle the infection rather well for long periods of time. Ultimately, however, the body will reject the prosthesis along with the infection, and this usually occurs by the presence of an erosion of the cuff into the urethra, or extrusion of the pump through the scrotal skin. One of the patients in this series developed an erosion of the pump through the scrotal skin, nine months following his implantation. There was no evidence of any erosion or signs of infection in any other area of the prosthesis, other than that associated with the pump erosion in the scrotum. It was my feeling that this patient had a contamination of the pump and that this smouldered for nine months before finally manifesting itself by an erosion. With the administration of prophylactic antibiotics, the signs of infections may be suppressed for some time following surgery. The earliest that an infection was apparent in this series was three weeks following surgery. Most patients who have a prosthesis-associated infection will present with an erosion within three months of their implantation.

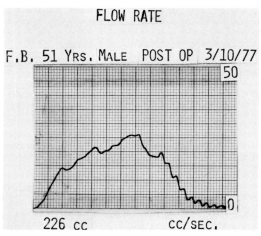

FLOW RATE

F.B. 51 YRS. MALE   POST OP 3/10/77

226 CC   CC/SEC.

Fig. 5. Postoperative flow rate shows no interference of flow by the artificial sphincter.

Urodynamics. Urodynamically, these patients have done excellently. Generally speaking, the voiding flow

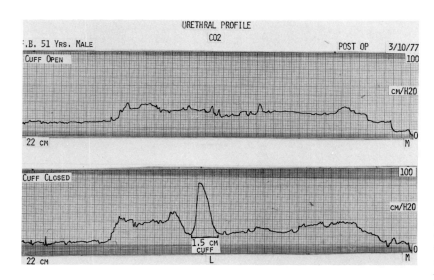

URETHRAL PROFILE
CO2

.B. 51 YRS. MALE   POST OP   3/10/77

CUFF OPEN   100

                                      CM/H20

22 CM   M   0

CUFF CLOSED   100

                                      CM/H20

1.5 CM CUFF

22 CM   L   M   0

Fig. 6. Urethral pressure profilometry shows the open, then occlusive pressures produced by the artificial sphincter. Note the maximum pressure applied to the urethra is less than the patient's diastolic blood pressure.

rates in these patients have been as good, or better, since surgery than they were before surgery. The flow rates that were obtained in these patients clearly proved that this prosthesis was effective in not only producing continence, but in doing so without interfering with urination, one of its unique advantages.

Long Range Results. I feel that all of the objectives stated in the introductory paragraph are being achieved by this prosthesis. More time will be required, however, to prove that the prosthesis has a long life reliability. The manufacturer has test-cycled the prosthetic device and has shown that the prosthesis can be cycled over 80,000 times without deterioration in its function. This would be equivalent to the patient urinating four times a day for over 50 years. This fact, coupled with the fact that one of the patients in this series has had the artificial sphincter functioning for four years and nine months, without any evidence of urethral necrosis, without any evidence of urethral obstruction, and with no problems of urinary tract infections, all suggests that this prosthesis should work indefinitely. Silicone rubber is nonreactive and one of the most inert synthetic prosthetic materials available for medical implantation. Since it has been in use for 15 to 20 years in other prosthetic implants, it can be assumed that it will probably continue functioning properly indefinitely.

Cost. The cost of the production of the prosthesis has been significant, and the manufacturer's charge for this prosthesis seems rather high, though by comparison to other prosthetic implants, as for example the cardiac pacemaker, the price does not seem out of line. It is hoped that the manufacturer will be able to reduce this price, should there be an increase in volume. Unfortunately, however, there does not appear to be a sufficient population that needs the artificial sphincter, for the cost to come down. With the additional requirements of fulfilling FDA regulations on devices, as well as product liability insurance requirements, it is likely that the cost of this prosthesis may indeed increase.

The results achieved in this series of patients have been most gratifying. Even greater has been the gratification received from the "thanks" expressed by the these patients, many of whom had undergone multiple prior operations before finally achieving successful continence.

ACKNOWLEDGMENTS

The development of these prostheses required the essential contributions of the engineering staff in American Medical Systems, both in new engineering design, as well as in new construction technology. These contributions include those especially made by G. W. Timm, J. H. Burton, and M. A. Mikulich.

REFERENCES

1. Burton, J.H., Mikulich, M.A., Timm, G.W., et al.: Development of urethral occlusive techniques for restoration of urinary continence. Med. Instrum., Vol. II, No. 4, July-August, 1977
2. Scott, F.B., Bradley, W.E., and Timm, G.W.: Treatment of urinary incontinence by an implantable prosthetic sphincter. Urology 1:252–259, 1973
3. Scott, F.B., Bradley, W.E., Timm, G.W., et al.: Treatment of incontinence secondary to myelodysplasia by an implantable prosthetic urinary sphincter. South Med 66:987–990, 1973
4. Scott, F.B., Bradley, W.E., and Timm, G.W.: Treatment of urinary incontinence by implantable prosthetic urinary sphincter. J Urol 112:75, 1974

Commentary: Surgery for Male Urinary Incontinence

Reg Bruskewitz and Shlomo Raz

The inflatable urinary tract artificial sphincter initially introduced by Brantley Scott, William Bradley, and Gerald Timm represents an outstanding innovation in the surgical treatment of urinary incontinence. The article selected is an update of the inventors' experience, which appeared in *Urologic Clinics of North America* in June 1978 under the title "The Artificial

Sphincter in the Management of Incontinence in the Male.'' This concise article evaluates the results of the treatment of incontinence in males using the AMS 721 and AMS 742 sphincters.*

SPHINCTER FUNCTION AND DYSFUNCTION

The sphincteric mechanism in the male urethra is composed of a proximal unit that is largely smooth muscle with a circular bulk concentration of tissue about the bladder neck with extension over the prostatic urethra to the verumontanum. The distal sphincteric mechanism is composed of an inner layer of smooth muscle tissue and the overlying urogenital diaphragm, which is a striated muscle component and under voluntary control. Both sphincters function in the prevention of incontinence during cough or stress. In the male, damage to or malfunction of both sphincter components, as may occur following open or transurethral surgery, generally results in total incontinence. Damage to either the proximal or distal sphincter alone does not. Preexisting damage to one component (which often is not appreciated preoperatively) may lead to incontinence when the other is surgically removed. For example, in the diabetic patient with peripheral neuropathy, after transurethral resection of the prostate and the bladder neck for obstructing prostatic adenoma, the distal sphincter is left intact. However, the distal sphincter may not function properly because of diabetic neuropathy, and the patient becomes incontinent postoperatively.

ETIOLOGY OF MALE INCONTINENCE

Scott notes that in the male, artificial urinary sphincters have their widest application in patients suffering from sphincter dysfunction following surgical injury to the urethral sphincters, including injury following prostatic surgery (either open or transurethral) or overvigorous Y-V plasty of the bladder neck. Patients who have suffered pelvic fracture with resulting incontinence and patients with myelomeningocele and low urethral closing pressures secondary to lack of urethral innervation are other patients in whom this device is frequently useful. Patients with other types of neurologic disease, such as paraplegia, are less frequently found to be suitable candidates for an artificial sphincter.

PREOPERATIVE PREPARATION AND SELECTION

It is necessary to have thorough preoperative evaluation and preparation before placement of an anti-incontinence device. The urodynamic evaluation includes a cystometrogram to evaluate bladder stability, capacity, and voiding pressure. Patients with stable bladders (no hyperreflexia) and normal detrusor contractions are good candidates provided they have no obstruction to voiding. Patients with detrusor hyperreflexia are less ideal in that the elevation of bladder pressure with each contraction may be greater than the presure with which the artificial sphincter compresses the urethra (*i.e.,* incontinence

* American Medical Systems, Inc., 3312 Gorham, Minneapolis, MN 55426.

will persist). The hyperreflexia must be abolished or greatly reduced, a task that is often difficult to accomplish. In bladder areflexia, the patient must be able to empty the bladder completely.

Cystometry may be performed in combination with pelvic floor electromyography (EMG) or cystourethrography to rule out obstruction to flow. Bladder pressure during voiding should not exceed 40 cm of water pressure, and the EMG should be electrically silent during voiding. Urethral resistance may be estimated by computing bladder pressure/flow^2 (P/F^2) at the moment of peak flow; P/F^2 should not exceed 0.5.

Despite the fact that these patients are incontinent, if there is any increased resistance to flow, increased postvoid residual urine, elevated detrusor pressures during voiding, a flow curve indicative of obstruction, or failure to open the external sphincter on EMG or radiographically, surgical procedures must be peformed to correct the situation.

In the male, transurethral resection of the bladder neck, external sphincterotomy, or both are indicated in cases where the sphincter is dyssynergic, fails to relax completely, or is fibrotic. In cases of previous external sphincterotomy or damage to the efferent pudendal nerves, fibrosis may be the cause of obstruction at the external sphincter. Anterior urethral stricture must be treated in appropriate fashion, again to diminish postvoid residual and improve the flow. Only after the patient has been rendered totally incontinent and voids with low resistance or residual urine can artificial sphincter placement be considered. Urodynamic studies should be repeated after the surgical procedures to ascertain that this result has been achieved and remains stable over time. External sphincterotomies must be complete, bladder neck contractures must not recontract, and anterior urethral strictures must not restricture. If obstruction recurs after insertion of the artificial sphincter, it can be disastrous.

We do not exclude patients with small bladder capacities from consideration for placement of a Scott prosthesis. Bladder capacity can be diminished secondary to longstanding urinary diversion and absence of normal daily bladder distantion by urine or secondary to continuous incontinence with negligible urethral closing pressures, resulting in insufficient regular bladder distention. Patients who have small bladder capacity for this reason generally respond to a program of progressive bladder distention using intermittent catheterization.

Patients with small bladder capacity due to a contracted bladder with diminished bladder compliance secondary to fibrosis or trabeculation of the bladder wall may occasionally have their bladder capacity enlarged with progressive distention. More frequently, however, such patients require enterocystoplasty. If the patients end up with a good flow of urine, persistent incontinence, improved bladder capacity, and low residual urines, they may be considered for placement of an artificial sphincter. If enterocystoplasty results in retention, intermittent catheterization should be instituted instead. Sphincters are usually not placed in patients who we anticipate will need intermittent catheterization, for fear of damaging the urethra at the level of the cuff.

Enterocystoplasty must be done as a staged procedure, with the enterocystoplasty and the sphincter placed in different operations to avoid contamination of the operative field by opening the bowel during the placement of the prosthesis. Mucous retention following enterocystoplasty is anticipated and managed by a generous bladder neck Y-V plasty at the time of the enterocystoplasty.

Patients with hyperreflexia can occasionally be considered for placement of a sphincter provided the hyperreflexia is well controlled. Initially, a trial of drugs (parasympatholytic agents or drugs with a combined alpha- and beta-adrenergic effect) is instituted to delay the onset of hyperreflexia and diminish the pressure of contractions (as documented on cystometrogram while the drug is administered).

If drug therapy fails, consideration may be given to a neural block, such as a percutaneous sacral rhizotomy. Neural blocks are not used in myelodysplastic patients because the alteration of bony and neural anatomy prevents accurate blocking. There appears to be no significantly increased risk of fecal incontinence or lower extremity paresis when limited levels of sacral roots are blocked unilaterally. However, unilateral saddle or paravaginal anesthesia may result. The question of impotence following percutaneous sacral rhizotomy is incompletely studied and may constitute a contraindication for sacral blocks in potent males with detrusor hyperreflexia. In the event of impotence, the man of course could be managed with an inflatable or semirigid penile prosthesis. If neural block results in urinary retention, intermittent catheterization may be employed.

If drugs and blocks fail to control hyperreflexia, enterocystoplasty may be considered as a last resort. (Enterocystoplasty for hyperreflexia may result in symptomatic improvement, but generally hyperreflexia persists.)

Most paraplegics have either a balanced bladder or marked detrusor–sphincter dyssynergia requiring an external sphincterotomy and condom drainage. However, a few patients with spinal cord injury have weak or absent detrusor contractions and may be considered for artificial sphincter implantation.

SPHINCTER PLACEMENT

Briefly, we would like to reemphasize two points. Our experience with the AMS sphincter parallels that of Scott with regard to the incidence of prosthesis infection. Patients who have urinary tract infection at the time of the surgical procedure are at a greatly increased risk of subsequent infection of the prosthesis, and it is mandatory that infection be cleared in advance of the operative procedure. Even though the infection lies within the urinary tract and the placement of the sphincter is outside the tract, there is a strong correlation between urinary tract infection and subsequent prosthesis infection.

In males with intact ejaculatory function, the prosthesis about the bladder neck should be placed with special care to avoid encirclement of the seminal vesicles, as emphasized by Scott. If the prosthetic cuff is placed about the bulbous urethra, ejaculation may be impaired with the 742 model, which automatically reinflates after a limited time. The older 721 model is perhaps more applicable in sexually active males, in whom it is necessary to place the cuff about the bulbous urethra. Ejaculation is unaffected, since the 721 will stay deflated until it is repumped, allowing sufficient time for emission and ejaculation.

RESULTS

Scott reports good results in 92% of his male patients who were given the AMS artificial sphincter. Reports by Kaufman of 60% improvement using the silicone gel prosthesis for male incontinence and 60% cure rate in patients treated with the Rosen prosthesis, by Rosen himself, do not compare. At University of California Los Angeles, the use of the AMS artificial sphincter has resulted in good results in about half the male patients with incontinence. Failures were secondary to continued unimproved incontinence, cuff erosion of the urethra, and infection of the prosthesis, necessitating its removal.

In patients suffering erosion, the pressure within the urethra under the cuff was in the range of 50 cm to 80 cm of water pressure postoperatively. High pressure does not seem to account for all cases of erosion. Previous irradiation of the pelvic area or pelvic surgery was also associated with an increased incidence of erosion, and fibrosis was apparent in the bulbous urethra at the time of placement of the sphincter in these cases. It does not seem apparent that most postsurgical incontinence is stress type and not total, so a sphincter that could have the cuff pressure adjusted postoperatively to the necessary level and be deactivated when the patient was supine or at rest would be beneficial in most patients in that it might allow a decrease in the incident of cuff erosion. The 721 sphincter does allow for long deflation of the cuff but does not permit adjustment of the cuff pressure once the operation is completed.

Male urinary stress incontinence after implantation of the sphincter can be distressing as well. We tested both the 742 and 792B models in the laboratory. Our testing suggests that there is delay in transmission of pressure from the balloon through the resistor to the cuff. Three patients with the 742 model with postoperative stress incontinence were likewise tested. Using simultaneous measurement of the pressures in the bladder and in the bulbous urethra under the cuff, we found that the urethral cuff pressure did not increase with coughing, while the bladder pressure did increase considerably. Based on this limited investigation, it seems that the AMS artificial sphincter does not transfer pressure to the cuff quickly enough to prevent incontinence with cough. Patients who do not experience stress incontinence following placement of the sphincter are likely to have some intact function of the external sphincter.

In the future, we anticipate that advances in artificial sphincters will allow a sphincter that will both have more complete transmission of fluid to the cuff during cough or abdominal strain and a sphincter that allows adjustment of the cuff pressures by external adjustment after the operation is completed. In recent years we have placed more AMS artificial sphincters than Kaufman silicone gel passive urethral compression devices. However, we still find the Kaufman device useful, particularly in the older male patients with postprostatectomy or posttraumatic incontinence and limited manual dexterity, that is, patients who could not be expected to work the pump of the Scott device correctly. With these exceptions, we believe the AMS artificial sphincter represents an advance over the passive urethral compression device.

ANNOTATED BIBLIOGRAPHY

Kaufman JJ, Raz S: Urethral compression procedure for the treatment of male urinary incontinence. J Urol 121:605, 1979

> This review of 184 patients primarily with incontinence after prostatectomy or sphincterotomy outlines indications for passive urethral compression in the treatment of male incontinence. Approximately 60% of patients have a good result. This procedure is an alternative to the AMS sphincter. Included is a description of the technique, wherein the straps of the silicone gel prosthesis are placed about staples placed in pubic bone. This allows better alignment of the silicone gel prosthesis against the bulbous urethra.

McGuire E: Urethral sphincter mechanisms. Urol Clin North Am 6:39, 1979

> This is a methodical, precise discussion of the relative contributions to continence in the male and female of the bladder neck and distal sphincteric mechanisms. The relative importance of each and the manner in which the urethra interacts with the bladder are discussed. Included is a discussion of the use of EMG and urethral profiles to evaluate distal sphincteric function objectively. When these are combined with radiographic studies of the bladder neck, adequate evaluation of the incontinent patient is accomplished.

Overview: Management of Incontinence by Implantation

F. Brantley Scott

The current results of those 104 males whom I have personally treated by implantation with the artificial sphincter model AMS AS791/792 are summarized in Tables 8 and 9.

The urodynamic test that I have used in all cases and found most helpful is uroflowmetry. Cystometry is unnecessary in the patient with postprostatectomy incontinence but imperative for a satisfactory evaluation of the patient with neurologic disease. The urethral pressure profile may indicate normal in an abnormal patient incontinent following prostatectomy; I prefer to examine such a patient's sphincter without anesthesia with the panendoscope where the absence of sphincteric closure confirms the diagnosis. Such patients can typically close the sphincter voluntarily but cannot hold it for more than about 20 sec before it opens despite voluntary intent. Pressure–flow studies need not be done if uroflowmetry is normal, but any

TABLE 8. Age Distribution, Male Incontinence, July 1980

Age (Yr)	No.
5–9	6
10–19	30
20–29	10
30–39	10
40–49	6
50–59	8
60–69	22
70–79	10
80–84	2
Total	104

TABLE 9. Male Incontinence, Results by Category

Etiology	Excellent	Acceptable	Improved	Failure
Myelomeningocele	24	0	4	2
Radical prostatectomy	21	0	1	2
Spinal cord injury	7	1	3	2
Transurethral resection of the prostate	11	1	1	0
Epispadias/exstrophy	8	0	0	0
Urethral injury	4	0	0	1
Pelvic fracture	1	0	1	2
Other	7	0	0	0
Total	83	2	10	9

obstruction of the lower urinary tract should be eliminated or at least reduced to an acceptable level. It is impossible to eliminate all obstruction in some patients, for example, those who have had pelvic trauma. Although at greater risk, such patients can get satisfactory results from the implantation of an artificial sphincter.

I no longer feel that hyperreflexia is a contraindication to implanting the artificial sphincter. A review of my patients who have a neurogenic bladder caused by myelomeningocele showed that 50% had bladder cystometry that indicated hyperreflexia, and yet 24 of 30 patients in this diagnostic category (Table 9) had excellent results. Once the obstructing neurogenic sphincter is ablated, infection eliminated, and repeated instrumentation (intermittent catheterization) stopped, the hyperreflexia, along with bladder trabeculation, disappears in most cases (Fig. 7).

BLADDER CAPACITY

In my experience, a program of progressive bladder distention to enlarge a defunctionalized bladder is a waste of time, even in patients with a neurogenic bladder. If a review of any study done before urinary diversion shows the bladder to be of normal capacity, for example, an old intravenous pyelogram showing a full bladder at rest, then the surgeon can anticipate a good bladder capacity after undiversion. If, on the other hand, the bladder is small as a result of extensive fibrosis and will not expand even under general anesthesia, a cystoplasty should be considered coincident with the implantation of the artificial sphincter. I prefer using lyodura, as popularized by Kelami, rather than bowel because it is a much simpler extraperitoneal procedure that is much less likely to lead to serious complications should there be failure. I have been pleased with this approach (Fig. 8).

NUMERICAL CODING SYSTEM

The first artificial sphincter implanted in June 1972 was called the AMS AS721. The first two numbers in the coding system used by American Medical Systems refer to the year in which the particular device evolved; for example, the AS721 was implanted in 1972. The AS741 (Fig. 9) was developed in 1974, as was the AS742 (Fig. 10). Another device evaluated in 1976 was called the AS761 (Fig. 11). The AS742 was a forerunner of the AS791/792 and is identical in concept, but because improvements completed in 1979 so improved the quality and reliability of this prosthesis, the newer form of this device was given the new designation AS791 or AS792. To further clarify, some surgeons know the AS742B and the AS742C as described in the article selected for this chapter from the *Urologic Clinics of North America;* these are now known as the AS791 and AS792, respectively. The only difference between the 791 and the 792 is that the AS791 has the ports that connect the cuff and pump on the same side opposite the balloon, whereas the AS792 has the pump connection on a side opposite the cuff and balloon. The AS791 is convenient for implantation around the bulbous urethra; the AS792 is appropriate for implantation around the bladder neck.

PERSONAL EXPERIENCE

From June 1972 to August 1980 I implanted approximately 350 artificial sphincters. During this period I had experience with two other types of artificial sphincters manufactured by the American Medical Systems that have not been heretofore reported.

Bruskewitz and Raz note distressing stress incontinence in some of their patients and indicated that the resistor interfered with transmission of fluid to the cuff with cough. They hoped that future advances would allow more complete transmission of fluid during cough. Theoretically, according to their reasoning, both the AS741 and AS761 would allow more transmission of intra-abdominal pressure. The AMS AS741 and the AS761 both had pressure control by means of a balloon, but these devices had the balloon directly connected to the cuff without an interposed resistor mechanism, as is the case with the AS742 and the current AS791/792. The AS761 also allowed

postoperative adjustment of pressure. The AS761 required a great deal of pumping to fill the cuff first and finally the balloon. Reducing the number of pumps on the inflationary mechanism would reduce the pressure actually rendered against the urethra, so depending on how many times it was pumped, the patient could regulate this pressure or leave the device open at night.

Thus, this device satisfied those requirements desired by Bruskewitz and Raz, namely, that intra-abdominal pressure could be transmitted directly to the cuff and the device pressure could be regulated subsequent to surgery. However, both these devices were determined to be inferior to the AS742 and AS791 for a variety of reasons. Even though the patient could regulate the pressure, he generally used all the pressure available to him to be "extra safe." Also, the dryness achieved during

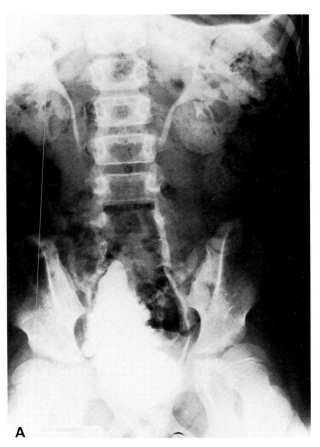

A

Fig. 7. (*A*) Before and (*B*) after bladder flap urethroplasty and artificial sphincter implant. (*C*) Post-voiding film. This young girl had a trabeculated neurogenic bladder due to myelomeningocele, but after her obstruction was relieved by a bladder flap urethroplasty, the bladder became smooth, she began to empty well, and her hyperreflexia disappeared. (*Figure continued on p 1492*)

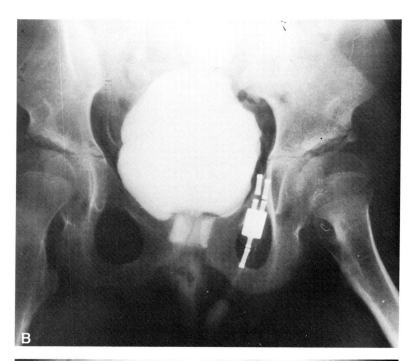

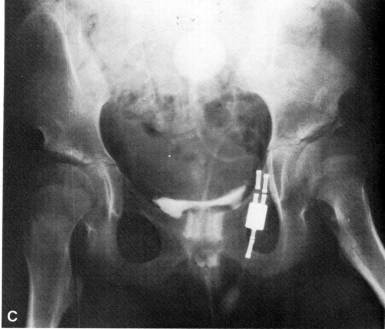

Fig. 7, continued

the day made most patients even more determined to be dry at night; they were not very cooperative.

Although these two devices had in common the fact that the balloon was in direct continuity with the cuff and had no resistor mechanism, the degree of continence achieved in those patients having these devices was definitely not as satisfactory as previously with the AS721 or subsequently with the 791/792. It appeared that any bladder contraction whatsoever caused leakage and some patients in whom I did not expect to see hyperreflexia did leak, seemingly because of uninhibited blad-

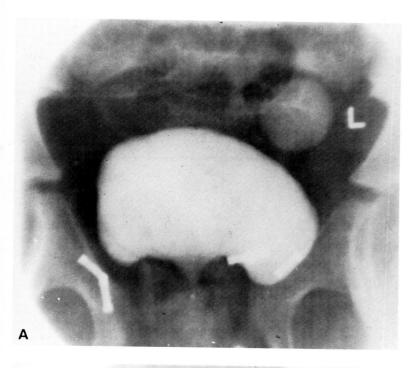

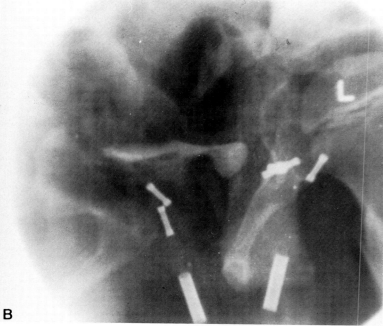

Fig. 8. (*A*) Before and (*B*) after voiding. A good bladder capacity was achieved in this young boy whose exstrophied bladder, previously closed, was quite fibrotic. This was accomplished by suturing a patch of lyodura to the dome of the bladder.

der contractions. Some of these same patients later had their devices changed to the 791/792 and were cured. Therefore, I believe the resistor mechanism tends to dampen the effect of a bladder contraction, yet still provides the safety of releasing pressures that are unphysiologic. Also, even though the intra-abdominal balloon was directly connected to the cuff, some of these patients had stress incontinence, even though the pressure of stress exerted against the balloon should have been transmitted immediately into the cuff.

These findings were difficult to explain, and since it was

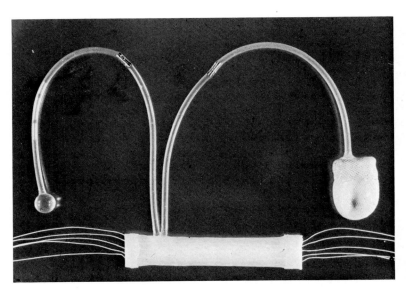

Fig. 9. The AS741 was a device with the cuff connected directly to the balloon. Squeezing the pump transferred enough fluid into the cuff and balloon to pressurize the cuff; a release valve on the pump allowed fluid to return to the pump when the patient wanted to urinate.

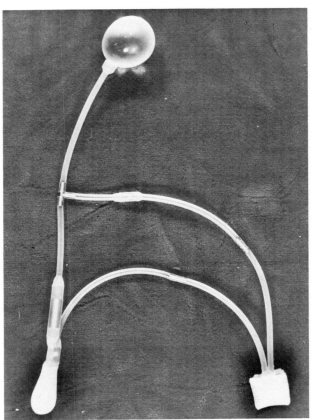

Fig. 10. Squeezing the pump of the AS742 transfers fluid from the cuff to the balloon. The resistor between the balloon and the cuff delays repressurization so the patient has time in which to urinate.

a problem seen only in those patients with the cuff around the bulbous urethra, I too thought that even though the balloon was connected directly to the cuff there must be a delay in pressure transmission, but finally other possible explanations became apparent. One patient was observed to be absolutely dry even though he strained as hard as he could, then he was seen to squirt some urine as he was putting on his trousers. When I called this to his attention, he responded by showing me that he could repeatedly expel squirts of urine and that he did so by contracting the perineal muscles. Since these muscles contract reflexly with coughing, I would expect that some stress incontinence might occur but not because of the absence of pressure transmission across the resistor into the cuff, but rather because the muscles trap and expel urine past the cuff from the posterior bulbous urethra. This experience convinced me that the cuff should be placed posteriorly on the bulbous urethra under the bulbocavernosus muscles. Also, in order to prevent the pressures of sitting on the perineum from displacing fluid from the cuff, a metal protector ("the perineal cuff enclosure," available from the manufacturer) should enclose the urethra.

OPERATIVE OBSERVATIONS

If the resistor between the balloon and the cuff prevented immediate transmission of the pressures of stress, as suggested by Bruskewitz and Raz, then the patient should be just as continent with the balloon placed inside the scrotum rather than intra-abdominally. But my intraoperative observations have shown just the opposite: a cuff enclosing the bulbous urethra was connected to the balloon in succession in the following three ways: (1) cuff to balloon directly with the balloon inside the scrotum, (2) cuff to balloon inside the scrotum but with an interposing resistor, and (3) cuff to balloon inside the abdomen with an interposing resistor. Then pressure was applied intermittently over the lower abdomen to simulate the pressures of coughing. The situation outlined in (1)

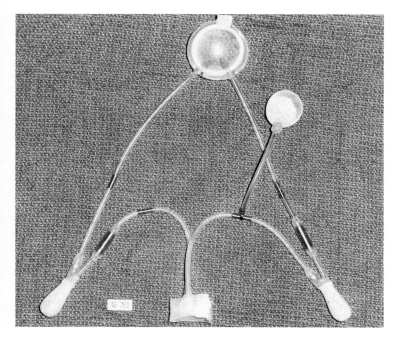

Fig. 11. The AS761 also had the balloon connected directly to the cuff without an intervening resistor. Many squeezes were required to fully inflate the cuff and the balloon; by decreasing the number of squeezes, the balloon could be inflated partially to have lower pressures in selected circumstances.

immediately resulted in leakage. The situation in (2) resulted in leakage but after several "coughs." The situation in (3) did not result in any leakage. Also, intraoperative measures in which simultaneous direct recordings of the pressures in the cuff, bladder, and the balloon indicated that the pressures of stress all changed equally (Fig. 12). Because of these observations, I believe the balloon should be located inside the abdomen, otherwise the pressures of stress will displace fluid from the cuff into the balloon causing the patient to leak. Also, the cuff should be placed around the posteriormost part of the urethra in order to avoid the accumulation of urine in a location where contraction of perineal muscles that normally occurs with coughing would otherwise expel this urine.

BALLOON PRESSURES

My preliminary data on patients with the AS791 around the bulbous urethra (as yet a fairly small group) indicates that the patients with a balloon pressure of only 50 cm to 60 cm of water are no more likely to have stress incontinence than those whose balloon pressures are 80 cm to 90 cm of water. I now routinely use balloons with pressures of only 50 cm to 60 cm of water on patients whose cuffs are placed around the bulbous urethra. If prior surgery prevents the optimal location of the cuff around a most posterior part of the urethra, I warn the patient that probably he will have some slight incontinence but that the degree of leakage is not likely to require the wearing of pads.

On close questioning some of the successful patients with the cuff around the bulbous urethra will state that they leak under certain circumstances—perhaps only when they sneeze, perhaps after a series of coughs, perhaps when they move a certain way, but the degree of this incontinence does not

require a pad. If the patient wears normal clothing and participates in normal physical activities, I consider him a success.

POSTOPERATIVE INCONTINENCE

There are multiple factors to consider in a patient who still has incontinence despite the implantation of the artificial sphincter: (1) there may be unhibited voiding contractions causing the sphincter to open, (2) the cuff size relative to the urethra may be too large, (3) the cuff may not be in a good position around the urethra, (4) the cuff may be too stiff and not efficiently rendering pressure (this was more of a problem with the old style cuff) (Fig. 13), or (5) there may be an urethral erosion. If there is an erosion, three causes should be considered: (1) the cuff pressure was excessive, (2) the urethra or its blood supply was injured at the time of surgery, or (3) the device was contaminated and is chronically infected. The latter diagnosis may not be easy to make, especially if the organism is a coccal organism, since the patient may have little in the way of physical findings even though his device is infected.

PRINCIPLES

There are a number of principles that I have formulated as a result of my experience with these devices. These principles are considered sufficiently important to emphasize by the following list:

1. Avoid any instrumentation of the lower urinary tract within 48 hr of implantation. For example, if urodynamic testing that requires catheterization is to be done, it should be completed and surgery should be delayed for 48 hr, during

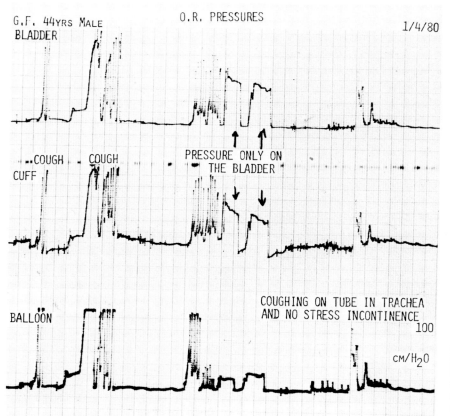

G.F. 44YRS MALE
BLADDER

O.R. PRESSURES

1/4/80

PRESSURE ONLY ON
THE BLADDER

··COUGH ·· COUGH

CUFF

BALLOON

COUGHING ON TUBE IN TRACHEA
AND NO STRESS INCONTINENCE

100

CM/H₂0

Fig. 12. Simultaneous pressure measurements in the balloon, the cuff, and the bladder show the pressures to rise equally in each. The pressures of stress impact against the bladder but also against the bulbous urethral cuff, which holds the urine. The pressures of stress never reach the bulbous urethra in the normal person because the intervening continent natural sphincter prevents this.

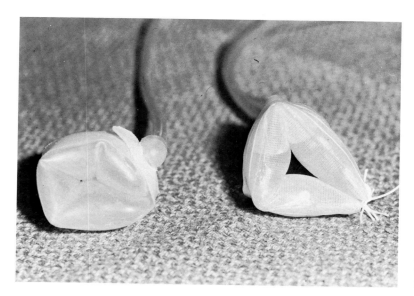

Fig. 13. Comparison of the older Dacron reinforced cuff to the newer pure silicone rubber cuff readily shows that the newer cuff would be more efficient. In some patients, the older cuff did not produce continence regardless of its pressure.

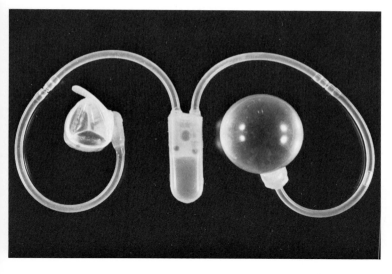

Fig. 14. The new AS800 incorporates the control assembly into the pump; this simplifies the device. Also, this device can now be locked and unlocked repeatedly into deactivated or activated positions by external manipulation.

which time antibiotics should be administered and urine cultures should ensure sterility of the urinary tract.

2. Make sure the patient has a protective blood level of antibiotics at the time of surgery, and this should be continued until there is no postoperative threat of wound infection.

3. Allow recent surgery to completely heal before proceeding with implantation; for example, if the patient needs a urethrotomy to relieve obstruction of a stricture, this should be done either coincident with the implantation or should be done only after complete healing. In other words, do not do a urethrotomy or sphincterotomy and then do the implant only a few days later.

4. Relieve all obstruction before the implantation, since the edema created at the time of the implantation may temporarily interfere with voiding in the early postoperative period. Under these circumstances, a patient who already has obstruction is more likely to have complications.

5. Measure the penile blood pressure, especially in the elderly male. If this pressure is considerably lower than the brachial blood pressure, consider using the lowest balloon pressure available (50 cm to 60 cm of water) and also consider doing the implant in stages by implanting the device but without connecting and pressurizing the cuff until later, after satisfactory recovery.

6. Do not use a balloon with a pressure greater than 90 cm of water, since the incidence of erosions is higher with pressures over 90 cm.

7. After dissection round the urethra, inflate the urethra and inspect carefully for injury before proceeding. If there is injury, repair it. The prosthesis can be implanted then, but not connected. A minor, second-stage procedure can be done later to pressurize the device after complete healing.

8. Avoid the use of surgical drains. The presence of drains provides a ready pathway for bacteria to gain entrance to the wound and contaminate the prosthesis.

The artificial sphincter model AMS AS791/792 appears to be reaching a pinnacle of success as a result of a significant research effort on the part of the engineering staff of the American Medical Systems. A significant improvement could still be made, however, if the device could be made so that it could be left open; this would facilitate healing after coincident reconstructive surgery that many of these patients need. At present, these operations must be done as two staged procedures. Such an improvement will no doubt come about. I hope this can be done without adding to the complexity of the operation. Meanwhile, this prosthesis is the most useful tool available in the treatment of urinary incontinence.

ADDENDUM

This article was written 1 year ago. As predicted, the device now has a modification that allows it to be locked in the open position. This device, which is now named the AS800 (Fig. 14), can be locked by externally squeezing on the upper part of the pump. This displaces a poppet into a locked position. To unlock and thus return the device to a functional condition, one needs only to give a quick squeeze to the lower part of the pump. One can feel a "pop" as the poppet moves out of its locked position.

I have found that the high-risk patient who has poor urethral blood supply can be taught readily to lock the device in the open position at night when the patient's blood pressure would be expected to be low. This may lower the incidence of urethral erosion in such patients. This new modification also now eliminates the need for an activation surgical procedure that many surgeons routinely used in the past.

PART FORTY-FOUR

SURGERY OF THE URETHRA IN THE FEMALE

115

DIAGNOSIS AND TREATMENT OF URETHRAL DIVERTICULA IN THE FEMALE

Joseph N. Ward, M.D., F.R.C.S.(Eng.), F.A.C.S.,
John W. Draper, M.D., F.A.C.S., and
Harold M. M. Tovell, M.D., F.A.C.S.

From the Department of Urology and of Obstetrics and Gynecology Women's Hospital, St. Luke's Hospital Center, New York.

Reprint from *Surgery, Gynecology & Obstetrics,* December, 1967, Vol. 125, 1293-1300

Diverticulum means a byroad or cul-de-sac and, by definition, is a herniation of the mucosa outward between muscle fibers. Diverticula occur in musculotubular organs such as the esophagus, duodenum, bladder, colon, and urethra and are usually classified into the congenital and acquired varieties. Urethral diverticula are most likely acquired. A diverticular wall has no muscle layer and, hence, has no expulsive power. The presence of a small aditus into a diverticulum associated with poor emptying of the diverticulum invariably leads to stasis and infection. Multiple theories as to the pathogenesis of urethral diverticula have been suggested, such as recurring infections in the paraurethral glands, meatal stenosis with increased intraurethral pressure, congenital weak points in the posterior urethral wall, and multiparity. The first theory is the most likely.

We have reviewed the presenting symptomatology, methods of diagnosis and differential diagnosis, complications, and treatment in 35 female patients with proved urethral diverticula. The youngest patient in the series was 19 years old, the oldest 69 years, and the average age at diagnosis was 42 years. Four patients were nulliparous, 2 had 1 child each, 19 had had 2 or more children, and the parity had not been recorded in 10 patients. Almost all patients presented with lower urinary tract symptoms. The average duration of symptoms was 5 years. The most frequently recorded presenting symptoms in the 35 patients were dysuria in 18, stress urinary incontinence in 14, urinary frequency in 14, dribbling incontinence in 10, urgency in 7, dyspareunia in 3, vaginal bleeding in 4, and urethral pain in 3.

In our experience, urethral diverticula will be found most often when the examining surgeon is constantly aware of their possible presence. Diverticula were palpable suburethrally in 21 patients, and pus could be expressed from the external urethral meatus by massaging the suburethral cystic swellings in 17 patients. The most commonly entertained differential diagnoses in these patients were cysts of the anterior vaginal wall or suburethral cysts, excess laxity of the vaginal wall rugae in the suburethral area, infected Skene's gland (Fig. 1), and urethroceles. The latter diagnosis should always be questioned to ascertain whether the existing condition is not really a diverticulum.

If the presenting symptoms are kept in mind, a high percentage of accuracy in diagnosis will be obtained if the gynecologist and urologist work in conjunction with each other. Many female patients with urethral diverticula will come for examination to either the gynecologic or the urologic clinic.

DIAGNOSIS

In our hands, the most definitive method of confirming the presence of urethral diverticula is by a combination of endoscopy and urethrocystography. While performing the endoscopic examination it is helpful to use a large panendoscope, as this will distend the urethral lumen and facilitate the diagnosis. A high level of irrigating fluid during the endoscopic examination will also aid in keeping the urethral lumen distended so that the mouths of diverticula may be identified more easily. As almost all diverticula are in the vaginal hemisphere of the urethra, a careful search should be made between 3 and 9 o'clock from the bladder neck to the external meatus. It is imperative to angulate the panendoscope during endoscopy in order that the lateral walls and posterior urethra are fully seen. In this way the urethral rugae will be temporarily obliterated and a diverticular opening more easily seen. Suburethral massage during endoscopy may also expel pus from a latent ostium and thus establish the diagnosis.

URETHROCYSTOGRAPHY

Roentgenographic studies are essential to confirm the size, position, and number of urethral diverticula. It is helpful to do a cystogram in conjunction with a urethrogram, as the presence of fluid in the bladder increases the tonicity of the bladder neck sphincter, and a greater intraurethral pressure can be exerted during urethrography. As a result there will be a greater likelihood of filling a urethral diverticulum. We have used a Brodny clamp or a regular 10 cubic centimeter plastic syringe with an attached urethral nozzle in performing urethrograms. Thixokon® and salpix® have given equally good roentgenographic results. Anteroposterior and lateral views are always taken of the bladder and urethral regions. In this way, it is possible to see that relationship of diverticulum to the bladder neck (Fig. 2), whether the diverticula are multiple (Fig. 3), bizzare in shape, or extend up behind the vesical neck.

These facts are of importance during subsequent diverticulectomy. Improved urethrograms may be obtained by emptying the diverticula before urethrography. This is helped by gentle suburethral massage. Should

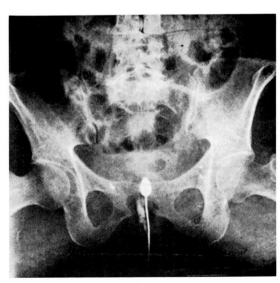

Fig. 1. Dye outlines an infected right Skene's gland. Bougie à boule lies in urethra.

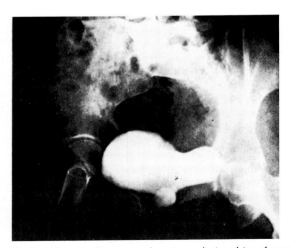

Fig. 2. Cystourethrogram showing relationship of urethral diverticulum to bladder neck.

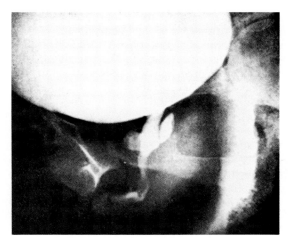

Fig. 3. Cystourethrogram showing 2 urethral diverticula.

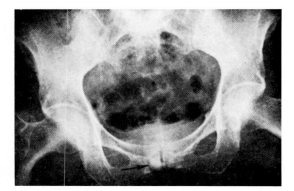

Fig. 4. Stone in a urethral diverticulum.

endoscopy and retrograde urethrography fail to reveal a suspected diverticulum, a voiding cystourethrogram may be rewarding. More recently, we have studied large urethral diverticula by cineradiography to observe the filling and emptying of the diverticula, as well as to exclude coexistent vesicoureteral reflux.

Urethral diverticula were incidentally found in 2 patients undergoing urethral dilatations. A double urethra was suspected in one patient and a false passage in the urethra in the other.

INCIDENCE OF CALCULI IN DIVERTICULA

In patients suspected of having calculi in urethral diverticula, lateral roentgenographic views should be taken of the urethral and bladder region. Such calculi may be easily overlooked on roentgenograms, especially if they are poorly calcified and are hidden behind the pubic rami. We had 2 patients with calculi in diverticula. The calculi were diagnosed preoperatively in one patient (Fig. 4) and at the time of operation in the second patient. Wharton and Kearns had a 10 percent incidence of calculi in urethral diverticula in their series of 30 patients.

URETHROVAGINAL FISTULAS

In the presence of a normal competent bladder neck, a small urethrovaginal fistula is of no significance and may go undiagnosed. When there is a coexisting urethral diverticulum, however, such fistulas may be symptomatic. Two patients in our series had a urethrovaginal fistula preoperatively. In one patient there was a coexisting calculus in the urethral diverticulum. In the second patient a urethrovaginal fistula was suspected because of a history of vaginal leakage of urine. The anterior vaginal wall was exposed by using a self-retaining weighted vaginal speculum. A fistula was then demonstrated by endoscopy in a darkened cystoscopy room. The most likely explanation of the urinary incontinence associated with urethral diverticula is that the diverticula fill during voiding. Between voidings the urine drips through the urethrovaginal fistula, with resulting urinary incontinence. In such patients, the most often entertained differential diagnoses are vesicovaginal or ureterovaginal fistula and stress urinary incontinence resulting from an incompetent bladder neck sphincter. A urethrovaginal fistula was demonstrated in a second patient at the time of operation. When methylene blue mixed with saline was injected into the urethra, the fistula was demonstrated at the apex of the diverticulum.

In our study urethrocystography confirmed the presence of urethral diverticula in 25 patients. The diagnosis, however, was missed in 3 patients in whom diverticula were subsequently found. Urethral diverticula were diagnosed in 26 patients by cystoendoscopy, but the diagnosis was missed in 2 additional patients. It would appear that the frequency of positive diagnoses of urethral diverticula is in direct relationship to the experience of the endoscopist. The mouths of all the urethral diverticula were on the posterior wall between 3 and 9 o'clock. Double diverticula were present in 3 patients and a horseshoe-shaped diverticulum was present in another (Fig. 5). In 1 patient, the urethra was transected during a difficult forceps delivery. The urethra was repaired at the time. Lower urinary tract symptoms associated with stress urinary incontinence subsequently developed. Endoscopic examination confirmed that the patient had a sacculation of the urethra, just distal to the bladder neck. This was not a true urethral diverticulum as it had no ostium and was comprised of all layers of the urethral wall. The urethral sacculation was excised and the bladder neck successfully plicated.

One patient was considered to have an infected

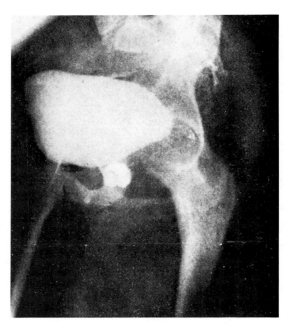

Fig. 5. Cystourethrogram showing a horseshoe type of urethral diverticulum.

urethral diverticulum. She was treated conservatively with antibiotics for some months, but eventually she was found to have an advanced urethral carcinoma. The importance of the differential diagnosis was only too obvious in this patient. Urethral diverticula were palpable suburethrally in 21 patients, and pus could be expressed from the external urethral meatus in 17 of these by gentle massage of the diverticula.

TECHNIQUES OF DIVERTICULECTOMY

It is advisable to remove urethral diverticula if they are causing symptoms, as most do, or if they are a source of recurring urinary tract infections. Diverticulectomy was performed on 33 patients in this series. Preoperatively, all patients had a full urologic work-up. This consisted of an excretory urogram, cystourethrogram, urine culture, and urine analysis. The two glass urinalysis test may be helpful. Theoretically, in the presence of urethral diverticula, the first voided specimen should contain many more pus cells than the second specimen. Patients were given a vaginal douche on the preoperative night. In the operating room a Foley catheter was placed in the bladder and the patient then put in the exaggerated lithotomy position. The anterior vaginal wall was exposed by placing a weighted self-retaining speculum in the vagina.

Better exposure can be obtained by stitching the labia laterally to the skin. The techniques of diverticulectomy differed in the type of incision used. In this series 2 methods were employed to expose the diverticula, a vertical vaginal incision and an inverted U-shaped vaginal flap.

VERTICAL VAGINAL INCISION

The anterior vaginal wall was brought into view by placing an Allis clamp at the external urethral meatus and another on the vaginal wall just below the diverticulum. A midline vaginal incision was made over the diverticulum. Blunt dissection facilitated the freeing and isolation of the diverticular sac. The diverticulum was then removed at its exit from the urethral canal. The ostium was closed with interrupted No. 0000 chromic catgut sutures, and an attempt was made to invert the urethral mucosa. The anterior vaginal wall was normally closed in 3 layers. The pubococcygeus muscles were sutured together suburethrally with interrupted No. 00 chromic catgut sutures thereby buttressing the urethra. It was often possible to obtain a second layer closure of the periurethral fascia. It was essential to have good hemostasis and adequate surgical exposure throughout the operation. Care was taken that the layers of surgical closure did not overlie each other, as this predisposed to fistula formation. The vaginal epithelial layer was closed with interrupted No. 0 chromic catgut sutures and any excess mucosa was removed before closure. Twelve patients were treated in this fashion. Two patients had to be reoperated upon because of persistence of symptoms due to incomplete removal of the urethral diverticula. The vaginal epithelial layer was closed by an overlapping method in 9 patients. In this method of closure the mucosal surface of one vaginal flap was then placed over the first, and both flaps were sutured together with interrupted No. 0 chromic catgut mattress sutures, as in a Mayo type of hernia operation (Fig. 6). The value of this type of vaginal closure lies in the fact that the suture lines are not superimposed, and that good suburethral buttressing is also obtained.

INVERTED U-SHAPED VAGINAL FLAP

Following the routine exposure of the anterior vaginal wall, an Allis clamp was placed at the external urethral meatus and one at either inferolateral angle of the anterior vaginal wall (Fig. 7). An inverted U-shaped flap of anterior vaginal wall was reflected downward. The incision was so placed that the diverticulum lay just beneath the flap. The diverticulum was isolated and removed as in the previous method. Following the closure of the first mucosal layer with No. 0000 chromic catgut

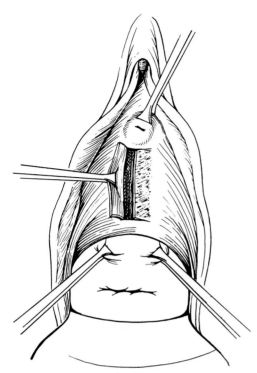

Fig. 6. De-epithelization of one vaginal flap with Mayo type of overlap closure.

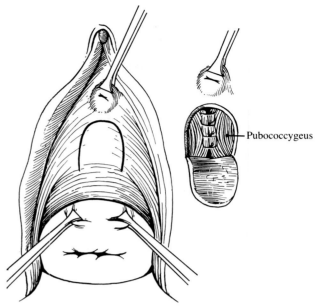

Pubococcygeus

Fig. 7. Reflection of unverted U-shaped flap. Buttressing urethra with pubococcygeus muscles.

sutures, methylene blue mixed with saline was injected into the urethra. This maneuver shows any defects in the urethral closure. It is most important to buttress the urethra during the second layer closure, by taking good bites of the pubococcygeus muscle and fascia which lie far laterally in the region of the subpubic rami (Fig. 7). The vaginal epithelial flap may require trimming before its replacement and suturing with interrupted No. 0 chromic catgut sutures. The vagina was packed with gauze in all patients for 24 or 48 hours postoperatively. An indwelling Foley catheter was left in position for approximately 10 days postoperatively. Twelve patients were operated upon by this method. Two patients had to be reoperated upon later because of continuing symptoms due to incomplete removal of the diverticula.

COMPLICATIONS

As in any surgical procedure the complications can be either immediate or delayed. During diverticulectomy, it is quite easy to extend the suburethral vaginal incision and enter the bladder. This complication occurred in 1 patient. The vesicovaginal opening was closed in 2 layers with interrupted No. 000 chromic catgut sutures. Meth-

ylene blue mixed with saline was then instilled in the bladder to confirm a watertight closure. The diverticulum could not be identified at operation in 1 patient, although it had been demonstrated preoperatively. The urethra was opened but the diverticular ostium could not be located. The periurethral tissues were removed at the site of the suspected diverticulum. The patient had a good postoperative result. It is often helpful to do a urethrotomy and try to locate the opening into a diverticulum, particularly when there is difficulty in defining the diverticulum from the outside.

One patient was found to have 2 calculi in the urethral diverticulum at time of operation. These were removed. A diverticulectomy was then performed and its difficulty was increased by the infection and adherence of the wall to the bladder neck. A urethrovaginal fistula developed in the post-operative period with an associated urinary incontinence. Endoscopy confirmed the presence of the fistula. The urinary incontinence was probably a result of too extensive dissection at the bladder neck. A urethroplasty was subsequently performed with no improvement in the urinary incontinence. The patient underwent a Marshall-Marchetti urethropexy some months later with a satisfactory result. In retrospect, it would have been wiser to have removed only the calculi initially, drained the diverticulum, and performed the diverticulectomy later. In a second patient also, a urethrovaginal fistula developed following the diverticulectomy. As it was asymptomatic, no further operative repair was undertaken. Two further patients developed stress-urinary incontinence following diverticulectomy, probably as a result of too extensive dissection at the bladder neck which caused damage to the bladder neck sphincter. Four patients had a recurrence of the lower urinary tract symptoms after diverticulectomy. Upon a urologic reassessment they were found to have had incomplete removal of the diverticula. They were reoperated upon subsequently, with satisfactory postoperative results. Of the 38 patients operated upon, a follow-up evaluation was obtained on 24. Seventeen patients were free of lower urinary tract symptoms within 1 year of operation. Seven patients were either not improved or still had symptoms at this time.

DISCUSSION

From our own observations and those of others, the most important point in the diagnosis of urethral diverticula is a constant awareness of their possible presence. Davis and Telinde noted that an increased interest in this condition had resulted in 50 new instances of urethral diverticula being diagnosed in 1 year, nearly as many as had been discovered in the preceding 60 years at Johns Hopkins Hospital. Our experience has been similar. In the majority of our patients with urethral diverticula, the diagnosis was made in the last 2 years. Multiple theories as to the pathogenesis of urethral diverticula have been suggested, but the one of recurring infections in the paraurethral glands would seem most tenable. Embryologically, the femal urethra is formed from the urinary part of the cloaca. In its 1½ inch course from the bladder neck to the external meatus, it lies in the anterior vaginal wall and traverses the urogenital diaphragm. It is lined with squamous epithelium in its distal part but this is replaced with transitional epithelium in the proximity of the bladder neck. The urethra is firmly attached to the back of the symphysis pubis but has little support in its posterior aspect. The numerous paraurethral ducts which open into the distal urethra are considered to be the homologue of the prostate in the male. The paraurethral ducts are visible during endoscopy, particularly so, if they are infected. It is quite conceivable how recurring infections of the paraurethral ducts eventually lead to the formation of suburethral diverticula. In our experience, endoscopy and urethrography were equally effective in confirming the diagnosis of urethral diverticula. Both diagnostic methods, however, should always be used to complement each other. Urethrography defines the size, number, and ramifications of the diverticula and when done in conjunction with a cystogram it establishes the relationship of the diverticular sac to the bladder neck. A surgical awareness of the proximity of diverticula to the bladder neck may avoid postoperative urinary incontinence. When diverticula are acutely infected or contain calculi it is wiser to drain the diverticula or remove the calculi and leave the diverticulectomy until later. In this way the surgical excision of the diverticula will be easier and the chances of urethrovaginal fistulas less.

The exact technique of diverticulectomy does not seem to be of importance. When an accurate preoperative assessment has been made, with regard to the number of diverticula, number of openings leading into a diverticulum, and their relationship to the bladder neck, then good results will be obtained. The basic surgical precepts must be observed, i.e., adequate exposure, good hemostasis, a watertight closure of the urethral canal, and satisfactory buttressing of the urethra. The diverticulum must be removed in toto, or if more than one be present, all must be removed. Patients will have a recurrence of symptoms otherwise, as happened in 4 patients in this series. When there is an associated stress urinary incontinence it is imperative to plicate the pubococcygeus muscles and fascia suburethrally and elevate the bladder neck at the time of diverticulectomy. If the diverticula are large and extend up behind the bladder neck or encircle the urethra, it may be more judicious to leave part of the diverticular sac behind, rather than risk causing incontinence or damaging the urethra. An attempt should be made, however, to remove the mucosal lining of the remnant of the diverticular sac left behind. The pathologic examination of the diverticula that were removed showed a relatively constant picture. Ulceration and squamous metaplasia were present in nearly all the specimens. No frank evidence of malignant change was ever found. Infected urethral diverticula may give a false impression of active urinary tract infections. This may be particularly so when urinalysis and urine culture are done on a voided or even clean catch urine specimens. While we agree with Beeson, the decision to catheterize does not seem warranted merely to obtain a clean specimen for routine analysis; it may be wiser to obtain catheter urinalysis and culture on female patients with persisting or recurring urinary tract infections, as the presence of infected urethral diverticula may give misleading impressions of upper urinary tract infections.

SUMMARY

Diverticula may be classified into congenital and acquired varieties; urethral diverticula are most likely acquired. Dysuria, stress urinary incontinence, frequency, dribbling incontinence, urgency, dyspareunia, vaginal bleeding, and urethral pain are the most common presenting symptoms.

A combination of cystoendoscopy and urethrocystography is a

valuable diagnostic method. The commonest site of urethral diverticula is between 3 and 9 o'clock.

A vertical vaginal incision over the diverticulum with blunt dissection and removal of the diverticulum at its ostium, or an inverted U-vaginal flap so placed that the diverticulum is beneath the flap, is the most successful technique for diverticulectomy.

Complications of diverticulectomy in 35 patients were urethrovaginal fistula, urinary incontinence, and incomplete removal of the diverticula.

REFERENCES

1. Beeson, Paul B. The case against the catheter. Am J Med 24:1, 1958
2. Davis, H. J., and Telinde, R. W. Urethral diverticula. J Urol Balt 80:34, 1958

3. Wharton, L. R., and Kearns W. Diverticula of the female urethra. J Urol Balt. 63:1063, 1950

Commentary: Urethral Diverticulectomy

Joseph N. Ward

The diagnosis of a urethral diverticulum in the female patient is usually suspected clinically and then confirmed either by cystoendoscopic examination or micturating cystourethrogram. The location, number, and relationship of the diverticulum(a) to the bladder neck should then be carefully studied.[1,2]

The surgical approach for diverticulectomy will depend on the above findings. The patient has a full urologic preoperative evaluation, including urinalysis, urine culture, and an excretory urogram. She is given a Betadine vaginal douche on the preoperative night. In the operating room, the patient is placed in the lithotomy position. A medium-sized Foley catheter is placed in the bladder.

Urethral diverticula can be removed by either a vertical vaginal incision or an inverted U-shaped vaginal flap.[3]

VERTICAL VAGINAL INCISION

The labia are stitched laterally to the skin. A self-retaining vaginal speculum is placed in position. The anterior vaginal wall is better exposed by placing an Allis clamp at the external urethral meatus and one each at either inferolateral angle of the anterior vaginal wall (Fig. 8). A midline vaginal incision is made over the diverticulum. It is important to enter the correct plane between the vaginal wall and submucosal tissues. Once in this correct plane, dissection is easy. The diverticular sac is freed from the surrounding tissues either by blunt dissection, using peanut dissectors, or by blunt scissor dissection (Fig. 9). The length of the vaginal incision must be adequate so that there is normal urethral canal both proximal and distal to the site of the diverticulum. Hemostasis can be controlled by either suture ligatures or coagulation. During the operation, the urethral canal is identified by palpating the urethral catheter.

The diverticulum is dissected down to its "takeoff" point from the urethral canal (Fig. 10). The diverticulum is then removed circumferentially (Fig. 11), using a small plastic scissors to trim the mouth of the ostium, which is then closed

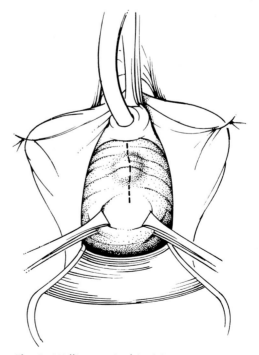

Fig. 8. Midline vaginal incision.

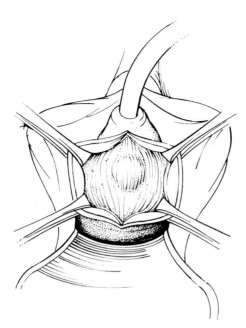

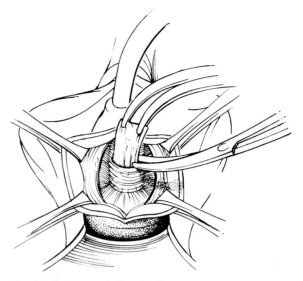

Fig. 11. Excision of diverticulum.

Fig. 9. Diverticulum covered by vaginal fascia.

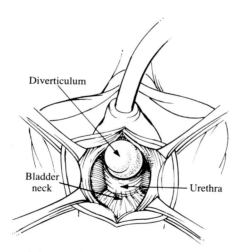

Diverticulum

Bladder
neck

Urethra

Fig. 10. Exposure of diverticulum.

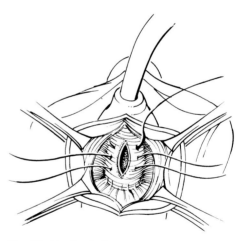

Fig. 12. Urethral closure.

with interrupted 4–0 chromic catgut sutures, and an attempt is made to invert the urethral mucosa. This should be a watertight closure (Fig. 12). This is best confirmed by injecting indigo carmine into the urethral canal with an Aseptosyringe, the Foley catheter having been removed previously.

The pubococcygeus muscles are then sutured together (Fig. 13) suburethrally, using 2–0 chromic catgut sutures. These muscles buttress the suburethral tissues and lessen the chance of stress urinary incontinence, which sometimes results from the suburethral and bladder neck dissection. The pubo-

coccygeus muscles are best sutured with a medium-sized Mayo needle. The vaginal epithelial layer is closed with interrupted 0 chromic catgut sutures. Any excess vaginal mucosa is trimmed off. The vagina is packed with gauze for 24 hr postoperatively. A Foley catheter drainage is maintained for 8 to 10 days.

INVERTED U-SHAPED VAGINAL FLAP

The anterior vaginal wall is exposed as in the previous technique. A U-shaped vaginal flap is positioned so that the diverticulum lies just beneath this flap (Fig. 14).[4] The diverticulum is isolated as previously and dissected down to the urethral canal. The ostium is then closed with 4–0 chromic

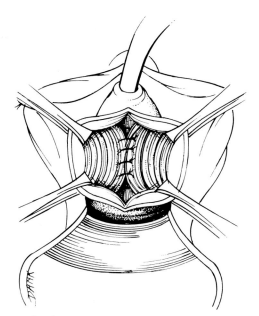

Fig. 13. Suture of pubococcygeus muscles.

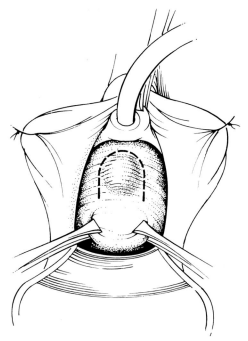

Fig. 14. Inverted U-shaped vaginal flap.

catgut sutures. A watertight closure again is confirmed by injecting indigo carmine into the urethral canal.

The pubococcygeus muscles, which are located laterally beneath the pubic rami, are sutured together with 2–0 chromic catgut sutures, using a Mayo-type needle. This technique of buttressing the suburethral tissues is important to prevent both stress urinary incontinence and the formation of urethrovaginal fistula.

Stress urinary incontinence may result from too vigorous a dissection in the region of the bladder neck. When urethral diverticula extend up behind the bladder neck, it is wiser not to pursue the dissection too vigorously, lest the sphincter muscles are damaged. An attempt should be made, however, to remove the mucosal lining of the diverticulum. Should a urethral diverticulum contain a calculus with an abscess formation or acute inflammation of the surrounding tissues, it is better to drain the diverticulum and remove the calculus first and later do an elective diverticulectomy when the infection has subsided.

A micturating cystourethrogram should be done when there is doubt about the diagnosis of a urethral diverticulum. This can be a most definitive method of diagnoses.

An extensive diverticulum, which extends subtrigonally, may be seen as a trigonal elevation at the time of cystoendoscopy. A cystic dilatation of the terminal suburethral part of an ectopic ureter may clinically present like a urethral diverticulum. Although uncommon, carcinoma can occur in urethral diverticula and must be dealt with accordingly.[5]

The most common cause of recurrence or persistence of symptoms of a urethral diveticulum is incomplete removal of the diverticulum or failure to diagnose other diverticula present.

The presence of a small fistula in a urethral diverticulum will give the patient symptoms of postvoiding urinary incontinence. This follows when the diverticulum, which fills during micturition, slowly leaks out the urine after micturition.

REFERENCES

1. Ward JN, Draper JW, Tovell HMM: Diagnosis and treatment of urethral diverticula in the female. Surg Gynecol Obstet 125:1293, 1967
2. Spence HM, Duckett JW Jr: Diverticulum of the female urethra: Clinical aspects and presentation of a simple operative technique for cure. J Urol 104:432, 1970
3. Busch FM, Carter FH: Vaginal flap incision for urethral diverticulectomy. J Urol 111:773, 1974
4. Sholem SL, Wechsler M, Roberts M: Management of the urethral diverticulum in women: A modified operative technique. J Urol 112:485, 1974
5. Cea PC, Ward JN, Lavengood RW, et al: Mesonephric adenocarcinomas in urethral diverticula. Urology 10:58, 1977

ANNOTATED BIBLIOGRAPHY

Ward JN, Draper JW, Tovell HMM: Diagnosis and treatment of urethral diverticula in the female. Surg Gynecol Obstet 125:1293, 1967

> This paper describes diverticula as possibly being classified into congenital and acquired varieties; urethral diverticula are most likely acquired. Dysuria, stress urinary incontinence, frequency, dribbling incontinence, urgency, dyspareunia, vaginal bleeding, and urethral pain are the most common presenting symptoms. A combination of cystoendoscopy and urethrocystography is a valuable diagnostic method. The most common site of urethral diverticula is between the 3 and 9 o'clock positions. A vertical vaginal incision over the diverticulum with blunt dissection and removal of the diverticulum at its ostium, or an inverted U-vaginal flap so placed that the diverticulum is beneath the flap, is the most successful technique for diverticulectomy. Complications of diverticulectomy in 35 patients were urethrovaginal fistula, urinary incontinence, and incomplete removal of the diverticula.

Spence HM, Duckett JW Jr: Diverticulum of the female urethra: Clinical aspects and presentation of a simple operative technique for cure. J Urol 104:432, 1970

> This well-written article discusses that the diverticulum of the urethra should be searched for in any woman with unexplained chronic lower urinary tract symptoms, that voiding cystourethrography is the most helpful diagnostic measure, that a simple surgical procedure has resulted in cure in a small series of patients and has been free from complications. It is recommended for further trial.

Busch FM, Carter FH: Vaginal flap incision for urethral diverticulectomy. J Urol 111:773, 1974

> A technique has been described to excise female urethral diverticula in order to improve ease of dissection and to lessen the risk of postoperative urethrovaginal fistulas. An inverted U-shaped vaginal flap is made over the diverticulum.

Sholem SL, Wechsler M, Roberts M: Management of the urethral diverticulum in women: A modified operative technique. J Urol 112:485, 1974

> Methods that have been used to diagnose and to surgically treat diverticula of the female urethra are briefly reviewed. The method in this article, which has been applied to 17 patients, consists of a submeatal, semilunar approach, and dissection along the urethra to the diverticulum followed by its excision. Complications have been minimal, and problems inherent in the transvaginal approach have been avoided.

Cea PC, Ward JN, Lavengood RW et al: Mesonephric adenocarcinomas in urethral diverticula. Urology 10:58, 1977

> This paper discusses that carcinomas arising in diverticula of the female urethra are rare neoplasms, approximately 30 of which have been presented since the first case report in 1951. The histologic appearance has not been documented in all these cases, but the classification of 21 tumors was 9 transitional carcinomas, 3 squamous carcinomas, and 9 adenocarcinomas. This variation suggests a diverse origin of these neoplasms. Two cases of adenocarcinoma with a mesonephric pattern that were found in urethral diverticula are reported herein.

Overview: Diagnosing and Managing Urethral Diverticulum

Stephen N. Rous

It has often been said that if one does not *think* of a given condition one will not make the correct diagnosis of that condition. Perhaps in no other aspect of adult urology is this more true than in diverticulum of the female urethra. Although this entity was first described in 1805 and although several hundred cases have been described in the literature since that time, most urologists think of diverticulum of the urethra only after treating a patient unsuccessfully for many weeks or even months with various therapeutic modalities.[1] In fact, the diagnosis of urethral diverticulum should readily and initially come to mind when one considers the differential diagnosis in any adult female complaining of dysuria, frequency, recurrent urinary tract infections, urgency, localized pain in the vicinity of the urethra, and incontinence of urine. Uncommonly, gross hematuria and dyspareunia may also be secondary to a urethral diverticulum. There are certain conditions in medicine, the frequency of which seem to be directly proportional to the diligence with which one searches for that condition, and this is clearly the case with diverticula of the female urethra.

It is probable that the "urethral diverticulum" is in fact neither a true nor a false diverticulum but a dilated periurethral duct communicating with the urethra. The mechanism of development is most likely an infection in the urethra that results in stenosis or occlusion of the opening of one or more of the periurethral ducts, and this in turn gives rise to dilatation of the duct, retention of secretions, and infection of the duct. This dilatation and infection of the periurethral duct or ducts may then result in perforation into the urethra either through the preformed duct or through a spontaneous point of entry into the lumen of the urethra.[2] It is obvious then that urethral diverticula are almost always acquired, and those situations thought to represent congenital diverticula may possibly be nothing more than a subvesical sacular dilatation of the urethra. Even though some diverticula may result from obstetrical trauma, the fact that these lesions are not infrequently found in nulliparous women tends to give credence to the fact that obstetrical trauma is at best a minor etiologic factor and that these diverticula really are, pretty generally, the result of retention cysts of the periurethral glands, which have become infected and have ruptured into the lumen of the urethra. Histologic examination of surgically removed diverticula rarely shows a diverticular wall consisting of all the urethral layers; most often the diverticulum is little more than an abscess cavity with the usual inflammatory constituents of such a lesion in the walls of the cavity and without any glandular or muscular components. At times calculi may be found in the diverticular cavity, although this is not common. The diverticula vary from the size of a pea to that of a hen's egg and about two thirds of the diverticula found are more than 2 cm in diameter. The ostia of these diverticula into the urethral lumen are usually in the 2-mm to 5-mm range.

It is interesting to note, in passing, that diverticula of the male urethra are usually acquired and caused by either obstruction in the urethra or destruction of the urethral wall through trauma or infection. The foregoing is applicable to diverticula of both the anterior and posterior urethra. Congenital diverticula, although very uncommon, tend to be found in the anterior urethra (bulbous and penile urethras). The most common causes of the acquired lesions found anywhere in the male urethra are stricture disease, periurethral abscess (usually secondary to an in-dwelling catheter and most commonly in the paraplegic) urethral trauma, and calculi in the urethra.[3]

Returning to the female urethra, once the diagnosis has been considered based on the patient's history, confirmation of the presence of a urethral diverticulum is usually not difficult. A majority of patients will have a definitely palpable mass on the anterior vaginal wall, and the mass itself can vary from the size of a pea to that of a golf ball or even larger. Upward pressure on this mass with the examining finger when the patient is in the lithotomy position will produce a discharge at the urethral meatus in a considerable number of these patients. A urethrocele is probably the primary entity in the differential diagnosis of a urethral diverticulum when palpated through the vagina, even though it is not nearly as discrete to the palpating finger as is a diverticulum. The absence of a palpable mass on the anterior vaginal wall does not, however, rule out a urethral diverticulum, since the diverticulum may be empty at the time and therefore not palpable or it may indeed be simply too small to indentify by palpation. If the condition is suspected, whether or not there is a palpable anterior vaginal wall mass, cystoscopy is indicated, and for this purpose I prefer the direct vision instrument such as the Frohmuller (Wolf Instrument Co.) or the Greene (ACMI). In some cases where the opening to the diverticulum is so minute that magnification is virtually a requisite for its visualization, the McCarthy panendoscope may be helpful. The usual right angle cystoscope is of little value in examining the urethra because the tissue to be observed is too close to the objective to allow for adequate visualization.

The urethra should be examined meticulously and repeatedly from the bladder neck to the distal portion of the urethra, and the vast majority (but not all) of the openings into the urethral diverticula will be found on the floor of the urethra between the 3 o'clock and the 9 o'clock positions. In addition to the direct visualization of the urethra, it is often helpful to visualize it with the index finger pressing upward on the anterior vaginal wall since small amounts of matter trapped within the urethral diverticulum will frequently be seen to squirt into the urethra and thereby confirm the location as well as the precise number of diverticular orifices present. To delineate the extent of the diverticulum after the orifice is found, a 4 French opaque ureteral catheter should be inserted into it through a direct vision cystoscope (or a panendoscope). If the ureteral catheter is placed in warm water for several minutes before use it will be sufficiently soft and pliable to enter into and coil within the diverticulum with minimal trauma to the urethra. Once the ureteral catheter is coiled within the diverticulum, radiopaque material is injected through the catheter to outline the diverticulum and to demonstrate its size and whether the diverticular pocket is single or multilocular.[4] Obviously, the urethra should be stripped and emptied as thoroughly as possible of all purulent material before the radiopaque material is injected. Additionally, it is necessary to keep the cystoscope firmly and gently in place in the urethra up against the diverticular orifice so that the coiled ureteral catheter is not inadvertently withdrawn from the diverticular cavity.

Alternative means of roentgenographically demonstrating the diverticulum(a) include voiding cystourethrography, in which the patient voids under fluoroscopic control with appropriate spot films being taken. The contrast medium may be introduced into the bladder in retrograde fashion, after which the catheter is removed and the patient voids, or, preferably, the contrast medium may reach the bladder physiologically following an excretory urogram. In the latter the contrast medium is usually in the bladder in sufficiently good concentration to delineate properly any diverticula that may be present. The additional advantage of this more physiologic approach is that the upper urinary tracts are visualized as well. Another means of visualizing urethral diverticula involves the placing of an Asepto-syringe just inside the urethral meatus and the injection of contrast medium into the urethra in the hope that the diverticula will be filled. Still another technique employs a specially prepared double bag catheter closed at the distal end. One bag is within the vesical neck, thereby occluding it, and the other bag is pressed snugly against the urethral meatus from the outside, so that the urethra itself becomes a closed tube. Contrast medium injected into a fenestrated catheter is thus trapped within the urethra under high pressure and will frequently be seen to enter any diverticular cavities that may be present.[5] This last approach is my least favorite, since it has not been too successful in my hands, but all approaches should be considered until accurate roentgenographic delineation of the diverticular cavities have been obtained. Although it is extremely doubtful that any of the foregoing studies could ever diagnose the extremely uncommon case of carcinoma in a urethral diverticulum, the condition itself should be borne in mind. In a recent review of my own series of carcinoma of the urethra, 2 of 22 patients were females with carcinoma found in a removed urethral diverticulum.[6]

Once the suspected diagnosis of urethral diverticulum(a) has been confirmed, the successful treatment of this condition is the next challenge, and it traditionally has been based on the complete excision of the diverticular cavity down to the neck of the sac, followed by closure of the defect in the urethral wall. The commonly accepted approach is a transvaginal one through a vertical incision over the main portion of the diverticulum with an 18 or 20 French Foley catheter in the urethra and bladder to give accurate definition to the urethra itself. The insertion of a coiled ureteral catheter in the diverticulum such as was placed for the purpose of filling the diverticulum with contrast medium keeps the diverticulum from collapsing during the dissection. In any case, dissection of the diverticulum is greatly facilitated by making certain *not* to empty the diverticulum inadvertently by pressure on it from within the vagina before surgery.

The longitudinal incision is made through the mucosa up the anterior vaginal wall from the most proximal margin of the diverticulum practically to the urethral meatus. The vaginal mucosa is separated from the cervicopubic fascia, and the latter is split longitudinally over the diverticulum. These layers may readily separate or there may be a considerable amount of difficulty in delineating the layers of tissue; the relative ease or difficulty of the procedure will depend on the amount of inflammatory reaction about the diverticular sac. In those cases in which there is considerable infection or calculi within the diverticular sac it may be best to simply marsupialize the sac and drain it, remove any calculi that may be present, and return some months later to excise the sac. Persistence in attempting a one-stage excision of the diverticular sac that is adherent to surrounding tissue, particularly if calculi are present, may result in a urethral–vaginal fistula. In the great majority of patients, however, the dissection will be easy with little or no inflammatory reaction noted.

Once the diverticulum is identified by palpation, dissection around it is begun next to the wall of the sac. An attempt is made to carry the dissection down on all sides to the diverticular orifice, and if this can readily be done the neck of the diverticulum is amputated and the ostium in the wall of the urethra is closed longitudinally with interrupted sutures of 4–0 chromic catgut; this is then reinforced, if possible, with a second imbricating layer in the urethral wall, taking care not to overlap the two suture lines. It is sometimes easiest to open the diverticular sac and dissect it from surrounding tissue using a peanut sponge with a finger in the sac itself, much as one does with an indirect inguinal hernial sac. If it is not possible to free all the sac from the urethra without damaging the urethra, then any adherent portion of the sac should be left attached to the urethra; the urethra is still closed as noted above. The fascia is next imbricated over the urethra with 3–0 chromic catgut, and again, if possible, the suture lines should not be superimposed one on the other. Finally, the vaginal mucosa is closed with interrupted sutures of 0 chromic catgut.

The reproduced article and the Commentary stress the importance of buttressing the urethra by bringing together the laterally located pubococcygeous muscles into the area of repair. I do not personally feel that this is necessary, but I certainly have no objection to this step and I feel that such a step is definitely warranted if any appreciable cystocele coexists.

Certainly repair of a significant coexisting cystocele should be included in the initial repair of the diverticulum. The reproduced article also suggests an inverted U-shaped incision in the vaginal mucosa. I do not see any advantage of this inverted incision over the longitudinal incision, and, indeed, my general tendency is to avoid mucosal flaps if possible so as to minimize the devitalization of tissue that may accompany the undermining of these mucosal flaps. In any case, I leave a large vaginal pack in place postoperatively for 48 hr to minimize oozing that might occur and also to apply uniform pressure over the operative region. A Foley catheter is left indwelling for 4 or 5 days. If the patient is unable to void following removal of this catheter or if a question of residual urine remains, the catheter should be reinserted with great care along the urethral wall opposite to the one that was the site of the repair.

The above represents the traditional manner of repairing urethral diverticula, but I think it important to note that there are other ways that are really simpler and quite possibly every bit as satisfactory. Saucerization as a definitive procedure has been recommended using a vaginal approach, and within the last year a series of patients have been very successfully treated using a transurethral approach with complete unroofing of the diverticlar cavities.[7,8] In this approach, urethroscopy with the insertion of the knife electrode through the diverticular stoma was used, and with this maneuver the sheath and resectoscope must be held at about a 45-degree angle to the urethra so that the tip of the curved knife electrode will slide along the urethral floor and slip through the opening into the diverticular cavity. The eyepiece end of the resectoscope is then lowered so that the sheath is parallel with the urethral floor, and the knife electrode is thusly brought into contact with the roof of the diverticulum. The resectoscope is elevated slightly so that the sac of the urethral diverticulum is pushed upward into the lumen of the urethra by the electrical knife, and this tented roof of the diverticulum is then incised with a cutting current. The procedure is repeated until the entire roof of the diverticulum has been divided, even though this may require extending the incision along most of the length of the urethra to the urethrovesical junction itself. Where multiple diverticula are present, each diverticular cavity is laid open in this manner and the urethral catheter is left inlying overnight. Although the technique just mentioned may not be ideal for the treatment of every patient with a urethral diverticulum, I feel that the concept is sound and the initial results reported are good enough to warrant more extensive use of this procedure with its significantly lowered morbidity and greatly decreased length of hospitalization.

In general, the results of treatment of urethral diverticula are good but certainly far from perfect. A small percentage of patients seem to have a troublesome and persistent inflammatory urethritis postoperatively; how much of this problem is due to the operation itself and how much to the longstanding preoperative inflammation in the urethral area is difficult to say. Certainly, the complication of incontinence is a real one and a feared one that may result if too-vigorous attempts are made at excising the entire diverticulum, particularly in those patients in whom the diverticula are too close to the vesical neck, under the trigone itself, or wrapped around the urethra toward the 12 o'clock position. In such cases, discretion is advised;

it is far better to leave behind portions of the diverticular sac than to render the patient incontinent. Other complications are failure to recognize and therefore failure to remove all the diverticular cavities present preoperatively and development of urethrovaginal fistulae. A meticulous diagnostic work-up preoperatively with as many cystoscopic examinations and as many roentgenographic studies as are necessary to document the exact number and precise location of the diverticular cavities will certainly minimize the first complication. Urethrovaginal fistulae can be kept to a minimum if meticulous closure of the diverticular neck in the urethral wall is carried out followed by meticulous closure of the overlying fascia and the vaginal mucosa, all of which should be done so that one suture line is not superimposed directly on the other.

REFERENCES

1. Hey W: Practical observations in surgery. Philadelphia, J. Humphrey, 1805. Cited by Linnet-Jepsen P, Danish Med Bull 7–8:204, 1960

2. Linnet-Jepsen P: Diverticulum of the female urethra. Dan Med Bull 7–8:204, 1960

3. Nickel WR, Plumb RT: Other infections and inflammations of the external genitalia. In Harrison JH, Gittes R, Perlmutter A, et al (eds): Campbell's Urology, Vol 1, p 678. Philadelphia, WB Saunders, 1979

4. Mackinnon M, Pratt JH, Pool TL: Diverticulum of the female urethra. Surg Clin North Am 39:953, 1959

5. Davis HJ, Cian LG: Positive pressure urethrography: A new diagnostic method. J Urol 75:753, 1956

6. Allen WR, Nelson RP: Primary urethral malignancy: Review of 22 cases. South Med J 71:547, 1978

7. Spence HM, Duckett JW Jr: Diverticulum of the female urethra: Clinical aspects and presentation of a simple operative technique for cure. J Urol 104:432, 1970

8. Lapides J: Transurethral treatment of urethral diverticula in women. J Urol 121:736, 1979

116

EXTERNAL URETHROPLASTY IN WOMEN: TECHNIQUE AND CLINICAL EVALUATION

Francis H. Richardson

1702 Washington Street, Waukegan, Illinois 60085

The Journal of Urology
Copyright © 1969 by The Williams & Wilkins Co.
Vol. 101, May
Printed in U.S.A.

External urethroplasty is for correction of distal urethral resistance to urination. Connective tissue which lies between the distal urethral mucosa and vaginal mucosa is excised to interrupt the continuity of the constricting ring of fibers surrounding the distal segment. The procedure results in decreased distal urethral resistance and improvement in urinary obstructive symptoms.

A brief description of the procedure is presented with the symptoms, diagnosis and clinical results obtained in 300 patients. The operation was performed in women (1) who had received no prior treatment, (2) in whom urethral dilatations had produced only temporary relief of symptoms or (3) who had not responded satisfactorily to other procedures such as internal urethrotomy or urethral meatotomy.

SURGICAL PROCEDURE

The principal features of external urethroplasty are illustrated in Figure 1. With the patient in the lithotomy

Accepted for publication September 18, 1968.
Read in part at annual meeting of American Urological Association, Miami Beach, Florida, May 13–16, 1968.

position, the perineum is prepared and draped in the usual manner. The urethra is calibrated with steel male urethral sounds to the size which causes visible blanching of the adjacent urethral mucosa. With the sound in the urethra, a posterior meatotomy is performed, if indicated, with a midline incision at the 6 o'clock position. The incision is made vertically, from below upward through the vaginal mucosa, subcutaneous tissue and the urethral mucosa for ⅛ to 3/16 of an inch, depending on the degree of stenosis. Progressively larger sounds are passed until the distal urethra fits snugly around the sound (usually 30 Fr.). The curvature of the sound is placed at the mid-portion of the urethra which draws the urethra away from the symphysis pubis and into the field of vision.

External urethroplasty is accomplished with a longitudinal midline incision through the anterior vaginal mucosa, extending proximally from the posterior edge of the meatus for a distance of ½ inch. The edges of vaginal mucosa are reflected laterally to expose the posterior portion of connective tissue surrounding the distal urethral segment. This tissue is grasped firmly with toothed forceps and pulled distally along the sound into view of the surgeon. A block of tissue is excised

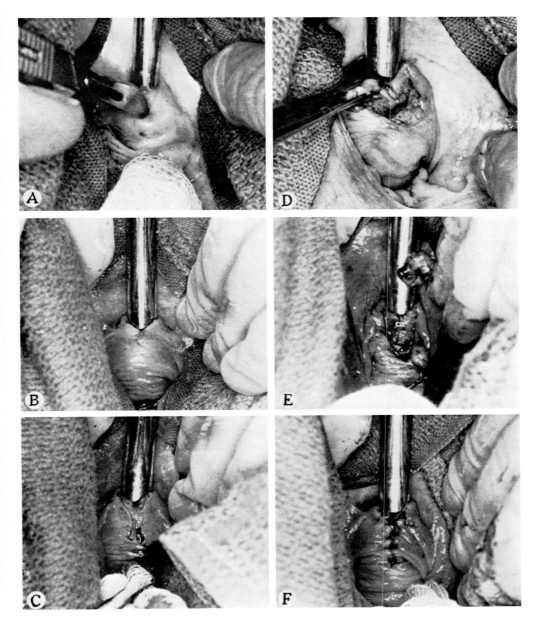

Fig. 1. (*A*) Scalpel in position for incision of meatus (with Fr. 22 sound in urethra). (*B*) Larger sound (Fr. 30) in urethra after meatotomy. (*C*) ½-inch longitudinal incision in anterior vaginal mucosa. (*D*) Subcutaneous tissue held by forceps during dissection. (*E*) Intact underlying urethral mucosa after excision of tissue (specimen in front of sound). (*F*) Vaginal mucosa is reapproximated and meatus is sutured transversely.

by sharp dissection with a No. 15 knife blade. No attempt is made during resection either to include or avoid Skene's glands.

Closure of the longitudinal vaginal incision is ac-

complished by approximating the edges of mucosa with 3 or 4 interrupted 3-zero chromic catgut sutures, using a curved, smooth, tapered needle. The steel sound is removed and the meatal incision is closed transversely with 3 or 4 interrupted 3-zero chromic catgut sutures placed in the edges of the urethral mucosa and vaginal mucosa.

When a meatotomy is not necessary, access to submucosal connective tissue is gained by a "T" incision in the vaginal mucosa. This approach consists of a transverse and a longitudinal incision. The transverse incision is ⅜ to ½ of an inch long, immediately inferior to the posterior edge of urethral meatus (short cross arm of "T"). The longitudinal incision (vertical arm of "T") is made ½ inch long, extending proximally from the mid-point of transverse incision. The edges of the vaginal mucosa forming the "T" incision are then reflected laterally to expose underlying connective tissue which is excised in the manner previously described.

Closure of the vaginal mucosa "T" incision is achieved by approximating the transverse and longitudinal incisions with interrupted 3-zero chromic catgut sutures before removing the sound from the urethra.

In selected cases, a repeat operation may be indicated to remove additional periurethral tissue. This operation is accomplished by a transverse incision through the vaginal mucosa at the junction of middle and distal third of urethra. After reflecting the edges of this incision, additional connective tissue can be excised from the sides of the distal urethral segment.

Bleeding during the operation has not been a problem. Some venous oozing occurs but seldom requires fulguration or ligation for hemostasis. A catheter is not used postoperatively since injury or stretching of the urethral mucosa is purposely avoided.

Surgical specimens: Gross examination of excised tissue has shown considerable variation in thickness (1 to 4 mm) of connective tissue between the urethral mucosa and vaginal mucosa. Ricci and associates have indicated from a histological study of the female urethra that ". . . the substantia propria becomes extremely thick and is a mass of fibrous tissue . . ." in the lower (distal) urethra.[1]

Histological examination of sectioned paraffin-embedded surgical specimens stained with hematoxylin and eosin revealed predominantly fibrous connective tissue, with occasional bands of smooth muscle fibers in the most proximal sections (Figs. 2 and 3). Many sections showed a number of pockets of mature epithelium. The epithelium was transitional, stratified squa-

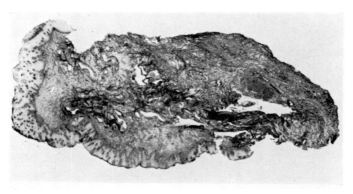

Fig. 2. Mid-sagittal section of surgical specimen from distal female urethra which includes narrow strip of vaginal mucosa for orientation purposes. Urethral meatus is at left. In right upper corner is area of smooth muscle. Darker area represents dense network of coarse elastic fibers. Lighter area is loose connective tissues with interweaving of fine elastic and collagen fibers. Verhoeff's counterstained with van Gieson's, 12×.

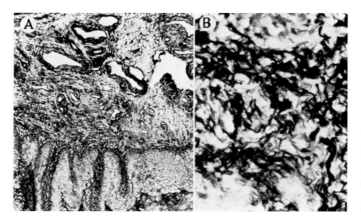

Fig. 3. (A) Representative section of medium magnification shows interstitial connective tissue containing abundant coarse elastic tissue networks and many plexuses of small veins. Immediately under vaginal mucosa there is dense network of fine elastic fibers; from here fine fibers run into loose network of collagen fibers and become condensed in walls of blood vessels. 200×. (B) High power magnification of connective tissue surrounding distal urethra shows dense network of elastic fibers. Lighter staining collagen fibers are intermixed with dark elastic fibers to form complex mesh. 480×.

mous in most areas and pseudo-stratified in others. In some microscopic fields there was a moderate degree of vascularity.

SYMPTOMS

Case records of 300 women treated by external urethroplasty revealed 1,494 symptoms, or an average of 4.9 per patient (see table). A history of recurrent cystitis was obtained in 121 of the 300 women. This was the sole complaint in 36 patients (29 percent) while the remaining 85 patients (71 percent) had additional symptoms such as frequency and nocturia. The average duration of recurrent cystitis was 6.1 years—78 women had symptoms for less than 5 years while 43 patients had had them between 5 and 30 years. No precipitating factor was elicited in 93 women; however, the onset followed pregnancy in 16 cases, marriage in 6 cases and operative procedures in 6 cases.

Symptoms of irritable bladder syndrome were encountered in 264 of the 300 women. Of this group, 179 women did not have a history of urinary infection.

Urinary symptoms were not characteristic of any particular age: 50 patients were between 18 and 29 years old, 65 between 30 and 39 years, 53 between 40 and 49 years, 55 between 50 and 59 years, 45 between 60 and 69 years, 26 between 70 and 79 years and 6 patients were more than 79 years old.

DIAGNOSIS

The diagnosis of distal urethral stricture due to extrinsic constrictive tissue often can be established by excessive resistance to the passage of steel sounds. By calibration, the distal urethra was less than normal size in 261 patients: 16 or 18 Fr. in 31, 20 or 22 Fr. in 96 and 24 or 26 Fr. in 134. Ten of the remaining 39 women who had no stenosis gave a history of urethral meatotomy.

Incidence of Symptoms in 300 Women Before External Urethroplasty

Symptom	No. Patients (%)
Urinary frequency	243 (81)
Nocturia	220 (73)
Slow stream	143 (48)
Bladder pain	127 (42)
Back pain	125 (41)
Recurrent cystitis	121 (40)
Groin pain	93 (31)
Urgency	85 (28)
Incontinence (dribbling, stress, etc.)	83 (27)
Leg pain	81 (27)
Flank pain	69 (23)
Dysuria	49 (16)
Dyspareunia	45 (15)

Distal urethral obstruction is commonly associated with cystoscopic findings such as trabeculation of the bladder wall, exudative trigonitis and polyps at the neck of the bladder. Residual urine was found in 49 cases. However, cystoscopic findings in all 300 patients were often minimal, even in those who had residual urine.

Almost half of the patients gave a history of a slow or intermittent flow during voiding. A helpful method for determining flow rate is to measure the voiding time for a known volume of water. The normal voiding time ranges from 12 to 20 seconds for 400 ml. water (average flow rate of 20 to 33 ml. per second). Voiding time was measured in 144 patients; the flow rate in milliliters per second was 1 to 5 in 41 cases, 6 to 10 in 50 cases, 11 to 15 in 31 cases, 16 to 20 in 17 cases and normal in 5 cases. Additional evidence for slow or incomplete emptying of the bladder is the presence of mucus and epithelial cells in a centrifuged catheterized specimen.

A history of temporary improvement of symptoms following a trial of urethral dilatation is a good indication that patients will benefit from an operation. One or more previous dilatations were noted in 74 cases. Additional evidence for diagnosis of urethral stricture included a history of urinary difficulties in childhood, during pregnancy and in other members of the family: 42 patients had urinary frequency during childhood (including 27 patients who had enuresis and 12 patients who had nocturia), 49 patients had had unusual urinary frequency, nocturia and urgency during pregnancy and 56 patients revealed that other members of the family had experienced urinary troubles.

CLINICAL RESULTS

Results of treatment by external urethroplasty were as follows: 90 percent had a good result or marked improvement in symptoms as early as 1 week and not later than 2 months postoperatively, 6 percent required postoperative urethral dilatation to maintain freedom from, or improvement of symptoms while 4 percent failed to improve or were lost to followup. Some of the latter group refused postoperative treatment of any kind. A repeat operation was performed in cooperative patients when preoperative symptoms and findings persisted, despite postoperative urethral dilatation.

Clinical results were not adversely affected by the age of the patient. Improvement was delayed in women with extremely large or small bladders and in women in whom residual urine had been present for several years. Improvement of symptoms of bladder irritation was slow in some patients whose stricture was adequately corrected. In such cases urethral dilatation was carried out at monthly intervals.

DISCUSSION

Postoperative complications have not been frequent or serious. Separation of edges of the sutured vaginal mucosa caused delayed healing in some patients. In some instances bleeding required resuturing of the mucosa. Postoperative urinary incontinence did not occur.

A modification of the operative procedure which may help to reduce complications involves an alternate technique for exposure of distal urethral connective tissue using a ⅛ inch posterior midline incision of the urethral meatus and 2 lateral incisions, each ¼ inch in length, on either side of the meatal incision. This modification is now being studied. The vaginal mucosa is reflected posteriorly from the distal urethra to expose the intervening connective tissue. Following excision of tissue, the intact vaginal mucosa is replaced in its original position and sutured.

Calibration of the urethra with steel sounds is not an infallible guide to diagnosis of stenosis since the ease with which they can be passed does not measure the caliber of the urethra during voiding or the degrees of resistance to urine flow. A voiding urethrogram, which is a useful diagnostic procedure to detect the distensibility of the urethral lumen during micturition, may show a long, tapering contour in the distal segment of the urethra. Visualization of narrowing in the distal lumen is further accentuated when there is concomitant dilatation of the proximal urethra and neck of the bladder. Unfortunately, voiding urethrograms are unsuitable as a routine procedure in women because they are inhibited about voiding for the examination. Thus, in women candidates for an operation, reliance must be placed on the history, symptoms, voiding pattern, urethral calibration and cystoscopic examination for making a proper diagnosis.

Some women have urethral stenosis without symptoms, whereas others may have urinary complaints with a normal size meatus. Immergut and Wahman found the urethral meatus in girls with recurrent cystitis to be actually larger than normal size.[2] The importance of the distal urethral segment as opposed to caliber of the urethral meatus is revealed in a report by McLean and Emmett, who observed that the healed scars following internal urethrotomy in women were limited to the distal third of the urethra.[3] Gleason and Bottaccini have shown in voiding cystourethrograms of children that the diameter of the distal urethral segment is the narrowest segment of the voiding urethra.[4] They believe this diameter has a crucial role in governing the rate of urine flow; whereas, configuration of the proximal urethra appears to be relatively unimportant.

In the author's experience, a small meatotomy which enlarges the meatus to normal size is not sufficient to produce consistent improvement in patients with stenosis. The clinical results of a large meatotomy (approximately 1 cm long) as reported by McAninch[5] are much better since most fibers of constricting connective tissue are divided. An aggressive meatotomy (i.e. a posterior urethrotomy) which divides the distal urethral segment produces the best clinical results. However, this procedure has the disadvantage of shortening and distorting the normal appearance of the urethra.

SUMMARY

External urethroplasty is done for treatment of distal urethral resistance to urination. The operation is designed to weaken the distal urethral segment by excision of posterior periurethral connective tissue, exposed through an incision of the anterior vaginal mucosa. The operative procedure has 3 advantages over other operations for correcting distal urethral obstruction: it is performed under direct vision, it is not traumatic to the urethral mucosa and it does not shorten the urethra.

Satisfactory relief of urinary obstructive symptoms was obtained in 90 percent of 300 women. A good result was obtained in an additional 6 percent of patients with postoperative urethral dilatations and, when indicated, a repeat urethroplasty. Clinical results were unsatisfactory in 4 percent of women who showed no improvement, were lost to followup or refused further treatment.

REFERENCES

1. Ricci, J. V., Lisa, J. R. and Thom, C.H.: The female urethra; a histologic study as an aid in urethral surgery. Am J Surg 79:499, 1950
2. Immergut, M. A. and Wahman, G. E.: The urethral caliber of female children with recurrent urinary tract infections. J Urol 99:189, 1968
3. McLean, P. and Emmett, J. L.: Internal urethrotomy in women for recurrent infection and chronic urethritis. J Urol 101:724, 1969
4. Gleason, D. M. and Bottaccini, M. R.: The vital role of the distal urethral segment in the control of urinary flow rate. J Urol 100:167, 1968
5. McAninch, L.N.: External meatotomy in the female. Canad J Surg 8:382, 1965

Commentary: Urethroplasty and Urethrolysis

Francis H. Richardson

A perplexing problem in modern urology is the treatment of recurrent urinary tract infections and the urethral syndrome in females. They suffer from a symptom complex that usually includes dysuria, frequency, nocturia, enuresis, urgency, incontinence, lower abdominal pain, and dyspareunia. Conventional therapy has traditionally consisted of antibiotics, periodic urethral dilatations, instillation of silver nitrate, internal urethrotomy, meatotomy, tranquilizers, psychiatric consultations, or some combination.

The Richardson urethroplasty is based on the premise that in a subset of the total population with the urethral syndrome, an outflow obstruction exists in the distal two thirds of the urethra.[1,2] The obstruction is formed by a congenital band of fibroelastic tissue, which produces a noncompliance in the urethra, resulting in a decreased flow rate. The decreased flow rate prevents a normal washout of urethral bacteria, thereby promoting recurrent infection and chronic urethritis. The irritable bladder symptoms and referred pain are a response to urethral obstruction by the same mechanism by which males have irritable symptoms and referred pain from urethral obstruction caused by meatal stenosis, congenital median bar, and prostatism. Excision or lysis of this tissue results in a increased flow rate by changing a noncompliant distal two thirds of the urethral into a passive conduit for urine, with subsequent alleviation of symptomatology.[3]

Etiology of distal urethral obstruction is multifactorial. Although I believe it to be primarily of congenital origin, chronic infection of the periurethral glands can also be responsible for dysuria, dyspareunia, and a reservoir of bacteria in certain patients. Onset of symptoms can appear spontaneously at any age, triggered by sexual intercourse, the birth of a child, catheterization, or anterior colporraphy.

Clinical data lend credence to support this basic premise. Lyon demonstrated the distal urethral ring in young girls, and he and other authors have reported success using urethral dilatations in controlling patients with recurrent urinary tract infections.[4-6] Numerous investigators have found marked success in management of lower urinary tract obstruction with meatotomy, internal urethrotomy, posterior urethrotomy, and anterior urethroplasty.[7-15] Other investigators, evaluating women with the primary complaint of urinary incontinence, have found large numbers of patients with urethral obstructions. Treatment to decrease urethral resistance has resulted in significant improvement.[16-19]

Some have questioned the existence of clinically significant outflow obstruction in the female or have shown that dilatation of the urethra has no influence on the number of recurrent infections in certain controlled studies.[20-23] In reviewing this literature I find it incongruous to deny the existence of urethral obstruction or to treat patients without first clinically showing that such urethral resistance does or does not exist. The methodology in the evaluation of urinary dysfunction in the cited studies has been of a static variety, using only urethral calibration in conjunction with voiding cystourethrograms. The use of the bougie à boule urethral calibration indicates only the passive urethral wall sensitivity and bears little significant relation to urethral dynamics during voiding. Severe urodynamic obstruction has been found in patients who calibrate easily to 30 French.[24] Although many workers have found VCUG helpful in making the diagnosis of urethral stricture, others will not make the diagnosis regardless of the urethral configuration.[25] Conversely, obstructed patients can have completely normal VCUG. Gleason provides an explanation for this when he points out that even a 1-mm decrease in the diameter of the distal urethral segment during voiding can significantly slow the flow rate.[26]

Nowhere is the battle between the advocates for the obstruction causality and those for nonobstruction more evident than in treatment of enuresis.[27-30] The latter group rarely if ever evaluates patients for distal urethral obstruction. Their mode of therapy is primarily medical or psychiatric. Success for them is when the patient stops wetting the bed. Switching an enuretic child to nocturia by waking her up every 2 hr, thereby giving the parents relief of social anxiety, can hardly be considered rational. The advocates for obstruction argue that they can help patients by relieving both nocturnal and diurnal symptoms. It is time that physicians cease to define "cure" by simply changing a child's lifestyle from a pattern of enuresis to nocturia.

Perhaps the primary reason for failure to accept the concept of urethral stricture has been the difficulty in obtaining data.[31] Neither the size of the meatal opening nor the dilatation of the urethra can be uniformly correlated with symptoms of obstruction. The flow rate, however, has proved to be an excellent test for assessing urethral obstruction. Given normal bladder function, the slower the average flow rate, the greater the obstruction. If one wishes to perform simple urodynamic studies without multiple pressure catheters in various orifices, it behooves the physician or technician performing the test to instruct properly the patient before examination that she is not to strain during voiding. Patients with mild or moderate urethral obstruction can be missed if testing is performed with abdominal straining during the examination.

The diagnosis of urethral obstruction cannot be made on history alone. Urodynamic studies should be performed; measurements are made of bladder capacity by retrograde filling, the average flow rate, and the presence or absence of residual urine.

CRITERIA

The Richardson urethroplasty does not claim to be a panacea for all urinary complaints in the female. As in all surgical procedures certain criteria must be met: The patient should have chronic symptoms of the urethral syndrome or repeated documented bouts of urinary tract infections or both. Before urodynamic study, any infection should be treated. If the patient is postmenopausal with atrophic urethritis, prior treatment with estrogen cream is indicated. Patients should demonstrate an average flow rate of less than 20 ml/s without straining. Several studies may be required to ensure proper patient compliance and reliability. The few patients with both an incompetent bladder neck and a stricture of the distal two thirds of the urethra present a difficult clinical problem and require treatment of both conditions. Stress urinary incontinence may be significantly improved by increasing the flow rate. The fear of producing incontinence with the urethroplasty procedure is unwarranted.

SURGICAL TECHNIQUE

The Richardson urethroplasty begins by measuring the length of the urethra with a foley catheter (Fig. 4).[32] The hymenal ring is sutured on either side to the thighs. A 2-mm to 3-mm posteroior meatotomy is performed unless the meatus is obviously larger than normal. A snugly fitting male sound is passed and held in a vertical position to stabilize the urethra. Two incisions 4 mm to 9 mm long are made on either side of the meatus along the hymenal ring. The vaginal mucosa is reflected off the periurethral tissue for approximately one half to two thirds the length of the measured urethra.

A suture holds the vaginal flap posteriorly. The periurethral tissue is grasped and pulled upward on the sound so the incision can be made under direct vision. A vertical 1-mm deep cut is made, and the knife is pushed against the sound. If the periurethral tissue is still soft, the cuts are repeated until the hardness of the sound can be felt through the urethral mucosa. Vertical incisions are made on either side and continued distally

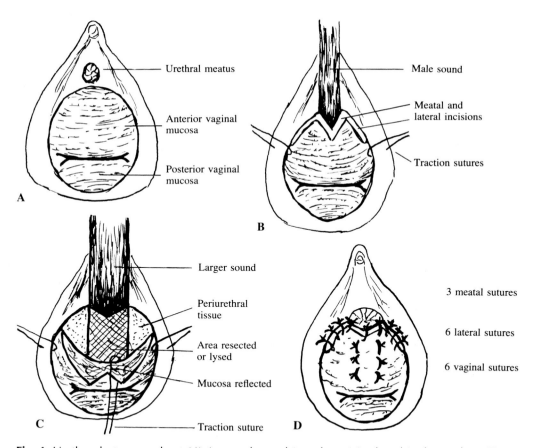

Fig. 4. Urethroplasty procedure. (*A*) A meatal sound (not shown) is placed in the urethra. (*B*) Two incisions are made: a transverse incision in the hymenal ring and a small midline posterior meatotomy. (*C*) The vaginal mucosa is reflected off two thirds of the urethra, exposing the periurethral tissue, which is excised or lysed down to the urethral mucosa but not through it. (*D*) The periurethral tissue retracts laterally after the lysis. The vaginal mucosa is replaced and sutured.

to the meatus (Fig. 4*C*). The specimen is then cut off the urethral mucosa. The specimen may be 2 mm to 5 mm wide. No attempt is made to control any bleeding until after the excision or lysis of tissue is finished. Two subcutaneous sutures (2–0 Dexon) are used for hemostasis. The vaginal mucosa is attached with 4 to 6 lateral sutures placed 0.5 cm apart for hemostasis and to close the dead space between the mucosal layers. The sound is removed, and the first suture of 4–0 Dexon is placed in the midline of the meatal incision to prevent the urethral mucosa from retracting. Sutures (4–0 Dexon) are placed 3 mm deep and 3 mm apart to close the meatus transversely and to reapproximate the lateral incisions (Fig. 4*D*).

ADVANTAGES

The advantages of the urethroplasty are as follows. Patients generally are provided with immediate relief of symptoms. Splatt has demonstrated well that the urethroplasty has the ability to increase the average flow rate postoperatively.[3] Postoperative urethral dilatations may be necessary at infrequent intervals. These are performed with sounds of 30 to 40 French without pain using lidocaine jelly because the circular continuity of the fibrous tissue has been interrupted posteriorly. Since bleeding points can be ligated under direct vision, postoperative bleeding is rarely a problem. Excision of periurethral tissue is performed under direct vision, and the amount excised can be varied according to the patient's clinical condition. The integrity of the urethral mucosa is not violated. If necessary, the urethroplasty can be performed under local anesthesia. No postoperative catheterizations or antibiotics are required. The urethroplasty has been used successfully after other procedures have failed.

RESULTS

Splatt has followed his 40 patients for 9 to 40 mo, showing clinical improvement in 38 of the 40. Improvement can be measured objectively by the increased flow rate postoperatively. Cooney, in his follow-up study of 375 patients and Clark's 25 patients present excellent results with almost no complications.[33,34] My own 6-yr to 10-yr follow-up study of patients with recurrent urinary tract infections or urethral syndrome or both has shown a significant improvement in 84% of the patients. Of the remaining 16%, 4% demonstrated no improvement postoperatively and 12% were asymptomatic or improved for periods of time ranging from 6 mo to 7 yr but have required postoperative dilatations.

CONCLUSION

Urethral outflow obstruction is a real entity. Without surgery, patients are condemned to a life of misery. Patients are subject to chronic pelvic pain with unremitting recurring bouts of cystitis. Dyspareunia can be so bad as to preclude a normal sex life. Frequency can interfere with school and work; nocturia will prevent patients from ever obtaining normal sleep. It is little wonder that these patients become neurotic and are known as hypochondriacs.

A cure for recurrent infection secondary to obstruction cannot be obtained by altering patients' hygiene or by long-term antibiotic therapy. Painful periodic urethral dilatations offer only transient relief. The Richardson urethroplasty can play a significant role in the management of females of all ages with symptoms of urethral syndrome or recurrent urinary tract infections or both. The Richardson urethroplasty should be part of the operating repertoire of every practicing urologist.

REFERENCES

1. Richardson FH: External urethroplasty in women: Technique and clinical evaluation. J Urol 101:719, 1969
2. Richardson FH, Stonington OG: Urethrolysis and external urethroplasty in the female. Surg Clin North Am 49:1201, 1969
3. Splatt AJ, Weedon D: The urethral syndrome: Experience with the Richardson urethroplasty. Br J Urol 49:173, 1977
4. Lyon RP, Tanagho EA: Distal urethral stenosis in little girls. J Urol 93:379, 1965
5. Wein AJ, Schoenberg HW: A review of 402 girls with recurrent urinary tract infection. J Urol 107:329, 1972
6. Graham JB, King LR, Kroop KA, et al: The significance of distal urethral narrowing in young girls. J Urol 97:1045, 1967
7. Halverstadt DB, Leadbetter GW Jr: Internal urethrotomy and recurrent urinary tract infection in female chilren. I. Results in the management of infection. J Urol 100:297, 1968
8. Keitzer WA, Benavent C: Bladder neck obstruction in children. J Urol 89:384, 1963
9. McLean P, Emmett, JL: Internal urethrotomy in women for recurrent infection and chronic urethritis. J Urol 101:724, 1969
10. Wyatt JK: Distal urethral stenosis in the female. Can Fam Phys 47, 1975
11. Harvard BM: Revision of the external urinary meatus in girls: A clinical appraisal. J Urol 103:236, 1970
12. Brannan W, Oshsner WE, Kittredge WE, et al: Significance of distal urethral stenosis in young girls. J Urol 101:570, 1969
13. Johnson EL: Evaluation of dorsal urethroplasty in female children. J Urol 109:113, 1973

14. Zimskind PD, Mannes HA: Approach to bladder neck and urethral obstruction in women. Surg Clin North Am 53:571, 1973
15. Vermillion CD, Halverstadt DB, Leadbetter GW: Internal urethrotomy and recurrent urinary tract infection in female children. II. Long term results in the management of infection. J Urol 106:154, 1971
16. Van Rooyen AJL, Liebenberg HC: A clinical approach to urinary incontinence in the female. Obstet Gyncol 53:1, 1979
17. Moolgaoker AS, Ardran GM, Smith JC, et al: The diagnosis and management of urinary incontinence in the female. J Obstet Gyncol Br Comm 79:481, 1972
18. Susset JG, Dutartre D, Leriche A, et al: Urodynamic assessment of stress incontinence and its therapeutic implications. Surg Obstet Gynecol 142:343, 1976
19. Susset JG, Shoukry I, Schlaeder G, et al: Stress incontinence and urethral obstruction in women: Value of uroflowmetry and voiding urethrography. J Urol 111:504, 1974
20. Lapides J, Diokno AC: Persistence of the infant bladder as a cause for urinary infection in girls. J Urol 103:243, 1970
21. Sanford JP: Urinary tract symptoms and infections. Ann Rev Med 26:485, 1975
22. Kaplan GW, Sammons TA, King LR: A blind comparision of dilatation, urethrotomy and medication alone in the treatment of urinary tract infections in girls. J Urol 109:917, 1973
23. Forbes PA, Drummond KN, Norgrady MB: Meatotomy in girls with meatal stenosis and urinary tract infections. J Pediatr 75:937, 1969

24. Farrar DJ, Osborne JL, Stephenson TP, et al: A urodynamic view of bladder outflow obstruction in the female: Factors influencing the results of treatment. Br J Urol 47:815, 1976

25. Shopfner CE: Cystourethrography: Methodology, normal anatomy and pathology. J Urol 103:92, 1970

26. Gleason DM, Bottaccini MR: The vital role of the distal urethral segment in control of urinary flow rate. J Urol 100:167, 1968

27. Arnold SJ, Ginsburg A: Enuresis: Incidence and pertinence of genitourinary disease in healthy enuretic children. Urology 2:437, 1973

28. Mahony D, Laferte RO: Studies of enuresis. VII. Results of distal internal urethrotomy in girls with juvenile urinary incontinence. Urology 4:162, 1974

29. Kass EJ, Diokno AC, Montealegre A: Enuresis: Principles of management and result of treatment. J Urol 121:794, 1979

30. Forsythe WI, Redmond A: Enuresis and spontaneous cure rate: Study of 1129 enuretics. Arch Dis Child 49:259, 1974

31. Walker D, Richard GA: A critical evaluation of urethral obstruction in female children. Pediatrics 51:272, 1973

32. Richardson FH, Stonington OG: Urethrolysis in girls and urethroplasty in women. Movie no. 789, Eaton Medical Film Library, Norwich, NY, 13815

33. Cooney CJ: Urethral meatoplasty in women. Paper read at the North Central Meeting of the American Urological Association, Oct. 6, 1975

34. Clark WE Jr, Borski AA: A clinical evaluation of urethrovaginal septoplasty. Kimbrough Urol Semin 4:48, 1970

ANNOTATED BIBLIOGRAPHY

Richardson FH: External urethroplasty in women: Technique and clinical evaluation. J Urol 101:719, 1969

This is the original description of the procedure by Richardson. The urethroplasty was performed on over 300 women with relief of urinary obstruction of 90% of patients. A major difference to be noted is that the surgical procedure has been modified slightly from the intitial vertical incision to a transverse one. This prevents breakdown of the suture line postoperatively. Suturing the vaginal mucosa to the periurethral tissue provided better hemostatis.

Clark WE Jr, Borski AA: A clinical evaluation of urethrovaginal septoplasty. Kimbrough Urol Semin 4:48, 1970

This article reports results of the Richardson urethroplasty on 25 women. The patients had previously been treated an average of 8 years with dilatations or antibiotics or both without relief. Postoperatively, surgical success rate was 80%. The authors recommend five criteria for urethrovaginal septoplasty: (1) symptoms of the urethral syndrome with concurrent negative urine, (2) nocturia times once or greater, (3) residual greater than 10 ml, (4) obstructive changes on cystoscopy, and (5) urethral calibration of 26 French on cystoscopy or greater. The patients classified as successful fulfilled at least four of these criteria. Failures fulfilled no more than three of the criteria.

Van Rooyen AJL, Liebenberg HC: A clinical approach to urinary incontinence in the female. Obstet Gynecol 53:1, 1979

The authors have treated 528 patients over the past 10 yr for urinary incontinence; 72% of the patients demonstrated urinary outflow obstruction. They treated patients primarily with internal urethrotomy, and 90% showed improvement. I feel that internal urethrotomy, although showing similarly gratifying short-term results, provides more long-term recurrences.

Arnold SJ, Ginsburg A: Enuresis: Incidence and pertinence of genitourinary disease in healthy enuretic children. Urology 2:437, 1973

Evaluating 200 children (85 girls) with a history of persistent nocturnal enuresis, 76% had significantly reduced bed wetting after surgical procedures for correction of distal urethral obstruction, 86% of 148 patients had relief of diurnal urinary symptoms after the procedures. Surgical procedures performed included meatotomy, urethral dilatation, and distal internal urethrotomy. At present, Dr. Arnold (personal communication) is performing the urethroplasty in approximately 40% of patients with obstruction and has found the procedure especially helpful in patients who failed to respond to internal urethrotomy.

Overview: Urethroplasty and Urethrolysis

John B. Nanninga

The procedure of external urethroplasty and urethrolysis is one that I or one of my associates has used in a relatively small series of 11 patients. The criteria for performing this operation are based on identifying the obstructing lesion in the distal urethra. The patient's symptoms should be those suggesting obstruction; namely, weak urinary stream, straining to urinate, prolonged urination, and perhaps a feeling of postvoiding retention. The above symptoms may not fit the term *urethral syndrome* completely, but they point to the obstructive component. Some patients will have increased frequency and urgency, but I feel that these are less specific symptoms of obstruction. If the symptoms of an intermittent stream is noted, it should alert the surgeon to possible sphincter spasticity, which may be on a neurogenic basis rather than from the stenotic meatus.

Objective findings include a markedly narrowed distal urethra (under 12 French). Actually, there is evidence that an orifice of only 9 to 10 French may provide satisfactory emptying.[1] Accompanying the narrowing should be a thickened, indurated urethrovaginal septum in the region of the stenosis. Bougie calibration may aid in defining the area of stenosis. The mean urinary flow rate should be less than 10 ml/sec with at least 200 ml voided. The mean flow rate, which the patient can perform at home, and peak flow rate will be approximately the same with marked obstruction because the stenosis acts as a sort of baffle and tends to dampen peaks of flow. Residual urine will vary, depending on whether there is adequate detrusor function. Residual urine itself is not an infallable guide as to the degree of obstruction.[2] Several of the patients discussed in this chapter demonstrated residual urine greater than 100 ml. One of my patients exhibited a large-capacity bladder (800 ml) that emptied poorly, partly from urethral obstruction, which the weak detrusor could not overcome. The cystometrogram will reveal the degree of detrusor weakness. A urethral pressure profile may be of use. There is some evidence that this test as performed by fluid perfusion is of little value with meatal stenosis.[3] Also, it is sometimes difficult to tell where sphincter ends and meatal stenosis begins.[3,4] Probably a voiding cystourethrogram is as helpful as the urethral pressure profile in certain patients.

With regard to infection, all patients in my small series had experienced at least one documented urinary tract infection. This was accompanied by dysuria and urgency as well as by obstructive symptoms. With elimination of the infection, the dysuria for the most part disappeared. Of interest was the finding by Splatt and Weedon that 8 of 40 patients had infection. I am skeptical that the stenosisis invariably directly related to infection or that correction of the narrowing will prevent future infections.[5] Nonetheless, there is evidence that removing an obstruction will eliminate turbulence in the stream and may reduce bacteria being washed into the proximal urethra and bladder.[6]

The surgical technique is relatively straightforward. The incisions, beginning on either side of the urethral meatus, will divide any urethrohymenal adhesions. I have not dissected further proximal than the distal third of the urethra for fear of sphincter damage. I leave an in-dwelling catheter in place for 24 to 48 hr unless the dissection was difficult and there was interruption of the urethral mucosa. Then the catheter is left in place for 5 to 7 days. The excised tissue will reveal scar tissue and periurethral glands with evidence of chronic inflammation. The surgeon should keep in mind other lesions that can produce some degree of urethral obstruction.[7]

Postoperatively, in my small series, there is definite improvement in flow rate (Fig. 5). There is symptomatic relief as well. Over a 2-yr period, however, 4 patients have experienced symptomatic bacteriuria. Consequently, I do not believe that near-perfect results can be expected in preventing urinary tract infection. One patient developed a hypospadic urethral meatus postoperatively from slough but has been asymptomatic. Postoperative scarring and recurrence of the stenosis has not

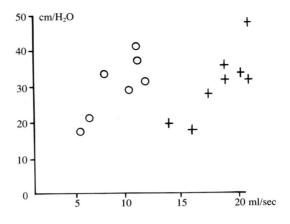

O = preoperative
+ = postoperative

Fig. 5. The maximum flow rate (*horizontal axis*) and bladder pressure (*vertical axis*) before and after urethrolysis. The bladder pressure was recorded by means of a 5F tube in the urethra in eight patients. In the other three patients, the urethral orifice was so stenotic that the urethral catheter was thought to obstruct the flow of urine.

been a problem, probably because, as pointed out, leaving the mucosa intact decreased the chance of scarring and stricture.

Patients with residual urine may benefit from the procedure if there is clear-cut evidence that obstruction is present. I have performed urethrolysis on a diabetic female with a large-capacity bladder and residual urine of 300 ml. She had a stenotic meatus, and an improvement in flow rate over a 2- to 3-week period occurred following urethral dilation. Subsequently, she underwent a urethrolysis with improvement; with straining, she could achieve a flow rate of 18 ml/sec, and the residual urine decreased to a range of 60 ml to 90 ml. She has intermittent episodes of bacteriuria, however. The fact that the patient can void so much more easily makes me cautious about extensive dissection in the midurethral area. I believe the spincter mechanism can be interrupted enough so that profound stress incontinence will occur.

In my small series of 11 patients, all met the rather strict criteria for distal urethral obstruction. Urethrolysis is relatively simple to perform and seems to correct a specific obstructing lesion. It need not be used for simple urethral meatal stenosis where meatotomy may suffice. Also, it need not be performed when the obstruction is not clearly present but urethral dilation affords the patient many months of symptomatic relief. The procedure does appear to have an advantage over internal urethrotomy in that specific obstructing tissue is removed and postoperative scarring has not been a problem. Finally, injudicious application of urethrolysis and external urethroplasty to patients with less than well-defined lesions will produce only sporadic satisfactory results.

REFERENCES

1. Backman K-A: Micturition in normal women; diameter and resistance of the urethra. Acta Chir Scand 132:413, 1966

2. Gleason DM, Bottaccini MR, Reilly RJ, et al: Urethral compliance and its role in female voiding dysfunction. Invest Urol 11:83, 1973

3. Hojsgaard A: The urethral pressure profile in female patients with meatal stenosis. Scand J Urol Nephrol 10:97, 1979

4. Tanagho EA, Miller ER: Functional considerations of urethral sphincteric dynamics. J Urol 109:273, 1973

5. Graham JR, King LR, Kropp KA, et al: The significance of distal urethral narrowing in young girls. J Urol 97:1045, 1967

6. Hinman F Jr: Mechanisms for the entry of bacteria and the establishment of urinary infection in female children. J Urol 96:546, 1966

7. Smith HW Jr, Campbell EW Jr: Benign periurethral masses in women. J Urol 116:451, 1976

PART FORTY-FIVE

SURGICAL TREATMENT OF CRYPTORCHIDISM

117

THE IMPALPABLE TESTIS: A RATIONAL APPROACH TO MANAGEMENT

Selwyn B. Levitt, Stanley J. Kogan, Rainer M. Engel, Robert M. Weiss, Donald C. Martin and Richard M. Ehrlich

The Journal of Urology, Vol. 120
Copyright © 1978 by The Williams & Wilkins Co.
Printed in U.S.A.

The impalpable undescended testis generally is considered briefly in discussions and publications on cryptorchidism. However, this entity poses unique clinical problems and was the subject of an in-depth discussion at the combined meeting of the Society for Pediatric Urology and the American Urological Association in May 1976. This review represents an updated, as well as a refined and expanded, version of that panel discussion.

Testes are impalpable when they are intracanalicular or intra-abdominal and never emerge through the external inguinal ring, or when they are atrophic, dysgenetic or absent. The incidence of clinically impalpable testes is approximately 20 percent of an undescended testis population (Table 1).[1-6] When an attempt is made to define the true incidence of impalpable testes though it is important to recognize that some analyses include retractile testes. The recently published results of a European collaborative study, comparing the effect of luteinizing-hormone-releasing factor with placebo on testicular descent, emphasize this problem.[6]

The incidence of impalpable testes among the 3 collaborating pediatric and 1 urology services varied from 14 to 43 percent. Placebo alone improved the position or resulted in complete testicular descent in 5, 43, 44 and 0 percent, respectively, in that study. Included among patients whose testis descended on placebo therapy alone were a number with impalpable testes. These data cast serious doubt on the accuracy of the reported incidence of bona fide impalpable undescended testes. Newborns have a poor to absent cremasteric reflex. Therefore, a non-palpable testis in newborns is never confused with a retractile testis. One can predict confidently that full descent will not occur in the full-term baby with an impalpable testis except in rare instances, although partial spontaneous descent is possible in the first few weeks to months of life. Full descent is possible within the first 3 months to 1 year in premature babies though.[7] Obesity and the rare perineal ectopic testis (0.6 to 1.3 percent)[3,8] represent other sources of error in any computation.

Impalpable undescended testes, as defined, differ

from other varieties of incomplete testicular descent in ways other than just their improbability of spontaneous descent. They usually are smaller than testes that have become arrested closer to the scrotum or that are ectopic. This may be the result of dysgenesis (gross deficiency in germ cells at the time of birth)[9,10] or be acquired secondary to their abnormal location. A higher incidence of associated clinically apparent hernias is noted.[3] Malignant degeneration is much more common.[1,11] In addition, surgical placement of the testis in the most dependent part of the scrotum is less frequently accomplished successfully.[2,3,10]

Few reports reveal the exact location of the non-palpable testis when it is actually found at surgical exploration. Jones found the testis to be intra-abdominal in 55 percent and intracanalicular in 45 percent of the cases at the time of the operation.[3] Flach, on the other hand, found 80 percent of the preoperatively non-palpable testes in the inguinal canal and only 20 percent in an intra-abdominal position.[5] Of greater import, though, is the incidence of unilateral and bilateral testicular absence (monorchism and anorchism) or severe dysplasia. A review of the literature indicates that monorchism can be expected in 4 percent of children explored for an undescended testis or testes (Table 2).[2,3,8,12–15] Most reports reveal that monorchism is more frequently on the left side. Anorchism (bilateral absence of testes) is much more rare and only occurred in 0.6 percent of 5,815 children with cryptorchidism (Table 2). The incidence has been estimated at 1 of 20,000 male subjects.[16] Campbell and Harrison did an autopsy study on 10,712 boys and found 26 cases of anorchism among 313 cryptorchids.[17] This finding represents an extraordinarily high incidence and is 50 times that noted in clinical studies. The reason for the discrepancy between the clinical and autopsy incidence of anorchism is not immediately apparent. One would expect the exact opposite in an autopsy series in which there are no restrictions to a complete search. Since the testis is impalpable in 20 percent of the undescended testis population (Table 1) one can feel confident that the testis or testes will be found in most cases (that is 80 percent) when exploration is undertaken.

Treatment of impalpable undescended testes, whether unilateral or bilateral, aims at accomplishing prepubertal scrotal placement of the testes, thereby enhancing germinal cell maturation and later fertility potential.[18] The psychologic and cosmetic sequelae of an empty scrotum or hemiscrotum are avoided also.[19,20] Testicular torsion and non-viability, which are particularly likely in the event of torsion of an impalpable testis, are prevented by early orchiopexy.[21,22] Exteriorization of the testis makes it accessible to examination and to early detection of malignant degeneration should it develop. The intra-abdominal undescended testis is particularly prone to malignant change and the probability of the malignancy ultimately proving fatal is significantly higher in these individuals.[1,11,22] Martin and Menck calculated the risk of death from an intra-abdominal testicular neoplasm in boys 15 years old to be 5.9 percent.[11] Optimum management of impalpable testes requires additional facts to be considered.

Endocrine Tests. These tests have added a new dimension in the management of boys with non-palpable gonads.[23] Hormonal assays can reliably predict the presence of functioning testes when the gonads are impalpable. Normal basal serum gonadotropins—follicle-

TABLE 1. Impalpable Testes: Compilation of 6 Series

References	No. Pts.	Testes Impalpable No.	Testes Impalpable (%)
Campbell[1]	176	33	(19)
Tibbs[2]	99	19	(19)
Jones[3]	500	102	(21)
Scorer and Farrington[4]	224	21	(9)
Flach[5]	2,319	499	(21.5)
Illig and associates[6]	112	20	(18)
Totals	3,430	694	(20)

TABLE 2. Incidence of Monorchism and Anorchism Among Cryptorchid Children

References	No. Pts. Operated	Monorchism No. (%)	Anorchism No. (%)	Monorchism or Anorchism No. (%)
Gross and Jewett[8]	988	27	6 (0.6)	33 (3)
Curtis and Staggers[12]	93	10	0	10 (10.8)
Tibbs[2]	108	12	1 (0.9)	13 (12)
Bill and Shanahan[13]	100	8	0	8 (8)
Jones[3]	500	13	1 (0.2)	14 (3)
Abeyaratne and associates[14]	304	12	4 (1.3)	16 (5)
	2,093			
Aynsley-Green and associates[15]	3,722	Not stated	21 (0.56)	
Totals	5,815	82/2,093 (4)	33/5,815 (0.6)	94/2,093 (4.5)

stimulating (FSH) and luteinizing (LH) hormones—and an appropriate increase in serum testosterone over basal values after a challenge with human chorionic gonadotropin (HCG) (1,500 units on alternate days for 3 doses) denote functioning testicular tissue and mandate a thorough and complete surgical exploration. In contrast, elevated basal levels of FSH and LH (LH may not be elevated in boys less than 9 years old with absent gonads) in association with failure of testosterone elevation over basal levels after an appropriate HCG challenge denote an absence of functioning testicular tissue. These endocrine findings in the clinical setting of a normal phenotypic male subject without palpable müllerian structures on rectal examination and with a normal 46-XY karyotype establish the diagnosis of congenital anorchism[15,23] (vanishing testis syndrome[14]). Surgical exploration is not necessary for confirmation in this syndrome. These children merely require placement of silicone gel-filled prostheses, preferably before they are 5 years old, since boys clearly are aware of their gonads by this age.[19,20] The endocrine parameters of testicular absence in adults more than 35 years old must be interpreted with caution since intra-abdominal testes may undergo premature failure of endocrine function.[24] Patients with hypogonadotropism and non-palpable testes may require prolonged HCG administration to elicit a testosterone response sufficient to diagnose the presence of functioning testicular tissue.[25] There is no reliable endocrine test that can differentiate monorchism from an impalpable normal, dysgenetic or atrophic testis.

HCG administration in individuals with bilateral impalpable testes not only allows one to predict that testes are present by their testosterone response but also may induce sufficient descent to allow palpation of one or both gonads.

Endocrine Therapy. The success rate (defined as complete or partial descent) of HCG in cryptorchids in general varies markedly in published reports.[26–31] However, even enthusiasts admit that impalpable intra-abdominal testes are particularly resistant to hormone therapy,[32] although Knorr reported complete descent in 32 percent of 93 intra-abdominal testes when HCG was administered in doses varying from 2,500 to 10,000 units (depending upon age) over a 5-week period.[33,34]

Other Methods. Other methods to differentiate impalpable undescended testes from monorchism or anorchism include pneumoperitoneography using nitrous oxide (andrography). When gas passes through the inguinal canal and fills the tunica vaginalis in an ectopic location[35] an ectopic location of the testis can be inferred. However, failure of the gas to pass into or through the inguinal canal does not differentiate the retained intra-abdominal

testis from a dysgenetic, atrophic or an absent testis. White and associates used positive contrast peritoneography (herniography) in an attempt to localize the impalpable testis.[36] They successfully located a third of their impalpable testes in an intracanalicular position with this method. However, this technique also does not differentiate monorchism from intra-abdominal retention of an atrophic, dysgenetic or even a normal testis. At present, ultrasound, radionuclide testicular scanning and thermography cannot be considered reliable in prospective assessment of the unilaterally or bilaterally impalpable testis. Aortography, selective gonadal angiography[37–40] and gonadal venography[39,41,42] have been tried to localize the position of non-palpable testes preoperatively as an aid in surgical management. Proponents of these tests claim that the exploration and search for testes after these procedures are more organized. Aortography alone generally does not allow for good visualization of the spermatic arteries in adults and usually fails to visualize testicular arteries in children. Therefore, selective gonadal angiograms are necessary for detailed visualization. However, because the origins of the testicular arteries vary considerably[43] and are particularly small in young children catheterization is difficult in this age group and, frequently, is unsuccessful.[42] Anesthesia may be necessary for the procedure and there also is the potential, albeit small, risk of causing arterial injury or thrombosis during transfemoral arteriography, particularly when the procedure is prolonged by difficult and time-consuming selective catheterization. Corriere and Lipshultz noted that arteriograms were not consistently helpful in determining the presence or predicting the quality of testicular tissue.[39] However, Vitale and associates successfully delineated the right internal spermatic artery and arterial plexus of the epididymis in a 5-year-old boy with prune belly syndrome and a right intra-abdominal testis who had been explored previously and in whom the right testis had not been found.[38]

Gonadal venography is safer and is performed more readily, particularly on the left side, where the gonadal vein enters the renal vein. Weiss and associates report no falsely negative results using gonadal venography in 9 children with 12 nonpalpable testes.[42] The identification of a gonadal vein that terminated in a pampiniform-like plexus indicated the presence and location of the testis. When the gonadal vein terminates intra-abdominally or when no veins are visualized they recommend a midline incision. Since routine inguinal skin crease incisions detect most impalpable testes in an intracanalicular position and since most intra-abdominal testes are found in immediate juxtaposition to the internal inguinal ring gonadal venography may not be required in the majority of instances. Irradiation exposure and the occasional need for anesthesia must be considered in determining the appropriate use of the procedure. All of the reported cases of total separation of a blind-ending partially descended vas and/or epididymis with an intra-abdominal testis were discovered during inguinal explorations.[44-48] Therefore, gonadal venography cannot be recommended routinely in cases of impalpable testes. It is useful though when local inguinal, retroperitoneal and intra-abdominal exploration fails to detect a testis and when no blind-ending spermatic vessels are found. If nothing further were done in these cases one could conceivably miss the rare high intra-abdominal testis with an absent vas as reported by Whitehorn[49] and Dickinson.[50] Positive identification of a testis by gonadal venography and/or angiography in this situation would justify a separate loin incision or abdominal exploration. Further exploration probably is unwarranted when venography indicates an absent testis and adequate local exploration already has been undertaken.

Surgical Considerations. The malignant potential and computed mortality rate in individuals with retained intra-abdominal testes are significantly higher than the risk of mortality from surgical exploration, at least in patients less than 50 years old.[11] A thorough organized surgical exploration seems warranted in all unilateral impalpable testes, at least in patients less than 50 years old, for this reason alone. When endocrine testing confirms the presence of a testis in the bilateral situation or when a negative endocrine test cannot be relied upon to definitively exclude markedly atrophic testes in the postpubertal man more than 35 years old, a careful and complete exploration is indicated.

The surgical considerations specific to the impalpable testis include (1) type of incision, (2) extent of the exploration and criteria of a negative exploration, (3) need for intraperitoneal exploration, (4) technique of orchiopexy when testes are found and (5) special considerations in bilateral cases before as well as after puberty.

We believe that an inguinal skin crease incision is the simplest, most cosmetic and most direct approach in most cases of unilateral impalpable testes. This incision allows satisfactory exposure and will detect a testis in 80 percent of the cases with initially impalpable gonads. It will allow access to and will locate blind-ending spermatic vessels or spermatic vessels plus a vas at the internal ring or below in 65 percent of patients with monorchism (Table 3).[2,14,51]

Blind-ending spermatic vessels are the sine qua non of testicular absence. No cases have been reported in which a testis was found after blind-ending spermatic vessels were identified. Therefore, a blind-ending tuft of spermatic vessels is the signal to terminate the exploration. A blind-ending vas or epididymis, which is found in approximately 11 percent of the explorations (Table 3), does not exclude complete separation of the vas or epididymis from a retained intra-abdominal testis. There are at least 5 well documented cases in the literature and many more that have not been published (Table 4).[4,44-50,52,53] Therefore, the finding of a blind-ending vas alone mandates further exploration, tracing the vas toward its origin proximally. It is important to emphasize that the findings are sometimes bizarre and misleading so that a thorough exploration in the region of the internal ring is necessary even when it appears that an atrophic testis has been located. Segments of the vas may be absent. A structure resembling the spermatic cord may suggest a scrotal testis when the testis actually is within the abdomen. Conversely, it is sometimes helpful to invaginate the scrotum into the inguinal incision to inspect its contents before proceeding to further exploration.[3] If no testis or definite blind-ending spermatic vessels are found the peritoneum is opened after transecting the epigastric vessels and incising the transversalis fascia. Extension of the incision superolaterally through the conjoined tendon and transection of the epigastric vessels allow wide exposure and easy intraperitoneal entry. The extended incision also allows for more adequate retroperitoneal exploration to at least the pelvic brim. The finding of no vas or vessels in the inguinal canal or retroperitoneally (23 percent) similarly mandates intraperitoneal exploration, since the testis may be so

TABLE 3. Operative Findings in Unilateral Absent Testis (Monorchism)

References*	No.	Vas Alone No. (%)	Vessels Alone No. (%)	No Vas No Vessels No. (%)	Vas or Vessels No. (%)	Vas Plus Vessels No. (%)
Tibbs[2]	12	1 (9)	0	0	12 (100)	11 (91)
Abeyaratne and associates[14]	12	0	0	1	11 (91)	11 (91)
Goldberg and associates[51]	39	6 (15)	3 (7)	14 (36)	25 (64)	16 (41)
	63	7 (11)	3 (5)	15 (23)	48 (77)	38 (60)

* Tibbs and Goldberg and associates explored through the inguinal incision with peritoneal extension if no testis was found. Abeyaratne and associates explored inguinally and retroperitoneally only.

Summary. Vas plus vessels is most frequent finding (60 percent). Unless spermatic vessels are identified when the vas is found a separate testis cannot be totally excluded. When no vas or vessels are found a testis could be present intra-abdominally.

TABLE 4. Abnormalities of Wolffian Duct Associated With Undescended Testes

References	Abnormalities	Incidence
Michelson, 1949 Young, 1949	Absent vas in fully descended testis	0.5–1%
Scorer and Farrington[4]	Epididymal or vasal abnormalities in undescended testis (mainly elongated or angled epididymis or long mesorchium)	24% (54/256)
Dean and associates[46] Scorer and Farrington[4]	Total separation—vas and epididymis in undescended testes	1.2% (3/245) 3% (9/256)
Badenoch[44] Lazarus and Marks[45] Dean and associates[46] Lythgoe[47] Nowak[48] Perlmutter[53]	Wide separation—intra-abdominal testis plus blind epididymis in canal or below	6 cases (5 published and 1 unpublished)
Dickinson[50]	Testis below left kidney (no epididymis or vas)	1 case
Dickinson[50]	Testis below kidney with vas plus epididymis plus hypertrophied vasal vessels (no spermatic vessels)	1 case
Whitehorn[49]	Testis in renal fossa, renal agenesis—absent vas and epididymis	1 case
Zelikovski and associates[52]	Testis plus vas plus epididymis in mesoappendix	1 case

well enveloped in peritoneum as to be an intraperitoneal organ, making it difficult to find by retroperitoneal dissection alone. Surgeons and urologists have long cherished the notion of the testis being a retroperitoneal organ. However, those organs that have invaginated the posterior parietal peritoneum sufficiently to acquire a mesentery are called intraperitoneal. When testicular descent fails altogether, as in the case of retained intra-abdominal testes, they are often intraperitoneal and do have a mesentery. Therefore, intraperitoneal exploration allows the testis to be identifed more readily than retroperitoneal dissection in these cases.

In bilateral situations we prefer a Pfannenstiel incision. The skin as well as Camper's and Scarpa's fascia is elevated and retracted to visualize the external rings that are incised, thus exposing both inguinal canals. As in routine unilateral explorations a patent processus vaginalis frequently is identified in the inguinal canal by this maneuver and incising the conjoined tendon superolaterally, thereby opening the internal ring, may suddenly allow the testis to descend from its intra-abdominal position down into the canal. When this occurs a long testicular mesentery usually is present. Routine separation of the peritoneum and high ligation of the sac, incision of the lateral spermatic fascia and the transversalis fascia medially with or without epigastric vessel transection and direct relocation of the spermatic vessels and vas through the external ring often allow adequate placement of the testis in a dependent scrotal position without tension. The easiest side is done first in these cases. When the testis does not descend readily on opening the internal ring the anterior rectus sheath and recti are divided between the 2 inguinal incisions and the peritoneum is opened. This allows wide exposure for either a more thorough bilateral exploration or for better planning of the bilateral orchiopexy when testes are found and do appear to have a short mesentery.

In patients with anorchism published reports indicate that 81 percent of patients have a blind-ending vas or a vas plus vessels on one or both sides.[2,14,15,51,54,55] These structures generally are found in the inguinal canal or below. Only a minority (19 percent) had no vas or vessels on one or both sides (Table 5).[2,14,15,51,54–56]

When testes are found intra-abdominally and appear to have short testicular vessels that will not allow tension-free scrotal placement using conventional techniques, one can select either staged orchiopexy or testicular vessel transection. The decision to transect the testicular vessels must be made early so that a wide peritoneal strip can be left attached to the vas and the testes distally to preserve the vasal vessels. Harrison, in fresh autopsy injections of vasal arteries in 24 men with fully descended testes, found retrograde filling of the testicular artery with anastomoses at the upper and lower pole of the testis in all subjects but only two-thirds had retrograde filling of the cremasteric artery.[57] However, the sum of the diameters of the vasal and cremasteric arteries was equal to the testicular artery in only a third of the cases, indicating that adequate functional collaterals in the normally descended testis was by no means universal. He speculated that boys with undescended testes might have even poorer collateral channels. Bevan advocated spermatic vessel transection for orchiopexy as early as 1903[58] but withdrew this recommendation in 1929[59] because of poor long-term results. Turner[60] and MacCollum[61] reported similar bad results using the technique. Interest in the maneuver was revived by Fowler and Stephens[62,63] in 1959 when they demonstrated by elegant intraoperative arteriograms that there was collateral arterial blood supply to undescended testes in those cases in which the vas loops into the scrotum and then returns to reach the testis situated at or near the internal ring (the long loop vas). They also pointed out the value of testing the adequacy of the collateral blood vessels by

TABLE 5. Operative Findings in Bilateral Absent Testes (Anorchism)

References	No. Pts.	Spermatic Cords No. (%)	Vas Alone No. (%)	Vas Plus Vessels No. (%)	No Vas No Vessels No. (%)
Tibbs[2]	1	2	0	2	0
Abeyaratne and associates[14]	4	8	0	8	0
Goldberg and associates[51]	9	18	5	13	0
Levitt and associates[56]	2	4	0	2	2
Reckler and associates[54]	1	2	2	0	0
Tosi and Morin[55]	1	2	1	0	0
Aynsley-Green and associates[15]	21	42	30	0	12
Totals	39	78 (100)	38 (49)	25 (32)	14 (19)

Most patients with anorchism have a blind-ending vas or vas plus vessels on one or both sides: 81 percent (63 of 78 sides explored). Usual site equals inguinal canal or lower. Minority (19 percent) have no vas or vessels on one or both sides.

TABLE 6. Results of Transection of Testicular Vessels: Compilation of 7 Series

References	No. Pts.	No. Cords Transected	Successful Result (No. Testes)
Fowler and Stephens*[62]	12	12	8
Jones†[3]	17	17	9
Brendler and Wulfsohn‡[64]	5	5	5 (5-month followup)
Barnhouse[65]	4 (all prunes)	7	7
Datta and associates[66]	3	3	3
Levitt and Kogan[67]	10 (6 prunes)	17	16
Ehrlich[68]	13 (9 prunes)	21	19
Totals	64	82	67/82 (82%)

* Long loop vas ensures vasal artery supply.

† Decision must be made early in dissection.

‡ All cases followed at least 6 months except those of Brendler and Wulfsohn.

82% successful gauged by size, consistency and position of testis.

TABLE 7. Results of Staged Orchiopexy Compilation of 9 Series

References	No. Cases	Successful Result No. (%)
Snyder and Chaffin[69]	7	6 (86)
Gross and Replogle[70]	24	24 (100)
Bill and Shanahan[13]	2	2 (100)
Williams and Burkholder[71]	3 (prunes)	3 (100)
Lynn[72]	2	2 (100)
Persky and Albert[73]	13	9 (70)
Piror[74]	32	30 (94)
Corkery[75]	5	5 (100)
Zer and associates[10]	62	48 (77)
Totals	150	129 (86)

temporary occlusion of the testicular artery followed by incision into the tunica albuginea to determine whether arterial bleeding was still present. A compilation of recent published as well as unpublished data indicates that when patients are selected carefully the procedure is successful in a high percentage of cases. Of 82 cases 82 percent maintained good size, consistency and a dependent position of the testis in the scrotum after testicular vessel transection (Table 6).[3,62,64–68] Staged orchiopexy is preferred by most authors and successful results are reported in 86 percent of the 150 reported cases (Table 7).[10,13,69–75] Redman, in a critical review of staged orchiopexy, stated that there was no accurate documentation for spontaneous spermatic cord elongation after surgical manipulation.[76] He implied that the good results attained by staged orchiopexy reflected an inadequate primary operation. However, our review of the literature and, in particular, of the largest series of planned 2-stage orchiopexies[10] does not support this statement.

The feasibility of microvascular anastomoses of spermatic arteries and veins to the inferior epigastric and pudendal artery and vein with preservation of testicular viability was demonstrated in dogs recently.[77] Moreover, Romas and associates reported successful autotransplantation of a high undescended testis in 3 children.[78]

A single stage orchiopexy that preserves the testicular vessels is the ideal operation and would seem to have the best prospect of maintaining testicular viability and, therefore, ensuring proper endocrine secretion and germinal cell maturation. Woodard and Parrott demonstrated that a single stage orchiopexy without testicular vessel transection was feasible in young infants with intra-abdominal testes who had the prune belly syndrome.[79] They suggested that an early operation increased the likelihood of a successful 1-stage procedure.

Whether 2-stage orchiopexies or testicular vessel transection actually preserves endocrine function and the potential for fertility despite the fact that the testis may appear grossly normal in size and consistency is unknown.

The location of the impalpable testis, as would be anticipated, does appear to influence the result of orchiopexy. When testes are found in an intracanalicular position Jones reported successful scrotal placement in 73 percent of the cases is compared to 59 percent when

TABLE 8. Results of an Operation on Impalpable Undescended Testes

References	Intracana-licular	Removed or Poor Result No. (%)	Brought Down Successfully No. (%)
Jones[3]	34	9 (27)	25 (73)
Intra-abdominal			
Tibbs[2]	14	7 (50)	7 (50)
Jones[3]	42	17 (41)	25 (59)
Zer and associates[10]	62	14 (23)	48 (77)

the testis was in an intra-abdominal position.[3] However, Zer and associates reported excellent results in 62 intra-abdominal testes when planned 2-stage procedures were used (Table 8).[2,3,10]

It is noteworthy that one authority recommended that bilateral intra-abdominal testes be left in situ for their endocrine function unless, as rarely happens, the spermatic cord is long enough to allow these testes to be brought to the bottom of the scrotal sac without tension on the cord. Sterility must be accepted in this unfortunate group in the light of present knowledge.[80]

Orchiectomy generally is recommended in postpuberal male subjects with a unilateral impalpable testis because of the risks of malignancy and because most of these testes are irreversibly infertile organs. Bilateral impalpable testes in the postpuberal male subject presents a much more difficult problem. Most authorities recommend accepting the risk of malignancy to preserve the endocrine function of these testes.[11] The testes may be brought out to a subcutaneous position for easy examination and earlier detection of malignancy should it occur. Hinman recently recommended unilateral orchiectomy as another option.[81]

CONCLUSIONS

Endocrine tests can reliably predict anorchism in normal phenotypic male subjects less than 35 years old with 46-XY karyotypes and no obvious müllerian structures on rectal examination, thereby avoiding the need for surgical exploration.

There are no reliable endocrine or other tests that exclude the presence of a testis when 1 gonad is impalpable. Surgical exploration will detect a testis in 80 percent of the cases in the inguinal canal or intra-abdominally.

Monorchism or anorchism is proved by definitive identification of blind-ending spermatic vessels. A blind-ending vas or epididymis in the inguinal canal or at the internal inguinal ring does not have the same connotation. A more extensive exploration is mandatory in this situation to exclude wide separation of the vas from an intra-abdominal testis.

Intraperitoneal exploration is essential when searching for a non-palpable testis that cannot be located retroperitoneally.

Gonadal angiography or venography is not recommended as a routine procedure in patients with impalpable testes. Gonadal venography is helpful in those situations in which local thorough retroperitoneal and intraperitoneal exploration is unrewarding and when a separate loin or abdominal incision is being contemplated. Identification of a pampiniform-like plexus is highly suggestive of a retained testis.

Preservation of testicular artery continuity appears preferable to transection and would seem to hold out the best hope for optimum testicular function. Early exploration in infancy appears helpful in this regard. When this is not possible a staged orchiopexy or testicular vessel transection in selected cases with a long loop vas generally is satisfactory. Microsurgical autotransplantation of the testis into the scrotum has been shown to be feasible in a small number of cases.

Retained intra-abdominal testes constitute a significant risk to the patient from mortality secondary to malignant degeneration. Exploration is mandatory and orchiopexy is recommended in the prepubertal boy. Unilateral non-palpable testes are best removed postpuberally. In bilateral cases the testes should be retained for their endocrine function. Scrotal placement is the preferred procedure when possible. Alternatively, subcutaneous orchiopexy will render these testes accessible to examination.

REFERENCES

1. Campbell, H. E.: Incidence of malignant growth of the undescended testicle. A critical and statistical study. Arch Surg 44:353, 1942

2. Tibbs, D. J.: Unilateral absence of the testis. Eight cases of true monorchism. Br J Surg 48:601, 1961

3. Jones, P. G.: Undescended testes. Aust Paed J 2:36, 1966

4. Scorer, C. G. and Farrington, G. H.: Failure of testicular descent. In: Congenital Deformities of the Testis and Epididymis. New York: Appleton-Century-Crofts, chapt. 3, p. 39, 1971

5. Flach, A.: Maldescensus testis. Colloquium at Tubingen. Baltimore: Urban and Schwarzenberg, 1977

6. Illig, R., Exner, G. U., Kollmann, F., Kellerer, K., Borkenstein, M., Lunglmayr, L. Kuber, W. and Prader, A.: Treatment of cryptorchidism by intravasal synthetic luteinising-hormone-releasing hormone. Lancet 11:518, 1977

7. Scorer, C. G. and Farrington, G. H.: The testis at birth and during infancy. In: Congenital Deformities of the Testis and Epididymis. New York: Appleton-Century-Crofts, chapt. 2, p. 21, 1971

8. Gross, R. E. and Jewett, T. C., Jr.: Surgical experiences from 1,222 operations for undescended testes. JAMA 160:634, 1956

9. Scully, R. E., Galdabini, J. J. and McNeely, B. U.: Case records of the Massachusetts General Hospital. New Engl J Med 296:803, 1977

10. Zer, M., Wolloch, Y. and Dintsman, M.: Staged orchiorrhapy. Therapeutic procedure in cryptorchic testicle with a short spermatic cord. Arch Surg 110:387, 1975

11. Martin, D. C. and Menck, H. R.: The undescended testis: management after puberty. J Urol 114:77, 1975

12. Curtis, M. S. and Staggers, F. E.: Treatment of the undescended testis with especial reference to pathological anatomy. J Urol 83:693, 1960

13. Bill, A. H., Jr. and Shanahan, D. A.: The management of undescended testicle. Surg Clin N Amer 44:1571, 1964

14. Abeyaratne, M. R., Aherne, W. A. and Scott, J. E. S.: The vanishing testis. Lancet 2:822, 1969

15. Aynsley-Green, A., Zachmann, M., Illig, R., Rampini, S. and Prader, A.: Congenital bilateral anorchia in childhood: a clinical, endocrine and therapeutic evaluation of twenty-one cases. Clin Endocrinol 5:381, 1976

16. Borbrow, M. and Gough, M. H.: Bilateral absence of testes. Lancet 1:366, 1970

17. Campbell, M. F. and Harrison, J. H.: Anomalies of the genital tract. In: Urology. Philadelphia: W. B. Saunders Co., vol. 2, p. 1625, 1970

18. Fonkalsrud, E. W.: Current concepts in the management of the undescended testis. Surg Clin N Amer 50:847, 1970

19. Smith, A. M., Lattimer, J. K. and Rezvan, M.: Current therapy for undescended testes. Rationale for treatment between ages four and five. NY State J Med 73:2557, 1973

20. Lattimer, J. K., Smith, A. M., Dougherty, L. J. and Beck, L.: The optimum time to operate for cryptorchidism. Pediatrics 53:96, 1974

21. Leape, L. L.: Torsion of the testis. Invitation to error. JAMA 200:669, 1967

22. Whitaker, R. H.: Management of the undescended testis. Br J Hosp Med 4:25, 1970

23. Levitt, S. B., Kogan, S. J., Schneider, K. M., Becker, J. M., Sobel, E. H., Mortimer, R. H. and Engel, R. M. E.: Endocrine tests in phenotypic children with bilateral impalpable testes can reliably predict "congenital" anorchism. Urology 11:11, 1978

24. Amelar, R. D.: Infertility in Men; Diagnosis and Treatment. Philadelphia: F. A. Davis Co., p. 120, 1966

25. Santen, R. J. and Paulsen, C. A.: Hypogonadotropic eunuchoidism. II. Gonadal responsiveness to exogenous gonadotropins. J Clin Endo Metab 36:55, 1973

26. Wespi, H.: Hormonal treatment of cryptorchidism. Praxis (Bern), 348, 1954

27. Webster: Zit nach H. Dettmar: Indication and timing of hormonal and surgical treatment of cryptorchidism. Therapiewoche 9:334, 1959

28. Laron, Z. and Levy, J.: Diagnosis, treatment and follow-up of 326 cases as referred as undescended testes. Acta Endocr suppl. 101:14, 1965

29. LeLong, M. P., Petit, P., Canlorbe, P., Cendron, J., Borniche, P., Gothie, S. and Lange, J. C. L.: Our experiences on the treatment and future of cryptorchids. Symposium International Fertility Association, Amsterdam, 1964

30. Lowsley: Zit nach H. Dettmar: Indications and timing of hormonal and surgical treatment of cryptorchidism. Therapiewoche 9, 1959

31. Ehrlich, R. M., Dougherty, L. J., Tomashefsky, P. and Lattimer, J. K.: Effect of gonadotropin in cryptorchism. J Urol 102:793, 1969

32. Bierich, J. R.: Treatment by human chorionic gonadotrophin in maldescended testes. In: Maldescendsus Testis. Colloquium at Tubingen, Baltimore: Urban and Schwarzenberg, 1977

33. Knorr, D.: Diagnosis and therapy of disorders of descent of the testicles. Paediat Prox 9:299, 1970

34. Knorr, D.: Diagnosis and therapy of disorders of descent of the testicles. Paediat Prox 10:635, 1971

35. Lunderquist, A. and Rafstedt, S.: Roentgenologic diagnosis of cryptorchidism. J Urol 98:219, 1967

36. White, J. J., Haller, J. A., Jr. and Dorst, J. P.: Congenital inguinal hernia and inguinal herniography. Surg Clin N Amer 50:823, 1970

37. Ben-Menachem, Y., de Berardinis, M. C. and Salinas, R.: Localization of intra-abdominal testes by selective testicular arteriography: a case report. J Urol 112:493, 1974

38. Vitale, P. J., Khademi, M. and Seebode, J. J.: Selective gonadal angiography for testicular localization in patients with cryptorchidism. Surg Forum 25:538, 1974

39. Corriere, J. N., Jr. and Lipshultz, L. I.: Endocrinologic and radiographic evaluation of cryptorchid testes. In: Birth Defects, Original Article Series XIII. New York: Alan R. Liss, Publisher, vol. 5, p. 275, 1977

40. Nordmark, L.: Angiography of the testicular artery. I. Method of examination. Acta Radiol Diag 18:25, 1977

41. Amin, M. and Wheeler, C. S.: Selective testicular venography in abdominal cryptorchidism. J Urol 115:760, 1976

42. Weiss, R. M., Glickman, M. G. and Lytton, B.: Preoperative localization of nonpalpable undescended testes. In: Birth Defects, Original Article Series XIII. New York: Alan R. Liss, Publisher, vol. 5, p. 273, 1977

43. Notkovich, H.: Variations of the testicular and ovarian arteries in relation to the renal pedicle. Surg Gynec & Obst 103:487, 1956

44. Badenoch, A. W.: Failure of urogenital union. Surg Gynec & Obst 82:471, 1946

45. Lazarus, J. A. and Marks, M. S.: Anomalies associated with undescended testis. Complete separation of a partly descended epididymis and vas deferens and an abdominal testis. J Urol 57:567, 1947

46. Dean, A. L., Jr., Major, J. W. and Ottenheimer, E. J.: Failure of fusion of the testis and epididymis. J Urol 68:754, 1952

47. Lythgoe, J. P.: Failure of fusion of the testis and epididymis. Br. J Urol 33:80, 1961

48. Nowak, K.: Failure of fusion of epididymis and testicle with complete separation of the vas deferens. J Ped Surg 7:715, 1972

49. Whitehorn, C. A.: Complete unilateral wolffian duct agenesis with homolateral cryptorchism; a case report, its explanation and treatment; and the mechanism of testicular descent. J Urol 72:685, 1954

50. Dickinson, S. J.: Structural abnormalities in the undescended testis. J Ped Surg 8:523, 1973

51. Goldberg, L. M., Skaist, L. and Morrow, J. W.: Congenital absence of testes, anorchism and monorchism. Urology 3:840, 1974

52. Zelikovski, A., Abu-Dalu, J. and Urca, I.: Meso-appendicular testis. Br J Urol 47:579, 1974

53. Perlmutter, A.: Personal communication, 1975

54. Reckler, J. M., Rose, L. I. and Harrison, J. H.: Bilateral anorchism. J Urol 113:869, 1975

55. Tosi, S. E. and Morin, L. J.: The vanishing testis syndrome: indications for conservative therapy. J Urol 115:758, 1976

56. Levitt, S. B., Kogan, S. J. and Schneider, K. M.: Unpublished data, 1974

57. Harrison, R. G.: The distribution of the vasal and cremasteric arteries to the testis and their functional importance. J Anat 83:267, 1949

58. Bevan, A. D.: The surgical treatment of undescended testicle: a further contribution. JAMA 41:718, 1903

59. Bevan, A. D.: The operation for undescended testis: a further study and report. Ann Surg 90:847, 1929

60. Turner, G. G.: Imperfect migration of the testicle: the surgical problem. Proc Roy Soc Med 30:1319, 1937

61. MacCollum, D. W.: Clinical study of the spermatogenesis of undescended testicles. Arch Surg 31:290, 1935

62. Fowler, R. and Stephens, F. D.: The role of testicular vascular anatomy in the salvage of high undescended testes. Aust New Zeal J Surg 29:92, 1959

63. Fowler, R. and Stephens, F. D.: The role of testicular vascular anatomy in the salvage of high undescended testes. In: Congenital Malformations of the Rectum, Anus and Genito-Urinary Tracts. Edited by R. Webster. London: E. & S. Livingston Ltd., 1963

64. Brendler, H. and Wulfsohn, M. A.: Surgical treatment of the high undescended testis. Surg Gynec & Obst 124:605, 1967

65. Barnhouse, D. H.: Prune belly syndrome. Br J Urol 44:356, 1972

66. Datta, N. S., Tanaka, T., Zinner, N. R. and Mishkin, F. S.: Division of spermatic vessels in orchiopexy: radionuclide evidence of preservation of testicular circulation. J Urol 118:447, 1977

67. Levitt, S. B. and Kogan, S. J.: Unpublished data

68. Ehrlich, R. M.: Unpublished data

69. Snyder, W. H., Jr. and Chaffin, L.: Surgical management of undescended testes. Report of 363 cases. JAMA 157:129, 1955

70. Gross, R. E. and Replogle, R. L.: Treatment of the undescended testis. Opinions gained from 1,767 operations. Postgrad Med 34:266, 1963

71. Williams, D. I. and Burkholder, G. V.: The prune belly syndrome. J Urol 98:244, 1967

72. Lynn, H. B.: Undescended testis. Canadian Family Phy 15:33, 1969

73. Persky, L. and Albert, D. J.: Staged orchiopexy. Surg Gynec & Obst 132:43, 1971

74. Firor, H. V.: Two-stage orchiopexy. Arch. Surg., 102:598, 1971.

75. Corkery, J. J.: Staged orchiopexy—a new technique. J Ped Surg 10:515, 1975

76. Redman, J. F.: The staged orchiopexy: a critical review of the literature. J Urol 117:113, 1977

77. MacMahon, R. A., O'Brien, B. McC. and Cussen, L. J.: The use of microsurgery in the treatment of the undescended testis. J Ped Surg 11:521, 1976

78. Romas, N. A., Krisiloff, M. and Janecka. I. L.: The role of microsurgery in orchiopexy. Read at annual meeting of American Urological Association, Chicago, Illinois, April 24–28, 1977

79. Woodard, J. R. and Parrott, T. S.: Reconstruction of the urinary tract in prune belly uropathy. J Urol 119:824, 1978

80. Myers, R. P. and Kelalis, P. P.: Cryptorchidism reassessed: is there an optimal time for surgical correction? Mayo Clin Proc 48:94, 1973

81. Hinman, F.: Endocrinology of cryptorchidism. Read at annual meeting of American Urological Association, Chicago, Illinois, April 24–28, 1977

Commentary:
The Impalpable Testis: A Rational Approach to Management

David M. Mazor

Over the years the various techniques for dealing with the diagnosis and surgical correction of the undescended testis have been refined and greatly improved. The major diagnostic problems at present surround the "impalpable testis", and it is to this problem that physicians address themselves. All physicians at one time or another are confronted with the child in whom a testicle cannot be felt. A precise regimen for the management of this problem is outlined in the preceding article, one that can easily be followed in the practice of clinical urology.

Before reaching the conclusion that one is dealing with a truly impalpable testis, a thorough physical examination is essential. This examination should be conducted with the child made to feel as relaxed as possible. Palpation should be carried out in both the supine and upright positions. Care should be taken to search for an ectopic testis. This includes careful examination of the perineum as well as the superficial inguinal and suprapubic areas. When dealing with the undescended

testicle, intravenous urography should be performed. This is necessary because of the possibility of associated urinary tract anomalies. However, the absence of the ipsilateral testicle in the scrotum does not preclude the presence of the testicle elsewhere.

In reviewing the indications for orchiopexy, one routinely finds reference to the increased incidence of neoplasms of the cryptorchid testis in the postpubertal state, particularly in the third and fourth decades of life. This has recently been reviewed in depth by Martin.[1,2] For these reasons, if none other, it is important that a thorough search be made for the impalpable testis.

The basic surgical principles involved in orchiopexy have been described by Fonkalsrud in his review article in the *Surgical Clinics of North America*.[3] Familiarity with the spermatic surgical triangles and lateral spermatic ligament will prove of great aid when conducting the retroperitoneal dissection, which can prove quite tedious when dealing with an impalpable testis.[4] Great care should be taken when dissecting so that there is no compromise to what may be a tenuous blood supply.

When dealing with an impalpable testicle, one must be prepared to meet the situation where, despite meticulous dissection, the necessary length of the spermatic artery cannot be obtained. With the triple blood supply of the testis, division of the spermatic artery can be considered and may be successful. Before division of the spermatic artery a rubber-shod clamp is applied. The clamp should be applied for approximately 10 min before a final decision is made. If the testicle becomes cyanotic, the collateral blood supply is not adequate to permit division of the spermatic artery. In addition to this maneuver, Levitt and coauthors refer to the success achieved with microsurgery by Romas and associates. As time passes, undoubtedly there will be more reports of success with microsurgical techniques. When faced with inability to achieve adequate arterial length through ordinary means, the testicle should be left as low as possible and a second procedure carried out at a later date. The procedure described by Persky and Albert may be of aid.[5] They suggest placing the testis transseptally in the contralateral hemiscrotum. At the second stage, the testis is placed in its proper position. In those cases where adequate length can be obtained, the involved testis should be fixed in the hemiscrotum using the Dartos pouch method. This relatively simple technique greatly enhances the probability of a successful result. The pouch acts as an additional safeguard against retraction of the testicle. The value of the use of traction is questionable. If adequate length has been obtained, traction should not be necessary. In the past, when dealing with bilateral undescended testicles, I have advocated that each side be operated on independently.[6] However, bilateral impalpable testicles should be approached surgically at the same time, as recently recommended by Levitt and associates.

Studies have demonstrated that up to the age of 9 or 10 yr, the cryptorchid testes have not undergone irreparable histological change.[7,8] Consequently, orchiopexy can theoretically be performed in the prepubertal male with the idea of obtaining a satisfactory functional result. In practice, however, as suggested by Gross, it is best that the procedure be carried out before the boy reaches school age, at approximately age 5 yr.[9] Studies done by Kiesewetter and associates showed that following orchiopexy there is improvement in the architecture of the involved testicle.[10] In this study, 96% of the testes revealed some improvement. The spermatogenic potential of the orchiopexed testis has been seriously questioned by Charney.[7] However, in most series, as quoted by Fonkalsrud,[3] there is a high degree of fertility in men who have undergone orchiopexy.[3] It remains to be shown whether this merely reflects good function in the normally descended contralateral testis.

With proper application of the diagnostic and surgical procedures outlined by Levitt and associates, successful diagnosis and treatment of the impalpable testis can be expected. The results obtained will be pleasing to both the surgeon and patient.

REFERENCES

1. Martin DC: Germinal cell tumors of testis after orchiopexy. J Urol 121:422, 1979

2. Martin DC, Menck HR: The undescended testis: Management after puberty. J Urol 114:77, 1975

3. Fonkalsrud EW: Current concepts in the management of the undescended testis. Surg Clin North Am 50:847, 1970

4. Prentiss RJ, Weickgenant CJ, Moses JJ, et al: Undescended testis: Surgical anatomy of spermatic vessels, spermatic surgical triangles, and lateral spermatic ligament. J Urol 83:868, 1960

5. Persky L, Albert DJ: Staged orchiopexy. Surg Gynecol Obstet 132:42, 1971

6. Mazor DM: In Whitehead ED (ed): Current Operative Urology, pp 1160–1167. Hagerstown, Harper & Row, 1975

7. Charney CW: The spermatogenic potential of the undescended testis before and after treatment. J Urol 83:697, 1960

8. Sohval AR: Histopathology of cryptorchidism: A study based upon the comparative histology of retained and scrotal testes from birth to maturity. Am J Med 16:345, 1954

9. Gross RE, Replogle RL: Treatment of the undescended testis. Postgrad Med 34:266, 1963

10. Kiesewetter WB, Shull WR, Fetterman GM: Histologic changes in the testis following anatomically successful orchiopexy. J Pediatr Surg 4:59, 1969

BIBLIOGRAPHY

Fonkalsrud EW: Current concepts in the management of the undescended testis. Surg Clin North Am 50:847, 1970

This is a well-written and concise review of the topic of the undescended testicle. All aspects of the topic are dealt with. This paper provides a good entry into research into the topic of the cryptorchid.

Martin DC: Germinal cell tumors of testis after orchiopexy. J Urol 121:422, 1979

The world's literature regarding the incidence of tumor in the cryptorchid is reviewed. Particular attention is paid to the age at which orchiopexy should be performed. Although it cannot be proved conclusively, it seems the earlier in life the procedure is performed, the less chance the boy has of developing a tumor.

Additionally, the various types of tumors are reviewed, and, contrary to common thinking, seminoma is not found in the vast majority of patients.

Prentiss RJ, Weickgenant CJ, Moses JJ, et al: Undescended testis: Surgical anatomy of spermatic vessels, spermatic surgical triangles, and lateral spermatic ligament. J Urol 83:868, 1960

In terms of surgical techniques this paper represents a basic building block. Thorough retroperitoneal dissection is of great importance in obtaining the necessary length of the spermatic cord. The surgical principles described are well illustrated with excellent drawings of actual and theoretic situations. The theoretic findings are substantiated clinically with a series of 75 cases done by the authors. There is a thorough, concise, step-by-step review of the necessary maneuvers that must be carried out to ensure success. This article is a must for every surgeon who undertakes an orchiopexy.

Lattimer JK: Scrotal pouch technique for orchiopexy. J Urol 78:628, 1957

Prevention of retraction of the involved testis due to contractions of the cremaster is the aim of the scrotal pouch. It has become almost a standard procedure. Lattimer provides a well-written, well-illustrated description of the technique.

Brendler H, Wulfsohn MA: Surgical treatment of the high undescended testis. Surg Gynecol Obstet 124:605, 1967

As described, the testis has a multiple blood supply with the spermatic artery having many collaterals. There is an excellent description of the vascular anatomy of the cord and testis. The operative technique employed is simple. The success rate is enhanced by applying a vascular clamp and observing color changes in the testis. Dissection of the cord can be undertaken provided meticulous care is taken not to injure any collateral vessels.

Persky L, Albert DJ: Staged orchiopexy. Surg Gynecol Obstet 132:43, 1971

When the surgeon is unable to obtain desired length to place the testicle into the scrotum, a two-stage procedure is suggested. The technique described has had good results. Fashioning of a subcutaneous pouch helps prevent retraction. (Placement of the testis into the scrotum in the described manner may have an additional physiologic benefit in that the temperature is certainly lower than within the inguinal canal). The ipsilateral hemiscrotum is left untouched until the second and final stage.

Overview: Orchidopexy

Selwyn B. Levitt

Orchidopexy is one of the most frequently performed pediatric urologic procedures. Hinman (based on an incidence of cryptorchidism of 1% to 2% in prepubertal males estimated that as many as 30,000 orchidopexies are performed each year in the United States.[1-8]

RETRACTILE TESTES

The retractile or pseudocryptorchid gonad, secondary to an overactive cremasteric reflex, is most frequently confused with true cryptorchidism.[9] Differentiation is important, since retractile testes do not require surgical correction. Puri and Nixon found testicular volume and fertility to be normal among a group of 43 adults who were diagnosed in childhood as having bilateral retractile testes.[10]

Retractile testes are usually bilateral, whereas most cases of true undescended testes are unilateral. It is important that the child be made to feel as relaxed as possible during the examination and that the clinician warm his hands before palpating the scrotum. A deliberate sweeping movement with the flat of the hand moving from the internal inguinal ring toward the pubic tubercle and scrotum will coax most retractile testes into the most dependent part of the scrotum, where the testis should rest comfortably without tension. Undue traction on the cord, or failure to bring the testis into the most dependent portion of the scrotum, signifies incomplete descent or ectopia within the superficial inguinal pouch rather than a simple retractile testis. The sitting position with the thighs abducted, and knees hugged against the chest, aids in inducing retractile testes back into the scrotum. A squatting position with the buttocks resting on the examining table, knees apart and hugged against the chest, is preferable in older boys.[11] A short course of gonadotropin injections may be used to distinguish the retractile from the true undescended testis when the clinical examination is inconclusive.

ASSOCIATED ANOMALIES: PREOPERATIVE EVALUATION

A higher incidence of associated upper urinary tract anomalies and contralateral inguinal hernias have prompted some authors to recommend routine intravenous urograms or herniograms followed by screening films of the upper urinary tract in children with cryptorchidism.[12] Watson and colleagues, in a critical review of 400 asymptomatic boys with cryptorchidism, confirmed the increased incidence of upper urinary tract anomalies.[13] However, the yield of clinically important abnormalities defined by Donohue and colleagues as "those abnormalities resulting in significant loss of renal substance or requiring surgical correction for conservation of renal tissue" did not exceed 3.75%.[13,14] They concluded that since the cryptorchid patient carries an above-average risk of silent upper tract disease, careful clinical consideration must be given to this possibility in every case.

Clearly, any additional evidence of upper tract disease or the presence of other congenital anomalies makes an intravenous urogram mandatory. However, routine urography in the otherwise asymptomatic patient should only be undertaken with the realization that, contrary to previous reports in the literature, this test will result in a relatively low yield of significant upper tract disease. In practice, screening is rarely performed. Ultrasonography, which is a noninvasive examination, would seem to be the ideal screening test.[15] Intravenous urography is reserved for those patients with cryptorchidism with abnormal sonograms or those with signs or symptoms suggestive of a urologic malformation. A similar approach has been advocated for boys with hypospadias, a condition where the yield of correctible anomalies is about the same as in cryptorchidism.[16] Protagonists of more invasive tests such as the herniogram must document a significant incidence of contralateral "clinical" hernias before recommending the study as a routine preoperative test. Indeed, Leape described herniography as "a test in search of a disease."[17]

NONPALPABLE TESTES: PREOPERATIVE EVALUATION

During the past decade a great deal of attention has been focused on the preoperative demonstration and localization of nonpalpable testes. This interest has been spurred by the expectation that an accurate and reliable test demonstrating testicular absence might obviate the need for surgical exploration in patients with proven congenital anorchia ("vanishing testis syndrome") or monorchia. In contrast, preoperative definitive delineation of impalpable testes would avoid the unfortunate sequelae of a negative limited surgical exploration.[18,19] Moreover, accurate localization would limit the extent of the exploration and might expedite the operative procedure. Furthermore, the recognition that a successful outcome following orchidopexy was less certain in patients with impalpable testes prompted a more critical appraisal of the available diagnostic studies and of their role in improving the surgical result. The application of microsurgical techniques to accomplish orchidopexy in patients with high intra-abdominal testes has further fueled interest and debate regarding the need and specific indications for more precise preoperative diagnosis.

Endocrine tests have added a new dimension to the management of boys with nonpalpable gonads. A negative human chorionic gonadotropin (HCG) stimulation test and hypergonadotropism in a normal phenotypic male with a 46XY karyotype, no obvious müllerian structures on rectal examination, and no utricular pouch on retrograde urethrogram is diagnostic of congenital anorchia. Surgical exploration for confirmation is unnecessary.[20,21] The advent of readily available radioimmunoassay techniques that allow accurate measurements of follicle stimulating hormone (FSH), luteinizing hormone (LH), and testosterone in small serum samples, even when in low concentrations, has eliminated the need for cumbersome urinary collections. A positive HCG test (a rise in serum testosterone after HCG stimulation to values exceeding the upper limit of the normal prepubertal range) mandates thorough and extensive abdominal exploration. These hormone determinations are only useful in patients with bilateral nonpalpable gonads, and although they establish the presence or absence of testes, they do not localize the position of the gonads. Endocrine tests do not differentiate the unilateral impalpable undescended testis from congenital monorchia, except when HCG administered empirically induces sufficient descent to allow palpation of the gonad.

Other methods that have been advocated to determine the presence or absence, as well as the location of an impalpable testis, include pneumoperitoneography, herniography, aortography and selective gonadal angiography, and venog-raphy.[23–30] These tests are discussed in detail in the review article. Gonadal venography, when technically successful, appears to be the most reliable method for positive identification and precise localization of the impalpable testis and has an acceptably low morbidity. However, since routine inguinal skin crease incisions detect most impalpable testes in an intracanalicular position, and since most intra-abdominal testes are found in immediate juxtaposition to the internal inguinal ring, gonadal venography is not required in *children* in the majority of instances. Radiation exposure and the need for anesthesia in young children must be considered in determining the appropriate use of the procedure. Gonadal venography cannot be recommended preoperatively as a routine in children, although there appears to be a more cogent argument for its routine use in the adult, where the exploration and search for an impalpable testis is a more formidable operative undertaking.

More recently, ultrasound and computed tomography (CT) scanning have been advocated for preoperative localization of the impalpable testis.[31–33] Ultrasound, although useful for localization of a testis within the inguinal canal, is not helpful for testis localization within the pelvis or abdomen. Moreover, experience with ultrasound at some centers has been disappointing.[34] Advocates of the CT scan claim that its advantages include a lack of discomfort, short procedure time (30 to 45 min), easy reproducibility, and interpretation that does not depend on operator skill.[31,33] It is important that the descended gonad be shielded to limit its exposure to radiation. Lee and colleagues correctly predicted the position of eight impalpable testes using the CT scan.[33] The patients ranged in age from 9 to 38 yr. Four testes were found at surgery in the inguinal canal, and four intra-abdominally at or close to the internal ring. Houttuin and associates compared the accuracy of the CT scan to gonadal venography.[32] The CT scan correctly localized the impalpable testis in 73% of their patients (8 of 11) ranging in age from 10 to 51 yr. Gonadal venography, which was performed in 7 of the 11 patients, was technically successful in only 4, although in 3 of the 4 technically adequate studies the gonadal venogram did accurately locate the testis. The lack of body fat in young children prevents accurate delineation by CT scanning in the upper pelvis and abdomen, thereby detracting from its clinical application in children.

At present, for the child with cryptorchidism, these tests are probably best reserved for those patients in whom thorough local retroperitoneal and intraperitoneal exploration fails to detect a testis and in whom no blind-ending spermatic vessels are found. Failure to demonstrate blind-ending spermatic vessels might conceivably miss the rare high intra-abdominal testis with an absent vas, as has been reported by Whitehorn and by Dickinson[35,36] Another indication for preoperative testing in children is when a second exploration is contemplated following a previously inadequate limited procedure.

Laparoscopy, first suggested by Stone in 1929 for identification of an intra-abdominal testis, is now recommended for accurate preoperative localization of high intra-abdominal testes.[37,38] Advocates of laparoscopy claim that it is the simplest, safest, and most reliable method for localizing high intra-abdominal testes and for selecting appropriate patients for microvascular autotransplantation.[38] Laparoscopy can identify intra-abdominal testes that lack a long loop vas and therefore that are likely to fail the Fowler–Stephens test or atrophy following testicular vessel transection because of tension on the vasal collateral blood supply following scrotal placement of the testis. Laparoscopy appears to have an acceptably low complication rate in experienced hands.[39] Further experience will determine its exact role and define more precise indications for its use.

Experimental studies using radionuclide-labeled imaging agents to identify testicular tissue provide an exciting glimpse into the future. Static radionuclide testicular imaging is potentially an ideal noninvasive means of identifying an impalpable testis. ^{131}I-labeled LH has been used to image the testis in rats, but the necessary dose of this isotope would result in unacceptable gonadal and total body radiation in humans.[40] The radiopharmaceutical thallium 201, which has been used successfully as a myocardial imaging agent, is concentrated in the testis. Despite its relatively low fractional uptake by the gonads, it is possible to visualize rabbit testes very clearly at 24 and 48 hr.[41] The average dose of this agent that would be required for imaging in children (1 mCi of thallium 201) results in a radiation dose to the testis of 0.59 rad. This radiation dose is within acceptable levels and is comparable to or less than that incurred by a three to four film gonadal venogram with fluoroscopic placement of the gonadal vein catheter. Clinical trials will ultimately determine its usefulness.

GONADOTROPIN THERAPY

There is a wide divergence of opinion on the indications, efficacy, dosage, and duration of gonadotropin therapy in cryptorchidism. Most authorities recommend a therapeutic trial of HCG in cases of bilateral undescended testes, although many feel that it has little value in unilateral cryptorchidism. Ehrlich and associates are among the most enthusiastic supporters of gonadotropin therapy in the U.S. literature.[42] In their retrospective review, testicular descent occurred in 33% of bilateral cases and in 16% of unilateral cryptorchid testes when a total dose of 10,000 U of HCG was administered. However, in a recent analysis of the original report, Ehrlich admitted that the study was flawed by the retrospective nature of the review, the reliance on multiple observers, and a lack of controls.[34] Furthermore, he stated that gonadotropin therapy had rarely been successful in his own practice and that he had abandoned its use in unilateral cases. Bierich has cited success rates in reported series ranging from 20% to 90%.[43] He himself observed a 50% descent rate in unilateral cases. This was almost certainly an overestimate, since 25% of the "successfully" treated gonads subsequently required further therapy because of retraction that occurred within a few weeks after terminating the therapy. Knorr and his group reported results similar to those of Bierich using a total of 10,000 U of HCG over a 5-wk period.[44,45]

Extensive experience has shown that an effective dose of HCG not high enough to cause gonadal damage is age dependent. A group of specialists invited to discuss the problem by the International Health Foundation in Geneva in 1973 recommended a total dose of 2500 to 3000 U for boys up to age 2 yr, 5000 U for children of 2 to 6 yr, and 10,000 units for boys more than 6 yr.[46]

Gonadotropin therapy is contraindicated in ectopic undescended testes (characterized by their extreme lateral mo-

bility), in cryptorchids with associated clinical hernias, in testicular retraction following herniotomy, and when sexual maturation is already well underway.

Some authors advocate gonadotropin administration to enlarge the underdeveloped scrotum as well as the testes and claim that this facilitates the subsequent surgery.[47,48] Lynch and Kaplan recently reported their results in two series of comparable patients undergoing orchidopexy procedures at different medical centers using different surgical approaches.[49] No beneficial effect of prior treatment with HCG was noted in either group of patients.

More recently, there have been reports of successful treatment with synthetic luteinizing hormone releasing hormone (LHRH) given intramuscularly, subcutaneously, or intranasally.[50–54] Success rates comparable to HCG have been achieved, although the convenient intranasal sprays required about 20 to 40 times the injected dose to achieve comparable LH blood concentrations. This renders the treatment very expensive. Higher doses of intranasal LHRH twice a day achieved a higher testicular descent rate at the end of 1 wk than lower doses given more frequently, suggesting that brief bursts of LH may be more important in initiating descent than prolonged stimulation with low concentrations.[54,55] Thus, LHRH does not appear to have any particular advantage over HCG in the treatment of cryptorchidism. Moreover, the convenient intranasal LHRH is not available commercially at present.

INDICATIONS AND TIMING OF ORCHIDOPEXY

Fertility. It is unanimously agreed that the testes should reside in the scrotum before puberty if optimum maturation of the germinal elements is to be expected. The optimum time for hormone administration or orchidopexy, however, remains controversial. Opinion has shifted somewhat toward earlier intervention. Detailed histologic and electron microscopic studies of testicular biopsy specimens from cryptorchid infants and young children indicate that maturation lag in the germinal epithelium as well as in Leydig cell development begins between 1 and 2 yr of age.[56–58] However, to date, an improved fertility rate has not been demonstrated in unilateral cryptorchids who have undergone earlier surgery.

Recent endocrine determinations and semen evaluations of men who have had prepubertal unilateral orchidopexies bring Charny's 1960 conclusions to mind: "Prevailing methods of treatment of cryptorchidism are not satisfactory and the operative techniques as practiced by most surgeons yield better cosmetic than functional results."[59,60] Despite this pessimistic statement there is some evidence to suggest that fertility potential is enhanced by successful prepubertal unilateral orchidopexy, even though testicular endocrine function and mean sperm counts remain significantly lower than normal adult controls. Review of the literature reveals that unoperated unilateral cryptorchid patients will demonstrate decreased fertility (46%) when compared to surgically treated patients (62%).[59] Bilateral untreated cryptorchidism is almost universally associated with infertility, whereas following orchidopexy, fertility rates ranging from 48% to 70% to 80% are reported.[61–63]

Based on current evidence, the optimum time for performing orchidopexy appears to be before age 5 yr and possibly as early as 1 to 2 yr. The decision to perform an orchidopexy at this young age in order to provide the conditions for optimal germ cell and interstitial cell maturation potential must be weighed against the increased risk of surgery to the delicate cord structures. This risk is minimized when early orchidopexy is performed by surgeons who operate frequently on babies and young children and who have the necessary training and experience required to deal with the more delicate cord structures.

Malignancy. It has long been held that orchidopexy does not afford any protection against subsequent malignant degeneration but merely renders the testis more amenable to examination and therefore presumably to earlier diagnosis of malignancy. Orchidopexy before age 5 yr, however, may reduce the incidence of malignancy, since only 6 cases of testis tumors have been reported where orchidopexy was performed before age 10 yr.[64] Many of the reported patients who developed malignant degeneration had orchidopexies after the age of 20 yr. The youngest age at which orchidopexy was performed in a patient who subsequently developed a testicular tumor is age 5 yr.[65]

The small number of tumors reported where the orchidopexy was performed before age 10 yr is encouraging, although it does not constitute convincing evidence of the protective effect of early orchidopexy. The long latent period before malignant degeneration, the fact that early orchidopexy has not been advocated or widely practiced until recently, and the lack of data regarding the numbers of patients at risk do not allow firm conclusions to be made regarding the protective effect of early orchidopexy.

A recent study by Batata, who reviewed the Memorial Hospital (New York) experience of malignancy in cryptorchid patients, suggests that scrotal placement of the testis did not even allow earlier detection of malignancy.[66] Untreated abdominal and groin testes and successfully placed scrotal undescended testes were found to have similar stages of malignancy at diagnosis, similar rates of metastasis after treatment, and similar 5-yr tumor-free survival rates after treatment. However, this report is marred by the fact that the patients referred to Memorial Hospital represent a highly selected group, frequently with advanced disease and with difficult and unusual problems. Such a referral center is not likely to encounter the patient who has had successful scrotal placement of an undescended testis, thereby allowing for early recognition of malignant degeneration, and who is cured of his tumor by early radical orchiectomy and appropriate adjuvant treatment. Moreover, the retrospective survey at Memorial was conducted before the modern era of highly effective multiagent chemotherapeutic treatment of testicular malignancies.

Torsion. The higher incidence of nonviability of the testis following torsion of an undescended testis results from the increased difficulty in diagnosis.[67] This is yet another reason to favor early orchidopexy.

Psychologic Factors. Recent psychiatric studies suggest that boys become aware of their genitalia between age 3 and 6 yr and show concern about any differences between themselves and their peers earlier than was previously suspected.[47] Early treatment would obviate any anxiety in this regard.

CONTRAINDICATIONS TO ORCHIDOPEXY

Orchidopexy postpubertally of a unilateral groin or intra-abdominal undescended testis should be avoided because it does not enhance fertility potential and leaves an organ that is at increased risk of malignant degeneration. These patients are best protected from malignancy and are offered the best cosmetic result at minimal risk by exploration, orchiectomy, and placement of a testicular prosthesis. The malignant potential and computed mortality in patients with retained intra-abdominal testes are significantly higher than the risk of mortality from surgical exploration, at least in patients of less than 50 yr.[68] The National Halothane study showed a 0.23% mortality for operations of comparable magnitude. Even the cosmetic result is inadequate in most cases, since the testis is usually smaller than normal. No treatment ignores the risk of malignancy and does not deal with the cosmetic and psychologic aspects.

The small atrophic or dysgenetic testis, at any age, is best excised. Hinman has argued for orchiectomy rather than orchidopexy, irrespective of testis size, even in prepubertal boys with unilateral intra-abdominal undescended testes.[69] I take strong exception to this recommendation and prefer to individualize treatment. Not all high undescended testes are structurally abnormal, and early orchidopexy may ultimately be shown to convey some protection against subsequent malignancy and may improve fertility potential. Prospective longitudinal studies are needed to determine a lower limit for testis size, beyond which orchiectomy would be more appropriate.

Hinman has also argued against surgical intervention in children with severe mental retardation, those with major endocrine and genetic disorders, and in boys who will be unable to ejaculate.[70] However, such determinations cannot be based solely on medical reasoning. Psychosocial factors and family considerations such as religious, moral, and social attitudes are probably more important in aiming at a satisfactory decision in these cases.

Children with prune-belly syndrome probably do not have an increased proclivity to malignant degeneration of their testes. Modern surgical techniques, particularly when applied in infancy, yield very satisfactory cosmetic results, and the psychologic satisfaction of having one's own organs rather than prostheses would seem to be an added advantage.[71] Moreover, the occasional patient without ejaculatory duct abnormalities may even be fertile. No treatment or placement of prostheses effectively denies fertility to all patients.

SURGICAL PRINCIPLES

The basic principles of successful orchidopexy include complete mobilization of the testis without damage to the associated vessels or vas, high ligation of the hernial sac, placement of the testis into the scrotum without tension, and fixation to prevent retraction. Ideally, these objectives are achieved in a single operation with preservation of the continuity of the testicular artery and vein.

Rosenmerkel reported the first attempt at orchidopexy, but Bevan in 1899 ushered in the modern era of orchidopexy by describing the fundamental technique of adequate testicular mobilization and high hernial sac ligation.[72,73] LaRoque emphasized the principle of greater exposure through retroperitoneal dissection.[74] Gross reemphasized the importance of thorough retroperitoneal dissection through a wide inguinal exposure, dividing the transversalis fascia and inferior epigastric vessels, thus moving the cord even closer to the midline, as had been suggested earlier by Davison and by Gessner.[75-77] Prentiss and associates supported this concept with elegant calculations made from cadaver and clinical dissections that demonstrated the actual increased length of the spermatic vessels obtained by obliteration of the frontal and sagittal spermatic triangles.[78] Torek, and later Ombredanne, described different techniques for testicular fixation.[79,80] Torek's method involves fixation of the testis to the fascia of the inner surface of the thigh. Ombredanne preferred contralateral scrotal fixation of the testis. Cabot and Nesbit described a more gentle and intermittent form of traction using rubber band fixation of the testis to the thigh in an effort to reduce the high incidence of testicular atrophy resulting from the aforementioned techniques of fixation.[81] Shoemaker and Petrivalsky both further refined the method of testicular fixation with their descriptions of the subdartos pouch technique.[82,83] This is the most widely used fixation procedure today and is the one I prefer.

Some surgeons advocate some or all of these maneuvers for routine conventional orchidopexy in palpable undescended testes. However, my own experience supports Koop's approach.[84,85] Most standard pediatric orchidopexies for palpable undescended testes can readily be accomplished through a small transverse inguinal skin-crease incision. A rolled towel placed under the lumbosacral spine produces lumbar lordosis, which stretches the inguinal skin crease and smoothes out its contour, thereby facilitating the incision. The external oblique aponeurosis is incised in the direction of its fibers through the external ring rather than leaving it intact, as Koop has suggested, since I prefer the exposure obtained and see no advantage in preserving the ring. The most important aspect of the operative procedure is careful and patient mobilization of the delicate hernia sac from the cord structures and high ligation of the sac. An intact processus vaginalis facilitates expeditious dissection, although this goal is not always possible to achieve. Entering the sac in no way represents a disaster. It merely makes the dissection a little more tedious, particularly in infants. This standard approach to orchidopexy will frequently suffice even in boys with nonpalpable undescended testes, provided that the mesorchium is sufficiently long to allow the testis to slide down into the processus vaginalis. After high ligation of the hernial sac, the testis is replaced in the tunica vaginalis and positioned in a subdartos pouch, securing the tunica albuginea loosely to the dependent portion of the scrotum with a simple absorbable suture. A subdartos pouch is routinely used; it prevents testicular retraction, which occasionally occurs despite adequate mobilization and cord length. The transverse scrotal skin incision for the subdartos pouch is made in the midscrotum, care being taken to develop the subdartos pouch sufficiently to allow the testis to be readily accommodated.

Orchidopexy for palpable undescended testes can usually be performed on an ambulatory basis, and most children do not require admission into the hospital. Nonpalpable undescended testes that do not require extensive dissection can be similarly handled. Should the dissection prove tedious, the child is kept overnight or admitted into the hospital.

When a long mesorchium is not identified using the standard inguinal skin-crease incision, the internal ring is opened laterally and the retroperitoneal space is widely developed. Some surgeons prefer a midline transabdominal or preperitoneal approach for the nonpalpable testis, whether unilateral or bilateral.[86-89] Keen judgment is required at this juncture to determine whether high ligation of the sac with obliteration of the frontal and spermatic triangles will allow adequate cord length for placement of the testis without tension into the scrotum. Any dissection of the hernial sac close to the testis at this stage will interfere with the collateral circulation through the vas and will preclude the possibility of a one-stage procedure by testicular vessel transection. Clatworthy has emphasized the importance of a "premeditated" and not a "salvage" Fowler–Stephens procedure.[90] His overall success rate was 85% when the procedure was premeditated. All intracanalicular testes and two of 14 intra-abdominal testes survived. However, salvage attempts using testicular vessel transection after efforts to bring the testicle down by dissection of the cord resulted in a viable testis in only 54% of cases (6 of 11). Gibbons and colleagues analyzed the factors that contributed to failure in their early cases of testicular vessel transection. They concluded that inexperience with the Fowler–Stephens procedure, extensive cord dissection, division of the spermatic artery and vein too close to the testis, and failure to leave a broad pedicle of vascularized visceral peritoneum overlying the vas were the main factors contributing to failure.[91] Segmental vas atresia or a detached epididymis was considered by these authors as a contraindication to the operation, since these conditions carry the uncertainty of an adequate collateral vascular supply. Identification of these errors and careful attention to detail resulted in no further instances of testicular atrophy in their subsequent ten patients treated by testicular vessel transection.

When testicular vessel transection is not feasible, a two-stage orchidopexy can be performed. Indeed, as is indicated in the review article, many authors prefer this approach. The reported results of two-stage procedures appear to be comparable to or better than those of testicular vessel transection. Firor recommended an interval of at least 6 mo between the first and second stage.[92] Corkery described a technique of placing the testis and spermatic cord in a Silastic envelope at the first operation in order to reduce the extensive adhesions between the testis and the inguinal tissues that usually make the second operation both tedious and excessively vascular.[93] However, some authors feel that the presence of the silicone sheath may deprive the testis and cord of important secondary neovascular collateralization, which ultimately may be essential to sustain the testis after the second stage.[91] Extreme caution is necessary to avoid injury to the vessels of the gonad during the second operation. Evans and colleagues report a high incidence of testicular atrophy following secondary orchidopexy, even when the procedure is performed by an experienced surgeon.[94]

The application of microvascular surgical techniques for anastomosis of the spermatic vessels to the vessels of the thigh or inferior epigastric vessels has introduced testicular autotransplantation into the armamentarium for managing high intra-abdominal undescended testes. The first successful case of microvascular autotransplantation of the testis in a boy aged 9 yr with prune-belly syndrome was reported by Silber and Kelly in 1976.[95] The publication, although interesting, did not meet with an early enthusiastic response.[91, 96] The intensive training and constant practice required to maintain the skill necessary for microsurgery, as well as the equipment, renders the procedure unrealistic for the majority of surgeons confronted intraoperatively with a high intra-abdominal undescended testis. The results of more conventional well-tried surgical techniques that are readily available to most surgeons that attain satisfactory results in at least 80% of cases seemed to relegate autotransplantation to the realm of the exotic.

MacMahon and colleagues reported five successful cases in eight autotransplants.[97] A recent compilation of seven series of microsurgical testicular autotransplants performed in the United States, including 19 published and unpublished cases, where the age range was from 20 mo to 30 yr, indicated a 100% success rate.[98] Skeptics are aware that surgeons tend to report successes and forget about their failures. However, this probably applies equally to the reports of success with testicular vessel transection as well as to staged orchidopexy. Evidence is accumulating that suggests that microsurgical autotransplan-

tation can be successful in a high percentage of patients. Moreover, it is frequently successful even in situations where conventional techniques are doomed to failure. Microsurgical autotransplantation appears to be the procedure of choice, at least on one side, in bilateral high intra-abdominal cryptorchidism when adverse circumstances are present. These include an inadequate or equivocal vasal collateral blood supply, such as when tension on the vas is likely, or when dissection of the hernial sac has been performed too close to the testis and a primary one-stage orchidopexy is elected.

COMPLICATIONS

Success rates vary widely in different published series and most patients have not been subjected to a prolonged period of observation. Success, defined by satisfactory scrotal placement of a grossly adequate testis, has been reported overall in 60% to 90% of cases.[94,99–101] Palpable testes fare much better than nonpalpable ones.

Testicular atrophy, when primary orchidopexy is performed by experienced surgeons, occurs in about 5% of cases.[102] Injury to the vas has been reported in approximately 1% of operations.[102] However, these figures are probably grossly inaccurate and do not lend themselves to verification.

REFERENCES

1. Buemann B, et al: Incidence of undescended testes in the newborn. Acta Chir (Suppl) 283:289, 1961

2. Johnson WW: Cryptorchidism. JAMA 113:25, 1939

3. Cour Palais IJ: Spontaneous descent of the testicle. Lancet 1:1403, 1966

4. Scorer GC: The descent of the testis arch. Dis Child 39:605, 1964

5. Ward B, Hunter WB: The absent testicle. A report on a survey carried out among school boys in Nottingham. Br Med J 1:1110, 1960

6. Hennessey J, Doyle CT, Brady MP: The effect of orchidopexy on the ectopic testis. Br J Surg 61:920, 1974

7. Evans JP, Rutherford JH, Bagskaw PF: Orchidopexy in prepubertal boys—five year survey. Urology 12:509, 1978

8. Hinman F Jr: Scientific background: Research grant application to National Institute of Health. Cryptorchism: Age, site, and histology, 1980

9. Charwey CW, Wolgin W: Cryptorchidism. New York, Harper & Row, 1957

10. Puri P, Nixon HH: Bilateral retractile testes—subsequent effects on fertility. J Pediatr Surg 12:563, 1977

11. Van Essen W: The retractile testis. Postgrad Med J 42:270, 1966

12. Engel RME: Cryptorchid testes. In Ehrlich RM (ed): Dialogues in Pediatric Urology, Vol 1, no 5., William J Muller, 1978

13. Watson RA, Lennox KW, Gangai MP: Simple cryptorchidism; the value of the excretory urogram as a screening method. J Urol 113:789, 1974

14. Donohue RE, Utley WLF, Maling TM: Excretory urography in asymptomatic boys with cryptorchidism. J Urol 109:912, 1973

15. Levitt SB: Cryptorchid testes. In Ehrlich RM (ed): Dialogues in Pediatric Urology, Vol 1, no. 5., William J Muller, 1978

16. Lutzker LG, Kogan SJ, Levitt SB: Is routine intravenous urography indicated in patient with hypospadias. Pediatrics 59:630, 1977

17. Leape L: Herniograms—a commentary. Surgery 83:361, March 1978

18. Levine LS: Preoperative detection of hidden testes. Am J Dis Child 121:176, 1971

19. Burns E, Segaloff A, Carrera GM: Follow up on previously reported congenital absence of gonads. J Urol 101:343, 1969

20. Aynsley-Green A, Zachmann M, Illig R, et al: Congenital bilateral anorchia in childhood: A clinical, endocrine and therapeutic evaluation of twenty-one cases. Clin Endocrinol 5:381, 1976

21. Levitt SB, Kogan SJ, Schneider KM, et al: Endocrine tests in phenotypic children with bilateral impalpable testes can reliably predict "congenital" anorchism. Urol 1:11, 1978

22. Lunderquist A, Rafstedt S: Roentgenologic diagnosis of cryptorchism. J Urol 98:219, 1967

23. White JJ, et al: Herniography: A diagnostic refinement in the management of cryptorchidism. Am Surg 39:624, 1973

24. Vitale PJ, Khademi M, Seebode JJ: Selective gonadal angiography for testicular localization in patients with cryptorchidism. Surg Forum 25:538, 1974

25. Ben-Menachem U, deBerardinis C, Salinas R: Localization of intraabdominal testes by selective testicular arteriography: A case report. J Urol 112:493, 1974

26. Corrierre J: Panel discussion on "cryptorchidism," presented at International Meeting of the Society of Pediatric Urologists, Philadelphia, 1976

27. Amin M, Wheeler CS: Selective testicular venography in abdominal cryptorchidism. J Urol 115:760, 1976

28. Nordmark L: Angiography of the testicular artery. 1 method of examination. Acta Radiol 18:25, 1977

29. Domellof L, Hjalmas K, Nordmark L, et al: Angiography of the testicular artery as a diagnostic aid in boys with nonpalpable testis. J Pediatr Surg 13:534, 1978

30. Weiss RM, Glickman MG, Lytton B: Venographic localization of the nonpalpable undescended testis. Presented at the Society of Pediatric Urologists, Las Vegas, 1976

31. Madrazo BL, Flugo RC, Parks JA, et al: Ultrasonographic demonstration of undescended testes. Radiology 133:181, 1979

32. Houttuin E, Hawathaneh IS, Gregory JG, et al: CAT scan cases search for undescended testes. Presented at American Urologic Association meeting, New York, 1979

33. Lee JKT, McClennan BL, Stanley RJ, et al: Utility of computed tomography in the localization of the undescended testis. Radiology 125:121, 1980

34. Ehrlich RM: Cryptorchid testes. In Ehrlich RM (ed): Dialogues in Pediatric Urology, Vol 1, no 5. William J Miller Associates, 1978

35. Whitehorn CA: Complete unilateral wolffian duct agenesis with homolateral cryptorchism; a case report, its explanation and treatment; and the mechanism of testicular descent. J Urol 72:685, 1954

36. Dickinson SJ: Structural abnormalities in the undescended testis. J Pediatr Surg 8:523, 1973

37. Stone ZE: Intraabdominal examination with the aid of the peritoneoscope. J Kansas Med Soc 24:63, 1929

38. Cohen R, Silber SJ: Laparoscopy for cryptorchidism. J Urol (in press)

39. Wheeless CR: Laparoscopy in operative gynecology. In Mattingly RF (ed): Operative Gynaecology. Philadelphia, JB Lippincott, 1977

40. Bruschini H, Hattner R, Okerlund M, et al: Feasibility of localizing ectopic testes by ^{131}-I labeled luteinizing hormone scintigraphy. Urology 9:657, 1977

41. Ongseng F, Chervu LR, Kogan SJ, et al: Static testicular imaging utilizing 201_{T11}. Invest Urol 16:451, 1979

42. Ehrlich RM, Dougherty LJ, Tomaskefsky P, et al: Effect of gonadotropin in cryptorchidism. J Urol 102:793, 1969

43. Bierich JR: Treatment by human chorionic gonadotropin in maldescended testes. In Bierich JR, Rager K, Ranke MB (eds): Maldescensus Testis. Baltimore, Urban & Schwarzenberg, 1977

44. Knorr D: Diagnose und therapie der Deszensustorungen des Hodens. Paediat Prax 9:299, 1970

45. Knorr D: Diagnose und therapie der Deszensustorungen des Hodens. Paediat Prax 10:635, 1971

46. Bay V, Bierich JR, Hecker W CHR, et al: Empfehlunger zur Behardlung des Hodenhochstardes. Dtsch Med Wochenschv 98:549, 1974

47. Lattimer JK, Smith AM, Dougherty LJ, et al: The optimum time to operate for cryptorchidism. Pediatrics 53:96, 1974

48. Thompson WO, Hecker WJ: Undescended testes: Present status of glandular treatment. JAMA 112:297, 1939

49. Lynch DF, Kaplan GW: Orchiopexy: Experience at 2 centers. Presented before The Society for Pediatric Urology, American Urological Association, meeting, San Francisco, May 1980

50. Bartsch G, Frick J: Therapeutic effects of luteinizing hormone releasing hormone (LHRH) on cryptorchidism. Andrologia 6:197, 1974

51. White MC, Ginsburg J: Treatment of cryptorchidism by synthetic luteinizing hormone-releasing hormone. Lancet 2:1361, 1977

52. Happ J, et al: Intranasal GNRH therapy of maldescended testes. Hormone metabolic Res 7:440, 1975

53. Illig R et al: Treatment of cryptorchidism by intranasal synthetic luteinizing hormone releasing hormone: Results of a collaborating double-blind study. Lancet 2:518, 1977

54. Pirazzoli P, et al: Luteinizing hormone-releasing hormone nasal spray as therapy for undescended testicle. Arch Dis Child 58:235, 1978

55. Cryptorchidism and gonadotrophin therapy. Lancet: 1344: 1978

56. Mengel W, Hienz HA, Sippe WG, et al: Studies on cryptorchidism: A comparison of histologic findings in the germinative epithelium before and after the second year of life. J Pediatr Surg 9:445, 1974

57. Hedinger CHR: The histopathology of the cryptorchid testes.

Chapter 4. Maldescensus testis (edited by Bierich JR, Rager J, Ranke MB):29, Munich 1977

58. Hadziselimovic F, Herzog B, Seguchi H: Surgical correction of cryptorchidism at 2 years, electron microscopic and morphologic investigation. J Pediatr Surg 10:19, 1975

59. Lipshultz LI, Caminos-Torres R, Greenspan CS, et al: Testicular function after orchidopexy for unilaterally undescended testis. New Engl J Med 295:15, 1976

60. Charney CW: The spermatogenic potential of the undescended testis before and after treatment. J Urol 83:697, 1960

61. Bramble FJ, Houghton AL, Eccles S: Reproductive and endocrine function after surgical treatment of bilateral cryptorchidism. Lancet 2:311, 1974

62. Scott LS: Fertility in cryptorchidism. Proc R Soc Med 55:1047, 1962

63. Gross RE, Jewett TC Jr: Surgical experiences from 1222 operations for undescended testes. JAMA 160:634, 1956

64. Martin DC: Germinal cell tumors of the testis after orchidopexy. J Urol 121:422, 1979

65. Grove JS: The cryptorchid problem. J Urol 71:735, 1954

66. Batata MS: Cryptorchidism with testicular cancer. Read at Annual Meeting. Clinical Society of Genitourinary Surgeons, New York, Feb. 9, 1979

67. Leape L: Torsion of the testis, invitation to error. JAMA 200:669, 1967

68. Martin DC, Menck HR: The undescended testis: Management after puberty. J Urol 114:77, 1975

69. Hinman F Jr: Unilateral abdominal cryptorchidism. J Urol 122:71, 1979

70. Hinman F Jr: Alternatives to orchidopexy. Presented before the Society for Pediatric Urology, May 12, 1979

71. Woodard Jr: The prune belly syndrome. Urol Clin North Am 5:75, 1978

72. Rosenmerkel JF: Ueber die Radicalcur des in der Weiche Liegenden Testikels bei nicht Descensus Desselben. Munich, J Lindauer, 1820

73. Bevan AD: Operation for undescended testicle and congenital inguinal hernia. JAMA 33:773, 1899

74. LaRoque GP: A modification of Bevan's operation for undescended testicle. Ann Surg 94:314, 1931

75. Gross RE: Undescended testicle (cryptorchidism). In The Surgery of Infancy and Childhood, p. 472. Philadelphia, WB Saunders, 1953

76. Davison C: The surgical treatment of undescended testicle. Surg Gynecol Obstet 12:293, 1911

77. Gessner HB: Davison's operation for undescended testicle. New Orleans Med Surg J 65:741, 1913

78. Prentiss RJ, Weickgenant CJ, Moses JU, et al: Undescended testis: Surgical anatomy of spermatic vessels, spermatic surgical triangles and lateral spermatic ligament. J Urol 83:686, 1960

79. Torek F: The technic of orchiopexy. NY J Med 90:948, 1909

80. Ombredanne L: Sur l'orchiopexie. Bull Soc Pediatr 25:473, 1927

81. Cabot H, Nesbit RM: Undescended testis. Arch Surg 22:850, 1931

82. Shoemaker J: Uber cryptorchismus und seine behandlung. Chirurg 4:1, 1932

83. Petrivalsky J: Zur behandlung des leistenhoden. Zentralbl Chir 58:1001, 1939

84. Koop CE: Inguinal herniorrhaphy in infants and children. Surg Clin North Am 37:1675, 1957

85. Koop CE: Technique of herniorrhaphy and orchiopexy. VI. Cryptorchidism. In Bergsma D, Duckett, JW (eds): Urinary Systems and Malformations in Children, p 303. New York, Alan R. Liss, 1977

86. Flinn RA, King LR: Experiences with the midline transabdominal approach in orchiopexy. Surg Gynecol Obstet 131:295, 1971

87. Berg OL: Editorial letter. J Urol 121 4:546, 1979

88. Lipton S: Use of Cheatle-Henry approach in the treatment of cryptorchidism. Surgery 50:846, 1961

89. Boley SJ, Kleinhaus SA: A place for the Cheatle–Henry approach in pediatric surgery. J Pediatr Surg 1:394, 1966

90. Clatworthy HW Jr, Hollanbaugh RS, Grosfeld JL: The "long loop vas" orchidopexy for the high undescended testis. Am Surg 38:69, 1972

91. Gibbons MD, Cromie WJ, Duckett JW Jr: Management of the abdominal undescended testicle. J Urol 122:76, July 1979

92. Firor HV: Two stage orchiopexy. Arch Surg 192:598, 1971

93. Corkery JJ: Staged orchiopexy—a new technique. J Pediatr Surg 10:515, 1975

94. Evans JP, Rutherford JH, Bagshaw PF: Orchiopexy in prepubertal boys—five year survey. Urology 12:509, 1978

95. Silver SJ, Kelly J: Successful autotransplantation of an intra-abdominal testis to the scrotum by microvascular technique. J Urol 115:452, 1976

96. Belker AM: Urologic microsurgery—current perspectives. 11. Orchiopexy and testicular homotransplantation. Urology 15:103, 1980

97. MacMahon RA, O'Brien B McC, Aberdeen J, et al: Results of the use of autotransplantation of the intraabdominal testis using microsurgical vascular anastomosis. J Pediatr Surg 15:92, 1980

98. Levitt SB: Presented in a discussion of the intra-abdominal testis, at the Society for Pediatric Urology and American Urological Association meeting. San Francisco, May 18, 1980

99. Gross RE, Replogle RL: Treatment of the undescended testis. Postgrad Med J 34:266, 1963

100. Scorer GC, Farrington G: Congenital Deformities of the Testis and Epididymis. New York, Appleton-Century-Crofts, 1971

101. Retief PJM: Fertility in undescended testes. South Afr Med J 52:610, 1977

102. Fonkalsrud WE: The undescended testis. Current Problems in Surgery, 15:5, 1978

PART FORTY-SIX

SURGERY OF TESTICULAR TORSION AND TORSION OF TESTICULAR APPENDAGES

118

TORSION OF THE TESTIS
Invitation to Error

Lucian L. Leape, MD

From the surgical services of the Alder Hey Children's Hospital, West Derby,
Liverpool, England.

Reprinted From The Journal of The American Medical Association
May 22, 1967, Vol. 200, pp. 669–672
Copyright 1967, by American Medical Association

One hundred forty-eight consecutive cases of scrotal pain and swelling in boys under
the age of 16 have been reviewed. Eighty-nine of these suffered from torsion, either of
the testis or appendix testis. Similarity in clinical history and physical findings makes
differentiation of torsion from epididymo-orchitis difficult. Operation in all appears to
be the only safe treatment. Delay in operation is disastrous with no testicular salvage
after 24 hours. On the other hand, 17 of 19 operated upon on the day of onset of
symptoms had viable testes.

When the surgeon operates for torsion of the testis, more
often than not he finds a black, necrotic organ. One of
the reasons for this is delay in operation—either on the
part of the patient or, more commonly, on the part of
the physician. Frequently the gradual onset of symptoms
lures the doctor into making a diagnosis of orchitis, and
only the failure of the patient to improve with time raises
the question of torsion—too late for salvage.

Because of a conviction that this tragedy can be
avoided by prompt diagnosis and operation, a retrospective study was made of boys admitted to the hospital

Read before the Society of Clinical Surgery, Kansas City, Kan,
Nov 12, 1966.

Reprint requests to University of Kansas Medical Center, Rainbow
Blvd at 39th St, Kansas City, Kan 66103 (Dr. Leape).

with scrotal swelling and pain. An evaluation has been
made of the effect of delay in definitive treatment. Signs
and symptoms in torsion of the testis are compared with
those in epididymo-orchitis. From this data two facts
clearly emerge: In many cases the diagnosis of orchitis
in a child can be made with confidence only at operation
when torsion of the testis has been ruled out. Secondly,
such exploration must be carried out on the day of onset
of symptoms if the twisted testicle is to survive.

MATERIALS AND METHODS

The clinical records of all boys under the age of 16
admitted to the Alder Hey Children's Hospital during
the ten-year period from 1956 to 1965 with pain and

swelling of the scrotum were studied. Because of the National Health Service system, over 90% of all children requiring hospitalization from this part of England and North Wales are treated in this hospital. Patients with hernia or hydrocele were excluded. The following data were tabulated on each patient: age, referring diagnosis, delay from onset of symptoms to operation, descent of testis, first symptom, nature of pain, history of trauma, redness of scrotum, tenderness, temperature on admission, urinalysis report, operative findings, pathology report, whether contralateral orchiopexy was performed, and results of follow-up examination.

RESULTS

The group totaled 148 patients. Of these, 89 suffered from torsion, either of the testis (spermatic cord) or of the appendix testis (hydatid of Morgagni). Thirty-one were diagnosed as having epididymo-orchitis, and 28 suffered from a variety of miscellaneous conditions.

Seven patients with torsion of the testis were seen in the neonatal period. All of these patients were operated on, and all proved to have a nonviable testis secondary to torsion. In one patient there were bilateral torsions and both testes were necrotic. In five of the seven, swelling and redness of the scrotum was noted at birth, which indicated antenatal torsion. Since there is no problem of differential diagnosis in these patients, they have been excluded from the remainder of the study.

Thirty-two patients were diagnosed as having torsion of the appendix testis or appendix of the epididymis, no distinction being made between these two entities in most clinical notes. The diagnosis was confirmed at operation in 27 patients. In the other five, tenderness and swelling was sufficiently confined and localized to permit treatment without operation.

Thirty-one patients had a diagnosis of epididymo-orchitis. This was established at operation in 16. In eight others there was good clinical evidence, such as bilateral symptoms, spreading inflammation, localization of tenderness in the epididymis, etc, to support the diagnosis, although actual histological proof is lacking. The remaining seven cases, in retrospect, are open to question, and several might well have had torsion of the testis.

MISCELLANEOUS SCROTAL SWELLINGS

Twenty-eight patients suffered from a variety of miscellaneous conditions (Table). Eight patients suffered from *idiopathic scrotal edema,* a condition described by Quist in 1955[1] and later by Essenhigh and Stewart.[2] In these patients there is local edema of the scrotum without testicular or epididymal tenderness. Infection with re-

Miscellaneous Scrotal Swellings

	No.	No. Operated On
Idiopathic scrotal edema	8	4
"Traumatic orchitis"	7	0
Scrotal infection	3	2
Exploration for torsion; no abnormalities found	4	4
Idiopathic partial testicular infarction	3	3
Torsion, not operated on	1	0
Hematoma	1	0
Spermatocele	1	1
Total	28	14

gional lymphangitis has been implicated as the cause but not proved. Some respond to antihistamines. Spontaneous remission is the rule, however, so the effect of treatment is difficult to evaluate. Four were operated on to rule out torsion of the testis.

Seven patients are listed as having *"traumatic orchitis."* These are patients who had a history of trauma prior to the onset of pain in the scrotum who, for one reason or another, were not operated on. The heading *scrotal infection* includes two cases of cellulitis and one case of a patient with a boil on the scrotum. Four patients underwent exploratory operations after the diagnosis of torsion of the testis had been made; no abnormalities were found. *Idiopathic partial testicular infarction* was found in three patients. In this condition the etiology is unclear. There is infarction of a portion of the testis without any evidence of occlusion of blood supply or of previous torsion of the spermatic cord. Johnston[3] has described several of these cases. One patient with clinical evidence of torsion of the testis was treated without operation since he was not referred to the hospital until a week after onset of symptoms. There was one case of *hematoma* and one of *spermatocele* also in this group.

THE EFFECT OF DELAY

Fifty non-neonatal patients were found to have torsion of the testis at operation. In 33, or two thirds, the testes were not viable. Experimentally, in dogs, tubular cells do not survive after the blood supply is occluded for six hours.[4] Just how long the testis will survive in humans is unknown. It undoubtedly varies.[5,6] The time elapsed from onset of symptoms in these patients until their operations is shown in Fig 1. Only 19 of the 50 patients were operated on within 24 hours after the onset of symptoms. In patients not undergoing surgical treatment on the day of onset of symptoms, delay was considerable, varying from 1 to 17 days with a median delay of three days. A similar delay was found in patients with torsion of the appendix testis, but, of course, in these cases

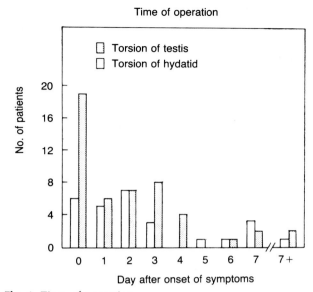

Fig. 1. Time of operation.

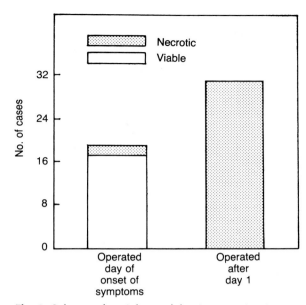

Fig. 2. Salvage of testicle *vs.* delay in operation in 50 cases of torsion of testis.

viability of the testis is not at issue. The effect of a delayed operation on testicular survival is dramatically illustrated in Fig 2. Of the 19 patients who were operated on on the day of onset of symptoms, a testis was viable in 17. However, of the 31 who were operated on after the first day of symptoms, not one testis was salvaged.

Analysis of records indicates that the cause for delay in treatment is *failure to suspect torsion of the testis.* The majority of these patients, even at the time of referral to the hospital, were not sent in with a diagnosis of torsion. Too often the label "orchitis" is attached to any testicular swelling, and symptomatic treatment or an antibiotic is given. The patient is sent to the hospital only when he fails to improve.

VARIABILITY OF SYMPTOMS

The major reason for diagnostic error is the failure of the majority of cases to conform to the accepted clinical picture of torsion of the testis. The usual textbook teaching is that pain in torsion of the testis has a sudden, sharp onset whereas that in orchitis is more gradual. Analysis of symptoms in our patients indicates that, in general, this is true for orchitis (Fig. 3). Less than 5% of patients with orchitis had sudden onset of pain. However, less than half of patients with torsion of the testis had a sudden, acute attack. The others had a gradual onset of pain indistinguishable from that of orchitis. Although pain was the first symptom in the majority of patients with testicular torsion, it was also the first symptom in 40% of patients with orchitis, and

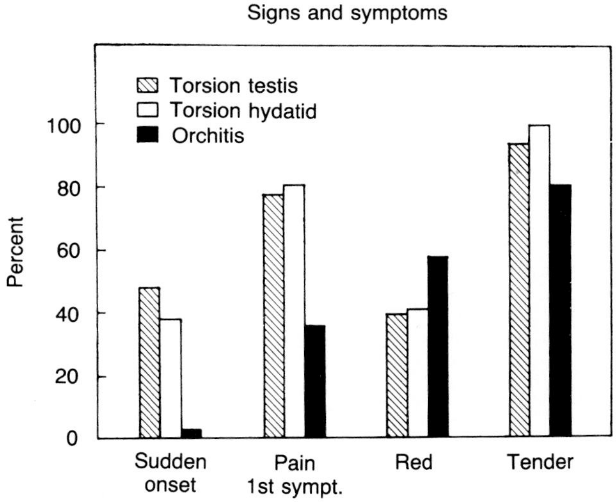

Fig. 3. Comparison of signs and symptoms in patients with orchitis, torsion of testis, and torsion of hydatid.

over 20% of patients with torsion of the testis did not have pain as their first symptom.

Physical examination is even more treacherous. There was no statistically significant difference in the frequency of redness or tenderness among the three groups with torsion of the testis, torsion of the hydatid, and orchitis. In some patients with torsion of the hydatid, tenderness or swelling was confined to this appendage;

in others it was indistinguishable from that of torsion of the testis. Although an experienced observer perhaps can differentiate torsion of the testis by the increase in pain with elevation of the testis or by noting the horizontal lie of the testis, the absence of such signs is common. Undoubtedly, it is the variation from the common pattern of symptoms and signs that leads to diagnostic error and delay.

THE RARITY OF ORCHITIS

Orchitis in childhood is a rare disease.[5,6] When all patients undergo exploratory operation, it is found that very few of them have orchitis. In this series 119 patients were operated on. Of these, only 16, or 13%, had orchitis. Analysis of discharge diagnoses of patients grouped according to five-year periods from 1951 through 1965 gives circumstantial evidence to support this. In the first five years (1951 through 1955) only 16 of 37 patients were diagnosed as having ''torsion'' (torsion of the testis or of the hydatid) as opposed to ''orchitis''— a ratio of 0.7:1. In the next quinquennium the diagnosis of torsion was made in 27 patients and that of orchitis in 18, a ratio of 1.5:1. In the final five-year period, however, the ratio climbed to 4.2:1, 55 patients with torsion and only 13 diagnosed as having orchitis. The changing ratios of diagnosis of torsion to the diagnosis of orchitis reflect the fact that as hospital physicians became more sophisticated in realizing that most patients with testicular swelling and tenderness have torsion and not orchitis, a higher percentage of patients were operated on and a higher percentage of torsions were found.

THE ROLE OF TRAUMA

In 21 patients there was a clear-cut history of injury prior to onset of symptoms. Fourteen underwent exploratory operation. Seven of these had a torsion of the testis, and five had a torsion of the hydatid. Thus, results of the exploration were normal in only two. From this we conclude that it is desirable to explore most of these patients. As with orchitis, it is of no harm to the few who have only a contusion of the testicle. Furthermore, incision of the tunica in these patients may prevent testicular damage if there has been internal bleeding.

TORSION OF THE UNDESCENDED TESTIS

Torsion has been said to occur with much greater frequency in the undescended testis.[7] This was true in this series. Eight of the 50, or 16%, had a torsion of an undescended testis. This figure is considerably higher than the incidence of cryptorchidism. Of even greater significance, however, is the fact that only one of these eight testes was saved (13%) as opposed to 18 (43%) in the patients with descended testes. This indicates the difficulty in diagnosis in the patient with undescended testis, and perhaps is one more reason for early orchiopexy. The number of patients with torsion of the hydatid is not as remarkable; only three of these 31 patients suffered from torsion of the hydatid in an appendage to an undescended testis.

COMMENT

The variability of symptoms in patients with testicular torsion has not been sufficiently emphasized. In this group of patients, the *majority* did not conform to the accepted clinical pattern of symptoms. Physical signs also were not clearly different from those in patients with epididymo-orchitis. Accordingly, the diagnosis was missed in many and operation was delayed, which led to loss of the testis. Epididymo-orchitis is rare in childhood. Barker and Raper[5] did not find any patients with epididymo-orchitis under the age of 18 in a series of 129 cases. Allan and Brown[6] found only one patient under the age of 20 in 64 cases of epididymo-orchitis. Quist,[1] however, found 14 cases in 97 children with scrotal swelling other than hernia, an incidence comparable to that in this series.

The infrequency of orchitis and the difficulty in differentiating it from torsion when it does occur make compelling arguments for scrotal exploration in every child presenting with localized pain and swelling. Only in this way can every case of torsion be treated in time to achieve testicular salvage. Putting it another way, the diagnosis of orchitis in a child is made at the operating table.

Many writers have commented on the need for urgency in operating on patients with torsion of the testis.[8] Although the details of history in these records did not permit a more accurate breakdown of time of operation according to hours after onset of symptoms, the division according to day is striking. In 50 cases, Allan and Brown[6] found 100% testicular survival in those patients operated on within ten hours, 50% survival in those operated on within 24 hours, and no testicular salvage after 24 hours. The safe period varies among individuals and may depend on the amount of twist the spermatic cord has undergone (360° vs 720°). Twenty-four hours appear to be a maximum length of time. The two patients in this series operated on within 24 hours who lost a testis were operated on considerably sooner than that—at 7 hours and at 15 hours. Obviously, the sooner the patient is operated on, the better. There is no place for a ''wait and see'' attitude.

Isabella Forshall, MB, FRCS, P. P. Rickham, MS, FRCS, J. H. Johnston, MB, FRCS, and Neil Freeman, MB, FRCS, gave permission to report the cases.

REFERENCES

1. Quist, O.: Swelling of the Scrotum in Infants and Children and Non-Specific Epididymitis, Acta Chir Scand 110:417–421 (March 10) 1955

2. Essenhigh, D.M., and Stewart, J.S.S.: Idiopathic Scrotal Oedema, Br J Surg 53:419–420 (May) 1966

3. Johnston, J.H.: Localised Infarction of the Testis, Br J Urol 32:97–99 (March) 1960

4. Smith, G.I.: Cellular Changes From Graded Testicular Ischemia, J Urol 73:355–362 (Feb) 1955

5. Barker, K., and Raper, F.P.: Torsion of the Testis, Br J Urol 36:35–41 (March) 1964

6. Alan, W.R., and Brown, R.B.: Torsion of the Testis. Br Med J 5500:1396–1397 (June 4) 1966

7. Abeshouse, B.S.: Torsion of Spermatic Cord: Report of Three Cases and Review of Literature, Urol Cutan Rev 40:699–714 (Oct) 1936

8. Lyon, R.P.: Torsion of the Testicle in Childhood: A Painless Emergency Requiring Contralateral Orchiopexy, JAMA 178:702–705 (Nov 18) 1961

Commentary: Management of Testicular Torsion

Stanley J. Kogan

Leape accurately identifies and analyzes the *key issues* concerning management of testicular torsion: confusion in arriving at the proper diagnosis and the effect of delayed diagnosis on testicular survival. In the 13 yr that have passed since he wrote the foregoing article, these very issues remain the essence of the clinical problem, since it is clear that testicular salvage relates to expediency in detorsion and restoration of normal blood flow. In this commentary, I will reexamine these two issues with a hindsight and advantage of 13 yr further experience with this problem.

Just how long can the torted testis survive without undergoing irreversible ischemic atrophy? In a review of 50 cases of testicular torsion, 17 of 19 boys operated on within 24 hr of symptom onset had their testes salvaged. Of 31 operated on beyond the first day, *no* testis survived. These findings are amply substantiated by considerable other experimental and clinical evidence. Various often-quoted experimental preparations using dogs with torted testes reveal that the "safe" period in which the tubules will recover is somewhere within 6 hr of complete torsion.[1,2] In several additional reviews maximal survival (70% to 95%) occurred in patients operated upon within 12 hr of symptom onset.[3–7] Survival dropped significantly within the next 12 hr but was still possible. Beyond 24 hr, testicular infarction is the rule. The degree of torsion as well as the occurrence of partial or complete *de*torsion influence these figures.[5] Whereas not all cases of testicular torsion are complete, explaining the occasional occurrence of testicular salvage after prolonged periods, these findings graphically illustrate the effect of delay in diagnosis and serve to reiterate Leape's admonition to have a high index of suspicion and to institute urgent therapy.

If time is so critical for testicular salvage, why is therapy often delayed? Two reasons contribute to delay in surgical intervention: failure to suspect torsion as the underlying cause of an acutely inflamed scrotum and confusion or delay resulting from confirmatory diagnostic testing done in an effort to exclude other inflammatory intrascrotal conditions.

In the first situation, lack of uniformity of symptoms and physical findings often suggest other diagnoses. The majority of Leape's patients failed to conform to the classic description of torsion: sudden onset of a painful testis, nausea and vomiting, and subsequent testicular swelling in the absence of fever and urinary symptomatology. The *painless* swollen testis, which occurs in 10% of cases (especially in newborns), is perhaps the most confusing presentation, often causing the physician to mentally exclude torsion in his differential diagnosis.[8] Failure to understand that torsion is the *leading cause* of the acutely inflamed scrotum in childhood,* being more common than epididymitis, orchitis, or testicular appendiceal torsion, also contributes to delay in treatment. In fact, the majority of Leape's patients were referred with diagnoses other than torsion. Physician education and maintenance of a high clinical index of suspicion should serve to minimize this cause of delay.

The second cause of delay in instituting surgical intervention points out the dual nature of the advances in diagnostic medical technology that have taken place since Leape's article was published. Whereas Leape states that every child having localized pain and swelling of the scrotum should be explored, various modalities have allowed physicians to become more discriminating than this uniform approach in an attempt to avoid operation in all but those who have documented torsion. Blind faith in these diagnostic modalities, failure to recognize that their accuracy is less than 100%, and conflict between clinical impressions and diagnostic testing have led to delay in exploration and even "missed" diagnosis of torsion in some cases.

Doppler ultrasonic examination of the intrascrotal contents, first introduced in the mid-1970s, has gained wide

* Bhat D, Varea E, Levitt SB: Unpublished date, 1980.

popularity as a tool in the diagnosis of testicular torsion. Using the Doppler stethoscope in the emergency room, the examiner can make a rapid distinction between *ischemic* conditions of the scrotum (*i.e.,* torsion) and those associated with an increased blood flow (epididymitis, orchitis, and sometimes late appendiceal torsion). This simple maneuver would seem to represent the ideal noninvasive diagnostic tool if it were not for the incidence of false-negative examinations that occur. A chronically torted testis often will develop a surrounding secondary hyperemic shell from collateral vessels from without the spermatic cord, causing a Doppler reading of "intact" blood flow. It was not originally recognized, however, that a similar Doppler false-negative determination might occur *early* in the course of testicular torsion. Scattered false-negative reports of this nature culminated in the publication of four false-negative Doppler cases, with one of the patients having had symptoms of 16 hr duration.[9] These observations would seem to limit the use of this examination as a surefire method of completely accurate determination, although it remains a valuable adjunctive diagnostic tool when interpreted in clinical context.

Radioisotopic nuclear imaging of the intrascrotal contents, first introduced in 1973, has also gained wide acceptance in the diagnosis of the acutely inflamed scrotum. Following intravenous injection of 99mTechnetium Pertechnetate, a blood flow agent, imaging of the scrotum with the Gamma Camera allows for rapid distinction between inflammatory conditions with an increase in vascularity demonstrated on the isotope scan and ischemic conditions such as torsion, where a cold "hole" in the isotope distribution in the scrotum will be noted. Whereas this technique is highly reliable, several potential drawbacks contribute to its lack of universal application. The examination is not available in all hospitals and is unavailable in some during all but routine working hours. Proper technical imaging of the scrotal contents is critical, especially the use of a pinhole converging collimator for achieving a distinct magnified image. Most important, skill and experience are needed for the interpretation of the images obtained. Even when all these factors are present, if the procedure cannot be performed on an *emergent basis* without contributing to any delay in the patient's care, its role in the diagnostic armamentarium should be questioned.

A recent collation of 594 cases derived from 16 published references in which the isotope scrotal scan was used to evaluate the various intrascrotal lesions reveals the accuracy of this diagnostic technique.* Of these 594 patients studied, 84 had testicular torsion. Only five false-negative examinations could be found: three associated with areas of increased perfusion, one with spontaneous detorsion noted at surgery, and one with the characteristics of an abscess. Thirteen false-positive examinations were found, usually associated with epididymo-orchitis.

A recent review contrasted the diagnostic accuracy of Doppler ultrasonic flowmetry with isotope testicular imaging in the diagnosis of testicular torsion.[10] Seven of 32 consecutive patients having an acutely inflamed scrotum were found to have testicular torsion. Five of the seven had the diagnosis

---

* Epididymo-orchitis is the most common cause when all ages are considered together.

confirmed by both positive Doppler flow studies and the technetium scan. Six of the seven Doppler examinations were consistent with torsion; five of the seven isotope scans were positive. The authors concluded that neither examination was sufficiently accurate to be used by itself but that both examinations were valuable when used alone or together to complement the clinical impression.

These findings vary somewhat with my experience, although the conclusions reached are similar. In my institution, experience with isotope scrotal imaging leads to routine use of this modality in the evaluation of the acutely inflamed scrotum. In the original published series in 1979, I used isotope scanning to predict the diagnosis of *non*torsion, that is, to confirm the clinical situation where surgical exploration was felt to be unnecessary.[11] Since I felt that testicular torsion itself was a clinical diagnosis and that diagnostic testing should not stand in the way of emergent surgery, all patients with a definite clinical diagnosis of torsion of the testis were explored immediately. In my original reported series, there were no false-negative determinations (scan evidence of no testicular torsion where torsion was actually present) in 19 patients studied. The scan accurately predicted the diagnosis of nontorsion in every instance. Similar accuracy in several additional patients studied each year since the original data were gathered has confirmed my original impressions. Therefore, in my institution, the scrotal scan is used to confirm the clinical impression of nontorsion, thereby adding further objective evidence allowing me to refrain from surgical exploration in those patients in whom a low index of suspicion or indeterminate clinical examination occurs. The patients with strongly suspected clinical evidence of testicular torsion undergo surgical exploration without other confirmatory testing. In this manner, I have found the isotope scrotal scan to be extremely helpful in complementing clinical impressions and in minimizing explorations in all but clear-cut necessary cases. Furthermore, delay from diagnostic testing of strongly suspected cases of torsion is eliminated.

As one can see, these examinations may sometimes "cloud the issue" and cause confusion, especially when the findings from diagnostic adjunctive tests conflict with the clinical impressions. The Doppler examination, although convenient, noninvasive, and simple to use does have a definite false-negative rate. The isotope scan requires skill and experience in interpretation and may similarly be a potential source of diagnostic error. The clinician, in seeking to be completely accurate in his diagnosis, should not allow either examination to dissuade him from his clinical impression or to cause a delay in instituting therapy: testicular atrophy will be the inevitable result.

If the differential diagnosis has been confusing, and the use of adjunctive diagnostic testing has been somewhat controversial, the *management* of testicular torsion is completely straightforward. Derotation of the involved testis should be done on an emergent basis. Manual derotation may be used as a temporizing maneuver. The recent suggestion that this be done under intravenous morphine analgesia (0.1 mg/kg body weight) is welcomed by the patient and apparently increases one's chance of success.[12] Efficacy of this maneuver usually is marked by relief of pain and may also be documented by

Doppler examination. Surgical fixation should follow promptly within 24 hr to prevent recurrence of torsion. Those cases that cannot be detorted manually should be urgently explored with derotation and fixation of the involved viable testis or excision if gangrenous. The contralateral symptomless mate should be simultaneously fixed to the surrounding dartos fascia to prevent subsequent torsion of this remaining testis, which distressingly has occurred 40% of the time when this is not done.[4,13]

There is now mounting evidence that contrary to previous suggestions, a severely impaired testis should not be left in place. On the one hand, review of existing data suggests that virtually all these testes undergo eventual atrophy; on the other hand, the incidence of morbidity (prolonged high fever, scrotal abscess, drainage of necrotic tubules through the scrotal incision and secondary orchiectomy) is high, approaching 22% in one recent series.[5] Furthermore, experimental and clinical observations of microscopic abnormalities in the *normal* (untwisted) testis and the presence of abnormal sperm analyses in patients who underwent previous unilateral testicular torsion suggests that the chronically twisted or necrotic testis may actually initiate damage within the remaining normal testis.[13,14]

What then constitutes the ideal approach to the management of the acutely inflamed scrotum? Acknowledgment of Leape's observations concerning failure to consider torsion as the primary process of concern and his appeals to expediate treatment must obviously form the basis for optimum treatment of this condition if testicular salvage is to be improved. A surgical exploration for suspected torsion, where torsion is not found, carries with it the minor morbidity of an "unnecessary" exploration. In none of the series reported to date has this been of any serious consequence. The morbidity resulting from failure to explore for a torted testis is inevitable testicular atrophy.

Adjunctive diagnostic testing can be helpful, but its use should be individualized according to availability and experience: the particular procedure that works best for the patient and surgeon should be the procedure used. In no case should conflicting evidence from adjunctive diagnostic testing stand in the way of sound clinical judgment when testicular torsion is suspected.

In the 13 years since publication of Leape's review, salvage following acute unilateral testicular torsion has improved somewhat; however, it still is somewhat disappointing.[5] Recognition of the issues raised in this review and implementation of the guidelines set forth would seem to maximize chances of improved testicular salvage in the future.

REFERENCES

1. Smith GI: Cellular changes from graded testicular ischaemia. J Urol 73:355, 1955

2. Sonda LP, Lapides J: Experimental torsion of the spermatic cord. Surg Forum 12:502, 1961

3. Allan WR, Brown RB: Torsion of the testis: A review of 58 cases. Br Med J 1:1396, 1966

4. Skoglund RW, McRoberts JW, Ragde H: Torsion of the testis: A review of the literature and an analysis of 70 new cases. J Urol 104:604, 1970

5. Williamson RCN: Torsion of the testis and allied conditions. Br J Surg 63:465, 1976

6. Williams JD, Hodgson NB: Another look at torsion of testis. Urology 14:36, 1979

7. Donohue RE, Utley WF: Torsion of spermatic cord. Urology 11:33, 1978

8. Kaplan GW, King LR: Acute scrotal swelling in children. J Urol 104:219, 1970

9. Nasarallah PF, Manzone D, King LR: Falsely negative Doppler examinations in testicular torsion. II. J Urol 118:194, 1977

10. Glazier WB, McGuire EJ, et al: Testicular torsion: Comparison of diagnostic procedures. Presented at the meeting of the Society for Pediatric Urology, San Francisco, May 1980

11. Kogan SJ, Lutzker LG, Perez LA, et al: The value of the negative radionuclide scrotal scan in the management of the acutely inflamed scrotum in children. J Urol 122:223, 1979

12. Betts JM, Cromie WJ, Duckett JW: Testicular detorsion: a temporizing manipulation. Presented at the American Academy of Pediatrics 48th Annual Meeting, Section on Urology, Program for Scientific Sessions, San Francisco, October 1979

13. Krarup T: The testes after torsion. Br J Urol 50:43, 1978

14. Chakraborty J, Jhunjhunwala J, Nelson L, et al: Effects of unilateral torsion of the spermatic cord on the contralateral testis in human and guinea pig. Arch Androl 4:95, 1980

ANNOTATED BIBLIOGRAPHY

Kaplan GW, King LR: Acute scrotal swelling in children. J Urol 104:219, 1970

This classic article reviews 63 cases of acute scrotal swelling over a 10-yr period admitted to a children's hospital. Incidence of each contributing cause and evaluation of frequency of various symptomatology (*i.e.,* pain, urinary findings) are discussed. The high frequency (25%) of previous episodes of pain in testicular torsion patients was first pointed out, as well as the absence of pain in 10%. The need for simultaneous contralateral orchidopexy is described. An aggressive surgical approach to acute scrotal swelling is stressed.

Williamson RCN: Torsion of the testis and allied conditions. Br J Surg 63:465, 1976

This is the largest contemporary review of acute scrotal swellings, with 293 cases of torsion of the testis, 55 cases of torsion of a testicular appendage, and 5 miscellaneous cases encountered over a 15-yr period. This is a comprehensive review paper investigating incidence, age, etiologic factors, clinical features, and differential diagnosis for each condition. A good discussion of testicular viability is included, with a summary table of various series of testicular torsion and testis survival reported over the years. Testicular viability is reported to depend on whether or not spontaneous reduction occurs, time between onset of symptoms and operation, the degree of torsion, and a frequently overlooked variable—adequate period of follow up to assess the occurrence of atrophy. The poor fate of nonviable testes replaced in the scrotum is graphically described, with a high incidence of complications encountered. The poor salvage in patients with torsion in an undescended testis is described.

Skoglund R, McRoberts JW, Ragde H: Torsion of testicular appendages: Presentation of 43 new cases and a collective review. J Urol 104:598, 1970

This article deals specifically with torsion of the testicular appendages and presents interesting anatomic data concerning the location and frequency of the various appendages. Pain, swelling, and an age distribution similar to the adolescent peak seen in torsion of the testis was noted. With the exception of the "blue dot" sign, which is pathognomonic of torsion of a testicular appendage, no definite distinguishing features from testicular torsion were noted.

Kogan SJ, Lutzker LG, Perez LA, et al: The value of the negative radionuclide scrotal scan in the management of the acutely inflamed scrotum in children. J Urol 122:223, 1979

This article describes a unique application of the isotope scrotal scan used in evaluation of the acutely inflamed scrotum in children. Patients with conditions suspected clinically of being other than torsion of the testis underwent scanning to confirm that they did not have testicular torsion. In this way, added objective confirmatory data was obtained, aiding in the decision to prevent surgical exploration. There were no false-negative determinations (scan indication that torsion was absent when subsequent surgical exploration or clinical follow up revealed it to be present). Patients with strong clinical suspicion of testicular torsion did not undergo isotope scrotal scanning but, rather, underwent direct surgical exploration.

Smith SP, King LR: Torsion of the testis: Techniques of assessment. Symposium on advances in imaging techniques. Urol Clin North Am 6:429, 1979

A brief review of the clinical aspects of torsion of the testis is followed by an extensive technical and clinical description of the techniques of Doppler ultrasonic scrotal examination and a similar description of the isotope scrotal scanning technique. The advantages of the Doppler examination, such as its noninvasive character and immediate availability, brevity in examination, and ability to perform serial examinations, are pointed out. The pathogenesis of false-negative examinations are described. The development and technique of the isotope scrotal scan is discussed in detail and the high accuracy rate reemphasized. The use of both of these techniques to complement the clinical impression is stressed.

Overview: Surgery of Testicular Torsion and Torsion of Testicular Appendages

Donald B. Halverstadt and Philip Mosca

Torsion of the testis or testicular appendages has long been a difficult diagnostic problem for the practicing urologist. Hugh Hampton Young offered a reasonable philosophy of approach to suspected testicular torsion when he wrote in 1926:

In the diagnosis, the picture is difficult to distinquish from acute epididymitis, in the case of a scrotal testis, or from a strangulated hernia, in the case of an inguinal testis. The history, the absence of urethral discharge, and the very sudden onset will help rule out the former. In the latter case the history is valuable. If, previous to the onset, there has been an undescended testis, but no hernia, the diagnosis should be suspected, although epididymitis is not ruled out. In strangulated hernia the general and abdominal symptoms are usually more severe, but may be deficient. Exploration is the safest method.[1]

Although substantial advances in the diagnostic armamentarium of the urologist have occurred in the past half century, Young's admonition is still pertinent in regard to the patient in whom testicular torsion is suspected.

A review of the anatomy and embryology of the testis and its appendages and investing layers is helpful to an understanding of the pathophysiology, diagnosis, and management of torsion of the testis or testicular appendages.

During the seventh week of embryogenesis, the undifferentiated gonad begins to assume the characteristics of a testis. At this time it is located in the area of the superior portion of the urogenital ridge. At the 26-mm stage, or third month of gestation, it is attached to the posterior abdominal wall by the genital mesentery. The superior portion of the testis is attached to the atrophying mesonephros and also to the diaphram by a suspersory ligament that shortly involutes. The caudad portion of the testis is continuous with a mesenchymal band that extends to the genital swelling and that eventually becomes the gubernaculum testis. By the end of the third month of gestation the testis lies in retroperitoneal position in the false pelvis. At the sixth month of gestation the processus vaginalis, which develops as a diverticulum of the coelom, has invaginated into the inguinal canal. At the seventh month of gestation the testis begins its decent through the inguinal canal and usually reaches the base of the scrotum during the eighth month. After the eighth month of gestation the caudadmost portion of the processus vaginalis remains as the tunica vaginalis testis, and the cephalad portion is usually obliterated.[2] Normally only the anterior half of the testis is covered by the parietal tunica vaginalis, and thus the posterior portion of the testis and epididymis are adherent to the internal spermatic fascia. However, if an excessive amount of parietal tunica vaginalis remains, the testis becomes less firmly attached to the scrotal tunics and hangs in the scrotal cavity with the so-called bell clapper deformity.[3] It is this anatomic variation that allows testicular torsion of the intravaginal type to occur. Extravaginal torsion, or torsion of the spermatic cord, occurs when the testicle and all its investing tunics become twisted at the level of the external inguinal ring. It has been postulated that a lack of adherence of the testicular tunics to the scrotal wall allows the testis and cord to rotate upon their long axis.[4]

The classification and location of the testicular appendages have been well described.[5] The appendix testis, a müllerian remnant, and the appendix epididymis, a mesonephric remnant, are the most important clinically, with torsion of the appendix testis occurring approximately three times more frequently than torsion of the appendix epididymis.

Clinically the problem of the acutely swollen scrotum may be approached according to the age of the patient at presentation, differentiating the newborn, child, adolescent, and adult.

In the newborn, the acutely swollen scrotum encountered within the first few days of life is usually due to one of three causative factors: birth trauma, intravaginal or extravaginal torsion of the testis, or infection.

Birth trauma as the cause of a swollen testis or scrotum is seen very infrequently. Usually there is a history of a difficult breech delivery. The infant is usually otherwise healthy, and physical examination reveals a swollen scrotum, often bilateral, with testes that feel normal to palpation. The diagnosis is usually easily made and conservative management with elevation is sufficient.

Neonatal torsion usually presents as a firm scrotal mass that does not transilluminate. The scrotum may be reddened and somewhat thickened to palpation. Frequently, the event has occurred *in utero* and the testis is found to be necrotic.[6] Immediate exploration is the rule, and if gross suppuration is not found at the time of exploration, fixation of the contralateral testis should also be performed. Experience over the past 10 yr at the Oklahoma Children's Memorial Hospital differs from the reports of other authors, with a preponderance of intravaginal neonatal torsion over torsion of the spermatic cord.[4]

Infection as the cause of a swollen testis or scrotum in the neonate is rare. We have seen one such an infant with generalized gram-negative sepsis and a swollen scrotum. The infant also had sickle cell disease, thalassemia, and respiratory distress. The child was not expected to survive, but with extensive care the child did recover and several weeks later the scrotum was explored to provide fixation for the contralateral testis. Normal testes were noted bilaterally at the time of exploration.

Clinical judgment is of paramount importance, and in all but the sickest of neonates exploration should be the rule. Recent experience with an infant of 18 hr with a swollen scrotum is instructive. In this child Doppler pulsations were noted to be present, and a nuclear scan performed 1 hr before surgery was interpreted as epididymo-orchitis with no evidence of testicular torsion. A necrotic testis with torsion was removed at exploration. Again, the general rule should be that the swollen scrotum in the newborn should be surgically explored without undue delay.

The child, age 1 mo to 9 yr, with the acute onset of a swollen scrotum usually does not present a difficult diagnostic situation. The differential diagnosis should include incarcerated hernia, torsion of the testis or testicular appendages, torsion of an undescended testis, and epididymo-orchitis either in the undescended or normally descended testis. Frequently this differential diagnosis can be shortened by a good history or a well-documented previous physical examination. Unless there are mitigating circumstances, however, the presumptive diagnosis should be confirmed by surgical exploration.[7]

In the adolescent, age 9 to 21 yr, testicular torsion is the most common cause of acute scrotal swelling. However, differentiation of testicular torsion from an inflammatory lesion is most difficult in this age group. Exploration should be carried out whenever the diagnosis of testicular torsion is entertained. Clinically the diagnosis of torsion should be strongly suspected when the scrotal swelling has not been preceded by irritative urinary symptoms. However, epididymo-orchitis is not always preceded by urinary symptomatology. Indeed, in Wright's series only 57 percent of his patients with epididymo-orchitis had preceding urinary tract symptoms.[8] Pyrexia when present is usually associated with epididymo-orchitis, although temperature elevation can occur with torsion. Classic physical signs of epididymo-orchitis such as significantly diminished pain with scrotal elevation are frequently difficult to interpret. The so-called transverse lie of the uninvolved testis is frequently of little diagnostic help. Perhaps the best indicators of probable epididymo-orchitis are pyuria or bacteriuria on urinalysis. However, these findings may not always be present. Even the "Doppler test" may be inaccurate, and it should be used only as an adjunct to the clinical impression.

Testicular scanning for testicular torsion was first introduced by Nadel and associates.[9] Several additional reports advocate the use of this test and are excellently reviewed by Dr. Kogan. Our own experience with radionuclide scanning has not been favorable. We recommend the radionuclide flow study should only be used as suggested by Dr. Kogan to confirm the impression that torsion does *not* exist.[10] If a significant doubt exists that the diagnosis may be testicular torsion, the patient should undergo surgical exploration.

Difficulty in establishing the diagnosis of testicular torsion by flow study may result from the pathophysiologic events following the torsion. After torsion occurs, arterial occlusion probably does not occur immediately. Indeed, venous and lymphatic occlusion first develop. Thicker-walled arteries remain patent so that edema and venous congestion are the first pathologic changes seen. It is only after some delay that the arterial supply becomes compromised. It is for this reason that the testis undergoing torsion usually exhibits hemorrhagic infarction. This sequence of events may also explain why the Doppler ultrasound test can provide misleading results if the examination is performed between the onset of venous congestion and the onset of hemorrhagic infarction.

In the adult male, over 21 yr of age, testicular torsion is much less frequent than in younger males, but it does occur and should be considered in the differential diagnosis of the acutely swollen scrotum. It is also in this group that intermittent torsion with spontaneous resolution may occur more commonly. It is also in this age group that greater success is possible with local anesthetic blockade of the spermatic cord and manual reduction of testicular torsion. Doppler ultrasound study or radioisotope flow techniques may also prove of greater value in this age group in confirming the absence of testicular torsion.

The diagnosis of torsion of the testicular appendages is

difficult to separate from that of testicular torsion itself. If the diagnosis of torsion of a testicular appendage is certain, conservative therapy may be considered. However, in the absence of the classical "blue dot" sign, this entity should be considered in common with testicular torsion and handled in similar fashion.[11,12]

Although diagnosis of testicular torsion may be difficult, surgical approach should not cause problem. The scrotum is explored, and the testicular torsion is reduced. If the testis becomes pink, it is fixed to the scrotum in at least two places and the scrotum is closed in layers without drainage. If the testicle fails to become pink and an incision in the tunic albuginea fails to bleed, an orchiectomy is performed. The contralateral testis is also explored and fixation carried out because of the high probability of torsion occurring in the contralateral gonad. We favor anchoring the tunic albuginea to the dartos layer using two sutures of nonabsorbable suture material. If absorbable suture material is used, sufficient scarring to provide stability of the testis may not occur, and reoccurrence of torsion may take place after dissolution of the absorbably suture. The "window" technique may also be used with good results.[14]

Fertility may be a problem in these patients. Even after successful salvage of testicular torsion, it appears that a large percentage of these testes will undergo atrophy. Even more distressing is the probability that fertility in these patients is reduced.[13]

Early diagnosis and prompt surgical exploration is critical in these patients to ensure salvage of the testis and attempt to maintain a reasonable probability of fertility.[7] Hugh Hampton Young's admonition of 1926 is still appropriate.

REFERENCES

1. Young HH, Davis DM: Young's Practice of Urology, p 64. Philadelphia, WB Saunders, 1926

2. Mitchell GAG: The condition of the peritoneal vaginal processes at birth. J Anat Lond 73:658, 1939

3. Parker RM, Robinson JR: Anatomy and diagnosis of torsion of the testicle. J Urol 106:243, 1971

4. Whitsell JA: Intrauterine and newborn torsion of the spermatic cord. J Urol 106:786, 1971

5. Rolnick D, Kawanoves S, Szanto P, et al: Anatomical incidence of testicular appendanges. J Urol 100:755, 1968

6. James T: Torsion of the spermatic cord in the first year of life. Br J Urol 25:56, 1953

7. Kaplan GW, King LR: Acute scrotal swelling in children. J Urol 104:219, 1970

8. Wright JE: Acute epididymo-orchitis with special reference to its differential diagnosis from torsion of the testes. Med J Aust 2:1110, 1960

9. Nadel ND, Gitter MT, Hahn LD, et al: Preoperative diagnosis of testicular torsion. Urology 1:478, 1973

10. Kogan SJ, Lutzker LG, Perez LA, et al: The value of the negative radionuclide scrotal scan in the management of the acutely inflamed scrotum in children. J Urol 122:223, 1979

11. Skoglund R, McRoberts JW, Ragde H: Torsion of testicular appendages: Presentation of 43 new cases and a collective review. J Urol 104:598, 1970

12. Dresner ML: Torsed appendage: Diagnosis and management; blue dot sign. Urology 1:63, 1973

13. Krarup T: The testes after torsion. Br J Urol 50:43, 1978

14. Moore TS, Hollabaugh RS: The "window" orchidopexy for prevention of testicular torsion. J Pediatr Surg 12:237, 1977

PART FORTY-SEVEN

SURGERY OF TESTICULAR TRAUMA

119

TRAUMATIC RUPTURE OF THE TESTICLE

J. L. McCormack, A. W. Kretz and R. Tocantins

From the Department of Urology, The Swedish Medical Center, Seattle, Washington

Reprinted from *Journal of Urology*, Vol. 96, pp. 80–82, 1966. Copyright 1966 by The Williams & Wilkins Company, Baltimore.

Testicular rupture by blunt trauma has been considered rare. Bronk and Berry suggest that one reason for the paucity of reported cases is that surgical exploration does not necessarily follow the diagnosis of hematocele.[1] Only 27 cases of traumatic rupture of the testis have been reported in the literature.[2–3] Five additional instances of testicular rupture have been treated in two Seattle hospitals during the past 10 years. In more than half of the cases previously reported injury occurred during participation in athletics. None of the reported injuries occurred in ectopic or undescended testes. In only 1 man (who had a seminoma) was testicular disease found to antedate the injury. None of the 5 patients to be described had pre-existing disease and all five were injured during sporting recreation.

Direct blunt trauma to the scrotum is required to rupture the tough, inelastic tunica albuginea. There may be two types of kinetic force which produce this injury. Three of the patients to be described experienced a crushing force to the scrotum where the testis was undoubtedly impinged against a ramus of the pubic bone. The other 2 patients were struck by missiles traveling at moderate velocity. In these latter instances one wonders if the testes were hanging loosely in the scrotum and literally exploded on contact or if the testis was forced against the ramus of the pubic bone allowing crushing to occur. In all cases the basic injury was rupture of the tunica albuginea.

CASE REPORTS

Case 1. While scuffling with a friend a 17-year-old boy was struck in the right groin and immediately experienced severe pain and swelling in the right testicle. Fifteen hours later examination showed a swollen, firm, red, tender mass in the right scrotum which did not transilluminate. The preoperative impression was acute torsion of the testis or testicular appendage or rupture of the testis. Immediate surgical exploration revealed a hematocele and a laceration of the tunica albuginea through which testicular tubules extruded. A portion of the tubules was exised permitting closure of the tunica albuginea. This reduced the total testicular mass by about 30 percent. One year later the injured testis felt smaller than the left but firm and viable.

Case 2. Three days following a fall from a bicycle a 13-year-old boy was seen by his family physician because of continued painful swelling in the left testis and

Accepted for publication July 9, 1965.
Read at annual meeting of Western Section, American Urological Association, Inc., San Francisco California, April 26-29, 1965.

fever of 104°F. For a presumptive diagnosis of acute epididymitis he was treated with penicillin and chloramphenicol. The fever subsided and the scrotal swelling seemed to decrease during the 7 days of his hospital care. After discharge the acute process recurred but did not respond to additional antibiotic therapy. A few hours prior to his second hospital admission, 22 days after injury, the large, swollen, scrotal mass spontaneously drained seropurulent matter. A culture of the drainage was sterile and no sperm cells were seen on smear. Surgical exploration through an extensively thickened and indurated scrotal wall showed a laceration of the tunica albuginea. The extruding tubules appeared macerated and the epididymis was indurated. An orchiectomy was performed and the microscopic study showed necrosis of all the testicular tubules. Convalescence was uneventful.

Case 3. A 19-year-old boy suffered an injury to the groin when his motor boat struck a piling and he was thrown across the gunwhale. He felt immediate pain and noted swelling with discoloration of the scrotal skin. During the next 8 days the swelling increased and the ecchymosis extended into the suprapubic and perineal areas. Surgical exploration 9 days after injury showed an extensive laceration of the tunica albuginea. There was a large hematoma in the scrotum containing an estimated 200 ml blood with blood extravasating along the cord. It was assumed that the laceration had extended into the tunica vaginalis allowing the extensive extravasation of blood. An orchiectomy was done. Convalescence was uneventful.

Case 4. A 23-year-old college football player was struck in the right scrotum with a baseball and immediately experienced moderately severe pain. Swelling soon developed. With conservative treatment, including a scrotal suspensory and ice packs, the patient was able to continue his usual school activities (no football) but after 8 days there was no reduction in the pain or scrotal turgor. Surgical exploration revealed a tense hematocele and a 2 cm laceration of the tunica albuginea with protrusion of some of the testicular tubules. The tubules were replaced and the tunica albuginea was closed. The tunica vaginalis was everted. Followup examination showed a testis normal to palpation.

Case 5. A 23-year-old medical student was struck in the left scrotum by a golf ball and experienced immediate pain with scrotal swelling and nausea. Despite conservative treatment, including ice packs, and scrotal support, the pain continued. On the third day following the injury he had a swollen, red, tense, tender mass in the left scrotum. Surgical exploration revealed a hematocele and

laceration of the tunica albuginea about 2 cm. long. The protruding testicular tubules were excised, the laceration was closed and the scrotum was drained. During the next 2 months he had constant drainage from the scrotum. At the end of this time no testicular tissue could be felt. He has subsequently married and has 2 children.

DISCUSSION

All 5 patients in the cases herein reported complained of testicular pain and turgor following trauma (Table 1). Ecchymosis was a prominent finding in 1 patient while in another, where exploration was delayed 22 days, systemic signs of inflammation were present. Acute epididymitis was the provisional diagnosis in four of the 5 cases and undoubtedly this erroneous impression led to the significant delay in definitive surgical treatment. Despite this delay a good result was ultimately obtained in one of the 4 patients. The remaining patient was seen and operated upon by a urologist 15 hours after injury. This testicle was salvaged and a good result was obtained.

Orchiectomy was the procedure chosen in 2 cases. In one the laceration of the tunica albuginea extended to involve the tunica vaginalis resulting in extravasation of blood along the spermatic cord and into the suprapubic and perineal areas. It is unlikely that the 9-day delay in his treatment altered the decision for orchiectomy. In the other patient who had an orchiectomy definitive treatment was delayed for 22 days. More immediate surgical treatment may have allowed salvage of the testicle rather than spontaneous evacuation of the infected hematocele.

In the other 3 patients who developed typical hematoceles an attempt was made to save the testicle. The technique used was surgical closure of the tunica albuginea after excision of the exposed and necrotic testicular tubules (Fig. 1). In 2 cases the maneuver was successful while in 1 case the remaining testicular tissue sloughed. In none of the 5 patients did the generally accepted measures for conservative treatment of testicular disease seem to alter the course of the process.

To be considered in the differential diagnosis of testicular rupture are those diseases which produce a painful, swollen, scrotal mass. When it is possible to

TABLE 1. Summary of Testicular Rupture

	Constant Pain and Turgor	Hema-tocele	Delay in Treatment	Result
17	×	Yes	15 hrs.	Salvage
13	×	No	22 days	Orchiectomy
19	×	No	9 days	Orchiectomy
23	×	Yes	8 days	Salvage
23	×	Yes	3 days	Sloughed

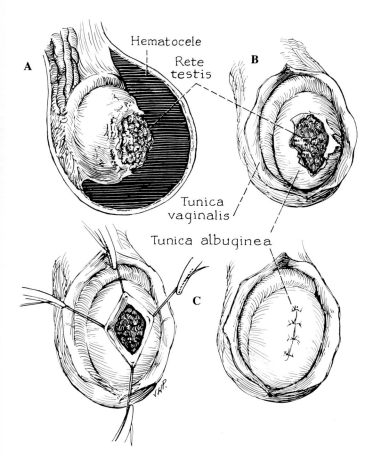

Fig. 1. (A) Diagram of hematocele. (B) Rupture of tunica albuginea. (C) Surgical repair.

exclude disease which pre-exists external trauma the remaining causes of this syndrome include acute epididymitis, torsion of either the testicle or a testicular appendage, or rupture of the tunica albuginea. Identification of bloody fluid by the aspiration of the hydrocele cavity should make surgical exploration mandatory. Sargent describes the result of neglect: "The delicacy of the spermatogenic tissue is such that severe injury almost inevitably terminates in complete testicular atrophy. Here secondary infection with abscess and sloughing is more prone to occur than in those injuries without frank rupture."[4]

However, of particular interest was Wesson's report in 1946 of his management of a patient with a traumatic rupture of a solitary testicle.[5] On 3 occasions he aspirated the hematocele. When surgical exploration was carried out on the twenty-third day yellow fluid filled the cavity and the necrotic slough was easily removed making closure of the lacerated tunica albuginea possible. The testicle was salvaged. We have had no experience with multiple aspirations of a hematocele.

Undoubtedly the extent of the injury influences the recovery of the damaged testis. Atwell and Ellis mention 3 patients with minor hematoceles in whom recovery was spontaneous, presumably by reabsorption of the blood and necrotic testicular tissue.[6] This may explain the atrophic testis sometimes found in older men during routine examination where there is only a vague history of testicular trauma.

One possible consequence of this type of injury to be considered is an auto-immune reaction to one's own sperm. Whether spermatic cells after extravasation of testicular tissue act as antigens and produce antibodies under these circumstances is not known. One patient of this group conceived 2 children after his injury. The fertility status of the other 4 patients in unknown.

CONCLUSION

Testicular rupture requires a non-penetrating external force to the testis to produce a tear of the tunica albuginea. Usually the laceration, limited to the tunica albuginea, produces a hematocele. The more promptly this condition is recognized and specific surgical repair of the laceration is effected, the less is the chance of complication and the greater is the opportunity for salvage of the testicle. The recognition of a hematocele by aspiration is suggested as one method of diagnosing testicular rupture. Early surgical exploration of the scrotum is recommended.

SUMMARY

The cases of 5 patients who had traumatic rupture of the tunica albuginea are described. When this condition is suspected surgical exploration of the testicle is recommended.

REFERENCES

1. Bronk, W. S. and Berry, J. L.: Traumatic rupture of the testicle: Report of a case and a review of the literature, J Urol 87:564, 1962
2. Counseller, V. S. and Pratt, J. H., Jr.: Rupture of the testicle: Report of cases and review of literature. J Urol 52:334, 1944
3. Senger, F. L., Bottone, J. J. and Ittner, W. F.: Traumatic rupture of the testicle, J Urol 58:451, 1947
4. Sargent, J. C.: Injuries of genital tract. In: Urology. Edited by M. F. Campbell, vol. 2: chapt. 4, pp. 926–951, Philadelphia, W. B. Saunders Co., 1954
5. Wesson, M. B.: Traumatism of the testicle; report of a case of traumatic rupture of a solitary testicle. Urol & Cutan Rev 50:16–19, 1946
6. Atwell, J. D. and Ellis, H.: Rupture of the testis. Br J Surg 49:345, 1961

Commentary: Management of Testicular Injury

John L. McCormack

Clinically significant trauma to the testis is uncommon. Due to the location and mobility of the testes these organs are relatively protected. When injury to the testicle does occur, it may take one of three forms. First, blunt trauma may cause rupture of the tunica albuginea. Second, laceration or foreign body penetration may involve the testicle. Third, the testicles may be displaced from their normal scrotal position when a direct squeezing force is applied.

Urologists generally agree that when testicular trauma is documented, surgical exposure of the injured organ may be indicated. Early exploration may salvage a testis that would be irrevocably damaged with delay.

A patient with traumatic rupture of the testicle presents with signs and symptoms of a painful hematocele. Needle aspiration of the bloody aspirate following a history of trauma may aid in diagnosis. The surgeon must not ignore the possibilities of acute epididymis, torsion of the testicle or its appendages, or trauma to a neoplasm in the differential diagnosis. None of these conditions should be significantly aggravated by surgical exploration.

Lacerations and penetration by foreign bodies are diagnosed by inspecting the scrotal injury. Because of mobility of the testes, involvement will not always correspond to the appearance of the superficial scrotal wound. A measurement of arterial flow to the testis by a Doppler unit may be helpful in assessing the extent of the damage. Lacerations in penetrating injuries require surgical exploration with debridement and closure.

Luxation of the testicle is uncommon, but several case reports appear in the literature. This type of injury is usually associated with more extensive trauma, such as fractures of the pelvic bones. The absence of a testicle in male patients with pelvic injuries should alert the physician to this possibility. The testis may be found in the fascial planes of the pubic or perineal area or internal to the internal inguinal ring. Surgical exploration with reposition of the testis should be done as soon as practical.

In none of the published articles on testicular trauma has a follow-up postoperative testicular biopsy been performed to evaluate spermatogenic function. Clinical follow-up study and physical examinations suggest that spermatogenic function as well as androgen secretion is preserved.

In summary, in all cases of scrotal trauma the examining physician should suspect testicular injury. Early surgical exploration offers the best opportunity to preserve testicular function.

ANNOTATED BIBLIOGRAPHY

Del Villar RC, Ireland GW, Cass AS: Early exploration following trauma to the testicle. J Trauma 13:600, 1973

These authors have reviewed 32 patients hospitalized for testicular trauma over a 10-yr period, and compared the management in terms of testicular salvage. Eight of the patients had a rupture of the tunica albuginea. The results of the first 7 yr, when few of the patients were treated by early surgical exploration, were compared to those patients later in the series managed by early surgical exploration. The etiology of the trauma was varied, but on the basis of this study the authors conclude that early exploration, with evacuation of the hematocele and repair of the testicular rupture, if present, resulted in a shortened hospital stay, reduced period of disability, and a faster return to normal activities.

Gross M: Rupture of the testicle; the importance of early surgical treatment. J Urol 101:196, 1969

This author analyzes his 5-yr experience with 8 patients with testicular rupture. He also combines his 8 cases with 34 previously reported ones, and concludes that *"few testicles are saved after the first three days posttrauma,"* strongly urging early surgical exploration.

Staff WG, Lomax AJ: Foreign bodies in the testis. Br J Surg 55:255, 1968

The authors report in detail on two patients who had missiles produce penetrating injuries to the testes. The first patient was injured when a piece of metal broke from a hammer and penetrated the scrotum. In the second case a piece of bolt that had been struck by a hammer penetrated the scrotum. The natural protection of the testis from external blunt injury due to mobility is discussed, but this does not apply to missile penetration. In both cases the injured testis was explored, the fragment removed, and the testis salvaged.

Merricks JR, Papierniak FB: Traumatic rupture of the testicle. J Urol 103:77, 1970

These authors use four case reports to describe their experience with unilateral testicular rupture. The details of the rupture varied from a straddle injury to injury from a moving missile (baseball) to a tractor injury and external blunt trauma. The ability of the testis to avoid injury is emphasized, along with the desirability of early exploration when the possibility of laceration or rupture exists.

Morgan A: Traumatic luxation of the testis. Br J Surg 52:669, 1965

This author described the occurrence of traumatic luxation of the testis, adding four additional cases that he has reviewed. In addition to the case reports, Dr. Morgan includes a classification of luxation depending on the eventual location of the disrupted testis. The author also discusses the mechanism for this displacement with a description of anatomic fascial planes that tend to impede spontaneous reduction of the luxated testis. The diagnosis of the condition can be aided by Brockman's sign, which he defines. Management of this problem is surgical replacement.

Umhey CE Jr: Experience with genital wounds in Vietnam: A report of 25 cases. J Urol 99:660, 1968

The author details his experience with 25 cases of genital wounds during the Vietnam conflict. Emphasis was placed on the importance of evacuating a soldier from the battlefield to a well-equipped surgical facility where primary care could be instituted. Of the 25 cases he describes, there were 20 injuries of the testis, most of which were produced by explosive fragments. The policy was to explore all penetrating injuries of the scrotum and all blunt injuries with hematocele. The techniques of salvage are discussed, especially emphasizing adequate debridement and careful hemostasis. Prophylactic antibiotics were used in all patients, and the salvage rate was high.

Warden S, Schellhammer PF: Bilateral testicular rupture: Report of a case with an unusual presentation. J Urol 120:257, 1978

This article gives a case report of a young man who was found to have bilateral testicular injury from blunt trauma to a retractile left testis. Exploration of the asymptomatic right testis revealed a laceration requiring repair. The authors discuss the etiology of testicular rupture and the necessity for surgical exploration to provide maximal salvage. Various methods used to repair rupture of the tunica albuginea are briefly discussed.

Overview: Testicular Trauma and Surgery of Testicular Trauma

Hubert Hecht

The true incidence of testicular rupture is unknown; reported cases of testicular rupture are rather rare.[1] Conservative management of nonpenetrating injuries may account for the relative infrequent diagnosis and reporting of testis rupture. Testicular trauma manifests itself soon after the injury by scrotal swelling and pain and must be considered a surgical emergency. The entity must be thought of in any patient who has an enlarging scrotal mass following blunt, nonpenetrating trauma to this region.

The mobility of the organ, toughness of the tunica albuginea, and anatomic situation all contribute, in a protective manner, to the rarity of the condition. Contrary to what one might expect, none of the reported cases involves injury to an undescended or ectopic testicle lying fixed in the groin. Direct trauma of considerable force is thought to be necessary to rupture the fibrous coat of the tunica albuginea.[2] Impingement of the testis against the pubic symphysis or pubic ramus probably contributes to the pathologic condition. The surgeon should be mindful of the fact that a relatively trivial injury may cause testicular rupture when associated with an underlying testicular neoplasm.[3]

The most consistent symptom of testicular rupture is severe scrotal pain, which may diminish in intensity with time. Fainting, nausea, and vomiting are commonly present. Typically there is gradual enlargement of the hemiscrotum involved due to bleeding into the tunica vaginalis. Ecchymosis and obliteration of the scrotal rugae may be a feature; transillumination is usually impossible. The differential diagnosis should include traumatic hydrocele, hematocele, epididymoorchitis, neoplasm, torsion of the cord, and torsion of appendix testis.

Perhaps the confusion that may exist in the clinical differential diagnosis of intrascrotal lesions can be lessened with the use of radioisotopic studies, particularly epididymitis and torsion. The technique described by Riley and other investigators monitors arterial blood flow through the testis.[4] Inflammatory lesions and some contusions will result in increased blood flow and a "hot spot" on the scan, whereas torsion interrupts blood flow and causes a "cold spot." This approach permits accurate interpretation and is highly reliable clinically. Its most dramatic value is in separating acute epididymitis and acute testicular torsion; however, its use in the diagnosis of testicular rupture is probably unreliable.[5]

In an effort to achieve a diagnosis of the "acute scrotum" with a minimum of delay, the use of the ultrasonic (Doppler) stethescope has been employed.[6,7] This is a rapid, easy, noninvasive means of evaluating testicular blood flow. Its usefulness is best appreciated in distinguishing torsion of the cord from that of the appendix testis. As to the use of this modality in cases of testicular rupture, the test of time and further experience will have to be the conclusive factor in judging its reliability. Miskin and Buckspan, in using ultrasonographic examinations of scrotal masses, have described distinct patterns attributable to hydrocele, abscess, spermatocele, epididymitis, hematocele, and testicular rupture.[8] With

testicular trauma and subsequent rupture and hemorrhage, the testis is found to be diffusely enlarged with an irregular outline. Scattered zones of lucency resulting from hemorrhage are apparent around the cluster of echoes, a representation of the disrupted testicular tissue. Admittedly, their experience with testicular rupture has been rather meager.[9]

With the laceration of the tunical albuginea, release of sperm will follow. The eventual production of sperm autoantibodies in both the blood and seminal plasma is a distinct possibility. The literature lacks any reference to studies in this regard in instances of testicular rupture with herniation of the seminiferous tubules.

The mobility of the testis can afford little protection against penetrating injuries. In situations where there has been penetration of the scrotal wall by a foreign body, and whether or not rupture is a consideration, the scrotum should be explored and the fragments removed. Preexploration x-ray study is, of course, obviously of value.[10,11]

In reviewing the surgical management, most authors agree that the scrotal incision is the one of choice unless the index of suspicion of the presence of an underlying testicular tumor is such as to consider the inguinal pathway with early mobilization of the cord structures. Debridement, evacuation of the hematocele, and evaluation of the damage to the tunica albuginea follow. Simple suture of the rent after excision of the herniated testicular tumor may suffice. However, doing so may create significant compression of the testicle. Should this be the case, then oftentimes the tear should remain unsutured, and, if indicated, relaxing incisions should be made elsewhere in the tunica albuginea. The alternative use of tunica vaginalis to cover the tear is also a distinct possibility. The surgeon should be certain to evert or excise the tunica vaginalis to prevent eventual secondary hydrocele. Where the testicle is found to be beyond salvage and an orchiectomy is performed, a testicular prosthesis should be considered.

Regardless of the diagnostic modalities employed, the basic tenet of prompt surgical exploration must be adhered to. Testicular salvage is a distinct function of time, and delay may result in an orchidectomy in a situation where early intervention may have meant salvage of the organ.[12,13]

REFERENCES

1. Bronck WS, Berry JL: Traumatic rupture of the testicle. Report of a case and a review of the literature. J Urol 87:564, 1962

2. Wesson MB: Traumatism of the testicle: Report of a case of traumatic rupture of a solitary testicle. Urol Cutan Rev 50:16, 1946

3. Cassie GF: Rupture of the testis: Seminoma. Br J Urol 28:283, 1956

4. Riley TW, Nosbaugh PG, Coles JL, et al: Use of radioisotope scan in evaluation of intrascrotal lesions. J Urol 116:472, 1976

5. Hahn LC, Nadel NS, Gitter MH, et al: Testicular scanning: A new modality for the preoperative diagnosis of testicular torsion. J Urol 113:60, 1975

6. Perri AJ, Slachta GA, Feldman AP, et al: The Doppler stethoscope and the diagnosis of the acute scrotum. J Urol 116:598, 1976

7. Levy B: The diagnosis of torsion of the testicle using the Doppler ultrasonic stethoscope. J Urol 113:63, 1975

8. Miskin M, Buckspan M, Bain J: Ultrasonic examination of scrotal masses. J Urol 117:185, 1977

9. Pedersen JF, Holm HH, Hald T: Torsion of the testis diagnosed by ultrasound. J Urol 113:66, 1975

10. Staff WG, Lomax AJ: Foreign bodies in the testis. Br J Surg 55:255, 1968

11. Umhey CE: Experience with genital wounds in Vietnam: A report of 25 cases. J Urol 99:660, 1968

12. Gross M: Rupture of the testicle. The importance of early surgical treatment. J Urol 101:196, 1969

13. Del Villar RC, et al: Early explanation following trauma to the testicle. J Trauma 13:600, 1973

PART FORTY-EIGHT

SURGICAL TREATMENT OF HYDROCELE

120

A BLOODLESS OPERATION FOR THE RADICAL CURE OF IDIOPATHIC HYDROCELE

Peter H. Lord

Smith and Nephew Research Fellow, Royal College of Surgeons of England

British Journal of Surgery, 1964, Vol. 51, No. 12, December

Postoperative haematoma seems to be an accepted risk following operations for the radical cure of idiopathic hydrocele.

Indeed, in some surgical firms it is the practice to warn the patient that he must not be dismayed if he wakes up with a scrotum as large as before, and that this postoperative swelling is merely blood which will eventually reabsorb.

The risk of postoperative haematoma is much reduced by meticulous attention to haemostasis at operation. This is time-consuming, and if diathermy is used extensively there is a theoretical risk of damage to the testicular artery, since all the current has to pass between the body and the scrotum through a narrow isthmus which consists of the neck of the scrotum and the spermatic cord on each side.

Some surgeons therefore feel that it is wise to avoid the use of diathermy as much as possible in this situation.

The work on which this paper is based was carried out when the author was Senior Surgical Registrar at St. George's Hospital, S.W.1. I am grateful to the consultant surgeons at St. George's Hospital for allowing me to operate on their cases and to the departments of photography of St. George's Hospital and the Royal College of Surgeons for their help with the illustrations.

Drainage of the wound has its drawbacks; haematoma may collect despite the drain, and there is always risk of infection.

The operation to be detailed avoids these troubles and would appear to give as satisfactory a cure of the hydrocele as any other operation at present in vogue.

THE OPERATION

It is carried out in seven steps. It is much easier to do the operation than to describe it.

The instruments used are: Scalpel and dissecting forceps; six Allis's forceps; diathermy and sucker; two lengths of O chromic catgut on 30-mm half-circle atraumatic needles; two Lane's tissue forceps; Michele clips and forceps and applicators.

1. The hydrocele is grasped in the left hand in such a manner as to put the scrotal skin on the stretch, and this grip is maintained until the third stage of the procedure. An incision, 1½ in. long, is made through the skin and dartos muscle, down to the hydrocele, getting as close as possible to the tunica vaginalis without actually opening it. The superficial vessels are easily seen through the stretched skin, and the incision is made where these appear to be fewest. The small amount of

bleeding seen at this moment should be the only bleeding seen during the whole operation. It is permissible to touch these bleeding points with diathermy. There are only five or six of them and they are small, but this is not absolutely necessary, and the operation can be successfully performed without them.

2. Three Allis's forceps are applied to each side of the wound; they grasp the skin and dartos and control the bleeding points until the end of the operation (Figs. 1, 2.)

3. The tunica vaginalis is incised and the hydrocele fluid is removed with the sucker. The grip on the scrotum can now be relaxed. A finger of each hand is inserted and the opening gently stretched. (Fig. 3.)

4. The testis is delivered through the opening, thus turning the hydrocele inside out. (Fig. 4.)

5. Using the atraumatic catgut suture, the peritoneum which forms the tunica vaginalis is plicated to form a collar around the junction of the testis and the epididymis. This is done by picking up the edge of the tunica on to the needle, and then taking a small bite of tissue on the shiny surface of the tunica, at 1-cm intervals, in a line from the cut edge to the junction of tunica and testis, a process known in needlework at 'gathering'. (Figs. 5, 6.)

6. This stitch is now tied and further stitches, 8–10 in all, are similarly inserted, working around the testis in a clockwise manner. As these sutures are tightened, they pull the cut edge of the tunica away from the skin and dartos, which are still held in the Allis's forceps. This exposes areolar subcutaneous tissue. Fortunately this tissue is able to stretch without tearing so that it does not bleed. (Figs. 7, 8.)

7. The testis is now returned to the scrotum. This may be difficult since the space from which the testis came has been obliterated, and as it is pushed back the scrotum has to stretch to accommodate it. The Lane's tissue forceps are now applied to each end of the wound in such a way as to maintain the eversion of the skin and dartos. The Allis's forceps are then removed two at a time, and as each pair is removed that part of the wound is closed with Michele clips. These clips are placed close together, and they take over from the tissue forceps the control of the bleeding points. The skin edge and dartos must be maintained well everted, so that if there is any oozing it is outwards on to the dressing and soon stops. (Figs. 9–11.)

The Michele clips are kept in for 5 days. It is fair criticism that clips in the scrotum are uncomfortable and difficult to remove, but if the scrotum is supported the clips seem to be well tolerated. Two patients who were self-employed were back at work on the second post-operative day.

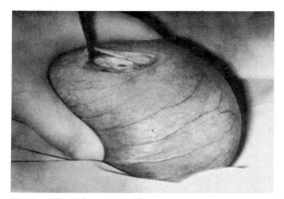

Fig. 1. Allis's forceps pick up all the incised tissues. Note that the scrotal skin is kept on the stretch by the left hand.

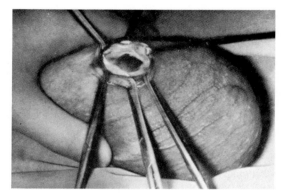

Fig. 2. Allis's forceps evert the cut edge. All bleeding is thereby controlled.

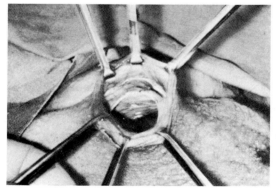

Fig. 3. The tunica vaginalis is incised and hydrocele fluid is removed.

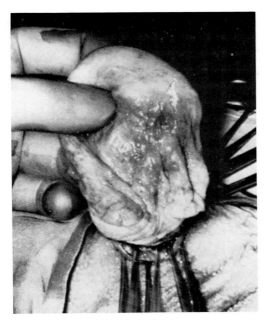

Fig. 4. The testis is delivered and the hydrocele turned inside out.

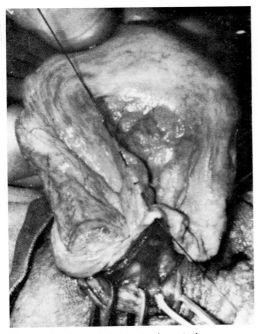

Fig. 5. The first of 8–10 similar stitches.

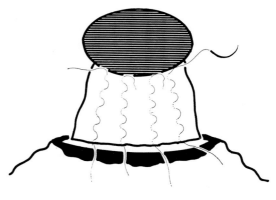

SIDE   VIEW

Fig. 6. Diagram representing half the stitches in position.

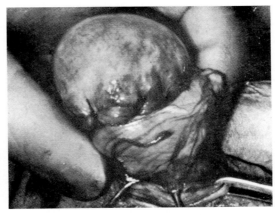

Fig. 7. The stitches have all been tied. The tunica vaginalis is gathered up at the junction of testis and epididymis.

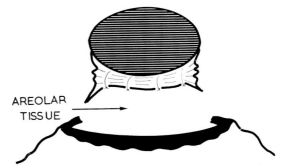

AREOLAR
TISSUE

Fig. 8. Diagrammatic representation of Fig. 7. The areolar tissue stretches without tearing or bleeding.

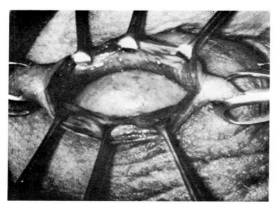

Fig. 9. The testis has been returned to the scrotum. The areolar tissue stretches to accommodate the testis.

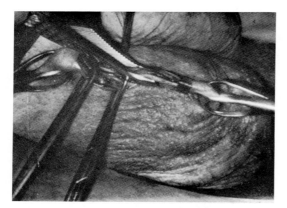

Fig. 10. Michele clips take over the control of the bleeding points and maintain the eversion.

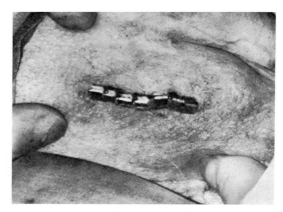

Fig. 11. The clips are close together; any oozing is outwards on to the dressing.

RESULTS

This operation has been performed twenty-two times without a trace of postoperative haematoma in any of the cases.

The first five of the series who have been followed for more than 3 years have not suffered from recurrence of their hydrocele.

Commentary: The Lord Procedure

Andrew J. McGowan, Jr.

Although no single method of surgical treatment of hydrocele has been universally accepted, the Lord procedure based on the principle of extrusion as described by Solomon in 1955 and applied by McGowan and Howley in 1969 continues to grow in popularity.[1,2] A hydrocele is an accumulation of serous fluid present within the two layers of the tunica vaginalis in abnormal amount. Embryologically the tunica vaginalis is an extension of peritoneum that has a serous surface that secretes and absorbs fluid. The mechanism of fluid accumulation in hydrocele is thought to be an imbalance in the interchange of production and reabsorbtion by the surfaces. That the imbalance is primarily a resorptive impairment can be proved by injecting indigo carmine into the hydrocele sac and comparing the resorption time to that of controls in producing renal excretion of the dye.

The resorption of hydrocele fluid takes place through the lymphatics of the parietal layer of the tunica vaginalis. In congenital hydrocele, lymphatics of the tunica vaginalis may mature after the closing of the patent processus. For this reason operative procedures are deferred for 1 yr to allow for spontaneous resorption of congenital hydroceles. Many acquired hydroceles are etiologically related to trauma, infection or inguinoscrotal operations that cause lymphatic obstruction.

The success of the Lord procedure is attributable to the fact that the visceral or secreting layer of the tunica vaginalis is placed outside the sac, enabling rapid absorption of fluid by tissue other than the resorptive parietal tunica, probably also contributing to a dimunition in the secretory mechanism itself. This repositioning of the secretory layer and elimination of the poorly functioning absorptive layer of tunica, either from its approximation to the testis or from the scrotum altogether, is also the crux of both the older ''bottle'' and ''excisional'' operations for hydrocele.

The Lord procedure is effected simply, rapidly, and efficiently. Extensive dissection is required for the other older methods. Because of the vascularity of the scrotal layers and the lack of tissue turgor in the redundant scrotal wall, any mobilization of transection of tunica results in production of multiple small bleeding points. Efron and Sharkey reported a 30% incidence of hematoma in patients treated by the bottle or excisional approach.[3] One more recent modification, and the only change in his technique, is the use by Lord of 3–0 polyglycolic acid suture in his more recent cases.[4] This suture is stronger, size for size, and causes much less tissue reaction than catgut. Indeed, it may be the early absorbtion of the catgut that accounts for the few recurrences of the hydrocele, attributed to the disruption of the anastomosis of the incised edge of the hydrocele sac to the epididymotesticular junction with reenvelopment of the testis by the tunica vaginalis.[5] The complication and recurrence rate with the procedure in the larger series has been 1% or less.[6] The operation has been carried out successfully on an ambulatory basis or with very short hospital stays as compared with a 5.9-day average hospital stay after other types of hydrocele repair.[7]

Although not applicable to the thick-walled fibrous hydroceles seen so commonly in the tropical countries, the procedure described by Lord based on the extrusion principle has become the procedure of choice in the cure of thin-walled hydroceles.

REFERENCES

1. Solomon AA: The extrusion operation for hydrocele. NY J Med 55:1885, 1955
2. McGowan AJ Jr, Howley TF: Experiences with the extrusion operation for hydrocele. J Urol 101:366, 1969
3. Efron G, Sharkey GG: The Lord operation for hydrocele. Surg Gynecol Obstet 125:603, 1967
4. Lord PH: Bloodless surgical procedures for the cure of ideopathic hydrocoele and epididymal cyst (spermatocoele). Prog Surg 10:95, 1972

5. McGowan AJ Jr: Hydrocelectomy—commentary. In Whitehead ED (ed): Current Operative Urology, p 1169. Hagerstown, Harper & Row, 1975
6. Haas JA, Carrion HM, Sharkey J, et al: Operative treatment of hydrocele. Urology 12:578, 1978
7. Dahl DS, Singh M, O'Conor VJ Jr, et al: Lord's operation for hydrocele compared with conventional techniques. Arch Surg 104:40, 1972

ANNOTATED BIBLIOGRAPHY

Solomon AA: The extrusion operation for hydrocele. NY J Med 55:1885, 1955

This is the first article in which the principle of extrusion is described. The author gives credit for the original verbal description and demonstration to Dr. Richard S. Muellner of Boston. He presents the method and the uncomplicated postoperative result in 42 cases.

Efron G, Sharkey GG: The Lord operation for hydrocele. Surg Gynecol Obstet 125:603, 1967

This article named the plicating procedure the ''Lord operation'' and was the first description and evaluation of the procedure to appear in the American literature. The authors listed one poor result in a series of 30 cases, that being a case of chronic epididymitis and thick-walled hydrocele sac. The plication produced a large scrotal mass that did not resolve. My feeling is that the presence of a thick wall of the hydrocele is a contraindication to this operation.

Haas JA, Carrion HM, Sharkey J, et al: Operative treatment of hydrocele. Urology 12:578, 1978

This largest reported series of cases confirms the significant advantages of the Lord procedure; 125 cases are reported with only 2 unacceptable results: poor resolution of a thickened sac (a contradiction to the procedure) and a postoperative hematoma.

McGowan AJ Jr, Howley TC: Experiences with the extrusion operation for hydrocele. J Urol 101:366, 1969

This is the only article to give proper recognition to Solomon's original description; it indicates that the critical step in both Solomon's and Lord's procedure is separation of the secreting layer from the faulty absorptive layer and exposure of the visceral tunica to the new absorptive surface in the scrotal compartment. The author does not advocate the use or necessity for the ''gathering'' stitches to collect the redundant sac.

Overview:
Surgery of Hydrocele

Bernard Fruchtman

Descriptions of operations for hydrocele date into antiquity and have been recorded on stone by aborigines. These have ranged from simple incision into the sac to packing of the sac or aspiration and injection of sclerosing agents or various methods of excision and suturing. The Lord operation is one of the newer procedures, and, as presented in the Commentary, it has been gaining popularity in the treatment of uncomplicated, acquired type of hydrocele. I have used this as the procedure of choice since 1968 and have been most gratified with the results. Hospitalization has been short, complications extremely few, and the recurrence rate almost nil. There are instances, however, in which this procedure cannot be used and may even be contraindicated:

Previously infected patients in whom there is an associated thickened tunica vaginalis

Patients with questionable testicular malignancy (An inguinal approach is mandatory.)

Patients with congenital hydroceles in whom a communicating tunica vaginalis must be ligated high in the inguinal canal or patients with an associated inguinal hernia

Patients with massive hydroceles in which the sac or tunica vaginalis is so large that imbrication leaves a very large, bulky mass (Some form of excision must be performed.)

Patients with recurrent hydroceles with much adherence to the scrotal wall

Patients with multiloculated hydroceles in whom some degree of excision is always necessary.

The first modern description of eversion of the sac has been ascribed to Winklemann and consists of suturing the bivalved tunic behind the epididymis.[2] Andrews in 1907 used the term *bottle operation,* in which he extruded the testicle through the scrotal incision and inverted the sac over the epididymis. This procedure has been popularly referred to in this country as the Winklemann or ''bottle operation.'' An alternative to eversion of the sac is simply suturing the edge or electrocauterizing it. Either of these operations would be applicable in the situations mentioned above, and the operative technique is described below.

After adequate preparation of the skin, a transverse incision is made in the scrotum, care being taken to avoid the superficial scrotal vessels. In congenital hydroceles or where there is a question of testicular tumor, an inguinal incision is made and the scrotal contents delivered into the inguinal wound after compression of the cord with rubber-shod bulldog clamps. Once the hydrocele sac is opened, and neoplasm has been ruled out, the clamp can be removed. With the inguinal approach, high ligation of the communicating sac can be easily performed.

In either of the above approaches it is important to attempt to preserve the sac without rupture so that the surrounding tissue can be bluntly dissected away without bleeding and delivered into the wound easily. The hydrocele sac is then opened at a point away from the testicle and epididymis and laid open. The excess sac is then excised as shown in Figure 12. At this point the surgeon can treat the sac in one of two ways. A running suture of 3–0 chromic can be taken around the entire edge as shown in Figure 13, or the surgeon can simply cauterize the entire edge after excising it close to the testicle and epididymis. The sac can be everted backward upon itself (''bottle operation'') as shown in Figure 14. In doing this, care must be taken not to close the sac too tightly at its upper end lest the blood supply to the testicle be compromised.

During excisional types of hydrocelectomy, meticulous hemostasis must be carried out in order to avoid the large serous or hemic collection so often associated with this type of repair. The surgeon must also be certain that conditions are not such that the opposing edges of the resected sac will coapt causing recurrence of the hydrocele.

The testis is then replaced in the scrotum, and the wound is closed in two layers with chromic catgut. I always leave a small Penrose drain in the scrotum for 48 hr. Fluff dressings are applied to the scrotum beneath a very snug scrotal suspensary. This is all the pressure that need be applied to the scrotum.

In the very elderly and poor-risk patient who has a

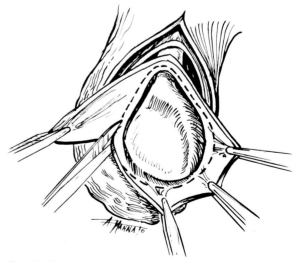

Fig. 12. Excision of excess tunica vaginalis.

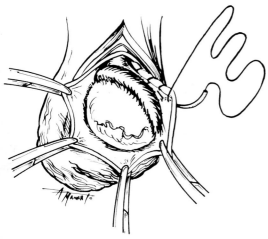

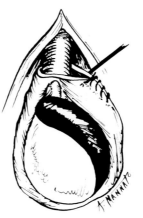

Fig. 14. Winkleman or "bottle" operation.

Fig. 13. Running suture placed around the cut edge of the tunica vaginalis.

symptomatic hydrocele, the surgeon should not eliminate the possibility of periodic aspiration. I have any number of patients who come to the office at 3- or 4-mo intervals to have their hydrocele aspirated and prefer this to entering the hospital for surgery. The hydrocele should be carefully transilluminated in a darkened room before the procedure in order to avoid puncturing the tunica albuginea with the aspirating needle.

This will result in severe pain as well as hematoma. After transillumination, the scrotum is carefully prepared with iodine solution. An 18-gauge needle is inserted into the most dependent portion of the scrotum. Local anesthesia is not necessary, as this is almost painless. While an assistant holds the needle in place with a hemostat, I completely aspirate the hydrocele. Fluid may be gently compressed toward the needle with one hand while aspirating with the other so that complete evacuation of the contents is obtained.

REFERENCES

1. Lander RR, Leonhardt KO: The history of hydrocele. Urol Surg 17:135, 1967
2. Winklemann O: Radial cure of hydrocele; Centrablatt Chirurg 44:1092, 1898
3. Andrews EW: The "Bottle operation" for radical cure of hydrocele. Ann Surg 46:915, 1907
4. Doyen E: Radical cure of hydrocele by inversion of the tunica vaginalis. Arch Proc Chirurg 4:706, 1895
5. Horwitz O: Hydrocele, its treatment, summary of 338 operations, description of a new method suggested by Doyen. Trans Coll Phys 1901

PART FORTY-NINE

SURGICAL TREATMENT OF CARCINOMA OF THE TESTIS, SCROTUM, AND URETHRA

121

IMPROVED MANAGEMENT OF NON-SEMINOMATOUS TESTIS TUMORS

John P. Donohue, J. Michael Perez and
Laurence H. Einhorn

From the Department of Urology, Indiana University Medical Center, Indianapolis,
Indiana

Journal of Urology
Copyright © 1979 by The Williams & Wilkins Co.
Vol. 121, April
Printed in U.S.A.

ABSTRACT—Two contributions to the management of non-seminomatous germinal
cell tumors of the testis are reviewed. First, a midline technique of extended retroperitoneal lymph node dissection has been developed, allowing good access to both
renal suprahilar zones as well as the traditional hilar and infrahilar areas. This
technique has been used at our medical center to stage embryonal carcinoma or
teratocarcinoma of the testis in patients who had negative preoperative chest tomography. Of 58 consecutive patients seen from 1965 to 1975, 30 had stage A disease
and 28 had stage B. All 30 patients with stage A disease survived (100 percent) and
24 of 28 patients with stage B disease survived (86 percent), for an over-all survival
rate of 93 percent.

The second contribution relates to the development of a new combination
chemotherapy protocol for patients with stage C disease. Preoperative stage C lesions
are treated with platinum, vinblastine sulfate and bleomycin. Patients who achieve
clearance of pulmonary tumors but who have anatomic or serologic evidence of
persistent retroperitoneal tumor after this chemotherapy are later treated with retroperitoneal lymph node dissection. Of 12 such patients 6 have been rendered free of
tumor and now enjoy complete remission. Furthermore, 33 of 50 patients (66 per-

Accepted for publication May 5, 1978.

cent) with disseminated stage C disease achieved initial complete remission using this drug combination. Of the 50 patients 26 remain in continuous complete remission with no evidence of disease for 2 to 4 years, 7 are alive and in partial remission and 17 are dead. Improved chemotherapy opens alternative methods to manage advanced testis cancer.

The management of non-seminomatous germinal cell testis tumors has improved dramatically in the last several decades because of advances in surgery, radiotherapy and chemotherapy (Table 1).[1–4] However, the biology of this tumor system lends itself to several treatment protocols. Our purpose is to review our own experience from 1965 to 1975. We shall describe our development of a bilateral dissection above the renal pedicles, our problems with radiotherapy and our success with our current protocol of surgery followed by no chemotherapy for stage A disease, single drug (actinomycin D) chemotherapy for stage B disease and a combination of chemotherapy for stage C disease.

MATERIALS AND METHODS

The classification of tumors used is that of Friedman and Moore.[5] Since we excluded pure seminoma from this series we are concerned here with embryonal carcinoma and/or teratocarcinoma and choriocarcinoma (Table 2). The staging used is: stage A—tumor limited to the testis, stage B—metastasis to regional lymph nodes and stage C—metastasis above the diaphragm (to lung) or disseminated. The patients described are 58 consecutive patients hospitalized from 1965 to 1975 for further staging and treatment of what was thought to be either stage A or B disease at the time of orchiectomy for primary diagnosis of testis tumor. All were non-seminomatous germinal cell testis tumors.

Preoperative evaluation for metastases included whole lung tomography. These 58 patients had negative whole lung tomograms at the time of retroperitoneal lymphadenectomy.

The method of radical retroperitoneal lymphadenectomy used is an extension of that described initially by Patton and Mallis,[6] Van Buskirk and Young[7] and later by Staubitz and associates[2,8,9] and Young.[10] It seemed to us that limitation of the procedure was the difficulty in equalizing the fine exposure in the suprarenal hilar areas provided by the thoracoabdominal approach.[11,12] Additional exposure and dissection in the areas above the renal hili were afforded by complete mobilization and elevation of the pancreas, using several techniques described in a separate report.[4]

The dissection was done en bloc. All lumbar arteries and veins were divided, and nodal and connective tissue was rotated under these and dissected off the posterior body wall in a continuous package. The lateral border of the dissection was either ureter, the inferior extent was each hypogastric artery (usually 2 to 3 cm beyond on the ipsilateral side) and the superior borders were the celiac axis, aortic crura, superior medial borders of both adrenals and retrohepatic inferior vena cava.

The tissue was placed on a diagrammatic template for the pathologist. More recently, it has been sectioned in the operating room and submitted in separate bottles of 10 percent formalin labeled: (1) right suprahilar nodes, (2) left suprahilar nodes, (3) periaortic nodes, (4) pericaval nodes, (5) right iliac nodes, (6) left iliac nodes and (7) ipsilateral (involved spermatic) vein and distal cord.

Each patient has been followed in our medical center. No patient with stage A disease received prophylactic chemotherapy. From 1965 to 1971 patients with stage B disease were given postoperative radiotherapy to the abdomen, mediastinum and supraclavicular area (4,500R in 5 weeks) and actinomycin D monthly for a year. Since then all patients with stage B disease have been treated only with actinomycin D chemotherapy monthly for a year.

TABLE 1. Comparison of Survival Rates in Series Using an Operation With or Without Radiation

| | Embryonal Ca | | Teratoca. | | Combined | |
	Stage A No. Pts. (%)	Stage B No. Pts. (%)	Stage A No. Pts. (%)	Stage B No. Pts. (%)	Stage A No. Pts. (%)	Stage B No. Pts. (%)
Walsh and associates[1]	15/16 (94)	2/7 (29)	26/28 (93)	10/13 (77)	41/44 (93)	12/20 (60)
Staubitz and associates[2]	27/30 (90)	14/17 (82)	15/15 (100)	1/3 (33)	42/45 (93)	15/20 (75)
Skinner[2]	8/11 (72)	16/18 (88)	31/32 (97)	13/18 (72)	39/43 (91)	29/36 (80)
Donohue[4]	17/17 (100)	16/19 (84)	13/13 (100)	8/9 (89)	30/30 (100)	24/28 (86)

RESULTS

Since 1965 more than 100 patients have had retroperitoneal dissections for non-seminomatous germinal cell tumors of the testis. This report includes 58 consecutive patients whose followup is 3 to 13 years. These 58 patients underwent formal retroperitoneal dissections for staging purposes (Table 3).

The over-all survival rate for these 58 patients is 93 percent (4 deaths). Thirty of these patients had negative nodes (stage A) and all are clinically free of tumor. In stage A disease no prophylactic chemotherapy or radiotherapy was given after node dissection. Three of these 30 patients subsequently suffered stage C disease: 8, 4 and 3 years ago. The first patient received actinomycin D for 2 years, radiation to the single lung lesion and a lobectomy (no viable tumor found). He remains free of tumor on no medication. The other 2 patients had multiple pulmonary lesions and are in complete remission after platinum, vinblastine and bleomycin chemotherapy. Therefore, 27 of 30 patients with stage A disease were never treated beyond retroperitoneal dissection and remain free of tumor. The other 3 patients are free of tumor after stage C disease developed and was treated. This gives us a 100 percent survival rate for our patients with stage A tumors.

Of the 28 patients with positive nodes 4 are dead, giving a survival rate of 86 percent for patients with stage B disease. This group includes every operated patient treated, even for massive disease. No patients have been excluded as inoperable. We divide these cases into 3 descriptive groups or substages: B1, B2 and B3. We arbitrarily segregate these subgroups according to degree of positivity. B1 represents little or no gross nodal tumor but histologic tumor and, as a rule, <5 positive nodes. B2 describes gross nodal tumor enlargement and/or >5 positive nodes. B3 indicates massive abdominal bulk tumor to or above the renal hilus. There were 14 patients in group B1, 11 patients in group B2 and 3 patients in group B3 (Table 4).

It is a practice in some series to exclude patients in our B3 category. Also, several (5) in our B2 group might have been excluded as having gross suprahilar nodes. Some consider these patients inoperable (effectively stage C) and, therefore, they do not submit the patient to retroperitoneal lymph node dissection. Our results suggest that such patients at great risk for subsequent stage C disease need not be excluded from possible benefits of effective and thorough node dissection.

Our 3 patients with B3 disease are well (Table 4). Postoperatively, 2 received radiotherapy and actinomycin D, and the third received actinomycin D only. While none suffered stage C disease we would recommend today combination chemotherapy postoperatively. These results encourage us to pursue our surgical and chemotherapeutic approach to these high risk patients. Three of our 11 patients with B2 disease are dead (Table 4).

TABLE 2. Cell Types*

	No. Pts.	Pos. Nodes	Neg. Nodes
Embryonal	33	20	13
Endodermal sinus	2	0	2
Teratoca.	21	7	14
Chorioca.	1	1	0
Teratoma (adult)	1	0	1
Totals	58	28	30

* Many cell types were mixed but the predominant cell type is listed for classification purposes.

TABLE 3. Survival After Retroperitoneal Lymph Node Dissection for Non-seminomatous Germinal Cell Testis Carcinoma

	No. Pts. (%)
Stage A	30/30 (100)
Stage B	24/28 (86)
Combined A + B	54/58 (93)

TABLE 4. Resuts of Operation

Stage*	Postop. Change of Stage				Present Status		
	Total Pts.	Remained Same	Recurrent Abdominal Tumor	Became Stage C Tumor	Living Complete Remission	Living Partial Remission	Dead
A	30	27	0	3	30	0	0
B1	14	10	0	4	13	0	1
B2	11	4	1	7	7	1	3
B3	3	3	0	0	3	0	0
	58	44	1	14	53	1	4

* Stage A—negative nodes gross and microscopic, stage B—microscopic + nodes or <5 and no tumurous enlargement, stage B2—grossly + nodes or >5 and tumorous enlargement and stage B3—massive disease, bulk tumor extending above renal hilus.

This group also is at high risk to suffer stage C disease. While 7 of our 11 patients had stage C disease only 3 of these are dead and 1 lives in partial remission. One of our 14 patients with B1 disease is dead (Table 4). Thirteen are free of tumor. Four of 14 tumors advanced to stage C but only 1 patient died. This excellent survival of patients with B1 lesions is reflected in other series also.[1,3,13,14]

Review of the present status of our 58 patients reveals that 14 tumors became stage C disease after retroperitoneal dissection but only 4 patients have died (Table 4). One patient, a B2 case, had a local recurrence. He seemed to be doing well off all therapy for more than 2 years after dissection. The serum human chorionic gonadotropin (β subunit and radioimmunoassay) became positive. Metastatic study was negative except for an abdominal ultrasound, showing a right iliac mass distal to the hypogastric artery and vein. This mass was resected (seminoma plus choriocarcinoma), the bed was radiated and the patient is well with negative serological testing. This case demonstrates the value of serological testing in the routine followup of patients with testis cancer.[15–19]

Postoperative chemotherapy is compared to postoperative radiotherapy for patients with stage B disease (Table 5). It is clear that, in our hands, postoperative radiotherapy is inferior to postoperative chemotherapy alone. There have been no deaths in the latter group but 4 deaths in the former. These 4 deaths are directly attributable to complications of radiotherapy (1 mesenteric radiation vasculitis with bowel segmental infarct, 1 radiation pericarditis and 2 bone marrow suppressions severely limiting use of chemotherapy for stage C disease). Two of these 4 patients were free of tumor postmortem. These events led us to adopt the alternative postoperative treatment for stage B disease of chemotherapy alone.

Also, the advent of effective combination chemotherapy for stage C disease was encouraging.[20–26] Our experience with combination chemotherapy for patients presenting with stage C metastatic non-seminomatous germinal cell testis cancer involved 2 protocols.[26,27] From 1973 to 1974 a combination of doxorubicin hydrochloride, bleomycin and vincristine sulfate was used in 10 patients with stage C disease and 9 responded; 5 with complete remission and 4 with partial remission. Of the 5 patients with complete remission 3 are well, in lasting complete remission, and 2 died of recurrent disease. All 4 patients with partial remission died. Since 1974 a second protocol has been followed, using combination platinum, vinblastine sulfate and bleomycin. Of the first 50 patients treated 33 achieved initial complete remission, 14 achieved partial remission and 3 died in the first month. These patients have been followed from 2 to 4 years and 33 are alive, while 17 are dead. Of the 33 patients who are living 7 are in partial remission with evidence of persistent disease, while the remaining 26 enjoy continuous complete remission with no evidence of disease. The 17 patients who died include 3 who died early before completing treatment, 4 who died with no evidence of disease and 10 who died of progressive disease. These patients are the subject of a separate report.[26,27]

DISCUSSION

When reporting any series of non-seminomatous germinal cell testis tumor one must be mindful of several variables at work over time. A favorable bias exists recently with the advent of truly effective combination chemotherapy. Also, the biology of the non-seminomatous testis cancer system clearly is amenable to several modalities of treatment. An operation alone,[8,28] radiotherapy alone,[29,30] sandwich therapy (preoperative radiation, retroperitoneal lymph node dissection and postoperative radiation)[31,32] and an operation combined with postoperative chemotherapy to all patients[2,3] have been effective and each has its supporters.

Certainly, improvements in chemotherapy are changing the surgical management of testis cancer. Second look resections of previously inoperable abdominal disease after medical bulk reduction by chemotherapy alone have become more common.[33,34] At least two-thirds of the specimens removed at a second look operation, after effective chemotherapy, show no viable malignant tumor.[34] Generally, the other alternative of primary cytoreductive operation before chemotherapy is not advisable.[25] While the rationale for this debulking seems good (reducing tumor burden for the drugs), in actual practice this works out less well than primary chemotherapy in most cases because (1) chemotherapy dramatically debulks mass by itself when used in effective dosage and combination, and (2) the operative morbidity is higher in the fresh cytoreductive surgical patient and is much less, in our experience, in the pretreated patient in partial remission on chemotherapy. Furthermore, combination chemotherapy toxicity risks are even greater

TABLE 5. Postoperative Treatment of Stage B Lesions

	Total Pts.	Living Complete Remission	Living Partial Remission	Dead	% Survival
Radiotherapy and chemotherapy	17	13	0	4	76
Chemotherapy alone	11	10	1	0	100

in the immediate postoperative patient and should post-operative medical or surgical complications develop the beginning of needed chemotherapy is delayed.

It is not our purpose to promote bilateral versus unilateral lymphadenectomy nor to champion extended bilateral suprarenal hilar versus the more common anterior retroperitoneal lymphadenectomy. However, we plan to continue a thorough and complete node dissection. Such dissection, in our opinion, includes a bilateral suprahilar dissection (extending widely 4 to 6 cm above each renal artery) and also is bilateral, extending beyond each hypogastric (internal iliac) vessel. We admit certain disadvantages to this approach, namely extra time of dissection and relatively few patients with only positive suprahilar nodes in the face of negative infrahilar nodes. While only 1 of our 28 patients had a solitary positive node above the left renal artery, 7 of 28 who had clearly positive infrahilar nodes also had positive suprahilar nodes. Some of these nodes might be left behind with other midline, less extensive lymphadenectomy techniques. Also, every patient has had ejaculatory impotence. Ganglia governing ejaculation are L1 and L2, as shown by Kedia and Markland.[35,36] However, all maintain erectile potency. The low incidence of isolated nodal metastases on the contralateral side is another argument against bilateral dissection.[37] The fact that this does occur, at least right to left, is enough to persuade us to continue our bilateral dissection for the present.

While an argument can be made that prophylactic chemotherapy could have prevented development of stage C disease in 3 of our 30 patients with stage A disease the fact is all survived in this series. Prophylactic chemotherapy series for patients with stage A disease, thus far, have not quite matched this (Table 6).

Clearly, our experience with retroperitoneal lymph node dissection followed by chemotherapy alone for patients with stage B disease is more favorable than our experience with retroperitoneal lymph node dissection followed by radiotherapy and chemotherapy (Table 5). The dramatic advances of combination chemotherapy for non-seminomatous germinal cell testis carcinoma far exceed any fundamental advance in delivery of radio-therapy in the last decade. It would appear that there will be a shift to chemotherapy (and away from radio-therapy) in the treatment of this metastatic testis disease.[38]

We estimate from patient history that half of our patients had a delayed primary diagnosis, many because of delayed referral to urologic surgeons by primary physicians who misdiagnosed testis tumor as epididymitis and treated the patient with antibiotics. This fact indicates a need for public, postgraduate and undergraduate medical education in the essentials of scrotal examination. The differential diagnosis of tumor and epididymitis is being taught with increasing vigor in our area at all levels.

Our plan of management for patients with non-seminomatous testis cancer differs from most other plans in the management of stage A cases (no prophylactic chemotherapy) and also in the use of extended suprarenal hilar lymph node dissection from the anterior approach. Also, we were the first to use platinum with the synchronized administration (8 hours apart) of vinblastine sulfate and bleomycin. The results in all stages indicate improved survivorship.

In summary, we present our 1965 to 1975 record in the management of non-seminomatous testis cancer. There is a 100 percent survival rate of patients with stage A disease (30 of 30 patients) and an 86 percent survival rate of patients with stage B disease (24 of 28 patients, including patients with massive suprarenal hilar disease). Also, 6 of an additional 12 patients with stage C disease, not herein reported, have been rendered free of tumor and survived in complete remission after removal of persistent retroperitoneal tumor after chemical cytoreduction by platinum, vinblastine sulfate and bleomycin chemotherapy. We are encouraged by these results.

Based on this experience our clinical impressions are: (1) A complete staging lymphadenectomy can be done through a midline anterior approach, provided care is taken to develop bilateral suprarenal hilar exposure. (2) While it is by no means clear that such extended dissection is necessary or even desirable, excellent survivorship and low operative morbidity of lymphade-

TABLE 6. Results of Operation Without Radiation but With Prophylactic Chemotherapy for Non-seminomatous Germinal Cell Testicular Tumors

| | Embryonal Ca | | Teratoca. | | Combined | |
	Stage A No. Pts.	Stage B No. Pts.	Stage A No. Pts.	Stage B No. Pts.	Stage A No. Pts. (%)	Stage B No. Pts. (%)
Walsh and associates[1]	10/10	2/3	14/15	1/1	24/25 (96)	3/4 (75)
Staubitz and associates[2]	27/30	14/17	15/15	1/3	42/45 (93)	15/20 (75)
Skinner[3]	7/10	6/7	30/30	7/9	37/40 (93)	13/16 (81)
Donohue[4]	17/17	7/7	13/13	4/4	30/30 (100)	11/11 (100)

nectomy suggest it may be of positive value at this time. However, more refined non-invasive staging techniques in the future may someday alter the role for such total lymphadenectomy, especially for presumed stage A cases. (3) Prophylactic chemotherapy does not appear necessary for stage A cases, particularly if a thorough node dissection has been done. Close pulmonary and serological testing followup and appropriate chemotherapy, only when indicated, can achieve equal, if not superior, results to prophylactic chemotherapy programs. (4) Current effectiveness of combined chemotherapy for metastatic testis cancer is changing our approach to advanced disease. Delayed second look operations for earlier inoperable disease is being used with increasing frequency and effectiveness. (5) More aggressive teaching of scrotal examination for tumor at all levels of medical and public education will serve to reduce delays in diagnosis of testis tumor.

REFERENCES

1. Walsh, P. C., Kaufman, J. J., Coulson, W. F. and Goodwin, W. E.: Retroperitoneal lymphadenectomy for testicular tumors. JAMA 217:309, 1971

2. Staubitz, W. J., Early, K. S., Magoss, I. V. and Murphy, G. P.: Surgical management of testis tumor. J Urol 111:205, 1974

3. Skinner, D. G.: Non-seminomatous testis tumors: a plan of management based on 96 patients to improve survival in all stages by combined therapeutic modalities. J Urol 115:65, 1976

4. Donohue, J. P.: Retroperitoneal lymphadenectomy: the anterior approach including bilateral suprarenal-hilar dissection. Urol Clin N Amer 4:509, 1977

5. Friedman, N. B. and Moore, R. A.: Tumors of the testis: a report of 922 cases. J Urol 57:1199, 1947

6. Patton, J. F. and Mallis, N.: Tumors of the testis. J Urol 81:457, 1959

7. Van Buskirk, K. E. and Young, J. G.: The evolution of the bilateral antegrade retroperitoneal lymph node dissection in the treatment of testicular tumors. Mil Med July, 1948

8. Staubitz, W. J., Magoss, I. V., Grace, J. T. and Shenk, W. G., III: Surgical management of testis tumors. J Urol 100:350, 1969

9. Staubitz, W. J., Early, K. S., Magoss, I. V. and Murphy, G. P.: Surgical treatment of non-seminomatous germinal testis tumors. Cancer 32:1206, 1973

10. Young, J. D., Jr.: Retroperitoneal surgery. In: Urologic Surgery, 2nd ed. Edited by J. F. Glenn and W. Boyce. New York: Harper & Row, Publishers, p. 848, 1975

11. Cooper, J. F., Leadbetter, W. F. and Chute, R.: Thoracoabdominal approach for retroperitoneal gland dissection: its application to testis tumors. Surg Gynecol & Obst 90:486, 1950

12. Skinner, D. G. and Leadbetter, W. F.: The surgical management of testis tumors. J Urol 106:84, 1971

13. Whitmore, W. F., Jr.: Treating germinal tumors of the adult testes. Contemp Surg 6:17, 1975

14. Fraley, E., Kedia, K. and Markland, C.: The role of radical operation in the management of non-seminomatous germinal tumors of the testicle in the adult. In: Controversy in Surgery. Edited by R. L. Varco and J. P. Delaney. Philadelphia: W. B. Saunders Co., chapt. 21, p. 479, 1976

15. Lange, P. H., Hakala, T. R. and Fraley, E. E.: Serum alpha-fetoprotein and beta-human chorionic gonadotropin levels in patients with non-seminomatous germ cell testicular cancer. Minn Med 58:813, 1975

16. Elgort, F. A., Abelev, G. I., Levina, D. M., Marienbach, E. V., Martochkina, G. A., Laskina, A. V. and Solovjeva, E. A.: Immunoradioautography test for alpha-fetoprotein in the differential diagnosis of germinogenic tumors of the testis and in the evaluation of effectiveness of their treatment. Intern J Cancer 11:586, 1973

17. Teilum, G., Albrechtsen, R. and Norgaard-Pedersen, B.: The histogenetic-embryologic basis for reappearance of alpha-fetoprotein in endodermal sinus tumors (yolk sac tumors) and teratomas. Acta Path Microbiol Scand 83:80, 1975

18. Vaitukaitus, J. L., Braunstein, G. D. and Ross, G. T.: A radioimmunoassay which specifically measures human chorionic gonadotropin in the presence of human luteinizing hormone. Am J Obst Gynec 113:751, 1972

19. Waldmann, T. A. and McIntire, K. R.: The use of a radioimmunoassay for alpha-fetoprotein in the diagnosis of malignancy. Cancer 34:1510, 1974

20. Li, M. C., Whitmore, W. F., Jr., Golbey, R. and Grabstald, H.: Effects of combined drug therapy on metastatic carcinoma of the testis. JAMA 174:1291, 1960

21. Samuels, M. L. and Howe, C. D.: Vinblastine in the management of testicular cancer. Cancer 25:1009, 1970

22. Samuels, M. L., Holoye, P. Y. and Johnson, D. E.: Bleomycin combination chemotherapy in the management of testicular neoplasia. Cancer 36:318, 1975

23. Monfardini, S., Bajetta, E., Musumeci, R. and Bonadonna, G.: Clinical use of adriamycin in advanced testicular cancer. J Urol 108:293, 1972

24. Kennedy, B. J.: Mithramycin therapy in testicular cancer. J Urol 107:429, 1972

25. Merrin, C., Takita, H., Beckley, S. and Kassis, J.: Treatment of recurrent and widespread testicular tumor by radical reductive surgery and multiple sequential chemotherapy. J Urol 117:291, 1977

26. Einhorn, L. H. and Donohue, J. P.: Improved chemotherapy in disseminated testicular cancer. J Urol 117:65, 1977

27. Einhorn, L. H. and Donohue, J. P.: Chemotherapy for disseminated testicular cancer. Urol Clin N Amer 4:407, 1977

28. Maier, J. G., Van Buskirk, K. E., Sulak, M. H., Perry, R. H. and Schamber, D. T.: An evaluation of lymphadenectomy in the treatment of malignant testicular germ cell neoplasms. J Urol 101:356, 1969

29. Caldwell, W. L.: Orchiectomy and irradiation in the treatment of testis tumors. Essay 3 of germinal tumors of the testis. In: Current Controversies in Urologic Management. Edited by R. Scott, Jr. Philadelphia: W. B. Saunders Co., p. 15, 1972

30. Blandy, J. P.: Testicular neoplasms. In: Urology. Edited by J. Blandy. Oxford: Blackwell Scientific Publications, p. 1203, 1976

31. Dykhuizen, R. F., George, F. W., III, Kurohara, S., Rotner, M., Sargent, C. R. and Varney, J. K.: The use of cobalt 60 telecurietherapy or x-ray therapy with and without lymphadenectomy in the treatment of testis germinal tumors: a 20-year comparative study. J Urol 100:321, 1968

32. Mittemeyer, B. T.: Management of testicular germ cell carcinoma. A prospective study comparing radiation alone to lymphadenectomy with pre and postoperative radiation. Walter Reed Army Medical Center, personal communication

33. Comisarow, R. H. and Grabstald, H.: Re-exploration for retroperitoneal lymph node metastases from testis tumors. J Urol 115:569, 1976

34. Merrin, C., Takita, H., Weber, R., Wajsman, Z., Baumgartner, G. and Murphy, G. P.: Combination radical surgery and multiple sequential chemotherapy for the treatment of advanced carcinoma of the testis (stage III). Cancer 37:20, 1976

35. Kedia, K. and Markland, C.: The effect of pharmacological agents on ejaculation. J Urol 114:569, 1975

36. Kedia, K. and Markland, C.: Alteration of ejaculation following surgical and chemical sympathectomy. Fertil Steril (in press)

37. Ray, B., Hajdu, S. I. and Whitmore, W. F., Jr.: Distribution of retroperitoneal lymph node metastases in testicular germinal tumors. Cancer 33:340, 1974

38. Skinner, D.: Advances in the management of non-seminomatous germinal tumors of the testis. Br J Urol 49:553, 1977

Commentary: Management of Testis Cancer

Stanley Brosman

Few advances in medicine have paralleled the significant improvement in survival that is seen in patients with testis cancer. The advent of effective chemotherapy and the discovery of specific tumor markers has altered physicians' approach to the staging and management of this disease. Donohue and colleagues have been in the forefront of this revolution and have contributed greatly to the successes obtained in dealing with testis cancer.

In the past, one of the most confusing aspects of this disease was the system of classification. Six classifications were developed for testis cancers. The system most commonly used in America was derived from the work of Dixon and Moore in 1952.[1] The other major system was described by the British Testicular Tumor Panel in 1976.[2] Both these systems can be correlated with each other.

It is interesting to note that although pathologists have eschewed allegiance to one system or another, clinicians have quietly adopted a totally new system based on therapeutic approach. No one has written about this new classification, but it has become a part of everyday thinking about this disease. Testis cancers in the adult are either seminomas or nonseminomas. They are no longer broken down into the particular kind of nonseminomas because the therapy is the same regardless of type. Donohue and colleagues, write about nonseminomatous testis tumors, and physicians understand what they mean. This change in the clinical classification of testis cancer has occurred so subtly and has been accepted so readily that most of the current literature uses these terms.

The role of retroperitoneal lymphadenectomy is controversial in patients with nonseminomatous cancer who have no evidence of distant metastases or large abdominal tumor masses. There is still discussion about the various surgical approaches and the need for bilateral or unilateral node dissection.[3-7] A comparison of survival between patients of similar stage indicates no significant differences attributable to surgical approach. Whether retroperitoneal lymphadenectomy is more useful for staging of the disease than for therapy is open for discussion.

Patients with stage A disease (tumor limited to the testis) have a 2-yr survival rate of 85% to 90%. Patients with the same stage of disease treated by surgery and radiation therapy,

or radiation therapy alone, have similar probabilities of survival.[8] Recurrent disease is found in 10% to 15% of these patients and is usually identified in the lungs within the first year. There were 30 patients in Donohue's series with stage A disease, and 3 developed metastases. All these patients responded to chemotherapy.

Donohue does not use prophylactic chemotherapy, nor does he advocate its use in patients with stage I disease. This opinion is not shared by others. Both Skinner and Staubitz have shown that actinomycin D can be an effective prophylactic agent and recommended this agent following lymphadenectomy.[9,10]

There is less disagreement about the management of patients with stage B disease. The presence of metastatic nodal disease indicates the need for chemotherapy. The types of chemotherapy protocols vary according to the amount of nodal disease present. Some believe that lymphadenectomy is sufficient therapy until other metastases have been identified. The use of effective chemotherapy and the availability of the tumor markers alpha-fetoprotein and human chorionic gonadotropin (HCG)-B can provide the means for early detection and treatment. Those patients whose tumor markers become negative after orchiectomy can be followed and chemotherapy initiated if the markers become positive. Despite this, most agree that some form of chemotherapy should be used in patients with stage B disease.

In order to facilitate comparisons in patients with stage B disease, they can be subdivided into three or four groups depending on the extent of their disease. Donohue and colleagues reported that the overall survival of stage B patients treated with monthly injections of actinomycin D for 1 yr following lymphadenectomy was improved. The authors indicate that this remains their treatment of choice in patients with small amounts of nodal disease, but they recommend combination chemotherapy in patients with large abdominal tumors.

The authors have had the opportunity to compare their results in stage B_1 and B_2 patients treated by chemotherapy or by irradiation. The comparison is historical and may be misleading, but they conclude that chemotherapy is more effective and point out that the "dramatic advances of combination chemotherapy . . . far exceed any fundamental advance in delivery of radiotherapy.'' The use of radiotherapy in nonseminomatous disease has decreased markedly with the advent of combination chemotherapy, and it may have little or no role in the management of stage B disease.

Other workers report an overall survival of 64% for patients treated by lymphadenectomy alone and 57% for patients treated with radiation therapy for stage B disease.[8] Adjuvant chemotherapy in several series indicates that the probability of 2-yr survival is increased to 86% when actinomycin D is the sole chemotherapeutic agent.[9] Currently combination chemotherapy using vincristine, bleomycin, and *cis*-platinum provides the maximum benefits to patients with stage B disease.

The greatest improvement in survival has occurred in patients with stage C or pulmonary metastases. Combination chemotherapy has been responsible for this success. Li and co-workers reported the first successful combination chemotherapy in 1960 in which 7 of 23 patients responded to actinomycin D, methotrexate, and chlorambucil.[11] The next major advance was reported by Samuels and colleagues in 1975.[12] They used a combination of vinblastine and bleomycin that was more toxic than previous regimens but produced a 39% complete response rate, which increased to 50% in previously untreated patients. The third major advance has been the introduction of *cis*-platinum used synchronously with vinblastine and bleomycin.[13] The Einhorn regimen, the VAB III, IV, and VI protocols at Memorial Sloan Kettering, and the regimens used at Roswell Park Memorial Institute consistently produce 50% to 75% complete response rates. Relapse rates run less than 25% with most tumor recurrences appearing within the first 12 to 15 mo. The most recent addition to the chemotherapy protocols is VP-16 (epipodophyllotoxin), an agent comparable in effectiveness to *cis*-platinum.

The results reported by Donohue's group indicate that 66% of patients achieved an initial complete remission and 28% had a partial remission. Thirty-three of these 50 patients remained alive 2 to 4 yr. The authors also noted that an additional six of 12 patients were rendered tumor free and in complete remission after chemotherapeutic cytoreduction and surgical removal of residual retroperitoneal tumor. The authors' experience in second-look resections is similar to others in that most surgical specimens show no evidence of viable tumor after effective chemotherapy, but surgery is beneficial in detecting the 16% of patients with residual tumor.

The improvements in chemotherapy are changing physicians' ideas on the surgical management of this disease. The authors conclude that it is not clear that extended node dissection is always necessary or desirable, particularlay if more refined noninvasive staging techniques become available. For the present, the use of lymphadenectomy remains a safe and valuable means of determining tumor stage and reducing the host tumor burden.

REFERENCES

1. Dixon FJ, Moore RA: Tumors of the male sex organs. Atlas of Tumor Pathology. Washington, DC, Armed Forces Institute of Pathology, sec. 8, Fasc. 31b and 32, 1952.

2. Pugh RCB (ed): Pathology of the Testis. Oxford, Blackwell Scientific Publications, 1976

3. Donohue JP: Retroperitoneal lymphadenectomy: The anterior approach including bilateral suprarenal-hilar dissection. Urol Clin North Am 4:509, 1977

4. Skinner DG, Leadbetter WF: The surgical management of testis tumors. J Urol 106:84, 1971

5. Whitmore WF Jr: Treating germinal tumors of the adult testes. Contemp Surg 6:17, 1975

6. Staubitz, WJ, Early KS, Magoss IV, et al: Surgical treatment of non-seminomatous germinal testis tumors. Cancer 32:1206, 1973

7. Fraley EE, Markland C, Lange PH: Surgical treatment of stage I and stage II non-seminomatous testicular cancer in adults. Urol Clin North Am 4:453, 1977

8. Williams C: Current dilemmas in the management of non-seminomatous germ cell tumors of the testis. Cancer Treat Rev 4:275, 1977

9. Skinner DG: Advances in the management of non-seminomatous germinal tumors of the testis. Br J Urol 49:553, 1977

10. Staubitz WJ, Early KS, Magoss IV, et al: Surgical management of testis tumors. J Urol 111:205, 1974

11. Li MC, Whitmore WF, Golbey R, et al: Effects of combined drug therapy on metastatic cancer of the testis. JAMA 174:1291, 1960

12. Samuels ML, Johnson DE, Holaye PY: Continuous intravenous bleomycin therapy with vinblastine in stage III testicular neoplasia. Cancer Chemother Rep 59:563, 1975

13. Einhorn LH, Donohue J: Cis-diammine dichloroplatinum, vinblastine and bleomycin combination chemotherapy in disseminated testicular cancer. Ann Intern Med 87:293, 1977

ANNOTATED BIBLIOGRAPHY

Donohue JP: Retroperitoneal lymphadenectomy: The anterior approach including bilateral suprarenal-hilar dissection. Urol Clin North Am 4:509, 1977

A description of the abdominal approach to retroperitoneal node dissection is presented. The author discusses the preoperative preparation, which is similar to that used for transplant donors. A mannitol diuresis is obtained during surgery, and the need for colloid replacement is emphasized. The bowel is mobilized by incising the right mesocolon into the foreman of Winslow, the root of the small bowel to the ligament of Treitz, and dividing the inferior mesenteric vein and right colic mesentery to the renal upper pole. The right suprahilar dissection extends up the aorta from the superior mesenteric artery, onto the crus of diaphragm, over to the medial aspect of the right adrenal gland about 4 cm to 6 cm above the right renal artery, then down the medial border of the right adrenal gland to the right renal artery and along the renal artery back to the aorta. The left suprahilar dissection extends from the superior mesenteric artery up the left side of the aorta, onto the crus, and up 4 cm to 6 cm above the left renal artery. The left renal vein and artery are mobilized caudad; the adrenal vein is divided. The infrahilar dissection involves the anterior longitudinal splitting of the nodal and vascular adventia over the vena cava and aorta, its lateral rotation, and the ''squaring out'' of the nodal package at each renal hilum at the renal vessels. Every lumbar vessel is divided to facilitate *en bloc* removal of posterolateral node tissue. Fifty-four of 58 patients with stage A or stage B disease have a cumulative 2-yr survival rate of 93%. There were 12 patients with stage C disease, of whom six remain clinically free of disease after surgery and chemotherapy. The abdominal approach is suitable for retroperitoneal lymphadenectomy and may be preferable for the management of right-sided lesions because of the need to dissect the left renal hilum and be able to extend the dissection to the diaphram on both sides.

Skinner DG, Leadbetter WF: The surgical management of testis tumors. J Urol 106:84, 1971

The authors report on a series of 58 consecutive radical retroperitoneal lymphadenectomies performed between 1953 and 1967. Nearly all the operations were performed through a thoracoabdominal retroperitoneal approach, excising the tenth rib. There were no operative deaths and negligible postoperative morbidity. The overall 2-yr survival rate was 74%. Stage B patients (27) had an overall survival of 58%. These patients were treated with antinomycin D. A description of the surgical technique is presented. The dissection extends between the crus of the diaphragm and the femoral canal on the involved side. Although not designed to be a bilateral procedure, this approach does permit dissection of the opposite renal hilum. There seems to be little difference in patient survival when the thoracoabdominal and abdominal approaches are compared.

Whitmore WF Jr: Treating germinal tumors of the adult testes. Contemp Surg 6:17, 1975

A general review of the diagnosis and management of testis tumors is presented. Radiation therapy is the mainstay of treatment for seminomas. Although nonseminomatous tumors are best managed by initial orchiectomy, retroperitoneal lymphadenectomy and chemotherapy are used for those patients with nodes containing metastases. The history of therapy of this disease is reviewed, and the author has played a major role in the understanding and management of testis cancer.

Staubitz WJ, Early KS, Magoss IV, et al: Surgical treatment of non-seminomatous germinal testis tumors. Cancer 32:1206, 1973

Bilateral retroperitoneal lymphadenectomy through a transabdominal approach was performed in 65 patients. Metastatic nodes were present in 30%. No other treatment was used. The 3-yr survival for stage I is 93%; Stage II, 75%. The authors conclude that lymphadenectomy is an essential part of the primary therapy for this disease. This is one of the few studies in which surgery alone was the treatment. The data tend to support the thesis that patients with stage I disease and normal markers do not need adjunctive chemotherapy, while all Stage II patients should receive adjunctive chemotherapy.

Fraley EE, Markland C, Lange PH: Surgical treatment of stage I and stage II non-seminomatous testicular cancer in adults. Urol Clin North Am 4:453, 1977

The authors present their philosophy and practise in the management of testis tumors. Patients with stage I disease, as determined by serum markers and histologic examination of the lymph nodes, are treated by surgery alone. Those with stage II disease (fewer than four positive nodes) and normal serum markers are followed frequently with serum markers and other diagnostic studies. If disease recurs, the patients receive a full course of therapy with Velban, bleomycin, and *cis*-platinum. Patients with Stage IIb disease receive chemotherapy postoperatively. The patients are treated for at least 2 yr. The authors do not believe in the use of preoperative irradiation and have discontinued the use of irradiation postoperatively except for special circumstances. They point out that there is no evidence that preoperative radiation therapy is of benefit, and it may in fact inhibit the subsequent use of chemotherapy.

Williams C: Current dilemmas in the management of non-seminomatous germ cell tumors of the testis. Cancer Treat Rev 4:275, 1977

The author of this paper is a medical oncologist who has reviewed the subject of testis tumors. He discussed the controversial areas in the management of this disease. He points out a number of inconsistencies and areas of confusion. He recommends controlled clinical trials to learn the best methods of treatment. In addition to standard evaluation, he recommends pedal lymphiography in all patients. Those with a positive study should have a blind supraclavicular node biopsy. Surgical staging is helpful, but the results and complications of surgery versus radiation therapy alone in stage I and II are not clear. The adoption of a single histologic classification is clearly overdue. The adoption of a universal staging system is necessary, taking into accord volume, state of fixation, and sites of tumor. He notes that surgeons, radiation therapists, and chemotherapists have yet to work together well enough to organize clinical trials, and without such investigative efforts, effective management will be hampered.

Skinner DG: Advances in the management of non-seminomatous germinal tumors of the testis. Br J Urol 49:553, 1977

This author devotes himself to a discussion of current dilemmas involved in the management of testis cancer. He believes that much of the confusion and controversy in the management of this disease stems from the facts that (1) the classification of these tumors has not been uniform and is inadequately understood, (2) it has only recently been demonstrated that lymph node dissection can effectively remove the retroperitoneal nodes, (3) the rarity of the tumors has made it difficult to develop a plan of management and there has been a tendency for one therapeutic modality to predominate; there is a need for combination surgery and chemotherapy, and (4) accurate staging is difficult unless surgical lymphadenectomy is performed. The author's experience with 146 patients is presented. Chemotherapy has proved to be the most important adjuvant, with postoperative radiation reserved only for patients with extensive retroperitoneal metastatic disease. The 3-yr crude survival for patients with all stages of disease was 78%, and in those in whom the disease was confined below the diaphragm, 85%.

Staubitz WJ, Early, KS, Magoss IV, et al: Surgical management of testis tumors. J Urol 111:205, 1974

A series of 72 patients with nonseminomatous cancer is reported. They were explored with the intent of performing a bilateral retroperitoneal lymphadenectomy. This was not accomplished in seven patients because of extensive disease above the renal pedicle. Metastatic nodes were found in 20 of the remaining 65 patients. The 3-yr survival rate in stage I was 93%; stage II, 75%. This study demonstrates the capability of surgery alone to control 70% of patients with retroperitoneal disease.

Li MC, Whitmore WF, Golbey R, et al: Effects of combined drug therapy on metastatic cancer of the testis. JAMA 174:1291, 1960

This article is now a classic in urologic oncology. This is the first major report indicating that nonseminomatous testis cancer can respond to chemotherapy. Twelve of 23 patients with advanced metastatic disease responded to a protocol using a 3-drug combination. Actinomycin D was found to be the active agent. This knowledge ushered in the era of adjunctive therapy with surgery and chemotherapy. Much has been accomplished since this pioneering effort.

Samuels ML, Johnson DE, Holaye PY: Continuous intravenous bleomycin therapy with vinblastine in stage III testicular neoplasia. Cancer Chemother Rep 59:563, 1975

The second major advance in chemotherapy was the discovery by these authors that bleomycin and vinblastine were effective agents in treating patients with stage III testicular neoplasia. Twenty-three patients were treated, and there were 17 responses, 9 of which were complete (39%). Eight of the complete responses were in patients with massive disease in whom a low response rate was expected. The authors discuss the toxicity of these agents. The increased knowledge of these agents has now reduced the toxicity and morbidity of this therapy.

Einhorn LH, Donohue J: Cis-diammine dichloroplatinum, vinblastine and bleomycin combination chemotherapy in disseminated testicular cancer. Ann Intern Med 87:293, 1977

Fifty patients with germ cell tumors of the testis were the subject of these studies. All had metastatic disease and were no longer amenable to attempts at surgical cure. A drug regimen of platinum + vinblastine + bleomycin was given:

1. Platinum, 20 mg/m² administered intravenously five times daily once every 3 wk for three courses

2. Bleomycin, 30 ml administered by intravenous push once weekly for 12 wk
3. Vinblastine, 0.2 mg/kg administered by intravenous push twice daily every 3 wk
   a. Vinblastine given 6 hr before bleomycin
   b. After 5 courses (12 wk) of vinblastine, maintenance therapy consisted of vinblastine, 0.3 mg/kg by intravenous push every 4 wk
   c. Therapy to be continued for 2 yr

Thirty-five of 47 patients (74%) who completed therapy achieved complete remission, and 29 of these were alive and disease free after 6 to 30 mos. There was partial remission in 26%. Five patients in partial remission became disease free following surgical removal of residual disease, producing an overall 85% disease-free status. Toxicity was manageable, and maintenance therapy was well tolerated. The Einhorn protocol is probably the most commonly used form of therapy for metastatic testis cancer. Recently, the authors have questioned the need for maintenance therapy, since those who are going to respond do so early in the course of treatment, and long-term survival may not be improved. This will be one of the issues to be resolved in the 1980s.

122

EXPERIENCE WITH PRIMARY CARCINOMA OF THE MALE URETHRA

Biswamay Ray,* Arturo R. Canto and
Willet F. Whitmore, Jr.

From the Urologic Service, Department of Surgery, Memorial Sloan-Kettering Cancer
Center, New York, New York

The Journal of Urology
Copyright © 1977 by The Williams & Wilkins Co.
Vol. 117, May
Printed in U.S.A.

ABSTRACT—We reviewed 23 cases of primary carcinoma of the male urethra and compared the clinical findings, treatment and results to the experiences previously reported. Patients with lesions of the pendulous urethra managed by appropriate amputation of the penis with ilio-inguinal node dissection for groin metastases had a good prognosis, whereas patients with lesions of the bulbomembranous or prostatic urethra had a poor prognosis. Despite occasional successful results with conservative surgical excision and over-all poor results with radical excision the generally extensive nature of such tumors necessarily makes radical excision the treatment of choice.

From 1940 through 1970, 34 patients with primary carcinoma of the male urethra were registered at our

Accepted for publication July 16, 1976.
Read at annual meeting of American Urological Association, Las Vegas, Nevada, May 16–20, 1976
*Requests for reprints: Division of Urology, University of Illinois Hospital, P. O. Box 6998, Chicago, Illinois 60680.

hospital. Eleven cases were excluded from analysis: 2 because the records could not be found and 9 because of a prior history of urothelial cancer (6 cases of bladder cancer and 3 cases of ureteral cancer). The remaining 23 cases were divided into 2 groups: group 1 consisted of 9 patients with carcinoma in the penile urethra and group 2 consisted of 14 patients with carcinoma in the bulbomembranous (13 cases) or prostatic urethra (1 case).

CLINICAL HISTORY

Of the 2 patients in group 1 with a history of instrumentation 1 had had intermittent dilatation for urethral stricture and the other had had transurethral resection for benign prostatic hypertrophy several years previously. Of the 14 patients in group 2, 9 had had instrumentation, usually dilatation for stricture, and 8 had had gonorrhea (Table 1). A more protracted course for patients in group 2 was evidenced by the fact that 5 had periurethral abscesses and ultimate fistulization before the diagnosis of urethral carcinoma was made. Patients in group 1 were generally less symptomatic than those in group 2. A palpable or visible urethral mass and a decrease in caliber of the urinary stream (with or without complete obstruction) were common, whereas urethral discharge (either serous or blood stained), hematuria and hemospermia were infrequent in both groups (Table 2).

CLINICAL INVESTIGATION

Investigation included urethrography, endoscopy, transurethral and open biopsies, and cytological examination of urethral secretions, washings or urine (Table 3).

TABLE 1. Significant History

	Group 1 (9 Cases)	Group 2 (14 Cases)	Totals (23 Cases)
Venereal disease	2	8	10
Urethral stricture	2	9	11
Post instrumentation or trauma	2	9	11

TABLE 2. Presenting Symptoms

	Group 1 (9 Cases)	Group 2 (14 Cases)	Totals (23 Cases)
Urethral mass	6	9	15
Obstructive symptoms (with or without retention)	4	9	13
Urethral fistula or periurethral abscess	—	5	5
Pain	1	5	6
Hematuria	1	4	5
Hemospermia	—	1	1

TABLE 3. Clinical Investigations*

	Group 1 (9 Cases)	Group 2 (14 Cases)
Urethrogram	—	4/7
Endoscopy	6/6	9/9
Transurethral biopsy	6/6	6/6
Open biopsy	4/4	6/6
Urinary cytology	3/4	4/4

* Number of examinations considered indicative of neoplasm per total number of examinations performed.

Although urethrograms and cytologic examinations were helpful diagnostic aids endoscopy, bimanual examination and biopsy were essential to diagnosis and to treatment decisions.

PATHOLOGY AND STAGING

One patient in group 2 had an adenocarcinoma, while the remaining patients had epidermoid carcinomas.

A method of staging male urethral carcinoma is proposed in Table 4. Although there is a logical reason for subdivision within several of the specified categories the limited experience does not justify a more elaborate staging classification. Patients necessarily were staged retrospectively, since many of them were first seen by us after primary treatment elsewhere. Staging was based on clinical and pathologic findings when we evaluated them before definite therapy. For example, 1 patient in group 1 had undergone transurethral biopsy of the urethral carcinoma elsewhere. Since there was no evidence of metastasis when we first examined the patient and the submitted slides of the urethral tumor revealed tumor invasion of the corpus spongiosum the clinical stage was B. The patient underwent radical amputation of the penis and the histologic findings of tumor invasion of the corpus spongiosum confirmed the final pathologic staging as B. One patient in group 2 had apparent tumor extension to the perineum without evidence of metastasis when he was referred to us and the clinical stage was C. He underwent total emasculation, radical cystectomy, bilateral pelvic lymph node dissection and ileal conduit and was found to have metastasis in the right external iliac nodes. Therefore, the final pathologic staging was D. There was no discrepancy between clinical and pathologic staging in group 1 patients but there was in group 2 patients (Table 5).

Group 1. The 9 patients were all white and ranged in age from 47 to 75 years (average 62, median 66). There were 7 meatal and 2 mid penile lesions, all of which were epidermoid carcinomas. Of the 6 cases in which information regarding grade of tumor was available 3 had grade II and 3 had grade III tumors. One patient

TABLE 4. Staging of Male Urethral Carcinoma

O—Confined to mucosa only (in situ)
A—Into but not beyond lamina propria
B—Into but not beyond substance of corpus spongiosum or into but not beyond prostate
C—Direct extension into tissues beyond corpus spongiosum, (corpora cavernosa, muscle, fat, fascia, skin, direct skeletal involvement) or beyond prostatic capsule
D_1—Regional metastasis including inguinal and/or pelvic lymph nodes (with any primary tumor)
D_2—Distant metastasis (with any primary tumor)

TABLE 5. Group II: Clinical Versus Pathologic Stage

	Pathologic Stage				
	O	A	B	C	D
Clinical stage:					
O	—	—	—	—	—
A	—	1	—	—	—
B	—	—	1	—	—
C	—	—	—	6	4
D	—	—	—	—	2

had local excision of the meatal lesion plus adjunct irradiation, 4 had partial amputation of the penis 2 cm proximal to the visible and palpable tumor, and 4 had radical amputation and perineal urethrostomy. Three of 4 men with clinically suspected inguinal node metastasis had bilateral ilio-inguinal lymph node dissection and proved to have metastasis. The fourth patient refused ilio-inguinal node dissection but the cytological examination of the groin sinus fluid was positive for malignant cells. One patient had right inguinal node metastasis 3 years after radical amputation and underwent right ilio-inguinal node dissection. One patient had right and left inguinal metastases 3½ and 5½ years, respectively, after radical amputation and underwent ilio-inguinal lymph node dissections at the respective times.

Of the 9 patients 6 are alive without evidence of neoplasm or dead of other causes, with survival ranging from 5 to 11 years from the time of initial treatment. Three patients have died: 2 of pulmonary metastases within 7 and 11 months, respectively, and 1 of bony metastases within 6½ years after the original treatment.

Group 2. The 10 white and 4 black patients ranged in age from 40 to 75 years (average and median 57). There were 3 bulbous, 8 bulbomembranous, 2 membranous and 1 prostatic lesions. One patient had an adenocarcinoma, while the remaining tumors were epidermoid carcinomas. Of the 9 patients in whom information regarding the grade of tumor was available 2 had grade II and 7 had grade III tumors. One patient with papillary epidermoid carcinoma of the bulbous urethra is well 8 years after transurethral resection and fulguration. He has had local recurrences similarly treated 3 times in this interval. Ten patients had radical excisions, including radical cystectomy, radical penectomy or total emasculation, bilateral pelvic node dissection and construction of an ileal conduit. Of these 10 patients 4 died postoperatively: 1 of myocardial infarction, 2 of upper gastrointestinal bleeding and 1 of delayed hemorrhage from the pelvic wound. Two of these 4 patients had clinically unsuspected distant metastases at autopsy: 1 had metastases in the pleura, lungs and left kidney and the other had metastases in the pleura, lungs, adrenals and stom-

ach. Of the 6 men who survived radical operations 5 died between 10 months and 3½ years postoperatively with local recurrence and/or distant metastases and 1 is well 6 years postoperatively, although he has had resections of lung metastases twice in this interval. Of 2 patients treated elsewhere by less radical excisions, including preserving the bladder and omitting inguinal and/or pelvic node dissections, 1 is living without evidence of neoplasm 12½ years postoperatively and the other died within 9 months of the operation with local recurrence and distant metastases. One patient who was found to have non-resectable disease (extensive bilateral pelvic node metastases) underwent palliative ileal conduit urinary diversion and died within 6 months of metastases.

DISCUSSION

Primary carcinoma of the male urethra is so rare that the literature on the subject consists primarily of periodic reviews accompanying case reports.[1-35] This fact suggests that primary carcinoma of the bulbomembranous urethra usually is diagnosed late in its course and has a poor prognosis despite radical treatment, whereas carcinoma of the penile (penulous) urethra can be treated more conservatively with reasonable prospects of survival. The experience at our hospital confirms these generalizations.

The clinical presentation and pathologic findings in our patients were similar to those described by others.[1-35] Patients ranged in age from 40 to 75 years, with an average of 60 years and a median of 59. The interval between the onset of symptoms and diagnosis was 6 weeks to 3 years in group 1 (average and median 11 months) and 6 weeks to 5 years in group 2 (average 18 months, median 6 months).

Cytological examination of urethral secretions, washings or urine, and transurethral biopsy were done in most patients and were positive in all cases studied except for a single falsely negative result in a patient from whom only a single specimen was obtained. The importance of cytological examination has been stressed by King.[21] Detection of urethral carcinoma by sponge biopsy or using a soluble swab has been described previously.[11,32] However, endoscopic and bimanual examinations and biopsy remain essential to diagnosis, staging and treatment planning.

As noted previously, there were no errors in the staging of group 1 patients, possibly owing to the small series, the submitted information from prior investigation and treatment, the accessibility to sight and touch of the primary lesion and of inguinal metastasis and 100 percent correlation between inguinal adenopathy and metastasis. The latter observation suggests that lymphadenopathy in group 1 patients is more apt to be caused by cancer than by infection, the reverse of the situation with cancer of the penis. Lymphangiography may prove useful in the staging of group 2 cases.

That patients in group 2 presented later in the course of the disease than did patients in group 1 was evident from a comparison of the stagings in the 2 groups (Tables 6 and 7).

A marked contrast is observed in the prognosis of patients in the 2 groups. Despite relatively conservative management 6 patients in group 1 survived without evidence of neoplasm from 5 to 11 years when radical ilio-inguinal dissection had been done only in the presence of clinically suspected inguinal metastasis. Furthermore, the only local recurrence occurred in a patient whose primary tumor was treated by radical amputation. The survival of patients in group 2 was poor, despite a distinctly radical over-all surgical approach. The postoperative mortality was excessive. The experience reported by Marshall is important and impressive, since it demonstrates that radical excision has the ability to control some locally extensive neoplasms, even when lymph node metastasis inside the pelvis or to the groin has occurred.[18] He reported 8 cases of carcinoma of the bulbous urethra, in each of which the prostate was invaded. Of the 4 survivors all were in the group of 5 patients who underwent a radical operation. Of these 4 survivors 2 had negative nodes, 1 had metastases in the groin and 1 had metastases in the external iliac nodes. Comparable results do not seem to have been obtained by other investigators with any method of treatment. In our series none of the patients with pelvic node metastases

TABLE 6. Group 1: 5-Year Survival With No Evidence of Neoplasm*

Clinical/Pathologic Stage	No. Pts.
O	—
A	1/1
B	3/4
C	—
D	2/4
Total	6/9

* Number of survivors per total number of cases.

TABLE 7. Group 2: 5-Year Survival With No Evidence of Neoplasm*

Clinical Stage	No. Pts.	Pathologic Stage	No. Pts.
O	—	O	—
A	1/1	A	1/1
B	1/1	B	1/1
C	1/10	C	1/6
D	0/2	D	0/6
Totals	3/14		3/14

* Number of survivors per total numbers of cases.

survived. Mandler and Pool claimed that for lesions of the bulbomembranous urethra radiotherapy gave results comparable or superior to those of radical excision.[23] However, radiation therapy alone generally has not been successful, since only a few patients in group 2 so treated were reported living,[7] and several patients in group 1 were cured, including 2 who were well at 5 and 14 years, respectively.[1,7,24] Radiotherapy may affect favorably the perineal mass lesions (secondary to urethral carcinoma)[23,29] and groin metastases,[9,14,17] at least temporarily.

Radical excision seems to offer the best chance of cure in group 2 patients. In order to extend the margins of surgical excision removal of the inferior pubic rami and lower half of the symphysis is being investigated. This method permits en bloc excision of the anterior perineum and may be expected logically to reduce the high local recurrence rate associated with the conventional radical excision. This technique was used in 1 patient but did not prevent perineal recurrence and subsequent death. Shuttleworth and Lloyd-Davies reported this technique in 2 patients with primary urethral carcinoma, both of whom were well 1 and 7 years postoperatively, respectively.[27] Of 14 patients in group 2 only 3 are free of disease; 2 following relatively conservative operations for relatively early lesions and 1 after a radical operation.

Reports in the literature indicate that early lesions have been treated successfully by transurethral resection (mostly in the prostatic urethra) or by resection of the involved segment of the urethra with end-to-end reanastomosis but these are certainly exceptional.[4,7,23,24] We have only 1 patient who survived after a radical operation and he has had metastases in both lungs requiring segmental (pulmonary) resections.

Among the 9 patients in group 1, 4 had stage D_1 groin metastases (successfully treated in 2) and 2 of the remaining 5 patients later had groin metastasis (successfully treated in 1). This limited evidence is consistent with the possibility that an early therapeutic ilio-inguinal dissection may be as effective in tumor control as a prophylactic one. Among the 14 patients in group 2, 2 had stage D groin metastasis that was not treated successfully and 2 had later groin metastases. These limited data suggest that the inguinal nodes are a less common site of drainage from lesions of the bulbomembranous urethra than from lesions of the more distal urethra. On the other hand, at least 4 of the 14 patients in group 2 had pelvic lymph node metastasis.

Optimal management of the regional (inguinal and/or pelvic) lymph nodes remains to be defined when clinical evidence of metastasis is lacking. In patients with pendulous, bulbomembranous or prostatic urethral tumors the precise propensity for involvement of the inguinal and/or pelvic lymph nodes is undefined. For all our patients our policy is to perform bilateral ilio-inguinal dissection only if the patient has proved unilateral or bilateral groin metastasis on presentation. Patients without clinical evidence of metastasis are followed at 2 to 3-month intervals and, if evidence of unilateral metastasis develops, then unilateral radical ilio-inguinal dissection is performed with careful observation of the contralateral groin in the subsequent followup. When a radical pelvic operation is done a bilateral pelvic node dissection is performed routinely.

Survival according to clinical and pathologic stages is summarized in tables 6 and 7. There was no correlation between age, duration of symptoms, histologic type or grade of tumor and survival. There is obvious correlation between the site and stage of the tumor and survival. Metastasis to the pelvic nodes had a grave prognosis and none of the 5 patients (1 in group 1 and 4 in group 2) with such metastases survived. The survival after the initial treatment of the patients who died of urethral carcinoma ranged in group 1 from 7 to 78 months, with an average of 32 and a median of 11, and in group 2 from 6 to 42 months, with an average of 19 and a median of 10.

REFERENCES

1. Kreutzmann, H. and Colloff, B.: Primary carcinoma of the male urethra, Arch Surg 39:513, 1939
2. Hickey, R. F. and Coleman, R. C., Jr.: Primary carcinoma of the anterior male urethra: case report. J Urol 51:643, 1944
3. Zaslow, J. and Priestly, J. T.: Primary carcinoma of the male urethra. J Urol 58:207, 1947
4. Lower, W. E. and Hausfeld, K. F.: Primary carcinoma of the male urethra: report of ten cases. J Urol 58:192, 1947
5. Gailey, H. A. and Best, J. W.: Primary carcinoma of the male urethra: report of two cases. J Urol 62:507, 1949
6. Kirkman, N. F.: Primary carcinoma of penile urethra. Br J Surg 37:162, 1949
7. McCrea, L. E. and Furlong, J. H., Jr.: Primary carcinoma of the male urethra. Urol Survey 1:1, 1951
8. Kimbrough, J. C.: Carcinoma of male urethra. Urol & Cutan Rev 55:78, 1951
9. Riches, E. W. and Cullen, T. H.: Carcinoma of the urethra. Br J Urol 23:209, 1951
10. Nansón, E. M.: Primary carcinoma of the male urethra. Br J Urol 23:222, 1951
11. Gladstone, S. A.: Cancer of male urethra diagnosed by sponge biopsy. JAMA 150:150, 1952
12. Scott, E. Van Z. and Barelare, B.: Adenocarcinoma of the male urethra. J Urol 68:311, 1952
13. Kaufman, J. J. and Goodwin, W. E.: Carcinoma of the male urethra. One stage surgical treatment by radical perineal excision and rectal transplantation of the divided trigone. Surg Gynecol & Obst 97:627, 1953
14. Hotchkiss, R. S. and Amelar, R. D.: Primary carcinoma of the male urethra. J Urol 72:1181, 1954
15. Baker, W. J. Graf, E. C. and Vandenberg, J.: Primary carcinoma of the male urethra. J Urol 71:327, 1954
16. Dean, A. L.: Carcinoma of the male and female urethra: pathology and diagnosis. J Urol 75:505, 1956
17. Flocks, R. H.: The treatment of urethral tumors. J Urol 75:514, 1956
18. Marshall, V. F.: Radical excision of locally extensive carcinoma of the deep male urethra. J Urol 78:252, 1957

19. Thompson, I. M. and Bivings, F. G.: Aspects of urethral carcinoma. J Urol 87:891, 1962
20. Howe, G. E., Prentiss, R. J., Mullenix, R. B. and Feeney, M. J.: Carcinoma of the urethra: diagnosis and treatment. J Urol 89:232, 1963
21. King, L. R.: Carcinoma of the urethra in male patients. J Urol 91:555, 1964
22. Howell, D. G.: Primary carcinoma of the male urethra. Proc Roy Soc Med 57:941, 1964
23. Mandler, J. I. and Pool, T. L.: Primary carcinoma of the male urethra. J Urol 96:67, 1966
24. Kaplan, G. W., Bulkley, G. J. and Grayhack, J. T.: Carcinoma of the male urethra. J Urol 98:365, 1967
25. Lee, D. A. and Bonney, W.: Carcinoma of the fossa navicularis of the male urethra. Am Surg 33:835, 1967
26. Pointon, R. C. S. and Poole-Wilson, D. S.: Primary carcinoma of the urethra. Br J Urol 40:682, 1968
27. Shuttleworth, K. E. D. and Lloyd-Davies, R. W.: Radical resection for tumours involving the posterior urethra. Br J Urol 41:739, 1969
28. Whitmore, W. F., Jr.: Tumors of the penis, urethra, scrotum, and testes. In: Urology, 3rd ed. Edited by M. F. Campbell and J. H. Harrison. Philadelphia: W. B. Saunders Co., vol. II, chapt. 30, pp. 1204–1208, 1970
29. Guinn, G. A. and Ayala, A. G.: Male urethral cancer: report of 15 cases including a primary melanoma. J Urol 103:176, 1970
30. Ogreid, P.: Development of carcinoma urethrae after operation for stricture of the urethra. Case report. Scand J Urol Nephrol 4:176, 1970
31. Milstoc, M.: New pathologic aspects of primary carcinoma of the prostatic urethra. J Am Geriatr Soc 19:80, 1971
32. Trott, P. A.: Detection of urethral carcinoma using a soluble swab. Br J Surg 58:66, 1971
33. Clark, M. O., Jr. and Kosanovich, M.: Primary carcinoma of the male urethra. South Med J 65:1339, 1972
34. Grabstald, H.: Tumors of the urethra in men and women. Cancer 32:1236, 1973
35. Mullin, E. M., Anderson, E. E. and Paulson, D. F.: Carcinoma of the male urethra. J Urol 112:610, 1974

Commentary: Surgical Treatment of Carcinoma of the Scrotum and Urethra

Biswamay Ray

PRIMARY CARCINOMA OF THE MALE URETHRA

Of the major genitourinary structures, the male urethra is the least often involved by primary carcinoma. Approximately 450 instances of carcinoma of the urethra in men have been reported in the literature.[1]

Classification and Location. Although the urethra in males is anatomically divisible into prostatic, membranous, and cavernous portions, for tumor location it is divided into prostatic, bulbomembranous, and penile sections (Fig. 1). Tumors in the prostatic and bulbomembranous urethra can be considered together, since primary tumors of the prostatic urethra are extremely rare and since tumors of the bulbo-membranous and prostatic urethra overlap in most instances. Accordingly, patients with carcinoma of urethra are classified into two groups: group 1, consisting of patients with carcinoma

of the penile, or anterior, portion of the urethra including the meatus and pendulous urethra, and group 2, consisting of patients with carcinoma of the bulbomembranous and prostatic, or posterior, urethra (Fig. 1). The bulbomembranous urethra is the most common, and the prostatic urethra is the least common, site of cancer of the urethra. In a collective review of 291 patients, 59% of tumors were situated in the bulbo-membranous urethra, 7% in the prostatic urethra, and 34% in the penile urethra.[1] Carcinoma involving both the anterior and posterior urethra was found in 5% of the patients reviewed by McCrea and Furlong.[2]

Most carcinomas of the urethra are of squamous cell type. Seventy eight percent of 262 patients reported had squamous cell carcinoma; 15%, transitional cell carcinoma; 6% adeno-carcinoma; and 1% undifferentiated tumors.[1] Squamous cell carcinoma occurred most commonly in the penile and bulbo-membranous urethra, and transitional cell carcinoma occurred

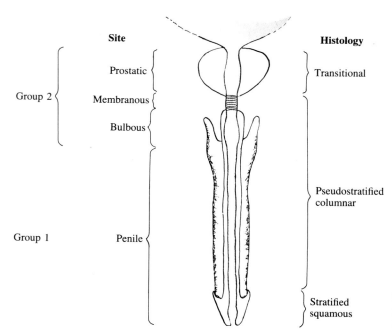

Fig. 1. Gross anatomy of the male urethra showing site of tumor origin and histology of specific areas.

most often in the prostatic urethra. Most squamous cell carcinomas are low grade tumors; however, in our series 33% were grade 2 and 67% were grade 3 carcinomas.[3,4]

Natural History. The onset of carcinoma of the urethra is usually insidious, and the symptoms of the disease are frequently attributed to a urethral stricture or an inflammatory lesion. The duration of symptoms varies greatly. Kaplan and associates reported symptoms between 1 day and 15 yr before diagnosis, with an average of 5 mo.[5] In our series the median interval between the onset of symptoms and diagnosis was 11 mo in group 1 and 6 mo in group 2.

The early lesion tends to spread by direct extension to the adjacent structures and usually involves the vascular spaces of the corpus spongiosum and periurethral tissue. Although the urethra is surrounded by the vascular corpus spongiosum, hematogenous spread is rare in either anterior or posterior tumors.

Metastasis usually occurs by lymphatic embolization to regional lymph nodes. The lymphatics from the anterior urethra drain into the superficial and deep inguinal lymph nodes and occasionally even to the external iliac lymph nodes, while the lymphatics from the posterior urethra drain into the external iliac, obturator, and hypogastric lymph nodes. Tumors of the anterior urethra usually metastasize to inguinal nodes, and tumors of the posterior urethra tend to metastasize to pelvic nodes; however, there are many exceptions. For example, metastasis to the inguinal nodes from tumors of the posterior urethra is not uncommon. Tumors of the posterior urethra that secondarily involve penile or perineal skin or both may metastasize to both the superficial and the deep inguinal lymph nodes. The incidence of pelvic nodal metastasis is undetermined, since few patients have undergone abdominal or pelvic exploration.

Distant metastasis is relatively rare. Kaplan and associates reported distant metastases in only 29 of 232 patients. Eighteen of these had invasion of the corpora cavernosa at the time of initial therapy.[5] Distal metastasis and extensive local spread occur more often in the patients with tumors of the posterior urethra.[2] Distant metastasis occurs more frequency to the lungs, liver, and bones. No spontaneous regressions of this tumor have been reported. Ninety six percent of the patients receiving either no therapy or palliative therapy died, with an average survival rate of 3 mo from the time of diagnosis.[5] Death is usually the result of chronic infection, sepsis, inanition, or hemorrhage.

Diagnosis. Although carcinoma of the urethra has been reported in males as young as 13 yr and as old as 91 yr, the vast majority occur in the 5th and 7th decades of life, with the peak incidence in the 6th decade. The signs and symptoms of urethral neoplasm are similar to those of urethral stricture. Urinary obstructive symptoms or a palpable mass or both are more common symptoms, followed by periurethral abscess, urethral fistula, pain, hematuria, and urethral bleeding or discharge.

Urethral bleeding or obstruction in a patient with no previous history of urethral disease or trauma, increasing difficulty in controlling a stricture, unusual bleeding during dilatation, or the appearance of a perineal abscess or fistula in an elderly male should always suggest the possibility of carcinoma. Only an awareness that the symptoms of benign diseases, such as urethral stricture, urethritis, prostatitis, and prostatic enlargement, are also those of carcinoma of the urethra can lead to early diagnosis. A tumor of the fossa navicularis may present as an ulcerating or papillary lesion with variable local induration. A lesion in the penile urethra may be palpable as a fusiform induration or a mass of varying dimensions. Lesions of the bulbomembranous urethra demonstrate variable degrees of local swelling, induration, and tenderness, which may progress to abscess formation or fistulization with involvement of the perineum or scrotum or both. Rectal and bimanual examinations are specifically important in patients with lesions of the bulbomembranous urethra to determine the extent of involvement of the prostate, anus, rectum, and urogenital diaphragm. Infiltrating lesions of the prostatic urethra may be palpable as a hard, nodular prostate with or without extension of induration in the periprostatic area, thus simulating adenocarcinoma of the prostate.

In addition to the diagnostic studies mentioned in the foregoing article, studies for metastases should include a roentgenogram of the chest, excretory urogram, skeletal survey or scan or both, liver scan, and liver profile studies. The usefulness of lymphangiography in defining the extent of regional lymph node involvement remains to be explored adequately. The differential diagnosis should include stricture, urethral rupture, periurethral abscess, tuberculosis, Peyronie's disease, foreign body, calculus, and carcinoma of the prostate. Differentiation between periurethral abscess or fistula and cancer is often difficult. The abscess should be opened widely, and multiple deep biopsy specimens must often be obtained before a clear-cut diagnosis of carcinoma can be made.

Treatment: General Considerations. *Group 1 Tumors.* Various methods, such as transurethral resection, local excision, segmental urethral excision with end-to-end anastomosis, partial or radical amputation of the penis, total emasculation, irradiation, or a combination of these, have been used to treat carcinoma of the distal urethra.

In general, for lesions localized to the distal half of the penis, a partial amputation of the penis 2 cm proximal to the visible and palpable tumor or induration is the best established form of treatment. Radical amputation of the penis and perineal urethrostomy are performed for more extensive lesions that preclude salvage of sufficient penile length for the patient to stand and direct the urinary stream.[5] The problem is somewhat analogous to that in the treatment of carcinoma of the penis. Radical removal of the penis gives no greater survival rate than conservative but adequate amputation. A total emasculation—removal of the penis and the scrotum and its contents—is indicated to minimize local recurrences only when there is extensive scrotal involvement.

The effectiveness of partial amputation in controlling the primary lesion was demonstrated by Mandler and Pool, by Kaplan and associates, and by our group, who observed no local recurrence in the urethral stump after partial penectomy in 4, 26, and 4 patients, respectively.[4,5] However, Kaplan and associates noted local recurrences in 3 of 22 patients treated by radical amputation and in 1 of 2 patients treated by emasculation.[5] We also observed one local recurrence in four patients treated by radical amputation. Further analysis of patients treated by radical amputation or emasculation in whom recurrence developed revealed that the lesion was in more proximal portions of the distal urethra, indicating a compromised surgical margin.[5]

Irradiation has little to offer in the treatment of male patients with tumors of the urethra. It is plausible that an early, small, superficial lesion in the region of the fossa navicularis could be irradiated. Although rare instances of tumor control by irradiation have been reported, such management could not be as definitive as a surgical procedure.[2,5] Radiotherapy has the advantage of preserving the organ; however, urethral stricture, chronic edema, and even penile atrophy may follow radiotherapy. A carefully planned partial penectomy may give a better chance for a functional organ than cancericidal doses of radiation.

Group 2 Tumors. Superficial lesions of the prostatic urethra are successfully managed by transurethral resection in more than 50% of patients.[3,5] However, in most instances, the tumor involves the bulk of the prostrate with variable extension to the bulbomembranous urethra, so that radical prostatectomy may not provide a tumor-free margin; in these instances anterior exenteration is the treatment of choice. Even with this aggressive approach, the prognosis is poor. Although my experience with carcinoma of the prostatic urethra has been limited, I believe that radical cystoprostatectomy with pelvic lymph node dissection is the treatment of choice in most infiltrating lesions.

Reports in the literature indicate that early lesions in the bulbomembranous urethra have been treated successfully by transurethral resection or by resection of the involved segment with end-to-end anastomosis, but these reports are exceptional. Most carcinomas of the posterior urethra are usually stage C or D lesions at the time of initial presentation and diagnosis, which frequently precludes anything but the most radical therapeutic effort, and even then the usual carcinoma of the bulbomembranous urethra has been surgically incurable. Treatment failures are caused by local recurrence and subsequent metastases. The high incidence of local recurrence even after such radical surgical treatment reflects the extensive nature of the disease and the inadequacy of initial surgical excision. This has led some investigators to explore the possibility of excision of inferior pubic and ischial rami to obtain a better

surgical margin and use of adjunct radiation therapy, usually preoperative irradiation followed by a radical surgical procedure. The radical operation I recommend includes anterior exenteration (removal of the bladder and prostate and a routine bilateral pelvic node dissection), total penectomy or urethrectomy or total emasculation (removal of penis and scrotum with its contents), and excision of inferior pubic and ischial rami when necessary. Preoperative external radiation therapy consisting of 2000 rads delivered over 5 days to large anterior and posterior portals is used before radical surgical treatment.

At present the following plans of therapy based on tumor site and stage of the disease are recommended because these factors have the most direct influence on the ultimate outcome of treatment.

Group 1 (anterior urethral) tumors
  Stage O, A—transurethral resection
        B—partial or radical amputation of the penis
        C—partial or radical amputation of the penis or total emasculation
        D—ilioinguinal lymphadenectomy in addition to the regimen recommended for stage C lesions
Group 2 (posterior urethral) tumors

Prostatic urethra
  Stage O, A—transurethral resection
  Small B—radical prostatectomy
  B, C, D—preoperative external irradiation, anterior exenteration with or without excision of inferior pubic and ischial rami.
Bulbomembranous urethra
  Stage O, A—transurethral resection
  B, C, D—preoperative external irradiation, anterior exenteration, total penectomy or total emasculation with or without excision of the inferior pubic and ischial rami.
Prophylactic inguinal node dissection is not performed for lesions in stage O, A, B, or C; inguinal lymphanectomy is performed for stage D lesions with metastases to the inguinal nodes

Results and Prognosis. The disease-free survival data according to the pathologic type and site collected from several series are presented in Table 8. The 5-yr survival rate without any evidence of disease for group 1 tumors was 43% and for

TABLE 8. Carcinoma of the Male Urethra: Type and Site Versus Survival*

Type	Location			
	Penile	Bulbo-membranous	Prostatic	Total
Squamous	12/27 (44%)	4/40 (10%)	0/1 (0%)	16/68 (24%)
Transitional	1.3 (33%)	0/4 (0%)	4/13 (31%)	5/20 (25%)
Adenocarcinoma		1/4 (25%)		1/4 (25%)
Undifferentiated		0/1 (0%)		0/1 (0%)
Total	13/30 (43%)	5/49 (10%)	4/14 (29%)	22/93 (24%)

* Ray B, Guinan PD: Primary carcinoma of the urethra. In Javadpour N (ed): Principles and Management of Urologic Cancer, pp 445–473. Baltimore, Williams & Wilkins, 1979.

group 2 tumors was 14%. Further analysis of the patients with group 2 tumors revealed a 10% and 29% 5-yr survival rate in tumors of the bulbomembranous and prostatic urethra, respectively. There is no significant difference in prognosis among lesions of different histologic types. In our series, the 5-yr disease-free survival rate for tumors of all sites was 100% for stage A, 80% for stage B, 17% for stage C, and 20% for stage D lesions.

Technique of Excision of the Inferior Pubic and Ischial Rami.

The operation is done with the patient in a modified lithotomy position, thighs being abducted 45 degrees, flexed 30 degrees (relative to the trunk) and externally rotated. Exploratory celiotomy is performed through a midline incision extending from 2 cm below the xiphisternum up to the symphysis pubis. Presence of lymph node metastases above the level of common iliac artery bifurcation or visceral metastases mitigates against any curative radical surgical procedures. If the lesion is judged resectable, the operation proceeds. After completion of bilateral pelvic node dissection, the branches of hypogastric arteries distal to the superior gluteal branch are divided between ligatures. Dissection of the posterior and lateral pelvic walls is carried out in the usual fashion for radical cystectomy, with complete mobilization of the bladder and prostate from their posterior and lateral attachments. If segmental excision of the inferior pubic and ischial rami is to be accomplished in conjunction with radical cystectomy and total emasculation, temporary packing is placed in the pelvis at this point and attention is diverted to the perineal area.

The penis is encased in a rubber glove (or a condom sheath) to prevent spillage of tumor cells during dissection. An elliptic incision is made encircling the penis and scrotum, starting anteriorly just above the root of the penis and ending posteriorly just below the perineal body in such a fashion to allow approximation of the lateral flaps without tension. The skin flaps are then dissected laterally up to the medial aspects of the thighs where Colles' fascia merges with the deep fascia of the thigh over the pubic and ischial rami. The spermatic cords are divided at the level of the external ring. Vertical incisions are then made in the deep fascia overlying the adductors of the thighs, and a transverse incision is made in the Colles' fascia overlying the transversus perinei muscles. This transverse incision is deepened until the pelvic cavity is entered, and the posteromedial border of the levator ani muscles is then divided from their attachment to the inferior pubic rami. Returning to the perineal approach the surgeon then prepares the pubic rami for their removal by dividing the adductors (longus, brevis, and magnus), obturators (externus and internus), and pectineus muscles close to their origins, exposing the lateral border of the inferior pubic rami and inferior ischial rami. The obturator foramina are identified, a Gigli saw is passed through the foramina, and a transverse cut is made through the upper part of the inferior pubic rami, hugging the inferior border of the symphysis pubis. The inferior ischial rami are then divided with a Gigli saw just distal to the crural attachments. The specimen is then quickly removed by dividing the puboprostatic ligaments and any remaining muscular attachments of the levator ani. Bone wax can be used to control bleeding from the cut ends of the bone (Fig. 2).

PRIMARY CARCINOMA OF THE FEMALE URETHRA

Malignant tumors of the urethra are reported to be twice as common in women as in men. This is a matter of some interest because of the greater length and complexity of the male urethra and the higher incidence of other tumors of the urinary tract in men. Primary carcinoma of the urethra in women accounts for less than 0.02% of all cancers occurring in women, 0.16% of gynecologic malignancies, and about 0.7% of all cancers of the female genital tract.[1]

Although carcinoma of the urethra has been reported in women as young as 29 yr and as old as 90 yr of age, the great majority occur in older, menopausal, multiparous women, three fourths of the patients being older than 50 yr of age. The most common type of carcinoma of the urethra is squamous cell carcinoma (70%), followed by transitional cell carcinoma (15%), adenocarcinoma (13%), and undifferentiated carcinoma (2%).[1]

Natural History. Carcinoma of the urethra in females is a locally destructive lesion that tends to spread by direct extension to involve the adjacent structures. If uninterrupted, the tumor may extend proximally to involve the vesical neck or distally to involve the vulva and may invade the vagina with ultimate urethrovaginal fistulization. Occasionally it is impossible on gross examination to differentiate malignant tumors of the urethra in their later stages from malignant tumors of the vulva, clitoris, vagina, or bladder.

Metastasis to the regional nodes is usually the next evidence of spread of this tumor. Although the exact route of lymphatic drainage from different parts of the urethra is not well defined, it has been generally accepted that the lymphatics from the distal urethra usually drain into the inguinal nodes, while the lymphatics from the proximal urethra drain into the pelvic lymph nodes. Twenty percent to 57% of patients have evidence of inguinal adenopathy when first seen, and, as with carcinoma of the male urethra, inguinal lymphadenopathy is usually indicative of metastatic disease rather than an infectious process.[1] Grabstald and associates reported clinical evidence of inguinal lymph node metastasis specifically recorded in 25 of 79 patients during the entire course of the disease.[6] Pathologic examination of these clinically enlarged nodes confirmed the presence of cancer in 88% (22 of 25 patients) and an overall incidence of 28% (22 of 79 patients) with inguinal lymph node metastasis during the entire course of the disease. In the same series, 13 of 26 patients for whom information was available regarding the status of the pelvic lymph nodes had metastasis to the pelvic lymph nodes. The incidence of the pelvic lymph node metastasis is more difficult to ascertain because pelvic node dissection is not systematically performed.

About 3% to 6% of patients have evidence of distant metastasis; however, distant metastasis was uncommon even in the patients who died of this tumor. In only 11 of the 79 patients were distant metastases diagnosed clinically at any time during the entire course of the disease as reported by Grabstald and associates.[6]

With persistence of active tumor, the clinical course of carcinoma of the urethra is apt to be short. Death usually occurs in 12 to 18 mo in untreated patients, and about 75% to 80% of unsuccessfully treated patients will die within 1 yr and

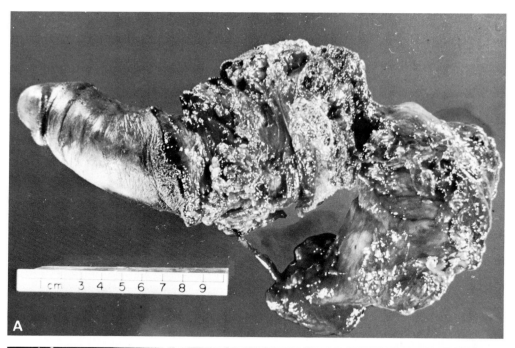

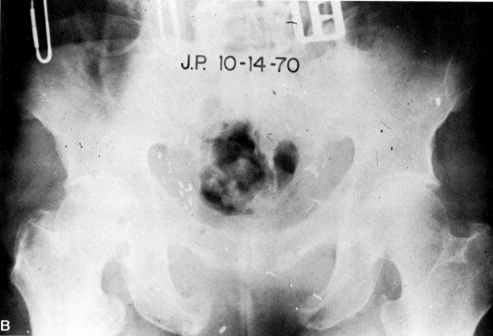

Fig. 2. (*A*) Extensive carcinoma of the bulbomembranous urethra treated by radical cystectomy, penectomy, and excision of inferior pubic rami. Excised specimen includes bladder, prostate, penis, urethra, and inferior pubic rami. (*B*) X-ray film of the pelvis showing skeletal defect following excision of the inferior pubic rami.

94% within 2 yr of diagnosis. The average duration of life after diagnosis of carcinoma of the urethra is 25 mo.[1] Death usually results from progressive incapacitation caused by regional spread, inanition, and sepsis.

Diagnosis. Regardless of the histopathology of the various types of carcinoma of the urethra, the symptoms are similar. Although no single symptom predominates, some form of bleeding is the most common presenting symptom. This may be bleeding or spotting from the urethra or vagina or hematuria. Dysuria and frequency are the next most common symptoms. Other symptoms include burning on urination or symptoms of urinary obstruction, such as difficulty in voiding or urinary retention, overflow incontinence, dyspareunia, or a palpable or visible mass. Late symptoms may include emaciation, weight loss, pelvic pain, periurethral abscess, or urethrovaginal fistulization with or without incontinence.

A variety of methods are useful in making the diagnosis of carcinoma of the urethra. These include inspection and palpation of urethra, vagina, and labia, cytologic examination of urethral secretions, washings, or urine, urethrogram, cystourethroscopy, bimanual examination, and open or transurethral biopsy. Because carcinoma of the urethra frequently masquerades as a urethral caruncle, polyp, prolapse, diverticulum, or urethrovaginal fistula, biopsy specimens must be obtained from all urethral lesions for proper diagnosis. As is true in carcinoma of the male urethra, although urethrograms and cytologic examinations are helpful diagnostic aids, endoscopic and bimanual examinations and biopsy are essential to diagnosis and to treatment decisions. Other investigations should include a roentgenogram of the chest, excretory urogram, skeletal survey or scan or both, liver scan, and liver profile studies. The usefulness of pedal lymphangiography is controversial, although routine lymphangiographic studies have been advocated by Antoniades and by Bracken and associates to determine the presence or absence of nodal metastasis and for more accurate clinical staging.[7,8]

Various forms of terminology have been used to describe the location of urethral tumors in women. A commonly used classification according to location is that of Grabstald and associates (Fig. 3).[6] Tumors are classified as ''anterior'' when limited to the distal third of the urethra and ''entire'' when more or other than the anterior third of the urethra is involved, that is, when the lesion is not clearly limited to the distal third of the urethra.

Grabstald and associates' clinical staging system is presented in a slightly modified form.[6]

Stage O—confined to mucosa only (*in situ*)

Stage A—into but not beyond lamina propria

Stage B—muscular—infiltrating into urethral muscle

Stage C—periurethral-infiltrating into adjacent structures such as the bladder, vagina, labia or clitoris

Stage D—metastasis

Stage D$_1$—regional metastasis including inguinal or pelvic lymph nodes or both (with any primary tumor)

Stage D$_2$—distant metastasis (with any primary tumor).

There is no significant correlation between location of the lesion and clinical staging, although lesions confined to the distal part of the urethra tend to be in lower clinical stages then those involving the proximal or entire urethra.[8]

Treatment. There is no universally accepted treatment for carcinoma of the urethra in the female, as is evidenced by the multiplicity of therapeutic modalities used to treat this cancer.

Before 1920, the treatment was usually an operation such as simple excision, partial urethrectomy, or total urethrectomy with suprapubic cystostomy or palliative permanent cystostomy in patients with advanced lesions and urinary obstruction. Disappointing surgical results and availability of radium and x-ray therapy led to radiation therapy becoming the treatment of choice in many centers. Radiation therapy still continues to be the primary and definitive form of treatment in several centers for all carcinomas of the female urethra.[9,10]

It became evident that the highest rate of local control by irradiation occurred in small lesions situated in the anterior urethra, whereas the poorest results of irradiation were obtained in patients with tumors of the posterior urethra or with large lesions extending into periurethral tissues or into the bladder or vulva or both. Similarly, surgical treatment alone results in poor survival when the carcinoma is in the ''posterior'' or ''entire'' urethra. However, radical surgical treatment alone usually results in a better prognosis than irradiation alone. Failure of either method of treatment alone was usually failure to achieve local tumor control.

Bracken and associates reported local recurrence in 64% of the patients treated by operation alone and in 46% of the patients receiving radiation therapy alone.[8] However, patients treated with combined surgical intervention and radiotherapy had a 22% incidence of local recurrence. The magnitude of the problem is evidenced by the fact that only 9% of patients with local recurrence were cured with secondary forms of treatment. Experience with preoperative irradiation combined with radical operation has been encouraging. Grabstald recently reported that 4 of 15 patients with epidermoid carcinomas of the entire urethra treated with preoperative radiation therapy combined with exenterative surgical procedures were alive and free of disease after 5 yr. Similar if not slightly better results were obtained in the treatment of adenocarcinoma.[3]

The observation that cancer of the urethra is usually a regional if not local disease, the relatively low incidence of distant metastases, the high incidence of local recurrence, and the extremely poor prospect of survival in patients with local recurrence or tumors of the entire urethra have led to a more aggressive surgical approach in therapy, including various exenterative procedures, with or without irradiation, especially for extensive tumors.[3,6,11]

The role of radical surgical treatment at present is possible salvage of patients with recurrent tumors after unsuccessful local excision or irradiation therapy or both and primary treatment in the majority of patients with lesions of the entire urethra or with high-stage lesions of the anterior urethra.

The management of the inguinal lymph node areas is essentially the same as that described for carcinoma of the male urethra.

A plan of therapy based primarily on tumor site and stage that I recommend follows.

Anterior Urethral Lesions. Partial urethrectomy is the treatment of choice for low stage lesions such as O, A, or B if it controls effectively the local tumor, although transurethral resection or local excision may suffice for stage O or A lesions. Because

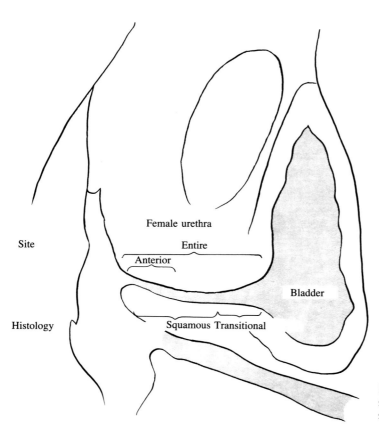

Fig. 3. Gross anatomy of the female urethra showing site of tumor origin, and histology of specific areas.

equally good results have been obtained with interstitial irradiation often supplemented with external and intracavitary irradiation, I conclude that adequate surgical treatment and carefully planned radiation therapy are equally effective in the management of lesions of the anterior urethra.

For stage C and D lesions, preoperative external radiation therapy and anterior exenteration are the treatment of choice. The operation includes removal of the bladder, urethra, anterior and lateral walls of the vagina, and the uterus and its appendages and a routine bilateral pelvic node dissection. For more invasive tumors the entire vagina and vulva are removed *en masse*. In addition, inguinal lymphadenectomy is performed for stage D lesions with metastasis to the inguinal nodes.

Prophylactic inguinal node dissection is not performed for cancer in stages O, A, B, and C. The patients are observed closely with examination at 2-mo intervals, and a node dissection is carried out only when there is clinical evidence of metastasis.

Patients with lesions of the anterior urethra in whom local recurrences develop after either partial urethrectomy or irradiation should undergo radical surgical treatment in the form of an anterior exenteration. Preoperative radiation therapy should be given if irradiation was not included in the initial treatment.

Entire Urethral Tumors. Early lesions in stage O or A may be treated successfully by transurethral resection, local excision, or interstitial radiation with or without local excision. A small lesion in stage B may be treated by interstitial radiation with or without local excision; however, these are certainly exceptions. The extensive nature of the tumor at the time of diagnosis frequently precludes anything but the most radical therapeutic effort. Accordingly, for stage B, C, or D lesions, I recommend preoperative external radiation therapy consisting of 2000 rad delivered over 5 days to large anterior and posterior portals followed by anterior exenteration with or without vulvectomy as treatment of most lesions of the entire urethra (Fig. 4). In addition, inguinal lymphadenectomy is performed for stage D lesions with metastasis to the inguinal nodes.

Lesions of either the anterior or entire urethra with distant metastasis cannot be cured and palliation only can be attempted.

Results. In a collective review it was noted that the 5-yr survival rate without evidence of disease for tumors of the anterior urethra ranged from 32% to 100%, with an average of 47%, and for tumors of the entire urethra the rate ranged from 0% to 21%, with an average of 11%. The overall 5-yr survival rate for lesions of all sites was only 29%.[1]

Survival rate according to stage for tumors of all sites as reported by Bracken and associates was 45% for stage A, 41% for stage B, 26% for stage C, and 18% for stage D lesions.[8]

Prognosis. The location of the tumor and stage are the most critical factors in the determination of prognosis. Prognosis

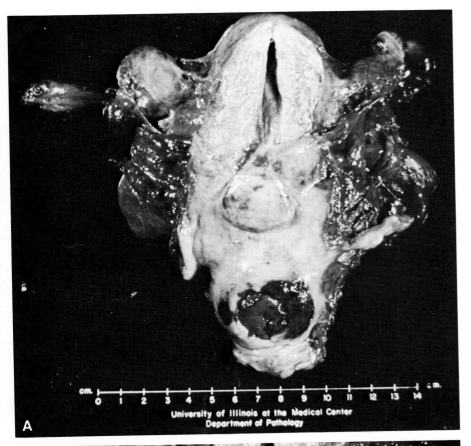

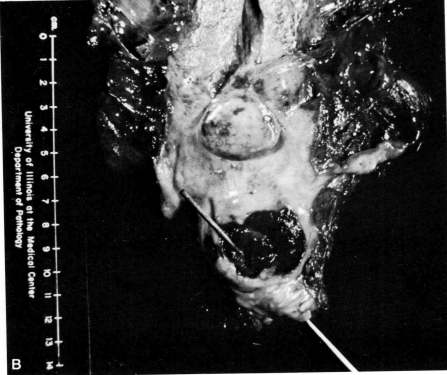

Fig. 4. (*A*) Advanced carcinoma of the posterior urethra with extension and fistulization into the vagina treated by anterior exenteration and excision of the anterior vaginal wall. The specimen has been opened through the posterior surface of the uterus. (*B*) Close-up view. A probe in the urethra defines the site of urethrovaginal fistula.

was worse for patients with lesions of the entire urethra than for those with tumors of the anterior urethra. Patients with tumors at the meatus or distal urethra have the best prognosis, since their tumors are diagnosed and treated earlier and tend to metastasize to the inguinal lymph nodes, whereas tumors in the proximal urethra metastasize to the deep pelvic nodes. Patients with higher stage lesions had a worse prognosis. There is some correlation between the size of the primary tumor and survival: lesions larger than 2 cm to 3 cm had a worse prognosis.[8,12] However, there was no significant difference in survival rates among patients with lesions of similar stage or similar size but different histologic types.

CARCINOMA OF THE SCROTUM

Carcinoma of the scrotum is rare. Five hundred and twenty-one men died of scrotal cancer in the United States between 1933 and 1948, averaging 32.5 deaths a year.[13] Twenty-three deaths were reported in 1965.[14] In 1977, we reported our experience with carcinoma of scrotum in 19 patients seen between 1948 and 1971 at the Memorial Sloan Kettering Cancer Center and reviewed the natural history, clinical presentation, management, and prognosis of this tumor.[15]

Natural History. Carcinoma of the scrotum usually begins as a small lesion that manifests itself as a small papule or wartlike growth or ulceration that is usually painless at onset. The lesions are usually unilateral, have no predilection for one side or the other, are usually situated on the anterior and lower part of the scrotum, and are most often solitary but may present as multiple or even bilateral tumors.[15] Simultaneous or sequential involvement of both sides was noted in approximately one third of the patients we saw.[15] With continued growth these lesions may reach a large size but even then tend to remain localized to the scrotal wall, occasionally involving the adjacent perineal skin but rarely involving the scrotal contents (i.e., testis, epididymis, or cord structures) and penis. Occasionally, the pubic bone is involved by direct extension. In the series of 141 instances reported by Southam and Wilson the testicles were involved in 6 and the penis in 3.[16] In our series there was local extension to the penis and perineum in one patient and to the perineum in another; however, neither testis nor cord was involved in any patient.[15]

Metastasis to the regional inguinal lymph nodes represents the earliest route of dissemination from carcinoma of the scrotum and usually occurs within 6 to 12 mo after the first symptom of the primary lesion. However, metastasis occurred as early as 4 mo or as late as 11 yr after the first signs of the tumor and provides an indication for long-term follow-up study.[15] Between one third and three fourths of patients will have inguinal lymph node metastasis.[13,17,18] Approximately one half to four fifths of patients with groin metastases have bilateral involvement; however, a much lower incidence of bilateral groin metastases has been noted in our series.[15,17,18] Thirteen of the 19 patients had groin metastases, 11 unilateral and 2 bilateral, 1 of which was a true crossed metastases.[15] Hematogenous spread with distant metastasis is rare. Patients with cancer of the scrotum have a high incidence of primary tumors in other sites, as reported by Dean (30%) and by us (47%).[15,17]

Diagnosis. Carcinoma of the scrotum occurs predominantly in the fifth and seventh decades of life, with the peak in the sixth decade. The average interval between onset of symptoms and diagnosis is reported to be about 10 to 12 mo.[16,17]

Physical examination usually reveals a growth or nodule or ulceration of varying size. The ulcerative lesion is characterized by raised and rolled edges with induration at its base and periphery and a granular and reddened floor with varying amounts of serosanguineous, foul-smelling drainage. A biopsy of the lesion, preferably including adjacent normal skin, is essential and usually will provide a definitive diagnosis. In addition to biopsy of the primary lesion, a roentgenogram of the chest, intravenous pyelogram, and bone survey or scan or both are indicated.

A staging system for carcinoma of the scrotum based upon the extent of the primary disease and the presence or absence of lymph node involvement or distant metastases as proposed by us is as follows:

Stage A_1—disease localized to the scrotum

Stage A_2—locally extensive disease involving adjacent structures, (penis, perineum, testis or cord structure, pubic bone) by continuity but without evident metastasis

Stage B—regional metastasis, (inguinal or ilioinguinal), resectable

Stage C—regional metastasis, nonresectable

Stage D—distant metastasis (beyond regional nodes)[15]

Treatment. *Of the Primary Tumor.* The primary lesion in the scrotum is treated best by wide local excision with a 2-cm to 3-cm margin of healthy skin peripheral to the tumor. Present and published experiences suggest that excision of the scrotal contents is rarely necessary for tumor control. Some investigators have recommended excision of the testis and cord structures on the involved side to facilitate closure of the remaining portion of the scrotum.[17,18] Two patients in our series underwent excision of the testis and cord structures when total scrotectomy was necessitated by the extent of the scrotal skin involvement. However, in neither of these patients was actual tumor extension into the testis, epididymis, or parietal tunica vaginalis demonstrated. Although wide excision usually is adequate in controlling the local tumor, occasionally there is local recurrence.[13] In our series 4 patients had local recurrence within 1 to 10 yr after excision of the original lesion; however, there is a real possibility that these may have represented new lesions rather than inadequate excisions of the original tumors.[15]

Of the Regional Lymph Nodes. Some authors advocate bilateral radical groin dissection either during or soon after excision of the primary scrotal tumor.[17,18] The rationale for contralateral radical groin dissection is the free communication between the lymphatics of the two sides of the scrotum. Dean, using data from a combined experience with penile and scrotal tumors, suggested that prophylactic groin dissection did not improve survival and might induce considerable disability.[19] He pointed out that only 50% of patients with inguinal adenopathy actually had metastases, suggesting that routine dissection would be useful in only half the patients with inguinal adenopathy. In addition, he pointed out that when dissection of regional nodes was delayed until histologic proof of cancer had been obtained, metastases subsequently did not develop beyond the groin. For these reasons he advocated bilateral groin dissection only for proved metastases.

Should one perform a node dissection in the absence of clinical evidence of metastases? Whether a routine prophylactic dissection increases survival rate in comparison with therapeutic dissection in the closely supervised patient is unanswered. Since the morbidity after regional node dissection is considerable, and since regional metastasis subsequently develops in approximately one third of patients presenting with clinical stage A disease, my present policy is to follow the patient at 2-mo intervals after excision of the primary lesion and to perform a regional node dissection only if there is clinical evidence of metastases as proved by biopsy. Evidence that inguinal lymph node involvement generally if not invariably precedes iliac lymph node involvement, that lymph node dissection limited to the inguinal node area has lower morbidity than a combined ilioinguinal dissection, and that, for carcinoma of the penis at least, a specific sentinel node in the superficial medial inguinal area may be consistently the first site of metastasis offers promise to exploration of a limited inguinal lymph node dissection as a logical compromise to the persisting problem of prophylactic versus therapeutic dissections.[20]

Should a regional node dissection be inguinal or ilioinguinal? In 13 patients who had regional metastasis, 8 metastases were localized to the inguinal nodes and 5 involved the iliac nodes (4 inguinal and iliac nodes and 1 apparently in iliac nodes only).[15] This 40% incidence of iliac node metastasis beyond the inguinal nodes and the 8% incidence of iliac node metastasis in the absence of recognized inguinal metastasis favor an ilioinguinal dissection if any dissection is performed. Although it is tempting to conclude that lymph node metastasis above the level of Poupart's ligament is an indication of surgical incurability, this conclusion must be tempered by the limited nature of the experience, the lack of detailed knowledge regarding the extent of the iliac node involvement, and uncertainties regarding the technical details of the surgical dissections.

Should contralateral ilioinguinal dissection be performed when there is ipsilateral regional metastasis? In our series bilateral metastases were found in 2 of 13 patients with nodal metastasis: 1 had a large tumor involving both sides of the scrotum, and 1 had a small tumor confined to one side of the scrotum.[15] Thus, the incidence of true crossed metastasis was only 1 in 13. Based on these admittedly limited data I defer contralateral inguinal dissection until there is clinical evidence of metastasis as proved by biopsy.

The nature of the ilioinguinal node dissection that I recommend is as follows: The pelvic portion of the dissection is performed through a lower midline extraperitoneal incision, such as is used in conjunction with a ^{125}I implantation for carcinoma of the prostate.[21] This permits bilateral extraperitoneal dissection of the pelvic nodes to the level of the common iliac artery bifurcation, including the obturator and external iliac nodes. This dissection is followed by inguinal node dissection through an incision parallel to Poupart's ligament and including an ellipse of skin and subcutaneous tissue immediately overlying the bulk of the inguinal lymph nodes.

For nonresectable regional metastatic disease no treatment of established effectiveness is available. Irradiation has proved to be beneficial on rare occasions, and hemipelvectomy may be considered in selected instances.[19,22]

Results and Prognosis. The prognosis for patients with carcinoma of the scrotum is markedly worsened by the presence of regional metastasis. Four of 13 such patients in our series survived, and 9 died of cancer or its treatment. Eight patients had metastases limited to the inguinal nodes, and four survived. None of the five patients who had metastases beyond the inguinal nodes (four ilioinguinal and one iliac only) survived. Survival according to the pathologic staging was as follows: five of seven patients with stage A_1, one of one patients with stage A_2, and four of nine patients with stage B survived. None of two patients with stage C disease survived. In total, ten patients were rendered free of evidence of cancer, nine living more than 5 yr.[15] The 5-yr survival rate has been reported by others as 8%, 18.5% and 70%.[13,17,18]

REFERENCES

1. Ray B, Guinan PD: Primary carcinoma of the urethra. In Principles and Management of Urologic Cancer, pp 445–473. Javadpour N (ed): Baltimore, Williams & Wilkins, 16, 1979

2. McCrea LE, Furlong JH Jr: Primary carcinoma of the male urethra. Urol Surv 1:1, 1951

3. Grabstald H: Tumors of the urethra in men and women. Cancer 32:1236, 1973

4. Mandler JI, Pool TL: Primary carcinoma of the male urethra. J Urol 96:67, 1966

5. Kaplan GW, Bulkley GJ, Grayhack JT: Carcinoma of the male urethra. J Urol 98:365, 1967

6. Grabstald H, Hilaris B, Heneschke U, et al: Cancer of the female urethra. JAMA 197:835, 1966

7. Antoniades J: Radiation therapy in carcinoma of the female urethra. Cancer 24:70, 1969

8. Bracken RB, Johnson DE, Miller LS et al: Primary carcinoma of the female urethra. J Urol 116:188, 1976

9. Chu AM: Female urethral carcinoma. Radiology 107:627, 1973

10. Taggart CG, Castro JR, Rutledge FN: Carcinoma of the female urethra. Am J Roentgenol 114:145, 1972

11. Peterson DT, Dockerty MB, Utz DC, et al: The peril of primary carcinoma of the urethra in women. J Urol 110:72, 1973

12. Blath RA, Boehm FH: Carcinoma of the female urethra. Surg Gynecol Obstet 136:574, 1973

13. Lione JG, Denholm JS: Cancer of the scrotum in wax pressmen. II. Clinical observations. Arch Indust Health 19:530, 1959

14. Cowdry EV: Etiology and Prevention of Cancer in Man. New York, Appleton-Century-Croft, 1968

15. Ray B, Whitmore, WF Jr: Experience with carcinoma of the scrotum. J Urol 117:741, 1977

16. Southam AH, Wilson SR: Cancer of the scrotum; the etiology, clinical features, and treatment of the disease. Br Med J 2:971, 1922

17. Graves RC, Flo S: Carcinoma of the scrotum. J Urol 43:309, 1940

18. Kickham CJE, Dufresne M: An assessment of carcinoma of the scrotum. J Urol 98:108, 1967

19. Dean AL: Epithelioma of scrotum. J Urol 60:508, 1948
20. Cabanas RM: An approach for the treatment of penile carcinoma. Cancer 39:456, 1977
21. Whitmore WF Jr, Hilaris B, Grabstald H, et al: Implantation of ^{125}I in prostatic cancer. Surg Clin North Am 54:887, 1974

22. Block NL, Rosen P, Whitmore, WF Jr: Hemipelvectomy for advanced penile cancer. J Urol 110:703, 1973

ANNOTATED BIBLIOGRAPHY

Marshall VF: Radical excision of locally extensive carcinoma of the deep male urethra. J Urol 79:252, 1957

Eight instances of carcinoma of the bulbomembranous urethra, in each of which the prostate was invaded, are reported. All three patients who underwent conservative surgical treatment died of their disease, whereas four of five patients who underwent radical surgical treatment (anterior exenteration and total penectomy or urethrectomy) survived 5 yr or more without any evidence of neoplasm. Two of these four survivors had negative nodes, one had metastases in the groin, and one had metastases in the external iliac nodes. The author concluded that locally extensive carcinoma of the deep urethra in men, even when pelvic lymph node metastasis is present, does not necessarily indicate hopelessness if a radical surgical procedure is performed. This is the most successful series of the treatment of carcinoma of the bulbomembranous urethra reported to date. The author demonstrated that radical surgical treatment has the ability to control some locally extensive carcinoma of the bulbomembranous urethra even when lymph node metastasis inside the pelvis or to the groin has occurred.

Mandler JI, Pool TL: Primary carcinoma of the male urethra. J Urol 96:67, 1966

Thirty-seven patients with primary carcinoma of the urethra seen at the Mayo Clinic from 1945 through 1964 are reported. Three of ten patients with lesions of the distal urethra had local excision, four had partial penectomy, and three had palliative radiation. Two of 20 patients with lesions of the bulbomembranous urethra had no treatment, 7 had surgical excision (only 2 had cystoprostatectomy), and 11 had radiation. One of seven patients with prostatic urethral lesions had cystoprostatectomy, and six had transurethral resection, with radiation in two instances. Local excision or partial penectomy proved to be adequate treatment for carcinoma of the distal urethra. For lesions of the bulbomembranous urethra, radiotherapy gave results comparable with or superior to those of radical excisional operation. Despite these results, radiation therapy for lesions of the bulbomembranous urethra generally has not been successful, since only a few patients so treated have been reported still living.

Kaplan GW, Bulkley GJ, Grayhack JT: Carcinoma of the male urethra. J Urol 98:365, 1967

These authors reviewed all instances reported in the literature and found 221 acceptable instances, to which they added 11 of their own. Lesions of the distal urethra are adequately treated locally by partial penile amputation provided a satisfactory margin of tumor-free tissue can be obtained. When this approach is used, recurrences are noted only when lesions of the proximal portion of the distal urethra are so treated. Lesions of the bulbomembranous urethra seem to carry an extremely poor prognosis and local recurrence is not infrequent after surgical therapy. However, because the disease is often locally confined at the time of death, it would seem that radical extirpation offers the best hope of cure. Superficial lesions of the prostatic urethra appear to carry a more favorable prognosis and are probably adequately treated by transurethral prostatic resection. More infiltrating lesions would seem to warrant prostatovesiculectomy or an extended

radical surgical procedure as described for lesions of the bulbomembranous urethra. Radiation therapy as the sole therapeutic modality has not generally been successful; however, radiation therapy as an adjunct to surgical extirpation seems worthwhile. Lesions of the distal urethra seem to carry the best prognosis, and lesions of the bulbomembranous urethra carry the worst prognosis. Sixteen of 71 patients with distal urethral lesions, 10 of 99 patients with bulbourethral lesions, and 4 of 16 patients with prostatic urethral lesions survived 5 yr. Most of the patients who died of carcinoma demonstrated only local invasion or spread to the regional lymphatics at death. Chronic infection from local ulceration and sepsis are frequently the cause of death. Distant visceral metastases are uncommon.

MacKenzie AR, Whitmore WF Jr: Resection of pubic rami for urologic cancer. J Urol, 100:546, 1968

For locally advanced urologic cancer, extended radical surgical treatment, including resection of the pubic rami, may provide a margin of normal tissue around the excised cancer and avoid spillage of cancer cells. Accordingly, the authors resected the pubic rami as part of operations upon five patients with carcinoma of the bladder, two patients with carcinoma of the penis, and two female patients with carcinoma of the urethra.

Shuttleworth KED, Lloyd-Davies RW: Radical resection for tumors involving the posterior urethra. Br J Urol 41:739, 1969

When periurethral abscess and fistula complicate carcinoma of the posterior urethra, the resection of the pubic arch is essential to remove the disease process *en bloc*. This resection aids the total eradication of the primary lesion, possibly preserving the integrity of the fascial planes surrounding the deep urethra and preventing local recurrence. Accordingly, the authors treated two patients with carcinoma of the posterior urethra by anterior exenteration with pubic arch excision. Both patients were well 1 and 7 yr postoperatively, respectively. The technique of pubic arch resection is described.

Grabstald H, Hilaris B, Henschke U, et al: Cancer of the female urethra. JAMA 197:835, 1966

An experience with 79 patients with cancer of the urethra seen between 1926 and 1965 at the Memorial Sloan-Kettering Cancer Center is reviewed. The tumors are classified as "anterior" or "entire" urethral, and a staging system is proposed to include all possible tumor stages for prospective treatment. This system of classification and staging currently is the most widely used. The overall incidence of inguinal lymph node metastases was 28% and of distant metastases was 14% during the course of the disease. The incidence of regional lymph node and distant metastases was sufficiently low to make probable a relatively high cure rate if the primary tumor were treated successfully. It was concluded that partial urethrectomy was usually successful in controlling tumors involving the anterior urethra, and equally satisfactory results may be achieved with irradiation. The prognosis for lesions involving the entire urethra was poor when radiation therapy or radical surgical treatment was used. However, the authors suggested that improved techniques of irradiation either alone or in combination with a radical surgical procedure may improve survival rate. Survival rate was determined chiefly by the extent of the neoplasm at the time of treatment.

Zeigerman JH, Gordon SF; Cancer of the female urethra. A curable disease. Obstet Gynecol 36:785, 1970

The authors review 230 histologically classified carcinomas of the female urethra reported since 1949 and add 7 patients of their own. They use the terms *gross cure rate* to indicate survival with the disease still present and *net cure rate* to indicate survival with no evidence of disease. The 5-yr gross cure rate for 181 evaluable patients was 21.5%, with a 5-yr net cure rate of 14.3%. These results are compared with Grabstald's survival statistics of a 5-yr gross cure rate of 19.4% and net cure rate of 16.4% in 70 patients. Fifty-three patients with cancer of the distal urethra had a 5-yr net cure rate of 50%. One hundred and twenty-eight additional patients with cancer of the entire urethra had a 5-yr gross cure rate of only 9.3%. Adenocarcinoma responded more favorably, with a 5-yr gross cure rate of 29% and a net cure rate of 20%. The 5-yr net cure rate for epidermoid carcinoma was 15% and for transitional cell carcinoma was 12.5%.

Grabstald H: Tumors of the urethra in men and women. Cancer 32:1236, 1973

Since Grabstald and associates' 1966 report, 17 additional patients with cancer of the urethra were seen, bringing the total to 96 patients. Since 1966, surgical treatment alone was not used for squamous cell carcinoma of the entire urethra. All patients with carcinoma of the entire urethra who underwent surgical treatment received preoperative radiation therapy. Four of 15 patients with squamous cell carcinoma of the entire urethra so treated were alive and free of disease after 5 yr, and the results with adenocarcinoma were about the same. Grabstald again concluded that adequate surgical treatment (partial urethrectomy) and carefully planned radiation therapy were equally effective in the management of tumors of the anterior urethra. Tumors of the entire urethra are best managed by preoperative irradiation and anterior exenteration. Overall, 27% of the patients in the entire series lived free of disease for more than 5 yr.

Peterson DT, Dockerty, MB, Utz, DC et al: The peril of primary carcinoma of the urethra in women. J Urol 110:72, 1973

This is a review of 49 instances of primary carcinoma of the urethra in women treated at the Mayo Clinic between 1916 and 1966. Twenty-five patients, including 2 with melanoma, had anterior urethral lesions, and 24 had entire urethral lesions. Only two patients had a recognizable distant metastasis when first seen, and only ten had enlarged lymph nodes. There was no correlation between the histologic type of the tumor and survival. Thirteen of the 23 patients with anterior urethral tumors and 5 of the 24 patients with entire urethral tumors lived 5 yr without any evidence of disease. Eighteen of the patients with entire urethral tumors died of disease within 2 yr of diagnosis. For carcinoma of the anterior urethra, local excision or partial urethrectomy alone or combined with irradiation is more effective than irradiation alone. Carcinoma of the entire urethra should be managed with anterior exenteration and radiotherapy as soon as the diagnosis is established.

Chu AM: Female urethral carcinoma. Radiology 107:627, 1973

This study reviews the survival periods of 22 patients seen between 1940 and 1970 who were treated primarily by radiation therapy. The author reports a 64% 5-yr disease-free survival rate for patients with anterior urethral lesions. None of the 11 patients with lesions of the entire urethra survived 5 yr, making the overall 5-yr survival rate only 32%. Anterior urethral lesions are effectively treated with interstitial irradiation. To reduce the likelihood of tumor implants being displaced by the tips of advancing needles, the author suggests a tumor dose of 2000 rad of external beam irradiation as a preimplantation dose, followed by interstitial therapy in the range of 5000 to 6000 rad. For lesions involving the posterior urethra or the bladder neck, 4000 to 5000 rad of external beam irradiation is given for 4 to 5 wk, followed by an additional 3000 to 4000 rads of interstitial implant delivered over 3 to 4 days. In these patients the author recommends suprapubic cystotomy at the time of radium implantation to allow proper and selective placement of needles. This article demonstrates the futility of irradiation as the sole method of treatment of carcinoma of the posterior (entire) urethra. None of the patients with urethral lesions with involvement of the vulva or bladder neck lived 5 yr. The techniques of treatment are discussed in detail. The open bladder implantation technique may carry a significant risk of tumor spillage.

Bracken RB, Johnson DE, Miller LS et al: Primary carcinoma of the female urethra. J Urol 116:188, 1976

The authors reviewed their experience with 81 instances of carcinoma of the urethra in women treated from 1950 to 1974 at M.D. Anderson Hospital. Fifty-three patients were treated with radiotherapy alone, 11 by operation alone, and 9 with a combination of radiotherapy and surgical treatment. Failure to achieve local tumor control was noted in 33 of 71 evaluable patients. Further analysis of this group of patients revealed recurrence in 64% of the patients treated by operation alone and in 46% of the patients receiving radiation therapy alone. This high incidence of local recurrence when single modality therapy was used led the authors to suggest preoperative irradiation followed by definitive surgical procedures. The overall 5- and 10-yr survival rate for the entire group was 32%. Prognosis was related directly to the clinical stage of the disease and the size of the primary lesion. The authors recommend interstitial irradiation with or without local excision for low-stage (O, A, and small B) lesions; preoperative external irradiation followed by anterior exenteration, and, if necessary, valvectomy for infiltrating lesions (stages B and C); inguinal lymphadenectomy for stage D lesions with metastatic inguinal lymph nodes in addition to the regimen recommended for stages B and C, and radiotherapy alone when pelvic lymph nodes are involved with the tumor.

Dean AL: Epithelioma of the scrotum. J Urol 60:508, 1948

An experience with 27 patients seen between 1926 and 1947 at Memorial Hospital, New York, is reported. Twenty-two patients were exposed to recognized carcinogens, 19 of which were occupational and 3 nonoccupational. All 27 patients had squamous cell carcinoma, and the majority of these tumors were low-grade lesions. Sixteen patients had groin metastases when first seen. The author advocates bilateral radical groin dissection only for proved metastases. The prognosis is poor. Only 4 of 11 patients without any demonstrable metastases when first seen and 2 of 16 patients with groin metastases when first seen are living 5 yr or more after treatment.

Tucci P, Haralambidis G: Carcinoma of the scrotum: Review of the literature and presentation of 2 cases. J Urol 89:585, 1963

The authors could find only two instances of carcinoma of the scrotum in black patients in 20 yr of experience at Harlem Hospital in New York, and neither had a known contact with a recognized carcinogen. The definite racial susceptibility to carcinoma of the skin holds true for carcinoma of the scrotum, which is extremely unusual in blacks.

Kickham CJE, Dufresne M: An assessment of carcinoma of the scrotum. J Urol 98:108, 1967

The authors reviewed their experience with 28 patients with carcinoma of the scrotum seen between 1930 and 1966. Twenty-two patients were exposed to occupational carcinogens. Epidermoid carcinoma was reported in 26 patients and basal cell carcinomas in 2 patients. Sixteen patients when first seen had palpable groin metastases, 13 of which were bilateral. The authors advocate bilateral radical groin dissection either during or soon after the excision of the primary scrotal lesion. Carcinoma of the scrotum is a highly malignant disease with a poor prognosis. Only 5 patients lived for more than 5 yr, 4 without any evidence of cancer.

Ray B, Whitmore WF Jr: Experience with carcinoma of the scrotum. J Urol 117:741, 1977

The natural history, management, and prognosis of carcinoma of the scrotum are reviewed in 19 patients seen between 1948 and 1971 at Memorial Sloan–Kettering Cancer Center, New York. Five patients were exposed to recognized carcinogens, one occupational and four nonoccupational. Only one of 19 patients was black. The authors propose a staging system for carcinoma of the scrotum for prospective treatment and to determine prognosis. Wide local excision of the primary lesion with radical ilioinguinal node dissection for proved inguinal lymph node metastases is recommended. Ten patients were rendered free of evidence of cancer; nine of these patients lived more than 5 yr. For nonresectable regional metastatic disease, no treatment of established effectiveness is availabale. Irradiation has produced benefit on rare occasions, and hemipelvectomy may be considered in selected instances.

OVERVIEW: CANCER OF THE SCROTUM, URETHRA, AND TESTIS

John P. Donohue

I agree entirely with Dr. Brosman's comments on the silent but universal adoption of functional classification of testis tumors as it relates to treatment. Physicians have more or less arbitrarily segregated germ cell tumors into seminomatous tumors and nonseminomatous tumors. The basic reason, as he indicates, is the different nature of these tumors, which allows and indeed requires different therapeutic approaches.

SEMINOMA

By and large, the seminomatous tumor is less inclined to metastasize. Eighty-five percent of seminomas are confined to the testis at the time of discovery and are therefore stage A. This greatly simplifies their treatment. The only requirement in staging, most would agree, is chest survey by whole lung tomography and retroperitoneal survey by lymphangiogram and, if available, computed tomography (CT) scan. Should the retroperitoneum appear benign and the chest survey be negative, the radiotherapist can draw his portals to exclude the left supraclavicular area and mediastinum. Many feel that 2500 rad is sufficient treatment in such cases. There are two other subsets of seminoma that deserve mention. The first is anaplastic seminoma, which implies more than five mitoses seen in a high-power field. Usually these are more aggressive in their biologic behavior and have a higher metastatic potential. Glenn and several others feel these should be treated aggressively just as nonseminomatous tumors. I agree with this if there is evidence of bulky retroperitoneal adenopathy by CT scan, lymphangiogram, or ultrasound. Ten percent to 20% of these metastases contain nonseminomatous tumor.[1] A very important point, yet to be published this year, is the value of combination chemotherapy (platinum, Velban, and bleomycin, four courses),

for disseminated seminomatous disease. The same survivorship can be achieved in this group of patients as with the nonseminomatous tumors. I have found in 19 such Stage C patients that two thirds can be salvaged in lasting complete remission should they present with metastatic seminoma. Usually these are anaplastic cases, which traditionally have had a poor survival if treated in the conventional manner with only 2500 rad to the retroperitoneal space. Merrin and Skinner have both reported survivorships ranging from 30% to 60% in this group of patients.[2,3] This simply is inadequate in today's world of improved chemotherapy for testis tumors. Sadly, alkylating agents and radiotherapy have been used even for advanced disease even in recent times for metastatic disease. I trust that the value of combination chemotherapy will become more widely recognized in advanced seminomatous disease.

The other subset of seminoma is spermatocytic seminoma, which generally occurs in the fifth or sixth decade, and there is only one report of metastasis from a spermatocytic seminoma.[4] Therefore, most feel that the orchiectomy alone is satisfactory treatment in such cases. I would follow orchiectomy with the usual diagnostic clinical checks, such as whole lung tomography and CT scan, to at least monitor the retroperitoneal space. Should there be question of metastasis in such a case, pathologic staging with removal of these suspicious enlarged nodes would be appropriate. This, however, should be a very rare instance, and again, I should underscore the success of conservative management of spermatocytic seminoma.

NONSEMINOMATOUS TUMORS

Nonseminomatous tumors are coming under control dramatically. In years past, just several decades ago, the survivalship of embryonal carcinoma was in the 30% range. Now with thorough retroperitoneal lymphadenectomy for staging I versus II disease and combination chemotherapy for disseminated III disease, nonseminomatous testis tumors have become the most effectively treated adult human solid malignancy. Several groups are reporting virtually 100% survival in the stage A case. The Minnesota group reported over 30 consecutive stage A cases without death several years ago.[5] The California group in recent years has compiled a 100% survivorship in stage A patients as well.[6] The only mild difference of opinion among several groups is whether to use some form of adjuvant or ''prophylactic'' chemotherapy in these cases without demonstrated pathologic condition and the lymph nodes removed from the retroperitoneal space. The Indiana and Minnesota groups have declined to use any chemotherapy in that group, fully aware that somewhere between 5% and 10% of these patients would subsequently appear to have relapsed as stage C patients. It is their view that combination chemotherapy can then be instituted in that small minority of patients relapsing to Stage C after lymphadenectomy. Fortunately, in each instance, in my experience, the patient has been salvaged; therefore, at the time of this writing, I have over 75 patients who were stage A, none of whom were treated with any form of chemoprophylaxis or radiotherapy following nodal surgical staging, and all have survived. Five patients in this group (from 1965) developed evidence of metastatic disease, and all enjoy a lasting complete remission without drugs. This means that 70 patients were spared the rigors of chemoprophylaxis that was, in retrospect, unnecessary in their case. ''One cannot do better than 100%'' in survival.

Hence, I feel comfortable in recommending no adjuvant or chemoprophylaxis in this stage A group, provided the patients are instructed in the importance of close follow-up study. By this, I mean monthly chest x-ray films in the first postoperative year as well as markers (beta-HCG, alpha-fetoprotein) every other month at least. Then, in the second postoperative year, I suggest a chest x-ray film every 2 mo and markers quarterly. My group's latest relapse following stage A lymphadenectomy was at 22 mo, and therefore I feel it important to follow these patients closely for the first 2 yr. In the third year I suggest a chest x-ray film every 3 mo, in the fourth year every 6 mo, and in the fifth year and beyond a yearly check-up. In over 10,000 collected cases, Mostofi has shown the rarity of late metastatic disease.[1] Far more likely would be a contralateral primary testis tumor, which occurs 1:100 times in patients with a prior germ cell tumor of the testis. Hence, this shows the importance also of stressing self-examination of the remaining contralateral gonad of any patient who has been treated for testis cancer.

This brings me to the management of stage B cases, those patients proved to have nodal metastasis from nonseminomatous germ cell tumors. I agree again with Dr. Brosman that most prefer to treat these patients with some form of adjuvant chemotherapy. Yet it is of great importance to note that randomized prospective protocols currently underway and already pilot studied by the Indiana group demonstrate that this form of management confers no survival advantage whatever. Indeed, in the Indiana experience, those who did not receive adjuvant chemotherapy did somewhat better! Clearly

this is at variance with the traditional teaching in the management of metastatic cancer. Nonetheless, these are the facts. Of 55 stage B patients followed here now with a minimum of 2 yr without treatment, I can say the following. Thirty-one patients received adjuvant actinomycin D for 1 yr in the usual dosage. Fourteen of these patients relapsed as stage C. Fortunately, all achieved a complete remission with platinum, Velban, and bleomycin, but one of these subsequently relapsed and died of metastatic testicular cancer. (This patient received three courses of the treatment regimen. It is my current experience that if these early stage C relapses receive four courses, further relapses are not seen.) Twenty-four patients who were stage B had no adjuvant chemotherapy whatever but were followed closely with monthly chest x-ray studies and serum markers. Interestingly, only 4 of these 24 patients relapsed as stage C cases. All were salvaged with platinum, Velban, and bleomycin chemotherapy and enjoy a lasting complete remission. Seven patients with grossly positive nodes received postoperative adjuvant chemotherapy with platinum, Velban, and bleomycin. They were given only two courses. None of the seven patients relapsed, and all are living and well.

This last small group was done as a pilot study for a proposed intergroup (SE Ca G) national adjuvant chemotherapy study for stage B nonseminomatous testicular cancer. Currently, the Southeastern cancer study group is following this protocol. Half the patients will receive no adjuvant chemotherapy following node dissection, and the other half will receive two courses of platinum, Velban, and bleomycin. On the basis of my own experience here, I would expect much the same survival in both groups provided the follow-up study is adequate and crossover to treatment is prompt in those who are randomized to the no-treatment arm in the event of relapse to stage C. There are now crude 3-yr survival rates for 112 consecutive patients who presented as stage I or A or stage II or B at Indiana University. One hundred and ten of these are presently alive and disease free. Furthermore, only one of these patients died of cancer. This data reemphasized my belief that cure for properly managed stage I and II disease should approach 100%. My primary philosophy in achieving this goal is as follows: (1) monthly follow-up study for 1 yr after retroperitoneal lymphadenectomy (whether stage I or stage II) with marker studies and chest x-ray films and the same studies every 2 mo during the second year of observation; surgical relapses beyond this point are uncommon, and the same studies should be done only every 4 to 6 mo thereafter, (2) avoid preoperative or postoperative radiotherapy in the nonseminomatous testicular tumors, since this will compromise chemotherapy and increase drug morbidity and mortality and those patients who relapse subsequently require full course chemotherapy, and (3) use effective chemotherapy if and when recurrent disease becomes manifest.

The role of radiotherapy is indeed contrasting sharply in the United States in the treatment of nonseminomatous testicular cancer. Yet in the United Kingdom, it is still used, and improved survivorship in this group can be anticipated, not so much from any fundamental change in the delivery of radiotherapy, but from the improved salvage of patients relapsing to stage C because of more effective chemotherapy. One might anticipate additional difficulty in administering chemotherapy in this group, particularly with myelosuppressive drugs such as vinblastine; hence, my preference for surgery and chemotherapy as the primary combination of treatment. Nonetheless, I must agree that radiotherapy has shown proven efficacy in treatment of nonseminomatous testicular cancer. If a group elects to abandon retroperitoneal lymphadenectomy entirely, an alternative method currently being used in the United Kingdom would be to radiate the retroperitoneal space in lieu of pathologic staging by lymphadenectomy. The Royal Marsden experience suggests that metastatic nodal disease less than 2 cm in diameter can be controlled with radiotherapy.[7] The European group is currently randomizing patients with nonseminomatous testicular tumor following orchiectomy to no treatment or radiotherapy in the United Kingdom and or retroperitoneal lymphadenectomy in other cooperating countries. It will be of interest to see how this group fares. My own bias is that there is no substitute for pathologic staging; furthermore, scientific analysis of survival data virtually requires this. Therefore, my view is that staging lymphadenectomy is appropriate, and, if done with experienced groups, the morbidity is very low indeed.

significant advance in the management of testicular cancer in the past decade has been improved chemotherapy. The dramatic improvement in stage C and disseminated bulky disease treated with combination chemotherapy, particularly platinum, Velban, and bleomycin, is remarkable. Dr. Brosman cites the literature in this area. A remarkable development also has been the great success of the four course regimen of platinum, Velban, and bleomycin in treating relapsing patients with stage B disease. Since initiating this there has not been a treatment failure in any patient with stage B relapse in the lungs, all of whom presented with relatively early disease because of their close follow-up study. In no case were the metastasis greater than 2 cm in diameter. Dr. Einhorn has treated 64 such relapsing B patients both from this institution and referred from elsewhere, and 63 achieved lasting complete remission.* The one who relapsed did not receive the four courses of platinum, Velban, and bleomycin, but three only. Therefore, those patients with nodular metastasis who are discovered early and have not achieved large bulky size have a good prognosis if the four courses of platinum, Velban, and bleomycin are initiated promptly.

Dr. Brosman points out an important concept in the management of bulky and massive metastatic disease. His statement that chemotherapy is the best initial mode of therapy is supported by my own experience in over 40 such patients as well as by the California experience and that of others. We have reported an 85% survival in this group of advance bulky massively metastatic cases.[8] How can this be achieved? By aggressive, initial combination chemotherapy, which usually will then clear the pulmonary structures and, in the cases of massive abdominal disease, reduce the tumor burden to a more operable size. Often the tumor may have cystic degeneration or a fibrous pseudocapsule. In any case, the resection of persistent abdominal metastases is greatly facilitated by prior combination chemotherapy.

* Einhorn L, Williams S: Personal communication.

Our patients fell into 3 groups. One third of them had fibrocystic disease only, one third had elements of teratoma remaining as well as fibrocystic change, and one third had persistent malignant elements remaining. The first two groups, fibrocystic or teratoma, did very well, and all survived without chemotherapy. The persistent cancer group did less well, and only half that group survived. But of my first 27 cases reported, 23 patients continue to enjoy a continuous complete remission without medication with over 2 yr of follow-up study for each patient. Those who would attack the bulky mass of disease with initial surgery are doomed to less favorable results. Merrin reported aggressive primary surgical debulking and had only a 43% survival in this group.[9] It is my impression that the agreement on this point is now completely shared by all. Bulky and disseminated metastatic disease should be treated at the outset with combination chemotherapy. (We suggest four courses of platinum, Velban, and bleomycin.) Then, surgical intervention would be warranted in those who show any evidence of persistent disease such as localized retroperitoneal mass or remaining pulmonary nodule. For tissue diagnosis this is essential. This will direct further therapy. Those patients with fibrocystic disease only can be followed without continued chemotherapy. Some may prefer to continue treatment in those with teratoma, although I have followed these people expectantly also. All would agree that those with persistent cancer require continued chemotherapy for an indefinite period. We would use additional courses of platinum, Velban, and bleomycin with the addition of VP 16 and adriamycin in those showing intolerance for cumulative doses of bleomycin or Velban.

I quite agree that physicians are entering an era where they must consider safe, effective alternatives to extended retroperitoneal lymphadenectomy. This is especially true for the stage A patient. The question is, Who is Stage A? Skinner and many others would suggest that it is precisely these people who need a thorough staging lymphadenectomy for pathologic staging.[6] In fact, he and Scardino reported that 38% of their patients with positive lymph nodes on dissection had negative preoperative markers. Clearly, there are no effective means of detecting intranodal disease at the present time. Markers, CT scans, and lymphangiograms become positive with more gross and extended disease.

Currently, my view is that retroperitoneal lymphadenectomy does provide valuable information regarding pathologic staging and, at times, reducing host tumor burden. Furthermore it tends to direct further therapy accordingly. Nonetheless, I am willing to concede that more limited resection of nodes in the primary zone of spread (*i.e.*, sentinel nodes in the primary drainage area of the internal spermatic vein) may be a suitable compromise and may also avoid the complications of ejaculatory impotence in those who receive a full retroperitoneal lymphadenectomy. We are considering this approach in staging as an alternative to the extended retroperitoneal lymphadenectomy in those patients who appear to be otherwise clinically stage A. Let me hasten to add that this limited resection does not apply to those who have evidence of gross or extensive disease, or to those who have a second-look operation following chemotherapy for extensive bulky disease that existed before chemotherapy. We have noted evidence of cancer in nodes far removed from the primary zone of spread in such patients and feel a thorough retroperitoneal dissection is required for both therapy and diagnosis in these instances.

Some would go so far as to eschew retroperitoneal lymphadenectomy altogether in clinical stage A disease (negative CT scan, whole lung tomography, lymphangiogram, serum markers). If they chose to do so, they must acknowledge a certain staging error rate by these clinical methods of 20% to 38%. Their hope now is that if the patients are followed closely on a monthly basis with chest x-ray films and serum markers, and perhaps with CT scans every several months, they might detect those with positive disease and convert them to the combination chemotherapy treatment group. In other words, the European group study would randomize the clinical stage A patients (as opposed to the pathologic stage A ones defined by nodal examination) to some form of treatment. In the United Kingdom, radiotherapy would be given, and in some other countries retroperitoneal lymphadenectomy would be done rather than radiotherapy. Those receiving no treatment would be followed equally closely as those treated. Treatment with chemotherapy would begin in either arm of the study only in the event of clinical evidence of metastatic disease.

It will be interesting to see how this study develops. I, for one, would be very uncomfortable with this in the no-treatment group because of personal experience with significant error rate in CT scans and serum markers in the nonsecreting tumors. Occasionally, we have found impressive retroperitoneal disease in people who are classified Stage A. Local growth in these people could be quite extensive before pulmonary disease becomes manifest. The salvage rate of chemotherapy treatment alone in this group is not encouraging. In my first 50 stage C cases we found that only half of the patients with such massive bulky disease could be salvaged with chemotherapy alone. I therefore would be reluctant to participate in such a study at this time. My own experience with clinical stage I and II cases (110 of 112 living and well from 1973 to 1978) suggests that the burden of proof remains on those who would alter what is clearly a highly successful management plan. Yet the alternatives mentioned above do provide other approaches to the management of stage I and II disease, and randomized prospective trials currently underway promise to shed light on what will be the most effective treatment.

Dr. Ray does a splendid job in covering a relatively difficult topic. The review of the pertinent literature is as complete as possible. The discussions of the pathologic states and clinical presentation are excellent. Further, I agree that the principles of treatment are also reasonably expressed. I agree that local control (excision) of distal primary cancers of the urethra is as good as radical treatment. In other words, partial penectomy in a distal lesion is as good as total peotomy. Furthermore, partial penectomy is better than radiotherapy in my experience because it allows a more functional organ both in terms of voiding and even in terms of erection. This can be ablated by high-dose radiotherapy, and the recurrence rate is unacceptable. There seems to be only one report in the literature by Marshall, cited by Dr. Ray, that supports the radical approach to bulbous urethral lesion. Of the eight cases noted, really five of that group had radical surgery and four survived. This is the one report that would support an aggressive approach

to primary bulbous urethral lesions. Dr. Ray's own data do not support the radical approach, since five of six patients treated by radical excision died and the survivor has had two thoracotomies for metastatic pulmonary disease. In any case, primary deep bulbous urethral lesions are difficult, and it seems reasonable to give them every chance of cure. As surgeons, it would not be unreasonable to do total pelvic lymphadenectomy and total *en bloc* cystoprostatourethrectomies. There is no conservative therapy on the horizon that appears promising. No radiotherapy or chemotherapy data support this. Patients with invasive and high-stage cancer in this area tend to die not only of metastatic disease but of local recurrent disease below the umbilicus. The complications of these are so great that every effort should be made to do a thorough pelvic cleanout, in my opinion. This would at least provide local control in most patients, and one can hope for the best regarding distant metastases.

In this era, adjuvant chemotherapy, particularly with platinum as one of the agents, would give some rationale to further medical treatment as experienced in several of my bladder protocols. It has been effective in two thirds of our patients with measurable metastatic transitional cell carcinoma with a median duration of 6 mo. Therefore, might it not be useful in patients with micrometastatic disease, particularly if transitional cell in origin?

Squamous cell carcinoma, to my knowledge, is not effectively treated by chemotherapy when metastatic. Dr. Ray's comments about excision of the pubic rami are interesting and well described. However, such a bony excision is usually not necessary unless a large local lesion requires this for exposure. I have found the combined abdominal perineal approach usually quite adequate without the need to remove bone.

Dr. Ray makes an important observation in discussing carcinoma of the female urethra. Preoperative radiotherapy in these cases of involvement of the mid- or proximal urethra requiring radical surgery has reduced the incidence of local recurrence. It would therefore be a strong recommendation for all clinicians to consider before embarking on radical pelvic surgery in such cases.

The discussion of carcinoma of the scrotum is also thorough and well balanced. The principles of wide local excision in most instances of small diameter are clearly supported by clinical data. Another important point is the need for follow-up study in such cases. My view is that groin dissection in such cases is indicated only if adenopathy persists after excision of the primary tumor. I recommend following such patients on a monthly basis. The complications of full bilateral groin dissection, including iliac continuation, are so great that they do not seem warranted at the time of initial local excision. If adenopathy persists following cessation of inflammatory changes and firm local nodes can be palpated a month or two postoperatively, then not only an inguinal dissection can be done but also an iliac continuation through two counterincisions as described by Fraley, which will spare the skin in the area of Poupart's ligament.[10]

The concept of a limited inguinal dissection of sentinel nodes is interesting and praiseworthy, particulary in the older patient. In many patients there seems to be a single suspicious node. I agree that local excision in such cases is reasonable.

Should the node be positive for cancer, my own view would be to extend the dissection, but I agree that bilateral dissection is not indicated in the case of a single unilateral suspicious nodal enlargement. The data cited are ample testimony that crossover is not frequent enough to warrant simultaneous bilateral inguinal dissection in such patients.

Dr. Ray is to be congratulated on a very thorough and carefully considered discussion of this relatively uncommon form of urologic cancer.

REFERENCES

1. Mostofi FV, Price EB: Tumors of the Male Genital System. Washington, DC, Armed Forces Institute of Pathology, 2nd Series, no. 8, 1973

2. Merrin C: Testis tumors: Seminoma. Urol Clin North Am 4(3): 379, 1977

3. Skinner DA: Surgical management of advanced testis tumors. Urol Clin North Am 465, 1977

4. Schoborg TW, Whittaker J, Lewis CW: Metastatic spermatocytic seminoma. J Urol (in press)

5. Fraley E, Kedia K, Markland C: The role of radical operation in management of NSGTT. In Varco RL, Deloney JP (eds): Controversey in Surgery, pp 479–488. Philadelphia, WB Saunders, 1976

6. Skinner DG, et al: Why retroperitoneal lymphadenectomy as a guide to future therapy. J Urol (in press)

7. Peckham MJ: Treatment of testicular tumors. Lancet (in press)

8. Donohue JP et al: Cytoreductive surgery: Considerations of timing and extent. J Urol (in press)

9. Merrin C, Takita H, Beckley S et al: Treatment of recurrent and widespread testicular tumor by radical reductive surgery and multiple sequential chemotherapy. J Urol 117:291, 1977

10. Hoppman HJ, Fraley EE: Squamous teratoma of the penis. J Urol 120:393, 1978

PART FIFTY

SURGERY OF MALE INFERTILITY AND FERTILITY

123

VARICOCELECTOMY: 986 CASES IN A TWELVE-YEAR STUDY

Lawrence Dubin, M.D., and Richard D. Amelar, M.D.

From the Department of Urology, New York University Medical Center, New York,
New York

Urology / November 1977 / Volume X, Number 5

ABSTRACT—Over a twelve-year period, surgical correction of varicocele was performed on 986 selected subfertile men. They were followed up for at least two years
after surgery. Semen quality was improved in 70 percent, and 53 percent of the wives
became pregnant. Statistically, the results were better in terms of semen quality
improvement and pregnancy for patients who had preoperative sperm counts over 10
million per milliliter (85 percent improved, 70 percent pregnancy rate) than for
patients who had preoperative sperm counts of less than 10 million per milliliter (35
percent improved, 27 percent pregnancy rate). The empirical use of postoperative
human chorionic gonadotropin therapy in this latter group improved results significantly (55 percent improved, 45 percent pregnancy rate).

Varicocele is a well-established cause of male infertility. Of 1,294 consecutive cases of male infertility seen from 1965 to 1970, we found 39 percent to be caused by varicocele.[1] Other authors have confirmed that the incidence is significant and deserves attention in the diagnosis and therapy of male fertility problems.[2–4]

Varicocele was noted as a cause of male infertility as early as the 1880s by Barfield,[5] a British surgeon. In 1929 Macomber and Sanders[6] reported restoration of fertility in men after bilateral varicocele surgery.[6] However, it was not until Tulloch's report in 1952[7] of restored spermatogenesis in an azoospermic man with varicocele that there was real notice of the problem. It is significant that, in general, therapeutic results in azoospermic men since that time have been poor.[3,8,9] Since Tulloch's work in the 1950s numerous reports of success after varicocele ligation have appeared in the literature.[7,10–16]

The seminal picture seen in subfertile men with varicocele was described in 1965 by MacLeod.[17] Oligospermia of varying degrees was noted, but of more importance were the signs of a marked impairment of sperm motility and a definite increase of immature and tapering sperm forms in the ejaculum. Indeed, although the sperm count frequently improves after ligation of the varicocele, the response is often limited to an improvement in sperm motility and a decrease in immature sperm forms.

Dubin and Hotchkiss in 1969[8] studied testicular

biopsies from subfertile men with varicocele and found germinal cell hypoplasia and a premature sloughing of immature sperm forms within the lumina of the seminiferous tubules. The testicular pathology was bilateral thus showing the effect to be bilateral in nature.

In 1970 we demonstrated that the size of the varicocele preoperatively had no effect on the results after ligation of the internal spermatic veins.[18] This corroborated the theory that varicocele is due to retrograde flow of blood down the internal spermatic vein from the renal vein to the scrotal circulation.[19–21] Comhaire and Vermeulen[22] have hypothesized that known testicular exposure to catecholamine-rich blood might explain the disturbance found in these patients. However, the theory that a change in heat counter current exchange in the scrotum is more prevalent at present.[13,23–25] Recently Kay and Alexander[26] reported increased scrotal temperature in rhesus monkeys with experimental creation of varicocele by partial occlusion of the left renal vein.

MATERIAL AND METHODS

We studied 986 men whom we had seen over a twelve-year period (March, 1963, to March, 1975). They had good follow-up for at least two years after varicocelectomy.

All patients were evaluated preoperatively and had normal thyroid, adrenocortical, and pituitary function test results. At least two semen specimens from each patient were checked prior to surgery; all had varying amounts of oligospermia, severely impaired mobility, and an increase in immature and tapering forms in the ejaculate. Azoospermic patients were eliminated from the study.

All patients had tried unsuccessfully to produce a pregnancy for at least one year prior to evaluation, and many had received previous therapy with medications elsewhere. The wives in all cases had been evaluated by their gynecologists.

Diagnosis of varicocele is not always a simple matter. The patient must be examined in the upright position since all but large varicoceles will be missed because of venous decompression with the patient in the recumbent position. Reflux of blood into the scrotum as detected by manual palpation should be determined with the patient performing Valsalva maneuver. This maneuver is extremely important for the diagnosis of small varicoceles.

The method of varicocelectomy used in all patients in this study was that of high ligation of the internal spermatic veins at the internal inguinal ring. This has been previously described by us in detail.[27]

RESULTS

Semen Quality. Nine hundred eighty-six cases were studied: 838 cases had unilateral varicocele and 148 (15 percent) bilateral varicoceles. Six patients had varicocelectomy on the right side; one had situs inversus, 3 had undergone previous left orchiectomy, and 2 had had previous left varicocelectomy. Semen quality improved in 690 (70 percent) while in 296 (30 percent) it did not; 523 pregnancies ensued with a resultant 53 percent pregnancy rate.

Of 416 men who had preoperative sperm counts of over 10 million per cubic centimeter, 354 (85 percent) has improved semen quality with 292 (70 percent) resultant pregnancies.

Of the 570 men who had preoperative sperm counts of less than 10 million per milliliter, 143 had no additional therapy; 50 (35 percent) of these had improved semen quality with 39 (27 percent) resultant pregnancies.

In our effort to improve on these results, 427 of the patients who had preoperative sperm counts below 10 million per milliliter were treated with varicocelectomy and postoperative human chorionic gonadotropin (80,000 units) for ten weeks: 235 men (55 percent) showed improved semen quality and 192 pregnancies (45 percent) resulted.

Of the 690 men who had semen quality improvement, all had improvement in sperm motility. There was improvement in count levels in 501 (73 percent) and improvement in sperm morphology in 435 (63 percent).

Pregnancies. The 523 pregnancies occurred at a mean of 4.4 month and a median of 5.3 month after varicocelectomy (Fig. 1). Five hundred twenty-three patients' wives delivered 637 babies; 322 were female and 315 male. There were 4 sets of twins, 31 miscarriages, and 5 ectopic pregnancies occurred.

Many of the patients fathered more than one child after varicocelectomy. Two patients have undergone subsequent bilateral vasectomy after each had fathered 3 children. Five men had improved semen quality and resultant pregnancy with an unexplained semen deterioration three years later.

It is noteworthy that pregnancy occurred after varicocelectomy in the wives of 7 patients who failed to demonstrate improved semen quality.

Postoperative Complications. The relatively few postoperative complications attest to the benign nature of the surgery (Table 1). Recurrence of the varicocele occurred in 1 patient. He and his wife had been trying for a pregnancy for four years. The patient's initial sperm count was over 10 million per milliliter, but semen

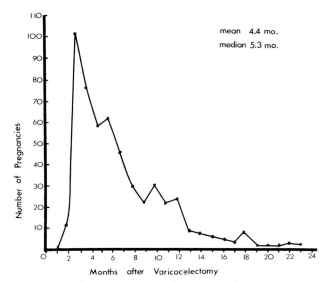

Fig. 1. Time between varicocelectomy and pregnancy.

TABLE 1. Postoperative Complications From Varicocelectomy in 986 Men

Complication	Number
Hydrocele not requiring surgery	25
Hydrocele requiring hydrocelectomy	5
Wound infection	7
Inguinal hematoma	10
Epididymitis	2
Atelectasis	2
Varicocele recurrence	1
Bladder hernia injury	1

quality was poor. A left varicocelectomy was performed on February 10, 1966; semen quality improved, and pregnancy occurred twelve months after surgery. A son was born on November 9, 1967. Difficulty in achieving a second pregnancy and poor semen quality were noted again three years after surgery. Examination revealed that the varicocele had recurred. Reflux of blood was again noted during scrotal palpation using the Valsalva maneuver. The patient was operated on again, and a large internal spermatic vein was ligated. Postoperatively a marked improvement in semen quality was noted, and pregnancy occurred three months after surgery. A daughter was born on August 10, 1970. A third pregnancy occurred and another son was born on January 6, 1972.

Thirty (3 percent) patients had hydrocele formation postoperatively. The exact etiology of this is unknown, but the low incidence is probably related to care in ligating the veins alone while trying to preserve all lymphatic channels. Three patients required operative hydrocelectomy.

We have also performed reoperations in 5 other patients who had previously had varicocelectomy by other physicians with recurrence: 3 of the 5 had improvement in semen quality and pregnancy. These cases are not included in this reported series.

COMMENT

The effectiveness of varicocelectomy in the therapy of male infertility has been demonstrated in this series. Surgery is indicated by poor sperm motility and immaturity. The presence of a varicocele with the absence of this combination of semen defects would not be sufficient indication for surgery.

Patients with initial sperm counts under 10 million per milliliter did not yield spectacular results. The empirical addition of gonadotropin therapy, however, almost doubled the pregnancy rates in a similar group of patients.

All the actual effects of varicocele on fertility are still unknown. Many men with varicocele have normal semen qualities and adequate fertility. The study of varicocelectomy failures does not reveal any preoperative differences between this group and the group which showed improvement. Nevertheless, the good results in semen improvement and pregnancy rate continue to make this form of therapy one of the most effective in the treatment of male infertility.

137 East 36th Street
New York, New York 10016
(DR. DUBIN)

REFERENCES

1. Dubin L, and Amelar RD: Etiologic factors in 1294 consecutive cases of male infertility. Fertil Steril 22:469, 1971
2. Russell JK: Varicocele in groups of fertile and subfertile men. Br Med J 1:1231, 1954
3. Stewart B: Varicocele in infertility: incidence and results of surgical therapy. J Urol 112:222, 1974
4. Lome LG, and Ross L: Varicocelectomy and infertility. Urology 9:416, 1977
5. Zorgniotti AW: The spermatozoa count: a short history. Ibid 5:672, 1975
6. Macomber D, and Sanders MB: The spermatozoa count. N Engl J Med 200:981, 1929
7. Tulloch WS: Varicocele in subfertility, results of treatment. Br Med J 2:356, 1955
8. Dubin L, and Hotchkiss RS: Testis biopsy in subfertile men with varicocele. Fertil Steril 20:50, 1969

9. Mehan DJ: Results of ligation of internal spermatic vein in the treatment of infertility in azoospermic patients. Ibid 27:110, 1976
10. Charny CW: Effect of varicocele on fertility. Ibid 13:47, 1962
11. Brown JS: Varicocelectomy in the subfertile male: a 10 year experience with 295 cases. Ibid 27:1046, 1976
12. Scott LS, and Young D: Varicocele, Ibid 13:325, 1962
13. Hanley HG, and Harrison RG: Nature and surgical correction of varicocele. Br J Surg 50:64, 1962
14. Dubin L, and Amelar RD: Varicocelectomy as therapy in male infertility: a study of 504 cases. Fertil Steril 26:217, 1975
15. Idem: Varicocelectomy as therapy in male infertility. J Urol 113:640, 1975
16. Stewart B: Varicocele in infertility: incidence and results of surgical therapy. Ibid 112:222, 1974
17. MacLeod J: Seminal cytology in the presence of varicocele. Fertil Steril 16:735, 1965
18. Dubin L, and Amelar RD: Varicocele size and results of varicocelectomy in selected subfertile men with varicocele. Ibid 21:606, 1970
19. Brown JS, Dubin L, Becker M, and Hotchkiss RS: Venography in the subfertile man with varicocele. J Urol 98:388, 1967
20. Brown JS, Dubin L, and Hotchkiss RS: Varicocele as related to fertility. Fertil Steril 18:46, 1967
21. El-Sadr AR, and Mina E: Anatomical and surgical aspects in operative management of varicocele. Urol Cutan Rev 54:257, 1950
22. Comhaire F, and Vermeulen A: Varicocele sterility: cortisol and catecholamines. Fertil Steril 25:88, 1974
23. Swerdloff RS, and Walsh P: Pituitary gonadal hormones in patients with varicocele. Ibid 26:1006, 1975
24. Zorgniotti AW, and MacLeod J: Studies in temperature, human semen quality and varicocele. Ibid 24:854, 1973
25. Comhaire F, Monteyner R, and Kunnen M: The value of scrotal thermography as compared with selective retrograde venography of the internal spermatic vein for the diagnosis of subclinical varicocele. Ibid 27:694, 1976
26. Kay RM, and Alexander NJ: Experimental creation of varicocele in rhesus monkeys. Presented IX World Congress on Fertility and Sterility, April 14, 1977, Miami Beach, Florida
27. Amelar RD, Dubin L, and Walsh PC: Male Infertility, Philadelphia, W. B. Saunders Co., 1977, p. 66

Commentary: Varicocelectomy

Stanley H. Greenberg

Although recognized as a clinical problem since at least the 16th century, varicosities of the scrotal veins are seldom severely painful or seriously deforming and consequently received little attention in the medical literature until a few decades ago. Before the development of satisfactory surgical techniques for the correction of varicoceles, patients with symptomatic varicoceles were generally treated by the application of suspensory garments. Early surgical approaches were exclusively through the scrotum, but because of poor results approaches for high ligation of the gonadal vein have been developed. These techniques are described and illustrated in detail below.

It was not until about 25 yr ago that physicians established a clear association between varicocele and subfertility. In 1952 Tulloch reported the appearance of sperm in the ejaculate of a previously azoospermic man after varicocele ligation. The preceding article by Drs. Dubin and Amelar documents their rather remarkable experience with varicocele ligation as a treatment in selected cases of male infertility.

Eighty percent to 98% of men with varicoceles have a unilateral left-sided lesion. The reported incidence of bilateral varicocele is 0% to 20%, but it is possible that many dilated right scrotal veins result from the presence of a primary left varicocele. Unilateral right varicoceles consistently comprise a small percentage (0% to 2%) of reported cases, and the presence of such a lesion should alert the examiner to the possibility of situs inversus, renal tumor, or retroperitoneal disease.

Recent venographic and anatomic studies clearly indicate that the left gonadal, or internal spermatic, vein is the vessel responsible for most instances of varicocele formation. Figure 2 shows the normal anatomy of the left renal vein and its major tributaries. The adrenal vein commonly joins the renal vein medial to the site of entrance of the gonadal vein. Typically, a gonadal vein valve is present at the right-angled junction of the renal and internal spermatic veins. When the gonadal vein valves are congenitally imperfect or become incompetent, varicosities of the vein occur in a process analogous to the development of varicose veins in the leg. Furthermore, because of the vertical course of the left gonadal vein and its compression between the aorta and the superior mesenteric artery, a prominent varicocele is likely to occur on the left side. The right gonadal vein, which drains obliquely into the vena cava, is less susceptible to the development of clinically obvious varicosities.

The testis has channels of venous drainage other than the internal spermatic vein. The vasal veins accompany the vas deferens and empty into the superior vesical vein. The cremasteric veins leave the spermatic cord at the external inguinal ring, communicate with the superficial and deep pudendal veins, and terminate in the deep epigastric vein. Extensive anastomoses between all the ipsilateral venous groups, as well as between the venous systems of the two testes, have been demonstrated in cadavers and in patients by dissection and radiographic techniques. This free venous communication explains how the effect of a unilateral left varicocele can be

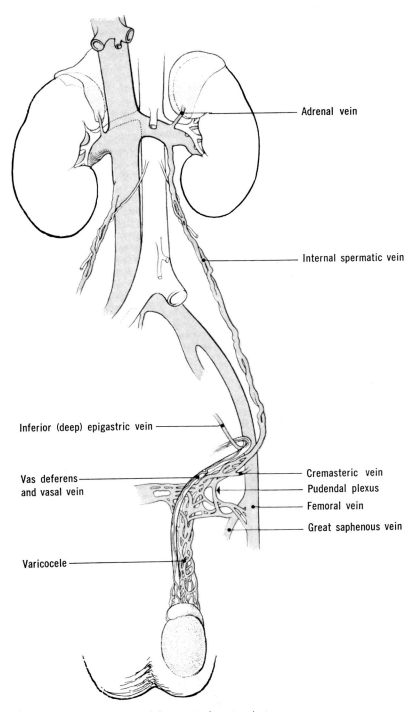

Fig. 2. Venous anatomy of the testicular circulation.

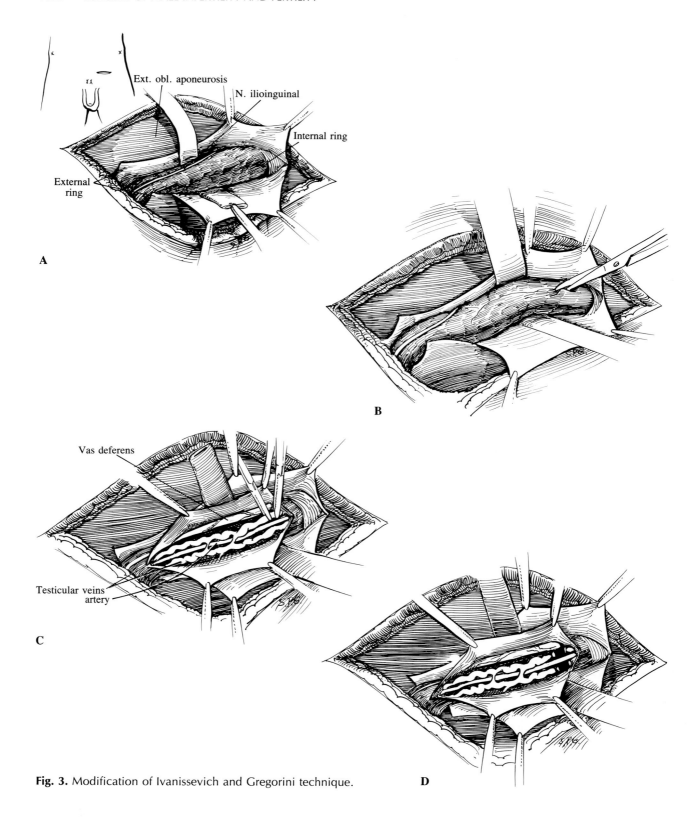

Fig. 3. Modification of Ivanissevich and Gregorini technique.

transmitted to the right side. It also allows for ligation of the gonadal vein with impunity. Although the primary communications between the veins of the two testes exist at the level of the pampiniform plexus, there is evidence that in some instances anastomoses also exist above the level of the internal inguinal ring. These anatomic considerations have implications for the techniques and the expected outcome of varicocele surgery.

Since approximately 15% of the general male population is thought to have some degree of varicocele, it is not surprising that even some varicocele patients with infertile marriages have normal semen quality. In these cases the varicocele is most likely coincidental, and surgery is probably not justifiable. However, when the semen quality is abnormal, especially when there is typical depression of the sperm count, motility, and morphology (*i.e.,* a "stress effect" or "varicocele effect"), then the prognosis for improvement in the seminogram and eventual pregnancy is good following varicocelectomy.

Varicoceles are generally classified according to size as follows: large, a scrotal mass that is visible as well as palpable; moderate, discrete, dilated, tortuous veins enlarging visibly with the Valsalva maneuver; small, usually a single convoluted supratesticular vein that enlarges with the Valsalva maneuver; and "impulse," grossly normal veins in the spermatic cord but a definitely palpable impulse produced by the Valsalva maneuver. At present it is controversial whether varicocele size governs the degree of "varicocele effect" or the prognosis for improvement if varicocele ligation is undertaken. For the proper diagnosis of the presence of a varicocele, it is important to examine the patient while he is standing, since a varicocele will decompress in the supine position. Failure to decompress is an indication of venous obstruction, and if the varicocele is of acute onset this finding should prompt a search for a renal or retroperitoneal tumor.

The most commonly used surgical approach to high ligation of the internal spermatic vein is probably a modification of the technique described by Ivanissevitch and Gregorini (Fig. 3). A herniorrhaphy incision is made, and the external oblique aponeurosis is incised so that the spermatic cord can be isolated. The veins are meticulously dissected at the level of the internal inguinal ring, where they may number between one and five,

and are individually ligated and divided. Placing the patient in a few degrees of the reverse Trendelenburg position often facilitates identification of the varicosities. The Palomo procedure (Fig. 4) requires dissection of the gonadal vein or veins above the level of the internal inguinal ring. An incision is made over the internal inguinal ring. The external oblique fascia is incised along the course of its fibers and elevated as it is incised to minimize injury to the underlying ilioinguinal nerve. The internal inguinal ring is identified with the index finger as a well-demarcated weakness in the internal oblique muscle. This is an important landmark. The internal oblique muscle is split in the course of the fibers just superior and lateral to the internal inguinal ring, and the transversalis fascia is incised. The peritoneum and contents are retracted superiorly and medially, and a retractor is also placed inferiorly. The internal spermatic vessels can now be identified easily. The vas and vasal vessels can often be identified, passing posteriorly as they exit from the internal inguinal ring. The peritoneum is usually adherent to the internal spermatic vessels, and it should be separated from these vessels by blunt dissection so that the internal spermatic venous system can be mobilized from the depth of the wound and elevated to the level of the skin. The internal spermatic vein or veins should be isolated from each other and from the internal spermatic artery, lymphatics, and nerves. An effort should be made to preserve the artery, lymphatics, and nerves. Segments of the skeletonized internal spermatic vein or veins are removed and their cut ends ligated. The wound is closed in the usual fashion.

The failure rate for varicocele ligation, defined in terms of recurrent or residually dilated scrotal veins, may be as high as 11%. Although some such "failures" may represent filling of the left scrotal veins from a normal right venous circulation, most result from the presence of small collateral branches of the left gonadal vein inadvertently left unligated. In some cases of recurrent or residual varicocele and unimproved semen quality following varicocelectomy, venography may be necessary to determine the proper approach for reoperation. At present it must be assumed that a man who has a good anatomic result but no improvement in semen quality after varicocele ligation either has suffered irreversible damage from the varicocele or has another cause for his subfertility.

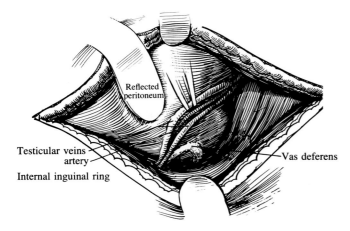

Fig. 4. The Palomo procedure.

BIBLIOGRAPHY

Greenberg SH: Varicocele and male fertility. Fertil Steril 28:699, 1977

This is an indepth review of the subject of varicocele and its relationship to male subfertility. The historical development of the discovery of varicocele as a factor causing depressed semen quality is traced. The contributions of the early British investigators, including Tulloch, Russell, and others, are discussed, and the findings of early American advocates of varicocelectomy for the improvement of fertility, including Charny, Hotchkiss, Brown, and Dubin and Amelar, are presented. The classic studies of John MacLeod demonstrating the ''stress effect'' in the seminograms of varicocele patients are reviewed.

Several theories of the etiology of the varicocele effect are discussed. Although the theory that efflux of hormones or toxins from the renal vein affects spermatogenesis is attractive, the relevant data are contradictory and none of the postulated mechanisms has been clearly demonstrated. An increase in scrotal temperature in varicocele patients has been documented, however, and this is the only proven effect of varicocele that is likely to cause a reduction in spermatogenesis. Data are also presented that point to a significant decrease in testicular size in men with asymptomatic and symptomatic varicoceles.

The results of numerous investigations of the outcome of varicocele surgery are presented. Generally, a 60% to 70% rate of improvement in semen quality is found in well-selected subfertile men who have undergone varicocele ligation. Pregnancy rates are variable, however. It is difficult to determine the true pregnancy rate following treatment of the male factor, since the contribution of the female factor to the infertility problem is often not apparent from the reports.

The extensive bibliography included with this review article should be helpful to the reader who has an academic interest in the subject of varicocele and the physiology of male reproduction.

Ivanissevitch O, and Gregorini H: A new operation for the cure of varicocele. Semona Med 25:575, 1918

This article describes the original ''Ivanissevitch procedure'' for high ligation of the gonadal veins. Drs. Ivanissevitch and Gregorini performed a very low retroperitoneal ligation of the gonadal veins immediately at the level of the internal inguinal ring. The herniorrhaphy type approach commonly used by present-day urologic surgeons is a modification of the Ivanissevitch technique.

Palomo A: Radical cure of varicocele by a new technique: Preliminary report. J Urol 61:604, 1949

This is the original publication of Dr. Palomo's technique of varicocele ligation. Thirty-eight patients, mostly military men complaining of pain from a varicocele during physical activity, underwent this procedure. The technique for exposure of the gonadal vessels is precisely that described in this chapter. Dr. Palomo advocated ligation of both the veins and the testicular artery, rightly pointing out in a discussion of testicular anatomy and vasculature that the vasal vessels, as well as the cremasterics, are often sufficient for testicular survival. However, in the treatment of subfertile varicocele patients it would seem extremely inadvisable to sacrifice the gonadal artery. In almost all cases it is possible to dissect the veins free from the artery and ligate them without disturbing the artery.

Tulloch WS: Consideration of fertility factors in light of subsequent pregnancies: Subfertility in the male. Trans Edinburgh Obstet Soc 59:29, 1952

This is Dr. Tulloch's ''classic'' article documenting an improvement in the fertility potential of varicocele patients following surgery. Actually, the subject of this report was an azoospermic man with chronic infertility who underwent a left varicocele ligation. Several months after the operation active sperm appeared in the semen, and eventually a pregnancy was documented. Although other factors are probably involved in most cases of azoospermia even when a varicocele is present, this report does provide evidence that the well-selected patient who seems to have a typical varicocele on scrotal examination and typical changes in testicular size and consistency can expect to benefit from varicocele surgery, no matter how poor the preoperative semen quality.

Overview: Varicocelectomy

Jordan S. Brown

Varicocelectomy performed in the select subfertile male is a widely accepted therapeutic measure. This procedure is considered by many to be the most effective treatment modality in the field of male infertility. Varicocelectomy is rarely, if ever, indicated for circumstances other than impaired fertility.

The operative correction of a varicocele may be performed in different ways. The most suitable method can be best determined by a fuller understanding of the anatomy and the pathophysiology of a varicocele. The left internal spermatic vein terminates in the left renal vein, and although the right internal spermatic vein generally ends in the inferior vena cava, 10% of the time this vein empties into the right renal vein in an anomalous fashion. Normally there is a large valve at the junction of the internal spermatic vein and the renal vein, and there are additional valves that vary in number and location that occur along the course of the internal spermatic vein (Fig. 5). These valves prevent the retrograde passage of renal venous blood (Fig. 6). When these valves are absent or become incompetent, renal vein blood passes in an abnormal manner down into the circulation of the testes (Fig. 7). The testicular

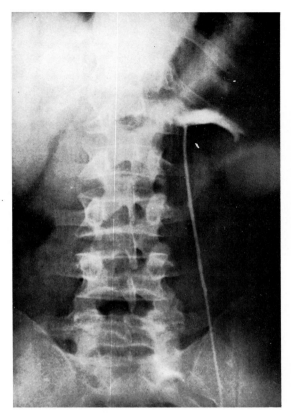

Fig. 5. Left internal spermatic venography in a subfertile man without a varicocele, demonstrating multiple venous valves.

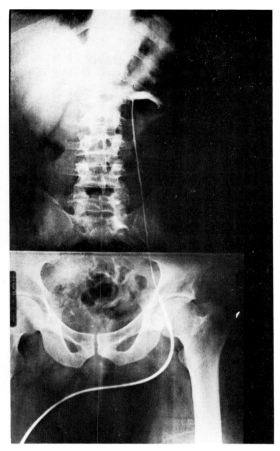

Fig. 6. Left internal spermatic venography in a subfertile man without a varicocele. Radiopaque medium is introduced in the direction of the kidney. Retrograde flow of blood is not demonstrated.

veins respond to the additional volume of blood by elongating, dilating, and becoming tortuous. These changes result in the formation of a varicocele. An operation designed to treat this condition successfully should prevent the renal vein blood from passing down the internal spermatic venous system into the scrotal veins. A complete ligation of the internal spermatic venous system would achieve this goal. This can be accomplished at different levels.

When varicocelectomy was initially introduced as an often successful therapeutic measure, there was a reluctance on the part of many to accept the surgery because they found it difficult to understand how a seemingly unilateral circulatory disturbance could have an adverse effect on both testes. Internal spermatic venography (Figs. 8 and 9) and anatomic studies have supported the potential bilaterality of the one-sided varicocele. In addition, biopsies in patients with unilateral varicoceles have demonstrated pathologic changes of equal magnitude bilaterally.

As indicated in the Commentary, the precise means by which varicoceles impair the spermatogenic process remains uncertain. The concensus currently supports the earlier speculation that varicocele alters the important thermoregulatory mechanism and by so doing raises the testicular temperature.

However, it is still not known whether the magnitude of the documented increase in temperature is in itself sufficient to alter spermatogenesis adversely. Abnormally high concentration of chemical and endocrine substances such as catecholamines and serotonin have also been demonstrated to be present in the venous circulation of the testes in patients with varicoceles. The mechanisms by which these substances can impede spermatogenesis have been postulated but conclusive evidence in this regard is still lacking. Although it is still important to determine the precise means by which varicocele is detrimental, and such knowledge would further promote the acceptance of the procedure, the gratifying experiences shared and reported by so many surgeons to date in itself recommends the operation.

Varicoceles occur more commonly in the subfertile population than in the fertile counterpart. However, many if not most men with varicoceles retain their reproductive ability, at least during that period in life when fatherhood is usually sought. Numerous examples of infertile men with varicoceles who have fathered children earlier in life during a prior marriage

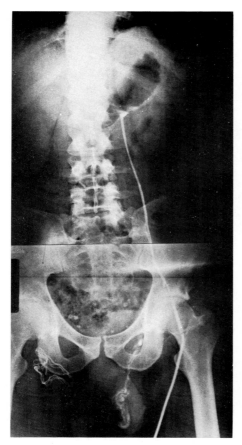

Fig. 7. Left internal spermatic venography in a subfertile man with a left varicocele. Radiopaque medium is introduced in the direction of the kidney. Retrograde flow of blood and the varicocele are demonstrated.

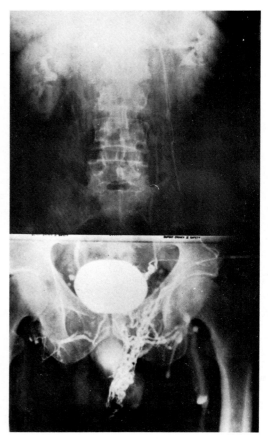

Fig. 8. Left internal spermatic venography in a subfertile man with a left varicocele. Cross-collateral channels and the varicocele are demonstrated.

are also encountered. Varicocelectomies performed in this group of men have similarly often restored their fertility potential. Experiences attained with these men would support the premise held by many that the detrimental effect of a varicocele is likely to be, at least in part, cumulative and time related.

As indicated earlier in the chapter, conflicting data exists on whether the size of the varicocele influences its deleterious effect or the prognosis following treatment. In my series, unlike that of others, those men with large and moderate-sized varicoceles fared significantly better following surgery than those with small varicoceles.

The clinical diagnosis of varicocele is not always a simple matter. Moderate and large-sized varicoceles are easily identified. There is not likely to be unanimity in regard to the presence of a small varicocele. Nonetheless, it is important in subfertile men to diagnose and treat small varicoceles. A carefully performed physical examination can be helpful in eliciting a small varicocele. Such an examination should be performed with the patient employing a Valsalva maneuver

while in the erect position. If during such an examination a varicocele appears to be questionable, a provocative or confirmatory test can be performed, which can prove to be helpful. This test is performed with the patient in the supine position. The scrotum is elevated, emptying the testicular veins. An attempt is then made to compress the testicular veins at their proximal extent, adjacent to the testis; while maintaining this compression the patient assumes an erect posture, and if the veins fill from above downward, a varicocelelike state is likely to exist. Venography is also helpful in clarifying matters of this nature, but it is an invasive study and its applicability in a clinical setting is more limited.

Ligation of the internal spermatic venous system is recommended for oligospermic males who have varicoceles and semen quality as defined by MacLeod that is consistent with the "varicocele effect." This operation is rarely successful when performed for azoospermia, even though one of the earliest reports of success was in such a man. Varicocelectomy is not recommended for the azoospermic male. It should be performed unilaterally for a single varicocele and bilaterally when two varicoceles are present. Although it is likely that in some men who have bilateral varicoceles the right varicocele

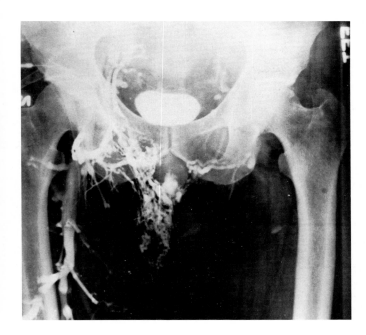

Fig. 9. Right internal spermatic venography in a subfertile man with a right varicocele. Cross-collateral channels and the varicocele are demonstrated. The left internal spermatic vein is also opacified.

is secondary to incompetency of the left internal spermatic veins, and as such, at least in theory, could be effectively managed with only a left internal spermatic ligation, bilateral operation is still recommended under these circumstances. Internal spermatic venography in the presence of bilateral varicoceles on more than one occasion has demonstrated that the right internal spermatic vein terminated in the right renal vein (Fig. 10), and in such a situation it is not likely that a left ligation would cure the right varicocele. Periodically, ligation of the internal spermatic veins in subfertile males who do not have varicoceles is advocated. Others, still, who are perhaps more scrutinizing, have endorsed the ligation in subfertile males without varicoceles who have the semen quality commonly seen in patients with varicoceles. The stress pattern of abnormal sperm quality that is commonly seen in the patient with a varicocele is not a specific pattern, since it is seen in many other conditions. There are no available data to support ligation in a man without a varicocele. On the other hand, based on personal experience, oligospermic males who have varicoceles but who do not have the semen quality suggestive of the "varicocele effect" should not necessarily be denied the ligation, provided all the other studies are normal and no other form of therapy is available. Candidates who fall into this category, although less optimal, have had semen improvement and produced progeny.

The best manner in which a teenager with a varicocele should be managed is often difficult to determine and at best speculative. Semen analyses in this group are difficult or impossible to obtain. Adolescents seeking medical advice usually have large varicoceles that are obvious to both the patient and his family. Varicoceles in this younger age group are also commonly associated with ipsilateral, smaller-appearing testis. Although it has not been proven, it is likely that these younger males are more apt to develop an impairment in their reproductive process. Parents of such children should be advised that although the need for a ligation is not established, it is nonetheless desirable. In general, youths with such varicoceles appear awkward and self-conscious regarding the matter and are most willing to have the condition corrected.

The principal objective of a successful varicocele operation is to ligate completely the internal spermatic venous system on the side or sides in question. The surgical approach can vary; it can be scrotal, inguinal, or at a level superior to the internal inguinal ring in the extraperitoneal space. The scrotal approach is justly and commonly condemned because any intraoperative arterial injury at this level will regularly result in testicular ischemia. The commonly employed inguinal approach is acceptable but it is thought to be less optimal than the low extraperitoneal approach. The occasionally encountered practice of performing the operation high in the retroperitoneal space in proximity of the renal hilum is not recommended and is thought to be unnecessary.

The ligation performed just superior to the internal inguinal ring in the extraperitoneal space is felt to be the preferable approach. This procedure technically remains easy and is associated with minimal morbidity. In this regard it compares favorably with the inguinal approach. There are fewer internal spermatic veins at this level, and it is more difficult to overlook a vein and perform an incomplete operation. It is also less likely that the single internal spermatic artery, lymphatics, and veins will be injured. On the other hand, if the gonadal artery is damaged at this more superior level, there is a good likelihood that an adequate, more distal collateral circulation will exist. Last, the anatomy of the inguinal canal is not violated, which may in time predispose the patient to a hernia.

The high ligation that is thought to be preferable is performed in the following fashion. A 5-cm to 6-cm incision is made parallel to and one fingerbreath medial to the inguinal

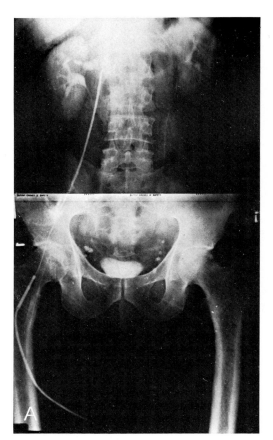

Fig. 10. Right internal spermatic venography in a subfertile man with bilateral varicoceles. Note that the right internal spermatic vein terminates in the renal vein.

ligament. The incision is made over the internal inguinal ring. In order to avoid injury to the ileoinguinal nerve, the external oblique fascia is grasped and elevated and then fully incised with the cutting surface of an open-bladed scissor. The internal inguinal ring is then identified as a well-demarcated weakness in the internal oblique musculature. The internal oblique muscle is then split with Kelly clamps just superior and lateral to the internal inguinal ring. The point at which this muscle is split is always in close proximity to the ileoinguinal nerve. The extraperitoneal space containing the internal spermatic venous system is then entered. The vas deferans can often be seen inferiorly in the depth of the wound coursing medially and posteriorly. The internal spermatic veins are then identified and superficially grasped with a Babcock clamp. The peritoneum, which is adherent, is identified and bluntly dissected off the veins with a moistened peanut dissector. Once the peritoneum is mobilized, the veins are more completely grasped. By mobilizing the peritoneum off the vessels, the internal spermatic artery, veins, associated nerves, and lymphatics can be drawn into the superficial aspect of the wound. All the internal spermatic veins, those appearing normal, and those dilated are isolated, clamped, segments, excised, and ligated. If all the veins are not ligated, the varicocele is not likely to be cured or in time may recur.

Unlike the technique described by Palomo, the internal spermatic artery, lymphatics, and nerves are preserved! The artery can usually be identified as a narrow, tortuous, pulsating vessel that courses along the wall of a vein. The wound is then closed in the usual fashion. Ligation of the internal spermatic venous system performed in this fashion is usually carried out under general anesthesia on inpatients, but it can also be done in select patients under local anesthesia as an outpatient procedure or with general anesthesia in an ambulatory care facility without the need for overnight hospitalization.

124

UROLOGIC MICROSURGERY—CURRENT PERSPECTIVES: I. VASOVASOSTOMY

Arnold M. Belker, M.D.

From the Department of Surgery, Section of Urology, University of Louisville School of Medicine, Health Sciences Center, Louisville, Kentucky

Urology / October 1979 / Volume XIV, Number 4

ABSTRACT—Microsurgical procedures are receiving increased attention in urology, and claims of improved results of vasovasostomy performed with operating microscope have been made. This review examines the available results, sometimes conflicting, of both macro- and microsurgical methods of vasovasostomy. The weight of the data leads to the conclusion that improved results of vasovasostomy will occur with use of the operating microscope regardless of the type of anastomosis performed bacause increased appreciation of the detail of the small vasal lumen is afforded by optical magnification.

Although microsurgery has been utilized by various specialists for many years, its use by urologists has increased only during the past few years. Because of reports of improved results in several urologic operative procedures,[1,2] a growing number of urologists have become interested in microsurgery.

In this report the various areas in which microsurgery may benefit the urologist are examined. As is true with many innovative techniques, enthusiasm and sometimes overutilization are replaced by a practical appreciation for the proper place of such new techniques. In certain urologic procedures, there are conflicting reports on whether or not microsurgery yields improved results. It therefore seems appropriate at this time to take a rational look at both sides of the controversies.

The time and effort expended in developing microsurgical skills must be evaluated not only in terms of benefits to patients, but also in its practical utility for the surgeon. If the reader concludes that microsurgery may benefit his performance of certain procedures, a word of caution is needed. Because considerable time is required to develop and maintain microsurgical skills, the urologist should consider both the benefits to be gained and the frequency with which he will use these skills clinically. If microsurgical skills are not maintained by constant practice or clinical performance, then surgical results will suffer. The surgeon should consider the wisdom of investing time to develop microsurgical skills if frequent and regular clinical use of these skills is not anticipated.

Although it is not within the scope of this review to discuss microsurgical instrumentation and technique, suggestions for further reading are provided for those interested.[3–10]

VASOVASOSTOMY

The number of divorced and remarried vasectomized men desiring vasectomy reversal is growing. Additionally, the report by Alexander and Clarkson[11] of increased diet-induced atherosclerosis in vasectomized monkeys compared with sham-vasectomized monkeys has received considerable attention. They theorized that the immunologic response to sperm antigens which often follows vasectomy may exacerbate atherosclerosis. If the results of this preliminary animal study should be substantiated in man, the demand for vasectomy reversal is likely to increase.

Controversy regarding the best method of vasectomy reversal has existed for many years. Excellent reviews regarding vasectomy reversal with comprehensive bibliographies are available for interested individuals.[12–18]

Historically, surgeons argued about the use or omission of stents for vasovasostomy as well as the proper type of stent. However, Fernandes, Shah, and Draper[18] demonstrated in dogs that obstruction often occurred at the site of exit of the stent through the wall of the vas deferens rather than at the anastomotic site (presumably due to sperm leakage with resulting spermatic granuloma). Schmidt[19] concurs with this adverse effect of externalized stents, even though he had experimented extensively with stented anastomoses.[20–23]

The use of absorbable intravasal stents was studied first in the canine model by Montie et al.,[24–25] who demonstrated no adverse effect of such stents. Although Urry, Thompson, and Cockett[26] found that such absorbable intravasal stents seemed to have adverse effects in dogs, preliminary clinical results encouraging the use of such stents have been reported by Rowland, Nanninga, and O'Connor.[27] Banowsky[28] believes that simplicity is an advantage of using minimal optical magnification (loupes), and he also employs absorbable intravasal stents to enhance mucosal alignment across the anastomosis. Certainly, the results of larger clinical studies in which absorbable intravasal stents are used will aid in resolving some current controversies concerning vasovasostomy.

Macrosurgical Results. The results of macrosurgical vasectomy reversal reported in the literature from 1948

to the present are summarized in Table 1. The results tabulated in the 1948 survey of O'Connor[29] and in the 1973 survey of Derrick, Yarbrough, and D'Agostino[30] are not as significant as those obtained by some surgeons reporting results of sizeable individual series. For many years, the best clinical results were those reported by the Phadkes,[31] who used externalized nylon stents. Rowland, et al.[27] have reported good results in a pilot series using absorbable intravasal stents. Schmidt[17–19] reported results comparable to, or better than, those of most other macrosurgical series, but he now uses a microsurgical adaptation of his previous macrosurgical method (full-thickness sutures at 120-degree intervals combined with muscular layer sutures). Amelar and Dubin[32,33] first used no optical magnification but then reported improved results with the use of 4× optical loupe magnification.

Middleton and Henderson[34–35] utilized macrosurgical placement of two full-thickness sutures (180 degrees apart) and very few interposed muscular layer sutures (6-0 or 7-0 Prolene used throughout), with encouraging results from this simplified anastomotic method.

Fallon, Jacobo, and Bunge[36] reported results obtained in a series of vasovasostomies performed by varied methods, while Glenn[37] reported excellent "sperm present" results and projected pregnancy results using externalized nylon stents and 2.5× ocular loupe magnification. Fitzpatrick[38] also reported excellent results in a small series using optical loupe magnification to anastomose fish-mouthed vasal ends.

Microsurgical Results. Silber[39] first attracted serious attention to the use of microsurgery for vasovasostomy (and other urologic procedures) in 1975. His[40–41] results have not been equaled as yet by other surgeons in this country (Table 2).

TABLE 1. Reported Results of Macrosurgical Vasovasostomy*

Author	No. of Cases	Sperm Present (%)	Pregnancies (%)
O'Connor (1948)[29]	420	35–40	Not stated
Phadke and Phadke (1967)[31]	76	83	55
Derrick, et al. (1973)[30]	1630	38	19
Schmidt (1978, 1975)[17,19]	45[17]	80–90[19]	42[17]
Rowland, et al. (1977)[27]	14	86	Too early
Amelar and Dubin			
(1963–1975)[32]	93	84	33
(1976–1977)[33]	26	88	53*
Middleton and Henderson			
(1978)[34]	72	95	39
Fallon, et al. (1978)[36]	41	83	40
Glenn (1978)[37]	100+	90+	50+*†
Fitzpatrick (1978)[38]	14	100	64

* Includes procedures performed with optical loupe magnification.
† Projected result.

TABLE 2. Reported Results of Microsurgical Vasovasostomy

Author	No. of Cases	Sperm Present (%)			Pregnancies (%)	
		<10 Yrs.	>10 Yrs.	All Patients	<10 Yrs.	All Patients
Owen (1977)[42]	50	—	—	98	—	72
Silber (1978)[40]	126	90*	35*	—	—	76
Sharlip (1979)[43]	17	91*	—	76*	64	47

* Over 20 million sperm/ml and over 50 percent motility.

In Australia, Owen[42] developed a similar two-layer microsurgical vasovasostomy technique concurrently with, but independently of, Silber and reported comparable results in patients undergoing unilateral vasovasostomy by this method. However, his series was biased because of the exclusion of at least a few patients having no sperm in the vas fluid at the time of planned vasovasostomy.

Sharlip[43] reported equal success with two different microsurgical methods. One method employed four equidistant, full-thickness 9-0 nylon sutures with interposed muscular layer 9-0 nylon sutures, while the other method was that used by Silber and by Owen. Although Sharlip's data were based on a small series of cases, they are supportive of the results of both Silber and Owen.

Importance of Leak-Proof Anastomosis. The ingenious experiments of Hagan and Coffey[44] demonstrated the adverse effect of sperm leakage on vasovasostomy results in rats. Irrigation of sperm out of the testicular end of the vas lowered the postanastomotic spermatic granuloma rate and increased the patency rate. If vasovasostomy was performed in the absence of sperm (by testosterone suppression of spermatogenesis in mature rats or by using immature rats in which spermatogenesis had not yet begun), patency rates were raised to 95 percent and spermatic granuloma rates were reduced to near 5 percent. Comparable results occurred if the vas was obstructed by division and ligature between the anastomosis and the testicle, thus preventing sperm from reaching the anastomosis. These experiments emphasize the need for a leak-proof anastomosis.

Quality of Sperm in Vas Fluid. *Interval Since Vasectomy.* The prognostic importance of sperm in the vas fluid at the time of vasovasostomy has been known for years. Silber[45] showed the absence of sperm in the vas fluid to become an increasingly adverse sign as the time between vasectomy and vasovasostomy increased. When the interval between vasectomy and its reversal was less than five years, he found only 2 patients with no sperm in the vas fluid at the time of vasovasostomy, and both

of these subsequently achieved normal sperm counts. When the interval was between five and ten years, 6 of 12 patients with no sperm in the vas fluid subsequently remained azoospermic. When the reversal was performed over ten years after vasectomy, 14 patients had no sperm in the vas fluid, and all remained azoospermic subsequently.

Gross Appearance of Vas Fluid. Silber[46] observed that if no sperm was present in the vas fluid at the time of vasovasostomy, patients with clear, translucent vas fluid seemed to have a much better prognosis than those in whom the vas fluid was thick, creamy yellow. The ultimate prognostic validity of this observation remains to be proved.

Sperm Antibodies and Sperm Granuloma. For years it was thought that the leak of sperm and resulting sperm granuloma which sometimes occurs after vasectomy were responsible for the formation of antisperm antibodies[47–48] which would impair fertility after reversal of vasectomy.[49]

The complex problem of sperm antibody formation after vasectomy, and the relationship of these sperm antibodies to fertility after vasectomy reversal have been omitted from this report. The interested reader is referred to the excellent article by Mumford,[50] who reviewed the entire development of immunity as it affects male fertility in a manner clearly understandable by the clinician who has little or no background in immunology. Extensive references are included in Mumford's review.

The occurrence of a sperm granuloma (whether located at the transected end of the vas or in the epididymis) after vasectomy has been considered an adverse prognostic sign regarding vasovasostomy results. However, Silber[51] demonstrated that a sperm granuloma at the transected end of the vas has a beneficial prognostic influence on the outcome of vasovasostomy. He observed that a sperm granuloma appears to have a pressure-releasing effect. He found that the lumen of the testicular end of the vas containing a sperm granuloma was minimally dilated when compared with the lumen of the testicular end of the vas not containing a sperm granuloma. Additionally, he found far better sperm quality in the vas fluid when a sperm granuloma was present than when it was absent.*

Vasoepididymostomy. As a result of vasal occlusion, in some individuals (and many animals) sufficient increased pressure develops to disrupt the epididymal tubule and cause resultant sperm granulomas in the epididymis. Sibler[46] recently showed such epididymal extravasation to be responsible for the absence of sperm in the vas fluid and to be the cause of poor results of vasectomy reversal in these patients. He presents a growing body of evidence to suggest that such patients may require vasoepididymostomy instead of vasovasostomy. The decision of which procedure to perform on a patient may be influenced by the elapsed time since vasectomy, or one could reserve vasoepididymostomy to be performed only if vasovasostomy fails in such patients.

The microsurgical method of vasoepididymostomy described in detail by Silber[52] is technically difficult compared to microsurgical vasovasostomy, but he has reported a high rate of success compared to other methods. This method involves anastomosis of the vasal mucosa to a single epididymal tubule rather than to the epididymal tunic and thus would appear to be more desirable than previously described macrosurgical methods.

COMMENT

My series of vasovasostomies is too small to be statistically meaningful. Yet, an intense interest in vasovasostomy and sufficient training and experience in microsurgical vasovasostomy lead me to believe that increased accuracy of approximation of the ends of the vas can be obtained with the optical magnification afforded by the operating microscope (5–25×), and that 2.5× optical loupe magnification does not afford sufficient resolution of the anatomy of the vas.[53,54]

The two-layer vas anastomosis is considerably more difficult than a one-layer anastomosis, and the former requires more microsurgical expertise. It will be interesting to see if the increased accuracy of anatomic approximation and the use of smaller sutures permitted

* These observations attesting to the pressure-venting effect of a sperm granuloma are currently being studied, and my preliminary data support Silber's finding.

by microsurgery will be sufficient to allow simpler (single layer and modified single layer) anastomoses to achieve results far better than identical anastomoses performed without magnification. Also, one awaits further reports of results of such simpler microsurgical anastomoses for comparison with the reported results of two-layer microsurgical vasovasostomy.[40–43,55–57]

Because no one surgeon in this country has accumulated cases of vasovasostomy at a rate comparable to that of Silber, a study group of surgeons using his method has been formed to pool data after a sufficient number of cases has been accumulated. Members of this group are: A. M. Belker (Louisville, Kentucky); A. J. Thomas, Jr., and J. E. Pontes (Detroit, Michigan); J. W. Konnak (Ann Arbor, Michigan); D. J. Albert (Buffalo, New York); and I. D. Sharlip (San Francisco, California). Results from this collaborative effort will not be available for at least two years.

Regardless of methods of anastomosis used, all surgeons are encouraged to report quality of sperm in the vas fluid at the time of reversal, the presence or absence of sperm granuloma, and to relate results to length of time since vasectomy was performed. Instead of "sperm present" rates, surgeons should use minimum cirtiera for normal semen analysis (sperm concentration of 20 million/ml and motility of 50 percent) so that more accurate assessment of results may be made. There can be no question that "success" can be measured better with the use of uniform criteria for normal semen analysis than by the use of either "sperm present" or pregnancy rates. This call for uniformity of criteria in reporting results of vasovasostomy has been made recently also by Wicklund and Alexander.[58]

The necessity of first learning and then practicing microsurgical skills has been reported. After such skills are mastered, they must be transferred to the operating room environment, and this requires considerable preparation. The skills which have been acquired must be practiced constantly. The "occasional" microsurgeon will meet with frustrations not encountered by the microsurgeon who keeps his skills at a high level by frequent practice or performance. A method of preserving vasectomized segments for use in microsurgical practice has been described previously.[54]

250 E. Liberty Street
Louisville, Kentucky 40202

REFERENCES

1. Silber SJ: Perfect anatomical reconstruction of vas deferens with a microscopic surgical technique. Fertil Steril 28:72, 1977
2. Owen ER: Microsurgical vasovasostomy: a reliable vasectomy reversal. Aust NZ J Surg 47:305, 1977
3. Daniel RK, and Terzis JK: Reconstructive Microsurgery. Boston, Little, Brown and Co., 1977
4. Acland RD: Instrumentation for microsurgery. Orthop Clin North Am 8:281, 1977

5. Idem: Microsurgery Practice Manual. Louisville, University of Louisville Publications, 1977

6. Idem: Factors which influence success in microvascular surgery. Louisville, University of Louisville Publications, 1978

7. Idem: Notes on the handling of ultrafine suture material. Surgery 77:507, 1975

8. Idem: A flat-bodied needle for microvascular surgery. Plast Reconstr Surg 61:793, 1978

9. O'Brien BMcC: Microvascular Reconstructive Surgery. Edinburgh, Churchill Livingstone, 1977

10. Silber SJ (Ed): Microsurgery. Baltimore, Williams & Wilkins, 1979

11. Alexander NJ, and Clarkson TB: Vasectomy increases the severity of diet-induced atherosclerosis in Macaca Fascicularis. Science 201:538, 1978

12. Davis JE, and Lubell I: Advances in understanding the effects of vasectomy. Mt Sinai J Med 42:391, 1975

13. Bradshaw LE: Vasectomy reversibility, a status report. Population Reports, Series D., No. 3 (May), Washington, D.C., The George Washington University Medical Center, 1976

14. Belker AM, Acland RD, Roberts TL, III, and Sexter MS: Vasectomy reversal: review and assessment of current status. J Ky Med Assoc 75:536, 1977

15. Silber SJ: Vasectomy and vasectomy reversal. Fertil Steril 29:125, 1978

16. Idem: Vasectomy and its microsurgical reversal. Urol Clin North Am 5:573, 1978

17. Schmidt SS: Vasovasostomy. Ibid 5:585, 1978

18. Fernandes M, Shah KN, and Draper JW: Vasovasostomy: improved microsurgical technique. J Urol 100:763, 1968

19. Schmidt SS: Principles of vasovasostomy. Contemp Surgery 7:13, 1975

20. Idem: Anastomosis of the vas deferens: an experimental study; I. J Urol 75:300, 1956

21. Idem: Anastomosis of the vas deferens: II. Successes and failures in experimental anastomosis. Ibid 81:203, 1959

22. Idem: Anastomosis of the vas deferens: III. Dilation of the vas following obstruction. Ibid 81:206, 1959

23. Idem: Anastomosis of the vas deferens: IV. The use of fine polyethylene tubing as a splint. Ibid 85:838, 1961

24. Montie JE, Stewart BH, and Levin HS: Intravasal stents for vasovasostomy in canine subjects. Fertil Steril 24:877, 1973

25. Montie JE, and Stewart BH: Vasovasostomy: past, present, and future. J Urol 112:111, 1974

26. Urry RL, Thompson J, and Cockett ATK: Vasectomy and vasovasostomy. II. A comparison of two methods of vasovasostomy: Silastic versus chromic stents. Fertil Steril 27:945, 1976

27. Rowland RG, Nanninga JB, and O'Connor VJ Jr: Improved results in vasovasostomies using internal plain catgut stents. Urology 10:260, 1977

28. Banowsky LH: Surgical alternatives in performing vasovasostomy (instructional course). Annual Meeting of American Urological Association, Inc., Washington, D.C., May 21, 1978

29. O'Connor VJ: Anastomosis of vas deferens after purposeful division for sterility. JAMA 136:162, 1948

30. Derrick FC Jr, Yarbrough W, and D'Agostino J: Vasovasostomy: results of questionnaire to members of the American Urological Association. J Urol 110:556, 1973

31. Phadke GM, and Phadke AG: Experiences in the reanastomosis of the vas deferens. Ibid 97:888, 1967

32. Amelar RD, and Dubin L: Vasovasostomy: How effective is it? Contemp Ob-Gyn 6:36, 1975

33. Idem: Vasectomy reversal. J Urol 121:547, 1979

34. Middleton RG, and Henderson D: Vas deferens reanastomosis without splints and without magnification. Ibid 119:763, 1978

35. Idem: Intravasal splints considered hindrance to vas reanastomosis. Urology Times, Oct 1977, p. 6

36. Fallon B, Jacobo E, and Bunge RG: Restoration of fertility by vasovasostomy. J Urol 119:85, 1978

37. Glenn JF: Vas reconstruction, Urologists' Letter Club, July 21, 1978

38. Fitzpatrick TJ: Vasovasostomy: the flap technique. J Urol 120:78, 1978

39. Silber SJ: Microsurgery in clinical urology. Urology 6:150, 1975

40. Idem: Vasectomy and vasectomy reversal. Fertil Steril 29:125, 1978

41. Idem: Microsurgery in urology, Presented at N.Y. Academy of Medicine, Section on Urology. New York, October 18, 1978

42. Owen ER: Microsurgical vasovasostomy: a reliable vasectomy reversal. Aust NZ J Surg 47:305, 1977

43. Sharlip ID: Microsurgical vasovasostomy: preliminary report of a new technic. Presented at Annual Meeting, American Fertility Society, San Francisco, California, February 6, 1979

44. Hagan KF, and Coffey DS: The adverse effects of sperm during vasovasostomy. J Urol 118:269, 1977

45. Silber SJ: Microscopic vasectomy reversal. Fertil Steril 28:1191, 1977

46. Idem: Epididymal extravasation following vasectomy as cause of failure of vasectomy reversal. Ibid 31:309, 1979

47. Alexander NJ: Immunologic and morphologic effects of vasectomy in the rhesus monkey. Fed Proc 34:1692, 1975

48. Alexander NJ, and Schmidt SS: Incidence of antisperm antibody levels and granulomas in men. Fertil Steril 28:655, 1977

49. Sullivan MJ, and Howe GE: Correlation of circulating antisperm antibodies to functional success in vasovasostomy. J Urol 117:189, 1977

50. Mumford DM: Immunity and male infertility. Invest Urol 16:255, 1979

51. Silber SJ: Sperm granuloma and reversibility of vasectomy. Lancet 2:588, 1977

52. Idem: Microscopic vasoepididymostomy: specific microanastomosis to the epididymal tubule. Fertil Steril 30:565, 1978

53. Belker AM, Acland RD, and Juhala CA: Microsurgical two-layer vasovasostomy: a word of caution. Urology 11:616, 1978

54. Belker AM, Acland RD, Sexter MS, and Roberts TL III: Microsurgical two-layer vasovasostomy: laboratory use of vasectomized segments. Fertil Steril 29:48, 1978

55. Silber SJ: Microscopic technique for reversal of vasectomy. Surg Gynecol Obstet 143:631, 1976

56. Idem: Perfect anatomical reconstruction of vas deferens with a new microscopic surgical technique. Fertil Steril 28:72, 1977

57. Silber SJ, Galle J, and Friend D: Microscopic vasovasostomy and spermatogenesis. J Urol 117:299, 1977

58. Wicklund R, and Alexander NJ: Vasovasostomy: evaluation of success. Urology 13:532, 1979

Commentary: Vasovasostomy and Vasoepididymostomy

Arnold M. Belker

VASOVASOSTOMY

The foregoing article was chosen to illustrate the controversy regarding the best method of anastomosis rather than emphasize a given technique. As the number of vasovasostomies increases because of the superimposition of the growing rate of divorce and remarriage on the popularity of vasectomy during the past few decades, the best method of vasovasostomy ultimately will become apparent.

Surgical Techniques. The reported methods of macrosurgical vasovasostomy are shown in Figure 1. Because prevention of sperm leakage at the anastomotic site is so important, the mucosal approximation obtained by the full-thickness suturing technique makes it the most attractive of these methods. In addition to their use in the technique shown in Figure 1B, full-thickness sutures may be used with the anastomotic techniques

depicted in Figure 1C to E. Schmidt, who popularized the full-thickness suturing technique, cautions against such sutures entering the lumen too far from the mucosal edge ("square sutures") because the mucosa will retract and the exposed muscularis will undergo cicatricial contraction (Fig. 2A).[1,2] He emphasizes that mucosal sutures should penetrate the lumen close to the transsected edge of the mucosa ("triangular sutures") to obtain the best mucosal approximation (Fig. 2B). The principle of full-thickness suture placement also has been adapted by many for microsurgical anastomosis.

The continued use of nonabsorbable, removable stents by some surgeons, despite their demonstrated adverse effect, does not seem rational. Assuming that stents are beneficial, a problem arises with their use when vasectomy has been performed in the convoluted portion of the vas because stents will not pass through the convolutions. Therefore, the surgeon who relies on stents to enhance apposition of mucosal edges

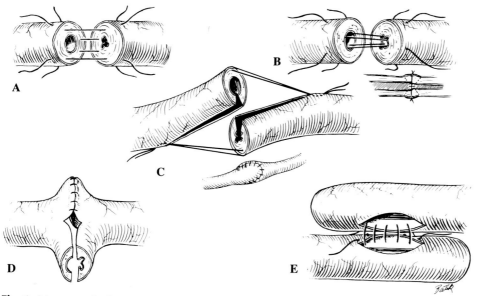

Fig. 1. Macrosurgical vasovasostomy techniques currently used. (A) Muscular layer sutures. (B) Full-thickness sutures. With this technique, interposed muscular layer sutures are also used. (C) Spatulation of opposite walls. (D) Fishmouth "flap" technique. (E) Side-to-side anastomosis. (Belker AM: Vasovasostomy. In Resnick MI (ed): Current Trends in Urology, Chap 2, pp 20–41. Baltimore, Williams & Wilkins, 1981. Reproduced with permission.)

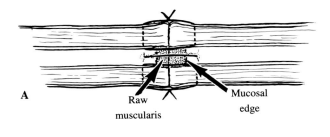

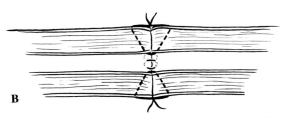

Fig. 2. Schmidt's full-thickness suturing method used for macrosurgical and microsurgical anastomoses. (*A*) "Square" sutures enter lumen at a distance from mucosal edge, allowing mucosal retraction. (*B*) "Triangular" sutures enter lumen near mucosal edge, assuring better mucosal approximation. (Belker AM: Vasovasostomy. In Resnick MI (ed): Current Trends in Urology. Baltimore, Williams & Wilkins [in press]. Reproduced with permission.)

will not be able to employ his preferred anastomotic method in the convoluted portion of the vas. Since vasectomy often has been performed at this level, it seems logical to use a method of anastomosis that achieves good mucosal apposition at any level of the vas. The inability to use stents in the convoluted vas applies to absorbable intravasal stents as well, even though ultimately they may prove useful for anastomoses in the straight portion of the vas.

An often-neglected but simple maneuver is the approximation of perivasal supporting tissues to relieve tension on the anastomosis. Until recently I believed that the strength of the anastomosis itself made this maneuver unnecessary. However, my recent observation of a disrupted microsurgical anastomosis convinces me of the importance of this maneuver.

Failure of a technically good anastomosis also may result when the surgeon does not resect an adequate length of the scarred end of the vas. The great distance between the two ends of the vas sometimes leads the surgeon to resect as little length as possible from each end. However, anastomosis of scarred tissues will result in a failed anastomosis. One must therefore mobilize enough length of each end of the vas so that each scarred end can be resected until healthy tissue is reached.

Silber envisioned numerous urologic applications of microsurgery, which he had used as a laboratory tool for experimentation in rat kidney transplants.[3] He not only introduced microsurgery to urologists, but he also demonstrated the practical clinical applications of microsurgery and popularized

its use by urologists. The urologist interested in microsurgery will find Silber's book invaluable to aid in understanding the history and principles of microsurgery in several areas of surgical specialization.[4]

The two-layer microsurgical vasovasostomy technique developed by Silber seems the best method of preventing sperm leakage and its devastating effects at the anastomotic site. However, this technique has not been universally accepted because of the necessity for the urologist to develop microsurgical skills and the technical difficulties experienced in performing the two-layer anastomosis, even after these skills have been mastered.

In the microsurgical two-layer vasovasostomy described by Silber, the entire mucosal layer is approximated before approximation of the muscular layer is begun. With this method, I experienced mucosal tears where previously placed and tied mucosal sutures were placed on tension during insertion of the final sutures in the mucosal layer.

Such problems led to the development of a simplified technique (Fig. 3) of microsurgical two-layer vasovasostomy using a hinged, folding vas-approximating clamp.[5] This method relieves tension during mucosal suturing by preliminary approximation of a portion of the posterior muscular layer. Also, all anterior mucosal sutures are cut long and left untied until the last suture in this layer has been placed, this avoiding the difficulties previously encountered when placing the final mucosal sutures. The details of this technique have been described elsewhere, but visual perception helps the appreciation of both the details of the technique and the match-up of the mucosal edges of unequal size lumina (Fig. 4).[5]

Figure 5 (corresponding to Fig. 3C) demonstrates placement of the first posterior mucosal suture (after approximation of the posterior muscular layer), and also shows the disparate luminal sizes. In Figure 6 (corresponding to Fig. 3F), all anterior mucosal sutures have been placed before any are tied. Note that the spacing between sutures is different on the abdominal end when compared to the spacing on the testicular end of the vas, so that after all mucosal sutures are tied the mucosal edge approximation will result in a leakproof anastomosis. Figure 7 shows that such a leakproof mucosal approximation will occur after the last anterior mucosal suture is tied.

Results. Since the original publication of the article reproduced in this book, other surgeons have reported results with a variety of methods of vasovasostomy. Results with macrosurgical spatulated anastomoses have been reported by Livingston and Weber and by Leadbetter.[6,7] The former reported 82% "sperm present" and 43% pregnancy rates after 28 cases, while the latter reported 85% "sperm present" and 50% pregnancy rates after 30 cases.

Using microsurgical technique for both methods, Sharlip compared results in 22 full-thickness anastomoses with results in 20 two-layer anastomoses.* "Sperm present" rates of 91% and 85% were obtained with the full-thickness and two-layer methods, while corresponding pregnancy rates were 55% and 70% respectively.

* Sharlip ID: Personal communication, Jan. 25, 1980.

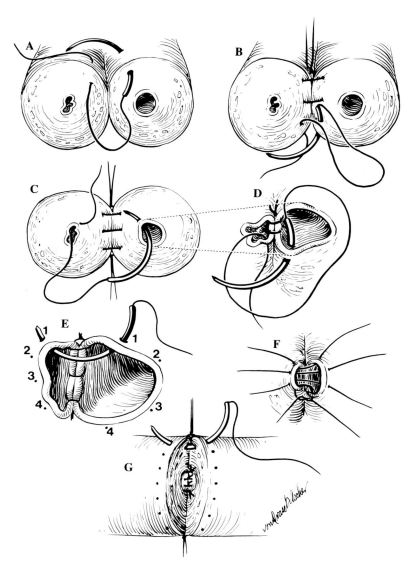

Fig. 3. Two-layer microsurgical vasovasostomy method using hinged folding vas approximating clamp. Note unequal luminal diameters. (*A* and *B*) Three posterior muscular layer sutures (knots outside) include only 90° of circumference, leaving access to mucosa. End sutures are tagged. (*C* and *D*) Three (sometimes two) posterior row mucosal sutures with knots extraluminal. Note change in magnification indicated by broken lines. (*E* and *F*) Four (sometimes three) anterior row mucosal sutures placed in order indicated by numbers, then tied in reverse order. (*G*) Anterior 270° (diagram depicts only 180°) of muscular layer sutures are placed, using tagged end posterior muscular layer sutures for traction. (Belker AM: Microsurgical two-layer vasovasostomy: Simplified technique using hinged folding aproximating clamp. Urology 16:376, 1980. Reproduced with permission.)

The most provocative data have come from Lee and McLoughlin, who compared results at one institution of an earlier series of 41 macrosurgical vasovasostomies with a later series of 26 microsurgical two-layer vasovasostomies.[8] They found "sperm present" rates of 96% and 90% and pregnancy rates of 54% and 46% with microsurgical and macrosurgical methods, respectively. It is possible that the much lower rate of follow-up study (68%) in the macrosurgical cases than in the microsurgical cases (100%) may reflect a spuriously high rate of success in the macrosurgical group. The authors conclude that there is little difference in patency and pregnancy rates resulting from macroscopic and microscopic vasovasostomies at their institution but favor use of the microscope so that skills will be available for exploration of the epididymis in cases where no sperm are found in the vas fluid.

VASOEPIDIDYMOSTOMY

Vasoepididymostomy may be considered in the treatment of both congenital and acquired obstructions of the epididymis. The procedure may be indicated in cases of azoospermia or severe oliospermia when other causes for these conditions have been ruled out and testicular biopsy demonstrates reasonably normal spermatogenesis.

In cases of azoospermia, seminal fructose should be determined first. Absence of fructose in the semen indicates congenital absence of the seminal vesicles (not remediable) or obstruction of the ejaculatory ducts (remediable by transurethral unroofing of the ejaculatory ducts).[9,10] If fructose is present in the semen but serum follicle-stimulating hormone (FSH) is over twice the normal level and the testes are small, there is

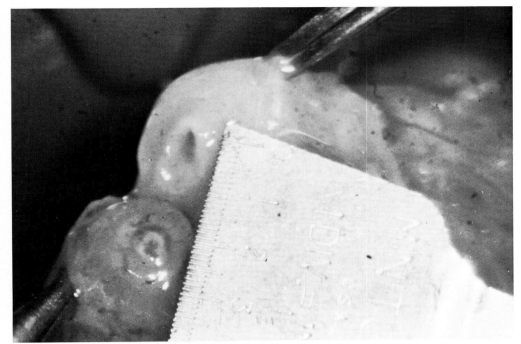

Fig. 4. Abdominal (*lower in photo*) and testicular (*upper in photo*) ends of vas at time of vasovasostomy. Numbered markings on ruler are 1 mm apart and subdivisions are 0.1 mm apart. (Belker AM: Microsurgical two-layer vasovasostomy: Simplified technique using hinged folding approximating clamp. Urology 16:376, 1980. Reproduced with permission.)

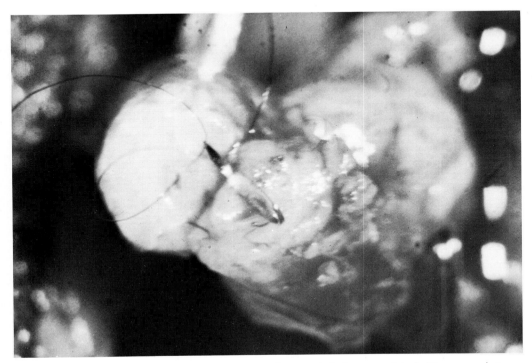

Fig. 5. Placement of the first posterior row mucosal suture is being completed. (Corresponds to stage of anastomosis in Fig. 3C. Belker AM: Microsurgical two-layer vasovasostomy: Simplified technique using hinged folding approximating clamp. Urology 16:376, 1980. Reproduced with permission.)

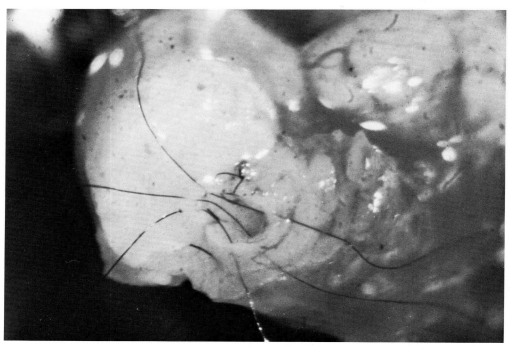

Fig. 6. All anterior row mucosal sutures (only three used here) have been placed, left untied, and cut long. Note that luminal diameter disparity necessitates wider spacing between sutures on testicular side (*larger lumen*) than on abdominal side (*smaller lumen*). (Corresponds to stage of anastomosis in Fig. 3F. Belker AM: Microsurgical two-layer vasovasostomy: Simplified technique using hinged folding approximating clamp. Urology 16:376, 1980. Reproduced with permission.)

good evidence that no remediable condition will be found and that further studies, including testicular biopsy, should not be performed.[11]

However, if fructose is present in the semen and serum FSH is not over twice the normal level, the urologist should perform testicular biopsy. I prefer to perform testicular biopsy as a separate outpatient procedure under general anesthesia. I do not explore the epididymis and vas at the time of biopsy. This allows me to use operating time more efficiently than when ''possible'' scrotal exploration and vasoepididymostomy are scheduled and performed at the time of biopsy, based on frozen section findings. This approach also allows the patient to schedule his time away from work when exploration and vasoepididymostomy ultimately are performed.

Surgical Techniques. Although congenital epididymal obstructions may be recognized by gross inspection relatively easily, I find acquired epididymal obstructions often difficult to recognize, even when the epididymis is inspected with high-power (20×) magnification through the operating microscope. It is difficult by mere inspection to appreciate at what level the epididymal tubule becomes dilated, and the surgeon should be prepared for the possibility that inspection alone will not reveal the level of obstruction. In this instance, one may partially transect the vas deferens until the lumen is entered.

Vasography may then be performed either toward the testis or toward the urethra, depending on the presence or absence of sperm in the vas fluid at this level, as suggested by Silber.[4] Alternatively, simple needle puncture vasography may be performed.

With vasoepididymostomy, the procedure may be performed as popularized by Hagner (Fig. 8) or as described by Silber (Fig. 9).[12,13] Hagner simply anastomosed the vas to a longitudinal opening in the epididymis, at the lowest point on the epididymis at which sperm were present in the epididymal fluid. As shown in Figure 9, Silber serially transsected the epididymis at 0.5-cm intervals, starting at the caudal end and proceeding toward the caput until sperm were found in the epididymal fluid. At the level at which sperm were present, he performed microsurgical anastomosis of the vas to the specific epididymal tubule from which the sperm-containing fluid was seen to flow.

Results. Using the method popularized by Hagner, Kar and Phadke reported that 49% of patients developed some sperm in the semen, but only 20% developed sperm counts above 20 million/ml; pregnancies occurred in only 14% of their wives.[14] Their series included patients with a variety of causes of epididymal obstruction.

In 14 patients on whom Silber performed microsurgical

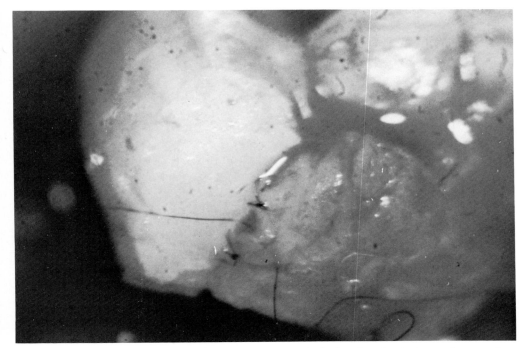

Fig. 7. The last anterior row mucosal suture remains untied, showing that leak-proof mucosal approximation will occur when this remaining suture is tied. Belker AM: Microsurgical two-layer vasovasostomy: Simplified technique using hinged folding approximating clamp. Urology 16:376, 1980. Reproduced with permission.)

vasoepididymostomy, 12 developed sperm counts over 20 million/ml, while two remained azoospermic.[13] All 14 of Silber's patients underwent vasoepididymostomy because of epididymal obstruction following previous vasectomy. Pregnancy rates were not reported because the group was not followed long enough for meaningful results to have occurred (2 yr).

CONCLUSIONS

The controversy regarding which method of vasovasostomy is best has not been resolved. At present, it seems that the surgeon's experience may be more important than the anastomotic technique used, because good results are being reported with a variety of techniques. I believe that optical magnification will improve results obtained with any anastomotic method. Increased appreciation of anatomic detail of the vas obtained with optical magnification enables one to approximate the ends of the vas more accurately. The two-layer microsurgical anastomosis requires considerable microsurgical training and practice and can be recommended only if more surgeons using this method obtain results comparable to those reported. It is anticipated that the Vasovasostomy Study Group will help resolve whether the time spent learning microsurgical technique is rewarded by significantly improved results.

Regarding vasoepididymostomy, the microsurgical method

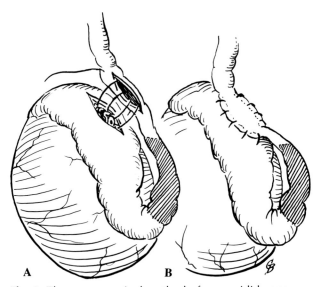

Fig. 8. The macrosurgical method of vasoepididymostomy popularized by Hagner. (Belker AM: Vasovasostomy. In Resnick MI (ed): Current Trends in Urology, Chap 2, pp 20–41. Baltimore, Williams & Wilkins, 1981. Reproduced with permission.)

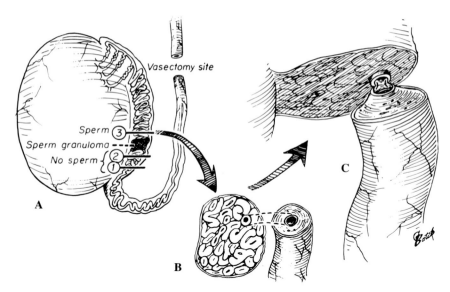

Fig. 9. The microsurgical method of vasoepididymostomy described by Silber. When a "blow-out" sperm granuloma obstructs the epididymis after vasectomy, sperm are not present in the epididymal duct at levels numbered 1 and 2, but are present above the "blow-out" sperm granuloma at level 3. (Belker AM: Vasovasostomy and vasoepididymostomy. AUA Update Series, Lesson 2, Vol. 1. Houston, American Urological Association, Inc, 1981)

described by Silber seems rational and attractive. However, it has failed in my few patients up through early 1980; therefore I cannot personally recommend it. Before undertaking this method of vasoepididymostomy, the surgeon should possess an advanced level of microsurgical expertise; otherwise, a successful operation will not be possible.

It is known that sperm must pass through the epididymis to acquire the ability for fertilization, but the exact length of epididymal passage required for this to occur has not been established. It also is known that vasoepididymostomy is increasingly successful the nearer the anastomosis is to the cauda (and the farther from the caput) of the epididymis. Silber recently reported encouraging results with vasoepididymostomy performed in the region of the caput of the epididymis.[15] Five patients who underwent anastomosis at this level achieved postoperative sperm counts of 50 million/ml or better but initially had less than 1% sperm motility after surgery. However, 1½ to 2 yr postoperatively they all achieved normal sperm motility. Whether such patients ultimately will be fertile remains undetermined, but his report is an encouraging development in the therapy of epididymal obstructive disease.

REFERENCES

1. Schmidt SS: Vas anastomosis: A return to simplicity. Br J Urol 47:309, 1975

2. Schmidt SS: Vasovasostomy. Urol Clin North Am 5:585, 1978

3. Silber SJ: Microsurgery in clinical urology. Urology 6:150, 1975

4. Silber SJ (ed): Microsurgery. Baltimore, The Williams & Wilkins Co., 1979

5. Belker AM: Microsurgical two-layer vasovasostomy: Simplified technique using hinged folding approximating clamp. Urology 16:376, 1980

6. Livingston WD, Weber CH Jr: The spatulated side-to-side vasovasostomy: A 5-year retrospective study. Read at the 27th annual James C. Kimbrough Urological Seminar, San Antonio, TX, Nov. 12–17, 1978

7. Leadbetter GW: Vasovasostomy without a microscope: Technique and results of ten years experience. Read at the annual meeting of the New England Section, American Urological Association, Dixville Notch, NH, Sept. 15–19, 1979

8. Lee L, McLoughlin MG: Vasovasostomy: A comparison of macroscopic and microscopic techniques at one institution. Fertil Steril 33:54, 1980

9. Amelar RD, Hotchkiss RS: Congenital aplasia of the epididymes and vasa deferentia: Effects on semen. Fertil Steril 14:44, 1963

10. Porch PP Jr: Aspermia owing to obstruction of distal ejaculatory duct and treatment by transurethral resection. J Urol 119:141, 1978

11. Hargreave TB, Jequier AM: Can follicle stimulating hormone replace testicular biopsy in the diagnosis of obstructive azoospermia? Br J Urol 50:415, 1978

12. Hagner FR: Sterility in the male. Surg Gynecol Obstet 52:330, 1931

13. Silber SJ: Microscopic vasoepididymostomy: Specific microanastomosis to the epididymal tubule. Fertil Steril 30:565, 1978

14. Kar JK, Phadke AM: Vaso-epididymal anastomosis. Fertil Steril 26:743, 1975

15. Silber SJ: Vasoepididymostomy to the head of the epididymis: Recovery of normal spermatozoal motility. Fertil Steril 34:149, 1980

ANNOTATED BIBLIOGRAPHY

Belker AM: Vasovasostomy. In Resnick MI (ed): Current Trends in Urology, Chap 2, pp 20–41. Baltimore, The Williams & Wilkins Co., 1981

This article is an effort to assess various methods employed for vasovasostomy and vasoepididymostomy. Uncontrollable effects of vasectomy and controllable surgical options are reviewed. A detailed description of all surgical techniques currently used and the results of these techniques is presented. Although a microsurgical bias is clearly stated, an effort is made to assess each anastomotic method relating ease of performance to results.

Belker AM: Microsurgical two-layer vasovasostomy: simplified technique using hinged folding approximating clamp. Urology 16:376, 1980

A method of two-layer microsurgical vasovasostomy using the Strauch hinged vas approximating clamp is described. This method simplifies performance of the anastomosis by lessening the danger of mucosal tears. The anastomotic technique, which is a modification of the method first reported by Strauch, is described in detail.

Silber SJ: Vasectomy and vasectomy reversal. Fertil Steril 29:125, 1978

Vasectomy is discussed briefly, with the conclusion that Schmidt's mucosal fulguration technique best prevents spontaneous recanalization. Arguments supporting the rationale for the leakproof microsurgical two-layer method of vasovasostomy are presented, and the surgical technique is described. Of 51 patients who had failures of macrosurgical vasovasostomy performed by other surgeons, 41 developed normal sperm counts after reoperation by the author with his microsurgical method. A 71% pregnancy rate occurred in the wives of the first 42 unselected patients.

The increasingly adverse prognostic significance of the absence of sperm from the vas fluid during vasovasostomy with the passage of time after vasectomy is shown in 121 consecutive patients. Also, the favorable pressure-releasing effect of a spermatic granuloma at the transected end of the vas after vasectomy is demonstrated by studies in 92 consecutive patients.

Species variability in the effects of vasectomy on the testis and epididymis are reviewed in depth. The significance of antisperm antibodies that may be present after vasectomy is discussed relative to possible influences of these antibodies on fertility after vasovasostomy.

Owen ER: Microsurgical vasovasostomy: A reliable vasectomy reversal. Aust NZ J Surg 47:305, 1977

The author describes his technique of two-layer microsurgical vasovasostomy and reports results of the procedure after performance unilaterally in 50 patients. Sperm were present in the semen postoperatively in 98%, and 72% of the wives achieved pregnancy. Unfortunately, the series was biased by exclusion from vasovasostomy of an unstated number of patients who had no sperm in the vas fluid at the time of surgery.

Schmidt SS: Vasovasostomy. Urol Clin North Am 5:585, 1978

The author, having devoted years of study to vasovasostomy, reports adaptation of his previously described full-thickness suturing technique to the operating microscope. Emphasis is given to the improvement in anastomotic results when optical magnification is used and to the "triangular" method of placement of full-thickness sutures to ensure better mucosal approximation than with the previously used "square" method of suture placement.

Lee HY, members of the Vasectomy Study Project: Observations on the results of 300 vasovasostomies. J Andrology 1:11, 1980

Experience with various anastomotic methods in many cases is reviewed. Success rates were better in patients under 40 yr of age and in a later group of patients in whom higher optical magnification and smaller sutures were used. Success rates decreased as the duration since vasectomy increased and if sperm were absent from the vas fluid during vasovasostomy. Sperm were absent from the vas fluid in only 30% of the patients whose vasa were obstructed less than 6 yr but in 70% of the patients whose vasa were obstructed over 9 yr. Either side-to-side or full-thickness end-to-end techniques are preferred by the authors.

Middleton RG, Henderson D: Vas deferens reanastomosis without splints and without magnification. J Urol 119:763, 1978

Over 6½ yr, 110 vasovasostomies were performed without optical magnification or stents. A very simple anastomotic technique was used. Two full-thickness sutures were placed, 180 degrees apart, and an additional muscular layer suture was placed in each of the remaining 2 quadrants. With this simple technique, 39% (28 of 72 patients available for follow-up study) achieved a pregnancy in their wives. An additional 35% (25 of the 72) had postoperative sperm counts above 25 million/ml. On the basis of these results, one could justify the technically demanding microsurgical methods of vasovasostomy only if the results with such methods are significantly better than the authors obtained with their simple method.

Lee L, McLoughlin MG: Vasovasostomy: A comparison of macroscopic and microscopic techniques at one institution. Fertil Steril 33:54, 1980

Between 1973 and 1977, 87 vasovasostomies were performed. Sixty-one were single-layer macroscopic anastomoses, and 26 were two-layer microscopic anastomoses. "Sperm present" rates of 90% and 96% and pregnancy rates of 46% and 54% were achieved with the macroscopic and microscopic techniques, respectively. Although a significantly lower follow-up study rate in the macroscopic anastomosis patients may have influenced results, the authors stress that results improve as experience with any anastomotic technique is gained. This is a provocative study. If similar results were to be obtained by other investigators, the advantages of microsurgical vasovasostomy would have to be questioned.

Silber SJ: Epididymal extravasation following vasectomy as a cause for failure of vasectomy reversal. Fertil Steril 31:309, 1979

In 28 patients, sperm were absent from the fluid obtained from the testicular end of the vas during planned vasovasostomy. This was true unilaterally in 17 patients and bilaterally in 11. When sperm were absent from the vas fluid, the corresponding epididymis was explored. Patients in whom the vas fluid contained no sperm but was crystal clear and colorless did not undergo epididymal exploration because the author previously had found that such patients develop a normal sperm count after vasovasostomy. When epididymal exploration was performed, the epididymis was transected transversely at 0.5-cm intervals from the cauda toward the caput. Abundant sperm were found in the fluid at variable levels in 33 epididymes, while no sperm were present in 6. Histologic examination revealed interstitial sperm extravasation and sperm granuloma formation in the epididymis distal to the level at which sperm were present in the epididymal fluid. The author establishes that obstruction of the epididymal duct (resulting from rupture due to increased back pressure after vasectomy) is responsible for the absence of sperm from the vas fluid during vasovasostomy in some patients and for persisting azoospermia after technically successful vasovasostomy in such cases.

Silber SJ: Microscopic vasoepididymostomy: Specific microanastomosis to the epididymal tubule. Fertil Steril 30:565, 1978

The author describes his innovative method of microsurgical anastomosis of the vas deferens to the specific epididymal tubule from which sperm-containing fluid effluxes on the transected surface of the epididymis. Preliminary results in 14 patients revealed that 12 had normal sperm counts (with sperm motility normal in 11 and impaired in 1); 2 remained azoospermic postoperatively.

Kar JK, Phadke AM: Vaso-epididymal anastomosis. Fertil Steril 26:743, 1975

The authors report a series of vasoepididymostomies performed for correction of congenital and acquired epididymal obstructions. The anastomotic technique consisted of side-to-side macrosurgical vasoepididymostomy. Operations were bilateral in 185 patients, unilateral by surgeon's choice in 47, and obligatorily unilateral because of the patient's disease in 49. Postoperatively, sperm were present in the semen of 55%, 25%, and 47%, while pregnancies occurred in 17%, 6%, and 10% of their wives for each of these categories. The authors indicated that the use of removable nylon stents influenced results favorably, but review of their data reveals conflicting results with nylon stents in different groups of patients. A review of the literature regarding vasoepididymostomy is included.

Overview: Management of Vasovasostomy and Epididymovasostomy

Richard D. Amelar and Lawrence Dubin

VASOVASOSTOMY

There has been a noticeable increase in the number of requests for vasectomy reversal in the past decade. It is our estimate that 2 of every 100 men who have been sterilized will seek to have his fertility restored. Indeed, the publicized fact that reversal operations can be often successful has led many men to consider this option.

The reasons for desiring vas reanastomosis and restored fertility are various: (1) a subsequent marriage (usually to a younger woman) with a desire to have children in this new union, (2) death or severe injury of children, (3) change of heart in a patient who thought as a young man that sterilization would aid society and zero population growth, (4) improvement in the economic situation of a couple, making children more desirable, and (5) psychologic inability to tolerate the concept of being sterile.

We recently have seen several patients who requested vasectomy reversal because they had exhausted the supply of their own semen, which had been frozen and stored in a commercial bank for fertility insurance before vasectomy. Their wives had failed to conceive by repeated inseminations with the stored frozen semen. More similar requests for vasectomy reversal are anticipated.[1]

Alexander and Clarkson have reported in a pilot study an increase in diet-induced atherosclerosis in monkeys after vasectomy.[2] If this preliminary study is confirmed in man the demand for vasectomy reversal would certainly increase markedly.

There have been significant recent advances in the surgical techniques for vasectomy reversal to restore fertility after previous voluntary sterilization by bilateral vasectomy, leading to improved results.

Anatomic and Physiologic Considerations. The vas deferens is usually palpable in the scrotum as a portion of the spermatic cord. It is about 35 cm long and 3 mm in diameter. The vas has a thick muscular wall, and the vas lumen has a mean diameter of 1 mm.[3] The vas extends from the cauda epididymis, where it originates as a convoluted structure, and after its proximal 2 cm it becomes straight and courses upward through the scrotum, the inguinal canal, retroperitoneum, and pelvis over the ureter and behind the bladder. The terminal portion enlarges to form an ampullary portion that joins the duct of the seminal vesicle, forming the ejaculatory duct. Histologically, the vas deferens is lined by mucosa and is surrounded by a wall composed of three layers of smooth muscle: longitudinal muscle in the outer and inner layers and circular muscle in the middle. This thick muscular wall affords powerful peristaltic motion. Exterior to this muscle layer is a sheath of connective tissue. The epithelial lining of the lumen varies along the length of the vas deferens. Near the epididymis the mucosa resembles the epithelium in the cauda epididymidis and is characterized by large columnar cells with regularly placed pairs of cilia that are actually stereocilia or microvilli that may have an absorptive function. These sterocilia do not move as do the cilia of the rete testis and the efferent ductules. Distally, the epithelial cells lining the lumen of the vas deferens become nonciliated and smaller.

Anatomically, the portion of the vas deferens of clinical interest for performing vasectomy is generally in the mid-scrotal portion.

The blood supply to the vas deferens is derived from the deferential artery, a branch of the inferior vesical artery, which provides an important collateral blood supply to the testis. At the time of vasectomy, if the deferential artery is not carefully ligated or coagulated, it may be a potential site of hemorrhage. The sheath of the vas deferens contains nerve fibers for pain and sympathetic fibers that release norepinephrine. These fibers may be responsible for the presence of the spontaneous motility of the human vas deferens that has been demonstrated *in vitro*. The presence of spontaneous motility *in vitro* leads to the working hypothesis that there is spontaneous motility of the human vas deferens *in vivo*. Tone in the sympathetic fibers innervating the vas deferens probably depends on the integrity of the spinal center. It is believed that the intrinsic rhythmicity of the vas deferens depends on the local concentration of norepinephrine. However, the powerful and coordinated series of contractions that propel sperm from the epididymis to the urethra during ejaculation are initiated and controlled by the release of substantial amounts of norepinephrine from the sympathetic nerve endings. It is well known that spermatozoa are expelled from the cauda epididymidis and vas deferens at ejaculation.

Vasectomy results in the division of the inferior spermatic nerve that runs parallel to the vas deferens and innervates it. Attempts at vasectomy reversal may fail to restore fertility because, although the sympathetic fibers are strongly regenerative and, consequently, if divided would probably grow from the vas deferens to reinnervate the lower vas and epididymis, iatrogenic surgical factors may prevent regeneration and restoration of the sympathetic nerve supply. These factors include the removal of a large segment of the vas, the placement of a suture or clip too close to the sheath around the stump of the vas, and an inflammatory reaction in scar tissue in response to the trauma of the operation. An intact sympathetic nerve supply probably is essential for the transport of sperm from the epididymis at the time of ejaculation. Without such a supply to the vas deferens and epididymis, complete recovery of sperm output is unlikely to be achieved after a functional vasovasostomy.

After vasectomy the lumen of the testicular side of the vas increases 70% in mean diameter because of the obstruction.[4] Silber believes that this dilatation on the testicular side can be reduced by purposely allowing sperm leakage from the testicular end of the vas at the time of vasectomy, but this suggestion has precipitated a great deal of criticism and Silber has since retracted this suggestion for use as a routine in performance of vasectomy until further experimental evidence is accumulated.[5,6]

The difference in the relative size of the two vas lumina requires that the anastomosis unite lumina of different diameters, and efforts should be made to avoid subsequent leakage of sperm at the site of the anastomosis, which can lead to the formation of granulomas with subsequent antibody formation.[7]

Results. In a review of the literature on reported experiences with vasectomy-reversal operations it can be found that after vasectomy, various authors have reported that sperm cells have returned to the ejaculate in 30% to 98% of the series. Pregnancy rates have varied widely from 10% to as high as 68%.[8]

O'Connor reported a survey of American urologists in 1948, with a success rate of 45% for 420 vasovasostomies accomplished by many different splinted and nonsplinted techniques.[9] However, there is a difference between sperm appearing in the ejaculate and the occurrence of pregnancy.

Hulka and Davis compiled the results from 705 vasovasostomies from the world literature.[10] In 60% of these cases reappearance of sperm was reported. Lee reported 156 cases of vas reanastomosis: 81% of these patients had viable sperm in the ejaculates, but there was a pregnancy rate of only 35%.[11]

Silber, in a series of 400 patients using the operating microscope and a two-layer anastomosis, reported excellent results with at least some sperm present in 94% of patients and a 71% pregnancy rate in the first 42 patients followed for 1½ yr.[5]

Middleton and Henderson used a simple nonmagnified technique with a 6–0 Prolene and reported the reappearance of sperm in 74% and a pregnancy rate of 39% in 110 vasectomy reversals in the last 6½ yr.[12]

In our own series of 93 vasovasostomies, which were performed *before* 1976 and followed for at least 2 yr, sperm were present in 78 men (84%). Thirty-one couples had children (a pregnancy rate of 33%). In 69 vasectomy reversals that we have performed using magnification from 1976 to 1978, sperm were found in 60 cases (87%) and pregnancies have occurred so far in 38 cases (55%).

It is of interest that spontaneous recanalization of the vas does occur in 1% to 2% of patients, after vasectomy.[13–16] Semen analysis should be performed before vas reanastomosis lest the operation not be necessary at all. It is amazing that even after a highly tortuous and scarified spontaneous reanastomosis, semen qualities of significant fertility potential may be present.

Surgical Technique. We are now using a nonsplinted technique with surgical ocular loupes of 6-power magnification (Fig.10) and eight 6–0 Prolene sutures. The increased magnification afforded by the expanded field surgical telescope (manufactured by Designs For Vision, Inc., 120 East 23rd St., New York, New York 10010) has contributed, we believe, to our recent better results, as compared to our results in the operations we performed before 1976.

The scrotum is well prepared with antiseptic and draped appropriately. The scrotum is then palpated to identify the scarred area or granuloma secondary to the vasectomy and the ends of the vas if possible. An incision of 5 cm to 6 cm is then made in the scrotum over this area, and the testis and spermatic cord are delivered from the scrotum. The fascia is incised to expose the scarred ends of the vas, which must be excised. The distal vas is incised, cannulated with a blunt needle, and tested for patency by injection of hydrogen peroxide dyed with methylene blue. Spatulation of the distal end may be necessary, since the proximal end usually is dilated and has a greater diameter. The proximal vas is then incised, and fluid from the vas is placed on a microscope slide and examined by an assistant for the presence of sperm. Efforts should be made to prevent spillage of vasal fluid containing sperm into the tissues to prevent granuloma or antibody formation.

Vasoepididymal anastomosis should be considered if no sperm are found in the proximal vas.

Using 6-power ocular loupe magnification, eight through-and-through 6–0 Prolene® sutures are placed with the knots on the outside of the lumen of the vas. The first four sutures are placed at each quadrant, and the remaining four are placed

Fig. 10. Surgical ocular loupes.

between the quadrant sutures (Fig. 11). This procedure gives a closure that aligns mucosa to mucosa and serosa to serosa. The closure is watertight and should not be under tension. Freeing the distal vas will often relieve any possible tension.

The fascia is then closed above the anastomosis. Small indwelling Penrose drains are left, depending on the extent of the operation, and the skin is closed with catgut sutures. A pressure dressing or scrotal support is then applied.

Schmidt uses a similar nonsplinted one-layer anastomosis, but he uses an operating microscope for the placement of 7–0 to 9–0 nylon sutures. Silber uses the delicate two-layer anastomosis with the operating microscope and emphasizes the importance of a precise watertight anastomosis.[5] Magnification of $16 \times$ or $25 \times$ is used with 9–0 nylon suture material.

The reasons for the marked discrepancy between the presence of sperm after vasovasostomy and the pregnancy rates remain obscure. Certainly, there may be a relationship between fertility and the presence of sperm-agglutinating and immobilizing antibodies in as many as 62% of men tested after vasectomy.[18–23] Significantly high titers (1:32 or greater) of antibodies also were found in 18 of 29 men (62.1%) with congenital bilateral absence of the vasa deferentia.[24] Such titers may be related to epididymal obstruction.

High antibody titers *per se* are not a contraindication to an operation, although they may be a poor prognostic sign. We have seen these titers return to normal in some patients after successful vasovasostomy. In others, the levels remained elevated and sperm motility was poor.

Semen analysis after vasovasostomy may show sperm as early as 1 mo postoperatively but sperm may not appear in some patients until 6 mo later. Poor sperm motility is likely to be noted in the early ejaculates but should be an adequate level by 6 mo. If the seman qualities are poor, further investigation of the patient for other causes in infertility (e.g., varicocele or hormonal imbalance) and appropriate therapy are indicated.

The improved results with vas reanastomosis recently reported by urologists using various techniques may be related to the elimination of the use of exteriorized intravasal splints that generally were removed several days or even weeks postoperatively. Such stents would often lead to sperm leakage and granuloma formation at the point of exit from the vas with subsequent obstructions and an increased incidence of antisperm antibody formation.[23] These exteriorized splints also could be a pathway for infection.

The consensus after a panel discussion on the various current techniques for vasectomy reversal by vasovasostomy (nonmagnified single layer, ocular loupe–magnified single layer, microsurgical singe layer, and microsurgical double layer) is that, at present, long-term comparative results are simply not available.[25] There were present a number of urologic surgeons who have acquired considerable experience with vas reconstruction, and they are having fair success in terms of subsequent pregnancies using a variety of surgical techniques with or without the operating microscope. Certainly, the more experience with a particular technique the surgeon has acquired, the better will be the results. This definitely is not an operation to be performed casually by the urologist who does not have a special interest and expertise in treating infertility problems.

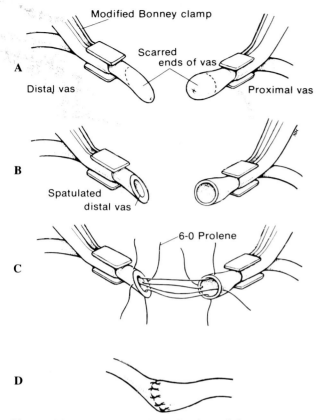

Fig. 11. Vasovasostomy. (*A*) Ends of vas deferens are exposed and scarred ends are excised. (*B*) After patency has been tested distal vas deferens may require spatulation. (*C*) Vasovasostomy with interrupted 6–0 prolene atraumatic sutures. (*D*) Completed anastomosis. (Reprinted with permission.)

The interval between vasectomy and vas reanastomosis usually does not appear to influence the rate of success in vasectomy reversal, but this interval may be critical in the patient who has suffered irreversible obstructive damage to the testes or epididymides after vasectomy. Schmidt has reported successful reanastomosis as long as 21 yr after vasectomy.[4] Phadke and Phadke also have reported success regardless of the time between vasectomy and reanastomosis.[26] Silber reported that he obtained poor results in patients who had vasectomies performed more than 10 yr before reanastomosis and excellent results when the vasectomy was performed within 2 yr of the reversal operation.[5] However, most patients who request vasectomy reversal within 2 yr probably should never have been sterilized in the first place. Silber believes that a prolonged duration of vas obstruction has a deleterious effect on the successful return of fertility after reconstruction of the vas deferens and that any series of vasovasostomies weighted toward patients whose vasectomies were performed more recently, no matter which surgical technique is used, will have a higher success rate than a series weighted toward patients whose vasectomies were performed more than 10 yr previously. The data that would allow conclusions with respect to a critical interval beyond which reconstruction of the vas should not be attempted are still not available.

EPIDIDYMOVASOSTOMY

When the seminal ejaculate is azoospermic but contains fructose, and the testicular biopsy has demonstrated normal spermatogenesis, epididymal obstruction is highly probable. Multiple cystic anomalies of microscopic size and other congenital defects are presently far more common causes of such obstruction than are postinflammatory obstructive lesions resulting from untreated gonorrhea. The fructose test serves to differentiate congenital absence of the ductal system from occlusions of the duct. Complete azoospermia due to tuberculosis is generally not amenable to surgical correction because of the extensive involvement of the epididymides, vasa, and seminal vesicles.

Robert Schoysman of Belgium suggests that there is no necessity for preliminary biopsy of the testis. He feels that the presence of an epididymis distended with sperm as seen under a microscope at the time of exploration is sufficient evidence of active spermatogenesis in the testis and obstruction of the epididymis.*

Postinflammatory lesions of the tail of the epididymis offer the best chance for cure. Among patients successfully undergoing this operation, about 20% have been able to achieve pregnancy, and these patients deserve the champagne. Sperm may appear in the ejaculate of a much higher percentage of the patients, however.

Only rare success has been reported in those cases in which azoospermia is due to congenital anomalies rather than to postinflammatory obstruction.

Hanley reported only 1 pregnancy after 83 vasoepididymal anastomoses.[27] In these patients sperm were found in the head of the epididymis and the vas was patent, but a congenital anomaly of the epididymis was present.

In our own series of 69 cases of azoospermia secondary to epididymal obstruction, all performed more than 1 yr ago, there were 24 patients with a definite history of epididymitis; the other 45 patients had congenital epididymal obstructions. Bilateral side-to-side epididymovasostomy on the 24 patients with epididymitis resulted in 14 patients able to produce sperm in their ejaculates (55%), but only 6 (20%) had good semen quality. Seven men caused pregnancies, which resulted in six normal children and one early miscarriage.

The procedure we have used in these cases is a modification of techniques first described by Hagner and colleagues.[17] The principle of this operation is the anastomosis of a minute elliptic opening in the vas to a similar opening in the epididymis where live sperm have been recovered.

In our operative technique the testes, epididymides, and spermatic cords are exposed through bilateral scrotal incisions. The straight portions of the vasa are identified and are freed from the other cord structures, taking care to avoid devascularization of the vasa. A sufficient length of vas is mobilized so that it can be easily approximated to the epididymis without tension.

* Schoysman R: Personal communication, 1974.

Using a no. 11 blade, an incision is made into the epididymis at the level of the globus minor on the border opposite its testicular attachment. Any fluid that escapes from the epididymal incision is collected on a sterile glass slide mixed with a drop of saline, and handed to an assistant outside the sterile field, who places it under the microscope. In favorable cases, many motile sperm will be identified. If sperm are few or absent, another incision is made into the more proximal parts of the epididymis, and the procedure is repeated until a satisfactory site is found for anastomosis.

By making the first exploratory epididymal incision at a point some distance from its proximal portion, part of the epididymis can be preserved for whatever function it affords the sperm. If the operation fails, a second attempt can be made at a later date, using the remaining proximal areas for a new anastomosis.

Once a favorable site in the epididymis has been selected on each side, the vas is brought adjacent to it and an incision is made into the vas. An invaluable surgical maneuver for making a clean and adequate incision is to support the vas on the index finger of the left hand while making the transverse incision through the upper portion of the tubular vas with the right hand. The incision should be just deep enough to expose the lumen, and care must be taken not to cut entirely through the vas (Fig. 12).

A no. 21 hypodermic needle, the tip of which has been honed to blunt its sharp edge, is inserted into the lumen of the distal segment of the vas. A few milliliters of hydrogen peroxide, which has been colored blue with a few drops of indigo carmine, is injected to ensure that the vas is patent. The tip of the needle is then withdrawn to a point 0.5 cm above the transverse incision. The point of the no. 11 blade is

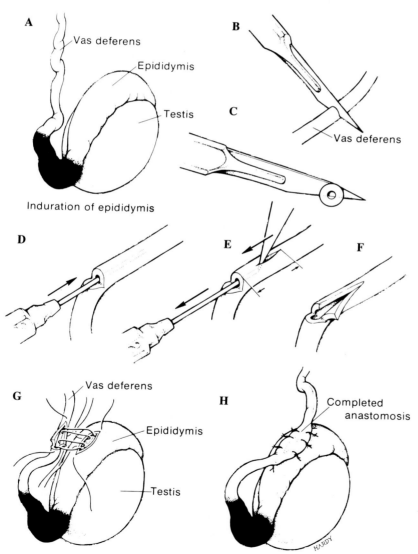

Fig. 12. Method of epididymovasostomy. (*A*) Exposure of anatomy and area of induration and obstruction. (*B* to *F*) Method of incision of vas deferens and preparation of the vas for epididymovasostomy. (*G*) Vasoepididymal anastomosis using interrupted 6–0 Prolene sutures. (*H*) Completed anastomosis. (Reprinted with permission.)

inserted into the wall of the vas so that it engages the lumen of the blunted end of the needle. Then, as the needle is pulled downward with gentle traction, the knife engaged in the tip of the needle cuts the desired uniform opening through the wall of the vas.

If the blue peroxide solution does not flow easily into the vas, or if there is any doubt about patency, a catheter can be passed into the bladder. If the vas is patent, the urine will be blue. If it is necessary to perform this procedure with the other vas, the bladder must be irrigated until the return fluids are clear.

If no solution can be injected into the vas, no. 1 nylon suture can be passed into the vas as a probe to locate the site of the obstruction. If the obstruction is in an accessible area of the vas, it may be possible to reenter the vas above the point of obstruction and make another test of patency. Occasionally, multiple points of obstruction may be encountered,

and if it is not feasible to detour them, the vasoepididymal anastomosis will have to be eliminated on that side.

Atraumatic 6–0 Prolene sutures are used for the anastomosis. The sutures are placed through each wall of the incised vas and then deeply into the epididymis so that all knots are outside the anastomosis. We have found it helpful to use an ocular loupe with 6-power magnification during the placing of these sutures.

At the conclusion of the anastomosis, the scrotal contents are replaced and the scrotum is closed in two layers with interrupted 3–0 chromic catgut sutures. Penrose drains are left in place for 24 hr. Sterile dressings and a scrotal suspensory or pressure drainage are applied. The patient may be discharged from the hospital on the third or fourth postoperative day.

The procedure of epididymovasostomy is performed on both sides unless the preliminary biopsy has revealed a hopeless condition in one of the testes. On occasion, when the testicle

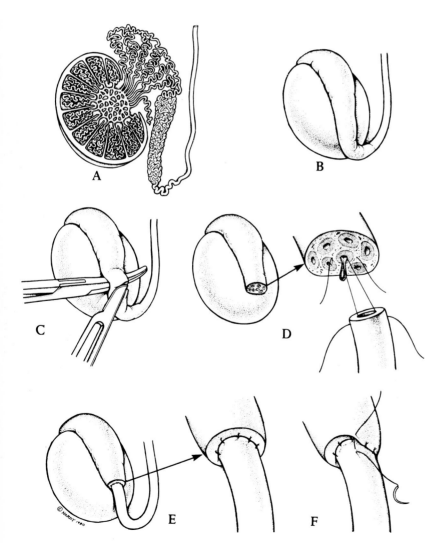

Fig. 13. Dubin and Amelar modification of epididymovasostomy. (*A* and *B*) Anatomy. (*C*) Epididymis is transected. (*D*) Tubule with sperm-rich fluid is identified. (*E* and *F*) Anastomosis. (Dubin L, Amelar RD: Magnified surgery of the vas deferens. In Reyniak JV, Lauersen NH (eds): Principles of Microsurgical Techniques in Infertility, pp 273–290. New YOrk, Plenum Press, 1982)

is normal on one side but its vas is occluded, and the opposite testicle is deficient but has a patent vas, a crossed anastomosis has been done successfully. In one such case the patient had unilateral testicular atrophy on the right side and an injured left vas incidental to a difficult low ureterolithotomy, resulting in sterility. At operation, the proximal left vas from the healthy testicle was anastomosed by crossover to the patent distal vas on the right side. He subsequently was found to have good semen quality and has since had two children.

In one case in which the point of obstruction on the right side appeared to be at the ejaculatory duct itself, an attempt was made to release the obstruction by forcible irrigation. All that we succeeded in accomplishing on this side was to blow up the seminal vesicle to enormous proportions, but the blue-tinted radiographic fluid still would not enter the bladder. The temporary seminal vesicle distention was confirmed by radiographic and rectal examinations immediately after the operative procedures. On the left side, however, there was congenital atresia of the epididymis and the convoluted lowermost segment of the vas; the remainder of the vas was patent. A crossed anastomosis was performed in this instance, and sperm were subsequently found in the ejaculum, but so far a pregnancy has not occurred.

When the anastomosis is successful, sperm may be found in the ejaculum within 3 to 6 mo, but occasionally it may require up to 1 yr before sperm appear. Periodic follow-up examination with semen analysis should be performed for at least 1 yr before it is determined that the procedure has not been successful.

In 1978 Silber proposed a new surgical approach to the problem of epididymal obstruction that may offer a much better prognosis than we have been able to achieve so far using the conventional technique we have just described.[28] The epidid-ymis is one tube 22 feet long coiled into a space 1½ inches long. After an incision is made into the epididymis, any sperm leaking out are indeed leaking out from only one of the many convolutions of the tube that has been cut. Careful inspection using magnification will reveal the specific epididymal tubule that is leaking sperm. Silber now employs a delicate micro-surgical technique to create an end-to-end anastomosis between the inner lumen of the vas and the one specific epididymal tubule after he has completely transected the vas and the epididymis.

We have modified Silber's technique of epididymovasostomy in our own practice and have used it with success, but it is too soon to cite our results with this technique. The concept of end-to-end anastomoses between the single leaking epididymal tubule and the vas seems to be an excellent one, and it offers hope for improved results. Our method is shown in Figure 13.

The testis is delivered as previously described. The distal vas is mobilized and cannulated. Dye or hydrogen peroxide is injected to prove distal patency. The epididymis is then transected. Observation with 6-power loupe or the microscope is now necessary to locate the tubule from which the sperm-containing fluid is flowing. The fluid should be checked for the presence of sperm with the light microscope if available. It is quite difficult to find the exact tubule, but one can locate the area of the epididymis from which the fluid is arising. Using magnification, an end-to-end anastomosis is performed using 6-0 Prolene® sutures. A second layer from the edge of the epididymis to the serosa of the vas can also then be performed. The testis is returned to the scrotum, and a Penrose drain is brought out through a stab wound. A pressure dressing is applied.

REFERENCES

1. Amelar RD, Dubin L: Frozen semen—a poor form of fertility insurance. Urology 14:53, 1979

2. Alexander NJ, Clarkson TB: Vasectomy increases the severity of diet induced atherosclerosis in macaca fascicularis. Science 201:538, 1978

3. Brueschke EE, Burns M, Maness JH, et al: Development of a reversible vas deferens occlusive device. I. Anatomical size of the human and dog vas deferens. Fertil Steril 25:659, 1974

4. Schmidt SS: Anastomosis of the vas deferens: An experimental study. II. Success and failures in experimental anastomosis. J Urol 81:203, 1959

5. Silber SJ: Vasectomy and vasectomy reversal. Fertil Steril 29:125, 1978

6. Stewart BH: Letter to the editor. Fertil Steril 29:472, 1978

7. Alexander NJ, Schmidt SS: Incidence of antisperm antibody levels and granulomas in men. Fertil Steril 28:655, 1977

8. Owen ER: Microsurgical vasovasostomy: A reliable vasectomy reversal. Aust NZ J Surg 47:305, 1977

9. O'Connor VJ: Anastomosis of the vas deferens after purposeful division for sterility. J Urol 59:229, 1948

10. Hulka JF, Davis JE: Vasectomy and reversible vasocclusion. Fertil Steril 23:683, 1972

11. Lee H: Technique and results of vasectomy in Korea. In Sciarra JJ (ed): Control of Male Fertility, pp 76–77. New York, Harper & Row, 1975

12. Middleton RG, Henderson D: Vas deferens reanastomosis without splints and without magnification. J Urol 119:763, 1978

13. Bunge RG: Bilateral spontaneous reanastomosis of the ductus deferens. J Urol 100:762, 1968

14. Blandy J: Vasectomy. Br J Hosp Med 9:319, 1973

15. Marshall S, Lyon RP: Transient reappearance of sperm after vasectomy. JAMA 219:1753, 1972

16. Schmidt SS: Technics and complications of elective vasectomy. The role of spermatic granuloma in spontaneous recanalization. Fertil Steril 17:467, 1966

17. Amelar RD, Dubin L, Walsh PC: Male Infertility. Philadelphia, WB Saunders, 1977

18. Phadke AM, Padukone K: Presence and significance of autoantibodies against spermatozoa in the blood of men with obstructed vas deferens. J Reprod Fertil 7:162, 1964

19. Rumke P: Sperm-agglutinating autoantibodies in relation to male infertility. Proc R Soc Med 61:275, 1968

20. Shulman S, Zappi E, Ahmed U, et al: Immunologic consequences of vasectomy. Contraception 5:269, 1972

21. Ansbacher R: Vasectomy: Sperm antibodies. Fertil Steril 24:788, 1973

22. Alexander NJ, Wilson BJ, Petterson GD: Vasectomy: Immunologic effects in rhesus monkeys and men. Fertil Steril 25:149, 1974

23. Alexander NS, Schmidt SS: Incidence of antisperm antibody levels and granulomas in men. Fertil Steril 28:655, 1977

24. Amelar RD, Dubin L, Schoenfeld C: Circulating sperm-agglutinating antibodies in azoospermic men with congenital bilateral absence of the vasa deferentia. Fertil Steril 26:228, 1975

25. Amelar RD, Alexander N, O'Connor VJ Jr, et al: Vasectomy reversal. Panel discussion presented at the annual meeting of the American Urological Association, Washington, DC, May 21–25, 1978

26. Phadke AM, Phadke AG: Experience in the reanastomosis of the vas deferens. J Urol 97:888, 1967

27. Hanley HG: The surgery of male subfertility. Ann R Coll Surg 17:159, 1955

28. Silber SJ: Microscopic vasoepididymostomy. Fertil Steril 30:565, 1978

125

PATHOLOGICAL ASPECTS OF THE INFERTILE TESTIS

Ting-Wa Wong, M.D., Ph.D.,* Francis H. Straus, M.D.,†
Thomas M. Jones., M.D., ‡ and
Nancy E. Warner, M.D.§

Urologic Clinics of North America—Vol. 5, No. 3, October 1978

In an age so preoccupied with the problem of birth control and the development of ever better contraceptives, it is an irony that a significant percentage of the married population is still suffering from an inability to procreate. In the United States, approximately 15 out of every 100 marriages are barren and do not produce progeny.[52] Defects in the husband's reproductive system are responsible for somewhat over 50 percent of the cases.[10] Male infertility is therefore a more prevalent problem than is perhaps appreciated generally.

Investigations into the pathogenesis of male infertility have relied predominantly on two types of analyses: histological evaluations of testicular biopsies and assays of those hormones thought to be responsible for the regulation of spermatogenesis. Many clinical syndromes of complete and partial gonadal dysfunction have been described based on combinations of histological and hormonal data. Other types of analysis such as chromosomal studies and biochemical determinations of ejaculate components have also played a role in characterizing male infertility.

CLASSIFICATION OF MALE INFERTILITY

Clinically, male infertility has been classified primarily on the basis of gonadotropin determinations. Depending on the levels of plasma gonadotropins, male infertility has been divided into three major categories: hypogonadotropic, hypergonadotropic, and normal gonadotropic. This essentially biochemical classification has been pivotal in clarifying in a broad sense the nature of the abnormalities encountered in the various types of infertile men.

Our experience in examining testicular biopsies for infertility studies in recent years has led us to believe that for the pathologist, a broad morphological-anatomical classification of male infertility paralleling the clinical-biochemical classification would be useful. Such a classification is presented in this review. It divides the different varieties of male infertility into three major categories: infertility due to pre-testicular, testicular, and post-testicular causes (Table 1).

An example of a pre-testicular cause of infertility is hypogonadotropism, whether of prepubertal or of postpubertal onset. As a result of the deficiency in

*Associate Professor, Department of Pathology, The University of Chicago, Chicago, Illinois.

†Associate Professor, Department of Pathology, The University of Chicago, Chicago, Illinois.

‡Assistant Professor, Department of Medicine, The University of Chicago, Chicago, Illinois.

§Professor and Chairman, Department of Pathology, University of Southern California, Los Angeles, California.

Supported in part by Grant CA 19265 from the National Cancer Institute.

TABLE 1. Classification of the Causes of Male Infertility

Pre-testicular causes
  Hypogonadotropism
    Prepubertal onset
    Postpubertal onset
  Estrogen excess
    Endogenous
      Estrogen-producing tumor (of the adrenal cortex, for example)
      Cirrhosis of the liver
    Exogenous
  Androgen excess
    Endogenous
      Adrenogenital syndrome
      Androgen-producing tumor
    Exogenous
  Glucocorticoid excess
    Endogenous
      Cushing's syndrome
    Exogenous
      Treatment for ulcerative colitis
      Treatment for chronic asthma
  Hypothyroidism
  Diabetes mellitus
Testicular causes
  Maturation arrest
  Hypospermatogenesis (proportional hypoplasia of all germ cells)
  Absence of germ cells (Sertoli-cell-only syndrome)
  Klinefelter's syndrome
  Other sex chromosomal anomalies and disorders of sex differentiation
  Cryptorchism
  Irradiation damage
  Mumps orchitis
Post-testicular causes
  Block of ducts leading away from the testes
    Congenital
      Atresia of the vas deferens or epididymis
    Acquired
      Infection
        Gonorrheal epididymitis
        Tuberculous epididymitis
        Others
      Vas ligation
        Voluntary
        Iatrogenic
  Impaired motility (sperm counts adequate, testicular biopsies normal; impaired sperm motility presumably due to faulty maturation or defective storage of spermatoza in the epididymides, or due to biochemical abnormalities of the seminal plasma)

TABLE 2. Causes of Male Infertility as Studied by Testicular Biopsy—A 20-Year Series at The University of Chicago

Causes	Number of Cases	Percent of Total Cases
Pre-testicular	15	10.7
Testicular	105	75.0
Post-testicular	20	14.3
Total	140	100.0

TABLE 3. Relative Frequencies of the Different Testicular Causes of Infertility in Our Series

Conditions	Number of Cases
Maturation arrest	45
Hypospermatogenesis	32
Absence of germ cells	11
Klinefelter's syndrome	7
Cryptorchism	
Unilateral	3
Bilateral	2
Irradiation damage	3
Mumps orchitis	2
Total	105

The posttesticular causes of infertility consist mainly of obstructions of the ducts leading away from the testes. Cases in which the spermatozoa are normal in number but greatly impaired in motility, presumably due to imperfect maturation of defective storage of the spermatozoa during their sojourn in the epididymides, or due to biochemical abnormalities of the seminal plasma (the nonspermatozoal portion of the semen), are also included in the post-testicular category.

In the remainder of this review, the pathological findings of testicular biopsies from patients with various causes of infertility will be presented. The cases were derived from a 20-year series of testicular biopsies performed at the University of Chicago for infertility studies or in association with orchiopexy for cryptorchism, the details of which have been reported elsewhere.[55–56]

TESTICULAR CAUSES OF INFERTILITY

As shown in Table 2, fully 75 percent of the cases of male infertility in our series belong to the testicular category. The conditions included in this group are listed in order of decreasing, frequencies in Table 3. They will be described in turn.

For reference, a section of normal adult testis is shown in Figure 1, showing the approximate size of the tubules and the thickness of the germinal epithelium. Because spermatogenesis normally proceeds in waves along the seminiferous tubules, various cell types may

gonadotropins, the testes fail secondarily. An excess of circulating estrogen, whether associated with an estrogen-producing tumor of the adrenal cortex, with cirrhosis of the liver, or with exogenous estrogen therapy, can also lead to suppressed gonadotropin production by the pituitary and secondary testicular failure, although an additional direct gonad-inhibiting action by the estrogen cannot be excluded. An excess of circulating androgen, whether endogenous or exogenous in nature, similarly has been shown to lead to secondary failure of the testes via its suppressive action on the pituitary. In short, any extra-gonadal endocrine disorder leading to defective spermatogenesis may be grouped under the pre-testicular causes of infertility.

The testicular causes of infertility are conditions in which the primary defects reside in the testes.

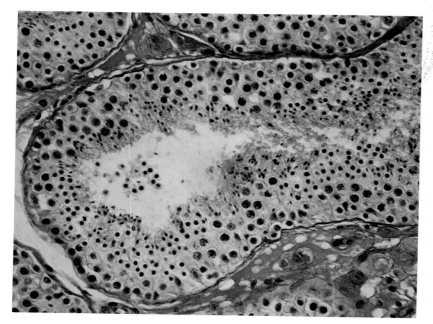

Fig. 1. Normal testis showing spermatogenesis proceeding in waves of activity along a tubule, with various cell types predominating in different portions of the circumference of the lumen. Thus, spermatozoa predominate at some stretches and spermatids at other stretches. Note the approximate diameter of the tubule and the thickness of the germinal epithelium. (Hematoxylin-eosin, ×250)

predominate in different portions of the circumference of the lumen. Thus, one may find many sperm heads embedded in Sertoli cytoplasm in one area and spermatids or spermatocytes in another area. On the whole, however, spermatozoa can be found in the majority of the tubules at the level of section in any normal adult testis.

Maturation Arrest. The most prevalent condition under the testicular causes of infertility in our series is maturation arrest (Table 3). Maturation arrest is a halt at some stage of spermatogenesis, an example of which is shown in Figure 2. In this biopsy, spermatogenesis stops abruptly with the formation of primary spermatocytes; scarcely any secondary spermatocytes, spermatids, or spermatozoa are present. The point of arrest is, as illustrated in this instance, reasonably constant in the individual biopsy, but varies from one patient to another. Failure of spermatogenesis to reach its usual conclusion appears to be the only defect in the testes. No abnormalities are detectable in the Sertoli cells, the tunica propria of the seminiferous tubules, or the Leydig cells. The diameter of the tubules is essentially normal.

Another point at which maturation arrest often occurs is the spermatid stage, with few spermatozoa formed.

Clinically, patients with maturation arrest in spermatogenesis are oligospermic or azoospermic, depending on the extent of the arrest. Plasma follicle-stimulating hormone (FSH) is often within normal limits, but may be elevated in severe maturation arrest, particularly when the arrest occurs at the spermatogonial or primary spermatocyte stage.[11] Plasma luteinizing hormone (LH) and testosterone are usually normal.

Hypospermatogenesis. The second most prevalent condition under the testicular causes of infertility in our series is hypospermatogenesis, or proportional hypoplasia of all germ cells. In this condition, all cell types, including spermatogonia, spermatocytes, spermatids, and spermatozoa, are present in approximately the usual proportion, but the number of each variety is decreased. The consequence of such a proportional hypoplasia is an overall thinning of the germinal epithelium, as shown in Figure 3. In contrast to maturation arrest, however, spermatogenesis does complete itself in the usual fashion in this condition. In most instances, some spermatozoa can be found. The tunica propria of the tubules is generally not thickened, and the Sertoli cells and Leydig cells are morphologically normal. The diameter of the tubules is within normal limits.

Clinically, patients with hypospermatogenesis are usually oligospermic. The majority of them have normal plasma FSH, LH, and testosterone.[10]

Absence of Germ Cells (Sertoli-Cell-Only Syndrome). In this disorder, the testicular tubules show a moderate decrease in diameter and are devoid of germ cells; they are lined by Sertoli cells exclusively, hence the other name for this condition, Sertoli-cell-only syndrome (Fig. 4). The cytoplasm of the Sertoli cells often contains a large number of fat vacuoles. Generally, there is no

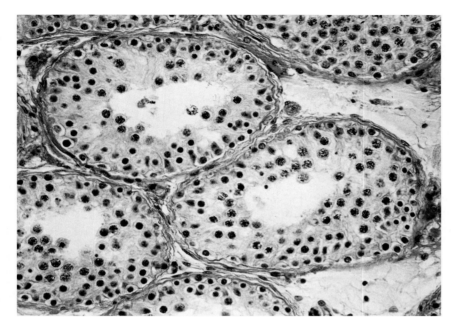

Fig. 2. Biopsy showing maturation arrest in spermatogenesis. In this instance, maturation stops abruptly at the primary spermatocyte stage; no secondary spermatocyte, spermatids, or spermatozoa are formed. The diameter of the tubules is within normal limits. This biopsy is from a 31-year-old man working in a petroleum cracking plant, with long-term exposure to gasoline, fuel oil, and other petroleum products, as well as litharge. (Hematoxylin-eosin, ×250)

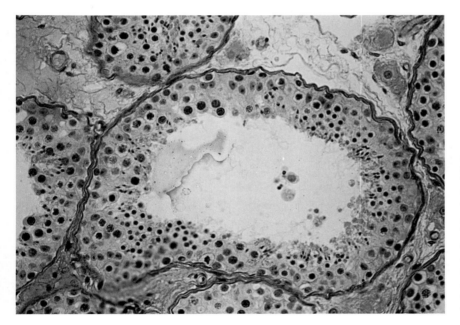

Fig. 3. Biopsy showing hypospermatogenesis. Note overall thinning of the germinal epithelium owing to proportional hypoplasia of all germ cells (compare with Fig. 1). Despite the thinning of the germinal epithelium, spermatogenesis does complete itself in the usual fashion, and a small number of spermatozoa can be found. The diameter of the tubules and the Leydig cells are usually normal. This is from a 27-year-old steelmill worker with daily exposure to high temperatures. (Hematoxylin-eosin, ×250)

thickening of the tunica propria of the tubules, and the Leydig cells appear normal.

In a rare biopsy, one or several tubules may contain some residual germ cells in various stages of maturation, amidst a lawn of tubules lined only by Sertoli cells (Fig. 5).

Clinically, patients afflicted with Sertoli-cell-only syndrome usually have well-developed secondary sex characteristics. The testes are somewhat decreased in size. Azoospermia on repeated semen analyses is the rule, although an occasional patient may have a few spermatozoa in the semen, corresponding to the rare tubules with some preserved germ cells seen in an occasional biopsy. Most patients have normal plasma

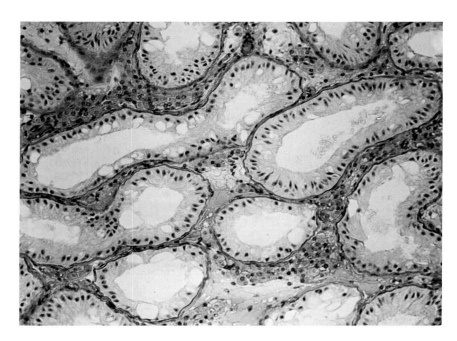

Fig. 4. Biopsy showing absence of germ cells. The seminiferous tubules are lined by Sertoli cells exclusively, hence the other name for this condition, Sertoli-cell-only syndrome. Many of the Sertoli cells have prominent cytoplasmic vacuoles. The tubular diameter is decreased. The Leydig cells appear normal. This biopsy is from a 29-year-old man with azoospermia but normal secondary sex characteristics. (Hematoxylin-eosin, ×150)

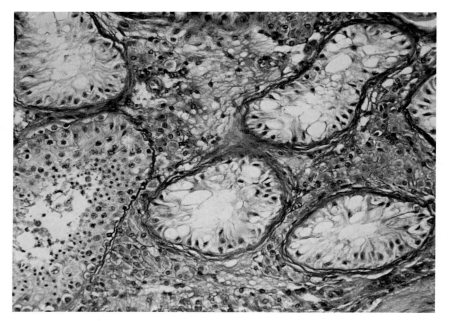

Fig. 5. An occasional testicular biopsy from patients with Sertoli-cell-only syndrome may have a rare tubule with preserved germ cells amidst a multitude of tubules lined only by Sertoli cells, as illustrated here. This biopsy is from a 28-year-old man with normal secondary sex characteristics, chromatin-negative buccal smear, and severe oligospermia bordering on azoospermia. (Hematoxylin-eosin, ×170)

LH and testosterone, indicating adequate Leydig cell function, but the plasma FSH is almost always elevated as a response to the absence or near absence of spermatogenesis.[10]

Klinefelter's Syndrome. The testis in classical Klinefelter's syndrome shows a progressive failure of spermatogenesis, accompanied by tubular sclerosis and a marked increase in the number of Leydig cells (Fig. 6). The earliest derangement is a reduction in spermatogenic activity, leading to gradual disappearance of the germ cells. In time, the loss of germ cells is followed by atrophy of the Sertoli cells and thickening of the tunica propria. Finally, both the germ cells and Sertoli cells

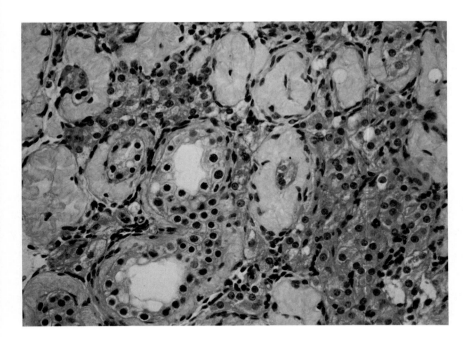

Fig. 6. Testicular biopsy from a 20-year-old man with Klinefelter's syndrome. A few tubules have sparse germ cells, atrophic Sertoli cells, and thickened, hyalinized, and contracted tunica propria. All tubules are markedly decreased in diameter. The Leydig cells are prominent and appear considerably increased in number focally. (Hematoxylin-eosin, ×250)

are absent, and the lumens of the tubules are obliterated by thickened, hyalinized, and contracted tunica propria. By this series of events, the tubules are converted into shrunken collagenous cords. At first, these changes do not affect all tubules equally, and indeed, in the early stage of the syndrome, the testicular involvement is uneven and patchy, with tubules in the same biopsy showing markedly different degrees of change. But ultimately the entire testis is sclerosed. The Leydig cells are characteristically increased in number, and often present a strikingly hyperplastic appearance.

The clinical signs of Klinefelter's syndrome generally appear sometime after puberty, when the intrinsically abnormal testes, unable to respond to pituitary gonadotropin stimulation, begin to undergo the typical pathological changes.[3] They fail to increase in size but instead become firmer and smaller because of progressive sclerosis of the seminiferous tubules. Leydig cell function is impaired to varying degrees despite the hyperplastic appearance of these cells seen on testicular biopsy. If plasma testosterone is low, the patient exhibits incomplete development of the secondary sex characteristics, a eunuchoid appearance, and gynecomastia. If plasma testosterone is normal or near normal, there is full development of the secondary sex characteristics. Semen analysis typically reveals azoospermia. Plasma FSH is characteristically high, reflecting the loss of germ cells. Plasma LH is similarly elevated, even in those patients with normal testosterone levels, and suggests an abnormality in the testosterone-LH feedback mechanism.[5,27]

In the classical form of Klinefelter's syndrome, the patient exhibits an XXY chromosomal pattern.

Cryptorchism. Cryptorchism has multiple causes. In some instances, a testis fails to descend into the scrotum because of a malformation of the fasciae of the inguinal canal, mechanically preventing descent. In other instances, the maldescent is due to insufficient gonadotropin stimulation, and in these cases, administration of gonadotropins or the normal onset of puberty may cause the testis to descend and develop properly. In still other instances, cryptorchism appears to be due to some inherent defect in the testis, uncomplicated by defective pituitary function. This inherent defect often exhibits itself in the form of germ cell hypoplasia.[6,19] It is this last variety of cryptorchism that is included in the testicular causes of infertility. All the patients with cryptorhism in our series had failed to respond to gonadotropin treatment before orchiopexy, and no anatomical abnormality of the inguinal canal was found during the surgical procedure. Because of the germ cell hypoplasia inherent in such cryptorchid testes, orchiopexy seldom brings about normal spermatogenesis in such cases, even when the orchiopexy is performed well before puberty.[6]

Histologically, a cryptorchid testis has small immature tubules with varying numbers of spermatogonia, depending in part on the severity of the intrinsic germ cell hypoplasia and in part on how long the testis has remained in the undescended position. After puberty,

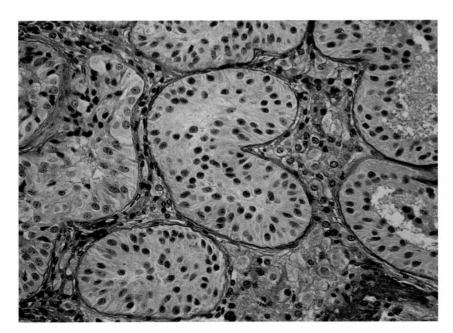

Fig. 7. Biopsy of a cryptorchid testis obtained during orchiopexy from a 15-year-old youth with bilateral cryptorchism that had failed to respond to gonadotropin administration. Note virtual absence of germ cells. The tubules are lined by Sertoli cells only. There is as yet no thickening of the tunica propria or tubular sclerosis. The Leydig cells are somewhat prominent. (Hematoxylin-eosin, ×250)

the germ cells in a cryptorchid testis gradually disappear until the tubules are lined by Sertoli cells only (Fig. 7). Later, the tubules become hyalinized and sclerotic. The Leydig cells, which are relatively resistant to elevated temperatures, develop properly as a result of gonadotropin stimulation and are often more prominent than usual. In some instances, the Leydig cells-show marked cytoplasmic vacuolation.

Clinically, patients with bilateral cryptorchism in the postpubertal period may have normal plasma LH and testosterone, indicating adequate Leydig cell function. But plasma FSH is increased, reflecting the loss of germ cells and the absence of spermatogenesis.

Irradiation Damage. Exposure to radiation above certain levels leads to permanent germ cell destruction. In contrast, Leydig cells are far more resistant.

Histologically, the germ cells undergo degeneration and are eventually lost. The tubules are lined by Sertoli cells only. Their diameter becomes smaller and their tunica propria is progressively thickened. In time, there is total sclerosis of the tubules. The Leydig cells are usually preserved.

Clinically, the patients are oligospermic or azoospermic. Plasma FSH is increased as a consequence of the loss of germ cells, but since the Leydig cells are usually preserved, plasma LH and testosterone are within normal limits.

A similar pattern of germ cell loss is seen in patients who have undergone prolonged chemotherapy for various lymphomas.[51]

Mumps Orchitis. Biopsies performed at one time on patients suffering from acute mumps orchitis revealed that at this stage, there is interstitial edema, mononuclear and leukocytic inflammatory infiltrate, and degeneration and sloughing of germ cells.[8]

After the acute inflammation has subsided, there are progressive chronic changes consisting of loss of germ cells and tubular hyalinization and sclerosis. Because of the progressive nature of the chronic changes, the full extent of the damage may not become apparent until 10 to 20 years after the acute infection.[40] Involvement is not uniform throughout the testis; some tubules are more affected than others. The Leydig cells seem by comparison far less susceptible than the germ cells to the action of the mumps virus and are usually preserved; often they are more prominent than usual, though seldom as striking as in Klinefelter's syndrome. A past history of acute mumps orchitis is necessary to confirm the histological diagnosis.

When the loss of germ cells is extensive, plasma FHS is increased. Generally, plasma LH and testosterone are normal, reflecting the preservation of Leydig cells.

Comments Regarding the Testicular Causes of Infertility. The testicular causes of infertility are essentially primary defects of the testis. Among such causes, maturation arrest and hypospermatogenesis represent the two most common conditions in our series; together they account for some 55 percent of the total cases. The patients so afflicted generally have no manifestations of extra-gonadal endocrine disorders, and no evidence of anatomical block is found on vasogram. The only abnormality seems to be a defect of spermatogenesis demonstrable on testicular biopsy, in the form of maturation arrest or hypospermatogenesis. For this reason, we have placed these cases in the testicular category. At present, they are the least understood of the conditions leading to male infertility, but unfortunately constitute the largest proportions of the cases. Most likely, there are a multitude of etiological factors that can lead to maturation arrest and hypospermatogenesis. A small number of the cases are potentially caused by noxious environmental agents, which may be chemical or physical. Among the chemical agents that have been implicated are various toxic industrial fumes, insecticides, and drugs.[29,55] Prominent among the harmful physical agents is heat. That heat has a detrimental influence on spermatogenesis is undoubted, as attested to by the degeneration of germ cells in cryptorchid testes, by the temporary or permanent sterility following prolonged febrile illness,[36] and by the reduction of sperm counts in normal men subjected to artificial fever.[31] Histologically, maturation arrest, as well as hypospermatogenesis of varying severity, has been reported as a consequence of exposure to elevated temperatures.[36] It is of interest that a number of patients in our series suffering from maturation arrest or hypospermatogenesis are steelmill workers or bakers whose occupations cause them to be exposed daily to the high-temperature environment of blast furnaces or baking ovens; a few other patients have well-documented severe and prolonged antecedent febrile illness.[55] Certain instances of hypospermatogenesis are associated with the presence of varicocele.[15] Excluding the above examples, however, there still remain a vast number of cases in which the maturation arrest or hypospermatogenesis has no obvious cause.

The disorder known as absence of germ cells or Sertoli-cell-only syndrome, despite having been recognized for three decades, has remained an enigma. Failure of migration of germ cells from the yolk sac entoderm into the embryonic gonads was initially proposed as the cause of this condition.[13] This theory, while attractive, lacks proof. Recently, there have been reports linking the Sertoli-cell-only syndrome with an XYY chromosomal anomaly.[45,53] The overall frequency of such an association will not be known until more testicular biopsies are subjected to chromosomal analysis in the future. Finally, ultrastructural abnormalities of the Sertoli cells have been reported in patients afflicted with this syndrome,[9] but whether such abnormalities play a role in the genesis of the disorder is not known.

In our present classification, Klinefelter's syndrome and other chromosomal disorders have been placed under the testicular category of infertility (Table 1). The reason for this is twofold. First, the plasma gonadotropins in these patients are generally high, indicating that the primary defects are in the testes. Second, there are variant forms of Klinefelter's syndrome that are now known to be due to chromosomal mosaicism, in which there is more than one stem cell line, as for example the coexistence of XY and XXY chromosomal patterns in the same individual.[40,41] The clinical and pathological manifestations in these instances depend largely on what tissue or tissues contain the abnormal stem cell line. Available data indicate that the presence of abnormal numbers of X chromosomes in the testicular tissue is the basis for the pathological changes observed in the seminiferous tubules and Leydig cells in Klinefelter's syndrome. Chromosomal analysis of the skin and peripheral blood from the same patient may reveal a normal sex chromosomal pattern, but if the testes contain a supernumerary X chromosomal complement, testicular dysgenesis typical for Klinefelter's syndrome develops.[40,41] The grouping of Klinefelter's syndrome under the testicular causes of infertility is therefore justified. The same may be said of other chromosomal disorders with testicular involvement.

As a group, the testicular causes of infertility offer little hope for treatment at the present, because the loss of germ cells accompanying most of these disorders is primarily irreversible. Maturation arrest and hypospermatogenesis, the two conditions in which the germ cells are by comparison far better preserved, have been treated empirically with hormone therapy, but the incidence of success is relatively low,[29] which is probably a reflection of the fact that the etiological mechanisms underlying most of these cases are not known; hence rational design of therapy is not possible. An exception to this pessimistic outlook is the hypospermatogenesis observed in patients with varicocele. While the mechanism by which varicocele exerts its deleterious effect on spermatogenesis is still open to question, it is indisputable that varicocelectomy leads to reversal of infertility in a high proportion of the cases.[14,25]

PRE-TESTICULAR CAUSES OF INFERTILITY

As shown in Table 2, 10.7 percent of the cases of male infertility in our series belong to the pre-testicular category. The various conditions included in the pre-testicular causes of infertility and their relative frequencies in our series are listed in Table 4.

Hypogonadotropism. Paramount among the pre-testicular causes of infertility is hypogonadotropism. Although the end result is testicular failure regardless of the cause of the gonadotropin insufficiency, it is important to separate cases of hypogonadotropism into those of prepubertal onset and those of postpubertal onset, since the two types of cases have entirely different morphological characteristics on testicular biopsies, depending on whether the gonads have undergone the normal development associated with proper gonadotropin stimulation at the time of puberty. As expected, the two types of cases also have different clinical presentation and prognosis.

TABLE 4. Relative Frequencies of the Different Pre-testicular Causes of Infertility in Our Series

Conditions	Number of Cases
Hypogonadotropism	
Prepubertal onset	
Craniopharyngiomas	1
Hypogonadotropic eunuchoidism	
Deficiency of FSH and LH	0
Deficiency of LH	2
Deficiency of FSH	0
Postpubertal onset	
Chromophobe adenoma	4
Estrogen excess	
Endogenous	
Tumor of adrenal cortex	1
Unknown source	4
Exogenous	0
Androgen excess	
Endogenous	0
Exogenous	0
Glucocorticoid excess	
Endogenous	0
Exogenous	
Treatment for ulcerative colitis	1
Hypothyroidism	1
Diabetes mellitus	1
Total	15

These patients were lost to follow-up before the source of their endogenous estrogen excess could be determined.

Prepubertal Hypogonadotropism. Patients with hypogonadotropism of prepubertal onset have small, immature seminiferous tubules resembling those seen in a prepubertal testis (Fig. 8). They are lined by essentially undifferentiated germinal elements and immature Sertoli cells. There is little evidence of maturation of germ cells beyond the stage of spermatogonium or primary spermatocyte. The tunica propria of the tubules is thin and delicate. As in the prepubertal testis, there are no peritubular elastic fibers demonstrable with special stains, since the development of such elastic fibers occurs only with proper stimulation by pituitary gonadotropins at puberty.[12] The Leydig cells are immature and poorly developed. They resemble undifferentiated mesenchymal cells.

Clinically, the gonadal failure arising from prepubertal hypogonadotropism may be caused by organic lesions in or adjacent to the pituitary, or due to genetic defects in gonadotropin secretion (Table 4).

The organic lesions include tumors, cysts, or trauma of the sella turcica or suprasellar area. Patients with such lesions eventually suffer from panhypopituitarism and exhibit sexual infantilism, lack of somatic growth, and varying degrees of thyroid and adrenal dysfunction.

By contrast, patients with genetic defects in gonadotropin secretion are generally tall and eunuchoid and exhibit no signs of deficiency of growth hormone, thyrotropin, or adrenocorticotropin. Hence the clinical syndrome embodied by such patients is referred to as hypogonadotropic eunuchoidism.[46,47] Characteristically, no organic lesion is demonstrable in or about the pituitary

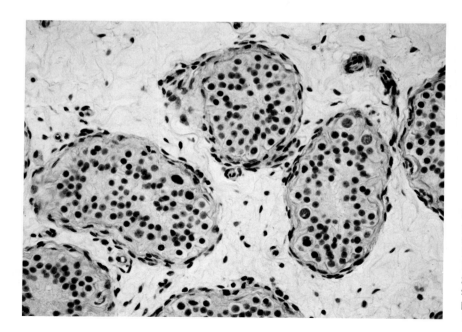

Fig. 8. Testicular biopsy from a 30-year-old man with hypogonadotropic eunuchoidism. The seminiferous tubules are small and immature. They are lined by Sertoli cells and spermatogonia; some of the latter are of giant size. Leydig cells are scarce and appear undeveloped. (Hematoxylin-eosin, ×250)

despite repeated searches. The syndrome is often associated with other congenital anomalies such as anosmia, harelip, cleft palate, and carniofacial asymmetry.[28,40] The patients show a deficiency of both FSH and LH and give a history of never having undergone a normal puberty. They are eunuchoid in build, with long legs, sparse facial and body hair, high-pitched voice, poor muscular development, small genitalia, and no ejaculations. Their testicular biopsies present a picture reminiscent of a prepubertal testis.[40,57] Recent reports indicate that in hypogonadotropic eunuchoidism, the primary abnormality may not reside in the pituitary but rather in the hypothalamus, and consists of a deficiency of LH-releasing hormone, a decapeptide of hypothalamic origin that has the ability to stimulate output of both LH and FSH by the pituitary.[54,58]

In an infrequent variant of hypogonadotropic eunuchoidism, FSH secretion is normal, but LH output is deficient to varying degrees. The amount of LH secreted by such patients, while insufficient to sustain a normal level of androgen production and to bring about full pubertal development of secondary sex characteristics, is apparently sufficient to assist FSH in promoting spermatogenesis to varying extents, so that spermatozoa are actually found in the seminal fluid of some such patients. For this reason, they are referred to as "fertile eunuchs."[35,40] Their testicular biopsies show a greater degree of development in the seminiferous tubules than in the Leydig cells.[57]

In the most recently reported variant of hypogonadotropic eunuchoidism, there is isolated FSH deficiency, associated with abnormal spermatogenesis, but since the plasma LH and testosterone are normal, the patients are well masculinized.[33]

Postpubertal Hypogonadotropism. If hypogonadotropism occurs in the postpubertal period, the seminiferous tubules, having once attained the full development associated with a normal puberty, do not revert to the prepubertal state. Instead, they show in succession maturation arrest, loss of germ cells, reduction in diameter, and progressive thickening and hyalinization of the tunica propria (Fig. 9). In time, the tubules are transformed into hyalinized collagenous cords. Special stains show that elastic fibers are present around these sclerotic tubules (Fig. 10), indicating that the tubules have been subjected previously to the normal stimulation by pituitary gonadotropins. The Leydig cells are generally shrivelled and inconspicuous; they often contain lipochrome pigment in their cytoplasm but scarcely any crystalloids of Reinke.

Clinically, the gonadal failure resulting from postpubertal hypogonadotropism may be due to space-occupying lesions in or near the pituitary, such as chromophobe adenomas and craniopharyngiomas. Acidophilic adenomas, which are generally accompanied by decreased gonadotropin secretion, similarly lead to hypogonadism (Figs. 9 and 10). Trauma to the pituitary fossa, as in basal fracture of the skull, can also lead to hypopituitarism and gonadal failure.

Estrogen Excess. Estrogen excess acts primarily by suppressing pituitary gonadotropin secretion,[30] leading to secondary testicular failure.[57]

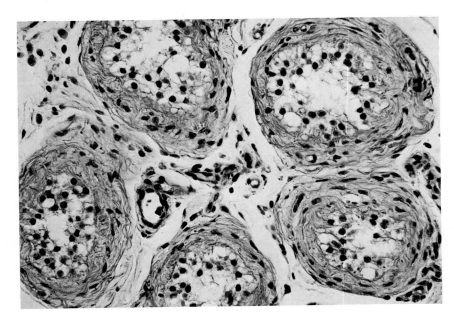

Fig. 9. Testicular atrophy in a 51-year-old man with an acidophilic adenoma of the pituitary, first discovered at age 39 and treated by x-irradiation, following which he developed panhypopituitarism. This patient was not from out biopsy series but is included here to illustrate the extent of loss of germ cells, seminiferous tubular sclerosis, and Leydig cell atrophy that postpubertal hypopituitarism is capable of causing. Only Sertoli cells persist in the tubules. (Hematoxylin-eosin, ×250)

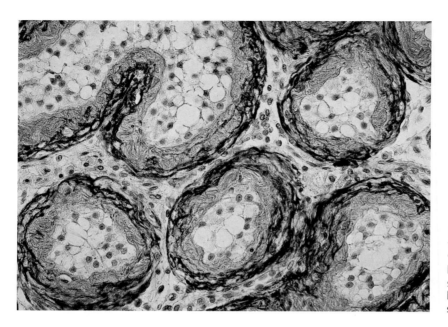

Fig. 10. Wiegert-Van Gieson stain of the same section of testis shown in Fig. 9. Elastic fibers (appearing as wavy black lines) are present around the sclerotic tubules, indicating that the tubular changes are postpubertal in onset. ($\times$250)

Endogenous estrogen excess may be associated with hepatic cirrhosis.[24] The excess may also be due to an estrogen-producing tumor, such as that originating in the adrenal cortex. A Sertoli cell tumor or interstitial cell tumor of the testis may also be estrogen-producing on occasions. Finally, administration of exogenous estrogen, as in patients with carcinoma of the prostate, similarly leads to testicular failure (Fig. 11), although such patients are seldom seen in infertility clinics.

Pathologically, the above disorders of estrogen excess, which occurs predominantly in the postpubertal period, lead initially to failure in germ cell maturation, followed by progressive thinning of the germinal epithelium, decrease in diameter of the seminiferous tubules, and thickening and hyalinization of the tunica propria. In time, there is complete sclerosis of the tubules. The Leydig cells are atrophied. These findings are identical to those caused by postpubertal hypogonadotropism, as anticipated from the mode of pathogenesis.

Androgen Excess. Androgen excess, like estrogen excess, acts by suppression of pituitary gonadotropin secretion, leading to testicular failure.[4,34]

Endogenous excess of androgen may be associated with the different biochemical variants of adrenogenital syndrome. In one such variant, a defect in 21-hydroxylation of adrenal steroids leads to reduced cortisol synthesis, which stimulates excessive adrenocorticotropic hormone (ACTH) production by the pituitary; a consequence of the latter is increased production of 17-ketosteroids by the adrenal cortex.[26] Such a surfeit of androgenic steroids leads to premature development of the secondary sex characteristics and abnormal enlargement of the phallus (virilism). The testes, however, do not mature and remain in the prepubertal state because of inhibition of pituitary gonadotropin secretion by the excess androgens. A much rarer biochemical variant of the adrenogenital syndrome, that of 11-hydroxylase deficiency, leads to virilism and hypogonadism by the same mechanism.[26] Treatment of the gonadal problems in both disorders consists of suppression of the excess ACTH secretion by cortisol.

Endogenous excess of androgen may also be due to an androgen-producing tumor of the adrenal cortex or the testis. The pathological findings in the testes depend on whether the tumor exists before or after puberty. If it is present prepubertally, virilism and failure of the testes to mature are the results. On the other hand, if the tumor develops postpubertally, the testes will undergo progressive loss of germ cells and tubular sclerosis; unless the androgenic tumor is eradicated before all spermatogonia are lost, no recovery is possible.

Exogenous excess of androgen behaves in a similar fashion as endogenous excess by inhibiting the pituitary.[4,34]

Glucocorticoid Excess. Glucocorticoid excess, whether endogenous as in Cushing's syndrome, or exogenous as in treatment for ulcerative colitis, rheumatoid arthritis, or bronchial asthma, can lead to decreased fertility, which is manifested by oligospermia on semen analysis and maturation arrest or hypospermatogenesis on testic-

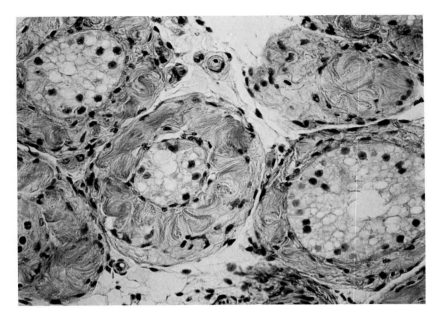

Fig. 11. The extent of damage that can be caused by estrogen excess is illustrated in this orchiectomy specimen for a 68-year-old man treated with stilbestrol for carcinoma of the prostate. The loss of germ cells, tubular sclerosis, and Leydig cell atrophy are similar to those caused by postpubertal hypopituitarism as illustrated in Fig. 9. This patient was not from out biopsy series. (Hematoxylin-eosin, ×250)

ular biopsy.[21,32,57] Improvement in sperm counts and fertility is observed when the glucocorticoid excess is corrected.

Hypothyroidism. Patients with proven hypothyroidism may have reduced fertility.[7] On testicular biopsy, the only abnormality appears to be a thinning of the germinal epithelium.[57] When thyroxine is supplied, fertility is often restored in such cases.[7]

Diabetes Mellitus. Patients with diabetes mellitus may have diminished fertility because of arteriosclerosis of the testicular arteries or their tributaries, leading to thinning of the germinal epithelium and thickening of the tunica propria of the seminiferous tubules. More commonly, however, the problem is one of impotence or retrograde ejaculation due to autonomic neuropathy associated with diabetes.[2]

Comments Regarding the Pre-testicular Causes of Infertility. The pre-testicular causes of infertility are endocrine problems primarily; hence any effective treatment must aim at removing such endocrine abnormalities. In recent years, the major share of the attention has been directed at patients afflicted with hypogonadotropic eunuchoidism, in whom the testes lie dormant indefinitely in the prepubertal state. Full spermatogenesis and fertility can be brought about by sustained treatment with chorionic gonadotropin (which mimics LH) and human menopausal gonadotropin (a preparation rich in FSH) to overcome the permanent endogenous deficiency of gonadotropic hormones.[43] Other pre-testicular causes of infertility, such as tumors in or about the pituitary, can be treated by surgery or radiation, and the accompanying hypogonadism or hypopituitarism may be remedied by hormone replacement therapy.[43] Testicular biopsy is of particular value in selecting patients who will respond to gonadotropin therapy. Other endocrine imbalances, such as those resulting from adrenal tumors or hyperplasia, may be eradicated surgically in certain instances, with restoration of fertility.

POST-TESTICULAR CAUSES OF INFERTILITY

As shown in Table 2, 14.3 percent of the cases of male infertility in our series belong to the post-testicular category. The various conditions which make up the post-testicular causes of infertility and their relative frequencies in our series are listed in Table 5.

Block of Ducts Leading Away from the Testes. Foremost in importance among the post-testicular causes of infertility is obstruction of the ducts leading away from the testes. The obstruction may be congenital or acquired.

Congenital Block. Congenital block is usually due to atresia of the vas deferens or the epididymis (Table 5). When bilateral, the atresia leads to azoospermia and sterility. Failure of anatomical union between the vas and the epididymis or between the testis and the epididymis has also been reported by others[39,49] but has not been observed in our series.

Acquired Block. The acquired obstructions are either due to infection or surgical interruption (Table 5).

Among the infectious causes, gonorrheal epididymitis is the most common; obstruction in such instances occurs most frequently in the tail of the epididymis and the adjacent proximal portion of the vas. Because of its tendency to be bilateral, azoospermia and sterility is a frequent sequela. Tuberculous epididymitis is another infectious disorder that may lead to sterility; the epididymal involvement usually follows a prostatic or seminal vesicle lesion, the scarring is apt to involve the vasa, seminal vesicles, and ejaculatory ducts in addition to the epididymides. Nonspecific pyogenic infections, often originating from a recalcitrant bacterial prostatitis, can also lead to scarring of the vas deferens and epididymis.

Surgical occlusion of the vas may be voluntary, as for contraceptive purposes, or iatrogenic; in which case the vas is inadvertently ligated during such surgical procedure as inguinal herniorrhaphy or correction of hydrocele or varicocele. Inadvertent bilateral vas ligation leads to sterility.

On testicular biopsy, regardless of the etiology, obstruction of the vas deferens or epididymis per se has no adverse effect on the germinal epithelium or the Leydig cells, as observed repeatedly by others.[1,37] and ourselves.[56] In cases of obstruction due to infection, if there is no accompanying orchitis, the germinal epithelium is preserved (Fig. 12). Similarly, in cases of surgical occlusion of the vas, unless some vasculature of the testis is ligated or transected simultaneously, the germinal epithelium is unaffected (Fig. 13). The preservation of the germinal epithelium appears to be due to the remarkable ability of the epididymis to become enlarged to accommodate the products of germ cell activity and its striking capacity in phagocytizing and resorbing disintegrated spermatozoa.[37,42] Clinically, the epididymal tubules are characteristically dilated proximal to a congenital or postinflammatory obstruction or following surgical interruption of the vas. An equilibrium is apparently established between the rate of spermatogenesis on the one hand, and epididymal enlargement, sperm flow, storage, and resorption on the other. Occasionally, slight dilatation of the seminiferous tubules and hypo-

TABLE 5. Relative Frequencies of the Different Post-testicular Causes of Infertility in Our Series

Conditions	Number of Cases
Block	
Congenital	
Atresia of vasa deferentia	3
Atresia of epididymides	2
Acquired	
Infection	
Gonorrhea	4
Tuberculosis	2
Nonspecific pyogenic	2
Surgical interruption of vasa deferentia	
Voluntary	1
Iatrogenic	1
Cause undetermined	2
Impaired sperm motility	3
(sperm count and testicular biopsy normal)	
Total	20

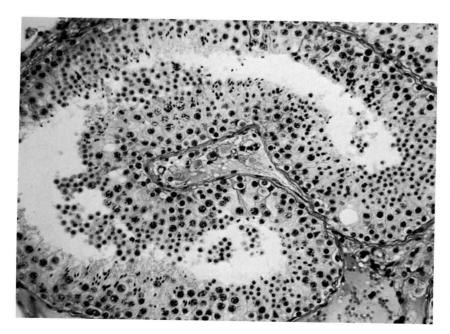

Fig. 12. Testicular biopsy from a 27-year-old man who had unilateral nephrectomy 13 years earlier for renal tuberculosis. Later, tuberculous involvement of the prostate and seminal vesicles was arrested by chemotherapy. When seen at the infertility clinic, he was azoospermic. Exploration revealed postinflammatory obstructions of the epididymides and vasa deferentia. Despite such obstructions, the vesticular biopsy showed normal spermatogenesis. (Hematoxylin-eosin, ×200)

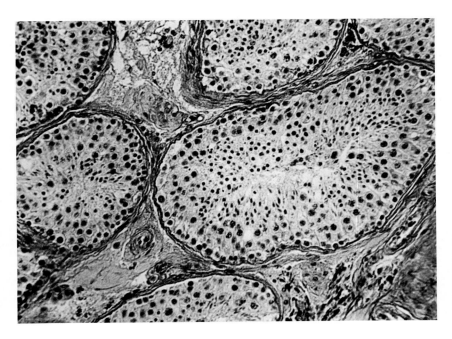

Fig. 13. Normal germinal epithelium and Leydig cells in a biopsy prior to bilateral vasovasostomy, from a 35-year-old man who had undergone bilateral vasectomy for contraception six years previously. (Hematoxylin-eosin, ×200)

spermatogenesis are observed in the testicular biopsies obtained from patients with known obstruction of the excurrent ducts of the testes. Conceivably, such findings may represent mild pressure atrophy of the seminiferous tubules when the rate of sperm production exceeds the rate of sperm resorption.

Impaired Sperm Motility. Reduced sperm motility is a frequent accompaniment of oligospermia, but in these instances, the overriding problem is the low sperm count, and the decreased motility is believed to be associated with faulty spermatogenesis in the testes. As used here, the term impaired motility refers specifically to those cases in which the sperm counts are adequate and the testicular biopsies are normal, yet the motility of the spermatozoa in the semen specimens is greatly impaired or absent (Table 5). At present, such cases are believed to be due to faulty maturation or defective preservation of the spermatozoa during their slow journey through the epididymides,[23] or due to biochemical abnormalities of the seminal plasma, the bulk of which is made up of secretions from the prostate and seminal vesicles.[16,17] An example of the testicular biopsies from such patients is shown in Figure 14, in which the germinal epithelium, the Sertoli cells, the size of the tubules, the tunica propria, and the Leydig cells are apparently normal.

Comments Regarding the Post-testicular Causes of Infertility. The two dominant problems in the post-testicular causes of infertility are obstruction and impaired sperm motility.

The treatment for obstruction is surgical correction. This treatment is feasible because the spermatogenic potential of the testes is preserved indefinitely despite obstruction of their excurrent ducts. Congenital blocks due to atresia, whether present in the vas deferens or the epididymis, are generally difficult to repair surgically; the absence of large segments of such structures makes anastomosis mechanically impossible.[49] Of the acquired blocks, those caused by gonorrheal epididymitis, tuberculous epididymitis, or other infections leading to scarring of the epididymis are also difficult to repair, because the epididymis is essentially a single tubular structure despite its highly serpentine and winding course, so that a block at any one point in effect represents a complete barrier to sperm transport. Results of epididymovasostomy in such patients have not been encouraging.[39,49] Cases of inadvertent ligation of the vas deferens resulting from inguinal herniorrhaphy likewise present obstacles to reanastomosis, because in such patients, the vas is most commonly occluded in the region of the internal inguinal ring, a difficult and inconvenient site for reanastomosis.[39] Instances of vas ligation or vasectomy performed for contraceptive purposes are generally far more amenable to surgical repair. The chances of restoring continuity are good if the original vasectomy was done in the straight portion of the vas without the excision of a segment of the vas. Successful vasovasostomy in terms of reappearance of motile spermatozoa in the semen is achieved in upward of 80 percent of the cases,[1,48] although the rate of restored fertility in terms of the ability to induce pregnancy is generally much

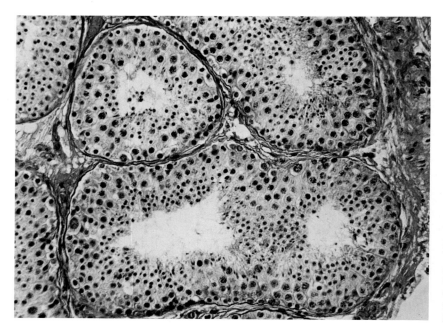

Fig. 14. Testicular biopsy from a 25-year-old man with normal sperm counts but greatly impaired sperm motility. The spermatozoa in the semen specimens consistently ranged from 60 to 80 million per cc, but only 10 to 20 per cent of them were motile, and the motility of these was rated as 1 to 2 + on a scale of 1 to 4 +. Note normal seminiferous tubules and Leydig cells. (Hematoxylin-eosin, × 200)

lower and ranges from about 25 to 30 percent of the cases, in part due to the development of sperm antibodies.[1,48]

Patients with adequate sperm counts and normal testicular biopsies but greatly impaired sperm motility offer an interesting challenge. Recently, the importance of the epididymis in sperm maturation and storage has been increasingly emphasized.[23] Because of the varieties of drugs that can lead to cytoplasmic degeneration of the epididymis,[22] the role of this accessory sex organ in male infertility is destined to become more prominent. The importance of the seminal plasma in preserving sperm motility is also well known.[16,17] In large part, the seminal plasma is made up of secretions from the prostate and seminal vesicles, with minor contributions from the epididymides, vasa deferentia, ampullae, and bulbourethral and urethral glands. In certain patients, the impaired sperm motility is apparently due to biochemical changes of the seminal plasma brought on by a bacterial infection of the prostate and seminal vesicles,[7,16] and in such cases, massage of these structures coupled with antibiotic therapy to eradicate the infection has been reported to be beneficial.[7] However, there still remain other cases in which the abnormalities of the seminal plasma are complex and poorly defined. The fact that such patients appear to have the potential for normal spermatogenesis based on hormonal and histological criteria renders the very low rate of successful treatment frustrating. Recently, patients with immotile spermatozoa

due to a congenital defect in the sperm tails were described.[18] Such observations added yet another facet to the problem of impaired sperm motility as a cause of infertility.

OVERVIEW

In this review, a 20-year series of testicular biopsies performed for infertility studies has been presented. The causes of infertility were divided into three categories: pre-testicular, testicular, and post-testicular causes. On theoretical grounds, one would expect the pre-testicular cases to be associated with a decrease in gonadotropin secretion. The decrease may be the consequence of primary pituitary or hypothalamic disease, or the result of feedback inhibition of the pituitary as in disorders associated with estrogen or androgen excess. The testicular cases, being due to primary defects of the testes, would be expected to have increased gonadotropin secretion (especially FSH) as a compensatory response to defective spermatogenesis. The post-testicular cases, which consist primarily of obstructions of the excurrent ducts of the testes, would be expected to have normal gonadotropin secretion, since obstructions per se do not affect the germinal epithelium.

The above correlations for the most part hold true in our series. The important exceptions are the cases of maturation arrest and hypospermatogenesis. The majority of patients suffering from either of these two testicular causes of infertility have normal gonadotropin levels, apparently because the extents of testicular damage are not sufficiently great to cause an increase in gonadotropin secretion. Only in those patients with severe hypospermatogenesis or maturation arrest involving the spermatogonial or primary spermatocyte stage are the FSH levels elevated, an experience well supported by others.[11,29,38] A rise of plasma FSH in patients with idiopathic oligospermia therefore portends extensive germ cell damage and a guarded prognosis in terms of restoration of fertility.

As a result of the rapid advances in hormone assays, it is becoming apparent that in addition to FSH and LH, prolactin may play a role in controlling the spermatogenic and endocrine function of the testis. Hyperprolactinemia, whether idiopathic or due to a prolactin-secreting tumor of the pituitary, has been linked with male infertility; treatment with bromocryptine, a substance that inhibits the release of prolactin by the pituitary, has been reported to be beneficial in such cases.[20,44,50] Thus far, few details concerning testicular biopsies in such patients have appeared. The precise nature of the interplay between prolactin and the testis awaits further study.

Along with the rapid advances in hormone assays, the increasing application of chromosomal analysis to testicular biopsies is contributing greatly to our understanding of the complex process of spermatogenesis. The XYY syndrome, for example, has been reported to be associated with a spectrum of abnormalities in spermatogenesis ranging from maturation arrest and hypospermatogenesis to complete absence of germ cells.[45,53] Often, tubules exhibiting these diverse patterns of abnormalities coexist within the same testicular biopsy. Such heterogeneity of morphological changes appears to be a characteristic of patients with chromosomal anomaly.[53] Because of the possibility of mosaicism, such chromosomal abnormalities may be difficult to detect unless the cytogenetic analysis is applied directly to the testicular biopsy.

The above examples point to the importance of correlating testicular biopsy findings with endocrinological data on the one hand, and with chromosomal analysis on the other. Such correlations are germane not only from a theoretical standpoint, but also in the practical sphere of devising therapy, since they help to pinpoint the source and nature of the difficulty and provide a sound base for therapy.

The pre-testicular causes of infertility are endocrine disorders or imbalances primarily, for which the pathophysiology is relatively well understood; hence their treatment rests on firm ground. In contrast, the testicular causes of infertility as a group offer considerably less hope for treatment at the present, because in these disorders, the primary defects are in the testes, most of which are permanent and irreversible; compounding the problem is their poorly understood etiology. Among the post-testicular causes of infertility, those due to obstructions of the excurrent ducts of the testes can be corrected surgically, though the rate of success is marred by the development of sperm antibodies in such patients; as for the problem of impaired sperm motility, its solution will only be forthcoming through a better understanding of the biochemistry and physiology of the accessory sex glands.

In conclusion, testicular biopsy is an important tool in the diagnosis and management of male infertility. The procedure is simple and safe in competent hands and yields information obtainable in no other way. The increasing use of this procedure has permitted a rational classification of the testicular lesions responsible for infertility and provides an intelligent basis for the institution of corrective measures or the withholding of therapy in cases in which the biopsy indicates a hopeless prognosis for fertility.

Department of Pathology
University of Chicago
950 East 59th Street
Chicago, Illinois 60637

SUMMARY

In this review, the pathological findings from testicular biopsies of men suffering from various types of infertility are presented. The causes of male infertility are divided into three major categories: pretesticular, testicular, and post-testicular causes. The pre-testicular causes of infertility may be defined as extra-gonadal endocrine disorders, such as those originating in the hypothalamus, pituitary, or adrenals, which have an adverse effect on spermatogenesis. The testicular causes of infertility are primary defects of the testes. The post-testicular causes of infertility consist primarily of obstructions of the ducts leading away from the testes. Cases in which the spermatozoa are normal in number but greatly impaired in motility, presumably due to faulty maturation or improper preservation of the spermatozoa during their sojourn in the epididymides, or due to biochemical abnormalities of the seminal plasma, are also included in the post-testicular category.

REFERENCES

1. Alexander, N. J.: Vasectomy: morphological and immunological effects. In Hafez, E. S. E. (ed.); Human Semen and Fertility Regulation in Men. St. Louis, C. V. Mosby Co., 1976, p. 308

2. Amelar, R. D.: Infertility in Men. Philadelphia, FA Davis, 1966
3. Becker, K. L.: Clinical and therapeutic experiences with Klinefelter's syndrome. Fertil Steril 23:568, 1972

4. Caminos-Torres, R., Ma, L., and Synder, P. J.: Testosterone-induced inhibition of the LH and FSH responses to gonadotropin-releasing hormone occurs slowly. J Clin Endocrinol Metab 44:1142, 1977

5. Capell, P. T. Paulsen, C. A., Derleth, D., et al.: The effect of short-term testosterone administration on serum FSH, LH and testosterone levels: evidence for selective abnormality in LH control in patients with Klinefelter's syndrome. J Clin Endocrinol Metab 37:752, 1973

6. Charny, C. W.: The spermatogenic potential of the undescended testis before and after treatment. J Urol 83:697, 1960

7. Charny, C. W.: Treatment of male infertility. In Behrman, S. J., and Kistner, R. W. (eds.): Progress in Infertility, Boston, Little Brown and Co., 1968, p. 649

8. Charny, C. W., and Meranz, D. R.: Pathology of mumps orchitis. Trans Am Soc Study Steril 3:167, 1947

9. Chemes, H. E., Dym, M., Fawcett, D. W., et al.: Pathophysiological observations of Steroli cells in patients with germinal aplasia or severe germ cell depletion. Ultrastructural findings and hormone levels. Biol Reprod 17:108, 1977

10. de Kretser, D. M., Burger, H. G., Fortune, D., et al.: Hormonal histological and chromosomal studies in adult males with testicular disorders. J Clin Endocrinol Metab 35:392, 1972

11. de Kretser, D. M., Burger, H. G., and Hudson, B.: The relationship between germinal cells and serum FSH levels in males with infertility. J Clin Endocrinol Metab 38:787, 1974

12. de la Balze, F. A., Bur, G. E., Scarpa-Smith, F., et al.: Elastic fibers in the tunica propria of normal and pathologic human testes. J Clin Endocrinol Metab 14:626, 1954

13. del Castillo, E. B., Trabucco, A., and de la Balze, F. A.: Syndrome produced by absence of the germinal epithelium without impairment of the Sertoli or Leydig cells. J Clin Endocrinol 7:493, 1947

14. Dubin, L., and Amelar, R. D.: Varicocelectomy as a therapy in male infertility: a study of 504 cases. Fertil Steril 26:217, 1975

15. Dubin, L., and Hotchkiss, R. S.: Testis biopsy in subfertile men with varicocele. Fertil Steril 20:50, 1969

16. Eliasson, R.: Biochemical analysis of human semen in the study of the physiology and pathophysiology of the male accessory genital glands. Fertil Steril 19:344, 1968

17. Eliasson, R., and Lindholmer, C.: Functions of male accessory genital organs. In Hafez, E. S. E. (ed.): Human Semen and Fertility Regulations in Men. St. Louis, C. V. Mosby Co., 1976, p. 44

18. Eliasson, R. Mossberg, B., Camner, P., et al.: A congenital ciliary abnormality as an etiologic factor in chronic airway infections and male sterility. New Engl J Med 297:1, 1977

19. Farrington, G. H.: Histologic observations in cryptorchidism: the congenital germinal-cell deficiency of the undescended testis. J Pediat Surg 4:606, 1969

20. Fossati, P., L'Hermite, M., Asfour, M., et al.: Infertility with hyperprolactinemia in a male displaying radiologic signs of pituitary microadenoma. In Hubinont, P. O., and L'Hermite, M. (eds.): Progress in Reproductive Biology, Vol. 1: Sperm Action. Basel, S. Karger, 1976, p. 153

21. Gabrilove, J. L., Nicols, G. L., and Sohval, A. R.: The testis in Cushing's syndrome. J Urol 112:95, 1974

22. Glover, T. D.: Investigations into the physiology of the epididymis in relation to male contraception. J Reprod Fert Suppl 24:95, 1976

23. Glover, T. D., and Nicander, L.: Some aspects of structure and function in the mammalian epididymis. J Reprod Fert Suppl 13:39, 1971

24. Gordon, G. C., Olivo, J., Rafii, F., and Southern, A. L.: Conversion of androgens to estrogens in cirrhosis of the liver. J Clin Endocrinol Metab 40:1018, 1975

25. Greenberg, S. H.: Varicocele and male infertility. Fertil Steril 28:699, 1977

26. Grumbach, M. M., and Van Wyk, J. J.: Disorders of sex differentiation. In Williams, R. H. (ed.): Textbook of Endocrinology. Edition 5. Philadelphia, W. B. Saunders Co., 1974, p. 423

27. Humphrey, T. J., Rosen, S., and Casey, J. H.: Klinefelter's syndrome. Experiences with 24 patients. Med J Austral 2:779, 1976

28. Kallmann, F. J., Schonfeld, W. A., and Barrera, S. E.: The genetic aspects of primary eunuchoidism. Am J Ment Defic 48:203, 1944

29. Keogh, E. J., Burger, H. G., de Kretser, D. M., et al.: Nonsurgical management of male infertility. In Hafez, E. S. E. (ed.): Human Semen and Fertility Regulation in Men. St. Louis, C. V. Mosby Co., 1976, p. 452

30. Kulin, H. E., and Reiter, E. O.: Gonadotropin and testosterone measurements after estrogen administration to adult men, prepubertal and pubertal boys, and men with hypogonadotropism: Evidence for maturation of positive feedback in the male. Pediat Res 10:46, 1976

31. MacLeod, J., and Hotchkiss, R. S.: The effect of hyperpyrexia upon spermatozoa counts in men. Endocrinology 28:780, 1941

32. Mancini, R. E., Lavieri, J. C., Muller, F., et al.: Effect of prednisolone upon normal and pathologic human spermatogenesis. Fertil Steril 17:500, 1966

33. Maroulis, G. B., Parlow, A. F., and Marshall, J. R.: Isolated follicle-stimulating hormone deficiency in man. Fertil Steril 28:818, 1977

34. Mauss, J., Borsch, G., Bormacher, K., et al.: Effect of long-term testosterone oenanthate administration on male reproductive function: clinical evaluation, serum FSH, LH, testosterone, and seminal fluid analysis in normal men. Acta Endocrinol 78:373, 1975

35. McCullogh, E. P., Beck, J. C., and Schaffenburg, C. A.: A syndrome of eunuchoidism with spermatogenesis, normal urinary FSH and low or normal ICSH ("fertile eunuchs"). J Clin Endocrinol Metab 13:489, 1953

36. Mills, R. G.: The pathological changes in the testes in epidemic pneumonia. J Exp Med 30:505, 1919

37. Moore, C. R.: Biology of the testes. In Allen, E., Danforth, C. H., and Doisy, E. A. (eds.): Sex and Internal Secretions. Edition 2. Baltimore, Williams and Wilkins Co., 1939, p. 353

38. Nankin, H. R., Castaneda, E., and Troen, P.: Endocrine profiles in oligospermic men. In Troen, P., and Nankin, H. R. (eds.): The Testis in Normal and Infertile Men. New York, Raven Press, 1977, p. 529

39. O'Conor, V. J.: Surgical correction of male sterility. Surg Gynecol Obstet 110:649, 1960

40. Paulsen, C. A.: The testes. In Williams, R. H. (ed.): Textbook of Endocrinology. Edition 5. Philadelphia, W. B. Saunders Co., 1974, p. 323

41. Paulsen, C. A., Gordon, D. L., Carpenter, R. W., et al.: Klinefelter's syndrome and its variants: a hormonal and chromosomal study. Rec Progr Hormone Res 24:321, 1968

42. Phadke, A. M.: Fate of spermatozoa in cases of obstructive azoospermia and after ligation of vas deferens in man. J Reprod Fert 7:1, 1964

43. Rosemberg, E.: Gonadotropin therapy of male infertility. In Hafez, E. S. E. (ed.): Human Semen and Fertility Regulation in Men. St. Louis, C. V. Mosby Co., 1976, p. 464

44. Roulier, R., Mattei, A., Reuter, A., et al.: Taux de prolactine dans les stérilités et hypogonadismes masculins. Nouv Presse Méd 5:1191, 1976

45. Santen, R. J., de Kretser, D. M., Paulsen, C. A., et al.: Gonadotropins and testosterone in the XYY syndrome. Lancet 2:371, 1970

46. Santen, R. J., and Paulson, C. A.: Hypogonadotropic eunuchoidism. I. Clinical study of the mode of inheritance. J Clin Endocrinol Metab 36:47, 1973

47. Santen, R. J., and Paulsen, C. A.: Hypogonadotropic eunuchoid-

ism. II. Gonadal responsiveness to exogenous gonadotropins. J Clin Endocrinol Metab 36:55, 1973

48. Schmidt, S. S.: Vas anastomosis: a return to simplicity. Br J Urol 47:309, 1975

49. Schmidt, S. S., Schoyman, R., and Stewart, B. H.: Surgical approaches to male infertility. In Hafez, E. S. E. (ed.): Human Semen and Fertility Regulation in Men. St. Louis, C. V. Mosby Co., 1976, p. 476

50. Segal, S., Polishuk, W. Z., and Ben-David, M.: Hyperprolactinemic male infertility. Fertil Steril 27:1425, 1976

51. Sherins, R. J., and DeVita, V. T.: Effect of drug treatment for lymphoma on male reproductive capacity. Studies of men in remission after therapy. Ann Intern Med 79:216, 1973

52. Simmons, F. A.: Medical progress. Human infertility. New Engl J Med 255:1140; 1186, 1956

53. Skakkebaek, N. E., Hultén, M., Jacobsen, P., et al.: Quantification of human seminiferous epithelium. II. Histological studies in eight 47,XYY men. J Reprod Fert 32:391, 1973

54. Snoep, M. C., de Lange, W. E., Sluiter, W. J., et al.: Differential response of serum LH in hypogonadotropic hypogonadism and delayed puberty to LH-RH stimulation before and after clomiphene citrate administration. J Clin Endocrinol Metab 44:603, 1977

55. Wong, T.-W., Straus, F. H., and Warner, N. E.: Testicular biopsy in the study of male infertility. I. Testicular causes of infertility. Arch Pathol 95:151, 1973

56. Wong, T.-W., Straus, F. H., and Warner, N. E.: Testicular biopsy in the study of male infertility. II. Posttesticular causes of infertility. Arch Pathol 95:160, 1973

57. Wong, T. W., Straus, F. H., and Warner, N. E.: Testicular biopsy in the study of male infertility. III. Pretesticular causes of infertility. Arch Pathol 98:1, 1974

58. Yoshimoto, Y., Moridera, K., and Imura, H.: Restoration of normal pituitary gonadotropin reserve by administration of luteinizing-hormone-releasing hormone in patients with hypogonadotropic hypogonadism. New Engl J Med 292:242, 1975

EDITORIAL COMMENTS

Dr. Wong and associates have provided us with a very lucid, comprehensive review of the histology of the infertile testis. Testicular biopsy can assist the clinician in making a diagnosis and rendering a prognosis for the infertile male. Unfortunately, the morphologic information obtained from a biopsy does not facilitate therapy; therefore, biopsies are not routinely indicated. Perhaps, in the future, as we garner more insight into the pathogenesis and treatment of male infertility, histologic studies will guide our therapy. Indeed, there is evidence from recent electron microscopic studies[9] and physiologic investigations (see *Physiology of the Male Reproductive System* in this symposium) that subtle abnormalities of the Sertoli cell frequently may cause male infertility.

Commentary: Testicular Biopsy

E. Douglas Whitehead

Shortly after Charny published the first article on testicular biopsy in 1940, crediting Robert S. Hotchkiss as the first to employ this procedure in man as a method to diagnose causes of male infertility, it became a practical method of selecting appropriate therapy and avoiding unnecessary therapy when the prognosis was poor.[1,2] In recent years, however, the status of testicular biopsy has been reviewed and reevaluated. As a result, there have been numerous efforts to identify subsets of male patients with subfertility and infertility in whom testicular biopsy might serve a useful purpose.[3–9]

The paper selected for reproduction *in toto* has been chosen because it is one of a series of three significant papers reporting a 20-yr experience of testicular biopsies.[5–7] The authors have divided their total series of 140 cases into pretesticular, testicular, and posttesticular etiologies. Eleven percent (15 cases) had pretesticular, 75% (105 cases) had

testicular, and 14% (20 cases) had posttesticular etiologies for the testicular biopsy studies. Today, it is generally agreed that testicular biopsy is unnecessary in many infertile patients. However, in properly selected patients with azoospermia and some patients with severe oligospermia (less than 10 million/ml), testicular biopsy offers a guide to diagnosis, prognosis, and therapeutic alternatives. The indications for testicular biopsy have been reduced because of extensive use of appropriate endocrinologic determinations such as radioimmunoassay quantitation of serum gonadotropins (follicle-stimulating hormone [FSH]) and luteinizing hormone [LH], testosterone and prolactin, gonadotropin-releasing hormone [GnRH] stimulation tests, chromosomal analysis of buccal smears, peripheral lymphocytes, serial semen analyses, seminal fructose determination, and careful physical examination including assessment of testicular size.[10–21]

INDICATIONS

Because small testes (less than 3.5 cm in greatest diameter) increase the likelihood of a hormonal abnormality and because impaired spermatogenesis associated with elevated serum FSH levels suggests primary damage to the seminiferous tubules, testicular size and serum FSH concentrations may be used to screen patients before testicular biopsy.[17] For example, testicular biopsy is not usually necessary diagnostically or prognostically in patients with Klinefelter's syndrome who have azoospermia, small testes, and high FSH levels (*i.e.,* indicating severe primary testicular damage for which no treatment is currently available). Similarly, it has been suggested that testicular biopsy can be avoided in patients with azoospermia, significantly small testes, and high FSH levels who have absence of germinal cells (Sertoli-cell-only syndrome) or severe maturation arrest.[11,16,18,19] Patients with high FSH levels and severe oligospermia usually have hypospermatogenesis or maturation arrest with varying degrees of seminiferous tubule hyalinization. In these patients and those referred to earlier who are azoospermic with high FSH levels, deKretser has recommended against testicular biopsy.[19] For these patients, however, as well as for those with ''end stage'' testes due a variety of etiologies, for example, irradiation, severe inflammatory disease, vascular compromise, testicular biopsy may be useful in verifying a hopeless prognosis. Azoospermic or severely oligospermic patients with normal or equivocal findings on testicular examination and normal, low, or only slightly elevated FSH levels may be offered testicular biopsy as a diagnostic and prognostic determinant.[20,21]

Patients with fructose-positive azoospermia and occasionally patients with oligospermia who demonstrate normal-sized testes and normal gonadotropins and testosterone concentrations may actually have ductal obstruction (*i.e.,* obstruction of the epididymides or vasa deferentia).[1] These men should undergo bilateral scrotal exploration and concomitant testicular biopsy. Even after long periods of obstruction, a favorable prognosis following vasovasostomy or vasoepididymostomy may be encountered if no adverse effects to the germinal epithelium or Leydig cells can be demonstrated.[7]

Testicular biopsy is not indicated in patients with azoospermia, absent vasa, and a negative seminal fructose determination. In patients with azoospermia and hypogonadotropic hypogonadism, testicular biopsy may be performed before a lengthy course of hormonal therapy to predict ultimate efficacy; frequently, however, hormonal screening may obviate the need for examination of testicular tissue. Gonadotropin concentration *per se* should not determine whether testicular biopsy is performed. Some patients with elevated FSH levels do not have irreversible testicular damage, while some Sertoli-cell-only patients may be eugonadotropic.[11]

The testes of infertile patients demonstrating oligospermia and a scrotal varicocele frequently have hypospermatogenesis with immature germ cell desquamation or a pattern of maturation arrest; however, testicular biopsy is infrequently necessary in these patients. It has been suggested that patients with cryptorchidism be considered for testicular biopsy of both the eutopic and dystopic gonads at the time of orchiopexy.[22,23] In addition, testicular biopsy has been recommended in patients with clinically suspected periateritis nodosum.[24] Ansbacher and Gangi have advised testicular biopsy before reanastomosis of the vasa after vasectomy in order to give the patient a more accurate prognosis; these results, however, have not seemed clinically useful.[25] Occasionally, data obtained from meiotic and nonmeiotic chromosome analyses and evaluation of androgen biogenetic pathways justify testicular biopsy, since more sophisticated use of the tissue can be offered.[26–29] Again, the clinical relevance of these procedures remains speculative. Finally, testicular biopsy is sometimes useful to correlate the response of an investigative treatment modality with the type of spermatogenic defect present.[30]

COMPLICATIONS

Complications from testicular biopsy are rare.[31] However, infection and hematocele have been reported, and potential anesthetic complications exist. Antibody formation has been described subsequent to testicular biopsy, but these findings have not been confirmed.[25,32,33] Although transient sperm suppression has been reported, this effect seems quite evanescent.[34,35]

HISTOLOGIC CLASSIFICATION

Because testicular biopsy is subject to individual interpretation and because there is not a uniform system of histologic classification, interpretations of biopsy findings have been difficult to compare. Suggestions have been made for the quantitative analyses of the germinal epithelium, for example, the use of a standardized method for differential cell counting or a scoring and rating scale for the entire specimen.[36–38] Some investigators maintain that in terms of fertility prognosis, testicular biopsy data in the oligospermic patient offer more than the interpretation of repetitive hormonal and semen analyses.[36]

Close examination of a testicular biopsy may reveal normal germinal epithelium demonstrating the six generations of germ cell development. However, frequently only four or five distinct cell types can be found. This is *not* a pathologic finding but rather a sequelae of the incomplete incorporation of *all* cell types within the six-cell association patterns demonstrated in the human testes. The more frequently encountered abnormal testicular biopsy findings may be further classified as maturation arrest, germinal cell aplasia (Sertoli-cell-only syndrome), and hypospermatogenesis with desquamation of immature cells; each may be associated with varying degree of peritesticular fibrosis. Less frequently one sees pathologic findings consistent with hypogonadotropic hypogonadism, that is, ''unstimulated cells'' due to failure of germinal and Leydig cell maturation following inadequate gonadotropin stimulation or findings consistent with Klinefelter's syndrome (marked hypospermatogenesis, normal or increased Leydig cell activity, and hyalinization of the tubules). In summary, however, the most common abnormal patterns seen in testicular biopsies are hypospermatogenesis and maturation arrest.[6]

SURGICAL TECHNIQUE

Bilateral testicular biopsy is preferred in patients with significant discrepancy in testicular size or consistency, but where possible, unilateral biopsy is recommended. If oligospermia is present and ductal obstruction unlikely, testicular biopsy can be performed in the office or hospital under local anesthesia. However, if azoospermia is present and ductal obstruction a possibility, general anesthesia is employed and the biopsy is performed in the hospital concurrently with corrective surgery, possibly microsurgery. In the former instance, scrotal exploration is not necessary and only a small incision is required; in the latter instance, scrotal exploration is necessary and the testes must be delivered into the operative field.

In a testis biopsy, the testis is immobilized and a transverse scrotal incision 1 cm to 2 cm long is made. The tunica vaginalis is exposed and incised parallel to the skin incision. The anterior surface of the testis is visualized, two stay sutures placed, and a 5-mm transverse incision made into the tunica albuginea. With gentle pressure, a small amount of testicular stroma is extruded through the incised tunic and atraumatically excised with either a sharp scalpel or razor. No forceps are used for this will crush the specimen which should be placed *directly* into the fixative. The edges of the tunica albuginea are then coapted using either 3–0 or 4–0 atraumatic chromic catgut.

The tunica vaginalis is similarly closed and the skin reapproximated in two layers with simple sutures of 3–0 catgut. A scrotal support is used for a few days. It is vital that the biopsy specimen be fixed in either Zenker's, Bouin's, or Carnoy's solution in order to preserve the delicate testicular architecture; formalin should always be avoided.

CONCLUSION

In summary, testicular biopsy is a safe and simple procedure that greatly aids in establishing the diagnosis and prognosis and, sometimes, directing the management of properly selected azoospermic or severely oligospermic patients. In recent years its judicious use in conjunction with endocrine evaluation and chromosomal analyses has greatly increased the number of successfully managed patients. As Robert S. Hotchkiss so sensitively noted, ''The boundless gratitude of those who are successfully treated is almost unparalleled in other fields of medicine, and this reward alone fully warrants continued trial and effort.''[39]

REFERENCES

1. Charny CW: Testicular biopsy: Its value in male sterility. JAMA 115:1429, 1940

2. Hotchkiss RS: Testicular biopsy in the diagnosis and treatment of sterility in the male. Bull NY Acad Med 18:600, 1942

3. Colgan TJ, Bedard YC, Strawbridge HTG, et al: Reappraisal of the value of testicular biopsy in the investigation of infertility. Fertil Steril 33:50, 1980

4. Meinhard E, McRae CU, Chisholm GD: Testicular biopsy in evaluation of male infertility. Br Med J 3:577, 1973

5. Wong TW, Straus, FH II, Warner NE: Testicular biopsy in the study of male infertility. III. Pretesticular causes of infertility. Arch Pathol 98:1, 1974

6. Wong TW, Straus FH II, Warner NE: Testicular biopsy in the study of male infertility. I. Testicular causes of infertility. Arch Pathol 95:151, 1973

7. Wong TW, Straus FH II, Warner NE: Testicular biopsy in the study of male infertility. II. Posttesticular causes of infertility. Arch Pathol 95:160, 1973

8. Schwarzstein L: Human menopausal gonadotropin in the treatment of patients with oligospermia. Fertil Steril 25:813, 1974

9. Levin HS: Testicular biopsy in the study of male infertility. Hum Pathol, 10:569, 1979

10. Franchimont P, Millet D, Bendrely E, et al: Relationship between spermatogenesis and serum gonadotropin levels in azoospermia and oligospermia. J Clin Endocrinol Metabol, 34:1003, 1972

11. Hargreave TB, and Jequier AM: Can Follicle Stimulating Hormone Estimation Replace Testicular Biopsy in the Diagnosis of Obstructive Azoospermia? Br J Urol 50:415, 1978

12. Hargreave TB, Kyle KF, Kelly AM, et al: Prolactin and gonadotrophins in 208 men presenting with infertility. Br J Urol 49:745, 1977

13. Hargreave TB, Kyle KF, Kelly AM, et al: Releasing factor tests in men with oligospermia. Br J Urol 51:38, 1979

14. deKretser DM, Burger HG, Hudson B: The relationship between germinal cells and serum FSH levels in males with infertility. J Clin Endocrinol Metabol 38:878, 1974

15. Pryor JB, Pugh RCB, Cameron KM, et al: Plasma gonadotrophic hormones, testicular biopsy and seminal analysis in the men of infertile marriages. Br J Urol 48:709, 1976

16. Pryor JT, Cameron KM, Collins WP, et al: Indications for testicular biopsy or exploration in azoospermia. Br J Urol 50:591, 1978

17. Snyder PJ: Endocrine evaluation of the infertile male. Urol Clin North Am 5:451, 1978

18. Smith KD, Tcholakian RK, Chowdhury M, et al: An investigation of plasma hormone levels before and after vasectomy. Fertil Steril 27:145, 1976

19. deKretser DM: Endocrinology of male infertility. Br Med Bull 35:181, 1979

20. Besser, GM, McNeilly AS, Anderson DC, et al: Hormonal responses to synthetic luteinizing hormone and follicle stimulating hormone-releasing hormone in man. Br Med J 3:267, 1972

21. Cunningham GR: Medical treatment of the subfertile male. Urol Clin North Am 5:563, 1978

22. Mininberg DT, Bingol MN: Chromosomal abnormalities in undescended testes. Urology 1:98, 1973

23. Pujol A, Rodriguez J, Bernat-Landoni R., and Serrallach, N.: The value of bilateral biopsy in unilateral cryptorchidism. Eur Urol 4:85, 1978

24. Amelar RD, Dubin L: Male infertility: Current diagnosis and treatment. Urology 1:1, 1973

25. Ansbacher R, Gangai MP: Testicular biopsy: Sperm antibodies. Fertil Steril 26:1239, 1975

26. Steinberger E, Fischer M, Smith KD: An Enzymatic defect in androgen biosynthesis in human testis: A case report and response to therapy. Andrologia 6:59, 1974

27. Steinberger E, Smith KE, Tcholakian RK, et al: Seroidogenesis in human testes. In Mancini RE, Martini L (eds): Male Fertility and Sterility, Proceedings of Serono Symposia, Vol 5, p 149. New York, Academic Press, 1974

28. Hendry WF, Polani PE, Pugh RCB, et al: Two hundred infertile males: Correlation of chromosome, histological endocrine and clinical studies. Br J Urol 47:899, 1976

29. Mehan DJ, Chehval MJ, Volk LR: Meiotic indices in the oligospermic male. Fertil Steril 29:952, 1977

30. Brannen GE, Roth RR: Testicular abnormalities of the subfertile male. J Urol 122:757, 1979
31. Ellis JD: Testicular biopsy. Hosp Med 2:654, 1968
32. Wortman JS, Sciarra JJ, Markland C: Control of male infertility: Report of a workshop. Contraception 10:561, 1974
33. Hjort T, Husted S, Linnet-Jepsen P: The effect of testis biopsy on autosensitization against spermatozoal antigens. Clin Exp Immunol 18:201, 1974
34. Gordon DL, Barr AB, Herrigal JE, et al: Testicular biopsy in man. I. Effect upon sperm concentration. Fertil Steril 1:477, 1950
35. Rowley MJ, O'Keefe KB, Heller CG: Decreases in sperm concentration due to testicular biopsy procedure in man. J Urol 101:347, 1969

36. Aafjes HA, van der Vijver JCM, Schenck CE: Value of testicular biopsy rating for prognosis in oligozoospermia. Br Med J 1:289, 1978
37. Zukerman Z, Rodriguez-Rigau LJ, Weiss DP, et al: Quantitative analysis of the seminiferous epithelium in human testicular biopsies and the relation of spermatogenesis to sperm density. Fertil Steril 30:448, 1978
38. Johnson SG: Testicular biopsy score count—a method for registration of spermatogenesis in human testis: Normal values and results in 335 hypogonadal males. Hormones 1:1, 1970
39. Hotchkiss RS: Fertility in men, p 203. Philadelphia, JB Lippincott, 1944

ANNOTATED BIBLIOGRAPHY

Pryor JT, Cameron KM, Collins WP, et al: Indications for testicular biopsy or exploration in azoospermia. Br J Urol 50:591, 1978

As a result of their experience with 311 azoospermic males, the authors report that estimation of testicular size and serum FSH levels allow accurate estimation of spermatogenic function, thereby avoiding testicular biopsy in patients with small testes and grossly elevated levels of serum FSH. In these patients they found absent or severely impaired spermatogenesis and, therefore, advised them of the options for adoption or artificial insemination. In patients with large testes (5 cm) or serum FSH levels that were not grossly elevated, they advise surgical exploration for possible correction of obstruction of the vasa deferentia or epididymides. In patients where no obstruction is found, the authors stress that testicular biopsy is essential because these patients may have spermatogenic arrest that might be amenable to hormonal therapy.

Wong TW, Straus, FH II, Warner NE: Testicular biopsy in study of male infertility III. Pretesticular causes of infertility. Arch Pathol 98:1, 1974

In this report the authors review their findings in 15 cases of testicular biopsies with pretesticular etiologies for infertility. The authors define these etiologies as extragonadal endocrine disorders or imbalances that have a detrimental effect on spermatogenesis. The most frequent etiology was hypopituitarism. Four cases of chromophobe adenoma with postpubertal onset were noted, two cases of hypogonadotrophic eunuchoidism with essentially normal FSH levels were present, and one case of craniopharyngioma was present. Both these entities were prepubertal in onset. There were five cases of endogenous estrogen excess. In four cases the source was unknown and in one case it was due to a tumor of the adrenal cortex. One case each was present of glucocorticoid excess as a result of ulcerative colitis, hypothyroidism, and diabetes mellitus.

Wong TW, Straus, FH II, Warner NE: Testicular biopsy in the study of male infertility. II. Posttesticular causes of infertility. Arch Pathol 95:160, 1973

This report is the second of 3 reports on causes of male infertility studied by testicular biopsy. In this study 20 of 140 patients had posttesticular causes for male infertility, representing 14.3% of the entire series. Most patients had acquired obstruction to the vasa deferentia or epididymides. The most frequent etiology was gonorrhea, followed by tuberculosis and nonspecific pyogenic etiologies. In two patients surgical interruption of the vasa deferentia was present, and in two patients the cause was undetermined. Five patients had congenital obstruction of the excurrent duct system. Three patients had atresia of the vasa deferentia, and two patients had atresia of the epididymides. The

authors indicate that such obstructive phenomena have no adverse effect on spermatogenesis and that treatment of choice is vasovasostomy or epididymovasostomy. In their series there were three cases of impaired sperm motility with normal sperm count and normal testicular biopsies. They postulate that this is a result of faulty maturation or storage of spermatozoa in the epididymis or of biochemical abnormalities of the seminal plasma.

Zukerman Z, Rodriguez-Rigau LJ, Weiss DB, et al: Quantitative analysis of the seminiferous epithelium in human testicular biopsies, and the relation of spermatogenesis to sperm density. Fertil Steril 30:448, 1978

This report concerns the authors' experience with a method of quantitative analysis of the seminiferous epithelium obtained by bilateral testicular biopsy from 14 patients. Their data were expressed either as numbers of cells per unit length of seminiferous tubule circumference or as number of cells per Sertoli cell. The results were correlated with sperm count (millions per milliliter), total sperm count (millions per ejaculate), and age. They found a significant correlation between sperm density and germ cell counts. In addition, they noted high coefficients of correlation when results were expressed per unit of tubular wall length. The authors conclude that quantitative analysis of spermatogenesis in testicular biopsies permits localization of the lesion to a specific cell type in the seminiferous epithelium. They speculate that such localization might, in the future, provide valuable information on etiopathogenesis and serve as a guide to therapy.

Narbitz R, Tolnai G, Jolly EE, et al: Ultrastructural studies on testicular biopsies from 18 cases of hypospermatogenesis. Fertil Steril 30:679, 1978

Electron microscopic studies were performed on biopsy material from 18 patients with hypospermatogenesis. Observations tended to exclude a diagnosis of "tubular disorganization" or "blockage." In addition, the authors noted that the Sertoli cells had normal cytologic characteristics and the normal amount of lipid droplets and microfilaments. Of unknown significance, in 6 patients, they noted thick banded collagen fibers in large numbers in substitution for the microfibriles usually found between the myoid in the tunica propria. The authors encourage further ultrastructural studies of patients with male infertility.

Taylor TA, Scott DG, Anderson CK, et al: Immunological studies of testicular tissue in oligospermic and azoospermic patients. Br J Urol 50:419, 1978

Eighteen patients underwent testicular biopsy. Six patients had oligospermia, and 12 patients had azoospermia. The specimens were examined histologically and immunohistologically. In all the oligospermic patients maturation arrest and type II allergic

stained DNA can be measured and used to describe relative quantities of haploid, S-phase, diploid, and tetraploid cells. The use of this precisely quantitative technique may in the future allow the separation of gross histologic patterns of testicular pathologic states into significant subgroups, thus allowing more precise diagnosis and, perhaps, even better prognostic capabilities.

In addition, recently published work on meiotic figure analyses may still enable yet a further subclassification of previously missed heterogenic "arrest" patterns. [10] The efficacy of such nuclear description depends on reproducible, standardized, and effective tissue processing; the use of plastic rather than paraffin embedding appears to be the technique of the future. Using this tissue-processing regimen, fixation is accomplished with either Clelono's or Zenker's formol solution with subsequent infiltration with glycol methacrylate. [11] This technique permits 2 μm sectioning, resulting in histologic specimens of increased clarity and nuclear detail.

As seen in Figure 16, routine paraffin embedding, although permitting recognition of morphologic cell types, does not allow the examination of nuclear detail seen with the paraffin technique. Only with precise nuclear staining can techniques such as meiotic figure analysis become a clinically important tool. Biopsy tissue can also be used for biochemical analysis and characterization. The recent work of several investigators in the evaluation of *in vitro* steroidgenesis using testicular tissue may direct future medical treatment for the correction of abnormal metabolic pathways in the testis and more clearly define that group of disorders now commonly referred in general as "primary testicular failure." [12]

Debate continues on when a testis biopsy is truly indicated. Scrotal exploration with concomitant testis biopsy is clearly necessary in the patient with azoospermia to differentiate ductal obstruction from an ablative testicular pathologic condition. A microsurgical setup should be available so that ductal surgery (*i.e.*, epididymovasostomy or vasovasostomy) can be instituted if obstruction is encountered. In addition, arguments can also be made to explore the scrotum of patients with severe, unexplained oligospermia, not only to establish a precise tissue diagnosis but also to direct the course of possible future medical treatment. Necessary gonadotropins (LH and FSH) and qualitative seminal fructose determination should be completed in this latter type patient before surgery to aid in the judicious use of adjunctive diagnostic procedures (*e.g.*, vasography). [13] The presence of seminal fructose merely indicates that the ejaculatory duct is patent and the seminal vesicle functioning, however; it tells nothing about ductal function proximal to the seminal vesicle. Scrotal exploration is needed to accurately define the point of ductal disease. Gonadotropin concentrations, moreover, should not determine whether a scrotal exploration and testis biopsy are performed. The previously held concept that an elevated FSH denotes irreparable testicular damage and obviates direct scrotal investigation is now being reexamined in view of the more recently defined role of FSH as reflecting negative feedback arm of the Sertoli cell system directly and of the spermatogenic process itself only indirectly. [14]

In summary, therefore, the testis biopsy remains a useful clinical tool. Coupled with sophisticated histochemical techniques allowing more precise nuclear investigation and even DNA quantitation, new categories of gonadal dysfunction in man may soon emerge. Only by more precise definition of testicular pathologic conditions, moreover, can specific treatment for the subfertile male be more rationally instituted.

REFERENCES

1. Charny CW: Testicular biopsy: Its value in male sterility. JAMA 15:1429, 1940

2. Hotchkiss RS: Testicular biopsy in the diagnosis and treatment of sterility in the male. Bull NY Acad Med 18:600, 1942

3. Simmons FA: Correlation of testicular biopsy material with semen analysis in male infertility. Ann NY Acad Sci 55:643, 1952

4. Roosen-Runge EC: Quantitative investigations on human testicular biopsies. I. normal testis. Fertil Steril 7:251, 1956

5. Mancini RE, Rosenberg E, Cullen M, et al: Cryptorchid and scrotal testes. I. Cytological, cytochemical and quantitative studies. J Clin Endocrinol 25:927, 1965

6. Clermont Y: The cycle of the seminiferous epithelium in man. Am J Anat 112:35, 1963

7. Steinberger E, Tjioe DY: A method for quantitative analysis of human semiferous epithelium. Fertil Steril 19:960, 1968

8. Johnsen SG: Testicular biopsy score count—a method for regis-

tration of spermatogeneses in human testes: Normal values and results in 335 hypogonadal males. Hormones 1:2, 1970

9. Clausen OPF, Purvis K, Hansson V: Quantitation of spermatogeneses by flow cytometric DNA measurements in endocrine approach to male contraception. Int J Andr. (Suppl) 2, 1978

10. Cheval MJ, Mehan DJ, Volk LR: Meiotic figures in the testicular biopsy of subfertile males. Fertil Steril 28:253, 1977

11. Chi EY, Smuckler EA: A rapid method for processing liver biopsy specimens for 2μ sectioning. Arch Pathol Lab Med 100:457, 1976

12. Rodriguez LJ, Tcholakian RK, Smith KD, et al: In vitro steroid metabolism studies in human testes. I. Effects of estrogen on progesterone metabolism. Steroids 29:771, 1977

13. Boreau J: Images of the Seminal Tracts. New York, S. Karger, 1974

14. Steinberger A, Steinberger E: Secretion of an FSH-inhibitory factor by cultured Sertoli cells. Endocrinology 99:918, 1976

126

VASECTOMY SHOULD NOT FAIL

Stanwood S. Schmidt, M.D.

Contemporary Surgery / Vol. 4 No. 5, 1974

In many areas of the world vasectomy is now the most common operation performed upon the adult male: It is also a little-studied and casually done surgical procedure. The results can be tragic when operative failure occurs or when the patient is not properly selected. Failures should never happen, because the fundamentals of the operation are simple and specific.

Vasectomy is most often done for sterilization. It also is done to prevent epididymitis secondary to prostatic infection or associated with prostatic surgery.[1,2] In either case the surgical technique is the same.

BASIC PRINCIPLES

The failure of vasectomy can be entirely psychological. Therefore, both the operation per se and its significance to the patient must be fully understood. When a sexually active man requests a vasectomy, the physician must be certain that his patient is making a mature, willing, informed decision— particularly if the man is unmarried or says he wishes never to father children. Resentment and disaster may follow a decision that is immature or made as a result of pressure from wife, family, or physician. Some physicians establish stringent conditions before they perform vasectomies. For example, they may not want to operate on any man under age 30 who

Dr. Schmidt is research associate in the department of urology at the University of California at San Francisco.

Please address reprint request to: M-478 (Dr. Schmidt), University of California, San Francisco, Calif. 94143.

has fewer than three children. In the author's view, setting up such specific criteria might force a man to adopt values or a life style alien to his own.

The popular press has done a great deal to explain vasectomy to the public, but most people still have doubts and questions regarding the operation. Indeed, some men considering the operation have been dissuaded by the teasing of their friends. Therefore it is the physician's responsibility to explain the procedure in terms that the patient can comprehend. For this purpose I used to conduct a personal interview and lecture that lasted between 30 and 45 minutes.[3] Now I use a printed brochure, which I mail to any patient interested in the operation; he is just as well informed and much time is saved.[4,5,6]

But I still insist on a preoperative interview with the prospective vasectomy patient and his wife. During this interview, I evaluate his decision, answer any last-minute questions, and build his confidence in me. This means he will be operated on by someone he has met and spoken with, rather than by a total stranger. The patient is asked to bring to the interview the brochure, which includes the consent to surgery. When this is sealed by the patient's signature, it becomes part of his record and is proof of an "informed consent."

Certain points are stressed in the brochure and in the interview. The patient should desire permanent— never temporary—sterility. It is possible to restore fertility by surgery, but the attempt sometimes ends in failure. I tell the man that postoperative testing must be done, assure him of my best efforts, but do not guarantee sterility, despite the fact that the technique has never failed in my hands.

It is valuable to use the analogy of the testis as a factory with two production lines, one for hormones and one for sperm. The operation creates a roadblock between the sperm factory and warehouse, and, as a result, no new shipments will be made. In addition, the warehouse must be emptied of sperm before a man can be accurately called sterile.

I assure the patient that no known physiologic changes follow vasectomy. A balance is reached between the production and absorption of sperm. Ejaculation still occurs after the operation, and sexual relations remain unchanged, except for being more carefree.

My approach to explaining vasectomy is serious but not grim. I make an appointment for the operation only after being satisfied that the patient understands the procedure and is making a wise decision. Friday afternoons and Saturday mornings are popular times among patients for such surgery, since rest is possible before work is resumed on Monday.

At this point, a little friendly humor goes a long way toward reassuring the patient. If I feel it appropriate, I refer to the testicles as the ''family jewels.'' Joking references to the shaven genitalia are apt to divert many patients' attention from the operation. Sometimes, and for some people, this form of therapy is quite effective. Different approaches are suitable to different people, and it is for the physician to assess which is the best, and when.

SURGERY

Most vasectomies are performed as office or outpatient procedures under local anesthesia. While the skin is prepped and the instruments laid out, I try to make the experience of surgery more familiar to the patient by explaining details like the noise made by the electro-surgical unit or the reason for postoperative ecchymosis. Such ground rules as the necessity for the patient to keep his hands out of the operative field and the need for me to relax the scrotum and stretch the cremaster also are stressed. The patient is encouraged to ask questions and, during the procedure, a conversation is continued about hobbies, occupations, or whatever. Many patients have assured me that this tactic calms them, keeping their thoughts away from the procedure.

Anesthesia should be complete, so that the patient has confidence that he will not feel pain during the procedure. I prefer lidocaine hydrochloride at a concentration of 1% or 2%, without the addition of epinephrine, since the spermatic artery and the artery of the vas are end arteries. The vas is grasped with the fingers and,

after infiltrating the skin, the anesthetic is injected into the area immediately surrounding the vas, where the nerves are located. Once the skin is open, the vas is clasped with an Allis clamp and additional anesthetic injected into the tissue surrounding the vas. Because the patient is awake and usually afraid of being hurt, one must proceed slowly, carefully, and use plenty of anesthetic.

Principles of Vasectomy. Since vasectomy is a relatively simple operation, it should not fail, provided a few principles are followed. Contrariwise, if these principles are ignored, the body will attempt to restore the continuity of the vas. And an unsuspected spontaneous vas anastomosis can result.

In 1924, H. C. Rolnick first cited the principles of vasectomy.[7] These are still basic, clear, and valid. Rolnick writes:

''The reproductive and regenerative capacity of the various epithelial lined structures, such as the bladder, urethra, ureter, and Fallopian tubes, is well known and forms a basis for much of the surgery of these structures. The vas deferens, an epithelial lined duct, follows the same law and has equal powers of regeneration . . .

''Even after extensive trauma, division or resection of the vas as much as from 3.7 to 5.0 cm of its length, regeneration and restoration of the continuity of the lumen can occur. This regeneration . . . is aided materially by the sheath of the vas deferens, the former acting as a splint promoting and directing the path for epithelialization. . . .''

The importance of the epithelium and of the sheath of the vas is clearly stated. If we are to outwit mother nature, the epithelium of the vas must be destroyed at its cut ends. Although this alone may be sufficient, closing the sheath of the vas assures success. With these fundamental principles in mind, we may now elaborate further.

Congenital Variations Exist. Congenital unilateral absence of the vas is rather common; it is seen in perhaps one in every 200 to 300 men. The vas varies somewhat in size from man to man but usually is distinct to palpation and easily recognized. However, if it is not readily palpable, it might be felt at its origin from the epididymis or at the external inguinal ring. If the vas still is not palpable, it is useless to incise the scrotum and institute a traumatic search of the spermatic cord. Instead, the vasectomy should be done on the other side (where the vas is palpable), and the patient should be warned to continue his birth control methods until tests for sperm in the semen become negative.

Congenital bilateral absence of the vas also occurs, but it is unlikely that a vasectomy will be requested by

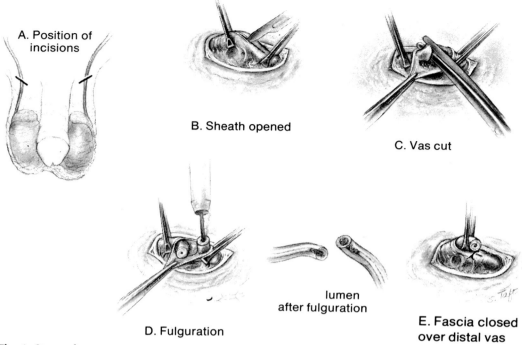

A. Position of incisions

B. Sheath opened

C. Vas cut

D. Fulguration

lumen after fulguration

E. Fascia closed over distal vas

Fig. 1. Steps of vasectomy.

a patient with this anomaly. Congenital duplication of the vas occurs very rarely but the possibility should be considered. Both vasa are thick-walled, just as the normal single vas is.

The vas should be divided in the upper scrotum. Two points are stressed here.

1. Ligation without division of the vas led to restoration of the lumen in every case in which catgut was used by Rolnick. It also followed in some cases where a nonabsorbable ligature was used. Thus, ligation in continuity should not be done. Rather, the vas should be divided (Fig. 1B & C).

2. The vas arises from the epididymis. At its beginning, it is small, thin, and convoluted. As it progresses, it thickens and straightens, becoming essentially straight at the top of the scrotum. Regardless of their motivation at the time of vasectomy, some men will wish their fertility restored in subsequent years. Vas anastomosis is relatively simple in the straight vas (Fig. 1A) but difficult and less successful in the convoluted vas. If my patient returns to me and requests restoration of his fertility, I don't want to work any harder than is necessary—and I want to succeed!

Excision Is Multilative and Without Merit. Rolnick stated that regeneration could occur even after resection of up to 5 cm of vas. The purpose of vasectomy is to permanently obstruct the vas not to secure a trophy! If a physician needs a pathologist to tell him that he has cut the vas, he should stop doing vasectomies. Resection of the vas does not guarantee operative success and in many cases simply amounts to mutilation. If excessive lengths are resected, it can make vas anastomosis impossible later.

Fulgurization, Not Ligation. In order to secure the best closure of the cut ends of the vas, the epithelium must be destroyed. Scar tissue, arising from the muscular wall, can obliterate the lumen. The best current technique utilizes a needle electrode inserted a short distance into the lumen. Coagulating current destroys the mucosa, leaving the muscular wall viable[8] (Fig. 1D).

Surgeons are so accustomed to using ligatures on blood vessels that they automatically think of ligatures and clips for the vas. This misjudgment can lead to operative failure. After a blood vessel is ligated, it thromboses back to the first branch and its intima vanishes into scar. All layers of the vas remain alive and patent up to the point of ligature. The tissue beneath the ligature necroses. Secretion of sperm continues, the lumen of the vas dilates, and peristaltic surges cause frequent blowouts from the ligated end[9] (Fig. 2). When performing

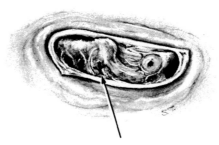

Blowout, ligature away from vas

Fig. 2. "Blowout": Ligature is now completely away from vas. This can lead to spontaneous reanastomosis.

vasovasostomies, one often finds silk or cotton ligatures in an area distant from the vas that they once occluded. Moreover, the danger of fistulas after ligation of the vas is just as real as after the ligation of a ureter.

Closing the Vas Sheath. The role the sheath plays in regeneration of the vas is not to be underestimated. At the time of vasectomy this sheath, the internal spermatic fascia, is opened to expose the vas. However the vas ends are treated, this sheath should be sutured over the upper cut end of the vas (Fig. 1E). An impenetrable wall of fascia is thus created, one which will prevent spontaneous anastomosis. With the sheath blocked, regeneration cannot occur.

Postoperative Testing. No matter how the vasectomy is performed, postoperative testing is advisable. If a vas is unobstructed, the semen will continue to show large numbers of sperm. If a spontaneous anastomosis occurs, sperm may completely disappear initially with frequent ejaculations—only to reappear a short while later. Thus two tests for sperm, both with negative results, one month or more apart, are highly desirable. Most reanastomoses occur in the immediate postoperative period, before firm scarring takes place.

COMPLICATIONS

Certain complications, such as wound infection, bleeding, or failure to find the vas are nonspecific, but there are a number of complications peculiar to vasectomy. These should be recognized and avoided whenever possible.

Ignorance, Superstition, and Fear. These can cause the most serious psychological complications. Most men are susceptible to wild rumors about unknown dangers to the testicles. Preoperative evaluation and calm, unhurried education are the best means of preventing these psychological complications, of which sexual disorders, even impotence, are typical.

Recanalization, or Spontaneous Anastomosis. This can have tragic effects if a man believes himself to be sterile, yet is not, and impregnates his sexual partner. Reanastomosis should never occur when the principles enumerated here are followed. None has occurred in my series of more than 1,500 consecutive cases.

Spermatic Granuloma.[10] This is a specific response to the extravasation of sperm. It occurs at the cut end of the vas in approximately 15% of patients in whom the vas has been ligated. Many of these granulomas are asymptomatic, but they can be extremely painful and often must be excised.

Spermatic granulomas also are seen in the epididymis, because of rupture of the postvasectomy dilated tubule. Insignificant trauma is sufficient to provoke this complication. When symptomatic, a granuloma of the epididymis can cause a persistently painful nodule and may require epididymectomy. Obstruction of the epididymis may result, thus preventing restoration of fertility.

Autoimmunity to Spermatozoa. Both immobilizing and agglutinating antibodies can appear—probably in response to extravasation of sperm. Their presence may persist for many months after the granuloma has been removed.[11] These antibodies are of concern only in the man who has undergone vasovasostomy and whose ejaculate contains nonmotile sperm or motile sperm which are agglutinated (Fig. 3).

"Congestive Epididymitis." This is my designation for an unusual variety of epididymitis in which the entire epididymis can be thickened and tender. A combination therapy of heat and scrotal support usually restores the structures to normal within a few days. I have never had occasion to explore or to biopsy the epididymis at the height of such swelling, but I have inspected several cases of "congestive epididymitis" in patients undergoing subsequent vasovasostomy. There was no evidence in these patients of the scarring that follows spermatic granuloma or of pyogenic epididymitis, and sperm were present in the fluid within the vas.

Funiculitis, to the point of vasectomy, is sometimes seen as a complication of prostatic infection. Rather than being a complication of vasectomy, it is a mark of the procedure's success. It proves that the ascending infection has been prevented from reaching the epididymis.

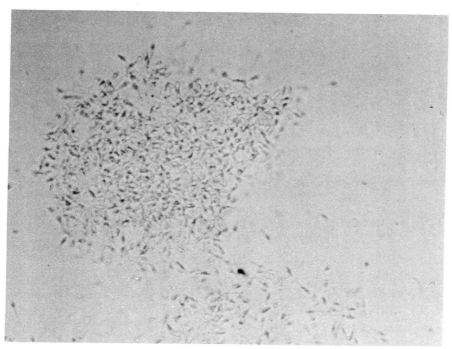

Fig. 3. Microphotograph shows sperm agglutinated, an autoimmune response that makes restoration of fertility unlikely.

REFERENCES

1. Abeshouse BS, Lerman S: Vasectomy in the prevention of epididymitis following prostatic surgery. Urol Cutan Rev 54:384, 1950

2. Schmidt SS, Hinman F: The effect of vasectomy upon the incidence of epididymitis after prostatectomy: an analysis of 810 operations. J Urol 63:872, 1950.

3. Schmidt SS: Vasectomy: Indications, technic and reversibility. Fertil Steril 19:192, 1968

4. Leader AJ: Elective Vasectomy. Eaton Laboratories

5. Klapproth HJ, Young IS: Vasectomy, vas ligation and vas occlusion. Urology 1:292, 1973

6. Leader AJ: Cited in Clinical Trends in Urology, 2:8, Nov–Dec. 1973

7. Rolnick HC: Regeneration of the vas deferens. Arch Surg 9:188, 1924

8. Schmidt SS: Prevention of failure in vasectomy. J Urol 109:296, 1973

9. Schmidt SS: Technics and complications of elective vasectomy. The role of spermatic granuloma in spontaneous recanalization. Fertil Steril 17:467, 1966

10. Schmidt SS, Morris, RR: Spermatic granuloma: the complication of vasectomy. Fertil Steril 24:941, 1973

11. Alexander: Personal communication. Nov. 30, 1973

Commentary: Vasectomy

Stanwood S. Schmidt

Vasectomy is the most commonly performed operation upon the adult male. Properly performed, on suitable patients, it is a simple, satisfactory procedure, one that answers a major human need. Improperly performed, it can be anywhere from distressing to tragic. Unfortunately, most vasectomists are self-taught and thus have poor teachers.

The article emphasizes patient selection, and rightly so. Any surgeon is entitled to set up criteria before he will perform an operation. Because of religious principles, some will refuse to do vasectomies. When the patient has other choices of surgeons, this is acceptable, but when he is denied by the only physician available to him, this may force him to have additional, unplanned children, whose lives may be ones of poverty and starvation.

When the criteria are rigid as to age, number of children, and so on, the surgeon may be forcing upon his patient a lifestyle that is entirely suitable to the surgeon's own life and totally unsuited to that of his patient. The criteria of "mature, willing, and informed" cannot be emphasized enough. This also means that each case is judged on its own merits and that no man is forced to comply with blanket, perhaps unsuitable, rules.

Before discussing elective vasectomy, a word about vasectomy to prevent epididymitis is in order. Articles continue to appear on this subject, even though the procedure had been proven years ago. With the advent of the newer antibiotics, vasectomy is uncommon as a preliminary to prostatectomy. It remains in limited use to prevent recurrent epididymitis. Having seen epididymitis at its worst, with suppuration and sloughing of both epididymis and testis, it seems a simple procedure to avoid a major complication. When so performed, however, it should be done in a failproof manner. Spontaneous reanastomosis can reopen the path so that bacteria may reach the epididymis at a later time. Thus, whenever a vasectomy is performed, and for whatever the reason, the technique should be the best.

This article presents the basic principles of the operation, after suitable patient selection has been carried out. They are that the vas should be divided in the upper scrotum, that resection of a segment of vas is without value and may be mutilative, that fulguration is the best method of sealing the vas ends, and that the sheath of the vas should be closed over the urethral end of the vas to create a barrier between the ends of the vas.

It is not enough to simply proceed knowing these principles. The nerves to the vas and to the testis accompany the vas, and thus the anesthetic should fill the sheath of the vas. It is important to realize that a greater depth of anesthesia is required against fulguration than against cutting; thus, additional anesthetic is always injected into the vas sheath before fulguration. Fulguration should destroy the mucosa of the vas but not the muscular wall from whence the fibroblasts will come to fill the lumen with scar tissue. If one is using a needle electrode from an electrosurgical unit for this purpose, the interior of the vas becomes opaque as the mucosa is fulgurated, and the outside of the vas should remain moist and glistening.

Because most elective vasectomies are performed under local anesthesia, and because the patient is seldom given preoperative sedation, this is an operation that calls for more than technical skill. The candidate for vasectomy is usually a very special person. He is a man who has agreed to take on the responsibility of birth control and who treats his wife as an important person rather than as a chattel. Vasectomy is rare in the land where women must be veiled when they leave their homes, while in the United States the man undergoing vasectomy is one who refuses to force his wife to undergo the more substantial, and less reversible, procedure of tubal interruption. At the same time, this is a man who is frightened of the procedure, a nervous person in a strange room. One must be both a competent surgeon, but also one should *be a physician!!* Talk to the patient—tell him that when he hears the sound made by the electrosurgical unit that the sound indicates that you and he are doing what you came there to do and that nothing is wrong. Tell him before you introduce the needle with the anesthetic, so that he is not startled (and do not stint on the anesthetic!). The considerate surgeon will employ verbal analgesia before and during the procedure and will be rewarded by a patient who asks "Is that all there is to it?" when the operation is finished.

Just as flying blind in an airplane is unwise, so is the failure to test, or to be tested, after vasectomy. Sperm disappearance is a function of the number of ejaculations after vasectomy, and most men will be aspermic after 15 postvasectomy ejaculations. The occasional case is seen, however, where a few sperm will remain in the semen 6 to 12 mo later. These are usually dead sperm, particularly when the vasectomy has been done properly, and seem to come from crypts in the ampulla. Nevertheless, there exists the possibility of a spontaneous reanastomosis. One should never be hasty in telling the patient that he may discontinue other contraceptive methods when sperm persist. One should examine a fresh semen specimen for motile sperm, and if none are seen, one should advise patience—and frequent ejaculations—to empty these crypts. One must also remember that a spontaneous anastomosis takes time to establish itself and that a sexually active man may empty his reservoirs of sperm and test negative for sperm and then have sperm reappear later as the anastomosis establishes itself. Also, he should know that the anastomosis may be temporarily open, only to subsequently scar shut. With this in mind, it is well to request at least two negative semen tests, with a time interval of at least a month between, before telling the patient that he is sterile.

The complication of spermatic granuloma of the vas is mentioned. Exploration of the vas ends at vasovasostomy has shown that this occurs in from 25% to 33% of men when the vas is ligated, but in only 1% of men when the vas is fulgurated. This granuloma is a means whereby the extravasated sperm are digested, but it is also an abscess. When the wall of the granuloma includes the spermatic nerve, agonizing pain can ensue either at ejaculation or by touching the area. This pain will occasionally mimic that of ureteral colic. Treatment is not excision of the granuloma, as is mentioned in the article, but evacuation of its contents when the granuloma is cystic and division and sealing of the vas proximal to the granuloma. When sperm are prevented from reaching the granuloma, it will disappear by scarring. Excision would unnecessarily disturb important vessels and nerves in the wall of the granuloma. An asymptomatic granuloma is best left alone.

Finally, I have used the technique described in the article in over 3300 consecutive cases without a failure. Although all men are told that a later vasovasostomy will often succeed, only 1 man in 300 requests this, usually in a second marriage. All cases have been done in an office surgery under local anesthesia. Postoperative complications are minimal in both numbers and degree. Neither preoperative sedation nor routine postoperative antibiotics are used. Codeine is requested postoperatively by only 1 man in 50, although all men are told that it is available if they wish it.

ANNOTATED BIBLIOGRAPHY

Rolnick HC: Regeneration of the vas deferens. Arch Surg 9:188, 1924

> This article is a classic. It should be compulsory reading for anyone contemplating performing a vasectomy, and particularly for the surgeon who has had a vasectomy fail by spontaneous reanastomosis. In dogs, regeneration of the vas occurred after cutting, ligating, and resecting the vas as long as the sheath of the vas was intact. Specifically, the body attempts to restore structures to their original condition, unless the surgeon prevents this.

Abeshouse BS, Lerman S: Vasectomy in the prevention of epididymitis following prostatic surgery. Urol Cutan Rev 54:385, 1950

> This is the classic on the subject of vasectomy to prevent epididymitis. It was written at a time when epididymitis was a common complication of prostatic surgery, a complication that caused a painful prolongation of hospitalization and disability and sometimes led to sloughing of the epididymitis and testis. These authors clearly show that vasectomy, properly performed, will prevent epididymitis as a complication of catheterization or prostatectomy. Having read this, it is difficult to understand why articles on this subject continue to appear and to understand the modern trend to discontinue vasectomy as a part of prostatectomy.

Smith KD, Tcholakian RK, Chowdhury M, et al: An Investigation of plasma hormone levels before and after vasectomy. Fertil Steril 27:145, 1976

> Testosterone, estradiol, FSH, and LH studies were done preoperatively and postoperatively on a series of men undergoing vasectomy. The levels of these hormones remained within normal ranges, thus showing that vasectomy produces no adverse hormonal changes.

Schmidt SS: Prevention of failure in vasectomy. J Urol 109:296, 1973

> Three series are compared, using different techniques for vasectomy. When the vas was cut, a section removed, and the cut ends ligated, failures occurred and spermatic granulomas were common. When interposition of fascia was added to the above technique, no failures resulted, but numerous spermatic granulomas occurred. When the vas was cut without removing a segment, the ends sealed by fulguration of the mucosa of the cut ends and fascia interposed between the cut ends, no failures occurred and spermatic granulomas were at a minimum. This showed the effectiveness of sealing the ends of the vas by fulguration and the value of fascial interposition in preventing spontaneous reanastomosis when the vas ends were not sealed.

Klapproth HJ, Young IS: Vasectomy, vas ligation and vas occlusion. Urology 1:292, 1973; Esho JO, Ireland GW, Cass AS: Vasectomy. Comparison of ligation and fulguration methods. Urology 3:337, 1974

> Both these articles compare the results of different techniques of vasectomy, finding the fulguration, fascial interposition technique superior.

Schmidt SS, Free MJ: The bipolar needle for vasectomy. I. Experience with the first 1000 cases. Fertil Steril 29: 676, 1978

> This article presents the satisfactory experience using a bipolar, battery-powered cautery specifically designed for fulguration of the vas lumen in vasectomy. A minimum of the muscular wall of the vas is destroyed.

Moss WM: Sutureless vasectomy, an improved technique: 1300 cases performed without a failure. Fertil Steril 27: 1040, 1976

> In this series, the mucosa of the vas is destroyed with a thermal cautery while the sheath of the vas is closed with a clip rather than a suture. This is another instrument that has proved satisfactory.

Albert PS, Seebode J: Nitrofurazone: Vas irrigation as adjunct in vasectomy. Urology 10:450, 1977

> This is an excellent addition to the present vasectomy technique. The authors injected 5 ml of a 1 mg/ml solution of nitrofurazone up the urethral side of the cut vas; 90% of their patients were azoospermic by the second postvas ejaculation, and no patient experienced discomfort attributable to the solution. Other authors have reported more rapid elimination of stored sperm following the instillation of euflavine, distilled water, and other solutions. A careful study is needed, comparing these and other solutions from the standpoint of effectiveness, lack of irritation, and so on. Additionally, physicians should know if the clearing is due to the volume of irrigant or to the chemical or osmotic quality of the solution.

Schmidt SS: Complications of vas surgery. In Control of Male Fertility. Sciarra JJ, Markland C, Speidel JJ (eds): Hagerstown, Harper & Row, 1975.

> The incidence of complications of vasectomy is detailed in different series at the hands of different authors. In particular, the techniques of fulguration and of ligation are compared and show the absence of failure and lessening of the incidence of spermatic granuloma following fulguration. There is no increase in the other complications of vasectomy following fulguration.

Schmidt SS, Morris RR: Spermatic granuloma: The complication of vasectomy. Fertil Steril 24:941, 1973

> Spermatic granuloma is a specific complication of vasectomy and occurs in the vas of at least 25% of patients having ligature vasectomy. It is the means whereby spontaneous reanastomosis occurs. Although often asymptomatic, it frequently involves the spermatic nerve in its inflammatory wall and may cause agonizing pain. Its incidence can be lessened by using fulguration to seal the vas. Granulomas also occur in the epididymis. Often painful, they may also cause an obstruction of the epididymal tubule, thus complicating the task of restoring fertility to a vasectomized man. Patient satisfaction is shown by the number of men who, having undergone the procedure, refer their friends and relatives.

Overview: Scrutiny of Vasectomy

Joseph E. Davis

Vasectomy, or more exactly, vas sectioning and occlusion, has become a popular elective procedure for permanent male contraception in the United States, Asia, and parts of Europe. Although cultural barriers to its acceptance currently exist in other parts of the world, vasectomy has been introduced into Africa, Latin America, and the Middle East. In spite of dire predictions that men will not accept the procedure for fear of loss of masculinity or castration, reports indicate that when properly presented, men in all societies will welcome the procedure when their concern for limitation of family size and economic and educational advancement outweigh desire for more children and when concern for risks of maternal morbidity and female contraceptive method failure is an overriding consideration.

As with many other contraceptive methods where popularity and acceptance preceded thorough scientific understanding of effects and sequelae, so the effects of vasectomy on the proximal genital tract have only come under scrutiny by serious investigators in the past 10 yr. Immunologic response, effects on lipid metabolism, effects on spermatogenesis, and epididymal function are under scrutiny. Such studies are necessary. Although millions of men have undergone uncomplicated vasectomies, and prospective studies of vasectomized and nonvasectomized matched controls have not as yet revealed significant differences in chemical or endocrine parameters, one cannot doubt that some changes, probably subclinical, do occur and that some men with as yet undefined diseases may be at greater risk if they undergo the operation. Intense study of the effects of vasectomy may lead to discriminants that assist the physician and family planning counselor in helping each man decide on the most appropriate contraceptive technique. The risk–benefit ratio of vasectomy, as with other contraceptive methods, will be better understood as a result of current studies.

The first reference to the occluded vas was made by John Hunter during his dissections in 1775. He observed a patient in whom the vas deferens was obstructed and replaced by a fibrous cord, while the corresponding testicle was of normal size and appearance.

The clinical development of vasectomy is historically linked with the course of experimental investigation. The first experiment in tying of the vas was reported as early as 1785, but it was not until the 1800s that several investigations into the effects of vasectomy were undertaken. Cooper is generally credited with initiating the first systematic experimental work in 1830 when he demonstrated that closing the duct of the testes (the vas) had no effect on the production of sperm by the testes for as long as 6 yr after the operation. Gosselin in 1847 and Simmonds in 1921 noted that even in men in whom the vas deferens had been occluded for many years, there was no apparent injury to the sperm-producing functions of the testicles.

In the late 1890s, the clinical uses of vasectomy were begun by surgeons in conjunction with operations on the prostate. Ochsner performed such operations in 1897 and reported in the *Journal of the American Medical Association,* April 22, 1899, that no change whatever had been noted in the sex lives of his patients following successful vasectomies. Although the operation gained in popularity over the years, it was the consensus among physicians that a vasectomy, once done, was irreversible.

Rolnick studied the regenerative power of the vas and its ability to resist trauma and restore continuity of its lumen.[1] He emphasized the importance of the blood supply and sheath of the vas acting as splints and making a path for epithelialization and recanalization after vas ligation. This classic work still has pertinence today in efforts to achieve successful vas occlusion, reducing the chance of failure and yet providing an opportunity for successful reanastomosis.

The popularity of vasectomy for contraception has increased sharply in the past decades. The Association for Voluntary Sterilization estimates that 75% of all voluntary sterilizations performed in the United States during 1970 were vasectomies, which represents a considerable upward trend in male sterilization from 10 yr earlier, when 60% of all voluntary sterilizations were on women.

Most men requesting vasectomies are over 30 and have 2 or 3 children. Most of the couples seeking vasectomy have used other forms of contraception. Some found them inconvenient, and others suffered ill effects such as hormonal or blood disturbances related to oral contraceptives or pelvic infections due to intrauterine devices. Other males suffer the consequences of failure, necessitating abortions or continued unplanned pregnancies.

Whereas failure rates of temporary methods of contraception are additive year by year, the 0.1% chance of recanalization decreases after the first year of vasectomy to virtually zero, making it, along with closure of the female tubes, the most effective method of contraception.

BIOLOGY OF THE VAS

Anatomy. The vas deferens is easily palpable in the scrotum as a portion of the spermatic cord. It is 35 cm long and extends from the tail of the epididymis to the prostate, where it forms the ejaculatory duct together with the duct of the seminal vesicle.

The vas deferens is composed of three layers of smooth

muscle: the outer and inner longitudinal and middle circular layers. It is capable of powerful peristaltic motion. The lumen of the vas, like the tubules of the epididymis, is lined with epithelium lying on a basement membrane arranged with submucosa and longitudinal folds. There is a thick sheet of connective tissue exterior to the muscle layer. The vas deferens may be divided into five portions: (1) the sheathless epididymal portion contained within the tunica vaginalis, (2) the scrotal portion, (3) the inguinal division, (4) the retroperitoneal or pelvic division, and (5) the ampulla. The portion of the vas of clinical interest for vasectomy is generally in the midscrotal portion.

The blood supply of the vas deferens is from the deferential artery, a branch of the inferior vesicle artery and an important collateral circulation for the testicle. It is also an important artery in terms of possible hemorrhage following vasectomy if it is not carefully separated from the sheath of the vas or suitably ligated or coagulated. The sheath of the vas in the scrotal portion contains pain nerves. Careful infiltration of the sheath mechanically limits long-acting local anesthetic agents and is valuable in limiting pain.

Histology. The human vas deferens is a firm, tubular structure about 3 to 4 mm in diameter. It is composed of epithelial mucosa, surrounded by a thick, muscular wall and adventitia. Collagen fibers are found interspersed in the muscle layers. The epididymis has two concentric smooth muscle layers that turn into three at the junction of the vas deferens. The middle layer of the three muscle layers gradually thickens as it approaches the urethra, whereas the innermost layer thins and disappears at the ampulla. In turn, these muscle layers are surrounded by adventitia, which contains small branches of the inferior spermatic nerve and blood vessels.

The epithelium and lamina propria of the vas deferens are folded into 8 to 12 longitudinal ridges. The epithelium, which is pseudostratified, is composed predominately of tall, thin principal cells extending from the base to the lumen and small, round, pyramidal basal cells. The principal cells have long stereocilia on their luminal surfaces. Scanning microscopy has revealed that the vas mucosa is carpeted with microvilli, which appear particularly tortuous in man. Surface blebbing of the epithelial cells is a further indication of secretory or absorptive processes.

Innervation and Theories of Sperm Transport. Innervation of the vas consists of short adrenergic postganglionic neurons.[2] The nerves of the testis, that is, the superior spermatic nerves, arise from the renal plexus and intermesenteric nerves and travel in association with the testicular arteries, whereas the inferior spermatic nerves arise from the hypogastric plexus and course around and along the vas deferens to innervate the epididymides. In man, the middle spermatic nerves arise from the hypogastric ganglia, whereas innervation to the testis is generally by classic long neurons. At the junction of the epididymis and vas deferens, the amount of adrenergic innervation increases. Histologic and pharmacologic studies indicate both adrenergic and cholinergic components. Adrenergic fibers, revealed by histochemical fluorescence methods for catecholamines and by electron microscopy, are found in both longi-

tudinal and circular muscles; these fibers are most likely the motor supply of the vas muscle.

Physiologic and structural studies have been conducted on the vas deferens. Generally, the vasa from most species respond similarly. Stimulation of the hypogastric nerve causes the isolated duct to contract longitudinally. If the vas is bathed in noradrenaline, the intensity of contraction increases.[3] If the tissue has been previously exposed to reserpine, the contractions diminish unless the nerve is again exposed to norepinephrine. phentolamine blocks contractions. Exposure to guanethidine or bethanidine, which especially damages the short adrenergic nerurons, greatly reduces or abolishes contractions. Thus, the pharmacologic evidence as well as the histochemical studies support adrenergic innervation.[4]

The mechanism of sperm transport through the vas deferens is still not totally understood. The heavy, smooth muscle layers equip the vas deferens for vigorous peristalsis. Several hypotheses have been advanced. Spermatic fluid could be transported by (1) pressure exerted by the epididymis, (2) peristalsis of the walls of the vas deferens, and (3) active contraction at ejaculation of the wall of the vas deferens constricting the lumen. A combination of propulsion mechanisms is probable.

Although there are different theories currently under consideration, the sequence of events in sperm transport probably includes (1) continuous movement of spermatozoa through the cauda epididymis and vas deferens due to peristalsis caused by contractions of smooth muscle, (2) emission that involves a coordinated contractile wave from the epididymis to the urethra, (3) strong adrenergically caused contractions of the wall that push the majority of the sperm of each ejaculate through the vas deferens, and (4) propulsion of the sperm to the ampulla and urethra by short, powerful, adrenergically mediated contractions of possibly the cauda epididymis and certainly the vas deferens.

CONTRAINDICATIONS TO VASECTOMY

Although vasectomy is a simple operation that can be performed almost anywhere, the more removed the setting is from medical back-up, the more important it is to screen out men who are likely to develop complications.

The major physical contraindications to vasectomy are local infections and systemic blood disorders. Local infections, which can prevent normal healing, are easily recognized and should be treated and cleared up before the operation is performed. Other local conditions which make vasectomy more difficult to perform include inguinal hernia or previous surgery for hernia or orchiopexy, hydrocele, varicocele, preexisting scrotal lesions, and a thick, tough scrotum.

Systemic blood disorders that call for special precautions would include any disease (*e.g.,* hemophilia) that interferes with normal blood clotting. In such cases, the technique used should minimize tissue trauma and emergency equipment should be available. The therapeutic use of anticoagulants may require the same precautions. Other systemic diseases such as diabetes or hypertension are not contraindications to vasectomy, but hospitalization may be advisable in case emergencies arise.

There is no physiologic basis for an adverse psychological response to vasectomy. Although there is a paucity of reliable information on the subject, available literature suggests that a normal, sexual well-adjusted male will experience no significant psychological changes following elective sterilization if he understands what he can expect during and after the procedure and if he is given an opportunity to express his fears and have his questions answered in advance.[5] When psychological problems do occur postoperatively, they can usually be explained by preoperative attitudes and conditions.

For the man with serious neuroses or sexual maladjustments, vasectomy may not be advisable. If professional counseling is available, vasectomy candidates with suspected psychological problems should be interviewed and evaluated individually. Tests measuring psychological adjustment indicate that postoperative problems can usually be traced to preoperative ones.[6]

PREOPERATIVE COUNSELING AND PREPARATION

A patient's request for vasectomy must be made voluntarily and must be accompanied by written, educated, and informed consent. The operative permission must include statements that the man seeking sterilization was given (1) a fair explanation of the surgical procedure to be followed, (2) a description of the attendant discomforts and risks, (3) a description of the benefits to be expected, (4) an explanation concerning appropriate alternative methods of family planning and the effect and impact of the proposed sterilization, including the fact that it must be considered to be an irreversible procedure, (5) an offer to answer any inquiries concerning the procedure, and (6) information that the man is free to withhold or withdraw consent to the procedure at any time before the sterilization.

In the counseling process, special attention must be paid to the fact that sterility is not guaranteed, to the immediate physical effects of the procedure, and to the possible long-range psychological reactions. Counseling may be done by a trained nonphysician; however, a physician must assume the responsibility for the content of the material provided by the counselor to the patient, for ascertaining that such counseling has been done before the procedure, for seeing that all the patient's questions have been satisfactorily answered, and for ensuring that informed consent has been obtained.

Consent of the spouse is not required by law, but inclusion of the spouse in the counseling and decision-making process is recommended when feasible.

There should be no rigid guidelines regarding waiting periods from the interview to the performance of the procedure. The physician should use his judgment based on evaluation of the patient (preferably the couple) as to a reasonable period in which the patient can reflect on this decision. In general, 2 or 3 wk is reasonable, but this should be individualized. The interview should include a general history, system review, attention to previous genital surgery, and adverse reactions to drugs. The patient should be examined following the interview. A complete physical examination is ideal. Attention to genital anomalies, individual characteristics such as associated hydrocele, undescended or retractile testes, scars, and thick scrotum should be noted so that the surgeon will be prepared to manage them. In some few instances the procedure may best be performed in the hospital under anesthesia. The patient should

be instructed on the area to be shaved. The hair from the penis extending onto the scrotum should be removed before surgery. Blood count, bleeding and clotting time, urinalysis, and semen analysis may be performed.

Preoperative sedation is not advised if the procedure is being performed on an outpatient basis. The outpatient facility should be equipped with emergency equipment, including oxygen, epinephrine, steroids, and other agents, consistent with local standards of ambulatory surgery and local statutory and health code requirements.

TECHNIQUE

Several general statements should be made about vasectomy techniques. Palpation and isolation of the vas from the spermatic cord is the first step in the performance of vasectomy—usually the vas can be identified as a firm cord, approximately 1 cm to 2 cm in diameter, unlike other structures of the spermatic cord. Relaxation of the scrotal wall can assist in this maneuver. A warm room and a relaxed patient are essential. The patient is usually apprehensive and appreciates reassurance and a friendly, relaxed attitude on the part of the surgeon. Downward displacement of the testicle assists the surgeon in localizing the vas. In the unusual situation, a thick, tough scrotum is encountered and vas isolation is difficult and indeed painful. In such instances, the procedure may more appropriately be performed in a hospital setting under general anesthesia.

Although reversibility should not be in the mind of the patient, it should, however, be in the mind of the surgeon. Vasocclusion by simple interruption of vas continuity, closure of the proximal (testicular) and by fulguration of the mucosal surface, or compression by tantulum clip or suture followed by fascial interposition describes the technique considered most acceptable today.[7-9] The danger of damaging the vital sympathetic innervation of the vas by removing a segment of the vas and accompanying nerves exists. An intact nerve supply may be vital to the transport of sperm from the epididymis at the time of ejaculation, should reanastomosis be performed.[10]

Pabst and colleagues prepared cross-sections of human spermatic cords and vasectomy specimens.[11] The number of and cross-sectional areas of nerves were determined. On average, about half of all nerves in the vicinity of the vas deferens were resected during vasectomy. The data support the hypothesis that removing nerves to the vas deferens during vasectomy could result in poor functional results after vasovasostomy; that is, that powerful contraction of the proximal vas deferens and epididymis could be lacking.

Other technical considerations that may improve chances of restoration of fertility include sectioning of the vas as high as possible away from the convoluted portion, careful preservation of the vas sheath, and preservation of the artery to the vas. Silber has suggested that fulguration of the distal end of the cut vas be performed rather than the proximal end, so as to allow sperm leakage to occur.[12] He feels that this will promote sperm leakage and sperm granuloma formation, thereby reducing intravasal and epididymal tubular pressure so as to prevent epididymal rupture. Although an increasing number of surgeons favor the Schmidt technique of mucosal fulguration describe above, there is no conclusive evidence that external compression, particularly with inert tantulum clips with fascial interposition, is in any way less effective or more apt to result in sperm granuloma or failure.

Routine resection of the vas for pathologic study is not essential, nor is it recommended. The presence of two vas specimens does not substitute for determining the end point of azoospermia. Since the same vas might have been sectioned twice, or a double vas may be present, the patient may still be fertile despite the fact that two separate specimens have been sent to the laboratory. Conversely, if the laboratory cannot confirm the presence of vasa on microscopic examination, the patient may still have had a successful procedure, since tissue can be distorted in removal or lost in transit to the laboratory. All patients must be followed carefully until fully healed and azoospermic, regardless of the pathology report.

Moreover, removal of a segment is no assurance that spontaneous recanalization could not occur. This unfortunate complication, although rare (3 to 4:1000 in large series), is more apt to be prevented by interposition of fascia between the cut ends of the vas and avoidance of the use of catgut suture material as the occluding material.

Silber has recently taken exception to proximal vas occlusion of any type, theorizing that sperm extravasation and granuloma formation may prevent elevated vasal and epididymal pressures.[13] This in turn could prevent intratubular rupture and occlusion in the proximal tract, making the success of vasectomy reversal more likely.

A percutaneous injection technique for vas occlusion, using a 4% formalin solution originally described by Coffey and Freeman, is currently under study by me.[14] Utilizing a no. 25 gauge needle, 0.5 ml of the agent is injected into the vas through the locally anesthetized scrotal skin. No attempt is made to find the vas lumen but simply to inject the agent into the vas wall. Very preliminary observations suggest that sperm transport can be affected by this technique, although several injections may be necessary to obtain azoospermia. Long-term follow-up study of semen analyses will be required.

EFFECTS AND SEQUELAE OF VASECTOMY

Disappearance of Sperm. Research into vasectomy and its sequelae and effects has resulted in better understanding of the mechanism of sperm transport during ejaculation. Formerly, urologists had advised a period of from 6 wk to several months of contraception following bilateral vasectomy or until two semen specimens without sperm had been produced. In a study performed by Freund and Davis to determine the exact end point in terms of the number of ejaculations after vasectomy required to render a patient's semen aspermic, it was apparent from the data, in which preoperative and consecutive postoperative semen specimens were studied, that approximately 60% to 70% of the sperm found in the normal ejaculate from an intact (*i.e.,* unoperated) man come from that part of the vasa proximal to the point of vasectomy and from the epididymis, since the first specimen after vasectomy consistently contained about 30% to 40% of sperm found in the preoperative specimen.[5] The constant percentage decrease in sperm output with successive specimens after vasectomy suggested that ejaculation is a true biologic emptying phenomenon and that at ejaculation

approximately 65% of the sperm distal to the point of vasectomy are expelled from the vasa. In over 100 patients studied, absence of sperm was noted after 6 to 10 ejaculations following vasectomy. By virtue of this technique, the urologist and the patient, with the cooperation of the laboratory performing the sperm counts, can determine within a relatively short period after the operation that aspermia has been produced and that the procedure has been successful.

This study was recently repeated and confirmed by Jouannet and David.[15] They also observed that motile sperm were not found in freshly ejaculated semen specimens 15 days after successful vasectomy. The reappearance of any number of motile sperm after vasectomy after 15 days strongly suggested failure or recanalization.

The absence of motile sperm in the third postoperative week after vasectomy was recently confirmed by Bedford and Zelikowsky.[16] To study the motility of residual spermatozoa, they examined ejaculates produced by 82 men between 6 and 19 days after vasectomy. In samples collected between days 6 and 8, the mean percentage motility fell from a preoperative value of $70 \pm 3.8\%$ to $34.4 \pm 5.2\%$. Mean total motile spermatozoa per ejaculate fell from $161 \pm 26.4 \times 10^6$ to $9.9 \pm 2.6 \times 10^6$. However, on the basis of total motile spermatozoa per ejaculate, 3 of the 23 men studied at this time were in the fertile range. Samples collected from 5 men on day 19 contained only immotile spermatozoa. No correlation was seen between the number of ejaculations since vasectomy and the total number of percentage of motile spermatozoa. The authors suggest that additional, extensive studies with observation periods of up to 3 wk be conducted to establish with greater certainty the limits of spermatozoa viability.

Vas irrigation during vasectomy, to effect immediate sterility or to shorten the interval between vasectomy and sterility, has provided an opportunity to study the distal male reproductive tract and to open up areas for further study. The numbers of sperm stored in the distal portion of the vas after vas occlusion differ enormously in different men.[17] The preoperative sperm count appears to be an inadequate indicator of the number of stored sperm that must be eliminated after vasectomy to achieve azoospermia. It appears that anatomic variation in the physical structure of the ampulla of the vas could account for the extremely wide variation in time after vasectomy to reach azoospermia in nonirrigated men. A knowledge of these anatomic variations could assist in answering a number of pertinent questions, such as (1) do sperm remain in the vas deferens proximal to the ampulla upon ejaculation? (2) Does the ampulla serve as a storage site for sperm in a manner that prohibits complete evacuation of all sperm at the time of ejaculation? (3) Are sperm regurgitated from the greatly narrowed portion of the vas distal to the ampulla, the ejaculatory ducts, or the prostatic urethra into the ampulla after ejaculation? (4) Are sperm regurgitated from the ejaculatory duct or prostatic urethra into the seminal vesicles after ejaculation? If sperm are regurgitated into the seminal vesicles, then the appearance of an occasional dead sperm in the ejaculate 6 to 15 mo after vasectomy may be explained by this fact alone.

Some spermicides acting as vas irrigants tend to produce azoospermia more quickly than others. Some agents such as nitrofurazone tend to penetrate outpockets and crevices of the ampulla better than others, killing all sperm immediately and making the dead sperm more vulnerable to being caught in the effluent of ejaculation shortly after irrigation.

Proximal Effects of Vasocclusion. Many investigators have been studying the anatomic, endocrine, immunologic, hematologic, and other systemic effects of occluding the vas in various animal models and in the human. One of the problems hampering research in this field is that various species used for vasectomy research respond differently to vasectomy. For example, vasectomy in rats invariably results in a granuloma formation at the surgical site. This phenomenon is much less common in other species. Even different strains of rats may differ in their antibody response to sperm antigens following vasectomy. Anatomic differences in vas structure and seasonal variation in testis–epididymis location due to scrotal–abdominal migration may introduce other factors that render findings in experimental vas occlusion not relevant to vas occlusion in man. Inasmuch as the ultimate objective is to understand human vas function better, much of the more meaningful experimentation will necessarily have to be done on larger animal models that more nearly approximate the human in regard to vas deferens physiology and anatomy.

Although prospective endocrine studies suggest that there is an increase in mean plasma levels of testosterone and LH and estradiol when compared with mean hormone levels measured before vasectomy, the changes were not found to be outside the normal range in adults.[18] An ongoing prospective study by the National Institute of Health, studying clinically significant parameters in vasectomized men matched with comparable nonvasectomized men, has failed to reveal any differences. Alexander and coauthors studied serum chemistry parameters as well as levels of FSH, LH, testosterone, and sperm-agglutinating and sperm-immobilizing antibodies before and at 1.5, 3, 6, 9, and 12 mo in 99 men; 40.5% of the men developed antisperm antibodies.[19] No significant changes in blood values were noted except that values for FSH were consistently slightly lower for those men who developed circulatory antisperm antibodies.

Morphologic of vasocclusion vary significantly from one species to another.[20] For example, sperm granulomas form rapidly in the rat vas and epididymis.[21] In biopsies of epididymal epithelium from the rhesus monkey, similarity of cellular organelles before and after vasectomy indicates that many functions of the epididymis, including secretion and resorption, continue and are probably not changed to any great extent.[22] The epithelial cells appear to remain metabolically active.

Kiviat and colleagues studied vas specimens obtained during vasovasostomy by scanning and transmission electron microscopy and compared them with vas specimens obtained during vasectomy.[23] Atrophy of microvilli were found in the vasovasostomy specimens on both the proxmal and distal sides of the occluded vasa, suggesting that the changes were not due to increased pressure but to a deprivational state of these cells in which androgenic steroids or some other trophic substance functioning to maintain the height of the epithelial microvilli and normally secreted into the ductal system are decreased or absent.

In men undergoing vasovasostomy, it has become possible to do ultrastructural studies of the testis and to study the long-term effects of vasocclusion upon human spermatogenesis.[24] To study the morphologic effects of vasectomy, testicular biopsy specimens from 3 to 7 yr after vasectomy were fixed, embedded, and stained for light and electronmicroscopic examination. Sections of the seminiferous tubules showed that the blood supply to the tubules was intact, the lumen of each tubule examined was patent, the Sertoli cells appeared to be intact, with elongated cell outlines, radially oriented, dense cytoplasm, prominent endoplasmic reticulum, lipid droplets, subsurface cisternae adjacent to Sertoli cell junction, and nuclei with characteristic clefts and large tripartite nuclei with characteristic clefts and large tripartite nucleolus. However, a large number of lysosomes were present in the area between the nuscleus and basement membrane as intact dense bodies and as membrane coated electron-lucent formations. Also, the germinal epithelium was present and showed normal stages of spermatogenesis, suggesting that vasectomy does not inhibit sperm formation. Spermatids were seen in the usual clusters of four to five. However, spermatozoa were not observed in their typical location close to the lumen, enwrapt by digitations of Sertoli cells, but rather appeared abutting the basal portion of Sertoli cells, often close to the basement membrane of the tubules. This peculiar location might indicate that these Sertoli cells were acting to absorb or eliminate the sperm. These ultrastructural findings suggest that the human testicle may actually deal with the sperm that are not ejaculated and that do not pass through the vas deferens. These studies are in progess and will be complemented by studies of a prospective nature in animals to determine ultrastructural and histochemical effects of vasectomy.

The question of immunologic consequences following vasectomy is of great interest today. No systemic diseases of an immunologic nature have been proven to be due to vasectomy, but Zappi and colleagues and Ansbacher have shown that in over 50% of men in the first year following vasectomy, factors in the serum will cause agglutination of donor sperm.[25,26] Normally, spermatozoa are sequestered behind a barrier limiting both their potential to immunize the male and their vulnerability to immune damage. Disturbances of this barrier might occur after vasectomy when massive sperm absorption may take place somewhere in the genital tract or as a result of testicular biopsy through a transient release of an immunizing dose of spermatozoa. This immunity usually is not a high titer response and may decline with time. The immunity following vasectomy or biopsy need not be deleterious. When the testis barrier is breached, however, a further possibility arises, namely autoallergic orchitis. Clinically, the incidence of orchitis following vasectomy is extremely low. Ansbacher has shown that the titers of humoral antibodies decrease 2 to 3 yr following vasectomy.[27] The mechanism of the humoral response is not yet known. It should be noted that the standard Kibrick test measures only IgG, while the sperm immobilization test measures both IgG and IgA. The origin of the immune response that may take place after vasectomy in man has not been demonstrated. Although antibodies have been reported in the blood of a certain percentage of men after vasectomy, the antigenic stimulus for antibody production has not been localized. Since the presence of such antibodies in only about half the vasectomy patients can be demonstrated, it is difficult to propose a unifying hypothesis. If the immune response is a classic pathophysiologic response in the epididymis to the presence of excess numbers of sperm that takes place weeks, or even months, after vasectomy, it should occur in all immunologically competent men. The verification of such a classic immune response requires the experimental demonstration of the steps involved, including the primary reticuloendothelial system response, the presence of 19S-containing lymphocytes, the secondary response in the epididymis, which involves macrophage activation with the stimulation of the large lymphocytes to produce the characteristic small lymphocytes, and the migration of the small lymphocytes to the testis. The experimental verification of such an immune response has not as yet been provided, and the need for such research work is urgent.

It is also necessary to characterize the specific immunoglobulins involved in the immune response. The basic research on immunology should have a high priority, since it is essential to understand the underlying phenomena involved in view of the anecdotal, unsubstantiated, and damaging reports in the lay press on the long-term sequelae of vasectomy that are attributed to the immune response.

In a recent review of the subject, Alexander and Anderson emphasized species specificity. Hypotheses mentioned to explain humoral immunologic reaction were leakage of sperm from the severed vas, sperm granuloma, epididymal degradation and leakage of soluble sperm antigens, rate of spermatogenesis (*i.e.,* higher antibody titers present in monkeys with higher sperm counts), and immune response genes. Also, since assays currently used for the detection of antisperm antibodies measure only free antibodies, it is possible that many vasectomized men and experimental animals without detectable antibody titers have high levels of antisperm antibodies circulating in the form of immune complexes.

As yet there is only indirect evidence of cell-mediated immunity as indicated by reports of lymphocytic infiltration of the testis and epididymis after vasectomy in guinea pigs, rabbits, and rhesus monkeys. Although more study of possible immune complex deposition in the human testis is needed, studies to date have not revealed significant intertubular testicular damage or changes in the function of hormone producing cells.

The pathogenicity of immune complex deposition (containing sperm antigen antibody) in the rabbit kidney has been demonstrated. However, urine from some long-term vasectomized rhesus monkeys has not revealed proteinurea, nor has Silber found any increase in urinary abnormalities in men undergoing routine pre-operative screening prior to vasovasostomy.[12,13]

Circulating immune complexes may become attached to the walls of blood vessels. They can bind complement and thereby cause local irritation to endothelial surfaces. Polymorphonuclear leukocytes attracted to endothelial surfaces by chemotactic complement components can release lysosomal enzymes that can also damage blood vessel endothelium. Arteritis resulting from circulating immune complexes, when associated with a high lipid diet, can experimentally produce arteriosclerosis in rabbits with plaques that resemble the type found in man.

Alexander and Clarkson studied cynomolgus monkeys on lipid diets and found a rapid development of arteriosclerosis in the vasectomized group.[29] The arteries from the vasectomized monkeys contained significantly more total and esterified cholesterol than those from sham vasectomized monkeys. Alexander and Anderson recently examined arteries from long-term vasectomized rhesus monkeys maintained on a normal monkey diet.[28] More severe arteriosclerosis was found in those animals than in age-matched nonvasectomized controls.

They found that monkeys lacking circulating antisperm antibodies had more extensive atherosclerosis than those with high levels of antibodies. It was postulated that those monkeys without detectable free antibodies were in a state of antigenemia and had higher levels of circulating immune complexes.

Kisker and Alexander studied vasectomized rhesus monkeys for changes in coagulation factors that might reflect an increased incidence of thrombosis.[30] The results of these tests were compared with nonvasectomized animals. There were no significant differences between the groups.

Perera found spermatogenesis to be qualitatively and quantitatively affected after vasectomy with associated epididymal changes, including development of spermatoceles and granulomas as well as disturbances in the process of sperm maturation.[31]

Wilson and associates found reduced cell-mediated immunity in vasectomized rhesus monkeys.[32] In this study, the longer an animal had been vasectomized, the more likely it was to have reduced mitogenic activity. These animals, however, did not manifest a higher incidence of infection or malignancy.

As yet there is little knowledge on the effects of vasectomy on the function of the human epididymis. Jones's studies in vasectomized rabbits suggested that the procedure does not seriously impair the capacity of the cauda epididymides to maintain a stable "milieu" in the lumen of the duct, and it seemed unlikely that the normal maturation and survival of spermatozoa would be affected.[33] He emphasized that if spermatocele formation occurred (due to epididymal rupture), then a different situation might arise and the function of the epididymis might then be impaired. Flickinger found species variation in the ability of the proximal vas and epididymis to distend following vasectomy.[34] Despite the distention, the epithelium of the epididymis and vas deferens of vasectomized rabbits remained columnar. The epithelium also continued to be functionally active as indicated by the persistence of the characteristic complement of cellular organelles, including vacuoles and lysosomes thought to be involved in secretion. Although the rabbit duct is more distendable and undergoes expansion for months, ultimately the epididymis may rupture and sperm escape. Thus, regardless of species, sperm at some point may reach the outside of the duct system and be phagocytosed by macrophages in connective tissue. Johnson and Howards measured intratubular hydrostatic pressure in the testis, caput epididymis, and cauda epididymis of the golden hamster.[35] Postvasectomy pressures in the cauda were significantly greater than the controls and reflected the accumulation of sperm and fluid. The high incidence of spermatic granuloma formation or rupture of the epididymis observed after vasectomy emphasized that in this species there are definite limits to both distensability and reabsorptive capacity. No similar experimental studies are available in humans, but clinical observation of thousands of vasectomized males over 10 yr rarely has revealed postvasectomy epididymal lesions, spermatoceles, or enlargement of the epididymis. Clinical epididymitis is rare. The mechanism whereby sperm can be accommodated in the epididymis is still not known, but at least clinicopathologically it does not resemble the events that occur in the rabbit, rat, and hamster.

At this time there does not appear to be any reason to limit vasectomy in men because of its occlusive effects on the testis or epididymis. The reasonable (and improving) success rates of reanastamosis suggest that in many instances, at least in the human, the vasocclusive effects are reversible.

Long-term epidemiologic studies in male populations in different societies, populations with large numbers of vasectomy acceptors, will be needed to determine if similar phenomena occur in the human. Alexander and colleagues have not found alterations in cholesterol metabolism in vasectomized and nonvasectomized males.[19] Kisker and colleagues found no changes in coagulation suggestive of a thrombotic tendency in a group of vasectomized men and age-matched controls, including eight patients undergoing total hip replacement, since these patients are known to have a higher risk of thrombotic complications.[36] Potts has proposed to study the incidence of arteriosclerosis found at autopsy in vasectomized and nonvasectomized men in developing countries where vasectomy has been popular.[37] It would also be valuable to study the structure of the vas occluded system in such groups.

Research in the human must be encouraged so that if some men for as yet undetermined reasons may be a greater risk if they undergo a vasoccluding procedure, this can be taken into consideration and weighed against the benefits and risks of other contraceptive methods and the risks of contraceptive failure.

COMPLICATIONS

Surgical complications are technique related, except where anomalous conditions or anatomic variations exist. The physician must pay particular attention to hemostasis and cannot hope for subcutaneous bleeding points to stop by themselves, since the complex scrotal fascial layers do not readily tamponade bleeding. Sterile technique is required. The occurrence of epididymitis, although rare, may be related to infection or may be a result of back pressure from the occluded vas. That this does not occur very often and that gross distension or pain from the epididymis is not noted clinically indicate some as yet unknown homeostatic mechanism in the human male not seen in other animals.

Sperm granuloma is an inflammatory response to the leakage of sperm from the vas or epididymis into surrounding tissues. It has been reported in 0.1% to 3% of vasectomy cases. Most granulomas are small and harmless, however, and would go unnoticed except in cases of later surgery. Thus, it is estimated that the true incidence may be as high as 20% in the vas and 15% in the epididymis. Some have been discovered only a few weeks after the procedure, others as long as 25 yr later. Although generally asymptomatic, sperm granulomas can be troublesome if they become infected, create vasocutaneous fistulae, cause recanalization of the vas through ducts formed within the granuloma, or prevent later surgical reanastomosis. In theory at least, an immune response may result from absorption of sperm from the granuloma.

A diagnosis of sperm granuloma should be considered if the man complains of pain and swelling at the site of vasectomy after 1 or 2 wk. Specifically, if the patient has been asymptomatic for some time after the operation, a sudden onset of pain suggests a granuloma, but because the symptoms are similar, cancer, tuberculosis, and neoplasms should first be ruled out. On gross examination, granulomas begin as an inflammatory response surrounding creamy-white, thick, seminal fluid. The initial lesion is usually pea sized. If the lesion becomes large and cystic, its contents may become tinged with blood. As the inflammation subsides, the lesion becomes yellowish brown and the walls become fibrous and sometimes calcified.

A sperm granuloma should be considered a complication and not a necessary sequela of vasectomy. Sperm extravasation and resultant granuloma formation may be preventable by the fulguration technique of Schmidt or by techniques of compression by inert instruments such as tantalum clips. Sutures, especially catgut, which cause pressure necrosis are more apt to be a setting for sperm leakage. As stated above, Silber feels that sperm granuloma should be allowed to occur to reduce proximal intravasal and epididymal pressure, anticipating the need for reversal. However, recanalization is more apt to occur in an area of sperm granuloma, according to Schmidt.

Rhodes and colleagues found evidence of recanalization through sperm granulomas that developed when the mucosa was incompletely fulgurated, in spite of fascial interposition, and suggest that interposing fascia may be irrelevant.[38] Cass found that proximal leakage led to failure, also, in spite of first interposing tissue.[39]

Although vasectomy is not completely foolproof, it is the most effective male method of fertility control now available, and it is becoming more effective as practitioners gain greater skill and experience. Studies conducted in the late 1960s reported failure rates up to 4:100 procedures performed. Recent studies show failure rates of less than 1:100 procedures.[40] This decline probably reflects the use of more effective and less traumatizing operative techniques as well as greater experience. Nevertheless, a vasectomy candidate should understand that a small possibility of failure exists.

Failure in vasectomy may or may not result in pregnancy in the female partner. Failure is usually discovered when semen examinations indicate the presence of sperm more than 3 mo after the operation or after 10 to 12 ejaculations, when there are motile sperm in the semen after a period of azoospermia, or when pregnancy takes place in the female partner. Although the female partner may have been impregnated by another male, pregnancy in the partner accompanied by the appearance of even a few motile sperm in a patient's semen is reasonably conclusive.

The likelihood of recanalization may be influenced by the vasectomy technique employed. For example, crushing and tying the vas, particularly with absorbable sutures, a widely used procedure, can lead to recanalization. Members of the workshop on clinical aspects of male sterilization at the 1973 Geneva conference on voluntary sterilization agreed that separating the treated vas ends with a barrier of fascia is an effective means of preventing vasectomy failure.[41]

The likelihood of operative failure is reduced if the surgeon performs the procedure frequently. The importance of frequent practice was emphasized by Sobrero and colleagues of the Margaret Sanger Research Bureau, New York.[42] They reported six failures in 236 procedures performed during the first year of the vasectomy service at the bureau. Four of these procedures were performed by physicians-in-training and two by general surgeons with little experience in the operation. Failure also results from inadequate occlusion of the vas ends. If ligatures or clips are applied too loosely, sperm continues to pass through the vas; if they are applied too tightly, they may cut through the vas wall and permit the sperm to exit.

REFERENCES

1. Rolnick HC: Regeneration of vas deferens. Arch Surg 9:188, 1924
2. Baumgarten HG, Owman C, Sjoberg NO: Neural mechanisms in male fertility. In Sciarra JJ, Markland, Spiedel JJ et al (eds): Control of Male Fertility. Hagerstown, Harper & Row, 1975
3. Ventura WP, Freund M, Davis JE: Influence of norepinephrin on the motility of human vas deferens. Fertil Steril 24:68, 1973
4. Batra SK, Lardner TJ: Sperm transport in the vas deferens. In Hafez (ed): Human Semen and Fertility Regulation in Men. St. Louis, CV Mosby, 1976
5. Freund M, Davis JE: A follow-up study of the effects of vasectomy on sexual behavior. J Sex Res 9:241, 1973
6. Ziegler FJ, Rodgers DA, Prentiss RJ: Psychosocial response to vasectomy. Arch Gen Psychiatry 21:46, 1969
7. Schmidt SS: Technics and complications of elective vasectomy: The role of spermatic granuloma in spontaneous recanalization. Fertil Steril 17:467, 1966
8. Leader AJ, Axelrod SD, Frankowski R, et al: Complications of 2,711 vasectomies. J Urol 111:365, 1974
9. Moss ___ : A sutureless technique for bilateral partial vasectomy. Fertil Steril 23:33, 1972
10. Freund M, Ventura W: Male sterilization—basic science aspects. In Schima ME, Lubell I, Davis JE, et al (eds): Advances in Voluntary Sterilization. Proceedings of the Second International Conference, Geneva, Feb. 25–Mar. 1, 1973, pp 338–345
11. Pabst R, Martin O, Lippert H: Is the low fertility rate after vasectomy caused by nerve resection during vasectomy? Fertil Steril 31:316, 1979
12. Silber SJ: Microscopic vasectomy reversal. Fertil Steril 28:1191, 1977
13. Silber SJ: Vasectomy and vasectomy reversal. Fertil Steril 29:125, 1978
14. Freeman C, Coffey DS: Sterility in male animals induced by chemical agents into the vas deferens. Fertil Steril 24:884, 1973
15. Jouannet P, David G: Evolution of the properties of seman immediately following vasectomy. Fertil Steril 29:435, 1978
16. Bedford JM, Zelikousky G: Viability of spermatozoa in the human ejaculate after vasectomy. Fertil Steril 32:460, 1979
17. Mumford SD, Davis JE: Flushing of distal vas during vasectomy. Urology 14:433, 1979
18. Smith KD, Chowdhury M, Teholakian RK: Endocrine effects of vasectomy in humans. In Sciarra JJ, Markland C, Spiedel J (eds): Control of Male Fertility, p 169. Hagerstown, Harper & Row, 1975
19. Alexander NJ, Free MJ. Paulsen CA, et al: A comparison of blood chemistry, reproduction hormones, and the development of antisperm antibodies after vasectomy in man. J Androl 1:40, 1980
20. Alexander NJ: Vasectomy: Morphological and immunological effects. In Hafez ESZ (ed): Human Semen and Fertility Regulation in Men. St. Louis, CV Mosby, 1976
21. Kwart AM, Coffey DS: Sperm granulomas: Adverse effects of vasectomy. J Urol 110:416, 1973
22. Alexander NJ: Immunologic and morphologic effects of vasectomy in the rhesus monkey. Fed Proc 34:1692, 1975

23. Kiviat MD, Eddy EM, Chapman WH: Changes induced in the epithelial surface of the vas deferens by vasectomy of long standing. Surg Gynecol Obstet 147:328, 1978
24. Hagedoorn JP, Davis JE: Fine structure of the seminiferous tubules after vasectomy in man. Physiologist 17:236, 1974
25. Zappi E, Ahmed U, Davis J, et al: Immunologic consequences of vasectomy. Fed Proc 29:728, 1970
26. Ansbacher R: Sperm agglutinating and sperm-immobilizing antibodies in vasectomized men. Fertil Steril 22:629, 1971
27. Ansbacher R: Vasectomy, sperm antibodies, Fertil Steril 24:788, 1973
28. Alexander NJ, Anderson D: Vasectomy: Consequences of autoimmunity to sperm antigens. Fertil Steril 32:253, 1979
29. Alexander NJ, Clarkson TB: Vasectomy Increases the severity of diet—induced antherosclerosis in macaca fascicularis. Science 201:538, 1978
30. Kisker CT, Alexander NJ: Coagulation changes following vasectomy: A study in primates. Fertil Steril 29:543, 1978
31. Perera BM, Oswin A: Changes in the structure and function of the testes and epididymides in vasectomized rams. Fertil Steril 29:354, 1978
32. Wilson BJ, Alexander NJ, Porter G, et al: Cell mediated immunity in vasectomized rhesus monkeys. Fertil Steril 28:1349, 1978
33. Jones R: Epididymal function in the vasectomized rabbit. J Reprod Fertil 36:199, 1973
34. Flickinger CJ: Fine structure of the rabbit epididymis and vas deferens after vasectomy. Biol Reprod 13:50, 1975
35. Johnson AL, Howards SS: Intratubular hydrostatic pressure in testis and epididymis before and after vasectomy. Am J Physiol 228:586, 1975
36. Kisker CT, Wu KK, Culp DA et al: Blood coagulation following vasectomy. JAMA 241:1595, 1979
37. Potts M: Personal communication
38. Rhodes DB, Mumford SD, Free MD: Efficacy of placing the cut vas in different fascial planes. Fertil Steril (in press).
39. Esho JO, Cass AS: Recanalization rate following methods of vasectomy using interposition of fascial sheath of vas deferens. J Urol 120:178, 1978
40. Hackett RE, Waterhouse K: Vasectomy—reviewed. Am J Obstet Gynecol 116:438, 1973
41. Schima M, Lubell I, Davis JE et al (eds): Advances in voluntary sterilization, p 232. Amsterdam, Excerpta Medica, 1974
42. Sobrero AJ, Kohli KL, Edey H et al: A vasectomy service in a free-standing family planning center: One year's experience. Soc Biol 20:303, 1973
43. Albert PS, Mininberg DT, Davis JE: Nitrofurans: Sperm immobilizing agents. Urology 4:307, 1974
44. Hulka JF, Davis JE: Sterilization of men. In Hafez, Evans (eds): Human Reproduction—Conception and Contraception. Hagerstown, Harper & Row, 1973
45. Jhaver PS, Davis JE, Lee H, et al: Reversibility of sterilization produced by vas occlusion clip. Fertil Steril 22:263, 1971

AUTHOR INDEX

SUBJECT INDEX